CAREERS 2015

11th edition

trotman t

Careers 2015

This eleventh edition published in 2014 by Trotman Education, an imprint of Crimson Publishing Ltd, 19–21c Charles Street, Bath BA1 1HX.

Contributors: Matthew Chorley, Victoria Daniel, Holly Ivins, Francesca Jaconelli, Elizabeth Mann, Lee Riley, Matt Russell, Sarah Skinner, Lucy Smith, Jessica Spencer, Charlotte Turner, Abigail Van-West and Libby Walden.

British Library Cataloguing in Publication Data
A catalogue record for this book is available from the British Library

ISBN: 978–1–84455–611–3

The information in this book was correct to the best of the publisher's belief at the time of going to press. However, if you would like to contact the publisher to report any recent changes please do so at the following address: info@crimsonpublishing.co.uk

Typeset by IDSUK (Data Connection) Ltd
Printed and bound in Malta by Gutenberg Press Ltd

CONTENTS

WELCOME TO *CAREERS 2015*

When you first start looking at the options for your future career, it can seem like a daunting and complicated process. With a vast range of opportunities within the current job market and new options emerging all the time, how do you begin to search for something that would suit you?

Careers 2015 is here to help.

By breaking down the job sector and grouping similar professions into 'families', we aim to give a clear and concise description of the jobs that may be of interest to you, as well as suggesting similar but alternative options that you may not have thought of before.

We understand that everyone has different values, interests, qualifications and ambitions so the job profiles within *Careers 2015* list the key aspects of each job to help you find the right one for you. Each one of the hundreds of job profiles within this book contains information on entry requirements, typical activities and working conditions, future prospects, advantages and disadvantages, salary information and a short description on the type of person suited for this position.

By annually researching and updating the content *Careers 2015* aims to give you an easy to use and accurate guide to the UK job market, helping you to find answers to the following questions.

- Which career will suit me?
- What qualifications will I need?
- How much can I hope to earn?
- What are the future prospects with that career?

There is a sample job profile overleaf to help demonstrate how you can use this book effectively, and get as much from the information included as you can.

We hope that you enjoy using *Careers 2015* and wish you all the best with your future career!

The Trotman team.

An example job profile

All of the job profiles in *Careers 2015* are laid out in the same style with the same sections. This is an example job profile showing you what each section refers to and the information it contains.

Heading/job title

This refers to the title of the job you will find on the page. In some cases, when two jobs are very closely linked, you will have two job titles listed in the heading and the profile will contain information on both.

CRCI

(Connexions Resources Centre Index)

These codes show you where you will be able to find additional information about the job title within school, college, university or community-based careers information areas.

Qualifications and courses

This section looks in detail at the most common ways to enter a profession and the qualifications and courses you will need. If there are different qualifications available depending on whether you live in England, Scotland, Wales or Northern Ireland, these variations will be listed here too.

As qualifications and courses often change, we recommend that you use the **Further information** section to get more detailed advice on which qualifications you will need in order to enter your chosen career.

What the work involves

This is a quick overview of what the job is like and typical tasks associated with the role.

ADMINISTRATION, BUSINESS, OFFICE WORK AND FINANCIAL SERVICES

CRCI: AA

QUALITY MANAGER — ENTRY LEVEL 2

Qualifications and courses

There are no set entry requirements although many entrants hold a degree or HND. The general entry requirements for a degree are 2 A levels/3 H grades and 5 GCSEs/National 5s (A*–C/A–C). HNDs usually require at least 1 A level/H grade and 4 GCSEs/National 5s. Depending on the industry that you want to move into, useful subjects may include business studies, engineering or physical, mathematical or applied sciences. Some areas require a technical background but others are open to all graduates. A pre-entry postgraduate qualification is not needed, although they are available.

You will need previous experience in quality control or management. Graduates can gain experience by trying to get a relevant summer job, arrange a work shadowing placement or seek out and talk to staff in supporting roles. You can also start in a technical job and progress to quality control.

Entry without a degree or HND is sometimes possible if an applicant has significant training and experience in a technician role, or is moving across from another vocational field involving quality or management. Having a relevant BTEC, HND, degree or professional qualification can boost your promotion prospects, so if you don't currently hold any higher qualifications it might be something to consider if you wish to progress. Providers of professional qualifications include the Chartered Quality Institute (CQI) and the Chartered Management Institute (CMI).

What the work involves

Quality managers are employed by an organisation to ensure that quality assurance aims are met in relation to products or services; this includes legal compliance levels and customer expectations.

Practices include monitoring and advising on existing systems in order to consistently improve current standards, and publishing data and reports that inform management.

Quality managers must ensure that the company they are working for is applying the required level of environmental and health and safety standards. Encouraging staff to adhere to new doctrines and legislation is fundamental.

Type of person suited to this work

This job is suited to someone who has an interest in securing and improving standards of quality. In order to do this, it is necessary to have good communication skills in order to influence and persuade others to follow set regulations and uphold required standards.

Problems may arise due to complicated legislation and staff lacking interest and so quality managers must be resilient and create ways in which models of quality can be easily understood and adhered to. An organisation's customers must be listened to and so quality managers must be adaptable and approachable.

Working conditions

Normal working hours apply when employed by the government or a bank, although a position in engineering, production or retail could involve shift work. Offices and laboratories are where most are based, although those with experience often become consultants to smaller firms once they have gained enough experience to be self-employed.

It may be necessary to travel to different clients during the working day, or even to stay overnight.

Future prospects

There are around 25,000 quality managers in the UK with employment opportunities in a wide range of industrial, commercial and public sector organisations. You can work for small companies or large multinational corporations.

Career development prospects are good. Experienced quality managers may be able to progress to senior management or director-level positions. It is possible to progress within the quality function or to go on to management jobs in other areas of the business. Some go on to become freelance consultants.

Advantages/disadvantages

Quality managers have high levels of responsibility and so the work they undertake can be both rewarding and respected.

Career progression or movement to self-employment is possible.

Quality legislation is constantly changing so entrants must be willing to remain up to date with developments in the field.

Money guide

Quality managers can expect a starting salary in the region of £18,000 to £25,000.

As you gain experience and progress to a senior role, you can achieve earnings of £35,000 to £70,000.

Salaries vary according to the sector you are working in, company size and geographical location.

Related opportunities

- Project Manager p43
- Quality Control Inspector p222
- Statistician p511

Further information

British Quality Foundation
www.bqf.org.uk

Chartered Management Institute
www.managers.org.uk

Chartered Quality Institute
www.thecqi.org

44

Type of person suited to this work

Within this category you will find lots of information to help you match your strengths, weaknesses, likes and dislikes to the individual job.

Sadly it is very common for someone to start a job not knowing what they will be expected to do. They might then be confronted with something they find either too hard or not enjoyable; this might mean leaving a job they studied a long time for. To make sure this doesn't happen to you, think carefully about the information provided here and whether it matches your skills, experience and personality. If you think it does, then you should also do some further research to get more detailed and comprehensive information.

Working conditions

This section explains where you can expect to be working, whether it's outside or inside, in an office or travelling around the country. It also tells you the typical working hours you can expect and whether you are likely to work at weekends, evenings and on shifts. This will give you a good idea of the day to day life you can expect on the job.

Entry level

This number corresponds to the *Careers 2015* level of qualification you need to start your career in a particular job. For more information about what the entry levels in *Careers 2015* mean, see the next page.

Future prospects

This section shows you where you could progress to within a certain career. This may be in terms of climbing the career ladder, or branching into new territory as a career sector develops and changes. Of course, no one can predict the future of any career sector completely but important changes to the economy, reductions and increases in the labour force as well as technological advances will have an impact upon how a sector develops. This information will give you a balanced view of what your future could be in any given career.

Advantages/disadvantages

It's important that, when choosing a career, you have a well-rounded and honest view of what the work will be like. This section gives you an idea of the most common good and bad points about a job so that you can decide if a job matches up to your expectations.

Money guide

For some people one of the most important things they'll consider before undertaking a new course, qualification or a career is 'how much can I expect to earn?'

To help you we have included:

- the most up-to-date information about pay scales
- where possible, what you can expect at entry, intermediate and senior levels
- any regional differences.

Related opportunities

This section lists jobs that are similar in style and the skills that they require to the job profile you are looking at. This is to give you lots of options to choose from if you haven't decided which career interests you the most.

You might not have considered or heard of some of these before, so it will help you to broaden out your ideas further.

Further information

Listed here are the websites of organisations that can help you continue your research into your chosen job areas.

Qualifications: what do the entry levels in *Careers 2015* mean?

You will see that every job profile in this book has an entry level number, ranging from 1 to 8, assigned to it. This refers to the lowest qualification level that you need to achieve in order to enter the profession.

The number shown indicates the level of qualification you are most likely to need:

- to enter the job and
- to enter the job and to train while working.

The qualifications grid

Opposite is a grid which shows what the levels in *Careers 2015* refer to in terms of qualifications that you can take in England, Wales, Northern Ireland and Scotland.

The information from three qualifications frameworks has been incorporated into this table: the Qualifications and Credit Framework (QCF), the Scottish Credit and Qualifications Framework (SCQF) and the Framework for Higher Education Qualifications (FHEQ).

Because the frameworks all have their own levels please be aware that this grid cannot accommodate subtle differences between the frameworks and you should refer directly to the websites below for more information.

The Qualifications and Credit Framework (QCF)

The QCF has now replaced the NQF (National Qualifications Framework) and is the basis of the qualifications grid on the following page. The framework contains both academic and vocational qualifications offered in England, Wales and Northern Ireland from Entry level to Level 8.

The Framework for Higher Education Qualifications (FHEQ)

The FHEQ includes higher education qualifications from Certificates of Higher Education through to Doctoral degrees. It applies to qualifications offered in England, Wales and Northern Ireland and includes five levels, each indicated by a letter corresponding with the initial of the main qualification offered at that level.

The Scottish Credit and Qualifications Framework (SCQF)

The SCQF is a 12-level framework including vocational, occupational and academic qualifications offered in Scotland. It covers all levels including further and higher education, from Access through to Doctoral degrees.

Further information

Each framework is under continuous review, but information in this book was correct at the time of writing.

For further details and the most up-to-date information, refer to the following websites:

- QCF: www.ofqual.gov.uk
  www.wales.gov.uk; www.ccea.org.uk
- FHEQ: www.qaa.ac.uk/en/publications/Documents/Framework-Higher-Education-Qualifications-08.pdf
- SCQF: www.scqf.org.uk

Key

Qualifications that are available in England, Wales, Northern Ireland and Scotland.

Qualifications that are available in England, Wales and Northern Ireland.

Qualifications that are available in Scotland*.

*In August 2013 Foundation, General and Credit Standard Grades were replaced with National 3, 4 and 5.

Careers 2015 level	**Rough equivalent framework level**	**General and academic qualifications**	**Vocational and occupational qualifications**
Entry level	QCF Entry Level Skills for Life at entry level SCQF Access Levels 1–3	**Entry Level Certificate** **National 1, 2, 3**	**National Progression Award (start at SCQF Level 2)**
1	QCF Level 1 SCQF Level 4	*GCSE grade D–G* *14–19 Foundation Diploma* *Skills for Life* *Key Skills Level 1* **Intermediate 1** **National 4**	NVQ/SVQ Level 1 *BTEC Introductory Certificate/ Diploma* *Level 1 Certificate* *Cambridge Nationals* **National Progression Award**
2	QCF Level 3 SCQF Level 5	*GCSE grade A*–C* *14–19 Higher Diploma* *Skills for Life* *Key Skills Level 2* **Intermediate 2** **National 5**	NVQ/SVQ Level 2 *Level 2 Certificate/Diploma* *BTEC Diploma/Extended Certificate/ Certificate* *Apprenticeship* *BTEC Nationals* *Cambridge Nationals* **National Progression Award**
3	QCF Level 3 SCQF Level 6	*A level* *Key Skills Level 3* *Advanced Extension Award Mathematics* *Extended Project* *International Baccalaureate* **Scottish Higher**	NVQ/SVQ Level 3 *A levels in applied subjects* *Level 3 Certificate/Diploma* *BTEC Extended Diploma/Diploma/ Subsidiary Diploma/Certificate* *Advanced Apprenticeship (England)* *BTEC Nationals* *Cambridge Nationals* *City & Guilds Level 3* **Modern Apprenticeship (Scotland, Wales, Northern Ireland)** **Professional Development Award**
4	QCF Level 4 FHEQ Level C SCQF Level 7	Certificate of Higher Education *Key Skills Level 4* **Scottish Advanced Higher** **Higher National Certificate**	NVQ/SVQ Level 3 *Level 4 Certificate/Diploma* *BTEC Professional Diplomas, Certificates and Awards* *City & Guilds Licentiateship* **Professional Development Award**
5	QCF Level 5 FHEQ Level I SCQF Levels 8 and 9	Bachelor's degree Diploma of Higher Education *Diploma of Further Education* *Foundation Degree* *Higher National Diploma*	NVQ/SVQ Level 4 Higher National Certificate/Diploma (HNC/HND) *BTEC Professional Diplomas/ Certificates/Awards* *National Diploma in Professional Production Skills* *Level 5 Certificate/Diploma* *City & Guilds Full Technological Certificate (FTC)* **Professional Development Award**
6	QCF Level 6 FHEQ Level H SCQF Level 10	Bachelor's degree with Honours Graduate Diploma Graduate Certificate	*NVQs* *Level 6 Certificate/Diploma* *BTEC Advanced Professional Diplomas/Certificates/Awards* *City & Guilds Graduateship* **Professional Development Award**
7	QCF Level 7 FHEQ Level M SCQF Level 11	Master's degree Postgraduate Diploma (PgDip) Postgraduate Certificate (PgCert) Integrated Degree *Diploma in Translation*	NVQ/SVQ Level 5 *Level 7 Diploma/Fellowship* *Level 7 Advanced Professional Certificate* *BTEC Advanced Professional Diplomas/Certificates/Awards* *City & Guilds Membership* **Professional Development Award**
8	QCF Level 8 FHEQ Level D SCQF Level 12	Doctorate	Specialist awards and diplomas from professional bodies *City & Guilds Fellowship* **Professional Development Award**

Job families

The jobs in this book have been divided into job families to make it easy for you to go straight to the right section and find the job you are interested in. At the beginning of each job family section is an introduction to the career sector and a list of all the jobs that will appear in the section. You will also find information on other similar job families and where to find them in the book.

There are 20 job families in *Careers 2015* which are:

- Administration, Business, Office Work and Financial Services
- Building and Construction
- Catering and Hospitality
- Computers and IT
- Design, Arts and Crafts
- Education and Training
- Engineering, Manufacturing and Production
- Environment, Animals and Plants
- Healthcare
- Languages, Information and Culture
- Legal and Political Services
- Leisure, Sport and Tourism
- Marketing, Advertising, Media, Print and Publishing
- Performing Arts
- Personal and Other Services including Hair and Beauty
- Retail, Sales and Customer Services
- Science, Mathematics and Statistics
- Security, Emergency and the Armed Forces
- Social Work and Counselling Services
- Transport and Logistics

What do the icons mean?

The icons used in this book are the same as those used in the CRCI (Connexions Resources Centre Index) and they will appear at the beginning of each section to make it easy and clear to see exactly which job families are being covered.

Administration, Business, Office Work and Financial Services

To work in this sector you often need to have a great head for numbers and be very good at managing your time effectively. The variety of jobs in this family is huge, so you could work in a large, busy office or you could work for yourself dealing with clients from a host of different professions. Many jobs require you to have an eye for detail as you could be compiling reports and advising organisations on how they could work more effectively or safely or organising other people's time and schedules. In all cases, you should be highly motivated and organised. If you enjoy this responsibility and like the idea of the challenge of keeping a business running like clockwork there are many jobs that would suit you in this sector.

For a full list of jobs in this section turn to page 1.

Building and Construction

The jobs in this sector are very varied; some require a high level of personal fitness, while for others, a creative flair is essential. You may be interested in working on a construction site with a team of people and for this you would need to demonstrate excellent personal safety and be happy to work outside in all weathers. Alternatively, maybe your interest lies in buying and selling property or maybe working in an office is more your sort of thing. All the jobs in the sector require someone with a great eye for detail who is very good at working with others.

For a full list of jobs in this section turn to page 55.

Catering and Hospitality

Working in this sector, you will meet a wide variety of people and probably need to be a very strong team player. For some of the jobs, you need to be outgoing, confident and sociable and may end up working early mornings or late nights. For many jobs in this sector you need to be very meticulous when it comes to standards of cleanliness and tidiness. Workers in the sector thrive on providing an impeccable service and ensuring customers are completely satisfied and are given a wonderful experience whether that be in a restaurant, hotel or bar.

For a full list of jobs in this section turn to page 119.

Computers and IT

This sector is still fairly new and so it is expanding all the time, creating new jobs for a whole range of people. You may have a mathematical brain or a real creative ability – or a bit of both! Essentially, you must be passionate about computers to consider working in this sector. You could be working directly with clients and customers, helping them to rectify problems with their computers or you could be researching and developing the latest console for the games market. In all cases you need to keep right up to date with the latest technologies and IT developments as well as people's tastes, interests and hobbies to enjoy working in this sector.

For a full list of jobs in this section turn to page 135.

Design, Arts and Crafts

The idea of turning your arts and crafts hobby into a career may be one you like the thought of. Jobs in this sector can involve working in any medium, from textiles to jewellery to metalwork or children's toys. Some jobs may involve you researching current styles and trends and creating your own designs whereas others will involve working to a set brief set out by your customer to create a bespoke product. You may find yourself working for a company but many people in this industry are self-employed, working for a range of clients. This means you need to be very organised and have brilliant communication skills to ensure you can give your clients exactly what they want. People working in this industry are extremely passionate about their careers and have a real sense of perfectionism to produce a beautiful finished article.

For a full list of jobs in this section turn to page 153.

Education and Training

To work in this sector you need to be motivated and enthusiastic about other people's learning, whether it's adults or children. There are jobs suitable for people with all levels of qualification, but whatever your entry level you will need to be interested in keeping up to date on the latest developments in education and will enjoy working with other people. If you choose to teach, the range of subjects available is huge so whatever your interest – languages, art, sciences, cooking, sports – you can become a teacher in that field. Jobs in this sector require a multitude of skills including: creativity, imagination, numerical skills, good communication and organisational skills and, in some cases, having a lot of patience!

For a full list of jobs in this section turn to page 175.

Engineering, Manufacturing and Production

There are a number of highly-skilled jobs available in this job family and workers need to be creative and methodical, combining brilliant technical skill with spatial awareness. Engineers are very well qualified indeed so you should be willing to study hard for good qualifications. Jobs in this sector can take you into a range of different fields, from scientific research to car production to working out at sea; there's something for anyone who has an inquisitive mind and a high level of technical capability. Another attractive element of this industry is that you can work with an enormous variety of different materials. You may be interested in food production but equally your passion could lie in working with aircraft or marine manufacture. People in these professions share the ability to concentrate for long periods of time and work meticulously on a job to finish it to a high standard. Some will also be highly trained with specialist equipment which may sometimes be hazardous to use so a high level of personal safety awareness is vital.

For a full list of jobs in this section turn to page 195.

Environment, Animals and Plants

Some people working in this sector spend a lot of their time outdoors. This means the jobs are perfect for those of you who don't want to spend every day behind a desk in an office, although this is not to say that you will not need to spend time writing reports and keeping a log of research findings or clients' information. Workers in this sector are passionate about animals or about caring for and maintaining the environment. You will sometimes work in unpredictable settings, especially if you are working outside or have close contact with animals. You should also have brilliant people skills especially if you find yourself responsible for the welfare of someone else's animal. You should be someone who is very observant and interested in the natural world, not just from a welfare point of view but also from an economic one; many jobs in this sector involve using the environment for financial gain but increasingly industry is interested in doing so responsibly.

For a full list of jobs in this section turn to page 233.

Healthcare

If you are keen to pursue a career in healthcare you must be compassionate and enjoy either caring for people or deciding what treatment they should receive. There is such a wide variety of jobs available in this sector simply because you can specialise in absolutely any aspect of human healthcare. Maybe you're interested in working with athletes or perhaps working with children interests you more. You could be part of the rehabilitation process after an illness or injury or find yourself working as a mental health nurse. Many jobs require a lot of training and you can expect to work in some highly pressurised and sometimes distressing situations. Workers in healthcare are extremely dedicated and enthusiastic about their careers, which rarely constitute a 9am–5pm job. You can expect every day to be different and you should relish the challenges working with people of all ages can bring.

For a full list of jobs in this section turn to page 267.

Languages, Information and Culture

If you are really interested in history or perhaps would like to use another language as part of your career, a job in this sector could be right for you. The jobs in this family are quite varied in terms of whether you would work with other people or by yourself. You could find yourself working in a range of different places, from museums to antiques fairs to conferences. Some of the jobs in this family are more unusual and are perfect for those of you who want a fascinating job that allows you to indulge in your passion for historic artefacts and artwork or languages and foreign countries. To excel in this sector you should have an inquisitive mind, be meticulous in your work and enjoy carrying out research. If you are keen to work with languages you should also be willing to travel in order to improve your language and your knowledge of the culture and history.

For a full list of jobs in this section turn to page 323.

Legal and Political Services

Are you interested in justice and fairness for all? Do you relish the opportunity to speak out for what's right and enjoy the challenge of persuading others that everyone needs an equal voice? Maybe you find the law a fascinating subject and you feel you would enjoy a challenging career where the rewards are a good salary and a real sense of achievement when your hard work pays off. If so, a job in this sector could be what you are looking for. Workers in this sector are fiercely passionate about their careers and have, more often than not, completed a lot of training and worked hard to establish themselves in this competitive field. You need to be driven and thrive on pressure and tight deadlines; this is a sector for someone who is ambitious and very talented at working tactfully with people.

For a full list of jobs in this section turn to page 339.

Leisure, Sport and Tourism

This sector relies on a motivated, upbeat and outgoing workforce for its success. You will need to show that you can work very well with other people, providing them with an excellent service when they want to enjoy themselves on holiday or if they are keen to improve their fitness and sporting ability. If you are keen to work with professional sports players or become one yourself you should be very aware of how to keep the body fit while avoiding injury. It's also important that you can keep a level head as you will often be responsible for other people's welfare. You should be warm and friendly but also able to maintain a high level of professionalism at the same time. You should also demonstrate you have patience and tact and be clued up on health and safety regulations.

For a full list of jobs in this section turn to page 357.

Marketing, Advertising, Media, Print and Publishing

Do you consider yourself to be a great communicator? Are you interested in working in an exciting and often fast-paced environment with passionate, driven and ambitious individuals? If so, a career in this industry could be right for you. People who work in this sector are exceptionally motivated and are willing to put in long hours often on low starting wages because of their love of the job. While you need to be good at preparing your work alone, people who work in this sector tend to be very good at working with others and build up strong professional relationships as part of their job. You should have a great sense of creativity and imagination and be good at putting your ideas on paper, but you will often also need strong business acumen as many of your decisions will be made from an economical point of view as well as a creative one.

For a full list of jobs in this section turn to page 375.

Performing Arts

This job family contains a wide range of exciting jobs for those of you who want to work in theatre, music, on screen or behind the scenes. People working in this sector do so because they are passionate and creative and love the arts. Jobs can be scarce, so you will need to demonstrate that you are willing to work very hard but the rewards of being part of a fantastic production can be huge. You won't necessarily be confined to working in one place as your job may take you on tour all over the world. There are also jobs available in this sector for those of you who are more technically minded – sound and lighting engineers also play a vital role in this industry as do people who have trained in fashion and textiles. Make-up artists also play an important part in theatre, television and music production.

For a full list of jobs in this section turn to page 407.

Personal and Other Services including Hair and Beauty

This is a very wide job family and covers everything from hairdressing and beauty to cleaning to wedding consulting. You can enter this career sector with a host of different skills and qualifications. What all of the jobs have in common is that they provide a particular service that a customer has asked for so you need to be good at listening to others and giving customers exactly what they want – people in this sector have a brilliant way with people. You should also demonstrate creativity and strong practical and technical skills as many of the jobs in this family require you to use specialist equipment, and have knowledge of health and safety.

For a full list of jobs in this section turn to page 429.

Retail, Sales and Customer Services

Jobs in this sector are suited to those of you who are very good at communicating with others and are interested in making your customers happy. Maybe you're interested in working with food and want to give your customers high quality, fresh produce. Your interest may lie in fashion retail and you could spend your time providing style advice. You should also be commercially minded and think about how your work relates to the success of the company you work for. Jobs in this sector also involve maintaining standards such as safety and quality to ensure guidelines are met, so a practical outlook can be useful.

For a full list of jobs in this section turn to page 449.

Science, Mathematics and Statistics

Do you have a very mathematical brain? Are you logical in how you approach tasks? Maybe you are fascinated by scientific advances and would like to be involved in future discoveries? People who work in this sector can spend long periods of time carrying out meticulous research. You may find yourself working for a variety of employers, from the health service to a cosmetics company or even a charity. You should be willing to work on your own but also be happy to present your findings in reports to others. People in this sector are very highly skilled individuals who have often been through a lot of training, and possess a questioning and inquisitive mind.

For a full list of jobs in this section turn to page 477.

Security, Emergency and the Armed Forces

Working in this sector may give you many incredible experiences and opportunities not open to most people. You need to be an excellent team player and in some instances you may find yourself in a potentially dangerous situation. Working in this sector you can expect to spend your day absolutely anywhere! Some roles involve a lot of office work whereas others can involve spending a lot of your time on the road, or even at sea. If you're looking for a job that will be exhilarating but are able to remain calm and professional under pressure this sector could offer you a lot of opportunities.

For a full list of jobs in this section turn to page 515.

Social Work and Counselling Services

People who work in this sector are dedicated to caring and talking through people's problems and anxieties to improve their general well-being and their future prospects in life. The work requires a lot of patience, an open mind and a friendly and approachable personality. You could be helping people who are distressed and need help and guidance but equally you may be helping people who want to move on to the next stage in their careers or educational choices. Either way, you should be someone who enjoys helping people change their lives for the better. If you are interested in working in this field you need to show that you are compassionate and very good at communicating with people from all walks of life and of all ages. You should also be someone who can maintain a strong sense of professionalism as you could be in a position of trust and you must be very respectful of your clients' privacy.

For a full list of jobs in this section turn to page 543.

Transport and Logistics

The jobs in this sector are immensely varied because of the wide range of transport and communication links that exist today to keep our lives running. You could need a high level of technical knowledge in this sector especially for jobs such as pilot or train driver. But you could also be great at keeping attention to detail and maintaining schedules if logistics is more where your interest lies. Jobs in transport and logistics require very efficient and practical people to ensure that our infrastructure continues to run smoothly and safely. You may need to cope well under pressure. As you will probably have contact with the general public you should be good with people, and have a calm, professional manner.

For a full list of jobs in this section turn to page 565.

Where to go for more help

Below is a brief explanation with some contact details of the main organisations that can help you find out more about the career you are interested in.

England

Speak to the careers adviser at your school or college. Alternatively there is a wide range of information on the National Careers Service website. You can also contact a trained careers adviser by phone, through their website with an email or by using the webchat service. The website also has moderated chatrooms and message boards.

Tel: 0800 100 900
Email: use the contact form on the National Careers Service website

https://nationalcareersservice.direct.gov.uk

Northern Ireland

If you want advice from a careers adviser you can attend one of the local careers offices throughout Northern Ireland. Here you will get information on all aspects of work, education and employment issues. Careers advisers visit schools regularly and you should speak to your careers teacher to arrange a careers interview. If you have left school you should contact your local JobCentre to make an appointment to speak to a careers adviser. The NI Government Careers Service website is also packed with information.

Tel: 0300 200 7820
Email: csni@delni.gov.uk

www.nidirect.gov.uk/careers

Scotland

Skills Development Scotland

Skills Development Scotland is available to both young people and adults looking for information about careers, education or employment options.

Tel: 0800 917 8000
Email: use the contact form on the Skills Development Scotland website

www.skillsdevelopmentscotland.co.uk
www.myworldofwork.co.uk

Wales

Careers Wales

Offering help to both young people and to adults, Careers Wales provides advice on any issues you have related to careers, work, education or training. The Careers Wales website offers a personalised career search with the option to create your own career profile, save your CV online, search and save career options and receive immediate advice from their online webchat service. Talk to your careers adviser in school or visit the website for more information.

Tel: 0800 028 4844
Email: use the contact form on the Careers Wales website

www.careerswales.com

England, Wales and Northern Ireland

learndirect

If you need advice on any aspect of your careers, training or educational options try contacting learndirect. learndirect has trained advisers who can discuss your options over the phone or you can attend one of the many learndirect centres available throughout England, Wales and Northern Ireland. Their help is available to anyone of any age, although it is mainly aimed at adults.

Tel: 0800 101 901

www.learndirect.com

Administration, Business, Office Work and Financial Services

To work in this sector you need to have a great head for numbers and be very good at managing your time effectively. Jobs in business and finance can be fast-paced and exciting and workers in all 4 of these areas are highly motivated and enjoy working in an office environment.

The jobs featured in this section are listed below. For similar jobs to this job family please go to the section: *Legal and Political Services* on page 339.

ACCOUNTANT

ENTRY LEVEL 6

Qualifications and courses

In order to practise, accountants will need to hold a qualification from one of the recognised accountancy bodies: Association of Chartered Certified Accountants (ACCA), Institute of Chartered Accountants in England and Wales (ICAEW), Institute of Chartered Accountants of Scotland (ICAS), Chartered Accountants Ireland (CAI) or Association of International Accountants (AIA). The websites for each organisation contain full details of the qualifications they provide.

You can qualify for these training programmes with or without a relevant degree, though having one is advantageous (usually 2.2 Honours degree or higher) and most accountants follow a graduate route. If your degree is in accounting or a related subject you may be exempt from certain papers of the professional qualifications so it is worth checking course details to see if this is the case. Owing to an increase in global companies, graduates with language degrees are in high demand.

The minimum entry requirements for a degree vary depending on the institution; however, they are normally 2 A levels/3 H grades and 5 GCSEs/National 5s (A*–C/A–C) including Maths and English.

Without a degree, you can qualify for the professional courses by following a vocational route provided by the above recognised bodies. For this it is useful to have a minimum of 3 GCSEs/National 5s and 2 A levels/3 H grades, in 5 separate subjects including maths and English, but there are still options even without these. Each body provides different options depending on the qualifications you already have.

To become a chartered management accountant, you are required to pass the Chartered Institute of Management Accountants (CIMA) Professional Qualification and complete a minimum of 3 years' relevant work experience. To become a chartered financial accountant you will need to study for the Charted Institute of Public Finance and Accountancy (CIPFA) Professional Qualification. This is made up of 3 parts and will usually take up to 3 years to complete.

It is becoming increasingly more competitive to secure a training contract with an employer that is approved by the institutes listed above so it is useful to gain pre-entry work experience.

What the work involves

Accountancy involves providing a company or individual with trustworthy information about their financial records.

By analysing a company's or individual's finances, accountants identify ways to maximise profits. They provide professional advice on financial planning and development, tax returns, future costs and budgets.

You will keep detailed accounts, carry out internal audits and produce regular statements on whether the company's systems are efficient and cost effective.

There are 3 main areas of accounting and within each sector you can become either a certified or chartered accountant. Chartered accountants work to a globally recognised standard and are often sponsored by their employer to achieve this qualification.

Industrial and commercial
Employed directly by a company, you will provide them with a range of services.

You will help to plan the company's development by predicting costs, benefits and risks.

You may be expected to make business decisions along with other managers.

Private practice
You will work for a specialist accountancy firm that offers services to clients.

Smaller practices usually work for local businesses. However, accountancy firms can be huge and some companies provide services to multinational corporations.

Your clients can vary from small businesses that do not employ their own in-house management accountant to large companies or wealthy individuals.

Public sector
Working for public bodies such as the NHS, universities and local authorities, you will offer advice on tax, financial problems, raising money, financial IT systems and management consultancy.

Your role will be to help provide an efficient, quality service that is within the budgets set by the government.

You will play an important part in making sure that public money is spent properly.

Type of person suited to this work

As you will be giving presentations and working with people at all levels, you will need excellent written and verbal communication skills.

Much of your work will involve dealing with confidential reports and financial information so reliability, honesty and integrity are essential attributes.

Time management and organisational skills are key as you must be able to work under pressure and meet deadlines.

As you are required to study whilst working and remain up to date with developments in the field, it is important to be self-motivated and committed to your career.

Confidence working with numbers and an interest in how businesses work is essential.

You will need problem-solving and research skills and the ability to process and analyse complicated financial information, therefore a good eye for detail is essential.

Working conditions

You could work in an organisation of any size and will generally be office based, spending a lot of time using IT, sitting at a desk or meeting clients. Smart dress will be required.

Depending on your role, you might have the opportunity to travel both in this country and abroad to meet clients so a driving licence could be useful.

Although you will normally work office hours from Monday to Friday, you might need to work extra hours at busy times, especially during February to April (the end of the financial year).

Flexible working is possible (once you are qualified) and there is the opportunity to set up as an independent practitioner.

Future prospects

The growing importance of information technology is having a major impact on the accountancy sector. Access to faster communication systems means that more companies are becoming global, which in turn will have an impact on the numbers required within the accountancy sector.

It is recommended that you think carefully about the area within accountancy that you would like to focus on at an early stage of your career as this may enable you to specialise in that field.

There are lots of structured routes for progression and an accountant can often become a manager after just 2 years and a senior manager 3 years after that. The next level is partner and although this is very competitive in certain firms, it is possible to achieve this 8–15 years after qualifying.

In the long term you could choose to become self-employed, offering consultancy services to clients.

There is also the opportunity to progress to general management roles within business.

Industrial and commercial
There is a high demand for trainees with opportunities throughout the country but as you would probably be working for a larger organisation you will probably be based in a city. Once you are qualified and experienced you could move into a highly paid senior management position, or you could choose to move to a larger multinational company for promotion.

Private practice
You could work for a small company, offering a personal service to local businesses and individuals or for a huge multinational firm. Job opportunities are good and there is high demand for qualified accountants.

After a time, you could set up your own private accounting practice or work independently by working on a freelance basis.

Public sector
The public sector covers a wide range of services, including education, healthcare and social services. Government changes mean that budgets are increasingly held at local level, opening up opportunities across the country.

If you do well, you can move into a high-level management position.

Advantages/disadvantages

Accountancy is a varied career and there are many opportunities both in this country and abroad.

You must be prepared to cope with a lot of responsibility, stress and pressure.

You will need to be committed and determined to manage training, studying and taking exams whilst you work.

Salaries in this field tend to be extremely high and progression can be quite rapid.

Money guide

During their training, graduates can earn between £15,000 and £27,000 a year, depending on the stage they have reached in their training, the sector and the location.

Recently qualified graduates can earn £20,000 to £50,000.

With experience accountants can earn £50,000 to £90,000. Directors can earn £140,000 and more.

Salary will depend on location and size of the organisation. The highest salaries are within London and the south-east of England; the lowest are in Northern Ireland, Scotland and the north-east of England. Graduates usually receive higher salaries than school leavers during their training.

Related opportunities

- Accounting Technician and Accounts/Finance Clerk p4
- Actuary p5
- Auditor p8
- Financial Adviser p26
- Insurance Broker p29

Further information

Association of Chartered Certified Accountants
www.accaglobal.com/uk

Chartered Accountants Ireland
www.charteredaccountants.ie

Institute of Chartered Accountants in England and Wales
www.icaew.com

Institute of Chartered Accountants of Scotland
www.icas.org.uk

Institute of Financial Accountants
www.ifa.org.uk

ACCOUNTING TECHNICIAN AND ACCOUNTS/FINANCE CLERK

ENTRY LEVEL 2

Qualifications and courses

There are no formal academic requirements to train to be an accounting technician although some GCSEs/National 5s (A*–C/A–C) would be an advantage, particularly English and Maths as they demonstrate a reasonable level of the essential literacy and numeracy skills. Other qualifications such as the Advanced Diploma in Business, Administration and Finance or A levels/H grades and BTEC Awards in subjects such as accounting, finance and business could also be useful.

You will need to train for a professional qualification with the Association of Accounting Technicians (AAT) or the Association of Chartered Certified Accountants (ACCA) to enter this profession. This is usually done on the job and studied part time via distance learning. The AAT Accounting Qualification provides flexible training and is comprised of 3 levels: Level 2 (L5 in Scotland), Level 3 (L6 in Scotland) and Level 4 (L8 in Scotland). You might be exempt from some levels if you have relevant qualifications or experience. To become a technician you will also need to complete 1 years' work experience. This is usually done while studying for the qualification part time. Once you have both the qualification and the experience you will be able to use the letters MAAT after your name.

Alternatively, the ACCA provides a Certified Accounting Technician (CAT) qualification. First you complete their 3 Foundations in Accountancy exams, followed by a year's practical experience, the Foundations in Professionalism module and 2 additional specialist exams.

What the work involves

Accounting technicians are responsible for financial issues including company expenditure, tax returns and payroll. Your work will include collecting and analysing information, controlling company budgets, keeping financial records and writing reports.

In a large firm, you will probably work as part of a team and support qualified accountants. In a smaller company, you might cover a wider range of tasks and be responsible for most of the finances.

Different financial sectors demand specialised knowledge and so, once you are qualified, you could choose to specialise in a specific financial area, for example insolvency or tax analysis.

Type of person suited to this work

You will need to be confident with numbers, and have the ability to gather, analyse and record information accurately when under pressure from deadlines. Good IT skills are also important, as most of the work is computer based.

Good verbal and written communication skills are essential, as you will often have to explain complicated financial issues to clients in a clear manner.

You must be willing and committed to further study in order to pass your technician exams. You will be expected to continue learning throughout your career, as it is important for accounting technicians to keep up to date with changes in financial law.

Working conditions

You will normally work standard office hours from Monday to Friday, however at busy times you might need to put in extra hours over evenings or weekends.

Most work will be office based, although you may also travel to meetings with clients within your working day so a driving licence could be useful.

Future prospects

Accounting technicians can progress to positions such as finance controllers, internal auditors, payroll managers, tax analysts and audit seniors. Many go on to become self-employed or become chartered accountants by studying for the qualifications of a chartered accountancy body. All of the chartered accountancy bodies offer fast-track routes for AAT and ACCA CAT qualified students.

Since the accounting technician qualifications are internationally recognised, it is also possible to work abroad.

Advantages/disadvantages

You will usually be working in a team environment, which means that you will build strong relationships.

The work can be slightly monotonous.

Money guide

As a trainee accounting technician you can expect to earn between £15,000 and £22,000 per year.

When fully qualified and with experience, earnings can be up to £32,000.

Salaries are geographically sensitive and tend to be higher in southern England, particularly in London.

Related opportunities

- Accountant p2
- Bank Cashier/Customer Adviser p9
- Pensions Administrator p40

Further information

Association of Accounting Technicians
www.aat.org.uk

Association of Chartered Certified Accountants
www.accaglobal.com/uk

ACTUARY

ENTRY LEVEL 6

Qualifications and courses

To enter the actuarial profession you should first study for a degree in a numerate subject, such as actuarial science, maths or economics, and join the Institute and Faculty of Actuaries (IFoA, also known as The Actuarial Profession) as a student member. Most employers prefer candidates to have achieved a 2.1 Honours degree or higher, as well as at least a B in A level/H grade Maths.

If you do not have the required entry requirements for the IFoA there is the option to take their Certificate in Financial Mathematics (CT1) exam which will enable you to become a member of the profession.

Once you have graduated, qualification as an actuary requires a further 3 to 6 years of studying for professional qualifications with the IFoA and on-the-job training. You should start looking to apply for graduate trainee positions in your final year of university, before October or November, as this is when most employers' deadlines will be and competition for places will be fierce.

While you train, you will study part time for the professional qualifications with the IFoA. There are 15 exams. It is possible to gain exemption from some exams, and therefore qualify faster, if you are a member of IFoA and have studied your degree at a university that holds exemption or accredited agreements or if you have a postgraduate qualification. If you did not, you may still be eligible for exemption from some exams depending on the subjects covered by your degree and your performance in them.

Pre-entry experience could also be useful. Some companies offer internships or work experience placements for students looking to become actuaries, and though this is not required to enter the profession, it may give you an edge when competing for graduate jobs. Talking with people already in the profession by approaching them at careers events or work shadowing can also be invaluable.

What the work involves

Actuaries evaluate, manage and calculate financial risks. Using statistics and knowledge of investments, law, business and economics, they make financial predictions to help design products such as insurance and pensions. They use their specialist economic and mathematical knowledge to assess situations in the financial world and relay reports and information to non-specialists.

As an actuary you would help set insurance premiums based on statistics, probability and risk. You would also use your knowledge to help companies make long-term financial decisions.

You might work in insurance, life assurance, pensions, investments or for the government.

Type of person suited to this work

You must be good with numbers and enjoy solving complicated mathematical problems. You should also be analytical, able to think logically, and be skilled at problem solving.

You will need to have excellent communication skills as you must explain complicated financial issues in a clear and understandable way to clients.

Actuaries must pay close attention to detail and work to deadlines. You must keep up to date with new developments, such as the laws governing the industry. You will be expected to have excellent IT skills.

Working conditions

Most actuaries work within life assurance companies and numbers in general insurance are increasing rapidly. You will normally work standard office hours, 9am–5pm, during the week and most of your work will be office based. Jobs are available throughout the country but most are based in large cities, such as Edinburgh and London, and the south-east of England.

As a trainee you will have to study in your own time but once you are qualified you could work abroad and might be able to work part time.

Future prospects

As a fully qualified actuary you can specialise in a particular field, work in a consultancy, or you could travel as your qualifications will be recognised all over the world. Within larger companies there are opportunities for promotion to very senior positions.

Advantages/disadvantages

Training after university takes up to 6 years and involves studying while working full time.

Actuaries have good long-term career prospects and opportunities for promotion.

UK qualifications are recognised worldwide giving you the opportunities and option to work abroad.

Money guide

The actuarial profession is one of the highest paid.

Starting salaries for graduates are around £25,000–£35,000. Once you are qualified this rises to between £40,000 and £55,000.

Senior actuaries with 10–15 years' experience usually earn in excess of £60,000 with senior directors often earning £185,000 or more.

Salaries vary based on location and specialty and are likely to be higher in London and the south-east of England.

Related opportunities

- Financial Adviser p26
- Risk Manager p49
- Stockbroker p52

Further information

Association of Consulting Actuaries
www.aca.org.uk

Institute and Faculty of Actuaries
www.actuaries.org.uk

Organisation Profile

Institute and Faculty of Actuaries

INSTITUTE AND FACULTY OF ACTUARIES (IFoA)

What do actuaries do?

Actuaries are experts in risk management. They use their mathematical skills to help measure the probability and risk of future events. This information is useful to many industries, including healthcare, pensions, insurance, banking and investments, where a single decision can have a major financial impact. An actuarial career can be one of the most diverse, exciting and rewarding in the world.

Where do actuaries work?

Actuaries provide commercial and financial advice on the management of assets and liabilities – especially where long term management and planning are key. Actuaries work in many areas such as finance and investment, risk management, general and life insurance, pensions and healthcare. Every area of business is subject to risks so an actuarial career offers many options. From working in risk, to retail banks, pension and investment firms there are no limitations to where an actuary can go; they can even be employed in the marketing and development of sophisticated financial products.

What is the salary like?

Salaries and benefit packages are excellent, even for those starting out in their career. In fact it's one of the highest paid professions wherever you go in the world. Trainees earn between £25,000 and £35,000 a year and newly qualified actuaries can earn up to £55,000. In later years, senior actuaries can earn six figure salaries. So despite the hard work, it is a very well rewarded job.

Who should become an actuary?

- A graduate typically with a 2:1 in a numerate subject (others may be suitable)
- Loves logic and problem solving
- Good communicator
- Excellent business acumen

How do you become an actuary?

Studying to become an actuary normally takes around three to six years. The exam programme is flexible, so you can study at your own pace while working for an actuarial employer – many employers give you time off to study. In addition to passing the profession exams, you'll work with your employer to meet the practical work-based skills requirement.

Where can you find out more information?

If you want to find out more about becoming an actuary, visit the IFoA website at www.actuaries.org.uk/becoming-actuary. Or visit our Facebook page, to engage with current student actuaries to discuss your future as an actuary.

International Actuarial Careers Network – IACN

The IACN is a global network of students who belong to an online community hosted on the Institute and Faculty of Actuaries website. Students are able to join together to discuss industry topics, network with students and employers, and find out firsthand what employers and the industry want from them. It is an opportunity to join like minded people to raise your profile within the Actuarial Profession and amongst employers to help you gain relevant industry knowledge and help you in your job search. To find out more about this opportunity see the IACN website: www.actuaries.org.uk/iacn.

Case Study

INSTITUTE AND FACULTY OF ACTUARIES (IFoA)

Institute and Faculty of Actuaries

Name: John Small
Job role: Actuarial Trainee
Company: First Actuarial LLP
Location: Tonbridge, Kent
Course: Actuarial Science
University education: University of Kent

I first heard of First Actuarial in my second year at the University of Kent, when I picked up a copy of the Directory of Actuarial Employers. In my third year, I went to a careers fair organised by the university and spoke to a guy called Tim (who I now sit next to!). He went through with me what they look for in a CV and covering letter.

I was fortunate enough to get invited to two interviews and was then offered the job during February. This gave me time to concentrate on my exams and enjoy my summer, knowing that I had a job lined up. There was obviously a bit of luck in this but if you can put in the legwork during the winter of your final year of university, it can definitely pay off.

Over the last three years I have gone back to the University of Kent for talks and careers fairs, hoping to recruit more graduates.

The biggest change I found when I started work was going from full-time study and part-time work, to full-time work and part-time study. When you start studying for the exams it can be nice having a day out of the office, doing something a bit different from your day-to-day work. However, it can get stressful nearer to the exam when you're spending a lot of time working and studying. An actuarial student needs to be able to work hard to pass the exams but, as long as you are organised and set time aside to study, it will be very rewarding, and you can still have a life at the same time!

Working for a consultancy, communication is a key skill and can be a great asset. If you come into the profession from a mathematical background, there may not have been many opportunities to establish this skill and so any opportunities at university or elsewhere should be taken. I have never been a fan of presenting to people, but I took some opportunities at university to go into local schools and talk about university life and I feel that this really helped me in my interview and has since helped me with my day-to-day work.

As you might expect, there are calculations to do. However, a lot of calculations are similar for different clients. Therefore, we have standard software and spreadsheets set up to do these more quickly.

A major part of what we do involves writing letters and reports. It's all well and good calculating the numbers, but we actually need to tell our clients what these numbers mean for them. To do this, we either use template documents or set them up from scratch. This can be a tricky skill at first, but it becomes easier with practice. An important skill is therefore being able to describe potentially complicated concepts in easy to understand language.

Overall, a consultant is giving advice. Initially, an actuarial student will have little practice of direct contact with clients, but as they get more senior, this becomes more of everyday work. This might involve emails and phone calls, or it might involve more face-to-face meetings.

AUDITOR

ENTRY LEVEL 5

Qualifications and courses

To become either an external or internal auditor you will usually hold a degree in a numerical subject, such as maths or finance. The minimum requirements for a degree vary depending on the institution, however they are usually 2 A levels/3 H grades and 5 GCSEs/National 5s (A*–C/A–C), including Maths and English.

To become an external auditor, you must first qualify as a chartered accountant with one of the main accountancy bodies: the Association of Chartered Certified Accountants (ACCA), the Institute of Chartered Accountants in England and Wales (ICAEW), the Institute of Chartered Accountants of Scotland (ICAS), Chartered Accountants Ireland (CAI) or the Association of International Accountants (AIA). Most students enrolling on these courses are graduates, though there are vocational routes in as well. Graduates will usually study for a professional qualification while working.

The National Audit Office runs an ACA School Leaver Scheme which is a 5-year fast-track scheme for school leavers to qualify as a chartered accountant with the ICAEW. Applicants need to have 5 GCSEs/National 5s (A*–C/A–C) including English and Maths, and a minimum of 300 UCAS points at A level or equivalent.

If you are a member of the Chartered Institute of Public Finance and Accountancy (CIPFA), you can only carry out audits in the public sector. If you have qualified with the Chartered Institute of Management Accountants (CIMA), you can only conduct internal audits unless you take audit training with another accounting body.

Candidates keen to work in internal auditing do not have to be a qualified accountant and can come from a variety of academic backgrounds, though experience in business or finance can be an advantage. Entry is with either a degree or recommendation by an employer and candidates can strengthen their application by taking the Chartered Institute of Internal Auditors' (IIA) Certificate in Internal Audit and Business Risk (IACert).

What the work involves

Specialising in audit work means exploring all aspects of a business, talking to staff and ensuring that the paperwork and accounts give a true picture of the company's finances.

Internal auditors work for a company preparing their accounts for external auditors to check. They are also responsible for assessing other risks, not just finances. Most businesses and government departments must be externally audited by law, with a few exceptions.

As an external auditor you will create an independent report for a company, stating that the accounts are true and accurate and recommending possible improvements to the business.

Type of person suited to this work

You must be happy working with numbers and interpreting statistics and be a thorough and methodical person with the ability to work independently. As you will be using your skills and experience to solve financial problems you need to enjoy researching all aspects of a business.

It is important that you have excellent communication skills so that you can present your findings clearly. You should also be able to work effectively as part of a team and with the company you are auditing. You should be well organised, able to work under pressure, meet deadlines and have excellent IT skills.

Working conditions

Large companies have internal auditors who prepare their accounts for inspection. External auditors are based temporarily in the firms they are auditing, so they may have to travel and stay away from home. A driving licence can be useful.

You will work normal office hours but might have to work evenings and weekends.

Future prospects

There is an increasing demand for qualified auditors. As an internal auditor you could work for a business or government department, work for yourself or as a consultant.

External auditors are employed by accountancy firms, the National Audit Office (the Accounts Commission in Scotland) auditing central government departments, or the Audit Commission working with public sector organisations such as local authorities or the NHS.

Advantages/disadvantages

Accountancy training takes 3–6 years and involves studying in your own time.

There are opportunities to work abroad during a secondment.

Money guide

Trainees on the National Audit Office's ACA School Leaver Scheme earn £22,274 per year if based in London or £16,973 if based in Newcastle.

Graduates and part-qualified auditors can earn £18,000–£25,000 a year during training, which could rise to £30,000–£45,000 once you are qualified.

A senior auditor can earn £50,000–£90,000. Audit directors or head auditors could potentially earn up to £150,000.

Related opportunities

- Actuary p5
- Chartered/Company Secretary p12
- Financial Adviser p26

Further information

Association of Chartered Certified Accountants
www.accaglobal.com/uk

Chartered Institute of Internal Auditors
www.iia.org.uk

Chartered Institute of Management Accountants
www.cimaglobal.com

BANK CASHIER/CUSTOMER ADVISER

ENTRY LEVEL 1

Qualifications and courses

Different employers have different entry requirements for this profession. Some may ask for a minimum of 4 GCSEs/National 5s (A*–C/A–C) including English and Maths. Others may not ask for qualifications but require you to pass an entry test upon application. Once employed you will take part in your employer's in-house training scheme and learn on the job.

Other useful qualifications include City & Guilds Award in Customer Service (Levels 1, 2 and 3), City & Guilds Certificate/Diploma in Business and Administration (Levels 2 and 3), the *ifs* Level 3 Diploma in Financial Studies, BTEC Nationals in Business or Personal and Business Finance, and the CCN Professional Bankers qualifications (Level 3).

Any customer service experience would be an advantage, as would cash handling experience and basic computer skills in any work environment. You can also enter this career by completing the Intermediate Level Apprenticeship in Providing Financial Services.

Employees will normally be required to undergo Disclosure and Barring Service (DBS) background checks.

What the work involves

Bank cashiers/customer advisers work for banks and building societies, and are the first point of contact for customers with enquiries or complaints.

You may be working in a branch dealing with customers face to face, or you could be based in a contact centre liaising with them over the phone or by email.

You will be handling customers' accounts, including the paying in and withdrawing of money using computerised systems. You will also be expected to sell the company's products and services, which will involve working to set sales targets.

Type of person suited to this work

You will need excellent customer service skills so that you can process customers' requests efficiently, and also gain their trust in order to advise them on a range of financial products.

You must be confident working with figures and IT, and working to targets. As you will be handling money, you should be trustworthy and able to work accurately, paying close attention to detail.

Since you will be working as part of a team, a helpful and positive attitude coupled with the ability to use your own initiative is valuable.

Working conditions

In a branch you will probably work normal office hours, and Saturdays if the bank is open. Call centres usually offer a 24-hour service, so you should expect to work shifts that include nights and weekends.

Part-time and flexible working hours are commonly available.

You should be well presented, and will usually be required to wear a uniform.

Future prospects

Despite the recent economic downturn, which has affected some areas of the financial sector, there are still opportunities in retail banking available, especially at entry level. Research suggests that there will be a growing demand for skilled people in all areas of customer service and relationship management. There has also been growth in Islamic banking.

You could progress to specialise in an area such as mortgages or pensions or into management, or gain further professional qualifications in order to train as a financial adviser or bank manager. Some banks offer internal fast-track management programmes. You might also be able to go into corporate or investment banking.

Advantages/disadvantages

Looking after customers and helping to solve their queries can be interesting and rewarding.

Banks offer well-structured training programmes on entry and you will have a clear route for career progression.

Due to the economic downturn, entry into this profession is more competitive than ever before.

Money guide

The starting salary for a trainee ranges between £12,000 and £18,000 a year. Apprentices can expect to earn between £11,000 and £15,000 once qualified.

With several years' experience and supervisory responsibilities you could be earning between £18,000 and £30,000 a year.

You may also receive bonuses for meeting sales targets and employers often offer packages that include cheaper mortgages, pensions, loans, shares and insurance.

Related opportunities

- Bank Manager p10
- Financial Adviser p26
- Pensions Adviser p41

Further information

***ifs* University College**
www.ifslearning.ac.uk

Financial Skills Partnership
www.financialskillspartnership.org.uk

BANK MANAGER

ENTRY LEVEL 1

Qualifications and courses

There are 3 main ways to become a bank manager. One is to join a bank or building society's graduate management scheme. These usually last 18–24 months and competition is high, so you will need at least a 2.2 Honours degree (some banks require a 2.1 Honours degree), ideally in business, finance, management or marketing. If you wish to apply to an international bank a foreign language qualification could be advantageous. Degree courses will usually require at least 2 A levels/3 H grades and 5 GCSEs/National 5s (A*–C/A–C). Pre-entry work experience can also help you get on a graduate scheme.

Another way to become a bank manager is by internal promotion from a customer service role via an in-house management training programme. Many banks have fast-track programmes. You will obviously need good job performance to be eligible for this, including supervisory experience, a good track record in meeting sales targets and the right drive and commitment.

A third way is, once you have completed the Advanced Apprenticeship in Providing Financial Services, progressing onto the Level 4 Higher Apprenticeship in Banking which will enable you to learn the management and leadership skills necessary for a bank manager position.

Qualifications studied part time from the Institute of Financial Services' School of Finance or the Chartered Banker Institute can also be useful.

Disclosure and Barring Service (DBS) checks and bankruptcy checks will normally be carried out.

What the work involves

Bank managers are responsible for running branches of retail, commercial or corporate banks. You will be accountable for staff recruitment, motivation and training, as well as meeting budget and sales targets for products and services.

You will be required to keep up to date with a range of financial products, and market your services to individuals and businesses.

Attending meetings and preparing reports on branch operations for both staff and head office will also be important tasks.

Type of person suited to this work

Bank managers work with people at all levels, so excellent verbal and written communications skills are essential.

You will be expected to deal with customers on a daily basis, as well as leading and motivating your team, both of which require confidence, organisation, negotiation skills, initiative and the ability to think on your feet.

You should be comfortable working with numbers as you will have to meet budget and sales targets, and calculate profits.

Working conditions

You will usually work normal office hours and occasional Saturdays, in keeping with the opening hours of your bank. If you manage a call centre, you will probably be required to work shifts in order to provide a 24-hour service to customers.

As well as working in an office, you will occasionally travel to visit clients at their business premises, so a driving licence could be useful.

Future prospects

Despite recent bank mergers and closures, branch management positions are still available. From branch manager you could progress to area and regional manager, and then into operations management or other areas such as risk or compliance. Sometimes you may be expected to relocate to other areas, usually within the UK. You may also move banks in order to progress.

More and more managers are completing technical qualifications for regulated financial products from organisations such as the *ifs* University College, the Chartered Institute of Bankers in Scotland and the Chartered Insurance Institute.

London is one of the leading financial centres of the world and offers the best opportunities for pursuing a high-level career. There are also numerous roles located overseas.

Advantages/disadvantages

This challenging, fast-moving industry offers roles in various sectors such as telephone and internet banking.

Most towns have bank branches so there are opportunities to work throughout the UK.

You will need to meet challenging targets in an increasingly competitive market which is sensitive to changes in the national and global economy.

Money guide

Graduates on bank management training schemes can make £18,000 to £24,000 a year. With extra training and experience this can increase to £26,000–£40,000.

Senior staff, such as branch managers, can earn salaries of £40,000–£60,000. Regional and head office managers may make in excess of £70,000.

You may also receive bonuses for meeting targets with additional benefits usually including cheaper mortgages, pensions, loans and insurance.

Related opportunities

- Accountant p2
- Bank Cashier/Customer Adviser p9
- Financial Adviser p26
- Insurance Broker p29

Further information

***ifs* University College**
www.ifslearning.ac.uk

Chartered Banker Institute
www.charteredbanker.com

BUSINESS ADVISER

ENTRY LEVEL 3

Qualifications and courses

There are no specific entry qualifications but advisers must have a proven track record in business. Many advisers have prior experience running a business or working as a management consultant. Others have expertise in a key area of business, such as project management, marketing, human resources or finance.

Employers are generally more interested in your experience than your qualifications; however, you may want to start off with GCSEs/National 5s and A levels/H grades in applied business or business studies before gaining practical experience in the industry. Business-related degree courses and diplomas that include a year in the industry may also be helpful.

The Institute of Consulting and the Chartered Management Institute provide various entry-level qualifications for those wishing to start a career as a consultant or adviser, such as Level 5 in Professional Consulting, Level 5 in Business Support and Level 7 in Professional Consulting.

Further business support and mentoring qualifications are provided by the Small Firms Enterprise Development Initiative (SFEDI) and include the Level 3 Certificate in Enterprise Coaching and the Level 3 and 4 Award/Certificate in Enterprise Mentoring.

You will be required to purchase professional indemnity insurance before becoming a business adviser.

What the work involves

Business advisers provide independent advice to an array of small- and medium-sized businesses or enterprises in order to improve their success.

You will provide advice on prospective business plans and recommend relevant specialist services and suppliers that could support the venture. You may run workshops and seminars that offer basic support and information for new or existing businesses.

You will need to be informed about numerous areas of business but you will often choose to specialise in a specific area, such as marketing and public relations (PR), accountancy and taxation or law.

Type of person suited to this work

You will need to have a good understanding of a variety of business environments and sizes. You must be able to use your knowledge to offer advice on current business issues, geographical trends and financial help available to support new or failing businesses.

You need to be logical and objective, yet approachable and enthusiastic. You will need the ability to manage a variety of projects whilst consistently meeting tight deadlines.

Working conditions

Hours tend to follow the national average of between 37 and 40 hours a week, working 9am–5.30pm, Monday to Friday. Occasionally you might be required to attend weekend or evening events.

You will be mostly office based, with occasional visits to clients' premises, suppliers or networking events. If you became a self-employed consultant then you would have the opportunity to work from home.

Future prospects

You can take further training throughout your career to enhance your prospects, such as an Institute of Consulting Certificate or Diploma in Business or a postgraduate course in Business Coaching and Mentoring.

If you take an IC qualification you automatically become a member. After 2 years' experience, members can choose to be assessed for the Certified Business Adviser Award and after 3 years they can apply for the Certified Management Consultant (CMC) Award. These give you independent recognition for your skills and competence.

Advisers with a Diploma in Business or the CMC Award can join the National Register for Business Support Professionals.

Business advisers can progress first to team manager and then to senior management positions, or else specialise in a particular area of business. They can also go on to become a self-employed consultant.

Advantages/disadvantages

Employment as a business adviser enables you to work autonomously and use your initiative.

You will work on a variety of projects and have the opportunity to build relationships with a range of people.

It is necessary to have a wealth of business experience before you can become a business adviser.

It is important to gain recognised awards, such as those offered by the Institute of Consulting, in order to prove to clients that you are a certified adviser.

Money guide

Business advisers can expect a starting salary of £20,000 a year. After several years' experience, salaries increase to around £35,000.

Those in senior positions can expect £50,000 or more.

Self-employed freelancers charge a daily rate, which could be between £150 and £500 a day.

Related opportunities

- Company Director p15
- Management Consultant p37
- Project Manager p43

Further information

Chartered Management Institute
www.managers.org.uk

Institute of Consulting
www.iconsulting.org.uk

National Enterprise Network
www.nationalenterprisenetwork.org

CHARTERED/COMPANY SECRETARY

ENTRY LEVEL 5

Qualifications and courses

While not required by law, the majority of companies will want someone with a degree, Foundation degree, HNC/HND or equivalent. At least 1 A level/2 H grades and 4 GCSEs/National 5s (A*–C/A–C) or equivalent are required for entry onto an HNC/HND course, while degree courses require 2 A levels/3 H grades and 5 GCSEs/National 5s (A*–C/A–C). This sector is open to all graduates but entrants with degrees in business, law, accountancy, politics or administration are preferred. A postgraduate degree is not necessary but could be useful.

Substantial relevant experience is essential to this role and it is possible to gain further qualifications if interested in becoming the secretary of a public company for which a registration with the Institute of Chartered Secretaries and Administrators(ICSA) is necessary. This is achieved by either completing the ICSA's Chartered Secretaries Qualifying Scheme (CSQS) or by undertaking an ICSA-approved postgraduate course.

The CSQS typically takes 1–3 years to complete and has 2 levels, each with 4 modules. Previous qualifications may lead to automatic exemption from some CSQS modules; you will need to consult the website for more details. When you complete CSQS you automatically become a graduate member of the ICSA. To become a full member at associate level you will need at least 3–6 years' further work experience, depending on whether or not you have a degree. You are eligible to become a Fellow of the institute when you reach a senior level and have 8 years' work experience.

What the work involves

This is a vital administrative and managerial role. You will have a high level of responsibility. You will be in a very senior position advising executives and directors on finance and company law.

You will be responsible for the legal reports all companies are required to keep, reporting to Companies House and other institutions such as the Stock Exchange.

You will be responsible for running board meetings and could be responsible for financial planning, accounts, wages, human resources and all administrative and IT systems.

Type of person suited to this work

You will need excellent communication skills to be able to work with people at all levels. You should be interested in business and have a thorough knowledge of how your organisation works. You will need to understand complicated legal and financial issues and be able to use your knowledge to solve problems, maximise efficiency and advise ways of improving and developing the company.

You should be highly organised, able to deal with several tasks at once and pay close attention to detail. You will analyse figures and accounts and work to strict legal guidelines. You must be confident giving presentations to high-level staff.

Working conditions

Most of your work will be office based, attending lots of meetings, including working at other sites and outside organisations, which could involve some travel and possibly going abroad.

You will normally work office hours but will have a heavy workload and a lot of responsibility; you will need commitment and dedication to work overtime and meet deadlines.

To be successful, a high level of personal and professional integrity is important.

Future prospects

The Companies Act 2008 means that private companies are no longer legally required to have a company or chartered secretary. Despite this change, businesses will still have to meet a range of legal requirements so most will continue to employ one.

An experienced company secretary will have opportunities to work in highly paid jobs in a range of organisations. Some move into senior management, some change to other sectors such as law and finance, and some go on to become a self-employed consultant or company formation agent. Further opportunities are within the public, voluntary and charity sectors, local and central government and educational institutions.

Advantages/disadvantages

This is a high-level career which is interesting, varied and challenging. You will use a wide range of skills and knowledge, prospects are good and earnings can be high. But you will have to take on a lot of responsibility and work long hours; you might have to prepare information for directors if the company is doing badly.

Money guide

Salaries vary depending on the job role, type of organisation and location.

A company secretarial assistant can earn between £35,000 and £55,000 per year. Senior company secretaries earn about £70,000.

Once fully qualified, a chartered secretary working in the private sector can achieve a salary of £100,000 to £150,000.

Experienced secretaries working for FTSE100 companies can earn up to £320,000.

Additionally, 68% of company secretaries receive annual bonuses.

Related opportunities

- Accountant p2
- Barrister/Advocate p341
- Company Director p15

Further information

Companies House
www.companieshouse.gov.uk

Institute of Chartered Secretaries and Administrators
www.icsa.org.uk

Skills CFA
www.skillscfa.org

CIVIL SERVICE ADMINISTRATIVE OFFICER

ENTRY LEVEL 2

Qualifications and courses

Each department within the civil service organises its own recruitment and sets its own entry requirements so you will need to consult each job description carefully when applying. Some departments do not require specific qualifications and instead prefer applicants to take aptitude tests in areas such as teamwork, communication skills or numeracy. You should also expect to be assessed on skills, competencies, knowledge and behaviour that fit in with the values of the civil service. Generally, administrative officers will need at least 5 GCSEs/National 5s (A*–C/A–C), including Maths and English with many applicants having 2 or more A levels/H grades or a degree.

Previous experience of clerical work is helpful.

A Civil Service Fast Stream scheme is open to all graduates, which allows a more focused and rapid career progression from administrative to management level.

To work for the civil service you will need to be a British national, a Commonwealth citizen or a national of the member states within the European Economic Area.

What the work involves

Administrative officers will often be the 'face' of a government department or agency, dealing with members of the public over the phone, via email, or in person. You may also be charged with reviewing and acting on recent cases, in accordance to the departmental rules and regulations.

You will often work alongside administrative assistants to research relevant information for your department, deal with paperwork (filing, photocopying, etc), update information on the department's general records and process benefit payments.

Civil service administrative officers will work either for specific national government departments, such as planning or environmental, or within the central administrative, policy and support services. If you work in local government, you are more likely to work across a range of areas such as leisure, environment and public health.

There are also some opportunities in departments such as human resources, neighbourhood renewal, social justice and European and international relations.

Type of person suited to this work

You will need excellent organisational skills as you will be responsible for administering numerous important projects at a time. The ability to use your initiative, prioritise your workload, and work on your own are also essential.

A high level of accuracy and attention to detail is required in order to keep good records and produce clear correspondence.

Since you will be liaising with team members and the public daily, excellent verbal and written communication skills are vital. You will also need to have an understanding of some specialist terminology.

Working conditions

You will mainly be office based, working normal office hours during the week, though some offices may operate a flexitime policy. Part-time, temporary work and job-sharing opportunities are widely available and you may be based in an office that is open to the public.

Future prospects

Although job opportunities may be affected by recent budget cuts to local government authorities, the civil service has an established training programme and a clear promotion structure that is based on merit. You will have several weeks of in-depth training when you start your job and may get the chance to take nationally recognised work-based qualifications such as NVQs in Business and Administration, and Customer Service. You will have access to in-house training and development throughout your career.

Progression is usually from administrative assistant to administrative officer, then to executive officer and beyond.

Advantages/disadvantages

Public sector work offers good holidays, flexible working hours and excellent perks.

Even without advanced qualifications there are opportunities to progress into higher level jobs.

In the initial stages of employment and training, work can be repetitive.

Money guide

You will often progress to an administrative officer from the position of an administrative assistant who start with an annual salary of £12,000 to £14,000 per year.

Administrative officers can expect to start with a salary of around £15,000 a year, rising to £20,000 with experience.

Typical salaries for middle management roles can range from £29,000 to £42,500.

Graduates on the Civil Service Fast Stream scheme receive a starting salary between £25,000 and £27,000. Increases in pay are based upon performance and if you are promoted, which generally takes about 4–5 years, graduates may earn over £45,000.

Related opportunities

- Personal Assistant p42
- Project Manager p43
- Secretary p50

Further information

Civil Service Fast Stream
www.faststream.civilservice.gov.uk

Local Government Association
www.local.gov.uk

CIVIL SERVICE EXECUTIVE OFFICER

ENTRY LEVEL 2

Qualifications and courses

Entrants may be recruited directly at executive level or can work their way up from the administrative grade. Entry requirements vary between the different departments and agencies so you should examine each job description carefully. Some departments require 2 A levels/3 H grades while others do not ask for formal qualifications but prefer to rely on performance in aptitude tests and interviews.

Prospective employees will be invited to attend an interview and may be required to complete a range of tests designed to highlight ability in numeracy, communication, interpersonal, decision-making and analytical skills. You will mainly be assessed on whether your natural values fall in line with those associated with the civil service.

Candidates who hold a 1st or 2nd class Honours degree can apply for the 4-year Civil Service Fast Stream scheme which allows a more focused and rapid career progression from administrative to management level. Applicants from all degree disciplines will be considered although some departments may prefer subjects relevant to their work. Competition for this scheme is fierce and you must pass a series of tests and interviews.

To work for the civil service you will need to be a British national, a Commonwealth citizen or a national of the member states within the European Economic Area.

What the work involves

There are around 170 different civil service departments and agencies you could be placed in, with each offering a different service and following different policies. A civil service executive officer helps to manage these departments in accordance with the government policies they adhere to.

Civil service executive officers will manage a small team of administrative officers and are expected to apply complex governmental policies and procedures to individual cases, enquiries or complaints, managing the expectations of and offering advice to the general public.

You will often have to prepare and present reports on specific projects and communicate regularly with senior managers.

Type of person suited to this work

You should have a neutral interest in governmental affairs, and enjoy providing a service to members of the public. You will need to understand government legislation and be able to explain it clearly to others.

Those wishing to become executive officers should have excellent management, leadership and communication skills, as much of the work requires liaising with your team and different departments.

Much of the information that you will be coming into contact with is of a confidential nature and so you must be appreciative of privacy rules.

Working conditions

Civil servants usually work between 35 and 37 hours a week, Monday to Friday, although hours may increase during busier periods. There are flexitime schemes in place for all government employees, which allow staff to work overtime to gain extra holiday time. Currently, 20% of employees work part time and job shares are also widely available.

These positions are office based, but it is occasionally necessary for executive officers to visit members of the public or organisations.

Future prospects

The civil service is committed to training and you will learn both on the job from more experienced staff and also from in-house training courses. Your individual training needs will be identified and your skills will be developed.

There is also a clearly defined promotion structure which is based on merit. Executive officers may work their way up through junior to middle management and then on to more senior roles. When an employee joins the civil service through the Fast Stream entry plan, promotion is often awarded after 3–5 years.

If an executive officer has at least 2 years of experience and was not employed through the Fast Stream service, they are eligible to be nominated as an applicant to the In-service Fast Stream system.

Advantages/disadvantages

There are various promotion opportunities on offer, alongside rewarding salaries and the opportunity to help members of the public.

Limited budgets sometimes mean an increased workload when colleagues go on leave or progress to other positions and funds are not available for their replacement.

Money guide

Starting salaries are £21,000–£24,000, depending on which department you work within, rising to around £30,000 with experience.

Those on the Civil Service Fast Stream scheme will commence their career with a salary of £25,000 to £27,000. After 4–5 years' service, candidates should expect a salary of £45,000.

All employees of the civil service receive a variety of benefits, such as a pension scheme and discounts on sports and social facilities.

Related opportunities

- Civil Service Administrative Officer p13
- Diplomatic Services Operational Officer p19
- Project Manager p43
- Quality Manager p44

Further information

Civil Service Fast Stream
www.faststream.civilservice.gov.uk

COMPANY DIRECTOR

ENTRY LEVEL 2

Qualifications and courses

There is no set route to becoming a company director but you will usually need experience at senior management level. You could enter the company at any level and then as you gain qualifications and work experience, you can progress up to management roles and eventually become company director. Alternatively, people who set up their own company may be appointed as director at the time their company is registered.

Entrants often have a degree, either in a business related subject or a specialist subject relevant to the company's business area. After completing a degree or Level 3 qualifications, candidates could start on a management trainee scheme.

The Institute of Directors (IOD) and the Chartered Management Institute (CMI) offer courses for the professional development of managers. The CMI offers both apprenticeships and higher level qualifications. The Certificate in Company Direction is one of the many courses available at the IOD.

What the work involves

As company director you will have responsibility for every aspect of your business. You will be responsible for setting the company's aims and policies and ensuring that it achieves these as efficiently as possible.

You might own the company or head a board of directors. In a large company you will probably lead a team of managers who specialise in specific areas such as sales, finance or product development but you will have overall responsibility.

Type of person suited to this work

The ability to analyse problems, find solutions, make decisions and think through their long-term effects is vital. You will need excellent communication skills to motivate staff and help sell your ideas, products and services to your customers and investors.

You should be highly motivated and prepared to work long hours. You must be able to prioritise, work to deadlines, supervise others, take advice and respond to change.

An excellent knowledge and understanding of your business and its markets will be necessary to make your company successful.

Although you will probably be advised by a team of experienced and knowledgeable managers, you will make the final decision and must be prepared to take risks and accept consequences.

Working conditions

You will probably be office based but will attend a lot of meetings with customers, financial and legal advisers and staff. You should be prepared to work long hours and to travel in the UK and abroad.

Future prospects

Once you are at manager level, you can take professional courses to develop your skills and become a member of the IOD. IOD members may become qualified as Chartered Directors. There is the opportunity for progression to chief executive and then chair of an organisation. You could also become a part-time non-executive director for other organisations.

If you are successful, there is no limit to what you can achieve.

Advantages/disadvantages

You can get enormous rewards and satisfaction from seeing the company grow and succeed.

You could start your own business based on a personal interest or skill.

You will have huge responsibility and need to be dedicated, hard-working and able to cope with failure as well as success.

Money guide

Earnings will vary enormously depending on the size and success of the business though salaries tend to be higher in London.

Directors can earn anything between £50,000 and £1.5 million a year plus huge bonuses and share options.

Related opportunities

- Accountant p2
- Financial Adviser p26
- Management Consultant p37

Further information

Chartered Management Institute
www.managers.org.uk

Institute of Directors
www.iod.com

COMPLIANCE OFFICER

ENTRY LEVEL 5

Qualifications and courses

While there are no set qualifications for this profession, most employers prefer candidates with a relevant degree and a background in accountancy, auditing or law. Professional qualifications in investments, insurance or banking are also useful. Entry requirements for financial degree programmes vary but are usually a minimum of 2 A levels/3 H grades and 5 GCSEs/National 5s (A*–C/A–C), including Maths and English.

There are a number of professional bodies that offer relevant qualifications, including the Chartered Insurance Institute's (CII) Award/Certificate/Diploma/Advanced Diploma in Financial Planning and the *ifs* University College's Level 3 Certificate for Financial Advisers or Level 4 Diploma for Financial Advisers. Several compliance qualifications are also available through the International Compliance Association (ICA). These vary from short introductory courses to a BSc degree in Management with Compliance.

The Financial Conduct Authority (FCA) offers 6 graduate programmes. The main Graduate Development programme has an intake of 40 to 50 graduates per year and requires a 2.1 degree in any subject, 300 UCAS points and the unrestricted right to work in the UK.

Many employers offer in-house training programmes. Trainees will work under the supervision of an experienced colleague, whilst gaining qualifications through part-time study or via distance learning.

What the work involves

Compliance officers work for financial services organisations, and are responsible for aiding senior management in ensuring that their firm is complying with the rules set by the FCA.

Alongside this you will investigate complaints from clients that relate to possible breaches of these rules.

You will explore the ways in which business efficiency can be improved within the FCA rules through the monitoring of sales processes, checking of paperwork and telephone recordings.

Type of person suited to this work

You will need to have an enquiring, analytical mind, enjoy analysing information and be interested in the legal aspects of selling financial products.

It is important that you are an easily approachable person with good communication skills and excellent report writing skills.

The job may be quite demanding and so you should be able to work well under pressure and be capable of working on a variety of projects at one time, whilst remaining organised and informed.

Working conditions

Compliance officers are generally office based, with attendance at meetings being a regular occurrence. They might have to travel around the country, or even overseas for an international company.

Generally, a compliance officer will work in the region of 37 hours a week, 9am to 5pm, Monday to Friday. However, changes to FCA policy may mean that extra hours need to be worked in order to implement changes.

Future prospects

Competition for FCA training posts is high, however you will be entering one of the fastest growing areas in financial services. There are around 9,000 compliance officers in the UK and many other positions involved with compliance, which highlights that the future is alive with prospects.

There are financial services companies in almost every town but most jobs are concentrated in the major financial centres, such as London, Manchester, Birmingham, Norwich, Bristol, Edinburgh and Glasgow.

As you progress within this role you will have the opportunity to experience greater levels of responsibility and roles within management.

Advantages/disadvantages

There are chances for progression within this vocation and opportunities to work from home as a consultant.

You may feel under pressure at times and will often be asked to explain changes to the financial system in a clear and concise way.

Money guide

Trainees or junior officers generally start at between £18,000 and £30,000 a year. The FCA Graduate Development Programme has a starting salary of £29,000 plus a £2,500 joining bonus and other benefits.

With experience compliance officers may earn between £30,000 and £60,000 a year. A head of compliance may earn up to £70,000.

Related opportunities

- Auditor p8
- Financial Adviser p26
- Risk Manager p49

Further information

***ifs* University College**
www.ifslearning.ac.uk

Association of Professional Compliance Consultants
www.apcc.org.uk

Chartered Insurance Institute
www.cii.co.uk

International Compliance Association
www.int-comp.org

CREDIT ANALYST

ENTRY LEVEL 6

Qualifications and courses

Credit analysts will usually have a degree (preferably a 2.1 Honours degree or higher) or HND and enter the profession through a graduate training scheme. Degree courses that include a high level of numerical content are often preferred, such as economics, finance, maths, accounting and statistics.

In order to be accepted onto one of the above degree courses, prospective students will need at least 5 GCSEs/National 5s (A*–C/A–C) and 2 A levels/3 H grades. However, most degree courses will ask for qualifications above this minimum suggestion.

Entry without a degree or HND is possible but generally larger companies will prioritise graduates in their selection process. Professional qualifications in areas such as accountancy will improve career prospects, as can experience in finance or insurance. Professional bodies that offer relevant qualifications include the *ifs* University College, the Chartered Financial Analyst Institute (CFA) and the Institute of Credit Management (ICM).

Competition for places is fierce as enhanced regulations and the more risk-aware banking sector invest heavily within risk analysis. Therefore pre-entry commercial experience and a relevant postgraduate qualification, such as an MSc in Risk Management, may improve chances of employment.

Once in employment, credit analysts are expected to take part in continuing professional development (CPD), which will involve reading relevant journals and undertaking skills-related courses.

What the work involves

Credit analysts deal with both personal and business credit. They assess the individual circumstances of the application, using statistical and accounting criteria in order to decide the extent of the risk involved when lending.

Much of the work involves administration and figure work, due to a need for the analysis of given data and the writing of reports and presentations.

To thoroughly assess an application, an analyst must have an understanding of legal, compliance and business issues. For instance, a business application would be considered against economic growth and the country's financial stability.

Type of person suited to this work

You should have an interest in the financial sector and have a general and varied knowledge of the business world. Much of the work deals with statistics and so analysts need computer skills and the ability to work with spreadsheets and specialist statistical software packages.

You need to have good organisational and both verbal and written communication skills so that you can explain concepts to non-specialists.

Working conditions

Daily working hours are from 9am to 5pm, Monday to Friday. There may be times when you will be required to work extra hours. However, there are also opportunities for part-time working.

Generally, credit analysts are based in offices, with much of their work involving computer-based activities and the monitoring of the financial markets, with the occasional need to present changes in the market to senior staff.

Future prospects

This profession holds many avenues for promotion or progression into other areas of banking. Prospects may be improved by professional qualifications. Many of the larger commercial and investment banks have graduate or career training programmes. There may also be the option to undertake higher-level qualifications such as a master's degree.

Most opportunities are available in London, West Yorkshire, Cardiff and Scottish cities.

Advantages/disadvantages

There are many opportunities for promotion and progression within this career.

Salaries tend to be very rewarding.

Credit analysts must be able to handle high levels of pressure and responsibility as they often have to make difficult decisions about awarding or denying credit.

Money guide

Credit analysts usually receive a starting salary of £22,000 to £25,000 a year.

Salaries rise to between £29,000 and £44,000 per year, with up to 6 years' experience.

A senior analyst or risk manager for a major corporation may earn up to £90,000.

Additional benefits could include monetary bonuses, subsidised mortgages, pensions and private healthcare.

Related opportunities

- Bank Manager p10
- Economist p20
- Insurance Broker p29

Further information

***ifs* University College**
www.ifslearning.ac.uk

Chartered Financial Analyst Institute
www.cfainstitute.org

Financial Skills Partnership
www.financialskillspartnership.org.uk

DEBT COLLECTOR

ENTRY LEVEL 2

Qualifications and courses

This role does not require specific qualifications as debt collectors normally train on the job. However, employers may look for GCSEs/National 5s (A*–C/A–C) in English and Maths.

Though it is not essential in this line of work, a degree with an element of credit management, such as business studies or finance, could be useful if you want to progress to management roles. For degree entry you will need at least 2 A levels/3 H grades and 5 GCSEs/ National 5s (A*–C/A–C) or equivalent.

Prospective debt collectors could take credit management training courses to enhance their employability. The Institute of Credit Management (ICM) offers short courses on cash collection, the psychology of a debtor and legal actions as well as the Level 4 Diploma in Credit Management which awards participants with first year membership of the Association of Credit Professionals. CILEx offers a Level 4 Diploma in Debt Recovery and Insolvency and the Credit Services Association (CSA) offers Awards/Certificates/Diplomas in Debt Collection. These courses include information on how to deal with abusive debtors and telephone collection techniques.

What the work involves

Debt collectors are employed to recover assets for the organisation that is owed the money. The debtor is firstly contacted by letter or telephone, they then receive a personal visit should this not work, and are finally contacted by a solicitor if the matter remains unresolved.

The 5 areas of specialism include consumer debt collection, commercial debt collection, international collection, legal collection and debtor tracing.

Specific activities include helping debtors by arranging payment through instalments and becoming involved with debt collections that have entered the legal system.

Type of person suited to this work

The job of a debt collector can often be challenging and sometimes confrontational, so a person entering this profession needs to be resilient, determined and skilled in all forms of communication. Empathy with the debtor's situation is required at times and is often just as important as assertiveness and the ability to negotiate a suitable solution for both parties.

Debt collectors require commercial awareness and an understanding of consumer and credit law, should they be involved in legal collections. Knowledge of the financial and credit industries, and numeracy and IT skills will also be of benefit.

Working conditions

Commercial debt collectors work from 9am to 5pm, Monday to Friday. It may sometimes be necessary to work extra hours, in this case in order to meet monthly collection targets.

In comparison, consumer debt collectors may work from 8am to 9pm, Monday to Saturday. However, these hours are usually part of a flexible shift system.

Most debt collectors will be office based and work in teams; in comparison field agents are often based at home and are self-employed, often visiting debtors' homes or places of work.

Future prospects

You will be entering an ever increasing profession that employs around 10,000 people, with employment opportunities existing throughout the UK.

Due to the UK being a capitalist, consumer society, overdue debt is a constant problem, with this allowing for good opportunities in the future of debt collecting.

This is one of few professions that will benefit from the current economic crisis.

Advantages/disadvantages

The job can often be confrontational and challenging, with consumer debt collectors sometimes working unsociable hours.

You may be working with clients who are quite emotional or aggressive which could create an uncomfortable working environment on occasion.

However, the salary is often rewarding and helping debtors arrange more manageable repayments can often be gratifying.

Money guide

The average starting wage for a debt collector is about £14,000 a year.

As you gain experience, your salary can increase to £25,000.

If debt collectors become self-employed and establish a successful business, they can earn in excess of £35,000 a year.

Debt collectors employed by a company can receive target-related bonuses or commission on top of basic salaries.

Related opportunities

- Bailiff/Enforcement Agent p340
- Debt Counsellor/Money Advice Caseworker p548
- Financial Adviser p26

Further information

Credit Management Training Ltd
www.cmtltd.co.uk

Credit Services Association
www.csa-uk.com

Institute of Credit Management
www.icm.org.uk

DIPLOMATIC SERVICES OPERATIONAL OFFICER

ENTRY LEVEL 6

Qualifications and courses

Operational posts within the Foreign and Commonwealth Office (FCO) are available to those with a minimum of a 2.2 Honours degree and candidates from all degree disciplines are considered. Entry onto a degree course usually requires a minimum of 2 A levels/3 H grades and 5 GCSEs/National 5s (A*–C/A–C). Entry with an HND only is not possible. Many entrants have a pre-entry postgraduate qualification, although this is also not essential.

All applicants into the Diplomatic Services must be British citizens and meet the FCO's residency requirements. You must be prepared to be placed anywhere in the world, pass a medical, and a stringent security vetting process which could take up to 9 months. As the job involves working abroad, language skills are beneficial but not essential.

One way to enter the FCO is through the graduate Civil Service Fast Stream scheme as a Policy Entrant. The application process has various stages which involve aptitude tests, assessment centres and interviews and opens for applications in mid-September. Competition for places on the scheme is tough so it is worth being persistent and applying again if you are unsuccessful. Previous applications will not be taken into account.

For the European Fast Stream, which will prepare you to work for the EU, you will also need French or German at A level/H grade (A–C). If you want to apply for a diplomatic placement within the Government Economic Service (GES), you must have a minimum of a 2.1 Honours degree in an economics-based subject.

What the work involves

Candidates on the Civil Service Fast Stream for Diplomatic Service will spend their first 2 years working at the Foreign and Commonwealth Office in the UK. The role involves delivering policy and delivering services. You could spend your time dealing with security issues, working to improve human rights abroad or assisting British citizens who are overseas.

Candidates will then work abroad, in one of the 200+ British embassies, for a 3–4 year posting. You will promote British interests overseas, providing advice and support to ministers developing UK foreign policy in many areas including politics and commerce.

For school leavers interested in joining the FCO, there are opportunities to work as an administrative assistant (providing clerical support) or an executive assistant (drafting letters, handling accounts and invoices, and providing clerical support).

Type of person suited to this work

An interest in foreign policy and international issues is essential, as is a willingness to work abroad.

You will need to have excellent organisational and communication skills and be able to prioritise conflicting tasks and deadlines.

You will need to be highly literate and numeracy is important for posts where you will be handling accounts. Strong customer service and IT skills are also essential.

It would be an advantage to speak another language or have the ability to learn new languages.

Working conditions

You work in the UK for the first few years of your career and then have the opportunity to work in various different countries. Most new entrants will be based in the FCO's London office, though there are some positions in Milton Keynes.

Approximately two-thirds of your career will be spent abroad and overseas postings will often last 3–4 years.

You would generally work normal office hours (9am to 5pm, Monday to Friday) but if you are working overseas these may vary according to the culture of the country.

Future prospects

Promotions are based on performance. Working in the Fast Stream Programme, you could reach senior management in as little as 4–5 years.

The British government is currently encouraging and promoting career opportunities for British Citizens at EU level.

Advantages/disadvantages

The government provides good benefit schemes and officers receive a range of allowances such as rent-free accommodation and travel expenses when posted abroad.

The regular hours in the UK allow for a good work–life balance.

You will have the opportunity to live in many different countries and cultures, although frequent relocation could be disruptive to family life.

Money guide

Administrative officers will start on £19,437 a year whereas an operational officer's starting salary will be around £22,000 per year.

Policy officers and graduates recruited from the Civil Service Fast Stream receive a starting salary of £25,000 to £27,000.

Salaries are often performance related.

Related opportunities

- Civil Service Administrative Officer p13
- Civil Service Executive Officer p14
- Politician p355

Further information

Civil Service Fast Stream
www.faststream.civilservice.gov.uk

Foreign and Commonwealth Office
www.fco.gov.uk

ECONOMIST

ENTRY LEVEL 6

Qualifications and courses

Candidates with a Foundation degree or HND only will not be able to enter this profession as a 2.1 Honours degree or higher, preferably in economics, is essential. A joint Honours degree in economics and another related subject, such as finance or maths, is also often acceptable, however you should ensure that the majority of your modules are in economics and that you study both microeconomics and macroeconomics. Many employers are also increasingly requiring candidates to hold a postgraduate economics qualification. A good Honours degree in a subject other than economics may be accepted if it is followed by a postgraduate economics degree.

Entry onto a degree course usually requires at least 2 A levels/3 H grades, including maths and preferably economics, and 5 GCSEs/National 5s (A*–C/A–C), including Maths and English. For entry onto a postgraduate degree you will need a 2.1 Honours degree.

If you meet the above criteria and have less than 3 years' professional experience, you can apply to the Government Economic Service's Fast Stream Economist programme. This is designed to develop your economic, managerial and communications skills to prepare you for early promotion to more senior jobs.

On top of academic achievement, knowledge of a foreign language may aid employment prospects (particularly for candidates who wish to work on secondment), as would relevant work experience. The Government Economic Service and the Bank of England offer work experience placements, internships, sandwich placements, gap year placements and vacation work placements for students and graduates.

What the work involves

Economists play a vital role in a country's financial stability, using their specialist knowledge to advise government and financial institutions and major businesses to help develop financial policy and strategy.

Economists research and analyse a variety of mathematical modelling techniques and data, with the information received being used to identify and predict economic changes. The work is diverse as research projects can cover a wide range of subjects: from the economic impact of major national events, such as the 2014 Commonwealth Games, to analysing a company's performance for fund managers and investors.

Many economists work alone, although much of their work will be through consultation with statisticians, civil servants and marketers.

Type of person suited to this work

Strong economic, business and financial understanding is essential as you will be required to analyse and apply economic theory to a variety of subjects. The work of an economist takes into account many factors and so it is also necessary for you to have an awareness of current affairs, politics and social welfare.

Much of the job centres on the research, analysis and prediction of market trends, so a good eye for detail and methodical nature is essential. Economists must be able to communicate their understanding of a situation in a clear and concise way as you will often be explaining complex economic procedure to non-economists.

Working conditions

Economists tend to work regular office hours, 9am–5.30pm, Monday to Friday. However, some related sectors could require extended hours due to the work topic being unpredictable. For those that work in the civil service and similar sectors, flexibility may be allowed in relation to hours worked, with part-time work and job sharing being an option.

Economists are mostly office based, with the occasional need to travel to meet clients or to be present at conferences and seminars, to which they may need to contribute.

Future prospects

This profession holds many exciting opportunities, such as the chance to progress to an economic adviser after 3–4 years, based on your ability and drive. Many economists choose to become self-employed or to work abroad with multinational companies after gaining experience and establishing a reputation.

Advantages/disadvantages

This job offers fantastic career prospects, with there being opportunities for progression in a short amount of time once training has been completed.

The salary is highly competitive, when compared with other professions, and the working hours are relatively average.

Tight deadlines, political pressure and the need to juggle different projects can make the job a demanding one.

Money guide

Economists will usually have a starting salary of £25,000–£35,000, rising to £40,000 with a few years' experience.

Those at senior level, with 10–15 years' experience, can achieve earnings of £60,000–£80,000 with earnings for the top economists in finance and consulting reaching up to £250,000.

Salaries vary greatly, with economists working in banking, consulting, industry and financial services sectors usually earning more.

Related opportunities

- Accountant p2
- Actuary p5
- Mathematician/Mathematics Research Scientist p503

Further information

Bank of England
www.bankofengland.co.uk

Government Economic Service
www.ges.gov.uk

Royal Economic Society
www.res.org.uk

EDUCATION OFFICER

ENTRY LEVEL 5

Qualifications and courses

In the role of an education officer you should be educated to degree or HND level. The normal minimum entry requirements for degrees are 2 A levels/3 H grades and 5 GCSEs/National 5s (A*–C/A–C), and for Foundation degrees or HNC/Ds, 1 A level/2 H grades and 3 GCSEs/National 5s (A*–C/A–C).

Though applicants may apply for an education officer position with any degree subject, it would be advantageous to have a degree relevant to the area you are applying to. For example, to work as an education officer in a museum or gallery, useful degree/HND subjects would include history, archaeology, anthropology, museum studies, cultural studies, history of art and education. For an environmental education officer position a degree/HND in a biological or environmental science, such as ecology, conservation or zoology, would be beneficial.

Qualifications and/or experience in teaching or community education, such as a PGCE or master's degree in education or education management, are useful and may be required. Relevant work experience is essential in order to secure a paid position.

Entry without a degree is possible but only if you have extensive voluntary experience. However, these positions are becoming increasingly difficult to find and career progression may be limited as degree-education candidates would take precedence for higher-level roles.

What the work involves

Education officers will prepare educational materials and resources to highlight and raise awareness for a particular issue or promote a certain gallery, museum or organisation. It will be your responsibility to increase public awareness about new exhibitions and/or events, and to update the educational sections of your website.

You will be responsible for teaching a wide range of age groups and liaising with communities and companies on a variety of topics. You will construct and be expected to run educational campaigns, talks, workshops and activities in line with the ethos of your organisation.

Type of person suited to this work

You will need self-confidence and an ability to talk to people in a way that will interest and excite them. You must be bright, interesting, humorous, have lots of patience and a willingness to listen.

You will always be busy, so you will need good organisational skills, as well as excellent written and verbal communication skills. An understanding of IT and confidence in handling budgets will also be useful.

Working conditions

Your time will be spent in an office, lecture room or working within the community where you will represent your organisation. You might be expected to wear a uniform or protective clothing.

Depending on your organisation you might spend some of your time outdoors in all weathers, for example at a zoo or community farm. You might do some evening work, especially if you work with community groups.

Future prospects

Entry to this profession is very competitive, but there is a steady increase in the number of educational jobs available in organisations.

Alongside traditional exhibits, learning through demonstrations, videos, talks and other presentations is being introduced by education officers as interactive experiences increase in popularity.

Advantages/disadvantages

This profession offers an opportunity to be involved in teaching without being in the classroom as well as learning effective marketing and events organisation.

You will help make a visit to your workplace a more memorable experience for everyone and create a positive public profile.

You will be juggling lots of different tasks at once which could be overwhelming.

Money guide

Starting salaries typically range from £15,000 to £23,000.

For senior level posts where officers have approximately 10 years' experience, salaries will rise to between £22,000 and £30,000.

For management positions within private organisations where you are responsible for developing policy and a multidisciplinary team, salaries can reach up to £50,000.

Related opportunities

- Arts Administrator/Manager p327
- Environmental Health Practitioner/Officer p22
- Learning Mentor p182
- Museum/Art Gallery Curator p335

Further information

GEM

www.gem.org.uk

ENVIRONMENTAL HEALTH PRACTITIONER/OFFICER

ENTRY LEVEL 6

Qualifications and courses

To become an environmental health practitioner you will need a BSc or MSc in Environmental Health, accredited by either the Chartered Institute of Environmental Health (CIEH) or the Royal Environmental Health Institute of Scotland (REHIS).

Entry to an undergraduate degree normally requires 2 A levels/3 H grades and 5 GCSEs/National 5s (A*–C/A–C) including English, Maths and a science. Appropriate GNVQ, BTEC or Foundation degrees may also be acceptable. Graduates who do not have an accredited undergraduate degree but one related to environmental health, such as a science, are able to enter an accredited MSc programme providing they have at least a 2nd class Honours degree.

After academic study, candidates need to complete a 9–12 month practical training course with the CIEH/REHIS. In England and Wales, this can be incorporated into an undergraduate degree through a sandwich year or completed after graduation. Candidates receive a Certificate of Registration from the Environmental Health Registration Board when they successfully complete the training requirements and professional exams.

In Scotland, the REHIS scheme consists of a 48-week placement with a local authority. Training may be undertaken during university holidays or after graduation. Successful completion of all the training requirements and professional exams leads to the REHIS Diploma in Environmental Health.

If you do not have a relevant degree, an alternate route to become an environmental health practitioner is to start work as an environmental health technician, study part time for a degree in Environmental Health and work your way up. For this you will need 5 GCSEs/National 5s (A*–C/A–C), or previous experience and qualifications in related work, such as health and safety.

A full UK driving licence is usually required for most positions.

What the work involves

Some environmental health practitioners are responsible for all aspects of environmental health in their local areas, while others specialise in either food safety, housing conditions, workplace health and safety, or environmental conditions.

Your tasks might include developing public health policies, carrying out inspections in premises such as restaurants, houses and workplaces to identify any hazards and ensure that relevant laws are being followed and educating and advising the public and businesses.

You will also carry out investigations of accidents or outbreaks and contaminations.

Type of person suited to this work

You must be interested in finding ways of improving public health, and will need a scientific and logical approach to collect and assess evidence and use it to identify and solve problems. Excellent written and verbal communication skills are vital for explaining regulations clearly and simply to a wide range of people.

You have to be able to handle challenging situations, for example when confronting noisy neighbours. You must be able to enforce the law when necessary.

You need to be comfortable working both alone and as part of a team.

Working conditions

You will be office based, but spend a lot of time visiting homes and businesses in your local area. Some of the places you visit will be smelly, dirty or potentially dangerous and you will sometimes have to wear protective clothing.

You will probably work a normal working week Monday–Friday, but you will occasionally need to work evenings and at weekends.

Future prospects

After 5 years of professional experience you can apply to the CIEH for Chartered Environmental Health Practitioner status.

Throughout your career you must keep abreast of all new developments in the industry.

In the public sector there is a clear promotion structure. With experience, you could progress to higher levels such as senior, principal or chief environmental officer. There are also promotion opportunities in the private sector. Self-employment and working abroad are also options.

Advantages/disadvantages

It can be challenging dealing with people who are angry, for example when enforcing regulations.

You will have the satisfaction of protecting the health and safety of people and improving their quality of life.

You may have to face some distressing sights.

Money guide

Starting salaries range from £25,000 to £35,000.

With experience, senior level salaries increase to £45,000–£60,000.

Environmental health practitioners working for private companies typically earn more than employees in the public sector.

Related opportunities

- Health and Safety Adviser p27
- Health Promotion/Education Specialist p286
- Trading Standards Officer p472

Further information

Chartered Institute of Environmental Health
www.cieh.org

Royal Environmental Health Institute of Scotland
www.rehis.com

EQUALITY AND DIVERSITY OFFICER

ENTRY LEVEL 5

Qualifications and courses

Most people enter this profession with a degree, HNC/HND or equivalent. While graduates in any subject can work in this field, degrees and HNCs/HNDs in education, law, business/management and human resources are useful.

Experience working in law, human resources, social work or teaching is very beneficial. Relevant experience can also be gained by getting involved in equality and diversity committees and societies at university, doing voluntary work or work shadowing. Many equal opportunities advisers are members of the Chartered Institute of Personnel and Development (CIPD). To work as an equality and diversity officer in schools you may have to train as a teacher first.

Relevant postgraduate courses include race relations or disability studies. These qualifications can be beneficial in acquiring a senior level position and for people whose first degree was not in a subject related to the field. There are part-time and full-time postgraduate courses in equality and diversity available at selected universities.

The CIPD offers short courses for further study, such as Discrimination and the Law and Managing Diversity.

What the work involves

Your role is to ensure that businesses and public organisations do not discriminate on disability, race, gender, sexuality, age or religion. You will make sure that services such as education and health are accessible to everyone.

You will promote positive images of all groups and promote diversity in all company literature.

You will advise on how to attract job applicants from all sections of the local community and ensure the company is following all the relevant legislation.

Type of person suited to this work

You should be committed to working for change, be persuasive and good at negotiating. At the same time you need to be a good listener, be sensitive and diplomatic in the way you deal with people and situations.

You will need excellent communication skills and should be confident in giving presentations, advising management and delivering training.

You will need to be able to understand all the relevant equal opportunities laws and regulations and be able to apply them to all policies and procedures within the company, offering advice on any new developments and how to implement them. For some jobs you might need specialist skills such as being able to speak another language.

Working conditions

Much of your time will be office based, working normal office hours. However, you will probably do quite a bit of evening and weekend work too, organising special events and working with community groups.

You may visit other businesses and organisations, so a driving licence may be useful.

Future prospects

Opportunities vary from employer to employer. Government departments, local authorities, universities, trade unions and large companies employ specialist equal opportunities advisers, and there may be more scope to develop your career within these types of companies by moving into management roles. In smaller companies the work is covered by the human resources department and you may need to move company to gain a promotion.

Employers will usually provide on-the-job training and you may be encouraged to work towards a relevant qualification such as a postgraduate degree or professional CIPD qualifications.

With significant experience you could work for yourself, offering a consultancy service to companies to ensure they are working within equal opportunities legislation. Some will go on to specialise in one particular area, such as disability, while others will continue to work across a range of areas.

Advantages/disadvantages

You will be working for a cause you feel passionately about and could be making a real difference to people.

The work can be stressful. You will be dealing with sensitive issues and may be working with people who do not share your beliefs or who have no desire to change.

Money guide

Starting salaries are between £17,000 and £25,000 per year.

With experience you can expect approximately £28,000 to £45,000.

Those in managerial roles within large companies can earn in excess of £50,000.

Related opportunities

- Human Resources/Personnel Officer p28
- Training and Development Officer p54
- Welfare Benefits Adviser/Welfare Rights Caseworker p562

Further information

Equality & Human Rights Commission
www.equalityhumanrights.com

Equality Commission for Northern Ireland
www.equalityni.org

ERGONOMIST

ENTRY LEVEL 6

Qualifications and courses

Entry to this profession requires an undergraduate degree in either Ergonomics or Human Factors that has been accredited by the Institute of Ergonomics & Human Factors (IEHF) or a degree in a related subject, such as biology, engineering, design, medicine or psychology, followed by an accredited postgraduate course in Ergonomics. For entry onto an undergraduate degree programme in Ergonomics you will need at least 3 A levels/4 H grades, with useful subjects including maths, physics, biology and psychology.

Graduates of degree courses accredited by the IEHF are then able to join the Institute as Graduate Members. This is a useful way to make professional contacts within the industry.

Entry onto degree courses and into the industry is very competitive, so an excellent academic record as well as recent, relevant work experience, paid or voluntary, is highly recommended. A relevant postgraduate qualification could help your employment prospects, even if you have an IEHF-accredited undergraduate degree.

It is possible to begin a career in ergonomics with an HND in a relevant subject, providing you have 4 years' experience and can demonstrate significant knowledge in the key ergonomics areas, such as physiology or psychology. You will probably have to take a relevant course to support any job applications but this may not necessarily be a degree-level qualification.

The IEHF encourages students and newly qualified ergonomists to take part in their Opening Doors work experience scheme. Many other organisations across the UK also offer schemes that are helpful to those entering the profession.

What the work involves

An ergonomist creates designs that aid society, such as a comfortable chair or a social environment that accounts for the disabled and the elderly.

People within this profession aim to improve the health, safety and efficiency of different equipment and systems.

Designs are informed by biomechanics, physiology, psychology, engineering, industrial design and IT. Ergonomists consult with other professionals including design/production engineers, health and safety practitioners, computer specialists and industrial physicians.

Type of person suited to this work

An interest in the human body and mind, and the ways in which designs can aid quality of life, is an important part of this profession. Ergonomists must be analytical, observant and able to conduct detailed research into the needs of society.

As the role involves creating high-quality designs and solutions, entrants need to have problem-solving skills, attention to detail and persistence.

Interaction with clients is frequent so good communication and negotiation skills are a must.

Working conditions

Those within the profession usually work normal office hours, 9am–5pm, Monday to Friday. However, overtime or weekend work may be required depending on the project and deadline.

Working environments are variable and involve a combination of office, laboratory and fieldwork.

Ergonomists are often required to travel within the working day, with occasional overnight stays and trips abroad.

Future prospects

Developing a specific area of interest early in your career can be useful and can lead to opportunities within specialist consultancies.

Self-employment as a consultant is a common option for ergonomists and it is also possible to move into a research role with universities or organisations.

Those keen to progress within the industry are more likely to gain promotion by changing employer and so a willingness to be geographically mobile is helpful.

Advantages/disadvantages

Ergonomics is a fairly small professional community so there are opportunities to become actively involved with industry bodies and network with your colleagues.

As the technology and industry is constantly changing, ergonomists must be willing to continue learning and training throughout their careers.

The work can be stressful as you are required to meet the varying demands and deadlines of your clients.

Money guide

Graduates entering the profession can expect to earn between £18,000 and £25,000 a year.

After about 5 years' experience, ergonomists have an average salary of £25,000 to £40,000.

If you reach a senior level within the field, you can achieve a salary in excess of £60,000.

Salaries vary with the size of the company, geographical location and terms of employment.

Related opportunities

■ Consumer Scientist p488
■ Health and Safety Adviser p27
■ Product Designer p169

Further information

Loughborough University
www.lboro.ac.uk

The Institute of Ergonomics & Human Factors
www.ergonomics.org.uk

ESTATES OFFICER

ENTRY LEVEL 3

Qualifications and courses

There are no set minimum entry requirements but it is still a good idea to get at least 5 GCSEs/National 5s (A*–C/A–C) and 2 A levels/H grades and an increasing number of applicants hold a relevant degree, often in surveying or a related subject.

You can work towards professional qualifications through the Royal Institution of Chartered Surveyors (RICS) or the Institute of Revenues, Rating and Valuation (IRRV). If you work in construction or estate management you can study remotely through the College of Estate Management.

There is also an Advanced Apprenticeship in Surveying that you can do.

Alternatively, another route in would be as a surveying technician. This would require an HND/HNC qualification, for which you will need a minimum of 1 A level/2 H grades or a BTEC National Diploma/Certificate plus 4 GCSEs/National 5s (A*–C/A–C).

What the work involves

Estates officers manage, refurbish and uphold land and property that belongs to private landlords, local authorities and organisations involved in land and property owning.

Specific activities include the management of an organisation's property portfolio, such as ensuring the amount of rent being paid is sufficient, dealing with tenancy agreements/applications, checking that properties are not being maltreated, and organising any necessary building repair or environmental work.

Letting, acquisitions and management are areas of specialism.

Type of person suited to this work

This job is suitable for someone who is able to communicate well in order to coordinate the work of colleagues, and has good negotiating skills when discussing tenancy agreements and the terms of a contract.

Organisation is of importance when overseeing a portfolio of properties for a client, with an appreciation for detail being paramount when examining a property, proposed legal documents or finances.

It is often necessary to be analytical when dealing with written and numerical information and the ability to write clear and concise reports and presentations is an important requirement of the job.

Working conditions

Working hours tend to be from 9am to 5pm, Monday to Friday.

As with many jobs, extra hours may need to be worked in order to attend committees or meet deadlines, although there are also opportunities for flexitime, job sharing and part-time work.

This job is mostly office based, although site visits to portfolio buildings may involve being outside in all weathers, a lot of walking, and the climbing of ladders.

Future prospects

Self-employment or employment with a commercial business may be the most sustainable career path for estate officers, due to local authorities privately contracting work to outside companies.

Health authorities, civil service departments, university estates departments, charities and the Office of Government Commerce also provide work opportunities.

Opportunity for promotion is more likely in larger estates businesses and departments, with progression leading to appointment as the head of a unit, a specialist area, or department.

Advantages/disadvantages

This position holds a fair amount of responsibility, with the use of leadership qualities and organisational skills on a regular basis increasing the chances of promotion.

Although mostly office based, estate officers often have to make visits to buildings within their remit, which may mean having to work outside in all types of weather.

Money guide

A junior estates officer can expect to earn £18,000 to £26,000 per year.

Through gaining experience and further qualifications, this amount may rise to £32,000–£35,000 per year.

Salary can vary widely depending on qualification and responsibilities.

Related opportunities

- Chartered Surveyor p68
- Facilities Manager p83
- Health Service Manager p288

Further information

Chartered Institute of Housing
www.cih.org

College of Estate Management
www.cem.ac.uk

Institute of Revenues Rating and Valuation
www.irrv.net

Royal Institution of Chartered Surveyors
www.rics.org

FINANCIAL ADVISER

ENTRY LEVEL 3

Qualifications and courses

There are no specific entry routes and qualification requirements depend on the employer, although it is common for employers to request a minimum of 2 A levels/3 H grades and 5 GCSEs/National 5s (A*–C/A–C), including English and Maths. In some cases, employers consider a background in customer or financial services and proven communication skills to be more important than formal academic qualifications but it is worth checking this with employers directly.

This area of work is open to graduates of all disciplines but graduates in finance, business management and accountancy may be at an advantage. Other useful qualifications include the Level 3 BTEC National Award in Personal and Business Finance, the Level 3 BTEC National Award in Business and the Level 3 BTEC Award in Providing Financial Advice. A pre-entry postgraduate qualification is not needed.

Whatever your academic background, to become a financial adviser you will be required to take one of a number of professional diplomas: the Diploma in Regulated Financial Planning from the Chartered Insurance Institute (CII), the Diploma in Investment Planning from the Chartered Banker Institute, the Level 4 Diploma for Financial Advisers from the *ifs* University College, the Investment Advice Diploma from the Chartered Institute for Securities and Investment (CISI) or the SQA/QCF Level 4 Diploma in Professional Financial Advice.

Prior experience through part-time or vacation work could be helpful and apprenticeships in Providing Financial Services are available.

Some banks, building societies and financial advice firms have graduate training schemes and trainees will usually begin as tied advisers.

What the work involves

Financial advisers offer client consultations on a wide range of financial issues including mortgages, pensions and investments.

You will also be producing reports and annual summaries for clients to keep them up to date with their financial situation.

Tied advisers work for a financial institution, such as a bank, advising clients on their services. Independent advisers sell products and services offered by a range of companies.

Type of person suited to this work

Good communications skills are essential in order to explain complex financial matters simply to your clients. You will need to enjoy working with numbers, and have the ability to analyse and understand technical financial information.

You should be honest and reliable. This will allow you to gain the trust of your clients and subsequently sell your products. You must be self-motivated and organised with good IT skills.

You will also need an understanding of the relevant financial laws and to keep up with changes in the industry.

Working conditions

You will usually work standard office hours but you should be prepared to work longer hours at busy times.

Tied advisers usually work some Saturdays. Independent advisers may have to work evenings and weekends to suit their clients.

You will be expected to dress formally, and to visit clients in their homes or offices so a driving licence would be useful. Jobs are available throughout the UK, but the majority are based within London and the south-east of England.

Future prospects

The demand for financial advisers is growing as people increasingly take charge of their own pensions and finances.

Financial advisers work in insurance companies, banks and other businesses, and there is also the option of being self-employed.

Promotion prospects are good, and there are opportunities to take additional qualifications and move into management jobs. You could also specialise in a particular area, perhaps training others or marketing products.

Advantages/disadvantages

Pay and prospects are good; you can specialise in specific financial areas, such as savings or pensions, or become self-employed.

The job comes with a high level of responsibility, and you will be under pressure to sell products and meet targets.

Money guide

Entry salaries at trainee adviser level vary from £22,000 to £30,000.

A typical salary for a qualified adviser is £30,000 to £45,000.

Senior level financial advisers can earn £50,000 to £70,000.

Bonuses or commission on mortgage or insurance products may also be offered and these can be uncapped.

Related opportunities

- Bank Manager p10
- Business Adviser p11
- Stockbroker p52

Further information

***ifs* University College**
www.ifslearning.ac.uk

Chartered Banker Institute
www.charteredbanker.com

Chartered Insurance Institute
www.cii.co.uk

Financial Skills Partnership
www.financialskillspartnership.org.uk

HEALTH AND SAFETY ADVISER

ENTRY LEVEL 3

Qualifications and courses

To enter this career you will need an industry-recognised professional qualification. These include a City & Guilds Level 3 NVQ in Occupational Health and Safety or a relevant course from either the National Examinations Board in Occupational Safety and Health (NEBOSH) or British Safety Council. You can study either full time before looking for work or part time while gaining experience in a related field.

There are an increasing number of entrants that now have an undergraduate degree or HND. Though the subject is not specified by the industry, graduates in health studies, occupational safety, engineering or life science would be at an advantage. Entry to a degree is usually with 2 A levels/3 H grades and 5 GCSEs/National 5s (A*–C/A–C), or equivalent, and for an HND 1 A level/2 H grades and 3 GCSEs/National 5s are often required. There are also industry-related Postgraduate Diplomas and Master of Science courses available.

Experience of working at an operational level within risk assessment, construction, engineering, manufacturing or scientific work can be very valuable when applying for jobs in health and safety. Knowledge of computer applications for preparing and analysing statistics is also desirable, as is physical fitness.

What the work involves

You will help maintain a safe workplace by developing and implementing health and safety policies and procedures.

You will inspect premises and ways of working, according to your industry knowledge of health and safety legislation, ensuring all relevant regulations are followed correctly. You will be committed to maintaining a working knowledge of all Health and Safety Executive (HSE) legislation and review company policy accordingly.

The work involves investigating and reporting on accidents and giving specialist advice and training to staff on health and safety issues, such as fire regulations and dealing with dangerous chemicals.

You may also be involved in carrying out risk assessments for companies, ensuring safe installation of new equipment and developing internal policies related to promoting workplace health and safety.

Type of person suited to this work

You must be investigative, diplomatic and able to visualise the big picture of how a company works and how it can improve.

You will need to understand technical and operational processes and be able to explain your findings and recommendations in a clear and straightforward way.

You should be thorough, methodical and able to understand and apply relevant regulations. You will also need good IT and administrative skills and need to be reasonably fit for working safely on large outdoor and industrial sites.

Working conditions

You will be office based but depending on where you work, may have to spend a lot of time visiting factories and building sites. This could mean having to wear protective clothing, working outdoors in all weathers and at heights or in hot, noisy conditions.

You will work normal office hours but may need to be on-call at other times in case of emergencies.

Future prospects

The government and European Union are producing more regulations and guidelines to help companies ensure a safe working environment for staff. This means that opportunities are increasing as employers need help implementing and monitoring new legislation.

Many health and safety advisers work in engineering, construction and manufacturing; there are also opportunities to specialise or do consultancy work. It might be necessary to switch jobs in order to be promoted.

Advantages/disadvantages

The work can be varied and you will be instrumental in helping to save people's lives.

You will be dealing with important issues that affect people's safety and wellbeing, so there is a lot of responsibility.

The conditions you have to work in will sometimes be dangerous, dirty and noisy. You may also have to work in extreme weather.

Money guide

Starting salaries can range from £18,000 to £25,000 per year.

After several years' experience, those at senior level should expect a salary of around £33,000 to £36,000 per year.

Levels do vary according to sector. However, generally graduates and those with a postgraduate degree often earn more than non-graduates, particularly if they are undertaking continuing professional development (CPD).

Benefits may include bonuses, a company car and medical insurance.

Related opportunities

- Human Resources/Personnel Officer p28
- Road Safety Officer p592
- Trading Standards Officer p472

Further information

British Safety Council
www.britsafe.org

Health and Safety Executive
www.hse.gov.uk

Institute of Occupational Safety and Health
www.iosh.co.uk

HUMAN RESOURCES/ PERSONNEL OFFICER

ENTRY LEVEL 3

Qualifications and courses

Whilst there are no formal entry requirements for this career employers are likely to expect candidates to have a minimum of 5 GCSEs/National 5s (A*–C/A–C), including English and Maths, and some A levels/H grades. Most human resources officers, however, will have a degree or postgraduate qualification in a relevant subject, such as business studies, human resource management, management, social administration and psychology. Entry onto a degree course will require a minimum of 2 A levels/3 H grades and 5 GCSEs/National 5s (A*–C/A–C).

Some employers prefer candidates to have a professional HR qualification accredited by the Chartered Institute of Personnel and Development (CIPD), such as the Level 3, 5 or 7 Certificate in Human Resources Practice or the Level 3, 5 or 7 Award in Human Resources Management, on application, whereas others will sponsor your studies part time whilst you work. Prior relevant work experience will improve your chances of securing a graduate job.

A common entry route is to start out in administration within an HR company and gain experience until a suitable internal vacancy arises. Alternatively, some companies offer a graduate training scheme. Usually you will need a minimum of a 2.2 Honours degree in any subject for these schemes, although degrees in human resources and business may be more relevant. Early application is advised as there will be a lot of competition.

What the work involves

Human resources officers are responsible for recruiting the right staff for jobs at all levels, developing company staff and recruitment policies and helping existing staff to get the appropriate training and development that they and the company need.

You will be charged with managing complaints and disciplinary procedure, administering and maintaining company payroll and staff records, devising and implementing personnel-related policies as well as advising on staff development.

There will be some involvement with negotiations between staff and trade unions on issues such as pay and conditions but this is dependent on the sector in which you are working. In large companies HR officers may specialise in one aspect of the role, whereas in smaller companies you would be expected to cover all aspects of the job.

Type of person suited to this work

You will work with people at all levels, including staff who could be angry or upset, so you will need excellent communication skills. You should be interested in people and be able to solve problems. You will need to help with negotiations between staff and managers over issues such as pay and conditions.

You may be involved with disciplinary procedures and redundancies which can be very stressful. In these situations you will need to be tactful and diplomatic.

You will have to understand and implement employment legislation, manage a budget, write clear and accurate reports, be organised and methodical and be able to work under pressure.

Working conditions

You will work standard office hours, 9am–5.30pm, Monday to Friday, although you might need to work extra hours during busy periods. You will visit the different locations and sites of your organisation so that people get to know and trust you, which could also involve being outdoors or in noisy, dirty places.

You must be able to work well with others as you will probably be working as part of a human resources team.

Future prospects

All types of businesses employ human resources staff but it's a popular and competitive career so work experience is vital. Many human resources personnel officers have a degree but you could work your way up from an administrative role.

You may get more responsibility in a small company but have better prospects in a larger one. You will need to take professional qualifications and could work abroad or become a self-employed consultant.

Advantages/disadvantages

This is a rewarding career if you are interested in people and helping them to develop their skills.

You can study for professional qualifications and gain promotion.

You will be involved in solving disputes between staff and the company, which can be stressful and you might have to make staff redundant.

Money guide

Salaries vary considerably between employers, sectors, office locations and job roles.

The average salary for a graduate-level human resources officer is £24,400 (though starting salaries may be lower).

The top human resources positions can be lucrative. Human resources managers earn on average between £25,000 and £50,000, and HR Directors can receive salaries of up to £100,000.

Related opportunities

- Recruitment/Employment Agency Consultant p46
- School Administrator/Secretary p187
- Work-based Training Instructor p193

Further information

Chartered Institute of Personnel and Development
www.cipd.co.uk

INSURANCE BROKER ENTRY LEVEL 3

Qualifications and courses

Although there are no formal entry requirements, most organisations prefer graduates with at least a 2.2 or, preferably, a 2.1 degree. Any subject area is accepted, though a degree in accounting, economics, maths, business or management would be advantageous. Larger companies offer specialised training schemes for graduates.

It is possible for non-graduates to gain entry-level positions in support or administration and progress to a broking career after gaining industry qualifications. For this you will need at least 2 A levels/H grades and GCSEs/National 5s (A*–C/A–C) in English and Maths.

Some previous work experience in customer service or finance, whilst not essential to a new entrant, will be looked upon favourably by employers. Many major insurance companies have summer internships and work experience schemes.

Apprenticeships at Levels 2 and 3 in Providing Financial Services are also available as an entry route with options to pursue financial advice, general insurance or long-term care insurance.

The Chartered Insurance Institute (CII), the Institute of Financial Services (*ifs*), and the British Insurance Brokers' Association (BIBA) run relevant courses for new entrants. Additional qualifications are offered by *ifs* University College, which are particularly relevant for those seeking to work in financial planning. Recruiters generally look for entrants with no criminal record.

What the work involves

Insurance brokers act as an agent between clients and insurance companies. You will advise on the best policies to meet the client's needs and negotiate deals. You could advise individuals or business clients.

You will have to research policies from many different insurance providers, and you will need to be impartial to ensure your client receives the best deal. You will have to negotiate with these insurance companies to get policies at the best terms for your client.

As a broker you could work in a small company, dealing with a wide range of services, or specialise in a specific area such as household or risk insurance within a larger organisation. You will also collect premiums and process all of your accounts.

Type of person suited to this work

Brokers need excellent verbal and written communication skills to negotiate deals, sell policies and explain complicated financial issues to clients in simple terms. It is essential to be detail oriented and good with numbers.

You will also need to be personable and trustworthy in order to gain the confidence of your clients. Good negotiating skills are imperative if you want to secure the best deal for your client. You should be able to manage your time well as you will work on multiple projects at once.

Working conditions

Brokers could work in a high-street location, selling policies to the public, or in an office where customers call for quotes or claims updates.

Although you will work normal office hours you might need to work the occasional Saturday to meet the needs of your clients.

Smart dress is important as you must be presentable when meeting with clients.

Future prospects

With experience you might choose to move into a management role or become an account executive dealing with more complex claims and visiting clients on their own sites. You also have the option to train further and become a chartered broker.

Eligibility for chartered status requires at least 5 years' experience. CII qualifications are very well regarded and have become essential rather than optional to ensure recognised professional status.

Advantages/disadvantages

The insurance industry offers good career prospects.

Insurance qualifications gained in the UK are respected worldwide allowing you to work abroad.

The work can involve a lot of responsibility and stress as you will be dealing with huge sums of money.

As this is a commission-oriented job you may experience extra pressure to perform and earn.

Money guide

Non-graduate trainee insurance brokers can expect to earn approximately £16,000 a year.

Graduates on training schemes may earn £22,000.

Over time and with experience you can progress to earning £80,000 or more, not including potential bonuses and other benefits.

Your pay may vary based on where you live, with higher salaries normally in London. Your salary may also be based on commission.

Related opportunities

- Financial Adviser p26
- Insurance Risk Surveyor p32
- Insurance Underwriter p33
- Loss Adjuster p36

Further information

***ifs* University College**
www.ifslearning.ac.uk

British Insurance Brokers' Association
www.biba.org.uk

Chartered Insurance Institute
www.cii.co.uk

Financial Skills Partnership
www.financialskillspartnership.org.uk

Organisation Profile

INSURANCE

CII

Insurance is about understanding risks around the world and managing them. Everything has a risk attached to it, from data to footballers' legs, from supertankers to climate change. Every risk also has a price and a context – and that's where sector professionals play their part.

The CII is the world's largest professional body for insurance, risk and financial services, with more than 115,000 members in over 150 countries.

The variety of roles is wide – brokers and underwriters negotiate on risks to be insured; claims experts and loss adjusters deal with the aftermath of local and global events; risk analysts and catastrophe modellers run complex programmes to understand the potential impact of events on people, businesses and the landscape; there are also professionals in marketing, IT, HR and other business support areas.

You can join from school, college or university. Wherever you start, there is nothing to stop you earning a very large salary and working anywhere in the world, since risk principles are global.

After school or college, you could take an Apprenticeship that includes a globally-recognised CII professional qualification at an SME or a huge brand like Aon, Lloyd's of London or Zurich. We've seen good growth in the number of openings like these over the last few years, across the country. Find out more by visiting www.cii.co.uk/apprenticeships. Remember, an Apprenticeship still offers a path to a degree – this way costs far, far less than three or four years full time at university.

If you are set on university, be aware that it's your personality – your communication, negotiation and problem-solving skills – and not the subject you study that will get you a place on a graduate scheme. That's why you find engineering, religious studies and fine art graduates working in risk alongside those with degrees in business, finance and law.

Larger employers have well-established graduate schemes that offer two approaches – the rotational scheme to expose you to different business areas; and the specialist scheme which builds expertise in one business area from day one.

Don't overlook smaller companies though – they may only offer one or two graduate roles but they will allow you to grow within a business and gain an understanding of broader business operations.

Being a professional includes completing professional qualifications and, in most cases, your company will pay for you to study CII programmes. Available at three levels – Certificate, Diploma and Advanced Diploma – many graduate schemes will fast-track to the Advanced Diploma in Insurance, completion of which gives you the designatory letters ACII. These letters are globally recognised and valued by employers. Find out more about CII qualifications by visiting www.cii.co.uk/qualifications.

With the ACII and five years' experience under your belt, you can apply for Chartered status, the pinnacle of a profession.

The CII's Discover Risk website www.discoverrisk.co.uk is an invaluable resource of case studies, jobs and employer information.

Email discover@cii.co.uk to find out more about this hugely rewarding and diverse profession.

Case Study

DISCOVERING RISK

Adam Marks' story

Adam works as an Account Handler at Willis, one of the world's largest brokers.

How did you get into risk?

Through a work experience placement after having been in contact with the Education Liaison team at Willis Ipswich for a number of years. I subsequently applied for the first apprenticeship scheme within Willis Ipswich and started in September 2012.

Why did you decide not to go to university?

I liked the idea of being in a position to 'earn while you learn'. I feel the Apprenticeship has helped me because of the qualification earned and the first-hand experience I have gained over the course of my employment. In my opinion, this qualification and experience increases my employability as it shows that I can manage and organise my workload whilst studying.

What do you do in a typical working day?

I facilitate and advise on the purchase and placement of Professional Indemnity insurance for our clients who work in a wide variety of industry sectors. I work on the high volume, small to medium enterprise book and these placements typically have a premium of under £10,000.

What do you enjoy most about your job?

I like the fast-paced nature of the job and the insurance industry in general. I enjoy interacting with the clients and communicating with insurers. Although the job is technical it is also a service industry and very people focused so I enjoy the balance of the more sociable side of the business which has included attendance at corporate events as well as business and networking lunches.

What is the most challenging part of your role?

As my job is to service a very high volume book of business, the most challenging part has to be the need to manage my workload and provide good client service to multiple clients at the same time. I found this particularly challenging in the beginning due to coming straight out of a college environment and into the full-time working environment.

What do you need to be successful in your role?

You need to be able to stick to tight deadlines and ensure every one of your clients has adequate cover at the right time. Organisational and time management skills are key, along with strong interpersonal skills and the ability to communicate clearly and articulately.

Have you taken any professional qualifications?

I have completed the Insurance, Legal and Regulatory (IF1) paper of the Certificate in Insurance as this was a requirement of my Apprenticeship. I am currently working towards my Diploma in Insurance (Dip CII) and will then progress onto the Advanced Diploma in Insurance (ACII).

What have been your career highlights so far?

Gaining a permanent position within my team in the summer of 2013 prior to completing my Apprenticeship in November 2013, is my career highlight so far.

Why did you choose a career in insurance?

I have always been interested in the business and finance sector. Since taking Economics in college I have learnt how certain factors can be detrimental or advantageous to the economy. Insurance helps to remove uncertainty for businesses, is a sustainable industry and so should continue to grow and provide jobs.

To find out more about other people working in the profession, email discover@cii.co.uk or visit www.discoverrisk.co.uk.

INSURANCE RISK SURVEYOR

ENTRY LEVEL 6

Qualifications and courses

This is not generally considered to be an entry-level position, although some large companies do run graduate trainee schemes. Normally you will need to have gained significant experience in the insurance industry, usually as an underwriter. Qualifications and experience in a related, specialised profession such as building surveying will also be accepted.

A degree or HND is increasingly normal among those entering the profession, usually a 2.1 degree qualification. Any subject is accepted but degrees in science, risk management, insurance or business studies will be useful. If you want to specialise in engineering insurance you will need an engineering degree. Although requirements vary between universities and colleges, most degree courses will require at least 2 A levels/3 H grades and 5 GCSEs/National 5s (A*–C/A–C).

Non-graduates who complete a Higher Diploma in Business, Administration and Finance may be able to get a job as a technician, risk assistant or claims handler and work their way up while studying for professional qualifications such as the CII Diploma in Insurance.

All trainees are expected to qualify as a Chartered Insurance Institute (CII) Associate. The qualifications can be studied at Diploma (Dip CII), Advance Diploma (ACII) and Certificate (Cert CII) level and many candidates will already be at this level through roles in underwriting.

What the work involves

You will provide insurance companies with relevant information about a site that may affect their decision to accept requests for insurance cover.

You will investigate sites that need to be insured and prepare reports detailing the risks and recommend ways underwriters can reduce these.

Your reports will enable underwriters to decide whether or not to accept these risks and what terms and conditions should go into their policies. You may specialise in 1 of 4 areas: engineering, fire and perils, burglary or liability.

Type of person suited to this work

You will come into contact with a diverse range of people and must be able to communicate complicated and technical information in a clear way. In order to obtain accurate information for your employer you should have excellent observational skills and be able to communicate well.

An investigative nature will help you survey a variety of risks and you will need to be able to pay close attention to detail and work efficiently under pressure when writing up your reports for insurance companies. Workloads can be heavy so you should be self-motivated and organised.

Good IT skills are essential.

Working conditions

Most of your time will be spent investigating a variety of sites which could include industrial plants, engineering plants, oil rigs and construction zones. These can be potentially dangerous and polluted and may require you to work at heights. You will need to wear business attire when in the office but change into protective gear when surveying the site.

You will most likely work Monday to Friday during normal office hours but might need to work evenings or weekends depending on the availability of sites to visit. Working from home will give you greater flexibility and is increasingly favoured over being office based.

Future prospects

Career prospects may be affected by the financial climate. However, insurance risks are a high priority for many companies and jobs are available.

You may choose to specialise in one area of risk such as business interruption or you may travel overseas to work for a global insurer dealing in international risks.

You could be promoted to corporate risk manager or head of department but this will mean a less hands-on role. Many surveyors also move out of insurance and into the public sector.

Advantages/disadvantages

You will always be developing and growing in knowledge as no two days will be alike. You also have the chance to meet new people and to travel the world.

Sometimes customers may prove difficult to work with. Visiting hazardous sites on a regular basis can be physically and emotionally demanding.

Money guide

Starting out, trainee insurance surveyors earn around £22,000 a year.

With a few years of experience and professional qualifications you can earn between £26,000 and £35,000.

At senior level, salaries range from £40,000 to £65,000, or £60,000 to £100,000 within London.

Many employers also offer additional benefits such as medical insurance.

Related opportunities

- Building Surveyor p63
- Civil/Construction Engineer/Civil Engineering Technician p69
- Insurance Broker p29
- Insurance Underwriter p33

Further information

Chartered Insurance Institute
www.cii.co.uk

Lloyd's of London
www.lloyds.com

INSURANCE UNDERWRITER

ENTRY LEVEL 3

Qualifications and courses

Many companies offer graduate training schemes that require a 2.1 degree for entry. All subjects will be accepted but degrees in business, statistics, law, accounting, financial services and economics are useful.

Non-graduates with A levels/H grades or equivalent qualifications, as well as GCSEs/National 5s (A*–C/A–C) in English and Maths, can join the industry in a support or assistant role while studying for the professional qualifications required to become an underwriter. It is also common for people to switch to underwriting from actuarial, risk management or claims management roles.

Although it is not essential, pre-entry work experience with an insurance company can be advantageous, especially when applying for graduate training schemes, as competition is fierce.

A Level 2 Apprenticeship and Level 3 Advanced Apprenticeship in Providing Financial Services are also available as entry routes with options to pursue general insurance.

The Chartered Insurance Institute (CII) offers certificates, diplomas and advanced diplomas in insurance for new entrants. The Edexcel BTEC Level 3 Award in Lloyd's and London Market Introductory Test (LLMIT) and the CII Level 3 Award in London Market Insurance are established qualifications for brokers working in London.

What the work involves

Underwriters decide whether applications for insurance cover should be accepted and under what terms. They assess the size of risks against the likelihood of claims in order to work out premiums for their prospective clients.

In all negotiations you should make a profit for your company and protect them from losses. You will often specialise in one type of insurance, either in general (home, pet, household, etc), life, commercial, or reinsurance.

You will be expected to conduct in-depth research, study insurance proposals, interview specialists, analyse statistics and write up policies, often inserting additional conditions. You will be expected to keep detailed reports and records of policies you have written and the decisions made in relation to them.

Type of person suited to this work

Underwriting is a specialist job that requires an in-depth knowledge of risk in order to make predictions from applications. You will need excellent attention to detail, along with numeracy skills, in order to solve complex problems and prepare accurate and detailed reports.

You must be able to work well under pressure and make quick, difficult decisions. You should have a good sense of judgement and be trustworthy when handling confidential information.

Negotiation and communication skills are essential when arranging deals with brokers.

Working conditions

Underwriters' work is mainly office based and travel is rare although commercial underwriters will occasionally travel to meet clients. You will work Monday to Friday but might need to stay late at the office to meet deadlines. Most underwriters do have the option to work on flexitime which means you can shape your hours around what works best for you.

You will spend most of your time at a computer researching and writing up reports. You may need to investigate dangerous or distressing situations at times.

Future prospects

As you gain experience you will attract more difficult and complicated cases, enabling you to earn a promotion or switch companies more easily. Many underwriters choose to move into management or training roles or specialise in one type of insurance such as aviation.

You may wish to set up your own broking company, switch to reinsurance or train in sales and sell insurance packages which can prove to be a profitable option.

Advantages/disadvantages

Underwriters are constantly researching risks and are therefore learning new information every day which makes the job diverse and exciting. It also offers excellent benefits, such as share schemes and bonuses.

You may feel under pressure as you must make difficult decisions regarding risks often at short notice. Insurance can be a tough industry to work in during a recession.

Money guide

If you start in a support role with the intention of taking professional qualifications in order to progress to an underwriter, you can expect to earn £14,000 per year.

Trainee underwriters on a graduate programme will earn around £25,000 a year.

Senior level salaries are generally between £40,000 and £65,000.

With the right experience qualified underwriters could earn £100,000 or more.

Benefit packages are also common including discounted personal insurance and subsidised mortgages.

Related opportunities

- Actuary p5
- Insurance Broker p29
- Insurance Risk Surveyor p32

Further information

Chartered Insurance Institute
www.cii.co.uk

Financial Skills Partnership
www.financialskillspartnership.org.uk

International Underwriting Association of London
www.iua.co.uk

INVESTMENT ANALYST

ENTRY LEVEL 6

Qualifications and courses

Entry to this profession is usually through a graduate programme. For this you will need at least a 2.1 degree in any discipline, though a qualification in a relevant subject such as economics, accountancy, maths or statistics may be advantageous. To qualify for a degree course most applicants will need at least 2 A levels/3 H grades and 5 GCSEs/National 5s (A*–C/A–C).

A relevant postgraduate qualification is desirable, though not essential. The internationally recognised Chartered Financial Analyst (CFA) qualification or a Master in Business Administration (MBA) are good options. Pre-entry work experience, such as summer internships, is beneficial; often as many as 60%–95% of interns will be offered full-time employment.

Should you choose not to study for a degree, another possible entry route is as a junior researcher or administrator, which allows for progression to a position as an analyst. Applicants should ensure that they have good A levels/H grades and relevant commercial experience.

A second language, particularly French, German or Japanese, can be useful.

What the work involves

The main job of an investment analyst is to inform other professionals, such as stockbrokers, traders and fund managers, about the best and worst investments for making a profit.

Sell-side analysts assess an individual company's financial output and report this to private investors and unit trust fund managers. Buy-side analysts research investment opportunities for pension funds, investment banks, and insurance and life assurance companies.

Activities include analysing the economic stability of various countries, predicting the movement of share prices and taking account of the economic implications of events, for example, warfare.

You might work for an investment management company where you will collate information to advise in-house fund managers. Alternatively, you could work for stockbrokers and investment banks where you will be assisting portfolio managers and the employer's clients.

Type of person suited to this work

This job is suitable for someone that has an interest in current affairs and the impact these have on the financial markets. A certain amount of research is required in order to make informed, accurate decisions on possible financial opportunities.

You will be expected to present your findings and this requires tenacity and self-belief. The pressured environment, and constant need to be reliable, requires someone who can be resilient and trustworthy when calculating risks and forecasting trends.

In order to present findings in an effective way, employees need to be good communicators who have initiative and are numerically skilled.

Working conditions

This profession requires employees to work long hours, often starting work before 7am in preparation for the opening of the London Stock Exchange and closure of Far Eastern markets, and working until after 6pm. These hours could change, or even increase, for analysts who need to cover markets operating in different time zones.

A lot of time is also spent in front of computer screens, which can be tiring.

Future prospects

Although employment prospects have been significantly affected by the recent economic downturn, there are still annual recruitment opportunities for graduates with large companies, particularly in London, Manchester and Edinburgh. Application deadlines will usually occur in between October and January of your final year of your degree.

Opportunities for promotion are related to individual performance, with 3 years of service seeing an analyst progress to associate level and a further 2 to 3 years to the position of company vice-president. Should an individual or team appear to perform extremely well, competing companies will often headhunt successful employees. Relocation to another country or city may be required to progress.

Advantages/disadvantages

This is an extremely well paid job that allows for progression within a relatively short period of time.

Due to the fast moving stock market and the responsibility for vast sums of money, this job can often be highly pressured, yet rewarding.

Long days and intense work can lead to high stress levels.

Money guide

Entry level graduate positions typically pay around £25,000, though salaries can be higher in London.

With 5–8 years of experience you could earn £50,000 to £70,000. Senior roles can pay more, for example £100,000.

In addition to this, analysts will often receive substantial bonuses, low-rate mortgages, medical insurance, and life and pension cover.

Related opportunities

- Credit Analyst p17
- Economist p20
- Stockbroker p52

Further information

Association of Certified International Investment Analysts
www.aciia.org

Financial Conduct Authority
www.fca.org.uk

The Chartered Institute for Securities & Investment
www.cisi.org

LEGAL SECRETARY

ENTRY LEVEL 3

Qualifications and courses

There are no set entry qualifications to become a legal secretary and requirements will vary among employers, though many will require a minimum of GCSEs/National 5s (A*–C/A–C) in English and Maths. A degree/HND in secretarial studies, law, business with a language or government/public administration can increase your chances of employment.

You can take an NVQ at Levels 1–4 or City & Guilds qualification at Levels 2 and 3 in Business. City & Guilds diplomas are also available in keyboarding, text production skills and office procedures, as well as the OCR Certificate in Text Processing.

More specific legal secretarial courses are also available. A course in conveyancing, family law or wills, probate and administration could be useful or The Institute of Legal Secretaries and PAs offers the Legal Secretaries Diploma. Additionally, the Institute of Legal Executives provides the Level 2 Certificate and the Level 3 Diploma for Legal Secretaries and Pitman Training has various relevant diplomas and courses.

Relevant experience is valued more highly by some employers than qualifications. This can be gained through working as a clerical assistant, temping through agencies or undertaking voluntary work. Apprenticeships are also available.

Having another language such as French, Italian or Japanese may also give you an advantage.

What the work involves

Legal secretaries deal with the day-to-day tasks of the law firm.

You will provide administrative support and carry out tasks such as arranging meetings, making travel arrangements and updating filing systems.

You will also help lawyers, legal executives and paralegals with specialist tasks such as studying different parts of the law for cases and making notes at court, police stations and appointments with clients.

You will be responsible for typing legal documents and arranging statements and paperwork for court. Secretaries may also manage cases in fields such as debt recovery.

Type of person suited to this work

You will need to be very organised, have fast typing skills and a good grasp of spelling, grammar and punctuation.

You must also have a good eye for detail as you will be checking and handling confidential legal documents.

A legal secretary will have to be aware of different legal terminology and processes and possess excellent research skills.

You should be able to work to tight deadlines and be friendly, polite and helpful at all times.

Working conditions

You will work normal office hours (9am–5pm) and will spend a great deal of time using a computer as well as other office equipment.

You may also have to attend court to make notes, make visits to police stations, deliver legal documents and attend meetings, and at all times you will need to be well presented.

Future prospects

After 2 years' experience, it is possible to become an associate member of the Institute of Legal Secretaries and PAs.

You could progress to a role as senior secretary, personal assistant or office manager. There is a higher chance of promotion into a senior role within a bigger organisation.

With further training, you can become a legal executive, paralegal or licensed conveyancer.

Some secretaries go on to study for a law degree in order to become a solicitor or barrister.

Advantages/disadvantages

You will often be entrusted to work on your own, so you can be independent.

With further qualifications, there is the opportunity to progress into related legal careers.

The job can be repetitive, particularly as you will be mainly at your desk. Tight deadlines and a heavy workload can be very stressful.

Money guide

Salaries will depend on the location and size of the employer. Higher salaries are often available in London and other big cities.

A legal secretary in their first job can expect between £17,000 and £22,000 within London, or between £13,000 and £18,000 elsewhere.

With experience, this can rise to £25,000–£30,000.

Legal secretaries with extensive experience and qualifications working in top law firms can earn up to £37,000.

Related opportunities

- Bilingual Secretary p328
- Personal Assistant p42
- Receptionist p45

Further information

Chartered Institute of Legal Executives
www.cilex.org.uk

Institute of Legal Secretaries and PAs
www.institutelegalsecretaries.com

National Association of Licensed Paralegals
www.nationalparalegals.co.uk

LOSS ADJUSTER

ENTRY LEVEL 3

Qualifications and courses

Loss adjustment is not normally an entry-level position although some larger companies do run graduate training programmes. Any degree subject may be accepted, although finance, business studies, construction or engineering are beneficial. Entry is usually with a 2.2 degree or higher.

Entry without a degree or HND is possible. Many candidates will start in the claims handling department of an insurance company and progress to loss adjusting. There are also some loss adjusting administrator/ assistant positions, which could be an entry point. All entrants must have GCSEs/National 5s (A*–C/A–C) in English and Maths. Entry to this career is feasible through a Level 2 Apprenticeship or Level 3 Advanced Apprenticeship in Providing Financial Services, taking the General Insurance pathway.

Relevant practical experience is just as important as academic qualifications. You could start out as a claims technician and, with experience and qualifications gained on the job, such as the Chartered Insurance Institute (CII) Level 3 Certificate, Diploma and Advanced Diploma in Insurance, progress to a loss adjuster position. If you are a graduate looking to get on a trainee scheme try to gain work experience in insurance through vacation work or work placements.

Most qualified loss adjusters will become associate members of the Chartered Institute of Loss Adjusters (CILA). To take the CILA exams, you will first need to be an ordinary member, have at least 2 years' work experience in the office of a member company and have a relevant professional qualification. To become an ordinary member of the CILA, you will need to be aged 21 or over and working for a company or an independent loss adjusting firm.

What the work involves

Loss adjusters are independent specialists who work for insurance companies, investigating and advising on large or complicated claims or where there is a dispute.

You will visit premises, check damage and inspect reports from other professionals such as the fire service or police force to assess whether loss resulting from an incident is covered by the insurance policy. On completing your research, you will recommend the size of payments and offer advice to both claimants and insurers.

You could be investigating numerous claims which can involve a lot of responsibility, dealing with huge sums of money and sometimes being drafted in following major incidents such as plane crashes.

Type of person suited to this work

You will need excellent communication skills for contact with distressed claimants in order to be sympathetic while maintaining a professional distance.

Part of your job will be resolving disputes between organisations and/or individuals, which will require you to be calm and focused in order to make impartial decisions based on evidence.

You could be dealing with a number of complex cases at once, so good time management and organisational skills are important.

Working conditions

You will usually work normal office hours, although you could be called to look at premises in the evening or at weekends in emergency cases.

The majority of work is office based but you will have to travel to sites within the local area or overseas to make assessments.

You may be asked to assess the potentially distressing aftermath of situations such as fires, robberies, and train crashes, in which case you must be emotionally prepared. You will be required to wear relevant safety equipment when on-site.

Future prospects

Loss adjustment is a highly competitive area of work but opportunities are increasing.

You could work in a large firm, which may allow you to focus on a particular area of interest and could create an excellent route of career progression into a management role.

Smaller insurance firms usually hire loss adjusters on a case-by-case basis, so there is the possibility to work on a freelance basis. With experience, you could set up your own firm.

Advantages/disadvantages

Loss adjusters who specialise in major risks can earn extremely high salaries.

Insurance is a major industry overseas, so this career offers plenty of international opportunities.

Money guide

The typical starting salary for a trainee loss adjuster can be anywhere between £15,000 and £25,000.

Typical salaries with 5 years' experience are £25,000 to £45,000.

With specialist skills or management duties and extensive experience this can increase to in excess of £80,000.

Additional benefits could include a pension scheme, bonuses, company car and medical insurance.

Related opportunities

- Accountant p2
- Actuary p5
- Financial Adviser p26

Further information

Chartered Institute of Loss Adjusters
www.cila.co.uk

Chartered Insurance Institute
www.cii.co.uk

Financial Skills Partnership
www.financialskillspartnership.org.uk

MANAGEMENT CONSULTANT

ENTRY LEVEL 6

Qualifications and courses

Entry to this profession will generally require a minimum of a 2.1 Honours degree. Any subject can be accepted but having a degree in either business, management, maths, economics, finance, engineering and science or a related area can be an advantage. The typical minimum entry requirements for a degree are 2 A levels/3 H grades and 5 GCSEs/National 5s (A*–C/A–C).

A postgraduate qualification, such as a Master of Business Administration (MBA), can be an advantage; entry will usually require a good first degree and substantial work experience may also be required.

Mature entry may also be possible with relevant work experience that shows evidence of analytical business skills. Some entrants have an accountancy qualification with one of the main accountancy bodies. The Institute of Business Consulting's (IBC) Certificate in Management Consulting Essentials is designed for people who want to move into consultancy from another area. You should have a degree and at least 2 years' business experience for this.

Pre-entry work experience is useful as competition is extremely intense. This can be acquired from part-time work, voluntary work or internships.

What the work involves

You will work with organisations and companies to help and advise them on developing and improving their efficiency, services, products or staffing.

This might involve observing and evaluating working practices, researching information, training staff or developing new ways of operating. You will need extensive knowledge of the sector you are working within.

Consultants can work for a private consultancy organisation, be members of a specialised team or be freelance/self-employed.

Type of person suited to this work

You must be dynamic, confident and self-motivated. You will need to be able to research information, talk to staff and develop a thorough knowledge of an organisation. You must be good at identifying problems and problem solving. You may need to develop training programmes.

You will need excellent communication skills for writing reports, dealing with staff and presenting information.

You may have to review budgets and make savings, which may result in redundancies or spending cuts. Therefore you will need to have good financial skills, be able to justify your decisions and cope with any criticism.

Working conditions

A lot of your time will be spent travelling to different companies, so you will probably have to spend time away from home.

Working to deadlines can be stressful. The work can be pressured as you will have to take responsibility for high-level decisions which could have far-reaching consequences.

You could be self-employed, work for a private consultancy service or be part of a team of company improvement specialists.

Future prospects

While the financial crisis initially caused a fall in revenue in 2009–10, the UK consulting industry has rebounded and is expected to continue to grow over the next few years.

Graduates tend to start out as analysts before progressing to the full consultancy role. The next step is usually to manager or senior consultant, which can be achieved in as little as 3 years. From there consultants can go on to become partner or director of a firm. Going freelance is also possible.

Advantages/disadvantages

This is a rewarding, varied and interesting career with lots of opportunities.

Salaries can be high and you may be able to travel.

This job can be stressful and demanding, and hours can be long and unpredictable.

Money guide

If you are freelance or self-employed you will probably be paid per day and your earnings will depend on your success.

Entry level consultants may earn from £25,000 to £30,000.

With several years of experience this can rise to around £50,000.

Senior consultants can earn much more and also receive commission and bonuses.

Related opportunities

- Equality and Diversity Officer p23
- Financial Adviser p26
- Human Resources/Personnel Officer p28

Further information

Chartered Management Institute
www.managers.org.uk

Institute of Consulting
www.iconsulting.org.uk

Management Consultancies Association
www.mca.org.uk

MEDICAL RECEPTIONIST

ENTRY LEVEL 2

Qualifications and courses

There are no minimum entry requirements, although employers sometimes ask for 5 GCSEs/National 5s (A*–C/A–C), including English and Maths.

Other qualifications that may be useful include Diplomas in Business Administration or Society, Health and Development, the City & Guilds Level 2 Certificate in Medical Reception or the Edexcel Level 2 NVQ in Support Services in Health Care.

Work experience in administration or in customer service is helpful. Apprenticeships in Business and Administration are available for candidates aged between 16 and 24.

Medical receptionists will be trained on the job and may be encouraged to undertake further training. The Association of Medical Secretaries, Practice Managers, Administrators and Receptionists (AMSPAR) offers several training courses that include the Certificate in Health Service Administration and the Level 2 and Level 3 Certificates in Medical Administration.

What the work involves

Medical receptionists book appointments for patients, organise the appointment diaries, answer the telephone and take messages.

You will be responsible for greeting patients when they arrive, making sure they are in the right place, and answering their queries.

You will also carry out some general administrative work, such as preparing patients' notes and files, dealing with post and typing letters.

Type of person suited to this work

It is important that you are well presented, friendly and reassuring. You will be the first point of contact for patients, so you will need to make a good first impression.

Excellent communication skills are required as you will be interacting with patients and other medical staff all day, in person and on the telephone.

Most receptionists are required to have a good working knowledge of basic computer programs as the majority of work is computer based.

You will need to be well organised and efficient, as you might be dealing with several queries at once and will need to make sure they are all dealt with as quickly and accurately as possible.

As you will be helping sick, ill or distressed patients it is important to be sympathetic when dealing with their problems.

You will often be dealing with confidential information and so it is important that you are respectful and professional.

Working conditions

You will be working standard office hours, Monday to Friday. However you may work shifts including the weekends and evenings if your place of work offers extended opening hours.

You will spend most of your time in an office, sitting at a desk, and looking at a computer screen.

Future prospects

Medical receptionists are needed all over the UK, so there are good job prospects. Most are employed by the NHS but there are opportunities in the private sector.

Progression in this career is relatively easy. With some training you could become a medical secretary or move into a supervisory or managerial role.

Advantages/disadvantages

Helping people who are sick or distressed will bring great job satisfaction.

You will have to deal with patients who could be angry or distressed which could be upsetting.

This job will be great for you if you enjoy meeting new people.

Part-time work is widely available.

You will work in accordance with surgery hours which can sometimes mean finishing late with extended opening hours and weekend work.

Money guide

Starting salaries on the NHS, coming under band 3 of the Agenda for Change pay scale, are £16,271 to £19,268.

With experience this would increase to between £18,000 and £20,000.

Those in senior positions or with extra responsibilities might be paid up to £22,000.

London pay rates are likely to be above the national rates.

Related opportunities

- Hotel Receptionist p128
- Personal Assistant p42
- Secretary p50

Further information

Association of Medical Secretaries, Practice Managers, Administrators and Receptionists
www.amspar.com

Skills CFA
www.skillscfa.org

PAYROLL MANAGER

ENTRY LEVEL 2

Qualifications and courses

You will not be required to have any specific qualifications to become a payroll clerk, supervisor or manager. However, employers prefer candidates with GCSEs/National 5s (A*–C/A–C) or equivalent, including English and Maths.

It is extremely unlikely that you will be able to go straight into a managerial role, as most employers will want at least 5 years' experience. Your skills, experience and industry knowledge are likely to be more relevant than any formal qualifications you may hold.

The Diploma in Business, Administration and Finance or the Levels 1–3 qualifications in Payroll from the International Association of Book-keepers (IAB) can both be useful for entry into this line of work.

Both intermediate and advanced apprenticeships are available in Payroll. Relevant experience in areas such as bookkeeping is welcome.

You will train on the job but there are also professional qualifications you can take while working, eg the Foundation degree in Payroll Management from the Chartered Institute of Payroll Professionals (CIPP).

What the work involves

Payroll managers are employed by organisations to arrange and manage employees' salaries. You will ensure that each member of staff receives the correct amount on the correct date. When doing this you will take into account laws regarding tax, national insurance, sick pay and maternity/paternity leave.

Your tasks will include keeping records of hours worked, calculating repayments for salary advances or student loans, calculating pay, pensions and tax deductions.

As you progress from payroll clerk to payroll supervisor and payroll manager you will gradually take on more responsibilities, such as managing and delegating tasks to a team of payroll clerks, and creating and documenting payroll policies.

Type of person suited to this work

As you will be in contact with many employees and work alongside other payroll staff, you must enjoy working with other people and be able to work in a team. You should be sensitive in your approach to discussing earnings with employees, and treat their information with confidentiality.

As you will be responsible for maintaining records and large amounts of information you must be organised and methodical in your work.

You will need strong numerical and IT skills as you will be working with figures and working on computerised systems. You should also be able to multi-task and work to tight deadlines.

Working conditions

From Monday to Friday you will work around 37 hours per week. You might have to work overtime, especially at the end of a financial year which can be a busy time.

You might have the option of working part time or flexible hours and there may even be opportunities for job sharing.

You will be largely office based. You will have a desk from which you will answer the phone, send emails and make calculations. You may have to attend meetings at times.

Future prospects

You will enter this profession as a payroll clerk and after you have gained a few years' experience and qualifications you will be able to progress to payroll supervisor and payroll manager.

These roles will involve more responsibility and managerial tasks such as liaising with HM Revenue & Customs, organising training for other members of payroll staff and being involved in business strategy.

Advantages/disadvantages

You will build relationships with a variety of people as you will potentially be working with each employee within an organisation.

At times the administrative nature of your work may become repetitive and monotonous.

Money guide

As a payroll clerk your starting salary can be around £14,000 per year.

With experience you can progress to a supervisory position and earn about £23,000 a year.

The salary for a payroll manager is dependent on the size of the team and your responsibilities. Starting salaries are likely to be between £25,000 and £35,000 with some positions available in excess of £40,000.

Related opportunities

- Accounting Technician and Accounts/Finance Clerk p4
- Bank Cashier/Customer Adviser p9
- Pensions Administrator p40

Further information

Association of Accounting Technicians
www.aat.org.uk

Chartered Institute of Payroll Professionals
www.cipp.org.uk

International Association of Book-keepers
www.iab.org.uk

PENSIONS ADMINISTRATOR

ENTRY LEVEL 2

Qualifications and courses

The entry requirements can vary widely but you will need a minimum of 4 GCSEs/National 5s (A*–C/A–C) including English and Maths.

It is highly likely that you will be expected to work towards a professional qualification as you work. The Pensions Management Institute (PMI) have numerous courses available, including an Award/Certificate in Pensions Essentials, a Certificate/Diploma in Pensions Administration and a Certificate in Pension Calculations (CPC). Advanced level apprenticeships in Providing Financial Services are available. Following this route can lead to a career as a pensions administrator, pensions team leader or pensions manager.

Previous experience in office work, an accounts role or a customer service role will be useful.

What the work involves

As a pensions administrator you will be responsible for the general management and maintenance of pension schemes and life insurance policies.

You will answer queries from customers by telephone or email and complete the necessary associated administration. This can include information on policies in general, tax relief entitlement, cash sums on retirement and options for benefit transfer.

You will undertake a variety of administrative tasks such as calculating pension forecasts, processing pension contributions and maintaining and updating accounts when, for example, someone retires. When a policy has to be paid out, in case of retirement or a death, you will organise all of the paperwork and arrange the payment of lump sums.

Type of person suited to this work

You should enjoy methodical, detailed work. You will need strong mathematical and IT skills in order to work out calculations and check databases for information.

As you will be dealing with the public a great deal you should be friendly and polite and be able to explain detailed policies in laymen's terms. You should have an interest in the financial sector and tax regulations and keep up to date with economic developments.

As you will be maintaining records and referring back to them frequently you must have excellent organisational skills. You must be able to multi-task and prioritise your workload.

Working conditions

You will work Monday to Friday, 35 hours a week. At times you may be required to work overtime at weekends or in the evenings. You are likely to be able to work part time with flexible hours or job sharing.

You will be office based, which will have certain benefits depending on the organisation you work for.

You will have a mainly sedentary working lifestyle, sitting at a desk using computers and answering the telephone.

A good deal of on-the-job assessment and training is required throughout your career, for example pensions companies must assess staff involved in pension schemes owing to the Financial Conduct Authority (FCA) requirements.

Future prospects

With experience and further qualifications you may be promoted to team leader or a management position.

There may also be opportunities to move across to pension advice or consultancy where you will provide information and guidance regarding financial planning and employee benefits.

Advantages/disadvantages

Each day you will have to deal with a variety of different queries from customers.

Although you may have to deal with stressed and annoyed customers, generally the work will be fairly unstressful.

Some aspects of your work may be repetitive and will include sitting at a desk and in front of a screen for much of your working day.

Money guide

As a trainee pensions administrator you can earn from £13,000 to £19,000 per year.

For experienced pensions administrators, annual salaries are typically between £20,000 and £35,000.

In a senior role or as a team leader you can earn up to £40,000 per year.

Benefits packages may be available, including pension, insurance and bonuses based on personal or company performance.

Related opportunities

- Bank Cashier/Customer Adviser p9
- Insurance Broker p29
- Pensions Adviser p41

Further information

Chartered Insurance Institute
www.cii.co.uk

Pensions Management Institute
www.pensions-pmi.org.uk

PENSIONS ADVISER

ENTRY LEVEL 2

Qualifications and courses

Most pensions advisers have a degree. It may be possible to enter this line of work through a graduate training programme, for example with a large pension or insurance company. You will ideally need a degree or HND in economics, business and finance, maths or management. Entry to a degree will usually be with 2 A levels/3 H grades and 5 GCSEs/National 5s (A*–C/A–C).

Graduate training programmes are very competitive, so prior experience in a customer-facing, sales or financial role can be useful.

Alternatively, many people in this job role start out as pensions administrators and work their way up to adviser while earning professional qualifications. To become an administrator you will need at least 4 GCSEs/National 5s, including English and Maths. Some employers may require a minimum of A level qualifications or equivalent. Pensions can also be a second career for people with a background in financial services or working with the public. Many employers consider a strong financial or sales background and good people skills to be more important than formal qualifications.

All pensions advisers will need to take professional qualifications before they can give advice. The Chartered Insurance Institute (CII) and the Pensions Management Institute (PMI) provide qualifications, including the CII Certificate in Life and Pensions and the PMI Certificate in Pensions Calculation.

There are also apprenticeships in Providing Financial Services or in Advising on Financial Products which may be useful.

What the work involves

Pensions advisers help individuals and organisations to choose, create and manage a pension plan that is most suited to their needs.

You will work in-house, or as a consultant for businesses and other organisations, to set up and maintain pensions that will suit all employees while remaining within budget.

Knowledge of the markets and government policy will help inform your decisions, along with an understanding of your clients' assets, circumstances, and financial situation.

Type of person suited to this work

As you will be working closely with the public you should have excellent communication and interpersonal skills in order to explain complex policies in laymen's terms in a polite, friendly manner. You should have a genuine interest in answering consumers' financial queries.

You must have strong numerical skills in order to make accurate financial estimates and economic forecasts and IT skills to keep records of current policies and procedures.

You must have excellent organisational skills and pay attention to detail.

An interest in financial markets and products could be beneficial, along with excellent concentration and attention span.

Working conditions

You will work around 40 hours a week, Monday to Friday. You may have to be flexible with your hours to suit clients who need weekend or evening appointments.

You will be mainly office based but you might occasionally have to travel within the UK to meet with clients and organisations or to liaise with other financial advisers.

Future prospects

As the financial sector is constantly changing and adjusting its regulations, and you must be aware of new developments, you will be subject to training and continuing professional development (CPD).

You may be promoted to senior roles, progress to other advisory roles in financial areas in actuarial firms, with accountants or solicitors for example. You may also be able to become self-employed.

Advantages/disadvantages

Your work will be diverse as you will meet with different customers on a daily basis and tailor your advice to each new client.

Some aspects of your work might be stressful, particularly if you are on performance related pay.

Money guide

With experience and qualifications advisers generally earn £25,000 to £50,000 a year.

If you work in a senior role for a large firm you can earn in excess of £80,000.

Performance bonuses are often available and benefits may include low rate insurance and mortgages.

Related opportunities

- Accountant p2
- Actuary p5
- Financial Adviser p26

Further information

Pension Careers
www.pensioncareers.co.uk

Pensions Management Institute
www.pensions-pmi.org.uk

PERSONAL ASSISTANT

ENTRY LEVEL 2

Qualifications and courses

There are no specific qualifications required but employers do want you to have a good standard of general education, including GCSEs/National 5s (A*–C/A–C) in English and Maths. A business-related BTEC or HND could help you find a position with greater responsibilities.

You may find it useful to have an NVQ Level 2 and/or 3 in Business and Administration or a City & Guilds Certificate/Diploma in Business and Administration. Advanced apprenticeships are also available.

Some employers may expect a bachelor's degree or equivalent. Any subject is acceptable but business, administration, secretarial studies and management degrees may increase your chances.

Previous experience, usually about 2 years, in other administrative or clerical roles is vital. For this reason graduates are unlikely to enter directly into a PA position. Since junior level administrative roles are very competitive, registering with temp agencies could be the best way to gain initial experience.

To show your commitment to the career, it may be beneficial to take the Private Secretary's Diploma offered by LCCI (London Chamber of Commerce and Industry) International Qualifications or Pitman Training's Executive PA Diploma. These are also useful for developing desirable skills such as shorthand and audio typing. A foreign language can also be helpful.

What the work involves

Personal assistants ease the workload of senior managers and directors, allowing businesses to run more efficiently.

They are responsible for administrative and secretarial duties.

You will work on a one-to-one basis with your manager, often making decisions on their behalf and representing them at events.

It will be your job to organise efficient administrative systems, both paper and IT based. You will maintain diaries, take minutes, answer phone calls, greet visitors, write letters and arrange meetings and travel.

Type of person suited to this work

Excellent organisational skills are essential. The role involves juggling several things at once so you need to be adaptable, efficient and able to work to deadlines. You will have to follow instructions but also use your initiative and manage your own workload.

You will need a good knowledge of the company you work for and you may have to deal with budgets. Strong written and verbal communication skills are a must.

You should be discreet and reliable as you may be dealing with confidential information. Excellent IT skills are essential in this role.

Working conditions

You will work in an office and your hours will mainly be 9am–5pm but occasionally you may have to work overtime to meet deadlines.

As the role involves frequent contact with colleagues and clients, you will be expected to dress quite formally.

Future prospects

With experience, PAs can progress rapidly to senior roles with increased responsibility and the possibility of managing junior employees.

PAs gain insight into all aspects of a business and these skills can be transferred to roles in other sectors, such as human resources or public relations.

There are opportunities to work throughout the UK and, if you have language skills, abroad.

Experienced PAs can become self-employed as 'virtual assistants', working from home for a range of clients.

Advantages/disadvantages

The job can be varied and interesting with a lot of responsibility.

If you have a good working relationship with your manager then the role can be very rewarding.

As you work in a support role, it can be frustrating if your contribution is not recognised within the company.

Money guide

Salaries vary according to the size and type of company you work for and your level of responsibility.

Wages tend to be higher in London and south-east England.

A starting salary tends to be around £18,000 to £25,000 per year.

A senior personal assistant in a large company could achieve a salary of up to £50,000.

Related opportunities

- Human Resources/Personnel Officer p28
- Public Relations Officer p396
- Receptionist p45
- Secretary p50

Further information

Institute of Administrative Management
www.instam.org

London Chamber of Commerce and Industry
www.londonchamber.co.uk

Skills CFA
www.skillscfa.org

PROJECT MANAGER ENTRY LEVEL 2

Qualifications and courses

There are no formal academic requirements but all entrants will need extensive experience in business, management, engineering, construction, IT, science, or whichever sector they are hoping to work in. Many project managers start in a project support team or gain experience managing smaller projects as part of another job.

A Foundation degree, degree or postgraduate qualification in project management, business management, IT or construction management would be an advantage. Entry onto degree courses requires at least 2 A levels/3 H grades and 5 GCSEs/National 5s (A*–C/A–C), or equivalent.

Knowledge of PRINCE2 and specialist software such as MS Project or Workbench could be an advantage, though not essential.

There are options to study while you are working by taking online or part-time courses. The Association for Project Management (APM), The Chartered Institute for IT (BCS) and the Project Management Institute (PMI) all offer a range of professional qualifications which are suitable for both entry-level and experienced project managers.

What the work involves

Many project managers specialise in a particular area, such as the managing of commercial business improvements.

As project manager, you will oversee all aspects of a project, from plans to budgets. In the course of a job, a project manager will liaise with the client, create a timescale, a budget plan that keeps to agreed standards, and choose a capable project team. Furthermore, you will report back to your line manager or senior manager and clients, updating them on the progress, scheduling, and difficulties of the project.

You will need to access specialist software for scheduling, risk analysis, costing and estimating.

Type of person suited to this work

The project manager is relied upon to coordinate the team's operations and solve any problems that may arise. Due to this, it is necessary for people thinking of entering this profession to enjoy teamwork and have strong people management, communication, and organisational skills. In order to solve any problems which may arise, a project manager must be logical and methodical, especially when under pressure.

In addition to this, the job of a project manager requires good computer skills and an ability to understand complex information and control budgets, whilst working on several other projects.

Working conditions

A certain amount of variation must be allowed for from these hours due to variety in projects. However, generally, hours range from 9am to 5pm, Monday to Friday. Like many jobs, the meeting of deadlines may mean these hours are occasionally increased.

Managers are often office based, with the occasional need to visit sites or clients to check progression. Should a manager be working on a project abroad, it may be necessary to spend prolonged periods of time away from home.

Future prospects

By becoming a project manager you will be joining a growing industry. Upon entering the profession, most people will make up part of the project support team, progressing to team leader after the gaining of experience, which gradually leads to a position as project manager.

There are opportunities for promotion to senior management posts, although this may mean changing companies, with some managers setting up their own consultancy business. There are opportunities to work abroad.

Advantages/disadvantages

This job allows for variety due to there being many different projects to work on. Although this may cause the employee to feel pressured, the rewards of the completed project may be of greater benefit.

Salaries are very rewarding and the expansion of the industry indicates that this is fast becoming a thriving industry with long term employment prospects.

Money guide

The starting salary for people joining the profession in a support role ranges from around £20,000 to £27,000 a year.

Earnings for experienced project managers can be between £30,000 and £60,000.

Top salaries can reach in excess of £75,000–£80,000.

Freelance project managers will be paid a daily rate.

There are often opportunities for bonuses when a deadline or objective has been met.

Related opportunities

- Business Analyst p136
- Construction Supervisor/Manager p74
- Risk Manager p49

Further information

Association for Project Management
www.apm.org.uk

Chartered Management Institute
www.managers.org.uk

Project Management Institute
www.pmi.org.uk

QUALITY MANAGER

ENTRY LEVEL 2

Qualifications and courses

There are no set entry requirements although many entrants hold a degree or HND. The general entry requirements for a degree are 2 A levels/3 H grades and 5 GCSEs/National 5s (A*–C/A–C). HNDs usually require at least 1 A level/H grade and 4 GCSEs/National 5s. Depending on the industry that you want to move into, useful subjects may include business studies, engineering or physical, mathematical or applied sciences. Some areas require a technical background but others are open to all graduates. A pre-entry postgraduate qualification is not needed, although they are available.

You will need previous experience in quality control or management. Graduates can gain experience by trying to get a relevant summer job, arrange a work shadowing placement or seek out and talk to staff in supporting roles. You can also start in a technical job and progress to quality control.

Entry without a degree or HND is sometimes possible if an applicant has significant training and experience in a technician role, or is moving across from another vocational field involving quality or management. Having a relevant BTEC, HND, degree or professional qualification can boost your promotion prospects, so if you don't currently hold any higher qualifications it might be something to consider if you wish to progress. Providers of professional qualifications include the Chartered Quality Institute (CQI) and the Chartered Management Institute (CMI).

What the work involves

Quality managers are employed by an organisation to ensure that quality assurance aims are met in relation to products or services; this includes legal compliance levels and customer expectations.

Practices include monitoring and advising on existing systems in order to consistently improve current standards, and publishing data and reports that inform management.

Quality managers must ensure that the company they are working for is applying the required level of environmental and health and safety standards. Encouraging staff to adhere to new doctrines and legislation is fundamental.

Type of person suited to this work

This job is suited to someone who has an interest in securing and improving standards of quality. In order to do this, it is necessary to have good communication skills in order to influence and persuade others to follow set regulations and uphold required standards.

Problems may arise due to complicated legislation and staff lacking interest and so quality managers must be resilient and create ways in which models of quality can be easily understood and adhered to. An organisation's customers must be listened to and so quality managers must be adaptable and approachable.

Working conditions

Normal working hours apply when employed by the government or a bank, although a position in engineering, production or retail could involve shift work. Offices and laboratories are where most are based, although those with experience often become consultants to smaller firms once they have gained enough experience to be self-employed.

It may be necessary to travel to different clients during the working day, or even to stay overnight.

Future prospects

There are around 25,000 quality managers in the UK with employment opportunities in a wide range of industrial, commercial and public sector organisations. You can work for small companies or large multinational corporations.

Career development prospects are good. Experienced quality managers may be able to progress to senior management or director-level positions. It is possible to progress within the quality function or to go on to management jobs in other areas of the business. Some go on to become freelance consultants.

Advantages/disadvantages

Quality managers have high levels of responsibility and so the work they undertake can be both rewarding and respected.

Career progression or movement to self-employment is possible.

Quality legislation is constantly changing so entrants must be willing to remain up to date with developments in the field.

Money guide

Quality managers can expect a starting salary in the region of £18,000 to £25,000.

As you gain experience and progress to a senior role, you can achieve earnings of £35,000 to £70,000.

Salaries vary according to the sector you are working in, company size and geographical location.

Related opportunities

- Project Manager p43
- Quality Control Inspector p222
- Statistician p511

Further information

British Quality Foundation
www.bqf.org.uk

Chartered Management Institute
www.managers.org.uk

Chartered Quality Institute
www.thecqi.org

RECEPTIONIST

ENTRY LEVEL 2

Qualifications and courses

There are no minimum entry requirements, although employers are likely to ask for 5 GCSEs/National 5s (A*–C/A–C), including English and Maths, or NVQs/SVQs at Levels 1 or 2.

IT skills such as word processing and previous office experience will be a distinct advantage. You can gain experience through temping for agencies. Foreign languages may also be useful if you're applying to an organisation that deals with international visitors and clients.

There are various relevant training options available that might give you an advantage. City & Guilds offer several courses such as the Diploma/Advanced Diploma in Reception Operations and Services. There is also an NCFE Level 1 NVQ Certificate in Customer Service and a Level 2 Certificate in Customer Service Knowledge.

An intermediate level apprenticeship in business and administration may be available for candidates aged 16–24 who are interested in becoming a receptionist.

Once entrants obtain a position, training will be provided on the job and many employers encourage further study.

What the work involves

You will be greeting visitors, signing them in and out of the building, checking they know where they are going and answering any queries.

Often based by the entrance, you will be the first point of contact for the organisation both for visitors and those phoning to make enquiries.

You will be responsible for answering the telephone, transferring calls and taking messages, as well as managing queries via email.

You may also manage incoming and outgoing post and handle cash transactions.

Type of person suited to this work

You will create the first impression of your organisation, so it is vital that you should be friendly, welcoming, outgoing and well presented.

Excellent communication skills are essential as you will be solving problems and queries for visitors and other members of staff.

You will need to be able to remain calm under pressure and balance a heavy workload, as the reception desk could get very busy at times.

Good organisation skills and efficiency are needed for dealing with visitors' queries swiftly and accurately.

Working conditions

Receptionists are based at a reception desk, with access to a phone and computer.

You will normally work standard office hours Monday to Friday, but this does depend on the opening hours of your place of work. You may need to work evenings and weekends.

How busy you are is entirely dependent on the size and nature of the organisation you work for.

There are usually opportunities to work part time or on temporary contracts.

Future prospects

All types of organisations employ receptionists including law firms, banks, garages, leisure centres and veterinary practices. There are therefore good job prospects across the UK.

Reception work offers progression into other areas such as office or customer service work; you will develop a good range of transferable skills.

You may be able to progress to a managerial role or supervisory position after a few years' experience and further training.

Once within a company, you may also be able to sound out other opportunities, even if unrelated to your field.

Advantages/disadvantages

This is a great job if you enjoy meeting people and providing good customer service.

Some people you encounter may be rude or angry if they have a problem with the company you work for.

There are good opportunities to enter other professions such as office or secretarial work.

Money guide

Starting salaries are around £12,000 to £15,000.

Senior receptionists with extra responsibilities may earn £25,000 or more.

Temporary and part-time receptionists can earn up to £10 an hour.

Related opportunities

- Medical Receptionist p38
- Personal Assistant p42
- Secretary p50

Further information

London Chamber of Commerce and Industry
www.londonchamber.co.uk

Skills CFA
www.skillscfa.org

RECRUITMENT/EMPLOYMENT AGENCY CONSULTANT

ENTRY LEVEL 2

Qualifications and courses

Employers are likely to ask for a minimum of 5 GCSEs/National 5s (A*–C/A–C), although many entrants are graduates. The general entry requirements for a degree are 2 A levels/3 H grades and 5 GCSEs/National 5s (A*–C/A–C). Graduate schemes are available and although most subjects are welcome, a degree in human resources, business or a subject related to the industry the agency recruits for may give you an edge.

While there are many entry-level and trainee vacancies available there is also a lot of competition for them, so prior experience in sales, human resources or another customer-oriented role will be an advantage.

Your skills and personality will often be more important than your academic qualifications. Good sales skills, an excellent telephone manner and a positive attitude are vital.

The Recruitment and Employment Confederation (REC) and the Chartered Institute of Personnel and Development (CIPD) both offer various courses to help you develop throughout your career.

What the work involves

As a recruitment consultant, it will be your job to match up candidates with jobs. Your clients will be both the companies you recruit for and the candidates you are recruiting.

You will help companies recruit the right staff for permanent and temporary jobs through advertising, networking, headhunting and referrals.

Your work will include carrying out a preliminary interview and background check and then helping suitable candidates to find work to suit their skills and experience.

You will assess people's skills to help them decide on the type of work they want, and may suggest further training, which could be available through your company. You will spend time making contacts with new companies to sell your agency's services.

Type of person suited to this work

You will be selling your agency's services so will need to be well presented with excellent sales ability.

You will probably be working on commission so should be able to remain calm when working to tight deadlines.

You will need to be persuasive as it is essential that employers continue to use your agency. You may need to be persistent if they do not respond after a first approach.

Working conditions

Office hours will often be long as you might have to speak to clients outside working hours.

You will be doing a lot of work on the phone and some agencies are internet based. You may need to visit employer premises, so a driving licence would be needed. You will probably work in a team and be expected to dress smartly.

Future prospects

Opportunities depend on the economy and which sectors are hiring new staff.

You could work for a specialist agency, for example supplying medical staff, but may need experience within that sector first. Some people work as 'headhunters', actively searching out people for specific high-level jobs.

With good results you could be promoted to senior consultant and then branch manager. You may go on to start your own agency or you could move into a related area such as human resources.

Advantages/disadvantages

You will meet people at all levels and will get satisfaction from helping them find the right job or career.

You will develop transferable interpersonal skills and a better understanding of the recruitment process if you ever decide to change careers.

Working on commission can be stressful and clients and businesses can be demanding.

This is a very competitive career and your success will depend on your sales ability.

There are often targets to hit which need to be balanced alongside finding the right candidate for the role.

Money guide

Recruitment consultants often work on commission and receive bonuses for meeting sales targets. This means that you can earn considerably more than your basic salary if you perform well.

Trainees usually start on a basic salary between £15,000 and £20,000 per year, plus commission.

Managers with 10–15 years' experience can achieve over £40,000 basic salary (£60,000 after commission).

Wages are higher in London and the south-east of England.

Related opportunities

- Human Resources/Personnel Officer p28
- Marketing Manager/Director p388
- Secretary p50

Further information

Chartered Institute of Personnel and Development
www.cipd.co.uk

Recruitment & Employment Confederation
www.rec.uk.com

REGENERATION MANAGER/ ECONOMIC DEVELOPMENT OFFICER

ENTRY LEVEL 2

Qualifications and courses

Entry without a degree is possible with significant skills and experience, although many entrants to this profession are graduates. Useful subjects include regeneration, housing, planning and surveying, and economics. Entry for a degree requires at least 2 A levels/3 H grades plus 5 GCSEs/National 5s (A*–C/A–C), including English and Maths. BTECs, HNC/HND qualifications and postgraduate study may all be beneficial as well.

You should also gain relevant pre-entry work experience in areas such as housing, planning, urban design or surveying or do voluntary environmental work in order to improve career and employment prospects. Job placements within regeneration are not recommended for new graduates as several years' relevant experience may be required.

Knowledge of government regeneration policy and the main sources of funding may also strengthen applications. Voluntary placements are available with organisations such as Groundwork and the Prince's Regeneration Trust.

You may start out as an administrator, assistant or researcher in an economic development unit and work your way up.

What the work involves

Regeneration managers aim to improve the living standards within their community by developing local projects with the aim to increase job opportunities and stimulate economic growth. The extent of involvement ranges from the presentation of an idea, to ensuring that the project is completed on time and on budget, and the generation of financial support and planning permission.

You will also be charged with improving relations between local businesses and government, improving business networks, setting up training schemes for the unemployed, applying for national and European funding as well as promoting the local area to tourists and new employers.

Typical areas you would be expected to help develop would include residential areas where local industries have closed down, areas of low income and high unemployment, and areas with poor access to healthcare and education.

Specialist fields include economic development, planning, surveying and housing.

Type of person suited to this work

It is necessary to have an interest in the ways in which communities and living environments can be managed and improved.

As this profession involves a lot of negotiation with a variety of people, you will need good communication skills and should be able to influence people towards contributing in a positive way.

Regeneration managers often need to be strict with budgets and able to solve problems that may arise; both of which need a strong will and an ability to deliver results in a set amount of time.

Working conditions

Working hours are typical of those for an office job, with the number of hours worked usually being around 37 a week. However, on occasion, you will be expected to attend a residency meeting during the evening or at weekends.

Employment with local councils tends to be employee focused, with most offering part-time or job sharing contracts, alongside flexitime schemes.

Although mostly based in an office, you will need to travel to sites that are undergoing the regeneration process in order to meet with residents, clients and agencies.

Future prospects

The government is currently committed to improving community areas through regeneration schemes, making this a very positive vocation to get involved with.

Opportunities are available within local authorities and government agencies, regional development agencies and English Partnerships and the government's national regeneration agency. There are also employment possibilities with private consultancies, housing associations and property developers.

Advantages/disadvantages

Both the public and private sector are becoming involved in regeneration projects, with opportunities opening up in senior management roles for those with experience.

You get to implement and oversee development and growth in local areas which will hopefully provide young adults especially with opportunities otherwise denied to them.

This job may be extremely challenging when you have to convince people that regeneration is positive, especially when they have lived in a location for a certain number of years.

Money guide

Initially regeneration managers can expect to earn approximately £22,000 a year.

Salaries steadily increase to around £26,000 to £35,000 as you gain experience.

Those in senior management roles can achieve a salary of up to £60,000 a year, depending on their level of responsibility.

Related opportunities

- Building Conservation Officer p61
- Chartered Surveyor p68
- Project Manager p43

Further information

British Urban Regeneration Association
www.rudi.net/partners/bura

Homes and Communities Agency
www.homesandcommunities.co.uk

Local Government Association
www.local.gov.uk

REGISTRAR OF BIRTHS, DEATHS, MARRIAGES AND CIVIL PARTNERSHIPS

ENTRY LEVEL 2

Qualifications and courses

There are no set entry requirements for this career, although candidates with 3 GCSEs/National 5s (A*–C/A–C, including English and Maths, would be at an advantage. Whilst training in registration law and procedures is given on the job, experience of dealing with a wide range of people and public speaking might be useful when making your application.

In England and Wales training is organised by the General Register Office and candidates can take the Registrar General's Certificate of Competence in Registration Law and Practice. In Scotland, training is organised by the General Register Office for Scotland and candidates take the Certificate of Proficiency in the Law and Practice of Registration, eligibility for which requires at least 2 years' work experience. The Local Registration Services Association (LRSA) launched the new National Qualification in September 2014, which brings together all local authorities under one unified set of standards and professional expectations.

Training in customer care and dealing with bereavement is also highly likely.

Applicants from certain professions are prohibited from becoming registrars, including doctors, midwives, ministers of religion, funeral directors and anyone working in the life assurance industry.

What the work involves

Registrars record all births, stillbirths, marriages, civil partnerships and deaths in their local area, making sure all details are accurate.

After a birth, you will interview parents, record the baby's name and date of birth and issue a birth certificate. After a death, you will interview relatives before providing a death certificate and informing the coroner or procurator fiscal if anything seems suspicious.

You will interview people planning to marry or enter a civil partnership to check that they are legally eligible to do so and you will conduct marriage and civil partnership ceremonies.

Type of person suited to this work

You will need to be a good listener and have the ability to communicate effectively with a wide range of people.

As you will often be dealing with people in difficult circumstances, discretion, tact and patience are essential attributes.

Confidence with public speaking is important for conducting marriages and civil partnerships.

Attention to detail, accuracy and the ability to work neatly are all vital when completing forms and ensuring that all legal requirements have been met.

You must be able to use your initiative and judgement to assess whether someone is withholding information.

Working conditions

You will be based in the registrar's office for your district and much of your day will be spent interviewing people by appointment.

You will work a 37 hour week which will often include Saturdays. You may also need to be on-call to work evenings, Sundays or bank holidays.

You will conduct ceremonies in various locations such as hotels, civic buildings and other public places so a driving licence is useful.

Future prospects

Vacancies within this field only arise occasionally.

In England and Wales the usual career path is from assistant registrar to deputy registrar, then to registrar and finally to superintendent. In Scotland there are only 2 grades: assistant registrar and registrar.

You will have opportunities for in-house training and you could move into other administration-based careers.

The increase in the number of civil ceremonies may present more opportunities for registrars to become celebrants, or those who are employed to conduct marriages and civil partnerships only. These jobs are often seasonal and part time.

Advantages/disadvantages

The work is varied and no two days are the same.

You have the opportunity to meet many different people who will be at their happiest or saddest moments.

You will work some weekends and bank holidays and may be on-call at other times.

This is regarded as an important community position to hold so you are likely to be well respected.

Money guide

Assistant registrars usually start on around £16,000 to £17,000.

Registrars can expect to earn £22,000–£25,000.

A superintendent registrar could earn around £40,000.

Part-time celebrants earn a set fee for each ceremony they conduct.

Related opportunities

- Court Administrative Officer p345
- Legal Executive p350
- Magistrates' Court Legal Adviser/Sheriff's Clerk p352

Further information

General Register Office
www.gro.gov.uk

Local Government Careers
www.lgjobs.com

The Association of Registrars of Scotland
www.aros.org.uk

RISK MANAGER

ENTRY LEVEL 3

Qualifications and courses

Entry without a degree is possible and entails following the career path from an administrative role to a risk assistant position and finally to a risk management role. Employers would require A level qualifications or equivalent for this route.

However, the majority of risk managers do have a degree. Some larger companies run graduate trainee schemes, which will usually require a 2.1 degree. Preferred degree subjects include risk management, economics, finance, management, building surveying, engineering, business studies or actuarial science, although graduates from other disciplines will be considered too. Graduates from risk management courses are particularly sought after. Entry to a degree will require a minimum of 2 A levels/3 H grades and 5 GCSEs/National 5s (A*–C/A–C). Prior work experience in insurance may also be required, which graduates can gain through summer placements.

If your first degree is not in a relevant subject, or as a way to strengthen your application, you can study for the Institute of Risk Management (IRM)'s Certificate in Risk Management or for a postgraduate degree. If you have not done so already, your employer will expect you to go on to qualify as an Associate of the Chartered Insurance Institute (ACII) by studying for their Advanced Diploma in Insurance.

What the work involves

Risk managers are responsible for assessing the viability and risks of a business or project within a business. They identify, analyse, control and monitor each risk for the safety of the business as well as develop coping strategies when issues arise or things go wrong.

Risks can be different in each organisation; financial companies are concerned with market risks and even the health service needs to identify risks to patients and staff.

You will be doing a variety of tasks including risk surveys, designing strategies to prevent risks, and presenting all of your findings to the head of the business. You will be charged with conducting policy audits, liaising with internal and external parties as well as making sure that the company complies with professional standards.

Type of person suited to this work

You will need to have in-depth knowledge of the organisation that you work for and excellent research skills to be able to identify potential risks.

Good problem-solving skills will be essential for creating strategies as will knowledge of regulations which are relevant to your company.

It is important to have excellent communication skills, both written and oral, as you will need to write up reports of your findings and present these back to your colleagues or clients. Being persuasive and tactful will help you convince people to support your view of how to deal with a potential risk.

Working conditions

You will be working around 37 hours a week, Monday to Friday, however a heavy workload might require longer hours.

Although the majority of your time will be spent in an office, you might need to visit sites which could be dangerous, or industrial locations such as engineering plants and building sites.

It would be helpful to have a driving licence and your own vehicle for travelling between sites.

Future prospects

There are jobs available across the UK, with risk managers being employed in both the private and public sector; employers may include banks, local authorities, engineering firms and the emergency services. There is currently a shortage of financial risk managers.

Promotions are possible from risk manager to chief risk officer; you might need to move around different companies though to gain enough experience. You can also go into self-employment as a consultant or trainer. There are promotional possibilities to senior positions through the gaining of experience, with opportunities increasing throughout the UK when specialising in a technical field or industry sector.

Advantages/disadvantages

This is an exciting and varied career as you can work in a range of sectors from financial to the emergency services.

There could be dire consequences if you make a mistake and neglect a risk.

There are opportunities to be self-employed as a consultant and to travel abroad.

Money guide

The typical starting salary for a risk assistant position is £16,000 to £22,000.

Experienced risk managers can earn £26,000 to £60,000.

At director level or as a highly experienced and specialised risk manager, it is possible to reach a salary in excess of £70,000.

Related opportunities

- Chartered Surveyor p68
- Insurance Broker p29
- Insurance Risk Surveyor p32

Further information

Association of Insurance and Risk Managers in Industry and Commerce
www.airmic.com

Institute of Risk Management
www.theirm.org

SECRETARY

ENTRY LEVEL 2

Qualifications and courses

Required qualifications vary depending on the employer and sector and there are vacancies for all levels of candidates from school leavers to those with a postgraduate degree. As a minimum you should have some GCSEs/National 5s (A*–C/A–C), including English, and a GCSE in Business Studies could be helpful.

Vacancies aimed at graduates may involve more responsibility. Although there are no specific degree subjects required, degrees in business with languages, government and public administration, business, management, law, and secretarial studies would be particularly useful.

Excellent IT skills are a must in this job role, including a typing speed of at least 50 words per minute. Other specific skills that are sometimes sought include shorthand and minute taking. A good way to gain these is by taking a secretarial course.

There are courses available for both school leavers and graduates. For example there are NVQs in Business and Administration at Levels 1–4 and also private colleges such as Pitman Training who do diplomas in secretarial studies. Foundation degrees in Business and Finance, BTEC National Certificates and apprenticeships are also available.

However, relevant experience is often more highly valued than specific, formal qualifications, especially since competition for vacancies is high. Part-time jobs and temping for employment agencies are a good way to start and can sometimes lead to permanent positions.

A second language, particularly French, Italian or Japanese, is often useful if you wish to work for an international company or explore opportunities abroad.

What the work involves

Secretaries are responsible for giving clerical assistance to professionals in order to ensure the efficient running of an organisation. They are responsible for the coordination of office procedures and are often in charge of monitoring certain projects or junior staff.

The role and the responsibilities associated with it are entirely dependent on the size, sector and nature of the company you work for. Typically, most secretaries will be expected to type letters, emails and reports, set up and update filing systems, take care of diaries and travel arrangements as well as coordinate meetings and appointments.

Type of person suited to this work

You must be highly organised, efficient and able to multi-task.

You will need a good grasp of spelling, grammar and punctuation as well as a fast typing speed. It is important that you are IT literate, have a good attention to detail and are able to work to tight deadlines.

You should have excellent communication skills and be friendly, helpful and discreet, especially when dealing with confidential information.

The ability to work on your own, as well as part of a team, is also essential.

Numerical skills are an advantage as your role may include dealing with financial tasks.

Working conditions

Your working hours will typically be from 9am to 5pm, with longer hours during busy periods.

You will probably be located in an office, spending the majority of your day on the phone and working at a computer.

Future prospects

You could progress in a bigger company to a job with a more senior manager, or to a role as a personal assistant.

You could find a role in human resources, sales or marketing.

With experience, many secretaries are working as a virtual assistant from home.

Advantages/disadvantages

You can use your experience in a particular company or department to gain a promotion.

Part-time and temporary work is widely available in this line of work.

This job could be a practical way of using your skills and interests.

Tight deadlines and a heavy workload can make this job stressful. It can be repetitive.

Money guide

You can expect a starting salary of between £14,000 and £18,000 when working outside London, and £17,000 to £22,000 within London.

After significant experience and responsibility salaries can increase to around £25,000 to £30,000.

Roles in banking, law and finance are more highly paid than those in the media, charities and smaller companies. Working for FTSE100 companies can lead to higher salaries. Annual and performance-related bonuses are possible in some sectors.

Related opportunities

- Bilingual Secretary p328
- Personal Assistant p42
- Receptionist p45

Further information

Institute of Chartered Secretaries and Administrators
www.icsa.org.uk

Skills CFA
www.skillscfa.org

STOCK MARKET TRADER

ENTRY LEVEL 6

Qualifications and courses

You will need at least a 2.1 degree or higher, preferably in subjects with a strong numerical focus such as actuarial science, economics, accountancy, maths or finance. Minimum requirements for degree courses are often at least 2 A levels/3 H grades and 5 GCSEs/National 5s (A*–C/A–C), including English and Maths.

You will also need a professional qualification that meets the Financial Conduct Authority (FCA)'s requirements and be registered with them as an 'approved person' before being allowed to trade.

Competition for positions is incredibly intense and the selection process is demanding, often involving psychometric tests. It is a good idea to try and gain an internship or financial work experience as networking is a large part of this industry. Alternatively, major investment banks offer graduate training schemes, which you will need to apply for by October/November the year before you plan to start.

Fluency in foreign languages is highly sought after within international companies and candidates will need to demonstrate strong skills in team-working, numeracy and communication skills as well as a decisive nature and ability to work under pressure.

Entry without a degree or HND is difficult, though possible if you work your way up through the administrative roles and make contacts.

What the work involves

Traders use their knowledge of the market to make the highest possible profit on behalf of investors by buying and selling shares, bonds and other assets.

There are 3 types: market traders operate on behalf of clients; sales traders highlight new financial ideas, but take direct orders from clients; and proprietary traders make investments for banks.

You will be dealing with large sums of money, so your decisions must be quick and well informed. You will need to build strong contacts in order to be successful in this business.

Type of person suited to this work

You should have enthusiasm for the financial sector and enjoy a working environment that is highly performance related.

Alongside this, you will need to be extremely confident and full of informed initiative, whilst having the ability to cope with the constant pressure of trading with large sums of money that belong to other people.

As well as demanding accuracy, skilled analysis and responsibility, the job also requires that you be forceful and competitive, an excellent verbal communicator and a team player.

Working conditions

Traders often need to begin work at 7am in order to be on top of overnight developments in foreign markets, ready for the 8am opening of the London Stock Exchange, often not finishing their working day until 5pm.

The highly pressurised trading arena involves the monitoring of markets on a screen and making deals over the phone. You have to be reactive to even the smallest of changes and so the work environment is very noisy as each trader is either on the phone or liaising with colleagues.

Future prospects

Given the current financial climate, opportunities for traders may be limited and competition high.

Once in the industry however, there are many opportunities for progression. With 2 years' experience and qualifications with either the Chartered Institute for Securities and Investment (CISI) or as a Chartered Financial Analyst (CFA), you can be promoted to an analyst or trader. After a further 5 years you will be put in charge of a team or gain the responsibility of a new trading desk. These positions often lead to associate, senior associate and director level.

International offices are common with investment banks, bringing an opportunity to work in foreign arenas.

Advantages/disadvantages

This is an exciting and rewarding job that changes on a daily basis due to the constant changes in the financial market.

The highly pressurised environment can be stressful and means the professional duration of a stock market trader is generally less than those in other professions.

Money guide

The starting salary for a stock market trader is usually £30,000–£45,000, plus a small signing-on bonus.

A typical, experienced trader will be earning £45,000–£150,000.

An associate with experience selling credits can expect a salary of around £140,000 per year in a top tier bank or around £230,000 if working in more lucrative markets. (These are figures for markets in London and other regions will sometimes pay far less than these top figures.)

In addition to these impressive salaries are large bonuses and other possible benefits including non-contributory pensions and mortgage subsidies.

Related opportunities

- Investment Analyst p34
- Risk Manager p49
- Stockbroker p52

Further information

Financial Conduct Authority
www.fca.org.uk

Financial Skills Partnership
www.financialskillspartnership.org.uk

London Stock Exchange
www.londonstockexchange.com

STOCKBROKER

ENTRY LEVEL 6

Qualifications and courses

You will normally need at least a 2.1 degree. Any discipline will be considered but employers prefer degrees in economics, business studies, maths, physics, accountancy or law. Entry onto a degree programme normally requires 2 A levels/3 H grades and 5 GCSEs/ National 5s (A*–C/A–C).

Possession of a postgraduate qualification such as a Master of Business Administration (MBA) or a master's in subjects such as business or economics has become increasingly common.

Graduate trainee positions are available. The application process may include psychometric and aptitude testing or making a presentation to a group panel. Pre-entry experience, such as internships, placements and vacation work, will give you a distinct advantage as competition for entry is intense. Many employers will offer full-time jobs to their interns.

Entry without a degree or HND is difficult, though it may be possible for individuals with A levels/H grades and relevant experience to move into stockbroking from administrative or research roles.

In order to trade, all stockbrokers require a professional qualification that meets the Financial Conduct Authority (FCA)'s requirements and be registered with them as an 'approved person'.

What the work involves

Stockbrokers work for individuals or companies investing their clients' money to make them a profit by buying and selling stocks, bonds and shares.

You will be managing investments, advising your clients on investing their money and trading on behalf of your clients, often dealing with huge amounts of money.

You will have to keep up to date with economic trends, interpret and analyse market information, and predict how a company's stocks and shares are likely to perform.

You will have to respond rapidly to changes in trends and stock market fluctuations.

Type of person suited to this work

To succeed as a stockbroker you must be confident, determined, competitive and outgoing.

You will have to predict trends in a constantly changing market and take risks with huge sums of money so must be decisive and able to remain calm under pressure. You will need to be personable, trustworthy and honest with a good reputation.

You will need excellent IT skills and will be expected to work long hours and to dress smartly.

Working conditions

You will be office based, acquiring much of your market information from computers and doing much of your work by telephone.

Hours are long: you will probably start early and finish late in order to accommodate international markets in different time zones. You will most likely work over the weekend as well. Much of your day will be spent in a very busy, tense and pressurised environment.

Future prospects

You could be working for a firm which specialises in this work or for other financial institutions such as banks or building societies. Your career will develop by taking on more responsibilities and more important clients.

Competition for jobs is intense so work experience is vital. Economic changes can happen fast so jobs are not always secure.

This is a high pressure job and many stockbrokers finish their careers in their 40s. You could move into other areas within finance such as fund management or become self-employed as a consultant.

Advantages/disadvantages

The hours are long and the work is very pressurised and stressful.

It is a very competitive job and you will need to be tough and determined to succeed.

The work can be very rewarding and is extremely well paid.

No two days will be the same, the market is in constant fluctuation and you will be required to respond accordingly. This gives a diverse and exciting environment to work in.

Money guide

In addition to their regular salary, stockbrokers receive bonuses on the trade they do and can earn substantially more.

As a basic salary, you could earn between £24,000 and £30,000 a year when you first start work and training after university.

With experience you could earn between £45,000 and £80,000. After many years of experience and depending on location, some stockbrokers can earn over £150,000, including bonuses.

Related opportunities

- Accountant p2
- Bank Manager p10
- Economist p20
- Stock Market Trader p51

Further information

Financial Conduct Authority
www.fca.org.uk

London Stock Exchange
www.londonstockexchange.com

TELEPHONIST

ENTRY LEVEL 2

Qualifications and courses

There are no formal entry requirements for this work, but 5 GCSEs/National 5s (A*–C/A–C), including English language and Maths, will be a distinct advantage. Many colleges offer relevant courses in customer service and telephone skills at Levels 1–3, including City & Guilds certificates and BTECs.

Basic computing skills or an IT qualification are useful, as is some basic experience in telesales or customer care. Temporary work is a good way to get experience and could lead to a permanent job offer. Apprenticeships are also available.

Being able to speak a foreign language may be an advantage depending on the organisation you're working for. Knowledge of alternative telephone systems, such as Type Talk, Meridian and Minicom, could also be helpful.

Most training is done on the job with a senior member of staff. Your employer may encourage you to study for NVQs such as Levels 1–4 in Customer Service, Levels 1 and 2 in Contact Centre Operations or Levels 2 and 3 in Contact Centre Professionals.

What the work involves

Telephonists work at a switchboard, answering calls, connecting callers to the right person and advising them on which department or person they need to speak to.

You will be responsible for a caller's first impression of your company.

Your job will include taking messages, testing phone lines and reporting faults. You may need to respond to out-of-office calls left on answering machines.

You might do other reception duties such as meeting and dealing with visitors, taking deliveries and other clerical work.

Type of person suited to this work

You will need a professional and friendly telephone manner, a clear and polite voice and good listening skills.

Excellent customer service is essential. You must be assertive with impatient and rude callers while at the same time remaining calm and understanding even when you are busy.

You should be someone who enjoys working with people in a team and who can work quickly and accurately.

It's also important to have a good understanding of how your organisation works in order to answer calls effectively.

Working conditions

Most of your work will be in an office or telephone room, probably with other people. You might be based at a reception desk.

Although you will probably work normal office hours, you might need to be at work to take calls before the company opens.

Some switchboards provide a 24-hour service which means working shifts including nights and weekends.

You will be wearing a headset and using computer databases and automated switchboards.

Future prospects

Most large or medium-sized companies need people to answer their phones and provide a reception service, so job opportunities are good.

You could work in finance, industry, schools, government, NHS, emergency services or transport companies and call centres.

You may lead a team of other telephonists or move into a job in telesales. You could become a senior telephonist receiving training in customer service skills and gaining administrative experience.

You could then move into a wide range of jobs working in business administration in offices or with the public.

Advantages/disadvantages

On a busy switchboard you will be working under pressure and could be working shifts.

Dealing with the public means staying polite and calm no matter what happens.

You will gain valuable customer service and administration skills to help you progress.

Money guide

As a trainee your starting salary is normally around £12,000 to £14,000 per year.

With more experience this can rise to between £14,000 and £19,000.

The average salary for a telephonist is £14,834, with salaries within London higher at £18,000.

Earnings for a senior telephonist with experience and more responsibility, such as supervising other staff, may reach £21,000 or more.

Related opportunities

- Court Administrative Officer p345
- Receptionist p45
- Secretary p50

Further information

e-skills UK
www.e-skills.com

Institute of Customer Service
www.instituteofcustomerservice.com

Skills CFA
www.skillscfa.org

TRAINING AND DEVELOPMENT OFFICER

ENTRY LEVEL 2

Qualifications and courses

With relevant experience and skills entry is possible with or without a degree or HND, although having one can be an advantage. Useful subjects include human resources, psychology, IT and business. Entry onto degree courses usually requires a minimum of 2 A levels/3 H grades or equivalent and 5 GCSEs/National 5s (A*–C/A–C). Entry onto HND courses requires 1 A level/2 H grades and 4 GCSEs/National 5s.

Postgraduate qualifications are not necessary, although a master's or a diploma recognised by the Chartered Institute of Personnel and Development (CIPD) can improve your chances. When you sign up to a CIPD course you become a student member and when you finish you can upgrade to associate membership or chartered membership, depending on how senior your job role is.

Graduates can boost their application by gaining relevant work experience through summer placements, work shadowing or voluntary work. Getting involved in university societies that allow you to develop organisational, teamwork or leadership skills can also help.

New graduates are not always recruited directly into training roles, though some companies may have graduate schemes. Many will start out as an administration assistant and work their way up to training officer. Training manager positions require significant experience in an officer role. Entrants without a degree can also work their way up this way.

What the work involves

You will be responsible for making sure your company's staff have the skills and knowledge they need to make the business as efficient as possible.

Some of your work will involve looking at how to provide the best training at the lowest cost – from different options such as in-house, distance learning, IT packages or college courses.

You will also deliver training yourself or organise other trainers to do this. You will have to write reports and make presentations assessing the value of training.

Type of person suited to this work

You should be interested in people and in helping them to develop and improve their skills. You will need to be able to pass on your knowledge and expertise in a lively, interesting way by designing imaginative and varied training that appeals to everyone.

You will need to be organised and able to plan ahead, meet deadlines and assess the effectiveness of training. To do this you will need excellent IT skills and an understanding of costs and budgets.

Working conditions

You will usually do normal office hours but may have to work longer at busy times or attend residential, evening or weekend events.

You will be based in an office, probably working as part of a team, but will spend a lot of your time out and about delivering training, finding training venues, going to meetings and visiting staff in their work places.

Future prospects

Training managers come from a variety of backgrounds as they often become experts in their own field before moving into training people within the industry, but it is possible to start as a graduate trainee.

There are opportunities all over the country as all types of organisations have training managers. Developments in new technology and more on-the-job training have increased the need for staff training. More companies are using consultants to deliver training to their staff so opportunities to become a self-employed consultant are increasing. It is also possible to gain promotion or move into related areas.

Advantages/disadvantages

The work can be varied and you will have the satisfaction of passing on your expertise to help people learn and develop.

You may need to work hard to motivate staff who are having to do training they are not interested in or do not feel they need.

Money guide

Starting salaries at officer level are typically £22,000 to £30,000.

Experienced and qualified training managers can earn up to £40,000. Senior training managers in large companies could earn £50,000 or more.

Salaries will vary depending on experience, responsibility level, location and the size of the company. CIPD qualifications could also help you get a higher salary.

Related opportunities

- Further Education Lecturer p181
- Human Resources/Personnel Officer p28
- Work-based Training Instructor p193

Further information

Chartered Institute of Personnel and Development
www.cipd.co.uk

Lifelong Learning UK
www.lifelonglearning.co.uk

Building and Construction

Are you interested in working on a construction site with a team of people? Maybe your interest lies in buying and selling property and working in an office is more your sort of thing. All the jobs in the sector require someone with a great eye for detail, creative flair and someone who is very good at working with others.

The jobs featured in this section are listed below. For similar jobs to the ones in this section why not have a look at *Engineering, Manufacturing and Production* on page 195.

ARCHITECT

ENTRY LEVEL 6

Qualifications and courses

Professional architects must have chartered membership of the Royal Institute of British Architects (RIBA) and registration with the Architects Registration Board (ARB). The main route to qualification is through a RIBA/ARB-recognised degree. Minimum entry requirements are 3 A levels/H grades which should be drawn from academic fields of study. In addition you must have passed at least 5 GCSEs/National 5s including English, Maths and Physics or Chemistry. Equivalent qualifications such as a BTEC certificate/diploma may be accepted. Potential students may also be expected to present a portfolio at the interview stage.

Candidates without the usual entry requirements for a degree may be able to take a Foundation year at a school of architecture instead. Mature students with relevant experience may also be accepted.

Training as an architect takes 7 years. Candidates spend 3 years studying for an undergraduate degree in architecture (RIBA Part 1) and then undertake 12 months of supervised practical training in an architect's office or in some sector of the building industry. Then 2 years are spent studying for a diploma, further degree (BArch) or Master of Architecture (MArch) (RIBA Part 2). After completing a further 12-month work placement, trainees are then eligible to complete the RIBA Part 3 Examination in Professional Practice and Management.

If you have passed Part 1, you may be able to work as an architectural technician.

Alternatively, an office-based route for people with experience is also available whereby candidates are able to self-study for the RIBA Examination in Architecture while continuing to work full time.

What the work involves

Architects design new buildings, the spaces around them as well as any proposed changes to existing buildings.

Your work will include agreeing design briefs with clients, researching development sites, deciding which materials to use for particular buildings and drawing technical plans. You will also be responsible for testing new ideas, obtaining planning permission and inspecting building work while it is in progress.

You could specialise in a particular field such as building heritage and conservation, sustainable and environmental design, or project management.

Type of person suited to this work

You must be able to produce creative, detailed designs that meet the needs of your clients.

You will need excellent verbal communication skills for working with other professionals and for presenting your ideas to them and your clients. You also have to be organised and have good research and problem-solving skills.

As you will use computer-aided design (CAD) in your work, IT skills are also useful.

Working conditions

Although architects are based in offices, you will go out to visit construction sites and meet clients. You will need to pay attention to health and safety regulations when on-site. A driving licence may be necessary.

You are likely to work regular office hours, although you might have to do some work at weekends and during the evenings.

Future prospects

Generally, you would start work in a private architect's practice to gain wide experience of the work, but you may also work for other employers later on.

Self-employment is common for experienced architects.

Your career will be dependent on your experience, ability and competence. If you decide to remain in private work you could progress to associate level and possibly become a partner. Some of the larger architectural practices win international contracts so you could work on projects abroad.

You could continue to develop your knowledge by completing a postgraduate course in a subject related to architecture, such as civil engineering, town planning, and surveying, among others. These courses are offered by most schools of architecture.

Advantages/disadvantages

There may be problems to overcome when making design decisions, such as conflicting views to deal with.

There is personal satisfaction in dealing with these problems and creating designs for buildings that will influence the landscape for many years to come.

Money guide

Graduates who have completed Part 1 of their training can expect a starting salary of up to £20,000.

Upon completion of Part 2, salaries rise to £20,000–£26,000.

Once fully qualified as an architect, you can earn £26,000–£35,000 a year.

Those who reach senior level or become a partner in a firm can achieve a salary of up to £80,000.

Related opportunities

- Architectural Technician p57
- Architectural Technologist p58
- Construction Supervisor/Manager p74

Further information

Architects Registration Board
www.arb.org.uk

Royal Incorporation of Architects in Scotland
www.rias.org.uk

Royal Institute of British Architects
www.architecture.com

ARCHITECTURAL TECHNICIAN

ENTRY LEVEL 5

Qualifications and courses

The most common route into this career is to complete an HNC/HND in Architectural Design or Architectural Technology or alternatively, to gain a Foundation degree in Architectural Technology. HNC/HND courses usually require applicants to have acquired at least 1 A level/2 H grades (relevant subjects include physics and maths) as well as a GCSE/National 5 (A*–C/A–C) in your A level/H grade subject. You should also have another 3 or 4 GCSEs/National 5s (A*–C/A–C) including Maths, English and a science subject. Some candidates may be considered on the basis of relevant experience rather than qualifications.

You can also complete a degree but most employers will not expect applicants to be graduates. Candidates with at least 4 GCSEs/National 5s (A*–C/A–C) may seek apprenticeship training provided by employers in the workplace. Apprenticeship schemes tend to award candidates a qualification such as a BTEC/SQA or NVQ/SVQ.

To become a qualified architectural technician you will need to apply to become an Associate Member of the Chartered Institute of Architectural Technologists (CIAT). To pass the required Architectural Technician Professional and Occupational Performance (POP) Record, candidates must undertake 2 years of supervised work experience and be assessed against CIAT's professional standards.

What the work involves

This is essentially a support role; you will be providing assistance to the other members of the team including architects, architectural technologists, surveyors and engineers enabling them to complete their work as efficiently as possible. You will be responsible for liaising between the construction and design teams, making sure everyone is up to date with the latest project developments.

You will gather and organise all of the technical information required throughout the project.

You will prepare drawings, plans and specifications using computer-aided design (CAD) software and also by hand.

Type of person suited to this work

You need good drawing skills, both hand and CAD. You will need an ability to visualise in 3 dimensions.

You must also be able to develop a scientific and technological knowledge of building materials. You will need to understand building regulations and techniques and be able to explain them to others.

You will need to be able to work well alone, as well as having good verbal communication skills for working with other professionals, such as architects, surveyors and engineers. Your organisational, research and problem-solving skills will need to be excellent.

Working conditions

Architectural technicians are based in offices, but you may visit sites to inspect work in progress so a driving licence might be useful.

You will need to be aware of health and safety regulations when on-site and will be expected to wear safety clothing. When working on-site you will be outdoors in all weathers and may need to climb ladders or scaffolding.

You are likely to work normal office hours (9am–5pm, Monday to Friday), although you might have to work late and at weekends on some projects.

Future prospects

An architectural technician may take further CIAT-accredited training to develop their skills and apply to work as an architectural technologist.

You could choose to work in private practice or alternatively within the public sector in an area such as local government, research, education or central government. You may need to change employers in order to progress.

There is also the possibility to work freelance or on short contracts.

Advantages/disadvantages

As you are the main point of contact between contractors and clients, you will be at the centre of any confrontations that arise.

If you work for a larger company you will have the opportunity to work on a range of projects which will keep your job interesting.

Money guide

Architectural technicians usually receive a starting salary of £15,000–£20,000.

With experience this could rise to between £30,000 and £45,000 a year.

Architectural technicians employed on a freelance/self-employed basis can expect to earn a higher hourly rate than those in full-time employment.

Earnings vary widely depending on location and the individual employer.

Related opportunities

- Architectural Technologist p58
- Surveying Technician p110
- Town Planner/Planning Technician p113

Further information

Chartered Institute of Architectural Technologists
www.ciat.org.uk

Chartered Institute of Building
www.ciob.org.uk

Construction Industry Training Board (CITB)
www.citb.co.uk

ARCHITECTURAL TECHNOLOGIST

ENTRY LEVEL 6

Qualifications and courses

The preferred route to becoming an architectural technologist is to complete a degree in Architectural Technology which has been accredited by the Chartered Institute of Architectural Technologists (CIAT). Admission to a degree course relies on candidates gaining at least 2 A levels/3 H grades and 5 GCSEs/National 5s (A*–C/A–C). There are currently over 30 accredited degree programmes and they are listed on CIAT's website. Candidates who take an accredited degree benefit from exemptions when they study for their Professional and Occupational Performance (POP) Record which is a necessary requirement when becoming a chartered architectural technologist (MCIAT).

There is also the opportunity to gain entry to the field for candidates who choose to complete a degree in a related area of the industry such as architecture, architectural engineering, building services engineering, building/construction, built environment studies, civil and structural engineering, computer-aided engineering or surveying.

Completion of an HNC/HND in Architectural Technology or a Foundation degree in Architectural Technology will enable you to become a qualified architectural technician. Once you have had more than 10 years' experience and after successful completion of CIAT's professional standards assessment you could become an architectural technologist. Those with a relevant HNC/HND may also opt to convert their qualification to a degree by completing a 1-year top up course or alternatively, may be granted acceptance onto the second year of a degree course.

What the work involves

You will be responsible for ensuring that the architect's design is translated into a functioning building. You will be involved right from the start, helping to liaise with the client and the architect and advise them on any issues that might affect the build.

You will make sure that the more practical elements of the build run smoothly, by ensuring that the right materials are used and that all legal requirements and building regulations are met.

You will have a leading role within the construction team including developing project briefs, coordinating, negotiating contracts and providing guidance.

Type of person suited to this work

You need good drawing skills, both hand and computer-aided design (CAD). You will need an ability to visualise in 3 dimensions.

You must also be able to develop a scientific and technological knowledge of building materials. You will need to understand planning regulations and construction law, and be able to explain them to others.

You will need good communication skills for working with other professionals. Your organisational, management, research and problem-solving skills will need to be excellent.

Working conditions

Architectural technologists are based in offices, but you may need to visit sites to inspect work in progress so a driving licence could be useful.

You will generally be working weekdays 9am–5pm, but you might need to work extra hours to meet deadlines.

You will need to be aware of health and safety regulations when on-site and will wear safety clothing. On-site work can be cold and wet or hot and dusty, as you will be outdoors in all weathers.

Future prospects

Architectural technologists, with CIAT qualifications and experience, may set up their own practice or work in a partnership with other architectural technologists or architects.

It is also possible to progress within private firms to more senior positions or move to other companies which attract larger and possibly international contracts. Promotion is generally easier within larger firms but you may still need to change employers in order to progress.

Advantages/disadvantages

There may be problems to solve at any time during the architectural process, for example, issues with the supply of the right materials.

It is rewarding to make your contribution to the design and construction of buildings that will influence the landscape for many years to come.

Money guide

Generally salaries are higher in London and the south of England.

A junior technologist typically has a starting salary of £15,000–£23,000 a year.

After 3 years' experience you should be earning between £24,000 and £28,000 a year.

Once you are in a senior position and have been working for 10 years, you could achieve a salary of £30,000–£45,000.

Higher salaries are also possible for people who acquire extensive experience. Benefits such as company cars and pension schemes may also be offered by some practices.

Related opportunities

- Architect p56
- Architectural Technician p57
- Cartographer p66
- Town Planner/Planning Technician p113

Further information

Chartered Institute of Architectural Technologists
www.ciat.org.uk

Construction Industry Training Board (CITB)
www.citb.co.uk

AUCTION PROPERTY CONSULTANT

ENTRY LEVEL 6

Qualifications and courses

There is no specific entry route for this career although you will need a degree in either land management or another property-related subject to join a company as a trainee. You could study for a degree in property and valuation accredited by the Royal Institution of Chartered Surveyors (RICS) and join a surveying firm or you could enter a different area, such as estate management, and train as a property consultant on the job. Entry to a degree is normally a minimum of 2 A levels/3 H grades and 5 GCSEs/National 5s (A*–C/A–C).

Training is carried out on the job under the supervision of a senior consultant. The National Association of Valuers and Auctioneers (NAVA) offers property auction workshops to help develop trainees' skills. The National Federation of Property Professionals (NFoPP) offers a Level 3 Technical Award in Real Property Auctioneering which is made available through distance learning. Completion of this is necessary for membership of NAVA.

It is important to commit to a continuing professional development (CPD) programme to keep your skills and knowledge of property law and auctioning methods up to date.

What the work involves

You will be responsible for valuing property and land, from listed buildings to new builds, assessing the current market and organising the property or land to be auctioned off.

You will be meeting prospective clients, researching their property or land, attending the auction and getting the best price for the client.

You will need to make detailed reports of the property you value, and report back to your client. You might also have other duties such as advising clients how auctions work and of any other services your company offers.

Type of person suited to this work

You will need excellent communication skills to successfully run an auction, and be firm when settling a bid.

Being lively, outgoing and confident will help when you have to address a large crowd of people; a clear and authoritative voice will be beneficial.

You will need good observational skills for valuing land and property, with a good knowledge of the property market. You will need to keep up to date with current property laws.

Working conditions

You will work around 37 hours a week, Monday to Friday, with the possibility of working evenings and weekends, depending on when the auction is.

You will spend a lot of time in an office, but you will be out and about on a daily basis, meeting clients and valuing properties. You will need to work in all weather conditions, and travel around regularly – a driving licence and vehicle will be very useful.

Future prospects

There are jobs available across the UK, with international auction houses being based in London. There is currently a need for property auctioneers due to the increase in popularity of property auctions, therefore job prospects are good.

You can progress into a senior auction role or managerial position. It may be possible to move into different areas of auctioning, such as livestock or antiques.

Advantages/disadvantages

Auctions are fast-paced and lively events; this job offers an exciting day's work!

It could be frustrating when an auction does not go the way you planned and profit is not made.

You get great job satisfaction when you successfully auction off a property.

Money guide

The amount that you earn depends on which type of organisation you work for and where it is located. For example, an auction house may pay less than a private chartered surveyor company.

Starting salaries tend to be between £23,000 and £26,000 a year.

With experience, earnings can rise to £27,000–£36,000.

Chartered land and property valuers can earn around £40,000 a year.

Those who choose to work freelance may charge fees according to their experience and the type of contract undertaken.

Related opportunities

- Auctioneer p451
- Surveying Technician p110

Further information

National Federation of Property Professionals
www.nfopp.co.uk

Royal Institution of Chartered Surveyors
www.rics.org

BRICKLAYER

ENTRY LEVEL 1

Qualifications and courses

The main route to entering the field is to train via an apprenticeship, splitting your time between working on-site and training for a qualification at college. In England and Wales, the Construction Apprenticeship Scheme (CAS) allows you to study for NVQ Levels 2 and 3 whilst in Scotland a modern apprenticeship offers trainees the chance to gain an SVQ Level 2. Northern Ireland offers 4 different types of apprenticeships for people in different circumstances, each leading to a qualification in your chosen trade. Apprenticeships normally require candidates to have some GCSEs/National 5s (A*–E/A–E) in subjects such as English, maths, a science and technology.

Many employers now require trainees to have a Construction Skills Certification Scheme (CSCS) card before working on-site, something that can only be achieved through a formal qualification, such as a BTEC Introductory Certificate and Diploma in Construction, BTEC Certificate and Diploma in Construction or a City & Guilds Certificate in Basic Skills (6081). Those without qualifications may work for an NVQ and a CSCS card via the ConstructionSkills' On-Site Assessment and Training (OSAT) programme.

New Deal offers taster courses and placements with an employer for at least 26 weeks. It may be possible to stay on and study for NVQs/SVQs. To qualify you must be aged 18–24 and unemployed for more than 6 months, or 25 or over and unemployed for 18 months.

What the work involves

Bricklayers build and repair external and internal walls.

You will use a range of materials including bricks, stones and mortar as well as specialist tools to build walls that often include ornamental and decorative effects.

Jobs include building houses as well as office buildings, other public venues, shopping centres and stadiums. You will spend a lot of your time outside doing manual work.

Type of person suited to this work

As the work requires you to move around a lot and lift materials, you must be physically fit and able to work at height.

You need to be able to follow plans and work with accuracy and attention to detail, so that the walls you build are structurally perfect and create the right visual effect.

You also need to work in a team with other bricklayers and those in other construction trades and professions.

Working conditions

You will often be working outdoors and in all weather conditions. This can mean being cold and wet in the winter and hot and dusty in the summer.

To keep yourself and others safe you will need to observe health and safety regulations, which will include wearing protective clothing.

You are likely to work a normal working week, although weekend and evening work is common.

Future prospects

Construction is one of the largest industries in the UK. Recent surges in demand for new housing has led to an increase in demand for bricklayers, but following the severe job losses during the recession, there are not enough bricklayers to keep up with demand. Between January and March 2014, 60% of firms said they had trouble finding bricklayers to employ. With a shortage of bricklayers, job prospects are promising, but the market is still volatile.

In the long term, you could progress to technical, supervisory and managerial roles or move into related areas such as estimating and construction management. Encouragingly, the number of managerial positions required by the industry is predicted to increase by 2016. You can also become an instructor in a training school.

The construction industry has one of the highest percentages of self-employment and bricklayers are no exception. Many have set up their own businesses, often working on smaller, local contracts. You may also opt to specialise in different trades such as stonemasonry, restoration or conservation.

Advantages/disadvantages

The work can be physically demanding for some people.

This is a great career if you like being outdoors, doing practical and creative work.

As you develop your skills there are great opportunities for progression.

Money guide

Trainees and labourers can earn up to £15,000 a year until they become qualified, when they can earn anything between £16,000 and £23,000.

Experienced bricklayers and instructors can earn up to £30,000.

Overtime is often available and on some projects there are bonuses based on fast outputs which can lead to higher earnings. If you are self-employed you have more freedom to negotiate your rate of pay with your clients.

Related opportunities

- Building Technician p64
- Dry Stone Waller p77
- Stonemason p108

Further information

Construction Industry Training Board (CITB)
www.citb.co.uk

Federation of Master Builders
www.fmb.org.uk

Scottish Building Apprenticeship and Training Council
www.sbatc.co.uk

BUILDING CONSERVATION OFFICER

ENTRY LEVEL 6

Qualifications and courses

Most entrants are graduates with a degree in a relevant subject such as building and construction, civil or structural engineering, surveying, architecture, or design. More specific courses in architectural heritage, conservation, building conservation, and management are offered by some universities. Many graduates will have an accredited or recognised postgraduate degree that meets the requirements of the Institute of Historic Building Conservation (IHBC). Membership of the IHBC is usually a requirement for jobs within this field.

Entry with an HND is possible, or alternatively you can enter as a planning technician after gaining considerable experience.

Training is usually provided on the job but employers do value candidates with demonstrable interest and experience within the field. Volunteering and work experience is particularly important if your degree is not directly relevant. The National Trust has around 47,000 positions available for volunteers.

The Society for the Protection of Ancient Buildings (SPAB) also runs a lecture series each year aimed at professionals in the industry which are useful in providing network-building opportunities. Once on the job, it is important to undergo continuing professional development (CPD) every 2 years. The IHBC offers its members numerous courses and seminars to ensure officers continue to enhance their skills.

What the work involves

Building conservation officers protect and restore buildings of special historical or architectural interest, such as houses, churches, windmills, factories and lighthouses.

You will be involved in planning the development of listed buildings and sites, recommending buildings for conservation, writing reports on their condition, making schedules and estimates for work required and giving advice to architects, local authorities or planning committees on building conservation.

You might have to source suppliers or craftspeople who work with specialised or traditional building materials.

Type of person suited to this work

You will be working to restore historic buildings and sites so it is important that you are interested in history, architecture and construction. An understanding of historical architecture, building methods and techniques would be very useful.

You will need excellent communication skills as you will coordinate the many different aspects involved in the development of one site. You must have excellent verbal and written skills to give presentations to planning authorities or government agencies to persuade them to follow your advice.

Working conditions

Your work is occasionally office based but much takes place outdoors on-site. This can be dusty and dirty, working at heights and confined spaces in adverse weather conditions. Protective clothing, including hard hats and safety boots, is necessary as you may be visiting buildings in poor repair.

Travel during the day with the occasional overnight stay may be necessary. Working as a consultant may involve travel all over the UK or visiting sites in remote areas so a car and driver's licence are useful. Working hours include regular extra hours but not weekends or shifts.

Future prospects

Positions as a historic building inspector or conservation officer can be found in local authorities, district and county councils. Within the private sector there may be opportunities for promotion, eg to senior conservation officer or managerial roles, but, due to the low turnover of staff, it may be necessary to relocate in order to achieve career progression. In small organisations, promotions may be limited.

There are many opportunities in national government organisations such as English Heritage and charities such as the National Trust, the Victorian Society or the Georgian Group.

As a qualified and experienced professional you can be self-employed. With substantial experience and industry contracts you can become involved in consultancy which focuses on advisory and design work. You may even opt to move into lecturing in universities.

Advantages/disadvantages

You will gain a great deal of satisfaction from working to ensure the survival of listed buildings.

Buildings are often in a poor state of repair and building sites may be hazardous.

Money guide

Starting salaries range from £18,000 to £26,000.

Experienced building conservation officers earn between £26,000 and £32,000.

Salaries at senior levels may rise to £40,000 or more after 10–15 years' experience.

Related opportunities

- Architect p56
- Architectural Technologist p58
- Building Surveyor p63

Further information

Institute of Historic Building Conservation
www.ihbc.org.uk

Society for the Protection of Ancient Buildings
www.spab.org.uk

BUILDING SERVICES ENGINEER

ENTRY LEVEL 6

Qualifications and courses

To enter this profession you will need a relevant degree in subjects such as building services engineering, mechanical engineering, maths or physics. Entry to a degree usually requires 2 A levels/3 H grades with Maths or a science and 5 GCSEs/National 5s (A*–C/A–C) including English and Maths. Gaining work experience during school holidays can be useful in enhancing future job applications and ensuring you secure important contacts.

Accredited HNDs or Foundation degrees in engineering or technology can be used to progress to full degree courses or trainee posts. Some apprenticeships may also be available through the modern apprenticeship scheme, SummitSkills.

As a trainee you will need to complete Initial Professional Development (IPD) to become a professional engineer. You can train for this through your employer. You can then work towards incorporated engineer (IEng) or chartered engineer (CEng) status by gaining membership of the Chartered Institution of Building Services Engineers (CIBSE). In order to do so, you will need a first in an accredited Master of Engineering (MEng) degree.

It is important that you commit to a continuing professional development (CPD) programme in order to keep your skills up to date.

What the work involves

Building services engineers are responsible for each aspect of energy-using building services such as lifts, lighting, heating, air conditioning, water supply, ventilation and electrical supply.

You will design and plan services that are efficient, cost effective, sustainable and in the interest of public safety. You will also be responsible for organising and supervising the installation and maintenance of these services, working with architects and clients to reduce the environmental impact.

Although the industry is becoming increasingly multidisciplinary, you will probably specialise in mechanical engineering, electrical engineering or public health.

Type of person suited to this work

You will need to be highly practical as well as having excellent problem solving, communication and interpersonal skills. Teamworking skills are essential so that you can work with those involved in other aspects of each project's design and construction.

You should have an aptitude for design and technical drawing, model-making and show proficiency working with computers and computer-aided design (CAD) software.

Working conditions

Your time will be divided between office-based work, such as planning, designing and estimating costs of projects, to spending time on-site, coordinating installation or managing existing systems.

You may work on sites such as airports, hospitals, industrial plants, domestic housing, leisure pools, hotels and cinemas; for this you might need specialist skills.

You will usually be expected to work more than the average office hours but not weekends or shifts. Some roles require on-call availability in case of emergencies. You may have to travel within a day but overnight stays are uncommon.

Future prospects

Opportunities in this field are numerous with demand for building services engineers usually exceeding supply.

Progression within the role is fairly scripted, with graduate engineers progressing to project engineers, associates, a director/partner and then a managing director. As a chartered engineer you may establish yourself as an independent consultant.

Your choice of specialism is important in determining your career development so it is important to decide early in order to gain as much practical experience as possible.

Training in design, installation or maintenance can increase your chances of progression as does training in new specialties such as intelligent buildings and organic lighting.

Advantages/disadvantages

The profession was traditionally separated into electrical and mechanical roles, but is now becoming increasingly multidisciplinary so you role may be more flexible and diverse.

This profession depends heavily on the economic climate of the construction industry, so you need to be aware of this as it will affect your chances of employment.

Money guide

Your starting salary could range from £20,000 to £24,000.

With experience this can rise to between £25,000 and £35,000.

At senior level it is possible to earn more than £45,000 and as a partner of a consultancy firm it is possible to earn between £65,000 and £85,000.

Salaries vary according to an engineer's experience rather than qualifications, therefore the more experience you gain, the higher your wage.

Related opportunities

- Architect p56
- Civil/Construction Engineer/Civil Engineering Technician p69
- Electrical Engineer p203

Further information

Chartered Institution of Building Services Engineers
www.cibse.org

Institution of Engineering and Technology
www.theiet.org

BUILDING SURVEYOR

ENTRY LEVEL 6

Qualifications and courses

You will be required to hold a relevant degree accredited by the Royal Institution of Chartered Surveyors (RICS) in a subject such as surveying, construction, civil or building engineering. The Chartered Institute of Building (CIOB), the Association of Building Engineers (ABE), and the British Institute of Facilities Management (BIFM) also offer professional qualifications. Completing a RICS-accredited degree course, however, will automatically qualify you to train as a chartered surveyor allowing you to carry out the Assessment of Professional Competence (APC), entitling you to RICS membership. The APC scheme allows you to train as you work and normally takes between 2 and 3 years.

Candidates with a non-accredited degree, or a degree in a non-vocational subject, can opt for a RICS-accredited postgraduate conversion course. It is also possible to enter the industry at technical surveyor level if you hold a relevant HNC/HND or Foundation degree. To reach the level of a building surveyor will require you to complete further qualifications whilst you work.

Alternatively, the Chartered Surveyors Training Trust offers work-based training for young people aged 16–24 in London and the south-east of England. Applicants must have 4 GCSEs/National 5s (A*–C/A–C) or equivalent, preferably in English, Maths and a science.

Graduates who have completed a year in the industry as part of their degree maintain a distinct advantage when seeking work.

What the work involves

Building surveyors work on new building projects as well as making suggestions on how to improve or enhance existing structures.

You could work on residential and commercial building projects, and will advise on a number of areas including design, restoration, sustainability and repairs.

You may also be responsible for ensuring that buildings meet health, safety and access regulations.

Type of person suited to this work

Since the job involves explaining ideas and negotiating with industry professionals and clients, good communication skills are vital. You will produce detailed reports, so a good standard of written English is required.

You will need excellent time management skills and a head for figures to ensure that projects come in on time and within budget.

You will need a logical, analytical and practical approach to work, along with the ability to organise and manage a team. As much of the work involves computers and electronic equipment, you will need to have good IT skills.

Working conditions

Working hours are normally 9am–5pm, although longer hours and evening meetings with clients are not uncommon.

Most surveyors divide their time equally between the office, external client meetings, site visits and surveys. These travel commitments mean it is helpful to have a driving licence and transport.

When on-site you will need to stick to health and safety regulations and be prepared for all types of weather.

You may occasionally be called to give evidence in court proceedings concerning a breach of building regulations.

Future prospects

Although the industry was affected by the recent financial crisis, the demand for building surveyors is on the rise alongside a possible shortfall in graduates.

You could work for a variety of employers including surveying practices, construction companies, government departments, and mortgage and property companies, both in the UK and abroad. Freelance and consultancy work are also a possibility. Gaining chartered status opens up further opportunities for career progression.

With experience, you could become a partner in a company or establish your own firm. You could also specialise in one area such as advising on the restoration and improvement of historic or architecturally valuable buildings.

Advantages/disadvantages

Surveying provides a varied career as each day is different and there is a range of areas to work in.

Many surveyors are self-employed and enjoy the flexibility of working freelance.

Sometimes you will need to work extra hours to meet deadlines.

Money guide

Graduate surveyors can expect a salary of £18,000–£26,000. Those with chartered status are more likely to start on a higher salary.

Experienced surveyors can earn between £23,000 and £38,000 whilst senior chartered surveyors can earn in excess of £50,000.

Becoming a partner in a firm will offer you a salary of £70,000 or more.

Benefits, such as a company car, mobile phone and pension scheme, are also available.

Related opportunities

- Civil/Construction Engineer/Civil Engineering Technician p69
- Quantity Surveyor p100
- Rural Property/Practice Surveyor p103

Further information

Chartered Institute of Building
www.ciob.org.uk

Royal Institution of Chartered Surveyors
www.rics.org

BUILDING TECHNICIAN

ENTRY LEVEL 3

Qualifications and courses

Building technicians normally need to train to NVQ/SVQ Levels 3 or 4. It is possible to train as a building technician with an employer as a construction apprentice. Apprenticeship schemes require a minimum of 4 GCSEs/National 5s (A*–C/A–C), including either Maths, a science, Design and Technology, or equivalent vocational qualification. Most apprentices start between the ages of 16 and 18, though entry is possible after this. In order to carry out an apprenticeship, you will need to find an employer who will sponsor your training.

HNDs in building studies or similar subjects can be studied over 2 years full time. Applicants should ideally have a science A level/H grade. Introductory courses to a career at technician level include BTEC Level 3 Diploma/Extended Diploma or Scottish Group Award in Construction.

You can apply for a ConstructionSkills Inspire Scholarship if you plan to pursue a construction-related degree. This includes a 10-week placement as well as a grant to support university study.

Many companies offer training schemes, day-release study (for HNC and Chartered Institute of Building exams), time spent on building sites, in-house training courses, and the Construction Industry Training Board (CITB) Technician Training Scheme.

Once qualified as a building technician, there are lots of opportunities to further your training whilst you work. You may for example, train for your NVQ Level 3 in Construction Site Supervision or NVQ Level 4 in Construction Site Management.

What the work involves

Building technicians support the work of construction professionals including surveyors and construction managers. They play an integral role in organising the construction of buildings by acting as a link between senior management and on-site labourers.

Your work will vary depending on your employer but might include planning work schedules, drawing up plans and estimating project costs and time scales. Knowledge of computer-aided design software (CAD) is necessary as technicians often have to make changes to plans and blueprints.

A building technician is also responsible for the negotiating and buying of materials, ensuring they are of good quality and are cost-effective. Another of your jobs will be to prepare sites prior to the commencement of a building project and later, to supervise staff whilst the work is being carried out. Monitoring building sites in terms of health and safety will be also be a high priority for you.

Type of person suited to this work

Organisational skills are essential as you ensure each construction job is completed accurately and efficiently.

Mathematical and IT skills are important for calculating costs, taking measurements and using CAD.

You must have an understanding of the technical aspects of construction. You must be dependable and will need strong communication skills for working with suppliers, site teams and other professionals.

Working conditions

When on site you will need to wear a safety helmet, overalls and boots at all times.

You are likely to work regular hours, but you may also have to start early, finish late or work at weekends on occasion as well as spend time away from home for various projects.

Future prospects

There is a steady supply of vacancies and a shortage of qualified applicants, particularly in London and Scotland.

Building technicians work for employers such as contractors, construction companies, property developers, surveyors' practices as well as within the public sector. You may also have the opportunity to work abroad.

There are vast opportunities for extending your responsibilities once employed. With experience and further qualifications, you may be promoted to a higher position such as building/construction manager. You may also choose to specialise in an area of expertise such as buying, drafting or estimating.

Advantages/disadvantages

It can be stressful having to work to deadlines.

Construction sites are dirty and dusty and some of your tasks may be dangerous.

Your work will be varied and interesting and you will be an integral part of the team producing all sorts of different buildings.

Money guide

Entry level salaries are typically £14,500–£16,500.

The average salary for a building technician ranges from £17,000 to £25,000.

Experienced senior building technicians can earn in excess of £30,000.

Related opportunities

- Architectural Technologist p58
- Construction Supervisor/Manager p74
- Surveying Technician p110

Further information

Chartered Association of Building Engineers
www.cbuilde.com

Chartered Institute of Building
www.ciob.org.uk

Construction Industry Training Board (CITB)
www.citb.co.uk

CARPENTER/JOINER

ENTRY LEVEL 1

Qualifications and courses

Although there are no formal entry requirements, GCSEs/National 5s in Maths, English and technology will be helpful for calculations, measurements and theory. Most employers will require some on-site experience so you may choose to shadow a professional or begin your career as a labourer. Your employer may then offer you training in carpentry.

Alternatively, another route into the industry involves attending college in order to gain a qualification. City & Guilds offer Certificates in Basic Construction Skills such as Carpentry and Joinery (6217-02) and Woodworking (6217-05) for young learners under the age of 16. By doing one of these, your chances of securing full-time work will be increased. Once employed, you can work towards NVQs/SVQs in Carpentry, both on the job and at college.

3-year Apprenticeships in Construction Building are available for school leavers. Diplomas and NVQs can be studied without an apprenticeship, or alongside practical work, by attending a training centre or college.

NVQs in Wood Occupations are available, such as the Diploma in Site Carpentry (Levels 2 and 3) and the Certificate in Shopfitting Site Work (Levels 2 and 3).

The Construction Awards Alliance (CAA) runs a Foundation Certificate in Building Craft Occupations. Young Apprenticeships for 14–16 year olds may be available through the Construction Industry Training Board (CITB).

What the work involves

Carpenters/joiners make, put in place or repair the wooden parts of buildings. You may be hired to make and install floorboards, skirting boards, cupboards, partitions, windows or doors. Other tasks may include fitting large wooden structures within the building trade, such as floor and roof joists or staircases.

You will work with different types of wood and use specialist hand tools such as hammers, chisels and planes, as well as power tools such as jigsaws and sanders. You will work either in a workshop or on-site with other building professionals.

Type of person suited to this work

You must have good practical skills and enjoy working with your hands and different tools.

You will be expected to follow plans and work carefully with attention to detail so that the structures you make fit into place correctly. As you will need to take measurements and calculate angles and dimensions, you will have to be good at maths and be accurate.

You should be physically fit in order to move around and lift materials. You must also be able to work in a team with other carpenters and those from the other construction trades.

Working conditions

You may work in a workshop or on construction sites, or divide your time between the two.

This can be heavy, dangerous and dusty work. You will need to keep to health and safety regulations, which may include wearing protective gear such as safety goggles and a mask. You are likely to work a normal working week, usually with an early start, although weekend work may also be required.

Future prospects

Across the UK there are around 240,000 carpenters/joiners, but employers are finding it difficult to recruit well-qualified and experienced workers. Many qualified carpenters are self-employed or work as sub-contractors.

With experience, you could move into a related occupation such as shopfitting, kitchen fitting or furniture making, or you may progress to technical, supervisory or managerial level. You may opt to specialise in one particular area, for example, in restoring old buildings or creating props. Alternatively, you might even consider instructing trainee carpenters in a college.

Advantages/disadvantages

Work can be seasonal: working fewer hours in the winter or having jobs cancelled is common.

You will develop a lot of new skills and you can specialise in certain areas such as listed buildings.

You get a sense of achievement when you see your woodwork in a building.

Money guide

Trainees start on a salary of £13,000–£16,000.

Qualified carpenters can earn anything in the range of £17,000–£23,000 per year.

Very experienced joiners may earn around £28,000 a year.

Skilled and experienced joiners could earn up to £40,000 per year.

The Building and Allied Trades Joint Industrial Council (BATJIC) agrees minimum wages annually.

Overtime is often available and on some projects you will receive bonuses based on output which can increase your earnings.

Self-employed carpenters will negotiate their own rates of pay.

Related opportunities

- Building Technician p64
- Construction Operative p72
- Window Fitter p117

Further information

British Woodworking Federation
www.bwf.org.uk

Institute of Carpenters
www.instituteofcarpenters.com

CARTOGRAPHER

ENTRY LEVEL 5

Qualifications and courses

The usual entry requirement for a cartographer is a relevant degree. Useful degree subjects include geography, geographical information systems, urban/land studies, surveying and mapping sciences. GCSE/National 5 English and Maths are generally needed for entry to these degrees and 2 A levels/3 H grades, including a science, Maths or Geography, would also be expected. Employers are increasingly seeking graduates with degrees in geographical information systems given the upturn in demand for digital map-making.

It may also be useful to hold a postgraduate qualification in a relevant subject, for example cartography, geographical information systems or remote sensing, if you are interested in more specialised areas.

Once employed, you will receive on-the-job training in relevant software and techniques. Government departments that employ cartographers have their own training schemes. It is also possible to work towards an NVQ/SVQ at Levels 3 and 4 in Spatial Data Management.

The Royal Air Force and Ordnance Survey may have opportunities for school leavers to study for a Certificate/Diploma or HNC/HND in Cartography by day release while training on the job.

The minimum entry requirements for a cartographic technician are 3 GCSEs/National 5s (A*–C/A–C), including Maths, English and occasionally a science. In practice, most entrants have A levels/H grades and some enter with a National Certificate/Diploma or HNC/HND in a relevant area.

Entry into the field is highly competitive, therefore by becoming a member of the Society of Cartographers and the British Cartographic Society, you will be able to secure important contacts and remain on top of current developments.

What the work involves

Cartography involves collecting, evaluating and displaying information gained from a variety of sources, including satellite technology, to create or update maps and navigation charts. This is achieved by using artistic, scientific, and technological methods.

Due to advances in information technology, geographical information systems and digital mapping techniques are now frequently used in this sector. You will use a range of sophisticated technology in all aspects of your work.

Type of person suited to this work

You will need to have strong IT, scientific and mathematical skills and an interest in geography.

Due to the nature of the work, it is essential that you have good spatial awareness, colour vision and an eye for layout and design. One sheet of a map can take months to produce, so you must be patient and dedicated to your work. A high level of accuracy and attention to detail is needed so that the map provides the best possible information for the user.

You must be willing to keep up with developments in the field and experiment with new ways of producing maps.

Working conditions

You are likely to work normal office hours at a workstation where you will have access to a computer.

At a senior level you will have more opportunity to meet and interact with colleagues and clients.

Part of your job will involve travelling around the UK to carry out surveys.

Future prospects

Most work is available in government departments, such as Ordnance Survey, the Hydrographic Office and the Meteorological Office. You could also work for local authorities, universities, councils, commercial map publishers, oil companies and motoring organisations.

With experience, you could become a freelance cartographer, provide consultancy services or work within higher education as a tutor.

Willingness to be geographically mobile can improve your chances of career progression.

If you are interested in living abroad, there are opportunities to work in cartography all over the world.

Advantages/disadvantages

Producing a map that looks good, is user friendly and likely to be used by many people is a very satisfying and rewarding experience.

As you near project deadlines, there is a higher level of pressure and you may be required to work late.

The work is varied and combines a variety of subject areas, from design to geography to maths.

Money guide

Starting salaries are usually between £16,000 and £20,000.

After 3–5 years' work experience, your earnings could increase to £20,000–£25,000.

It is possible for experienced or senior cartographers to achieve a salary of £30,000–£47,000.

Earnings vary depending on the size of the company and whether you work in the public or private sector.

Related opportunities

- Geographer p495
- Land/Geomatic Surveyor p92
- Town Planner/Planning Technician p113

Further information

Association for Geographic Information
www.agi.org.uk

British Cartographic Society
www.cartography.org.uk

The Survey Association
www.tsa-uk.org.uk

CEILING FIXER

ENTRY LEVEL 1

Qualifications and courses

No specific qualifications are required, although GCSEs/National 5s or a BTEC in Construction and the Built Environment may be helpful. Useful GCSE/National 5 subjects include maths, design and technology, a science and English.

You could approach companies directly in order to seek work as a trainee. You will be trained on the job whilst working towards qualifications. This may also involve going to a college or training centre on day or block release. Prior construction experience, for example as a labourer or tradesperson, may support you in your search for work.

Alternatively, you could develop your skills by completing an NVQ/SVQ in Interior Systems (Construction) Ceiling Fixing (Levels 1–3). The Construction Specialist Apprenticeship may also be available for those aged 16–24 who are looking to become a ceiling fixer.

You can also train by carrying out one of the Construction Industry Training Board (CITB)'s ConstructionSkills Apprenticeships which involves both studying and on-site experience.

Many employers require you to have the CSCS card issued by the Construction Skills Certification Scheme as proof of your competence working on-site. This can only be granted if you hold a valid qualification or have on-site experience.

What the work involves

As a ceiling fixer you will fit suspended ceilings into new and existing commercial or public buildings.

Your work will involve fitting a ceiling grid in place and inserting tiles by using tools such as metal cutters and screwdrivers. The ceiling is fitted to the concrete floor of the room above and may hide wiring and air conditioning systems.

As the job requires you to work at heights and on construction sites, your safety training must be up to date.

Type of person suited to this work

You will need to be comfortable working at heights and you must be physically fit to do the necessary climbing, carrying and bending.

You need to be thorough and accurate. An understanding of technical plans is essential and you must be able to follow instructions but also use your initiative. Numeracy skills are important to measure materials and calculate weights. As you will work alongside other ceiling fixers, electricians, heating and ventilating fitters, painters and decorators you need to be a good team player.

Working conditions

You will need to travel to various construction sites so a driving licence will be useful. The sites you work on will mainly be indoors and you will most likely work from a ladder in confined spaces.

You will need to take safety precautions for yourself and your colleagues and you will be expected to wear protective clothing such as a hard hat, boots and overalls. You are likely to work Monday to Friday, normal office hours, although overtime may be available at the weekends.

This could be dusty work which might be difficult if you suffer from some allergies.

Future prospects

Demand for qualified ceiling fixers in the construction industry is expected to increase over the next few years, with job opportunities likely to be available once trained.

You will most likely start out as a tradesperson. With experience, you may progress to a supervisory or managerial position, or perhaps run your own company. You could also become a subcontractor.

Advantages/disadvantages

Working at heights and in confined spaces may be stressful for some people.

It is satisfying to see the transformation that takes place when you have worked on fitting a ceiling.

You will have the opportunity to work on a variety of projects in different types of buildings.

Money guide

Trainees can earn up to £13,000 a year.

Once qualified as a ceiling fixer, you can expect to earn anything between £16,000 and £22,000.

Highly skilled and experienced workers within the role can earn in excess of £27,000.

Those who do contract/temporary work may receive a higher hourly/daily rate than those in full-time employment.

There are often opportunities to increase your earnings through shift allowances, working overtime and receiving performance-related bonuses.

Related opportunities

- Construction Operative p72
- Plasterer p97
- Roofer p102

Further information

Association of Interior Specialists
http://aisfpdc.org

Construction Industry Training Board (CITB)
www.citb.co.uk

CHARTERED SURVEYOR

ENTRY LEVEL 6

Qualifications and courses

You must become a member of the Royal Institution of Chartered Surveyors (RICS). For this you must complete an RICS-accredited degree course or a postgraduate conversion course. Degree entry requires 5 GCSEs/ National 5s (A*–C/A–C) and 3 A levels/4 H grades, or the relevant BTEC/SQA national awards. After completing an RICS-accredited course you must gain practical experience and undertake training before you will be fully qualified.

If you do not have the appropriate A levels or GCSEs you can take HNC/HND courses or Foundation degrees which can then be supplemented by an RICS-accredited degree course.

You can also train on the job as part of the Chartered Surveyors Training Trust scheme. This is available to those aged 16–24 who have 4 GCSEs/National 5s (A*–C/A–C) or equivalent. This programme involves a 2-year apprenticeship which will grant you Associate membership of the RICS. You then have the option to study for an accredited degree and take the RICS Assessment of Professional Competence to become a chartered surveyor.

You will be required to undertake continuing professional development (CPD) to keep up to date with surveying trends and skills.

What the work involves

As a chartered surveyor you will offer professional advice within the field of surveying in which you choose to specialise. This can be in building, construction, planning, the environment or quantity surveying. You will also spend time negotiating and explaining design/construction issues to clients.

You will have a variety of tasks to do such as examining plans, designs and project briefs, taking measurements, recording and analysing data and interpreting it through charts, maps or diagrams.

You may oversee entire construction projects, where you will ensure that specifications are met, calculate supplies needed and advise clients on the purchase, sale or development of property or land.

Type of person suited to this work

You should have an interest in construction, architecture, landscape and the environment.

As you are required to liaise with construction workers and clients, you must have excellent communication, negotiation and problem-solving skills and the ability to delegate tasks.

You need to be highly organised, methodical in your work and have a keen eye for detail as you may be coordinating several complex projects at the same time.

Working conditions

You will probably work 9am to 5pm, Monday to Friday. You may have to work longer hours to meet deadlines. Part-time work is available.

You will primarily be based in an office but you will also spend a considerable amount of time on-site.

Depending on your field of specialisation, you might have to work in various weather conditions and wear protective clothing when on-site.

You may have to travel for your work, both abroad and within the UK. For this reason a driving licence is strongly recommended.

Future prospects

There are good prospects for people training as chartered surveyors as the current demand for them exceeds supply.

You may follow a formal promotion structure to gain senior management roles.

You could choose to become self-employed or to join a private practice.

As a qualified chartered surveyor and member of the RICS you will have to take part in continuing professional development (CPD). For this you must accumulate 60 hours of CPD every 3 years.

Advantages/disadvantages

Employers may provide benefits such as a company car, mobile phone, bonuses and pension scheme.

There is significant competition for graduates wishing to gain entry to some areas of chartered surveying.

Money guide

As a graduate your starting salary may range from £18,000 to £26,000 a year.

Within 5 years of qualifying, you can expect to earn up to £45,000.

Senior chartered surveyors or those who are partners in firms have the potential to reach 6 figure salaries.

Geographical location does have an effect on how much chartered surveyors can earn with the highest wages typically found in London.

Depending on the type of project you are working on, very generous bonuses may be available.

Related opportunities

- Land/Geomatic Surveyor p92
- Surveying Technician p110
- Town Planner/Planning Technician p113

Further information

Chartered Association of Building Engineers
www.cbuilde.com

Chartered Surveyors Training Trust
www.cstt.org.uk

Royal Institution of Chartered Surveyors
www.rics.org

CIVIL/CONSTRUCTION ENGINEER/ CIVIL ENGINEERING TECHNICIAN

ENTRY LEVEL 5

Qualifications and courses

Entrants to civil engineering are usually graduates, although there are opportunities to progress from a craft or technical level.

The main route to becoming an engineer is a degree in the relevant branch of engineering or a closely related subject. It is recommended that you study a civil engineering course which is accredited by the Institution of Civil Engineers (ICE). The normal minimum entry requirements for an engineering degree are 3 A levels/5 H grades including Maths and a science, usually Physics or Chemistry. Equivalent qualifications such as BTEC/SQA Level 3 Certificates or Diplomas may be accepted.

Candidates who do not have the relevant A levels or equivalent may gain entry to an engineering degree by taking a 1-year Foundation course. Foundation courses are offered by universities and are sometimes taught at local partner colleges.

Once you have gained your degree you may then join a company's graduate scheme whereby you train alongside and with the support of a professional mentor for 1 to 2 years.

It is possible, however, to enter engineering after taking GCSEs/National 5s and progress to technician or professional level by studying part time for an HNC/HND or NVQ/SVQ Levels 4 or 5. You will need GCSEs/National 5s (A*–C/A–C) in English, Maths and a science. There are also BTEC and SQA Level 3 Certificates or Diplomas which will give you the relevant qualifications and can be studied at any age.

Alternatively, some engineering technicians gain entry to the career by firstly working through an engineering apprenticeship scheme. To gain a place you may need 4 GCSEs/National 5s with grades (A*–C/A–C) in subjects including maths, a science or design and technology, or equivalent qualifications. The availability of apprenticeship schemes depends on the job market of your local area and on the skills required by your local employers.

Professional engineers can work towards becoming chartered or incorporated members of one of the engineering professional bodies, such as ICE or the Chartered Institution of Building Services Engineers (CIBSE). The usual requirement for chartered status is an accredited MEng degree or equivalent. For incorporated status, a 3-year accredited BEng or BSc degree or an HND or equivalent, plus an additional period of learning, is required.

Undertaking a summer work experience placement or choosing a degree course with a year in industry can be useful ways to develop contacts within engineering and extend your knowledge.

What the work involves

Civil engineer (consulting)
You will be designing and developing plans for construction projects such as roads, tunnels, bridges, railways, reservoirs, pipelines and major buildings.

Your work could span many areas including waste management, coastal development and geotechnical engineering.

Your job will involve communicating with clients and once you have gained significant experience, you can run projects as a project manager.

Civil engineer (contracting)
You will take the consulting civil engineer's designs and make them into a reality at ground level, overseeing and managing the construction project.

This will include recruiting a team, sourcing materials, managing budgets and ensuring that the project is completed on time.

Contractors will sometimes create a design and build a team themselves. The roles of consultants and contractors are therefore not always entirely different from one another.

Civil engineering technician
You will be responsible for providing technical support to the civil engineer, which may include producing costing and timing estimates for a project and helping with recruitment.

The role will also include aspects of land and quantity surveying, as well as the production of design drawings.

Projects in which you are involved will fall under the categories of structural, transportation, environmental and maritime.

Type of person suited to this work

Regardless of the area you decide to work in, you will need to enjoy finding creative but workable solutions to problems.

You will need to be confident when using computers to produce designs, work out budgets and undertake research.

You should also be good at maths and science so that you can make accurate calculations and understand the different building materials available to you.

You must be able to think 3-dimensionally so that you can visualise and design different buildings and structures.

Written and verbal communication skills are important as you will have to write reports, explain your designs to clients and other professionals and supervise construction staff. You will work as part of a team so you must be able to communicate and cooperate with people at all levels.

An understanding of environmental building issues, such as the use of energy efficient materials and land protection, is of increasing importance.

Working conditions

Working hours are typically longer than the average working week and can include early morning and evening work on-site.

Weekend or shift work is rare for civil engineers, although civil engineering technicians can be required to remain on 24-hour call for some projects.

Your work will involve being both indoors and out on-site. When working on-site you will need to stick to health and safety regulations and be aware of your own and colleagues' safety. You will have to wear safety clothing including a helmet.

You could spend time in dangerous places or in difficult environments, for example you may have to work at height, up ladders or on scaffolding.

When you are in your office, you will be based at a workstation where you will use a computer with specialised software and possibly a drawing board. You will attend meetings and speak to clients on the phone or in person.

It is also likely that you will have to work away from home occasionally, both within the UK and abroad, but the extent of this will depend on the size of the company you work for and the type of contracts they attract.

Future prospects

Job prospects for civil engineers tend to remain steady, and are promising. Around 100,000 professional civil engineers work in the UK for a range of employers including health trusts, local authorities, central government and energy suppliers (including water, gas, nuclear and electricity companies), contractors, consultancies and transport networks.

Work is available on a variety of projects including the building of new schools, hospitals and the upgrading of public transport networks.

Many UK civil engineering companies also operate globally, increasing the opportunities to work overseas. The range and size of opportunities open to you will depend on the size of the company you work for and the types of contracts won.

Civil engineering technicians can undertake job-related training and study for more qualifications to become a civil engineer.

There is scope to undertake further study and specialise in areas such as environmental engineering, coastal and marine engineering, geotechnics or tunnelling.

With experience, you can progress into management or possibly associate/partnership positions within UK or international companies. Within the public sector, there are opportunities for management and chief engineer jobs. Another career option is to become self-employed or to provide training or consultancy services.

Advantages/disadvantages

You will play an important part in the design and construction of buildings and structures throughout the world so you are likely to be well respected.

Seeing a project come to completion can be very satisfying.

Having an engineering background and qualifications opens up opportunities to enter other non-engineering careers at senior levels.

There is the opportunity to become self-employed or work overseas.

Work is varied, each day is different and you will be meeting and dealing with a wide range of people.

The pace of work varies quite extensively as you will alternate between a heavy workload and quieter periods.

There is a high level of responsibility in this field so the work can be demanding and occasionally stressful.

Money guide

Civil/Construction engineer

Starting salaries for civil engineers, either contracting or consulting, are between £17,000 and £25,000.

With more experience, engineers can earn anything between £25,000 and £40,000 a year.

Qualifying as a member or fellow of the Institution of Civil Engineers (ICE) can see salaries for civil engineers rise to between £60,000 and £100,000.

Civil engineering technician

Civil engineering technicians start on about £13,000–£19,000.

With experience, earnings increase to £20,000–£35,000 a year.

Senior technicians can earn £37,000 or more and if you train as a civil engineer your earning potential will increase as above.

Earnings are likely to be considerably higher in London and they vary depending on the size of the company.

Many employers offer additional benefits including a pension scheme, life insurance, a healthcare package and possibly a company car.

Related opportunities

- Architect p56
- Building Surveyor p63
- Insurance Risk Surveyor p32
- Town Planner/Planning Technician p113

Further information

Engineering Council UK
www.engc.org.uk

Institution of Civil Engineers
www.ice.org.uk

WISE
www.wisecampaign.org.uk

CONCRETER

ENTRY LEVEL 1

Qualifications and courses

There are no formal qualifications required in order to become a concreter. After you have completed school you may choose to seek employment within the industry. Training is usually available on the job.

An increasing number of employers require their employees to hold a Construction Skills Certification Scheme (CSCS) card to show proof of their competence working on-site. This can only be gained by having completed or, in the process of completing, a vocational qualification and health and safety test.

Apprenticeships are a common route into the construction field. It would be useful to have GCSEs/ National 5s (A*–E/A–E) including Maths, Design and Technology and English. You may be required to complete a test in order to secure your apprenticeship.

As a trainee, you can work towards NVQs in Trowel Occupations (Levels 1 and 2), Erection of Precast Concrete (Level 2) and Specialist Concrete Occupations such as Concrete Repair, Sprayed Concrete or Concrete Drilling (Level 2).

Alternatively, Foundation Construction Awards in Trowel Occupations are available if obtaining experience in the workplace for NVQs is a challenge. Colleges offer these awards alongside an apprenticeship.

What the work involves

Your job will include initially levelling and compacting the ground to prepare it for concreting and then the construction of drives and pathways, floor slabs, foundations, columns and beams.

You will be working as part of a construction team, working with other specialists on building projects.

You will take early-morning deliveries of concrete, dig foundation trenches, mix, lay and level the concrete on the prepared ground, vibrate it to remove air trappings, and wrap it in polythene sheeting in order to cure it.

As well as laying fresh concrete you may also be required to reinforce existing concrete structures, repair cracks that have been caused by moving ground and create different styles and effects within the setting concrete for aesthetic purposes.

Type of person suited to this work

You should have a careful, methodical approach to your work and have good hand skills.

Maths skills are important as you will be calculating quantities for materials.

You should enjoy working outdoors, as part of a team or on your own. Being fit and active is essential as you will be required to work long and at times hard hours.

You need to be aware of health and safety requirements when working on-site.

Working conditions

Your work will be site based, largely undertaking manual labour in dirty or dusty surroundings.

You will work 37 hours a week, including some early mornings and late nights.

You could work on a building site, motorway, private driveway or the interiors of large buildings.

Protective clothing is needed, as the work is messy and at times, potentially dangerous.

You will use traditional hand tools such as shovels as well as machinery such as cement mixers and drillers.

Future prospects

You can move into specialised areas of work such as concrete spraying or concrete repair. It is also possible to progress to a managerial or supervisory role.

After gaining experience, many concreters choose to become self-employed. You could start your own company or work on a labour-only basis for a contractor.

You can work for building and engineering contractors, local authorities and public organisations. Job opportunities are also available abroad, as well as throughout the UK.

Advantages/disadvantages

You have the opportunity to earn good money if you work hard.

There is an increased risk of injury on construction sites. The cement in concrete can cause burning or inflammation and you should avoid contact with the skin.

The work is physically draining, as it involves a great deal of practical work and, at times, heavy lifting.

Money guide

As a trainee you can expect to earn around £12,500.

With experience this can rise to £20,000–£25,000.

Concrete sprayers with a lot of experience can earn £30,000.

Salaries can be boosted by bonuses and overtime.

You may earn more if you set up your own contracting firm.

Related opportunities

- Bricklayer p60
- Construction Operative p72
- Plasterer p97

Further information

Chartered Institute of Building
www.ciob.org.uk

The Concrete Centre
www.concretecentre.com

Women and Manual Trades
www.wamt.org

CONSTRUCTION OPERATIVE

ENTRY LEVEL 1

Qualifications and courses

Your training will take place mainly on the job by experienced labourers/construction operatives and tradespeople. Employers may ask for a number of GCSEs/National 5s in subjects such as English, maths and technology or equivalent qualifications. Once employed, there may be opportunities to study for NVQs/SVQs (Levels 1 and 2) in Construction and Civil Engineering or in Specialised Plant and Machinery Operations.

Many employers require you to hold a CSCS card issued by the Construction Skills Certification Scheme as proof of your competence working on site. A health and safety test and evidence of a vocational qualification is usually necessary in order to qualify for one of these.

City & Guilds offer Certificates in Basic Construction Skills (6217) for young learners under the age of 16 and an Award/Certificate/Diploma in Basic Construction Skills for 14–19 year olds. BTEC Certificates and Diplomas are available in Construction as well as a Foundation Certificate in Building and Craft Occupations.

You can also train to be a construction operative via a 2-year Construction Civil Engineering Apprenticeship scheme and choose to complete an extra year for a Level 3 Construction Diploma.

If you are a full-time student doing a construction-related course you can qualify for a programme-led apprenticeship (PLA) and gain experience up to NVQ Level 2.

What the work involves

Construction operatives support the work of other construction workers by doing various practical tasks.

Your work might include digging trenches, moving building materials and tools, putting up signs and safety barriers, helping to lay drains, and paving roads.

You will also mix and lay cement as well as operate construction equipment and vehicles.

Type of person suited to this work

As the work requires you to lift heavy materials and be on the move a lot you must be physically fit. You must also not mind working at great heights or depths.

You need to be able to follow and carry out instructions and work well in a team with other labourers and professionals.

It is essential to be hands on, flexible and trustworthy.

Working conditions

You will be working both indoors and outdoors in all weather conditions.

The work is often dusty and dirty and may be difficult for people suffering from allergies.

You will need to pay attention to both your own and your colleagues' health and safety. You will be expected to follow procedures for each type of work you do, including the wearing of protective clothing.

You may work a normal week, although evening and weekend work may also be available, and you might need to start early or finish late for some projects as well as work away from home at times.

Future prospects

Building projects, new builds and renovations cannot happen without construction operatives so they are in strong demand when business is doing well.

You could work for contractors or local authorities.

You may progress to a specialist craft career such as carpentry or bricklaying or advance to a supervisory role. You also have the option of becoming self-employed or finding work abroad.

Advantages/disadvantages

The work can sometimes be physically demanding.

You have the opportunity to learn a wide range of skills and work on a different project every day.

Your role on-site is important as you pave the way for tradespeople to complete their tasks.

Money guide

As a trainee starting out you can expect a salary of up to £15,500 per year.

As a qualified construction operative you could earn £17,000–£20,500.

Depending on the project they are working on, skilled operatives may receive up to £24,000 a year.

Overtime is often available for those who wish to increase their earnings.

On some projects there are bonuses based on outputs which can lead to higher earnings.

Related opportunities

- Bricklayer p60
- Building Technician p64
- Mastic Asphalter p93

Further information

Construction Industry Training Board (CITB)
www.citb.co.uk

Federation of Master Builders
www.fmb.org.uk

Women and Manual Trades
www.wamt.org

CONSTRUCTION PLANT OPERATOR

ENTRY LEVEL 1

Qualifications and courses

There are no set academic entry requirements, although GCSEs/National 5s or equivalent in English, Maths and a science or technology are useful, alongside any equivalent vocational qualifications. It is also possible to take NVQs/SVQs in Specialised Plant and Machinery Operations (Levels 1 and 2) and Foundation, Intermediate and Advanced certificates in Maintenance of Construction Plant.

The minimum age to operate plant and equipment is 18 but 17-year-olds may work under supervision while they are training.

Construction civil engineering apprenticeships may be available for those over the age of 16 who wish to train as a construction plant operator. Another option is to train as an apprentice in Crane Operation or Plant Operations with the National Construction College. This route involves practical training and studying for the NVQ Diploma and Certificate in Plant Operations (Level 2).

The Construction Plant Competence Scheme (CPCS) card is required in order to operate most categories of plant, including cranes. New applicants must pass a health and safety test and technical test for a red CPCS card which allows trainees to work on-site. After working 300 hours and completing an NVQ/SVQ you can obtain a blue card.

What the work involves

Construction plant operators operate and maintain different forms of plant (machinery) used for tasks such as moving soil and building materials, flattening the earth and preparing concrete.

You may operate bulldozers, excavators, diggers, cranes and fork-lift trucks.

In larger organisations you may specialise in operating one type of plant. For example, crane operators control the machine to load and unload materials, working in conjunction with a signaller on the ground.

Type of person suited to this work

As you will often handle large and complex machines, you need to be good with your hands and have keen safety awareness. You will also need good mechanical knowledge.

You need to stay focused and communicate with your workmates so that you can operate safely. If you are working on cranes, you need to be comfortable working at heights, be alert and be a skilled driver.

Working conditions

You will work outdoors and on a variety of sites. Expect to get hot, dusty and dirty in the summer and cold, muddy and wet in the winter. You will have to stick to health and safety regulations and wear a protective helmet and boots.

You are likely to work a normal working week from Monday to Friday but you may also work extra hours at weekends. Some construction firms operate longer hours during the summer months and shorter during the winter. You might have to travel away from home on some contracts.

A driving licence (often a large goods vehicle category C licence) is essential for crane operators.

Future prospects

Work is available across the UK with crane-hire companies, manufacturers, local authorities and construction companies. For operators specialising in engineering work there is a high concentration of jobs available in the Midlands and in the north of England.

With experience, you may progress to using a wider range of plant and you may supervise or train plant operators or work as a safety inspector. You may also choose to specialise in operating one type of plant.

With experience and financial backing, it may be possible to start your own construction plant operation or hire business.

Advantages/disadvantages

Working on construction sites can be noisy, dusty and dirty although you will have safety equipment/clothing such as ear protectors. Working at heights may be demanding for some people.

It is a skilled and varied career where you are responsible for some impressive machinery. It can be satisfying to be able to control the machinery efficiently and safely.

Money guide

Trainee construction plant operators typically have a starting salary of £13,000.

As you gain qualifications, your earnings can increase to £15,000–£19,000 a year.

Very experienced plant operators or those with specialist skills can achieve £20,000–£26,000.

It is possible to increase your earnings through bonuses and working overtime.

Related opportunities

- Construction Operative p72
- Demolition Operative p76
- Highways Maintenance/Road Worker p89

Further information

Chartered Association of Building Engineers
www.cbuilde.com

Construction Industry Training Board (CITB)
www.citb.co.uk

CONSTRUCTION SUPERVISOR/ MANAGER

ENTRY LEVEL 5

Qualifications and courses

The normal entry qualification required to be a construction manager is a degree, HND or Foundation degree. Relevant subjects include construction project management, building services engineering and building technology. For entry to a degree, 5 GCSEs/National 5s (A*–C/A–C) including Maths and a science and 2 A levels/3 H grades are normally required. You could seek financial sponsorship from an employer whilst you complete your studies and then go on to work for them after you graduate.

If you chose a degree unrelated to the construction industry, you may still be able to enter the field by completing a Graduate Diploma Programme offered by the Chartered Institute of Building (CIOB).

Alternatively, it may be possible to work your way up from technician level, as an estimator or as a site supervisor. The NVQ/SVQ in Construction Site Supervision (Level 3) and Construction Site Management (Level 4) are open to anyone with experience in building site supervision and management. Technicians can also study part time towards an HNC or degree.

The Chartered Institute of Building (CIOB) offers qualifications at Levels 3 and 4 in Site Management and Site Supervisory Studies which could improve your career prospects.

Recently qualified graduates are likely to continue training on programmes designed for professional and managerial staff. The CIOB runs a professional development programme (PDP) leading to chartered membership of the Institute.

What the work involves

Construction supervisors/managers run both new build and maintenance construction sites. Your duties will include planning the build, preparing the site, arranging deliveries, and checking quality and cost of building materials and equipment.

You will also have the responsibility for overseeing the construction project, hiring and managing staff, making sure everyone is safe on-site, and solving problems when they arise.

You will need to report directly to whoever is paying for the work to be done and keep them updated on progress.

Type of person suited to this work

You have to be able to plan ahead and have good management and problem-solving skills so that projects run smoothly. Numeracy skills are important in order to budget your projects.

You need to be a good communicator, energetic, hard working and diplomatic in order to motivate and manage your staff effectively. You must be able to develop an in-depth knowledge and understanding of all aspects of the construction business. You will use computer software packages to plan workflow, so IT skills are also useful.

Organisational skills are essential and you should be prepared to take responsibility for anything that happens on your site.

Working conditions

You will be based on construction sites and are likely to work from a portable office. You will work outdoors in all weathers.

You may work a normal working week, but you may also have to start early, finish late or work at weekends on some projects. As some companies win contracts all over the UK, you might have to work away from home.

Future prospects

Demand in the construction industry does seem to be on the increase again after a few years of uncertainty. A rise in construction means that there are good opportunities for construction supervisors on a wide range of builds, including multi-million pound projects as well as opportunities abroad.

You may work for contractors, construction companies, project management companies, surveyors' practices, public services, utility companies or retailers.

With experience, you may be promoted to work as a contract manager on bigger and more prestigious projects. You could go into teaching the trade or work as a health and safety inspector.

Advantages/disadvantages

There is a great deal of satisfaction to be obtained from knowing that you have the ability to begin with an empty piece of land and leave a finished construction behind.

When there is a tight deadline to meet and a problem arises, the work can be stressful; particularly as many projects are on large but tightly planned budgets.

Money guide

Trainee construction managers usually have an annual salary of around £20,000.

Once you have gained experience as a manager, your earnings can rise to between £27,000 and £45,000.

For managers running the largest projects, a salary in excess of £70,000 is possible.

Earnings vary depending on geographical location and your particular employer.

Related opportunities

- Architectural Technician p57
- Building Surveyor p63
- Civil/Construction Engineer/Civil Engineering Technician p69

Further information

Chartered Institute of Building
www.ciob.org.uk

Construction Industry Training Board (CITB)
www.citb.co.uk

DAMP PROOFER

ENTRY LEVEL 1

Qualifications and courses

There are no set academic requirements. However GCSEs/National 5s in English and Maths (A*–E/A–E) are an advantage as you will need to calculate quantities, form estimates and maintain written records.

Currently, there are no colleges that provide apprenticeships specifically for those wishing to go into the field of damp proofing. Some private companies, involved in Investors in People, may offer apprenticeships however.

On-the-job training is provided by experienced damp proofers. Damp-proof installer companies may also provide courses on safety awareness.

Technicians can take short courses at the British Wood Preserving and Damp Proofing Association. You can study for the Level 2 NVQ in Insulation and Building Treatments, a course developed by CITB ConstructionSkills. Courses accredited by the CITB are recognised throughout the industry.

In order to work on a building site, you must also hold a Construction Skills Certification Scheme (CSCS) card which acts as proof of your competency. Completing a vocational qualification before or whilst you train will qualify you for one of these.

What the work involves

You will provide guidance and solutions to people in residential or commercial properties who experience damp problems.

As a damp proofer, you inspect and assess properties using moisture meters to aid you in your discovery of a client's damp problems. Drawing on your knowledge and experience within the industry, you will provide your clients with recommendations as to how to eradicate their damp issues and suggest a suitable price at which to do so.

You also may need to install damp-proof courses to buildings. This is a horizontal layer of water-repellent/proof material that prevents moisture rising from the ground up the walls. This involves drilling holes in walls to inject mortar or creams/gels at varying pressures.

Type of person suited to this work

As you will be working on buildings or engineering projects, you should have an interest in construction and architecture. You should also be in good health and have an understanding of health and safety protocol.

You should have good problem-solving skills and relish new challenges. You should be able to work in a team and cooperate with colleagues and customers. You will need good written and communication skills to give and follow instructions and guidelines.

You need to have a keen eye for detail and have good practical skills to operate drills and specialist machinery such as moisture meters to check damp levels. You should also be willing to travel.

Working conditions

You will usually work 38 hours a week, Monday to Friday. You may have to work overtime and this could include evenings and weekends. These hours will vary depending on where you are working, who you are working for and even the weather.

You will have to do a lot of travelling to each new site. A driving licence and car would be useful.

Your work will be largely outdoors, so can be affected by the weather.

Future prospects

You can find job opportunities with the 1,500 damp proofing contractors across the UK. You can also find employment in related fields such as timber treatment, waterproofing and pest control.

With experience you will be eligible for promotion to remedial treatment surveyor or supervisory posts. The Wood Protection Association (WPA) runs its own training courses for surveyors and technicians and with an NVQ/SVQ Level 2 in Insulation and Remedial Maintenance you can apply for occupational assessment under the CSCS.

You could become self-employed.

Advantages/disadvantages

As a damp proofer you will have plenty of opportunities to travel around the UK and abroad.

Bonus payments are extremely common within this field of work.

You may have to work in uncomfortable weather conditions and antisocial working hours.

The work is very physical and demanding and a lot of your time will be taken up travelling between different work sites and projects.

Money guide

Starting salary can range between £12,000 and £15,000 a year.

With experience, this can rise to £25,000 a year.

With specialised skills and training you can earn in excess of £35,000.

Related opportunities

- Building Technician p64
- Concreter p71
- Thermal Insulation Engineer p112

Further information

Institute of Specialist Surveyors and Engineers
www.isse.org.uk

Wood Protection Association
www.wood-protection.org

DEMOLITION OPERATIVE

ENTRY LEVEL 1

Qualifications and courses

No formal qualifications are required to be a demolition operative. However GCSEs/National 5s (A*–E/A–E) in Maths, science subjects and English or a background in general construction may be useful for calculations, measurements and theory. The BTEC Diplomas (Levels 1–3) in Construction and the Built Environment may also be relevant for this job.

You can enter via the CITB ConstructionSkills Apprenticeship in Demolition Plant Operation, if you are under 16, but you need to be at least 18 to work as a demolition operative. There is also a specialist apprenticeship for people who work in demolition but do not handle machinery.

Most training is done on the job, with special attention given to health and safety – including accident prevention, manual handling, noise control and fire control/prevention. You can study for the NVQ Level 2 in Demolition and Demolition Plant. Other NVQs are available for specialist work such as the Level 2 in Removal of Hazardous and Non-Hazardous Waste.

You will need a Certificate of Competence of Demolition Operatives (CCDO) card to prove you are qualified to carry out the job safely. To qualify for one of these, you are normally required to have completed or signed up for a vocational qualification.

What the work involves

Demolition operatives demolish or dismantle buildings and structures. The job can be highly dangerous if the right precautions are not taken so you will be responsible for assessing structures and planning for the safest and most efficient way to demolish them.

You will clear and prepare sites, put up fencing and scaffolding, strip out fittings, and remove, sort and grade reusable materials.

You will use a variety of tools such as chisels, crowbars and axes for hand demolition of brick and stone and you may also use specialised machinery including pneumatic drills, steel girders, chainsaws and even explosives for bigger jobs.

Type of person suited to this work

As you will be involved in the construction industry you should have an interest in building, construction and the environment.

You should have a high level of fitness as your work will be quite physical a lot of the time, involving lifting and carrying, and you should be able to work at heights. You will also need good manual skills to operate equipment and tools and an aptitude for more delicate tasks such as hand demolition.

You should have a strong eye for detail and be able to follow health and safety instructions rigorously.

You should be willing to work as part of a team and be conscious of your safety and that of those around you.

Working conditions

You will normally work 39 hours per week. This will frequently include weekends and overtime.

As you will be working on construction sites you should be willing to work outdoors in dirty, dusty, noisy conditions in all weathers. This will also involve lifting, bending and working at heights.

You will need to wear protective equipment including helmets, boots, gloves and goggles which will be provided by the employer. You may also be required to wear breathing equipment for some jobs.

Future prospects

There are opportunities for demolition operatives on many building and development projects throughout the UK. You can find employment in specialist companies which may be based nationally but many companies are based in urban and traditionally industrial areas of the UK.

If you work hard and commit yourself to the job, there are fantastic opportunities for progression and personal achievement.

Advantages/disadvantages

Although it is unusual to be self-employed in this profession, with experience you can set up your own contracting business.

At times your work can be strenuous and potentially hazardous if you do not follow safety procedures.

Money guide

Demolition operatives have nationally recommended minimum rates of pay.

The starting salary for a trainee is around £12,500 a year.

Once qualified as a demolition operative, your salary will rise to anything between £13,000 and £18,000. As a senior operative you can earn up to around £23,000.

You may earn significantly more with overtime or for carrying out specialist responsibilities such as operating plant machinery or handling explosives.

Related opportunities

- Construction Operative p72
- Quarry Worker p224
- Scaffolder p104

Further information

Construction Industry Training Board (CITB)
www.citb.co.uk

National Federation of Demolition Contractors
www.demolition-nfdc.com

DRY STONE WALLER ENTRY LEVEL 1

Qualifications and courses

No specific qualifications are necessarily required in order to become a dry stone waller. You can train with an experienced professional or do a land-based training course that includes dry stone walling.

The Dry Stone Walling Association of Great Britain (DSWA) runs a National Certification scheme at 3 levels (Initial, Intermediate and Advanced), which is open to anyone, including complete beginners. Completion of these usually leads to the DSWA Master Craftsman Certification. These qualifications are available through some colleges and across the DSWA branch network, including Scotland and Wales. These branches also offer short courses and practice days aimed at improving the skills of beginners and are usually led by a DSWA instructor over a period of one weekend.

Alternatively, you may choose to go down the apprenticeship route. A number of colleges across England offer Lantra Certificates in Dry Stone Walling (Levels 1 and 2) as part of a more general Diploma in Environmental Conservation. You will need sponsorship from an employer in order to complete this.

What the work involves

Dry stone walls are built as boundaries in rural landscapes, and sometimes in gardens and parks. Unlike other walls, they are built without the use of mortar or cement.

As a dry stone waller, you will build new walls and maintain and rebuild existing walls, using the existing or newly quarried stone.

You will prepare foundations, set up a frame and lay stones, as well as strip out any existing wall or stones. You will need to be able to use tools such as hammers, sledgehammers, pick axes and tape measures.

Type of person suited to this work

You need to be thorough, methodical and good with your hands.

Being physically fit is essential as you will be lifting and carrying heavy stones. You will also need endurance and self-motivation as you will most likely be self-employed.

An eye for design is useful for creating decorative effects. You may also need to work in a team with other dry stone wallers.

You will need to respect the plants, animals and insects that live within, on or around the walls and other parts of your working area so having an interest in conservation and the environment is useful. You should also be aware of health and safety regulations.

Working conditions

Your work will be physically demanding and take place outdoors in most weather conditions. The work may also be dusty and dirty.

You will need to wear protective gear such as boots, strong gloves and safety goggles.

Your working hours are likely to vary according to daylight hours and when the work is available. You may need to work weekends.

Future prospects

Dry stone walling is prospering due to the increased interest in conserving walls and the growth in artistic landscape projects. Given that dry stone walls are composed of natural materials, they are highly valued in a society increasingly concerned about its environment.

As a highly important feature of the British landscape, there is a demand for the maintenance, repair and creation of dry stone walls in farms, parks and gardens. Work is available in all rural areas of the UK for skilled members of the profession.

Employment is possible with organisations such as National Parks and The National Trust – although most experienced dry stone wallers are self-employed.

You can begin by working for an experienced dry stone waller and gain the necessary skills before working for yourself.

Many experienced wallers travel around the UK to complete projects. A few wallers combine this work with traditional bricklaying projects.

Advantages/disadvantages

The work can be physically demanding.

It is rewarding to use craft skills to build dry stone walls that are not only functional, but also enhance the landscape and become part of our heritage.

You also have the chance to be creative when producing decorative effects.

Money guide

The normal starting point for new entrants is around £8,000 per year.

For dry stone wallers with some experience, earning between £10,500 and £14,500 is possible.

Very skilled dry stone wallers with a lot of experience and contacts are able to earn up to £21,000, however earnings vary widely across the UK.

Related opportunities

- Blacksmith p198
- Construction Operative p72
- Stonemason p108
- Thatcher p111

Further information

Dry Stone Walling Association of Great Britain
www.dswa.org.uk

Lantra
www.lantra.co.uk

ELECTRICIAN

ENTRY LEVEL 3

Qualifications and courses

An industry-recognised Level 3 NVQ qualification and a technical certificate are required in order to become a qualified electrician. Examples of these Level 3 qualifications include: a City & Guilds/EAL-approved Level 3 Diploma in either Electrotechnical Services (Electrical Maintenance) (2357), Installing Electrotechnical Systems & Equipment (Buildings, Structures and the Environment) (2357) or Electrical Installations (Buildings and Structures) (2365).

The most common route to training as an electrician is by undertaking an electrotechnical advanced apprenticeship. This route will involve working towards a Level 3 NVQ Diploma in the workplace whilst studying for a technical certificate one day a week at college. You will be required to secure employment prior to signing up for the apprenticeship and typical entry requirements include 3 GCSEs/National 5s (A*–C/A–C) including English, Maths and a science. You must be 16 or over.

The City & Guilds Certificate in the Requirements for Electrical Installations helps to ensure that those practising in the electrical industry are up to date with the latest safety regulations.

Those experienced in areas such as electronics may qualify for entrance onto a training course. Colleges and private organisations offer their own courses but candidates must show practical work ability. Other qualifications include the City & Guilds NVQ in Engineering Maintenance and the BTEC Certificates/ Diplomas in Engineering.

Entry to the profession is quite competitive and you must pass a colour vision and selection test.

What the work involves

Electricians install and inspect the wiring systems in all kinds of buildings (residential and commercial) and mechanical equipment.

You will follow detailed diagrams and plans when checking and installing new systems. Once installed you will test them to make sure they are safe.

You may work on quite complex wiring systems, ranging from security circuits and computer networks to traffic lights and other street lighting.

Type of person suited to this work

You must have the practical skills to be able to use tools such as pliers, screwdrivers and drills as well as the ability to follow wiring diagrams and work within strict safety regulations. Knowledge of maths and physics is therefore beneficial.

You will need to be physically fit as the work involves bending, stretching, kneeling and generally being active. It can also involve working at heights, so you must be comfortable with this.

You may work alone or in a team but either way you will be talking to customers and explaining electrical problems, so good communication skills are an asset.

Working conditions

You may work a normal working week from Monday to Friday, but most electricians work 37–40 hours including evenings and weekends to accommodate the needs of their customers.

Electricians work in a variety of locations from people's homes to offices or building sites. You will almost certainly need a driving licence. The work can be dusty and dirty.

You will need to keep to health and safety regulations otherwise working with electricity can be exceedingly dangerous.

Future prospects

Employment prospects for new trainees are good as demand remains consistent.

Work is extremely varied and available in all kinds of environments including in housing associations, general building companies and public services such as local authorities and health trusts.

Most large employers have a formal progression structure, therefore, as you gain more experience, opportunities for supervisory and managerial responsibilities will become available and you may even move into consultancy work or training. Owning your own company and working abroad are also possible.

Advantages/disadvantages

You are providing a vital service and it is particularly rewarding to solve problems for people.

Many electricians are self-employed so you could have increased control over your work–life balance.

You may be required to work long hours and sometimes in physically difficult circumstances.

Money guide

The Joint Industry Board (JIB) for the Electrical Contracting Industry sets salary rates for apprentices and qualified electricians.

Trainee electricians may begin on around £8,000.

Once qualified, salaries rise to between £17,000 and £20,000.

Earnings increase with experience and those who specialise in a certain area can make £23,000–£30,000 a year.

Overtime and bonuses are also possible.

Related opportunities

- Bricklayer p60
- Carpenter/Joiner p65
- Plumber p98

Further information

Scottish Electrical Charitable Training Trust
www.sectt.org.uk

Organisation Profile

NICEIC

About NICEIC

NICEIC is the UK's leading voluntary regulatory body for the electrical contracting industry. It has been assessing the electrical competence of electricians for over 50 years and currently maintains a roll of over 26,000 registered contractors.

Choosing an NICEIC registered electrician is a householder's best way to ensure a safe job. Electricians registered with NICEIC are assessed on a regular basis to ensure high standards and their work is checked against the IEE Wiring Regulations BS7671 as well as other standards.

Why choose an NICEIC registered electrician?

NICEIC operates an independent complaints procedure governing the technical standards of its Approved Contractor and Domestic Installer Schemes. If the work of a registered contractor is found to be below the accepted technical standard, NICEIC can require the contractor to correct the work at no additional cost to the customer.

Approved contractors undergo a rigorous assessment process, covering a representative sample of their work, their premises, documentation, equipment, and the competence of their key supervisory staff. They are then re-assessed on a regular basis to ensure continued compliance.

Once registered with the NICEIC, contractors can access a range of support services, including technical advice, industry recognised training, industry literature and contractor insurance.

NICEIC regularly promotes the importance of employing an approved contractor to homeowners. Aside from the assurance of safety and competence of work, additional benefits to the consumer include guaranteed compliance with building regulations, an insurance-backed warranty and access to an independent complaints procedure, should a problem arise.

Looking after the industry

NICEIC is committed to improving standards within the industry and in September 2010 NICEIC set up an apprenticeship scheme as part of its commitment to training the workforce of the future.

NICEIC believes apprenticeships make industries more effective, productive and competitive by addressing the skills gap directly. They are the proven way to train the workforce of the future.

The NICEIC Apprentice Academy gives those just starting out on their careers the knowledge to complete electrical installations in line with current and future working practices. Run in partnership with Bedford College, trainee electricians complete a series of fortnightly courses over 2 years before embarking on a final year of professional development under the guidance of NICEIC.

NICEIC is also committed to improving opportunities for women in the electrical contracting industry. Women are severely under-represented in most trade professions with less than one in every thousand electricians a female – despite there now being a valid business case to employ more women.

In response to this NICEIC launched its Jobs for the Girls campaign. Through its extensive media coverage the campaign has raised awareness of the opportunities available to women in the industry. It also garnered the support of a cross party band of MPs and in 2011 NICEIC was invited to Westminster to host a parliamentary reception about the campaign. You can find out more at www.jobsforthegirls.com.

For more information or to find a qualified electrician in your area, visit www.niceic.com.

Case Study

ELECTRICIAN

Steven Bastien, NICEIC Approved Contractor

When I was younger, during the weekends I would accompany my electrician uncle on his jobs in London, to earn extra pocket money. I was about 14 and I found it interesting working in different types of buildings and areas. The excitement and adventure of going to different places and meeting different people made it enjoyable.

Until the age of 16 I continued working with my uncle at weekends. I learnt how to install new electrical installations and rewire properties. At first, the jobs I did were mainly manual, moving furniture, lifting up carpets and floorboards etc. Sometimes I would get the opportunity to chase out walls to bury cables. I also had to pack away the tools at the end of the day, and make sure none were missing!

As time went on, I realised I really enjoyed electrical work. It made me feel important and made me feel valued. I felt good about myself. I felt I was doing something which was a skilled trade … so becoming an electrician was a straightforward choice. I was advised by my careers adviser and teachers what subjects would be best to study; these subjects were science, maths, English, history and geography.

After leaving school, I studied at college for two years, taking relevant City & Guilds qualifications. I studied very hard to make sure I would pass – which I did with a distinction and passes. I then applied to electrical companies for an electrical apprenticeship. I was successful and offered a 5-year JIB Apprenticeship. It was here I gained a vast amount of experience in the electrical field, working in offices, schools, factories and shops. I carried on at college where I continued my studies to gain more qualifications in Electrical Installations.

Three years later I became a Qualified Electrician. I then decided to become even more adventurous by becoming self-employed. This gave me the opportunity to work on major building projects throughout the UK. I worked in a variety of places such as Fleet Street working for different newspapers. I even worked on a building which had a helicopter pad on top of it. That was quite exciting! I also worked on the first tower block of Canary Wharf. I worked on Tower Bridge, the NEC in Birmingham, the first Toyota car factory in the UK, and many more.

I then started working for local authorities, carrying out maintenance work as well as emergency callouts. Callouts give you a good feeling as you have helped someone.

Recently, I have formed my own company – Facelift Electrical Services Ltd – and successfully became an NICEIC Domestic Installer. I then became an NICEIC Approved Contractor which involved me taking more qualifications.

I can now say to any young person who would like to become an electrician, that it's a very enjoyable and satisfying career. It's great when you see the beginning of the project and see it through to the end. It's great to know you were part of that project being completed.

For further information visit www.niceic.com or call 0870 013 0382.

ESTATE AGENT

ENTRY LEVEL 3

Qualifications and courses

No formal qualifications are required to become an estate agent. It is useful for entrants to have 5 GCSEs/National 5s (A*–C/A–C). Most entrants start as a trainee negotiator and undertake an NVQ in the Sale of Residential Property (Level 2). A degree, Foundation degree or HND in subjects such as property management, urban and land studies or civil and structural engineering, may increase your chances of employment in a competitive industry or a background in sales, customer service or administration could be advantageous.

Training is mostly carried out on the job. It may involve studying for Technical Awards offered by the National Federation of Property Professionals (NFoPP), such as the Sale of Residential Property, Residential Letting and Property Management and Commercial Property Agency. NFoPP also offer Certificates in these subjects which are intended for those with around 3 years' experience. Both the Technical Awards and the Certificates may be studied by distance learning or part time at a college. Further training may qualify you to become an energy assessor or surveyor.

School leavers looking to become an estate agent administrator can enrol on the Intermediate Level Apprenticeship in Property Services and those who want to become an estate agent could consider the Advanced Apprenticeship.

As an estate agent, you will be required to hold a valid driving licence.

What the work involves

Estate agents are responsible for selling or letting residential or commercial properties on behalf of their clients.

Properties are valued based upon factors such as their condition, location, comparison with other properties and the current housing market.

Estate agents market a property, show prospective buyers around and negotiate prices to ensure the best deal for their client.

During the selling process you will have to liaise with banks, surveyors, mortgage brokers and solicitors.

Type of person suited to this work

You will need excellent speaking and listening skills so that you can recommend suitable properties to potential buyers. You also have to be good at negotiating so that you can help buyers and sellers to agree prices for properties.

You must be confident dealing with people and prepared to work hard to achieve sales.

As you will be dealing with the figures when valuing properties or negotiating prices, you will need numeracy skills and an interest in keeping up to date with what is happening in the housing and property markets.

Working conditions

Some of your time will be spent in the branch office, and the rest of the time you will be visiting properties, so a driving licence is needed.

Estate agency branches are often modern and open plan with up-to-date equipment. You will spend a lot of your time working at a computer and speaking to your customers on the phone.

This can be very stressful work as you will have sales targets to reach and your earnings will depend on your selling ability. You are likely to need to work at the weekends and evenings (with some time off during the week instead).

Future prospects

Estate agents are located throughout the UK but there tend to be fewer opportunities in a poor housing market and within rural areas. Positions are not always advertised, therefore you may need to make general enquiries.

With experience and qualifications, there are opportunities for promotion, especially in larger companies. You may move from trainee to negotiator, then to senior negotiator and on to branch manager. If you established a substantial client base, you may opt to become self-employed or to carry out freelance work. You could set up your own agency or become a partner in a firm.

Advantages/disadvantages

The work can be stressful if you are finding it hard to meet sales targets, especially if you are working on a commission-only basis in a slowing housing market.

When the property market is booming, or for those who are very skilled in sales, the financial rewards can be high.

Money guide

Estate agents' earnings are usually a combination of a basic salary plus commission based upon their sales figures. Some estate agents work for commission only.

Starting salaries for new entrants are between £12,000 and £20,000.

With experience you can expect to earn around £25,000 a year.

Those employed at a managerial level can achieve up to £55,000.

Related opportunities

- Auction Property Consultant p59
- Planning and Development Surveyor p96
- Property Valuer p99

Further information

National Association of Estate Agents
www.naea.co.uk

FABRICATOR

ENTRY LEVEL 1

Qualifications and courses

Whilst there are no specific entry qualifications to becoming a fabricator, GCSEs/National 5s (A*–E/A–E) in English and Maths are useful. A science and Design and Technology are also beneficial as you must have an understanding of calculations, measurements and theory.

Many trainees develop their profession through an apprenticeship scheme. The Level 3 Advanced Apprenticeship in Metal Processing will give you a broad understanding of the metal industry as well as the opportunity to develop and make a range of metal products, including structural steelwork. Construction apprentices learn practical skills under the supervision of skilled fabricators, as well as taking courses at a college or training centre. These relevant courses include NVQs/SVQs such as Level 1 in Construction and Civil Engineering Services, Fabrication and Welding Engineering (Levels 2 and 3), Carpentry and Joinery (Levels 2 and 3), and Level 4 in Construction Site Management.

A Construction Skills Certification Scheme (CSCS) card is needed to work on a building site as it acts as proof of your competence within the field. In order to qualify for one of these, you must have completed or be registered with a scheme that offers you an industry recognised qualification. CSCS cards are granted in accordance with your qualifications and experience.

What the work involves

Fabricators manufacture, assemble and install structural frames of buildings.

You will extend and adapt existing buildings or work on manufacturing the entire framework for new ones. This may include houses, public buildings, swimming pools, airport terminal buildings and caravans.

Your work will be influenced by architectural demands and advances. The need for thermal performance, speed and versatility in architecture means that traditional forms of construction such as concrete, steel and glass are being replaced with new, more efficient materials. You will probably work with a diverse range of materials such as aluminium, PVC foam, timber, natural stone and fibreglass.

Type of person suited to this work

As a fabricator you should have an interest in machinery and the construction industry.

You will be working on-site or in a manufacturing plant; as this may include physical labour you should be fit and have good manual skills.

You should also enjoy working in a team and have excellent knowledge and awareness of health and safety practices. You should be organised and know how to plan ahead.

Working conditions

You will typically work 39 hours per week, Monday to Friday. This may vary depending on the project you are working on.

You may also be required to do shifts and overtime or work evenings and weekends.

You may work in a variety of locations; outdoors, indoors and at heights. Weather conditions may make this work uncomfortable or delay work.

As a fabricator you might have to operate machinery such as mobile cranes.

Future prospects

As you gain experience you will have the opportunity to specialise in a certain area of fabrication. This could be as an aluminium fabricator (curtain walls, windows and frames), a conservatory fabricator (working with timber, aluminium or PVC to erect conservatories), or a window fabricator (working with frame makers and door makers building off-site manufactured rooms that can be assembled on-site).

As you accumulate experience you can progress to a higher level position such as a supervisor or you may also choose to become self-employed. There are also fantastic opportunities to take your skills abroad.

Advantages/disadvantages

New and exciting developments and improvements in materials and technology mean that your work is likely to include scope for diversity and creativity.

Your work at times may be very physically demanding.

Money guide

The wages of fabricators are normally paid according to the nationally recommended industry rates. Earnings of trainees are graded to a nationally agreed minimum rate.

Your starting salary may be around £13,000 a year.

With experience, you could earn between £18,000 and £25,000 per year.

Highly experienced fabricators may earn in excess of £35,000 a year.

Wages will increase in the event of overtime and shift allowances.

Related opportunities

- Building Technician p64
- Carpenter/Joiner p65
- Ceiling Fixer p67

Further information

Construction Industry Training Board (CITB)
www.citb.co.uk

National Association of Shopfitters
www.shopfitters.org

FACILITIES MANAGER

ENTRY LEVEL 4

Qualifications and courses

You can become a facilities manager by completing a degree in any discipline although many entrants are graduates of property or land-based subjects such as building management or surveying. Others gain experience in relevant fields such as construction, building services engineering or hospitality in order to acquire the necessary skills to become a facilities manager. Postgraduate diplomas and master's degrees in facilities management, although not a prerequisite, can be particularly useful in aiding career progression, especially if you want to gain chartered status later on in life.

Alternatively, you can take vocational courses in facilities management. These include appropriate NVQs/SVQs or professional qualifications from the British Institute of Facilities Management (BIFM). You can also study for a Foundation degree (developed by Asset Skills), or an HND in Facilities Management. Entry into the field with these qualifications will usually be at a lower level however.

Work experience is recommended and employers will seek candidates with good experience. For graduates, year-long placements are invaluable.

What the work involves

Facilities managers are responsible for the management and administration of premises, including offices, schools and commercial properties. You will provide a safe and efficient work environment for staff by implementing procedures to improve facilities, reduce costs and increase productivity.

Your day-to-day work will depend on the type of organisation you work for, but will include a broad spectrum of tasks such as coordinating and managing central services, organising mail receipt and despatch, arranging contractors for security or supervising cleaning and catering.

You must be able to respond to all problems that arise unexpectedly, and react to them appropriately and efficiently.

Type of person suited to this work

As you will be coordinating many different aspects of an organisation, or many organisations in one location, you need to be highly organised. You should be able to meet deadlines and have strong problem-solving skills.

You will lead a team so you should have excellent negotiation skills and strong written and verbal communication ability. As you will be working with a variety of different people you should have good customer service skills.

You should also be aware of environmental issues affecting premises and how budgets are planned and controlled.

Working conditions

Your hours will vary depending on the organisation you work for but on average you will work from 9am to 5pm. You will mainly be office based, but you will move around a lot to inspect and supervise various projects throughout the location you work in.

You may have a permanent contract or work on a fixed-term contract. At times you may be required to be available at any time in the event of emergencies.

Future prospects

You may begin as an assistant in a particular support field such as IT, HR, finance, purchasing or health and safety and then progress to functional manager, senior manager and director positions.

You can work as a facilities manager in-house or join a facilities management provider or consultancy. This will provide a variety of projects and responsibilities but will not have the same level of stability.

It is recommended that you seek opportunities in different organisations to secure promotion.

Advantages/disadvantages

Prospects for career development can be excellent. If you are hardworking, flexible, and efficient, have commercial acumen and the ability to juggle tight budgets you can progress to higher level management jobs.

You may find it difficult to move from an in-house role to a position with a service provider as there is a perceived difference in outlook and experience.

Money guide

A starting salary for an entry-level assistant role may range from £18,000 to £22,000 per year.

An experienced facilities manager can earn between £25,000 and £35,000 a year.

Senior and regional facilities managers can earn in excess of £60,000.

Wages are typically higher in the south-east of England and in the capital. Financial bonuses may also be available.

Related opportunities

- Building Services Engineer p62
- Health and Safety Adviser p27
- Quality Manager p44

Further information

British Institute of Facilities Management
www.bifm.org.uk

Chartered Management Institute
www.managers.org.uk

FLOOR LAYER/FINISHER

ENTRY LEVEL 1

Qualifications and courses

No specific qualifications are required, although a common route of entry is through an apprenticeship scheme where GCSEs/National 5s (A*–E/A–E) in Maths, Design and Technology, a science and English might be a requirement.

As an apprentice you will be trained on the job while working towards vocational qualifications. You may go to a college or training centre on day or block release. The Construction Industry Training Board (CITB) offers an apprenticeship scheme in Floor Covering, which will provide you with a Level 2 Construction Diploma in Floor Covering and a Level 2 NVQ Diploma in Flooring Occupations.

Alternatively, fast-track short courses from independent providers such as the Flooring Industry Training Association and NVQs/SVQs in Floor Covering at Levels 1–3 are available. These awards allow you to specialise in impervious coverings, textile carpeting or wood block flooring. You may also be able to acquire some of the necessary skills to become a floor layer by completing a BTEC Level 2 or 3 Certificate or Diploma in Construction.

Many employers on construction sites require workers to have a Construction Skills Certification Scheme (CSCS) card. This demonstrates that the holder has health and safety training. In order to be granted one of these, you must have completed or be registered with a scheme that awards you an industry recognised qualification.

Once employed, you may be required to hold a valid driving licence in order to commute between projects.

What the work involves

Floor layers fit various rooms and buildings with many different types of flooring, such as vinyl, wood, carpet, tiles, rubber or plastic. You will often work with materials chosen by the client but on occasion may be asked to make recommendations on the best material to use for the particular type of floor.

You will use various tools to prepare the surface, cut the flooring material to size and lay the floor.

You will work from technical plans and diagrams in order to lay and fit each floor correctly.

Type of person suited to this work

To do this work you will need accurate numerical skills in order to calculate the exact amount of flooring material you will need for each job.

You should be physically fit as you will spend a lot of time lifting and carrying materials, or working on your hands and knees.

You may work alone for some smaller jobs, but you must also be able to work in a team with other construction professionals for larger jobs. Good planning skills are helpful when organising your workload, and you should be happy meeting and talking to lots of different people.

Working conditions

You will usually work normal Monday to Friday office hours, but you may also need to work through the night or over weekends on some contracts, so that you can lay floors without disrupting the work of shops and businesses.

Most of your work will be spent indoors in a variety of locations including people's homes, hospitals, offices and construction sites, some of which will be dirty and dusty.

Some contracts may involve absence from home overnight or for longer periods of time.

Future prospects

Employment for floor finishers is expected to remain relatively steady given the variety of industries readily employing the small number of people within the profession.

Once you have qualified, work will be available within small or large flooring companies or contractors across the UK. You could work across numerous industries including construction, retail trade and manufacturing.

You may choose to specialise in using one type of flooring material such as tiles or laminates.

With experience, you can progress to supervisory or managerial posts. Alternatively, you could set up your own business as a self-employed floor layer.

Advantages/disadvantages

An attractive and well-laid floor can transform a room. The ability to use your skills and a range of materials to create this effect can give you great job satisfaction.

You will spend a lot of time travelling to and from jobs, and may need to spend time away from home on big flooring projects.

Money guide

The salary of a trainee ranges from £12,500 to £16,500 per year.

As a fully qualified floor layer you could earn £20,000 to £25,000.

Highly skilled, experienced floor layers can earn salaries of up to £30,000 a year.

Many floor layers are self-employed and earnings will depend on the ability to win contracts.

Related opportunities

- Carpenter/Joiner p65
- Plasterer p97
- Roofer p102

Further information

Construction Industry Training Board (CITB)
www.citb.co.uk

Flooring Industry Training Association
www.fita.co.uk

Case Study

THE FLOORING TRADE

Matthew Blackbourn's Story

On the job training has formed a key part of 27 year old Matthew's journey into the flooring trade fitting all types of flooring in the domestic and commercial sectors. He firmly believes that ensuring you begin your working life with a reputable, established company is vital. Matthew has supplemented the experience he has gained on site with training courses through FITA, after which he applied to become a 'Master Fitter' in Carpet via the NICF. Although he has a passion for installation and gets a true buzz from a job well done, Matthew hopes to grow more in to the management side. However, his positive experience of training has also led him to have ambitions to become an instructor and put something back in the industry.

For Matthew the future in flooring is bright and full of opportunity.

- Master Fitter in different disciplines other than carpet e.g. Vinyl Tiles & Laminate, also a fitter in Wood & Resilient;
- QA card accredited, leading to more work e.g. M&S and also contractors looking for quality commercial installers;
- Training to be a FITA Instructor;
- Training two apprentices with our company;
- Being part of the NICF has got me involved with some very interesting installation such as London Fashion Week. Also a carpet company who make handmade 100oz luxury carpets with borders for very wealthy clients around the country;
- Now doing more with the day to day running of our company, working with customers, selling in the showroom, estimation and quoting, site surveys etc.;
- Installing a wide range of floor coverings for the family business.

What the job entails

Working for a small business in the domestic market, means that the range of tasks involved are enormous. 'I generally find myself fitting floors during the day and find the diversity of products and skills I have to employ really interesting. I also like working with the public and when we are busy I tend to help out with measures in the evenings. More recently, I have started to get involved with pricing and ordering stock etc.'

The commercial sector is of course slightly different with work typically taking place in offices, hospitals and schools. Generally on a bigger scale, some of the contracts involved have materials worth many thousands of pounds. Main contractors are often working to tight timescales and obviously floor layers have to enjoy working in a team in what is often essentially a construction environment. As well as a craft and a skill, floor laying is increasingly technical and finding the solution to meet the needs of a client (many working on fast track projects) is among the demands and challenges of the 'on site' role.

What you need to succeed

Flexibility, good communication, as well as an obvious natural tendency towards good practical skills, are all qualities required to succeed in the flooring industry. The ability to use your own initiative, as well as work in a team, is often an advantage.

Practical on site experience will always be required, but formal qualifications such as an NVQ level 2 in floor laying are recognised qualifications that can currently be gained through a number of routes including a modern apprenticeship. This can be supplemented with short training courses through organisations such as FITA as both an introduction, as well as a career building strategy.

For further information or advice contact:
The Contract Flooring Association (CFA)
Telephone: 0115 941 1126

The Flooring Industry Training Association (FITA)
Telephone: 0115 950 6836

The National Institute of Carpet & FloorLayers (NICF)
Telephone: 0115 958 3077

CONTRACT FLOORING ASSOCIATION cfa

n i c f
national institute of carpet & floorlayers

fita
THE FLOORING INDUSTRY TRAINING ASSOCIATION

GAS SERVICE TECHNICIAN

ENTRY LEVEL 2

Qualifications and courses

At least 4 GCSEs/National 5s (A*–C/A–C) including English, Maths and sometimes science or technology subjects are normally required to enter this career. Practical subjects such as metalwork and woodwork are also useful.

Apprenticeships are available for people aged 16–24. An Advanced Level Apprenticeship in the gas industry is a good route for those who wish to become a gas service engineer. Apprentices work towards the NVQ/SVQ in Domestic Natural Gas Installation and Maintenance and Emergency Services Operations (Levels 2 and 3) awarded by City & Guilds (6034). You will normally need to be employed by a company willing to sponsor you prior to signing up to an apprenticeship. Gas service companies also run their own apprenticeship schemes.

Trainees must gain registration with the Gas Safe Register. To become registered, you will need to work towards the above City & Guilds NVQ/SVQ or complete equivalent in-house training with a company. Technicians with qualifications or training other than the NVQ/SVQ must complete Accredited Certification Scheme (ACS) assessments.

Gas service technicians have to demonstrate their gas safety competence on a 5-year cycle by successfully completing nationally agreed ACS assessments.

A valid driving licence is essential to allow travel between clients' premises.

What the work involves

Your job will be to install, maintain, repair and test gas appliances such as fires, cookers, heating systems, shower units and industrial equipment. You will carry out scheduled maintenance checks on systems and equipment.

You could work in private homes or on business premises.

You may also have to give customers quotes for costs and timescales, sell additional company services and deal with complaints.

As a trained professional, you will be required to give advice on the safety and efficiency of gas systems and equipment.

Type of person suited to this work

You will need excellent practical and problem-solving skills as you will be required to investigate and fix faults.

Gas appliances are potentially dangerous so you should be very thorough, reliable and aware of safety practices.

As you will be visiting clients' homes, you should be personable and presentable.

Working conditions

Working hours are generally 8am to 5pm, Monday to Friday. However, if your employer offers 24-hour emergency cover, you may have to undertake shift work.

Although most of your work will take place in customers' homes or business premises, you will also need to work on many different construction sites. You will need to wear protective clothing, such as a hard hat, goggles and gloves.

You will be required to travel to jobs in a van which stores your parts and equipment.

Future prospects

Job prospects for gas service technicians are favourable given the national shortage of trained personnel. There are opportunities for work throughout the UK.

You can work for national or private companies. In larger companies you can apply for training posts at local colleges or within private organisations.

Once you have gained enough experience, you could progress into gas engineering, a supervisory/management role or become self-employed. Your employer may even sponsor you to study further qualifications.

You could also choose to specialise in a specific area such as energy efficiency, oil-fired equipment or environmental technologies.

Advantages/disadvantages

If your employer offers 24-hour emergency cover, you may have to work some unsocial hours.

The job can be strenuous and can involve working at heights or in confined spaces.

There is a high demand for gas service technicians and career progression opportunities are good.

Successfully repairing a potentially dangerous gas leak can be a rewarding experience.

Money guide

During your apprenticeship, you can expect your salary to start from between £12,000 and £15,000 per year.

Salaries for qualified gas service technicians range from £19,000 to £30,000.

Those who become self-employed and manage their own company and employees can achieve in excess of £40,000.

It is also possible to increase your earnings through overtime and shift work.

Related opportunities

- Gas Network Engineer p210
- Heating and Ventilation Engineer p88
- Plumber p98

Further information

Energy & Utility Skills
www.euskills.co.uk

Gas Safe Register
www.gassaferegister.co.uk

GLAZIER

ENTRY LEVEL 2

Qualifications and courses

GCSEs/National 5s (A*–C/A–C) or relevant vocational qualifications can improve your chances of getting work in the industry. Maths, English and technology-based subjects are useful for the areas of the job that involve measurements and calculations and for theoretical training.

You can train and gain vocational qualifications while you work by completing an apprenticeship. You will be taught practical skills by an experienced professional and may spend time off-site at a college or training centre. Apprenticeships in the Glass Industry are available at both Intermediate and Advanced Levels and last for 2 to 3 years. You are likely to work towards NVQs in glass-related subjects. These include Glazing Installation and Maintenance, Automotive Glazing, and Fenestration Installation and Surveying at both Levels 2 and 3. You will have to complete an aptitude test and have a selection interview prior to acceptance onto an apprenticeship.

Glass Training Limited (GTL) also provides flexible learning schemes that offer candidates in full-time employment the opportunity to gain an NVQ/SVQ through a distance learning programme.

To work as a glazier you need to have a Construction Skills Certification Scheme (CSCS) card or be registered with an affiliated scheme. This scheme requires an NVQ Level 2 and the completion of a health and safety test.

What the work involves

Glaziers use specialist cutting and fixing tools to cut glass to the correct size and fit it into place.

You might fit glass into houses, shop fronts, office blocks or roofs.

You might be working on new buildings or replacing existing or broken glass.

You will use your knowledge to choose a suitable type of glass for each job.

Type of person suited to this work

You should be able to follow technical drawings accurately and have a good eye for detail when measuring the materials for a job.

As you will be using different hand tools a practical ability will be necessary. You will also need to be physically fit so that you can carry glass and be comfortable working at heights (sometimes extreme heights).

You may work alone for some jobs, such as in people's homes, but you must also be able to work and communicate with other glaziers, especially when working on large jobs with big, heavy panes of glass.

Working conditions

You will work indoors and outdoors in many different locations. A driving licence may be useful.

You will need to work safely and be aware of your own, the public's and your colleagues' safety when carrying, cutting and fixing glass.

You may work normal working hours during the week, but you may also need to work at weekends and during evenings, possibly offering emergency cover for households and businesses when replacing broken glass.

Future prospects

Work is available with glazing and construction companies throughout the UK and the demand for trained glaziers is high.

The range of jobs in glazing work is also increasing to include specialist areas, for example automotive glass repair and replacement.

After gaining sufficient experience, you may progress to technical or supervisory levels, or you could decide to start your own glazing business. The majority of glaziers are self-employed.

Advantages/disadvantages

Working at extreme heights may be demanding for some.

You will get to work in a variety of locations on a wide range of projects.

Cutting tools and glass can be dangerous, so you will have to be aware of health and safety regulations.

You could be called out at all hours for emergency jobs but the rates of pay for this type of work will be higher.

Money guide

Starting salaries can be between £13,000 and £16,000.

With qualifications, glaziers can expect to earn up to £18,000.

Those who are highly skilled, with experience and extra responsibilities such as emergency call-outs, might achieve anything from £20,000 to £35,000.

Shift allowances and the opportunity to work overtime can supplement your income.

Related opportunities

- Building Technician p64
- Ceiling Fixer p67
- Window Fitter p117

Further information

Glass and Glazing Federation
www.ggf.co.uk

Glass Qualifications Authority
www.gqaqualifications.com

Proskills UK
www.proskills.co.uk

HEATING AND VENTILATION ENGINEER

ENTRY LEVEL 2

Qualifications and courses

To become a heating and ventilation engineer, you will need to work towards an NVQ Diploma in Heating and Ventilation (Level 2 or 3). Most entrants to the profession study for these qualifications during an apprenticeship scheme. Apprenticeships in Heating and Ventilation are available at Intermediate and Advanced Level with 5 GCSEs/National 5s (A*–C/A–C) including Maths, English and a science subject required for entry. You will also need to pass a colour vision test and selection test.

Apprenticeships involve being trained by and working alongside a professional engineer whilst also attending college on day or block release. You may therefore be required to secure employment prior to signing up. NVQs/SVQs cover industrial, commercial, ductwork installation, service and maintenance of components. It usually takes 2 to 4 years to become fully qualified.

Other options for training include a City & Guilds Certificate in Energy Efficiency for Domestic Heating (6084) if you seek to become a domestic fitter and the Oil Firing Technical Association (OFTEC)'s training scheme for those who wish to work with oil-fired equipment.

It is also possible to achieve higher level qualifications including NVQ Level 4, Foundation or master's degree which can lead to professional membership of the Chartered Institution of Building Services Engineers (CIBSE).

What the work involves

Heating and ventilation engineers install equipment such as pipework and boilers for systems including central heating, hot and cold water services, and gas supplies in industrial and commercial buildings.

Your work will include cutting, bending and joining pipes that will need to withstand high pressures, so welding is an important part of the work.

When you have installed a system, you will test it to make sure that everything is working properly.

Type of person suited to this work

You must be a practical person so that you can use the equipment for the job. Understanding and following diagrams is an essential part of the work, so you need a logical, mechanically minded approach to your work. You will also need to be good at maths for making calculations.

It can be physically demanding work, as you will be bending, kneeling and working in tight spaces. You also need a head for heights and a safety-conscious attitude, because you will often be working from ladders and scaffolding.

Teamwork and communication skills are also important when you are installing large systems.

Working conditions

A lot of your time will be spent indoors, but you will also need a driving licence to travel between various construction sites, where you will need to wear safety protective clothing.

You may work a normal working week, but there may be times when you will work weekends and evenings to avoid disruption to clients or if you provide emergency cover. You may also be expected to work away from home.

Future prospects

There is currently a shortage of skilled heating and ventilation engineers with around 56,000 currently working in the UK.

Once you are qualified, work will be available with specialist heating and ventilation companies, or organisations such as the NHS or local authorities. With the government targeting greater energy efficiency, you may also opt to complete training that will allow you to install and maintain renewable energy technologies, eg solar powered heating systems. Some qualified fitters become self-employed, joining up with other engineers to offer sub-contracting services.

There are good prospects for advancement to supervisory roles and it is possible for you to become a heating and ventilation technician. If you take additional qualifications and higher education, progression to professional engineering level is also possible. There are also opportunities to work overseas.

Advantages/disadvantages

Working in cramped and awkward spaces can be uncomfortable.

Transforming a building from an empty shell into a warm, comfortable environment can be rewarding.

Career progression opportunities are excellent and there is demand across the country for work in this area.

Money guide

As an apprentice your starting salary could be between £9,100 and £11,250.

A newly qualified engineer could expect to earn up to £20,000.

With experience, you could achieve £22,000–£24,000.

Working overtime and receiving bonuses could increase your pay.

Related opportunities

- Gas Network Engineer p210
- Gas Service Technician p86
- Thermal Insulation Engineer p112

Further information

Building and Engineering Services Association
www.b-es.org

Building Engineering Services Training
www.best-ltd.co.uk

HIGHWAYS MAINTENANCE/ROAD WORKER

ENTRY LEVEL 1

Qualifications and courses

There are no formal entry requirements for this work but GCSEs/National 5s in Maths, English and Design and Technology may be helpful. Personal skills and physical fitness are usually more important than qualifications. Employers may also want you to have some on-site experience, for example, as a construction labourer.

Your training will mainly be given on the job by experienced road workers. After you have secured employment, you may be able to study at a local college on day or block release to progress. You could work towards an NVQ Level 2 Certificate in Construction and Civil Engineering, an NVQ Level 2 Certificate/Diploma in Highways Maintenance, an NVQ Level 2 Diploma in Roadbuilding or a City & Guilds Level 2 Award in Winter Maintenance Operations. Your NVQ may cover areas such as excavation, re-surfacing, drainage, kerb laying and pavement construction.

Alternatively, you may opt to gain relevant skills prior to accepting full-time work by completing a City & Guilds (6217) Basic Skills in Construction course or a BTEC Level 2 in Construction.

To become a fully qualified site operative, you need to register with the Street Works Qualifications Register (SWQR) by studying for either a City & Guilds Certificate in Streetworks Excavation and Reinstatement, an SQA national award in Excavation and Reinstatement or a Street Works Excavation and Reinstatement qualification awarded by CABWI.

If working with plant machinery, you will need to be 18 or over. A driving licence will also be required and an LGV licence may be needed for some jobs.

What the work involves

Road workers' tasks include building new roads, re-routing or widening existing roads, and repairing potholes and cracks in roads.

You will also have other duties such as putting up warning signs and barriers, controlling the movement of traffic near the work site, laying kerbstones and pavements, and gritting roads in the winter.

You will work with numerous building materials including concrete, tarmac and paving slabs. You will use a range of tools and equipment in your work, including specialised, heavy machinery such as diggers and rollers.

Type of person suited to this work

You must have a good standard of fitness, as the work involves a lot of hard, physical work and requires you to lift and carry heavy materials.

Practical ability with tools such as picks and shovels is useful, as is experience of operating equipment such as cement mixers, diggers and rolling machines.

As much of your work will be undertaken as part of a team of road workers and supervisors, it is important that you can get along with colleagues at all levels.

Working conditions

You are likely to work a normal 37 hour working week, although you may also work weekends and evenings to avoid disrupting traffic.

You will need to be aware of the danger of traffic and mindful of health and safety for yourself and your colleagues. On-site, you will wear protective clothing such as a safety helmet, fluorescent jacket and boots.

Future prospects

Road workers may work for local authorities or, as work is increasingly contracted out, for specialist road-building or civil engineering companies.

Work is available across the UK. Some work is short term or seasonal. You could become self-employed and work on a contract basis.

As you develop and gain experience and qualifications, you may go on to lead a small team or become a supervisor.

Advantages/disadvantages

You will be helping to maintain and improve the safety of the roads in your local area which can be personally rewarding.

You will be carrying out physically demanding work outdoors during all weathers so you can expect to get hot in the summer and cold in the winter.

Money guide

Trainee road workers have a starting salary of £12,000–£14,500.

As you gain experience, you could earn around £18,000.

Road workers with additional responsibilities, such as supervisory duties, can achieve a salary of £24,000.

Qualified operatives can earn up to £40,000 a year.

Those who operate plant machinery may receive additional payments and you can increase your earnings with overtime and shift work.

Related opportunities

- Bricklayer p60
- Concreter p71
- Construction Operative p72

Further information

Construction Industry Training Board (CITB)
www.citb.co.uk

Street Works Qualification Register
www.swqr.org.uk

HOUSING OFFICER

ENTRY LEVEL 2

Qualifications and courses

It is possible to enter at an administrative level with GCSEs/National 5s (A*–C/A–C) and work your way up to housing officer. Personal qualities and pre-entry experience in housing or customer service is highly valued and, at times, more sought after by employers than qualifications.

Larger housing associations are, however, more likely to recruit graduates, therefore you may choose to study a degree or postgraduate qualification in a relevant subject such as housing, social policy, town planning or urban studies. You will need 2 or 3 A levels/H grades to be accepted. Those with an unrelated degree can complete the Chartered Institute of Housing (CIH) Level 4 Certificate in Access to Housing before progressing to the postgraduate diploma or master's degree in housing.

Housing officers whose degrees do not include a work placement will be expected to gain industry experience before they become a member of the CIH. Voluntary work in local authority housing departments, experience in a customer service role or as a member of a tenants' committee could all be useful when seeking employment.

The CIH also offers courses which can be studied part time and through distance learning; these include the Certificate in Housing Practice (Level 2–4).

What the work involves

You will manage and maintain rented housing, usually for a housing association or local authority. Tasks include assessing housing needs in an area and making policies to provide for them, allocating housing to applicants and planning property maintenance and repair.

You will also need to set rent rates, deal with tenants who are behind with their payments, resolve neighbourhood disputes and answer tenants' enquiries.

You will find yourself working with a variety of different people, ranging from vulnerable members of the community to those in challenging economic situations.

Type of person suited to this work

As most of your work will involve talking and listening to people, you will need excellent communication and negotiation skills. You should have an interest in working with diverse social groups and be sensitive to the needs of tenants and colleagues.

Maths and numeracy skills are useful for dealing with rental payments, maintenance and repair costs, and budgets.

It is important to keep up with developments in a range of housing and tenant welfare issues, be flexible and have the ability to solve problems as and when they arise. You will also need to be capable of working both independently and as part of a team.

Working conditions

Many housing officers are based in an office but regularly travel to make property inspections, visit tenants or attend meetings. As some of your work will involve travelling, a driving licence and your own vehicle is often required. Although you will normally work standard office hours, you might have to do some weekend work or unsocial hours.

You should be prepared to deal with rude and aggressive tenants.

Future prospects

Social housing is currently a growth area, with organisations taking on a number of new trainees as well as experienced staff.

Most housing officers work for local authorities and housing associations but you may also work for voluntary organisations, property companies, private landlords and housing trusts. You can work in various other sectors such as finance, IT, PR or law and with different groups of people, eg the homeless or elderly, students or people with disabilities.

With experience, you may specialise in one area, for example, homelessness assessment, special needs housing, urban renewal or tenant support. Alternatively, you may become a team leader or housing manager. Housing managers are particularly in demand in London and the south-east of England.

Housing associations have a strong tradition of developing the talent of their staff so there are great opportunities for progression.

Advantages/disadvantages

You will be responsible for resolving complicated issues, such as misuse of property, and disputes between residents.

Helping people find a home can be personally rewarding.

Money guide

Salaries for those in housing assistant/customer service positions reach about £18,500.

Housing officers usually have a starting salary of £20,000–£27,000.

Those who become housing managers can expect to earn £28,000–£32,000.

At senior manager level, you can achieve earnings in excess of £50,000.

Related opportunities

- Residential Support Worker p556
- Social Worker p557
- Welfare Benefits Adviser/Welfare Rights Caseworker p562

Further information

Chartered Institute of Housing
www.cih.org

Scottish Federation of Housing Associations
www.sfha.co.uk

LAMINATOR

ENTRY LEVEL 2

Qualifications and courses

No formal qualifications are normally required, however some GCSEs/National 5s in subjects such as maths or design might be useful as you must have an understanding of design technology and calculations. Other relevant qualifications include a BTEC Diploma Level 2 in either Manufacturing and Product Design, Engineering or Construction and the Built Environment.

Some employers will take on school-leavers as technician apprentices. Apprenticeships require 4 GCSEs/National 5s (A*–C/A–C) in Maths, a science or technology. A GCSE/National 5 in Manufacturing or Engineering may also be appropriate for this entry route. Apprentices are usually aged between 16 and 24.

As an apprentice, on-the-job training is provided by experienced professionals. You will also undertake further training at college through courses that focus on the safety requirements of your job, for example First Aid and health and safety. You can train for an NVQ Level 2 in Polymer Processing Operations or Performing Engineering Operations, an NVQ Level 3 in Polymer Processing and Related Operations or BTEC Level 3 Certificates/Diplomas in Polymer Processing and Materials Technology. If the training does not include NVQ Level 3, a workplace assessment will be carried out to check competence at this level.

Companies also tend to use a series of short course programmes with a specialist training provider to gradually build up the skills and knowledge required of a laminator.

Once technician status has been achieved it is possible to combine studying with further experience to gain an HND in Manufacturing Engineering (Metallurgy and Materials), Polymer Science or Polymer Technology.

With 4 years' experience, relevant NVQs/SVQs or a BTEC certificate/diploma, you could apply for membership of the Institute of Materials, Minerals and Mining.

What the work involves

Laminators work with polymer composite materials to make a variety of products such as hockey sticks, snowboards, canoes, car bodies, yachts and aircraft cabin interiors.

You will follow a brief for the design of a product, taking into consideration any requirements regarding strength, colour and finish. You will then choose the appropriate material to be pressed, sprayed or poured into a mould, prior to it being shaped into the final product.

You will work with traditional materials such as wood laminates, fibre glass and resin, and new products such as Kevlar.

Type of person suited to this work

You should have a keen interest in design and technology, engineering and materials science.

You should like practical work and have practical skills to handle tools and use specialist machinery. You need to be reasonably fit and have good vision for monitoring quality and noticing detail.

You should have initiative, follow a brief and work to a deadline. You should also be interested in, and keep up to date with, technological advancements in laminate materials. You should like to work in a team.

Working conditions

Your working hours will depend heavily on the project you are working on. Typically they can range from 37 to 40 hours but will vary according to the rate of your work and deadlines.

You will usually work in an environmentally controlled building. This means that the temperature is controlled and maintained to help resin harden quickly. Air is changed frequently to remove dust and the strong smell of resin.

You will be required to wear full protective clothing.

Future prospects

You may be employed by an engineering consultancy that undertakes installation projects for companies.

With experience and training there are opportunities to be promoted to roles such as technician and senior technician, or to move into design, research or development work for specialist composite laminate manufacturers.

Advantages/disadvantages

You may have the opportunity to work on products that are on the cutting edge of design such as speedboats, Formula 1 racing cars and craft for the military.

Your environment will frequently be dusty and involve the use of strong industrial chemicals which may be hazardous if handled incorrectly.

Money guide

A salary for an apprentice laminator starts at around £10,000 per year.

With further experience and qualifications this may increase to £25,000 per year.

A senior laminator can earn up to £30,000 per year.

Related opportunities

- Carpenter/Joiner p65
- Marine Craftsperson p214
- Polymer Technologist p221

Further information

British Plastics Federation
www.bpf.co.uk

Institute of Materials, Minerals and Mining
www.iom3.org

LAND/GEOMATIC SURVEYOR

ENTRY LEVEL 6

Qualifications and courses

Most entrants have completed a Royal Institution of Chartered Surveyors (RICS) accredited degree in subjects such as surveying and mapping science, geomatics or geographic information systems as well as a period of supervised instruction. If you wish to specialise in a particular area, such as hydroinformatics or environmental management, or if you are a graduate with a non-accredited degree, a postgraduate qualification may be required.

It may be possible to enter the industry at a lower level, for example, as a digital mapping assistant or as a computer-aided design (CAD) technician, with an HND or Foundation degree in a related area such as applied science, civil engineering or land/estate surveying.

Alternatively, apprenticeships for school or college leavers in land/geomatics surveying are also available. You will begin as an assistant surveyor and progress through a combination of training on the job and studying for an NVQ. GCSEs/National 5s (A*–C/A–C) in English, Maths and IT are usually required.

Once qualified, many surveyors work towards achieving chartered status and undertake further courses and assessment through bodies such as the Chartered Institution of Civil Engineering Surveyors (ICES) and the Royal Institution of Chartered Surveyors (RICS). This usually takes between 4 and 5 years. Regardless of your position, it is advisable to become a student member of RICS or ICES in order to keep up to date with developments in the industry and to support you in your continuing professional development.

What the work involves

Land/geomatic surveyors collect and analyse information to map the land and/or sea, which is then used when planning construction and civil engineering projects.

You will use satellite images, GPS, digital mapping and other equipment to produce surveys that record features such as contours, materials below the Earth's surface and man-made objects.

You will use technical software such as computer-aided design (CAD) to record and present the data you have gathered. You will also have to interpret data from maps and plans and explain it to clients.

Type of person suited to this work

You will be working with clients and other professionals on a daily basis, so excellent verbal and written communication skills will be needed to present and explain complex information.

As much of the work involves using technical equipment and producing maps, plans and reports using specialist computer software, you will need to have very strong analytical and IT skills with specific knowledge of geographical information systems (GIS) and AutoCAD.

Working conditions

Working hours are usually 9am to 5pm, but you may need to work unsocial hours to ensure projects are finished on time. Weekend or shift work may also be needed for certain projects.

As you will often work away from home, you will be paid more for overseas work and most contracts are on a short-term basis, although multinational companies offer good long-term opportunities.

Self-employment is an option, but finding work is not always easy so most surveyors choose to work in salaried employment.

Future prospects

As a result of the changing nature of mapping and spatial data management, there continues to be a current shortage of land/geomatic surveyors.

Most graduates start as a junior surveyor, from which there is a natural progression to surveyor and then on to a team management position. You could undertake further study and gain a qualification as a chartered surveyor as this can enhance opportunities for progression and improve pay. Ease of progress will depend on professional qualifications and the size of your employing organisation. Geographic mobility can also be helpful to career development.

Alternatively, you may decide to specialise in different areas such as offshore engineering and exploration or cartography and it is also possible to move between the public and private sectors.

Advantages/disadvantages

You will have the opportunity to travel throughout the UK and overseas.

You could be playing a key role in land and environmental development.

A considerable amount of time is spent outdoors so be prepared to get cold, wet and muddy.

Money guide

Starting salaries for non-graduates are around £14,500.

For newly graduated land surveyors salaries may be between £19,000 and £25,000.

With chartered status, your salary would rise to £27,000–£34,000.

At a senior level, either as a manager or a partner, salaries can reach £72,000.

Related opportunities

- Planning and Development Surveyor p96
- Rural Property/Practice Surveyor p103
- Town Planner/Planning Technician p113

Further information

Chartered Institution of Civil Engineering Surveyors
www.cices.org

Chartered Institution of Water and Environmental Management
www.ciwem.org

MASTIC ASPHALTER

ENTRY LEVEL 1

Qualifications and courses

To train in this field, it is useful to have some GCSEs/ National 5s (A*–E/A–E) in English, Maths, Design and Technology. Alternatively, vocational qualifications such as the BTEC Level 1 or 2 Certificate/Award/ Diploma in Construction, the Foundation, Intermediate and Advanced Levels in Construction Awards and the Scottish Progression Award/Skills for Work Award in Building Crafts may prove useful for introducing you to the basics of the industry.

Most entrants complete the Construction Industry Training Board (CITB) Construction Apprenticeship Scheme in Mastic Asphalting. This scheme takes 2 to 3 years to complete and apprentices study either an NVQ Level 2 or 3 in Mastic Asphalting or the Cskills Awards Level 2 Diploma in Mastic Asphalting. You may be required to complete an aptitude test prior to your acceptance. Training typically involves a combination of block-release training at an approved college or training centre, alongside on-the-job training from an experienced professional.

Additionally, if you decide to specialise in roofing, it would be useful to undergo examinations offered by the Institute of Roofing.

Mastic asphalters employed on construction sites require a Construction Skills Certification Scheme (CSCS) card. This demonstrates that the holder has health and safety training, as well as aiming for competence in a particular occupation. You will need to have or be working towards an NVQ or equivalent in order to be granted a CSCS card.

What the work involves

You will work with material called mastic asphalt, a mixture of limestone and bitumen which turns to liquid when heated. You will inspect a site, clean it, lay out membranes and guides and then spread hot liquid asphalt onto the area. It will cool into a protective waterproof surface.

You will work on surfaces such as dams, landfills, riverbank protection, car parks, bus stations, pathways and the roofs of buildings.

You will use various specialised tools such as boilers, mixers and cylinders in order to prepare surfaces and apply the asphalt.

Type of person suited to this work

You need to have good practical skills to be able to spread and form the mastic asphalt. Maths skills will be useful too, for calculating quantities of materials.

It is important to be able to understand plans, follow instructions and work well in a team.

As it is an active job you must be physically fit, and you must be happy climbing and working at heights. Agility is essential and you should be able to work quickly but accurately.

Working conditions

You will mainly work outdoors, although some of the work may be under cover. You will travel regularly between sites. You will need to wear protective gear such as a safety helmet, gloves and boots.

If you suffer from claustrophobia, vertigo or breathing problems, this work might be difficult for you.

You are likely to work a normal working week, although you might need to work evenings and weekends as well.

Future prospects

Most opportunities are with specialist mastic asphalt contractors. Self-employment is also common if you are skilled.

You can work your way up to become a supervisor, manager or trainer in large companies. Alternatively, you could set up your own contracting business.

You may need to move between employers for promotion.

Advantages/disadvantages

Working at heights on roofs, or in cramped conditions when working in tanks or underground spaces, can be demanding for some people. There is the possibility of fumes and accidental burns in this line of work.

You will develop a range of skills and work on a variety of surfaces.

Money guide

The average wage for a trainee starting in this line of work is £10,000 per year.

Once qualified, your wage may rise to around £16,000 a year.

With experience, your salary could reach £31,000.

Overtime is often available, and on some projects there are bonuses based on outputs, which can lead to higher earnings. Travelling expenses will be reimbursed.

Related opportunities

- Floor Layer/Finisher p84
- Roofer p102
- Thatcher p111

Further information

Construction Industry Training Board (CITB)
www.citb.co.uk

Mastic Asphalt Council
www.masticasphaltcouncil.co.uk

NAVAL ARCHITECT

ENTRY LEVEL 6

Qualifications and courses

In order to become a naval architect, you will need to gain a degree in a relevant subject such as naval architecture, ship science or ocean, offshore or marine engineering, ideally one accredited by the Royal Institution of Naval Architects (RINA). Newcastle University, University of Southampton and University of Strathclyde are the main institutions offering a degree specific to naval architecture, which may increase your chances. Typical entry requirements for a degree course include 2 A levels/3 H grades, including Physics and Maths, and 5 GCSEs/National 5s (A*–C/A–C). A postgraduate qualification may also be useful, particularly when later seeking chartered status.

If you have work-based qualifications, eg a BTEC, HND or HNC, you can transfer to an engineering degree. Alternatively, you may be able to join a marine engineering apprenticeship after school through the Royal Navy or local ship builders.

As a graduate, you will carry out a RINA-accredited training scheme within the workplace where you will be trained by experienced professionals in areas including design, engineering practice and management services. Alternatively, the Ministry of Defence offers a Defence Engineering and Science Group Graduate Scheme, although it is competitive.

With 2 years' work experience and the relevant qualifications, full membership of RINA and registration as a chartered (CEng) or incorporated (IEng) engineer are possible.

What the work involves

As a naval architect you will be responsible for the design, construction and repair of marine vessels and offshore structures, including merchant ships, submarines and offshore drilling platforms. You will have to coordinate a team of engineers working on a project.

You will ensure that the structure you are working on is safe and seaworthy, within budget and to the designated specifications.

Your work will depend on the specialism you choose, but you could prepare architectural designs, work with computer or 3D models, source materials or evaluate the safety of the design.

Type of person suited to this work

As you will be working with others and as part of a team you will need to have good written and verbal communication skills.

You will be coordinating various aspects of a project such as budget, location and facilities, so you must be organised and efficient in your work. You must also be able to lead a team and work to a deadline.

Strong IT and numeracy skills and a keen eye for detail are also necessary.

Working conditions

You will work average office hours, 5 days a week. However you might have to work extra hours to meet deadlines.

You may be office based while working on design work, or visiting construction sites, docks and shipyards within the UK or overseas. Your surroundings may be noisy and dirty. If you are working on-board a craft you may encounter fumes, heat and noise and you will have to work in all weather conditions. You may have to wear protective clothing.

Future prospects

As a naval architect you can become self-employed, work for a company or as a design consultant. Given the small size of shipyards in the UK, there are limited openings for naval architects to work on the construction of new ships but you could find work in the design and production of small crafts and yachts or in maintenance and repair.

You can move up from technical roles to general management and on to senior roles. With chartered status, you can specialise in particular areas such as design, research or consultancy. Alternatively, you could work as a ship surveyor, assessing the safety of ship and marine structures. You may even opt to instruct at universities.

Organisations such as RINA provide continuing professional development (CPD) courses which cover areas such as new technologies, management systems and communication.

Advantages/disadvantages

There are lots of opportunities to work abroad for a ship surveying company, or you may work on a large scale project abroad.

Competition for jobs as a naval architect is high.

Some aspects of the work may involve working in difficult and physically demanding conditions.

Money guide

Your starting salary as a graduate can range from £22,000 to £28,000 a year.

With experience this can increase to £30,000–£50,000.

You could earn in excess of £50,000 if you are highly experienced and working for a large organisation.

Your income will vary when undertaking freelance or contract work.

Related opportunities

- Aerospace Engineer p196
- Marine Engineer p215
- Merchant Navy Engineering Officer p583

Further information

Defence Engineering and Science Group
www.gov.uk/defence-engineering-and-science-group

Royal Institution of Naval Architects
www.rina.org.uk

WISE
www.wisecampaign.org.uk

PAINTER AND DECORATOR

ENTRY LEVEL 1

Qualifications and courses

It is useful to have some GCSEs/National 5s (A*–E/A–E) in subjects such as maths, design and technology and English. Numeracy skills are particularly important as calculating area and quantities will be a large part of your job.

Vocational qualifications, such as the City & Guilds Level 1 Certificate/Award in Basic Construction Skills may also offer you opportunities to grasp the basic skills required by the industry. Working as a decorator's labourer may also allow you to do this.

A common route of entry is a construction apprenticeship which leads to an NVQ/SVQ Level 3. As an apprentice, most of your training is carried out on the job whilst taking day or block release at college in order to obtain qualifications such as an NVQ/SVQ Diploma in Decorative Finishing – Painting and Decorating (Construction) (Level 2 and 3) and Cskills Diplomas in Decorative Finishing and Industrial Painting Occupations (Level 1 and 2). You can also apply for a construction craft apprenticeship from Construction Skills, which involves an aptitude test.

Those interested in heritage work can also train in graining, marbling and gilding, by completing the NVQ Level 3 in Heritage Skills (Construction).

A Construction Skills Certification Scheme (CSCS) card is mandatory in order to work on-site. You will need to have a relevant NVQ qualification and pass a health and safety test. A trainee card is available for those working towards a qualification.

A driving licence is also necessary in order to transport materials and equipment.

What the work involves

Painters and decorators improve the interior and exterior of people's homes and other buildings. On occasion, they may also be required to paint larger structures such as bridges.

Your work will include preparing surfaces by making sure they are clean and smooth, applying primers, undercoats and topcoats of paint and putting up wall coverings such as wallpaper.

You will use a range of tools including brushes, rollers and spraying equipment.

Type of person suited to this work

You need to be good with your hands, and particularly skilful when using fine decoration techniques. You will also need an eye for colour and design and an interest in décor.

You need to be friendly, personable and able to work well in a team. You will need to be fit and active as you will have to climb ladders and carry tools. You should not mind working at heights.

You must be able to measure accurately so that you can work out how much paint and other material you will need.

Working conditions

Most of the work is indoors, but some is outdoors. You will regularly work on ladders or on scaffolding. You might have to wear a mask to prevent you from breathing in paint fumes.

You are likely to work a normal working week, although weekend work and overtime is common. You may need a driving licence.

Future prospects

The building and construction industry is the largest employer in the UK and whilst there may be a shortage of skilled painters and decorators, the demand for people in this profession largely depends on the state of the economy.

You can work for painting and decorating companies or building contractors, local authorities or the NHS. Painting and decorating companies may offer a range of work or may specialise in work such as domestic, commercial, new build or industrial.

After gaining experience, it is possible to progress to a supervisory role or transfer into related areas such as estimating or contract management, particular in the larger organisations. With further training, you may opt to specialise in restoration or even instruct on a college course as a lecturer or craft teacher.

A popular option is to become self-employed and work on a sub-contract basis. Alternatively, you could take your skills abroad.

Advantages/disadvantages

Working at extreme heights may be difficult for some people.

It can be rewarding to see the improved look of a newly painted building or structure and you have the opportunity to be creative.

Money guide

New entrants/trainees can expect to earn between £14,500 and £17,000 per year.

NVQ Level 2 or 3 qualified painters and decorators can earn between £17,000 and £23,000.

Decorators with specialist skills and supervisory duties can earn £23,000 or more.

Overtime is often available, and on some projects there are bonuses based on outputs. Those who are self-employed set their own rates of pay.

Related opportunities

- Construction Operative p72
- Plasterer p97
- Wall/Floor Tiler p114

Further information

Painting & Decorating Association
www.paintingdecoratingassociation.co.uk

PLANNING AND DEVELOPMENT SURVEYOR

ENTRY LEVEL 6

Qualifications and courses

In order to enter this profession, you will need a Royal Institution of Chartered Surveyors (RICS) accredited degree in a relevant subject such as surveying, estate management, economics or land and property development. Entry requirements for most degree courses are a minimum of 3 A levels/H grades and 5 GSCEs/National 5s (A*–C/A–C), or the relevant BTEC/SQA National Awards (or equivalent).

For graduates without an accredited degree or with a non-property related degree, a postgraduate conversion qualification approved by RICS is essential. Some large surveying firms may support you in your conversion training through a distance learning graduate traineeship or alternatively, you may complete this full time prior to employment.

Those with a relevant HND/HNC or NVQ/SVQ, plus significant work experience may be able to enter the field as a surveying technician. With further training, you could qualify as a planning and development surveyor.

Once employed you will continue to update your skills by working towards chartered status. In order to do so, you will be required to complete the Assessment of Professional Competence with the RICS or register with the Chartered Institute of Building's (CIOB) Faculty of Architecture and Surveying. Subject to a minimum of 2 years' experience and your performance in an interview, you will gain chartered status.

What the work involves

Planning and development surveyors develop and manage new building or refurbishment projects. You will create proposals and oversee projects from conception through to completion.

You will be responsible for recruiting team members for each project, as well as liaising with external industry professionals throughout.

You will also give valuations on properties and developments, advise clients on financing options for their building plans, and prepare their applications for planning permission.

Type of person suited to this work

As you will be managing team members, briefing other professionals and dealing with clients, well-developed communication and negotiation skills are required.

Good numeracy skills, coupled with scientific aptitude, are essential to successfully write proposals and manage financial details within a project. An understanding of legal matters within the building and construction industries is helpful, as is an interest in the architecture, history or preserving the natural landscape.

Working conditions

You may have to work longer than the standard 35 hour week, but weekend and shift work is unusual.

Work exists in a variety of areas including local authorities, construction firms, property developers and building conservation.

Although there is some day to day travelling involved, overnight stays are uncommon.

Most jobs are found in cities where there is a high level of commercial activity. You could work for public sector or private companies, which range in size from very small practices up to large multinational firms. Work in the public sector is becoming increasingly flexible, with part-time work and career breaks available.

Future prospects

As a graduate trainee you can progress to surveyor, to senior surveyor, and up to associate or partner with several years' experience. If you progress to become an equity partner you will earn a high salary and also get a cut of the company's profits.

If you work in the public sector, you could enhance your career prospects with a Royal Town Planning Institute (RTPI) qualification, or develop a more specialised career in one area of surveying. Specialist knowledge in regeneration, conservation or land management is particularly useful in a society where sustainable development is growing in importance.

You may also consider transferring to other areas of surveying, eg waste management, arts and antiques or telecommunications. You could even take your skills abroad, eg to assist disaster-relief projects.

Advantages/disadvantages

Work is varied and you have the opportunity to travel within the UK and overseas.

Although you might need to work extra hours, weekend work is rare.

You will have a lot of responsibility which can be stressful at times.

Money guide

New graduates will earn £20,000–£24,000.

Fully qualified and experienced surveyors can earn £24,000–£38,000 per year.

Chartered surveyors can achieve a salary over £50,000.

Partners in a surveying firm often earn £70,000–£80,000, with an additional share of profits on top.

Related opportunities

- Land/Geomatic Surveyor p92
- Rural Property/Practice Surveyor p103
- Town Planner/Planning Technician p113

Further information

Chartered Institute of Building
www.ciob.org.uk

Chartered Institution of Civil Engineering Surveyors
www.cices.org

Royal Institution of Chartered Surveyors
www.rics.org

PLASTERER

ENTRY LEVEL 1

Qualifications and courses

A common route of entry into the plastering industry is to serve an apprenticeship. In order to be eligible for the Construction Apprenticeship Scheme (CAS) you will need some GCSEs/National 5s in English, Maths, and Design and Technology and an employer to sponsor your training.

Apprenticeship schemes are available at both Intermediate and Advanced Levels and offer a structured training programme leading to an NVQ/SVQ Level 3. Trainees will follow routes in solid plastering, fibrous plastering or dry lining. Programmes are validated by the Construction Industry Training Board (CITB) and last 2–3 years in England and Wales, and 4 years in Scotland. Most training is done on the job whilst attending college to obtain qualifications such as NVQs/SVQs in Plastering (Levels 1–3) or the City & Guilds Certificate in Basic Construction Skills – Plastering (6217-04). Further options available through City & Guilds include the Foundation/Intermediate Construction Awards. If you wish to specialise in the repair and conservation of historic buildings, you could also take an NVQ Level 3 in Heritage Skills (Construction).

Construction Skills Certification Scheme (CSCS) cards are required by plasterers employed on construction sites as proof of your competency on-site. You will need to have gained or be working towards a formal qualification, eg an NVQ, in order to qualify for one of these.

What the work involves

There are 3 types of plastering that you could do: solid, fibrous or dry lining. Solid plastering involves the application of plaster or cement to internal and external walls, ceilings and floors.

Fibrous plastering involves making ornamental plaster work, such as the kind you see on decorative ceilings.

Dry lining involves the use of plasterboard to construct walls or partitions and then skimming over the joins with plaster making them ready for decoration.

Type of person suited to this work

To be able to use your tools skilfully, you need to be good with your hands. An ability to use basic maths for calculating the amounts of materials you will need for a job is also helpful.

You will need to be able to work in a team with other plasterers, and with those in other construction trades.

You should be physically fit, as the work is very active. It can also be dusty when working with the plaster powder; this may be difficult if you suffer from certain allergies. You will be climbing ladders and possibly scaffolding, so you must be fine with heights.

Working conditions

Solid/dry lining

Most of the work for solid plasterers and those doing dry lining work is indoors, although you might have to work outdoors if working on exteriors. You will work from ladders and scaffolding.

Fibrous

Most fibrous plasterers work in workshops, although you may also install your work on-site.

All plastering requires an understanding and appreciation of health and safety regulations, which includes wearing protective gear. You may work a normal working week, although you might need to start early or finish late, and weekend work may also be available.

Future prospects

The building industry is cyclical therefore during a recession, there may be less of a demand for plasterers. Shortages of qualified plasterers do exist however, particularly in the domestic market and as a fibrous plasterer.

Besides being employed by specialist plastering firms and building contractors, you can also work in the cultural heritage or public sectors, conserving and restoring historic buildings. Due to its rapid expansion, many plasterers are also moving into the related area of dry lining. Opportunities to diversify and move into tiling, estimating or site management are also possible.

After you have gained sufficient experience, you could progress to technical, supervisory or managerial roles or alternatively, you may opt to become self-employed. You may even be able to seek contract work overseas.

Advantages/disadvantages

Working at heights may be difficult for some people.

You will be able to work in a variety of locations and those in fibrous plaster work have opportunities to be creative.

Money guide

As a trainee you could earn around £14,000–£17,000.

Once qualified, salaries can rise to £17,000–£25,000. High earning plasterers could earn upwards of £35,000.

Overtime, shift allowances and performance-based bonuses can increase earnings. Self-employed plasterers negotiate their own rates.

Related opportunities

- Building Technician p64
- Mastic Asphalter p93
- Wall/Floor Tiler p114

Further information

Construction Industry Training Board (CITB)
www.citb.co.uk

Federation of Plastering and Drywall Contractors
http://aisfpdc.org

Scottish Building Apprenticeship and Training Council
www.sbatc.co.uk

PLUMBER

ENTRY LEVEL 2

Qualifications and courses

To grasp some of the basic practical skills, you might first complete a course relevant to the industry such as the City & Guilds Certificate Level 1 in Introduction to Plumbing, the City & Guilds Diploma Level 2 in Access to Building Services Engineering or the City & Guilds Diploma Level 2 in Plumbing Studies. These courses could be used as the first step towards a higher level qualification or as support when seeking employment.

A very common route of entry into plumbing is through an apprenticeship, lasting 2 to 3 years. This would involve a combination of learning on the job from experienced professionals whilst studying at a college for a qualification, eg an NVQ. In order to become a qualified plumber you will need to complete an industry-recognised qualification at Level 2 or 3, something you can do whilst taking part in an apprenticeship. Typical qualifications include City & Guilds NVQ Diploma in either Plumbing and Heating or Installing and Maintaining Domestic Heating Systems, the Excellence, Achievement & Learning Limited (EAL)'s NVQ Diploma Level 2 in Plumbing and Heating and NVQ Diploma Level 3 in Domestic Plumbing and Heating. Entrants for apprenticeships or training schemes need to pass a selection test and have their colour vision tested.

Once you have passed recognised qualifications and gained practical experience, it is possible to become a member of the Chartered Institute of Plumbing and Heating Engineering (CIPHE).

Gas Safe registration and possession of a Gas Safe ID card is a legal requirement for anyone installing or repairing gas fittings or appliances.

What the work involves

Plumbers install, maintain and repair plumbing, heating and water systems in various locations including people's homes and public buildings. You will also be responsible for routine check-ups on appliances such as boilers.

You will use a range of hand and power tools, such as wrenches, cutters and welding equipment.

When you have completed a job, you will need to test the system to make sure that everything is working properly.

Type of person suited to this work

Good practical skills are essential. You must be careful, accurate and follow instructions to ensure that systems work properly and safely. Analytical and problem-solving skills are also important.

You might be bending, kneeling and squeezing into tight spaces so it would help if you were physically fit. You need to be comfortable working at heights.

You need to be a team player but also willing to work alone. You should keep a good appearance and have excellent communication skills when dealing directly with customers.

Working conditions

You will work both indoors and outdoors, possibly within confined spaces and at heights. Travelling will be required for jobs so it would be useful to have a driving licence and your own vehicle.

You may work a normal working week but, if your organisation offers a 24/7 call-out service, you need to be available at all times of the day or night, any day of the week.

Future prospects

Work is available across the UK, though the job market is more competitive in London.

As a plumber, you can use your skills in a variety of areas, including heating and ventilation, refrigeration, air conditioning, gas servicing, kitchen and bathroom fitting. With additional training, you could move into gas central heating installation and repair. You may also opt to install and maintain renewable energy technologies, solar water heating systems and ground source heat pumps given the increasing importance placed on sustainable systems.

You can progress to supervisory, training or managerial positions or move into estimating or contract management. Self-employment is also available, with lots of plumbers opting to set up their own businesses.

Advantages/disadvantages

You could be called out any time of day to deal with plumbing emergencies, which can be difficult for those with family commitments.

Being able to solve a difficult problem and make a customer happy can be very rewarding.

Money guide

Trainee plumbers typically start on £10,000–£15,000 per year.

Newly qualified plumbers' earnings increase to £16,500–£21,000.

Experienced plumbers can expect £21,000–£35,000.

Earnings for self-employed plumbers can be much higher as they negotiate their own rates of pay.

Overtime is often available and those who attend emergency call-outs can receive higher pay for working unsociable hours. Self-employed plumbers negotiate their own rates.

Related opportunities

- Gas Network Engineer p210
- Heating and Ventilation Engineer p88
- Refrigeration Engineer/Technician p101

Further information

Chartered Institute of Plumbing and Heating Engineering
www.ciphe.org.uk

SummitSkills
www.summitskills.org.uk

PROPERTY VALUER

ENTRY LEVEL 5

Qualifications and courses

Although entry requirements vary depending on employer, in order to become a property valuer you would normally hold a degree or professional qualification accredited by the Royal Institution of Chartered Surveyors (RICS) in a relevant subject such as residential surveying and valuation, building surveying, law or real estate management.

If you hold an HND or HNC you could enter the profession as a surveying technician and after further training and experience, you could progress from associate level to chartered status.

Once employed within the industry, you should work towards gaining chartered membership of a professional body such as the RICS or the Institute of Revenues Rating and Valuation (IRRV). Graduates of an RICS-accredited degree are required to complete the Assessment of Professional Competence (APC) in order to do so. Subject to 2 years' postgraduate work experience and your performance in an interview with a panel of assessors, you can gain chartered status.

Those who have not studied a degree in a relevant subject can take an RICS-accredited postgraduate degree or diploma course in an auctioneering/valuation subject. You may have to combine these courses with work experience and further professional qualifications.

It is important that you update your skills throughout your career. The IRRV offers qualifications and training that cover the valuation, legal and taxation aspects of your job, ensuring continuing professional development.

Given the nature of your work, it is likely that you will require a driving licence.

What the work involves

As a property valuer you will assess the value of property (buildings, land or personal items) for a client and advise them on how the property may be sold, loaned, taxed, acquired by a company or made part of a compensation claim. Local authorities also use these valuations to help set council tax and rating levels.

You will assess new commercial and industrial property and reassess existing property that has been altered.

You will provide reports on your valuations which may be important if property becomes part of legal negotiations or insurance claims. You may have to run live auctions where you will sell items that you have valued or you may pass them to a specialist.

Type of person suited to this work

You should have a keen interest in property valuation, law and taxation. You must have strong numerical skills to make accurate calculations, such as working out taxes or analysing accounts. As you may be hired by a company on a freelance basis, you will also need to be organised and able to use your initiative.

You need to have excellent written and verbal communication skills in order to communicate with clients, employers and government bodies.

Working conditions

You will work about 35–40 hours per week, Monday to Friday. You may have to work weekends depending on the project or your employer.

You will mainly be office based but will frequently have to visit and inspect properties or meet clients. As you might need to travel locally, a driving licence is recommended.

Future prospects

There are many opportunities in the UK. You could work in an estate agency valuing property that is being sold, rented or mortgaged. You may find work in the Valuation Office Agency assessing property for local authorities and government departments.

Valuers are also required by HM Revenue & Customs (HMRC) where you will value property and land that must be taxed when it is sold or bought.

Once you have gained sufficient experience, you could become a project manager, company partner or work as a freelance consultant.

Advantages/disadvantages

The job tends to be diverse and interesting as you will usually combine your role as a valuer with other areas such as estate management, surveying and even auctioning.

Property and land valuations may become part of compensation claims which involve a lengthy legal process.

Occasionally, property viewings and auctions will take place in the evenings and at weekends.

Money guide

Your starting salary may be £23,000–£26,000. With experience, earnings can increase to between £27,000 and £36,000.

A property valuer with chartered status can earn in excess of £40,000 a year.

Freelance property valuers negotiate their own wage.

Related opportunities

- Auction Property Consultant p59
- Insurance Risk Surveyor p32

Further information

Institute of Revenues Rating and Valuation
www.irrv.net

National Association of Valuers and Auctioneers
www.nava.org.uk

Royal Institution of Chartered Surveyors
www.rics.org

QUANTITY SURVEYOR

ENTRY LEVEL 5

Qualifications and courses

This career requires a degree or professional qualification accredited by the Royal Institution of Chartered Surveyors (RICS). If, however, you hold a non-accredited degree, or you opt to study a subject other than quantity surveying, you will be required to complete a 1-year postgraduate conversion course that is recognised by the RICS. Other first degree subjects which may be relevant include geography, maths, urban and land studies, economics, construction, civil and structural engineering. Entry to a degree will require a minimum of 2 A levels/3 H Grades and 5 GCSEs/National 5s (A*–C/A–C).

An HND in a related subject is also valued by employers and may gain you employment as a surveying technician. You can then progress to quantity surveyor level by studying, either part time or via distance learning, for RICS-recognised qualifications.

Once you are in employment, you should work towards gaining membership of the RICS or the Chartered Institute of Building's (CIOB) Faculty for Architecture and Surveying in order to become a fully qualified chartered surveyor. To gain chartered status, you must complete a 2-year training programme called the Assessment of Professional Competence (APC). Subject to you having gained a RICS-accredited degree, 2 years' work experience and your performance in an interview with assessors, you will gain chartered status.

What the work involves

Quantity surveyors are responsible for calculating costs, issuing contracts, keeping projects to time and within budget, managing subcontractors and arranging payments for work.

You will need a good understanding of building regulations to ensure that projects meet the required standards of quality and safety.

You could work on a wide variety of projects from residential developments to hospitals or sports stadiums.

Type of person suited to this work

You must have a high level of numeracy and the ability to manage financial projects as you will be responsible for all the financial details of projects. Good negotiation skills are also important, as you must agree contracts and prices with workers and contractors.

Excellent verbal and written communication skills are vital for leading and motivating the on-site team, liaising with clients and subcontractors, and producing accurate and detailed progress reports.

Finally, a good understanding of business and legal matters in relation to the building and construction industry is needed, since you will be responsible for ensuring that all projects meet current regulations and standards.

Working conditions

Working hours are slightly longer than average and will include early starts, late evenings and weekend work.

You will usually be office based, although it is not uncommon for the office to be in the form of a temporary hut on-site. Travel to client meetings and other projects is also expected.

Self-employment is possible, and many companies use freelance quantity surveyors on projects. There is also the opportunity to travel overseas.

Future prospects

Your opportunities are likely to lie within local authority or government departments, private practices, building contractors, property companies or commercial organisations both in the UK and abroad.

With experience, you can undertake a more comprehensive project management role and have the satisfaction of taking a job through from conception to completion. You may opt to specialise in certain areas such as value engineering, risk assessment, capital allowances or supply chain management or, alternatively, you could become self-employed.

There is usually a natural progression from quantity surveying to commercial management. Gaining chartered status will aid you in your bid for career progression.

Advantages/disadvantages

Working on numerous projects and with a range of people makes the job varied.

There are good opportunities for career progression and specialisation.

Hours are longer than average, with occasional weekend work.

Money guide

Starting salaries for quantity surveyors can range from £20,000 to £25,000, rising to £30,000–£45,000 a year with experience.

Senior surveyors can earn £50,000–£60,000 and partners in private firms can expect considerably more.

With chartered status, extra responsibilities or further qualifications, your earnings can significantly increase.

Benefits include shift and site allowances, pension schemes, healthcare packages and a company car.

Related opportunities

- Civil/Construction Engineer/Civil Engineering Technician p69
- Insurance Risk Surveyor p32
- Town Planner/Planning Technician p113

Further information

Construction Industry Training Board (CITB)
www.citb.co.uk

Royal Institution of Chartered Surveyors
www.rics.org

REFRIGERATION ENGINEER/ TECHNICIAN

ENTRY LEVEL 2

Qualifications and courses

The most common form of entry into the refrigeration engineering industry is by undertaking an apprenticeship. In order to be considered, you are likely to need 4 GCSEs/National 5s (A*–C/A–C) in English, Maths, Physics and Design and Technology.

Apprenticeships offer candidates the opportunity to gain the appropriate NVQs/SVQs required of a qualified refrigeration engineer/technician. As an apprentice, you will work towards either an NVQ in Servicing and Maintaining Refrigeration Systems (Level 2 and 3), an NVQ in Refrigeration/Air Conditioning Equipment Engineering Technology (Level 2 or 3) or, in Scotland, an SVQ in Install, Commission and Maintain Refrigeration Systems (Level 2 or 3). Alongside gaining an industry recognised qualification, you will also be educated in the necessary health and safety procedures.

Apprenticeships are open to people aged 16 or over and take 2 to 4 years. A combination of on-the-job training from experienced professionals and day or block release formal instruction at a college takes place. There are limited places available to candidates over 25.

Further qualifications such as HNCs/HNDs in Refrigeration and Air Conditioning and Foundation degrees in Building Services Engineering are also available. Alternatively, if you wish to specialise in fluorinated gas (F gases) or ozone depleting substances (ODS), you could complete the City & Guilds Level 2 Award in F-gas and ODS Regulations (2079). You may also apply to be a member of the Institute of Refrigeration which offers a variety of continuing professional development (CPD) workshops as you progress throughout your career.

What the work involves

Your work as a refrigeration engineer will involve the design, installation and repair of refrigeration equipment and air conditioning systems. You will be called out to undertake repairs and maintenance, estimate costs of construction and installation projects, inspect existing equipment, and give advice on adjustments and improvements.

Refrigeration engineers aim to create and maintain comfortable working/living environments in offices and homes that are both energy-efficient and safe.

Your work in commercial buildings and factories will be to provide refrigeration systems that keep food at the correct, safe temperature.

Type of person suited to this work

It is important that you like hands-on work and have a practical approach to problem solving.

You should be interested in the building services industry and keep up to date with relevant developments in legislation and technology.

Written and spoken communication skills are important as you will be in contact with clients and planning projects. You should also have an aptitude for maths and physics and have strong technical skills.

Working conditions

You will normally work around 37 hours a week and how this is spread over a week may vary. However you might have to work longer hours during the summer which is peak time for refrigeration engineers.

You will be office based to plan visits to sites and organise jobs, but you will also visit various locations such as offices, shopping centres or factories. This will be to complete practical jobs such as maintenance, repair and installation.

You may also work in refrigeration transport, on specially adapted vehicles such as trucks, aircraft and fishing vessels or in vehicle workshops. On certain visits you might have to wear protective clothing or equipment.

Future prospects

As you gain experience in the field you will find opportunities for progression to supervisory and managerial roles.

To improve your skills you may take further qualifications such the NVQ in Building Services Engineering (Level 3 and 4) or in other refrigeration and air conditioning specific topics. Such courses act as a stepping stone to membership of the Chartered Institution of Building Services Engineers (CIBSE).

You can add further experience with further qualifications and work towards becoming an incorporated or chartered engineer. Alternatively, you may opt to become self-employed or move into teaching.

Advantages/disadvantages

There are opportunities to work abroad as UK qualifications are internationally recognised.

You may also be required to do overtime work and to be on-call overnight and at weekends.

Money guide

Trainees can earn around £11,000 to £19,000 a year, depending on the stage.

Starting salaries once you have qualified are around £20,000 to £25,000 a year.

This can increase to around £35,000 with experience, supervisory responsibilities and qualifications.

There are also opportunities for bonuses and overtime pay.

Related opportunities

- Civil/Construction Engineer/Civil Engineering Technician p69
- Electrical Engineer p203
- Electrician p78

Further information

Institute of Refrigeration
www.ior.org.uk

ROOFER

ENTRY LEVEL 1

Qualifications and courses

In order to train as a roofer it may be useful to have some GCSEs/National 5s (A*–E/A–E) in relevant subjects such as maths, English, craft, design and technology or a vocational qualification, eg a BTEC Certificate/Diploma in Construction and the Built Environment or a City & Guilds Certificate in Basic Construction Skills (6218). Introductory vocational qualifications are available at some schools and colleges and act as a foundation for further training or preparation for first employment.

One means of entry into the roofing industry is to find work post-secondary school as an entry-level roofing labourer. This way you will gain both valuable on-site experience and opportunities for further training in roofing techniques.

Alternatively, you could enter the profession through an apprenticeship programme with a building or roofing company. ConstructionSkills offers specialised roofing apprenticeships through the National Construction College (NCC) that lead to NVQ/SVQ Level 2 qualifications. Most training is carried out on the job whilst attending college to obtain qualifications such as NVQs/SVQs in Roofing Occupations and Mastic Asphalting.

You will need a Construction Skills Certification Scheme (CSCS) card in order to work on-site. The purpose of this card is to demonstrate that the holder has health and safety training and maintains professional competency. You will normally have to have completed, or be in the process of completing, an industry recognised qualification as proof of your capability.

You could later gain membership of the Institute of Roofing (IOR) which offers numerous continuing professional development (CPD) schemes that update your skills.

What the work involves

Roofers remove old roofs and replace them, fit new roofs and repair existing ones. You will have a choice of roofing materials to work with, such as tile, slate, felt, thatch and sheet. You could specialise in flat or pitched (sloping) roofs or work on both.

When working on flat roofs you will need to spread a waterproof bitumen layer. On all types of roofs your work will involve measuring and cutting materials, layering them on the roof and using mortar or cement to seal it.

You could also carry out lead work or liquid applied roofing.

Type of person suited to this work

You need to have good practical skills and be physically fit, so that you can climb ladders and scaffolding and carry roofing materials. You must be comfortable working at heights.

It is important to be able to understand plans and follow instructions. You should be a team player with good communication skills when dealing with customers.

It will also be useful to be interested in building construction and to enjoy being outdoors.

Working conditions

You will work outdoors on roofs in various locations from people's homes to historic cathedrals and construction sites. The work can be dusty and dirty.

As you will be working up ladders, on scaffolding or on the roof itself, you will need to pay close attention to all health and safety procedures, which includes wearing protective gear such as a safety helmet and boots.

You are likely to work a normal working week, although extra work may be available at weekends.

Future prospects

There is a good demand for qualified roofers across the UK at the moment. Work is available within roofing companies, contractors, roofing material suppliers, local authorities and other public organisations.

You can decide to specialise in using one type of roofing material, such as slate, or you can train to become skilled in several types.

You may work your way up to technical, supervisory and managerial levels. After you have gained enough experience, you could start your own roofing company or seek contract work abroad.

Advantages/disadvantages

Working at heights may be difficult for some people.

You could get to work on some impressive projects such as fitting the roof on a new football stadium. It is satisfying to produce a lasting structure that is functional and looks good.

You will gain an understanding of other construction work, such as joinery.

Money guide

Trainee salaries are about £13,500–£15,000 a year.

As a qualified roofer you can earn £16,000–£24,000.

With experience, your salary can increase to £31,000.

Self-employed roofers negotiate their own rates.

Overtime and bonuses are often available.

Related opportunities

- Construction Operative p72
- Scaffolder p104
- Thatcher p111

Further information

Construction Industry Training Board (CITB)
www.citb.co.uk

Institute of Roofing
www.instituteofroofing.org

RURAL PROPERTY/PRACTICE SURVEYOR

ENTRY LEVEL 6

Qualifications and courses

This sector normally requires a Royal Institution of Chartered Surveyors (RICS) accredited degree in a related subject such as agriculture, forestry, estate, land or property management and surveying. Most degree courses require 5 GCSEs/National 5s (A*–C/A–C), 2 A levels/3 H grades or relevant BTEC Diplomas/Certificates (or equivalent).

If your first degree was in an unrelated or unaccredited subject, a postgraduate conversion course offered by the College of Estate Management (CEM) can be studied via distance learning. It is also possible to take a degree or postgraduate course at a college recommended by the Central Association of Agricultural Valuers (CAAV).

If you have a relevant HND or Foundation degree then you can qualify for Associate/RICS status. However, you will usually have to top up your qualifications to degree level in order to become a fully chartered surveyor.

Once qualified, you will need to complete the Assessment of Professional Competence (APC) during your first 2 years of employment, in order to gain chartered status.

Competition for training places in the industry is fierce and pre-entry work experience may increase your chances of employment. By completing work experience during your undergraduate year, not only are you developing your confidence in dealing with members of the rural community, but you are also enhancing your career prospects. Relevant work experience placements may include a working farm or estate agent.

It is highly recommended that you also gain a valid UK driving licence.

What the work involves

Rural property/practice surveyors manage properties in the countryside such as farms and estates. You will give professional and technical advice to rural landowners on how to develop their assets – land and property – as well as providing business and resource management and consultancy for land, construction and property industries.

Giving advice on the buying and selling of properties, on farming grants and subsidies and how national and EU law affects clients' businesses is a typical example of work involved.

However, jobs do vary between those who work for corporations who deal with several clients and those who manage estates. You can also choose to specialise in specific areas, such as auctioneering or environmental sustainability, but this can limit employability to an extent.

Type of person suited to this work

Excellent communication skills are needed as you will need to negotiate and liaise with people of all ages and backgrounds.

You must have an analytical mind and a clear, concise writing style in order to explain detailed statistical information.

A good understanding of rural issues, including knowledge of crops, is essential in order to assess a client's economic viability with accuracy. Problem-solving and forward-planning skills are also essential to keep on top of a heavy workload.

Working conditions

The average working week can reach over 40 hours and early morning and weekend work is common as you need to adapt around clients as well as rural events such as harvests.

You will mostly work outdoors, regardless of the weather. If you are office based, it will usually be in rural market towns or villages. You should be prepared to drive and travel regularly as work will often cover a large geographical area.

Future prospects

Your career path is narrowed but progression can occur very quickly. In larger companies, there may be the opportunity to specialise in areas such as pure agriculture or renewable energy use. By contrast, a smaller company could give you a greater range of projects which will build broader experience but with fewer opportunities for specialising.

With 10–15 years of experience, you could become a partner in a firm.

Advantages/disadvantages

You will be based in peaceful rural locations.

You will be instrumental in developing the future of the countryside and rural industries.

Hours can be long and you should expect to regularly work early mornings and weekends.

Money guide

Average earnings for new graduates are £20,000–£25,000.

With experience, this can increase to £38,000.

A senior chartered surveyor can receive a salary in excess of £40,000.

Additional benefits such as bonuses, a company car or health insurance are sometimes offered and subsidised accommodation may be available for surveyors managing a farm or estate.

Related opportunities

- Auction Property Consultant p59
- Building Surveyor p63
- Civil/Construction Engineer/Civil Engineering Technician p69

Further information

Agricultural Development and Advisory Service
www.adas.co.uk

Department for Environment, Food and Rural Affairs
www.defra.gov.uk

Royal Agricultural College
www.rac.ac.uk

SCAFFOLDER

ENTRY LEVEL 1

Qualifications and courses

There are no set entry requirements but some GCSEs/National 5s (A*–E/A–E) in subjects such as English, maths, a science and Technology or a vocational qualification, such as the BTEC Introductory Certificate or Diploma in Construction (Level 1) are useful.

In order to become a scaffolder, you will normally be trained on the job whilst studying for industry recognised qualifications part time at a college or training centre. Employers often expect some on-site experience so it may be useful to develop your skills by working first as a labourer.

The Construction Industry Scaffolders Record Scheme (CISRS) operates a systematic card system at all levels, ie labourer, trainee, scaffolder and advanced scaffolder, and is the recognised qualification for scaffolding. The CISRS card system ensures that operatives are properly trained and sufficiently experienced to work safely and competently. After on and off-site training and an NVQ Level 2 in Accessing Operations and Rigging, you can apply for a Scaffolder card. This will allow you to carry out basic scaffolding tasks as part of a scaffolding gang.

For the Advanced CISRS Card, scaffolders must have a Scaffolder Card, 12 months' subsequent experience and complete the 10-day Advanced Scaffolding course provided by CISRS and the NVQ Diploma in Accessing Operations and Rigging (Construction) (Level 3).

What the work involves

Scaffolders put up scaffolding so that new constructions, or the maintenance of existing buildings and structures, can take place. You will put together metal tubes, fittings and wooden or metal platforms to create the scaffolding.

You will use tools such as swivel spanners and spirit levels in your work.

You may also put up spectator stands, stages and rigging for outdoor concerts and events.

Type of person suited to this work

Safety is the main priority in scaffolding. You need to ensure that it is safe for the people who will be working on it, passers-by, workmates and yourself. For this reason, you have to be able to keep your concentration, have good practical skills, be well organised and be able to follow instructions and take measurements accurately.

You must be physically fit so that you can lift and carry equipment up and down ladders and, of course, you must be happy working at heights.

You also need to be able to work as part of a team of scaffolders.

Working conditions

You will be working mainly outdoors in most weather conditions, often at great heights.

You will need to wear protective equipment such as a hard hat, boots and a safety harness.

You may work a normal working week from Monday to Friday, although you might need to start work early or finish late. Extra hours at weekends may also be available.

Future prospects

There is currently a good demand for scaffolders across the UK. There are lots of opportunities within specialist scaffolding firms and building contractors as well as in oil and power companies, particularly in the east of England and Greater London.

You may progress from basic to advanced scaffolder, and then on to supervisory and managerial positions where you might move into estimation or construction management. The CISRS offers supervisors/managers training in health and safety, risk assessment, design and resource management. If you possess computer-aided design skills, progression to project design and management is possible.

With experience you may set up your own business or take up contract work overseas.

Advantages/disadvantages

This job can be physically challenging and working at heights can be demanding for some people.

You will get to work in a variety of locations and you might have the chance to put up scaffolding for major sports and music events or for film sets.

Money guide

Starting as an apprentice or trainee, you can earn up to £13,000 per year.

Once qualified as a scaffolder, salaries range from £17,000 to £38,000 depending on experience.

Self-employed or contract scaffolders can often negotiate higher rates of pay.

Overtime is frequently available and on some projects there are performance-related bonuses which can lead to higher earnings.

Related opportunities

- Building Technician p64
- Construction Operative p72
- Roofer p102

Further information

Construction Industry Training Board (CITB)
www.citb.co.uk

National Access and Scaffolding Confederation
www.nasc.org.uk

SHOPFITTER

ENTRY LEVEL 1

Qualifications and courses

No formal academic qualifications are required but some employers might expect entrants to have GCSEs/National 5s (A*–E/A–E) in English, Maths and a science. GCSEs/ National 5s in Art, Design and Technology might also be useful. The BTEC Certificate and Diploma in Construction (Levels 1 and 2) and City & Guilds (5782) NVQ in Woodmachining (Levels 2 and 3) are also relevant.

In order to become a shopfitter, you could begin as a trainee in a relevant area of the industry such as a shopfitting joiner, wood machinist or metal fabricator.

Alternatively, you could serve an apprenticeship with a shopfitting company. As an apprentice, you will experience a combination of work-based training from professional shopfitters and a series of day or block release at a college studying for qualifications. NVQs/ SVQs in Shopfitting (Levels 2–4) or an NVQ Diploma in Wood Occupations (Levels 1–3) which will include training, on-site work, bench work and site management are typically studied as part of an apprenticeship.

With experience you can apply for membership of the National Association of Shopfitters (NAS) for further training in areas such as contract law, estimation and site management, provided by the Shopfitting Independent Training Forum (SITF).

Many employers require you to have the CSCS card issued by the Construction Skills Certification Scheme as proof of your competence and a skills card distributed by the Shopfitting and Interior Contracting Competency Scheme (SICCS) specific to shopfitters. In order to obtain these, you will have to have completed or be in the process of completing an industry recognised qualification.

What the work involves

As a shopfitter you will create and install the interiors and exteriors of commercial buildings such as shops, banks, offices, restaurants and hotels. You may be working from designs made by an architect or designer, or you might have to research and prepare your own design drawings.

You will prepare, assemble and finish joinery and metalwork according to the design, before bringing each part together and assembling them on-site.

You will probably specialise in a particular area. These include a metal fabricator, cutting and shaping metal components; a wood machinist, using specialist machinery to cut precise parts for joiners.

Type of person suited to this work

As you will be working in a workshop or on-site you should have a keen interest in practical work and have good hand skills. You should also be interested in design and construction.

You should have an eye for detail and a high level of concentration, but you will also need a certain level of fitness as you will be required to work long and at times, hard hours.

As you will be taking measurements and making calculations frequently you should have good spatial awareness and an aptitude for maths.

Working conditions

You will work around 40 hours per week, with overtime often required, in a variety of locations. You may have to travel to work on-site and this may involve working away from home at times.

You may have to work irregular hours, overnight or at weekends to accommodate clients – work may need to be done during the night when premises are closed.

On-site work may be dusty, dirty and noisy and usually involves physical work such as lifting and bending.

Future prospects

Once you are qualified and have built up experience, you could progress to a supervisory or managerial role, ensuring your team's work meets the necessary standards. Experienced shopfitters may be able to apply to become masters of their trade through the Institute of Carpenters.

It is possible to establish your own shopfitting business.

Alternatively, the skills that you develop as a shopfitter could be utilised in various other building trades.

Advantages/disadvantages

Shopfitting is a diverse profession as your work will change according to the project that you are working on as well as the materials you will work with.

You will meet and work with many other professionals involved in construction such as engineers, architects, electricians and plumbers.

The job is physically demanding and you may be required to work long or unsocial hours.

Money guide

Your starting salary may be around £13,500 to £16,000.

With experience and qualifications, earnings can rise to between £17,000 and £22,000.

As a shopfitter with supervisory duties you may earn around £30,000 per year.

Related opportunities

- Builders' Merchant/Assistant p453
- Carpenter/Joiner p65
- Furniture Manufacturing Operative p209

Further information

Construction Industry Training Board (CITB)
www.citb.co.uk

Institute of Carpenters
www.instituteofcarpenters.com

National Association of Shopfitters
www.shopfitters.org

SITE MANAGER/ CLERK OF WORKS

ENTRY LEVEL 2

Qualifications and courses

There are no set qualifications to become a site manager/clerk of works. Experience in a relevant industry however, is necessary, perhaps at craft or technician level in construction or civil engineering. It is not normally a profession that you can enter when you first leave school.

As well as experience, you may need certain construction and civil engineering qualifications. You may decide to seek employment at trainee level and work your way up after completing some introductory courses. These might include a City & Guilds Award/Certificate/ Diploma in Basic Construction Skills (Level 1), NVQs Level 2 or 3, a BTEC/SQA Level 2 or 3, a BTEC Higher National Diploma (HND) or Higher National Certificate (HNC) or a Foundation or Honours degree. Graduates may be taken on by companies as apprentices where they will learn on the job.

Once in employment, you can gain NVQs in Site Inspection (Levels 3 and 4) which will cover areas such as health and safety, inspecting property, planning, monitoring and maintenance of projects in construction.

As you accumulate qualifications you can achieve different levels of membership with the Institute of Clerks of Works and Construction Inspectorate (ICWCI). Although this membership is not essential, it is increasingly sought after by employers and beneficial to your career progression. To enter each level of membership you will need to have a relevant qualification, a report of your professional history, a professional practice interview and a materials identification test.

You may be required to obtain a Construction Skills Certification Scheme (CSCS) card as proof of your competency working on-site. Subject to your qualifications, your membership with ICWCI and an examination, you will be eligible for a CSCS card.

What the work involves

As a site manager/clerk of works you will be responsible for supervising all the on-site aspects of a construction contract.

You must ensure that good standards are maintained and that work is carried out efficiently and on time.

You will inspect and monitor materials, procedures and work so that the client is guaranteed quality and value for money. You will also act as a superintendent, advising contractors about aspects of work and solving problems as they arise.

Type of person suited to this work

You should have an interest in construction and should enjoy working outdoors and in all weather conditions. You will need to be physically fit and have a head for heights.

You need to be responsible, organised and honest as you may be in control of projects involving large teams of workers and a variety of materials. You will need a keen eye for detail and to be thorough and vigilant in maintaining quality standards of work and materials.

You should have excellent communication skills, be able to lead a team and to establish appropriate working relationships with contractors' staff.

Working conditions

You will usually work around 40 hours a week, Monday to Friday. However you will frequently have to work at the weekend and during the evening depending on deadlines.

You will be based in a site office which will usually be a temporary structure. You will have to spend much of your time outdoors in all weather conditions.

You may have to climb ladders and scaffolding or in tunnel construction, work underground. When you are inspecting a site you might have to wear protective clothing such as a hard hat and work boots.

Future prospects

There is currently a shortage of site managers in the UK. As an experienced clerk of works you must undertake continuing professional development. This is so that you can keep up to date with advances in areas such as new materials, practices, law and regulations, and health and safety issues.

Clerks of works can move up to roles in site management or other management roles in the construction industry.

You may have the opportunity to specialise in your chosen field or become self-employed. You may even take your work abroad.

Advantages/disadvantages

You can choose to specialise in particular areas such as building, civil engineering or mechanical and electrical installations.

On-site inspection may be dusty, dirty and noisy.

Money guide

The starting salary for a clerk of works can be between £21,000 and £40,000 a year.

With experience, your salary can be in excess of £50,000 depending on the contract undertaken.

Related opportunities

- Building Surveyor p63
- Civil/Construction Engineer/Civil Engineering Technician p69
- Construction Supervisor/Manager p74

Further information

Chartered Institute of Building
www.ciob.org.uk

Institute of Clerks of Works
www.icwgb.org

STEEPLEJACK

ENTRY LEVEL 1

Qualifications and courses

There are no formal entry qualifications for this job but you will find it useful to have GCSEs/National 5s (A*–E/A–E) in Maths, English, a science and Technology. Pre-entry experience within the construction industry, as a labourer or tradesperson, may be advantageous.

Young entrants can train on the job with an employer or as an apprentice within an approved apprenticeship scheme. CITB and the Steeplejack and Lightning Protection Training Group provide opportunities for apprenticeships. Entrants will be required to take aptitude tests in maths and problem solving and will be assessed in literacy and their ability to work at heights. Apprentices are sponsored by an employer and spend 6 months out of a 2 year period at the residential National Construction College.

Candidates will work towards NVQs/SVQs Levels 2 or 3 in Accessing Operations and Rigging – Steeplejacking and various other CITB-accredited courses such as Health and Safety, First Aid, Mobile Towers, Fire Fighting, Safe Use of Ladders and Industrial Rope Access.

Many employers require you to have the CSCS card issued by the Construction Skills Certification Scheme as proof of your competence working on-site. You will need to have completed or be working towards an industry recognised qualification in order to be granted one.

In order to remain up to date with current issues within the industry, you may find it useful to gain membership with The Association of Technical Lightning and Access Specialists (ATLAS).

What the work involves

Steeplejacks work on high structures including power station chimneys, cooling towers, oil refineries, factories and church spires. Your work on these structures will involve climbing to high places with your tools to complete routine maintenance, repairs or renovation projects.

You will plan each job carefully. To ensure a safe and accessible working environment you will put in ladders, specialist scaffolding or industrial rope access (abseiling), work platforms (cradles) and bosun's seat (harness) and fall-arrest devices.

You will be working on both historic buildings and modern constructions, in urban and rural areas.

Type of person suited to this work

You should be organised as you will have to make sure in advance that you have the right safety equipment and tools to complete the job. The ability to work well as part of a team is also important.

You must be comfortable working at heights or in confined spaces, have a good sense of balance and be physically fit. Good coordination and practical skills are required to use the tools of the trade.

You should enjoy working outdoors in all weather conditions and you must be very conscious of, and committed to, health and safety procedures.

Working conditions

Your working hours and shifts can vary and you might have to work during the evenings and weekends.

Your work will be physically demanding as it will involve rigging, climbing, carrying ladders and tools and working with your hands. You will need to wear protective clothing and headgear. You may have to work on industrial chimneys which can be extremely dusty, requiring respiratory equipment.

A driving licence is useful as you may have to travel.

Future prospects

As a steeplejack you will probably work for construction firms that specialise in steeplejacking. These tend to be based in the major UK cities such as London, Manchester, Nottingham, Bristol, Cardiff, Edinburgh and Glasgow, and tend to seek local employees.

With experience you will be eligible for promotion to a role as a supervisor or manager within a firm. With significant experience you can become self-employed, although this is not particularly common.

There are, however, increasing opportunities to work abroad.

Advantages/disadvantages

There are currently between 800 and 1,000 steeplejacks in the UK. As a qualified steeplejack you may find work easily and there are plenty of opportunities in this area.

Your work may be hampered by weather conditions, for example, high winds may prevent access to structures and delay completion of projects.

Money guide

Trainee steeplejacks over the age of 21 can earn between £15,000 and £17,000 a year.

Once qualified, your salary may increase to £20,000.

With experience, advanced skills and extra responsibilities, senior engineers can earn in excess of £25,000 a year.

Your wage can significantly increase with overtime and shift allowances.

Related opportunities

- Bricklayer p60
- Scaffolder p104
- Stonemason p108

Further information

Association of Technical Lightning and Access Specialists
www.atlas.org.uk

Construction Industry Training Board (CITB)
www.citb.co.uk

STONEMASON

ENTRY LEVEL 2

Qualifications and courses

There are no formal entry requirements to train as a stonemason but an interest in art and design is desirable and it may also be useful to have GCSEs/National 5s (A*–C/A–C) in English, Maths, Design and Technology in order to calculate areas and volumes. Pre-entry on-site experience, as a labourer for example, is highly valued by potential employers and may offer you a route in for subsequent stonemasonry training.

Another common form of entry is via an apprenticeship with a building or stonemasonry firm. Training is provided on the job by experienced professionals and combined with part-time attendance at college or training centre in order for you to gain relevant NVQs/SVQs, for example, in Stonemasonry Levels 2 and 3. Candidates will have to complete an aptitude assessment and may have to secure employment prior to acceptance.

As an apprentice you may work towards relevant qualifications in stonemasonry offered by the Construction Awards Alliance (CAA). NVQ Diplomas in Heritage Skills (Construction) – Mason (Level 3) or the City & Guilds NVQ in Stonemasonry (Levels 1–3) are available. Courses cover estimating, planning and setting out projects, as well as understanding product information and tools.

You might opt to complete a relevant course full time at college but you may find that future employers do value on-site experience.

Many employers on construction sites require workers to have a Construction Skills Certification Scheme (CSCS) card as proof of one's competence working on-site. A driving licence may also be useful, particularly for fixer masons, who will be required to travel between jobs.

What the work involves

There are 3 types of stonemason. Banker masons cut, shape and carve the stone, fixer masons assemble and fix stones into place and monumental masons make things such as plaques and headstones.

While the work is manual and strenuous it is also highly creative. You may work on new buildings but could also work on restoring and repairing old buildings.

Type of person suited to this work

Banker mason
As a banker mason, you have to be good with your hands to cut, shape and carve stone accurately. You also need artistic skills for producing decorative finishes.

Fixer mason
You must be physically fit so that you can lift the stones, although you will use special equipment to lift the heaviest ones. You must not mind working at heights.

Monumental mason
In this sector, you will be working closely with the funeral industry, so you need to be sensitive to people's requirements and have a good eye for design. It is also useful to be interested in architecture and history, as much of the work involves restoring old buildings.

Working conditions

Banker masons mainly work in a workshop, while fixer masons work on-site in all weather conditions and restoration masons work on monuments and listed buildings, often at heights.

All masonry work can be dusty, noisy and unsuitable for people who have allergies. You will need to follow health and safety procedures and wear protective clothing.

You will normally work a 39-hour week but overtime may be required when nearing a project deadline.

Future prospects

There is good demand for stonemasons in the UK given the shortage of traditional craft skills.

You can choose to work for stonemasonry firms and larger building contractors. If you work for a small stonemasonry company you are likely to have to do both banking and fixing work. There are fewer opportunities in small, family run businesses however.

With experience, you may wish to specialise in restoration work or new buildings or to take on supervisory roles. You may even opt to instruct at a college or to become self-employed.

Advantages/disadvantages

The physical nature of the job, including working at heights, may be strenuous for some people.

You may have the opportunity to work on impressive restoration projects, for example in cathedrals or stately homes.

It can make you proud to produce work on a building that will be admired for many years.

Money guide

Starting salaries can range between £15,000 and £18,000 a year.

With experience, your salary could rise to between £20,000 and £30,000.

Overtime and bonuses are often available. Self-employed stonemasons negotiate their own rates.

Related opportunities

- Bricklayer p60
- Building Technician p64
- Dry Stone Waller p77

Further information

National Heritage Training Group
www.the-nhtg.org.uk

Stone Federation Great Britain
www.stonefed.org.uk

STRUCTURAL ENGINEER

ENTRY LEVEL 5

Qualifications and courses

Entrants normally have gained an accredited degree and/or postgraduate qualification in structural or civil engineering. Those who have studied another engineering subject or a highly numerate science degree may be able to enter the profession but their career progression may be slower and increasingly limited. In order to be accepted onto a degree course in engineering, you will normally be required to have achieved 2 A levels/3 H grades and 5 GCSEs/National 5s (A*–C/A–C). This should include maths and any science subject, although physics is at times specifically requested by certain universities.

It is possible to enter this career after studying for an HNC/HND or Foundation degree in Engineering. You will have to enter at technician level (TIStructE) and work your way up to engineer status by training on the job and gaining further qualifications. The Initial Professional Development (IPD) scheme lays out the skills you need to prove your ability as an engineer and work towards incorporated or chartered status. This takes 3 to 4 years before being completed with an exam and interview, the Professional Review Interview (PRI). Success will allow you to become a professional Chartered Structural Engineer (MIStructE) or Incorporated Structural Engineer (AMIStructE).

Graduate structural engineers are advised to pursue membership with the Institution of Structural Engineers (IStructE) and the Engineering Council as this can greatly improve your employability, salary and progression into senior or specialised roles.

You may opt to study for a master's prior to securing employment in order to work towards chartered status immediately, or alternatively, your employer may sponsor your studying whilst you work at associate level, for example, through a graduate training scheme.

What the work involves

Structural engineers design structures that are able to withstand the high pressure they are placed under.

You will work with architects on the design and construction of a variety of structures including bridges, tunnels, domestic houses, office blocks or sports stadia.

Among other tasks you will calculate the loads and stresses of a structure, analyse potential problems and test digital models to examine how they will endure influences such as wind, gravity and earth tremors. You will investigate soil conditions, visit construction sites, and undertake projects that involve demolition or repair of a structure.

Type of person suited to this work

You will need to be good at technical drawing and have 3D concept skills. You must have a keen eye for detail and accomplish your work efficiently and with the utmost accuracy.

You should have an aptitude for problem solving and analytical thinking. You should also have strong skills in maths, physics and IT.

You must be able to work in a team as well as being able to work with other professionals from across the construction industry.

Working conditions

You will work a total of approximately 40 hours a week, Monday to Friday. At times you might have to work at the weekend.

You will work both in an office and on-site. This can be in all weather conditions and you will have to wear protective clothing such as a hard hat.

You will frequently have to travel from site to site and a driving licence may be useful for this.

Future prospects

Many employers provide training schemes for new structural engineers which allow you to work towards achieving professional status. You may follow a formal progression structure beginning as a construction designer before becoming a project manager.

You may work in an engineering consultancy or construction company and later, specialise in a specific type of work, such as concrete buildings or refurbishment.

With chartered status you could become self-employed or move into research or lecturing. You could also find contract work abroad or go on to become a Fellow of the IStructE, a recognition of excellence in structural engineering.

Advantages/disadvantages

You should be prepared to work in all weather conditions.

Travel within a working day is common and you may be required to work away from home sometimes.

This is an important job with high levels of responsibility so you are likely to be well respected.

Money guide

Graduate trainees have a starting salary of £18,000–£23,000.

With experience, you could earn £24,000–£40,000.

A senior employee with chartered status could receive up to £50,000, with top positions attracting more than £70,000.

Related opportunities

- Architect p56
- Quantity Surveyor p100
- Surveying Technician p110

Further information

Association for Consultancy and Engineering
www.acenet.co.uk

Construction Industry Training Board (CITB)
www.citb.co.uk

Institution of Structural Engineers
www.istructe.org.uk

SURVEYING TECHNICIAN

ENTRY LEVEL 3

Qualifications and courses

There are a number of routes of entry into this profession, one being completing a relevant course at college to gain the basic skills required by the job. Introductory courses that are suitable include the Level 3 Diploma in Construction and the Built Environment or Civil Engineering for Technicians. These courses provide candidates with a useful foundation of knowledge which they can draw upon when training for more advanced qualifications such as a BTEC HNC/HND in Construction or a Foundation degree in Surveying, Construction or Civil Engineering.

Alternatively, the Chartered Surveyors Training Trust (CSTT) offers work-based training for young people aged 16–24, living in England. Applicants must have a minimum of 4 GCSEs/National 5s (A*–C/A–C) or equivalent. CSTT apprentices train for 2 years and, upon completion, have the option to study for a Royal Institution of Chartered Surveyors (RICS) accredited degree.

Another route for school leavers is to apply for the Advanced Level Apprenticeship in Surveying. Apprentices will typically work towards gaining an industry recognised qualification, for example, an NVQ/SVQ Level 4 in either Quantity Surveying Practice, Valuation, Spatial Data Management or Town Planning.

Once you have acquired the relevant qualifications and secured employment, you can work towards becoming a technical member (TechRICS) of RICS. In order to do so, you will need to complete a 2-year Assessment of Professional Competence (APC) which involves a period of structured training and practical experience followed by a technical assessment interview known as the Assessment of Technical Competence. Those with an NVQ/SVQ Level 4 and substantial work experience may proceed to the technical assessment interview.

Once you have qualified as a surveying technician, further training is possible in the form of NVQs. This may lead you to specialise in a particular area of surveying.

What the work involves

Surveying technicians work alongside chartered surveyors, providing hands-on support across the full range of surveying specialisms including building, land, rural and commercial.

You will be expected to carry out a range of administrative tasks associated with each project, such as putting together contracts and writing reports.

You will also be using complex computer programs and technical equipment both on-site and in the office in order to create reports and survey drawings, and to assess various aspects of each project.

Type of person suited to this work

You will be working closely with other professionals and clients at all levels, so the ability to communicate both orally and in writing is vital.

Because you will be dealing with very specific technical issues in each project, you will need to have an accurate and methodical approach to work, good numerical skills and the ability to multi-task.

You will need a good level of IT skills, and confidence in using the wide range of sophisticated equipment required for the job. Knowledge of business, law and health and safety-related regulations is also desirable.

Working conditions

Working hours usually follow those of a normal office job, but you will occasionally be called to work early mornings, evenings and at weekends during busy times or for certain site visits.

Most of the work is office based, but you will also spend time working on-site. This means you must be prepared for all weathers and wear appropriate safety equipment at all times.

You could work with a variety of contractors, ranging from central or local government to smaller surveying companies or even financial businesses and auction houses.

You will be carrying out a lot of complex technical tasks which require excellent concentration and can be quite tiring.

Future prospects

You could progress to become a consultant, a partner in a firm or even move into related sectors such as town planning or chartered surveying with the right qualifications. Self-employment is also an option.

Advantages/disadvantages

Job satisfaction is likely to be high as you will provide invaluable support on a number of important projects.

There is the opportunity to become self-employed or work overseas.

Earning potential is not as high as in some other roles in surveying and hours can be long and unpredictable at busy times.

Money guide

Salaries start from £18,000 to £22,000 per year.

With experience, you can earn £30,000 and more.

Salaries are generally higher in London.

Related opportunities

- Civil/Construction Engineer/Civil Engineering Technician p69
- Construction Supervisor/Manager p74
- Quantity Surveyor p100

Further information

Chartered Association of Building Engineers
www.cbuilde.com

Chartered Surveyors Training Trust
www.cstt.org.uk

Royal Institution of Chartered Surveyors
www.rics.org

THATCHER

ENTRY LEVEL 1

Qualifications and courses

There are no set entry requirements for this profession, however, it may help to have GCSEs/National 5s (A*–E/A–E) in English, Maths and IT. The BTEC Diploma/Certificate in Construction and the Built Environment offered by some schools and colleges may also be relevant to the skills of a thatcher.

There are no formal apprenticeship schemes for thatching, therefore it is recommended that you contact experienced senior thatchers or thatching companies to try and secure a training or apprentice role. In order to make the necessary contacts within the industry, you may find it useful to seek the help of the National Society of Master Thatchers, the National Council of Master Thatchers Associations or the Thatch Advice Centre. The National Society of Master Thatchers in particular offers a membership scheme, training courses and advice on technical issues, that could help you develop your career, ensure your skills are up to date and ultimately, enhance your career progression.

As a trainee thatcher you may be able to apply for the New Entrants Training Scheme, which takes 2 years to complete both on the job and at Knuston Hall in Northamptonshire. On completion you will gain an NVQ in Roofing Occupations (Thatching). This scheme is run by Herefordshire and Ludlow College.

An NVQ in Roofing Occupations (Thatching) at Level 2 or 3 familiarises candidates with health and safety procedures and equips candidates with the skills and specialist knowledge necessary to prepare and construct roofs and thatching materials.

The Traditional Building Skills Bursary Scheme seeks to address skill shortages in traditional crafts by offering bursaries and work experience placements for eligible applicants.

What the work involves

Thatching is the covering of roofs with plant stems such as water reed, combed wheat reed and long straw. Your tasks will include thatching new roofs and repairing or re-thatching existing thatched roofs.

Your work will involve using many different tools, including mallets, hooks, needles, knives and shears.

As thatchers work outside all year round, your hours will differ depending on the season.

Type of person suited to this work

You need to have good practical skills to use the specialised equipment and to develop an expertise in the craft. You must be physically fit so that you can climb ladders and scaffolding whilst carrying thatching materials. You will need to be comfortable working at heights.

It is important to be able to measure roofs accurately in order to calculate the required amount of thatching material so strong numerical skills are required.

Working conditions

You will work outdoors on roofs in rural locations in most weather conditions. The work can be dusty, which can be difficult if you suffer from certain allergies.

It is important that you follow health and safety procedures closely when working on roofs.

Your working hours are likely to vary according to when the work is available. This can be seasonal work, meaning you will be busiest during the spring and summer months when the weather is best.

Future prospects

There are approximately 500 thatcher businesses in the UK and, as about half of all thatched buildings need to be re-roofed every 15–20 years, there is a steady demand for thatching work. Conservation regulations do not allow owners of thatched properties to replace their roofs with any other material, therefore the number of thatched buildings requiring repair/replacement remains reasonably stable.

There is fierce competition for training vacancies and some thatchers have another job to supplement their income. Not all areas of the UK have thatched buildings so you may find you will need to relocate to an area where the skills are more in demand, ie in rural areas.

Your work opportunities are likely to be on a self-employed basis. It can take a number of years to become highly skilled.

Advantages/disadvantages

It is rewarding to practise an ancient craft and create thatched roofs that are both functional and decorative.

The job involves being active and working outdoors.

Working at heights may be demanding for some people and potentially dangerous.

You may need a second job to supplement your earnings.

Money guide

The starting salary for a qualified thatcher ranges between £13,000 and £16,000.

With experience, your salary is likely to rise to £17,000–£22,000 a year.

Self-employed thatchers who have established a good reputation with their clients can achieve around £35,000.

Related opportunities

- Roofer p102
- Stonemason p108

Further information

Lantra
www.lantra.co.uk

National Heritage Training Group
www.the-nhtg.org.uk

Thatching Advisory Services
www.thatchingadvisoryservices.co.uk

THERMAL INSULATION ENGINEER

ENTRY LEVEL 1

Qualifications and courses

There are no formal entry requirements for this profession and a common route of entry is through a 3-year Thermal Insulation Apprenticeship accredited by the Insulation and Environmental Training Agency (IETA). You will have to pass an entry test assessing your ability to work at heights and a medical screening, after which you will undertake on-the-job training by experienced professionals and a period of off-the-job instruction at college.

Apprentices will work towards an NVQ/SVQ Level 2 in Thermal Insulation Engineering, complete a Level 2 Certificate in Thermal Insulation and a course in Employment Rights and Responsibilities.

Once employed, you may opt to complete short training courses offered by the Asbestos Control and Abatement Division (ACAD) of IETA if you are an engineer working closely with asbestos.

Many employers on construction sites require workers to have a Construction Skills Certification Scheme (CSCS) card and a CCNSG Safety Passport. This demonstrates that the holder has health and safety training and is competent working on-site. You will need to have gained or be working towards completing an NVQ in order to be granted a CSCS card. If you are working without qualifications, the On-site Assessment Workshop or Experienced Worker Practical Assessment schemes will help you gain the qualifications required.

What the work involves

You will use various types of insulation to either prevent heat loss or keep heat out within different types of products and equipment, such as boilers, pipework, refrigeration or air conditioning. The types of insulation you will use will be dependent on the actual project but could involve silicate or foam.

You will measure, cut and shape insulating materials to fit around pipes, boilers and duct work. Once the item is insulated, you will cover it using sheet metal or another cladding material.

You will assess clients' needs and advise them on the best plan to solve their insulation problem.

Type of person suited to this work

You may be exposed to some potentially dangerous materials, so you must follow health and safety regulations carefully.

You should be able to understand instructions, have a practical approach to your work and enjoy using manual skills, particularly for cutting and fitting materials. Mathematical skills are useful for measuring and working out quantities.

Much of the work involves strenuous lifting, balancing and climbing up scaffolding, so you will have to be physically fit, as well as able to work within confined spaces and at height.

The ability to work in a team and get on with other people will be important as you will often work alongside other professionals from the construction and engineering industries.

Working conditions

You could be working indoors or outside at heights, in places that are cramped or difficult to access.

You may be exposed to harmful substances and be working in dusty and dirty environments, so you will wear protective clothing, such as goggles and sometimes a face mask.

You will normally work a standard 38-hour week, but overtime and evening or weekend work might be required. Travelling around the country to visit different sites and projects may be necessary.

Future prospects

There is currently a growth in the demand for qualified thermal insulation engineers given the increasing focus on environmental conservation.

After gaining training and experience, you could find a job within building, building service engineering or specialised energy conservation companies or you could move into related areas such as heating and ventilation engineering or refrigeration.

Within the larger companies it might be possible to progress into technical, supervisory or managerial posts such as a site safety officer or contracts manager.

Advantages/disadvantages

You will be working alongside people from different industries. Opportunities are good and overseas work may be possible.

You will need many different skills to complete one job.

You may need to work away from home which could be difficult if you have family commitments.

Money guide

Apprentices usually earn £10,000–£16,000 a year, depending on the stage of training.

With qualifications this rises to £17,000–£22,000.

Senior thermal insulation engineers can earn up to £30,000.

Contract work is common and allowances could be made for working away from home.

Related opportunities

- Damp Proofer p75
- Gas Network Engineer p210
- Heating and Ventilation Engineer p88

Further information

Construction Industry Training Board (CITB)
www.citb.co.uk

Thermal Insulation Contractors Association
www.tica-acad.co.uk

TOWN PLANNER/PLANNING TECHNICIAN

ENTRY LEVEL 5

Qualifications and courses

Town planner

You will need to have a Royal Town Planning Institute (RTPI) accredited qualification such as a degree or a postgraduate qualification. For degree entry you will need at least 2 A levels/3 H grades. For entry to a postgraduate course, a degree in a related subject such as geography, architecture or urban studies is required. To ensure chartered status, it is recommended that your qualifications be completed on a combined level of study, meaning both spatial planning and a specialist area of planning are covered.

Chartered (MRTPI) membership of the RTPI is available after completion of an accredited qualification and 2 years' relevant work experience.

Continuing professional development (CPD) forms an essential part of advancement in your career. You will be expected to undertake relevant courses and maintain an annual professional development plan.

Town planning technician

There are no set qualifications, but at least 4 GCSEs/ National 5s (A*–C/A–C) including English and Maths, are usually required. Many entrants also have A levels/ H grades, Foundation degrees or other relevant qualifications, such as a Scottish Group Award (SGA) in Construction, a HND in Planning or a graphic design or IT qualification. You may also find having relevant work experience, preferably in a planning office, advantageous when seeking employment.

Planning technicians are trained on the job by experienced professionals whilst studying part time or via distance learning for an NVQ/SVQ in Town Planning Support (Level 3–4).

Technical Membership (TechRTPI) of the Royal Town Planning Institute (RTPI) requires a recognised qualification at NVQ Level 3 or higher and 2 years' work experience.

What the work involves

Town planner

You will manage and develop urban or rural areas to best serve the population. When deciding how to use the land you will take into account commercial, social, environmental and heritage needs.

Town planning technician

You will support the work of town planners.

You will carry out surveys, map areas, record information, analyse and present reports and provide advice on planning permission.

Type of person suited to this work

You will need excellent communication skills as you will need to explain your ideas clearly and produce comprehensive written reports.

You must be organised with good research, problem solving and analytical skills to investigate the potential effects of different proposals for land use.

Specialist skills required include competency in graphic design, desktop publishing and familiarity with computer-aided design (CAD), geographical information systems (GIS) and cartography.

Working conditions

Regular office hours are likely, although you may sometimes need to attend meetings in the evening.

Most town planners are based in offices but often go out on-site visits. A driving licence might be necessary.

Future prospects

There is a huge demand for more qualified planners in the UK and overseas.

Most employers are local authorities and planning consultancies, but opportunities also exist within central government, construction companies and environmental organisations.

With experience and chartered status, you may be promoted to senior or county planning officer or you could specialise in areas such as urban design or conservation. Alternatively, you could move into related careers such as recreation management, market research or property development.

Advantages/disadvantages

It is satisfying to deal with public problems and to improve the environment in which people live and work.

It can be frustrating to compromise on planning initiatives.

Dealing with angry or upset members of the public can be difficult.

Money guide

Newly graduated town planners could earn between £16,000 and £28,000. This will be more if you are a registered member of the Royal Town Planning Institute (RTPI).

Senior planners can earn up to £34,000, with extra responsibilities can earn £41,000.

Chief planning officers, heads of department and company directors can earn between £55,000 and £80,000.

Technicians can start on £14,000 a year and earn up to £28,000 with experience and supervisory experience.

Related opportunities

- Land/Geomatic Surveyor p92
- Planning and Development Surveyor p96
- Quantity Surveyor p100

Further information

Royal Town Planning Institute
www.rtpi.org.uk

WALL/FLOOR TILER

ENTRY LEVEL 2

Qualifications and courses

A common route of entry into this industry is to complete an apprenticeship with a building or tiling firm. There are no specific qualifications required, although GCSEs/National 5s (A*–E/A–E) in subjects such as maths, technology or English may be required by some employers and are helpful when dealing with calculations, measurements and theory. Similar subjects or equivalent vocational qualifications such as the BTEC Introductory Certificate/Diploma in Construction may also be useful in introducing candidates to the basic skills required in the industry.

An apprenticeship is a possible route into this career, where you will receive on-the-job training and working towards industry recognised qualifications. These qualifications include an NVQ/SVQ in Wall and Floor Tiling at Levels 2 and 3. Apprenticeships are available to those aged 16–24 and may involve a skills learning exercise prior to your acceptance. You will have to secure employment prior to starting an apprenticeship and employers often value people with some on-site experience. You might first, therefore, gain experience as a labourer before applying for a formal training scheme.

It is becoming increasingly necessary to have a Construction Skills Certification Scheme (CSCS) card to work in construction as proof of your competency. You must have gained or be working towards an NVQ in order to be granted one.

What the work involves

You will fit tiles in various locations, from bathrooms and kitchens to hospitals and swimming pools. You may work with many kinds of tile including ceramic, stone, glass, terracotta, granite, marble and mosaic.

First you will set out (known as marking) an area by calculating the amount of tile and adhesive needed. You will then use bench-mounted or hand tools to cut the tiles to the correct size and shape.

You will level the surface with plaster, cement or sand, fix the tiles in the correct position and then fill in the gaps with grout.

Type of person suited to this work

Maths skills are essential as you will need to measure and calculate how much material you will need. You must work carefully and accurately. It is important to match colours and patterns, so a flair for design is useful.

You need to be physically fit for carrying the materials and for working on your hands and knees.

You need to be able to work on your own initiative as well as in a team. You should be presentable and pleasant when dealing with customers.

Working conditions

You will work mainly indoors in a variety of locations, ranging from a client's home to offices, factories and construction sites. A driving licence might be useful.

You may work a normal working week, but you may also need to work evenings or weekends so that you can tile walls and floors without disrupting businesses.

As you will use special cutting tools and adhesives you will need to be aware of health and safety procedures.

Future prospects

Work is available with specialist tiling companies and building contractors, or you may choose to become self-employed, providing services to individuals or sub-contracting for organisations. Demand for tilers very much depends on the current state of the economy.

It is possible to specialise in one type of tiling, for example flooring tiles, mosaic work or bathrooms.

With experience and further training, you may be able to progress into technical, supervisory or managerial positions. You could even move into college instruction.

Advantages/disadvantages

You will be on your hands and knees, sometimes working in dusty, dirty or cramped conditions.

The work is varied and you can achieve spectacular results using coloured and textured tiles to decorate walls and floors.

Money guide

Salaries for trainee tilers can be up to £14,000 a year.

With experience, this can rise to £17,000–£23,000.

Tilers with supervisory duties can earn between £25,000 and £30,000.

Overtime is often available, and on some projects there are bonuses based on outputs, which can lead to higher earnings.

Related opportunities

- Building Technician p64
- Construction Operative p72
- Floor Layer/Finisher p84

Further information

Construction Industry Training Board (CITB)
www.citb.co.uk

The Tile Association
www.tiles.org.uk

WASTEWATER TREATMENT PLANT OPERATOR

ENTRY LEVEL 1

Qualifications and courses

There are no formal academic qualifications required to become a wastewater treatment plant operator. Some companies, however, do seek employees with a minimum of 4 GCSEs/National 5s (A*–E/A–E) in Maths, English and a science or technology subject. The BTEC Diploma in Engineering or Environmental and Land-based Studies may also be relevant for this type of work.

The most common form of entry into the industry is by a water industry apprenticeship. The minimum age for apprentices is generally 18 and applicants will normally be required to pass a medical examination prior to acceptance. Previous work experience on a building site or within plant maintenance may be advantageous, not only in introducing you to the basics of the industry but in your bid to secure an employer to sponsor your training.

As an apprentice, you will combine on-the-job training from experienced professionals with a series of day or block release instruction at a college or training centre where you will work towards achieving an industry recognised qualification. Courses include the NVQ/SVQ Level 2 in Operating a Process Plant (Water/Waste Water/Sludge), the City & Guilds Level 2 Certificate in Water Sector Competent Operators or Water Engineering.

To further your career, you may also choose to pursue an HNC/HND or degree which will qualify you for more senior roles.

In order to work as an operator, employers may require you to register with an appropriate safety passport scheme, eg the Energy and Utilities Skills Register (EUSR).

What the work involves

Water treatment plant operators monitor wastewater as it goes through various treatment processes which remove harmful substances. They ensure that treated water is returned to the water cycle and that waste is removed and destroyed as appropriate.

You will be responsible for the operation and maintenance of the plant, ensuring that septic tanks, filters and screens are disinfected, checking water samples, and adding treatment micro-organisms and chemicals to the water when necessary.

You will conduct tests on samples, take readings from monitors and adjust treatment equipment as necessary. You will work with a team composed of a supervisor, senior technicians, engineers and a manager.

Type of person suited to this work

You need to have a passion for the environment, science and technology. You also need to be happy to work with new technology which you will use on a daily basis.

You must be able to communicate effectively and work well in a team. You will have to follow health and safety regulations. It is important that you are fit and active as you may be doing practical, strenuous work at times, such as cleaning and maintenance.

You must be organised and methodical as you will be testing samples to ensure that harmful substances are removed from the water cycle.

Working conditions

You will work approximately 37 hours a week. Overtime may be possible but part-time work is rare. You will probably have to work shifts as water treatment plants operate 24 hours a day. You may have to join a call-out rota to cover nights and weekends.

You will be based indoors in control rooms but some of your work will involve being outside in all weather conditions. You may also have to carry out work at heights or in confined spaces.

Protective clothing is provided. This may include a breathing apparatus, and should be worn to prevent contact with harmful substances.

Future prospects

After gaining experience, you could progress to a role as a supervisor and from there, on to roles as an inspector, a superintendent or a plant manager. You may also choose to move into a related area such as treatment plant design.

Advantages/disadvantages

You may find opportunities to increase wages by taking extra shifts, going on stand-by and doing overtime.

Your working environment in the plant may be smelly and wet.

You may sometimes be called into work if there is an emergency situation.

Money guide

Your salary as a trainee can start at around £12,000 a year.

With experience and qualifications you can earn between £18,000 and £25,000.

Supervisors and department leaders can earn between £25,000 and £32,000.

Overtime and extensive shift work can greatly increase salary.

Related opportunities

- Brewery Worker p199
- Energy Engineer p205
- Water/Sewerage Network Operative p116

Further information

City & Guilds
www.cityandguilds.com

Energy & Utility Skills
www.euskills.co.uk

Water UK
www.water.org.uk

WATER/SEWERAGE NETWORK OPERATIVE

ENTRY LEVEL 2

Qualifications and courses

There are no formal academic requirements needed to become a water/sewerage network operative but a number of GCSEs/National 5s (A*–C/A–C) including Maths, English, a science or technology may be useful in supporting your search for employment as is a history of relevant work experience, in site maintenance for example. Equivalent vocational qualifications such as the BTEC Diploma in Engineering may also be relevant to this line of work.

The most common route of entry is via an apprenticeship. Entrants combine on-the-job training from experienced professionals with a series of day or block release instruction at a training centre or college where you will work towards industry recognised qualifications. The Certification and Assessment Board for the Water Industry (CABWI) offers a range of relevant awards, including Level 2 Diplomas in Distribution Control and Operating Process Plant (Water) and Level 3 Diplomas in Leakage Control, Controlling Process Operations and Network Construction Operations.

An alternative route to an apprenticeship is work experience in a related area, such as road working, construction or plant machine operation.

Registration with an appropriate safety passport scheme, such as the Energy & Utilities Skills Register (EUSR), may be required by some employers for you to be able to work on-site. The passport acts as proof of competency to work on the water network.

A driving licence may be useful for some roles.

What the work involves

Water/sewerage network operatives lay, maintain and repair the pipework that carries drinking water, waste water and sewage.

Your tasks might include digging trenches in roads and relaying them afterwards, putting up barriers and warning signs, laying pipes, repairing leaks, clearing blockages and installing water meters.

You will use a range of tools such as welding equipment to join pipes together and machinery such as mechanical diggers.

Type of person suited to this work

You must have good practical skills and be mechanically minded so that you can use tools, equipment and machinery effectively. You must be able to follow health and safety regulations as working on-site can be dangerous. You will have to follow plans and instructions accurately, so that systems are installed correctly and safely.

You must be fit and active for bending, kneeling and carrying materials and equipment.

You will have to deal with complaints from the public, who might be upset that their water services are disrupted.

You must also be able to work in a team with other water/sewerage network operatives.

Working conditions

You will work outdoors in all weather conditions. The work can be dusty, dirty and wet, as well as smelly.

You will need to follow strict health, safety and hygiene regulations, which may include wearing a breathing apparatus, a safety helmet, boots and gloves.

You may work normal working hours or shifts, but the particular hours you work will vary according to the needs of the job and the hours of daylight available. You may be on-call 24/7 in case of the need for emergency repairs.

Future prospects

There is currently a strong demand for water/sewerage network operatives because the privatised water companies, who manage water supply and sewerage disposal, are investing money in developing their systems. The industry currently maintains an ongoing system of construction, operation and maintenance of water and waste water infrastructure, thus there is a steady supply of jobs available.

You can find work with water companies and construction firms across the UK. After gaining experience, you could progress to a role as a team leader or in senior management and with further training, as an engineering technician or incorporated/chartered water engineer.

You could move into related areas such as water distribution inspection work.

Advantages/disadvantages

The work can be physically demanding and it can get smelly if you are working on sewerage systems.

Helping to provide people with an essential service can be rewarding.

Money guide

Apprentices earn around £12,000 a year.

Once qualified, this can rise to between £17,000 and £25,000.

Your salary can rise with overtime and shift allowances.

Related opportunities

- Construction Operative p72
- Gas Network Engineer p210
- Plumber p98

Further information

Energy & Utility Skills
www.euskills.co.uk

Water UK
www.water.org.uk

WINDOW FITTER

ENTRY LEVEL 1

Qualifications and courses

There are no formal entry requirements but you might find employers value candidates with some GCSEs/National 5s in subjects such as English, technology and, particularly, maths, as calculations and measuring are important aspects of your job. Equivalent qualifications, such as a BTEC Certificate/Diploma in Construction, may introduce you to some of the basic skills required in the industry.

Previous experience within related areas of the field, in carpentry or joinery for example, may be helpful if you decide to seek entry-level employment as a fitter's 'mate' or labourer.

The most common route of entry, however, is via an apprenticeship with a glazing company. An apprenticeship will typically involve a combination of on-the-job training from experienced professionals and a series of day or block release instruction at a college or training centre in order for you to work towards industry recognised qualifications. Applicants normally need GCSEs/National 5s (A*–E/A–E), or an equivalent qualification and may be required to pass an aptitude test prior to entry.

Whilst you train, you will have the opportunity to work towards gaining vocational qualifications such as NVQs/SVQs in either Fenestration Installation (Level 2–3) or Fire Resistant Glazing and Glazing Installation (Level 2–3). Your training will cover areas such as the removal and fitting of window frames, health and safety, customer relations and relevant paperwork.

The Glass Qualifications Authority offer many NVQs related to the manufacture and installation of glass and other products.

Many employers require their staff to hold a Construction Skills Certification Scheme (CSCS) card as proof of one's competency working on-site. You normally have to be working towards or have gained an NVQ in order to be granted one.

A driving licence may also be required in order for you to travel between clients.

What the work involves

Window fitters install windows into new and existing buildings.

You will use hand and power tools to take out any old windows and fit new ones. You will work with materials such as glass, plastic and wood.

Once you have fixed a new window into the allocated space, you will need to give it a weatherproof seal. Your job may also involve fitting doors, conservatories and weatherboarding.

Type of person suited to this work

You will need good practical hand skills for using tools and you will need to be physically fit as you will be lifting and carrying windows. Maths skills are essential in order to make accurate calculations and fit frames properly.

You should be safety conscious and comfortable working on ladders.

You may work on your own for some jobs, but you will often work with one other window fitter, or in a small team so you must be able to work with others. You should also be able to get on with customers because you will spend a lot of time on their premises.

Working conditions

You will work indoors and outdoors in a variety of locations, and you will be working in most weather conditions.

You will need to pay attention to health and safety, especially when working with glass, and be happy clearing up after your work has finished.

You are likely to work normal working hours during the week, but overtime may be available at weekends.

Future prospects

Work is available throughout the UK. There is an increasing demand for double-glazed windows and for conservatories so job prospects are good.

You may find opportunities for work within large national firms or smaller local companies and you could go on to specialise in fire-proof glazing or film application (applying film to glass for privacy). There are also openings within the sales and marketing sides of the industry.

After gaining sufficient experience, you may progress to team leader or supervisory positions or move into window surveying or estimating. You may even opt to become self-employed and run your own window-fitting business.

Advantages/disadvantages

Lifting and carrying windows and working at heights is physically demanding.

It is satisfying to make customers happy by improving the appearance, value and function of their buildings by installing and repairing windows.

Money guide

As a trainee, you can expect a salary of £14,000.

Once qualified, your salary will increase to around £16,000 and £25,000 a year, depending on your experience.

Overtime and shift allowances may increase your earnings. Self-employed fitters negotiate their own rates.

Related opportunities

- Carpenter/Joiner p65
- Ceiling Fixer p67
- Glazier p87

Further information

Glass and Glazing Federation
www.ggf.co.uk

Proskills UK
www.proskills.co.uk

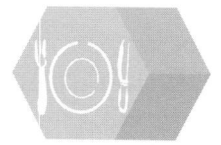

Catering and Hospitality

Working in this sector, you will meet a wide variety of people and probably need to be a very strong team player. Workers in the sector thrive on providing an impeccable service and ensuring customers are completely satisfied and are given a wonderful experience whether that is in a restaurant, hotel or bar.

The jobs featured in this section are listed below. For similar jobs to the ones in this section why not have a look at *Leisure, Sport and Tourism* starting on page 357 and *Retail, Sales, and Customer Services* from page 449.

BAR MANAGER/LICENSEE/ PUBLICAN

ENTRY LEVEL 1

Qualifications and courses

There are no formal entry requirements, although a degree or HND in subjects such as business and hospitality or hospitality management may help you progress faster.

There are several possible entry routes. You could start as a bar person and train on the job to progress to a supervisory or management position. Alternatively, school leavers may be able to enter through an Apprenticeship in Hospitality and Catering (Food and Beverage Services).

Some larger companies have graduate training schemes. You would enter as an assistant manager and train on the job before taking the licensing exams. There are no specific degree subjects required but you must have previous customer service experience in a pub, bar or food establishment, preferably at supervisory level.

To be a bar manager/publican you will need a personal licence, for which you will need to be at least 18 years old and have an accredited licensing qualification from the British Institute of Innkeepers Awarding Body (BIIAB). In England and Wales this means passing the Level 2 Award for Personal Licence Holders. In Scotland it's the Scottish Certificate for Personal Licence Holders. You will also need an in-date Disclosure and Barring Service (DBS) check.

What the work involves

Your duties will include the recruitment, training and management of staff. You will also deal with the accounts, stock replenishment, maintaining links with suppliers, and business development.

You will need to keep up to date with any changes to licensing laws and other legal requirements such as health and safety or fire safety regulations, and ensure that your customers and staff adhere to them.

In addition, you will demonstrate a high level of customer service to ensure client satisfaction.

Type of person suited to this work

It is essential to have excellent communication skills and to enjoy meeting and speaking to people of all ages. A confident, professional attitude is needed to deal with customer or supplier problems.

Being physically fit and able to stay on your feet all day is helpful. You should be practical, flexible and good at multi-tasking.

Good numeracy skills are expected as you will be managing cash on a daily basis. You should keep up to date with legal requirements, and ensure that those that affect you are enforced within your establishment.

Working conditions

Although pubs, clubs and bars can remain open for 24 hours a day, most only extend their hours at weekends or for special events.

You will work long hours in an environment which can be busy, noisy and hot. You will be required to stand for lengthy periods and lift and carry heavy items such as barrels.

You may have to deal with demanding or difficult customers who are intoxicated. Changes to smoking legislation have resulted in the expectation of the provision of outside facilities, where problems are more likely to occur.

Future prospects

The number of pubs has been gradually decreasing for some time now, with approximately 2 closing every day, so the availability of publican jobs has been decreasing as well. However, recent changes to duty on alcohol could provide the industry with a much needed boost. There has been a reported boost in the number of managerial roles available in the sector already.

Bar manager jobs at other types of establishments, such as bars, hotels, high street chains, restaurants and clubs, are still available but may have been affected by the industry only having had slight growth in recent years.

Managers could progress to larger or different types of establishments, become area managers for a chain, open their own premises or move into a different area of hospitality.

Advantages/disadvantages

The hours will be long and irregular which might affect your personal life.

You will have to deal with drunk customers, who may be difficult or aggressive, on a fairly regular basis.

The working atmosphere is informal and enjoyable.

You may have the opportunity to live on the pub premises which can reduce your living expenses.

Money guide

Assistant managers can expect a starting salary in the region of £15,000 to £20,000 per year. Once you reach manager or licensee level, you could earn £25,000 to £35,000.

Those who work in a very successful or large establishment, or become area managers for a pub company, can achieve earnings of £50,000 or more.

Earnings vary according to the type, size and location of the premises you work in. Benefits can include pension schemes, health insurance and cheap or free accommodation.

Related opportunities

- Brewery Worker p199
- Hotel Manager p126
- Waiting Staff p132

Further information

British Beer and Pub Association
www.beerandpub.com

Wine & Spirit Education Trust
www.wset.co.uk

CATERING/RESTAURANT MANAGER/ MAÎTRE D'HÔTEL

ENTRY LEVEL 1

Qualifications and courses

There are no formal entry requirements for this profession. School leavers could start as a kitchen assistant, waiter/waitress or chef and gradually progress to management level. Studying for relevant qualifications, such as NVQs and diplomas in hospitality and catering, could help you progress.

Many hotel and restaurant chains offer training schemes. It may be possible to join a scheme with A levels/H grades or equivalent but the usual requirement is a degree or HNC/HND in a relevant subject, such as hospitality management, hospitality and catering, hotel management or international hospitality management. The minimum requirements for degree entry are usually 5 GCSEs/National 5s (A*–C/A–C) and 2 A levels or 3 H grades.

Relevant work experience is important, for example through part-time or seasonal work or an Apprenticeship in Hospitality.

What the work involves

You will manage, train and employ staff in a kitchen or restaurant. A maître d'hôtel is specifically responsible for running a hotel restaurant.

Part of your work will involve planning menus, checking stocks of food and drink and ordering fresh supplies when needed. You will be expected to handle paperwork, manage budgets and organise staff rotas.

You will be responsible for the health and safety of both your staff and customers.

Type of person suited to this work

You will be dealing with kitchen staff, suppliers and other business professionals so you must be confident and have excellent communication skills. It is essential to provide good customer service at all times.

As you will be involved in an industry centred on preparing food for the public, you will be required to follow and keep up to date with health and safety laws. You will also need an interest in service delivery and food.

Good management skills, including an understanding of the different roles undertaken by your staff, are essential. Exceptional organisational abilities and good numeracy skills are also important.

Working conditions

Much of your time will be spent in your kitchen or restaurant, which can get very hot and busy. Expect to be on your feet for long periods of time.

You might wear a uniform or protective clothing and regularly work unsocial hours. It is important to follow high standards of food safety and hygiene.

It is possible to work as a catering manager in the armed forces, in which case you might find yourself working in challenging environments, anywhere in the world, in a variety of climates.

Future prospects

Some restaurant/catering managers move on to running their own businesses, either a restaurant or private contract catering company. Managers of single restaurants may progress to area manager for a particular chain.

There are opportunities to work abroad, possibly within the same company. Some managers may also move into hotel or leisure management.

Advantages/disadvantages

You will be working in a fun and lively atmosphere and you might have the chance to organise the catering for special events such as weddings or parties.

This can be a very busy job where you will be doing several tasks at the same time.

Hours are long and will include weekend or evening work.

Money guide

Salaries vary significantly depending on the type of establishment you work in. The highest salaries are in London and the south of England.

As the manager of a casual dining restaurant, you could earn between £18,000 and £30,000 a year.

In a fine dining establishment, your salary could be between £20,000 and £40,000.

Senior managers could make up to £60,000 a year.

Related opportunities

- Events and Exhibition Organiser p384
- Food Safety Officer p125
- Kitchen Assistant/Supervisor p131

Further information

Institute of Hospitality
www.instituteofhospitality.org

People 1st
www.people1st.co.uk

CELLAR TECHNICIAN ENTRY LEVEL 2

Qualifications and courses

There are no required qualifications to become a trainee cellar technician, although some employers prefer you to have GCSEs/National 5s (A*–C/A–C) in Maths, a science or technology subjects, or a BTEC, NVQ or City & Guilds qualification in engineering.

Experience working in a bar is useful and many cellar technicians work their way up from bar staff level. Cask Marque offers a 1-day course in Cellar Management Training for those already employed in the sector. Experience in engineering or electrical work is also an advantage.

Employers provide training that covers areas such as health and safety, customer care, refrigeration, checking systems and working with equipment. They may also expect you to study for a British Institute of Innkeeping Awarding Body (BIIAB) Certificate in Cellar Service, Installation and Maintenance (Level 2). This involves classroom and on-the-job training while candidates study for 5 units.

Once you have acquired the BIIAB certificate, you could take other qualifications such as an NVQ/SVQ Level 2 or 3 in Drinks Dispense Systems.

What the work involves

You will set up and maintain the systems that keep alcoholic and soft drinks at a consistent quality in pubs, hotels and other sites.

Visiting a range of locations, you will install equipment such as high-pressure gas systems, and check that they are compatible with existing water, electricity supply or drainage systems.

You will undertake regular maintenance checks to make sure that everything works properly, train the staff in how to operate it and deal with any problems.

Type of person suited to this work

You will need good practical skills and the confidence to work and operate different systems quickly and efficiently.

As you will be handling heavy equipment, a good level of physical fitness is helpful.

Good communication skills are useful, as is a confidence in your ability to do the job well.

As you will be providing a service on behalf of your company for lots of different licensed premises you will need to have excellent customer care skills.

Working conditions

You will spend lots of time driving from site to site.

Some of your work will be attending emergency call-outs which could include evenings and weekends. The extended pub opening hours might mean this includes 24-hour call-out duties.

You will work in dark, cramped conditions using specialist tools and equipment such as electrical testing devices.

Future prospects

There is a steady demand for experienced cellar technicians.

The main employers are breweries, drink-dispensing equipment manufacturers and soft drinks manufacturers.

Many applicants come from the licensed trade who have watched the job and become interested. It is therefore useful to have pub experience or relevant qualifications before applying.

With experience you can apply for senior/managerial posts or move into other areas of the licensed or food and drink sector such as sales.

Advantages/disadvantages

This job combines meeting and training people with lots of practical work.

You might have to travel long distances to reach customers.

You might work in uncomfortable conditions, for example when fitting a new dispensing system in a cellar.

Money guide

Starting salaries for cellar technicians range from £15,000 to £18,000 per year.

With experience, earnings can increase to around £20,000 to £30,000.

The highest salary for a cellar technician is about £35,000.

You may be paid overtime for emergency call-out duties or for working evenings/weekends.

Related opportunities

- Bar Manager/Licensee/Publican p120
- Brewery Worker p199
- Plumber p98

Further information

British Soft Drinks Association
www.britishsoftdrinks.com

People 1st
www.people1st.co.uk

CHEF/SOUS CHEF

ENTRY LEVEL 1

Qualifications and courses

Academic qualifications are not essential to enter this profession as a trainee (commis) chef, although some employers prefer you to have a good general standard of education and possibly qualifications in hospitality or catering. Most training is on the job and you will be taught by an experienced chef whilst you work in the kitchen. It is possible to work your way up to chef level with enough experience.

There are a number of qualifications available that could give you an advantage, for example GCSEs in Hospitality and Catering, a City & Guilds Diploma in Professional Cookery (Levels 1–3) or an NVQ Diploma in Professional Cookery (Levels 2 and 3). Further qualifications are also available, including degrees, Foundation degrees and HNC/HNDs in Professional Culinary Arts and Culinary Arts Management.

Intermediate and advanced apprenticeships may be available.

Many employers will require you to have health and safety and/or food hygiene certificates so it would be useful to study for these while training as a chef.

What the work involves

Chefs and sous chefs cook for restaurants, cafés, bars, cruise ships and catering firms. Some also work for specialist food companies, helping to create new products. You will coordinate kitchen activities and supervise the preparation of food by your team of kitchen staff.

Commis chefs are trainee chefs. Sous chefs are second-in-command of the kitchen. They will be required to recruit and train kitchen staff.

Planning new menus and dishes, checking stocks of food and drink and dealing with suppliers are also included in the sous chef role.

Type of person suited to this work

Kitchens can be hot and hectic environments, therefore you need to be able to remain calm under pressure.

Good teamwork, communication and multi-tasking skills are important to ensure the smooth running of the operation. As you are responsible for the health and safety of your team, you must also be vigilant at all times.

You should have excellent cooking skills, be very creative and have a passion for food. This role would suit someone who is keen to try out new things and set trends. Good numeracy skills are also required to manage budgets and stock levels.

Working conditions

Most of your work will be in a kitchen which will be hot, busy and noisy. You will be required to use equipment that can be dangerous if not used correctly.

As you will be preparing food, you will need to wear protective clothing and pay attention to health and hygiene.

Hours are typically 40 per week in a shift pattern and include evenings and weekends. Part-time work can be found.

Future prospects

There is currently a shortage of qualified chefs in many areas of the UK.

Starting as a commis chef you will help in different sections of the kitchen. With experience you can progress to sous chef, where you act as deputy to the chef and manage your own section, and then to head chef.

Gaining significant experience may allow you to open your own business or even become a lecturer.

Advantages/disadvantages

Preparing high-quality food that your customers enjoy is very rewarding.

You will have the opportunity to combine creativity with practical skills.

You will work long, unsocial hours when you will be on your feet in a hot and busy environment.

Money guide

A commis chef may earn around £13,000 per year.

Section chefs (chef de partie) earn an average of £16,000.

Sous chefs usually earn £30,000.

A head or executive chef could earn anything from £40,000 to £50,000, depending on their skills and the style of hotel or restaurant.

Salaries vary significantly depending upon the size, reputation and location of the restaurant, with the highest salaries in London and the south-east of England.

Related opportunities

- Catering/Restaurant Manager/Maître d'Hôtel p121
- Food Safety Officer p125
- Kitchen Assistant/Supervisor p131

Further information

Institute of Hospitality
www.instituteofhospitality.org

People 1st
www.people1st.co.uk

CONCIERGE

ENTRY LEVEL 1

Qualifications and courses

There are no required academic qualifications for this profession, however useful qualifications may include the BTEC Award in Principles of Customer Service in Hospitality, Leisure, Travel and Tourism (Level 2) or an NVQ/SVQ in either Hospitality and Catering (Level 2) or Multi-skilled Hospitality Service (Level 2). The ability to speak a foreign language would also be very beneficial.

You will usually start in a front-of-house role, such as a porter, bellboy or receptionist, and progress to the role of concierge with experience. You could train in-house or through an Apprenticeship in Hospitality.

You will learn and train as you work. This may include gaining knowledge of the establishment's policies and techniques in waiting and room service. It is also important that you have good knowledge of the local area.

Previous work experience in reception is recommended, particularly when applying for 4 or 5 star hotels.

What the work involves

Concierges work as part of the front-of-house team in a hotel, apartment block or corporate organisation. You will be responsible for greeting guests, assisting with their baggage, answering questions, giving advice or directions and generally making them feel as comfortable as possible.

If you work in a hotel you must keep up to date with events and functions in the hotel and you may be asked to book tickets or organise travel for guests.

You may manage a team of other concierges, reception or door staff. Some organisations may require you to undertake extra services such as shopping and pet walking/sitting.

Type of person suited to this work

As you will be the first point of contact for guests and visitors to the establishment, you should look presentable, enjoy meeting new people and thrive in a busy environment.

You must be polite, friendly, helpful and informative at all times. You should have an interest in the catering and hospitality industry.

You need to have a practical approach to problem solving and be able to remain calm. As you will be entrusted with important errands and messages, you must be responsible, reliable and trustworthy.

You should also have a certain level of strength and fitness to carry bags and work long shifts.

Working conditions

On average, you will work 40 hours a week. This will mainly be shifts of 12 hours and will include working at night, early mornings and weekends.

You may have a desk or an office where you will use the telephone or computer but you will spend the majority of your time on your feet in the reception area, meeting and helping guests or running errands within the establishment or around the local area. You may be required to lift heavy bags.

Your employer will usually provide you with a uniform.

Future prospects

The hospitality industry has had only very small growth in recent years, which could affect the number of positions available.

Establishments may have formal progression routes that could involve moving up from a position as a porter to deputy head concierge, head concierge and then up again to front office management positions.

You could transfer to another discipline within hospitality or even set up your own business.

There are international opportunities within certain establishments so you may be able to live abroad.

Advantages/disadvantages

You will have the opportunity to meet a variety of new people from different countries each day.

You will be responsible for a wide variety of guests or visitors and their requirements.

You may have to work long and unsociable hours.

Money guide

Your starting salary as a concierge can be around £12,000 per year. As you gain experience you can earn up to £20,000.

If you reach the position of head concierge in a 4 or 5 star establishment, you could achieve £25,000 or more.

Salaries can be boosted by tips, although if you are required to live in the hotel your salary may be reduced to cover accommodation and food costs.

Related opportunities

- Customer Services Assistant/Manager p456
- Personal Assistant p42
- Receptionist p45

Further information

Institute of Hospitality
www.instituteofhospitality.org

People 1st
www.people1st.co.uk

FOOD SAFETY OFFICER

ENTRY LEVEL 6

Qualifications and courses

To become a food safety officer you will first need to train as an environmental health officer. There are 2 routes you could take.

The first is an undergraduate or postgraduate degree in environmental health/science which has been accredited by the Chartered Institute of Environmental Health (CIEH) in England, Wales and Northern Ireland, or the Royal Environmental Health Institute of Scotland (REHIS) in Scotland.

Entry to a degree normally requires 2 A levels/3 H grades including a science subject, plus 5 GCSEs/National 5s (A*–C/A–C) including English, Maths and a science. Entry to a Master of Science (MSc) requires a degree in a relevant science or technology subject.

Before qualifying as an environmental health officer, graduates must complete an Experiential Learning Portfolio (ELP) by undergoing a period of work-based learning through a placement with an approved organisation and by passing professional exams.

The second route is to train as an environmental health technician, working your way up through a local council. This route requires a minimum of 4 GCSEs, including Maths, English or a science, relevant qualifications or previous experience. Your employer could offer you the chance to take a degree while you work.

CIEH also offers a wide range of food safety qualifications at Levels 1–4 which may be useful. These awards cover food safety issues within catering, manufacturing and retail.

Food safety officers in Scotland must meet the requirements of the Scottish Food Safety Officers' Registration Board. Candidates for the Higher Certificates in Food Premises Inspection and Food Standards Inspection must have a minimum of an HND in Food Science or Food Technology. Candidates undertake 6 months' structured practical training with a local authority and complete written assessments.

What the work involves

You will advise those working in catering/food premises by providing information on the safe presentation, preparation and storage of food for public consumption.

Your role will be to investigate outbreaks of food-related illnesses and implement hazard warnings in places such as butchers, retailers and restaurants.

You will enforce accurate food labelling. You will also advise schools and businesses on food regulations as well as nutritional awareness.

Type of person suited to this work

You need excellent communication skills as you will be advising and educating people on food safety and nutrition. You should be able to explain technical information in a simple and clear way. You must also be tactful when investigating food poisoning and other hazardous issues.

It's important to be analytical and methodical in your work. Good attention to detail is essential. You need to be able to juggle many different jobs at once and be a confident decision maker.

Working conditions

Although you will be office based, most of your time will involve travelling to businesses, following up complaints and giving advice. A driving licence is essential.

The places you investigate may be smelly and unpleasant at times. You will need to wear protective clothing such as masks, hair protection and boots. You will work normal office hours, but some evenings and weekends may be required.

Future prospects

You may be employed by a local authority or by a food company.

Outside of Scotland, most food safety officers begin as environmental health officers and specialise later. In Scotland, inspection and food hygiene is undertaken by registered food safety officers.

With experience you can progress to senior positions within food safety or return to other areas of environmental health. You could also set up your own consultancy.

Advantages/disadvantages

This job offers flexibility (with opportunities available for part-time work or job shares) and variety (as you will be visiting a range of different premises).

You have a chance to make a difference to public health.

Investigations can occasionally be stressful if you have to enforce regulations or close down a business.

You will sometimes have to visit dirty or unpleasant establishments.

Money guide

Starting salaries for environmental technicians are usually £17,500 to £22,000 per year.

Fully qualified officers can earn from £25,000 to £35,000. Food safety officers employed at a senior or managerial level can achieve up to £45,000.

Those employed by private companies earn more than workers in the public sector.

Related opportunities

- Environmental Health Practitioner/Officer p22
- Health and Safety Adviser p27
- Meat Hygiene Inspector p462

Further information

Chartered Institute of Environmental Health
www.cieh.org

Royal Environmental Health Institute of Scotland
www.rehis.com

HOTEL MANAGER

ENTRY LEVEL 1

Qualifications and courses

No specific academic qualifications are required as it is possible to enter the industry at a lower level and work your way up. However it is possible to enter as a management trainee if you have a relevant degree or HNC/HND qualification. Relevant subjects include hotel and hospitality management, business with languages and travel, tourism or leisure studies.

Knowledge of a foreign language could be useful. If you are entering as a graduate you should have some prior work experience as well as your degree. Experience in a hotel is desirable; however other customer-oriented work such as bartending or retail work would also be considered highly relevant.

School leavers could apply for an Advanced Apprenticeship in Hospitality Catering, which involves on-the-job training and the opportunity to study for relevant NVQs.

Existing employees, graduates or those with previous hotel experience may be eligible for one of the fast-track training schemes offered by some of the larger hotel companies.

The Institute of Hospitality provides a range of qualifications for those pursuing a management or leadership role within the hospitality industry.

What the work involves

You will manage the services and staff of your hotel, ensuring that it is a successful business and gains new customers to make a profit.

You will be responsible for checking that the buildings and grounds of your hotel meet health and safety regulations and other professional standards.

Your work could involve promoting and developing the hotel to increase numbers of customers. You could work in all types of hotel, from a small private one up to large national or international chains.

Type of person suited to this work

As you will manage budgets and cash flow, you will need a good level of numeracy and the confidence to handle large amounts of money. Communication skills are very important as you will be organising staff and dealing with guests. You will be working in a sociable and busy environment, so you will need to enjoy meeting lots of different people.

You should be well organised and able to meet targets. Strong customer service and good business skills are essential, as is flexibility, as you will be working long and unsocial hours.

An interest in local tourism may also be useful.

Working conditions

This work involves working long hours that include evenings and weekends. You might spend some of your evenings living-in so you can be on-site in case of emergencies. You are also likely to work shifts.

Some members of the public can be rude and aggressive so you will need to maintain a calm professional manner at all times.

You will need to have a smart appearance and you might have to wear a uniform.

Future prospects

The workforce in the hotel industry is often young and there is a high staff turnover. Depending on the size of the hotel and job performance, graduate trainees could progress from assistant managerial roles to deputy or head of department roles within 2 years, and then to general manager within a further 5 or 6 years.

With experience, you could work overseas, open your own hotel or progress from hotel management into other areas of a company such as human resources, finance and IT.

Advantages/disadvantages

There are opportunities to travel and work overseas.

You can progress to be a manager of a large hotel relatively quickly.

As you are responsible for the welfare and happiness of the guests, there will be a lot of pressure and demands.

Money guide

Salaries will depend on the size, reputation and location of the hotel in which you work.

Assistant or trainee managers can earn £19,000 per year.

Managers of small hotels or deputy managers of large hotels could earn £20,000 to £35,000. Typical general managers' salaries are around £21,000 to £55,000.

Senior managers can achieve £60,000 or more and salaries for those employed in large, global hotels can be considerably higher.

Benefits can include pension schemes, healthcare, live-in accommodation and discounts on staying in other hotels. If the manager is required to live at the hotel, the salary could be reduced to cover accommodation and food costs.

Related opportunities

- Bar Manager/Licensee/Publican p120
- Holiday Representative p364
- Housekeeper/Accommodation Manager p130

Further information

Institute of Hospitality
www.instituteofhospitality.org

Springboard UK
www.springboarduk.net

HOTEL PORTER

ENTRY LEVEL 1

Qualifications and courses

There are no minimum entry requirements for this job but some employers prefer individuals with a good general education. Good English and maths and basic IT skills are preferred and previous experience in a customer service field may also be required.

You may be able to enter this profession through an Apprenticeship in Hospitality and Catering. Professional qualifications, such as the City & Guilds Level 2 Award in Introduction to Employment in the Hospitality Industry, may be an advantage.

Many hotels will provide training to new staff, whether or not they have previous experience. This is usually gained over a period of several weeks or longer, under the supervision of a more experienced member of staff. As you are required to lift and carry luggage, some of the training may be concerned with health and safety and risk assessment for manual handling.

What the work involves

As a porter, you will greet hotel guests, answer the phone, take reservations and deal with general enquiries.

You will also be responsible for moving guests' luggage to and from rooms.

If you work as a night porter, you will look after the security and safety of the hotel site.

As a head porter in a large hotel, you will be responsible for a team of porters that will include night, conference and kitchen porters.

Type of person suited to this work

You will need excellent customer service skills, a smart appearance and extensive knowledge of the local area.

Strong communication skills and the ability to work as part of a team are highly sought after and, as you may be asked to undertake duties at short notice, you will need a flexible and enthusiastic attitude.

You must be fit and active as you will do a lot of lifting and carrying.

Being responsible for the security of the hotel site and guests' belongings means that you must be honest, reliable and aware of security issues.

Working conditions

The work can be physically demanding as you will spend a lot of time on your feet and lifting luggage. You will primarily be based inside the hotel but you may be required to greet guests outside in all weather conditions.

You may work shifts or standard hours. If you work as a night porter your working hours may affect your personal life. If you live in the hotel you might be on-call.

You might have to wear a uniform which should be provided by your employer.

Future prospects

You can work in hotels all over the country and possibly abroad. Part-time and seasonal work is also available.

Smaller hotels tend to employ one porter so you would need to move to larger hotels if you want to progress. For this reason, willingness to be geographically mobile could be helpful.

In larger companies, you could work towards a job as a head porter or a reception-based role.

Advantages/disadvantages

In some hotels you would be required to live on-site.

If you find a seasonal position this job can fit around educational commitments but some hotels prefer to employ mature individuals.

You will have the opportunity to meet and help many different people so your work will be rewarding and interesting.

Money guide

Salary levels vary according to the type of hotel you work for and geographical location.

Starting salaries are about £12,000 per year.

As you gain experience, your annual earnings can increase to about £16,000.

Head porters in large hotels can achieve £18,000 or more.

Shift allowances, overtime work and tips from guests can all increase your earnings. Salaries may be reduced if the porter is living in the hotel. Benefits can include staff meals and free or discounted use of hotel facilities.

Related opportunities

- Concierge p124
- Hotel/Accommodation Room Attendant p129
- Receptionist p45

Further information

Institute of Hospitality
www.instituteofhospitality.org

People 1st
www.people1st.co.uk

HOTEL RECEPTIONIST

ENTRY LEVEL 1

Qualifications and courses

There are no minimum entry requirements, although employers may ask for GCSEs/National 5s (A*–C/A–C), including English and Maths. They will usually also want to see evidence of communication skills so having some office or customer service work experience would be helpful for this career.

The Intermediate Apprenticeship in Hospitality would also be useful for those seeking a reception role and candidates keen to progress to head of reception could take the Advanced Apprenticeship.

There are various qualifications available that might help your employment prospects and give you more insight into the industry. These include a City & Guilds Level 1 Certificate in Hospitality Services and an NVQ Level 2 in either Front of House Reception or Hospitality Supervision and Leadership.

Further training is usually provided by the employer and new entrants often work under the supervision of more experienced reception staff.

What the work involves

You will be responsible for welcoming guests to the hotel, checking them in and out, managing any requests and allocating them a room. You will also prepare guests' bills, take payments and handle foreign exchange. You will answer the telephone, take messages and bookings and inform guests about the local area.

Hotel receptionists work closely with other members of staff to ensure the smooth running of the hotel. In a large hotel you might work within a team of receptionists whereas in a small hotel you may work alone and have extra duties including housekeeping and waitressing.

Type of person suited to this work

You should be a friendly, welcoming and well-presented person as you will be the first point of contact for hotel guests.

Good communication skills are essential as you will be interacting with all types of people and a polite telephone manner will be necessary when making calls and taking messages.

You will be very busy at times but will have to stay calm and polite even under pressure, making sure that each guest gets the service they expect.

It would be helpful to be knowledgeable about the local area and the hotel. Being able to speak a foreign language would also be desirable, as you might have foreign guests staying at the hotel or you may want to work overseas.

Working conditions

Hotels are open 24/7 so you will probably do shift work to ensure the reception desk is manned at all times. There are opportunities to work part time or seasonally.

You will work behind the reception desk the majority of the time, where you will have access to a computer and a telephone. You might be provided with a uniform.

Future prospects

The tourism industry has had only slight growth in recent years and job opportunities may be affected. While vacancies are available throughout the UK, the majority of hotels are in the south-east of England, Scotland and the west country.

As a hotel receptionist you could progress to being a supervisor or manager of a team of receptionists, or move to a different area of the hotel industry, such as event organisation.

Your transferable skills would enable you to work as a receptionist in other sectors.

Advantages/disadvantages

You will be responsible for dealing with complaints and disturbances which could be stressful or frustrating.

This is a varied and active role which will suit those who like to keep busy and meet new people.

You could have the opportunity to work in hotels overseas.

Money guide

Your salary may depend on the location and size of the hotel you work for.

Starting salaries range from £12,500 to £14,500 per year.

Senior receptionists or those in supervisory roles can achieve £15,000 to £18,000. As front desk manager, you can expect to earn up to £23,000 a year.

Additional benefits may include meals and accommodation. Overtime pay and allowances for working unsociable hours may be available.

Related opportunities

- Personal Assistant p42
- Secretary p50
- Travel Agent p374

Further information

Institute of Hospitality
www.instituteofhospitality.org

People 1st
www.people1st.co.uk

HOTEL/ACCOMMODATION ROOM ATTENDANT

ENTRY LEVEL 1

Qualifications and courses

There are no minimum entry requirements for this job. Employers are more concerned with hiring people who are honest, reliable and hardworking. Some relevant cleaning experience could be useful but is not essential.

The intermediate level Apprenticeship in Hospitality could provide a route into this line of work.

While not required, there are pre-entry qualifications available that could be helpful. City & Guilds run an Entry Level Award and a Level 1 Certificate in Introduction to the Hospitality Industry. Edexcel offer a Diploma in Hospitality and there is an NVQ/SVQ Level 2 in Hospitality and Catering also available.

Once you find a position as a room attendant you will receive on-the-job training, usually under the supervision of a more experienced member of staff. This could include aspects such as safe lifting methods and furniture and carpet cleaning.

What the work involves

You will clean, tidy and prepare guest rooms to a high standard. This could include cleaning bathroom and toilet areas and other parts of the hotel.

Work involves stocking up levels of supplies as they are used and keeping records of any items of lost property left in rooms.

Using a trolley or cart, you will move supplies of linen, towels and other items around the hotel. You will also check for maintenance problems or damage to hotel property.

Type of person suited to this work

As much of the work involves cleaning areas of the site and moving supplies around, you will need a good level of physical fitness.

You must be well organised, enthusiastic and able to work quickly to get all your tasks completed on time. In order to keep up standards of cleanliness, you need a good eye for detail.

A polite and friendly manner when liaising with guests is essential. As you will be cleaning areas around guests' personal belongings, it is important to respect their privacy.

Working conditions

This is physical work so expect to be on your feet for much of the time, using cleaning equipment and pushing a cart from room to room.

You will be working with cleaning fluids and other cleaning equipment on a daily basis which could affect those with skin problems.

You will probably work shifts and may need to work early mornings, late at night and at weekends.

Future prospects

You could work in a hotel, bed and breakfast or leisure facility. Larger employers provide staff with good training and development support.

You may have opportunities to work abroad for an international hotel or in a resort.

With experience, you could go on to work as an accommodation manager or housekeeper and have responsibility for other staff.

Advantages/disadvantages

Some employers allow you to live on-site and will provide your meals.

There are opportunities to gain seasonal/holiday work and this type of job is available on a part-time basis.

The work is quite physically demanding and involves bending, stretching and some heavy lifting.

During busy periods when many guests are staying at the hotel, you will have to work efficiently to meet tight deadlines.

Money guide

Earnings vary according to employer and location.

Some room attendants may receive an hourly rate which can start at National Minimum Wage. Based on a 37 hour week, this works out at around £7,254 per year for under 18s, £9,808 for 18–20 year olds and £12,304 for 21 year olds and up.

Salaries can rise to £15,000 with experience.

Guests often leave tips for room attendants. Overtime work or shift allowances could also increase earnings.

Related opportunities

- Cleaner p436
- Hotel Manager p126
- Hotel Porter p127

Further information

Institute of Hospitality
www.instituteofhospitality.org

People 1st
www.people1st.co.uk

HOUSEKEEPER/ACCOMMODATION MANAGER

ENTRY LEVEL 1

Qualifications and courses

It is possible to enter this career without academic qualifications by working your way up from a room attendant position. Employers will want to see evidence that you are organised and have good customer service skills.

Any professional qualifications you have gained while working at a lower level can also help you achieve promotion to manager. You can study for qualifications through the Institute of Hospitality. There are also various City & Guilds awards and NVQs available.

HNCs/HNDs, Foundation degrees or degrees in subjects such as hospitality or hotel management can be useful. Large hotels sometimes run management training schemes, for which you will need a degree.

Previous work experience, perhaps from part-time or holiday work, is preferred for entry, as is supervisory experience. Intermediate or Advanced Apprenticeships in Hospitality can also be a good entry route.

What the work involves

You will be in charge of a team of cleaners and will ensure that all rooms on your premises are clean, tidy and hospitable.

You may work in hotels, conference centres, private households, hospitals, care homes and university halls of residence.

You will manage a housekeeping budget, recruit and train staff, and organise work rotas and duties.

On a day-to-day basis you will inspect rooms, take care of repairs, and ensure linens, soaps, towels and other necessities are always in stock.

You will also be responsible for sorting out lost property and filing maintenance reports.

Type of person suited to this work

As you will be in charge of a team, good organisational, delegation and management skills are essential, as is the ability to motivate and encourage staff. You should be capable of managing budgets and solving problems.

Strong verbal communication skills are important as you will interact with both customers and staff.

Working conditions

Although you will have an office, you will be on your feet for the majority of the time.

Some establishments will require you to live on-site and you might have to work shifts or unsocial hours.

Future prospects

There is scope to develop a career in management in this area but you have to work your way from junior or deputy housekeeper to senior housekeeper.

In larger hotels, you could progress to a role in head office, in areas such as human resources or training. There are also opportunities in facilities management.

International companies could provide the opportunity to work overseas.

With enough experience, you could go on to own and run your own cleaning service company or even your own hotel.

Advantages/disadvantages

Larger hotel and leisure companies often provide staff with leisure and restaurant discounts.

You will be responsible for generating customer satisfaction which can be very rewarding.

Depending on the size and location of the establishment, the work may be seasonal.

Money guide

Salaries vary significantly depending on the size, reputation and location of the establishment.

A graduate trainee accommodation manager will start on £17,000 to £22,000 per year.

Senior housekeepers can expect to earn £22,000 to £40,000 or more.

If accommodation is provided, salaries might be reduced to cover rent and living expenses. Benefits can include pensions and free or discounted accommodation or meals.

Related opportunities

- Cleaner p436
- Hotel Porter p127
- Hotel/Accommodation Room Attendant p129

Further information

Institute of Hospitality
www.instituteofhospitality.org

People 1st
www.people1st.co.uk

Springboard UK
www.springboarduk.net

KITCHEN ASSISTANT/ SUPERVISOR

ENTRY LEVEL 1

Qualifications and courses

Kitchen assistant
There are no minimum qualifications but a good general secondary education and previous catering or kitchen experience are helpful. Most employers provide on-the-job training.

Qualifications such as a GCSE/National 5 in Food Technology, the City & Guilds Level 1 Certificate in Food Preparation and Cookery and City & Guilds Level 2 Diploma in Food Service are useful. In Scotland the SQA National Qualification in Health and Food Technology is available. There may also be apprenticeships in hospitality and catering available in your area.

Kitchen supervisor
To become a supervisor you will ideally have health and safety or food hygiene qualifications and previous experience working in a kitchen, possibly as a kitchen assistant or commis chef. Management experience also helps.

Sometimes employers will ask for Level 2 qualifications, such as the City & Guilds Diploma in Professional Cookery, an NVQ in Kitchen Services or even the City & Guilds Level 3 Diploma in Hospitality Supervision and Leadership. HNC/HND and degree qualifications in hospitality will also increase your chances of getting a job.

What the work involves

Kitchen assistant
You will keep the kitchen clean, wash up equipment, peel and chop fruits, vegetables and meat and check on stock levels. You will also prepare quick, simple dishes.

Kitchen supervisor
Kitchen supervisors are experienced, trained chefs who oversee the running of a kitchen and hire, train and manage all kitchen staff.

You will plan menus, order ingredients, oversee food preparation, presentation and quality control and contact suppliers to place orders and negotiate prices.

Type of person suited to this work

Kitchen assistants need to be on time for work, able to follow directions and to work efficiently at a fast pace.

As a supervisor you need to be assertive, patient and composed as you will have to delegate tasks, resolve disputes, negotiate prices, keep records and stay in control of a team. You also need to have good teamwork, communication and multi-tasking skills and must adhere to and impose strict health and safety procedures and hygiene standards.

Working conditions

Most kitchen assistants work part time on a shift system including split shifts and overtime. Supervisors generally work a 40-hour week. All kitchen staff should be prepared to work holidays and weekends.

Kitchens can be noisy, hot and cramped places to work. You will need to wear protective clothing to ensure food is not contaminated.

While both kitchen assistants and supervisors will spend most of their time standing and lifting heavy items, supervisors will also have a small office in which they organise their paperwork.

Future prospects

Kitchen workers are constantly in demand. You may work in a wide range of settings from restaurants, bars and hotels to hospitals, schools or the armed forces.

Kitchen assistant
You may progress to an assistant chef position or move into food service or bar work.

Kitchen supervisor
You may be promoted to general manager or head office manager. You may also choose to set up your own independent restaurant or catering company.

Advantages/disadvantages

Working with a team in a fast-paced kitchen can be fun and exciting.

You may need to work long shifts at unsocial times.

The work can be stressful and physically demanding.

Money guide

Kitchen assistant
If you work a 40-hour week your salary can range from £11,500 to £12,500 per year. With experience you may earn up to £15,000.

Kitchen supervisor
Kitchen supervisors can earn £16,000 to £35,000.

Related opportunities

- Catering/Restaurant Manager/Maître d'Hôtel p121
- Chef/Sous Chef p123
- Waiting Staff p132

Further information

Institute of Hospitality
www.instituteofhospitality.org

WAITING STAFF

ENTRY LEVEL 1

Qualifications and courses

Waiter/waitress

No minimum qualifications are required, however communication and numeracy skills are important and some previous experience is often preferred. School leavers could apply for an Intermediate Apprenticeship in Hospitality and Catering.

While looking for work you could study for qualifications such as an NVQ/SVQ Level 2 Diploma in Hospitality and Catering or the City & Guilds Certificate/Diploma in Professional Food and Beverage Service (Levels 1 and 2). These are not essential but could give you an advantage.

High profile restaurants, those with Michelin stars for example, may require staff with experience in fine dining and silver service. The Academy of Food and Wine Service provides short courses such as the Licence to Work in Banqueting Service.

Butler

Qualifications in general hospitality and catering are not required but are well regarded. These may include an NVQ Level 2 in Food and Beverage Service or Level 3 in Hospitality Supervision and Leadership. The City & Guilds Diploma for Butlers (Levels 2 and 3) would also be a useful qualification.

Significant hospitality experience is essential. This could be from working as a houseman, footman or under-butler, or you could transfer from a hotel or catering background.

Some large institutions such as hotel chains provide formal training and there are private butler training schools, although these are expensive. You will probably need a driving licence and a second language may be useful.

Sommelier

There are no minimum qualifications required, however relevant experience working in a bar or restaurant is desirable and fluency in a foreign language, especially French, is useful.

The Wine & Spirit Education Trust (WSET) offer qualifications in wines, spirits and wine service ranging from Level 1 Awards up to a Level 5 Honours Diploma. Employers may require you to have completed some of these courses.

The Academy of Food and Wine Service offers specialist training sessions in this sector, including the one-day Licence to Work in Wine Service course.

School leavers have the option of entering through an Apprenticeship in Hospitality and Catering (Drinks Service Route).

What the work involves

Waiter/waitress

You will take food orders from customers and provide meals through table or counter service. You will supply accurate bills for meals and take payment from customers. Before and during your shift you will probably have to keep the eating area clean and prepare tables for customers.

Butler

You will work in a private household where you will be responsible for arranging travel and security, providing and serving food and welcoming visitors. You will usually work within a wealthy household, including those of celebrities or royalty.

Sommelier

You will be responsible for the provision of wines or other alcoholic beverages such as spirits. You will be expected to attend tastings and to design a wine list or cocktail menu. It is important to understand how beverages complement food in order to aid customer selection. You will need to serve beverages correctly at the expected temperature.

Type of person suited to this work

Waiter/waitress

As you will be working with the public, you should possess a polite attitude, a neat appearance and good customer service skills. You may have to explain parts of the menu to customers so an interest in food and drink is useful.

You will need a good memory and communication skills to take food orders correctly from customers and pass them on to kitchen staff. You should be happy to work as part of a team.

The ability to work with numbers and deal with cash is important. You must work to a high standard of health and hygiene at all times.

Butler

In addition to the above skills, you should be impeccably presented, honest and reliable. Your employers will expect you to be dedicated, loyal and discreet as you will be responsible for their day-to-day security, their home and their personal affairs.

Sommelier

It is essential that you are enthusiastic about wines and have an interest in food. You should understand tasting notes, have a good palate and demonstrate a thorough knowledge of wines and beverages from all over the world.

Working conditions

Waiter/waitress

This role involves shift work and you will have to work unsocial hours including evenings and weekends. It is essential to have lots of energy as you will be on your feet most of the time, carrying heavy plates and dishes.

Most waiting staff serve a number of tables at once and have to remember different customer requests. It is important to have the ability to remain calm in the face of customer complaints.

You will be required to wear a uniform and may be exposed to a hot, noisy kitchen environment. You will be expected to work to a high standard of cleanliness at all times.

Butler

You will probably work within luxurious surroundings in the UK or abroad and will normally live-in and have your own quarters.

You may be required to care for the home whilst your employer is away and you may also escort them overseas.

Sommelier
You will probably wear a uniform and work shifts, including weekends and evenings, until the early hours of the morning.

You will spend most of your time front of house and should be energetic and have high hygiene standards.

You may have the opportunity to travel domestically and internationally to attend tastings.

Future prospects

Waiter/waitress
The hospitality industry in the UK has had only slight growth in the past few years so vacancies may be affected, particularly at entry level. Opportunities to work abroad are available.

If you do not already have them you may be encouraged to take Level 2 or 3 qualifications, such as the City & Guilds Level 3 Certificate in Food and Beverage Service Supervision. You may also receive training in food safety and food hygiene.

Once you gain experience, you could become junior or head waiter. Larger employers such as hotel chains increasingly provide formal training and support for staff and may allow inter-departmental movements, such as stock control or purchasing. You could also move into more specialist posts such as sommelier.

Butler
The popularity of *Downton Abbey* has caused the demand for butlers to more than double in the past few years. English butlers are particularly in vogue among foreign employers.

You are more likely to get a job if you are willing to be flexible and take on other responsibilities, such as those of a personal assistant or providing some childcare services. Many catering firms have butler services and there is demand from contract caterers, hotels and financial institutions.

Many of the jobs are overseas and the most successful butlers are willing to be geographically mobile.

Sommelier
There are opportunities to work in a variety of outlets in the UK and abroad. Traditionally a man's profession, an increasing number of women are now becoming sommeliers.

With experience it is possible to progress to a higher managerial position in the hospitality industry, start your own business in the wine sector or become a wine taster or manager for an importer or manufacturer. Qualifications from the Court of Master Sommeliers or the Institute of Masters of Wine may increase promotion prospects.

Advantages/disadvantages

Waiter/waitress
Catering staff are often provided with uniforms, free meals and accommodation.

The role can be physically draining.

Butler
Your job could include lots of travelling and the opportunity to live in the luxurious homes of the rich and famous.

This job can affect your personal life as it is difficult to be off-duty.

Sommelier
You may have the opportunity to travel within the UK and abroad.

Working long and unsociable hours can affect your personal life.

Money guide

Waiter/waitress
Salaries will depend on the location, size and reputation of your employer.

Starting salaries are often minimum wage and can range from £7,254 to £12,304 per year depending on your age.

With experience and extra responsibilities you can achieve £18,000 or more.

Your income can be supplemented by tips from customers. Benefits include free meals while on duty.

Butler
Your salary will depend on your experience and your employer.

Starting salaries are around £15,000.

This will increase as you gain experience and the most successful butlers working in the private sector can receive £50,000 to £75,000 or more.

You may also be provided with free accommodation or a car.

Sommelier
Salaries will depend on the location, size and reputation of the organisation you work for.

A trainee can expect around £13,000 per year.

Salaries increase to £30,000 as you gain experience.

A head sommelier could earn £45,000 or more.

Benefits may include tips, bonuses, free meals and accommodation.

Related opportunities

- Concierge p124
- Cruise Ship Steward/Purser p573
- Housekeeper/Accommodation Manager p130
- Kitchen Assistant/Supervisor p131

Further information

Institute of Hospitality
www.instituteofhospitality.org

Springboard UK
www.springboarduk.net

Wine & Spirit Education Trust
www.wset.co.uk

Computers and IT

This sector is still fairly new and so it is expanding all the time, creating new jobs for a whole range of people.

You may have a mathematical brain or a real creative ability – or a bit of both! Essentially, you must be passionate about computers to consider working in this sector. You need to keep right up to date with the latest technologies and IT developments as well as people's tastes, interests and hobbies to enjoy working in this industry.

The jobs featured in this section are listed below. For similar jobs to the ones found in this section have a look at *Administration, Business, Office Work and Financial Services* on page 1 and *Retail, Sales and Customer Services* starting on page 449.

BUSINESS ANALYST

ENTRY LEVEL 5

Qualifications and courses

Most entrants have a degree, Foundation degree or HNC/HND in a relevant subject, such as software engineering, business studies, IT or computer science. Entry for degrees usually requires 2 A levels/3 H grades and 5 GCSEs/National 5s (A*–C/A–C). For Foundation degrees or HNCs/HNDs, 1 A level/2 H grades and 3 GCSEs/National 5s (A*–C/A–C) are necessary. Maths might be a required subject. Degree courses usually last 3 to 4 years or 4 to 5 years for sandwich courses. Although not essential, a postgraduate qualification may be advantageous.

BTEC Level 3 qualifications in an IT or business-related subject could also be helpful. The Chartered Institute for IT (BCS) offers business analysis certifications at various levels. There are also specialist training centres, such as Business Analyst Solutions, that provide short courses in a variety of business analysis certifications as well.

A sponsored degree in Information Technology Management for Business (ITMB) from e-skills UK is available. This is focused on learning through project work in teams with external mentors from sponsoring organisations such as BT, Ford, IBM, Deloitte, the BBC and Asda. The opportunities to network with industry professionals could be invaluable when pursuing a graduate career.

There may be relevant apprenticeships available as a funded route and these can lead on to a full Honours degree in addition to vocational, technical and Key Skills qualifications and work experience.

Business analysts are required to undertake continuing professional development (CPD) in order to keep up to date with industry developments.

What the work involves

You will be responsible for inspecting businesses, to see if there are any improvements to be made or current problems that can be solved using information technology. Your aim is to generate higher efficiency and profits for the company.

You will work with managers in order to learn more about the organisation structure and the technology it uses. You will map out a new business plan and train staff on how to implement it.

You will ensure that project deadlines and budgets are met on time.

Type of person suited to this work

Your understanding of how businesses work is the key to being a successful business analyst – you will be aware of the need to balance costs with solutions.

You will also need to be a good negotiator, able to influence managers who may not understand how the new solutions or products you are suggesting can benefit their businesses.

Excellent communication skills are crucial because you will need to put across your ideas in meetings and in written reports. You will also need a strong knowledge of what is available in the technology market and how it works in order to develop project briefs.

Working conditions

You will work standard office hours, although work in the evenings and at weekends will be necessary when projects are near to completion. You will spend a lot of time working with other members of the project team.

It is likely that your job will also involve travelling to meet clients at all stages of the project.

Future prospects

There are vacancies in all areas of business including finance and retail. Employers also include specialist management consultancies, software houses and computer companies.

There is a growing market for business analysts with the right combination of skills and talents. Analysts with e-commerce technology skills and experience are in particular demand, due to the continued growth of internet use in business.

Progression is possible into senior analyst jobs and on to project management or consultancy work.

Advantages/disadvantages

You can get a real sense of satisfaction from producing successful solutions that transform a business.

There often has to be a trade-off between the solution you would like to recommend and the limitations set by your client's budget.

Entry to this profession can be quite competitive.

You will have the opportunity to meet a range of people and gain exposure to various business sectors.

Money guide

Starting salaries can range from £17,000 to £25,000.

Earnings rise to £30,000–£45,000 with experience.

Senior business analysts can achieve £60,000–£80,000.

Salaries vary greatly depending on location and are highest in London. Additional benefits may include profit sharing, performance-related pay and a company car.

Related opportunities

- Software Developer/Programmer p145
- Systems Analyst p147
- Technical Sales Specialist p148

Further information

BCS, The Chartered Institute for IT
www.bcs.org

e-skills UK
www.e-skills.com

COMPUTER GAMES DESIGNER

ENTRY LEVEL 5

Qualifications and courses

Many employers will ask for a minimum of a degree and although entry into the industry is possible with a HND, many developers are graduates. A portfolio of game projects or designs is also beneficial although this is largely dependent on the kind of job you apply for; depending on either artistic or programming requirements. Relevant industry experience is a must and many people work initially as a tester of quality assurance in a games studio. The Chartered Institute for IT (BCS) offers the Professional Certification in Software Testing at Foundation, Intermediate, Practitioner or Higher level for quality assurance testers which may also help your application.

Useful degree subjects include computer games technology, computer arts or computer animation. The computer games industry is constantly developing, and as games grow closer to traditional cinema, developers may value knowledge of cinematography or a flair for storytelling. At least 2 A levels/3 H grades are required for entry to related degrees. A relevant postgraduate qualification may also prove advantageous in this increasingly competitive industry.

A funded route that may be on offer in your area is the Higher Apprenticeship in IT. This can lead on to a full Honours degree in addition to vocational, technical and Key Skills qualifications in addition to much valued work experience. Apprenticeships in Quality Assurance and Games Production are also available. Training programmes are on offer for graduate entrants from any discipline.

What the work involves

Using storyboards and flowcharts, you will present your ideas for a new computer game to a panel for acceptance or rejection.

If it is accepted you will manage all aspects of the playing experience, from scripts to programming and from animation to sound effects and music.

You will work with a team of specialists, such as programmers and graphic artists, to produce a prototype. Once a computer games playtester has picked out any flaws and if the panel think it is a winner, it will go into full development by your team.

Type of person suited to this work

To be a top-class computer games designer you will need creativity and an ability to see how ideas fit together. You will also have a passion for and knowledge of the computer games market.

Your ideas need to be technically viable and cost effective, so you will need a broad understanding of computers and games consoles, multimedia and the internet.

You will need to be a team player to work with specialists such as graphic designers to make sure that their part of the project fits in with the final version of the game.

Working conditions

You will be mainly based in an office or studio working with other members of the games project team.

Although you will work Monday to Friday, you might need to work overtime in the evenings and at weekends to meet deadlines.

Future prospects

Employers are specialised companies producing games for computers or games consoles such as Wii U, Xbox One or PS4. This market is expected to grow as the computer games industry continues to be a profitable global business.

It is a popular career choice so entry is competitive. You will need talent and project/people management skills in order to be promoted from junior to designer and then to lead designer.

There may be opportunities to work abroad. Progression is possible into management or consultancy work.

Advantages/disadvantages

Games designers say it is enjoyable creating entertainment for a living, and there is the opportunity to be creative.

It is a young, vibrant business and the rewards can be high.

It can be tough when a game does not sell or receives poor reviews.

It is stressful producing a game for a timed release such as the Christmas market.

Money guide

£18,000 to £25,000 per year is the usual starting/training salary for designers with prior industry experience. This can then rise to between £30,000 and £50,000 with more experience.

Senior or lead games designers can go on to earn between £35,000 and £55,000.

Additional benefits usually include profit sharing and performance-related pay or a bonus.

Related opportunities

- Interactive Media Designer p141
- Online/Web Content Manager p144
- Software Developer/Programmer p145

Further information

BCS, The Chartered Institute for IT
www.bcs.org

Learning and Performance Institute
www.learningandperformanceinstitute.com

COMPUTER HARDWARE ENGINEER

ENTRY LEVEL 5

Qualifications and courses

Whilst it is possible to start at basic technical support level and work your way up, the majority of employers look for prospective employees to have a degree when recruiting for this position. The normal minimum entry requirements for degrees are 2 A levels/3 H grades and 5 GCSEs/National 5s (A*–C/A–C). Useful degree subjects include computer systems engineering or electronic engineering and for technical degrees A levels/H grades in Maths, technology or a science subject may be required.

You may choose to enter this career through an Apprenticeship in IT and Telecoms Professionals. Getting a Level 2 Diploma in Consumer Electrical and Electronic Product Servicing or equivalent could help get you a job as a technician. You could then look to build your qualifications while working.

Training programmes are on offer for graduate entrants from any discipline. Engineers must ensure their technical knowledge is always up to date by completing continuing professional development (CPD) courses. Once qualified, computer hardware engineers register with the Engineering Council as an incorporated engineer (IEng) or chartered engineer (CEng). Registration can aid career advancement and CPD, as it can expose you to networking, training and job opportunities.

What the work involves

You will be responsible for developing, installing and repairing computer hardware – the computer itself rather than the applications or software.

You will be designing computer components, including microchips and circuit boards, and testing these systems.

When repairing a fault or upgrading a machine you will open up the computer and use tools to install upgrades or replace faulty parts.

You may specialise in installing new computer systems and training the people who use them.

Type of person suited to this work

You will need both technical skills and practical ability. Building your own computer system and repairing friends' machines is something you will probably already be doing in your spare time.

You should be a good problem solver. You will need to be able to identify what is wrong and put it right within a strict deadline, especially as your customer may be losing money while you do the repair.

It is important to be inquisitive and adaptable as you will need to absorb new information quickly in order to make many repairs.

You should pay close attention to detail and be thorough and accurate in your work. Often working on your own, you will also need to be reliable and able to work unsupervised.

Working conditions

You might be based in a workshop or in an office, but many engineers travel to individual customers' premises or homes.

Computer hardware engineers are employed by computer manufacturers, computer service firms and by a range of large organisations such as banks, hospitals and universities.

You will work a 37 to 40 hour week, but as businesses generally need major work to be done in the evenings and at weekends, you will have to work shifts or be on a call-out rota.

Future prospects

The IT industry is constantly expanding and is therefore a stable area of work as computers require regular repair and upgrading to improve performance and/or capacity.

Promotion could be to team leader or supervisor and then on to senior engineer. Self-employment as a freelance/consultant engineer is possible.

Advantages/disadvantages

Your job will be varied as few technical problems are ever the same.

It is rewarding to get a computer up and running again.

Your customer may have a service agreement requiring you to put the problem right in a fixed period of time, which can be stressful.

Money guide

When you begin work as a computer hardware technician you can expect your starting/trainee salary to be around £18,000 per year.

This could then increase once you have experience to between £25,000 and £40,000.

Salaries can rise to between £40,000 and £50,000 at senior level.

Related opportunities

- Computer Technical Support Person/Helpdesk Adviser p139
- Software Developer/Programmer p145
- Software Engineer p146

Further information

e-skills UK
www.e-skills.com

Tomorrow's Engineers
www.tomorrowsengineers.org.uk

COMPUTER TECHNICAL SUPPORT PERSON/HELPDESK ADVISER

ENTRY LEVEL 2

Qualifications and courses

It is possible for school leavers to enter this profession via an Intermediate Apprenticeship for IT, Software, Web and Telecoms Professionals. Those with limited IT experience can also obtain qualifications in customer service and support from the Help Desk Institute (HDI). However, some employers may prefer you to have relevant qualifications, such as a BTEC Level 3 in IT, or a HNC/HND or degree in computing or a related subject. Applicants for degree programmes usually require at least 2 A levels/3 H grades or equivalent qualifications.

For computer technical support staff, the Computer Technology Industry Association (CompTIA) provides the A+ Certification and the Service Desk Institute (SDI) also offers qualifications suitable for both entry level and experienced IT support workers.

Other acceptable entry qualifications include the City & Guilds NVQ for IT Practitioners/Professionals (Levels 1–4), the Certificate/Diploma in ICT Systems and Principles (Levels 2 and 3), the Diploma in ICT Systems Support (Levels 1–3), and the Diploma in ICT Professional Competence (Levels 1–4). BTECs are also available. There is also the OCR iPRO Certificate and Diploma in ICT Systems Support and the Chartered Institute for IT (BCS) offers various courses.

Microsoft, Linux, Unix, Oracle and Cisco offer certification courses in their own products, such as the Microsoft Certified Solutions Associate (MCSA) and the Microsoft Certified Solutions Expert (MCSE). These qualifications are the most broadly accepted technical certifications.

What the work involves

Computer helpdesk advisers answer telephone calls or emails from computer users who are having technical problems and will advise the customer on how to correct the fault.

A computer technical support person will also try to solve customers' technical problems by phone or email, and will also go to the user's workstation to fix the problem if it is more complex. You might also install new systems and upgrades and train staff in their use.

Type of person suited to this work

You will need to be both technical and practical to resolve hardware or software problems.

You will also need to be a good communicator and be able to explain technical language to inexperienced users.

You need to cope well with stress and deadlines. You will be under pressure to get the problem sorted quickly so that staff can get back to work. A keenness to stay up to date is vital – you will be expected to be the expert.

Working conditions

You will probably be based in an office with a technical workshop attached.

You may have to work shifts to cover your employer's hours of operation, which may be 24/7, or to install or repair equipment outside office hours.

Computer helpdesk advisers are mostly employed by computer hardware and software manufacturers or internet service providers, who offer support to their customers. The main employers of computer technical support staff are large organisations such as banks, retail chains and hospitals.

The employers of computer technical support staff may have several sites you need to travel between, sometimes in different parts of the UK.

Future prospects

The number of technical support positions has reduced, due to the shift in IT companies offering remotely managed services and the recession. Similarly, employers sometimes source helpdesks outside the UK to reduce costs.

However, with experience and a good working reputation, promotion for a computer technical support person could be to team leader, network manager/administrator or on to network development. You could also become self-employed. For a computer helpdesk adviser, promotion to supervisory and management work is possible.

Advantages/disadvantages

It is a rewarding experience to help people and solve problems.

The job can be stressful because customers might be angry and frustrated.

Money guide

Starting salaries for computer helpdesk advisers range from £17,000 to £21,000.

With experience this can rise to £27,000 and those in managerial or supervisory roles can earn between £30,000 and £42,000 a year.

Related opportunities

- Computer Hardware Engineer p138
- Network Manager p143
- Technical Sales Specialist p148

Further information

BCS, The Chartered Institute for IT
www.bcs.org

e-skills UK
www.e-skills.com

Learning and Performance Institute
www.learningandperformanceinstitute.com

DATABASE ADMINISTRATOR

ENTRY LEVEL 2

Qualifications and courses

Entrants to this work normally have a degree, Foundation degree or HNC/HND in a relevant subject, such as computer science, software engineering, operational research, e-commerce, technology or maths. The normal minimum entry requirements for degrees are 2 A levels/3 H grades and 5 GCSEs/National 5s (A*–C/A–C). For Foundation degrees or HNCs/HNDs you will need 1 A level/2 H grades and 3 GCSEs/National 5s (A*–C/A–C). For technical degrees, an A level/H grades in maths or science may be required. Other qualifications may be acceptable, such as BTEC Level 3 qualifications and NVQs/SVQs.

Entry without a degree may be possible if you have significant programming experience and knowledge. A funded route for school leavers is the Advanced Apprenticeship for IT, Software, Web and Telecoms Professionals. Entrants will receive practical and technical training in database administration and have the opportunity to work towards relevant qualifications.

Once employed, database managers may also take courses in particular operating systems/packages offered by the manufacturers.

Industry bodies also provide professional development awards. These include the e-skills UK Professional Programme, the BCS Certificate, Diploma and Professional Graduate Diploma, and the IMIS programmes.

Software development companies also offer database certification programmes, including the Microsoft Certified Database Administrator, the Oracle PL/SQL Developer, the Sybase Adaptive Enterprise Server, and the IBM Certified Database Administrator.

Database administrators also need to know structured query language (SQL) and database management systems (DBSM).

What the work involves

Your job is to ensure that databases are accurate, accessible and secure. A database will be used if a huge amount of information needs to be stored with the capacity to search and access specific parts of the data. For example, a hospital uses a database to manage information about its patients.

To keep the data secure you will back up the content regularly, train users and issue them with passwords.

You may also be responsible for setting up and testing a new database.

Type of person suited to this work

Databases function to provide people with the information they require to do their jobs, so you will need effective communication skills.

You should be a good negotiator. To train users to input or access a new or modified database you will need to be able to convince them that these changes will benefit them.

To set up or develop a database you will need to be very technical with a high level of programming knowledge. You will also need to be a good listener, able to find out what the database users want including the new design they wish to achieve.

Working conditions

The main employers of database administrators are large organisations, such as banks and retailers. You could also work for a specialist IT firm providing a complete database service to customers.

You will be based mainly in your own office although in some cases the work can be carried out at home or in a place of your choice using laptops and broadband wireless technology.

Your employer may have several sites you need to travel between, sometimes in different parts of the UK.

You may have to be on-call to deal with problems outside your normal working hours.

Future prospects

This is a growth area because increasing numbers of businesses are developing databases for their websites to allow customers to look at information about their goods online and then go on to buy them.

With experience, you could specialise in network development or move into consultancy work.

Advantages/disadvantages

If you are methodical and analytical you will enjoy the complex job of creating a new database.

It can be frustrating when database users cause problems by not keeping their information up to date or by leaving out vital parts.

The job can be flexible as there are often opportunities for freelance and part-time work, self-employment and working from home.

Money guide

Starting salaries for graduates in this field can be up to £22,000 a year. As you gain experience, your earnings will increase to about £35,000 a year.

The average salary for a database administrator with several years' experience is £45,000.

Those employed at a senior level can achieve up to £55,000.

Related opportunities

- IT Trainer p142
- Network Manager p143
- Software Developer/Programmer p145

Further information

BCS, The Chartered Institute for IT
www.bcs.org

e-skills UK
www.e-skills.com

INTERACTIVE MEDIA DESIGNER

ENTRY LEVEL 5

Qualifications and courses

Entrants often have a Foundation degree, Diploma, HNC/HND, or degree in interactive media design or an art and design-related subject such as graphic or multimedia design. The normal minimum entry requirements for degrees are 2 A levels/3 H grades and 5 GCSEs/National 5s (A*–C/A–C). For Foundation degrees or HNCs/HNDs you usually need 1 A level/2 H grades and 3 GCSEs/National 5s (A*–C/A–C). For entry onto a technical degree course, an A level/H grade in Maths or a science may be required.

Entry without a degree, Foundation degree or HNC/HND is possible for those with IT skills and creative talent. The BTEC Level 3 qualifications in Interactive Media could be beneficial. Other useful qualifications include NVQs/SVQs at Levels 3 and 4 in Communication and Technology, the A level in applied art and design, and the BTEC Level 3 qualifications in subjects such as e-business, and IT practitioners (software development).

Alternatively, you may choose to do the Advanced Apprenticeship for IT, Software, Web and Telecoms Professionals to gain qualifications and practical training.

All entrants should try to get as much experience in the field as possible and it is essential that you compile a portfolio with relevant samples of your interactive media work, produced either at home or during a work placement.

The Chartered Institute for IT (BCS) and the Institute for the Management of Information Systems (IMIS) also offer qualifications which may be useful.

What the work involves

Interactive media designers will usually work as part of a product development team.

You will use a mix of visuals, sounds, animation, text and effects to produce multimedia and communication tools such as apps and content for phones and tablets, interactive websites and DVDs.

You will work with a team to develop a brief, finding out what your client wants and determining how to find the best solution. You will create simulations along the way to show the client your ideas.

Your role will also involve planning, coordinating and overseeing the whole project as well as testing, integrating and, if needed, installing at the customer's site.

Type of person suited to this work

Your creative skills need to be outstanding for this job. Every project will be different and you will need the vision to be able to think about what a client wants to achieve with a multimedia project and then develop ideas to produce a solution.

You need to be good at working in a team and motivating others to meet tight deadlines. You must be organised, have a keen eye for detail and possess good drawing skills.

You should have excellent presentation and communication skills, as you might need to bid against other designers to win contracts for new projects.

Working conditions

Employers include specialist multimedia consultancies, internet service providers, e-learning specialists, mobile phone companies, software houses and hardware manufacturers.

You will spend time at your workstation, working in an office or studio, but you will also be working with your project team and meeting customers and may also have the opportunity to work from home.

You may have to travel regularly to clients, to meet and present your solutions to them.

Although you will work normal hours from Monday to Friday, you may need to work overtime when a deadline is approaching.

Future prospects

Interactive media is an incredibly fast growing industry with various platforms to work on. Competition for jobs though is very high with applicants outnumbering the number of places. In spite of this, skilled media designers are constantly in demand at the moment with over 50,000 people currently working in the interactive media sector.

Once experienced, you could become self-employed, or work on a contract or consultancy basis.

Advantages/disadvantages

This is a young, vibrant industry where you will be using cutting-edge technology.

Seeing people use apps and websites that you have created is very rewarding.

The fast pace of development in this field means that you will have to continue learning to remain up to date.

Money guide

Starting salaries are usually between £15,500 and £22,000.

Experienced interactive media designers can expect an average salary of £31,800.

Those who are highly experienced could earn in excess of £45,000.

Salaries are usually higher in London and the south-east of England.

Related opportunities

- Online/Web Content Manager p144
- Software Developer/Programmer p145
- Software Engineer p146

Further information

British Interactive Media Association
www.bima.co.uk

e-skills UK
www.e-skills.com

IT TRAINER

ENTRY LEVEL 3

Qualifications and courses

To work as an IT trainer you need to first gain the relevant skills and experience in IT. There are no set qualifications required, but it might be advantageous to have a degree, Foundation degree or HNC/HND in a relevant subject, such as computer science, e-business/commerce or software engineering. The normal minimum entry requirements for degrees are 2 A levels/3 H grades and 5 GCSEs/National 5s (A*–C/A–C). For Foundation degrees or HNC/HNDs you need 1 A level/2 H grades and 3 GCSEs/National 5s (A*–C/A–C). You could enter this job without a degree if you have got significant experience and training in IT.

Other useful qualifications that may benefit entry into this industry include the BTEC Certificate/Diploma for IT Practitioners and the OCR Certificate/Diploma for IT Users (Levels 1–3). There are also qualifications in specific desktop applications and technical areas, such as the Microsoft Certified Trainer (MCT), Technology Specialist (MCTS), Systems Engineer (MCSE), and Systems Developer (MCSD) certifications.

The Institute of IT Training is the certification awarding body for a range of courses in e-learning training skills offered by the Training Foundation. Through the Institute of IT Training you can qualify as Certified Training Practitioner.

Once you have qualified, it is advisable that you join the Chartered Institute for IT (BCS), giving you the opportunity to interact with others in the industry and pursue courses to continue your professional development and knowledge in what is a continually evolving industry.

What the work involves

IT trainers give people user skills, for example, in applications such as Word, Excel or desktop-publishing packages. You may also train people in advanced computer skills such as programming languages.

Planning courses, preparing learning materials and setting up the computers ready for a session will be part of your typical day. You will give presentations and network some materials. You will demonstrate the software being taught and assist students with any problems.

Evaluating clients' existing knowledge and developing future learning materials as required will also be part of your job.

Type of person suited to this work

The constant release of new IT products guarantees a future for trainers but only if you are keen to stay up to date. For example, social media courses are becoming increasingly popular and relevant qualifications may broaden your job opportunities. City & Guilds and BTEC offer a Level 3 qualification in Social Media for Business.

You will need lots of self-discipline to do research and prepare learning materials.

As e-learning and virtual classroom technology expands, more students are being taught over the internet. Therefore, you will need to be up to date with e-learning tools, technologies and processes.

This job is about helping others to learn. Whether you train face to face or by virtual technology, you will need strong interpersonal and communication skills. Students can be sensitive to criticism and need to be motivated and encouraged.

Working conditions

Employers such as hardware and software manufacturers, IT consultancies, training organisations and colleges employ IT trainers. There is a strong demand for trainers, especially in the south-east of England.

You may be based in a training centre or you may travel to clients' premises to train their staff on-site.

Although your hours will be usually Monday to Friday, you will need to spend time preparing learning materials and working some evenings and weekends to fit in with students' timetables.

Future prospects

This is not considered to be an entry-level post. Most trainers have gained experience in other areas of computing first.

Experienced IT trainers can move into self-employment as consultants. Promotion into supervisory or management roles may be possible.

Advantages/disadvantages

It can be personally rewarding when you succeed in making a student understand a difficult subject.

This job can be affected if the economy is depressed as training is often the first thing businesses cut back on in difficult times.

Money guide

Graduate IT trainers usually earn around £18,000. Experienced trainers can earn between £19,000 and £26,000 a year. Those with management responsibilities can earn around £30,000.

Salaries can be higher for trainers in specialised or technical areas of work. For example, experienced legal IT trainers earn £38,250 per year on average.

Freelance or self-employed trainers might charge a daily rate of £300 to £450.

Related opportunities

- Business Analyst p136
- Secondary School Teacher p189
- Work-based Training Instructor p193

Further information

BCS, The Chartered Institute for IT
www.bcs.org

Learning and Performance Institute
www.learningandperformanceinstitute.com

NETWORK MANAGER

ENTRY LEVEL 5

Qualifications and courses

To become a network manager you will need experience within the sector, for example as a network engineer or in more general IT management and work your way up. Entry at this lower level is usually by means of a degree, Foundation degree or HNC/HND in a relevant subject, for example control and network computing, software engineering, artificial intelligence or computer science. The normal minimum entry requirements for degrees are 2 A levels /3 H grades and 5 GCSEs/National 5s (A*–C/A–C), and for Foundation degrees or HNC/HNDs, 1 A level/2 H grades and 4 GCSEs/National 5s (A*–C/A–C). For entry onto a technical degree, an A level/H grade in Maths or a science may be required.

Other useful qualifications include the City & Guilds Level 4 Higher Professional Diploma in Information Management using IT, the Institute for the Management of Information Systems Foundation Diploma and the Network/Telecoms Manager Higher Apprenticeship.

Training programmes on offer to graduates from any discipline include the Graduate Professional Development Award. This offers training and accreditation to IT professionals in work.

Many accredited courses are offered by various professional bodies. For example, Cisco offers the Cisco Certified Network Associate (CCNA), Certified Network Professional (CCNP), and Certified Internetwork Expert (CCIE) qualifications, whilst Microsoft offers the Certified Systems Engineer (MCSE) and Certified Systems Administrator (MCSA) qualifications.

You may also need to train in specialist areas such as wireless networking or satellite communications. For example, Cisco offers the CCNA Wireless or CCNP Wireless qualifications and the Lever Technology Group offer many different courses, including Understanding Satellite Communications Systems and the Certified Wireless Network Administrator (CWNA) certification.

What the work involves

You will design, set up and maintain a network of computers and any linked equipment such as printers. This could be in just one building or extend across different sites around the UK or perhaps the world. It will be your responsibility to solve the network users' problems.

Managing access to and the security of your network, you will put in place and monitor firewalls, password systems and antivirus software.

In large organisations you could manage a team of IT technicians and carry out duties such as training staff, organising work rotas and allocating staff duties.

Type of person suited to this work

You need to have excellent communication skills in order to explain technical issues clearly and simply to computer users who need to get back onto the network.

Technical ability and determination are needed for this job. You might develop and write software programs for your network and need to be logical to work out how to sort out any problems.

Network solutions are developing very quickly so you will need to be prepared to carry on learning to keep up your expert status.

Working conditions

You will work standard office hours, though longer hours can be required when installing systems or on-call.

You will use a computer to manage the system. You may need to work in the same room as a noisy mainframe server.

You may have to move around your company's site to attend meetings, train staff and resolve problems.

Future prospects

Most organisations use networks to enable their staff to work together, communicate and share resources from their own workstations. Employers include industry, retailers, schools and universities, hospitals, local and central government and financial companies. You could work within an organisation as a network manager, or as part of an external IT agency and work in many different companies.

Promotion could be into the job of senior network manager and then project manager. A talented network manager could also move into freelance or network design consultancy work. Other possibilities include lecturing or training.

Advantages/disadvantages

You will feel valued because communication and the sharing of information are central to the effective running of any organisation.

This job can be stressful as problems will need to be solved quickly so that users can go back to work.

Money guide

Starting salaries are usually from about £24,000 per year. Salaries in the private sector, however, may be slightly lower.

With experience you could earn from £30,000 to £50,000.

Senior network managers can earn in excess of £70,000.

Additional benefits may include profit sharing or performance-related pay.

Related opportunities

- Computer Hardware Engineer p138
- Computer Technical Support Person/Helpdesk Adviser p139
- Database Administrator p140

Further information

BCS, The Chartered Institute for IT
www.bcs.org

e-skills UK
www.e-skills.com

ONLINE/WEB CONTENT MANAGER

ENTRY LEVEL 3

Qualifications and courses

There is no fixed entry route into this industry. You may wish to pursue a degree, Foundation degree or HNC/HND in a relevant subject, such as e-systems design/technology, graphic design, computer science, e-business/commerce, journalism, publishing, media and communications, or marketing. The normal minimum entry requirements for degrees are 2 A levels/3 H grades and 5 GCSEs/National 5s (A*–C/A–C). For Foundation degrees or HNCs/HNDs you will be expected to have 1 A level/2 H grades and 3 GCSEs/National 5s (A*–C/A–C). Postgraduate degrees may help your application.

Experience in writing is essential and can be achieved in voluntary work or writing a personal online blog. Training will be provided on the job but any experience that you have working with HTML, web content management systems (Drupal, Convio, Kintera, etc) or particular programs (eg Adobe Creative Suite), packages or operating systems, search engine optimisation (SEO), web analytics and social media platforms may prove advantageous. A portfolio of previously developed or published content may also help.

Vacation work or voluntary placements within the sector would also provide useful experience and enable you to develop industry contacts.

A funded route that may be on offer for school leavers is the Advanced IT Application Specialist Apprenticeship. Entrants will gain practical training and relevant qualifications which will help them to secure a suitable role within this industry.

What the work involves

You might work in or supervise a team of staff who design, programme and maintain the various pages that make up an internet site. This may include the company's various social media platforms.

You might write or develop content or develop a content management program for authorised staff to contribute material. You may also have to copy-edit and proofread content. Search Engine Optimisation (SEO) techniques could be beneficial here.

Content is typically required to fit within a marketing strategy and marketing ability is one of the most consistently required skills in relevant job advertisements.

Many jobs combine management with writing and web design. In a small company, you might be the programmer, designer and master/manager of the site.

Type of person suited to this work

You must have good attention to detail and be able to carefully check your work. You will need to set up secure data entry checking systems and regularly test them for faults. You must be able to respond quickly and calmly when faults occur, such as the wrong prices being matched to the wrong products on a shopping site, and be able to work efficiently to fix them.

It will be your responsibility to create your own website or maintain one from the group of sites you work with. Creativity is important, as is accuracy; you need to make sure the site is easy to use.

Excellent management and communication skills are vital as you may be required to lead a project team at senior level.

Working conditions

You will mainly be office based, using a computer to manage the website. You may have to move around your company's premises to train, meet with managers and discuss website improvements.

You could work for web-based retailers, travel companies, the multimedia industry, local and central government and financial companies.

You will work a 37–40 hour week, normally Monday to Friday, but if you are working to maintain and support a 24/7 site you will work shifts as part of a team to cover all hours.

Future prospects

Websites are big business, with growing numbers of organisations using them to share information, market themselves, sell goods or services and advertise jobs.

After gaining experience, you could progress to project management level. A talented web content manager could move into freelance or website development consultancy work.

Advantages/disadvantages

This is an expanding market with high rewards on offer if you are creative and have technical skills.

As you are responsible for your company's website, the work will sometimes involve high levels of pressure.

The skills that you will develop in this role are transferable and could open up opportunities to work for a variety of companies.

Money guide

The starting salary for a web content manager would usually be in the region of £24,000.

Those with experience in the field could expect to earn £25,000–£35,000 a year.

Senior web managers with additional responsibilities could achieve £40,000–£50,000.

Related opportunities

- Database Administrator p140
- Network Manager p143
- Software Developer/Programmer p145

Further information

British Interactive Media Association
www.bima.co.uk

e-skills UK
www.e-skills.com

SOFTWARE DEVELOPER/ PROGRAMMER

ENTRY LEVEL 5

Qualifications and courses

Entry is usually by means of a degree, Foundation degree or HNC/HND in a relevant subject, for example programming, software engineering or computer science, or a degree with modules in computer graphics or HTML and Java programming. The normal minimum entry requirements for degrees are 2 A levels/3 H grades and 5 GCSEs/National 5s (A*–C/A–C), and for Foundation degrees or HNC/HNDs 1 A level/2 H grades and 3 GCSEs/National 5s (A*–C/A–C) are typically required. For entry onto a technical degree, an A level/H grade in Maths or a science may be required. You could also complete a postgraduate degree and specialise in a specific branch of IT or computer science, such as artificial intelligence.

Entry with a degree in an unrelated subject area is possible; larger employers recruit graduates from all disciplines. However as the industry is competitive it may be beneficial to take a conversion course or postgraduate course in a computing subject.

Entry without a degree, Foundation degree or HNC/HND is unusual unless you have substantial experience in programming work and experience of designing or programming websites using new media. A strong portfolio will be required.

Further study is available, from in-house training to professional qualifications. These include the BCS Professional Certification, Diploma and Professional Graduate Diploma in IT and the Institute for the Management of Information Systems (IMIS) Foundation Diploma, Diploma and Higher Diploma.

Software companies also offer training courses, which include the Microsoft Certified Solution Developer (MCSD) and Certified Applications Developer (MCAD) certifications, the Sun Microsystems Java Certified Programmer (SCJP) and Developer (SCJD) certifications, and the Oracle PL/SQL Developer (databases) certification.

What the work involves

You will be designing, developing and testing computer software for your clients to improve their business's productivity and efficiency.

You may also improve existing software by analysing and fixing any problems.

Your clients could be companies from the finance, insurance, retail or building industries.

You will work closely with a team of other programmers and designers to develop a detailed specification for the software and present this back to your client.

You will write the programming code for the new software from scratch or adapt an existing code.

You will then be responsible for testing and maintaining the software, and making sure your client is happy with the new system.

Type of person suited to this work

You will need to have excellent IT skills, with an in-depth knowledge of up-to-date packages and software coding techniques.

You must be a good communicator, as you will be working with other IT professionals and members of staff.

Being logical and having a knack for problem solving will be vital in this work, as you will need to come up with new programming codes and restore existing ones.

Working conditions

Most software developers/programmers work normal office hours. If there is a deadline to meet you might work overtime or at the weekend.

Software developers/programmers are employed by a variety of industries; these include retail, finance, engineering and government bodies.

You will be based in an office, but you might need to travel around the country when meeting clients.

Future prospects

You can progress into senior or management roles, or work as a contracted IT consultant.

Some software developers/programmers become self-employed or become trainers.

Advantages/disadvantages

You will need to keep up to date with new and developing IT techniques; this could prove difficult if you wanted a career break.

There are great opportunities for promotion, leading to senior management roles and consultancy.

Money guide

Starting salaries may be around £20,000–£26,000.

This can increase to £28,000–£40,000 once you have gained several years' experience.

Senior and management roles can pay over £50,000.

Related opportunities

- Interactive Media Designer p141
- Online/Web Content Manager p144
- Website Designer p150

Further information

British Interactive Media Association
www.bima.co.uk

SOFTWARE ENGINEER

ENTRY LEVEL 6

Qualifications and courses

The usual entry qualification is a degree or a master's in a relevant subject, for example software engineering, computer science, or electronic engineering. The normal minimum entry requirements for degrees are 2 A levels/3 H grades and 5 GCSEs/National 5s (A*–C/A–C). Required subjects usually include maths and physics. IT conversion courses are available for those without a computing degree.

Pre-entry experience is advantageous in this competitive industry. There are sandwich degrees containing 1-year work placements, and voluntary work and internships are also possible.

Should you have no formal qualifications, there may be the opportunity of an apprenticeship in IT.

In the past, engineers just designed software to meet a business's needs, but you now generally need to know how to perform a computer programmer's work as well. Most companies offer employees ongoing training, but you will need experience using different programming languages, real-time operating systems (RTOS), embedded systems, microcontrollers, device drivers, microprocessors or system-on-chip technology etc.

Companies such as Apple, Oracle and Microsoft offer appealing certifications in their own products. For example, Microsoft offers the Microsoft Certified Solutions Developer (MCSD) and Certified Solutions Expert (MCSE). Experience in business, management and finance may also prove advantageous.

Software engineering is a constantly evolving profession and you must ensure you keep up to date by completing continuing professional development (CPD) courses available from institutes such as the Chartered Institute for IT (BCS).

What the work involves

Software engineers test and evaluate software that helps computers to run effectively. You will then debug faulty software and constantly research new technologies to find the best solutions.

You may also develop new software such as computer games, operating systems and business applications.

As well as providing technical support to businesses and organisations, you may also build new computer systems for them from scratch.

You will work with computer codes and will usually specialise in either systems or applications.

Type of person suited to this work

You will need technical, practical and creative ability. It will be useful if you have a personal interest in writing your own programs or have built your own computer system.

You should be an excellent problem solver. You will need to be able to anticipate problems and work out ways to prevent them.

You must be patient and methodical to be able to produce accurate work when your deadline is close and your tests are not going well.

Your teamwork and communication skills should be strong as you will be working with a project team. At higher levels you will be giving presentations or lectures.

Working conditions

You may be based in a laboratory, a research and development unit, or a workshop.

At project management level you may travel nationally and internationally to meetings and conferences.

You will work a 37 to 40 hour week but you will need to be flexible and put in extra hours at key times.

Future prospects

Talented software engineers are increasingly in demand, and so job prospects are good in many sectors, including academia, government research, computer manufacturing, software development and electronics and telecommunications.

You will have more opportunities if you are both creative and technical.

You will start work as a junior member of a project team. With experience you could move into lecturing or project management. You might also choose to become an IT consultant or work as a contractor.

Advantages/disadvantages

Your team's work could make the headlines. New products and cutting-edge research, such as the building of world-class supercomputers, are of international interest.

Solutions to problems do not happen quickly. It can be really frustrating to retest hundreds of times and still not get the result you are looking for.

Money guide

The starting salary for a graduate software engineer is typically around £21,000.

With experience this can rise to between £25,000 and £38,000. The average salary in this field is £30,000 a year.

Senior software engineers and those with managerial responsibilities usually earn over £45,000.

Related opportunities

- Computer Hardware Engineer p138
- Interactive Media Designer p141
- Software Developer/Programmer p145

Further information

e-skills UK
www.e-skills.com

Institution of Analysts and Programmers (IAP)
www.iap.org.uk

SYSTEMS ANALYST

ENTRY LEVEL 5

Qualifications and courses

A degree, Foundation degree or HNC/HND is usually required. Useful degree subjects include computer science, information technology and e-systems design and technology. Minimum entry requirements for these degrees are usually 2 A levels/3 H grades (including Maths) and 5 GCSEs/National 5s. Work experience is important to enter this profession, so taking a course with a placement year could prove advantageous. Entry to the profession is open to those with unrelated degrees but a postgraduate conversion course in IT may be needed.

A sponsored degree in Information Technology Management for Business (ITMB) from e-skills UK is available. This is focused on learning through project work in teams with external mentors from sponsoring organisations.

Alternatively, entrants can gain industry experience through a Higher Apprenticeship for IT, Software, Web and Telecoms Professionals which combines practical training with a professional qualification. For entry onto a Higher Apprenticeship you will need qualifications such as A levels/H grades or a Level 3 NVQ. As part of your apprenticeship you may study an NVQ in Communication Technology for Practitioners and Professionals (Levels 1–4), the City & Guilds Advanced Diploma for IT Professionals (Level 3), or the BTEC Level 3 qualifications in IT.

You will be expected to have a working knowledge of programming skills and analysis methods. Industry bodies such as the Chartered Institute for IT (BCS), e-skills, and the Institute for the Management of Information Systems (IMIS) offer relevant development courses that can be completed whilst working. Certifications are also available from program vendors such as Microsoft, IBM and Oracle.

What the work involves

You will prepare a brief of what your client wants a computer system to do and then translate this brief into recommendations for IT solutions.

To determine the system needed you will use performance monitoring or sizing tools. You will then design, cost and recommend suitable hardware/software solutions.

If purpose-built software is needed, you may write it or brief a programmer on your team. You will go on to install and test the configuration you have developed.

Type of person suited to this work

An excellent all-round knowledge of IT, including hardware and software, is vital. You will also have to keep up to date with new IT products as you will be expected to be the technical expert.

Your teamwork and communication skills will need to be good as you will be working with business clients and colleagues such as business analysts and programmers to produce the best value system as a team.

To make systems that work well and enhance profitability and efficiency for your customer, you will also need to be a problem solver who understands how businesses work.

Working conditions

Employers include software and systems houses, IT consultants as well as organisations in sectors such as commerce, finance and banking, retail and health.

You will be mainly based in an office, working with other members of the project team. You will have to travel to clients at all stages of the project and may be away for several days when installing and testing the new system.

Although your hours will be usually Monday to Friday, you will need to work some evenings and weekends to meet deadlines.

Future prospects

You could move from this broad-based job either to specialise in offering IT solutions for business, or into a technical area such as software or website development.

Progression is possible into a senior analyst role, project management or consultancy work. The speed of advancement depends upon the size and type of organisation you work for. You could also become an independent consultant.

Advantages/disadvantages

It is rewarding to combine hardware and software to create a unique solution designed for your customer.

You will have the opportunity to meet a range of people and work on a variety of IT projects.

Trying to work to strict deadlines and a tight budget can involve high levels of pressure.

You have full responsibility for meeting your clients' needs which could be stressful.

Money guide

Graduates usually receive a starting salary of £20,000–£27,000.

Experienced systems analysts can expect to earn £30,000 to £45,000. The average wage is currently £40,000.

Project managers can earn up to £60,000.

Salaries tend to be higher in London, the south-east of England and the Midlands.

Related opportunities

- Database Administrator p140
- Network Manager p143
- Software Developer/Programmer p145

Further information

BCS, The Chartered Institute for IT
www.bcs.org

e-skills UK
www.e-skills.com

Learning and Performance Institute
www.learningandperformanceinstitute.com

TECHNICAL SALES SPECIALIST

ENTRY LEVEL 5

Qualifications and courses

You will usually need a degree, Foundation degree or HNC/HND in a computer-related subject to enter this job. The normal minimum entry requirements for degrees are 2 A levels/3 H grades and 5 GCSEs/National 5s (A*–C/A–C), and for Foundation degrees or HNC/HNDs, 1 A level/2 H grades and 4 GCSEs/National 5s (A*–C/A–C). Maths and physics are often required subjects for entry.

A funded route that may be on offer in your area is the IT and Telecoms Professionals Apprenticeship.

Experience in sales is extremely useful. If you have a sales or telesales background and want formal IT training you can pursue a City & Guilds Level 4 Higher Professional Diploma in Information Management using ICT or a BTEC Level 3 qualification in IT Practitioners. Recently, a new degree course has been founded in partnership with several successful IT companies; the Information Technology Management for Business (ITMB) BSc integrates a BSc Honours degree with learning, teaching and assessment aspects.

Initial training is usually intense as you will need to gain a thorough technical knowledge of your employer's products and their preferred communication style.

The IT industry is constantly developing and it is essential you keep up to date with new technologies. Professional qualifications may prove useful and can be obtained from the various professional bodies, such as the Chartered Institute for IT (BCS). IT companies such as Microsoft also offer sales workshops.

What the work involves

You will talk to customers interested in your product, finding out what they are looking for, answering technical questions and explaining how the product works.

You will then present what the client requires to an in-house technical team and work on adapting the product to suit the client.

Presentation of the finished product to your client is an important part of making the sale.

Type of person suited to this work

It is essential to be personable and persuasive. You will also need good oral and written communication skills as you will be dealing with customers as well as writing up reports and proposals.

You must be able to clearly explain technical jargon to customers who may have no technical knowledge. Equally, you will need to understand all the technical specifications of your products as some of your customers will be experts.

It is a competitive market so you will need to be good at selling, negotiating and building customer loyalty. You will also need to be up to date with all the products out there so that you know the competition.

Working conditions

Employers include large IT companies producing and retailing products such as mobile phones, computer hardware and software. Large specialist IT retailers also employ technical sales staff.

You might be based in an office, dealing with customers by phone or email, or in a retail outlet selling directly.

If you specialise in selling to retail chains or organisations, you will spend a lot of time driving and in meetings. A driving licence will be useful.

Your hours will depend on your customers. Your employer may operate a shift system to deal with queries and sales from early until late, 7 days a week.

Future prospects

The demand for new IT products continues to grow but new competitors are always entering the market. Strong areas of demand include secure wireless broadband and mobile working.

You might be able to gain promotion to a supervisory or sales management role, or work as an IT consultant, a lecturer or contractor.

Advantages/disadvantages

If you close a deal at a good price or sell extras such as a service contract, you could be paid a bonus.

Selling can be very stressful, with high sales targets to achieve.

It can be frustrating if you spend a lot of time with a customer without it resulting in a purchase.

Money guide

Starting salaries are usually £20,000–£30,000 per year.

As you gain experience you could earn £35,000 or more.

Sales managers can earn up to £80,000.

Additional benefits may include profit sharing, performance-related pay, mobile phone, laptop and a car.

Related opportunities

- Business Analyst p136
- Computer Technical Support Person/Helpdesk Adviser p139
- IT Trainer p142

Further information

BCS, The Chartered Institute for IT
www.bcs.org

e-skills UK
www.e-skills.com

Institute of Sales & Marketing Management
www.ismm.co.uk

TELECOMMUNICATIONS TECHNICIAN

ENTRY LEVEL 2

Qualifications and courses

You can enter this profession as an apprentice, where you will be supervised by a qualified telecommunications technician. Apprenticeships usually last for 2 years, giving you practical work experience as well as the opportunity to work towards a relevant professional qualification such as an NVQ/SVQ Level 2 or 3.

The IT and Telecoms Professionals Apprenticeship requires that candidates have 4 GCSEs/National 5s (A*–C/A–C) which must include English, Maths, a science and technology, or a BTEC Level 2 qualification in a relevant subject. There are Intermediate (Level 2), Advanced (Level 3), and Higher (Level 4) Apprenticeships available.

HNCs/HNDs, undergraduate or postgraduate degrees are available in subjects such as telecommunications, communications engineering, computing, electrical engineering, data communications and digital communications. The normal minimum entry requirements for a degree are 2 A levels/H grades, including Maths, Electronics or a physical science, and 5 GCSEs/National 5s (A*–C/A–C). HNCs/HNDs and Foundation degrees typically require 1 A level/H grade and 4 GCSEs/National 5s (A*–C/A–C), including English and Maths.

There are also various vocational qualifications available, including the City & Guilds Level 2 Award in Communications Cabling and Level 3 Diploma in ICT Communications Systems, the NVQ Level 3 in Engineering Maintenance (Communication Electronics), and the BTEC Level 3 qualifications in Communications Technology.

Depending on the company you work for, continuing in-service training may be available. This can be combined with specific manufacturers' courses and vendor qualifications such as the networking qualifications offered by Cisco and Microsoft.

You may also be expected to hold a full driving licence.

What the work involves

Telecommunications technicians install, test and repair networking and communications technology and systems across a range of applications, including mobile phones, telephones, satellite and radio networks and aerials.

Your day to day tasks will vary but you may be assembling, installing and testing telecommunications equipment; laying copper and fibre optic wire in the street or other sites; setting up or repairing networks.

You may also be involved in designing or consulting on plans for telecommunications systems.

Type of person suited to this work

You should be interested in maths, IT, electronics and communications.

As you will be working in a team and explaining technical terms to customers you should have good communication and customer service skills. You should also have good writing skills to write up reports and produce statistics.

As you may be installing systems and laying wires which may involve heavy lifting and carrying, digging or using ladders, you should be fit and have a good head for heights.

Working conditions

You will work between 9am and 5pm, Monday to Friday. You may be required to work shifts which may include evenings, weekends or to be available on-call. Overtime may be necessary to complete projects or meet deadlines.

You may be based in a factory workshop or in a control centre from where you will travel to complete projects. These may be in homes, offices or outdoors.

Future prospects

To progress as a telecommunications technician you can apply to become a professionally recognised engineering technician (EngTech) or ICT technician (ICTTech) with an industry body, which include the Engineering Council and the Institution of Engineering and Technology (IET). You need to possess at least a Level 3 BTEC, NVQ or equivalent qualification.

With experience and qualifications you may be promoted to senior technician or supervisor. With further experience, qualifications and skills you can apply for incorporated and chartered engineer status.

You can become self-employed, or work on a contract basis. There are also numerous opportunities to work abroad.

Advantages/disadvantages

You may be in a diverse working environment as new and exciting developments in technology are occurring rapidly.

You may have to work outdoors in uncomfortable weather conditions.

Money guide

Your starting salary will be around £12,000–£15,000 a year.

With experience and qualifications you can earn up to £25,000.

The most experienced technicians can earn in excess of £30,000.

Earnings can increase with shift allowances and overtime.

Related opportunities

- Computer Hardware Engineer p138
- Electrical Engineer p203
- Network Manager p143

Further information

Institute of Telecommunications Professionals
www.theitp.org

Institution of Engineering and Technology
www.theiet.org

WEBSITE DESIGNER

ENTRY LEVEL 3

Qualifications and courses

There are no specific qualifications needed to become a web designer, although most designers have experience in other design fields or have taken training in web design. Most employers will expect you to have some experience and to have a related qualification such as a Foundation degree, computer related Honours degree or HND that covers internet technology, graphic or interactive design. To gain entry to a degree you will need 2 A levels/3 H grades and 5 GCSEs/National 5s, whilst Foundation degrees or HNDs require 1 A level/2 H grades and 4 GCSEs/National 5s (A*–C/A–C) or equivalent qualifications.

A good working knowledge of HTML is essential. It could be useful to have experience working with Dreamweaver, Photoshop, Flash and Fireworks, CSS, Javascript and .Net. Professionally accredited training courses and online tutorials are also available from a number of recognised institutions such as the Chartered Institute for IT (BCS).

On-the-job training is common, but you will also need to keep updated with the latest developments in the field.

You could also study for qualifications such as the BTEC Interactive Use of Media Level 1–3, OCR ITQ Levels 1 to 3, OCR Creative iMedia Levels 1 to 3 and City & Guilds E-Quals IT Users awards Level 2 (Diploma) and Level 3 (Advanced Diploma).

Organisations such as the Certified Internet Web Professional (CIW) also offer industry certifications you could work towards, such as the CIW Web Specialist course.

What the work involves

Web designers build new or improve existing websites. You will be responsible for dealing with the visual image of the website but you will not necessarily be involved with coding the website or making it function.

You will need to ensure your websites are designed to be accessible through different, evolving platforms, such as PCs, Macs, mobile phones, tablets, and digital television.

You will meet with clients and discuss what they want their website to look like and who it is aimed at. You will then have to use their requirements to create the design.

Type of person suited to this work

You will need excellent communication skills, as you have to understand the requirements of your client and create a design from their instructions.

You will need a great deal of creativity, to make the site as attractive as possible, but it is also essential to have a good understanding of consumer needs, in order to make the design comprehensible and functional.

Good time management is necessary, as you will be working to very strict deadlines.

Working conditions

You will usually work 37 to 40 hours a week, Monday to Friday, although you will sometimes have to work extra hours to meet a deadline, or when problems occur with a website.

Most of your time will be spent indoors in an office, or at home on your own computer if you are self-employed. When meeting clients, it may sometimes be necessary to travel.

Future prospects

You could work for web design companies, in the IT departments of large public and private organisations, or as a freelance designer.

Working for a company could give you the opportunity to work your way up into a design team management post, or expand your skills to become a web content manager.

Once you have gained enough experience, you could set up your own web design business.

Advantages/disadvantages

If you enjoy being creative, web designing will give you the opportunity to express your passion on a daily basis.

You will also feel a sense of achievement when you are able to see your finished piece being put to use.

Your clients could be relying on you to create a website that will generate them more business which could mean a lot of pressure to do an excellent job.

You will have to work to strict deadlines and this could mean working extra hours.

Money guide

Starting salaries begin at around £15,000 to £20,000 a year.

The average salary for this line of work is £30,000, with experienced designers earning up to £37,500.

Senior designers and those with specialist skills can earn in excess of £40,000.

Related opportunities

- Business Analyst p136
- Interactive Media Designer p141
- Online/Web Content Manager p144
- Website Developer p151

Further information

BCS, The Chartered Institute for IT
www.bcs.org

British Interactive Media Association
www.bima.co.uk

e-skills UK
www.e-skills.com

UK Web Design Association
www.ukwda.org

WEBSITE DEVELOPER

ENTRY LEVEL 4

Qualifications and courses

Many who are just starting out in this career now have either a Foundation degree, BTEC, HNC/HND award or degree in web development or web design, multimedia design, digital media development, computer programming or a related subject.

Alternatively, there are various vocational qualifications you could complete, such as the BTEC Level 3 qualifications in Art and Design (Multimedia), Computer Studies or IT. Applicants typically need 4 GCSEs/ National 5s (A*–C/A–C) for entry. Alternatively, NVQs/ SVQs are available in IT practitioner subjects, including website development, and there are HNCs/HNDs in various IT and design related subjects. Entry to these courses typically requires at least 1 A level/2 H grades and 4 GCSEs/National 5s (A*–C/A–C).

It is possible to become a web developer without qualifications, but employers will want evidence of your experience and employability. You should therefore keep a portfolio of your work. Developing and designing sites for local community groups or voluntary agencies could be a useful way to get your portfolio started.

It is important to be familiar with a number of areas, including the various computing languages, common operating systems and servers, databases and web programming, networking and security, graphics, animation and web design software. Training courses are available from national bodies and program vendors such as Microsoft and ORACLE.

You should also have an understanding of the World Wide Web Consortium (W3C) standards for website accessibility.

Due to the evolving nature of the IT industry generally, you should try to keep up to date with industry developments, and continuing professional development (CPD), through courses run by larger companies or membership of The Chartered Institute for IT, is advised.

What the work involves

As a web developer, you will be in charge of working with a client, learning what they require from their website and then programming the website to make sure it functions as it should.

You will often work alongside a web designer to work on the site's appearance.

You will have to make sure that the site can be smoothly integrated into the client's existing network and also find and fix any 'bugs' before the site goes 'live'.

Type of person suited to this work

Excellent web and database programming skills are essential. These should coincide with good problem-solving skills.

You will need to be committed to working to deadlines and to keeping up to date with developments in the latest technology.

It is also very important to have good communication skills, as you will be working with clients and listening to their requirements, before ensuring that their website functions in the way they desire.

Working conditions

Normal working hours are 37 to 40 hours a week, Monday to Friday. Near to deadlines some evening and weekend work may be necessary. As this is an industry with a large proportion of workers who are self-employed, working hours can be also be very flexible.

Work is mostly office based. If you work for a company, this will usually mean working on one site, but self-employed web developers will often have to work from home or from the client's premises.

Future prospects

The internet and e-commerce are constantly expanding and consequently, you could find opportunities in a range of industries.

Once you have gained enough experience, you could specialise in a particular area, such as e-commerce.

You could also progress to more senior roles, such as project leader or lead programmer. Alternatively you could work for yourself and run your own company.

Advantages/disadvantages

It is extremely satisfying to see your finished website up and running.

You need to make sure you are up to date with new design trends and software, which could be challenging.

You will also face a lot of pressure from clients, who wish to see their website completed to a deadline and to a high standard.

Money guide

Salaries start at between £19,000 and £22,000 a year.

With experience this can rise to between £25,000 and £35,000.

Lead developers could earn up to £45,000.

Related opportunities

- Interactive Media Designer p141
- Software Developer/Programmer p145
- Website Designer p150

Further information

BCS, The Chartered Institute for IT
www.bcs.org

e-skills UK
www.e-skills.com

Design, Arts and Crafts

The idea of turning your arts and crafts hobby into a career may be one you like the thought of. Jobs in this sector can involve working in any medium, from textiles to jewellery to metalwork or children's toys. You may find yourself working for a company but many people in this industry are self-employed working for a range of clients. This means you need to be very organised and have brilliant communication skills to ensure you can give your clients exactly what they want.

The jobs featuring in this section are listed below. For similar jobs to these have a look at these sections: *Marketing, Advertising, Media, Print and Publishing* on page 375 and *Performing Arts* starting on page 407.

ANIMATOR

ENTRY LEVEL 5

Qualifications and courses

Entry requirements vary, however you will usually need an HND, Foundation degree or degree in animation, art and design or a related area for an entry level position. A relevant postgraduate qualification can also be an asset.

A portfolio of relevant work demonstrated by a show reel is essential. Some people study a Foundation course in art and design before starting their degree in order to develop a portfolio. 5 GCSEs/National 5s (A*–C/A–C) are usually required for this. Unpaid work experience as a general or animation assistant is also a good way to build up relevant skills, as is applying for a residency.

The usual entry position for animators is studio runner. There are no entry requirements for this position, so candidates without a degree/HND who are particularly talented may still be able to break in, but in practice most runners are graduates. Progression could then be to a junior role such as assistant animator, storyboard artist, inbetweener or digital painter.

Entering animation competitions, submitting short films and ideas to broadcasters or visiting festivals are all good ways to show enthusiasm, develop your reputation and increase your chances of finding work. Building a network of contacts can help you get started and find work in the future.

What the work involves

Animators produce images that appear to come to life on the screen, both creatively and commercially, for use by TV companies, games developers, in advertising, on websites and in films.

There are 4 specialisms: traditional (2D drawn), 2D computer generated, 3D computer generated and stop frame or stop motion. In all of these styles you will work to create a continuous story.

Type of person suited to this work

You will need strong creative flair and imagination to develop new ideas for animated stories and characters.

You must have excellent computer skills; a knowledge of software such as Flash, Maya and After Effects is essential. However modelling and life drawing are still important.

You must be patient, have a keen eye for detail and be able to work in a team as well as under pressure. Problem-solving skills are also necessary in a job where you might need to adapt to technical challenges.

Working conditions

Your working environment will depend on the type of animation you do. In some jobs, you will work with tools to hand-create images or forms in different materials and you could be on your feet (using your hands) all day: bending, lifting and shaping models.

On the other hand, many new animation jobs involve work with specialist computer-aided design (CAD) packages at a computer console; this can be done individually or as part of a team.

Most of your work will be done during normal office hours except when projects have tight deadlines!

Future prospects

This is a highly competitive field. Although there are still some opportunities for traditional drawing-based animators, the main area of growth is in computer generation.

The UK is good for stop motion and children's animation opportunities and the video games industry is also doing very well, however you may have to move abroad for opportunities in other types of animation. The USA has a lot of the largest CGI (computer-generated imagery) companies and East Asia does a lot of 2D animation. Within the UK the best places for opportunities are London, Bristol, Cardiff, Dundee and Manchester.

Once in the industry, contracts are usually short term, but it is possible to move from working as a key animator to an animation director role. At senior levels, you would have more creative input and be less directly involved with the technical side. With experience, you could set up as a freelance animator or start your own company.

Advantages/disadvantages

This type of work can be highly satisfying, providing opportunities to develop your own creative ideas and style. Animation is rising in popularity amongst the public with many animated films being highly successful at the box office.

In more commercial jobs, you would need to produce work under pressure to meet a client's requirements.

Money guide

The Broadcasting, Entertainment, Cinematograph and Theatre Union (BECTU) sets minimum wage guidelines. Beyond these, animators negotiate their own rates and may receive more depending on the project. In the computer games industry bonuses at the end of a project are common.

A new animator can expect a starting salary between £12,000 and £20,000 per year.

An experienced animator could earn up to up to £30,000 and senior animators can expect in excess of £40,000.

Contact BECTU for details of current freelance salaries.

Related opportunities

- Cartoonist p155
- Fine Artist/Sculptor p158
- Graphic Designer p161

Further information

Broadcasting, Entertainment, Cinematograph and Theatre Union
www.bectu.org.uk

Creative Skillset
www.creativeskillset.org

CARTOONIST

ENTRY LEVEL 4

Qualifications and courses

A strong portfolio and relevant experience are usually more important than formal qualifications. However, most entrants have an HNC/HND or degree in an art and design subject, such as graphic design, illustration or fine art. A minimum of 1 A level/H grade in an art and design subject, a relevant BTEC award or a BTEC Diploma in Foundation Studies (Art and Design) are usually needed for entry to an HND/HNC.

In England, Wales and Northern Ireland, many students preparing for a degree also take the art Foundation course. In Scotland the first year of an art and design degree equates to the Foundation year. 5 GCSEs/ National 5s (A*–C/A–C) and a relevant A level/H grade are usually required for entry to both the Foundation course and the degree.

Sometimes well-established cartoonists run workshops for both adults and young people. These may be at the Cartoon Museum in London, at conventions or privately. The Cartoonists' Club of Great Britain and the Professional Cartoonists' Organisation (PCO) also run training events. These are good for honing your skills and keeping up to date with the industry.

Cartoonists are required to convey a message with humour, and are increasingly required to have websites that show examples of their work so a qualification in IT could be very useful.

What the work involves

You will plan and draw original cartoons and captions. These can be single images, whole cartoon strips or entire books. You will promote and market your work, for example by sending out samples to newspapers and advertising through the internet.

Cartoonists create images for greetings cards, adverts, book illustrations, magazines, newspapers and websites.

A small number of cartoonists are employed to run regular cartoon features in newspapers or other media whereas others maintain a web comic of their work.

Type of person suited to this work

Creativity and an excellent sense of humour are essential. You should have a wild imagination and be up to date with current trends. Cartoon ideas often draw on situational humour or arise in quick response to headline news.

Even if you use a software art package, good drawing skills and a developed, individual style are very important. You may have to work to deadlines so need to be well organised, with good business management skills. Self-motivation is important.

As you will be sending out examples of your work to potential employers, you will need to be able to deal with rejection and have the confidence to persevere.

With commissioned work you will need to be able to stick to a design brief and show awareness of the target market as well as incorporating your unique flair.

Working conditions

Most professional cartoonists work on a freelance basis, either in a studio or from home. This can be isolating as many work alone. Much of your time will be spent at a drawing board or a computer where you will either sit or stand using the materials required.

If you are self-employed you will have the freedom to set your own working hours. You might need to attend meetings with clients or potential employers, which could involve travelling long distances and working longer hours.

Future prospects

With a good reputation and popular style or cartoon character, you could be employed by publishers, advertising agencies, television studios, newspapers, magazines or theme parks. With experience you could run workshops in schools, libraries and museums.

You could also specialise in one form of cartoon such as political satire or comic strips, or move into other areas such as illustration or graphic design.

Advantages/disadvantages

As cartoonists are usually paid for individual pieces of work they have little job security, especially at the start of their careers.

You would have the satisfaction of creating original work and seeing it in print.

If you are working from home, set up costs are relatively low.

Money guide

Salaries vary greatly due to the freelance nature of the industry and cartoonists are usually paid for each piece of commissioned work. A skilled, established cartoonist may charge £300 per picture.

As a guide, new cartoonists with regular work could earn up to £15,000 per year. Established, well-known cartoonists whose work is in demand could earn up to £50,000.

It is possible to earn higher levels of pay by doing commercial work for greetings cards and adverts. Cartoonists creating work to illustrate books can earn royalties from sales.

Related opportunities

- Animator p154
- Fine Artist/Sculptor p158
- Graphic Designer p161

Further information

Arts Council England
www.artscouncil.org.uk

Creative and Cultural Skills
www.ccskills.org.uk

The Cartoon Art Trust
www.cartoonmuseum.org

COSTUME DESIGNER ENTRY LEVEL 4

Qualifications and courses

Entry without qualifications may be possible, however most people have a Foundation degree, degree or postgraduate diploma in a relevant subject, such as art, costume design, fashion, theatre design or performing arts (production). Entrants commonly begin their career as a wardrobe assistant or costume maker and progress to designer as they develop experience and build contacts.

Useful training courses include the City & Guilds qualification in Design and Craft – Fashion (Theatre Costume) (Levels 2 and 3), the Royal Academy of Dramatic Art (RADA)'s 2-year vocational course in Theatre Costume, and various awards from the National Open College Network (NOCN).

Work experience is invaluable as it helps you to build up a portfolio or 'showreel' of your design work. As well as contacting theatres and film and TV companies, you could become involved in student productions or amateur theatre, or possibly undertake a work placement as part of your degree. Those interested in costume design for film and TV could apply for the BBC Design Trainee Scheme. There are also Apprenticeships in Costume and Wardrobe available.

Joining the Society of British Theatre Designers or the Costume Society might facilitate networking and lead to work experience opportunities.

What the work involves

You will design, buy or hire the clothes and accessories worn by casts in films, plays and TV shows.

You will read scripts, research the period and setting of a production and come up with original sketches to best represent the director's vision. You will then decide which fabrics and materials to use. You could also be involved with making costumes or overseeing costume production.

You will be responsible for organising fittings and ensuring that costumes are delivered on time, are comfortable and within budget. Depending on the size of the production, you may also manage a team of costume professionals.

Type of person suited to this work

Creativity and originality are essential. Having the skills to draw designs by hand and to use specialist computer-aided design (CAD) software when required is also important.

You should have a meticulous eye for detail and demonstrate a passion for costume history, fashion and the arts. It is important to be a good communicator and to work well in a team.

You must be organised to ensure that projects are carried out on time, within budget and as requested. As deadlines can be tight, you need the ability to work well under pressure.

Working conditions

Hours are long and irregular, including evenings and weekends. It is possible to work for production companies but most costume designers are freelancers who travel around the UK and sometimes overseas.

You will normally work in a studio using drawing tables, computers, cutting tables and sewing machines.

It is likely that you will be standing for long periods of time and you may do some heavy lifting.

Future prospects

Costume designer vacancies are rarely advertised and most work is centred in major cities such as London and Manchester. It is essential for costume designers to have a strong portfolio and to build up good contacts.

If you work for a large organisation such as the BBC you could progress to head of department or to head of wardrobe for a theatre company.

Advantages/disadvantages

It is rewarding to see your original work on the stage or screen, providing enjoyment for viewers.

You might be able to work flexible hours but they could also be unsocial.

You will often be required to work to tight deadlines which could be stressful.

Money guide

Industry salaries vary depending on the type of employer and geographical location. Earnings in film and TV are generally higher than in theatre.

The starting salary for a costume designer is typically between £18,000 and £28,000 per year.

Established designers can earn £30,000 to £40,000 with senior costume designers receiving salaries in excess of £40,000.

The Broadcasting, Entertainment, Cinematograph and Theatre Union (BECTU) website lists guidance on the rates charged for freelance work dependent on the budget and seniority involved.

Related opportunities

- Fashion Designer/Milliner p157
- Tailor/Dressmaker p227
- Visual Merchandiser p173

Further information

Costume Society
www.costumesociety.org.uk

Department for Culture, Media and Sport
www.gov.uk/government/organisations/department-for-culture-media-sport

Design Council
www.designcouncil.org.uk

FASHION DESIGNER/ MILLINER

ENTRY LEVEL 4

Qualifications and courses

Entrants to this profession usually have a degree, Foundation degree or HNC/HND in a relevant subject such as fashion, textiles or millinery. City & Guilds and the National Open College Network provide other general design courses whereas a postgraduate degree may help those who wish to specialise in a particular area or whose first degree was in an unrelated subject.

Candidates without a degree or graduates from non-related subjects can sometimes enter this industry but they must have relevant work experience and be able to demonstrate expertise and interest in fashion.

All entrants are strongly advised to pursue work experience, either voluntary or paid, to build up their portfolio of designs, technical drawings and garments. Placements show commitment to the profession and provide opportunities to make industry contacts. Some graduates choose to gain international experience with European or American designers before looking to break into the UK market.

New designers are normally selected based on their portfolio and an interview. Your portfolio should include technical drawings, mood boards and designs. Some interviews may require evidence of actual garments you have made. Networking is also a very important tool when trying to find work, so it is important during your education to make as many contacts with people in the industry as possible.

What the work involves

Using your design sense and knowledge of textiles and other materials you will develop clothing, shoes and accessories. A milliner specialises in creating headwear.

You could work in haute couture, ready-to-wear or high street fashion. You will be responsible for analysing trends in fabrics, colours and shapes.

As well as creating initial designs by hand and with computer-aided design (CAD), you may also oversee the manufacture of these items.

Type of person suited to this work

It is essential to have the creativity and the imagination to develop original designs as well as the foresight to read future fashion trends.

Having the skills to draw designs by hand and to use specialist CAD software is also important, as are technical skills, such as pattern cutting, and a good eye for design, colour and detail. These abilities should be balanced with good business sense and the competence to see a project through.

You will also need excellent communication, negotiation and organisational skills to ensure that projects are carried out on time, within budget and as requested.

Working conditions

You will usually work alone or in a small team in a studio. The environment can be dusty and you will be using specialist equipment such as cutting tools and sewing machines.

Hours could be irregular including overtime in the run-up to shows when changes to designs might need to be made at the last minute.

You will also spend some of your time visiting textile producers and clients at their premises which could be overseas.

Future prospects

Most designers work in and around the fashion hub of London.

Career progression depends upon the individual's talent and reputation. You will most likely start as a design assistant and progress to a role as a designer. With experience, it is possible to become a senior or head designer or work in an area such as style consultancy or fashion journalism. There are fewer opportunities for promotion in millinery owing to the smaller size of the industry.

The UK fashion industry has an excellent international reputation, offering the chance to work overseas if desired.

Advantages/disadvantages

Seeing your original ideas in the public eye is satisfying.

You will have the opportunity to travel and meet interesting people of different nationalities.

Working to tight deadlines in the lead-up to shows can be stressful.

Money guide

Salaries vary according to the company type and location.

Newly qualified designers can expect to earn £18,000 to £22,000 per year.

After 3 to 4 years of experience, you could have a salary of £25,000 to £40,000. Senior designers can achieve more than £60,000.

Your salary will be determined by your success and the most famous designers have very high incomes. Rates for freelance designers vary widely and if they have an agent, that agent will generally take up to 30% of earnings.

Related opportunities

- Illustrator/Technical Illustrator p162
- Interior Designer p163
- Visual Merchandiser p173

Further information

Design Council
www.designcouncil.org.uk

FINE ARTIST/ SCULPTOR

ENTRY LEVEL 1

Qualifications and courses

There are no specific entry requirements, artistic talent being the most important attribute. However, the majority of artists choose to pursue formal qualifications to increase their chance of success. A degree or HNC/ HND in fine art, art and design or a related subject would be useful. Postgraduate qualifications in fine art are also available. Sculptors usually have a fine art degree with a specialisation in sculpture. Entry requirements for degree courses vary. Some institutions require A levels/H grades in relevant subjects, some want the student to have completed a Foundation degree and others accept students solely on the strength of their portfolio.

Artists without a degree often take short courses, including evening or weekend classes, one-week intensive classes, certificates and diplomas. Entrants who undertake voluntary work experience or work shadowing in the creative industries can improve their employment prospects.

It is up to artists and sculptors to create their own opportunities for showcasing their work. Gallery owners and curators are always looking for new artists but you can also display your work online through your own website or established ones. Networking is important and having an agent may be useful.

What the work involves

Fine artists work with various media such as oil paints and charcoal to create 2D pieces of various sizes. Sculptors create 3D pieces and use materials such as clay, stone and metal.

You will be responsible for promoting your work to sponsors, galleries and other organisations by networking or issuing publicity material.

You might organise solo or joint exhibitions in a variety of venues to showcase your work. Some residencies are available in institutions such as schools and prisons.

Type of person suited to this work

You will be creating original works of art so need strong artistic and technical skills, well-developed powers of observation and a vivid imagination.

Self-belief and motivation are important as it takes perseverance to turn an original idea into a finished piece. Sculptors will also require a high level of manual dexterity.

Many artists are self-employed, necessitating good business sense and organisational skills. Strong communication skills will help you to negotiate exhibitions with galleries and network with contacts in the art world.

Working conditions

You will work in a studio, on location or teach workshops at a residency. Much of your time will be spent alone and you will set your own hours.

Many artistic materials are dusty, oily or may stain and, even wearing overalls, you can expect to get dirty. You might have to work with solvents and other chemicals.

Sculptors will work with dangerous tools such as knives, chisels and welding equipment.

Future prospects

This job demands confidence and persistence as few artists and sculptors earn their living from art alone. You could earn additional income by working in related areas such as arts education, community development and in art galleries.

A developing artist should join networks to make contacts. It is possible to sell your work through a number of galleries, shops, workshop co-operatives, studios and the internet. You could progress from showcasing your work in a group exhibition to securing a solo exhibition. You could eventually have your own studio, secure an agent and have your work displayed in national and international art fairs.

Advantages/disadvantages

The job is fulfilling as you will have the pleasure of seeing customers enjoy and appreciate your art.

It can be an isolated way of life and you may not always receive recognition for your work.

Money guide

Artists' earnings vary depending on their talent, experience and reputation.

While it is possible to earn a regular income from your work, many artists have another job to provide a more stable source of income.

The Artists Information Company have an artist's fees toolkit on their website which provides guidance on the rates artists should charge for their work.

New artists displaying at degree shows should expect no more than £1,000 for a BA-level piece of work or £2,000 for MA work.

Related opportunities

- Cartoonist p155
- Graphic Designer p161
- Illustrator/Technical Illustrator p162

Further information

Arts Council England
www.artscouncil.org.uk

Department for Culture, Media and Sport
www.gov.uk/government/organisations/department-for-culture-media-sport

Scottish Arts Council
www.creativescotland.com

GEMMOLOGIST

ENTRY LEVEL 4

Qualifications and courses

Some people enter this profession with relevant experience in areas such as cutting or retailing gems, dealing, mining or auctioneering, however there are no set entry requirements. Some entrants are graduates of relevant subjects such as art, craft, earth sciences, geology, science (physics in particular) and technology. Other useful qualifications include a degree in a geoscience subject, such as geology, geophysics or geochemistry, and an HND in Gemmology is available from Birmingham City University.

Entrants are most likely to train on the job and study for qualifications on a part-time basis. The Gemmological Association (GEM-A) offers qualifications which combine theoretical and practical work. These generally take 3 months to a year to complete. Jewellery courses and qualifications are available in many institutions throughout the UK.

What the work involves

Gemmologists work with diamonds, gems, precious stones and other ornamental materials. You will identify such materials and examine their quality. This may involve assessing or grading the cut of the stone, or identifying flaws or imitations (stones that are made of synthetic or artificial materials).

You are likely to work for a jewellery house where you will be involved in making valuations for customers and clients, and buying and selling stones.

You may also be employed by an insurance company where you will make appraisals for those who wish to insure their jewellery.

Type of person suited to this work

It is important that you have an interest in rocks, gems and crystals, design, the earth sciences and geology. You should also have a keen eye for detail as you will have to look for the slightest qualities to make valuations and identify stones.

As your work will mainly be hands on, you should be good with your hands and have good eyesight and memory.

You should be trustworthy and happy to work in high-security environments.

Working conditions

Your working hours will depend on the type of organisation that you work for. If working for a retail jeweller, you might work around 40 hours a week, including weekends.

You could work in an office, laboratory, workshop or studio. If you become involved in mining or travelling to gem markets you might have to work in remote and uncomfortable conditions.

You will use specialist equipment such as lenses, refractometers, spectroscopes and microscopes to examine gemstones. Owing to the nature of your work, you will have to adhere to strict security protocol, including locked doors, barred windows, armed guards, CCTV surveillance and alarm systems.

Future prospects

After you have finished your training and gained qualifications and experience, you may move up to senior management positions.

You may find opportunities in wholesale organisations, retail operations such as jewellery houses, and insurance companies. There may be opportunities to work abroad.

With significant experience and good contacts you may become self-employed, work as a consultant or jewel sourcer.

Some gemmologists, after years of experience, decide to combine their market knowledge with a more creative output by setting up their own business as a jewellery maker or designer.

Advantages/disadvantages

As a self-employed gemmologist your work may involve travel to mines, markets and international gem-selling centres such as Africa, Russia, Australia, Thailand, Brazil or Madagascar.

As you may be working with valuable materials you might have to work in restricted, high security environments.

Money guide

Starting salaries for gemmologists are around £16,000 per year.

As an experienced gemmologist you can earn between £20,000 and £30,000.

A stone buyer at a wholesaler could earn £35,000 a year, rising to £40,000 for managerial roles.

Self-employed gemmologists' salaries vary.

Related opportunities

- Gold/Silversmith/Engraver p160
- Jeweller p460
- Materials Scientist p502

Further information

GEM-A The Gemmological Association of Great Britain
www.gem-a.com

Jewellery and Allied Industries Training Council
www.jaitc.org.uk

GOLD/SILVERSMITH/ ENGRAVER

ENTRY LEVEL 4

Qualifications and courses

No formal qualifications are required but it may be usual to have an artistic background or art and design qualification. GCSEs/National 5s in Art and Design or Design and Technology are useful.

Many different qualifications in design crafts and art and design are available. Entrants could take BTECs, Foundation degrees or NVQ/SVQ courses in art and design or 3D design.

For the creative side of engraving, there are degrees and master's degrees in metalwork, jewellery making, goldsmithing and silversmithing. Entry for a degree usually requires a portfolio of work, an art and design Foundation course and/or a relevant BTEC National Diploma. Whilst a candidate's creative ability and potential, as displayed in their portfolio, is valued highly, degree courses usually also require a minimum entry requirement of 2 A levels/3 H grades and 5 GCSEs/ National 5s.

The National Association of Goldsmiths (NAG) has created many distance learning courses which would be very useful. The course fees are cheaper for NAG members.

Some employers offer training positions, working with an experienced goldsmith, silversmith or engraver. Alternatively, the Goldsmiths' Company offer official apprenticeships which combine practical training with the study towards professional qualifications, for those aged 16–21. Apprenticeships last up to 5 years.

A portfolio of work will be useful as evidence of your work and skill level.

What the work involves

Gold/silversmiths create large and small items such as boxes, figures, picture frames and clocks in gold and silver. You will also be expected to undertake repair work on existing items.

Engravers will create and insert or engrave images, words or patterns onto stone, glass, metal or wood. You will be required to work with your hands and use specialist equipment.

You may create objects commissioned by jewellers or individual clients, or develop your own craft pieces to sell through galleries and craft shops.

Type of person suited to this work

This job demands dexterity and conscientiousness. A technical and creative approach is useful to help you plan a piece and decide on the amount of material needed.

An artistic flair is essential in this type of work, as is the ability to see a project through from start to finish. You will need considerable patience to undertake delicate and sometimes repetitive work with specialist materials and equipment.

If you run your own business you will need a confident and determined approach in order to promote yourself and your products. Financial and business skills are also needed.

Working conditions

You will probably work in a workshop or studio – either with other craftspeople or on your own. You may work in a shop and have meetings with customers to discuss pieces of work.

You will use specialist tools for heating, cutting, bending and shaping the metals, tools which can be dangerous if used incorrectly. You will therefore need to wear eye, face, hand and possibly ear protection for some jobs.

Future prospects

Most gold/silversmith employers are based in London, Birmingham, Sheffield, Glasgow and Edinburgh. Entry level and apprenticeship positions are very competitive.

Once in the profession you may progress to become a workshop supervisor, international buyer or manager, or become self-employed.

For engravers, promotion to senior engraver, supervisor or manager may be possible within larger companies.

Engravers may also become self-employed.

Advantages/disadvantages

This type of work provides the intense satisfaction of creating attractive and lasting objects.

Working with expensive materials such as glass and metal can be challenging, time-consuming and allows little room for mistakes.

Money guide

It is quite common for a gold/silversmith or engraver in the early stages of their career to supplement their income with another job.

Trainee gold/silversmiths could expect to earn about £10,000. Graduates may start at £15,000.

With experience, your earnings might rise up to £25,000 and with extensive experience could potentially increase to £50,000 a year.

The salary for engravers starts at around £11,500 and could climb to £30,000 or more for experienced, self-employed engravers.

Earnings for those who are self-employed will vary depending upon their sales and reputation.

Related opportunities

- Gemmologist p159
- Jewellery Designer p164
- Model Maker p166

Further information

British Jewellers' Association
www.bja.org.uk

Crafts Council
www.craftscouncil.org.uk

Institute of Professional Goldsmiths
www.ipgoldsmiths.com

GRAPHIC DESIGNER

ENTRY LEVEL 5

Qualifications and courses

The majority of entrants have a degree in a visual arts subject such as graphic design, fine art, illustration or 3D design. Entry without a higher education qualification is possible if you have an exceptional portfolio but progression is difficult without formal training. The minimum requirements for a degree are usually 2 A levels/3 H grades, including an art-related subject, and 5 GCSEs/National 5s. It is also recommended to complete a Foundation diploma or BTEC National in art and design, as entry to an undergraduate art degree without these qualifications is rare.

School leavers have the option to apply for an apprenticeship in design and train to become a graphic design assistant or junior graphic designer.

Competition within this industry is strong so pre-entry experience, for example from work experience placements or internships, is essential. Work experience will also allow you to build up a portfolio of your design work which is essential for interviews, and networking with graphic designers during a placement could help you to secure employment in the future. Creating a website to showcase your work is also advised.

A working knowledge of computer design software such as QuarkXPress, FreeHand, Illustrator or Photoshop is beneficial.

What the work involves

Graphic designers produce original images and designs for use in published or other materials such as leaflets, brochures, websites, logos and stationery. Most work is now done on computer, although manual techniques are occasionally used.

You will need a thorough understanding of clients' needs in order to develop appropriate designs for specific projects.

You will be responsible for producing time and budget schedules and ensuring that they are adhered to.

Type of person suited to this work

It is essential to have a strong creative flair, the imagination to develop original designs and a good eye for layout. Having the skills to draw designs by hand and to use industry-specific graphics or multimedia software packages is also important.

You need good communication skills and the confidence to present ideas to colleagues and clients. It is likely that you will work in a fast-paced environment with tight deadlines so you need to be able to multi-task and work well under pressure.

Organisational skills are essential to ensure that projects are carried out on time, within budget and as requested.

Working conditions

Most of your work will take place at a computer and drawing board within a studio. However, you may undertake external research in order to gain inspiration for a project and you will also be required to attend client meetings to present your ideas.

The majority of graphic designers work 37 hours a week, Monday to Friday. You will be expected to work overtime in order to meet deadlines. Part-time work is available and many experienced designers become freelancers.

Future prospects

In the UK there are about 18,000 businesses in this sector, with about 34% of its workforce in London and the south-east of England. The diversity of graphic design qualifications available has resulted in increased competition for positions.

There is the possibility to work for a range of clients in an agency or in-house for a large organisation such as a bank. Junior designers in larger organisations can progress to senior level and eventually a director role.

In smaller companies, many designers will decide to become self-employed within 5 to 10 years in order to progress and diversify their workload.

With experience there are many freelance opportunities.

Advantages/disadvantages

Creating original work and seeing your ideas being used in the public eye is satisfying.

Competition is becoming increasingly fierce as the number of available qualifications in this field rises.

Money guide

Earnings vary according to the type and size of employer and geographical location. Salaries tend to be higher within in-house design teams than in design agencies.

A junior designer can expect to earn £14,000–£17,000 at the start of their career.

As you gain experience in the field, your salary could increase to £18,000–£30,000.

Senior graphic designers or creative directors can earn up to £50,000.

Freelance designers could be paid hourly or daily, which could range from £200 to £300 a day.

Related opportunities

- Advertising Art Director p377
- Animator p154
- Illustrator/Technical Illustrator p162

Further information

D&AD
www.dandad.org

Department for Culture, Media and Sport
www.gov.uk/government/organisations/department-for-culture-media-sport

Design Council
www.designcouncil.org.uk

ILLUSTRATOR/ TECHNICAL ILLUSTRATOR

ENTRY LEVEL 3

Qualifications and courses

While a higher education qualification is not needed for this profession, most professional illustrators have an HNC/HND, Foundation degree or a degree in art and design related subjects. A postgraduate qualification but may also be useful, particularly for illustrators who are also interested in teaching or those who do not have a design-related first degree.

A strong portfolio is essential, and an excellent portfolio can be a substitute for academic qualifications.
The ability to produce work in multimedia format is increasingly sought after.

Technical illustrators are required to demonstrate a good knowledge of science and/or technology depending on your desired specialisation.

The Association of Illustrators (AOI) offers practical advice to illustrators and runs training seminars on business and computer related subjects.

What the work involves

You will create original illustrations for published material such as books, magazines and greetings cards. You may also create images for TV and the internet.

You will work with specialist design software, pen and ink and other media to develop strong designs. Your work will include attending client meetings, agreeing payments and contracts, and working to fulfil specific clients' requirements.

Technical illustrators design accurate graphics or illustrations to accompany and clarify often complex technical information in product and systems manuals, training materials, presentations and technical websites.

Type of person suited to this work

You will need strong design skills, a creative flair and imagination for illustration work. You should also be able to work well with computer design software. You will require a good knowledge of legal issues in order to protect your copyright and licence rights.

Technical illustration necessitates high attention to detail and strong technical drawing skills to plan and create accurate images.

Sharing ideas and working around another person's vision or 'brief' demands good communication skills. As many illustrators/technical illustrators work on a self-employed basis, you will need the confidence to promote your services as well as good business and financial sense.

Working conditions

You are likely to work in a shared studio or at your own premises. Technical illustrators occasionally work in offices, and some illustrators are employed in publishing or design houses, but freelancing is becoming increasingly more common.

You will probably use paints and adhesives which may cause respiratory problems or skin allergies for susceptible people.

Future prospects

The internet and email have made it easier for illustrators to promote themselves and find work, and it is now possible to gain work from clients based overseas.

More illustrators are now using agents to find work for them. Agents used to mostly take on clients who were already established in the field but more of them are now taking on new talent.

Some people choose to specialise in competitive areas such as medical, botanical or technical illustration.

To subsidise their income, some illustrators also teach, lecture or work in other related areas. A small number write and illustrate their own books. Others supplement their salary by selling illustrations, prints and paintings through galleries.

Advantages/disadvantages

This type of work provides the satisfaction of seeing your work in print and often in the public domain.

Working on a freelance, job-by-job basis can be an insecure way to make a living. Generally, illustrators have a second job to support them during quiet periods.

Money guide

Salaries vary according to employers and individual projects. Projects can range from one image to a series of illustrations. The NUJ Freelance Fees Guide website has guidelines on freelance fees for various types of projects.

Income for employed new entrants is around £14,000 to £19,000 per year.

Experienced illustrators could earn £20,000–£30,000.

With experience the best known can earn in excess of £40,000 per year.

Starting salaries for technical illustrators tend to be around £20,000–£25,000. With experience this can increase up to £40,000.

Related opportunities

- Cartoonist p155
- Graphic Designer p161
- Medical Illustrator p165

Further information

Association of Illustrators
www.theaoi.com

Institute of Scientific and Technical Communicators
www.istc.org.uk

INTERIOR DESIGNER

ENTRY LEVEL 5

Qualifications and courses

The preferred route is to take a degree or HND/HNC in interior design, interior architecture or spatial design. Other related subjects are also acceptable. Two relevant A levels/3 H grades and 5 GCSEs/National 5s (A*–C/A–C) are usually required for degree entry, or 1 A level/H grade and 4 GCSEs/National 5s for HNC/HNDs. Many applicants also complete a Foundation Diploma in Art and Design before applying for higher education.

Entrance in the absence of formal qualifications may still be possible for an applicant with relevant experience, enthusiasm and an exceptional portfolio.

Regardless of qualifications held, prior voluntary or part-time work experience is usually imperative to securing full-time employment. Placements will enable you to become familiar with computer design software and build up your portfolio of design work. The British Institute of Interior Design, the Chartered Society of Designers and the Directory of Design Consultants provide contact details for interior designers which may be useful when looking for work placements. Competition is fierce so networking and sending speculative applications are recommended. Traineeships are unusual and many designers take other jobs before starting in design.

The City & Guilds Award/Certificate/Diploma in Creative Techniques – Interiors (Levels 1–3) would be useful for developing practical skills.

What the work involves

Interior designers create specific, coordinated styles for homes, commercial spaces and other buildings.

You will be required to assess spaces, produce detailed designs, be familiar with computer-aided design (CAD) software, and choose suitable materials for the project which may include upholstery, wallpaper, furniture and decorative objects.

You will need to get a good understanding of the client's needs and negotiate fees with them. You will provide supervision to ensure that the project is completed accurately and in accordance with the budget and schedule.

Type of person suited to this work

It is essential to have a strong creative flair and the imagination to develop original designs. Having the skills to draw designs by hand and use specialist CAD software is also very important.

You will be required to keep up to date with changes in design and architecture, and to understand building regulations. You also need good business sense and the competency to see a project through.

You should have good communication, negotiation and organisational skills to ensure that projects are carried out on time, within budget and as requested.

Working conditions

The main employers in this sector are design and architectural firms. However, many designers are self-employed and part-time work is possible.

Client meetings often occur in the evenings and at weekends. You could be working on several contracts at the same time and tight deadlines can result in overtime.

Your work will be divided between meeting clients in their own premises and working in your studio or other work space. Smart dress is expected and protective clothing may be required on-site.

Future prospects

There is a growing demand for good interior designers but the sector is intensely competitive.

Although many interior designers work for design and architectural companies, some are freelance and many choose to start up their own design companies, either immediately after graduation or once they have gained experience.

There is no established career structure; however it is possible to progress to a partner role in a consultancy.

Working for a smaller company can lead to more responsibility than a larger consultancy. The UK industry has an excellent international reputation so you could work overseas.

Advantages/disadvantages

Creating original work and seeing your ideas being used in a practical or decorative way is satisfying.

Working as a freelance designer can result in greater flexibility.

Meeting deadlines and budgets can be stressful.

Money guide

A junior/trainee interior designer would usually start on £18,000–£22,000.

Those with experience can expect to earn £24,000–£40,000 a year.

Senior designers can achieve £45,000 and up. Directors may earn up to £75,000.

Freelance designers set their own rate based upon their reputation and experience.

Related opportunities

- Illustrator/Technical Illustrator p162
- Model Maker p166
- Visual Merchandiser p173

Further information

British Institute of Interior Design
www.biid.org.uk

Chartered Society of Designers
www.csd.org.uk

Design Council
www.designcouncil.org.uk

JEWELLERY DESIGNER

ENTRY LEVEL 2

Qualifications and courses

Most jewellery companies ask entrants to the industry to hold a degree in jewellery design, although it is still possible to enter this career through skill alone.

GCSEs/National 5s and A levels/H grades in Art and Design or Design and Technology may help you to gain entry to this profession or to higher level courses as they demonstrate both creativity and commitment. Other useful qualifications include HNDs, Foundation degrees or degrees in art and design or more specific subjects such as goldsmithing, silversmithing and jewellery design.

However, qualifications are not as important as craft skills. Work placements can help you to accumulate experience of the jewellery industry and build up a network of contacts which will help you to develop skills and find buyers and sellers for your work. If you do not have higher qualifications you will normally need to do an apprenticeship, such as the Goldsmiths Company's 5 year scheme for example.

It is common for designers to take other jobs in related areas first in order to build experience. It may be possible to move across from another relevant subject such as fashion design, textile design, fine art or applied arts if you build up a suitable portfolio.

What the work involves

Jewellery designers are involved in each aspect of the production of decorative pieces of jewellery of various types, including the selection of materials such as gold, silver, precious metals and stones.

You will research the design and the function of a piece; its symbolism, the materials used, the cost, the potential buyer and even current trends.

You will prepare detailed drawings which you or a craftworker will create using traditional crafting methods or using high-tech machinery. A design may be for a one-off piece or part of a range of pieces. You will undertake tasks such as stone cutting and setting, model-making, mounting, engraving, enamelling, welding, chain-making, cleaning and polishing.

Type of person suited to this work

You should have a strong interest in art, design, fashion and craftwork. As your sales may be influenced by the current design marketplace, you should keep up to date with jewellery fashion and design trends.

Reputation is increasingly important for developing and sustaining a successful career. You should be skilled at marketing and self-promotion and willing to visit trade fairs, enter competitions and write articles for trade magazines to establish your brand.

You must have a keen eye for detail and patience as you will be working with small scales and intricate and delicate designs.

You will need to be organised and self-motivated as you will probably be working on a variety of projects at the same time. You should also be able to visualise 2D designs as 3D objects.

Working conditions

If you are employed by a company you will usually work 35–40 hours a week, Monday to Friday, including late nights or weekend work when deadlines are approaching.

You can also work on a freelance basis which will involve working on commission and producing designs specifically tailored to the client's requirements.

You may work in a studio which can be bright and airy or in a large workshop, which may be noisy and dusty. You must wear protective clothing.

Future prospects

Salaried positions for graduates are limited and you will probably need to start as a freelancer or run your own business. This could involve selling your designs to manufacturers or making the items and selling them yourself through galleries, shops or online. To stay ahead in the industry you should attend trade fairs and exhibitions.

Specialising in creating products for a particular market is important. In order to keep up to date with trends and techniques you should also be willing to continuously research and retrain, either through postgraduate or specialist short courses.

Advantages/disadvantages

You may be able to work from your own designs and see your creations become popular pieces.

As a self-employed jewellery designer you may find that without the right support system in areas such as promotion, marketing and sales it can be difficult to become established.

Money guide

As a graduate in an employed position your salary can start at around £16,000 per year.

This can increase to anywhere between £20,000 and £50,000 with experience.

Your salary will depend greatly on factors such as whether or not you are self-employed, experienced and have enough success to gain a reputation within the industry.

Related opportunities

- Fashion Designer/Milliner p157
- Gold/Silversmith/Engraver p160
- Product Designer p169

Further information

Crafts Council
www.craftscouncil.org.uk

MEDICAL ILLUSTRATOR

ENTRY LEVEL 5

Qualifications and courses

Entry into this profession is not possible without a relevant degree or HND. Desirable degree subjects include medical illustration, clinical photography, and photography with typical entry requirements being 2 A levels/3 H grades, often including Biology and Photography, and 5 GCSEs/National 5s.

Medical illustrators usually enter the profession as trainees and learn on the job while working towards a medical illustration qualification. Students on a recognised course of study or training are entitled to become a student member of the Institute of Medical Illustrators (IMI).

A voluntary national register for medical illustrators was formed in 2010 by the Committee for the Accreditation of Medical Illustration Practitioners (CAMIP). The register was formed with the aim of regulation and maintaining high standards in the profession.

You will need to have a good portfolio of work to help you stand out in a specialised field. Pre-entry work experience in a placement, project, or in a caring capacity would be useful. It may lead to freelancing opportunities for medical books.

What the work involves

Medical illustrators create annotated or labelled images to provide visual information to professionals and trainees working in medical care, research and education.

You may also work as a medical photographer or video producer (digital technician), or combine all these functions in one role.

You will have to record images of patients and develop graphics for health/medical publications such as information leaflets and websites. You could work in wards, operating theatres, pathology labs, mortuaries and clinical exam centres.

Type of person suited to this work

Good visual sense and attention to detail is very important. You should have excellent technical skills to work with equipment such as videos and cameras, and will have to work creatively yet accurately with computer design packages.

As you will have to record images of patients, a sensitive, tactful and ethical approach is necessary. You should also have a knowledge of physiology and anatomy.

Also required is the ability to communicate with all sorts of people, some of whom could be very ill. You must be able to cope with upsetting situations and sights, for example, if visiting someone who is terminally ill.

Working conditions

You may be based within a group of hospitals and other centres and have to travel regularly between these. During the day you will visit theatres, wards, training centres and mortuaries – all of which could involve distressing sights and intense odours. You may have to be on-call at night to photograph emergency operations.

Using a computer and software design packages, you will work within an office or studio to prepare and produce images and visual information. You may also have to record laboratory results.

Future prospects

This is a small and specialised profession, with great competition for jobs. There is, however, great opportunity to train and further specialise in niche fields.

Gaining a range of technical skills and experience rather than specialising in one area could open more opportunities.

After training, it is possible to progress within one organisation to head of department or you could go on to provide freelance services for medical establishments or medical and scientific publications.

Advantages/disadvantages

This job gives the satisfaction of providing valuable visual information to help medical professionals and their patients.

You may have the opportunity to freelance, which offers flexibility.

You will work with sick and sometimes distressed patients and may have to deal with upsetting sights. You may also have to be on-call at night in order to photograph emergency operations.

Money guide

The Agenda for Change (AfC) NHS pay structure means medical illustrators start on band 5, earning between £21,388 and £27,901 a year.

With experience, senior medical illustrators progress to band 6, earning between £25,783 and £34,530.

When in charge of a team you progress to Band 7, which pays between £30,764 and £40,558.

Medical illustrators in large university teaching hospitals could be employed on a number of pay scales covering technicians, medical laboratory officers, or sterile services technicians. Check with the university teaching hospitals for more details. Freelance work in photography or illustration for medical books can supplement income.

Related opportunities

- Fine Artist/Sculptor p158
- Graphic Designer p161
- Photographer p392

Further information

Association of Illustrators
www.theaoi.com

Health and Care Professions Council
www.hpc-uk.org

Institute of Medical Illustrators
www.imi.org.uk

MODEL MAKER

ENTRY LEVEL 2

Qualifications and courses

There are no formal entry requirements to this industry, however, the ability to work with your hands and use specialist tools is very important. It would be important to note that most entrants complete a model-making course and have a strong portfolio of work.

With an increasing emphasis on computer-aided design, there are a wide variety of courses available to help improve knowledge and skills including a City & Guilds Level 2 Certificate in Engineering, ABC Level 3 Award in Visual Art (Exploratory Model Making), Foundation degrees in 3D design and degrees in design modelling. Entry requirements vary but most institutions will expect some GCSEs/National 5s in subjects such as maths, design and technology, and physics. For entry onto a degree course, you will need at least 2 A levels/3 H grades and 5 GCSEs/National 5s in relevant subjects.

Entry via an Engineering Manufacture (Craft and Technician) Apprenticeship may be possible in your area, which would combine the practical work experience of a job with the study of a professional qualification. You will need to be employed to qualify for an apprenticeship and work experience in areas such as engineering, electronics, carpentry or furniture making may help with finding work.

Professional bodies such as the Design Council and the Design and Art Direction (D&AD) provide various opportunities for continuing professional development. The New Bloods scheme in particular includes awards, exhibitions, workshops and intense training courses in order to get under-24s noticed by the industry. The Institution of Engineering Designers operates a membership scheme with events and classes which are useful to share ideas and network.

What the work involves

Working with materials such as fibreglass, resin, wood and rubber you will create 3D images or models.

You will construct detailed and accurate models of buildings, prototypes of items, engineering products and figures for museums and TV or film companies.

You will work with clients to develop their ideas into a convincing and practical model, deciding which materials to use. You will plan the model using technical drawings or computer software.

Type of person suited to this work

You will need a strong creative flair to visualise and develop models. Producing detailed models out of fragile materials demands tremendous patience and good technical skills. You should have a logical approach in order to plan and create accurate work.

The tasks will demand great attention to detail and good eyesight. A feel for, and interest in, design will enable you to create well-planned models.

You will also need a basic knowledge of maths and the ability to understand technical drawings. The capacity to work effectively with computer design packages is increasingly important in this area of work.

Working conditions

Most model makers work within London and the south-east of England. There is still a demand for traditional model makers but often this is combined with computer-aided design (CAD).

Most model makers work standard office hours, but evening and weekend work may be required to meet deadlines.

Your work will be carried out in a studio, where you will wear protective clothing to suit the materials and tools you are using. Sometimes you may be based in an office, planning models with specialist design software.

You may need to travel around the UK or overseas to meet clients and assemble or install models for them.

Future prospects

The majority of model makers are self-employed and move from project to project as required in sectors such as architecture, film and TV and engineering. Often this type of business is set up after developing a strong portfolio, gaining a good reputation and undertaking courses on running a small business.

A high level of experience in the industry could lead to a management position where you would manage a team of model makers within an organisation or your own team/ company.

Advantages/disadvantages

This job can provide the satisfaction of developing original work.

You will need to create highly detailed work to fairly limited deadlines, which can be stressful.

Some of the materials you work with may produce unpleasant or dangerous fumes.

Money guide

Starting salaries are around £19,000 per year.

With experience this rises to between £23,000 and £30,000.

At senior level, with many years of experience, you could earn £42,000 or more.

Freelancers negotiate a set fee for each project.

Related opportunities

- Fine Artist/Sculptor p158
- Graphic Designer p161
- Toymaker/Designer p172

Further information

Creative and Cultural Skills
www.ccskills.org.uk

D&AD
www.dandad.org

Design Council
www.designcouncil.org.uk

MUSICAL INSTRUMENT MAKER/REPAIRER

ENTRY LEVEL 2

Qualifications and courses

There are no set qualifications for this type of work; however you will require the specialist skills to make/repair your particular type (family) of instruments.

BTEC awards in Music Technology are available and courses in musical instrument making are available up to degree level from specific colleges and universities, such as London Metropolitan University. Entry requirements for these courses vary, but it will be necessary to have relevant GCSEs/National 5s and A levels/H grades for some courses. Others will accept you without these if you have relevant practical experience. For full details of course providers visit the National Association of Musical Instrument Repairers website.

When you begin employment you may receive on-the-job training from an experienced instrument maker/repairer and develop skills through part-time, specialist courses.

What the work involves

You will make, repair and service musical instruments such as pianos, flutes and violins but normally will specialise within one family of instruments.

The work will include building new instruments and working with specialised equipment and materials, replacing worn-down or broken parts and checking for the cause of specific faults by undertaking assessments. This could range from fine tuning to significant maintenance work.

You will work with customers, dealing with repair requests or commissions for new instruments.

Type of person suited to this work

A passion for music and a practical understanding of how musical instruments function is essential. They are complex objects so you will need a good eye for detail, excellent hearing and a patient approach.

Strong technical skills will enable you to design, create or repair instruments. You will need to be dexterous and confident in working with your hands and in using materials such as wood and glue.

You need to have excellent communication and interpersonal skills in order to deal with customers, particularly if you are self-employed.

Working conditions

This is a specialised area of work, but you could work for educational music departments, major orchestras, opera houses and theatres, rehearsal studios, retailers, and individual musicians.

You will work with a range of specialised tools in the workshop of a specialist company or from home if self-employed.

You will normally work a 40-hour week, Monday to Friday, however if you are self-employed you will often have to adapt your working hours to meet demand and clients' timetables.

With larger instruments, such as pianos, organs or timpani, you will need to visit private homes and other locations (such as concert halls, theatres or music studios) to do repairs on-site.

It would be useful to have your own driving licence and transport.

You need to have strong manual handling skill. This job may be difficult for people with skin or respiratory conditions owing to some of the specialist materials used.

Future prospects

Specialising in a specific area such as classical guitars or making unusual instruments from commissions can enhance your reputation and build a strong client base in niche markets.

You may also be able to sell instruments to enhance your income as you will have ready access to the market.

A lot of people are self-employed and some music shops will publicise local repairers, instrument makers and tuners, rather than employing their own.

Advantages/disadvantages

Many musical instrument repairers/makers are freelance and work on a project-by-project basis, which can create some job insecurity.

This career has excellent fringe benefits as you could work for some of the best musical talents in the UK.

Money guide

In some parts of the country there is not sufficient work for full-time employment so most musical instrument makers and repairers are self-employed. Earnings will depend on your location, the local music scene and your specialism.

Work permitting, you could earn around £15,000–£20,000 per year once trained.

The most experienced people can earn up to £30,000 a year.

Related opportunities

- Art Therapist p272
- Musician p418
- Private Music Teacher p186

Further information

British Violin Making Association
www.bvma.org.uk

Crafts Council
www.craftscouncil.org.uk

Institute of Musical Instrument Technology
www.imit.org.uk

National Association of Musical Instrument Repairers
www.namir.org.uk

PICTURE FRAMER

ENTRY LEVEL 1

Qualifications and courses

There are no formal educational requirements, though you should have a good standard of general education and gaining relevant qualifications will help you to learn the specific skills and techniques that the job requires. Courses are available from local colleges and education services. These could be residential, weekend or part-time courses and they might last from 8 weeks up to a year.

An interest and experience in woodwork, metalwork or textiles would be useful. GCSEs/National 5s, A levels/H grades, certificates, diplomas, NVQs, Foundation degrees or degrees can also be an advantage; relevant subjects include art and design, creative arts and contemporary crafts.

Training is usually done on the job alongside an experienced professional. In order to work with high-value items, framers need to be trained to conservation standards.

Picture framers are able to work towards the Guild Commended Framer (GCF) qualification from the Fine Art Trade Guild, which involves both practical and written assessments. This qualification sets an internationally recognised standard for picture framers.

What the work involves

You will plan and create attractive and protective surrounds or frames for prints, paintings, photographs and 3D objects. Working with specialist equipment and materials you will create strong, high-quality frames.

Helping customers choose the most suitable style and size of frame will be part of your job and you will advise them on the most practical and appropriate method of framing and glazing the artwork.

If you work on a self-employed basis you will need to promote your services to potential customers.

Type of person suited to this work

Creativity is essential in order to design the frame. You will also need good customer service skills. Technical skills and the ability to work safely with potentially dangerous equipment are highly important.

Paying attention to detail and taking a pride in your work will ensure that you produce high-quality frames. You will need to be able to work under pressure as short deadlines can be a part of this job. You should also be commercially aware. If self-employed, you will require business, financial and marketing skills to be successful.

Working conditions

You could work in a shop or workshop. When working in the shop you will have to deal with customers who can sometimes be rude or confrontational if dissatisfied. Workshops can be noisy and busy.

Picture framers generally work 40 hours a week, with weekend work often needed and overtime during busy periods. Many picture framers work on a part-time basis.

Picture framers work with potentially dangerous equipment such as specialist cutting machinery so you will need to be aware of health and safety requirements and wear protective clothing.

Future prospects

Success depends upon the skills and reputation of the individual.

Many picture framers set up their own studios or shops where they also sell works of art and artists' materials. Others work solely in framing and are employed in larger workshops, mass-producing framed prints and mirrors. There is the possibility of promotion to a supervisory or managerial role in bigger companies. Some picture framers take additional training so that they can teach part time.

Advantages/disadvantages

This job provides the satisfaction of creating enduring and high quality items.

If you are employed in a gallery or museum, you will have the opportunity to work with famous and valuable pieces of art.

The nature of the work requires you to be precise, careful and patient.

Money guide

The starting salary for a trainee picture framer is usually about £12,000.

With experience, your earnings could rise to £17,000 or more.

Specialists who work with high value artwork in a gallery or museum could achieve £25,000.

Earnings for self-employed framers vary depending on location, expertise and the success of their business.

Related opportunities

- Conservator/Restorer p329
- Gold/Silversmith/Engraver p160
- Model Maker p166

Further information

Fine Art Trade Guild
www.fineart.co.uk

Institute of Conservation
www.icon.org.uk

PRODUCT DESIGNER ENTRY LEVEL 5

Qualifications and courses

Entry without a HNC/HND, Foundation degree or degree in product design, industrial design or a related subject is unlikely. Design courses can be centred on the art or engineering sides of product design. Students should check which universities offer modules in areas they would like to specialise in. Those choosing the art-based route sometimes take a 1-year Foundation course in art and design before their degree. A portfolio of design work is essential to prove creative skill, knowledge and the ability to work to a brief.

Entry requirements for degree programmes are usually a portfolio and 2 A levels/3 H grades and 5 GCSEs/ National 5s (A*–C/A–C). For an HND you need 1 A level/H grade in an art and design subject and 3 GCSEs/ National 5s. A BTEC qualification in art and design or 3D design could also be useful.

A postgraduate qualification enables you to specialise in a specific area and may provide an advantage when working with certain European clients.

Previous experience through industrial placements, freelance work or design competitions is invaluable. This sector is very competitive so you should make contacts during work placements or by joining the Chartered Society of Designers. Employers will look for a strong portfolio which showcases your design work.

What the work involves

Product designers create new products and improve the design, functionality or cost efficiency of existing products. These could be day-to-day products such as tables or specialist ones such as medical equipment.

You will decide upon a design brief with your client and carry out research into similar products and consumer behaviour. You will use both traditional drawing techniques and specialist computer software to develop appropriate designs.

You will select materials, produce prototypes and ensure that the project is completed on time and to budget.

Type of person suited to this work

This job requires both creativity and technical expertise. You should have a good eye for design as well as technical drawing and IT skills. It is important to understand how different materials and production methods function.

You need good communication skills and an understanding of clients' needs and consumer behaviour.

Problem-solving and organisational skills are essential to ensure projects are completed on time and within budget.

Working conditions

Product designers work in manufacturing firms and design companies which produce material for a variety of sectors. Employment is available all over the UK but most design consultancies are based in London and the south-east of England.

The majority of product designers work 37 hours a week, Monday to Friday. You will be expected to work extra hours in order to meet deadlines. Part-time and freelance work is quite common.

Most of your work will take place in a bright, clean studio or office. However, you will undertake some experiments and material testing in lab conditions, using specialist tools and equipment. You might also have to visit production factories which may be dusty and noisy.

Future prospects

There is strong competition for entry level jobs but there is significant demand for experienced product designers with a high level of technical expertise, particularly in niche areas.

Experienced designers may have the opportunity to work abroad or freelance. You could progress to a senior or managerial level.

Advantages/disadvantages

You will have the opportunity to use your imagination and technical skills.

Creating original work that is used by the public is satisfying.

Competition for entry level jobs is fierce.

Working to tight budgets and project deadlines can be stressful.

Money guide

Earnings vary according to the geographical location, type and size of employer.

Starting salaries for junior designers are around £17,000–£25,000.

Those with experience typically earn £30,000–£40,000 per year.

Senior product designers can achieve up to £50,000.

Contract or freelance designers set their own rates depending upon their reputation and client contacts.

Related opportunities

- Manufacturing/Production Engineer p213
- Toolmaker p230
- Toymaker/Designer p172

Further information

Chartered Society of Designers
www.csd.org.uk

SIGNWRITER/ SIGNMAKER

ENTRY LEVEL 1

Qualifications and courses

There are no formal educational requirements for either role, but GCSEs/National 5s in art or relevant vocational qualifications can be useful. You can specialise in signwriting after completing a BTEC or HNC/HND in Graphic Design.

Training is usually done on the job, especially in the case of signwriting. Many employers offer apprenticeships for people aged between 16 and 24 for signmaking which can combine employment with the study of a relevant, professional qualification. Applicants normally require 4 GCSEs/National 5s (A*–E/A–E), including Maths, English language, a science and an art and design subject, or other evidence of aptitude.

It is possible to take a full- or part-time course in signwriting and signmaking, such as the NVQ Level 2 or 3 in Signmaking. There are specialist courses available, such as gold leaf gilding, that can improve your skills and job prospects.

Due to having to work on site, as a signmaker you will need to gain a Constructions Skills Certification Scheme (CSCS) card as a Sign Installer–Illuminated/ Non-Illuminated. This card acts as a passport to work and is proof of an NVQ and having passed a health and safety test. The Prefabricated Access Suppliers' and Manufacturers' Association (PASMA) or the International Powered Access Federation (IPAF) provide accreditation for working at heights.

What the work involves

You will design, plan and produce signs with graphic images, lettering and logos to publicise companies, attract customers and draw attention to specific locations.

You will work closely with customers to develop appropriate, appealing designs that match their requirements.

You could work with any number of different materials and methods; from plastics to glass to sketching as well as computer-aided design (CAD).

You will produce signs for shop fronts, roadsides, hospitals, vehicles and even boats!

Type of person suited to this work

As you will be creating signs to interest or warn people, you will need strong graphic design skills. A creative flair and drawing skills are also important.

You will need an understanding of the materials you work with and good manual skills.

You must be methodical and have strong attention to detail. Technical skills will allow you to work with a range of equipment. IT skills and an ability to use programs such as Omega are becoming increasingly important.

Good written and verbal communication skills, along with excellent people skills, will help you to meet client requirements accurately and avoid expensive errors.

Working conditions

You could work within a studio or manufacturing site, which can get messy and noisy.

You might attend meetings with customers and make site visits. Much of your time will be spent drafting signs at a computer using special software.

You may work with large or small-scale specialist equipment, with printing inks and chemical finishes, which can affect people with skin or respiratory conditions.

Future prospects

You could work in the more commercial side of signwriting, within a specialist company on the design or manufacturing side, or you could work within the more creative, hand-crafted side of the industry.

Some signwriters go into set or prop design for theatre, film or TV programmes.

With experience, you could start your own business – perhaps specialising in pub or restaurant signs.

Despite being a declining industry, signmaking is still a fairly competitive area; the demand from a range of organisations for high-quality signs means that there are opportunities throughout the country.

Advantages/disadvantages

This kind of work can provide opportunities to be creative and to use your imagination to help customers, for example when designing a company logo.

You might need to travel frequently to a range of locations in order to take measurements or photographs. There is the option of working abroad.

Money guide

Trainee and apprentice signmakers are likely to start with an income of around £12,000.

This can rise with experience to £17,000–£30,000 a year.

Signwriters are usually self-employed and their earnings vary depending on demand and their own level of success in the market.

Related opportunities

- Cartoonist p155
- Fine Artist/Sculptor p158
- Graphic Designer p161

Further information

British Sign and Graphics Association
www.bsga.co.uk

Creative and Cultural Skills
www.ccskills.org.uk

Faversham House Group
www.favershamhouse.com

STAGE/SET DESIGNER

ENTRY LEVEL 4

Qualifications and courses

It is possible to enter the industry without any formal qualifications as a designer's assistant or prop maker in the theatre or as a runner or art department trainee in film and TV and then work your way up. The Key Skills of creativity, vision and design are essential.

Most people, however, have a HND, degree or postgraduate diploma. Specialist courses include theatre design, performing arts (production) and design for film and television, but other art and design related subjects such as architecture, interior design and fine art can be useful too. For a degree you should have 2 A levels/3 H grades or a HNC/HND in a relevant subject, 5 GCSEs/ National 5s (A*–C/A–C) and a good portfolio. For an HNC/ HND you are normally required to have 1 A level/H grade.

A design qualification is useful as it enables you to further build your portfolio which will be essential when securing employment. You also must demonstrate a passion and commitment to stage and set design.

It is helpful to obtain experience before entering this highly competitive profession as it highlights commitment and helps you build contacts as well as skills. Experience can be achieved by means of an unpaid placement, freelance work and involvement in student productions, amateur theatre, independent films or design competitions. There are also apprenticeship schemes available, such as the BBC's Design Trainee Scheme, a year-long contract that builds professional contacts and establishes your career.

What the work involves

Stage/set designers are responsible for the visual elements of a theatre (stage designer), TV or film production (set designer) including sets, locations and possibly props and costumes.

From background research, you will be required to create original ideas which accurately reflect the relevant style and historical period of the piece.

Working closely with the production team, you will oversee the development and installation of the sets and ensure that everything is delivered on time and within budget.

Type of person suited to this work

It is essential to have a strong creative flair and a good eye for design. Having the skills to use specialist computer-aided design (CAD) software, to draw designs by hand and to create scale models when required is also very important.

You should be detail orientated and demonstrate a passion for history, culture and the performing arts. These abilities should be balanced with good communication skills to aid leadership and self-promotion.

Organisational skills are important to ensure that projects are carried out on time, within budget and as requested. As deadlines can be tight, you should also have the ability to work well under pressure.

Working conditions

Designers work either directly for the production company or freelance. Working hours are long and unsociable and you will be expected to work supplementary hours in order to meet deadlines.

Your work will be divided between being in a studio designing and building models of the sets, and then supervising in their creation on-set. Normally this happens behind the scenes in theatres, television studios or purpose-built warehouses.

You will work on large pieces, which necessitates the use of ladders and scaffolding.

Future prospects

Stage designers work for theatres and opera houses and may have the opportunity to oversee a travelling production. There is fierce competition for entry-level positions.

Set designers can work for the BBC or one of the 1,500 production firms in the country.

Part-time work is difficult to find and although there are many freelancers in the industry, work can be sporadic.

Advantages/disadvantages

The creation of original work and seeing your ideas being used in the public eye and in high profile productions is satisfying. Working as a freelancer can also result in greater flexibility.

Competition for entry-level jobs is fierce and a strong portfolio and good networking skills are important.

Meeting tight deadlines can result in high stress levels.

Money guide

Most designers work freelance as very few companies have resident designers now. Earnings will be dependent on individual ability, location and the contract size.

The Independent Theatre Council recommends a design fee of £2,410 in 2015/16 and a weekly fee for set building and other duties to be £472.

Contact the Broadcasting, Entertainment, Cinematograph and Theatre Union (BECTU) for information on minimum pay guidelines.

Related opportunities

- Costume Designer p156
- Interior Designer p163
- TV, Film and Radio Production Assistant/Runner p405

Further information

Broadcasting, Entertainment, Cinematograph and Theatre Union
www.bectu.org.uk

Design Council
www.designcouncil.org.uk

Society of British Theatre Designers
www.theatredesign.org.uk

TOYMAKER/ DESIGNER

ENTRY LEVEL 3

Qualifications and courses

There are no formal entry requirements but many entrants have a background in art and design. An HND or degree can be an advantage and relevant subjects include art and design, product design, graphic design or 3D design. Qualifications in child behaviour and psychology may also be useful. Higher education institutions sometimes have links with toy manufacturers which can provide a useful first step into the industry.

Minimum entry requirements for a degree are usually 2 A levels/3 H grades or equivalent, 5 GCSEs/National 5s (A*–C/A–C) and a portfolio of work. In England, Wales and Northern Ireland many students take a 1-year Foundation course as preparation for entry to an art and design degree. In Scotland, the first year of a 4-year degree equates to the Foundation year.

Alternatively, those who do not wish to pursue a degree could take relevant courses such as the City & Guilds Award/Certificate/Diploma in Creative Techniques (Levels 1–3), the Edexcel BTEC Level 3 Award/Certificate/ Diploma in Design Crafts or the BTEC Higher National in 3D design (Levels 4 and 5).

Product design experience is useful. Toymakers involved in market research with children may need to undergo a Disclosure and Barring Service (DBS) check. You will also have to be aware of toy safety regulations as well as legislation, for example in relation to toy guns.

What the work involves

You will design, plan, test and create toys for babies, children and, possibly, adults.

As a traditional toymaker, you could make toys by hand, such as doll houses and rocking horses. If you work for a large manufacturer you will develop new products based on original ideas and sketches.

You will spend time promoting your work and design services to clients and customers. Your work could be sold in shops or at craft and toy fairs.

Type of person suited to this work

You will need creative flair to develop original ideas and a genuine interest in how individuals respond to toys. Practical design skills and an active imagination will help you create long-lasting and functional toys.

If creating objects by hand, you will need good manual skills and an understanding of the materials you work with. Knowledge of 3D design is fast becoming essential.

If self-employed, you will also need good business and financial skills and the confidence to promote your work.

Working conditions

Most toymakers/designers spend a lot of time in a workshop, planning and developing their products.

If employed as a toy designer by a manufacturer, you may work purely with computer design software and create, rather than construct, your designs.

You could work on a self-employed basis, making and designing toys. A small number of toymakers also restore antique toys.

Future prospects

There are limited opportunities in established companies for toymakers and designers. Mass production of toys normally takes place overseas and UK-based businesses tend to be small with fewer than 5 employees.

Toy design in the UK, however, is still strong and there is a growing market in toys with 'green' designs that are ethically created from renewable materials.

Some toymakers/designers own shops where they sell their own handmade toys and a growing number sell their products at craft fairs, on the internet or by mail order.

Within larger companies it may be possible to progress from junior to senior design roles. You can also move into development, buying and marketing.

'Techno toys' as well as sporting events can help to provide interest and growth in the toy industry.

Advantages/disadvantages

Creating fun, attractive toys to be enjoyed by children and adults alike is a rewarding career.

It is satisfying to see your original designs come to life as a finished product.

Competition is high and vacancies for toy designers are limited at manufacturing companies.

Those who become self-employed can expect it to take time and hard work to establish a business.

Money guide

Starting salaries for toy designers working for toy manufacturers range from £10,000 to £15,000 per year.

Those with experience who work in a large company can expect £23,000–£35,000.

The most successful designers of popular toys can achieve in excess of £45,000.

Traditional toymakers are usually self-employed and salaries will depend on the success of the business.

Related opportunities

- Animator p154
- Carpenter/Joiner p65
- Picture Framer p168

Further information

British Toymakers Guild
www.toymakersguild.co.uk

Crafts Council
www.craftscouncil.org.uk

Design Council
www.designcouncil.org.uk

Qualifications and courses

You could start as an in-store sales assistant and work your way up to trainee visual merchandiser. If you want to start out as a visual merchandiser, there are no formal entry requirements but many employers will look for relevant qualifications in design or retail.

Many different courses are available at Level 5 in display or design, marketing or retail. Degree courses in visual merchandising usually require 2 A levels/H grades and 5 GCSEs/National 5s (A*–C/A–C) or equivalent. Foundation degrees typically require 1 A level/H grade and 4 GCSEs/National 5s (A*–C/A–C) or equivalent.

Other relevant qualifications include the Fashion Retail Academy's Visual Display and Retail Branding for Fashion Retail Diploma (Level 4) and the distance learning Certificate in Display and Visual Merchandising from the British Display Society. ABC also offers a Level 3 Diploma in Retail Skills (Visual Merchandising).

The Intermediate Level Apprenticeship in Retail involves training for the visual merchandiser role and you can progress to the level of visual merchandiser supervisor by taking the Advanced Apprenticeship. Apprenticeships combine practical work experience with the opportunity to study for a relevant, professional qualification. Applicants for an apprenticeship often require a minimum of 1 A level/H grade or strong GCSEs/National 5s, typically within a design-related subject.

A portfolio of art and design work is usually required by employers. Experience in display and the retail/exhibition sector can also be helpful.

What the work involves

Using your technical design skills, you will plan and design eye-catching window or shop front displays for shops, businesses and other organisations. You will work closely with clients to make sure that your designs meet their requirements.

Once you have identified materials and props for a window display, you will design an arrangement to create a striking theme or effect.

You might also provide advice to other shop branches or organisations on successful display design.

Type of person suited to this work

It is important to have strong creative ability, as well as excellent technical drawing and computer-aided design (CAD) skills. You need to have excellent communication skills to be able to balance your vision with that of your client and work with a wide range of people.

Certain roles will require you to keep up with new trends and products in fashion and culture. You must also be numerate, as one of your responsibilities will be to manage project budgets. A good level of fitness is also needed as assembling displays can be tiring.

Working conditions

Normally, you will be working indoors with different hand tools, materials, fabrics and the products to be displayed in the window or display. The work can often be pressured due to strict deadlines. You might have to work late especially in the build up to holiday seasons such as Christmas.

The job can involve a great deal of manual work. You will do lots of lifting and be on your feet for long periods, which can be very tiring. A driving licence would be useful as you will have to travel to meet suppliers and visit exhibitions and different company stores.

Future prospects

There are a range of opportunities, for example working for specialist display consultancy firms, large retailers, museums and other visitor attractions.

You will probably start as a junior and progress to a more senior position as supervisor, head designer, merchandiser and possibly department manager.

If you work for a multinational company, the opportunity may arise to work abroad. You could also go on to teach or lecture in design-related subjects. With experience, some display designers set up their own businesses or provide consultancy support to other organisations.

Advantages/disadvantages

This type of work can involve high levels of pressure due to tight deadlines.

You will have the satisfaction of seeing people enjoying your displays and giving you positive feedback.

You could have the opportunity to work with special effects such as animatronics.

Money guide

Starting salaries are usually in the range of £12,000 to £16,000.

Once you have gained experience, your salary could rise to £20,000 to £25,000.

Visual merchandising managers or designers can earn £25,000 to £55,000.

At director level you could achieve up to £60,000.

Related opportunities

- Interior Designer p163
- Model Maker p166
- Retail Buyer p465

Further information

British Display Society
www.britishdisplaysociety.co.uk

Design Council
www.designcouncil.org.uk

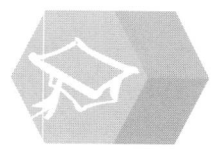

Education and Training

To work in this sector you need to be motivated and enthusiastic about other people's learning, whether it is adults or children. If you chose to teach, the range of subjects available is huge so whatever your interest – languages, art, sciences, cooking, sports – you can become a teacher in that field. Jobs in this sector require a multitude of skills including: creativity, imagination, numerical skills, good communication and organisational skills and, in some cases, having a lot of patience!

The jobs featured in this section are listed below. For similar jobs to the ones in this sector turn to *Social Work and Counselling Services* on page 543.

COMMUNITY EDUCATION OFFICER

ENTRY LEVEL 5

Qualifications and courses

You can gain entry to this profession with a degree, a diploma or an HND/Foundation degree. A qualification in a relevant subject such as community education, sociology, social sciences, educational studies or youth work may improve your chances of employment. Some undergraduate and postgraduate courses offer part-time or distance learning options which will enable you to work/volunteer alongside your studies and some employers will offer formal support for students.

Employers usually seek candidates who have combined their qualification with paid or voluntary community experience. Some entrants come from a teaching background, while others have experience in the youth and community sector. Information and advice about voluntary work is available from YouthNet, the Workers' Educational Association (WEA) and local volunteer centres. Paid vacancies could arise from voluntary placements.

If you have no qualifications but you have accumulated significant experience then it may be possible for you to secure a post in the voluntary sector. However, it is likely that you will be required to have academic qualifications to reach a senior level. Some postgraduate courses will accept candidates with extensive experience as a substitute for qualifications and others offer the opportunity for those already employed to obtain a postgraduate qualification whilst working, both of which significantly improve your career prospects.

Depending on whether you specialise within certain demographics, or work with certain organisations, you could need Disclosure and Barring Service (DBS) clearance.

What the work involves

Community education officers provide all members of the community with information on, and access to, educational and developmental programmes. You may work in areas of social deprivation or high unemployment, or with certain disadvantaged groups such as ethnic minorities or the homeless.

You will identify the needs and interests of the community, and sensitively and creatively organise a variety of suitable activities and courses to improve learning, career and personal development opportunities.

You will plan projects and outreach programmes, liaise with community and local authority groups, and recruit and train staff. At a senior level your job will involve developing policies and negotiating funding.

Type of person suited to this work

You should have a genuine interest in helping people and charitable work. As you will be liaising with communities, government departments and voluntary bodies, you must be able to communicate with a variety of different people, in both casual and formal situations, whilst maintaining a professional approach.

You should be a good listener and have a practical, optimistic approach to problem solving.

You will need to show initiative and be able to work as part of a team. Patience is essential as many projects are long-term developments rather than quick-fix solutions.

Working conditions

Many posts are short-term contracts because their existence is heavily dependent on funding. This can be difficult as projects often require long-term support. There is plenty of opportunity for part-time work and flexible hours but these may involve working during the evening and at weekends.

You will have an office based in a community centre, a local authority or a college, from which you will travel to the surrounding region. A driving licence is useful.

Future prospects

Once you have secured a post you will receive formal training consisting of short courses that will develop skills or examine new issues such as health development.

You may find that postgraduate programmes in community studies and education are beneficial to your progress. NVQs and diplomas in relevant subjects such as youth and community work will boost your opportunities for progression.

Willingness to be geographically mobile will greatly enhance your career prospects.

Advantages/disadvantages

Providing communities with the educational opportunities they require for personal or career growth can be highly rewarding.

You will have the opportunity to work with a variety of people from different backgrounds.

Limited funding may prevent you from providing the courses and programmes that you wish to which can be frustrating.

Money guide

Starting salaries are usually between £23,500 and £28,000.

Those employed at a senior level can achieve more than £30,000.

Salaries in the voluntary sector are usually lower than in the public sector.

Related opportunities

- Social Worker p557
- Volunteer Manager p561
- Youth and Community Worker p563

Further information

Workers' Educational Association
www.wea.org.uk

DANCE TEACHER

ENTRY LEVEL 5

Qualifications and courses

The usual entry route for a dance teacher is to study for a degree, HND or Foundation degree in a dance-related subject.

If you want to teach dance in a state school you will need to reach Qualified Teacher Status (QTS). This can be achieved by doing a Postgraduate Certificate in Education (PGCE) after your degree or, alternatively, some undergraduate degrees in dance subjects incorporate study for QTS.

Those who wish to become a dance teacher in the private sector can take vocational qualifications available at certain dance and performing arts institutions. The Royal Academy of Dance (RAD) offers diplomas, bachelor's degrees and master's degrees which provide students with RAD Registered Teacher Status (RTS). The Imperial Society of Teachers of Dancing (ISTD) also has teaching qualifications at both initial and advanced level. These schools are both accredited by the Council for Dance Education and Training (CDET), as are some courses taught at colleges and professional schools. The list of all accredited schools are on CDET's website.

Once you have qualified you could apply for the CDET Recognised Awards scheme, which will help demonstrate a commitment to safe and professional standards of teaching.

As well as having qualifications, you will need to maintain a high standard of personal performance. Many who have forged successful careers as performers, opt to go into private dance teaching later on in their career.

Joining the National Dance Teachers Association (NDTA) will ensure you remain up to date with new training, developments and teaching resources.

What the work involves

You will plan dance lessons for pupils that adhere to a syllabus or curriculum set out by a school. In the private sector you will train and prepare pupils for dance exams.

You will help your pupils to develop their fitness and agility, ensuring that they do so safely without causing injury to themselves or others.

You will choreograph dance routines, as well as choosing music and costumes.

Type of person suited to this work

You need to have a high level of fitness and be able to demonstrate complicated dance moves and positions to your pupils.

You should also be very enthusiastic about music and the performing arts in general and possess good rhythm and balance.

As a teacher of any subject it is imperative that your communication skills are impeccable but for dance teachers this is especially important because you need to ensure that everyone in your class is dancing safely.

Creativity and self-discipline are very important traits to possess as well.

Working conditions

If you are employed in the state school sector you will be working during the school day but it is likely that you will also run classes after school in the early evening. This is certainly true of the private sector.

If you are a freelance teacher you can expect to travel as you will work at a variety of different venues; from schools and colleges to theatres and community centres.

Future prospects

As a dance teacher you can progress to becoming self-employed and even to running your own dance school.

There are also other performing arts sectors you could branch into such as choreography.

For experienced dance teachers there is the possibility to move into community work as a dance therapist.

Advantages/disadvantages

The job is very active so you will stay fit and healthy.

Your work will often be fun as it is a very creative and expressive art form.

You may injure yourself from constantly dancing and this could jeopardise how much you can work.

Preparing for a big performance can be stressful, especially if you are working with children who can be unpredictable!

Money guide

Earnings vary according to what sector you work in and location.

Newly qualified teachers in state schools start on a salary of around £21,500.

As state teachers gain experience and increased responsibilities, they can earn up to £31,500.

Earnings for dance teachers in the private sector depend upon the size, type and reputation of the dance school.

Self-employed dance teachers charge an hourly rate which can range from £12 to £50. These fees have to cover the cost of hiring a venue.

Related opportunities

- Choreographer p410
- Dancer p413
- Primary School Teacher p185

Further information

Council for Dance Education and Training
www.cdet.org.uk

Imperial Society of Teachers of Dancing
www.istd.org

National Dance Teachers Association
www.ndta.org.uk

EARLY YEARS SPECIALIST/ NURSERY NURSE

ENTRY LEVEL 3

Qualifications and courses

It is best to check with the nursery you want to work for about the qualifications they require, as each nursery may differ. However, recent government proposals are demanding that all childcare professionals have sufficient professional qualifications in order to better deal with the increasing number of children any one member of staff is responsible for at any one time.

To become a nursery nurse, you must hold a full and relevant Level 3 qualification. For example, a CACHE Level 3 Diploma in Children and Young People's Workforce; an NVQ Level 3 in Children's Care, Learning and Development; and a BTEC National Diploma in Children's Care, Learning and Development should be accepted. From September 2014, there will also be a new Level 3 Early Years Educator qualification which will replace existing ones.

It may be useful to start out as a nursery assistant while working towards these qualifications. At least 4 GCSEs/National 5s may be required for some of the qualifications, and certainly ones at grade C or above in English and Maths.

In Scotland, registration of nursery workers has been introduced. Early years practitioners with qualifications such as SVQ Level 3 or an HNC can register to work with the Scottish Social Services Council (SSSC).

To be an Early Years Specialist, you will need at least an NVQ Level 4 in Early Years Care and Education or a Diploma in Early Childhood Studies. In order to progress, you may opt to complete higher qualifications such as a BTEC HNC/HND in Advanced Studies in Early Years or a Foundation degree or degree in early childhood studies during your career.

All applicants must pass a Disclosure and Barring Service (DBS) check to work with children.

What the work involves

Within a nursery or private home, early years specialists/ nursery nurses look after young children, from newborn babies up to the age of 8, ensuring they are safe and comfortable.

Much of your work will involve feeding, changing, dressing and bathing babies, and helping older children to develop in areas such as language, art, practical skills and music.

You will plan the day to include play, exercise, meals and rest, to keep children healthy and mentally stimulated.

Type of person suited to this work

It is essential to enjoy caring for young people and to be outgoing, with a friendly manner towards children and adults alike. You also need to be patient and tolerant to deal with different types of behaviour.

Planning activities needs imagination, and it is helpful to be good at art, practical tasks and singing.

You will need to be flexible, enjoy working in a team and be comfortable working with many different types of people from all cultures and backgrounds.

You will also need excellent diplomacy and communication skills as you will need to discuss the children's development and progress, and any other issues, with their parents or carers.

Working conditions

The majority of nursery nurses work 40 hours a week, however hours can vary depending on parents' requirements.

Most of your work will be indoors in a nursery, school, hospital or private home. You may 'live-in' if you are a nanny in a private home.

The work involves playing with children, bending and lifting so you need to be physically fit.

Future prospects

Nursery nurses work in nurseries, schools and hospitals, and as nannies in private homes. You can start to train straight from school or after gaining experience in other types of work.

With the large rise in working mothers, there is high demand for qualified childcare staff throughout the UK.

Promotion prospects are limited. After gaining experience and further specialist qualifications you could become a nursery manager or you could take further training to enter paediatric nursing or primary school teaching. Sometimes, there are opportunities to travel, particularly in private work.

Advantages/disadvantages

The work is varied and rewarding.

You will have the opportunity to work with a wide variety of children, all at different stages of development which makes for an exceptionally diverse work environment.

The hours can be long, particularly in nanny work, and you might have to work shifts and weekends.

Money guide

As a nursery nurse, expect to start on around £11,000.

With experience earnings can increase to £14,000–£18,000.

Salaries can rise to between £22,000 and £30,000 for a nursery management post.

Related opportunities

- Childminder p545
- Children's Nurse p274
- Teaching Assistant/Learning Support Assistant p192

Further information

CACHE
www.cache.org.uk

Care Inspectorate
www.careinspectorate.com

EDUCATION AND CHILDCARE INSPECTOR

ENTRY LEVEL 6

Qualifications and courses

Registered inspectors in England and Wales, and inspectors in Scotland, must be qualified as teachers and have 5 years' experience working in education.

Qualified Teacher Status (QTS) is gained through Initial Teacher Training (ITT). The 2 main routes are a first degree followed by a Postgraduate Certificate in Education (PGCE), or a first degree (BEd/BA/BSc) leading to QTS.

Registered inspectors also need to have completed 3 years' experience in a leadership or a managerial role. Many inspectors are ex-head teachers or childcare managers. An understanding and up-to-date knowledge of the curriculum and the latest developments within the education sector is vital.

Training for inspectors is provided by the Office for Standards in Education (Ofsted) in England, Estyn or the Care and Social Services Inspectorate in Wales (CSSIW), HM Inspectorate of Education in Scotland, and the Department of Education for Northern Ireland. This includes, in England, additional courses which continue into the first year of employment.

In Wales, candidates undertake a 3-day course on which they are taught and assessed on the Common Inspection Framework. You can then undertake a further 2 days' training in a chosen specialism.

You will need a current and up-to-date Disclosure and Barring Service (DBS) check in order to work alongside children and vulnerable adults. Access to transport is also recommended.

All assessors, throughout the UK, will be expected to keep their knowledge up to date through a series of continuing professional development (CPD) courses.

What the work involves

You will use your extensive experience gained from working in schools, colleges, nurseries or youth service settings to conduct inspections.

You might inspect early years learning, or focus on secondary education and preparation-for-work organisations. Inspections cover special schools and out-of-school learning units.

Inspectors look at the quality of teaching, curriculum, standard of leadership and pupils' achievement levels. During the visit you will contribute to the inspection report, which is then made publicly available on the internet.

Type of person suited to this work

You must be knowledgeable about the types of organisations you will be inspecting. You should be observant and possess a high level of integrity. Strong analytical skills are essential. You will be gathering evidence and interviewing a variety of people so you need to be an effective communicator and be able to make appropriate and fair judgements.

It's important to work to a high standard but also to work quickly and to deadlines. Good IT and report writing skills are also important.

Working conditions

You will visit organisations across the country and will need to spend long periods of time away from home.

Most of the work takes place in classrooms or offices where you will speak to head teachers, pupils, parents, governors and the other professionals linked to the organisation.

Most inspectors are freelance.

Future prospects

You could be working for Ofsted, Tribal Inspections, Serco Education and Children's Services or the Centre for British Teachers Education Trust. These organisations have offices in London, Bristol and Manchester although most inspectors work from home.

Inspectors working for Ofsted are called HMIs (Her Majesty's Inspectors). AIs (Additional Inspectors) work for other organisations under contract to Ofsted. Early years inspectors specialise in education for under-5s. AIs can apply to be HMIs, and early years inspectors can be promoted to adult and senior children's services. There is also the chance to be promoted to managerial level in all groups.

Advantages/disadvantages

This job offers you the chance to use your experience to make sure that the right quality of provision is in place in an institution.

You have the chance to travel around the country.

It's challenging when you need to give an 'inadequate' judgement to an institution.

Money guide

Early years inspectors are usually employed by private organisations; salaries vary but as a guide starting salaries are between £24,000 and £27,000 a year.

HMIs can earn £48,500–£61,000 per year for full-time employment, pro rata for part-time work.

AIs can earn £300–£500 per day and have expenses paid.

Related opportunities

- Education Officer p21
- Secondary School Teacher p189
- Work-based Training Instructor p193

Further information

Care and Social Services Inspectorate in Wales (CSSIW)
http://cssiw.org.uk

Department of Education, Northern Ireland
www.deni.gov.uk

HM Inspectorate of Education in Scotland
www.educationscotland.gov.uk/inspectionandreview/index.asp

Ofsted
www.ofsted.gov.uk

EDUCATION WELFARE OFFICER

ENTRY LEVEL 3

Qualifications and courses

There are a number of routes into this profession though candidates generally have relevant work experience in areas such as special education, teaching, counselling or youth work.

Employers often expect you to have, or be studying for, a qualification in social work. Qualifications in education welfare, teaching or youth and community work may also help you gain entry to this profession. Degree courses usually require a minimum of 2 A levels/3 H grades and 5 GCSEs/National 5s (A*–C/A–C) or equivalent including English and Maths.

Those without a professional qualification who have extensive experience working with children/young people and their families may be accepted into assistant level positions but they will usually be expected to have at least A levels/H grades or equivalent. You could work towards an NVQ in Learning, Development and Support Services for Children, Young People and Those who Care for Them (Levels 3 and 4) whilst you work.

Regardless of qualification level, all candidates are advised to gain as much experience as possible by seeking opportunities through Community Service Volunteers (CSV). Experience in caring for people or advising/counselling work and skills in communication, IT and teamwork would also be valuable. You will need Disclosure and Barring Service (DBS) clearance to work with children.

Once employed, you will work closely with more senior colleagues, receiving ongoing training and professional development throughout your career.

What the work involves

You will work with young people who are not attending school, and their families, to support them back into education.

It will be your responsibility to issue education supervision orders, school attendance orders and truancy schemes. You may have to prosecute parents of children who continue to play truant despite your efforts to help the children return to school.

You will help families get all the benefits they are entitled to, such as free school meals, clothing or transport. As a link between families and schools, you will try to improve existing relationships – writing reports, attending meetings and case conferences.

Type of person suited to this work

As there can be many reasons for poor attendance at school, such as fear of bullying, caring responsibilities at home or difficulty in coping with school work, it is important to be open minded and impartial. You will also need to be strong enough to prosecute a family if it becomes necessary.

You must enjoy working with young people and have a strong conviction as to the value of education as you may have to spend time convincing parents who do not share your views.

You will also have to keep up to date with legislation and you must be able to work on your own and as part of a team.

Working conditions

You will have an office base, but most of your time will be spent visiting young people and their families at home or looking for young people in the local area, so a driving licence is useful.

You may go to other agencies' offices to attend meetings and case conferences.

Families may view your interventions as interfering rather than assisting; you must always consider your safety.

Future prospects

There are about 4,500 education welfare officers in England, Wales and Northern Ireland. In Scotland, they are called attendance officers.

There is a promotion structure within local authorities and you can become a senior education welfare officer, team leader or manager.

There is the opportunity to become a specialist, for example dealing only with primary school pupils.

With further training, you can do similar work in care and social services.

Advantages/disadvantages

You will have the satisfaction of helping people – sometimes quite profoundly.

You may have to work in the evenings to meet parents when they are available.

Some people may be abusive and you could find yourself in stressful situations.

Money guide

Wages vary depending on your geographical area and the local authority you work for.

You should expect a starting salary of around £22,000 per year.

With experience, this could rise to over £30,000.

Those with relevant qualifications are likely to receive higher salaries.

Related opportunities

- Careers Adviser p544
- Social Worker p557
- Youth and Community Worker p563

Further information

Health and Care Professions Council
www.hpc-uk.org

Northern Ireland Social Care Council
www.niscc.info

FURTHER EDUCATION LECTURER

ENTRY LEVEL 5

Qualifications and courses

New entrants need a relevant degree, Foundation degree or HND in the subject you wish to teach. You can also apply if you have significant work experience and at least a qualification at Level 3 in your chosen subject. You will need to register with the Institute for Learning (IfL) in order to practise as a lecturer.

In England and Wales, within 5 years of commencing further education teaching, you will need to have worked towards either a Certificate in Teaching in the Lifelong Learning Sector (CTLLS), a Diploma in Teaching in the Lifelong Learning Sector (DTLLS), a Certificate in Education (Cert Ed) or a Postgraduate Certificate in Education (PGCE) in order to qualify. You will generally need a QCF Level 4–6 qualification for entry to the DTLLS or Cert Ed programme and a degree for entry to a PGCE. To qualify as an associate teacher with fewer responsibilities you need the CTLLS.

Those who secure a lecturing position without a teaching qualification must gain a minimum of a Preparing to Teach in the Lifelong Learning Sector (PTLLS) Award within their first year.

Relevant classroom experience gained through voluntary work shadowing will help you come to an understanding of the skills required of a further education lecturer as well as improving your chances of securing employment.

Within 5 years of starting to teach, all new lecturers must pass a process of Professional Formation monitored by the IfL. Evidence of your teaching qualification together with proof of your continuing professional development (CPD) will lead to confirmation of Qualified Teacher Learning and Skills (QTLS) or Associate Teacher Learning and Skills (ATLS) status.

What the work involves

You will teach students aged 16 and over on vocational or academic courses at a further education college.

Your work will involve planning and preparing lessons, setting assignments and marking pupils' work. You will also undertake administrative tasks and keep records of students' progress.

As well as teaching your main subject, you will arrange work placements, visit students to assess their progress, act as a student mentor and meet colleagues to develop courses.

Type of person suited to this work

Lecturers need to be interested in teaching people of all ages. You must be comfortable talking to large groups of students.

You need extensive knowledge of your subject and the ability to explain things to students at a level that they will understand.

You should be creative to devise lectures, activities and materials which will interest your students. Planning and organisation skills are essential.

Working conditions

Further education lecturers mostly teach in classrooms, labs or workshops. If you teach a practical subject you may work outdoors. Occasionally you might take students on field trips.

When you are not teaching, you will be researching, writing papers and marking students' work. Consequently, you will have to work some evenings and weekends.

Depending on the institution you are employed by, you will usually work during term-time and have school holidays off.

Future prospects

Further education lecturers could progress to more senior roles such as senior lecturer, curriculum manager, head of department or divisional manager. However, tight college budgets have led to a reduction in the number of management positions. For this reason, you will need a willingness to be geographically mobile if you are keen to gain a promotion.

You could move into other areas of education, for example, you could take further training to become a higher education lecturer.

You could also progress to a non-teaching position in college management.

Advantages/disadvantages

You are able to teach in a less formal environment than a school.

Witnessing students' progression is rewarding.

You will be required to spend a lot of time planning lessons and marking work, which may interfere with your personal life.

Money guide

Salaries are dependent on your experience and expertise, and the size and status of your college.

Starting salaries for full-time, qualified lecturers start from around £22,000 and could rise to around £36,000 depending on experience.

Salaries are typically £3,000 per year higher in London.

Leadership and management jobs could potentially reach up to £80,000.

Related opportunities

- Primary School Teacher p185
- Secondary School Teacher p189
- Work-based Training Instructor p193

Further information

Lifelong Learning UK
www.lifelonglearning.co.uk

University and College Union
www.ucu.org.uk

LEARNING MENTOR ENTRY LEVEL 3

Qualifications and courses

Whilst there are no formal entry requirements for this career, nearly all entrants have a degree, HND or equivalent vocational qualification with relevant degree subjects including social sciences, early childhood studies, psychology and any of the National Curriculum subjects. Typical entry requirements for a degree subject include 2 A levels/3 H grades and 5 GCSEs/National 5s.

The NVQ Level 3 in Learning, Development and Support Services for Children and Young People is the minimum requirement for many local authorities, but not all.

The NVQ/SVQ Level 4 is normally required to become a learning mentor coordinator.

Experience of working with young people is normally required, and time spent volunteering in a related area such as social work, counselling or teaching may improve your chances of securing employment within a somewhat competitive industry. Some universities offer the opportunity to participate in mentoring schemes.

The majority of newly appointed learning mentors will participate in a standardised induction programme aimed at support staff in education. You will also receive specific mentor training, usually from the area learning mentor coordinator. It is also common for newly appointed mentors to keep a portfolio of evidence detailing their work.

All candidates are required to undergo a Disclosure and Barring Service (DBS) check in order to practise as a learning mentor.

What the work involves

Your work will be complementary to teachers and other school support staff as you support students while they are learning to overcome obstacles and meet their learning objectives.

Working on a one-to-one basis, you will listen to your mentee's difficulties and offer various solutions, covering a range of topics from bullying to abuse to gifted and talented students.

You will help everybody you work with to succeed in and enjoy their learning experience.

Type of person suited to this work

To be a good learning mentor, you will need to have experience of the subject you mentor, along with an understanding of different styles of studying.

You should enjoy helping and listening to people and have good communication skills. You should be patient and willing to listen.

The best mentors are those who can be a critical friend, know the benefits of learning and can explain them to the people they work with.

You should be able to handle emotional stress, be adaptable, non-judgemental and encouraging.

Working conditions

You can work on a part- or full-time basis with people at school, home or sometimes at a college, university or training centre.

You might be employed on a term-time only basis or all year round. Some of your work might involve weekends and evenings – this will depend on the organisation you work for.

You will meet in a quiet, confidential area where you will examine workbooks and essays, talk over any issues and offer help.

Future prospects

There are opportunities to progress to management roles or even to head of year at some schools.

You may choose to study further and become a teacher, youth worker or social worker.

You could also specialise in various areas including working with refugee families or children with behavioural disorders.

As the profession is still developing, current learning mentor coordinators have often come from other professions such as careers advisory roles or social work but it is possible to progress from a learning mentor to coordinator through experience and further training.

Advantages/disadvantages

This job involves a variety of roles – friend, confidence builder and motivator.

Results have shown how important this job can be in helping learners to succeed.

You will be working with students without being a teacher.

Money guide

Within schools, salaries for newly appointed mentors range between £15,000 and £17,000 per year.

With experience, you can expect this to increase to between £20,000 and £24,000.

£30,000 is possible with managerial responsibilities.

The salary can vary a lot between different employers. The professional status of the role is in contention, as some employers recognise the expertise as similar to a new teacher or social worker (and this is reflected in the salary offered) whereas other employers only view the position in a supporting capacity.

Related opportunities

- Careers Adviser p544
- Learning Disabilities Nurse p294
- Special Educational Needs Teacher p190
- Youth and Community Worker p563

Further information

Mentoring and Befriending Foundation
www.mandbf.org

NVQ/SVQ ASSESSOR ENTRY LEVEL 3

Qualifications and courses

It is necessary to have between 2 and 4 years' occupational experience, and often a Level 3 vocational qualification in the subject or work area to be assessed. For this reason it is not possible for school or college leavers to enter this profession straight away.

It is also necessary to have an assessor qualification. You may study for a Level 3 Award in either Assessing Competence in the Work Environment or Assessing Vocationally Related Achievement, or a Level 3 Certificate in Assessing Vocational Achievement. Each of these will include a knowledge and understanding unit (Level 3 Award in Understanding Principles and Practices of Assessment) and a practical application unit. The qualification you choose to complete will depend on the environment in which you wish to assess, ie in the workplace, in a college or both. You can also study for a Training Assessment Quality Assurance (TAQA) award from City & Guilds.

Qualified assessors can carry out further training to work as an NVQ/SVQ verifier, a post that ensures assessment methods meet quality standards. A number of Level 4 Awards and Certificates are available for both internal and external verifiers.

Once you begin your training you can join the Institute of Assessors and Internal Verifiers (IAV) as an Associate member. After gaining 12 months' experience you can apply for Licentiate membership and you will be added to the IAV's National Register. After 5 years you can apply for Fellowship.

The work involves a great deal of travelling between test centres and places of employment so a driving licence is essential.

What the work involves

NVQ/SVQ assessors work alongside trainees to ascertain their current knowledge and formulate a plan for their development.

You will offer feedback on their progress as they gain experience and take their NVQ/SVQ qualifications.

You will observe how trainees perform different tasks and measure their achievements against the standards for the qualification. You will also read through each trainee's portfolio of evidence, checking that tasks are undertaken.

Type of person suited to this work

It is essential to demonstrate an interest in other people and a commitment to helping them to progress. You will need to motivate and encourage all kinds of individuals – some of whom will not have enjoyed school and find training difficult.

Excellent communication skills are important for the amount of speaking, questioning, listening and reporting that is involved.

You should be organised and able to interpret the different standards in ways that are helpful to those who are learning. You should also have an interest in the area you are assessing.

Working conditions

You will have access to an office where you will use a computer to update learner records and check portfolios. You will also spend lots of time travelling to meet employers and trainees at their places of work.

Depending on your specialist area you could have very early starts (for example assessing bakers at work) or late finishes (assessing car finishers working nights).

It is necessary to keep up to date with the changes and developments in your occupational area.

It is possible to work freelance.

Future prospects

The government is currently focussed on encouraging learning through work-based qualifications and school/college leavers now have more opportunities to pursue apprenticeships or national traineeships.

Therefore, there is currently a national shortage of skilled professionals in this area, and there will be increasing need for NVQ/SVQ assessors in the future.

It is possible to expand your role by becoming an internal or external verifier. With experience, it is also possible to move into further education teaching or training.

Advantages/disadvantages

This work involves being at the centre of improving the skills levels of the workforce. You will spend lots of your time meeting, speaking to and getting to know other people.

Depending on your specialist area, you might have to work unsociable hours in order to assess candidates in their workplace.

It can be challenging to motivate and encourage candidates who do not enjoy learning towards a qualification.

Money guide

Average starting salaries are between £18,000 and £24,000.

With experience and responsibilities, this can reach £30,000 a year.

Related opportunities

- Education and Childcare Inspector p179
- Further Education Lecturer p181
- Training and Development Officer p54

Further information

Chartered Institute of Personnel and Development
www.cipd.co.uk

Lifelong Learning UK
www.lifelonglearning.co.uk

The Institute of Assessors and Internal Verifiers
www.iavltd.co.uk

PLAY WORKER/HOSPITAL PLAY SPECIALIST

ENTRY LEVEL 3

Qualifications and courses

Most people enter this career as a play assistant for which you will need an NVQ Level 3 in Childcare.

There are apprenticeships available in health and social care and children's care which may also be useful when entering this career. Apprenticeships offer entrants the chance to combine practical work experience with study towards a professional qualification, such as the Council for Awards in Care, Health and Education (CACHE) Certificate in Playwork and NCFE Certificate in Playwork, both at Level 2, and the CACHE Certificate and Diploma in Childcare and Education.

You might still be able to work as a playworker without the qualifications, under the supervision of a senior playworker. You would also have to demonstrate some commitment to attaining the qualifications in future.

To become a registered hospital play specialist, you must be aged 20 or over and have a Foundation degree in a hospital play specialism, approved by the Hospital Play Staff Education Trust (HPSET). To be accepted onto the Foundation degree course applicants must have an appropriate Level 3 qualification in a subject such as childcare, nursery nursing, teaching or social work, and at least 2 years' experience working in a related field. GCSEs/National 5s (A*–C/A–C) in English and maths and a pre-organised hospital placement will also be required.

The 2-year Foundation degree course is delivered by means of formal teaching and practical experience with a mentor. Once this is completed you can apply for a licence to practise from the HPSET. You will have to re-register with the HPSET every 2 years thereafter. In order to do so, you will need to show evidence of your continuing professional development (CPD).

What the work involves

Play workers and hospital play specialists are responsible for ensuring that children between the ages of 5 and 15 play in a safe environment.

You will encourage children and young people to learn through play by giving them the freedom to explore and get to know themselves.

Hospital play specialists use play to entertain children and help them to deal with their experiences in hospital. This includes using play to prepare them for treatments and diverting their attention from unpleasant procedures. You may work with severely disabled children.

Type of person suited to this work

Imagination and creativity are needed to do this job well. It is essential that you like being with children of all ages, understand what they like to do and recognise how they change as they develop.

You should be positive and patient with lots of energy and stamina. As the safety of the children will be your responsibility, you will need high levels of concentration and an awareness of any health and safety issues in the surrounding environment.

A hospital play specialist needs to be sympathetic to the needs and issues of each child, have some understanding of medical conditions, and must be able to cope with distressing situations.

Working conditions

You will normally work in the early evening, at weekends and in school holidays, as many jobs are seasonal and most are part time.

Hospital play specialists work in children's hospitals, children's wards and out-patient clinics. You may take children on trips or visit them in their homes, so you might need a driving licence.

Future prospects

This area of work is rising in importance and is part of the National Childcare Strategy, which recognises the significance of giving young people opportunities to improve their lives through education, sport and leisure.

With the increased number of working parents, the need for out-of-school carers has grown.

There is currently an increase in the number of hospital play specialist posts available nationally. Most opportunities are with NHS hospitals but you could also work in hospices or community paediatric teams.

With at least 2 years' experience, it is possible to move into senior or managerial roles.

Advantages/disadvantages

Helping children who are ill to enjoy themselves can be extremely rewarding.

You will receive immediate feedback from the children which will help you develop and adapt to different situations quickly.

Hospital play specialists may have to deal with distressing situations and face challenging children.

Money guide

Starting salaries for hospital play specialists range from £13,000 to £15,000.

With experience or promotion, salaries can increase to between £18,800 and £22,000.

As a senior manager, it is possible to achieve salaries up to £34,500.

Related opportunities

- Childminder p545
- Teaching Assistant/Learning Support Assistant p192
- Youth and Community Worker p563

Further information

CACHE
www.cache.org.uk

National Association of Health Play Specialists
www.nahps.org.uk

PRIMARY SCHOOL TEACHER

ENTRY LEVEL 5

Qualifications and courses

You can enter this career with a Bachelor of Education (BEd) degree or a BA/BSc degree with Qualified Teacher Status (QTS).

If you have obtained an Honours degree in an unrelated degree subject, you could complete a Professional Graduate Certificate in Education (ProfGCE) or a Postgraduate Certificate in Education (PGCE). In Scotland you can complete a Professional Graduate Diploma in Education (PGDE). Whilst these courses are open to all graduates, those with a degree in a National Curriculum subject will be at an advantage given the competitive nature of entry into these courses.

Alternatively, you could gain qualifications whilst working. In England and Wales, if you have a degree, it is possible to apply for School Direct, school-centred initial teacher training (SCITT) or Teach First programmes where students are employed by a school and earn a salary while they train. Competition for the limited places available on employment-based schemes is high so entrants are advised to gain as much classroom experience as possible.

All entrants are required to have GCSEs/National 5s (A*–C/A–C) in English, Maths and a science subject and a history of relevant experience. Prior to your acceptance, you must also pass numeracy and literacy skills tests and obtain clearance from the Disclosure and Barring Service (DBS). Knowledge of a foreign language is important given its compulsory inclusion in the National Curriculum.

As a newly qualified teacher (NQT) you will undertake a 1-year probationary period where you will be continually monitored and supported. You will undergo continuing professional development (CPD) throughout your career in order to remain on top of new developments in the curriculum.

What the work involves

You will teach young children the key subjects of English, maths and science as well as IT, history, religious education, geography, art, languages and physical education.

Primary schools admit pupils aged 5–11 and have children of a wide range of abilities in the same class.

In a state school, you will teach children reading, writing and numeracy following the frameworks outlined in the National Curriculum. Private schools can set their own teaching guidelines.

You will prepare resources for structured play and social development work as well as conducting individual assessments on the students in your care.

Type of person suited to this work

You should be assertive and able to uphold discipline within the class. It is also important to be able to encourage and motivate your students – no matter how small their achievements are.

Planning activities requires creativity. You need to have excellent organisational skills and be able to communicate with children, parents and colleagues.

Working conditions

The majority of primary school teachers work over 50 hours a week with 12–13 weeks' holiday per year when the school closes. Preparation for lessons and marking is often completed during holiday time, as well as in the evenings and at weekends during term-time. Extra responsibilities include parents' evenings, after-school activities and school inspections.

You will be based in a classroom and will have a great deal of freedom over your teaching timetable for the day. It is also possible to gain part-time supply work.

Future prospects

You could become a coordinator of your subject or work with teachers in nearby schools as an advanced skills teacher (in England and Wales) or a chartered teacher (in Scotland).

The National College for Leadership of Schools and Children's Services provides programmes which offer greater salaries and responsibilities to gifted teachers.

Progression to deputy head teacher/head teacher can be achieved in 10 years.

Other options include jobs in local or national government, such as an Ofsted inspector. Some teachers offer private tutoring or prepare educational texts.

Advantages/disadvantages

Being responsible for your students' educational development can be very rewarding.

The job is demanding as you will have to carry out many duties, such as marking and preparing lessons, and you will be required to complete this work in the evening and at weekends.

Money guide

The main pay scale for qualified teachers in England and Wales ranges from £21,804 to £31,868 a year.

Teachers on the main pay scale move up to the next point each year if their performance has been satisfactory.

Those who take on additional responsibilities can earn up to £36,756.

Advanced skills teachers have a salary of £37,461–£56,950 and those in senior roles can earn considerably more.

Related opportunities

- Secondary School Teacher p189
- Teaching Assistant/Learning Support Assistant p192

Further information

Department for Education
www.gov.uk/dfe

PRIVATE MUSIC TEACHER

ENTRY LEVEL 5

Qualifications and courses

For private music teachers there are no set qualifications, however most do have a degree. It is also useful to study for further teaching and performance and theory qualifications. The most important qualification, however, is excellent musical competence and knowledge of your instrument, usually at a grade 7/8 from an Associated Board on a first instrument and grade 6 on a second.

Private music teachers can join the Incorporated Society of Musicians (ISM) Music Directory which lists available teachers and their credentials. The ISM awards Approved Private Teacher status to those members who have obtained a clean Disclosure and Barring Service (DBS) check, a good reference from a current pupil or their parent/guardian and actively adhere to the ISM Code of Practice for Private Music Teachers.

There is also a wide range of courses available for music teachers. Rockschool offers a music educator course and a Diploma and Licentiate in Music Teaching (Levels 4 and 6). The Associated Board of the Royal Schools of Music (ABRSM) also offers introductory and continuing professional development (CPD) courses at various levels. You could even work towards a postgraduate qualification in instrumental teaching.

For private music teachers who want to work in state schools, Qualified Teacher Status (QTS) could improve your chances of securing employment. QTS can be achieved through a first degree followed by a Postgraduate Certificate in Education (PGCE) or a Professional Graduate Diploma in Education (PGDE) in Scotland or a Bachelor of Education (BEd) degree that includes QTS.

Practical experience and a demonstrable passion for music will not only enhance your applications but help you to establish a client base. Take every opportunity to raise your profile through giving local performances, networking with local musicians and gaining membership with professional bodies such as the Musicians' Union (MU), as customers are usually secured through personal recommendation and advertising.

What the work involves

Private music teachers provide vocal, instrumental and theoretical music training for a range of people and ages. You will work at a variety of different levels.

Your teaching may take place in a classroom, in either a primary or secondary school, in a community setting, at your pupil's home or in your own home. You will be expected to plan lessons, organise groups such as orchestras, and you might have to prepare students for external exams.

You may be hired by a particular local authority music service, schools, a music centre or be self-employed and many private music teachers work in a combination of these settings and roles.

Type of person suited to this work

You should be patient, have a caring attitude towards others and an interest in drawing out and developing an individual's potential in learning about music.

Excellent communication skills are important, as are firmness and commitment, imagination and creativity. You have to be well organised, flexible and able to change plans and the sequence of lessons to accommodate unexpected events.

It is important to be comfortable in maintaining discipline and be confident when speaking to large groups of young people and also to other professionals.

Working conditions

Music teachers work indoors in all kinds of settings within public and private sector schools and learning centres, and in their own or pupils' homes as tutors.

Work in schools will usually be between 8.45am and 3.45pm, with some evening and weekend work required for tuition, rehearsals and concerts.

It is likely that you will work evenings and weekends, and part-time work is common. You should expect to carry out some travelling and you may be expected to lift and carry heavy musical instruments.

Future prospects

Many private teachers combine their teaching work with composing, performing or directing choirs/orchestras, and career breaks are common. If you can play the piano and have excellent sight reading, you could accompany students at examinations and recitals.

Advantages/disadvantages

Teaching is a rewarding profession in which you can witness a student's progression.

You will be kept very busy with preparation, classes, assessing your students, communicating with examining bodies, meetings and ordering materials.

Money guide

For private teachers the Musicians' Union recommends a rate of £29 an hour.

For teachers visiting schools pay varies between £24 and £35 an hour, depending on reputation, location and qualifications.

After considerable experience, at least 10–15 years, private music teachers can expect to earn in the range of £30 to £50 an hour.

Related opportunities

- Dance Teacher p177
- Primary School Teacher p185
- Secondary School Teacher p189
- Teaching Assistant/Learning Support Assistant p192

Further information

Incorporated Society of Musicians
www.ism.org

Musicians' Union
www.musiciansunion.org.uk

Rockschool Ltd
www.rockschool.co.uk

SCHOOL ADMINISTRATOR/ SECRETARY

ENTRY LEVEL 2

Qualifications and courses

There are no formal entry requirements but many employers value 5 GCSEs/National 5s (A*–C/A–C) or equivalent and a good standard of maths and English. Adult entry is common and many candidates have several years of office experience.

You will need keyboard and word-processing skills. Other IT skills such as an ability to maintain databases, spreadsheets and to manage accounts computer packages is useful, as is knowledge of shorthand. Training is mostly on the job however, and some schools will require you to undergo external instruction via courses and workshops.

If you do not have sufficient office experience, you might consider starting out as a clerical assistant in a school before working your way up to a post with more responsibility.

Once employed, you may be encouraged to work towards work-based qualifications such as the Institute of Administrative Management (IAM)'s National Level 3 Certificate in Educational Administration at the School of Educational Administration (SEA). This course can be undertaken in 1 year by distance learning and it covers topics such as government policies, education and the law, and business management.

In addition, an NVQ in Business and Administration (Levels 1–4) is available, and City & Guilds offer an Award/Certificate/Diploma in Support Work in Schools (Levels 2 and 3).

You will need to gain clearance from the Disclosure and Barring Service (DBS) in order to work alongside children.

What the work involves

School administrators/secretaries are responsible for greeting visitors and answering telephone calls.

You will develop administrative systems (both paper and IT based) to keep information organised and easily accessible.

In some schools you might also collect money for lunch and school trips and you could be in charge of the medical room.

Type of person suited to this work

You will be highly organised and efficient with excellent written and verbal communication skills. You should be confident dealing with people at all levels, including teachers, students and their guardians. You might need to work with people who are ill, angry or upset.

You should have an excellent telephone manner and possess keyboard skills and knowledge of IT packages and information systems.

You must be responsible, flexible, and able to prioritise your workload and use your initiative. You should also be able to work calmly under pressure, meet deadlines and handle confidential information discreetly.

Working conditions

You will usually be office based, doing normal school hours (8.30am–4pm). You will use a range of office equipment, including computers, photocopiers, telephones and fax machines.

School offices are open to visitors and pupils and can be very busy. On a reception desk you will be responsible for greeting visitors and showing them to their meeting room or contacting colleagues. Business dress is often required.

Many school secretaries work part time and do not work at all during the school holidays.

Future prospects

In the UK there are about 55,000 administrators employed in nursery, primary and secondary schools. There are job opportunities in all areas of the country, although entry can be competitive as the working hours and holidays are appealing.

Much of the work is part time and there are not many opportunities for promotion. However, you could work your way up to become a school business manager/bursar or move into secretarial work outside the education sector.

Advantages/disadvantages

The working hours, holiday allowances and opportunities for part-time work make this job ideal for someone with family commitments.

You will learn key, transferable skills that could be used in many other jobs and sectors.

The work can be routine and repetitive.

Money guide

In a state school, you would usually receive a starting salary of £15,000–£19,000.

With experience in the role, or if you take on additional responsibilities, your earnings could increase to £22,000.

Salaries in large secondary schools and private schools may be higher.

Related opportunities

- Arts Administrator/Manager p327
- Personal Assistant p42
- Receptionist p45
- School Business Manager/Bursar p188

Further information

School of Educational Administration
www.admin.org.uk

SCHOOL BUSINESS MANAGER/ BURSAR

ENTRY LEVEL 4

Qualifications and courses

Most entrants have experience in a related field and many hold a degree or professional qualification in a business or finance-related subject. Management experience in the education, accounting or personnel sectors would be useful. Those seeking entry to this career may find it an advantage to study for the NVQ/SVQ in Business and Administration (Levels 1–4) or the NVQ/SVQ in Management and Team Leading (Levels 2–5).

You could start out as a school administrator or secretary and work your way up to school bursar/ business manager.

Alternatively, for those already employed as a school business manager, the National College for School Leadership offers a professional development programme. The Certificate of School Business Management (CSBM) is an entry-level qualification aimed at newly appointed bursars or those in school administration posts, and the Diploma of School Business Management (DSBM) is intended for experienced bursars/business managers. An Advanced Diploma of School Business Management (ADSBM) is also available, as is a School Business Director Programme aimed at managers seeking to reach the highest levels of the profession. Each qualification consists of an 8–15 month period of short courses and distance learning, eventually leading also to Institute of Administrative Management qualifications and membership.

The Independent Schools' Bursars Association also offers induction courses for new bursars working in independent schools and a series of professional development seminars.

With experience, the appropriate qualification and membership of The National Association of School Business Management (NASBM), you may consider the MSc in Educational Leadership (School Business Management).

What the work involves

You will be responsible for the financial and strategic planning, human resources and environmental issues of a school or college.

The term 'bursar' is common in independent schools; in the state sector you might be called a school business manager or finance manager.

Your role will involve organising staff pay and recruitment, as well as managing contracts with maintenance companies. You will have to keep all the school premises' insurance documents up to date. In independent schools, you will also set fees and distribute bursaries, scholarships and awards.

Type of person suited to this work

You will need a polite yet firm approach and excellent communication skills as you will deal with the head teacher and senior staff, other professionals (auditors, company managers, etc) as well as parents and students.

You should have a head for figures and be happy using computers and financial software. You need to be very organised in order to oversee all of your responsibilities.

Working conditions

Usually you will work in an office sitting at a desk. You will have access to a computer and spend lots of time talking to people – both in or outside of your organisation.

You will attend lots of meetings with the head teacher and other professional staff – sometimes staying late to give reports to your school's governing body.

You may also need to work during the evenings and school holidays.

Future prospects

Most bursars progress to the role after working in a private financial organisation or as an accountant. Some bursars work their way up within a school, possibly from secretary level.

With experience, bursars can move to larger organisations or return to the private sector. You could also work in British schools overseas.

Posts are advertised in local and national publications such as the *Times Educational Supplement*. Jobs are also posted on the National Association of School Business Management (NASBM)'s website.

Advantages/disadvantages

The role is varied and allows you use your initiative.

You will have the opportunity to work with people of all ages and backgrounds.

You are usually required to work during the school holidays.

There is a high level of responsibility involved in this job so your work may occasionally be stressful.

Money guide

Salaries for bursars vary greatly depending on the size, type and location of the institution you work in.

The average starting salary in a state school or college ranges from £16,000 to £25,000.

As you gain experience, you could expect to earn between £30,000 and £50,000.

Salaries are higher in the independent sector and it is possible to achieve up to £90,000.

Related opportunities

- Accountant p2
- Accounting Technician and Accounts/Finance Clerk p4
- Financial Adviser p26

Further information

Independent Schools' Bursars Association
www.theisba.org.uk

National Association of School Business Management
www.nasbm.co.uk

SECONDARY SCHOOL TEACHER

ENTRY LEVEL 5

Qualifications and courses

To enter this profession you will need to hold either a Bachelor of Education (BEd) degree, a BA/BSc degree with Qualified Teacher Status (QTS) or, if you wish to teach in Scotland, a teaching qualification (TQ). Alternatively, you can complete an undergraduate degree followed by a Postgraduate Certificate in Education (PGCE) or a Professional Graduate Diploma in Education (PGDE) if you live in Scotland. You should study for a degree related to the subject you wish to teach.

Employment-based routes are also available for those who want to work in a school whilst they qualify. The school-centred initial teacher training (SCITT) is a 1-year course open to graduates who hold a degree in the subject they wish to teach. Alternatively, the School Direct programme involves training graduates in a classroom environment with the expectation that candidates will go on to work in that same school once qualified. Teach First offers a 2-year Leadership Development Programme in which graduates study for a PGCE whilst training on the job.

All entrants must have GCSEs/National 5s (A*–C/A–C) in English and Maths and Disclosure and Barring Service (DBS) clearance. Literacy and numeracy skills tests must also be passed prior to acceptance. Relevant work experience will improve your chances of securing entry onto a programme.

As a newly qualified teacher (NQT), you will serve a 1-year probationary period of assessment, monitoring and support until QTS is confirmed.

What the work involves

You will be a specialist in 1 or 2 subjects and teach students aged 11–19.

You will also take on the role of form tutor and be responsible for encouraging personal development and good behaviour.

In state schools, you will follow the National Curriculum. Private and independent schools are free to set their own educational standards.

Type of person suited to this work

You must be patient, caring and have excellent communication skills in order to relate to and teach your pupils. You should also be assertive and able to maintain discipline with large groups of young people.

You must be imaginative and creative to design lessons which capture your students' attention.

It is important that you are highly organised as this job involves a lot of marking and lesson planning.

Working conditions

You will be based in a classroom and will teach classes from about 9am until 4pm. However, you will have to come in early, stay late and work from home in order to carry out preparation for lessons and finish marking pupils' work.

Schools are usually open for 39 weeks of the year but teachers often carry out preparatory work during the holidays.

Teachers sometimes go on school trips or visit students on work placements. Modern foreign language and PE teachers should be prepared to go on school trips overseas.

Future prospects

There are shortages teachers of science, maths, modern foreign languages, design and technology (food and textiles or resistant materials) and computing with IT in secondary education and many universities offer attractive bursaries in order to encourage graduates to train in these areas. There is a serious fear that by 2015, there will be a nationwide shortage of 15,000 teaching staff.

As you gain experience, you could move into a role as a Key Stage coordinator, a head of a department or year group, or work with teachers as an advanced skills teacher. You could also go into teacher training, advisory work or become a school inspector. The National College for School Leadership provides opportunities for gifted teachers to develop skills and improve their leadership.

You should undertake continuing professional development (CPD) throughout your career so as to remain on top of any curriculum changes. Curriculum changes are occurring both in GCSEs and A levels. The replacement of IT with a new computing curriculum means teachers need to be increasingly confident in elements of computer science.

Advantages/disadvantages

Helping your students to learn and progress can be very rewarding.

The holiday allowance is very generous.

Pupils can sometimes be difficult and disruptive.

You will have to work from home in order to finish marking and preparing lessons.

Money guide

Qualified teachers in England and Wales earn £21,804–£31,868. London wages are higher.

With additional responsibilities, you can earn £34,181–£36,756.

Advanced skills teachers typically earn £37,461–£56,950 and those in senior roles can earn considerably more.

Related opportunities

- Education and Childcare Inspector p179
- Primary School Teacher p185
- Teaching Assistant/Learning Support Assistant p192
- Work-based Training Instructor p193

Further information

Department for Education
www.gov.uk/dfe

General Teaching Council Scotland
www.gtcs.org.uk

SPECIAL EDUCATIONAL NEEDS TEACHER

ENTRY LEVEL 5

Qualifications and courses

It is generally necessary to have teaching experience in a mainstream school before you can work as a teacher for pupils with special educational needs. In England and Wales you must have Qualified Teacher Status (QTS) and in Scotland you should have a teaching qualification (TQ). In order to obtain these you should have a Postgraduate Certificate in Education (PGCE) or a Postgraduate Diploma in Education (PGDE), a Bachelor of Education (BEd), or a BA or BSc with QTS. Employment-based training programmes such as SCITT or Teach First are also available.

It may be possible to secure work first as a special needs teaching assistant before working your way up to the position of a special educational needs teacher, although this is rare.

The Training and Development Agency for Schools provides courses that cover ways of teaching different subjects, such as maths and science, to children with special educational needs. It also offers courses which raise awareness of special educational needs (SEN) teaching methods and practices.

Postgraduate qualifications are available in subjects such as special educational needs, specific learning difficulties (dyslexia), and visual impairment. You can study part time or by distance learning.

You must have relevant qualifications if you are teaching children with visual, hearing or multi-sensory impairments. Qualified teachers of hearing impaired pupils are required to have a Stage 1 qualification in sign language, or equivalent, from the Council for the Advancement of Communication with Deaf People (CACDP). Qualified teachers of visually impaired pupils must be proficient in Braille.

You will be required to gain clearance from the Disclosure and Barring Service (DBS) in order to work with children and vulnerable adults.

What the work involves

Teachers for special educational needs help children with disabilities, learning difficulties or emotional or behavioural problems to achieve their best. You might also work with exceptionally gifted children.

Working with educational psychologists, social workers, other teachers and learning support workers, you will assess each child's individual needs and draw up an Individual Education Plan (IEP).

In each of these teaching jobs, you will accompany students on visits and trips, help them understand the world around them, and teach life skills to give them greater independence.

Type of person suited to this work

You must be patient and determined in order to deal with challenging behaviour and solve communication problems with pupils. You should be observant and must be able to recognise and praise efforts and achievements, however small.

You need to be kind and have excellent communication skills as well as a commitment to drawing out and developing individuals' potential in learning. You have to be well organised, flexible and able to change plans and the sequence of lessons to accommodate unexpected events.

Working conditions

There are opportunities all over the UK. You may be based in one school or work in teams covering a number of institutions. Part-time work is possible if you are registered with your local authority. Freelance or self-employment is less common.

You will work 39 weeks a year in school. Hours are usually 9am to 4pm, Monday to Friday. Additional hours will be required to create lesson plans and attend meetings.

Future prospects

There are over 150,000 SEN teachers in the UK. Most work in mainstream schools, whilst others work in special schools such as hospital schools, pupil referral units, youth custody centres and community homes. There is a shortage of skilled candidates.

SEN teachers working in a mainstream school may have the opportunity to be promoted to special education needs co-ordinator. You could also progress to a role as a special needs assessor in a local education authority.

Advantages/disadvantages

Helping children with disabilities, learning difficulties or emotional or behavioural problems and knowing that you helped them to progress is extremely rewarding.

You will be kept very busy with duties including preparation, classes, marking and assessing, analysing coursework, communicating with examining bodies, meetings and ordering materials, which can be stressful.

Money guide

Salaries are based on the teaching pay scale and range from £21,804 to £31,868. An additional allowance ranging from £2,001 to £3,954 for teachers working in the SEN field is allocated.

Once you reach the top of the main salary scale you can apply to be assessed for the upper salary scale which ranges from £34,523 to £37,124.

Salaries in central London are usually higher.

Related opportunities

- Education and Childcare Inspector p179
- Further Education Lecturer p181
- Work-based Training Instructor p193

Further information

National Association for Special Educational Needs
www.nasen.org.uk

TEACHER OF ENGLISH TO SPEAKERS OF OTHER LANGUAGES

ENTRY LEVEL 5

Qualifications and courses

It is becoming increasingly necessary to have a degree to enter this occupation, especially in England. Useful degree subjects include English, linguistics, modern foreign languages and education.

In addition, you will need the Level 5 Certificate in Teaching English to Speakers of Other Languages from either Cambridge ESOL (CELTA) or from Trinity College London (CertTESOL). These are the most commonly recognised qualifications and allow you to teach English as a foreign language worldwide. Certificates are also available from the same organisations for those wishing to specialise in the teaching of English to children or young learners (aged 4–18).

Higher-level courses are also available for people with an initial language qualification (such as CELTA or CertTESOL) and at least 2 years' Teaching English as a Foreign Language (TEFL) or Teaching English to Speakers of a Other Languages (TESOL) experience. Cambridge ESOL offers the Level 7 Diploma in Teaching English to Speakers of Other Languages (DELTA) and Trinity College London provides the Level 7 Licentiate Diploma in Teaching English to Speakers of Other Languages (DipTESOL). These courses are aimed at people seeking career progression.

You will generally need to be aged 18 or over in order to gain entry onto a course with good A levels/H grades and an excellent standard of English. Pre-entry experience gained through overseas voluntary work or home tutoring, is also desirable. Employers tend to favour accredited courses that encompass both theory and teaching practice in classrooms.

Experienced teachers with a degree and/or TESOL qualification can also study for a master's in TESOL.

Candidates who wish to teach in a state school must have Qualified Teacher Status (QTS) which can be obtained from studying for a BA/BSc with QTS or a Postgraduate Certificate in Education (PGCE) or a Postgraduate Diploma in Education (PGDE) in Scotland.

What the work involves

You may be based in the UK or overseas and will teach English to students who are not native speakers. The term TESOL is only used when the students are in the UK. Teaching English as a Foreign Language (TEFL) is used if you are teaching students abroad.

You will teach pupils of all ages who want to learn to speak English for educational, cultural or business reasons.

You will want to demonstrate your passion for the English language as well as inspiring and encouraging your students.

Type of person suited to this work

It is essential that you have an excellent grasp of the English language. You should be patient and have an interest in developing individuals' learning potential. Good communication skills are important, as is commitment and imagination.

You have to be well organised and flexible. You must be able to recognise and praise efforts and achievements.

You should be comfortable in maintaining discipline and be confident when speaking to large groups.

Working conditions

If you teach English as a foreign language, you may work in this country or abroad, teaching in community and learning centres or commercial and industrial settings.

Hours vary according to the employer, however evening and weekend work is common.

Future prospects

There is always a need for English language teachers to cope with the high demand of people who wish to learn English. However, competition is fierce for full-time positions.

Most English language teachers are employed overseas on temporary contracts during the academic year. They may return to the UK to teach during the summer.

It is possible to progress to become a course director or course co-ordinator. With experience, you could get involved in teacher training or set up your own private language school.

Advantages/disadvantages

This is a very busy and demanding job as you will have to deal with preparation, teaching, marking and different examining bodies.

Teaching is a rewarding profession in which you can witness a student's progression and know that you played a major role in helping them master the English language.

Money guide

Teaching English in a UK commercial language school, you can expect a starting salary of £14,000–£25,000.

Experienced teachers or those in a senior role can earn £25,000–£38,000.

Those who work on a part-time or seasonal basis usually receive an hourly or weekly rate.

If you work outside the UK, your salary is likely to be much lower.

Incentives offered by overseas language schools may include flights and accommodation.

Related opportunities

- Education and Childcare Inspector p179
- Further Education Lecturer p181
- Teaching Assistant/Learning Support Assistant p192

Further information

Cambridge ESOL
www.cambridgeenglish.org

TEACHING ASSISTANT/LEARNING SUPPORT ASSISTANT

ENTRY LEVEL 3

Qualifications and courses

There are no specific academic requirements for entry to this career as local education authorities set their own requirements, however employers typically expect candidates to have GCSEs/National 5s (A*–C/A–C) in English and Maths. You need to be at least 18 years old to apply and must obtain clearance from the Disclosure and Barring Service (DBS). Previous relevant experience or qualifications, for example in nursing, childcare or youth work, is an advantage when seeking employment as competition for posts is fairly strong.

The Council for Awards in Care, Health and Education (CACHE), NCFE and Edexcel (BTEC) offers the Level 2 Award/Certificate/Diploma in Support Work in Schools which may be useful for those new or not yet employed in a teaching assistant role. The Apprenticeship in Supporting Teaching and Learning in Schools is available to school leavers at both Intermediate and Advanced level and leads to NVQs at Levels 2 or 3.

Once employed, you will be trained on the job and local authorities in England and Wales may encourage you to study for professional qualifications while you work. Upon entry you can study for the NVQ in Supporting Teaching and Learning in Schools (Levels 2 and 3) or the SVQ in Supporting Teaching and Learning in Schools (Classroom Assistants) (Levels 2 and 3). Another option is the City & Guilds (7329) vocational Certificate in Supporting Teaching and Learning in Schools (Levels 2 and 3).

Experienced teaching assistants in England can work towards Higher Level Teaching Assistant (HLTA) status. Alternatively, you may opt to gain a Foundation degree. These 2 qualifications will not only enable you to take on extra responsibilities, but they can significantly improve your career prospects and salary.

What the work involves

Teaching/classroom assistants help pupils to learn by supporting the teacher and, sometimes, by describing the work in a more visual way or reading questions aloud.

You may be required to plan and deliver parts of a lesson for the main teacher, working together to make the best use of time and resources.

Some teaching/classroom assistants will offer one-to-one support to students with learning difficulties or disabilities.

Type of person suited to this work

In this work, you need to like children to help them make the most of their time in school.

You will need lots of patience and possess the ability to stay calm, as all pupils have their off-days when they are noisy or upset.

Sometimes, you will work with students who need extra help so you should have an interest in young people who have special needs.

Working conditions

Many learning support assistants work in mainstream schools, but some are employed in independent schools, in residential institutions for students with special needs or specialist colleges.

You will normally work between 8.30am and 4.30pm, although you might have to attend meetings after this and sometimes at weekends.

Future prospects

Recent changes to teachers' workload have involved freeing them from some administrative tasks so they have more classroom time. This has increased the need for teaching assistants working across the UK although competition for posts is strong.

You can progress to become a Higher Level Teaching Assistant (HLTA), which involves increased responsibility.

Experienced teaching assistants often train to become teachers themselves and there are Initial Teacher Training courses especially for teaching assistants.

Special needs learning assistants may specialise in helping young people with a particular disability.

Advantages/disadvantages

This can be a very rewarding job as you will witness students' educational development and growth.

You might help students take steps towards independent living.

You will be very busy and will have limited time to hold meetings with colleagues.

Money guide

Wages are set by local education authorities so the rates can vary across regions.

The starting salary for a teaching assistant ranges from £12,000 to £17,000.

Experienced HLTAs can achieve £16,000–£21,000 per year.

Related opportunities

- Childminder p545
- Play Worker/Hospital Play Specialist p184
- Primary School Teacher p185

Further information

CACHE
www.cache.org.uk

Department for Education
www.gov.uk/dfe

WORK-BASED TRAINING INSTRUCTOR

ENTRY LEVEL 3

Qualifications and courses

Whilst there are no set entry requirements, training instructors must maintain a high level of knowledge and experience of the skill which is being taught and therefore many have completed academic or vocational qualifications relevant to that skill. Although there is no minimum age limit, it is likely that you will not have developed the sufficient level of knowledge and experience required to become an effective instructor until the age of 21.

Many who have secured work as a work-based training instructor have worked their way up from other positions in the same organisation, eg in a customer services team or as a supervisor on a production line.

Others train specifically for a career in work-based training. In order to secure employment in a training consultancy, you will typically be required to hold a recognised training qualification. NVQs/SVQs in Learning and Development (Levels 3–5) are available. The Chartered Institute of Personnel and Development (CIPD) also offers a host of qualifications at Foundation, Intermediate and Advanced Levels that aim to prepare candidates for a career in training and development. You would normally start by completing a CIPD Level 3 Certificate or Diploma in Learning and Development Practice which is equivalent to an NVQ/SVQ Level 3. Upon completion, you can apply for Associate Membership of the CIPD and work your way up to higher qualifications appropriate for those seeking training manager positions.

Postgraduate qualifications are also available in subjects such as education and training management, training and development, mentoring and coaching. These can usually be studied part time or by distance learning. Entry requirements are a degree or equivalent professional qualification.

Training practitioners can also work towards gaining NVQ assessor qualifications. Entry requirements are at least 2 years of occupational experience in the subject or work area to be assessed.

Associate teachers at further education colleges or organisations funded by the government need a Certificate in Teaching in the Lifelong Learning Sector. Full teachers need to take a 1-year course to obtain the Diploma in Teaching in the Lifelong Learning Sector.

What the work involves

You will work alongside employees, in their workplace or in a training centre, and teach them new skills or develop existing skills.

You will liaise closely with the employer's training or human resources manager in order to ascertain the type of training needed.

It is likely that you will specialise in an area such as IT, management, personal development, customer service or craft.

Type of person suited to this work

It is essential to demonstrate a real interest in helping people to learn and progress.

You must be patient, organised and up to date with the latest developments in your occupational area. Good IT skills will also be helpful.

Excellent communication skills are important for the large amount of speaking, questioning, listening and reporting that are involved.

Working conditions

You will work in an office where you will use a computer to prepare lessons and update learner records. However, you will also spend lots of time travelling to meet employers and learners at their workplaces.

You will work normal office hours, Monday to Friday.

Future prospects

New media and different ways of working mean that there is a continual need to help businesses and industry develop the right people to carry out new work tasks.

All companies today are expected to develop their workforces and the government is currently encouraging learning through work-based qualifications. Additionally, school/college leavers now have a wider range of opportunities to pursue such as apprenticeships.

Promotion to a training manager or consultant post is possible with experience and further qualifications such as NVQs at Levels 4 and 5.

Advantages/disadvantages

This work involves being at the centre of improving the skills levels of the workforce.

You constantly have the opportunity to learn new things.

It can be challenging to motivate trainees who do not have an interest in studying towards a qualification.

Money guide

Salaries vary depending on the type and size of employer and location. Larger salaries are possible if the specialised skill you teach is in high demand.

Starting salaries are about £16,000 a year.

With experience this can rise to between £18,000 and £20,000.

Top earners can expect £30,000.

Related opportunities

- Further Education Lecturer p181
- Human Resources/Personnel Officer p28
- Training and Development Officer p54

Further information

Chartered Institute of Personnel and Development
www.cipd.co.uk

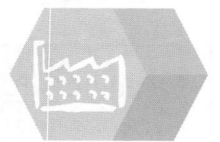

Engineering, Manufacturing and Production

There are a number of highly skilled jobs available in this job family and workers need to be creative and methodical and combine brilliant technical skill with spatial awareness. You may be interested in food production but equally your passion could lie in working with aircraft or marine manufacture. People in these professions share the ability to concentrate for long periods of time and work meticulously on a job to finish it to a high standard. Some will also be highly trained with specialist equipment which may sometimes be hazardous to use so a high level of personal safety awareness is vital.

The jobs featured in this section are listed below.

AEROSPACE ENGINEER

ENTRY LEVEL 5

Qualifications and courses

Most entrants are graduates of an aeronautical/aerospace engineering degree although employers may accept those who have gained a bachelor's in other relevant disciplines, such as electrical, mechanical or manufacturing engineering, computer software, physics or maths.

A Bachelor of Engineering degree (BEng) lasts 3 years whilst a Master of Engineering degree (MEng) lasts 4. You will need at least 2 A levels/H grades, including Maths and Physics, and 5 GCSEs/National 5s (A*–C/A–C) in order to ensure entry onto a degree course. Completing a postgraduate qualification is advantageous, as well as being particularly useful to those whose first degree was in a different subject.

Many companies offer graduate training schemes and some are accredited by professional bodies such as the Royal Aeronautical Society. Your scheme may offer you a placement overseas and the chance to work towards an engineering licence accredited by the Civil Aviation Authority (CAA). Employers often value graduates with prior work experience, therefore completing a voluntary work placement or sandwich placement as part of your degree may improve your employability.

It is possible to enter the industry at a lower level by training as a craft or technician straight from school but you will have to complete further qualifications in order to become an engineer. Apprenticeship schemes offered by airline operators, manufacturers or with a service engineering company usually require good GCSEs/National 5s in English, Maths and Physics. A HNC/HND in Aeronautical or Aerospace Engineering, Avionics, or Air Transport Engineering may improve your chances of employment at technician level.

To enhance opportunities for progression, you may decide to work towards incorporated or chartered status further on in your career whilst undergoing a series of continuing professional development (CPD) courses.

What the work involves

Aerospace engineers research, design and manufacture space vehicles, satellites, missiles and aircraft. You can specialise in mechanical, electrical or electronics engineering, and within these areas you can focus on airframes, hydraulics, materials and structures, or engines.

Your work might involve research, design and manufacture, or experimenting with new materials.

You may also undertake flight test programmes, and maintain and improve fleets of aircraft all over the world.

Type of person suited to this work

You should have a logical mind and be good at problem solving. You should also be good at maths, and be able to produce good drawings and diagrams, as well as being able to interpret them well.

Your oral and written communication skills should be good as you will need to communicate ideas effectively. Teamworking skills are essential but you must also be able to take on responsibility and work independently.

You will be expected to keep up to date with new technology and developments in the industry, and for some roles you will need to have normal colour vision.

Working conditions

It is usual to work 37–40 hours a week, but this depends a lot on project deadlines and what is currently taking place: hours can be longer.

Work usually takes place in clean quiet laboratories, but visits to production areas are essential and these areas are usually dirty and noisy.

Visits to airfields also take place, where you might be required to inspect and test the functions of the aircraft.

Future prospects

There are good opportunities for promotion in aerospace engineering with the industry maintaining a strong record of investing in its workforce. The skills you will acquire will make you suitable for higher positions even in other branches of engineering, and many move into consultancy, management or research roles as their career progresses.

Some aerospace engineers work independently as consultants, and others find work abroad for foreign governments or aircraft construction companies. With chartered status, your earnings and responsibilities will increase.

Advantages/disadvantages

You may have to work long hours, evenings and weekends. Stress levels can also be high if you are trying to meet deadlines.

The starting salary is relatively high, and you can work your way up to a good wage with time and experience.

Money guide

Starting salaries for graduates tend to range from £20,000 to £26,000 per year.

Depending on your professional status, your earnings will increase to £28,000–£45,000.

Senior engineers might earn in excess of £65,000.

Related opportunities

- Electrical Engineer p203
- Marine Engineer p215
- Mechanical Engineer p217

Further information

Institution of Engineering and Technology
www.theiet.org

Royal Aeronautical Society
www.aerosociety.com

ASSEMBLER

ENTRY LEVEL 1

Qualifications and courses

There are no formal entry requirements for this line of work. However, GCSEs/National 5s in English, Maths, Design and Technology or equivalent vocational qualifications in engineering/manufacturing are valued by employers.

The most common route of entry is via an apprenticeship where you will undertake a combination of on-the-job training from experienced professionals and a series of day or block release instruction at a college or training centre in order to work for industry recognised qualifications. NVQs/SVQs in Performing Manufacturing Operations (Levels 1 and 2), Performing Engineering Operations (Levels 1 and 2) and Electrical Assembly/ Installation (Levels 2 and 3) are available.

As a new recruit you will learn about the company's health and safety policies, welfare and conditions of employment whilst being trained under the supervision of a more experienced colleague in the use of appropriate tools and machinery and the ability to read assembly diagrams. You may also acquire the skills necessary to inspect the quality of finished products and, in the event that new working methods are introduced, you will receive further training.

In order to secure a trainee position within the industry, you may have to undertake an entry test and an interview that will assess your reading and writing skills and your practical aptitude, eg your ability to work quickly and accurately with your hands. Normal colour vision is a requirement for work involving electrical and electronic assembly.

What the work involves

You will work on an assembly line within a factory or workshop, or at a bench. You could work on products within sectors as diverse as: engineering, furniture production, soft furnishings, domestic electrical equipment, vehicles or electrical circuit boards.

Assembly line
You will assemble products or components as they arrive at your work area. Sometimes they may not stop, but keep moving along a belt or route in the factory. As the line needs to keep going at a set speed, you will be required to work at the same pace as everyone else.

Bench
Using hand tools, and in some cases simple machinery, you will carry out specific assembly tasks or create a finished product.

Type of person suited to this work

You will need to have practical skills and enjoy making or repairing items. In order to construct your product or components, you will have to follow diagrams and instructions and be able to work quickly and precisely.

You need good interpersonal skills and a solid work ethic.

Whilst carrying out repetitive tasks, you must be able to concentrate and maintain a fast pace of work for long periods of time.

Working conditions

Assembly line
You can expect to be in a large factory – in some sectors this could be noisy, dirty and busy and in others, such as the electronics industry, it would be clean and dust-free.

Some assembly lines require 24/7 production; if so, you will normally work a shift pattern.

Bench
You will be sitting or standing using the tools and machinery positioned around you. If you need to use a soldering iron for assembly it can be hot work and may cause fumes. You can also work part time.

Future prospects

The largest employers of assemblers are the electrical, electronic and information technology industries.

As machines are increasingly replacing some of the assembly work that used to be done by people, jobs are reducing. However, there is still demand for assemblers to work on the assembling of products that are too intricate to be done by machine, or on small batches of goods.

With experience, you may be able to progress into a team leader or supervisory role or within other areas of manufacturing such as quality control. You could also go on to train as an engineering craft worker.

Advantages/disadvantages

Your surroundings may be dirty and noisy.

Due to advances in technology, the need for workers will continue to drop.

Part-time work is also available, which is attractive to people with families wanting to supplement their income.

Money guide

Starting salaries for assemblers are around £12,000.

With experience, salaries can range from £13,500 to £17,000.

Very skilled and experienced assemblers in certain parts of the industry, such as automotive assembly, or those with supervisory responsibilities can earn around £20,000 a year.

Related opportunities

- Food Processing Operative p208
- Mechanical Engineer p217
- Welder p232

Further information

Proskills UK
www.proskills.co.uk

Semta
www.semta.org.uk

BLACKSMITH

ENTRY LEVEL 1

Qualifications and courses

One route of entry is via an apprenticeship. As an apprentice you will typically experience a combination of on-the-job training from professionals and a series of day or block release at a college or training centre in order to work towards industry recognised qualifications, such as an NVQ/SVQ in Fabrication and Welding. There are no specific academic qualifications required for entry, however you will need to approach individual employers in order to see if they are willing to take you on as an apprentice. Availability is not always guaranteed and will depend on your local jobs market.

Alternatively, you may opt to complete a full-time college course with a focus on either traditional blacksmithing skills or design. Courses such as a BTEC Level 3 in Blacksmithing and Metalworking may require specific GCSEs/National 5s and forge-work experience. HNDs and degrees in creative aspects of blacksmithing are also available. To gain entry, you will need 2 A levels/3 H grades and 5 GCSEs/National 5s (A*–C/A–C), an understanding of design and a portfolio of artwork.

Herefordshire and Ludlow College offers a degree in artist blacksmithing and diplomas in blacksmithing and metalwork as well as a Farriery Access course. As contacts are so important in securing work, it may be beneficial to join the British Artist Blacksmiths Association (BABA) in order to attend relevant courses and meet new people. Awards distributed by the Worshipful Company of Blacksmiths are also available.

What the work involves

You will shape and join metals such as steel, iron, copper and bronze to produce decorative pieces, such as gates and furniture or functional objects for use by companies, such as fire escapes and security screens. You may also restore antique ironwork.

You may create specially commissioned pieces such as a stairway for a building project or specialise in an area such as agricultural engineering or security.

If you specialise in artistic work, you are likely to be self-employed. Your job will therefore include all of the administrative tasks needed to run a business, alongside the general work as a blacksmith. You will have to actively promote your services in order to gain customers and this may involve attending craft shows and fairs.

Type of person suited to this work

Much of your time will be spent on your feet using different hand tools, often near to the forge which will be very hot. You will need to be very responsible, as the tools and materials that you will be working with can be dangerous.

Having a creative flair will help you to use your materials imaginatively and you will need an understanding of the way products function and how different metal properties will affect the end product.

Working conditions

You will work with various metals and use different hand and bench tools and a forge. This will result in conditions that can be noisy, dirty and sometimes cramped. You will spend much of the time on your feet and you will wear protective clothing such as gloves, ear protectors and goggles.

You could work in rural areas or in mines, docks and with engineering companies. Artist blacksmiths are less restricted geographically and can be based within both larger cities and rural communities.

Future prospects

The demand for industrial blacksmiths working in mining sites, docks and engineering is decreasing but, due to an increased interest in decorative metalwork, the skills of artistic blacksmiths are often in demand for commission work.

Working under commission is unreliable and so many blacksmiths are forced to accept other types of work in order to earn a living wage.

Most blacksmiths are self-employed but there are still opportunities for work within small, usually family-run businesses, though positions are very limited in number. With experience, you might progress into supervisory or managerial posts or you may opt to work for a museum or heritage centre.

Entry into trainee positions is competitive and you may need to relocate in order to find one. Future success will rely on your ability to build a reputation.

Advantages/disadvantages

Much of the work is done alone and can be isolating.

The work is tiring, but when you have created what a customer requires it can be satisfying too.

If you are involved in a creative project such as a commissioned sculpture, it can be very rewarding.

Money guide

Starting salaries generally range from £12,000 to £16,000 a year.

Once training has been completed you could earn in excess of £25,000.

Earnings tend to vary as most blacksmiths, being self-employed, are free to negotiate their own rates.

Related opportunities

- Bricklayer p60
- Farrier p247
- Sheet Metal Worker p226

Further information

British Artist Blacksmiths Association
www.baba.org.uk

British Farriers and Blacksmiths Association
www.forgemagazine.co.uk

Worshipful Company of Blacksmiths
www.blacksmithscompany.org

BREWERY WORKER

ENTRY LEVEL 1

Qualifications and courses

There are no set entry requirements for this career. GCSEs/National 5s in English, Maths and a science may be useful though, particularly when seeking work. Employers often value those with qualifications when promoting workers to supervisory and management positions. Sometimes it is possible to enter the industry in a related area such as in a manufacturing, processing or packaging operations environment, whilst later progressing to the role of brewery worker.

Alternatively, there may be an apprenticeship available in your area in food manufacturing which leads to this career. Apprenticeships typically involve a combination of on-the-job training and assessments from experienced professionals covering all stages of the beer-making process, with a series of day or block release instruction at a college or training centre in order to gain industry recognised qualifications. NVQs/SVQs Levels 1–3 in Food Manufacture are usually the qualifications trainee brewery workers work towards achieving. It may be helpful to complete the NVQ Level 3 in Food Manufacture if you wish to progress to a supervisory post.

Brewing Research International (BRI) offers the opportunity to progress into the more technical side of the industry, although this requires you to be educated to degree level. The Institute of Brewing and Distilling also offers courses, such as the General Certificate, Fundamentals or Diplomas in Brewing, Distilling and Packaging.

What the work involves

You will make and package beer, stout and lager for a variety of outlets including shops and pubs.

You could be involved in the whole beer making process or just certain stages.

You will work as part of a team supervised by a technical brewer. Your jobs will include weighing and mixing ingredients, monitoring quality, labelling and packing the product and loading the beer ready for dispatch.

Type of person suited to this work

You will need to enjoy working in a team, and be aware of the health and safety regulations to keep yourself and others safe at work.

The work is quite physically demanding; you will be lifting and operating heavy machinery so will need to be fit and healthy.

Good numeracy skills will be helpful when measuring out ingredients and checking the amount of products produced.

Working conditions

Most large breweries have a shift system in place for their workers. You will usually work around 40 hours a week, and can work overtime if necessary.

You will be working with machinery and fermenting ingredients, therefore overalls, gloves and goggles may be worn to limit contamination and to keep you safe.

You will have to work through all weather conditions, loading products and unloading raw materials.

Future prospects

Due to the increasing usage of machinery and automated processes in the mass production of beer and the decline in the number of large breweries in the UK, there are fewer industry vacancies available to brewery workers.

However, there has been a significant rise in micro-breweries producing craft beer in the last few years which has created over 900 jobs in 2013 alone, due to a large change in consumer behaviour. With 1,147 micro-breweries in operation in the UK, you may find yourself working for a more specialised employer, in a supervisory or management role, or opening your own once you have specialist training and gained technical brewing status.

Advantages/disadvantages

Due to the decline in multinational brewing companies across the UK, it can be difficult to find work and many smaller micro-breweries are family run, employing very few staff with limited promotional opportunities.

Working in a brewery can be smelly, hot and physically demanding; this may be stressful or tiring at times. However, working in a team of other brewery workers creates a lively and fun atmosphere.

Making beer, stout and lager is a satisfying job role as you know you are creating beverages that people enjoy drinking.

Money guide

The amount you earn does depend on the location and size of the brewery you work for.

Average starting salaries can be up to £15,000, with this rising to £22,000 with a few years' experience.

Senior brewery workers or those in supervisory roles may earn in excess of £29,000.

Those working within a shift system may get a shift allowance.

Related opportunities

- Cellar Technician p122
- Craft Technical Brewer p202
- Food Processing Operative p208

Further information

Campaign for Real Ale (CAMRA)
www.camra.org.uk

Campden Brewing Research International
www.campdenbri.co.uk/brewing-services.php

Institute of Brewing and Distilling
www.ibd.org.uk

CAD DRAUGHTSPERSON

ENTRY LEVEL 2

Qualifications and courses

One route of entry into this industry is to begin as a trainee technician, developing your skills via an Advanced Apprenticeship in Engineering Manufacture (Craft and Technician). The Engineering Construction Industry Training Board (ECITB) offers a 3-year apprenticeship for design and draught technicians.

As an apprentice, you will typically experience a combination of on-the-job training from skilled professionals and a period of day or block release instruction at a college or training centre. You are likely to work for industry-recognised qualifications; the actual subjects you study will depend on your employer's business. They may include an NVQ Level 1 and 2 in Performing Engineering Operations, an NVQ Level 2 and 3 in Engineering Technical Support, a City & Guilds Certificate or BTEC Certificates/Diplomas. Applicants for an apprenticeship will require 4 GCSEs/National 5s (A*–C/A–C) or equivalent including Maths and science or technology.

Alternatively, you may opt to study relevant pre-entry qualifications at college, such as the City & Guilds Awards and Certificates in Computer-Aided Design and Manufacturing (Levels 1–3), the City & Guilds Award in Computer-Aided Design and Parametric Modelling (Levels 1–3), the BTEC Certificate/Diploma in Engineering (Levels 2–3) or the BTEC Level 3 Certificate/Diploma in Mechanical, Manufacturing or Civil Engineering.

Upon completion of your training, CAD draughtspeople are encouraged to seek engineering technician (EngTech) registration with the Engineering Council UK in order to improve your career prospects. As technology changes, you should update your skills throughout your career through a series of continuing professional development (CPD). Employers may offer you the chance to gain further qualifications such as HNCs/HNDs or training in your company's specific software.

What the work involves

You will produce the drawings and instructions that will enable others to create structures, equipment or components.

Using a computer-aided design (CAD) workstation you will draw up technical drawings for components or sections of a structure, or for different products.

Depending on the specialism of the company you work for, you may design part of a structure as large as a factory or bridge, or a component as small as an electronic circuit.

Type of person suited to this work

You should be patient, accurate and have a good understanding of different production processes.

You need to be organised and methodical in your work and able to work to tight deadlines.

Good IT, technical drawing and numerical skills are essential.

You will need to be able to solve design problems in a creative way and you should be comfortable communicating your work to others.

Working conditions

Most of your work will be done sitting in front of your computer or drawing board in an office or design area.

You will work normal office hours but you might need to work overtime when deadlines are close.

Sometimes you will visit the shop floor or factory area where the product you are designing is being made and conditions could be noisy, hot and dirty. However, your own workspace will be quiet as a lot of concentration is required.

Future prospects

All construction and manufacturing companies across the UK need trained draughtspeople which means they are in constant demand, however, your job prospects may also depend on the economic state and the fluctuating nature of the construction and manufacturing industries.

You may work within fields including aeronautical, civil, electrical, mechanical and marine engineering companies, central and local government and public utilities.

You can progress to senior, supervisory and team-leader work and with further qualifications you could become an architect or a chartered engineer. There are also opportunities to work abroad or work freelance.

Advantages/disadvantages

As much of your work involves using your drawing board or computer, your eyes could get tired and strained.

If you want to progress, you can move to supervisor level within your own company or elsewhere.

With experience, it may be possible to work on a freelance basis, being contracted by smaller companies who do not employ their own draughtsperson.

Money guide

Starting salaries are typically between £15,000 and £20,000 per year.

With experience, you can expect to earn £23,000–£30,000.

High earners employed at a senior level can achieve up to £40,000.

Related opportunities

- Architectural Technician p57
- Architectural Technologist p58
- Graphic Designer p161

Further information

Chartered Institute of Architectural Technologists
www.ciat.org.uk

Tomorrow's Engineers
www.tomorrowsengineers.org.uk

CHEMICAL ENGINEER

ENTRY LEVEL 6

Qualifications and courses

Ideally you should gain an Institution of Chemical Engineers (IChemE) accredited degree or postgraduate qualification in chemical, biochemical or process engineering. Other relevant degree subjects such as chemistry, polymer science, environmental or nuclear engineering may be considered, but an accredited postgraduate qualification, such as an MSc in Process Engineering, will significantly improve your chances of both employment and chartered status further on in your career.

HNDs in similar subjects are also considered although you may have to start your career as a technician and work up to the position of chemical engineer as you gain further qualifications. You will need a minimum of 3 A levels/H grades and 5 GCSEs/National 5s (A*–C/A–C), including English, Maths and a science, in order to gain a place on an engineering or related degree/HND course.

Entry without a degree or HND is uncommon, although you may be able to secure an Apprenticeship in Engineering, which could lead to a role as an engineering technician, providing you with the opportunity to study for a relevant degree.

Many companies offer graduates internal training programmes, some of which are IChemE certified. These Accredited Company Training Schemes (ACTS) ensure graduates become competent professional engineers whilst covering the requirements of chartered status. Employers are placing increasing value on candidates with appropriate work experience, thus, carrying out voluntary work may enhance your employability.

Chemical engineers need to commit to a programme of continuing professional development (CPD) to make sure their skills are kept up to date throughout their career.

What the work involves

You will devise low-cost, safe and environmentally friendly methods that will transform raw materials into products such as fuel, pharmaceuticals, plastics and toiletries.

You might research ways to improve the future of our planet which could include discovering renewable energy sources or producing replacement human organs.

You might work in manufacturing and help to design and construct plants for mass production of products. You will then oversee the running of the plant and the quality of its products.

Type of person suited to this work

You will need to have good oral and written communication skills in order to brief colleagues and compile extensive reports from research you have undertaken. Project management skills are also very important.

An analytical mind and the ability to problem-solve are helpful when designing and testing products or equipment in the plant itself.

You will also need to be creative in order to come up with cost-effective products and solutions to problems.

An aptitude and interest in chemistry are also recommended, as is a good understanding of engineering and maths.

Working conditions

Working hours are normally standard office hours from Monday to Friday, although you might have to work overtime on occasion (including evenings and weekends), particularly if you are developing a new product.

You will usually work in a plant, laboratory or research establishment so conditions can vary from peaceful, sterile labs to noisier factory floors.

You might need to wear appropriate safety equipment for certain aspects of the job.

Future prospects

Jobs are available across the UK in a range of industries, from pharmaceuticals to oil and gas.

Opportunities for progression and promotion are good; you could obtain a position in senior management or a project leader role.

Chemical engineers are encouraged to achieve chartered or incorporated status.

Advantages/disadvantages

You will continue to learn new skills and gain qualifications throughout your career.

You will have the opportunity to work in a range of industries and possibly abroad.

Some of the conditions that you work in could be distracting or challenging.

Money guide

Salaries are likely to vary according to the sector, size and location of the industry in which you work, however a typical graduate starting salary is around £28,000.

Experienced engineers can expect to earn £50,000 a year.

Senior chemical engineers with chartered status can achieve in excess of £60,000.

Related opportunities

- Environmental Engineer p207
- Manufacturing/Production Engineer p213
- Mechanical Engineer p217

Further information

British Chemical Engineering Contractors Association
www.bceca.org.uk

Institution of Chemical Engineers
www.icheme.org

Semta
www.semta.org.uk

CRAFT TECHNICAL BREWER

ENTRY LEVEL 5

Qualifications and courses

Trainee technical brewers are usually required to have a degree or postgraduate qualification. Heriot-Watt University offers a specialist degree in brewing and distilling through their International Centre for Brewing and Distilling (ICBD) but other subjects such as food studies, chemical and mechanical engineering and biology will also provide you with some of the relevant skills required in the industry. Entry requirements for a degree are typically 2 A levels/H grades and 5 GCSEs/National 5s. Those whose first degree is not related to the field of brewing may benefit from completing a postgraduate qualification in brewing science or biotechnology.

Alternatively, you could begin you career as a brewery worker or production assistant before progressing to technical brewing roles by gaining further qualifications as you train. Usually a number of GCSEs/National 5s grades are needed to be accepted onto an Apprenticeship in Food Manufacturing.

After completion of your degree, graduate training schemes may be offered by some of the larger brewery companies but competition is fierce. You may find pre-entry experience, eg work placements or shadowing opportunities in a brewing environment, advantageous as employers often look for candidates who can demonstrate a familiarity with technical language, teamwork skills, management experience and a logical approach.

Once employed, you are likely to undergo a series of continuing professional development (CPD) programmes in order to update your skills and qualifications. The Institute of Brewing and Distilling offers a range of courses for general brewing and specialist subjects; these include a general certificate in brewing, distilling and packaging, a diploma in brewing modules and master brewing modules.

What the work involves

You will be overseeing the whole brewing process, managing the brewery workers and monitoring the condition of the brewing equipment.

Technical brewers are responsible for checking the quality of raw materials and testing the product regularly for texture, taste and appearance.

In a large brewery you may specialise in a certain area of brewing, such as fermentation, packaging or quality control, whereas in a small brewery you are likely to be involved with all aspects of the brewing process.

You will be responsible for developing new brewing methods, and designing and developing new beers, stouts and lagers.

Type of person suited to this work

You will need to be scientific, with an enquiring mind and a particular interest in biochemistry. Both a practical ability and an interest in engineering are also useful.

Leadership and interpersonal skills are needed as you will be managing a team of brewers. Good communication skills are also needed as you will be responsible for writing reports, keeping records and presenting new brewery methods to your colleagues.

Working conditions

As brewing is a continuous process, you will work shifts including nights and weekends. Usually you will work no more that 40 hours a week.

Some technical brewers will need to be on their feet all day, checking the brewing process, in hot and noisy conditions.

Some time will be spent in an office organising paperwork and making reports on production, stock quality and budgets.

Future prospects

The number of large breweries in the UK is in decline and the increased use of machinery and automated processes means that competition for positions will be high. The majority of available industry jobs are concentrated around the east of England, the London area, Glasgow and Aberdeen.

With experience you can progress to managerial roles and senior brewer positions in a large brewery, such as a head brewer or technical director where you will lead a team of specialist staff. Alternatively, you could move into related areas such as research and development, quality control, distribution, sales or personnel.

The number of UK micro-breweries and market demand for craft beer have risen dramatically in the last few years and diversified the opportunities available for craft technical brewers. You could work within a very small, specialised team or open your own micro-brewery.

Advantages/disadvantages

This is an interesting and diverse role, which can lead to good promotions and self-employment.

Working night shifts in a hot and smelly environment may be tiring and stressful.

Money guide

Starting salaries are generally between £17,000 and £24,000 per year.

With experience this is likely to increase to £25,000–£33,000.

Senior brewers may earn in excess of £40,000.

Related opportunities

- Biotechnologist p483
- Brewery Worker p199
- Cellar Technician p122

Further information

Campaign for Real Ale (CAMRA)
www.camra.org.uk

Campden Brewing Research International
www.campdenbri.co.uk/brewing-services.php

Institute of Brewing and Distilling
www.ibd.org.uk

ELECTRICAL ENGINEER

ENTRY LEVEL 6

Qualifications and courses

You will need a degree or postgraduate qualification in a subject such as electrical or electronic engineering, mechanical engineering, applied physics or computer science. For degree entry you will need at least 2 A levels/H grades and 5 GCSEs/National 5s (A*–C/A–C) including Maths and a science. Relevant HNDs or Foundation degrees, in Electrical, Mechanical or Building Services Engineering for example, may also be considered, although employers often place value on those who have studied at degree level. Some universities may offer those diplomates with relevant work experience the opportunity to accelerate into the final year of a degree programme.

Alternatively, you could enter the field at a lower level by first training as an electrical engineering technician and working your way up by gaining experience and higher qualifications. Advanced Apprenticeships in Engineering Manufacture (Craft and Technician) or the Higher Level Apprenticeship in Engineering Manufacture (Senior Technician) are available. You will need good GCSEs/National 5s (A*–C/A–C) in English, Maths, a science or technology in order to be considered. You will need to study for a degree, however, if you wish to become a professional electrical engineer.

Many companies offer graduates training schemes post-university. Programmes vary according to the size of the company but typically involve a series of on-the-job training and structured continuing professional development (CPD). Undertaking work experience or a vacation placement will benefit your application as employers often like to see evidence of a candidate's enthusiasm, ability to work in a team and commercial awareness.

Those with a bachelor's degree in engineering (BEng) or equivalent can apply for incorporated engineer (IEng) status via the Engineering Council and those who have studied to master's level can gain chartered engineer (CEng) status further on in their career.

What the work involves

Electrical engineers research, design and develop a range of electrical equipment. You will be making, testing and servicing all types of electrical equipment and machinery, and as such you will be involved in projects from conception to completion.

You will usually work on projects with a team of professionals, including contractors and engineers from other industries.

You will also be liaising with clients and contractors about the development of each project, which will involve preparing reports and giving presentations.

Type of person suited to this work

You should have excellent mathematical ability and a very analytical mind in order to successfully design and develop complicated new electrical systems. A logical approach to problem solving is also beneficial.

You will need good communication skills, both oral and written, for working alongside team members and clients. This will involve explaining and talking through projects, as well as compiling written reports and leading presentations.

You must have normal colour vision and natural manual dexterity.

Working conditions

Although electrical engineers usually work within the normal working week, you may find that you need to work additional or unsocial hours in order to solve problems and meet project deadlines.

Your time will be divided between office-based and on-site work. You can expect to travel on a daily basis so a driving licence is useful.

Conditions on-site can often be dirty, cramped and potentially hazardous so you should be prepared to get your hands dirty and wear safety equipment.

Future prospects

There are no set pathways of career progression for electrical engineers and many decide to stay in a purely engineering role for the duration of their working life.

Alternatively, there are possibilities to move into project management, become a consultant or take on a more managerial role within a company.

Advantages/disadvantages

Your work will be undertaken at a variety of indoor and outdoor locations so you will not be confined to an office environment.

You will play an instrumental role in developing new and increasingly safe electrical equipment for a variety of important functions.

Hours can be long and unpredictable, especially when nearing completion of a project.

Money guide

The starting salary for a graduate electrical engineer can range from £20,000 to £25,000.

Experienced or incorporated engineers are likely to earn £28,000–£38,000 a year, with chartered engineers usually receiving a salary of £40,000–£55,000 or more.

Some companies offer excellent benefit packages and bonus schemes in addition to a basic wage.

Related opportunities

- Civil/Construction Engineer/Civil Engineering Technician p69
- Mechanical Engineer p217
- Telecommunications Engineer p228

Further information

Institution of Engineering and Technology
www.theiet.org

ELECTRICITY DISTRIBUTION WORKER

ENTRY LEVEL 2

Qualifications and courses

The most common route of entry into a career as an electricity distribution worker is via an apprenticeship, for example the Advanced Apprenticeship in Engineering Manufacture (Craft and Technician) may be available. Although there are no set qualifications required to gain access to a training scheme, most employers seek a minimum of 4 GCSEs/National 5s (A*–C/A–C) including English, Maths and a related subject such as a science, Design and Technology or Engineering.

Apprenticeships are open to those aged 16–24 and typically take 4 years in which to become fully qualified. You are likely to undertake a combination of on-the-job practical training from experienced professionals and college-based instruction where you will work towards achieving industry recognised qualifications, such as a City & Guilds NVQ in Electrical Power Engineering (Levels 2 and 3) with options in overhead lines or underground cables or the BTEC Level 3 Certificate/Diploma in Electrical/Electronic Engineering. Short courses in areas such as high voltage safety are also possible options to further your career.

On completion of your training, you could work towards becoming a registered engineering technician (EngTech) with the Engineering Council, which will improve your earning potential and career prospects. Appropriate qualifications, 3 years' experience, membership of the Institution of Mechanical Engineers (IMechE) or the Institution of Engineering and Technology (IET) and a professional review are required.

As proof of your competency working on-site, your employer may need you to be registered in an appropriate safety passport scheme.

What the work involves

Electrical distribution workers are responsible for installing, checking and maintaining all machinery and equipment that supplies electricity to commercial and residential properties. You will be working on a variety of projects from small-scale domestic problems to regional electrical concerns.

You will be working on the overhead lines, masts and underground cables that run from power stations and connect all the electricity networks together.

You could work as a cable jointer who mainly works on the underground cables, an overhead line worker or an electrical fitter who installs, tests and repairs equipment in the regional electricity substations.

Type of person suited to this work

You will need to be practical and good with your hands as you will be using a variety of tools and undertaking fiddly tasks. You must have normal colour vision and pay meticulous attention to detail.

You should be reasonably fit with a head for heights, as some jobs may require lifting and carrying heavy equipment or working high above the ground.

Since you will be working with live electricity, you must be aware of your own safety and that of others around you. You may need to wear protective equipment at times.

Working conditions

Although you will usually work an average of 37 hours a week, these may involve shift patterns including evenings and weekends. You should also expect to work overtime on occasion in order to complete projects on time.

The work can be physically demanding as you will be bending and carrying large cables and equipment. You may work outdoors in damp and muddy trenches and you can expect to be carrying out tasks in cramped conditions sometimes.

Future prospects

As an electricity distribution worker, you will have various options available as you progress in your career. You may go on to become a supervisor or manager and be responsible for a team of workers. Alternatively, you could move into another related job within the industry.

Your career prospects could be improved by studying for additional qualifications as you work, such as an NVQ Level 4 in Electrical Engineering, or even a relevant degree.

Advantages/disadvantages

You will be on-site for the majority of your time so you will not be confined to an office environment.

Possibilities for career progression or diversification are good.

Conditions can be unpleasant owing to extreme weather or space constraints.

You may have to work irregular/unsocial hours.

Money guide

Apprentices typically earn between £11,000 and £15,000 per year, depending on the stage of their training.

You can expect your salary to increase to between £20,000 and £45,000 a year, depending on your qualifications and experience.

Related opportunities

- Electrical Engineer p203
- Electrician p78
- Gas Network Engineer p210

Further information

Engineering Council UK
www.engc.org.uk

Institution of Engineering and Technology
www.theiet.org

ENERGY ENGINEER

ENTRY LEVEL 6

Qualifications and courses

This career is open to graduates of a relevant accredited engineering degree, such as environmental, petroleum, electrical, mechanical or chemical engineering as well as other science-related subjects such as chemistry, physics or earth science. Due to an increase in profile and application of renewable and sustainable energy solutions, a number of specialist degrees have become increasingly available, such as energy engineering, sustainable energy and climate science.

Entry requirements for engineering or related degrees are a minimum of 2 A levels/3 H grades and 5 GCSEs/ National 5s (A*–C/A–C) including English, Maths and a science. Alternative entry qualifications may include relevant BTEC Diplomas or Access courses.

For those with non-accredited degrees, you will need to complete a postgraduate conversion course in renewable energy engineering, sustainable energy systems or energy futures, in order to upgrade your qualifications. A postgraduate course in engineering may be beneficial to all candidates however, as this will enhance your career prospects and support your pathway to gaining chartered status.

Graduate training programmes are available to those post-university. Most entrants for schemes within the larger oil companies will have gained a 2.1 in their degree subject, but postgraduate qualifications are generally preferred. Experience is also valued by employers so work placements may be worthwhile in a somewhat competitive jobs market.

Becoming a member of relevant organisations will also ensure you remain up to date with the latest developments in the industry, allow you to make essential contacts and inform you of new training courses. To improve your prospects further, you could work towards gaining chartered status via the Institution of Engineering and Technology (IET).

What the work involves

You will be involved with the extraction of oil and gas and the production of energy from renewable or sustainable sources, such as wind power, solar power or biofuels.

You will have to calculate how much oil or gas a well will produce and decide how to extract as much as possible and also oversee the drilling operations on an offshore rig.

You could also have to research new ways of generating energy, whilst developing ways of improving existing processes.

Type of person suited to this work

Excellent communication and interpersonal skills are needed for teamwork and to build strong relationships with other professionals and clients.

You should have a high level of numeracy and good IT skills, as well as scientific understanding of related fields such as geology and chemistry.

You will need to have excellent planning, organisational and problem-solving skills to successfully run a project.

Working conditions

If you become involved with power plant or drilling operations, you could work on a 7-day shift system, which would include nights and weekends, whereas working in design, research and development will mean working more standard office hours.

The work is both mentally and physically demanding and conditions on-site are often noisy, wet, cold and inhospitable.

Some jobs may involve international travel and long stays away from home.

Future prospects

The renewable energy industry is rapidly expanding, due to an increased interest in environmental issues, the rise in demand for oil and gas and the pressure on businesses to reduce their carbon footprint.

Renewable and sustainable energy has become a government priority and so job prospects for energy engineers are very good with growth areas including corporate social responsibility (CSR), teaching roles and positions in research and development.

You could be employed in the oil and gas industry, energy production companies or you could move into the education field by teaching or conducting university research.

With experience, you could move into planning, policy development, or freelance consultancy.

Advantages/disadvantages

Oil drilling in particular operates in some of the most dangerous and hostile areas of the world, so your safety could be threatened on a daily basis.

It will be rewarding to know that you have helped to minimise environmental damage.

You will have to be prepared to spend some time away from home.

Money guide

Salaries for graduates typically range from £20,000 to £30,000, with the larger earnings coming from the big oil companies.

Those with experience or in senior management roles could earn between £35,000 and £80,000.

Related opportunities

- Civil/Construction Engineer/Civil Engineering Technician p69
- Environmental Engineer p207
- Mechanical Engineer p217

Further information

Engineering Council UK
www.engc.org.uk

Oil Careers
www.oilcareers.com

ENGINEERING CRAFT MACHINIST

ENTRY LEVEL 2

Qualifications and courses

The most common route of entry into this career is via an Advanced Apprenticeship in Engineering Manufacture (Craft and Technician). Most employers require candidates to have 5 GCSEs/National 5s (A*–C/A–C) in subjects including, English, maths, a science and either technology or Engineering. Employers value candidates who have shown demonstrable interest within the engineering field, by either completing work experience in the sector, carrying out a 14–19 Young Apprenticeship in Engineering or Manufacturing or completing the Intermediate Level Apprenticeship in Engineering Manufacture.

As part of the selection process, you may be required to complete basic literacy, numeracy, communication skills and spatial awareness tests and an interview prior to being accepted.

As an apprentice, you will undertake several months of training away from the workplace to develop specialist skills. You will then spend 2–3 years working for a company whilst also attending college and studying towards relevant professional qualifications. There are several possible pathways leading to careers in different areas of the field, such as fabrication and welding, electronics, aerospace or marine engineering, therefore the qualifications you study will be vital in determining your chosen pathway. These qualifications could include the BTEC Level 2 Certificate/Diploma in Engineering, the NVQ/SVQ in Mechanical Manufacturing Engineering (Levels 2–3), the BTEC Level 3 Certificate/Diploma in Mechanical Engineering or Manufacturing Engineering or the City & Guilds Certificate/Diploma in Engineering. More specialist qualifications such as an NVQ/SVQ in either Engineering Woodworking, Pattern and Model Making, Marine Engineering or Toolmaking (all Level 3) may be encouraged by your employer.

What the work involves

Engineering machinists make engineered parts from various materials, such as metals or heavy and lightweight plastics. You could make parts for a variety of products, from domestic appliances and machines to wind turbines and aeroplane engines.

You will be using a range of machinery, including grinding and cutting machines, drills and presses. Increasingly, computer numerically controlled (CNC) machinery is being used which combines some of the manufacturing processes.

You will need to interpret complicated engineering drawings in order to assess which materials, tools and machines to use to produce each part.

Type of person suited to this work

You will need to have good eyesight, excellent coordination and sound practical ability in order to operate machinery safely and accurately.

Good mathematical skills and the ability to read complicated engineering drawings and interpret them into a 3D part are essential.

You should have strong communication skills as you will mainly be working in a team environment. A good level of physical fitness is also beneficial as the job involves lifting heavy materials and standing or bending over machinery for the majority of the day.

Working conditions

Working hours are usually around 38 hours a week, Monday to Friday, although you will usually start early in the morning and finish early in the afternoon.

Some larger companies operate 24-hour production and would require you to work shifts including evenings and weekends. Conditions in factories and workshops are usually fairly pleasant, although it can be noisy at times.

As you are operating machinery, you will need to wear appropriate safety equipment at all times.

Future prospects

Job prospects are good as there is currently a shortage of skilled machinists in the engineering sector. There are jobs available for machinists throughout Britain, although the majority are found in larger cities and within general mechanical engineering companies. You could work in mechanical engineering, automotive or aerospace industries or within shipbuilding.

With experience, you could be promoted to team leader or supervisor and if you gain further qualifications you could move into engineering technician roles such as design.

Advantages/disadvantages

Jobs are available throughout the UK and there is little travelling involved so you will rarely be absent from home.

It is a physically demanding role, with large amounts of time spent standing or bending over machinery and lifting heavy materials and equipment.

You may have to work unsocial hours owing to early starts or unpredictable shift patterns.

Money guide

Starting salaries for trainees are usually between £12,000 and £15,000.

With experience, your earnings can rise to £17,000–£25,000.

Those employed in a senior position with supervisory responsibilities can achieve up to £30,000 a year.

Related opportunities

- Motor Vehicle Technician p218
- Sheet Metal Worker p226
- Toolmaker p230

Further information

Semta
www.semta.org.uk

ENVIRONMENTAL ENGINEER

ENTRY LEVEL 5

Qualifications and courses

Most employers require candidates to have a good degree, usually a 2.1 minimum, or postgraduate qualification in a relevant subject such as civil or environmental engineering. You will need at least 2 A levels/H grades and 5 GCSEs/National 5s (A*–C/A–C), including Maths and Physics, for degree entry. You may be considered if you have studied another engineering subject, or something related such as physics, applied physics or maths but the field is highly competitive and you may have to supplement your degree with a postgraduate qualification. Candidates are encouraged to complete a master's degree as this will be beneficial further on in your career when seeking chartered status.

Alternatively, it may be possible to enter the field with an HND in a relevant subject such as general engineering, civil engineering, environmental engineering, applied physics or computing and IT. As some employers prefer graduates, supplementing your HND with work experience is highly recommended.

Some companies offer a sponsorship scheme for candidates who have completed their A levels/H grades. This sponsorship consists of financial support to the candidate throughout their degree programme and the offer of an apprenticeship upon graduation.

Many employers offer graduates opportunities to enter structured graduate development programmes once in employment. With the training and supervision of senior mentors, graduates will work towards becoming professional engineers of either incorporated (IEng) or chartered (CEng) status or becoming specialists in their individual fields.

What the work involves

Environmental engineers work on projects concerning waste management, land reclamation and pollution control, and liaise with a variety of clients from local authorities to private property developers.

You will visit and assess numerous sites in relation to their environmental impact, and will explain your findings to clients via presentations and reports.

You may also communicate the environmental issues of a project or site to the general public, green groups and regulatory authorities.

Type of person suited to this work

You should have excellent mathematical ability and a very analytical mind in order to successfully carry out complicated procedures and calculations to assess sites and projects. A swift and logical approach to problem solving is also needed when dealing with often unforeseen environmental complications.

Good oral and written communication skills are essential for working alongside team members and clients.

Negotiation skills are also helpful as you might need to reach compromises over projects with local government officials, residents or clients.

Working conditions

You will usually work 35–40 hours from Monday to Friday, although additional or unsocial hours are not uncommon should problems occur or if deadlines need to be met on a project.

Your time will be divided between office-based and on-site work, so you can expect to travel on a daily basis. A driving licence is essential.

You will work in all weather conditions on-site, so should be prepared to get cold and muddy. You will also have to adhere to site safety regulations and wear relevant protective clothing.

Future prospects

As environmental concerns become an increasingly important aspect of construction projects across the globe, there are good prospects and opportunities within this field for career progression.

With experience, you could move into consultancy and set up your own firm. Alternatively, you could specialise in an area such as treatment of industrial waste, or provision of drinking water in developing countries.

You could work in a small company, or in much larger multinational firms. There are also numerous opportunities to work on projects abroad.

Advantages/disadvantages

You will be responsible for minimising the environmental impact of building projects and protecting the wellbeing of the natural surroundings, which will be rewarding.

Working on potentially controversial developments could lead to confrontations with local residents or clients.

There are excellent opportunities to work overseas, or set up your own company.

Money guide

The starting salary for an environmental engineer can range from £17,000 to £25,000.

With a few years' experience, you can expect to earn anything up to £55,000 a year.

Senior environmental engineers with chartered or incorporated status could earn £90,000.

Related opportunities

- Environmental Health Practitioner/Officer p22
- Marine Engineer p215
- Mechanical Engineer p217

Further information

Chartered Institution of Water and Environmental Management
www.ciwem.org

Engineering Council UK
www.engc.org.uk

FOOD PROCESSING OPERATIVE

ENTRY LEVEL 1

Qualifications and courses

There are no set qualifications required for this profession though some employers may ask for basic levels of literacy and numeracy and, depending on the shift patterns and machinery involved, some employers will require employees to be at least 18 years of age.

A common route of entry into the industry is via an Apprenticeship in Food Manufacture. Apprenticeships are structured training schemes that typically combine on-the-job training with a series of day or block release instruction at a college or training centre where you will work towards gaining industry-recognised qualifications. Depending on the area of the sector in which you work, your employer may encourage you to work towards awards such as an NVQ/SVQ in Food and Drink Manufacturing Operations (Levels 1–4), an NVQ/SVQ in Chemical, Pharmaceutical and Petrochemical Manufacture (Levels 1–4) or a BTEC Level 3 Certificate/Diploma in Food Science and Manufacturing Technology. Practical skills as well as general health and safety with food will be taught.

With time, you can work towards progressing to a management role or supervisory position. In order to do this, you might need GCSEs/National 5s (A*–C/A–C) in English, Maths, a science or Food Technology in order to be considered later on in your career. At an operative level, you can choose to move to different areas of food production, such as baking, freezing or brewing.

What the work involves

Food processing operatives can be involved in one of many areas of food processing. These include freezing, canning, baking, drying, cooking, chilling, pasteurising or a combination of several of these processes.

Since much of the work above is carried out by machines, you may be involved in operating the machinery and you might also be expected to carry out basic maintenance on it.

You might be involved in the production of the food, for example placing different components of foodstuffs in containers. Packaging and labelling are other tasks that you might be required to carry out.

Type of person suited to this work

It is helpful if you have an interest in food and food processing.

You should be good at working in a team, and be able to respond quickly to problems that may arise. You need to be able to stay alert and perceptive at all times, even if tasks are mundane or boring. A good ability to concentrate and observe what is going on around you will really help with this.

Good literacy and numeracy skills are also essential, and you will need to be able to follow instructions easily, both written and spoken. A thorough understanding of health and safety requirements is also an advantage.

Working conditions

You will be working in a factory environment most of the time. This will involve standing in a production line, as well as bending and lifting. Temperature in the factory varies according to the processes taking place.

You will almost certainly be required to wear protective clothing, such as overalls and hats, and a high level of personal hygiene is essential.

You can expect to work 37 to 40 hours a week, usually on a shift system which may include weekends. Overtime is often available.

Future prospects

The food and drink manufacturing industry is extremely large, employing more than 500,000 workers in over 30,000 companies. The sector is currently set to expand, thus there are good job prospects for food processing operatives.

Many industries are now shifting to automated processes, higher value products and niche markets, such as organic food production and processing, therefore, if you hold qualifications or specific technical skills, you will maintain a distinct advantage.

Progression within the food and drink industry is relatively common and, if committed, you stand a good chance of moving up in your company or moving on to others. You can progress to supervisory and management positions quite quickly and opportunities for work within quality control roles are common. Most managers in this sector started out as a food processing operative or something similar.

Advantages/disadvantages

The working environment may not always be pleasant: it can be very hot or very cold. Work may be mundane at times, and the salary is not very high.

There are usually plenty of jobs available in this sector, and prospects for promotion are good. If you work your way up jobs become more interesting and better paid.

Money guide

Salaries typically start at £11,900 per year.

This can rise to £16,500 as you gain experience.

Supervisors and managers can earn in excess of £18,000.

Related opportunities

- Brewery Worker p199
- Food Safety Officer p125
- Meat Process Worker p216

Further information

Food and Drink Federation
www.fdf.org.uk

Improve Ltd
www.improveltd.co.uk

Scottish Food and Drink Federation
www.sfdf.org.uk

FURNITURE MANUFACTURING OPERATIVE

ENTRY LEVEL 1

Qualifications and courses

Most employers do not require furniture manufacturing operatives to hold any specific academic or vocational qualifications, but a number of GCSEs/National 5s (A*–C/A–C) may be valued and could support you in your search for employment. You may need to pass an eyesight and colour vision test in order to be considered for work.

The most common route of entry into this industry is via an Apprenticeship in Wood Making or Making and Installing Furniture. As an apprentice, you will typically experience a combination of on-the-job training from professionals in a furniture manufacturing or other relevant company, and a series of day or block release instruction at a college or training centre where you will work towards gaining industry recognised qualifications.

Awards such as a City & Guilds Certificate in Furniture Production (Levels 1–3) or an NVQ/SVQ Level 1 in Supporting the Production of Furniture and Furnishings, a Level 2 in Making and Installing Furniture, a Level 3 in either Making and Repairing Hand-Crafted Furniture and Furnishings or Making and Installing Production Furniture, and a SQA HNC in Furniture Construction and Design may also be available.

What the work involves

Furniture manufacturers construct pieces of furniture; they may either use machinery, or construct furniture by hand.

This involves cutting and shaping individual parts of each piece, then assembling them to make a finished item. You may then have to smooth and finish items, getting them ready for sale.

You will usually then be asked to add handles and hinges, and sometimes to upholster the furniture too.

Type of person suited to this work

You must be practical and good with your hands.

You should also have excellent eyesight and full colour vision. Hand-to-eye coordination is a must.

Some jobs will also require artistic ability. You must be accurate, careful, and above all patient.

Your physical strength should be reasonably good, as you will need to lift and carry things.

You must be able to take orders, and work under supervision. It is also important to be able to work in a team.

Tasks may become repetitive, but you need to be able to stay focused at all times.

Working conditions

You will be working in a factory, so the environment may be noisy. Most jobs require you to stand in a production line all day, and the air may be dusty and smell strongly of the products used to treat finished furniture.

Protective clothing is usually worn, including ear protectors and face masks for many jobs. Many jobs involve standing for long periods, lifting heavy weights, and bending.

It is normal to work a 39 hour week. Shift work might be required and overtime is common during seasonal peaks or when the factory has a delivery deadline.

Future prospects

The furniture manufacturing industry currently employs around 150,000 workers within 7,600 businesses, alongside a further 12,000 related companies offering opportunities for operatives to work across the UK. You may have to relocate to areas where companies are more concentrated, for example in the major UK cities, the Midlands, the north-west of England, Edinburgh and Aberdeen.

With the increased mechanisation and use of technology, employees with good IT skills who can operate specialist machinery and understand complex systems, are rapidly replacing the need for those workers with physical strength.

Promotion is a possibility, and many manufacturers move into more senior roles within companies, managing projects and gaining responsibility. Others choose to specialise in specific areas of furniture manufacture, for example furniture restoration, craft cabinet making or even furniture design.

More furniture manufacturers are now choosing to teach their craft or set up their own business by becoming self-employed.

Advantages/disadvantages

If you are interested in your craft and willing to put a little time in, a career in furniture manufacture can really grow, and so can your salary.

This job can be satisfying if you enjoy building and making things and are good at DIY.

Working on constructing the same item over and over again can get repetitive.

Money guide

Most operatives start on a salary of around £12,000 per year.

With experience, this might increase to £15,000.

If you become highly skilled, you can expect to earn in excess of £25,000.

Related opportunities

- Carpenter/Joiner p65
- Ergonomist p24
- Shopfitter p105

Further information

Association of Master Upholsterers and Soft Furnishers
www.upholsterers.co.uk

British Furniture Manufacturers
www.bfm.org.uk

British Woodworking Federation
www.bwf.org.uk

GAS NETWORK ENGINEER

ENTRY LEVEL 2

Qualifications and courses

The most common route of entry into a career as a gas network engineer is via an apprenticeship. There are no formal qualifications required for traineeships but a good standard of education would be expected. For entry you will need a minimum of 4 GCSEs/National 5s (A*–C/A–C), in Maths, a science, English and a practical technical subject such as Engineering or Design and Technology.

Once employed in a company as an apprentice, you will experience a combination of on-the-job training from professional engineers and a series of day or block release instruction at a college or training centre where you will work towards achieving industry-recognised qualifications. NVQs in Gas Network Operations (Mains Laying, Service Laying or Craft) (Levels 1–3) and an NVQ Level 3 in Gas Emergency Service Operations are some of the qualifications available to study. These awards are often undertaken on a progressive basis, meaning the more experience and skills which you develop, the more equipped you are to gain the higher level qualifications.

After completing an NVQ Level 3, it is possible to apply for a HND/degree or higher level NVQs. Graduate engineering and management training schemes are also available. It is also possible to undertake a 3-year National Grid Advanced Apprenticeship.

Employers will consider it necessary for you to have a safety passport from an appropriate industry scheme, with Energy and Utility Skills for example, in order to demonstrate your competency working on-site.

What the work involves

Gas is transported from its supply points (called beaches) to domestic and industrial customers by a network of pipes and meters that will be your responsibility to fit and maintain.

To gain access to pipework you will probably need to dig a hole in a road, garden or pavement. This can be a physically demanding job. You will be using digging and excavating tools and pipe-laying equipment.

You will be responsible for the safety of yourself and others when carrying out work. This will include putting up warning signs, barriers and traffic control if needed. You may have to deal with emergency gas leaks.

Type of person suited to this work

You will normally work in a small team, so you should enjoy working with and be able to get on with people. You will be meeting new customers each day, so being polite and courteous are also important skills.

An ability to follow instructions and an understanding of technical language and drawings is essential as these will be used to tell you what you need to do on a daily basis.

When the job is complete, you will have to ensure the finished surface is safe and as good as it was when you started, so you should be tidy and efficient.

Working conditions

You will be working in a team outdoors in all weathers. You will normally work 37–40 hours a week; overtime and weekend work will be expected on a rota basis.

You will be using equipment which can be physically demanding and you will get dirty. As this can be dangerous work you will wear protective clothing such as high-visibility and fireproof clothing, steel toe-capped boots and headgear.

Future prospects

The National Grid coordinates and monitors the gas distribution network in the UK. There are 4 gas distribution companies: National Grid Distribution, Wales and West Utilities, Northern Gas Networks and Scotia Gas Networks (operating in the south of England as Southern Gas and in Scotland as Scotland Gas Networks).

There is currently a high demand for gas network engineers due to both an extensive 30-year pipeline replacement programme and an ageing workforce, particularly in the north of England. You could find work in one of the regional gas distribution companies, for a utility contractor or a construction company building new developments.

With experience and training, you could progress from craftsperson status to a technician, team-leader or management position where you would be responsible for managing a number of teams.

Advantages/disadvantages

You will be working outside in all weathers.

You may have to deal with complaints from angry customers about holes in their road.

Giving the public a gas supply for their homes and businesses can be rewarding.

Money guide

Whilst training, workers can earn around £11,000 per year.

With qualifications and experience this can rise to £18,000–£25,000 per year.

As a team leader or with more responsibility you can expect your salary to increase to £25,000–£32,000 per year.

Related opportunities

- Construction Operative p72
- Construction Plant Operator p73
- Water/Sewerage Network Operative p116

Further information

Energy & Utility Skills
www.euskills.co.uk

Energy & Utility Skills Register
www.eusr.co.uk

Northern Gas Networks
www.northerngasnetworks.co.uk

Scotland Gas Networks
www.sgn.co.uk

LAND-BASED ENGINEER

ENTRY LEVEL 6

Qualifications and courses

This career is open to all graduates with a degree in engineering and specific degree qualifications in subjects such as agricultural engineering, environmental engineering, electrical engineering, ergonomics, off-road vehicle design or mechanical engineering may improve your chances. HNDs in similar subjects are also considered for entry level, technician, positions and some employers may be willing to support further study to take you to degree level. You will need a minimum of 2 A levels/3 H grades and 5 GCSEs/National 5s (A*–C/A–C) including English, Maths and a science, for degree entry.

Your degree or HND must be accredited by the Institution of Agricultural Engineers (IAgrE), or a similar licensed body of the Engineering Council, if you would like to progress to incorporated (IEng) or chartered (CEng) engineer status. Those with an accredited bachelor's degree or HND are eligible for IEng status and those who have studied to master's level can pursue CEng status. These qualifications will significantly enhance your career prospects and earning potential.

For those looking to work as a technician, the Intermediate or Advanced Apprenticeship in Land-based Engineering may be available. However, if you wish to become a fully qualified engineer, you will need to study for a degree.

Some larger organisations may offer graduate training schemes post-university. When seeking employment as a graduate, you will be at a distinct advantage if you have had some pre-entry experience within the field as employers often look for candidates who can show evidence of teamwork, an ability to record and analyse data and an understanding of equipment. Some university courses may include a year of paid, practical work experience.

What the work involves

Land-based engineers design, develop, test and modify agricultural and horticultural equipment in order to ensure that these industries stay up to date.

You will need to carry out extensive research into the needs of those using the equipment you are producing, as well as assessing and limiting the environmental impact of your projects.

You will also be required to compile reports, present your findings and offer expert advice to colleagues, clients and other professionals.

Type of person suited to this work

You will need great ingenuity in order to find solutions to problems or design new equipment to aid agricultural and horticultural processes.

Excellent communication skills are required to understand the needs of your clients and translate them into designs and instructions for your team.

Good IT skills, problem-solving abilities and a flexible approach to work are also essential in order to cope with the various demands of differing projects.

Working conditions

You will usually work a normal working week, although occasional overtime may be necessary to meet project deadlines.

Although you will be office based for the majority of the time, there will be some work on-site and fieldwork so that you can assess projects and carry out tests on equipment.

You may find that you have to work outdoors in unpredictable weather or cold, wet and muddy conditions. You will also need to wear relevant safety equipment whilst on-site.

Future prospects

There are opportunities for land-based engineers to work all over the world, undertaking a variety of projects from food production in the UK, dealing with natural disasters and war, to creating effective water supplies in areas of the developing world. There is currently a national shortage of professional engineers; therefore, job prospects are good.

Larger firms offer greater scope for career progression and you could soon be managing your own projects. You could specialise in design or testing and development where it is also possible to become self-employed. Alternatively, you could move into sales and marketing or even research and teaching. Smaller firms offer less opportunity for progression, so you might have to move to another company to develop in your field.

Advantages/disadvantages

Each day will present new problems and challenges so the work will always be interesting and stimulating.

You will be working with a variety of people from many professional sectors and areas of the community.

On average, you will earn less than engineers in other industries.

Money guide

Starting salaries are usually between £19,000 and £25,000.

Once you have gained 10–15 years' experience, you could expect earnings in the range of £35,000–£50,000.

Chartered land-based engineers can earn in excess of £60,000.

Related opportunities

- Agricultural Scientist p235
- Environmental Engineer p207
- Land/Geomatic Surveyor p92

Further information

British Agricultural and Garden Machinery Association
www.bagma.com

Engineering Council UK
www.engc.org.uk

LOCKSMITH

ENTRY LEVEL 2

Qualifications and courses

There are no specific educational requirements but most applicants will be expected to hold GCSEs/National 5s (A*–C/A–C) in English, Maths and preferably a practical subject such as craft or technology.

There are no formal apprenticeship schemes for locksmithing but you may be able to enter the industry as a trainee within a company. Candidates are advised to approach local locksmiths and ask if there are any trainee positions available. The 'Find a Locksmith' database on the Master Locksmiths Association (MLA)'s website is a useful resource. As a trainee, you would receive on-the-job instruction from experienced professionals and you may also be offered the chance to develop your skills by completing short courses accredited by the MLA.

Alternatively, the MLA, the recognised authoritative body for locksmithing, offers a General Locksmithing Course at their training centre in Northamptonshire. As part of this course, candidates will study industry recognised qualifications such as the City & Guilds Award in Basic Locksmithing. To apply for training you must be a member of the British Locksmiths Institute (BLI). Individuals over the age of 16 can apply for student membership without any prior experience. Advanced Student membership is for those who have 12 months' practical training in locksmithing and have passed the entry exam.

An NVQ in Providing Security, Emergency and Alarm Systems (Levels 2 and 3) and City & Guilds vocational courses in security and alarm systems are also available.

What the work involves

You will sell, install and fix the locks of houses, cars and businesses for your customers.

You will use specialist machinery to cut replacement keys for locks.

Advising on, repairing and installing security and closed-circuit television systems may be part of your job.

Type of person suited to this work

As a locksmith you will have to be calm and patient – reassuring your customers, who may be distressed, whilst providing a prompt and reliable service. Good communication skills are important in this job.

Your customers and employer will also expect you to be totally trustworthy and honest.

To do this job you will have to enjoy using your hands, different tools and equipment. You should enjoy practical tasks and be able to offer solutions to security problems. Carpentry or general engineering skills are also helpful.

Working conditions

Employers include independent small locksmiths, larger national companies offering a 24-hour call-out emergency service, specialist security companies, DIY hardware stores and shoe repairers that offer a key-cutting service.

If you work in a shop you will probably have a 40-hour, Monday–Saturday week. Self-employment is possible.

If you or your employer offer a 24-hour call-out service, you could be working at all times of the day or night.

You will mainly operate from a van that holds your tools so a driving licence is essential.

Future prospects

Progression for locksmiths is mainly achieved by becoming self-employed and building up a profitable business.

It is also possible to progress into more specialist areas of work such as safe engineering.

Advantages/disadvantages

This can be a varied job as your work and location will change with each customer.

You will have the opportunity to meet many people and have the satisfaction of helping them.

Working unsocial hours/during the night can affect your personal life.

Call-outs to replace locks after burglaries can be distressing.

Money guide

Trainee locksmiths can expect a starting salary of about £13,000.

As you gain experience, you could achieve earnings of £14,000–£25,000 and over.

You will usually receive bonuses or higher rates for emergency call-outs.

Self-employed locksmiths establish their own rates based upon their company's success and reputation.

Earnings can vary with geographical location.

Related opportunities

- Carpenter/Joiner p65
- Glazier p87
- Shoe Repairer p469

Further information

Master Locksmiths Association
www.locksmiths.co.uk

Skills for Security
www.skillsforsecurity.org.uk

MANUFACTURING/ PRODUCTION ENGINEER

ENTRY LEVEL 6

Qualifications and courses

The most common entry route is with a relevant degree in an engineering subject. For degree entry, you will need 2 A levels/3 H grades (including Maths and Physics) and 5 GCSEs/National 5s (A*–C/A–C). It is becoming increasingly common for candidates to obtain a master's degree as this will be benefit you when seeking chartered engineering (CEng) status further on in your career. HNDs in similar subjects are also considered by employers, but you will have to undertake further study towards degree level qualifications whilst working.

It is recommended that your degree be accredited by the Engineering Council as this will make the process of gaining incorporated (IEng) or chartered (CEng) engineering status quicker. The most direct way to reach incorporated engineer (IEng) status is through obtaining a relevant degree, but it can also be achieved through a HNC or Foundation degree in Engineering or an appropriate NVQ Level 4 or SVQ Level 4 qualification. A postgraduate qualification or an MEng is required in order to become a chartered engineer.

You may be able to secure a graduate training scheme or in-house training programme, post-university. These offer recently qualified engineers the opportunity to gain experience within several departments of a company whilst working towards professional engineering status. When seeking work, academic qualifications are not always considered essential, but you must be able to show good problem-solving and project management skills, leadership, an ability to work to deadlines and have an awareness of health and safety issues in the workplace. Work experience within the manufacturing industry will improve your chances of gaining employment.

What the work involves

Manufacturing engineers design, implement and maintain manufacturing processes. You will be consulting with other professionals, such as design engineers, in order to produce high quality products efficiently and with minimum cost.

You could work in a variety of industries, including food and drink, fashion, and pharmaceuticals. You could work widely across a project, from design and research to after-sales care. Therefore, you will be using a variety of manufacturing equipment and computer systems on a daily basis.

Type of person suited to this work

You should be able to work as part of a team, as you will be liaising with other professionals on a daily basis to discuss product ideas and manufacturing solutions.

You should be good at analysing and solving problems in order to understand and stay ahead of potential manufacturing issues. The ability to prioritise your workload is also beneficial. Strong numerical skills are essential.

Working conditions

You will usually work 37 hours a week, but this often includes evening and weekend work. Extra or unsocial hours can be expected when a new production process is being tested, or if the company you are working for operates a shift system.

You will divide your time between office-based work, meetings and time spent on the shop floor or in the factory. When on the shop floor, you might have to wear safety equipment or protective clothing.

Future prospects

It is encouraged that you join your relevant professional body, dependent on your specialism, once you have qualified. These include the Institution of Mechanical Engineers (IMechE) and the Institution of Chemical Engineers (IChemE). This also lets you keep your training up to date through the continuing professional development (CPD) courses many of them run. You could work in a variety of manufacturing sectors, building diverse experience that will help you move across industries and sectors within manufacturing, taking up managerial or marketing roles.

Alternatively, you could specialise in a certain area (such as pharmaceuticals or clothing) and move into production management or consultancy; here you would draw upon your knowledge and experience to motivate and advise others.

There are also numerous short-term contracts available for manufacturing engineers, which would allow you to become self-employed.

Advantages/disadvantages

Manufacturing engineers enjoy one of the most creative roles in the engineering sector, with great input into product design and final function.

If you work in a large company, there may be opportunities to travel.

You may work evenings and weekends on a regular basis.

Money guide

The average graduate starting salaries, on completion of initial training, range from £24,000 to £28,000.

With 5–10 years' experience, you could earn up to £40,000.

Senior manufacturing engineers can expect to earn £40,000–£60,000.

Related opportunities

- Electrical Engineer p203
- Mechanical Engineer p217
- Textile Operative p229

Further information

Institution of Engineering and Technology
www.theiet.org

Institution of Mechanical Engineers
www.imeche.org

Semta
www.semta.org.uk

MARINE CRAFTSPERSON

ENTRY LEVEL 3

Qualifications and courses

Many employers ask for GCSEs/National 5s (A*–C/A–C) in English, Maths, a science and another related subject, such as Engineering or Design and Technology. Sometimes employers will ask for further qualifications, or even require candidates to complete an aptitude test.

The most common route of entry into a career as a marine craftsperson is via an apprenticeship within a firm of shipbuilders, repairers or boat builders. As an apprentice, you will undertake a combination of on-the-job training from experienced marine craftspeople with a series of day or block release classroom-based instruction, which most employers will be willing to fund. Training usually begins with health and safety regulations and an induction course, followed by basic skills including selecting materials, interpreting drawings and how to use relevant tools, before practising and furthering your abilities by working towards industry recognised qualifications.

Possible boat-building courses that may be available to you include an NVQ Level 3 in Engineering Maintenance, in Marine Engineering (Levels 2–3), Level 2 in Boat Production and Support Services and a City & Guilds Certificate/Diploma in Marine Construction, Systems Engineering and Maintenance (Levels 2–3). You could also take a specialist degree in Leisure Boat Design and Construction.

Alternatively, you could develop your skills by studying general engineering college courses full time. Some colleges situated in coastal, boatbuilding areas may run introductory courses in marine crafts. BTEC Certificates/Diplomas in Mechanical, Electrical or Electronic Engineering are available, as are higher-level qualifications, such as HNCs/HNDs in Marine Engineering. Experience working in other related craft industries, such as welding, plumbing or joinery, may also support you in your search for employment.

What the work involves

A marine craftsperson takes part in the building and repair of many different kinds of ships and boats.

Repairers and shipbuilders work with big vessels such as ferries, dredgers, tugs, submarines, tankers and warships. Boat builders work with smaller boats, such as wooden dinghies, sailing boats, narrow boats and powerboats.

Both crafts require you to work from a design to create the ship or boat. This has usually been created on a computer, and you work at marking and cutting out shapes, welding, and cutting and bending steel and other materials.

Type of person suited to this work

You should be a good teamworker, and a good communicator.

A practical, logical and problem-solving mindset is essential, as you will not only be required to interpret drawings and plans but will also need to solve problems on the job quickly and intelligently.

You should also be good with numbers, and have good eyesight and good physical fitness.

Working conditions

Marine craftspeople tend to work a normal 37-hour week, but overtime is usually available. Some urgent repair jobs may take place overnight and during weekends, but this is relatively rare.

Working at heights is normal, and you will probably spend the majority of your time indoors.

Future prospects

Opportunities for boatbuilding and repair work are more likely to be found in coastal areas, therefore you may have to relocate in order to secure employment. Work in shipyards, building larger vessels is found in Scotland, Northern Ireland and the north of England.

As you gain experience, it may be possible to progress to a position such as supervisor or inspector. You could also work towards becoming workshop manager.

Another option is to use your experience to become self-employed in areas such as boat building and repair.

Some people choose to gain further qualifications and become a marine engineering technician, move into marine design or specialise in equipment sales and support. You may even opt to transfer your skills into the wider engineering or construction industries.

Advantages/disadvantages

If you have an interest in practical work and building things, and in ships and maritime matters, then this job can be really enjoyable. It can be really satisfying to create something you are passionate about.

The dirty working conditions might not sit well with everybody, so if you want to work in a clean and tidy environment your skills may be better suited elsewhere.

Money guide

Starting salaries range from around £13,000 to £17,000 per year.

Once qualified you could earn between £18,000 and £23,000.

As a senior craftsperson you could earn more than £25,000 a year.

Related opportunities

- Civil/Construction Engineer/Civil Engineering Technician p69
- Marine Engineer p215
- Merchant Navy Engineering Officer p583

Further information

British Marine Federation
www.britishmarine.co.uk

Semta
www.semta.org.uk

The Institute of Marine Engineering, Science and Technology
www.imarest.org

MARINE ENGINEER

ENTRY LEVEL 5

Qualifications and courses

Entry to this career is usually with a degree or a BTEC HNC/HND in a relevant subject such as marine engineering, naval architecture, marine technology or offshore engineering. Entry to a degree course usually requires at least 2 A levels/3 H grades, including Maths, English and a science subject, and 5 GCSEs/National 5s (A*–C/A–C). Entry requirements for an HND course are usually 1 A level/Higher or a BTEC Level 3 Certificate/ Diploma in a relevant subject.

When seeking employment, you may be able to secure a graduate apprenticeship scheme post-university, provided by some companies, where you will receive training on the job. The Royal Navy also accepts applications for engineering officers from candidates in their final year of university. Upon completion of your service, you could then move into the commercial marine engineering industry.

Alternatively, you could enter the industry at a lower level by undertaking an apprenticeship as a marine engineering technician and then later working your way up to marine engineer by undertaking additional training and qualifications on the job.

The Merchant Navy Training Board also offers a number of training and sponsorship schemes for entrants at 3 stages, the GCSE/National 5 and A level/H grade stage, the undergraduate stage and the graduate stage. All entrants should be in good health and will be required to pass a statutory medical exam prior to being employed at sea. You must also seek sponsorship from a shipping company or training provider prior to acceptance. Trainees will spend alternate periods at college and at sea, whilst working towards industry recognised qualifications and professional maritime certificates. Each route provides opportunities for progression through the ranks, eventually reaching chief engineer level.

To update your skills, improve your career prospects and ensure a salary increase, you may wish to work towards securing incorporated (IEng) or chartered engineering (CEng) status.

What the work involves

Marine engineers design, construct and maintain ships' seafaring equipment, as well as developing and preserving offshore systems.

You could work in a shipbuilding company, on-board ships and submarines, in marine surveying, in an oil company or in the leisure industry.

You will work across a range of engineering disciplines, including electrical, construction and mechanical. You will work closely with naval officers, architects, other professionals and team members.

Type of person suited to this work

You will need excellent communication skills, both oral and written, in order to manage and lead your team as well as liaise with other professionals and clients.

Excellent maths and IT skills are essential, as is an ability to solve problems under pressure. Prioritising your workload through careful planning and project management is also very important.

You should be good at working within a team, especially as you might have to live and work with colleagues in confined areas when undertaking projects on boats or submarines.

Working conditions

You could work anywhere from an office to a boatyard, or even on a submarine, and many jobs involve a combination of office-based and on-site work.

If you are working on projects on a ship or offshore installations, living accommodation can be tight and you will probably need to spend time away from home.

The job involves climbing and lifting equipment so you will need to be physically fit.

Future prospects

Prospects are good for marine engineers. You could work for a variety of companies, from small shipping businesses, to leisure cruise liners, through to joining the Royal Navy.

When you have gained skills and experience, you could go on to specialise in project management or marine research, or even work as a consultant.

There are plenty of opportunities to work abroad.

Advantages/disadvantages

There are a huge variety of employment options available to you, from conservation projects to defence systems.

You will work in numerous diverse areas, and with many different people, so the work will always be interesting and fresh.

You may be working in cramped, uncomfortable conditions for long periods of time. This includes living and working with colleagues 24 hours a day on certain projects.

Money guide

As a graduate marine engineer, you could expect to earn around £23,000.

Experienced marine engineers can expect a salary of between £28,000 and £55,000 a year, depending on experience and responsibilities.

Related opportunities

- Electrical Engineer p203
- Marine Craftsperson p214
- Mechanical Engineer p217

Further information

Engineering Council UK
www.engc.org.uk

Merchant Navy Training Board
www.mntb.org.uk

The Institute of Marine Engineering, Science and Technology
www.imarest.org

MEAT PROCESS WORKER

ENTRY LEVEL 1

Qualifications and courses

Whilst there are no formal entry qualifications needed to work as a meat processor, some employers value GCSEs/National 5s in English and Maths, particularly when considering candidates for supervisory, inspection or technical levels.

One route of entry into the industry as a meat process worker is via an apprenticeship. The most relevant apprenticeships available include the Improve Proficiency Apprenticeship in Food and Drink (Meat and Poultry Industry Skills) and the Improve Proficiency Apprenticeship in Food and Drink (Food Manufacturing Excellence).

As an apprentice you will typically experience a combination of on-the-job training for professional meat process workers with a series of day or block release instruction at a college or training centre where you will work towards gaining industry-recognised qualifications. The courses that may be available to you include the NVQs/SVQs in Meat and Poultry Processing or Food Manufacturing Excellence (Levels 2–3) and then on to an NVQ/SVQ Level 4 in Meat Processing Management or Food Safety Management. The Meat Training Council (MTC) also offers a number of further education courses, such as the Intermediate Certificate in Meat and Poultry. Your training will cover health and safety procedures, food hygiene and quality assurance. Alternatively, you could opt to complete courses such as these full time at college before seeking employment.

To work at an abattoir or meat processing plant you must be aged 18 or over, and hold a Certificate of Competence in the Protection of Animals at Time of Killing. A driving licence may be required, particularly in operating forklift trucks.

To enhance your contacts and ensure you remain up to date with any industry developments, you may opt to register with the Worshipful Company of Butchers Guild.

What the work involves

Meat process workers do everything from herding animals, to slaughtering, to cutting up carcasses, to packaging and grading meat and ensuring it is free from contamination and ready to sell to the public. A meat process worker could specialise in either of the following roles.

Abattoir operative
You will slaughter animals for food.

After the animals have been humanely killed, you will separate the edible meat from the waste.

Meat manufacturing operative
You will manufacture meat products.

You may also weigh, wrap and label the meat.

Type of person suited to this work

This can be distressing work, so you should be prepared to cope with blood and mess.

As you will have to do lots of lifting and operating machinery, you will need to be physically fit.

You should have a responsible attitude as you may use dangerous knives and machinery. You also need to be aware of your personal cleanliness as you are part of a food production process.

Working conditions

Refrigerated areas are cold and all areas need frequent cleaning and so may be wet. You will be expected to wear protective clothing, including footwear and hairnets.

You will normally do a 40-hour week, usually from 7.30am to 3.30pm although shift and part-time work are possible.

Future prospects

Abattoir operative
With experience you could apply for senior positions or look to move to related areas such as butchery, retail or food marketing. Other options are jobs in quality control, health and safety consultancy or self-employment.

Meat manufacturing operative
With experience you could apply for supervisory, quality control and management jobs or move into related areas of work such as retail butchery.

With the right experience, qualifications and training you may be able to progress into work on the meat inspection teams employed by the Meat Hygiene Service (MHS) – part of the Food Standards Agency.

Advantages/disadvantages

This can be cold, smelly and dirty work. The job can be repetitive and monotonous.

You will be part of a team and often there is a good working atmosphere.

Money guide

Abattoir operative
The minimum salary for trained adults is around £12,000 per year (although apprentices may receive less). With experience this can rise to between £15,000 and £22,000 a year.

Meat manufacturing operative
The starting salary is usually around £12,000 per year. Experienced meat manufacturing operatives can expect a salary of between £14,000 and £20,000.

Related opportunities

- Butcher p454
- Kitchen Assistant/Supervisor p131
- Meat Hygiene Inspector p462

Further information

Department for Environment, Food and Rural Affairs
www.defra.gov.uk

Food Standards Agency
www.foodstandards.gov.uk

Meat Training Council
www.meattraining.org.uk

MECHANICAL ENGINEER

ENTRY LEVEL 5

Qualifications and courses

Most employers require candidates to have completed a degree in a relevant subject such as mechanical, nuclear, aeronautical, civil or computer-aided engineering. For entry on to a degree course you will need at least 2 A levels/3 H grades, including Maths and Physics, and 5 GCSEs/National 5s (A*–C/A–C). An accredited Foundation degree or BTEC HNC/HND can also provide a path into the industry with further training later. Some employers place as much emphasis on general communication skills and commercial awareness as they do on a candidate's degree class, but if you wish to seek chartered status (CEng) later on in your career, a postgraduate qualification or a Master of Engineering (MEng) is recommended.

Some employers recruit graduates only, therefore you may struggle securing employment as a diplomate. However, diplomates are considered for technician level posts which are entered via an apprenticeship. To apply for an apprenticeship you will need GCSEs/National 5s (A*–C/A–C) in English, Maths and a science. You will work towards an NVQ in Performing Engineering Operations, Mechanical Manufacturing Engineering or Technical Services (Levels 1–3). In order to progress however you will need to take a top-up course to convert to degree level.

Some companies may offer graduate training schemes for newly qualified engineers. If you aim for incorporated (IEng) or chartered (CEng) status, it is important that your training scheme be accredited by the Institution of Mechanical Engineers (IMechE). A mentor will monitor the early stages of your development while you undertake a structured programme of training. With appropriate experience and the necessary qualifications, you will gain professional status, significantly improving your prospects and salary as a result.

What the work involves

Mechanical engineers design, develop and maintain the moveable parts of all equipment, ranging from those in small household appliances up to large machinery.

You will probably work on a project from start to finish, so will be involved with all aspects from design and development through to manufacture.

You could work in a number of industries, including manufacturing, sport, medicine or transport.

You will also have to manage budgets, resources and people on each project.

Type of person suited to this work

You will need an exceptionally high level of scientific knowledge and technical ability in order to design mechanisms and solve practical problems as they occur in the development process.

Good communication skills, both oral and written, are essential for dealing with colleagues, other professionals and clients on a daily basis. You will also be required to produce detailed reports and presentations.

Excellent organisational skills and the ability to work under pressure are a must, as are good IT skills including knowledge of computer-aided design (CAD).

Working conditions

You will usually be required to work longer hours than those of the average working week, but evening or weekend work is rare.

You will be based mainly in an office although you will also spend a good amount of time on site, whether in a factory, workshop, hospital or other building. Despite this travel, overnight absence from home is uncommon.

You will need to wear a smart suit while in the office, but appropriate safety equipment when on-site.

Future prospects

Job opportunities for mechanical engineers are found throughout the UK, particularly in cities. There are also excellent opportunities for working abroad.

With experience, you will be able to qualify for chartered engineer (CEng) status. You could become self-employed and undertake freelance work which will give you greater flexibility over your work–life balance. Alternatively, you could go on to increasingly senior engineering posts, or even set up your own consultancy.

Some engineers choose to move into a more business-orientated role within their company such as sales.

Advantages/disadvantages

It is exciting to be at the forefront of creating new products and finding solutions to mechanical problems across numerous industries. You will be working on a variety of projects and meeting a range of people, so the work is rarely boring.

There are excellent opportunities for career development, including the option of working overseas.

You may have to work long hours to meet project deadlines.

Money guide

Starting salaries can range from £20,000 to £28,000 and, with experience, could increase to between £35,000 and £50,000.

Engineers with chartered status/10–15 years' experience can earn up to £55,000.

Related opportunities

- Clinical/Biomedical Engineer p276
- Electrical Engineer p203
- Marine Engineer p215

Further information

Engineering Council UK
www.engc.org.uk

Institution of Mechanical Engineers
www.imeche.org

MOTOR VEHICLE TECHNICIAN

ENTRY LEVEL 2

Qualifications and courses

Although you do not need any formal qualifications to begin training as a motor vehicle technician, most employers, particularly larger companies, value those candidates with 4 GCSEs/National 5s (A*–C/A–C) in English, Maths and a science.

There are several ways to enter the industry at a trainee level. A common route is via an Intermediate or Advanced Apprenticeship in Vehicle Maintenance and Repair. This scheme involves learning on the job while gaining qualifications at college.

Another option is to study full time at college for relevant qualifications. Many training centres have links with local employers which could be a route into work experience or employment. City & Guilds provide the NVQ in Automotive Maintenance and Repair, Body and Paint, Vehicle Fitting and Roadside Assistance (Levels 1–3). IMI Awards offer the NVQ Level 2 in Vehicle Maintenance and Repair specialising in either Motorcycle or Auto Electrical and the NVQ Level 3 in Vehicle Fitting Operations. Those who wish to pursue higher qualifications could take the BTEC Level 3 Certificate/Diploma in Vehicle Technology, the BTEC Higher National Certificate/Diploma in Automotive Engineering (Levels 4 and 5) or the City & Guilds Level 4 Certificate in Advanced Automotive Diagnostic Techniques.

To enable career progression, you may later opt to complete a qualification that allows you to specialise in a particular area, such as in MOT testing, air conditioning or LPG conversions.

You are likely to require a driving licence for the type of vehicle you work with. You also need good colour vision.

What the work involves

Motor vehicle technicians are responsible for the maintenance and repair of all vehicles, including cars, motorbikes, lorries and coaches.

You will need to carry out routine jobs, such as servicing a vehicle, and identify technical problems, advising customers which repairs are necessary and the costs involved.

You will work on a variety of different mechanical and electrical systems and use a range of tools and equipment.

Type of person suited to this work

You need an excellent technical and mechanical knowledge of most motor vehicles and you will be expected to build on this knowledge throughout your career to ensure that you are familiar with technological changes.

Strong communication skills are required for advising customers and you must be able to work well within a team.

Full colour vision, a good level of fitness and the ability to think quickly and work methodically are all essential. You will also need good IT skills in order to understand and fix the computerised equipment in vehicles.

Working conditions

You will usually work 40 hours a week, just above the national average. Most of your work will involve regular hours but occasionally, depending on your employer, you may be expected to work shifts, weekends and overtime.

If you specialise in repairing broken-down vehicles, you might have to travel to their location at any time of the day or night.

You will usually work in a garage, which can be noisy, and cold in winter. You will need to wear overalls and use other safety equipment to protect you while you work.

Future prospects

Being a motor vehicle technician provides good career opportunities as there is currently a shortage of skilled technicians across the UK. The variety of work available is good with opportunities possible in garages, freight transport, construction, vehicle hire or breakdown companies, car dealerships as well as in local authorities.

Within a larger organisation, you could progress to a senior or supervisory level as a technician, or alternatively move into a management or training role. You could also specialise in a specific type or make of vehicle.

There is also the option of setting up your own repair business, although the initial costs of hiring and equipping premises can be high.

Advantages/disadvantages

There is demand for technicians throughout the UK so you should be able to find a job in the location of your choice.

The hours are fairly regular and it is unlikely that your work will involve absences from home.

You may have to work in cold or cramped conditions which can be unpleasant.

Money guide

Trainee motor vehicle technicians may have a starting salary of £10,500–£11,000.

Once qualified, you could expect £15,000–£20,000.

Those with extensive experience in the industry can achieve in excess of £25,000.

Garage owners and self-employed technicians can earn considerably more.

Related opportunities

- Electrician p78
- Highways Maintenance/Road Worker p89
- Sheet Metal Worker p226

Further information

GoSkills
www.goskills.org

The Institute of the Motor Industry
www.theimi.org.uk

NUCLEAR ENGINEER ENTRY LEVEL 6

Qualifications and courses

Candidates seeking to become a nuclear engineer require a degree in mechanical, electrical or chemical engineering but you could still enter with a related degree subject such as maths, physics or science. Some universities offer specialist degrees in nuclear engineering and the Nuclear Industry Association (NIA) provides further information on these courses. For degree entry you will need at least 2 A levels/3 H grades, including Maths and a science subject, and 5 GCSEs/National 5s (A*–C/A–C). A postgraduate qualification, although not a requirement, may give you an advantage when looking for work and will make the process of seeking chartered engineer (CEng) status easier.

You can also enter the industry with an HND in a relevant subject such as General Engineering, Civil Engineering, Maths or Physics. Entry requirements are usually 1 A level/2 H grades or a BTEC National Certificate in a relevant subject.

When you are seeking employment, some companies offer opportunities for apprenticeships or training schemes which combine study at degree or postgraduate level with work-based learning. The Nuclear Technology Education Consortium (NTEC) offers professional development courses which your employer may encourage you to undertake. Entry requirements are usually a minimum of a 2.2 degree in a relevant subject.

Once experience has been gained, nuclear engineers with a Master of Engineering (MEng) can apply for chartered engineer (CEng) status with the Engineering Council and those with a bachelor's degree are eligible for incorporated engineer (IEng) status. Professional membership with the institutional body relevant to your role will significantly improve your career prospects and earnings.

What the work involves

Nuclear engineers work mainly in the large-scale production of nuclear energy, although they can be involved in smaller industrial or medical projects.

Alternatively, you could work in developing effective nuclear waste management systems.

You might lecture and train other people on the subject of nuclear power.

Type of person suited to this work

You will need excellent communication skills, both oral and written, in order to manage and lead your team, and liaise with other professionals and clients. The ability to work effectively as part of a team is also important.

You should possess an analytical mind and a logical approach to problem solving. Excellent maths and IT skills are also essential.

As you will be working with nuclear hazards, you must be able to take responsibility for your own safety and that of your colleagues.

Working conditions

You will usually work a normal 37-hour week, although you may be required to work additional hours as project deadlines approach. If you work in a nuclear power station, your hours will usually adhere to a 7-day shift system.

The majority of the work will be indoors in a power plant, laboratory, office or factory.

You may have to work in hot, cramped conditions and you will have to wear protective clothing in certain situations. As you will be working with radioactive substances, you will also need regular medical check-ups.

Future prospects

Prospects are good for nuclear engineers. In 2013, the government outlined an initiative to develop the UK's nuclear energy programme. It is thought this could generate up to 40,000 new jobs for workers. The strategy has proposed to make the UK the leading civil nuclear energy nation.

With continued study and increased experience, you can move into more senior positions within any company or discipline.

Advantages/disadvantages

Nuclear power is a growing industry so employment opportunities will increase accordingly.

You have the opportunity to work freelance after building significant experience so you can achieve a suitable work–life balance.

You will be working in an environmentally controversial industry which could potentially upset your friends and family.

Money guide

Graduate nuclear engineers typically have a starting salary of £20,000–£25,000.

With increased experience, earnings rise to between £30,000 and £50,000.

Senior engineers with chartered status could achieve £55,000–£65,000.

Some companies offer excellent benefit packages and bonus schemes.

Related opportunities

- Aerospace Engineer p196
- Chemical Engineer p201
- Mechanical Engineer p217

Further information

Nuclear Industry Association
www.niauk.org

Semta
www.semta.org.uk

PAPER MANUFACTURER/ TECHNOLOGIST

ENTRY LEVEL 1

Qualifications and courses

There are no formal entry requirements in order to become a paper manufacturer, but having some GCSEs/ National 5s (A*–E/A–E) in English, Maths and a science will be useful.

You can usually enter the field straight from school, working your way up whilst training on the job as an apprentice. Apprenticeships typically involve a combination of on-the-job training and formal instruction at a college or training centre where you will work towards industry-recognised qualifications.

Courses that may be available include an NVQ in Combined Working Practices (Levels 2–3), Performing Manufacturing Operations (Levels 1–2), Fibreboard Operations (Levels 2–3) or a Certificate in Paper Technology (Levels 2–3). There are also short courses and workshops in paper technology offered by the Confederation of Paper Industries (CPI). Your employer will also offer you additional training in health and safety, the operation of machinery and possibly, in forklift truck driving.

To become a technologist, you will need a BTEC HNC/ HND in Applied Science (Chemistry) or a relevant degree in a science or engineering discipline. You will gain experience and training within different departments once employed and you may be offered the opportunity to study at postgraduate level, for example in paper science or packaging technology.

To improve your prospects, membership with the Paper Industry Technical Association (PITA) is advised.

What the work involves

Paper manufacturers/technologists work with the equipment and systems that turn wood pulp and other materials into many different kinds of paper.

As a manufacturer, you might be operating the machine that breaks down the raw materials, managing what is going on inside, checking consistency, adjusting the controls or managing the steam system that dries the paper, or overseeing the packaging process.

As a technologist, you would design and test the equipment used in the manufacturing process. You may trial new products, ensure the quality and safety of materials, write technical reports or supervise the work of manufacturers.

Type of person suited to this work

You need to be good with your hands, and good at team-working and communication with others.

Being able to act on your own initiative is important, and you should have an accurate and methodical mindset.

Following plans and diagrams is a big part of the job, so you should be confident in this, and the ability to work with chemicals is also important.

A lot of the work will involve using computerised machinery. You must be capable of adapting to new equipment and learning to use it safely and accurately.

Working conditions

This kind of work usually takes place in shifts. You could be working daytimes, evenings, nights or weekends depending on your company, and it may well be a combination of them all.

It is normal for you to work 38 to 40 hours a week. Overtime is usually available and often encouraged.

You will be working on the factory floor most of the time or in the control room. This is so that you can monitor the processes being carried out by the machines you are looking after.

It will sometimes be necessary to work outdoors in order to load and unload delivery wagons.

Future prospects

As a manufacturer or technologist, you could find work within the paper mills and paper recovery plants based in Scotland and the north-west, south-west and south-east and Yorkshire areas of England.

With experience you can apply for positions at technician and supervisor level, which can turn into engineering roles. As a technologist, it may be possible to move into research posts in universities or with companies overseas.

You could also move around in the industry, changing to a career such as management or sales.

Advantages/disadvantages

Opportunities to progress are good in this job, and even if you come straight from school and work on the factory floor, you could move up to sales or management relatively quickly.

The work may be a little mundane to start with.

Conditions inside the factory can be noisy, hot and humid.

Money guide

A trainee manufacturer can earn around £12,000 and with experience, this can increase to between £14,000 and £21,000.

Starting salaries for paper technologists are between £17,000 and £20,000, with £25,000 being possible after experience.

Related opportunities

- Chemical Engineer p201
- Manufacturing/Production Engineer p213
- Textile Operative p229

Further information

Confederation of Paper Industries
www.paper.org.uk

Paper Industry Technical Association
www.pita.co.uk

Proskills UK
www.proskills.co.uk

POLYMER TECHNOLOGIST

ENTRY LEVEL 5

Qualifications and courses

Most entrants to this profession have a degree in a related subject such as polymer science, materials engineering, materials technology or materials science. For entry onto a degree course you will need at least 2 A levels/3 H grades in subjects including chemistry, maths or physics and 5 GCSEs/National 5s (A*–C/A–C). A 1-year Foundation degree may be available for those who wish to take a relevant degree but do not have the required scientific subjects. Several universities provide their students with first-hand experience of polymer processing equipment and small-scale production.

A postgraduate qualification, in materials engineering or polymer technology for instance, is recommended to those candidates whose first degree was in a broad engineering or science subject.

It may be possible to gain entry into this profession with an HNC/HND in polymer technology or manufacturing engineering. Given the variety of skills required of a polymer technologist, entrants with relevant experience are welcomed.

Some companies offer training programmes in engineering that combine study at degree or diploma level with structured work-based learning. Entrants are paid in terms of how much time is spent in the workplace and this could offer an effective way of securing employment once qualified.

The British Plastics Federation (BPF) provides professional development for those within the industry, offering both short courses and the master's level Materials for Industry (MfI) programme.

What the work involves

Polymer technologists use polymer materials, such as plastics, rubber, adhesives, resins and fibres, to manufacture products. You will utilise these materials to make a wide range of products including toys, casings for mobile phones, medical devices, tyres, wetsuits and hoses.

You might also use composite polymer materials when manufacturing car bodies or aircraft wings instead of traditional materials such as metal.

You will be responsible for developing the moulds used to form materials during manufacture. This is a job that requires specialist skills as a minor flaw could ruin an entire batch of products.

Type of person suited to this work

You should have a strong interest in materials science, chemicals, engineering and design technology. A good understanding of manufacturing processes and construction methods is also important.

Familiarity with computer-aided design and developed IT skills would be beneficial.

Analytical and numeracy skills are required for analysing projects or problems that arise.

You must be able to communicate effectively with people as you will be working within, and possibly leading, a team.

You should be able to take initiative, use your creativity and find a solution when you are confronted with a problem.

Working conditions

You will work between 35 and 40 hours per week, Monday to Friday. It may be necessary for you to work additional hours to meet deadlines. Overtime and weekends will increase your pay accordingly.

Your time may be divided between the office, the laboratory and the factory. As you will be required to travel, it would be useful to have a driving licence.

You will be expected to wear protective clothing in some of your working environments.

Future prospects

Polymer science is a growing industry with a shortage of qualified staff. As new uses are found for plastic, rubber and composite materials, the industry will continue to develop. There are many opportunities for promotion within the field.

You could work for a variety of companies including manufacturers of medical equipment, toy companies and aerospace engineering firms. Smaller businesses tend to specialise in the manufacturing of electrical switches and light fittings, whilst the larger companies produce goods such as food packaging and fragile components.

Alternatively, you could choose to specialise in a specific area such as vehicle manufacturing, aviation or medical equipment.

Advantages/disadvantages

You may have the opportunity to travel locally and abroad as part of your work.

The factory or laboratory conditions that you work in may sometimes be noisy and messy.

Money guide

Starting salaries are around £14,000–£18,000.

With experience, you can expect to earn £20,000–£25,000.

Those at senior level or who work as a specialist technologist can achieve £35,000 or more.

Related opportunities

- Aerospace Engineer p196
- Chemical Engineer p201
- Manufacturing/Production Engineer p213
- Materials Scientist p502

Further information

British Plastics Federation
www.bpf.co.uk

Institute of Materials, Minerals and Mining
www.iom3.org

QUALITY CONTROL INSPECTOR

ENTRY LEVEL 2

Qualifications and courses

Most entrants have prior experience in a relevant industry. For example, you might have started your career in a production role and then progressed to the level of quality control inspector. Employers usually seek applicants with 4 GCSEs/National 5s (A*–C/A–C) including Maths, English and a science subject or equivalent vocational qualifications in engineering or food science.

As a quality control inspector you could specialise in a particular sector such as aerospace or pharmaceuticals. For this you may require A levels/H grades, a BTEC/SQA National qualification, an HNC/HND or a degree in science, technology or quality management.

Engineering apprenticeships may offer an alternative route of entry for a career as a quality control inspector. Intermediate Apprenticeships in Improving Operational Performance or the Intermediate and Advanced Apprenticeships in Food and Drink are available. You will experience a combination of on-the-job training from professionals and formal instruction at a college or training centre where you will work towards industry-recognised qualifications in quality control or management. Awards available include an NVQ in Food Manufacture (Levels 1–3), a Diploma in Engineering Inspection and Quality Control, and a Chartered Quality Institute (CQI) Certificate/Diploma in Quality or Quality Management (Levels 3–5).

To enhance your career prospects, it is recommended that inspectors gain membership with the CQI. By doing so, you can apply for Chartered Quality Professional (CQP) status and significantly increase your earning potential.

What the work involves

Quality control inspectors work in a variety of industries such as engineering, food, pharmaceuticals and clothing, where manufacturing procedures must be monitored to ensure that products meet specified standards.

You will test products as they go through each stage of production by observing, measuring and weighing samples, and comparing results with specified requirements. You will also work to ensure that quality and safety standards are maintained by checking and testing materials sourced from external suppliers.

You will write reports on the tests that you carry out and help to come up with solutions to any problems or inconsistencies that arise.

Type of person suited to this work

As you will be regularly inspecting products and manufacturing processes, you must be highly organised and methodical with a keen eye for detail.

You should be responsible, thorough and able to solve problems efficiently.

You will have an aptitude for communicating with others and for advising and persuading people to improve standards.

Good written communication skills are required for writing up reports on testing methods and results.

You should have an interest in the science and technology of the industry that you are monitoring.

You also need a keen awareness of health and safety procedures.

Working conditions

You will work 35–40 hours a week and this will often include shift work, weekends and nights.

You could be based in a laboratory or an office. You will also frequently visit factories or warehouses to monitor production processes or meet with staff. These locations may be clean and bright or noisy and dirty. Protective clothing is often required.

Future prospects

Though quality control is an important part of company competitiveness, sophisticated equipment that can identify faults in products means that there are usually fewer jobs available. With greater emphasis on workers taking responsibility for the quality of their output, inspection activities, generally, are less in demand.

However, there are opportunities to work in many different sectors such as cosmetics, textiles and electrical goods.

When you have some experience you may progress to become a team leader, supervisor or quality manager. You could also move into technical sales or production management.

Advantages/disadvantages

There may be opportunities to travel and work abroad as a quality control inspector.

You could become self-employed.

Due to developments in technology, companies are increasingly using advanced equipment to monitor quality standards.

Money guide

Starting salaries are £15,000–£20,000.

Those with experience can expect to earn around £24,000 a year.

With responsibility, you can earn £30,000 to £35,000.

£40,000–£60,000 is possible for freelance inspectors who specialise in high-technology disciplines.

Related opportunities

- Laboratory Technician p500
- Quality Manager p44
- Trading Standards Officer p472

Further information

Chartered Quality Institute
www.thecqi.org

Semta
www.semta.org.uk

QUARRY MANAGER

ENTRY LEVEL 5

Qualifications and courses

You will need a degree or HND in a relevant subject such as minerals engineering, environmental sciences, geology or mining engineering, although candidates with degrees unrelated to engineering or mining are sometimes considered. You will typically need at least 2 A levels/3 H grades in sciences and 5 GCSEs/National 5s (A*–C/A–C) in order to gain entry onto a degree course. Postgraduate qualifications, although not essential, are available in quarry management and may enhance your career prospects. You could also take a year-long industrial placement with a large organisation as part of your degree which will support you post-university, in your search for employment.

Graduate management schemes with large organisations are available and employers often seek candidates with a degree in quarry engineering, IT or business. Trainees gain experience within a variety of company departments before deciding on which function to work in permanently. You may be offered support when studying for further management qualifications. Work experience on a quarry site would be very useful as employers often seek candidates who can show evidence of an ability to communicate effectively, have knowledge of health and safety and a strong level of technical understanding.

The Mineral Products Qualifications Council (MPQC) offers many useful qualifications in risk assessment, supervising safety in quarries, quarry safety inspections and understanding quarries regulations. Entrants will typically acquire professional accreditation with the Institute of Quarrying or the Institute of Materials, Minerals and Mining.

What the work involves

Quarrying involves opencast mining to extract minerals and other materials to manufacture goods such as chemicals. Your job will involve managing staff in the office and quarries.

On-site you will inspect the quality of the minerals and other products mined as well as ensuring production is on schedule and checking equipment.

In the office you will manage the sales department, look after the budget, produce performance reports and plan changes to the production system when different materials are needed.

Type of person suited to this work

You will need to have good communication skills as you will be liaising with a wide range of people. You must also have a good technical knowledge of the production system in quarries. You should be business minded with excellent management skills.

You will need to be aware of health and safety legislation as well as government regulations and ensure that these are followed on-site. It is important to have a good understanding of technical drawings and plans.

Working conditions

You will be on-call in case of emergency. You will typically spend 2 days on-site and 3 days based in an office.

You must wear protective clothing such as helmets and ear protectors when on-site and be prepared to work in all weathers.

Future prospects

The variety of different areas within the quarrying sector means that there is a great deal of work available to quarry managers within a strong industry that offers workers a well-established career route and a comparatively low level of job competition.

After gaining experience, it might be possible to progress into a managerial role in area operations but you may have to relocate in order to increase your level of responsibility. The type of quarry you specialise in, eg hard rock quarrying or sand and gravel, will impact your career progression and the skills which you will need to develop.

It would be helpful to become a member of the Institute of Quarrying. It has a professional development system which ranges from student to fellowship levels. Career prospects can be improved by further qualifications in management and quarry legislation. It will be necessary to take jobs at different quarries to improve career progression, unless you work for a big company. However, personal development generally remains in the hands of the individual.

Advantages/disadvantages

You will have a high level of responsibility.

You will spend time working outdoors. Long hours, including work at weekends, are common in this industry.

Working conditions on sites are dirty, dangerous and noisy, with sites often based in rural areas.

Money guide

A new assistant quarry manager can earn £23,000 or more.

£35,000 is a typical starting salary for a quarry manager.

A unit manager who is in charge of a number of quarries or a big quarry can earn in excess of £50,000.

Salaries will depend upon the location of the site and the employer. Benefits such as private healthcare and bonuses may be offered.

Related opportunities

- Construction Operative p72
- Demolition Operative p76
- Quarry Worker p224

Further information

Institute of Materials, Minerals and Mining
www.iom3.org

Institute of Quarrying
www.quarrying.org

Proskills UK
www.proskills.co.uk

QUARRY WORKER

ENTRY LEVEL 2

Qualifications and courses

This job does not have any formal educational requirements. Some employers do, however, generally seek candidates who hold at least 5 GCSEs/National 5s (A*–C/A–C) in relevant subjects such as English, maths, a science and technology. The Diploma in Engineering or Construction and the Built Environment could be useful when seeking employment, as is any experience of construction, mining or mobile plant machinery operation.

Apprenticeships in Extractive and Mineral Processing Operations may offer a route of entry into the industry. Construction companies and quarrying firms offer school-leavers both on-the-job training and the opportunity to study for work-based qualifications accredited by the Mineral Products Qualifications Council (MPQC). Courses you may work towards include a Level 3 Certificate/Diploma in the Extractive and Minerals Processing Industries, an NVQ Certificate in Processing Operations for the Extractive and Minerals Processing Industries or an NVQ Diploma in Complex Processing Operations for the Extractive and Minerals Processing Industries. Short courses in risk assessment and hazards, safety passports, quarry regulations and competency schemes are also available.

Once on the job, you could also work towards an NVQ in either Specialised Plant and Machinery Operations (Levels 1–2) or Level 2 in Drilling Operations. An NVQ Level 3 in Blasting Operations or equivalent is needed to work with explosives. If you wish to progress into managerial jobs, a bachelor's degree will normally be required.

A LGV licence would be helpful, but some vehicles can be driven on a full category B driving licence.

What the work involves

There are many types of quarry worker. A machine operator controls heavy equipment whilst a plant and process operator is focused on the screening plant.

Shotfirers are responsible for explosives and drillers are responsible for creating holes for explosives and investigation.

Truck drivers, maintenance workers and laboratory technicians are also needed to undertake quality control and investigate samples from the site.

Type of person suited to this work

You need to be strong, fit and active to do this job.

You must also follow safety regulations at all times owing to the dangers that could arise when using heavy machinery.

You need to be able to work well with others as teamwork is a big part of this job.

An interest in mechanical work is also crucial. Quarry workers should enjoy working outdoors and be prepared to do so in all weathers.

Working conditions

You will often work in shifts, which will include early mornings and late nights. Floodlights will be switched on during these periods.

You should be prepared to travel for long periods of time to reach sites, as they are predominantly located in rural areas.

Working conditions are often dirty, noisy, muddy and dangerous. Protective clothing such as helmets and ear protectors must be worn at all times. Work will often include a lot of carrying and climbing.

Future prospects

Roughly 1,000 quarries exist in the UK. Although each local authority will have a quarry, the majority of them are located in the East Midlands and south-west of England.

After gaining experience and the necessary further qualifications, you may be able to progress into a role as a supervisor, manager, laboratory or quality control technician or health and safety inspector.

Drivers, mechanics and fitters can undergo training to become drillers or shotfirers.

Advantages/disadvantages

You could use powerful machines such as drills and excavators or explosives.

You will work outdoors. Working conditions are muddy, noisy and dangerous.

Travel times to work can be fairly long as sites are often located in remote, rural areas.

Money guide

Salaries will depend upon the location of the site and the employer. They can also be boosted by extra payments from overtime, bonuses and shift work.

The starting salary for an operator is about £12,000.

After gaining experience and training this could rise to between £17,000 and £23,000.

If you are a specialist with significant experience, or progress to a role as a manager, you could earn up to £40,000 a year.

Related opportunities

- Construction Operative p72
- Demolition Operative p76
- Quarry Manager p223

Further information

Institute of Materials, Minerals and Mining
www.iom3.org

Institute of Quarrying
www.quarrying.org

Proskills UK
www.proskills.co.uk

RAILWAY FITTER/ ELECTRICIAN

ENTRY LEVEL 2

Qualifications and courses

The typical entry route into this profession is through an apprenticeship scheme or a training scheme with one of the major rail engineering firms, such as Network Rail. The Advanced Apprenticeship in Rail Traction and Rolling Stock Engineering is available. Entry requirements are usually 3–5 GCSEs/National 5s (A*–C/A–C) including English, Maths, a science and technology. It would be very beneficial if you have experience working as a mechanical fitter, electrician or craftsperson in another industry.

The selection process for employment involves a medical exam that aims to test candidates' physical fitness, eyesight and hearing. An aptitude test may also be set in order to assess your existing skills and knowledge.

As an apprentice, you will first be trained in basic engineering craft skills before experiencing a combination of on-the-job practice alongside professional fitters and technicians and a series of day or block release instruction at a college or training centre where you will work towards gaining industry recognised qualifications. Relevant qualifications include the NVQ Level 2 in Rail Transport Operations and the NVQ in Railway Engineering (Traction and Rolling Stock) (Levels 2 and 3). These awards cover areas such as safe working, maintaining equipment, testing systems and preventative maintenance.

An ability to drive and access to personal transport is often required, as is a track safety card. Your employer will put you through a Personal Track Safety (PTS) course in order to gain one of these.

What the work involves

A mechanical fitter will maintain and service the traction and rolling stock, plant, machinery and passenger coaches.

You could also repair station equipment such as customer lifts and hoisting equipment.

An electrical fitter will work alongside mechanical fitters and other engineers, specialising in the electrical side of the maintenance and servicing work on the traction and rolling stock, plant machinery and passenger coaches.

A multi-skilled fitter will possess the skills held by both mechanical and electrical specialists so they will be able to work in all aspects of railway maintenance.

Type of person suited to this work

You should enjoy working with your hands, diagnosing faults and working out solutions. You will be comfortable using different hand tools and equipment and enjoy working in a team alongside other fitters.

Physical fitness is important as you will be on your feet, working at your bench or directly within the various railway stock.

You should be happy to follow verbal and written instructions, be able to read and understand technical drawings and diagrams and have a responsible attitude to health and safety.

Working conditions

Much of your work will take place within heated workshops or depots. Sometimes you will have to visit jobs which are outdoors, for example near railway sidings or within a station. On these occasions it might be cold and dark.

As many of the work places are in remote areas, it is often essential to have your own transport.

You will have to wear protective clothing and be prepared to work in cramped places, engaging in lots of bending and lifting.

You will have a 37-hour working week with shifts that cover early, late, evening and weekend hours. You might also need to be on-call for emergencies that occur outside your working hours.

Future prospects

The rail industry is one of the largest industries in the passenger transport sector and is continuing to expand, therefore the demand for new recruits is increasing.

Well-developed promotional and in-service training programmes exist which help fitters to progress to supervisor, technician, team leader and management levels.

Many specialist maintenance companies carry out work for operating companies and engineering companies, making new traction units and carriages.

Advantages/disadvantages

Owing to the range of jobs within the railway industry, it is possible to move sideways into other related job areas.

Working on the railway tracks is hazardous so you must be aware of health and safety procedures.

Money guide

Trainees will usually earn £12,000–£15,000 per year.

Those with experience and relevant qualifications can achieve a salary ranging from £18,000 up to £30,000.

Further benefits include increased pay for working overtime and free or discounted rail travel.

Related opportunities

- Mechanical Engineer p217
- Rail Signalling Technician p588
- Rail Track Maintenance Operative p589

Further information

Engineering Council UK
www.engc.org.uk

GoSkills
www.goskills.org

Network Rail
www.networkrail.co.uk

SHEET METAL WORKER

ENTRY LEVEL 2

Qualifications and courses

Entry into a career as a sheet metal worker is usually via a training scheme. The Apprenticeship in Engineering Manufacture (Craft and Technician) is available at Advanced Level. To qualify for an apprenticeship, you will need to have at least 5 GCSEs/National 5s (A*–E/A–E) in subjects including maths, English and a science. Vocational awards in engineering drawing, metalwork or other practical subjects may also be considered by employers.

The Engineering Construction Industry Training Board (ECITB) offers a fast-track Advanced Apprenticeship under the National Apprenticeship Scheme for Engineering Construction (NASEC). This scheme takes approximately 3 years to complete, with up to a year of college-based learning, followed by practical work on-site and study for professional qualifications. Relevant courses for sheet metal workers include an NVQ in Fabrication and Welding Engineering (Levels 2 and 3) and the BTEC Level 3 National in Manufacturing Engineering. The Welding Institute (TWI) also offers qualifications for those who wish to specialise in welding techniques.

You will be required to hold a Client Contractor National Safety Group (CCNSG) Safety Passport in order to work on-site.

What the work involves

Sheet metal workers produce parts for a number of important items ranging from vehicles and aeroplanes, through to electrical equipment and common domestic appliances.

You will be using complex engineering drawings as a guide for marking out and cutting each piece.

You will also be operating a variety of machines including hand-powered tools, cutting and pressing devices and computer numerically controlled (CNC) devices.

Type of person suited to this work

You should have good communication skills and be able to build strong relationships with colleagues as you will be working within a team.

Good numerical skills and the ability to interpret complicated technical drawings are essential for making accurate calculations and creating precise parts. You should also have good IT and technical skills as computer-operated machinery is increasingly being used in this role.

You need a fairly high level of fitness as you will be expected to lift large items and operate heavy machinery. Good eyesight and excellent practical skills are also required in order to use tools and equipment safely.

Working conditions

You will usually work a 37–39 hour week but shift work and overtime is common. If you are producing bespoke items for a customer to a tight deadline, you may be required to work overnight on occasion.

Work is usually undertaken in a factory or workshop. You will spend the majority of your time at a bench so you will be bending over for most of the day. The work also involves lifting and spending hours on your feet.

You will be required to wear appropriate safety clothing at all times.

Future prospects

Prospects are good for sheet metal workers.

Once your initial training is completed, you could work towards qualifying as an engineering technician.

Alternatively, you could become a supervisor/manager of an engineering workshop which would increase your responsibility and salary.

Owing to demand, opportunities are available on small and large projects both in the UK and overseas.

Advantages/disadvantages

You will work with a variety of materials and tools, enabling you to build specialist understanding and knowledge quickly.

With overtime, it is likely that you will work considerably longer than the average working week.

Money guide

Starting salaries for trainees within this sector are usually £14,000–£17,000.

With experience, you can expect to earn between £17,000 and £23,000.

Workers with supervisory responsibilities or those who are highly skilled in using computer-controlled equipment can achieve in excess of £25,000.

Shift allowances and overtime can increase earnings.

Related opportunities

- Assembler p197
- Blacksmith p198
- Welder p232

Further information

Engineering Construction Industry Training Board
www.ecitb.org.uk

Semta
www.semta.org.uk

Qualifications and courses

If you wish to become a tailor or dressmaker, you can seek employment or a trainee scheme as a school leaver. A history of work experience is not required as you will be provided with on-the-job training from more experienced colleagues or a master tailor, however a demonstrable aptitude for design, sewing and art is usually highly valued by employers. GCSEs/National 5s (A*–C/A–C) in English, Maths, Textiles or Art will also be valuable in securing entry-level employment.

To increase your employability, you may opt to gain some of the skills required in the industry by completing a course such as the City & Guilds Award/Certificate/ Diploma in Creative Techniques in Fashion (Levels 1–3), the ABC Awards in Fashion and Textiles, the BTEC Certificate/Diploma in Art and Design (Levels 2–3) and the BTEC Higher National in Fashion and Textiles (Levels 4–5). These courses are available on a full or part-time basis or via distance learning.

If you are specifically looking to train as a prestigious Savile Row tailor, you could join the Bespoke Tailoring Apprenticeship programme run by Newham College in partnership with Savile Row Bespoke. This scheme teaches all the skills and knowledge you need to become a top tailor, including pattern cutting, garment construction and sewing by both machine and hand. The intensive programme could lead to an NVQ Level 3 in Bespoke Cutting and Tailoring. The number of opportunities is limited so competition for places is very strong.

Once you are qualified, you could continue developing your skills by working towards higher level qualifications such as an HNC, Foundation degree or degree in fashion or textile design. These qualifications would allow you to move into other sectors of the industry. Alternatively, it may be useful to complete an ABC Level 4 Diploma in Business for Creative Practitioners if you aim to become self-employed.

What the work involves

Tailors and dressmakers design and make made-to-measure, bespoke items of clothing. They may also be called upon to alter, repair or duplicate certain existing pieces.

Tailors usually make structured items such as suits, jackets and coats. Dressmakers can make a range of clothing, from day dresses and casual trousers to ball gowns and wedding dresses.

You will be working with numerous materials including silk, linen, cotton and polyester and you will also use equipment such as sewing machines, scissors, tape-measures and pins.

Type of person suited to this work

Since you will be dealing with a range of people, including clients and suppliers, you will need to have excellent interpersonal and verbal communication skills.

Understanding how different cuts, styles and colours flatter various shapes and figures is important for customer satisfaction, as is maintaining a smart/fashionable appearance.

You must be creative and innovative to produce fashion designs.

Working conditions

You can expect to work 37–40 hours a week. Weekend work is common as that is when most of your clients will be available for meetings and fittings. You could be situated in a workshop, small factory or work from home if you are self-employed.

A reasonable level of physical fitness and flexibility is required, as you will be bending and kneeling when measuring customers and fitting clothes. You may also need to lift and carry heavy rolls of fabric.

A lot of the work is very detailed so you will need a high level of accuracy and good eyesight.

Future prospects

You could work for a small or large company and create high fashion or more classic pieces. You can also opt to be self-employed.

In larger companies, you may be promoted to a supervisory position and there may also be the opportunity to diversify into pattern cutting or design.

There are opportunities to travel and work overseas, especially if you are involved in fashion and haute couture tailoring or dressmaking.

Advantages/disadvantages

You will be undertaking very creative work with lots of scope to use your talent and imagination on a daily basis.

Fashion is a fast-paced, interesting and potentially lucrative industry to be working in.

Making clothes requires many hours of concentration and patience.

Money guide

The average starting salary for both tailors and dressmakers ranges from £11,500 to £13,500.

With experience, your salary could rise to £14,000–£20,000.

Senior tailors or dressmakers, especially those located on Savile Row or who work in high fashion, could earn up to £50,000.

Self-employed tailors establish their own rates based upon their experience and reputation.

Related opportunities

- Costume Designer p156
- Fashion Designer/Milliner p157
- Textile Operative p229

Further information

ABC Awards
www.abcawards.co.uk

Newham College of Further Education
www.newham.ac.uk

TELECOMMUNICATIONS ENGINEER

ENTRY LEVEL 5

Qualifications and courses

Most employers require an accredited degree in a relevant subject such as telecommunications, electronic engineering, computer science, information technology, physics or maths. You will need at least 2 A levels/3 H grades, including Maths and a science, and 5 GCSEs/ National 5s (A*–C/A–C) to be accepted onto a degree course.

It is possible to enter this sector with an HND in a relevant engineering subject but you will only be able to work at technician level. You could complete a 'top-up' course to convert it into a degree or you may be able to supplement your on-the-job experience with further qualifications at degree level.

Many employers also look for candidates who have a postgraduate qualification such as a Master of Science (MSc). Those with master's level qualifications and extensive industry experience are eligible to apply for chartered engineer (CEng) status through the Institution of Engineering and Technology (IET) which could improve long-term career prospects. Alternatively, you could gain incorporated engineer (IEng) status with a bachelor's degree.

A doctorate could help you to enter the industry at a more senior level or specialise in a particular area.

Post-university, you could seek an IET-accredited graduate training scheme offered by some companies, although competition is fierce and many employers value candidates with evidence of a technical ability, a good understanding of networks, teamwork skills, an ability to adapt and a commercial awareness. Gaining relevant work experience is a useful way to develop these skills and build contacts within the industry.

What the work involves

Telecommunications engineers are responsible for designing, testing and overseeing the installation of all telecommunications equipment and facilities.

You could work across a variety of engineering fields, including electronics and construction, providing technical guidance and offering solutions to other professionals and clients.

You will be responsible for the management of telecommunications projects which includes planning budgets, recruiting a team and implementing on-site safety. You will also produce written reports and verbal presentations in order to keep both your team and your clients up to date on how each project is progressing.

Type of person suited to this work

Good communication skills are essential for managing and briefing your team, as well as negotiating with clients and explaining complex technical information to them in a clear and simple manner.

You should have an analytical mind and be excellent at problem solving. The ability to work efficiently under pressure and organise your workload effectively is also essential.

Working conditions

You will usually work a normal week of about 37 hours, Monday to Friday. Occasionally additional hours may be required, particularly as you progress to more senior positions.

Your working hours may be fairly flexible and you will not always be office based as the industry is seeking to promote working from home and part-time opportunities.

You will sometimes work on-site, checking and overseeing the installation of telecommunications equipment. In these instances, you may find yourself working outdoors or in cramped conditions. You will usually be required to wear appropriate safety equipment as well.

Future prospects

As the telecommunications industry is continually expanding, particularly due to customer demand for wireless services, job prospects for engineers in this sector are good.

Working in this fast-paced industry will require you to undertake further training throughout your career in order to stay up to date with new products, techniques and developments. Pursuing incorporated (IEng) or chartered (CEng) engineering status will significantly improve your prospects and earnings.

As you gain experience, you could move into senior or management positions. Alternatively, you could become a specialist in a particular sector, start your own company or move into training or consultancy.

Advantages/disadvantages

Hours are generally regular and there are increasing opportunities to work from home or undertake part-time hours.

In such a rapidly changing industry, you will be learning continually throughout your career.

You will have to spend time on-site which may involve working in cold, muddy conditions, at heights, or in cramped and uncomfortable surroundings.

Money guide

Starting salaries are typically £22,000–£27,000.

Once qualified, you could earn £35,000–£45,000.

At senior level and with chartered status, you could earn in excess of £60,000.

Related opportunities

- Civil/Construction Engineer/Civil Engineering Technician p69
- Electrical Engineer p203
- Electrician p78

Further information

Institution of Engineering and Technology
www.theiet.org

TEXTILE OPERATIVE

ENTRY LEVEL 1

Qualifications and courses

There are no specific entry requirements as training usually takes place once employed under the supervision and mentoring of experienced professionals. The best way to get a position would be to apply directly to textile manufacturers.

Employers may, however, value candidates who have trained in some of the skills required in the role. Courses that may improve your employability include a GCSE/ National 5 in Art and Design (including a textiles module), Edexcel BTEC Introductory Certificate/Diploma in Art, Design and Media, and Edexcel BTEC Level 1 Certificate in Art and Design. The Textile Centre of Excellence also offers a Technical Certificate in Textiles that provides a flexible, distance learning programme.

Alternatively, apprenticeships with textile manufacturers may also be available. These training schemes combine on-the-job training with college instruction, offering you the chance to work towards gaining relevant work-based qualifications such as the NVQ Level 2 Award in Manufacturing Sewn Products and the Level 3 Award in either Manufacturing Textile Products or Apparel Manufacturing Technology. As an apprentice, you will cover areas such as health and safety, the industry history, understanding materials, manufacturing techniques, the use of machinery and quality standards.

The Textile Institute (TI) also offers a range of globally recognised qualifications for professional development for those already working in the sector from licentiate to fellow level. ABC Awards offers a variety of courses in sewing, manufacturing and textiles, as do City & Guilds at Levels 1–3.

What the work involves

Textile operatives manufacture carpets, prepare the yarns of fibres to be woven or knitted (which may involve carding and combing or chemical processing), spin yarn on a machine or even make fabric on a loom.

You will carry out basic maintenance on your machinery, make sure you have a supply of raw materials and keep your work area clean and tidy in accordance with health and safety regulations.

You may also work on finishing processes such as dyeing or waterproofing fabrics.

Type of person suited to this work

You will need to be practical in order to operate the machinery skilfully and responsibly. In keeping with this, you should have good concentration as you will be doing repetitive tasks for long periods of time.

Manual dexterity and good spatial awareness, coupled with excellent eyesight and, usually, full colour vision, are also requirements for carrying out tasks such as spinning or weaving textiles.

A reasonable level of personal fitness, an understanding of, and adherence to, workplace health and safety rules, and enjoyment of working in a team are also relevant attributes.

Working conditions

Although you will work an average 37 to 40 hours a week, you will usually be doing shift work which is likely to involve early mornings or late evenings. Overtime and part-time work are also available.

You will usually work in a textile factory, which should be light and well ventilated, although the machines can be noisy and you will have to wear relevant safety equipment at all times.

It can be physically tiring, as you will spend the majority of your time standing over your machine or walking between the various pieces of equipment you are using.

Future prospects

Transfer of textile production abroad, along with the increased use of machinery, means that there are potentially fewer textile operative jobs. However, as the textile industry has a prominently mature workforce, retirements from the industry mean jobs will continue to be available. To improve your chances of employment, you should be skilled in as many aspects of textile production as possible.

If you gain experience in using a variety of machines and performing a range of tasks, you will find your prospects improve accordingly.

You could also choose to move into quality control or sales once you have gained a full knowledge of the textile industry.

Advantages/disadvantages

You will be putting your practical skills to good use creating a range of textiles for various purposes.

The work can become monotonous.

Hours can involve unsocial shift work in the early morning or evening.

Money guide

Starting salaries are about £12,500. With experience and diverse skills, you could earn between £14,000 and £17,000.

Once you have become a multi-skilled senior operative you could earn up to £20,000.

If you work shifts, or undertake overtime, earnings could be higher. Piecework payments (awarded for high production volume) can also boost earnings.

Related opportunities

- Costume Designer p156
- Fashion Designer/Milliner p157
- Tailor/Dressmaker p227

Further information

Society of Dyers and Colourists
www.sdc.org.uk

Textile Institute
www.textileinstitute.org

TOOLMAKER

ENTRY LEVEL 2

Qualifications and courses

One route of entry into a career as a toolmaker is via an apprenticeship. You will need at least 5 GCSEs/National 5s (A*–C/A–C) or equivalent, in relevant subjects including maths, English, a science, engineering, and design and technology in order to be considered.

Most people start on the Advanced Apprenticeship in Engineering scheme on completion of school or college either as an apprentice machinist or multi-skilled apprentice. You will typically experience a combination of on-the-job training from your employer and formal instruction in a college environment. Here you will also work towards gaining industry-recognised qualifications such as an NVQ Level 2 in Performing Engineering Operations, or Mechanical Manufacturing Engineering (Levels 2–3) or Level 3 in Engineering Toolmaking. Qualifications such as these will instruct you in turning, milling, grinding and drilling and your employer may also train you in the use of CNC machines.

Many companies aim to train multi-skilled craftspeople rather than specialists. Apprentices may learn fabrication skills (welding and metalwork), computer-aided design (CAD) or computer-aided manufacturing (CAM). Only exceptional trainees are encouraged to focus completely on toolmaking.

Alternatively, you may opt to gain some of the skills required of the profession by studying full time at college. Courses available include a BTEC Certificate/Diploma in Engineering (Levels 1–3), a City & Guilds Certificate in Engineering and an EAL Certificate/Diploma in Engineering (Levels 2–3).

What the work involves

Toolmakers make specialist tools and devices that are used to cut, shape, mould and form various materials for use in the production of all items; ranging from domestic appliances to aeroplanes. You will work with a range of materials, including metals and plastics.

You will also be using complex engineering drawings as a guide to marking out and cutting each piece.

You will be operating a variety of machinery including drills, grinding and milling machines, cutting and pressing devices and, increasingly, computer numerically controlled (CNC) equipment.

Type of person suited to this work

Good hand-to-eye coordination and a keen eye for detail will be beneficial, both when operating machinery and to check the quality of the tools produced. You will be making extremely precise devices, so it is essential to be able to spot any faults or errors before the tools are despatched to customers.

Good numerical skills and the ability to interpret complicated technical drawings are essential, both for making accurate calculations and creating precise parts.

Finally, you should have good IT skills as computer-operated machinery is increasingly used in this role.

Working conditions

You will usually work 39 hours a week, Monday to Friday. Although some larger companies operate shift patterns so evening and weekend work may be necessary.

Work is usually undertaken in a tool room within a factory or workshop. This means that you will be working in a fairly quiet environment, away from the main factory machinery.

You will normally stand for the duration of your working day, which can be tiring. You will be required to wear appropriate safety equipment at all times.

Future prospects

You will find your chances of securing work are enhanced if you have CNC machine skills as there is currently an increase in the number of computer-controlled machinery and precision casting techniques being used within the industry. The number of toolmakers in the industry has fallen due to this growth as workers struggle to deal with the introduction of new equipment and processes.

After gaining experience, you could move into a supervisory role within a company. This would involve overseeing production within a tool room or workshop. This could then lead into a senior or management position.

You could also undertake further qualifications in order to work towards employment as an engineering technician. This could then lead to you undertaking a degree course in order to become an engineer of some kind.

Advantages/disadvantages

You will be making tools which are vital for the construction of important equipment; these range from aeroplanes to washing machines.

You will be using both your practical skills and your mental abilities daily.

The work can be physically exhausting, as you will spend the majority of your day on your feet.

Money guide

Starting salaries range from £15,500 to £17,500 a year.

With experience, this can rise to £18,000–£24,000.

Highly skilled toolmakers, who are fully trained in using computer-controlled equipment, can earn £25,000–£35,000.

Related opportunities

- Motor Vehicle Technician p218
- Sheet Metal Worker p226
- Welder p232

Further information

Engineering Council UK
www.engc.org.uk

Semta
www.semta.org.uk

VEHICLE MAINTENANCE PATROLLER

ENTRY LEVEL 2

Qualifications and courses

Vehicle maintenance patrollers are qualified vehicle technicians, and as such must hold NVQ Levels 1 and 2 in Motor Vehicle Maintenance and Repair along with having a minimum of 3 years of relevant experience in motor vehicle repair.

You will need a clean driving licence, and will have to pass a driving assessment, aptitude test and medical exam. For some positions, a LGV licence may be required. Most employers will expect you to have at least 4 GCSEs/National 5s (A*–C/A–C), including English, Maths and a science.

Some of the larger organisations such as vehicle breakdown companies, dealerships and garages offer apprenticeship programmes that allow new entrants to train on the job and learn skills such as customer service techniques, road safety and use of communications equipment, alongside building their technical knowledge. Employers may also support you in your study of relevant industry recognised qualifications such as NVQs in Roadside Assistance and Recovery (Levels 2–3), City & Guilds Level 4 Certificate in Advanced Automotive Diagnostic Techniques (4121) or the IMI Awards Level 4 Diploma in Automotive Master Technician.

Your career prospects and earnings will be significantly enhanced if you work towards Institute of the Motor Industry's Automotive Technician Accreditation (ATA). You would be required to complete a number of practical and theory exams in order to gain status as a Roadside Assistance Diagnostic Technician or Roadside Assistant Master Technician.

What the work involves

Vehicle maintenance patrollers travel to motorists who have broken down in order to diagnose the problem with the vehicle and fix it if possible. If repair is not possible, you will need to tow the vehicle to the nearest garage.

You will be responding to urgent calls from a central control centre, and may need to reassure worried or shaken motorists.

You will be driving a van or truck, and operating a range of electronic equipment alongside general tools and car parts.

Type of person suited to this work

You will need excellent communication skills in order to explain to motorists what is wrong with their vehicle and what can be done to fix it. You may be required to reassure people who are distressed or upset following an accident.

The ability to think quickly when assessing vehicles at the roadside is necessary.

You should be good with your hands as you will be operating various tools and machines and undertaking repairs within the small space of an engine.

Working conditions

An average working week comprises around 39 hours, usually worked on a shift system including evening, night and weekend work. You may also be required to remain on standby on occasion.

Since the majority of work is undertaken on the road, a driving licence is essential. Depending on the vehicle you drive, you may also need an additional HGV or LGV licence. You will be working on the roadside in all conditions, including hazardous weather such as snow and fog, so must wear relevant safety equipment at all times.

Future prospects

Vehicle maintenance patrollers enjoy a variety of employment options. You could work for a large, well known national organisation such as the Royal Automobile Club (RAC) or the Automobile Association (AA), or for a smaller garage providing a localised breakdown service.

With experience you may progress to a supervisory role in a larger organisation, in which you will oversee and develop the performance of a number of breakdown engineers across a region.

In larger organisations, you could also move into a managerial or senior administrative position.

Advantages/disadvantages

You will be providing a valuable and appreciated service to people every day.

There is great job satisfaction in being able to repair a vehicle at the roadside and send a happy customer on their way.

You will spend long periods of time on your own, which can get boring and lonely.

Money guide

The starting salary for a qualified vehicle breakdown engineer is around £13,000 to £18,000 per year.

With 3 to 5 years' experience, you could expect to earn in excess of £30,000.

The specialist skills you acquire, such as the ability to use lifting equipment to move a stranded vehicle, are likely to increase your pay. Shift work and overtime can also affect your earnings.

Related opportunities

- Assembler p197
- Highways Maintenance/Road Worker p89
- Motor Vehicle Technician p218

Further information

Royal Automobile Club
www.rac.co.uk/careers

The Automobile Association
www.theaa.com

The Institute of Vehicle Recovery
www.theivrgroup.com

WELDER

ENTRY LEVEL 2

Qualifications and courses

One route of entry into a career as a professional welder is via an Apprenticeship or Advanced Apprenticeship in Engineering. Most employers expect you to have least 5 GCSEs/National 5s (A*–C/A–C) or equivalent, including Maths, English and a science subject. You may have to pass a competency test prior to entry.

As an apprentice, you will experience a combination of on-the-job training from experienced professionals and a series of day or block release instruction at a college or training centre where you will work towards gaining industry recognised qualifications. Relevant courses include NVQs in Performing Engineering Operations (Levels 1–2) and in Fabrication and Welding Engineering (Levels 2–3). Your training will cover areas such as how to read technical drawings, how to select materials and tools whilst also teaching you the relevant welding methods required of your specific job role.

Alternatively, you may opt to study for related qualifications full time at college in order to gain knowledge prior to entering the industry. Relevant qualifications include the ABC Certificate in Fabrication and Welding Practice (Levels 1–3), the BTEC Level 3 Diploma in either Manufacturing Engineering (Fabrication & Welding) or Mechanical Engineering, the City & Guilds Award in Welding Skills (Levels 1–3), the City & Guilds Certificate in Engineering (Levels 1–3), the Welder Approval Certificate and the EAL Award in Welding.

To enhance your career prospects and future earnings, you may decide to seek membership with The Welding Institute (TWI) which offers professional welders the chance to apply for chartered (CEng) or incorporated (IEng) engineering status or registration as an engineering technician (EngTech).

What the work involves

Welders work with metals and heavy duty plastics, which they join together using heat to form plates, pipes and other items.

You could use a number of welding techniques that are classed as either manual, semi-automatic or fully mechanised. You will most likely specialise in one of these areas as opposed to working across all 3.

You may have to work from technical drawings, using them as a guide by which to weld components together.

Type of person suited to this work

You will need good hand-to-eye coordination, coupled with manual dexterity, to successfully operate your tools and machinery.

You should be willing to work responsibly within strict health and safety guidelines, and to look out for the safety of others in your team. This will prove especially important when you work unsupervised.

Working conditions

Hours are usually 37 a week, often operating on a shift pattern, and opportunities for overtime are common.

You could find yourself working in almost any location, from standard factory or workshop roles to on-site jobs which could be outdoors or even under the sea. This means you might have to work in confined spaces which can be uncomfortable.

You will also need to wear safety equipment, including protective goggles to shield your eyes from UV light and sparks, and also fire-resistant aprons and gloves.

Future prospects

There are excellent employment opportunities for welders throughout the UK due to a shortage of skilled welders, although the majority of jobs are found in the more industrial areas.

There is a great variety of industries in which you could work, including civil engineering, agricultural engineering, shipbuilding and vehicle maintenance and repair. As your skills are transferable, you will find it easy to move between different fields of work as well as overseas.

As you gain experience within a company, you could move into a supervisory role such as a foreman/forewoman or a fabrication workshop manager. Alternatively, you could undertake further qualifications in order to specialise in a particular area of welding, move into inspection and quality control or work towards a career as an engineer.

Contract work and self-employment are also common.

Advantages/disadvantages

Practical work, where you can see the result of your efforts, is extremely rewarding.

Career prospects are good, with opportunities throughout the UK.

You will be operating machinery that is potentially dangerous.

Money guide

Starting salaries are usually between £12,500 and £17,000.

With experience you could earn in the region of £18,000–£26,000 a year.

If you are working as a specialist welder you could earn in excess of £30,000 a year.

Related opportunities

- Blacksmith p198
- Civil/Construction Engineer/Civil Engineering Technician p69
- Sheet Metal Worker p226

Further information

Engineering Construction Industry Training Board
www.ecitb.org.uk

The Welding Institute
www.twi-global.com

Environment, Animals and Plants

Jobs in this sector are perfect for those of you who do not want to spend every day behind a desk in an office, although this is not to say that you will not need to spend time writing reports and keeping a log of research findings or clients' information. Workers in this sector are passionate about animals or about caring for and maintaining the environment. You should also have brilliant people skills especially if you find yourself responsible for the welfare of someone else's animal. You should be someone who is very observant and interested in the natural world, not just from a welfare point of view but also from an economic one; many jobs in this sector involve using the environment for financial gain but increasingly industry is interested in doing so responsibly.

The jobs featured in this section are listed below. For similar jobs to the ones in this section turn to *Leisure, Sport and Tourism* starting on page 357.

AGRICULTURAL INSPECTOR

Qualifications and courses

The entry requirements vary depending on the specific role you wish to apply for. Some employers will expect you to have A levels in subjects such as a science, technology or engineering, or equivalent qualifications such as the BTEC Level 3 in Agriculture or City & Guilds Awards in Agriculture (Levels 2–3). At least 2 years' relevant work experience would also be beneficial. Extra qualifications that may be useful include the City & Guilds Level 4 Award/Certificate in Work-based Agricultural Management (Livestock or Crop Production) or City & Guilds Level 4 Diploma in Work-based Agricultural Business Management.

For other roles you will be required to hold a degree or equivalent professional qualification. Subjects which may be beneficial for this career include environmental health, engineering and science. For degree entry you usually need a minimum of 2 A levels/3 H grades and 5 GCSEs/National 5s (A*–C/A–C) including Maths and English.

Once you have secured employment, training is provided on the job, usually over a 2-year period in which you accompany experienced inspectors onsite visits and attend short courses.

Relevant professional qualifications include the NVQ in Occupational Health and Safety (Levels 3–5) and the BGAS-CSWIP Agricultural & Environmental Inspector course offered by TWI Training.

To work in a specialist sector, such as the Sea Fisheries Inspectorate, you may need relevant industry qualifications such as a degree in marine sciences, oceanography or fisheries studies. A competency certificate or naval qualification to act as an officer on a merchant ship or a mate of a fishing vessel would also be necessary.

What the work involves

You will be responsible for monitoring standards within agriculture and ensuring that regulations are followed. You are likely to be employed as one of the following:

Health and Safety Executive (HSE) inspector
You will be concerned with occupational health and safety and required to visit premises to check machinery, investigate accidents, write reports and at times give evidence in court cases.

Department for Environment, Food and Rural Affairs (DEFRA) inspector
You will enforce UK and EU legislation. This will involve collecting and analysing data, issuing certificates and planning for the prevention and control of animal and poultry disease.

Food assurance scheme inspector
You will check that agricultural practice meets the Assured Food Standards. You will also inspect the health and living conditions of livestock.

Type of person suited to this work

You must have knowledge and experience of agriculture and be able to carry out the inspections with impartiality, consistency and sound judgement. You need up-to-date knowledge of relevant laws.

Much of your job will involve monitoring others so observational and problem-solving skills are essential.

You will also need good written and spoken communication skills, as well as confidence using IT.

Working conditions

Normal working hours will be 9am to 5pm, Monday to Friday, although extra hours will sometimes be necessary.

You will have an office base but at least half your time will be spent visiting workplaces. You will therefore travel often and overnight stays may sometimes be required.

The job can involve a great deal of pressure as it will be your responsibility to ensure that legal requirements are followed effectively within agriculture. Your actions could determine the health and welfare of both people and livestock.

Future prospects

Once you have several years' experience, you could progress to a senior position or work as a consultant in occupational health.

With enough experience and training, you could move into education, becoming a lecturer in occupational health and safety.

Alternatively, you could work in public health or conservation.

Advantages/disadvantages

The job involves inspecting others and pointing out violations of the law so you may encounter confrontation.

It will be rewarding to know that you have ensured that livestock are treated correctly and people are working in a safe environment.

Money guide

Trainee inspectors could expect a starting salary between £18,000 and £26,000.

As you gain experience, your salary may increase to £35,000.

Those working in a specialist area could achieve up to £50,000.

Related opportunities

- Countryside Ranger p241
- Farm Manager p243
- Farm Worker p244

Further information

Assured Food Standards
www.redtractor.org.uk

Department for Environment, Food and Rural Affairs
www.defra.gov.uk

Health and Safety Executive
www.hse.gov.uk

AGRICULTURAL SCIENTIST

ENTRY LEVEL 6

Qualifications and courses

To enter this profession you will need a degree in a subject such as agriculture, biological science, horticulture, soil science or animal nutrition. Entry requirements for a degree are typically a minimum of 2 A levels/3 H grades, including Maths and Chemistry or another science, as well as 5 GCSEs/National 5s (A*–C/A–C) including English, Maths and a science. Equivalent qualifications may also be accepted.

It can be useful to have a postgraduate qualification in a specialist area, for example, a master's degree in animal production, soil science, poultry science or seed and crop technology.

It will also be necessary to have some work experience on a farm or in horticulture and the City & Guilds Certificate/Diploma in Agriculture (Levels 2–3) may be useful.

Those with an accredited master's degree and at least 4 years of work experience may be eligible to become a chartered scientist (CSci), a qualification which provides international recognition of your experience and expertise within your field.

What the work involves

Agricultural scientists carry out research to improve current farming techniques in crop production and the breeding and managing of livestock.

Using biology, biochemistry or chemistry, you will become a specialist in an area such as the study of soil, viruses, fungi, pests or genetics.

You will conduct tests, analyse the information and write reports. You could also teach farmers and companies that sell seeds or chemicals about your findings.

Type of person suited to this work

You must have an aptitude and a passion for science and the environment, especially biology and chemistry.

You will need strong communication skills as you will liaise with farmers and other growers to find out about their agricultural problems. You should be innovative and have strong research skills as you will spend much of your time in a laboratory or in the field, developing new solutions.

It is important to be patient, methodical and organised as progress in some research projects can take a very long time.

Working conditions

You will work 35–39 hours a week. It may be necessary to work early mornings, late evenings and weekends.

You will be based in either an office or a laboratory. Shift work could be needed when conducting experiments in the laboratory.

This job may be unsuitable for those with hay fever, dust allergies or animal allergies. A driving licence would be helpful as you might have to travel to farms or greenhouses.

Future prospects

Opportunities for general research are declining, although they are rising in some fields such as genetic engineering. There is strong competition for jobs.

Vacancies are available with local and national government bodies, research organisations, and manufacturers of animal feed, fertilisers and chemicals.

After gaining experience, you could become a lecturer in a university, school or college. You may be able to move into sales-related work for production companies.

Advantages/disadvantages

This job is perfect for those with a passion for plants and wildlife.

Conducting scientific research and practical work can be interesting and varied.

Job opportunities are falling in some areas.

It can take a long time to see any progress in some research projects.

Money guide

Salaries will depend on your location and employer.

Certain private companies and the majority of public organisations have a structured pay scale.

The starting salary for an agricultural scientist is £17,000–£22,000.

With experience, earnings can increase to £26,000–£35,000.

Those in a senior role, including those with chartered status, could earn considerably more.

Related opportunities

- Botanist p484
- Chemist p485
- Ecologist p490

Further information

Department for Environment, Food and Rural Affairs
www.defra.gov.uk

Lantra
www.lantra.co.uk

Society of Biology
www.societyofbiology.org

AGRONOMIST

ENTRY LEVEL 6

Qualifications and courses

Most entry-level candidates to this industry have a degree in a relevant subject, such as agriculture, ecology or biosciences. Typical entry requirements to a degree course are a minimum of 2 A levels/3 H grades, including at least one science, and 5 GCSEs/National 5s, including Maths, English and a science. Work experience on a farm is very useful in giving you an insight into the industry you will be working closely with. Those candidates who wish to specialise in a particular area of agronomy typically take a postgraduate qualification, such as a master's degree in soil science or seed and crop technology.

Other relevant qualifications include the FACTS Certificates, the BASIS Advanced Certificate or BASIS Diploma in Agronomy, and the Graduate Diploma in Agronomy with Environmental Management. The BTEC Level 1 in Land Based Studies (Agriculture) or BTEC in Agriculture (Levels 2–3) may also be helpful. On-the-job training is provided and a driving licence is often needed.

Alternatively, you can enter the profession in other ways, including as a field trials officer. As part of your career progression you can, with experience and training, become a senior field trials officer, assistant agronomy assistant, eventually rising to become a fully fledged agronomist.

Entry with only a Foundation degree/HND is limited, but does allow you enter as a technician or fields trials officer, which can be an excellent way of gaining experience in the industry.

What the work involves

As an agronomist you will develop and implement production systems for the maximum economical production of high quality crops without harming the environment.

You will become an expert in areas such as irrigation, drainage, plant breeding, soil classification and soil fertility.

You will study any factors which could affect the crop, including the weather and water supply. You will carry out experiments, examine the results and then complete reports.

As a field trials officer you will need to organise different trials, either in the field or laboratory. You will be expected to write research proposals, record trial results accurately, developing experiments and ensuring government legislation is correctly followed. Other duties in support of the agronomist will also be expected.

Type of person suited to this work

You need to be good at problem-solving and have excellent research skills. You should be comfortable working on your own and as part of a team.

You must have strong analytical and communication skills in order to turn your research into practical solutions and explain them to farmers or businesses. It is important that you are methodical, practical and patient as it may take a long time to conduct successful experiments.

Working conditions

You will spend a lot of time working outdoors. You will also carry out experiments and tests in laboratories and write up reports in an office.

Hours are generally between 9am and 5pm, Monday to Friday, although you might have to work extra hours to complete some experiments.

Travelling to different locations such as farms can be necessary for some agronomists. Protective clothing is needed as you will probably work with hazardous equipment. This job may not be suitable for those with pollen or dust allergies. Good colour vision may be needed for certain jobs.

Future prospects

Job prospects are good. There is a lack of young people in the profession and companies are recruiting. Agronomists that specialise in certain fields, such as genetic engineering, are also desired.

A lot of agronomists work for the government, research organisations and agricultural development organisations as well as businesses that produce seeds, chemicals or food products.

After gaining experience, it is possible to become self-employed and work as a consultant. Lecturing in universities is another option. You could also progress to a role such as a manager in a research agency or a project supervisor.

Advantages/disadvantages

You will have the opportunity to work outdoors.

This role combines scientific research with practical work, making for a diverse work environment. Conducting successful experiments can take a long time and requires patience.

Money guide

The starting salary for an agronomist, and similar roles including a field trials officer, is between £16,000 and £20,000.

After gaining experience, salaries can range from £25,000 to £35,000. If you progress to a senior role, you can expect a salary of £45,000 or more.

Related opportunities

- Botanist p484
- Chemist p485
- Ecologist p490

Further information

British Agrochemical Standards Inspection Scheme (BASIS)
www.basis-reg.com

Department for Environment, Food and Rural Affairs
www.defra.gov.uk

Lantra
www.lantra.co.uk

Society of Biology
www.societyofbiology.org

ANIMAL PHYSIOTHERAPIST

ENTRY LEVEL 6

Qualifications and courses

There are several ways to qualify as an animal physiotherapist. The most typical is for a candidate to undertake a degree in human physiotherapy followed by a 2-year Postgraduate Diploma or Master of Science (MSc) in Veterinary Physiotherapy at either the Royal Veterinary College (RVC) or University of the West of England. You will need the highest level A levels/H grades in Maths and a science for entry onto an undergraduate degree course and entry onto a postgraduate course requires a suitable first degree, in equine sciences for example, of at least a 2.1 standard, however veterinary nurses with 4 years' experience are also considered. Upon completion, you can then become a member of the Association of Chartered Physiotherapists in Animal Therapy (ACPAT).

Alternatively, you can train for 2 years with a fully qualified member of ACPAT and complete the ACPAT education course or complete an animal physiotherapy course, such as the Certificate in Animal Physiotherapy offered by the National Association of Veterinary Physiotherapists (NAVP).

The College of Animal Physiotherapy also offers a Diploma in Animal Physiotherapy. This course lasts 1 to 2 years, part time. If you successfully complete this course you will be accepted into the International Association of Animal Therapists (IAAT).

The Canine and Equine Physiotherapy Training (CEPT) offers an Advanced Certificate in Veterinary Physiotherapy. This course also lasts 2 years, part time, and entry requires a good working knowledge of animal care and a relevant higher or further education qualification.

What the work involves

Animals suffer from joint and muscular pain in the same way that humans do. As a result, animal physiotherapy has become a regular part of animal care.

You would be used by many domestic pet owners and even more so by horse owners.

Techniques you will use may include soft tissue mobilisation, ultrasound (including long-wave), neuromuscular stimulation, joint mobilisation, magnetic field therapy, hydrotherapy and massage.

Type of person suited to this work

You must love animals and want to help in their recovery process. Whilst you will spend a vast majority of your time working closely with animals, this job does also involve working alongside veterinarians and owners so you will have to be able to communicate clearly with people too!

Working with animals can be messy and smelly, so you must be prepared to get dirty. You should expect the work to be occasionally distressing, especially if the animal is injured or dies.

You will need to have good dexterity and be physically fit. You should have experience of working with animals and the ability to match treatments with problems.

Working conditions

You will be working in clinics, clients' homes, farmyards and/or stables. You could be indoors or outside in all weathers.

A driving licence is essential for some posts and you will normally wear protective clothing. This job will probably involve some heavy lifting and you will need to be physically fit.

Some assignments will involve evening and weekend work, especially if you visit your clients and animals in their own homes. As most animal physiotherapists are self-employed, working hours must be flexible to suit the client.

Good business skills are essential if self-employed.

Future prospects

This profession is extremely competitive and employs very small numbers. Work experience will improve your chances of employment.

Some of the larger animal welfare charities and veterinary surgeries employ animal physiotherapists; however most are self-employed running their own practices. To be successful you will need to build up a client list and have good business skills. There is not a structured career path in place.

With experience you could work as a lecturer or consultant.

Advantages/disadvantages

You will be working with animals, perhaps helping them to have a better quality of life. Some aspects of the job may be messy and smelly.

There is the opportunity for self-employment.

Some heavy lifting will be required.

Money guide

Many working in this area are self-employed; average fees are around £35 to £70 for each hourly consultation.

The average starting salary is about £18,500 per year; this can increase to around £20,000–£25,000 with experience.

As a senior animal physiotherapist or consultant you could earn up to £65,000 a year.

Related opportunities

- Pet Behaviour Counsellor p259
- Physiotherapist p310
- Veterinary Surgeon p263

Further information

Association of Chartered Physiotherapists in Animal Therapy
www.acpat.org

National Association of Veterinary Physiotherapists
www.navp.org.uk

The College of Animal Physiotherapy
www.tcap.co.uk

ANIMAL WELFARE OFFICER

ENTRY LEVEL 2

Qualifications and courses

There are no formal entry requirements required to become an animal welfare officer but experience of working with animals is, unsurprisingly, expected. Opportunities for voluntary work are available on the Do-it website and through the RSPCA and the SSPCA. The City & Guilds Award/Certificate/Diploma in Work-Based Animal Care (Levels 1–3) may also be advantageous.

To be recruited by the RSPCA and SSPCA you will need a full UK driving licence and 5 GCSEs/National 5s (A*–C/A–C). A pre-entry NVQ/SVQ Level 3 in Animal Care or Level 4 in Animal Care and Management is also desirable. Physical fitness is also highly important; you must be able to swim 50m fully clothed and pass a medical examination.

Once employed by the RSPCA as a welfare officer you must complete their training course, with a view towards becoming an inspector. This course must be completed within 3 years. Successful trainees become probationer inspectors for 6 months before confirmation as a full inspector.

The SSPCA training course lasts 6 months. After 2 years an intermediate examination is taken, and after 3 years you are required to sit the SVQ Level 3 in Animal Welfare.

Offers of employment are subject to passing the Disclosure and Barring Service (DBS) check.

What the work involves

You will work for an animal protection organisation or local authority offering a 24/7 service. You will undertake rescue work, visit and advise pet and animal owners, investigate cases of abuse and, when abuse is found, complete legal procedures.

You will be on-call to collect stray and injured animals or animals at risk from dangerous situations.

You will promote animal welfare in your area and you may be responsible for caring for any animals taken in by the organisation you work for.

Type of person suited to this work

You will find yourself in situations that could be potentially dangerous so you will have to be aware of your own, the public's and the animal's health and safety. Some work will be distressing, especially if the animal is in pain or has been mistreated.

Although you will often work on your own, you may well work within a team, especially in rescue situations.

Strong interpersonal skills are one of the RSPCA's key requirements and you must be able to handle confrontational situations in a calm and assertive manner. Accurate report writing ability is also important.

Working conditions

Each day will be different; you could be in a factory, private house, animal establishment or outdoors up to your waist in water.

You will spend a lot of time travelling around the local area in a van so a driving licence is essential. You will probably have to work shifts including evenings and weekends.

Animals can bite and kick, especially when they are frightened, so you will have to use your skills to make sure they remain safe and that you do not put yourself at risk. You will not be able to do this work if you suffer from animal or dust-related allergies.

Future prospects

You could work for a number of animal charities such as the RSPCA, SSPCA or the Blue Cross, or for a local authority. Within the RSPCA you can be promoted from animal welfare officer to inspector, with increased responsibility for animal cruelty cases. Further progression to chief inspector or superintendent level is possible.

You may be able to work overseas, providing support to local people in disastrous events, such as earthquakes, or informing local people about animal welfare.

You can also move into other related jobs as a local authority dog and animal warden, or kennel and cattery work.

Advantages/disadvantages

You will have the satisfaction of rescuing animals that are being abused and improving their quality of life.

There will be opportunities to work with a range of wild animals, farm animals and pets.

Some people will be abusive and you may encounter dangerous situations.

Money guide

Starting salaries for a trainee animal welfare officer are around £15,000. Once qualified, you will earn about £18,000.

In the RSPCA, the starting salary for a student inspector is £22,322, rising to £24,246 and then a maximum of £27,078.

In the SSPCA, a probationary inspector earns £19,293 and a qualified inspector's salary begins at £22,792 along with a housing allowance.

After several years' experience, you could achieve up to £28,000.

Related opportunities

- Dog Trainer/Handler p242
- Veterinary Nurse p262

Further information

Royal Society for the Prevention of Cruelty to Animals
www.rspca.org.uk

Scottish Society for the Prevention of Cruelty to Animals
www.scottishspca.org

ARBORICULTURAL WORKER/ TREE SURGEON

ENTRY LEVEL 2

Qualifications and courses

There are no set academic requirements for this job but some employers do prefer people to have some GCSEs/ National 5s. Entry is through a combination of work experience, on-the-job training and qualifications.

There are NVQs/SVQs available in Tree Work (Arboriculture) (Levels 1–2) which include workplace assessments. The BTEC qualifications in Forestry and Arboriculture (Levels 2–3) and the Royal Forestry Society Level 2 Certificate in Arboriculture are also available.

The National Proficiency Training Council (NPTC) also offers various short part-time and full-time courses at colleges of further education. Qualifications include the NPTC Level 2 Awards in Chainsaw Maintenance and Cross Cutting and Felling and Processing Small Trees 200mm–380mm, and the Level 3 Awards in Felling and Processing Trees over 380mm, Operate a Chain Saw from a Rope and Harness, Aerial Tree Pruning, Assisted Fell Operations and Preparing, Agreeing Emergency Treework Operations, and Installation and Maintenance of Structural Tree Supports. These could be completed pre-entry or on-the-job.

The Royal Horticultural Society also offers short courses leading to Arboricultural Association certificates and Lantra-accredited apprenticeships.

A Competency Certificate from the National Proficiency Training Council or Scottish Skills Testing Service is needed to work on your own or with machinery.

The National Trust can help in organising work experience placements. The Woodland Trust and the British Trust for Conservation Volunteers also provide volunteer opportunities.

What the work involves

You will carry out all kinds of work on the trees, shrubs and hedgerows in private and public gardens, parks, roadsides and on paths.

You will be responsible for planting new trees and shrubs, taking direction from a landscaper or garden designer.

Using chainsaws, hand tools, ladders and other specialised climbing equipment, you will use your knowledge of trees to make them safe, help them grow or increase the light available for other species.

Type of person suited to this work

You must have practical skills and be happy using potentially dangerous machinery and tools. You will also have to be interested in trees and the problems that can occur with them and be good with your hands.

This job is physically demanding and will include lifting, cutting and climbing so you will need to be strong and agile and good with heights. You will need to observe health and safety rules and be happy working in a team or on your own.

You will need excellent communication skills to deal with customers and explain what work needs to be done.

Working conditions

You will be outdoors in all weathers, hanging from ropes and using dangerous tools such as a chainsaw.

If you suffer from pollen and dust allergies or vertigo, this work will be difficult for you.

You will have to wear protective clothing and be very safety conscious.

Future prospects

Demand for experienced workers has risen due to greater public interest and concern for the environment. Opportunities are available with the National Trust, contractors, landowners or private employers.

With further qualifications you could enter senior or managerial positions, but this might involve moving to larger organisations.

With experience you could set up your own business.

Advantages/disadvantages

The work can be hazardous so you must obey safety regulations.

You will be outside working in all weathers.

You could do very long hours in the summer and shorter hours in the winter, which may affect your earnings.

Money guide

Salaries will depend on whether you are working for a contractor or are self-employed, however you will probably earn more in the south-east of England.

The starting salary for a junior arboricultural worker is around £12,000.

After further experience, and accreditation from the Arboricultural Association, salaries can rise to between £18,000 and £24,000.

Those who are self-employed can earn in excess of £30,000.

Related opportunities

- Countryside Ranger p241
- Gardener/Garden Designer p251
- Horticultural Worker/Manager p254

Further information

Institute of Chartered Foresters
www.charteredforesters.org

Lantra
www.lantra.co.uk

Royal Forestry Society
www.rfs.org.uk

COUNTRYSIDE MANAGER/ OFFICER

ENTRY LEVEL 3

Qualifications and courses

Whilst most entrants have completed a degree, it is still possible to enter this profession with a HND, Foundation degree or A levels/H grades. Every candidate, independently of formal qualifications, will have to demonstrate a commitment to this career by completing work experience placements within conservation groups or wildlife trusts such as the National Trust. However, generally, degree programmes require applicants to have achieved at least 2 A levels/3 H grades and 5 GCSEs/ National 5s (A*–C/A–C).

A postgraduate qualification may be beneficial as this field is becoming increasingly competitive. Subjects such as environmental science, biological sciences (such as zoology), environmental conservation, countryside management and earth sciences (such as geography) would all be relevant.

An alternative route into this industry is to start as a ranger or warden, gather experience and then apply for a countryside officer post. There are apprenticeships available, such as the Environmental Conservation Apprenticeship, and groups such as The Countryside Management Association or The National Trust offer a range of short courses and events – ranging from ecology and habitat management to the identification of fungi – to help you gain expertise and develop your career.

What the work involves

Countryside officers/managers preserve and protect important wildlife areas, including nature reserves and sites of special scientific interest. You will achieve this through methods such as raising awareness of the issues that affect the natural environment, monitoring species to see which require protection, and gathering evidence of pollution.

You will advise authorities and communities on the effect developments will have on the natural environment. Managers are responsible for the hiring, training and supervising of staff. You will also be in charge of the way budgets are spent.

Type of person suited to this work

In order to pursue this career you must have an interest in, and a passion for, environmental conservation.

You should have strong observational skills. You will also need to be physically fit. You should be capable of conducting research, have strong communication and negotiation skills, both in person and on paper, and the ability to speak in public.

You might have to be involved in enforcing environmental laws and so you will have to be able to remain calm and logical.

Working conditions

You will spend some of your time in an office environment and the rest working outdoors.

Working hours will vary depending on the season, but the average is about 40 hours a week. This is not a 9am to 5pm job; working weekends, evenings and bank holidays is common.

You might be required to travel between sites and so a driving licence may be useful. As an officer you may be provided with protective clothing.

Future prospects

Officers may progress into a managerial position, for example countryside manager or senior officer. In order to gain this kind of promotion you will need to gather qualifications and experience. However, promotion opportunities can be hard to come by.

You may also be able to specialise in a specific area of conservation such as rivers, coasts or access and recreation for the general public. Each of these could increase your employment potential.

Advantages/disadvantages

You will have to work outside in all weathers.

This job has many elements to it and so every day will be different.

You will have to enforce environmental legislation which might place you in heated situations.

Money guide

These figures will vary depending on location, employer and sector.

Your salary will increase as you gain responsibility.

The average starting salary for a countryside officer is between £18,500 and £21,500 a year.

With experience this can increase to between £24,000 and £32,000.

Those who excel in the field can earn up to £36,000.

Related opportunities

- Countryside Ranger p241
- Landscape Architect/Designer p256
- Landscaper/Landscape Manager p257

Further information

The Conservation Volunteers (TCV)
www.tcv.org.uk

The Countryside Management Association
www.countrysidemanagement.org.uk

COUNTRYSIDE RANGER

ENTRY LEVEL 2

Qualifications and courses

Relevant courses include the NVQ/SVQ in Environmental Conservation (Levels 2–3), BTEC Level 2 Certificate/Extended Certificate/Diploma in Countryside and Environment, and BTEC Level 3 in Environmental Conservation and Countryside Management. BTEC/SQA Higher National Certificates and Diplomas in Environmental Conservation and Countryside and Environmental Management are also available. You will require 1 A level/Higher and relevant work experience to gain entry to these. The Environmental Conservation Apprenticeship is also available.

Relevant degrees include countryside management, conservation and environment, and environmental studies. You will require at least 2 A levels/3 H grades, and 5 GCSEs/National 5s (A*–C/A–C). Postgraduate qualifications are also available.

Most training is done on the job. Courses for professional development are provided by Lantra National Training Organisation.

A driving licence is essential. Employers prefer applicants aged 21 or over. This can be a very competitive area to enter so unpaid experience can be vital. Most entrants have completed at least 6 months of voluntary work, which may be possible at the Wildlife Trust, the National Trust and Groundwork.

Membership of relevant professional bodies such as the Countryside Management Association may enhance job prospects.

Once employed it will be necessary to further your knowledge by completing short courses with organisations such as The Conservation Volunteers (TCV) and the Field Studies Council (FSC). Subjects include coppicing, species identification and habitat management.

What the work involves

By patrolling the countryside throughout the year you will monitor the success and progress of the plants/animals and the integrity of the fencing and buildings in your care. You will also perform practical tasks such as tree planting and pond management, as well as plan and create habitats for animals and plants.

You will manage exhibitions and resource centres, take part in community projects, give talks, lead guided walks and be responsible for the safety and enjoyment of any visitors, answer their queries and help them get the most from their visit.

You will keep a record of any work that is carried out, along with inspections, accidents and incidents.

Type of person suited to this work

You will need to enjoy being outdoors and have a strong interest in wildlife and the countryside.

To ensure the future of your area you will need to provide information to the public which could include talking to potential funding organisations or local politicians. You will therefore have to be confident speaking in public and have excellent written and spoken communication skills. You might have to write reports and sometimes undertake research.

To find work you might have to start with some voluntary or community-based work, so it is important that you are keen and willing.

Working conditions

Most of your work will be outdoors, driving or walking around your area. You will be working in all weathers and despite protective clothing you will be, at times, cold and wet or hot and dusty. This is physically demanding work and is likely to involve walking over difficult terrain.

You are likely to work longer hours during the spring and summer, especially if there are animals or plants that require protection.

This work can be difficult if you suffer from pollen or dust allergies.

Future prospects

Once employed within the industry it is likely that you will need to move from employer to employer in order to progress.

After gaining experience, it is possible to enter lecturing, consultancy or research work. You could also progress to the role of officer or a more managerial position, which would be more office based. You might choose to move to leisure management, agriculture or horticulture work.

Advantages/disadvantages

You will spend a lot of time in the open air combining your interest in the countryside with work!

You could be working in remote areas.

Many jobs are offered on temporary contracts or on a seasonal basis.

Money guide

Initial salaries are from around £13,000 per year.

With experience this can rise to around £20,000 a year.

The most senior countryside rangers can earn over £30,000 per year.

You may also be given additional payments if you are required to work unsocial hours.

Related opportunities

- Countryside Manager/Officer p240
- Farm Manager p243
- Gamekeeper p250

Further information

Lantra
www.lantra.co.uk

Natural England
www.naturalengland.org.uk

The Conservation Volunteers (TCV)
www.tcv.org.uk

DOG TRAINER/ HANDLER

ENTRY LEVEL 2

Qualifications and courses

Dog handler
Dog handling is usually a second career. Employers such as the UK Border Agency, the police, the army and the fire service expect you to start in mainstream work in the service before applying. For example, the police force requires you to have at least 3 years of police work experience. The security industry requires you to have a Security Industry Authority (SIA) licence.

The National Search and Rescue Dog Association (NSARDA) requires at least 12 months of experience as a full-time member of a rescue team. You could also volunteer as a 'dogsbody', where you act as the victim being searched for and, after 6 months of experience, you could move into dog support/navigation work, complete First Aid, radio and equipment training, and then apply for dog handling training.

You could start as an apprentice and work towards a Diploma in Work-Based Animal Care. There is also an ASET Level 2 National Award for General Purpose Security Dog Handlers, and a HABC or BTEC Level 2 Certificate in Providing Security Services, which include training with guard dog options.

Dog trainer
After working as a handler you can then apply to become a trainer. Some organisations, such as the police, require 3 GCSEs/National 5s (A*–C/A–C), including English and Maths. Voluntary work is recommended.

Foundation degrees and degrees are available in animal behaviour and training and animal studies. Typical entry requirements for a degree course include 2 A levels/3 H grades and 5 GCSEs/National 5s. It is also recommended that as a dog trainer you join a professional body through which you can pursue your continuing professional development (CPD).

What the work involves

Dog handler
Working as a team, you will search buildings, vehicles and open spaces for such things as people, illegal drugs, firearms or evidence. You may protect property including private property or military establishments.

You might attend large-scale disturbances to control crowds or search for casualties at disaster scenes.

Dog trainer
You could support security staff, the police force or animal charities such as the Guide Dogs for the Blind. Your work will be divided between training the dogs and their human carers.

You might run one-to-one and group classes on obedience training for dogs.

Type of person suited to this work

You may need to house and care for your dog from puppyhood right to the time it retires 7–10 years later. You will require a stable home environment.

Most police dog work involves attending incidents, so you will need to be able to stay calm in an emergency. You will need to be patient, self-confident, alert and observant.

Much of your time will be spent on your feet and may involve running, so a high level of fitness is required.

Dog trainer
You will need to be patient, firm and a good teacher. You will need to have a good imagination to make classes fun and also be physically fit.

Working conditions

If you work with domestic owners you will probably be self-employed and work from a community setting such as a village hall.

Dogs are used in dangerous situations and so you will be at risk of injury.

Future prospects

The main employers are the police, armed forces and customs and excise. Some other organisations employ a few dog handlers, for example the fire service, security companies and search and rescue services.

This job is fiercely competitive as many handlers stay in the job for life.

There is also the option of self-employment or lecturing on dog training courses.

Advantages/disadvantages

You may at some point be bitten or scratched.

You will form a strong bond with your dog. It is really rewarding when the dog you have trained catches a criminal, or finds dangerous drugs or explosives.

Money guide

On average dog handlers earn between £15,000 and £25,000 a year depending on experience. Extra allowances are paid when the dog lives with and is cared for by you.

Domestic dog trainers earn around £15,000 a year. Police dog trainers make about £21,000 which can rise to £30,000 with experience. If you are self-employed your earnings will depend on your success.

Related opportunities

- Pet Behaviour Counsellor p259
- Police Officer p529
- Racehorse Trainer p260

Further information

Army
www.army.mod.uk/join

Association of Pet Dog Trainers
www.apdt.co.uk

Police Recruitment
www.policecouldyou.co.uk

FARM MANAGER

ENTRY LEVEL 3

Qualifications and courses

There are no formal entry requirements but most people who enter this area have a HND, degree or other higher level qualification.

Courses are available in agriculture, agricultural science, land and property management, and agricultural engineering. A levels/H grades or their equivalent, often including a science subject will be required. Postgraduate courses are also available which will require a relevant degree or HNC/HND and experience.

Previous experience of farm work is as important as qualifications, and most degree-level courses include sandwich placements for this purpose. Organisations such as Velcourt, Sentry Farms, MDS and the JSR Farming group also offer graduate training schemes. A driving licence is essential.

It is possible to enter with an NVQ/SVQ Level 3 in either Agriculture Crop Production or Livestock Production, and/or a Level 4 in either Agriculture (Livestock Management) or Agricultural and Commercial Horticulture (Crop Management).

Apprenticeships are also available through organisations such as Co-operative Farms.

What the work involves

You will be responsible for the overall running of a farm. This includes making the decisions about which crops to grow or livestock to raise. You will supervise the work of your staff, keep up to date with farming developments and oversee the financial side of the business whilst satisfying the regulations set by the Department for Environment, Food and Rural Affairs (DEFRA).

You will have to communicate with government officials, farming suppliers and feed merchants and your customers who could be major supermarkets or small local shops.

You will keep farm records up to date such as the budget and where crops and livestock are sold to and bought from.

In recent years smaller farms have started offering more activities and products to increase income. Farm managers can now be expected to run accommodation and camping sites, offer field sports, fishing and other rural activities.

Type of person suited to this work

You should have a passion for science, the environment and business, combined with a strong understanding of farming and a desire to learn.

You will also need an appreciation of health and safety and the ability to recruit, develop and retain your staff, as well as run the business of the farm.

You should be capable of motivating staff, be computer literate and work well when under pressure.

Working conditions

Farm managers tend to work long hours, with early morning starts as the norm. Particular times of year are exceptionally busy, such as harvest or lambing season.

Managers will spend a lot of their time doing accounts and making sure the farm is operating profitably, but will also need to participate in general farm work during busy periods. On smaller farms this may be a regular occurrence. The outdoors work will involve heavy lifting and will be dirty, smelly and/or dusty.

Future prospects

Competition for jobs is intense and career progression is likely to involve moving between farms and from one part of the country to another.

With substantial experience and qualifications it is possible to progress into other related areas of agriculture such as plant breeding, crop protection, plant trials or genetics. These opportunities are available within private companies or academic/research organisations.

Training or research opportunities are also possible, as well as consultancy or civil servant work with DEFRA. There could be the chance to work abroad.

Advantages/disadvantages

You will spend a lot of time in the open air caring for living and growing things. You will get to combine business acumen and an understanding of nature.

At some times of the year your social life may be restricted.

Your future can depend on factors outside of your control such as bird flu or foot and mouth disease.

Money guide

There is a set minimum wage, decided upon each year by the Agricultural Wages Boards for England and Wales, Scotland and Northern Ireland.

Assistant or trainee farm managers earn between £16,000 and £21,000. With experience this can increase to between £24,000 and £30,000.

Managers of a large farm, with at least 10 years of experience, may earn over £50,000.

Some jobs include rent-free accommodation and a vehicle.

Related opportunities

- Farm Worker p244
- Fish Farmer p248
- Parks Officer p258

Further information

Department for Environment, Food and Rural Affairs
www.defra.gov.uk

Lantra
www.lantra.co.uk

National Federation of Young Farmers' Clubs
www.nfyfc.org.uk

FARM WORKER

ENTRY LEVEL 1

Qualifications and courses

There are no set entry requirements but many employers will expect you to have some form of work experience. An Advanced Apprenticeship in Agriculture is available for formal training. GCSEs/National 5s in English, Maths and a science may also be useful for gaining promotion and higher pay.

Candidates may choose to specialise in either livestock or crop agriculture.

Livestock

Lantra offers a variety of livestock courses including Herdsman Foot Trimming, Sheep (lambing) and Dairy (calf-rearing). You can train while on the job and work towards an NVQ in Livestock Production (Levels 1–3) or a Diploma in Animal Care.

You may choose to do an HNC in Poultry Production at the Scottish Agricultural College. Poultry husbandry courses are also available at many other colleges.

Crops

The Royal Agricultural College offers degrees in crops, sustainable soil management and agricultural science. You could also take a National Proficiency Tests Council accredited course in Tractor Driving or Pesticide Use.

Many employers will allow you to train on the job and undertake qualifications such as the NVQ in Agriculture, Mixed Farming and Crop Production (Levels 1–3), the BTEC in Agriculture (Levels 2–3) or the City & Guilds Diploma in Agriculture (Levels 2–3).

What the work involves

Livestock

You will work on farms or estates caring for livestock. You will need to feed and handle the animals, clean their living spaces, and prepare them for transport. You may need to milk cows and shear sheep.

You will tend to ill livestock, give them proper medication and help out with birthing procedures. You may be required to keep track of animals' breeding cycle and care for the animals through pregnancy and the birthing process.

Crops

You will work on arable farms, ploughing, planting, sowing, fertilising, spraying and harvesting a variety of crops. You will either handpick crops or use machinery.

You could work with crops such as wheat, barley and oats, non-food crops such as linseed and flax, or energy crops used for heat and power generation. You will also be responsible for general maintenance and upkeep of the farm.

Type of person suited to this work

You should be practical and have a passion for the outdoors and environmental issues. You should be strong, active and adaptable and prepared to work very long hours.

A good knowledge of plant and/or animal care is important. You may need to work out weights and other calculations so good numeracy skills are also useful. You also need to be able to follow instructions and work with care and caution.

Working conditions

Farm work is seasonal so you will be busier at certain times of the year, when you may need to work 16 hour days.

You will normally work 40 hours a week, including evenings, early mornings and weekends. You will work in all weathers and will often be expected to live on or near the farm.

The work on livestock farms can be dirty so you will need to wear protective clothing and footwear.

People with allergies such as hay fever may also find the work difficult.

Future prospects

You could be promoted to supervisory roles or train further and become farm manager. Most farms are small so you might need to move farms in order to be promoted. There are also opportunities to work overseas.

Livestock farms are mostly found in western parts of the UK. A rise in farmers' markets means that demand for meats is high and interest in organic foods has left ample opportunity.

Crop farms are mostly found in eastern parts of the UK. You could specialise in non-food crops such as pharmaceuticals, oils or materials such as hemp.

Advantages/disadvantages

Working on a farm, especially during busy seasons, can be exhausting and at times dirty.

It is an amazing experience to tend to and watch an animal give birth and rewarding to reap an abundant harvest.

Money guide

Many farm workers are paid per hour on a flexible or part-time basis. You can earn from £6.25 to £9 per hour. Apprentices earn between £139 and £232 per week.

If you start out as a trainee aged 16, you may earn around £9,977 a year. If you are 18 or older you may earn between £12,000 and £16,690. When you reach 20 this may increase to £20,000.

Many employers will provide you with free or low-rent accommodation. Overtime pay is also common.

Related opportunities

- Farm Manager p243
- Fish Farmer p248
- Gamekeeper p250

Further information

Department for Environment, Food and Rural Affairs
www.defra.gov.uk

Lantra
www.lantra.co.uk

National Federation of Young Farmers' Clubs
www.nfyfc.org.uk

Organisation Profile

BRIDGWATER COLLEGE

BRIDGWATER COLLEGE

Learning in the Somerset countryside

The Cannington Centre at Bridgwater College has been delivering land-based education for almost 100 years. Somerset Farm Institute, as it was first known, opened its doors in 1921, and as Cannington College, it went on to achieve a national reputation as one of the leading providers in the sector. In 2004, it merged with local tertiary education provider Bridgwater College, a move which secured a substantial investment package to significantly improve the facilities.

The countryside location of the Cannington Centre makes it an ideal choice for students wanting to pursue a land-based education. The rural environment creates a calm and relaxed atmosphere, which students find very satisfying and conducive to learning. The teaching facilities consist of a range of purpose-built accommodation within beautifully maintained grounds. Many students opt to live on site and the College recently achieved an overall rating of 'outstanding' in its recent Social Care inspection by Ofsted. The inspectors summarised, 'The College provides excellent support for learners while they are living in residence. Arrangements for safeguarding are outstanding reflecting the College priorities for the safety of learners.'

The Student Liaison Team makes sure there is plenty of entertainment for day and residential students. Typical activities might include paintball and laser quest trips, DVD nights, various sports activities, pool competitions, College parties and the College Young Farmers' Club. The common room has a pool table, jukebox, games machines and much more. The team is on duty 24 hours a day, Monday to Friday, providing help and support to all students.

Facilities at the Centre include a 200 hectare farm with a new £1 million milking parlour, a £2 million new animal management centre with dog grooming salon, a fully refurbished BHS approved equestrian centre, beautiful walled gardens and botanical glasshouse, new activity centre with high and low rope challenges, a nine hole, 18 tee golf course – and much, much more. The recently opened Agricultural Innovation Centre will enable continued growth of research provision at the College, further to its first PhD being appointed (in conjunction with Oxford Brookes University) and the development of a new commercial forage trial plot in association with Mole Valley Farmers.

There is also a dedicated Learning Resources Centre, with a library and access to over 20,000 books, journals, newspapers, DVDs and CDs, and a careers library. Our Virtual Learning Environment allows students 24 hour access to course materials, assignments and other resources. The Centre has its own restaurant offering breakfast, lunch and dinner, with a College shop selling groceries and stationery.

The provision is comprehensive – offering everything from agriculture to sports turf management, and from floristry to equine studies. Class sizes and tutor groups are usually small, which allows every student to have individual attention from their lecturers and tutor groups tend to form strong units and many lasting friendships are established.

The College hosts regular open days and evenings throughout the year, which are ideal opportunities to view the facilities, find out more about the courses, and speak to staff and students.

For more information, visit www.bridgwater.ac.uk or call 01278 441234. You can also keep up-to-date with new events and information by following Bridgwater College on Facebook, Twitter and Flickr.

Case Study

BRIDGWATER COLLEGE

Faye Broad

Which course are you studying?

I am studying an Animal Management BTEC Level 3 Extended Diploma at Bridgwater College's Cannington Centre in Somerset.

Why did you choose this course?

I have always had a love of animals and wanted to learn more about them. This course allows me to keep my options open and provides me with the knowledge required for a variety of different careers.

What would you usually do on a typical day?

The Animal Management Centre at the College is great for learning all the practical skills of caring for the huge variety of animals we have there. Our lessons are a mixture of these practical tasks and theory; no lessons are ever the same. We also have our duties of cleaning out the animals, feeding them and generally caring for them, so this all adds to our knowledge and really supports our learning. I live on site and there are also lots of social activities to get involved in during the evenings!

What do you enjoy most about the course?

I just love working with the animals and learning about them on a daily basis. The fact that we are learning and caring for anything from snakes to alpacas is fantastic and I feel I'm gaining so much experience from all the tutors. I also really enjoyed the time we spent at the College farm during lambing season.

What are the main benefits of studying a course in Animal Management?

The course covers so many aspects of Animal Management including animal nutrition and business management; it really does allow you to progress onto many different careers and courses. We've taken part in lots of study visits including a trip to Crufts, during which we learnt all about genetics and breeding, which was fascinating. As part of the course you have to take part in a work experience placement. I worked in a kennels and this then led to me having a part-time job, which will be great to put on my CV.

What do you hope to progress on to on completion of this course?

On completion of my course, I am hoping to train as a dog handler for the Police or Mountain Search and Rescue.

FARRIER

ENTRY LEVEL 3

Qualifications and courses

To train as a farrier you must be at least 16 years old and will need to take an advanced apprenticeship with a training farrier approved by the Farriers Registration Council (FRC). Only 80 to 100 apprenticeships are offered each year and they cost approximately £12,000 if you are not eligible for grant aid funding.

To be accepted for the advanced apprenticeship, you will need a minimum of 4 GCSEs/National 5s (A*–C/A–C), including Maths and English Language, or an NVQ Level 2 and the Level 2 Key/Functional Skills of Communication and Application of Number, or a BTEC Diploma and the Key/Functional Skills. As part of the entry requirements you will also have to pass a medical examination and complete a practical forging test. City & Guilds offer preparatory courses and certificates.

The apprenticeship takes 4 years and 2 months. The course combines on-the-job training with periods at a college. At the end you will also be awarded a NVQ Level 3 in Farriery and the Diploma of the Worshipful Company of Farriers. To work as a farrier you must register with the FRC. A driving licence is required.

For those who cannot satisfy the academic and/or practical entry requirements, an Access to Farriery Course is available at colleges such as Oatridge, Chichester and Enniskillen.

A Foundation degree in Farriery at Myerscough College is also available for those who are already qualified and working. It is also possible to learn farriery with the Royal Horse Artillery whilst serving with the army.

What the work involves

Farriers shoe, trim and care for the feet of horses.

As well as the skills of removing and fitting new shoes, you will have to keep up to date with new practices and know about horse anatomy and illnesses that can affect horses' feet.

You would often work in partnership with vets to treat leg and joint problems.

Type of person suited to this work

You should enjoy being around horses and have the right temperament to handle them. You will need to get on with your customers and deliver high-quality care to them and their horses.

You will have to enjoy being outdoors working in all weathers, often in a muddy environment.

This work is both practical and physical, so you will need to be strong to do manual work using lots of hand tools and have good metalworking skills.

Working conditions

Weekend work is common and emergency cover can be needed at any time.

Your days will involve driving to each customer, working with the horses and returning to your forge to prepare shoes and collect materials. In the summer months your hours will be long, especially when more people are riding their horses. This can be hot, tiring work, especially if fitting shoes to a difficult horse.

You could work from a blacksmith's forge or travel to farms and stables and work out of a mobile workshop.

Future prospects

Riding is a very popular activity and there are stables all around the country.

There are about 2,500 farriers who are mostly self-employed. There is high competition for each apprenticeship. Larger riding schools, stables and horse breeders can offer permanent jobs. You could progress to become a senior farrier, 1 of only 300 current farrier trainers or into a managerial role.

Some farriers supplement their earnings by undertaking blacksmithing whilst they build up their farriery client list.

Advantages/disadvantages

This is a great job if you want to work with horses without riding.

Using your hands is a satisfying skill to have.

The work is physically demanding and can result in back injuries.

Money guide

Apprentices who start work aged between 16 and 17 are not entitled to the full national minimum wage until they are 19. Those who start aged between 18 and 25 will be paid a percentage of the national minimum wage for the first 12 months of their apprenticeship.

Once qualified, you can earn between £16,000 and £25,000, depending on your success and the number of customers you have.

Some experienced and popular farriers can earn £30,000 or more.

Related opportunities

- Farm Manager p243
- Pet Behaviour Counsellor p259
- Racehorse Trainer p260

Further information

Farriers Registration Council
www.farrier-reg.gov.uk

Worshipful Company of Farriers
www.wcf.org.uk

FISH FARMER

ENTRY LEVEL 2

Qualifications and courses

Applicants do not necessarily need formal educational qualifications but most employers require GCSEs/ National 5s (A*–C/A–C). The BTEC Level 2 Certificate in Fish Husbandry is available to those with 4 GCSEs/ National 5s (A*–C/A–C). Students can then progress to the BTEC Level 3 Certificate in Fish Management. SQA also offer a National Progression Award (NPA) in Aquaculture (Levels 4–5).

Training can be done on the job with attendance at short courses. Entrants may study via distance learning for the Certificate or Diploma in Fisheries Management offered by the Institute of Fisheries Management (IFM).

In Scotland you may be able to enter through a Level 3 Modern Apprenticeship.

Those who would like to begin their career as a manager or assistant manager may require a degree in a relevant subject such as aquaculture and fishery management, biology or marine and freshwater biology.

Once you are employed in this sector, you may be expected to take industry recognised qualifications in emergency First Aid, food hygiene and sea survival. A full driving licence is also required and you must be able to swim.

What the work involves

As a fish farmer you will raise fish from small (juvenile) fry until they reach saleable size. The most common fish to raise are salmon and trout. You will feed them, check and treat for disease, clean tanks and protect them from predators. The final stage of the process is to net the catch, harvest and pack them for market.

Some farms specialise in producing the breeding stock – the tiny fish that other farmers bring to saleable size – known as fingerlings. Some shellfish farms in coastal locations also produce oysters, scallops and mussels.

Type of person suited to this work

You must be a practical person, willing to get wet and dirty. You need a good knowledge of fish which you will develop throughout your career. Much of this work is scientific in approach, so you should have good observational skills to be able to identify anything that might affect the quality and success of the fish in your care.

You should be patient, hard working and able to persevere in challenging situations. This work is difficult and long-term security is not guaranteed.

Entrants to this profession must be comfortable working within a team and independently.

If you become a manager you will also require good business and administrative skills.

Working conditions

Working with fish is the same as any animal-based work, which means they need care and attention 24/7. You are likely to work on a rota basis with 2 days off every week. You will work very long hours including early mornings, late evenings and weekends.

Fish farms are usually isolated, and you will be outdoors in damp, cold conditions having to cope with all types of weather.

Some of the work will be unpleasant and will involve the sight of blood.

Future prospects

Fish farming is becoming quite important due to the problems with sea fish stocks.

Like other farming enterprises, fish farms are vulnerable to price fluctuations, so predicting the future is difficult. In the UK, there are around 1,100 fish farms employing 7,500 people, most of whom are based in Scotland.

With experience you may move into a research-related role involving scientific and technical work. You could also start up your own fish farm or work abroad.

Advantages/disadvantages

You will spend a lot of time in the open air.

You will have the satisfaction of producing an in-demand product.

There are only limited areas of the UK where the work is available.

Having to work unsocial hours could interfere with your personal life.

Money guide

Fish farm workers may have a starting salary of £10,000–£13,000.

As you gain experience, you could expect to earn around £18,000.

Experienced managers of a fish farm can achieve up to £38,000, whilst regional managers can earn even more.

Related opportunities

- Countryside Ranger p241
- Farm Manager p243
- Skipper/Deckhand p261

Further information

British Trout Association
www.britishtrout.co.uk

Institute of Fisheries Management
www.ifm.org.uk

FOREST WORKER/ OFFICER

ENTRY LEVEL 2

Qualifications and courses

Forest worker

There are no formal entry requirements but at least 2 GCSEs/National 5s (A*–C/A–C) or a forestry qualification would be an advantage. Relevant qualifications include the City & Guilds Certificate in Forestry and Arboriculture (Levels 2–3), the City & Guilds Diploma in Work-based Trees and Timber (Levels 2–3), BTEC in Horticulture and Environmental and Land-based Studies (Levels 2–3), the BTEC Level 3 Extended Diploma in Forestry and Arboriculture or Countryside Management, the Diploma in Environmental Land Based Studies, the NPTC Diploma in Work-based Trees and Timber (Levels 2–3), the ABC Certificate in Practical Environmental and Conservation Skills (Levels 1–3), and the LANTRA Awards Level 2 Certificate in Land-based Activities.

Alternatively, an Apprenticeship in Trees and Timber is available at Intermediate and Advanced Level.

The National Proficiency Tests Council (NPTC) and Lantra award certificates of competence in skills such as operating chainsaws and carrying out chemical spraying. A full driving licence is also required.

Forest officer

Entry is with a Foundation degree, HND, degree or postgraduate qualification in forestry, land management, horticulture or environmental science. For entry to a degree a minimum of 2 A levels/3 H grades, normally including Maths or a science, and 5 GCSEs/National 5s are required. At least 1 A level/H grade and 3 GCSEs/National 5s are required for entry to an HND or Foundation degree. It may be useful to gain some experience before applying for a course.

What the work involves

Forest worker

Work includes planting and felling trees, managing weeds, maintaining fencing and carrying out tree surgery. In addition, you will use tools, drive vehicles and repair any broken fences.

Forest officer

You will plan and manage the annual programme of your forest. This includes organising the clearing of areas, planting and felling trees, and overseeing general maintenance.

Type of person suited to this work

Forest worker

It is important that you can follow instructions and safety procedures as the work is dangerous. You should enjoy being outdoors.

Forest officer

You must be organised as you will plan jobs months in advance. You need both technical skills and theoretical knowledge of forests and wildlife.

Working conditions

Forest worker

You will probably work a standard Monday to Friday week with overtime and weekend work during the busier summer months. You will have to be aware of health and safety legislation as this can be dangerous work, using potentially hazardous tools.

Forest officer

Much of your time will be spent outdoors but you will also work indoors planning duties for your staff. You are likely to do a lot of travelling whilst you check the different areas under your responsibility. A driving licence would be helpful as many of these places are isolated.

Future prospects

The range of employers includes the Forestry Commission, private landowners and estates, local authorities and large companies.

Career progression is likely to involve relocating as promotion is rare unless you work for a large company. Many contracts are seasonal or short term, so you need to have a flexible approach to employment opportunities. Consequently, around 50% of forest workers are self-employed.

With significant experience, self-employment as a consultant or trainer is possible.

Advantages/disadvantages

It is a perfect job if you love the outdoors.

As with all land-based careers, you are often at the mercy of the weather.

Money guide

Forest worker

You are likely to earn around £12,000 per year when starting out in this career.

With experience, salaries increase to around £18,000.

A supervisor could earn up to £26,500.

Forest officer

Starting salaries for this role are usually between £19,000 and £30,000.

An experienced forest officer could achieve in excess of £35,000.

Forest workers and officers employed by private estates may have accommodation provided.

Related opportunities

- Countryside Ranger p241
- Gardener/Garden Designer p251
- Rural Property/Practice Surveyor p103

Further information

Forestry Commission
www.forestry.gov.uk

Institute of Chartered Foresters
www.charteredforesters.org

GAMEKEEPER

ENTRY LEVEL 1

Qualifications and courses

No formal qualifications are needed for this role, however, 3 GCSEs/National 5s (A*–C/A–C) may be an advantage. Relevant GCSE/National 5 subjects include design and technology, mechanics, geography, environmental or rural studies, and business studies.

Voluntary or relevant work experience is very useful for gaining insight into the industry and relevant apprenticeships may be available for those aged between 16 and 24.

Whilst training is usually done on the job, there are some courses available to applicants who wish to progress. Such courses include the City & Guilds Level 1 Award in Land-based Studies, the Level 2 Certificate in Countryside and Environment Management, and the Level 3 Certificate in Countryside Management. They also offer the Diploma in Work-based Game and Wildlife Management (Levels 2–3).

Other courses include NVQs/SVQs in Gamekeeping and Wildlife Management (Levels 2–3), the BTEC in Gamekeeping and Countryside Management (Levels 2–3), and the HNC in Gamekeeping with Wildlife Management, for which candidates would need practical experience and/or the Extended Diploma in Gamekeeping.

Foundation degrees are available in countryside and environment (gamekeeping) at several colleges if you wished to specialise your learning. These generally require a Level 3 qualification or 2 or more A levels/H grades for entry.

If you deal with specific animals, such as deer, then further qualifications may be prove helpful. For example, the British Deer Society offers deer management courses. You may also have to operate chainsaws or use pesticides and will be required by law to gain certificates in competence from the National Proficiency Test Council (NPTC).

What the work involves

As a gamekeeper you will work on a large country estate, where shooting for sport is part of the estate business. You will also play an important role in managing the land.

You will be responsible for providing birds and other animals such as deer or hares for the clients to shoot, or possibly fish to catch. This is achieved by raising game birds and releasing them into the wild once they are mature enough, and protecting game from its natural predators such as magpies and rats.

You will also have to patrol the land at night to help protect game from poachers.

Planting and protecting crops, clearing the land, and keeping rivers clean may also be necessary.

Type of person suited to this work

You must have an unsentimental approach to wildlife as this job involves the killing of animals for sport.

To enable the clients to get the most from their day, you will need to be a good communicator and be able to offer advice about gun usage and how to hit targets successfully.

Physical fitness and stamina are essential. You must be alert and possess excellent practical skills. You must be happy to work on your own for long periods of time.

Working conditions

You will be outdoors in all weathers and seasons. Your hours will be flexible and will involve weekend working and late or early starts. You will spend long periods of time on your own, doing lots of walking to check the estate and the progress of the game.

You will be handling and using guns, traps and poisons so will have to be confident using them and very aware of your own safety and that of others.

This work will be difficult for those who suffer from allergies to animals, pollen or dust.

Future prospects

Most of this work is within remote parts of the country or on large country estates.

There is strong competition for jobs, so it is best to take a few training courses before applying.

With further skills in shoot or land management you can be promoted to head of estate; with experience and dedication you can advance from trainee to head keeper quickly.

Advantages/disadvantages

This job combines outdoor physical work with lots of practical skills.

You will spend a lot of time alone.

You might be provided with a house.

Money guide

Starting salaries for new entrants are around £11,000 per year.

With experience you may earn between £13,000 and £18,500.

Head gamekeepers can expect up to £21,500.

Related opportunities

- Countryside Ranger p241
- Farm Manager p243
- Farrier p247

Further information

British Association for Shooting and Conservation
www.basc.org.uk

Game and Wildlife Conservation Trust
www.gwct.org.uk

National Gamekeepers' Organisation
www.nationalgamekeepers.org.uk

GARDENER/GARDEN DESIGNER

ENTRY LEVEL 1

Qualifications and courses

Gardener
There are no set requirements for entry to this career, however some GCSEs/National 5s (A*–C/A–C) may be sought by some employers. Some specialist courses are available to those who wish to progress and these include the City & Guilds Level 2 Certificate in Gardening and in Horticulture. The Royal Horticultural Society (RHS) also runs the Advanced National Certificate in Horticulture and the Kew Royal Botanical Gardens offers a Diploma in Horticulture.

Apprenticeships in Horticulture are also available with various organisations, such as B&Q, the National Trust and Royal Parks, Capel Manor College, and Kew Gardens.

Garden designer
Although there are no formal requirements for this job, a design-orientated qualification is a definite advantage.

Many garden design courses are offered at land-based colleges and some art colleges. Courses include the Edexcel Diploma in Environmental and Land-based Studies (Levels 1–3), the BTEC Level 3 in Horticulture, the BTEC HNC in Horticulture (Garden Design), and the BTEC HND in Landscape and Garden Design, Horticulture and Plantsmanship, and Horticulture. NVQs/SVQs in Horticulture (Levels 1–4) are also available.

Foundation degrees in garden/landscape design and management, and degrees and postgraduate degrees in garden design and related subjects are also available.

The Institute of Gardening also offers a Diploma in Horticulture which can be studied at home.

Courses in computer aided design may also be beneficial. A driving licence will also be necessary.

What the work involves

Gardener
Gardeners work in a wide range of settings, from large gardens such as those in stately homes and National Trust properties, to small urban parks and private gardens.

Garden designer
You will advise clients on how to improve the look and planting of their garden. You will present your ideas as a series of plans, and supervise a landscape contractor to turn your design into reality.

Type of person suited to this work

Gardeners need to be physically fit and confident in using hand tools.

You must be creative and be able to picture how a piece of bare or neglected ground can be transformed into something beautiful.

As a garden designer, drawing and IT skills will be useful, as will an extensive knowledge of plants and the environments they need.

Good business and maths skills are necessary in order to keep to your clients' budgets. You will also have to keep to deadlines.

Working conditions

Gardeners mostly work outdoors. There will be a lot of physical work, lifting large pots and bags of peat, and digging and clearing beds.

Garden designers will spend most of their time in a studio designing and researching garden plans. You will spend some time outdoors overseeing practical tasks.

Future prospects

Gardener
Many gardeners are self-employed offering services to both the public and private sectors. If you work for a local authority, with experience, you could move on to supervisor or manager jobs, especially if you gain further qualifications. Gardeners can also train to be garden designers.

Garden designer
Half of all designers work in private practice. Some specialise in certain types of design such as planting, landscaping, etc. Some designers choose to be self-employed offering services to private home owners.

Advantages/disadvantages

Designers can mix creative, practical and outdoor work.

Your work will depend on the weather.

You may work in beautiful places (or create them if you are a designer).

Money guide

Gardener
Gardeners working for a local authority start at around £11,000–£12,000 per year. With experience this can rise to £20,000, especially if you have management duties. If self-employed you will agree an hourly rate with your customer.

Garden designer
As a guide, trainee rates start at between £10,000 and £15,000 per year. Designers' pay will depend entirely on how well they can market themselves and generate work; many are self-employed and charge around £30–£60 per hour.

Related opportunities

- Groundsperson/Greenkeeper p253
- Horticultural Worker/Manager p254
- Landscape Architect/Designer p256

Further information

Royal Horticultural Society
www.rhs.org.uk

GROOM/STABLE HAND/ STUD HAND

Qualifications and courses

Groom/stable hand
You must be at least 16 years of age and ideally you should have experience working with horses. Useful courses include the NPTC NVQ in Horse Care (Levels 1–3), the City & Guilds Certificate and Diploma in Horse Care and Management (Levels 2–3), the BTEC Level 2 in Horse Care, the BTEC Level 3 in Horse Management, and the BTEC Level 4 HNC and Level 5 HND in Equine Management. The Association of British Riding Schools (ABRS) offers the Grooms Certificate and Grooms Diploma, and the British Horse Society (BHS) have exams in Horse Knowledge Care and Riding at stages 1 to 4.

The British Racing School in Newmarket and the Northern Racing College in Doncaster offer a 9-week residential course, during which you could complete the Level 1 Diploma in Work Based Racehorse Care and Riding. Upon completion you can take another 9-week course and gain the Level 2 Diploma in Work Based Racehorse Care before undertaking the 18-month Advanced Apprenticeship Level 3 Diploma.

Stud hand
There are no formal entry requirements. Some knowledge of stable work and horse care is expected. The National Stud in Newmarket offers a free apprenticeship for school leavers. This involves 10 weeks of training at a residential centre and the opportunity for a 10-month placement. Those over the age of 18 with experience working with horses can apply for the free Diploma in Stud Practice and Management with the National Stud. Students spend 5 months undertaking practical training, attending lectures and workshops, and completing projects and exams.

What the work involves

Groom/stable hand
You will be responsible for the health and welfare of the horses in your care. You will groom, feed, muck out and tack up the horses. You could be based within a riding school, competition or livery yard, racing stable or veterinary hospital.

Stud hand
This is a specialised area of work as you will be working with stallions, brood mares and young stock. You will use your understanding and knowledge of breeding lines to help owners breed a foal that meets their requirements.

Type of person suited to this work

You must be comfortable and competent riding and working with horses. Good observation skills and patience are essential when caring for animals.

You need strong communication and teamworking skills to work with your colleagues, the horse owners and stable visitors.

You should be a practical person, physically fit and willing to work in messy conditions.

Working conditions

You will spend most of your time outdoors lifting heavy bags of feed, hay and bedding. You will carry tack, clean up the yard or ride. In the summer the work can be hot, dusty and smelly. In the winter it is cold, wet and muddy.

You will wear protective clothing and, as this work can be dangerous, you must be aware of your own and others' safety. Horses can kick and bite.

You can expect to work 24/7, including some holidays and weekends, especially if you live-in.

A driving licence is useful.

Future prospects

Groom/stable hand
With experience it is possible to specialise. Competition grooms (show-jumping, dressage and eventing) are in demand. Gaining your HGV driving licence can increase opportunities. Most grooms progress to more successful yards that compete internationally or keep more expensive and higher quality horses.

Stud hand
Interest in breeding quality British horses and ponies has increased due to European competition. Stud work is therefore rising in importance and those with skills are in demand.

Advantages/disadvantages

This is the perfect job for a horse lover.

The pay is relatively low for such a demanding job.

Injury risks are high in all horse activities and this could affect your long-term career security.

Money guide

The horse industry has a reputation for low salaries and long hours.

Starting salaries are usually around £12,500.

With experience, you could earn £14,000–£16,000.

A head groom could achieve up to £20,000.

Free or subsidised accommodation is common for those living on the premises.

Related opportunities

- Farm Manager p243
- Farrier p247
- Racehorse Trainer p260

Further information

British Horse Society
www.bhs.org.uk

GROUNDSPERSON/ GREENKEEPER

ENTRY LEVEL 1

Qualifications and courses

There are no set entry qualifications for this role and training generally takes place on the job. The Apprenticeship in Horticulture is available at Intermediate and Advanced Levels.

Relevant qualifications offered by City & Guilds are the Award in Work-Based Horticulture (Levels 1–3), the Level 2 Certificate in Sports and Amenity Turf Maintenance, and the Diploma in Horticulture (Levels 2–3). Other courses include the BTEC Level 2 Diploma in Horticulture, the BTEC Level 3 in Horticulture, and the BTEC HNC and HND in Horticulture (Sports Turf Management).

Degrees and Foundation degrees in sports turf and golf course management are available. Entry requirements are 2 A levels/3 H grades and 5 GCSEs/National 5s (A*–C/A–C) including English and Maths.

The Institute of Groundsmanship (IOG) offers short courses in areas such as generic sports turf management, basic lawn care and synthetic surfaces.

The British and International Golf Greenkeepers Association (BIGGA) also have a range of qualifications, including the Master Greenkeeper Certificate for those with experience and expertise.

What the work involves

Your main role will be to prepare and maintain the grounds used for different sports. Although you might work on synthetic surfaces for games such as hockey, most of the time you will be working with grass. You will cut, treat, weed and prepare the surface before each game, match or event.

You will be responsible for outlining the playing areas with tape or marking compound, ensuring that they adhere to the regulations of the appropriate governing body.

You will put up posts, nets and other equipment where needed.

Type of person suited to this work

You need specialist horticultural knowledge, combined with an understanding of the different sports and what the competitors of each sport need.

You should be good with your hands and have a working knowledge of machinery maintenance.

You will require lots of stamina and physical fitness to do a variety of jobs.

Working conditions

You will have to work flexible hours including evenings and weekends.

The role involves a lot of physical labour such as carrying heavy items and bending. This work may be unsuitable for those who suffer from hay fever or allergies to chemicals.

You will spend a lot of your time working outdoors, although you will probably be in a workshop when repairing and maintaining the equipment. You will need to wear protective clothing.

Future prospects

The range of potential places for you to work is increasing. You could work in a professional sports club, local authority education or sports and leisure department, hotel, university or college.

With additional qualifications and experience you could apply for promotion to team leader or supervisor, head groundsperson and then area manager. Bigger companies offer greater promotion opportunities.

It is possible to progress into a position in leisure management or estate management.

Advantages/disadvantages

This job provides the satisfaction of knowing that your work will be seen by thousands of people.

Sports fans will have the opportunity to work in a sector that they are passionate about.

You will spend most of your time working outside in all weather conditions.

Money guide

As an untrained groundsperson, you can expect to earn up to £18,000 a year.

An experienced and skilled groundsperson/greenkeeper could receive between £18,000 and £24,000.

A head groundsperson could achieve £25,000–£33,000.

Staff responsible for major sporting venues can receive higher salaries.

Employers may also offer on-site accommodation or bonuses for overtime.

Related opportunities

- Countryside Ranger p241
- Gardener/Garden Designer p251
- Horticultural Worker/Manager p254

Further information

British and International Golf Greenkeepers Association
www.bigga.org.uk

Institute of Groundsmanship
www.iog.org

HORTICULTURAL WORKER/ MANAGER

ENTRY LEVEL 2

Qualifications and courses

There are no formal entry requirements for horticultural work, but some employers will prioritise candidates who have GCSEs/National 5s (A*–C/A–C), including a science, a BTEC in Horticulture (Levels 2– 3), or the City & Guilds Certificate in Horticulture (Levels 2–3). Certificates of competence from the City & Guilds may also be required if your job involves dangerous tasks such as operating chainsaws or pesticide use. Work experience may also prove helpful.

There are a number of useful vocational qualifications that can enhance your skill set, such as the NVQ/SVQ in Horticulture (Levels 1–4) or a qualification in horticulture from the Royal Horticultural Society (Levels 1–3). There are also Foundation degrees and degrees in horticulture available.

A Kew Diploma from the Royal Botanical Gardens can be obtained after 3 years. They also offer a 3-year Kew Apprenticeship and the International Diploma in Botanic Garden Management. Both the Royal Botanical Gardens and the Royal Horticultural Society, amongst others, offers work placements with accreditation.

What the work involves

You will undertake a variety of horticulturally related tasks and have a number of different responsibilities such as mowing lawns and tidying flowerbeds. You will also need to maintain equipment and tools and look after plants by checking for disease, feeding, watering, pruning and spraying them. To produce new stock, you will plant out cuttings and seedlings. You will also pot-up and pack plants for selling and shipping.

You may also be asked to strategically place plants in order to create naturalistic settings if employed by a botanical garden.

As a manager you will supervise, train and recruit staff and look after the day-to-day running of the organisation. You will decide which plants to grow, manage the budgets, ensure deliveries are despatched on time and develop a business plan for now and in the future.

Type of person suited to this work

Much of your day will involve carrying, bending and working with the plants, so you will need to be physically fit.

You will be outdoors for much of the time working in all weathers, doing dirty work.

These jobs could be difficult if you suffer from pollen or dust allergies.

Working conditions

You will normally work a 40-hour week and could be based at a garden centre, plant nursery, in a park or public garden. You will often have to work weekends and late evenings.

Work could be seasonal with more hours required at certain times of the year. You will spend much of your time outdoors, in all weathers.

Future prospects

There is a constant demand for workers, especially for those with experience.

Horticultural jobs are available within major plant producers, national parks, public gardens and local and national garden shops/nurseries.

After gaining experience and qualifications you could progress to a role as supervisor or manager, freelance work or start up your own shop. There is the opportunity to undertake training to help career development. The British Agrochemical Standards Inspection Scheme (BASIS) offers a number of courses on a range of technical subjects including fertilisers, pesticides and cultivation.

Advantages/disadvantages

There is a good mix of practical and managerial work.

These jobs combine lots of skills and can be very rewarding.

This is an expanding market with lots of opportunities.

Money guide

Starting salaries are between £12,000 and £15,000 per year.

With experience, this rises to between £18,000 and £20,000.

Salaries for a managerial role are around £16,000 per year, rising to £21,000 for graduates.

Qualified and experienced managers can earn between £30,000 and £40,000.

Related opportunities

- Arboricultural Worker/Tree Surgeon p239
- Gardener/Garden Designer p251
- Groundsperson/Greenkeeper p253

Further information

British Agrochemical Standards Inspection Scheme (BASIS)
www.basis-reg.com

Institute of Horticulture
www.horticulture.org.uk

KENNEL WORKER

ENTRY LEVEL 1

Qualifications and courses

There are no formal educational requirements although some employers will favour candidates with GCSEs/National 5s (A*–C/A–C) in English and/or Maths. As a practical vocation, paid or unpaid experience working with animals will vastly improve your chance of employability – most local organisations, as well as the RSPCA and Dogs Trust, require volunteers.

The Guide Dogs for the Blind Association can provide work experience for applicants aged over 18 and also offer the Dog Care Technician Training Programme for candidates who have 5 GCSEs/National 5s (A*–C/A–C) and 2 A levels/H grades. Hearing Dogs for the Deaf also recruit volunteer puppy socialisers from people who have experience of looking after young dogs and have an approved home.

Other relevant qualifications include the NVQs/SVQs Levels 1–3 and the BTEC Level 2 Certificate/Extended Certificate/Diploma in Animal Care, and the City & Guilds Advanced National Certificate in Animal Care and Management. There is also the BTEC Level 3 Certificate/Subsidiary Diploma/Diploma/Extended Diploma in Animal Management. The Animal Care College also offers training programmes which may prove helpful.

There are several apprenticeship schemes for those aged between 16 and 24, such as the Apprenticeship in Animal Care. Training takes place on the job and is given by the manager or an experienced staff member and you are given the opportunity to combine practical work experience with study for a professional qualification.

What the work involves

There are lots of types of kennels including boarding, pet sanctuary, breeding and quarantine kennels for animals brought from overseas.

Administrative skills may be useful as you might need to answer the phones, take payments and keep records when medicine is administered or if any behavioural problems are displayed. As well as cleaning the kennels, you will feed, exercise and check on the general health of the dogs and cats.

In a pet sanctuary you might be required to show prospective owners around and answer any questions they have on animal care.

Type of person suited to this work

You will need to enjoy spending time outdoors and not mind getting dirty. Some of the animals you will be working with might have behavioural problems or nervous dispositions and so you will need to be calm and patient. A good knowledge of small pet care is vital.

You will require a good level of fitness as you will spend a large part of the day being active.

You should have strong communication skills and the ability to work well alone or as part of a team.

Working conditions

This is physically demanding work involving walking dogs and cleaning the kennels. You may work shifts and your hours will probably include evenings, weekends and public holidays.

Many animals will be frightened and confused so they could be aggressive; you will therefore have to be aware of not only your own, but the safety of those around you.

You will spend a lot of time outdoors in all weathers and the work can be smelly, dirty and noisy.

Future prospects

There are approximately 3,500 kennels in the UK, although the number of jobs available does not tend to fluctuate much. However, you could work for national charitable organisations such as the RSPCA, Guide Dogs for the Blind Association or a private breeder.

The army and police recruit service and civilian kennel staff, and it may be possible to use your experience to enter associated professions, such as dog trainer, RSPCA or SSPCA inspector or veterinary nurse.

In larger kennels there may be the opportunity to progress to the position of supervisor or manager.

Advantages/disadvantages

This is not a 9am–5pm job and the unsocial hours may affect your social or family life.

There is the possibility of being attacked by an animal.

There is an opportunity to become self-employed by opening your own kennels.

Many kennels may only ask you to work part time or seasonally.

Money guide

Pay will depend on the nature of your employer.

If you are working for a private kennels £12,000–£16,000 is likely. For animal charities and larger organisations you may get more. The RSPCA offers a minimum of £10,500 to its kennel workers (known as Animal Care Assistants).

You may be provided with accommodation and extra pay could be offered for overtime.

Related opportunities

- Dog Trainer/Handler p242
- Veterinary Nurse p262
- Zookeeper p265

Further information

Animal Care College
www.animalcarecollege.co.uk

Guide Dogs for the Blind Association
www.guidedogs.org.uk

Lantra
www.lantra.co.uk

Royal Society for the Prevention of Cruelty to Animals
www.rspca.org.uk

LANDSCAPE ARCHITECT/ DESIGNER

ENTRY LEVEL 5

Qualifications and courses

You will need a bachelor's degree in landscape architecture that has been accredited by the Landscape Institute (LI) or, if not, a relevant first degree followed by a LI-accredited postgraduate qualification will qualify you for this profession. In order to gain entry to a degree course you will usually need at least 2 A levels/3 H grades and 5 GCSEs/National 5s (A*–C/A–C), or a diploma in an environmental or land-based subject. In order to gain entry to a postgraduate course you will usually need to complete an Honours degree in a relevant subject. It is not possible to gain accreditation with only a HND or Foundation degree.

Entrants who have completed an LI-accredited course can work towards chartered membership of the LI through the Professional Practice Examination.

Courses are also available at land-based colleges of further education, which offer a range of BTEC qualifications in relevant subjects.

Practical experience in a landscape-related field is very useful when applying to postgraduate courses.

What the work involves

You will design or develop a new or existing outside space. You will then make a plan, saying what plantings should be included, and calculate the cost. You will then see the project through to completion by supervising the work on-site.

Although you will understand garden design, you will also have to understand civil engineering, horticulture and planning law.

You could work on projects aimed to regenerate towns and cities and developments to combat climate change.

Type of person suited to this work

You will have to enjoy being outdoors and want to make a difference to the environment. You will need to be happy in the open in both the summer and the winter and be prepared to spend time away from home on some jobs.

You will have to be creative and have excellent design and drawing skills that may require computer-aided design (CAD).

You will be interested in making, building and constructing hard landscaping but will appreciate and understand the impact that different plants can have.

You should be physically strong and able to use machinery and hand tools. You must be creative, artistic and have strong computer skills. You should have solid communication and negotiation skills.

The profession welcomes mature applicants.

Working conditions

Landscape architects spend a lot of time in the design studio sitting at a computer and drawing board or attending meetings on-site at clients' premises.

You could spend about a quarter of your time at the project site, supervising operations. Some of your time will also be spent on the phone dealing with contractors and suppliers.

Site work will involve being outdoors in all weather. Average hours are about 37 per week, Monday to Friday. You may spend some time away from home.

Future prospects

Due to the impact of home improvement programmes, designing and developing gardens is now a popular and growing business. However, it can be a competitive area so many choose self-employment.

Organisations who recruit landscape staff include local authorities, botanical gardens, large private estates, the National Trust, English Heritage, building contractors and landscape design houses.

If you choose to become self-employed your success will depend upon finding customers, the quality of your work and how quickly you can build your reputation.

Advantages/disadvantages

There is a good mix of practical hands-on work with planning, design and meeting people.

You will get satisfaction from knowing your work will have an impact on future generations.

You could get wet, cold, hot and dusty.

You will not be able to do this work if you suffer from pollen or dust allergies.

Money guide

Starting salaries for a graduate landscape architect are around £20,000 per year.

Once you have become fully qualified as a chartered landscape architect salaries could range from £25,000 to £45,000 a year.

If you work in private practice these figures could increase substantially, especially if you become partner.

Related opportunities

- Architect p56
- Landscaper/Landscape Manager p257
- Town Planner/Planning Technician p113

Further information

Landscape Design Trust
www.landscape.co.uk

Landscape Institute
www.landscapeinstitute.org

LANDSCAPER/LANDSCAPE MANAGER

ENTRY LEVEL 1

Qualifications and courses

Landscaper
There are no required qualifications but relevant GCSEs/National 5s, the National Proficiency Tests Council (NPTC) Certificates, the RHS Certificates/Diplomas in Horticulture (Levels 1–3), and the BTEC in Horticulture (Levels 1–5) are useful.

A driving licence is often required.

Landscape manager
Although there are no set qualifications this is still an extremely competitive industry. A HNC/HND, degree or postgraduate qualification in a relevant subject, such as garden design, would prove valuable. An NVQ Level 4 in Amenity Horticulture Management or a Level 3 Diploma in Work-Based Environmental Conservation may also be useful.

The Landscape Institute (LI) has accredited some degree courses, the completion of which can then offer you a pathway to chartership. Many employees may expect you to already be or working towards being a chartered member of the LI. While undertaking the pathway you will be mentored by a fully qualified professional member of the LI for 2 years before completing an oral exam.

Experience with computer-based design applications is also advisable.

For both positions it is possible to obtain a ROLO card. This entitles you to membership of the Register of Land Based Operatives. To qualify for this you will need a Level 2 or 3 Work Based Diploma (a new NVQ course), and accredited health and safety training. More information is available on the British Association of Landscape Industries (BALI) website.

What the work involves

Landscaper
You will do the practical work of turning a landscape architect's plan into reality.

You will operate machinery, carry out planting schemes, put up fences, create ponds, lay paths, construct decking and make terraces.

Landscape manager
You will use your specialist knowledge to advise others on the development and maintenance of a wide range of landscapes such as historic gardens, motorway verges and public parks. You will decide where to place features such as footpaths and play areas, oversee the people contracted to carry out work, complete reports and manage budgets.

Type of person suited to this work

You must enjoy working outdoors and want to make a difference to the environment. You will be interested in making, building and constructing hard landscaping but will also appreciate and understand the impact that different plants can have.

Landscaper
You will need to be physically strong in order to use machinery and hand tools, be fit and enjoy the physical demands of this manual profession.

Landscape manager
An understanding of the laws surrounding the environment and the countryside is essential.

Working conditions

Landscaper
You will be outdoors in all weathers creating the design and working on landscape maintenance. There is a lot of physical labour involved such as heavy lifting, operating machinery and digging. You will need to wear protective clothing.

Landscape manager
You will work in an office for a lot of your time, but you will also go out for meetings to check and supervise work on-site. On average you will work 37 hours a week, though overtime may be required. You may need to spend time away from home.

Future prospects

Landscape staff work for local authorities, botanical gardens, large private estates, the National Trust, English Heritage, building contractors and landscape design houses.

Landscape managers in government can follow a structured career path; in other organisations you may find yourself moving companies in order to progress.

Self-employment is also an option.

Advantages/disadvantages

You will get satisfaction from knowing your work will have an impact on future generations.

You could get wet, cold, hot and dusty.

You will not be able to do this work if you suffer from pollen or dust allergies.

Money guide

Landscaper
Starting salaries are around £15,000 per year increasing to £19,000–£20,500 for those with experience.

Landscape manager
Starting salaries are around £20,000 rising to between £25,000 and £45,000 with experience.

Related opportunities

- Gardener/Garden Designer p251
- Groundsperson/Greenkeeper p253
- Landscape Architect/Designer p256

Further information

British Association of Landscape Industries (BALI)
www.bali.org.uk

Landscape Institute
www.landscapeinstitute.org

PARKS OFFICER

ENTRY LEVEL 1

Qualifications and courses

No formal qualifications are required for this work although 5 GCSEs/National 5s (A*–E/A–E) may be helpful. The Advanced Apprenticeship in Horticulture provides a good route to training as a parks officer.

Many people begin their career as gardeners/horticulturists. NVQs/SVQs in Amenity Horticulture (Levels 1–2) are available and useful qualifications to take at the early stages of your career. City & Guilds also offer several relevant courses such as the Level 1 Award in Practical Horticulture Skills, the Award in Work-Based Horticulture (Levels 1–3), the Level 2 Certificate in Horticulture, and the Level 3 Certificate in Horticulture.

Other training options include the BTEC qualifications in Horticulture or Countryside Management (Levels 2–3), the BTEC Level 4 HNC in Horticulture, and the BTEC Level 5 HND in Horticulture. Due to job competition a Foundation or Honours degree in horticulture, landscape design, landscape management or a related subject may be required. The minimum requirements for entry on to a Foundation degree or HND are normally 1 A level/2 H grades and 4 GCSEs/National 5s (A*–C/A–C); for a degree course the minimum requirements are normally 2 A levels/3 H grades and 5 GCSEs/National 5s (A*–C/A–C), usually including English and Maths, or equivalent.

The Royal Horticultural Society (RHS) also provides courses from entry to degree level, such as the Level 1 Award in Practical Horticulture, the Diploma in the Principles and Practices of Horticulture (Levels 2–3) and the Master of Horticulture (RHS) Award.

What the work involves

You will supervise the gardeners and horticulturists who maintain and look after local parks, sports and recreation centres, gardens and public places. As well as planning new planting schemes you will organise staffing rotas and annual work programmes. You will be responsible for the recruitment and monitoring of your team, as well as budget control.

You will have to liaise with your employer (normally your local government) and other department colleagues.

Type of person suited to this work

To do this work you must be organised, able to plan ahead and capable of managing people. You will need technical and practical horticultural skills, an understanding of budgets and you should be an effective negotiator.

You must have a good understanding of plants and how to present outside spaces so they look good throughout the year.

To do this job you will need to be physically fit and passionate about your work.

Working conditions

You will normally work Monday to Friday but at busier times, particularly in the spring and summer, you may do extra hours.

You will be provided with protective clothing and you will have to ensure that health and safety rules are followed by your teams. This work might be unsuitable if you suffer from asthma, pollen allergies or some skin conditions.

A small part of your job will involve working in an office at a computer where you will spend time ordering plants and materials.

Future prospects

Most parks officers are employed by a local or county council. A small number work for companies who win park management contracts. Some jobs have been hit by cutbacks from the recession, and cutbacks are still occurring, most recently at the Snowdonia National Park Authority. This may affect the number of jobs available.

It is likely that you will start your career as a gardener or horticulturist and then progress to a parks officer role once you have gained sufficient experience.

You may also move into department or divisional management within local/county authorities.

Advantages/disadvantages

This is a mixture of indoor and outdoor work, using a variety of skills.

You will use your experience and knowledge to make a difference in your local community.

You might have to wait for opportunities to become available or be willing to relocate to progress in this career.

Money guide

Your earnings depend on the size and location of your local authority employer, and the number of staff and sites that you are responsible for.

Starting salaries are usually around £17,000.

Experienced parks officers could earn up to £27,000.

Those employed in a senior role could achieve in excess of £30,000.

Related opportunities

- Countryside Ranger p241
- Groundsperson/Greenkeeper p253
- Horticultural Worker/Manager p254

Further information

Chartered Institute for the Management of Sport and Physical Activity
www.cimspa.co.uk

Convention of Scottish Local Authorities
www.cosla.gov.uk

Local Government Careers
www.lgjobs.com

PET BEHAVIOUR COUNSELLOR

ENTRY LEVEL 5

Qualifications and courses

There is no specific route into this career but a degree is required to either join the Association of Pet Behaviour Counsellors (APBC) or to be registered as a Certified Clinical Animal Behaviourist by the Association for the Study of Animal Behaviour (ASAB). Candidates are advised to take a degree in one of the following subjects: biological science, behavioural science, animal behaviour or equine science. ASAB and APBC provide lists of approved courses.

Typical entry requirements for an appropriate Honours degree are 2 A levels/3 H grades (which should include Biology and/or another science subject) and 5 GCSEs/National 5s (A*–C/A–C).

Those who are already employed within the animal care industry, for example as an animal welfare officer, may be able to progress into a role in pet behaviour counselling. Short training courses and diplomas are available from the Canine & Feline Behaviour Association (CFBA) and VetNet's Courses in Animal & Veterinary Education (CAVE).

It is essential that all entrants to this profession have practical experience working with animals. Opportunities to volunteer with animals in your local area are available on the Do-it website and through the RSPCA, SSPCA and the Blue Cross.

What the work involves

Pet behaviour counsellors advise owners whose pets have developed inappropriate and dangerous behaviour.

Although working with all domestic animals, you will probably focus on dogs, cats and horses. Typical problems include aggressive behaviour, soiling or destructiveness. You will also aid owners in achieving general control over their pets.

You could be connected to a veterinary practice, work in kennels, catteries and welfare societies or be freelance.

Type of person suited to this work

You will need a strong interest in animals, their care and welfare. As this job also involves working with the owner, you will have to be able to communicate with people too! You need to be tactful but also assertive.

Working with animals can be messy and smelly work, so you must be prepared to get dirty. You will also need to have lots of patience and the ability to remain calm.

You should be good at science, especially biology, and have a certain degree of business acumen along with the ability to keep records and accounts.

Working conditions

This work takes place in clinics and often in clients' homes so a driving licence would be beneficial. You could be indoors or outside in all weathers.

Some jobs will involve evening and weekend work, especially if you visit your clients and animals in their own homes. Most pet behaviour counsellors are self-employed and set their own hours.

The work can be dusty, dirty and physically demanding, so you will need to be fit and active. This profession is unsuitable for those with animal allergies.

Future prospects

Although demand across the canine and equine areas has increased due to television programmes and press coverage, there are still very limited career opportunities for this job.

Some of the larger animal welfare charities are starting to employ staff with these skills but most pet behaviour counsellors are self-employed and running their own practices.

Few people are able to work full time, so expect to supplement your earnings by teaching, lecturing and writing papers on animal behaviour.

Advantages/disadvantages

You will have the satisfaction of working with animals and improving their quality of life.

Some owners may be resistant to changing the way they deal with their pets which could be challenging.

This job offers the opportunity for self-employment but it can be difficult to establish a client list.

Money guide

Most pet behaviour counsellors are self-employed and charge fees of £85–£250 per consultation, depending on their experience and the size of the business.

Newly qualified pet behaviour counsellors can expect to earn around £15,000 per year.

With experience, you could achieve £25,000–£35,000.

Few people make a full-time living from this industry. Many supplement their income by lecturing or writing articles.

Related opportunities

- Animal Physiotherapist p237
- Animal Welfare Officer p238
- Dog Trainer/Handler p242
- Veterinary Surgeon p263

Further information

Association for the Study of Animal Behaviour
asab.nottingham.ac.uk

Association of Pet Behaviour Counsellors
www.apbc.org.uk

RACEHORSE TRAINER

ENTRY LEVEL 3

Qualifications and courses

Racehorse trainers need to be licensed with the British Horseracing Authority with one of the 3 types of licence: a Combined Licence (which permits the training of horses for both flat and jump races), a Jump Only Licence and a Flat Only Licence.

All candidates for a trainer's licence must have the QCF Level 3 Diploma in Work Based Racehorse Care and Management and they need to attend 3 week-long courses in Racehorse Management, Business Skills for Racehorse Trainers and Staff Management.

The British Horseracing Authority also requires all applicants to have at least 5 years' experience working in training establishments which should include at least 2 years in a senior position, such as assistant trainer in a racing yard. Those who have been a successful jockey will often become a racehorse trainer later in their career.

What the work involves

Trainers usually own or lease their stables and train horses for owners as well as owning horses themselves. Most trainers start as a jockey or assistant trainer and progress to running their own yard.

You will have to prepare the horses for races by increasing their stamina, technique and fitness. In order to do this you will have to create training regimes.

To be successful you will work closely with everyone in your team including other professionals such as vets and farriers.

Type of person suited to this work

You should have a strong interest in horse racing, a flair for business and an inherent talent for training horses. You will need the ability to communicate well and be a strong leader and manager of people.

This role is ideal for people who love caring for horses, have the right temperament to work with them and plenty of patience.

You will need to enjoy working outside in all weathers as this is where most of your duties will take place. You should be a practical person who is willing to get their hands dirty. You will require a certain level of physical fitness.

You need to be able to foster and build strong relationships with clients, particularly if self-employed. Creating and developing a good reputation is essential in order to get new business, and how you interact and present yourself to clients will be an important facet of that, as well as your skill as a trainer.

Working conditions

Much of your work will take place outdoors. In the summer months it may be hot, smelly and dusty, whereas in winter it could be cold, wet and muddy. You will also spend some time in an office environment.

When riding you will wear a hard hat and a body protector. Horses can be unpredictable and so there is a certain level of risk involved.

The hours are long and include weekends. There will also be some travel involved if you are required to attend race meetings. A driving licence would be useful.

Future prospects

There are around 600 licensed trainers in the UK.

Before you are granted a licence, you need several years' experience as an assistant trainer. Your success will then depend on attracting and retaining the owners of good quality horses, and lots of luck! You will need to build up a strong client base in order to progress.

Managing your own successful yard may enable you to employ staff to complete some of the more mundane tasks.

Advantages/disadvantages

This can be an extremely lucrative profession if you are successful.

Injury risks are high in all animal-related careers. This could affect your long-term career security.

Looking after horses is not a 9am to 5pm job and the hours may affect your social or family life.

Money guide

As you are likely to be self-employed, your earnings will depend on the size, success and reputation of your yard. Most yards are usually fairly small or modest in size, but large trainers can be responsible for up to 150–200 horses.

You will establish your own fees and these will be influenced by a variety of factors including costs and the market rates.

As a guide, a trainer can earn anything from £15,000 per year to over £50,000 if they are very experienced and have a good record of winning.

Related opportunities

- Farm Manager p243
- Farrier p247
- Groom/Stable Hand/Stud Hand p252

Further information

Association of British Riding Schools
www.abrs-info.org

British Horse Society
www.bhs.org.uk

British Racing School
www.brs.org.uk

SKIPPER/DECKHAND ENTRY LEVEL 2

Qualifications and courses

There are no formal academic requirements to become a deckhand but you must be at least 16 years old. School leavers have the option to apply for the Apprenticeship in Sea Fishing. Alternatively, Seafish offer the Introduction to Commercial Fishing course and the Maritime Skills Alliance run a Sea Fishing Apprenticeship programme.

New entrants must take the Marine Coastguard Agency (MCA) approved basic safety training course. This programme consists of 4 days of training in sea survival, First Aid, fire fighting and basic health and safety.

To become a skipper, you must have at least 2 years' experience working as a deckhand. Those who wish to be a limited area skipper (working around the UK coastline) must be over the age of 20 and have Seafish's Deck Officer (Fishing Vessel) Class 2 certificate. To work as an unlimited area skipper (fishing beyond UK coastal waters) you need to be at least 21 years old and study for Seafish's Deck Officer (Fishing Vessel) Class 1 certificate.

For those who wish to develop further skills and knowledge, Seafish offer various short courses on topics such as basic seamanship, net repair, navigation, engineering and stability awareness.

What the work involves

Deckhands are crew members on sea-going fishing vessels. You will spend anything from a few days to several weeks at sea. You will drop the nets, wind them in, sort the catch and then box it up. If your vessel has the facilities on-board, you might help to process fish by gutting and filleting. You might keep watch, steer the ship and use winching gear. Duties may also include vessel maintenance and cooking.

Skippers are in charge of fishing vessels. Their role includes overseeing health and safety, navigation, paperwork and crew management. They also manage the business arrangements to ensure that fishing trips return a profit.

You may also choose to work with holiday companies who run independent boat charters, sea safari or wildlife trips for tourists.

Type of person suited to this work

This work is suited to someone with practical skills and a high level of physical fitness. You should be able to cope with challenging conditions while remaining positive and focused.

A deckhand needs teamwork skills and the ability to follow instructions. Skippers should be comfortable managing and leading a team of people and able to take control of situations.

Due to the physicality of the industry, you should be physically fit and comfortable with working manually for long periods of time.

Working conditions

This is a very tough outdoor job. You will work in cold, wet and rainy conditions during the winter and hot weather during the summer.

Fishing is the most dangerous industry in the UK, with big machinery and rough seas producing a combination of risks which must be treated with great caution.

You will have to work long hours at sea, often for substantial periods away from home, and conditions below deck may be basic and cramped. There could also be some heavy lifting and carrying.

Future prospects

The career progression route is from deckhand to ship's mate and then skipper with most jobs being located around the coasts of Scotland and the south-west and east of England.

Many jobs are within family-owned businesses which have been in existence for generations, making it difficult to find work. Some are seasonal, meaning long-term security can be difficult.

Advantages/disadvantages

This job is ideal for those who love working outdoors.

You will have the opportunity to develop strong relationships with the other crew members.

Your social and family life may be difficult as you could be away at sea for extended periods of time.

Jobs are limited to certain locations in the UK.

Money guide

Earnings from fishing can vary extensively as you are often paid a share of the total value of the catch. For this reason, pay depends upon the type of boat you work on, the amount of fish caught and the weather conditions.

New entrants can expect to receive around £10,000 per year as a starting salary.

With experience, earnings can rise to £25,000.

Skippers are generally self-employed so their earnings depend on the success of their team.

Skippers who work for large companies could achieve up to £65,000.

Related opportunities

- Coastguard Watch Assistant/Officer p520
- Fish Farmer p248
- Merchant Navy Deck Officer/Rating p582

Further information

Maritime and Coastguard Agency
www.dft.gov.uk/mca/

Scottish Fishermen's Federation
www.sff.co.uk

Seafish
www.seafish.org

VETERINARY NURSE

ENTRY LEVEL 3

Qualifications and courses

You usually enter this profession through work-based training. For those aged 16–24, the Apprenticeship in Veterinary Nursing is available at Advanced Level.

Alternatively, you can study for the Level 3 Diploma in Veterinary Nursing from the Royal College of Veterinary Surgeons (RCVS). This can be completed on a full-time basis or alongside work in a veterinary practice. Qualifying takes 2–3 years and involves practical training and college-based learning.

Entry requirements for the RCVS scheme are 5 GCSEs/National 5s (A*–C/A–C) including English, Maths and 2 science subjects. Trainees must be at least 16 years old and there is strong competition for places. For those without these qualifications, an alternative route may be through the ABC Level 2 Certificate for Animal Nursing Assistants, the City & Guilds Level 2 Diploma for Veterinary Care Assistants, the CQ Level 2 Diploma in Veterinary Nursing, or the BTEC Level 3 Certificate in Animal Management.

You could also complete an RCVS-approved veterinary nursing degree or Foundation degree. Entry requirements are 2 A levels/3 H grades, ideally in Biology and Chemistry, and 5 GCSEs/National 5s (A*–C/A–C).

Work experience with a veterinary practice or an animal charity would be helpful in supporting any job or course application.

What the work involves

Veterinary nurses assist vets in their work by helping to treat animals suffering from disease and injury. Most nurses also undertake the day-to-day care of animals recovering from treatment within veterinary hospitals.

As well as carrying out simple procedures, such as changing dressings and nail trimming, you will also examine blood and urine samples, give injections, prepare and help in the theatre and sterilise the instruments after use. You might also work in reception, giving an initial assessment of animals, ordering drugs and arranging future appointments.

Type of person suited to this work

You will have to be passionate about animals and want to help them. You need the capacity to learn scientific information about different diseases and treatments.

Although lots of animals recover, some of this work will be distressing. This means you will have to work in a practical and unsentimental way.

As you will work closely with animal owners, you will also need to have excellent communication skills to explain what is happening to their pet.

You may need administrative and IT skills to complete duties on reception.

Working conditions

Depending on the type of practice you are employed by, your role may involve working with small animals, horses, farm animals, or even zoo animals.

Most of your work will take place indoors, possibly in a treatment room, operating theatre or on the reception desk. If you work with large animals, you may have to travel to visit farms or zoos.

Working with animals can be noisy and dirty. This job would be unsuitable for those with animal allergies or a fear of blood. You will usually be provided with a uniform and you will be expected to wear protective clothing during some procedures.

Future prospects

You could be employed by zoos, wildlife centres, animal welfare centres, veterinary hospitals and charities such as the People's Dispensary for Sick Animals (PDSA).

With experience, you could progress to become a supervisor, practice manager or head nurse, or move into related areas such as research.

You could also lecture, specialise in an area such as animal behaviour or become a representative for a veterinary drugs company.

Advantages/disadvantages

Helping sick animals is very rewarding.

The role is interesting, with lots of variety and the chance to meet many people and animals.

You will deal with illness and death which can be stressful and upsetting.

You may have to work irregular hours which will affect your social life.

Money guide

You can expect a starting salary of £10,500–£14,000.

As you gain experience, your earnings can increase to £22,000.

Head nurses or supervisors can achieve £25,000 or more, depending on the size and type of the practice they work for.

Related opportunities

- Dog Trainer/Handler p242
- Veterinary Surgeon p263
- Zookeeper p265

Further information

British Veterinary Nursing Association
www.bvna.org.uk

People's Dispensary for Sick Animals (PDSA)
www.pdsa.org.uk

VETERINARY SURGEON

ENTRY LEVEL 6

Qualifications and courses

In order to practise as a vet, all candidates are required to have a degree in veterinary science/veterinary medicine and register with the Royal College of Veterinary Surgeons (RCVS). Degrees approved by the RCVS are currently available at 7 institutions in the UK. Normal minimum entry requirements for a degree are 3 A levels/4 H grades including Biology and 1 or 2 from Chemistry, Physics or Maths. Depending upon the individual university, you will be expected to have either 2 A grades and a B or 3 A grades (or equivalent). A good range of GCSEs/National 5s (A*–C/A–C) required. For the University of Cambridge, an additional admissions test, the BioMedical Admissions Test (BMAT), will need to be sat.

Degree courses usually last 5 years but courses may include an optional additional year in which students gain an Honours degree in a related science subject. All courses include the 38 weeks of practical experience required by the RCVS.

All universities expect applicants to demonstrate their passion for animals and commitment to a career as a veterinary surgeon by undertaking relevant work experience. Candidates could work on farms, in stables, kennels or vets and opportunities to volunteer with animals are available on the Do-it website or through the RSPCA, SSPCA and the Blue Cross.

What the work involves

Vets treat animals that are suffering because of disease or injury. They administer vaccinations, prescribe drugs and deliver newborn animals. They also advise owners on caring for their animals. You might carry out surgical operations and be involved in the inspection of livestock and meat.

You could work in local practices and become a specialist carrying out complex surgery on a certain part of the anatomy or become an expert on a particular animal.

Type of person suited to this work

You must have the capacity to learn large amounts of complex scientific information and apply this in a practical way to treat animals.

Some of your work will be sad or distressing, so you will have to work in a practical and unsentimental way. You must have good communication skills to talk to the owners.

Working with large animals is physically demanding so you will need to be in good health. This job will not suit those who dislike the sight of blood or suffer from animal allergies.

Working conditions

Your working conditions will depend on the type of practice that employs you. In veterinary practices for small animals, you will spend a lot of time in the surgery. Working with farm livestock and horses, you will travel to visit your patients.

Some of this work will be unpleasant or smelly and involve travelling long distances. A driving licence is required.

Your job may be dangerous as animals can be unpredictable. You will work long hours and be on-call to cover emergencies 24/7.

Future prospects

With a strong record of work experience, there are still jobs and practices to join upon graduation, although it is not as easy as it was owing to an increased intake of veterinary science students by RCVS-accredited institutions.

As a graduate, you will normally join an established practice. With experience, you could progress to become a partner (effectively part-owner) of a practice.

There are around 20,000 registered vets in the UK. The majority of these work in private practice. Some vets work for the government or for firms researching and producing animal pharmaceuticals.

Advantages/disadvantages

The training is long and very competitive to enter. In this career you will never stop learning – more experience will make you a better vet.

It can be a very stressful but rewarding job, with lots of responsibility.

You will have to deal with the death of some of the animals you treat, including times when you put them down.

Money guide

Salaries vary according to experience, specialisations, and the size, type and location of the practice you work in.

Newly qualified vets have a starting salary of £20,000–£30,000.

As you gain experience, your earnings can range from £35,000 up to £48,000 for a senior vet.

A senior partner in a veterinary practice can achieve in excess of £50,000.

Employers may include accommodation and a company car within your benefits package.

Related opportunities

- Farm Manager p243
- Hospital Doctor p292
- Veterinary Nurse p262

Further information

British Veterinary Association
www.bva.co.uk

People's Dispensary for Sick Animals (PDSA)
www.pdsa.org.uk

Royal College of Veterinary Surgeons
www.rcvs.org.uk

WATER BAILIFF/FISHERIES OFFICER

ENTRY LEVEL 2

Qualifications and courses

Fisheries officers generally enter with a degree/HND in subjects such as marine sciences, environmental sciences, and land management. Gaining a relevant postgraduate qualification may help candidates. If you do not possess these qualifications you could build up relevant work experience as a water bailiff.

In England and Wales, there are no set requirements for those wishing to become a water bailiff. In Scotland, you have to pass a training module set by the Institute of Fisheries Management and in Northern Ireland, you need at least 5 GCSEs/National 5s at C grade or above, including English and Maths.

Basic practical fishery experience is essential as competition is fierce. Many people work unpaid for angling clubs or undertake voluntary work on fishing boats. The Environment Agency (EA) also offers a summer placement programme.

The Scottish Institute of Fisheries Management (IFM) offers a course in Fisheries Management. You can choose between a 1-year certificate or 2-year diploma, covering all aspects of working with fish and pond life. You can also follow an NVQ in Fisheries Management if you choose to do so.

This is a popular second career, and if you want to get into the field then any experience you can gain in gamekeeping, security work, police work or farm work will be advantageous. Medical examinations usually need to be passed.

What the work involves

Water bailiffs work outdoors, maintaining lakes or rivers and everything that lives in them, for the purpose of legitimate recreational use.

You will confront 2 main problems in your work: breaches of the law and ecological problems.

You will basically be a gamekeeper for water. Water bailiffs have the same powers of search and arrest as police officers. You would mostly be looking out for poachers and lawbreakers, and you will be granted a warrant by the Environment Agency.

Type of person suited to this work

Ideally, you should be a friendly yet firm person, able to deal with members of the public effectively and politely, sometimes in difficult disciplinary situations.

An interest in the environment and working outdoors is really useful, as is knowledge of waterways. You need to be aware of the main environmental threats, understand the basics of how ecosystems maintain themselves and know about fish diseases and biology.

You also need to know about fishery law, not only in the UK (although this is most useful), but also at EU level. Be aware that it may even be different at local level, for example if you live in Scotland.

Working conditions

You will spend the majority of your time outside, patrolling areas either in a car, by boat or on foot.

You will usually work between 37 and 39 hours per week, which will involve night shifts and weekends. Part-time or seasonal work is also available.

The work is physical and tiring. You may have to pursue offenders across rough terrain on foot, and could find yourself wading through cold rivers and ponds. For this reason, you will probably spend your days in waterproofs, wellies and even lifejackets.

Future prospects

The public sector provides well-defined career paths, although you may choose to move into private consultancy. The Centre for Environment, Fisheries and Aquaculture Science, and Marine Scotland are possible public organisations to work for, but it is likely you will end up with the Environment Agency in some capacity.

Once you are working for the Environment Agency, many possibilities arise. You will have the opportunity to become a team leader within the agency, and this may lead to promotion and managerial opportunities.

Another option would be to move into related areas of work, such as fish farming or gamekeeping. Once you have a little experience in the area it will be possible to choose what interests you most, and in which direction you want your career to progress.

Advantages/disadvantages

This can be a really satisfying and exciting job, and if you enjoy being outside, you will probably thoroughly enjoy the job.

It can be lonely, and conditions can be hard if you are not naturally a country person.

You need to be prepared for all weather conditions, and work can be cold, wet, and tiring.

Money guide

Salaries vary, and can range from £14,500 to £26,500 upwards per year.

With 10 to 15 years' experience you can expect to be earning up to £34,000.

Those in the most senior positions earn around £40,000 per year.

Related opportunities

- Countryside Ranger p241
- Fish Farmer p248
- Gamekeeper p250

Further information

Environment Agency
www.gov.uk/government/organisations/environment-agency

Institute of Fisheries Management
www.ifm.org.uk

ZOOKEEPER

ENTRY LEVEL 2

Qualifications and courses

No specific qualifications are required for entry although GCSEs/National 5s (A*–C/A–C), especially in English and science subjects, will be useful. It is, however, becoming increasingly necessary to gain higher level qualifications as this is a very competitive area.

Foundation degrees or Honours degrees in subjects such as zoology are also available. Typical entry requirements for a degree course are 2 A levels/3 H grades, including a science, and 5 GCSEs/National 5s (A*–C/A–C). Sparsholt College in Hampshire offers a Foundation degree in Zoo Resource Management for people in relevant employment.

General animal care and management courses are available and include the NVQ in Animal Care (Levels 1–3), the ABC Award and Diploma in Work-based Animal Care (Levels 1–3), the City & Guilds Level 2 Certificate in Animal Care, the City & Guilds Level 3 Certificate in Animal Care, the Advanced National Certificate in the Management of Zoo Animals, and the Advanced National Level 3 Diploma in Animal Management. Alternatively, there are the BTEC qualifications in Animal Management (Levels 2–3), and the BTEC Level 4 HNC and Level 5 HND in Animal Management.

Experience, proven interest and interaction with animals is incredibly important, sometimes favoured over qualifications, but often a requirement of application. Volunteering at a zoo or animal sanctuary would be beneficial, but these programmes are very popular and you may be placed on a waiting list. Apprenticeships may be available if you are aged 16–24.

What the work involves

You could work in a zoo, safari, wildlife or birdlife park or aquarium where you will care for animals (ranging from mammals to birds, reptiles to amphibians, fish to invertebrates etc) and their surroundings.

You will provide food, water and fresh bedding for the animals in your care. You will clean out enclosures and check the animals for signs of injury or disease, keeping records of feeding, health and behaviour and informing veterinary staff if there are any issues.

Many zoos stress the importance of conservation and education and some of your work may involve leading tours and giving presentations to visitors.

Type of person suited to this work

You need to be passionate about the care and wellbeing of animals in your care. This requires patience, observation and the desire to handle and be around animals.

Most of this work is done outdoors and can be physically demanding so a fit, active person who is not afraid of physical work would be well suited to the job.

Some animals you will work with could be dangerous, so you will have to respect them and be aware of your own and others' safety.

Working conditions

Animals require 24/7 care so you will be expected to work 5–6 days a week. This is normally organised on a shift system which includes early mornings, late evenings, weekends and bank holidays, especially during busy periods.

Your work will be physically demanding and often dirty. A uniform will be provided. If you suffer from allergies, this work will be difficult for you.

Work could be seasonal as some centres close for part of the year.

Future prospects

There are over 350 zoos and wildlife parks throughout the UK, although the number of stand-alone zoos, rather than those as part of a larger complex, is significantly lower. Jobs can be hard to find and competition for employment will be high so be prepared to move for work or promotion.

You may choose to specialise and work with one species. You could also be promoted to senior keeper or head keeper.

You may also choose to move into related work such as becoming an RSPCA inspector.

Advantages/disadvantages

This can be difficult work to enter and progress in and the financial rewards can be small.

You will be working with some unusual or exotic animals, with some opportunity to specialise.

A variety of tasks with lots of different animals can keep the job interesting.

The role of zoos as centres of breeding and supporting conservation has increased recently, so you could undertake important work.

Money guide

Pay will depend on your location and type of zoo or animal park. Many jobs include free or subsidised accommodation.

Trainees can start at about £10,000–£13,000 per year.

With experience, this can rise to £16,000.

Senior keepers earn around £17,000–£30,000 a year.

Related opportunities

- Animal Welfare Officer p238
- Dog Trainer/Handler p242
- Veterinary Surgeon p263

Further information

Association of British and Irish Wild Animal Keepers
www.abwak.co.uk

British and Irish Association of Zoos and Aquariums
www.biaza.org.uk

Healthcare

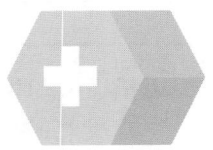

If you are keen to pursue a career in healthcare you must be compassionate and enjoy either caring for people or deciding what treatment they should receive. There is such a wide variety of jobs available in this sector simply because you can specialise in absolutely any aspect of human healthcare. Many jobs require a lot of training and you can expect to work in some highly pressurised and sometimes distressing situations. Workers in healthcare are extremely dedicated and enthusiastic about their careers, which rarely constitute a 9am–5pm job.

The jobs featured in this section are listed below. For similar jobs to the ones in this section turn to *Science, Mathematics and Statistics* on page 477 and *Social Work and Counselling Services* on page 543.

ACUPUNCTURIST

ENTRY LEVEL 5

Qualifications and courses

Careers in acupuncture are open to all graduates and diplomates although a degree or HND in a related subject such as life or medical sciences may increase your chances of employment.

Degrees are not compulsory though and experience and determination is just as important. Previous experience of advice work or counselling may enable entry into the profession.

Acupuncture is currently only regulated by voluntary agreement but the British Acupuncture Council (BAcC) works with the British Acupuncture Accreditation Board (BAAB) to offer training courses. The courses generally take 2–3 years to complete full time. Entry onto one of the courses requires at least 2 or 3 A levels/H grades, science subjects preferred, and 5 GCSEs/National 5s. The British Medical Acupuncture Society (BMAS) also offers a Certificate of Basic Competence (COBC) and a Diploma in Medical Acupuncture (DipMedAc).

These accredited training courses lead to professional membership of the BAcC which offers protection and public liability insurance. You are also required to register with your local authority.

Courses vary, but generally cover topics such as anatomy and physiology, techniques and acupuncture points, ethical issues, clinical experience, and advice on setting up a practice.

Some courses are even available at postgraduate and doctorate levels.

What the work involves

Acupuncturists work from ancient Chinese holistic guidelines. They treat medical illnesses and imbalances by inserting very fine needles into identified pressure points on the human body.

You will need to talk to patients about their problems, taking plenty of notes, in order to explore their lifestyle and emotional state, and then assess all of these factors to determine a suitable treatment.

In addition you may carry out procedures such as burning herbs on needles, and passing small electric currents through them.

Type of person suited to this work

You must be very personable, with excellent communication skills in order to elicit trust and personal information from your patients, as well as being able to explain the techniques you are using to them.

You will need an analytical mind in order to understand each patient's problem and formulate a beneficial course of treatment. Being comfortable with close and physical contact is also important when examining and treating your patients.

As you will probably be running your own business, you will need excellent business acumen in order to successfully take on aspects such as marketing, accounting, and administrative tasks.

Working conditions

Hours vary and tend to fit around the needs of clients. This usually involves evening and weekend work.

You could work from your own rented treatment room, from home, in your patients' homes, or in hospices, health clinics and addiction treatment centres. As you may work across a number of locations, a driving licence is useful.

You will usually be working on your feet, standing and bending a lot. Conditions have to be clean and sterile, and there are strict health and safety guidelines to adhere to.

Future prospects

Most acupuncturists are self-employed, although a few find work at medical centres or centres which specialise in complementary medicine.

If you are self-employed, the success of your career depends on your reputation and marketing skills. If you build up a strong client base there are plenty of opportunities for expansion and even setting up your own health clinic.

Many practising acupuncturists choose to teach their subject, or carry out research and write articles for books and magazines.

Advantages/disadvantages

This can be a really rewarding career, especially if you like being with people and enjoy helping them.

You may hear distressing stories and have insight into some upsetting personal lives, so you need to be able to leave work at work.

Money guide

Earnings in acupuncture depend a lot on your situation, marketing ability, experience and how many patients you treat. As a newly qualified acupuncturist starting up your own practice, you will probably earn around £12,000 per year.

Once you have started to build up clients and gain experience, you can expect to earn up to £30,000 a year.

If you grow your business into a large established practice, your earnings may rise to about £40,000 a year.

Per session, acupuncturists charge around £40, although this can rise to up to £90 in London.

Related opportunities

- Chiropractor p275
- Counsellor p547
- Homeopath p291

Further information

British Acupuncture Accreditation Board
www.baab.co.uk

British Acupuncture Council
www.acupuncture.org.uk

The Acupuncture Society
www.acupuncturesociety.org.uk

ADULT NURSE

ENTRY LEVEL 6

Qualifications and courses

You must hold a degree in adult nursing which has been approved by the Nursing and Midwifery Council (NMC). Minimum entry requirements for a degree are usually 2–3 A levels/H grades, ideally including a science-based subject, and 5 GCSEs/National 5s (A*–C/A–C) including English, maths and a science subject. All applicants must obtain clearance from the Disclosure and Barring Service (DBS) before commencing their training.

If you do not have the required GCSEs/A levels, some universities will accept other qualifications, such as the BTEC Level 3 qualifications in Health and Social Care (Health Sciences), or an Access to Higher Education Diploma in a science or health-related subject. Check your desired university for their specific entry requirements.

Graduates with a degree in a health-related subject such as human biology, life and medical sciences or biomedical science, may be eligible to enter the nursing profession by taking an accelerated 2-year programme which leads to a Master of Science (MSc) or Postgraduate Diploma.

Pre-entry experience is not essential, but relevant experience as a care worker or in some other work with people is good preparation.

You are eligible to register as a nurse with the NMC once you have completed an approved nursing degree. Nurses are expected to engage in continuing professional development (CPD) throughout their career to keep their skills and knowledge up to date.

What the work involves

Adult nurses assess the needs of each patient in order to plan a care programme for them. You will work alongside doctors and other medical practitioners to observe how patients progress on treatment plans and modify them as necessary. You will also give patients practical care such as administering medicines and injections, changing dressings and checking blood pressure.

You could work in a variety of positions, such as a community nurse, occupational nurse or healthcare assistant.

Type of person suited to this work

You will be working with patients from all parts of the community who will have a wide range of problems, so it is essential to remain non-judgemental and sympathetic. A clear understanding of confidentiality is essential.

You will need excellent communication skills in order to interact with patients, explain care plans and illnesses, and calm those who are angry or distressed.

You will also need to be very practical with good manual dexterity for undertaking precision jobs such as taking blood.

Working conditions

You will usually work 37.5 hours per week but overtime is available for those who want it. If you are working in a hospital, these hours will include night and weekend shifts.

You could work in a number of locations including hospitals, GP surgeries, prisons, hospices and in patients' homes. If you are required to travel around in the local community, a driving licence is useful.

Adult nurses in hospitals work in specific wards, such as intensive care or accident and emergency.

Future prospects

Despite student numbers increasing, there is still a shortage of trained adult nurses. Over the past 4 years, around 4,000 senior nursing jobs have been cut, but employment prospects generally remain good.

The majority of job opportunities lie within the NHS, although other employers include private hospitals, the armed forces, hospices and nursing homes, and the prison service.

With experience and additional qualifications, you could specialise in a subject of interest such as neurology or cardiology, and go on to become a nurse consultant.

UK nursing qualifications are recognised across the globe so there are opportunities to work abroad.

Advantages/disadvantages

Helping a wide range of people to get better or become more independent is both rewarding and enjoyable.

There are opportunities to work flexible hours or part time. Career breaks are common and the NHS runs specialist courses to get nurses who have had a break back up to speed quickly.

You may have to deal with distressed, angry or violent patients.

Money guide

Nurses' salaries follow a rising scale divided into 9 bands. As a fully qualified nurse you could start in band 5, which pays between £21,178 and £27,625. Those who take on a senior position with additional responsibilities can advance towards band 6, which pays up to £34,189.

If you specialise in a particular area and undertake the training to become a nurse consultant, you could advance towards band 7, which pays £30,460–£40,157, band 8, which pays £38,851–£67,805.

Related opportunities

- Hospital Doctor p292
- Learning Disabilities Nurse p294
- Mental Health Nurse p297

Further information

NHS Careers
www.nhscareers.nhs.uk

Nursing and Midwifery Council
www.nmc-uk.org

Royal College of Nursing
www.rcn.org.uk

ANAESTHETIST

ENTRY LEVEL 8

Qualifications and courses

Candidates must first train as a hospital doctor by completing a medical degree which is approved by the General Medical Council (GMC). Entry requirements for medical school are very high A level/H grade results including relevant subjects such as science and maths. You may also be asked to take the UK Clinical Aptitude Test (UKCAT) when you apply for your degree.

After completing a medical degree, candidates undergo 7 years of specialist postgraduate training. Stage 1 involves a 2-year Foundation Programme of general training. This acts as the bridge between medical school and specialist training. The second stage is 3 years of core training in acute care and candidates then move on to the final stage: higher specialty training in anaesthesia, intensive care medicine and pain management.

After successfully completing the higher specialty stage, trainees receive a Certificate of Completion of Training (CCT) and become eligible to join the GMC Specialist Register.

Anaesthetists must engage in continuing professional development (CPD) throughout their career to ensure that their skills and knowledge are up to date. The Royal College of Anaesthetists provides information on available training.

What the work involves

Anaesthetists are qualified hospital doctors who have undergone further training in anaesthesia. You will prepare and administer drugs to make patients unconscious and pain free during surgery. You will monitor patients during the procedure and bring them back to consciousness afterwards. You will also give local anaesthesia to specific areas of the body.

In addition, you will give pain relief after surgery to seriously ill patients or during procedures such as childbirth. Anaesthetists also work in intensive care, resuscitation and pain management.

Type of person suited to this work

Anaesthetists need excellent communication skills: you must be reassuring and a good listener in order to gain patients' trust and explain procedures to them. You should work well in a team and be able to give and follow instructions.

You must be able to stay calm in an emergency and make decisions under pressure. You will need the confidence and skill to use complicated equipment and administer powerful drugs safely and accurately. You should have a strong sense of the responsibility involved in this job.

You will need to be prepared to undergo a long programme of education and training in order to gain the in-depth knowledge and skills necessary to become an anaesthetist.

Working conditions

Anaesthetists work in operating theatres, wards, clinics and accident and emergency departments within hospitals.

You will work shifts as part of an on-call rota, which includes working at nights, weekends and on bank holidays.

You will handle potentially dangerous drugs and equipment.

Future prospects

There are opportunities throughout the UK, mainly within the NHS but also in private hospitals and clinics.

Promotion to consultant posts is very competitive. Anaesthetists may work in sub-specialities such as paediatrics, obstetrics, cardiac surgery, resuscitation or intensive care.

Once fully qualified you will probably be expected to teach and examine students and trainees and to carry out research.

Advantages/disadvantages

Being responsible for the safety of patients in your care and dealing with emergency situations makes this a very demanding job.

It is rewarding to be able to help patients through surgery and other medical procedures by providing pain relief.

Money guide

Salary levels in the NHS may vary in different locations.

Junior doctors have a starting salary of £22,000–£28,000 during the 2-year Foundation Programme.

When undertaking the specialty training, you can expect to earn between £28,000 and £46,000 a year.

Consultant anaesthetists can achieve salaries ranging from £74,000 up to £170,000 for those in the most senior positions.

Earnings are often higher in private practice work.

Related opportunities

- Doctor (GP) p285
- Hospital Doctor p292
- Pathologist p305

Further information

British Medical Association
www.bma.org.uk

The Association of Anaesthetists of Great Britain and Ireland
www.aagbi.org

The Royal College of Anaesthetists
www.rcoa.ac.uk

AROMATHERAPIST

ENTRY LEVEL 3

Qualifications and courses

There are no formal academic requirements for aromatherapists. Professional training courses are the standard method of entry and you usually have to be at least 18 years old to enrol.

The General Regulatory Council for Complementary Therapies (GRCCT) has devised National Occupational Standards (NOS) for aromatherapy. If you wish to operate as a professional aromatherapist, you must ensure that you choose a course which meets the NOS. Courses which conform to the standards are offered at diploma, Foundation degree or degree level. Short courses are only advised for those with a personal (rather than professional) interest in aromatherapy. The Aromatherapy Council provides information on choosing a course. Prior experience in a related profession, such as massage, will help your application.

Most courses include modules on anatomy, physiology, pathology, therapeutic relationships and the theory and practice of aromatherapy. You will also consider the practicalities of being a professional aromatherapist, covering topics such as legal and ethical issues and business studies.

Once qualified, you can improve your career prospects by registering with the Complementary & Natural Healthcare Council (CNHC).

What the work involves

Aromatherapists use essential oils to improve the health and wellbeing of clients.

You will be required to look into the medical history of all your clients, discussing their lifestyle, diet, exercise, allergies and stress levels. Using the information gathered, you will decide on blends and mixes of oils appropriate for the needs of the client.

You will administer oils to the skin by massage, provide instructions for aftercare and maintain records of each of your clients.

Type of person suited to this work

You must be very personable with excellent communication skills in order to explain the techniques you are using and elicit trust and personal information from your patients. Being comfortable with close and physical contact is also important when examining and treating your patients.

You need an analytical mind in order to understand each patient's problem and formulate a beneficial course of treatment.

As you will probably be self-employed, you need excellent business acumen to undertake marketing, accounting and administrative tasks.

Working conditions

Aromatherapists tend to run their own businesses so working conditions vary. You could rent a treatment room in a health clinic, gym or leisure centre, work from home or travel to patients' homes to provide treatment. Hours depend on individual schedules and the needs and demands of clients. You should expect to work evenings and weekends. Part-time hours are a possibility.

Rooms and workspaces must be clean and quiet, and most aromatherapists tend to wear white clothes.

You will be bending, stretching and spending most of the day on your feet.

Future prospects

Success in aromatherapy depends on effective business skills. If you build a strong client base and market your services well, your practice will grow into a successful business.

You could train in another relevant therapy such as homeopathy, reflexology or counselling, which could attract more clients.

If you like the idea of working abroad, you could take your skills overseas. You must ensure that the country you choose recognises your qualifications.

Advantages/disadvantages

This can be a really rewarding career, especially if you are sociable and enjoy helping people.

There is a lot to remember in aromatherapy so it requires a calm and intelligent person to be familiar with all the oils and administer them carefully.

Money guide

Most aromatherapists are self-employed and charge a fee of between £20 and £50 per session.

Income will depend upon your experience, reputation and the number of clients you treat.

During the process of building up your practice, earnings can be quite low – possibly ranging from £2,000 to £10,000 a year. Many aromatherapists have another job to supplement their income.

With experience and an established business, you could achieve between £15,000 and £30,000.

Related opportunities

- Acupuncturist p268
- Beauty Therapist p431
- Homeopath p291

Further information

General Regulatory Council for Complementary Therapies
www.grcct.org

Institute for Complementary and Natural Medicine
http://icnm.org.uk

ART THERAPIST

ENTRY LEVEL 7

Qualifications and courses

To work as an art therapist you must complete a postgraduate qualification that has been approved by the British Association of Art Therapists (BAAT). It is also possible to specialise in music or drama therapy and for these roles you would need to complete a course by their specific approved association.

Although arts-based first degrees are preferred for entry to postgraduate courses, other subjects such as psychology, education and nursing may all be acceptable. To apply for a master's you will need a strong portfolio, and at least a year's experience in working in health, education or social care. Substantial clinical work experience, a relevant HND may also be considered for entry.

A master's degree course lasts 2 years full time, or 4 years part time. Many areas are covered, including psychodynamics, psychopathology of art, contemporary art therapy and practice skills.

You will have to have therapy yourself as part of training, and will also be expected to spend 120 days on clinical placement during the course.

Once you have qualified, you need to register with the Health Professions Council (HPC).

What the work involves

Therapists use a range of mediums of art to help clients who may have difficulty in expressing themselves through words.

You may work closely with people suffering from mental health problems, emotional problems, or those with drug and alcohol addiction, helping them to recover. People with speech and language difficulties also benefit from art therapy.

You will create a safe environment where patients feel free to express themselves and their feelings and move on positively.

Type of person suited to this work

If you want to work with people with emotional and psychological difficulties, you need to be a calm, caring, understanding and trustworthy person. You will need a lot of patience, excellent communication skills, and a very sensitive nature.

These skills need to be combined with strong artistic ability: you have to be a creative thinker prepared to take on the responsibility of helping clients who may be in a great deal of emotional pain. An interest in all forms of art is also essential.

If you plan on starting your own business, you will need good marketing and accounting skills.

Working conditions

Conditions depend on who you choose to work for. If being employed by the NHS appeals to you, you are likely to work 37.5 hours per week, with weekends free. If you work in private practice, your hours will vary and will probably include evenings and weekends.

As a therapist, you will probably have to travel around to give therapy, so a driving licence is really useful. You could work in hospitals, prisons, clinics and community centres.

Surroundings for therapy must always be warm, light and comfortable, so you can expect this to be your working environment.

Future prospects

There tend to be few advertised vacancies for art therapists. If you work for yourself, you can grow and expand your business by building up a solid client base and making good contacts.

If you choose to work for the NHS, you could be promoted to management positions; becoming a specialist, head of profession, or consultant.

You might decide to specialise within a particular area, such as mental health or palliative care. Alternatively, you could combine art therapy with another complementary treatment such as psychotherapy.

Advantages/disadvantages

If you have both a love of art and a desire to help people this will prove a very rewarding career.

Opportunities for progression are good, and experiences can be enriching and very fulfilling; there will never be a boring day at work.

You will have to deal with people who are in pain or mentally unstable, which can be extremely upsetting.

Money guide

As a newly qualified art therapist working for the NHS your salary will typically reach £25,472–£34,189.

If you set up your own practice your initial salary will probably be less.

As you gain experience this figure can rise to about £40,000 a year.

If you get into a management or supervisory role, you can earn around £46,600 a year.

Related opportunities

- Clinical/Health Psychologist p546
- Counsellor p547
- Learning Disabilities Nurse p294

Further information

British Association of Art Therapists
www.baat.org

Health and Care Professions Council
www.hpc-uk.org

NHS Careers
www.nhscareers.nhs.uk

AUDIOLOGIST

ENTRY LEVEL 5

Qualifications and courses

The professional qualification for audiologists is a 4-year degree in audiology. The typical entry requirements for a degree course are 2 A levels/3 H grades, including at least one science subject, maths or psychology. You will spend the first 2 years of the course at university. During year 3, you will work in a placement in an audiology setting. The final year will be spent back at university learning about more advanced aspects of audiology.

It is also possible to enter this profession with a degree in another appropriate subject if you complete a Master of Science (MSc) in Audiology. Most people who follow this route work towards registering as audiological scientists.

The NHS Practitioner Training Programme (PTP) is also available. You will train as a healthcare science practitioner by completing a full-time (usually 3-year) accredited, integrated Bachelor of Science (BSc) degree in healthcare science at university. The NHS Scientist Training Programme (STP), specialising in neurosensory sciences, is available to those already with a relevant degree awarded at 2.1 classification.

If you want to practise as an audiological scientist or clinical scientist in audiology you will need to undertake a Higher Training Scheme (run by the British Academy of Audiology (BAA)). This involves on-the-job training and clinical supervision.

You will be expected to engage in continuing professional development (CPD) and to conduct ongoing research.

No pre-entry experience is required for audiology but experience working with young and elderly people is an advantage.

What the work involves

Audiologists examine patients to identify and assess hearing and balance disorders. You will usually work in one of 4 main areas: paediatrics, adult assessment and rehabilitation, special needs groups, and research and development.

As an audiologist, you will use specialist equipment to test patients and assess their problems and needs.

You will also fit hearing aids and give treatment and advice to patients on how to improve and manage their conditions.

Type of person suited to this work

As an audiologist you will need to speak clearly and be easily understood by people who are lip reading. You should also be flexible and able to work as part of a team.

You will need to be a caring person with excellent communication skills to deal sensitively with patients of all ages and backgrounds, listening to them and explaining the tests and procedures you are doing.

You will need to be practical to operate specialist equipment and take a logical, scientific approach to your work and be able to assess patients' needs and conditions correctly, keep accurate records and provide solutions and practical help.

Working conditions

Most audiologists work as part of a hospital team but you could also be based in a clinic or visit patients in their homes or in care homes or schools.

You could also be involved in teaching and research work in a university.

You will probably work Monday to Friday but could have to be on-call and cover shifts including nights, weekends and bank holidays.

Self-employment or freelance work, part-time hours and career breaks are all possible.

Future prospects

Audiology is a rapidly developing area of healthcare, there is a shortage of qualified staff so job prospects are good, although there are now more students training. There are opportunities within the NHS throughout the UK. There are also jobs available in research and in private hospitals.

You could specialise in one area such as paediatrics or adult rehabilitation.

Within the NHS you could progress to higher grades, where you will have more responsibility including managing and training others.

Advantages/disadvantages

You may need to deal with people suffering from an illness or disorder, such as those with dementia, and this can be emotionally draining at times.

It is fulfilling to know that you are using your skills to improve people's hearing and balance, providing them with a better quality of life.

Money guide

The NHS sets rates for audiologists. There are extra payments available, for example, if you work in London.

Trainees start on NHS band 5 and salaries range from £21,176 to £27,625 per year. Once qualified and registered as an audiological scientist you can reach NHS band 7 and earn between £30,460 and £40,157.

Senior posts have a salary range of £38,851 to £97,478 at bands 8 and 9.

Related opportunities

- Occupational Therapist p299
- Physiotherapist p310
- Speech and Language Therapist p318

Further information

British Academy of Audiology
www.baaudiology.org

British Society of Audiology
www.thebsa.org.uk

NHS Careers
www.nhscareers.nhs.uk

CHILDREN'S NURSE

ENTRY LEVEL 6

Qualifications and courses

All children's nurses must hold a degree in child nursing which has been approved by the Nursing and Midwifery Council (NMC). Minimum entry requirements for degree courses are usually 2 A levels/3H grades, ideally including a science-based subject, and 5 GCSEs/ National 5s (A*–C/A–C) including English, maths and a science subject. All applicants must obtain clearance from the Disclosure and Barring Service (DBS) before commencing their training.

If you do not have the required A levels/H grades or GCSEs/National 5s, some universities will accept other qualifications, such as the various BTEC Level 3 qualifications in Health and Social Care (Health Sciences) or an Access to Higher Education Diploma in a science or health-related subject.

Graduates with a degree in a health-related subject such as human biology, life and medical sciences or biomedical science, may be eligible to enter the nursing profession by taking an accelerated 2-year programme which leads to a Master of Science (MSc) or Postgraduate Diploma.

You are eligible to register as a nurse with the NMC once you have completed an approved nursing degree. Nurses are expected to engage in continuing professional development (CPD) throughout their career to keep their skills and knowledge up to date.

What the work involves

Children's nurses work specifically with babies and young people up to the age of 18. You will also work closely with the parents and families of your patients, providing support, education and advice on treatment and care plans.

You will take medical histories from children and their families, devise a care plan for them with the help of other medical professionals and record their treatment procedures and outcomes in detailed records. You will also have to carry out procedures such as checking blood pressure, taking temperatures, dressing wounds and taking blood samples.

Type of person suited to this work

You will need to be a very warm, approachable person in order to gain the trust of young patients and their families. At the same time, you must be highly professional and authoritative to deal with difficult children and situations.

You should be patient when teaching others, as you will need to demonstrate treatment techniques to both your patients and their parents or carers. You will also need to motivate them to continue treatment at home.

You must be observant, capable of making decisions and able to respond quickly to changes in children's health.

Working conditions

On average, you will work 37.5 hours per week and this will usually include early morning, evening, night and weekend work as part of a shift-based rota. Part-time and flexible hours are often available.

You could work on paediatric wards within NHS hospitals, specialist hospitals, hospices and GP surgeries. You may also work throughout the local community, visiting patients at home, in care homes or at school.

You will usually be required to wear a uniform and suitable sterile clothing, such as gloves and an apron, for certain procedures.

Future prospects

As you gain experience, you can undertake further training and specialise in a particular area such as neurological or cardiovascular conditions in children. You could eventually become a nurse consultant.

Alternatively, you could apply for team leadership roles such as staff nurse or sister. You could also move into general NHS management.

Advantages/disadvantages

Working with children, helping them to get better, managing their treatment and easing their suffering is extremely rewarding.

There are plenty of opportunities to work part time in order to fit your job around your family commitments.

It can be upsetting to deal with distressed or very ill children.

Money guide

A newly qualified nurse can expect a starting salary of £21,200.

As you gain experience, your earnings can increase up to about £28,000.

Those who take on a senior position with additional responsibilities can achieve £30,000–£40,000.

If you specialise in a particular area and undertake the training to become a nurse consultant, you could earn up to £56,000.

Related opportunities

- Adult Nurse p269
- Learning Disabilities Nurse p294
- Speech and Language Therapist p318

Further information

NHS Careers
www.nhscareers.nhs.uk

Nursing and Midwifery Council
www.nmc-uk.org

Royal College of Nursing
www.rcn.org.uk

CHIROPRACTOR

ENTRY LEVEL 5

Qualifications and courses

Entrants must complete a degree course that has been accredited by the General Chiropractic Council (GCC). There are currently 3 institutions in the UK offering the GCC-recognised Master of Chiropractic (MChiro), which takes 4–5 years to complete. Upon graduation, candidates are eligible to register with the GCC, which is a legal requirement for anyone wishing to practise as a chiropractor.

You must be at least 18 years old to start training. Minimum entry requirements are 3 A levels/H grades or equivalent qualifications, including biology and another science subject. For candidates who do not meet these requirements, year-long preliminary chiropractic courses are available as an entry route to the full degree.

More mature applicants looking to move into chiropractic as a second career are considered for degree courses without the usual entry qualifications, providing they have relevant experience or knowledge of science.

You must undergo a Disclosure and Barring Service (DBS) check prior to training as you will be working with children and vulnerable adults.

Registered chiropractors must undertake continuing professional development (CPD) throughout their career.

What the work involves

Chiropractors work with joints, bones and muscles, using their hands and other physical tools, as opposed to drugs, in order to treat patients. Techniques include massage, movement and applying ice or heat to troublesome areas.

You could treat a variety of ailments including back and neck problems, joint stiffness, postural and muscular complaints, headaches and sports injuries.

You will also need to carry out full patient examinations, listen to their concerns and complaints, and record detailed notes of each consultation.

Type of person suited to this work

You should have exceptional communication skills as you will need to listen to patients carefully in order to understand their complaint and to explain the techniques you are using to treat it.

You will need to be professional and approachable in order to inspire confidence and trust in your patients.

Good organisation and commercial awareness are essential if you are to run your own business.

Working conditions

Working hours are usually 9am–5pm, Monday to Friday, although some flexibility may be required to suit the needs of clients. Many clinics and practitioners are increasingly offering early morning, evening and weekend appointments.

Most chiropractors work either in a specialist clinic, a doctor's surgery, at home or at the homes of their clients. This means you could be working alongside other chiropractors/ healthcare professionals or alone.

It is a physically demanding job so you will have to ensure that your own fitness levels remain high in order to avoid work-related injuries.

Future prospects

The chiropractic profession continues to grow and develop. However, there are also many graduates competing for clients.

Most chiropractors are self-employed or work in private practice. A few are employed by the NHS.

Numerous options are open to you as you gain experience. You could choose to specialise in a specific area, such as children or sports injuries, you could set up your own practice or you could teach.

Advantages/disadvantages

Each day you will meet new people and relieve their physical aches and ailments which gives great job satisfaction.

Being self-employed can be extremely stressful as you are responsible for your own business administration and your earnings are dependent on the number of clients you attract.

Money guide

Most chiropractors are self-employed so their earnings depend upon the size, location and reputation of their practice, as well as how many clients they have.

Newly qualified chiropractors can expect a starting salary of between £20,000 and £22,000 per year.

With experience, your earnings could rise to £40,000.

Once you are in a senior position within your own practice, you could achieve £50,000 to £70,000.

Related opportunities

- Massage Therapist p295
- Osteopath p303
- Physiotherapist p310

Further information

British Chiropractic Association
www.chiropractic-uk.co.uk

General Chiropractic Council
www.gcc-uk.org

CLINICAL/BIOMEDICAL ENGINEER

ENTRY LEVEL 6

Qualifications and courses

You will need either a 1st or 2.1 degree in a subject such as mechanical, electronic or electrical engineering or biomedical science/engineering. You should choose a degree which is accredited by the Institution of Engineering and Technology (IET) or the Institution of Mechanical Engineers (IMechE). For degree entry you will need at least 3 A levels/4 H grades, including maths and physics.

Mature students without relevant qualifications may be considered if they have significant work experience in this area or complete an Access to Higher Education course.

Those who wish to work in the public sector can apply for the graduate NHS Scientist Training Programme (STP) which is offered in conjunction with the Institute of Physics and Engineering in Medicine (IPEM). Training takes 3 to 4 years and involves both work-based learning and studying for a master's degree in your chosen specialism.

You will need to commit to a programme of continuing professional development (CPD) throughout your career.

What the work involves

Clinical engineers design and maintain medical equipment such as scanners, X-ray machines, pacemakers, heart rate and blood pressure monitors, equipment for surgery and instruments used in medical research.

All kinds of engineers, from physicists to computer scientists, work on many different parts of the process.

You would test equipment and collaborate with hospital staff, installing equipment and teaching them how to use it.

Type of person suited to this work

If you are looking to go into this field, you need to have a natural interest in both electronic and mechanical engineering, and in health and medical issues. You must also be skilled in engineering and have in-depth knowledge of your subject.

You should be good at problem solving and willing to keep up to date with developments in science, medicine and engineering.

You need organisational skills to effectively prioritise and plan your workload and the ability to work within a budget.

Communication and teamwork skills are also essential.

Working conditions

You could work in a hospital or laboratory, depending on the nature of the work.

Those working in hospitals might have to work shifts and are often on standby for call-outs. Laboratory hours tend to be more fixed.

The usual working hours for clinical engineers are Monday to Friday and you would normally be working 37.5 hours a week.

Future prospects

There are good opportunities for progression and promotion for clinical and biomedical engineers.

With the right experience, you can move into management and senior management jobs, and if you work for the NHS you could be promoted to consultant level.

For those who do not wish to work for the NHS, other opportunities may be available in the private sector. For example, you could be employed by a medical equipment manufacturer.

Advantages/disadvantages

This career requires very skilled and well-educated professionals, and building up this knowledge, studying for your degree and putting it into practice can be a really rewarding experience.

You will be doing a worthwhile job as you will help many people by building and maintaining medical equipment.

The role can be stressful at times and involve high levels of pressure.

Working in a hospital environment will not suit everyone.

Money guide

In the NHS, entry-level engineers earn between £21,176 and £27,625.

Specialists can earn between £25,528 and £34,189, and those with significant experience and/or a team manager position can earn between £30,460 and £40,157.

An engineer with chartered status, who is employed by the NHS in a senior position, can achieve £49,000–£61,000.

Salaries in the private sector are comparable to those in the NHS and may be higher.

Related opportunities

- Biotechnologist p483
- Clinical Scientist p487
- Medical Physicist p296

Further information

Association of Clinical Scientists
www.assclinsci.org

NHS Clinical Scientists Recruitment
www.nhsclinicalscientists.info

CRITICAL CARE TECHNOLOGIST

ENTRY LEVEL 5

Qualifications and courses

To enter this profession, you will need either a 1st or 2.1 degree in a relevant subject such as biochemistry, biomedical sciences, physics, engineering or another science subject related to these disciplines. A 2.2 degree or alternate Higher Education qualification will suffice if followed up with a relevant postgraduate degree. For degree entry you will need 3 A levels/4 H grades, including maths and a science subject (preferably physics), and 5 GCSEs/National 5s including English language, maths, and 2 sciences.

Following your degree, you will have to complete the NHS Healthcare Scientist Training Programme (STP). The STP is a workplace-based salaried learning programme, which results in accreditation in one of nine themed pathways, including critical care science. Applications for a place on the STP are incredibly competitive, so relevant work experience and voluntary work can greatly enhance your chances. Contact hospitals and try and get a role involving patient contact. Contact your course provider for more directed guidance on what to aim for.

Once qualified, you could become a member of the Society of Critical Care Technologies (SCCT) which is the governing body for critical care technologists, where you would have access to opportunities to develop your professional career.

You might also decide to study further and gain a PhD or join the NHS Higher Specialist Scientific Training Programme (HSST).

What the work involves

Critical care technologists support other medical staff caring for critically ill patients by maintaining and operating life-support equipment in intensive care units.

You will work with equipment such as ventilators, brain monitors, blood filtration machines, electrocardiograms (ECGs) and infusion devices. Your job will involve setting up this equipment, taking readings, checking the equipment is working correctly, repairing it and ordering more supplies.

You will use diagnostic techniques to help the medical team assess a patient's needs and condition. You will also be required to keep detailed reports of all your work for patients' records.

Type of person suited to this work

You should have an interest in electronics, science and medicine, with a willingness to keep your skills and knowledge up to date.

You must be a practical person with good technical skills and the ability to work accurately and precisely when under pressure. Good problem-solving and decision-making skills are essential. You should have a responsible attitude to your work as patients' lives will depend on you.

You will need compassion and excellent communication skills to work with patients and their relatives at a time of intense stress, and to be able to explain things simply and clearly.

Working conditions

Critical care technologists work as part of a team in the intensive care unit of a hospital using specialist equipment and machinery.

You will need to follow strict health and safety regulations to ensure that infections and diseases are safely contained.

You will normally work shifts which include nights, weekends and bank holidays.

Future prospects

The requirement for a degree is a recent one and as such, competition for jobs may change in the near future. Job prospects are currently good though as there is a shortage of qualified applicants.

You could specialise in a particular area such as cardiology or respiratory units.

Many critical care technologists are involved in research and teaching, as well as in practice.

Advantages/disadvantages

Working under pressure in emergency situations will be emotionally and physically demanding.

It is extremely rewarding to help patients recover from illnesses.

You will have a varied working day which will involve using your technical skills and having contact with patients.

Money guide

The NHS sets pay rates for critical care technologists.

The current starting salary for someone on the STP is £25,000 plus a location allowance where valid.

A qualified critical care technologist would move into the NHS wage band 6 and could earn £34,530 with the potential to move up to Band 7 as a manager and earn £40,558.

If you work in London, you may receive an additional allowance and wages may be higher in the private sector.

Working overtime or being on-call can increase your earnings.

Related opportunities

- Audiologist p273
- Operating Department Practitioner p300
- Sterile Services Technician p320

Further information

NHS Careers
www.nhscareers.nhs.uk

Skills for Health
www.skillsforhealth.org.uk

Society of Critical Care Technologists
www.criticalcaretech.org.uk

DENTAL HYGIENIST

ENTRY LEVEL 5

Qualifications and courses

To practice as a dental hygienist you will need to register with the General Dental Council (GDC) and have completed a GDC-approved course. This can be either a 2-year full-time Diploma in Dental Hygiene and Therapy, a Foundation degree in Oral Health Science, or a 3-year full-time BSc degree in Oral Health Science. Minimum entry requirements for these courses are 2 A levels/3 H grades and 5 GCSEs/National 5s (A*–C/A–C), including English, maths and a science related subject, and an interview is typically arranged before an offer to study is made. Relevant work experience may also be advantageous.

Many institutions also accept a GDC-recognised qualification in dental nursing as long as it is accompanied by other qualifications such as an AS level in biology or human biology (A–D). Equivalent qualifications may also be considered, such as an advanced GNVQ, BTEC, Access to HE Diploma or Advanced Diploma, all of which must be in a science-related subject.

Prior to their place at the dental school being confirmed, all potential students are required to pass a medical test and undergo screening for blood borne viruses, such as Hepatitis B and C, and HIV.

As you will work with children and vulnerable adults you will also need a Disclosure and Barring Service (DBS) check prior to training.

What the work involves

Dental hygienists are predominantly concerned with oral hygiene and help prevent tooth decay and gum disease in their patients whilst working closely with and under the instruction of dentists.

Your work will include scaling and polishing teeth, putting in temporary fillings, taking impressions and X-rays, and applying protective coatings to teeth to prevent decay. You will require sufficient bi-manual dexterity to simultaneously treat patients with the necessary equipment whilst using a dental mirror.

You will be using a range of instruments, including scraping devices and drills. You will instruct patients on the appropriate way to floss and brush as well as advise them on their diet.

Type of person suited to this work

You will need to have excellent communication skills and be warm and reassuring as you treat patients of all ages, advising them on oral care.

You will need to combine good scientific knowledge with a personable approach to your work in order to motivate patients and convince them to stick to dental routines. A genuine desire to help people is essential.

You will need good eyesight and precise manual skills so that you can carry out detailed dental work with delicate instruments. An ability to stay focussed for long periods of time is also important.

Working conditions

You will usually work a 37-hour week from Monday to Friday, although occasional evening and Saturday morning work may be required according to practice opening hours. Part-time work is also available.

If you work for a community dental service you may travel to see patients in various locations such as schools and residential homes. You may also work out of a mobile clinic.

Surgeries are clean and well-lit. You will need to wear a white coat, surgical gloves, a face mask and eye protection for various procedures.

Future prospects

There is not the shortage in the industry that there was a few years ago, but demand is still strong and job prospects are good.

Despite the majority of hygienists working in dental surgeries, you could also work for a community dental service, in a hospital or for the Defence Dental Agency (DDA), providing dental treatment for the British armed forces around the world.

You may be promoted to practice manager or go on to become an orthodontic therapist.

You could also become self-employed and work across several practices, undertaking part-time hours in each or teach a dental hygiene training course.

Advantages/disadvantages

You will meet all kinds of people, which can create a diverse and interesting working day.

It is satisfying to see a patient's condition improve based on your advice.

You may come across anxious patients who are difficult to calm down.

Money guide

Dental hygienists usually start in the NHS wage band 5 which means a starting salary of between £21,388 and £27,901 per year.

Moving up to band 6 could mean earnings between £25,783 and £34,530.

If you work in private practice, have considerable experience and a good reputation, you could earn up to £48,000 per year.

Related opportunities

- Dental Therapist p281
- Dentist p282
- Orthodontist p302

Further information

British Dental Association
www.bda.org

British Society of Dental Hygiene & Therapy
www.bsdht.org.uk

General Dental Council
www.gdc-uk.org

NHS Careers
www.nhscareers.nhs.uk

DENTAL NURSE

ENTRY LEVEL 3

Qualifications and courses

Typically there are no academic entry requirements to work as a trainee dental nurse but in order to progress you will need to study a recognised qualification in dental nursing before becoming a dental nurse. These qualifications need to be approved by the General Dental Council (GDC) and many of these courses require GCSEs/National 5s (A*–C/A–C) in English, maths and a science subject for entry.

Qualifications recognised by the GDC are the Certificate of Higher Education in Dental Nursing, City & Guilds Level 3 Award in Dental Nursing, SQA Level 3 in Dental Nursing, National Examining Board for Dental Nurses (NEBDN) National Certificate or a Certificate of Proficiency in Dental Nursing from a recognised dental hospital.

Alternatively, you could complete an Advanced Apprenticeship and will allow you to register with the GDC. The apprenticeship lasts 18 months and you will study for either a QCF Level 3 Diploma in Dental Nursing, NEBDN National Diploma in Dental Nursing, NVQ Level 3 in Dental Nursing, or Level 3 VRQ in Dental Nursing.

You will also need to be registered with the GDC in order to work.

The armed forces also offer several routes into dental nursing.

What the work involves

Dental nurses assist dentists in all aspects of clinical work and patient treatment.

You will be expected to prepare the surgery each day and for each patient, ensuring that all instruments are to hand and sterilised ready for use. You will also assist in dental procedures by holding suction devices in the patient's mouth, ensuring that they are comfortable throughout their treatment, and giving patients pre- and post-operative advice.

You may also take responsibility for the day-to-day running of the surgery, including maintaining stock and ordering equipment, and undertaking some administrative duties.

Type of person suited to this work

You should have excellent interpersonal skills as you will be dealing with patients on a daily basis, many of whom may be anxious about forthcoming treatment and in need of kindness and reassurance.

Good eyesight and manual dexterity are helpful when aiding in procedures, as is a calm approach to jobs and the ability to react quickly and calmly to unforeseen situations. As you will be working closely with a dentist and other colleagues, you will need to enjoy being part of a team environment.

Good time management and organisational skills are necessary in order to fulfil the range of duties you will be expected to undertake.

Working conditions

You will usually work from 8am to 5.30pm, Monday to Friday, and some evening or weekend work may be required. Part-time work is often available. If you work in a hospital, you may be asked to remain on-call over weekends and provide emergency cover at any time of day or night.

Dental nurses are also employed by the Salaried Primary Care Dental Service (SPCDS) to work in local communities, assisting with patient care in various locations such as mobile clinics, schools and residential homes.

You will have to wear a uniform, and relevant safety equipment such as surgical gloves and a face mask.

Future prospects

Once qualified, you could continue your studies in order to gain further qualifications that will allow you to take on additional responsibilities such as sedation of patients and radiography.

Another option is to train to become a specialist orthodontic dental nurse, or a dental hygienist.

Some dental nurses also move into teaching roles and train student nurses.

Advantages/disadvantages

You will be working in pleasant, clean environments helping to treat patients and maintain a high standard of dental care across the UK.

Hours are usually standard and regular, with the opportunity to work part time for a better work–life balance.

Money guide

Entry level dental nurses start in NHS band 3 and so can earn from £16,271 to £19,268.

With more experience this could rise to £22,016.

Specialists and team leaders could earn up to £27,901.

A dental nurse manager is under band 6 which goes up to £34,530.

These figures are based on the NHS' Agenda for Change pay rates. The exact rate of pay could depend on your location and employer. Private dental nurses may earn more.

Related opportunities

- Adult Nurse p269
- Dental Hygienist p278
- Dentist p282

Further information

British Association of Dental Nurses
www.badn.org.uk

General Dental Council
www.gdc-uk.org

DENTAL TECHNICIAN

ENTRY LEVEL 4

Qualifications and courses

Before working as a dental technician you will have to pass a qualification recognised by the General Dental Council (GDC) and then register with them. Relevant qualifications include the BTEC Level 3 Extended Diploma/Subsidiary Diploma, Foundation degree and degree in dental technology.

Entry requirements for the BTEC Level 3 Extended Diploma/Subsidiary Diploma are at least 4 GCSEs/National 5s (A*–C/A–C), including English, maths and a science. For a Foundation degree in dental technology, you will need an A level/H grade and 4 GCSEs/National 5s (A*–C/A–C). Typical entry requirements for a degree course are 2 A levels/3 H grades, including a science, and 5 GCSEs/National 5s (A*–C/A–C).

You can work as a trainee in a laboratory or hospital whilst you study to obtain a relevant qualification that will enable you to register as a practising dental technician.

The armed forces also recruit dental technicians, but you will need to be fully qualified at the time of applying, and be under 33 years of age.

It is important to commit to a programme of continuing professional development (CPD) to keep your skills up to date.

What the work involves

Dental technicians can work within 3 different areas: prosthodontic technicians specialise in designing and making dentures and implants; conservation technicians specialise in crown and bridge work; orthodontic technicians produce braces. Some technicians may specialise in one discipline whilst others may work in all 3.

You will follow detailed prescriptions, written by a doctor or dentist, in order to create individual, patient-specific appliances.

You will use a variety of materials for crafting each device, including gold, steel, porcelain and plastic. You will also use numerous technical instruments in order to accurately carve, mould or wire each accessory.

If you train as a healthcare scientist in reconstructive science via the NHS Scientist Training Programme (STP) or complete a Diploma or Master of Science (MSc) in Maxillofacial Technology you can also become a maxillofacial technician and help reconstruct the faces of patients damaged by accident or disease.

Type of person suited to this work

You will be producing extremely delicate, precise devices so you will need excellent manual dexterity, good eyesight and full colour vision. It also helps to have some artistic ability so that you can make items such as false teeth and crowns look as natural and aesthetically pleasing as possible.

You will need to be able to concentrate on a task for lengthy periods of time, and maintain a high level of accuracy throughout.

You should also be comfortable understanding and interpreting complex technical instructions in order to create them as 3D devices.

Working conditions

You should expect to work between 37 and 40 hours per week. Hours usually fall on weekdays but if you work in a hospital dental unit you might have to work evenings and weekends to cover emergency clinics.

Dental technicians usually work for commercial laboratories that produce equipment for a number of different practitioners in an area. These range in size from smaller businesses to large companies.

You will be working in a laboratory, either within a hospital, dental practice, or independent commercial facility.

You will be expected to wear protective clothing and safety equipment when undertaking certain tasks.

Future prospects

Alternate employers include hospital dental units, the Royal Army Dental Corps (RADC), the Royal Air Force, and the Royal Navy. There is also the option to be self-employed, although this is relatively uncommon.

Within larger companies, prospects for promotion are good.

Advantages/disadvantages

You will have job satisfaction in knowing you are producing high quality dental devices to improve a patient's dental health or appearance.

It is not a very sociable job. Although you will be working in a laboratory with other professionals, you will be responsible for your own projects and have no patient contact.

Money guide

Dental technicians for the NHS start in the NHS wage band 5, earning between £21,388 and £27,901.

With experience you could gain a position as a dental technician specialist increasing your salary to between £25,783 and £34,530.

Dental lab managers could earn between £39,239 and £67,805.

These figures are based on the NHS' Agenda for Change pay rates. Private dental technicians may earn more.

Related opportunities

- Dental Hygienist p278
- Dental Nurse p279
- Dental Therapist p281

Further information

British Institute of Dental and Surgical Technologists
www.bidst.org

General Dental Council
www.gdc-uk.org

DENTAL THERAPIST

ENTRY LEVEL 5

Qualifications and courses

You will need to register with the General Dental Council (GDC) prior to working as a dental therapist. To do this, you will need either a Diploma in Dental Therapy (often combined with a Diploma in Dental Hygiene) or a GDC-approved degree in Oral Health Sciences. Minimum entry requirements for these courses are 2 A levels/3 H grades and 5 GCSEs/National 5s (A*–C/A–C), including English, maths and biology. Some schools may accept a GDC-recognised qualification in Dental Nursing in place of A levels.

In addition to all of the training applied to a dental hygienist you will also need clinical skills training in how to do fillings and extract deciduous (milk) teeth. As a student you can join the British Association of Dental Therapists (BADT) which can give you access to relevant job adverts as well as help you network.

Qualified dental hygienists and dental nurses can also become therapists either by completing a conversion course or studying a Foundation programme in science and dental therapy at the University of Portsmouth.

Qualified therapists need to complete 150 hours of professional development activity every 5 years in order to remain registered with the GDC.

You will need a Disclosure and Barring Service (DBS) check prior to training.

What the work involves

Dental therapists, or oral health practitioners, perform both clinical and educational dental tasks.

You will not only perform a hygienist's role such as scaling and polishing teeth, but you will also remove plaque from the root surface of the teeth and carry out fillings and nerve treatments on both adult and deciduous teeth.

You will educate patients on proper diet and ways to brush and floss their teeth. You could also need to administer a supervised local anaesthetic.

Type of person suited to this work

As you will treat everyone from children to the elderly you will need to be adaptable, good-natured and encouraging. Your patients must feel comfortable with you and trust you.

You need to be a clear and motivational communicator in order to educate patients on proper dental care.

It is essential to have both a solid understanding of biology as well as a sincere interest in the wellbeing of your patients. You will need endurance, the ability to focus for long periods of time and a precise hand for carrying out detailed procedures.

Working conditions

You will work in a clean and bright environment. Your hours will be standard Monday to Friday but you might need to work the occasional Saturday morning or evening surgery, depending on the opening hours of your dental practice. It might be possible to work freelance or on a part-time basis.

You might need to travel to schools or residential homes to visit patients if you are employed by a community dental service. This may include working from a mobile clinic.

For most procedures you will need to wear protective gloves, a facemask and uniform.

Future prospects

Good job opportunities exist for dental therapists throughout the UK. You may be employed by a general practice (private or NHS), a dental school, a cosmetic surgery, a Salaried Primary Care Dental Service or with a Primary Care Trust.

You could be promoted to a dental practice manager or become a researcher or lecturer. With further training you could also specialise in health promotion.

You might choose to set up your own dental practice.

Advantages/disadvantages

It is rewarding to see a patient satisfied at the end of their treatment.

Your work will be varied as each patient's case will be unique.

The job can be demanding as you must deal with the public all day and you might find it difficult to win a patient's trust.

Money guide

The starting salary for a therapist in the NHS is between £21,478 and £27,901 a year. As a specialist you may earn up to £34,530 a year.

Advanced therapists may earn up to £40,558 a year.

Your salary may increase based on your employer and where you live. If you are self-employed you will be able to negotiate your fees. These figures are based on current NHS wage bands.

Related opportunities

- Dental Hygienist p278
- Dental Nurse p279
- Dentist p282

Further information

British Association of Dental Therapists
www.badt.org.uk

General Dental Council
www.gdc-uk.org

NHS Careers
www.nhscareers.nhs.uk

DENTIST

ENTRY LEVEL 5

Qualifications and courses

To become a dentist, you need to complete a degree at one of the British Dental Association (BDA) schools. The standard programme lasts 5 years. You will need at least 3 good A levels/H grades, including chemistry and biology, and 5 GCSEs/National 5s (A*–C/A–C). Though not essential, work experience may be advantageous as competition for degree places is fierce. Some universities also require candidates to complete the UK Clinical Aptitude Test (UKCAT) or the Graduate Medical School Admissions Test (GAMSAT).

If you have good A level/H grade results, but not in the required subjects, you can apply for a 6-year programme that includes an initial 30-week Foundation course that will get you up to speed in chemistry, physics and biology.

If you already have a degree in another subject it is possible to take an accelerated degree lasting only 4 years. To qualify you will need a 2.1 classified degree, and have relevant qualifications (usually high quality A levels/H grades) in biology and chemistry.

Once you have completed your degree you will have 1 or 2 years of vocational training and will also need to commit to a programme of continuing professional development (CPD) to remain registered with the General Dental Council.

What the work involves

Dentists are trained to recognise, diagnose and treat all problems that affect the teeth, gums and mouth.

You will examine teeth and carry out appropriate treatments, such as fitting or replacing fillings, scraping away plaque, polishing and removing teeth, as well as educating patients about good oral habits in order to prevent disease or decay.

You will also need to keep detailed dental records for each patient, alongside managing your staff and, if you are a practice manager, looking after the practice budget.

Type of person suited to this work

You will need to have excellent communication skills in order to inspire your team and build good relationships with your patients, who will represent all ages and backgrounds.

You should also be compassionate and sympathetic, as you will encounter patients who are nervous or anxious about their treatment and you will need to be able to soothe and reassure them.

You will need good eyesight, concentration and manual dexterity to successfully carry out complicated and delicate procedures. If you intend to run your own practice, you will also need good business acumen.

Working conditions

If you work in a dental surgery, you should have regular Monday to Friday hours, and may even enjoy some flexibility within this framework. Dentists who work in hospitals will usually work longer hours, including weekends, and will have to adhere to an on-call rota.

You could work across the community, travelling to provide treatment in locations such as schools and retirement homes.

You will need to wear protective, hygienic clothing such as a white coat and surgical gloves when dealing with patients.

Future prospects

Most dentists are self-employed, working in general practice across the UK. Some work for the NHS, and some take on a mixture of private and NHS patients. You could also work for the armed forces.

A recent surge in dental graduates has increased competition in this sector. There is still demand for graduates across the UK, but this is mostly within the NHS which is viewed by some as a less lucrative career move than private practice.

You could undertake further training to specialise in a field such as orthodontics, maxillofacial surgery or dental public health, which is a relatively new and expanding specialty with a shortage of consultants.

Advantages/disadvantages

The majority of dentists are self-employed and work in the private sector, so you have a good amount of control over the hours you work and the patients you see.

There are excellent opportunities for rapid career progression or further training if you want to specialise in a specific area.

You will mainly be undertaking routine check-ups and very standard procedures, so work can feel monotonous at times.

Money guide

Salaries for recently graduated, trainee dentists in general practice start at around £30,000 to £40,000 per year. If you start your career in the NHS, your salary may be slightly lower.

Experienced dentists in general practice can earn between £50,000 and £110,000. Salaries can be even higher if you run your own surgery.

If you reach consultant level working for the NHS, your salary could exceed £100,000.

Related opportunities

- Dental Hygienist p278
- Dental Therapist p281
- Orthodontist p302

Further information

British Dental Association
www.bda.org

General Dental Council
www.gdc-uk.org

NHS Careers
www.nhscareers.nhs.uk

DIETITIAN

ENTRY LEVEL 5

Qualifications and courses

To become a dietitian, an approved degree or postgraduate qualification in dietetics or human nutrition and dietetics is required. You must then register with the Health & Care Professions Council (HCPC) in order to practise. You will need 2 A levels/3 H grades, including chemistry and another science, and 5 GCSEs/ National 5s (A*–C/A–C), including English and maths, for entry to a degree in dietetics. Entry requirements for a postgraduate diploma are typically an Honours degree in a science subject with an acceptable level of biochemistry and human physiology, along with a good command of spoken and written English.

The approved degree is usually a full-time course that lasts 3 or 4 years, while the postgraduate diploma takes 2 years. Both routes include practical training in a hospital or community setting.

Some institutions expect applicants to have undertaken some work experience with a dietetic department or related hospital setting before applying for a place.

Mature applicants can complete an Access course in science to be accepted onto a degree programme. If you don't have an approved degree or postgraduate diploma, entry is only available at assistant level.

Dietitians are regulated by the HCPC and are required to continue their professional development (CPD).

What the work involves

Dietitians use their scientific knowledge of food to provide advice and information about diet and nutrition. Dietitians might work in industry developing food products and even in the media.

You will give advice to a broad range of people, such as hospital patients, caterers, sports professionals and the general public.

You will help people improve their health and prevent disease by making changes in their diet.

Type of person suited to this work

You will need expert knowledge of the science of food and nutrition, and how this relates to the body.

You must have excellent communication skills to be able to give practical information and advice to a range of people, from school children to food manufacturers. You will need to be caring, supportive and non-judgemental, and able to understand the needs and issues of individuals, especially if you are working with sick people.

You should have good motivational skills so that people can follow your advice and make the changes that you recommend.

Working conditions

You could work in a range of locations such as hospitals, laboratories, offices and sports centres.

You are likely to work a standard working week from Monday to Friday, although in hospitals you may be called in to work at weekends and on bank holidays.

In most jobs you will be working directly with people who can be ill, distressed or reluctant to take your advice.

Future prospects

The British Dietetic Association has over 5,000 members and the profession is growing around the world. There are opportunities across the UK and abroad, but competition for jobs is fierce.

Most dietitians work in the NHS, but there are also many opportunities in areas such as sports nutrition, the food and pharmaceutical industries, scientific research, education and journalism. You could become self-employed working as a consultant or see private clients.

In the NHS, you could go on to specialise in areas such as cancer care, or with particular groups such as children or the elderly. You could also move into management.

Advantages/disadvantages

People might be unable or unwilling to take on your advice, which can be frustrating.

It is rewarding to see improvements in people when they put into practice the information and advice you have given them.

Money guide

NHS dietitians start work on the NHS wage band 5 and earn between £21,478 and £27,901 per year.

Specialist dietitians work in band 6 and earn from £25,783 to £34,530.

Salaries for senior grade dietitians working in band 7 can be between £30,764 and £40,558.

There are higher grades for chief members of staff, or for work outside the NHS, although salaries are not necessarily higher in private work.

You may earn more if you work in London or the south-east of England. In addition, salary premiums are offered where there are recruitment issues or for specialist positions.

Related opportunities

- Food Scientist/Technologist p493
- Health Promotion/Education Specialist p286
- Health Visitor p289

Further information

British Dietetic Association
www.bda.uk.com

NHS Careers
www.nhscareers.nhs.uk

Skills for Health
www.skillsforhealth.org.uk

DISPENSING OPTICIAN

ENTRY LEVEL 5

Qualifications and courses

You must be registered with the General Optical Council (GOC). To qualify, you must complete an appropriate training course, pass the Professional Qualifying Examinations of the Association of British Dispensing Opticians (ABDO), and undergo a pre-registration year working under the supervision of a qualified optician.

The GOC has approved 3 routes into the profession: a 3-year degree course in optical management, ophthalmic dispensing or a related area; a 3-year distance learning course, including a 4 week residential block, is also offered by ABDO; a 2-year diploma course or Foundation degree in ophthalmic dispensing, followed by one year of supervised work.

Typical entry requirements for a degree or Foundation degree are 2 A levels/3 H grades, normally including relevant science subjects, and 5 GCSEs/National 5s (A*–C/A–C), including English, maths and science. For a diploma, you will need at least 5 GCSEs/National 5s (A*–C/A–C), including English, maths and a science.

You could also start as a trainee with a qualified optometrist and work part time towards qualifications. High street companies such as Specsavers and Boots also offer training programmes and certain colleges offer a 3-year day-release programme for those in suitable employment.

Relevant pre-entry experience is also desirable as many individuals who enter the profession already have experience as an optical assistant or other relevant professions, or in company positions such as receptionists or sales assistants.

What the work involves

Dispensing opticians use prescriptions from optometrists to supply and fit glasses.

The work you will do includes measuring the patient's face to ensure the glasses will fit and advising on lenses and frame styles to suit them and their prescription. You will check that the finished glasses meet the original specifications and supply them to the patient. You will also do repairs.

Some dispensing opticians take further training to supply and fit contact lenses.

Type of person suited to this work

Interpreting prescriptions requires specific scientific expertise.

You will be advising and listening to customers of many different ages and backgrounds, and working as part of a team with other professionals, so you will need excellent communication skills. It will be your responsibility to take measurements and repair glasses so manual skills are necessary.

You will need to be interested in fashion, as well as have strong commercial awareness and product knowledge.

You will need to be business minded if you choose to set up your own practice.

Working conditions

Most dispensing opticians work in high-street opticians. Financial and management challenges may arise if you are self-employed.

You may work 35–40 hours a week from Monday to Saturday (with some time off during the week instead).

You may have to work on Sundays and bank holidays or in shifts, including weekends, in big chains.

Future prospects

Most dispensing opticians work for high-street companies. Some work is available in hospitals. Registration with the GOC will allow you to work in other countries.

With experience you may specialise, for example in supplying and fitting contact lenses or low vision aids. You could also train new entrants.

You may also be promoted into a management position within a high-street optical chain.

With experience, some opticians choose to run their own practices, however, increasing numbers of dispensing opticians are choosing to work for established franchises rather than run an independent practice. This is due to the growing threat from big high street chains as well as online alternatives.

Advantages/disadvantages

It can be stressful having to meet sales targets in some opticians.

If you enjoy combining scientific knowledge with working with the public, this job could be good for you.

Money guide

Salary levels vary enormously and are usually higher for opticians with management responsibility.

Starting salaries are around £12,000 to £17,000 per year.

Practice managers or those who are qualified to fit contact lenses can earn between £28,000 and £35,000 per year.

Related opportunities

- Optometrist p301
- Pharmacist p306
- Sales/Retail Assistant p468

Further information

Association of British Dispensing Opticians
www.abdo.org.uk

General Optical Council
www.optical.org

NHS Careers
www.nhscareers.nhs.uk

DOCTOR (GP)

ENTRY LEVEL 8

Qualifications and courses

To become a General Practitioner (GP) you must first complete an degree in medicine that is recognised by the General Medical Council (GMC). The standard programme lasts 5 years and you will require at least 3 good A levels/H grades, including chemistry and biology, for entry. Some medical schools also require applicants to sit the UK Clinical Aptitude Test (UKCAT) or BioMedical Admissions Test (BMAT), which not only test academic ability but behavioural characteristics. It is now common, and expected, for applicants to have some work experience in healthcare, for example, as a care assistant in a nursing home or hospital.

If you do not have science A levels, some universities offer a 6-year programme that includes an initial 'pre-medical' year that will get you up to speed. If you already have a 2.1 degree in another subject, some medical schools offer an accelerated degree in medicine lasting only 4 years.

Once you have a degree in medicine, you will need to complete a 2-year Foundation programme with specialist training in general practice before you can qualify as a GP. At the end of the Foundation programme you would choose to train in general practice. This second stage of specialist training takes around 3 years to complete and will include at least 12 months working as a GP registrar in the NHS.

What the work involves

General practitioners (GPs) diagnose various health problems, physical or emotional, within their local community.

You will be talking to and examining patients in order to find out what is wrong with them, and then deciding on how to treat them. This could include giving them advice, prescribing medicine or referring patients to a specialist doctor.

You may occasionally have to perform minor surgery such as removing moles or warts. You are responsible for educating your patients about how to live a healthy lifestyle and prevent illness.

Type of person suited to this work

You will need to have excellent communication skills in order to gain the trust of your patients and build good relationships with them. You should be able to put them at their ease quickly whilst maintaining a professional attitude.

You must have excellent scientific and medical knowledge in order to assess problems quickly and reach a suitable diagnosis, all within the time limit of a 10 minute appointment.

You should have an enquiring mind as you will need to continually update your knowledge and learn about new techniques and medicines in order to keep up to date in this fast moving discipline.

Working conditions

You will usually work normal hours from Monday to Friday, although increasingly surgeries are offering evening and weekend appointments which you might have to cover on a rota basis. You may also have to spend some time on-call, visiting patients at home at any hour of the day or night.

GPs are practice based in small or large surgeries within cities, towns and rural areas. GPs have to adhere to time and budget constraints, which can make the work stressful and demanding.

Future prospects

The healthcare system is changing and the NHS will need more GPs in the future. Therefore, the number of training places is increasing and job prospects are promising.

As a general practitioner you will be able to work anywhere in the UK, in a larger practice with healthcare professionals from a number of disciplines, or a smaller surgery.

You could undertake work for the NHS, enjoy the freedom of self-employment, or opt for a combination of the 2.

Advantages/disadvantages

The training period prior to qualifying as a GP is, on average, 10 years.

As a full-time GP 52-hour weeks, which could include evening and weekends as well as out-of-hours emergency work, are not uncommon.

Dealing with patients with varying complaints each day can be stressful, but helping them to recover is rewarding.

The work is varied and you will meet lots of different people on a daily basis.

Money guide

For a doctor in training, the basic salary is £22,636, rising to £28,076 in the second year of training. In the first year of specialist training, you can expect a salary of £30,002.

You may get overtime pay for working more than 40 hours a week or outside the hours of 7am to 7pm. This could be as much as 50% of the basic salary.

As a fully-qualified GP your earnings could be between £54,319 and £81,969 a year.

Independent GPs are self-employed and have an NHS contract. As such they can earn more than salaried GPs, depending on the specialism, the services provided and the practice.

Related opportunities

- Hospital Doctor p292
- Pharmacist p306
- Surgeon p321

Further information

British Medical Association
www.bma.org.uk

General Medical Council
www.gmc-uk.org

Royal College of General Practitioners
www.rcgp.org.uk

HEALTH PROMOTION/EDUCATION SPECIALIST

ENTRY LEVEL 5

Qualifications and courses

Entrants to this profession need a degree in a relevant subject such as health studies or public health. Subjects such as psychology, social science or education can also be useful. Entry requirements for degrees are usually a minimum of 2 A levels/3 H grades and 5 GCSEs/National 5s (A*–C/A–C) or alternative qualifications such as a BTEC in Health and Social Care. More senior posts generally require a Postgraduate Diploma or Master of Science (MSc) in health promotion. If you have a nursing diploma or a related Foundation degree, there is the option to take a top-up degree course in health promotion.

It may be possible to train on the job for recognised qualifications. The Open University offers a certificate in Health Promotion. Some colleges run a Health Studies Access course for candidates without the necessary entry requirements. The Royal Society for Public Health (RSPH) also offers the Level 1 Award in Health Awareness and the Level 2 Award in Understanding Health Improvement.

It is possible to enter the profession through related fields though it is advisable to undertake relevant voluntary work or short courses in areas such as stopping smoking and working with patient groups in order to demonstrate your commitment to the profession.

The Public Health Register maintains a voluntary register for specialists in this field, and recommends degree and postgraduate courses to its members.

What the work involves

Health promotion/education specialists aim to promote and improve public health in line with national recommendations. This could be done by running training courses and workshops, public health campaigns such as screening and immunisation, and producing publicity materials.

You could work with organisations such as schools or directly with individuals, groups or communities.

Your work might include advising individuals on how to make lifestyle changes, such as taking more exercise or giving up smoking, encouraging organisations such as workplaces, schools and hospitals to improve diets and promote health or developing partnerships with communities to improve public health. Your role might also involve liaising with the press and compiling features to encourage healthy living.

Type of person suited to this work

You must be able to encourage individuals and communities to change their lifestyles. It is important to have excellent communication and negotiation skills as a large part of your job will involve dealing with people from all age groups and all walks of life.

You will need to be creative to find different ways of persuading people and organisations to make changes. Good research and writing skills are also necessary in order to put together clear reports.

You will need to be supportive and non-judgemental and able to relate to the needs of a wide range of people, communities and cultures. You must have good organisational skills to run and manage projects.

Working conditions

You could work in many different places such as health centres, local authority buildings, hospitals, workplaces and fitness centres.

You are likely to have a normal working week, Monday to Friday. Some employers offer flexible working schemes.

Travel within a working day is common as you will need to attend meetings, for example at local schools or community groups.

Future prospects

This is a very competitive industry and you will probably need to do work experience.

Most health promotion/education specialists work for the NHS, health promotion agencies, local authorities or in social and community settings.

You can progress to management roles or go into research and lecturing in health promotion.

Advantages/disadvantages

Changing people's habits can be difficult and take a long time.

Working to tight deadlines and targets can be very stressful.

Seeing improvements in public health when people put into practice the information and advice you have provided is very rewarding. You will have the opportunity to work with many different people.

Money guide

Salary levels are largely dependent on which health sector you work in and which health authority you work for.

In the NHS, the Agenda for Change salary bands states health promoters should start on NHS wage band 5, earning between £21,388 and £27,901.

More experienced and senior staff could progress to band 7, earning between £30,764 and £40,558.

Related opportunities

- Dietitian p283
- Health and Safety Adviser p27
- Youth and Community Worker p563

Further information

Faculty of Public Health
www.fph.org.uk

NHS Careers
www.nhscareers.nhs.uk

HEALTH RECORDS CLERK

ENTRY LEVEL 3

Qualifications and courses

Most employers require candidates to have at least 5 GCSEs/National 5s (A*–C/A–C), including English and maths. Other relevant qualifications include the NVQ Level 1 or 2 in Business and Administration and the BTEC qualifications in Business (Levels 1–2). Previous administrative experience would also be advantageous.

Training is mostly done on the job, however you may also be offered the chance to formally study for professional qualifications such as the NVQ Level 2 in Support Services in Healthcare or the Level 3 in Business Administration. The Institute of Health Record and Information Management (IHRIM) offers several courses in healthcare administration including the Certificate in Health Records Management. If you have 12 months' experience, the Foundation degree in Health Informatics is available through the University of Central Lancashire.

Apprenticeships might enable you to enter this role for candidates aged 16–24.

As you will be working with children and vulnerable adults, you will need to pass a Disclosure and Barring Service (DBS) check.

What the work involves

Health administrators and records clerks are responsible for preparing and maintaining records of patients' medical notes, including details about the medicines they take and any other care needs.

You will be collating, organising and archiving relevant notes and documents in each patient's file, and also ensuring that they are easily accessible for other healthcare professionals.

You will be working with both paper documents and electronic records, which will include using equipment such as computers, photocopiers and scanners. You will also undertake other administrative duties, such as making and rearranging patients' appointments, sorting incoming correspondence and covering reception from time to time.

Type of person suited to this work

You will be working within a team of healthcare professionals as well as dealing with patient enquiries, so you should be personable and have excellent communication skills.

You will need good numeracy and IT skills. As you will be dealing with a variety of tasks each day, you will also need good organisational skills and the ability to prioritise your workload.

You will be working with confidential information so you must be discreet.

Working conditions

You could work in an office, a reception area, filing room, medical records library or a hospital ward. You will usually work a 37-hour week from Monday to Friday, although occasionally some jobs require employees to work shifts. Part-time opportunities are common.

As you will be moving and transporting large, heavy piles of paper files around the hospital or practice, you will need to be reasonably strong and fit.

The majority of the work is office based, although you might need to courier documents to various departments within your building. You will be expected to look fairly smart, although a business suit is unnecessary.

Future prospects

Although the NHS is the biggest employer of administrative staff, there are also opportunities in private hospitals and voluntary organisations.

Increasingly, the NHS is providing a structured career path for their administrators. With the correct training and experience there are positions within every NHS pay band. For example, you could progress towards a supervisory or managerial role within your department, become head of communications, or support a specialist area such as neurology or gastroenterology. You could also transfer to other similar departments, such as the clinical informatics or the information management staff, where there are a variety of more specialist roles.

Repercussions from the recession is still affecting the NHS and job opportunities may be harder to come by.

Advantages/disadvantages

You will be providing an essential service to both patients and other healthcare professionals by ensuring the smooth running of behind-the-scenes operations.

You can expect to have a heavy workload at times.

Hours are regular and there is plenty of opportunity for part-time work which fits in around family commitments.

Money guide

The salary for a health records clerk usually starts at between £13,000 and £17,000.

As you gain experience this should rise to between £16,000 and £19,000, whilst team leaders can earn up to £22,000.

If you move into a more senior supervisory or management position, you can expect to earn up to £30,000.

Salaries do vary according to your employer, where you work in the UK and the additional benefits on offer, such as a pension scheme.

Related opportunities

- Adult Nurse p269
- Health Visitor p289
- Pharmacy Technician p308

Further information

Institute of Health Records and Information Management
www.ihrim.co.uk

HEALTH SERVICE MANAGER

ENTRY LEVEL 3

Qualifications and courses

A typical way to enter into health service management is by starting out as an administrator and working you way up to a management role. For entry-level positions 5 GCSEs/National 5s (A*–C/A–C) or, more commonly, 2 A levels/3H grades are needed.

Once you are in an administrative post you can study for relevant management training courses, such as those offered by the Institute of Healthcare Management (IHM). The Association of Medical Secretaries, Practice Managers, Administrators and Receptionists (AMSPAR) offers a Level 5 Certificate/Diploma in Primary Care and Health Management in association with City & Guilds.

One of the most direct routes into health service management is through the NHS Graduate Management Training Scheme. There is a choice of 4 specialisms: finance management, general management, HR management or informatics management. Entry is with a 2.2 degree in any subject or equivalent qualifications that are health or management-related, including the NVQ Level 5 in Management and the Diploma in Management Studies (DMS). The recruitment process for this 2-year graduate scheme is fiercely competitive and involves a variety of aptitude tests and rounds of interviews.

The private sector also has graduate management schemes. To apply for a position with BUPA and BMI Healthcare you will need a 2.1 in any degree or equivalent.

What the work involves

You will help run GP surgeries, hospitals and other health centres, either working for the NHS or within the private sector.

Your job will be varied; you might be controlling finances, managing staff, producing reports on performance, overseeing buildings and buying equipment.

There are specific areas that managers can work in, such as clinical, financial, human resources, IT and facilities. You could also be a practice manager who runs GP surgeries.

Type of person suited to this work

Strong leadership skills and a likeable personality will be essential for managing your team. Good communication skills are important as you will be interacting with a variety of people including professionals and patients.

You should be comfortable making important decisions, be logical in your approach to problems and have good negotiation skills.

You must have excellent written communication skills to produce detailed reports and you should be comfortable working with figures, as you may be responsible for budgets and resources.

Working conditions

You will work standard office hours, Monday to Friday, but you could be on-call for emergencies or required to work weekends.

Most of your time will be spent in an office within hospitals, GP surgeries or health centres.

As a manager, you will be expected to dress smartly.

It is useful to have a driving licence as you might travel between sites or to attend meetings.

Future prospects

The NHS Graduate Management Training Scheme is fiercely competitive and changes in the NHS structure means that job numbers fluctuate due to the constant possibility of cutbacks.

There is a structured career path if you are employed by the NHS and promotion is gained by moving into different departments and areas of management.

The NHS Gateway to Leadership is available for managers with substantial experience. This fast-track programme enables you to become a chief executive within 5 years. In private healthcare there are stages of promotion which can also be followed.

With experience you may choose to take your managerial skills into another industry or become a consultant.

Advantages/disadvantages

You will be in a very responsible position which could be daunting and stressful.

You will gain valuable management skills which are transferable to many other industries.

Meeting and helping lots of different people provides a strong sense of job satisfaction.

Money guide

On the NHS pay scale, Agenda for Change, graduates on the NHS training scheme have a starting salary of about £22,444.

Once qualified, you are placed on either NHS wage band 6, earning between £25,783 and £34,530 or band 7, between £30,764 and £40,558.

Those in the most senior positions will be on band 9, earning between £77,850 and £98,453.

Salaries in the private sector could be higher.

Related opportunities

- Accountant p2
- Archivist/Records Manager p326
- Human Resources/Personnel Officer p28

Further information

Institute of Healthcare Management
www.ihm.org.uk

NHS Careers
www.nhscareers.nhs.uk

NHS Graduate Management Training Scheme
www.nhsgraduates.co.uk

HEALTH VISITOR

ENTRY LEVEL 6

Qualifications and courses

All health visitors must be registered nurses or midwives, but there is no minimum length of pre-entry experience required. To become a nurse or midwife, you must complete a degree in nursing or midwifery that is recognised by the Nursing and Midwifery Council. Generally, you will need 2 A levels/3 H grades and 5 GCSEs/National 5s (A*–C/A–C) to apply for a 3- or 4-year degree course.

Pre-entry experience may be useful and should be relevant to the work of a health visitor and demonstrate a desire and commitment to working in the community. More specialised experience, such as working with children, obstetrics or midwifery would also be advantageous.

Once you have completed your training as a nurse, you will need to complete the Specialist Community Public Health Nursing Health Visiting (SCPHN/HV) programme. This is qualification usually consists of 45 weeks of study that must be completed within a 156 week period; part-time study should be completed within 208 weeks.

You will be required to undergo a series of pre-employment checks including occupational health and Disclosure and Barring Service (DBS).

What the work involves

Health visitors work with people of all ages, backgrounds and cultures in various settings such as residential homes, schools, GP surgeries and village halls.

You will provide advice on issues ranging from problems in children's sleep or feeding patterns, to postnatal depression, bereavement or relationship problems and your primary patients will be parents with babies and young children.

You will also be involved in organising community events designed to promote health and wellbeing.

Type of person suited to this work

You will be working closely with patients so you will need excellent communication skills.

You must be trustworthy, understanding, reassuring and professional in order to inspire confidence in your patients, mainly parents, and allow them to share their problems and concerns with you openly. You should also be able to motivate them to make important lifestyle changes on occasion.

You must be able to prioritise a heavy workload, and maintain discretion when dealing with confidential information.

Working conditions

You will usually work a 37-hour week from Monday to Friday, and flexible hours or part-time work are often available.

You will work in a variety of locations, including schools, GP surgeries, health centres and residential homes. Because this will require a good deal of travelling within the local area, a driving licence is usually required.

You will encounter patients who are extremely difficult or distressed at times, which can be upsetting.

Future prospects

All health visitors work for the NHS, and they can be based in larger areas such as cities and towns, or work across villages and rural communities.

Due to a shortage of NHS health visitors the government has committed to the creation of 4,200 new jobs by 2015, a target they are currently working towards. Job opportunities in this sector are therefore on the increase.

Career progression could take the form of managing a team of health visitors, moving into a role as a consultant nurse, specialising in a particular area of nursing, education or research, or even taking up a position in general management within the NHS.

Advantages/disadvantages

You will be offering healthcare advice and treatment across the community, including to those who may otherwise not be able to reach a doctor or hospital very easily such as the elderly.

There are opportunities to work part time or on a job share basis, which would allow you to work around other commitments.

You may have to deal with difficult, potentially threatening patients, which can be frightening and upsetting.

Money guide

Qualified health visitors can earn between £25,783 and £34,530, with team managers earning up to £40,558.

Extra allowance can be made for added duties, location and experience.

Related opportunities

- Adult Nurse p269
- Children's Nurse p274
- Midwife p298
- Occupational Therapist p299
- Paramedic p304

Further information

Nursing and Midwifery Council
www.nmc-uk.org

Royal College of Nursing
www.rcn.org.uk

HEALTHCARE ASSISTANT

ENTRY LEVEL 1

Qualifications and courses

There are no fixed entry qualifications for this job, however previous experience caring for people, either through paid or voluntary work, may be expected by some employers.

All entrants to this profession will be required to pass a medical test and obtain clearance from the Disclosure and Barring Service (DBS).

The Apprenticeship in Health and Social Care offers an ideal route into this career for school leavers and is available at both Intermediate and Advanced Levels. This gives candidates the opportunity to combine practical work experience with the study towards a relevant professional qualification. These courses could include a BTEC in Health and Social Care (Levels 2–3), an A level/H grade in Health and Social Care, NVQs/SVQs such as the Level 3 Health and Social Care, and QCF qualifications in Healthcare Support Services or Clinical Healthcare Support (Levels 2–3). Entry for an apprenticeship usually requires 4 GCSEs/National 5s (A*–C/A–C) or a BTEC Level 1 Certificate/Diploma.

Once you secure employment as a healthcare assistant, you will receive on-the-job training covering topics including hygiene, health and safety, personal care and communication skills. You could go on to take a Foundation degree or degree in a subject such as nursing, mental health or applied health and social care.

What the work involves

Healthcare assistants help people who find it difficult to look after themselves with everyday tasks. Your clients could be children, elderly people or people with disabilities living in residential care or in their own homes.

You will help them to bathe, dress and use the toilet or commode, as well as assisting them with eating, washing, ironing, cleaning and shopping.

Part of your time will be spent talking to your clients, helping them to write letters, budget their money or pay bills.

Type of person suited to this work

Healthcare assistants need to be cheerful, outgoing and friendly, as their clients may be lonely or depressed.

As the job involves working with people who need individual support, you will have to work out what help they need and provide it in a sympathetic and tactful way.

You must be trustworthy, discreet and able to keep clients' confidential information private, as you will handle money, and write and read personal/business letters.

The job usually includes domestic work so you need to be happy and skilled at doing housework and laundry.

Working conditions

Many healthcare assistants work in residential homes and day-healthcare centres, but more people are being cared for in their own homes.

As the main employers are health authorities, social services, private homes and voluntary agencies, most of your work will be looking after clients from the time they wake up to the time they go to bed, with the chance to supervise on hospital appointments or outings. You might have to live-in for some jobs.

You will usually work on a shift system which will include early mornings, evenings, weekends and bank holidays.

You need to be physically fit and capable of heavy lifting as you may need to help people who are unable to move around themselves.

You will be expected to be very careful about health and safety issues, such as fire and hot water.

Future prospects

There are over a million healthcare assistants in the UK and demand is increasing as the NHS evolves due to cutback in other roles. The 2013 Cavendish Report makes several recommendations as to how healthcare assistants can receive training and their role in the NHS.

Promotion depends on qualifications and experience. With experience in healthcare work, you could train for related jobs such as social work or nursing.

Advantages/disadvantages

It can be satisfying to help people in need.

Working on public holidays, such as Christmas Day, can interfere with your personal life.

Some jobs can be messy and unpleasant.

Money guide

Salaries start between £14,000 and £17,000 a year.

With experience and relevant qualifications, you can expect to earn approximately £19,000 a year.

Allowances for working shifts and unsocial hours can increase your income.

Related opportunities

- Adult Nurse p269
- Childminder p545
- Social Worker p557

Further information

NHS Careers
www.nhscareers.nhs.uk

HOMEOPATH

ENTRY LEVEL 3

Qualifications and courses

Although it is not compulsory to hold a qualification, most patients would not feel comfortable seeing you if you are not registered with one of the UK regulatory bodies, the best known of which is the Society of Homeopaths (SOH).

In order to register, you will need to complete an accredited degree or licentiate diploma in homeopathy from a private college. Entry requirements for these courses are usually 2 A levels/3 H grades and 5 GCSEs/National 5s (A*–C/A–C). Degree courses can be taken full time over 3 years or part time over 4. Most private colleges may require 2 A levels/H grades, including a science subject, but your life and work experience and your interest in homeopathy are usually more valued.

Qualified healthcare professionals can undertake shorter accredited courses in homeopathy at various universities, each of which is regulated by the British Homeopathic Association (BHA).

What the work involves

Homeopaths use highly diluted doses of natural remedies to treat patients for a variety of ailments, ranging from simple headaches to complicated emotional issues, addiction and disease.

You will need to take into account not only patients' physical symptoms, but also their psychological and emotional state, as well as their lifestyle.

You will be working with a variety of patients of all ages, backgrounds and cultures. You could undertake general cases, or specialise in areas such as fertility and drug addiction.

Type of person suited to this work

You will need excellent communication and listening skills in order to quickly build a rapport with patients and encourage them to discuss their problems and concerns honestly.

As you will need to build your own practice and find clients from scratch, you must have good business acumen, confidence and motivation.

You should also be well organised and methodical, as you will need to undertake your own administration and keep detailed, informative patient notes.

You will be in charge of storing confidential information about patients and should be professional in your approach to each client.

Working conditions

You will be self-employed and reliant on your clients, so will find that you mainly work in the evenings and at weekends (especially when newly qualified) in order to fit around their lifestyles.

You could work in a clinic with other healthcare professionals, in an alternative therapy centre, in your own home, or you could travel to see patients in their homes.

Patient appointments can take anywhere between 45 minutes and an hour and a half. The work is therefore mentally and emotionally draining as it requires long periods of concentrated work and, because of this, most homeopaths only work part time.

Future prospects

Alternative therapy has increased in popularity in recent years. This means that there are more people willing to explore it as a means of treatment, but also that there are an increasing number of practising homeopaths. Competition for clients, especially in the early years, can be great.

The majority of homeopaths are self-employed, although there are opportunities in independent surgeries, private hospitals and in one of the 5 homeopathic NHS hospitals in the UK.

With experience you could use your knowledge to teach in a university or college, or write related books and articles.

Advantages/disadvantages

Spending time talking to patients about their concerns and alleviating their ailments is extremely rewarding.

If you are self-employed, overheads such as renting clinic space and buying remedies and other equipment will eat into your earnings.

You must be commercially aware in order to successfully market your business, and be prepared to do your own complicated tax forms.

Money guide

Most homeopaths charge their patients directly by appointment. They usually charge between £40 and £100 per session, with higher fees being found in London and the south east.

A newly qualified homeopath who is just starting to build a reputation and attract clients could earn about £6,000 a year.

For top earning homeopaths with lots of experience, salaries can rise to £30,000.

Related opportunities

- Aromatherapist p271
- Chiropractor p275
- Osteopath p303

Further information

Alliance of Registered Homeopaths
www.a-r-h.org

British Homeopathic Association
www.britishhomeopathic.org

Society of Homeopaths
www.homeopathy-soh.org

HOSPITAL DOCTOR

ENTRY LEVEL 8

Qualifications and courses

To become a hospital doctor, all entrants need to hold a degree in medicine which has been accredited by the General Medical Council (GMC). Courses normally last 5 years and entry requirements are usually at least 3 very high A levels/H grades including chemistry and biology, and good GCSEs/National 5s (A*–C/A–C), including English, maths and science. Competition for places on medical degrees is very high and undertaking relevant pre-entry work experience as a care assistant, for example, may benefit your application. You may also be asked to take the UK Clinical Aptitude Test (UKCAT) to substantiate your suitability for a career in medicine.

For those without the relevant A levels or equivalent, some universities offer a 6-year medical degree, in which the first year is a preliminary course in chemistry, physics and biology lasting 30 weeks.

Graduates of a science-related subject (minimum 2.1) can apply for a 4-year, fast-track medical degree programme. Some universities will consider applications from non-science graduates.

Upon completion of your degree in medicine, you will need to complete 2 further stages of vocational training to qualify as a senior doctor or consultant in your chosen field. The first stage is the 2-year Foundation Programme which forms the bridge between medical school and specialist/general practice training. The second stage is specialist training in an area of medicine which particularly interests you and the length of time this takes depends upon the area you choose.

What the work involves

Hospital doctors work in either NHS or private establishments, diagnosing illnesses, treating patients and monitoring their care.

You may treat patients yourself or, having assessed them, refer them to their General Practitioner (GP) or another healthcare professional. You will work in one of over 60 specialisms which include cardiology, general medicine, paediatrics, orthopaedics and psychiatry.

You will also be required to carry out surgical operations within your specialism, for example fitting a pacemaker if you are in cardiology. You may be responsible for teaching medical students.

Type of person suited to this work

You must have excellent communication skills as you will be dealing with patients and healthcare professionals on a daily basis.

When handling patients, you should be empathetic, non-judgemental, professional and calm.

You should be good at working under pressure, making sensible, but sometimes difficult, decisions and solving problems.

Working conditions

Generally you can expect to work longer hours than in most other professions, although new guidelines prohibit junior doctors from working more than a 48-hour week. You will usually work on a shift pattern of days and nights which will sometimes involve being on-call.

You will work in a consulting room, on the wards and in operating theatres. Conditions are usually quiet and clean, although things can get very fast paced during times of emergency.

You will also be required to attend numerous meetings and conferences across the UK, Europe and perhaps worldwide.

Future prospects

Junior doctors can choose to specialise in an area such as gastroenterology or geriatric medicine. Once they have completed a training programme in their specialism and passed the necessary exams, they will become a consultant.

Increasingly, senior level hospital doctors undertake managerial responsibilities, alongside teaching and mentoring work with students or junior doctors.

Advantages/disadvantages

You will be responsible for helping patients get better and making them comfortable throughout their illness which is very rewarding.

Hours can be long (reportedly over 100 hours a week sometimes) and unpredictable so it can be difficult to get a satisfactory work–life balance.

Constant developments in medicine and medical technology mean that you will be continually learning and developing throughout your career.

Money guide

As a junior hospital trainee, the basic salary starts at £22,636 and rises in the second year of foundation training to £28,076.

A doctor in specialist training has a starting salary of £30,002. Trainee doctors also receive extra pay for working more than 40 hours a week or outside of the normal working hours, 7am to 7pm, Monday to Friday.

Specialist doctors can earn £37,176 to £69,325, while consultants can earn a basic salary between £75,249 and £101,451.

Doctors in the private sector can earn more.

Related opportunities

- Children's Nurse p274
- Doctor (GP) p285
- Surgeon p321

Further information

British Medical Association
www.bma.org.uk

NHS Careers
www.nhscareers.nhs.uk

HOSPITAL PORTER

ENTRY LEVEL 1

Qualifications and courses

There are no formal entry requirements for this job, but applicants must be literate and have good all-round communication skills as well as good physical fitness.

There is no set minimum age, but most applicants are at least 18 years old, and there are good opportunities for mature entrants.

You will undergo a short induction once you start and then training is generally on the job. However, in order to strengthen your application or even, once you have started work, you work towards several formal qualifications such as an NVQ Level 2 in Support Services in Health Care, the Level 3 Diploma in Healthcare Support Services or a BTEC in Health and Social Care (Health Sciences) (Level 2–3).

Previous experience of volunteer hospital work, or previous work with the public in a caring role, can be useful to your job application and a health and safety qualification may also be beneficial. Alternatively, apprenticeships in health and social care are available and will prepare you to be a hospital porter and other related roles.

Candidates usually have to pass a medical examination, and may be required to take a physical fitness test. A driving licence may be required so that you can work at a range of different sites.

What the work involves

Hospital porters transport patients, equipment and other items to where they need to go within the hospital.

One of your main tasks will be to move frail and ill patients between departments and wards, while keeping them safe and comfortable.

You will transport patients using wheelchairs and trolleys.

You may also have a variety of other tasks such as delivering mail and moving medical equipment and supplies.

Type of person suited to this work

Hospital porters need to be responsible and reliable with a positive attitude to make sure that people and equipment are transported to the correct part of the hospital on time.

You should be able to follow instructions and work well as part of a team.

Patients may be distressed or in pain so you must be caring and sympathetic and be able to reassure them and keep them comfortable. You must be able to cope with sickness and death.

Physical fitness is important, because you will walk long distances during your shift and you will have to lift and move patients and equipment.

Working conditions

You will work with patients and other staff, mainly indoors, although you might need to travel to other hospital sites to make deliveries.

You will need to pay attention to health and safety when lifting and handling people and equipment.

Porters usually wear a uniform and often need to work shifts, which includes working nights, weekends and bank holidays.

You may assist with hospital security which could involve working on reception.

Future prospects

Most jobs are within NHS hospitals, although there are also posts within private hospitals.

There are opportunities throughout the country but they can be competitive in some areas.

With experience you could become a supervisor and then take management qualifications for promotion to head porter or porter manager.

You could also do further training to move into related careers, such as healthcare assistant or ambulance work.

Advantages/disadvantages

The work can be physically demanding and stressful at times.

You will meet a variety of people and the job is active and busy.

It is satisfying to play a vital role within a hospital; without porters a hospital would not be able to function.

Money guide

The NHS sets national pay rates for hospital porters, with salaries in private hospitals being similar to those of the NHS.

Earnings start at around £14,294 per year and can rise to £17,425.

There are additional payments for overtime and additional duties.

Related opportunities

- Hotel Porter p127
- Paramedic p304
- Sterile Services Technician p320

Further information

NHS Careers
www.nhscareers.nhs.uk

Skills for Health
www.skillsforhealth.org.uk

LEARNING DISABILITIES NURSE

ENTRY LEVEL 6

Qualifications and courses

Learning disabilities nurses must hold a degree in nursing which has been approved by the Nursing and Midwifery Council (NMC). Minimum entry requirements for degree courses are usually 2 A levels/3H grades, ideally including a science-based subject, and 5 GCSEs/ National 5s (A*–C/A–C), including English, maths and a science subject. All applicants must obtain clearance from the Disclosure and Barring Service (DBS) before commencing their training.

If you do not have the required GCSEs/National 5s or A levels/H grades, some universities will accept other qualifications, such as a BTEC in Health and Social Care (Levels 2–3) or the Access to Higher Education Diploma in a science or health-related subject.

Graduates with a degree in a health-related subject such as human biology, life and medical sciences or biomedical science, may be eligible to enter the nursing profession by taking an accelerated 2-year programme which leads to a Master of Science (MSc) or Postgraduate Diploma.

For this branch of nursing, you will usually be required to have relevant experience working with people with learning disabilities. Opportunities to volunteer may be available through the Charity Choice website.

Postgraduate courses are also available in topics such as mental health practice, cognitive behaviour therapy, forensic mental health practice, and acute and psychiatric intensive care settings.

What the work involves

Learning disabilities nurses work with people with learning disabilities in order to teach them new skills and support them in becoming as independent as possible.

You will be assessing patients and devising suitable care plans for them, as well as supporting their families or carers by helping them implement development strategies and arranging for them to take a break from their responsibilities when necessary.

You will work in a range of locations, including patients' homes, care homes and schools.

Type of person suited to this work

You will need excellent communication skills in order to develop a good relationship with patients and colleagues alike. To successfully help people to learn new skills, you must be a patient teacher.

You should be compassionate and empathetic in understanding your patients' feelings and frustrations, whilst maintaining a professional attitude so that you can distance yourself from your work at the end of the day.

You will need both physical and mental stamina to support your patients fully.

Working conditions

You will usually work 37 hours a week including evening, night and weekend work. Part-time work and flexible hours are frequently available.

As you will be working in the community, you will spend time travelling to and from patients' homes, schools, clinics and residential homes. A driving licence would be useful.

You may also accompany and support clients as they undertake everyday tasks such as going to the shops or the gym, booking a holiday, travelling on public transport or even going to work.

Future prospects

Most learning disabilities nurses are employed by the NHS, although there are also opportunities in the private sector and with local authority healthcare teams. The governments Strengthening the Commitment review of learning disability nurses makes many recommendations on career choices and developing new roles to fill skill gaps.

You may undertake further training that could allow you to specialise in an area that particularly interests you, such as education or cognitive disability.

You could go on to become a team leader, supervisor, or even a nurse consultant. Alternatively, you could move into research or teaching.

Advantages/disadvantages

You will be providing a life enhancing service for a number of people in your local community.

There are good opportunities for career development or diversification, as well as the option of flexible working hours to suit your lifestyle and family commitments.

You may encounter difficult or abusive patients which can be distressing and unpleasant.

Money guide

A newly qualified nurse can expect a starting salary of £21,388.

As you gain experience, your earnings can increase to about £28,000.

Those who take on a senior position with additional responsibilities can achieve £25,500–£40,500.

If you specialise in a particular area and undertake the training to become a nurse consultant, you could earn up between £39,000 and £67,000.

Related opportunities

- Adult Nurse p269
- Children's Nurse p274
- Health Visitor p289

Further information

NHS Careers
www.nhscareers.nhs.uk

Nursing and Midwifery Council
www.nmc-uk.org

Qualifications and courses

There are no set requirements to enter this profession, but many professional bodies recommend you take an in-depth course of at least 6 months full time or 12 months part time. You will need at least 5 GCSEs/ National 5s to enrol on a course. Relevant qualifications include the NVQ Level 3 in Beauty Therapy (Massage), the VTCT Level 3 Diploma in Body Massage, Swedish Massage or Remedial Massage, the ITEC Level 3 Diploma in Massage or Massage Techniques, the ITEC Certificate in Anatomy and Physiology, and the City & Guilds Level 3 Diploma in Anatomy, Physiology and Pathology for Complementary Therapies.

The course you choose will need to be recognised by the General Council for Massage Therapy, and include beauty therapy, Swedish massage, holistic massage, and anatomy and physiology. Awarding bodies include the International Therapy Examination Council (ITEC) and Vocational Training Charitable Trust (VTCT). Once you start training you will cover not only massage itself but also First Aid, health and safety, employment law, and assessing clients.

You could begin on the path to massage by following an Apprenticeship in Beauty Therapy. If you already have experience of work in health and beauty, you can enter this field as a second career; many people choose to do this.

Once you are fully qualified you can choose to become a member of a professional body and register with the Complimentary and Natural Healthcare Council. The Council runs best practice, protects the public and manages complaints.

To specialise in a particular form of massage, such as baby and infant massage or sports massage, you will need to enroll on additional, specialist training courses.

What the work involves

A massage therapist uses massage as a therapy to relieve clients of pain or stress. Some practitioners specialise in specific areas of the body, whilst others work on the entire body. Many practitioners are self-employed and either work from home or run their own salons.

As a massage therapist, you are trained in techniques and movements that have proven therapeutic effects and aid the healing process.

Type of person suited to this work

You will need to be good with people and have a reassuring friendly manner.

You will need to be able to explain what you are doing clearly, and have to be able to respond to your client effectively and calmly. You should be very comfortable with close physical contact, and have good manual dexterity.

You should have excellent concentration skills, as the work demands great physical and mental energy. You will also need good organisational skills, as you may well end up running your own business. This will also require confidence and good business acumen.

Working conditions

If you work in a beauty clinic or spa, you will usually do a 40-hour week, whilst self-employed massage therapists can opt for fewer hours. Either way, you will have to work around your clients' lifestyles, which means working evenings and weekends.

You could work in hospitals, beauty salons, health spas, care homes, leisure centres, and clients' homes. You could also work from home, or even set up your own clinic.

Treatment rooms should be (and usually are) clean, warm and peaceful. You may often play calming music or use aromatherapy oils to add to the experience.

Future prospects

Once you have gained some experience you could set up your own practice, provided you have the business sense to do so.

Physiotherapy, sports or alternative medicine clinics are the biggest employers of massage therapists. You might also decide that you would like to learn about a similar profession such as reflexology or aromatherapy so that you can offer your clients a wider range of services.

You could even teach massage, if you are prepared to study for a teaching qualification.

Advantages/disadvantages

If you like working with and helping people you should really enjoy this work.

It is a good opportunity to use your skills, and you can really see the results.

The work can be tiring, and you need to be physically fit to do a good job and enjoy it properly.

Money guide

Many massage therapists are self-employed and charge by session or hourly rate. This could be between £25 and £60 an hour, depending on location.

A skilled therapist who has built a large, dependable client base could earn between £20,000 and £40,000. This could be supplemented through the sale of beauty products.

Related opportunities

- Acupuncturist p268
- Aromatherapist p271
- Physiotherapist p310

Further information

CIBTAC
www.cibtac.com

Complementary and Natural Healthcare Council
www.cnhc.org.uk

General Council for Massage Therapy
www.gcmt.org.uk

International Therapy Examination Council
www.itecworld.co.uk

MEDICAL PHYSICIST

ENTRY LEVEL 6

Qualifications and courses

Candidates will need a 1st or 2.1 degree in a subject such as physics, medical physics, physical science or electrical engineering. Entry to a relevant degree course requires at least 2 A levels/3 H grades, usually including physics and maths, plus 5 GCSEs/National 5s (A*–C/A–C), including English and maths. A postgraduate qualification or industrial experience may also be useful to enter this career.

Candidates go into the profession as trainees and the competitive NHS Healthcare Scientist Training Programme (STP) is the specified entry route. Your application will be strengthened with work experience in a hospital medical physics department, which should also help you decide on a specialist area. The training programme lasts 3 years and you will study for a Master of Science (MSc) in medical physics. If you already have an MSc qualification, you need only to complete a 15-month training period based in a hospital.

Advanced trainee medical physicists undertake 2 years of training in a specialist field. You can then apply for an Academy for Healthcare Science Certificate of Attainment or Certificate of Equivalence. On completion, candidates are eligible for registration with the Health & Care Professions Council (HCPC) to work in unsupervised situations and in the NHS and apply for Membership of the Institute of Physics and Engineering in Medicine (IPEM), which is the professional body for this area of clinical science.

What the work involves

Medical physicists use their expert knowledge of physics to diagnose, prevent and treat disease.

You will be using specialist equipment and techniques to investigate patients' illnesses, this includes X-rays, radiography, ultrasounds, MRI machines, radiotherapy, and laser therapy.

You may be designing, developing and maintaining equipment, and advising medical staff on its use or planning the correct treatment for a patient using specific equipment. Your role may also involve patient contact, explaining procedures and results.

Type of person suited to this work

Medical physicists need to have expert skills in physical sciences and the ability to use their skills to solve problems and improve the diagnosis and treatment of disease.

You should have excellent research skills, be able to work accurately and be willing to take responsibility for decisions which will have a direct effect on patients.

You will need good communication skills to explain complex procedures clearly to patients, and to work as part of a team. You must also be prepared to keep up with the latest developments and continue to learn new skills.

Working conditions

Most medical physicists work in hospitals and laboratories and some have contact with patients on wards or in clinics.

You will need to work safely with equipment and chemicals in the laboratory, some of which can be hazardous.

You will normally work from Monday to Friday, but work outside normal hours and travel to conferences will sometimes be necessary.

Future prospects

The number of medical physicists is increasing, although trainee posts are competitive and you might have to relocate for some specialist roles.

Most jobs are in the larger NHS hospitals throughout the UK. There are also some opportunities in the nuclear energy industry, medical equipment industry, private hospitals and medical research institutes.

Within the NHS there is a recognised career path and you could even reach consultant level. Employment in the private sector is less structured.

There are plenty of opportunities for continuing professional development (CPD) which will improve your career prospects. IPEM also offers formal development courses in skills such as management, and once these have been completed you will have the opportunity to become a chartered scientist (CSci).

Advantages/disadvantages

Some of the work could be routine at times.

You will be playing an important role in the overall healthcare of the patients, as you will be contributing to the diagnosis and treatment of their diseases.

Money guide

In the NHS trainees could expect a starting salary of around £25,000.

Medical physicists working for NHS usually start on the NHS wage band 6 of the Agenda for Change pay structure, earning between £25,783 and £34,530.

Team leaders could advance to band 7, £30,764 to £40,558. A healthcare consultant could earn up to £67,805 on band 8.

Salaries will differ if you work for private companies outside the NHS.

Related opportunities

- Physicist p509
- Radiographer p316
- Radiologist p317

Further information

Institute of Physics and Engineering in Medicine
www.ipem.ac.uk

NHS Careers
www.nhscareers.nhs.uk

Skills for Health
www.skillsforhealth.org.uk

MENTAL HEALTH NURSE

ENTRY LEVEL 6

Qualifications and courses

All mental health nurses must hold a degree in mental health nursing which has been approved by the Nursing and Midwifery Council (NMC). Minimum entry requirements for degree courses are usually 2 A levels/3 H grades, ideally including a science-based subject, and 5 GCSEs/National 5s (A*–C/A–C) including English, maths and a science subject. All applicants must obtain clearance from the Disclosure and Barring Service (DBS) before commencing their training.

If you do not have the required GCSEs/National 5s or A levels/H grades, some universities will accept other qualifications, such as the BTEC qualifications in Health and Social Care (Levels 2–3) or an Access to Higher Education Diploma in a science or health-related subject.

Graduates with a degree in a health-related subject such as human biology, life and medical sciences or biomedical science, may be eligible to enter the nursing profession by taking an accelerated 2-year programme which leads to a Master of Science (MSc) or Postgraduate Diploma. Part-time programmes are also provided by some universities and normally last for 5 or 6 years.

For this branch of nursing, it would be useful to have relevant experience working with people who use mental health services.

Once qualified, the NMC requires you to keep yourself up to date with healthcare issues and practice through continuing professional development (CPD).

What the work involves

Mental health nurses care for people with mental health problems both in hospitals and within the wider community. They help patients come to terms with their problems and overcome their limitations by listening to them as they discuss their illness and anxieties.

You will also work with a patient's friends and family where possible to create a stable and proactive network around the individual and also to provide support to those closest to him/her.

You could encounter patients with problems including stress-related conditions, eating disorders, drug and alcohol dependency, and personality disorders.

Type of person suited to this work

You will need excellent communication skills in order to develop a good relationship with patients, their families and other healthcare professionals.

You must be extremely observant so that you can spot any minor changes in a patient's condition and manage them before they trigger undesirable results.

You should be non-judgemental and empathetic in order to understand your patients' feelings and frustrations. In a difficult situation, you must be able to remain calm and assertive.

Working conditions

You will usually work 37 hours a week, including evenings and weekends.

You could work in a hospital, in the community, or undertake a mixture of both.

If you work across the community, you will travel to a variety of places including patients' homes, hostels, day centres and drug dependency units. A driving licence may be required.

Future prospects

Most mental health nurses are employed by the NHS, although there are also opportunities in the private sector and in local social services teams. Changes to legislation and funding means new roles are being established, such as basing mental health nurses in police stations.

You may undertake further training to specialise in an area that particularly interests you, such as drug abuse.

You could go on to become a team leader, supervisor or nurse consultant, or you may progress to a general management position within the NHS. Alternatively, you could move into research or teaching.

Advantages/disadvantages

Providing a life enhancing service for a number of people in your local community is highly rewarding.

After gaining a few years' experience, you should have the option of flexible working hours that will suit your lifestyle and personal commitments.

You may encounter difficult or abusive patients which can be distressing and unpleasant.

Money guide

A newly qualified mental health nurse can expect a starting salary of £21,388.

As you gain experience, your earnings can increase up to about £27,901.

Those who take on a senior position with additional responsibilities can achieve between £25,500 to £40,500.

If you specialise in a particular area and undertake the training to become a nurse consultant, you could earn up to £67,000.

Related opportunities

- Health Visitor p289
- Learning Disabilities Nurse p294
- Occupational Therapist p299

Further information

NHS Careers
www.nhscareers.nhs.uk

Royal College of Nursing
www.rcn.org.uk

MIDWIFE

ENTRY LEVEL 6

Qualifications and courses

All midwives must hold a degree in midwifery which has been approved by the Nursing and Midwifery Council (NMC). Entry requirements for degree courses depend upon the individual university but you will usually need 2 A levels/3 H grades, ideally including a science-based subject, and 5 GCSEs/National 5s (A*–C/A–C), including English, maths and a science subject. Relevant pre-entry experience is a distinct advantage. A degree in midwifery lasts 3 years when studied on a full-time basis and all applicants must obtain clearance from the Disclosure and Barring Service (DBS) before commencing their training.

If you do not have the required GCSEs/National 5s or A levels/H grades, some universities will accept other qualifications, such as a BTEC in Health and Social Care (Levels 2–3) or an Access to Higher Education Diploma in a science or health-related subject.

Those who have already qualified as an adult nurse and are currently registered with the NMC have the option of taking a shorter 18-month course to become a midwife.

You are eligible to register as a midwife with the NMC once you have completed an approved midwifery degree. Midwives are expected to engage in continuing professional development (CPD) throughout their career to keep their skills and knowledge up to date.

What the work involves

Midwives help and support women and their partners from early pregnancy, through the antenatal period, during the labour and birth, and also for up to a month after the baby has been born.

You will be responsible for monitoring your patient throughout her pregnancy, providing advice and support on issues including nutrition, methods of childbirth and breastfeeding.

You will deliver babies or assist in the birthing process. You will also be responsible for identifying high risk pregnancies and arranging specialist care and provisions where necessary.

Type of person suited to this work

You must be an excellent communicator as it is essential to form a good relationship with patients, their partners and other healthcare professionals. You need to be friendly and caring in order to gain the trust and confidence of the women under your guidance.

As childbirth is strenuous, messy and unpredictable, you should be able to stay calm under pressure, think on your feet and have good mental and physical stamina.

You need careful attention to detail when carrying out your work and completing patient notes.

Working conditions

You will usually work 37 hours a week and these will include evening, night and weekend work. You may also be on-call at times. Part-time work and flexible hours are frequently available.

You could be based in the maternity unit of a hospital or in a birth centre. Midwives are also increasingly affiliated with GP surgeries and other health centres.

You will probably spend time travelling from your place of work to your patients' homes so a driving licence would be helpful.

Future prospects

The effects of the recession is affecting the number of midwife jobs and cuts are expected to continue as the NHS is restructured. Midwifery 2020, a government evaluation of the sector, notes a change of working patterns from full time to part time.

In the NHS, midwives can progress to a senior level as a team leader or midwife consultant. You could take further training which would allow you to specialise in an area that particularly interests you, or to move into a related profession such as neonatal nursing.

Other opportunities include undertaking research, or training and teaching student midwives.

Advantages/disadvantages

Supporting women and families through pregnancy and childbirth is both rewarding and fulfilling.

This job can be distressing as you will have to deal with complications in pregnancy and labour.

Money guide

The starting salary for a newly qualified midwife is between £21,388.

As you gain experience, you can expect to earn up to £34,500.

Those in a senior position, such as a midwife team manager, typically earn £30,000 to £40,000.

If you specialise or become a midwife consultant, you could earn up to £67,000.

Salaries are usually higher in London and allowances for on-call duties can increase earnings.

Related opportunities

- Adult Nurse p269
- Children's Nurse p274
- Occupational Therapist p299

Further information

Nursing and Midwifery Council
www.nmc-uk.org

Royal College of Midwives
www.rcm.org.uk

discover risk .co.uk
Do you have an ENQUIRING mind?
Have you got an enquiring mind?
Do you ask more questions than you can answer?
Want to know more?

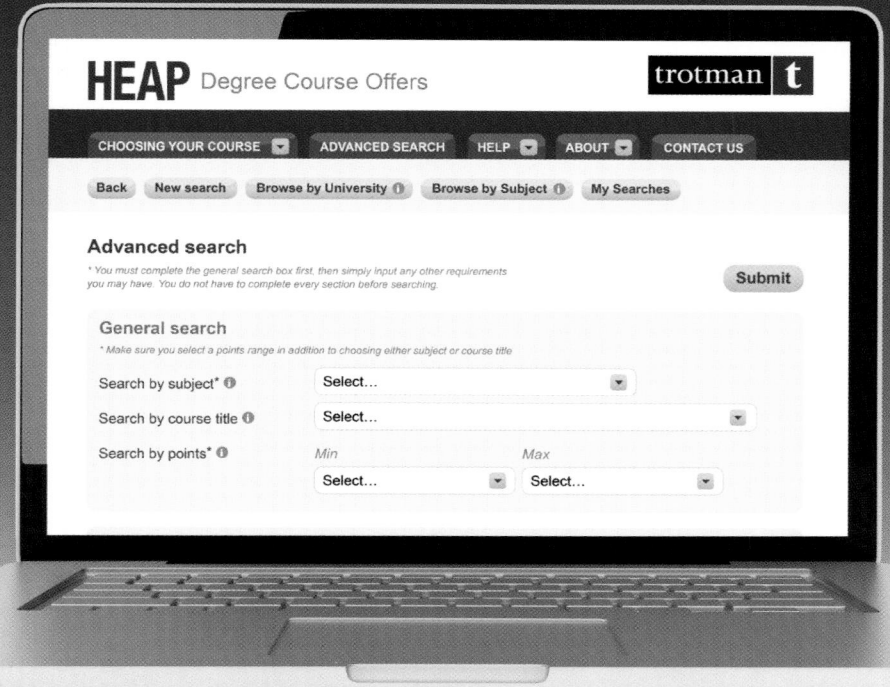

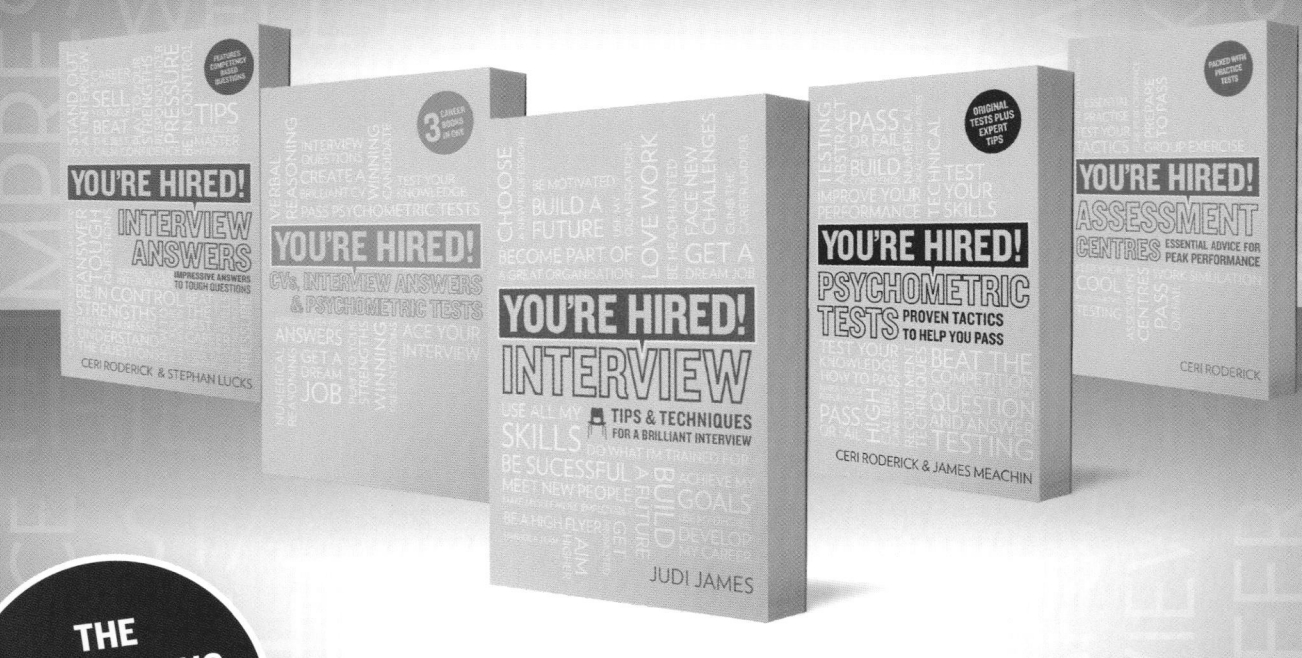

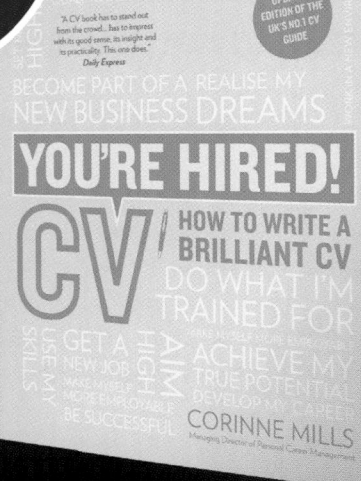

OCCUPATIONAL THERAPIST

ENTRY LEVEL 6

Qualifications and courses

To become an occupational therapist, you will need a degree or postgraduate diploma in occupational therapy that has been approved by the Health and Care Professions Council (HCPC).

For degree entry, you will normally need at least 2 A levels/3 H grades including a science, preferably biology, human biology or psychology, and 5 GCSEs/National 5s (A*–C/A–C). The Advanced Diploma in Society, Health and Development may also be relevant. A degree in occupational therapy normally takes 3 years, however there is an accelerated 2-year diploma programme available to graduates from other degree disciplines who have experience in health or social care.

In-service courses are available for those employed as occupational therapy support workers or technical instructors. Courses are studied part time and lead to professional qualification as an occupational therapist.

Before you can register with the HCPC, you must undergo a Disclosure and Barring Service (DBS) background check.

To remain registered with the HCPC, occupational therapists must carry out continuing professional development (CPD) throughout the course of their career. You can do this by joining the British Association of Occupational Therapists (BAOT).

What the work involves

Occupational therapists help people overcome physical, psychological or social problems arising from illness or disability.

You could see patients with problems stemming from conditions such as multiple sclerosis or Parkinson's, those with physical and mental disabilities or issues, and those who are affected by drug and alcohol use.

You will help patients with everyday tasks such as washing, cooking and even going to work. Your care will focus on what patients can achieve, rather than on their disabilities. Your job will also include writing treatment plans, giving advice on practical issues such as disability equipment, teaching coping strategies and using activities to stimulate your patients.

Type of person suited to this work

You must have excellent interpersonal skills as you will need to inspire trust and confidence in patients with a range of problems, including some who are difficult, anxious or unpredictable. You will need to be patient, caring, and sensitive to your patients' needs, concerns and expectations.

You should have both mental and physical stamina as you will need to provide hands-on support to patients as well as coping with their emotional issues.

You should be a natural problem solver with a flexible and creative approach to your work. The ability to motivate your patients and other professionals is also essential.

Working conditions

Most occupational therapists work a normal working week from Monday to Friday, although you might have to work evenings and weekends to provide a 24-hour community service.

You could work in a variety of locations, such as hospitals, a patient's home, residential homes, prisons and workplaces, so a driving licence would be useful.

Future prospects

Demand for occupational therapists is high, but you may still find that there is competition for jobs in certain areas.

You could be employed by the NHS, private hospitals, local authorities, charities or voluntary agencies. There are also opportunities to work abroad.

With experience, you could move into a more clinical position, take up a research post or set up your own practice. Alternatively you could progress to a managerial role within the NHS or opt to teach within your field.

Advantages/disadvantages

It is very rewarding to be able to help people to overcome difficulties and achieve their goals.

You could specialise in a variety of areas such as rehabilitation, learning disabilities or paediatrics.

The work can be emotionally and mentally demanding.

Money guide

Starting salaries for newly qualified occupational therapists are around £21,388.

With further experience this can rise to between £25,500 and £34,500.

In a more senior role that includes supervisory and managerial responsibilities or consultancy your earnings could rise to £40,000.

Related opportunities

- Health Visitor p289
- Learning Disabilities Nurse p294
- Mental Health Nurse p297

Further information

British Association of Occupational Therapists and College of Occupational Therapists
www.cot.co.uk

NHS Careers
www.nhscareers.nhs.uk

OPERATING DEPARTMENT PRACTITIONER

ENTRY LEVEL 5

Qualifications and courses

Entry into this profession requires a Diploma of Higher Education (DipHE) in Operating Department Practice approved by the Health and Care Professions Council (HCPC). Courses are available throughout the UK and generally last 2 or 3 years with normal minimum entry requirements being 5 GCSEs/National 5s (A*–C/A–C) preferably in English, maths and/or a science based subject or equivalent, but some institutions might require AS levels or A levels/H grades. Access courses may be taken prior to Diploma programmes.

The minimum age for entry into this line of work is 18, and mature candidates are very common as many have experience of other types of hospital work, for example as a healthcare assistant, and apply to become operating department practitioners later.

A small number of universities also offer an undergraduate degree in Operating Department Practice, with entry requirements typically including 2 A levels/3 H grades and 5 GCSEs/National 5s (A*–C/A–C). Again, pre-entry work experience may be necessary for a successful application.

Once qualified, you will need to undergo a medical test, an occupational health screening and Disclosure and Barring Service (DBS) check. You can then be accepted on to the state register and be a member of the College of Operating Department Practitioners (CODP).

What the work involves

Operating department practitioners work alongside surgeons, anaesthetists and other staff before, during and after operations.

Before surgery you will help calm a patient's anxiety, plan treatment, sterilise equipment and bring the patient to the operating theatre. During surgery you will monitor effects of the anaesthetic, pass tools to surgeons, take care of surgical wounds and dispose of soiled dressings.

After surgery you will bring patients to the recovery unit, monitor their wellbeing, provide pain relief and evaluate care.

It will be your responsibility to anticipate the needs of your colleagues and respond effectively.

Type of person suited to this work

You will need the scientific knowledge and practical skills to prepare specialist equipment and drugs. You will be helping with operations so you cannot be squeamish.

You must pay close attention when monitoring patients because their lives depend on it. You need to be able to react quickly and accurately if the patient experiences any complications.

Excellent communication skills are essential and you will need to be caring and sensitive.

Working conditions

You will mainly work in operating theatres, anaesthetic areas and recovery rooms in hospitals. However, operating department practitioners are increasingly being recognised for their skills in other critical areas.

You will need to follow hygiene procedures closely, wear a sterile gown and gloves during operations and be able to stand for long periods.

You will usually work shifts which may include working at nights, at weekends and on bank holidays. You might also have stand-by or on-call duties.

Future prospects

Demand for qualified operating department practitioners remains high, both within the NHS and the private health sector.

Most employment is available with the NHS throughout the UK. There are also opportunities in private hospitals.

You could progress into higher grade posts which involve more responsibility for managing and training others. It is possible to become a senior operating department practitioner or run your own theatre.

There are also opportunities to enter research or teaching.

Advantages/disadvantages

The work can be stressful at times and you will see some unpleasant things.

It is rewarding to be part of a team improving people's health and saving lives.

You could work in a range of areas, such as resuscitation, intensive care or day surgery.

Money guide

Starting salaries for qualified staff in the NHS is £21,176, rising to £27,625.

With experience you can earn up to £34,189.

It is possible for a higher-level theatre practitioner to earn up to £34,189.

Related opportunities

- Critical Care Technologist p277
- Paramedic p304
- Sterile Services Technician p320

Further information

NHS Careers
www.nhscareers.nhs.uk

Skills for Health
www.skillsforhealth.org.uk

OPTOMETRIST

ENTRY LEVEL 6

Qualifications and courses

In order to become an optometrist, you must obtain a degree that has been accredited by the General Optical Council (GOC). Degrees accredited by the GOC are offered at several universities and entry requirements may vary according to the institution. For entry onto a degree course, students are normally expected to have 2 A levels/3 H grades, including at least 2 from biology, maths, physics and chemistry, and 5 GCSEs/National 5s (A*–C/A–C), including English, maths and physics or double award science.

Graduates with a 2.2 degree or higher and a valid Certificate of Clinical Competency, which is awarded on graduation and valid for 2 years, must then follow a pre-registration year of supervised clinical experience. Successful completion of this year of work-based training and completion of the final assessment examination from the College of Optometrists will enable you to register as an optometrist with the GOC.

If you did not achieve a 2.2 at undergraduate level, or if your Certificate of Clinical Competency has expired, you will need to complete the GOC's Optometry Progression Scheme before progressing onto the pre-registration year.

To remain registered with the GOC, continuing education and training (CET) is mandatory.

There are many advanced courses that allow qualified optometrists to specialise in other areas, such as paediatric vision, vision therapy and sports vision. Postgraduate qualifications are also available.

What the work involves

Optometrists examine the eyes of their patients for disease or abnormalities and carry out vision tests.

Your work will include shining a light on the retina, and using reading charts and other instruments to diagnose the needs of the patient.

You will determine prescriptions and may also supply and fit glasses or contact lenses. You will look out for signs of diabetes and eye diseases and refer patients to surgeons when needed.

Type of person suited to this work

Examining eyes and diagnosing problems requires a high level of scientific knowledge and a high attention to detail. Fitting contact lenses and handling instruments require good technical skills.

You need to have excellent communication and listening skills to deal with patients of all ages and backgrounds. You will need to put patients at ease and explain procedures simply and clearly to them.

You should have good interpersonal skill as you will have to work as part of a team with other professionals.

Working conditions

Optometrists work in high-street opticians and hospitals, in examination rooms which usually have no natural light and often have to be quite dark.

You will undertake 10 to 20 half-an-hour eye examinations per day.

You will probably have a normal working week from Monday to Friday, but may need to work on Saturdays as well.

Future prospects

Job prospects are good but vary throughout the UK.

You may work for a chain of opticians, an independent practice or a hospital. You could also do related work with lens manufacturers.

With experience you may specialise, for example, in children's vision, low vision or contact lenses. You could choose to run your own practice. There are also opportunities to move into research and university teaching.

Advantages/disadvantages

The work can be routine and repetitive at times.

If you enjoy combining scientific knowledge with working with the public, this job could be good for you.

Working closely with patients can be demanding.

Money guide

In private practices, trainees may earn between £17,000 and £21,000 during their one year pre-registration period. NHS trainees on the Agenda for Change pay scheme will earn at NHS wage band 4 (£18,838) at the same stage of training.

Once qualified starting salaries in the private sector begin at around £28,000 and in the NHS £25,783 to £34,530.

With specialist training, optometrists can earn and £40,558.

Consultants can progress to NHS wage band 8, with an income of £81,618.

Related opportunities

- Dentist p282
- Dispensing Optician p284
- Hospital Doctor p292

Further information

College of Optometrists
www.college-optometrists.org

General Optical Council
www.optical.org

ORTHODONTIST

ENTRY LEVEL 7

Qualifications and courses

All orthodontists must first qualify as a dentist. The standard degree programme lasts 5 years and you will need at least 3 good A levels/H grades, including chemistry and biology. GCSE/National 5 results may also be taken into account, and at least 8 passes (A*–C/A–C) are required for consideration. You may be asked to take the UK Clinical Aptitude Test (UKCAT) as part of your university application and pre-entry interviews are common.

If you have good A level/H grade results, but not in the required subjects for entrance onto the degree course, you can apply for a 6-year degree programme that includes an initial 30-week course that aims get students up to speed with the sciences.

Owing to the competitiveness of dentistry degrees, students are sometimes choosing to do an initial degree before their dental degree or embarking on extensive work experience before applying to a course.

Once you have qualified as a dentist, you will need to gain 2 years of clinical experience before being able to apply for a postgraduate Master of Science (MSc) in Orthodontic Dentistry. Orthodontic training combines academic study with hands-on training in a hospital, and lasts 3 years full time. You will then sit the Membership in Orthodontics (MOrth) exam to qualify as an orthodontist.

If you are looking to progress to become a hospital consultant, you will need to undertake a further 2 years training and pass the Intercollegiate Specialty Fellowship Examination.

What the work involves

Orthodontists examine and treat dental problems. These problems may be an aesthetic correction or a more serious dental issue, such as jaw realignment.

Treatment will usually involve correcting irregularities or abnormalities in terms of teeth growth or jaw position. Through treatment, you will be responsible for improving the patient's quality of life.

The most common procedures for an orthodontist are usually the fitting and maintaining of braces, and the extraction of teeth. You may occasionally have to carry out jaw surgery. You will also need to examine the mouths and teeth of your patients, take X-rays and impressions, and keep detailed medical records of their treatment. Owing to the further education, an orthodontist's remit extends beyond that of a dentist's.

Type of person suited to this work

You will need to have excellent communication skills in order to gain the trust of your patients and build good relationships with them.

You will be working with and possibly managing other professionals, so you should also enjoy working in a team environment and motivating those around you.

Good eyesight and manual dexterity are essential for undertaking fiddly tasks such as fitting and tightening braces or performing jaw surgery. The ability to maintain your concentration during occasionally lengthy procedures is also important.

Working conditions

If you work in private practice you can generally expect to do normal office hours, although some orthodontists choose to work evenings and weekends to suit their patients' lifestyles.

Those working in hospitals must be more flexible, occasionally undertaking emergency shifts and being on-call.

You will need to wear protective clothing, along with surgical gloves and a mask when working on patients in order to maintain high levels of hygiene and safety.

Future prospects

There is a constant demand for orthodontists in both the private and public sector, so career prospects are good.

Jobs can be found across the UK in both large cities and smaller towns. You could work in the NHS or as a self-employed professional.

There are opportunities to specialise in certain areas of orthodontics, such as adult cosmetic dentistry or children's corrective orthodontics.

Advantages/disadvantages

Many orthodontists are self-employed and work in the private sector. This provides more control over working hours and salary.

Orthodontic treatment for one patient can often last a few years; you get to build up a relationship with your patients. This can also make the process of improving their health and their smile all the more rewarding.

Despite the costs of education, it is a reliable source of income.

It can be a demanding and stressful job, with the need to work unorthodox hours at times.

Money guide

Generally, salaries start at around £28,000 to £30,000.

Working in a specialist private practice, you could earn anything from £40,000 to £90,000.

If you run your own practice you could earn in excess of £150,000.

Related opportunities

- Dental Hygienist p278
- Dentist p282
- Surgeon p321

Further information

British Dental Association
www.bda.org

British Orthodontic Society
www.bos.org.uk

NHS Careers
www.nhscareers.nhs.uk

OSTEOPATH

ENTRY LEVEL 5

Qualifications and courses

All osteopaths must be registered with the General Osteopathic Council (GOsC) before they are legally allowed to practise. In order to register, you must hold a qualification in osteopathy from one of the 11 osteopathic educational institutions currently providing courses recognised by the GOsC.

Most recognised courses are at bachelor or master's degree level. Each course takes 4 years when studied full time, and 5 years on a part-time basis. For entry onto these courses, most of the universities require a minimum of 2 A levels/3 H grades, with chemistry or biology preferred and 5 GCSEs/National 5s (A*–C/A–C). If you do not have a science degree or appropriate A levels, you may still be considered but will have to take an intensive science course before beginning to train.

Though not essential, it may be advantageous to gain pre-entry experience by shadowing a practising osteopath or by working in a caring role.

Many people train in osteopathy as a second career. If you have relevant experience in healthcare or hold medical-related qualifications prior to commencing your degree, you may be exempt from parts of the course. Short courses are available for fully qualified healthcare professionals.

As part of your registration with the GOsC you will also have to pass a Disclosure and Barring Service (DBS) check and, once qualified, the GOsC requires you to complete 30 hours of relevant learning each year as part of the continuing professional development (CPD) scheme.

What the work involves

Osteopathy is considered a complementary medicine. It does not use surgery or drugs. Osteopaths usually work on the patient's musculoskeletal system. You may use medical techniques such as X-rays, as well as physical exams, observation, and talking with your patient to understand their ailment.

You will then use hands-on treatment such as massage, joint mobilisation and deep pressure to help the treat the problem. You may also advise on aspects of their lifestyle or diet to help remedy the problem.

Type of person suited to this work

You will need a highly developed sense of touch and strong observational skills in order to identify points of slight weakness or pain in your patients. Logic and problem-solving abilities will also help you diagnose correctly and treat the problem creatively where necessary.

Excellent communication skills are also essential to develop a good relationship with patients and in order to explain their treatment to them.

The work can be very physical, so you should also have a good level of fitness.

Working conditions

You could practise in a variety of locations including leisure centres, therapy centres, private clinics, hospitals and even your own home. You will probably have a treatment room in which to see patients.

Most professionals offer evening and weekend appointments as well as those during the day, as these tend to be more convenient for patients.

Future prospects

As awareness of osteopathy grows, there is increasing demand for qualified and registered professionals, so career opportunities are correspondingly positive.

Most osteopaths are self-employed, and usually start out by working as an associate in a practice to establish a reputation and solid client base. After a few years, many then go on to set up their own practice or become involved in the training of future osteopaths.

You could also choose to specialise in an area of particular interest to you, such as treating sports injuries or problems resulting from childbirth.

Advantages/disadvantages

As an osteopath, you will encounter a variety of complaints and challenges on a daily basis, which can be both refreshing and intellectually stimulating.

You provide an alternative to medicine and surgery for patients.

If you are self-employed, income might not be quite so predictable as for other medical professions, which can cause stress having to manage it on your own.

The work can be physically demanding.

Money guide

As the majority of osteopaths are self-employed and work varying hours, it is difficult to predict an exact level of earnings at any stage. Generally, most charge between £35 and £50 for a 30–45 minute session.

Newly qualified osteopaths in a practice can expect to earn between £15,000 and £20,000 in their first couple of years.

With experience, you could see this increase to around £40,000.

If you run your own practice or work in a well-established one, your salary could rise to £50,000 per year.

Related opportunities

- Acupuncturist p268
- Chiropractor p275
- Physiotherapist p310

Further information

British Osteopathic Association
www.osteopathy.org

British School of Osteopathy
www.bso.ac.uk

General Osteopathic Council
www.osteopathy.org.uk

PARAMEDIC

ENTRY LEVEL 3

Qualifications and courses

There are 2 approved routes you can follow. You could apply to an ambulance service trust for a role as a student paramedic, and they will put you through an approved course. Training takes between 2 and 5 years to complete and you will need at least 5 GCSEs/National 5s (A*–C/A–C), including English and maths, in order to apply.

Alternatively you could take an approved degree course in paramedic science which can take from 2 to 4 years to complete. Entry requirements are usually 2 A levels/3 H grades and 5 GCSEs/National 5s (A*–C/A–C), including English and maths or a science subject.

Alternatively, some ambulance service trusts are approved by the Health and Care Professions Council (HCPC) and provide training for the Institute of Healthcare Development (IHCD) Paramedic Award, leading to registration. You will need to possess a current IHCD Technician Certificate/BTEC Certificate to apply.

Useful pre-entry experience includes completing First Aid certificates and voluntary experience, both of which are available with organisations such as St John Ambulance, St Andrew's Ambulance Association and British Red Cross. You could also volunteer as a community 'first responder' with a local ambulance service and gain experience in lifesaving techniques.

A full clean driving licence, that allows you to drive larger vehicles and carry passengers, is essential. You will also need to pass a Disclosure and Barring Service (DBS) check, fitness test, and medical assessment before working and if you are employed with the NHS, you will need to be registered with the HCPC.

What the work involves

Paramedics provide a rapid response to 999 calls reporting medical emergencies.

You will usually be the first healthcare professional to reach a patient, and often the most senior one, and as such must assess their condition and administer immediate treatment.

Working either alone or with another healthcare professional, you will stabilise patients using a variety of methods, including oxygen, drugs, and sometimes minor operations such as tracheotomies. You will also ensure notes are made to brief hospital staff.

Type of person suited to this work

You must have good communication skills and a caring disposition to successfully soothe and comfort patients. You should be mature, responsible and non-judgemental so that you can relate to people from a wide range of ages, backgrounds and cultures.

You must be able to keep calm in a crisis, as you will be making life and death decisions on a fairly regular basis.

A good level of physical fitness is required for lifting and carrying both patients and equipment. Mental stamina is also essential for coping with occasionally horrific and frightening circumstances.

Working conditions

You will work 37.5 hours a week on rotational shifts. This means you will work nights, weekends and on public holidays regularly. Part-time work is commonly available.

You will either work for a local ambulance service or be based at a hospital, but you will travel to a range of locations in response to emergency calls. You should be prepared to undertake treatment of patients in unfamiliar and potentially dangerous situations.

Because you will be responsible for full or shared driving responsibilities of your vehicle, you need a full, clean driving licence.

Future prospects

Career prospects for paramedics are good. Once you have completed your training and gained 3–5 years' experience you could be promoted to a team leader.

Further promotion can take you into management posts within the ambulance service, although you will need to supplement your work experience with further relevant qualifications to achieve this level.

You could also move into related careers such as nursing or occupational therapy.

Advantages/disadvantages

Providing rapid response in emergency situations means that you really will be responsible for saving lives on a weekly basis.

You could find yourself confronted with very difficult patients; those who are frightened, angry or under the influence of drugs and alcohol may be violent and hostile to treatment.

You will have to work unsocial hours fairly regularly.

Money guide

Salaries for student paramedics vary depending on the ambulance trust you train with.

Once qualified, salaries range from £21,478 to £27,901.

As a team leader or senior paramedic you could earn up to £34,530.

Related opportunities

- Adult Nurse p269
- Hospital Doctor p292
- Midwife p298
- Occupational Therapist p299

Further information

College of Paramedics
www.collegeofparamedics.co.uk

NHS Careers
www.nhscareers.nhs.uk

NHS Confederation
www.nhsconfed.org

PATHOLOGIST

ENTRY LEVEL 8

Qualifications and courses

Before becoming a pathologist, candidates must be qualified as a hospital doctor by completing a General Medical Council (GMC) approved medical degree. Entry requirements for medical school include very high A level/H grade results, including subjects such as science and maths. Competition for places on medical degrees is tough and it is strongly advised that you have undertaken relevant pre-entry work experience.

After studying for a medical degree, graduates will take the 2-year Foundation programme of general training which acts as the bridge between medical school and specialist training. Candidates then progress to 5–6 years of specialty training in a particular area of pathology, such as histopathology or chemical pathology.

After successfully completing the specialty stage, trainees receive a Certificate of Completion of Training (CCT) and become eligible to join the GMC Specialist Register. It is then possible to apply for a post as a consultant.

Pathologists must engage in continuing professional development (CPD) throughout their career to ensure that their skills and knowledge are up to date. The Royal College of Pathologists provides information on available training.

What the work involves

Pathologists are doctors who have undergone further training to specialise in pathology.

As a pathologist you will detect and diagnose diseases, help to identify sources of disease and reduce the risk of them spreading further.

You will spend a lot of time in a laboratory but you will also work directly with patients.

You could work in one of many branches including haematology (studying diseases of the blood), histopathology (studying tissue samples removed for diagnosis, and determining cause of death by performing post-mortems and autopsies) and immunology (studying diseases and conditions of the immune system).

Type of person suited to this work

To be a pathologist you should be able to use your medical knowledge and training to diagnose patients' conditions. You must have problem-solving skills and pay close attention to detail when carrying out laboratory assessments.

You should be kind and caring in order to gain your patients' trust. Excellent communication skills are required to listen to patients carefully and explain their conditions and treatments in a clear, simple way.

Working conditions

You will normally work within a hospital as part of a medical team, working both in a laboratory and with patients.

You will need to work safely in the laboratory and wear protective clothing such as a lab coat and gloves.

There will be long hours and you are likely to work shifts and be on an on-call rota, which includes working at nights, weekends and on bank holidays.

Future prospects

Most pathologists work within the NHS throughout the UK. There are also opportunities in industry, working for private companies.

You could decide to specialise further in particular areas of the work such as forensic pathology or transfusion medicine. You could also move into academic work, carrying out research or teaching students.

There are also similar careers in pathology for clinical and biomedical scientists but they do not treat patients.

Advantages/disadvantages

The work can be emotionally demanding because it involves dealing with patients who have life-threatening conditions.

As your role is to make accurate and early diagnoses for patients, you will help to save their lives.

Money guide

Salary levels in the NHS may vary in different locations.

Earnings are often higher in private practice work.

Junior doctors have a starting salary of between £22,000 and £28,000 during the 2-year Foundation programme.

When undertaking the specialty training, you can expect to earn between £28,000 and £46,000 a year.

Consultant pathologists can achieve salaries ranging from £74,000 up to £170,000 for those in the most senior positions.

Related opportunities

- Anaesthetist p270
- Psychiatrist p315
- Radiologist p317

Further information

NHS Careers
www.nhscareers.nhs.uk

Royal College of Pathologists
www.rcpath.org

Skills for Health
www.skillsforhealth.org.uk

PHARMACIST

ENTRY LEVEL 7

Qualifications and courses

All candidates who wish to become pharmacists need to study for a 4-year Master of Pharmacy (MPharm) degree. Throughout the UK there are 26 pharmacy schools offering degrees which have been accredited by the Royal Pharmaceutical Society (RPS).

Most universities require a minimum of 2 A levels/3 H grades, including chemistry and one from biology, maths or physics, and at least 5 GCSEs/National 5s (A*–C/A–C) including English, maths and science. Most universities will accept other qualifications for entry, such as HNCs/Ds, International Baccalaureate Diplomas and Access qualifications, but it worth checking with them directly regarding their entry policies.

It is not possible to start work as a pharmacist with an HND only but you could gain employment as a pharmacy technician. This would enable you to build up experience whilst you study for an MPharm degree.

Once students have completed their pharmacy degree, they need to apply for a 1-year pre-registration training course in community, hospital or industrial pharmacy. This enables you to train on the job with experienced professionals. A pre-entry postgraduate qualification is not needed, but a Clinical Diploma or Master of Science (MSc) may give you an advantage when applying for hospital pharmacist positions. Upon completion, candidates must then pass the General Pharmaceutical Council (GPhC)'s registration examination to become a fully qualified, registered pharmacist.

What the work involves

Pharmacists work in one of 3 areas: hospital, community or industry.

Hospital pharmacists are responsible for buying, manufacturing, dispensing and supplying medicines to in-patients and out-patients. You will ensure that patients receive the most appropriate treatment in the correct dosage.

Community pharmacists work in high-street pharmacies in both cities and towns. You will supply medicines over the counter, prepare doctors' prescriptions and advise people on general health-related queries.

Industrial pharmacists work for pharmaceutical companies. You will be discovering, developing, manufacturing, testing and marketing new drugs.

Type of person suited to this work

You should be a strong communicator as you will be advising patients on medications and explaining how to administer them. You must be comfortable working in a team with other pharmacy staff or healthcare professionals.

You need in-depth medical knowledge and problem-solving skills in order to identify treatment solutions and prepare medications for patients. You should be committed to keeping your knowledge up to date. Accuracy and attention to detail are essential when selecting, preparing, measuring and labelling medicines.

Working conditions

Hours will depend on where you work. Community and industrial pharmacists will usually work 39 hours per week, from Monday to Friday, although Saturday work is increasing in order to meet patients' requirements. Hospital pharmacists may need to work shifts in order to provide a 24-hour service. There are opportunities to work part time.

You could be working in a shop, hospital or laboratory and you may occasionally be required to travel to nursing homes and community health centres/clinics.

Future prospects

Over the past 10 years there has been a rise in the number of students staying to become a pharmacist. Until recently, there was a national shortage of pharmacists, so currently the opportunities to find employment should be good.

You will have the option of working in a range of different environments including community shops and large hospitals.

As you gain experience, you could choose to combine your work with other responsibilities such as teaching. You could also go on to research or write about pharmaceutical matters.

Advantages/disadvantages

Your role will be varied and rewarding as you endeavour to help a diverse range of patients.

It is not as stressful as some other medical jobs.

You may have to work unsocial hours which could disrupt your personal life.

The job can be quite repetitive and requires standing on your feet for long stretches.

Money guide

Pharmacists employed by the NHS during their pre-registration training have a starting salary of £21,388.

Once qualified, you can expect earnings ranging from £25,528 to £34,530.

Those employed in a senior or managerial role could achieve between £38,000 and £67,000.

Specialist pharmacists could earn up to £80,000 a year.

Those who are employed by smaller, independent pharmacies may receive lower salaries.

Related opportunities

- Biochemist p481
- Pharmacologist p307
- Pharmacy Technician p308

Further information

NHS Careers
www.nhscareers.nhs.uk

Royal Pharmaceutical Society
www.rpharms.com

PHARMACOLOGIST

ENTRY LEVEL 5

Qualifications and courses

Owing to the scientific nature of this work, most entrants to pharmacology either have a pharmacology degree or a degree in a similar subject such as biomedical sciences, biochemistry, molecular and cell biology, physiology or microbiology. Entry for a degree requires 2 A levels/3 H grades, including chemistry and biology, and at least 5 GCSEs/National 5s (A*–C/A–C).

Competition for jobs within this industry is high so candidates may benefit from a postgraduate qualification such as a Master of Science (MSc) in Pharmacology or a relevant PhD. Qualifications at this level are likely to be essential for a research and development role or to gain employment with a major pharmaceutical company. Undertaking a PhD gives candidates essential lab experience which is viewed favourably by employers.

Pre-entry work experience within a pharmaceutical company is also desirable as it demonstrates your enthusiasm and commitment. A sandwich degree with a year-long placement would enable you to make industry contacts.

If you do not have a degree, it is still possible to enter this profession, working your way up from a lower position in the industry. Having a relevant HNC/HND would allow you apply for an entry level position, and give you the opportunity to learn on the job as you gain valuable work experience and the chance to gain further qualifications as you work.

If you work in research and development and carry out tests on live animals and humans then you will be required to hold a Home Office licence.

What the work involves

Pharmacologists study the impact of drugs and chemical substances on various living organisms, including on humans, animals, natural environments and cells.

This will involve potentially discovering, researching, developing and testing new drugs and medicines, so suits somebody with a creative as well as analytical mind.

You will study the actions of drugs via computer simulations, in tests on cells and tissues, and on animals and human volunteers.

There might be the opportunity to specialise in areas of pharmacology, such as neuropharmacology.

Type of person suited to this work

You should be a strong communicator with the ability to work within a team whilst also leading and motivating your colleagues in order to drive projects forward.

You will need excellent analytical skills as you will be gathering and interpreting complex information. Since the majority of equipment used to undertake experiments is computer-based, it is essential to have good IT skills.

To design and modify experiments, you will require problem-solving skills, creativity and flexibility. Patience and perseverance is essential as projects may involve many months of research and change.

Working conditions

You will normally work from 9am to 5pm during the week. Occasionally you may have to work evenings and weekends in order to monitor the more complex experiments.

You will work in a laboratory environment, usually within a university, government or commercial research centre, or a pharmaceutical company. The environment is generally clean and quiet, and you may be required to wear protective clothing when undertaking certain experiments.

Future prospects

Although the industry is competitive, once you have gained a position as a pharmacologist the opportunities for career progression are good.

You could work within a university, undertaking research and gaining a PhD, and then perhaps moving into a position as a lecturer.

Within commercial laboratories, experience will lead to increased responsibility and managerial opportunities.

Advantages/disadvantages

Gaining an entry-level position in this competitive industry is difficult but once you have secured a job, prospects are excellent and career progression rapid.

You will have the satisfaction of knowing that the new drugs you develop will enhance the quality of life for thousands of people worldwide.

Potential choice of career paths and specialties.

You will probably have to experiment on animals which may be upsetting and controversial.

Money guide

Starting salaries range from £23,000 to £28,000.

As you gain experience, you can expect to earn £30,000–£40,000.

Pharmacologists employed in senior roles can achieve between £35,000 and £80,000.

Commercial pharmaceutical companies tend to offer higher salaries than academic institutions.

A PhD will increase your earning potential by approximately 25%.

Related opportunities

- Biochemist p481
- Pharmacist p306
- Toxicologist p512

Further information

British Pharmacological Society
www.bps.ac.uk

PHARMACY TECHNICIAN

ENTRY LEVEL 3

Qualifications and courses

The Pharmacy Services Apprenticeship is available at Advanced Level for those who wish to become a pharmacy technician. The apprenticeship typically lasts 2 years and involves training on the job with a practising pharmacist whilst studying for relevant qualifications. Another route into the industry is to obtain a trainee post within either a community pharmacy or a hospital. Most employers will expect apprentice/trainee applicants to have 5 GCSEs/National 5s (A*–C/A–C), including English, maths and at least one science subject.

To register as a qualified pharmacy technician you must meet the requirements of and be registered with the General Pharmaceutical Council (GPhC). Entrants must complete one of the GPhC-accredited competency-based qualifications, such as the NVQ Level 3 in Pharmacy Services Skills, and one of the knowledge-based qualifications, such as the City & Guilds Level 3 qualifications in Pharmacy Services Skills or BTEC Level 3 Diploma in Pharmaceutical Science. These can also be achieved via on-the-job training as a trainee technician. It is also possible to take a single qualification that combines the knowledge and competency elements, such as the Buttercups Training Level 3 or National Pharmacy Association Level 3 qualifications. Candidates must also complete 2 years of work experience with a qualified pharmacist before they are eligible for GPhC registration.

All pharmacy technicians are required by the GPhC to undertake continuing professional development (CPD) throughout their career to keep their knowledge up to date.

What the work involves

Pharmacy technicians will assemble and supply medication to patients, as well as provide advice regarding the medication. Technicians operate under the supervision of a qualified pharmacist.

You could work in a retail environment as a community pharmacy technician, within a hospital or in a commercial pharmaceutical lab. You will be responsible for monitoring stocks of medicines, checking expiry dates and reordering supplies as necessary.

You will be working with a variety of healthcare professionals including pharmacists, doctors and nurses, and you will also have considerable contact with patients and customers.

Type of person suited to this work

You will need to be a strong communicator as you will advise patients on medications and clearly explain how to administer them. You will also need to be comfortable working in a team and following instructions.

You should be good with numbers and calculations. Accuracy and attention to detail are essential to ensure that you are making and labelling medications correctly, and keeping detailed records of each patient's medication needs.

You must be mature, tactful and non-judgemental when dealing with patients, who will present a variety of complaints.

Working conditions

Hours will depend on where you work. Community pharmacy technicians usually work 39 hours a week from Monday to Saturday. Industry and hospital technicians work a 37-hour week but may be required to cover evening and weekend shifts on occasion.

You could work in a shop, hospital or laboratory and you may occasionally be required to travel to nursing homes or community health centres and clinics.

Future prospects

You could work in a community context, within a small local pharmacy or a larger well-known chain. Alternatively, you could be employed by an NHS or private hospital, be based in a prison or work for the armed forces.

If you work in a hospital you could move into a specialised, supervisory role after gaining a few years' experience.

Additionally, many clinical pharmacy technicians in hospitals are now more involved with patients, undertaking ward rounds and other such duties.

Advantages/disadvantages

You will meet and help a range of patients and colleagues so your work will be varied and rewarding.

You can choose to work in a more relaxed retail environment, in the bustle of a hospital or in a professional industrial setting.

You may have to work evenings and weekends in order to provide a good level of service to patients and healthcare professionals.

The work can be very repetitive.

Money guide

Starting salaries for pharmacy technicians are usually between £18,000 and £22,000.

Experienced pharmacy technicians employed in a senior position could expect earnings of between £21,000 and £28,000.

If you become a team manager or specialist your salary could reach £40,000.

Related opportunities

- Health Records Clerk p287
- Pharmacist p306
- Sterile Services Technician p320

Further information

Association of Pharmacy Technicians UK
www.aptuk.org

Royal Pharmaceutical Society
www.rpharms.com

PHLEBOTOMIST

ENTRY LEVEL 2

Qualifications and courses

There are no formal entry requirements for this job, but 4 or more GCSEs/National 5s (A*–C/A–C), including English, maths and science, may be an advantage for applicants for entry-level positions and are essential for more advanced work.

Other useful qualifications include the BTEC qualifications in Health and Social Care (Levels 2–3) and the Diploma in Society, Health and Development. HNC/HND or degrees in chemistry, physics, biology and materials science/technology are not essential but may improve your chances for employment.

Pre-entry work experience in a caring role or laboratory and a familiarity with lab procedures could also prove advantageous.

Training is usually done entirely on the job and organisations such as Phlebotomy Training Services (PTS) and Medicare Phlebotomy Trainers offer short introductory and advanced training courses for potential phlebotomists. After training, you may be awarded a Certificate of Competence, which will allow you to work without close supervision throughout the hospital. You will be trained to National Occupational Standards.

Phlebotomists may be able to work towards related qualifications, such as an NVQ/SVQ in Clinical Healthcare Support (Levels 2–3), or an NVQ in Health (Blood Donor Support) (Levels 2–3).

The National Association of Phlebotomists offers short training courses and workshops for qualified phlebotomists.

What the work involves

Phlebotomists are specialist medical laboratory assistants who collect blood samples for analysis to help diagnose diseases.

You will take blood samples from patients as painlessly as possible, label samples and make sure they are taken promptly and safely to a laboratory for examination.

You will need to keep accurate records and enter data in a computer system. It is your responsibility to ensure samples are not mixed up or contaminated.

Type of person suited to this work

Phlebotomists need to be practical and good with their hands to take blood without harming the patient or disturbing nursing care.

Good colour vision is essential.

You need to pay close attention to detail and work carefully as any errors could affect results.

It is important that you are able to communicate well with a range of people from children to the elderly. Some people are scared of having their blood taken, so you need to be able to reassure them.

Working conditions

You will carry out your work in hospital wards, out-patient departments and in the community. You will also spend time working in laboratories.

You will need to pay close attention to health and safety to prevent infection, and will wear a uniform and protective clothing such as gloves.

You are likely to work a normal working day during the week, but you may also need to work at weekends.

Future prospects

Most employment is available in NHS hospitals throughout the UK. There is also similar work available in blood transfusion services, government research departments and university laboratories. However, many phlebotomists work part time, and some support workers or assistant healthcare scientists perform phlebotomy as part of their role.

Currently there is a shortage of skilled phlebotomists in certain areas, including London, and opportunities for phlebotomists are increasing as more health screening initiatives are introduced.

Phlebotomists can progress into managerial and senior roles.

Although there is no route for phlebotomists to progress to a career as a biomedical scientist, you may be encouraged to gain the qualifications that you need to train as one. You can also train to enter other areas of healthcare, such as nursing.

Advantages/disadvantages

Some of your patients will be scared of blood and needles which can make your job difficult.

It can be rewarding to work with patients and play a vital role in helping to diagnose illnesses.

Money guide

The NHS sets national pay rates for phlebotomists each year; those listed below are a guide only.

Salaries start at £14,000 per year and generally go up to £17,000.

Senior level phlebotomists can earn between £17,700 and £21,400, with managers earning up to £33,500.

If you work in the private sector or in London you may be paid more.

Related opportunities

- Biomedical Scientist/Medical Laboratory Assistant p482
- Immunologist p499
- Laboratory Technician p500

Further information

National Association of Phlebotomists
www.phlebotomy.org

NHS Careers
www.nhscareers.nhs.uk

Skills for Health
www.skillsforhealth.org.uk

PHYSIOTHERAPIST

ENTRY LEVEL 6

Qualifications and courses

All chartered physiotherapists must hold a degree in physiotherapy that has been recognised by the Health Professions Council (HPC). Full-time and part-time courses are available. Once you have completed your degree you are then eligible to apply to be a member of the Chartered Society of Physiotherapy (CSP).

Entry requirements for a degree course vary according to the university, but you will usually need 3 A levels/H grades including biology or similar, and 5 GCSEs/ National 5s (A*–C/A–C), including English, maths and science. You may also be considered if you possess a BTEC Level 3 qualification in Science, Applied Science, or Health Sciences, an Advanced GNVQ/GSVQ in Health and Social Care or Science, or an NVQ Level 3 in a related subject.

Graduates with a related science degree could opt for a 2-year fast-track postgraduate course, and Access courses are available for entry onto a degree programme for candidates without the relevant science qualifications.

It is recommended to get work experience prior to applying for your degree, as universities look favourably on this and physiotherapy courses are very competitive.

What the work involves

Physiotherapists treat patients with problems affecting their muscles, bones, heart, circulation and lungs that have been caused by accident, illness or ageing.

You will assess patients, then decide on an appropriate course of treatment for them. This could include exercise, movement, hydrotherapy, massage or manipulation.

Sports physiotherapists use the same techniques as those above, but focus solely on treating sports-related injuries.

Type of person suited to this work

You must have excellent communication skills as you will be dealing with both patients and other healthcare professionals on a daily basis. When treating patients, you will need to be able to listen to their concerns, explain the best course of treatment, and motivate them to persevere with their programme.

You will need to have a practical, logical mind in order to think around problems and solve unusual complaints in a creative way.

You must be physically fit, as much of the work can be strenuous and involve a good deal of hands-on contact and muscle manipulation.

Working conditions

You will generally work a 37-hour week, although you should expect to work evenings and weekends to fit in with your clients' lifestyles.

You could be employed by the NHS, private practices and health centres, residential homes, or sports centres and specialist clinics. A good number of physiotherapists opt for self-employment and work in a mixture of locations.

You will need to wear practical clothes, and certain employers may require you to wear a uniform.

Future prospects

Over half of physiotherapists are employed by the NHS, although this is significantly lower for those who have specialised in sports physiotherapy. There are opportunities with numerous other employers such as health clinics and sports centres, and you can be self-employed.

In recent years there have been a shortage of junior level physiotherapy positions but this situation is improving and job prospects are still good.

You could go on to specialise in an area such as orthopaedics or geriatric care, or pursue more senior positions. The NHS now offers consultant-level posts for experienced physiotherapists.

Advantages/disadvantages

You will have a great deal of contact with patients and other healthcare professionals so the job is varied and rewarding.

If you opt for self-employment, you have control over your working hours and the patients you decide to take on.

It is physically demanding work, and working with injured or ill people can also prove emotionally draining.

Money guide

Starting salaries for newly qualified physiotherapists depend on your employer, or whether you are self-employed but private sector salaries are generally quite similar to the NHS.

In the NHS, physiotherapists start at NHS wage band 5 which ranges from £21,388 to £27,901.

With a few years' experience, this can rise to between £25,472 and £34,500.

For specialist and advanced physiotherapists, salaries are between £30,460 and £40,157.

Consultant physiotherapists in the NHS earn in excess of £50,000, and those who have specialised in sports physiotherapy can earn up to £55,000.

Related opportunities

- Acupuncturist p268
- Chiropractor p275
- Hospital Doctor p292

Further information

Chartered Society of Physiotherapy
www.csp.org.uk

Health and Care Professions Council
www.hpc-uk.org

NHS Careers
www.nhscareers.nhs.uk

PODIATRIST

ENTRY LEVEL 6

Qualifications and courses

To work as a podiatrist, you need to have gained an Honours degree in Podiatry (lasting 3 or 4 years) that has been approved by the Health and Care Professions Council (HCPC).

There are currently 13 institutions in the UK offering approved courses. For degree entry you are generally required to have a minimum of 2 A levels/3 H grades, one of which should be a science subject, preferably biology, and 5 GCSEs/National 5s (A*–C/A–C). Competition for places on podiatry courses is fierce and it is advisable that you demonstrate your commitment to the subject by completing pre-entry, relevant work experience.

There are currently no fast-track degrees or qualifying postgraduate podiatry courses available for those who already possess a degree in a different subject, but experience or qualifications in subjects such as nursing, biology, physiology and physiotherapy may increase your employment chances.

You must be registered with the HCPC in order to practise as a registered podiatrist. In order to remain registered you must show evidence of continuing professional development (CPD). The Society of Chiropodists and Podiatrists (SCP) is the main provider.

Once qualified you can then take a whole range of specialist training.

Entry to the profession is subject to an occupational health clearance and a Disclosure and Barring Service (DBS) check may also be required.

What the work involves

Podiatrists (also commonly known as chiropodists) are healthcare practitioners responsible for assessing, diagnosing and treating problems relating to the feet and lower limbs.

The work involves using medical braces to correct deformities, administering local anaesthetics to enable pain free specialist foot treatment, wound care, neurological assessment, skin, nail and bone surgery, care planning and health promotion.

You will treat a variety of people including those with disabilities and long-term illnesses, children and people with sports related injuries.

Type of person suited to this work

Podiatrists need to be caring and understanding. You should be able to reassure patients of all ages who could be in pain and explain their treatment clearly and simply.

You will also need good communication skills to be an effective part of a healthcare team. You should be able to apply your skills and knowledge to diagnose and solve problems.

You should be good with your hands as you will be using a range of equipment and techniques.

Working conditions

You will most likely work in a clinic but may visit patients in their own homes or in residential care homes at times. You might also need to attend sporting events to treat injured players.

If employed by the NHS you will work 37 hours per week, Monday to Friday. Self-employed podiatrists can work flexible hours, including evenings and weekends.

Future prospects

Podiatry offers excellent employment flexibility with the opportunity to work in the NHS, private practice, commerce, leisure, education and occupational health sectors to name but a few.

With experience you might choose to specialise in one area of podiatry such as biomechanics (musculoskeletal disorders), forensic podiatry, working with children or surgery.

You could also go on to teach and research in a university or move into management. Many podiatrists even set up their own small private practices.

Advantages/disadvantages

The idea of working with other people's feet and lower limbs may not appeal instantly, but podiatrists generally get great satisfaction from their work.

The NHS and Scottish Funding Council (SFC) cover the tuition fees for all 13 accredited podiatry courses.

You will have to deal with people who may be badly injured, very ill and in pain, which could be distressing.

You will be helping people to deal with pain and issues that could be affecting their mobility which can be rewarding.

Money guide

In the NHS, starting salaries typically range between £21,388 and £27,901, while experienced specialist lead podiatrists can earn between £30,460 and £40,157.

Private podiatrists can charge hourly, but their income is dependent on the number of patients they have and the location of their practice. That said, earnings should be similar to, or possibly more than, earnings in the NHS. Typically, initial assessments cost patients around £40, whilst basic treatment charges are around £32.

Related opportunities

- Doctor (GP) p285
- Physiotherapist p310
- Prosthetist/Orthotist p314

Further information

NHS Careers
www.nhscareers.nhs.uk

Skills for Health
www.skillsforhealth.org.uk

Society of Chiropodists and Podiatrists
www.feetforlife.org

Organisation Profile

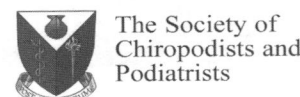

The Society of Chiropodists and Podiatrists

THE SOCIETY OF CHIROPODISTS AND PODIATRISTS

Interesting facts about The Society of Chiropodists and Podiatrists

- The Society of Chiropodists and Podiatrists came into being in 1945 when five United Kingdom chiropody organisations amalgamated. The oldest of the constituent bodies and the first such organisation in Europe was founded in 1912.
- The Society of Chiropodists and Podiatrists is the largest organisation representing the podiatry profession. It has an educational as well as trade union function. While the society acts as the focus for the corporate identity of practitioners, the college maintains and develops the systematic body of knowledge and skills that define the profession and on which the practice of podiatry is based. It does this by accrediting undergraduate honours degree courses in podiatry which are offered at 13 universities.
- Podiatrists are also required to keep themselves abreast of developments in their particular field. The college helps them by providing opportunities to update their skills and knowledge and developing postgraduate training and qualifications, for example in local anaesthesia, medicines and podiatric surgery. The college therefore not only reflects the established traditions and contemporary definitions of podiatry education and research in the UK, but offers opportunities for continuing professional development.
- The head office is in London and there are currently 25 members of staff, some of who work in other locations around the country including an office in Edinburgh.
- The society is governed by a council who are responsible for the conduct of the business of the society. The council is made up of 24 members, all chiropodists/podiatrists elected by members of the society.
- The council meets four times a year. Members of the council are working clinicians, educators and managers who work in the NHS, private practice, higher education and other areas of practice.
- The mission of the society is 'looking after the interests of members, enabling them to practise more effectively'. The society's five year strategic plan for 2007–2012 focused on growing our presence and influence, developing the profession, improving member services and extending democracy in the organisation.
- The key roles of the society are education, guidance on professional practice, raising foot health awareness, representing members on a wide range of national bodies, influencing the influencers, working with other professional bodies, trade unions and membership organisations. The society offers a range of membership services including professional indemnity insurance, legal advice, trade union support, a monthly journal and e-newsletter and a website that reports all the latest podiatry and society news together with an extensive library of resources.
- The majority of members are practising chiropodists and podiatrists working in both the public and private health care sectors in clinical, educational or managerial capacities. The society also offers associate membership to orthotic technicians and podiatry assistants.
- The society has an active student body and almost all students graduating from the 13 recognised courses run by universities join the society on completion of the honours bachelor degree in podiatry.

www.careersinpodiatry.com

The Society of Chiropodists and Podiatrists
1 Fellmongers Path
Tower Bridge Road
London
SE1 3LY
www.feetforlife.org/careers

Case Study

PODIATRIST

The Society of Chiropodists and Podiatrists

Here's Joe Parker's story

After graduating from his BSc in Podiatric Medicine, Joe started out as a community podiatrist working in a local health centre dealing with the foot disorders and complaints of the local community. He did this for three years before being moved on to a promoted post where he specialises in children, working in different health centres and hospitals.

What the job entails

'Working with children is a specialist area which covers a variety of foot and gait (walking) complaints. I get referrals from health visitors, GPs, physiotherapists and other podiatrists. My referrals include children with in-grown toenails, verrucae and curly toes, but mostly I get children who have flat feet, in-toeing gait or other unusual walking/ development problems. I also go out to schools and give health promotion talks to pupils on foot health.'

A bad day in the office for Joe

'When a child comes into the clinic with a really sore toe and it's so sore that they don't want you to even touch it. Most children don't like getting an injection so won't let you give them a local anaesthetic and it can take you a long time to try and persuade them that you will be able to make them feel better. The parents can put pressure on you also as they know how sore it has been and know that it has become infected.'

What makes Joe good at his job

'You need to be very patient and sympathetic towards the children to make them feel relaxed with you to allow you to assess and treat them. Good communication skills are vital to be able to decipher what is wrong. Problem-solving skills help you to be able to come up with a management plan that suits you, the patient and the parents.'

What Joe personally gets out of it

'It is really rewarding working with children, when that crying child with the sore toe comes back to you smiling as the pain has gone and their foot is better it makes it all worthwhile. Also working as part of a team with the health visitors, GPs, physiotherapist etc. is interesting as you are all working together to help your patient.

'No two days are the same in this job, there is always something different to do, i.e. one day you could be treating ingrowing toenails, the next you are giving exercises to help correct a child with an in-toeing gait. You could also be in the lab making specialist insoles to fit into someone's shoes then going off to give a talk to children in a primary school – there is never a dull moment!'

www.feetforlife.org

The Society of Chiropodists and Podiatrists
1 Fellmongers Path,
Tower Bridge Road,
London
SE1 3LY

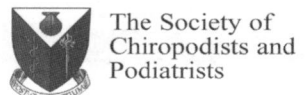

PROSTHETIST/ ORTHOTIST

ENTRY LEVEL 6

Qualifications and courses

Training to become a prosthetist and orthotist takes 4 years, leading to a BSc Honours degree recognised by the British Association of Prosthetists and Orthotists (BAPO) and the Health and Care Professions Council (HCPC). Approved degrees are offered by either the University of Strathclyde or the University of Salford, and they also offer further qualifications such as a Postgraduate Certificate/ Diploma or Master of Science (MSc) in Prosthetics and/or Orthotics Rehabilitation Studies.

Entry requirements are usually 240 UCAS points with 2 A levels/3 H grades, including maths or physics as well as either biology or chemistry, plus 5 GCSEs/National 5s (A*–C/A–C). Entry could be granted with alternate qualifications such as AS levels, BTEC Nationals and Higher Nationals or the International Baccalaureate but you will need to check university entry policies individually.

Graduates can either specialise in one area or practise both specialities. You must also register with the HCPC, undergo a Disclosure and Barring Service (DBS) check and pass a medical.

HCPC registration also requires prosthetists and orthotists to undertake continuing professional development (CPD).

What the work involves

Prosthetist
Prosthetists design and fit artificial limbs for patients who have lost a limb, have a deformity or who were born without a limb.

Work will include taking a cast of the area where the artificial replacement limb will fit and modelling it so that it will be safe and comfortable for the patient. You will also fit and adjust the replacement limb and teach the patient how to use it.

Orthotist
Orthotists provide surgical appliances such as arm and leg braces, collars, splints and special footwear for patients.

Work will include assessing the patient's problem, designing, fitting and adjusting the orthosis, and helping the patient to use it.

Type of person suited to this work

You must have a good technical knowledge of and aptitude for biomechanics and movement. You need to have excellent manual skills in order to take measurements, design devices and do fittings and make adjustments.

You should be practical and have a high attention to detail as each device is made to perfectly fit each patient.

It is important to have excellent communication skills and be caring and tactful as you will have to reassure, encourage and explain procedures to your patients.

Working conditions

Opportunities are available in hospitals, clinics and centres for people with disabilities.

Some time will be spent in workshops where the prostheses and orthoses are made.

You will generally work normal hours from Monday to Friday, although extra hours are required at busy times. A driving licence is useful if you are working in many different locations.

Future prospects

With a shortage of prosthetists and orthotists, job prospects are generally excellent across the UK. Most prosthetists and orthotists work within the NHS but there are also opportunities in private practice, in charities such as the Red Cross and with commercial companies that make devices for NHS hospitals.

With experience, you may specialise in an area such as upper or lower limb prosthetics or spinal orthotics; you could also move into management or carry out research and teaching.

There are also many opportunities to work all over the world – especially in the USA. Prosthetic and orthotic work is especially important in development programmes which work with communities affected by war.

Advantages/disadvantages

Working with patients who are upset and in pain can be emotionally demanding.

It is satisfying to be able to see the positive effects that the artificial limbs and surgical appliances have on people's lives.

You get to work with a diverse range of people from all age groups.

Money guide

There is no set salary scale for NHS prosthetists and orthotists, but salaries tend to be similar to those in commercial companies.

The starting salary for prosthetists and orthotists is around £21,200 to £27,500 per year.

Experienced prosthetists and orthotists can earn between £30,000 and £40,000.

Some senior practitioners in the NHS or those who work for manufacturers can earn up to £67,000.

Earnings are generally higher in London.

Related opportunities

- Medical Physicist p296
- Occupational Therapist p299
- Physiotherapist p310

Further information

British Association of Prosthetists and Orthotists
www.bapo.com

Skills for Health
www.skillsforhealth.org.uk

PSYCHIATRIST

ENTRY LEVEL 7

Qualifications and courses

Candidates must initially train as a hospital doctor by completing a medical degree which is approved by the General Medical Council (GMC). The entry requirements for medical schools are very high A level/H grade results including relevant subjects such as science and maths. Competition for places on medical degrees is very high and so undertaking relevant pre-entry work experience will not only benefit your application but is becoming increasingly expected.

After studying for a medical degree, graduates will then undertake the 2-year Foundation programme of general training which acts as the bridge between medical school and specialist training. Candidates then progress to 5–6 years of specialty training in a particular area of psychiatry, such as general adult, forensic or geriatric psychiatry.

After successfully completing the specialty stage, trainees receive a Certificate of Completion of Training (CCT) and become eligible to join the GMC Specialist Register. It is then possible to apply for a post as a consultant.

Psychiatrists must engage in continuing professional development (CPD) throughout their career to ensure that their skills and knowledge are up to date. The Royal College of Psychiatrists provides information on available training.

What the work involves

Psychiatrists are doctors who have undergone further training in psychiatry.

As a psychiatrist, you will diagnose mental health problems by talking to patients and carrying out tests. You will then decide on a course of treatment which could include prescribing drugs and talking to patients to help them deal with their problems.

You will treat people with a range of mental health problems and often conduct specialist research, depending on your areas of professional interest. These include depression, schizophrenia, eating disorders, anxieties, phobias, drug and alcohol abuse, and post-traumatic stress disorder.

Type of person suited to this work

As a psychiatrist you need to be patient and caring. You will need excellent communication skills to listen carefully to people who might be confused or withdrawn. You will help them discuss and come to terms with their problems or illness and you should be able to explain their conditions and treatment in a clear, simple way.

You will work with relatives and carers, and as part of a team with other medical staff such as psychiatric nurses and occupational therapists.

Working conditions

You could work in a range of locations including hospitals, patients' homes, schools, residential homes and prisons.

Some psychiatrists have standard office hours. Others work shifts and are on an on-call rota which includes working nights, weekends and on bank holidays.

You will work as part of a team of healthcare professionals.

Future prospects

Most psychiatrists work within the NHS throughout the UK. There is also a small amount of work available in private hospitals, care homes and rehabilitation centres. The armed forces also employ psychiatrists.

There are 6 specialist areas of psychiatry that you may work in: adult, child and adolescent, forensic, the psychiatry of learning difficulties, geriatric, and psychotherapy. Entry to psychotherapy is competitive.

You could move into academic work, either carrying out research or teaching medical students.

Advantages/disadvantages

Your patients could be confused or aggressive with a range of difficult problems so the work can be demanding.

Getting patients to open up and talk may be difficult, particularly if they have a distressing personal history.

It is rewarding to be able to make a difference to people's lives by helping them to regain their self-respect and happiness.

There is the opportunity to work in different environments, but usually in calm environments.

Money guide

Salary levels in the NHS may vary in different locations and earnings are often higher in private practice work.

Junior doctors have a starting salary of between £22,000 and £28,000 during the 2-year Foundation programme.

When undertaking the specialty training, you can expect to earn between £28,000 and £46,000 a year.

Consultant psychiatrists can achieve salaries ranging from £74,000 up to £170,000 for those in the most senior positions.

Related opportunities

- Doctor (GP) p285
- Hospital Doctor p292
- Psychoanalyst/Psychotherapist p554

Further information

British Medical Association
www.bma.org.uk

NHS Careers
www.nhscareers.nhs.uk

RADIOGRAPHER

ENTRY LEVEL 6

Qualifications and courses

All radiographers need a degree approved by the Health Professions Council (HPC). You must decide which branch of radiography you wish to practise in before university as they require different qualifications so it is worth visiting radiography and radiotherapy centres before applying to help with the decision.

Most universities expect you to have previous work experience in a radiography department and to have observed radiography in practice. All radiography degrees involve spending 50% of your time doing academic work and 50% undertaking practical placements. Courses usually last 3 years and the minimum entry requirements for a degree are usually 2 A levels/3 H grades, including a science-based subject (preferably biology or physics), and 5 GCSEs/National 5s (A*–C/A–C).

Diagnostic radiographer
You must hold a degree in diagnostic radiography. Radiography assistants who wish to qualify as radiographers could study for in-service or Foundation degrees.

Therapeutic radiographer
You will need a degree in radiotherapy or therapeutic radiography. Alternatively, those who already have a degree in a science or health-related subject, such as life and medical sciences, biology or health studies, may be eligible for a 2-year postgraduate training course.

What the work involves

Diagnostic radiographer
You will help doctors and surgeons to diagnose diseases and injuries as an essential step towards treating a patient. You may use a variety of methods such as X-ray, computed tomography (CT) scanning and ultrasound to create images of body parts and organs.

Therapeutic radiographer
Working with an oncology team, you will use doses of radiation to control or kill cancerous cells. You will be involved in every aspect of the treatment, including pre-treatment preparation, planning, the delivery of the radiation and follow-up care of patients.

Type of person suited to this work

You should be warm, understanding and adaptable. You must be able to work with both children and adults who are extremely ill. Communication skills are vital for listening to patients and explaining their treatments.

You need to be a quick thinker and be detail-oriented in order to produce accurate images. Confidence to operate sophisticated computerised equipment is essential.

Working conditions

Diagnostic radiographer
You will be based in accident and emergency, operating theatres, wards or imaging units. These departments need to be staffed 24 hours a day so you will work a shift system including nights and weekends. You should work a total of 37.5 hours a week.

Therapeutic radiographer
You will be based in radiotherapy or oncology centres, out-patient units or at charities such as Macmillan Cancer Support.

Future prospects

You could work for the NHS in a clinic, hospital or oncology centre, or work for the armed forces or a private practice.

You could be promoted to management roles or become an instructor or researcher. UK radiography qualifications are recognised internationally so you could choose to work overseas.

Diagnostic radiographer
You could specialise in areas such as magnetic resonance imaging (MRI), ultrasound or nuclear medicine.

Therapeutic radiographer
You could specialise in anything from quality management to treatment planning or palliative care.

Advantages/disadvantages

Each of your patients will be unique, keeping your work interesting.

It is satisfying when you capture the best image possible and contribute to your patients' wellbeing.

Rota work can be difficult as you may be required to work bank holidays and nights.

Money guide

Starting salaries for NHS radiographers are between £21,388 and £27,901.

An experienced specialist could earn from £25,528 up to £34,500.

Senior radiographers can achieve up to £40,000 and consultants could reach £67,000.

Salaries may be higher in private practice.

Related opportunities

- Critical Care Technologist p277
- Medical Physicist p296
- Radiologist p317

Further information

Radiography Careers
www.radiographycareers.co.uk

Society and College of Radiographers
www.sor.org

RADIOLOGIST

ENTRY LEVEL 8

Qualifications and courses

To become a radiologist, you must initially train as a hospital doctor by completing a medical degree which is approved by the General Medical Council (GMC). Entry requirements for medical school include very high A level/H grade results within relevant subjects such as science and maths. Competition for places on medical degrees is tough and pre-entry work experience is becoming increasingly expected. Universities offer 30-week 'pre-medical courses' in sciences for those applicants without science A levels/H grades.

After studying for a medical degree, graduates undertake the 2-year Foundation programme of general training which acts as the bridge between medical school and specialist training.

Candidates then register as Members of the Royal College of Radiologists (RCR) and begin 5 years of speciality training in clinical radiology. At least 4 years of the training are spent in clinical posts and 6 months research in any aspect of diagnostic imaging is also included. Trainees must pass all 3 parts of the Fellowship of the Royal College of Radiologists (FRCR) examination before receiving a Certificate of Completion of Training (CCT) and becoming eligible to join the GMC Specialist Register.

RCR operates a continuing professional development (CPD) scheme for qualified radiologists to update their knowledge and skills.

What the work involves

Radiologists are doctors who have undergone further training in radiology. Radiologists increasingly perform interventional procedures such as biopsies using image guidance.

As a radiologist, you will diagnose patients' diseases by using information gained from images such as X-rays, and computed tomography (CT) or magnetic resonance imaging (MRI) scans.

You will also play an important role in identifying sources of disease and reducing the possible risks of them spreading further.

Type of person suited to this work

As a radiologist, you must care about patients and be sensitive to their situation. You need strong communication skills to explain things to patients simply and clearly so that they understand their health conditions and any treatments they may require.

You must be comfortable working as part of a team with other medical staff.

Scientific and technical knowledge and an ability to diagnose patients' conditions accurately are also necessary. You should be willing to continue learning throughout your career.

You will need good eyesight and excellent attention to detail so that you can interpret images. Practical skills are required when caring for patients and operating equipment.

Working conditions

You will work within a hospital, mainly in the radiology department but you will also spend time visiting patients on their wards.

You will use a range of sophisticated equipment and you will be required to wear protective clothing when operating it.

Your working hours will vary and you will be expected to work shifts, evenings and weekends in order to provide a 24-hour service for patients.

Future prospects

Career prospects are excellent due to an international and domestic shortage of radiologists.

Most radiologists work within the NHS throughout the UK, however there is also some work available in private hospitals.

You may decide to specialise further in a particular area or you could progress to a management role. You could also move into academic work, either carrying out research or teaching medical students.

Advantages/disadvantages

The role can be emotionally demanding because you will be dealing with patients who have life-threatening conditions.

Your work is vital in finding an accurate and early diagnosis for patients, which can help to save lives.

Money guide

Salary levels in the NHS may vary in different locations.

Earnings are often higher in private practice work.

Junior doctors have a starting salary of £22,000–£28,000 during the 2-year Foundation programme.

When undertaking the specialty training, you can expect to earn between £28,000 and £46,000 a year.

Consultant radiologists can achieve salaries ranging from £74,000 up to £170,000 for those in the most senior positions.

Related opportunities

- Anaesthetist p270
- Hospital Doctor p292
- Radiographer p316

Further information

British Medical Association
www.bma.org.uk

NHS Careers
www.nhscareers.nhs.uk

Royal College of Radiologists
www.rcr.ac.uk

SPEECH AND LANGUAGE THERAPIST

ENTRY LEVEL 6

Qualifications and courses

All speech and language therapists must be registered with the Health and Care Professions Council (HCPC). In order to qualify for registration, you must either have a speech and language degree that has been accredited by the Royal College of Speech and Language Therapists (RCSLT) or complete postgraduate study (a good healthcare-related undergraduate degree and relevant work experience is necessary for a postgraduate application).

For entrance onto a degree course you will need 2 A levels/3 H grades, and 5 GCSEs/National 5s (A*–C/A–C) including English, science and maths.

There are also Foundation courses available for those who do not have the relevant qualifications to go straight onto a degree programme, and accelerated 2-year degree courses for students who already have a health-related degree. All courses combine academic study with on-the-job training.

As you will be working with children and vulnerable adults, you will need to undergo a Disclosure and Barring Service (DBS) check and pass a medical screening.

What the work involves

Speech and language therapists work with patients who have problems speaking, chewing or swallowing.

You will be responsible for assessing patients, and prescribing a suitable course of treatment.

You will work with a range of patients including children who need help in developing their speech, people with a speech defect such as a stammer, and those who have trouble eating because of an accident or illness. You will also work with each patient's family, partner or carer in order to show them how to support your patient at home.

You will liaise with professionals in education and social services.

Type of person suited to this work

You will need excellent communication skills in order to develop a good relationship with patients and colleagues alike. You will also need to be a patient teacher in order to successfully help your patients learn new skills to overcome their problems.

You should be mature and non-judgemental in your approach to patients as you will be dealing with people of varying ages, backgrounds and cultures.

You will work both on your own and within a wider team of healthcare professionals, so you must have plenty of initiative coupled with a good approach to working within a team.

Working conditions

Speech and language therapists usually work 37.5 hours per week from Monday to Friday. Evening, weekend or shift work is rare.

There are plenty of opportunities to work part time.

You could work in one or several of a variety of locations, including hospitals, schools, residential homes, health centres, young offenders' institutions and in patients' homes. Since local travel in the community is required, it is useful to have a driving licence, particularly in rural areas.

Future prospects

There is a current shortage of registered speech and language therapists, so job opportunities outweigh the number of candidates.

Most therapists are employed by the NHS and work throughout their local community. Others work for social services, local education authorities, charities and schools. There is a growing trend amongst therapists to be self-employed and treat patients privately.

You could progress to more senior supervisory positions, specialise in an area that particularly interests you, or move into research.

Advantages/disadvantages

Speech and language therapists are in great demand, so you will have a greater choice of job opportunities open to you than in some other health-related professions.

Working closely with patients and seeing them improve under your care and guidance is rewarding.

You may have to work with difficult patients in unfavourable conditions on occasion, such as young offenders' institutions or prisons.

Money guide

As a newly qualified speech and language therapist, you could expect to earn around £21,000. This is in-line with the National Health Service pay scale, which consists of 9 bands.

This usually rises quickly to £27,000 and then, as you gain experience, it can increase up to £34,000.

Senior therapists start at around £35,000 and can earn up to £46,374. If you take on significant supervisory and management responsibilities as well you could expect to earn in excess of £50,000.

Other employers, outside of the NHS, such as charities and local education authorities, offer comparable pay.

Related opportunities

- Health Visitor p289
- Learning Disabilities Nurse p294
- Occupational Therapist p299

Further information

NHS Careers
www.nhscareers.nhs.uk

Royal College of Speech and Language Therapists
www.rcslt.org

Qualifications and courses

Most entrants to this profession have a degree in sports science, but degrees in psychology or any kind of physical education are also relevant.

The entry requirements for a degree in sports science are usually 2 A levels/3 H grades, including a science, particularly sought after in biology, and 5 GCSEs/National 5s (A*–C/A–C). There is also the option of following an Access course before taking a degree, or doing a postgraduate degree in sports science after a degree in a related subject.

Once you have a relevant degree, you can seek accreditation through the British Association of Sport and Exercise Sciences (BASES) and it may be necessary to gain some relevant practical experience in the fitness or leisure industry to increase your chances of employment.

Continuing professional development (CPD) and keeping your skills up to date is really important, and there are plenty of opportunities to do this through the BASES.

What the work involves

Sports scientists work either with athletes to help build their performance or with people who need or wish to improve their health. Clients may also be recovering from illness or injury and need guidance on how to get back to their level of fitness.

As a sport or exercise scientist, you require a lot of scientific knowledge, including an understanding of human biology, biomechanics and physiology. You also need to have an understanding of psychology, in order to assess the mental state of some athletes.

It is typical practise to spend time on performance analysis (usually done with video footage) and work with clients on perfecting performance and fitness.

You will spend some time outside of the office with clients and may conduct research on areas of professional interest or sports you wish to specialise in.

Type of person suited to this work

If you want to be a sports and exercise scientist, above all you need to be a good communicator. Your work will centre on building relationships with people, and you have to be good at listening and aware of your clients' needs.

Aside from this, you need to have a clear writing style to communicate findings, and be good at research and problem solving.

You should be good with numbers and statistics, well organised, accurate and good with computers.

You will also need a scientific and analytical mind to help your clients improve their sporting potential.

Working conditions

You will usually work in leisure and sports centres and gyms, for around 38 hours a week.

If you are a sports scientist, some clients may require you outside regular working hours, and part-time work is also available.

You will also spend a lot of time outdoors, and probably travel too. For this reason, a driving licence is an advantage.

Future prospects

Although there is no specific career path for this job, progression is possible.

Building a list of contacts is important, and with the right experience you may be able to work your way up to helping people who play sport at an international level.

You could also teach, or if you are an exercise scientist, you might be able to move into a specific area such as cardiology.

Advantages/disadvantages

This job is really rewarding for those who are interested in exercise and science, and like to be out and about being active rather than sitting still.

You have to use your brain and your body, and the job is unlikely to become boring as you will be working with so many different people.

It can be tiring, and you need quite specialist knowledge that has to be constantly maintained.

Money guide

As a newly qualified sports and exercise scientist, you will probably earn around £20,000 a year.

As you gain experience, this may rise to about £40,000.

If you work with top athletes in competitive sport, you might earn in excess of £60,000 a year.

Related opportunities

- Leisure Centre Assistant/Manager p365
- Sports Coach p368
- Sports Development Officer p369

Further information

British Association of Sport and Exercise Sciences
www.bases.org.uk

English Institute of Sport
www.eis2win.co.uk

SkillsActive
www.skillsactive.com

STERILE SERVICES TECHNICIAN

ENTRY LEVEL 2

Qualifications and courses

There are no set minimum qualifications to begin work in this position. However, employers will expect you to have a good general standard of education, with strong reading skills and neat handwriting (in order to label materials and equipment clearly and correctly).

Some employers may specifically request that you have 5 GCSEs/National 5s (A*–C/A–C) before applying and other qualifications, such as the BTEC Level 3 in Applied Science or the BTEC Level 3 in Applied Science (Medical Science), could also be advantageous.

Once you secure a position as a sterile services technician, training is provided on the job by experienced colleagues. You may also be encouraged to study for an ASET Level 2 Certificate in the Control of Infection and Contamination or NCFE Prevention and Control of Infection Level 2 Award.

Gaining the NVQ Level 3 in Health (Decontamination) would allow you to register with the Institute of Decontamination Sciences (IDSc). This could help you to progress and gain a management position. The IDSc also offers useful training programmes. Supervisors generally need an SVQ/NVQ Level 3 in Supervisory Management or the First Line Management Certificate from the Institute of Leadership Management (ILM). Further qualifications, such as NVQ Level 4 in Management or the ILM Diploma in Management may also prove advantageous to job progression.

What the work involves

Sterile services technicians work as part of a team responsible for helping to prevent the spread of infections by making sure that hospital equipment is sterile.

Your work will involve collecting and cleaning a range of instruments. You will have to operate a steam sterilising machine, such as an autoclave.

You will dismantle and examine certain instruments through a microscope before sterilising them and then reassembling and testing them. Once the equipment is reassembled and sufficiently cleaned, you will follow set procedures to repackage, seal and label the equipment.

You will work to national standards, operating highly technical machines, and you must keep accurate records of your work.

You will also be expected to deliver sterile supplies by trolley to wards and departments and restock supplies of items such as dressings, needles and syringes.

Type of person suited to this work

You will need to be good with your hands, work accurately, pay attention to detail and follow instructions and set procedures carefully.

Sterile services technicians should be very vigilant about hygiene and interested in keeping hospitals and equipment clean and safe for patients and staff.

You will work in a team so you will need good communication skills. You should also be well organised and able to keep clear, detailed records.

You will be collecting and dismantling machinery so you will need to be physically fit.

Working conditions

You will work in a hospital as part of a team and will have contact with doctors, nurses and other staff.

Based in the sterile services department, you will collect equipment from all parts of the hospital and this will involve lifting and pushing trolleys.

You will have to wear protective clothing and you may have to work shifts. People with skin conditions may find this job difficult.

Future prospects

Most jobs are in NHS hospitals throughout the UK but you could also work in a private hospital. Opportunities are good as there is a shortage of applicants for vacancies.

With experience, you could be promoted to senior technician or supervisor. You could then take professional qualifications and become a sterile services manager.

As a manager you could move into management in other areas of the NHS.

Advantages/disadvantages

The work can be routine and physically demanding.

The working conditions can be humid and uncomfortable as protective clothing is essential and steam sterilising machines are often required.

You will be making a vital contribution to controlling the spread of potentially deadly infections which is very rewarding.

Money guide

Starting salaries for sterile services technicians, in NHS wage band 2, are between £14,294 and £17,425 per year.

Those employed as a supervisor can expect to earn from £16,110 to £19,077.

Related opportunities

- Biomedical Scientist/Medical Laboratory Assistant p482
- Hotel Porter p127
- Operating Department Practitioner p300

Further information

Institute of Decontamination Sciences
www.idsc-uk.co.uk

NHS Careers
www.nhscareers.nhs.uk

Skills for Health
www.skillsforhealth.org.uk

SURGEON

ENTRY LEVEL 8

Qualifications and courses

To become a surgeon, you must initially train as a hospital doctor by completing a medical degree which is approved by the General Medical Council (GMC). Degrees usually take 5 years and entry requirements include very high A level/H grade results, including relevant subjects such as science and maths. Some universities offer a foundation or pre-medical year in addition to the 5-year medical degree course, lasting 30 weeks, for candidates without science A levels/H grades.

Competition for places on medical degrees is very tough, so undertaking relevant pre-entry work experience may benefit your application and is becoming increasingly expected. You may also be required to take the UK Clinical Aptitude Test (UKCAT).

After studying for a medical degree, graduates undertake the 2-year Foundation programme of general training which acts as the bridge between medical school and specialist training. Candidates then progress to 5–6 years of specialty training in a particular area of surgery, such as neurosurgery, paediatric surgery or plastic surgery.

After successfully completing the specialty stage, trainees receive a Certificate of Completion of Training (CCT) and become eligible to join the GMC Specialist Register. It is then possible to apply for a post as a consultant surgeon.

Surgeons must engage in continuing professional development (CPD) throughout their career to ensure that their skills and knowledge are up to date. The Royal College of Surgeons of England provides information on available training.

What the work involves

Surgeons work in hospitals, operating on patients in order to remove or prevent the spread of disease, treat injuries, and fix other complaints.

You will specialise in operating on specific conditions or diseases relating to a particular system of the body, such as neurological, gastrointestinal or cardiovascular. You will also be responsible for diagnosing problems, taking case histories, talking patients through surgical procedures and advising them on post-operative care.

You will see patients on ward rounds and in out-patient clinics, as well as undertaking administrative work such as updating patient records.

Type of person suited to this work

You need excellent communication skills in order to develop a good relationship with patients and colleagues alike. You will be required to direct your team through complex surgical procedures in the operating theatre, as well as explaining them to patients in simple terms.

You should have excellent manual and technical skills in order to operate with precision and confidence. As you will be working under immense pressure, you should also be able to think quickly and clearly when solving problems.

You must be prepared to break bad news to patients and relatives on occasion, which requires sensitivity and diplomacy.

Working conditions

Surgeons work extremely long hours which often include nights and weekends.

Most of your work will take place in hospitals, working with health professionals including other surgeons, nurses, anaesthetists and GPs. You could work in the NHS or in private hospitals, although the majority of surgeons divide their time between the 2.

The work is mentally and physically exhausting as you will need to concentrate for hours at a time and spend a lot of time on your feet.

Future prospects

There are many opportunities to work abroad, particularly in conjunction with specialist charities operating in developing countries.

You will continue to train and learn new skills throughout your career as technology and techniques develop, change and improve.

Once you have qualified as a surgeon, you can become a consultant and work within the NHS or in private practice, both of which are lucrative options.

Advantages/disadvantages

You will be personally responsible for transforming and saving a number of lives throughout your career.

The training period is extremely long, often in excess of 12 years, so you have to be extremely dedicated.

You will work long and unpredictable hours which can have an adverse effect on your personal life.

Money guide

Salary levels in the NHS may vary in different locations.

Junior doctors have a starting salary of between £22,000 and £28,000 during the 2-year Foundation programme.

When undertaking the specialty training, you can expect to earn between £28,000 and £46,000 a year.

Consultant surgeons can achieve salaries ranging from £74,000 up to £170,000 for those in the most senior positions.

Related opportunities

- Dentist p282
- Doctor (GP) p285
- Hospital Doctor p292

Further information

British Medical Association
www.bma.org.uk

NHS Careers
www.nhscareers.nhs.uk

Royal College of Surgeons of England
www.rcseng.ac.uk

TRICHOLOGIST

ENTRY LEVEL 3

Qualifications and courses

The main route into trichology is to complete the Institute of Trichologists' 2-year training course. There are no set minimum entry requirements but the course is academic and scientific in nature and the progress of students is closely monitored through exams and practical placements.

Successful completion of the Institute's course makes you eligible for admission as an Associate Member of the Institute (AIT). Progression to full membership (MIT) is available upon further study and a minimum of 2 years' professional practice as a trichologist.

Another option is to study for the Diploma in Pure-Trichology offered by the Trichological Society. This is a distance learning course which lasts up to 3 years and involves practical clinical experience, a dissertation and an oral exam.

Those who already have medical qualifications may be eligible to take shortened versions of the above courses.

Some trichologists do not have formal qualifications as the profession is unregulated, though it is highly recommended if you want to begin a career and attract clients. Some people gain the NVQ in Hairdressing (Levels 3–4), which contains some trichology teaching, before starting their training.

What the work involves

Trichologists help people who have issues with their hair or scalp. A trichologist diagnoses and treats diseases and disorders of the scalp and hair, such as hair loss and dandruff.

Patients might complain of sudden hair loss all over the scalp, excessive itching and scaling, or bald patch, among other problems.

You will talk to patients about their medical history, health and diet, and thoroughly examine their hair and scalp.

You will give advice and recommend treatment, such as using special creams or shampoos. You might also refer patients to other healthcare professionals or a specialist if appropriate.

Type of person suited to this work

Trichologists need excellent communication skills to speak to patients about their problems and explain the treatments they have recommended.

You should be sympathetic, tactful and able to reassure patients, put them at their ease and gain their trust.

You will need to have a methodical approach to your work and pay close attention to detail so that you can assess patients' conditions accurately and plan appropriate treatment.

Working conditions

Most trichologists work in clinics treating patients and if you are self-employed you will rent your own premises.

You will usually have normal working hours from Monday to Friday. If you work in private practice you might need to work in the evenings or occasionally at weekends to treat people at times that suit them.

The work involves close contact with patients and hands-on treatment.

You are likely to wear a uniform and those employed in a research role may need protective clothing for laboratory work.

Future prospects

Many trichologists are self-employed, so you should expect to start up your own business.

Some trichologists will become involved in teaching and will work in universities and colleges (often in hair and beauty departments).

There are also a number of opportunities to work in research for pharmaceutical and cosmetics companies. Research positions may require further qualifications, such as a medical degree and training in dermatology.

Advantages/disadvantages

Working with patients who are distressed can be challenging and stressful for both parties.

It is rewarding to be able to use your knowledge to treat patients successfully.

Potential for quite a varied workload.

Money guide

Self-employed trichologists charge clients by the session.

Earnings vary widely, depending on your location, experience and the number of clients you have.

Newly qualified practitioners may charge about £30 per consultation.

Experienced practitioners may earn up to £90 for a session.

Trichologists who work in a clinic can earn from £20,000 to £60,000 with experience.

Related opportunities

- Dietitian p283
- Hairdresser/Barber p441
- Hospital Doctor p292

Further information

Institute of Trichologists
www.trichologists.org.uk

The Trichological Society
www.hairscientists.org

Languages, Information and Culture

The jobs in this family are quite varied in terms of whether you would work with other people or by yourself. You could find yourself working in a range of different places, from museums to antiques fairs to conferences as an interpreter. Some of the jobs in this family are more unusual and are perfect for those of you who want a fascinating job that allows you to indulge in your passion for historic artefacts and artwork or languages and foreign countries. To excel in this sector you should have an inquisitive mind, be meticulous in your work and enjoy carrying out research.

The jobs featured in this section are listed below. For similar jobs to the ones in this section please see *Design, Arts and Crafts* on page 153 and *Marketing, Advertising, Media, Print and Publishing* on page 375.

ANTHROPOLOGIST

ENTRY LEVEL 6

Qualifications and courses

Entry to this area is usually gained with a relevant degree or postgraduate qualification. Voluntary or paid work experience can be useful. There are limited opportunities to gain qualifications in this area before degree level. A level/H grade Sociology covers some aspects of anthropology and for biological anthropology an A level/H grade in biology may be useful.

Access and degree courses in this area cover subjects such as social anthropology and physical/biological anthropology. Anthropology can also be studied as part of a combined Honours degree with subjects such as archaeology or psychology. It is also possible to study for a master's or other postgraduate degree in anthropology following a first degree in any subject.

The Association of Social Anthropologists based at the University of Birmingham runs seminars and conferences, and has information on bursaries and awards for anthropology students.

Professionals using their anthropology training in another area such as archaeology are likely to have gained a qualification or degree in their specialist subject. Researchers in this area are often required to have a relevant postgraduate qualification or the equivalent practical experience. Higher education lecturers are usually required to have, or be working towards, a doctorate (PhD) and are expected to have experience in, or show potential for, teaching.

What the work involves

You will study and research the origin and cultural, physical and social developments of humans. You will investigate human culture across the world, in terms of its beliefs, values, traditions, social structure and language.

You will also apply specialist knowledge and research skills to find out about the differences between human cultures.

Anthropologists undertake their research in a wide range of areas such as archaeology, the arts, the environment, biology and religion.

You may use technology such as facial recognition software or carbon dating to get a more accurate idea of your subject, particularly if it is a historical one.

The increased use of technology to communicate means that the development of social interaction and the reliance on media have become large aspects of anthropological study and significance.

Type of person suited to this work

Whatever job you do as an anthropologist, you will need a strong interest in people and a respectful, flexible attitude to other people's beliefs and customs. You should also enjoy meeting new people and entering different social situations.

Good communication skills are also very important. Strong research skills and an organised approach are useful. IT skills and a good level of numeracy are also helpful.

You will need an observant approach with an interest in a wide range of subjects.

Working conditions

For research-based work, you might need to visit and stay in different areas. Spending time in other places means that anthropology is not generally a 9am to 5pm, office-based job.

The work can involve travel in the UK and overseas.

Some physical or biological anthropologists work in laboratories analysing and researching samples.

Forensic anthropologists is often a part-time job and involves fieldwork.

Future prospects

You could gain employment as a researcher on specific projects. Many anthropologists progress within academia by undertaking research and teaching around their specialist interests.

You could also work for government bodies and charities and there are some opportunities to work overseas.

Anthropologists also apply their research skills and training to their work in other areas such as social care, teaching and the health service.

Advantages/disadvantages

This job can provide opportunities to develop and research theories about people and cultures.

Anthropology can also provide the chance to meet a variety of people and visit different places.

Field research can be physically demanding and spending time away can be difficult if you have family commitments.

Money guide

Anthropologists work in a range of sectors, so salaries vary.

Starting salaries for graduates are around £21,000 per year, rising to £26,000 for research assistants/researchers.

Between £33,000 and £43,000 per year is usual for lecturers, with the expected salary for senior lecturers lying between £28,000 and £55,000.

Related opportunities

- Archaeologist p325
- Archivist/Records Manager p326
- Historian p331

Further information

Association of Social Anthropologists
www.theasa.org

Royal Anthropological Institute of Great Britain and Ireland
www.therai.org.uk

ARCHAEOLOGIST

ENTRY LEVEL 6

Qualifications and courses

Most professional archaeologists have a degree, BTEC HND, or postgraduate qualification. Degree entry usually requires 2 A levels/3 H grades and 5 GCSEs/National 5s (A*–C/A–C). There are a number of relevant degree subjects, including ancient history, anthropology and conservation, which can be studied in combination with archaeology. A number of different degrees, ranging from geography or history to computer science and geology, can also be good preparation for a career in archaeology. A small number of Foundation degrees are also available in archaeology.

There is intense competition for jobs and postgraduate degrees are becoming increasingly common and are available in a variety of specialist subjects, such as the archaeology of specific regions or time periods (Egypt etc), bioarchaeology, osteoarchaeology, and landscape archaeology. Entry usually requires a good first degree and a history of relevant work experience.

Skills with computer-aided design (CAD) or geographical information systems (GIS) software could be very useful owing to the increasing use of technology in archaeology.

It is possible to enter this profession without a degree, although this is becoming increasingly uncommon. The Diploma in Environmental and Land-based Studies could be useful. An NVQ in Archaeological Practice (Levels 3–4) is also available.

Voluntary experience on digs is very useful. The key professional bodies can provide details of holiday work experience opportunities. The Archaeology Training Forum (ATF) develops and offers short courses in continuing professional development (CPD), and similar options are offered by English Heritage and the Society for the Protection of Ancient Buildings (SPAB).

What the work involves

Using your specialist knowledge and skills you will investigate and record physical evidence of the past.

You will provide practical support on archaeological excavations or 'digs', which might include undertaking basic digging work, project-managing a team or researching evidence found on sites.

You will develop public understanding of history through presentations, the publication of your findings or teaching in universities or schools. You could also provide information and advice on how to protect and maintain historical sites.

Type of person suited to this work

You will need a strong interest in history and past cultures.

For practical work you will need a patient and careful approach. You should also be observant with an eye for detail. A good level of physical fitness and manual dexterity will be needed when working on digs and handling objects.

The ability to work as part of a team is useful. In more senior jobs, you will need to explain your work to others so communication skills are important. Writing skills will help you to be able to write up reports and keep detailed records. IT skills are also useful.

Working conditions

Archaeologists often work on sites or digs that are outdoors. Varying weather conditions and the nature of the work make this job physically demanding.

Some archaeologists are based in offices within government bodies, heritage organisations and museums.

Much of your work will be on temporary contracts.

Future prospects

Whatever route you follow, this is a very competitive area in which to develop a career, and may be tough to get into.

You will need to gain practical experience on a voluntary or paid basis. With further experience you could project-manage site excavations or work as a researcher analysing excavation findings.

Some archaeologists work for heritage organisations to help preserve historic monuments and buildings. Others go into teaching or follow an academic career.

Advantages/disadvantages

It is likely that you will need to move around different geographical areas to gain practical experience.

There are opportunities to work overseas.

It's rewarding to discover artefacts that can shed ground-breaking light on the past.

Money guide

Salaries can vary dependent on location, sector and size of your employer.

The starting salary in an excavatory role is around £15,500 a year, whilst graduate archaeologists earn between £18,700 and £20,100 at a practitioner level.

Experienced archaeologists with the relevant qualifications can earn around £30,000.

Senior archaeologists can expect a salary of £32,000–£37,000.

Related opportunities

- Archivist/Records Manager p326
- Conservator/Restorer p329
- Further Education Lecturer p181

Further information

Council for British Archaeology
new.archaeologyuk.org

Creative and Cultural Skills
www.ccskills.org.uk

Institute for Archaeologists
www.archaeologists.net

Society for the Protection of Ancient Buildings
www.spab.org.uk

ARCHIVIST/RECORDS MANAGER

ENTRY LEVEL 7

Qualifications and courses

Archivist
Entrants to this profession need a 2.1 Honours degree followed by a postgraduate qualification in archives and records management or archival studies. Your postgraduate degree must be recognised by the Society of Archivists. Useful first degree subjects include history, classics, languages and information science. You will need at least 2 A levels/3 H grades and 5 GCSEs/National 5s (A*–C/A–C) for degree entry.

Relevant work experience is an advantage and is considered a necessity for entry onto a postgraduate course. This experience must be of good quality and cannot be undertaken in a library. See the Society of Archivists website for opportunities.

Records manager
You will normally require both an Honours degree and a postgraduate qualification in records management or in archives and records management. You will need at least 2 A levels/3 H grades and 5 GCSEs/National 5s (A*–C/A–C) for degree entry. Relevant experience is also important. Visit the Society of Archivists website for opportunities.

Both archivists and records managers may start out as assistants without a degree but will need to study for a degree and postgraduate qualification in order to become professionals.

Continuing professional development (CPD) is important and, once you are fully qualified and have at least 3 years of industry experience, you are encouraged to complete the Archives and Records Association (ARA) registration scheme, which takes 3 years to complete.

What the work involves

Archivist
You will manage and organise stored sets of archives, including records such as documents, maps, films and other items.

Many archivists deal with information enquiries and advise on the availability of records. You will ensure that archives are maintained in an appropriate way. You may also conserve documents and prepare them for storage.

Records manager
You will be responsible for organising records and information and advising your organisation as to which should be classified, stored or destroyed. You could be dealing with paper-based or electronic records.

Type of person suited to this work

Both records managers and archivists manage information, so a well-organised and methodical approach is essential. They need strong analytical and IT skills.

Archivists will need an interest in preserving historical records. You may provide information and advice to members of the public, so strong communication skills are useful.

Working conditions

Record/archive centres can be modern and spacious, but if based in older buildings, space may be limited.

Accessing records from cramped storage rooms or high shelves can be physically demanding. This job may not suit people with dust allergies.

In dealing with enquiries from visitors, the working environment can be very busy.

Future prospects

Archivist
Public records offices, private companies and other organisations need skilled information professionals.

With experience, you could progress from an assistant archivist role into senior management.

Records manager
Records managers may need to change employers in order to progress. Consultancy work is an option.

Advantages/disadvantages

Archivist
This job allows you to preserve and protect historical documents.

Employers often offer short-term contracts which can create job instability.

Records manager
You may have to change employers in order to progress.

You will constantly be learning as computer software and legislation are always changing.

Money guide

Archivist
A salary between £17,000 and £24,000 a year is typical as a starting salary (before gaining a professional qualification) for archivists.

When qualified and with some experience you could earn between £21,000 and £30,000.

As a senior archivist it is possible to earn between £30,000 and £55,000.

Records manager
Records managers receive a starting salary of between £21,000 and £30,000.

With some experience this can increase to between £30,000 and £55,000.

Related opportunities

- Antiques Dealer p450
- Bookseller p452
- Librarian/Library Assistant p334

Further information

Society of Archivists
www.archives.org.uk

ARTS ADMINISTRATOR/ MANAGER

ENTRY LEVEL 5

Qualifications and courses

There are no specific entry requirements, but most arts administrators have a degree or HND in an arts subject or business studies.

At degree level, arts management can be studied on its own, or in combination with a related subject such as events management and heritage management. The minimum entry requirements for a degree course are 2 A levels/3 H grades and 5 GCSEs/National 5s (A*–C/A–C).

Postgraduate courses in arts administration/arts management are available. A degree and/or relevant work experience is required for entry to these programmes. NVQs are available in Cultural Venue Operations and Support at Level 2 and Cultural Venue Administration or Cultural Heritage Operations at Level 3, Cultural Heritage at Level 4 and Cultural Heritage Management at Level 5. Another possible entry route is a creative apprenticeship as it covers community arts management.

Experience in the arts, in administration or business, and good IT skills will be an advantage. It is crucial to gain experience in the arts sector by undertaking work experience, voluntary work, internships or temporary work.

What the work involves

You will support the development and operation of activities and events in areas such as visual arts, drama and music.

You will undertake a range of administrative tasks including coordinating facilities and office management. You may be responsible for booking artists, refreshments, security and ticket sales. Your job could also involve managing funding applications and budgets or writing press releases.

Arts administrators are employed in many different organisations including arts centres, museums, community arts groups, local authorities and theatre companies. If you work for a bigger organisation, you will probably specialise in one administrative field such as public relations or sponsorship.

Type of person suited to this work

Enthusiasm for the arts is essential for this role, and a knowledge of the area of art or organisation you will be working for will be important. You will need a committed approach and be able to take initiative. A good range of administrative, office and IT skills are also essential.

You should be able to communicate well in person and in writing. As you will probably have to manage project budgets, numeracy skills are also useful.

Good organisational and multi-tasking skills are essential. You should enjoy working with a range of people, including artists and members of the public. You should be able to work equally well independently or as part of a team.

Working conditions

Working hours can vary but it is likely that you will need to work some evenings and weekends to attend events.

Working environments vary according to employer. You might be based in a spacious office or have to work in more cramped conditions.

You might be required to travel to meet with artists and to attend performances.

Future prospects

This is a competitive area to get into. Developing expertise in a specific area such as community arts or theatre can be helpful.

With experience, you could progress from an assistant administrator role into a more senior job such as general manager or director.

With higher levels of experience, you could provide freelance support or specialise in a particular area such as arts marketing.

Advantages/disadvantages

This job provides the satisfaction of working in the arts.

Get to see potentially exciting exhibitions before the public.

Many roles are available on a part-time or on a project-by-project basis which can create job insecurity.

You may have to move geographic areas to gain work.

Money guide

Salary levels vary according to the type of organisation you work for.

Assistants and trainees typically have a starting salary of between £15,000 and £18,000 which rises to £21,000 a year once qualified.

With further experience and more responsibilities you could earn up to £30,000.

Senior managers could earn between £30,000 and £60,000.

Salaries are higher in London and in other large cities.

Related opportunities

- Events and Exhibition Organiser p384
- Museum/Art Gallery Curator p335
- Personal Assistant p42

Further information

Arts Council England
www.artscouncil.org.uk

Scottish Arts Council
www.creativescotland.com

BILINGUAL SECRETARY

ENTRY LEVEL 3

Qualifications and courses

To work as a bilingual secretary it is necessary to be fluent in at least one foreign language and the majority of entrants have this language as their mother tongue with English as their second language.

For those who are not native speakers, employers will usually expect you to have at least an A level/H grade in your chosen foreign language. A degree in languages or a joint Honours degree in languages and business studies may be useful but is not essential. Degree entry requirements are usually 2 A levels/H grades, including your chosen language, and 5 GCSEs/National 5s (A*–C/A–C).

Employers may also look for qualifications in administration or secretarial skills such as the NVQ/SVQ in Business and Administration (Levels 1–4). A GCSE/National 5 in Business Studies could be useful. OCR also offers Entry Level and Levels 1–3 Certificates in Business Language Competence for French, German, Italian or Spanish.

An Advanced Apprenticeship in Business and Administration is also available for those seeking to develop the required secretarial skills.

The ABC Awards in Practical Languages and the OCR qualifications in Asset Languages are aimed at those looking to use their language skills in a work-based context. NVQs are also available from Levels 1 to 4 in a variety of languages, and The LCCI International Qualifications and the Chartered Institute for IT (BCS)'s European Computer Driving Licence (ECDL) may give entrants an advantage.

What the work involves

Bilingual secretaries use their language skills to provide administrative support to professionals.

You will deal with incoming and outgoing telephone calls, emails and faxes in a foreign language, translate reports and take on the role of an informal interpreter.

It will also be your responsibility to coordinate travel arrangements for visits overseas and make arrangements for foreign visitors.

Type of person suited to this work

You must have the ability to write and speak fluently in English and at least one foreign language, as well as having a good grasp of spelling and grammar. It is necessary to have excellent IT and keyboard skills.

You should be extremely organised, able to multi-task and have good attention to detail. You must be friendly, helpful and polite and be able to work well as part of a team or independently. You should be able to remain calm under pressure.

Working conditions

You will work standard office hours but overtime may be required during busy periods. You could find part-time or temporary work. Job sharing is also available.

Bilingual secretaries share an office and spend a lot of time on the phone, working on a computer, and reading and translating documents. It could be your responsibility to deal with members of the public.

At senior levels, you might get the opportunity to travel abroad.

Future prospects

Western European languages such as Spanish, French and German are most sought after by employers, although there is growing demand for other languages including Chinese, Arabic and Japanese.

You could work for an international organisation or any companies which conduct business abroad, although most vacancies are in London and big cities.

You can progress to working for a more senior member of staff or to a supervisory role in a bigger company. This job can be a stepping stone into a career in marketing or human resources. You could also work overseas. After gaining more qualifications, you could become a translator or interpreter.

Advantages/disadvantages

You will get the opportunity to use your language skills on a daily basis.

It is possible to use the experience you have gained in a specific company or department to gain a promotion.

This job can be repetitive.

Tight deadlines and a heavy workload can be stressful.

Money guide

Salaries vary with geographical location and are likely to be highest in London.

Jobs in banks or other financial organisations tend to be higher paid than those in the media or charity sectors.

Bilingual secretaries can expect a starting salary of £18,000–£20,000.

Those with experience can earn between £20,000 and £35,000.

Taking on additional responsibilities may increase your salary further.

Related opportunities

- Personal Assistant p42
- Receptionist p45
- Secretary p50

Further information

Institute of Administrative Management
www.instam.org

Institute of Chartered Secretaries and Administrators
www.icsa.org.uk

CONSERVATOR/ RESTORER

ENTRY LEVEL 6

Qualifications and courses

The most common route into this profession is through a degree or postgraduate qualification in conservation. Entry requirements for a degree are 2 A levels/3 H grades, including chemistry, and 5 GCSEs/National 5s (A*–C/A–C). Some candidates may choose to take a Foundation degree in an art or furniture-related subject before their undergraduate degree and entry requirements for these courses are 4 GCSEs/National 5s (A*–C/A–C) and at least one relevant A level/H grade.

Graduates from relevant disciplines such as fine art, textile technology, ceramics, art history or chemistry can also enter this profession but they will need a postgraduate qualification in conservation. Details of approved courses are available from the Institute of Conservation (ICON).

An alternative route for school leavers looking to specialise in stonemasonry conservation or other crafts is to apply for an apprenticeship.

Work experience in a museum or gallery is useful and opportunities to volunteer are available through the National Association of Decorative and Fine Arts Societies (NADFAS). Internships, lasting between 8 weeks and one year in length, are also available with museums and are listed on the Museums Association website.

Restorers/conservation officers can work towards NVQs in Cultural Heritage (Levels 2, 3 and 5) or the EDI Level 4 Diploma in Conservation that is offered by the Victoria & Albert Museum.

Once you have several years of experience you can be accredited as a fully-qualified conservator/restorer by applying for the Professional Accreditation of Conservators-Restorers (PACR) scheme.

What the work involves

You will manage the preservation of historical objects and artwork, as well as the care of historic houses and stately homes, applying your specialist knowledge of subjects such as textiles and furniture.

You will undertake conservation work, treating objects to protect them against wear and tear or restoring objects to as close to their original state as possible.

Your job might involve managing freelance restorers/ conservators.

Type of person suited to this work

The role of preserving valuable collections or buildings requires a sound knowledge of culture and history.

You will need good practical skills, attention to detail and normal colour vision and have a patient and methodical approach to your work.

Strong communication skills, the ability to clearly explain complex issues and confidence speaking at public events are important. You should be comfortable working both independently and as part of a team. Those who are self-employed need business and administration skills.

Working conditions

Your work is likely to involve handling and treating fragile objects and you will usually be based in a clean workshop or laboratory. Conservators of stonework or other outdoor exhibitions may have to work outside in all weather conditions.

If you are employed by a museum or gallery you will work regular office hours Monday to Friday. Some conservators/ restorers are self-employed and may have to work additional hours to suit the needs and deadlines of their client.

You might have to work with specialist materials and equipment which can affect people with skin conditions.

Future prospects

Restoration/conservation officers work in museums, galleries and historic houses, often with alternative job titles such as collections manager or curator. Many will have worked as craft conservators/restorers or have gained extensive experience in caring for collections.

You have the opportunity to work anywhere in the world. A willingness to be geographically mobile may improve your career prospects.

With experience, you could progress to managing a historic house or managing a team in a museum or gallery. It is also possible to become self-employed.

Advantages/disadvantages

This type of work offers the chance to care for valuable and rare historical collections and artwork.

Most galleries/museums employ only one person in this role so you might have to relocate to progress in this career.

Money guide

Starting salaries are usually between £18,000 and £22,000.

Once you have gained experience, you can expect earnings of £20,000–£35,000.

Those who are employed in a senior or managerial role can achieve up to £40,000.

Salaries vary according to the quality of your work and your employer and earnings are likely to be higher in London and large cities.

Related opportunities

- Architect p56
- Archivist/Records Manager p326
- Museum/Art Gallery Curator p335

Further information

Creative and Cultural Skills
www.ccskills.org.uk

Institute of Conservation
www.icon.org.uk

National Association of Decorative and Fine Arts Societies
www.nadfas.org.uk

GENEALOGIST

ENTRY LEVEL 5

Qualifications and courses

Direct entry to this profession is unusual. Entrants normally have qualifications and experience in a related field such as archive administration, librarianship or historical research. A knowledge of social and local history sources is necessary, and training in palaeography (the study of ancient writing and scripts) and Latin is also essential.

A history degree provides a useful first step into this profession and the University Campus Suffolk offers a specialised degree in Family, Local and Community History. Typical entry requirements for a degree course is usually 2 A levels/3 H grades with 5 GCSEs/National 5s (A*–C/A–C). Blackpool and The Fylde College also runs a Foundation degree in History and Heritage Management Studies, which contains modules in genealogy, and the University of Strathclyde offers a postgraduate Certificate, Diploma and Master of Science (MSc) in Genealogical, Palaeographic and Heraldic Studies which may be useful to progression within the industry.

The relevant institutions related to genealogy may be a good place to look for continued professional development (CPD) and further training. The Society of Genealogists offers short courses in genealogy and palaeography for beginners and those already working in the field, whilst the Institute of Genealogical Studies offers short courses at Basic, Intermediate and Advanced Levels. The Institute of Heraldic and Genealogical Studies (IHGS) provides qualifications including a Certificate, Higher Certificate and Diploma in Genealogy. Those over the age of 25 who have completed the Diploma and have at least 5 years of experience in research are eligible to apply for Licentiateship of the IHGS.

What the work involves

You will organise and plan research into the history or ancestry of individual families (genealogy) and write reports from your findings.

You will work with a range of historical information such as newspapers and directories to trace specific facts about family histories. Your work could also involve liaising with or supervising the work of researchers.

Meeting with clients and keeping them updated with your research would also be part of your job.

Type of person suited to this work

As you will be investigating family history, an enthusiasm for historical research is essential. You will also need excellent research skills and the ability to understand and interpret detailed information.

IT skills will help you work with information management software. You will also need excellent writing skills to produce reports.

You should enjoy meeting a range of people and working with them to understand and manage their expectations.

You will need a good knowledge of historical resources and subject areas and an organised, thorough approach to your work is important.

Working with unique historical documents demands careful handling skills.

Working conditions

Most genealogists are self-employed and work from home or in offices. However, they spend a lot of their time undertaking research in public records buildings.

The job can involve travel, for example to visit archive collections. A driving licence would be useful.

You will spend a lot of time reading and assessing detailed information.

Future prospects

Genealogy is usually followed as a hobby rather than as a profession and the number of formal employment opportunities are small.

Most genealogists work on a self-employed basis, as a sole trader or part of a small partnership while a small number work for specialist research companies.

You can develop knowledge on a specific subject or geographical area and then undertake additional work such as teaching.

Advantages/disadvantages

As the work is often project based, it can create some job insecurity.

This work gives the satisfaction of providing people with information about their family history and it can be both fascinating and rewarding to tell people the information you find out.

Money guide

Freelance genealogists are usually paid at an hourly rate which can range from £15 to £25. This fee can increase for more complex projects.

You could also charge a fixed rate for each piece of information you find.

Annual income varies considerably, but may be between £15,000 and £25,000 a year.

Genealogists with a postgraduate qualification can expect to earn between £26,500 and £35,000 per year.

Related opportunities

- Archivist/Records Manager p326
- Librarian/Library Assistant p334
- Registrar of Births, Deaths, Marriages and Civil Partnerships p48

Further information

Creative and Cultural Skills
www.ccskills.org.uk

Institute of Heraldic and Genealogical Studies
www.ihgs.ac.uk

Society of Genealogists
www.sog.org.uk

HISTORIAN

ENTRY LEVEL 7

Qualifications and courses

A master's degree or alternate postgraduate qualification in history or historical archaeology is usually required for work as an archival or historical researcher.

Typical entry requirements for postgraduate degrees include a strong undergraduate degree (2.1 or higher) in history or related subject, such as ancient world studies or politics, as well as significant work experience within the historical field, such as archive work for a museum or collector. Entry requirements for an undergraduate degree are generally 2 A levels/3 H grades, including history, and 5 GCSEs/National 5s (A*–C/A–C).

For a position in a university faculty, a doctorate (PhD) is usually required.

Training courses in historical research are available through the Institute of Historical Research, the Society of Genealogists and the Institute of Heraldic and Genealogical Studies.

What the work involves

The type of work you will undertake depends who you work for. Most jobs will require some form of historical research, either for the public or for academic circles, and this may be done through a variety of resources, including internet research (using academic resources such as online journals), paper-based information (journals, books), and hands-on research with historical objects. This could involve work from home, library, museums, or wherever necessary.

You can choose to teach and lecture on specific historical subjects, and you might write articles for professional journals and other publications.

Heritage organisations sometimes employ historians for research purposes.

Depending on your specialism, you could spend a lot of time searching for and analysing primary documents in archives and museums.

Type of person suited to this work

You will need a strong enthusiasm and love for history. You should also have a good knowledge of your specialist subjects.

Research skills are essential and will develop over the course of your study. You should pay close attention to detail and be accurate in your work.

Excellent verbal communication skills are important for explaining facts to people. Good writing skills are needed for writing up research and articles.

Historians need to consider a wide range of theories, so an open-minded approach is important.

You should also be well organised to manage and plan your research.

Working conditions

You will spend time in libraries and archive centres. This will involve reading and assessing information.

Some historical researchers are based in public records offices.

Historians in an academic role are based in universities.

You can also become the specialist historian for a wide variety of organisations, businesses or groups such as a football club, a military formation or think tank.

Undertaking historical research on a self-employed basis can create some job insecurity.

Future prospects

As a professional historian you could go into historical research or follow an academic career path.

Many historians combine both roles; they write, teach and carry out research on their specialist area of interest. Others combine historical research with other related areas such as genealogy.

A small number of historians are employed by heritage organisations to provide expert advice and support.

Some historians go into more media-based roles, such as a researcher, consultant, author or television presenter.

Advantages/disadvantages

This type of work provides the satisfaction of undertaking original research and finding out about the past.

There is the opportunity to remain in education, which will provide a rewarding opportunity to educate others.

It takes time and dedication to get established as a specialist on a specific historical period or subject.

Money guide

Earnings vary according to your job. Historical researchers usually charge by the hour; rates vary from £16 to £50.

Starting salaries for academic posts range from £21,000 to £25,000 per year.

With experience this rises to around £35,000.

At senior academic levels this could increase to between £35,000 and £55,000.

Related opportunities

- Archaeologist p325
- Genealogist p330
- Museum/Art Gallery Curator p335

Further information

Creative and Cultural Skills
www.ccskills.org.uk

Institute of Historical Research
www.history.ac.uk

Royal Historical Society
www.royalhistoricalsociety.org

INFORMATION OFFICER

ENTRY LEVEL 6

Qualifications and courses

Most professional information officers (sometimes called information scientists) have an undergraduate degree in an industry-related subject, such as information management, information studies and information and library studies, that has been accredited by the Chartered Institute of Library and Information Professionals (CILIP). Entry onto most degree courses usually requires 2 A levels/3 H grades and 5 GCSEs/National 5s (A*–C/A–C).

An alternative route to professional qualification is through a degree in a non-related subject, followed by a CILIP-approved postgraduate qualification. This is particularly beneficial for information services provided in scientific or technical contexts.

Experience of information-related work is advantageous, and may be a requirement for some postgraduate courses. Graduate training opportunities are available for people who wish to pursue a career in this area, and need to gain relevant experience before studying for a postgraduate qualification. Details are available through CILIP.

It is also possible to become a qualified information scientist from a library/information assistant post. CILIP offers a certification scheme for people with 5 years' experience of information work, or 2 years' experience plus relevant work-based training.

Entrants through both the educational and certification routes may have the opportunity to work towards Chartered membership of CILIP. Candidates for Chartership must have completed an approved period of professional experience.

What the work involves

You will develop, manage and coordinate both electronic and paper-based information systems for a range of organisations and companies. You will be working to ensure the information is accessible and relevant.

Your job will involve cataloguing, indexing and archiving information. You will also respond to research enquiries, manage intranets and ensure all of your information is up to date.

You could work in a range of sectors, including law, education and business and be employed in a variety of roles. For example you could be an analyst or a librarian. You will produce reports, graphs and briefings based on your findings.

Type of person suited to this work

You should be able to work with different forms of information such as databases, the internet and paper resources.

You may provide information for members of the public or staff within an organisation so strong communication skills are important. An interest in customer service is useful.

Writing skills and IT skills are increasingly important. Managing information demands an organised, methodical approach. A good level of numeracy can be useful. You will need to be resourceful and pay close attention to detail.

Working conditions

Information scientists work in offices, resource centres, libraries and other sites.

You will be working standard hours, Monday to Friday, and can also be hired on short-term contracts for specific projects.

You could work face to face with members of the public or staff within your organisation. You could also deal with information enquiries over the phone and through email.

Self-employed or freelance work is possible.

Future prospects

Information science is a very broad area. You could begin in an assistant or junior information job and with experience you could progress to working in a management role.

With experience you could specialise and work on a consultancy basis. At the moment there is a demand for specialists in science and computer science.

There are also opportunities to work abroad.

Advantages/disadvantages

Depending on the sector you work in, this job can be very fast paced.

Information science skills are transferable to a wide range of job areas.

Money guide

Salaries range quite widely for this role. Starting salaries are between £17,000 and £26,000.

With experience or at senior level this rises to between £26,000 and £50,000 or maybe more.

Salaries at £70,000 per year and above are possible at senior levels in large organisations, particularly private sector companies such as legal and finance sectors and sometimes in consultancy.

Specific salary guides for some sectors are available from the Chartered Institute of Library and Information Professionals (CILIP).

Information consultants can earn around £400–£500 a day.

Related opportunities

- Archivist/Records Manager p326
- Media Researcher p389
- Museum/Art Gallery Curator p335

Further information

Arts and Humanities Research Council
www.ahrc.ac.uk

Association for Information Management
www.aslib.com

Chartered Institute of Library and Information Professionals
www.cilip.org.uk

INTERPRETER

ENTRY LEVEL 6

Qualifications and courses

Fluency in English and at least one foreign language is a prerequisite for those looking to work as an interpreter. Most entrants have a degree in either a modern language, translation and interpreting, or British Sign Language (BSL) and interpreting. Entry requirements for a degree usually include 2 A levels/H grades, including your chosen modern language, and 5 GCSEs/National 5s (A*–C/A–C). A postgraduate diploma or master's degree in interpreting techniques is normally required.

Joint Honours degrees in science, engineering, the environment, business or politics with your chosen language can be useful for jobs where you will be expected to understand specialist vocabulary and concepts.

The Chartered Institute of Linguists (CIOL) offers vocational qualifications including the Level 3 Certificate in Bilingual Skills, the Level 6 Diploma in Public Service Interpreting and the Level 7 Diploma in Translation. Candidates are expected to have achieved the required level of competence in their language. CILT, the National Centre for Languages, has developed National Occupational Standards for professional linguists.

To become an accredited freelance interpreter for the EU you will have to pass an inter-institutional accreditation test, whilst a short training course is also available in conference interpreting from the European Commission in Brussels.

Qualified interpreters can work towards membership of the IoL or the Institute of Translation and Interpreting (ITI). These professional bodies provide further training and development opportunities.

What the work involves

Interpreters convert words spoken in one language into conversation or speech in another language. Using your knowledge of foreign languages, you will enable speakers of different languages to communicate with each other.

You could interpret while a person speaks or make notes and then interpret their statements.

Interpreters provide services for international political conferences, court hearings, business meetings and public services.

Type of person suited to this work

You must be fluent in at least one, or preferably 2, foreign languages. It is also important to be aware of the culture and country of your chosen language. You must have excellent listening skills and the ability to speak clearly.

Interpreting at courts and conferences requires a confident manner. You should keep up to date with current affairs as you may interpret on subjects including business and law, or if an alternative field, ensure you are up to date with the latest news in that field.

Dealing with confidential information may be part of your job so you will need discretion.

Working conditions

Interpreters have to concentrate continuously for long periods which can be physically demanding.

You will need to travel to different locations at fairly short notice, either abroad or within the UK.

Interpreters work in a range of environments, including high-profile conferences and formal meetings.

Hours vary according to clients' needs and are likely to include evening and weekend work. Freelance interpreters may find the demand for work irregular.

Future prospects

This area of work is very competitive with a limited number of full-time opportunities. A small number of interpreters work for international or European agencies. Others are employed by local governments and interpret in courts, hospitals and police stations.

You can choose to work within community organisations, helping people gain access to public services. Many interpreters work on a freelance basis.

There is a growing demand for Chinese, Urdu, Punjabi and eastern European languages.

Advantages/disadvantages

This type of work provides the opportunity to travel and live abroad.

Due to tight schedules and extensive travelling, this can be a pressured and demanding job.

Freelance interpreters often need to take on additional work to support themselves.

Money guide

Newly qualified interpreters can expect a salary of around £17,000–£21,000 per year. With experience, your earnings can rise to between £26,000 and £35,000.

Senior interpreters working for international or European agencies can achieve up to £60,000.

Many interpreters work freelance and charge a daily rate of £110–£500, depending on their experience, the level of demand for the language they speak and the type of interpreting required.

Related opportunities

- Importer/Exporter p579
- Secretary p50
- Teacher of English to Speakers of Other Languages p191

Further information

Chartered Institute of Linguists
www.iol.org.uk

CILT, the National Centre for Languages
www.cilt.org.uk

Institute of Translation and Interpreting
www.iti.org.uk

LIBRARIAN/LIBRARY ASSISTANT

ENTRY LEVEL 2

Qualifications and courses

The entry requirements to become a library assistant are usually at least 5 GCSEs/National 5s (A*–C/A–C), including English. Commercial or industrial libraries may require A levels/H grades, and university libraries may need a degree so check requirements carefully before applying.

The Apprenticeship in Libraries, Archives, Records and Information Management Services is available at Intermediate and Advanced Level and may help yo gain on-the-job experience whilst studying for a relevant professional qualification.

The fastest route to becoming a qualified librarian is through a degree in librarianship or information management that has been accredited by the Chartered Institute of Library and Information Professionals (CILIP). The usual entry requirements for a degree are 2 A levels/3 H grades and 5 GCSEs/National 5s (A*–C/A–C) but people with experience as library assistants are often admitted to the degree courses with vocational qualifications.

An alternate route can be to take a CILIP-accredited postgraduate qualification in librarianship or information management. Depending on your first degree subject, it may be possible to work in a more specialist library, such as science or art. Prior experience of library or information work is advantageous and some institutions will expect you to have up to one year's experience in a role such as library assistant before applying.

Senior library assistants can study for a librarianship qualification (degree or postgraduate qualification) accredited by CILIP if they wish to progress to librarian level.

What the work involves

Librarian

You will manage collections of books, newspapers, documents and IT resources in libraries and information services to make them available to visitors. You may choose new resources to suit the library or information service you work in. You will also help visitors look for information and use IT and other resources.

Library assistant

You will organise and reshelve books and other resources. You may also work on the library counter to help visitors with enquiries and check books in and out of the library. You might deal with petty cash, catalogue new library resources and maintain databases.

Type of person suited to this work

You should have good customer care skills and enjoy helping people with enquiries. The ability to undertake research and use resources to locate information is essential. You must be able to work with IT software, the internet and databases and be confident in explaining these to others.

Librarians should be comfortable working in a team and managing people. Financial skills will help you monitor budgets. You will need an organised approach to your work.

Working conditions

You are likely to work face to face with members of the public or staff within an organisation.

Working on a counter, dealing with information enquiries and lifting and carrying books can all be physically demanding.

Library work can be pressured as you will need to locate and provide information to meet specific requests.

Future prospects

Librarians could progress to a senior level, meaning they would manage a branch library or department.

Some librarians move into information management roles within public services or private companies.

Library assistants are employed in library and information services in businesses, community library services and government. Larger organisations provide opportunities to progress into senior roles and take on additional responsibilities.

The worst of the library closures are over, though jobs may still be tough to get.

Advantages/disadvantages

You will be able to exercise your creativity by thinking up ways to promote the library and its resources.

You may need to move geographic locations to develop your career.

This type of work provides the satisfaction of helping people access information and other services.

Money guide

Salaries vary according to the sector in which you are employed and CILIP provide recommendations for minimum salaries.

Most library assistants start on £15,000 a year. With experience, earnings can increase to £18,000, and senior assistants earn over £20,000.

Starting salaries for librarians range from £20,000 to £24,000.

At chartered librarian level, you could expect earnings of £24,000–£33,000.

A senior librarian can receive up to £40,000 and a head of service can achieve £55,000 and above.

Related opportunities

- Archivist/Records Manager p326
- Arts Administrator/Manager p327
- Information Officer p332

Further information

Chartered Institute of Library and Information Professionals

www.cilip.org.uk

MUSEUM/ART GALLERY CURATOR

ENTRY LEVEL 6

Qualifications and courses

Entrants to this profession are required to have a relevant degree in a subject such as archaeology, history of art, heritage management, fine art or archive and museum studies. Typical degree entry requirements include 2 A levels/3 H grades and 5 GCSEs/National 5s (A*–C/A–C).

As competition for entry-level jobs is very high, many candidates increasingly have a postgraduate qualification in museum, gallery or heritage studies. To study at this level you will need at least a 2.1 in your undergraduate degree.

Employers will also require you to have relevant paid or voluntary work experience. Details of opportunities to volunteer are available through the Museums Association, the National Trust and English Heritage.

Many curators continue their studies while working and undertake a master's degree or doctorate (PhD) in their specialist area, such as egyptology. Short training courses and professional development schemes are often provided by museums, galleries and the Museums Association (MA). The Victoria and Albert Museum also runs a graduate training programme which lasts 5 years and involves training while working as an assistant curator. Once employed you may also wish to study for the NVQ in Cultural Heritage (Levels 2, 3 and 5).

What the work involves

You will manage and maintain collections of artworks, historical objects or documents. Curators usually have specialist knowledge of a specific historical or cultural field such as women's history, textiles or archaeology. You will research and write about the collections in your care.

You might be responsible for thinking of ways in which you can gain funding for your museum/gallery. You will also organise exhibit loans with other museums/galleries.

You will work with other museum/gallery staff to plan exhibitions using items and information from your collection. You may also give talks to members of the public at special events.

Type of person suited to this work

You will need a good knowledge of history and of your specialist area of art/culture. You must be able to communicate this information to other staff and be a confident public speaker. You may lecture at educational events so enthusiasm for your subject is essential.

You will need good written communication skills for writing reports. IT skills are increasingly important in this area, for example when managing collection information through specialist databases. You should be organised, careful and have good attention to detail.

Working conditions

Curators generally work 37 hours a week, however these hours may be extended for special exhibitions and private showings.

This job will probably involve weekend or evening work. You may have to be on-call to respond to emergencies at the gallery/museum.

Working environments vary depending on the size, location and popularity of the gallery/museum. You will work indoors on a daily basis. There may be some heavy lifting and carrying involved when exhibits need to be moved.

Future prospects

Museum/gallery work is a competitive area in which to develop a career as staff turnover is low, but it offers a variety of interesting roles.

You could work your way up in some larger organisations but often you will need to move employers or geographical location in order to move up the career ladder.

From working as an assistant curator, you could progress into a curator's role. You could then move on to work as a senior curator or go into managing museums/galleries or historic buildings.

Advantages/disadvantages

This job provides the satisfaction of working closely with works of art and historical objects, some of which can be very valuable.

You will help create exhibitions and then watch the public enjoy them.

Gaining necessary funding may be difficult.

Money guide

Salaries vary according to the location, size and type of employer.

A museum or art gallery curatorial assistant can expect a starting salary of £16,000–£19,000, whilst curators can earn up to £23,000.

Once you have gained experience in the role, curators could earn between £26,000 and £35,000 a year.

A senior curator with high levels of responsibility could achieve up to £60,000.

Related opportunities

- Arts Administrator/Manager p327
- Events and Exhibition Organiser p384
- Museum/Art Gallery Technician p336

Further information

Museums Association
www.museumsassociation.org

MUSEUM/ART GALLERY TECHNICIAN

ENTRY LEVEL 3

Qualifications and courses

Experience of working with the public and enthusiasm for museums/galleries are often valued more by employers than academic requirements. However, many large galleries/museums will require at least 4 GCSEs/National 5s (A*–C/A–C) and some may expect A levels/H grades. Vocational qualifications in subjects such as carpentry, engineering, or computing may prove advantageous due to the work involved when setting up some exhibitions. The Victoria & Albert Museum also offers the Museum Technician Awards at Levels 3 and 4.

Studying for a Foundation degree or degree in museum and gallery studies may improve your career prospects. Other useful subjects are history of art, heritage management and arts and cultural management. You will need at least 2 A levels/3 H grades and 5 GCSEs/National 5s (A*–C/A–C) for entry to a degree.

The Apprenticeship in Cultural and Heritage Venue Operations is offered at Advanced Level and provides school leavers with the opportunity to train for a museum assistant position. Once employed, you could then work your way up to technician level through the study of professional qualifications, such as an NVQ/SVQ Level 2 in Heritage Care and Visitor Service or in Cultural Heritage Venue Operations (Levels 2–3).

Relevant work experience is recommended and may help you secure a permanent position. Details of volunteering opportunities are available from the Museums Association, and internships are available with organisations such as the Contemporary Art Society.

What the work involves

You will help prepare gallery and museum spaces for temporary exhibitions and collection displays.

Your work will involve installing audio-visual equipment to suit specific exhibitions. You will also transport objects and artworks to and from exhibition spaces. You will provide general technical support to the museum/gallery team as required.

You might be responsible for maintaining files, mending and cleaning exhibitions, and labelling and storing specimens.

Type of person suited to this work

You will need a good range of technical skills to meet the varied practical demands of a museum/gallery environment.

As well as providing support in setting up new exhibitions, you will have to deal with practical problems as they arise. The ability to handle fragile or valuable objects and artworks carefully is essential.

You will need a good knowledge of building security and maintenance. You may also be responsible for the fire safety of the gallery/museum. You will be a good team player and have a strong interest in helping people get the most out of their visits to galleries and museums.

Working conditions

Although you may spend some time in an office environment, the majority of your work will take place around the museum/gallery.

Generally technicians work about 36 hours a week but you might have to be on-call to respond to emergencies at the gallery/museum. You might also have to work longer hours when setting up or dismantling exhibitions. You may have to work some weekends, evenings and bank holidays.

You will usually be required to wear a uniform and/or name badge.

Future prospects

Museum/gallery work is a competitive industry and permanent jobs are relatively rare due to low staff turnover. However, freelance opportunities are common, especially with smaller galleries.

It is possible to progress to working as a senior or head technician. In larger organisations, you could manage a team of technicians.

It may be possible to start your own technician business and you could even run your own gallery.

Advantages/disadvantages

This job provides the satisfaction of working closely with works of art and historical objects, some of which can be very valuable.

This is a competitive area of work so you might have to change jobs to gain a promotion.

You may have to work some unsocial hours which could disrupt your social or family life.

Money guide

These figures are only approximate and may vary depending on location and employer. Larger galleries and museums may pay a higher rate.

Starting salaries are between £13,000 and £16,000.

With experience, you can expect to earn about £19,000 a year.

Senior technicians with additional responsibilities can achieve up to £25,000.

Related opportunities

- Archaeologist p325
- Events and Exhibition Organiser p384
- Museum/Art Gallery Curator p335

Further information

Association of Independent Museums
www.aim-museums.co.uk

Creative and Cultural Skills
www.ccskills.org.uk

Museums Association
www.museumsassociation.org

TRANSLATOR

ENTRY LEVEL 6

Qualifications and courses

Most translators will have a relevant degree in either one or more foreign languages (preferably applied), a foreign language combined with a specialist subject such as business, law or European studies, translation or interpreting.

For modern language degrees a minimum of 2 A levels/3 H grades, with one in a language, and 5 GCSEs/National 5s (A*–C/A–C) are normally required.

Postgraduate courses in translation are available, and usually require a degree in a modern language. The Chartered Institute of Linguists (IoL) offers vocational qualifications in a wide range of languages, including the Certificate in Bilingual Skills (equivalent to A level/H grade), the QCF Level 6 Diploma in Public Service Interpreting and the Level 7 Diploma in Translation. Examinations are open entry, but candidates are expected to have achieved the required level of competence before sitting an exam.

Fluency in 2 or more languages is required to work as a translator. You may also be expected to have a thorough knowledge of the culture and country of your chosen languages, usually gained by living and working there. Qualified translators can work towards membership of the IoL or Institute of Translation and Interpreting. These professional bodies provide further training and development opportunities.

To apply for translator posts in a European Union (EU) institution, you must be fluent in at least 2 languages in additional to your mother tongue, possess a relevant degree and pass an exam.

What the work involves

You will convert written text such as letters, reports, leaflets and brochures from one language to another. You will ensure that your translation matches the tone and style of the original text and has a high standard of grammar.

Your work will also involve meetings with employers to agree projects.

Translators provide services to specialist translation agencies, private companies, local government bodies and international organisations.

Type of person suited to this work

Translators must work to a high standard of accuracy, so attention to detail is important.

The ability to write in your chosen languages in a range of styles is essential. You should also be able to understand and translate complex documents. IT skills are very useful.

Discretion is important as you may translate confidential information. Being well organised will help you to meet project deadlines. You will need a confident approach to work on a freelance basis and promote your services. Numeracy skills are also useful.

Working conditions

Translators are usually self-employed and based in offices at home, but there are opportunities for translators in companies.

You might attend meetings with employers and colleagues.

This type of work involves close working at a computer and the use of resources such as dictionaries and technical reference books.

Future prospects

As a translator you could work for a variety of employers, translating medical, technical, legal and other documents.

Many translators work on a freelance basis.

There are opportunities to work for private companies and international organisations on a permanent basis, in the UK or abroad. Demand for translators is growing, as the markets become more global and large multinational events are held, such as the World Cup.

Advantages/disadvantages

This area of work can provide opportunities to travel and work abroad.

Working on a self-employed project-by-project basis can create some job instability.

Translation can be very demanding owing to short deadlines and the constant demand for accuracy.

Money guide

Translators may be paid between £75 and £180 per 1,000 words, depending on the language they are translating.

Most positions pay between £18,000 and £21,000 per year.

With experience, generalist translators earn around £30,000 and senior translators can earn up to £60,000.

The EU generally provides the best pay. Translators earn between £3,800 and £4,300 a month to begin with, whilst senior translators with sufficient experience can earn between £14,800 and £16,000 a month.

Related opportunities

- Importer/Exporter p579
- Secretary p50
- Teacher of English to Speakers of Other Languages p191

Further information

Chartered Institute of Linguists
www.iol.org.uk

CILT, the National Centre for Languages
www.cilt.org.uk

Institute of Translation and Interpreting
www.iti.org.uk

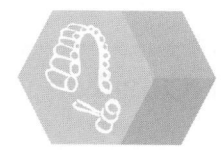

Legal and Political Services

If you find the law a fascinating subject and you feel you would enjoy a challenging career where the rewards are a good salary and a real sense of achievement when your hard work pays off, a job in this sector could be what you are looking for. Workers in this sector are fiercely passionate about their careers and have more often than not, completed a lot of training and worked hard to establish themselves in this competitive field. You need to be driven and thrive on pressure and tight deadlines; this is a sector for someone who is ambitious and very talented at working tactfully with people.

The jobs featured in this section are listed below. For similar jobs to the ones in this section turn to *Administration, Business, Office Work and Financial Services* on page 1.

BAILIFF/ENFORCEMENT AGENT

ENTRY LEVEL 3

Qualifications and courses

Employers prefer candidates to have 5 GCSEs/ National 5s (A*–C/A–C), including English and maths. Applicants must be aged between 21 and 62 but mature candidates, without a criminal record or debt, are often preferred because their life experience may help them deal with difficult situations.

To become a certificated bailiff, candidates need to obtain a Bailiff's General Certificate. This is issued by a circuit judge and needs to be reapplied for every 2 years. The necessary legal knowledge can be gained by taking the examinations of the Certificated Bailiffs Association (CBA). With a certificate, you are eligible to join Her Majesty's Court Service's Certificated Bailiff's Register.

In Scotland, to be commissioned as a sheriff officer, candidates need to pass the examinations of the Society of Messengers-at-Arms and Sheriff Officers. The minimum age to be commissioned is 20, but training, which normally takes 3 years, can begin earlier.

You will need a security bond up to the value of £10,000, plus 2 references for insurance purposes.

In England and Wales training is done mostly on the job where you learn the laws and procedures before applying for the Certificate. However it is possible, upon gaining enough experience and having passed the relevant exams, to join the Association of Civil Enforcement Agencies (ACEA) or the Enforcement Services Association (ESA) in order to aid continuing professional development (CPD).

In Scotland, training is done under an appointed mentor. After 2 years of experience has been gained you can apply to become a messenger-at-arms.

What the work involves

Court bailiffs deliver legal documents, such as a court summons, to people who owe money and might also take steps to ensure payment. Certificated/private bailiffs visit people in debt to recover the money they owe, arranging for removal of their property where necessary.

In Scotland, officers of court deliver legal documents to people who owe money and take all the legal steps required to get the money paid.

You may also give advice on how to pay debts.

Type of person suited to this work

As there are strict legal procedures connected with recovering debt, you will need to be completely up to date with legislation to conduct your work correctly and within legal guidelines.

The work will bring you into contact with many different people, so it's important that you are able to deal with all members of the public.

You will need to be assertive to deal with people's resistance and persistent to get the job done. Being tactful and able to cope with people under stress is also essential.

Working conditions

You will spend a lot of time travelling and so will need a clean driving licence.

Although you will be based in an office, you might have to visit people's homes in the evenings and early mornings to make sure that someone is there.

If you have to remove furniture in payment of debt, you could have to do a lot of heavy lifting, so you will need to be physically fit.

In England and Wales, court bailiffs generally work for the county courts and private bailiffs with magistrates' court orders.

In Scotland, officers of court are called sheriff officers in the sheriff court and messengers-at-arms in the Court of Session.

Future prospects

Opportunities for work as a bailiff/enforcement agent depend very much on the current economic climate. Despite improving economic situation, factors such as council tax support cuts mean prospects remain good. Job prospects for bailiffs are usually stable.

Self-employment is also an option.

If you work for the county court you can progress into management or switch to a private firm in which you would also have opportunities to progress into management roles.

Advantages/disadvantages

The work is varied and in different locations; no two days will be the same.

You will meet many different people, some of whom may be difficult to deal with and threatening.

The hours can be long and unsocial.

Money guide

Starting salaries range between £13,000 and £15,000.

With experience this can rise to between £16,000 and £25,000.

£50,000 per year is possible for the very capable and highly experienced.

In Scotland you could earn between £17,000 and £28,000.

Related opportunities

- Police Officer p529
- Police Support Worker p530
- Security Officer/Manager/Door Supervisor p541

Further information

Civil Enforcement Association
www.civea.co.uk

Society of Messengers-at-Arms and Sheriff Officers
www.smaso.org

BARRISTER/ ADVOCATE

ENTRY LEVEL 6

Qualifications and courses

England and Wales

You will need either an approved law degree or another degree (minimum 2.1 Honours for both), followed by a postgraduate law conversion course, known as the Common Professional Examination, or a Graduate Diploma in Law (GDL).

Following this, you must complete the vocational stage of qualification by becoming a member of one of the 4 Inns of Court where you will undertake the Bar Professional Training Course (BPTC). This will prepare you for completion of 2 6-month pupillages (a mix of work and training taking place in chambers). Training for the 'bar' continues for 3 years, working in one of the Inns of Court.

Once you have qualified, you will be required by the Bar Standards Board (BSB) to undertake at least 45 hours of continuing professional development (CPD) per year. This must include at least 9 hours of advocacy training and 3 of ethics. After the first 3 years, the amount of annual CPD you are required to take will drop to 12 hours.

Scotland

You will need either an Honours degree in Scottish Law from a Scottish university (minimum 2.1 Honours); an Ordinary degree in Scottish Law from a Scottish university with an Honours degree from a UK university (minimum 2.1 Honours); or a Scottish Ordinary degree with distinction. You must also undertake a 1-year full-time Postgraduate Diploma in Legal Practice at a Scottish university.

For vocational entry, you will need to work for 12–21 months in a solicitor's office and 'devilling' (training with) a member of the bar for nine and a half months, before taking the entry examinations of the Faculty of Advocates.

Advocates will normally practise as a solicitor for 10 years, prior to acting as an advocate.

What the work involves

Barristers/advocates give legal advice to other legal professionals and act for clients in certain cases in the high courts. You will research information and past cases before giving advice to solicitors on whether a case should go to court.

In court, you will examine witnesses and present the case for the prosecution or the defence.

You will also act for clients at tribunals or enquiries if asked to do so by a solicitor.

Type of person suited to this work

You will need to research large amounts of information before giving legal advice. You will need to be able to think logically to work out what is important in the case and apply the law to it.

You will need to be confident to speak in court, to convince a jury with your arguments, and able to think quickly when questioning witnesses or defendants.

Excellent written and public speaking skills are needed in order to prepare your case. Keeping an open mind is important and you must be able to gain people's confidence.

Working conditions

Barristers usually work in offices called 'chambers', and advocates in groups known as 'stables' in the Advocates' Library in Edinburgh.

If you specialise in criminal law, you will spend more time in court than civil law specialists would.

Future prospects

Most barristers/advocates are self-employed and it can take around 5 years to establish a practice and become known.

After 10–15 years' experience you can apply to 'take silk' to become a Queen's Counsel. This is essential if you want to become a judge in the higher courts.

Some people work in central or local government where there is a clear promotion structure.

Advantages/disadvantages

The work is varied and you will get satisfaction when you win a case.

Some cases may put you under pressure, particularly if they attract media attention.

You will sometimes work long hours to meet deadlines.

Money guide

Salaries during pupillage are around £12,000 and first year salaries can range from £12,000 to £42,000.

Earnings between £28,000 and £60,000 are normal in the Crown Prosecution Service in England and Wales.

As an advocate in Scotland you may start at around £11,000; moving up to between £24,000 and £56,000 in the Procurator Fiscal Service.

Generally, salaries range from £25,000 up to £210,000 with experience.

Many barristers in England and advocates in Scotland are self-employed. Earnings can reach up to £300,000, however this is entirely dependent on experience, location and reputation.

In private practice top earnings can be in excess of £750,000.

Related opportunities

- Barrister's/Advocate's Clerk p342
- Crown Prosecutor/Procurator Fiscal p348
- Paralegal p353

Further information

Faculty of Advocates
www.advocates.org.uk

Skills for Justice
www.sfjuk.com

The Bar Council
www.barcouncil.org.uk

BARRISTER'S/ADVOCATE'S CLERK

ENTRY LEVEL 3

Qualifications and courses

In England and Wales, barrister's clerks usually require a minimum of 4 GCSEs/National 5s (A*–C/A–C), including maths and English. A levels/H grades are an advantage and relevant work experience, in a business or legal environment for example, would increase your chances of securing employment.

Some individual chambers offer their own work experience schemes which are useful in developing your interpersonal skills, telephone manner, computer literacy and commercial awareness, amongst other skills vital to the role.

You are likely to enter employment at a junior clerk level and work your way up to deputy senior or senior clerk.

You may choose to join the Institute of Barristers' Clerks (IBC). The IBC offers a 1-year BTEC Advanced Award in Chambers Administration for Barristers' Clerks which is aimed at clerks with 5 years' service in chambers. Upon completion you can apply for qualified membership of the IBC. Graduates do not need to take the BTEC but must have 3 years' service in chambers.

The IBC also offers a number of topical seminars and an annual conference which it is important to attend as you must maintain a firm grasp on current legal issues.

In Scotland, advocate's clerks require a minimum of an H grade in English and evidence of computer literacy and numeracy. More advocate's clerks are now entering with a HNC/HND or degree. Most training is on the job but you are encouraged to take courses organised by Faculty Services Ltd.

What the work involves

Clerks manage the day-to-day work for a group of barristers (England and Wales) or advocates (Scotland).

An important task will be liaising with solicitors to encourage them to give work to your business. You will estimate how much work is involved in a case to see how much time it will take, allocate cases to barristers/advocates and negotiate fees.

When you first enter this career, you will mainly be preparing accounts, filing and photocopying, and answering the phone.

Type of person suited to this work

As your work will involve meeting lots of people, you will need excellent speaking skills. Good writing skills are needed for writing letters and preparing notes and reports.

Being good with figures is essential when negotiating fees and preparing accounts. You will need to be business-like and have good negotiating skills to bring in work, and confidence to deal with solicitors, court officials and clients.

Your work will involve handling confidential information, which means discretion and tact are necessary. It is also important to be a good teamworker and flexible in your approach to work.

Working conditions

You will work mainly indoors in an office, using computers and spending a lot of time on the telephone. However, you might travel in connection with your work so a driving licence is useful.

Some chambers are based in historic buildings with difficult working conditions and limited access.

You will typically work standard office hours, Monday to Friday. However, you might have to work evenings and weekends during busy periods.

One clerk will serve more than one barrister at a time, with most offices in London or other large cities. Advocates work in groups known as 'stables' in the Advocates' Library in Edinburgh.

Future prospects

Competition is high for entry to this profession.

You would start as a junior clerk and progress to clerk with experience. Training will be ongoing throughout your career.

With experience you could train for another legal profession or move into general administrative work.

Advantages/disadvantages

Your work will be interesting and varied and you will have a lot of responsibility.

Work in the evenings and long hours are necessary when deadlines are approaching.

After further training, you can move into other legal careers.

Money guide

Starting salaries range between £12,000 and £14,000 for a junior clerk or clerk's assistant.

Clerks with more than 5 years' experience can earn between £25,000 and £55,000. Senior clerks with a high level of responsibility, in busy chambers, can earn up to £100,000.

There is also the opportunity for bonuses directly related to the income of the barristers.

In Scotland you can earn between £22,000 and £28,000. As a senior clerk, you can earn up to £45,000.

Related opportunities

- Barrister/Advocate p341
- Court Administrative Officer p345
- Paralegal p353

Further information

Faculty of Advocates
www.advocates.org.uk

Institute of Barristers' Clerks
www.ibc.org.uk

Skills for Justice
www.sfjuk.com

CONSTITUENCY AGENT/POLITICAL RESEARCHER

ENTRY LEVEL 6

Qualifications and courses

There are no set academic requirements but entry is very competitive and many employers expect candidates to have a 2.1 degree or above. Valued degree subjects include politics, law, social policy, economics, marketing, public relations or journalism. You will need at least 2 A levels/3 H grades and 5 GCSEs/National 5s (A*–C/A–C) for degree entry.

A postgraduate qualification such as master's degree in public affairs and lobbying, politics or political communications may improve employment prospects.

Experience of working for your chosen political party on a voluntary basis is often valued more than academic qualifications as formal on-the-job training is rarely offered as there is an expectation that candidates will have already acquired the skills necessary for success within the job. Work experience also demonstrates your commitment to the industry and will significantly improve your career prospects. It is also possible to develop relevant skills through other opportunities, for example, involvement with a trade union, holding office in a students' union or campaign work for a charity group.

There are limited opportunities for graduate training programmes offered by some large political consultancies.

In general, candidates must be at least 20 years of age and should remain up to date with current developments within politics by reading journals, newspapers, attending workshops and conferences offered by Capita Learning and Development or the Chartered Institute of Public Relations.

What the work involves

Constituency agent
Your job will be to organise the running of the constituency for your political party, including election campaigns. You will arrange meetings, coordinate PR and marketing, and deal with enquiries.

As secretary to the local office, your duties will include managing local membership, fundraising and organising volunteers.

Political researcher
You will research information on political subjects and provide your employer with a coherent briefing of your conclusions. Your duties may include helping to write political speeches, finding sources of expertise on a specific issue and monitoring parliamentary reports.

Type of person suited to this work

You will need a solid understanding of the political system, along with a genuine interest in and love of politics.
It is important to have strong political opinions while understanding that sometimes you must look at the bigger picture.

Key skills for constituency agents are communication, information handling, IT, money management, teamwork and leadership and supervisory skills.

Key skills for political researchers include tact, resourcefulness, debating abilities, IT and research skills, resilience, communication, articulation and analytical abilities.

Working conditions

Constituency agent
Most of your work will be based in the party office which will be open to the public. However, you will be expected to do lots of travelling both locally and nationally, so a driving licence and car would be useful. You could work evenings, weekends or during the day. Hours could increase during national or local events such as elections.

Political researcher
You will be working in an office, normally 9am–5pm although some longer hours might be required to meet specific deadlines. You may need to travel.

Future prospects

Constituency agent
Your prospects could depend on the size of the party you support. Later, you could become a local councillor or Member of Parliament.

Political researcher
This is an excellent starting point for a career in politics. Progression may include becoming an MP. You could take on extra responsibilities and move between public affairs firms in order to achieve promotion.

Advantages/disadvantages

You will get considerable job satisfaction as your work will make a difference to citizens and the local community.

You may find this career stressful, particularly when you have to meet project deadlines or when there are elections.

Money guide

Constituency agent
Your starting salary is likely to be between £17,000 and £21,000.

With experience and increased responsibilities, you could earn £25,000–£30,000.

Political researcher
Starting salaries range from £17,000 to £22,000.

Those with considerable experience can achieve £27,000–£35,000.

Related opportunities

- Media Researcher p389
- Politician p355
- Welfare Benefits Adviser/Welfare Rights Caseworker p562

Further information

Association of Professional Political Consultants
www.appc.org.uk

Chartered Institute of Public Relations
www.cipr.co.uk

CORONER

ENTRY LEVEL 8

Qualifications and courses

Following the Coroners and Justice Act 2009, the coroner service is undergoing reforms regarding the recruitment and training of coroners. New coroners must be qualified solicitors, barristers or a Fellow of the Chartered Institute of Legal Executives (CILEx) with at least 5 years' experience. The usual entry route is to find a coroner who is willing to appoint you their deputy or assistant deputy coroner.

To train as a lawyer you need either an approved law degree, or a non-law degree followed by either the Common Professional Examination (CPE), the Postgraduate Diploma in Law (PgDL) or the Senior Status Law degree. Candidates must then complete a Legal Practice Course (LPC). To be accepted onto a law degree you will usually require 2 A levels/3 H grades and 5 GCSEs/National 5s (A*–C/A–C).

A number of existing coroners have a medical degree, while some have both a medical and law degree. Law changes mean that a law qualification is essential, but it can be useful to have a medical degree.

In order to qualify as a doctor you must complete an undergraduate course which leads to a degree in medicine. To do this you will need very high results in 3 A levels/H grades including chemistry and biology, and at least 5 GCSEs/National 5s (A*–C/A–C).

Aldermen and councillors of local authorities are not eligible for appointment as coroners in their counties or districts until 6 months after the end of their service.

Once employed, you will be provided with training from the Coroners Division of the Ministry of Justice. Throughout your career you will be expected to undertake continuing professional development (CPD) so as to remain up to date with changes in law, medical and administrative practices.

What the work involves

You will investigate sudden and suspicious deaths, determining if an inquest or post-mortem is necessary. Coroners preside at inquests and make decisions on whether or not further action is required.

You will need to work with police and medical services to determine whether or not a person died of natural causes and keep detailed records of all proceedings.

Once you have completed your investigations you must provide families or the relevant authorities with your report.

Type of person suited to this work

Preparing cases involves looking at statements and reports so you need to be able to read and analyse large amounts of information. You might need to check points of law and request further information so you must pay attention to detail.

Much of your work will involve talking to people and writing reports so you need to have excellent verbal and written communication skills. Being confident to speak in court and argue logically are also important.

You must be organised, able to meet deadlines and handle distressing situations calmly.

Working conditions

You will work indoors and outdoors, as you will primarily be based in an office but will also spend time in court, at crime scenes and in hospitals.

You will usually work normal office hours but you will also fulfil on-call duties as each county is required to provide a 24-hour service.

Most coroners work part time and spend the rest of their time working in private legal practice.

Future prospects

Coroners are appointed and paid for by local councils but hold office under the Crown.

Once employed as a deputy or assistant deputy coroner, with experience you can progress to coroner level. Although there is currently no further promotion route, the Coroners and Justice Bill has proposed that posts such as senior coroner and chief coroner should be made available in the future.

Advantages/disadvantages

The work is varied, carries responsibility and can be satisfying.

You will have the opportunity to meet a wide range of people.

The role involves extensive administration and paperwork.

You will be on an on-call rota for evenings, weekends and bank holidays.

Money guide

If you work full time as a deputy coroner, your starting salary will be around £25,000.

As a full-time coroner you can expect earnings between £83,000 and £104,000 a year, depending on the population size of the area you cover.

Part-time coroners are paid according to the number of cases they undertake. As a guide, you could receive salaries ranging from £10,000 for 200 cases to £50,500 for 2,000 cases a year.

Related opportunities

- Barrister/Advocate p341
- Hospital Doctor p292
- Solicitor/Notary Public p356

Further information

Coroners' Society of England and Wales
www.coronersociety.org.uk

Ministry of Justice
www.justice.gov.uk

COURT ADMINISTRATIVE OFFICER

ENTRY LEVEL 3

Qualifications and courses

Qualification requirements vary within different regions and according to the type of court, however most employers expect candidates to have at least 2 GCSEs/ National 5s (A*–C/A–C), including maths and English, for an administrative assistant role and 5 GCSEs/National 5s (A*–C/A–C) for a more senior position such as an administrative officer.

Some areas require administrative, typing, office or computing experience while others also expect a minimum of one year of relevant office-based experience. City & Guilds offer several courses which enable candidates to develop their administrative skills such as word processing, typing and shorthand.

Applicants without formal qualifications but with relevant administrative experience may be able to sit computer and communication aptitude tests in order to gain entry to this profession.

Once employed, you will typically experience a combination of on-the-job training and a series of in-house or external short courses that offer you the opportunity to work towards industry-recognised qualifications. The Apprenticeship in Court, Tribunal and Prosecution Administration is available at Intermediate Level and the NVQ/SVQ Level 2 in Court Tribunal Administration may be beneficial for those already working as an administrative assistant and looking to progress to the role of officer.

What the work involves

You will organise all the papers and information for a court hearing so that everything is ready for the judge or magistrate when the court session begins.

Booking dates, times and courtrooms for court hearings will be part of your job and you will prepare the timetable for each day. You will ensure that everyone arriving at court knows where to go and receives the relevant paperwork.

After the hearings, you will carry out court orders such as endorsing driving licences, writing adoption orders or collecting fines.

Type of person suited to this work

As you will be responsible for making sure that court hearings run smoothly and everything is ready on time, it is important to be methodical, organised and pay close attention to detail.

You must be polite and helpful so that you can put people at ease and explain things clearly to them. Tact and an understanding of confidentiality are essential.

If you are working in a finance section, you must have good numeracy skills to be able to calculate fines and costs. You should be confident using computers.

Working conditions

Most of your time will be spent indoors in courtrooms and offices in the court. You may have to travel to different courts so a driving licence is useful.

You will be working around 37 hours a week, however overtime may be necessary if there is a hearing in the evening or at the weekend. Part-time work is often possible.

Future prospects

Court administrative officers in England and Wales are employed by Her Majesty's Courts Service (HMCS) and move through promotion grades. In Scotland they are often known as court officers and are employed by the Scottish Court Service.

Most training is on the job. It is possible to start as a court administrative assistant and work your way up to officer level.

You may have to move courts to widen your experience. You could move into similar work in the legal field, such as legal executive roles, or into general administrative work. Promotion to senior administration roles is possible.

Advantages/disadvantages

The work is often quite steady and, with strong organisation, often it's not too stressful.

Dealing with members of the public means that you will meet and work with many different people, which can mean a diverse work environment but some people may be aggressive and threatening which can be difficult to deal with.

Work might be monotonous, despite the variety of cases that will be dealt with.

Money guide

Salaries vary depending on your employer and geographical location.

Those beginning their career as an administrative assistant can expect to earn between £12,824 and £14,912 a year.

An administrative officer will have a starting salary of about £14,551.

Earnings can increase to £19,200 as you gain experience.

If you progress to become a senior clerk or team leader you could earn in excess of £22,000 per year.

Related opportunities

- Barrister's/Advocate's Clerk p342
- Civil Service Administrative Officer p13
- Court Usher/Officer/Macer p347

Further information

HM Courts and Tribunals Service
www.justice.gov.uk

Scottish Court Service
www.scotcourts.gov.uk

COURT REPORTER/VERBATIM REPORTER

ENTRY LEVEL 3

Qualifications and courses

Candidates are usually required to have 3–5 GCSEs/ National 5s (A*–C/A–C), including English, and many entrants also have A levels/H grades. Thorough knowledge of the English language and a high standard of spelling, grammar and punctuation is expected but computer keyboard skills and knowledge of traditional shorthand are often valued above any formal academic qualifications.

To begin work as a court reporter in England and Wales, you must be certified as competent by the British Institute of Verbatim Reporters (BIVR). In order to become certified, you will need to acquire competency on a stenotype machine, reach a typing speed of at least 180 words per minute and experience as a trainee court reporter. After the correct training and 3 years' experience you may apply to become a qualified member of the BIVR by taking an examination. As a member, you can aid your career progression by completing training in real-time reporting or Speech-to-Text (STT) reporting.

Sorene Court Reporting & Training Services offer a distance learning course which lasts 1–2 years and teaches candidates how to use the stenotype machine.

In Scotland, all training is undertaken on the job with a mentor and regular tests will be set to monitor progress.

What the work involves

Your job could involve attending court hearings, listening and reporting on what is said. Using a stenotype machine, or sometimes other recording equipment, you will write down everything a witness says. You may asked to edit other speakers in order to correct their grammar.

Mostly you will work on your own but in complex cases where lawyers may want a daily transcript of proceedings you will work in a team of 3, on a rota basis.

You could also record proceedings within other legal forums such as industrial tribunals.

Type of person suited to this work

You need to have excellent listening skills and the ability to concentrate for long periods of time.

A fast typing speed, strong attention to detail and a good grasp of punctuation and grammar are needed to ensure that your record is accurate. Manual dexterity and keyboard skills are essential for operating the stenotype.

You must speak clearly when reading back what you have written. If you do not hear what is said or you fall behind in your transcription, you must have the confidence to stop proceedings or ask for something to be repeated.

Working conditions

You will operate a stenotype machine with computer aided transcription systems, a machine with a keyboard layout which enables whole words and phrases to be typed with one stroke.

There is a growing trend in Scotland for court cases to be taped and transcribed afterwards.

You might have to travel to different courts so a driving licence and access to or ownership of a car is useful.

Future prospects

You could attend criminal cases in the Crown Court or civil cases in the high courts. You will also be present at other events, including industrial tribunals, public enquiries and in Parliament to record proceedings for Hansard.

Most court reporters are self-employed and there is no defined promotion ladder. Others work for companies contracted to service courts.

In England and Wales there is a shortage of trained staff. In Scotland vacancies may decrease due to the shift to taping court proceedings.

Reporters also have the option to work in the media industry, providing subtitles for viewers with hearing impairments.

Advantages/disadvantages

You will have contact with a wide range of people.

You will have to concentrate for long periods so the work is demanding.

Work in the evenings is possible to complete reports for the next day.

Money guide

Starting salaries in London and large cities are between £18,000 and £28,000.

Those based in other locations can expect a lower salary of between £12,000 and £20,000 a year.

With experience, your earnings can increase to £25,000–£50,000.

Many court reporters work on a freelance basis so earnings vary according to the number of days worked.

Daily rates can range from £40 to £200.

Real-time reporters are likely to earn more and could receive £300 a day for private sector work.

Related opportunities

- Court Administrative Officer p345
- Paralegal p353
- Receptionist p45

Further information

British Institute of Verbatim Reporters
www.bivr.org.uk

Sorene Court Reporting & Training Services
www.sorene.co.uk

COURT USHER/OFFICER/ MACER

ENTRY LEVEL 2

Qualifications and courses

Whilst no formal qualifications are required, a minimum of at least 2 GCSEs/National 5s (A*–C/A–C), including English, is strongly recommended. A qualification in or possession of computer skills is also highly desirable.

Employers often value one's personal qualities and life experience above any formal academic qualifications however. A background in administration or a customer service environment can be advantage, as is experience within the police or armed forces. A history of working closely with the public will improve your chances of securing employment.

Training is conducted on the job and new entrants will work alongside an experienced usher. Employers may also provide short courses covering topics such as equality awareness, security and dealing with challenging situations.

You may also have the opportunity to work towards industry recognised qualifications such as the NVQ/SVQ Level 2 Certificate for Court Ushers, the Level 2 Certificate in Knowledge of Court/Tribunal Administration, the Diploma in Court Tribunal Operations (Levels 2–3) and the Level 3 Certificate in Witness Care.

You will need to obtain clearance from the Disclosure and Barring Service (DBS) before becoming a court usher.

The stated minimum age for entry to this profession is 21 (16 in Scotland), but most courts prefer to recruit mature people under the age of 63 (60 in Scotland).

What the work involves

Court ushers make sure that everything in the courtroom is ready for proceedings to begin, for example that all papers are ready, glasses and water are on tables, and fire exits are clear.

When people arrive at court, you will meet them and direct them to the right courtroom. In court, you will tell people to stand when the judge comes in, call witnesses and administer the right oath to them. You will have to label the evidence and give it to the judge and jury. You will also pass messages between lawyers and legal advisers.

In Scotland, you will be known as a court officer in the sheriff court and a macer in the supreme courts.

Type of person suited to this work

As courtrooms must be prepared at the beginning of the day, court ushers need to be thorough in their work and pay attention to detail. You must be logical and organised.

You need to be able to work with people of all ages and backgrounds. Some may be nervous so it is important to have good communication skills to explain what is happening and put them at ease. You will also need to be confident and sound in control in court.

It is important to stay calm at all times and be impartial when dealing with people from both sides of a case. You will come into contact with a great deal of confidential information so trustworthiness and professionalism are essential attributes.

You need to be able to work well as part of a team to ensure the smooth running of the court case.

Working conditions

You will spend most of your time in a courtroom but you might also have an office in the courthouse, as your job will involve entering data into the computer system, filing and photocopying.

In certain jury cases, you might have to stay away from home overnight. A driving licence would be useful if you are required to travel between courts.

As you represent the court, you must be smartly dressed at all times.

Future prospects

There are few jobs for court ushers and entry to the career can be competitive.

You can be promoted to senior and supervisory grades. You could also progress into other administrative jobs within the legal profession or another sector.

Advantages/disadvantages

The job will be varied and no two days will be the same.

You might have to stay late or start early if proceedings overrun.

You will meet many different people, some of whom may be difficult to deal with.

Money guide

Earnings vary with location and tend to be higher in London.

Starting salaries for ushers range from £11,500 to £14,000. Although in London, it is possible to earn up to £17,000.

At a senior level you may be able to achieve a salary of up to £22,412.

You may receive overtime payments for late nights or early starts.

Related opportunities

- Bailiff/Enforcement Agent p340
- Civil Service Administrative Officer p13
- Court Administrative Officer p345
- Receptionist p45

Further information

HM Courts and Tribunals Service
www.justice.gov.uk

Scottish Court Service
www.scotcourts.gov.uk

Skills for Justice
www.sfjuk.com

CROWN PROSECUTOR/ PROCURATOR FISCAL

ENTRY LEVEL 5

Qualifications and courses

Crown prosecutor
If you are a qualified solicitor or barrister then you can apply directly to the Crown Prosecution Service (CPS). In Northern Ireland, public prosecutors are employed by the Public Prosecution Service (PPS). Lawyers must have completed their Legal Practice Course (LPC) and 2-year training contract and barristers must have finished their Bar Professional Training Course (BPTC) and 12-month pupillage.

Alternatively, law students can apply for the CPS Legal Trainee Scheme (LTS) in the year that they are due to complete their vocational training. The CPS offers 10 candidates a training contract each year.

Once employed you will be trained on the job and supervised by a more experienced colleague before progressing into a more senior crown prosecutor role. This can take between 6 months and 2 years depending on your level of experience prior to entry. The Law Society and the Bar Council run a series of continuing professional development (CPD) schemes vital to aid career progression.

Procurator fiscal
Candidates are solicitors qualified in the Scottish legal system. An LLB degree in Scottish law (or 3 years of pre-diploma training and a pass in the Law Society of Scotland's exams) is required, followed by a Diploma in Professional Legal Practice (PEAT 1) and a 2-year training contract with a practising solicitor in Scotland (PEAT 2).

Alternatively, those who have completed an LLB at a Scottish university can apply for one of 25 places available on the 2-year traineeship offered by the Crown Office and Procurator Fiscal Service (COPFS).

What the work involves

Crown prosecutor
You will look at reports from the police and other agencies and decide whether or not crimes in England and Wales should be prosecuted.

You will take statements from witnesses before a trial and examine witnesses in court, guiding them through their evidence. You will then sum up the case for the prosecution.

Procurator fiscal
You will work in the Scottish legal system, carrying out similar duties to crown prosecutors in England and Wales. In Scotland, the Crown Office and Procurator Fiscal Service (COPFS) investigates and prosecutes all crime.

Type of person suited to this work

Preparing cases involves looking at statements so you must be able to read and analyse a lot of information. Attention to detail is essential.

You must have excellent verbal and written communication skills as you will deal with other professionals and the public. You should be confident making clear and logical arguments in court and have the ability to make unbiased decisions.

Working conditions

You will be based in an office but you will also spend time in court. You might also work outdoors at scenes of crime and accidents.

You will work 37–42 hours a week, including covering weekends and bank holidays on a rota system.

Future prospects

Crown prosecutor
There is a clear promotion structure within the service but very few posts at the most senior levels. Competition in the CPS is high.

Procurator fiscal
Candidates start as a depute, working under the guidance of senior colleagues and gradually taking more responsibility. After a few years, they can apply to become procurators fiscal but promotion is not automatic.

Crown prosecutors and procurators fiscal can transfer into other areas of law such as private practice.

Advantages/disadvantages

The job is interesting, carries responsibilities and can be rewarding.

You will encounter different cases in terms of type and difficulty.

You will have contact with many different types of people, some of whom may be difficult to deal with.

Working on a rota system may disrupt your personal life.

Money guide

Crown prosecutor
Crown prosecutors have a starting salary of £27,393–£31,002.

As a senior crown prosecutor, you can earn up to £42,500.

Earnings will be higher in London.

Procurator fiscal
Fiscal deputes are likely to earn between £27,300 and £33,600 a year.

With experience and extra responsibilities, a senior procurator fiscal can expect a salary of around £56,000.

Related opportunities

- Barrister/Advocate p341
- Paralegal p353
- Solicitor/Notary Public p356

Further information

Crown Office and Procurator Fiscal Service
www.crownoffice.gov.uk

Crown Prosecution Service
www.cps.gov.uk

JUDGE/SHERIFF

ENTRY LEVEL 7

Qualifications and courses

Candidates looking to become a judge must be a qualified solicitor or barrister with 5–7 years' legal experience. The Lord Chancellor requires that candidates should normally have previous judicial experience in a part-time role such as deputy district judge, recorder or tribunal judge. District or circuit judges are usually appointed after 10–15 years' court experience and applications are made through the Judicial Appointments Commission (JAC).

To qualify as a solicitor or barrister, you will need either an approved law degree, or a non-law degree followed by the Common Professional Examination (CPE), the Postgraduate Diploma in Law (PgDL) or the Senior Status Law degree. Solicitors must then complete a Legal Practice Course (LPC) followed by a 2-year training contract and barristers must undertake the Bar Professional Training Course (BPTC) and a 12-month pupillage.

In Scotland, candidates for a sheriff's position must be a fully qualified solicitor or advocate with at least 10 years' experience. Applications are made through the Judicial Appointments Board for Scotland.

To become qualified in the Scottish legal system it is necessary to have an LLB degree in Scottish law (or 3 years of pre-diploma training and a pass in the Law Society of Scotland's exams), followed by a Diploma in Professional Legal Practice (PEAT 1) and a 2-year training contract with a practising solicitor in Scotland (PEAT 2).

What the work involves

Judges (sheriffs in Scotland) preside over courts and make judgements on what should happen based on the evidence from 2 opposing parties. You will listen to all the evidence and decide on procedures, including whether a piece of evidence can be used, whilst keeping order in court.

In jury cases, you will instruct and advise the jury on the strength of the evidence before the jury leaves court to consider the verdict.

You will decide on penalties in criminal courts and on settlements in civil cases.

Type of person suited to this work

As judges make the final decision in a court case, it is important to be able to grasp facts quickly and analyse the evidence to help make your decision. Judges must think logically and not become emotionally involved.

You should have excellent communication and public-speaking skills. You also need to be a good listener and pay careful attention to the evidence.

It is important to have the confidence to make difficult decisions and stand by them. Discretion is needed to deal with confidential information.

Working conditions

You will spend much of your time in court but you will also have an office with support staff to help you. You will travel between courts and may have to spend time away from home.

You will dress smartly at all times and wear robes in court. Courts are very formal and have traditions which you must observe.

Future prospects

There are very few openings for judges and sheriffs, which means entry is competitive. Successful candidates have normally followed a long career in law as a barrister/advocate or solicitor.

Most judges work in one type of court, such as a Crown Court or Court of Appeal. Senior positions, such as Lord Chief Justice and Master of the Rolls, are made on the recommendation of the Prime Minister.

In Scotland, most sheriffs work in sheriff courts. A few with experience become supreme court judges in the High Court of Justiciary or the Court of Session.

Judicial office holders are legally required to retire at the age of 70.

Advantages/disadvantages

The work is varied and no two days will be the same.

This is a very responsible job which requires a high amount of intellect and dedication.

You will meet many different people and hear some cases which will have a high media interest or involve distressing evidence.

Some courts work into the evenings.

Money guide

The lowest starting salary currently for a district judge is £104,990.

You could earn £130,875 as a circuit judge.

As a High Court judge you can achieve in excess of £170,000.

The Lord Chief Justice, the highest legal position in England and Wales, earns £239,845 a year.

In Scotland, sheriffs have a salary of £128,296–£138,548.

Related opportunities

- Barrister/Advocate p341
- Crown Prosecutor/Procurator Fiscal p348
- Legal Executive p350

Further information

Judicial Appointments Commission
www.judicialappointments.gov.uk

Judicial Communications Office
www.judiciary.gov.uk

Skills for Justice
www.sfjuk.com

LEGAL EXECUTIVE

ENTRY LEVEL 5

Qualifications and courses

You need to undertake 2 levels of academic and practical training in order to become a legal executive. These qualifications are set by the Chartered Institute of Legal Executives (CILEx) and include the CILEx Level 3 Professional Diploma in Law and Practice and the CILEx Level 6 Professional Higher Diploma in Law and Practice. Once completed, you will need to gain 5 years' work experience to become a fully qualified Chartered Legal Executive.

The minimum requirements for the Level 3 training are 4 GCSEs/National 5s (A*–C/A–C), including English. City & Guilds/CILEx Level 2 Certificate in Legal Studies is a suitable alternative. Students will train for their Level 3 Diploma under the supervision of a solicitor or senior legal executive. Study is carried out on day release or at evening classes and will take 1–2 years to complete.

Full training at Level 6 takes 2 years (while working full time) and leads to CILEx Membership. CILEx qualifications can also be taken as part of a Modern Legal Apprenticeship scheme.

Certain qualifications, such as an undergraduate law degree, may provide exemption from some academic parts of the qualifications. People with relevant experience can also apply to have their experience approved by CILEx.

In Scotland, there is no direct equivalent to legal executive; staff are known as paralegals or solicitors' assistants. Generally 4 GCSEs/National 5s (A*–C/A–C), including English and maths, followed by office experience is required for entry.

What the work involves

Legal executives work with solicitors, preparing complex cases for them and dealing with straightforward cases themselves.

You will interview clients, asking questions to help you give them legal advice and explain legal points to them clearly. You will write letters on their behalf, draft contracts and wills and prepare other documents.

In certain cases, you may represent clients in court or at tribunals.

Type of person suited to this work

Excellent written and verbal communication skills are essential.

Clients will give you confidential information so it is important to be discreet and tactful. You will also need patience as legal points can be difficult to grasp.

When preparing cases, you will be handling large amounts of information, which means it is useful to be a thorough and well organised worker.

Working conditions

Most legal executives work 37 hours a week, Monday to Friday but you will probably be expected to work additional hours on a regular basis including evenings and weekends.

You will be based in an office but you may need to attend court and as such you will be expected to dress smartly.

You might have to travel to visit clients or legal libraries, so a driving licence is useful.

Future prospects

You could work in a private practice for a solicitor or in local and central government and industry. Legal executives usually specialise in one area, for example property or business law.

You can train to qualify as a legal executive advocate or as a solicitor, which allows you to follow a case right through to court.

This is a very competitive career, and the majority of entrants are now graduates.

Advantages/disadvantages

You will have the chance to work in a legal environment while studying part time and earning a good salary.

You might have to work under pressure to meet deadlines and work unsociable hours.

Money guide

Starting salaries for trainee legal executives vary from £15,000 up to £28,000 per year of training.

Once you have the CILEx qualifications you can earn up to £38,000, depending on where you work.

Legal executives with more experience (it takes 5 years to become a fully qualified Legal Executive) can earn between £35,000 and £55,000 and in big city firms the salary potential is even higher.

Due to increasing demand for legal executives the salary range has broadened considerably depending a lot on experience, skills and location.

Related opportunities

- Barrister's/Advocate's Clerk p342
- Civil Service Administrative Officer p13
- Solicitor/Notary Public p356

Further information

Chartered Institute of Legal Executives
www.cilex.org.uk

Law Society of England and Wales
www.lawsociety.org.uk

Law Society of Northern Ireland
www.lawsoc-ni.org

LICENSED CONVEYANCER

ENTRY LEVEL 6

Qualifications and courses

England and Wales
Candidates must pass the Council for Licensed Conveyancers (CLC) training and exams which are typically undertaken in employment. To begin training applicants must have a minimum of 4 GCSEs/National 5s (A*–C/A–C), including English, and an A level/H grade in law is useful. You may be accepted without minimum qualifications if you have relevant work experience within a solicitor's or licensed conveyancer's office.

However, many applicants will already hold a law degree or might have taken either the Chartered Institute of Legal Executives (CILEx) course or the Legal Practice Course (LPC) for trainee solicitors. Applicants must have at least 2 years' practical training with a 'qualified employer' and pass the CLC examination. Many students take this as a correspondence course. It is also offered on a part-time basis.

Once completed, candidates can then apply for a limited licence and after a further 3 consecutive years you can apply for a full licence. An Apprenticeship in Business, Administration and Law may also be available.

Scotland
Entrants require a degree in law from a Scottish university or a Diploma/Certificate in Legal Studies which takes at least 2 years.

They then undertake a 1-year training contract with an independent qualified conveyancer. After 6 months of training, a Professional Competence Course which comprises 36 hours of core requirements and 18 hours of electives, must be completed.

For a law degree you need 5 GCSEs/National 5s (A*–C/A–C) and 3 A levels/H grades. Some universities require applicants to take the National Admissions Test for Law.

Northern Ireland
The job of a licensed conveyancer is carried out by a solicitor. Solicitors must complete an apprenticeship programme of 2–4 years, combined with a vocational course. You can complete either a Certificate in Professional Legal Studies or a Postgraduate Diploma in Professional Legal Practice.

What the work involves

Licensed conveyancers deal with the legal side of buying, selling, renting and mortgaging of houses, flats, business premises and other property.

You will draw up the legal documents, known as contracts, that buyers and sellers exchange to make a sale legal.

Other work includes liaising with lawyers and estate agents involved in the sale and researching details in the contract.

Type of person suited to this work

You will need excellent communication skills to explain complicated legal matters to clients. Being a good teamworker is useful to liaise with others involved in a contract.

As legal contracts must be completely accurate, you must be thorough and able to process large amounts of information.

You will need good organisational skills to deal with several properties simultaneously.

Working conditions

You will work standard office hours, but may be required to work some late evenings or weekends to meet clients.

Your job may be salaried or commission only.

Many licensed conveyancers are self-employed.

Future prospects

There are only around 1,000 licensed conveyancers in England and Wales, and very few qualified conveyancers in Scotland. Job opportunities are mainly with legal practices, although since the recession there are fewer places for trainees.

Training is ongoing to cover developments in property law. You could progress into other legal professions, a managerial role or run your own business.

Changes in the law now allow conveyancers to take an additional qualification, to add to their licence, and deal with probate. Probate is the legal procedure of administering the money, property and possessions of a person after they die.

Advantages/disadvantages

The work is varied. You will meet different people, though some may be difficult.

You will get satisfaction when clients get their dream home.

You might find it stressful when trying to meet deadlines or clients feel things are moving too slowly.

Money guide

A trainee should expect a salary of between £15,000 and £20,000 per year.

With experience, this rises to £25,000–£50,000.

At the more senior levels you might earn £35,000–£55,000 per year.

It is possible to earn in excess of £60,000 per year as a partner or an owner of a conveyancing firm.

Related opportunities

- Barrister/Advocate p341
- Surveying Technician p110

Further information

Council for Licensed Conveyancers
www.conveyancer.org.uk

Law Society of Scotland
www.lawscot.org.uk

MAGISTRATES' COURT LEGAL ADVISER/SHERIFF'S CLERK

ENTRY LEVEL 6

Qualifications and courses

Magistrates' court legal adviser (England and Wales)
Candidates must be fully qualified as either a barrister or solicitor. You will start as a trainee legal adviser following a structured on-the-job induction programme organised by the associated court.

You need an approved law degree, or a non-law degree followed by the Common Professional Examination (CPE) or a Graduate Diploma in Law (GDL). You should then have completed either the Legal Practice Course (LPC) or the Bar Professional Training Course (BPTC).

Sheriff's clerk (Scotland)
There are no minimum entry requirements but it would be helpful to have National 5s (A–C) in maths and English. You could start as an administrative officer and then progress to a role as sheriff's clerk.

Fast-track entry to a position as sheriff's clerk deputy is sometimes available to those with a law degree, the Diploma in Legal Practice and 2 years' training with a solicitor.

What the work involves

Magistrates' court legal adviser (England and Wales)
You will be a qualified solicitor or barrister with responsibility for advising magistrates in court.

You will advise on points of law, procedures, penalties and other issues.

Magistrates are volunteer civil officers that deals with minor offences among other tasks, who will not necessarily be trained in the law. A court legal adviser, or court clerk as it is sometimes known, will therefore advise the magistrate on the law, the proper procedures, and may advise on sentencing, but will never carry out any sentencing.

Sheriff's clerk (Scotland)
You might advise on points of law and procedures in any court (civil or criminal).

You could have a more general administrative role such as handling court complaints and providing statistics for court staff.

Type of person suited to this work

You must have a strong interest in the law and excellent communication skills as you will be expected to advise on a wide range of issues.

You must be organised, reliable and able to work quickly and accurately under pressure.

It's important to be impartial and remain detached from emotionally demanding cases. You will need to be discreet to deal with confidential information.

Working conditions

You will normally be located in one court building and will generally work a 37-hour week, from Monday to Friday. However, your working hours may, at times, be irregular due to complex cases.

Some courts also open as early as 8am and you might need to work weekends.

You might travel to different courts so a driving licence is useful.

Future prospects

Her Majesty's Court and Tribunal Service has a set career structure. You could progress to a role as a justices' clerk or a justices' chief executive. You could go on to a role where you train magistrates or manage a team of legal advisers.

In Scotland, sheriff's clerks are employed by the Scottish Court Service. Small rural courts may have only one clerk, while a court in a big city will have several.

There is a clear promotion structure within the Scottish Court Service.

Advantages/disadvantages

The work is often varied with new cases being presented before the court, even if minor cases.

Less stressful than working on bigger cases, usually less riding on it.

You might have to work unsocial hours at times.

A strictly advisory role may get frustrating.

Basic administrative tasks such as preparing courtroom schedule could become dull.

Money guide

You can expect around £20,500 as a trainee adviser, having completed either the LPC or the BPTC.

Those who have completed a training contract in addition, can expect to earn around £29,000.

An experienced magistrates' legal adviser can earn between £30,000 and £43,000.

Starting salaries for sheriffs' clerks are about £12,211. This can rise to between £28,000 and £35,000.

Related opportunities

- Barrister/Advocate p341
- Legal Executive p350
- Solicitor/Notary Public p356

Further information

HM Courts and Tribunals Service
www.justice.gov.uk

Scottish Court Service
www.scotcourts.gov.uk

PARALEGAL

ENTRY LEVEL 3

Qualifications and courses

You do not need any specific qualifications to become a paralegal and, with exceptional work experience, may begin employment in this position as a school leaver. However, most employers will prefer you to have some relevant qualifications, such as relevant GCSEs/National 5s (A*–C/A–C), a BTEC/HNC in Legal Studies, an NVQ in Business Administration, a legal secretary qualification at Level 2 or 3 or a Foundation degree in law.

It is important to note that becoming a paralegal is now a popular option for those who have graduated in law but do not have a training contract to become a solicitor. Therefore, as competition is high, some employers ask for a HND or degree in law, and others even request the LPC (Legal Practice Course) postgraduate qualification.

For those who have not studied law previously, you should seek employment within an administrative role in a law firm and study for paralegal qualifications whilst working.

Training usually takes place on the job, and you will be supervised by experienced lawyers. Employers may well encourage you to follow courses in legal training; these are widely available. They might include BTEC in Law and Legal Work (Levels 2–3) or City & Guilds Level 2 Award/Certificate/Diploma in Legal Studies.

Membership of the National Association of Licensed Paralegals (NALP) offers the opportunity to work towards a degree-level qualification and provides increased recognition in the industry. As a member, you must take part in continuing professional development (CPD) programmes. The Institute of Paralegals also offers relevant qualifications and training schemes and is the only government approved organisation that independently regulates paralegals.

What the work involves

A paralegal is somebody who is not a qualified lawyer, but whose job involves dealing with a lot of legal issues.

You may have legal training or experience, and will work in a law firm or similar organisation. Your duties will be varied, but will probably involve legal research and drafting documents, as well as other administrative tasks.

You will also interview witnesses and clients, and appear in court, often acting on behalf of lawyers. You might specialise in a specific area of law.

Type of person suited to this work

You should have a natural interest in law and current affairs and be discreet in your work, as you may frequently be dealing with confidential information.

Attention to detail is essential. Equally, a good command of English and the ability to communicate well with everybody, from the lawyers you will be working with to all of their clients, is vital. You should also be patient, understanding, tactful, sympathetic and be able to work well under pressure.

Organisational skills are essential, as is computer literacy, excellent concentration and a good memory. You also need to be able to understand and absorb a lot of information.

Working conditions

You'll probably be working in an office for about 37 hours a week. However, some of these will be spent visiting clients, which means that a driving licence is useful.

You may spend time in police stations and court, occasionally out of office hours.

You may be required to work weekends and bank holidays.

Future prospects

Future prospects for a paralegal are good. You can use the knowledge you gain on the job to develop your legal career.

If you have the necessary qualifications, you can become a solicitor or barrister, and even work your way up to partner.

With experience, you can take on additional responsibilities and move up within the firm. You may choose to move on to freelance work.

Advantages/disadvantages

Working as a paralegal is stimulating and rewarding, especially if you have an interest in or study law.

It can really give your law career a nudge in the right direction, and is a great option if, for example, you are training to be a solicitor and want to take a gap year or year out.

Occasionally tasks may be a little mundane and meeting with clients can be stressful.

Money guide

As a paralegal who is starting out, you may earn between £10,000 and £25,000 a year.

This can grow, with experience, to £40,000.

As a senior paralegal, you might be earning over £70,000 a year.

Related opportunities

- Barrister's/Advocate's Clerk p342
- Court Administrative Officer p345
- Legal Executive p350

Further information

Chartered Institute of Legal Executives
www.cilex.org.uk

Institute of Paralegals
www.theiop.org

National Association of Licensed Paralegals
www.nationalparalegals.co.uk

PATENT ATTORNEY/ EXAMINER

ENTRY LEVEL 6

Qualifications and courses

Patent attorney
All patent attorneys need a degree related to science, engineering or maths. The general entry requirements for a degree are 2 A levels/3 H grades and 5 GCSEs/National 5s (A*–C/A–C), including maths and English. Entry to the profession is competitive and most employers will expect candidates to have a minimum of a 2.1 Honours degree. While a postgraduate qualification is not obligatory, it may improve your chances of securing employment.

Patent attorneys receive specialist training in intellectual property law. Qualified solicitors with experience of working in an intellectual property department or those training to become patent agents may apply to join the Chartered Institute of Patent Attorneys (CIPA).

A high level of skill in the English language is required, and fluency in foreign languages, especially French and/or German, is a bonus. This is a requirement in order to become a European patent attorney, as is a period of 3 years' training under the supervision of an experienced professional.

A training period and the successful completion of examinations is required for admission to the Register of Patent Attorneys and the Register of Trade Mark Attorneys. It usually takes 4 to 5 years to qualify. The Certificate in IP Law offered by several universities (typically a 1- to 3-month course) provides candidates with exemptions from all the Foundation Papers of the CIPA examinations.

Examiner
You must have a good Honours degree in science, maths, engineering or technology. An equivalent professional qualification or corporate membership of a relevant major professional institution may be accepted. It is also essential that you meet the nationality and residency requirements as specified by the civil service.

What the work involves

Patent attorney
You will advise clients on the law of intellectual property.

The work involves checking that an invention is a new one and does not already exist.

You will prepare specifications for the Patent Office, carrying out any negotiations required and representing the client before the patent examiner.

Examiner
You will examine patent applications submitted by patent agents for new inventions, trademarks or designs.

You must ensure that patents are granted for new inventions.

You will conduct a study of each application to check that it is clear and that it meets legal requirements.

Type of person suited to this work

You will need a thorough knowledge of applying intellectual property to inventions and of the laws regarding this sector.

You should have strong research skills and a high attention to detail. You must have excellent communication skills in order to explain complex legal issues to your clients.

You must be highly organised, decisive and able to multi-task.

Working conditions

You will be based in an office, although patent agents do some travelling in the UK and abroad; a driving licence would be useful.

The majority of your time will be spent researching and writing reports on the computer.

Just over 2000 patent attorneys are registered in the UK with CIPA. Around 80% work in private practices, mostly in the larger towns and cities. Around 20% work with industrial companies or local government agencies.

Patent examiners are civil servants, mostly based in the Patent Office in Newport with a few working in London.

Future prospects

While there has been an increase in demand for trainees given that the age of those within the profession at present is rather high, the demanding standards required of entry are expected to remain firm.

The civil service has a formal promotion structure culminating in the successful candidate becoming a senior patent examiner.

Advantages/disadvantages

This job has a high level of responsibility and is intellectually demanding.

You will get satisfaction from helping new inventions become recognised and being involved from an early stage in the process of creation.

Money guide

Trainee patent attorneys earn around £25,000, rising to £32,500 with experience.

Once qualified you could earn between £50,000 and £60,000, reaching in excess of £400,000 for senior partners in private practices.

Patent examiners earn between £22,808 and £42,250 a year, plus £1,500 Recruitment and Retention Allowance (RRA).

Related opportunities

- Barrister's/Advocate's Clerk p342
- Legal Executive p350
- Solicitor/Notary Public p356

Further information

Chartered Institute of Patent Attorneys
www.cipa.org.uk

Intellectual Property Office
www.ipo.gov.uk

POLITICIAN

ENTRY LEVEL 1

Qualifications and courses

Any British citizen may stand for election as long as they are over 18 years old. There are no formal minimum educational requirements, however commitment to a political party is the most important criterion.

Typically, owing to the competitive nature of this field, many Members of Parliament (MPs) are graduates or hold other professional qualifications. The general entry requirements for a degree are 2 A levels/3 H grades and 5 GCSEs/National 5s (A*–C/A–C).

Active involvement in a political party is essential and experience as a trade union activist may be useful. Some people work their way up from being a politician's assistant or political researcher. Many people enter politics after a career in medicine, law or education.

There are a series of selection interviews before candidates can be 'adopted' by their party and their local constituency to stand for election. Candidates must then carry out a successful campaign and be elected by the votes of the local people. In order to stand for election, you must pay a £500 deposit and submit nomination papers signed by 10 electors from the constituency which you aim to represent.

Those disqualified from standing for election are undischarged bankrupts, prisoners of more than one year, members of the House of Lords and people holding offices listed in the House of Commons Disqualification Act 1975.

If elected, you will learn on the job with the help of experienced MPs and party whips and via training workshops that will instruct you in presentation and communication skills, election procedures and dealing with the media.

What the work involves

MPs represent the people in their local constituencies in Parliament, usually as a member of a political party. You will hold 'surgeries' in your local constituency and deal with issues raised by local people at local and national level.

MEPs (Members of the European Parliament) deal with European legislation. In Parliament, you will join committees, attend meetings and take part in debates. You will also vote on new policies or laws.

You may specialise in a particular area and you may hold office in the government or for the opposition.

Type of person suited to this work

You should be passionate about politics and have strong social beliefs, along with a desire to represent the people of your constituency. Key skills include: communication, decision making, information handling, supervisory and management skills. A pleasant manner and the ability to gain people's confidence are also important.

You will be expected to keep up to date with party policies and legislation, which requires being able to process large amounts of information quickly and thoroughly.

You will need plenty of stamina to cope with the long hours and high levels of pressure.

Working conditions

Your time will be divided between your local constituency and Parliament/Scottish Parliament/Welsh Assembly. MEPs spend one week a month in Strasbourg and much of their remaining time in Brussels.

Politicians tend to work very long hours when parliament is sitting. From the end of July to the beginning of October parliament breaks so that politicians can spend time in their constituencies. This is an extremely demanding job with a great deal of responsibility.

There is a lot of travel involved both at home and overseas.

Future prospects

Your job in any parliament will depend on being re-elected, which means it is important to have another career option to fall back on.

Although most MPs represent the local people in their constituencies, they are also involved in the government of their country.

You could be offered a post in a ministry, which may lead to appointment as a minister in a particular area. In exceptional circumstances, you could become the leader of your party and maybe even the Prime Minister.

Advantages/disadvantages

The work is varied and challenging, and no two days will be the same.

You will get a sense of satisfaction if your party is in power but also frustration when votes are not in your favour.

Money guide

The basic salary for an MP in the House of Commons is £67,060, however you could earn £134,565 as a cabinet minister.

The Prime Minister currently takes an annual salary of £142,500.

MEPs are paid the same salaries as national MPs in their own countries.

Additional allowances/expenses are available for travel and communications.

Related opportunities

- Public Relations Officer p396
- Trade Union Official p559
- Welfare Benefits Adviser/Welfare Rights Caseworker p562

Further information

National Assembly for Wales
www.wales.gov.uk

Scottish Parliament
www.scottish.parliament.uk

UK Parliament
www.parliament.uk

SOLICITOR/NOTARY PUBLIC

ENTRY LEVEL 6

Qualifications and courses

England and Wales
You will need either an approved law degree, or a non-law degree followed by a one-year conversion course, either the Common Professional Examination (CPE) or the Graduate Diploma in Law (GDL).

Alternatively, candidates without a degree can qualify through 1 of 2 routes offered by the Chartered Institute of Legal Executives (CILEx), the CILEx Fellowship route or the CILEx Membership route. Following this, you may have to complete a 1-year conversion course, although exemptions may be available.

All candidates much then complete a 1-year Legal Practice Course (LPC). This is followed by a 2-year training contract and a Professional Skills Course. Those having opted for the CILEx Fellowship route, however, are exempt from this training contract.

Scotland
You will need either an approved LLB degree in Scots Law or a good non-law degree followed by an accelerated 2-year graduate law degree. Candidates without a degree can take 3 years' Pre-Diploma training with a qualified solicitor, where you will also take the Law Society of Scotland exams. Very few solicitors offer this contract however.

Entrants must then complete a 1-year Diploma in Legal Practice followed by a 2-year training contract with a practising solicitor.

Northern Ireland
You will need to obtain a Qualifying Law Degree (QLD), or a non-law degree followed by a postgraduate law conversion degree known as the Masters in Legal Science (MLegSci).

Potential solicitors must then complete an apprenticeship programme of 2 years, combined with a vocational course at the Institute of Professional Legal Studies or at the Graduate School of Professional Legal Education. You can opt for either a Certificate in Professional Legal Studies or a Postgraduate Diploma in Professional Legal Practice. In order to do so, you must be registered with the Law Society and have a master.

Notary public
In England and Wales, qualified solicitors who hold a current Certificate of Exemption from the Faculty Office of the Archbishop of Canterbury may take a 2-year distance learning course in Notarial Practice. Candidates will then be approved by the Master of the Faculties but will continue to be supervised for a further 2 years.

In Scotland and Northern Ireland, solicitors can apply to enroll as notaries upon qualifying as solicitors.

What the work involves

Solicitor
You will advise clients on legal matters, such as making a will or setting up a business. In certain circumstances you may represent clients in court, or you might have to instruct a barrister or advocate to act for your client.

Notary public
You will certify deeds and other documents so that they will be accepted by judicial and public authorities as authentic and legally binding. Notaries public are generally solicitors who combine this function with other legal work.

Type of person suited to this work

You must be able to examine and analyse vast amounts of information and pay close attention to detail.

You will need to possess good communication and interpersonal skills.

You will need to be discreet when dealing with confidential information. It is important to remain impartial.

Working conditions

Most of your work will be in an office and you will often be under a lot of stress to meet deadlines.

You might spend time in court or have to visit clients, therefore you will need to dress smartly.

Future prospects

There is keen competition for traineeships, but when qualified there are good prospects in private practice, government and industry. You can specialise in one area of law and may eventually become a partner in a firm or even a judge.

As a notary public you may decide to start your own company.

Advantages/disadvantages

The work is varied and no two days will be the same, although some people may be difficult or unpleasant to work with.

You might have to work long hours.

Money guide

As a trainee, you can earn £16,650 in England and Wales, £16,200 in Scotland, and in Northern Ireland your salary ranges from £10,600 to £18,000.

With experience, you can earn £25,000–£75,000.

A senior partner in a legal practice can earn in excess of £100,000.

Notaries public are paid set fees for individual cases.

Related opportunities

- Barrister/Advocate p341
- Crown Prosecutor/Procurator Fiscal p348
- Legal Executive p350

Further information

Law Society of England and Wales
www.lawsociety.org.uk

Law Society of Northern Ireland
www.lawsoc-ni.org

Law Society of Scotland
www.lawscot.org.uk

Leisure, Sport and Tourism

This sector relies on a motivated, up-beat and out-going workforce for its success. You will need to show that you can work very well with other people, providing them with an excellent service when they want to enjoy themselves on holiday or if they are keen to improve their fitness and sporting ability. If you are keen to work with professional sports players or become one yourself you should be very aware of how to keep the body fit while avoiding injury. You should be warm and friendly but also able to maintain a high level of professionalism at the same time. You should also demonstrate you have patience and tact with people of all ages and be clued up on health and safety regulations.

The jobs featured in this section are listed below. For similar jobs to the ones in this section turn to *Catering and Hospitality* on page 119.

BETTING SHOP CASHIER/ MANAGER

ENTRY LEVEL 3

Qualifications and courses

There are no formal entry requirements although maths skills are important and many betting shop chains may ask for a GCSE/National 5 (A*–C/A–C) in that subject. You may have to take a basic maths test as part of the recruitment process, focusing on the calculation of percentages, odds and payments. By law, you must be 18 years of age to work in a betting shop and at least 20 years old to start as a manager.

Experience working in a customer service role is an advantage. Betting shop employees may have opportunities to work towards the NVQ Level 2 Diploma in Gambling Operations or the Level 2 Award in the Principles of Customer Service in Hospitality, Leisure, Travel and Tourism.

Training is provided on the job and covers areas such as calculating betting odds and payouts, administration, customer service, business skills, managing staff, betting laws and company policies.

Managers will be expected to have betting shop experience. Some universities have degrees and Foundation degrees in gambling and leisure management which may improve employment prospects and aid job progression.

What the work involves

You will take bets from customers on the outcomes of sporting events and contests, and pay out winnings. You will work out and betting odds for your customers, often using an electronic system. This could include unusual bets that might be difficult to establish.

For both positions, you will also explain bets and promotions, balance the day's takings, maintain the shop, and also ensure that nobody under-aged tries to bet or use in-store gambling machines.

Cashiers will update display boards with betting opportunities, oversee betting terminals, balance the books at the end of each shift and look out for fraud.

Managers ensure that the shop meets Gambling Commission regulations, deal with disputes and complaints, and control profits and costs.

Type of person suited to this work

You need to be alert to gather vital information about race entrants' recent performance ratings and handicaps. You should have a good understanding of sports.

Customers will keep coming back to place bets in your shop if you are friendly and service-oriented. You need to be good with numbers and money.

Confidence and good verbal and negotiation skills are vital in order to handle difficult customers. Being able to work well under pressure is essential.

Working conditions

You will most likely work up to 40 hours a week although part-time work may be available. Betting shops are open 7 days a week year-round and are usually open until 10pm. Your busiest day will be Saturday and you will need to be prepared to work evenings, weekends and holidays.

You will need to wear a uniform or dress smartly.

An independent bookmaker will travel long distances to attend all major sporting events and much of the work will be outdoors.

Future prospects

You have the opportunity to work for a chain, an independent shop, a bookmaker business at a racecourse or a national regulatory body such as the Gambling Commission. With experience, you can be promoted from cashier to manager.

You could become a multi-site manager of about 15 shops within a city or even an area manager looking after 50 or more shops.

Successful bookmakers often prefer to move into self-employment and may work well beyond normal retirement age.

Advantages/disadvantages

Being involved with people taking risks can create a high-pressure atmosphere and may lead to confrontations.

The long hours may disrupt your personal life and commitments.

You have the opportunity to build a good rapport with customers which can make for an enjoyable workplace.

Money guide

Full-time starting salaries for a cashier are between £11,500 and £13,500.

Deputy managers can expect about £15,500.

Betting shop managers usually earn £20,000–£30,000.

An area manager for a large chain could achieve £45,000 plus bonuses.

If you are a self-employed bookmaker your salary will depend on racing conditions, the number of entrants and gamblers, and the number of events in the calendar.

Related opportunities

- Accounting Technician and Accounts/Finance Clerk p4
- Croupier p360
- Entertainment Manager p362

Further information

Association of British Bookmakers Ltd
www.abb.uk.com

Gambling Commission
www.gamblingcommission.gov.uk

National Association of Bookmakers
www.nab-bookmakers.co.uk

CINEMA PROJECTIONIST

Qualifications and courses

Owing to film classification laws, you must be at least 18 years of age to work as a projectionist but there are no formal academic requirements for entry to this career. Instead employers may give you a simple entry test to determine your technical ability.

It is useful to have some knowledge or experience of working with electronics, cameras or sound equipment. Joining a film club can help develop your knowledge of projection equipment and film formats. You could also work part time as an assistant projectionist for a few months. Alternatively, working as a cinema attendant is a good way to gain further insight into the industry while you wait for a trainee projectionist role to become available.

All employers look for candidates who can demonstrate a real enthusiasm for the moving image.

There are also short and part-time courses available which could give you the experience needed to go straight into employment as a projectionist. The Moving Image Society (BKSTS) offer courses in both film-based and digital cinema projection.

What the work involves

Projectionists work in cinemas and are responsible for operating film screening equipment, ensuring that everything runs smoothly throughout the feature.

You will also be required to monitor other technical equipment in the cinema, including lighting, heating and ventilation systems, and electrical and gas supplies. You may be responsible for ensuring that all fire alarms and extinguishers are in good working order.

You may work with traditional 20-minute reels of film or modern digital versions that are stored on a hard drive. Most cinemas now use digital versions instead of film reels, although some smaller and independent cinemas may still use reel.

You will be expected to check that the sound on each film is operating properly and the volume is correct.

Type of person suited to this work

You should enjoy working independently and have a strong interest in film and cinema, as the majority of your time will be spent alone operating machinery in the projection room. You will need good IT skills in order to use increasingly complicated film screening technology and equipment.

You must be alert and observant so you can identify problems quickly, and also have the practical skills and knowledge to solve these issues effectively and under pressure. Good eyesight, hearing and coordination are essential.

You should be able to adhere to the strict timings given on schedules to ensure that each film runs according to plan.

Working conditions

You will work 5 days a week but hours are generally long and irregular as most cinemas screen films from the afternoon up until late in the evening.

Shift work, weekend work and overtime are common.

You will spend most of your time in a projection room. Most of these do not have windows but in modern cinemas they are usually air conditioned. You will be working alone in the projection room for the majority of your shift.

Future prospects

The ongoing switch over from the old 35mm projectors to new digital ones is changing the job role of the projectionists. The rise in higher quality 3D films is furthering the need for good IT skills. Fewer staff are now needed and projectionists often take on other duties within the cinema as well.

Opportunities can be found in large cinema chains or in smaller and often more specialist independent theatres.

In larger organisations, you could be promoted to senior projectionist or an administrative role. Small independent cinemas offer scope for experienced staff to become more involved with the running of the business.

Advantages/disadvantages

If you love cinema, you will enjoy being able to watch films for free.

You will have the opportunity to work for a number of employers, ranging from large multiplexes screening major blockbusters, to small independent cinemas which may specialise in art-house or international films.

You will be working alone for the majority of the time.

Your hours will be unsocial, including evenings and weekends.

Money guide

Salaries for cinema projectionists start at around £12,000.

With experience this can rise to around £17,000 a year.

Chief projectionists in larger cinemas can achieve up to £22,000.

Related opportunities

- Actor p408
- Arts Administrator/Manager p327
- Lighting Technician p416

Further information

BKSTS
www.bksts.com

British Film Institute
www.bfi.org.uk

CROUPIER

ENTRY LEVEL 2

Qualifications and courses

You must be 18 years old to work in a casino and obtain clearance from the Disclosure and Barring Service (DBS), as you are unable to work as a croupier if you have a criminal conviction. All entrants to this profession need to apply for a personal functional licence (PFL) from the Gambling Commission.

There are no specific academic requirements but many employers ask for at least 3 GCSEs/National 5s (A*–C/A–C), including English and maths. You may have to pass various assessments at interview, including mental arithmetic and manual dexterity tests. Normal colour vision, good hearing and clear speech are required. It could also help to have experience of working with the public and handling money.

Most major casino operators run training schemes for entrants, both in-house and externally. You can also gain an NVQ Level 2 in Gambling Operations (Casino) by attending an 18-week course available at Blackpool and The Fylde College, the London Gaming College and North Warwickshire and Hinckley College.

The National Gaming Academy offers a Foundation degree in Gaming Technology which could improve your long-term career prospects.

What the work involves

Croupiers work in casinos and are responsible for setting up gaming tables, preparing packs of cards and selling gaming tokens to customers.

You will be greeting customers, inviting them to join games of roulette, blackjack or baccarat and explaining the rules if necessary. Spinning the roulette or money wheel, shuffling and dealing cards, shaking mini dice cages and encouraging players to place their bets will be part of your role.

You will also be responsible for announcing and paying out wins, and collecting in lost bets.

Type of person suited to this work

You should have an engaging personality, good interpersonal skills and possess the ability to make customers feel happy and relaxed. Confidence in front of an audience is essential.

Appearance is highly important. You must be smartly dressed, clean and manicured, with immaculately groomed hair.

There might be difficult moments when people are distressed or angered by losing so you must be confident and assertive.

Fluency in another language is an asset.

Working conditions

Casinos open 7 days a week and on bank holidays from 12pm to 6am. Many are now open 24 hours a day. This means that staff work shifts including evenings, weekends and bank holidays.

On cruise liners, croupiers spend up to 12 months on-board, with about 6 weeks vacation. Casinos close when in port so you do get time ashore in exotic locations!

Future prospects

Britain currently has 140 casinos, which is a figure that is unlikely to change substantially any time soon. Gambling has become better regulated in recent years and employers really value good staff.

Significant numbers of croupiers are needed to fill jobs on cruise liners and this can be a favourite choice for experienced croupiers seeking management-level experience.

As a croupier with 2 years of experience, you can progress to supervising a number of gaming tables after undertaking further training. Promotion could be to inspector, pit boss and, finally, manager of a casino.

Advantages/disadvantages

If you are quick and ambitious, you can make rapid progress from croupier to casino manager.

If you work as a croupier on a cruise ship, there will be the opportunity to visit new countries, especially as ship casinos are usually not allowed to be open when ships are in port.

Standing for hours and concentrating on running the games without error, while talking to customers, can be tiring.

Casino-goers drink alcohol which exacerbates the emotional tension during gaming. Arguments often break out which you must be able to handle according to the rules and regulations governing gaming.

Money guide

Starting salaries can range from £11,500 to £18,500. Salaries in London are generally higher.

Those with experience who are employed in a senior position can achieve £25,000–£30,000.

Recent changes to the law has allowed for croupiers to earn tips, which may increase your salary.

Pay scales on cruise liners are similar, however meals and accommodation are provided and the tips are generally higher.

Related opportunities

- Cruise Ship Steward/Purser p573
- Entertainment Manager p362

Further information

National Casino Industry Forum
www.nationalcasinoforum.co.uk

DIVER

ENTRY LEVEL 1

Qualifications and courses

To become a professional diver or diving instructor you will need a qualification approved by the Health and Safety Executive (HSE). There are no formal academic requirements for these courses, although basic maths and English may be tested. You must also obtain a valid certificate of medical fitness from a doctor approved by the HSE and pass a medical every year during your diving career.

Certain types of divers may need extra qualifications: most scientific divers have a degree in oceanography or marine biology, offshore divers may need a degree in surveying or engineering, construction divers might need qualifications in welding or non-destructive testing, and divers for the police or armed forces must already be serving in the force. Divers who intend to work offshore must have an up-to-date HSE First Aid at work qualification.

All divers must meet the Diving at Work Regulations 1997 (DWR) established by the HSE.

What the work involves

As a diver you will work either at sea or inland (ie rivers and reservoirs). Your tasks will depend on the industry you choose to work in and the type of diving you specialise in.

You could choose to become a diving instructor. Diving instructors teach a variety of skills from entry level diver training to technical diving for more experienced divers. They often operate from dedicated dive centres at coastal sites or through holiday resorts or local swimming pools.

Professional divers are often used in several industries, such as offshore oil and gas, civil engineering, fish farming, media, scientific research, underwater archaeology or police diving, and undertake a variety of specialist tasks.

A civil engineer diver is employed for underwater repairs and demolition. Divers employed in media will be required to participate in stunts or underwater filming. Police divers are responsible for searching for and recovering missing persons or evidence. Offshore divers recruited in the oil and gas industries will be employed for exploration and surveying, or building and maintaining drilling rigs and pipelines.

Scientific diving is the use of diving techniques by scientists to study underwater what would normally be studied by scientists on land. Examples of disciplines pursued include underwater archaeology, marine biology and geology.

Type of person suited to this work

You must be fit, active and a very strong swimmer as diving is extremely physically demanding.

You must be able to follow health and safety regulations. You should work well in a team and on your own.

You need to be able to concentrate and cope with diving conditions that could be dangerous and have quick reactions to deal with emergencies.

Working conditions

Underwater working conditions are cold, dark and may be cramped. It is necessary to wear protective clothing and breathing apparatus.

Working hours for divers are irregular and depend on the job. A lot of divers work just 120–180 days per year. Jobs may be located abroad.

Future prospects

Divers who pursue higher education have good prospects because they can combine subject expertise with practical skill. For example, a diver with a qualification in forensics would be more likely to be involved with police diving.

Experienced, senior divers may become self-employed, either as contractors or as operators of diving schools or equipment stores.

The growth of offshore wind farms and the oil and gas sector has led to a rise in the demand for experienced offshore divers around the world. However, those with experience already will be favoured.

Advantages/disadvantages

There is a strong demand for experienced, offshore divers.

The high levels of fitness and health needed for diving can make this a short career.

There is a risk of accidents when underwater and there are potential long-term health hazards which include a number of specific acute and chronic medical conditions.

Money guide

Most divers are paid daily. Earnings can be between £120 and £1,000 a day, depending on the type of diving and work involved.

An inshore or civil engineering diver could earn between £120 and £250 a day, for up to 200 days a year.

An offshore North Sea diver could expect £450 a day for 150 days a year.

Divers in the army or Royal Navy can earn an extra £4.24 per day or up to £1,000 per month on top of their basic salary.

Police divers can earn anything from £12,000 to over £100,000 per year.

Related opportunities

- Marine Engineer p215
- Royal Navy Officer p539
- Sports Coach p368

Further information

International Marine Contractors Association
www.imca-int.com

PADI
www.padi.com/scuba

Underwater Centre
www.theunderwatercentre.co.uk

ENTERTAINMENT MANAGER

ENTRY LEVEL 1

Qualifications and courses

There are no formal entry requirements for this career. Experience, enthusiasm and personality are more important than qualifications. Some employers may expect you to have previous experience working in the entertainment industry or a relevant sector such as hospitality, customer service or events management. Foreign language skills are useful for those looking to work abroad, and a good knowledge of contract law may be useful.

Degrees, Foundation degrees and HNDs are not essential but it could be useful to have one in a related subject such as event management, performing arts or business studies. Degree courses usually require at least 2 A levels/3 H grades and 5 GCSEs/National 5s (A*–C/A–C). There are also various NVQs, City & Guilds Awards and other professional qualifications available.

To become a manager in a holiday resort you will need at least 2 years' entertainment or performing experience. Relevant apprenticeships may be available.

If you are working with children or vulnerable adults you will need a Disclosure and Barring Services (DBS) check.

What the work involves

Entertainment managers take responsibility for the schedule of visiting entertainers to a venue, achieving a balance of activities that engage the age, gender and cultural interests of the audience.

You will plan, organise, advertise and oversee the running of a full calendar of social events.

You will contact acts and agents, and negotiate the best possible prices with them. When the events listing is finalised, you will promote the programme on a weekly and daily basis. You will also be responsible for costing out the entertainment.

Type of person suited to this work

Entertainment managers are people who are talkative, outgoing and vivacious. People have to be a central focus, whether it's the needs of artists, stage managers or the audience. They must remain cool under pressure, think on their feet and be flexible without being weak.

You will need excellent interpersonal and communication skills. Confidence speaking in public is essential.

Your organisation depends on you to find reliable acts, possibly at short notice. You have to make quick appraisals to drive home a deal. You need persuasive powers, imagination and considerable personal initiative.

Working conditions

You could be permanently based in a grand hotel or located in a popular resort, on a cruise liner, or with a large company that frequently entertains important clients.

Entertainment managers work in an office during the day and emerge after 6pm to manage the flow of evening entertainment and introduce the artists.

There is seasonal work for entertainment managers in all the major holiday centres. Travel may be required so a driving licence would be useful.

Future prospects

The travel and tourism industry in the UK continues to grow, so the job market for entertainment managers should at least remain steady if it doesn't expand.

A willingness to be geographically mobile could be important if you are looking to progress in this career.

With experience, you could move into other managerial roles within the hospitality industry.

You will have the opportunity to travel both around the UK and overseas. Those employed on a cruise liner may spend extended periods of time away from home.

Advantages/disadvantages

You will meet some interesting and entertaining artists, perhaps developing lifelong relationships with them.

You may have the opportunity to travel, such as on cruise ships or for certain seasons.

You will have to work evenings, weekends and bank holidays.

Pressure can build if an act does not show up so you might occasionally need to fill a gap and prevent the audience from getting irritable.

Money guide

Generally, travel and recreation work is not well paid.

New entertainment managers can expect a starting salary of £12,000–£15,000.

With experience, you may receive £18,000–£20,000 per year.

If you are an entertainment manager for a large international company, pay and prospects could be much higher, with possible earnings of £30,000.

Related opportunities

- Croupier p360
- Holiday Representative p364
- Theme Park Assistant/Manager p371

Further information

NCFE
www.ncfe.org.uk

People 1st
www.people1st.co.uk

FITNESS INSTRUCTOR/ PERSONAL TRAINER

ENTRY LEVEL 1

Qualifications and courses

No formal academic qualifications are required for this career but an industry-recognised qualification approved by the Register of Exercise Professionals (REPs) can be beneficial. This can be completed prior to becoming an instructor or as part of a work-based training scheme. You need to be aged 16 or over to be an assistant instructor and at least 18 to become a full instructor.

The most popular REPs-approved qualification is the Level 2 Certificate in Fitness Training available from City & Guilds. During this course you can choose to specialise in gym-based exercise, exercise to music, water-based exercise or physical activity for children. A full list of all REPs-approved courses is available on their website.

An alternative route is to take the Instructing Exercise and Fitness Apprenticeship which is available at both Intermediate and Advanced Level.

Before you can work as an instructor, you will also need to hold public liability insurance, a First Aid certificate and, if you intend to work with children or vulnerable adults, undergo a Disclosure and Barring Service (DBS) check. Applicants will, of course, need to be physically fit.

Personal trainers are normally experienced fitness instructors who then take a Level 3 Award in Conversion of Advanced Fitness Instructor to Personal Trainer Status. This changes your membership status on REPs to Personal Trainer.

Further courses are available, in yoga or zumba for example, which may help further your career.

What the work involves

Fitness instructors/personal trainers teach people how to exercise in a safe and effective manner, whilst also helping them work towards personal fitness targets.

You could provide a one-on-one service to your clients, direct and choreograph group fitness activities and classes, or undertake a mixture of the 2. You could work in a health club, community gym, leisure centre or private gym.

Other duties may include writing individual training programmes for clients, showing them exercise techniques and how to use equipment, and offering advice on nutrition and other lifestyle-related issues.

Type of person suited to this work

You will need excellent interpersonal skills so that you can attract new business opportunities, chat to clients and advise them on fitness and dietary requirements, and build good relationships with other team members.

You must be very enthusiastic about training and fitness in order to motivate your clients, be sensitive to their needs and, sometimes, persuade them to persevere with exercise.

You should look smart and fit yourself to promote a good image to existing and potential clients.

You must be innovative in your approach to keeping fit, thinking up new routines for classes or creating diversity in one-on-one clients' training programmes so people remain enthused and interested in their activities.

Working conditions

Fitness instructors work longer than average hours – between 38 and 40 hours per week – and these often include early mornings, evenings and weekends to suit the needs of their clients.

Most instructors work on a part-time basis and are affiliated to one or a number of gyms in their local area.

Future prospects

As society has become increasingly aware of health and fitness issues, the demand for fitness instructors has grown. This trend is set to continue for the foreseeable future so employment prospects are good.

In certain areas and in popular high street gyms, competition for jobs can be tough.

With experience, you could move into roles such as fitness manager or sports facility manager. Alternatively, you could build your own fitness consultancy.

Advantages/disadvantages

You will play an active role in enhancing many people's lives by introducing them to exercise and ensuring they continue with it.

You will see tangible results of your efforts and guidance as people become fitter and slimmer during the course of your work with them.

You will have to work unsocial hours.

Money guide

Earnings usually depend on your reputation, client base and location.

Fitness instructors usually have a starting salary of around £13,000. With experience, earnings can increase up to £20,000 and freelance instructors may charge an hourly rate of £10–£20.

Personal trainers in full-time employment can receive a salary ranging from £12,000 up to £20,000. Self-employed personal trainers are likely to earn £20–£40 an hour and those working with high profile clients can achieve an hourly rate of £50–£100.

Related opportunities

- Leisure Centre Assistant/Manager p365
- Outdoor Pursuits Instructor p367
- Sports Coach p368

Further information

Register of Exercise Professionals
www.exerciseregister.org

HOLIDAY REPRESENTATIVE

Qualifications and courses

You will normally need to be aged 20 or over to be a holiday representative, although some children's representatives may be accepted at 18 or 19. Academic qualifications are not essential as most employers place higher value on customer service experience, however, GCSEs/National 5s (A*–C/A–C) in subjects such as English, maths and geography can be useful. Competency in a foreign language, such as Spanish, French, Italian, Portuguese, Greek or Turkish would be particularly beneficial if you wished to work in these countries.

A degree is not required but may still be useful. Relevant subjects include leisure and tourism, modern languages and international tourism management. Entry to a degree usually requires a minimum of 2 A levels/3 H grades and 5 GCSEs/National 5s (A*–C/A–C).

Other relevant qualifications include the online Holiday Rep Ticket Diploma, an NVQ in Travel and Tourism Services (Levels 2–3) from City & Guilds and the NCFE Level 2 Award for Resort Representatives.

Training is usually provided on the job, both in the UK and at the holiday resort. In some roles you might need specialist knowledge in an area such as archaeology, scuba diving or history.

To work with children, you will need 6–12 months of practical experience, a childcare qualification and clearance from the Disclosure and Barring Service (DBS).

What the work involves

Holiday representatives have many duties including meeting holidaymakers at airports and other terminals, helping them to locate their luggage and directing them towards the transport that will take them to their accommodation. You will be responsible for checking all the details of each passenger's transport and accommodation to ensure that everything is in place for their stay.

You will inform customers of important information, including local bus routes, recommended restaurants and sites of interest. You will also sell excursion tickets. You may be expected to accompany tourists on expeditions and provide them with holiday entertainment.

You may be required to specialise in certain activities, such as running the kid's club or a particular sport.

You will usually be based in certain places or countries, but travel will be part of the job.

Type of person suited to this work

You will need to look smart and have a pleasant, approachable attitude so that holidaymakers are comfortable speaking to you. You will need to be sociable and very patient as you will deal with guests 24 hours a day for the duration of the holiday season.

You should have a methodical approach to your work and excellent organisational skills as you will be coordinating lots of details for numerous people at one time.

Fluency in the language of the country in which you are working is also an asset.

Working conditions

Working hours vary from day-to-day but are usually long and unpredictable. Most representatives only have one day off a week and even then they will be on-call in case of an emergency.

The work is seasonal, although there are opportunities all year round with beach holidays in the summer months and ski work during winter. You could work indoors or outdoors. You will usually have to wear a uniform.

Future prospects

You could work for a large international travel company or a smaller, more specialist firm. Most opportunities are overseas, although there are a few jobs available in the UK.

With experience, you could move into a supervisory or managerial position. Some representatives also branch out into another area of travel and tourism, such as hotel management or working on a tourist board.

Advantages/disadvantages

You will have plenty of opportunities to work abroad in a number of diverse and exciting areas.

You will deal with a range of people from all ages and backgrounds on a daily basis, making the work diverse and challenging.

You will have to work long hours which can make the job both physically and mentally exhausting.

Money guide

Holiday representatives often work by season, with a first season's pay starting at around £550 to £650 a month plus accommodation. This gives a starting salary of £6,000 to £7,800 a year. An experienced representative working both the summer and winter season could earn £11,000 to £14,000 a year.

Salaries can be boosted by commissions from selling services and company benefits such as free flights, meal allowance and use of facilities.

Salaries and commission structures improve as you progress to more senior roles, such as team leader or resort manager. The benefits package varies but can include company cars, discounts for bars and restaurants, free or discounted excursions and more.

Related opportunities

- Air Cabin Crew p566
- Tour Guide/Manager p372
- Travel Agent p374

Further information

Career in Travel
www.careerintravel.co.uk

LEISURE CENTRE ASSISTANT/MANAGER

ENTRY LEVEL 1

Qualifications and courses

Assistant

Although there are no formal entry requirements, some employers prefer applicants with GCSEs/National 5s (A*–C/A–C) in maths, English and a science and an A level/H grade or a BTEC National qualification in sport or leisure. Previous experience working in customer service is also helpful and a Disclosure and Barring Services (DBS) check is required.

Specialist qualifications may be needed to work in certain areas, such as lifeguard qualifications for swimming pool attendants.

Training is often given on the job, although many courses are offered by the Institute for the Management of Sport and Physical Activity (IMSPA). A First Aid certificate would be useful.

Manager

There are a few routes to becoming a manager. One is to study for a relevant degree, HND or Foundation degree and enter onto a graduate trainee scheme where you will gain the necessary experience. If you have pre-entry experience you may be able to apply for the role directly or work your way up from a lower position by studying for professional qualifications.

Relevant degree subjects include sports science, physiology and sport, leisure or recreation management. The general entry requirements for a degree are 2 A levels/3 H grades and 5 GCSEs/National 5s (A*–C/A–C).

Professional qualifications should be recognised by the Register of Exercise Professionals (REPs) and can be in areas such as fitness instruction, pool operation or sports coaching. A First Aid certificate and a DBS check are usually required.

What the work involves

Assistant

You will help run sports activities, set up equipment and demonstrate its safe use to leisure centre users.

You will also work on the reception desk issuing tickets, taking bookings, answering enquiries and performing other tasks specified by your manager.

It is important to maintain, set up and tidy equipment, and to monitor all activity to make sure everything is running smoothly.

Manager

You will oversee the day-to-day work and recruitment of all leisure centre staff, and deal with queries.

You will meet with company or council reps to discuss budgets, funding sources, marketing issues, and new developments.

You will ultimately be responsible for the health and safety of those working in and using the leisure centre. Organising external activities, ensuring the enjoyment of your customers, and overseeing the schedule will all come under your remit.

Type of person suited to this work

You will need to be friendly and helpful with excellent interpersonal skills.

A role as manager will require proven leadership skills. As you will be working within or leading a team you must be able to communicate well.

Assistants should be fit and pro-active with customers.

Working conditions

Most of your time will be spent indoors – at the poolside, in a sports hall, at reception or in the office.

You should expect to work unsocial hours; early starts and late finishes.

Future prospects

Interest in leisure and fitness centres are popular, so demand is likely to, at the very least, be steady.

You could progress from a role as an assistant to supervisor and then become a manager. After gaining more experience, you could go on to become an area or regional manager.

There are greater opportunities for promotion in large organisations.

Advantages/disadvantages

Most leisure centres have a relaxed working atmosphere.

It is possible to work a variety of shifts and hours can be flexible.

Earnings can be low unless you start on the trainee management route.

Money guide

Starting salaries for leisure centre assistants are around £12,500 per year, rising to £19,000 with qualifications and experience. This can be boosted by overtime and bonuses related to membership as well as weekend and shift work.

The starting salary for managers is between £15,000 and £25,000 a year. Managers at senior levels with 10–15 years' experience can earn around £35,000 with a few reaching £40,000.

Salaries could be higher with professional qualifications. Bonuses can include use of leisure centre facilities outside working hours and target-related bonuses.

Related opportunities

- Fitness Instructor/Personal Trainer p363
- Lifeguard p366
- Outdoor Pursuits Instructor p367

Further information

Chartered Institute for the Management of Sport and Physical Activity
www.cimspa.co.uk

LIFEGUARD

ENTRY LEVEL 1

Qualifications and courses

Pool lifeguard

You must be over 16, physically fit and a strong swimmer to qualify to become a poolside lifeguard. There are no specific academic entry requirements but a good standard of English and maths is preferred and a qualification in Physical Education (PE) or fitness would be a bonus.

Lifeguards must be in possession of either a National Pool Lifeguard Qualification (NPLQ) from the Royal Life Saving Society UK or a NaRS Pool Rescue Qualification from the Swimming Teachers Association (STA). You could take a job as a pool attendant or assistant and study for the qualifications part time.

The NPLQ training covers 3 assessed units: The Lifeguard and the Law, Intervention and Rescue and Emergency Action Plans, and Cardiopulmonary Resuscitation, AED and First Aid. This training can only take place in a centre approved by the Institute of Qualified Lifeguards.

Both the NPLQ and NaRS qualifications are valid for 24 months. After this you must have your lifesaving and First Aid skills assessed before your qualification is renewed.

Beach/ocean lifeguard

You must be aged over 18, physically fit and a strong swimmer to qualify to become a beach lifeguard.

Lifeguards must be in possession of the National Beach Lifeguard Qualification (NBLQ) from the Royal Life Saving Society UK or the NaRS Beach Lifeguard Award run through clubs by the Surf Life Saving Association of Great Britain. These courses cover practical ocean rescue skills involving the use of boards and tubes. Training is also provided by the Royal National Lifeboat Institution.

All lifeguards need to hold a valid First Aid Worker Certificate. Lifeguard qualifications must be renewed every 2 years.

What the work involves

Lifeguards are responsible for patrolling and monitoring the water and weather conditions where people are swimming, surfing or boating. You will keep watch on public swimming pools or stretches of shoreline to reduce the risk of tragic accidents occurring and take rapid action to alert the public to danger.

Your role could involve rescuing people at risk from drowning, assisting them ashore and administering First Aid including mouth-to-mouth or CPR (cardiopulmonary resuscitation).

You will also be involved in informing the public about water safety.

Type of person suited to this work

You must be fit and active, with a full understanding of the level of danger in all water activities.

You should be a strong swimmer (able to cover 400 metres of a pool in less than 8 minutes) and have good vision and hearing. The ability to work within a team is also essential. It's important to be observant and be able to respond quickly.

You must be assertive in order to take command and manage dangerous incidents and be able to stay calm in emergencies.

Working conditions

You will work either on the beach or poolside and work could be offered on a seasonal basis or full time. Either way, you will need to cover early morning and later shifts as part of your hours in order to provide a full emergency service to water users.

You must keep alert and vigilant at all times as when emergency strikes, you have to be ready to act in seconds – not minutes.

Overseas work is possible with holiday companies.

Future prospects

Interest in water sports has grown, although the demand for lifeguards has always been fairly consistent.

You could progress into a managerial role such as a pool supervisor, duty manager or general pool manager.

You could also qualify as a swimming teacher to boost your income.

Advantages/disadvantages

Pools and beaches have a relaxed, upbeat atmosphere.

There can be periods of boredom that you have to work through, maintaining vigilance. Accidents can happen at any time.

If working outdoors you could be in danger of overexposure to sunlight.

Money guide

Starting salaries for full-time lifeguards are around £11,500–£15,000 per year. With experience, pay can rise to £15,000 or over.

Many lifeguards work for local authorities on a part-time basis and rates of pay can vary from £6 to £10 per hour. Seasonal lifeguards earn around £200 a week.

Pay can be increased by overtime and taking on extra responsibilities such as coaching duties.

Related opportunities

- Fitness Instructor/Personal Trainer p363
- Outdoor Pursuits Instructor p367
- Sports Coach p368

Further information

Royal Life Saving Society UK
www.rlss.org.uk

Saltwater Training
www.saltwatertraining.com

Surf Life Saving Great Britain
www.slsgb.org.uk

Swimming Teachers Association
www.sta.co.uk

OUTDOOR PURSUITS INSTRUCTOR

ENTRY LEVEL 3

Qualifications and courses

No formal academic qualifications are required to work as an outdoor pursuits instructor and requirements will vary depending on the role and the employer. You will however need a coaching or proficiency qualification in at least one activity. The more activities you can offer the better.

These qualifications should be recognised by the relevant national governing body for that activity. Examples include the Sports Leaders UK Basic Expedition Leadership Award (BEL), British Canoe Union Level 1 Coach Award and the Mountain Leader Training UK Single Pitch Award. You would usually need 12 months' experience in the activity before you can take the courses. There are also full-time college courses and degrees available that provide relevant qualifications.

A First Aid certificate is required, as is a Life-Saving certificate if your activities are water-based.

Candidates are also expected to be able to demonstrate a history of leading and taking responsibility for others. This could be through volunteering at outdoor activities centres, involvement in activities such as the Duke of Edinburgh's Award or membership of activity clubs. Experience of youth work, teaching or coaching can also be useful.

You will need to be 18 years old before you can work as an instructor (21 if you will be driving a minibus). If you will be working with children or vulnerable adults you will need to undergo a Disclosure and Barring Service (DBS) check.

What the work involves

Outdoor pursuits instructors lead groups of people through a range of challenging activities, designed to help them bond, have fun, learn more about themselves and develop new skills.

You will work with people of all ages and backgrounds, including those with disabilities, children with special needs, adult recreation groups, and business professionals. You will be responsible for guiding these groups though a range of activities.

You will also be responsible for checking safety equipment, ensuring that group members are comfortable with each activity, and giving practical demonstrations.

Type of person suited to this work

You should have strong leadership skills as you will be required to persuade a group of people who have never met you before to undertake activities that are frightening and push them out of their comfort zone.

You must have an excellent level of physical fitness, alongside good eyesight and hearing.

You must be responsible and maintain continual awareness of the safety of both yourself and those around you. You should have good communication skills and a personable manner to explain activities clearly.

Working conditions

Hours are generally long and irregular, usually falling over evenings and weekends, including bank holidays. Much of the work is seasonal. Part-time hours are commonly available.

Many outdoor pursuits centres are located in the countryside, so a driving licence may be useful in order to travel to and from work with ease. Holding a licence for a passenger carrying vehicle (PCV) may also be helpful.

You should expect to be working outdoors in all weather conditions. Long treks may also involve spending evenings away from the centre, camping in a tent.

Future prospects

Although the outdoor leisure industry is growing, there is still a lot of competition for jobs.

Most opportunities are in independently run activity centres, or those owned by local authorities and charities. There are also jobs available with expedition companies who organise overseas excursions.

Many instructors specialise in a particular discipline, such as canoeing or abseiling, and work freelance across several activity centres.

Advantages/disadvantages

You will be helping people to break down boundaries and overcome fear, which will increase their self-reliance and self-confidence.

You will be working with a wide range of people, from all backgrounds and ages, which will give great diversity to your working day.

You will have to work unsociable hours.

Money guide

As an outdoor activities instructor, you could expect to earn £9,000 to £12,000 as a starting salary.

As your experience grows, this could increase to around £18,000.

Once you have reached the level of a more senior instructor, perhaps also developing specialist skills, you could earn up to £25,000.

Food and accommodation are sometimes provided.

Related opportunities

- Holiday Representative p364
- Sports Coach p368
- Sports Development Officer p369

Further information

British Activity Providers Association
www.thebapa.org.uk

Institute for Outdoor Learning
www.outdoor-learning.org

SPORTS COACH

ENTRY LEVEL 4

Qualifications and courses

All sports coaches must hold a qualification that has been accredited by the National Governing Body (NGB) of their chosen discipline. You can start working towards recognised qualifications at the age of 16, but must be 18 or over to work as an independent coach.

Accredited courses are available directly from the NGB, or you can undertake a college or university course. NGB qualifications are equivalent to studying for NVQs from Level 1 to 4, and no academic qualifications are required (except for the golfing qualification which requires 4 GCSEs/National 5s (A*–C/A–C)), although sometimes a First Aid certificate is essential and you will need a Disclosure and Barring Service (DBS) check to work with children. NGBs are usually studied on a part-time basis.

Relevant courses at college include BTEC HNC/HNDs in sports coaching or leisure studies and Foundation degrees in sports coaching are available. Typical entry requirements for these courses include 1 A level/H grade and 4 GCSEs/National 5s (A*–C/A–C). Degrees in sports science, sports coaching, health science, and sports management may improve employment prospects and degree courses usually require 2 A levels/3 H grades and 5 GCSEs/National 5s (A*–C/A–C), including English and maths, for entry.

You could start out as an assistant coach on a voluntary basis, then take a Level 1 qualification to progress to higher levels. Coaching is also often a second career for ex-professional sportspeople.

What the work involves

Sports coaches provide specialist support, motivation and knowledge to athletes in order to help them attain their best performances and achieve personal goals.

As a competitive coach, you could work with a variety of levels of athlete, ranging from children's football or netball teams, through to professional and even world class sports professionals.

At a non-competitive level, you will focus on providing fun and accessible exercise sessions for participants with a range of abilities and fitness levels.

You will usually coach one specific sport.

Type of person suited to this work

You will need excellent communications skills. You will also need to have good motivational abilities in order to inspire and encourage sports players to push themselves.

You will need an in-depth knowledge of your chosen sport, and an understanding of nutrition and physiology is also useful.

It is also essential that you understand a variety of training methods and principles so that you can provide an informed and beneficial service to your clients. Patience and determination are also vital qualities.

Working conditions

You will usually work early mornings, evenings and weekends. This is when the majority of your athletes will be available.

If you are working in a seasonal sport such as cricket or football, you might have to supplement your income with another job during the quiet months.

You will spend hours on your feet, and might also have to undertake activity in order to demonstrate methods and principles to athletes.

Future prospects

The vast majority of sports coaches working in the UK work on a voluntary or part-time basis. Competition for full-time positions is fierce.

Career prospects will depend on the level of success you achieve in your work. If you gain credibility, you could move into a related development or management position.

You could be self-employed, work for a local authority, or in a school, gym or professional sports club.

Advantages/disadvantages

You will be teaching the sport you love to a range of people and developing their interest in it.

You may have the opportunity to work with talented athletes.

You will have to spend long periods of time standing outside in all weather conditions.

Money guide

As a newly qualified coach working for an employer, you could earn between £12,000 and £25,000, depending on experience and employer.

Experienced coaches who work for a NGB or professional association can earn between £30,000 and £35,000.

If you work at the highest level of your sport, such as coaching Premiership football players, you could earn in excess of £100,000.

Coaches working with amateur teams or individuals can earn £15 to £60 per hour.

Related opportunities

- Fitness Instructor/Personal Trainer p363
- Outdoor Pursuits Instructor p367
- Sports Professional p370

Further information

SkillsActive
www.skillsactive.com

Sports Coach UK
www.sportscoachuk.org

SPORTS DEVELOPMENT OFFICER

ENTRY LEVEL 5

Qualifications and courses

Although there are currently no specific academic requirements, new entrants to the profession are usually graduates.

Relevant first degree subjects include sports science/studies, physical education, recreation/leisure management, and health and exercise sciences. Most universities require candidates to have 2 A levels/3 H grades, one in a related subject such as biology, and 5 GCSEs/National 5s (A*–C/A–C), including English, maths and a science. Some employers will also accept entrants with relevant BTEC or HNC/HND qualifications in sport, sports science, sports development or another related subject.

Entry without a degree is still possible if you have coaching qualifications and start out as a sports development assistant. Pre-entry work experience is always essential with or without a degree. Many employers will require 2 years' experience in sports development, for example at a leisure centre, a holiday camp or summer school. Coaching experience is also desirable.

A Disclosure and Barring Service (DBS) check is usually required.

What the work involves

Sports development officers are responsible for ensuring that sports and related activities are available to people of all ages and abilities. You will be promoting the benefits of exercise and encouraging people to live a healthy lifestyle by devising simple but effective strategies that increase participation in sport.

You will work within the local community, liaising with schools, gyms and social clubs, and also have involvement with larger agencies such as sports national governing bodies (NGBs).

You may work closely with groups who are usually excluded from sports-related activity, such as disadvantaged youths, prisoners and disabled people.

Type of person suited to this work

You will need a positive attitude and a clear commitment to sport that will help you to persuade local community members and service providers to back your initiatives.

You will need excellent verbal and written communication skills in order to illustrate your objectives to other professionals. This includes strong persuasive and negotiating skills.

Good IT and administrative ability will be essential for creating reports, producing material to support your ideas, and keeping accurate records.

Working conditions

You will usually work a 36-hour week within normal office hours. Flexible hours and overtime are often available.

It is not unusual to have to work additional hours during evenings and weekends, attending meetings or networking events.

You will work in an office environment, and also spend time at local schools, clubs and community venues. Since a good deal of travelling is required each day, a driving licence can be helpful.

Future prospects

You will most likely be working for a local authority, county sports partnership, or NGB. A few opportunities are available in specialist sports colleges.

Career progression for sport-specific development officers is fairly limited; you could be promoted to the role of sports development manager, or become more involved with other community initiatives. The Institute for the Management of Sports and Physical Activity (IMSPA) offers a number of different courses aimed at continuing professional development (CPD) and similar courses are available through Sports Coach UK.

Advantages/disadvantages

You will play an active role in enhancing many people's quality of life by providing them with access to sport in their local area.

You will be liaising with a variety of people on a daily basis, which should make the work dynamic and interesting.

You will need a resilient approach to your work, as suggestions and plans will often be knocked back or fall through.

Money guide

The starting salary for an assistant sports development officer is £13,000 to £18,000.

Sports development officers have a starting salary of between £18,000 and £20,000 per year, which can rise to around £35,000 with experience.

If you reach a management position, you could potentially earn up to £50,000.

Related opportunities

- Fitness Instructor/Personal Trainer p363
- Outdoor Pursuits Instructor p367
- Sports Coach p368

Further information

Chartered Institute for the Management of Sport and Physical Activity
www.cimspa.co.uk

Sports Coach UK
www.sportscoachuk.org

Sports Leaders UK
www.sportsleaders.org

Qualifications and courses

You do not need any academic qualifications for most sports as ability, dedication and determination to succeed within your chosen sport are the key requirements to become a sports professional. Joining a club or amateur organisation would be beneficial in terms of receiving instruction and training. Some sports have specific entry requirements, such as height and weight restrictions for boxing and horse racing.

Talented athletes aged 16–18 could apply for the Advanced Apprenticeship in Sporting Excellence. This structured training and development programme is for young people who show the potential to reach Olympic/Paralympic level or to gain a professional contract. Depending on which of the 2 pathways you choose, this could lead to either an NVQ Level 3 Diploma or a Level 3 Certificate. The Diploma can be used to move on to other Level 3 qualifications.

Across the UK, there are opportunities to gain additional help and support if you are a promising young athlete. In England, for example, the Talented Athlete Scholarship Scheme (TASS) awards funding of up to £3,500 for sports training to those over the age of 16. Details of national governing bodies (NGBs) are available from the Sport England website.

What the work involves

Sportsplayers are paid professionals who compete across the globe in their chosen sport, often in front of an audience. You could compete individually in sports such as boxing, swimming, golf and athletics, or alternatively with a team in sports such as football, hockey, cricket and rugby.

You will need to spend a great deal of time training in order to maintain a high standard of general fitness, alongside honing your skills in your chosen sport.

You may also be required to attend social events, give interviews and promote the companies that provide you with sponsorship.

Type of person suited to this work

First and foremost, you will need to have an outstanding natural ability in your chosen sport. You must also have the necessary commitment and self-discipline to maintain a continuous training schedule and strict healthy diet.

You will need to have a highly competitive nature but also a polite and pleasant manner in order to get on with team members, fellow players and coaches.

As well as being physically fit, you must be mentally stable so that you can cope with the pressure of competition, defeat and disappointment.

Working conditions

Competitions and matches usually fall on weekends, although qualifying rounds may take place during the week.

You will usually need to travel to reach competitions, which may involve overnights away from home. If you are competing at an international level, you could be away for weeks at a time.

You will need to train most days and if you are supplementing your professional sports income with a regular job, this will mean exercising either early in the morning or in the evening.

Future prospects

Most professional sportsplayers are spotted at an early age by a talent scout or coach. From this point, they build up skills and a reputation through competitions.

Unfortunately, the majority of professionals cannot earn a living playing their chosen sport alone, so you might have to supplement your income with full- or part-time work.

Sports professionals rarely continue to compete once they have reached their mid-30s but there are plenty of opportunities to work as a coach or manager, commentator, or even earn money as a TV personality.

Advantages/disadvantages

Pursuing your dream as a professional sportsplayer is much more exciting than a conventional job.

The hard work and dedication you put in should be repaid in the form of sporting achievements and acclaim.

The profession is unpredictable and is an unstable job to pursue as a bad injury or a bad game has the potential to ruin your career.

Money guide

If you start your professional career as an apprentice, you may earn less than £10,000, plus accommodation and food allowances.

Once you are established as a professional, competing in and winning competitions regularly, you should earn £20,000 as above.

Successful sports professionals may make extra money by advertising products or through sponsorship.

Highly successful sports professionals working in well-supported sports, such as tennis and football, can earn anything up to £3,000,000 a year.

Related opportunities

- Fitness Instructor/Personal Trainer p363
- Outdoor Pursuits Instructor p367
- Sports Coach p368

Further information

SkillsActive
www.skillsactive.com

Talented Athlete Scholarship Scheme
www.tass.gov.uk

THEME PARK ASSISTANT/ MANAGER

ENTRY LEVEL 1

Qualifications and courses

You have to be at least 18 years old to start work in a theme park, though it may be possible for entrants to begin at the age of 16 if working on children's rides. No formal academic qualifications are required to be an assistant but if you intend to become a supervisor or manager then it would be beneficial to have some GCSEs/National 5s in maths, English, IT and possibly design technology. A degree in business, management or leisure/travel/tourism management may also increase your chances.

Once you are employed you will receive on-the-job training from more experienced staff, in areas such as customer care and health and safety.

NVQs/SVQs and other qualifications in customer care, catering and sales could be relevant, along with qualifications in Leisure & Tourism.

With experience as a theme park assistant, you could progress to a role as a team leader or manager, possibly by taking relevant qualifications. You could start out as a manager if you have previous customer service and management experience.

If the theme park you work for is registered with the British Association of Leisure Parks, Piers and Attractions (BALPPA) then you may be able to attend specialist training schemes and seminars.

What the work involves

As a theme park assistant you will greet customers, check ticket holders' ages and heights, and operate and supervise rides. You may also sell merchandise.

You must always observe safety rules and ensure that there are no hazards. Assistants are also required to carry out repairs and maintenance on machines each morning and evening.

If you are a manager you will need to oversee all the different operations within a theme park, ensuring the smooth running of the amusements and catering facilities. You will be responsible for the maintenance, cleaning and surveillance of the park.

You will also be involved with recruiting and training staff, managing the budget of the park and handling any problems that arise.

The manager must inspect the whole site before opening time, taking responsibility for checking that all the necessary safety checks have been done and that the rides and other facilities are fully staffed.

Type of person suited to this work

Theme park workers should be comfortable talking to the public and keen to ensure that they have an exciting and memorable time.

You must be trustworthy and dependable, with good practical and mechanical skills, and the ability to follow instructions carefully. Awareness of health and safety practices is essential.

Working conditions

Theme parks are open 7 days a week and on bank holidays. You are likely to work shifts and have one full day off each week. This work may be seasonal and could involve travelling to different locations.

As a theme park assistant, you will work outdoors in a variety of weather conditions. Managers will spend some of their time in an office environment.

Assistants may be required to wear a uniform and managers should dress smartly.

Future prospects

There is always a high turnover of staff in theme parks but a core group of workers stay on, benefiting from training and increased responsibility which allows them to gain certificates as evidence of their skills.

There is more work in Europe for trained, experienced theme park workers so learning to speak a foreign language may improve future prospects.

Advantages/disadvantages

This is a specialised line of entertainment and leisure work so it may be difficult to progress to roles in other sectors.

You have the opportunity to work anywhere in the world such as Legoland Denmark or Disneyland USA.

Money guide

Theme park assistants can expect a starting salary in line with the national minimum wage.

For managers, typical starting salaries are around £19,500 to £30,000. After about 10 years this could increase to between £35,000 and £75,000.

Salaries tend to be higher at large, corporate-owned parks. Benefits may include pension, health insurance and free or discounted park tickets.

Related opportunities

- Customer Services Assistant/Manager p456
- Entertainment Manager p362
- Leisure Centre Assistant/Manager p365

Further information

British Association of Leisure Parks, Piers and Attractions
www.balppa.org

Equity
www.equity.org.uk

TOUR GUIDE/ MANAGER

ENTRY LEVEL 2

Qualifications and courses

Most tour guides and managers are aged 18 or over. Although no formal academic qualifications are required, you will need a good standard of general education. Some GCSEs/National 5s (A*–C/A–C) might be useful, particularly in subjects such as English, maths and languages. A levels/H grades and degrees, while they may also be useful, are not essential.

Fluency in another language is important if you intend to work abroad or work with foreign tourists in the UK. Competition is strong, so experience of dealing with the public and presentations are an advantage. Tour guiding is often a second career for people from other backgrounds.

A professional qualification may be useful as a way of enhancing your employability. The Institute of Tourist Guiding runs courses for tour guides at Levels 2, 3 and 4. You do not need any prior tour guiding experience or academic qualifications to enroll on these courses as entry will be based on interview and a location knowledge test. Some employers, such as Westminster Abbey, require a Level 4 Blue Badge qualification.

Once hired as a tour guide there are other professional qualifications you can work towards, which include NVQ in Travel and Tourism (Levels 2–3).

Professional courses for tour managers include full-time HND and degree courses in travel and tourism management, City & Guilds HLQ Level 3 in Travel and Tourism, and a range of related Northern Advisory Council for Further Education (NACFE) certificates.

What the work involves

Tour guides are responsible for meeting and greeting parties of people who are taking a holiday, cultural visit or tour together. You will accompany the sightseers on their journey and inform them of the historical/environmental/cultural interests of the area they are visiting. You will also assist them if they encounter problems or difficulties.

Tour managers are responsible for putting together proposals for day trips and excursions in order to attract holidaymakers to the company.

You will visit destinations to assess their potential as a tour venue, and may also assist tour guides with the delivery of the trip itself.

Type of person suited to this work

Tour guides and managers need excellent communication skills and an infectious enthusiasm and interest for areas or venues you work in. You will need good stamina in order to keep up a high level of energy and interest throughout tours.

You will need to have excellent customer relations skills in order to soothe any disgruntled holidaymakers and reach amicable solutions to problems.

Tour managers should also be methodical in order to put together logistically plausible, suitably detailed plans for excursions.

Working conditions

You may work long hours, and when out on a tour you will be on-call for customers 24 hours a day should they need anything.

You could work for a large international company, or a small independent tour provider, but either way your focus will be on promoting the company image and following their tour policies carefully.

You will be expected to wear a uniform when on duty, which usually includes a shirt and tie.

Future prospects

The government has committed to a £90 million investment, over the next 2 years, to VisitBritain's GREAT campaign, after a record-breaking year for UK tourism in 2013. As a result, prospects for tour guides, although competitive, should be good.

You could work in a large international company that runs tours throughout the UK and overseas, or a smaller provider that focuses on specific tourist areas in the UK such as Bath or London.

Competition for work as a tour manager is tough, but if you have built up good skills and knowledge as a tour guide first, you will be in a good position for promotion.

Advantages/disadvantages

You will be dealing with a variety of people of all ages and backgrounds on a daily basis, educating them about areas in which you have an interest.

It can get monotonous as you will be repeating the same information over and over again for weeks, months and even years.

Money guide

Tour guides can expect to start on around £11,900. With experience this could rise to up to £25,000 for those with specialist knowledge. Many tour guides are self-employed.

Tour managers are on short-term contracts, mostly in the summer, and have other jobs the rest of the year. There are some full-time positions available however, particularly in mainland Europe and Asia.

Salaries generally start at around £15,000 to £20,000. At senior level this can rise to over £30,000.

Related opportunities

- Holiday Representative p364
- Tourist Information Centre Assistant p373
- Travel Agent p374

Further information

Institute of Travel and Tourism
www.itt.co.uk

International Association of Tour Managers Limited
www.iatm.co.uk

VisitBritain
www.visitbritain.org

TOURIST INFORMATION CENTRE ASSISTANT

ENTRY LEVEL 1

Qualifications and courses

No formal academic qualifications are required for this career, although employers prefer a good standard of general education. GCSEs/National 5s (A*–C/A–C) might be an advantage, although personal qualities are usually more important. Acute listening and clear speaking skills are essential and it is very helpful if assistants can use IT to research information and respond to enquiries sent via the internet.

A number of tourist information centres (TICs) are close to international airports or in popular destinations for overseas visitors. Modern foreign language skills are valuable in order to help newly arrived tourists, business travellers and foreign visitors and a knowledge of British Sign Language would also be an advantage.

Though not essential, having relevant qualifications can enhance your employment prospects. A levels/H grades, BTECs, City & Guilds Diplomas and NVQs are all available in Travel and Tourism. Previous experience handling cash or working with the public is desirable.

Working as an assistant, most training will be on the job, although you can be assessed for NVQs/SVQs in Tourist Information and Customer Service. Many employees within tourist information centres work towards these awards.

Part-time HLQ Level 4, BTEC or SQA HNC qualifications in Leisure and Tourism might be useful for career progression to become a tourist information centre manager. However, it is possible to move into supervisory and managerial positions with extensive experience alone.

What the work involves

You will be answering questions in person, over the phone or via the internet from UK and foreign tourists, business people, local young people and researchers.

You will provide information, make bookings and reservations, locate accommodation, restaurants or sites of interest. You will also be expected to inform people about forthcoming shows and events in the local area.

You will hand out leaflets and sell maps, postcards and items of interest from the local area and region. You may also operate a bureau de change, depending on the services offered by your employer.

Type of person suited to this work

You need to have an interest in local matters and in promoting your local area. Good, up-to-date knowledge about places of interest is useful. You should be friendly with good interpersonal skills.

A methodical approach to researching difficult questions is an asset. Relevant skills include customer-service experience, the ability to research information using the internet and good verbal communication skills.

It is important to be a good team player and assist your colleagues, even if you are busy.

Working conditions

You will usually work shifts which include the weekends and bank holidays.

Tourist information centres are modern, bright spaces that make pleasant work surroundings.

There is quite a lot of standing at the counter and moving to and from storage areas with piles of information, leaflets and stock items. You may spend some hours sitting at a computer, researching routes or B&B facilities in distant locations.

Future prospects

Tourist information centres are located across the whole of the UK, so you should have one local to you.

You could move from a part-time contract into a full-time one and with experience progress to a managerial or supervisory post. You could also choose to become a travel agent or tour guide.

Advantages/disadvantages

There are both busy and quiet times at the counter in tourist information centres.

You could spend a long time on the phone which could get dull.

You will play an important role in promoting both the local region and helping its economy.

Money guide

The starting salary for full-time staff is around £14,000 to £17,000 per year.

With experience, this can rise to £20,000.

You can earn up to £28,000 as full-time manager of a tourist information centre.

Your salary will most likely be higher in and around London.

Related opportunities

- Holiday Representative p364
- Tour Guide/Manager p372
- Travel Agent p374

Further information

VisitBritain
www.visitbritain.org

VisitEngland
www.visitengland.com

VisitScotland
www.visitscotland.com

VisitWales
www.visitwales.com

TRAVEL AGENT

ENTRY LEVEL 2

Qualifications and courses

No formal academic qualifications are needed for entry into this profession, though it is useful to have a good standard of education with GCSEs/National 5s (A*–C/A–C) in English and maths. Other languages and experience working in a customer service or sales role would also be beneficial.

The Apprenticeship in Travel Services is available in the Leisure and Business pathway, which trains entrants for a customer-facing role as a travel agent, or the Tour Operator (Head Office) pathway, where you would be based at a call centre and assist customers with booking their holiday over the phone.

Training is provided on the job by employers but you could take relevant qualifications to help you secure a position. These include A levels/H grades, BTECs, City & Guilds awards and degrees in travel and tourism. The general entry requirements for a degree are 2 A levels/3 H grades and 5 GCSEs/National 5s (A*–C/A–C).

What the work involves

You will sell holiday packages to the public and try to meet your company's sales targets. You could be based in a high street travel agency or work in a call centre, assisting customers with online and telephone bookings.

You will put together individual holidays for an independent customer or for an organisation that seeks travel, accommodation and entertainment arrangements that are distinct from the travel companies' normal holiday packages.

You will need to contact airline, ferry and rail sales operatives to arrange transport and make reservations for accommodation, meals, hire cars and entertainment, both in this country and abroad. There are numerous details to check over the phone and tickets, booking confirmations and insurance notes to post out to customers.

Type of person suited to this work

You will need excellent administrative and research skills to quickly track down, assemble and book all the parts needed for each customer's ideal journey or holiday. You must have excellent listening and questioning skills in order to find the right holiday package for each individual customer.

If you are friendly, communicative and methodical, with excellent IT skills, you will suit both your customers' and your employers' needs. It helps if you have a real interest in exploring new places yourself.

Working conditions

You will work indoors, mainly at a desk or behind a counter. Almost all the work is done using a computer and telephone.

All travel agents tend to work 35–40 hours a week. If you work in a travel agency, it can be very busy at lunchtimes, near to closing time and on Saturdays, particularly leading up to the peak holiday season. Those working in a call centre are likely to work shifts including evening and weekend work.

Travel agencies usually provide staff with a uniform.

Future prospects

The travel industry has changed as more people now book their holidays via the internet. For this reason, many travel agents work in call centres, selling holiday packages over the phone and assisting customers with online bookings and queries. However, opportunities do still exist in high street travel agencies as some customers still prefer to book a holiday face-to-face with an agent's help.

With experience, you could progress to a managerial position. You can also move into other areas of tourism work, such as work as a holiday representative or tour guiding, which may give you to opportunities to travel the world.

Advantages/disadvantages

A perk of this career is that you may receive free or discounted holidays.

Working to meet performance targets can be stressful.

It can be satisfying knowing that you have helped a customer to find and book their ideal holiday.

Money guide

Starting salaries are usually £11,000–£13,000.

With experience, your earnings can increase to £13,000–£25,000 and senior travel agents can achieve over £40,000.

Benefits can include target-based commission and discounted holidays.

Related opportunities

- Holiday Representative p364
- Tour Guide/Manager p372
- Tourist Information Centre Assistant p373

Further information

Association of British Travel Agents Limited
www.abta.com

Institute of Travel and Tourism
www.itt.co.uk

Marketing, Advertising, Media, Print and Publishing

Do you consider yourself to be a great communicator? Are you interested in working in an exciting and often fast-paced environment with passionate, driven and ambitious individuals? If so, a career in this industry could be right for you. People who work in this sector are exceptionally motivated and are willing to put in long hours often on low starting wages because of their love of the job. You should have a great sense of creativity and imagination and be good at putting your ideas on paper, but you will often also need strong business acumen as many of your decisions will be made from an economic point of view as well as a creative one.

The jobs featured in this section are listed below. For similar jobs to the ones in this section turn to *Design, Arts and Crafts* on page 153 and *Performing Arts* on page 407.

ADVERTISING ACCOUNT EXECUTIVE

ENTRY LEVEL 5

Qualifications and courses

Given the highly competitive nature of the advertising sector, most entrants are graduates. Large agencies usually expect candidates to have a degree or HND. A range of courses is available at universities and colleges at HND, Foundation degree, Honours degree and postgraduate levels. Although employers consider graduates of all disciplines, those who have gained qualifications in a relevant subject such as advertising, marketing, English, communications or business/ management will be at a distinct advantage. The general entry requirements for a degree are 2 A levels/3 H grades and 5 GCSEs/National 5s (A*–C/A–C).

Entry without a degree is sometimes possible in smaller or specialist agencies. Applicants will be expected to have relevant work experience and it is likely that you will be employed in a junior administrative role whilst you work your way up to account executive level.

Work experience or volunteering work within a commercial context is an excellent way to develop your knowledge and build a network of industry contacts, crucial when securing employment. Vacation work, job shadowing or taking a sandwich degree course are all useful. Some larger agencies offer formal work experience or internships during the summer.

Post-university, you may seek a graduate training scheme offered by many larger agencies where you will be trained on the job by experienced professionals. Employers may encourage you to study for qualifications offered by the Chartered Institute of Marketing (CIM), the Institute of Practitioners in Advertising (IPA) and the Communication, Advertising and Marketing (CAM) Education Foundation whilst you work. These will ensure career progression and higher earnings.

What the work involves

You will plan, develop and oversee strategies for campaigns to suit different clients' requirements, working for advertising, PR or media agencies. It will be your responsibility to ensure that all the campaigns arrive in on budget and to schedule.

You will use a variety of different mediums to run campaigns from TV to newspapers, radio and direct mail to viral and online marketing. Social media work is an increasingly integral part of the job role.

Your work will involve liaising between clients and the agency staff, including designers and budget planners.

Type of person suited to this work

As much of your work involves discussions with clients and agency staff, you will need to be flexible with good communication skills. Having a well organised approach is essential because you could be running a number of campaigns at the same time.

You will need a strong creative flair and a resourceful attitude. A key ability will be to manage clients' campaigns within budget.

Being a confident team player with an enthusiastic attitude and strong negotiating skills is essential.

Working conditions

You will be based in an office, spending a lot of time at your computer, though at times you will be expected to travel to visit clients and attend meetings.

At times you will have to work under pressure to complete projects within limited time scales. You will work standard office hours but during busy periods you will have to work late if required.

Future prospects

It can be difficult to progress due to a lack of higher-level opportunities. The majority of agencies have fewer than 100 employees and competition for jobs is tough.

The speed and extent of your career progression will depend on the outcome of your different advertising strategies. With experience, it is possible to progress into a role as account manager and then to account director, where you would have control of the account management department. Another option would be to work as a freelancer or open your own agency.

Your training will be relevant to the related industries of marketing, market research, business or retail and commerce.

Advantages/disadvantages

The job is fast paced with hectic periods of work.

There are opportunities to meet and work with a wide range of people.

It is rewarding to create successful campaigns.

Money guide

Earnings vary according to employer and geographical location, with the highest salaries in London.

Starting as a graduate you can expect to earn £18,000–£25,000 a year.

An experienced account executive is likely to receive £30,000–£35,000.

Those employed at a senior level, as an account manager or account director, can achieve between £45,000 and £90,000.

Related opportunities

- Advertising Art Director p377
- Advertising Media Planner p379
- Marketing Manager/Director p388

Further information

Advertising Association
www.adassoc.org.uk

Communication, Advertising and Marketing Education Foundation
www.camfoundation.com

Institute of Practitioners in Advertising
www.ipa.co.uk

ADVERTISING ART DIRECTOR

ENTRY LEVEL 5

Qualifications and courses

While there are no specific entry requirements, art directors usually have an HND, degree or postgraduate qualification in graphic design, advertising design, illustration, advertising and marketing or fine art. Employers will consider graduates of other disciplines who can demonstrate knowledge of design and advertising, but gaining a qualification in a relevant subject will significantly increase your chances. If your degree subject is unrelated, you may decide to supplement your degree with a relevant postgraduate qualification.

For degree entry, students generally require at least 2 A levels/3 H grades, 5 GCSEs/National 5s (A*–C/A–C) and a portfolio of work. Foundation courses in an art-related subject are also available.

Work experience is an excellent way to develop your knowledge and build a network of industry contacts. Vacation work, job shadowing or taking a sandwich degree course are all useful ways to show evidence of your enthusiasm, your ability to offer new ideas and your teamwork skills. Employers also look for candidates with a strong portfolio of design work and ideas, which should include both print and digital work and proof of working with software packages such as Photoshop or Illustrator. Design & Art Direction (D&AD) run workshops in which participants develop relevant skills and build up a portfolio.

It can take a few years before securing your first job as you are normally required to establish a team of people first. Once employed, training is normally carried out on the job. Your employer may also encourage you to take a course offered by the Institute of Practitioners in Advertising (IPA) so as to remain up to date in a constantly evolving industry.

What the work involves

You will design and create effective brand styles and images for advertising campaigns in accordance with clients' requirements.

Working with specialist software, you will develop new designs, often at short notice, to convey the required mood or tone of a particular campaign. In close collaboration with colleagues, especially copywriters and reprographic specialists, you will make sure your ideas are realised.

You might also be involved in selecting photographers and other professionals to create additional visuals for use in a campaign.

Type of person suited to this work

You will need visual design skills and creative strengths but also the skills to develop commercial ideas. The capacity to adapt to a client's requirements is also important.

As you will be using software to create new designs, you will need to have up-to-date computer skills.

Much of your time will be spent working in a team so you will need excellent communication and people skills. Your ideas could be rejected or changed so a flexible yet confident attitude is essential.

It is important to be able to work to exacting standards, paying close attention to detail.

Working conditions

Most of your tasks will be office based, sometimes in a studio. Your job will also involve travelling to visit clients and attend shoots.

You will be seated for long periods at a workstation using a number of computers and you may often be on the phone.

The majority of your work will be done in normal office hours. However, there will be pressure to complete jobs as you near deadlines and at these times you will be expected to work late.

Future prospects

This is a highly competitive area of work to enter. Although newer agencies exist in some of the larger cities (Manchester, Bristol and Newcastle), the number of creative art directors employed is still low. Job opportunities are increasing at the fastest rate in digital/viral marketing.

Normally agencies hire a team consisting of a copywriter and an art director so finding a good partner is essential. You will start as a junior creative team member and then could progress to becoming a middleweight art director.

With experience you could move up to senior art director level. Some very established art directors go on to work on a freelance basis although this can be an often precarious way of earning a living given the industry's competitive nature.

Advantages/disadvantages

This job is rewarding as it offers individuals the chance to influence the images of major companies and brands.

The constant need to develop new ideas can be stressful at times.

Money guide

Starting salaries at junior level are around £18,000–£25,000.

With experience earnings can range from £25,000 to £50,000.

Those in senior positions can achieve a salary between £45,000 and £120,000.

Related opportunities

- Advertising Media Planner p379
- Copywriter p383
- Graphic Designer p161

Further information

Communication, Advertising and Marketing Education Foundation
www.camfoundation.com

Institute of Practitioners in Advertising
www.ipa.co.uk

ADVERTISING MEDIA BUYER

ENTRY LEVEL 5

Qualifications and courses

A career as an advertising media buyer is open to graduates of all degree or diploma disciplines. As a result of the media industry becoming more global, business qualifications and a commercial awareness are becoming increasingly valued, therefore a degree in a relevant subject such as marketing or communications, media studies, statistics or business management may increase your chances of employment. Entry to an HND is with 1 A level/2 H grades and 4 GCSEs/National 5s (A*–C/A–C). Requirements to study for a degree are 2 A levels/3 H grades and 5 GCSEs/National 5s (A*–C/A–C).

Building up a portfolio of work experience through work placements or volunteering will increase your chances of employment, whilst helping you to develop your skills and experience in media buying, negotiation and sales.

Few jobs are advertised within this fiercely competitive industry, therefore it may pay to make speculative and persistent applications or to accept other relevant posts in order to gain entry into the profession. Once you are in employment, some advertising and media agencies offer structured training programmes. Here you are likely to be recruited into a planner/buyer role in order to gain experience of the company's departments whilst being trained by senior professionals. There will be a focus on developing your IT and presentation skills at this stage.

Your work-based training may be supplemented by external instruction via seminars and workshops delivered by industry bodies such as the Media Research Group (MRG) and the Institute of Practitioners in Advertising (IPA).

What the work involves

Advertising media buyers research, identify and negotiate the purchase of media space (eg advertising time on television or radio).

Working for an advertising agency, you will work from a brief laid out by your clients, taking into consideration target audiences, media events and activities, schedules and budgetary constraints.

You will present proposals, advise creative teams, estimate costs and profits, and monitor and keep records of the progress of your media campaigns.

You will make media contacts and liaise with other media companies in order to get the best deal and most exposure on behalf of your client.

Type of person suited to this work

You should have a keen interest in media, marketing and advertising and be constantly thinking of new creative ways to approach your work. As you will need to have a good understanding of your target audiences and markets, you should also be interested in the reasons why people purchase certain products or use certain media channels.

You must have good communication skills as you will have to make presentations, draw up proposals and correspond with contacts on a regular basis. You should have strong organisational skills and be able to work under pressure and within tight deadlines.

You will need to have initiative, drive and be able to work in a team.

Working conditions

You will work around 40 hours a week, Monday to Friday. You may have to work longer hours to meet deadlines. Part-time work or flexible hours may be possible.

You will be mainly office based but as you gain experience you will spend more time meeting with clients, making presentations and discussing proposals. You may have to travel away from home with some overnight stays.

The majority of your correspondence with media owners and companies is conducted on the phone, by email or by socialising.

Future prospects

You will usually progress to a permanent position after 1 year in a junior role. Your promotions will depend largely on personal performance and successful campaigns. You may have to move between agencies in order to progress.

You can take postgraduate qualifications to increase your knowledge about specific aspects of your job such as business or marketing.

After 3–5 years you may gradually take on more account management responsibilities or you may take a position in data management or account planning.

Advantages/disadvantages

Advances and changes in the media industry mean that you will find new and exciting opportunities to work with multimedia technologies.

This is a highly competitive industry and your work may involve long and stressful hours.

Money guide

As a junior, your starting salary may be £18,000–£26,000.

With experience, your earnings may increase to between £26,000 and £35,000.

At a senior level you can achieve up to £50,000 a year.

Related opportunities

- Advertising Account Executive p376
- Market Research Executive p386
- Marketing Manager/Director p388

Further information

Account Planning Group
www.apg.org.uk

Institute of Practitioners in Advertising
www.ipa.co.uk

The Advertising Association
www.adassoc.org.uk

ADVERTISING MEDIA PLANNER

ENTRY LEVEL 5

Qualifications and courses

Although there are no minimum educational requirements for a role as an advertising media planner, competition is high and most entrants will have either an HND or a degree. Relevant subjects such as media studies, business management, marketing, advertising, operational research and English will increase your chances of securing employment. The general entry requirements for a degree are 2 A levels/3 H grades and 5 GCSEs/National 5s (A*–C/A–C).

Most agencies tend to require relevant work experience and undertaking a sandwich course can be a particular advantage. Work experience will help you to develop the necessary skills and knowledge vital to an advertising media planner, whilst also introducing you to industry contacts crucial in a fiercely competitive industry. Internships are also effective in demonstrating to potential employers that you have a history of strong interpersonal communication skills, a commercial flair and an ability to work with numbers.

Once in employment, you will normally be trained on the job by senior planners. New account planners may train with the Account Planning Group (APG) or the Market Research Society (MRS). At this stage of your career, your focus will be on gaining an understanding of audience research figures, how best to make use of IT resources and how to communicate presentations effectively. Alongside your internal training, employers may also encourage you to study for qualifications offered by the Institute of Practitioners in Advertising (IPA), the Communication, Advertising and Marketing (CAM) Education Foundation or the Media Research Group (MRG).

What the work involves

You will research public opinion and interest in a client's product or service to develop new advertising and media campaigns. Market research, both positive and negative, will form a starting point from which you will plan and develop new advertising strategies for your clients.

You will need to be very clear when interpreting your clients' intentions. The work will require close cooperation with your clients and your creative team in order to create strong and successful advertising.

Type of person suited to this work

As you will be developing new advertising ideas, you will need a high level of creativity.

To understand and make use of a range of facts and figures in support of your work, you will need an ability to interpret and analyse trends in data.

As you will have to make presentations to your clients and colleagues at progress meetings, excellent oral and written communication skills will be essential. Being self-motivated and confident is also important.

Good business skills are helpful and you will need to use clear verbal reasoning when stating your point of view.

Working conditions

Most of your work will be undertaken in an office or at clients' premises. You will be expected to dress formally and be well presented at all times.

Although you will mainly work normal office hours, you can expect to work overtime and at weekends during busy periods.

You will have to travel to attend meetings on a regular basis, perhaps staying overnight.

Future prospects

The majority of job opportunities in advertising are based in London, although the number of companies in other large cities is growing. Despite this, entry is highly competitive and trainee posts sparse. Realistically, account planning makes up only a very small part of the overall advertising/media sector.

If employed by one of the few larger companies, career progression is largely based on performance but is normally rapid with promotion to a senior or management position common after one year. Headhunting is also common so a good reputation is important.

With experience, you could work on a freelance basis or move into market research, design or management. Sometimes you can 'invent' new roles given the dynamic nature of the industry and eagerness to remain up to date with the ever evolving requirements of clients.

Advantages/disadvantages

This type of work can provide the opportunity to work for high-profile companies with a Europe-wide or global reach.

You will have to develop new ideas, often at relatively short notice.

This is a very competitive career and only the most determined will succeed.

Money guide

Starting salaries for a junior media planner range from £18,000 to £24,000 per year.

Experienced advertising media planners can earn between £25,000 and £45,000.

Those employed in the most senior positions can achieve £60,000–£80,000.

Related opportunities

- Market Research Executive p386
- Marketing Manager/Director p388
- Media Researcher p389

Further information

Account Planning Group
www.apg.org.uk

Communication, Advertising and Marketing Education Foundation
www.camfoundation.com

Institute of Practitioners in Advertising
www.ipa.co.uk

AGENT/LITERARY AGENT

ENTRY LEVEL 5

Qualifications and courses

Most entrants will have a degree but enthusiasm, good industry knowledge and the ability to make good contacts are equally important. For entry onto a degree course you will usually need a minimum of 2 A levels/3 H grades and 5 GCSEs/National 5s (A*–C/A–C).

Most entrants to this work will have previous experience and qualifications in related fields such as sales, business, music, performing arts or publishing.

It is also possible to start out as an assistant or administrator and then work your way up to an agent or manager.

Contract law knowledge and a second language may be useful in the negotiation of rights deals. Knowledge of the existing client lists, up-and-coming industry figures and working knowledge of the industry in which you wish to work will always be beneficial, for example as a literary agent you should have a strong knowledge of the genre of books you wish to specialise in (eg business books, children's fiction, commercial fiction, etc).

What the work involves

Agents represent and promote artists and creatives in the film, television, radio, theatre, music and publishing sectors. They can also play a similar role for sporting professionals. You will be expected to work proactively to enhance your client's career by securing work and negotiating to ensure that the client attains the best work at the highest fee.

Literary agents are responsible for assessing the quality and commercial potential of manuscripts submitted by authors. They will work with a selected author to create a more polished manuscript that would be marketable enough to send to publishers under their recommendation.

You will also have to develop publication and rights agreements with publishers and TV, radio and film producers on their behalf.

Type of person suited to this work

As you will be acting as the link between your client and the world they work in, you will need excellent communication skills. The ability to develop good contacts and a name for reliability is essential. It is also important to develop good working relationships with clients.

You should have a good head for business and an assertive approach will be helpful when it comes to agreeing contracts on behalf of clients.

You should have a good knowledge of the law and how it applies to your client's sector, as they will rely on you for professional advice in this area.

Working conditions

Agents are office based and can be self-employed or work for agencies.

Although, theoretically, they could work anywhere, most agents are based near London. Literary agents can also be found in Edinburgh, which is an important centre for the UK publishing industry.

Travel is common and you should expect to work 30–40 hours a week, including evenings and weekends, as some of your work will involve attending performances and social events to network and raise the profile of your clients.

Future prospects

This is an extremely competitive profession, made increasingly more difficult to gain employment in due to the rise in opportunities for digital and self-publishing meaning agents are less in demand. Agencies are constantly being set up but few stand the test of time. Most agencies, particularly literary agencies, are relatively small, although there are a few large ones. However publishers increasingly prefer to respond to new publication ideas through agents.

Your success will be determined partly by the standard of the clients you represent but, also, by the quality of the advice you can provide to them.

With sufficient experience you might have the opportunity to work abroad in entertainment and publishing hubs such as New York.

Advantages/disadvantages

You will have the satisfaction of supporting new artists and helping them to succeed.

As you will earn your income from commissions, you will be under pressure to identify and promote new artists.

Unsociable hours and extensive travelling can affect your personal life.

Money guide

Salaries vary widely according to the nature of the agent, the number of artists they work with and the success they have in their field.

Literary agents are paid commission which is usually between 10% and 25% of authors' earnings.

New entrants can expect to earn £15,000 in a large agency, progressing to £30,000 with experience.

Top agents with prestigious clients can earn in excess of £100,000.

Related opportunities

- Marketing Manager/Director p388
- Public Relations Officer p396
- Publisher/Commissioning Editor p397

Further information

Association of Authors' Agents
www.agentsassoc.co.uk

The Agents' Association (Great Britain)
www.agents-uk.com

AUTHOR/ SCRIPTWRITER

ENTRY LEVEL 1

Qualifications and courses

There are no specific qualifications required in order become an author, although it is important to note that many writers are graduates in a relevant degree subject, such as English language, literature or creative writing. There are a variety of courses available that are designed to improve a writer's technique, ranging from evening classes to a postgraduate course, however it is style, originality of ideas, imagination and use of language that is the most important aspect of this profession.

It is a fiercely competitive industry and few authors reach the level of commercial success required to earn a living wage. For this reason it is often necessary to obtain a second job.

If you wish to write for the media, short courses in script or creative writing, practical television or film may be useful. Work experience within the media industry may also help if you intend to write for television, film or radio. The BBC offers work experience schemes for budding writers.

Competitions may help you to break into the profession and attending conventions such as the Winchester Writers' Conference or Crimfest, alongside membership of The Writers' Guild of Great Britain, are useful ways to network. Arts Council grants may also be available to new authors for work in literature and drama.

What the work involves

Authors write the text for books, magazines, IT resources and more. This can involve developing initial ideas to create a complete piece, or simply rewriting sections.

Scriptwriters create text for TV, film, radio and theatre productions.

As part of the work, you will undertake research using resources such as the internet and libraries.

Authors often specialise in a particular subject area such as technical writing, science, medicine, cookery, travel or education. A small number of authors write and publish creative works of fiction, poetry or drama.

Type of person suited to this work

It is essential to have command of the English language and the ability to write with your audience in mind. Having a good imagination and a creative approach is important.

As you will be pitching project ideas to the industry, you will need strong communication skills. Whilst commissions are exciting you should be resilient enough to handle rejection.

As you will be working with publishers and/or agents, it might be useful to have some business awareness and numeracy skills are very helpful when working out royalties against advancements.

You will be working independently a lot of the time and this can mean long periods of solitary work so you should be self-motivated and committed to the job.

Working conditions

As the majority of authors and scriptwriters are self-employed, you will usually work from home. Most of your time will be spent researching and writing, whilst sitting at a computer for long periods.

It may be necessary to juggle deadlines with other part-time employment taken on to supplement income. Most authors/scriptwriters are employed on a project-by-project basis, so the work provides very little job security.

Future prospects

Making a living as a professional author can be challenging. Having an established network of contacts helps and you must look for opportunities to publicise yourself. A variety of support groups and courses exist to help people develop their writing skills and are important ways to remain up to date with new technologies and programs available.

Self-publishing is steadily becoming more common amongst new writers wishing to reach a wider audience and demonstrate their motivation and pro-active nature to potential agencies.

At present, short dramas for radio broadcast are actively sought and many radio and television companies are happy to accept unsolicited scripts to read.

Advantages/disadvantages

This type of work can provide the satisfaction of being creative and seeing your work in print and in the public domain.

Not all authors succeed in publishing their work and you might need to take on other types of work to make a living.

Money guide

Earnings vary depending on the nature of the writing project, your experience, and your popularity as a writer.

Publishers may give a one-off payment for a piece of work or will pay you royalties.

Salaries can be £15,000–£30,000 for authors employed in a commercial environment but you may have a higher income if you are well known.

For freelance writers in screen and television, you will negotiate your own fees but salaries at a senior level can reach £120,000.

Related opportunities

- Copywriter p383
- Journalist p385
- Technical Author/Medical Writer p399

Further information

BBC Writersroom
www.bbc.co.uk/writersroom

Society of Authors
www.societyofauthors.org

Writers and Artists
www.writersandartists.co.uk

COPY EDITOR/SUB-EDITOR/ PROOFREADER

ENTRY LEVEL 6

Qualifications and courses

Although there are no set formal entry qualifications, most copy editors are graduates. Relevant degree subjects such as English, publishing studies, media and journalism will provide you with the basic skills required by the industry and you will need at least 2 A levels/3 H grades and 5 GCSEs/National 5s (A*–C/A–C) for degree entry. For financial journalism, a business studies degree would be useful and to work in technical publishing a science-related degree is recommended. Studying for a postgraduate qualification in publishing may also increase your chances of employment.

Entry with an HND or Foundation degree alone is rare, unless candidates can provide evidence of an aptitude for the work and/or some highly relevant experience.

Candidates may first be taken on as an editorial assistant or trainee before working your way up to copy editor. Building a portfolio of work and experience is very important during this early stage of your career. In order to secure employment as a trainee, it is likely that you will need pre-entry experience. Working on your university magazine or time spent in a bookshop or library are invaluable as employers often seek those candidates who can demonstrate their enthusiasm and knowledge of the English language, good communication skills and great attention to detail. This also allows you to build crucial contacts within a highly competitive industry.

The Society for Editors and Proofreaders (SfEP) and the Publishing Training Centre offer introductory and advanced courses on topics such as copy editing and grammar skills, allowing you to remain up to date with new developments in technology. The National Council for the Training of Journalists also offers an introductory sub-editing qualification.

What the work involves

Copy editors prepare manuscripts for publication by checking for grammatical and punctuation errors, spelling mistakes and inconsistencies in style. You might also be responsible for checking the legality of the text.

Sub-editors are copy editors who work in newspapers and magazines. You may also create headlines and captions and manipulate text to fit a word count.

Proofreaders carry out the final quality checks on texts, including e-books now, before publication. You will use a recognised set of symbols and normally mark changes on a hard copy, but sometimes make alterations on screen using specialist software.

Type of person suited to this work

As you will be responsible for preparing texts for publication, you will pay great attention to detail. An excellent knowledge of the English language and strong writing and communication skills are expected. Patience and a methodical approach to your work are also helpful.

If you are working in-house for a publishing or other company, you will need good teamworking skills. In addition you will need to be able to deal tactfully with people, for example when explaining changes to authors' manuscripts.

The ability to manage budgets is useful, as is the ability to work to tight deadlines and cope with pressure.

Working conditions

These jobs tend to be largely solitary. Most copy editors work within offices or are self-employed and work from home. You can spend some time attending meetings with authors, designers, printers, illustrators and colleagues.

At the busiest times you might have to work late to meet copy or production deadlines, but mostly you will work normal working hours.

Future prospects

This is a very competitive area and many copy editors start off in an administrative or related role and work their way up.

It may be necessary for in-house copy editors to change their job frequently to aid career progression. With experience you could become a project manager or commission new publications.

With the rise of digital and self-publishing, copy editors who work on a freelance basis are increasingly in demand.

Advantages/disadvantages

The work provides the satisfaction of shaping and improving the style and tone of manuscripts.

You will work with many different types of people.

As you will be making sure a publication is produced on time, this can be a high-pressured job.

Money guide

Starting salaries are between £16,000 and £22,000.

Salaries for experienced editors employed in-house vary between £23,000 and £40,000.

The most senior editors can earn up to £60,000.

Freelance rates vary between £12 and £25 an hour, with higher rates for more complex project management editorial work.

As a freelancer you may charge a page or word rate.

Related opportunities

- Copywriter p383
- Journalist p385
- Publisher/Commissioning Editor p397

Further information

National Union of Journalists
www.nuj.org.uk

Society for Editors and Proofreaders
www.sfep.org.uk

COPYWRITER

ENTRY LEVEL 6

Qualifications and courses

There are no formal requirements for this profession but most entrants have a degree or HND. Students generally require at least 2 A levels/3 H grades and 5 GCSEs/ National 5s (A*–C/A–C) to get a place on a degree course and relevant degree subjects, such as advertising design, English, public relations or media studies, will increase your chances of employment. A postgraduate qualification in copywriting or creative advertising can be useful for graduates without a relevant academic background.

You will require determination to enter this highly competitive industry and you are likely to have to complete several unpaid work experience placements before being taken on.

The most common entry route involves producing a high-quality portfolio and presenting this to agencies in the hope that they might offer you a work placement. Some employers often value high quality and innovative portfolios over qualifications. Given that entry-level jobs and graduate training schemes are rarely advertised, you will need to ensure your portfolio makes you stand out. Occasionally, employers may attend graduate shows or seek out talent via competitions and showcases such as the Design & Art Direction (D&AD) New Blood Exhibition.

Once employed, you will usually be hired in a pair, ie a copywriter and an art director. You will learn on the job from experienced professionals but you may also be encouraged to study for industry recognised qualifications throughout your career offered by the Institute of Practitioners in Advertising (IPA), the Communication Advertising and Marketing (CAM) Education Foundation and the Design & Art Direction (D&AD).

What the work involves

Copywriters create informative, well-constructed text (or 'copy') on a wide range of subjects, from a range of perspectives and for a variety of audiences.

Advertising copywriters produce text for TV, film, radio, press and internet advertisements. You will create copy for websites, company publications, direct mail, brochures and product information guides.

Design companies, sales promotion organisations and other companies employ copywriters to write text that promotes their services or products and helps to increase sales.

Type of person suited to this work

As you will be writing copy for a range of uses, you will require excellent writing skills, a strong creative flair and a good imagination. The ability to describe a subject concisely is also important.

In discussing innovative ideas with your colleagues and clients, you will make valuable use of your oral and written communication skills. You will have to be flexible and willing to alter what you think are good ideas to meet clients' requirements.

It is essential to have good organisational skills, to be able to work well under pressure and to meet tight deadlines.

Working conditions

Many copywriters work on a freelance basis for a number of employers. In-house copywriters will work 9am–5pm from Monday to Friday, within an office or studio environment.

You will spend long periods of time sitting typing, which can be tiring. You will also be expected to attend client meetings, which may involve overnight stays. You will have to work long hours to meet project deadlines, which can be stressful.

Advertising copywriters normally work with an art director, who creates the visual aspect of the campaign.

Future prospects

There are interesting opportunities available as an increasing number of organisations find freelance copywriters online via established sites.

Competition is fierce but with good contacts, a strong writing style and knowledge of your market, it is possible to make a living.

With experience, some copywriters become freelancers or set up agencies in partnership with other creatives. Others go on to work in related areas such as public relations and publishing.

Advantages/disadvantages

This job provides the satisfaction of seeing your work in print and in the public domain.

You will be working alongside imaginative colleagues, which can be stimulating.

Copywriting can be stressful because of the need to produce new ideas to tight deadlines.

There may be some job instability if working on a self-employed basis.

Money guide

Starting salaries are around £18,000–£22,000.

With experience, you could earn £25,000–£40,000.

Senior level salaries can range between £45,000 and £100,000.

Self-employed copywriters negotiate their own rates.

Related opportunities

- Author/Scriptwriter p381
- Journalist p385
- Technical Author/Medical Writer p399

Further information

Institute of Copywriting
www.inst.org/copy

Institute of Practitioners in Advertising
www.ipa.co.uk

EVENTS AND EXHIBITION ORGANISER

ENTRY LEVEL 6

Qualifications and courses

Whilst there are no set entry requirements for this profession, many entrants hold degrees and/or postgraduate qualifications in a variety of disciplines. For entry to a degree course, you will need at least 2 A levels/3 H grades and 5 GCSEs/National 5s (A*–C/A–C), including English and Maths. Relevant degree courses include events management, conference and exhibition management, and hospitality management. A Diploma in Hospitality is also available and a postgraduate qualification in events management may be recommended if your first degree is unrelated.

The Northern Council for Further Education Certificate in Events Management is also relevant, and is good if you want to work at a supervisory level or if you are already in the industry and wish to develop your career.

The best advantage you can have when you are looking to enter the industry is to gain as much experience as you can of organising events as employers highly value those candidates who can demonstrate their organisation, time management and problem-solving skills. Try to help with the organisation of charity events, local festivals or university society outings as this will not only develop your skills but also provide you with crucial industry contacts useful when seeking work.

Once you are in the industry, you will experience a combination of on-the-job training from experienced professionals and external instruction. Your employer may encourage you to train in courses such as planning techniques, marketing, customer care, sales and sponsorship and crowd safety offered by industry recognised bodies such as the Chartered Institute of Marketing (CIM) or the Society of Event Organisers (SEO).

What the work involves

As an events and exhibition organiser, you will be planning and organising events of varying sizes and ensuring that they run to plan on the day. You could find yourself organising anything from conferences, seminars and meetings to parties, ceremonies or weddings.

The nature of your role will depend on the event itself, but you might be researching, planning, marketing the event, setting the budget, and sorting out all of the little details that go into planning an event.

Hours can be late and involve working at weekends – but you may get to attend a free party or 2!

Type of person suited to this work

You need to be incredibly well organised. Work can be tough and stressful, so you need energy and stamina: you should relish taking on a heavy workload, not crumple beneath it.

You should be a team player, an effective communicator and reliable. More often than not you will be organising events that aim to give people fun experiences, an attitude you should also exude at work.

You need to be creative and have a good imagination, but also have a business mind. Your project management and problem-solving skills should be very good, and you must be able to market, sell and negotiate.

Working conditions

You will be extremely busy and rushing to and from various locations.

You will usually work office hours, although additional hours are common when events require extra last-minute work.

Your time will be divided between the office, events venues and client meetings. You may well have to travel away from home, sometimes abroad.

You will be working both indoors and outdoors, and may find yourself in hotels, museums, castles, showgrounds – the list is endless!

Future prospects

By starting off in roles such as assistant events organiser, you are paving the way and can aim towards positions such as event organiser or manager. From this level you can progress to event director, or even start up your own company.

It is often necessary to move company more than once to progress in this industry.

Advantages/disadvantages

This is an exciting job, and the sense of achievement when an event you have planned is a success is a great feeling.

Planning an event can be stressful, and you might have to work flat out to meet deadlines and make your event a success, sacrificing your evenings and weekends in the process.

Money guide

As you start out, you might earn between £18,000 and £25,000.

With experience this can grow to between £25,000 and £45,000.

Within a senior role, you can expect to earn £50,000–£70,000 a year.

Your earnings may increase as a result of performance-related pay. Commission and bonuses are fairly common within this profession.

Related opportunities

- Catering/Restaurant Manager/Maître d'Hôtel p121
- Entertainment Manager p362
- Hotel Manager p126

Further information

Association of British Professional Conference Organisers
www.abpco.org

JOURNALIST

ENTRY LEVEL 5

Qualifications and courses

The most common route into this career is with pre-entry qualifications. The National Council for the Training of Journalists (NCTJ), the Broadcast Journalism Training Council (BJTC) and the Periodicals Training Council (PTC) all accredit HNDs, Foundation degrees, degrees and postgraduate courses. Taking a course that has been accredited will demonstrate your commitment to the profession and if you have an unrelated degree you must supplement it with an accredited 1-year or fast-track postgraduate conversion course.

The NCTJ offers the Diploma in Journalism, a new qualification aiming to prepare trainees for multimedia journalism, as well as distance-learning courses in both newspaper and magazine journalism. Those looking to work in the magazine sector could take professional qualifications from the Professional Publishers Association (PPA).

Those with 18 months' work experience who have gained the Diploma in Journalism can take the NCTJ's National Certificate Examination (NCE) which enables candidates to achieve senior status as a journalist.

The industry is highly competitive and there are limited opportunities on graduate training schemes. It is advisable to get as much work experience as possible, either within the industry or for student newspapers and magazines, in order to build up a portfolio of your writing and establish contacts. Employers value candidates with strong communication skills, good grammar and attention to detail. Web-editing skills along with a social media presence is useful, and setting up your own blog is a good way to start developing a portfolio. Broadcast journalism is fiercely competitive and entrants should have a strong show reel and work experience in student or community media.

Membership of the National Union of Journalists (NUJ) is recommended as it advertises work experience placements, job opportunities and training courses.

What the work involves

Journalists research and write stories on subjects such as current affairs, business, health and culture. Broadcast journalists also present these features on radio, television or the internet.

These stories can immediately become live news articles or features for local and national newspapers, magazines, TV, radio and online broadcasts.

You will be planning, writing and editing articles in accordance with a house style, usually to very tight deadlines.

Type of person suited to this work

As you will be producing articles on a regular basis, you will need to thrive on working under pressure.

Strong written and oral communication skills are essential for this job and broadcast journalists should have a clear and professional voice.

You should be a highly organised multi-tasker with a good instinct for a potential story and the ability to undertake research through interviews and contacts. You will be expected to research difficult stories and meet hostile people, which can be stressful.

Working conditions

Your work will be dictated by the story you are following. You could visit a range of locations in the working day, often at short notice as news stories unfold.

You will have to work long, sometimes irregular hours in order to meet publication deadlines, including public holidays.

While you may be part of a wider team, you could work alone for much of the time, or in the company of a photographer. If freelancing, you will have to take the initiative on stories and work patterns could be irregular.

Future prospects

This is a highly competitive area to enter and many people undertake unpaid work experience before securing a job. Approximately a third of all journalists work freelance. Many journalists started work as freelancers to establish their reputations.

It is possible to cross over from newspaper/magazine journalism into broadcast journalism as a reporter or presenter.

Advantages/disadvantages

You will create features that could be read, heard or seen by thousands of people – often beyond the UK.

This profession offers exciting, varied work.

Owing to tight deadlines, you will have to regularly produce work under pressure, and deal with potentially difficult people.

Money guide

Starting salaries for trainees are usually £12,000–£18,000.

An experienced newspaper or magazine journalist can expect to earn £21,700–£39,000.

In broadcast journalism, you can achieve up to £40,000.

Newspaper/magazine editors and television newsreaders can receive in excess of £85,000.

Related opportunities

- Copywriter p383
- Media Researcher p389
- Newspaper/Magazine/Web Editor p391

Further information

Broadcast Journalism Training Council
www.bjtc.org.uk

National Council for the Training of Journalists
www.nctj.com

National Union of Journalists
www.nuj.org.uk

MARKET RESEARCH EXECUTIVE

ENTRY LEVEL 5

Qualifications and courses

There are no set qualifications for this role but most employers will expect you to hold a relevant HND or degree. Useful subjects are those which develop skills in communication and analysis, such as English, maths, marketing, psychology, statistics, business management and social sciences. If you wish to take on specialist industrial market research positions, a degree in the subject most linked to that industry is an advantage, for example in engineering or science. A postgraduate qualification may improve your chances of employment and later career prospects, although it is not essential.

Employers also perceive an outgoing personality and enthusiasm for the job to be as important as academic qualifications.

Competition for places on graduate training schemes is fierce and you may consider applying for research assistant posts before working your way up. Pre-entry voluntary or vacation work experience in research, statistical data analysis or interview techniques is often desired by employers as they like candidates who can show evidence of good interpersonal skills, analytical and numerical abilities, a business awareness and effective teamwork.

Once employed, you will receive a combination of on-the-job training and external instruction. The Market Research Society (MRS) offers the Advanced Certificate in Market and Social Research Practice and, at a higher level, the Diploma in Market and Social Research Practice for those with experience in the industry. Once candidates have completed the Diploma, they are eligible for full membership of the MRS. An NVQ in Marketing (Levels 2–4) is also available and the Social Research Association (SRA) runs short courses on survey design and quantitative data analysis, useful to ensure continuing professional development (CPD).

What the work involves

You will undertake research to obtain people's opinions on specific products, services or issues and then analyse the results.

Developing surveys to analyse public opinion on a wide range of subjects or issues will be part of your job. You may also interview small groups of people, known as focus groups or panels, to assess their views on a specific topic in more detail.

You will compile the results of your research in the form of detailed reports or summary analyses to be used by your clients, businesses and other organisations.

Type of person suited to this work

This job is all about people and their opinions, so verbal communication skills are essential. You will also need strong writing skills to create surveys, plan interviews and write reports.

You will need to understand exactly what your client wants to know and think up ways to get this information. A logical and deductive approach to your work is important. You should be interested in human psychology and behaviour.

Also, as you will be working with a lot of paperwork, you will need to be well organised. Confidence working with numbers will be useful in helping you to perform statistical analyses. Being aware of the marketplace and what sells is also important.

Working conditions

Market researchers work from offices and attend meetings, presentations and interviews. You could work in a specialist market research agency or a marketing department within a larger organisation. Some market researchers work freelance.

The job can involve frequent daily and overnight stays. You will usually work standard office hours, Monday to Friday, with occasional overtime if necessary to meet project deadlines.

Future prospects

The market research industry is worth well over £1 billion a year. As well as businesses, many other organisations increasingly depend on market researchers to provide up-to-the-minute facts and figures concerning public opinion on everything from train services to trainers!

After gaining experience as a market research interviewer, you can move up to research executive, and then progress to senior research executive.

With sufficient experience you could enter a senior management role or set up your own agency.

Advantages/disadvantages

The role is interesting as you will work on a variety of projects and meet many different types of people.

The public may not want to speak to you and getting the required information needed may be difficult.

This job is fast paced and can involve high levels of pressure near deadlines.

Money guide

Starting salaries are typically between £18,000 and £25,000.

With experience, earnings increase to £25,000–£35,000.

A very experienced market researcher employed in a senior position could achieve £40,000 to £80,000.

Related opportunities

- Marketing Manager/Director p388
- Media Researcher p389
- Statistician p511

Further information

ESOMAR

www.esomar.org

Market Research Society

www.mrs.org.uk

MARKETING ASSISTANT/ EXECUTIVE

ENTRY LEVEL 5

Qualifications and courses

Marketing is a highly competitive industry and while you may become an assistant/executive with relevant work experience or a dynamic personality, you will have an advantage if you are a graduate. A degree, Foundation degree or HND in a relevant subject such as marketing, communications or business/management may improve your chances of either initially securing employment or progressing within a company. Entry requirements vary between universities but are usually 2 A levels/3 H grades and 5 GCSEs/National 5s (A*–C/A–C).

BTEC offers the Certificate in Principles of Marketing (Levels 2–3) which may be useful. School leavers and graduates of non-related disciplines could take the Introductory or Professional Certificate in Marketing provided by the Chartered Institute of Marketing (CIM).

Owing to the competitive nature of this sector, you are advised to undertake vacation work or an internship in order to build a network of contacts and develop your skills and experience. You could also take on administrator or assistant positions within a company's marketing department in order to work your way up from there.

Once employed, perhaps in a graduate training scheme, you will normally experience a combination of on-the-job training from experienced professionals and external instruction. Employers may encourage you to study for industry recognised qualifications provided by accredited bodies such as the CIM or the Communication, Advertising and Marketing (CAM) Education Foundation to improve your career and promotion prospects.

What the work involves

Marketing assistants/executives (under the direction of a marketing manager or director) need to promote and raise the profile of ideas, products and services for their clients or organisation.

You will use a variety of techniques to do this including writing press releases and brochures, advertising, developing promotional material for the web or for TV and radio, poster campaigns or events. Use of social media is becoming increasingly important within this field.

You will need to conduct market research which could involve writing surveys and setting up consumer focus groups. You will network (sourcing new clients and gaining contacts) regularly and update customer databases with new client details.

Type of person suited to this work

You must be commercially aware and in-tune with consumer behaviour. It is important to understand what motivates people. Imagination and initiative are essential when developing innovative marketing techniques.

Excellent communication and persuasion skills are necessary. You need to be confident, adaptable and ambitious in order to succeed.

You should be organised as many projects will require you to multi-task, working quickly and to a high standard.

Working conditions

You will spend most of your time in an office working normal hours from Monday to Friday. However, you might need to work evenings and weekends when running events and campaigns. Most companies will provide you with time off in lieu for working overtime.

You will travel to meet clients and attend exhibitions or launches. You will probably be expected to dress formally.

Future prospects

The majority of marketing vacancies are centred in cities such as London, Manchester and Birmingham.

You will work either in-house with a company or for a specialist agency.

With 3–10 years' experience you may be promoted to marketing manager. You could also choose to focus on a particular area such as social media, public relations or advertising. It may be necessary to transfer to a new company in order to increase your chances of promotion.

Advantages/disadvantages

You will be inspired working alongside lively and creative people.

It is rewarding when your campaigns are successful and impact the public or profit your company.

A deadline-driven environment can be stressful and demanding.

You could have many campaigns running at once which can be difficult to balance.

Money guide

Salaries vary with geographical location and tend to be higher in large cities.

As a marketing assistant, you can expect to earn £18,000–£22,000.

Salaries rise to between £25,000 and £40,000 as you gain experience.

Marketing directors can earn in excess of £50,000 a year.

Salaries tend to be lower in the public sector. Bonuses can increase your earnings.

Related opportunities

- Advertising Account Executive p376
- Marketing Manager/Director p388
- Public Relations Officer p396

Further information

Chartered Institute of Marketing
www.cim.co.uk

Communication, Advertising and Marketing Education Foundation
www.camfoundation.com

MARKETING MANAGER/ DIRECTOR

ENTRY LEVEL 6

Qualifications and courses

For entry to management positions, employers want to see a good track record, sufficient industry knowledge and previous experience in marketing. Most managers begin as marketing assistants or executives and work their way up to senior level.

Most employers prefer candidates to have completed the 1-year Professional Diploma in Marketing from the Chartered Institute of Marketing (CIM). This course is aimed at those wishing to pursue marketing management and you will need either a degree in a related subject, such as marketing or business studies, or the CIM Professional Certificate in Marketing in order to apply.

If you want to work at a strategic, directorate level then a postgraduate qualification may be useful. Your employer may sponsor you if you opt to study for the Chartered Postgraduate Diploma in Marketing offered by the CIM. Entry requirements are a degree in marketing or the CIM Professional Diploma in Marketing, and significant experience working as a manager.

Alternatively, the Institute of Direct and Digital Marketing (IDM) accredits relevant courses such as the IDM Diploma in Direct and Digital Marketing and an MSc in Marketing Management.

NVQs/SVQs in Marketing (Levels 2–4) are also available from City & Guilds.

What the work involves

You will analyse markets and evaluate the competition in order to develop marketing strategies that will promote and increase sales of products, services or ideas.

You will be responsible for post-campaign evaluations, assessing past strategies and overseeing product branding. This information will help you to come up with innovative campaigns in the future. You will also be in charge of product development and budgeting.

You will oversee a team of assistants and executives.

Type of person suited to this work

In order to work at a strategic level, you must have vision and be a confident and creative decision-maker. You should be diplomatic and persuasive in order to manage your team effectively.

Good business sense and consumer knowledge are essential. You need to have excellent communication and presentation skills. Enthusiasm and imagination will help you to stay ahead of your competitors.

Analytical and numerical skills are also important as you will be responsible for a project's success and ensuring it is within budget. You must be able to cope under pressure.

Working conditions

You will usually work a 37-hour week, Monday to Friday, but you may often work overtime in order to meet deadlines.

As the manager of a campaign you will be in regular contact with the press, printers and designers and will need to travel often. International travel may also be required and you may spend long periods of time away from home. Otherwise you will be office based, developing strategies and supervising staff.

Future prospects

With 10–15 years of experience you may be promoted from marketing manager to marketing director.

Taking postgraduate qualifications or moving to another company could increase your chance of promotion.

Directors may choose to become self-employed or work as freelance marketing consultants. Alternatively, if you work for a global organisation you may choose to take up a leadership role in an office overseas.

Advantages/disadvantages

It is rewarding to see your strategies and campaigns increase profits and raise awareness for your clients.

You have the freedom to be creative and innovative in your role.

Clients might dislike your ideas and can be difficult to please.

Working overtime to meet deadlines is stressful and demanding.

Money guide

The starting salary for a marketing manager is around £25,000.

As you gain experience in the role, your earnings can increase up to £40,000.

Senior managers and marketing directors can achieve in excess of £50,000.

Earnings are higher if you work in the private rather than public sector and many companies offer additional benefits such as bonuses, medical insurance and a company car.

Related opportunities

- Advertising Account Executive p376
- Marketing Assistant/Executive p387
- Public Relations Officer p396

Further information

Chartered Institute of Marketing
www.cim.co.uk

Communication, Advertising and Marketing Education Foundation
www.camfoundation.com

MEDIA RESEARCHER ENTRY LEVEL 5

Qualifications and courses

There are no formal educational requirements to become a media researcher but owing to the competitive nature of the industry, many entrants have a degree or HND in a relevant subject, such as journalism, English, media studies and broadcasting. Depending on the type of programmes you will be working on, a degree in a specialist subject, such as politics, history or legal studies may be useful. Typical entry requirements for a degree course include 2 A levels/3 H grades and 5 GCSEs/National 5s (A*–C/A–C).

Those without a degree could start their career as a production assistant or runner and work their way up to become a researcher. Personal qualities, confidence and relevant skills are often valued as much as academic qualifications.

Pre-entry work experience is essential as it helps you develop your skills and build crucial industry contacts. Volunteering for student film/TV productions, hospital or community radio stations, local newspapers or TV/radio production companies would be useful. Some media production courses offer their students the chance to gain practical skills via a variety of work placements. A good knowledge of current affairs and media practice would also be an advantage.

Many researchers gain experience as print or broadcast journalists first. If you have undertaken research in a non-media field, such as social or political research, then your skills would also be relevant.

You should continue to update your skills throughout your career by taking short courses offered by film schools, private training companies, TRC media and the Producers' Alliance for Cinema and Television (PACT).

What the work involves

Researchers develop TV and radio programmes and documentary films by gathering and checking information on specific subjects, people or places.

You will use the internet and phone, conduct face-to-face interviews and visit different locations to do your research. It will be your job to research guests and programme contributors as well as to find relevant images, film clips and music. You could also write and edit programme scripts.

You will brief the production team on the specific subjects covered by your research in preparation for filming.

Type of person suited to this work

The ability to find accurate, relevant information quickly is central to this role. You will need to be creative and resourceful in order to find the best story angles possible. Strong IT skills are required.

You should be persistent, confident and an excellent communicator. You will work to strict deadlines and must be able to stay calm under pressure. A flexible approach will help you balance varied tasks and unsocial hours.

Organisational skills are also important. As you will be responsible for gaining permission to access and make use of information, you will need a clear understanding of the law.

The ability to network and build good relationships with contacts is essential.

Working conditions

You will be based in offices or studios to undertake desk research. You will also spend time on research trips to locations in the UK or overseas. A driving licence would be useful.

The hours tend to be long and it is likely that you will have to work weekends and evenings on a regular basis.

Future prospects

While this is a competitive area to get into, researchers are employed in many areas of the media including radio, production companies, TV and film companies. Many opt to work freelance and hence, there is strong competition for work.

Researchers are currently being employed less in some broadcasting companies due to the introduction of assistant producers. However, those employed are increasingly being given more hands-on responsibilities.

With experience, you could progress into a role as an assistant producer and then on to working as a producer/ programme director. Many researchers work freelance, getting paid on a contract-by-contract basis.

Some specialise in areas such as documentaries on wildlife, architecture, social history or travel, whilst others concentrate on picture research.

Advantages/disadvantages

You will have to work long and often unsocial hours, which can affect your personal life.

You could get the opportunity to travel to a range of places.

Money guide

Starting salaries are usually around £19,000 a year.

An experienced media researcher can expect to earn £29,000–£32,500.

Many researchers work on a freelance basis and could receive £650 a week, depending on their employer and the number of hours worked.

Related opportunities

- Archivist/Records Manager p326
- Historian p331
- Journalist p385

Further information

Creative Skillset
www.creativeskillset.org

TRC media
www.trcmedia.org

MODEL

ENTRY LEVEL 1

Qualifications and courses

There are no formal entry qualifications to become a model but you will need to possess the right 'look' and modelling agencies will expect to see a portfolio of photographs before taking you on. You should not have to pay an upfront fee to join an agency and be wary of paying for portfolio pictures; most reputable agencies will cover these costs if they think you have potential.

Female fashion models should be at least 5 feet 8 inches (1.72m) tall and should measure no more than 34–24–34 inches (86–61–86cm). Male fashion models should be at least 6 feet (1.83m) tall and have a 38–40 inch chest (97–102cm) and a 30–32 inch waist (76–81cm). However, some photographic models are required to be smaller or larger than the usual sizes, depending on employer requirements.

Your agency may send you on courses which focus on diet, health, deportment, fashion coordination, grooming, catwalk turns and movements, photographic modelling techniques and how to work with agents. Some independent modelling schools provide similar courses although they do not offer any guarantee of work.

You will need to be licensed by your local Education and Welfare Authority in the event that your modelling career takes off before the legal school leaving age.

What the work involves

You could be involved in different types of modelling, such as fashion, photographic or demonstration work. You could work in a studio, on location outdoors, at fashion shows or at events such as car shows or conventions.

It is necessary to build a good portfolio of your work and establish a good reputation within the industry.

Your job will be to show off new clothing or products to their best advantage in order to help potential customers visualise them being worn or in use.

Type of person suited to this work

This is a very competitive area to find work. You will have to be determined and prepared to deal with disappointment if contracts do not come your way.

Most fashion model agencies have set physical requirements that you will have to meet before you are accepted onto their books. There is also scope for models with one particularly good feature, such as hands, feet, eyes or hair, to model specific items.

During your work you will meet different types of people, so you will have to be confident and have good communication skills.

Working conditions

The places you will work will depend on the type of modelling that you do and the nature of the contracts you are offered. You might work indoors within a studio, or you could be on location doing catalogue work. This can involve many hours of work to get the correct shot.

You will be on your feet for long periods at a time and will always have to look your best, even if you have been travelling.

The work can be physically demanding; hours spent walking back and forth and posing in awkward positions for long periods can take their toll.

Future prospects

Only the most successful models are always in work. Most are self-employed and have to take on alternate temporary or part-time work when necessary in order to boost earnings.

To build your reputation, you will have to create a portfolio of work using photos from previous contracts. Your portfolio will need to have a distinct edge to help you win contracts and work.

While top models are very famous and can be rich, there are hundreds more who work for smaller companies and businesses who may earn a lot less. Most models finish their career in their early 30s.

Advantages/disadvantages

Only a few models get the top contracts.

You could get to travel around the world.

You will be posing for long periods which could be tiring.

Modelling can be a very glamorous and confidence-boosting career although you will also have to take criticism.

Modelling can be quite a short career.

Money guide

You will probably be self-employed so your earnings will depend on your success in finding regular, well-paid work.

Most agencies keep 20% of earnings as commission.

You can expect to start on around £50–£200 per booking, rising to up to £1,000 per booking for models with experience.

Models working for particular fashion houses can earn between £12,000 and £18,000 a year.

Well-known models can earn very high wages.

Related opportunities

- Beauty Consultant p430
- Fashion Designer/Milliner p157
- Wardrobe Assistant p427

Further information

Alba Model Information
www.albamodel.info

Association of Model Agents
www.associationofmodelagents.org

Equity
www.equity.org.uk

London College of Fashion
www.arts.ac.uk/fashion

NEWSPAPER/MAGAZINE/WEB EDITOR

ENTRY LEVEL 5

Qualifications and courses

Most newspaper, magazine or web editors have extensive journalistic experience. To become a journalist you usually need an HND, Foundation degree or degree accredited by the National Council for the Training of Journalists (NCTJ) or the Periodicals Training Council (PTC). Alternatively, you could complete an unrelated degree, followed by an accredited 1-year postgraduate course or a fast-track postgraduate course lasting 18–20 weeks. Editors of specialist publications may have qualifications or experience in that particular field, for example a degree in science or art.

The Diploma in Journalism or other distance-learning courses in newspaper and magazine journalism from the NCTJ and professional qualifications from the Professional Publishers Association (PPA) may also be useful.

Those with 18 months' work experience who have gained the Diploma in Journalism can take the NCTJ's National Certificate Examination (NCE) which enables candidates to achieve senior status as a journalist.

Developing a strong portfolio by writing for student publications, local newspapers or online magazines is important as the industry is fiercely competitive. Employers seek candidates who can show evidence of their creativity, persistence, excellent writing skills and an ability to accept criticism, so gaining a variety of work experience is highly recommended. Knowledge of HTML code and photography could also make your application stand out given the rapid increase in digital publishing.

As you build experience and contacts, you may be offered a journalism position where you will work your way up to editor status.

What the work involves

Newspaper/magazine/web editors are responsible for the coordination of each aspect of a publication or website.

You will understand the readership of the publication or website and include informative, newsworthy articles, entertaining features and high quality images. You will work with the editorial, design and advertising departments, as well as journalists, printers, web developers and publishers.

Tasks include editing and proofreading articles and features, assigning journalists to cover stories, commissioning freelance writers for features, meeting with photographers and conducting interviews.

Type of person suited to this work

You should be able to demonstrate excellent writing skills and a creative flair. You must have a strong interest in current affairs.

You will have a practical approach to problem solving and remain calm in stressful situations. You need to show initiative, persistence and decisiveness. You must pay attention to detail, be meticulous in your organisation and time management, and be able to work to a deadline.

You must have excellent communication skills to be able to delegate tasks and persuade others to meet deadlines.

Web editors must possess good IT skills and feel comfortable using a content management system, monitoring online message boards and dealing with enquiries. You must also keep track of developments within web technology and legal requirements.

Working conditions

You will probably work around 40 hours a week which may include early starts, late nights and weekend work to cover a breaking story. Some large newspapers may offer shift work.

You will mainly be based in an office which could be noisy and busy. You may be required to meet with other editors, journalists or photographers outside the office.

Future prospects

Journalism is a very competitive industry. Work experience, published articles and evidence of commitment to journalism are as important as qualifications.

The typical route to becoming a newspaper/magazine/web editor is to begin in a junior role as a journalist or editorial assistant and work your way up through the editorial department until you are in charge of the content of the magazine, website or newspaper.

You could later work in PR, website development or on a freelance basis.

Advantages/disadvantages

Your work will be diverse and stimulating as it will involve constantly creating new content.

You may work in a highly stressful environment, working long and unsocial hours.

Money guide

Earnings depend on the type, size and location of your employer.

The salary for a newspaper editor can range from £30,000 to £80,000. Higher salaries are possible with extensive experience.

As a magazine editor, your salary is likely to range between £25,000 and £40,000, with £65,000 possible when experienced.

A web editor is likely to earn £25,000–£38,000.

Related opportunities

- Copy Editor/Sub-editor/Proofreader p382
- Publisher/Commissioning Editor p397
- Website Developer p151

Further information

National Council for the Training of Journalists
www.nctj.com

Newspaper Society
www.newspapersoc.org.uk

PHOTOGRAPHER

ENTRY LEVEL 3

Qualifications and courses

There are no set academic requirements to become a photographer but the following courses may be useful to gain relevant knowledge: an A level/H grade in Photography; a City & Guilds Certificate in Photo Imaging and Photography (Levels 1–3); an HNC/HND in Art and Design or a relevant degree. The content of a photography degree can vary significantly, with some having greater emphasis on artistic aspects and others more focused on commercial concerns.

Given photography's competitiveness, a postgraduate qualification may be advantageous, particularly those that promote contact with the industry. A master's degree may benefit those who seek to work in very specialist areas such as fashion, advertising or photo-journalism. These courses will also help develop and demonstrate key technical skills.

Candidates wishing to pursue careers as police, medical or press photographers will need 5 GCSEs/National 5s (A*–C/A–C) including English and Maths. It is necessary for medical photographers to have a degree or postgraduate certificate in clinical photography and forensic photographers to have an A level/H grade in a science.

It is generally accepted that prior work experience is a necessary requirement, with perseverance and patience essential. Visit galleries, volunteer in museums and find any way to get your work published as you will need a strong portfolio comprising between 10 and 15 shots and knowledge of a variety of software packages.

Depending on the area of photography in which you work, your training will vary. Many photographers are self-employed and learn on the job whilst medical and press photographers often follow a recognised training pattern.

The British Institute of Professional Photographers (BIPP) provides a variety of 1-day courses which cover a wide range of photography disciplines and business skills. These may be useful should you choose to become freelance or set up your own photography business. The BIPP also offers a tiered professional training route which could result in your gaining Licentiateship, Associateship or Fellowship qualifications. The Association of Photographers (AOP) hosts discussions and workshops which could also help you further your skills.

What the work involves

Photographers capture images using technical lighting and equipment. Using your eye for design and knowledge of photographic techniques you will create images for a specific brief.

Many photographers work with digital enhancing techniques to modify and improve, or add interest and illusions to the images they produce.

Type of person suited to this work

You will need a strong visual sense and an eye for what makes a good picture. You will need technical knowledge and skills to get the most from lighting, studio set-ups and camera equipment. The use of editing software means that IT skills are increasingly important.

Strong communication skills and a flexible attitude come in useful when discussing projects with clients, or calming nervous subjects.

To work on a freelance basis, business skills and self-confidence are essential.

Working conditions

You will either be based in a studio or work on location. In a studio you could work with still life and portraiture. Lighting equipment can be heavy and the work can be physically tiring as you will be on your feet for long periods.

If you work outdoors you could record images for advertising and photo-journalism. This may require patience if the weather or light conditions are not correct for your shot.

Commercial photography is completed to tight deadlines, which can be stressful.

Future prospects

In order to gain the essential skills and an understanding of your specialist type of photography, you could work as a photographer's assistant.

With experience you could progress into freelance work or specialise in a particular area such as press, medical or food photography.

Nowadays, positions are even more limited as digital photography has reduced the work of professionals.

Advantages/disadvantages

There is the potential for public acknowledgement and personal satisfaction for using your creativity and technical skills to create original images.

It takes time in this competitive industry to develop contacts, so you might need a second job to support yourself.

Money guide

As an assistant photographer you can expect to earn around £12,000.

Depending on your experience and popularity, this can rise to £25,000–£65,000 once established.

Earnings will vary if you are self-employed or freelance.

Related opportunities

- Graphic Designer p161
- Illustrator/Technical Illustrator p162
- TV and Film Camera Person/Operator p400

Further information

British Institute of Professional Photography
www.bipp.com

The Association of Photographers
www.the-aop.org

PHOTOGRAPHIC STYLIST

ENTRY LEVEL 3

Qualifications and courses

There are no formal qualifications required in order to become a photographic stylist, however many people who enter into the role do have an art or design related qualification or experience as a photographer's assistant. If you wish to work in food styling then you should have a background in catering.

Several relevant further education courses are available, such as the London College of Fashion's Foundation degree in Fashion Styling and Photography. A BTEC National Diploma in Fashion or Photography may also provide you with some of the skills required in the industry.

Only a few HNCs and HNDs, degree courses and postgraduate qualifications are directly related to this area (for example, in fashion styling, visual merchandising or fashion promotion) but many fashion or photography courses include the relevant module. The skills used in interior or exhibition design or home economics (food styling) could be useful. Some courses also include work placements which are invaluable in ensuring you build contacts within the competitive industry.

It is essential that you secure as much relevant work experience as possible. You must remain determined and proactive in order to secure placements. It is useful to compile a portfolio of any work you do in order to show potential employers.

Once employment is secured, you will normally be trained on the job as an assistant to a stylist or photographer, or as a fashion/editorial assistant on a magazine, before working your way up to photographic stylist.

What the work involves

Photographic stylists work closely with photographers to design the look and mood of a photo shoot.

It would be your responsibility to arrange and dress the set, to find appropriate props and to organise any work that needs to be done behind the scenes.

Typically, you would receive a brief from the photographer or director of the shoot and then come up with creative ideas to fulfil the brief. Sometimes you will have a lot of freedom for your own ideas but at other times the brief will be very strict.

It is useful to build up a collection of accessories that you can bring to shoots.

Most stylists specialise in a particular area, such as fashion, food or interior photography.

Type of person suited to this work

You will need to be creative with a good eye for design and understand what makes a good picture. You will also need to have a sound understanding of photography and lighting.

Good communication skills are essential as you will need to coordinate with a range of people on each shoot.

You must be able to stay calm under pressure.

An understanding of the latest fashion trends is important as is commercial awareness.

Working conditions

You will need to have an office base but will spend the majority of your time out on location and in photography studios.

Working hours will be varied and days will often be long and often extremely pressurised. You will probably need to work some evenings and weekends.

You will probably work freelance and as you build up contacts and experience you may secure work with magazines, photography studios and design houses.

It is useful to have a full driving licence as you will need to drive between shoots and transport props which could be large or delicate.

Future prospects

The industry is competitive and tough to enter, attracting more people than jobs available. Most photo stylists are self-employed and work on a per-assignment basis, but there is the opportunity for more secure work through agency representation.

Advancement generally comes through producing work on a bigger platform and developing your reputation.

Advantages/disadvantages

Working as a photographic stylist is a very creative job where you can see your ideas brought to life on camera.

Hours are long and the work can be stressful as you will have to work to very tight deadlines.

Pay can be low to start with and competition is fierce.

Money guide

Starting salaries vary, but are typically around £12,000. With experience, this can rise to £35,000 a year.

Top stylists who have built up a reputation can earn considerably more.

As most stylists work freelance, incomes vary considerably depending on how much work you have. Daily rates vary between £200 and £400.

Related opportunities

- Fashion Designer/Milliner p157
- Photographer p392
- TV and Film Camera Person/Operator p400

Further information

British Display Society
www.britishdisplaysociety.co.uk

British Institute of Professional Photography
www.bipp.com

The Association of Photographers
www.the-aop.org

PRINTER

ENTRY LEVEL 2

Qualifications and courses

Although there are no set entry requirements for this career candidates with GCSEs/National 5s (A*–C/A–C) in English, Maths, a science and technology subjects would be at an advantage. The Diploma in Manufacturing and Product Design might also be useful or you can study a relevant college course prior to entry. Many people enter these professions by means of an apprenticeship.

Machine printer

Most employers will expect a good level of education, particularly GCSEs/National 5s in English, Maths, a science and IT. General art and design courses may teach you the basics of screen printing and you will also need to have good colour vision.

As an introduction you may take a 10-day course run by the Institute of Paper, Printing and Publishing. Alternatively, you might opt to study other printing courses such as the City & Guilds Certificate in Printing and Graphic Communications or the ABC Level 3 Diploma in Print Media, full time at college.

Apprenticeships may be available. As an apprentice you will experience a combination of on-the-job training and a series of day or block release instruction at college where you might work towards an NVQ in either Machine Printing, Mechanised Print Finishing and Binding, Digital Print Production, Envelope Manufacture or Carton Manufacture (Levels 1–3).

Screen printer

You can choose to do a college course in printing and graphic communications, printmaking skills, screen printing, graphic printmaking or print media.

It is also possible to attain City & Guilds Certificates in Printing and Graphic Communications (Levels 2–3), an NVQ in Screenprinting (Levels 2–3), or an ABC Level 3 Award in Printmaking Skills, Screen Printing and Screen Printing Skills.

The majority of training takes place on the job with experienced colleagues and many companies provide in-house training schemes.

The Digital and Screenprinting Association and specialist schools, such as the London College of Communication, also run courses in this area.

Bookbinder

You do not need formal qualifications to be a machine bookbinder as on-the-job training is provided, however it may be advantageous to have GCSEs/National 5s particularly in English or Maths.

Specialist NVQs are available such as the NVQ in Mechanised Print Finishing and Binding (Levels 2–3) and the Level 3 NVQ in Hand Binding. It is also possible to enter the profession through an apprenticeship scheme.

To work as a craft bookbinder you will need certain skills. Craft bookbinding is often a second career path. Courses, degrees and diplomas are available in fine bookbinding and repair.

To enhance your prospects, you may seek membership of the Society of Bookbinders (SoB). With experience you may be encouraged to apply for Licentiateship or Fellowship.

Print production planner

This area of printing is open to graduates and diplomates of a variety of disciplines. Those who have studied a relevant subject such as print management, graphic communications, business studies or publishing may be at a distinct advantage however. Courses such as these will help develop skills including production management, print processes, digital pre-press and total quality management. Postgraduate qualifications are available, although not essential.

For a degree, entry requirements are usually 2 A levels/3 H grades and 5 GCSEs/National 5s (A*–C/A–C). For an HND, you should have 1 A level/2 H grades or a BTEC National Diploma in a related subject. You can study for an NVQ Level 3 in Print Administration, which includes modules on health and safety.

It is also possible to enter without a degree or HND and employers are willing to provide release from work for training. If you have any qualifications in art, design, communications or IT, this will help your search for employment.

This job requires maturity and practical industry experience. It is possible to commence as a machine printer and work your way up to this position.

Once employed, your training will take place on the job. Your employer may encourage you to further your skills by completing external short courses such as those offered by the British Printing Industries Federation (BPIF).

What the work involves

Machine printer

Machine printers oversee the production of printed items on machines of various sizes for products such as newspapers, posters, books, etc. You will set up the printing press correctly for the specific job. This includes ensuring that the appropriate plates, paper and inks have been selected.

You will trial the print run, check for errors and ensure that the quality is up to standard.

Screen printer

Screen printers create visual images by organising and operating hand- or power-driven screen printing machines which print graphics onto fabrics and paper by forcing ink through a delicate mesh overlay of the stencil design.

You will be required to prepare the stencils, inks and print processes.

Bookbinder

Bookbinders are responsible for transforming the printed material into the finished product. Nowadays the majority of bookbinding is a machine orientated process, which involves stitching, stapling, collating, cutting, binding and coating.

Print production planner
Print production planners are responsible for workflow in the printing firm and ensuring that the efficiency is maximised by checking orders, creating schedules, allocating work, supervising and quality control. It will be your responsibility to liaise with other production departments.

Type of person suited to this work

Printing requires good teamwork and communication skills. It is usual that your work will involve computers and other types of machinery and equipment so you will need good practical skills and an understanding of IT.

It is important to have normal colour vision, good hand-to-eye co-ordination and a high level of physical fitness.

You should have a meticulous eye for detail, and you will need to demonstrate design skills to convince customers that you can make aesthetically pleasing finished products, from CD covers to full-text pages or full-colour brochures.

As print runs do not always go smoothly you will need to be adept at problem solving, have a long concentration span and the ability to work under pressure.

Furthermore you should be flexible as some print companies run 24-hour operations and you might have to work shifts at night and at the weekends. Print production managers should also have good multi-tasking skills, a good head for numbers and the ability to influence people.

Working conditions

In smaller print companies you will normally work office hours, that is 9am to 5pm, but during busy periods you could do additional hours in order to ensure that projects are completed on time. Larger companies tend to run 24-hour operations and you will be expected to work shifts and weekends. Overtime is widely available.

Bookbinders may also have the opportunity to work part time.

Your working environment will depend on your role and the size of the firm. Printshops can be dirty and noisy when machines are functioning. Hazardous chemicals are used in finishes and to wash inks from the press but there is good ventilation to cope with the resulting fumes.

You will be required to adhere to health and safety regulations at all times and use protective gear such as overalls, boots, gloves and ear protectors.

It is necessary to have a good level of physical fitness as you will be standing for long periods of time. Upper body strength is also important as you may be required to carry out some heavy lifting.

Print production planners will work in an office but will also carry out work on the production floor and may have to travel to attend meetings with clients.

Future prospects

At present in the UK there are approximately 10,500 print companies which employ about 140,000 people, although changes in costs and technology means that small printing firms are in decline.

The majority of the industry comprises small, family-owned enterprises. The industry is sensitive to wider economic issues, such as cheaper rates from foreign print companies, increasing use of electronic resources and seasonal order variations.

Opportunities will depend on your skills and the size and type of your company. Although printers cover all the stages of production, the job of folding machine operator (at the finishing end of the process) is becoming a skills shortage area.

With experience and additional design skills, you could work for a specialist press production company, a design or reprographic house or general printers. To run a printing business takes a high level of business skills, including accounting and sales.

Advantages/disadvantages

This job combines creative and artistic skills with technical and computer-aided design.

There are good entry opportunities for some printing jobs such as specialist print finishers, which have become skills shortage areas.

Owing to the nature of the industry, you might have to move to other parts of the country for promotion.

Many companies now produce high quality publications in-house, so printers need to work with large volumes or specialist niche markets to make a profit.

Money guide

Machine printer
Newly qualified printers can expect to earn £16,000–£19,000.

With experience, this can rise to £40,000.

Additional payments for shift allowances and bonuses are also possible and the highest salaries in this profession can be up to £60,000.

Screen printer
Screen printers can expect to start on £16,000, rising to £24,000 with experience.

Top earners can reach salaries of up to £36,000.

Bookbinder
Bookbinders can expect to earn £14,000.

This can rise to £16,000–£35,000, depending on your experience and responsibilities.

If you are a self-employed craft bookbinder earnings can vary depending on the amount of work you have.

Print production planner
New entrants can expect £20,000–£25,000.

With experience, you can earn between £30,000 and £40,000.

Senior planners can expect £45,000–£56,000.

Related opportunities

- CAD Draughtsperson p200
- Publisher/Commissioning Editor p397
- Quality Control Inspector p222
- Signwriter/Signmaker p170

Further information

British Printing Industries Federation
www.britishprint.com

Institute of Paper, Printing and Publishing
www.ip3.org.uk

Society of Bookbinders
www.societyofbookbinders.com

PUBLIC RELATIONS OFFICER

ENTRY LEVEL 6

Qualifications and courses

There are no formal academic requirements but most entrants to this profession are graduates or diplomates. An HND or degree in a relevant subject, such as public relations, marketing, business, English or media studies is highly likely to increase your chances of employment. You could enter the industry at a junior level as a PR assistant and work your way up or you may try to secure a place on a graduate training scheme offered by some large organisations. As entry to the profession is highly competitive, a postgraduate qualification may improve your career prospects.

Employers often expect candidates to undertake pre-entry work experience in PR, communications or marketing or, alternatively, you could develop relevant skills by volunteering at a charity or writing for a student newspaper.

Membership of the Chartered Institute of Public Relations (CIPR) is useful as it often advertises placements, training courses and encourages you to build contacts within the industry. The CIPR also offers professional qualifications which are becomingly increasingly sought after by employers. Entry requirements for the CIPR Advanced Certificate in Public Relations are a relevant undergraduate degree or 2 years' PR experience and 5 GCSEs/National 5s (A*–C/A–C) including English Language.

The Diploma in Marketing Communications available from the Communication, Advertising and Marketing (CAM) Education Foundation could also be beneficial.

The Public Relations Consultants Association (PRCA) have a range of qualifications at different levels suitable for new entrants, experienced PR officers or managers.

What the work involves

Public relations officers work in public relations or communications departments in large organisations and for PR companies. Some work on a freelance basis.

You will manage the image and reputation of organisations by writing publicity materials, studying and advising clients, and responding to enquiries or complaints.

It will be important that you develop and maintain positive working relationships with reporters and other members of the press.

You will need to monitor media coverage to gauge perception of your company. Social media is particularly important now as it offers an opportunity for the public to interact directly with companies.

Type of person suited to this work

You must be confident and have a smart appearance.

You need to have strong communication skills and enjoy liaising with a wide range of people. Written communication and research skills are essential, as are good IT skills.

You must be able to work effectively to tight deadlines and be flexible when managing several projects at once. Financial management skills are also useful.

Working conditions

Most of your work will be office based and although you will work normal office hours, longer working days are common, particularly during busy periods.

You will have meetings with clients, colleagues or other professionals. You will need to travel to attend meetings, special events and presentations on a regular basis. Working for global companies or high-profile charities may mean some overseas travel.

Future prospects

PR is a growing industry. However, there is strong competition, often with hundreds of well-qualified applicants for one post.

You will typically start your career as a PR assistant and then progress to a role as an account executive, followed by a move into a senior role.

There could be various opportunities to work abroad. With experience, some PR professionals set up their own companies or work freelance for other organisations.

Advantages/disadvantages

You can be part of high-profile campaigns.

This job can be pressured due to the speed of press releases and the range of activities you will have to juggle.

If working for a high-profile organisation, you might have to be on-call to respond to unexpected situations.

Money guide

Starting salaries are around £18,000 to £28,000.

With experience, this can increase to around £30,000.

Those in senior positions can achieve £40,000–£100,000.

The private sector usually pays more than the public sector.

Benefits such as private health insurance, bonus schemes and a company car may be offered.

Related opportunities

- Advertising Account Executive p376
- Advertising Media Planner p379
- Journalist p385

Further information

Chartered Institute of Public Relations
www.cipr.co.uk

Communication, Advertising and Marketing Education Foundation
www.camfoundation.com

International Public Relations Association
www.ipra.org

PUBLISHER/COMMISSIONING EDITOR

ENTRY LEVEL 6

Qualifications and courses

The majority of new entrants are graduates with a degree in a relevant subject such as publishing, English language or literature. Specialist publishers, such as those in the academic field or journals, will expect candidates to have more subject-specific degrees related to the academic areas in which they publish, such as maths or science. You will need at least 2 A levels/3 H grades and 5 GCSEs/National 5s (A*–C/A–C) for degree entry. A relevant postgraduate qualification, such as a master's in publishing, is not essential but may be beneficial given the competition for places.

As this is a senior role, it is unlikely that a recent graduate would begin their career at a publisher/commissioning editor level. Most entrants begin as an editorial assistant before being promoted to an editor position and then going on to secure a publisher/commissioning editor role.

Entry into the industry is highly competitive and it is important to learn as much as possible about publishing from trade magazines or people in the industry before applying. Experience of writing or editing at a non-professional level can be useful as employers often value those candidates who can provide evidence of good research skills, an ability to think creatively, effective communication and teamwork skills. Gaining work experience will also ensure you form industry contacts which are crucial when seeking employment as few trainee publishing jobs are formally advertised.

Specialist centres such as the Publishing Training Centre provide short courses on different areas of publishing such as commissioning and list management, financial planning and managing publishing strategy.

What the work involves

Publishers/commissioning editors plan and manage the range or list of books, magazines or IT resources produced by their department or company. This includes researching consumers' needs and identifying gaps in the company's list of publications.

You will develop ideas for new publications and respond to proposals from authors. You will also oversee the entire process of developing new publications from an original idea to completed manuscript.

In a small organisation you might also be responsible for liaising with copyeditors and proofreaders. You may also be responsible for developing marketing strategies to increase publication sales.

Type of person suited to this work

You will need a strong interest in producing products that have extensive commercial appeal and you will have relevant market knowledge and experience in order to identify gaps in the market.

As you will liaise closely with authors and colleagues, you should enjoy meeting and working with a variety of people.

You will also need strong written and oral communication skills and the ability to encourage people to complete tasks to deadlines. You must be well organised and able to plan ahead.

Working conditions

Most of your work will involve attending meetings or working at a computer within the office of a company or organisation.

You will be expected to liaise with authors, colleagues, designers and IT specialists either face to face, by email or on the phone.

Although your working week will comprise normal office hours, you can expect to work late in order to meet strict publication deadlines or to attend evening events. Business trips, including overnight stays, are a possibility and you could travel abroad.

Future prospects

This is a competitive profession to enter. The main employers are publishing houses, specialist businesses, and professional and educational organisations.

Sales and marketing experience can facilitate entry to this sector. It is possible to set up your own publishing company, although the market is well covered and profit margins narrow.

Currently, the area of greatest expansion is that offered by the internet and digital publishing.

Advantages/disadvantages

You will meet and work with an interesting cross-section of people.

You will be responsible for creating strategies to increase sales of publications, which can be stressful.

Developing new publications can be a lengthy process and requires patience.

Seeing the finished publication that you have helped to develop is highly satisfying.

Money guide

The average starting salary for an editorial assistant is £18,000.

As a commissioning editor, your salary is likely to be around £26,450 and, with experience, this could increase to £40,000–£50,000.

Senior managers, publishers and directors of large publishing companies can earn up to £80,000.

Related opportunities

- Copy Editor/Sub-editor/Proofreader p382
- Copywriter p383
- Newspaper/Magazine/Web Editor p391

Further information

Publishers Association
www.publishers.org.uk

Publishing Training Centre
www.train4publishing.co.uk

RECORDING INDUSTRY PRODUCER

ENTRY LEVEL 3

Qualifications and courses

Although there are no specific qualifications for entry into this profession, formal music training of some kind is recommended and practical work experience or voluntary work for a studio or record company is extremely important.

Courses that may help you develop skills and experience include Foundation degrees and degrees in music production, music technology, music practice and music industry management. You will need at least 2 A levels/3 H grades and 5 GCSEs/National 5s (A*–C/A–C) for degree entry. Other useful courses include the BTEC Level 3 Extended Diploma in Music Technology, or the HNC/HND Level 5 in Music Production.

It is unlikely that as a graduate you will enter a recording industry producer position straight away, therefore you will have to work your way up from lower level roles such as studio assistant or assistant engineer. Job vacancies within this fiercely competitive industry are rarely advertised and most producers are self-employed. Networking, establishing contacts and building a reputation are key to securing work.

Short music courses are available for young professionals beginning in the music industry, such as the BPI seminar 'Music, It's the Business'. The Music Producers Guild (MPG) have also created a Knowledge Band and Members' Directory to encourage debate and facilitate future recording industry producers' networking within the industry. The MPG, in association with the Association of Professional Recording Services (APRS), has set up the Joint Audio Media Education Services (JAMES) to allow new entrants to learn from experienced professionals.

What the work involves

Recording industry producers are employed by the artists and repertoire (A&R) department of a recording company to work with artists to produce successful music tracks or demos.

You will discuss ideas with artists and their management, plan new projects, listen to existing tracks and identify areas for improvement.

You will be involved in the organisation of each stage of the recording process, including rehearsal time, recruitment of sound engineers, booking studio time, directing the artists and suggesting alterations that will produce the desired sound.

Type of person suited to this work

You must have excellent communication skills to give instructions to others, persuade people to try your ideas and to build up a good network of contacts.

As you will have to spend long hours in the studio you should have a good ear for music, high stamina, self-discipline and patience.

You should also have good planning skills to work out budgets, organise time scales for recording studios and estimate production and post-production costs.

Working conditions

You will work long, irregular hours. This may include working late into the night and at the weekends.

Your work may not always be constant and you might have to find other methods of earning money.

You may have to travel within the UK and abroad.

Future prospects

You will probably progress to a production position after several years of working in an assistant sound engineer or engineer role.

At first, you will approach A&R departments with your services until you establish your reputation, usually by producing music that is commercially successful.

As a top record producer, work abroad with international artists is possible. Some go on to establish their own recording studios, supplying facilities, equipment and sound production teams to other producers.

Advantages/disadvantages

You may have the opportunity to work with a diverse range of artists and to be a part of the creative process of making music.

You may produce music which becomes very successful and gains you national, or even international, acclaim.

Prolonged exposure to loud music may damage your hearing.

Artists can be independent-minded and sometimes difficult.

Money guide

You can expect a starting salary of around £15,000 per annum, which can rise to over £30,000 with experience and constant work. The top recording industry producers can earn in excess of £100,000.

You may be paid 'on spec' if you work with an unsigned band, being paid if and when the artist is successful.

Usually you will be paid a flat fee, but this will also be supplemented by an agreed percentage of the sales income. This can be minimal or thousands of pounds.

Very few self-employed producers maintain a consistent level of work throughout the year; therefore you may have to secure a second job in order to supplement your income.

Related opportunities

- DJ p414
- Musician p418
- Sound Engineer p422

Further information

BPI The British Recorded Music Industry
www.bpi.co.uk

Music Producers Guild UK Ltd
www.mpg.org.uk

TECHNICAL AUTHOR/ MEDICAL WRITER

ENTRY LEVEL 6

Qualifications and courses

Many entrants have a degree or qualification in either a general subject, such as English, journalism or media studies, or a more specific qualification in the area in which they wish to specialise, engineering or computer science for example. Minimum degree entry requirements are usually 2 A levels/3 H grades and 5 GCSEs/National 5s (A*–C/A–C).

The University of Portsmouth offers a master's degree in technical communication which is suitable for graduates in science and technology who wish to improve their writing skills. The Institute of Scientific and Technical Communicators (ISTC) provides a further list of approved specialist courses that may improve employability and enhance your skill set.

It is possible to enter this profession without an HND or degree but a demonstration of extensive specialist knowledge within your chosen field and experience utilising a range of software packages will be required. It is common for mature adults to enter this profession as it necessitates expert knowledge. There is the possibility to take an open-learning course in Communication of Technical Information at the ISTC, which may be beneficial for mature entrants.

Gaining pre-entry practical experience will support you in your search for work as employers often seek candidates who can show evidence of a feel for words, an appreciation of tone and style, editorial judgement and creative thinking. While competition for trainee vacancies is moderate, they can be difficult to come across. Cherryleaf and Ecademy are useful groups of which to gain membership as they offer opportunities to network and search for employment, alongside further training courses.

What the work involves

Technical authors/medical writers interpret technical information and communicate it in written language which the intended audience can understand. Technical authors work in various sectors from medicine and defence to business and finance.

You will create content, commission images, organise and design the layout of any given document.

You should be an expert in your specialist sector, but your audience may be novices as well as specialists. For example, you may write mass market instructions for a mobile phone or a medical writer may create a report on clinical trial results for the medical community.

Type of person suited to this work

It is essential to have an excellent command of English and the ability to write concisely and convincingly, with your audience in mind. You should also be detail driven and have a good eye for design.

Having a passion for your specialist sector and an enquiring mind is a necessity. The ability to solve problems, multi-task and to work to deadlines is also important.

Good communication and teamworking skills are required as you will have to work closely with technical colleagues, such as doctors, as well as liaising with suppliers including printers and translators.

Working conditions

The majority of work will take place at a computer within normal office hours. However, supplementary hours may be required in order to meet tight deadlines. Also, you might have to travel to meet clients.

Having gained experience, many people decide to start up their own business or go freelance, especially as the pay is more attractive.

Future prospects

Increasingly complex systems and applications are being produced which has led to a greater need for technical writers in a variety of sectors, such as aerospace, finance and technical publishing.

The demand for technical authors is expected to increase due to the continuing expansion of scientific and technical information which needs to be communicated. With increasingly complex developments and discoveries comes a demand for people who can interpret technical information for a wide audience.

As a junior technical author you can progress into senior roles and later, project leader or editor positions. Moving to different organisations may be the key to career progression as there are very few workers in any one company.

Freelance or consultancy work is also popular.

Advantages/disadvantages

This type of work can provide the satisfaction of seeing your completed work in print and, sometimes, in the public domain.

The work can be quite arduous having to familiarise yourself with difficult concepts.

Money guide

You can expect to earn £23,000–£40,000 depending on your experience.

Those in senior roles with extensive experience can achieve in excess of £40,000.

Freelance authors negotiate their own rates.

Related opportunities

- Copy Editor/Sub-editor/Proofreader p382
- Journalist p385
- Publisher/Commissioning Editor p397

Further information

e-skills UK
www.e-skills.com

Institute of Internal Communication
www.ioic.org.uk

Institute of Scientific and Technical Communicators
www.istc.org.uk

TV AND FILM CAMERA PERSON/ OPERATOR

ENTRY LEVEL 3

Qualifications and courses

To be a TV/film camera operator you do not need any specific academic qualifications although GCSEs/ National 5s (A*–C/A–C) in English, Maths and a science might be useful. Many camera operators do have higher level qualifications, however, such as HNDs, Foundation degrees or degrees in relevant subjects (media production, photography or media studies for example) as this can help improve chances of employment.

Courses which may help you to develop the necessary skills required in the industry include the City & Guilds Level 3 Diploma in Media Techniques, the BTEC Level 2 Certificate/Diploma in Creative Media Production, the BTEC Level 3 Certificate/Diploma in Media Production – Television and Film and the BTEC HNC/HND in Creative Media Production – Moving Image (Levels 4–5).

The industry is competitive and appropriate experience is often valued more than formal qualifications. Employers seek candidates with a demonstrable interest in photography, typically in the form of showreels, amateur films and videos, film stills or a collection of images. Large companies, such as the BBC, offer work experience placements that provide opportunities to work with camera equipment or in a set-up studio. Experience with community film projects or working for a camera equipment hire company could also be useful. You could apply for the Advanced Apprenticeship in Creative and Digital Media which trains apprentices in the skills required of an assistant to a camera crew.

Work experience offers you the opportunity to establish industry contacts crucial when seeking work as few entry-level jobs are formally advertised. The Guild of Television Cameramen (GTC) provides networking opportunities and workshops in camera techniques, lighting and editing as does the BBC Academy and the National Film and Television School.

What the work involves

Camera operators use digital, electronic and film cameras to capture images for use in films, TV programmes or other broadcasts.

You will work closely with a director or director of photography and will be helped by a 'grip' (a camera assistant) and other crew members such as pullers, clappers, sound engineers and lighting technicians.

You will understand the technical and creative aspects of filming, including how to work with a script or list of shots, planning shots and shooting images.

You will have an in-depth knowledge of the equipment you work with and how best to use, maintain and repair it.

Type of person suited to this work

You must be interested in photography, camera technology and video, film and TV production.

You will be required to have a certain amount of physical fitness as your work may involve carrying heavy equipment for long periods of time.

As you will be working in a creative environment, you will need to have a good imagination and at times an abstract approach to problem solving.

You should be patient, have good concentration and work well under pressure.

Working conditions

Your working hours will vary greatly. You may be required to work irregular hours. Shooting may be long and run over planned schedules.

Your work may be affected by weather, for example some shoots may be cut short, or extended, if they depend on natural light.

You may have to work with cameras on cranes, scaffolding, in moving vehicles or in venues such as concert halls, theatres and sports grounds.

Camera operators usually learn most of their skills on the job. Regular training in health and safety is also required.

Future prospects

You will typically start your career as a trainee, runner or camera operator's assistant and learn on the job. Experience leads to becoming a camera operator, and then director of photography among other senior roles.

Geographical mobility will be important to progress your career.

Advantages/disadvantages

You may work on exciting projects, including big budget films or breaking news programmes.

Working on location may be dangerous at times, especially if it involves shooting footage for news broadcasts.

Money guide

A starting salary for a camera operator ranges from £11,500 up to £40,000, depending on your experience.

Most camera operators work on a freelance basis so rates of pay vary according to the type of production you are working on.

As an example, you could earn £285 for working a 10-hour day on a TV documentary, £411 for a 10-hour day filming commercials or £227 for TV news.

Related opportunities

- Lighting Technician p416
- Photographer p392
- TV, Film and Radio Director p402

Further information

BBC Training and Development
www.bbc.co.uk/careers/why-join-us/training

TV FLOOR MANAGER ENTRY LEVEL 3

Qualifications and courses

There are no set academic qualifications required for entry into this profession, although it might be useful to have GCSEs/National 5s (A*–C/A–C) and A levels/H grades in subjects such as maths, English, languages or theatre and drama studies.

Degrees or HNDs in relevant subjects such as media studies, drama, photography, film and television will give you an advantage over other candidates as competition for entry to the industry is fierce. The general entry requirements for a degree are 2 A levels/3 H grades and 5 GCSEs/National 5s (A*–C/A–C). Other qualifications that may help include the BTEC Level 2 Certificate/Diploma in Creative Media Production, the BTEC Level 3 Certificate/Diploma in Creative Media Production – Television and Film and the City & Guilds Level 3 Diploma in Media Techniques.

Creative Skillset have formed a network of Media and Film Academies which offer film and television training, with the option to work towards vocational qualifications. The BBC and Channel 4 also run training schemes.

Employers seek candidates with a proven commitment to the job and the industry. It is advisable to undertake voluntary pre-entry work experience as you are likely to start your career as a runner or production assistant and securing this type of junior role is usually a combination of luck, timing and networking. A portfolio of work is likely to be required and once employed, you will be trained on the job whilst you work your way up the ladder to TV floor manager.

Some independent companies may offer graduate training schemes but, again, competition is fierce. Your employer may encourage you to undertake short courses such as those offered by the Broadcasting, Entertainment, Cinematograph, and Theatre Union (BECTU) in order to develop your skills throughout your career.

What the work involves

TV floor managers are responsible for the coordination of many aspects of the filming process.

You will ensure that all sets, props and technical equipment are working, in place and set up correctly.

In situations where the director is away from the set (in the gallery or a broadcast vehicle) you will wear headphones to relay instructions from the director to the crew, actors or audience members. You will make sure that everyone involved in the production process knows what to do so that everything runs according to schedule.

Type of person suited to this work

You must be passionate about the media industry and TV production in particular.

You should be very organised and able to work under pressure and to a tight schedule.

As you will be working with a variety of people, from directors to the most junior crew members, you will need to have good communication skills to create an efficient working environment.

You must have an understanding of the technical and creative aspects of production to ensure that you can deal with problems encountered during the filming or recording stage.

Working conditions

Hours are likely to be long and irregular, including early starts, late nights and weekend work. If you work on feature films, 6-day weeks are common.

You will probably work on a freelance basis, which may involve periods of unemployment between jobs.

You will spend most of your time at work on your feet. You will mainly work in studios but sometimes you may be required to work outdoors in all weather conditions.

You might have to travel within the UK or abroad, at short notice and for varying periods of time.

Future prospects

There are not a great number of positions available but with experience you may find it possible to move up into a position as first director, producer or director.

You could move across into other aspects of the industry such as production or broadcasting.

As you will be working on a freelance basis most of the time, you will depend on having a strong portfolio of your work, an excellent reputation and good contacts within the industry to guarantee work.

Advantages/disadvantages

Your work will involve a diverse range of projects including creative, practical and technical tasks.

Your working hours may be long, stressful and unsocial which could disrupt your personal life.

Money guide

Starting salaries are usually between £15,000 and £22,000.

Those with experience can expect to earn in excess of £25,000.

Many floor managers work on a freelance basis and receive an hourly, daily or weekly rate. Daily rates could range from £150 to £400.

Related opportunities

- TV and Film Camera Person/Operator p400
- TV, Film and Radio Director p402
- TV, Film and Radio Production Assistant/Runner p405

Further information

Creative Skillset
www.creativeskillset.org

National Film and Television School
http://nfts.co.uk

TV, FILM AND RADIO DIRECTOR

ENTRY LEVEL 6

Qualifications and courses

There are no specific entry requirements but most entrants have a drama or media-related degree or postgraduate qualification.

GCSEs/National 5s or A levels/H grades in media-related subjects would demonstrate an early interest in this industry and studying these subjects at BTEC National, HND, degree or postgraduate level would be beneficial when applying for entry-level positions. The general entry requirements for a degree are 2 A levels/3 H grades and 5 GCSEs/National 5s (A*–C/A–C). For an HND, you should have an A level/H grade in an art and design-related subject. Specialist postgraduate courses in directing are offered at the National Film and Television School (NFTS).

Practical work experience is often valued more than formal qualifications, however, and most budding directors create a showreel to promote their work. Taking part in student or community film and TV activities are good ways to show your commitment to the media. Some production companies, such as the BBC, offer work experience placements which could lead to full-time employment. Work experience is particularly useful in that it provides you with opportunities to establish a network of contacts, crucial considering the competitive nature of the industry.

Directors often begin as runners and work their way up to become floor managers or assistant directors. Others break into directing through competitions, film festivals or marketing short films to agents. You will develop your skills throughout your career by combining learning on the job with external masterclasses such as those offered by the Directors' Guild of Great Britain.

What the work involves

Directors manage the process of creating films, radio and TV programmes. This involves commissioning each project and overseeing the work and schedules of the entire production team.

You will define the presentation and style of films and productions by making decisions about content, scripting, camera work, editing and acting.

You will also be required to handle any problems with presenters, actors or production staff, as well as editing the final 'cut' of the show you have directed.

Type of person suited to this work

Working in these competitive sectors can be very demanding and stressful. You should be confident and able to react quickly and calmly to any crises that may arise.

Good verbal communication, interpersonal and teamworking skills are important, especially as you could be away from home on location for weeks at a time.

In addition, you should have good organisational skills to ensure that projects are carried out on time and within budget.

Working conditions

Contrary to popular belief, this is not glamorous work! A good level of physical stamina and fitness is required as this job involves lengthy days spent standing up and carrying heavy equipment.

In TV and film you will work on set and on location. You will have to cope with changeable outdoor conditions.

You will also be expected to be flexible and work at night and weekends, both during and post-production.

Future prospects

In the UK there are over 80,000 people working in television and film. Investment in British film rose by 14% last year following a fall in 2012, as more Hollywood films are being filmed in the UK again.

Entry to the industry is very competitive and excellent technical skills and a well-established network of contacts are required in order to be successful. It is unlikely that you will enter the industry as a director straight away. Most work their way up from runners to floor managers until finally reaching director status. Your reputation will play a vital role in ensuring career progression.

It is possible that you might work freelance on specific contracts for production companies or you may fund and develop your own projects.

Advantages/disadvantages

This role provides the satisfaction and excitement of seeing your work in the public sphere.

The work is fast paced and varied.

Directors are often employed on a freelance or contract basis which can lead to job instability.

Money guide

Earnings in this sector vary greatly according to media, location, employer and project.

New entrants can expect to earn about £20,000.

With experience, your salary can rise to £40,000.

The most successful directors can earn anything up to £200,000.

Freelancers negotiate their own fees.

Related opportunities

- Artistic/Theatre Director p409
- TV, Film and Radio Producer p404
- TV, Film and Radio Production Assistant/Runner p405

Further information

BBC Careers
www.bbc.co.uk/careers

Creative Skillset
www.creativeskillset.org

TV, FILM AND RADIO EDITOR

ENTRY LEVEL 6

Qualifications and courses

There are no specific academic requirements but many entrants have either a degree or a degree and postgraduate qualification in a relevant subject such as film, IT, media studies and visual art. The general entry requirements for a degree are 2 A levels/3 H grades and 5 GCSEs/National 5s (A*–C/A–C) and for a postgraduate course you will usually need at least a 2.1 Honours in your bachelor's degree.

Entry-level training courses may be beneficial in gaining industry knowledge and are available through the BBC as well as independent organisations such as Cyfle, Creative Scotland or Screen Yorkshire. Alternative qualifications include the City & Guilds Level 3 Diploma in Advanced Media Techniques, the BTEC Level 3 Certificate/Diploma in Creative Media Production specialising in Radio or Television and Film and the BTEC Higher National in Creative Media Production specialising in Moving Image or Radio (Levels 4–5).

It is common to start out as a runner or editing assistant before working your way up to editor status. Practical work experience is essential for entry-level jobs as it demonstrates pre-entry industry interest and is a good way of building a network of contacts. This is important considering that job vacancies are rarely advertised within this somewhat competitive industry. Employers will seek evidence of a candidate's use of appropriate editing software packages, a keen eye for detail and creativity, often requesting a showreel of your work, eg short films, amateur videos and photography.

You will continue to develop your skills throughout your career by completing short courses such as those offered by the Broadcasting, Entertainment, Cinematograph, and Theatre Union (BECTU). It is important that you remain up to date with any new technologies or equipment.

What the work involves

Editors play a key role in the post-production process by assembling the final product from captured footage and additional sound and graphics. They are also responsible for storing the footage.

You will fulfil a brief and liaise closely with the director. You will monitor and correct the flow and pace of a production by using specialist IT editing equipment to put shots together in a smooth sequence.

You will ensure the continuity and order of these productions, which may include TV and radio programmes, films, music and corporate videos, and advertisements.

Type of person suited to this work

It is essential to be creative and to have a passion for your chosen medium.

You should have good attention to detail, plenty of patience and the ability to identify good storytelling techniques.

You will be expected to be well versed in the latest technological advances in the field, as well as possessing advanced IT skills and a willingness to try new techniques.

Working conditions

Hours vary depending on workload but are typically 9am–5pm, Monday to Friday. Your personal life may be affected during busy periods as you will be expected to work long and unpredictable hours in order to meet tight deadlines.

The majority of the work takes place at a computer in an editing suite and may be carried out alone or with a director.

Freelance editors with their own equipment may work from home.

Future prospects

It is thought that there are at least 10,000 people working in post-production roles in the UK. This profession is fast-paced and there is fierce competition for entry-level positions.

The majority of roles are based in London in post-production companies, independent production firms, broadcasters, and companies in the film and computer software sectors. However, big broadcasting firms such as ITV and the BBC have moved a lot of their operations up to Salford, and opportunities continue to grow there.

Having gained experience, many editors choose to go freelance. This involves working on several projects simultaneously and the workload may be irregular, with both busy and quiet periods.

Advantages/disadvantages

You will have the satisfaction of seeing the results of your work in the public domain.

This is a fast-moving and varied industry with exciting opportunities.

Editors are often employed on a freelance or contract basis which can lead to job instability.

Money guide

Earnings in this sector vary greatly according to employer and project.

New entrants can expect to earn £18,000–£25,000. With experience, you can earn £20,000–£35,000. Those in senior positions can achieve up to £70,000.

Freelancers negotiate their own fees but tend to follow those set by BECTU.

Related opportunities

- Media Researcher p389
- TV and Film Camera Person/Operator p400
- TV, Film and Theatre Special Effects Technician p426

Further information

Broadcasting, Entertainment, Cinematograph and Theatre Union
www.bectu.org.uk

Creative Skillset
www.creativeskillset.org

TV, FILM AND RADIO PRODUCER

ENTRY LEVEL 6

Qualifications and courses

There are no specific academic requirements but producers need extensive experience in both the creative and business sides of the industry.

Given the competitive nature of the industry, many entrants have a Foundation degree, degree or HND in a related subject, such as film production, communications, broadcasting, media studies or drama. You will need at least 1 A level/2 H grades and 4 GCSEs/ National 5s (A*–C/A–C) for entry to a Foundation degree or HND and 2 A levels/3 H grades and 5 GCSEs/ National 5s (A*–C/A–C) for a degree.

As this is a job that requires experience, you will normally have to work your way up from the bottom – first as a runner, assistant producer and film production manager until finally reaching producer status. Gaining experience in a junior role provides a well-rounded view of the industry, invaluable knowledge and the opportunity to develop a network of contacts. Jobs are rarely advertised, therefore work experience may offer you a way of entry into the industry through the contacts you make at each placement.

You should create a showreel/portfolio so as to promote your work and demonstrate your aptitude to prospective employers. You may wish to seek an apprenticeship or course that incorporates practical work experience in order to show evidence of your creativity, leadership skills and an ability to cope under pressure. The Advanced Apprenticeship Programme in Digital and Creative Media may be available in your area or, if you have a degree, graduate training schemes are offered by some independent television companies.

If you are a radio producer working on news and current affairs shows you will need to have journalistic training. The Broadcast Journalism Training Council (BJTC) provides further information on accredited institutions and courses.

What the work involves

A producer develops ideas, employs key team members, has creative input, gets involved in casting decisions and script editing, and generally oversees the complete production. Many producers also play a financial role by approaching initial backers, securing rights and managing the budget throughout production.

You will be the lead person in TV, film and radio production. Producers have a detailed knowledge of the industry, coupled with sound business skills. You may also need to oversee the final editing process, as well as marketing and distribution plans.

Type of person suited to this work

It is essential to have a strong creative flair and a passion for your chosen medium. A well-rounded knowledge of your sector, spanning technical, creative and commercial aspects is also required.

Excellent communication skills are important and you should have the ability to provide inspiration and motivation for team members. You should be a competent problem solver who works well under pressure.

You also need strong negotiation, numeracy, multi-tasking and organisational skills to ensure that projects are carried out on time, within budget and according to the original plan.

Working conditions

Producers work in a variety of environments including offices, studios and external filming locations.

Your working day is determined by the demands of the filming schedule and as such the role requires a great deal of flexibility. Working hours can be long and erratic, with travel often required.

Future prospects

Over half of the UK's TV and film workforce are situated in south-east England with the rest spread across major cities such as Manchester and Glasgow.

The main employers are well-known broadcasters such as the BBC, TV and film production firms, and production and facilities houses.

Establishing good contacts throughout your career will ensure job progression as positions are rarely advertised and are awarded based on the reputation of the producer.

Advantages/disadvantages

You will have the satisfaction of seeing the results of your work in the public domain.

This is a fast-moving and varied industry which can provide exciting opportunities.

Producers are often employed on a freelance or contract basis which can lead to job instability.

Money guide

New entrants can expect to earn £18,000–£25,000 per year and, with experience, this can increase to £40,000–£55,000. Senior producers can achieve £60,000–£80,000.

Almost half of all producers in the industry are freelancers and daily rates are typically between £237 and £437.

Rates of pay are set by the Broadcasting, Entertainment, Cinematograph and Theatre Union (BECTU).

Related opportunities

- Media Researcher p389
- TV Floor Manager p401
- TV, Film and Radio Production Assistant/Runner p405

Further information

BBC Careers
www.bbc.co.uk/careers

Creative Skillset
www.creativeskillset.org

UK Film Council
www.ukfilmcouncil.org.uk

TV, FILM AND RADIO PRODUCTION ASSISTANT/RUNNER

ENTRY LEVEL 3

Qualifications and courses

Runner

There are no formal entry requirements as this role is a starting point in the TV and film industry. It may be advantageous to have a degree in TV/film/radio production or a media-related subject as competition for entry-level jobs is fierce but this is not expected. The Apprenticeship in Creative and Digital Media would be an excellent way of combining practical work experience with a relevant industry qualification and will enhance your skill set.

Given the competitive nature of the industry, enthusiasm is essential and you may have to carry out a significant amount of unpaid work experience in order to succeed. Building a network of contacts via work experience is particularly important as securing a position as a runner is often a combination of luck and timing. You should also build a portfolio of your work to show potential employers or for entry into competitions.

Production assistant

No formal qualifications are required but entry is highly competitive and many entrants are graduates of a relevant degree or have a postgraduate qualification. The BTEC Level 3 Certificate/Diploma in Creative Media Production (radio or TV and film) may also be useful. It is important that your course is accredited and offers opportunities for direct contact with the industry.

An understanding of the production process developed through relevant work experience is very important. As vacancies in this field are rarely advertised, it is important to be proactive and network to self-promote. Many production assistants begin as runners and work their way up. You should demonstrate your talents by way of a portfolio.

The UK Film Council and Creative Skillset have collaborated to open specialist training academies and offer advice on professional development.

What the work involves

Runner

You will provide a wide range of practical help and support to all members of the production team. As well as some administrative work, you will pass messages on and carry equipment and scripts between offices and sets – often with no prior notice.

Production assistant

Production assistants provide support to the producer and director to help ensure that productions run smoothly and to schedule. You will manage a range of key administrative activities, such as organising scripts and updating filming schedules, booking hotels and hiring equipment. You may also be responsible for managing budgets for productions.

Type of person suited to this work

It is essential to be enthusiastic, be willing to learn and to have a passion for your chosen medium.

You should be interested in learning about all areas of the field and be well versed in recent trends in the industry.

You should also enjoy problem solving and have the ability to work well under pressure and adhere to strict deadlines.

Working conditions

There are no standard hours in this profession as they vary depending on the project you are working on. During production, hours can be long, unpredictable and include evening and weekend work. Shift work is common and you may be required to be on-call at all times.

Many runners and project assistants work as freelancers. This means you will have to manage your own work schedule, often working on several projects simultaneously, and the workload may be irregular, with both busy and quiet periods. You will work in offices, studios and editing suites, as well as on location.

Future prospects

Most opportunities are in London and the south-east of England, where over half of the TV and film industries are based. This profession is fast-paced and there is fierce competition for entry-level positions.

With experience, you might look to become a researcher, working on programme development, or become a senior producer or editor in TV, film or radio.

Advantages/disadvantages

This is a fast-moving and varied industry with exciting opportunities.

Entry-level positions are very demanding and can affect your social life.

Money guide

Earnings in this sector vary greatly according to experience, media area, employer and project. Mostly people are employed on a freelance or contract basis.

Runner

New entrants can expect to earn £10,000–£12,000.

With experience, salaries can rise to £20,000.

Production assistant

Starting salaries are typically about £15,000 and those with more experience earning up to £25,000.

Senior production assistants can achieve up to £30,000.

Related opportunities

- TV and Film Camera Person/Operator p400
- TV Floor Manager p401
- TV, Film and Radio Producer p404

Further information

Broadcasting, Entertainment, Cinematograph and Theatre Union
www.bectu.org.uk

Creative Skillset
www.creativeskillset.org

Performing Arts

This job family contains a wide range of exciting jobs for those of you who want to work in theatre, music, on screen or behind the scenes. People working in this sector do so because they are passionate and creative and love the arts. Jobs can be scarce, so you will need to demonstrate that you are willing to work very hard but the rewards of being part of a fantastic production can be huge. There are also jobs available in this sector for those of you who are more technically minded – sound and lighting engineers also play a vital role in this industry as do people who have trained in fashion and textiles.

The jobs featured within this section are listed below. For similar jobs to the ones in this section turn to *Design, Arts and Crafts* on page 153 and *Marketing, Advertising, Media, Print and Publishing* on page 375.

ACTOR

ENTRY LEVEL 1

Qualifications and courses

Although there are no specific academic requirements to enter this profession and there is a variety of different routes into the industry, it is still incredibly competitive and a lot of actors have taken some formal training in order to hone their skills and prepare for the demands of the job.

Acting degrees are offered at both drama schools and universities. The National Council for Drama Training (NCDT) and the Conference of Drama Schools accredits full-time 3-year vocational drama school courses and degrees. Entry to these courses is by audition, and A levels/H grades or a BTEC Level 3 in Performing Arts are often required. Further study, such as a master's degree or postgraduate diploma in acting, is also available and can offer more opportunities to make contacts and develop your skills.

Graduates of NCDT-accredited courses who are legally entitled to work in the UK are eligible for Equity membership.

However, experience in the industry is more beneficial than qualifications. It can be helpful to join a local amateur dramatics group and undertake relevant work experience. The BBC, for instance, runs a number of work placement schemes which provide an insight into how the industry works.

Some actors gain experience working at holiday camps in entertainer roles. This is a good way of getting paid work and experience at the same time.

Networking is extremely important as a lot of actors secure roles through contacts they have made.

What the work involves

Actors perform in front of audiences and this can sometimes include dancing and singing as part of the role. There are opportunities for parts in dramatic plays, comedies and musicals on stage as well as on TV and in films.

You will research your characters, rehearse lines and attend auditions.

You will also attend costume fittings and make-up sessions.

Type of person suited to this work

Acting is a very competitive area so you should be truly dedicated to this career path. A good memory is important as you will have to learn lines.

There will be many times when you will be rejected at auditions mainly because you are just not the right face for the part, and so you will need to be able to cope with this and keep trying.

Adaptability, self-confidence and creativity are essential.

Working conditions

You will work mainly indoors, in theatres, halls and sometimes studios.

Your hours will be long and irregular, including evenings and weekends.

You could have to travel to different venues for your performances where you might spend time waiting for your part in the performance.

Future prospects

Prospects for success as an actor depend on talent, hard work and a bit of luck.

Some actors go on to work as writers or directors, while others train to teach drama in schools and colleges.

Advantages/disadvantages

Sometimes work can be irregular so you will not necessarily have a stable income.

The nature of the work means that you will experience a lot of rejection which may be hard to take.

It is a tough, demanding career to enter and to stay in, but once you get regular work it can be very satisfying.

Money guide

Basic rates of pay depend on experience and reputation. It is important to join Equity, the union for the world of entertainment – as this can help you negotiate fair rates of pay, terms and conditions. Union-negotiated pay scales are on the Equity website.

The minimum pay for theatre workers (as set by Equity) is £373 per week although this can increase if the actor has to relocate. The salary in the West End tends to be higher and you are guaranteed a minimum salary of £470 a week. The wages for TV and film work vary considerably and are dependent on how well known you are as an actor.

Although there are a few (very famous) actors who earn huge salaries, the majority of actors have to take on second employment to support themselves and raise their income. Only 6% of actors receive more than £30,000.

A lot of actors have an agent to help them secure work but also to help them negotiate higher wages. However, although agents can obtain higher wages they will also take a cut of your earnings, generally between 10% and 25%.

Related opportunities

- Artistic/Theatre Director p409
- Dancer p413
- Entertainer p415

Further information

Creative and Cultural Skills
www.ccskills.org.uk

Equity
www.equity.org.uk

National Council for Drama Training
www.ncdt.co.uk

Royal Academy of Dramatic Art
www.rada.ac.uk

ARTISTIC/THEATRE DIRECTOR

ENTRY LEVEL 6

Qualifications and courses

Most artistic directors hold a relevant degree in either English, creative/performing arts, drama or theatre studies on entry to the industry. HNDs and Foundation degrees in creative/performing arts or drama/theatre studies are available and may also be useful qualifications to hold prior to entering the theatre.

If you are looking to move into the industry after completing your first degree, Birkbeck, the Royal Academy of Dramatic Art (RADA) and Mountview Academy of Theatre Arts offer postgraduate courses in theatre direction.

Entry without any FE/HE qualifications is possible as the industry is reliant on reputation which you can gain through experience in acting, directing, writing and producing.

Of equal importance to professional qualifications are practical skills, acquired through work experience and involvement in school, college, university and community productions. Since few theatre companies offer in-house training, gaining this practical experience prior to applying for positions is vital.

The Arts Council England runs assistant director schemes for new entrants to the profession, and a few theatres and regional arts councils also offer training bursaries for candidates with exceptional potential. Competition for the bursaries is fierce.

What the work involves

Artistic and theatre directors have control over the artistic interpretation of plays, ballets, operas and other performances.

You will be responsible for coordinating all the creative elements of each production, including set and costume design, stylistic presentation, the interpretive work of artists, and any musical or choreographic sequences.

You will liaise with a number of other professionals on a daily basis, including producers, musical directors, technicians, theatre managers, financial backers, performing artists and writers.

You will select each production, oversee casting, and appear at performances and press events to help generate publicity around each show.

Type of person suited to this work

You will need fantastic artistic and creative vision, that you are able to express both verbally and in written documents. You will also need to have the courage and tenacity to make your vision a reality and present it to an audience.

You must be an excellent leader with the ability to inspire and motivate others. Being able to negotiate with writers, actors and other professionals is an asset.

You should have an in-depth knowledge of the theatre, including productions past and present, theatrical trends, and the history of the industry.

Working conditions

Hours can be irregular and you will be employed on a freelance basis through which contracts can be short. Longer fixed-term contracts are available, but they usually only last 3–5 years.

You will be mainly working in theatres and other performance venues. Although the final production may take place on a large stage, you could spend a great deal of time directing scenes in small, off-site rehearsal rooms.

You will mainly work indoors, although certain venues will require you to work outdoors in occasionally inhospitable conditions.

Future prospects

Competition in the theatrical industry is fierce, so you will need talent, dedication, good qualifications and experience.

Since the majority of theatrical work takes place in London you can expect to be based there for some or all of your career. The city is a base for most freelance directors, although there are opportunities in regional theatres.

As an experienced and admired artistic director, you could set up your own theatre company through which you can stage your performances. Other directors move from theatre into film or television work.

Advantages/disadvantages

Your creative ability will be the driving force behind the production of visually and technically beautiful or unusual performances.

The industry is extremely competitive so you might have to spend long periods of time working for free or at a minimal wage in order to build enough experience to work as an artistic director.

Money guide

Salaries are dependent upon the length and type of contract, for example if you were working freelance, touring or repertory.

Theatre directors who are working regularly can earn around £19,000.

Reaching the level of artistic director should increase your salary to about £23,000.

Well-established artistic directors who have built up a good reputation and are in demand across the industry can earn in excess of £40,000.

Related opportunities

- Actor p408
- Stage Manager p423
- Stagehand p424

Further information

Arts Council England
www.artscouncil.org.uk

Directors Guild of Great Britain and Directors Guild Trust
www.dggb.org

CHOREOGRAPHER

ENTRY LEVEL 1

Qualifications and courses

There are no formal academic entry requirements for this career, however GCSEs/National 5s and A levels/H grades are available in Dance, and some institutions offer BTEC Level 3 in Performing Arts.

Most choreographers have experience as dance performers prior to becoming choreographers and aptitude, commitment and ability are often valued more highly than formal qualifications.

Choreography can be studied as an option on some full-time vocational dance courses accredited by the Council for Dance Education and Training. Falmouth University, the University of Winchester and Northumbria University also offer specialised choreography courses. Entry onto these courses usually requires at least 2 A levels/3 H grades, one of which should be in Dance or a related subject, and 5 GCSEs/National 5s (A*–C/A–C), including English and Maths. You will also be expected to audition/perform and prove your choreography and dance skills.

Postgraduate courses in choreography are also available at several institutions, including the Laban Trinity Conservatoire of Music and Dance in London, London Contemporary Dance School and University of Roehampton.

Work experience alongside an experienced practitioner offers a good introduction to choreography and will certainly be taken into account if applying for a dance or choreography-related course.

What the work involves

As a choreographer, you will create and develop new dance movements for productions such as ballets, opera and musicals.

Creating a dance means planning the way dancers move to perform beautiful and exciting routines which interpret the music.

Choreographers work closely with performance artists, musical directors, ballet dance teachers and trainers.

Type of person suited to this work

You will need to have a keen, lively interest in music and movement, and a very well-developed sense of rhythm and timing.

Developing new routines requires an excellent knowledge of past and present pieces, understanding of how the body works and of possible movements to interpret the significance of events and mood changes through physical expression.

Choreographers have the responsibility of developing and teaching complicated movements and routines. You will need a good memory, clear communication skills, patience and an ability to get on well with others.

Working conditions

You will mainly work indoors in dance studios, theatres, TV or film studios.

Your initial contacts are likely to be producers, directors and musical conductors. Some choreographers work directly with modern composers, interpreting their music.

As production plans progress, you will start working directly with the performers. To do this you will travel frequently.

Future prospects

Jobs and opportunities can be limited as this is a highly competitive area of work, where experience counts.

Most choreographers work on a freelance or a fixed-term basis. There will be some full-time opportunities, particularly with larger dance companies, but these are likely to be competitive.

It is possible to find opportunities outside mainstream ballet; for example in modern dance companies and developing international venues.

Opera and musicals are becoming reinvigorated through audience demand and both performance areas require choreographers to interpret dance music and contextual pieces as dance routines. You may choose to set up your own dance company.

Advantages/disadvantages

Many hours are spent travelling to different venues – even overseas.

Seeing your finished routine beautifully performed will boost your morale.

Enthusiastic reviews will help your career progression.

It will be hard going and you will need patience and enthusiasm to get the best from dancers.

Money guide

Equity, the performing arts union, recommends a minimum daily sum of up to £130.

You could earn around £12,500 per year if you have just finished at a dance college, completed a degree or other college courses.

With experience, your salary could increase to £20,000 if you have moved into choreography as an experienced dancer.

Established, well-known choreographers can earn £50,000.

Related opportunities

- Artistic/Theatre Director p409
- Dancer p413
- Make-up Artist p417

Further information

Council for Dance Education and Training
www.cdet.org.uk

Creative and Cultural Skills
www.ccskills.org.uk

Dance UK
www.danceuk.org

Equity
www.equity.org.uk

COMPOSER/ SONGWRITER

ENTRY LEVEL 4

Qualifications and courses

Useful qualifications include GCSEs/National 5s and A levels/H grades in Music, BTEC Level 3 in Music Practice or Popular Music, and relevant degree courses. The Institute of Contemporary Music Performance offers a specialised course on songwriting and more institutions are investing in similar courses.

For entry onto a BTEC Level 3 course you will need 4 GCSEs/National 5s (A*–C/A–C) including Music or an equivalent qualification. Degree courses usually require 2 A levels/3 H grades, preferably with one in Music or a related subject, and 5 GCSEs/National 5s (A*–C/A–C). Candidates who have reached grade 8 in an instrument as classified by the Associated Board of the Royal Schools of Music are usually preferred.

A wide variety of postgraduate courses is also available. If you are looking to break into the world of classical composition, you are strongly advised to attain a postgraduate qualification.

It is possible, but extremely rare, to achieve success without having undertaken some of the relevant qualifications for this industry provided you have an exceptional reputation and vast experience.

What the work involves

Composers and songwriters create original music for a variety of uses. You could sell your songs to or be approached to write for an established commercial talent, or you could work within TV, film, computer games and radio. An understanding of the business and current trends may prove essential.

You could use a variety of tools and instruments when composing or writing, from a pen and paper to advanced computer software programs. You may also be expected to understand music production and recording practices.

You may also perform your compositions and songs, although this is most common for composers who are just starting out and those writing for individuals or small groups.

Networking is integral. The more people you know in the industry, the more options and chance you have of finding professional paid work.

Type of person suited to this work

You will need to have outstanding musical or lyrical talents.

You will need dedication, determination and self-discipline as the music industry is extremely tough and disappointment may well be frequent.

You should have a flexible attitude to your work and be willing to take on a range of commissions and assignments in order to build up your experience and reputation.

Working conditions

Composers and songwriters (the former in particular) can expect to work long and unsocial hours writing, rehearsing and performing their work.

Most composers and songwriters have other jobs in order to fund themselves whilst they establish a name in the music industry.

Future prospects

The music industry is highly competitive, so it can take a long time to gain any recognition for your work. This makes composing a challenging profession to choose and you will need to be extremely resilient.

Most composers or songwriters are self-employed. Although opportunities are available with theatrical companies, music publishers and universities.

You could gain great critical acclaim and commercial success, although the majority of work completed by composers and songwriters stems from smaller commissions within the media.

Advantages/disadvantages

You will be working in a job that you are passionate about, which will be immensely satisfying.

If you gain recognition the personal and financial rewards can be excellent.

The industry is highly competitive and chances of success are relatively slim. You may earn little money to begin with as a lot of early work could be done with small bands or amateur filmmakers (when creating soundtracks) etc, for the exposure and not the money.

Money guide

It is very hard to gauge salaries in this industry as so many composers and songwriters are freelance.

If you are commissioned by a large company or orchestra, as a composer you can expect to earn around £500 to £1,000 for each minute of music you create.

Songwriters could earn around £300 per minute. For title music, jingles and commercials both composers and songwriters can earn about £350 per minute.

You could also be entitled to royalties from your work.

Related opportunities

- Conductor p412
- Musician p418
- Singer p421

Further information

Arts Council England
www.artscouncil.org.uk

Sound and Music
www.soundandmusic.org

The British Academy of Songwriters, Composers and Authors
basca.org.uk

CONDUCTOR

ENTRY LEVEL 6

Qualifications and courses

Entry to this profession usually starts with a degree in music. Most universities require at least 2 A levels/3 H grades and 5 GCSEs/National 5s, as well as the ability to play an instrument to grade 8, for entry onto a music course. Upon completion of a degree, the majority of candidates go on to study for a postgraduate qualification in conducting. The Conservatoires UK Admissions Service (CUKAS) lists all the schools and conservatoires offering undergraduate and postgraduate courses.

Those who achieve good marks may be eligible for a scholarship offered by institutions such as the Royal Opera House, the Royal College of Music and the Guildhall School of Music and Drama.

Whilst studying, it is advisable to seek work experience as a deputy or assistant conductor. Working as a répétiteur in opera may also be beneficial, as you can watch and learn from highly skilled and experienced conductors.

Most conductors speak at least 2 European languages fluently, with the most useful being English, German, French and Italian.

Attending seminars run by the Association of British Orchestras (ABO) is a useful way to learn about current areas of interest in the sector. Qualified conductors are expected to engage in continuing professional development (CPD) throughout their careers to ensure that their knowledge of music theory and practice is up to date.

What the work involves

Music conductors work with musicians and singers to help shape their performance and make sure each musical piece is performed the way it should be.

You will be responsible for preparing musical scores for the performance and making decisions about how each musical piece should sound.

You need to understand the role of each performer and make sure every musician knows which part to play and does so correctly.

You may work with a wide variety of musicians, both amateur and professional, and these could include choirs and choruses, music students, youth groups and professional artists.

Type of person suited to this work

You must have a strong interest in music and extensive knowledge of the subject. You need to be able to play an instrument, preferably the piano, to a very high standard.

Good communication skills are vital, as is the ability to remain calm under pressure and work flexibly and with lots of different creative people.

You must be comfortable both taking control of a performance and being centre stage performing in front of an audience.

Working conditions

Working hours for conductors are varied, and you must be prepared to work whenever and wherever the opportunity arises. Hours include evenings and weekends for both rehearsals and performances.

You will divide your time between working in rehearsal rooms, concert halls, churches, theatres, opera houses and other venues.

Conductors often spend a lot of time away from home, both within the UK and abroad. The places where you stay will vary in standards.

A driving licence is useful as travel is often required.

Future prospects

A successful career in conducting is entirely dependent on your reputation and ability to build it up.

You may begin your career conducting small community or youth orchestras.

Once you have proved yourself and become established, opportunities to conduct large, high profile orchestras may become available.

Advantages/disadvantages

This job is ideal for those who are musically talented and like a balance between working with people and independently.

Producing a performance that audiences enjoy is incredibly satisfying.

In the early stages of your career it may be difficult to secure work and you could experience a sense of job instability.

Money guide

Conductors tend to be paid a fee for each concert.

At the start of your career, you may earn £380 per concert, but this could be lower.

With experience, you are likely to receive approximately £1,000 per concert.

The most successful conductors can achieve up to £5,000 per concert.

Related opportunities

- Composer/Songwriter p411
- Musician p418
- Private Music Teacher p186

Further information

Association of British Orchestras
www.abo.org.uk

Incorporated Society of Musicians
www.ism.org

International Artist Managers' Association
www.iamaworld.com

DANCER

ENTRY LEVEL 5

Qualifications and courses

Most professional dancers take classes in at least one form of dance from a very young age. Completing graded exams from awarding bodies such as the British Ballet Organisation or the Royal Academy of Dance will help you hone your skills and prove your desire to dance.

Entrants to this career usually undertake a 3-year vocational diploma or degree at a specialist school such as the Royal Academy of Dance (RAD). Entry is by audition, interview and a medical, and 5 GCSEs/National 5s (A*–C/A–C) are usually needed. For ballet, there are also physical requirements, including height and body proportion requirements.

The Council for Dance Education and Training (CDET) accredits full-time courses at vocational dance schools. Some universities or colleges of higher education offer degrees in dance but these courses tend to be more theoretical than performance based. A levels/H grades are usually required and candidates attend an audition. For those without the relevant qualifications, BTEC Level 3 in Performing Arts – Dance may be accepted instead. Postgraduate courses in professional dance or musical theatre are also available.

Some courses include a teacher training element. RAD and the Imperial Society of Teachers of Dancing (ISTD) provide specialist teacher training programmes. The British Ballet Organisation (BBO) and the British Theatre Dance Association (BTDA) also offer qualifications in dance and teacher training.

What the work involves

Dancers use the movement and language of their bodies as a way of expressing ideas and emotions to an audience, often accompanied by music.

You will focus on any number of styles including street, cultural, modern, contemporary, classical ballet, jazz or tap dance.

You might find work in theatres, cabaret clubs, cruise ships or video/TV studios. In addition to performing, you may use dance as a form of education or therapy.

Type of person suited to this work

Anyone entering this area of work must enjoy performing and be very talented to succeed. You must be dedicated to improving your technique through daily practice – sometimes for as long as 10 hours each day.

To be a successful dancer, you need a good sense of rhythm and timing. Being creative and imaginative with routines and choreography is desirable. It is important that you can cope with setbacks and remain positive and focused.

The majority of your time will be spent dancing in a group so you must enjoy working with others.

Working conditions

Most of your rehearsals and performances will take place indoors in studios, schools, theatres or other venues.

The job is physically demanding and requires working long hours, including evenings and weekends. Frequent travel is often required.

Future prospects

Your future prospects as a dancer will largely depend on talent, hard work and luck; competition is always strong. Only a few individuals become top performance artists in solo roles.

If you are employed by a dance company you can progress from chorus to solo parts, but this will depend on your skills and dedication.

Although dancing is a career for younger people, dance teachers can continue long after they finish as professional performers, and many set up private dance schools.

With experience you could also become a choreographer or take extra qualifications and undertake complementary professions such as dance movement therapy.

Advantages/disadvantages

Dance can be a fantastically rewarding career.

A career as a top soloist can be finished by the age of 30.

You will need to stay fit and healthy as injuries can necessitate a complete career change.

Money guide

Salaries for dancers depend on the length, type and location of the job.

Dancers usually work on a freelance basis and as such most dancers are members of Equity, the trade union for the performing arts.

Equity have established minimum weekly rates of £400 for dancers.

Experienced dancers can expect to earn £450 to £500 a week.

Those working on a West End show can achieve a weekly rate of £550.

Dance teachers are mainly self-employed and receive remuneration dependent on the type and size of dance school they work in.

Related opportunities

- Actor p408
- Choreographer p410
- Stagehand p424

Further information

Council for Dance Education and Training
www.cdet.org.uk

Equity
www.equity.org.uk

Royal Academy of Dance
www.rad.org.uk

Royal Ballet School
www.royalballetschool.org.uk

DJ

ENTRY LEVEL 2

Qualifications and courses

There is no specific entry route to this job and no formal qualifications are required.

Work experience is highly advisable in order to gain industry contacts and get valuable experience on the equipment. Those looking to work in radio can gain practical experience by volunteering at student, hospital or community radio stations. To work as a club DJ you need to develop your skills using decks, mixers and sampling equipment. Some top DJs offer masterclasses or allow work-shadowing; this can also help you develop useful industry contacts. You need to produce a demo CD to showcase your DJing abilities and style.

There are some qualifications that may help you with industry training such as the BTEC Level 3 in Music Technology specialising in DJ Technology, the Level 3 in Creative Media Production (Radio) and the Level 3 in Performing Arts. These courses are offered at some colleges of further education and the normal entry requirements are 4 GCSEs/National 5s (A*–C/A–C).

Other qualifications which may be useful include the City & Guilds Certificate and Diploma in Sound Engineering and Music Technology (Levels 1–3), the NCFE Award and Certificate in Music Technology (Levels 1–2) and the NCFE Award, Certificate and Diploma in Radio Production (Levels 1–3). Training in radio skills is also offered by CSV Media which runs Media Clubhouses around the UK. Radio DJs may also find qualifications in journalism, broadcasting or media advantageous.

Though not essential, Foundation degrees and degrees in subjects such as music technology, audio technology, sound engineering and electronics may enhance your technical skills and increase your job opportunities.

What the work involves

You will play and mix music for audiences at live venues or on the radio. You could use vinyl, CDs, MP3s, turntables, mixers, microphones and amplifiers.

Club DJs keep people dancing in bars and clubs. You will create your own sounds and mixes and use lighting and visual effects in time to the beats.

Mobile DJs play at weddings and other social occasions.

As a radio DJ, you will work in a studio playing records, interviewing musicians and chatting to listeners.

VJing (video jockeying) is an alternative form of artistic expression, using a good computer and software to mix/inter-splice sounds with images, from video clips and loops, in real time.

Type of person suited to this work

You must have a passion for music, excellent coordination, good communication and listening skills, and a lively outgoing personality.

You need advanced technical skills as DJs use the latest in turntables, amplifiers and multimedia, and practise techniques such as mixing, scratching and cross fading to make their performance interesting.

Hard work and persistence are key to success. As most DJs are self-employed, basic business skills are an advantage.

Working conditions

As a DJ, you could work in clubs, on radio, in hotels, in holiday camps or at festivals and gigs. You will work long, irregular hours including weekends.

You will be required to travel to different venues so a driving licence is useful.

High noise levels are an occupational hazard for DJs; you need to take steps to protect your hearing.

Future prospects

Some DJs stay in the job only a short time before moving on. Many work part time alongside a daytime job.

You have to be a self-starter and seek out opportunities as jobs are rarely advertised. Experienced DJs can get seasonal work in holiday camps. Some move into careers in music production or retail.

Increasingly, DJs are finding opportunities working with VJs who create pop videos.

Advantages/disadvantages

DJs are usually passionate about music, so you get to work with what you love.

There can be heavy equipment to move around, often in the early hours.

Over time you will buy new technology and update your deck and equipment. Start-up costs are likely to be high (in excess of £1,500).

Money guide

Your earnings will depend on the event, venue and your reputation and experience. At the start of their career, DJs often do unpaid work to gain experience.

Your starting fee per session may range from £50 to £300 with very established and experienced DJs going on to earn £500 to £1,000 for a session.

Top club DJs with celebrity status can achieve an annual salary in excess of £100,000, however most DJs have another job to supplement their income.

Related opportunities

- Musician p418
- Private Music Teacher p186
- Sound Engineer p422

Further information

Access to Music
www.accesstomusic.co.uk

SAE Institute
www.sae.edu

ENTERTAINER

ENTRY LEVEL 1

Qualifications and courses

Entertainers do not need to hold any academic qualifications as the most important requirement is to have a skill or talent that will entertain audiences. Specific training and courses may be beneficial in developing your skills and proving your ability and commitment to potential employers. Previous experience, such as acting in school or community shows, could also prove advantageous.

Entry routes are numerous and varied and could include entering talent competitions, working in holiday centres, performing in local clubs and bars or undertaking professional training courses.

Courses that will lead to useful qualifications include the BTEC Certificate in Performing Arts (Levels 2–3) and the BTEC HNC/HND in Performing Arts (Levels 4–5). You could also take an HNC/HND in Acting and Performance or a Foundation degree/degree in performing arts. BTEC entry requirements are usually 4 GCSEs/National 5s (A*–C/A–C) and all degree courses require at least 2 A levels/3 H grades, with one in a related subject.

If you are intending to work with children and/or vulnerable adults, you will also be required to obtain clearance from the Disclosure and Barring Service (DBS) before entering this profession.

What the work involves

Entertainers perform amusing or amazing acts in front of audiences. They include comedians, circus performers, street artists, cabaret performers, dancers, musicians and magicians.

You could specialise in one area or skill, or you might have several skills that you can combine into one act.

You will have to source your own props and costumes, attend regular auditions, book venues, rehearse your routine and also carry out your own promotional work.

Type of person suited to this work

You will need natural confidence and a very outgoing nature in order to present a lively and entertaining act to your audience. You will need to be extremely talented in your chosen field.

You should be good with a wide range of people, as your audience could include members of all ages and backgrounds.

You should have good business awareness, be entrepreneurial in your approach and creative in marketing yourself in order to attract interest in your act and increase your bookings. You must be extremely punctual and reliable so as not to disappoint or annoy a venue or your audience.

Working conditions

Working hours vary. Most performances take place during evenings and weekends, with occasional daytime work. You can choose to work full time if you have a number of bookings, or part time in order to supplement your income with another job.

You could have regular weekly, fortnightly or monthly jobs but a great deal of work is on a one-off basis.

You may work across numerous venues throughout the UK (and abroad) so a driving licence would be useful.

Future prospects

The majority of entertainers are self-employed, although there are employment opportunities with circuses, theme parks, holiday parks and cruise ship companies.

Some may also work with one or more agents, who help with promotion and finding bookings in return for a small fee or commission from earnings.

Overseas work is possible, especially if you work for a cruise ship company or if you have an act that is appreciated across a variety of cultures.

Advantages/disadvantages

You will travel across the UK, and even the world, showcasing your talent to a variety of people to entertain and amaze them.

If you are self-employed, you have the opportunity to choose your hours and bookings to fit around other commitments.

The industry is competitive and few entertainers are able to pursue their career on a full-time basis.

Money guide

Salaries for entertainers vary depending on your act, reputation and level of success.

New entrants who have regular work can expect around £10,000 a year.

With experience, you could earn between £12,000 and £20,000.

Well-established entertainers, such as those with regular bookings at reputable venues, or regular TV appearances, can earn over £30,000.

In a recent Equity member survey however, only 6% of those in the entertainment industry earned over £30,000 the previous year, and nearly half had earned under £6,000.

Related opportunities

- Dancer p413
- Musician p418
- Singer p421

Further information

Equity
www.equity.org.uk

National Centre for Circus Arts
www.nationalcircus.org.uk

Spotlight
www.spotlight.com

LIGHTING TECHNICIAN

ENTRY LEVEL 3

Qualifications and courses

All lighting technicians must be fully qualified electricians. The Advanced Level Electrotechnical Apprenticeship may be available or you could study for the NVQ Level 3 in either Electrotechnical Services or Electrotechnical Systems and Equipment.

Colleges, universities and drama schools offer courses in subjects such as lighting technology, lighting design and technical theatre, film, theatre design and theatre production, which include the study of lighting. Many of these are accredited by the National Council for Drama Training (NCDT). There is also an NVQ in Film and Television Lighting (Lighting Technician) (Levels 3–4) for those wishing to specialise in TV and film.

A degree in theatre practice specialising in production lighting is available at the Central School of Speech and Drama and Rose Bruford College offers degree programmes in lighting design or creative lighting control. The general entry requirements for a degree are 2 A levels/3 H grades and 5 GCSEs/National 5s (A*–C/A–C). The Association of British Theatre Technicians (ABTT) also provides the Bronze, Silver and Gold Awards for Theatre Electricians.

An alternative route which may be available is the Apprenticeship in Technical Theatre at both Intermediate and Advanced Levels which would combine practical work experience with the study towards professional qualifications.

Experience is necessary and may be accumulated within amateur dramatic companies or drama societies at university etc. This will allow you to train, network and prove your proficiency to potential employers.

The BBC offers a work experience scheme but places are limited. Volunteering with student or community film projects, theatres or concert venues would be useful.

What the work involves

Lighting technicians are responsible for creating stage lighting effects, working closely with the set designer and producer. It is important to visit venues before productions start and watch rehearsals to get the lighting effects right for live performances.

You will do lighting for advertising sets, in video production, theatre and broadcasting work.

You will be responsible for rigging and setting up the lighting, and plotting and programming the lighting requirements.

Type of person suited to this work

Anyone entering this career must have an interest in electrical work and electronics, combined with a strong interest in theatre and performance or live concerts.

Lighting technicians need to have a creative flair as the main aim of this job is to create the atmosphere required by the producer.

You will also need to be physically fit and work well in a team.

In some situations, for example changing or operating spotlights, the tasks could involve working at heights, and would not suit a person who suffers from vertigo.

Working conditions

You will work indoors and outdoors, usually working afternoons, evenings and weekends.

You will work with lots of heavy equipment and you may sometimes need to wear protective steel toe-capped boots.

You may have to work in cramped spaces with computerised control systems.

You will often be away from home for weeks and months if you are travelling with a roadshow.

Future prospects

Theatre lighting is usually provided by specialist companies which employ technicians on a short-term contract basis.

However, once you are experienced and known in the trade, your opportunity to join the backstage crew of a particular theatre group increases.

Progression as a lighting technician relies on skills and dedication. When in demand, you can become a senior or chief lighting technician and, in some cases, technical manager.

Advantages/disadvantages

You will have irregular working hours, including evening and weekend work, and you will frequently be away from home.

Seeing your skills and experience light up a set or production will be a great confidence booster.

Money guide

Trainee technicians start on around £9,500 per year.

Experienced lighting technicians working in theatre can earn between £15,000 and £25,000.

Earnings are higher in film/TV and you could receive up to £30,000.

Many lighting technicians work on a freelance basis, earning a daily or weekly rate which ranges widely.

The Broadcasting, Entertainment, Cinematograph and Theatre Union (BECTU) recommends a daily rate of £250.

Related opportunities

- Electrician p78
- Stage Manager p423
- TV, Film and Theatre Special Effects Technician p426

Further information

Association of British Theatre Technicians
www.abtt.org.uk

National Electrotechnical Training
www.netservices.org.uk

MAKE-UP ARTIST

ENTRY LEVEL 2

Qualifications and courses

Make-up artists in theatre/TV/film are usually trained in beauty therapy or both hairdressing and make-up. Relevant qualifications include NVQs in Beauty Therapy (Levels 1–3) and BTECs in Beauty Therapy (Levels 2–3). In Scotland there is also the HNC/HND in Beauty Therapy.

There is a range of specialist further education courses in theatrical and/or media make-up, including both short courses and diplomas. Relevant qualifications are available from the Vocational Training Charitable Trust (VTCT), the International Therapy Examination Council (ITEC) and the National Association of Screen Make-Up Artists and Hairdressers (NASMAH). City & Guilds also offer a Diploma in Hair and Media Make-Up (Levels 2–3).

A number of universities and colleges run HND courses in theatrical and media make-up or make-up artistry. A Foundation degree in Hair and Make-Up for Film and TV and a degree in make-Up and prosthetics for performance are available at the London College of Fashion. Degrees and diplomas in subjects such as fine art, visual art, fashion design or graphic design can be useful.

Relevant experience is desirable and can be accumulated via working with amateur dramatic companies or by working in beauty salons.

What the work involves

Your work will involve applying make-up and arranging hair to produce the right look for male and female artists and performers in films, TV and stage productions. You will need to listen to the director in order to create the desired look for the individual characters or troupe.

You could be employed in TV, by a video production company, as a specialist in wedding and occasion make-up, by a theatre or film company, or be self-employed, perhaps as part of a backstage team.

Type of person suited to this work

Anyone who considers doing make-up work needs to be creative, with the imagination to visualise the finished effect. You will have to pay great attention to detail. The job requires excellent communication skills, as you will need tact to advise colleagues or clients on their image.

At times, there will be many people needing to be made up for a particular scene and you could be working under intense pressure. Self-confidence and an outgoing personality are positive factors in building relationships and succeeding at work.

Working conditions

Most of your work will be undertaken indoors in theatres, studios, beauty salons and, at first, possibly in retail outlets.

Long hours and weekend work are common. Doing make-up involves spending extended periods of time standing over customers and you will need to be physically fit.

If you are self-employed, you will need to provide your own cosmetics and you will need carry all your equipment and materials with you.

A driving licence would be useful for travelling to different jobs.

Future prospects

Although this is not a huge area for employment, there will always be a demand for make-up artists. The larger towns and cities present the best opportunities. Although limited, some work could be available in hotels or on cruise ships.

Once you have gained experience, you can secure regular work in TV or video, on a cruise ship, in a hotel, a retail store or with a theatre company. You could set up your own beauty salon.

Competition is strong and progression depends upon the reputation, contacts and talent of the individual.

Advantages/disadvantages

Working hours may be irregular and unsocial, especially if you do make-up both before and during performances.

It is highly satisfying to see your work on stage or set, or to make people look nice for a special occasion.

Tools and cosmetics may be provided, but it is often expected that you will have your own make-up kit with you. Professional kits can cost up to £1,500.

Money guide

Most make-up artists work on a freelance basis and their earnings depend on their reputation, experience and the project they are working on.

Recommended rates of pay are set by the Broadcasting, Entertainment, Cinematograph and Theatre Union (BECTU).

A make-up artist assistant should earn between £178 and £198 for a 10-hour day.

The daily rate for a make-up artist is between £206 and £257.

A chief make-up artist can achieve £268 to £289 for a 10-hour day.

Related opportunities

- Beauty Consultant p430
- Beauty Therapist p431
- Hairdresser/Barber p441

Further information

British Association of Beauty Therapy and Cosmetology
www.babtac.com

Greasepaint
www.greasepaint.co.uk

Make Up Artist magazine
www.makeupmag.com

MUSICIAN

ENTRY LEVEL 4

Qualifications and courses

Classical musicians undertake extensive musical training and academic qualifications with most taking all the graded examinations in their chosen instrument/s, as well as further related courses. These courses include GCSEs/National 5s and A levels/H grades in Music and the HNC Level 4 and HND Level 5 in Music or Music Technology.

Some musicians also pursue music degrees at university, specialist courses at music colleges (conservatoires) and relevant postgraduate qualifications. For entry to a music degree you usually need a minimum of 2 A levels/3 H grades, including Music, 5 GCSEs/National 5s (A*–C/A–C) and grade 8 in your chosen instrument or voice. Postgraduate programmes require entrants to hold a relevant first degree.

Popular musicians do not need to hold any qualifications for entry to the industry. However, undertaking training may prove your ability and dedication to prospective employers. Any of the qualifications mentioned above would be useful for popular musicians. There is also the option to study for a degree in popular music.

Armed forces musicians do not need to hold any formal qualifications and aptitude in your chosen instrument/s will be assessed during an audition.

What the work involves

Whether you work as a classical, popular or armed forces musician, your main responsibility will be to perform to and entertain an audience.

You will spend the majority of your time practising in order to develop and strengthen your ability on the instrument/s you play.

You could compose your own material or play existing music from a variety of genres.

Type of person suited to this work

You must be extremely musical, particularly if you are looking to work as a classical musician. You will need to be very confident in yourself and your abilities, as well as having considerable stage presence to hold the attention of an audience.

Throughout the music industry, there is intense competition for jobs. You will need determination, tenacity and resilience in order to cope with knock-backs and persevere.

Working conditions

You must be prepared to work long, unsocial hours in a variety of environments including clubs and bars. You may have to work away from home for long periods of time.

Classical musicians tend to work in locations such as concert halls, theatres, parks and recording studios.

Musicians employed by the armed forces usually perform for military parades, regimental dinners, state occasions, sporting events and other special occasions.

Future prospects

Classical musicians may rise to enjoy success as solo artists or may work in group ensembles, such as orchestras, in which there are chances for promotion. Diversifying into teaching is also common.

Prospects for popular musicians are varied and depend a great deal on how successful you become. Many decide to move into a business role, for example as a manager or representative for a recording company. You could also become a music teacher.

Armed forces musicians usually move across various bands throughout their career, whilst also progressing up through the standard ranks as they gain relevant management, leadership and military skills.

Advantages/disadvantages

As a musician, you could work in a variety of disciplines and with a range of different people, so the job will be stimulating and interesting.

Competition is intense in the music industry so you will have to work incredibly hard.

Money guide

Classical musicians employed by an orchestra usually receive a salary of between £22,000 and £26,000 with principal players earning from £25,000 up to £50,000.

Session musicians could receive £120 to £350 for a 3-hour job.

Solo musicians can achieve £500 to £2,000 a week, depending on their popularity.

Armed forces musicians have a starting salary of about £14,000, rising to £18,000 upon completion of training.

Army musicians on a fast-track scheme can earn over £23,000 after 2 years.

Pay in the army will increase as you gain experience and promotions.

Related opportunities

- Composer/Songwriter p411
- Entertainer p415
- Singer p421

Further information

Arts Council England
www.artscouncil.org.uk

Associated Board of the Royal Schools of Music
gb.abrsm.org/en/home

Royal Military School of Music
www.army.mod.uk/music

PROPS MAKER/ ASSISTANT

ENTRY LEVEL 3

Qualifications and courses

There is no standard route into this career and it is possible to enter without academic qualifications. However, to be employed as an assistant you will be expected to have at least GCSEs/National 5s (A*–C/A–C) in English, Maths and Art. You will also need a good history of relevant work experience, possibly from student productions or amateur theatre, and a lot of talent and dedication.

Most prop makers have relevant qualifications, such as the BTEC Level 3 Certificate in Production Arts, specialising in Stage Management or Set Design and Construction, or the BTEC HNC/HND in Performing Arts specialising in Production. The Royal Academy of Dramatic Art (RADA) offers a specialist course in Property Making and the Central School of Speech & Drama provides a degree in Theatre Practice (Prop Making).

Degrees, Foundation degrees and postgraduate courses are available in set design, prop making and stage management. Other useful subjects include art and design, fine art, 3D design and model-making. Entry requirements for a degree are usually at least 2 A levels/3 H grades, including Art, and 5 GCSEs/National 5s (A*–C/A–C). Most course providers also ask candidates to present a portfolio of work for entrance assessment.

You may be able to receive apprenticeship-style training at the start of your career with the BBC's Art Department Training Scheme, which lasts 12 months. Apprenticeships may also be available with regional screen agencies or media training organisations.

What the work involves

Props makers and their assistants are responsible for designing, changing, making and finishing the props used in theatre, video, film, TV or circus work.

Working closely with set designers, prop makers help create the right atmosphere within particularly stages/scenes by creating relevant and necessary set dressings and items for actors to interact with.

You will spend a considerable amount of time researching the historical and cultural background of the props to ensure that they have the look and feel the era they represent.

You will be working with different materials, such as wood, fibreglass, fabric and metal, and you will use a range of practical skills including carpentry, modelling and painting.

Type of person suited to this work

You will need to have a mixture of practical and artistic skills in order to have the vision to design props and the ability to make them yourself.

You will be taking direction from theatre/TV producers, so you must be able to listen carefully to their briefs and ideas, and translate them into actual props. You will need good problem-solving skills so that you can balance meeting people's expectations and working to a budget.

The ability to use a variety of IT packages, including computer-aided design (CAD), is useful.

Working conditions

Working hours vary but you can expect to work long hours over evenings and weekends in order to meet deadlines now and again. You will be working in small studios and prop rooms and these locations can often be cramped.

You may also spend time visiting suppliers for equipment and travelling to libraries and museums to carry out research.

You will have to wear relevant safety equipment when dealing with materials such as wood, metal, fibreglass and any chemical products.

Future prospects

The majority of props makers are freelance so you will be employed on short-term projects most of the time. These could be for film studios, theatres, TV companies or museums.

Career progression is dependent upon building a good reputation and an excellent portfolio of work.

With experience, you could move into set design or take a more general role in stage management.

Advantages/disadvantages

Working in a creative industry such as theatre or film provides challenging, exciting work opportunities.

You will be using a mixture of artistic, practical and intellectual skills which will be tiring but rewarding.

Working freelance can create a sense of job instability and it can be difficult when you have a period of time without work.

Money guide

As an assistant to a props maker, you can expect to earn about £12,000.

Props makers who are just starting in the industry usually receive an annual salary of around £15,000.

If you gain a good reputation and start to work on large productions with big budgets, you could earn in excess of £40,000.

Many props makers work on a freelance basis and negotiate fees dependent on the project and their reputation. The Broadcasting, Entertainment, Cinematograph and Theatre Union (BECTU) suggest a daily rate of between £190 and £375.

Related opportunities

- Make-up Artist p417
- Stage Manager p423
- Wardrobe Assistant p427

Further information

Creative and Cultural Skills
www.ccskills.org.uk

Royal Academy of Dramatic Art
www.rada.ac.uk

Stage Management Association
www.stagemanagementassociation.co.uk

ROADIE

ENTRY LEVEL 1

Qualifications and courses

There are no formal entry qualifications. Most people enter this career through experience of working with a friend or other contacts and the majority of roadies will learn the trade from working with other more experienced people. Helping small local bands and school productions is a good way to start and gain some experience; however, if you are under 18 you may not be able to work in some licensed premises.

Though not essential, GCSEs/National 5s and A levels/H grades in Music or Music Technology may prove advantageous. Qualifications in technical procedures such as electronics, music rigging, sound production, lighting and pyrotechnics could set you apart from the intense competition, and there are various BTECs, HNCs/HNDs, NVQs/SVQs, City & Guilds courses, degrees and postgraduate courses available. The Creative & Cultural department of the National Skills Academy also provides relevant courses and the Creative Apprenticeship in Music.

Useful skills and qualifications include a First Aid certificate and the ability to speak one or more foreign languages. The Production Services Association (PSA) operates a Safety Passport scheme that deals with issues including manual handling, transport and general safety precautions.

A full driving licence is helpful and a large goods vehicle (LGV) licence or passenger carrying vehicle (PCV) licence could be useful if you need to drive the tour bus or larger vehicles to transport heavy equipment.

What the work involves

Roadies are responsible for setting up a range of equipment for music concerts and events including amplification systems, electrical cabling, stage and special effects lighting.

You will have to move and set up heavy equipment, load and unload vans and trailers and do lots of driving around. You will need to maintain and fine-tune your equipment on a regular basis.

Your work could include handling pyrotechnics, laser displays, computer/live film feeds and video links.

Type of person suited to this work

You will need to have a strong interest in music, technology and electronics. It is essential to have good communication skills and an interest in people, and be creative and practical.

Physical fitness and stamina will be essential, with a sense of humour a bonus. Sets will have to be assembled and disassembled safely to tight deadlines so you should be able to work whilst under pressure.

As most roadies are self-employed, a well-organised person with some business skills will do well by maintaining their accounts and keeping records of bookings.

Working conditions

You will have exceptionally long working hours, mainly evenings, nights and weekends. If you are on a tour you might be working 7 days a week. Three-month contracts are typical in this line of work.

The work is very physical and there is lots of heavy lifting involved. Sometimes you could be working at heights on electrical cabling.

Future prospects

There is strong competition for jobs. The work is unpredictable and you might need another job to boost your income. Work can be seasonal, with more roadies needed for summer events.

Marketing your services will be essential for getting gigs; many roadies now use websites to advertise.

A wide range of technical skills such as stage lighting and management or sound engineering will improve your chances of employment and could enable you to secure lighting or sound jobs in film, television or theatre.

The HND in Music Industry Management and other relevant qualifications could also allow you to work in promotions, productions or band management.

Advantages/disadvantages

Roadies work long unsociable hours and there is lots of travelling.

Very loud sounds will damage your hearing if your ears are unprotected.

You will get to attend many gigs and concerts for free.

Money guide

Most roadies work freelance and your pay will depend on the gig, your experience and general availability of roadies.

As a starter, with regular work, you could earn around £12,000 per year.

A roadie with electrical, audio or video skills can earn in excess of £21,000. With excellent technical skills, pay can rise to £30,000.

On contract to a big touring band, you could earn in excess of £35,000.

Related opportunities

- Large Goods Vehicle Driver p580
- Lighting Technician p416
- Sound Engineer p422

Further information

National Skills Academy for Creative & Cultural
http://ccskills.org.uk/network

Production Services Association
www.psa.org.uk

Stage Management Association
www.stagemanagementassociation.co.uk

SINGER

ENTRY LEVEL 1

Qualifications and courses

Academic qualifications are not strictly required in order to become a singer, but they often demonstrate honed talent, commitment, and the necessary expertise to succeed in the music industry to potential employers or clients.

Relevant qualifications include the national exams in singing (grades 1 to 8) from the Royal Schools of Music, and GCSEs/National 5s and A levels/H grades in Music. There are also BTEC courses in music, performing arts, music performance, music practice and music technology, and HNC/HND courses and degrees in popular music and related subjects. Entry requirements for these courses vary; BTECs usually require 4 GCSEs/National 5s (A*–C/A–C) or equivalent, while HNC/HND programmes require an additional A level/H grade, and degree programmes require at least 2 A levels/H grades, often including Music, and 5 GCSEs/National 5s (A*–C/A–C). Specialist singing degrees are also available from institutions such as the Academy of Contemporary Music.

You could perform with choirs or in amateur productions and talent contests as this will help you develop as a rounded performer who can hold the attention of an audience.

Networking is essential and an understanding of marketing and social media may help you get noticed and help build a fanbase.

Classical singing is formally taught at a number of different institutions. As part of a much longer preparation process, singers take postgraduate courses in either opera or oratorio, dependent on their repertoire, alongside short courses.

What the work involves

Singers perform in front of an audience in clubs, at gigs, on television or radio, in a recording studio or in an opera house. They work as solo artists, or as part of a backing group, choir or chorus.

You will spend many hours practising in order to develop and strengthen your breathing and vocal ability. You will need to have good diction, have a good grasp of language and may even be asked sometimes to perform in a variety of languages, including Latin and French.

You will work with a variety of musicians and music industry professionals, including orchestras, bands, session musicians, sound engineers, and maybe a manager.

Type of person suited to this work

You will need to have an exceptional talent for singing in order to get noticed in the music industry.

Owing to the intense competition in this area, you will also need determination, self-discipline and resilience in order to cope with disappointments and to persevere in order to achieve your goals.

You will need to be very confident in yourself and your abilities. It is difficult to hold an audience without stage presence and charisma.

Working conditions

As a singer you can expect to work long and unsociable hours, over evenings and weekends, as this is when the majority of your audience will be free.

You may have to travel long distances for gigs and rehearsals.

You could work in a variety of locations, from small clubs and theatres to large concert halls and even outdoor venues.

Future prospects

Singing is a highly competitive industry, and opportunities for full-time work are extremely limited. Most professionals supplement their income with another job, so you could look into teaching, or writing songs and jingles for other artists.

Most successful singers move to London to pursue their careers, as this is where the majority of opportunities lie.

You may well work with an agent or manager at some point in your career. Their purpose is to offer you career advice and to find you singing opportunities.

Advantages/disadvantages

You will be fulfilling a passion while also doing your job, which is rare and satisfying.

You will be bringing pleasure to the people in your audience, no matter how big or small.

You will have to work long and unsociable hours.

You will have to be resilient in order to persevere despite negative feedback on occasion.

Money guide

As a solo singer, you could earn between £150 and £450 per concert.

Chorus singers usually earn between £70 and £100 and backing singers on albums are paid £110 or more for a 3-hour recording session.

If you become a commercial success you could earn significantly more, especially if you write your own songs and earn royalties.

If you go on to perform in the theatre, there are set rates of pay that employers must adhere to. For example, chorus members command £650 per week for performances onstage in London's West End.

Related opportunities

- Composer/Songwriter p411
- Entertainer p415
- Musician p418

Further information

BRIT School for Performing Arts and Technology
www.brit.croydon.sch.uk

Creative and Cultural Skills
www.ccskills.org.uk

SOUND ENGINEER

ENTRY LEVEL 2

Qualifications and courses

Sound engineers can work within several different industries, such as music, film, TV, computer games and theatre. It is possible to become a sound engineer without gaining any relevant qualifications, as many companies take on trainees as runners or assistants, and you can build your knowledge whilst you work.

However, job competition is intense and larger studios and companies prefer candidates to hold relevant qualifications. These could include: GCSEs/National 5s or A levels/H grades in Music, Maths and Physics; BTEC HNCs in Live Sound, Stage Sound, or Light and Sound; HNDs in Sound Technology or Sound Engineering and Electronics; Foundation degrees and degrees in music production or audio technology. Entry requirements for a degree course are typically 2 A levels/3 H grades and 5 GCSEs/National 5s (A*–C/A–C), and HNDs usually require 1 A level/H grade and 4 GCSEs/National 5s (A*–C/A–C). Organisations such as the Association of Professional Recording Services provide a list of current accredited short courses that will allow you to develop your skills.

Pre-entry experience is essential and can be accumulated by volunteering with recording studios, working with local bands and working on school plays or with amateur dramatic companies.

Postgraduate qualifications are also offered by a limited number of providers. The University of Westminster runs a master's degree course in audio production, and the National Film and Television School offers a Diploma in Sound Recording for Film and Television or a Master of Arts degree in Sound Design for Film and Television.

For theatre sound engineers, many drama schools offer courses in theatre lighting and sound which may be useful. All good programmes are accredited by the National Council for Drama Training.

What the work involves

Sound engineers set up, operate and maintain a range of technical equipment that is designed to capture, magnify and manipulate words and music.

Theatrical sound engineers create 'sound plots', choose equipment and insert sound effects according to the instructions of the director of the production.

Sound engineers working in the recording industry capture speech, music and other sound effects and modify them using sophisticated electronic equipment for a number of purposes including creating pop songs, adverts or computer game soundtracks to name but 3 possible outlets for your work.

Type of person suited to this work

You will need a good musical ear and excellent sense of timing in order to put together pleasing and appropriate soundtracks/background audio to a range of productions.

You should also have knowledge of both electronics and IT systems.

Recording industry sound engineers must also have a good knowledge of both recording and post-production processes.

Working conditions

Sound engineers working in both theatre and the recording industry should expect to work varied hours that will encompass day, evening and weekend commitments.

Theatre sound engineers will spend the majority of their working day confined to a small control box which may be cramped and often is plunged into semi-darkness.

Recording sound engineers work in studios, some of which are large and air-conditioned, whilst others can be small and cramped. You will usually be working in artificial light and the atmosphere can be stressful when working against deadlines.

Future prospects

Competition for jobs is intense, and you may spend a long while proving your credentials as a runner or gofer.

You could work for a variety of employers, including theatres, opera and ballet houses, commercial recording studios or media post-production departments.

Theatre sound engineers may go on to become sound designers with greater creative input in productions, whereas many recording sound engineers move into roles as producers.

Advantages/disadvantages

You will work with a variety of people on diverse projects, so each day will bring new challenges and rewards.

Theatre and media are exciting industries to work in as there is constant cultural and technical development.

You will have to work long hours that will often fall over evenings and weekends.

Money guide

Starting salaries for sound engineers, whether they work in theatre or the recording industry, range from £15,000 to £18,000 per year. With experience, this could rise to £30,000.

Sound engineers working on large productions, with big companies or well-known artists, can earn in excess of £40,000.

Related opportunities

- Lighting Technician p416
- Musician p418
- TV, Film and Theatre Special Effects Technician p426

Further information

National Film and Television School
http://nfts.co.uk

Professional Lighting and Sound Association
www.plasa.org

STAGE MANAGER

ENTRY LEVEL 3

Qualifications and courses

Practical experience is often valued as highly as formal qualifications by employers and can be gained through volunteer work with local theatres or student productions. You could also begin your career as part of the stage crew and progress up to the position of stage manager. However, as this is a competitive industry, you may find that qualifications will help prove your proficiency and improve your future prospects.

You can complete a BTEC Level 3 Certificate in Production Arts specialising in Stage Management which lasts 2–3 years when studied full time. The selection process involves an interview and providing a portfolio of your practical work.

Drama schools such as the Royal Academy of Dramatic Art (RADA) and the London Academy of Music and Dramatic Art (LAMDA) offer Foundation degrees and degrees in stage management and theatre production. The general entry requirements for a degree are 2 A levels/3 H grades and 5 GCSEs/National 5s (A*–C/A–C), as well as a demonstrable interest in theatre production. HNCs/HNDs are also available in Performing Arts (Production), Technical Theatre and Theatre Production. The National Council for Drama Training (NCDT) accredits vocational stage management courses.

You could also undertake a Creative Apprenticeship (Technical Theatre Pathway) and specialise in stage management.

The Stage Management Association (SMA) runs a variety of short courses for people already working as stage managers or assistant stage managers.

What the work involves

Stage managers work with designers, directors and producers, assessing and discussing what props, lighting and other stage support are needed for the production.

You are the link between the artistic and technical aspects of all productions, as you are in charge of everything that happens on stage including calling actors, giving technical cues and moving scenery.

You could work on numerous types of production, such as theatrical performances, opera, ballet and even music festivals.

Type of person suited to this work

You will need to have artistic flair, be practical, communicate instructions clearly and manage others confidently.

Good time management skills are crucial.

The work is demanding as the successful running of the backstage support for the performance rests with you. A cool head and a sense of humour – while still being assertive – will make the work easier for you. An excellent stage manager can help create a good team atmosphere backstage between artists, prop managers and stagehands.

Working conditions

You will spend long hours in theatres and studios, sometimes working into the night to meet deadlines. In addition, you will have to travel to different venues so a driving licence would be useful.

Finding work is not easy and can take up a huge amount of your time, so you should be prepared for rejection and periods without work.

Future prospects

The employment demand for stage managers currently remains relatively stable, and opportunities for full-time or regular work are better than on the performing side.

This is a competitive area of work and the opportunities for employment are not extensive. Work can be found in theatre companies, opera, theatre in education and touring companies.

You could be promoted to a nationally recognised position or become a company stage manager where you would do publicity and finance work as well.

You could also choose to move into TV or film, becoming a director or producer.

Advantages/disadvantages

You will work long, unpredictable hours to meet the deadline of the production.

Permanent contracts are difficult to find so you may experience a sense of job insecurity.

The work is both creative and practical.

There is a great sense of achievement at the end of a successful run when everything has operated smoothly.

Money guide

Starting out as a trainee or assistant stage manager, you will earn between £16,000 and £17,000 per year.

With experience, your annual salary can rise to between £20,000 and £26,000.

The most successful and experienced stage managers can achieve up to £40,000.

Many stage managers work on a freelance basis.

Minimum rates of pay are negotiated by Equity, the performers' and entertainment workers' trade union.

Related opportunities

- Entertainment Manager p362
- Props Maker/Assistant p419
- Wardrobe Assistant p427

Further information

Equity
www.equity.org.uk

Stage Management Association
www.stagemanagementassociation.co.uk

STAGEHAND

ENTRY LEVEL 1

Qualifications and courses

There are no formal qualifications necessary to work as a stagehand.

Usually you will begin casual work backstage and you are more likely to secure this work if you have previous experience and some practical skills. It would therefore be useful to have worked backstage at school or college, or as part of an amateur dramatics society.

Skills in carpentry, electrics or sound and lighting are all advantageous for securing work. There are various qualifications available in these areas, such as BTECs and qualifications from the City & Guilds and the Association of British Theatre Technicians.

If you eventually want to progress into stage management, there are some relevant courses that may be useful, including BTECs in subjects such as production arts (stage management) and performing arts (Levels 1–4), and Foundation degrees and degrees in stage management with drama schools such as the Central School of Speech and Drama. Entry requirements for a degree course are typically 2 A levels/3 H grades and 5 GCSEs/National 5s (A*–C/A–C), and HNDs usually require 1 A level/H grade and 4 GCSEs/National 5s (A*–C/A–C).

What the work involves

Stagehands (also known as stage technicians or crew) work backstage as part of the production team.

You will provide assistance with props, scenery and special effects in either theatres, concert halls or at TV/film studios.

Your tasks will involve handling the equipment, helping to assemble and move scenery, opening and closing the theatre curtain between acts (when working on live plays or shows) and clearing the stage or studio at the end of each performance.

The work is normally completed as part of a team of stagehands under the supervision of the stage manager.

Type of person suited to this work

You will need to be physically fit to work as a stagehand as the work will involve a lot of heavy lifting. It will also be important to have good stamina as working hours will be long and you will probably work 6 days a week on a show.

As the work is normally team based, you will need to work well as part of a team and have a flexible attitude as you may be required to do a wide range of tasks, some at short notice. You must also be able to cope under pressure as the shows will be live and things can go wrong.

You must have a head for heights as well as a good understanding of health and safety.

A passion for theatre and live performance, as well as for stage and set design, is also essential.

Working conditions

You will be working irregular hours, including evenings, weekends and bank holidays.

You must be prepared to work at short notice and work overtime as productions can overrun.

You may be based in one venue, or have to travel to different venues if the production goes on tour.

You should wear black, comfortable clothing for making scenery changes during a production.

Future prospects

This is a popular and competitive area to work in.

With experience, you could go on to a supervisory or management role, leading a crew of stagehands.

You could also specialise in a certain area such as carpentry and become a production carpenter.

Eventually, after working your way up, it may be possible to progress to tour manager or stage manager.

Advantages/disadvantages

The work is often quite casual, so you may not have a steady income.

You will work irregular and unsocial hours as most performances will be in the evening and at weekends and you may have to work away from home on location for days or weeks at a time.

Working in theatre is an exciting and challenging job role; you will get to be part of a glamorous industry.

Money guide

The salary for stagehands is fairly low, and many roles are often on a low or no pay basis with profits shared among those involved afterwards.

Starting salaries are around £250–£300 per week or around £12,000 per year. This could rise to £15,000 with experience.

The majority of stagehands work on a freelance or casual basis though so pay rates vary considerably. You may be able to negotiate a higher rate if you have extensive or specialist experience.

Related opportunities

- Artistic/Theatre Director p409
- Stage Manager p423
- TV, Film and Radio Producer p404

Further information

Association of British Theatre Technicians
www.abtt.org.uk

Creative Skillset
www.creativeskillset.org

National Council for Drama Training
www.ncdt.co.uk

Stage Management Association
www.stagemanagementassociation.co.uk

STUNT PERFORMER

ENTRY LEVEL 1

Qualifications and courses

There are no academic entry requirements for this work but you must be over the age of 18 in order to be employed. Equity (the trade union for the performing arts) recommends that film and TV producers only employ stunt performers who are on the Joint Industry Stunt Committee (JISC) Stunt Register.

To join the JISC register you are required to prove that you have at least 1 year's experience and qualifications in a minimum of 6 sports across the following categories: fighting, falling, riding/driving, agility/strength and water. You must have experience in at least 4 of these categories and you cannot have more than 2 sports from the same category. For example, you could be skilled in martial arts, high diving, horse riding, gymnastics, rock climbing and swimming.

When registering these qualifications they must not be more than 5 years old. You will also need to give the JISC evidence that you have spent a minimum of 60 days in front of the camera either as an actor or walk-on artist.

Organisations such as the British Academy of Dramatic Combat (BADC), the British Academy of Stage and Screen Combat (BASSC) and YoungBlood offer a range of courses, workshops and classes in stage combat for practising actors.

What the work involves

Stunt performers plan, design, practise and perform stunts in areas such as motorbike riding, car driving, diving, flying, paragliding, bungee jumping, skiing and horse riding.

Standing in for actors in TV, film or video productions, you will enter flaming buildings, crash vehicles, drive at speed or do dangerous stunts at sea. Sometimes, performances are in front of live audiences.

You could advise other performers on health and safety issues.

Type of person suited to this work

Stunt performers are dedicated to their art and committed to ensuring that their skills are highly developed. A high level of stamina and fitness is essential. You should be a risk taker with an adventurous spirit.

You need to be happy to practise every aspect of your stunts over and again until they are reproducible in all aspects, so you must be a perfectionist. You must always be aware of the dangers you face, practising long hours to make the performance appear easy!

Working conditions

Part of your working day could be spent within a studio, on location or on a film set.

You could be working indoors or out, in cramped spaces, at heights or sometimes in bad weather conditions.

The hours will be very long, often up to 16 hours per day depending on the production, with frequent weekend work and travel to distant places.

Future prospects

Opportunities for live stunt work are decreasing, as digital graphics and new media can simulate stunts, so competition for work is growing increasingly fierce.

Stunt artists work anywhere in the world, with the main employers being film, TV and video production companies.

You could progress into advisory work, helping film directors or advising and training other stunt artists. You could also direct action scenes.

Advantages/disadvantages

You will have the opportunity to travel the world and no two days will be the same.

Seeing the finished product on screen is rewarding.

This is difficult, dangerous work involving many risks.

Entry to this sector is very competitive, and it may be difficult to remain in the industry as you grow older owing to fitness levels.

Money guide

There is no formal pay scale for stunt performers and income varies greatly.

Equity establishes minimum rates for stunt work with TV companies and independent producers.

Recommended daily rates are £250 to £370 for TV work and £425 a day for film work.

Although the majority of stunt artists are freelance, you might enter full-time employment with a salary of about £12,000.

A very experienced performer may earn £25,000 and above per year.

Related opportunities

- Actor p408
- Choreographer p410
- Entertainer p415

Further information

British Academy of Stage and Screen Combat
www.bassc.org

Equity
www.equity.org.uk

YoungBlood
www.youngblood.co.uk

TV, FILM AND THEATRE SPECIAL EFFECTS TECHNICIAN

ENTRY LEVEL 3

Qualifications and courses

There is no specific entry route into this profession. Although a degree is not essential, it is becoming increasingly common for employers to expect candidates to have a degree or diploma in a relevant art subject, such as stage craft, animation or technical arts. The general entry requirements for an arts degree include 2 A levels/3 H grades and 5 GCSEs/National 5s (A*–C/A–C) and to pass a portfolio interview for entry. Most applicants take a Foundation Art and Design course prior to entry.

There are some courses available to improve your skillset, for example the Association of British Theatre Technicians runs day courses in specialised subjects such as pyrotechnics. For more courses, visit The BFI/Skillset Media Courses Directory, which lists many UK courses that are related to visual effects.

There are very few permanent posts within large broadcasting houses, mostly found in London, so relevant work experience is essential for learning new skills and gaining contacts. These skills can be in any aspect of special effects, from theatre stage crafts to pyrotechnics and working with explosives. Learning computer aided-design could help give you a broader portfolio, and keeping on top of new techniques and technological developments is advisable.

When you gain employment, you will be trained whilst shadowing an experienced technician. This trainee period often lasts 5 years, though this is reduced to 2 for visual effects.

What the work involves

As a technician you will work to create special effects in the TV and film industry. You might work with either physical effects, pyrotechnic, or visual. The first involves robotics, the second explosions, and the third superimposes images after filming.

You will work with colleagues to plan effects, create them, test them, and oversee their staging during filming.

You will adhere to strict health and safety regulations, update detailed logbooks of work done and the methods used and prepare the work area by setting up explosives for a gun battle or preparing materials for prosthetic work for example.

Type of person suited to this work

An interest in films and TV is useful for this profession. You need to be creative and imaginative, but at the same time practical and logical.

A visual mind is important as you'll need to imagine how things will look on screen as well as having a sense of drama and the desire to create a feeling of authenticity in screen shots through detailing. You should also be resourceful as you'll be working to a budget.

A strong awareness of health and safety issues is paramount as you will be working with props and explosives that can pose a threat to others if used improperly. You will often have to help with the equipment and this often includes heavy lifting so a level of fitness would be required.

You'll be working under pressure, both with others and on your own, so need to be good at adapting to different situations and finding solutions to problems quickly.

Working conditions

Hours are flexible, and you should be prepared to fit around filming schedules. This may mean late nights, early mornings and weekends.

You could work freelance, which may well mean you are very busy for a while, then unemployed for a long period of time. When you're working, you could be travelling anywhere, sometimes for quite a while. Be prepared to stay away from home often.

Work takes place wherever filming takes place – in a studio or workshop, outdoors in the sunshine, outdoors in the rain, on location etc.

Future prospects

Although there will probably be only average growth in this line of work, there could be increasing breadth within the role as new techniques and technology are developed.

After working for about 10 years, you can advance to a senior technician position, and following this, a supervisory role.

Progression is much easier when you've built a list of contacts, and vacancies in this industry are often only advertised internally.

Advantages/disadvantages

This is a really exciting job, and seeing your hard work on the big screen can be really rewarding.

It's a fiercely competitive profession, and you might have to face periods of unemployment.

Money guide

As a trainee, you can expect to earn between £200 and £500 a week, depending on how advanced your skills are.

Once you are a technician this can rise to about £1,250 for a week of work.

If you make it to a senior technician role, this might rise to between £2,000 and £3,000 or more a week.

Related opportunities

- Animator p154
- Lighting Technician p416
- Props Maker/Assistant p419

Further information

Association of British Theatre Technicians
www.abtt.org.uk

Broadcasting, Entertainment, Cinematograph and Theatre Union
www.bectu.org.uk

WARDROBE ASSISTANT

ENTRY LEVEL 3

Qualifications and courses

There are no formal entry requirements for this career but it is an absolute necessity that you possess the practical skills of hand and machine sewing, pattern cutting and dress making. The best way to get a job is to gain practical experience and applying to local theatre companies or to student productions as a volunteer is a good place to start.

As competition is fierce many people study for qualifications in costume-related subjects. Courses include the City & Guilds Certificates and Diplomas in Creative Techniques (Levels 1–3), the BTEC Level 3 in Production Arts (Costume) or Level 2 in Fashion and Clothing, the HNCs/HNDs in Fashion and Textiles, and the BTEC Level 5 Professional Diploma in Costume Management. Also available are Foundation degrees in Fashion and Costume Craft and costume for the Stage and Screen, and degrees in performance costume. The general entry requirements for a degree are 2 A levels/3 H grades and 5 GCSEs/National 5s (A*–C/A–C). Postgraduate degrees in costume design are also available.

Apprenticeships are available within large corporations such as the BBC and regional screen agencies but again competition is very fierce. Details of available schemes can be found on the Creative Skillset website.

Most training is done on the job, under the supervision of a senior wardrobe assistant. It is important to develop your skills by taking short courses in costume assembling or by joining a professional association.

What the work involves

You will be responsible for assembling and sourcing the costumes needed for TV, film and theatre productions. You will be buying or hiring accessories and costumes and making sure they are correctly stored and transported.

You will be responsible for altering, repairing, cleaning and fitting costumes as well as looking after them in between scenes/takes.

You will need to keep a detailed record of the different costumes worn by each performer and make sure they are ready to be worn for each stage of the production.

Type of person suited to this work

You will need to be organised, accurate and be able to remain calm under pressure, especially when dealing with costume emergencies during a live performance when you must use your initiative.

It is important to have good communication and interpersonal skills as you will be working with a range of people; colleagues and professionals.

A good eye for detail, practical sewing skills and creative flair are all useful when assembling costumes. A solid working knowledge of design, fashion and fashion periods will be advantageous.

Working conditions

You will be working unsocial and long hours the majority of the time. In film and television most of the work is during the daytime whereas in theatre you will be expected to work before and after both matinee and evening performances, usually 6 days a week.

Film and television production companies may need you to work away from home for long periods of time.

You will be sitting down, sewing and fitting costumes or running around a set helping to dress performers.

Future prospects

Most work can be found in London and other major cities with theatres, touring companies and film/TV production companies. It is important to gain as many contacts as possible by undertaking work experience and working for free as competition for jobs is fierce.

You can gain promotion to wardrobe supervisor and short courses are available which can enable you to acquire the right skills to switch between theatre and film/TV work; you usually start off specialising in one area.

Some wardrobe assistants move into specialist areas such as costume/set design or stage management.

Advantages/disadvantages

This is an exciting job in a glamorous industry; no two days will be the same and you may get to work with celebrities.

The pay is low for such an important role.

You can gain good insight and experience into a competitive industry enabling you to progress to senior positions.

Money guide

You could start out doing work experience where only travel expenses or lunch are paid for; £30 per day is the average amount.

Your starting salary may be around £10,000, which could rise to between £12,000 and £17,000. Senior wardrobe assistants could earn in excess of £25,000.

Freelance rates do vary greatly depending on the job you are doing and your reputation.

Related opportunities

- Costume Designer p156
- Fashion Designer/Milliner p157
- Museum/Art Gallery Curator p335

Further information

Costume Society
www.costumesociety.org.uk

Creative Skillset
www.creativeskillset.org

Society of British Theatre Designers
www.theatredesign.org.uk

Personal and Other Services including Hair and Beauty

This is a very wide job family and covers everything from hairdressing and beauty to cleaning to wedding consulting. You can enter this career sector with a host of different skills and qualifications. What all of the jobs have in common is that they provide a particular service that a customer has asked for so you need to be good at listening to others and giving customers exactly what they want – people in this sector have a brilliant way with people. You should also demonstrate creativity and strong practical and technical skill as many of the jobs in this family require you to use specialist equipment and to have knowledge of health and safety.

The jobs featured in this section are listed below. For similar jobs to the ones in this section turn to *Catering and Hospitality* on page 119.

BEAUTY CONSULTANT

ENTRY LEVEL 2

Qualifications and courses

Although formal qualifications are not generally required, GCSEs/National 5s (A*–C/A–C) may prove useful, particularly in Maths and English. Previous experience in a retail, sales or customer service role would be beneficial and you must be over 18 years old if you wish to be self-employed.

The Vocational Training Charitable Trust (VTCT) offers a Level 2 Certificate in Cosmetic Make-Up and Beauty Consultancy, and NVQs/SVQs are available in Retail Skills, Beauty Therapy (general or specialising in make-up) and Customer Service (Levels 1–3). City & Guilds and BTEC both provide Level 2 qualifications in Retail Knowledge (Beauty). These courses may be taken prior to employment or while working and, although they are not essential, they will help to show prospective employers that you are committed to the industry.

An alternative training route to becoming a beauty consultant is to apply for the Beauty Therapy Apprenticeship at Intermediate Level.

Once you secure employment, training is generally provided in-house and may cover topics such as sales techniques, skincare and make-up techniques, and stock recording and ordering.

What the work involves

You will work in department stores and other public locations, promoting and selling beauty products on behalf of cosmetics companies.

You will provide product demonstrations to individual customers or groups, including facials, make-up applications and manicures. You will give advice and information on cosmetic products. Your work may involve selling items and taking payments, managing stock levels and keeping the demonstration area attractive and presentable.

If you are self-employed, you will have to control every aspect of your business including sales, finances and marketing.

Type of person suited to this work

A sociable and professional approach is important because you will meet many customers. You should have a smart appearance.

Working on a store counter can be fast paced so you should be able to stay calm in busy situations. You will use your communication skills to encourage customers to find out more about your products.

You should also have a strong interest in helping people make the best of themselves. For applying make-up and other products, you will need an eye for design and good practical skills. Numeracy skills will help you manage stock and take payments. You should enjoy the challenge of working towards sales targets.

Working conditions

You could work between 37 and 40 hours a week, with some weekend and evening hours. If you are self-employed, the majority of your hours will be in the evening.

You may have to do some lifting and carrying from the stockroom.

Depending on where you work, you may wear a uniform and you will normally be expected to wear the cosmetics that you are selling.

Future prospects

Beauty consultancy offers a flexible career for people who want to combine their interest in beauty with working in sales.

As well as employment within department stores, there are opportunities to work in airports and hotels. You may choose to promote and sell products from your own home.

With experience, you could progress to working as a team manager and then move on to an area management role. Progression might involve changing employers and moving to a larger company.

Advantages/disadvantages

This type of work is often available on a part-time or flexible basis which would suit people with other commitments.

You might spend a lot of time on your feet which could prove tiring.

You may receive a product allowance of either discounted or free cosmetic products.

Money guide

Starting salaries are usually between £12,000 and £13,000.

Experienced beauty consultants can expect to earn from £19,000 to £23,000.

Those employed in a senior or managerial position could achieve up to £30,000 a year.

Many beauty consultants receive commission based upon their sales figures.

Related opportunities

- Beauty Therapist p431
- Hairdresser/Barber p441
- Nail Technician p442

Further information

Hairdressing and Beauty Industry Authority
www.habia.org

People 1st
www.people1st.co.uk/retail-apprenticeships

BEAUTY THERAPIST ENTRY LEVEL 3

Qualifications and courses

To work as a fully qualified beauty therapist, you will need to be qualified to at least a Level 3 standard in beauty therapy and you will usually be expected to have some GCSEs/National 5s (A*–C/A–C).

Suitable courses include the City & Guilds Level 2 Diploma in Beauty Consultancy, the Diploma in Beauty Therapy (Levels 2–3), and the specialist Level 3 Diplomas in subjects such as advanced beauty therapy, body massage, and Indian head massage. There is also the NVQ Diploma in Beauty Therapy (Levels 2–3), the BTEC Level 2 qualifications in Beauty Therapy, the Vocational Training Charitable Trust (VTCT) Diploma in Beauty Therapy Treatments, and the International Therapy Examination Council (ITEC) Diploma in Advanced Beauty Therapy.

An alternative route for those aged 16–24 is to take the Apprenticeship in Beauty Therapy which is available at Intermediate and Advanced Levels.

Some universities and higher education colleges will offer HNCs/HNDs, Foundation degrees, degrees and postgraduate degrees in cosmetic science, beauty therapy, and spa management. The general entry requirements for a degree are 2 A levels/3 H grades and 5 GCSEs/National 5s (A*–C/A–C).

Beauty therapists often extend their knowledge into holistic or alternative treatments such as massage and aromatherapy. The International Federation of Professional Aromatherapists (IFPA) accredits courses at private schools and colleges in the UK.

What the work involves

You will provide a range of face and body treatments, including facials, massages, electrolysis and waxing treatments.

Your work will also involve preparing, cleaning and tidying the treatment room before and after each client. You may have to take payments and bookings, undertake some general administrative duties and maintain client records.

Beauty therapists are often employed by and provide services in beauty salons, health clubs and hotels. You may choose to work on a self-employed basis in rented treatment rooms or from your own home.

Type of person suited to this work

People often choose to have a treatment to help them relax so you will need a calm, confident approach.

An interest in helping people with a range of therapies is essential. You will need good communication skills when advising clients about the treatments they can have.

A well-presented appearance and a good level of physical fitness are also important. You will work to a high standard of health and hygiene.

Working conditions

You will generally work 37–40 hours a week, including weekends and evenings to accommodate customers' needs, and you will usually wear a uniform.

Therapy rooms or cubicles are usually private, clean and warm, however if you are self-employed you may need to visit clients in their own homes and adapt your services within different environments.

This can be quite a physically demanding job as you will spend the majority of your day standing and bending.

Future prospects

Future prospects in this line of work are good with a variety of other career paths to potentially choose from, including spa management and sales.

Your location can vary from being based in a beauty salon to working in a hotel or spa and opportunities are generally good across the country.

With experience you could progress into a management role or choose to set up your own beauty therapy business. You could also go on to training and lecturing in beauty therapy after extensive professional experience and further training.

There are opportunities to work on cruise ships and in resorts overseas.

Advantages/disadvantages

Therapists working in health and beauty companies or clubs may be provided with free club membership and discounted treatments.

You might find some treatments difficult to carry out if you are not comfortable seeing people's bodies.

You can feel proud knowing that you have made a customer happy after completing their chosen treatment.

Money guide

Salaries vary depending on location and employer.

Once qualified as a beauty therapist, you could receive a starting salary of between £11,000 and £13,000.

With experience, earnings increase to about £17,000 a year.

In a senior or managerial position, you could achieve in excess of £20,000 per year.

Tips and commission from the sale of products can supplement your income.

Related opportunities

- Beauty Consultant p430
- Hairdresser/Barber p441
- Nail Technician p442

Further information

British Association of Beauty Therapy and Cosmetology
www.babtac.com

Hairdressing and Beauty Industry Authority
www.habia.org

CAR VALET

ENTRY LEVEL 1

Qualifications and courses

No formal qualifications are required for entry to this job, however valets are usually aged 17 or over as a full driving licence is often required. Qualifications in practical or technical subjects and previous experience in the motor trade, industrial/office cleaning or dry cleaning can also be an advantage.

Once you secure employment, you will undertake training on the job and learn about cleaning techniques and health and safety procedures from an experienced colleague. You could also be sent on short courses run by the manufacturers of cleaning products as part of your training and development.

The British Institute of Cleaning Science (BICSc) provides a Car Valeting Certificate scheme for candidates interested in more formal training. Topics covered include interior cleaning, exterior cleaning, engine cleaning, pressure washing, stain removal, upholstery cleaning and polishing and waxing.

The City & Guilds Certificate and Diploma in Vehicle Valeting Principles (Levels 1–2), the NVQ in Vehicle Maintenance and Repair (Levels 1–3), and the NVQ in Cleaning and Support Services (Level 1–3) are also available for those who wish to take a relevant qualification.

Apprenticeships in Cleaning and Environmental Services, Vehicle Body and Paint Operations, and Vehicle Maintenance and Repair can give you the relevant skills and knowledge for this career.

What the work involves

Car valets clean and finish car exteriors and interiors using specialist equipment.

You could work for vehicle service centres, car showrooms, garages, crash repair centres or valeting companies.

Depending on the services offered by your employer and the client's wishes, you may be expected to clean a vehicle both internally and externally, the exterior only or just the engine. You might be hired by a garage to help clean up cars after bodywork repairs.

Typical tasks include clearing the interior of rubbish, polishing the surfaces and windows, cleaning the seats and removing any stains. For exteriors, you will clean the wheels and polish and wax the bodywork.

Type of person suited to this work

You should be physically fit as jobs can take between 1 and 4 hours and involve a lot of bending, stretching and lifting.

You should be able to use different types of cleaning equipment and apply your knowledge of health and safety to your work.

As you will be providing a service to customers, you will need to be a quick but thorough worker with good attention to detail.

You need strong people skills and the ability to work both independently and as part of a team.

You should be able to cope with dirty working conditions.

Working conditions

The work is very hands on and can be tiring because it involves spending a lot of time on your feet.

You might be based outside cleaning cars on a forecourt or in a car park so you need to be prepared to work in all weather conditions.

This job requires regular contact with cleaning chemicals, so it might not suit people with allergies or skin conditions. Sometimes you will be required to wear protective clothing including gloves and safety glasses.

Future prospects

Car valeting is a key part of the sales and services sector of the motor vehicle industry.

You could work for a large vehicle repair company or service centre as part of a valeting team.

With experience and further training, you could progress to a supervisory or managerial role or move into sales.

Alternatively, you could choose to set up your own valeting company offering a mobile service or going out to visit customers at their premises.

Advantages/disadvantages

Car valeting jobs may include regular travel, either when providing services to customers on their premises, or when returning vehicles to customers.

This type of job offers the chance to work in close contact with a range of cars and other vehicles.

Money guide

Trainee valets have a starting salary of around £10,000 per year.

Fully trained valets can earn between £12,000 and £18,000.

Overtime and shift payments can increase your income.

Related opportunities

- Cleaner p436
- Motor Vehicle Technician p218
- Vehicle Parts Operative p473

Further information

British Institute of Cleaning Science
www.bics.org.uk

The Building Futures Group
www.thebuildingfuturesgroup.com/sector-skills-council

CARETAKER

ENTRY LEVEL 1

Qualifications and courses

No formal qualifications are required for entry to this job as hands-on skills and experience in basic DIY, carpentry or painting and decorating are deemed more important than academic credentials. However, some GCSEs/ National 5s (A*–C/A–C), particularly English, Maths and practical subjects, may be an advantage when applying for jobs. Experience in maintenance or security work is useful, as is a driving licence, and within some areas, for example schools, you will need to pass a Disclosure and Barring Service (DBS) check.

Maturity is an advantage and employers often prefer older applicants with relevant experience.

It may be possible for entrants to work towards an NVQ Level 1 and 2 in Cleaning and Support Service but mostly caretakers are trained on the job. The Cleaning Supervisory Skills Certificate offered by the British Institute of Cleaning Science (BICSc) or a Diploma in Construction and the Built Environment could also be useful, as well as training in specific areas, such as dealing with asbestos and other substances that are hazardous to health. The Chartered Institute of Housing (CIH) also offers a Level 3 Certificate in Housing and Housekeeping, which includes a caretaking option, and the Chartered Institute of Building runs a Level 3 Certificate in Housing Maintenance.

Studying for an NVQ Level 3 in Property and Caretaking Supervision and the NVQ Level 4 Certificate in Housing Maintenance Management can speed up career progression and a full driving licence may be required if you become a mobile caretaker who looks after a number of different sites.

What the work involves

Caretakers manage the security, cleaning and general maintenance of sites such as schools, colleges and office blocks.

In some jobs, you might be expected to combine caretaking duties with other roles such as cleaner, gardener, porter or security attendant.

You will be responsible for opening and locking the premises, checking building security and the overall management and upkeep of the site. You will repair broken equipment, either yourself or booking in and managing a maintenance team, as well as reordering the necessary supplies for your job.

Type of person suited to this work

Caretakers need good communication skills as they interact closely with the people based on their premises.

You may be responsible for the security of an entire site, so it's important to have a mature, honest attitude and a full understanding of emergency procedures.

The ability to work independently is essential, as you will often be working on your own initiative and sites usually only employ one caretaker. You should also be able to work as part of a team when necessary though, for example when having to manage larger repairs.

Physical fitness is essential for work such as moving equipment and gardening. You will work to a high standard of health and safety at all times.

Working conditions

A 37-hour working week, which could encompass early mornings, evenings and weekends, is normal in this line of work. In some cases, you may be living on-site or nearby so expect working hours to be more flexible.

Caretaking work is physically demanding as you will be spending the majority of your time on your feet, doing general maintenance and using ladders and other tools.

Caretakers work with cleaning chemicals and wear protective clothing such as overalls. The job might not suit people with allergies or skin conditions.

Future prospects

Many locations only employ one caretaker, so you might need to move to a bigger site to progress.

In larger establishments, senior caretakers have the responsibility of managing a small team of caretakers or other staff such as cleaners.

You could progress to a management position in a private cleaning company.

Advantages/disadvantages

As the premises keyholder, you could be on-call for emergencies.

This job can be sociable and caretakers often build up a good working relationship with the people based on their premises.

Money guide

The starting salary for an assistant caretaker is around £12,000 per year, which will increase to roughly £16,000 after experience.

You could earn £25,000 as a senior or mobile caretaker.

In some work areas, such as education, caretakers are offered on-site subsidised housing as part of their contract.

Related opportunities

- Cleaner p436
- Hotel Porter p127
- Refuse and Recycling Operative p444

Further information

Chartered Institute of Housing
www.cih.org

The Caretakers' website
www.thecaretakers.net

CARPET/UPHOLSTERY CLEANER

ENTRY LEVEL 1

Qualifications and courses

There are no formal qualifications for this career and you will usually be trained on the job by an experienced colleague in the practice of cleaning as well as health and safety regulations. It might also be helpful to have basic numeracy and literacy skills to calculate correct quantities of chemicals and writing quotes for customers.

Once employed, you may decide to undertake specialised training such as the NVQ in Cleaning and Support Services (Levels 1–2), which contains one unit specifically for carpet and soft furnishings, the City & Guilds Certificate in Cleaning Science, the Level 2 Certificate in Cleaning Principles, or the British Institute of Cleaning Science's Cleaning Operators Proficiency Certificate.

The National Carpet Cleaners Association also offers regular specialist cleaning courses in subjects such as carpet cleaning, commercial carpet maintenance, upholstery and fabric cleaning, leather identification and cleaning, hard floor cleaning, and advanced spot and stain treatment and removal. Relevant repair courses are also available and may improve your business opportunities if self-employed. Courses include water damage restoration, carpet colour repair and carpet repair and reinstallation.

Apprenticeships may be available for people aged between 16 and 24 in Cleaning and Support Services, which features modules on soft floor and furnishings cleaning.

Knowledge or qualifications in business might be useful if you wish to run your own cleaning business, as well as the Level 3 City & Guilds Diploma in Cleaning Services Supervision.

What the work involves

Carpet and upholstery cleaners clean soft furnishings, including curtains, tapestries, antique fabrics, rugs, seat covers and carpets, using specialist equipment.

These fabrics and carpets need special cleaning to remove dirt, smoke and grease that build up on them daily and your job is to determine and implement the best method for removing the dirt.

You will work in a variety of private and public buildings, dealing with large and small orders. If the job is big, you will be expected to visit the cleaning site first to assess what needs to be cleaned and what sort of equipment and chemicals you might need.

Each job will be assessed on face value and costed according to size, equipment required and time it will take you.

Type of person suited to this work

You will have an in-depth knowledge of different types of fabrics and their make-up in order to determine the best way to remove stubborn stains.

You will need good practical skills to be able to use specialist cleaning equipment and an understanding of the different types of chemicals you will use.

Excellent communication skills and an understanding in the importance of good customer service will be essential when dealing with clients and colleagues. You should be able to work equally well alone or as part of a team.

Working conditions

You may need to work evenings and weekends. Most of your time will be spent on your feet and carrying around heavy equipment. You will normally be based indoors, in people's homes or public buildings.

You are likely to need to drive around to work at different locations so a driving licence will be useful. You should also be physically fit.

You might have to wear protective clothing to protect you from dust and chemicals which may irritate your skin.

Future prospects

Carpet and upholstery cleaners are needed throughout the UK, meaning there will be lots of job opportunities wherever you live.

You might work for a general or specialist cleaning company or be self-employed.

With experience, you can move into managerial or training roles or start your own cleaning business.

Advantages/disadvantages

This work brings good job satisfaction; you will be pleasing people by restoring their carpets and upholstery to perfect condition.

You could find some aspects of cleaning messy or dirty which could be unpleasant.

You have the opportunity to work for yourself and run your own business.

Money guide

The starting salary is around £12,000 per year.

With experience this can increase to £14,500.

You may be able to earn up to £25,000 if you specialise in antique or tapestry cleaning.

Related opportunities

- Car Valet p432
- Caretaker p433
- Cleaner p436

Further information

British Institute of Cleaning Science
www.bics.org.uk

National Carpet Cleaners Association
www.ncca.co.uk

CHIMNEY SWEEP

ENTRY LEVEL 1

Qualifications and courses

There are no formal entry requirements as you will normally be trained on the job by an experienced chimney sweep. Basic qualifications in English and maths are useful and previous experience of manual work, such as construction, is an advantage.

Trainee chimney sweeps can work towards membership of the National Association of Chimney Sweeps (NACS), the Association of Professional Independent Chimney Sweeps (APICS), or the Guild of Master Chimney Sweeps. This would allow you to register with HETAS, which is the official government-recognised body of chimney sweeps, and registration is particularly important if you wish to be self-employed.

NACS offers a 3-day induction course which covers industry techniques and health and safety. On completion of the training, candidates become probationary members of NACS until they have gained sufficient experience and on-site training to work as professional sweeps. NACS also provides an NVQ Level 2 in Chimney Engineering and several other HETAS-approved training courses in subjects such as solid fuel, chimney and flue maintenance, fire safety, and rooftop and ladder safety.

Alternatively, the Guild of Master Chimney Sweeps offers an intensive 2-day training course covering both theory and practical elements, and the Institute of Chimney Sweeps (ICS) offers a 2-day chimney sweeping course, as well as 1-day courses in practical flue lining installation, twin wall insulated flue installation and a stove refurbishment course.

To be qualified to carry out inspections and work on gas appliances, you need to gain a certificate of competence through the Accredited Certification Scheme (ACS), leading to registration with Gas Safe.

What the work involves

Chimney sweeps help prevent chimney fires and dangerous fuel emissions by inspecting and cleaning chimney and flue systems, heating appliances and vents.

Your work will involve cleaning sites and using brush and vacuum equipment to clear chimneys and vents of blockages.

You will provide information and advice to customers on the repair and maintenance of their chimneys.

Type of person suited to this work

Chimney sweeps combine their professional knowledge with practical skills to protect public safety. You will need a good knowledge of different types of chimney and flue systems.

Operating brush and vacuum chimney cleaning equipment requires good manual skills and a good level of physical fitness and stamina is essential as the work is demanding and potentially strenuous.

You will visit customers in their homes so you should have a friendly, professional attitude.

You should be comfortable working at heights and able to work independently without supervision.

Working conditions

Most of your work will take place at people's homes but you could also work on heating systems in commercial or industrial premises.

Travel to different locations is a regular part of the work so a driving licence is essential.

When clearing chimneys, you will wear protective clothing, such as overalls, gloves, a helmet, eye guards and respiratory protection.

You will usually work normal hours Monday to Friday but you may also be required to work unsocial hours, including weekends and evenings, to suit customers.

Future prospects

Chimney sweeping is a specialist but essential service. After gaining the relevant experience and professional qualifications, you could set up your own business, providing services within your local area.

Most chimney sweeps build up a network of loyal and regular customers.

You could go on to expand your services into roofing or ventilation, with opportunities to work with another professional or to join a small specialist company.

Advantages/disadvantages

Most chimney sweeps work on a self-employed basis, which can lead to some job insecurity, particularly at the start of their careers.

You will have the opportunity to meet a variety of people.

Money guide

The majority of chimney sweeps are self-employed and establish their own rates of pay for each job they undertake.

Earnings vary according to the hours spent on a task and the speed at which you work.

You could charge between £35 and £55 for a full sweep.

For a more specialist task, you could receive £70–£75.

Those working full time can expect to earn between £16,000 and £25,000 per year.

Related opportunities

- Cleaner p436
- Roofer p102
- Steeplejack p107

Further information

Guild of Master Chimney Sweeps
www.guildofmasterchimneysweeps.co.uk

HETAS
www.hetas.co.uk

National Association of Chimney Sweeps
www.chimneyworks.co.uk

CLEANER

ENTRY LEVEL 1

Qualifications and courses

There are no formal qualifications required for this job, although it may be helpful to have basic literacy and numeracy skills. Once employed, cleaners usually receive on-the-job training in health and safety and how to use the necessary cleaning materials and equipment in order to deliver a good service.

School leavers could apply for the Intermediate Apprenticeship in Cleaning and Environmental Services which combines practical work experience with the study of a professional qualification. Courses available include an NVQ in Cleaning and Support Services (Levels 1–2), a Level 2 NVQ in Cleaning Building Interiors, the City & Guilds Level 2 Award in Cleaning Principles, or the Award in Practical Cleaning Skills (Levels 2–3).

Alternative professional qualifications are offered by the British Institute of Cleaning Science (BICSc) and you could work towards the Cleaning Operators Proficiency Certificate (COPC), the BICSc Level 1 Certificate in Cleaning, or the Cleaning Professionals Skills Suite, which includes a wide range of training options to suit the type of cleaning and environment you wish to work in.

Experienced cleaners who wish to progress to a supervisory level can study for the BICSc Cleaning Supervisory Skills Certificate or the City & Guilds Level 3 Diploma in either Cleaning Services Supervision or Cleaning Supervision Skills.

If your job involves contact with hazardous waste, such as sharps and syringes, you will need vaccinations against hepatitis B and C. This is most likely to be necessary if you work in a hospital.

What the work involves

You will be responsible for cleaning and tidying a variety of places including people's homes and places of work.

Industrial cleaners work in public buildings, such as hospitals, prisons, schools and health centres, and work to the highest standards to reach health and safety requirements.

Domestic cleaners work in people's homes and may have additional tasks such as ironing and washing up.

You will use a range of cleaning materials and equipment such as hoovers, mops, dusters and brooms.

Type of person suited to this work

You will need to be honest and trustworthy, as you will be entering people's homes and workplaces where valuables could be on display.

Being fit and mobile is important, as you will be on your feet for long periods, bending, stretching and carrying heavy equipment.

Good communication skills are required to interact with colleagues and clients, especially if you run your own cleaning business.

You will need a good knowledge of the cleaning chemicals you use and the ability to decide which chemical should be used in each situation. It will also be necessary to adhere to health and safety regulations when using hazardous chemicals.

Working conditions

You will usually work 35–40 hours a week in a full-time job but hours vary. You may be required to work weekends, evenings and early mornings when public places or offices are closed. If you clean private homes, you will normally work during the day when the owner of the home is out. Hospitals need to be kept clean 24/7 so shift work is common. Part-time work is often available.

Many cleaners are self-employed and work for several different clients in one day. It would be useful to have a driving licence. Most cleaners wear a uniform or protective clothing.

Future prospects

There is a great demand for cleaners in all sectors.

You could choose to work for a cleaning company or be self-employed.

Many cleaners decide to set up their own small business or move into other roles as a caretaker or supervisor of a team of cleaners.

Advantages/disadvantages

You can work different shifts that fit in well with other jobs or family commitments.

You can progress to being the owner of your own cleaning business.

Owing to the chemicals used in cleaning, this job would not be suitable for those with breathing problems or skin allergies.

Money guide

Earnings vary according to your employer and the number of hours you work.

Most cleaners are paid hourly, with rates ranging from the national minimum wage to £10 an hour.

If you are employed on a full-time basis you can expect a starting salary of £11,000–£12,000.

Earnings are higher for specialist cleaners or those employed in a supervisory role.

Related opportunities

- Caretaker p433
- Pest Control Technician p443
- Window Cleaner p448

Further information

British Institute of Cleaning Science
www.bics.org.uk

The Building Futures Group
www.thebuildingfuturesgroup.com/sector-skills-council

CREMATORIUM TECHNICIAN

ENTRY LEVEL 1

Qualifications and courses

There are no formal entry requirements for this type of work and training is done on the job, although some employers require candidates to have a GCSE/National 5 in English (A*–C/A–C) as good reading and writing skills are important. Basic administrative and computer skills are also valued.

Trainees may follow the Crematorium Technicians' Training Scheme (CTTS) provided by the Institute of Cemetery and Crematorium Management (ICCM) which will lead to the study of both the BTEC Intermediate and Advanced Certificate. Another work-based training route is provided by the Federation of Burial and Cremation Authorities' (FBCA) TEST scheme.

If your work involves ground maintenance you may also receive training in practical areas such as how to safely use chainsaws and pesticide sprayers. Employees may also work towards NVQ/SVQ Level 2 in Amenity Horticulture (Cemeteries and Graveyards).

Once you have the relevant experience you may be able to work towards ICCM qualifications for crematorium managers. These qualifications can be taken in 3 stages – ICCM Certificate for Cemetery and/or Crematorium Management, ICCM Diploma and finally ICCM Diploma with Honours. These can be studied by distance learning.

The ICCM also operates a continuing professional development scheme for crematorium staff at all levels.

What the work involves

Crematorium technicians assist with the running of the crematorium and cemetery premises.

Your work will involve operating cremation equipment to a high standard of health and safety. You will ensure that the cremated remains are stored and disposed of correctly. You will help manage the chapel and cemetery and attend cremation ceremonies.

You will also assist with other cemetery duties, such as excavating graves and grounds maintenance. However, grave digging work is mostly undertaken by contractors working for local authorities.

Type of person suited to this work

Meeting with bereaved people requires a mature, sympathetic attitude. You will use your communication skills to help people understand the process of cremation ceremonies so they know what to expect.

A good level of physical fitness is helpful in a role that covers a wide range of activities.

You will need to keep accurate records so must have good attention to detail.

It's important that cremations are undertaken to a high standard of health and safety, so you should be able to follow strict working guidelines. The ability to work as part of a team is also useful.

Working conditions

This can be a tiring job due to the range of activities involved and the physical requirements of operating cremation machinery. You will be on your feet for long hours.

You will need to be smartly dressed when facing the public and your outfit will usually be provided for you.

When operating machinery you will need to wear protective clothing.

Crematorium technicians are usually employed by local councils and you will normally work 37–40 hours a week, with some overtime including Saturdays.

Future prospects

The Church of England is set to make cremations cheaper than burials, so the number of cremations, and need for skilled professionals, may consequently increase.

There is also the opportunity to progress into an administrative position within the cemetery.

With experience, you could progress to working as a senior crematorium technician and manage a team of technicians.

Advantages/disadvantages

This role provides the opportunity to provide support to people at an important and challenging time.

The nature of the job means this work can sometimes be distressing.

Money guide

Starting salaries vary between £11,000 and £13,000 per year.

With experience you could earn up to £17,000.

At senior management level you could earn in excess of £20,000.

Salaries are often dependent on local authority rates so may be higher in areas such as London. There may also be the opportunity for additional money through overtime.

Related opportunities

- Cleaner p436
- Embalmer p439
- Funeral Director p440

Further information

Federation of Burial and Cremation Authorities
www.fbca.org.uk

Institute of Cemetery and Crematorium Management
www.iccm-uk.com

Local Government Careers
www.lgjobs.com

The Cremation Society of Great Britain
www.cremation.org.uk

DRY CLEANER

ENTRY LEVEL 1

Qualifications and courses

There are no formal qualifications needed for this work, although good numeracy and literacy skills will be useful. Some previous experience working in a laundry, customer service and/or retail skills would also be an advantage.

You will be trained on the job by an experienced dry cleaner. Many employers offer opportunities to study for qualifications part time. These include Level 2 NVQs in Dry Cleaning Operations, Dry Cleaning Service Support, and Textile Care Services, an NVQ in Customer Service (Levels 1–4), and the BTEC Level 2 Certificate in Laundry and Dry Cleaning Technology. The Skillsfirst QCF Award in Retail Skills (Levels 1–3) may also be useful.

The Guild of Cleaners & Launderers (GCL) awards certificates as part of their Qualification Star Scheme. Candidates can undertake exams in retail sales, stain removal, garment finishing, dry cleaning practice and wet cleaning. Modern apprenticeships (equivalent to an NVQ Level 3 qualification) are also available.

The SATRA Technology Centre also provides dry cleaning courses at their training centre in Kettering.

All dry cleaners who intend to use solvents must be registered and hold a permit.

What the work involves

You will be cleaning clothes and fabrics which are delicate or sensitive to being washed in water; using chemicals and steam to clean items instead. You might be cleaning specialist fabrics or garments such as wool, suede, bridal wear, suits and beaded fabrics.

You will look for any stains and treat them individually before cleaning the item. You might use potentially hazardous chemicals, although many dry cleaners now use safe and environmentally friendly products. You will press and package the garments after cleaning.

You will assist customers at the counter, take payments, complete paperwork and operate the cleaning machinery.

Type of person suited to this work

You will need to have good communication skills for dealing with customers and practical skills for handling the cleaning machinery.

A good level of fitness would be helpful for bending, carrying heavy items of clothing and organising cleaned garments.

You will be dealing with payments and paperwork so it is important to have good numeracy skills and an organised approach to your work.

Working conditions

You will most likely work standard hours from Monday to Saturday, usually with 1 day off during the week, however, dry cleaners are increasingly staying open in the evenings and Sundays to accommodate customers' needs. You are likely to work shifts to accommodate these hours. Part-time work is often available.

You will be working in the store, both at the counter and with the cleaning machines.

You might be exposed to some chemical fumes and there is a danger of burning yourself on pressing machines. This work would not be suitable for people with skin allergies.

Most stores will supply you with a uniform.

Future prospects

There are jobs available across the UK in high street dry cleaning stores or industrial cleaning plants which clean for hospitals or factories. Though there is no longer the shortage there was a few years ago, there will still be plenty of positions available within the industry.

You can progress from an assistant position to a supervisory or managerial role; gaining a qualification in team leading might help you to progress more quickly.

After developing extensive experience and knowledge of dry cleaning, you could choose to open your own store.

Advantages/disadvantages

This is a good career if you enjoy practical work and providing a service.

You could be affected by the chemical fumes which would be unpleasant.

There are opportunities to run your own business.

Money guide

The starting salary for a dry cleaner is usually between £10,000 and £12,000.

Once you have undertaken training and gained experience, you can expect to earn approximately £14,000 a year.

If you are employed in a senior or managerial position, your salary could range from £15,000 to £30,000, depending on the reputation and performance of the store.

Related opportunities

- Car Valet p432
- Cleaner p436
- Textile Operative p229

Further information

Guild of Cleaners and Launderers
www.gcl.org.uk

Textile Services Association
www.tsa-uk.org

EMBALMER

ENTRY LEVEL 1

Qualifications and courses

There are no formal entry requirements for working as an embalmer but GCSEs/National 5s in English, Maths, Chemistry, Biology and Religious Studies may be useful.

To achieve professional qualifications, you must first secure a job and register with a tutor approved by the British Institute of Embalmers (BIE). You will then undertake on-the-job training, with part-time or distance learning tuition from your tutor.

Most embalmers work for qualifications awarded by the International Examinations Board of Embalmers (IEBE). The IEBE training is modular and trainees must pass the foundation unit before proceeding with the rest of the training. You are eligible to register with the BIE as a student member upon completion of the foundation unit.

The main IEBE training involves modules in anatomy, physiology, bacteriology and practical embalming. Assessment is via exams and practical work. Once you have passed these modules, you can apply for full membership of the BIE.

You could develop your skills by taking courses in facial reconstruction, hair and make-up or airbrushing. Some embalmers train to work in specialist areas, for example with the bodies of disaster victims.

What the work involves

Embalmers prepare the bodies of deceased people for funerals and for viewing by their relatives. They preserve the body in the most life-like way.

You will wash and disinfect the deceased person's body. You will use specialist equipment to remove all liquids and gases from the body and replace these with injected preservatives which help prevent infection.

Part of preparing the body will involve washing and arranging the person's hair and applying cosmetics. If the deceased has any injuries, you will use plaster of Paris or wax to restore their body.

Your work will also include setting up and cleaning the embalming equipment and treatment area.

Type of person suited to this work

You must be able to cope with working with the bodies of deceased people. A respectful approach to your work is essential. You might have to deal with distressing sights so a mature, detached and down-to-earth attitude is very important.

Embalming work involves presenting a deceased person in the most positive way for grieving relatives. A creative flair and attention to detail will help you to achieve this. You should be sensitive to people's feelings.

Working conditions

Embalmers work in operating rooms within funeral parlours. These are maintained to a very high standard of hygiene and kept at a low temperature.

Whilst embalming you will wear protective clothing such as latex gloves, rubber boots and a theatre gown. Regular contact with chemicals means that this job may not suit people with skin conditions or allergies. You will spend most of the day on your feet and the work is physically demanding.

You will usually work normal hours from Monday to Friday, with occasional weekend and overtime work during busy periods. Some employers will require you to be on-call for emergency work.

Future prospects

There are over 1,000 qualified embalmers in the UK but the industry has a relatively slow turnover of staff.

Embalming is an integral part of the funeral care process, so qualified workers will always be needed. You could gain employment with a funeral care company or you may choose to work on a self-employed basis, providing services to a number of funeral companies. There are opportunities to work abroad.

With extensive experience there may be the opportunity to go into teaching, at a place such as Salisbury College of Funeral Sciences and Embalming, but opportunities here are likely to be rare too.

Advantages/disadvantages

You have the option of working on a freelance basis for a number of employers at the same time.

There are opportunities to work overseas.

This can be distressing work, so you will need to be able to stay detached and professional.

Money guide

Starting salaries are typically around £12,000.

With experience, an embalmer could earn £18,000–£28,000 per year.

Very experienced embalmers, or those who offer specialist services, can achieve in excess of £30,000.

Related opportunities

- Crematorium Technician p437
- Funeral Director p440
- Hospital Porter p293

Further information

British Institute of Embalmers
www.bioe.co.uk

Federation of Burial and Cremation Authorities
www.fbca.org.uk

FUNERAL DIRECTOR

ENTRY LEVEL 1

Qualifications and courses

There are no minimum academic qualifications to work as a funeral director. However, GCSEs/National 5s (A*–C/A–C), or relevant qualifications, in English, Maths, Chemistry, and Biology may prove advantageous. You will normally start as an assistant and undertake on-the-job training, however funeral operatives/assistants with driving duties will require a full driving licence.

The National Association of Funeral Directors (NAFD) also offers the Foundation Certificate in Funeral Service, Diploma in Funeral Directing (DipFD), and the Diploma in Funeral Service Management (DipFSM). They also offer work-based vocational qualifications for those who are currently employed in the funeral industry. The Advanced Certificate in Funeral Service is an entry-level course suitable for funeral assistants, funeral operatives, drivers and bearers. Those who have progressed to a role as a funeral arranger or administrator can study for the Advanced Diploma in Funeral Arranging and Administration.

NAFD also has a Certificate of Training in Funeral Service Awareness which is aimed at people considering entering this line of work.

Co-operative Funeral Services, through the Co-operative College, run specialised courses including the BTEC Level 3 Advanced Certificate in Funeral Services, the BTEC Level 3 Advanced Diploma in Funeral Arranging and Administration, and the BTEC Level 4 Professional Diploma in Funeral Directing. Short courses are also available in a variety of subjects, such as understanding bereavement.

The British Institute of Funeral Directors (BIFD) provides several qualifications, ranging from entry-level courses to a Diploma in Funeral Service Management.

What the work involves

Funeral directors coordinate funeral arrangements for burials and cremations.

You will liaise with the family of the deceased, offering advice and taking note of the details they would like included in the ceremony.

You will arrange the date and location of the funeral, and also arrange transport and death notices. You will also attend the funeral and ensure that everything runs smoothly during the ceremony.

You may be asked to prepare the body for the funeral, though this is usually done by the embalmer.

Type of person suited to this work

You need to have a sensitive and mature attitude to your work. Excellent communication skills and a high standard of health and safety are essential. You must also be well organised with a good eye for detail.

For liaising with local authorities and completing paperwork you will need a good knowledge of the relevant legal issues.

If you are self-employed, you will require good office and budgeting skills.

A thorough knowledge of different cultures and religions is also helpful.

Working conditions

Funeral directors work in funeral homes or centres based within high-street outlets or other areas. Attending funerals will involve working outdoors in all weather conditions.

Your working hours will vary. Most of your administrative work will be undertaken during office hours from Monday to Friday but you may need to visit clients at weekends and in the evenings. You will also have to be on-call, possibly working on a rota system and you may be required to work extra hours during busy times.

It is imperative that funeral directors dress smartly due to the nature of the industry.

Future prospects

Most people start a career in this area by gaining experience as a funeral operative or assistant. They learn the varied aspects of the job from more experienced colleagues and work towards professional qualifications.

You could work for one of the large funeral services companies or for a smaller independent firm.

With experience, you could work as a funeral director abroad. After several years in the industry, you could set up your own funeral services company.

Advantages/disadvantages

Depending on the size of the funeral company you work for, you may be on-call on a regular basis, which can affect your personal life.

Providing a professional and sympathetic service to people experiencing a very difficult time can be rewarding.

Money guide

Starting salaries are typically £15,000 per year.

With experience in the sector, you can expect to earn up to £25,000.

Those employed in a senior position can achieve £30,000 a year.

Self-employed funeral directors could earn considerably more.

Related opportunities

- Crematorium Technician p437
- Embalmer p439
- Management Consultant p37

Further information

British Institute of Funeral Directors
www.bifd.org.uk

National Association of Funeral Directors
www.nafd.org.uk

HAIRDRESSER/ BARBER

ENTRY LEVEL 2

Qualifications and courses

You can either train as a hairdresser full time at college or you can start as an assistant/trainee in a salon and attend college on day release. You could take the Edexcel NVQs in Hairdressing or Barbering (Levels 1–3), the City & Guilds NVQ Level 1 Certificate in Hairdressing and Barbering, the NVQ Level 1 Diploma in Hairdressing and Beauty Therapy, or the NVQ Diploma in Hairdressing or Barbering (Levels 2–3). Those who wish to specialise in African-Caribbean hair could take the NVQ Diploma in Hairdressing (Combined Hair Types) (Level 2–3).

Another route into this career is to apply for an apprenticeship, either in hairdressing or barbering, both of which are available at Intermediate and Advanced Level.

Those with NVQ Level 2 can register as a state-registered hairdresser with the Hairdressing Council (HC). The Freelance Hair and Beauty Federation (FHBF) runs courses for hairdressers on establishing and managing their own business, as well as continuing professional development (CPD) courses.

Qualified hairdressers can take more specialised courses through part-time study, such as the BTEC HNC/HND in Hair and Beauty Management (Levels 4–5) or various Level 4 qualifications in Technical Salon Management from City & Guilds. Foundation degrees in subjects such as hairdressing, salon business management, and hair and beauty management, as well as degrees in fashion styling and salon business management, are also available. Entry usually requires at least 1 A level/2 H grades and a Level 3 BTEC, NVQ or equivalent qualification in a hairdressing/barbering subject.

For those wishing to work in theatre, film and TV, there are degrees in subjects such as theatre arts (make up and hair for theatre and media).

What the work involves

Hairdressers shampoo, cut and style clients' hair to a range of modern or classic looks. You could also provide dry or wet shaves to male clients.

You will discuss hair treatments with clients and may carry out colouring, tinting, perming and fixing hair extensions. You will also give advice on general haircare and hair products.

At senior levels, you could provide training to junior hairdressers.

Type of person suited to this work

Cutting and styling hair involves close personal contact with clients so hairdressers need good communication skills and a friendly manner.

You should have an interest in fashion, a creative flair and an eye for detail. You will need manual dexterity when using specialist chemicals and equipment required to style, perm and colour customers' hair. You should be willing to learn new techniques and methods throughout your career.

Sometimes you may work on reception, booking appointments and taking cash, so you will have to be efficient, confident and numerate.

Some salons require staff to be able to offer a wider choice of services, such as nail and beauty treatments.

Working conditions

Most hairdressers and barbers are based in salons in high streets and other areas. Some work as mobile hairdressers, providing services to clients in their own homes, so a driving licence would be required.

You will do a 40-hour week, which may include working Saturdays. A lot of salons remain open in the evening once or twice a week. Certain salons also open on Sunday. Part-time work is often available.

Future prospects

In a salon, you could progress to a role as senior stylist or manager. Alternatively, you could set up your own business.

As a mobile hairdresser, you could provide services to people in hospitals, care homes or prisons, as well as private clients.

There are opportunities to work on cruise ships. With further beauty therapy training you could work in film, TV or theatre.

Advantages/disadvantages

As a profession, it gives you the chance to be creative on a daily basis.

It is a very sociable profession as you meet new people on a daily basis.

You are on your feet for most of the day so it can be tiring.

Regular contact with beauty products and chemicals means that this type of work may not suit people with skin conditions or allergies.

Money guide

As a trainee you can expect to earn the national minimum wage, which varies according to your age. Earnings also vary with employer and geographical location.

Fully qualified and experienced hairdressers can expect to earn up to £20,000 a year.

Top professional hairdressers can achieve in excess of £30,000.

Related opportunities

- Beauty Therapist p431
- Image Consultant p459
- Nail Technician p442

Further information

Hairdressing and Beauty Industry Authority
www.habia.org

NAIL TECHNICIAN

ENTRY LEVEL 1

Qualifications and courses

There are no formal entry requirements for this career, however, in many areas nail technicians require a licence from the environmental health department of their local council. To obtain a licence you will need to have nationally recognised qualifications and you should check which qualifications your local council will accept.

Relevant courses include the City & Guilds NVQ Diploma in Nail Services (Levels 2–3), the Vocational Training Charitable Trust (VTCT) Level 2 Certificate in Nail Technology or Nail Treatments and the VTCT Level 3 Diploma in Nail Technology. You could also complete a Level 2 Certificate in Nail Technology or a Level 3 Diploma in Nail Technology from the International Therapy Examination Council (ITEC). The Confederation of International Beauty Therapy & Cosmetology (CIBTAC) offers a Level 3 Certificate in Nail Technologies and a Level 3 Diploma in Nail Tech Services.

The NVQ/SVQ Level 3 in Beauty Therapy, BTEC Level 3 qualifications in Beauty Therapy Sciences and the Foundation degree in Salon Business Management in Beauty Therapy also contain specialist units on nail techniques.

Private organisations also offer various courses and qualifications. For example, the Nail and Beauty Academy offers short courses in subjects such as nail art, acrylic nail and airbrush nail art, which can be combined and completed as a Basic, Intensive, Professional and Masters Diploma in Nail Technology.

An option for those aged 16–24 is to apply for the Apprenticeship in Nail Services which is available at Intermediate and Advanced Levels.

What the work involves

Nail technicians provide a range of nail treatments to clients, including manicures, nail extensions, nail art and nail jewellery. Depending on the treatment you are providing, you will work with a range of beauty products and equipment such as brushes, stencils and airbrushes.

You will discuss with clients their intended treatment and check their hands for skin or nail disorders. You will provide advice about aftercare and recommend products for nail care and maintenance.

Your work will also include cleaning and tidying the treatment area before and after each client.

Type of person suited to this work

Nail technicians work with many people so you should have good communication skills. A professional appearance and high standard of hygiene is very important.

You will need excellent manual handling skills to undertake nail design work. A good knowledge of nail and beauty products is important. An eye for design and an interest in fashion are essential.

If you work as a freelance technician you will need good business skills.

Working conditions

Nail technicians work in nail or beauty salons and other locations. Mobile nail technicians provide treatments to clients in their own homes. A driving licence would be useful for travelling to your clients.

Salon-based technicians usually work between 30 and 40 hours a week with some evening/weekend work.

Nail technicians come into regular contact with chemicals so the job might not suit people with skin conditions or allergies.

Future prospects

Nail technology is a popular area of beauty, and treatments are now available in nail salons, department stores and beauty and hairdressing salons. Job opportunities are consequently currently steady.

You could work as a freelance nail technician, providing services to care homes and hotels as well as private clients. If you gain additional professional qualifications you could offer other therapies.

There are opportunities to work abroad or on cruise ships.

You could choose to teach nail treatments or become an NVQ assessor.

Advantages/disadvantages

Working as a freelancer can involve unsocial hours which may disrupt your personal life.

Benefits available from working in a salon include bonus schemes, commission payments for product sales and free or discounted beauty treatments.

Money guide

Starting salaries in this career are between £8,000 and £12,000.

With increased experience, your earnings will rise to about £16,000.

At senior/management level, you could receive £18,000–£25,000 a year.

Some nail technicians either work on a freelance basis or are self-employed and charge per job.

Rates vary from £10 to £50 depending on the type of treatment.

Related opportunities

- Beauty Therapist p431
- Hairdresser/Barber p441
- Make-up Artist p417

Further information

British Association of Beauty Therapy and Cosmetology
www.babtac.com

International Therapy Examination Council
www.itecworld.co.uk

PEST CONTROL TECHNICIAN

ENTRY LEVEL 2

Qualifications and courses

A good standard of education is required for entry as you will be expected to undertake professional qualifications as part of your training and will need to be able to measure correct chemical quantities on the job. It is therefore recommended that candidates have GCSEs/National 5s (A*–C/A–C) in English, Maths and a science, although this is not essential.

Training is given on the job and you will be supervised by an experienced technician. There might be opportunities to attend training courses although some larger companies will have an in-house training programme that you will automatically be signed up to when you join. As the job involves using specialist equipment and dangerous substances, some employers prefer candidates to be over 18 years old.

The Royal Society for Public Health (RSPH), British Pest Control Association (BPCA) and the National Pest Technicians' Association (NPTA) offer various courses. The entry-level qualification is the BPCA/RSPH Certificate in Pest Management, which equates to NVQ Level 2. You could then complete the RSPH/BPCA Level 3 Diploma in Pest Management or a Level 3 NVQ/SVQ in Pest Control Supervision. The BCPA also offers a Technical Inspector Certificate, as well as specialist short courses in fumigation, rodents, insects, bird management and field biology. The NPTA also offers various short courses, whilst the Property Care Association offers short courses covering insect infestation, and the National Proficiency Training Council (NPTC) offers Certificates in Competence in the use of pesticides in rural areas.

Once qualified, you can join a professional registration scheme such as the NPTA Professional Pest Technician Registration Scheme (PPTRS) where you can document your level of training.

What the work involves

Pest control technicians protect public health by treating and eradicating infestations of insects and vermin such as cockroaches and rats, working on site in private homes, offices, shops and other locations.

Your job may involve investigating or monitoring a site to check for pests. You will use a range of specialist chemicals and equipment. Your work might involve fitting traps or spraying areas with chemicals.

In some situations you will provide advice to customers on the prevention of pest problems.

Type of person suited to this work

This job is all about protecting public health so you should be able to work to a high standard of health and safety. Working with chemical treatments and specialist equipment demands a professional approach.

You will need to be calm when dealing with large numbers of insects and rodents. A strong stomach will also help you cope with working in unpleasant conditions.

Physical fitness and good manual handling skills are essential. You will need to be able to communicate and have a tactful approach when providing advice to customers. You will use your writing skills to keep records and write reports.

Working conditions

Whilst not all pest control work is unpleasant, dealing with dirty or unhygienic situations is a likely part of the job.

You will travel to different locations on a regular basis. A driving licence is essential.

You must wear protective clothing, such as overalls and eye goggles, as you will be working with a range of chemicals. The job might not suit people with skin conditions or allergies.

You may choose to specialise in one type of pest once you have gained some experience.

Hours will normally be longer during the summer months when there are more problems with pests.

Future prospects

Pest control technicians provide an important service to domestic homes, factories, offices and other locations in cities and rural areas.

You could run your own business or work with local councils or specialist companies.

With experience you could progress to supervising teams of staff, managing a large pest control company or working in a management role for local councils.

Advantages/disadvantages

Your day-to-day work will be varied so no two days will be the same!

The work is quite solitary; you will often drive alone to jobs in a van containing the specialist equipment.

You might be faced with unpleasant situations.

Money guide

As a trainee you could start at between £13,000 and £16,000 per year.

With experience and qualifications, this rises to £25,000.

There may be the opportunity for additional income depending on your employer, such as commission or bonuses.

Related opportunities

- Environmental Health Practitioner/Officer p22
- Refuse and Recycling Operative p444
- Toxicologist p512

Further information

British Pest Control Association
www.bpca.org.uk

National Pest Technicians Association
www.npta.org.uk

REFUSE AND RECYCLING OPERATIVE

Qualifications and courses

There are no formal academic entry requirements but you will need to be at least 18 years old and drivers must hold a large goods vehicle (LGV) licence. When you secure employment you will receive on-the-job training in health and safety, manual handling and the disposal of hazardous items.

The Apprenticeship in Sustainable Resource Management, available at both Intermediate and Advanced Levels, offers an ideal route into this career as you will be combining practical work experience with formal training. The Apprenticeship in Driving Goods Vehicles may also equip you with useful skills.

Those who wish to gain relevant qualifications could take the NVQ in either Waste Management Operations or Recycling Operations (Levels 1–2), for which there are different pathways. There is also the City & Guilds Diploma in Sustainable Recycling Activities (Levels 1–2).

People looking to progress to supervisory or managerial roles could study for the NVQ Level 3 in Waste Management Supervision or Management Recycling Operations, the NVQ Level 4 in Managing Waste Collection Operations or the Management of Recycling Operations, or the City & Guilds Level 3 Diploma in Sustainable Recycling Activities, or Level 4 Diploma in Management of Sustainable Recycling Activities.

Although not essential, voluntary work may prove beneficial and opportunities can be found on websites, such as Do-it.

What the work involves

You will collect rubbish and unwanted items and take them to an official rubbish tip or recycling depot.

Working as part of a team, you will travel around your area emptying bins, removing plastic sacks of waste or picking up recyclable waste.

Recycling operatives may have additional duties, such as sorting rubbish or collecting hazardous waste. Recycling technicians also work in recycling facilities, sorting through recycled materials in preparation for re-use.

Type of person suited to this work

A strong stomach is useful when dealing with rubbish. You should also be able to cope with getting your hands dirty.

Most companies are required to complete their rounds to deadlines so you should be able to work under pressure. You will also need manual handling skills to lift and move recycling collections. For work in a recycling sorting facility, you will require good eyesight and attention to detail.

Excellent people skills are necessary as you will work as part of a team and encounter members of the public.

Working conditions

You will wear protective clothing, such as gloves and overalls, and you will come into contact with dirt and rubbish on a regular basis. The work will involve nasty smells and some unpleasant sights.

The hours are generally around 6am–3pm from Monday to Friday. You may be required to work overtime during busy holiday periods when the amount of rubbish increases.

You will work outdoors in all weather conditions and the role involves bending, lifting and carrying heavy rubbish bags.

This type of work might not suit people with skin conditions or allergies.

Future prospects

Loaders will always be in demand as even recyclable rubbish has to be collected. You could work for a contracting company providing services for a local authority and there are some jobs with specialist companies which collect paper or food waste.

Current recycling targets may be changed with the EU continuing to look to set more ambitious ones. There will be a growth in the number of jobs in the industry; the exact rate of growth will depend on the ambition of the recycling targets and legislation.

With experience, you could progress to supervisory or management work.

Advantages/disadvantages

Your working day usually finishes early so you will have your entire evening free.

The work is physically demanding and potentially unsafe.

Money guide

Starting salaries usually range from £11,000 to £14,500.

With experience in the role, you could expect to earn £16,500–£18,000 a year.

Drivers receive slightly higher earnings, usually between £15,000 and £20,000.

A recycling or refuse collection manager can achieve up to £25,000 per year.

There are usually opportunities to increase your income by working overtime or during holiday periods.

Related opportunities

- Delivery Driver p574
- Large Goods Vehicle Driver p580
- Removals Operative p591

Further information

Waste Management Industry Training and Advisory Board
www.wamitab.org.uk

SPA THERAPIST/ TECHNICIAN

ENTRY LEVEL 3

Qualifications and courses

Spa therapists must have qualifications in the treatments or therapies they wish to offer before practising and will often be trained in a combination of therapies.

One route into this career is to take an apprenticeship in Spa Therapy. This is an advanced apprenticeship so candidates are required to have already completed a Level 2 qualification in another subject, such as beauty therapy or nail services, before applying.

You could choose to study for a BTEC in Beauty Therapy (Levels 1–2) or Level 3 in Beauty Therapy Sciences, a City & Guilds NVQ Diploma in Beauty Therapy (Levels 1–2) or the Level 3 in Spa Therapy. The Vocational Training Charitable Trust (VTCT) offers a Level 3 Award in Spa Treatments and a Level 3 Diploma in Spa and Body Treatments.

The industry's main governing bodies also offer qualifications in association with approved colleges. The International Therapy Examination Council (ITEC) offers a Level 3 Diploma in Spa Treatments and Spa Therapy, whilst the Comité International d'Esthétique et de Cosmétologie (CIDESCO) offers the Spa Therapy Diploma. For entry you must possess the CIDESCO Diploma in Beauty Therapy or Postgraduate Diploma in Beauty Therapy.

Courses are also available in related, specialist subjects such as aromatherapy and Indian head massage.

If you wish to progress into management then a Foundation degree/degree in beauty and spa management will give you an advantage. ITEC also offers a Level 4 Diploma in Spa and Salon Management. Entry is usually with a BTEC Level 3 qualification in Beauty Therapy Sciences, or an NVQ/SVQ Level 3 in Spa Therapy, plus at least 3 GCSEs/National 5s (A*–C/A–C), including a science subject.

What the work involves

Spa therapists provide various treatments which are designed to enhance appearance, reduce stress or improve wellbeing.

The treatments you offer could include facials, manicures and pedicures, massage, body treatments such as wraps, and exfoliation and specialist treatments such as light therapy and lymphatic drainage.

You will be required to talk to your clients in order to discover their specific health needs and personal expectations. You will ensure that they are comfortable at all times and provide them with any necessary aftercare advice.

You will also be expected to keep the salon clean and tidy.

Type of person suited to this work

You will need a caring manner and the ability to make people feel at ease. You should be discreet and understand the role of confidentiality within the industry.

It is important that you are able to work effectively as part of a team. You should have excellent dexterity, outstanding attention to detail and good time management skills.

You will need to have strong personal hygiene and a smart appearance. A sound understanding of health and safety requirements would also prove beneficial.

Working conditions

Most of the work will be based in private treatment rooms which will be warm and clean but you may be required to complete some treatments in wet rooms.

A great deal of time will be spent standing and bending. Some products may irritate your skin, particularly if you are prone to such reactions. Most spa therapists wear a uniform.

Full-time hours are usually between 37 and 40 hours a week and often include evening and weekend work.

Future prospects

You will have the possibility of working in various beauty-related professions such as beauty therapist and nail technician.

You may choose to progress to a supervisory or management post which introduces more administrative and managerial work to your role. There is also the option of becoming a trainer or lecturer.

There are numerous opportunities for overseas work, for example on a cruise ship or in a hotel.

Advantages/disadvantages

The unusual working hours may prove inconvenient.

Opportunities within this industry are varied so you will have many options regarding which environment you wish to work in.

Being on your feet all day could be tiring.

You may receive bonuses, discounted/free products and the use of spa facilities.

Money guide

Salaries vary depending on location, employer and number of hours worked.

Starting salaries for spa therapists are usually £12,000–£14,000.

With several years' experience, earnings can increase up to £19,000.

A spa manager may earn £18,000–£30,000 a year.

Related opportunities

- Beauty Consultant p430
- Beauty Therapist p431
- Nail Technician p442

Further information

Guild of Professional Beauty Therapists
www.beautyguild.com

TATTOOIST

ENTRY LEVEL 2

Qualifications and courses

Tattooists typically start their career through an apprenticeship which can last between 1 and 3 years. There is no formal training scheme so the only way to get a traineeship is by approaching a working tattoo artist and applying for a training position with them. There are no formal qualifications required to become a tattooist's apprentice, however it is advisable to compile a portfolio of any artwork and experience you have to present to any future employers.

Over time greater responsibility will be granted and, once you can tattoo unsupervised, you will become a trainee tattooist. It can take about 5 years to become fully competent and able to carry out the various styles of tattooing.

Once your teacher deems you ready, a licence to practice must be obtained from your local environmental health department and then you will be qualified to work as a professional tattooist. Working without a licence incurs a heavy penalty.

You can get details of registered tattooists from the Tattoo Club of Great Britain or from the environmental health department of your local council. Some environmental health departments also offer short training courses for experienced and practising tattooists.

What the work involves

Tattooists, also referred to as body artists, apply permanent images onto their clients' bodies, using needles and ink to draw images, symbols or words onto the skin.

As a tattooist you will have to advise clients on suitable tattoos, ensuring that the chosen design is exactly what the client wants and that they understand the permanent nature of a tattoo.

You will create the tattoo either by drawing freehand on the customer's skin or by using a transfer.

When not tattooing, you will clean and sterilise tattoo equipment and work areas, keeping up to date with the latest health and safety procedures and devise new and interesting designs.

Type of person suited to this work

A tattooist ought to possess a flair for design, raw talent as an artist and an excellent attention to detail.

You must have good hand–eye coordination, a steady hand and feel comfortable using different equipment depending on the type of tattoo. Tattooists should also possess the ability to communicate with customers both in the consultation process and during the tattoo itself.

Owing to strict regulation, tattooists must maintain high standards of cleanliness and constant awareness of the need for hygiene and an up-to-date knowledge of health and safety.

Working conditions

You will generally work 5 or 6 days a week, including Saturdays. Studio hours are usually 9am to 5pm, but you may schedule your work into short sessions during the day because of the level of concentration and attention to detail you need.

Tattoo artists usually work from a tattoo studio, which must be registered by the local environmental health department.

Tattoo studios are fitted out with books of designs, all the hygiene equipment necessary and dedicated work and preparation spaces, whilst tattooists must provide their own inking equipment.

Future prospects

Once a subject of taboo, the alternative culture of tattoos has become more mainstream and tattooing is increasingly regulated, creative and popular.

You could work as a tattooist in tattoo studios around the UK. Some of these are part of beauty salons offering other similar services such as body piercing.

Once you have experience as a tattooist you could become self-employed.

Advantages/disadvantages

The job is very artistic and poses new challenges of creation with each customer.

As a tattooist you will come into contact with many different people; some of these may be difficult to deal with.

Hours are long and mistakes are out of the question, so working as a tattooist can be mentally exhausting.

Money guide

Many tattoo artists are self-employed and remuneration varies widely depending on the amount of trade they receive. Summer months are traditionally the busiest.

As an apprentice you are likely to work for free and some tattoo studios require apprentices to pay for their training. Apprentices must also provide their own equipment and sterilising kit.

A trainee tattooist can earn around £12,000 a year, while an experienced tattooist can earn between £15,000 and £30,000.

A tattoo artist owning his or her own business and employing others could earn in excess of £50,000 although again, this varies considerably.

Related opportunities

- Cartoonist p155
- Fine Artist/Sculptor p158
- Graphic Designer p161

Further information

Arts Council England
www.artscouncil.org.uk

Tattoo Club of Great Britain
www.tattoo.co.uk

WEDDING PLANNER

ENTRY LEVEL 1

Qualifications and courses

There are no set entry requirements for this career, however a background in hospitality, event planning, catering or marketing will be useful, especially if you want to work for a large events company. BTECs, HNDs, Foundation degrees and degrees in events or hospitality management may help to give you a pre-entry understanding of industry processes.

An alternative way to start a career in the industry is to work your way up from an administrative position in a wedding planning or event management company then progress as your experience grows. The UK Alliance of Wedding Planners' 2-day course with an optional work placement may also be helpful.

The UK Academy of Wedding and Event Planning also offers Level 3 Certificates in Wedding Planning and Event Planning, a Level 4 Certificate in Event Design, a Level 4 Diploma in Wedding Planning, Styling and Design, and a Level 4 Advanced Diploma in Special Event Planning and Design.

Those with proof of more than 3 years' business trading, 3 client references and a satisfactory quality inspection can become members of the National Association of Professional Wedding Services which offers an Advanced Certification in Wedding Design and Management.

What the work involves

Wedding planners organise ceremonies, receptions and other events to suit a client's plans and budget. You will liaise with florists, caterers, photographers, musicians, venues and hair stylists, negotiating prices, booking and confirming with all suppliers and keeping a detailed record of costs.

You will help come up with creative ideas and themes, as well as advise the couple on wedding customs and etiquette. You will help organise transport, stag and hen weekends, wedding attire and accommodation for out-of-town guests.

After all the preparations are in place, you will also be charged with managing the running of the wedding day itself. It will be your job to make sure everything happens according to schedule and that the day is exactly what the bride and groom requested.

Type of person suited to this work

You need to be enthusiastic and approachable. You should be a good listener and always take into account your client's ideas and wishes. You will need the initiative and creativity to develop these dreams into a reality. A good sense of style and attention to detail is essential.

It's important to have both financial and crisis management skills. It's your job to ensure the wedding stays within budget and runs smoothly so you should be confident and effective in negotiations.

In order to keep track of multiple clients and the variety of tasks involved you must possess strong organisational skills and be adept at multi-tasking.

You will have to be able to work with sensitivity if your client's wishes are unrealistic or not feasible for their budget and be able to offer suitable alternatives.

Working conditions

It is common to work 12-hour days, especially in the period leading up to the wedding. Although you can generally plan your own hours you will most likely need to meet your clients during evenings and weekends.

The busiest months for weddings are July to September, with about 42% of the year's weddings happening in that 3 month period. During peak wedding season you will often work at weekends, attending clients' weddings to ensure the day runs smoothly.

You could work from home or out of an office but most of your time will be spent visiting venues, suppliers and clients. A driving licence is essential.

Future prospects

You might work for a hotel or event-management company and start out temping as an assistant. You could also offer to plan weddings for friends, helping you to build up a portfolio.

Most wedding planners are self-employed. Your success will depend on your reputation and how well you market yourself.

You could choose to specialise in destination weddings or work overseas.

Advantages/disadvantages

It's rewarding when you make a bride and groom's dream wedding come true.

You will be under a lot of pressure to deliver perfection.

Money guide

If you work for a wedding and events planning company your starting salary is typically between £16,000 and £20,000 and, with experience, this can rise to £25,000–£40,000.

If you are freelance you can charge either a percentage of the total cost of the wedding, an hourly rate or a flat fee. Your salary will be dependent on how many weddings you organise a year.

Related opportunities

- Entertainment Manager p362
- Events and Exhibition Organiser p384
- Image Consultant p459

Further information

National Association of Professional Wedding Services
www.theweddingassociation.co.uk

UK Alliance of Wedding Planners
www.ukawp.com

WINDOW CLEANER

ENTRY LEVEL 1

Qualifications and courses

There are no formal qualifications needed for this job, although basic numeracy skills for calculating prices are useful. Most training is done on the job by a senior window cleaner as both the trade and health and safety issues will need to be fully understood for you take on jobs independently.

If you are using ropes and access equipment you will need to be insured. The Industrial Rope Access Trade Association offers rope access courses at trainee, operative and supervisor level.

The British Window Cleaning Academy offers courses covering window cleaning skills, water-fed pole instruction and health and safety. Theses courses are aimed at both new and experienced window cleaners in subjects and although the courses lead to a certificate in their own right, they also provide evidence for the NVQ/SVQ Level 2 in Cleaning and Support Services or Cleaning Principles.

The Federation of Window Cleaners also offers courses in cleaning windows safely and risk assessment.

With some experience you might want to study for an NVQ in either Team Leading or First Line Management (Levels 3–4). If you are self-employed then qualifications in business or a related subject may prove beneficial.

What the work involves

You will be cleaning internal and external windows and other glass surfaces, using detergents, in private and public buildings.

You will be using ladders to reach high windows or platforms and ropes for very tall office buildings. Recently the use of water pumping poles has reduced the use of ladders for health and safety reasons.

Customers may ask you to complete other tasks, alongside cleaning their windows. This could involve clearing gutters and cleaning paintwork or UPVC window frames.

If you are self-employed you might need to organise paperwork and collect payments.

Type of person suited to this work

Practical skills are very important for this job as you will be working at heights and with equipment. Having a good level of fitness will help with lifting and carrying heavy equipment.

You need to be aware of health and safety issues and you will have to learn to safely use power-operated lifting equipment for high level cleaning.

It is important to respect your customers' privacy especially when cleaning windows at people's homes.

Good communication skills are needed for dealing with customers, in particular if you want to run your own business.

Running your own business will require you to be organised, as you will have to plan your own work schedule, keep your accounts in order and chase payments. In order to maintain a successful business, you must be capable of advertising your services, which will require you to be persuasive.

Working conditions

The hours you work will vary greatly. You may be contracted to work about 40 hours a week, in daylight hours, or if self-employed, you can choose which jobs you take.

Be prepared to work in all weathers and at great heights. It is useful to have a driving licence and access to your own vehicle.

Health and safety regulations have been introduced to help prevent accidents at great heights.

Future prospects

There are jobs available across the UK, with demand in towns and cities. Smaller rural areas also require window cleaners, so job prospects are potentially good.

However, if self-employed, it will be important to establish a reputation and try and get your name into the community, often working locally.

If you have access to stabilising equipment it can help you win large contracts and more work.

Advantages/disadvantages

You may have to work in poor weather conditions or at great heights which could be demanding.

You will get to meet all types of people and establish contacts.

You can set up and run your own business.

Money guide

If you are employed by a contract cleaning company, you could earn between £15,000 and £20,000.

If you are a self-employed window cleaner your earnings will depend on how many customers you have and your reputation. With a good reputation you could earn over £20,000.

Related opportunities

- Car Valet p432
- Caretaker p433
- Pest Control Technician p443

Further information

Federation for Window Cleaners
www.f-w-c.co.uk

The Building Futures Group
www.thebuildingfuturesgroup.com/sector-skills-council

Retail, Sales and Customer Services

Jobs in this sector are suited to those of you who are very good at communicating with others and are interested in making your customers happy. Maybe you are interested in working with food and want to give your customers high quality, fresh produce. Your interest may lie in fashion retail and you could spend your time providing style advice. You should also be commercially minded and think about how your work relates to the success of the company you work for. Jobs in this sector also involve maintaining standards such as safety and quality to ensure guidelines are met, so a practical outlook can be useful.

The jobs featured in this section are listed below. For similar jobs to the ones covered in this section turn to *Administration, Business, Office Work and Financial Services* on page 1.

ANTIQUES DEALER

ENTRY LEVEL 1

Qualifications and courses

No formal qualifications are needed, but employers often seek candidates with sales skills and demonstrable enthusiasm, for example those that have collected and researched antiques or bought and sold products on a market stall or via the internet. GCSEs/National 5s (A*–C/A–C) in subjects such as art, design and history are also an advantage as they demonstrate an interest in history and/or aesthetics.

Entry is normally through having completed relevant work experience within an antiques shop, salesroom or auction house as a trainee or within a junior role. Here you begin as a general worker, assistant, cataloguer, porter or valuer within an auction house, learning on the job from experienced professionals, before working your way up to a position as an antiques dealer.

Alternatively, you may wish to study for an industry recognised qualification, such as an NVQ/SVQ in Retail Operations, or a diploma, degree or postgraduate award in a relevant subject such as fine arts, applied arts or history of art. Upon graduation, you may decide to apply for one of the relevant graduate training schemes offered by large auction houses such as Sotheby's, Christie's and Bonhams.

You can add to your skills throughout your career through extensive self-study or by taking one of the privately run short courses available from institutions such as Christie's and Sotheby's. Information and advice about careers in antiques dealing and current vacancies with dealers may be available from the British Antique Dealers' Association (BADA) or the Association of Art and Antique Dealers (LAPADA).

What the work involves

You will be buying and selling things such as furniture, clocks, jewellery and pictures, which are either old or which people collect. You will go to auctions and fairs to buy things to sell in shops, markets or antique salerooms.

You will need to develop specialist knowledge so that you can assess the age of an object, its value and whether it will sell at a profit.

You will advise customers on the value of their antiques.

Type of person suited to this work

You should be fascinated by antiques and working out where they come from and what they are worth.

You will need to be interested in history and dedicated enough to travel and visit fairs and auctions all over the country, and possibly abroad, searching out bargains and objects to sell. You will need to develop good specialist knowledge, know what is likely to be popular and sell quickly at a profit.

Antiques do not have fixed prices, so you will need to be able to make quick decisions and cope with the stress of buying things at auction. You will need to have good all round business skills.

Working conditions

You will work in a shop, in an antiques saleroom or on a market stall. You could be outside in all weathers and will probably have to travel to different markets.

You could be dealing with heavy objects such as furniture or dusty and dirty things such as clothes and books.

Your working hours will vary a lot. Shops and stalls will be open at fixed times and on public holidays, and you could be visiting auctions or customers at any time.

Future prospects

Most antique dealers are self-employed or work in a family business, but you could start in an auction house or as a sales assistant in a larger shop.

Once you have developed contacts and knowledge of antiques and their value, you could work for yourself, perhaps starting with a market stall and expanding your business from there. You will have to stay ahead of industry developments, such as the rapid rise in online auctions, in order to secure deals.

Most dealers specialise in a particular period of history or type of antique or move into valuing or auctioneering.

Advantages/disadvantages

You will be working with things that you love and have the thrill of finding bargains or rare items.

It can be a very uncertain business and prices will rise and fall as things go in and out of fashion. You can make a lot of money, but you can also lose a lot.

Money guide

An assistant earns around £15,000 per year.

Between £20,000 and £30,000 is usual for a dealer with a flair for the trade and considerable experience.

In excess of £50,000 is possible for successful dealers, or people with a high level of specialist knowledge.

Related opportunities

- Auctioneer p451
- Museum/Art Gallery Curator p335
- Sales/Retail Assistant p468

Further information

British Antique Dealers' Association
www.bada.org

Sotheby's
www.sothebys.com

AUCTIONEER

ENTRY LEVEL 2

Qualifications and courses

There are no set entry requirements for this profession, but most employers prefer candidates with good communication skills and GCSEs/National 5s (A*–C/A–C), particularly in English and Maths.

One way of entering the profession is to start your career in a junior role such as a salesroom assistant before progressing to the position of auctioneer. If you want to go into property auctioneering, you could start out by gaining experience in valuation work. Some employers will be willing to take you on as a trainee.

However if you want to work for an international auction house you will need either a degree in a related subject, such as history of art or fine arts conservation, or a degree in property or valuation that has been accredited by the Royal Institution of Chartered Surveyors (RICS). You can also follow a Foundation degree in Auctioneering and Valuation, or a degree in the arts market. Sotheby's Institute of Art also offers a postgraduate qualification in art business.

Upon graduation, you may opt to complete a graduate training scheme offered by some large London auction houses such as Sotheby's and Christie's, although competition is fierce. Relevant art or business work experience may improve your chances of securing a place on one of these training programmes.

Once employed, you will experience on-the-job training from experienced auctioneers and external instruction via short courses and workshops. You may even be encouraged to work towards gaining incorporated or chartered membership of RICS which would significantly improve your career prospects and salary. In order to remain up to date with current developments, such as the rise in online auctions, it is recommended that you join the National Association of Valuers and Auctioneers.

What the work involves

Auctioneers sell items at auctions, getting the best market price possible for the items they are selling.

It is your responsibility to make sure the item sells for the best price, both by selling well on the day and by organising and publicising sales in advance. You will be inspecting and valuing items and coming to price agreements with the sellers, making sure that reserves are appropriate.

On auction days, you will run through the items on sale, observe customers, and take bids. You may specialise in a particular area, and could be working on anything from antiques and property to livestock and motors.

Type of person suited to this work

You will need to be good with people and communicate well, so that you can interact with customers and successfully sell goods. In addition, you should be outgoing and confident, with excellent knowledge of what you are selling.

You should have excellent observational skills and a good attention to detail; valuing objects is also a big part of the job. For this reason you also need to be able to think on your feet, and work well under pressure.

You must have shrewd business sense and a good head for figures, as much of your day will revolve around numbers.

Working conditions

You will usually be working in an auction house, or an office or auction room within. Normal working hours are 9am–5.30pm Monday to Saturday, but be prepared to carry out viewings and valuations during evenings and weekends.

A driving licence is useful as travel may be necessary, for example if you're selling the contents of a large house clearance.

You may also sell livestock and motor vehicles outdoors.

Future prospects

Career development relies on building a list of contacts, and working towards moving to larger more prestigious auction houses.

You may want to become self-employed, or work towards a management position or partnership.

You may also have the chance to travel, as some auction houses have offices abroad.

Advantages/disadvantages

This work is stimulating and challenging, and especially rewarding if you choose to work with items or goods you have a genuine interest in.

Every day will be different, and you will constantly be interacting and communicating with people.

It can be tiring work, and much of the day will be spent on your feet. As the person leading an auction, you have to be 100% alert all the time.

Money guide

Starting salaries for trainees are around £15,000 a year.

With experience, this may rise to between £30,000 and £40,000.

If you become a business partner, you might earn over £60,000.

Related opportunities

- Antiques Dealer p450
- Chartered Surveyor p68
- Rural Property/Practice Surveyor p103

Further information

Livestock Auctioneers' Association Limited
www.laa.co.uk

National Association of Valuers and Auctioneers
www.nava.org.uk

National Federation of Property Professionals
www.nfopp.co.uk

BOOKSELLER

ENTRY LEVEL 2

Qualifications and courses

There are no formal qualifications to enter this work, but most employers look for candidates with GCSEs/ National 5s (A*–C/A–C) in English and Maths. A degree/ HND/Foundation degree in English, retail or business management or retail marketing may increase your chances of employment. If you wish to work in specialist academic bookshops, a degree in a subject similar to that being sold in the store is recommended, as is a postgraduate qualification for those working in antiquarian bookselling.

Other relevant further education courses include NVQs/ SVQs in Retail Operations at Levels 2–3, Customer Service at Levels 2–4, Visual Merchandising at Level 2 and BTEC qualifications in retail and distribution.

Pre-entry experience in retail is highly valuable as competition for posts is strong. Employers often seek candidates who can provide evidence of excellent communication skills, a passion for literature, effective teamwork and an interest in and knowledge of the bookselling industry. An understanding of e-commerce is becoming increasingly desired by employers given the rise in online ordering and e-books.

Some larger employers offer fast track structured training schemes or trainee manager schemes whilst new recruits of smaller branches are trained by experienced colleagues and through external instruction. Membership of The Booksellers Association (BA) or The Antiquarian Booksellers Association (ABA) is recommended in order to remain up to date with new developments and training courses.

What the work involves

Front of house duties often include serving customers, taking money, answering enquiries, giving advice and ordering books. You might also be expected to liaise with publishers and stockists, ordering books and keeping stock information up to date.

You will be expected to undertake shop floor work which will include stock replenishment, recommending books to customers, arranging displays and keeping shelves tidy. Depending on the size and type of shop you may also be responsible for shop maintenance and undertake cleaning duties after hours.

Behind the scenes you will also have to deal with deliveries, update the stock list, repackage returns and cash up the till. You might work with local colleges or universities to make sure you have got the books needed for their courses and sometimes organise book sales and events with them.

Type of person suited to this work

You need to have a genuine interest in books and to be able to keep up to date with new publications, so that you can help and advise customers.

You will need excellent communication skills for dealing with customers and sales representatives. You will work as part of a team, but should also be able to use your own initiative. It is important to remain calm and polite when the shop is busy.

Basic numeracy and IT skills will be useful when using the tills for payments and computers for stock orders.

You should be able to use your initiative, especially when ordering stock. You should be able to identify customer demand for certain titles and order books accordingly.

Working conditions

You will be working in either an independent bookshop or one that is part of a larger chain.

You will be on your feet all day, at a till, carrying heavy books and assisting customers.

You will work 39–40 hours a week, which may include weekends and evenings on a rota basis.

Future prospects

The number of small independent bookshops is currently in decline due to competition from larger stores and online sales along with the rise in e-books, so the majority of opportunities are with the big chains.

You can progress to a supervisor role or be in charge of a specific section of books. You can go on to management level or to work for head office.

With considerable experience and good finances you might open your own shop or choose to specialise in certain types of books such as antique or second hand.

Advantages/disadvantages

You will be using your knowledge and love of books to help other people and to keep up to date with new publications.

You could develop specialist knowledge, for example in children's books.

You will be dealing with the public, which can be rewarding but also stressful.

Money guide

Salaries vary a lot depending on the size of the shop. With large chains, you may get bonuses for high levels of sales or for meeting targets.

You can expect £12,000–£17,000 per year when you start.

With experience and/or managerial responsibilities, you can expect £20,000–£40,000.

Related opportunities

- Librarian/Library Assistant p334
- Publisher/Commissioning Editor p397
- Sales/Retail Assistant p468

Further information

Booksellers Association
www.booksellers.org.uk

British Independent Retailers Association
www.bira.co.uk

BUILDERS' MERCHANT/ ASSISTANT

ENTRY LEVEL 1

Qualifications and courses

Although there are no entry requirements most employers prefer applicants to have a number of GCSEs/National 5s, particularly in subjects such as English and maths.

Previous experience within the construction or retailing industry is beneficial however, as many employers view experience and personality as being more important than academic qualifications. Having said this, the BTEC Level 1 Diploma in Construction might be a useful qualification in introducing you to some of the basic skills required in the industry.

You may opt to complete an apprenticeship with a DIY store or building suppliers. Here you are likely to experience a combination of on-the-job training from professionals and a series of day or block release instruction at a college or training centre where you will work towards gaining industry recognised qualifications.

Your employer may encourage you to work towards specialist courses in areas such as central heating, bricks, mortar and bathrooms, as well as a Diploma in Merchanting, offered by the Builders Merchants Federation (BMF). NVQs/SVQs also accredited by the BMF in subjects such as business administration, customer service, retail, team leading and management or warehousing and storage may also be available to you.

A forklift truck and/or LGV licence may improve your chances of securing employment as will short courses in management, operations, product knowledge and sales, also provided by the BMF.

What the work involves

You will be dealing with building materials and bathroom fittings. You will keep track of stock using computer or paper systems, order new stock and take deliveries.

You will supply goods to building firms and individual contractors – plumbers, electricians or plasterers – and members of the public. As part of this you will take payments and use tills.

Assistants will work for a builders' merchant looking after the stock.

Assistants will also handle a range of building materials, take deliveries, store deliveries properly, keep the yard clean and deal with customers.

Type of person suited to this work

You will need to have a certain level of physical fitness for both of these positions, as there will be heavy lifting and carrying involved. Candidates with asthma and/or allergies to dust and chemicals may not be suitable for this type of work.

You will need solid communication skills for dealing with customers and suppliers. You should have good numeracy and computer skills and the ability to handle money and paperwork efficiently.

Customer service skills will also be useful.

Working conditions

You will work about 40 hours a week, usually on Saturdays and sometimes Sundays. You may start at about 7.30am so that builders can buy their materials on the way to their work.

You may also need to use a forklift truck and climb ladders, which could be dangerous. You will be wearing overalls and protective boots or shoes.

You could be working outside in all weathers.

Future prospects

There are job opportunities in all areas of the country, but these vary depending on the strength of the building trade within the current economic climate. Firms are most concentrated within the south of England for example.

Although the number of small builders' merchants is declining, there are still many specialist and larger firms recruiting workers regularly. A growing specialist area is the sale of reclaimed building materials, eg roof tiles, slates, staircases and window frames.

You could choose to work part time, and if you work for large merchants or a chain you could progress to become a supervisor or manager. You could also work for a supplier or as a sales representative.

Those employed in smaller companies may have to transfer between employers in order to ensure promotion.

Advantages/disadvantages

The work can be a great way of using your interest in building and knowledge of materials, tools and equipment.

There is a lot of paperwork involved in keeping track of the stock.

You could be starting early in the morning and working outside.

Money guide

An assistant at a builders' merchant could start on around £12,000 a year.

Once you have built up your experience and have additional responsibilities you can expect to earn up to £20,000.

You could earn more as the manager of a department or store. Managers of large companies could earn up to £50,000 a year.

Related opportunities

- Building Surveyor p63
- Sales/Retail Assistant p468
- Warehouse Worker/Manager p597

Further information

Builders Merchants Federation
www.bmf.org.uk

BUTCHER

ENTRY LEVEL 2

Qualifications and courses

There are no formal qualifications required to become a butcher and most people train on the job. Many employers will want proof, however, of a certain standard of literacy and numeracy skills. They may require employees to have acquired English, Maths and science GCSEs/National 5s (A*–C/A–C) and some even set aptitude tests. Work experience in the food and drink industry is also beneficial.

A good way to begin in this career is through an apprenticeship scheme, the most suitable being the Improve Proficiency Apprenticeship in Meat and Poultry Industry Skills. Many employers provide entrants with the opportunity to study towards industry recognised qualifications including food safety awards and NVQs/SVQs in Meat and Poultry Processing at Levels 1 and 2.

The Meat Training Council (MTC) offers a range of qualifications which include the Intermediate Certificate in Meat and Poultry, the Intermediate Certificate in Management and the Intermediate Certificate in Hazard Analysis Critical Control Points (HACCP). Courses such as these cover topics including food labelling, the displaying of meat products, food safety, the production of cooked and raw meat and boning, cutting and trimming operations.

It is advised that you become a member of the professional body for butchers, the Worshipful Company of Butchers, which would demonstrate to customers that you work to high professional standards.

What the work involves

You might prepare an assortment of meat and poultry products. This could involve cutting, de-boning, trimming and slicing. You could offer advice to customers about varieties of meat available and preparation techniques involved with them. Some butchers offer a delivery service.

You will take part in the everyday running of the business, visiting markets, ordering stock, taking deliveries from suppliers, organising displays and selling the products.

Butchers can also work in the wholesale area of the industry, receiving the meat from the abattoir, then preparing and storing it for sale to the retailers or wholesale customers.

Type of person suited to this work

You will have to be meticulous and practical. You will need to have a strong understanding of and a professional approach to health and hygiene. Owing to the fact you will be using sharp tools and machinery you need to be safety conscious.

You should be personable, maintaining a high level of customer service. You need to have an outstanding knowledge of the various products and cuts of meat.

You should have strong mental arithmetic skills in order to value a sale quickly and correctly and be confident handling cash.

Working conditions

A retail butcher works in a shop environment with a chilled storage area. You will be expected to prepare meat in front of customers, using knives, cleavers and saws and will therefore be required to wear protective clothing, such as disposable gloves and an apron. Wholesale butchers also work in chilled environments and wear protective clothing.

This profession involves a great deal of standing, lifting and carrying as butchers are required to transport joints of meat.

You will work, on average, 40 hours a week, including Saturdays and sometimes evenings and Sundays. Work starts as early as 7am.

Future prospects

With a large number of local butchers having closed down and the ones left being small businesses, prospects are becoming somewhat limited. Supermarkets have however resurrected the idea of the meat counter over simply selling packaged meats and promotion opportunities within these chains are plentiful.

Once you have gained experience there is the option of setting up your own retail outlet. Other options include making the move into meat catering, meat hygiene, meat wholesale or meat-product manufacture.

Advantages/disadvantages

You will have a great deal of customer contact and the opportunity to share your knowledge.

The amount of time spent on your feet, heavy lifting and in cold temperatures may cause discomfort.

Money guide

Typically, a butcher will earn a starting salary of between £12,500 and £16,000 a year.

With experience, earnings will increase to between £16,500 and £22,000 a year.

A butchery manager could make up to £30,000 per year.

If an individual chose to open their own shop this may increase further.

Related opportunities

- Food Processing Operative p208
- Kitchen Assistant/Supervisor p131
- Meat Process Worker p216

Further information

Meat Hygiene Service
www.food.gov.uk/enforcement/monitoring/meat

CALL CENTRE OPERATOR

ENTRY LEVEL 2

Qualifications and courses

There are no formal entry qualifications but employers generally look for at least 5 GCSEs/National 5s (A*–C/A–C) including English and Maths. You can enter and train in this career with qualifications at Levels 1 or 2. Previous experience of working with the public or in a customer service role is helpful as employers often seek candidates with a confident telephone manner and good keyboard skills.

You may decide to gain some of the skills required of a call centre operator full time at college prior to employment. Courses such as a BTEC Level 1 Award in an Introduction to Contact Centres, a BTEC Level 2 Award in Contact Centre Skills or a BTEC Level 3 Award in Contact Centre Supervisory Skills may be useful. City & Guilds also offer relevant qualifications such as the Level 1 Certificate for Introduction to the Contact Centre and the Level 2 and 3 Technical Certificate in Contact Centre Operations. Apprenticeships might also be a possibility.

If you wish to work in more specialist call centres, such as an IT support helpline, you should be willing to work towards certain qualifications such as a computer maintenance award.

Once you have secured employment in a call centre, you may wish to undertake further study to enhance your career progression prospects. City & Guilds provide the NVQ Award, Certificate and Diploma in Contact Centre Operations (Levels 1–4), the NVQ for Contact Centre Professionals (Levels 2–4) or the NVQ in Sales and Telesales (Levels 2–4). The Chartered Institute of Marketing (CIM) offers a 1-day course in the Fundamentals of Outbound Calling.

What the work involves

You will be dealing with customers over the phone and using a computer to log details or find information. You might do telesales or telemarketing, selling, mail ordering, banking, or promoting goods and services, which could involve 'cold calling'.

You could be doing market research, asking about people's buying habits or what services they would like from a company.

You might be providing a service – receiving calls from customers who are ordering goods, making a complaint or accessing their bank accounts.

Type of person suited to this work

You should have good spoken English, with a clear voice and good hearing. You will need excellent customer service skills and you must be polite and calm when dealing with difficult callers.

For telesales or telemarketing, you will need to be motivated, persuasive and persistent. Good IT skills are also important.

You will probably work to targets and you are likely to be very busy, so you must be comfortable working under pressure and using your initiative. The ability to work successfully as part of a team is also required.

Working conditions

You will be office based, usually working about 40 hours a week. You might work shifts which could include nights, weekends and evenings.

Call centre staff have their own workstations with a headset and computer and work as part of a team.

You will be given targets which you are expected to meet. For this reason, calls are often monitored by supervisors and staff turnover can be fairly high.

Future prospects

There has been a huge growth in call centres recently as more services are available over the phone – such as mail order and banking – and more companies are using telesales and marketing to sell their goods and services.

You could become a team leader or supervisor.

You could also work abroad or establish new contact centres.

Advantages/disadvantages

There are lots of job opportunities and flexible working hours are possible.

You could utilise your customer service and sales skills to move into related areas such as marketing or human resources.

Trying to reach sales targets can be stressful and the work can be repetitive.

Money guide

Earnings vary with employers and financial services call centres tend to pay the highest wages.

Starting salaries for call centre operators range from £12,000 to £15,500.

A team leader is likely to receive £18,000–£24,000 a year.

Those employed in a managerial role usually earn in excess of £25,000.

If you meet your targets you may receive commission on sales or bonuses which will increase your income.

Related opportunities

- Customer Services Assistant/Manager p456
- Marketing Assistant/Executive p387
- Sales/Retail Assistant p468

Further information

Institute of Customer Service
www.instituteofcustomerservice.com

Institute of Direct and Digital Marketing
www.theidm.com

CUSTOMER SERVICES ASSISTANT/ MANAGER

ENTRY LEVEL 1

Qualifications and courses

Assistant
You can enter this profession without any formal qualifications. However, certain employers look for at least 3 GCSEs/National 5s (A*–C/A–C), including Maths and English. Progression to a senior role might be faster with A levels/H grades.

The most important entry requirement is to have strong people skills and experience of dealing with customers, either face to face or over the phone.

You could improve your chances of employment by taking a college course such as a BTEC Award in Introduction to Customer Service (Level 1–2), a BTEC Level 1 Award/ Certificate in Principles of Customer Service or a BTEC Level 2 Certificate in Contact Centre Operations. If you wish to specialise in the customer service of a specific industry, you could take the BTEC Level 2 Award in Cultural Awareness for Customer Service in Hospitality, Leisure, Travel and Tourism or the Level 2 Certificate in Customer Service for the Automotive Industry.

Once you secure employment, you will be trained in company procedures and customer service standards. Your employer may even encourage you to work towards an NVQ in Customer Service (Levels 1–4).

Manager
A degree or Foundation degree can increase your chances of direct entry into a managerial position. Relevant degree subjects such as business studies, marketing or management studies may increase your chances of employment. Competition amongst graduates is high so a history of working closely with customers may give you an advantage when seeking work or training schemes.

However, many entrants start as a customer services assistant and progress to a role as manager, obtaining qualifications while they work. You could study for the NVQ Level 4 in Customer Service.

What the work involves

Assistant
You will be liaising with customers, either face to face or by phone and email, in order to sell products and services such as retail goods, insurance or holiday packages. You could be responsible for dealing with customer enquiries, problems or complaints.

Manager
Your role will include hiring and training customer services assistants. You will need to establish targets and implement different motivational techniques to ensure that staff reach them.

Type of person suited to this work

Assistant
You need to have good people skills and to be polite and helpful. You must remain calm and patient when faced with difficult customers. You should be able to work well as part of a team and independently.

Manager
A manager needs to have excellent leadership skills and to be able to motivate his or her team. Managers must also be organised, decisive and able to work under pressure.

Working conditions

You will typically work a 37-hour week, although this could be on a rota system that includes early mornings, evenings or weekends. If your company provides 24-hour assistance, you might have to work nights. There is also the opportunity to work part time.

You could spend the majority of your time dealing with customers face to face, or at a desk with a computer or telephone headset.

Future prospects

Vacancies are available throughout the UK, especially in big cities and towns. You could work in shops, call centres, banks, airports or tourist information centres.

Assistant
After gaining experience and further qualifications, you could progress into a role as team leader, supervisor and then manager.

Manager
You could move into a head office role or take a job with a higher salary and responsibility. You can go on to train staff or take further qualifications and work as a staff assessor.

Advantages/disadvantages

Difficult customers or problems can make the work stressful.

This job can be repetitive.

There are good prospects for promotion within this sector.

Money guide

Opportunities for bonuses or commission will increase your income.

Assistant
Starting salaries are about £12,500–£14,000.

With experience, you could earn £16,000–£19,000 a year.

Manager
Starting salaries for trainees are £16,000–£23,000.

With experience, you can expect £30,000–£45,000.

Senior managers can achieve up to £60,000.

Related opportunities

- Receptionist p45
- Retail Manager p466
- Sales/Retail Assistant p468

Further information

Institute of Customer Service
www.instituteofcustomerservice.com

FISHMONGER

ENTRY LEVEL 2

Qualifications and courses

You do not need any formal qualifications to enter this industry. However, most employers will expect a good standard of general education including English and Maths. The Apprenticeship in Retail offers an ideal route into this career and is available at both Intermediate and Advanced Levels. Competition for places is fierce so good GCSEs/National 5s (A*–C/A–C) would be beneficial.

You will normally begin at counter assistant level and train on the job. Whilst working you will need to attain your basic food hygiene certification, followed by Hazard Analysis and Critical Control Point (HACCP) training.

It may be useful to work towards the City & Guilds Award in Retail Skills (Levels 1–2) or the Certificate in Retail (Sales Professional) at Level 3. These qualifications have a wide selection of optional units so you can choose to specialise in relevant areas.

The Billingsgate Seafood Training School offers 1-day courses on topics such as Introduction to Fishmongering, Get into Fishmongering and Knife Skills. The City & Guilds Seafood Profile of Achievement is a 2-day course which equips candidates with skills in cutting, displays, selling techniques and quality assessment.

What the work involves

Fishmongers prepare and sell fish, offering advice to customers on how to store and cook it. They can work in various environments including shops, supermarkets and market stalls.

You will be required to provide customers with information such as how the fish was caught, the sustainability of its stock and whether it has been previously frozen.

You will buy fish from the wholesaler and prepare it for retail sales. This preparation includes removing bones, skin and scales then gutting the fish and maybe cutting it into portions.

Type of person suited to this work

You will require good hand–eye coordination as you will be using sharp knives to complete detailed jobs such as filleting and taking out small bones. You will have to carry out messy tasks such as cleaning and gutting fish.

You should be able to stand for long periods of time. You need a strong level of personal hygiene and an awareness of food safety procedures.

You will need to be personable as customer service is extremely important for this role.

Working conditions

The conditions in this industry can be cold and wet. You will be expected to spend a great deal of time on your feet, moving between the counter and storage areas.

Most fishmongers work for approximately 40 hours a week. Your working week will usually include Saturdays, with a day off during the week to compensate.

You will frequently have to work early mornings to sign for stock deliveries.

Protective clothing and footwear are required. If you suffer from skin allergies then this work may not be suitable for you.

Future prospects

Fishmongers work in many different environments including supermarkets, small local stores and mobile fish units so you may choose to move between them.

You may have the opportunity to work overseas.

Other possibilities for progression might involve supplying fishmonger stores with fresh fish or moving into other industries which require food preparation, for example working with meat.

You can also work your way up to a management position or open your own shop.

Advantages/disadvantages

You will have to work early mornings.

You will have the opportunity to be creative, both in the preparation of the fish and in providing customers with advice on how best to prepare or cook it.

Spending all day on your feet and in cold temperatures can be uncomfortable.

Money guide

Pay rates vary depending on location and employer.

Fishmongers usually have a starting salary of £11,000–£14,000.

With experience in the role, earnings increase to about £20,000 a year.

Fishmongers who are self-employed and own a shop are likely to have a higher income.

Related opportunities

- Butcher p454
- Kitchen Assistant/Supervisor p131
- Shopkeeper p470

Further information

Sea Fish Industry Authority
www.seafish.org

FLORIST

ENTRY LEVEL 1

Qualifications and courses

There are no specific academic qualifications for this career. Candidates can either find work and train on the job or study at college prior to securing employment. Those seeking work in a florist shop should demonstrate an interest in floristry, possibly through joining a local flower arranging club or doing a course in flower arranging.

Available qualifications include the BTEC Certificate in Floristry (Levels 2–3), the City & Guilds Diploma in Floristry (Levels 2–3) and the City & Guilds Level 3 Advanced National Certificate in Floristry. Those who are currently working at a florist shop could study for the City & Guilds Diploma in Work-based Floristry (Levels 2–3). The entry requirements for these courses vary, however GCSEs/ National 5s (A*–C/A–C) in subjects such as English, maths and art would be beneficial. Any other relevant experience and skills might be taken into account so work experience in a florist shop would be valuable.

Another option is the Apprenticeship in Floristry which is available at both Intermediate and Advanced Levels. With experience, you could work towards an NPTC Level 4 Higher Diploma in Floristry (HDF), an NPTC Master Diploma in Professional Floristry (MDPF) or an NVQ Level 4 in Floristry Business Management. Foundation degrees and degrees in floristry are also a possibility.

What the work involves

Florists combine creativity with knowledge of plants and flowers to design and create floral displays that are then sold in shops and/or on market stalls.

You will be responsible for ordering and caring for the plants and flowers, aiding customers in choosing flowers suitable for specific occasions and creating floral displays. You may also be required to deliver flowers to customers and set up displays at events.

You will be expected to handle money, complete regular stocktakes and help with the day to day running of the business.

Type of person suited to this work

You will need to be extremely creative, with an understanding of shape, colour and design. As a great deal of this job is hands on, you must be dexterous.

A strong knowledge of plants and flowers and the care required for them is essential, along with a desire to expand your knowledge. You should be patient, with good customer service skills and sensitivity to the needs of the client.

You will be expected to have brilliant telephone communication skills and the ability to work within tight deadlines, particularly if you have to fulfil last-minute or online orders. Administration and sales skills are also important.

Working conditions

Florists usually work inside in a shop environment. Those who work on a floristry stall will spend most of their time outdoors.

This job involves a great deal of standing at the work bench/ counter.

Working hours usually vary between 35 and 40 hours per week, and shop opening hours are normally 9am to 5pm. Some travel may be required when making deliveries so a driving licence might be needed.

Some shops provide uniforms or aprons. This job will not be suitable for people who suffer from pollen allergies.

Future prospects

Those with experience may progress to a managerial role. Once you have the required skills, there is also the possibility of becoming self-employed and opening your own business.

Another progression option is to work as a freelance florist for a variety of businesses on a contract basis.

You could also teach floristry or become a professional demonstrator.

Advantages/disadvantages

You can combine creativity, skill and knowledge to create floral displays.

You will be on your feet for a great deal of time and those who work on florist market stalls will be outdoors in all weathers.

Every day will be different as you will work with a wide range of customers for a variety of events.

Money guide

Earnings vary depending on location and employer.

At the start of their career, a florist usually receives the National Minimum Wage. As you gain experience, you can expect your salary to increase to £16,000–£18,000 a year.

Those employed in a managerial role can achieve up to £25,000.

Related opportunities

- Gardener/Garden Designer p251
- Landscaper/Landscape Manager p257
- Visual Merchandiser p173

Further information

British Florist Association
www.britishfloristassociation.org

Flowers and Plants Association
www.flowers.org.uk

IMAGE CONSULTANT ENTRY LEVEL 2

Qualifications and courses

While there are no set academic qualifications for this career, related experience in areas such as fashion, hair, beauty, retail, consultancy, sales and marketing or public relations is useful.

The City & Guilds Level 2 Diploma in Beauty Consultancy or the BTEC Level 2 Certificate in Retail Beauty Consultancy may be a good starting point. Some entrants hold a Foundation degree, HND or degree in a subject such as beauty therapy, cosmetic sciences, business studies or sales and marketing. For HND courses you will need at least 4 GCSEs/National 5s (A*–C/A–C) and for degree entry you are required to have at least 2 A levels/3 H grades and 5 GCSEs/National 5s (A*–C/A–C).

Entrants to this profession are recommended to take a course in image consultancy approved by the Federation of Image Professionals International (FIPI). Courses involve training in the 4 core areas of image consultancy: colour analysis, women's style, men's style and cosmetic application and tuition. Upon completion of this training, you can become a Registered Affiliate of FIPI.

To improve your skills and marketability, you could work towards the FIPI/City & Guilds Masters Certification Award in Image Consultancy. You are eligible to become a Master of FIPI once you hold this qualification. You could enhance your skills throughout your career by attending seminars and workshops also offered by the FIPI.

What the work involves

You will advise individuals and companies on branding, impact and appearance. This can include style analysis, make-up advice, wardrobe management and personal shopping. Part of your job might involve speaking on the radio as a way of promoting your business.

When working with private clients you will discuss fabrics, styles, patterns and colours that will suit your client's body shape, hair and eye colour and skin tone.

When working with corporate clients you may advise on body language, etiquette, first impressions and branding. You could also coach executives and run workshops.

Type of person suited to this work

You must be aware of current fashion trends, possess a good sense of style and a great eye for colour and detail. Creativity and communication skills are essential in order to inspire clients to believe in their image. You want clients to trust you so you should be easy to talk to, uplifting and sensitive.

Self-motivation is important when running your own business. You should be able to budget well and to organise your time effectively.

The ability to network and market your brand is essential.

Working conditions

You can choose to work from home or out of a studio. Your hours will vary depending on how many clients you see and could include evenings and weekends.

You will need to travel at times to a client's home or company so a driving licence would be useful.

You should dress smartly when meeting clients.

Future prospects

You could be an independent image consultant or work for an organisation such as First Impressions who will provide you with business support. As a result of the rise in technology, many image consultants are also moving into online consultancy, offering highly personalised shopping experiences to customers on the internet.

With experience, you can progress from working solely with private clients to setting up your own image consultancy business or moving into corporate work. Developing a good reputation is key to a thriving business.

You might specialise in one area, such as working with brides, or, if one area of your job particularly interests you, you could move into life coaching, retail or hairdressing. Opportunities to work abroad are also available.

Advantages/disadvantages

It is rewarding to help clients with low self-esteem gain confidence in their personal or professional brand.

The job can be glamorous as you may work with well-known people.

Setting up your own business and building up a client base can be difficult.

You might need to supplement your income when first starting out.

Money guide

Whilst establishing your business, you could earn between £10,000 and £15,000 per year.

With experience and a regular client base, you may earn up to £30,000.

If you work in the corporate sector you could earn in excess of £40,000.

As most image consultants are self-employed, your income will depend on your location, skills and how well you market yourself.

Related opportunities

- Beauty Consultant p430
- Fashion Designer/Milliner p157
- Make-up Artist p417

Further information

Federation of Image Professionals International
www.fipigroup.com

Hairdressing and Beauty Industry Authority
www.habia.org

People 1st
www.people1st.co.uk/retail-apprenticeships

JEWELLER

ENTRY LEVEL 2

Qualifications and courses

Although there are no specific entry requirements, many employers will expect GCSEs/National 5s (A*–C/A–C), in subjects including English, maths, and art or design and technology. Previous work experience in a retail or customer services role would also be beneficial, as is a background in metalwork.

Candidates looking to take relevant qualifications should consider studying for a City & Guilds Level 2 Award in Retail Principles, the City & Guilds Award in Retail Skills (Levels 1–2) or the City & Guilds Level 3 Diploma in Retail (Sales Professional) full time at college.

Alternatively, you could work towards any one of these awards whilst completing an Apprenticeship in Retail, available at both Intermediate and Advanced Levels. Here you will be trained on the job by experienced professionals in the relevant skills required of a retail jeweller whilst attending a series of day or block release instruction at a college or training centre.

Alongside working towards qualifications offered by City & Guilds, your employer may also encourage you to gain awards run by the The National Association of Goldsmiths (NAG). The Professional Jewellers' Diploma (JET 1–2), an 18-month course which covers topics such as design, manufacture, hallmarking, gemstones, silverware, horology, antiques, legal matters, repair handling, selling techniques and window displays, is available. NAG also runs short courses in valuation and window displays.

Senior staff, managers and business owners may wish to extend their knowledge by studying for the NAG Business Development Diploma (JET Pro) further on in their career.

What the work involves

Retail jewellers work in shops, selling jewellery and sometimes watches, clocks and silverware to customers. Other services they offer might include valuation, alteration and repair.

You will advise customers on the available products and help them to choose an appropriate item. You will package the customer's goods and process their payment.

As part of the day-to-day running of the shop, you will arrange window displays, ensure that the shop is presentable and carry out stock control procedures.

You may work for a company which specialises in selling a particular gemstone, such as diamonds. You could focus on one area, for example casting or enamelling, or learn a variety of techniques.

Type of person suited to this work

An interest in precious metal, gemstones, jewellery or fashion is essential.

As you will be interacting with customers, you need excellent communication skills, with a polite and friendly manner. You should be comfortable working independently and as part of a team.

You must be extremely trustworthy and conscious of security procedures when handling valuable goods. Numeracy skills are important for processing payments and dealing with money.

If your role involves carrying out repairs or alterations, you should have practical skills, patience and good attention to detail.

Working conditions

Retail jewellers work indoors in shops and spend the majority of the day standing up.

You will work 37 to 40 hours per week including weekends. Sometimes you may be required to work overtime during evenings and bank holidays. Part-time work is often available.

You will be expected to look smart and some stores may provide a uniform.

Future prospects

There are opportunities to work for independent jewellers or large high street chains. You could progress to become a supervisor, assistant manager or even a manager.

Specialist skills can improve your prospects, so learning how to value or alter items may lead to higher paid roles.

With extensive experience, you could open your own jewellery shop or enter into gemmology or jewellery design.

Advantages/disadvantages

You will have the opportunity to meet a wide range of people and help them choose jewellery for special occasions.

Working on your feet all day can be demanding and tiring.

Money guide

Your starting salary is likely to be around £16,000 a year.

Working within a luxury retail jewellers will increase your salary to £30,000.

Your income will be significantly higher if you earn commission for your sales.

Related opportunities

- Gold/Silversmith/Engraver p160
- Jewellery Designer p164
- Sales/Retail Assistant p468

Further information

British Jewellers' Association
www.bja.org.uk

The Goldsmiths' Company
www.thegoldsmiths.co.uk

MARKET TRADER

ENTRY LEVEL 1

Qualifications and courses

There are no formal entry requirements but you will need to have basic maths and English skills. Your personality and ability as a salesperson are the most important attributes required of a market trader. Any previous experience working in a retail or customer service role would be highly beneficial.

Most of the training is done on the job, learning from more experienced market traders. As markets have their own culture, and often their own language, it's beneficial to learn directly from an established trader.

There are some short courses you can take, usually run by the local authority, and the National Market Traders Federation (NMTF) can give advice on which ones are most beneficial to you. Small business advice services provide short courses on starting or running your own business which may also be useful.

To become a market trader you must be 17 or 18 years old and you are likely to need a driving licence, a vehicle/van and public liability insurance. The NMTF can provide appropriate insurance. You will also need to apply for a market licence and a pitch from your local authority. Competition for pitches can be strong so you may have to start your career by helping out on other stalls or working parttime as a casual trader, arriving early and queuing for an available pitch, before securing a regular stall.

What the work involves

Market traders buy goods from a wholesaler or manufacturer and then sell them from a market stall which they rent in an open-air or covered market. Alternatively, you might sell things you have made yourself at specialist craft markets.

You will be dealing with customers, encouraging them to buy items on your stall, weighing and wrapping goods, and taking cash and possibly credit and debit payments.

As well as setting up the stall in the morning, arranging your things and keeping the stall clean and tidy, you will also pack up and clear away in the evenings.

Type of person suited to this work

You will need to be friendly, outgoing and enjoy working with the public in an informal way, persuading them to buy your goods.

Market traders have to be fit and active to transport their goods, be on their feet all day and then pack up when the market closes.

When you are buying goods, you need to know what will sell and negotiate a good price. If you make your own products, you should be creative and able to produce attractive items.

You must have good numeracy and business skills for dealing with money and, if you are self-employed, doing your accounts. You should also be self-motivated and hardworking.

Working conditions

You will probably have a very early start and work from about 5am to 6pm. You will usually work Saturdays and often Sundays.

You could work on your own or with a few other people. You might work at the same market every day or move round to several different markets during the week. You will work outdoors in all weather conditions.

You might have to travel to a wholesale supplier to buy your goods and transport them to your stall so a driving licence is essential.

Future prospects

It can be hard to do well with a market stall: there is a lot of competition and you will need good products.

At craft markets, it can be difficult to sell things at a competitive price.

Most market traders are self-employed and you could expand by taking on staff to run extra stalls or opening a shop.

Advantages/disadvantages

You will be your own boss, working outside in an active, practical job with lots of contact with the public.

The hours can be long and strenuous.

You earnings are entirely dependent on market trends and being able to anticipate them which can make for an unstable income.

Money guide

When starting your career as an employee on a market stall, you are likely to earn the National Minimum Wage.

As an experienced market trader who runs a stall several days a week, your earnings can range from £15,000 up to £26,000 a year.

Market traders who sell specialist goods tend to have a higher income and the most successful traders can achieve £30,000–£50,000 a year.

You will be required to pay for your stall rent, stock and vehicle out of your income.

Related opportunities

- Customer Services Assistant/Manager p456
- Sales/Retail Assistant p468
- Shopkeeper p470

Further information

British Independent Retailers Association
www.bira.co.uk

National Market Traders Federation
www.nmtf.co.uk

MEAT HYGIENE INSPECTOR

ENTRY LEVEL 4

Qualifications and courses

To qualify as an official meat inspector, you are required to hold the Royal Society for Public Health (RSPH)'s Level 2 Certificate for Proficiency in Poultry Meat Inspection and the Level 4 Diploma for Proficiency in Meat Inspection. For entry to these qualifications you will need to have at least 5 GCSEs/National 5s (A*–C/A–C) including English and either Maths or a science and a proven history of working in the meat industry. In order to complete the RSPH courses, you need access to practical work placements.

An NVQ in Food Manufacture Meat and Poultry Processing Skills (Levels 1–3) is available and can equip you with relevant skills and knowledge for this profession.

The RSPH also provides a Level 3 Award in Food Safety Supervision for Manufacturing and a Level 4 Award in Food Safety Management for Manufacturing.

The Apprenticeship in Food and Drink is available at Intermediate, Advanced and Higher Levels and involves both on-the-job and off-the-job training to develop the required technical and practical skills.

Once employed, you will shadow experienced inspectors whilst receiving practical training in slaughterhouses and other meat plants until fully qualified.

What the work involves

Meat hygiene inspectors visit slaughterhouses and meat stores to check that meat is being processed and produced safely and hygienically, following relevant laws and regulations.

You will check that live animals and poultry are healthy and disease free, and do post-mortems on diseased carcasses. You will check that animals are cared for and transported safely, that meat plants and deliveries are run safely and hygienically, and that unwanted meat or carcasses are destroyed properly.

You will write detailed reports and make sure that any action you have recommended is carried out quickly and to the right standards.

Type of person suited to this work

You will be dealing with people in lots of different organisations and at all levels, so you will need to be able to establish good working relationships and deal with problems calmly.

You must have strong written and communication skills, good attention to detail and the ability to understand and apply laws and regulations.

It is a fairly active job so you will need to be fit and healthy, practical and good with your hands.

Working conditions

You will spend most of your time travelling to farms and processing plants so a driving licence is usually required.

You will be wearing protective clothing, using tools and equipment and handling heavy meat carcasses.

Slaughterhouses can be cold, noisy and smell strongly, and on farms you will be working outdoors in all weathers.

Meat inspectors usually work normal office hours but might need to work evenings, weekends and at short notice if there is a hygiene emergency.

Future prospects

Most meat inspectors work for the Meat Hygiene Service which is part of the government's Food Standards Agency. Others work for companies producing or selling food and meat products.

You will need experience in the industry before you can become an inspector. You can then progress to be a supervisor or manager for the Meat Hygiene Service or go into management in a large food company.

In the wake of the 2013 horse meat scandal, it is becoming increasingly important that inspectors are held accountable for their professional practice. A new non-statutory register has been put into place which ensures all newly qualified workers and those in the industry who volunteer to register with the new list, have their work regulated. This provides assurance to the public that inspectors are demonstrating the necessary professional conduct and undergoing continuing professional development (CPD).

Advantages/disadvantages

You need to be flexible with your working hours as you may be asked to respond to an emergency at any time.

You will feel satisfied that you are doing an important job in ensuring that food standards are met and the meat is safe for the public.

Money guide

You can expect to earn around £16,000 per year as a trainee inspector.

Once you have qualified and gained experience in the role, your salary is likely to be £20,000–£25,000.

Those employed as a senior meat inspector can earn up to £30,000.

Related opportunities

- Butcher p454
- Health and Safety Adviser p27
- Trading Standards Officer p472

Further information

Food Standards Agency
www.foodstandards.gov.uk

Meat Hygiene Service
www.food.gov.uk/enforcement/monitoring/meat

MERCHANDISER

ENTRY LEVEL 5

Qualifications and courses

Competition for entry to this career is fairly high so most entrants have a degree, Foundation degree or HND. Larger companies will accept degrees in any subjects, although degrees in retail management, marketing, business studies, economics, accounting or maths may improve your chances of employment. Entry requirements for a degree are usually 2 A levels/3 H grades and 5 GCSEs/National 5s (A*–C/A–C), including English and Maths.

The London College of Fashion offers a 2-year Foundation degree in Fashion Buying and Merchandising or a 15-week Postgraduate Certificate in Fashion: Buying and Merchandising. NVQs/SVQs in Supply Chain Management (Levels 2–5) and an ABC Level 4 Diploma in Buying and Merchandising for Fashion Retail are also available and may prove beneficial.

Those aged 16–24 may gain entry to a trainee post through a relevant apprenticeship, for example in purchasing and supply management. However, competition for a position would be very high and you would usually need retail experience.

Once employed, you are likely to be trained on the job starting in a more junior position whilst you work your way up. Competition for graduate training schemes and relevant vacancies is fierce however, so it is advised that you undertake work experience in order to demonstrate your interest and understanding of the industry.

Throughout your career you could work towards professional qualifications from the Chartered Institute of Purchasing and Supply (CIPS) or the Chartered Institute of Marketing (CIM).

What the work involves

You will ensure that stores are stocked with products at the right quantity and price.

You will work with retail buyers who choose different lines and then calculate the quantities of products required and the amount of money to be spent. It will be your responsibility to decide upon the selling prices of goods and any special offers.

You will put together budgets and sales targets, analyse sales trends, negotiate with suppliers and ensure that goods are displayed and presented in an attractive way that is consistent throughout the company.

Type of person suited to this work

You will need to be interested in your product and in predicting what will sell and how best to display it. Merchandisers must be creative and self-motivated, with initiative and confidence, because they make decisions involving large amounts of money and have to present their ideas to managers and staff.

You should be able to work well in a team and deal with people at all levels, for example when negotiating prices and arranging deliveries. The job involves analysing statistics and sales figures and working under pressure to meet targets and deadlines.

Working conditions

You will mainly be based in an office in a large store or in a head office, and you will probably visit other stores in your region.

You will also travel to suppliers and manufacturers, possibly staying away from home regularly. It is necessary to have a driving licence.

You will probably work normal office hours but you might have to work much longer at busy times.

Future prospects

Most opportunities are in the south-east of England and big cities such as London. There are also opportunities for work overseas given the rise in retail firms maintaining and dealing with international outlets.

You will usually start as an allocator, distributor or merchandise administrative assistant and advance to a role as an assistant merchandiser and then to merchandiser. In a large company, you could progress to a role as senior merchandiser and then possibly manager or director.

Progression depends on the talent of the individual. After gaining experience, you could become self-employed and work as a retail consultant, or you could move into a related role such as a business analyst.

Advantages/disadvantages

This job can be stressful as you will be making decisions which will directly affect the image of your company and what the public can buy.

Keeping your finger on the pulse of fashion and future trends is exciting.

Money guide

Salaries depend on the size and location of the employer, and are typically higher in high street chains.

Starting salaries for assistant merchandisers are usually £18,000–£20,000.

With experience, your earnings can increase to between £28,000 and £36,000.

A senior merchandiser is likely to receive a salary of £45,000 to £65,000.

Those employed in the most senior positions can achieve up to £85,000.

Related opportunities

- Purchasing/Procurement Manager p587
- Retail Buyer p465
- Retail Manager p466

Further information

British Independent Retailers Association
www.bira.co.uk

Chartered Institute of Marketing
www.cim.co.uk

POST OFFICE CLERK

ENTRY LEVEL 1

Qualifications and courses

There are no set requirements for this role but you will normally have to complete an aptitude test prior to entry so GCSEs/National 5s (A*–E/A–E), particularly in English and Maths, may be useful. An aptitude for languages may also be beneficial.

Most people enter directly into employment with training completed on the job. As a trainee, you will need to complete 2 weeks in a training centre followed by 2 further weeks being supervised at a counter and be instructed in areas such as customer care and the Post Office computer system.

Any experience of working in a customer service industry would be particularly advantageous, as would experience of handling money. This experience might involve working in a shop as a sales assistant, working in a restaurant as a waiter/waitress or maybe as an assistant in a launderette.

Your employer may encourage you to work towards further qualifications such as NVQs/SVQs in Customer Service (Levels 1–3) in order to develop your communication skills, ability to promote and sell products and your understanding of customer needs throughout your career.

What the work involves

Post Office clerks provide customers with a variety of postal services along with banking services, bill payment, lottery sales, passport applications and offering advice to customers on these services.

Tasks you will complete on a daily basis include sending important and expensive mail, selling stamps, weighing, measuring and mailing letters and parcels and dispatching mail abroad.

You might also be required to complete administrative work such as keeping accounts.

Type of person suited to this work

A Post Office clerk should be able to work within a team and without supervision. You should have excellent communication skills, being both polite and helpful with the ability to adjust to the needs of each client.

You should have a certain level of numeracy and be able to handle money with confidence and accuracy. You will be able to cope under pressure.

You should have an interest in the numerous services you will be offering along with a willingness to learn about the various forms that clients may require information on. You should have a keen eye for detail and the ability to sustain concentration.

Working conditions

If you work for a sub-Post Office you might be working in a newsagent, stationer or village shop, for example WH Smith has opened franchise Post Offices in many of its high street stores.

You will be working mainly at a counter but could also do some behind-the-scenes work in an office environment. You may be required to wear a uniform. The job will probably involve some lifting of heavy parcels.

You will usually work 35 hours per week, Monday to Friday and occasionally Saturday mornings. Part-time and flexible working hours may be arranged.

Future prospects

The Post Office is currently in a state of transformation, with some branches being partnered with high street retailers. There is a fear that there will be a loss of jobs, although this has not yet been confirmed.

Once employed, you could progress to the role of postmaster or training officer.

Experienced Post Office clerks may have the opportunity to work on the Post Office helpline. Within this role you would answer any queries customers or sub-postmasters/mistresses had regarding the products and services that the Post Office offers.

The skills you acquire in this role stand you in good stead to move on to careers within other industries such as banking.

Advantages/disadvantages

You may, at times, find this role stressful particularly when the Post Office is especially busy.

You might be able to work flexible hours which suit you.

There may be some heavy lifting involved.

Money guide

The rate of pay will vary depending on the location and the employer.

Post Office clerks generally start on a salary of around £13,000. After experience this may increase to £17,500 a year.

A promotion to the role of postmaster or training officer would result in a pay increase. Post Office managers can earn around £24,000.

Related opportunities

- Accounting Technician and Accounts/Finance Clerk p4
- Bank Cashier/Customer Adviser p9
- Customer Services Assistant/Manager p456

Further information

People 1st
www.people1st.co.uk/retail-apprenticeships

Royal Mail
www.royalmail.com

Royal Mail Group
www2.royalmailgroup.com

RETAIL BUYER

ENTRY LEVEL 5

Qualifications and courses

Entry is usually with a degree, though an HND or equivalent may also be considered. Relevant degree subjects including business, management, purchasing, logistics and marketing may increase your chances of employment. The minimum entry requirements for a degree course are normally 2 A levels/3 H grades or equivalent.

Although degree subjects are generally non-specific, entry into fashion retail does require a relevant qualification in fashion buying. It is possible to take a 2-year Foundation degree in Fashion Buying and Merchandising at The London College of Fashion.

Some companies offer their own graduate training schemes, but entry is highly competitive. Gaining work experience within the retail industry is invaluable in supporting your applications. If unsuccessful, you could try to work your way up from a more junior position until gaining an internal promotion to retail buyer.

Once employed, you could enhance your career progression by studying for a professional qualification offered by the Chartered Institute of Purchasing & Supply (CIPS). CIPS offers a Certificate and Advanced Certificate for people employed in purchasing at a clerical level. Entrants with an HND or degree study towards the CIPS Graduate Diploma. CIPS-accredited degrees in purchasing or business are available at some institutions, and give exemption from part or all of the Graduate Diploma.

Other relevant qualifications also include an NVQ/SVQ in Supply Chain Management (Levels 2–5) or the Level 4 Diploma in Buying and Merchandising for Fashion Retail.

What the work involves

You will probably work in the merchandising and marketing team of a large retail company, looking for products which fit the company image and will appeal to its customers. You will be responsible for reviewing current stock and sourcing new stock to ensure the products sold by your company remain competitive.

You will visit manufacturers and suppliers to negotiate prices and decide on quantities and colours. You will also check on the quality of the products.

You will help to predict and set trends. This could involve analysing sales figures and researching competitors to see what customers are buying and why.

Type of person suited to this work

You will need to be confident and decisive because you will be dealing with large budgets. You will need to be assertive with good communication skills to negotiate prices and make presentations to staff.

Numerical skills are important as you will need to be able to analyse figures and use them to set prices and targets and check stock levels.

You should be creative, well organised and good at planning ahead, and have an eye for detail.

Working conditions

You will be office based but spend a lot of time visiting suppliers and manufacturers in this country and abroad, so will probably have to spend time away from home.

You will work standard hours but will need to work late at busy times and to meet deadlines.

Future prospects

There are job opportunities all over the country but most will be in London and the south-east of England. Typical employers include high street stores, online sellers, supermarkets and niche retailers.

In a small company there may not be much chance of promotion, but in a larger company prospects are good. You would normally begin as a buyer's assistant before progressing to junior buyer, assistant buyer, senior retail buyer, trading manager and buying controller.

It is possible to work as a buyer in other areas, including manufacturing, the civil service and local government.

Alternatively, you could set up your own retail outlet.

Advantages/disadvantages

This can be an exciting job and the decisions you make will affect what the public can buy and the image of the stores.

You will have a lot of responsibility and tight deadlines which can be very stressful.

Money guide

Junior retail buyers typically earn between £18,000 and £25,000 a year.

Experienced buyers can earn between £35,000 and £60,000 a year.

Senior buyers can earn between £55,000 and £70,000, more if working for large organisations with multiple retail outlets.

Salaries will vary depending on the size and location of the company you work for and your buying specialism.

Related opportunities

- Marketing Assistant/Executive p387
- Purchasing/Procurement Manager p587
- Retail Manager p466

Further information

British Independent Retailers Association
www.bira.co.uk

Chartered Institute of Marketing
www.cim.co.uk

Chartered Institute of Purchasing & Supply
www.cips.org

RETAIL MANAGER

ENTRY LEVEL 3

Qualifications and courses

There are no set requirements in order to become a retail manager but many stores will require candidates to have at least 5 GCSEs/National 5s (A*–C/A–C), including Maths and English. Previous experience of working in a retail or customer service role, be that through paid employment or work experience, is highly beneficial and usually favoured above formal academic qualifications. Experience of stock management, pricing, merchandising and finance will ensure your application stands out.

You may however opt to pursue an Edexcel BTEC Certificate in Retail or a Foundation degree, degree or postgraduate qualification in retail management, marketing, business studies or accounting and finance in order to develop your skills and knowledge of the industry. If you are planning to work within a specialist field, such as a builders' merchant, a qualification in a subject relevant to that retailer may give you an advantage in securing employment.

Advanced Apprenticeships in Retail Management may also be available. As an apprentice you are likely to experience a combination of on-the-job training and day or block release college instruction where you will work towards gaining qualifications such as NVQs/SVQs in Retail Operations (Levels 2–3), BTEC retail qualifications (Levels 2–3) or the City & Guilds Level 4 Higher Professional Diploma in Retail Management.

Many retailers offer graduate trainee management schemes and if you have a suitable degree you could pursue this fast-track option, although competition is fierce. Here you will experience in-house training, work shadowing and supplementary courses. Your employer may even encourage you to gain further professional qualifications.

What the work involves

Unlike a shopkeeper who owns the store and deals with manufacturers, you will be running the shop on a day-to-day basis. This could be a small or a large department store, chain, independent store or a supermarket. Managers recruit, train and supervise staff, encouraging them to develop their skills and meet targets.

You will monitor sales looking at ways of improving them and oversee supplies by checking stock, placing orders and making sure you do not run out or over-order.

The store manager has overall responsibility for everything that happens in the shop and must deal with any problems or complaints.

Type of person suited to this work

As you could be dealing with customers and complaints you will need excellent negotiation skills. You will also need to motivate, train and sometimes discipline staff.

You should be energetic, able to take responsibility and make quick decisions. You will need an understanding of business and of relevant laws.

You should be able to analyse sales figures and have creative ideas for selling and promoting goods to improve profits. You will have to be organised whilst working to targets and deadlines.

Working conditions

Many stores are open long hours, at weekends and overnight, so you will probably have to work shifts, usually over 5 days.

You will be on your feet a lot as well as doing administration and paperwork.

You may be based in one store, or be visiting several that you have responsibility for.

Future prospects

Out of the 2.5 million people employed in retail, only 18% are in management or senior positions. Despite the fall in retail shops however, the number of people employed in the UK retail sector is expected to rise by 6% by 2017.

With a large retail chain your prospects can be good and you can quickly take on more responsibilities. You could move into other areas of the company, for example, marketing or buying and might be able to work abroad. With experience, regional management is also possible.

You could work for yourself, but will need money to start up your own store.

Advantages/disadvantages

Retail is an expanding, developing business and can offer you an exciting career with good promotion prospects.

You will have a lot of responsibility quite early in your career.

Working with the public can be demanding and stressful.

Money guide

The typical starting salary ranges between £21,000 and £28,000 but depends largely on the organisation in which you work.

With experience, this can rise to between £34,000 and £60,000.

A salary in excess of £70,000 is possible in large retailers and supermarkets.

You are likely to be offered discounts, commission and bonuses related to sales.

Related opportunities

- Distribution Manager p575
- Merchandiser p463
- Retail Buyer p465

Further information

British Independent Retailers Association
www.bira.co.uk

Chartered Institute of Purchasing & Supply
www.cips.org

SALES REPRESENTATIVE

ENTRY LEVEL 1

Qualifications and courses

There are no specific entry requirements but if you choose to work in pharmaceutical or engineering sales, a relevant degree is likely to be required. However, employers are often more interested in your sales and communication skills rather than any formal academic qualifications.

You may be able to become a sales representative by working your way up from an administrative position in a sales office, though additional experience of retail or customer service will be beneficial if you opt to take this route.

Alternatively, before entering employment you may find it useful to complete a qualification from a professional body such as the Institute of Sales and Marketing Management (ISMM) which offers qualifications in both Sales Skills and Sales/Marketing (Levels 1–6). The Managing and Marketing Sales Association (MAMSA) offers a Standard Diploma in Salesmanship and an Advanced Diploma in Sales Management and the Chartered Institute of Marketing (CIM) offers a Certificate in Professional Sales Practice.

Alongside these qualifications NVQs/SVQs in Sales are also available at Levels 2–4, which you may be able to study as part of an apprenticeship scheme. As an apprentice you will be trained on the job by experienced professionals in a company's products and systems, whilst at the same time, you will work towards gaining industry recognised qualifications on day or block release at a college or training centre.

You may find a full driving licence is essential for most positions.

What the work involves

You will be responsible for selling your company's products or services to existing clients and creating relationships with new clients.

You will most likely specialise in a particular market, such as pharmaceuticals, medical equipment, engineering or consumer goods.

Your responsibilities will include meeting with customers and maintaining good relationships with them, promoting new products, meeting sales targets and reporting sales trends.

You will be in charge of agreeing sales, organising the delivery and signing of contracts as well as checking payments have been made. You will also be responsible for providing after-care sales service by recording orders, advising customers about delivery schedules and receiving feedback.

Type of person suited to this work

You must have good people skills as much of your success will depend on how you interact with customers and your ability to maintain relationships with them.

Excellent communication and negotiation skills are essential, as are organisational and time management skills as much of your work will be self-motivated.

You must have the ability to gain and maintain an in-depth knowledge of the product you are selling and the markets you are selling to.

Working conditions

You will most likely be working for a large company.

As much of your work will involve meeting with customers, you may be able to choose your hours to a certain extent, as long as you are meeting sales targets.

You will usually be responsible for sales in a geographic area, and will spend a lot of time driving to meet customers in that area.

You may have to put in long hours, depending on your appointment schedule and travel time. When not in transit, you could be based in an office or at home.

Future prospects

Opportunities are available throughout the UK as the work is often based on a geographical area.

With experience and success, you could be promoted to sales team leader or a national sales manager.

You could also be headhunted from one company or region to another.

Advantages/disadvantages

Your job will vary from day to day, and you will be constantly interacting with people.

Your performance will be tangibly rewarded through commission bonuses.

You will spend a lot of time travelling which can be lonely and increase the time you spend away from home.

Money guide

You will often earn a basic salary plus commission, which will be based on meeting and exceeding targets.

You could start at around £15,000–£20,000 per year plus commission.

This can rise to between £35,000 and £40,000 with experience.

Top salespeople can make over £100,000 per year.

Related opportunities

- Customer Services Assistant/Manager p456
- Recruitment/Employment Agency Consultant p46
- Retail Buyer p465
- Sales/Retail Assistant p468

Further information

Institute of Sales & Marketing Management
www.ismm.co.uk

Managing and Marketing Sales Association
www.mamsasbp.org.uk

SALES/RETAIL ASSISTANT

ENTRY LEVEL 1

Qualifications and courses

There are no minimum entry requirements for this work as training is provided by employers. However, larger companies may ask for 2–4 GCSEs/National 5s (A*–C/A–C), particularly in English and Maths given that communication and working with money are important aspects of the job. You may be required to pass tests in basic maths and English but retail or customer service experience is often valued above qualifications.

Many shops employ temporary staff for busy periods such as at Christmas and for sales and this can be a good way of securing work experience and/or permanent work.

You could take part in a retail apprenticeship if aged 16–24. As an apprentice, you will be trained on the job by experienced professionals whilst working towards industry recognised qualifications such as Certificates and Diplomas Levels 1 and 2 in Retail Skills offered by City & Guilds, Edexcel and OCR. The Level 3 Diploma also allows you to complete specialist modules in management, visual merchandising and sales professional. Depending on your role, you may have to complete other training such as food hygiene or health and safety.

If employed in a large company, you are likely to follow a structured in-house training scheme in order to progress.

Degrees in business or retail management are also available and can speed up entry into management roles. The general entry requirements for a degree are 2 A levels/3 H grades and 5 GCSEs/National 5s (A*–C/A–C).

What the work involves

Shops range from small specialist outlets to huge department stores, so your duties will vary. You will deal with customers, offering them a polite, helpful and speedy service and sell them a range of goods.

You will help keep the shop tidy and well stocked, answer questions, deal with complaints and give suggestions and advice.

When you are working on the till you will take payments, give change, deal with refunds, wrap goods and arrange orders and deliveries.

Type of person suited to this work

You will need to be well presented, outgoing, friendly, polite, and able to deal with awkward customers and stay calm when you are busy. Sales assistants have to learn about the things they are selling, which could involve in-house training, and they must be able to help and advise customers to find what they want.

You could be working to targets and earning bonuses according to how much you sell, so will need to be persuasive but not pushy.

You should be responsible and trustworthy, and fit and active to cope with being on your feet all day. You should be able to work within a team and on your own when required.

Working conditions

In small shops you could spend most of the time at the till/checkout. In large stores you could be working on the shop floor, helping and advising customers and fetching goods from stockrooms.

You might have to carry heavy items. You will keep the shop clean and tidy and might wear a uniform.

You could work early or late shifts and at weekends and in the evenings. There are many opportunities for part-time work.

Future prospects

There are shops in all areas of the country, though large retail parks and shopping centres have meant that some smaller shops in town centres have closed.

Working in a small shop you may get to know your regulars well and be given responsibility quite quickly, but promotion prospects can be limited.

In large stores and chains you will probably get training and can quickly become a supervisor and then move into management jobs. Depending on your employer, you might have to move around from shop to shop gaining experience within different-sized shops and departments.

With significant retail experience, some sales assistants progress to occupations such as merchandising or buying.

Advantages/disadvantages

There are lots of opportunities and you will be meeting new people.

The hours can be long and the work can be stressful if you have to reach sales targets.

The work environment is constantly changing as you will have both very busy and very quiet times.

Money guide

Wages vary a lot depending on the type and size of the shop and its location.

Salaries at entry level are around £11,000 to £15,000 per year.

As a supervisor you could earn up to £20,000.

You will get discounts and may get bonuses and commission on what you sell. You may also get more money for working shifts.

Related opportunities

- Bank Cashier/Customer Adviser p9
- Customer Services Assistant/Manager p456
- Receptionist p45

Further information

British Independent Retailers Association
www.bira.co.uk

British Retail Consortium
www.brc.org.uk

SHOE REPAIRER

ENTRY LEVEL 1

Qualifications and courses

There are no minimum qualifications for this job but you should be able to take measurements, handle money and work with numbers. Some employers require entrants to take an aptitude test to assess their abilities in English, basic maths and practical skills. Experience in a retail/customer services role or any qualifications in leatherwork would also be useful.

One form of entry into a career as a shoe repairer is via an apprenticeship. As an apprentice, you will be trained on the job whilst working alongside an experienced shoe repairer. Your employer may also encourage you to work towards industry recognised qualifications, such as the BTEC Level 2 Certificate in Apparel, Footwear, Leather or Textile Production or the BTEC Level 3 Diploma in Apparel, Footwear or Leather Production. For those employed in a shoe repair shop offering several services, the ABC Level 2 Certificate in Shoe Repair, Key Cutting and Associated Multi Services would be appropriate.

The City & Guilds Level 2 Award in Retail Principles or the Diploma in Retail Skills (Levels 1–3) may also be beneficial.

What the work involves

Shoe repairers mend and repair shoes and other footwear. They also repair belts, bags and briefcases using tools and materials including nail and staple guns and stitching machines. A lot of shoe repairers use specialist machinery to cut keys and do metal engraving.

You will replace soles and heels by stitching or gluing on new ones and finishing them off neatly.

You will be serving customers, labelling the shoes they leave, issuing customers with tickets, taking payments, using a till and probably selling things such as shoe dyes and polishes.

Type of person suited to this work

It is important to be practical, good at working with your hands and able to do detailed work quickly and neatly. As the machinery and tools can be dangerous, you will need to be responsible, able to work safely and happy to get your hands dirty. You might be dyeing shoes so good colour vision is essential.

You should enjoy meeting people and be able to cope with working whilst customers wait for their repairs. You must be comfortable working on your own or in a small team, and be able to work out costs and deal with money and payments. You will need to have good communication skills and, if you are self-employed, business skills.

Working conditions

You will be on your feet a lot, using a range of tools, equipment, dyes and glues. The work can be smelly, noisy and dirty so you will wear overalls.

Shoe repairers usually work around 40 hours a week, including weekends.

You will typically be based in a small high street store. Some shoe repairers work in factories repairing goods which customers have returned.

Future prospects

There are around 8,000 shoe repairers in all areas of the country but job opportunities can be limited as most are small shops only employing a few people. Shoe repairers also work in small outlets in supermarkets or department stores.

You will learn at least one skill, and possibly more, so you would be equipped to open your own business. You would need some money to start up and business skills to plan your work and keep accounts.

In a large chain you could progress to management roles.

Advantages/disadvantages

You do not need qualifications and you will be doing a practical, hands-on job.

You could work for yourself, running your own shoe repair outlet.

The work can be repetitive and demands long periods of concentration as repair work can be fiddly.

Money guide

Those entering this profession can expect a starting salary of around £12,000.

With experience, your earnings could be between £13,000 and £17,000.

A shop manager is likely to receive £21,000 per year.

Many shoe repairers are self-employed so income depends upon the size, location and success of the shop.

Some employers offer a target-based bonus scheme.

Related opportunities

- Locksmith p212
- Sales/Retail Assistant p468
- Shopkeeper p470

Further information

MultiService Association
www.msauk.biz

SHOPKEEPER

ENTRY LEVEL 1

Qualifications and courses

There are no formal academic requirements but it is essential that you have strong numeracy, business and people skills. Experience working in a customer services, sales, administrative or managerial role would be highly beneficial.

One route into this career is to undertake the Apprenticeship in Retail, which is available at both Intermediate and Advanced Levels, and then work your way up to become a shopkeeper. As an apprentice you are likely to experience a combination of on-the-job training from experienced professionals and a series of day or block release college instruction where you will work towards gaining relevant qualifications.

NVQs/SVQs in Retail Skills (Levels 1–3), the NVQ/SVQ in Customer Service (Levels 1–4) and the City & Guilds Level 2 Certificate in Retail Principles may be available. City & Guilds also offer an Award in Retail Skills (Levels 1–2) and a Level 3 Diploma in Retail Management.

Once you are running your own shop, you will be responsible for ensuring your own development, therefore those who wish to study at a higher level should consider studying for a Foundation degree or degree in retail management.

Some local colleges offer evening courses in marketing and sales skills. Local training facilities also provide courses in all aspects of self-employment including starting up a business, marketing and VAT. You could consult an organisation such as the National Enterprise Network for advice.

What the work involves

A shopkeeper owns or manages one or more shops that specialises in selling a product or range of products, such as greengrocers, bakeries, newsagents, supermarkets, fishmongers, fashion retailers, jewellers and florists.

You will find manufacturers and suppliers in order to stock your shop with products. For stores that sell foodstuffs, this may mean sourcing local produce and purchasing it for the best price.

As well as keeping the shop tidy and well stocked, you will pay staff wages and keep books and accounts.

Type of person suited to this work

You need to be determined and motivated, with a real passion for the products you stock. You should be prepared to work long hours and to travel in order to find good suppliers and stock at the right price for your market.

You will need to be able to sell and market your goods and be confident about finding products that people want to buy.

Excellent communication skills are essential. Having good business sense and the ability to plan your finances and keep accounts is also important. You should be well organised and have some marketing, business and sales skills to succeed in this area of work.

Working conditions

Your hours and conditions will depend on what you are selling and how well you do.

Shops usually open at weekends and often in the evenings, with newsagents and convenience stores opening early and closing late.

Shops vary in size and appearance, and how pleasant the working environment is will depend on their staff and clientele.

You might wear a uniform and do some heavy lifting.

Future prospects

The trend towards large multi-product shops and online purchasing has meant that lots of smaller shops have been forced to close. This is a very competitive sector so you will need to find products that sell well in your chosen location and demographic.

One option is to operate a franchise, such as a local convenience store, paying a larger company to use their name and sell their products.

If you are successful, you could expand by opening more or larger stores.

Advantages/disadvantages

There is a lot of freedom and satisfaction in being your own boss: you do not have to answer to anyone else and you can make all your own decisions.

It can be a daunting prospect as success will entirely depend on your business acumen and selling abilities.

Money guide

Earnings vary significantly and depend upon your success and reputation, the size and location of the business, and the products you sell.

When you first enter this profession, you may have a relatively low salary of £13,000–£15,000.

With experience, you are likely to earn up to £34,000.

Related opportunities

- Merchandiser p463
- Retail Buyer p465
- Sales/Retail Assistant p468

Further information

British Franchise Association
www.thebfa.org

National Enterprise Network
www.nationalenterprisenetwork.org

STOCK CONTROL/REPLENISHMENT ASSISTANT

ENTRY LEVEL 1

Qualifications and courses

No formal qualifications are necessary, however some employers might expect applicants to have GCSEs/National 5s (A*–E/A–E) in Maths and English. Most employers will want candidates to have solid communication skills, a can-do attitude and a basic level of numeracy in order to know how much of each item needs to be restocked.

Previous experience dealing with the public within a relevant industry such as retail would prove beneficial when applying for a post in stock control/replenishment.

One route of entry into a career as a stock control/replenishment assistant is via an apprenticeship. As an apprentice, training is typically carried out on the job by experienced professionals. Training may be in a formal, traditional manner or individually through specially designed computer programs. A number of different subjects are covered, including health and safety, company policies, customer care, pricing or stock rotation. If you decide to work with specialist products such as unwrapped food, dairy produce or meat, you will also receive further training in order to equip you with the skills necessary to replenish this kind of stock.

Whilst you train, your employer may also encourage you to work towards industry recognised qualifications at a college or training centre. Edexcel BTEC Awards in Retail (Levels 1–3) may be available.

What the work involves

You will work in a supermarket or retail environment refilling the shelves. You must be aware of where each product is, both for when you need to restock it and for when a customer enquires about the whereabouts of an item.

Your duties will include checking to see which goods need replacing, adding labels to products, tidying the display areas and shelves and transporting goods from the stockroom.

You may be required to order stock, take deliveries and serve customers.

Type of person suited to this work

This role involves physical activity and so you will need to have a certain level of fitness.

You will be expected, at times, to work alone and unsupervised and so you must be trustworthy. You will also spend some time working as part of a team so you will need to be comfortable working with others.

You must have an approachable and friendly disposition as you might need to advise customers. You might use a battery-hand terminal (BHT) or hand-held terminal (HHT) in order to keep track of stock or print labels and so you should be comfortable working with computerised equipment.

Working conditions

You will be working in a retail environment; your surroundings will vary depending on which area you choose to work in.

Supermarkets can sometimes be cold.

You will be on your feet for most of the day; you will be lifting and transporting sometimes heavy stock.

Typical working hours are about 37 to 40 a week; you will probably be on a rota and so could be working at any time of the day or night. Part-time work and flexitime are available and you might be asked to wear a uniform.

Future prospects

Working in stock control/replenishment stands you in good stead to move into other retail positions such as sales assistant or checkout operator. Your skills will be transferable to other retail environments. However, if you have not completed any qualifications progression may prove difficult.

You might be able to complete extra training whilst working which would enhance your chances of promotion.

There is a possibility, with training and/or qualifications, that you could progress into a supervisory or managerial position.

Advantages/disadvantages

You may find the physical nature of this job tiring.

You might find this role repetitive.

Your job will allow you to be active.

Money guide

These figures are only approximate and will vary depending on location and employer.

Typically the starting salary for this role will range from £10,000 to £11,500 per year. This amount could increase to approximately £15,000 with experience.

If you reach the role of supervisor you can expect to earn up to £18,000 per year.

Related opportunities

- Retail Manager p466
- Sales/Retail Assistant p468

Further information

British Independent Retailers Association
www.bira.co.uk

British Retail Consortium
www.brc.org.uk

TRADING STANDARDS OFFICER

ENTRY LEVEL 4

Qualifications and courses

To become a qualified trading standards officer, you need a Diploma in Consumer Affairs and Trading Standards (DCATS) awarded by the Trading Standards Institute (TSI). You must be working for a local authority in order to achieve this.

Prior to this, you can follow a relevant degree course, such as a degree accredited by the TSI. The normal entry requirements for a degree in trading standards or consumer protection are 2 A levels/3 H grades and 5 GCSEs/National 5s (A*–C/A–C). The degree provides exemption from certain parts of the DCATS.

Graduates from an unrelated degree subject can apply to do a Graduate Diploma in Trading Standards at Manchester Metropolitan University. A 2.2 Honours degree in any subject is a minimum requirement for entry onto this course.

Non-graduates can join as an enforcement officer or consumer adviser with a local authority and follow the Accreditation of Prior and Experiential Learning route (APEL) before studying for the DCATS. The Trading Standards Institute also offers a 5-level qualification framework which people in these positions can work towards. This allows trainees to combine study with paid employment, undertaking the various levels of training in accordance with your existing qualifications, experience and needs of your employer.

Throughout your career you may opt to undertake continuing professional development (CPD) offered by the TSI and run in-line with the qualification structure. You will collect evidence of your development in a portfolio of research and work completed during seminars, workshops and work shadowing.

A driving licence is recommended.

What the work involves

Trading standards officers work for local government to protect consumers. You will check that any individual or company selling products or services is keeping to the law and providing a fair service.

You will be working with a range of people and organisations. You will travel to check premises, or to follow up on a complaint from the public.

You will be enforcing the law, leading to prosecutions but also giving help and advice to companies and consumers.

Type of person suited to this work

You will be enforcing laws and regulations so will need to be able to take in and apply a lot of complex information. You must have an eye for detail and make sure the reports you write are accurate because they could be used in court.

Excellent communication skills are vital because you will be dealing with lots of different people, advising them and enforcing the law. You will need to be forceful but not aggressive.

You will need to be efficient at using computers and be good at maths as you will be dealing with lots of statistics.

Working conditions

You will probably work for local government but could work for private industry advising on relevant legislation.

You will be office based but will spend time visiting places such as shops, factories, pubs and clubs which could be dirty or cold.

Trading standards officers work normal office hours, Monday to Friday and possibly evenings and weekends. This is largely dependent on when different business premises are open.

Future prospects

There are jobs all over the country and the work varies from cities to rural areas. You could move from local government to central government or into retail and manufacturing companies.

There is currently a shortage of qualified staff but trainee jobs are competitive.

It might be possible to progress to senior officer and managerial positions. As relevant laws and regulations are increasing, opportunities in private industry are growing.

Advantages/disadvantages

This can be an interesting and satisfying job where you are helping the public to get a fair deal.

You could be dealing with difficult or aggressive people.

Money guide

As a new enforcement officer or a trainee, you could expect between £16,000 and £22,000 per year.

You would start on between £24,000 and £34,000 when newly qualified.

You could go on to earn between £35,000 and £50,000 as a senior trading standards officer.

Depending on the size of the local authority for which you work, in excess of £70,000 is possible for the head of a service.

Related opportunities

- Environmental Health Practitioner/Officer p22
- Police Officer p529
- Quality Control Inspector p222

Further information

Trading Standards Institute
www.tscareers.org.uk

VEHICLE PARTS OPERATIVE

ENTRY LEVEL 2

Qualifications and courses

There are no formal entry requirements for this line of work as a positive attitude, enthusiasm for the job and a demonstrable interest in practical work is often valued above any formal academic qualifications, however GCSEs/National 5s (A*–E/A–E) in English, Maths, IT and a science may be a useful.

In order to gain some of the skills and understanding required in the industry, you may consider completing one of a range of vocational awards or applying for more formal industry training. Those aged 16–24 could apply for the Vehicle Parts Apprenticeship which is available at both Intermediate and Advanced Levels. As an apprentice, you will typically receive a combination of on-the-job training from experienced colleagues and a series of day or block release college instruction where you will work towards gaining industry recognised qualifications such as NVQs/SVQs in Vehicle Parts Operations at Levels 2 and 3.

Trainee parts operatives can also study for the Institute of the Motor Industry (IMI) Awards Level 2 Certificate in Vehicle Parts and Level 3 Diploma in Vehicle Parts Principles. Alternatively, those who have secured employment could work towards the NVQ/SVQ in Vehicle Parts Operations (Levels 2–3) or the NVQ/SVQ in Automotive Maintenance and Repair, Body and Paint, Vehicle Fitting and Roadside Assistance (Levels 1–3).

It may also be beneficial to take the IMI Awards Level 2 Certificate in Customer Service for the Automotive Industry and Level 3 Certificate in Customer Service for the Motor Industry.

What the work involves

This job involves ordering and looking after vehicle parts and accessories and selling them to the public, garages and mechanics. You need specialist knowledge of stock, and when ordering or supplying parts you have to know the exact make, model and year of the vehicle.

You will undertake stock control using computerised systems or possibly keeping paper records, and reorder from warehouses or manufacturers when stocks are low. You will check off parts that arrive against delivery notes before placing them in a stock room.

As well as processing deliveries and taking orders over the phone and in person, you will use tills, take payments and sometimes invoice customers.

Type of person suited to this work

You should be interested in cars, know about a wide range of parts and accessories, and which makes of vehicles they are for. You will need to be well organised and able to research where to find more unusual parts.

You will also deal with the public over the phone and in person, so you will need the ability to explain technical information clearly and simply.

You must have strong communication skills, be a good team player and able to work on your own. The job involves being on your feet a lot so you will need to be fit and active.

Working conditions

You could be working in a large shop open to the public or a warehouse used by the motor trade. You could be in a fairly small, local garage or work for a large dealership.

You might have to lift heavy parts, move trolleys and climb ladders to reach high shelves. You will work with the public and staff from the motor trade.

Normal hours are Monday to Friday from 8.30am to 6.00pm but you may be expected to work evenings and weekends with time off in lieu.

Many employers provide a uniform.

Future prospects

If you work for a smaller company your promotion prospects might be limited but in larger companies you could get additional responsibilities more quickly and move into supervisory and managerial roles.

You could become a trainee manager in other areas of the retail trade or move into car sales.

Advantages/disadvantages

This is a skilled job which enables you to undertake training and use your knowledge of, and interest in, cars and the motor trade.

There is a lot of information to remember and the work can be repetitive.

This is an ideal career for those wanting to work with vehicles who do not want to be mechanics.

Money guide

During your training you can expect to earn between £9,000 and £14,000.

Once you are qualified and have gained experience, your salary could range from £16,000 to £18,000.

Those employed as a senior vehicle parts operative can achieve in excess of £25,000 a year.

Overtime work and sales-based bonus schemes may increase your income.

Related opportunities

- Motor Vehicle Technician p218
- Stock Control/Replenishment Assistant p471
- Vehicle Sales Executive p474

Further information

Retail Motor Industry Federation
www.rmif.co.uk

VEHICLE SALES EXECUTIVE

Qualifications and courses

You do not need formal qualifications to enter and train in this career but employers will expect candidates to have GCSEs/National 5s (A*–C/A–C) in Maths and English. Good communication skills and previous experience of working in a sales or customer service environment will improve your chances of securing employment.

Most entrants to this profession are at least 21 years old, as insurance companies will not insure younger people to conduct test drives.

The Apprenticeship in Vehicle Sales, available at both Intermediate and Advanced Levels, offers an ideal route into this career. As an apprentice you will typically receive on-the-job training whilst also working towards NVQs/SVQs Level 2 and 3 in Vehicle Sales or the Institute of the Motor Industry (IMI) Awards Level 2 Certificate and Level 3 Diploma in Vehicle Sales. Upon completion of the Certificate you can apply for the grade of Licentiate Member of the IMI and those who achieve the Diploma are eligible to become an Associate Member.

Those who have studied to degree level have the option to apply for a graduate training scheme run by one of the larger car manufacturers. Entry is usually with good A levels/H grades and at least a 2.1 in your degree.

Once employed, you may opt to complete continuing professional development (CPD). This is important in not only ensuring you maintain an up-to-date knowledge of new vehicle models, features and special promotions but to encourage career progression. The Institute of Sales and Marketing Management (ISMM) offers relevant qualifications that could lead to a promotion.

What the work involves

You will be selling new or used cars, motorbikes or vans. Your role will involve greeting customers, advising them, explaining different models, features and prices, and demonstrating cars by going out on test drives.

Your job will include arranging finance for customers and doing paperwork for the sale and the finance.

Garages promote their cars through advertising, special events and direct contact with customers, which may also be part of your work. Sales staff help keep the forecourt, salesroom and cars clean and tidy.

Type of person suited to this work

You will need to be smart, confident and outgoing with a polite, friendly manner. You must have the ability to deal with all types of people and be persuasive without being pushy. You will need good negotiation and numeracy skills. You should be able to work without supervision.

You must be interested in cars, know a lot about the ones you are selling and be able to explain technical features clearly and simply.

Your wages will depend on how much you sell so you will need to be motivated, determined and able to deal with stress and pressure. You need good attention to detail to complete forms and paperwork accurately.

Working conditions

You could be working in a small, local garage selling used cars or for a large dealership. You will be based in a showroom but will also be outside on the forecourt and going on test drives. A driving licence is essential.

You will usually work a 40-hour week which includes evening and weekend work.

Future prospects

There are currently good opportunities in all parts of the country. But, this is a popular industry with strong competition for jobs, especially with the main dealers.

In larger dealerships you can progress to senior salesperson, sales manager or dealer principal. At management level you will probably earn bonuses linked to the sales of the whole team.

With extensive experience, you could establish your own dealership.

Advantages/disadvantages

It can be rewarding when you help a customer to purchase the car they want/need.

You can progress well in this industry and earn a high salary.

Working on commission and having to meet targets can be very stressful and often requires long working hours.

Money guide

Wages vary considerably.

Employees in this sector usually receive a basic salary which is supplemented by commission on sales and bonuses for achieving sales targets.

You could expect to earn between £10,000 and £13,000 as a starting salary.

With experience, you are likely to receive £14,000–£25,000 a year.

The most successful vehicle sales executives can achieve £35,000–£40,000.

In a senior role, you could earn up to £50,000.

Related opportunities

- Customer Services Assistant/Manager p456
- Motor Vehicle Technician p218
- Retail Manager p466

Further information

Retail Motor Industry Federation
www.rmif.co.uk

The Institute of the Motor Industry
www.theimi.org.uk

WINE MERCHANT

ENTRY LEVEL 3

Qualifications and courses

There are no formal academic requirements but many new entrants will have a degree or vocational qualification. Some employers require candidates to have 5 GCSEs/National 5s (A*–C/A–C) and experience in the retail industry. You must be at least 18 years old to sell wine.

It is possible to study for the Wine and Spirit Education Trust (WSET) qualifications, which range from the Level 1 Award in Wines to the Level 5 Honours Diploma.

Other relevant qualifications include the BTEC HNC/HND in Hospitality Management specialising in Licensed Retail (Levels 4–5) and a Foundation degree in Wine Business or Hospitality Management. It is also possible to take a degree in hospitality and licensed retail management. As a graduate, you may be able to secure employment within a large wine retailer as a management trainee.

It may be possible to enter the trade without qualifications and work your way up, beginning first as a sales assistant in an off-licence, department store or supermarket, and later progressing to department manager. To work as a manager, buyer or importer, a driving licence is recommended, as is the ability to speak another language.

To become an independent wine merchant, you will need a premises licence and a personal licence to sell alcohol. In England and Wales, candidates are required to take the Level 2 National Certificate for Personal Licence Holders from the British Institute of Innkeeping Awarding Body (BIIAB). In Scotland, you must take the BIIAB Scottish Certificate for Personal Licence Holders (SCPLH).

Once in a position of wine merchant, you could progress to become a Master of Wine (MW), the highest recognised qualification in the British wine industry.

What the work involves

You will use your knowledge of wine to buy from vineyards and suppliers and sell to the public or shops, pubs and restaurants. If you manage your own shop or an off-licence, you will also be responsible for supervising staff and maintaining profitability. If you sell wine over the internet or by mail order, you could be doing your own deliveries.

You could also act as a buyer for a supermarket or wine retailer. You will probably spend a lot of time abroad finding and tasting new wines, agreeing prices and checking quality.

As an independent merchant, you will probably go to wine tastings to make selections and buy wine from companies who import their product to the UK.

Type of person suited to this work

Wine merchants are keen to develop their knowledge, find new wines and growers, and keep up to date with developments and tastes.

A good sense of taste and smell is needed to judge the quality of a wine. You should be able to advise people on specific wines to complement different foods.

You must have excellent communication and customer service skills as dealing with the public and negotiating prices with growers and suppliers will be an important part of your job.

Working conditions

If you are self-employed, you will have freedom and flexibility but you will probably work long hours. If you work in retail, wine shops are often open until 10pm so you might work shifts including weekends. You will be on your feet a lot and could be lifting heavy boxes.

If you become a buyer you may travel frequently, both within the UK and abroad, or you could be based in a head office.

You could be working with the public, sometimes even travelling to people's homes to sell wine.

Future prospects

As supermarkets have become the biggest retailers of wine, it is increasingly difficult for small shops to succeed.

Large chains offer good promotion prospects. You could progress to a store manager role and then to area manager.

To start your own business you will need experience, a good knowledge of wine and money to buy stock and premises.

Advantages/disadvantages

This job will allow you to use your expertise and passion for wine.

You might get to travel and work abroad.

There are few vacancies for buyer positions and competition is high.

Money guide

Starting salaries for this profession are typically about £17,000.

With experience, you can expect to earn up to £28,000.

Wine merchants who are self-employed or employed in a senior position by the largest companies can achieve in excess of £35,000.

Related opportunities

- Bar Manager/Licensee/Publican p120
- Importer/Exporter p579
- Retail Buyer p465

Further information

British Independent Retailers Association
www.bira.co.uk

Wine & Spirit Education Trust
www.wset.co.uk

Science, Mathematics and Statistics

Do you have a very mathematical brain? Are you logical in how you approach tasks? Maybe you are fascinated by scientific advances and would like to be involved in future discoveries? People who work in this sector can spend long periods of time carrying out meticulous research. You may find yourself working for a variety of employers, from the health service to a cosmetics company or even a charity. You should be willing to work on your own but also be happy to present your findings in reports to others. People in this sector are very highly skilled individuals who have often been through a lot of training, and possess a questioning and inquisitive mind.

The jobs featured in this section are listed below.

ACOUSTICIAN

ENTRY LEVEL 6

Qualifications and courses

Most entrants to this profession are graduates from relevant disciplines such as acoustics, maths, physics, environmental science, mechanical engineering and subjects related to construction. For degree entry, you usually need at least 2 A levels/3 H grades including Maths and a numerate science/physics and 5 GCSEs/National 5s (A*–C/A–C). There are also specialist postgraduate courses available in subjects such as environmental or architectural acoustics.

The Institute of Acoustics offers a Postgraduate Diploma in Acoustics and Noise Control for graduates with a degree in a science, engineering or construction-related subject. The Certificate of Competence in Workplace Noise Risk Assessment and the Certificate of Competence in Environmental Noise Measurement are also available.

Once you secure employment, you will usually undertake a training programme or graduate scheme.

You can also become a member of the Institute of Acoustics and take part in its continuing professional development (CPD) scheme. There are several levels of membership, ranging from student members to fellows, who are over the age of 35, have at least 7 years' experience working in acoustics and have made a significant contribution to the industry.

What the work involves

An acoustician is an expert on sound waves and how they interact with the environment around them. The environment can range from office buildings to nature, and you could be looking to improve the quality of sound, reduce the noise pollution, or monitor and analyse the sound waves.

You will manage, regulate and control sound and vibrations in various environments. You could work on projects for defence, music, healthcare or telecommunications.

Your work can include many kinds of noise, from building acoustics, architectural acoustics and aerodynamic noise to electroacoustics, environmental issues and even therapeutic uses of ultrasound, as well as diagnostic techniques.

In your daily work you could be doing anything from advising on sound insulation to researching new ways to reduce the noise levels created by machinery. You might use computer modelling software to design ways to reduce or eliminate noise.

Type of person suited to this work

If you want to be an acoustician, you should have an interest not only in how sound behaves, but also in problem solving and environmental science. You need to understand sound and acoustics, and be good at physics and maths.

You must be creative and innovative in your approach to problem solving. You will require good skills in technology for testing and planning any designs that you or others create. You should be organised, with the ability to design and plan projects methodically.

Excellent communication, project management and people skills are essential.

It is important that you understand environmental legislation and standards. IT, budgeting and negotiation skills are also required for this role.

Working conditions

Working conditions and hours vary depending on the sector in which you work.

Those employed in a research role in a laboratory will usually work 9am to 5pm but unsocial hours may be required when working on some projects.

You will mainly work at a desk with a computer but you will also frequently visit laboratories, studios and sites.

The work involves standing and bending, and you may occasionally be required to lift and install heavy instruments.

You may spend time away from home and travel both within the UK and abroad.

Future prospects

Registering with the Institute of Acoustics could significantly improve your career prospects.

Possibilities for promotion include moving into supervisory or managerial roles, or specialising in a particular area. You could work freelance, or even consider setting up your own company.

Advantages/disadvantages

Depending on where you specialise, you could get the opportunity to be involved in exciting projects, whether it is the design of a concert hall or monitoring the sounds of whales.

Your work could be something varied and interesting.

You will have the opportunity to travel to some very interesting locations but this means that you will frequently be away from home.

Money guide

When you start out, you can expect to earn between £20,000 and £25,000 a year.

With increased experience in the role, your salary could rise to about £35,000.

Senior acoustics consultants can achieve in excess of £50,000 a year.

Related opportunities

- Aerospace Engineer p196
- Physicist p509
- Sound Engineer p422

Further information

EngineeringUK
www.engineeringuk.com

Institute of Acoustics
www.ioa.org.uk

Semta
www.semta.org.uk

ASTRONOMER

ENTRY LEVEL 6

Qualifications and courses

A degree in physics, maths, astrophysics, geophysics or a related science is required, usually at a minimum of a 2.1 Honours degree. Specialist degrees are available in astronomy, astrophysics and space science, and you often have the option to study for either a single Honours degree or joint Honours combined with a related subject such as maths, physics or another science. The Royal Astronomical Society (RAS) provides details of relevant degree courses, as well as pre-entry work experience opportunities. Due to the profession's competitive nature, being able to show your astronomy aspirations from a young age may be advantageous.

Entry requirements for a first degree are usually 2 A levels/3 H grades, including Physics, Maths and another science, as well as 5 GCSEs/National 5s (A*–C/A–C), including English and possibly Chemistry.

Most entrants to this career also have a master's degree or a doctorate (PhD) and jobs may be limited if you do not. To work as a research astronomer, candidates should have a first or 2.1 Master of Science (MSc) or Master of Physics (MPhys), followed by further study for a PhD in their specialist area of interest. University physics departments may include astronomical research groups and some universities offer PhD programmes specifically in astronomy.

Astronomy is becoming increasingly globalised, and so foreign language skills may prove beneficial.

You may also be encouraged to register as a chartered scientist (CSi), which would require a commitment to continuing professional development (CPD).

What the work involves

Astronomers investigate and study the universe. Astronomy covers a wide range of areas and astronomers usually focus on a specific subject, such as planets or stars.

You will mainly use maths, physics and specialist computer software to examine the images and information collected by observatories.

You will plan and coordinate projects using specialist equipment, such as telescope systems, to observe the skies and collect information. Your work can include constructing new observational instruments and software to improve your knowledge about the universe.

Type of person suited to this work

As a professional astronomer you should have a keen interest in the natural world. You will also need a good understanding of the sciences. Whether you are observing the skies or analysing detailed information, you should be able to take in a range of facts and figures.

You will use your decision-making skills to make informed conclusions from the information you work with.

A patient, logical and organised approach to your work is essential as projects can last several years. You should be confident in working with computers to complete a range of tasks. You will also need strong communication skills and an aptitude for numbers.

Working conditions

Late or antisocial working hours can often be a feature of this type of work, whether you are based in a university, observatory or research centre.

You will spend a great deal of your time working with computers.

The job may involve frequent work away from home as many of the major telescopes are in remote locations.

Close observation is often part of this job so it may be unsuitable for people with visual impairments.

Future prospects

Employment as a professional astronomer is very competitive and demands a great deal of academic study. Entry into the field still remains competitive and a lot of astronomers find work outside the profession in associated jobs. Funding and turnover are increasing slightly though.

If you followed the academic route, you could undertake original research combined with a PhD-level qualification and then progress to lecturing.

You may choose to work as part of a technical team providing support for astronomy research projects.

You could progress into related jobs such as a software or electronics engineer.

Advantages/disadvantages

This job provides the opportunity to increase public understanding of the natural world.

You might have to spend a lot of time undertaking observations which requires patience and commitment.

Carrying out research on-site can be physically tiring.

Money guide

A junior researcher can expect to earn between £20,000 and £30,000 per year.

With experience in a postdoctoral research post, your salary can increase to £36,000.

Senior researchers and lecturers can achieve £50,000 to £60,000 per year.

Related opportunities

- Geophysicist p497
- Mathematician/Mathematics Research Scientist p503
- Physicist p509

Further information

British Astronomical Association
www.britastro.org

Institute of Physics
www.iop.org

Royal Astronomical Society
www.ras.org.uk

BACTERIOLOGIST

ENTRY LEVEL 6

Qualifications and courses

To work as a bacteriologist, a first or 2.1 degree in a relevant subject such as biochemistry, physiology or microbiology is required. Entry to a degree is usually with a minimum of 2 A levels/3 H grades and 5 GCSEs/National 5s (A*–C/A–C). Entry may also be possible by completing a Foundation degree course in a science which normally requires 1 or 2 A levels/H grades.

A Master of Science (MSc) or doctorate (PhD) is an advantage as a postgraduate qualification is required for entry to an academic research post. Applicants without a PhD may start as a research assistant and work towards a PhD.

Alternatively you could enter as a laboratory assistant; for this you will need a minimum of 4 GCSEs/National 5s, including 2 sciences, Maths and English.

Bacteriologists are given regular on-the-job training to learn new laboratory techniques and keep up to date with IT developments and health and safety regulations. You might also receive training for personal development, management or supervisory responsibilities.

Registration with professional bodies, such as the Association for Clinical Biochemistry (ACB) will allow you to continue your professional development (CPD).

What the work involves

Bacteriologists study and analyse single-celled micro-organisms, particularly ones that cause disease. Their research provides important information on protecting against illnesses and caring for people with specific kinds of diseases.

In industry bacteriologists work in companies manufacturing pharmaceuticals, agrochemicals, food and drink, home and personal care products and consumer goods.

Research bacteriologists study a particular genus or species. This work may be new and untried, and often techniques are selected by the researcher. Researchers may work in hospitals, universities and private companies.

In all areas the work involves the interpretation and analysis of findings, and will include designing and conducting experiments, making observations and drawing conclusions from your findings. You must enjoy writing reports and scientific papers and presenting them to other scientists.

Type of person suited to this work

You need to be scientifically capable. You need to be meticulous, practical and logical in your approach to work and should be patient as you may have to repeat tests.

You should have an enquiring mind and good problem-solving skills and be able to work to tight deadlines when required.

You must also be able to work well alone and as part of a team, have good communication skills and be highly safety conscious.

Working conditions

You are likely to work in a multidisciplinary team with other scientists, including geneticists, microbiologists and chemical engineers.

You will usually work from 9am to 5pm, Monday to Friday. Evening and weekend work may be required for fieldwork or some experiments.

You will work in laboratories or factories or out on location. You must wear protective clothing in laboratories. Microbes are classified as bio-hazardous substances so you must follow strict health and safety regulations. The job might require you to travel to meetings and conferences.

Future prospects

Promotion prospects vary depending on the type of organisation. Some bacteriologists may need to change employer to gain promotion.

Career prospects may be improved with additional qualifications or experience. This could allow you to work in associated fields such as microbiology, virology, mycology and parasitology.

There may be opportunities to work abroad, especially for clinical bacteriologists involved in healthcare projects.

Advantages/disadvantages

There are opportunities to visit different types of outside locations on research trips.

Employers such as the National Health Service can offer the chance to gain experience in different departments and provide well-structured career paths.

You will be handling potentially dangerous substances and experiments can take a long time to complete and some aspects might become tedious.

Money guide

If you begin your career as a laboratory assistant you can expect to earn between £13,000 and £19,000 a year.

Newly qualified bacteriologists can expect between £20,000 and £38,000 a year.

Top salaries for bacteriologists are about £65,000 a year.

Related opportunities

- Biochemist p481
- Clinical Scientist p487
- Microbiologist p506

Further information

Health and Care Professions Council
www.hpc-uk.org

Institute of Biomedical Science
www.ibms.org

NHS Careers
www.nhscareers.nhs.uk

BIOCHEMIST

ENTRY LEVEL 6

Qualifications and courses

A degree in biochemistry or a related subject is required for entry to this profession. Many posts also require a postgraduate qualification.

The minimum entry requirements for a biochemistry degree are 2 A levels/3 H grades, including Chemistry and/or Biology, and 5 GCSEs/National 5s (A*–C/A–C), including science subjects, English and Maths. Some universities offer a Foundation or 'bridging year' as a pre-degree course for applicants who do not have the required scientific qualifications.

Biochemists with a degree and relevant work experience are eligible to join a professional body, such as the Biochemical Society or the Society of Biology.

Biochemists continue their training while working. Those with a first degree are encouraged to study part time for a Master of Science (MSc) or doctorate (PhD) as competition for work is fierce. Accredited MSc degrees in Clinical Biochemistry are currently offered by 4 universities: Birmingham, London, Surrey and Manchester.

If you want to work with the National Health Service (NHS) as a clinical biochemist you will need a 1st or 2.1 degree and to follow the Scientist Training Programme (STP). The programme is very competitive with many more applicants than there are places. This is a 3-year work-based learning programme that leads to a master's degree in your specialist subject. Upon successful completion, after 4 years of work experience and by attaining the certificate of competence offered by the Association of Clinical Scientists (ACS), you will be able to register with the Health and Care Professions Council (HCPC) and be called a clinical biochemist. The HCPC will require you to undertake continuing professional development (CPD).

What the work involves

You will research a range of living organisms and processes, using specialist equipment. Your work may involve collating detailed information and producing reports.

Biochemists investigate the chemistry of living organisms. They use their investigations to plan experiments and solve problems.

Biochemists can specialise in particular fields, such as endocrinology, toxicology, paediatrics, immunology, and molecular biology, and apply their knowledge and skills in many areas, including food and nutrition, agriculture, medicine, plant research and brewing.

Type of person suited to this work

You will need to be curious about biological organisms and interested in improving systems and products. You will constantly use problem-solving skills in this job. Your excellent observational skills will also be very useful. You should enjoy working as part of a team.

You will be confident in using a range of scientific equipment with a patient and methodical approach for sometimes repetitive but important activities. Your strong communication skills will help you explain and record your work. Confidence in working with numbers and detailed information is also essential.

Working conditions

You would normally work in a laboratory as part of a team. You may also do some of your work in an office environment. In some sectors, biochemists work on a shift system.

The job involves the regular use of specialist equipment which requires good manual handling skills. Protective equipment will also have to be worn.

As you become more senior, it is likely you will be involved with managing staff or projects.

Future prospects

Many of the products you use on a daily basis have been developed by biochemists. Biochemists have an important role in organisations ranging from research institutes to multinational companies.

If you go into research and development, you would start by working as part of a team. With further training and experience you could gain membership of The Royal College of Pathologists (MRCPath) or a PhD, which allows biochemists to advance to higher post-registration positions and consultancy work.

You may choose to undertake academic research and go into lecturing or teaching.

Advantages/disadvantages

You may have to work very long hours in this job.

This type of work is often project based which provides job variety.

Biochemistry offers a wide range of areas in which to specialise.

Money guide

The starting salary on the NHS's Science Training Programme is around £25,000, while post-registration trainees could earn £30,764 (NHS wage band 7), which increases with experience.

Consultant clinical scientists can earn in excess of £54,998.

Salaries tend to be higher in industry compared with the NHS and universities, especially at junior levels.

Related opportunities

- Biomedical Scientist/Medical Laboratory Assistant p482
- Biotechnologist p483
- Chemist p485

Further information

Biochemical Society
www.biochemistry.org

Institute of Biomedical Science
www.ibms.org

The Association for Clinical Biochemistry and Laboratory Medicine
www.acb.org.uk

BIOMEDICAL SCIENTIST/MEDICAL LABORATORY ASSISTANT

ENTRY LEVEL 3

Qualifications and courses

Biomedical scientist
To become a biomedical scientist you must register with the Health and Care Professions Council (HCPC). Registration can be achieved by completing a HCPC-approved biomedical sciences degree accredited by the Institute of Biomedical Science (IBMS), one year's training in a laboratory (which could be undertaken as part of a sandwich degree), and by completing the Registration Training Portfolio. You will then achieve the IBMS Certificate of Competence and be eligible to register with the HCPC.

Alternatively, those with A levels/H grades in Life Sciences can start work as a trainee biomedical scientist if their employer is willing to allow them to study part time for a relevant degree. Entry requirements for a biomedical science degree are 2 A levels/3 H grades, including Biology and Chemistry and 5 GCSEs/National 5s (A*–C/A–C), including Maths and English. Alternative qualifications such as BTECs may also be accepted. Biomedical scientist graduates can then apply for the NHS Scientist Training Programme (STP) in life sciences.

Pre-entry experience and postgraduate qualifications are not essential but may prove advantageous.

Medical laboratory assistant
There are no formal entry requirements but 4 or more GCSEs/National 5s (A*–C/A–C) in English, Maths and a science, or an equivalent qualification such as a BTEC First in Applied Science (Level 2) may be valuable. Laboratory assistants can work towards qualifications such as NVQs/SVQs.

What the work involves

A biomedical scientist carries out laboratory tests on bodily fluid and tissue in order to help doctors assess what is wrong with their patients. They use a range of specialist equipment to carry out tests.

Medical laboratory assistants support the work of biomedical scientists. As a medical laboratory assistant, you will carry out a variety of tasks including sorting and labelling tissue samples, sterilising and disinfecting equipment, making up chemical solutions, separating blood serum and plasma from samples, and recording and analysing information.

Type of person suited to this work

Biomedical scientist
You must be interested in science and medicine and have strong scientific skills. You should be practical and responsible, with good IT skills. You need the ability to supervise junior members of staff and to follow complex instructions.

Medical laboratory assistant
You need a careful, methodical approach to your work. You should be able to concentrate and pay attention to detail. You will work accurately under pressure to meet deadlines. Solid communication skills are essential.

Working conditions

You will mainly work in pathology laboratories within hospitals but sometimes you will have direct contact with patients.

You will work a 37-hour week which could involve shift, evening, weekend and on-call work.

You will be required to wear protective clothing.

Future prospects

Biomedical scientist
You will probably specialise in a specific area. You might need higher qualifications in order to progress. Within the NHS, you could move up to a managerial role.

Jobs in the NHS are still fiercely competitive.

Work abroad is a possibility, especially within developing countries.

Medical laboratory assistant
Most employment is available in NHS hospitals. You may specialise or move to a related career such as a pharmacy technician. To train as a clinical or biomedical scientist you will need to study for a relevant degree which may be available for part-time study.

Advantages/disadvantages

Providing an essential service within a hospital, by helping to diagnose patients' illnesses, is incredibly rewarding.

You may have to deal with angry doctors/patients who want results sooner than you can deliver them.

Money guide

Rates of pay in this sector are established by the NHS.

A medical laboratory assistant will have a salary of £16,271 to £19,268.

A biomedical scientist will have a starting salary of £21,478 to £27,901.

As a team leader or specialist, you could earn from £25,783 to £34,530.

Those who reach an advanced level or are employed as a team manager can achieve from £30,764 to £40,558.

Related opportunities

- Chemist p485
- Clinical Scientist p487
- Laboratory Technician p500

Further information

Institute of Biomedical Science
www.ibms.org

NHS Careers
www.nhscareers.nhs.uk

BIOTECHNOLOGIST ENTRY LEVEL 6

Qualifications and courses

The entry requirements for this profession are a degree in biotechnology, bioscience or a related subject, such as microbiology, biochemistry or chemical engineering. Requirements for a degree are usually 2 A levels/3 H grades, including Chemistry or Biology, and 5 GCSEs/ National 5s (A*–C/A–C), including English, Maths and a science.

For research posts you will be expected to have a postgraduate qualification, experience working in the sector, and be studying for a doctorate (PhD). Entry to a postgraduate course is with a minimum of a 2.1 in a relevant bachelor's degree and courses typically last 1–3 years.

Although rare, it is possible to become a biotechnologist with an HND or Foundation degree in chemical or manufacturing engineering by working your way up from trainee technician level.

The majority of employers look for relevant work experience, such as a vacation placement or a sandwich degree course with a year in industry.

Once you have secured employment, you will learn on the job, possibly through a structured in-house training programme. NVQs/SVQs in Laboratory and Associated Technical Activities (Levels 2–4) are also available.

What the work involves

You will use biological organisms and processes to develop and adapt products. Biotechnologists work in a range of areas such as genetic engineering, electronics, food science and microbiology. Biotechnology provides the scientific basis for agriculture, pharmaceuticals, waste management, food and medical care.

You could work in research and development or in aspects of production such as quality control.

Your work might involve enhancing existing products or developing new types of organisms.

You could work within government research institutions or play a central role in developing and enhancing products in commercial biotechnology companies.

Type of person suited to this work

You will need a keen interest in science for working in any area of biotechnology. Strong observational skills and an organised approach are also essential.

You should be confident working with scientific equipment and computers to manage information and undertake research. Most biotechnologists are employed as part of a group so the ability to work within a team is helpful.

If you work as a technician, you should be able to cope with undertaking routine but required testing activities. Biochemists in industry also need to understand the commercial applications of their work.

Working conditions

Biotechnologists usually work in a laboratory or research centre in sterile conditions to undertake experimental and testing work.

You will work normal office hours but you may occasionally be on-call during evenings and weekends. Protective clothing is needed when working with micro-organisms and dangerous chemicals.

Your work is likely to involve using microscopes and electronic testing equipment, and spending time on a computer doing analysis work.

Future prospects

The job market is improving, but slowly and the jobs remain competitive if steady. Jobs are available abroad, particularly in the USA, but these are also very competitive.

You could progress to a supervisory role.

There is also the option to develop an academic career – this may provide additional opportunities to undertake commercial research. You can use this research to move into sales, marketing or production roles.

Advantages/disadvantages

Laboratory work, particularly at technician level, can be time consuming and requires a lot of patience.

You will be researching and learning new things every day.

Job prospects are good as there is a range of sectors in which you can work.

Money guide

Earnings vary according to the type of employer and tend to be highest in industry.

Starting salaries for graduates are usually between £19,000 and £24,000 per year.

With experience, you can expect to earn from £30,000 to £45,000.

Those employed in a senior position with high levels of responsibility can achieve up to £60,000 a year.

Related opportunities

- Biochemist p481
- Biomedical Scientist/Medical Laboratory Assistant p482
- Chemist p485

Further information

BioIndustry Association
www.bioindustry.org

Biotechnology and Biological Sciences Research Council
www.bbsrc.ac.uk

Society of Biology
www.societyofbiology.org

BOTANIST

ENTRY LEVEL 6

Qualifications and courses

Botanists may enter this career as laboratory technicians or technical assistants. Most entrants have a degree in a relevant subject such as botany, plant biology, plant science, environmental science and ecology. Entry into a degree programme requires 2 A levels/3 H grades in Biology and another science, often chemistry, and 5 GCSEs/National 5s (A*–C/A–C).

It may also be a good idea to complete some voluntary work in related organisations and to acquire relevant skills such as plant identification.

The Field Studies Council, the Botanical Society of the British Isles (BSBI) and local wildlife trusts offer a wide range of training programmes, such as the Field Identification Skills Certificate, which grades your skill level on a scale from 1 to 5.

To work as a teacher or researcher, a postgraduate course is required. Candidates may enter with a Master of Science (MSc), doctorate (PhD) or enter as a trainee researcher in a university department who is working towards a PhD. In order to apply for a postgraduate qualification you will need to successfully complete an undergraduate degree, usually with 2.1 Honours or higher.

What the work involves

Botanists study all kinds of plant life and plant biology. They are increasingly employed within industry and research in areas such as plant-cell technology and genetic engineering.

Your work could involve managing rare plant collections, environmental conservation, horticulture, agriculture and other areas. You will use specialist equipment such as electron microscopes and satellite imaging technology.

You might look into how human activity affects plants in farming, or you may try and discover useful chemicals produced by plants.

Type of person suited to this work

As a botanist you should have a real interest in science and plants. This interest should stretch to a particular field of work such as conservation.

This profession will involve detailed analysis so you will need strong observational skills. You must also have a methodical approach to your work activities.

You should be comfortable working with a range of scientific equipment and be happy undertaking practical research work, sometimes outdoors and in unpleasant weather conditions. You may also need to be a good leader as you might be in charge of junior staff, students and volunteers.

Working conditions

You could be working in one or more of the following environments: laboratories, classrooms, lecture theatres, offices and outdoors. Hours will vary, but within research and higher education you will work about 37 hours a week.

Field work takes place in all weather conditions and you may find it physically demanding.

Whilst working in a laboratory you will be using specialist equipment and might be required to wear protective clothing. A driving licence may be required if you need to travel between locations.

Future prospects

Within conservation and fieldwork, progression would entail taking on more responsibility and possibly managing others.

Within the higher education sector there is a set career path leading from researcher to head of department or professor.

Within industry there is the possibility of promotion. You also have the option of working as a freelance consultant and therefore being self-employed. There is the potential to work overseas in most areas of botany.

Advantages/disadvantages

There are opportunities to visit different types of outside locations on research trips.

Research jobs are often offered on a short-term basis, which can create job insecurity.

You will have the opportunity to combine your love of plants with your passion for science.

Money guide

These figures will vary depending on location, sector and employer. Salaries within private industry will vary considerably.

Starting salaries are around £16,000 to £22,000 a year.

Botanists in research jobs can expect to earn up to £30,000 a year.

In a senior role, such as a senior lecturer at a university, you could earn around £55,000 per year.

Related opportunities

- Ecologist p490
- Entomologist p491
- Microbiologist p506

Further information

Botanical Society of Britain and Ireland
www.bsbi.org.uk

Society of Biology
www.societyofbiology.org

The Conservation Volunteers (TCV)
www.tcv.org.uk

CHEMIST

ENTRY LEVEL 5

Qualifications and courses

You will usually require a degree in chemistry, applied or analytical chemistry, biochemistry or a related scientific subject to enter this profession. For entry to one of these degrees you will need 2 A levels/3 H grades in Chemistry and one other science or Maths and 5 GCSEs/National 5s (A*–C/A–C) including Maths, 2 sciences and English.

Many institutions offer 1-year Foundation courses for candidates who do not have the necessary academic science background.

The majority of chemists also have a postgraduate qualification in chemistry or in a specialist area such as materials chemistry, medicinal chemistry or pharmaceutical chemistry. You can also work towards professional membership of the Royal Society of Chemistry.

Alternatively, it is possible to enter as a technician with a minimum of 4 GCSEs/National 5s (A*–C/A–C), including English, Maths and 2 sciences. A levels/H grades, BTEC Level 3 qualifications, or a HNC/HND in a science subject may also be required. Technicians may have the opportunity to study for NVQs/SVQs in Laboratory Skills (Levels 2–4), or the NVQ/SVQ Level 5 in Analytical Chemistry. With further training and qualifications they may be able to progress to the job of a chemist.

What the work involves

Chemists work in many different sectors, undertaking the analysis and use of complex scientific processes and substances on a detailed molecular level.

As well as engaging in research and development, chemists also check that products are developed to a safe standard.

Professional chemists are employed in a wide range of sectors, including the oil industry, pharmaceuticals, medical research and academia.

Type of person suited to this work

Chemists need strong observational, numerical and technical skills. You must have an enquiring mind with a logical approach and desire to solve complex scientific problems.

You will have good dexterity for undertaking research and experiments with a range of scientific equipment. The ability to interpret and analyse data is vital and you must have good written and verbal communication skills to convey complex problems.

Often you will be working as part of a team so you must be comfortable working with other people as well as having the patience and confidence to take the lead within certain projects.

Working conditions

The average chemist works about 37 hours a week. Your job could involve working in a laboratory as part of a research centre, but you may also undertake research outdoors on-site.

You may have to wear protective clothing such as lab coat, protective glasses and gloves.

If you are employed by a private company you may be required to work shifts organised by a rota. At senior levels, you may be involved with business development and managerial activities.

Future prospects

Professional chemists play an important role in developing and updating products and systems and job opportunities are good.

Public research institutes, academic institutions and private companies employ chemists. There are also opportunities in government research, health and education. Some chemists move into areas such as law, IT, science journalism and marketing.

With experience you could enter a supervisory role. There are also opportunities to teach in schools and universities. Postgraduate qualifications may improve your chances for progression.

Advantages/disadvantages

Low numbers of entrants taking chemistry degrees means that there are many opportunities.

Laboratory tasks can sometimes be repetitive and time-consuming.

Many large companies employ chemists, so promotion can be possible without moving employers.

Money guide

These figures are only approximate and will vary depending on sector, employer and location.

Salary levels should increase with the level of academic qualification. At graduate entry you can earn between £16,000 and £22,000 per year.

With experience, and when established, you can expect £35,000 a year.

With added responsibility, such as if you are in charge of a team or project, you could expect to earn between £35,000 and £60,000 a year.

Related opportunities

- Biochemist p481
- Biotechnologist p483
- Cosmetic Scientist p489

Further information

Association of the British Pharmaceutical Industry
www.abpi.org.uk

Royal Society of Chemistry
www.rsc.org

CLINICAL GENETICIST

ENTRY LEVEL 6

Qualifications and courses

To become a clinical geneticist with the National Health Service (NHS) you will need to complete their 3-year Scientist Training Programme (STP). Entry requires a degree (first or 2.1) in either biomedical sciences, biology, microbiology, genetics or biochemistry, and 2 A levels/3 H grades in the sciences, Chemistry and/or Biology may be specified, and 5 GCSEs/National 5s (A*–C/A–C). You can also gain entry with an accredited master's degree.

You must then work towards state registration as a clinical geneticist with the Health & Care Professions Council (HCPC). This requires you to have completed a further 4 years of pre-registration work experience, during which you should have completed part 1 of the membership of the Royal College of Pathologists (MRCPath) and been awarded the certificate of competence by the Association of Clinical Scientists (ACS).

Career advancement depends on further experience and/or qualifications, including specialised postgraduate research. Completion of part 2 of the MRCPath, resulting in full membership, allows post-registrants to apply for consultancy and head of laboratory posts.

It is also possible to enter the profession at technician or trainee level with GCSEs/National 5s and A levels/H grades in subjects such as biology, other sciences, maths and English. To advance you must gain the relevant qualifications whilst working.

It is essential for all healthcare professionals to undertake continuing professional development (CPD) to maintain their registration with the HCPC.

What the work involves

Clinical geneticists are responsible for identifying and diagnosing genetic disorders by testing samples from patients, recording their findings and drawing a conclusion from them. They also supervise the work of others.

Geneticists analyse and modify human, animal or plant DNA. If working as a human geneticist, you could be involved with medical genetics or human genetic research.

You could undertake genetic engineering in agricultural research.

There are 2 other main jobs in this field that may be of interest: cytogeneticists (who study chromosomes which contain genes) and molecular geneticists (who study DNA exclusively).

Type of person suited to this work

You should be an excellent communicator, both verbally and in writing. You will need to be able to work accurately and meticulously, whilst keeping to deadlines.

You must have a good understanding of computers. You will need to be discreet as you will be dealing with confidential medical information.

You should be able to work effectively as part of a team and be able to take on the role of a supervisor when training junior staff. You must have strong problem-solving skills.

Working conditions

You will be based in a sterile laboratory. You will have to wear protective clothing such as overalls, laboratory glasses and gloves.

You will also have to ensure that you reach all health and safety standards.

As a clinical geneticist within the NHS you will be working about 37.5 hours per week, from Monday to Friday. There may also be a rota in place which covers bank holidays and weekends.

Future prospects

Genetics is a developing area of science that offers the chance to work directly with patients as a medical geneticist within the NHS or directly within research in research centres and universities.

You could also go on to work in research and development in industry.

In order to be promoted you will need to gather experience, responsibility and training. Once you have worked for 2 or 3 years as a registered geneticist you can begin to apply for more senior positions.

Advantages/disadvantages

You may have to repeat procedures, which could become tedious.

This job involves a great deal of responsibility.

You will be working with a wide range of samples and so every day will be different.

Money guide

These figures will vary depending on sector, location and employer.

The average starting salary for a graduate clinical scientist trainee is about £24,000 per year.

Once registered, you can expect to earn £29,000–£38,352.

If you reach the level of principal clinical scientist you could earn up to £44,527.

As a consultant you can earn between £65,270 and £93,098.

You may also receive an additional allowance if you work in London.

Related opportunities

- Clinical Scientist p487
- Forensic Scientist p494
- Laboratory Technician p500

Further information

British Society for Genetic Medicine
www.bsgm.org.uk

Genetics Society
www.genetics.org.uk

NHS Careers
www.nhscareers.nhs.uk

CLINICAL SCIENTIST

ENTRY LEVEL 6

Qualifications and courses

Entrants to this profession require a first or 2.1 Honours degree in a relevant subject, such as biochemistry, biology, chemistry, engineering, genetics, microbiology, physics or physiology. Entry to a degree typically requires a minimum of 2 A levels/3 H grades, including a science subject, as well as 5 GCSEs/National 5s (A*–C/A–C) including English and Maths. Equivalent qualifications may also be relevant, but please check with your preferred university. Some universities also offer a 1-year Foundation course for those without an academic background in science.

After your degree you will need to find a trainee clinical scientist job. A relevant Master of Science (MSc) or doctorate (PhD) may help your application.

The National Health Service (NHS) offers the Scientist Training Programme (STP) in many of the different disciplines a clinical scientist can specialise in, such as life sciences (embryology, pathology, genetics and haematology) physiological sciences (audiology, cardiac physiology), and clinical engineering. These programmes can last up to 4 years and lead to a specialist diploma or MSc. Clinical scientists start as Grade A trainees and, upon completion, candidates are eligible for state registration with the Health and Care Professions Council (HCPC), for which you also need a Certificate of Attainment from the Association of Clinical Scientists (ACS). You could then work towards passing parts 1 and 2 of the Membership of the Royal College of Pathologists (MRCPath) exams. This enables you to apply for Grade C consultancy jobs.

Once qualified, clinical scientists are required to undertake continuing professional development (CPD).

What the work involves

Clinical scientists work mainly for the NHS but are also employed in the Health Protection Agency, research centres and industry.

Your work may involve supporting doctors, suggesting suitable tests for diagnosing patients, reporting on results and recommending treatments. You may also research and test new methods of treatment and make recommendations on the best equipment or test materials.

You might specialise in a particular area such as clinical embryology (the study of infertility), or clinical microbiology (identifying infections in patients caused by bacteria, fungus or parasites).

Type of person suited to this work

You should have a keen interest in medicine and science, alongside a desire to help others. You should have excellent observational skills.

You need technical skills and the ability to use scientific equipment to get results. You will need an organised approach for undertaking practical work and the ability to work to set deadlines. You should be able to interact well as part of a team.

As a scientist you will get results by combining a logical approach with a creative flair. You should have strong computer skills.

Working conditions

You might work around 37.5 hours a week, usually from Monday to Friday, although these hours could vary depending on your specialty. You may need to work some evenings and weekends if you are on-call.

You will usually work in a laboratory or within a specialist department. You may have some contact with patients.

You will be working in a sterile environment, which may demand that you wear protective clothing. You might need to use ionising radiation.

Future prospects

As progression is performance based, you will need to accept more responsibility and/or take part in research and development projects to reach a more senior level.

As a consultant, you would be responsible for a large department and have the chance to make important contributions to your area of expertise.

There is also the option of moving between departments to gain further training. You could move into lecturing or training. There is the possibility of working abroad.

Advantages/disadvantages

You will be helping to diagnose patients and suggest treatments which will improve their quality of life.

Mistakes could lead to an incorrect diagnosis and so you will be working under a lot of pressure.

Money guide

Salaries vary depending on employer and location. If you work in London you will be given an additional allowance.

As a trainee clinical scientist within the NHS you could earn about £21,000 per year.

Once registered, you could earn between £30,000 and £40,000.

This could increase to £97,478 if you become an advanced practitioner, clinical scientist or consultant clinical scientist.

Related opportunities

- Hospital Doctor p292
- Medical Physicist p296
- Radiographer p316

Further information

Association of Clinical Scientists
www.assclinsci.org

NHS Clinical Scientists Recruitment
www.nhsclinicalscientists.info

The Association for Clinical Biochemistry and Laboratory Medicine
www.acb.org.uk

CONSUMER SCIENTIST

ENTRY LEVEL 5

Qualifications and courses

For entry, you will be expected to have an HNC/HND or degree in a relevant subject such as consumer studies/science, food studies/science, food and nutrition, food and marketing or food technology. Degrees are also available in specialist areas of consumer science, such as consumer protection or consumer psychology.

To gain acceptance on to an HNC/HND course you will usually require at least 4 GCSEs/National 5s (A*–C/A–C) and 1 A level/H grade. Most degree courses expect candidates to have at least 2 A levels/3 H grades and 5 GCSEs/National 5s (A*–C/A–C). These requirements may vary so be sure to check with the institution.

Some employers may also prefer you to have a postgraduate qualification in a relevant subject such as health promotion or consumer behaviour. For entry to a postgraduate course you will need a good undergraduate degree, usually at 2.1 class or higher.

Experience in the food manufacturing industry or within market research can also offer an alternative way of entering the field or act as an advantage when applying for jobs.

It is also possible to enter the profession with NVQs/SVQs in Food Preparation and Cooking, Proficiency in Food Industry Skills, or Food and Drink Manufacturing Operations, or with a BTEC/SQA Level 3 qualification in a hospitality or catering subject. You may be able to gain these whilst working, as well as take relevant courses in many of the occupational areas in which a consumer scientist may work, such as health promotion, social policy, business, marketing and journalism.

What the work involves

Consumer scientists or home economists provide support, information and specialist services related to healthy living and eating.

You will be the point of communication between consumers and manufacturers. You will study what the consumer needs and provide advice on how to develop it. Your work could involve developing new food products, educating people about healthy eating or assessing new cookery equipment.

Jobs are available within quality assurance, marketing, media and journalism, food product development, education, government, product and service development and catering.

Type of person suited to this work

You will need to have strong communication skills, which allow you to talk to people of all ages and backgrounds.

You should also have an interest in food and how people live their lives within the domestic environment.

You should have good computer skills and the ability to impart information in a clear, concise manner, both orally and in writing. You must be creative and have proficient design skills.

Working conditions

This role may involve travelling to meetings, conferences and other environments in the UK and abroad.

Your working environment will vary according to which industry you work within. You could be in an office, kitchen, classroom, laboratory or a selection of these.

You will be working about 35 to 40 hours per week, usually from Monday to Friday.

Future prospects

Consumer scientists can move between industries as their services are always required. Specific industries include retail chains, marketing bodies, local authorities, magazines, television and newspapers, health authorities, producers of food, advisory and consumer organisations, hotels and restaurants, consumer pressure groups, schools, colleges and universities and many others.

In most areas there is the opportunity to progress to managerial level.

Promotion may involve moving to a new location within the country.

Advantages/disadvantages

You may find it frustrating when asked to complete tests in the later stages of the factory process.

This profession will give you the opportunity to move into a number of industries, such as retail or food manufacturing, which will aid your career progression possibilities.

You may have to complete reports in your free time.

Money guide

Salary levels vary according to employer, sector and location.

Starting salaries range from £17,000 to £22,500 per year.

With experience, you could earn up to £30,000 a year.

Managers at a senior level earn between £40,000 and £50,000 per year.

Consumer scientists working on a consultancy basis can earn £150–£500 a day.

Related opportunities

- Dietitian p283
- Environmental Health Practitioner/Officer p22
- Market Research Executive p386

Further information

Improve Ltd
www.improveltd.co.uk

Institute of Food Research
www.ifr.ac.uk

Institute of Food Science & Technology
www.ifst.org

COSMETIC SCIENTIST

ENTRY LEVEL 5

Qualifications and courses

Career entry can be achieved at more than one level, including a degree in a relevant subject, such as cosmetic science, chemistry, chemical engineering, biology, microbiology, physics, medicine and pharmacy, Foundation degree or HNC/HND. Most degree courses require applicants to have achieved a minimum of 2 A levels/3 H grades, which should include at least 1 science (particularly Chemistry) and 5 GCSEs/National 5s (A*–C/A–C), including English and Maths.

Many colleges offer students who have not studied the requisite science subjects at A level/H grade a 1-year introductory (Access) course. For Foundation degrees and HNC/HND qualifications, applicants are normally expected to have achieved at least 1 A level/H grade.

Postgraduate degrees are also available in cosmetic science and related subjects.

The Society of Cosmetic Science (SCS) offers the Diploma in Cosmetic Science for those working in the industry. This can be attained by distance learning after approximately 300 hours of study. The Principles and Practice of Cosmetic Science course is a shorter course, which is particularly useful for those who have been in the industry for a while and are looking to move into supervisory or managerial roles.

What the work involves

The cosmetics industry requires scientists to help develop, test and produce new and existing cosmetics and beauty products, such as make-up, perfumes and haircare products.

There are various elements to this profession, including researching new ingredients, developing cosmetic products, developing the processes used to create the product, quality control, safety testing, packaging development and regulatory affairs which involves ensuring the product meets all legal requirements.

Type of person suited to this work

You will have an interest in the science of cosmetics, along with knowledge and skill in chemistry and biology. You will need to be meticulous, accurate and able to work at speed.

You will need to understand statistics and have the ability to use the relevant computer software. You should have an extremely methodical approach to your work and the ability to follow instructions effectively.

You must have strong communication skills, to convey information to your colleagues and clients effectively.

Working conditions

Most of your work will take place in a sterile, laboratory environment. Your job may involve handling potentially dangerous materials, so you will need to wear protective clothing.

In addition to hands-on experimental work, your work may include using computers. Your job might involve travelling to meetings, conferences and other events in the UK and abroad.

Future prospects

Progression generally comes in the form of moving to a supervisory or managerial role, which could allow you to spend more time with the client.

Alternatively, you might consider changing departments and moving into a sales or marketing position, where the scientific knowledge you have acquired would be extremely relevant.

There is also the option of self-employment by working as a consultant and providing specialist support to cosmetic companies. You might also consider lecturing on cosmetic science courses.

Advantages/disadvantages

You may find some elements of the job extremely repetitive and monotonous.

Your work will be directly influenced by the fashion industry; you will be working to predict the latest trends, which could be exciting.

This profession can be fast paced and you may find it stressful.

Money guide

Salary levels will vary according to employer, sector and location.

Starting salaries are roughly between £16,000 and £23,000 per year. De Montfort University states that within 6 months of completing their cosmetic science degree, graduates earn an average salary of £23,265.

With experience and training this will increase and you could earn from £25,000 to £45,000 a year.

At senior levels, such as within management, it is possible to earn over £50,000 a year.

Related opportunities

- Biochemist p481
- Laboratory Technician p500
- Pharmacologist p307

Further information

Cosmetic, Toiletry and Perfumery Association
www.ctpa.org.uk

Royal Society of Chemistry
www.rsc.org

Society of Cosmetic Scientists
www.scs.org.uk

ECOLOGIST

ENTRY LEVEL 5

Qualifications and courses

Entrants normally require a degree in a relevant subject such as ecology, environmental biology/management, conservation or marine biology. The general entry requirements for a degree are 2 A levels/3 H grades and 5 GCSEs/National 5s (A*–C/A–C).

Many employers require pre-entry experience (as a research assistant or a conservation project volunteer), and postgraduate qualifications are increasingly advantageous. A driving licence may also be useful when travelling to conduct fieldwork.

NVQs/SVQs are available in Environmental Conservation at Levels 2 and 3 and Environmental Management at Level 4.

Ecologists with relevant qualifications and experience can become members of the Institute of Ecology and Environmental Management (IEEM). Different levels of membership are available depending on your qualifications and experience. The IEEM, the Field Studies Council and the Botanical Society of the British Isles also provide many short professional development courses for their members.

Once you have enough experience you could apply for chartered environmentalist (CEnv) status with the Society for the Environment, for which you are expected to undertake continuing professional development (CPD).

What the work involves

Ecologists help to protect the natural world by investigating the relationship between living organisms and their environment. Ecologists usually work within a specialist area such as freshwater, marine or fauna.

You will undertake ecological surveys of animals and plants and monitor the state of urban and rural environments. You may also write reports and analyse statistical information.

You may also advise on legal regulations, manage wildlife conservation areas and present your research at conferences or educational seminars.

Type of person suited to this work

A keen interest in the natural world is essential. It's important to be observant and methodical in your work. You will also need to be organised and work to a high standard of accuracy when collating statistics.

You will need to be comfortable working outdoors, sometimes in poor weather conditions. You must have a good knowledge of environmental policies and legislation. Good manual handling skills are important.

You will be presenting your research on a regular basis so excellent written and communication skills are essential.

Working conditions

Ecologists work in laboratories or research centres when undertaking analysis activities.

You would work outside in all kinds of weather conditions when undertaking fieldwork such as surveys of plants or animals.

For fieldwork you would need a good level of physical fitness and good observational skills. This may make the job unsuitable for people with visual impairments.

Future prospects

Ecology offers a wide range of job opportunities; you can shape your career according to your interests. However, there is strong competition for jobs; some are available only on a contract basis and it can take time to find a permanent role.

Despite the recent recession, the demand for ecological assessment and consulting services has increased by an average annual rate of 8.6% since 2006 and job opportunities are available.

Many types of organisations employ ecologists. You could go into scientific research, environmental management, teaching or conservation for organisations such as environmental consultancies, research bodies and private companies.

Advantages/disadvantages

This job provides the satisfaction of having a positive impact on the natural environment.

You may need to move around employers to develop your career.

You can choose to work in your specialist area, and develop your career around something you are passionate about.

Money guide

Salaries vary according to the type of organisation you work for.

Starting salaries range from around £20,000 to £27,000 per year.

With experience you could earn from £35,000 to £40,000.

Senior or management roles in larger organisations can pay in excess of £45,000.

Related opportunities

- Countryside Manager/Officer p240
- Countryside Ranger p241
- Environmental Scientist p492

Further information

British Ecological Society
www.britishecologicalsociety.org

Chartered Institute of Ecology and Environmental Management
www.cieem.net

Institution of Environmental Sciences
www.ies-uk.org.uk

ENTOMOLOGIST

ENTRY LEVEL 6

Qualifications and courses

An Honours degree in a relevant subject is required for entry to this profession. There are no entomology degree courses available but biology, zoology, environmental science and biological sciences would all be appropriate as these typically include modules in entomology. For entry to a degree course, candidates usually need at least 2 A levels/3 H grades, including Biology, and 5 GCSEs/National 5s (A*–C/A–C). However, entry requirements vary between universities so it is worth checking with each institution before applying.

Many employers will also expect applicants to have a postgraduate qualification in entomology. Postgraduate courses are available at several universities throughout the UK and you must have achieved a minimum of a 2.1 in your first degree to be eligible for a place. To secure a research post you will need to have or be studying for a doctorate (PhD).

Entry at technician level requires GCSEs/National 5s and A levels/H grades. Useful subjects include biology (and other sciences), maths, English, geography and geology. Foreign language qualifications may also prove beneficial.

Experience within the field is valued by employers and candidates can develop relevant skills through voluntary work in museums or with conservation organisations.

What the work involves

Entomology is the study of insects, including how they live and how they interact with their environment. Entomologists also observe the behaviour of insects to gain valuable information on the state of specific natural areas.

As an entomologist, you could analyse and assess the effects of insect life on agriculture. Entomologists are also employed to undertake research in medicine or to support ecological and environmental conservation work.

Work in the field might include searching for new species or studying insect ecology. In the laboratory, you could be developing insecticides or classifying insects.

Type of person suited to this work

You should have a methodical, logical and meticulous approach to your work and the ability to be patient and persevere when you encounter problems. You will also require good communication, computer and leadership skills.

You must be able to work effectively both alone and within a team. As you will need to remember a great deal of information, such as insect names and classifications, you should have an excellent memory.

Working conditions

Working hours and environments will depend upon the area of entomology you work in.

Entomologists working in research and higher education usually work regular hours from Monday to Friday. In a research post, you will spend your time in a laboratory, whilst a lecturer will also work in classrooms, lecture theatres and an office. Those working in conservation or field research will often work irregular hours and be outdoors in all weather conditions.

Future prospects

Entomologists work in a wide range of areas, including agricultural research and development, ecological protection and conservation, forensics and pest control. Others go on to develop their research interests as academic professionals after gaining postgraduate qualifications.

Progression within conservation and field research will depend on merit and responsibilities such as managing others. Within universities there is a progression path from researcher to head of department. Within industry, promotion opportunities to senior positions are available.

Self-employment is a possibility.

Advantages/disadvantages

It could be frustrating when an experiment or investigation does not go according to plan.

Your work could take you all over the world.

There is a wide variety of career options available.

If you work in the field or within conservation, you might have to live and work in inhospitable environments.

Money guide

Salaries vary depending on location, sector and employer.

Starting salaries for entomologists are around £16,000.

With experience, you should expect to earn £35,000 a year.

The most senior and highly regarded entomologists can achieve over £60,000 per year.

Related opportunities

- Agricultural Scientist p235
- Ecologist p490
- Environmental Scientist p492

Further information

British Entomological and Natural History Society
www.benhs.org.uk

Natural History Museum
www.nhm.ac.uk

Royal Entomological Society
www.royensoc.co.uk

ENVIRONMENTAL SCIENTIST

ENTRY LEVEL 5

Qualifications and courses

Most employers expect candidates to have completed either an environmental science degree or one in a relevant subject such as sustainable development, environmental management, chemistry, geophysics and environmental engineering. Graduates with a first degree in a science subject can take a postgraduate course in a specialist area of environmental science.

For entry to an undergraduate degree, most universities require applicants to have 2 A levels/3 H grades and 5 GCSEs/National 5s (A*–C/A–C). Relevant subjects at A level include biology, chemistry, physics, geography, English, maths and geology. Some admissions tutors will also favour foreign languages.

Candidates without a degree may gain entry to this profession by starting as a technician and working their way up to an environmental scientist position. In order to do this you will need at least 4 GCSEs/National 5s (A*–C/A–C), which should include 2 sciences, English and Maths or Technology. Equivalent qualifications, for example a BTEC First in Applied Science (Level 2), might be considered. Many technicians also complete A levels/H grades.

Relevant work experience would be beneficial and some degree courses include a placement.

What the work involves

Environmental scientists apply scientific techniques to study and protect the natural environment. You might look for ways to ensure sustainable development by discovering and experimenting with methods to reduce the damage caused to the world and our natural resources.

You could work in pollution monitoring, conservation, energy engineering, environmental consultancy and research or other areas.

You will probably be advising colleagues and clients, some of whom may not have a scientific background, on the damage particular developments could cause to the environment.

Type of person suited to this work

To work in this industry you should have an interest in geography, science and environmental issues.

You will need to be practical and methodical, as well as having the ability to think outside the box in order to solve problems. You must be meticulous in your approach to work, as the results you find could have an impact on whether developments go ahead.

You should be comfortable working independently and as part of a team. Communication, presentation and IT skills are required.

Working conditions

Your working hours and conditions will depend on the specific role you take and the sector you are employed in. Some environmental scientists work 9am to 5pm, Monday to Friday, but others involved in fieldwork will have to work overtime in order to meet deadlines.

For fieldwork you will be outside in all weather conditions and are likely to travel both within the UK and abroad. You will also spend a considerable amount of time in an office and/or laboratory.

Future prospects

There is a growing demand for environmental scientists, owing to the increasing concern about climate change and environmental issues along with a shortage of skilled people who can translate environmental knowledge into action.

You can progress to team manager or project manager, which will involve taking on more responsibilities. You could also become self-employed, working as a consultant and advising clients on a variety of environmental issues.

You might consider lecturing in environmental science.

Advantages/disadvantages

Your work will have a positive impact on the environment.

There could be opportunities to work abroad in unusual environments, such as rainforests and deserts.

You might face animosity if you refuse to approve a development.

You will often be required to spend time away from home which could disrupt your personal life.

Money guide

Earnings typically vary depending on sector, employer and location.

Starting salaries range from about £15,000 to £22,000.

With increased experience and training, you could expect up to £30,000 a year.

As a senior environmental scientist with managerial duties, it is possible to earn between £35,000 and £50,000.

Related opportunities

- Botanist p484
- Environmental Health Practitioner/Officer p22
- Oceanographer p507

Further information

Environment Agency
www.gov.uk/government/organisations/environment-agency

Institution of Environmental Sciences
www.ies-uk.org.uk

StudentForce for Sustainability
www.studentforce.org.uk

FOOD SCIENTIST/ TECHNOLOGIST

ENTRY LEVEL 5

Qualifications and courses

Entrants to this profession usually have a degree, HNC/HND or Foundation degree in a subject such as food science or food technology. For degree entry you will need 2 A levels/3 H grades, including Chemistry and Biology, and 5 GCSEs/National 5s (A*–C/A–C). HNC/HND programmes usually require 1 A level/2 H grades and 3 GCSEs/National 5s (A*–C/A–C). Pre-entry experience is also valued by potential employers.

Graduates with a degree in an unrelated subject could take a postgraduate course in subjects such as food safety, food quality management, advanced food manufacture, food production management, nutrition or food management. Some food technologists have a Postgraduate Diploma or a Master of Science (MSc) in Food Sciences.

You can enter this profession with lower qualifications as a laboratory technician/assistant and then work your way up as you gain more training and experience. Typical entry requirements at this level are 4 GCSEs/National 5s (A*–C/A–C), including English, Maths, Chemistry and Biology, or an A level/H grade in Applied Science. Technicians can work towards an NVQ/SVQ in Food Manufacture (Levels 1–3) or in Laboratory and Associated Technical Activities (Levels 2–4). They can also study part time for an HND or degree to gain promotion to a role as a food technologist.

Once qualified, candidates can apply for registration with the Institute of Food Science and Technology (IFST), which will give access to their continuing professional development (CPD) scheme. The Apprenticeship in Food and Drink may also equip you with relevant skills.

Once employed, most food scientists/technologists continue to update their skills by completing courses in specific areas such as meat safety, or subjects such as advanced baking.

What the work involves

Food scientists undertake research, as well as production and quality assurance work in all areas of the food industry. You could apply your knowledge of food, chemistry, biology and nutrition to analyse food products, set up manufacturing processes and develop food labelling.

Your research may involve ensuring that food is safe to eat by testing it under different conditions. Alternatively, you might decrease the risk of contamination by analysing the food safety systems.

You will be using both laboratory and computer equipment to carry out your work.

Type of person suited to this work

You will need to have a high level of ability in biology and chemistry and an interest in food and its production. You should also possess a good knowledge of maths and physics.

You will require strong communication and teamwork skills. You should be meticulous, with a keen eye for detail. You will need to be organised and able to manage your workload.

Good problem-solving skills are key and you will need to be extremely logical. You should be able to follow strict health, safety and hygiene rules.

Working conditions

You could be working in research units, laboratories or within the quality department in a factory. The working environment will always be clean to prevent the food being contaminated and you will be required to wear protective clothing.

You will typically work between 35 and 40 hours per week and if your employer operates a shift system, you might need to work weekends.

This role may include travel to warehouses, factories and distribution centres. A driving licence would be useful.

Future prospects

You might be offered the opportunity of promotion to team leader, technical director or project coordinator if you work within a larger organisation. You could also become a supervisor of research programmes or manager of food production activities, among other possible jobs.

Your skills would be transferable to several related sectors such as production management, marketing and buying raw materials. You could also become a specialist in a certain area.

Working abroad may be a possibility, especially within larger companies.

Advantages/disadvantages

You will be able to combine your love of food with your scientific background.

You may find some aspects of the job tedious, for example if you need to repeat the same tests over a period of time.

This career has the possibility of leading to roles in a number of areas.

Money guide

Starting salaries range from £18,000 to £26,000.

With several years' experience and increased responsibilities, you could expect to earn £30,000–£45,000 a year.

Those employed in a senior management role can achieve £55,000–£65,000.

Related opportunities

- Chef/Sous Chef p123
- Dietitian p283
- Microbiologist p506

Further information

Food and Drink Federation
www.fdf.org.uk

Improve Ltd
www.improveltd.co.uk

Institute of Food Science & Technology
www.ifst.org

FORENSIC SCIENTIST

ENTRY LEVEL 6

Qualifications and courses

Entry requires a good Honours degree in biology, chemistry, forensic science or a related subject. The Chartered Society of Forensic Sciences accredits university courses so it might be worth looking out for these at an early stage. For degree entry you will usually require at least 2 A levels/3 H grades, including Biology and/or Chemistry, and 5 GCSEs/National 5s (A*–C/A-C) including Maths, English and a science.

Many entrants to this profession have a postgraduate diploma, master's or doctoral degree in forensic science or a related subject. This is becoming increasingly important to employers, who may also expect you to have at least 6 months' experience working in a laboratory. Some employers may accept an equivalent professional qualification.

To enter as an assistant forensic scientist in England and Wales, you will need 4 GCSEs (A*–C), including English, Biology, Chemistry or Maths, and an A level in Chemistry or Biology. In Scotland, an H grade in Chemistry, Biology or a related subject is normally required. Assistant forensic scientists usually cannot progress to a higher level without at least a degree or postgraduate qualification.

Once you secure employment as a trainee forensic scientist, you will receive on-the-job training from experienced colleagues. The Chartered Society of Forensic Sciences also provides qualifications in areas such as fire investigation, firearms examination, courtroom skills, statement writing, and interpretation skills. If you want to specialise in electronic casework, you need a qualification in computing, electrical engineering or electronics.

A Disclosure and Barring Service (DBS) check may be required.

What the work involves

You will use your skills to provide important scientific information and help resolve legal and criminal cases. By analysing samples and assessing accident and crime scenes, you will support the work of police and lawyers.

Your role will involve identifying anything that may be used as evidence from a crime scene, including organs, blood, bodily fluids, illegal drugs, firearms and explosives, DNA and even paint or fragments of glass. You will carry out the necessary tests to extract the information required by the police.

You will use techniques including photography, DNA profiling, chromatography and metallurgy.

Type of person suited to this work

You need strong scientific skills and the desire to help solve crimes. Confidence is essential, as you might have to make court appearances.

You should be able to handle distressing situations well. You will need to pay great attention to detail whilst in the field, in the laboratory and when producing reports. Good colour vision is required.

You will require the ability to clearly explain scientific findings to people without a scientific background. You should be able to use statistics to interpret your findings. You must be a great communicator.

Working conditions

You will spend the majority of your time in the laboratory but you will also need to visit crime scenes. You might have to deal with unpleasant or upsetting sights.

You may also be outdoors in all weathers. You could be standing or crouching for long periods of time to examine evidence. You might have to travel with some absences from home.

The average forensic scientist works about 35 to 37 hours per week. You may also have to spend time on-call.

Future prospects

The job market is highly competitive, with scientists being employed by organisations such as the Centre for Applied Science and Technology, the Defence Science and Technology Laboratory and some of the police forces.

Promotion to management is generally based on appraisal reports and experience. You could become self-employed by working as a forensic consultant. You might also have the opportunity to work abroad.

Advantages/disadvantages

You will be using your scientific knowledge and applying it to real life situations in order to help the police catch criminals, which would be extremely rewarding.

This job comes with a lot of responsibility as your evidence may be the reason behind someone's conviction or acquittal.

This is a varied job and no two cases will be the same.

Money guide

Earnings vary according to employer and location.

Starting salaries for trainee or assistant forensic scientists are between £16,000 and £20,000.

Once you have gained 2–3 years' experience, earnings can increase to between £25,000 and £35,000 a year.

As a senior forensic scientist you could achieve £45,000 to £60,000 a year.

Related opportunities

- Biomedical Scientist/Medical Laboratory Assistant p482
- Clinical Scientist p487
- Microbiologist p506

Further information

Chartered Society of Forensic Sciences
www.forensic-science-society.org.uk

Skills for Justice
www.sfjuk.com

GEOGRAPHER

ENTRY LEVEL 6

Qualifications and courses

An Honours degree in geography is usually required but it is also possible to gain entry with an bachelor's degree in a related subject, such as oceanography or global change. Geography-based degrees cover varied aspects of human, economic and physical geography, knowledge of which will be useful in your working life.

Entry requirements for geography degrees vary but are usually 2 A levels/ 3 H grades, including Geography, and 5 GCSEs/National 5s (A*–C/A–C). For science-based geography courses (BSc) an A level/H grade in a science will also be needed.

Graduates who wish to secure a role as a researcher in academia will need to continue their studies to master's and doctorate (PhD) level. You will need a minimum of a 2.1 in your first degree to progress to a master's degree. To obtain funding for a PhD, you will be required to have achieved a high level on your master's course.

The Royal Geographical Society (RGS-IBG) offers opportunities for A level/H grade students to carry out sponsored fieldwork, and also provides gap year scholarships and several short courses.

What the work involves

You will be undertaking research, using IT, fieldwork and paper-based resources to broaden public and academic knowledge of your specific field of geography.

You can choose to specialise in either physical geography – the study of the earth, rivers, climate, land formation and oceans – or human geography – the study of humans in their environment. There are also several other branches of geography within these 2, including environmental, health, historical, geomatics and pedology.

You could use your skills in a range of industrial fields, from government bodies to private consulting firms. As a researcher for a university, you will also lecture and contribute as a writer to geographical journals or articles while studying for a PhD or similar.

Type of person suited to this work

You need to have a good knowledge of your area of geography, with a genuine interest in and love for what you study. You will need excellent research and communication skills to be able to thoroughly understand and lecture on your chosen area of study.

Being flexible, approachable and hardworking will assist your progression to becoming an expert in your specialist geographical subject.

You will need a good level of physical fitness for fieldwork, as you will be working long hours in unusual conditions, spending a lot of time on your feet.

Working conditions

You could be based in a research centre, university, office or on location during fieldwork. Travel within the UK and abroad is frequently required.

You might need to work unsocial hours and weekends during fieldwork. Lecturing and office-based research tend to have more standard working hours, Monday to Friday. Although when doing academic research your hours will probably align with normal working hours, but you will have some flexibility to work the hours you want.

You will have access to a computer and a library to assist with research. You might need to use special equipment while in the field.

Future prospects

It is important to get some work experience in a research position before applying for a fully paid job, as the competition for research positions can be fierce. You can progress from research assistant to head researcher.

If you are following an academic route, you can start off as an assistant lecturer, working with undergraduate and master's studentsand progress to professor after completing a PhD and contributing significantly to your field of geography.

Advantages/disadvantages

You can work overseas, often for long periods of time, when doing field-based research.

The work is interesting and varied.

You will be required to constantly keep up to date with any changes or developments in your geographical field of expertise.

Money guide

Earnings vary according to your experience and employer.

As a research assistant, you can expect a starting salary of between £17,000 and £26,000.

With increased experience and recognition in your chosen area of expertise, your earnings could rise to £30,000–£45,000.

Professors contributing significantly to their field can earn in excess of £50,000.

Related opportunities

- Planning and Development Surveyor p96
- Secondary School Teacher p189
- Town Planner/Planning Technician p113

Further information

Geographical Association
www.geography.org.uk

Royal Geographical Society with IBG
www.rgs.org

GEOLOGIST/GEOLOGICAL TECHNICIAN

ENTRY LEVEL 3

Qualifications and courses

Geologist
To enter this profession you need a degree in a relevant physical science subject such as geology, geophysics or geochemistry. Typical entry requirements for a degree course are 2 A levels/3 H grades from subjects such as physics, chemistry, biology, geology and maths and 5 GCSEs/National 5s (A*–C/A–C), including English. The Geological Society website provides details of approved courses which meet the first stage requirements for becoming a chartered geologist (CGeol) which may be of interest when choosing a university course.

Many entrants will have studied for a master's degree or doctorate (PhD) in a relevant area of geoscience, such as geophysics, petroleum geology or sedimentology. As competition for jobs is strong, a postgraduate qualification and pre-entry experience may improve your career prospects.

Geological technician
The usual minimum entry requirements for a junior technician are 4 GCSEs/National 5s (A*–C/A–C) including a science and Maths, and some employers may also require A levels/H grades. A BTEC National Level 3 in Applied Science may be accepted. Some employers may ask for a HNC/HND or a degree.

Once you secure employment, it is possible to work towards further qualifications, such as a degree, HND or the NVQ/SVQ in Laboratory and Associated Technical Activities (Levels 2–4).

What the work involves

Geologist
Geologists analyse and study the planet Earth, including its materials, structure and history. Your work may involve organising practical field and laboratory research to gain specific information. You may use your skills to support development work, for example mineral mining and the oil industry.

Geological technician
You will work closely with geologists, undertaking practical research work in the field and laboratory. You will collect and examine samples and produce test results. You will use other sources, for example surveys, to provide detailed information on specific geological features and aspects.

Type of person suited to this work

You should have the ability to pay close attention to detail. You will need to be meticulous, practical and logical in your approach to work. You will have to work with technical equipment so you should have high levels of dexterity. You must be able to uphold health and safety regulations.

Geologists need to be able to make important decisions and communicate well, both orally and in writing. A geological technician requires good graphical skills, including computer-aided design, to help produce maps.

Working conditions

The hours and working conditions of a geologist will vary considerably depending on the sector they work in.

Geological technicians normally work 9am–5pm, Monday–Friday, with some exceptions when they have approaching deadlines.

The majority of work will take place in labs, often with specialist equipment. Protective clothing might need to be worn for certain tests.

Future prospects

Geologists could progress to a managerial role, although this may involve relocating. There is also the possibility of becoming self-employed if you work as a consultant. Alternatively, you could work as a university lecturer.

There are more promotion opportunities for geological technicians within larger organisations. If you choose to work for a smaller company, you might need to change employers to progress. Training to become a geologist is possible.

Advantages/disadvantages

You may have difficulty gaining enough money to fund your research or projects.

There are job opportunities within multinational corporations which would allow you to use the latest technology and travel.

Employers generally prefer geologists who have completed postgraduate study.

Money guide

Geologist
Starting out as a graduate you can expect a salary of between £20,000 and £30,000.

With experience, you could earn from £40,000 to £50,000 a year.

Senior geologists with extensive experience can receive a salary ranging from £70,000 to over £100,000.

Geological technician
Starting salaries are between £12,800 and £16,000.

With experience, you can expect to earn from £20,000 to £32,000 a year.

At senior levels, salaries can increase to £40,000.

Related opportunities

- Ecologist p490
- Geophysicist p497
- Oceanographer p507

Further information

British Geological Survey
www.bgs.ac.uk

Cogent Sector Skills Council Limited
www.cogent-ssc.com

GEOPHYSICIST

ENTRY LEVEL 6

Qualifications and courses

A degree in geophysics, geology, physics or a related subject is required for entry to this profession. For entry onto a geophysics degree, you will usually need at least 2 A levels/3 H grades, including Maths and Physics, and 5 GCSEs/National 5s (A*–C/A–C). Other useful subjects to study at A level/H grade are biology, chemistry, geography and geology.

Many entrants also have a postgraduate qualification and relevant courses include a Master of Science (MSc) in Petroleum Engineering, Petroleum Geoscience or Exploration Geophysics. It is also possible to study at doctorate level in a specialist area of geophysics.

Pre-entry work experience, from a vacation placement or internship, is desirable and will provide opportunities to make contacts within the industry, which could lead to freelance work in the future.

For entry at technician level, an A level/H grade in Physics is normally required. It may be possible to enter with an SQA National in Physics at Intermediate 2 or a BTEC National Level 3 Certificate/Diploma in Applied Science.

The Apprenticeship for Laboratory and Science Technicians is available at both Intermediate and Advanced Levels and for entry to an apprenticeship you will need 4 GCSEs/National 5s (A*–C/A–C).

What the work involves

Geophysicists apply physics-based investigation techniques to analyse the nature of the rocks, structures and minerals below the Earth's surface. You will spend a lot of time undertaking practical work and writing up results.

Most geophysicists and field seismologists are involved with helping companies locate oil and gas. You will plan and organise exploration work and interpret detailed geological information.

Geophysicists work in research in universities, research institutes and for companies involved in oil and mineral exploration. You will work as part of a team of geologists, engineers and/or engineering geologists.

Type of person suited to this work

You should have an interest in rock structures and a desire to travel. Your scientific and technical skills will be of a high quality. You should pay excellent attention to detail and have a methodical and meticulous approach to solving problems.

You will need to have strong numeracy skills and the ability to use software packages which may be extremely complex. You should be able to communicate well, both in person and in writing.

Working conditions

You will spend some time in an office or laboratory and the rest in the field. If you are involved in data collection you will travel the world, operating from base camps.

You might also work offshore (at sea) on oil or gas platforms or ships. This work will involve being away from home for long periods of time in a confined space, living and working with the same people.

In a UK office-based role, hours are generally 9am–5pm but you will be expected to be flexible. At sea, the working day is 12 hours. You may also be called on during your free time if there is an urgent need.

Future prospects

Skilled geophysicist professionals are in demand with construction, fuel and mineral exploration and development organisations within the public and private sectors.

Developing a career in industry may involve moving around to gain the relevant professional experience. In some jobs you might work overseas.

As you develop appropriate contacts, you have the option of becoming self-employed or doing consultancy/freelance work.

Advantages/disadvantages

The work can be physically demanding and may involve visiting potentially hazardous sites.

You may have the opportunity to study and observe the natural world in a variety of locations.

Some employment in this area is offered on a short-term basis, which can lead to job insecurity.

Money guide

Earnings vary depending on location, employer and the sector you work in.

Graduates with a first degree have a starting salary of between £22,000 and £25,000, whilst those with postgraduate qualifications can expect to earn between £24,000 and £30,000.

With experience, you could earn between £30,000 and £45,000 a year.

In a senior position, you could achieve over £60,000 per year.

Related opportunities

- Energy Engineer p205
- Environmental Scientist p492
- Oceanographer p507

Further information

British Geological Survey
www.bgs.ac.uk

British Geophysical Association
www.geophysics.org.uk

Geological Society
www.geolsoc.org.uk

HYDROLOGIST

ENTRY LEVEL 6

Qualifications and courses

The minimum requirement for entry to this profession is an Honours degree in a subject such as geography (focusing on physical science), environmental science, civil engineering or environmental management. For entry onto a degree course, students usually need a minimum of 2 A levels/3 H grades and 5 GCSEs/National 5s (A*–C/A–C). Useful subjects to study at A level/H grade include maths, science, geography and geology.

Owing to the high level of competition for positions in this sector, a postgraduate qualification is strongly recommended. Possible subjects to study are water resources, engineering hydrology and water management. Entry onto a postgraduate course is with a minimum of a 2.1 in a relevant first degree.

The Chartered Institution of Water and Environmental Management (CIWEM) accredits a number of undergraduate and postgraduate courses in the field which may be worth looking out for when considering degree courses.

Pre-entry work experience is a useful way to develop your skills and build contacts within this competitive industry. You should consider undertaking placements during your holidays or as part of a sandwich degree.

Hydrologists are expected to engage in continuing professional development (CPD) throughout their career.

What the work involves

As an invaluable natural resource, water needs to be monitored and managed by hydrologists. You will help ensure that safe drinking water is available when and where it is needed.

Your work could involve measuring river flows, rainfall, evaporation and groundwater. You may assess water use in agriculture and forestry, or deal with water-management emergencies, for example in droughts.

Your research might involve working out potential flood risks, designing water supply systems or developing resources such as reservoirs. You will work with civil engineers, freshwater ecologists, chemists and other professionals.

Type of person suited to this work

You will need to have an interest in environmental protection and management, and an understanding of how a water supply affects a society. You should have strong geographical, scientific, mathematical and technical capabilities.

This role requires the ability to think creatively and solve problems. You will also need to be confident in using and creating maps and other ways of portraying a landscape.

The job demands excellent observational skills and attention to detail. You must be able to work with detailed factual information and communicate your findings.

Working conditions

Most hydrologists work conventional hours within an office environment. If there is an emergency or a deadline approaching, you might need to work some evenings and weekends.

You might also be required to spend time in the field. You will be working outdoors in a variety of weather conditions and using heavy equipment, so you will need to have a certain level of physical stamina.

This job might involve travel within the UK and abroad.

Future prospects

The opportunities available for promotion will vary according to the organisation and employer. Progression also depends on experience, skills, responsibility and merit. You may be able to increase your chances of promotion by moving to another team or geographical location. To progress, you should be able to manage people, projects and budgets.

Self-employment is possible if you become a consultant and there are many opportunities to work overseas for international organisations.

Advantages/disadvantages

You can live and work abroad while you undertake research work.

You may have to work outdoors in the wind and rain.

Some employment in this area is offered on a short-term basis, which can lead to job insecurity.

If you work within consultancy, you will have a wide variety of work available to you.

Money guide

Earnings vary according to sector, location and employer.

Starting salaries range from £17,000 to £25,000.

With experience, your earnings can rise to £32,000 a year.

Those employed in a senior role can earn between £35,000 and £45,000.

Related opportunities

- Geophysicist p497
- Meteorologist p505
- Oceanographer p507

Further information

British Hydrological Society
www.hydrology.org.uk

Chartered Institution of Water and Environmental Management
www.ciwem.org

IMMUNOLOGIST

ENTRY LEVEL 5

Qualifications and courses

All immunologists hold a relevant degree in immunology or a related science subject such as medical microbiology, biomedical science, or genetics. These should be accredited by the Institute of Biomedical Science (IBMS) and most institutions require at least 2 A levels/3 H grades (including Biology) and 5 GCSEs/ National 5s (A*–C/A–C) for entrance.

The National Health Service (NHS) offers graduates the chance to study on the Scientist Training Programme (STP) in clinical immunology. This takes 3 years and leads to a master's degree. Entry requires that you have a relevant degree with a minimum of a 2.1 classification. Pre-entry laboratory experience may also prove advantageous.

Outside of the NHS, most job candidates possess a relevant master's degree or doctorate (PhD), which are necessary for research positions. Many employers, such as universities, may expect you to work towards a PhD as part of your ongoing training. After at least 4 years of training you will be eligible for mandatory registration with the Health & Care Professions Council (HCPC), which requires you to undertake continuing professional development (CPD) throughout your career.

You can also enter the profession by working in a pathology laboratory straight from school, after A levels/ H grades, but this route is less common. Mature students can also enter this profession by completing an Access course, which can help those who are out of practice at education prepare for a degree.

What the work involves

Immunologists work with the body's immune system. They study functions and use the knowledge gained to treat and control illness and disease.

You might work on developing vaccines against diseases such as HIV or meningitis.

You could also find yourself studying the causes of allergies and looking at ways to stop the human body rejecting transplanted organs.

Type of person suited to this work

If you are thinking of becoming an immunologist, you naturally need to be interested in medicine and healthcare, and the way the body works.

You should have a logical, scientific mind and be good at solving problems, as well as being good at biology and scientific subjects in general. You may spend years researching one area or topic, and so will need to be patient and enjoy in-depth research work.

You will often have to work in teams, so you should enjoy this but equally be able to use your initiative and work independently. If you choose to lecture, your communication skills need to be excellent.

Working conditions

Working hours will vary depending on your employer, but will generally fall into the average 9am–5pm Monday to Friday pattern. During busy periods you may be required to work overtime.

Work tends to take place in a laboratory environment, often in sterile conditions. You will probably be required to wear appropriate clothing, and this often includes a white coat, face mask and rubber gloves.

If you choose to lecture, the environment will be very different, and you will spend most of your time in classrooms and lecture theatres.

Future prospects

If you choose to work as a lecturer, once you are a researcher you can work your way towards a promotion to lecturer, then senior lecturer and so forth, up to professor and head of department.

If you follow the NHS pathway, the career progression structure is very clear. You basically work your way up the grades, from A to C.

Other options to consider include scientific writing and publishing, or working on drugs trials and quality assurance. You could also progress to sales, finance and management positions within the biotechnology industry.

Advantages/disadvantages

This is a skilled profession, and training and progression can be really rewarding, especially in such an interesting job.

There is also the added advantage that you will be helping people.

The job can be stressful and demanding, and the work is by no means easy.

Money guide

As a new graduate in an NHS training post you will start on wage band 6 which is £25,783 a year.

After considerable experience this can gradually rise to wage band 9 which is up to £98,453 a year.

Outside of the NHS, starting salaries range from £22,000 to £30,000. Once you gain experience, this rises to between £28,000 and £37,000 and senior immunologists can earn between £40,000 and £60,000 a year.

Related opportunities

- Biomedical Scientist/Medical Laboratory Assistant p482
- Clinical Scientist p487
- Hospital Doctor p292

Further information

British Society for Immunology
www.immunology.org

NHS Careers
www.nhscareers.nhs.uk

LABORATORY TECHNICIAN

ENTRY LEVEL 3

Qualifications and courses

Entrants need at least 4 GCSEs/National 5s (A*–C/A–C), including English, Maths and a science. Equivalent qualifications such as a BTEC Level 2 Certificate in Applied Science may be accepted. Pre-entry laboratory experience is not necessary but may help your application.

Qualifications at a higher level such as A levels/H grades, a BTEC Level 3 qualification, NVQs/SVQs, an HNC/HND or a degree in a science subject might be required, especially if you wish to advance during your career.

The majority of laboratory technicians are trained on the job, and may be able to study towards NVQs/SVQs in Laboratory and Associated Technical Activities (Levels 1–4) or Level 2 in Clinical Laboratory Support. NVQs/SVQs are also available in more specialist subjects, such as laboratory operations specialising in water, chemicals and pharmaceuticals, metal industry laboratory services, and forensic science.

You could take the Institute of Science & Technology's Certificate in Laboratory Technical Skills (Levels 1–3) or their Higher Diploma in Analytical Chemical, Biochemical or Microbiological Laboratory Techniques.

Apprenticeships are available in England. They last 1 year and you gain the Laboratory Technician Certificate. Scotland also offers a 2-year Modern Apprenticeship in Laboratory Technician work, during which you would gain the HNC Applied Science and SVQ Level 3 in Laboratory Techniques. Entry requires a minimum of 4 National 5s (A–C) or above including Maths, English and Chemistry. Higher maths or chemistry qualifications are also considered desirable.

What the work involves

You will analyse samples of different types of substances and materials using specialist equipment. You could specialise in a particular area, such as microbiology or clinical chemistry.

Your work may involve recording detailed information and developing and maintaining microbiological or other cultures.

Laboratory technicians apply their scientific analysis and measurement skills in organisations such as the military services, the National Health Service (NHS), industry and scientific research institutions.

Type of person suited to this work

You will provide important factual information, so must work to a high standard of accuracy. Your patient attitude will help you undertake sometimes repetitive but important laboratory activities.

Good manual handling skills will be needed to organise laboratory equipment. You will also need good communication skills and normal colour vision.

Good IT skills will help you record and analyse a range of information. As your work may involve tasks that are potentially dangerous, such as handling bacteria and working with radiation, you must work to a good standard of health and safety at all times.

Working conditions

You will most likely have standard working hours, although some employers do work on a shift or rota basis which includes early mornings, evenings and weekends. Your working day will be spent in a clean and sterile laboratory.

You will work with specialist computer software to complete your research and record activities.

You could also have to carry out fieldwork at various sites outside the laboratory.

Future prospects

You will play an important role in protecting public health and research what makes the high-quality products that many of us use every day safe.

With further experience, you could progress to supervising a team of technicians or managing a laboratory.

Medical laboratory technicians can advance into a role as an education laboratory technician, phlebotomist, cardiographer, physiologist or research positions.

Advantages/disadvantages

Laboratory tasks can be repetitive, time-consuming and require patience.

Because of the transferable nature of lab skills, you could move from one organisation to another quite easily.

In some organisations you would work on a shift basis.

Money guide

Starting salaries are generally between £14,000 and £19,000 per year.

With experience and qualifications, you could earn between £20,000 and £25,000.

As a very experienced laboratory technician, team leader or laboratory manager, it is possible to earn from £30,000 to £40,000.

Related opportunities

- Biochemist p481
- Biomedical Scientist/Medical Laboratory Assistant p482
- Pharmacy Technician p308

Further information

Biochemical Society
www.biochemistry.org

Science Council
www.sciencecouncil.org

Semta
www.semta.org.uk

MARINE BIOLOGIST ENTRY LEVEL 6

Qualifications and courses

To enter this profession you require a degree in a relevant subject such as marine biology, marine science and oceanography. Minimum entry requirements for a degree are usually 2 A levels/3 H grades in relevant science subjects such as biology along with 5 GCSEs/National 5s (A*–C/A–C). A levels/H grades in Maths, technological subjects or languages would also be beneficial.

Gaining some work experience during the summer break or by taking a gap year could also be useful. There are organisations such as the Earthwatch Institute or the Sea Turtle Protection Society of Greece (STPS) who offer various camp-based or expedition projects.

Due to the fierce competition within this industry postgraduate qualifications are a distinct advantage. For postgraduate study you will normally require a minimum of a 2.1 in your first degree.

If you want to apply for a technological support role you should have achieved A levels/H grades in Biology, Maths or Geography and another science subject.

Experience with scuba diving might also prove necessary if you wish to study animals first hand.

Once qualified you will need to continue learning. The Marine Biological Association (MBA) runs advanced courses on specific areas of marine science.

What the work involves

You will undertake practical research and analysis into animal and plant life in the world's seas and oceans. As well as academic research, you could apply your skills in fisheries, research or fish-farming development.

You may undertake research trips above or below the sea's surface and keep detailed research records. By increasing understanding of the sea you will be able to make predictions about the effects man will have on the marine ecosystem and how it will cope with these changes.

You may provide specialist advice to organisations such as governments or environmental pressure groups.

Type of person suited to this work

You should have a strong interest in science with a particular interest in marine life. You will require both a scientific understanding and practical ability. You will need to be meticulous and extremely patient.

You should have good numerical and computer-based skills. You must be observant and have a questioning mind. You will need to be able to analyse and interpret data effectively. You should have a certain level of physical stamina.

You will need a desire to travel and not mind being at sea. You should be highly organised and able to work autonomously and as part of a team.

Working conditions

You will spend time in an office environment, laboratory and researching in the field. While in the laboratory or office you will usually work normal office hours, however some projects and deadlines may require overtime. Laboratory work will usually involve working with hazardous organic materials as well as chemicals.

When working on projects at sea you will probably be working longer hours. Operating at sea might mean you are away for long periods of time, in cramped and possibly uncomfortable conditions. You will be subject to changeable weather conditions and potentially hazardous work environments. Fieldwork may also involve being inside aquariums.

Future prospects

Competition for jobs remains high. Gaining a good level of practical experience in addition to the relevant training shows commitment and provides useful skills. Once you have gathered enough field experience you could go freelance or set up your own consultancy.

You could lecture students, which you could combine with undertaking your own research.

Working abroad, where many institutes are based, is a distinct possibility.

Advantages/disadvantages

A lot of your research in the field will depend on the tides and weather conditions, which could slow down your progress.

You will use your skills and knowledge to increase public understanding of the natural environment.

Finding funding for your projects may prove problematic.

Money guide

Starting salaries for graduates are usually between £18,000 and £24,000 although they vary greatly depending on the employer and location of the work.

With experience, and for those with a PhD, you could earn from £26,000 to £34,000.

The highest earning marine biologists, who are at the top of their field, can earn around £50,000 a year.

Related opportunities

- Ecologist p490
- Environmental Scientist p492
- Oceanographer p507

Further information

Centre for Environment, Fisheries and Aquaculture Science
www.cefas.defra.gov.uk

Marine Biological Association
www.mba.ac.uk

National Oceanography Centre, Southampton
www.noc.soton.ac.uk

MATERIALS SCIENTIST

ENTRY LEVEL 6

Qualifications and courses

Candidates typically hold a relevant degree, often in metallurgy, materials science, materials technology or materials engineering. It is also possible to enter with a degree in a general science subject. A Foundation year is available at some institutions for candidates without the required scientific background. HNC/HNDs in Engineering, Construction and the Built Environment and Manufacturing and Product Design may be relevant for this type of work.

Most degree courses expect applicants to have achieved at least 2 A levels/3 H grades, including Maths and a science, and 5 GCSEs/National 5s (A*–C/A–C), including Maths and English. The Advanced Diploma in Engineering is often accepted, whilst Level 3 NVQs, BTECs and City & Guilds qualifications may also be accepted when combined with other qualifications. The Apprenticeship in Engineering and Manufacturing Technologies is also available.

To become a chartered materials engineer with the Engineering Council, you need to have studied an accredited 4-year Master of Engineering (MEng) degree, or a 3-year bachelor's degree followed by a period of professional development. Postgraduate courses are available, and may be studied prior to entry, or through company training schemes. In order to be accepted you must have successfully completed a first degree. Many employers prefer candidates to have a Master of Science (MSc) or to be working towards a doctorate. Professional bodies also expect you to undertake continuing professional development (CPD).

It may be possible to enter the profession at technician level. Often technicians are studying part time for their doctorate. Applicants usually need at least 4 GCSEs/National 5s (A*–C/A–C), including 2 sciences (or Double Science), Maths and English, or equivalent qualifications such as BTEC Level 2 qualifications in science.

What the work involves

Materials scientists measure, define and process materials. They help decide the types of materials to use in engineering, construction and product processing work.

You will use your knowledge of the properties of metals and alloys, glass, ceramics and other materials in many areas of industrial research, development and production. You will research how and why materials react to certain conditions and how they can be used in our everyday lives.

You will use technology and computer equipment to carry out tests on different materials, keep records of your findings and draw conclusions from the results.

Type of person suited to this work

You will need to have creative flair and you should have an inquisitive and logical mind. You will need to be meticulous.

You will be able to write coherent reports and be a good public speaker, as you might need to give presentations. You will need solid computer skills. You should work well in a team environment.

You should have dexterity as you will be working with a range of test equipment. You will need good eyesight (including colour vision for some projects).

Working conditions

Materials scientists in industry work normal office hours or shifts, however the more senior your role is, the longer you will have to work.

You could be working in a sterile laboratory or an industrial environment. The most common working environments for materials scientists are laboratories and offices.

There is a possibility you will have to complete work in the field. You may have to wear protective clothing.

Future prospects

You will have the option to change industries and purchase raw materials, work in sales, management or marketing. You could progress to become a project manager or a technical director, meaning you would be leading people in developing new products.

Alternatively, you could move into a career in teaching.

Opportunities for self-employment are limited but you could work in non-destructive testing (NDT) or failure analysis. There may be the possibility to work abroad.

Advantages/disadvantages

You will have the opportunity to apply your skills and knowledge to develop new products and provide new scientific information.

Scientists are constantly in demand in most areas of industry.

This can be a highly lucrative career.

Money guide

On entering this career as a graduate you can expect to earn around £21,000 per year. Entry salaries tend to be higher if you have a postgraduate qualification, from £25,000 to £35,000 per year.

Once you have reached a senior role, as a professor for example, you could earn in excess of £50,000 per year.

Salaries are usually higher within large companies in the private sector.

Related opportunities

- Biochemist p481
- Chemist p485
- Laboratory Technician p500

Further information

Institute of Materials, Minerals and Mining
www.iom3.org

Semta
www.semta.org.uk

UK Centre for Materials Education
www.materials.ac.uk

MATHEMATICIAN/MATHEMATICS RESEARCH SCIENTIST

ENTRY LEVEL 6

Qualifications and courses

A degree in maths is essential to work as a professional mathematician in industry, business/finance, education or research.

Degrees are available in general maths or in specific areas, such as financial or business maths. Entry onto maths degree courses usually requires at least 2 A levels/3 H grades, including Maths, and 5 GCSEs/National 5s (A*–C/A–C), including English and Maths. A science and/or computing-related subject are also viewed favourably.

Maths graduates are recruited directly by some companies. Most mathematicians have postgraduate qualifications, which require a first degree in maths, physics or another subject with a high mathematical content. Entry is possible with an undergraduate degree only but progression is significantly limited unless you hold a further qualification, particularly within academia.

It is possible to become a chartered mathematician with the Institute of Mathematics after gaining an Honours degree in maths and 3 years in employment.

What the work involves

Research is conducted using mathematical theory in order to solve problems in areas such as science, engineering, finance, government and IT. You could work at all levels of industry, research and education and help to inform the work of different organisations.

You could study and teach pure maths in an academic environment or work in job roles requiring mathematical skills and knowledge, for example actuary, operational researcher or statistician.

Your work may involve undertaking research and analysis, setting up research programmes and assessing research findings. In a business, you will work on a specific project such as predicting future trends in population growth or financial markets.

Type of person suited to this work

You must have a strong interest in working with numerical information to solve complex problems. You need to be logical and methodical, as well as flexible and innovative to analyse a range of problems.

Your work could help shape the activities of your company so you must have good attention to detail and be able to record your work accurately.

Strong communication skills will help you explain mathematical ideas to people without a maths background. As maths-related research can take time to set up, a patient attitude can be helpful.

Working conditions

For many roles, you would work in an office and use computers to analyse information. Long hours are common in this role.

If you work in education, you will spend time teaching in classrooms and in lecture rooms. You could also spend time undertaking research.

Mathematicians who work in business, such as accountants, will spend time in meetings with their clients.

Future prospects

There is a high demand for professional mathematicians in areas such as business, finance or industry, and in companies that develop new products such as new computer software and pharmaceuticals. Graduates have fared fairly well in the labour market in recent years.

After gaining experience, you could progress into a managerial role.

In an academic environment, progression depends on your research accomplishments. Academic jobs may not necessarily have as high a turnover as jobs with corporations.

Advantages/disadvantages

Mathematical skills apply to many different sectors, so you could move across a range of areas.

A shortage of qualified mathematicians means that there are a variety of opportunities.

A second degree could be needed to follow your chosen career.

Tight deadlines and the uncertainty in being able to find a solution to problems can make this line of work stressful.

Money guide

Salary levels vary widely according to employer and sector, although on average larger companies will pay more than smaller companies.

Starting salaries range from £25,000 to £35,000 per year. With several years' experience you could earn from £29,000 to £38,000 per year.

At senior level, expected earnings would be from £30,000 up to £70,000, depending on sector and level of responsibility. These figures apply to professors within academic settings and team leaders within industrial settings.

Related opportunities

- Actuary p5
- Stockbroker p52
- Systems Analyst p147

Further information

Institute of Mathematics and its Applications
www.ima.org.uk

Mathematical Association
www.m-a.org.uk

Maths Careers
www.mathscareers.org.uk

METALLURGIST

ENTRY LEVEL 5

Qualifications and courses

The usual entry qualification required for a career as a metallurgist is a degree. Degrees are available in metallurgy and in materials science, materials technology and materials engineering. Entry to a relevant degree course usually requires a minimum of 2 A levels/3 H grades and 5 GCSEs/National 5s (A*–C/A–C). The Advanced Diploma in Engineering and BTEC/SQA Level 3 qualifications might be offered as alternatives. Knowledge of foreign languages may also prove advantageous within this globalised industry.

For those seeking entry to the profession by first becoming a technician or with an HNC/HND or Foundation degree (in a subject such as metallurgy and materials, metals technology, manufacturing engineering or applied science) then at least 1 science A level/H grade will be required.

You could apply for one of the graduate training programmes offered by several industry employers. This can lead to membership with a professional institution such as the Institute of Cast Metals Engineers (ICME), which could increase job prospects.

Once you have qualified, continuing professional development (CPD) is encouraged. Once you have gained 2 years of relevant experience you will be given the opportunity to join the Institute of Materials, Minerals and Mining (IOM^3). Membership will give you an opportunity to attend conferences and network with others in the industry. If you have a relevant master's degree and 4 years' experience you will be able to become a professional member of IOM^3. You can then apply to gain chartered engineer (CEng) status.

What the work involves

Metallurgists apply their materials science and engineering knowledge to support product and process development in areas such as aerospace, rail, construction and oil and gas.

You may be involved with the metal extraction process (chemical metallurgy), designing metal components (process metallurgy), managing projects, or investigating metals and materials (physical metallurgy). You might help develop practical solutions for production problems.

It is likely that your role will involve aspects of quality control, project management and process/product development.

Type of person suited to this work

Metallurgists need an excellent knowledge of metals and related materials, whatever area they work in. They must also be able to understand the uses for different materials.

You will need to have good communication and teamworking skills. You will also have to be confident in making decisions that could affect major industrial processes and understand the commercial impact of your work.

Your flexible approach and attention to detail will help you adapt to the demands of different projects. Your IT and numeracy skills will also be important. Because you could work with potentially dangerous materials you must have a good knowledge of health and safety.

Working conditions

You might have to work in a noisy location if you are employed by a large manufacturing company. In other roles you could be based in a laboratory-style setting.

Hours vary from employer to employer, but they can be long especially if you are working to complete a specific project to a set deadline.

In many roles, you will be part of a team and could also meet with clients on a regular basis. In some roles you may be required to write detailed reports.

Future prospects

There are job opportunities at various companies, from steel producers to those who need metal composites.

You could undertake project management for individual companies. You might work for companies that develop materials for industries such as automotive and aerospace engineering.

There may be the opportunity for you to directly manage the process of mining and extracting materials.

Advantages/disadvantages

The role can provide the satisfaction of developing new products and materials.

There are opportunities to work abroad and this usually pays well.

You might need to work unsocial hours for various projects.

If you specialise in a particular field, job choices could be narrow.

Money guide

Starting salaries range from around £18,500 to £28,000 per year. Those with chartered engineer status are likely to earn more.

With experience and at a senior level it is possible to earn £40,000.

As a senior manager and with chartered engineer status and considerable experience you could earn in excess of £50,000.

Related opportunities

- Aerospace Engineer p196
- Laboratory Technician p500
- Materials Scientist p502

Further information

Engineering Council UK
www.engc.org.uk

Institute of Cast Metals Engineers
www.icme.org.uk

Institute of Materials, Minerals and Mining
www.iom3.org

METEOROLOGIST

ENTRY LEVEL 6

Qualifications and courses

Entrants to this profession need a degree accredited by the Royal Meteorological Society (RMetS) and postgraduate degrees are often necessary for employment. Degrees in meteorology are available, but other suitable subjects include physics, maths, computer science, oceanography and environmental science. The general entry requirements for a degree are 2 A levels/3 H grades and 5 GCSEs/National 5s (A*–C/A–C) and some employers may also require A levels/H grades in Maths and Physics.

Relevant postgraduate courses are available and a requisite of research posts. Subject areas include meteorology, climatology and atmospheric science. There are also opportunities to do a research doctorate at some institutions which may improve employment prospects.

The Met Office provides initial training for new entrants without a postgraduate qualification. The training consists of an 18-week Initial Forecasting Course, followed by practical training at a weather station, and a 3-week Forecasting Consolidation Course. You will generally need a first or 2.1 and a good grade in at least A level/H grade Physics to apply for a post at the Met Office. During your training you will work towards NVQ/SVQ Level 3 in Meteorological Observing or the Level 4 in Meteorological Weather Forecasting. Once employed, you may also be expected to work towards a QCF Level 5 Diploma in Meteorological Forecasting.

You can also enter work at the Met Office in a supporting role, for which you will generally require at least an HNC/HND or 2 A levels/H grades at grade C or above in Maths and Physics. Relevant work experience would be extremely valuable, and the RMetS offers a few work experience placements every year.

What the work involves

Information gained from observing the sky, the atmosphere and natural phenomena gives a picture of everyday weather conditions.

As well as providing weather forecast information that is used throughout the media and to inform industries such as fishing, meteorologists undertake research into the Earth's atmosphere. You could be employed by the Royal Navy, the Royal Air Force, the Met Office or other employers.

You will be using specialist computer programs and mathematical techniques to gather information, which you will combine in order to form a weather picture. Within meteorology you can work as a forecaster or a researcher.

Type of person suited to this work

You should have a strong interest in the environment, science, research and climate change. You will need to excel in maths and physics.

The job calls for the ability to problem solve and think creatively to resolve specific issues. You should be happy to work in various locations, however remote. The job demands excellent observational skills and attention to detail.

You should be able to comprehend and evaluate complex information. You must be able to communicate effectively, both in person and on paper. You will be computer literate, and work well as part of a team.

Working conditions

You will generally conduct your work from an office environment, using specialised computers.

When you are working in the field you could be living and working in extremely isolated areas with basic living conditions.

Researchers generally work ordinary office hours. Forecasters and observers however will usually work in shifts. When working in the field you will not usually have set hours.

Future prospects

There are 3 main areas that a meteorologist can work in; these are forecasting, research and teaching. You may wish to move between them in order to progress.

Once you have gained experience as a forecaster you might be able to move into broadcasting, research or consultancy work.

There could be the possibility of working abroad.

Advantages/disadvantages

You may have the opportunity to study and observe the natural world in a variety of locations.

You might have to work inconvenient shifts.

There is a wide variety of work within this industry so you shouldn't get bored.

Employers increasingly require applicants to have a postgraduate qualification in a relevant subject.

Money guide

Starting salaries are usually between £21,000 and £27,000 per year.

Experienced meteorologists can earn between £25,000 and £35,000 a year.

As a manager you could earn from £38,000 to £60,000 per year.

Related opportunities

- Geophysicist p497
- Oceanographer p507
- Physicist p509

Further information

Met Office
www.metoffice.gov.uk

Royal Meteorological Society
www.rmets.org

MICROBIOLOGIST

ENTRY LEVEL 6

Qualifications and courses

Most entrants have at least a degree in microbiology or another biological science. To get onto a degree course in microbiology you will usually need at least 2 A levels/3 H grades, including Biology and preferably Chemistry, and 5 GCSEs/National 5s (A*–C/A–C), including a science, English and Maths. A Master of Science (MSc) or doctorate (PhD) in microbiology will increase your job opportunities. Work experience will prove advantageous when applying for jobs. This may be possible via a work placement as part of a sandwich degree course, or by arranging work experience during the holidays. For example, the Society for Applied Microbiology provides student work schemes, and the Society for General Microbiology funds research projects for penultimate-year undergraduate students.

The National Health Service (NHS) offers graduates the chance to study on the Scientist Training Programme (STP), specialising in clinical science. The programme lasts 3 years and you would achieve an MSc in Microbiology. After another 2 years of lab experience you can gain the Association of Clinical Scientists Certificate of Attainment and apply for the mandatory state registration with the Health & Care Professions Council (HCPC).

It is also possible to get into microbiology by working your way up from laboratory technician by working and studying part time for a relevant degree. NVQs/SVQs are available in Laboratory and Associated Technical Activities (Levels 2–4).

Once you are working as a microbiologist, you will receive on-the-job training in areas such as lab techniques, technology and management skills.

What the work involves

Microbiologists study micro-organisms such as bacteria and viruses.

As a clinical microbiologist in a healthcare setting, you would aim to identify diseases and protect the community from the spread of infection. Alternatively, you could work in research and development for the pharmaceutical and food industries, in agriculture, the environment or in education.

Duties include presenting the findings of your research, supervising the work of support staff and carrying out administrative work. If you worked as a researcher and lecturer in a university or teaching hospital, you would also be involved in tutoring, mentoring and supervising students.

Type of person suited to this work

You will need to be scientifically capable. You must also have good problem-solving skills and the ability to work with statistics and relevant computer packages.

You will require a high level of dexterity and need to be meticulous, practical and logical in your approach to work. You should also be patient as you might find you have to repeat tests.

Microbiologists should be able to work equally well independently or as part of a team. They must be able to keep careful records and to communicate their ideas and findings to others.

Working conditions

Most microbiologists spend at least part of their time in laboratories. Some microbiologists spend part of their time in classrooms and offices.

The work week for many microbiologists is generally 40 hours. Some overtime may be necessary when a project must be completed or when an experiment must be monitored around the clock.

Microbiologists usually spend some time reading and studying to keep up with the newest findings of other scientists.

Future prospects

There is considerable competition for research positions. Nonetheless, increased public awareness in preserving the environment, providing sanitary food production and storage, and finding cures for such diseases as AIDS, cancer, and heart disease could provide the stimulus for increased spending by private companies.

Opportunities for those with doctoral or master's degrees in microbiology are expected to be better than the opportunities for those with bachelor's degrees.

Advantages/disadvantages

There are opportunities to visit different types of outside locations on research trips.

Experiments can take a long time to complete and some aspects might become tedious. You will also be handling potentially dangerous substances.

Employers such as the NHS can offer the chance to gain experience in different departments and provide well-structured career paths.

Money guide

If you begin your career as a laboratory assistant you can earn between £13,000 and £19,000.

In the NHS you would have a starting salary of around £25,000 to £35,000.

If you work in research and development for a pharmaceutical firm, salaries are generally higher and start from £27,000 to £37,000.

Top salaries for microbiologists can reach £60,000.

Related opportunities

- Biochemist p481
- Immunologist p499
- Pharmacologist p307

Further information

NHS Careers
www.nhscareers.nhs.uk

Society for General Microbiology
www.sgm.ac.uk

OCEANOGRAPHER

ENTRY LEVEL 6

Qualifications and courses

The majority of entrants within this profession will hold a degree. Degrees are available in oceanography and related areas, such as marine biology, and other relevant subjects include biology, chemistry, physics, maths and geology. For degree entry, candidates usually require 2 A levels/3 H grades, including Maths and a science, and 5 GCSEs/National 5s (A*–C/A–C). Relevant GCSE/National 5 subjects include sciences, English and maths along with foreign languages, IT and geography.

Most employers expect candidates to hold an A level/H grade in Maths. It is possible to join the Merchant or Royal Navy without a degree and then undertake the necessary studying and training to become an oceanographer.

Having a postgraduate qualification in oceanography is very common and also will increase your employability. You could also study for a course in related/specialist areas. In order to be accepted onto a master's degree you will usually need a first degree in a science-based subject. Some master's programmes will accept graduates without a scientific background, though this is very uncommon. It is also possible to do a research-based doctorate, which some employers may expect you to already have or be working towards.

Entry without a degree or HND/HNC qualification is possible but support and technical roles are rare and a willingness to pursue in further study later on would be expected.

What the work involves

Oceanographers investigate how ocean organisms and structures work together.

Your work could involve undertaking fieldwork above and below the surface of the sea. You may also interpret the information you find and write research reports.

The information you produce could be used by government and/or industry.

Type of person suited to this work

You will require a passion for the environment and ocean life, along with an interest in maths, science and engineering. You will need to be prepared to travel and spend time working at sea.

As you may be working in the field you will need to be physically fit. You should have strong verbal and written communication skills. You will be carrying out detailed research and so will need to be meticulous, logical and practical.

You will also need to be able to present your findings in front of an audience and so should have a certain level of confidence. Good teamwork is essential.

Working conditions

Much of your time will be spent working in a laboratory or an office, with typical office hours from Monday to Friday.

Fieldwork may be carried out at sea or along the coastline.

When working at sea you might be required to spend 6 weeks or more away from home. You will be living and working with the same people.

Future prospects

Most oceanographic work is structured around fixed, short-term contracts and so progression can prove tricky.

You might find that you have to move between employers in order to achieve a promotion. Progression is based on merit and taking on more responsibilities, such as leading a team.

It is possible to become self-employed and work as a consultant. Another option might be university lecturing, where progression opportunities are easier to come by.

You may choose to undergo further training in order to specialise in several associated areas, such as marine geology (the study of the ocean floor), marine chemistry (the study of the chemical composition of water and/or sediment), marine physics (measuring the properties of currents etc), or marine biology (the study of the plants and animals in the sea).

Advantages/disadvantages

You will be able to combine your love of the environment with your scientific ability.

Some employers may expect candidates to hold a postgraduate qualification.

You will have the opportunity to travel.

Money guide

These figures are only approximate as salaries will vary depending on location, sector and employer.

Starting salaries are between £18,000 and £25,000 per year.

Those with a PhD could start on £20,000–£25,000.

Once you have gained experience as an oceanographer you could earn between £33,000 and £44,000 a year.

As a senior oceanographer, with management responsibilities, you could earn up to £60,000. Consultants can earn between £35,000 and £50,000; senior consultants could earn more.

Lecturers can earn upwards of £30,000.

Related opportunities

- Diver p361
- Ecologist p490
- Marine Biologist p501

Further information

Centre for Environment, Fisheries and Aquaculture Science
www.cefas.defra.gov.uk

National Oceanography Centre, Southampton
www.noc.soton.ac.uk

OPERATIONAL RESEARCHER

ENTRY LEVEL 6

Qualifications and courses

The entry requirement for this profession is a 2.1 Honours degree or higher in a relevant subject such as maths, statistics, economics, management science or business studies. Specialist degrees in operational research are available at some institutions and are usually offered as a joint Honours degree with a subject such as maths or statistics.

Entry to a relevant degree course is with a minimum of 2 A levels/3 H grades, including Maths, and 5 GCSEs/ National 5s (A*–C/A–C). It may be possible to become an operational researcher with a degree in a non-mathematical subject if you have a good A level/H grade in Maths.

Some employers may expect candidates to have a postgraduate qualification, for example a master's in operational research or management science. Entry onto a postgraduate course is dependent on a candidate's experience and a minimum of a 2.1 class in a relevant undergraduate degree.

Opportunities for graduates are available through the Civil Service Fast Stream programme. The Government Operational Research Service (GORS) recruits candidates with a minimum of a 2.1 in a numerate degree or a postgraduate degree in operational research.

The Operational Research Society organises an annual careers open day for undergraduates who are considering working in this sector and also offers a wide range of training courses and in-house training services.

What the work involves

Operational researchers use mathematical, scientific and other analytical methods to help improve the performance of organisations in business, industry and government.

You will work closely with managers and other staff to create practical solutions to different management and organisational issues.

You will develop analytical models or strategies to improve a specific area or aspect of an organisation. You might also be involved with putting your ideas into practice within companies.

Type of person suited to this work

Operational research is all about getting practical results from in-depth analysis. Consequently, you should enjoy solving problems and applying your analytical and mathematical abilities to find solutions.

You will have a strong interest in helping organisations develop and you will put your understanding of each company to practical use. You will need excellent communication skills for working closely with managers and other staff.

Your flexible approach will help you cope with the varied demands of each project. While you will need strong IT skills, a creative flair can also benefit you in this job.

Working conditions

You will usually work a 37-hour week, Monday to Friday, with some overtime required if projects are nearing deadlines.

You will undertake most of your work in an office setting and meetings with managers, technical specialists and staff are likely to be a regular part of your job. You will also be required to visit clients so a driving licence would be useful. Travel both within the UK and abroad is possible.

Future prospects

Operational researchers help many different organisations to develop successfully. There are increasing opportunities in manufacturing, finance and other sectors.

You could move into managing an operational research team or work in areas such as marketing. With more experience, you could develop a career as a consultant.

The civil service offers a well-structured career path and a range of opportunities in operational research.

Advantages/disadvantages

Strong demand in many sectors means that you can develop your career in various types of companies.

Operational research work is fast moving and you will always be learning something new.

Resolving production, resource or staffing problems for a company can be stressful and confrontational.

Money guide

Salary levels depend on location, the sector you work in and your academic background.

Earnings tend to be highest for those employed by management consultancies.

Starting salaries range from £20,000 to £28,000.

With experience and a more senior position, you can expect to earn between £40,000 and £80,000.

At operational research consultant level, you could achieve up to £100,000 a year.

Related opportunities

- Actuary p5
- Mathematician/Mathematics Research Scientist p503
- Statistician p511

Further information

Government Operational Research Service
www.operational-research.gov.uk

Operational Research Society
www.theorsociety.org.uk

PHYSICIST

ENTRY LEVEL 6

Qualifications and courses

For entry to this profession you need to have a relevant degree in either physics or applied physics. Entry requirements for a degree course are usually at least 2 A levels/3 H grades, including Physics and Maths, and 5 GCSEs/National 5s (A*–C/A–C) including English, Maths and a science, typically Physics.

Many institutions offer 1-year science Foundation courses for candidates who do not have the necessary scientific background to directly enter a science-based degree course.

Some employers may also expect you to have a relevant postgraduate qualification such as a Master of Science (MSc) or doctorate (PhD). Entry onto a postgraduate course requires a minimum of a 2.1 in your first degree and pre-entry work experience is increasingly requested.

Physicists are trained on the job and often study for a PhD or the membership exams of relevant professional bodies alongside their professional work. For example, medical physicists must work towards the Clinical Science Diploma of the Institute of Physics and Engineering in Medicine (IPEM).

For entry at technician level, an A level/H grade in Physics, or equivalent qualifications such as a BTEC Level 3 qualification in Applied Science or SQA National in Science, is required. Some technicians may hold a science-based degree. Technicians who have secured employment can take the NVQ in Laboratory and Associated Technical Activities (Levels 2–4).

What the work involves

Physicists apply their understanding of the relationship between matter and energy to their work in industry, government research, academia and medicine.

You could use your specialist skills and knowledge to investigate diverse subjects, including space research, nuclear energy, electronics, defence technology and materials for industrial use.

You might be involved with research and development work or with designing projects and experiments. Your role could also include developing products and systems in areas such as computing, aeronautics, transport and medicine.

Type of person suited to this work

Physicists must combine their scientific knowledge with strong problem-solving skills.

You will need the confidence to work with complex numerical information. You should have excellent attention to detail and a patient approach for undertaking research.

IT skills are also important. Good written and oral communication skills are needed for you to be able to explain your work clearly.

Working conditions

You will usually work Monday to Friday from 9am to 5pm. If you are employed by the NHS as a medical physicist, you are likely to work shifts and fulfil on-call duties.

You will be based in a laboratory, workshop or office, using specialist equipment and computers. This work can involve handling dangerous chemicals so you will need to wear protective clothing.

For some jobs you will be required to travel to meetings and conferences so a driving licence would be useful. If you are undertaking research in the field, you may be away from home for extended periods of time.

Future prospects

Physicists work at the cutting edge of science and industry. They apply their skills in areas as varied as electronics, power, communications and defence. They are employed by research institutions, government bodies and private companies to improve and develop products and systems.

You will be able to progress to supervisory or management roles, or enter into the training and teaching of physics.

Advantages/disadvantages

Physics offers the chance to develop public understanding of important scientific questions.

Working with detailed information for long periods of time can be very tiring.

You might have the chance to work abroad.

Money guide

Salary levels vary according to employer and sector, however a relevant PhD may increase your income.

Starting salaries are usually between £21,000 and £25,000.

A qualified and experienced research physicist can expect to earn between £24,000 and £35,000.

Senior physicists with increased responsibilities typically receive a salary ranging from £40,000 to £50,000.

In academia, a senior higher education lecturer can achieve £55,000 to £60,000 a year.

Related opportunities

- Aerospace Engineer p196
- Astronomer p479
- Meteorologist p505

Further information

Institute of Physics
www.iop.org

Institute of Physics and Engineering in Medicine
www.ipem.ac.uk

Physics World
www.physicsworld.com

SEISMOLOGIST

ENTRY LEVEL 6

Qualifications and courses

Depending on their interests, seismologists can come from the fields of geology, geophysics, physics or applied maths.

A bachelor's degree in a scientific discipline is necessary for entry into this profession, and a master's degree or doctorate are significant assets for more advanced research. Available bachelor's degrees usually include geophysics, computer science, chemistry, and other mathematical and science subjects and the general entry requirements are 2 A levels/3 H grades and 5 GCSEs/National 5s (A*–C/A–C). Pre-entry work experience is also desirable and many companies offer summer internships.

While lecturers and researchers often continue with their studies at the postgraduate level, seismologists who work for private companies will often undertake additional specialised training in the area required.

Continuing professional development (CPD) is advised, but there are no formal methods through which to do this. Membership of a relevant professional body, such as the Society of Exploration Geophysicists (SEG), may be advantageous as it would allow you to keep up to date with the latest developments in your chosen specialism.

Initial training is usually provided on the job. This includes health and safety, field training and data entry. There may be a probationary period during which you will be mentored by a more experienced colleague.

What the work involves

Seismologists are earth scientists, specialists in geophysics, who study seismic waves in geological materials. Their research aims at interpreting the geological composition and structure of the Earth. In the case of earthquakes, seismologists evaluate the potential dangers and seek to minimise their impact through the improvement of construction standards.

Some of a seismologist's typical tasks may include monitoring, maintaining, testing and operating seismological equipment, documenting data, supervising preparation of test sites, managing equipment and maintaining safety standards.

Most seismologists work for petroleum or geophysical companies, and data processing centres. Government jobs in geology and earthquake surveying are also available. Some seismologists even teach, or work on their own as private consultants.

Type of person suited to this work

As with any earth scientist, curiosity and a thirst for knowledge are essential traits. You will also need a meticulous nature and an interest in computer science. In certain cases, an interest in outdoor activities would also be advantageous.

Though often called upon to work alone, seismologists must also be able to work within teams to solve problems.

Developed written and oral communication skills are important in order to communicate the results of their research.

Working conditions

Hours of work may vary depending on your role.

A scientist who specialises in earthquake seismology may work in a university or a laboratory, keeping a standard work week.

Alternatively, a seismologist who works for an earthquake monitoring facility or a petroleum company may work hours that vary. Some seismologists may even be on-call, which requires their availability at a moment's notice.

Future prospects

Though the need for experts in earthquake seismology is typically slim, employment prospects for seismologists are generally strong in the oil and gas industries.

Seismologists who acquire a postgraduate degree are often able to secure employment more easily than those with only a bachelor's degree.

Growing needs in the fields of resource management, environmental protection, and energy may also increase the demand for seismologists.

Advantages/disadvantages

You must live and work closely with a small team of scientists and other staff away in the field or offshore for long periods of time.

It is possible to work as a freelancer or you could set up your own consultancy firm.

It may be possible to move between seismology and engineering geology or hazard prediction.

Money guide

Salaries vary depending on the industry, with earnings often 10%–30% higher in commercial companies, such as oil service firms.

A typical starting salary for a seismologist is £22,000–£25,000.

Candidates with a relevant postgraduate qualification can expect an increased salary of between £24,000 and £30,000.

With experience, the typical salary of a senior level seismologist, where the post holder is in charge of one or more major projects, is between £40,000 and £65,000.

Related opportunities

- Cartographer p66
- Geologist/Geological Technician p496
- Hydrologist p498

Further information

British Geophysical Association
www.geophysics.org.uk

Energy & Utility Skills
www.euskills.co.uk

STATISTICIAN

ENTRY LEVEL 6

Qualifications and courses

The usual entry requirement for this profession is a degree in statistics or another quantitative subject such as maths, economics or operational research. The general entry requirements for a degree are 2 A levels/3 H grades and 5 GCSEs/National 5s (A*–C/A–C).

As well as 3-year degrees, there are also 4-year sandwich degree courses that include a year-long work placement, which may help when applying for your first job. Master's degrees in subjects such as statistics or medical statistics may be an advantage and entry is with a 2.1 or above in your first degree. Foundation degrees and HNDs may also be accepted by potential employers.

The professional examinations of the Royal Statistical Society (RSS) provide an alternative entry route for mature candidates or those already in relevant employment. Courses are available at 3 levels and can be studied by day-release, at evening classes or by distance learning. The Graduate Diploma is the highest level qualification and is equivalent to an Honours degree.

The Government Statistical Service (GSS) offers a Fast Stream recruitment programme. Candidates must have at least a 2.1 in a numerate degree with a high statistical content or a postgraduate qualification in statistics in order to be considered for entry.

Chartered statistician (CStat) status is awarded by the RSS to those with an approved degree and a minimum of 5 years' experience in the field. Graduates of an approved degree who have not yet undertaken the required training and experience are eligible for graduate statistician status.

What the work involves

Statistics involves the use of mathematical techniques to collect, analyse and present large quantities of factual information.

You will plan and undertake surveys using a range of mathematical research methods. You could apply your skills to investigate diverse subjects such as population levels, patterns of illness or national shopping habits.

Statistical research plays a vital role in informing the activities of many areas such as government, advertising, medicine and scientific research.

Type of person suited to this work

Strong mathematical skills are essential for producing and analysing a range of statistical information. You will also need excellent problem-solving abilities to create practical solutions and collect information on specific issues.

Excellent IT skills are needed as it is likely that you will use specialist computer software.

Your findings could help to shape the work of different organisations, so you must have a high standard of accuracy and pay close attention to detail at all times.

The ability to communicate with managers, staff and clients is essential.

Working conditions

You will be based in an office environment and spend a lot of time using computers. Depending on the sector you are employed in, you may undertake practical projects in a laboratory or research centre. You will sometimes be required to travel to meet colleagues and clients so a driving licence would be useful.

You will usually work 37–40 hours a week from Monday to Friday, with some overtime as project deadlines approach.

Future prospects

Statisticians investigate and research issues within the environment, medicine, business, social science and many other areas.

You could develop a career in the Government Statistical Service. There are many opportunities in scientific and medical research and pharmaceutical development. Alternatively, you could choose to work in academia, researching and lecturing on statistics. Self-employment as a consultant is also possible.

Advantages/disadvantages

Working to a high level of accuracy at all times can be very demanding.

You are likely to need a postgraduate qualification for roles in environmental or forensic statistics.

As the job is often project based, it offers variety through different projects.

Money guide

Earnings vary depending on your location, employer, qualifications and experience, with the highest salaries offered in London.

Employees in the private sector tend to earn more than those working in the public sector.

Starting salaries outside of London typically range from £22,500 to £31,000. In London, the average starting salary is between £22,500 and £39,000.

With experience, you can earn between £30,000 and £50,000.

Those employed in the most senior positions can achieve up to £70,000 a year.

Related opportunities

- Actuary p5
- Economist p20
- Mathematician/Mathematics Research Scientist p503

Further information

Office for National Statistics
www.statistics.gov.uk

Royal Statistical Society
www.rss.org.uk

TOXICOLOGIST

ENTRY LEVEL 6

Qualifications and courses

You will need a degree in a science subject in order to become a toxicologist. Relevant degree subjects include pharmacology or biochemistry and you will need at least 2 A levels/3 H grades, including Maths and Chemistry, and 5 GCSEs/National 5s (A*–C/A–C) for entry.

Following your degree, it may be possible to take up a post that offers training as you work, but the usual route is to take a postgraduate qualification. Entry requirements for postgraduate courses are at least a 2.1 classification for your bachelor's degree in a subject such as biomedical sciences, forensic sciences or toxicology. Other related acceptable subjects include pharmacology, food safety and environmental management. Your master's degree should be chosen in accordance with the area of toxicology you wish to work in, with available specialities including industrial, pharmaceutical, forensic, clinical, regulatory and occupational toxicology.

After completing a master's degree, you could choose to study further by carrying out a research doctorate in a specialist area of toxicology. There are postgraduate diplomas offered by many institutions in the subject, and you may even choose to go into ecotoxicology or study pollution or pesticide science.

The National Health Service (NHS) offers graduates the chance to study on the Scientist Training Programme (STP), which would allow you to train as a clinical scientist specialising in toxicology. The course typically lasts 3 years and entry requires a relevant first degree with a minimum 2.1 classification.

Organisations such as the British Toxicology Society (BTS) and Federation of European Toxicologists offer various qualifications and the chance for continuing professional development (CPD) with membership.

What the work involves

As a toxicologist, you will study the effects of chemicals on the environment and everything within it, from humans and animals to plants. Some toxicologists work for the government.

Work is very varied and you may find yourself working on the development of products, on testing new drugs, or lecturing and carrying out your own research.

You may deal with poisons and drugs.

Type of person suited to this work

You should have a strong interest in the environment, science, and public health and safety. For forensic toxicology, an interest in law is also useful.

Your level of scientific and technical knowledge should be high, and you need an excellent eye for detail as well as the ability to work carefully and accurately.

You should be able to apply scientific knowledge to practical work, and have excellent communication skills in order to explain technical and scientific information to others both orally and in written reports. You will also need good IT skills.

Working conditions

The hours worked by toxicologists usually follow the standard 9am to 5pm, Monday to Friday working week pattern. This does not tend to vary too much. However, if you are carrying out experimental work you might be expected to be more flexible. You might be on-call on occasional weekends and evenings in case emergencies occur.

You will spend most of your time working in a laboratory, but may sometimes have to visit scenes where incidents have taken place.

Expect to wear protective clothing most of the time, and be prepared to work occasionally with animals.

Future prospects

Job opportunities are good, as the number of available positions is about equal to the number of those applying.

You can work towards being promoted to a more senior position such as project manager. This will involve spending less time with hands-on toxicology, and more on tasks such as administration and supervision. If you decide that this does not suit you, it is possible to become self-employed and/or work on a freelance basis.

Advantages/disadvantages

Toxicology is an interesting and challenging profession, and you may be involved in exciting cases. You will continually be learning and expanding your knowledge.

It can be difficult, and you may see some distressing things. You also need to be constantly alert and cannot afford to make mistakes.

Money guide

When you start out in toxicology, you can earn about £21,500 to £26,500 a year.

This can increase to around £40,000 with experience.

In clinical toxicology salaries can rise to up to £65,000 and in other fields this can reach £100,000.

Related opportunities

- Biochemist p481
- Chemist p485
- Clinical Scientist p487

Further information

Association of the British Pharmaceutical Industry
www.abpi.org.uk

British Toxicology Society
www.thebts.org

ZOOLOGIST

ENTRY LEVEL 6

Qualifications and courses

The most common route into this profession is to obtain a degree in zoology or a related subject, such as wildlife biology, marine biology, parasitology, animal behaviour, animal ecology or wildlife conservation. The typical entry requirements for a degree course are 2 A levels/3 H grades, including Biology, and 5 GCSEs/National 5s (A*–C/A–C). Some courses also require an A level/H grade in Chemistry. Pre-entry volunteer work in conservation may also help your application.

Some people undertake a degree after gaining practical experience working as a zookeeper or laboratory technician. Admissions tutors often grant these candidates a place, regardless of their formal qualifications.

Many candidates also have a relevant postgraduate qualification and entry is with at least a 2.1 in your first degree. To work in research, you would initially secure a post as a trainee researcher within a university research department and work towards a doctorate in your specialist area.

It is also possible to enter the profession at technician or trainee level with good GCSEs/National 5s and A levels/H grades, including Biology, Maths and English. In order to progress, you should be prepared to study towards relevant qualifications whilst working. Courses may include the NVQ/SVQ Level 3 in Zoo Animal Management, the BTEC Level 3 qualifications in Animal Management, or the Foundation degree in Zoo Resource Management.

Zoologists are expected to engage in continuing professional development (CPD) throughout their careers and there are various professional organisations that offer this, such as the Institute of Zoology (IoZ) and the Society of Biology.

What the work involves

Zoologists classify, study and research all kinds of animal life. You could be involved with protecting endangered species through practical work and raising public awareness.

Some zoologists work within industry, developing pharmaceuticals or enhancing agricultural products. Others are involved with research in their specific area of interest in academic or research institutions.

You may choose to specialise in an area such as mammalogy (mammals), entomology (insects) or herpetology (amphibians and reptiles). You could work in a variety of environments including safari parks, wildlife centres and zoos.

Type of person suited to this work

You will need to have a passion for environmental issues and a love of science.

For some roles in this sector, you will need to feel comfortable dissecting animal cadavers for research purposes. You must be meticulous, logical, practical and patient in your approach to your work.

The ability to solve problems is a key feature of this role. Communication skills are important as you might need to share your findings with people who lack scientific knowledge. Leadership and computer skills are also essential.

Working conditions

If you are working in the field, you will have to base your hours upon the animals you are studying, for example, you will have to work nights if you are researching nocturnal animals.

Your working environment will also vary depending on your area of interest.

Many zoologists spend the majority of their time in laboratories or teaching in lecture theatres but outdoor work is also common.

Future prospects

Whilst this is a specialist area, zoologists work for a variety of organisations such as environmental consultancies, conservation bodies, animal charities and local authorities. Others go into research and development in industry.

Many choose to work in universities, which have a set progression path from researcher to head of department. Promotion within industry and government is also clearly defined. Within other areas such as conservation, progression is more limited and you may need to change employers in order to achieve promotion.

Advantages/disadvantages

There are opportunities to travel and visit various locations on research trips.

You will use your skills and knowledge to increase public understanding of many aspects of the natural environment.

When undertaking fieldwork, you may find yourself in inhospitable environments.

Money guide

Earnings vary depending on sector, location and employer, although a relevant postgraduate qualification may increase your income.

Your starting salary will probably be in the region of £17,000 to £20,000.

With experience, earnings can increase to between £25,000 and £35,000 a year.

As a senior zoologist, you could achieve in excess of £50,000 per year.

Related opportunities

- Ecologist p490
- Veterinary Surgeon p263
- Zookeeper p265

Further information

British and Irish Association of Zoos and Aquariums
www.biaza.org.uk

Institute of Zoology
www.zsl.org/science

Society of Biology
www.societyofbiology.org

Security, Emergency and the Armed Forces

Working in security and the armed forces may give you many incredible experiences and opportunities not open to most people. You need to be an excellent team player and in some instances you may find yourself in a potentially dangerous situation, therefore it is essential that you are a great communicator. Working in this sector you can expect to spend your day absolutely anywhere! Some roles involve a lot of office work whereas others can involve spending a lot of your time on the road, or even at sea. If you are looking for a job that will be exhilarating but are able to remain calm and professional under pressure this sector could offer you a lot of opportunities.

The jobs featured in this section are listed below. For similar jobs to the ones in this section turn to *Legal and Political Services* on page 339.

ARMY OFFICER

ENTRY LEVEL 3

Qualifications and courses

Entrants must have 35 Advanced Level Information System (ALIS) points from 7 GCSEs/National 5s subjects, including at least a C in English language, maths and either a foreign language or a science; as well as 240 UCAS points from 2 or more A levels/H grades (A*–E/A–E). Though a degree is not a requirement in most regiments and corps, over 80% of cadets accepted each year are graduates, and a few corps specifically ask for a degree.

For the army you will need to be aged between 18 and 26 years old, whereas for the army reserve you can join at up to 35 years old. Officers can be male or female but some units are still male-only.

You will need to pass rigorous medical and fitness entrance tests, as well as a range of interviews and written tests during the selection process. Upon entry into the army you will undertake the 44-week Commissioning Course of intensive training at Sandhurst, in both practical and academic subjects. Once you have completed your initial training you will go on to specialist training to prepare you for your first appointment.

The University Officer Training Corps (UOTC) can help with funding part of your degree course by offering a bursary of £6,000–£8,000. If successful, you will have a provisional place at Sandhurst and be expected to serve as a Regular Officer for at least 3 years.

There is the opportunity for some professionals, such as dentists, nurses, lawyers, physiotherapists and chaplains, to become officers by fast-track training which lasts 10 weeks.

What the work involves

Army officers lead, command and train a team of soldiers on day-to-day activities, either on training exercises or on a range of combat, peacekeeping, humanitarian operations or disaster-relief missions.

Your platoon's training, welfare and discipline will be entirely your responsibility. You will work within a specific professional or skill area such as medicine, dentistry, engineering, intelligence or combat.

Type of person suited to this work

You will need to have excellent self-discipline, confidence and a natural ability to lead and motivate your team, which will consist of soldiers, non-commissioned officers and junior officers.

You must be able to keep a clear head and make sensible decisions under pressure in order to take responsibility for the safety of your team.

Initial training, with its physical and mental challenges, often comes as a shock. You will need to have determination, courage and resilience as well as a good level of physical fitness in order to get through the training stages.

Working conditions

Your hours will depend upon which specialty you have chosen to work in. Some officers work within a normal office timeframe, whilst others are required to work shifts. Hours may also be long and irregular when away on training or taking part in field-based operations.

You could be stationed anywhere in the world, and have to travel to destinations at short notice. Officers must wear a uniform at all times.

Future prospects

You will take further leadership training throughout your career in order to improve your promotion prospects and keep your skills fresh.

Most will start out as a second lieutenant before being promoted to lieutenant after 12–25 months. You can expect to be promoted to captain after 5 years in service (or 3 years if you have a degree).

Although prospects for new and existing recruits may be affected by defence budget cuts, there are still good opportunities if you meet the selection criteria.

Advantages/disadvantages

You will be working within a close-knit team of professionals, so will build strong personal and working relationships within the job.

You may be involved in implementing large-scale peace initiatives which would be rewarding.

You may be posted overseas for long periods of time which can be disruptive to your personal life.

Money guide

Officer cadets joining the programme straight after their A levels/ H grades can expect to start on £16,073 during training, rising to £24,900 once you are commissioned as a second lieutenant.

Graduate entrants start on £24,615 and can earn a minimum of £29,586 once they leave Sandhurst.

Salaries gradually increase as you rise through the ranks. After serving for 5 years you could be earning at least £37,915 as a captain.

If you are away from your base for more than 7 days there is also an allowance of up to £28.24 per day, with a further £18.16 if conditions are unpleasant. You will receive subsidised accommodation and food, medical and dental care, discounted rail fares and subsidised nursery facilities.

Related opportunities

- Army Soldier p517
- Police Officer p529
- Royal Navy Officer p539

Further information

Army
www.army.mod.uk/join

Welbeck College
www.dsfc.ac.uk

ARMY SOLDIER

ENTRY LEVEL 1

Qualifications and courses

There are no formal qualifications for entry as a soldier, although some technical jobs require certain GCSEs/National 5s. You must be aged between 16 years and 32 years and 11 months on the day you enlist, as well as meet the army nationality and residency requirements. Applicants under 18 must have parental consent.

You will need to undergo a number of interviews, during which you will take the British Army Recruit Battery (BARB), literacy and numeracy tests. Once these stages are completed, you will take a physical assessment, a medical and attend 2 days at an assessment centre.

Upon acceptance you will begin phase 1 of training. If you are under 17 years and 5 months old this will be either a 6- or 12-month course at Harrogate. If you are older you will do a 14-week package at either Pirbright or Winchester. After initial training you go on to do phases 2 and 3 in particular trades, such as aviation and engineering. This can take between a few months and a year.

Adult infantry soldiers, after initial training, go to the Infantry Training Centre to complete a 24-week Combat Infantryman's Course (CIC).

What the work involves

The army is responsible for defending the UK and its allies across the world, as well as taking part in peacekeeping and humanitarian operations.

You will be involved in regular training exercises to ensure you maintain a high level of fitness and military skills so that you are ready for combat at any time.

You will also choose to train and work within one of more than 130 different trades. You may be posted to dangerous areas and inhospitable environments at any time, whether for peacekeeping and aid missions or to engage in warfare.

Type of person suited to this work

You should be able to work within a team, reacting quickly to orders, working on your own initiative where necessary, and supporting other team members both professionally and emotionally at times.

You must be extremely disciplined and responsible, with the ability to think and act logically under pressure.

You must be physically fit with excellent stamina. You should be practical, with good manual dexterity, so that you will be able to operate various machines and equipment.

Working conditions

Some soldiers work normal office hours, whilst others are expected to undertake shifts that encompass night and weekend work.

You could be stationed in the UK or overseas, and must be prepared for life in a number of environments including deserts, war torn cities, and mountains.

Future prospects

Although prospects for new and existing recruits may be affected by defence budget cuts, the army still represents a solid career path. Provided you meet the selection criteria, there are still good opportunities available.

You will sign up for an open engagement lasting 22 years, but you can leave after serving 4 years. You must give 12 months' notice prior to leaving.

All soldiers start as a private and are awarded promotion according to their increasing levels of skill and commitment.

Advantages/disadvantages

You will be meeting new challenges each day and adapting to unusual and inhospitable situations, which will ensure the work never gets dull.

You will be working within a close knit team, supporting their work both in training and actually out on operations.

You are continually on-call, and could be sent anywhere in the world at a moment's notice.

Money guide

Soldiers can expect to receive £14,300 per year during initial training. This rises to a minimum of £17,700 per year once you are qualified as a private.

Some roles receive additional specialist pay, which can be up to an extra £19 a day.

If you move up the ranks to sergeant, you can expect to earn up to £32,756.

All staff receive an annual salary increase, regardless of promotion or additional responsibilities. There is also a scheme which offers additional pay for spending longer than 7 days away from your base where you will be entitled to an allowance of up to £28.24 per day with a further £18.16 if conditions are unpleasant.

In addition to a basic salary, you will receive subsidised accommodation and food, medical and dental care, discounted rail fares and subsidised nursery facilities.

Related opportunities

- Army Officer p516
- Royal Air Force Airman/woman p535
- Royal Marines Commando p537

Further information

Army
www.army.mod.uk/join

Welbeck College
www.dsfc.ac.uk

BODYGUARD

ENTRY LEVEL 3

Qualifications and courses

All bodyguards are legally required to hold a Security Industry Authority (SIA) licence, which lasts for 3 years (before it needs to be renewed) and covers other security sectors that also require a licence, such as security guarding and door supervision. To obtain an SIA licence you must be over 18, hold a recognised First Aid certificate, have a clean identity with no criminal record and a Level 3 SIA-approved qualification. The SIA website has a list of all approved courses which cover topics such as risk assessment and surveillance.

A driving licence will be necessary and you will need to be physically fit and have good eyesight. Knowledge of foreign languages may be useful as you might need to accompany clients abroad.

Being a bodyguard is usually a second career for people who used to be in the armed forces or the police. While this is not essential, employers will be looking for relevant experience and you will usually need to have been in the Special Forces or specialist police units to work in the most high-risk areas of the industry.

What the work involves

You will be guarding your client or group, keeping them safe from harm or unwanted attention. You might also be known as a personal protection officer or a close protection officer (CPO).

Protecting an executive on a business trip to a dangerous region of the world, an overseas royal visiting the UK, or a celebrity during an autograph-signing session could all be part of your work.

You will be responsible for making a preliminary sweep of premises before your client arrives, setting up surveillance equipment, assessing potential threats and driving your client around. It is possible to be a specialist in areas such as close protection, surveillance or defensive driving.

Type of person suited to this work

This is not a first job – most have related experience and the most lucrative contracts go to those who have worked in the Special Forces or specialist close-protection police units. Most of the work is on a self-employed basis, so you need to have a flair for business because you will need to network and keep your accounts.

Exceptional planning skills and quick responses are essential to ensure that your client is free from harm or unwanted attention. You will also need to be confident, physically fit to cope with the demands of the work, and have good eyesight and hearing.

Your appearance, diplomacy and communication skills also need to be top level, because you will be with your client and need to blend into the background to observe at high profile events.

Working conditions

Your work will be wherever your client goes and so this could mean lots of travelling.

You could be at risk as you need to protect your client – if necessary with your own body – but this is more an issue when working in dangerous areas of the world.

You will work long and irregular hours during a contract as some clients may need 24-hour protection and there will be long periods of inactivity.

Future prospects

You can progress to become a leader of a team of CPOs on assignment or establish your own business.

Very few officers are in long-term employment. The vast majority are self-employed. The profession is male-dominated but the demand is present and growing for female bodyguards.

Some progress into more mainstream security work, for example security guard or security manager. There may be opportunities to specialise in areas such as driving and residential security.

Advantages/disadvantages

You will get to enjoy a fast-paced lifestyle and travel frequently.

Training courses are residential and expensive.

The work can be dangerous.

Money guide

Most bodyguards are self-employed, earning daily or hourly rates for specific contracts. These could range from £100 to £150 a day for low risk work to £1,000 a day in a very hostile environment or for protecting a key principal.

For those bodyguards contracted to a particular company, a new entrant can earn over £18,000 per year. With experience this can rise to £24,000 to £30,000 per year.

In high risk areas, with considerable experience, you could earn up to £100,000 per year.

Related opportunities

- Army Officer p516
- Police Officer p529
- Royal Marines Officer p538

Further information

British Security Industry Association
www.bsia.co.uk

Security Industry Authority
www.sia.homeoffice.gov.uk

CIVIL ENFORCEMENT OFFICER

ENTRY LEVEL 2

Qualifications and courses

There are no specific entry requirements for employment as a civil enforcement officer, although some employers may ask for a minimum of 4 GCSEs/National 5s (A*–C/A–C), including English and Maths. Experience of working with the public or in a customer service role would also be beneficial.

Your employer will provide introductory training on the job which must be completed before you can work unsupervised. Training will cover on-street enforcement activity, car park patrolling and enforcement, clamping and tow-away, and CCTV operation. Civil enforcement officers need to keep their knowledge of traffic laws and regulations up to date.

To further your career or improve employability you could complete a relevant course such as a NVQ Level 2 in Controlling Parking Areas or a City & Guilds Level 2 Award for Civil Enforcement Officers (Parking). You could then go on to an Award and Certificate in Leadership and Management for Parking Operations (Levels 3–5).

Applicants may be required to undergo a Disclosure and Barring Service (DBS) check. A full driving licence is also needed for some positions. Good fitness levels will also be necessary.

What the work involves

You will be enforcing parking regulations for a local authority or contractors working on their behalf, patrolling and checking for illegal parking and non-payment of parking fees.

Using a hand-held computer you will regularly check details of vehicles parked in limited-stay parking areas and issue fixed penalty tickets. You will take pictures of any illegally parked vehicles.

You will need to arrange for vehicles to be clamped or sent to the pound. You will attend court to give evidence if any prosecution results from your work. You will have to report any suspected abandoned or stolen vehicles to the police.

Type of person suited to this work

All employers look for a polite but firm manner as well as good communication skills. You will need to be very good at dealing with people, many of whom could be feeling irate about the ticket you have just given them. Patience and calmness will be vital assets in dealing with people making things difficult.

You need to be a good observer and able to follow rules and instructions. You will have to watch out at all times for illegal parking, enforce the rules and keep record for official use.

You will meet a lot of people but you will also be working unsupervised and independently so you need to be confident, self-disciplined and reliable, as well as comfortable working on your own.

Working conditions

You will be working in the streets, in all seasons and weathers.

You will need to wear a uniform and carry a hand-held computer.

You will work shifts to a total of 37–40 hours a week, including early mornings and late evenings. You might also have to work at weekends.

Future prospects

Civil enforcement officers are now carrying out most of the duties that were formerly assigned to traffic wardens.

Parking contractors are working with over 100 local authorities to enforce parking legislation. Vacancies are available with numerous main contractors.

With experience, progression is possible into a role as supervisor or trainer and then into management if suitable. However, prospects may be more limited in more rural areas.

Advantages/disadvantages

You will keep fit, walking an average of 10 miles a day, 5 days a week carrying a 5kg pack (including your computer, printer and radio).

It can be an enjoyable job if you enjoy or prefer to work outdoors.

There is no doubt that civil enforcement officers are not always popular and you might have to deal with some aggressive people.

Illegal parking can cause real problems for most law-abiding motorists and many attendants feel a sense of satisfaction from keeping the roads clear.

Money guide

Starting pay is about £12,000 to £13,000 per year. In certain places, salaries for civil enforcement officers can reach up to £18,000.

Civil enforcement managers can expect £26,000 to £30,000 a year.

Some jobs pay an hourly rate, which is usually between £7 and £10.

Related opportunities

- Bailiff/Enforcement Agent p340
- Police Community Support Officer p528
- Train Conductor/Guard p595

Further information

British Parking Association
www.britishparking.co.uk

COASTGUARD WATCH ASSISTANT/OFFICER

ENTRY LEVEL 1

Qualifications and courses

There are no minimum entry qualifications, but GCSEs/ National 5s (A*–C/A–C) including English and Maths may be required by some employers as you should have clear literacy, numeracy and IT skills.

Most people join HM Coastguard as a volunteer before becoming a coastguard watch assistant (CWA). You must be aged 16 or over to apply. A few join at coastguard watch officer (CWO) level if they have a good standard of education and either a coastal skipper licence or a yachtmaster certificate from the Royal Yachting Association (RYA).

You will need a good standard of hearing and eyesight and a high level of fitness. You must have significant seagoing experience, for example from the Royal Navy, working as a coastguard rescue officer volunteer or anything else that involves boat work and navigation.

Training as a CWA lasts for 10 months. Initial training is conducted at the Maritime and Coastguard Agency Centre at Highcliffe, Dorset. The second stage is part on-the-job and part classroom-based. CWO training lasts between 9 and 12 months, depending on whether you have already worked as an assistant. You must pass an exam at the end of your training.

Volunteers will also be expected to attend regular training.

What the work involves

You will work as part of a team responding to vessels and people in distress.

You will be dealing with 999 coastguard calls and radio distress calls, and will direct the efforts of the volunteer coastguard rescue officers. You may also work alongside the services of the Royal National Lifeboat Institution (RNLI).

You will keep records of all activity and weather conditions, giving information to vessels and reporting anything unusual. Part of the role will also require providing safety information to the public about the sea, as well as give advice on safety procedures to those operating small craft/boats.

Type of person suited to this work

You must have excellent computer skills, the ability to concentrate for long periods and a clear voice to make sure that you send rescuers to the right place.

Active search and rescue work involves carrying heavy equipment, climbing and working out at sea, all of which require a high level of physical fitness.

Watch officers need good management and teaching skills to lead and train groups of auxiliary coastguards.

The ability to deal with distressing or pressurised situations, along with a patient and calm manner will be invaluable.

Working conditions

You will be located in an operations centre, using a computer and talking to others using hands-free communications equipment.

Search and rescue work involves working outside in dangerous conditions.

Coastguards operate 24/7 – you will be working shifts that include evenings and weekends and will often work over a 42-hour week.

Future prospects

Coastguard numbers have reduced slightly over the past few years, and there could still be moves to lower the number further. Volunteer numbers will remain steady though. Consequently, a lot of coastguards are now spending their time supporting those volunteers.

Progression is generally from assistant to officer, then to watch manager and finally to sector manager.

If you have experience and a degree, you could go on to a job in marine surveying within the Maritime and Coastguard Agency.

Advantages/disadvantages

With the use of satellite technology, it is possible to coordinate the rescue of someone hundreds of miles away from your control centre.

The sea is dangerous and you may arrive too late, which is an upsetting event for the whole team.

Money guide

Starting out as a coastguard watch assistant you could earn £15,000 per year. After gaining experience, this can rise to £17,800.

The starting salary of a coastguard watch officer is £18,100 and can increase to £23,200.

Volunteers are unpaid but may be reimbursed for expenses. All coastguards receive an allowance for the purchase of uniforms and footwear and those working in the Scottish islands or other very remote areas can receive additional allowances.

Related opportunities

- Air Traffic Controller p567
- Merchant Navy Deck Officer/Rating p582
- Royal Navy Officer p539

Further information

Maritime and Coastguard Agency
www.dft.gov.uk/mca/

Maritime Skills Alliance
www.maritimeskills.org

Port Skills and Safety Ltd
www.portskillsandsafety.co.uk

CRIME SCENE INVESTIGATOR/ SCENES OF CRIME OFFICER

ENTRY LEVEL 3

Qualifications and courses

Individual police forces have different entry requirements. As a minimum you should have 3–5 GCSEs/National 5s (A*–C/A–C) but many require applicants to have at least A levels/H grades and increasingly a degree in a science-related subject. Various universities offer degrees or Foundation degrees in subjects such as forensic science and criminology and you will need at least 2 A levels/3 H grades, including a science, for entry to these degrees.

You will need to be able to show you have scientific ability and possibly photographic ability as well, either from employment or education. Previous work experience dealing with the public would also be an advantage.

You will need to undergo a medical exam, have full colour vision and a driving licence for this role.

In some forces you would start as an assistant crime scene investigator (CSI) or scenes of crime officer (SOCO) before undertaking further training to become fully qualified. You might be enrolled in the Foundation Crime Scene Investigators Learning Programme at the College of Policing's Forensic Centre. This could take up to 12 months to complete.

Once in the job you will have an introductory period with your force. Upon completion you are qualified to undertake volume crime scene investigation. It is then possible to do a further 5-week training programme which qualifies you as a full CSI/SOCO.

You, and possibly your close family members, will be subject to a background and employment check.

What the work involves

You will be collecting, storing and recording evidence such as fibres, hair and blood to help investigate crimes such as burglary, accidents and suspicious deaths.

You will use equipment and materials to lift, package and preserve evidence, such as biological samples, paint, tyre marks and fingerprints.

Your job will involve taking photographic and video evidence of both crime scenes and victims of crime. You will also need to keep thorough records and attend court when required to give evidence.

Type of person suited to this work

Sifting through evidence is the main aspect of this job so you will need to be able to pay attention to detail. You will also need to be methodical and patient.

This job can be very distressing. You will need to be able to distance yourself emotionally from the crime, and be able to record the scene and collect evidence in an analytical, scientific way. Good teamworking skills are essential as you may be working on a project with many others.

An interest in science and technology is essential. You will need to keep up to date with developments in forensic science and technology as they will affect how well you do your job.

Working conditions

You will work both outside at crime scenes and inside at base.

You will do a 37-hour working week, including shifts, but hours might be longer at times. You could also be on-call 24-hours.

Conditions at crime scenes can be very difficult and unpleasant but you will be provided with protective clothing.

Future prospects

Crime scene investigators are recruited by all regional police forces. Some forces only recruit civilians to do this work but a few also recruit specialist police officers. There are 43 police forces in the UK, all of whom employ CSIs, but competition for vacancies is high.

It is possible to move into more specialised areas of work, such as the investigation of suspicious fires or scenes where firearms have been used.

There may be opportunities for promotion to senior investigator with management responsibilities. You can study for further qualifications and become a forensic scientist or specialise in fingerprint technology.

Advantages/disadvantages

Although this job has an exciting image, fuelled by popular television shows, the work can be routine, repetitive and quite shocking at times.

You will have the satisfaction of working with a team of investigating officers and forensic scientists to gather evidence needed to trace, arrest and convict offenders.

Money guide

Starting salaries for assistants are around £16,000. Once fully qualified, salaries vary from £17,000 to £26,000 per year.

This rises to in excess of £35,000 for experienced and senior investigators, depending on your local police force and responsibility level.

There may also be on-call, weekend or shift allowances.

Related opportunities

- Forensic Computer Analyst p525
- Forensic Scientist p494
- Private Investigator p533

Further information

Police Recruitment
www.policecouldyou.co.uk

CUSTOMS AND EXCISE OFFICER

ENTRY LEVEL 3

Qualifications and courses

While it is possible to join at officer level it is more common to start as an administrative assistant or assistant officer and work your way up.

You will usually need 2 GCSEs/National 5s (A*–C/A–C), including English and Maths, to start as an administrative assistant; 5 GCSEs/National 5s to start as an assistant officer; and 5 GCSEs/National 5s and 2 A levels/3 H grades to start at officer level.

Entry without these qualifications may sometimes be possible with a test to prove your abilities in areas such as teamwork and communication.

If you have a degree at 2.2 or above, you could join the Civil Service Fast Stream graduate recruitment scheme, although opportunities may not be specifically for customs officer roles but rather for other positions in Her Majesty's Revenue & Customs (HMRC).

All candidates must be UK nationals, Commonwealth citizens or European Union nationals.

What the work involves

You will be working as a civil servant for HM Revenue & Customs, enforcing tax regulations on all goods entering and leaving the country and all goods bought and sold in the UK.

You could specialise in customs: checking for anyone either not paying tax or smuggling in illegal items and substances.

You could specialise in excise work: visiting traders, manufacturers and importers to check licences and accounts to make sure that the right duties are being paid on goods such as petrol, alcohol and tobacco.

You could specialise in VAT: visiting businesses to check their accounts and that the right amount of VAT is being collected.

Type of person suited to this work

If you are part of front-line detection work, investigating the entry of illegal goods into the UK, you will be involved in observing, questioning and challenging people.

You will need top-notch communication and observation skills. You must be intuitive and persistent. Knowledge of or a willingness to learn a foreign language is useful.

If you work in VAT or excise, an aptitude for numbers and computers is a must, because you will be checking business accounts and watching out for sometimes quite sophisticated cover-ups.

Working conditions

Customs and immigration officers mainly work in airports, seaports and freight terminals but also may need to do outdoor surveillance work. You will wear a uniform if you are a front-line detective.

Excise and VAT officers are based in offices but also travel around their local areas carrying out checks and interviews. You will generally work office hours, Monday to Friday.

Customs officers work shifts.

Future prospects

There are about 23,000 staff based all over the country. Customs specialist staff are mainly located at air and seaports and the Channel Tunnel.

Training lasts for around 9 months and is usually on the job through a combination of learning from experienced staff and residential training courses. There will also be ongoing training throughout your career.

There is a clear promotion structure within the civil service and it is possible to move on to senior or management posts. There are also specialist areas within customs that you may decide to move into, for example in detection, operations and intelligence units and dog units.

Advantages/disadvantages

When dealing with front-line detection work you might have to question or detain angry or abusive people. It can be a high-pressure job at peak times.

No two days are ever the same, especially in detection work.

It can be very rewarding to know that you have prevented dangerous items such as drugs and firearms getting into the country.

Money guide

Starting out at administrative or assistant level you could earn around £15,600 a year.

As an officer you could be earning between £20,175 and £26,570 a year.

After promotion to higher officer grades salaries increase to between £25,248 and £38,861 a year.

There can also be extra allowances for working unsocial hours (eg evenings, weekends and public holidays) and people working in London generally earn more.

Related opportunities

- Army Officer p516
- Civil Service Executive Officer p14
- Police Officer p529

Further information

Chartered Institute of Taxation
www.tax.org.uk

General Fast Stream Programme
www.faststream.gov.uk

EMERGENCY PLANNING/ MANAGEMENT OFFICER

ENTRY LEVEL 6

Qualifications and courses

Typically entrants to this role have a degree and whilst all graduates with a relevant degree will be considered, some subjects, such as disaster management, international security, business continuity and environmental hazards, are considered more desirable. The general entry requirements for a degree are 2 A levels/3 H grades and 5 GCSEs/National 5s (A*–C/A–C).

Individuals without a relevant degree will need a postgraduate qualification, such as a Master of Science (MSc) in Disaster Management.

There are more specific courses available which are geared towards a job in emergency planning but these do not guarantee a job in the sector.

Candidates who have extensive previous experience of working in this sector or a related career may be able to enter the industry without the usual necessary qualifications. For example, working in international relief and development, either as a volunteer or professional, could provide the necessary experience and skills. Even getting volunteer work in international relief can be difficult though.

Previous work experience in an emergency planning related role or practical experience such as voluntary work for a humanitarian organisation may be an advantage when applying for a first job.

What the work involves

Emergency planners and managers work primarily in local government as part of a larger team to help maintain public safety, especially at times when this is threatened by an external force. Although there are opportunities to work abroad.

You will be required to respond quickly to and learn from emergency situations that have arisen from natural disasters, outbreaks of serious contagious diseases, industrial accidents and terrorism.

You will compile reports from lengthy research and planning on the most efficient ways to protect the general public should an emergency situation arise.

You will carry out risk assessments, write safety briefs to train emergency response services and help with the recovery process after an incident has occurred.

Type of person suited to this work

You will need to enjoy working in a high pressure situation as part of a large team. You should be enthusiastic about helping to provide better public safety.

You will also need to respond quickly and calmly in an emergency and keep a level head in what may be a dangerous situation.

The job requires someone willing to work long hours, sometimes at unsociable times as well as a neat and organised person who can take comprehensive notes and present their findings accurately.

Working conditions

You may often find yourself in a highly pressured situation especially in the aftermath of a major incident so you could find yourself in danger or not knowing when you will finish the job.

You can expect travel to feature heavily as part of your job with many trips away from home a distinct possibility.

Future prospects

If you enter the career as an assistant you can expect to progress, with experience, to a management or senior role if you show signs of willingness to go where the work takes you and put in long hours.

Once you reach a more senior role you will not be working in such a hands-on environment but would provide more managerial support to your team.

Advantages/disadvantages

Your future prospects could take you all over the world to work with individuals who enjoy working as part of a close-knit team.

Humanitarian work such as this can be immensely rewarding. However, it also has the potential to be highly distressing since you could be one of the first people on the scene after a major natural disaster or a terrorist attack.

Travelling and working on intense projects can take up much of your life and be very draining.

Money guide

A typical starting salary in the profession is likely to be £22,000 to £28,000.

Senior roles come with a lot of responsibility but you could expect to earn £34,000 or more.

The profession is still relatively new so salaries vary widely between jobs. Private sector jobs are often more highly paid than in the public sector.

Related opportunities

- Environmental Health Practitioner/Officer p22
- Firefighter p524
- Police Officer p529

Further information

Emergency Planning Society
www.the-eps.org

The Emergency Planning College
www.epcollege.com

FIREFIGHTER

ENTRY LEVEL 1

Qualifications and courses

To be considered for selection as a firefighter you must be at least 18 years old and preferably have a full UK driving licence. No formal qualifications are required, though you should have a good general standard of education and any qualifications you bring with you may help with future promotion. Firefighters need a reasonable level of fitness and good eyesight.

Entrance is dependent on performance within practical and written tests, including psychological tests, as well as a medical and an interview. Some colleges offer a fire service pre-recruitment course. This does not guarantee entry but aims to prepare candidates for the entrance tests. Health and safety restrictions means that it may not be possible to do work experience as a firefighter, however you would be able to volunteer or work in related jobs such as station clerk or control room operator.

As a new firefighter you will be required to undergo full-time induction training which lasts between 12 and 16 weeks (18 weeks in Northern Ireland). You will learn basic firefighting skills, fire safety and the importance of educating the public about fire safety.

What the work involves

You will be dealing with a range of emergencies, not only fires but also helping at other incidents such as rescuing trapped animals and people, handling chemical spillages and assisting at road, rail or air crash scenes.

If your team arrives on the scene before the paramedics you will be expected to have the knowledge and practice to administer First Aid if required.

You might give advice to organisations on fire safety and check that buildings or public events meet fire regulations.

Type of person suited to this work

You will need to stay calm in dangerous situations. People in danger tend to react in extreme ways and you will need to be good at talking to them, giving instructions, reassuring them and leading them to safety.

You need to be an excellent team player. You will be assigned to a 'watch' (a team) and need to work together to keep yourself and others safe.

You will need to be able to deal with very stressful and disturbing situations.

Working conditions

You will be based at a fire station but will go out to attend incidents.

Working conditions can often be unpleasant and dangerous. You will wear a uniform and, when needed, protective clothing and equipment.

You will work an average of 42 hours per week, which will be divided into day and night shifts. You can also work as a retained firefighter which means you will be on-call. Many retained firefighters have other full-time or part-time occupations.

Future prospects

The main employers are regional fire services but airports, the Ministry of Defence, the RAF and the Royal Navy also recruit firefighters.

Some firefighters start their career as retained firefighters to gain experience. There are around 18,000 retained firefighters in the UK, mostly in rural areas. Entry is competitive.

You will undergo regular training throughout your career and could work towards specialising in a particular area of the services. For example you could specialise in driving fire trucks by taking a large goods vehicle (LGV) licence. Promotion to supervisory and management roles is by clear grades and given on ability, but exams must also be passed.

Advantages/disadvantages

This job can be very stressful and you cannot just leave an emergency situation if your shift has ended.

You will get to know your watch very well; firefighters say they really enjoy the team spirit at work.

You need to pass demanding training successfully to qualify, and keep up a rigorous fitness and training schedule.

Money guide

The fire service is subject to a nationally agreed salary structure.

Full-time firefighters can expect a salary of £21,583 as a trainee which will increase to £28,766 with experience.

Crew and watch managers can earn between £30,574 and £35,664, whilst a station manager will earn £37,096–£40,915.

With experience you may become a group manager and your salary will increase to £42,723 to £47,361.

Area managers will earn between £50,156 and £55,018.

Retained (on-call) firefighters earn a fee of around £2,100 to £2,800 per year. They also receive additional payments, according to their rank, for attending fires and carrying out extra duties.

Related opportunities

- Paramedic p304
- Police Officer p529
- Royal Navy Officer p539

Further information

Defence Fire Training and Development Centre
www.gov.uk/defence-fire-training-and-development-centre

Fire Service Recruitment Information
www.fireservice.co.uk

FORENSIC COMPUTER ANALYST

ENTRY LEVEL 6

Qualifications and courses

Most people who enter this career have completed a degree in IT or equivalent computing subject. If your degree is not IT-based you can take an IT conversion course. Some universities offer specific degrees in forensic computing and information security. In order to gain a place on a degree course you will normally need at least 2 A levels/3 H grades and 5 GCSEs/National 5s (A*–C/A–C). Computing, Maths and sciences are all relevant A level/H grade subjects. Alternatively, you could complete a Foundation degree in an IT subject. The Diploma in Information Technology might also be of interest.

Some employers may ask for a postgraduate degree or an industry qualification. Entry to postgraduate programmes is reliant on the successful completion of a first degree. The National Skills Academy for IT offers relevant professional qualifications. Courses that include industry placements are particularly valuable as they will help you build up work experience as well as making relevant contacts.

A strong background working in IT is also usually required. You could start out by working as a network engineer or developer and taking professional qualification courses while working your way up.

Applicants may have to undergo a Disclosure and Barring Service (DBS) check.

What the work involves

You will be responsible for inspecting computers (and other technology such as mobile phones) for criminal activity. You might be looking for evidence of identity theft, child abuse, hacking, phishing and other illegal activity.

Even if evidence of the crime has been deleted or corrupted you will need to retrieve it without altering it in any way.

You might be using specialist software and working with the police to look through files, photographs, emails and phone conversations in order to discover evidence of criminal activity. You may need to appear in court to relay your findings.

Type of person suited to this work

You will need to have a certain level of skill using computers, as well as an interest in detecting and preventing crime.

You should be a patient and determined person as some investigations may take place over a long period of time. You might come across unpleasant or even horrific material and you must be able to distance yourself and deal with it objectively.

You will need to be able to record your findings in a clear, coherent and logical manner. You should be able to understand the law in relation to IT crime. Articulacy and strong communication skills are essential.

Working conditions

You will spend most of your time in an office using a computer.

You will generally work standard office hours (9am–5pm from Monday to Friday), however you might need to be on-call over weekends and public holidays or work overtime to meet deadlines.

You might also have to attend court to give evidence and will be expected to dress accordingly.

Future prospects

Postgraduate qualifications will enhance your chances of promotion (particularly if you work within the commercial world).

You could progress to the level of supervisor or line manager.

You may have to change employers in order to progress. Jobs are available with the police force, MI5, government, the National Crime Agency and IT firms which specialise in computer security.

Advantages/disadvantages

Your workload will be varied and opportunities are available in many different sectors.

You will spend a lot of time hunched over a computer.

If you work within a police or government sector you might help to send criminals to jail.

Money guide

As a trainee you can expect to earn around £20,000 per year. After some experience, this can rise to somewhere between £25,000 and £35,000.

A senior forensic analyst might earn in the region of £40,000 to £60,000.

These figures are only approximate and will vary depending on location, sector and employer.

Related opportunities

- Forensic Scientist p494
- Information Officer p332
- Software Engineer p146

Further information

BCS, The Chartered Institute for IT
www.bcs.org

Skills for Justice
www.sfjuk.com

Qualifications and courses

Immigration officers need no formal qualifications, although many applicants will be educated to A level standard or higher. Graduates in any discipline are welcome. Applicants with a minimum of a 2.2 Honours degree can apply for the Civil Service Fast Stream scheme. This is for entry into all civil service departments and, although a preference can be expressed, entry into immigration is not guaranteed.

All applicants must be 18 or older and be either a British citizen or a British subject who has lived here continuously for 5 years and have no restrictions on their stay in the UK. Security clearance and possibly health checks will be necessary.

Foreign language skills can be an advantage.

Application usually involves attendance at an assessment centre to be tested on your communication skills, conflict management, judgement and awareness of equal opportunity and diversity. There is a period of 9 weeks' initial training, which will take place at Heathrow, Stansted, Gatwick or Manchester airports or at the port at Dover. This will be partly classroom-based and consists of partly mentored practical work.

What the work involves

You will be working as a civil servant for the Home Office; you will be controlling the entry of people into the UK by checking the passports and visas of passengers arriving at ports, airports or via the Channel Tunnel. You could ask questions to find out more about them and, if suspicious, conduct a more detailed interview.

As an assistant officer you would refer to a more senior officer if you are concerned about documentation or answers to questions.

You might work in an office processing immigration applications, dealing with appeals and conducting intelligence-based activities.

Type of person suited to this work

You will need to be confident, assertive, have the ability to work under pressure and to deadlines.

You will need to be well organised, reliable and have good report-writing skills. You will need an ability to get on with people from across the world.

You should enjoy investigating and collecting information. You will need the ability to write up and pass on your concerns to others in your team or colleagues from other professions.

Working conditions

You could work in a range of places such as ports and airports where you will have access to a desk, computer, phone and interviewing area.

Some immigration officers have to undertake surveillance duties and work with other intelligence officers, but normally you will check documents and interview individuals within your office or interviewing booth.

You will work shifts that will include out-of-office hours and weekends.

Future prospects

Half of all immigration staff are employed in London and the south-east of England, at Heathrow, Gatwick and the Channel ports.

The numbers of people entering the UK and asking for asylum has increased over recent years. This has impacted on the service, which has grown in size. Entry is competitive at officer level and the majority of entrants are graduates.

It is possible to enter at assistant grade and work up to officer grade. Placements are also possible, for example, to Immigration Visa sections at the British Deputy High Commissions overseas or to police forces around the UK.

Advantages/disadvantages

You will play an important role in helping protect national security.

This job is part of the civil service, so entry can be competitive.

The civil service offers excellent conditions of service and training.

Money guide

When starting out as an assistant officer, you can earn around £16,500 a year within London or £15,300 elsewhere.

Salaries for immigration officers start at around £21,900 within London and £21,500 elsewhere. With experience this can increase to £30,000 for operational managers.

All staff working shifts or unsocial hours are paid additional allowances. Those working in and around London receive London weighting.

Related opportunities

- Civil Service Executive Officer p14
- Equality and Diversity Officer p23
- Police Officer p529

Further information

General Fast Stream Programme
www.faststream.gov.uk

Home Office
www.gov.uk/government/organisations/home-office

Home Office UK Border Agency
www.gov.uk/government/organisations/uk-visas-and-immigration

INTELLIGENCE OFFICER/ ANALYST

ENTRY LEVEL 5

Qualifications and courses

While some employers will accept non-UK citizens who have the right to live and work in the UK, applicants for any post within Government Communications Headquarters (GCHQ), the Security Service (MI5) and the Secret Intelligence Service (MI6) must be a British citizen and one or both of your parents must also be British or have substantial ties to the UK. You normally will have to have lived in the UK for 9 out of the 10 years prior to applying. MI5 applicants must also be aged 18 or over.

Entry requirements vary. Most police forces will require GCSEs/National 5s (A*–C/A–C), especially in English and Maths, though some departments also ask for A levels/H grades or degrees. To work for MI5, MI6 or GCHQ you will need to have at least a 2.1 degree. Any subject is welcome although criminology, technology and/or language subjects may be an advantage. Some agencies may consider significant work experience within an intelligence environment in lieu of a degree qualification.

Computer skills are essential for intelligence officers in any area, and you should be skilled in using databases, spreadsheets, internet and word processing.

There is a rigorous vetting procedure, known as Developed Vetting (DV) clearance. This includes medical and security clearance, as well as possible background checks on family and friends. These checks may feel intrusive. Recruitment can take many months and includes competency tests, telephone interviews and attendance at an assessment centre.

What the work involves

In most cases you will work for one of the UK's 3 intelligence and security agencies: GCHQ, MI5 and MI6.

Your job is to protect the UK from attack and terrorism, to protect its economic wellbeing as well as to prevent organised crime such as drug trafficking. You may be involved in helping to build up intelligence pictures by identifying targets, evaluating the reliability of source information and validating data, and then formally delivering information to the government.

You will also develop expertise in particular areas.

You might be involved in military operations, counter-espionage, detecting weapons of mass destruction, and identifying agents and targets.

Type of person suited to this work

This job requires you to use your initiative and be aware of the big picture, sometimes across agencies. You should be a confident decision-maker, flexible and adaptable with an exceptional eye for detail. You must be persevering, diligent and work well under pressure.

Motivation, inquisitiveness and cultural sensitivity are essential. You need to be able to recall events accurately and analyse information and data efficiently with the ability to convey your findings effectively.

Some of your work will include informing and working alongside professionals from other national and international security services so you should be a good team player.

You must keep up to date on current affairs and communications technologies.

Working conditions

Some of the posts operate shifts, which might include weekends.

Starting out you will be required to work at headquarters. GCHQ is based in Cheltenham and MI5 and MI6 are based in central London. You could also be required to travel both nationally and internationally. It might be possible to work from home for some posts.

This job can become more of a way of life than a career so you should be completely dedicated and be able to keep information totally confidential.

Future prospects

You will usually work for up to 3 years in your first role. Based on your performance and your potential you may be promoted to a more specialist role which will include more responsibility.

You could be responsible for a wider geographical region or for specific analytical techniques. You could also move into policy work, projects, personnel or finance.

Advantages/disadvantages

It's satisfying to know you are helping to protect national security.

Background checks in the recruitment process can be long and very intrusive.

The need to maintain secrecy may be difficult and sometimes it can be lonely as you will not be allowed to talk about your work with friends and family.

Money guide

If you work for MI5, MI6 or GCHQ your salary will start at around £24,000. With experience you could earn up to £43,000.

Outside of these agencies a junior analyst will earn around £16,000 a year. With experience this can rise to £18,000 to £26,000 and once you reach senior/management level you can expect a salary in excess of £30,000.

Related opportunities

- Army Officer p516
- Customs and Excise Officer p522
- Private Investigator p533

Further information

GCHQ
www.gchq.gov.uk

MI5 Careers
www.mi5careers.co.uk

Secret Intelligence Service
www.sis.gov.uk

POLICE COMMUNITY SUPPORT OFFICER

ENTRY LEVEL 1

Qualifications and courses

Applicants must have indefinite leave to live in the UK but beyond that a diverse range of backgrounds are encouraged to apply in order to get a good representational mix across the force. You must be at least 18 years old to become a police community support officer (PCSO).

People with criminal records may be ruled out depending on the severity of the offences. All prior offences must be declared when applying.

There are no specific academic entry requirements. You should have good spoken and written communications skills and it may strengthen your application if you have experience in community service (paid or unpaid) or if you have undertaken a relevant course. This could be an NVQ Level 2, BTEC National Diploma or HNC/HND in Public Services or a Foundation degree in Police Studies or Public Services. Entry onto HND and Foundation degree courses usually requires 1 A level/2 H grades and 3 or 4 GCSEs/National 5s (A*–C/A–C).

During the application process, you will be required to take written, fitness and role-play tests, as well as undergo medical, financial and security checks. Upon entry you will undertake between 3 weeks and 3 months of classroom training. Areas covered will include law, self-defence, First Aid, interviewing skills and using police communication equipment.

What the work involves

Police community support officers are uniformed members of the force whose role is to work within their local community, supporting the activities and initiatives of police officers.

You will be part of the group of officers that provides visible police presence on the streets and in other public areas. You will be on the front line, offering help and advice to members of the public, as well as tackling antisocial behaviour.

Everyday duties could include crowd-control and traffic directing, dealing with minor offences, checking out abandoned vehicles, or imposing fines for acts such as littering or dog fouling.

Type of person suited to this work

You will need to be an excellent communicator, as you will encounter a range of people in your work. You must also be able to remain calm but authoritative when confronted with potentially difficult or violent members of the public.

You must be able to work effectively within a team. This means you should be able to take orders but also act on your own initiative when necessary.

You should have good, accurate writing skills, as you will need to produce reports on events and deal with complex paperwork at times.

Working conditions

You will work up to 40 hours on a shift basis, encompassing night and weekend work. Flexible or part-time hours are available.

Although you will be based at a police station, you will work in a variety of locations including patrolling the streets, within people's homes, or in public places such as train stations.

You will be required to wear a uniform, which includes a high visibility jacket and protective hat. Additional protective equipment may need to be worn or carried on occasion.

Future prospects

Experienced PCSOs are often responsible for teaching, training and guiding new recruits. There are also opportunities to move into supervisory or managerial roles within the PCSO contingent.

PCSO is a good role to start in if you would like to become a police officer.

Prospects for this role may be affected by budget cuts.

Advantages/disadvantages

You will play a direct role in protecting your local community and finding solutions to problems and crime in the area.

There are good opportunities for career development, including progression to become a police officer.

You may be confronted with difficult and dangerous situations, which can be both frightening and unnerving.

Money guide

As a new recruit to the force you could expect to earn around £17,000 (although those working in London will earn more).

If you are working specifically for the British Transport Police, your basic starting salary will be slightly higher at £18,933. There is also an additional 15% shift allowance and PCSOs based in London will receive £2,245 London weighting.

If you reach a supervisory or managerial role, your earnings can reach about £25,000.

Similar to police officers, community support officers are eligible for certain benefits such as free London travel, flexible hours and key worker housing.

Related opportunities

- Army Soldier p517
- Police Officer p529
- Prison Officer/Instructor p532

Further information

Police Recruitment
www.policecouldyou.co.uk

POLICE OFFICER

ENTRY LEVEL 1

Qualifications and courses

There are no specific academic requirements but you must be aged 18 years or older and be a UK, European Union or Commonwealth citizen or a foreign citizen with indefinite leave to stay in the UK. Beyond that a diverse range of backgrounds are encouraged to apply in order to get a good representational mix across the force.

The police force operates an intensive selection process and you will need to pass medical, fitness, eyesight, literacy and numeracy tests. You will also be assessed using a variety of scenario exercises by which your communication, decision-making and problem-solving skills will be judged. The fitness tests are among the most rigorous, as it can be a very physically demanding job. You will also need to pass a Disclosure and Barring Service (DBS) check. Minor cautions or offences may not necessarily affect your eligibility.

A relevant qualification may enhance your application. Examples include BTEC qualifications at Levels 1–3, an HNC/HND in Public Services or a degree or Foundation degree in police studies or criminology. Voluntary police or community work, for example as a special constable, could also be useful experience. Specials work unpaid (with expenses covered) but after full training they will have the same powers as regular police officers.

Upon entry you will be a probationary officer for 2 years while you undergo further officer training through the Initial Police Learning and Development Programme (IPLDP).

What the work involves

Police officers are responsible for safeguarding communities from crime by apprehending criminals and maintaining order.

You will spend your time on patrol, responding to any situation that occurs whilst you are on shift. You will keep records, take statements and write reports. You may need to give evidence in court on occasion, and may also give educational talks in community venues.

Once trained, you work within specialised departments such as the criminal investigation department (CID), the mounted police, child protection services, the drugs squad or traffic police.

Type of person suited to this work

You must have excellent communication skills in order to deal with a variety of people on a daily basis whose position could range from that of a criminal who needs restraining, to a victim who needs careful treatment.

You will need to be non-judgemental, and have the ability to view situations from different perspectives.

You will need courage, initiative and common sense in order to deal with many of the circumstances you will be presented with. You will also need to have good problem-solving skills.

Working conditions

You will be required to work 40 hours a week, covering early, late and night shifts 7 days a week. Part-time or flexible working hours can usually be accommodated.

You will be based at a police station, but the majority of your time will be spent on patrol, either on foot or by car. This means you will be out in all weather conditions, and will travel to many different locations.

Future prospects

You can move upwards to the level of sergeant and inspector. These promotions are subject to examination and interview. To progress further you must demonstrate your skills to a board of judges.

Government cuts led to some widespread job losses over the past few years. The occasional cutback still occurs, but the job market has become more stable recently.

Advantages/disadvantages

You will be meeting new challenges each day and adapting to unusual environments, which will keep you mentally and physically alert and ensures the work never gets dull.

You will be responsible for promoting safety and wellbeing in the local community, which is rewarding.

You will be required to work unsociable hours including nights and weekends.

You will have to deal with difficult, distressed and occasionally violent members of the public.

Money guide

The starting salary varies between forces. For instance, salaries tend to be higher in the Metropolitan Police.

A typical constable starting salary is £23,000. Once you have completed your initial training this rises to £25,300 to £26,000.

For senior officers, such as sergeants and chief inspectors, salaries can rise to between £35,610 and £53,919.

London weighting of up to £6,501 is available for all ranks and key benefits can include free London travel, flexible hours and key worker living benefits.

Related opportunities

- Police Support Worker p530
- Road Safety Officer p592
- Security Officer/Manager/Door Supervisor p541

Further information

Civil Nuclear Constabulary
www.cnc.police.uk

Police Oracle
www.policeoracle.com

Police Recruitment
www.policecouldyou.co.uk

POLICE SUPPORT WORKER

ENTRY LEVEL 2

Qualifications and courses

There are no specific academic requirements for entry to the police force as a support worker, but most employers prefer that you are educated to GCSE standard or equivalent. You must also be aged 18 or over, a UK or European Union national, or come from within the European Economic Area.

There are several qualifications that would be viewed favourably by employers. These include an NVQ Level 2 or BTEC First Diploma in Public Services, and the BTEC National Diploma in Uniformed Public Services. Entry requirements for these courses are usually 5 GCSEs/ National 5s (A*–C/A–C) or equivalent, including English and Maths.

If you reach interview stage, you will need to have medical, criminal record and other background checks to assess your suitability for the role. You must declare any previous convictions prior to this stage.

Once you have been accepted onto the force, your training will be provided by a more experienced support worker and you will learn on the job. Training usually lasts between 3 weeks and 3 months.

What the work involves

Police support workers are the first point of contact for members of the public in a police station.

You will be responsible for answering and directing calls, passing walk-ins to appropriate members of staff, and carrying out general administrative tasks within the station.

You will be on the front desk, so will receive firearms, knives, driving licences and any other paraphernalia seized by police whilst on patrol. You will also be the first point of contact for missing persons and lost property enquiries. You will need to look after victims and witnesses when they come into the station, which may require providing First Aid on occasion.

Type of person suited to this work

You must have excellent communication skills in order to deal with a wide variety of people on a daily basis, ranging from victims to aggressive detainees. Assertiveness, confidence and sensitivity are all desirable personality traits.

You should be happy working within a team, supporting your colleagues, taking directions, and working on your own initiative when required.

You will also need to adhere to confidentiality, diversity and data protection issues.

Working conditions

You will usually work a 37-hour week based on a shift pattern, which will require early morning and weekend work. Part-time and flexible working hours are commonly available.

You will be based within a police station, and will spend most of your time on the front desk answering queries or updating information on a computer. It is unlikely that you will need to travel in the course of your working day.

Stations can get very busy at times, so you should expect to work in pressurised and potentially stressful conditions at times.

Future prospects

The police force operates throughout the length and breadth of the UK, so there are opportunities in all regional forces.

Opportunities for promotion within a station are limited by its size. Larger establishments may have room to move you to a more senior, supervisory role whereas the smaller ones will not be able to.

You could move to a more specialised area of support work, such as manning the crime helpdesk, or working in an enquiry centre. It is possible to train as a police officer from a support role.

Advantages/disadvantages

You will be working within a close-knit team, so your support work will be essential to the successful running of the station.

You will encounter a wide variety of people and stories so your working day will be very diverse with no two days being the same.

You will have to deal with difficult, distressed and occasionally violent members of the public which can be stressful.

Money guide

The starting salary for an entry-level police support worker is about £15,500 per year.

With a couple of years' experience, this should rise to around £19,000.

If you pursue promotion and attain a high level administrative role, or become a police officer, you could earn in excess of £40,000.

Related opportunities

- Civil Service Administrative Officer p13
- Police Community Support Officer p528
- Secretary p50

Further information

Police Oracle
www.policeoracle.com

Police Recruitment
www.policecouldyou.co.uk

PRISON GOVERNOR/OPERATIONAL MANAGER

ENTRY LEVEL 3

Qualifications and courses

Most prison governors enter the profession as a prison officer. Generally, requirements for candidates include good health and physical fitness, Commonwealth, British or European Union citizenship and, if you are going to work with inmates under 18 years of age, Disclosure and Barring Service (DBS) clearance.

Training is largely on the job and would be tailored to individual needs to take into account any previous and relevant work experience.

Once you have gained experience as a prison officer you will need to work your way through supervisory and senior positions, taking relevant work-related qualifications as you go, in order to become a prison governor.

In England and Wales, the National Offender Management Service (NOMS) provides a graduate training scheme as an alternative route into the profession. It is designed to encourage rapid progression through the grades into a management position. To follow this route you will need at least a 2.1 degree.

On the NOMS graduate programme you would complete full prison officer training followed by up to a year working as a prison officer. You may then progress to a senior role with responsibility for other staff members before taking up an operational management post.

In Scotland, prison officers are able to apply for promotions once they complete their 1-year probationary period. Applications are assessed based on individual merit and ability.

What the work involves

Prison governors/operational managers are responsible for the overall running and security of the establishment.

You will supervise security measures, make inspections, carry out disciplinary procedures, and advise both staff and inmates on behavioural standards and guidelines. You will also be dealing with each prisoner's casework and administration. This will include processing parole applications and complaints, and require liaison with other social and healthcare professionals.

You will be working within strict parameters set out by the government, and must ensure that you meet their targets on service, health and safety, and prisoner welfare and development.

Type of person suited to this work

You will need excellent communication skills, including confidence, assertiveness and a motivational ability, all of which will be essential when managing and inspiring staff, and also for building effective relationships with inmates.

You must have integrity and be committed to working with vulnerable people with various social issues. This should include respect for those in your care, and for the other professionals working around you.

Working conditions

You will be expected to work on a shift basis, including night and weekend hours, in order to meet the 24-hour needs of the prison. On average, you will work a 39-hour week.

You could work in a modern prison with excellent facilities, or an older, more austere establishment that will come with maintenance problems and perhaps a less comfortable working environment.

Future prospects

Prisons are located in large cities, towns and very rural locations, so you have a good range of options regarding the working environment that would most suit you.

Prison governors are at the top of their sector, so only sideways movements are possible. You could opt to work in a specialist institution, such as one dealing with inmates with specific medical needs. Extra qualifications may be required for this.

Vacancies may possibly be affected by budget cuts. Although these cuts have mainly taken place, a lot of prisons are still trying to reduce costs.

Advantages/disadvantages

You could be responsible for turning the lives of inmates around, both by providing them with opportunities whilst serving their sentence, and also by encouraging them to pursue better lives when they leave.

You may have to control difficult and violent situations at times.

Money guide

On gaining the full title and responsibilities of a prison governor, you could earn between £47,000 and £83,000.

Related opportunities

- Police Community Support Officer p528
- Police Officer p529
- Prison Officer/Instructor p532

Further information

HM Prison Service
www.gov.uk/government/organisations/hm-prison-service

Scottish Prison Service
www.sps.gov.uk

PRISON OFFICER/ INSTRUCTOR

ENTRY LEVEL 2

Qualifications and courses

There are no specific academic requirements in England and Wales, although some GCSEs (A*–C), including English and Maths, could be useful. In Scotland you need to have 5 National 5s (A–C), including English and Maths, and/or experience in a people-facing role.

You will need to pass an entrance test, assessment day, medical examination, fitness test and a Disclosure and Barring Service (DBS) check, as well as meet the nationality criteria outlined on HM Prison Service's website. You must be at least 18 years old, not an undischarged bankrupt or a member of a group or organisation that the Prison Service considers racist.

Before you can start work as a prison officer you will need to undergo an 8-week entry-level training course. During your probation period you will also be expected to complete a NVQ Level 3 in Custodial Care.

For graduates in England and Wales there is a National Offender Management Service (NOMS) Graduate Programme which aims to fast-track competent graduates into managerial roles. You must have a 2.1 degree or higher in order to qualify.

If you are hoping to become a prison instructor you will need a recognised teaching qualification, a Level 3 vocational qualification and experience in the field you will be teaching. You may also need to hold a qualification in health and safety and be able to demonstrate teaching or supervisory experience.

What the work involves

Prison officers are responsible for supervising inmates within a secure institution. Prison instructors undertake the same duties as prison officers, but are also responsible for training prisoners in order to help them develop new skills and gain qualifications.

You will need to build positive relationships with the prisoners in your care in order to educate and encourage them to pursue a law-abiding life.

You could work with a variety of inmates, ranging from high risk criminals in top security institutions, to those with minor offences in low security prisons.

Type of person suited to this work

You should have excellent communication skills and be a confident person so that you can interact positively with inmates whilst also retaining your authority when necessary.

You must be non-judgemental and have respect for the prisoners in your care. The ability to remain calm in pressurised or uncomfortable situations is also an asset.

Prison instructors should be approachable and patient. You will need to be understanding and encouraging in order to help prisoners learn and progress.

Working conditions

You will usually work 39 hours a week. Prison officers will work on a shift basis including night and weekend shifts, but prison instructors usually only work during the week.

Most work is indoors and within a prison. Prison officers will also be responsible for supervising outdoor exercise and patrolling the prison grounds. Prison instructors will work in a setting suitable for their subject, for example a workshop within the prison, or in the grounds if they are teaching horticulture.

Some travel between prisons may be expected to provide extra staffing on occasion. Prison officers may also have to escort prisoners to and from court appearances.

Future prospects

Prison officers and prison instructors can move into a position as a senior officer or principal officer of a prison. Promotion is based solely on merit, so the more you put in the more you can get out of this career.

The number of vacancies available may have been affected by budget cuts and the drive to reduce prison costs.

Advantages/disadvantages

Helping to rehabilitate and educate prisoners can be rewarding, and you will be providing an important public service.

Working in a prison environment can be claustrophobic and stifling.

You may be faced with difficult and occasionally violent prisoners, which can be both stressful and unpleasant.

Money guide

The national starting salary for officers in England and Wales is £18,720, which includes a base salary and 17% addition for working unsocial hours. You can also opt to commit to working an additional 4 hours a week on an ongoing basis at an enhanced rate, increasing the starting salary to £20,796.

Senior managers with significant experience can earn up to £82,892.

In Scotland, the starting salary is £16,081. Good performance can increase your salary to £21,400 within 5 years.

Instructors can earn between £19,500 and £25,260 a year.

Related opportunities

- Police Officer p529
- Police Support Worker p530
- Social Worker p557

Further information

HM Prison Service
www.gov.uk/government/organisations/hm-prison-service

Qualifications and courses

There are no formal entry qualifications for this work. However, while it is possible to be taken on by an investigations company in a junior role and train on the job, it is difficult as many entrants have had previous relevant experience in a related job such as the police, law, customs and excise or security work.

Therefore applicants new to the role will benefit from having a relevant qualification. This could be a degree in subjects such as investigative studies or crime and investigation, an Association of British Investigators (ABI) membership qualification or the online Foundation Private Investigation Course from the Institute of Professional Investigators (IPI).

Whatever your training, it should be accepted by the Security Industry Authority (SIA) and include topics on the law, investigative methods and equipment. The SIA are in the process of considering a new regulation system for private investigators (PIs) which may involve needing a licence to practise. Check with the SIA directly for the latest developments.

Candidates who are just starting out can try approaching companies about work shadowing. Another option is to start out working on a freelance basis. Let local investigators know in case any opportunities arise.

You will need a driving licence.

What the work involves

You will be collecting information for a private client or a solicitor by asking questions, researching, obtaining evidence and making sense of what you find out.

PIs do a variety of different jobs such as surveillance, tracing people, serving legal documents or investigating road accidents, suspected fraud and employee backgrounds.

You could be recording your findings using a computer, and you may be asked to present your findings in court or to a large company. You will probably take witness statements, attend court hearings and give evidence.

Type of person suited to this work

Much of the day-to-day work of this exciting-sounding job is actually quite routine, so you will need to be patient and persistent and be happy with your own company as you will be predominantly working independently.

You need to have a keen interest in developing a working knowledge of the law.

You will need to have excellent communications skills, both spoken and written in order to write reports and take witness statements. You may need to calm down anxious or aggressive people when you serve legal papers or repossess belongings in order to pay a debt.

Working conditions

Most of your working hours will be spent driving or walking around. You could be in your vehicle for hours or out in all weathers.

Hours are irregular and in some cases they could be long and include evening and weekend work.

You will be at risk of assault from aggressive individuals who you are serving with legal papers.

Future prospects

With the introduction of licensing there may be more opportunities for those with licences. A lot of the work is for legal, insurance or financial companies.

Some private investigators go on to take further qualifications and specialise in areas such as commercial piracy or insurance fraud. A few set up their own agencies and others move into supervisory or security management work.

There is the opportunity to progress into a managerial or senior investigator role at bigger agencies.

Advantages/disadvantages

PIs are usually self-employed and so need to buy their own equipment. Licences and training will also add to the expense.

A lot of the work is routine, but PIs say that there is a lot of satisfaction when after months of patient work you manage to find the evidence your client needs.

Money guide

Starting salaries range between £12,500 and £15,000 per year.

Well-qualified specialists working in corporate investigation can earn between £50,000 and £100,000.

Clients may pay for some expenses, such as hotel or restaurant bills, and PIs who work for companies or agencies may get a vehicle allowance.

Related opportunities

- Forensic Computer Analyst p525
- Police Officer p529
- Store Detective p542

Further information

Academy of Professional Investigation
www.pi-academy.com

Institute of Professional Investigators
www.ipi.org.uk

Security Industry Authority
www.sia.homeoffice.gov.uk

The Association of British Investigators
www.theabi.org.uk

PROBATION OFFICER

ENTRY LEVEL 6

Qualifications and courses

You will need to work as a probation service officer (PSO) before training to be a probation officer. Pre-entry experience of working with offenders or other vulnerable groups, for example with prison visiting services, victim support services or community payback teams, is often required when applying for PSO jobs.

Once you are in a PSO position, there are 2 ways to train to work as a probation officer in England and Wales. The first is to undertake a 3-year Honours degree in Community Justice and a Level 5 Vocational Qualification Diploma in Probation Practice (VQ5).

The second way, if you already have an Honours degree that includes at least 50% criminology, community justice, criminal justice or police studies, is to take the work-based Graduate Diploma in Community Justice as well as the VQ5.

In Scotland, in order to join the Probation Service you must complete a 4-year Honours degree in social work which has been approved by the Scottish Social Services Council (SSSC), and gain relevant experience. Alternatively there is a postgraduate scheme available for candidates with a degree in a different subject. Northern Ireland has a similar approach, with candidates needing a degree in social work and experience working with offenders.

What the work involves

Probation officers protect the public by assessing the risk that offenders pose to the community and working out how to limit that risk.

You will work with offenders before, during and after their sentencing. This will include ensuring they carry out their punishment, making them aware of the consequences of their offences and helping them back into the community. You will construct and deliver programmes to change offenders' behaviour and attitude.

You will prepare pre-sentence reports (PSRs) to advise judges on sentencing and prepare risk assessments for prisons and parole review boards, which may then contribute towards a decision on the early release of an offender.

Type of person suited to this work

You will need to have the ability to gain the trust and confidence of offenders and have a fair and non-judgemental approach. Good communication skills will be helpful.

Organisational skills are essential as you will often be planning your own workload. An ability to write clearly and accurately will be needed for reports and risk assessments. Employers also look for good teamwork skills and experience of the criminal justice system.

As you may face stressful situations and setbacks, strong motivation and commitment is important.

Working conditions

Typically you will work between 37 and 40 hours a week. Hours are not always regular and you may have to work in the evenings and at weekends, but you will usually get extra time off to make up for unsocial hours.

You will work from an office but will also be expected to travel to courts and prisons and community programmes on a regular basis.

Future prospects

You can specialise in areas such as managing approved premises, which provide accommodation for people on bail, or drug treatment and testing orders. Probation officers are offered frequent opportunities for training.

With experience there is a possibility of moving to a managerial role as a senior probation officer. Eventually you may become an area manager.

Recruitment may be affected by budget cuts. Most cuts have already happened, but plans to cut £215 million from the annual budget for legal aid and to privatise and outsource 70% of probation services mean the future state of the job market could be uncertain.

Advantages/disadvantages

Providing a public service and helping to rehabilitate prisoners can be deeply rewarding.

You may meet difficult or violent offenders which could be stressful or distressing.

Money guide

Salaries differ between probation trusts, but probation service officers typically earn between £21,000 and £27,000 a year.

Qualified probation officers usually earn between £28,000 and £36,000.

Salaries for assistant chief officer posts start at around £50,000.

Related opportunities

- Prison Officer/Instructor p532
- Social Worker p557
- Victim Care Officer p560

Further information

Ministry of Justice
www.justice.gov.uk

Probation Board for Northern Ireland
www.pbni.org.uk

Skills for Justice
www.sfjuk.com

ROYAL AIR FORCE AIRMAN/WOMAN

ENTRY LEVEL 2

Qualifications and courses

The Royal Air Force (RAF) has detailed eligibility requirements. Entrants need to be at least 15 years old (those under 18 must have parental consent) and you must be a British Citizen, British National, British/Dual National, Commonwealth Citizen or Irish Republic National. There are further requirements for residency, health and fitness. Details of the exact criteria you must meet can be found on the RAF Careers website.

Educational requirements vary depending on the type of job. Some positions, such as physical training instructor or flight operations assistant, only require GCSEs/National 5s, whereas some others, such as registered nurse, will require a degree. Whatever the role, you will need to pass rigorous medical and health tests as well a range of interviews and written tests during the selection process.

Once accepted into the RAF you will complete a 9-week training course at RAF Halton in Buckinghamshire, which will cover fitness and weapons training. On completion of these general elements you will then start on more specialised training for your chosen trade, which can take between 3 weeks and 18 months.

What the work involves

The RAF is responsible for protecting UK airspace, performing search and rescue missions offshore and on land, transporting aid to the victims of war and natural disaster, and pursuing military action in a war situation. Opportunities include positions in catering, aircrew, engineering, protection and medical support.

You will work within a team of other RAF professionals, under the guidance of an officer.

You will also be expected to undertake general military duties, such as guarding RAF bases, and taking part in training exercises and military initiatives.

Type of person suited to this work

You should be able to work well within a team. This includes being able to follow orders, work calmly under pressure, support colleagues and use your own initiative when necessary.

You should be self-disciplined in order to maintain high levels of fitness, mental agility and a positive attitude to your work.

You should be good at interpreting and analysing information, both oral and written.

Working conditions

Airmen/women usually work regular office hours, but you are required to be available for duty at all times in case of an emergency. There are also occasional social functions or other duties that need to be fulfilled over weekends.

You will be stationed at an RAF base, many of which have all the amenities of a small town.

You should be prepared to be posted overseas at short notice, and to spend long periods of time away from friends and family.

Future prospects

On joining the RAF as an airman/woman you will usually be asked to stay for between 6 and 12 years, though many people stay longer.

After 6 months, or on completion of specialist training, you should be promoted to leading airman/woman and from there you can work up the ranks to the position of corporal or higher. Promotion is based on merit, so you will be rewarded for the hard work that you put in.

Prospects for new and existing recruits may be affected by defence budget cuts with an aim to reduce personnel by about 1,500 by 2020. Nevertheless, there are still good opportunities if you meet the selection criteria.

Advantages/disadvantages

You will work on a wide variety of assignments within a supportive team environment, so each day will be both diverse and interesting.

There are good training schemes and potential for promotion and career progression within the RAF.

You may have to enter war situations, which can be traumatic and stressful.

Money guide

There is an established pay structure for RAF airmen/women.

During training you can expect to be paid £14,348 per year. Once you are fully qualified your salary will increase to £17,767.

Senior level airmen/women will earn between £18,245 and £29,357 per year. Corporals can expect to earn between £26,785 and £33,660, and sergeants between £30,445 and £37,461.

Related opportunities

- Air Traffic Controller p567
- Army Soldier p517
- Royal Air Force Officer p536

Further information

RAF Careers
www.raf.mod.uk/careers

RAF Halton
www.raf.mod.uk/rafhalton

ROYAL AIR FORCE OFFICER

ENTRY LEVEL 3

Qualifications and courses

The Royal Air Force (RAF) has detailed eligibility requirements concerning age, nationality, residency, health and fitness. Details of the exact criteria you must meet can be found on the RAF Careers website. All RAF roles are now open to both men and women except for regiment officer and regiment gunner, which remain open only to men.

Educational requirements vary depending on the type of job. Some positions, such as regiment officer or pilot, require 5 GCSEs/National 5s (A*–C/A–C) and 2 A levels/3 H grades. Some others, such as medical officer, will require a degree.

Whatever the role, you will need to pass rigorous medical and health tests, as well as a range of interviews and written and aptitude tests during the selection process. This will take place at the RAF College Cranwell in Lincolnshire.

For entrance onto related degree courses, you will need 3 A levels/H grades and at least 5 GCSEs/National 5s (A*–C/A–C) or equivalent, including English, Maths and a science. The RAF also offers sponsorship to sixth form and university students.

As a new recruit you will have to complete a 30-week initial officer training course at Cranwell where you will be taught a variety of skills such as service knowledge and leadership skills. If you join the RAF with a professional qualification this initial training may be reduced to 12 weeks. You will then go on to specialise.

What the work involves

The RAF is responsible for protecting UK airspace, performing search and rescue missions offshore and on land, transporting aid to the victims of war and natural disaster, and pursuing military action in a war situation.

RAF officers are responsible for managing, leading and inspiring a team of airmen.

You will occupy a specialist post within the RAF, such as that of a pilot, engineer, catering manager or medical officer.

You will be involved in planning and implementing various procedures from rescues to humanitarian aid drops.

Type of person suited to this work

You must have excellent communication skills as you will be responsible for briefing, leading and motivating your team. This also includes being able to listen to and get on with all team members.

You will be called upon to make difficult decisions in highly pressurised situations, so must be able to think on your feet in order to reach mature, responsible conclusions.

You must be physically fit and mentally alert.

Working conditions

Officers usually work regular office hours, but you are required to be available for duty at all times in case of an emergency.

There are also occasional social functions or other duties that need to be fulfilled over weekends.

You will be stationed at an RAF base, many of which have all the amenities of a small town, including shops, banks, a gym and childcare facilities.

You should be prepared to be posted overseas at short notice, and to spend long periods of time away from friends and family.

Future prospects

On joining the RAF as an officer you sign up to a minimum length of service that ranges from 6 to 12 years according to your specialisation.

There is defined career progression through the ranks from flying officer to flight lieutenant, squadron leader, wing commander, group captain and further if you wish.

The training, qualifications and personal skills that come with being an RAF officer are easily transferred to a number of civilian positions.

Although prospects for new and existing recruits may be affected by defence budget cuts, there are still good opportunities if you meet the selection criteria.

Advantages/disadvantages

You will be responsible for training and organising a team that will carry out essential defence and humanitarian functions for the UK and the world.

You may have to enter combat situations which can be distressing and unpleasant.

Money guide

There are different pay scales for some specialist officers and for people who join as graduates or with professional qualifications.

Entering the RAF without a degree, a pilot officer can expect to earn £24,615 as a starting salary. If you hold a degree and enter as a flying officer, your starting wages will be £29,586 to £32,702 per year.

On promotion to flight lieutenant your salary will increase to £37,915 to £45,090 per year.

Squadron leaders can earn between £47,760 and £57,199.

Related opportunities

- Air Traffic Controller p567
- Royal Air Force Airman/woman p535
- Royal Navy Officer p539

Further information

RAF College Cranwell
www.raf.mod.uk/rafcranwell

ROYAL MARINES COMMANDO

ENTRY LEVEL 1

Qualifications and courses

The Royal Navy has detailed eligibility requirements. Only men can serve in the Royal Marines at this time and they must be least 16 years old to be a commando (those under 18 must have parental consent). You must be a British Citizen, British National, British/Dual National, Commonwealth Citizen or Irish Republic National. There are further requirements for residency, health and fitness. Details of the exact criteria you must meet can be found on the Royal Navy Careers website.

There is a rigorous selection process. You will need to pass a recruit test, which covers English, maths, mechanics and problem solving, attend an interview and pass medical and fitness examinations.

You will also have to undertake the Potential Royal Marines Course. This lasts 2.5 days and is designed to test your fitness, determination, stamina and mental ability. This is a gruelling assessment designed to push you to your limits, so you will have to train and prepare for it for a number of months.

There are no academic qualification requirements for entry but a career in the Royal Marines offers the opportunity to gain qualifications related to your area of specialism as your career progresses.

What the work involves

The Royal Marines are a specialist, highly trained, amphibious division of the Royal Navy. They carry out operations on land, at sea or in the air. They operate in combat, peacekeeping and humanitarian situations, and also as a law enforcement agency at sea.

You will be a commando and rifleman, working within an operational commando unit. You will be ready to take immediate action in any emergency or threat to national security, and this means performing to a very high standard at all times whether on land or at sea.

You will specialise either in general duties or in one of 26 trades, including assault engineer, mountain leader or swimmer canoeist.

Type of person suited to this work

You will need high levels of fitness, discipline, commitment and self-confidence in order to get through one of the most demanding and gruelling training programmes in the armed forces prior to qualifying as a commando.

You must be able to work well within a team and also use your own initiative when required. The ability to lead and motivate others is also an asset.

You should be level-headed and be able to react quickly and logically when under pressure. Courage and determination are also necessary in order to head into combat situations.

Working conditions

You will usually work 37 hours a week, unless you are on an operation or in training. In these instances, you could expect to work long, unpredictable hours. Even if you are not at work, though, you will always be on-call in case of emergency.

You could be stationed or deployed anywhere in the world at short notice, including undertaking operations in areas of desert, jungle, and even out in the Arctic.

You will be expected to wear a uniform.

Future prospects

Within the UK, you are most likely to be stationed within the south-west of England or in Scotland, as that is where the majority of naval bases are located.

You will be expected to serve with the Royal Marines for 22 years, although you can leave at any point after completing the minimum 3 years of service and giving 12 months' notice.

You will be promoted on merit, so hard work should be rewarded. You could move up the ranks from lance corporal right up to warrant officer 1.

Although prospects for new and existing recruits may be affected by defence budget cuts, there are still good opportunities if you meet the selection criteria. Most of the job cuts have already occurred with the Royal Navy and any further cuts are unlikely to come from the Royal Marines. Consequently, the job market should be quite steady.

Advantages/disadvantages

You will be operating at your optimum level of mental and physical fitness, meeting new challenges each day and adapting to unusual and inhospitable situations.

You will be working within a close-knit team, providing essential services such as delivering aid or maintaining order in areas across the globe.

You are continually on-call, and could be sent anywhere in the world at a moment's notice.

Money guide

New entrants to the Royal Marines as general duties Marines receive a starting salary of around £14,492, rising to between £17,945 and £29,651 on completion of initial training.

If you move up the ranks and reach the level of warrant officer 1 you should earn £39,548 to £47,902.

Related opportunities

- Army Officer p516
- Army Soldier p517
- Royal Marines Officer p538

Further information

Royal Marines
www.royalnavy.mod.uk/royalmarines

ROYAL MARINES OFFICER

ENTRY LEVEL 4

Qualifications and courses

The minimum criteria for entry to officer training in the Royal Navy are 5 GCSEs/National 5s (A*–C/A–C), including English and Maths, and 180 UCAS points from the UCAS tariff table (including 2 non-overlapping A level/H grade subjects with each subject providing at least 45 UCAS points). Graduates in any subject are welcome and have more opportunities open to them than non-graduates. It is also possible to study for a fully funded Honours degree while working for the Royal Navy.

Only men can serve in the Royal Marines at this time and you must be between 17 and 25 years old to enter. You must also meet particular nationality, residency, health and fitness criteria, which are outlined on the Royal Navy's website.

You will attend a 3-day Potential Officers Course, which is a gruelling assessment designed to push you to your limits. If you successfully complete the assessment you will be invited to sit tests in maths, reasoning, accuracy, written communication, spatial orientation, leadership and problem solving, and undergo a series of interviews.

If you are selected to train as an officer, you will then have to complete a further 15-month programme prior to being given your own team to lead.

What the work involves

The Royal Marines carry out operations on land, at sea or in the air. They operate in combat, peacekeeping and humanitarian situations, and also as a law enforcement agency at sea.

You will be responsible for leading and managing a team both on training operations and on real missions including combat situations and peacekeeping tasks. You will be in charge of training your team, keeping them disciplined and looking out for their welfare.

You will be given the opportunity to specialise in 1 of 10 areas, including weapons training, signals, physical training, or as a pilot.

Type of person suited to this work

You will need high levels of fitness, discipline, commitment and self-confidence in order to get through the demanding and gruelling training programme prior to qualifying as an officer.

You must be able to lead and motivate your team, looking out for their welfare and making decisions for them in dangerous and stressful conditions.

You should be able to focus fully on the operations you undertake in order to function at your maximum level of mental and physical capacity.

Working conditions

You will usually work 37 hours a week, unless you are on an operation or in training. In these instances, you could expect to work long, unpredictable hours. Even if you are not at work, you are always on-call in case of emergency.

You could be stationed or deployed anywhere in the world at short notice, including undertaking operations in areas of desert, jungle, and even out in the Arctic.

You will be expected to wear a uniform, and specialised clothing when required.

Future prospects

Competition for entry as a Royal Marines officer is fierce. You will be expected to join on a 12-year commission and must serve at least 3–5 years of this. 12 months' notice is required prior to departure.

You will normally move appointments every other year, so you will be able to experience numerous areas of work in various locations throughout your career.

Promotion is awarded based on merit and you could work through the ranks from 2nd lieutenant right up to major-general.

Although prospects for new and existing recruits may be affected by defence budget cuts there are still good opportunities if you meet the selection criteria.

Advantages/disadvantages

You will be operating at your optimum level of mental and physical fitness, meeting new challenges each day and adapting to unusual and inhospitable situations.

You will be working within a close-knit team, leading them through essential operations such as delivering aid or maintaining order in areas across the globe.

Money guide

Entrants who do not have a degree can expect a starting salary of £16,073 at the start of their training, rising to £25,220 once qualified.

Graduates can expect a starting salary of between £29,587 and £32,703.

With experience those who rise to captain/colonel could earn £81,310 to £89,408.

Related opportunities

- Army Officer p516
- Army Soldier p517
- Royal Marines Commando p537

Further information

Royal Marines
www.royalnavy.mod.uk/royalmarines

ROYAL NAVY OFFICER

ENTRY LEVEL 4

Qualifications and courses

You will need to be at least 151.5cm tall, be of proportionate weight and, upon entry, you must be aged 16 or over. A medical, with strict eyesight standards, must be passed and you must meet the Royal Navy nationality and residence requirements. Both men and women are accepted in most roles.

The minimum requirements for officer entry are 5 GCSEs/National 5s (A*–C/A–C), including English and Maths, and a minimum of 180 UCAS points (each A level/H grade subject must be allocated at least 45 UCAS points). Some officer roles have more specific qualifications, details of which can be found on the Royal Navy's website.

Prospective entrants who want to go to sixth form college or university may be able to acquire a Royal Navy-funded scholarship or bursary to help pay for their study. Those who have already graduated from university can apply to the Royal Navy through Direct Graduate Entry.

All candidates undergo selection interviews, tests and a medical examination before they reach the Admiralty Interview Board (AIB) stage. The tests include mental agility, physical fitness, communication and maths.

Upon entry, there are 2 phases of officer training. Initial training lasts for 30 weeks, first at Dartmouth and then at sea. You then go on to professional training, the length and location of which depends on your job.

What the work involves

You will command and train ratings, looking after their welfare, development and discipline.

Your day-to-day work will involve you managing operations in 1 of 4 areas of duty: warfare officer, engineer officer, supply officer or specialist officer (for example chaplain, doctor or dentist).

Your ship may be sent into combat or on peacekeeping duties.

You may be tasked to do a specific job such as policing the North Sea fishing grounds or helping out in a disaster situation.

Type of person suited to this work

Officers especially need top-level leadership and communication skills as well as good judgement.

You will be required to inspire ratings, be resourceful and have excellent communication skills. You should have good levels of physical fitness and stamina.

You should also have a very strong sense of responsibility as your decisions may impact upon your colleagues' safety as well as your own. You should display a very high level of personal awareness and a keen sense of personal safety.

Working conditions

Most of your work will be on-board a ship or submarine, or at land-based establishments in Britain or overseas. At sea, conditions can be cold, cramped and damp. You will need to wear a uniform, and protective clothing when necessary.

Hours vary but you will usually work 8-hour turns of duty on a shift rota including weekends and holidays.

You may find yourself working in a dangerous or highly unpredictable situation.

Future prospects

There are annual vacancies but some specialisms are more competitive than others.

A naval college entrant usually starts out as midshipman, rising to sub-lieutenant after 2 years. A graduate starts as sub-lieutenant, rising to lieutenant commander by their early 30s. If you have the right qualities you can progress on to the ranks of commander, captain and, for a few, admiral.

Although prospects for new and existing recruits may be affected by defence budget cuts there are still good opportunities if you meet the selection criteria.

Advantages/disadvantages

You will be trained to a high level and will be offered a resettlement package to help you find work in civilian life when you leave.

You will be living in cramped conditions with lots of other people. However, most officers say that they enjoy the feeling of camaraderie on-board and make life-long friendships.

Money guide

Entering this career without a degree you can expect to start on £16,073 per year, rising to £25,220 once you complete your training.

Graduates entering this career can start on £29,587 to £32,703.

As you rise through the ranks and gain experience, your salary can range from £37,916 to £89,408 per year.

Related opportunities

- Army Officer p516
- Royal Marines Officer p538
- Royal Navy Rating p540

Further information

Royal Navy Careers
www.royalnavy.mod.uk

Welbeck College
www.dsfc.ac.uk

ROYAL NAVY RATING

ENTRY LEVEL 1

Qualifications and courses

There are no formal qualifications for entry but holding at least 2 GCSEs/National 5s (A*–C/A–C) or equivalent is helpful. Typically, you must be 16 to 37 years of age to apply. Some specialist trades have specific entry requirements and a higher age for admission.

Selection takes place at local armed forces careers offices, where you will be required to take several tests including numeracy, English language, reasoning and mechanical comprehension. If you are successful you will be invited for an interview and be expected to pass a medical assessment and fitness test.

After passing the recruitment process you will attend a 4-day induction course. Upon entry you will undertake 10 weeks' basic training, followed by specialist training in your chosen trade.

You will join the Royal Navy on a Full Career, which lasts 18 years. You can leave after completing 2.5 years but must give 12 months' notice.

What the work involves

The Royal Navy protects the UK's ports and coastline, and also undertakes international missions such as delivering humanitarian aid, entering combat and enforcing the law on the seas.

Royal Navy ratings work on-board a ship, submarine or onshore, and are responsible for operating, maintaining and repairing technical equipment.

You will specialise in one of the 6 main trades: medical, warfare, logistics, engineering, fleet air arm, or submarine. These inevitably encompass a wide range of roles from overseeing electrical systems and sensors to providing a medical service for the Royal Navy personnel and their families.

You will also take part in naval exercises and operations in both UK and overseas waters.

Type of person suited to this work

You should be able to work within a team, reacting quickly to orders, working on your own initiative where necessary, and supporting other team members both professionally and emotionally at times.

You must be responsible and decisive and find solutions to problems under difficult or pressurised circumstances. You should also have a methodical and logical approach to your work.

You will need to have a good level of fitness, including the ability to swim and tread water for a number of minutes.

Working conditions

You will usually work 37 hours a week, which can include weekends and public holidays. You will also be on-call at all times, in case of an emergency.

You could be based at sea on a ship or submarine, or in a naval station onshore. Living conditions on ships and submarines tend to be basic, and men and women always sleep in separate accommodation.

You will have to spend long periods of time away from friends and family, and may be posted overseas at a moment's notice.

Future prospects

The career progression for a Royal Navy rating is clearly mapped out. Promotion is awarded based on merit so the harder you work the faster you will progress. The grades that you will move upwards through are able rating, leading rating, petty officer, chief petty officer and warrant officer.

If you have the necessary qualifications you could apply to become an officer. This is a popular route of career progression amongst ratings.

Although prospects for new and existing recruits may be affected by defence budget cuts, there are still good opportunities if you meet the selection criteria.

Advantages/disadvantages

You will be meeting new challenges each day and adapting to unusual and inhospitable situations, which will keep you mentally and physically alert and ensures the work never gets dull.

You will be working within a close-knit team, supporting it both in training and when out on real operations.

As you are continually on-call you could be sent anywhere in the world at a moment's notice.

Money guide

You will enter the Royal Navy as a rating on a starting salary of £14,145.

Once you have completed your training and have qualified as an able rating, you could earn between £17,515 and £28,940.

If you work your way up to warrant officer 1 you could earn between £38,600 and £46,753.

Related opportunities

- Army Soldier p517
- Royal Air Force Officer p536
- Royal Marines Commando p537
- Royal Navy Officer p539

Further information

Royal Navy Careers
www.royalnavy.mod.uk

SECURITY OFFICER/MANAGER/ DOOR SUPERVISOR

ENTRY LEVEL 1

Qualifications and courses

Officer
There are no specific academic qualifications needed, although a good standard of general education would be helpful, as would previous experience of working in the police or armed forces. Employers will carry out personal, work history and possibly criminal records checks.

Security guards must have an industry licence approved by the Security Industry Authority (SIA), unless you are carrying out in-house security for your employer on your employer's premises. You will need to be 18 years old, pass identity and criminal records checks and complete an SIA-approved course. A full list of these can be found on the SIA's website. If the role involves monitoring CCTV you may need an SIA Public Space Surveillance (CCTV) licence.

Manager
In addition to needing the SIA licence, specialist managers or prospective managers can take further part-time courses including Foundation degrees, degrees and postgraduate qualifications in security and risk management. The Security Institute offers a Certificate and Diploma in Security Management.

Door supervisor
You will need an SIA licence, an SIA-approved Level 2 Certificate in Door Supervision and to pass a Disclosure and Barring Service (DBS) check. There are no academic requirements for entry onto the course. Some employers may take you on as a trainee and support you through the training.

What the work involves

Security work is about protecting organisations, people, places, valuable goods or money.

Officer
You might work at reception monitoring visitors and deliveries or you might patrol a site, checking for intruders or fire risks. You might also monitor CCTV footage and respond to any issues noticed through it.

Manager
You will manage a team and be responsible for their work, training and supervision. You will do security surveys, give advice on improvements and liaise with other organisations such as the emergency services.

Door supervisor
You will stand at the entrance to a building and help control people entering and leaving, judging whether or not they should be allowed on the premises. You could also search bags for potentially dangerous items and assist the police if trouble breaks out.

Type of person suited to this work

You will need to be a mature, responsible and honest person. You should be keen on technology and keep up to date with new security systems. You will also have to keep records of all incidents, so you must be happy to do paperwork.

For certain types of security work, you will need to be physically fit and healthy. You will also need to be able to remain calm in the face of confrontation.

To become a manager you will need a great deal of experience in security work as well as a talent for motivating a team of staff.

Working conditions

If you are a door supervisor you will be based in one location which could be inside, or outside in all weathers. Many security officer/manager jobs involve driving and you will spend a lot of time in a security van.

You will probably be working shifts of up to 12 hours covering days, nights and weekends. Some door supervisors or security officers work permanent nights. You may work a 48-hour week although part-time work is available.

Future prospects

This work will increasingly use sophisticated technology, computer security systems and also biometrics (fingerprint recognition systems) to control access to buildings and other secure areas.

With the right training and technical ability you are likely to be in demand in this growing industry.

Advantages/disadvantages

Your promotion and earnings prospects are excellent.

You could often work alone and be put in vulnerable situations.

Money guide

Officer
Starting out, officers are paid between £12,000 and £15,000 per year. With experience this can rise to £20,000.

Manager
On entry, managers earn around £25,000. With experience, senior managers can earn £50,000 or more.

Door supervisor
Door supervisors tend to be paid by an hourly rate of around £8 to £12 (£15,600 to £23,400 per year). With experience this can rise to £15 per hour for a part-time supervisor.

Related opportunities

- Bodyguard p518
- Police Officer p529
- Prison Officer/Instructor p532

Further information

Security Industry Authority
www.sia.homeoffice.gov.uk

STORE DETECTIVE

ENTRY LEVEL 1

Qualifications and courses

There are no formal entry requirements but you will need to be able to write clearly and accurately. A GCSE/ National 5 in English or a Key Skill in Communication may be useful.

A Security Industry Authority (SIA) licence may be required if you are employed by an agency or contractor. For this you will need to be aged 18 or older, pass an identity check and a Disclosure and Barring Service (DBS) check, and have completed relevant training approved by the SIA. Training can be completed before beginning work or undertaken part time while working at your first job. An additional SIA licence may be required if your job involves using CCTV equipment.

Previous relevant work experience is preferred, especially within the police, armed forces or security industry. An Apprenticeship in Providing Security Services could be helpful.

Once you start work, training is primarily done through courses and on the job with the support of a more experienced store detective. Most companies run an induction course for new employees covering topics such as relevant criminal law and principles of investigation.

Store detectives can work towards a BTEC Level 2 Certificate in Providing Security Services or a City & Guilds Level 3 Award in Security Operations.

What the work involves

You will be preventing and detecting theft or fraud in a retail outlet. You might need to chase the suspected offender, search them and make arrests. You will then need to contact the police and describe your observations.

Working undercover, wearing plain clothes, you will merge with shoppers, looking out for suspicious behaviour or theft.

Using a radio you will call for assistance and listen for alerts from other staff about known offenders entering the store.

You will make notes of any incidents and may need to use these if a decision is made to prosecute. Occasionally you will have to give evidence in court. If trouble does break out, you may also need to take evidence from any witnesses.

You may also be involved with preventing the use of stolen credit cards.

Type of person suited to this work

You need to have excellent communications skills as it will be your responsibility to deal with customers who have become anxious or aggressive when challenged.

Your written reports will be used in court if you prosecute and you will need to be fluent and precise to get a conviction.

You must have good observation skills in order to spot suspicious behaviour and also remember the faces of known shoplifters.

You should be able to plan and think ahead so that when needed you can act quickly.

You will need to be mature, responsible and be able to handle difficult situations sensitively.

Working conditions

You will spend the majority of your time on your feet, in the store.

A 40-hour week is common and you may work shifts to cover long opening hours and weekends.

You might wear a uniform but the majority wear their own clothes to blend in.

Future prospects

Shoplifters cost retail businesses more than £2 billion a year so most large shops in the UK employ store detectives to minimise their losses.

Some retail chains employ their own detectives, while others use agencies on a contract basis.

After gaining experience, you could become a supervisor or move into more general security management.

Advantages/disadvantages

Apprehending shoplifters can be dangerous.

This job can be a good stepping stone into jobs such as security management.

Money guide

Starting wages are usually between £13,000 and £16,500 per year.

Experienced store detectives generally earn around £18,000. £30,000 is possible for top earners.

Store detectives are sometimes paid hourly with the rate ranging from £6 to £8 per hour. Working overtime can boost wages.

Related opportunities

- Police Officer p529
- Private Investigator p533
- Security Officer/Manager/Door Supervisor p541

Further information

British Security Industry Association
www.bsia.co.uk

Security Industry Authority
www.sia.homeoffice.gov.uk

Social Work and Counselling Services

People who work in this sector are dedicated to caring and talking through people's problems and anxieties to improve their general wellbeing and their future prospects in life. The work requires a lot of patience, an open mind and a friendly and approachable personality. You could be helping people who are distressed and need help and guidance but equally you may be helping people who want to move on to the next stage in their careers or educational choices. Either way, you should be someone who enjoys helping people change their lives for the better. If you are interested in working in this field you need to show that you are compassionate and very good at communicating with people from all walks of life and of all ages. You should also be someone who can maintain a strong sense of professionalism as you could be in a position of trust and you must be very respectful of your clients' privacy.

The jobs featured in this section are listed below. For similar jobs to the ones covered in this section turn to *Healthcare* on page 267 and *Education and Training* on page 175.

CAREERS ADVISER

ENTRY LEVEL 4

Qualifications and courses

There are 2 main routes into this profession: the study of the Qualification in Careers Guidance (QCG) or gaining relevant qualifications through work-based study.

The QCG is a 1-year full-time or 2-year part-time course that combines academic study with work-based learning and leads to the Postgraduate Diploma in Careers Guidance. You normally need a degree to take this course but applicants with significant and relevant work experience would also be able to follow this route. Relevant degree subjects include social work, counselling and psychology and the general entry requirements for a degree are 2 A levels/3 H grades and 5 GCSEs/National 5s (A*–C/A–C).

If you go the work-based route you will need to study for either the OCR Level 4 Diploma in Career Information and Advice or the OCR Level 6 Diploma in Career Guidance and Development while working in an organisation that offers advice or guidance services to clients.

You may choose to study qualifications such as the OCR Level 3 Award for Supporting Clients to Overcome Barriers To Learning and Work or the Level 3 NVQ Certificate in Advice and Guidance as a way of gaining basic sector knowledge before embarking on more formal, specialised training.

You do not always need a professional careers qualification to work as a careers adviser in higher education, although most successful candidates do have one. They also often have experience working in careers or have knowledge of their subject from teaching or industry.

It is common for people to enter this profession after gaining experience in another field, such as social work or teaching.

You will need a Disclosure and Barring Service (DBS) check to work with young people or vulnerable groups.

What the work involves

Researching information about job opportunities in different sectors from newspapers, books, the internet or through visits to employers is all part of the role.

You will help people make realistic choices about education, training and work by listening to their ideas, discussing their interests and skills, and providing information on different jobs. Advisory work is often one to one, but you could also work with large groups. Increasingly advice is being delivered over the phone or via email and instant messaging services.

Careers advisers work with young people in schools/colleges, but also with higher education students or adults.

Type of person suited to this work

Since much of the work involves talking with and listening to people, careers advisers need to have excellent communication skills. You will need to be impartial, allowing people to come to their own decisions rather than making up their minds for them.

Careers information and guidance is largely IT-based, so computer skills are essential, along with the ability to write reports and perform administrative tasks.

You will need to enjoy researching, as you will need to keep up to date with any changes in skills and opportunities available, and with any new qualifications and training routes.

Working conditions

Most of your work is office based, in either a careers centre open to the public or an educational establishment. You would normally work 9am–5pm, Monday to Friday but occasional evening work may also be required.

You may need to travel between different educational establishments and visit employers and training organisations, which means that a driving licence may be required.

Future prospects

Careers advisers work in schools, colleges, universities and adult guidance services – some will be based in one institution, others will work for several organisations.

You could move into a managerial-level post in a careers service, work for a large company as a careers manager or you could become self-employed as a consultant or researcher.

Cutbacks in 2010 led to reduced career services in some areas, which may still be affecting the number of jobs available.

Advantages/disadvantages

The work is varied and can be highly satisfying.

You will work some evenings or weekends to attend school/college parents' evenings and for careers events.

The job also includes a great deal of administrative work.

Money guide

Starting salaries range from £18,000 to £20,000 a year.

With experience and qualifications salaries can increase to £20,000–£27,500.

As a senior manager you could earn around £35,000.

Salaries in London are often higher.

Related opportunities

- Counsellor p547
- Debt Counsellor/Money Advice Caseworker p548
- Youth and Community Worker p563

Further information

CRAC: Career Development Organisation
www.crac.org.uk

CHILDMINDER

ENTRY LEVEL 1

Qualifications and courses

Childminders must register with Ofsted in England, the Care Commission in Scotland, the Care and Social Services Inspectorate in Wales and the local Health and Social Services board or trust in Northern Ireland. You need to take an introductory childminding training course and be prepared for a registration visit. A Paediatric First Aid certificate is also required.

Candidates must be aged 18 or over. They, and everyone in their households over 16, must be police checked.

There are no essential academic requirements for becoming a childminder but qualifications in childcare may be useful. These include BTEC Certificates and Diplomas in Children's Care, Learning and Development, the Diploma in Society, Health and Development and the Oxford Cambridge and RSA Examinations (OCR) Entry Level Certificate in Child Development.

You will have to contact the Family Information Services for a pre-registration meeting and details on the Early Years Foundation Stage (EYFS). The EYFS provides the framework and standards expected from childminders.

All childminders are inspected by the authorities which oversee the registration in that country and inspections are usually carried out every 2 to 3 years.

It could be useful to have previous relevant experience, such as working in a crèche, playgroup or nursery.

What the work involves

You will care for children in your own home, ensuring they are comfortable and happy. You will plan activities and tasks for your charges and keep their parents informed about what they have done during the day, what they have eaten and if there have been any problems.

You could accompany the children to and from playgroup, nursery or school or spend time arranging and managing transport to extra-curricular activities or play dates.

For children aged under 5, you will have to follow the guidelines set by the Early Years Foundation Stage for play-based learning.

Type of person suited to this work

As a childminder you must be patient, caring and excellent with children. Creativity and ingenuity is needed to plan varied activities for children of different ages. You must also be adaptable and prepared to change your plans at short notice to meet the changing needs of the children in your care.

You need to share information with parents on a daily basis which means that good observation and communication skills are important.

As you will be self-employed, you will need to be organised, with good administrative and numeracy skills to work out tax returns and invoices. IT skills are useful.

Working conditions

You are allowed to care for up to 6 children, including your own, under the age of 8 providing that only 3 are less than 5 years old.

You will work in your own home which may have to be altered to meet childminding standards by fitting equipment such as stairgates and socket covers.

A driving licence is useful as you may take children to playgroup or school. You will do a lot of lifting and clearing up. A working day of 8am to 6pm is usual and you will need to do other administrative tasks outside of this time.

Future prospects

Although the minimum age for entry is 18, most childminders are older and are parents themselves or have experience of care work.

The demand for childminders can vary regionally and at different times of the year.

Childminders can become care assistants or home care assistants, or can go on to train for similar work as a nursery nurse or registered nurse.

Advantages/disadvantages

The work is varied, fun and working from home often suits people who have young children themselves.

The hours can be very long and it can sometimes be hard work for low pay.

Money guide

In 2012 the Professional Association for Childcare and Early Years reported that average fees charged by childminders ranged between £3.63 and £5.42 per child, per hour, depending on the area of the country. The highest salaries were in London.

You can expect an income of around £6,000–£10,000 per year when starting out, rising to £15,000 when experienced.

Top hourly rates are charged in London where experienced, full-time childminders can earn up to £20,000 a year.

Childminders are self-employed so they need to arrange their own tax payments and insurance, and pay for training and extra costs such as public liability insurance.

Related opportunities

- Children's Nurse p274
- Early Years Specialist/Nursery Nurse p178
- Play Worker/Hospital Play Specialist p184

Further information

Northern Ireland Childminding Association
www.nicma.org

Professional Association for Childcare and Early Years
www.pacey.org.uk

Scottish Childminding Association
www.childminding.org

CLINICAL/HEALTH PSYCHOLOGIST

ENTRY LEVEL 8

Qualifications and courses

In order to become a qualified clinical or health psychologist you must have Graduate Basis for Chartered Membership (GBC) with the British Psychological Society (BPS). This can be obtained by achieving a BPS-accredited Honours degree in psychology. Entry to the degree is usually with 5 GCSEs/National 5s (A*–C/A–C), including Maths, and 2 A levels/3 H grades, including a science. If you already have a degree that is not in psychology you can do a BPS-accredited conversion course, as relevant postgraduate study will then be needed in order to specialise.

Clinical psychologist
To become a clinical psychologist you will need to complete a doctorate in clinical psychology that has been approved by the Health & Care Professions Council (HCPC). Entry to a doctorate course is usually dependent on achieving a BPS-accredited degree with a 2.1 classification or above, although some courses will accept a 2.2 with a master's degree.

Relevant work experience is necessary to gain a training contract. Typical applicants have completed 2 years' experience. This can take a range of forms including working as a psychological assistant or volunteering with the National Health Service (NHS).

Health psychologist
A BPS-accredited master's degree in health psychology is required in order to become a health psychologist. This should then be followed by Stage 2 of the BPS qualification in health psychology which involves 2 years' supervised practice. Some universities run doctorate programmes in health psychology which combine a master's degree and supervised practice.

To use the title health psychologist you will need to register with the HCPC after completing all your training.

A Disclosure and Barring Service (DBS) check will be required as you will be working with children and vulnerable adults.

What the work involves

Clinical psychologist
You will work with people whose health problems affect their behaviour, to learn what they do and why they do it.

Health psychologist
This is a new and rapidly growing field of applied psychology which promotes changes in people's attitudes, behaviour and thinking about health.

Type of person suited to this work

An interest in people, their personalities, abilities and interests is essential.

The work involves contact with many different types of people which means you must be good at relating to others and have excellent communication skills.

Psychologists must think logically, analyse data and statistics. They need administrative and IT skills for writing reports and analyses, and presenting information at case conferences or company meetings.

Working conditions

Clinical psychologist
Your work will take you to schools, colleges, hospitals and health centres. You may find yourself working with social services or with adolescent and child mental health services. Most clinical psychologists are employed by the NHS.

Health psychologist
Health psychologists work in a number of settings, such as hospitals, academic health research units, health authorities and university departments.

Future prospects

Entry to psychology degrees is competitive and it takes a long time to become a chartered psychologist. For both clinical and health psychology the jobs available tend to be within government services, education and health, in the public and private sectors. Ongoing professional development will be important throughout your career.

Advantages/disadvantages

The work is varied, interesting and challenging.

You will meet many different types of people.

Some people may be aggressive or even violent and you may sometimes have difficulty remaining impartial.

Money guide

Clinical psychologist
Trainee clinical psychologists can expect to earn £25,500, which is the current NHS wage band 6. Once qualified, this rises to roughly £30,500. As you gain experience salaries can rise to £46,600 and in top-level positions you can earn in excess of £80,000.

Health psychologist
Salaries start from around £18,600 for trainees. Upon qualification pay rises to between £21,700 and £35,500 and as a senior health psychologist with the NHS salaries can reach £89,000.

For both positions, salaries depend on geographical location. The NHS pays a London high cost area supplement. Private hospital and practice salaries vary.

Related opportunities

- Educational Psychologist p549
- Occupational Psychologist p553
- Psychoanalyst/Psychotherapist p554

Further information

British Association for Counselling and Psychotherapy
www.bacp.co.uk

Health and Care Professions Council
www.hpc-uk.org

NHS Careers
www.nhscareers.nhs.uk

COUNSELLOR

ENTRY LEVEL 5

Qualifications and courses

Counselling is open to all graduates and those with an HND qualification but a pre-entry qualification in counselling is almost essential. This could be a master's degree or a professional certificate or diploma. First degree subjects such as psychology, social studies or education are most useful for entry onto a master's course.

The British Association for Counselling and Psychotherapy (BACP) runs various certificate and diploma courses, which tend to last either 1 year full time or 2 to 3 years part time. Diploma courses usually require a degree, although sometimes they may also accept a relevant certificate in counselling. Certificate courses are more flexible and entry without an HND or degree is common. Membership with UK Council for Psychotherapy (UKCP) can also help your prospects.

Previous counselling experience and skills are just as important for getting onto the courses as qualifications. This could be gained through volunteering or pre-arranged work experience programmes.

It is rare for someone to enter a full-time position in this field before their mid-20s. Counselling is often a second career, and maturity and experience are beneficial.

Government legislation means a new system to accredit registers of counsellors is being introduced by the Professional Standards Authority for Health and Social Care.

A Disclosure and Barring Service (DBS) check will be necessary if you want to work with children or vulnerable adults.

What the work involves

Counsellors listen to what their clients say and ask questions in response, to help them explore, talk about and eventually resolve their problems.

You will help your clients to see things more clearly, perhaps from a different point of view. You will not tell people what to do but will help them work out their next steps themselves.

You might work with people with a range of problems or specialise in a particular area, such as bereavement, gambling, relationship difficulties or eating disorders.

Type of person suited to this work

As most of the work involves interacting closely with people, excellent communication and listening skills are essential.

Counselling workers may not always agree with the views held by their clients, which means they have to be open minded and tolerant. You must also be highly discreet as you will be given a lot of confidential information.

You need to be interested in how the mind works, and in people's welfare.

Working conditions

You will work indoors, usually sitting in a quiet, comfortable room in places such as advice centres, schools, colleges, out-patient clinics and health centres. If you are self-employed, you might work from home, visit your clients at home, or both. Some counselling work is done exclusively over the phone.

You will work mainly with people on a one-to-one basis but also, on occasions, with couples, families or groups. Most counselling sessions last 50 minutes.

You may work in the evenings and at weekends and many counsellors work part time.

Future prospects

Larger units may have limited opportunities for you to move into management roles but on the whole counselling units tend to be flat structures with not much room for promotion.

It is possible to go on to specialise in a particular area of counselling, such as bereavement, family therapy or substance abuse. Experience in more than one area is beneficial for career development.

Self-employment is also possible once you have significant experience and training, and can be combined with voluntary or part-time work.

Advantages/disadvantages

The work can be very rewarding but also highly stressful.

You must be able to take constructive criticism from an experienced counselling worker, therapist or psychoanalyst – both during and after completing training.

Some clients may become dependent on therapy or analysis sessions and will have to be carefully assisted to refocus.

Money guide

Starting salaries range from £19,000 to £26,000 per year when newly qualified (but this can vary considerably).

Experienced counsellors or those with supervisory or managerial responsibility can earn between £30,000 and £40,000.

Counsellors in private practice can charge £30–£50 an hour. A lot of counsellors combine part-time employment with private practice and voluntary work.

Related opportunities

- Careers Adviser p544
- Debt Counsellor/Money Advice Caseworker p548
- Mental Health Nurse p297
- Psychoanalyst/Psychotherapist p554

Further information

British Association for Counselling and Psychotherapy
www.bacp.co.uk

Counselling & Psychotherapy Central Awarding Body
www.cpcab.co.uk

DEBT COUNSELLOR/MONEY ADVICE CASEWORKER

ENTRY LEVEL 2

Qualifications and courses

There are no fixed entry requirements but you will need a good standard of English and maths, so GCSEs/National 5s in those subjects would be useful.

Experience is considered more important than qualifications and many applicants have training and/or experience in finance or accounting, consumer advice or have worked as a volunteer for at least a year in an advice centre.

You need to undergo a Disclosure and Barring Service (DBS) check to work with vulnerable adults.

Once you have secured employment, you will receive on-the-job training. You could also study for an NVQ Level 3 Certificate and Level 4 Diploma in Advice and Guidance. Alternatively, you could take a diploma, Foundation degree or degree in advice or legal advice work.

The Money Advice Trust (MAT) and the Citizens Advice Bureau (CAB) also provide training programmes for debt counsellors.

What the work involves

It will be your responsibility to give free, impartial and confidential advice to people in serious debt.

You will have to guide your clients through the legal procedures and represent them if they are being taken to court.

To ensure that clients are claiming available and applicable tax allowances and benefits, you will calculate your clients' income and expenditure and work with them to devise an achievable budget to live by.

By liaising with creditors, you will try to arrange realistic repayments over a reasonable timescale.

Type of person suited to this work

People experience money problems for reasons such as unemployment and bad money management. You will need to work with very different people and be non-judgemental about their circumstances. You will require good communication skills and a confident manner so that people trust you and the advice you give them.

Much of the work involves figures, so you should have strong numeracy skills. It is also important to be a good negotiator in order to get the best repayment plans for your clients from creditors.

Good time management is essential, as are excellent IT skills. This job suits people who have worked in financial services or have a financial background.

Working conditions

You could meet your clients face to face in an office or advise them through a telephone helpline. You could also spend time in court or at meetings.

You might travel around locally so a driving licence is useful.

You will usually work 9am to 5pm from Monday to Friday. In order to suit your clients' needs, you will sometimes have to work Saturdays and evenings, perhaps doing shift work.

Future prospects

Although money advisers are in demand, there are more applicants than jobs. Most openings are town or city based, in the Citizens Advice Bureau, advice centres or money advice units.

As funding is provided by local authorities or voluntary organisations, the majority of vacancies are for 2-year contracts.

You could move into specialist casework or there could be opportunities for progression into a role as team leader or supervisor. You could enter other social care jobs or change to work in the financial sector.

Charities such as Debtline have recorded large increases in numbers of people seeking out help over debts with an increase of over 140% from 2007 to 2014. With an increase in demand, the job market should at least be stable, if not soon to expand.

Advantages/disadvantages

Helping clients to manage and get rid of their debt can be rewarding.

You may have to deal with rude and difficult people.

Evening and weekend work is possible in this job, but there may also be opportunities for part-time work.

Money guide

Starting salaries are usually between £19,000 and £20,000.

An experienced caseworker can expect to earn £22,000–£24,000.

Those employed in a senior position as a supervisor or manager can achieve £28,000–£30,000 a year.

Earnings vary with location and tend to be higher in London.

Related opportunities

- Accountant p2
- Financial Adviser p26
- Welfare Benefits Adviser/Welfare Rights Caseworker p562

Further information

Advice UK
www.adviceuk.org.uk

Citizens Advice Bureau
www.citizensadvice.org.uk

Financial Skills Partnership
www.financialskillspartnership.org.uk

EDUCATIONAL PSYCHOLOGIST

ENTRY LEVEL 8

Qualifications and courses

In order to become a qualified educational psychologist you will need to gain an Honours degree in psychology accredited by the British Psychological Society (BPS) at a 2.1 or higher. The general entry requirements for a degree are 2 A levels/3 H grades, including a science, and 5 GCSEs/National 5s (A*–C/A–C). If you already have a degree that is not in psychology you can do a BPS-accredited conversion course to gain the right academic knowledge to progress in your career.

Once you have graduated you can register for Graduate Basis for Chartered Membership (GBC) with the BPS. This is required to progress to the next level of training.

You must then undertake a BPS-accredited doctorate in educational psychology. In Scotland only, it is possible to take a BPS-accredited master's course in educational psychology followed by the BPS Award in Educational Psychology (Stage 2).

Finally you need to register with the Health & Care Professions Council (HCPC) in order to be able to use the title 'educational psychologist'. In Scotland you must also be a member of the Scottish Division of Educational Psychology or the Division of Educational and Child Psychology.

As you will be working with vulnerable groups and young people, you will need to undergo a Disclosure and Barring Service (DBS) check.

What the work involves

You will work with children with social, behavioural or learning difficulties to assess their progress and their academic and emotional needs. You will give help and guidance, and design activities which will enable them to learn and develop.

Your role will also involve working closely with parents and teaching professionals to broaden their understanding of children's psychological needs and the difficulties they face.

You will carry out research and you will be required to remain up to date with new government policies and measures that have been brought in with regard to assessing a child's psychological progression.

Type of person suited to this work

You must enjoy working closely with children. You will need to be sensitive, tactful, assertive and persuasive. You should be prepared to work with pupils who are finding school difficult and may not be very receptive to your help.

You will need excellent communication skills as you will be working regularly with both children and adults. You should ensure that you are good at explaining procedures and assessment methods in a way that is easy to understand.

You need administrative and IT skills for writing reports and analyses, and presenting information.

Working conditions

You will usually work 35–37.5 hours a week from Monday to Friday, with some evening work required to attend parent–teacher meetings.

You will spend time in an office, as well as visiting schools and colleges, meeting clients, writing reports and assessing your findings. You will also run training sessions for parents and teachers.

You will probably have to travel between different locations so a driving licence is useful.

Future prospects

Most educational psychologists work for local authorities but an increasing number are self-employed as independent consultants. You will be more restricted in the way you can progress while working for a local authority as there are only a certain number of positions you can work up to. However, you may become a senior officer in a local authority children's services department.

Being an independent consultant will give you more opportunity to branch out into different areas of psychology such as occupational psychology.

Advantages/disadvantages

The work is varied and interesting.

Helping children to learn and develop is incredibly rewarding.

Dealing with difficult children, and parents who are not willing to accept that their child has a psychological problem, can be stressful and challenging.

Money guide

In England, Scotland, Wales and Northern Ireland educational psychologists are usually paid in accordance with the Soulbury Agreement.

As a graduate trainee you can expect to earn between £21,800 and £29,700 per year. Once qualified, your annual salary can range from £33,900 to £50,200. Senior educational psychologists can achieve £42,500–£62,900 a year.

In Scotland, pay scales are set by the Scottish Negotiating Committee for Teachers (SNCT). Educational psychologists can expect between £39,800 and £48,800 a year, with senior, depute principal and principal psychologists earning £51,800 to £60,000.

Related opportunities

- Clinical/Health Psychologist p546
- Counsellor p547
- Youth and Community Worker p563

Further information

Association of Educational Psychologists
www.aep.org.uk

Children's Workforce Development Council
www.cwdcouncil.org.uk

FORENSIC PSYCHOLOGIST

ENTRY LEVEL 8

Qualifications and courses

To become a qualified forensic psychologist you will need to have a degree in psychology that has been accredited by the British Psychological Society (BPS) with a classification of 2.1 or higher. Entry to the degree is usually with 5 GCSEs/Nationals (A*–C/A–C), including Maths, and 2 A levels/3 H grades, including a science. If you already have a degree that is not in psychology you can do a BPS-accredited conversion course in order to gain the right academic knowledge so you can to progress.

Once you graduate the next step is to register for Graduate Basis for Chartered Membership (GBC) with the BPS. You will then need to undertake a BPS-accredited master's degree in forensic psychology, followed by the BPS qualification in forensic psychology (Stage 2) which involves 2 years of supervised practice. Some universities run doctorate programmes in forensic psychology that combine a master's degree and Stage 2 of the BPS qualification.

Registration with the Health & Care Professions Council (HCPC) is then required for you to be able to use the title forensic psychologist.

It is an advantage to have previous work experience when applying for the master's degree as competition is strong. Pre-entry experience will often be required once you start looking for work after registering with the HCPC. Options include working as an assistant forensic psychologist, psychological assistant or doing voluntary work with witness and victim support organisations. Some prison service positions are only available to people with experience as a psychological assistant.

What the work involves

You will apply psychology to the criminal and civil justice systems. Your job will involve direct contact with offenders to carry out assessments and you may design programmes to help in their rehabilitation.

You may be required to present your findings on a criminal case in court.

Your work will also include carrying out detailed research into what provokes people to commit crimes. You will analyse the behavioural patterns and personality traits of offenders.

Type of person suited to this work

You need brilliant communication skills and the ability to work with people from a wide variety of backgrounds. You must be prepared to work with criminals and be enthusiastic about helping them during their rehabilitation process. You should not be a judgemental person and you must hold no prejudice against the people you are working with, even if they have committed an awful crime.

You should be very good at reading people's subconscious behaviour and taking detailed notes of your findings to present in reports. You must be organised and able to manage your workload. Research and IT skills are necessary.

Working conditions

You will spend a lot of time working in prisons, secure hospitals, police stations and mental health rehabilitation units. You may be employed by a variety of organisations; from the National Health Service to the prison service to the police force. If you are working in a prison you will need to become adjusted to the conditions and regulations.

A driving licence would be useful for travelling between locations.

You will typically work a 37-hour week from Monday to Friday and some evening/weekend work will be expected. Part-time work may be available.

Future prospects

The job market for psychologists continues to remain relatively good. As this particular role is in a fairly new and emerging sector, there should be opportunities to progress and branch into different areas of psychology and forensics once you have some experience.

If you achieve chartered status as a forensic psychologist, you may have the chance to move into a senior role. In this position, you could be in charge of creating a complete rehabilitation scheme for a certain type of offender.

With experience, you will have the option of working for a consultancy.

Advantages/disadvantages

You may find yourself working with people who have committed very serious crimes which can be distressing.

Helping to rehabilitate offenders back into society can be immensely rewarding.

You will learn new things all the time which will make the job exciting and fulfilling.

Money guide

In the prison service, trainee forensic psychologists can earn £24,200 to £27,400. Chartered forensic psychologists can expect £26,200 to £38,000, with senior level salaries reaching £63,000.

In the NHS starting salaries for trainees are £25,528 to £34,189. Qualified forensic psychologists earn from £30,460 to £40,157. Senior level positions can reach £97,478.

Related opportunities

- Clinical/Health Psychologist p546
- Counsellor p547
- Forensic Computer Analyst p525

Further information

Division of Forensic Psychologists
www.bps.org.uk/dfp

HM Prison Service
www.gov.uk/government/organisations/hm-prison-service

FUNDRAISER

ENTRY LEVEL 1

Qualifications and courses

The popularity and competitiveness of the not-for-profit sector means that most entrants to this role are now graduates. Useful degree subjects include business studies and sales and marketing and for entry to a degree course you will need at least 2 A levels/3 H grades and 5 GCSEs/National 5s (A*–C/A–C) including English and Maths.

However, having skills and significant experience is usually considered more important than formal qualifications. Experience in marketing, events, advertising, sales, public relations or finance would be beneficial.

Most entrants undertake voluntary fundraising work to demonstrate their commitment to the not-for-profit sector and to help develop a network of industry contacts. The majority of charities run unpaid internships and large organisations, such as Cancer Research UK, offer graduate training schemes. You could also work as an assistant fundraiser.

Short courses for people working as fundraisers/fundraising managers are available.

What the work involves

Fundraisers raise money for their charity by targeting donors and organising activities such as publicly sponsored events, membership schemes with various benefits and corporate sponsorship.

You will represent your charity at public events such as dinners, giving talks to possible supporters.

You will write strategies, reports for trustees and donors, and proposals for grants.

You will prepare publicity material and liaise with the media, always keeping your charity in the public eye.

Type of person suited to this work

It is essential that you are enthusiastic and committed to your charity. You must be good with all types of people. You should be an excellent communicator and an engaging and confident public speaker, able to persuade people to support your charity.

You will need to be a good negotiator, with effective writing skills to produce noteworthy publicity material. You will have to be imaginative and creative to come up with innovative fundraising ideas.

You must be able to organise your time and workload so you can keep running costs down to a minimum and save money for your charity.

Working conditions

You will normally be based in an office working on a computer, but you could be based at home, particularly if you work for a very small charity. You might spend time outdoors at fundraising activities.

You will work about 35–40 hours a week and weekend/evening work is common when arranging and attending events.

You will travel fairly widely so a driving licence is useful.

Future prospects

It is not usual to become a charity fundraiser straight from school – most entrants have experience in sales or marketing and voluntary fundraising.

Most jobs are with charities, pressure groups and other not-for-profit organisations, including hospitals.

It may be necessary to move around – possibly to larger organisations – to progress in your career. With experience you could move into management, become self-employed or offer consultancy advice.

Advantages/disadvantages

It is satisfying to see your charity flourish with the money that you have helped to raise.

There could be pressure to meet fundraising targets and deadlines for organising events.

People who do not support your charity can be unpleasant at times.

You will need to work evenings and weekends.

Money guide

Earnings vary according to the size and location of the charity.

Starting salaries for an assistant role can start at £13,000, rising to £24,000 with experience.

Typical salaries for a fundraiser with a few years' experience could be £25,000 to £32,000.

Senior level salaries are around £28,000 to £40,000 and if you become director or head of fundraising in a large charity you could achieve up to £70,000.

Related opportunities

- Advertising Account Executive p376
- Events and Exhibition Organiser p384
- Public Relations Officer p396

Further information

Association of Chief Executives of Voluntary Organisations
www.acevo.org.uk

Directory of Social Change
www.dsc.org.uk

Institute of Fundraising
www.institute-of-fundraising.org.uk

LIFE COACH

ENTRY LEVEL 1

Qualifications and courses

There are no specific requirements to enter this area of work as it is not a regulated field, but clients tend to prefer coaches who have relevant qualifications and professional organisation memberships. You also need to have gained a great deal of life experience and have the right skills and qualities.

A degree in human resources, sociology or psychology would be helpful starting points. The general entry requirements for a degree are 2 A levels/3 H grades and 5 GCSEs/National 5s (A*–C/A–C). If you already have a degree in an unrelated subject, some universities offer postgraduate degrees in coaching that may be useful.

There are a number of private agencies and academies offering training in life coaching. For example the Coaching Academy has a free 2-day certificate that covers the basics of coaching, as well as other more specialised courses. The Coaching and Mentoring Network website contains a full list of coaching courses.

You could also work towards accreditation from one of the recognised bodies for life coaches, such as the International Coach Federation (ICF), which would give you greater credibility with clients.

What the work involves

You will help people, both independent clients or employees, to recognise and develop their special attributes and skills.

You will coach individuals to become more successful in career matters, fitness levels, financial affairs or personal relationships. You will also help in boosting self-esteem.

You will discuss values, attributes and beliefs and set goals with your clients for them to work towards. At a later stage you will review and revise the action plans you have created.

Type of person suited to this work

A bond of trust needs to be established for you to be an effective life coach. You must be non-judgemental and exude a trustworthiness that will allow clients to open up and reveal their present feelings and frustrations, their future ambitions and their perceived restrictions to progress.

Besides integrity and discretion, life coaches need excellent interpersonal skills, patience and perseverance to allow clients the time to set themselves goals for change.

Working conditions

You will agree timetables with clients for coaching sessions and hold one-to-ones at their work-base or in a neutral location. Later sessions are often by phone or email.

Many life coaches work with busy, highly successful chief executives, usually outside normal business hours.

Coaching sessions can be weekly, fortnightly or monthly; the frequency may change.

Future prospects

Life coaching is a relatively new field in the UK (although it has been around for longer in the USA), but interest has increased as more attention is paid to developing the whole person – both within and outside the workplace.

The industry is currently growing although to be picked up as an independent consultant it usually helps to have qualifications.

Life coaches work as independent consultants or for business consultancy agencies. If you network and market yourself well you can build up a substantial client base.

You could choose to specialise in one area such as spiritual coaching or executive coaching.

Advantages/disadvantages

There is great satisfaction in observing changes in your clients.

If clients fail to implement action plans, it can be dispiriting and frustrating.

You could have long-term coaching relationships with clients who want to work on different aspects of their lives.

Money guide

Life coaches earn an agreed rate per session and may take the client's financial circumstances into account when charging.

Working for an agency, you can earn around £40–£75 per session plus expenses.

You could charge up to £250 a session if you are working with corporate clients.

The median full-time salary for a life coach in the UK is £30,000, although this is based on a very small sample.

Life coaches who become well known and sought after can charge higher fees for periods of life coaching lasting 6 months or longer.

Related opportunities

- Careers Adviser p544
- Counsellor p547
- Social Worker p557

Further information

Association for Coaching
www.associationforcoaching.com

Chartered Institute of Personnel and Development
www.cipd.co.uk

International Coach Federation
www.coachfederation.org.uk

The Coaching Academy
www.the-coaching-academy.com

OCCUPATIONAL PSYCHOLOGIST

ENTRY LEVEL 7

Qualifications and courses

To become a qualified occupational psychologist you will need a 2.1 or higher Honours degree in psychology that has been accredited by the British Psychological Society (BPS). Entry onto a degree course usually requires 2 A levels/3 H grades, including a science and 5 GCSEs/ National 5s (A*–C/A–C), including Maths. If you already have a degree that is not in psychology you can do a BPS-accredited conversion course in order to gain relevant working knowledge of the subject.

Once you graduate the next step is to register for Graduate Basis for Chartered Membership (GBC) with the BPS which is required in order for you to progress to the next level of training.

You must then undertake either a BPS-accredited master's degree in occupational psychology or complete stage 1 of the BPS's qualification in occupational psychology. These are followed by stage 2 of the BPS's qualification, which involves 2 years of supervised practice for master's graduates or 3 years for those who completed stage 1. Registration with the Health & Care Professions Council (HCPC) is then required for you to be able to use the title 'occupational psychologist'.

It is an advantage to have previous work experience when applying for the master's degree as competition is strong. Pre-entry experience will also often be required once you start looking for work after registering with the HCPC. This could be in personnel/human resources or business/management, or you could work for a psychometric test publisher.

Some positions may require competence in psychometrics or statistical analysis.

A Disclosure and Barring Service (DBS) check will be needed for working with vulnerable adults.

What the work involves

You will explore how organisations function and how people behave at work to improve an organisation's efficiency and employees' job satisfaction.

You will help managers plan how they recruit and train staff. You will give advice on matters concerning communication between individuals in the workplace, the most effective working environment and coping with change.

Part of your job may involve helping to recruit the right person for a particular role as well as offering support to those facing redundancy. You will also be working with bosses and managers to help them to understand the psychological needs of their staff, so that they can maintain a stress-free environment for them as much as possible.

Type of person suited to this work

You should have a great interest in how organisations function and what makes people tick in the workplace.

You should be comfortable working with adults and also be happy to help them progress professionally.

You must be a brilliant communicator and it will also be very useful for you to have strong business skills because you will have been employed to improve the overall efficiency of a company.

Working conditions

Much of your work will take place in offices and business premises of the companies you are working for. This may involve working by yourself or as part of a team.

You can expect to work around 37 hours a week from Monday to Friday but you may run or attend courses that require you to travel away and stay overnight.

There is the opportunity to be self-employed but this is often after working for an organisation and building up your work experience.

Future prospects

Occupational psychologists work in large companies in the public and private sectors.

They can work with government and public services as private consultants.

Some specialise in a certain area, for example ergonomics (the interaction of people with where they work), or health and safety – studying the causes of accidents and how to prevent them.

Once you have progressed to a senior role you may set up your own consultancy.

Advantages/disadvantages

Your work will really make a difference to people's day to day lives at work which will be very rewarding.

You may be working with unmotivated or stressed individuals.

You may find that bosses are not willing to take on your advice for their staff.

Money guide

As a starting salary you can earn anything from £18,000 to £32,000.

This can progress to between £35,000 and £80,000 with experience in a senior position.

Private sector organisations tend to pay more than public sector.

Related opportunities

- Educational Psychologist p549
- Health and Safety Adviser p27
- Recruitment/Employment Agency Consultant p46

Further information

Health and Care Professions Council
www.hpc-uk.org

Occupational Psychology Services
www.opsltd.com

The Association of Business Psychologists
www.theabp.org.uk

PSYCHOANALYST/ PSYCHOTHERAPIST

ENTRY LEVEL 7

Qualifications and courses

Psychoanalyst
Most people enter psychoanalysis as a second career after they have gained experience in a related field such as psychology, psychiatry, counselling or social work.

To qualify as a psychoanalyst, candidates must undertake a training course approved by the International Psychoanalytical Association (IPA) or the Institute of Psychoanalysis (IoP). Training takes 4 years and entry is with a first degree, for which you will need at least 2 A levels/3 H grades and 5 GCSEs/National 5s (A*–C/A–C). The IoP also offers a 1-year Foundation course for people with experience in a related field with alternative professional qualifications.

Psychotherapist
Psychotherapy is often a second career for people in a related field. You will need a degree in a relevant subject, such as psychology, nursing, medicine, social work or sociology. A postgraduate qualification in psychotherapy which has been approved by the UK Council for Psychotherapy (UKCP) or the British Psychoanalytic Council (BPC) will usually be required. Pre-entry experience in mental health professions, psychology, psychiatry or social work is expected.

Training courses usually last 4 to 6 years when studied on a part-time basis and include personal therapy, theory and supervised clinical work. A Disclosure and Barring Services (DBS) check may also be required.

What the work involves

Psychoanalyst
You will help people uncover their deep-rooted insecurities, thoughts and behaviours which are disrupting and negatively affecting their daily life. You will see your patients 4–5 times a week over an extended period of time. You will listen during the sessions and then write down your observations after your patient has left. Your goal is to help patients achieve self-awareness.

Psychotherapist
You will explore a person's inner conflicts and feelings in order to help alleviate their distress. Your goal is to help patients feel happy or better. Your treatment will be non-medical, focussing on talking through problems. Your treatment approach may include cognitive behavioural therapy, hypno-psychotherapy and psychodynamic therapies.

Type of person suited to this work

You need to be positive, empathic and a great listener. You want to build a good bond with your patients so you should respect confidential information.

Your work can be intense and you will need to sympathise with your patients' problems whilst remaining emotionally resilient. You should be observant and have a genuine interest in feelings and emotions but able to professionally distance yourself from personal situations that may be distressing.

Working conditions

You will work in a consulting room that is comfortable, quiet and welcoming for your patients.

You will most likely work Monday to Friday but you may need to work weekends and evenings to suit your clients' needs. You can choose your own hours if you work for a private practice.

This work can be emotionally demanding and you are advised to be involved in a support network, especially if you are self-employed.

Future prospects

Psychoanalyst
Most psychoanalysts are self-employed and you may choose to work part time for a prison, school or child guidance clinic. You could become a lecturer, train graduate entrants or specialise in a particular area such as adolescent psychoanalysis.

Psychotherapist
With experience, you could go on to become a manager or supervisor of other psychotherapists, although this will mean you will have less clinical work. You could also become a consultant for community organisations or specialise in an area such as psychodrama.

Advantages/disadvantages

It is rewarding to see a patient overcome their problems.

You will constantly be learning more about the human mind which can benefit you as well as your patients.

Your patients might struggle with upsetting issues and this can be emotionally taxing for you.

Money guide

Psychoanalyst
Psychoanalysts are normally self-employed and earnings depend on their rate per session, which is normally between £45 and £70 a session, and how many patients they see.

You can expect a starting salary of £40,000 when you are newly qualified. With experience, you can achieve £50,000–£60,000 a year.

Psychotherapist
National Health Service trainees can earn between £21,200 and £27,500 a year. Once qualified and with experience, your salary can range from £35,000 to £45,000.

In private practice hourly rates can be anything from £40 to £100 per hour.

Related opportunities

- Counsellor p547
- Educational Psychologist p549
- Psychiatrist p315

Further information

British Association of Psychotherapists
www.bap-psychotherapy.org

REHABILITATION OFFICER

ENTRY LEVEL 1

Qualifications and courses

Visually impaired
You will need a qualification in rehabilitation work (visual impairment) to specialise in this particular field. A relevant 2-year Foundation degree is available and involves both work-based training through an employer and distance learning. Entry requirements are at least 1 A level/2 H grades and 3 GCSEs/National 5s (A*–C/A–C), or good BTEC qualifications.

There are also Advanced Apprenticeships in Health and Social Care available for school leavers.

All entrants must undergo a Disclosure and Barring Service (DBS) check.

Hearing impaired
There are no set entry requirements for this career. However, some employers will look for GCSEs/National 5s (A*–C/A–C) and relevant experience, whether paid or voluntary. It might also help to have the Signature Level 1 Award in British Sign Language (BSL). The Apprenticeship in Health and Social Care may also equip you with relevant skills for this profession.

Training is on the job, possibly with the chance to study for further qualifications such as the City & Guilds Level 2 Certificate in Supporting Users of Assistive Technology.

What the work involves

Rehabilitation officers train people with visual and hearing impairments to use their existing skills in new ways that will help them lead a normal life.

You will assess your patients' needs before making a detailed action plan to teach them new skills. You will also provide financial and employment information and advice.

Part of your role will be liaising with other medical professionals to follow up on reports you have made about your patients' quality of living. You might also be responsible for providing training to other social and healthcare workers about sensory loss and awareness.

Type of person suited to this work

You will need to be aware of the issues that affect visually and hearing impaired people. It is important to have good communication skills as your patients may rely on other senses to understand you.

You will be in contact with people of all ages and backgrounds, so it is essential that you are friendly and approachable. Good organisational, problem-solving and assessment skills are required for report writing and devising action plans for patients.

Working conditions

You will divide your time between working in an office and visiting patients' homes to assess their living space and daily routines. It is useful to have a driving licence as you might be travelling around on a regular basis.

You might need to work outdoors when training a patient to use a new piece of assistive equipment or if you are escorting them somewhere.

You will work around 40 hours a week, Monday to Friday, although you might need to visit your patients during the evenings and weekends.

Future prospects

Most positions are with local authority social care departments, voluntary services such as the Royal National Institute of Blind People (RNIB) and educational institutions.

Although there is no set career path in rehabilitation work, you can be promoted to supervisory and managerial roles in sensory support or you can choose to train other people. There are postgraduate qualifications available which would speed up your career progression.

Advantages/disadvantages

This is a very rewarding career as you will be helping people who are in a vulnerable position.

You need to stay emotionally detached from your patients, which could be difficult as you will be spending a lot of time with them.

Money guide

Visually impaired
Starting salaries are around £23,000.

With experience, you can expect £27,000–£30,000 a year.

Team leaders can earn in excess of £35,000.

Hearing impaired
Your starting salary could range from £16,000 to £18,000.

Earnings can increase to £20,000 with experience.

Those in more senior positions can earn up to £26,000.

Related opportunities

- Careers Adviser p544
- Healthcare Assistant p290
- Social Worker p557

Further information

Royal National Institute for Deaf People
www.actiononhearingloss.org.uk

Royal National Institute of Blind People
www.rnib.org.uk

Skills for Care and Development
www.skillsforcareanddevelopment.org.uk

RESIDENTIAL SUPPORT WORKER

ENTRY LEVEL 1

Qualifications and courses

If you want to be a residential childcare worker you must be educated to at least Level 3 qualification level. For all other areas of residential support work there are no particular qualifications necessary, though some could be useful.

You can study for qualifications in health and social care, youth work or childcare. For instance, it may be helpful to complete the BTEC National Certificate or Diploma in Health and Social Care. NVQs/SVQs in Care, as well as a First Aid certificate, are also useful. A Level 2 QCF Diploma in Youth Work Practice, an NCFE Level 2 Certificate for the Children and Young People's Workforce, and Level 2 QCF Diploma in Work Preparation for Health and Social Care can all be beneficial too. Courses usually include work placements, which can make them beneficial for building skills and experience.

Previous paid or voluntary experience of social work or caring for people is essential for all candidates. This could include nursing, working with the disabled, elderly or homeless, working as a social work assistant or even caring for a family member.

If you will be working with children or vulnerable adults you will need to undergo a Disclosure and Barring Service (DBS) check.

Once hired you will receive induction training and learn on the job from more experienced staff.

What the work involves

Residential workers look after the welfare of people living in supervised accommodation, including the elderly, people with disabilities, temporary hostel residents, students and young people.

You will make sure that meals are organised, cooked and served at set times, and that cleaning and maintenance are up to standard.

It will be your responsibility to make sure health and safety standards are met, insurance is up to date and that security is effective. You will also collect rents and fees and organise social events, and sort out any disputes.

Type of person suited to this work

As you may be responsible for the accommodation of many different groups of people, it is important to be friendly and outgoing. You will also need to be understanding, patient and tolerant.

There are likely to be crises in the job so it is important to be able to cope under pressure and make decisions quickly. Problem-solving skills are useful in these situations.

If you are dealing with rents and fees, being good with figures is helpful. There will be a lot of administrative work which needs a well organised and methodical approach.

Working conditions

Most of your work will be indoors, but you may handle maintenance and repair work, using tools and climbing ladders.

Many residential support workers live on-site or in the grounds, but you might travel locally, so a driving licence is useful. You will be constantly on the go, responding to alarm calls at any hour of the day or night.

You will use IT for administration and record-keeping.

Future prospects

Although there are opportunities throughout the UK, there are few vacancies for residential workers. Most jobs are in cities and major towns.

The main employers are local authorities, housing associations, private companies, voluntary organisations, universities and colleges.

Promotion is likely to be to a senior support worker. You might have to move jobs to progress your career. It is also possible to train for a related field such as social work. Once you have experience, your employer may sponsor you to train part time for the social work degree.

Advantages/disadvantages

The work is varied and no two days will be alike.

You will get great job satisfaction from helping people.

Some residents may be difficult to deal with or particular situations may be distressing.

You will work long hours, evenings and weekends, and may have to live on-site.

Money guide

Starting salaries are usually between £15,000 and £18,000 per year.

Senior support workers can earn between £19,000 and £25,000 a year.

Part-time workers may be paid hourly rates, which range between £7 and £14 an hour.

Accommodation and food may also be provided. Salaries in the private sector are often lower than those in the public sector.

Related opportunities

- Caretaker p433
- Cleaner p436
- Hotel Manager p126

Further information

Chartered Institute of Housing
www.cih.org

Scottish Social Services Council
www.sssc.uk.com

SOCIAL WORKER

ENTRY LEVEL 6

Qualifications and courses

Qualification is with the Honours degree in social work that has been approved by the Health & Care Professions Council (HCPC) or Scottish Social Care Council (SSCC). The degree takes 3 years full time (4 years in Scotland) and at least 200 days of the course will be work-based training. There are also options to study part time. Entry requirements are usually 2 A levels/3 H grades and 5 GCSEs/National 5s (A*–C/A–C), including English and Maths.

If you already have a different degree you can take an HCPC- or SSCC-approved postgraduate course in order to gain the appropriate knowledge required. You will need a minimum of a 2.2 Honours degree to be accepted onto this.

Both the degree in social work and the postgraduate degree usually require relevant work experience for entry. This can be gained through paid positions in community care centres or by volunteer work. Some universities request a specific period of experience and some may be willing to accept you on the basis of your experience alone, without the academic qualifications.

To work as a social worker you will need to pass checks from the Disclosure and Barring Service (DBS) and register with either the HCPC or the SSCC. In England, Wales and Northern Ireland registration with the HCPC takes place after completing your degree. In Scotland you will need to register with the SSCC when you are accepted onto the degree and then again when you finish.

Other routes include the Step Up to Social Work programme, which is an accelerated route combining work and study.

Some local authorities may also sponsor employees working in a social care support role to take a social work degree part time or as part of a distance learning programme.

What the work involves

Working at a senior level, you will interview your clients and assess their complex problems and needs.

You will then advise on the best package of care for your client.

Your goal is to support people to live independently and thrive in their surroundings. This might involve helping families to stay together, protecting vulnerable people or helping the excluded to be a part of their community.

You will keep detailed records of all your work.

Type of person suited to this work

You should be culturally aware, non-judgemental and able to engage with clients of all ethnicities, religions and backgrounds.

Caseloads can be heavy, so you need to be organised and able to multi-task effectively. Excellent communication skills are important.

At times your clients may become difficult and you must be confident at resolving conflict. You also need to remain professionally detached in emotionally tense circumstances.

Working conditions

You will often work within a team from other disciplines including psychologists and therapists and will be office based. Most of your time however will be spent visiting clients at their homes.

A driving licence is essential.

You will work 37 hours a week but this may include evenings, early mornings and weekends.

Future prospects

There is currently a demand for qualified social workers so job prospects are high. You will most likely work for a local authority social services department or for children's or adult services departments within the National Health Service. Jobs may also be available with armed forces support groups.

After gaining experience you can vary your role by changing your specialty or by moving on within your specialty. For example you could move from child protection into foster care.

You could also become a senior practitioner or manager but this will mean you will deal more with finances and bureaucracy rather than directly with clients. Lecturing and self-employment opportunities are also possible.

Advantages/disadvantages

No two cases will be the same, keeping your work interesting.

It is rewarding to see people reach their full potential, solve their own problems and improve their lives.

Social work systems can be bureaucratic and frustrating at times.

Your work can be emotionally distressing and may put you in vulnerable situations.

Money guide

Starting salaries vary between £19,500 and £30,000 per year, depending on where you are working.

With experience you could earn up to £40,000. Managers can earn £42,000 or more.

Many employers offer additional benefits such as car allowances and child care.

Related opportunities

- Counsellor p547
- Healthcare Assistant p290
- Youth and Community Worker p563

Further information

British Association of Social Workers
www.basw.co.uk

Skills for Care
www.skillsforcare.org.uk

SUBSTANCE MISUSE WORKER

ENTRY LEVEL 1

Qualifications and courses

There are no set minimum entry requirements and each employer will have their own specifications. Previous experience in social care, youth work, criminal justice or counselling would be beneficial and some jobs are only open to qualified nurses, counsellors or youth workers.

Most employers require you to be at least 21 years old, as they are looking for maturity and life experience. Some will welcome applications from people who have been through addiction or dependency themselves and successfully come through treatment.

Employers may also ask for a relevant qualification, such as the NCFE Certificate in Drug Awareness or an NVQ/SVQ or BTEC Certificate in Health and Social Care. You could also enter the profession through an Advanced Apprenticeship in Community Justice (Drug and Alcohol Pathway).

Volunteering for organisations that offer support to people with drug and alcohol problems would also be beneficial, as it helps you gain an understanding of the issues people with substance misuse problems face, how experienced members of staff go about offering support and will help you build the necessary skills for the job.

If you want to work in a specialist role you may need job-specific experience and relevant professional qualifications.

Once employed, either in a paid position or as a volunteer, you will receive on-the-job training. This will usually include studying for qualifications up to a minimum of Level 3.

A Disclosure and Barring Service (DBS) check is necessary.

What the work involves

You will help people who misuse harmful substances, including drugs and alcohol, to overcome their dependencies.

You could provide support in one-to-one or group sessions. This can include counselling and care planning.

You could offer drug treatment options to prisoners, advise on detox methods in a rehabilitation centre, prescribe drugs and give medical advice in a clinic or run educational workshops in schools and youth centres. You could also help substance users find housing and temporary accommodation. You might accompany police patrols around clubs doing street outreach work.

Type of person suited to this work

You want your clients to trust you so you should be understanding, warm and a good listener. You need to be patient and non-judgemental as it may take substance users a long time to recover. If your clients know that you believe in them, they will develop confidence to change.

You could work with many clients at any given time and should be organised. An ability to stay calm under pressure and to maintain professional boundaries is essential.

Good communication skills are important as your role may involve educating others about the dangers of substance abuse.

Working conditions

You could be based in a drop-in centre, a clinic, prison or other community site. A lot of your time will be spent visiting substance users in their homes or other venues such as shelters as many clients may be homeless. A driving licence will therefore be useful.

You will most likely work 35 to 40 hours a week but these could be irregular hours including evenings and weekends. You might need to be on-call throughout the night.

Part-time work is available.

Future prospects

Your job prospects are high as there are a variety of opportunities across the UK for substance misuse workers. You could work for drop-in centres, local authorities, housing associations, private rehabilitation centres, the National Health Service, the prison service, police services, charities or drug and alcohol organisations.

With experience, you could become a supervisor or manager, specialise in one area of treatment such as psychological intervention or drug and alcohol testing or even specialise in one user group such as young people.

Advantages/disadvantages

You have the opportunity to build meaningful relationships with clients and colleagues.

It's rewarding when you help a client overcome an addiction.

You might need to be on-call 24-hours a day which can be demanding.

It can be frustrating to work with uncooperative clients who don't believe they have a problem.

Money guide

You can start out earning between £15,000 and £20,000 per year.

With experience and team leader responsibilities this may increase to between £21,000 and £28,000 a year. At project manager level you may receive in excess of £40,000.

Volunteers may be reimbursed for expenses such as travel costs.

Related opportunities

- Adult Nurse p269
- Counsellor p547
- Social Worker p557

Further information

Federation of Drug and Alcohol Professionals
www.fdap.org.uk

National Treatment Agency for Substance Misuse
www.nta.nhs.uk

TRADE UNION OFFICIAL

ENTRY LEVEL 1

Qualifications and courses

Many officials have degrees in social sciences, economics, law or politics, although there are no formal academic requirements for entry. To become a paid official at a union's branch or regional office, candidates will normally need to have previous experience working unpaid as a local representative, shop steward or administrator.

You may be able to work as a paid union learning representative without completing unpaid experience first if you have an adult education or training and development background.

If you want to work at national head office level, you will need experience or a degree in the particular area you wish to specialise in, eg law, media, education and training, research, trade union legislation or economics. Alternatively, it is possible to work your way up to national office from branch or regional level. Entry by either route requires relevant work experience, paid or unpaid.

Training is mainly on the job. The Trades Union Congress and commercial training organisations run regular short training programmes in a range of different skills.

What the work involves

Trade union officials negotiate with employers over pay, working conditions, health and safety, dismissal and redundancy.

Working in regional offices, you will recruit members, train shop stewards, support local officials and negotiate individual cases with employers. At head office, you will work on national policies and negotiate at national level.

At all levels your role will be to bring about the best deal for the workforce by finding common ground between employers and employees.

Type of person suited to this work

It is important to have a genuine interest in people's welfare and to believe in the aims of your union. You will need to see issues from different viewpoints.

You will spend time dealing with individuals or groups, which requires good speaking, listening and negotiating skills. Speaking in public requires confidence.

Union matters involve problem solving and negotiation which needs a patient, methodical approach and the ability to research and analyse information.

Working conditions

As a local shop steward you will have another job and attend to union business part time. Paid officials at regional and national level are office based.

You could travel quite extensively to meetings, tribunals and conferences so a driving licence is useful.

You will spend a lot of time answering queries either online, by email or by phone – sometimes after normal work hours.

In response to any major policy shifts or events, you might be expected to offer comment or advice at relatively short notice.

Future prospects

Your prospects depend very much on the size of the union, ie they are greater with the large unions which are never out of the news.

Head-office posts are usually in London. After gaining experience it is possible to progress to a regional role, as organiser or secretary, or a national role.

Some people move from union work into politics by becoming councillors or MPs.

Advantages/disadvantages

The work is varied, but you may be working on one theme in preparation for a meeting.

Negotiating better pay and working conditions can be very rewarding.

Some people might be unpleasant and sometimes you have to support people you do not agree with.

You might have to work long and unsocial hours.

Money guide

Local shop stewards and union representatives are generally unpaid. As a paid official you can expect a starting salary of between £20,000 and £25,000 per year.

As an experienced regional or national official you could earn £30,000 to £50,000.

In senior positions such as a general secretary, salaries can rise to as much as £80,000.

Related opportunities

- Equality and Diversity Officer p23
- Health and Safety Adviser p27
- Human Resources/Personnel Officer p28

Further information

Scottish Trades Union Congress
www.stuc.org.uk

Trades Union Congress
www.tuc.org.uk

VICTIM CARE OFFICER

ENTRY LEVEL 1

Qualifications and courses

Formal qualifications are not essential to enter this field. Qualifications in subjects such as psychology, counselling, criminal justice and law can be useful but experience is more highly valued. You will however need a good standard of English and it may be helpful to be fluent in a foreign language.

You will need about 1 or 2 years' voluntary experience in order to find paid work as a victim care officer. There are no entry requirements for a voluntary post but you must be at least 18 years old.

As a volunteer you will undergo basic training, after which you have the option to specialise in supporting victims of particular crimes, such as domestic abuse, or families of homicide victims. Day to day activities may include working on the victim supportline, supporting witnesses at court or work with victims in your community, which will help develop your listening and communication skills.

It is also possible to move into victim support from another related area, such as social services.

A Disclosure and Barring Service (DBS) check will be made if you are volunteering and if you are applying for paid work.

Once you are working as a victim support officer, you will receive further on-the-job training combined with subject-specific sessions run by external agencies. You may also be encouraged to work towards Level 3 NVQs/SVQs if you do not already have them. Suitable courses include the Level 3 in Witness Care and Community Justice: Work with Witnesses, Survivors and Victims (Levels 3–4).

What the work involves

Victim care officers help victims to deal with the aftermath of crime and come to terms with events.

Your work may be focused on a particular group such as victims of domestic abuse, serious sexual assault or antisocial behaviour.

You will listen carefully to victims and provide objective support. You may provide information on legal procedures and relevant services and agencies.

Practical support for victims may involve arranging visits from a police community support officer (PCSO), organising repairs to damaged property or obtaining a personal attack alarm for the victim.

Type of person suited to this work

You will need to be patient, understanding and possess the ability to remain objective and to relate to people from all walks of life.

Excellent listening and communication skills, including telephone skills, are imperative.

There may be tight deadlines which you will have to meet, so organisational skills are important.

You will need to have the energy and ability to assess clients' needs and be able to create solutions for them.

The ability to keep strict confidentiality is essential.

Working conditions

You will work from 37 to 40 hours a week and may often work in the evening and at weekends as required by clients.

Support of victims may take place over the telephone. You may also visit the victim at their home; it will usually be whichever the victim prefers.

The time between the incident and you meeting the victim will vary dependent on the victim's wishes, police advice and severity of the incident.

Future prospects

With time and experience as a victim care officer you may become a victim care team leader and eventually a victim care manager.

Recruitment for this role may be affected by local authority budget cuts.

Advantages/disadvantages

You will have the satisfaction of helping people through difficult stages and experiences in their lives.

Part-time and job share opportunities are often available.

If the victim has not spoken about their feelings before, a lot of emotions may come to the surface, such as distress, confusion or anger, which may become directed at you.

It can be emotionally draining having to handle such delicate situations.

Money guide

Starting salaries for victim care officers working full time are between £15,000 and £20,000 per year.

With experience this can rise to between £22,000 and £24,000.

Related opportunities

- Counsellor p547
- Police Support Worker p530
- Social Worker p557

Further information

Skills for Justice
www.sfjuk.com

Victim Support
www.victimsupport.org.uk

Qualifications and courses

There are no set qualifications required to enter this career but many employers will ask for a degree in a relevant subject such as business studies, human resource management or social care. Relevant experience organising and managing people or working as a volunteer is essential and extensive experience could be an alternative to qualifications.

A postgraduate degree is not usually needed but could offer you an advantage if you are working in the creative industries or for an international development project, as these fields are becoming increasingly competitive.

You could begin as a volunteer and move into managing other volunteers before progressing to a paid role as a manager. There aren't many graduate training schemes but some larger charities run internships.

To work for an international organisation you should have voluntary experience overseas, international contacts and a second language.

The National Council for Voluntary Organisations (NCVO) has established Working for a Charity, a project which provides training for those in the not-for-profit sector. Volunteers may benefit from completing the Award Scheme Development and Accreditation Network (ASDAN)'s Community Volunteering Qualifications (Levels 1–3).

What the work involves

You will recruit, train and organise volunteers to assist hospitals, social service departments, charities and other volunteer organisations.

After interviewing volunteers, you will match them to the kind of work that would suit them. Once you have selected the volunteers, you will provide them with training and mentor them in their position. You will then offer ongoing advice and support.

You will deal with administration, budgets, correspondence and report writing.

You could also prepare publicity material and liaise with other agencies.

Type of person suited to this work

You will work with volunteers from many different backgrounds so you must be personable, as well as a good motivator.

You will need tact and patience, as not all volunteers are suited to the kind of role they wish to have.

It is essential to be confident and have good communication skills to sell placements to volunteers and volunteers to placements. You will need to be flexible and adaptable.

The job will demand a good deal of administration and record-keeping, which requires excellent organisational and time-management skills.

Working conditions

You could work out of an office or from home, depending on the size of the organisation.

You will need to travel locally to arrange placements and visit volunteers, so a driving licence will be useful.

You will most likely work 40 hours a week from Monday to Friday but you may need to work evenings and weekends to meet deadlines.

Future prospects

You are unlikely to enter this career straight from school.

Opportunities are good but there is keen competition for jobs and you might have to move to another organisation or charity to gain promotion. A willingness to be geographically mobile would be useful.

Volunteer management provides useful experience if you would like to transfer into a career such as social work or other management posts in the not-for-profit sector.

You will have opportunities for further training, mainly through short courses.

Advantages/disadvantages

This work is varied and challenging.

The job is fulfilling; by helping volunteers find placements you will be making a difference to people in need.

You might have to work long hours.

As with any management role, some people may be hard to work with and difficult to please.

Money guide

Starting salaries are usually between £16,000 and £26,000 per year.

With experience, you can expect to earn £21,000 to £38,000.

Senior staff who have substantial supervisory experience and are employed in large organisations can achieve £40,000 or more.

Salaries tend to be higher in larger charities, hospitals and the private sector than in smaller charities, educational institutions and the creative industries.

Related opportunities

- Fundraiser p551
- Social Worker p557
- Substance Misuse Worker p558
- Welfare Benefits Adviser/Welfare Rights Caseworker p562
- Youth and Community Worker p563

Further information

Association of Chief Executives of Voluntary Organisations
www.acevo.org.uk

Directory of Social Change
www.dsc.org.uk

National Council for Voluntary Organisations
www.ncvo.org.uk

Scottish Council for Voluntary Organisations
www.scvo.org.uk

WELFARE BENEFITS ADVISER/ WELFARE RIGHTS CASEWORKER

ENTRY LEVEL 1

Qualifications and courses

There are no set minimum entry requirements but a good standard of English and maths is necessary to do the job. Many welfare benefits advisers have a degree in a subject such as social science, law or sociology but this is not essential. Having prior relevant experience is deemed more important than formal qualifications.

Many entrants to this profession begin their career as a volunteer in an advice centre. Once you have gained experience in general advice, you can choose to specialise in welfare rights and benefits. You will usually need to work on a voluntary basis for about a year to be qualified for a paid job.

Undertaking training with the Citizens Advice Bureau (CAB) or other community advice centres would equip you with relevant skills. Speaking a minority language is also an advantage and you will usually need to undergo a Disclosure and Barring Service (DBS) check.

Once you have secured employment, you will attend in-house training and continuing professional development (CPD) courses. The CAB has a nationally recognised training programme for their paid employees. There is also an NVQ Level 3 Certificate and Level 4 Diploma in Advice and Guidance available from City & Guilds which may be useful.

What the work involves

In this sector, you will help people to cope with problems by listening, asking questions and giving impartial and confidential advice.

Benefits advisers may represent their clients at tribunals or act as advocates in a court of law.

Welfare rights caseworkers explain people's rights on matters such as tenancy, employment, conflicts with neighbours, consumer law and finance; sometimes referring clients to other professionals.

You will help people fill in forms to claim benefits and make phone calls on their behalf.

Type of person suited to this work

As the work is mainly about dealing with people, you must have excellent interpersonal skills and the ability to remain impartial and non-judgemental. In order to explain issues very clearly to your clients and help them to complete forms and documents, you will need excellent verbal and written communication skills.

You will be handling large amounts of information, often to find answers to queries, which means you must enjoy research and be able to grasp facts and analyse data quickly.

You need to be understanding and tactful when dealing with clients who are upset and stressed.

Working conditions

Benefits advisers are based in an open-access centre within a local community, town or city. You will see clients on a one-to-one basis by appointment and you will also liaise with colleagues and other professionals, such as social workers and solicitors.

You will usually work standard office hours from Monday to Friday with occasional shift work including Saturdays and evenings.

You will use IT to consult client records, access email and the internet, and undertake research.

Future prospects

Advice centre work is not open to school-leavers – it suits mature people who are experienced in other fields. Entry is competitive; you should gain experience in helping people through voluntary work.

Most jobs are with local authorities or charities. There are a few paid jobs with the CAB but many posts are voluntary. Training will be given in areas such as counselling skills and benefits.

Promotion prospects are limited, although every advice centre has a manager.

Advantages/disadvantages

You will get the opportunity to work with many different people.

You will have to deal with angry and upset clients; some may even have mental health problems.

Helping clients resolve their problems can be personally rewarding.

Money guide

Earnings vary with location and employer.

Starting salaries are usually around £19,000 to £20,000 per year.

With experience and increased responsibilities, you are likely to earn between £22,000 and £30,000.

Related opportunities

- Counsellor p547
- Equality and Diversity Officer p23
- Solicitor/Notary Public p356

Further information

Advice UK
www.adviceuk.org.uk

Citizens Advice Bureau
www.citizensadvice.org.uk

Citizens Advice Scotland
www.cas.org.uk

YOUTH AND COMMUNITY WORKER

ENTRY LEVEL 6

Qualifications and courses

Entry to this profession is with an Honours degree in youth or community work which has been validated by the National Youth Agency (NYA). The requirements for a degree course are usually 2 A levels/3 H grades and 5 GCSEs/National 5s (A*–C/A–C), though these may be waived for mature applicants with relevant experience.

Many employers request a postgraduate certificate, diploma or master's degree endorsed by the Joint Negotiating Committee (JNC) for Youth and Community Workers. These qualifications vary in length, are available in full-time or part-time study options and include work placements. Graduates with a degree in a non-related subject can also take these courses to gain the appropriate knowledge required for entry.

Significant experience in youth and community work, whether paid or voluntary, is essential for entry onto the postgraduate courses. A second language may be useful.

You will need to pass a check from the Disclosure and Barring Service (DBS).

What the work involves

Youth workers are mainly involved with young people while community workers try to make sure that people of all ages in the local community have access to opportunities.

You will work with people in their local area, encouraging them to take part in learning opportunities and community activities.

You could be in charge of a community centre, arranging activities for people of all ages, such as youth clubs, over-60s lunch clubs and playgroups.

You will keep records, manage budgets and try to obtain grants and funding.

You will work alongside other professionals including social workers, teachers, probation officers and the police.

Type of person suited to this work

As the work involves contact with all sorts of people, it is important to be able to get on with everyone and earn their trust. You also need to be genuinely interested in the local community and in equal opportunities.

Local people have a say in what they want in their area, so you must be a good listener, with the ability to balance the ideas of the community with local and national government policies.

Working conditions

You might be based in a community centre, drop-in centres, cafés and youth clubs or in an area office. Depending on your job, you could also work in a school or college.

You will usually work 35 to 37 hours a week and this includes attending evening and weekend sessions.

Youth/community workers often travel around their local area so a driving licence is useful.

Future prospects

Youth and community work is an area that is doing quite well at the moment. As well as roles in youth club and community centre management, there are new strands to the work with developing music, drama, art or sporting groups. Local lifelong learning adult centres also require youth and community workers.

Local authorities have a defined promotion structure but in some jobs you might have to move around to widen your experience. You could progress to working for voluntary organisations or for a specific young people's service.

Advantages/disadvantages

This work provides variety and challenge.

You will play a major part in developing your local community and/or the lives of young people.

You might have to work evenings, weekends and public holidays.

Money guide

Earnings vary with location and tend to be higher in London.

Starting salaries for qualified youth and community workers are about £20,000 per year.

With experience, you can expect to earn £27,000 to £34,000.

Those employed in managerial positions are likely to receive in excess of £35,000.

Related opportunities

- Education Welfare Officer p180
- Further Education Lecturer p181
- Social Worker p557

Further information

Council for Wales of Voluntary Youth Services
www.cwvys.org.uk

National Youth Agency
www.nya.org.uk

Transport and Logistics

The jobs in this sector are immensely varied because of the wide range of transport and communication links that exist today to keep our lives running. You could need a high level of technical knowledge in this sector especially for jobs such as a pilot or a train driver. But you could also be great at keeping attention to detail and maintaining schedules if logistics is more where your interest lies. Jobs in transport and logistics require very efficient and practical people to ensure that our infrastructure continues to run smoothly and safely. You may need to cope well in pressurised situations as well as be very good at communicating so that any problems can be sorted out quickly.

The jobs featured in this section are listed below. For similar jobs to the ones in this section see *Security, Emergency and the Armed Forces* on page 515 and *Leisure, Sport and Tourism* on page 357.

AIR CABIN CREW

ENTRY LEVEL 3

Qualifications and courses

Entry requirements depend on the individual airline. Employers often expect 3–5 GCSEs/National 5s (A*–C/A–C) including English and Maths and although a degree is not required, having one in languages, hospitality management or travel may be useful.

You will need to be at least 18 years old (sometimes 21), physically fit and within height and weight restrictions. You will also need a valid passport allowing unrestricted world travel, or at least, with no restrictions to the countries the airline travels to. Most airlines will expect you to be able to swim at least 25 metres. Previous experience in a customer service role, the ability to speak another language (essential if you are looking to be based abroad) and training in First Aid would all be beneficial.

There are various qualifications that could be useful for people looking to become an air cabin crew member. These include a GCSE/National 5 or A level/H grade in Leisure and Tourism, BTECs in Customer Service or Aviation Operations and NCFE Airline Cabin Crew courses. While these qualifications may give you an edge over other candidates, they don't guarantee you a job and are not required by airlines.

Some airlines may want relevant work experience rather than qualifications, so it is a good idea to do part-time or temporary work in customer service roles or anything that demonstrates teamwork and communication skills.

Once accepted by an airline you will take part in their 4–6-week training course which covers areas such as First Aid, safety and emergency procedures, security regulations and customer care.

What the work involves

When you have prepared the cabin, you will welcome your passengers on-board and make sure that they are comfortable.

You will be responsible for checking that customers are wearing their safety belts when required and that their bags are stored away. You will demonstrate safety procedures before take-off.

During the flight you will help to care for any young children and sick passengers, giving First Aid if needed. You will also serve food and drinks, sell duty free items, ensure that passengers are ready for landing and see them all safely off the plane.

Type of person suited to this work

You will need to be welcoming, friendly, well-groomed, confident and caring.

You should be happy working in a team with the rest of the crew.

Common sense and tact are important when dealing with a variety of situations ranging from nervous or unruly passengers to medical emergencies. It is essential to stay calm under pressure and to have a reassuring attitude.

Working conditions

You will work in a cabin, which can sometimes be cramped and unstable. You will spend the majority of your time standing up and the work may affect your health, for example ear pain from cabin pressure or jet lag from long flights.

Planes fly 24/7 which means unsocial working hours. You will work different shifts on a rota system. You might work on short flights within the UK/Europe or you could fly long-haul with frequent periods of time away from home.

You will be provided with a uniform and you must have a smart appearance at all times.

Future prospects

There is strong competition for jobs and the assessment process can be very tough.

With experience, you could progress to working as a purser (looking after a particular cabin such as first class) and then to cabin service director or crew controller. You could also go on to train new cabin crew.

Advantages/disadvantages

You will travel to dream destinations, but on short flights you will not always get off the plane!

No two working days will be the same.

While working with people can be very rewarding, you may have to deal with difficult passengers.

Money guide

Starting salaries for air cabin crew are usually between £12,000 and £20,000.

With 5 or more years' experience, earnings can rise to £18,000 to £25,000. Senior members of the crew with 10 or more years' experience can earn £25,000 and up.

Benefits include meals, free or discounted flights and allowances for working unsocial hours or working away from home. Air cabin crew can often boost their income with commission on in-flight sales.

Related opportunities

- Holiday Representative p364
- Tour Guide/Manager p372
- Travel Agent p374

Further information

EAL
www.eal.org.uk

NCFE
www.ncfe.org.uk

AIR TRAFFIC CONTROLLER

ENTRY LEVEL 3

Qualifications and courses

To enter this profession you will need to complete a training course approved by the Civil Aviation Authority (CAA) in order to obtain the required Air Traffic Controller's (ATCO) Licence. Course providers include Resource Training, Global ATS and National Air Traffic Services (NATS).

Applicants for an air traffic control course must be at least 18 years old and have a minimum of 5 GCSEs/ National 5s (A*–C/A–C), including English and Maths. A degree is not needed to apply; however, having one in a numerical or technical subject may help you on the job. You will need a good standard of health, hearing, colour vision and a clear voice.

There is strong competition for places and the application process involves attending assessment days and a formal interview, completing online and written tests and receiving security and medical clearance.

Candidates will initially learn in the classroom and through practical exercises using computer simulators. There are ongoing exams and assessments throughout the course which you need to pass in order to progress to the next stage, a process that may take up to 11 months.

After graduation, trainees go on to an operational air traffic control unit for validation training under the supervision of an experienced instructor. The ATCO licence is awarded upon successful completion of the training.

What the work involves

Air traffic controllers issue pilots with instructions and advice to ensure that planes take off, fly and land safely.

When using radar, you will be in control of a specific section of airspace, keeping air traffic flying safely and expeditiously. In a control tower, you will be responsible for the safe movement of aircraft on the ground both arriving and departing from an airport.

You will have to make quick but safe decisions at all times, particularly in emergencies or difficult weather conditions.

Type of person suited to this work

You must speak clearly and confidently when passing instructions to pilots. It is essential to stay alert at all times and pay close attention to detail. You must be able to make quick and logical decisions and stay calm in an emergency situation.

Whilst controlling you will need to have good spatial awareness and the ability to multi-task and operate safely in a 3D environment.

The technology and software used is regularly upgraded to improve safety, so you will need to be willing to train on new equipment and procedures during your working life.

Working conditions

You will work around 40 hours a week at an air traffic control centre or in an air traffic control tower. As this is a 24/7 job, you will work shifts including early mornings, nights, weekends and public holidays. Hours are strictly regulated to provide rest periods during your shifts.

You will use radar displays, radio headphones and computer tools. The lighting in the control room is kept at the right level to help you read the radar screens.

Future prospects

Most UK air traffic controllers are employed by the NATS. Most of the NATS controllers work in one of 2 main area control centres (Swanwick near Southampton and Prestwick in Scotland) and others work at airports where NATS are contracted to provide air traffic control.

Air traffic controllers are also employed by other companies/ councils at other airfields.

With experience, you could manage and train other air traffic controllers.

Advantages/disadvantages

No two working days are the same and your job will remain interesting and challenging.

You will be paid well for the level of responsibility you take on.

This job can involve high levels of stress.

Money guide

If you study with NATS, your basic salary during the college part of the training will be around £11,967 a year, plus benefits that include a contributory pension scheme and very good annual leave.

Whilst undertaking the validation training you can expect to earn between £17,066 and £20,479 depending on where you're placed.

Once you are fully qualified as an air traffic controller you will receive an annual salary of £32,522 to £36,247.

Those employed in a senior position at Swanwick or Heathrow could potentially earn over £100,000.

Related opportunities

- Airline Pilot p568
- Helicopter Pilot p578
- Royal Air Force Officer p536

Further information

Civil Aviation Authority
www.caa.co.uk

National Air Traffic Services Ltd
www.nats.co.uk

AIRLINE PILOT

ENTRY LEVEL 3

Qualifications and courses

You must be aged at least 16 to begin training for a 'frozen' Airline Transport Pilot Licence (ATPL), which allows you to become a first officer. After you have accumulated enough flying hours you can unfreeze your licence and work towards becoming a captain. You will need to be over the age of 21 to hold a full ATPL.

There are various entry routes to getting an ATPL. You can train full time over around 18 months with a flying school. Entry is with at least 5 GCSEs/National 5s (A*–C/A–C) in English, Maths and a science. This route usually costs at least £60,000 for the training.

Another option is to undertake modular training. The first stage is to apply for a Private Pilot's Licence (PPL) and then gain an extra 150 hours' flying experience to be eligible for an ATPL. This method usually costs at least £25,000.

Alternatively, you could train as a pilot in the armed forces, serve for a time and then take a conversion course to get a commercial pilot's licence. Or you may do a degree course in pilot training at university, which will take you to frozen ATPL status.

Sponsorship for your course is possible and organisations such as the Air League offer scholarships. You will have a medical to assess your physical fitness, hearing, eyesight and colour vision.

What the work involves

You will be responsible for the safety of your passengers, crew and cargo and will need to carry out a range of safety, route and fuel checks before each flight.

When flying you will keep in radio contact with air traffic controllers, inform and direct the crew, plan your route and use computer systems to control and monitor the aircraft.

After each flight you will need to write a report and record any problems that occurred.

Type of person suited to this work

You will need to be confident and responsible enough to take charge of your aircraft and follow the exact instructions of air traffic control. You must have the ability to read maps and 3D displays.

Good communication and teamwork skills are essential.

You must stay composed under pressure and in emergency situations. Quick thinking and good coordination are also important.

Once you have earned your full licence, you will still be regularly assessed on your health, skills and competencies so you must be keen to keep on learning.

Working conditions

You will wear a uniform and carry company ID at all times.

You will work shifts which will include weekends, nights and public holidays. If a flight is delayed you may work much longer hours than anticipated. The hours you are allowed to work are strictly regulated.

You must be prepared for jetlag and spending time away from home if piloting a long-haul flight. You will spend the majority of your time sitting in a small flight deck.

Future prospects

Competition for vacancies for new pilots is intense.

You could be promoted to co-pilot on a long-haul flight after you have about 5 years of experience on short-haul flights. In order to be promoted to captain level you will need to fly 5,000 hours, which can take up to 10 years to achieve.

You could become a manager or an instructor or even work up to a senior position within a major airline.

Advantages/disadvantages

The training to qualify as a pilot is incredibly expensive.

You will be at the mercy of the weather and you may not always be able to minimise turbulence.

You will have the opportunity to travel to exotic locations. Often, you will be able to travel for free or at reduced rates.

Flying a plane is a thrilling experience so your day-to-day work will be exciting.

You will spend a lot of time away, which can severely affect your personal life.

Money guide

Salaries vary depending on the airline you are employed by and the type of aircraft you are flying.

A newly qualified first officer working for a small airline could earn £18,000 to £20,000. This can go up to about £43,000 with experience.

Captains can earn from £55,000 to £80,000 with the potential for even more with experience.

Experienced captains flying long-haul aircraft can earn up to £140,000.

Salaries usually increase with each year of service with a company. Benefits include free or discounted flights.

Related opportunities

- Air Traffic Controller p567
- Helicopter Pilot p578
- Royal Air Force Airman/woman p535

Further information

British Airline Pilots' Association
www.balpa.org

The Honourable Company of Air Pilots
www.airpilots.org

AIRPORT BAGGAGE HANDLER

ENTRY LEVEL 1

Qualifications and courses

There are no minimum entry requirements for this job but employers often expect a good standard of literacy and numeracy. You will usually need to be at least 18 years old, be physically fit and pass medical and vision tests and a Disclosure and Barring Service (DBS) check. You will also need a clean driving licence and in some cases a large goods vehicle (LGV) or forklift licence. Previous experience working in a warehouse may be an advantage.

The Apprenticeship in Aviation Operations on the Ground is available at both Intermediate and Advanced Levels and may equip you with relevant skills for this profession.

Once you secure employment you will receive training from an experienced colleague in areas such as health and safety, security procedures, using luggage conveyor belts and lifting equipment, and driving airport vehicles.

You can also study for relevant qualifications whilst you work. There are City & Guilds Diplomas, NVQs and BTEC certificates available in Aviation Operations on the Ground (Levels 2–3).

What the work involves

You will be responsible for safely loading, unloading and transporting baggage, cases and freight.

By checking the baggage against flight lists, you will sort items to make sure you get the baggage to the right place on time. You will then lift the baggage onto the ramp or conveyor belt to move it onto the plane or into the baggage hall.

If you spot any unusual or suspicious baggage, you will need to report it immediately.

You may also help de-ice the plane or keep the runway clear of debris during particularly busy periods.

Type of person suited to this work

You need to be alert and pay close attention to detail when checking labels against flight lists and looking out for suspicious baggage. As you will be handling passengers' belongings, you must be honest and reliable.

In order to get aircraft loaded and unloaded on a short timescale, you will need to be physically fit, fast moving and accurate.

Flexibility and a willingness to get your hands dirty are also vital, as you might need to carry out jobs such as cleaning the aircraft and keeping runways free of hazards such as snow and birds. You should enjoy working as part of a team.

Working conditions

You will mainly work outdoors in all weathers, as well as in cramped spaces such as cargo holds.

You will work around 39 hours per week, usually on a shift system which includes evenings, weekends and public holidays. It is advisable to live near the airport and have your own transport so that you will arrive on time for early shifts.

Working near aircraft can be noisy but you will wear ear protectors.

Your job will involve a lot of bending, lifting and carrying and you will be required to wear protective boots and a high visibility jacket.

Future prospects

Heathrow and Gatwick airports are among the largest employers in the UK but there are vacancies at many regional airports as well, particularly the larger ones such as Birmingham and Manchester.

Seasonal work will be on offer during busy holiday periods.

You may be promoted to a supervisory role or manage ground transport on the runways. With further training and qualifications you could also work in cargo services or aviation management.

Advantages/disadvantages

This is a very active, fast-paced and busy role.

If you are working for an airline, one of the perks may be subsidised travel.

You may have to work outside in poor weather conditions and be on your feet hauling heavy baggage.

Money guide

Starting salaries are usually between £10,000 and £15,000 per year.

With a few years' experience in the role and supervisory duties you could expect to earn about £16,000 or more.

Team leaders may earn £18,000 a year or more.

Some workers are paid by the hour and rates are typically between £6 and £9.

Allowances for shift work and overtime pay can increase your income.

Related opportunities

- Hotel Porter p127
- Removals Operative p591
- Warehouse Worker/Manager p597

Further information

International Air Transport Association
www.iata.org

Royal Aeronautical Society
www.aerosociety.com

BUS/COACH DRIVER

ENTRY LEVEL 1

Qualifications and courses

There are no specific academic requirements for this profession, though some employers will expect you to have a good standard of literacy and numeracy.

You must hold a passenger carrying vehicle (PCV) licence and obtain the Driver Certificate of Professional Competence (Driver CPC). You need to have a full EU driving licence and be at least 18 years old to train for your PCV. You have to be over the age of 21 to drive on major bus and coach routes.

If you already have a full EU driving licence then many companies, including National Express, will be willing to employ you and fund your training for the PCV. Others require you to already have one, with no more than 6 points on it. You can train independently by taking private lessons through a local driving school. Application forms for PCV licences can be obtained from your local Post Office.

PCV training lasts between 1 and 6 weeks and includes a theory test, a practical driving test and a medical. During your training period your company will teach you about customer care, disability awareness, defensive driving and health and safety.

The CPC can be obtained by taking an approved training course, a list of which can be found in the Driving, Transport and Travel section of the gov.uk website.

What the work involves

Bus/coach drivers provide a transport service for passengers making short or long journeys.

You will be responsible for the safety and comfort of your passengers throughout their journey, which includes ensuring that passengers are safely on or off your vehicle before pulling out, and that they are wearing seatbelts when applicable.

If you do not have a conductor, you might have to work out passenger fares and issue tickets and passes. You will also be responsible for checking your vehicle, coping with breakdowns and other emergencies, and driving safely at all times.

Ensuring all baggage is safely loaded and that there are no obstructions inside the bus will be important on coaches.

Type of person suited to this work

You will need to be an extremely competent driver.

You should have a polite and approachable manner when dealing with passengers, but have the confidence to handle disagreements or other situations which may arise on journeys.

You will need good eyesight and excellent concentration in order to remain alert for very long periods of time. Quick reactions are also useful in case you need to respond to an unforeseen event on the road.

You should be a punctual person as you will have to adhere to a strict timetable.

Working conditions

You will work on a shift pattern including evening, overnight and weekend work. You cannot work more than 56 hours a week, or 90 hours over 2 weeks. You are also required, by law, to take a 45 minute break every 4.5 hours.

Coach drivers are expected to provide assistance to disabled travellers and help passengers with luggage so your role could involve heavy lifting. You will have to wear a uniform.

Not all buses have air conditioning, so can become quite hot inside, particularly when the bus is crowded during summer.

Future prospects

Over 80% of the workforce is employed by 1 of 6 companies: Stagecoach, First, National Express, Transdev, Arriva and Go-Ahead.

You could work anywhere in the UK, undertake long distance tour driving or provide a transport service for specific groups such as the elderly or disabled.

You can progress to become a supervisor, service controller or instructor within your company.

Advantages/disadvantages

You will be providing an essential public service.

Part-time and flexible hours are available so you can fit your work around other commitments.

You may have to deal with difficult or distressed passengers.

Driving the same route or for long periods of time can become monotonous.

Money guide

As a trainee driver working towards your PCV licence you could expect to earn between £11,000 and £14,000 a year.

With experience your salary is likely to be £15,000 to £20,000. Coach drivers for specialist tours can earn around £25,000 a year.

You could supplement your income with overtime and shift work.

Related opportunities

- Driving Instructor p576
- Large Goods Vehicle Driver p580
- Taxi Driver p594

Further information

Driver and Vehicle Standards Agency
www.gov.uk/government/organisations/driver-and-vehicle-standards-agency

CHAUFFEUR

ENTRY LEVEL 1

Qualifications and courses

You will not need any specific academic qualifications to become a chauffeur. The only necessity is that you hold a full driving licence. Most employers will expect this to be clean but some do consider candidates with penalty points. You may benefit from holding an advanced driving certificate, details of which can be found through the Institute of Advanced Motorists. This demonstrates an enhanced driving ability and additional skills that may be valued by some employers.

It is beneficial to have several years' driving experience. Not only does this demonstrate a proven ability behind the wheel, but if you are over 21 years old you will cost your employer less to insure. Previous experience in a related driving job, such as a taxi driver, can be an advantage.

There are professional courses that you could take to enhance your application and understanding of the job, for example, NVQs in Road Passenger Vehicle Driving. The British Chauffeurs Guild offers a Security Chauffeur Training Course which covers the fundamental areas of chauffeuring: theory, practice, protocol, security and etiquette.

Some employers may also require you to pass a medical assessment and a Disclosure and Barring Services (DBS) check prior to taking you on. Others may have specific requirements such as car maintenance skills, the ability to speak a foreign language or to be a non-smoker.

What the work involves

Chauffeurs are responsible for driving their client to and from appointments or events, as well as the maintenance of the vehicle.

You will have to clean the vehicle regularly, inside and out, and also undertake any minor maintenance work when necessary, or book it in to be seen by a mechanic.

You will be providing a personal service to your passengers, including opening and closing doors for them, assisting them in and out of the vehicle, and carrying and loading their luggage or shopping. You might also be required to provide a low level of security protection to your client, as well as maintaining confidentiality at all times.

Type of person suited to this work

You must be an excellent driver who observes the law and keeps cool under pressure, even when faced with endless traffic jams or unpredictable clients. You will also need to have a good awareness of safety and security, both on the road and with regard to your client.

You should have excellent interpersonal skills. You must be punctual, respectful and polite.

Good map reading skills, knowledge of basic vehicle maintenance, and a reasonable level of fitness are also helpful.

Working conditions

It is unlikely that you will work regular hours as a chauffeur, as most clients will require your services during the evenings and at weekends. Split shifts are common, where you will find yourself with 2 or 3 free hours in between appointments.

You may be required to spend nights away from home on occasion.

You will need to wear a uniform in most instances.

Future prospects

Most chauffeurs are employed by limousine companies, but there are opportunities with hotel groups, car-hire companies, park and ride schemes, tour operators, businesses and private employers.

The British Chauffeurs Guild operates a specialist employment agency for its members, through which they can find suitable opportunities.

With experience, you can command a higher salary, or you could branch into a related career such as that of a taxi driver or driving instructor.

Advantages/disadvantages

You could work for some interesting, high profile clients.

The work offers some flexibility with hours.

There is a lot of waiting around for clients, which can get boring and frustrating.

Money guide

Salaries vary depending on your employer but typically average the starting wage for a chauffeur is between £12,500 and £18,000 a year. With a few years' experience this could rise to £25,000.

An experienced chauffeur could earn £30,000 or more.

Chauffeurs can earn extra money in overtime, bonuses and tips.

Related opportunities

- Driving Instructor p576
- Motor Vehicle Technician p218
- Taxi Driver p594

Further information

British Chauffeurs Guild
www.britishchauffeursguild.co.uk

Institute of Advanced Motorists
www.iam.org.uk

COURIER

ENTRY LEVEL 1

Qualifications and courses

There are no formal qualifications needed to become a courier but most employers will look for candidates with strong literacy and numeracy skills.

You will need a full driving licence and so will need to be at least 17 years old, though high insurance costs for young drivers mean that most driver couriers are over 21. School leavers could start as bicycle couriers.

Motorcycle couriers will need the Compulsory Basic Training (CBT) qualification issued by the Driver and Vehicle Licensing Authority (DVLA).

Commercial driving experience or knowledge of vehicle maintenance could help when looking for work.

Some courier firms may also offer apprenticeships which would enable you to combine on-the-job training with the study of an industry-related qualification, such as a BTEC in Carry and Deliver Goods (Levels 1–2) or an NVQ/SVQ in Driving Goods Vehicles (Levels 2–3).

What the work involves

You will collect fragile, valuable or urgent packages and letters and deliver them within an agreed time limit.

Once you have been allocated your job, you will travel to a collection point for pick-up. You will load up the goods and then take them to the drop-off point where you will obtain a signature for delivery.

Motorcycle couriers may travel long distances and van couriers carry larger parcels in a town or city.

Type of person suited to this work

Map-reading skills are essential. You may only be paid for the number of deliveries you do so you need to be quick and know where you are going.

You will be in constant contact with customers; collecting items, asking for instructions and getting signatures for deliveries, so you need to be good with people.

You should be very reliable, with excellent time-keeping skills, as you will often be handling high value or very urgent items.

Working conditions

You will spend a lot of time travelling as courier services operate 24/7 with many couriers working on overnight deliveries. Long distance or overseas deliveries might mean time away from home.

Motorcycle and bicycle couriers will be out in the weather at all times.

You might have to provide your own car or van and motorcycle or bicycle couriers usually use their own bikes. You will also be responsible for the maintenance of your vehicle and will be expected to check the lights, brakes and tyres of your motorbike, van or bicycle regularly.

Future prospects

The continued growth of online shopping and customer online tracking means that the demand for same and next day courier delivery is high. There are around 90,000 couriers working in the UK and almost 11,000 workplaces as competition among companies is fierce. This means there remains a demand for reliable couriers.

You could improve your prospects by becoming a member of the Institute of Couriers, the Despatch Association or the National Courier Association.

Promotion generally depends on the size of the courier company – large companies may have sales and management opportunities.

It might be possible to become self-employed and start your own courier service. You could also train further and move into a related area such as large goods vehicle driving, freight planning or distribution.

Advantages/disadvantages

Pay rates are good but if you are using your own transport you will have running, insurance and maintenance costs.

Making up to 20 journeys a day and possibly working 50-hour weeks make this a stressful job.

Most couriers take up the job because they are attracted to the freedom of travel. However most couriers do lots of repeat deliveries in a small, often congested, urban area.

Money guide

Couriers are often self-employed and paid for each delivery they make, so earnings vary. Some companies offer bonuses for delivering a certain number of items or for full attendance.

New couriers can earn between £12,000 and £14,500 a year.

Experienced couriers could earn £25,000 a year or more.

Motorcycle couriers in London can earn up to £23,000 a year, though part of that will go towards fuel, equipment and insurance.

Related opportunities

- Airport Baggage Handler p569
- Delivery Driver p574
- Warehouse Worker/Manager p597

Further information

Driver and Vehicle Standards Agency
www.gov.uk/government/organisations/driver-and-vehicle-standards-agency

Institute of Couriers
www.instituteofcouriers.com

CRUISE SHIP STEWARD/ PURSER

ENTRY LEVEL 1

Qualifications and courses

Steward

There are no formal entry requirements for this work, but relevant experience in the leisure and hospitality industry is normally required.

Training is provided on the job and will cover areas such as safety, health, environment, survival and rescue, fire, First Aid as well as company-specific training.

Qualifications such as a BTEC Level 2 in Hospitality and Catering Principles or a NVQ Level 2 Diploma in Housekeeping could help.

Purser

Good A levels/H grades are normally required, and many employers prefer a degree in a related subject such as hospitality or travel and tourism. The normal entry requirements for a degree in a travel- or hospitality-based subject are 2 A levels/3 H grades and 5 GCSEs/ National 5s (A*–C/A–C).

Related experience is normally required for employment as it demonstrates pre-entry commitment to the hospitality industry. For senior positions, managerial experience or a degree in hotel management may be required.

Knowledge of a language other than English is an advantage.

What the work involves

Steward

You will be responsible for keeping the public and private areas on a cruise ship clean and serviced to a very high standard. Duties may include making beds and vacuuming.

You may serve passengers drinks in the bar area, wash glasses and keep the bar stocked and tidy.

Purser

Pursers provide the administrative support necessary to ensure the ship operates smoothly and that passengers have a good holiday. You might work in the reception area, do secretarial duties or order various items of stock.

As well as providing passenger services you might also support crew members by paying their salaries or updating and maintaining immigration records.

Type of person suited to this work

As you will have contact with passengers, you should be happy meeting, talking with and helping people of all nationalities.

You should be polite and happy to help, and have good customer service skills.

You will need to be a dedicated employee as the work can be hard at times.

Working conditions

You will be expected to work long shifts, which for some posts can last up to 10 hours. Although cruise ships appear to be glamorous, you might work in cramped conditions or during rough weather.

You might have to share your accommodation with other members of staff.

Short-term, holiday and summer work is available.

Future prospects

In the last 7 years the cruise ship industry has become the second fastest growing sector in the UK and USA, so prospects are good.

There is a clear process of career progression. You will start as a member of crew then rise to officer as you gain skills and responsibilities.

The skills gained on-board will also be useful on land in many areas of hospitality and catering (steward) or the business sector (purser).

Advantages/disadvantages

You will be away from home for months at a time so your personal life will be affected.

You will be able to visit lots of places around the world.

Your accommodation could be cramped and you might have to share with other crew members.

Pay is very good; accommodation and food are free while on-board, and usually your salary is tax free if on a 6 month contract or longer.

Money guide

Salaries for all on-board positions are higher than for comparable jobs ashore. Salaries vary with company and liner, so contact companies directly for their earnings guide.

Stewards typically earn around £12,000 per year; this may increase slightly with experience. Free accommodation and food, as well as tips from passengers, boost the value of earnings.

The purser can expect a varying salary dependent on experience and responsibility. Salaries generally start from £19,000 to £21,000 per year as an assistant purser.

With experience and increased responsibility as the administration purser, this can increase to between £33,000 and £37,000.

A chief purser can earn between £45,000 and £55,000.

Related opportunities

- Holiday Representative p364
- Housekeeper/Accommodation Manager p130
- Tourist Information Centre Assistant p373

Further information

Springboard UK

www.springboarduk.net

DELIVERY DRIVER

ENTRY LEVEL 1

Qualifications and courses

No specific academic qualifications are required for delivery drivers but some employers prefer candidates with some GCSEs/National 5s (A*–E/A–E) or equivalent, including English and Maths. They also require good eyesight and perfect colour vision.

You will need to hold a good driving record and the appropriate driving licence for work as a delivery driver. Drivers also need a Driver Certificate of Professional Competence (CPC) which, to achieve, involves passing a short course.

If you gained your licence after 1 January 1997 you cannot drive vehicles over 3.5 tonnes. Acquiring an additional licence for category C1 will allow you to drive vehicles up to 7.5 tonnes and may increase opportunities. For this you will need to be at least 18 years old, pass a medical and take a large goods vehicle (LGV) theory and C1 practical test.

Training providers for both the CPC and the LGV can be found on the Joint Approvals Unit for Periodic Training (JAUPT) website.

Additionally, if you plan to work for a company that transports large sums of money or valuable items you will also need a Security Industry Authority (SIA) licence. This can be obtained on completion of the National Open College Network (NOCN) Level 2 Award in Cash and Valuables Transit.

What the work involves

You could be responsible for the safe transportation and delivery of a variety of goods, including food and drink, parcels and domestic appliances.

You will be loading and unloading goods from your vehicle, and making sure that your load is secure prior to starting on your journey. You will also be responsible for ensuring that your van is well maintained and roadworthy.

You will need to organise your own delivery schedule in order to meet strict distribution times each day.

Type of person suited to this work

You will need to be an extremely competent driver and be able to focus for long periods of time.

You should have a polite manner in order to build good relationships with colleagues and customers. You should be physically fit, as you might need to load and unload heavy items from your van.

Good map reading and navigational skills are helpful for finding your way round new and unfamiliar areas on a delivery. It is also important to be reliable and to stay calm in hazardous situations.

Working conditions

You might need to work 37–40 hours in shifts over evenings and weekends. Other companies will only deliver goods during standard working hours. Part-time work is often available.

You might work on your own or with another person who will help navigate and plan your route, and assist with loading and unloading goods.

You will spend the majority of your time in the van, and will have to drive and meet time-restricted schedules no matter what the weather. You might have to wear a uniform.

Future prospects

The rise of internet shopping has resulted in an increase in opportunities for delivery drivers and there is demand for drivers all over the UK, so you could work anywhere, although most opportunities are found in larger towns and cities.

You could work for a variety of companies, including retail, manufacturing and supermarkets, or you could opt for self-employment or start up your own delivery company.

You could choose to move into a related area in transport, such as an administrative or transport manager post.

Advantages/disadvantages

Part-time and flexible hours are available so you can fit work around other commitments.

You will be providing a valuable service to people, either delivering food or appliances to their homes, or transporting parcels or money safely around the UK.

The work can be quite lonely as you may work for long periods on your own.

Money guide

Starting salaries for full-time van drivers are usually around £11,000 to £13,000.

With experience this could rise to between £15,000 and £26,000.

Most van drivers earn around £19,000 to £21,000. You can increase your wage by working overtime and some employers give bonuses for attendance or reaching work targets.

Related opportunities

- Chauffeur p571
- Large Goods Vehicle Driver p580
- Train Driver p596

Further information

Driver and Vehicle Standards Agency
www.gov.uk/government/organisations/driver-and-vehicle-standards-agency

National Open College Network
www.nocn.org.uk

DISTRIBUTION MANAGER

ENTRY LEVEL 2

Qualifications and courses

It is possible to enter this role without a degree by working your way up from a transport clerk position, however an increasing number of candidates are graduates with either degrees, Foundation degrees or HNCs/HNDs. Any subject can be accepted but some employers may specifically prefer candidates with a degree in logistics and/or transport and distribution management. There are only a few undergraduate degrees in this subject but a growing number of postgraduate courses. Degrees in areas such as geography and supply chain management can also be useful.

The general entry requirements for a degree are 2 A levels/3 H grades and 5 GCSEs/National 5s (A*–C/A–C). Entry for an HNC/HND requires a minimum of 4 GCSEs/ National 5s (A*–C/A–C) and 1 A level/2 H grades, a related BTEC National Certificate/Diploma or equivalent.

Most companies are unlikely to take on new graduates in managerial roles, preferring several years' experience within the industry, however some larger organisations do have graduate recruitment schemes. Competition for these can be high so relevant work experience in areas such as retail, storage, warehousing or administration may be useful.

Apprenticeships are available in Traffic Office, Logistics Operations Management and Warehousing and Storage.

People working in the industry can study for the Chartered Institute of Logistics and Transport's (CILT's) professional qualifications. The Level 2 Certificate in Logistics and Transport is suitable for employees new to the profession. The Advanced Diploma is intended for recent graduates and is meant to be between undergraduate and postgraduate level.

What the work involves

You will be responsible for overseeing the control and movement of goods or raw materials held in stock.

Using IT, you will manage stock levels and monitor the ordering and storage of goods.

You will also manage staff and carry out their recruitment and training.

Type of person suited to this work

Distribution is a fast-moving industry and IT is at its centre, so you will need excellent computer skills. Like the computer programs you will use, you will need to be systematic and logical.

Brilliant communication skills are also a necessity as you will have to deal with people at different levels. It might be that the goods you have to order come from far-flung places. This means that the supply chain you will be managing might be very complex.

You will also need to be able to deal with the stress of making sure that you get the goods at the best price and supply them in the right condition.

Working conditions

Most of your work will be in an office, but you will also travel to meetings with suppliers or customers and visit storage depots.

Your hours will be mainly office hours, Monday–Friday, but you might have to do shift work or work weekends and evenings on a rota system.

There could be travel away from home and, for some, travel overseas.

Future prospects

Career development opportunities are good at the moment and there is a demand for experienced managers. You could work for a wide range of companies, including warehouse and distribution firms but also manufacturers, major retail companies, the armed forces and central and local government.

With experience, you could progress into a senior role in business development or undertake consultancy work.

Advantages/disadvantages

As a key figure in your company, you will have the satisfaction of making sure your supply chain works and that your customers are happy.

The demands of coordinating vehicles, products, people and tight deadlines, can make this a stressful role.

Money guide

Salaries for new graduates start at around £15,000 to £18,000 per year.

More experienced employees with management duties can earn £19,000 to £22,000, possibly more in larger companies. Graduates can double their starting salary after 5 years.

Senior distribution managers responsible for transport schedules can earn £45,000 to £60,000 per year. More is possible depending on the company size and various other factors. Managers often receive performance-related bonuses, health insurance, company cars and other benefits.

Related opportunities

- Freight Forwarder p577
- Importer/Exporter p579
- Warehouse Worker/Manager p597

Further information

Chartered Institute of Logistics and Transport
www.ciltuk.org.uk

Freight Transport Association
www.fta.co.uk

DRIVING INSTRUCTOR

ENTRY LEVEL 1

Qualifications and courses

You must be registered with the Driver & Vehicle Standards Agency (DVSA) as an Approved Driving Instructor (ADI). You will need to be 21 years old or over and have held a full clean driving licence for at least 3 years, with no disqualifications, criminal or motoring convictions and no more than 5 penalty points.

Before you register with the DVSA you must get a Disclosure and Barring Service (DBS) check for driving instructors. After registering you need to take 3 qualifying tests: an IT-based multiple choice theory test and video-based hazard perceptions test; a practical driving test; and a practical teaching test. Parts 2 and 3 must be completed within 2 years of completing part 1. You can take part 1 as many times as necessary but you must pass the others within 3 attempts each. If not you will have to wait 2 years from when you took part 1 and start again.

After you have passed the first 2 exams you could apply for the trainee licensing scheme. This is not essential but you will gain experience of driving instruction, for which you will have the right to receive payment. Once you pass all 3 tests you can apply for your first ADI badge.

The majority of entrants join a training organisation or an organisation which provides franchise prospects if you complete the training. Most trainees fund the training themselves, which can be expensive.

What the work involves

You will teach people how to drive safely, and well enough to pass their driving test. You will explain basic motor and road skills as well as safe and courteous driving.

Your role will include making your pupils aware of all aspects of the Highway Code, helping to develop observation skills and teaching manoeuvres such as reverse parking.

It will be your responsibility to plan driving lessons to suit your pupil and give constructive criticism.

Type of person suited to this work

Not only will you need to be a good, safe driver, you will also need teaching skills. People learning to drive are often nervous, susceptible to stress and anxious, so you will need to be calm, steady and very patient.

Instructors need to plan lessons to cover individual weaknesses. You will need to have quick reactions in order to prevent your pupils from causing any accidents.

As many instructors are self-employed, you will need to have a good business sense and the ability to manage your own finances.

Working conditions

Instructors can spend more than 8 hours a day sitting in the car ready to operate the dual controls to avert problems.

Early morning, evening and weekend work is common as you will teach lessons at times that suit your pupils.

Instructors with lots of experience can work a 35 to 40 hour week. However, you might have to work longer hours to keep a steady income. This can restrict the times and lengths of holidays for self-employed or franchised instructors.

Future prospects

Driving instructors could work for driving schools, operate under a franchise, or have their own businesses. Opportunities are also available with big transport companies, the emergency services, local authorities and the armed forces.

Around 80% of instructors are self-employed. There are no restrictions on the numbers of instructors meaning there is sometimes strong competition for pupils.

You could undertake fleet driver training and instruction in driving large goods or passenger-carrying vehicles. You could also progress to a role as a trainer for new driving instructors or a driving examiner.

Advantages/disadvantages

It can be very rewarding to enable learners to become safe, qualified drivers.

Many driving instructors are self-employed so you can choose your own working hours.

If you run your own car to give lessons you will have to pay for your fuel, insurance and maintenance costs.

It may be a challenge to maintain a steady income.

Money guide

Fees charged by instructors vary greatly because of competition in the industry, but they generally charge £15 to £30 per hour for a driving lesson. Your income will be reduced by the costs of running and maintaining your vehicle or paying a franchise fee.

Full-time driving instructors could earn £15,000 to £16,000 as a starting salary. With several years' experience this can rise to around £23,000 to £25,000.

It is possible for full-time, experienced driving instructors to earn over £30,000. Salaries are higher in London.

Related opportunities

- Chauffeur p571
- Taxi Driver p594
- Work-based Training Instructor p193

Further information

Driving Instructors Association
www.driving.org

Motor Schools Association of Great Britain Ltd
www.msagb.co.uk

UK Driving Instructors Confederation
www.ukdic.co.uk

FREIGHT FORWARDER

ENTRY LEVEL 2

Qualifications and courses

Entry requirements vary between employers but you will need a minimum of 4 GCSEs/National 5s, including English and Maths. Some employers may also ask for A levels/H grades or the BTEC Level 3 Certificate in Road Freight Logistics. Other useful qualifications might be a City & Guilds Level 2 Certificate in International Trade and Logistics Operations or a QCF Level 3 Certificate in Transporting Freight by Road.

Larger employers may expect a degree, HND or Foundation degree in a related subject such as logistics, supply chain management, economics or modern languages.

Entry to degree courses will require a minimum of 2 A levels/3 H grades and 5 GCSEs/National 5s (A*–C/A–C). For HNC/HND courses you will normally need at least 1 A level/2 H grades and 4 GCSEs/National 5s (A*–C/A–C).

The Apprenticeship in International Trade and Logistics can also be an entry route and some larger haulage companies run graduate training schemes for entry level candidates.

Language skills are useful and may lead to opportunities to work abroad. Previous experience in the freight industry is not required but experience in an office or in any area with a similar skill set to the freight industry is an advantage.

Edexcel Key Skills qualifications in Communication, IT, Problem-solving and Working with Others could be useful.

Professional bodies such as the British International Freight Association (BIFA) and the Chartered Institute of Logistics and Transport (UK) offer industry training programmes and qualifications that you might be encouraged or expected to take.

What the work involves

You will organise the transport of goods across the world for importers and exporters. Your role will involve working out if the freight needs special handling and whether it should go by sea, road or air.

Arranging the packing, carriage, collection and storage of the goods will be part of your job.

You will be responsible for dealing with paperwork, applying for customs clearance and calculating insurance, transport and customs costs.

Type of person suited to this work

As you will deal with lots of different customers, some of whom may not speak fluent English, you must have excellent communication skills.

You need to be determined and have excellent bargaining skills to get the best prices and terms. You will also be a good problem solver. For example, you might have to work out how to transport a valuable racehorse from Hong Kong to the UK.

You will require strong basic maths skills as you will be asked to calculate exchange rates, or work out if a large piece of cargo will fit into the cargo hold of a small aircraft.

Working conditions

Most of your work will be in an office at a workstation using a telephone, computer and fax machine. You will also need to travel to meet customers and contractors, within the UK and possibly abroad, so you will sometimes be away from home. A driving licence would be useful.

Depending on your employer, you might work normal office hours from Monday to Friday or you might work shifts and extra hours to cover urgent deliveries and world time zones.

Future prospects

Freight forwarding offices are usually in cities and near airports and ports. Opportunities are growing but it is a competitive industry and it helps if you have related work experience.

As you progress, there are opportunities to specialise in specific countries and industries. You could work within the entertainment industry, shipping film and concert sets around the world, or with medical and pharmaceutical supplies.

After gaining experience, you could progress to become a senior freight forwarder and then to a managerial role such as export office manager.

Advantages/disadvantages

This role offers varied opportunities – you could specialise in moving film and TV crews and their equipment or handling perishable goods such as fruit.

You might get a chance to travel or work overseas.

Working to meet tight delivery deadlines can be stressful.

Money guide

Starting salaries range from £16,000 to £25,000.

With 3 to 5 years of experience you could expect to earn £25,000 to £28,000 a year.

As a senior freight forwarder, manager or director you could achieve £35,000 to £40,000.

Related opportunities

- Distribution Manager p575
- Importer/Exporter p579
- Warehouse Worker/Manager p597

Further information

Chartered Institute of Logistics and Transport
www.ciltuk.org.uk

Institute of Export
www.export.org.uk

HELICOPTER PILOT

ENTRY LEVEL 3

Qualifications and courses

To fly commercially and charge for your services you will need to be over the age of 18 and hold the Joint Aviation Authority (JAA)'s Commercial Pilot Licence (CPL(H)), which is issued by the Civil Aviation Authority (CAA).

There are 2 main routes to obtaining a CPL(H). There is an integrated course that involves full-time training for 12 months to complete 500 hours of theoretical study, 135 hours of flight training, 9 exams and a flight skills test.

Alternatively, if you already have a Private Pilot's Licence for helicopter flying (PPL(H)), you may undertake modular training and qualify for your CPL(H) with 155 hours of flying experience, 500 hours of theoretical study, a 35-hour commercial flying course and 9 exams.

For both of these routes you will need at least 5 GCSEs/National 5s (A*–C/A–C) including English, Maths and a science (preferably Physics). You need to pass aptitude tests and a medical exam and raise money for training as sponsorships for helicopter pilots are rare. Courses cost in the region of £45,000. You can take a trial lesson with a flight school before committing to the full course.

If you have trained as a pilot in the armed forces you can take a conversion course to get a commercial licence. To pilot a 2-crew helicopter you will need an ATPL(H) (Advanced Airline Transport Pilot Licence).

What the work involves

You will most likely pilot a helicopter alone and you will be responsible for the safety of your passengers. You will carry out fuel, weather and route checks before taking off and you will keep in contact with air traffic controllers whilst navigating and monitoring the helicopter during the flight.

After landing you will log your hours and details from the flight.

You may fly for a variety of purposes including searching for missing persons, emergency work, crop spraying, photography, leisure trips or ferrying supplies.

Type of person suited to this work

You must be good with maths and physics, an excellent problem solver and a quick thinker in order to control your helicopter in all weather conditions and emergency situations. Strong communication and teamwork skills are essential.

Good coordination, spatial awareness and attention to detail are also important. You could be flying long hours and you will need stamina, forward-thinking skills and the ability to stay focused on your work.

As a pilot you are responsible for other people's safety so you must be reliable.

Working conditions

Helicopter pilots are usually provided with a uniform. If you fly over the sea for emergency services you will wear a survival suit. Most of your time will be spent sitting alone in a small space.

Your helicopter will be single or multi-engine and it will take time to adjust to the noise and sensation.

If you are a pilot within the leisure and tourism industry, you will most likely work during the daytime only. Emergency and business services may require you to fly through the night and at weekends. If you undertake long journeys, you may spend time away from home.

Future prospects

There are opportunities to work in emergency services, the armed forces and for commercial companies but competition is intense for newly qualified helicopter pilots.

With 1,000 hours of flight experience and 350 hours as 'pilot in command', you can go on to get your Advanced Airline Transport Pilot Licence (ATPL(H)). You can then fly multi-engine, multi-pilot helicopters for commercial air transport.

You could also set up your own air taxi service company or become self-employed.

Advantages/disadvantages

Helicopter training is expensive and you will need to raise a lot of money if you are unable to gain sponsorship.

Commercial piloting could lead you to be away from home for prolonged stretches of time, which could put a strain on your personal life.

You can meet new and interesting people during the course of your career, perhaps even celebrities.

No two days will be the same and it is exciting to be unaware of what each flight will hold.

Money guide

Newly qualified commercial helicopter pilots can earn between £20,000 and £25,000 per year.

Pilots with extensive experience captaining passenger-carrying helicopters can achieve between £45,000 and £65,000.

Allowances may be paid for overnight stays or flying to inhospitable areas.

Related opportunities

- Air Traffic Controller p567
- Airline Pilot p568
- Royal Air Force Airman/woman p535

Further information

British Helicopter Association
www.britishhelicopterassociation.org

Civil Aviation Authority
www.caa.co.uk

IMPORTER/ EXPORTER

ENTRY LEVEL 2

Qualifications and courses

There are no minimum qualifications to enter this industry but most employers will expect 4 GCSEs/National 5s (A*–C/A–C), including English and Maths. Others will ask for A levels/H grades or a relevant HND, Foundation degree or degree. Any subject that covers logistics, marketing, international trade, business or languages would be relevant at this level, although proficiency in a language subject is particularly in demand.

Entry onto degree courses requires 2 A levels/3 H grades and 5 GCSEs/National 5s. HNC/HND courses normally ask for 1 A level/H grade and 4 GCSEs/National 5s.

Many entrants start in a junior administration or sales position within an import/export or freight-forwarding company and work their way up, though larger companies may offer graduate training schemes.

Apprenticeships in Logistics Operations Management, Business and Administration or Sales and Telesales may equip you with relevant skills for this profession.

The Institute of Export (IOE) offers professional qualifications in international trade. You can take the Advanced Certificate in International Trade, which leads to associate membership of the IOE, or the Diploma in International Trade, which leads to graduate membership. Candidates must be at least 18 years old to take these courses.

What the work involves

You will organise all aspects of exporting or importing goods for companies which source or sell them overseas.

Liaising with shipping and forwarding companies, you will get the best prices, sources, quality and delivery services.

You will deal with all the necessary financial paperwork, including invoicing and checking, and issuing letters of credit so that payment can be made. You will also work out accurate costings, customs duties, insurance and forwarding charges.

Type of person suited to this work

You should have an interest in business and trade, as well as other countries and cultures.

As you will be making arrangements with a wide range of customers, you need to be confident, tactful and an excellent communicator. Language skills are a real advantage.

Dealing with numbers will be another of your key strengths because you will be responsible for working out currency exchanges and import and export duties.

You must be a good negotiator as you will need to bargain with shipping and distribution companies, as well as your customers and suppliers.

In addition, problem solving, IT and organisational skills are vital.

Working conditions

Most of your work will be in an office using the telephone, computer and fax machine.

You will usually work standard office hours from 9am to 5pm, Monday to Friday. You might need to work early mornings or late evenings if your customers or suppliers operate in a different time zone.

You may travel to meet suppliers or customers. At a senior level, you are likely to work overseas on a regular basis in order to maintain your network of business contacts.

Future prospects

As more products are bought and sold in a global market, the number of companies employing an import/export specialist has increased.

Freight-forwarding, industrial, retail and specialist companies such as flower, jewellery or fruit distributors all offer potential jobs.

Vacancies are competitive and usually require work experience in a related area.

Some import/export specialists move into overseas sales management or take up consultancy work.

Advantages/disadvantages

This job is satisfying as you are helping to make the global supply chain work.

You could be under a lot of stress to meet tight deadlines and budgets.

You might have the opportunity to travel overseas.

Money guide

Starting salaries at clerk level range from £11,000 to £15,000 per year.

Experienced staff with increased responsibilities can expect to earn up to £35,000.

Import or export managers of companies with global interests can achieve between £40,000 and £65,000 a year.

Related opportunities

- Freight Forwarder p577
- Road Transport Manager p593

Further information

Institute of Export
www.export.org.uk

LARGE GOODS VEHICLE DRIVER

ENTRY LEVEL 1

Qualifications and courses

No formal academic qualifications are required, although most employers prefer candidates who have GCSEs/ National 5s (A*–E/A–E) in English and Maths.

You need to be over 18 years old, have a full clean UK driving licence, pass a medical exam, have good eyesight and hold a large goods vehicle (LGV) licence. There are 3 categories of LGV licence: a C1 licence allows you to drive a truck up to 7.5 tonnes, a C licence is for rigid vehicles of over 7.5 tonnes, and a C+E licence is for vehicles with trailers. In order to obtain an LGV licence you need to pass both a theory and a practical driving test.

All drivers need to also train for the Driver Certificate of Professional Competence (Driver CPC) which involves passing a short course. To keep your licence, you are required to do 35 hours of training every 5 years. Training providers for both the CPC and the LGV can be found on the Joint Approvals Unit for Periodic Training (JAUPT) website.

If you want to carry dangerous goods you will need to undertake training to obtain an International Carriage of Dangerous Goods by Road (ADR) certificate, which is valid for 5 years before it must be renewed.

The Apprenticeship in Driving Goods Vehicles, which is available at both Intermediate and Advanced Levels, is a possible entry route into this career.

What the work involves

You will transport thousands of tonnes of cargo in your LGV. You could carry loads such as livestock, fuel, chemicals, food or construction equipment.

Your job is to deliver the cargo to its destination on time and you will work with your transport manager to find the best, most efficient route to do so.

You will sometimes help load and unload cargo, keep the goods safe, and refuel and clean your lorry after each journey.

Type of person suited to this work

You must be an excellent driver with good maths skills as you will be navigating long distances and calculating mileages. You should be able to use your initiative and follow safety precautions.

Quick reactions, good eyesight and colour vision are useful in case you need to respond to an unforeseen event on the road. It is essential that you can stay alert for long periods of time.

Overall, you need to be an experienced, confident and punctual driver. You should be polite when dealing with customers and also be content working on your own.

Working conditions

LGV cabs are cosy and quiet, equipped with cooking facilities, bunks, air conditioning and heating. These comforts are important as you will spend hours by yourself in your lorry, eating and sleeping in the cab.

On average, you will work 48 hours per week and legislation prevents you from exceeding 60 hours. Ten hours of night driving is the maximum you may do in a 24-hour period.

Your shifts will include evenings, nights and weekends.

Future prospects

If you work for a road haulage firm you will transport loads for multiple companies. You could also work for farms, transporting livestock, or move sporting goods for retailers. You could be employed by manufacturers, for example moving fleets of cars.

You could be promoted to a supervisor, become an instructor or move into driving hazardous goods. With further training you could become a manager or start up a company, operating your own lorry.

Advantages/disadvantages

You have freedom and flexibility in your work.

The job can be adventurous as you travel to different locations.

You might need to spend long periods of time away from home which can be difficult.

It can be frustrating when you are stuck in traffic and have a deadline to meet.

Money guide

Earnings vary by geographical location and employer.

Starting salaries are typically £14,000 to £17,000 per year.

With experience and increased responsibilities you could expect to earn £25,000 to £30,000.

If you choose to drive a specialist fuel or chemical tanker then your salary can increase up to £35,000.

Overtime pay can supplement your income.

Related opportunities

- Driving Instructor p576
- Taxi Driver p594
- Train Driver p596

Further information

Driver and Vehicle Standards Agency
www.gov.uk/government/organisations/driver-and-vehicle-standards-agency

Freight Transport Association
www.fta.co.uk

Road Haulage Association
www.rha.uk.net

LIFT TRUCK OPERATOR

ENTRY LEVEL 1

Qualifications and courses

There are no minimum entry qualifications for this job but basic maths is useful to work out safe loads and weights. English skills are also useful for paperwork and record keeping. You may have to pass a medical exam and an aptitude test as part of the application process and it is important to be in good physical condition.

You will need to be at least 18 years old to work without supervision, although you can start training at the age of 16. A driving licence is required if the truck is to be used on public roads.

Many employers require lift truck operators to have a Construction Plant Competence Scheme (CPCS) card before starting work. To qualify you will need to pass the NVQ Level 2 in Plant Operations, as well as the Construction Skills Health and Safety Test.

Direct entry to this career is possible but it may be advantageous to have experience of working in a warehouse. An Apprenticeship in Warehousing and Storage may provide you with relevant skills for this career and would lead to relevant NVQs/SVQs at Levels 2 and 3.

Lift truck operators can also work towards the National Proficiency Tests Council (NPTC) Level 2 Certificate of Competence in Forklift Truck Operations or an NVQ/SVQ Level 2 in Specialised Plant and Machinery Operations.

What the work involves

Operating a lift truck with a special fork and carrying platform, you will load, unload, move and stack heavy goods.

You will activate the controls so that your fork or lifting gear is under the load, usually stored on pallets, in cages or cases, to raise it safely. This may require manoeuvring at considerable heights.

You will then drive the goods, being careful not to damage them, to their destination. This could be a transport vehicle, a depot or a warehouse. You will also need to perform routine maintenance checks to your truck.

Type of person suited to this work

An aptitude for driving is vital. You will need to be focused and alert when manoeuvring your truck in narrow spaces, always on the lookout for potential hazards. A responsible, mature outlook is required for working to strict safety rules.

You will need to be physically fit and have good coordination. You might be working for a prolonged period so good concentration and care will be needed.

Although you will operate the truck on your own, you will also need to be a team player, working alongside warehouse operatives and large goods vehicle (LGV) drivers.

Working conditions

At times you will work inside a warehouse or factory and at other times outside in loading bays. While some trucks will have cabs offering protection from the weather, you need to be prepared to get cold and wet when working outside.

Operating your equipment will mean sitting in a driving seat for long periods.

Hours vary depending on your employer. You may work regular hours from Monday to Friday, but many jobs include shift work covering evenings and weekends.

Future prospects

There are about 100,000 lift truck operators in the UK. You may be employed by the manufacturing, transport, haulage, warehouse or retail industries.

With experience, you can move into supervisory or management roles in areas such as warehousing. You could go on to train new lift truck operators.

Some large employers may train you to become an LGV driver or instructor.

Advantages/disadvantages

You may have to work unsociable hours in shift patterns that vary from week to week, which can make it hard to organise your time.

Equally, this type of shift pattern can be flexible and fulfilling.

It can be stressful to get a load out quickly but it is very satisfying when transport leaves on time.

Money guide

Starting wages are about £12,000 per year. With some experience, you could expect to earn £16,000.

The most experienced operators can achieve a salary of £20,000 or more.

Shift allowances and the opportunity to do overtime can increase your income.

Related opportunities

- Airport Baggage Handler p569
- Construction Plant Operator p73
- Delivery Driver p574

Further information

Association of Industrial Truck Trainers
www.aitt.co.uk

Fork Lift Truck Association
https://fork-truck.org.uk

National Plant Operators Registration Scheme
www.npors.com

MERCHANT NAVY DECK OFFICER/RATING

ENTRY LEVEL 2

Qualifications and courses

You will need to be over 16, in good health with good eyesight, and pass a medical in order to join the Merchant Navy.

To become a rating most companies will expect you to have at least 3 GCSEs/National 5s, preferably in English, Maths and a science. If successful you will be sponsored through a training programme lasting 12 to 18 months.

Entrants wishing to become officers need either a Foundation degree/Scottish Professional Diploma in Nautical Science or Marine Operations, an HNC/HND in Nautical Science or an Honours degree in nautical science, merchant ship operations or marine studies. The general entry requirements for a degree are 2 A levels/3 H grades and 5 GCSEs/National 5s (A*–C/A–C). Full details of entry requirements can be found on the Merchant Navy Training Board website.

If successful in your officer application you will be trained over 3 to 4 years and study for academic qualifications whilst gaining on-the-job experience. Completion of training leads to the Maritime and Coastguard Agency Officer of the Watch Certificate of Competency.

You may also be considered for an officer role if you have previous relevant experience or if you were formerly a Royal Navy officer. For graduates, having evidence of teamwork, for example through activities such as the Duke of Edinburgh's Award, Sea Cadets, boating or sailing, will give you an advantage when applying.

What the work involves

The Merchant Navy consists of thousands of civilian ships, operated by individual shipping companies. They include fuel tankers and cargo ships, as well as ferries and cruise liners.

Merchant Navy deck officers are responsible for navigating ships, as well as being involved in communications and cargo handling.

Deck ratings are responsible for supporting the ship's officers by helping to navigate and steer the ship, as well as carrying out maintenance tasks and helping to load and unload cargo.

Both jobs will involve using satellite and radar systems to navigate the ship, maintaining machinery and safety equipment, and training and support of junior officers and ratings.

Type of person suited to this work

Both officers and ratings need to have good social skills in order to work successfully as part of a team. You will also need to be calm and logical in the face of emergency situations.

In addition, officers will need to have excellent numeracy skills and be able to use complex technology in order to successfully make navigational calculations.

Officers will also need to have good leadership qualities, so that they inspire respect and dedication from their crew members.

Working conditions

You will expect to work shifts, known as 'watches'. These can vary in length from 4 hours on and 4 hours off, to 6 hours on and 6 hours off, or even 12 hours on and 12 hours off at times. These shifts can take place at any time.

Ratings can expect to live in close proximity to their colleagues, often in fairly cramped accommodation. Officers typically have their own private, en-suite cabin.

Generally, good leisure facilities are provided on-board so that crew can make the most of their time off.

Future prospects

Ratings can progress to seaman (Grade 2) or take a conversion course to become an officer. However, only a small number of companies offer places for trainee ratings, so there are relatively few opportunities to enter the Merchant Navy through this route.

There are around 800–900 places for new officers every year and competition is quite high. Officers may move into related onshore work, including shipbuilding, maritime law and ship and fleet management.

Advantages/disadvantages

You will be working within a strong team environment, so will build excellent relationships with colleagues from a variety of backgrounds.

Shift work can be exhausting.

You will have to spend long periods of time away from your family and your personal life will be severely affected.

Money guide

Trainee Merchant Navy ratings can expect to earn around £15,000 to £16,000 per year. This can increase to up to £30,000 with experience.

For officers, trainee salaries for cadets are around £7,000 to £15,000. Newly qualified deck officers may have a starting salary of £23,000 to £27,000. Senior officers' salaries can rise to £60,000.

Your employer will pay for food and accommodation while at sea and holiday allowance is usually very generous. For every month you spend at sea you can get a month's paid leave.

Related opportunities

- Marine Engineer p215
- Merchant Navy Engineering Officer p583

Further information

Marine Society & Sea Cadets
www.ms-sc.org

Merchant Navy Association
www.mna.org.uk

Merchant Navy Training Board
www.mntb.org.uk

MERCHANT NAVY ENGINEERING OFFICER

ENTRY LEVEL 5

Qualifications and courses

You will need to be at least 18, be in good health with good eyesight and pass a medical to join the Merchant Navy. You will also need to secure sponsorship from a shipping company who will provide you with work placements whilst you are at sea.

There are 4 educational routes to becoming an engineering officer, depending on your current qualifications.

The first is to study for an Honours degree in marine engineering, marine operations or nautical science. Entry requirements vary but 2 A levels/3 H grades, including maths and/or a science, and 5 GCSEs/National 5s (A*–C/A–C) are often the minimum required. Secondly, if you already have a science-based degree but it is not specifically directed towards this line of employment you will need to complete a relevant postgraduate course to boost your employability.

The third route is to study for an HNC/HND in Marine Engineering, for which you will need GCSEs/National 5s (A*–C/A–C) in English, Maths, a science and at least one other subject. Alternatively, you can study for a Foundation Diploma in marine or mechanical which requires the same GCSEs along with 2 A levels/H grades.

Whichever training route you follow, you will need to take and pass an exam for the Certificate of Competency (also known as the Officer of the Watch Certificate), which is distributed by the Coastguard and Maritime Agency.

Evidence of teamwork, for example through activities such as the Duke of Edinburgh's Award, Sea Cadets, boating or sailing, will give you an edge when applying for positions.

What the work involves

The Merchant Navy consists of thousands of civilian ships, operated by individual shipping companies. They include fuel tankers and cargo ships, as well as ferries and cruise liners. Merchant Navy engineering officers work with all the mechanical and electrical equipment on-board ships.

You will work on areas of the ship such as the engines, the computer-controlled engine management systems, and the pumps and fuel systems.

Engineering officers are based in the engine control room of a ship. They are responsible for assisting in the repair and servicing of technical equipment.

Type of person suited to this work

You will need to be interested in working with very high-tech machinery and enjoy learning about new, state-of-the-art technology.

You will also need to be very practical and logical so that you can work quickly and efficiently to rectify problems that occur with the equipment.

You should enjoy working as part of a close-knit team and have a high level of self-discipline. Impeccable communication skills are essential for these roles.

Working conditions

You will expect to work shifts, known as 'watches'. These can vary in length from 4 hours on and 4 hours off, to 6 hours on and 6 hours off, or even 12 hours on and 12 hours off at times. These shifts can take place at any time, day or night.

You will spend the majority of your time in the engine control room or the engine room itself, where it will be hot and noisy. As an engineering officer you could be responsible for all of the ship's systems.

Generally, good leisure facilities are provided on-board so that crew can make the most of their time off.

Future prospects

Opportunities for work are good as the marine sector is growing. Most people who undertake officer training programmes are employed at the end of it.

Officers may rise through the ranks to reach the level of chief engineer. Alternatively, there are also opportunities in related areas such as ship surveying or ship management.

There are also opportunities to work for companies based overseas.

Advantages/disadvantages

You will be working within a strong team environment, so will build excellent relationships with colleagues from a variety of backgrounds.

The relentless nature of shift work can be exhausting.

You will have to spend long periods of time away from your family so your personal life is severely affected.

Money guide

Sponsored trainee salaries are roughly £7,000 to £8,000 per year. Once you are qualified this jumps significantly to around £25,000 to £27,000 a year.

Chief engineers can earn up to £60,000.

Whilst at sea, your food and accommodation will be paid for by your employer. Holiday leave is usually very generous. For every month you spend at sea you will get a month's paid leave.

Related opportunities

- Marine Engineer p215
- Mechanical Engineer p217
- Motor Vehicle Technician p218
- Royal Navy Rating p540

Further information

Merchant Navy Association
www.mna.org.uk

Merchant Navy Training Board
www.mntb.org.uk

PASSENGER CHECK-IN OFFICER

ENTRY LEVEL 2

Qualifications and courses

Entry requirements vary, but many employers prefer applicants with 3–5 GCSEs/National 5s (A*–C/A–C), including English and Maths. Some companies may require you to be at least 18 years old.

Employers may ask for experience of working in a customer service role or the ability to speak another language. As shifts will often be at unsocial hours you will need to live near the airport and possibly have your own transport.

You may be able to get into this role through an Apprenticeship in Aviation Operations on the Ground which combines professional work experience with the study of an industry-related qualification, such as a GCSE/National 5 or A level/H grade in Leisure and Tourism, a BTEC or NVQ/SVQ in Travel and Tourism, Customer Service or Aviation Operations, or Key Skills in Communication or Information Technology.

Once employed you will be trained for 4 to 8 weeks in all aspects of the job.

What the work involves

You will be responsible for making sure that passengers and their baggage board the right aircraft.

You will greet passengers, provide information, ask security questions and check tickets and passport details. You will also handle passenger enquiries.

Once you have weighed and put luggage on the conveyor belt, you will issue boarding passes and prepare paperwork for customs. You could also work at the flight gate, making announcements and checking boarding cards.

If a passenger is late, you may need to contact boarding staff to let them know and assist the passenger in reaching the gate quickly.

Type of person suited to this work

As the public face of your airline, you will need a pleasant, confident and helpful manner with a well-groomed appearance.

You need to be confident with IT as you will use a sophisticated computer system to allocate seats, print boarding cards and baggage labels and produce post-flight figures.

You must be friendly and approachable as you will be helping passengers, including those with disabilities and unaccompanied children, from check-in, through security, and onto their flight. You will also need to be able to deal with difficult situations. Good communication skills are essential for working with your colleagues and other airport staff.

Working conditions

You will wear a uniform and work indoors at an airport. When you are working at the check-in desk you may sit behind a counter for long periods.

If you are escorting passengers or helping with boarding at a gate, you will spend periods of time on your feet, sometimes walking quite long distances and carrying luggage.

Hours will include shifts covering evenings, weekends and holidays. This is done to cover all the times the airport is open.

Future prospects

Employers are either airlines or the ground handling companies that work on their behalf.

There are currently around 138,000 people working in this sector in total and opportunities for work increase dramatically if you live within travelling distance of one of the big 4 UK airports – Heathrow, Gatwick, Stansted and Manchester. There is a lot of competition for jobs, many of which are seasonal.

You could progress to be a member of the air cabin crew or a supervisor within passenger services.

Advantages/disadvantages

You will get to meet all types of new people from across the world.

If there is a delay to their flight, you might have to deal with difficult or demanding passengers.

If you are keen to work as a member of air cabin crew or similar role, experience in this work will be a big advantage.

Money guide

Starting salaries are between £12,000 and £14,000 per year.

Experienced passenger check-in officers can earn between £15,000 and £20,000.

In a supervisory or management post you could earn more.

Shift allowances are usually paid for working unsocial hours and there may be opportunities to earn overtime pay or increased salaries for candidates with a special skill such as fluency in a foreign language.

Some airline companies grant their employees free parking and concessions on flight costs and at retail outlets at the airport.

Related opportunities

- Air Cabin Crew p566
- Holiday Representative p364
- Tour Guide/Manager p372

Further information

GoSkills
www.goskills.org

Royal Aeronautical Society
www.aerosociety.com

PASSENGER TRANSPORT CLERK

ENTRY LEVEL 2

Qualifications and courses

There are no formal qualifications required to enter this profession, however GCSEs/National 5s in English and Maths (A*–C/A–C) may be useful.

You will learn largely on the job, although some training might be provided and many companies will provide their own in-house training, or organise day-release training for clerical staff.

If you are going into a position as a rail passenger transport clerk or a member of telephone enquiry bureau staff, you will be trained in fare structures, customer care, railway geography and computerised ticket systems.

You may also be provided with training from bus and coach companies which will involve learning how to use timetables, and ticket systems, and understanding price structures and customer care information.

What the work involves

As a passenger transport clerk you will deal with customer enquiries regarding departure times, fares, routes, connections and disruptions on bus and rail services.

You will use computerised systems to organise the purchase or refund of tickets and in order to issue travel cards.

You will research the best rail or coach fares for a customer and ensure that their transport is as efficient and affordable as possible.

You may specialise in either sales or customer enquiries but usually members of staff share these responsibilities amongst themselves.

Type of person suited to this work

You should be friendly and polite and have a genuine interest in travel, customer service and working with the public.

Some maths and IT skills will be necessary as you will be dealing with fares and payments.

You must be able to work quickly and efficiently so that passengers are not delayed getting to their train/bus.

As you might have to deal with customers at busy times or times when there are unexpected delays, you need to have patience and the ability to deal with frustrated or angry customers. Good oral communication skills are therefore important.

Working conditions

You will work an average of 37 to 40 hours each week. This may include shift work, evenings, weekends and even public holidays.

You may have the opportunity to work part time, overtime and flexible hours.

You will be based in stations, or travel centres which will function essentially as an office, but you will deal with customers on the phone or as they come to the ticket office or information desk you are based at.

Future prospects

Further training and qualifications will aid future progression. You may gain NVQs/SVQs as you work in order to progress to supervisory and managerial roles.

You may be employed by any bus or coach operator or private rail companies, train operating companies throughout the UK, the London Underground or Eurostar.

Advantages/disadvantages

You will have the opportunity to work in an ever-changing environment as bus and rail services are constantly updated.

Assisting members of the public with their queries can provide variety, but delays and cancellations can also create a stressful situation having to deal with customer anger.

Your work is likely to often be repetitive, doing similar tasks on a daily basis.

The opportunities for progression without further training and qualifications are not great.

Money guide

Your starting salary as a transport clerk may be around £14,500 a year.

With some experience this can increase to £17,000.

With several years' experience and qualifications, you can earn between £19,500 and £22,500.

Related opportunities

- Customer Services Assistant/Manager p456
- Passenger Check-in Officer p584
- Train Conductor/Guard p595
- Travel Agent p374

Further information

Customer Contact Association
www.cca.org.uk

GoSkills
www.goskills.org

POSTAL DELIVERY WORKER

ENTRY LEVEL 1

Qualifications and courses

No specific qualifications are required for this job, however candidates should be aged 18 or over. Selection for employment is by an aptitude test, a fitness assessment and interview. You might need to pass a medical examination or test to ensure that you can read addresses properly and spot any mistakes.

The ability to ride a bicycle and/or possession of a driving licence with no more than 6 penalty points may also be required.

Apprenticeships are available from the Royal Mail and these combine professional work experience with the opportunity to study for an industry-related qualification such as an NVQ/SVQ Level 2 in Mail Services.

Once employed you will receive induction training, with further training done, mostly, on the job and lasting 18 months. Once you have gained a minimum of a year's experience, you can seek advancement to supervisory or managerial levels.

What the work involves

You will sort and deliver post to homes, shops, factories and offices in your area.

Your day will start at the sorting office, getting your deliveries ready for transporting and packing your bag in the best order for your route.

You will then deliver the post by foot, bicycle or, in rural areas, by van. If working in a rural area you may also be responsible for delivering other goods such as milk. You might also be responsible for collections from post boxes and places of work.

Ensuring that packages are received safely, and that large packages are either left in a safe area or signed for will be important. If the recipients are not in, you will have to document and record time of delivery and reason for not delivering, if applicable.

Type of person suited to this work

Your round could include several hundred addresses and cover several miles a day so you will need to be fit, especially if you are doing the job on foot or by bicycle. You should also enjoy being outdoors as you will be expected to deliver the mail in all weathers.

Honesty and reliability are vital qualities in this job. You will be carrying lots of valuable and urgent post around and you will be responsible for delivering it to the right place.

Good customer service skills and a friendly attitude are important.

Working conditions

Most of your work will be outside in all weathers. A uniform, footwear and protective clothing will be provided. If on foot, you might have to carry your deliveries in bags, though there will be arrangements to transport you and your post out to the start of your route.

Shift work with an early morning (5am) start or late evening (10pm) finish is usual. You will often work on a Saturday.

You might have to walk up steep hills and deal with minor hazards.

Future prospects

Postal delivery workers mainly work for the Royal Mail.

Recruitment tends to be steady and there are opportunities in urban and rural areas throughout the UK.

Postal work can be seasonal, particularly over the Christmas period. Some workers start out with temporary work over the Christmas period and are retained.

It is possible to move into parcel deliveries, supervisory or managerial work.

Advantages/disadvantages

With a regular round you will really get to know your customers.

There might be some hazards on your round, however all the walking or cycling will keep you fit.

Although you will have to start work by 5am if you are on the early shift, you will finish at around lunchtime.

Even if you drive for your rounds, you will still be subject to the weather conditions.

Money guide

Starting pay for staff over 18 is £13,312 a year.

After a year's experience you can expect to earn between £14,820 and £16,172.

With further experience postal delivery workers outside of London can expect to earn £19,280 and £20,405 is common for those working within London.

There are additional payments for overtime and sometimes for shift work which takes place during unsocial hours.

Related opportunities

- Courier p572
- Delivery Driver p574
- Freight Forwarder p577

Further information

Royal Mail Group
www2.royalmailgroup.com

Skills for Logistics
www.skillsforlogistics.org

PURCHASING/PROCUREMENT MANAGER

ENTRY LEVEL 4

Qualifications and courses

Entry requirements vary but employers usually ask for a degree, though it may be possible to enter at an administrative level and progress with experience and on-the-job training. Whilst this field is open to all graduates, a degree in business studies, operations management, retail management, purchasing and logistics or purchasing and supply may be beneficial.

To progress you will need Chartered Institute of Purchasing & Supply (CIPS) professional qualifications. You can study at all levels from a Level 2 Introductory Certificate up to a Level 7 Executive Diploma. The Introductory Certificate has no formal entry requirements and once you have completed it you can progress to higher level qualifications. The CIPS diplomas are usually in Procurement and Supply or Procurement and Supply Operations at the lower levels.

Most employers will want their purchasing managers to be full members of the CIPS or working towards it. For this you need to either have a CIPS-accredited degree or have worked for 3 years and completed the Level 6 Graduate Diploma. Entry onto the diploma course requires at least 2 A levels/3 H grades and 3 GCSEs/National 5s (A*–C/A–C), or equivalent qualifications.

What the work involves

You will be responsible for buying the goods or services needed by a business, and providing the best value for money.

Your first job is to find out what your employer wants to buy and how much the budget is.

An important aspect will be to find the best suppliers and negotiate with them to get products or services at the right conditions and price. You will then be responsible for quality checks to make sure that the goods or services provided are of the standard agreed.

Type of person suited to this work

You must have excellent negotiation and communication skills in order to get the best quality and lowest priced goods and services for your company.

IT and numerical skills are essential for researching, calculating costs and managing a budget.

You will need to be organised and analytical and have a good business-sense, as you will evaluate the multiple deals available to work out which is the best fit for your company.

As a result, you will also need to be decisive, making informed decisions confidently.

Working conditions

You will work Monday to Friday, from 9am to 5.30pm although longer hours may occur if you work in the manufacturing industry or if your suppliers are in a different time zone to the UK, which can mean early mornings or late nights.

You will be located in a busy office, although you may travel to meet suppliers and customers which can mean time away from home.

Future prospects

Jobs are available in nearly all areas of the business sector including manufacturing, retailers, wholesale and government organisations. There is a lot of competition for jobs but not as much as in related areas such as marketing.

Some buyers move into specialist areas, for example construction or chemicals. IT purchasing is a new specialism and is predicted to grow with the expansion of e-business.

Promotion prospects are good, especially in large organisations. It may be possible to progress to a role as director. Increasing numbers of experienced managers are choosing to become self-employed and work as consultants or contract workers.

Advantages/disadvantages

If successful, you can reach high levels of responsibility, and even travel overseas, early in your career.

This job is stressful. Businesses spend over half their money on the goods and services they need to buy, so mistakes could be expensive.

Money guide

Entry-level graduates may earn around £18,000. Junior managers can earn £20,000 to £25,000 and with time and promotion to higher levels you could earn £30,000 to £40,000. £50,000 to £100,000 or more is possible for senior managers and directors.

Members of the CIPS tend to earn more than non-members.

Related opportunities

- Distribution Manager p575
- Importer/Exporter p579
- Warehouse Worker/Manager p597

Further information

Chartered Institute of Purchasing & Supply
www.cips.org

Skills for Logistics
www.skillsforlogistics.org

RAIL SIGNALLING TECHNICIAN

ENTRY LEVEL 2

Qualifications and courses

Network Rail operates a 3-year advanced apprenticeship programme for those aged between 16 and 24, as do many other employers of rail signalling technicians. Candidates usually need to have 3 to 5 GCSEs/National 5s (A*–C/A–C), including English, Maths and a science, to apply. Apprenticeships combine professional work experience with the opportunity to study towards an industry-based qualification, such as the NVQ/SVQ in Railway Engineering (Signalling) (Levels 2–3).

Most employers operate their own selection process on top of these academic requirements. This usually consists of a medical test, which will assess your fitness, eyesight and hearing, as well as drug and alcohol screening. Occasionally you may also have to sit an aptitude test.

You will be expected to work towards an Institution of Railway Signal Engineers (IRSE) licence while you're training and you will also be put through the Personal Track Safety (PTS) course, after which you will receive a safety card and be passed to work on the railway tracks.

You can also enter this profession after gaining experience as a mechanical or electrical technician in another industry. Electrical or electronics engineers with an HNC/HND and at least 3 years' experience can take Network Rail's Signal Engineering Conversion Programme.

A double GCSE/National 5 in Engineering or a related technical subject would also be helpful in finding work.

What the work involves

Rail signalling technicians are responsible for installing and repairing all of the signalling and telecommunications systems that are used to support the railways.

Equipment that you will be working on will include signal boxes, warning systems, manual lever frame boxes and coloured light signals.

You will also install new signalling equipment, such as GSM-R communication masts, and update existing systems.

Type of person suited to this work

You should have good manual dexterity in order to operate a range of tools and machines.

A logical approach to your work will help when tracing faults, as will the ability to understand technical drawings and engineering instructions when repairing systems. You will need good eyesight and full colour vision.

You should have a reasonable level of numeracy and good IT skills so that you can operate computerised machinery. You will also need to be physically fit, as the work can include lifting and carrying heavy equipment, as well as working up ladders or in awkward places.

Working conditions

You will work around 37 hours a week, most likely in a shift pattern that could include early morning, evening and weekend work. You may also be expected to work overtime fairly regularly.

Your time will be divided between working outside, carrying out repairs trackside, and undertaking maintenance near signal boxes or within stations. You should be prepared to work in any weather conditions.

You may well have to travel to various different locations each day; overnight absence from home is common.

Future prospects

You could be employed by Network Rail, working on the UK's commercial railway tracks, or by a number of underground, metro or light rail operators such as London Underground, Metronet, Translink and the Docklands Light Railway.

It is important to continue to develop your skills throughout your career, for example by taking training courses and development programmes. With experience you can become a member of the Institution of Railway Signal Engineers, which offers a route into becoming a registered engineering technician.

You could end up as a team manager or even move into a consultancy role.

Advantages/disadvantages

You will be playing an essential role in maintaining and developing the infrastructure of the UK.

Promotion opportunities are good, and there is also the chance to undertake extra training to drive forward your career.

Working in all weather conditions and cramped surroundings can be uncomfortable and extremely unpleasant at times.

Money guide

Network Rail's apprenticeship scheme starts out on a salary of £8,400, plus a £1,150 bonus when you successfully complete the first year. They also pay for your accommodation, food and work clothing. In the second year the salary rises to £11,750 and in the third year to £14,000.

If you become a senior technician or move into a consultancy role your salary could reach in excess of £40,000.

Related opportunities

- Electrician p78
- Electricity Distribution Worker p204
- Telecommunications Technician p149

Further information

Railway-technology.com
www.railway-technology.com

RAIL TRACK MAINTENANCE OPERATIVE

ENTRY LEVEL 3

Qualifications and courses

There are no formal entry requirements, however Network Rail and other employers may look for candidates with a minimum of 4 GCSEs/National 5s (A*–C/A–C) or equivalent, including English, Maths, a science and one other technical subject. Previous experience in construction or civil engineering would be an advantage.

Qualifications in related subjects, such as a GCSE/National 5 or A level/H grade in Engineering or the City & Guilds NVQ Level 1 in Basic Track Maintenance or Level 2 Certificate in Engineering, may be helpful in demonstrating your enthusiasm for the role and securing employment.

Network Rail operates a large apprenticeship programme for those aged 16–24, which provides another possible route into the profession by combining professional work experience with the opportunity to study for an industry-related qualification.

You will have to be physically fit and most employers will ask you to take a medical assessment to measure your fitness, stamina, hearing and eyesight. You will also have to take tests for drugs and alcohol.

Some employers require candidates to go through a Disclosure and Barring Service (DBS) check, as the role of a maintenance operative is critical in ensuring railway safety.

Your employer will send you on the Personal Track Safety (PTS) course to earn a safety card, which you will need before you can work on the tracks.

What the work involves

Rail track maintenance workers are responsible for building, repairing and maintaining the rail track network across the UK.

You will use a variety of manual and automated tools including welding equipment, clamping machines and cement mixers.

You will also be responsible for inspecting the track in order to spot potential faults, which will involve walking along live tracks, with trains passing nearby.

Type of person suited to this work

You will need to be fit and strong to undertake this work, as you will be lifting and moving heavy pieces of track, as well as operating powerful machinery at times. You should also have good manual skills in order to use tools effectively and safely.

You must be a good communicator so you can work effectively within a team. You should be able to listen to instructions and take direction, whilst also having the confidence to use your own initiative and help colleagues when necessary.

You should have a good awareness of on-site safety practice and a responsible attitude to your work.

Working conditions

You will work an average of 35 hours per week on a shift system. You will have to work nights, weekends and bank holidays regularly, as these are the times at which maintenance work causes least disruption to the train timetable.

Work usually takes place outdoors, in all weather conditions. You should be prepared to get cold and wet working in muddy conditions, and also extremely hot in the summer months.

You will have to wear protective clothing; including a hard hat, high visibility jacket and reinforced boots.

Future prospects

Network Rail employs almost all the rail track maintenance workers in the UK and they continuously update track all around the country.

There are also opportunities with rail employment agencies, who recruit workers for specific projects managed by rail engineering contractors.

With experience, you could progress to a supervisory role or become a specialist in a technical area such as line-laying or welding.

Advantages/disadvantages

The work is physically tiring but rewarding, as you will be working towards maintaining the infrastructure of the UK.

You will be working in a team, so the job will be sociable and you will build strong relationships with your colleagues.

Working in all weather conditions can be uncomfortable and extremely unpleasant at times.

Money guide

Your salary as an apprentice rail track worker will be between £8,400 and £14,000 per year, depending on which year of the apprenticeship you are in.

The average starting pay for a rail track worker is about £14,000 per year.

Once you have spent a few years in the role and built up your skills you could be earning £20,000 or more.

Rail track workers with additional supervisory responsibilities can earn up to £30,000.

Related opportunities

- Bricklayer p60
- Rail Signalling Technician p588
- Stonemason p108

Further information

Institute of Mechanical Engineers
www.imeche.org

Network Rail
www.networkrail.co.uk

RAILWAY STATION ASSISTANT

ENTRY LEVEL 2

Qualifications and courses

You must be at least 18 years of age to do this job. Good communication skills and numerical ability are viewed as extremely important by employers, so most train operating companies (TOCs) require candidates to have 4 GCSEs/National 5s (A*–E/A–E), including English and Maths. You may be tested on these skills during interviews as well as being required to pass medical assessments, which will include eyesight, colour vision and hearing tests, and having to have occasional drugs and alcohol testing.

Employers favour candidates who have previous experience in customer relations roles, whether paid or voluntary.

Candidates usually apply directly to TOCs or Network Rail. Once employed as a railway station assistant, you will have to undergo a short training period that will encompass classroom-based learning programmes including health and safety, customer care, railway operating systems and coping in emergency situations. This will be followed by practical training in the station. Some TOCs also encourage employees to work towards a NVQ Level 2 in Rail Services as part of their training.

What the work involves

Railway station assistants work within train stations, assisting customers, dealing with queries and ensuring that passengers are happy.

You may work behind a ticket desk, on an information stand, or on the station platforms so that you are accessible to passengers.

You will need to provide assistance to wheelchair users and other people who require help boarding or disembarking from a train. You will check tickets, and be on the lookout for any security threats or other problems within the station.

You will also keep up to date with arrivals information, directing passengers to the correct platform and informing them about delays and possible other routes they can take.

Type of person suited to this work

You will need to be a confident communicator so that you can impart information to passengers, and also field any negative comments that might be directed towards you.

You should be polite and approachable, and maintain a clean, smart appearance. You will need good hearing and eyesight, as well as a high level of fitness in order to physically assist customers and move around the station quickly when necessary.

You should be able to work well within a team, taking instructions and helping colleagues, but also enjoy working autonomously and using your initiative.

Working conditions

You will usually work 37 hours per week, and this will include early morning, late night and weekend shifts.

There are usually opportunities to undertake paid overtime work.

You will also be working within ticket offices or passenger information areas in the station. You will have to wear a uniform so that you are easily recognisable to passengers.

Future prospects

You could work either for a train operating company or for Network Rail, within large or small train stations across the UK.

There are also opportunities to work for underground or metro operators in some cities.

You could progress as a ticket inspector, conductor or driver, move upwards to become assistant station manager or even reach the position of station manager.

Advantages/disadvantages

You will be working in a variety of roles each day so work should not get monotonous.

You will spend a lot of time on freezing station platforms in the winter.

You may have to deal with aggressive passengers at times.

Money guide

Your starting salary as a railway station assistant is likely to be about £12,500 to £13,500 per year.

As you gain experience and knowledge, you could earn from £14,000 up to around £21,000. If you are promoted to team leader your salary will increase to £21,000 or more.

Overtime is always available, so your wages could be increased if you are willing to work extra hours. Benefits can sometimes include free or reduced travel.

Related opportunities

- Rail Track Maintenance Operative p589
- Train Conductor/Guard p595
- Train Driver p596

Further information

National Rail Enquiries
www.nationalrail.co.uk

Network Rail
www.networkrail.co.uk

Qualifications and courses

No formal academic qualifications are required, although GCSEs/National 5s (A*–E/A–E) in English and Maths are useful. While some firms will accept you at 16 years old, many specify a minimum age of 18 or even 21. It is important that you are physically fit and you may need to pass a medical in order to be successfully employed.

To work as a removals operative driver you will need a large goods vehicle (LGV) licence, as well as a Driver Certificate of Professional Competence (Driver CPC). You must be at least 18 years old to train for an LGV licence and you will be required to undertake both a theory and a practical driving test.

Edexcel offers an Award, Certificate and Diploma in Commercial Moving (Levels 1–3) which may be useful or you can enter this job through the Intermediate Apprenticeship in Commercial Moving. Experience in delivery driving, warehousing or other related areas can give you an advantage when applying for this course or apprenticeship scheme.

Most entrants are trained on the job by experienced colleagues. Some firms send employees on courses run by the British Association of Removers (BAR). Statutory training covers topics such as health and safety, manual handling and risk assessment, while skills training is offered in areas including fragile, commercial and specialist packing. You may be able to take NVQs/SVQs in Warehousing and Storage (Levels 1–2) or in Driving Goods Vehicles (Levels 2–3).

What the work involves

Removals operatives move furniture, garden, household and office items into storage or to new sites. This involves carefully packing goods and taking apart large items to fit into the removals van.

You must plan how you will pack the van in advance to make the most of the space and to prevent damage to the goods during transit. You will also need to unload and unpack as well as placing them in specific places on arrival, at the customer's direction.

Type of person suited to this work

Your customers will most likely be stressed about moving and will rely on you to remain calm and cheerful. You should be friendly and personable.

An honest and careful approach to your work is vital as you will be dealing with valuable and fragile items on a regular basis. You should also be a team player and able to follow instructions.

It is important that you are physically fit and enjoy practical work. You will be lifting and carrying large items and sometimes removing door or window frames to get items out of or into a property.

Working conditions

You will spend the majority of your time in the cab of your van. Your job may sometimes involve overnight and long-distance journeys and you should be prepared to spend time away from home.

Removals operatives usually work a 40-hour week but some days will require working overtime until the job is finished. A lot of moves take place at weekends.

All the lifting, carrying and bending involved may put you at risk of back injury.

Future prospects

Although you will find removals companies throughout the UK, urban areas are the best places to look for vacancies as thousands of people and businesses are constantly on the move in these hubs.

You may find that drops in the housing market and the condition of the economy can affect the number of jobs available.

With further training, such as the management courses offered by BAR, you may be promoted to specialist packer, foreperson, removals estimator, supervisor or manager.

You could also buy or lease a van and set up your own removals service.

Advantages/disadvantages

You might need to start early and work late, especially when legal processes can delay house removals.

You will be satisfied by your efforts and professionalism when you finish a move.

Happy customers may reward you with tips!

Money guide

Starting salaries range from £10,000 to £15,000 per year.

Experienced removals operatives earn an average of £20,000 per year. Senior staff can receive up to £30,000.

Overtime pay, shift allowances and tips can all increase your income.

Related opportunities

- Airport Baggage Handler p569
- Delivery Driver p574
- Roadie p420

Further information

British Association of Removers
www.bar.co.uk

Skills for Logistics
www.skillsforlogistics.org

ROAD SAFETY OFFICER

ENTRY LEVEL 5

Qualifications and courses

Although there are no formal entry requirements to this job, most entrants are graduates who hold qualifications in subjects such as transport management and transport safety. The general entry requirements for a degree are 2 A levels/3 H grades and 5 GCSEs/National 5s (A*–C/A–C). It is important to note, however, that experience and personal qualities are as important, if not more important, to employers and a driving licence is essential.

The Manchester College (MANCAT) is the only college in the UK that offers a BTEC Professional Development Diploma in Accident and Safety Management. For entry to the course you will need at least 1 A level/H grade and GCSEs/National 5s (A*–C/A–C) in Maths and English. It is also possible to work towards an NVQ/SVQ in Transportation (Levels 3–5).

The National Staff Training Group offers a training programme for road safety officers. Phase 1 provides training for newly appointed officers, phase 2 consists of a residential short course and phase 3 involves a series of seminars. Completion of phase 2 training can lead to Associate Membership of the Institute of Road Safety Officers (IRSO).

Requirements for becoming a member of IRSO are a relevant degree, a BTEC Professional Development Diploma in Accident and Safety Management, or NVQ/SVQ in Road Safety (Levels 3–4).

What the work involves

You will be working to reduce the number of motorists, cyclists and pedestrians injured or killed on the roads in your area.

You will educate the public by giving presentations to groups, particularly children and primary schools. Promoting national road safety campaigns by distributing leaflets and running exhibitions could also be part of your job.

You will collect information about traffic accidents and make recommendations about how to prevent them.

Type of person suited to this work

As this job involves a lot of marketing and raising public awareness through presentations, you will need to be an excellent communicator in all areas. You will use these skills to develop publicity materials and encourage people to behave more responsibly on the roads.

Self-confidence is vital to build good working relationships with safety engineers, police officers and local councillors.

To persuade others, you may find that an aptitude for teaching may be useful when working with all age groups. You could give advice outside supermarkets on fitting child car seats, or teach small groups of young children how to cross the road safely.

You will need to be conscientious and diligent to help push and promote the importance of road safety.

Working conditions

Most of your work will be office based, but you will also visit schools and other locations. You will usually work 37 hours a week, Monday to Friday. Some evening work is required.

When working on-site with engineers, or when investigating accidents, you must wear high visibility clothing.

Your office work will involve using a computer to collect and analyse information.

Future prospects

Road safety officers are usually employed by local authorities. Some jobs are temporary as they are paid for by short-term government funding.

You could be promoted to manager or to a specialist post, for example, in publicity or working with schools. You might also find a job coordinating national safety and environmental initiatives, for example, the National Walk to School Campaign.

Cuts reduced the number of road safety officers by a third in London in 2012, but the market has stabilised since then.

Advantages/disadvantages

You will receive great satisfaction in saving lives and seeing death and injury figures reduced in your area.

There may be chances to implement your own initiatives and campaigns, and the opportunity to inspire children and improve their awareness of road safety is particularly rewarding.

There might be delays or obstacles to putting in place the safety improvement work you have recommended, which can be frustrating.

Money guide

Newly qualified officers earn £18,000.

With experience you can earn up to £25,000 a year.

Officers with management responsibility can earn £40,000.

If you are a senior manager this can rise to over £50,000.

Local authorities may offer essential car user allowances as well as bonuses.

Related opportunities

- Community Education Officer p176
- Health and Safety Adviser p27
- Police Officer p529

Further information

Institute of Road Safety Officers
www.irso.org.uk

Workforce - Local Government Association
www.local.gov.uk/workforce

ROAD TRANSPORT MANAGER

ENTRY LEVEL 2

Qualifications and courses

It is possible to enter the transport industry with qualifications ranging from a few GCSEs/National 5s, including English and Maths, to a degree. Some companies offer Apprenticeships in Logistics Operations Management which will combine professional work experience with the opportunity to study for an industry-relevant qualification. Alternatively, you can also start out as a driver, administrator or team leader and work your way up.

Some companies recruit graduates to management trainee programmes and it is possible to enter these with a degree in any subject although there are specialist degree courses available in transport management, transport planning and logistics. The general entry requirements for a degree are 2 A levels/3 H grades and 5 GCSEs/National 5s (A*–C/A–C).

Once working you can study for a variety of other qualifications, including NVQs/SVQs in Road Passenger Transport (Passenger Work) or Traffic Office (Freight Work) (Levels 2–3). Postgraduate courses are available as well, for example the Chartered Institute of Logistics and Transport (CILT) offers master's programmes in partnership with different universities.

By law, each road transport business has to have at least one member of staff who has a Certificate of Professional Competence (CPC). This would normally be the manager, so you should train for this as soon as you start work if you want to progress.

What the work involves

You will work for a business that moves goods or passengers, planning the routes and work timetables of your drivers.

You will oversee the day-to-day movement of your vehicles, checking that they are in the right places at the right times.

Implementing health and safety regulations, and monitoring compliance, will be part of your role. Your job will include checking costs to make sure that your company makes a profit.

Type of person suited to this work

Planning timetables, journeys and loads means that you will need to be organised. You should also be logical and enjoy using computers to manage and develop information.

You will cost up journeys, work out timetables and stick to a strict budget, so you must enjoy working with figures.

You will need to have motivational and leadership skills, as it is your responsibility to take care of your drivers.

Working conditions

Most of your work will be based in an office. You will also spend time at vehicle depots, and might need to travel to carry out spot checks on your drivers.

Transport is a 24/7 business, so you might need to work shifts and weekends, or be called out in emergencies.

A passenger service vehicle or large goods vehicle licence will be useful.

Future prospects

Transport is a large and changing industry, and passenger transport will continue to expand. You could work for a range of employers such as logistics and distribution companies, road haulage firms, manufacturers, retail chains or coach and bus operators.

It is possible to be promoted to area or general manager. Prospects are better if you are flexible about moving to a larger company or into other modes of transport. With multinational companies there may be opportunities to work abroad.

Graduate schemes will allow for fast-track progression and moving into management.

Advantages/disadvantages

No two days are the same – traffic levels, problems and weather conditions vary from day to day.

You will have the satisfaction of seeing an instant result when you make decisions. The way you manage a problem can mean happier customers.

The job is not wholly office based, and so you could be working outside in bad weather.

Shift work can affect your social life.

Money guide

Starting salaries are usually between £15,000 and £24,000 per year.

Experienced managers can earn between £25,000 and £45,000, though this is largely dependent on the size of the company. Senior managers can earn up to £65,000.

Allowances are usually paid for shift work and unsocial hours.

Related opportunities

- Distribution Manager p575
- Freight Forwarder p577
- Warehouse Worker/Manager p597

Further information

Chartered Institute of Logistics and Transport
www.ciltuk.org.uk

TAXI DRIVER

ENTRY LEVEL 1

Qualifications and courses

It is not necessary to have any formal qualifications to become a taxi driver but you must fulfil the conditions set out by your local licensing authority prior to them granting you a licence to work.

Criteria vary across the different licensing authorities but all require applicants to have held a full driving licence for at least 12 months (3 years in London), pass an enhanced Disclosure and Barring Service (DBS) check and a medical assessment, and be over the age of 18 (21 in some areas, including London).

The strictest local licensing authority is London, which requires all registered taxi drivers to pass an extensive geographical test known as 'The Knowledge'. It can take 2 years or more to accumulate and learn all the necessary road information to pass, which includes 400 routes through London and the locations of all places of interest, including hospitals and police stations.

The Driver and Vehicle Standards Agency (DVSA) has developed a Hackney Carriage/Private Hire Test Assessment, which some licensing authorities use.

What the work involves

Taxi drivers pick up and transport passengers between destinations in a licensed vehicle for an agreed fee.

You could either drive your own black cab (also known as a hackney carriage) or operate a private hire vehicle (more commonly called a minicab).

If you drive a black cab, you will be able to pick up people who are waiting at a taxi rank, in the street, or those who have pre-booked. Minicabs are only allowed to carry pre-booked passengers. You will also need to assist passengers in and out of your vehicle, and help them with bags as necessary.

Type of person suited to this work

You will need to be personable and pleasant to passengers but also have the confidence to handle difficult or aggressive customers should the need arise. You should be numerate, as you will be handling money regularly and you will need to ensure that you give passengers the correct change.

You must have an extensive knowledge of the local area in which you operate so you will need a good memory and sense of direction.

Working conditions

Your working hours will vary according to your employment terms. If you work for a company, you may undertake shifts that include night and weekend hours whereas self-employed drivers can choose their own hours.

Most work is available in larger towns and cities, and taxi drivers are busiest on Friday and Saturday nights when people are looking to go home after a night out.

You will spend the majority of your time in your vehicle, either driving passengers to their destination, or waiting for a job to come up.

Future prospects

Smartphone apps, satnavs and new start-up companies are increasing and the ways people get taxis are changing, meaning that competition is potentially broadening among taxi firms.

Although you can work anywhere in the UK, the majority of work is focused within the larger towns and cities.

Many taxi drivers are self-employed. With experience and knowledge you could gain an operator's licence and build up your own company.

Advantages/disadvantages

You will be dealing with a variety of people and different routes on a daily basis so the work is sociable and interesting.

You will be confined to your vehicle for most of your working day, and you may spend long periods of time waiting around between jobs.

You will occasionally have to deal with drunk, aggressive or distressed passengers.

If self-employed, you often have the freedom to choose your own hours.

Money guide

Taxi drivers who work around 40 hours a week in a major city and take a good amount of fares could earn between £12,000 and £20,000 a year.

Some drivers can achieve up to £30,000 a year but you must be prepared to work long hours.

Long distance driving or night work may earn higher fares. Drivers have to pay for fuel, car insurance, licensing and maintenance, though this may be paid for by your employer if you work for a taxi or private hire firm.

Related opportunities

- Chauffeur p571
- Driving Instructor p576
- Tour Guide/Manager p372

Further information

Driver and Vehicle Standards Agency
www.gov.uk/government/organisations/driver-and-vehicle-standards-agency

Licensed Taxi Drivers Association
www.ltda.co.uk

TRAIN CONDUCTOR/ GUARD

ENTRY LEVEL 1

Qualifications and courses

Although there are no set qualifications to become a train conductor, train operating companies (TOCs) usually look for candidates with good basic maths and English skills, so GCSEs/National 5s (A*–C/A–C) or equivalent in those subjects would be ideal.

You will need to be 18 years of age before you are legally allowed to work on-board a train but you can work within a railway station from the age of 16, which could help you build up the customer service skills that employers desire in candidates applying for conductor roles.

When you apply to be a conductor, you will need to pass a series of tests designed to assess your suitability. These include a full medical to gauge your level of fitness, eyesight, colour vision and hearing. You might also need to pass memory, comprehension and concentration tests, as well as a Disclosure and Barring Service (DBS) check. There is also a strict safety policy with regard to drugs and alcohol abuse for anyone working on a train and you may be asked to take random drugs tests throughout your career.

What the work involves

Train conductors work on passenger trains, checking and issuing tickets, and ensuring that passengers are enjoying a comfortable and pleasant journey.

You will mainly focus on providing an excellent level of customer service to those travelling in the train. This will include fielding any queries or complaints, and handling rowdy passengers at times.

You will be responsible for making announcements to notify passengers about approaching stations, times of arrival, and any delays in the journey. You may also need to look after passengers with special requirements, such as assisting the elderly and disabled, and keeping an eye on children travelling alone.

Type of person suited to this work

You must have excellent interpersonal skills in order to advise passengers about their journey, answer queries, deal with complaints calmly and professionally, and to maintain authority when dealing with aggressive or difficult passengers.

You should be very confident, as you will be working alone as the first point of contact for all train passengers.

You must be able to quickly and effectively deal with a number of unexpected situations. It is also beneficial to be medically fit, and have good eyesight and hearing.

Working conditions

You will usually work 37 hours per week, according to a shift rota that will include early morning, night and weekend work. Overtime opportunities are regular. If you work on long distance routes, you may be required to stay overnight at the destination on occasion.

Although most of your time is spent walking through the train, you will usually also have a small, private office on-board. This will have equipment for making announcements, CCTV and usually a computer terminal.

You will be expected to wear a uniform and maintain a clean, smart appearance at all times.

Future prospects

Job opportunities for conductors have decreased slightly in recent years with the introduction of driver-only trains on shorter routes. Nowadays roles are concentrated on cross-country trains.

Most train conductors are employed by a TOC that specialises in passenger transportation. TOCs operate throughout the UK, so there are opportunities in most towns and cities.

Promotions can include titles such as senior conductor or train manager and there may also be opportunities to move into general management within the rail sector.

Advantages/disadvantages

You will be dealing with a variety of people on a daily basis, so work is rarely monotonous or boring.

You will be providing an important and valuable service to railway passengers.

You may have to deal with drunk, aggressive or distressed passengers from time to time.

Money guide

The starting salary for a trainee conductor is about £12,000 per year.

This will rise to around £18,000 to £21,000 once you are qualified. With experience and extra supervisory responsibilities you could earn £25,000.

Earnings can be increased by overtime payments, allowances and benefits.

Related opportunities

- Air Cabin Crew p566
- Rail Signalling Technician p588
- Train Driver p596

Further information

National Rail Enquiries
www.nationalrail.co.uk

TRAIN DRIVER

ENTRY LEVEL 2

Qualifications and courses

Although there are no set qualifications to train as a driver, almost all train operating companies (TOCs) look for candidates with a good general standard of education, including GCSEs/National 5s (A*–C/A–C) or equivalent in English, Maths and a science subject.

You will need to be 21 years of age before you are legally allowed to train as a driver but you can work in a station when you are 16 years old and on-board as a conductor when you are 18. These are good ways to gain beneficial experience of dealing with railway passengers and learn how the industry works prior to applying to be a trainee driver. Candidates aged 18 and over could also gain experience working as a shunter.

When you apply to become a driver, you will need to pass a series of tests in order for your suitability to be assessed. These include operating hand and foot controls, concentration skills, basic mechanical knowledge and staying calm under pressure. You will also need to pass a medical assessment that will encompass fitness, hearing, eyesight and colour vision, and possibly a Disclosure and Barring Service (DBS) check. Additionally, companies will do random drug and alcohol screening.

Once you have gained a position as a trainee driver, you will undergo 9–18 months of training prior to becoming qualified. This will take the form of both classroom-based learning and practical experience of driving trains.

What the work involves

Train drivers are responsible for safely operating trains that carry both passengers and goods around the UK.

You will drive the train on set routes aiming to arrive punctually at your destination, as long as there are no interferences with signalling or other unforeseen problems.

You must check your route carefully prior to setting off to ensure that it is still viable. You should also carry out safety-related checks on the train itself. You will provide a safe and efficient service by observing railway signs, signals and speed limits, and staying alert at all times.

Type of person suited to this work

You will need to have excellent concentration and good observational skills, coupled with a responsible attitude towards safety, so that you can effectively operate a train. You must be happy working alone for long periods of time.

You will need good eyesight and hearing, as well as quick reactions in order to respond to unexpected situations. Being able to keep calm under pressure is also an asset as difficult circumstances can arise during journeys.

You should have some mechanical or engineering knowledge so that you can carry out the necessary safety checks on the train.

Working conditions

You will usually work 35–40 hours per week on a shift system, which will include early morning, late night, and weekend work. Overtime is commonly available, and part-time work can be an option.

Occasionally you might need to stay overnight at a destination if it is a long way from home, although this is more common for freight train drivers than those providing passenger services.

You will usually work alone, operating the train from the driver's cab. You may occasionally have company in the form of a driver inspector or trainee driver.

Future prospects

Most train drivers are employed by a TOC, of which there are 24 in the UK. These consist of passenger operators, light rail companies that provide underground services, freight companies and engineering supply organisations.

With experience you could become a trainer or an inspector of other drivers. Your company would probably fund your studies towards gaining a professional qualification in this area.

It may also be possible to move into a management role within your company or elsewhere in the rail sector.

Advantages/disadvantages

It can be very peaceful and pleasant driving through the British countryside on journeys.

You may have to work nights and weekends on a fairly regular basis.

It can get quite lonely being on your own in the driver's cab for long periods of time.

Money guide

Starting salaries for trainee drivers are usually about £17,500 to £22,000. This should rise to £25,000 to £30,000 once you are fully qualified.

Experienced drivers could earn £35,000. A salary of £40,000 per annum is possible if you work on mainline or high-speed passenger services.

Benefits can include free or reduced-price travel.

Related opportunities

- Delivery Driver p574
- Rail Signalling Technician p588
- Train Conductor/Guard p595

Further information

National Rail Enquiries
www.nationalrail.co.uk

WAREHOUSE WORKER/ MANAGER

ENTRY LEVEL 1

Qualifications and courses

For employment as a warehouse worker you will need to be physically fit with normal colour vision. A medical assessment may be required to test these. There are no formal qualifications needed but basic English, maths and IT skills are useful so many employers look for GCSEs/National 5s in these subjects. A forklift licence may be needed for some jobs.

The Apprenticeship in Warehousing and Storage may be available for which applicants should have a least 3 GCSEs/National 5s (A*–C/A–C), including Maths and English.

Most training takes place on the job, although your employer may put you on a forklift course if you do not already have a licence.

It is possible to start as a warehouse worker, gain NVQs/ SVQs or the professional qualifications of the Chartered Institute of Logistics and Transport (CILT) and progress to supervisory or management roles. Some employers may require qualifications such as A levels/H grades or degrees for management positions.

Some companies run graduate management trainee schemes. Degrees in subjects such as logistics or supply chain management are ideal. CILT offers various qualifications which could also be useful for people entering the profession, such as an Advanced Diploma in Logistics and Transport.

What the work involves

Warehouse workers are responsible for making sure that goods from a delivery or dispatch are in the right condition and quantity. They then input details into a hand-held computer terminal. If trained, you may also drive a lift truck.

Managers will be in overall charge of the warehouse, responsible for maintaining stock levels, storing the goods safely and dispatching them onwards when needed. You will have to manage a team of staff and ensure that they adhere to health and safety regulations.

You will use a computer to monitor stock levels and orders, and to check the times when deliveries are due in and dispatches due out of your warehouse. You may also need to keep up to date and trained on new software designed to improve efficiency of warehouse operations such as digital records of warehouse documents and computerised warehouse management systems (WMS).

Type of person suited to this work

You must be honest and security conscious as warehouses often store valuable stock. You will need to work well in a team to get goods in and out of the warehouse quickly.

The use of machinery to move and stack goods at heights can be dangerous, so you should be able to follow or implement safety regulations.

You will need excellent IT skills as deliveries and dispatches are recorded and monitored on the warehouse's computer tracking system.

Working conditions

You will work a 37–40 hour week. Shift work and overtime are typical and include working nights and weekends.

Workers spend a lot of time on their feet and might need to lift heavy items and climb ladders. Managers work at a computer in an office and out in the warehouse.

Future prospects

Warehouses are owned and managed by companies which either store large quantities of goods for their own businesses or charge customers to store their goods. The biggest employers of warehouse staff are retail and manufacturing companies, logistics and distribution service providers and specialist freight and haulage companies.

Warehouses are becoming more computerised and some of the heavier work is being automated. This is likely to change the job in the future. Some warehouses will have fewer operatives and some are already 'lights out' warehouses with no human workers at operative level.

After gaining experience you can progress to a role as team leader or supervisor. With additional qualifications you can move into warehouse management.

Advantages/disadvantages

You will be working to tight deadlines which can be stressful.

Working together to finish a job can foster an excellent team spirit.

Heavy workloads are common at certain periods such as Christmas, although you will receive overtime pay.

Money guide

Starting salaries for workers are usually £12,500 to £13,500 per year. With experience, this can increase to £17,000 to £18,000. A warehouse team leader may earn over £20,000.

Graduate warehouse managers start on between £17,500 and £31,000 per year. Experienced senior managers can achieve £36,000 to £60,000 a year.

Bonuses and overtime pay can increase your income and benefits can include pension, company car, life insurance and staff discount.

Related opportunities

- Airport Baggage Handler p569
- Distribution Manager p575
- Freight Forwarder p577

Further information

Chartered Institute of Logistics and Transport
www.ciltuk.org.uk

United Kingdom Warehousing Association
www.ukwa.org.uk

INDEX OF LEVELS

Level 1

Level 2

Level 3

Level 4

Level 5

Level 6

Level 7

Level 8

INDEX

INDEX OF ADVERTISERS

A HISTORY OF
TECHNOLOGY

A HISTORY OF
TECHNOLOGY

EDITED BY

CHARLES SINGER · E. J. HOLMYARD
A. R. HALL and TREVOR I. WILLIAMS

ASSISTED BY

Y. PEEL · J. R. PETTY · M. REEVE

VOLUME IV

THE INDUSTRIAL REVOLUTION
c 1750 TO *c* 1850

OXFORD
AT THE CLARENDON PRESS

Oxford University Press, Walton Street, Oxford OX2 6DP

London Glasgow New York Toronto
Delhi Bombay Calcutta Madras Karachi
Kuala Lumpur Singapore Hong Kong Tokyo
Nairobi Dar es Salaam Cape Town
Melbourne Auckland

and associates in
Beirut Berlin Ibadan Mexico City Nicosia

ISBN 0 19 858108 4

First published 1958
Reprinted from corrected sheets of the first edition
1965, 1967, 1975, 1979, 1982

Printed in Great Britain
at the University Press, Oxford
by Eric Buckley
Printer to the University

PREFACE

THE present volume covers a period of exceptional, indeed unique, importance in the history of technology, for within it occurred what is generally known as the Industrial Revolution. That title is not altogether apt, for it suggests changes more sudden and violent than in fact took place; the varying dates that historians assign to this period of rapid change themselves suggest that neither its beginning nor its end is susceptible of sharp definition. Nevertheless, the hundred years from 1750 to 1850 with which we are here concerned saw technological developments that profoundly affected the whole pattern of civilization, first in Britain, then in continental Europe and in the North American continent, and ultimately in much of the rest of the world. During this period man's relationship to natural resources became utterly changed.

Britain, as the cradle of the new inventions and technical innovations, and for the time the undisputed industrial leader of the world, necessarily figures largely throughout this volume. By 1850 the end of her supremacy in a number of fields was within sight, but the story of the successful challenges that other countries made to British industrial leadership, and of the complex factors that made them possible, belongs to the next and final volume of our work. For that volume, too, we reserve all discussion of the profound economic and social changes that resulted from this tremendous technological progress.

In 1750 the industrial state, as now understood, did not exist, although, as our previous volume made clear, the foundations for it had been well laid. Britain was then essentially an agricultural and mercantile nation. Napoleon could refer to England as 'a nation of shopkeepers', but by 1815 Britain, and Britain alone, was so far industrialized as to deserve the title of the workshop of the world. By 1851 she could stage the Great Exhibition, which brought together a profusion of machinery, and of the products of machinery, unimaginable in 1750.

But the wide use of power-driven machinery, although a basic factor in the Industrial Revolution, was not all-important. The application of science to technology played an increasingly effective part. Science did not become a major force in industry as a whole until after our present period, although it had become significant even in the seventeenth century. Nevertheless, as the final chapter in this volume shows, the transition from craft-mystery to science as a basis of technology was becoming increasingly evident. While many branches of technology were virtually unaffected by the ferment of new scientific ideas, some were receptive of them. Thus the chemical industry (ch 8), which was closely linked with textile manufacture, made increasing use of the new theoretical ideas of the age; the development of the steam engine (ch 6) owed much to Black's conception of the idea of latent heat; and the making of optical glass for special purposes was rendered possible by researches such as those of Faraday at the Royal Institution. Again, the safety lamp, an invention of profound significance for the increasingly important coal-mining industry (ch 3), was the direct fruit of laboratory investigation, while instruments for navigation and map-making—important factors in the great expansion of shipping that was an essential concomitant of industrial development—were based upon new scientific discoveries as well as upon improved craftsmanship.

That the seeds of the Industrial Revolution lay dormant for many years before they sprang into such prodigious growth in Britain was no chance event but the natural consequence of several factors. Britain not only had inventive genius and commercial enterprise, but was in fact the only country in a position to take great material advantage of the opportunities of the age. The wars that tore Europe in the second half of the eighteenth century and continued into the first part of the nineteenth, had indeed borne heavily upon her. But her commitment in terms of man-power was always relatively small and she had always retained command of the seas. With the latter went the wealth conferred by freedom to trade without restriction in any part of the world—to import the raw materials vital for the new industries and to export the manufactured products. Coal and iron ore she had in abundance and conveniently situated within her own frontiers. Britain emerged potentially wealthy from the wars that impoverished the rest of Europe.

Though the main initiative in these changes was with Britain, other European countries, especially France, made notable contributions, and we can also glimpse in this volume the beginnings of the tremendous developments that were to take place in North America. The revolution in thought that established chemistry as a formal science, with all that this subsequently entailed, was mainly of French origin. Moreover, the violent political changes of the French Revolution—shocking though their excesses were—disseminated new conceptions of individual freedom that played their role also in the Industrial Revolution. With no liberty to change employment or to seek other centres of work by the new modes of transport, with no belief that the existing order was susceptible of radical change, the growth of the new industrial towns would have been impossible. Countries that remained feudal also remained technologically backward.

Editorially, the tremendous increase in the pace of discovery and application has presented great problems of selection. Our first volume covered the whole of technological history before 500 BC; the second, the following two millennia. In the third volume the principal technological events of no more than two and a half centuries could be recounted, and for the present one the span is virtually but a hundred years. Even so the limitation of space has obliged us to omit altogether, or to discuss but briefly, many interesting topics. We have sought throughout to follow the main lines of evolution and to avoid the by-ways and blind alleys, however tempting their exploration may be. To those who find the absence of particular topics disappointing, we can but say that they could have been included only at the cost of displacing other material of at least comparable importance. While the main span of the volume is the period 1750 to 1850 we have had frequent occasion, as in earlier volumes, to interpret the time-frontiers elastically, and to look backward or forward in order to avoid artificial breaks in the thread of discussion.

A further editorial difficulty—which we have found still more acute in the preparation of our fifth and final volume—lies in the rapidly increasing complexity of the subject. As long as ideas and machines remain relatively simple—springing from common experience and fertile imagination rather than from specialized knowledge—the nature of new inventions is relatively easily expounded. We now, however, enter a period in which there is an acceleration in the complexity of machines and in the use of processes depending upon less familiar principles and concepts. Detailed explanation is often not feasible without interrupting the discourse and occupying space essential for discussion of other topics. We are grateful to our authors for the trouble they have taken in seeking a compromise between these two opposing obligations, and for their guidance in selecting appropriate illustrations for their chapters. Those who wish for more detailed accounts than it is possible to give here will find them in the works cited in the bibliographies at the end of each chapter.

We have again some changes in our staff to record. Mrs A. Clow left us at the end of 1956, and we are glad to take this opportunity of acknowledging her assistance in the collection of illustrations for many of the chapters of this volume. Mrs E. Harrison remained with us until virtually all the material for this volume had gone to press, but has now taken up another appointment, and we are happy to put on record our appreciation of her painstaking work over nearly three years. To the other members of our team—Mrs D. A. Peel, Miss J. R. Petty, Miss M. Reeve, and Miss J. V. Woodward—we once again express our thanks. It is perhaps not easily comprehended how great an amount of meticulously careful work, other than editorial, is entailed in such a project as this. We must also acknowledge part-time help given by Mrs S. Withers in collecting material for illustrations and bibliographies for this volume. The work has demanded close collaboration between editors and publisher and we should like to put on record our appreciation of the patient co-operation of the staff of the Clarendon Press.

As with earlier volumes, much recourse has had to be made to large libraries and we once again express our thanks to the officials concerned. We have mainly relied on the British Museum Library, the Bodleian Library, the Cambridge University Library, the library of Imperial Chemical Industries Limited, the London Library, the Patent Office Library, the Science Library, and the library of the Warburg Institute. As previously, Mr D. E. Woodall has been responsible for most of the drawings, and we much appreciate the trouble he has taken in meeting our rather exacting requirements. The indexes were prepared by Miss M. A. Hennings. The list of abbreviations was compiled by Mr F. H. Ayres.

Finally, we would again express our warm appreciation of the patronage of Imperial Chemical Industries Limited, without which this project, now near completion, would never have been started. In this connexion we must in particular thank Sir Walter Worboys, a director of the Company, for his unfailing support and encouragement.

CHARLES SINGER
E. J. HOLMYARD
A. R. HALL
TREVOR I. WILLIAMS

CONTENTS

ILLUSTRATIONS AND TABLES

TEXT-FIGURES*

* The names at the end of entries are those of the artists who drew the illustrations.

4. PART I. EXTRACTION AND PRODUCTION OF METALS: IRON AND STEEL
by H. R. SCHUBERT

8. PART II. THE CHEMICAL INDUSTRY: INTERACTION WITH THE INDUSTRIAL REVOLUTION *by* A. and N. L. CLOW

9. GAS FOR LIGHT AND HEAT *by* SIR ARTHUR ELTON, BT

13. PRECISION MECHANICS *by* MAURICE DAUMAS

14. MACHINE-TOOLS *by* K. R. GILBERT

15. BUILDING AND CIVIL ENGINEERING CONSTRUCTION *by* S. B. HAMILTON

PLATES

ABBREVIATIONS OF PERIODICAL TITLES

(AS SUGGESTED BY THE WORLD LIST OF SCIENTIFIC PERIODICALS)

Agric. Hist.	Agricultural History. Agricultural History Society. Washington
Amer. Mach., N.Y.	American Machinist; Magazine of Metalworking Production. New York
Ann. Sci.	Annals of Science. A quarterly Review of the History of Science since the Renaissance. London
Apothekerztg, Berl.	Apothekerzeitung. Standeszeitung deutscher Apotheker. Berlin
Arch. Eisenhüttenw.	Archiv für das Eisenhüttenwesen. Fachberichte des Vereins Deutscher Eisenhüttenleute und des Max-Plank Instituts für Eisenforschung. (Ergänzung zu 'Stahl und Eisen'.) Düsseldorf
Archaeol. Rev.	Archaeological Review. London
Beitr. Gesch. Tech. Industr.	Beiträge zur Geschichte der Technik und Industrie. Jahrbuch des Vereins Deutscher Ingenieure. Berlin
Bijdr. Gesch. Overijssel	Bijdragen tot de Geschiedenis van Overijssel. Zwolle
Bull. Instn Metall.	Bulletin of the Institution of Metallurgists. London
Bull. Soc. industr. Mulhouse	Bulletin de la Société industrielle de Mulhouse. Mulhouse
Chron. méd.	La Chronique médicale. Revue de médicine scientifique, littéraire et anecdotique. Paris
Civ. Engng, Lond.	Civil Engineering and Public Works Review. London
C.R. Acad. Sci., Paris	Comptes Rendus hebdomadaires des Séances de l'Académie des Sciences. Paris
Discus	Discus. Imperial Smelting Corporation Ltd. Bristol
Econ. Hist.	Economic History. A Supplement to Economic Journal. Royal Economic Society. London.
Econ. Hist. Rev.	Economic History Review. Economic History Society. Cambridge.
Edgar Allen News	Edgar Allen News. Allen, Edgar and Co. Ltd. Sheffield
Edinb. new phil. J.	Edinburgh New Philosophical Journal. Edinburgh
Emp. Surv. Rev.	Empire Survey Review. London
Engineer, Lond.	Engineer. London
Expositor	The Expositor. An illustrated Recorder of Inventions, Designs, and art Manufactures. London
Fmrs' Mag.	Farmers' Magazine. London
Geogr. J.	Geographical Journal. Royal Geographical Society. London

Hist. Acad. R. Sci.	Histoire de l'Académie royale des Sciences avec les Mémoires de Mathématique et Physique. Paris
Ill. Lond. News	Illustrated London News. London
Imago Mundi	Imago Mundi. A Review of early Cartography. Stockholm
Industr. text.	Industrie textile. Paris
Ingenieur, 's Grav.	De Ingenieur. The Hague
Iron Coal Tr. Rev.	Iron and Coal Trades Review. London
J. Chem. u. Phys.	Journal für Chemie und Physik. Nuremberg
J. Inst. Navig.	Journal of the Institute of Navigation. London
J. Paris	Journal de Paris. Paris
J. R. agric. Soc.	Journal of the Royal Agricultural Society (of England). London
J. Soc. Bibl. nat. Hist.	Journal of the Society for the Bibliography of Natural History. London
J. Soc. chem. Ind., Lond.	Journal of the Society of Chemical Industry. London
Mariner's Mirror	Mariner's Mirror. Journal of the Society for Nautical Research. London
Mechanic's Mag.	The Mechanic's Magazine. London
Mém. Acad. Sci. Sav. étrang.	Mémoires de Mathématique et de Physique présentés à l'Académie Royale des Sciences par divers Savants [étrangers]. Paris
Mem. Manchr lit. phil. Soc.	Memoirs and Proceedings of the Manchester Literary and Philosophical Society. Manchester.
Milit. Engr, Wash.	Military Engineer. Society of American Military Engineers. Washington
Min. Proc. Instn civ. Engrs	Minutes of Proceedings of the Institution of Civil Engineers. London
Nature, Lond.	Nature. London
Nieuwe Verh. proefonderv. Wijsbeg.	Nieuwe Verhandelingen. Bataafsch Genootschap der proefondervindelijke Wijsbegeerte. Rotterdam
Obsns Phys.	Observations sur la Physique, sur l'Histoire naturelle et sur les Arts. Paris
Phil. Mag.	Philosophical Magazine; a Journal of theoretical, experimental and applied Physics. London
Phil. Trans.	Philosophical Transactions of the Royal Society. London
Post Man	Post Man and the historical Account. London
Proc. Amer. Soc. civ. Engrs	Proceedings of the American Society of Civil Engineers. New York
Proc. Instn civ. Engrs	Proceedings of the Institution of Civil Engineers. London
Repert. Arts Manufact.	The Repertory of Arts and Manufactures. London
Road Tar	Road Tar. British Road Tar Association. London

Schweiz. Z. Strassenwesen	Schweizerische Zeitschrift für Strassenwesen und verwandte Gebiete. Solothurn
Sci. Amer. Suppl.	Scientific American Supplement. New York
Strasse	Strasse. Berlin
Struct. Engr	Structural Engineer. Institution of Structural Engineers. London
Suisse horlog.	La Suisse horlogère. La Chaux-de-Fonds
Surveyor, Lond.	Surveyor and Municipal and County Engineer. London
Tijdschr. Inst. Ing. 's Grav.	Tijdschrift van het Koninklijke Instituut van Ingenieurs te 's Gravenhage. The Hague
Trans. Instn Min. Engrs	Transactions of the Institution of Mining Engineers. London
Trans. Instn wat. Engrs	Transactions of the Institution of Water Engineers. London
Trans. Newcomen Soc.	Transactions. Newcomen Society for the Study of the History of Engineering and Technology. London
Trans. roy. Soc. Edinb.	Transactions of the Royal Society of Edinburgh. Edinburgh
Trans. Soc. Arts	Transactions of the Society [afterwards Royal Society] of Arts. London
Univ. Mag. Knowledge Pleasure	Universal Magazine of Knowledge and Pleasure. London
Verkündiger	Der Verkündiger, oder Zeitschrift für die Fortschritte und neuesten Beobachtungen, Entdeckungen und Erfindungen in den Künsten und Wissenschaften. Nuremberg
Wat. Pwr	Water Power. London
Yale J. Biol. Med.	Yale Journal of Biology and Medicine. New Haven
Z. öst. Ing.- u. ArchitVer.	Zeitschrift des österreichischen Ingenieur- u. Architektenvereins. Vienna

I

PART I

AGRICULTURE: FARM IMPLEMENTS

OLGA BEAUMONT AND J. W. Y. HIGGS

1. INTRODUCTORY

THE century from 1750 to 1850 saw considerable activity and expansion in British agriculture. The new interest in farming under the influence of the great improvers; the opportunity to adopt new ideas resulting from enclosure; the continually increasing population leading to additional demands for food; better means of communication; and the stimulus of the Napoleonic wars, all led to great developments in farming techniques (ch I, pt II). More effective equipment was invented and brought into use, and ideas which had been put forward many years earlier found practical expression for the first time. Without any doubt the main incentive to advance in Britain was to be found in enclosure; machinery or equipment that would have been worthless on strips could be used effectively on the new commercial farms. In the rest of Europe, where enclosure lagged behind that in this country, the introduction of new equipment was slower and was confined to the larger estate-farms.

Although changes in the farmer's implements had become inevitable, the actual time of the change was to some extent conditioned by contemporary industrial progress. In 1750 most tools used by the farmer were made either locally by the village blacksmith or carpenter or, in a cruder form, by the farmer himself. In 1850 the equipment of the farm was coming in ever increasing quantities from the factories of industrial Britain. The village craftsman worked largely in wood and wrought iron, whereas the factory was able to make use of new materials and techniques. Cast iron, for example, because of its cheapness of manufacture and its durability, quickly replaced not only wrought iron but wood. Many of the leading manufacturers of agricultural machinery of the nineteenth century developed from the more enterprising craft-establishments of the eighteenth century. Despite the advantages of manufactured goods, however, the farmer continued to remain faithful to the craftsman for some implements until well into the twentieth century, and although much equipment was bought from the big firms some continued to be made in the village (vol III, ch 5).

A time-lag of up to a century could occur between the invention of a machine and its adoption for general use. The small tenant-farmer, even with his land consolidated, often lacked the capital to change to more advanced methods and had of necessity to continue to use old-style implements. During the period now under review, however, the big landowners and the farmers with capital never hesitated to take advantage of the great technical changes of the times. In fact, the changes in the equipment available between the beginning and the end of the period amounted to no less than a revolution. A countryman living on one of the more progressive farms between 1770 and 1850 might have witnessed a complete transformation of farming during his lifetime. The factory-made plough would have replaced the one made locally; seed formerly broadcast would be sown in rows by drills and the plants hoed by horses; intricate machines would have replaced the sickle or scythe for harvesting and the flail for threshing.

II. CULTIVATING IMPLEMENTS

Important developments in the design and construction of ploughs took place in the eighteenth and nineteenth centuries. The Rotherham plough (plate 2 A), built according to principles brought from Holland, was smaller and lighter than older ploughs and required fewer draught-animals. It was a swing-plough with a curved mouldboard which turned the earth well over, but the main innovation was a rearrangement of the parts of the main frame involving the substitution of a triangle for the quadrilateral of the seventeenth-century plough and earlier forms. This change was the first significant development in plough design in the eighteenth century.

The Rotherham plough was widely used in the northern and eastern counties of England. It inspired men such as John Arbuthnot and James Small to consider principles of plough design and to discuss in books the relative merits of the various ploughs in use. They produced plans, tables, and detailed descriptions from which ploughs could subsequently be built. James Small introduced the Rotherham plough into Scotland about 1767, and his book 'A Treatise on Ploughs and Wheeled Carriages' (1784) has an important place in the history of plough design. Competition between designers was intensified by the offer of premiums by the Royal Society of Arts, founded in 1754.

The close of the eighteenth century and beginning of the nineteenth century is the period during which the change from wooden ploughs to iron ploughs occurred. The mouldboard of the Rotherham plough was of wood partly covered with an iron plate. It also had an iron coulter and share. In 1763 James Small brought out the Scotch swing-plough, an improvement on the Rotherham with a wrought iron beam and handles. While working at a foundry at Norwich in 1785, Robert Ransome, founder of the firm of that name, took out a patent for hardening cast iron shares. Four years later he established a factory at Ipswich and patented chilled cast iron shares. The under surface of the share was cooled more quickly than the upper surface, thus making one side harder than the other and the share self-sharpening. Shares had previously been filed in the

FIGURE 1—*Crosskill's clod-crusher.*

field or taken back to the forge for sharpening. When chilled cast iron shares came into use a permanently sharp edge was ensured. The principle of manufacture of self-sharpening shares is still the same today.

A third important patent was taken out by Ransome in 1808; this was for a plough-frame of iron to which standardized replaceable parts could be fitted. This plough was constructed in such a way that it could be taken to pieces with ease and fresh parts substituted for those worn or broken. Since that time no very radical changes have been made in the principles governing the construction of horse ploughs.

It must not be assumed that the ideas of Ransome and other prominent ploughwrights were at once adopted throughout Great Britain. In the mid-nineteenth century, every available type of implement was in use from the *caschrom*[1] in the west of Scotland to the Rotherham and other improved forms of general purpose ploughs. By 1840 Ransomes were making as many as eighty-

[1] A tool used by Highlanders for cultivating stony ground. The word is Gaelic.

six distinct types of plough in order to suit the requirements of local markets. Some village craftsmen continued to produce implements of traditional regional design long after manufacturers were making all-metal ploughs. Throughout the northern counties variations of the Rotherham plough were important, but in Kent and Sussex a turnwrest (plate 2B) plough was widely used. This was an old form of the one-way plough and had been little altered in basic design

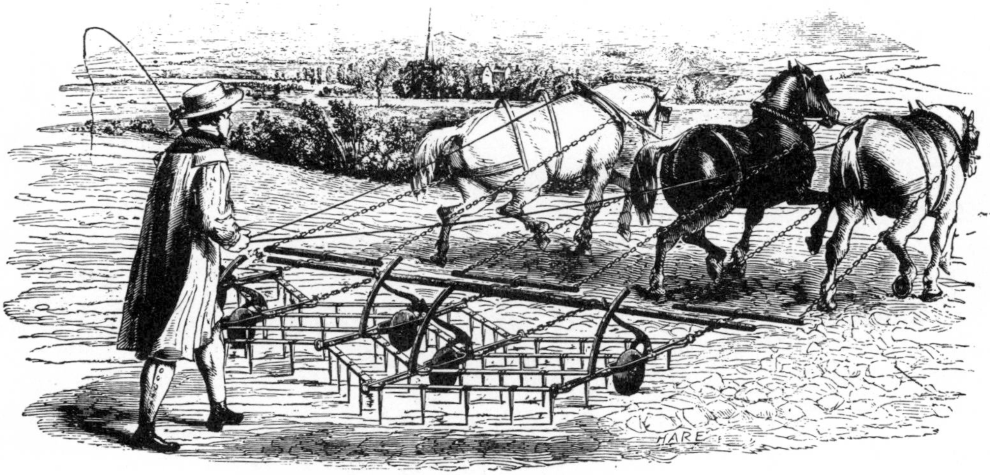

FIGURE 2—*Coleman's patent expanding lever harrow: a mid-nineteenth century zigzag harrow.*

over a period of 300 years. At the end of the furrow the mouldboard was removed and replaced on the other side, so that the plough could return down the same furrow.

Changes in other cultivating implements were equally important. Some entirely new equipment was introduced in addition to improvements in the design of old implements. Rollers were originally made of wood or stone, but smooth cast iron rollers appeared in the early nineteenth century. When constructed in two sections rotating independently, such rollers had less tendency to pull the plants out of the soil in turning on the headland. Later, rollers were manufactured consisting of a number of cast iron wheels mounted closely together on an axle to permit independent movement of each segment. Rollers were used both for consolidation of the soil and for breaking down the clods. The heaviest varieties were known as clod-crushers. The famous Crosskill clod-crusher of 1841 (figure 1) consisted of numerous serrated disks on a central axle.

Harrows were made in many sizes and weights. They were square, triangular, or rhomboidal in shape. In some places iron tines had replaced wooden spikes as early as the sixteenth century, and soon after 1800 frames also came to be made of iron. Finally the zigzag form of harrow was invented. This design overcame the troublesome swinging from side to side which had impaired the efficiency of early harrows. The distance between tines was reduced and individual tines were less likely to become clogged. Zigzag harrows (figure 2) were made up of two or more sections attached to a bar; the form patented by Armstrong in 1839 was the prototype of modern tined harrows.

Increased population at the end of the eighteenth century and the need for additional home-grown food supplies during the Napoleonic wars made the cultivation of new land imperative and led to the invention of a number of heavy implements capable of deep penetration. Previously, several ploughings had sufficed. Cultivators, which came into use at that time, were built more heavily than harrows and were often mounted on wheels. They had strong curved tines capable of stirring the land to a considerable depth. After 1850 tines mounted on springs which imparted a vibrating action were introduced.

III. SOWING IMPLEMENTS

Jethro Tull's seed-drill, invented in 1701, and made public in his book 'Horse-Hoing Husbandry' in 1731, was not only the first practical drilling machine produced in England but the first important step towards the elimination of manual labour in farm operations in Britain. Tull (1674–1741) made a number of varieties of his drill. The type for sowing wheat may be considered typical. It sowed three rows at a time and was drawn by one horse. After 1780 many other varieties of drill were produced, but some were not very successful. James Cooke's drill, brought out in 1782 and later improved, was the real ancestor of the modern machine. A feature of this drill was the use of gears instead of belts and chains to turn the dropping-mechanism. Improved forms of Cooke's drill were the most important type in England in the early nineteenth century. They formed the basis for Salmon's Bedfordshire and Smyth's Suffolk drill, which were first produced about 1800.

Drilling was not widely adopted until long after Jethro Tull's death, and even then the use of drills was limited to larger farms. The surveys made by the first Board of Agriculture reveal that at the turn of the nineteenth century progress in drilling was greatest in Norfolk and Suffolk. Travelling drills went from Suffolk into the midlands to serve scattered farms. Arthur Young noticed that the use of drills was most widespread on lighter soils. Drilling spread gradually into grain-growing areas as the number of machines available increased. John Morton, writing in his 'Cyclopedia of Agriculture' in 1851, remarked: 'Drilling corn . . . is steadily progressing in every district of England where high farming and improved cultivation prevail.'

Early drills were designed for sowing light, small seeds such as sainfoin, but machines were later produced that could be adjusted to sow most sizes of seeds. Drills or spreaders with special mechanisms were used for distributing manure and artificial fertilizers. The Suffolk corn and manure drill built by the Smyth brothers was probably the first combined commercial drill on the market. Other contemporary improvements included the invention of different mechanisms

FIGURE 3—*Garrett's general purpose cup-feed drill.*

for adjusting sowing rates. The leading manufacturers in Britain in the mid-nineteenth century were Garrett (figure 3), Smyth, and Hornsby. Seed was conveyed from the dropping-mechanism to the ground by pipes which were normally made of loose, telescoping, metal sections. In 1850 Hornsby invented indiarubber seed-pipes.

The horse-hoe was introduced by Jethro Tull early in the eighteenth century. He tried to impress upon farmers the necessity for cleaning between rows of crops, and it was to simplify the work of hoeing that he advocated the use of mechanical drills which sowed seeds in parallel rows. James Sharp's catalogue, published in 1777, showed a horse-hoe very similar to Tull's original design. It had three blades and was intended for use with a drill-plough. By 1830 hoes were being made in a wide variety of forms. They often hoed only one row at a time, but some types possessed several rows of blades, and could hoe a number of rows of crop in one operation.

IV. HARVESTING IMPLEMENTS

Before the introduction of mechanical reaping, more labour per unit was required for harvesting than for any other task on the farm. It was customary to hire extra labour every year to harvest the crops. Many reaping machines were invented in England and America between 1780 and 1850. The mechanisms brought into use were many and varied, but few of the machines were successful. The first patent for a reaping machine in England was issued to Joseph Boyce in 1800. For cutting, his machine used a series of scythes projecting from a circular disk. James Smith of Deanston in Perthshire adopted a circular

FIGURE 4—*Patrick Bell's reaping-machine.*

cutter which operated horizontally; this design was first tested in 1811. John Common submitted a reaper for a prize offered by the [Royal] Society of Arts in 1812.

The first really successful reaper was brought out in 1826 by Patrick Bell of Forfarshire (figure 4). The cutting apparatus consisted of a series of scissors which worked with a clipping action, and the grain was brought on to the cutter by sails. Later the now universal knife and cutter-bar principle was used in Bell's machine. His reaper was pushed by horses and not pulled behind them. It was exhibited in Scotland and awarded a prize of £50 by the Highland and Agricultural Society. It came into use in Scotland, but was not at first in sufficient demand to justify manufacture on a commercial scale.

The first reaper to be generally adopted was invented in America by Cyrus McCormick in 1831 (figure 5), when he was only twenty-two. Cutting was done by a knife and cutter-bar and the machine was pulled, not pushed. McCormick's reaper, together with a design by another American, Hussey, and also one of

Bell's, aroused much interest at the Great Exhibition in 1851. Trials were frequent after this date, and both Bell's reaper and that of the American design came into wider use.

In the eighteenth century little was done to assist haymaking by mechanical means. Throughout the British Isles hay was made entirely with hand tools before 1850, and methods were not revolutionized until the latter half of the nineteenth century. The earliest mechanical invention in connexion with haymaking was the horse-rake, which appeared early in the nineteenth century. It consisted of long metal teeth placed a short distance apart and mounted on a framework with wheels. When pulled along, this simple device gathered up loose

FIGURE 5—*Cyrus McCormick's American reaping-machine.*

hay; it has altered little in general design since its first introduction. The use of a lever by which the tines could be raised and the hay freed at regular intervals was an effective improvement.

A simple haymaking machine or tedder was designed by Robert Salmon of Woburn about 1800. It consisted of an axle with wheels at each end; attached to the axle were a series of iron tines which scattered the hay in all directions. It can be considered the forerunner of the present day haymaker and was remarkably similar to the rotary tedder now in use.

In England contemporary agriculturists thought in terms of arable rather than pastoral farming. Consequently the mowing machine, which replaced the scythe in the late nineteenth century, developed as a by-product of the invention of corn harvesters. Mowing machines left hay in straight swaths and therefore made easier the invention of machinery for tedding and collecting.

V. THRESHING MACHINERY

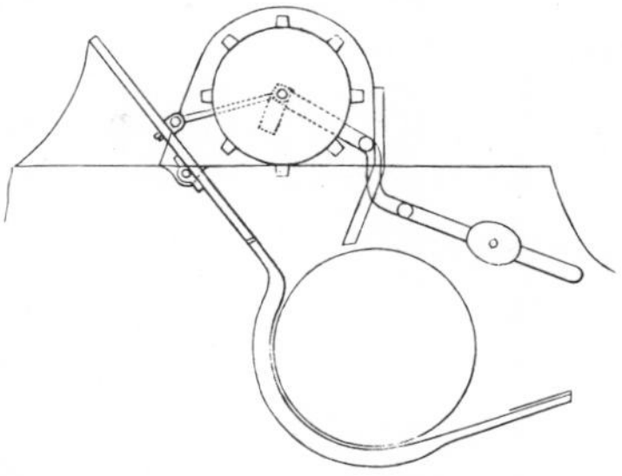

FIGURE 6—*A section of Fison's drum guard, showing the drum and concave principle.*

Attempts to produce a device that would reduce the time and labour involved in the arduous work of flailing were made as early as the seventeenth century, but few of the machines produced were of any value. Many of them, in fact, worked on the flail principle. In 1732 Michael Menzies, for example, invented and patented a machine which consisted of a number of flails on a shaft operated by water-power in such a manner that they struck grain laid out on the floor beneath them. Another method, tried by William Winlaw, consisted of a rubbing-mill, not unlike a corn-mill in action; the corn had first to be pulled by hand through a comb in order to free the ears from the straw. The method which was ultimately successful, and which was to become universal, was that employing the drum and concave (figure 6). A metal or wooden drum was made to rotate at speed inside a fixed concave with only a small clearance between the two;

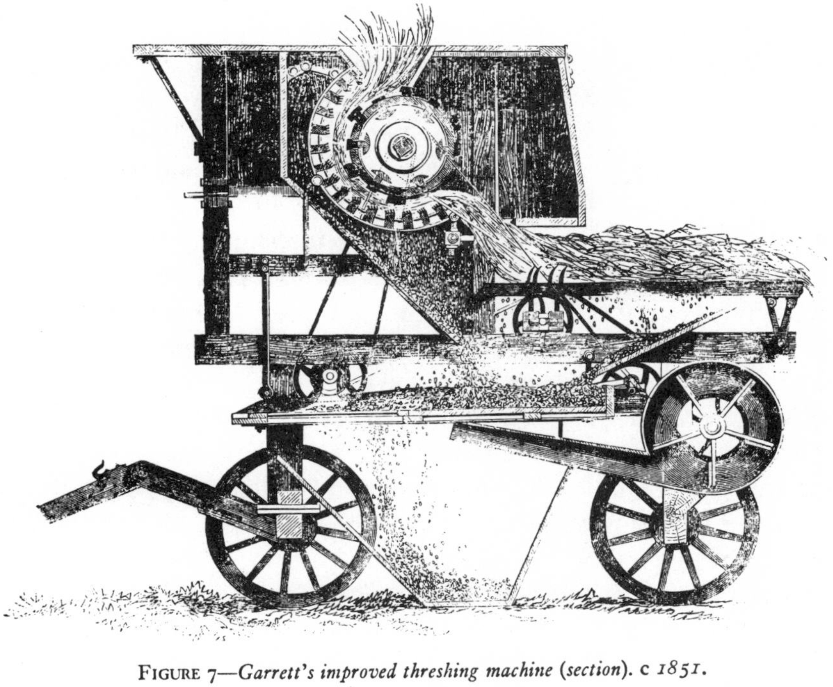

FIGURE 7—*Garrett's improved threshing machine (section). c 1851.*

the corn was then fed in and the grain removed by the rubbing action of the drum.

It is not possible to discern who first thought out this principle, for many people appear to have tried it, but it is clear that the first successful machine embodying it was built in 1786 by Andrew Meikle of the East Lothians of Scotland. Meikle's machine was a simple one consisting of drum and concave only; it had none of the elaborate cleaning equipment of later days. It did a more successful job of threshing than any of the previous devices, and the result was not only that his machines were in great demand in Scotland and on the border, but that other manufacturers began producing machines embodying the same idea. These machines were generally driven by water or by horses, but sometimes by hand. The most common type was driven by four horses walking round a central geared wheel from which the drive was transmitted by shafting to the thresher. So great were the advantages of the machine over the flail that its use spread rapidly. A survey of the reports to the Board of Agriculture reveals that many were at work on farms by the early years of the nineteenth century. For example, Bailey and Culley, in their survey of Northumberland in 1805, state that threshing machines were then coming into general use. Arthur Young, in his Norfolk survey of 1804, described several different types of threshing machines then working in the county. It is fair to say that, by the middle of the nineteenth century, machine threshing (figure 7) had become the normal method on all larger farms and on many small ones.

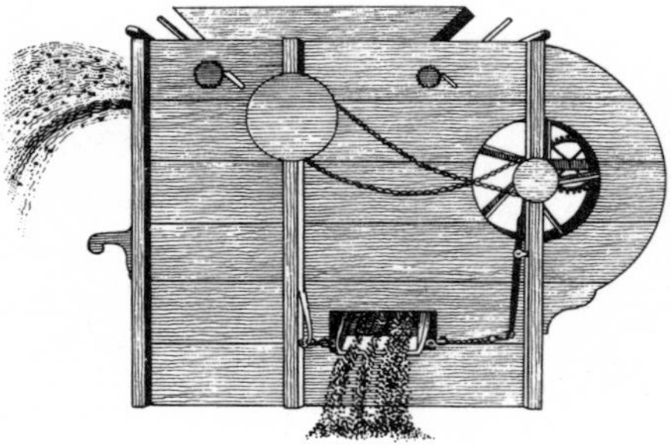

FIGURE 8—*Winnowing machine. Late eighteenth century.*

The grain had still to be separated from the chaff by hand, and in 1750 the most advanced tool for the purpose was a crude implement consisting of a central axle and arms to which sacks were attached. By 1777 James Sharp, a London manufacturer, was selling a self-contained winnowing machine (figure 8) very similar to many still in common use on farms today. A fan within the machine was rotated by a handle which also oscillated some cleaning sieves. Corn and chaff were thrown into the top of the machine, which cleaned the grain and delivered it into a sack.

From this stage it was not difficult to combine the functions of threshing and cleaning in one machine, and such a piece of equipment is said to have been produced at Thetford, in Norfolk, as early as 1848. Numerous other devices were added after 1850, such as rotary grading screens for sorting the corn. As a result the threshing machine grew into the rather complex mechanism that we know today. With the advent of the steam-engine it became possible for it not only to be steam-driven but also to be hauled from farm to farm by the engine. In the late nineteenth century few but the largest farms would own their threshing equipment. Most farms would use the services of a contractor, who would visit them with his travelling 'drum'.

VI. BARN EQUIPMENT

Barn equipment included chaff cutters, root cutters, linseed-cake crushers, and grinding mills. Forage crops and roots, such as turnips, mangolds, and swedes, had become increasingly important after 1750, and numerous different machines were produced to prepare them for consumption.

FIGURE 9—*Ransome and May's chaff cutter.*

Early chaff cutters consisted of a three-legged wooden trough with a knife at the end which was used with a guillotine action. In 1794 James Cooke brought out a design which may be considered the prototype of modern chaff cutters. It consisted of a rectangular trough along which straw was moved by hand. As the straw reached the end of the trough it was cut by blades attached to a wheel. Ransome and May's chaff cutter is shown in figure 9.

The root slicer developed in the same period, but not so rapidly. One form, consisting of a lever hinged to a trestle, appeared after 1800. This implement acted by downward pressure of the lever on to knives fitted to the trestle. Rotary root cutters, consisting of fluted rollers or incised disks placed under a hopper, appeared after 1830.

The equipment in the barns of large farms was very elaborate by 1850, and remained so until the end of the nineteenth century. Contemporary accounts of farm buildings are illustrated with pictures that include the huge barns which the wide variety of barn machinery made necessary. All this machinery would be driven from shafting by a stationary steam-engine.

Agriculture in Great Britain was gradually mechanized in the late eighteenth and early nineteenth centuries and the foundations were laid for the developments of the late nineteenth and twentieth centuries. The progress made in technology and industry after 1750 was followed by the gradual use of machinery in agriculture, which assisted all the operations of the farming year. This machinery, though opposed by workers and treated with indifference by less enlightened farmers, played an important part in the movement for increasing productivity and helped the practice of farming to go hand in hand with scientific developments. Credit for most of the inventions made before 1850 must be given to Britain, but after 1850 America and the countries of the British Empire began to play an increasingly important part.

BIBLIOGRAPHY

BEECHAM, H. A. and HIGGS, J. W. Y. 'The Story of Farm Tools.' Young Farmers' Club Booklet, No. 24. Evans, London. 1951.
FUSSELL, G. E. 'The Farmer's Tools, 1500–1900.' Melrose, London. 1952.
LOUDON, J. C. 'An Encyclopaedia of Agriculture' (5th ed.). London. 1844.
MORTON, J. C. 'A Cyclopedia of Agriculture.' London. 1855.
PASSMORE, J. B. 'The English Plough.' Oxford University Press, London. 1930.

Ploughing scene, eighteenth century.

PART II

AGRICULTURE: TECHNIQUES OF FARMING

G. E. FUSSELL

BEFORE 1750 farmers in the countries of western Europe had already begun to break away from the age-old traditional methods, but most arable land was still cropped under the ancient rotation of winter corn, spring corn, fallow. The livestock grazed on the wild grass pastures of the waste, on the fringes of the woodland, on the fallow, and on the stubble after harvest. During the winter they subsisted on a little hay and the straw of the corn-crops, often supplemented by leaves and branches of trees and vines.

The cattle did not fare well. Only small numbers—and those of inferior breeds—could be kept. The mid-eighteenth century farmer lacked two things: adequate feed for his stock and consequently adequate manure for his crops. The result was that crop-yields were low, and animals and their products were small.

The great problem was to increase supplies of animal feed for use in winter. In some of the earliest printed books on farming, didactic writers in many countries had recommended the cultivation of fodder crops, but with little immediate result, and it is now difficult, if not impossible, to determine where such crops were first grown. In the mid-seventeenth century clover (*Trifolium* spp) and turnips were already well established in the district between Antwerp and Ghent, and clover was grown in north Italy. In France some sainfoin (*Onobrychis viciifolia*) was grown, and perhaps in southern Spain some lucerne (*Medicago sativa*). Buckwheat (*Fagopyrum esculentum*) was important in most continental countries for both man and beast. From Flanders, clover spread southward into Germany and westward into England. By the mid-eighteenth century, clover, sometimes mixed with ryegrass (*Lolium perenne*), was grown in many parts of England, and the so-called Norfolk four-course rotation (p 18) was spreading through the country.

The introduction of fodder crops called for new implements, or improved implements, and created the need for the seed-drill (p 5) and the horse-hoe (plate 2 C and p 6). It also enabled more animals to be kept, and more manure and livestock-products to be produced. Having these things to hand the farmer was obliged to consider the best and most economical way of using them. He had to employ his supply of organic manure to the best advantage for his crops, and his supply of feeding-stuffs to produce the maximum improvement in his animals, without wasting either of these precious materials.

Here the nascent science of his time came to his aid, though much of the recondite work done on plant physiology and nutrition, farriery or veterinary science, animal nutrition, and so on, was long in becoming part of the working knowledge of the ordinary farmer. It was, however, in this period that the foundations of modern agricultural science were firmly laid.

Z. W. Sneller has said that the new impulses in farming of the eighteenth century were derived from England, but, true as this may be, England herself had earlier learned much from the Low Countries, where the development of agriculture between the sixteenth and the nineteenth centuries was an example to the whole of Europe (vol III, ch 1). There were wide variations in the systems followed in the comparatively small area comprising the present-day Belgium and Holland, where differences in the soils and the level of the water-table make such variations necessary. It was the treatment of the light sandy soils that excited so much admiration in foreign visitors, and this system played a great part in the development of modern farming in Britain and in other countries.

As practised on the sandy land of the Low Countries, it was a form of what is now called mixed husbandry, but in Flanders it did not depend upon the sheep-fold. Its fundamental principles were the careful accumulation of manure, and the provision of green and root crops for animal feed. It was a sort of ley husbandry. Originally the arable rotation was the simple one practised almost everywhere on the open fields. Rye was the main winter grain, often grown for two years in succession, followed by buckwheat. For centuries, however, a part of the land was laid down with hay-seeds, occasionally sown under spring grain but also upon the fallow. The length of time the so-called 'dries' remained in grass varied in different parts of the country. It might be anything from two to six years.

During the first year the weeds and grass were cut green for feeding cattle kept in the cow-sheds, under the summer stall-feeding system. This was general all over the light-land farms throughout the Low Countries. Early in the seventeenth century clover took the place of the hay-seeds, and became one of the main crops. It is estimated that in parts of Belgium up to two-thirds of the arable area was ley. Some part of the produce was made into hay for use in winter. When the ley was broken up, and the turf turned under, it improved the soil; oats were then sown by some farmers.

Sir Richard Weston (1591–1652) observed long rotations in the mid-seventeenth century, and there was little change in the following 200 years. All the cereals had been grown from time immemorial and the ley system was very old, but this was modified before the sixteenth century, when 'the Flemish landowners allowed their tenants to grow crops besides the winter and summer corn. The tenant was free to replace the cereals by flax, weld, rape seed or hemp, at his own risk.' From this time onwards cole-seed, beans, clover, flax, and later potatoes, gradually took up the fallow land. Turnips were grown as a catch-crop and for fodder; carrots and spurrey (*Spergula arvensis*) were sown with corn or flax. Mixed grains also were grown.

Throughout the period every effort was being made to extend the area of arable, and the sandy lands were laboriously reclaimed. Broom was planted to bind the soil after it had been dug with the spade. The broom was cut, possibly after two years, and dug in, the loamy sub-soil being raised and mixed with the surface. Rye was then grown, and soon a regular rotation could be introduced.

Much the same system was followed in Holland at the end of the eighteenth century. On the light land in that country, the improved three-course rotation was generally followed; rye, rye, and buckwheat. On the unploughed stubble of the second-year rye, spurrey was sown as green fodder for cattle or to be ploughed in as green manure, and turnips also were grown. The fallow year had long since vanished. Pulse, carrots, and cole were grown in gardens where fruit trees flourished. Hemp and flax were cultivated on separate small pieces of land heavily manured, but the true Flemish husbandry was practised only in north Brabant, in the neighbourhood of Breda.

A very rough division of types of farming in the Low Countries has been made by Slicher Van Bath. Cattle-breeding was found chiefly in Groningen, Friesland, Holland, and west Utrecht, which turned over to arable farming in the nineteenth century. Commercial crops, fibre-plants, and oil- and dye-plants flourished in Flanders, west Brabant, and the islands of Zeeland and south Holland. There was an area of perpetual rye-growing without fallow in the east Netherlands, and a grain area with fallow in the south Netherlands and east Belgium, where fodder-crops were grown on the fallow after 1800. Market gardens developed near the towns, and fruit- and bulb-growing became important.

The summer stall-feeding of cattle and the housing of sheep produced accumulations of organic manure. The animals often stood upon their droppings, to which were added layers of sand and peat to absorb the liquid manure. This material was applied to arable, and especially to industrial, crops, and so much improved yields of grain and fodder that the animals were better fed and yielded more livestock-products. Turf-ashes from Holland were imported into Belgium, and town wastes—including sewage, referred to as 'beer'—were brought to the farms along the canals. This material was known to the French in the early nineteenth century as Flemish manure. Part of this system was adopted in Great Britain, where peace enabled the mixed husbandry to develop into the so-called high farming of the period 1840–80; in Flanders, however, it was on the small peasant-holdings that it was first perfected.

From the Middle Ages an important dairy industry had flourished in Holland because the country was so rich in cattle. It suffered many set-backs through floods and war in the seventeenth century. These disasters were so destructive that the original Dutch red cow, very similar to the German one, almost disappeared. Black and white Jutland cows were imported from Denmark for use as a cross, but on the lighter land of the south and east the farmers, who had less capital, imported cheap, small Munster cows. From these crosses the present breeds of Dutch cattle have developed, mainly distinguished by their markings: the black and white Friesian breed now seen on many British farms, the red and white breed, and the black-and-white-faced Groningen breed. In spite of outbreaks of disease there was a large export of butter and cheese, which continued throughout the century under consideration. Both were sent, not only to the countries that had long obtained them—France, Germany, south Netherlands, Spain, and Portugal— but in increasing quantities to England, where the growth of population and the progress of the industrial revolution created a larger demand for all sorts of agricultural produce.

By the end of the eighteenth century the flourishing business of cattle-breeding and dairying was begining to change. Improved drainage made more land dry enough to plough, and cattle disease had reduced the number of beasts. Both factors persuaded the Netherlands farmers to turn to arable, but the dairy industry nevertheless remained the main source of income. Fat cattle for slaughter were also exported. The potato became important and madder was extensively grown.

It was the ley farming which he saw between Antwerp and Ghent that so greatly impressed Sir Richard Weston. He tried it out in St Leonard's Forest and at Worplesdon, Surrey, in the seventeenth century. This rotation was flax, turnips, and oats with clover bush-harrowed in and grazed until the following Christmas, mowed three times the following year, and left as ley for four or five years. Though quite different from the four-course system eventually evolved in Britain, that system owes its origin to Weston perhaps more than to any other individual. There had, however, been commercial contact between eastern

England and the Low Countries for centuries. There is some similarity too, between the light lands of Norfolk and Suffolk and the sandy lands across the sea. Merchants and traders must have discussed farming, and it is not unlikely that the English light-land farmers learned something of the Flemish methods in this way as well. A good deal of clover was grown on the light lands of Norfolk and Suffolk by the late seventeenth century, as well as in Kent and elsewhere; turnips were grown and used as a fodder crop in several counties before the end of the century.

Then, too, Jethro Tull at Howberry designed a seed-drill that worked (p 5); this was not the first but was the one that gained most reputation. He also developed his horse-hoeing husbandry (p 6), though his book on the subject was not published until the 1730s. Clearly the stage was set by this time for the new crops and the new system of alternate husbandry, but in a large part of Britain, as in other countries, there was one insuperable obstacle to the cultivation of green crops. Where the intermixed farming of the ancient open fields was carried on, as in the midlands, all the village farmers had the right to graze the fallow and the stubble field after the grain-harvest. Consequently no one could grow fodder crops on his scattered acres in the fallow field, for they would merely be eaten by other people's animals as well as his own (plate 3). It was possible to grow clover on the fallow if all the farmers agreed to do so, and in one or two places this was certainly done, but in the majority of open-field villages there were too many objectors.

The enclosure and rearrangement of the open fields in enclosed farms was undoubtedly stimulated, in part at least, by this factor, as well as by the desire to keep good livestock apart from the common herds and flocks that grazed the waste in summer, bred promiscuously, and contracted each other's diseases. Some less admirable human traits, too, helped to urge the movement on. After 1760, enclosure both of open arable fields and of the wild grass pasture of the waste proceeded rapidly. Between that date and 1840 about 6 million acres were dealt with by private Acts, and a substantial acreage without that formality. On these enclosed farms the occupier could use what rotation of crops he wished, subject to climate, elevation, and soil. He could also choose the better of his animals to breed from in the certainty that his plans would not be ruined by haphazard mating.

During the second half of the eighteenth century the alternate husbandry spread over large areas of Britain. Some of the open arable fields that were enclosed had soils suitable for it, though a good deal of heavy clay went down to grass. It was used as a means of improving the light lands of East Anglia, already in individual occupation, and then spread to the Lowlands of Scotland, the wastes of Northumberland, and the Yorkshire and Lincolnshire wolds. Much of this was new land that had never before been ploughed.

The alternate husbandry, which came to be known as the Norfolk four-course, became standard practice by 1850, although naturally there were local variations. Some farmers preferred to leave the seed-leys down for two years, and in the south-west it was adapted to sheep-husbandry by growing two grain-crops in succession, followed by a series of catch-crops to feed the sheep.

The advantages of the system are obvious. Instead of having one-third of the arable, as in the open fields, without a crop of any kind, all the fields carried something useful. The former system of winter corn, spring corn, fallow gave place to the wheat–turnips–barley–clover rotation. Not only was the land thus continually cropped, but conditions for growth were improved. If cereals are cultivated in unbroken succession a very heavy crop of weeds appears. The grain-crops do not stifle them, especially when the land is not well worked, and eventually would be completely overpowered. For this reason the triennial fallow was necessary on the open fields, and an occasional bare fallow long remained essential on the heavier soils which were too much for implements drawn by animal traction. When seeded grass and roots were grown in alternation with the cereals there were two advantages. The roots had to be hoed to cut out competing weeds until the crop had developed enough leaf to smother them. This destroyed unwanted natural growth and kept the top soil in a fine state of comminution. Again, the clover crop fed the soil, as the farmers knew without being able to explain: only comparatively recently has science discovered that bacteria in the nodules on the roots of leguminous crops fix atmospheric nitrogen.

The natural fertility of the soil was supplemented by the larger quantities of organic manure produced by the more numerous and superior livestock that could be maintained on the new fodder crops. If sheep were folded on the roots their urine and droppings manured the land, or if part of the crop were drawn and fed to cattle in yards large stocks of rich dung were accumulated. Sheep could also be folded on the clover, or it could be cut for hay and the aftermath grazed, again an extra source of winter feed and of larger supplies of manure. The system promised an indefinite continuance of fertility and improved livestock. It was a simplified form of the Flemish seven-course rotation, but omitted the industrial crops and long ley of that system. Concentration was on the production of grain for human needs and of forage for animal needs, so that there would be continual production of meat, milk, and other livestock products. Another advantage of the system was that it enabled wheat to be grown where formerly only rye was a possible crop.

The Norfolk four-course rotation exercised great influence on continental farming in the latter part of the eighteenth century and during the nineteenth century. An analogous system, though not so highly organized, had also developed elsewhere. Tarelli, a Venetian, recommended the cultivation of fodder crops in the sixteenth century, and in the eighteenth a four-course rotation was said to be already old-established in part of Italy. This was winter grain–clover–fodder grass–fallow. Though including two years of animal-feed production it did not eliminate the break for fallow, so that here a quarter of the arable remained bare every year. Turnips were included in some rotations in Italy. Again, von der Goltz (1765–1832), on the authority of Johann Nepomick von Schwerz (b 1759), believed an alternate husbandry to have been practised in scattered places along the Moselle for many years. von Schwerz travelled widely over Germany in search of agricultural information, and visited Brabant and Flanders as well. The four-course system may have developed here because the holdings were distributed between two or four fields, and in the earlier days the rotation may have been grain-crop and fallow alternately, or possibly three grain-crops and fallow. The fallow in time began to be cultivated partly with clover and partly with roots, and eventually these alternated in the series between the two cereal crops. It is quite possible that the grasses and roots could have reached the area, because there the rivers formed an ancient and important means of communication between southern and northern Europe, and the forage crops could have been introduced from either Italy or Flanders.

The preoccupation of all farmers with winter feed had led in Britain to the introduction, between 1650 and 1700, of sainfoin as a long ley on the chalk downs that stretch from East Anglia to Wiltshire. The making of water-meadows, which began in the seventeenth century, was directed to the same end. They spread from Hampshire and Wiltshire into Berkshire, Gloucestershire, and Devon, and even into Nottinghamshire and Norfolk, where suitable streams and rivers could be stopped and their waters diverted on to the riparian meadows. Such works continued to be constructed until well into the nineteenth century. Concurrently the search for new fertilizing materials went on.

The practice of marling was revived in Norfolk in the early eighteenth century. This was in effect the same sort of soil-mixing which characterized Flemish husbandry, and was extremely ancient, having been known to the Romans. It may have fallen into desuetude in Britain and have been revived after the sixteenth century, but there is reason to believe that it was uninterrupted in Cheshire, where it replaced some of the soil-elements removed by the dairy industry, and in Kent. The clay under the peat of the fens was laboriously excavated and spread on the surface. Old turf and even clayey soil were burned to form a fertilizer. Both these last processes remained popular until 1850.

Soap-boilers' waste and tailors' shreds were two industrial by-products pressed into service. Peat-ashes were burned near Newbury and sent to other districts. Stable and cow-shed manure was collected in towns and carried by barge or cart to farms within reach. Towards the end of the eighteenth century cutlers' waste from Sheffield began to be used in the neighbouring countryside: this consisted of scraps of horn and bone resulting from the manufacture of knife-handles and so on. The good effects of this material on pasture were readily observable, and a large demand for crushed bones arose. Some farmers installed grinding machinery; others bought the material ready crushed. Later, bones were dissolved in sulphuric acid, and demand for the product became so great that the battlefields of Europe are said to have been searched for material. Late in the 1820s the first cargo of Peruvian guano arrived, to be followed not much later by shipments of Chilean nitrate. These were extensively used by the British farmers during the following decades. When Sir John Bennet Lawes (1814–1900) began to manufacture calcium superphosphate in 1842 the artificial fertilizer industry may be said to have been established.

The general preoccupation with fodder crops led agricultural writers of the eighteenth century to recommend lucerne, sainfoin, and burnet (*Poterium polygamum*), as well as clover. Ray- or rye-grass seed was collected on the Chilterns and sown in Oxfordshire about 1700. It was thereafter very usually sown with red clover. Lucerne has never come into general use, though sainfoin was accepted by the chalk-land farmers, and Jethro Tull tested his seed-drill with this crop. Burnet was tried by experimental farmers and found good for sheep, but never became general. It was a natural constituent of downland pastures. One of the greatest difficulties in grassland improvement was the want of pure seeds. Thomas Coke (1752–1842), who did so much to introduce the new husbandry, organized bands of school children to go out into the fields to collect grass seeds in their several sorts. The [Royal] Society of Arts supported the scheme, but it is doubtful whether anything much came of it, though some pure strains may have been developed. Besides the grasses, root-crops and brassicas of several kinds came into use. Three sorts of turnips were recognized. The mangold was discussed in the 1780s, but did not gain acceptance by practical farmers until the 1830s. The Swedish turnip or swede (*Brassica napus* var. *napobrassica*) was introduced towards the end of the eighteenth century. Rape (*Brassica napus* var. *arvensis*) had come to the Fenland with the Dutch drainers in the seventeenth century, and spread thence to other districts. Cabbage became a field crop, possibly first in Yorkshire, and kohlrabi was grown in the nineteenth century. Carrots were recommended as a forage crop in the 1780s, though they had long been grown in one part of Suffolk.

By the end of the eighteenth century very considerable improvements had been made in the management of both arable and grassland. This had been assisted by the design of new and improved implements, not the least of which was the Rotherham plough (p 2), innumerable horse-hoes and seed-drills, and the threshing machine (p 9), which was slowly coming into use.

The new wealth of feed enabled farmers all over the country to maintain their flocks and herds in good condition through the winter, and encouraged breeders to devise methods of selective breeding to create better types. Great breeders were numerous, but little is known of their methods. Robert Bakewell (1725–95) of Dishley, Leicestershire—who produced improved Longhorn cattle, created the New Leicester sheep, and bred fine horses—is possibly the most famous. The Colling brothers and Bates of Kirklevington are associated with Shorthorn development. Coke at Holkham experimented with Devon cattle and Shorthorn sheep. The Quartleys bred fine Devons in their own county. Ellman of Glynde produced the improved Southdown sheep. Other names are associated with Hereford cattle; the Ayrshire owes its place to the efforts of Dunlop, who is said to have imported Dutch cattle to improve the breed. Similar work was done on pigs, often with an admixture of Chinese blood. Horses for the plough, the wagon, and the coach, for riding, racing, and the cavalry, were essential in that age. Of these the plough- and cart-horse had the least attention, but the Shire horse, Suffolk Punch, Cleveland Bay, and Clydesdale all received careful attention during the century.

In the main the technical progress in British farming made in the late eighteenth century was achieved by practical landowners and farmers, but it could not have been made without propaganda. Arthur Young (1741–1820) was the untiring advocate of new methods through nearly sixty years. William Marshall (1745–1818) undertook a one-man survey of English farming. The Board of Agriculture, established in 1792, did the same on a more elaborate scale. Great landowners, like Coke of Norfolk and the Duke of Bedford, held annual sheep-shearings where fine animals, new implements, and improved varieties were to be seen, as well as the most modern methods of farming. Visitors came to such gatherings from all over the country, and even from many continental countries. Foreign princes and potentates visited Bakewell and other leading farmers. British farming had become the pattern for Europe, though similar developments were taking place elsewhere.

The French wars were a great stimulant, and the arable area was increased, often to an uneconomic extent; consequently there was a great set-back when the wars ended and prices fell. For twenty years farming was in the throes of despair, but in the late 1830s conditions began to improve. The Board of Agriculture had ceased to exist in 1821, though private agricultural associations, great and small, had survived. Prominent amongst them were the Bath and West of England Society, the Highland and Agricultural Society, and the Smithfield Club. Then in 1839 the English (later Royal) Agricultural Society was formed with very influential support.

The eighteenth century saw the improvement of light land, the nineteenth that of heavy land. Light land does not need a great deal of drainage; heavy land does, and this was one of the problems not finally solved until the invention of the tubular drain-pipe, about 1800, and of the method of making it mechanically, in the 1840s. This work was largely done with the assistance of government and private loans after 1850. By that date, too, the mobile steam-engine had been adapted for farm purposes.

It was the English system of alternate husbandry, combined with selective animal-breeding, that made so great an impression on the European continent after about 1800, though there were other influences, internal as well as external, that stimulated its adoption, especially in eighteenth-century Germany. There, as in the Low Countries, usually only grain was grown in the open fields. Hemp, flax, cole, and other industrial crops were cultivated on special pieces of land outside the three fields. In western Germany the crops grown were wheat or rye or winter spelt, with stubble-grazing after harvest. The following spring, oats and barley were grown, with stubble-grazing after 24 June. Peas and field-beans were also grown as spring crops. The land was ploughed only twice to make a seed-bed for winter corn. Implements were simple and hauled by weak cattle. The land was heavily infested with weeds and what little manure it received was of poor quality. As elsewhere, this system provided inadequate forage. The livestock grazed on the waste in summer and in winter were fed on straw, chaff, and leaves, and—in the vine-growing areas— on vines and on grapes too poor to use. They were half starved in winter and in spring were often too feeble to stand up. Milk yields were very low. Conditions were almost exactly those of Britain under the open-field system.

Much of Germany was completely devastated in the Thirty Years War (1618–48), when the population was greatly reduced. From this and subsequent wars a recovery did not take place until the nineteenth century. The land reverted to grass and forest. Migration had to be arranged to colonize the waste areas anew.

Nevertheless, the three-field system prevailed, but by the beginning of the nineteenth century it had been subjected to some modifications.

Perhaps the most important change was the adoption of three important crops introduced from America: tobacco, maize, and potatoes (vol III, ch 1). By 1730 potatoes were grown in many parts of Germany, where the crop was encouraged by Frederick the Great. At about the same time red clover, and later lucerne and sainfoin, began to be grown in the fields as fodder crops. These formed part of an improved three-field system in which part of the fallow field—a half or three-quarters—was devoted to fodder crops, red clover, potatoes, roots, and pulse, though a part was preserved as fallow because people could not convince themselves that fallow could be completely dispensed with. This change took place alike on village farms, peasant-owned lands, and great estates. Out of it developed long rotations of six, nine, and twelve courses, including an occasional fallow, which continued until the beginning of the present century on peasant farms where the holding was in scattered pieces. The advantages of this system were more feed for livestock, of which the numbers and quality could be improved, and, when combined with summer stall-feeding as it frequently was, much larger supplies of organic manure for the arable.

Besides the improved three-field system, two other systems of cultivation were followed in Germany at the end of the eighteenth century. One was the true alternate husbandry of straw crop–green crop regularly, or nearly regularly. The other was a type of convertible husbandry: some years of cropping with cereals followed by some years under grass. On the larger Mecklenburg farms there were often two rotations. The fields nearer the house were under a system whereby cereals were more frequent and were grown on a larger area than the fodder crops, including clover and peas, which were grown after a summer half-fallow. These fodder crops were used for the stall-feeding of cattle, and often included rape. The more distant fields were under a 'sheep' rotation, in which grain-crops were less frequently cultivated than green crops.

The regular alternate husbandry was not adopted in north-east Germany because it did not include enough pasture for sheep and cattle. On the large estates the convertible husbandry (*Koppelwirtschaft*) in some form spread all over this part of Germany between 1800 and 1850. The peasants here followed the three-field or alternate husbandry. Very long rotations were found in Pomerania in 1850, including lupins for green manure, and oil-plants, as well as all the cereals, pulses, roots, clover for hay, and a two-year clover ley. Potatoes were frequently included in such rotations.

By 1850 a revolution had taken place in German agriculture. The ancient three-field system had completely disappeared. In its place farmers were practising the improved three-course, which included some fodder crops on the fallow, or the alternate husbandry combined with several years of ley. In the deeper soils and better climate of western Germany the three-field system had given place to the alternate husbandry. On the poorer soils the change had been to the improved three-field system or to the system of a few years of judicious cropping and a long ley. In the east, near the towns and on good soils, the alternate husbandry

FIGURE 10—*Seed-drill in use, 1846. This machine required three horses and three men. Another man harrows in the seed in the distance.*

had frequently been adopted, but more on small and medium holdings than on large. The last adopted the combined alternate husbandry and long ley system, while the peasant proprietors preferred the improved three-field system. Cattle were seldom grazed where the farmers practised the alternate husbandry or long ley system. Where there was grassland that could not be cultivated, as subject to common rights, open-air grazing continued.

New and better implements were adopted during the same time. The great landowners led the way, the peasants being slower to follow, but drills (figure 10), harrows, horse-hoes, extirpators, various rollers, subsoil ploughs, feed-preparing machines, steam-ploughs (figure 11), and threshers (figures 12 and 13) formed the equipment of many German farms by 1850, as they did in England.

In Britain, the change from the old three-course system to the new husbandry in all its variations was made on the initiative of individuals. The government played no part, except in so far as the great landowners who led the movement were members of the governing class. In many of the German states it was at least partly imposed by statute. For example, clover was introduced to the Palatinate by Walloon immigrants, and was first known as Brabant or Spanish clover. It did not spread far, and was not widely cultivated until after 1750, when

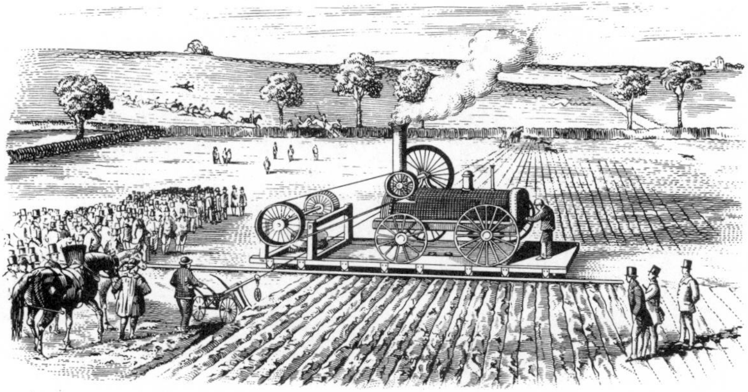

FIGURE 11—*Steam-ploughing demonstration.* c *1851.*

it was carried to other west-German districts. In 1771 Prince Karl Theodore ordered it to be grown on the summer fallow; other princes did the same. Frederick the Great promoted it in central and east Germany, together with flax, woad, hops, madder, caraway, and, especially, potatoes. He ordered orchards to be established in 1740, and brought from the Palatinate instructors in the art of growing fruit-trees. He was also interested in forestry, and the sand and heath of east Germany were planted with Scots pine. This and other soft woods were also grown in various elevated and rather sterile districts of west and south Germany. Viticulture was continued along the Moselle and Rhine.

In spite of the increased supplies of feeding-stuffs, animal breeding did not make the same progress as arable farming, with which it was so intimately bound up. Frederick the Great, under whose régime much of east Germany had been recolonized, had cows bought in Holland and sold to the settlers at low prices. Selected bulls had to be used for mating. Frederick also brought instructors in dairy husbandry from Holland, and bought cattle in Friesland, Holstein, and Holland. These efforts had some effect, and the herds of east Germany based on this new stock achieved some reputation. Cavalry horses, too, were supplied to the peasants for breeding, and stud-farms were set up, for no great state could then afford to be without adequate supplies of horses for military purposes.

Frederick the Great made another effort to improve livestock. In 1747 he imported Spanish merino rams, whose fine wool was widely famous. In their native country there were two classes of merino. One spent its life on the same farm, or in the same district, wherever there was sufficient feed; this was the breed kept

FIGURE 12—*Manual threshing-machine. England, early nineteenth century.*

in Segovia and the neighbouring mountains. Merinos of the other class were migratory, and travelled for wintering from the mountains of northern Spain, where they passed the summer, to the plains of the south. There was a further breed of sheep in Spain, larger and bearing coarser wool. This is supposed to have resulted from crossing the merino with some English sheep in the Middle Ages. It was the true merino that Frederick imported, though how he did so in face of the strict Spanish prohibition of export is not known.

Some years previously a small flock of these sheep had been imported into Sweden by an 'improver' named Alstroemer. The government supported him after some sixteen years, and offered premiums to breeders of the Spanish sheep. By 1765 there were some 65 000 pure merinos in Sweden, and 23 000 of a cross between merinos and the native breed. In this year Frederick, who had imported more flocks in 1751–2, sent 230 of his best merino sheep to the Elector of Saxony. The Elector became enthusiastic and made a further import of 300 in 1778. Though he encountered some opposition, he was able to establish the merino firmly on Saxon farms, and by the end of the century the Saxon merino was famous. The Empress Maria Theresa of Austria imported some in 1775; Frederick did the same in 1778; and by the beginning of the nineteenth century sheep-breeding had become the most important branch of animal husbandry on many large farms in northern Germany. It declined only with the growth of foreign competition from the Antipodes.

FIGURE 13—*Mobile steam-engine driving a threshing-machine.* c *1840.*

France showed a similar interest in merinos. A few were brought in in the early years of the eighteenth century, but owing to the stubborn opposition of the farmers this enterprise came to nothing. L. J. M. Daubenton (1716–1800), the famous French naturalist and agriculturist, favoured the production of Spanish wool, and by Turgot's orders a few rams were imported secretly in 1776. The results were so good that Louis XVI secured Spanish agreement to the importation of 334 ewes and 42 rams in 1786. Kept as a pure breed at Rambouillet these sheep had a great influence on the national flock. Fresh merino blood was again introduced in 1801 by Napoleon, under a secret clause of the Treaty of Basle. From that time onwards French flocks in Provence, Champagne, and other districts took much of their character from merino crosses, but here again interest in the breed faded away when faced with the competition of Antipodean wool in and after the 1840s.

England, too, had her enthusiasts. Some merinos were imported for George III through Sir Joseph Banks, and a Merino Society was formed, but proved a failure. The sheep was not suited to the requirements of English breeders, having little capacity for putting on flesh. The home market was for mutton as well as wool, and the native breeds suited it best. By the 1840s there were few flocks of pure merino in this country, and those declining. However, there was probably some effect on our breeds from the large amount of crossing that was done.

The sudden interest in merino sheep (figure 14) all over western Europe is an example of how economic considerations affect farming. Most of the importing countries wanted to produce fine Spanish wool themselves rather than buy it from Spain. They also wanted to improve their own breeds of sheep by crossing, but, owing to the production of large quantities of fine merino wool in Australia in the nineteenth century, the economic advantage disappeared within a century or so. Other kinds of livestock were sent from one country to another for similar purposes, but not perhaps to the same extent as the merino sheep.

FIGURE 14—*Merino sheep.*

Many crops travelled in the same way, as has already been shown; among them the sugar-beet, now cultivated in almost all countries, is a remarkable example. In 1747 Marggraf discovered that sugar could be extracted from beet, and half a century later (1799) Franz Achard told Frederick William III that he could produce from beet all the sugar necessary in his kingdom. Achard built the first sugar-beet factory in the world at Gut Gunern, in Silesia, in 1801–2, but seems to have extracted only 2–3 per cent sugar. He published the results of his work in 1809. Another factory was built by Freiherr von Koppy in Krain bei Strahlen in 1805. In Britain, Sir Humphry Davy was antagonistic; his opinion was that it was impossible to found such a sugar industry.

Napoleon, however, was very much alive to the importance of the new industry and supported it in Germany. He ordered a certain acreage of beet to be grown in the Low Countries, and factories to be built for sugar-manufacture, but after his fall both the cultivation of beet and the industry declined. Napoleon had also ordered beet-cultivation and the erection of factories in France, where the business continued to develop without interruption. By 1840 there were 58 factories there.

A marked fall in prices in the 1820s led the Germans to seek new crops. A commission went to France to investigate the sugar-beet industry and their report led to the re-establishment of the industry in Germany. It made rapid progress—in beet-growing, in weight handled in the factories, and in the percentage of sugar extracted. The sugar-beet also became important in Italy in the nineteenth century.

In France under Louis XV, farming methods (figure 15) still remained the same as in the Middle Ages, all the emphasis being upon cereals, wheat, rye, maslin (mixed grain), oats, barley, sarrasin (*blé noir*, buckwheat), beans and peas, and a little hemp and flax. The same difficulties as in other countries confronted the open-field farmer, whose holdings comprised scattered strips intermixed with those of his neighbours, where all had the right to graze their livestock on the stubble after harvest and on the fallow field.

Except occasionally in French Flanders, in Alsace, and in Normandy, the bare fallow year was general, and in a large proportion of the country the ancient system of crop, fallow, crop, fallow was followed. It was general from the south, on the central massif, in Poitou, and even farther to the north, from Strasbourg to Wissembourg, in Franche-Comté, and in Brittany. More to the north the three-course system—winter corn, spring corn, fallow—was usual. In the Vosges and Ardennes the convertible husbandry flourished, namely a few years of arable followed by several years of grass. A large area of the country was agriculturally useless, being covered with oak forest, broom, bramble, and gorse.

France possesses widely varying soil-conditions, elevation, and climate. By 1760 maize had taken the place of the fallow in the crop-and-fallow rotation of the Mediterranean littoral. In 1789 Young was very enthusiastic about this innovation, though some French authorities think he was over-impressed. Maize may also have been grown in Burgundy. The crop had been introduced to Béarn in the seventeenth century, as it had to Spain and Italy. Growing maize on the fallow modified the old rotations used as a staple by the peasants, and paved the way for other fodder crops, the area of which expanded a little in the second half of the eighteenth century. The olive and the vine flourished on the southern slopes of the Alps. Water-meadows had been constructed in the foothills of the Pyrenees, as they had in Germany and in the foothills of northern Italy.

The central massif and Armorica were still medieval, although some wheat was exported. Relatively little was produced in the valleys of the Loire and the Orne, where oaks and chestnuts flourished. In parts of Brittany, Maine, and Anjou briars, bracken, and gorse covered very large areas. The grassland was

FIGURE 15—*Farming in France, 1755. Ploughing, hand broadcast-sowing, and harrowing-in the seed.*

neglected, and only cereals—oats, barley, and wheat—were cultivated. Normandy was more advanced. Fodder crops were introduced about 1750, and there was good pasture in the valley of the Auge. Here cider was beginning to take the place of wine as the common drink. Picardy had absorbed some of the Flemish husbandry and grew successful crops of flax on its heavily manured soil. Haricot beans were grown, and carrots for cattle. In Artois, spring wheat was sown after mustard. Cole was grown near Lille in 1758–9, and the haulm used as straw. The crop was fertilized with sewage and liquid manure from the cowshed. Hops were grown. The Île de France and the Paris basin grew rape and turnips for cattle-feed and for pigs. Carrots were grown here for human consumption, as well as asparagus and other market-garden crops. Vines were cultivated on the Mediterranean, in Alsace, between Orleans and the sea, and particularly in Burgundy. Anjou peasants grew vines when they could obtain chestnut poles to support them. The vine requires a dry soil, deeply dug; not much manure is necessary, but porous stones, or bits of broken pots, were placed in the soil to allow air to circulate among the roots. The vines themselves had to be carefully tended and pruned.

In general, agricultural progress was slow in France, though successive governments tried to stimulate it in the last decades of the old régime. Bertin in 1759 organized what was, in effect, a ministry of agriculture and created local agricultural societies for educational purposes. Some great landowners undertook the direction of their own estates, made experiments, tried to overcome the peasants' suspicion of any departure from traditional routines, introduced new crops and breeds of livestock, and undertook the reclamation of waste land and the improvement of soils. The exchange of scattered strips in order to make compact holdings was speeded, as well as the abolition of common grazing. All feudal remnants disappeared with the Revolution in 1789, as they did with the French annexation of the Low Countries and Germany. There was, however, no pressure of population in France—as there was in Flanders and in England—to enforce progress by an insistent demand for a more intensive system of agriculture.

Conditions in France at the end of the century are described by J. Meuvert. The large farms often had a big proportion of uncultivated land. The limit was imposed by the power of animal-draught and the distance to the fields from the buildings. If not true meadow, the waste grassland was nevertheless useful land more often in individual use than is commonly thought. Small pieces near the buildings could be well worked and manured. A variety of crops, in addition to the cereals, were grown, including vines, hemp, flax, saffron, tobacco, and perfumery plants. Sainfoin and lucerne were often grown, and the fallow in some places was cultivated with legumes and roots. Progress was delayed by the weight of tradition and by the wars. French farming, in which livestock were secondary to corn-growing, advanced more slowly in the eighteenth century than did that of the Low Countries and England.

The Normandy oxen were powerful, and the Norman and Breton cows had much in common with those of the Channel Islands. All over the country the cattle were normally grazed on pasture during the summer. Winter feed was the problem here as elsewhere. To add to the stores of hay and straw, leaves of trees were collected and dried. The beasts ate the leaves and the branches fed the fire. Vine-foliage was often mixed with small and waste grapes. As the century advanced potatoes were fed to stock, but were found unsuitable for cows.

Both flocks and herds were ravaged by disease. Between 1740 and 1750 a 'putrid' disease carried off the horned cattle. A contagious sickness destroyed many sheep in 1746, 1754, 1761, and 1762. In the following year a 'mouth' disease affected sheep, pigs, horses, and poultry, and there was another disastrous outbreak in 1773. These diseases affected all Europe, including England. The French government intervened; it had the buildings disinfected and the bodies buried, the owners being partly indemnified by the state. Perhaps it was this long series of disasters that encouraged C. Bourgelat (1712–99) to establish the first veterinary school at Lyons in 1762, an example followed by d'Alfort in 1765–6.

Particular attention was naturally paid to horse-breeding for saddle-horses, cavalry chargers, and army transport, but there were heavy breeds of strong farm-horses, especially the Normans. Limousin produced fine hackneys. Serviceable horses were bred in Auvergne, in Burgundy, and in Poitou. Pigs, as in most countries, were abundant, and supplied much of the peasant's food.

During this period much land was reclaimed by drainage. In England, the drainage of the Fens was a great enterprise. Large-scale drainage in the Low Countries was a centuries-old undertaking (vol III, ch 12). In France, Gascony was a vast marsh with scrub gradually being overwhelmed by drifting sand from the coast. The area was grazed by a few small sheep, over which impoverished shepherds mounted on stilts kept guard while industriously pursuing a handicraft of some kind. When they grew a patch of grain it had to be covered with branches to prevent the seed from being blown away. The invasion of the sand was comparatively recent, apparently dating only from the fourteenth century, but nothing was done about it until the latter part of the eighteenth century, when some slight attempts were made to stem the torrent. Under Napoleon the government decided in 1800 to afforest the area. Following the theories of

Charlevoix, tested practically by Bremontier from 1788 to 1793, the coast dunes were planted with reeds, gorse, broom, and pine trees (*Pinus maritima*). The reeds were necessary near the coast to fix the sand, and the leguminous plants, as was recognized only in recent times, supplied the trees with nitrogenous nutriment, indispensable in those very poor soils. The subsoil was impermeable, and it was only some fifty years later that the necessity for breaking it up, in order to drain the land properly, was realized by Chambrelent, a civil engineer; he worked out a general scheme of drainage for the area. The afforestation was considered complete in 1873, when some 800 000 hectares had been planted. The whole district had been made healthy and productive: where trees were not planted, good sheep-pasture had been made.

Napoleon also encouraged the cultivation of chicory, from the dried and ground roots of which a substitute for, or an addition to, coffee could be made. It flourished on sandy soils, like those between Dunkirk and Calais, where sugar-beet would not grow. Tobacco, too, came to be widely grown. Cole, linseed, poppy, and the oil-plants covered no fewer than 300 000 hectares in 1860.

Progress in French livestock husbandry did not keep pace with the arable. Much more progress had been made in the United Kingdom, but after the restoration of the monarchy it became the fashion in France to purchase expensive cattle, sheep, and pigs from famous British flocks to improve the native breeds. To what extent this was done is not clear: some royal cattle-farms were set up in unsuitable places, where beasts rapidly developed tuberculosis.

A measure of success was achieved in 1850. The good qualities of the Durham Shorthorn were added to those of the native cattle in parts of Brittany, Armorica, Maine-Anjou, and other places. The New Leicester sheep was crossed with the merino by Yvart to produce the Île de France breed. The Yorkshire pig was introduced.

In Spain the feudal system prevailed until the end of the eighteenth century. No measures had been taken—as they had in Germany, in the Low Countries, and even in France—to modify the pressure of this kind of tenure upon the peasants. The English had the advantage of being finally free from these burdens a century or more earlier. The result was general stagnation in Spain, and there was no progress in farming, though a wide variety of crops was grown. The peasants neglected manure and their methods were often irrational, but some research in irrigation was made. The rotations were often lengthy, such as wheat, rice, chick-peas (vetches), haricots and beans, potatoes. Other crops grown were flax, hemp, saffron, and vines, the last yielding excellent wines. Cotton was grown in Andalusia, olives and sugar-canes flourished in the south and east; sunflowers were grown; figs, oranges, lemons, and almonds had a place.

The merino sheep was the source of wealth best known outside the country; it was estimated that there were some 5 m of them in 1796. The Spanish horses had a great reputation, and the stud-farms were carefully managed. The mules, too, were often fine animals. Many goats were kept, as well as cattle and pigs, but nothing outstanding was done in Spain to develop livestock or tillage.

Though a great deal of agricultural technique had necessarily been learned in Italy from classical times onwards, and progress there compared favourably with that in Spain, Italian farming-methods did not advance so rapidly as those in some other countries. An estimate that the total output rose by 75 per cent during the eighteenth century is probably over-optimistic. Tarelli had preached the need for forage crops in the sixteenth century, by which time rice-growing was practised. Maize and potatoes were relatively early introduced. There were fine water-meadows around Milan, and irrigation-works were constructed in Piedmont and elsewhere. Five cuts of hay every year were made from the Milanese water-meadows and at Lodi; those of Parma yielded a little less. Between Bologna and Tortona two hay-harvests a year were obtained, but Istria remained dry and arid and the Campagna consisted of little but unhealthy marshes. The lowlands about Siena were also marshy, though some wheat was grown.

Rotations varied. A species of four-course was already ancient in the eighteenth century, but there were others. Tuscany cultivated wheat in two successive years, next rye or maize, then beans, millet, or haricots—or rye if the second crop was maize—and finally a fallow before wheat. A wheat–beans–fallow rotation was favoured on heavy soils, as in England. Sometimes a wheat or turnip crop was followed by beans or fallow, or there were different combinations of wheat, turnips, and beans. Maize and a fallow were introduced occasionally. Citrus fruits and bergamots were grown in the warmer south, and vines flourished everywhere. The wine was naturally good, but the viticulturists did nothing to improve it. Some flax, hemp, and oats were grown all over the country. Buckwheat was important in Italy, as in France, the Low Countries, and Germany.

Legumes and maize grew well, but despite the culture of clover, rye grass, and turnips the shortage of winter fodder apparently limited livestock husbandry. The oxen in the Roman Campagna were fed on turnips, roots, and leaves in winter; the leaves of trees and vines, with the small sour fruit, were collected and preserved as fodder in pit silos. Furze was cut for both cattle and sheep. However, in spite of the difficulties of forage-supply, it had always been possible to maintain cattle more or less successfully through the winter in Lombardy,

Tuscany, and the valley of the Po. The milch kine here compared favourably with those of other countries.

A new agricultural literature appeared in Italy during the eighteenth century, but it is very doubtful whether it was read by the peasants. They had their ideas, but did not derive them from books. In Piedmont they began to grow such things as buckwheat on the fallow because they did not like to see land not bearing a crop, but the practice was not widely adopted. Maize began to take the place of rye in the food of the poor in the early eighteenth century. Rape, too, began to be cultivated then, but was not extensively grown until after 1800. Other crops were kidney- and broad-beans, chick-peas, spelt, barley, lupins, hemp, and oats. The potato, though introduced early, did not become a staple of diet until the nineteenth century.

The plains of Piedmont and Lombardy were famous for their farming in the mid-nineteenth century, but were not self-supporting in grain. Supplies were imported from the Black Sea and the Danube through Venice. The south produced silk, oil, madder, liquorice, and cotton, as well as cereals and wine. The coastal belt on the Adriatic produced a surplus of wheat that was carried over the mountains on mule-back, but in spite of the interest of capitalists in the late eighteenth century wide areas of unreclaimed land remained.

Denmark and Schleswig-Holstein were handicapped in the eighteenth century by the heavy incidence of feudal rights and dues, though some reforms took place towards its end. A Danish agricultural society was founded in 1769, and a veterinary school at Copenhagen in 1773, both marks of liberalism in ruling circles, possibly due to the influence of the French physiocrats. It was not, indeed, till well on in the nineteenth century that these countries, with the final abolition of serfdom and the rise of the co-operative movement, began to win their modern reputation for outstanding farming.

Swedish society, too, was influenced by the physiocrats. The importation and breeding of the merino sheep showed that there was an interest in improving breeds, but farming in general remained rather primitive. The implements were crude and rather inefficient, but cereals and pulse were cultivated: rye, oats, beans, peas, and, in the south, a little barley. The potato was introduced in 1738, but remained unfamilar for a century. Only with great difficulty could a second cut of hay be mown on the natural pastures. Leaves helped to eke out winter feed for the cattle, as in other countries.

As has been shown, progress in farming technique was very remarkable during the century 1750–1850, and it took a similar form in many countries. The great need was to increase supplies of winter feed, thus enabling livestock to be maintained in good condition the whole year round, and consequently to supply larger quantities of organic manure. Coupled with this there was a need for better implements, with which a finer seed-bed could be prepared. These things were achieved over wide areas, mainly by the example of Flemish husbandry. The improvement was not effected, however, without changes in social organization and land tenure, which on the continent took the form of the gradual extinction of feudalism. This system had already vanished from the English scene by the

FIGURE 16—*Manure conservation on an advanced farm in England,* c *1756. The dung is carted from stable and cow-shed and deposited in the pit, and drains from these buildings carry the liquid into it.*

eighteenth century, and during that century serfdom was gradually wiped out elsewhere, being finally extinguished during the course of the French wars and the annexation of most of western Europe by France. In England the land was redistributed in separate holdings under the Enclosure Acts, and much of the waste was brought into cultivation by the same method, so that the introduction of the new crops and new methods was made easy. In the Low Countries, the peasants were encouraged to exchange their scattered strips and to enclose and distribute the common waste. Common grazing was done away with by a Prussian order of 1811, but the old arrangements of strips remained in much of the west, as it still does. France made little change in this way, in spite of the abolition of feudal rights. The serious problem there was the repeated reduction of the size of holdings by reason of the co-heir system of inheritance.

New plenty raised new questions for agricultural science to answer, in addition to those it was already attempting. How much of the new kind of fodder-crops ought the different kinds of animals to eat daily? What was the most effective quantity that ought to be given to a cow in calf? How should a working horse or ox be fed? Again, we have seen that feeding and fattening store-cattle in yards during the winter in England, and summer stall-feeding in the Low Countries and later in Germany, provided more ample supplies of manure (figure 16). This was supplemented by organic waste, by marl, chalk, lime, and so forth. Which of these things, and in what quantity, ought to be used on the land prepared for the different crops? How much seed of each plant should be sown per acre to secure the optimum yield?

Aristotle was responsible for the system of thought that ruled scientific ideas of plant-nutrition until the sixteenth century. It was that plants obtained their food through their roots from the soil already elaborated or ready to be assimilated. In 1563 Bernard Palissy (1510–88) published careful observations of the importance of salts in plant-nutrition, and formulated for the first time the idea that the minerals removed from the soil ought to be replaced if fertility was to be maintained. His work was overlooked for centuries, and, like most of the early scientific work, had no influence on practical farming.

Van Helmont (1577–1644), whose work was first published by his son in 1652, made a famous and protracted experiment from which he concluded that 'all vegetables do immediately and materially proceed out of water alone'. J. Woodward (1665–1728), who made similar experiments, believed in 1699 that the water absorbed by the plants he used carried the necessary soil-matter, presumably in solution. Marcello Malpighi (1628–94) learned experimentally in 1671 that the leaves played a part in nutrition, and thought that the action of sunlight on the leaves caused a fermentation of the nutrient sap. Nehemiah Grew (1641–1712), at about the same time, believed that the leaves played a part, as the roots and trunk had done earlier, in purifying the sap for absorption by the fruit, flower, and seed.

Edmé Mariotte (1620–84) observed the result of various grafts, and studied the composition and circulation of sap; he thought that the leaves absorbed and expelled gases and that different plants found, in the same soil, substances from which they could form the wide variety of materials of which they were composed. Early in the eighteenth century Stephen Hales (1677–1761), by his experiments, explained the movement of the sap and transpiration through the leaves, and demonstrated that air, as well as water and substances in solution, was taken in by the plant and used to build its structure. The science of his time regarded light as a substance, and he carried Malpighi's theories a step farther by suggesting that the absorption of light by the leaves was an important function in plant nutrition.

Duhamel du Monceau made experiments with the Tullian drill-husbandry and on the growth of trees, but he was influenced a good deal by Tull's theory that the more the soil is comminuted the more it becomes available as plant food; in other respects his ideas about the effect of fertilizers upon the growth of plants were those common to practical men of the time.

No further progress was made until the composition of air was known. In 1754 Joseph Black discovered 'fixed' air, which Lavoisier (1743–94) renamed carbonic acid in 1781. Joseph Priestley (1733–1804) discovered oxygen in 1774, and Lavoisier demonstrated the composition of water and of atmospheric air. He carried out experiments on his estate at Freschines, where in ten years he doubled the yield of wheat and increased by fivefold the number of livestock carried.

Priestley noticed that plants confined in an atmosphere rich in carbon dioxide produced large quantities of oxygen, and thought that this was caused by the growth of the plant. Jan Ingenhousz (1730–99), a Dutch physician who emigrated to London, was stimulated by Priestley's discoveries and studied the relation between air and plant; he was finally able to demonstrate that green shoots give off oxygen in sunlight and carbon dioxide in darkness, while non-green parts always give off carbon dioxide. This, with Priestley's work, was critically examined by Senebier (1742–1809), a Swiss, who made careful and exhaustive experiments. He proved that light, not heat, is the effective agent in the fixation of carbon dioxide, and that oxygen is liberated only when carbon dioxide is present. A decade or so later de Saussure demonstrated that green plants cannot live without some carbon dioxide. This they obtain from the small amount of carbon dioxide normally present in the atmosphere. He also showed that plants fix water coincidentally with carbon, and that oxygen is freed only as an accompaniment of the fixation of carbon dioxide. Perhaps his most important finding was that plants are dependent upon the nitrogen in the soil, which was confirmed by Boussingault almost fifty years later.

In view of these results, how did the humus theory of nutrition come to the fore? It was chiefly advocated by Albrecht Daniel Thaer (p 41) and Mathieu de Dombasle, whose opinions carried great weight with practical men. In their belief, plants, like animals, utilized carbon in the organic form, obtaining it from partially decomposed animal and vegetable matter in the soil. The inorganic salts, the significance of which could not be absolutely denied, were said to act merely as stimulants.

In 1840 Liebig proved this view false by showing that the insolubility of humic acid made it impossible, under the most favourable conditions, for more than a small fraction of the carbon found in the growing plant to have been obtained from this source. He asserted that plants were nourished by carbonic acid, ammonia, water, phosphoric, sulphuric, and silicic acids, lime, magnesia, potash, and iron. He further demonstrated that nitrogen was absorbed through the roots as ammonium salts or nitrates.

Little of this early work can have reached the ordinary farmer, who would have found it remote from his daily practice even had he been acquainted with it. Agriculture was indeed, as Francis Home said in the introduction to his book 'Principles of Agriculture and Vegetation' (1757), hardly sensible of its dependence upon chemistry.

Home made the first attempt to give practical application to the principles discovered up to his time. He adopted the nutrition of plants through their roots as basic, and divided his subject into five parts: (1) the nature and qualities of different soils, (2) the nature and qualities of different composts, (3) the action of composts on vegetation, (4) tillage and cultivation, (5) weeds and other impediments to the growth of crops.

Wallerius, a Swedish physician, under whom Gustavus Adolphus Gyllenborg produced his *Agriculturae fundamenta chemica* in 1761 (English translation 1771), pronounced that 'manuring is that operation by which land receives substances that nourish plants', and discussed the effects of using chalk, lime, marl, and clay, and of mixing soils, all matters of immediate practical value to farmers. He subscribed to the humus theory and declared that plant nutrients, to be absorbed, must be exceedingly fine, liquid, or gaseous. Making the soil 'fat' was for him the basis of nearly all agriculture. It is worth while noting that these and other agricultural chemists, before the nineteenth century, confined their inquiries to the composition of the soil, to its preparation and manuring, and to plant nutrition; they took little interest in the problems of animal nutrition.

But it was the great landowners and farmers—who carried out field-scale experiments, who tested the often peculiar, and occasionally fantastic, recommendations of the innumerable 'book farmers' of the time, and who made demonstration-farms of their land—rather than the scientists who influenced the development of farming in western Europe in the second half of the eighteenth century. Arthur Young enthusiastically described the work of many of these men. 'Turnip' Townshend and Robert Walpole were exponents of the new husbandry in the early eighteenth century; Coke of Norfolk and the Duke of Bedford in the later years. There were many others who won less fame but whose influence on their own estates and the surrounding districts was no less marked. The normal farming of various districts and the improvements which might be of service to others were described by William Marshall in his 'Rural Economy' series, and in the county reports undertaken by surveyors appointed by the Board of Agriculture after 1793. Much was written about marling, chalking, and liming, about drainage and new implements. Animal breeding and feeding were developed by practical farmers like Fowler of Rollright, Bakewell of Dishley, Ellman of Glynde, and many others, but few details of their methods remain to us. These pioneers were secretive, realizing the advantages to be gained from a monopoly of their own methods.

The Society of Arts, founded in 1754, offered prizes for agricultural experiments and inventions. Voluntary organizations of landowners and farmers did the same sort of thing and usefully published results. Innumerable smaller groups formed societies to conduct local competitions in growing both unfamiliar and familiar crops, in manuring, and in animal breeding, and served for the exchange of ideas. In France, many of the nobility set up model farms similar to those in England (figure 17), to demonstrate the economic value of the new methods.

The enthusiasm for progress was very great, though the new methods spread very slowly, at a rate of not more than a mile a year from their place of origin. Many farmers declared that they were only for gentlemen who had money to burn, and that ordinary farmers must keep to the old ways. Marked advances were made nevertheless, and this was vitally important because even by 1770 Britain had become a grain-importing country. A tentative measure of these advances is given by the rise in the yield of wheat from an average of 16 bushels an acre in the late sixteenth century to about 20–22 bushels an acre 200 years later. There was an increase, too, in the average size of livestock and their productivity, but exact figures of the increase are difficult to compute.

Examples of the new farming were not wanting in late eighteenth-century Germany. C. Reichart (1685–1775) cropped a plot of land for eighteen years in succession, applying dung only once at the rate of 24 three-horse loads because he thought different crops took different food from the soil. A change of crops therefore allowed better plant nutrition. He made personal observations and experiments, and concluded that three kinds of 'artificial grasses' were valuable —lucerne, sainfoin, and Spanish or red clover—but he did not consider the connexion of animal husbandry with tillage. Johann Christian Schubert (1734–86) grew as much clover and beet as possible upon his own estate, as well as madder and tobacco, and the cultivation of these crops involved a new rotation.

Albrecht Daniel Thaer (1752–1828) was physician in ordinary to George III, King of England and Hanover. In 1784 he joined the Royal Agricultural Society at Celle and bought an estate which in 1802 he turned into an agricultural institute. Thaer's published work had very great influence on the practical side. The management of farmyard manure, composting, and the use of lime, marl, and gypsum are well described. In the field of animal nutrition he tried to assess the value of different feeding-stuffs by reference to a 'hay unit'; this was an unfortunate choice because 'hay' is so extremely variable in composition. This was, however, the first attempt to express animal feeding-requirements quantitatively.

FIGURE 17—*Model farm, England, 1859. Note the elaborate and extensive range of buildings.*

In England, Humphry Davy's lectures on 'Agricultural Chemistry' for the Board of Agriculture were published in book form (1813). But the Board was at that time already in a decline, and was dissolved in 1821. A beginning had, however, been made towards formal agricultural education by the establishment of a chair of agriculture at Edinburgh in 1790, and of a chair of rural economy at Oxford in 1796, though both were very inadequately endowed. Much more was done on the continent. Besides Thaer's institute, a school had been founded by von Voght in Holstein in 1803; the famous Hohenheim institute was established through the efforts of von Schwerz in 1818; and schools for peasants were opened in Bavaria a little later. In France, de Dombasle formed a school of agriculture at Roville, near Nancy, in 1819, and ten years later Bella, with funds provided by large landowners, founded a similar school at Grignon. In 1836

Boussingault built in Alsace an agronomic institute devoted to the study of plants and of animal nutrition. Two years previously, Lawes had entered into occupation of Rothamsted, where he was joined by Gilbert in 1835. They did work of immense importance during their long collaboration, and the Rothamsted Experimental Station soon became famous. Altogether, the first half of the nineteenth century was a time of enormous activity in the theory and systematic practice of agriculture all over western Europe. In every country the foundations of centres of agricultural research and education were being laid—many by voluntary effort, some with government assistance—and the way lay open to the astonishing achievements that now supply the world's vast population with its daily bread.

BIBLIOGRAPHY

BATH, B. H. S. VAN. 'Agriculture in the Low Countries (*c* 1600–1800).' Relazione del X Congresso Internazionale delle Scienze Storiche. Sansoni, Florence. 1953.

BOURDE, A. J. 'The Influence of England on the French Agronomes 1750–1789.' University Press, Cambridge. 1953.

BROWNE, C. A. 'A Source Book of Agricultural Chemistry.' Chronica Botanica, Waltham, Mass. 1944.

DEMOLON, A. 'L'Évolution scientifique et l'agriculture française.' Flammarion, Paris. 1946.

FUSSELL, G. E. "The Size of English Cattle in the Eighteenth Century." *Agric. Hist.*, **3**, 160–81, 1929.

Idem. "Eighteenth Century Estimates of British Sheep and Wool Production." *Ibid.*, **4**, 131–51, 1930.

Idem. "The Technique of Early Field Experiments." *J. R. agric. Soc.*, **96**, 78–88, 1935.

Idem "Animal Husbandry in Eighteenth Century England." *Agric. Hist.*, **11**, 96–116, 189–214, 1937.

FUSSELL, G. E. and COMPTON, M. "Agricultural Adjustments after the Napoleonic Wars." *Econ. Hist.*, **4**, 184–204, 1939.

FUSSELL, G. E. and GOODMAN, CONSTANCE. "Crop Husbandry in Eighteenth Century England." *Agric. Hist.*, **15**, 202–16, 1941; **16**, 41–63, 1942.

GOLTZ, T. VON DER. 'Geschichte der deutschen Landwirtschaft' (2 vols). Cotta, Stuttgart. 1903.

GROMAS, R. 'Histoire agricole de la France dès origines à 1939.' Published by the author, Mende. 1947.

KRZYMOWSKI, R. 'Geschichte der deutschen Landwirtschaft.' Ulmer, Stuttgart. 1939.

LARGE, E. C. 'The Advance of the Fungi.' Cape, London. 1940.

LINDEMANS, P. 'Geschiedenis van de landbouw in België' (2 vols). De Sikkel, Antwerp. 1952.

MEUVRET, J. "L'agriculture en Europe au XVIIe et XVIIIe siècles." Relazione del X Congresso Internazionale delle Scienze Storiche. Sansoni, Florence. 1953.

ORWIN, C. S. "Agriculture and Rural Life", in TURBERVILLE, A. S. (Ed.), 'Johnson's England', Vol. 1, p. 261. Clarendon Press, Oxford. 1933.

PRATO, G. 'L'evoluzione agricola nel secolo XVIII.' Accademia delle Scienze, Turin. 1910.

PROTHERO, R. E. (LORD ERNLE). 'English Farming Past and Present.' Longmans, London, 1932.

PUGLIESE, S. 'Due secoli di vita agricola: produzione e valore dei terreni, contratti agrarî e prezzi nel Vercellese nei secoli XVIII e XIX.' Bocca, Torino. 1908.

REED, H. S. 'A Short History of the Plant Sciences.' Chronica Botanica, Waltham, Mass. 1943.

SALAMAN, R. N. 'The History and Social Influence of the Potato.' University Press, Cambridge. 1949.

SHERMAN, CAROLINE C. "Theories on the nutrition of plants from Aristotle to Liebig." *Yale J. Biol. Med.*, **6**, i, 43–60, 1933.

SNELLER, Z. W. 'Geschiedenis van de Nederlandse landbouw 1795–1940.' Wolters, Groningen. 1951.

SOREAU, E. 'L'agriculture du XVIIe siècle à la fin du XVIIIe'. Vol. 4 in the collection: 'L'agriculture à travers les âges.' Boccard, Paris. 1952.

WATSON, J. A. S. and HOBBS, MAY E. 'Great Farmers.' Faber, London. 1937.

YOUNG, A. 'Arthur Young's Travels in France during the Years 1787, 1788, 1789' ed. by Miss BETHAM-EDWARDS. Bell, London. 1905.

Agricultural labourer, eighteenth century.

2

FISH PRESERVATION

C. L. CUTTING

FISHING, with its offspring whaling (p 55), is the last survivor of the food-gathering stage (vol I, ch 8) of any economic importance. The flesh of fish is rapidly affected by microbial spoilage and is therefore more perishable than other fresh animal protein foods. Thus at all times it has needed special treatment to preserve the surpluses (vol I, pp 264–5, vol II, pp 120, 123), and until the days of rapid transport most fish could be eaten only in a preserved state (figure 18). Effective preservation was the condition of its usefulness. Though the principal methods of preserving adopted in Bronze Age and classical civilizations were based on salting, drying in the sun, smoking over fires, or a combination of some of these processes, there were notable minor developments in technique in the fourteenth century or thereabouts. These maintained edibility sufficiently long to permit widespread distribution of products, thus bringing the new foods within reach of the majority. The rules of the Church concerning fasts added religious emphasis to the economic dependence on fish. It may be here interpolated that though fishing has been world-wide since early times, the North Sea was by far the most important fishing-ground in the western world until the twentieth century, and that an account of the treatment of its products affords something more than a mere sample of the European fish-industry.

During the Middle Ages and for long after, fresh fish was mostly of fresh-water origin and very expensive. Every river-species was eaten; ponds were kept artificially stocked for the rich; and coarse fish were transported alive by road, notably to London. Sea-fish were also brought to port alive in boat bottoms whenever possible. Most of the population, however, ate only hard-dried, salted, and smoked products, and though at coastal villages mildly cured varieties were consumed the slowness of transport by land and sea confined trade to products that could be kept for several months without going bad. Practically all species of sea-fish and shell-fish were preserved for eating, but the main catches were (*a*) of white fish, such as cod and related species, which are plentiful in the North Sea and adjacent waters and can be taken all the year round, and (*b*) of the herring family, the capture of which is seasonal. Of the two, the herring catches were the more important.

Herring, as also salmon, are rich in oil and prone to oxidation, with resulting rancid flavour. They could not therefore be preserved for long by simple drying, even with salt, such as was suitable for the leaner, white fishes. As the Egyptians had long before discovered, an oily fish could be better preserved in a jar by covering with a salt brine, which, as we know, impedes the access of atmospheric oxygen. Rancidity could also be greatly retarded by the anti-oxidant effects of wood-smoking.

Salt herring were first prepared on a large scale at the western end of the Baltic during the twelfth century. This trade was organized by merchants from the ports of the Hanseatic League. The quality was strictly regulated by their

FIGURE 18—*Preparation of fish for preservation. Sixteenth century.*

supervision of the process of salting and packing. After landing, the fish were gutted, washed in sea-water, mixed with salt, and finally packed in barrels made of wooden staves and hoops (figures 18, 19). When full, these stood closed for ten days, during which the herring sank a little owing to osmotic shrinkage. The barrels were then reopened, filled, and closed again. Hanseatic laws forbade placing small or inferior fish in the middle of the barrel, and the fish had all to be salted alike and packed in regular layers. 'Full' herring, containing roes and in prime condition, were distinguished from spawned fish, which are meagre and deficient in oil.

This trade was, in fact, basic for the League, which did not long survive the decline in the Baltic fishery about 1400. The Netherlands then assumed supremacy in the trade and retained it until nearly 1700. Their process, which derived much from the Hanseatics, also depended on adherence to a precise specification formulated over the years and enforced by inspection and penalties.

Herring, mostly caught off the British coast, were salted at sea aboard the herring-busses (figure 20), which accommodated empty barrels and carried provisions for about 15 men, including skilled salters and coopers. These busses were sturdy broad-beamed two- or three-masted decked ships, mostly of 80 to 100 tons, capable of prolonged sojourn at sea. Large drift-nets (figure 26), 50 to 60 fathoms in length, which trapped the herring by the gills, appeared about 1416. Immediately the herring were shaken out of the net their gills and viscera were

FIGURE 19—*Packing salted herring into wooden barrels. The Dutch laws were very strict and the packing had to be done on the street or quayside.*

removed and they were first sprinkled with salt, then turned over and over, and finally sorted and packed head to tail in barrels with salt sprinkled between the layers, which were arranged alternately across each other (figure 21). Finally, the barrels were topped up with brine, made air-tight, and branded with the date of catch. Packing bad herring with good was severely punished. An ordinance issued in 1651 forbade putting old fish under new, or laying the sickly, or those bitten by dogfish, next the good, or mixing those caught on one night with those of another taking. There were also minute regulations governing mesh-size, the quantity and type of salt used, the time and place of fishing, and the making and branding of barrels—including even the number and size of staves and the nature and quality of the wood. The use of old barrels was strictly prohibited. The proportion of salt specified, about one of salt to three of fish, would result in roughly a saturated solution in the flesh, which is essential for proper keeping. A brine-tight barrel was necessary to prevent rancidity.

The fishing started off the Shetland Islands at the end of June, though the date varied from year to year, probably on account of natural variations in the

FIGURE 20—*A fleet of herring-busses returning to harbour. These were larger than the hoys and had two or three masts.*

movements and condition, particularly the oiliness, of the fish. It continued off north-east Scotland until September. In the autumn it reached to near East Anglia and ended in the Thames estuary about Christmas. After that, ships returned home to refit. The barrels were taken to Holland for branding, and could not be sold at sea or shipped direct to foreign markets. Fresh-caught herring had to be in pickle for at least ten days before sale. At sea, herring already barrelled were moistened with sea-water every fortnight. Repacking on shore had to be completed within three weeks of landing. No herring could be 'heightened' by fresh pickle, or repacked except in the public street or on the quays (figure 19). This carefully controlled technique resulted in a keeping-quality of 12 months in any climate. The Dutch could distribute fish up all the principal rivers of Europe. Thus pickled herring was one of the first foodstuffs to become a major item of international commerce, and helped to revolutionize the economic conditions of the time.

Smoked herring. Herring had been widely preserved by smoking as early as the thirteenth century, from the Baltic to France. The special type of *red herring* cured at Yarmouth had acquired a reputation by about 1350. Ungutted herring

FIGURE 21—*A hulk or great hoy at the fishing-grounds. The drift-net is being pulled in, and the men on the deck are gutting and packing the fish.*

were first hard-salted for a week, then washed to remove surface salt and hung up in a tall kiln over smouldering fires of sawdust for several weeks (figure 22). In this process they became very hard and dry and thoroughly impregnated with smoke. After being taken down from the kiln they were packed in barrels and distributed.

Stockfish is a word used for fish that are dried but not salted or smoked. Cod and members of the cod family were being dried in northern Norway as early as the twelfth century, merely by hanging up the eviscerated fish in the open air for several weeks until it was quite hard (figures 23 and 24). The Hanseatic merchants monopolized this trade from about 1350 until 1550 by their control of Bergen.

Salt cod was prepared at sea early in the fifteenth century by English fishermen from Scarborough, Cromer, and Bristol, fishing off Iceland in two-masted ketches holding 5 to 10 men. They salted their catch in the summer months and

FIGURE 22—*A kiln showing the preparation and smoking of red herring. The salted ungutted herring were hung over smouldering sawdust fires for several weeks. When smoked hard they were packed into barrels.*

returned with cargoes of about 30 tons in the autumn. These operations are sometimes confusingly described as the 'Iceland stockfishery', despite the facts that the salted product was kept in the wet state on the ship and that the Icelanders produced true stockfish, which they exported to England.

The discovery in 1497 of Newfoundland and its prolific cod-fishery led to intense rivalry between France and England. The French had access to plenty of salt formed by solar evaporation on the Biscay coast. They split their cod and wet-salted it in barrels for sale either in that condition if the fish were large, or, if smaller, after drying in the open. British salt was for many centuries too impure to be suitable for fish curing. Bay salt, so called from La Baie (now Bourgneuf) at the mouth of the Loire, was therefore imported into Britain but used sparingly there. To ensure adequate preservation, drying-grounds were essential, and English fishermen from south-west ports occupied suitable sites in Newfoundland, New England, and Nova Scotia, while the French took over the Gaspé Peninsula.

The cod were caught on baited hooks cast from small boats. Stony beaches were preferred for drying, otherwise hurdles had to be erected to keep the fish off the damp sand or grass. French practice at Cape Breton, as described in the

FIGURE 23—*The preparation of stockfish. The fish, with their heads still on, were split open and spread out to dry on the rocks.*

second half of the seventeenth century, was typical. The fish were first dressed by slitting the throat, heading, and splitting open. They were then piled in layers, flesh-side uppermost, with salt in between, and left for five or six days, after which they were washed in the sea to remove surplus salt and piled again to drain. After this they were spread out on the beach, flesh up during the day, flesh down at night, for some weeks. Finally they were stacked in piles to 'sweat', that is, to even out moisture-gradients (figure 25). A typical ship for a salting-expedition was of 200 to 300 tons burthen, and carried a crew of 70 and 14 small boats as catchers. There were numerous variants of this process over the North Atlantic seaboard, depending on local conditions and circumstances. As a result of observation, various refinements were introduced and passed on by tradition. Thus, certain impurities in the salt produced what was termed salt-burn; if the fish had too much sun, the skin lifted off; fish bled immediately they were caught produced a whiter product. At the end of the nineteenth century various types of artificial dryer, using fans and heating, were introduced.

Fresh fish. The products described above are tough, salty, and highly flavoured. In the industrial era successful attempts to transport and market fish in the fresh state had converted it by 1850 from a luxury article into one within reach of the bulk of the population.[1] The chief factors responsible for this dietary revolution were: (*a*) improvement in communications, culminating in railways (vol V); (*b*) use of ice to preserve fish by chilling; and (*c*) vast increase in production,

FIGURE 24—*Smaller fish were headed and hung by their tails. Slatted huts gave shelter whilst permitting free ventilation.*

resulting from more efficient ways of fishing, particularly trawling, finally combined with steam-propulsion.

All these factors reacted on one another as population and the demand for food rose rapidly in the nineteenth century. The use of ice to delay spoilage permitted voyages farther from port, and resulted in the discovery of new and more prolific fishing-grounds, thus leading to increased supplies and cheaper fish. Although the following account relates to western Europe, and Britain in particular, the same general pattern of development was followed in North America.

Live fish. Keeping sea-fish alive developed into a large industry at North Sea ports, particularly Harwich and Grimsby, in the eighteenth and nineteenth centuries. The fish were caught on lines by special tackle with a gorge, to prevent injury from the hook. Well-vessels of some 50 tons carried a tank about 20 ft

[1] Canning (vol V, ch 2) was the result of another attempt to vary the diet. The traditional products of the old methods continued to be exported to less industrialized countries.

long amidships, into which the fish were thrown tail first so that they did not break their necks. The well was perforated for continuous replenishment of the sea-water. Flat-fish, which would lie on the bottom and block the holes, were stowed in boxes. Large predatory fish such as skate and halibut were tethered by a cord at the nose and tail respectively. Fish normally arrived at the surface with their swim-bladders inflated by the rapid change in pressure, so that these had to be punctured before they could swim in a natural position. Cod and haddock could normally be kept alive at sea for a week or two, the dead being removed

FIGURE 25—*In preparing salt cod, the fish were split open and laid in piles with dry salt between each layer. After five to six days they were washed, spread out to dry, and then again stacked to allow them to 'sweat'.*

daily. At port, the fish were transferred to large floating crates which were anchored in the dock until the fish were required for sale.

Trawling, or fishing by dragging a net over the sea-bottom, was reported from time to time between the fourteenth and seventeenth centuries, chiefly in sheltered waters such as the Thames estuary and the Zuider Zee. By the end of the eighteenth century the fishermen of Barking and Brixham were having success in coastal waters with a much larger net of this type, kept open by a beam of wood. They extended their operations to the North Sea and, by the middle of the century, settled at Hull and Grimsby for proximity to the prolific Dogger Bank area. Trawling was a more productive method of fishing than lining. The fish, however, were mostly dead when landed on deck and could be distributed to consuming centres in sound condition only if handled expeditiously, as by fleeting (p 53), or if chilled by means of ice.

Fleeting. The use of specially swift ships to carry the catches from the busses to the harbour was practised by the Dutch from at least 1600. In Britain, the firm of Samuel Hewett (1797–1871) of Barking, which owned a number of North Sea sailing trawlers, first organized the system of fishing as a fleet, under an 'admiral'; the catch from every ship was collected daily and sent to Billingsgate market in London by special, swift, cutter-rigged carrier-vessels which, after 1864, were steam-powered. The trawlers themselves continued for some time to be sail-driven, despite a number of attempts to apply steam-power to them from 1860 onwards. About 1877 converted paddle-tugs began to be used for trawling, and steam-powered capstans and winches for hauling the nets. The first successful steam-trawlers were built about 1883 and steam-drifters for herring soon after.

FIGURE 26—*Small boat preparing to take in drift-net.*

Refrigeration. The first use of ice to preserve fish during transport in Britain was in 1786, following a report that it was common practice in China. Salmon from the north of Scotland were thereafter sent to London packed in ice in boxes. The ice was collected from lochs during the winter and stored in earth houses. Such ice is also reported to have been used for herring just before 1800, and it was becoming common in the normal fresh-fish trade by about 1820. About the middle of the century it began to be used systematically by Hewett's for the preservation of fish at sea. Ice from the Thames marshes was collected as a crop by the farmers and brought in carts to a large store at Barking. Ice-lugs then took it out to the cutters in the river. The supplies of ice were scarcely adequate for requirements; it had to be used sparingly, and only on the most valuable species. 'Offal fish', including plaice and haddock, often had to be thrown overboard. Hull and Grimsby trawlers first started using ice about 1860, relying on imports from Norway. More ample supplies made it possible for trawlers to go farther afield in search of fish, thus developing new trawling grounds off Iceland (1883) and later farther away still. Larger steam-trawlers with improved fishing-gear, such as the otter-trawl and steel warps, brought back ever-increasing quantities. By 1900 factories were erected for making ice artificially for the trade. The limited preservative properties of ice, however, set a corresponding limit to the distance ventured from port, and this is still a major problem in the twentieth century.

Mildly smoked fish. The advent of railways made possible the distribution of less heavily cured products. Red herring gave way to Yarmouth bloaters (1835) and Newcastle kippers (1843). Finnon haddocks, originally a local product cured on a domestic scale at Findon, near Aberdeen, provided an outlet for surplus trawled haddock landed at London, Hull (1847), and Grimsby (1856). On the continent a preference developed for hot-smoked products, such as the *Bückling*, which was probably a descendant of a much earlier Baltic product. In all these products the chief purpose of smoking is to impart an attractive flavour. The degree of preservation is inadequate for a delay of more than a few days between production and consumption.

BIBLIOGRAPHY

ALWARD, G. L. 'The Sea Fisheries of Great Britain and Ireland.' Gait, Grimsby. 1932.

BEAUJON, A. "The History of the Dutch Sea Fisheries" in 'International Fisheries Exhibition Literature', Vol. 9, Pt II: 'Prize Essays.' London. 1884.

CUTTING, C. L. 'Fish Saving.' Hill, London. 1955.

HERBERT, D. (Ed.). 'Fish and Fisheries. A Selection from the Prize Essays of the International Fisheries Exhibition, Edinburgh, 1882.' Edinburgh. 1883.

HOLDSWORTH, E. W. H. 'Deep Sea Fishing and Fishing Boats.' London. 1884.

INNIS, H. A. 'The Cod Fisheries.' Yale University Press, Newhaven. 1940.

JENKINS, J. T. 'The Herring and the Herring Fisheries.' King, London. 1927.

POWER, E. and POSTAN, M. M. (Eds). 'Studies in English Trade in the Fifteenth Century.' Routledge, London. 1933.

SAMUEL, A. M. 'The Herring; its Effect on the History of Britain.' Murray, London. 1918.

A NOTE ON WHALING

L. HARRISON MATTHEWS

UNTIL recent times, whales have been valued for their oil and certain other products for industrial and domestic use rather than for their meat as food. Their immense size and the rapidity with which their flesh undergoes decomposition have made it necessary to cut them up and carry out the preliminary processing 'in the field' immediately after capture, thus combining in a single enterprise the techniques of fishing, processing, and preserving.

Whales are mammals, not fish, though they have no legs and their arms are modified to fin-like flippers. They are warm-blooded, breathe air, and bear living young which they suckle. The larger sorts are the largest animals that have ever existed—a large blue whale is nearly 100 ft long and weighs about 150 tons. No animal of such size whose body was not supported by immersion in water could exist. But not all members of the whale tribe are of gigantic size, and the porpoises and dolphins are comparatively small.

There are many species of whale, but they fall naturally into two main groups, the whalebone whales (Mystacoceti) and the toothed whales (Odontoceti). The latter have uniform peg-like teeth for seizing their prey, which consists of fish and, probably even more important, squids and cuttlefish.

The feeding-mechanism of the whalebone whales is quite different. They do not catch individual animals for food, but filter the sea-water to extract in bulk the vast numbers of minute organisms that are collectively termed plankton. This consists of small plants and animals, many of microscopic size, which float in vast numbers in the upper layers of the sea. The largest whales feed on little else. The apparatus of the whalebone whales for filtering plankton out of the sea is most peculiar. These creatures have no teeth, but hanging from the upper jaw is a series of many fibrous horny plates set crosswise on each side, where the upper teeth are placed in ordinary mammals. These plates are known as baleen, or, incorrectly, 'whalebone'. The inner edges of the plates are frayed out into separate fibres, so that a sort of hairy mat, supported by the inner edges of the plates, is formed in the mouth. When the whale is feeding it takes in a mouthful of sea-water together with its contained plankton, shuts the mouth, and raises the tongue so that the water is driven through the mat, between the plates of whalebone, and out between the lips at the side. The plankton thus left stranded on the mat of whalebone fibres is then swallowed.

Even primitive man appreciated the value of whales, as is shown by the bones sometimes found in ancient kitchen-middens and hut-sites. A stranded whale (figure 27) must have been a godsend to dwellers near the coast—a position now curiously reversed when the responsibility for removing a malodorous dead whale as a serious public nuisance devolves on the owners of foreshore-rights. In far-off days the meat provided by a whale was doubtless a great attraction, but for many centuries the main value of whales has been their yield of oil.

The oil was used for illumination and for lubrication up to the middle of the last century, and it was not until about the beginning of the twentieth century that the process of hydrogenation was applied on a large scale to it. Chemically, whale-oil is a mixture of the esters of unsaturated fatty acids with the trihydric alcohol glycerol, and is liquid at ordinary temperatures; after hydrogenation it is a solid fat extensively used in the manufacture of margarine and soap. The oil is extracted partly from the thick heat-insulating coating of blubber that envelops the whale's body beneath the skin, partly from the bones, and partly from the meat. After the oil has been extracted by boiling (nowadays in steam-heated open boilers for blubber, and superheated steam-digesters for meat and bones), the meat and bones are kiln-dried and reduced to meal, the better

FIGURE 27—*An old woodcut showing a stranded whale being cut up on the beach. The pieces were then carried away in carts, 200–300 journeys often being needed. Olaus Magnus, 1555.*

grades being compounded in food for pigs and poultry, and the poorer used as fertilizers. The horny plates of baleen find a limited use in the manufacture of brushes and sieves. Whalebone was formerly used extensively for making umbrella-ribs, corset 'bones', hoops for crinolines, and the handles of punch-ladles; for springs in light mechanical devices; and, when frayed out into its component fibres, for the plumes on soldiers' helmets. Occasionally whale bones were used for building (figure 28).

The oil of the sperm whale and some of the smaller toothed whales differs from that of the whalebone whales, as does a second substance, spermaceti, that separates from the oil as a solid when it cools. Chemically, both are esters produced by combination of fatty acids with monohydric alcohols, and are liquid waxes that cannot be hydrogenated into edible fats. Both are liquid at the temperature of the sperm whale's body, but, on cooling, the spermaceti solidifies whereas the sperm oil remains fluid. They are mixed together in the tissues of the whale, but the proportion of spermaceti greatly preponderates in the head, where, in front of the brain-case, there is a series of spaces filled with it and surrounded by a network of fibres and tendinous tissue. From this hollow part, the 'case', spermaceti can be baled out or poured off. Spermaceti sets to a white wax on cooling and was formerly the base of the best quality of candles. It is still used for candles for religious ceremonial purposes, and in making cosmetics. The unit candle-power was originally defined as the light emitted by a standardized spermaceti candle burning at a specified rate.

Ambergris is a substance obtained from the intestines of some sperm whales, but its physiological origin is unknown; it is said to be a pathological concretion found only in whales that are sickly. It is a black greasy substance with a horrible smell when found in the whale, but when exposed to the air it becomes harder, and lighter in colour, and exchanges its bad odour for a characteristic faintly aromatic, earthy smell. The best sort is found floating in the sea or washed ashore; it has then had ample time to undergo its natural refining-process, probably an oxidation. Ambergris is used in cosmetics to fix and intensify perfumes, and commands a very high price.

FIGURE 28—*Whale bones were sometimes used in the north, where timber was scarce, for building such things as gates and seats. Whale ribs are not large enough to make a house like that illustrated, but jaw bones would be suitable. Olaus Magnus, 1555.*

It was discovered at some early date that fortuitous strandings of whales could be improved upon by deliberately driving the animals ashore. This primitive way of hunting was practised in Scandinavia in the Middle Ages and still survives in the Faeroe Islands, where schools of a rather small species are annually driven ashore by the hundred and slaughtered, cut up, and boiled down for their oil. A similar fishery lasted into the present century in Orkney and Shetland.

During the Middle Ages the Basques carried on a profitable fishery by attacking in small boats the rather slow-moving and coast-frequenting Atlantic 'right' whales, which they exterminated locally. They evolved the technique of harpooning them with barbed spears attached to the boat by a line, and playing them until they could be approached and killed by stabbing with a lance. The dead whales were towed ashore to be cut up. When the number of whales declined through over-fishing these enterprising men fitted out ships to go farther afield in search of their quarry. The base of operations was thus merely transferred from shore to ship, for the actual hunting was done as before in small boats which were now lowered from the larger vessel. As the right whales became rare in temperate European waters, lengthy voyages into high latitudes became the practice.

Here the whalers found a further reward for their boldness, for within the Arctic circle they discovered another sort of whale, the Greenland right whale, which yielded a greater quantity of oil than any other (plate 4 A). Throughout the seventeenth and eighteenth centuries a large fleet of whalers—French, Dutch, English, and Scandinavian—was regularly engaged in voyages to the north. Some ships boiled out their oil at such places as Spitzbergen, Jan Mayen Island, or Bear Island, but others merely casked the blubber after cutting it into small pieces and brought it back to be boiled out at home. The chief British ports concerned were Whitby, Hull, Peterhead, and Dundee. The 'Greenland' fishery was for long carried on almost entirely at Spitzbergen, but later it was extended also to Davis Strait and Labrador.

After the mid-nineteenth century, northern whaling steadily declined, for Greenland whales were becoming scarce, and towards the end of the century it was only the high value of the whalebone that kept it going. The passing of the crinoline, together with the introduction of steel busks for corsets, dealt the final blow to the industry. With the twentieth century sailing-ships ceased to hunt the right whales of the Arctic.

On the Connecticut and other New England coasts of America a similar evolution of whaling took place during the eighteenth century, but the pursuit was directed not only towards the right whales of the Arctic but towards the sperm whales of temperate and tropical seas. In the first half of the nineteenth century Yankee whalers sailed the seven seas from such ports as New Bedford, Nantucket, New London, Fairhaven, Mattapoisett, Stonington, and Sag Harbor, but during the American civil war (1861–5) many of the whale-ships were sunk as block-ships, and others captured and burned. At the same time the rise of the petroleum industry (vol V, ch 5), which substituted paraffin for whale-oil as an illuminant, started the ruin of American whaling. The first decade of the present century saw its end.

During the second and third quarters of the nineteenth century whaling-voyages got longer and longer. They ultimately extended up to five years, during which there would be visits to the Arctic and Antarctic, as well as months of cruising after sperm whales in the tropics. If the ship filled her holds before the end of the voyage she forwarded her full barrels home by freighter from some convenient port and then continued her hunting. The crews were paid by shares in the profits of the voyage, but few of a crew lasted out a five-year voyage. Unscrupulous skippers and mates sometimes gave their crew such a rough time that sooner or later practically every hand would have deserted the ship at intermediate ports, thus forfeiting their shares. Even those that returned home as crew often found themselves so much in debt to the ship for advances of pay and credit from the slop-chest that they received only a few dollars at paying-off.

On these long voyages the Americans developed the practice, adopted by whalers of other nations, of stripping the blubber from the dead whales in the water alongside the ship and extracting the oil by boiling the finely minced blubber in a series of cauldrons set in brickwork (plate 4 B). The fuel used was the oil-soaked fibrous scrap remaining after the oil had been boiled out of the blubber. Despite the danger of such operations on a wooden ship there was no unduly high loss from fire.

This industry was carried on by spearing the whales with harpoons hurled from small

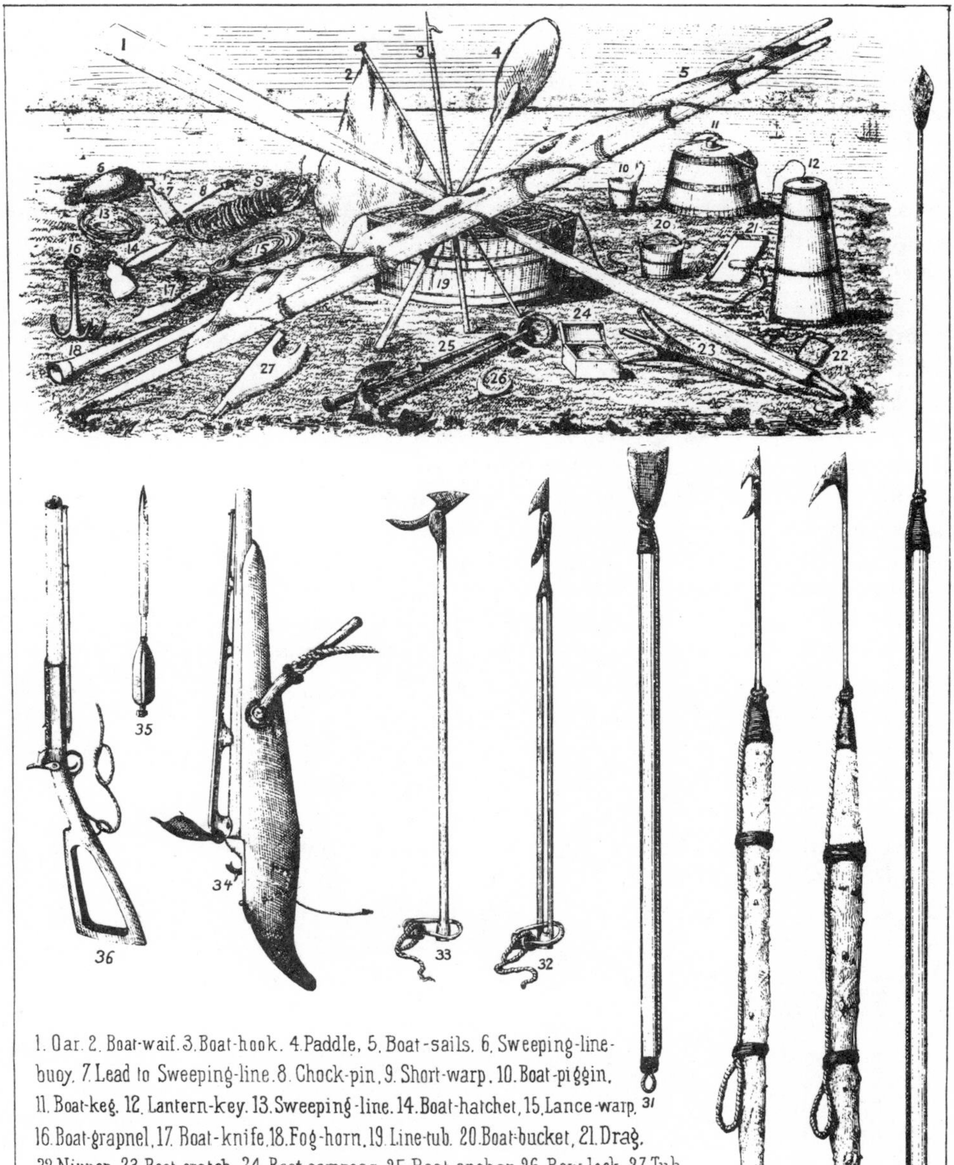

FIGURE 29—*Some of the gear provided for each boat lowered from a nineteenth-century sailing whale-ship.*

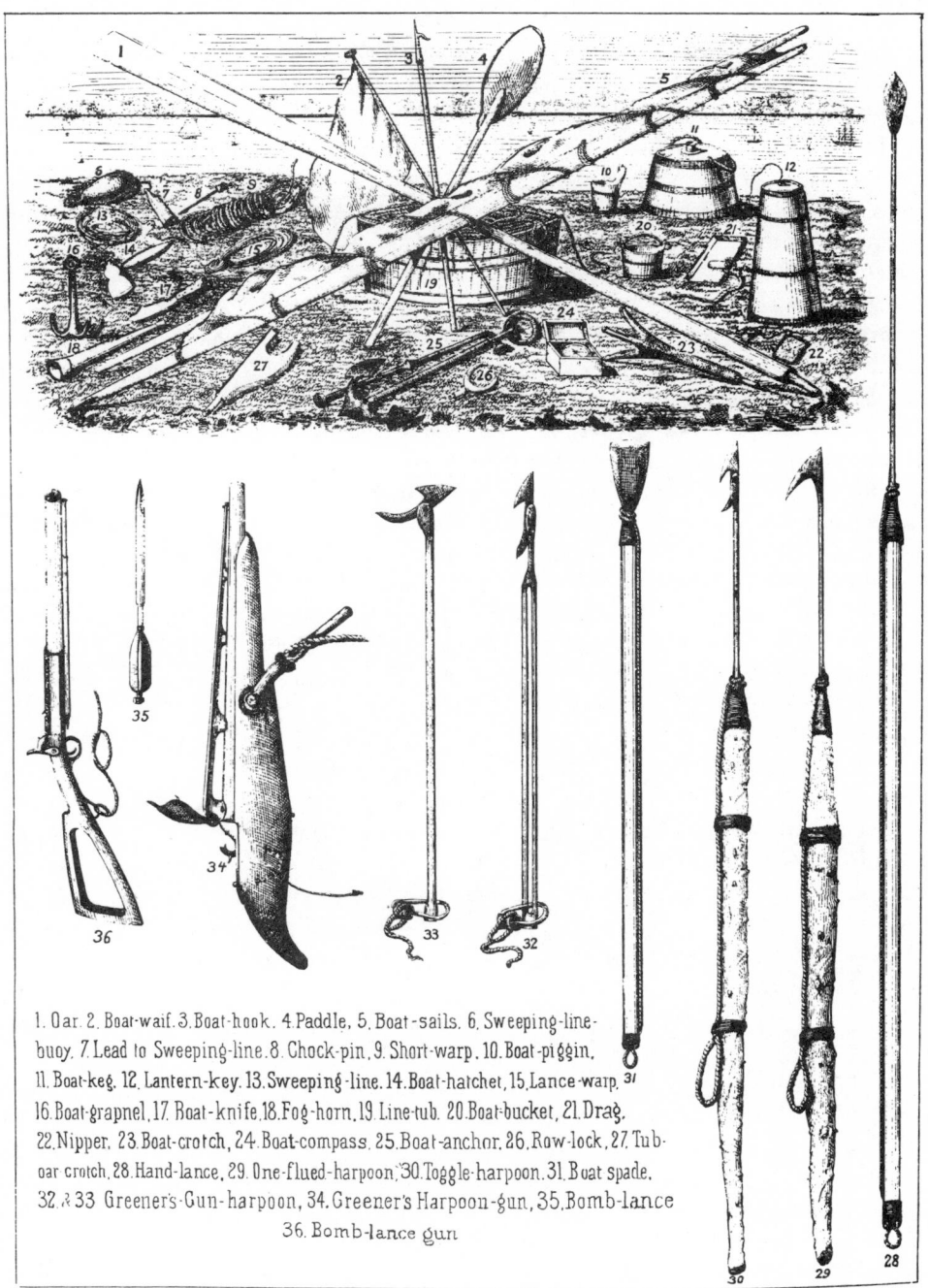

boats lowered from sailing-ships. The harpoon was secured to the boat by a long line, and once harpooned the whale towed the boat until it was so exhausted that the boat could approach closely by hauling in the line. The whale was then dispatched by stabbing with long lances mounted on poles. About 1850 the bomb-lance was invented. It was an explosive dart fired from a heavy shoulder- or swivel-gun. This saved time and damage to whale-boats and their crews, but met with little success and was not extensively used. Some nineteenth-century whaling gear is shown in figure 29.

Such whaling was restricted to the few species of whale, mainly right and sperm whales, that float when dead. Other and larger species were inaccessible to this technique because they are so large and active that the danger of attacking them, and the difficulty of even approaching them, were too great. Further, when dead they sink and would drag down any boat made fast to them. But about 1860 the existence of large numbers of the larger kinds of whalebone whales, the blue, the fin, the humpback, and the Sei whales, all immune from attack, attracted the attention of Svend Foyn, an inventive Norwegian. He realized that entirely new methods were required to capture these commercially desirable species, and invented a very large harpoon fired from a cannon mounted in the bow of a small steamer and attached to a stout rope (figure 30). The steamer had the speed required to approach the whales, and the heavy harpoon with its thick whale-line gave sufficient strength to hold them when struck. He also devised an explosive head, fused to explode a few seconds after the harpoon entered the whale, which was usually killed at once. The line ran over a system of movable pulleys that could compress a series of heavy steel springs alongside the ship's kelson when great strain came upon it. This arrangement had a 'give' to prevent the line from being broken by the first rushes of the whale and to compensate for the rise and fall of the ship in a seaway; it was in fact analogous to the flexible rod of the angler.

The dead whale sank, but was brought to the surface by means of a steam-winch to haul in the line. It was then made buoyant by inflating it with air pumped in through a hose fastened to a pointed pipe plunged into the body-cavity. The carcass could now be towed home to be cut up and boiled down at leisure. This method of whale-hunting is the basis of the modern whaling-industry, and is in use on a large scale at the present day. Foyn's methods of hunting were used in conjunction with shore-stations—factories at the water's edge in a sheltered harbour—where the dead whales were hauled out on to the land and the products extracted with the aid of machinery.

The exploitation of these hitherto untapped resources led to the establishment in many parts of the world of whaling-stations, in which the management and practically all the skilled labour were Norwegian; in the tropics the same methods were adopted for the pursuit of sperm whales. A prosperous industry became firmly established, though after some years the numbers of whales were obviously falling.

At the end of the nineteenth century much attention was being directed towards the exploration of the Antarctic, the last great unknown region of the world. In 1902–3, the veteran whaling-captain C. A. Larsen, commanding the Swedish South Polar expedition's ship the *Antarctic*, noted the abundance of whales and the suitability of many of the islands of that region for whaling-stations. His ship was lost, but after his rescue and return he found financial backing in South America to organize a whaling expedition on modern lines.

In 1904 he started the first Antarctic whaling-station in a sheltered cove on South Georgia. Whales were abundant and the enterprise was a great success; it paid a dividend of 70 per cent in its first year. The then recent invention of the hydrogenation process for converting oils into fats (p 56) had created a demand for animal oils in the margarine and soap trades. A rush for the new El Dorado started, and within a few years many whaling companies were working on this island and on the South Orkneys and South Shetlands farther south. A quarter of a century later, the introduction of pelagic floating

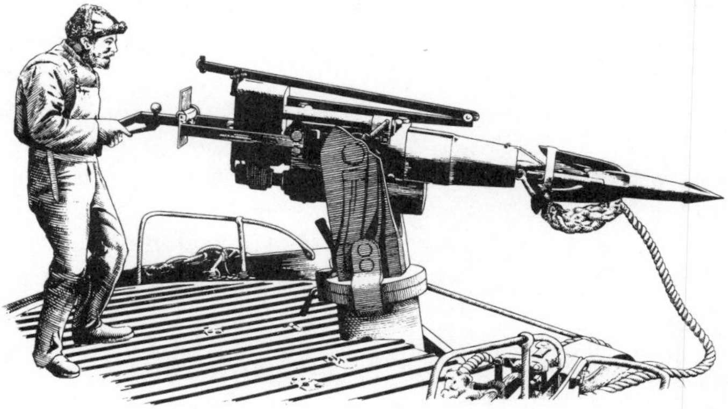

FIGURE 30—*Modern version of Svend Foyn's harpoon cannon, which is mounted in the bow of the whale-catcher. The shank of the harpoon is pushed into the barrel of the cannon, and the head, which has arms that open like an umbrella, projects. The rope runs over pulleys in the bow.*

factories freed the industry from dependence upon land-bases and from the attentions of the colonial tax-gatherer. These great self-contained ship-borne factories—which can haul the carcass of the largest whale on deck for processing—with their attendant fleets of whale-catchers seek out whales wherever they are most abundant. Many of the ships now carry aircraft to locate the whales. In recent years the world catch has varied from 24 000 to 44 000 whales annually, producing from about 400 000 tons to over 540 000 tons of oil. To prevent the destruction of the basic stock of whales the catch is now limited by international agreement.

Europeans and Americans are not the only peoples that have developed highly specialized techniques for the capture of whales. The Japanese were carrying on a prosperous whaling industry before the end of the eighteenth century. Several species of whalebone whales regularly come close inshore among the Japanese islands on their annual migrations, and the fishery for them was efficiently organized. Barbed harpoons were used in the hunt, and lances for the death blow, but the method differed fundamentally in that the initial stages of the capture were made by nets. As soon as whales were sighted from the look-out stations, a fleet of boats put out to sea across the path of the approaching whales and laid a series of nets, somewhat like the drift-nets of the North Sea herring-fishermen on a gigantic scale. Once the whale was entangled, other boats attacked with harpoons and lances, and naked men plunged into the sea and mounted on the back of the wounded whale to make fast ropes passed through incisions cut in the blubber with cutlasses carried in the mouth. The most usual quarry was the humpback whale, which generally sinks when dead; the hunters therefore brought two barges alongside and secured them to the animal before death to support it and carry it to the shore-station.

When the dead whale was brought to the factory it was dismembered, and the oil was boiled out of the blubber. The meat was cut up for human consumption, and many by-products were manufactured from the bones, sinews, intestines, and other parts. The industry was the monopoly of certain feudal landowners, and was carried on by great numbers of serfs.

A more primitive technique of whaling was in use until recently off the coasts of the Malayan islands. Whales such as humpbacks were harpooned from canoes, but the line instead of running was made fast to the boat. On striking a whale the crew jumped into the sea and swam about until picked up by their companion boats. The whale took the canoe down with it and dragged it about as a sort of sea-anchor until it was so exhausted that it could be killed with lances. The main object of this fishery was to obtain the meat for human consumption.

When the American whalers set off on their lengthy voyages they obtained the basic elements of their crews by 'shanghai'-ing the dockside scum of the New England ports and the 'hick hayseeds' from the Middle West who had come to the coast to seek their fortunes. The first part of the cruise, in search of the comparatively small blackfish or pilot whales, took them across the Atlantic, and they then put into the Azores or the Cape Verde Islands to complete their crews and engage skilled harpooners for the main voyage. The hand-harpoon technique of whaling from sailing-ships still lingers in the Azores, where it is carried on from shore-stations. A sperm-whaling industry of some importance is even yet preserved there. Look-out stations, like those formerly maintained by the Japanese, keep watch for the whales and signal the waiting boats when the quarry is sighted. The boats, and all the whaling-gear, are exactly as those used by the Yankee whalers of a century ago, and even the old American-English technical terms are in vogue, modified into the Portuguese speech of these hardy islanders. Their only concession to modernity is that the boats are towed out to the whaling-grounds by motor-launches, which also tow in the dead whales. But the boats are propelled by oar and sail, and all the ancient technique is retained.

The demand for fresh meat led to the development of a minor branch of whaling immediately after the 1939–45 war. Whale-meat is coarse, though palatable enough if removed from the whale soon after death, and it quickly becomes tainted by the incipient decomposition of the oil if it is not quite fresh. Whale-meat has always been used by whalers to supplement preserved foods, and has long been marketed in Scandinavia. Before the Reformation the flesh of the small kinds of whale, the porpoises and dolphins, was considerably esteemed because it was regarded as fish, and so could be eaten during Lent and on fast-days.

BIBLIOGRAPHY

AAGAARD, B. 'Den gamle Hvalfangst. Kapitler av dens Historie.' Hvalfangstmuseet, Publ. no. 13. Sandefjord. 1933.

JENKINS, J. T. "Bibliography of Whaling." *J. Soc. Bibl. nat. Hist.*, **2**, 71–166, 1948.

RISTING, S. 'Av Hvalfangstens Historie.' Christensens Hvalfangstmuseet, Publ. no. 2. Sandefjord. 1922.

SCAMMON, C. M. 'The Marine Mammals of the North-western Coast of North America together with an Account of the American Whale-fishery.' San Francisco. 1874.

STARBUCK, A. 'History of the American Whale Fishery from its Earliest Inception to the Year 1876.' Waltham, Mass. 1878.

Hand-harpooning from open boats, nineteenth century.

3

METAL AND COAL MINING, 1750–1875

J. A. S. RITSON

ALTHOUGH the mining of metalliferous ores and of coal have many features in common, they differ in two major respects. First, deposits of coal commonly have a great horizontal extension, whereas mineral deposits tend to follow a near-vertical course. Secondly, coal-mining practice has to pay great attention to the possibility of the presence of explosive or poisonous gases and of explosive dust, which are not normally encountered in metal mines. Like most generalizations both these have exceptions—some of which will be noted later—but they are of sufficient force to make it appropriate to discuss the two subjects separately.

METAL-MINING

I. LOCATION OF MINERAL DEPOSITS

In the middle of the eighteenth century mining was confined mostly to western Europe. Small mining enterprises were developed in other regions, but these were mostly concerned with the working of surface deposits. It is true that great quantities of precious metals came to Europe from Central and South America, but much, indeed most, of this supply had been laboriously won from the earth by the natives before their conquest. After the decline of the Roman Empire, when much mining was done by slave labour, mining languished in Europe. There was slight activity in the ninth and tenth centuries, but it was not until the fifteenth century that the Germans, Saxons, and Bohemians staged a full revival (vol II, ch 1). This is clearly shown in central Europe and in the near East, where there is evidence of mining (said to be by Saxon miners) up to the time of the Turkish conquest. After this, the operating mines show evidence of having been abandoned until they were rediscovered and reopened in the twentieth century.

An example of the vicissitudes a mine can pass through is well illustrated by Parys Mountain in Anglesea. This is said to have been exploited originally by the Romans, then for 1700 years it lay idle until the 1780s, when it became for a few years, in the hands of Thomas Williams, the largest copper mine in the world, 1000 tons of copper being smelted annually at the mine's own works in Lancashire. After Williams's death in 1802 it languished, but came to life for a time in 1850 and again languished. In 1956 it underwent still another reopening.

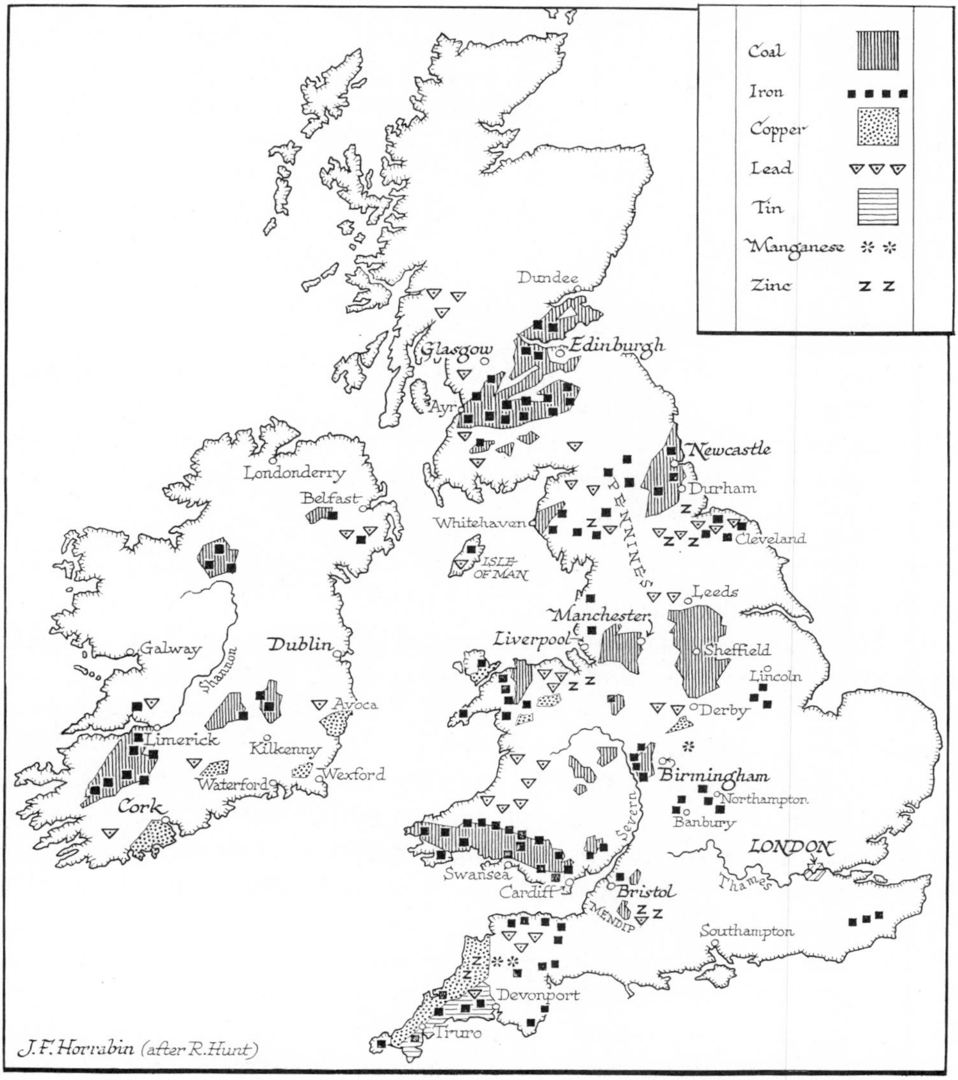

FIGURE 31—*Mineral map of the United Kingdom, 1851.*

During the late eighteenth and early nineteenth centuries there was great metal-mining activity in Britain (figure 31), Sweden, Bohemia, and Spain. In the middle of the nineteenth century, after the discovery of gold in California, American prospectors began to uncover the mineral riches of the western States; they were followed by British and American engineers, who developed the finds.

Up to the time of the industrial revolution, the demand for the base metals had been limited to the requirements of agricultural communities and the demands of war, but once new uses for such metals became apparent there was a rush to find new sources of raw materials. These were found in the American and Canadian Rocky Mountains, Australia, South Africa, and many other places. As a result of the development of rich deposits of lead in the United States and Australia, and of tin in Malaya and Nigeria, the older and less rich deposits of Britain and western Europe could not be worked cheaply enough to secure a sale for their products in the industrial markets.

Discovery can be divided into two sections:

(i) discovery of surface outcrops; that is, the mineral deposit actually shows on the surface of the land;
(ii) discovery of deposits that do not show on the surface but whose possible existence can be deduced from local geological evidence. Their actual presence must be proved by boring and other means.

Many of the most famous deposits have been found by chance, and up to about 1750 most known deposits were adventitious finds. The lead-zinc deposits of Broken Hill, New South Wales, for example, formed a rough black ridge like a reef rising above the level of a dusty plain and were ignored for years by the boundary riders of a sheep station near by. When they at last began to feel an interest in the ridge, they took samples and sent them to be analysed for tin, but with negative results. Nevertheless, a small syndicate was formed and a shallow shaft was sunk, which proved the presence of lead carbonate. The sinking was continued, and rich silver, lead, and zinc ores were discovered.

The famous Comstock lode is another example of fortuitous discovery. In 1851 two men were panning for gold along a small stream in what is now Nevada. They found a little gold and silver but complained about the presence of a heavy black mineral which fouled their pan, and they abandoned the area. Eight years later another party visited it and, after some very questionable behaviour, became the owners of a 500-ft strip of outcrop which subsequently developed into the fabulously rich Comstock mine: the heavy black mineral was silver sulphide.

During the period 1750–1850 there does not appear to have been any remarkable discovery of further mineral deposits. After 1850, discoveries of many kinds were made in various parts of the world; for example, gold in California and Australia, nickel in Canada, lead in Missouri, and diamonds in South Africa, and most of these again were found by pure chance.

Chance has done much, but properly directed efforts can do more. The indications that guide a prospector are natural features such as form of the ground, colour, nature of decomposed outcrop, mineral springs, special plants, altered flora, burrows of animals, old workings, slag heaps, bygone records, and the chemical contents of vegetation. If the mineral deposit is harder or softer than the surrounding ground, the process of geological weathering will leave either a projecting wall or a hollow. The reefs of Western Australia, the Mother lode of California, and the quartz reefs of Wales are examples of hard rock left exposed.

Until about 1875, the ancient methods of prospecting for a deposit whose presence was suspected from evidence such as the above were still in common use. They included shoading, trenching, and hushing. Shoading involves walking up a stream and examining the pebbles by hand and eye, and also washing samples of the finer sands on a prospector's pan. As the seeker travels up the stream the 'show' pieces become more and more numerous and more and more angular until at last they cease altogether. Somewhere nearby is the outcrop. Cross-trenches a yard or so wide are dug to bed-rock across the supposed line of outcrop, and then, with luck, the vein will be laid bare. Hushing, no longer practised in civilized countries, consists of damming a stream near the top of a hill or valley to form a small reservoir. When a sufficient volume of water has been collected, the dam is breached and the water rushing downhill removes the top soil and lays bare the rock below. Search is then made for a mineral vein.

II. PROSPECTING BY BORING

Surface boring tools are used for many reasons, such as to ascertain the nature of a mineral deposit, its depth from the surface, thickness, angle of dip, and direction of strike, or to obtain liquid minerals such as oil and brine. During the period now under discussion three principal methods of boring were in use. They were, respectively, (*a*) by rotation, (*b*) by percussion with rods, and (*c*) by percussion with ropes.

Soft rocks such as clay, soft shale, sandy clay, and sand were bored by an open auger, resembling the familiar carpenter's tool. The auger was attached to a wooden or iron rod and was fitted with a capstan head, which was rotated by hand. As the hole became deeper, more and more rods were added until the required depth, or the limit of human strength, was reached. Such hand-bored holes rarely exceeded 200 ft in depth. For deeper boring, horses were used to rotate the drill, and these in turn were superseded by machines. A wooden tripod was erected over the hole and a small hand-operated winch was used to raise and lower the rods.

In the middle of the nineteenth century a great improvement in rotary drilling for prospecting purposes was effected, namely the application of industrial diamonds, or bort, as the cutting agent. This not only increased the speed and reduced the cost of drilling but provided a solid sample of all rocks passed through. The drill rods consist of a string of hollow tubes, to the lower end of which is attached a soft metal ring into which diamonds are fixed. The ring is rotated and cuts out a cylinder of the rock through which it passes. This cylinder is gripped within another hollow tube, called the core-barrel, and at suitable intervals is drawn to the surface and removed for examination. Hence a complete visual record is obtained of all rocks passed through, which can be retained for further examination. In the early days a small number of diamonds of several carats each were used, but owing to their cost and the difficulty of finding stones without too pronounced cleavage planes, the more modern diamond 'crowns' were introduced. These consist of a multitude of small stones or chips embedded in a matrix of cast metal. Alternatively, and particularly where no accurate record is required, three conical serrated wheels of very tough steel are used to grind the rock to powder. This powder is washed out of the hole by a continuous stream of water which flows down the inside of the hollow rods, round the cutting or pulverizing wheels, and up the outside of the rods, carrying the dust and sand with it.

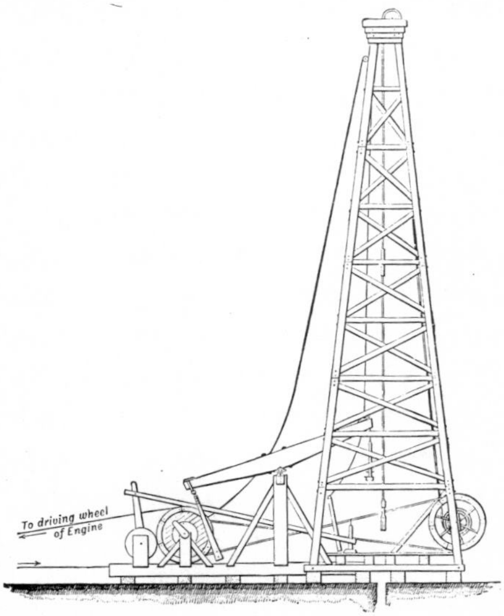

FIGURE 32—*'American rig' for boring by percussion with rope. The high derrick enables the whole string of boring tools to be extracted from the hole without disjointing. The power for this rig was provided by a 15-hp steam-engine.*

In the eighteenth century, drill-holes for proving minerals were also made by means of chisels attached to iron or wooden rods. The latter were raised and then allowed to drop vertically, the rods being slightly rotated between successive blows so as to ensure symmetrical working. The bore-hole was kept full of water and the soft paste of debris was removed from time to time. This method was very slow.

Percussion with ropes is one of the earliest forms of boring and was practised more than a thousand years ago in China, when putting down bore-holes for the purpose of dissolving rock-salt into brine. It resembles percussion boring with rods, save that the chisel is raised and lowered by means of a rope. It was not practised much in Europe and America, however, until the nineteenth century, when it was brought to great perfection in the United States for tapping oil and gas, hence its common name, the 'American rig' (figure 32).

III. APPROACH OR METHOD OF ENTRY

In the early days the limiting factor to successful working at any depth below the surface was water; adequate pumps were not then available. Luckily, many of the mineral deposits of the world are found in or close to hard rock such as igneous rock or limestone, and the surrounding country is hill and dale. Consequently it was possible to drive level or slightly rising roads into the hillside, thus allowing any water encountered to run away. Then all useful minerals above this level could be mined.

When the more easily accessible deposits of minerals showed signs of exhaustion, the possibility of direct extraction diminished and shaft-sinking was begun. At first the shafts were close together and regularly spaced along the outcrop of the vein. As there is rarely any poisonous or inflammable gas in a metal-mine, only a single shaft was sunk in each unit area, fresh air for ventilation being allowed to find its own way to the workers. Usually a stream of fresh cold air crept along the floor of the levels and the warmer vitiated air flowed out close to the roof. It is said that a road could be driven 400 yds from a shaft, but the conditions at the far end must have been unpleasant. To improve conditions the custom grew up of sinking rectangular shafts divided into two sections by a wooden partition. The underground road also was divided into two sections by wooden or canvas partitions, and thus fresh air had a way in and foul air a way out. As the workings became deeper, two levels were utilized, one above the other, either in or parallel to the vein. The fresh air then entered by the lower level and returned by the upper.

It became the practice to sink rectangular shafts almost exclusively; the sides were supported by local timber, since the metal-miners, usually being pioneers in opening up a country, often had no other material for lining the shaft. The space within a rectangular shaft could all be put to a directly useful purpose. In a three-compartment rectangular shaft, for example, one compartment could contain the ladderways, and the other two be used for hoisting. The rectangular shaft is still in common use, but where the mine has been worked to a great depth, say 6000 ft, the rock pressure on the long sides of such a shaft becomes excessive and circular shafts are sunk. At great depths the need for cooling air becomes increasingly important, and unused space in a circular shaft serves for ventilation.

IV. BREAKING GROUND

Most of the rock underground was won manually with the aid of a pick, crow-bar, and wedge (plate 5 A). Many of the mines were shallow and above the level of the water-table: consequently the rocks were weathered and fissured. Hand tools could therefore make some impression upon them. The form of these tools

FIGURE 33—*Splitting rocks by fire.*

has not altered very much with the passage of time, except that hardened steel has now superseded cast iron in the picks, and plate iron has replaced wood in the shovels.

Where the ground was too hard to bore, so that explosives could not be used profitably, fire-setting was practised. It was in use in Saxony, Hungary, and the Harz during the latter half of the eighteenth century. In this process horizontal layers of billets of firewood, disposed crosswise one above the other, were piled up in a nearly vertical position so as to present four free vertical faces (figure 33). They were then set on fire. The flame played on the face of the ore, which became shattered; when cooled it was easily broken up with a pick or bar. The splitting of the rock was increased by pouring cold water on to it while still hot. At

Goslar, in the Harz, the fires were lighted on Saturday night and kept burning until Monday morning. Early on Monday water was poured on the rock so that it was cooled and broken up before the miners arrived for their fresh week's work.

At this time ordinary black gunpowder, in granulated form, was in common use, for high explosive was available only at the extreme end of the period now under consideration. Holes 3 to 4 ft in depth and 1 to 3 inches in diameter were bored by hand. A quantity of loose powder was poured or pushed to the back of the holes, and a thin copper bar or pricker was then inserted. The remainder of the hole was filled with plastic clay, hammered well home, and the pricker was withdrawn. Straws, preferably wheaten, were filled with powder and pushed into the hole so that a continuous train of powder reached to the back. A piece of touch paper or a slow match was fastened to the outer end and ignited from the miner's lamp.

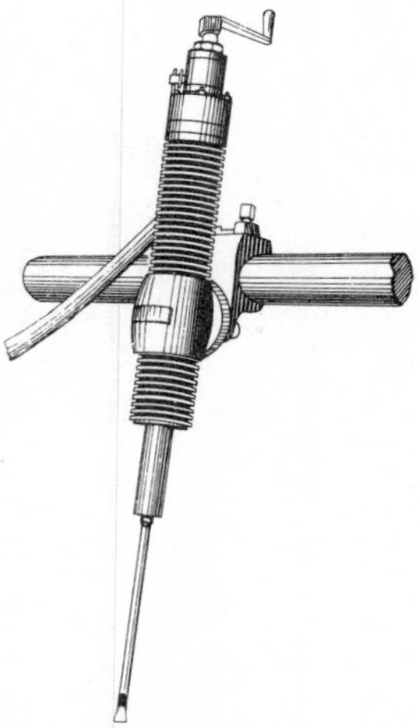

FIGURE 34—*Single-acting pneumatic drill mounted for quarry work.*

All this was very laborious work and many attempts were made to ease it. Rotary rock drills were tried, but being manually operated and constructed of indifferent steel they were unsuccessful. The inventor of the first mechanical rock-boring machine (1813) is said to have been the Cornish engineer Richard Trevithick (1771–1833), but it was forty years before the boring of shot-holes by machinery became practicable, with the invention by Bartlett of a steam rock-boring machine which was used in the Mont Cenis tunnel. Later, Sommelier showed how a similar machine could be worked by compressed air; a single-acting pneumatic drill is shown in figure 34. In the United States, Fowle produced a similar steam-operated drill, but the modern prototype, the Ingersoll drill, was not made until 1871. The principle upon which the earlier machines were based was the boring of a hole either by the continuous motion of a rotating drill or by intermittent blows delivered by a pointed tool striking the rock.

Low's machine, made by the Turner firm at Ipswich (figure 35), attempted a combination of these operations. It consisted of a cylinder into which the tool, similar to the hand-held chisel, was inserted. This cylinder was housed within another cylinder in which it was made to rotate slightly but continuously between each blow of the drill, the latter striking between 300 and 500 blows per minute. The whole machine was carried on a trolley and driven by compressed air.

Later, a light drill which could be held by one man was produced. This consisted of a cylinder in which a piston travelled backwards and forwards at a high speed, up to 1500 times a minute, and delivered a series of blows on a chisel inserted in the bore-holes. After each blow the chisel or 'steel' automatically turned through a small arc, allowing the succeeding blow to strike new ground. To clean the hole the chisel had a small tubular passage down its centre through which water or air was forced in order to remove the cuttings.

FIGURE 35—*Low's rock-boring machine. This was driven by compressed air at a pressure of 70–90 lb per sq in. It was capable of working at a distance of more than a mile from the compressor.*

V. METHODS OF MINING

Extraction of ore was effected in two operations. First, the mine was divided up into large square or rectangular blocks: secondly, the blocks were removed. The first operation consisted of driving levels in the deposit at a definite vertical distance apart, say 300 ft, and constructing small connecting shafts, raises or winzes (figure 36), at intervals of 300 to 600 ft. The object of these roads was twofold: (*a*) to probe the deposit and prove whether it continued to be valuable, and (*b*) to provide routes for subsequent extraction of ore. Although the fissures, into which seeped the mineral-bearing solutions from which the ore derives, may persist for long distances both horizontally and vertically, it does not follow that the entire area will be equally mineralized. It is common experience to find some sections much richer than others, and hence thorough exploration is necessary.

When sufficient exploratory roads had been driven to make certain that an adequate tonnage of valuable ore was available, extraction was put in hand. What is considered an adequate tonnage varies with each mine, and depends, among other factors, upon the capacity of the ancillary plant available and how much ore it is considered should be in reserve to enable the mine to continue operation even if further exploration runs into barren ground. It was, and still is, good practice to have three years' work blocked out in advance whenever possible. Exploratory work is expensive and unremunerative; many mining companies at

FIGURE 36—*Winze-shaft in a Cornish mine.*

this time could not afford it and consequently often worked from hand to mouth. Profits therefore fluctuated widely and failures were common. This was particularly so where the so-called cost-book system was prevalent. Under this system, mines were opened by a small group of adventurers with limited capital. At the end of a given period, say one month, the accounts were made up. So much was then paid to the mineral owner, say one-tenth to one-seventh; the tributers or bargain men were paid their share; and what was left over was divided amongst the adventurers. As a rule little or nothing was put to reserve. Consequently the amount of development possible was limited; if the mine ran into a poor stretch of ground there was no money available to carry it on except by a fresh call on the adventurers. In time this system gave way to the institution of limited liability companies, which resulted in a more cautious and stable method of working.

The cost-book system was adopted in Cornwall during the period when the

FIGURE 37—*Working by descending levels, as practised in Saxony, Hungary, and Rhenish Prussia in the early nineteenth century.*

upper portions of the veins were being worked. These contained copper which persisted down to about 1000 ft; below this there came a poorly mineralized zone, below which again was tinstone. The cost-book mines made a regular profit while in the region of copper ore, but with no reserves could not weather the unprofitable barren zone.

The method of extraction of the ore pillars was overhand or underhand stoping, that is, working in steps. To open a new underhand stope a pillar of solid ground was, or was not, left below an upper level carrying the road for haulage and the travelling road. If no pillar of solid ground was left, an artificial floor of wooden planks was laid and work started beneath this. A slice of the pillar the width of the lode and roughly 6 ft high was taken right and left from one of the connecting winzes. Bore-holes were made either vertically downwards or horizontally, charged with gunpowder, and fired. The broken ground was then shovelled to the winze, where it fell to the level below and was thence transported to the shaft. When the first levels had travelled a few yards, two more were started below them, so that in time there was a series of descending levels travelling in echelon outward from the winze (figure 37). If barren or poor ground was encountered, the valueless material was piled on scaffolds carried by timbers fixed between the walls of the lode, or else was left *in situ* as a support. In overhand stoping (figure 38) the procedure was reversed, except that driving was almost always horizontal and rarely vertically upwards. The coming of mechanical drills, with the consequently easier work, allowed of variations in these basic methods—such as rill-stoping to reduce the labour involved, or flat-back stoping to enable mechanized haulage devices such as scrapers to be used—but there was no fundamental change.

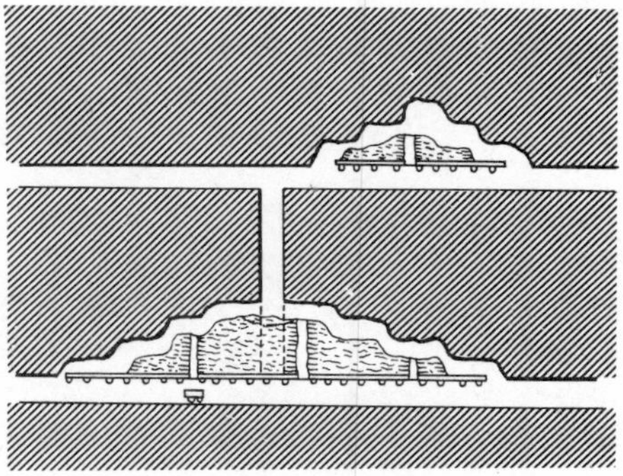
FIGURE 38—*Overhand stope, with ascending levels.*

When the walls of the lode or vein were strong, little or no support was needed, but in thicker veins, or in those with soft and slabby walls, precautions had to be taken. Where timber was plentiful and cheap, or the vein of material very rich, the open space left after the removal of the mineral was sometimes filled with frames of timber cut and fitted together into hollow cubes on the surface and then fitted into the open space underground. These were known as square sets. A simpler, and possibly more satisfactory system, used whenever possible, was to run down—through old workings from the surface or some other convenient spot—barren material from which all valuable ore had been extracted. When in place underground, any water in this rubble drained out and the material set hard. It was kept so close up to the face of the stopes that the men could stand on it to work. Another variation, developed towards the end of this period for working very thick deposits, was the removal of pillars by taking thick slices and allowing the worked space to cave in. The area above what had already been worked usually caved in also, but the descent of the caved-in material was regulated by placing thick layers of timber on the floor of the section being extracted. These timber mattes fell with the rest but had a restraining influence on the broken rock.

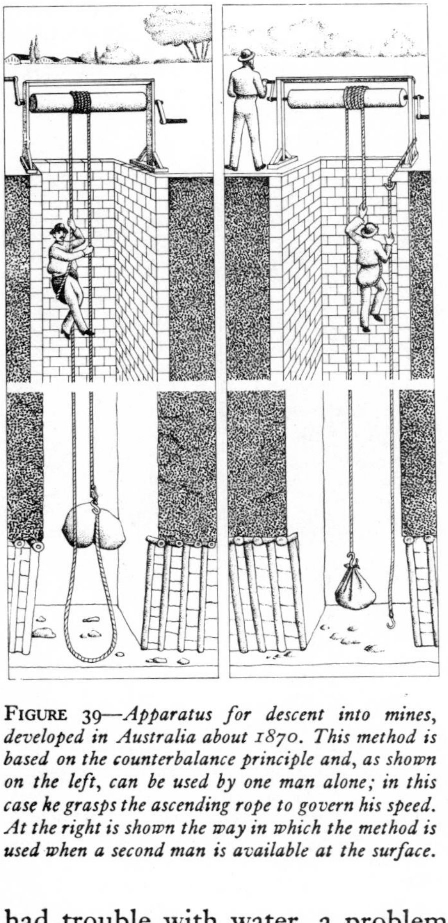

FIGURE 39—*Apparatus for descent into mines, developed in Australia about 1870. This method is based on the counterbalance principle and, as shown on the left, can be used by one man alone; in this case he grasps the ascending rope to govern his speed. At the right is shown the way in which the method is used when a second man is available at the surface.*

VI. RAISING AND LOWERING OF MEN AND MATERIALS

Before the days of the steam-engine workmen went underground by ladders—a method that continued long after the introduction of steam hoisting-engines. As long as the mines were shallow, this was no great hardship, but to climb 600 ft or more up ladders at the end of a hard day's work was very wearisome. Sometimes counterpoise methods were used when no power was available (figure 39). From very shallow mines mineral was raised in baskets by hand-worked windlasses or even cast by shovel from stage to stage. For deeper mines the horse-whim (figure 49) was common if no water-power was available.

An interesting device for bringing miners up and down was the man-engine (figure 40 and plate 5B), which persisted into the twentieth century. To understand the working of this engine it must be remembered that nearly every mine had trouble with water, a problem that was dealt with by a surface pumping-engine which transmitted vertical motion by rods down the shaft to a stationary pump at or near the bottom. These rods had a stroke of 6 to 12 ft, with a pause at the end of the stroke while the valve-gear reversed at the pumping-engine.

At the side of the shaft, exactly opposite the point of the end of the stroke of each rod, and spaced the distance of the stroke apart, were fixed strong platforms to hold a man, or possibly two men in an emergency. At corresponding points on the pump-rods smaller platforms were fixed. Suppose that a man wanted to go to the surface. At the bottom of the shaft, when the pump-rod momentarily halted between strokes, he stepped on to the attached platform. As the rod ascended the man was carried up and when it stopped at the end of its stroke he stepped on to the convenient platform fixed to the shaft. The rods descended again, stopped, and the man stepped on to the next platform on the rods and so was carried up another stage when the rods ascended. At the end of the shift in a deep mine there might be a hundred men side-stepping between rods and shaft platforms at each stroke of the pumping-engine. This device was known as the man-engine; its use is particularly associated with Cornwall, but it was used all over the world until more efficient hoisting-systems came into general use.

VII. HAULAGE

Haulage in metal-mines has never been so important as in coal-mines, because veins of metal ore tend to be more or less vertical and do not extend horizontally for great distances. Exceptions are the sedimentary gold-mines of the Transvaal, the bedded copper-mines of Northern Rhodesia, and a few others. The little haulage normally necessary was provided during this period by men or animals, who either carried the load on their backs, or pushed or pulled a wheeled tram. In the early days wheelbarrows with a low centre of gravity were often used. The sequence in a new mine was first, human porters, then wheelbarrows, and, finally, tracked vehicles pulled by horse or mule.

FIGURE 40—*Form of Cornish man-engine.*

VIII. REMOVAL OF WATER

Nearly all mines, and metalliferous mines in particular, have a water problem, and in many instances this represents a major item in the cost of operation.

Before the development of efficient steam-power many mines could not cope with the problem at all and had to close down. This was particularly, but not exclusively, true of the mines in Central and South America, which were extensively worked before and after the Spanish conquest; it was true also of the Cornish copper-mines. Many remained idle until after Boulton and Watt developed their steam-powered pump and engine.

The oldest way, and still the best way when practicable, to drain a mine is by means of an adit; this is a tunnel driven from the lowest possible point in a valley at a slightly rising gradient, say 1 in 300, into a hillside so as to penetrate a mineralized area. There are adits today in Cornwall, the Harz Mountains, and many other places, which with their side-shoots extend to a total of 40 to 50 miles each. Some are 200 years old and are still being extended. Naturally, adits can drain only the workings above them, but they are invaluable even in deeper mines because they reduce the head against which the water has to be pumped.

In 1778 W. Pryce wrote in his *Mineralogia Cornubiensis*, 'with all the skill and adroitness of our miners they cannot go to any considerable distance below the adits before they must recourse to some contrivance for clearing the water from their workings'. During this period the rag-and-chain pump was not wholly discontinued, although it was falling into disfavour on account of the great expense and heavy labour involved. According to Pryce, the rag-and-chain consisted of 'an iron chain with knobs of cloth stiffened and fenced with iron, seldom more than 9 ft asunder. The chain is turned round by a wheel 2 to 3 ft in diameter furnished with iron spikes to enclose and keep steady the chain so that it may rise through a wooden pump 3, 4, or 5 inches bore and from 12 to 22 ft long and by means of the knobs bring up with it a stream of water.' These pumps, mounted on timbers set across the shaft, were placed in series down it, each lifting water from and to a wooden box or sump also fixed to the side of the shaft. The pumps were worked by manual labour and the work was so hard that it was the cause of many deaths (cf vol II, figure 21).

When water-power was available, water-driven whims were used to draw water in barrels to the surface. Water-wheels were also used where circumstances allowed. These water-wheels were fitted with cranks, attached by a straight balk of wood to heavy 'bobs' pivoted at the centre. As the cranks revolved the ends of the bobs rose and fell. One end of the bob was over the shaft and was fitted with a heavy iron chain which passed over an arc to give it a vertical motion. This chain was attached to a vertical piece of timber hanging in the shaft; at the lower end was a piston fitting into a cylinder on the shaft. For example, the water-wheel at the Cook's Kitchen mine in Cornwall was 48 ft in diameter and worked tiers of pumps of 9-in bore. There were four lifts, enabling water to be raised from 480 ft and delivered into an adit (cf vol II, figure 20).

When water-power was not available, steam-engines (plate 7 A) were extensively used. In 1778 more than 70 Newcomen engines were working in Cornwall, but by 1790 all but one of them had disappeared, having been replaced by the much more economical Boulton and Watt engine. As an example of the kind of economy thus effected, it may be mentioned that when seven Newcomen engines were replaced by five of Boulton and Watt's at the Consolidated mines, Cornwall, in 1781, the consumption of coal was reduced from 19 000 tons a year to 6100 tons. This represented a yearly saving of £10 830, at the price of coal then ruling. By 1798 there were forty-five Boulton and Watt pumping-engines in use in Cornwall alone. Such engines, commonly known in mining as Cornish engines, continued in use well after electricity became common in mines. The popularity they achieved in their day is easily recognized by the great number of gaunt, tall buildings which housed the engines and which still dot the landscape of any old metal-mining district.

However, the size of these machines, the amount of room the rods took in the shaft, the great engine-houses, and the cost of new parts all spelt their doom. Their place was taken by smaller reciprocating or centrifugal pumps electrically driven.

COAL-MINING

By 1750 coal-mining had become a well established industry in Britain and western Europe, and had reached its highest development on the north-east coast of England. In Britain during this period coal output rose from 7 m to 150 m tons annually. This was before the days of the general use of steam, but the stage of manual labour was nearing its end and the mechanical age was looming ahead. Little power except water-, animal-, and man-power was used in coal-mines at the beginning of this period, but during the century 1750–1850 manual labour gave way to steam-power and mechanization began in earnest. Shallow mines were becoming exhausted, but the availability of power enabled larger and deeper mines to be developed to meet the growing demand for coal as the industrial revolution progressed (figure 41).

The early years of the eighteenth century saw the introduction into mining of Savery's 'fire' engine and Newcomen's 'atmospheric' engine. Newcomen's invention not only solved the water-problem of many collieries and metal-mines but marked a new and great demand for coal as a source of power. The use of this engine in the north brought into production large areas that were previously considered unworkable because of the difficulties with water. In 1769, 120 Newcomen engines were in use in coal-mines. The introduction of surface-railways, at first horse-drawn on wooden rails, and underground wagon-ways added a further impetus to the development of mining. Where practicable, tracks were so laid that the full wagons gravitated to staithes on the river, whence the empty ones were pulled back by horses. Watt's double-acting steam-engine began to replace water-wheels for driving the hoisting-engines, and trams came into use underground in place of sleds.

I. COAL-GETTING: TOOLS AND MACHINES

The usual methods of coal-getting during this period were by hand-pick (figure 42) and crowbar, and by blasting with gunpowder. The miner cut a groove under the coal close to the floor to a depth of 2 to 4 ft and broke the coal down

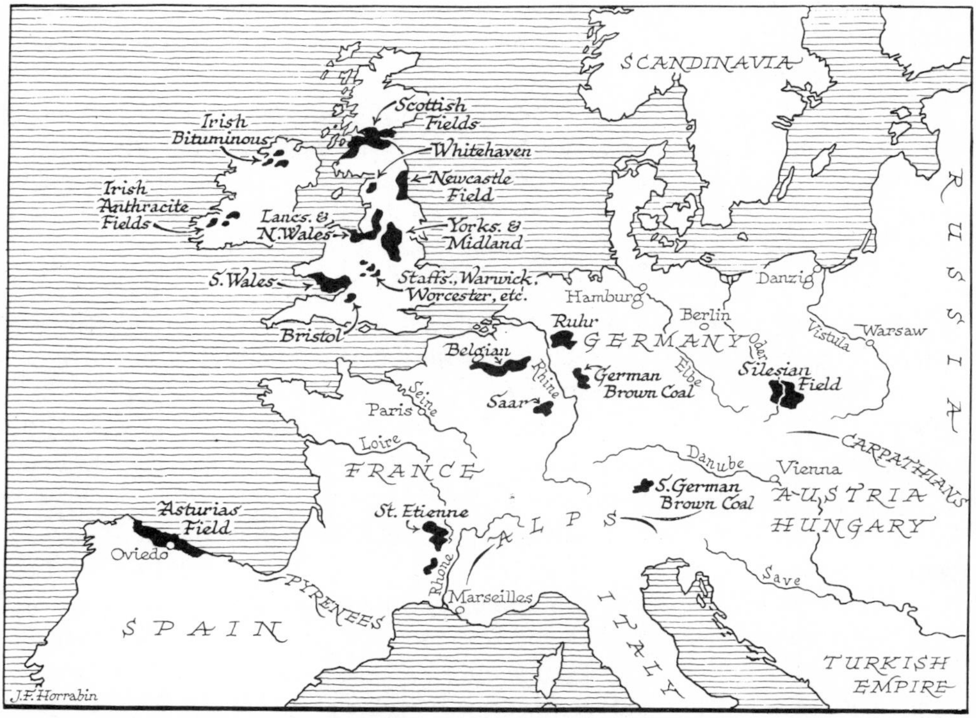

FIGURE 41—*Coalfields of the United Kingdom and western Europe, 1851.*

either with a pick, a crowbar, or a wedge. In the harder coals a hand-worked rotary drill was used to bore a hole 1–1½ inches in diameter, into which was put a charge of loose black powder. The method of firing the charge has been described already in connexion with metal-mining (p 71).

Towards the end of the period William Bickford, of Tuckingmill, Cornwall, invented a form of safety-fuse that made the operation of blasting much less hazardous, but black powder was still used. Undercutting the coal by hand was very hard and slow work, and early attempts to mechanize this operation were made. Even today, however, no coal-mine is completely mechanized. Coal is undercut by machines, broken down by explosives or other means, and loaded at the coal-face on to conveyors of various kinds, which deliver it into trams on the haulage-roads or at the shaft itself; but the actual loading of the broken-down coal on to the conveyor is still done by manual shovelling.

Many attempts have been made to produce an economical and mechanically satisfactory combined cutter-loader, but so far complete success has not been attained. Up to about 1850 all coal was cut by hand and loaded by means of shovels or forks (to eliminate small coal) into small trams taken right up to the coal-face. In thin, hard seams this was very laborious work. In the early nineteenth

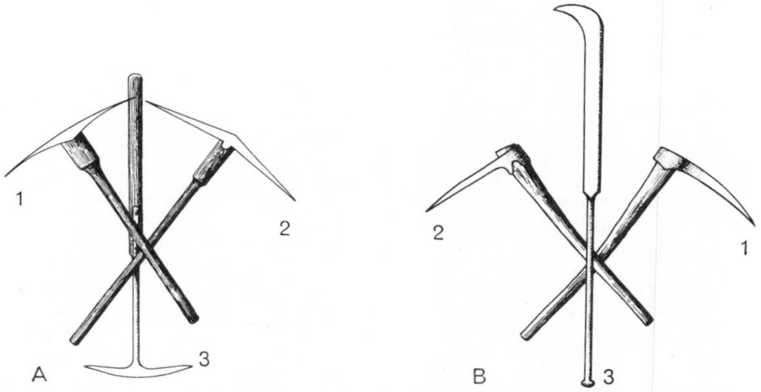

FIGURE 42—*Tools used in coal-mining about 1880.* (A) (1) *Holing pick, north Staffordshire,* (2) *anchored pick, Durham,* (3) *pick from Rivelaine, Belgium.* (B) (1) *Pembrokeshire coal-pick,* (2) *Westphalian pick,* (3) *Liége pick.*

century a machine with an arc-like motion, imitating the swing of a pick by man, was made. This 'iron man' cut as much coal as a single efficient miner, but several men were needed to work it, so the invention was dropped.

A later device, the disk-machine, was based on a circular saw, but nothing of any value materialized until improved metallurgy gave a steel pick that would not wear away after a few hours' work and, equally important, until a form or forms of power had been developed that could be used both safely and economically underground. The later growth of mechanism in the mines ran parallel with the development of compressed air and electricity, particularly the latter, as sources of motive-power.

The invention of the steam-engine, which did so much to mechanize other branches of industry, had little effect on coal-mining, except for machinery on the surface, where it was rapidly and skilfully applied, especially for pumping, hauling, and hoisting (figure 43). Attempts to use steam underground, except close to the bottom of the shaft, were not successful. If power had to be used in the working, it could be applied only through the medium of rigid iron rods running on small rollers alongside the main roads, or by endless ropes, chains, or bands. None of these methods proved satisfactory.

Thomas Harrison made the first practical coal-cutter in 1863. It consisted of a toothed wheel fitted to the spindle of a compressed-air turbine, driving, through gearing, 'a circular revolving cutter or disk having a serrated edge like

FIGURE 43—*Steam winding-gear for mines*, c *1880*.

a circular saw but stronger, or, alternatively, a hollow circular box or frame' into which were fitted any required number of cutting-tools. This machine exemplified the transition from reciprocating motion to the rotary motion which characterized the development of all subsequent coal-cutting machinery.

The introduction of the principle of rotary or continuously moving cutters opened the way to an enormous increase in capacity for cutting, and by multiplying the number of cutting picks made it possible with a single machine to apply greatly increased power to the operation. Development was slow but there emerged three well defined types of machine (figure 44):

(A) The disk, whose cutting-member consists of a disk or wheel armed at its periphery with cutters.

(B) The chain, whose cutting-member consists of a projecting arm or jib carrying an endless chain, the links of which are armed with cutters.

(C, D) The bar, whose cutting-member consists of a projecting, rotating bar armed with cutters throughout its length.

These machines were at first driven by reciprocating compressed-air motors, and later by compressed-air turbines. Unfortunately, while compressed air is a

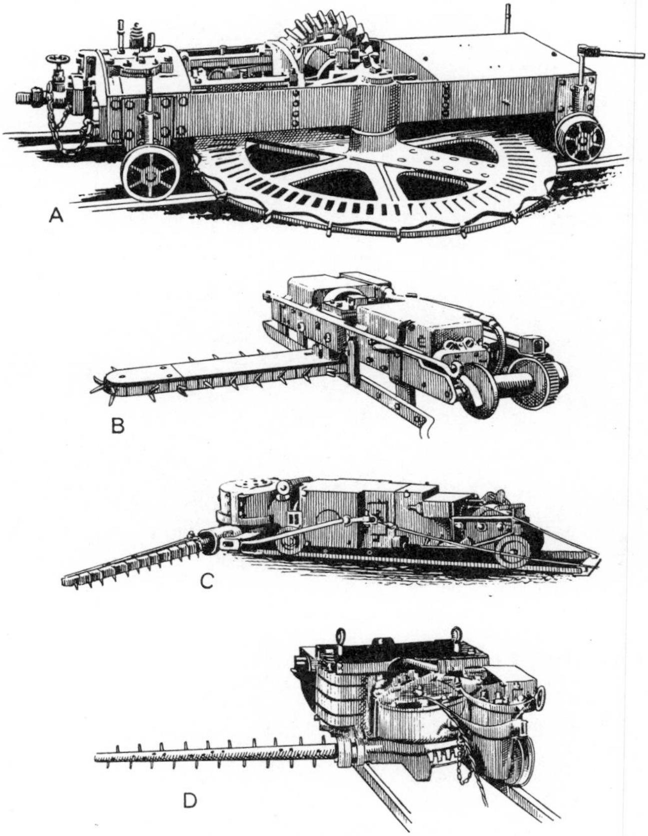

FIGURE 44—*Three types of coal-cutter:* (A) *disk,* (B) *chain,* (C) *and* (D) *bar.*

very safe form of power to use underground, where precautions have to be taken against the danger of gas or coal-dust explosions, it is uneconomical, mainly because of transmission-losses from the compressor to the machine. With the coming into general use of electricity, first as direct and then as alternating current, smaller, more powerful, and more economical machines were constructed. Except for the addition of more safety-devices, electrical coal-cutters have not altered materially in design during the last fifty years.

II. HAULAGE

In the eighteenth century haulage of coal underground was effected by wooden sleds on which were placed wicker baskets. These were at first pulled along the roads by men or women, but by 1763 ponies began to be used underground. By 1789 wheeled trams were introduced into mines, and later they were adapted to light rails of malleable iron. These enormously eased the heavy toil:

> God bless the man wi' peace and plenty
> That first invented metal plates.
> Draw out his years to five times twenty
> Then slide him through the hevenly gates.[1]

FIGURE 45—*'Putters' or trolley-boys moving a coal tram from the face. Early nineteenth century.*

Ponies still formed the motive-power, but self-acting inclines were coming into use.

The first record of the use of steam-power for haulage is in 1812, when George Stephenson altered a pumping-engine to make it haul coals from a dip-road. Between 1820 and 1840 the use of steam-engines for hauling from the dip became more common, and in many cases both engines and boilers were placed underground. The use of mechanical haulage on the level roads came later. An early record states that in 1841 'at Peacock Mine, Hyde, a stationary engine is used to draw the wagon along the main level'. In 1844 John Buddle introduced the slow-moving continuous or 'endless' rope haulage at Wallsend, and in the same year the 'main and tail' system[2] was installed at Haswell, Co. Durham.

These forms of haulage were employed only on the main roads. On subsidiary roads and face-roads, animal or manual labour still served (figure 45).

[1] 'The Pitman's Pay', by Thomas Wilson, *c* 1799.
[2] Full wagons were drawn by the main rope and empty ones returned by the tail rope.

At the end of the nineteenth century all coal was loaded on to wheeled trams (figure 46), except in a few isolated cases where it was still first loaded on sleds and dragged along the coal-face. This meant either that tram-rails had to be laid along the coal-face, which could be done only in seams 3 ft or more in thickness; or that roads had to be made partly in the coal and partly in the roof at intervals of 12 to 15 yds, so that the hewer could fill the tubs without having to cast his coal along the face more than once, or occasionally twice. In highly inclined seams the coal was induced to slide along the floor to the road, where it was loaded.

FIGURE 46—*Coal in baskets being loaded underground on to a tram.*

The first satisfactory coal-face conveyor was invented by W. C. Blackett at Durham in 1902. In the specification of his patent Blackett set out the advantages of face conveyors. These are, *inter alia*, the avoidance of the necessity of forming, and maintaining at comparatively short distances apart, gate-roads for the transport of coal from the working-face, thus avoiding the heavy cost of such ancillary work in thin seams; reduction of the physical labour of filling tubs by hand; and the avoidance of breakage.

Blackett's conveyors consisted of a steel trough laid alongside a longwall face (p 87), usually extending for *c* 100 yds. In this trough moved an endless scraper-chain, driven by a machine at one end, which carried the coal to the waiting tub. After each cut by the machine, the coal was stripped and loaded into the conveyor; when all was cleared, the conveyor was advanced the distance of a cut ready for the next stripping. Since that time several types of conveyors have been produced, such as the shaking-conveyor, which jerks the coal along a trough, and the endless belt. The latter, of which there are several varieties, is in common use today.

III. METHODS OF WORKING

As the majority of the mines were shallow, the workings were entered by drifts or tunnels from the surface wherever possible. When this could not be done, shallow shafts were sunk from the surface and as much of the coal as possible was worked away from the sides of the shaft. It had been found that if all the coal was worked, the roof collapsed, and so the practice was developed of leaving pillars of coal *in situ* to hold it up. These pillars were irregular in pattern and shape and resulted in much coal being lost.

The next stage was the recognition that it was both practicable and economical to divide the seams of coal up into large pillars from 22 to 60 yds square by roads driven at or near right-angles (the 'whole' workings), and subsequently to 'follow up' by extracting the pillars or 'broken' workings. At first the whole area was worked into pillars, but the ventilation was then difficult to control; later, the practice of dividing the area into small areas or panels by leaving solid ribs of coal was found very advantageous. This system divided the mine into separate compartments, each self-contained, with the result that any misadventure in one panel did not necessarily affect any other area. It was found to be more economical, and much safer, to extract the pillars shortly after they were formed.

The extraction of each individual pillar is done by taking slices about 6 yds wide off one side. One slice is extracted, the roof meanwhile being supported by vertical timber props which are set under horizontal planks and bars, usually made of round props sawn into halves longitudinally down the centre. When the slice has been removed, the timber supports are withdrawn and the roof is allowed to collapse. After complete collapse another parallel slice is started, and so on until the whole pillar is extracted. With good management, and a certain amount of luck, at least 90 per cent of the pillar is removed. One important point, which was early noted, is that the line of the removed pillars or fallen roof should make an angle of about 45° with the main natural 'slips' or breaks in the roof. By this means the danger of an unexpected collapse is minimized and usually averted.

This method, which is technically known as bord-and-pillar working (bord is a Saxon word meaning road), is, in effect, extraction in two operations. It has been found to be an excellent system where the workings do not lie under too great a thickness of overlying rocks. The maximum permissible depth is of the order of 900 ft, but the figure is very variable. Where the depth is greater, the weight of the overlying rocks tends to crush the pillars as, or sometimes before, they are removed. As a consequence some coal is lost or, alternatively, crushed into small pieces or slack. To overcome the drawback, extraction in one operation was developed; this is technically known as the longwall method (figure 47). When the mines were shallow, or where the coal was thick, clean, and strong, this system was not used, and it did not come into common use elsewhere until after 1850. Longwall working has many advantages where it is practicable. It is an excellent system for mechanical coal cutting in dirty seams, that is, seams with a layer of stone or shale within them; or where the seam is hard, because, if properly worked, the weight of the overhanging roof will assist in breaking down the coal. In this system a wall of coal about 100 yds long is won out and removed bodily in line. As the coal is removed any stone available is built into dry stone walls or packs some 6 to 21 ft wide, arranged in parallel lines at right-angles to the advancing wall or face. The purpose of these walls is to cushion the lowering of the roof after its supporting coal is removed and thus preserve as far as possible its unbroken state, especially at the face itself.

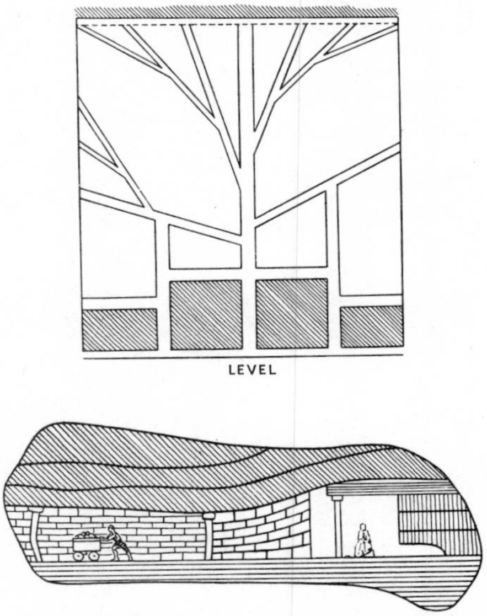

FIGURE 47—*Longwall mining, as practised in Shropshire in the late seventeenth century.* Above, *plan;* below, *elevation.*

Naturally these two methods—bord-and-pillar and longwall—do not cover every eventuality encountered in practice, and hybrids were developed to cover varying conditions. The most common was the Welsh stall system, in which a short longwall face of some 10 to 20 yds was driven in one direction, after which the miners turned round and removed a similar and parallel slice back to the main road.

IV. WINDING OR HOISTING

When shafts had to be sunk to reach the deeper coals, some form of machinery had to be developed to replace the women and boys who carried coals on their

FIGURE 48—*Women coal-bearers, Scotland, early nineteenth century. Coal was often carried in this way from depths exceeding 100 ft.*

backs in wicker-work baskets up ladders round the edges of the shafts (figure 48). The hand-windlass was first used, but was replaced by the horse-whim or -gin (figure 49 and plate 6B). This consisted of a horizontal rope drum, 12 to 16 ft in diameter, built round a vertical axis, the foot of which turned on a stone or an iron casting and the head pivot of which was supported by a long span-beam resting at its end upon inclined legs. The horses were attached at one or both ends of a strong horizontal beam, generally 30 to 36 ft long, which embraced the vertical axis close to the drum. The ropes passing off the opposite sides of the drum were conducted over small pulleys overhanging the shafts.

With the introduction of the steam-engine, the modern horizontal drum was developed, but this was originally driven by a large low-pressure single-cylinder vertical engine with hand-operated valves. The winding was slow and very wasteful of steam. One of the difficulties experienced arose from the necessity of overcoming the unbalanced weight of the rope hanging in the shaft. Various forms of counterbalance were tried, but no satisfactory solution was developed in this period.

The ropes originally used were round and made of hemp. They consisted of several strands wrapped to form a composite rope. Instead of forming the strands into a round rope, many preferred to lay them side by side and stitch each strand to its neighbour to form a flat rope. This had the advantage that during winding the rope could be wrapped layer upon layer on a narrow drum or pirn, thus varying the leverage. The heavy load at the bottom of the shaft corresponded to the smallest radius of the drum and the empty cage or basket at the top to the largest.

At first the wicker baskets were lifted from the trams, hitched to the rope, and raised up the shaft. Owing to the twist in the rope, however, they spun round and round and also swayed from side to side. Consequently the speed of winding

FIGURE 49—*Horse-whim, c 1820.*

was slow and accidents in the shaft were frequent. Iron-wire ropes were first tried in 1829 and came into general use about 1840.

To overcome the oscillation, shaft-guides were introduced in 1787. The baskets were suspended from cross-bars which were fixed to wooden guides attached to the sides of the shafts. Later, tubs or corves with wheels securely attached were made, and at the same time cages or open boxes running on guides were introduced into the shafts. By this means a load of coal could be hauled on wheels from where it was filled at the face, run into the cage, safely hauled to the surface, and there emptied before the cage was returned underground (figure 50).

V. MINE-GASES AND EXPLOSIONS

In the earlier part of the eighteenth century, most of the coal-mines were shallow, and the only mysterious gas or vapour with which the miners had to contend was 'stythe', now known to mining engineers as black-damp. It consists essentially of air deficient in oxygen, and is a variable mixture of carbon dioxide, nitrogen, and some oxygen. Another name is choke-damp, because its presence in large quantities may choke or suffocate all coming in contact with it. In most coalfields, however, the term choke-damp denotes the products of incomplete combustion more commonly known as after-damp; this contains varying percentages of the most poisonous gas met with in mining, namely carbon mon-

FIGURE 50—*Bottom of pit shaft, showing loaded trams waiting to be hauled to the surface.*

oxide. The word damp in this context derives from the German *Dampf*, meaning fog or vapour.

No flame will burn when the percentage of oxygen in the air falls below a certain limit. The miner therefore had ample warning of the presence of black-damp because his light gradually became dimmer and dimmer before finally dying out; this gave him time to retire to fresher air and safety.

Choke- or after-damp was understandably feared, but because carbon monoxide has neither smell nor taste, and is a cumulative poison, the concentration in the blood gradually rising without warning until the victim becomes unconscious, little was known about it.

Later, as the mines became deeper and more extensive, fire-damp—a mixture of methane and air—began to be encountered, and the era of serious mine explosions began. Though the explosiveness of fine coal dust was suspected, it had not been proved, and all explosions were attributed to fire-damp.

Fire-damp is produced during the decay of vegetable matter. During the conversion of vegetation into coal, the gas given off is occluded in the cleavage-planes of the coal and also in the rocks of the roof and floor. When the coal is worked the gas is driven out into the air, with which in certain proportions it forms an explosive mixture. The explosive limits of the mixture are between 5·4 and 13·5 per cent of methane under normal atmospheric conditions.

At this time mines had little or no artificial ventilation and the light gas tended to collect in stagnant ends and disused parts of the mine, particularly in old workings. When the atmospheric pressure began to fall, the gaseous contents of these old workings expanded and flowed into the active areas, where the fire-damp could ignite at the flame of an open lamp.

At times practically pure methane flows out of the rocks in the form of a concentrated jet or blower. Thus the miner may suddenly, almost without warning, become surrounded by an explosive mixture, and an explosion may follow. Towards the end of the eighteenth century and in the early years of the nineteenth, explosions—in some cases of great violence—became common, especially in the north of England (p 94), and gave rise to national concern.

The general use of a safety-lamp (p 95), though the lamp was not at that stage truly safe, reduced the incidence of explosions, but every few years the world was shocked by a catastrophe involving the death of a hundred or more miners. Towards the middle of the nineteenth century explosions became less frequent, but their magnitude and violence increased. Thus in 1860 145 men were killed in the Risca mine at Newport; in 1867 178 lives were lost at the Ferndale colliery in the Rhondda Valley. Such explosions have since been proved to be due to the ignition of fine coal-dust, and today steps are taken to combat this risk.

An interesting side-light on the daily life of the coal-miner in those days is shown by the origin of the term 'fireman'. Today, a fireman in a mine is a junior official in charge of a section of a mine, where he is responsible essentially for the safety of the workmen under his charge. In the days of small mines, and before the invention of the early safety-lamps, it was the custom for one of the more resolute of the miners to wrap himself from head to foot in damp sackcloth and to arm himself with a pole some 10 ft long on the end of which he stuck a lighted candle (figure 51). With this in his hand he travelled the underground workings. When he came to a working face he crawled on his hands and knees into the face with the candle close to the ground. When he arrived at the face itself he buried his face in the wet sacks, raised the end of his stick, and ignited any gas present. The place was then considered safe for the ordinary miner to come to his work.

VI. VENTILATION

No attempts were at first made to induce a flow of fresh air round the mine to dilute and render harmless any noxious or inflammable gas. As mines became

FIGURE 51—*Fireman, swathed in damp sacking, igniting fire-damp to clear workings.*

more extensive, however, something had to be done to ward off the possibility of disastrous explosions.

The first step in more up-to-date practice was to make two roads into the mine, one by which the air went in and the other by which it came out. This provision did not become compulsory until after a disaster at Hartley, Northumberland, when a large pump on the surface broke, fell down, and blocked the only shaft, with the result that many men lost their lives.

If there are two roads into a mine, and if in one of them the temperature is higher than in the other, a flow of air will take place from the region of lower to that of the higher temperature, because the density of air decreases as the temperature rises. In shallow mines this variation in temperature is slight and the flow of air small. Further, the temperature differential is apt to reverse between night and day, and between summer and winter, so that the rate of flow of air is also variable and may often be negligible. To overcome this unsatisfactory circumstance and produce a steady flow, fire-buckets were lowered into one entrance-shaft, thus producing an artificial temperature difference. As the mines became larger, something better than fire-buckets became necessary, and furnaces were constructed at the foot of the rising or up-cast shaft. If the mine gave off dangerous quantities of inflammable gas, the furnace was fed with fresh air from the down-cast shaft and the products of combustion were admitted into the up-cast shaft at a temperature below the ignition point of a mixture of fire-damp and air. Steam-jets were also tried but were not satisfactory. Extracted fire-damp was often burned at the surface (plate 6A).

The first known mechanical ventilator was an air-pump used by Buddle at Hebburn colliery in 1807. It was a suction-pump consisting of a wooden piston 5 ft sq with a stroke of 8 ft, working in a wooden-lined chamber. At 20 strokes a minute it exhausted 6000 cu ft of air in that time; this figure may be compared with 600 000 to 1 000 000 cu ft a minute in today's mines. The air-pump principle was extensively adopted at the same time both in Belgian coal-mines and in the lead-mines of the Harz. At first, all efforts were devoted to the improvement of the air-pump; Struvé's ventilator was an example largely adopted in south Wales. The piston of this device was a wrought iron bell, closed at the top, of 12 to 22 ft diameter, working up and down in water. By means of ranges of valves above and below, placed in the walls of the piston-chamber, it drew in and forced out air at each up and each down stroke respectively. When worked in pairs these pumps could displace as much as 100 000 cu ft of air a minute.

Another pump was Nixon's ventilator. This had a horizontal piston, in some cases as large as 30 ft by 22 ft, supported on wheels. The chambers were fitted with flap-valves, as in Struvé's machine. When doing nine 7-ft strokes a minute it was reputed to displace 160 000 cu ft of air in that time.

About 1830, successful attempts were made to develop fans. The idea was not new, for Agricola had discussed their use nearly three centuries earlier. Typical early types were designed by Waddell, Guibal (Belgium), and Fabry; these were all centrifugal fans. The general idea was a drum made to rotate horizontally by a steam-engine. Air from the mine was drawn into the centre of the drum, and then expelled to the outer air from its circumference. It reached the outer air through a widening chimney, which diminished the velocity at which the expelled air regained the open. This was the *évasé* chimney of later years.

In addition to the production of a ventilating current, changes occurred in the method of conducting the air round the workings. In the beginning, when mines were small, no attempt appears to have been made to guide the air. It went where it listed and probably in most cases it went nowhere very useful. Then parallel, instead of single, roads were driven, with connecting roads between them. As a new connexion was completed, the previous one was blocked up, thus forcing the air to travel up one road and down the parallel one. Where connexions had lagged behind the working faces, a temporary circuit was made by dividing the road into two, either by a wooden partition or by tarred canvas (brattice cloth).

FIGURE 52—*Flint-and-steel mill*, c *1813*.

When connecting-roads were required for traffic and could not be permanently blocked up, temporary blocks (doors or stoppings) made of canvas sheets were hung from the roofs of the roads; for permanent working hinged wooden doors were used. These were opened and closed by small children (trappers) as traffic required.

At first the air travelled round the mine in one circuit, but this was found to have many disadvantages, such as excessive friction, contamination, and leakage. Later, the main current of air was divided so that each section of the mine received a separate fresh supply. The air was split, but the separate streams all reunited at or near the up-cast shaft. In order to control the quantity of air entering each district of the mine, artificial resistances or regulators were inserted into the low-friction areas. Further, in order to make sure that no accumulation of gas lurked in an unused portion of the mine, the air was coursed through all the open workings.

VII. LIGHTING: DEVELOPMENT OF THE SAFETY-LAMP

Owing to the exhaustion of the best seams close to the surface in the vicinity of the rivers Tyne and Wear, mining engineers in this district had to sink shafts as deep as 600 ft to reach unworked areas. The increase in depth brought in its train an increasing volume of methane. Consequently, the number of underground explosions began to assume very serious dimensions. As these explosions all originated at the unprotected flame of a candle or oil-lamp, some alternative system of underground lighting had to be found. One of the earliest expedients used was the phosphorescent glow from decaying fish, but this was unsatisfactory as a luminant and also, with the limited ventilation then prevalent, decidedly unpleasant.

Between the years 1740 and 1750 a flint-and-steel mill (figure 52) for miners was invented by Charles Spedding of Whitehaven, Cumberland; the first allusion to this instrument was made in a poem by John Dallin, published in 1750. The machine was strapped to a man's chest; by rotating the handle he produced a steady stream of sparks which could, however, have given only a poor light. The sparks gave indications of the presence of inflammable air by an increase in their size and luminosity; on approaching the explosive points they assumed a liquid appearance and adhered closely to the periphery of the wheel, giving off a bluish light. This device was also known and used on the continent of Europe. However, it could and did cause explosions, so the problem was not fully solved.

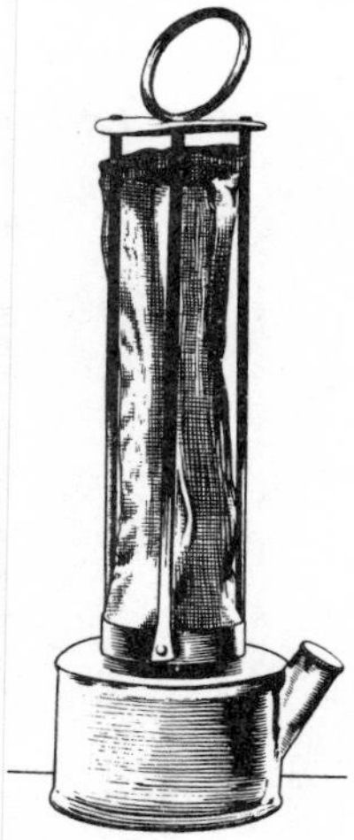

FIGURE 53—*One of the first Davy lamps to be taken underground, 1816.*

Reflection of light from the surface by mirrors was tried, but abandoned as unsatisfactory, except in sinking shafts in which blowers, or continuous evolutions of gas in the form of jets, were encountered.

About 1812 explosions became so frequent and, with the increasing size of mines, so disastrous to life, that the Sunderland society for preventing accidents in coal-mines was formed in 1813, largely through the efforts of the Rev. John Hodgson, rector of Jarrow-on-Tyne. The Sunderland society determined to interest the leading scientists in the country in the problem, and decided first to approach Sir Humphry Davy. Davy was at that particular time (August 1815) shooting in Scotland, but he was intercepted at Newcastle on his way south and steps were taken to interest him. After visiting several mines, and discussing the problem with people on the spot, he had some specimens of the gas sent to him at the Royal Institution in London. By November in the same year he had discovered the conditions under which fire-damp explodes, its degree of inflammability, and its behaviour when mixed with certain quantities of air. He also studied the passage of flames through tubes of varying diameter, and observed that metal was more effective than glass in retarding it. He found wire gauze to be an effective barrier. On 9 November 1815 he published his results and showed three lamps incorporating his findings (figure 53). The third lamp included the principle upon which modern safety-lamps depend. On 1 January 1816 he wrote to Newcastle announcing his discovery of the 'absolute safety' of a wire-gauze cylinder surrounding a naked or unprotected flame. The gauze was made from iron wire ranging from 1/40th to 1/60th of an inch in diameter, and containing 28 wires to the inch, or 784 apertures to the square inch.

While Davy was busy in London, other experiments were being carried out on Tyneside by George Stephenson and by W. R. Clanny (1776–1850), an Irishman from County Down who was practising medicine in Sunderland. Stephenson's first lamp was based on the principle that if a number of candles were held to the windward side of burning blowers of gas, the blowers were extinguished by 'the burnt air which was carried towards them'. He also noticed that when fire-damp was ignited an appreciable time was necessary for the flame to travel from one point to another, and he concluded that 'if a current of air could be produced in the opposite direction at a greater velocity than that at which the burning fire-damp travelled it would be possible to arrest it and prevent the flame from passing at all'. Hence he conceived the idea that if a lamp could be made to contain the burnt air above the flame and to permit the fire-damp to come in from below and to be burnt as it came in, 'the burnt air would prevent the passing of the explosions upwards and the velocity of the current from below would prevent it passing downwards'. The result was his first lamp, the 'tube and slider'. After further experiments underground, in which no accident occurred, Stephenson arranged the admission of air through small circular holes in the side, not the bottom, of the oil-vessel and then through more small holes, 2/25ths to 1/22nd inch in diameter, into a space between two plates, and finally to the flame through a further series of holes 1/12th to 1/18th inch in diameter (figure 54).

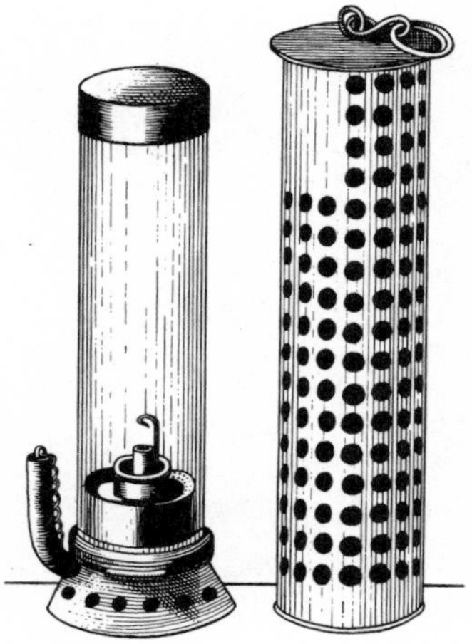

FIGURE 54—*George Stephenson's third safety lamp, 1816.*

Clanny's first lamp was the 'blast' lamp; this preceded Davy's idea by two years, but was never developed (figure 55). Later, Clanny surrounded the flame with a glass cylinder surmounted by a Davy gauze. The first lamp had a cistern of water above and below the flame, through which the outer air was forced by a hand-bellows. The South Shields committee for investigating the cause of accidents in mines expressed the opinion in 1843 that 'Dr Clanny, in this country, appears to have been the first man of science that conceived it possible to enter into a contest with the destructive element [fire-damp] and has never ceased for 35 years to devote his talents and exertions to mitigate the horrors consequent upon the explosions'.

The first real proof that a safety-lamp had been produced was made at Hebburn colliery in January 1816, with the Davy lamp, when Buddle reported: 'to my astonishment and delight, it is impossible for me to express my feelings when I first suspended the lamp in the mine and saw it red hot. If it had been a monster destroyed I could not have felt more exultation than I did. I said to those around me "we have at last subdued this monster".'

FIGURE 55—*Clanny's blast-lamp, second form, 1816. The lamp was carried on a belt worn by a boy, who also worked the bellows.*

In point of fact Buddle was too optimistic, because the early lamps were not wholly safe and the volume of light they gave was meagre. The chief defect of the Davy gauze was that when it became red hot flames could pass through it, as heat could not be carried away quickly enough. This was overcome by the use of two gauzes, one inside the other. The quantity of light given out was improved by surrounding the flame with a glass cylinder, allowing the air to enter through gauzes either below or above the flame. It was later noticed that increased safety was obtained if the circular gauzes were surrounded by a bonnet to shield them from the current of the ventilating air, which in unprotected lamps tended to blow the flame against the gauze, causing it to become red hot and thus allow the passage of flame.

During the next thirty years many alterations and improvements were made, notably by Meuseler in Belgium in 1840. His lamp was about 10 in high, including the oil-vessel. Round the flame was a very strong glass. Above the glass, and forming a continuation of it, was a wire-gauze cylinder $4\frac{1}{2}$ in high and $1\frac{3}{4}$ inches in internal diameter, having a brass top full of minute perforations. The glass and the wire gauze, closely united, made a continuous cylinder about 8 in high, having a piece of wire gauze stretched across the junction of the two materials, above the top of the glass. Through the centre of this piece of horizontal gauze was a small metal chimney to convey the smoke and 'de-oxygenated air' away from the flame. The chimney passed down to within an inch of the wick; it was

4 in high, about 0·7 inches in diameter at the bottom, and tapered to 0·4 in at the top. Subsequently, further improvements were made by Marsaut, in France, and others, but no fundamental change was made.

BIBLIOGRAPHY

FORDYCE, D. W. 'A History of Coal, Coke, Coalfields.' London. 1860.

HAIR, T. H. 'Views of the Collieries in Northumberland and Durham.' Madden. 1860.

HUNT, R. 'British Mining.' London. 1884–7.

MINING ASSOCIATION OF GREAT BRITAIN. 'Historical Review of Coal Mining.' Fleetway Press, London. 1928.

PRYCE, W. *Mineralogia Cornubiensis.* London. 1778.

SIMONIN, L. 'Mines and Miners; or Underground Life' (trans. from the French and ed. by H. W. BRISTOW). London. [1869.]

SMYTH, W. 'A Rudimentary Treatise on Coal and Coal-Mining' (5th ed., rev. and enl.) London. 1880.

Transactions of the Institution of Mining Engineers.

Female coal-bearer. Seventeenth century.

4

PART I

EXTRACTION AND PRODUCTION OF METALS: IRON AND STEEL

H. R. SCHUBERT

THE period from 1750 to 1850 was marked by fundamental changes in the iron industry. Coke and coal were substituted for charcoal as a fuel. Water was replaced by steam as a motive-power. Cast iron, which hitherto had constituted less than 5 per cent of furnace-production, was produced in increasing quantities for machinery and constructional purposes. Production of wrought or bar iron also increased considerably after Henry Cort's invention of puddling and of the grooved rollers which made it possible to produce wrought iron more cheaply and in larger masses than with the hearths and hammers of the older forges. A more homogeneous steel was produced by the crucible process invented by Benjamin Huntsman.

Until about 1800, however, all these changes and improvements were only in the initial stage of development and were confined mainly to Britain. Thus the whole period may be subdivided into two consecutive phases, roughly corresponding to the last half of the eighteenth and the first half of the nineteenth centuries respectively.

In the first of these two phases development proceeded very slowly, even in Britain. Attempts to smelt iron ore with coke or coal instead of charcoal had been made long before. Best known in this respect is Dud Dudley (1599–1684), who claimed that as early as 1619 he had with coal successfully produced cast iron in the blast-furnace as well as wrought or bar iron in the forge. His claims to have succeeded where all others before him had failed were, and still are, generally rejected. The only way of utilizing coal for smelting was to produce coke first, since coking eliminates the sulphur content of raw coal, which tends to weaken the metal. The first successfully to smelt iron ore with coke was Abraham Darby (1677–1717) in 1709, at his Coalbrookdale works in Shropshire.

Darby's success was in part based on the nature of the clod coal found near the surface at Coalbrookdale. It contains a very low proportion of sulphur, the presence of which had been the principal obstacle in all the previous attempts.

As a fuel, coke had distinct advantages over charcoal, first because it was obtained from mineral coal, of which there were abundant resources; this was in marked contrast to charcoal, the demand for which was rapidly depleting the woodlands. Thus coke was available at a very much lower price than charcoal. Secondly, coke was less friable, so that a greater burden could be charged into the furnace without the danger of the fuel being crushed and the draught blocked. As a result, it was possible to use larger furnaces, by which production was increased (plate 7 B). The greater height of the furnace made the ore remain longer in contact with the incandescent fuel. The stronger blast that coke could stand without destruction caused a greater reduction, so that the iron became more liquid in the smelting process than did charcoal-produced iron. On account of its increased liquidity the metal was able to run into smaller channels in the moulds, so that castings of a lighter and more delicate design could be produced. The sphere of the operations conducted by the founder was thus enlarged. At the start of the coke-smelting at Coalbrookdale, Darby's main production was cast ware of a fine type, such as his bellied pots and other utensils. Since they were much superior to the heavy products hitherto produced by casting in iron derived from the charcoal-fired blast-furnace, an open market was secured to him.

On the other hand, the use of coke had distinct disadvantages. Coke contains more impurities than charcoal, which, being made from vegetable matter, contains only traces of minerals. The quantity of ash is smaller (0·011 per cent) than in coke (about 0·029 per cent) and, in consequence, very much less phosphorus is present. Phosphorus contributes to the fluidity of iron, but it adversely affects the strength. In England the presence of phosphorus was an additional disadvantage, since many of the iron-ore deposits exploited in the eighteenth century were themselves of a phosphoric kind. Moreover, not all the mineral coal used for coking had the low sulphur-content characteristic of the clod coal of Coalbrookdale.

It is, therefore, not surprising that in the early years smelting with coke was confined to Coalbrookdale and a very limited number of furnaces outside the area, and that in all these furnaces coke was used only intermittently, alternating with charcoal. The main product consisted of small cast iron ware. Pig iron made by smelting with coke was defective on account of the brittleness caused by impurities; it could be sold only because of its cheapness, and it served mainly for the manufacture of nails. Coke-produced pig iron did not rival charcoal iron until at least 1750, but after that date the forge-masters in Worcestershire began to accept it.

About that time several innovations were introduced, and smelting with coke was improved considerably. Closed coking-ovens of brick, in shape resembling a beehive, began to be used in place of open piles similar to those in which charcoal was made (figure 56). Of greater importance was wider adoption of foundry furnaces for the remelting of coke-produced iron. Remelting for foundry purposes was already no novelty; small movable furnaces used to remelt cast iron for making bullets were described by the French scientist R. A. F. de Réaumur in 1722. In the English iron industry the use of remelting furnaces began about 1702. The furnace was an improved form of a reverberatory furnace, in which the iron did not come into immediate contact with the coal used as fuel, so that impurities in the latter could not exert any detrimental effect upon the metal. The invention of an improved furnace of this type is ascribed to Edward Wright, a physician and chemist in London. From 1696 he carried out experiments on the smelting and refining of lead in north Wales. The successful outcome of these, in 1701, led to the erection of a lead-smelting works equipped with a furnace of Wright's improved type to which the name 'cupola' was given. It was the first time that the term was used and Wright was subsequently regarded as the inventor, but the exact nature of his improvements is not known. It is supposed that Abraham Darby used such a cupola furnace when he started the casting of iron wares at Bristol before he settled at Coalbrookdale. An English foundry furnace was depicted and described by the French engineer Gabriel Jars (1732–69), who visited England in 1764–5 (figure 57).

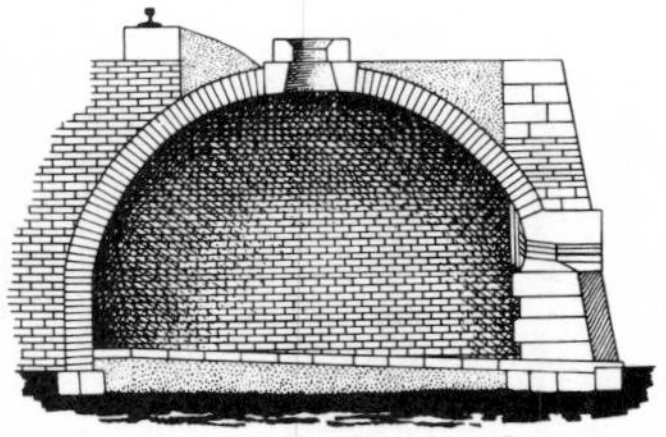

FIGURE 56—*Brick-built 'beehive' coking-oven.*

By remelting, the coke-smelted iron obtained from the blast-furnace was greatly improved in respect of both homogeneity and purity. This improvement was of national importance, since the casting of better-quality cannon, in particular for the Royal Navy, was made possible. The advantage of the process for naval purposes was greatly appreciated by a French brigadier, M. de la Houlière, who in 1773 had made some moderately successful experiments in smelting iron ore with coke and came to England two years later to study the English methods. On a visit to works at Bersham, in Denbighshire, managed by William Wilkinson, he was greatly impressed by the product of the foundry furnaces, and particularly by the casting of cannon. In his report to the French government he summarized his experiences and pointed out that during the twenty years that had elapsed since the adoption of the foundry furnace not one English naval cannon had burst, while in the French navy such accidents were so common that the sailors 'fear the guns they are serving more than those of the enemy' [1]. William Wilkinson subsequently went to France and was manager of the state ironworks and cannon-foundry on the island of Indret, near Nantes, from 1777 to 1780. There he installed two small cupola furnaces.

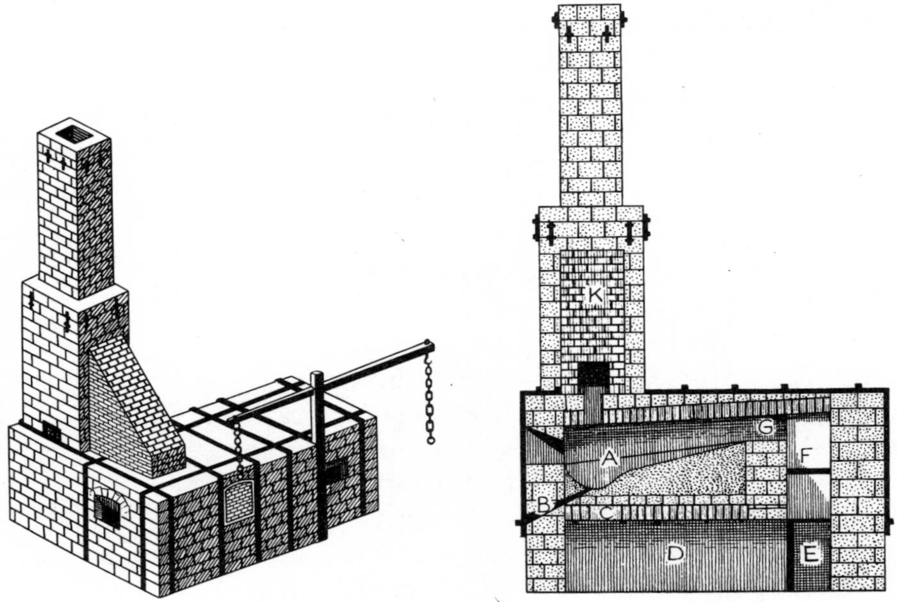

FIGURE 57—*Foundry furnaces (external view and elevation) near Newcastle upon Tyne, 1765. In these the ignited fuel was on a grate* (F) *above the ash-pit* (E). *The flame passed (through* G) *into the main basin* (A) *of the furnace, the bottom of which was filled with sand laid upon the brick roof* (C) *of a vault* (D). *The molten metal was let out into the moulds for casting through a channel* (B). *The smoke escaped through a chimney* (K).

Despite the increasing use of cupola furnaces, castings continued also to be produced directly from the blast-furnace. The old furnace at Coalbrookdale was rebuilt in 1777 for casting the 378½ tons of bridge-members for the local bridge over the Severn (p 455). In contrast to the older pattern, the shaft was made very wide and short and the hearth or crucible very deep, so as to accumulate a larger mass of liquid metal for casting.

The desire to lower the high cost of production resulting from this double process, conducted first in the blast-furnace and afterwards in the cupola, led Wilkinson to construct a new type of cupola resembling a small blast-furnace. The new cupola, larger than the old one, was not a success, but is historically noteworthy as a precursor of the modern cupola furnace.

The use of coke, which was less easily burned than charcoal, made it necessary to apply a stronger air-blast. For the charcoal-furnace, motive-power was produced by a water-wheel which operated a pair of wood and leather bellows supplying an intermittent blast into one *tuyère* and thence into the furnace. The diameter of the water-wheels did not exceed 22 ft even in the early seventeenth century, but the desire to obtain a stronger blast when coke was introduced led to the wheel at some ironworks being of a diameter of 30 to 40 ft. The blast

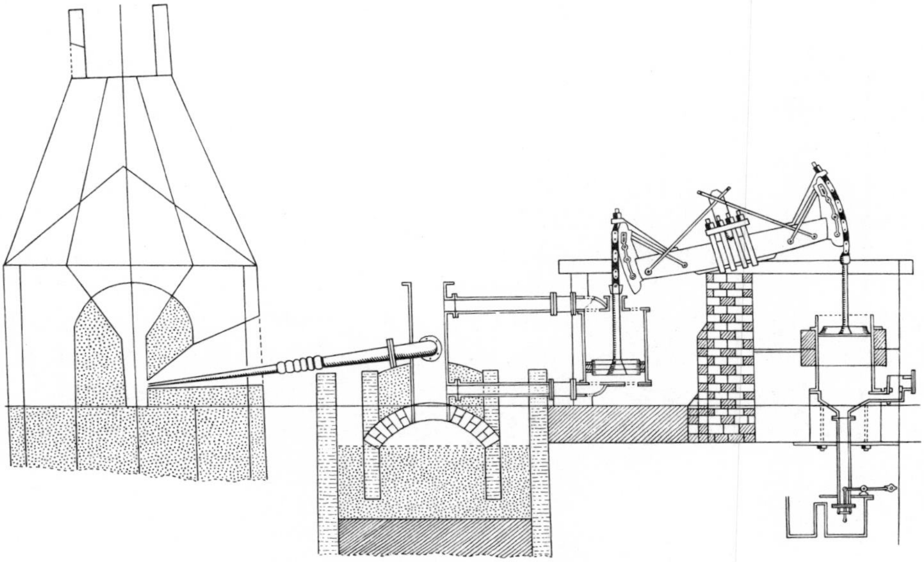

FIGURE 58—*Arrangement of blowing-engine, water-blast regulator,* tuyères, *and furnace.*

obtainable from water-driven bellows, however, was insufficient to obtain the full benefit of Darby's invention.

In 1762 a new type of blowing-apparatus began to appear. Shortly after this date John Smeaton (1724–92) introduced his blowing-cylinders, the use of which ensured a more complete combustion. Water-power, however, still remained the motive-force. It was not until James Watt's steam-engine was applied to blowing-cylinders that the final victory of coke over charcoal was won.

The early cylinders delivered to Watt for his steam-engines were not satisfactory, since they were not sufficiently accurate in bore to prevent leakage of steam. It was John Wilkinson (1728–1808) who produced the first completely satisfactory cast iron cylinders for steam-engines by a new method he had invented for boring cannon and had patented in 1774 (p 421). The improvement in the steam-engine was tremendous.

In 1776 a steam-engine was used for the first time for purposes other than pumping water. This engine, which had a 38-in cylinder, was used to blow Wilkinson's furnace at Willey in Shropshire. Four years later, Wilkinson had four engines employed in producing blast for iron-smelting. The success of Watt's invention soon led other ironmasters to order furnace engines, which were installed in a wide area extending from Yorkshire to south Wales (figure 58).

The substitution of the steam-engine for the water-wheel not only caused an increase in the output of the blast-furnace, but made it possible to develop the potentialities of the rolling- and slitting-mill. The improved technique of rolling wrought iron plates, which developed in the later years of the eighteenth century, favourably affected the manufacture of tinplate (p 125).

In the seventeenth century a tinplate industry flourished round Dresden in Saxony. Tinplate, a cheaper material, was beginning to replace pewter for domestic utensils. Attempts to create a tinplate industry were made in both France and Britain towards the end of the century; Britain then had the materials for manufacture, but was nevertheless completely dependent upon import from Germany. In Britain, tinplate was first successfully manufactured at Pontypool, probably in the 1720s. In 1745 the use of a separate grease-pot to prepare the plates for tinning was introduced. Before going to the tin-pot the plates remained in the grease for an hour, a method which continued to be employed under the name of the Welsh dipping-process and is to some extent still used for the tinning of prefabricated articles of steel. In 1800 eleven tinplate works are recorded as working in Britain; they were located in south Wales, Monmouthshire, and Gloucestershire, and their products had begun to be exported [2].

The next important step was the application of steam-power to forging. Water-driven hammers were in use (p 116), but the first forge-hammer driven by a steam-engine was erected only in 1782, for John Wilkinson at his forge at Bradley in Shropshire; this hammer could strike 30 blows a minute. Its head weighed $7\frac{1}{2}$ cwt and was raised 2 ft 3 in before each blow. A hammer of this type used in Yorkshire in the 1820s is shown in the accompanying illustration (figure 59).

The effect of all these various improvements is reflected in the increased number of coke-fired furnaces. In Britain the rate of increase was slow at first, but from 1775 onwards became rapid. In 1760 not more than 17 coke-furnaces were in operation, and only 14 more were established in the following 15 years; but, by 1790, 81 out of 106 blast-furnaces in Britain were operated with coke, almost half of them in the Midlands (Shropshire 24, Staffordshire 11).

Outside Britain the adoption of coke-furnaces proceeded very slowly. The first continental one for iron-smelting was erected at the French state ironworks at Le Creusot built by William Wilkinson in association with de Wendel and Toufaire in 1781–5. The next country was Prussia, where, at the invitation of the Prussian government, William Wilkinson unsuccessfully tried to smelt iron with coke at Friedrichshütte, in Silesia, in 1789. In 1791–2 a German engineer, T. F. Wedding, successfully used coke for smelting at Malapane, and in 1794–6 another coke-furnace was erected at Gleiwitz; both these places are in Upper Silesia. In the coal-basin of the German Ruhr smelting with coke did not start earlier than about 1850. In Belgium the coke-furnace was introduced by John Cockerill at Seraing, near Liége,[1] in 1823. Five years later a coke-furnace was established at Wilkowitz, now in Czechoslovakia. It was the first in the whole of the former Austrian Empire.

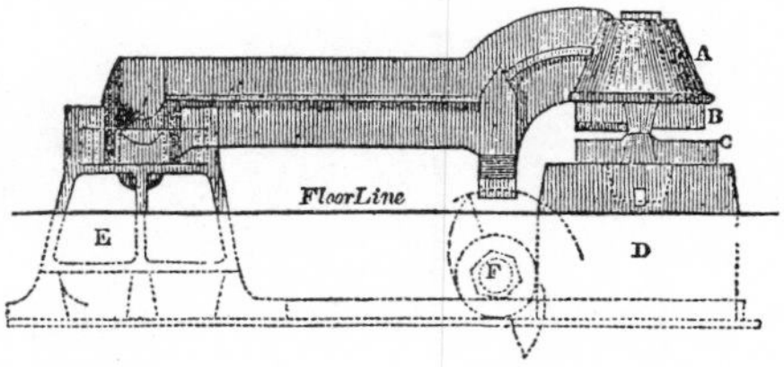

FIGURE 59—*Helve-hammer used at Milton ironworks, Yorkshire. The helve was of cast iron weighing about 6 tons.* A *is the hammer head and* B *the hammer. The anvil* (C) *was fitted into a cast iron block* (D), *which weighed upwards of 4 tons. The hammer was lifted by a cam or lifter* (F). *The helve worked in a frame* (E) *which was of iron, so that the cumbersome wooden frame of the old forge hammer was disposed of.*

As late as 1813, however, the use of coke for smelting and of the steam-driven blowing-cylinders instead of water-driven bellows was still almost completely confined to England. According to a statement made in 1813 by Thomas Cooper, professor of chemistry and mineralogy at Carlisle in Pennsylvania, nine-tenths of all the iron then produced in England was made with coke. In the United States, as well as on the continent of Europe, charcoal was still almost exclusively used [3].

The increase in the production of cast iron does not alone explain the rapid rise of the British iron industry in the last quarter of the eighteenth century, although cast iron was more in demand than at any time previously. An extensive replacement of other metals and of wood by cast iron took place in building (ch 15) as well as in the construction of machinery (ch 14). In 1760 the Carron Ironworks in Scotland began to cast iron cog-wheels. The first all-iron plant was designed by John Rennie for the Albion Mill in London in 1784. It had, as has been indicated, become possible to make quite large castings, such as those for the Severn bridge at Coalbrookdale (plate 30 A) and the steam-hammers.

[1] Since 1945 Liège, although its inhabitants are still Liégeois.

Despite all these remarkable achievements, however, the demand for cast iron was still smaller than that for wrought or bar iron. Wrought iron, although now an unimportant commodity, was still the principal metal in use about 1800, and remained so for at least half a century (plate 9).

Pig iron made by smelting with coke was found unsuitable for conversion into wrought iron because of the impurities introduced into the iron by the coke; these made wrought iron so brittle that it crumbled under the hammer. The problem of producing a pig iron suitable for conversion into wrought iron seems to have been solved about 1749–50 by Abraham Darby II (1711–63), but unfortunately nothing is known about the technique he applied. After him, the brothers Cranage, skilled iron-workers at Coalbrookdale, made iron in a reverberatory furnace using raw coal alone. The credit for final success is generally given to Henry Cort (1740–1800) of Gosport, who in 1784 obtained a patent for the conversion of pig iron into malleable, that is wrought, iron by puddling. Peter Onions, however, used a process which was essentially that of puddling and had been patented a year earlier.

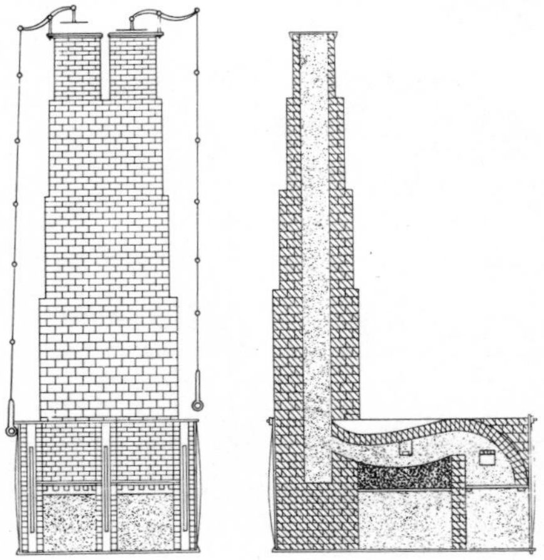

FIGURE 60—*Puddling-furnace;* (left) *external view;* (right) *vertical section.*

The process of puddling used by Cort consisted essentially of stirring molten pig iron on the bed of a reverberatory furnace. The puddler turned and stirred the molten mass until, through the decarburizing action of air which circulated through the furnace, it became converted into malleable iron. In this process contact between the metal and the raw coal that served as fuel was avoided, and the need for blowing-machinery was dispensed with. How Cort's method was superior to those of his predecessors, in particular that of Onions, is not known. Perhaps it was the use of dampers on top of the furnace (D, D in the accompanying illustration) for regulating the heat (figure 60).

Cort is also credited with the invention of grooved rollers (figure 61), patented in 1783. There too, however, he had predecessors; Christopher Polhem, in Sweden, apparently constructed a rolling-mill equipped with similar rolls in 1745. Previously, bars had to be made either by hammering, or by cutting hot strips from a rolled plate with a slitting-mill. With grooved rollers 15 tons of iron could be dealt with in 12 hours, whereas it was difficult to produce one ton in the same time with the forge-hammer.

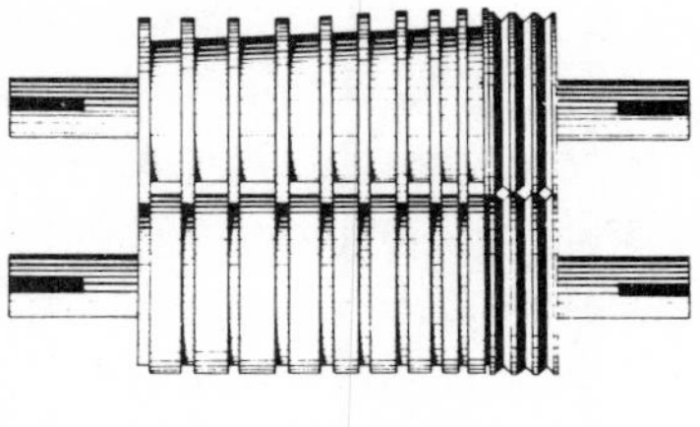

FIGURE 61—*Grooved rollers for bar-making.*

Cort's success was immediate, owing to the combination of the two processes he introduced. He achieved a simplification that resulted in lower cost of production. Although puddled iron was inferior in quality to charcoal iron, it was very much cheaper. His success was reflected in a tremendous increase in the production of British pig iron required for making puddled iron. This increase is demonstrated by a graph illustrating development between 1740 and 1840 (figure 62) [4].

One branch of the industry not affected by the great increase in production in Britain was steel manufacture. The quality of steel produced mainly depended upon the ores employed, and for this reason steel produced from German manganiferous ores still enjoyed the highest reputation in the eighteenth century. Attempts to make England independent of foreign steel led to improvements in the cementation process. The greatest development in the production of steel took place shortly before 1750: it was the invention of crucible or cast steel, which was more homogeneous in composition and more free from impurities than any steel produced previously. The inventor of this process was Benjamin Huntsman (1704–76), an Englishman of Dutch descent. As an instrument-maker at Doncaster he started experiments with the object of producing a more uniform steel for the springs and pendulums of clocks. At Handsworth, near Sheffield, where he settled between 1740 and 1742, he finally found, after many failures, a method by which steel could be produced in a molten state (figure 63). He melted bars of blister steel, with the addition of fluxes, in closed clay crucibles; the intense heat necessary was generated by coke. The two crucibles were placed in a chamber lined with fire-brick. The top of the furnace was closed by a cover of fire-brick, which was level with the floor of the melting-house. A vaulted cellar gave access to the ash-pit.

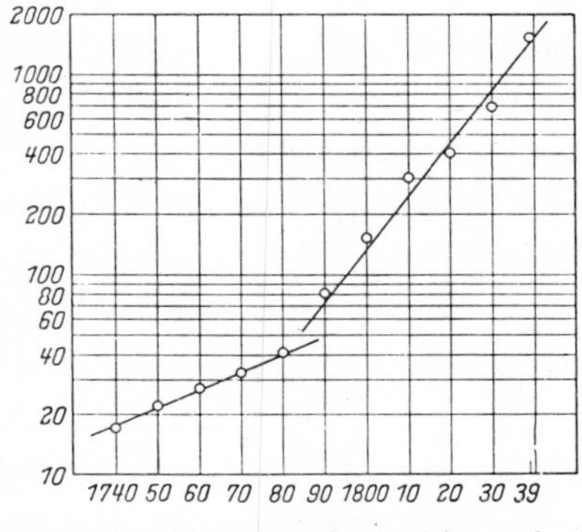

FIGURE 62—*Pig iron production (thousands of tons) in England, 1740–1839.*

Huntsman's process was less complex than those previously used for the production of steel. As a result, costs of production were reduced and output was increased. A difficulty, however, was that cast steel could not be welded, since it would not bear more than a red heat (*c* 900° C).

The invention was appreciated first in France. The manufacturers of cutlery at Sheffield, who in the beginning considered Huntsman's steel too hard, did not accept it until the competition of imported French cutlery forced them to do so. In England the production of cast steel increased very slowly before 1770, and even then some further decades elapsed before Huntsman's invention was adopted more widely.

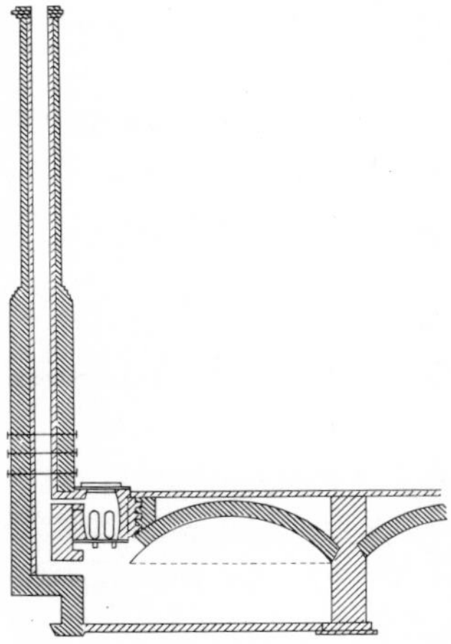

FIGURE 63—*Cross-section of Huntsman's melting-furnace, showing two crucibles in position.*

On the continent cast steel was first manufactured by Johann Conrad Fischer, one of Switzerland's leading industrialists, at Schaffhausen about 1802. Since Huntsman's process was kept secret, Fischer had to invent the method for himself. He also invented copper-steel and nickel-steel alloys, which he called 'yellow steel' and 'meteor steel' respectively. Fischer soon extended his industrial interests beyond Switzerland by setting up steel works and engineering-shops in Austria and France.

In the whole of the period with which we are now concerned cast iron remained superior to every other material for the construction of ordnance. Attempts were indeed made to substitute cast steel for cast iron in the manufacture of artillery. Thus Krupp proposed the use of cast steel, but his first gun, a three-pounder with a tube of cast steel inside an outer tube of cast iron, finally burst under the severe tests to which it was submitted in Berlin in 1849. A committee of Prussian artillery officers expressed doubts about the production on this principle of heavy ordnance of uniform quality, and criticized the high cost involved. About the same time, a cast steel gun weighing 5 tons was sent from Essen to Woolwich, but when tried it burst on the first time of firing.

The influence of the carbon-content of steel upon its hardness was not realized before 1750. The first to analyse carbon in iron was the Swedish metallurgist T. O. Bergmann (1735–84). He, and after him Guyton de Morveau (1737–1816), arrived at the conclusion that the conversion of iron into steel was due to its combination with carbon. Simultaneously with Guyton de Morveau, Priestley (1786) derived the same conclusion from experiments on nails at Birmingham.

The great inventions and improvements that caused a revolution in the iron industry, and a completely new orientation, had almost all been made by the close of the eighteenth century. After the end of the Napoleonic wars in 1815, when the demand for war material ceased, a temporary depression affected the iron trade, but after 1830 a tremendous growth occurred in every branch of British manufacture, including iron-making. There was a period of unusual prosperity, which culminated in 1835. Production of iron increased rapidly as a result of improvements in the processes conducted in both the furnace and the forge.

Perhaps the greatest of the improvements was the application of a hot instead of a cold blast in the smelting of iron. The first idea that a higher temperature in the furnace could be achieved by heating the blast before its entrance through the *tuyères* was due to James Beaumont Neilson (1792–1865), manager of the Glasgow gas-works. He obtained a patent in 1828, and early in the following year his invention was applied in the Clyde Ironworks at Glasgow.

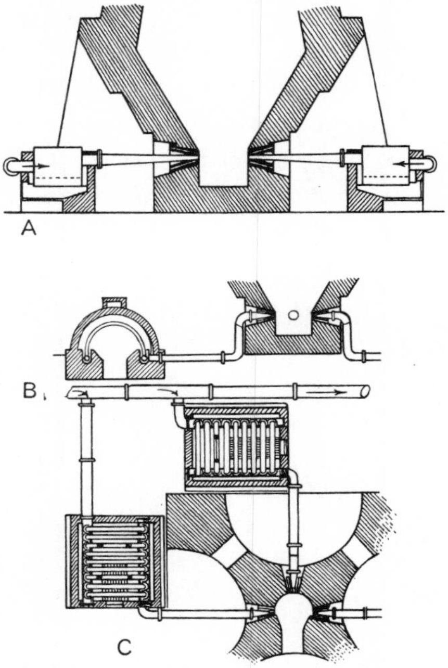

FIGURE 64—*Elevation* (A) *of Neilson's hot-blast stove erected at the Clyde works, Glasgow, in 1832. It consisted of a wrought iron chamber 4 ft long, 3 ft high, and 2 ft wide, similar to the wagon-head steam-boiler, and set in brickwork over a grate. A cold blast entered at one end and passed out to the* tuyère *at the other end, the temperature being raised to* c 200° *F. Below is the elevation* (B) *and plan* (C) *of an improved device in which the iron chambers were replaced by cast iron retort-shaped vessels enclosed in brick. Subsequently, water-cooled* tuyères *were introduced by John Condie (not illustrated).*

The apparatus first used by Neilson consisted of a small chamber of wrought iron set in brickwork, with a grate below. The cold blast entered at one end, above the grate, and passed out into the *tuyère* at the other end after having attained a temperature of about 200° F. Each *tuyère* had one heating chamber. It was found that iron chambers of this kind soon succumbed to heat and oxidation, so Neilson replaced them by cast iron retort-shaped vessels completely enclosed within a brick casing. By this means waste of heat was prevented, and the temperature could be increased to 280° F. After several further improvements an oven was erected at the Clyde works in 1832 which represents the first practical realization of the cast iron tubular stoves (figure 64).

Here, the cold blast was supplied to each oven by a pipe branching off the large main from the blast-engine. The blast entered the oven at the end remote from the *tuyère* and passed through the arched tubes over the fire into the pipe on the other side of the grate, whence it passed into the *tuyère*. The whole apparatus was enclosed in an arched oven, so as to retain and reflect as much heat as possible. While traversing the two longtitudinal pipes and the connecting arched pipes the blast was heated directly and was raised to a temperature of 600° F, about the melting-point of lead.

This increase in temperature required protection of the *tuyères*, which entered the furnace at its hottest part. It was achieved by the water-cooled *tuyère* invented by John Condie of the Blair ironworks in Scotland, and commonly known as the Scottish *tuyère*. This consisted of a coil of wrought iron tubing embedded in a short cast iron cone. Both ends protruded from the base of the cone, one at each side. Water entered at one end of the protruding pipe, passed straight to the narrow end of the *tuyère*, circled back through the coil, and finally escaped through the opposite protruding pipe.

By the time that stoves generating a temperature of 600° F had been constructed, it was recognized that with them the same amount of fuel produced three times as much iron as before, and that the same amount of blast acted twice as powerfully as a cold blast. Realization of the enormous potentialities of smelting with a hot blast led the majority of the ironmasters to accept it, although there was some resistance in the beginning. By 1835 the use of a hot blast had become general.

Neilson's invention resulted in a great increase in the output of iron. Application of hot blast not only made it possible to smelt a greater quantity of ore with the same amount of fuel but to build larger furnaces. A further advantage was that with the higher temperature generated by a hot blast not only coke but raw coal could be used as a fuel. This was of great importance in Scotland, since very few of the Scottish coals made good metallurgical coke. It also rendered it possible to make use of the black-band ironstone which had been discovered in Scotland at the beginning of the century but was almost useless for iron-smelting until the hot blast was introduced.

By the invention of the hot blast yet another important source of fuel was made available for smelting, namely the anthracite coal of south Wales and Pennsylvania. The idea of using anthracite with hot blast first occurred to an American of German descent, W. Geissenheimer. He was a Lutheran pastor in New York, where he used a small experimental furnace in the winter of 1830–1. After obtaining a patent in 1833, he erected the Valley furnace on Silver Creek, Pennsylvania, and then successfully smelted iron ore with anthracite and hot blast. Unfortunately, working ceased after two months because of an accident.

Independently of Geissenheimer, George Crane and his employee David Thomas put the same idea into practice in Britain in 1837; his works was at Ynyscedwin in the anthracite-bearing region of south Wales. After Geissenheimer's death his American patent was bought by Crane in 1838; in the summer of that year Thomas settled in the United States and began to erect an anthracite furnace at Catasauqua in Pennsylvania. It initiated a new era, in which the large deposits of anthracite—already well known but of little use—were made available for the American iron industry. Thomas's activity had far-reaching consequences in another respect, for he was the first in America completely to realize the immense value of powerful blowing-engines. About 1852 he introduced engines by which the pressure of blast was increased to double that customary in England at the time.

In the United States the flourishing state of the iron industry based on anthracite retarded the development of smelting with coke. Since anthracite and hard coal were available in large quantities they were naturally preferred to coke. Although attempts to smelt with coke were made as early as 1819, it was not until after 1850 that coke was used on a large scale in the United States.

The use of blowing-cylinders for supplying air to the furnace made bellows unnecessary. As a result, the large aperture in the outer casing of the furnace through which the nozzles of the bellows were inserted could be replaced by smaller apertures for the pipes that conducted the blast from the cylinders. Consequently there was sufficient room for two or three *tuyères*. More *tuyères* could not be employed as long as the old quadrangular shape of the furnace-shell was retained. The desire to employ a greater number of *tuyères*, stimulated by the necessity of generating more blast in order to increase production, led to important alterations in the exterior form of the furnace. The outer casing was given a round shape and was placed on five strong brickwork pillars. This innovation, which started in the 1820s, did not, however, allow more than four *tuyère* openings. Since a greater number became desirable to obtain the full benefit of hot blast after its introduction about 1830, the hearth was laid completely free. By placing the outer casing of the furnace upon cast iron pillars, the hearth was made accessible from all directions, so that the number of *tuyères* could easily be increased. The stone walls of the shell were made considerably thinner and were bound by wrought iron hoops, later replaced by a casing of boiler-plates. Furnaces of this type were known as Scottish furnaces, because the first was erected at Dundyvan, in Scotland, in the early 1830s (figure 65). Not long afterwards the new type was introduced on the continent, first at Hayange in France, where a furnace of this type was operated from 1838. The

Dundyvan type represented a considerable step forward in development towards the modern form of the blast-furnace, but the change did not affect the interior of the furnace.

The internal cavity was circular in section as far down as the hearth; this shape was first introduced about 1650 and gradually extended to the vast majority of furnaces. Despite this, the ironmasters clung to rectangular hearths

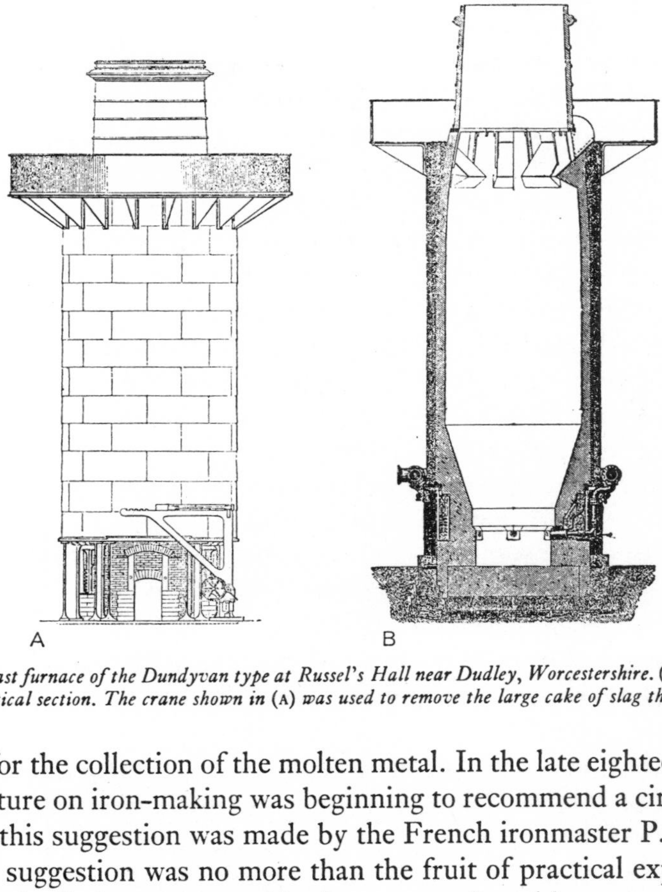

FIGURE 65—*Blast furnace of the Dundyvan type at Russel's Hall near Dudley, Worcestershire.* (A) *Front elevation,* (B) *vertical section. The crane shown in* (A) *was used to remove the large cake of slag that formed.*

or crucibles for the collection of the molten metal. In the late eighteenth century French literature on iron-making was beginning to recommend a circular shape; for example, this suggestion was made by the French ironmaster P. C. Grignon in 1775. The suggestion was no more than the fruit of practical experience, for the hearth gradually became round in the course of smelting on account of the destructive effect of the fire. It was, however, not until 1832 that such a shape was accepted and deliberately put into practice. The change took place in south Staffordshire in a new furnace built by T. Oakes at Corbyn's Hall, Brierley Hill, for the ironmaster John Gibbons (figure 66).

The immediate effects of Gibbons's alterations were a distinct acceleration of the smelting process, a considerable saving of fuel, and, in consequence, an increased output of metal. Gibbons's furnace set the pattern for the further development of the blast-furnace. It was first taken up by the ironmasters of the Black Country. The furnaces, which before 1832 had an average height of 35 to 40 ft, increased to a height of 50 to 60 ft.

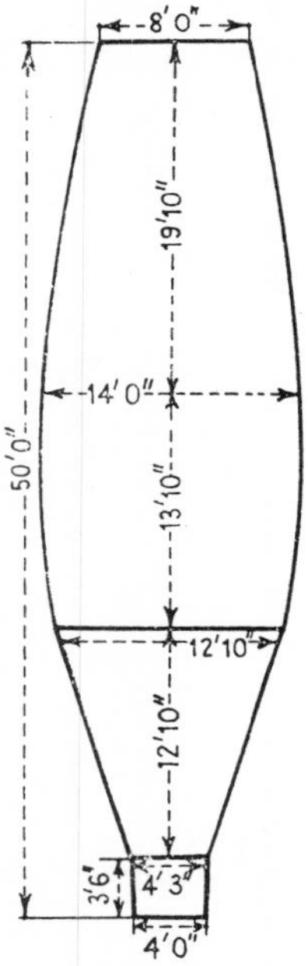

FIGURE 66—*Diagram of Gibbons's furnace at Corbyn's Hall. Gibbons modified the internal measurements of the furnace so that its life was longer.*

Further innovations affected the top aperture or 'mouth' of the blast-furnace. For several centuries this aperture had been left open, so that the gases escaped. The burning gases rising high into the air presented a spectacular sight, especially at night, but their free escape represented a waste. Attempts to utilize the waste gases were made in Württemberg, Germany, by A. C. W. F. Faber du Faur in 1831. The first practical success was achieved in 1832 at the ironworks of Schopfheim, in Baden. The gases were taken off the top of the furnace and conveyed through pipes to the hot-blast stoves (cf. figure 67). In England the first attempt to utilize the furnace-gas for heating the hot-blast stoves was made by Lloyds, Fosters and Company of the Old Park ironworks at Wednesbury, Staffordshire, in 1834. The heat produced, however, was so small that a supplementary oven near the *tuyère* was required for raising the temperature of the blast still further before it entered the furnace. Utilization of furnace-gas spread rapidly, and the method was improved on the continent, but in England it did not come into general use until the device introduced by James Palmer Budd, of the Ystalyfera ironworks near Swansea, and patented in 1845, became more widely known. This cup-and-cone device for feeding the blast-furnace was first used by George Parry at the Ebbw Vale ironworks in Monmouthshire in 1850 (figure 67). The simplest form had a fixed cup and a movable cone which could be raised or lowered. The device guaranteed a more even distribution of the charge than that attainable in furnaces in which the top was open.

Improvements in the early nineteenth century extended also to the forge and to the practice of making malleable or bar iron. A drawback in the process of puddling resulted from the use of sand for the bottom of the puddling-furnace. Combination between the silica of the sand and oxidized iron was liable to form a slag too acid to take up the phosphorus contained in pig iron made from ordinary phosphoric ores. The resulting corrosion of the bed of sand caused considerable loss through repairs and made the furnace less productive. A remedy was found by Samuel Rogers of Nant-y-Glo, Monmouthshire, who substituted a cast iron bottom plate. During the years 1816–18 he tried hard to make his invention acceptable to the ironmasters in south Wales, but his efforts were ridiculed and earned him the nickname of 'Mr Iron Bottom'; it was some years before Rogers's cast iron bottom plate was universally adopted.

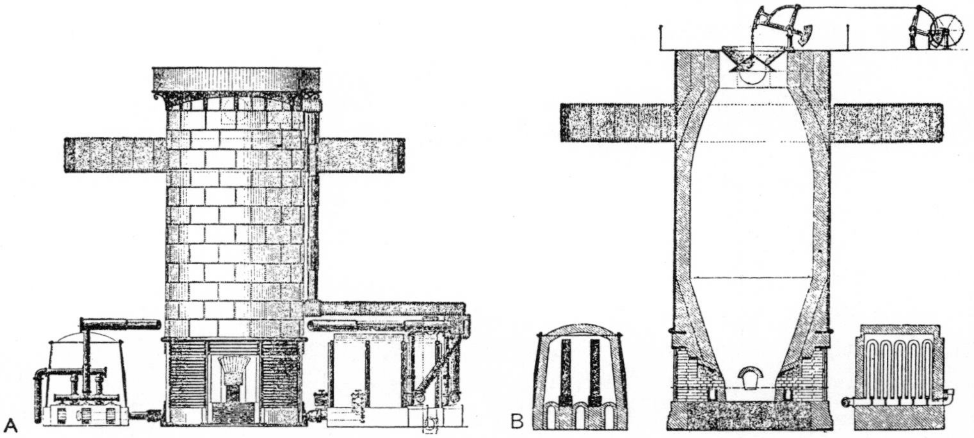

FIGURE 67—*Blast-furnaces at Ebbw Vale, Monmouthshire.* (A) *Front elevation showing hot-blast stoves;* (B) *vertical section. The mouth of the furnace is fitted with a 'cup-and-cone'. There is a circular opening for taking off the hot gases, which are then conveyed by pipes to the hot-blast stoves.*

Not only the furnace but the process of puddling itself was materially altered. Since Cort's invention almost all wrought iron had been produced by 'dry' puddling; this was slow, because it necessitated stirring the metal with iron bars in order to expose it to atmospheric action. An acceleration of the process was achieved by Joseph Hall of the Bloomfield ironworks at Tipton, in Staffordshire. In 1839 he obtained a patent for calcining 'top cinder' or 'bull dog'—the slag from puddling-furnaces—in kilns. After calcination the 'bull dog' was allowed to cool, broken into small pieces, and used for coating the floor of the furnace. The oxide of iron contained in 'bull dog' combined with the carbon in the charge and produced carbon monoxide below the surface of the molten metal; in escaping, this gas created the appearance of boiling, which gave the process the name of pig boiling. From the liquid nature of the slag, which was absent in the old method of puddling on sand bottoms, the name of 'wet' puddling is derived. By the new method, in which the iron was melted in a single stage, the process was greatly accelerated and was quickly adopted.

In the second quarter of the nineteenth century British puddlers migrated to the continent and went from factory to factory in Belgium and Germany instructing foreigners in their craft. They came mostly from south Wales, then the centre of puddling and rolling. The first puddling- and rolling-plants in France were installed in 1818–19, at Hayange (near Thionville) and St-Étienne (Loire). In Germany, Cort's puddling-process (p 106) was first introduced in 1824–5 at Rasselstein, near Neuwied, and at the Hoesch ironworks at Lendersdorf-Krauthausen, near Düren. At both these works British puddlers were employed,

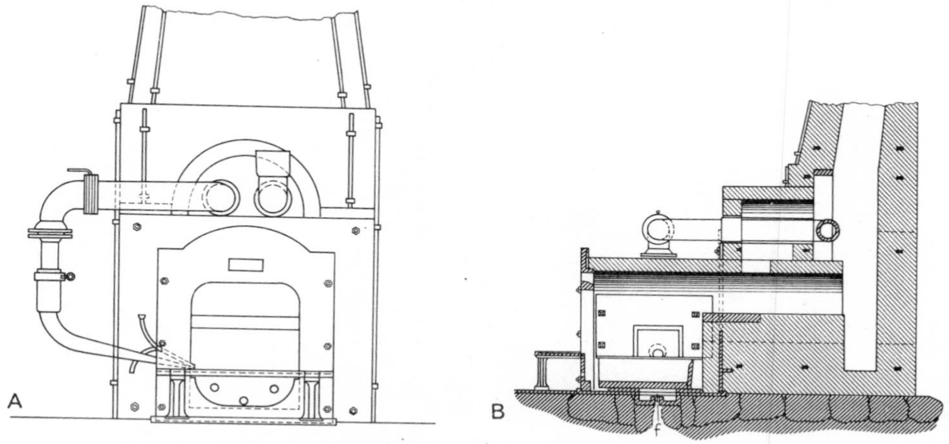

FIGURE 68—*Swedish Lancashire hearth.* (A) *Front elevation,* (B) *longitudinal section.*

and nearly all of them came from south Wales or Monmouthshire. Skilled workers from south Wales were also engaged in 1829 for the manufacture of charcoal-plate in Sweden. They introduced into Sweden a refining-hearth which developed into the so-called Swedish Lancashire hearth (figure 68). These workers evidently came from Pontypool, Monmouthshire, which at that time was the only place in the south-west of Britain where the old method of refining iron was still employed. The forges at Pontypool obtained their pig iron from Lancashire, which may have given rise to the name 'Lancashire' hearth. There is no evidence that such a hearth was used in Lancashire. There were three main characteristics in which the Lancashire hearth differed from the usual hearth employed for the refining of pig iron. Firstly, the chimney was not above the hearth, but set right at the rear. Secondly, and in consequence, the hearth itself was covered with an arched roof that reflected the heat and thus caused a notable economy in fuel. Thirdly, a shallow cast iron box (f in figure 68 B) was placed beneath the hearth. During the process of refining, water continually flowed through the box so that the bottom of the hearth was cooled. From Sweden the Lancashire hearth was reintroduced into England; it was also adopted in Germany.

The invention of a practical steam-hammer by Nasmyth was of immense importance. His hammer was a simple, direct-working machine which dispensed

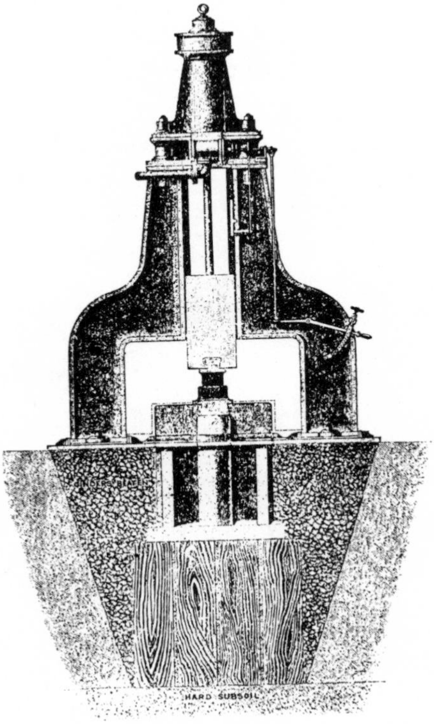

FIGURE 69—*Double-acting steam-hammer erected at the Atlas works, Sheffield. The steam-hammer was originally suggested by Watt in 1784 and afterwards planned by Deveral in 1806, but it was Nasmyth who developed it for practical use. Originally steam was used only to lift hammers, but by using it on both the up and down strokes the power of the hammer was increased.*

with much of the cumbrous wheel-work required with the old-fashioned trip-hammer (p 431) (figure 69 and plate 24 A). A further advantage was the ease with which the strokes could be regulated according to the size of the object and the force of the blow required. This was of particular importance in small works (plate 8 B), in which it was not practicable to have a number of different sizes of hammer according to the sort of work in hand. A modification of Nasmyth's hammer was the steam-hammer invented by John Condie and patented in 1846.

REFERENCES

[1] LA HOULIÈRE, M. DE. "Report to the French Government (1775)", ed. by W. H. CHALONER in *Edgar Allen News*, December 1948 and January 1949.
[2] HOARE, W. E. *Bull. Instn Metall.*, **8**, 1–23, 1951.
[3] COOPER, T. 'The Emporium of Arts and Sciences', p. 19. Philadelphia. 1813.
[4] SCHULZ, E. H. *Arch. Eisenhüttenw.*, **26**, no. 7, 370, 1955.

BIBLIOGRAPHY

ASHTON, T. S. 'Iron and Steel in the Industrial Revolution' (2nd ed.). University Press, Manchester. 1951.
GILLE, B. 'Les origines de la grande industrie métallurgique en France.' Collection d'histoire sociale, no. 2. Domat Montchrestien, Paris. 1948.
HENDERSON, W. O. 'Britain and Industrial Europe, 1750–1870.' University Press, Liverpool. 1954.
JOHANNSEN, O. 'Geschichte des Eisens' (3rd ed.). Stahleisen, Düsseldorf. 1953.
KARSTEN, C. J. B. 'Handbuch der Eisenhüttenkunde' (3rd ed.). Berlin. 1841.
PERCY, J. 'Metallurgy', Vol.: 'Iron and Steel.' London. 1864.
SCHUBERT, H. R. 'History of the British Iron and Steel Industry, *c* 450 B.C.–A.D. 1775.' Routledge & Kegan Paul, London. In the press.
SWANK, J. M. 'History of the Manufacture of Iron in all Ages.' Philadelphia. 1892.

The 'Old Furnace' at Coalbrookdale, rebuilt by Abraham Darby III in 1777. One of the iron beams seen above the tapping-hole is dated 1658. From this furnace the metal for the iron bridge was cast.

4

PART II

EXTRACTION AND PRODUCTION OF METALS: NON-FERROUS METALS

F. W. GIBBS

A GREAT change of outlook occurred in the whole field of metals during the century or so with which this chapter deals. Developments in engineering —the introduction of railed ways for haulage, and of steam-driven machinery for pumping water from mines and for blowing air into blast-furnaces—made possible deeper and larger workings and helped to increase greatly the whole scale of operations throughout the metal industries. A great change, too, had been brought about by advances in physics and chemistry (ch 8) which improved beyond measure the understanding of the traditional processes by which metals were won from their ores. The new field of electrometallurgy had acquired considerable industrial importance by 1850–70. Above all, the remarkably rapid development of analytical chemistry (p 221) in the later eighteenth century led to the discovery of a large number of metals that had not previously been characterized. Many of them were mixed with the commoner metals in their ores, and this made improvements possible in methods of separation and purification. Work on the new metals was also made easier by the invention of the oxy-hydrogen blowpipe, with which small quantities of materials could be heated to much higher temperatures than ever before.

Manufacturers, however, at first showed little inclination to test these new methods and materials, and the metal industries were not greatly affected by them for a considerable time. A writer in 1828 said that a number of the new metals were little better than hypothetical assumptions; some of them, such as potassium and sodium, were so different from the popular conception of a metal that 'nothing but the rage of the day for the invention of new metals could have prompted their insertion in the list'.

In the main, the methods used for the extraction of the non-ferrous metals in the early nineteenth century were the same as had been found satisfactory in the early eighteenth. Thus the extraction of copper, one of the most difficult processes, still remained somewhat haphazard, and the product was often brittle.

If a reliable grade of the metal was required for some purpose, copper coins were sometimes used; for example, the silver-platers of Birmingham are said to have sought for copper coins issued during and since the reign of Queen Anne, as these were easier to work than much commercial copper made in the later eighteenth and early nineteenth centuries.

In the principal mining-centres of Germany, however, improvements in analysis were put to good account, and operations were often carried out with exceptional skill and care, particularly when local ores contained several elements for each of which a good market could be found. In many other parts of the continent, and in Britain, older and often wasteful methods at first prevailed, and this sometimes meant that only the richest ores could be successfully worked on the commercial scale.

Among the new metals of the period, special mention must be made of zinc and the platinum metals. Zinc was by this time being extracted direct from its ores by a method apparently brought to this country from China and first used in Europe on the commercial scale at Bristol. Among other metallic products of the Far East, Malacca tin and Chinese sheet lead became well known. Platinum, iridium, and rhodium were obtained from the *platina* brought to Europe from Spanish America. Platinum was especially prized; it was much used for laboratory vessels and for stills with a capacity of 35 gallons or more. Little use was found for many of the other new metals; yet by 1830 it was known, or claimed, that cadmium, iridium, nickel, osmium, and palladium could be worked into plates or drawn into wire, and that tellurium could be cast. The furnaces then available could not produce temperatures high enough to permit the easy working of cerium, chromium, cobalt, columbium (now known as niobium, but then sometimes confused with tantalum), manganese, molybdenum, rhodium, tungsten, titanium, and uranium, and only a few of these metals found occasional use in alloys.

Thus, apart from iron and steel and the useful half-metals arsenic, antimony, and bismuth, the commercially important metals of the period were lead and tin; copper and zinc; mercury, silver, and gold; the platinum metals; and cobalt, nickel, and manganese. Their extraction, production, and chief alloys will be described in that order. Lead and tin were among the easiest to smelt, whereas copper and silver offered some of the most difficult metallurgical problems. The use of mercury for the extraction of silver and gold makes it convenient to treat them together; they and the platinum metals played an important role in the history of Spain and of the Spanish possessions in South America. Cobalt, nickel, and manganese had not yet assumed the importance they were later to have in the steel industry.

I. BISMUTH, ANTIMONY, AND ARSENIC

No outline of the technology of the non-ferrous metals would be complete without some mention of these important elements, which, unlike most metals, lack true permanence in air and are easily calcined, melted, and vaporized. They were used in numerous alloys and in many arts, as well as for the manufacture of several compounds widely needed in industry. They all occur native to some extent, and were often found together in German and Scandinavian ores used for the extraction of other metals.

Bismuth was the easiest to obtain. This was done by liquation; that is, by heating the ore and allowing the liquid metal to run off into a receiver. Normally, cast iron retorts placed obliquely in a furnace were charged with about ½ cwt of ore and heated, when the liquid bismuth ran down the retorts and out into iron pans. As the pans filled, the bismuth was ladled out and cast into bars of 20 to 50 lb each. In the middle of the nineteenth century, about 10 000 tons were prepared annually by this method at Schneeberg, wood still being used as fuel.

Pure bismuth for medicinal purposes was prepared chemically on a laboratory scale, the bismuth of commerce being largely used for the production of alloys. With tin it gave bell metal; two parts of bismuth with one of tin and one of lead gave 'fusible metal', so called by Sir Isaac Newton; one part of bismuth, two of tin, and one of lead gave soft solder for use with pewter. The oxide and nitrate were also made on a large scale.

Antimony occurs naturally as the sulphide, stibnite, European deposits of which are found in Czechoslovakia and Yugoslavia. Antimony sulphide is also often present in ores of other metals. It is easily fusible, and was therefore separated from such ores, or from gangue in the case of stibnite, by liquation. The metal was then extracted by a two-stage process, in which the sulphide was first heated with free access of air to give the oxide, and this was then reduced to metal by heating with crude tartar. In Germany, antimony was sometimes obtained in one operation by heating the sulphide with scrap iron, which combined with sulphur, and an alkali carbonate: later this became the chief method. The impure antimony thus obtained was purified by fusion with a little antimony sulphide and sodium carbonate. On partial cooling the metal separated from the slag, and the process was repeated if necessary.

Antimony was used chiefly in alloys, such as the two common type-metals (70 or 75 per cent tea-lead,[1] 25 or 20 per cent antimony, 5 per cent tin) and

[1] As the name suggests, this was sheet lead used to line tea-chests. It was made in China by hand, molten lead being pressed between flat stones, and was used for some purposes in preference to European lead as it was relatively hard and stiff.

stereotype metal (112 lb tea-lead, 18 lb antimony, and 3 lb tin). Britannia metal, used for table-ware, was 90 per cent tin and 10 per cent antimony. Antimony was also used for concave mirrors required to take a high polish; in bell metal to

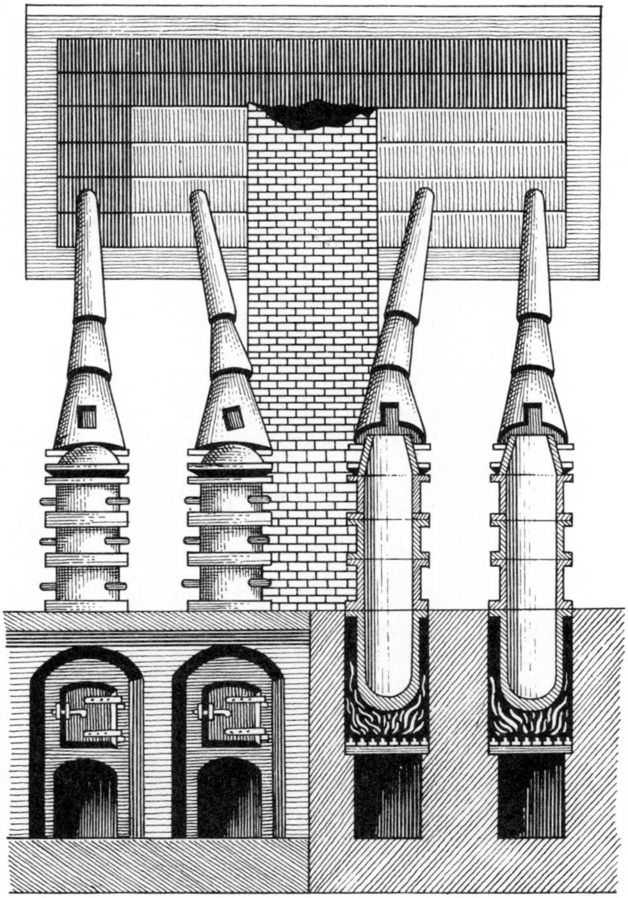

FIGURE 70—*Purification of white arsenic by sublimation, at Reichenstein.* (Left) *Front elevation;* (right) *vertical section.*

give a stronger and clearer sound; and to improve the fusibility of metals used for casting, such as that for cannon-balls.

Arsenic, unlike bismuth and antimony, was obtained chiefly from native arsenic or the ores containing it, particularly mispickel (arsenical pyrites), by sublimation in earthenware retorts and collection of the solid in large receivers, in which it was allowed to settle on pieces of sheet iron. Again unlike bismuth, arsenic was widely used in the arts, chiefly in the form of compounds. These included the oxide (white arsenic); the sulphides (orpiment and realgar, or red orpiment); and salts, such as the copper compounds known as Scheele's green (1778) and Schweinfurth green (1814). White arsenic was obtained from arsenical ores by carrying out a similar sublimation, but with the admission of air to effect oxidation. A typical sublimation furnace of the period is shown in figure 70.

II. LEAD

Lead occurs widely as the sulphide, galena, but also as sulphate, carbonate, phosphate, chloride, and other forms. Throughout this period, however, it was

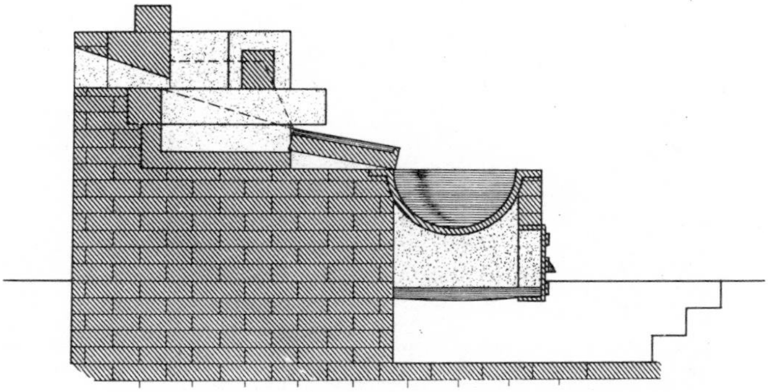

FIGURE 71—*Smelting lead in the ore-hearth (section).*

smelted chiefly from galena. In the nineteenth century several methods, traditional and new, were in use, in which either reverberatory or blast furnaces were employed. Among the most important of the former were the Flintshire, Spanish, and Bleiberg types. The first two were similar in that the lead was allowed to accumulate in the furnaces, whereas the metal ran out of the Bleiberg furnace as it was formed. The ore, after grinding and washing, was first converted to sulphate by gentle roasting in the molten state with free access of air. It was then mixed with a roughly equal amount of sulphide and reduced by strong heating without air, the furnace gases passing directly over the hearth on their way to the flue.

Blast-furnaces were used mainly with very rich ores. The most important types were the ore-hearth (figure 71), or Scotch furnace, and the American blast-furnace, the latter introducing the important innovation of pre-heating the air used in the blast by leading the pipes round the back of the hearth (figure 72). In the Scotch furnace the ore was placed on a cast iron hearth, and heated sufficiently to effect a partial oxidation without melting the galena. When the ore began to soften it was rabbled to produce a fresh surface. After about half the ore had been oxidized it was all drawn out into water and then dried. It was then returned to the hearth, mixed with coal and peat, and heated, the blast being forced in by a condensing-engine or by a fan worked by steam. At frequent intervals the slag was separated, the lead was run off into the vessel seen on the right of figure 71, and fresh fuel and ore were added. The process was continued without interruption for about 15 hours, when the hearth was emptied.

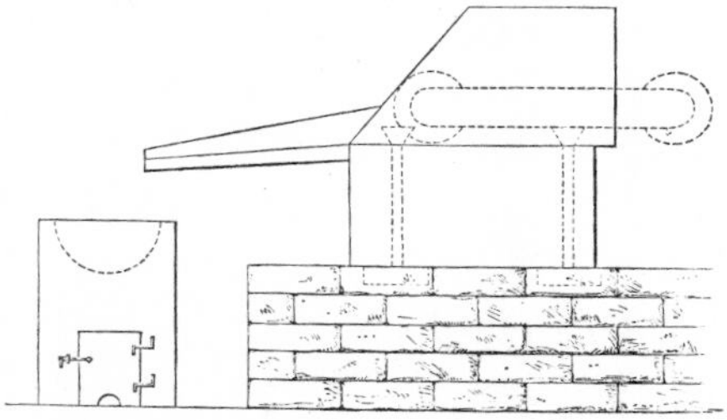

FIGURE 72—*Smelting lead in the American ore-hearth (side elevation).*

By these methods very large quantities of lead were produced in England and Wales, Spain, Germany, Sardinia, France, Belgium, Greece, and Austria-Hungary—in that order of importance. In the early part of the period some lead was used as sheets for sheathing the bottoms of ships, but copper was preferred in the eighteenth century. Sheet lead was also required for roofing and other purposes. At first such sheets were made by pouring molten lead on to a large stone and pressing another over it, but later grain rolls were employed, the former method being retained only for a few special purposes, such as making plates of metal. Much lead was required in the nineteenth century for water- and gas-pipes, but for the so-called composition pipes the tea-lead from China was sometimes used. At Birmingham, antimony was added to lead to impart hardness. Considerable quantities of the purest lead were also used in sulphuric acid chambers and for the manufacture of white lead and red lead.

III. TIN

In the eighteenth and nineteenth centuries nearly the whole of the tin of commerce was smelted from tinstone (tin oxide), with which sulphide ores containing copper and iron pyrites were often associated, as for example in Cornwall (plate 6B). The ore was first broken up and sorted into heaps of various qualities and then reduced to powder in a stamping-mill, driven by a water-wheel or by steam. After further sorting and purification by washing, any arsenic and sulphur compounds were removed by roasting in a reverberatory furnace. Later a special furnace was used, called Brunton's calciner after its inventor. This was provided with a hopper fitted in the arch over the bed, which consisted of a revolving cast iron table kept turning throughout the calcination. Oxides of sulphur passed out through the wide flue, in which the arsenic was retained in a number of chambers. The tin oxide was allowed to fall off the table into a lower compartment.

After about 1840, acids also were used for the purification of the ore—hydrochloric acid when the chief impurities were iron compounds and sulphuric acid for the separation of copper. Tungsten, too, was being removed at this time, the ore being first fused with alkaline salts: in Oxland's process crude soda was added, but by 1850 the more economical saltcake (sodium sulphate) was being used in Cornwall.

When the tin ore was ready for smelting, it was placed in a reverberatory furnace, together with a little lime or powdered fluorspar to combine with any silica still present. After six to eight hours, it was well rabbled and any metal formed was run off. It was then reheated and the floating scoria removed in stages. The first portion of the scoria was thrown away; the second was stamped to permit the recovery of pieces of metal spread through it; and the final skimmings, together with the recovered pieces, were kept for smelting with the next charge. The clean metal was then run out through a gutter into a cast iron pot, the slag and other impurities rising to the surface were skimmed off, and the tin was poured into moulds holding up to 3 cwt each.

Metallic impurities, usually iron and lead, but sometimes also copper, tungsten, and cobalt, had now to be removed. This was done in a number of ways. In 'boiling', a bundle of green-wood billets was lowered by a crane into a pot of molten tin. A great deal of seething took place, and the impurities were oxidized by the steam generated. In 'tossing', melted tin was lifted in ladles and allowed to fall again; this led to the formation of a small amount of oxide, which on mixing with the mass lost its oxygen to the more easily oxidized metals, thus causing them to rise as a slag. A further method was liquation. In this operation the blocks of metal were heated slowly in a reverberatory furnace until the tin began to melt, and the temperature was then kept constant until no more tin would run off. The impurities remained in a solid alloy of higher melting-point.

In Germany, and particularly at Altenberg, small blast-furnaces (figure 73) were preferred to reverberatories, and with them very good metal was produced, though the loss of tin was estimated at 15 per cent and the fuel consumed was nearly twice as much as in a reverberatory furnace.

Tin was used in large quantities for the production of alloys, such as bronze, bell metal, and solder, and for the manufacture of tinplate, tin-foil, and a number of compounds for use in pottery, glazes, and colours and as mordants in cloth-printing. Tin-foil, like lead-foil, was made by passing a thin slab backwards and forwards between rollers.

The manufacture of tinplate grew to large proportions during the final half-century of the period; for this purpose iron was required in sheets. The iron for 'charcoal' plates was prepared in a charcoal-fired refinery, whereas a light spongy coke was used for preparing 'coke' plates. During the nineteenth century these terms lost their significance and 'coke' plates were made from puddled iron. The prepared iron was heated and worked into blooms, which were cut and rolled into bars; the bars were sheared into lengths suitable for rolling into sheets.

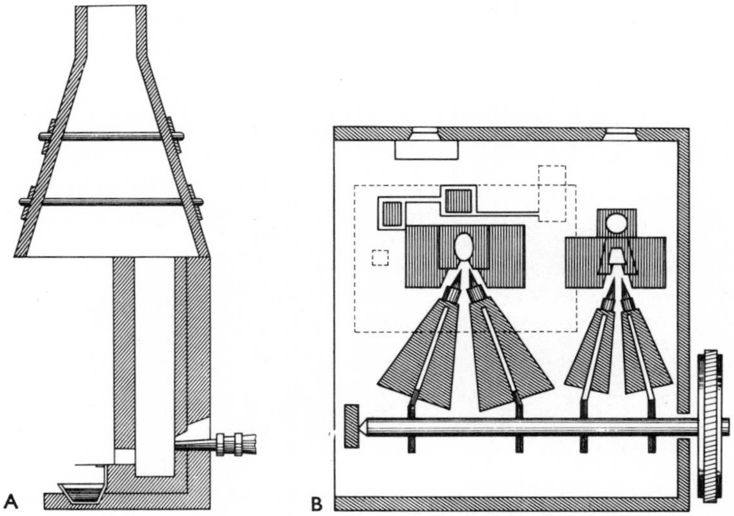

FIGURE 73—*Smelting tin by bellows-blown blast-furnace, at Altenberg.* (A) *Vertical section,* (B) *plan: (the right-hand furnace was for re-smelting slags).*

Scale was removed by pickling in an acid liquor and rubbing with sand and water, and the plates were then annealed and again pickled before tinning in a stow. This consisted of a row of baths of molten tin and of grease with fires below. The plates were first dipped in grease and then in tin. In a divided compartment the plates received a longer immersion to complete the tinning, and then, after brushing with hemp to remove any surplus, a short immersion in the purest tin. They were immediately placed in a grease pot to prevent the tin cooling more quickly than the iron and so cracking the surface of the plate. They were next immersed in melted tallow at a lower temperature. In the final bath, the list-pot, the plates were dipped in about a quarter of an inch of molten tin to remove the 'wire' of tin formed on the edges.

IV. COPPER

Copper occurs widely as sulphide, but considerable amounts of oxide and carbonate ores were also used in this period, particularly in Germany. Traditional methods of extraction were followed with little change until the nineteenth century, when the scale of the industry greatly increased.

In Britain the chief extraction centres were Neath and Swansea, with Bristol and parts of Lancashire important in the eighteenth century. The ores were obtained mainly from Cornwall and Ireland, but some came from Anglesey. By 1830–50 ores were being obtained mainly from South America, Canada, Cornwall, Ireland, and Wales. Low-grade sulphide ores were also being imported by

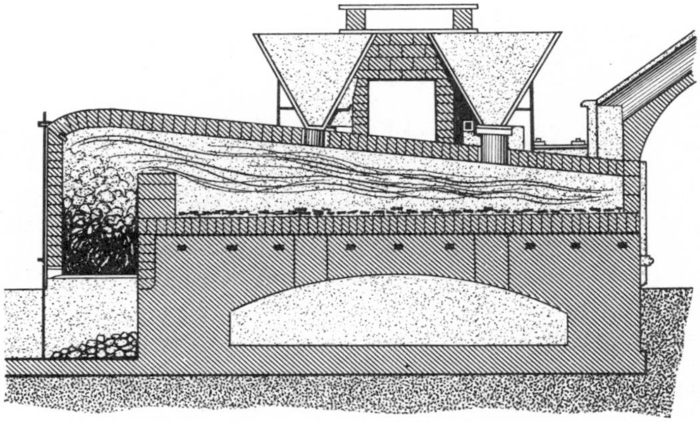

FIGURE 74—*Roasting furnace for sulphide ores of copper* (*vertical section*).

chemical manufacturers for the sake of the sulphur, and these were afterwards sold to the copper-smelters. Normally, reverberatory furnaces were used, though in other parts of Europe blast-furnaces were preferred. The methods of extraction, particularly from sulphide ores, were somewhat complicated; they derived from methods that in the sixteenth century took as long as eighteen months for their completion. Some makers recognized fourteen stages, but during the nineteenth century the work was considerably simplified, and the Welsh process, with its six major operations, will be described here.

(i) The ore was first roasted, in quantities of about three tons, and after 12 to 24 hours was raked into holes at the side of the bed and cooled with water (figure 74).

(ii) The brownish-black material was melted in the ore-furnace with 'metal slag' from process (iv). This gave 'coarse metal' containing about 35 per cent copper, which was separated from the slag. When the bed was full the coarse metal was granulated by running it into a pit filled with water (figure 75).

(iii) The granulated coarse metal was then calcined for 24 hours with frequent stirring, the temperature being gradually raised towards the end.

(iv) The calcined coarse metal was melted with the slag from (v) and (vi) or with ores rich in copper oxide. This gave metal containing about 75 per cent copper, and 'metal slag'.

(v) The metal was run out of the furnace and made into pigs (figure 76),

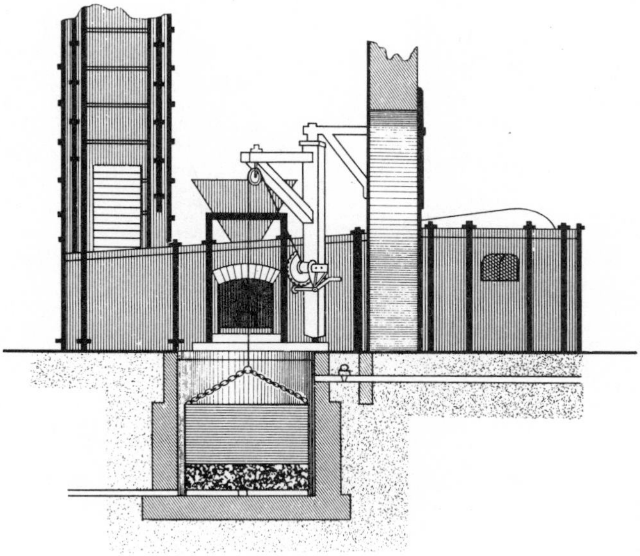

FIGURE 75—*Side view of melting furnace for sulphide ores of copper, showing water tank. The fused matte flowed into the tank from the furnace, and was thus granulated.*

which were transferred to a melting-furnace and heated, with air passing freely over the fire-bridge. The products were 'blister copper', containing 95 per cent copper, and 'roaster slag'. During this process the melt appeared to boil owing to the liberation of gases in the reaction. After removal of the slag the copper was tapped into sand-moulds.

(vi) The product was then further refined to give marketable copper and 'refinery slag'. This was done in a melting-furnace having an inclined bottom. About 6 to 8 tons of blister copper were melted and allowed to oxidize for about 15 hours in the air entering the furnace; the slag was then skimmed off. The copper was next toughened by throwing charcoal or anthracite on the surface and poling with green wood. In poling, the thick end of a long birch or oak pole was pushed into the melt and kept depressed by means of a prop. Much gas and vapour were evolved, and the metal was splashed about and exposed to the reducing action of the charcoal or anthracite. The copper, now in the state of 'tough pitch', was ladled out and quickly cast into moulds (figure 77), poured

FIGURE 76—*Copper furnaces at St Helens, Lancashire, in the nineteenth century. Tapping copper to make into pigs.*

into hot water to give 'bean shot', granulated for 'feather shot', or mixed with lead if intended for rolling into sheets.

Two enterprising methods of further simplifying the process of extraction may be mentioned. In 1846 James Napier patented a process, used near Swansea, that followed the four stages in the Cornish method of assay. It involved adding saltcake in the melting-furnace (stage ii) and afterwards breaking up the mix in water to separate impurities such as tin and antimony. The separation was not, however, complete, and the method was later abandoned. In 1859 Henry Hussey Vivian (1821–94) took the calcination direct to stage iv to obtain metal with 70 per cent copper. As a result large quantities of copper-rich slag were formed, which was the reason why this part of the process was normally stopped at about 35 per cent copper. Vivian smelted the slag separately in a blast-furnace, thus following the method customary on the continent.

All these processes were used with fairly rich sulphide ores. The Swedish ores, such as those smelted at Åtvidaberg, the chief centre of the industry there, were

FIGURE 77—*Casting purified copper in moulds. St Helens, Lancashire.*

in comparison very poor. As in France and Germany, blast-furnaces were used, and by 1861 the blast was being pre-heated by the waste gases. The ore was first roasted in kilns or in heaps. It was then fused, after mixing with slag rich in iron oxide, to give 20 to 30 per cent copper and a slag of iron silicate, the lower half of which contained sufficient copper to make it worth while using again. The furnace was tapped every two or three days. The coarse metal or regulus was then roasted and afterwards fused to give 'black copper' (95 per cent), which was refined in the blast-furnace to give 99·5 per cent copper.

Apart from its use for a great variety of vessels and utensils, copper was sold in very large quantities to the brass-makers, while a high proportion of the copper sheet made was used for sheathing the bottoms of ships. It was first used on warships about 1761, all ships being so sheathed by about 1780. Though later superseded in the merchant service by Muntz's metal (a brass containing about 3 parts of copper to 2 of zinc patented in 1832 by G. F. Muntz of Birmingham), copper sheet was still used in the Royal Navy long after this time. Both kinds of sheet often corroded rapidly and had to be replaced at frequent intervals.

Copper, together with silver, was also used in the eighteenth century for 'Sheffield plate', introduced about 1742 by Thomas Bolsover, a Sheffield cutler. Bolsover discovered that a billet made by fusing or soldering a thick sheet of copper to a thin one of silver could be rolled or flattened without unequal spreading of the metals. He applied this process to button-making and was thus able to supply the market at much below the usual prices. About 1758 Joseph Hancock used the new material to make household goods, such as coffee-pots and candlesticks, and soon afterwards the method spread elsewhere. Matthew Boulton of Birmingham entered the field about 1762, and after 1770 there were several firms of platers in Birmingham. One of the difficulties with Sheffield plate was the adequate protection of exposed edges, and Boulton was one of the first to use sterling silver thread, soldered on, for this purpose.

V. ZINC

In 1702 Abraham Darby I and a number of merchants formed the British Brass Battery and Copper Company to exploit the calamine (zinc carbonate) deposits on Mendip, and by 1730 there were several works at Bristol and to the east of the city. John Champion (1705–94) and his brother William (1709–89) are credited with being the first in Europe to manufacture zinc from calamine and zinc blende (zinc sulphide) respectively. William is said to have learned of the Chinese method of obtaining zinc from calamine (vol III, p 691), possibly by way of the Dutch trading-posts in the Far East and Holland. By 1737 he had worked out a commercial process on these lines and he patented it in the following year. Later he had 31 furnaces producing copper, zinc, and brass, with associated rolling-mills and wire-mills. The machinery was run by water-power, a steam-engine being used to return the water to the pond. His interest in these ventures was eventually sold to the Bristol Brass Wire Company.

John Champion also built a works to produce zinc, and introduced a method for using blende instead of calamine, the ore being roasted to oxide before reduction. Other patents acquired by the brothers covered the removal of arsenic from copper and the production of alloys containing antimony and bismuth.

In the middle of the nineteenth century the extraction was carried out in a similar manner by the 'English' process, for example at Swansea. The ore was

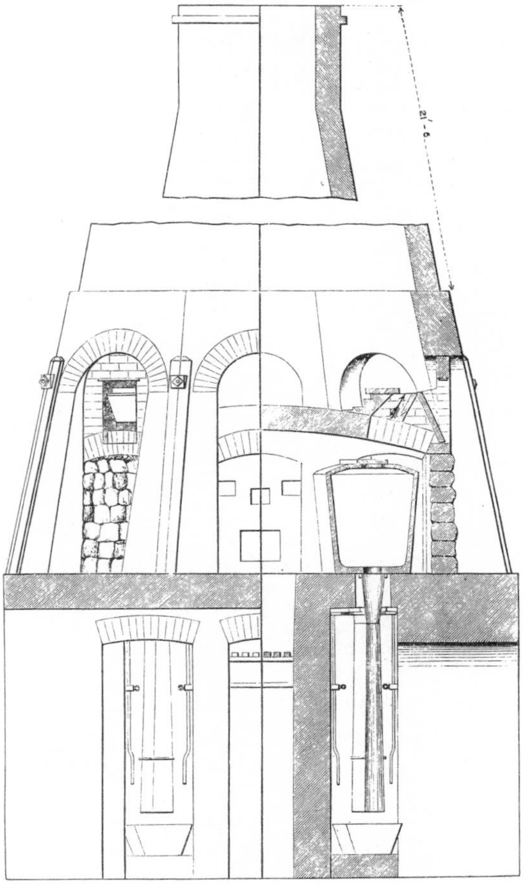

FIGURE 78—*Zinc reduction house; English process,* c *1850, showing two vertical sections at right angles.*

crushed between iron rollers and then, after washing, roasted on a flat-bedded calciner. Sometimes double-bedded calciners, heated by the waste gases from the reduction furnace, were used. The reduction house (figure 78) had two storeys; in the upper the roasted ore and coke were heated, and in the 'cave' below the zinc vapour was condensed. Barrel-shaped pots, with holes at the top and bottom, were made from Stourbridge clay, glasshouse potsherds, and old spelter-pots. Over the bottom hole were placed plugs of old wood, then coke, then quantities of calcined blende and coke alternately. A short tube was fitted below the hole. On heating, the flame issuing beneath was watched until it

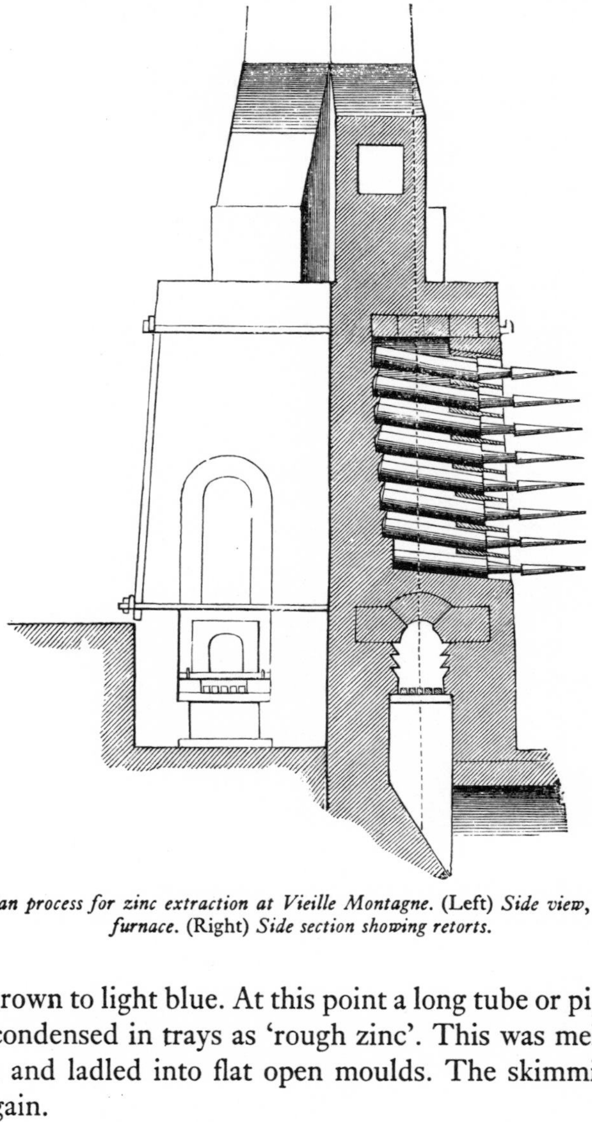

FIGURE 79—*Belgian process for zinc extraction at Vieille Montagne.* (Left) *Side view, showing position of furnace.* (Right) *Side section showing retorts.*

changed from brown to light blue. At this point a long tube or pipe was attached, and the metal condensed in trays as 'rough zinc'. This was melted in cast iron pots, skimmed, and ladled into flat open moulds. The skimmings or 'sweeps' were worked again.

Other processes employed on the continent differed from the English one mainly in the design of the reduction plant. In the Silesian process the vapour was taken off from the upper part of the retort and condensed in tubes. In the

Belgian process, introduced in the region of Liège in the early nineteenth century, parallel rows of retorts were placed over a fire in a narrow arched chamber (figure 79). The retorts were cylindrical vessels of refractory clay fitted with clay nozzles or condensers.

VI. BRASS

In the early eighteenth century Bristol was an important centre of the brass industry, but Birmingham later held pride of place, 1000 tons being put to use there in 1795. Brass, an alloy of copper and zinc, was much prized for its resemblance to gold when polished. A number of alloys were distinguished, with colours varying from yellow to burnished gold. In the range of 70 to 85 per cent copper were Prince's metal, Mannheim gold, and Dutch metal. In the lower range came Muntz's metal (p 130), containing 50 to 63 per cent copper.

Two methods of production were employed. Either the two metals were alloyed in the required proportions, or 'calamine' brass was prepared without melting the copper. In the direct method the metals were melted in crucibles or reverberatory furnaces, skimmed, and poured into sand-moulds or rolled into sheets. If rolled, the sheets were afterwards pickled in sulphuric acid to remove scale and then washed in water. Considerable quantities of wire were also made.

For calamine brass, copper was heated in pots with calamine and charcoal. The product was not homogeneous, but it had a characteristic appearance when polished and was much in demand in the eighteenth century for 'gilt' objects, such as the buttons for which Birmingham became famous. By the end of the period we are now considering, however, the manufacture had ceased.

The consumption of brass was further increased by reason of the variety of surface effects that could be produced by chemical and other means. For example, dead-dipping or etching the surface of finished goods with nitric acid to give a pale yellow subdued appearance was for some time a very popular treatment. In other brass-work the colour was heightened by lacquering with shellac dissolved in proof spirit and coloured with the resin known as dragon's blood, obtained from a species of *Dracaena*. Sometimes the brass was 'bronzed' by dipping into a solution of arsenious acid in hydrochloric acid, by dilute platinum chloride solution, by a solution of mercuric chloride mixed with vinegar, or by rubbing with plumbago. The bronze-like tint was made permanent with lacquer.

VII. MERCURY

The principal ore of mercury, cinnabar (mercury sulphide), has been known from very early times. The liquid metal is readily separated from several of its compounds and often occurs dispersed through the ore. Mercury was also found in parts of South America as an amalgam with silver, as in the rich mines of Arqueros, or with gold, as mixed with some platinum ore in Colombia. On the large scale, however, mercury was prepared from cinnabar.

In the nineteenth century the most important mercury mine was that at Almaden in Spain, where the traditional method of extraction was still carried out in aludel furnaces (figure 80). The ore was heated with admission of air, which was sufficient to oxidize the sulphur and liberate the mercury as vapour;

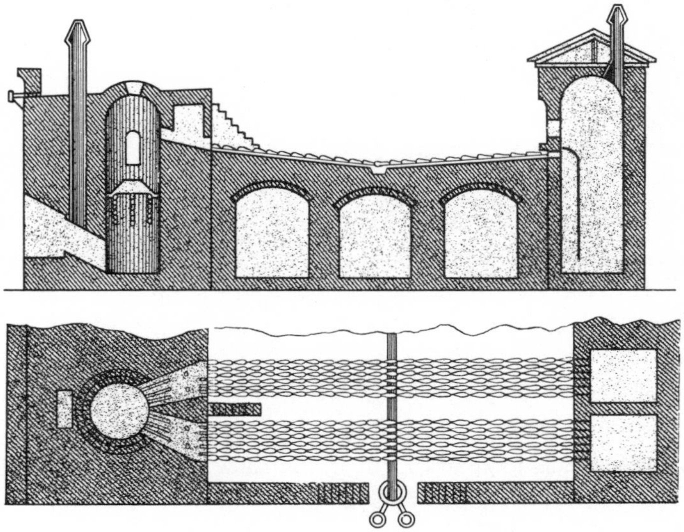

FIGURE 80—*Aludel furnace for extraction of mercury at Almaden.* (Above) *Vertical section.* (Below) *Plan. Note long files of aludels to condense the mercury.*

this was led away with the other gases through long files of earthenware condensers (aludels). The aludels were detached and emptied after two weeks.

Another mine that became famous was that worked at Idria in Italy, where the Almaden system was adopted in 1750 as an improvement on the crude method previously followed. However, towards the close of the century a large distillation furnace of a new pattern was erected (figure 81). Here the vapours emerging from the furnace were led alternately downwards and upwards through communicating compartments on either side. In the last compartment water was made to fall on a series of inclined boards fitted from one wall almost to the opposite one, so as to condense the last traces of mercury. The metal flowed out from each chamber into a receiver and thence to the main tank. After filtering through ticking it was put into cast iron bottles for sale and export.

At works in the duchy of Deux-Ponts (Zweibrucken) the ore was heated with quicklime to avoid using extensive condensing equipment. Up to 52 earthenware retorts (cucurbits) were arranged in double rows in a gallery over a coal fire, and the metal was collected in earthenware receivers.

A new method used at Lansberg in Bavaria was designed by Andrew Ure (1778–1857) on a principle resembling that employed for coal-gas manufacture (figure 82). The plant was erected in 1847 and consisted of a series of cast iron retorts arranged in threes under arches of masonry. A pipe from each retort led

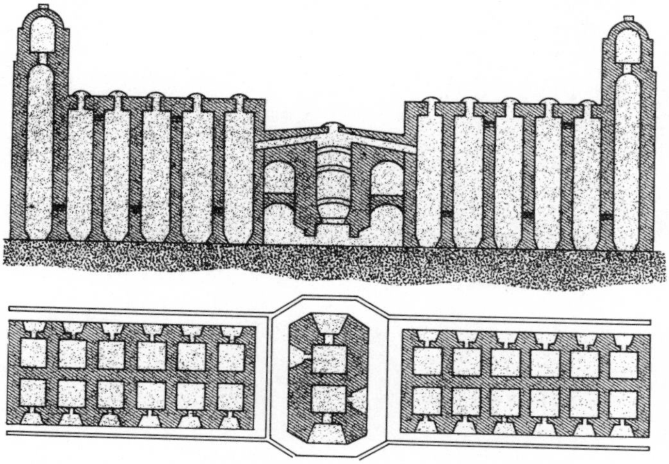

FIGURE 81—*Mercury distillation furnace at Idria, c 1800.* (Above) *Vertical section.* (Below) *Plan.*

down to a wide condenser-pipe cooled with water. In this way a charge of 6 to 7 cwt of coarsely powdered ore and quicklime was worked off in a few hours.

About 1844 some Mexicans attempted to obtain gold from the red earth of a cave in California. This led to the discovery of another important source of mercury and to the opening up of the mine at New Almaden by Barrow, Forbes & Company. By 1853 nearly 20 000 bottles, each containing 75 lb of mercury, had been exported from New Almaden through the port of San Francisco, some 20 miles away. In 1856 there were 14 smelting-furnaces with condensing chambers; these were very similar in principle to the furnaces introduced at Idria some fifty years earlier.

VIII. SILVER

The metallurgy of silver, according to Percy, was 'the most extensive, the most varied, and the most complicated of all'. Although silver could be obtained fairly readily from its compounds, the high value of the metal meant that it was profitable to extract it from other metals, such as copper and lead, with which it was often mixed in relatively small amounts. Though in the earlier part of this period silver occurring in copper was in part removed by liquation, the

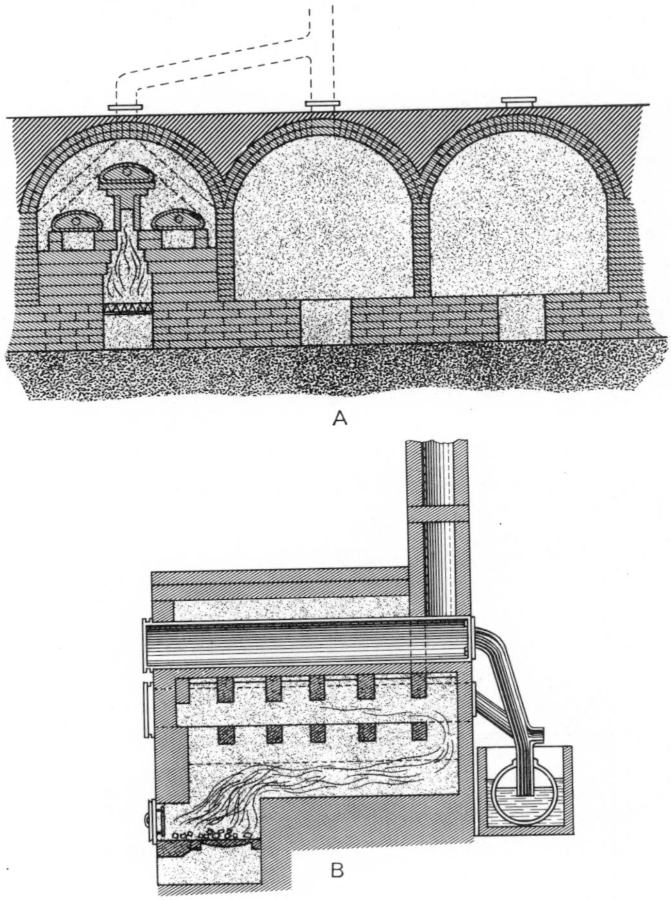

FIGURE 82—*Mercury extraction at Lansberg, Bavaria, in 1847.* (A) *Vertical section;* (B) *section through a retort. The mercury liberated in the triple stills in* (A) *is condensed in the condenser seen in the bottom right of* (B).

later method was to remove it at the reguline stage. It was fused with a large excess of lead at a temperature below the melting-point of copper; the lead flowed off, carrying with it most of the silver. The lead was then removed by cupellation (p 137). The copper that remained was impure, being always contaminated with lead and retaining some of the silver.

The most important developments in the extraction of silver, however, were two processes introduced by H. L. Pattinson (1796–1858) and Alexander Parkes (1813–90) respectively for the removal of the metal from lead. Until 1833 this was done by cupellation, in which under the action of an air-blast the lead was converted to litharge and blown out in the molten state. This was continued until the lead–silver alloy contained about 8 per cent of silver, when it was tapped out. It was then refined again in a similar way, the fire being increased towards the

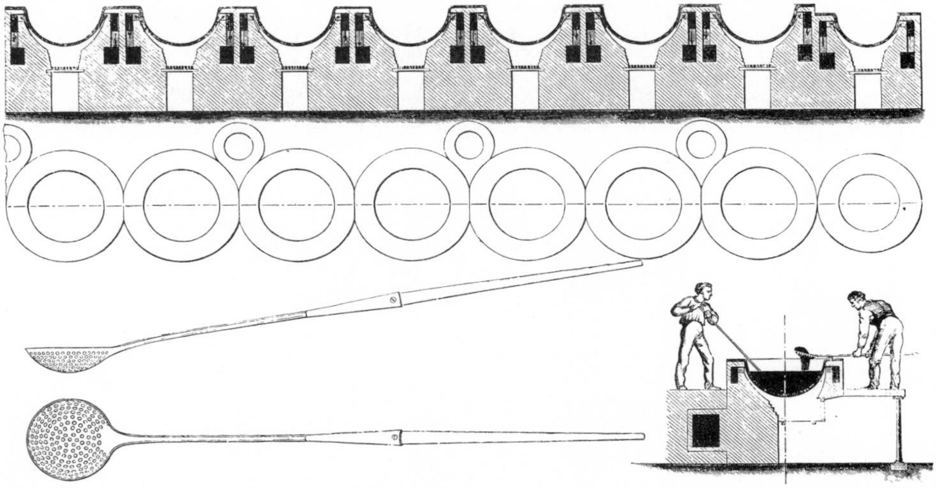

FIGURE 83—*Pattinson's process, 1833.* (Above) *Section and plan of cast iron pots and fires.* (Below) *Removal of lead crystals with perforated ladles. The small pot on the right was for melting pure lead.*

end of the operation and the silver kept molten until all the lead had been removed.

A much greater recovery of the silver became possible after 1829. In that year Pattinson, of Newcastle upon Tyne, discovered that when molten argentiferous lead is cooled until it begins to crystallize, the first crystals to separate are of pure lead. From this observation a new process of separation was worked out and patented in 1833 (figure 83). A row of eight or ten cast iron pots, each large enough to contain 5 tons of molten lead, was arranged in a brickwork gallery with a fire under each pot. The lead was put into the middle pot, melted, skimmed, and allowed to cool with constant stirring. The crystals were removed in a perforated ladle, from which any molten metal was shaken off, and this was continued until about three-quarters to four-fifths of the original lead had been removed. The enriched lead that remained was then transferred to the next pot on the one side and the crystals to the next on the other side. The middle pot was recharged and the process was repeated until the pot of enriched lead was nearly full. This enriched charge was heated, and the process was repeated until 'lead riches', with 300 oz silver per ton, were obtained. They were then purified by cupellation in a reverberatory furnace. The new method was soon in use throughout the United Kingdom, and about 1850 was adopted in the lead foundries of France, Spain, and Prussia.

A further process, patented by Alexander Parkes of Birmingham in 1850, was based on the observation that when zinc and lead are melted together and

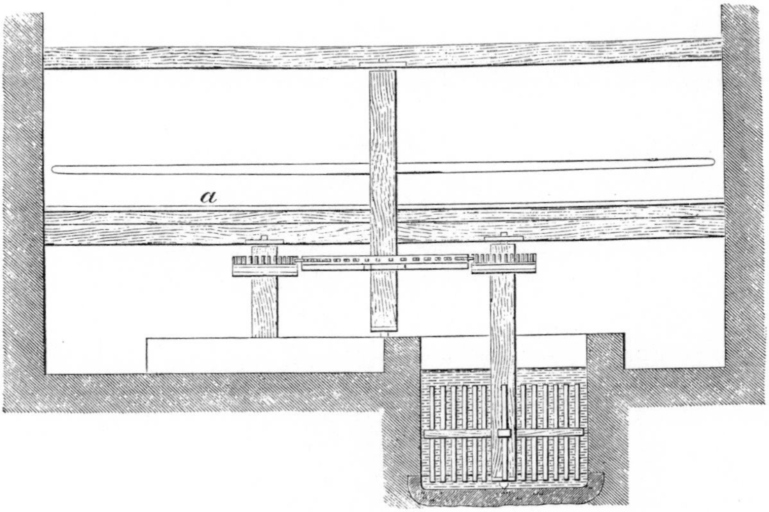

FIGURE 84—*Extraction of silver amalgam by washing*, c *1840. The stirring apparatus is worked by mules, walking on platform* (a). *The amalgam is taken out from the bottom of the vat* (bottom right).

allowed to cool, any silver present becomes concentrated in the zinc. The method used in 1851 was to add 22·4 lb zinc for every 14 oz silver in each ton of lead to be treated. On cooling the melt, the zinc–silver crystals that rose to the surface were drawn out in a perforated ladle. Lead and zinc were removed by heating to dull redness in air, skimming, and then removing the remaining zinc by means of acid or by distillation. The zinc in the impoverished lead left in the pot was separated by poling with green wood. By Parkes's method almost complete separation of the silver was effected, and it eventually superseded Pattinson's process. The method was not successfully operated in Germany until 1866.

Poor ores, worked for their silver content only, were often extracted by the amalgamation process, introduced in Mexico by Bartolomeo Medina, a miner of Pachuca, in 1557. This was a considerable achievement, for it was an intricate process, but the only one possible in a country deficient in both fuel and water-power. The method was taken to Peru in 1570, when the Spaniards were beginning to exploit the mercury in the area of Huancavelica. The amalgamation method was introduced into Hungary in 1786, and thence carried to Saxony,

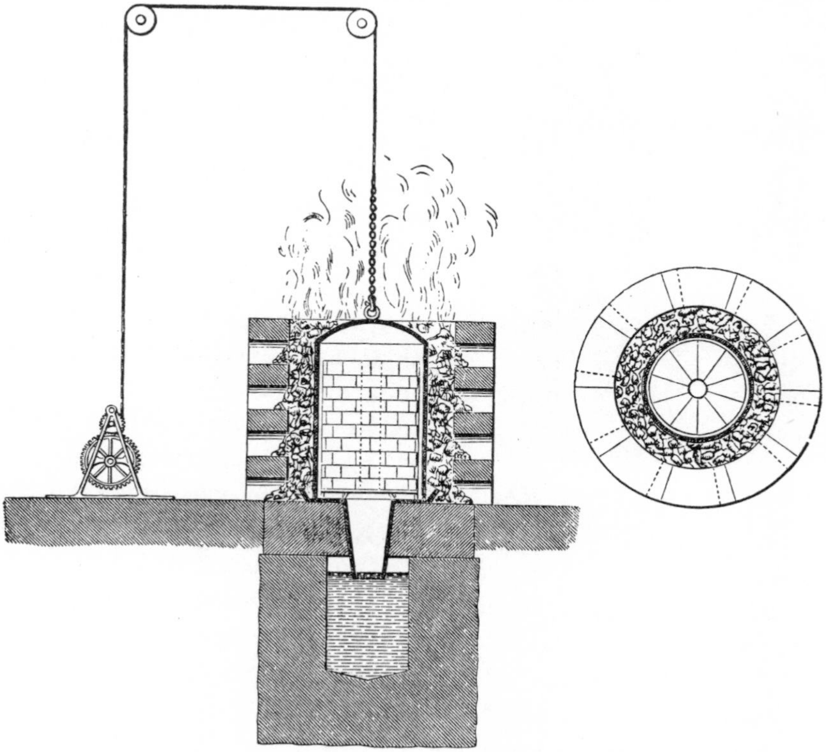

FIGURE 85—*Furnace for the pressed amalgam distilling, seen in section and plan. The amalgam was stacked in the centre of the apparatus and the mercury collected in the reservoir beneath it.*

when it was found that some Freiberg ores could be treated similarly to those of Oaxaca and other parts of Central America.

In America the ore was first stamped, and then pulverized with the addition of water until a mud or soft paste was formed. The fine state of division so obtained was essential to avoid great loss of mercury during the amalgamation. The paste was then placed in pits to dry. The amalgamation-floor was a flat, open space on which several heaps of crude sea-salt were arranged and covered with quantities of the paste. The materials were thoroughly mixed by turning over with shovels and prolonged treading by mules. Roasted and pulverized copper ore, such as copper pyrites, was then added and intimately mixed. Mercury was afterwards sprinkled over the heap by straining it through coarse cloth. Turning over and treading were repeated for several days until all the mercury had been incorporated.

The salt and copper ore reacted to give copper chloride, which in turn acted on the silver ore to give silver chloride. This with mercury gave mercury chloride, which was lost, and silver. Further quantities of mercury were then added so as to form an amalgam with the silver. The material was next transferred to large vats for washing, the earthy matter being separated from the heavy amalgam by constant stirring (figure 84). After all the earthy matter had flowed away, the amalgam was strained through leather to remove excess of mercury, and the semi-solid amalgam was distilled to liberate the silver (figure 85). The excess mercury contained some silver and was used again.

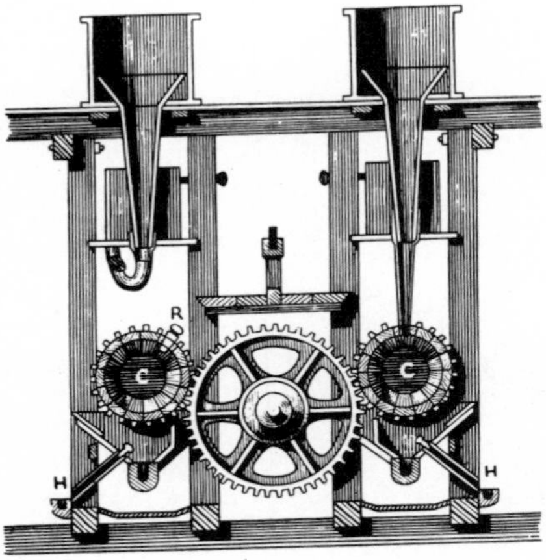

FIGURE 86—*Silver extraction by amalgamation in Saxony.*

When the method came to Europe in the late eighteenth century, fuel and water-power were used whenever possible to replace human and animal labour. The ore was mixed with iron pyrites and pulverized. Salt was then added and the mixture roasted in a reverberatory furnace. After grinding to a powder, the material was placed with mercury in casks arranged so that they could be rotated mechanically (figure 86). During the reaction the temperature rose and had to be controlled to prevent loss of mercury in a fine state during washing. After the amalgamation was complete, the casks (C) were filled with water and turned for two hours. The bungs (R) were then removed, stop-cocks were inserted, and the amalgam was run out into gutters (H) leading to a reservoir. The mercury was next distilled off by placing the amalgam in flat iron dishes and heating under a bell-shaped apparatus. The remaining silver was melted in open crucibles and cast into ingots containing about 80 per cent of silver, the remainder being mainly copper.

The chief methods of refining are mentioned later (p 142).

IX. GOLD

The only gold of commercial importance was the native metal, most commonly obtained by washing sand and gravel from the beds of streams and rivers and alluvial deposits in general. Plentiful supplies of water were necessary for this purpose, but not much equipment. The discovery of rich new sources of gold in California (1847) and eastern Australia (1851) caused world-wide excitement. In 1860 it was considered that a sand containing 1 part of gold in 36 000 was

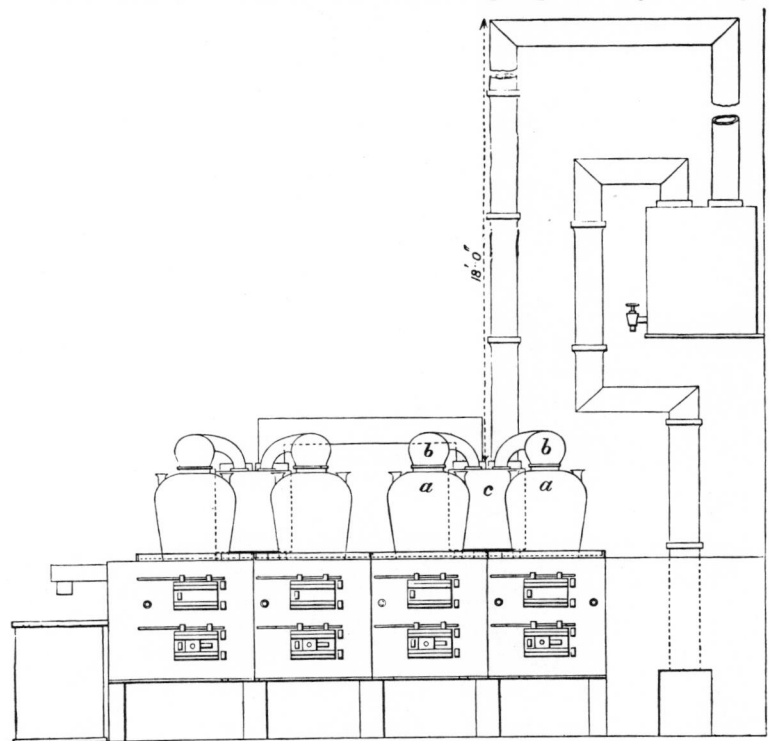

FIGURE 87—*Parting with nitric acid in platinum vessels, with arrangements for carrying off nitrous fumes: Johnson Matthey & Company,* c *1850. Each platinum vessel* (aa) *is set over a separate furnace;* bb, *still-heads. The receivers* (c) *are of earthenware.*

worth working; with modern chemical methods it later became profitable to extract gold occurring to the extent of only 1 part in 100 000 of quartz and 1 part in 3 000 000 of sand.

The process of amalgamation was introduced primarily to extract the fine particles of gold from the quartz in which it was often found dispersed, and by 1850 it was becoming generally realized that amalgamation was advantageous also in working alluvial sands.

Not much gold was obtained in Europe, the most important sources there being Hungary and Russia. For a time a novel method was used to extract gold from the arsenical pyrites at Reichenstein in Silesia: it was suggested by the analyst C. F. Plattner and earned a medal at the Great Exhibition of 1851. After roasting to remove arsenic, a current of chlorine was passed through the ore and the chlorides of iron and gold were removed with water. Hydrochloric acid was then added and hydrogen sulphide was passed through to precipitate the gold. The iron remained in solution.

X. REFINING PROCESSES FOR SILVER AND GOLD

Neither the silver nor the gold from the processes so far described was pure.

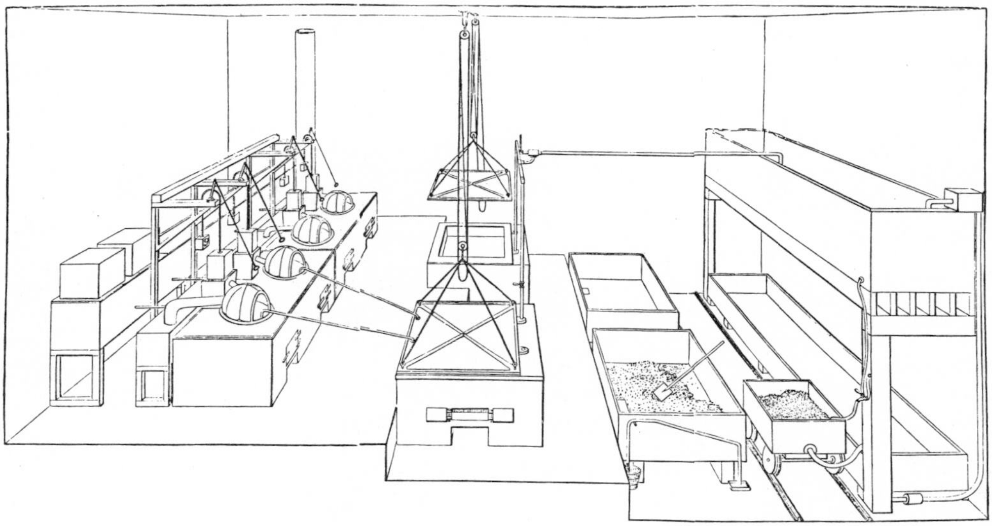

FIGURE 88—*Plant for parting silver bars with sulphuric acid by Gutzkow's method. San Francisco, c 1867.*

Silver often contained copper and some gold, while gold was frequently admixed with copper, silver, and the platinum metals. For some purposes the presence of copper in silver was not a serious disadvantage, but if necessary the silver could be melted with excess lead; the lead was removed by cupellation, carrying the copper with it. Similarly, although a number of chemical methods for detecting and separating platinum, which was sometimes used to debase gold, were worked out in the eighteenth century, they were not often conducted on a large scale. The most important operations were those used to separate silver and gold.

Several such methods were in use before 1700: for example, 'parting' with nitric acid, and with sulphur, sulphur and iron, sulphur and litharge, and antimony sulphide, in addition to the 'cementation' process. Parting with nitric acid was commonly carried out in platinum vessels (figure 87) when that metal became available, all the metals other than gold and platinum dissolving. When required free from copper, the silver was sometimes precipitated from the solution with salt.

A cheaper but nevertheless efficient method of parting, with sulphuric acid, was introduced about 1840 and was soon in use at the Royal Mint and in some refineries on the continent. By 1870 it was widely practised in Europe and

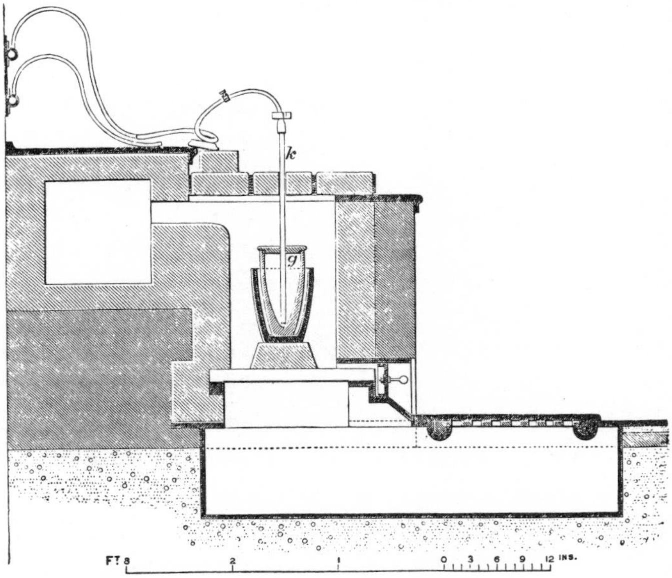

FIGURE 89—*Purification of gold by chlorine at Sydney,* c *1867. The gold is melted in the crucible* (g) *and chlorine is admitted through the pipe* (k).

America (figure 88). Vessels of cast iron were employed at first; after a time a change was made to platinum, but later there was a return to cast iron. The silver was dissolved in strong boiling sulphuric acid (figure 88, left), when the gold and any platinum formed a sediment. Copper, lead, and tin also dissolved but they could be largely removed by throwing the mass into water. Before 1830 the limit to parting by any of the methods then available was 0·08 per cent of gold; with the sulphuric acid method it was 0·03 to 0·05 per cent, a considerable advantage with such a valuable metal.

By the end of our period two other methods had been developed. In the first, which was adopted at the Sydney mint, gold was refined by chlorine in special crucibles (figure 89) made by Payen of Paris and Morgan of Battersea. The gold was melted and borax added. On passing chlorine through, fumes consisting of the volatile chlorides of the baser metals were emitted. After a time these fumes ceased and chlorine was then absorbed until all the silver had been acted upon: the operation was known to be complete when free chlorine passed through. The melt was then cooled until the gold solidified, when the liquid silver chloride was poured off. The chloride was made into slabs and arranged alternately with slabs of iron or zinc in a vessel containing acidulated water. This was fitted up as a cell, and the silver was purified electrolytically.

XI. THE PLATINUM METALS

The name 'platina' (a diminutive form of the Spanish *plata*, silver) was given in South America to the very heavy metal, somewhat resembling silver, that was sometimes found alloyed with gold. It was first reported in Europe in 1736 by Antonio d'Ulloa (1716–95) and was much studied by chemists throughout the second half of the eighteenth century; this led to the discovery of other metals that occurred with it—palladium, rhodium, iridium, osmium, and ruthenium. At first platinum was obtained solely from South America, but during the nineteenth century alluvial deposits were worked in the Urals, and other sources were discovered in Germany, France, Spain, Hungary, and the Ratoo mountains in Borneo. Platinum washings were established on the western slopes of the Urals in 1824, the ore containing 70 to 88 per cent of platinum.

Platinum was freed from the other metals it contained as follows. To remove gold the metal was dissolved in *aqua regia*, the excess acid boiled off, and ammonium chloride added. This precipitated the platinum, and the gold chloride was separated by washing. Baser metals, such as iron, copper, and manganese, were removed by treating the metal grains with strong nitric and hydrochloric acids alternately until the base impurities were removed. The platinum was then redissolved in *aqua regia*, precipitated with ammonium chloride, and reduced, the latter merely by gradually raising the temperature to red heat. To prevent precipitation of the other metals of the platinum group, the solution in *aqua regia* was freed as much as possible from excess acid, and nitric acid was added before precipitation with ammonium chloride. The platinum black, or powder, obtained in this way, was pressed and beaten into sheets.

At St Petersburg (Leningrad) ore from the Urals was treated in a number of open platinum basins ranged on a sand-bath and covered with a glazed dome surmounted with a ventilator-pipe. It was heated for 8 to 10 hours with *aqua regia* and subsequently decanted, the platinum salt then being precipitated with aqueous ammonia. After settling, it was again decanted and cooled, when the iridium salt crystallized out. The precipitates were evaporated in porcelain vessels and heated to redness. The platinum powder was placed in a mould and pressed with a rammer; it was then baked in a porcelain kiln for 36 hours, after which it could easily be forged as required. This was a modification of the process known as Wollaston's method, which was also arrived at independently by L. N. Vauquelin (1763–1829).

Crucibles and other laboratory wares were manufactured by means of special moulds into which the powder was rammed. It was afterwards heated in an air-furnace, then in a very hot blast, and finally finished off on the anvil. In addition, the metal was employed for the equipment used in sulphuric acid rectifiers, in the construction of electric batteries, and in dentistry. It was not, however, used at this time for jewelry.

XII. COBALT AND NICKEL

The metal cobalt was obtained by the Swedish chemist Brandt in 1733 from the mineral cobalt or zaffre, long used to give a blue colour to glass. Until the second half of the nineteenth century the metal was scarcely more than a laboratory curiosity and was not extracted on the large scale. Some of its compounds, however, were in frequent use. The chloride, nitrate, and sulphate were sometimes employed as sympathetic inks, while the phosphate was used as the pigment known as Thenard's blue. Cobalt oxide and cobalt silicate (smalt) were in large demand and were prepared on the commercial scale in the following way. The ore was smelted and the regulus calcined, and the product was then dissolved in concentrated hydrochloric acid. After removing iron with milk of lime, copper and some other impurities were precipitated by means of a stream of hydrogen sulphide. The cobalt was then precipitated with bleaching-powder and the solid was dried and heated to red or white heat, giving blue oxide or 'prepared' oxide respectively. In England these oxides were made chiefly at Birmingham by the nickel refiners.

Smalt was obtained, mainly in Germany, by a method not greatly different from that practised in earlier times (vol III, p 703), by roasting the ore to impure oxide and then vitrifying it with pulverized quartz and calcined potash in an oven resembling a glass-furnace.

Nickel was recognized as a distinct metal by Axel Cronstedt (1722–65) in 1751. He obtained it from *Kupfernickel*, or false copper, an ore resembling one of copper but from which copper could not be obtained. It was chiefly extracted from this ore, mined in Germany and Norway, or from ores containing nickel and cobalt. *Kupfernickel* was first roasted to remove arsenic, and was then mixed with sulphur and potash and fused in a large earthenware crucible. After this treatment warm water was added, when arsenic and sulphur, which had reacted with the potash, were removed. The nickel sulphides, usually contaminated with iron, were then dissolved in sulphuric acid and a little nitric acid. The nickel and iron were precipitated from the solution as carbonates and treated with oxalic acid. The nickel oxalate was separated by dissolving it in ammonia, and on evaporating the solution to dryness and strongly heating the residue in a luted crucible a globule of nickel was obtained.

In the nineteenth century a different method was used at Birmingham. The ore or speiss was fused with chalk and fluorspar, powdered, and then roasted to expel arsenic. The residue was dissolved in hydrochloric acid, and the iron was oxidized with bleaching-powder and precipitated with milk of lime. The liquid was next treated with hydrogen sulphide to remove impurities such as copper, bismuth, and lead. This left cobalt and nickel in solution. On adding bleaching-powder, the cobalt was precipitated. Milk of lime was then added to the remaining solution until no more precipitate was given.

Nickel was used mainly in alloys, the chief of which was German silver, sometimes used as a substitute for silver or for cheaper plated articles. The normal composition was 1 part nickel, 1 part zinc, and 2 parts copper, but if the alloy were intended for rolling the proportions of nickel and copper were raised somewhat, a common formula being 5 parts of nickel to 4 of zinc and 12 of copper. For casting, a small amount of lead was added to the latter. By 1860 a number of alloys were distinguished in the English midlands, having the following approximate compositions:

	Copper per cent	*Nickel per cent*	*Zinc per cent*	*Use and chief characteristics*
Common German silver .	60	15	25	Cheap wares. Minimum nickel feasible to avoid tarnishing.
Good German silver . .	55	20	25	Better wares, near silver in appearance.
Electrum (normal) . .	51·5	26	22·5	Slight blue shade, like polished silver. Better wares.
Electrum (richest) . .	46	34	20	Highest proportion of nickel feasible. Best wares only.
Tutenag (Chinese alloy) .	46	17	37	For casting; very hard and fusible.

At this time nickel-plated articles were coming into favour, the metal being deposited electrolytically with a nickel slab as anode and nickel chloride as electrolyte.

XIII. MANGANESE

Though the character of manganese compounds was known in the eighteenth century through the work of C. W. Scheele (1742–86) and J. G. Gahn (1745–1818), the extraction of the metal was difficult and it remained a laboratory process until late in the nineteenth century. Some manganese compounds were, however, widely used, particularly the common black oxide. This and other oxides were required in large quanitites for making glass and pottery and for preparing chlorine for the manufacture of bleaching-powder. Manganese sulphate was used in dyeing and calico-printing.

BIBLIOGRAPHY

Much information for this period is collected in the following works, among others:

DUPORT, H. ST CLAIR. 'De la production des métaux précieux au Mexique.' Paris. 1843.
GRAY, S. F. 'The Operative Chemist.' London. 1828.
MUSPRATT, J. S. 'Chemistry, Theoretical, Practical, and Analytical as applied and relating to the Arts and Manufactures' (2 vols). Glasgow. 1853, 1861.
PERCY, J. 'Metallurgy', Vols 1, 3, 5. London. 1861–80.
URE, A. 'A Dictionary of Arts, Manufactures and Mines.' London. 1837–9.

The following illustrate various aspects of the subject:

'Copper through the Ages.' Copper Development Association, London. 1934.
DICKINSON, H. W. 'Matthew Boulton.' University Press, Cambridge. 1937.
GUILLET, L. 'L'Évolution de la métallurgie.' Alcan, Paris. 1928.
HAMILTON, H. 'The English Brass and Copper Industries to 1800.' Longmans, London. 1926.
'History of Henry Wiggin & Company, Ltd., 1835–1935.' Henry Wiggin & Co., Birmingham. 1935.
LIPPMANN, E. O. VON. 'Die Geschichte des Wismuts zwischen 1400 und 1800.' Springer, Berlin. 1930.
MCDONALD, D. 'Percival Norton Johnson: The Biography of a Pioneer Metallurgist.' Johnson Matthey, London. 1951.
PAIRPOINT, F. 'Antique Plated Ware' (4th ed.). Pairpoint Brothers, London. 1925.
PURSEY, L. N. W. "The Champions of Bristol." *Discus*, 11, 1955.
'The Platinum Metals Exhibition.' Institution of Metallurgists, London. 1953.

Chilian mill for crushing silver ores.

5

POWER TO 1850

R. J. FORBES

I. THE INDUSTRIAL REVOLUTION

During the last 250 years five great new prime movers have produced what is often called the Machine Age. The eighteenth century brought the steam-engine; the nineteenth the water-turbine, the internal combustion engine, and the steam-turbine; and the twentieth the gas-turbine. Historians have often coined catch-phrases to denote movements or currents in history. Such is 'The Industrial Revolution', the title for a development often described as starting in the early eighteenth century and extending through much of the nineteenth [1]. It was a slow movement, but wrought changes so profound in their combination of material progress and social dislocation that collectively they may well be described as revolutionary if we consider these extreme dates.

The roots of this revolution stretch back into the sixteenth century, when important technological changes slowly began to take place. These had gained momentum by the middle of the eighteenth century. Outside Britain the revolution was far from complete even by 1880; thus Germany cannot be said even to have entered the industrial stage before the 1870s. In the United States, though it began early in the 1860s, it did not obtain a firm grip until the turn of the century. Economically the basic factor in the industrial revolution was the remarkable expansion of overseas trade in the seventeenth and eighteenth centuries. The new markets came first, the inventions followed. Unconsciously, the successful inventors worked within the limits laid down for them by the changing society in which they dwelt and the new materials that were becoming available.

That the industrial revolution first gained momentum in the British Isles and that its results first began to become most clearly visible in Scotland and the midland counties of England may be ascribed to many fortuitous factors. Britain, by conquering the seas, established the largest foreign markets; she had the necessary capital for industrial experiments, a currency firmly based on gold, an efficient banking system, political and social stability, abundance of iron ore and coal, a humid climate suitable for textile manufacture, and social circles interested in scientific knowledge. The economic demands were met by scientific and technological advances of an increasingly high standard. Much of the new science of the seventeenth century had from the beginning stressed the importance of practical aims.

From the days of Stevin (1548–1620) and Galileo (1564–1642) the science of mechanics yielded fresh understanding of machines, particularly when, in the eighteenth century, mathematics came to be constantly applied to the theory and practice of their construction. That century also saw the start of experiment on the strength of materials, and thus notably contributed to practical mechanics

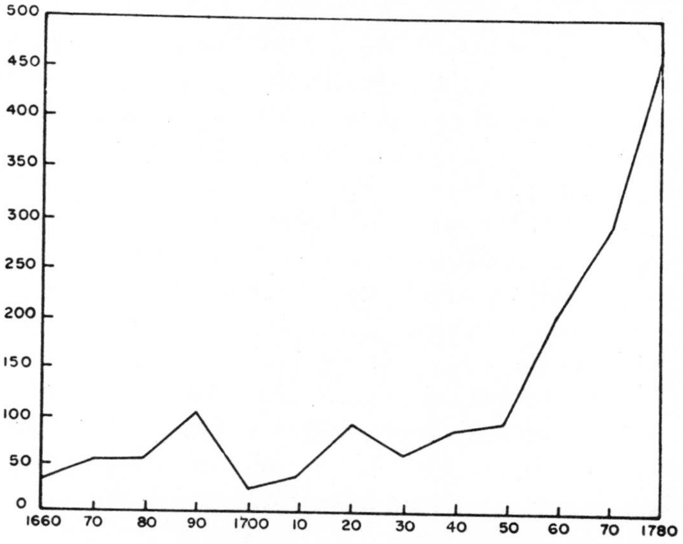

FIGURE 90—*Numbers of patents of inventions, 1660–1780.*

and the design of well built engines. Exact measurement, the very basis of science, was becoming ever more important for the design and maintenance of all complex mechanisms. Moreover, practical engineering itself had gained momentum [2]. The classical world had been seriously concerned with the study and control of motion, though several factors, notably slave labour, had kept power resources at a low level (vol II, ch 17). Subsequent developments had involved changes in scale rather than in principle. In the words of Usher, 'these developments may seem to be little more than a diffusion of knowledge already attained. For a long time, no additional theoretical knowledge would have been of much practical use. It would be an error, however, to minimize the magnitude of the technological changes that opened up the first extensive applications of power. It was the beginning of an essentially new stage in mechanical technique' [3].

By the mid-seventeenth century there were many who saw clearly that co-operation between science and practical engineering formed the essential basis of technical improvements. In this century and the following one there was a notable rise in the number of patents (figure 90). Adam Smith (1723–90) realized that these improvements were not only the work of practical engineers but that 'some came to be by the ingenuity of those men of speculation, whose trade it is not to do anything, but to observe everything; and who, upon that account, are often capable of combining together the powers of the most distant and dissimilar objects'.

The four basic technical achievements of the industrial revolution were:

1. *Replacement of tools by machines.* Both enable man to perform certain operations more dextrously than with the bare hand. The chief difference is that the tool is set in motion by man's physical strength, the machine by some natural force. The word machine is here used in the eighteenth-century sense, for both then and long afterwards no proper distinction was made between prime movers and other machinery. This is clear from the definition given in 1875 by Reuleaux [4]: 'A machine is a combination of solid parts so contrived that by means of it natural forces can be made to cause certain definite motions.'

2. *The introduction of new prime movers.* The new machines demanded a new prime mover, for the older ones had grave limitations. Wind was cheap but unreliable, water was limited by local conditions, but steam suffers neither disadvantage. It is independent of the weather and the seasons. The invention of the steam-engine is the central fact in the industrial revolution.

3. *The universally available prime mover.* The power of the steam-engine could be created where needed. This mobility is the most characteristic feature of the Machine Age, and made possible the industrialization of many countries that had no great resources of water-power. Moreover, the steam-engine proved capable of producing much more power than the older prime movers, and thus in time it raised energy-output to a significantly higher level.

4. *The factory as a new form of organization of production.* Factories were built long before the advent of the steam-engine. Thus the early textile mills and ironworks were of this type, rather than of the workshop type so characteristic of medieval and earlier technology. In the eighteenth century, however, the word factory was not used in its present sense. A factory then was merely a shop, a warehouse, or a depot, and only by the end of the century was the word used for mills or machine-factories. The word mill was much more common, for the machine that first caught the eye was usually the great water-wheel. Not only the flour mills but the ironworks and foundries with their hammers and bellows

were worked by water-wheels in sixteenth-century England, and so were the first cotton mills. The first legal use of the word factory is in the Textile Factory Act of 1844. The concentration of machines driven by steam-engines had become a characteristic feature of the industrial revolution by 1800, but certainly not the only one; much of the manufacturing still took place in workshops, and the part of factories in the industrial revolution has been overstressed.

II. THE EARLIER COMPETITORS OF THE STEAM-ENGINE

The steam-engine did not rapidly displace the earlier prime movers. It was some time before it had been sufficiently developed as a prime mover with an appreciably higher average energy-output. Mobility alone was not enough to displace the treadmill, the water-wheel, and the windmill. In fact, the earlier phase of the industrial revolution was certainly not characterized by the steam-engine. Windmills still dotted many a landscape. Water was the main source of power in eighteenth-century England, driving fulling-stocks, millstones, saws, bellows, and ore-crushers. The new textile inventions came in an area of hills, valleys, and streams, and the early mills were built on river-banks. The pioneers of the industrial revolution hardly thought in terms of steam-engines. Wyatt pictured the mechanized textile industry as a kind of mill with wheels turned either by horses, by water, or by wind. Lewis Paul (d 1759) and he used two donkeys for their first machines; Cartwright drove his invention with a cow; Arkwright speaks of a 'water-frame'; and the first two power-looms in Scotland (1793) were worked by a Newfoundland dog.

For many industries in the sixteenth and seventeenth centuries, the obstacles to the use of power were cost and physical availability rather than the mechanical difficulty of application. The capital involved was large relative to the amount of power generated, so that power-using devices were not generally preferred to mechanisms actuated by the workman. Much early machinery was concerned with exchanging low intensities exerted through long distances for high intensities exerted through short distances. Many machines were designed so as to make it a simple matter to arrange for them to be driven by any prime mover capable of producing rotary motion. But until power became cheap, reliable, and generally available, there was no purpose in attempting to run them from a specialized power-plant.

In the eighteenth century no factory could be established far from a stream powerful and swift enough to work its machines. Mill-owners therefore crowded in narrow valleys, where an artificial fall could be secured by using dams. Hence the importance of the valleys of the Pennine range for eighteenth-century British industry. This continued as long as water was the driving-power of machinery, but the introduction of steam gradually brought industrial ruin to those districts where no coal was available locally.

In many other parts of England the water was mostly slow-flowing. Even the

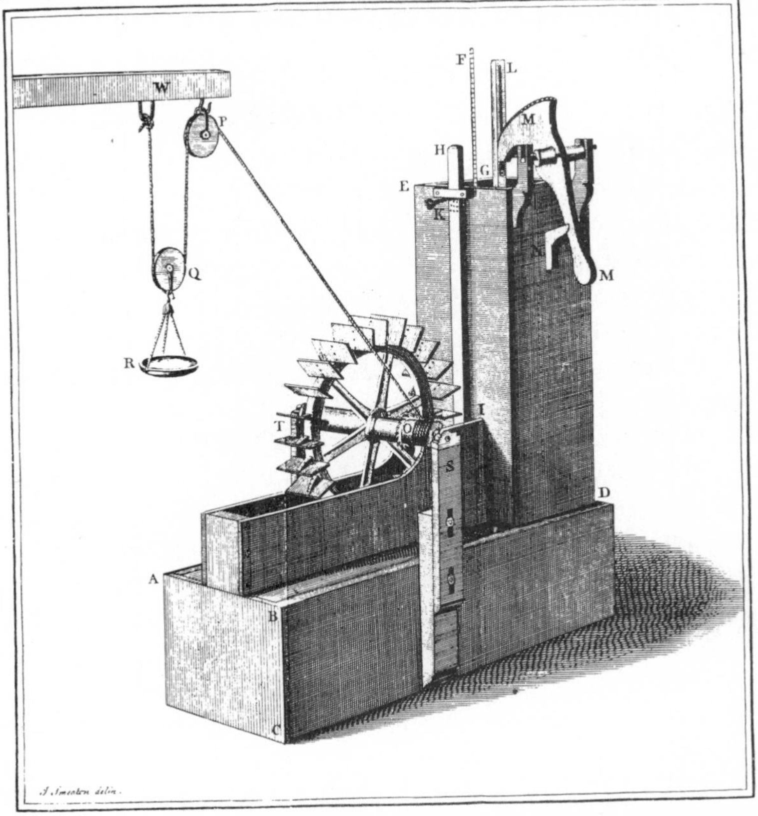

FIGURE 91—*Smeaton's model for measuring the power of undershot water-wheels.* ABCD, *cistern to receive water;* DE, *cistern to receive water raised by pump;* FG, *float marked in inches;* HI, *rod to open sluice;* K, *peg to hold* HI; GL, *upper part and pump;* MM, *handle for pump;* N, *catch to check* MM; O, *cylinder with cord that goes over pulleys* P *and* Q *to raise* R, *the pan with weights;* W, *beam;* S *and* T, *devices to adjust level of wheel.*

little water-power that was available was wasted by the clumsy systems of wheels and troughs used to collect and transmit it. The only practicable method was to create artificial waterfalls. The water had then to be raised to the level of a reservoir by a pump. It was for raising water that the first steam-engines came into use.

In the eighteenth century, competition for available water-supplies became very keen, notably in the midlands. In the seventeenth century the rolling-mills, paper-works, and similar enterprises began to congregate about the Tame and Stour. Arthur Young (1741–1820) commented at the end of the eighteenth century on the small use of water at Birmingham and other metallurgical centres in the midlands. He was surprised at the amount of work done by hand without

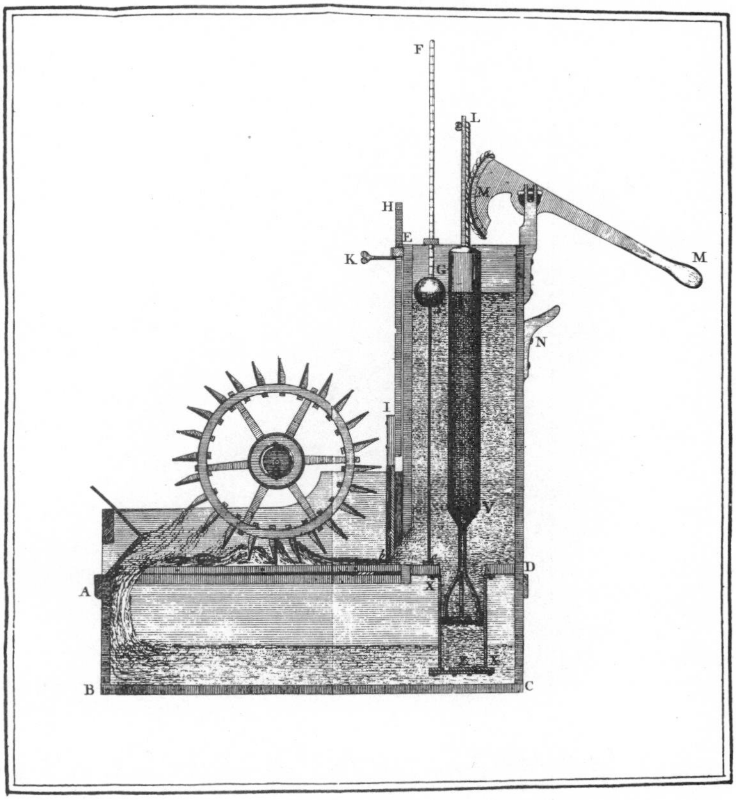

FIGURE 92—*Cross-section of Smeaton's model for measuring the power of undershot water-wheels, cf figure 91.* XX, *pump-barrel 5 inches in diameter and 11 in long;* V, *piston;* Z, *valve. By a modification of the model the power developed by an overshot wheel could be calculated.*

the aid of machinery. The midlands were badly in need of water-power, and this need, combined with the needs of the collieries, stimulated the search for a new source of power.

About the middle of the eighteenth century the combined use of Newcomen engines and water-wheels was found everywhere. Early Watt engines were similarly used. Indeed, the steam-engine would have remained an accessory to the water-mill, pumping up the water that worked the wheel, had not Watt by his invention of the 'sun-and-planet motion' and his 'parallel motion' (ch 6) solved the problem of converting the oscillation of the beam into rotary motion. About 1780 Richard Arkwright used a Newcomen pump as an accessory to his 'hydraulick machine', and the first steam spinning-mill was set up for Robinson at Papplewick, Nottinghamshire, in 1785.

FIGURE 93—*Water-wheels at Marly-la-Machine for supplying the fountains at Versailles, 1725.*

It would be interesting to establish the energy-output from the water-wheels with which the steam-engine had to compete in its early stages, but unfortunately the data are very meagre. No theoretical calculations or considerations entered into the construction of the first water-wheels. With experience in the construction of gears and transmission of power during the sixteenth and seventeenth centuries, water-wheels became more efficient and attempts were made to calculate their capacities. Most of them in the sixteenth century were undershot; Olaus Magnus (1555) is among the few who illustrate overshot wheels. The first to make serious attempts at measuring the power-output of water-wheels was John Smeaton [5] (figures 91, 92). In 1759 he laid down certain rules for the determination of the theoretical energy-output and the amount of energy consumed in overcoming the friction of the wheel's parts (p 203). He showed on theoretical grounds that 'the effect therefore of overshot wheels, under the same circumstances of quantity and fall, is at medium double that of the undershot.

FIGURE 94—*Inside the wheel-house at Marly-la-Machine as reconstructed in the mid-nineteenth century.*

The higher the wheel is in proportion to the whole descent, the greater will be its effect.'

From the figures available for eighteenth-century water-wheels we can conclude that their energy-output was seldom better than 10 hp, and on the average only 5 hp. This poor record was mainly due to the limitation of water-power in Britain and to the primitive gearing and consequent loss of power in transmission. The largest series of water-wheels was the colossal 'machine of Marly' built for Louis XIV by the Liège carpenter Rennequin in 1682 (figures 93, 94). It had a potential capacity of 124 hp and delivered at least 75 hp in actual work, but owing to faulty maintenance it had less than one-fortieth of its original capacity by 1796. Nevertheless, even when the output of the steam-engine rose above the average of 10 hp, it did not quickly displace the water-wheel. Water-wheels continued to play an important part in the mechanized industries of England till at least 1850. Cotton, the steam industry *par excellence*, still drew a quarter of its power from water in 1830 and one-seventh in 1850. The other textile industries drew even more of their energy from water. Only where there was no water-power was the steam-engine rapidly adopted.

The windmill was not a popular prime mover in eighteenth-century England, but it played an important part on the coasts of the North Sea and the Baltic. Since the windmill came to western Europe many improvements had been made in it [6] (vol III, ch 4). It was used not only for grinding corn but in mining, especially in central Europe. This was not something novel, for a fifteenth-century manuscript from Bohemia shows a hoist in a mine moved by a windmill. The sixteenth century saw many new applications of the windmill. Cornelis Dircksz Muys invented (1589) a marsh-mill with an inclined shaft rising from a low point, where it drove an Archimedean screw, to the necessary height. The *tjasker* still popular in Friesland is probably derived from this invention (vol III, figure 204).

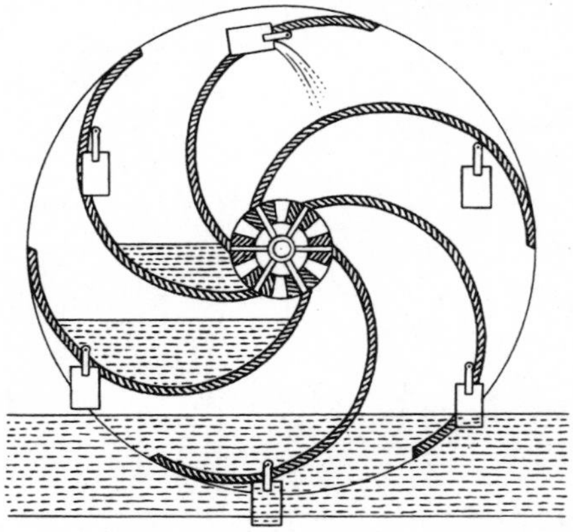

FIGURE 95—*Scoop-wheel for raising water. Early nineteenth century.*

Certain districts were favoured by nature. The banks of the river Zaan, west of Amsterdam, were flat, windy, and easily approached by water. This became the main industrial district of Holland. By the end of the seventeenth century it had 900 windmills (marsh-mills included). Wind-driven mills were built in the Zaan district after the French war of 1672, when paper-making in the eastern provinces became too dangerous. Other industrial districts deriving their power from windmills were around the towns of Leiden, Rotterdam, and Dordrecht [7]. Many towns had windmills on their city-walls and fortifications, to raise water in war-time. Altogether the United Provinces had some 8000 windmills, 2000 of which survived in the year 1900. 1306 were still in existence in 1950, but many in a damaged state.

The introduction of the windmill as a prime mover did not proceed smoothly. The craftsmen's guilds of Holland protested against them in 1581, claiming that they would throw many craftsmen out of work. A mechanical saw worked by a windmill was built in 1766 at Limehouse, east of London, but was destroyed by a riotous mob two years later.

We have very few data on the energy-output of these windmills. The capacity of a mill depends on the velocity of the wind and the span of the sails. Taking a windmill with a span of 100 ft and modernized sails, we estimate the following figures for the power at the windshaft:

Velocity of wind (m/sec)	*Energy-output in*	
	hp	*kwh*
3	10	7
4	22	16
5	42	31
6	68	50
7	108	79
8	159	117
9 and over	227	167

Whereas modern windmills respond to a wind of 3 m/sec, the eighteenth-century form required one of at least twice this.

The standard works of the Dutch millwrights of that century [8] contain only constructional detail. The only early attempts at the calculation of windmill capacities concern marsh-mills. Simon Stevin wrote on them about 1590, when he was at work on improving the gearing and scoop-wheels of such mills. He not only obtained patents, but actually engaged in certain experiments with mills built according to his plans. In his account of this work, which was not printed until nearly 300 years later, he tried to calculate the amount of water thrown out by the scoop-wheel and the pressure on the sails needed to raise this water, but he omitted many factors. About 1600 Jan Adriaanszoon Leeghwater (1575–1650) measured the output of two marsh-mills, expressed as the fall of the level of the lake they pumped. Similar measurements, comparing a marsh-mill turning a scoop-wheel with one turning an Archimedean screw, were made near Leiden in 1763 [9]; the output in cubic feet of four marsh-mills near Rotterdam was measured in 1774–6 [10]; and a comparison of the efficiency of scoop-wheels (figure 95) and Archimedean screws was carried out in 1821–4 [11]. None contains accurate measurements of wind-velocities.

In 1759 John Smeaton reported [12] on his experiments on windmills and different forms of sails. He used windmill-models having a span of about 3½ ft, acted on by an artificial wind (figure 96). He thus avoided consideration of the turbulence of the wind, though he published a table giving a rough scale of winds expressed in feet per second. His experiments certainly established the changes with wind-velocity of the capacity of a known mill; but they told little of the actual capacity of windmills, for he lacked the proper instruments, and even units, with which to evaluate and express this energy.

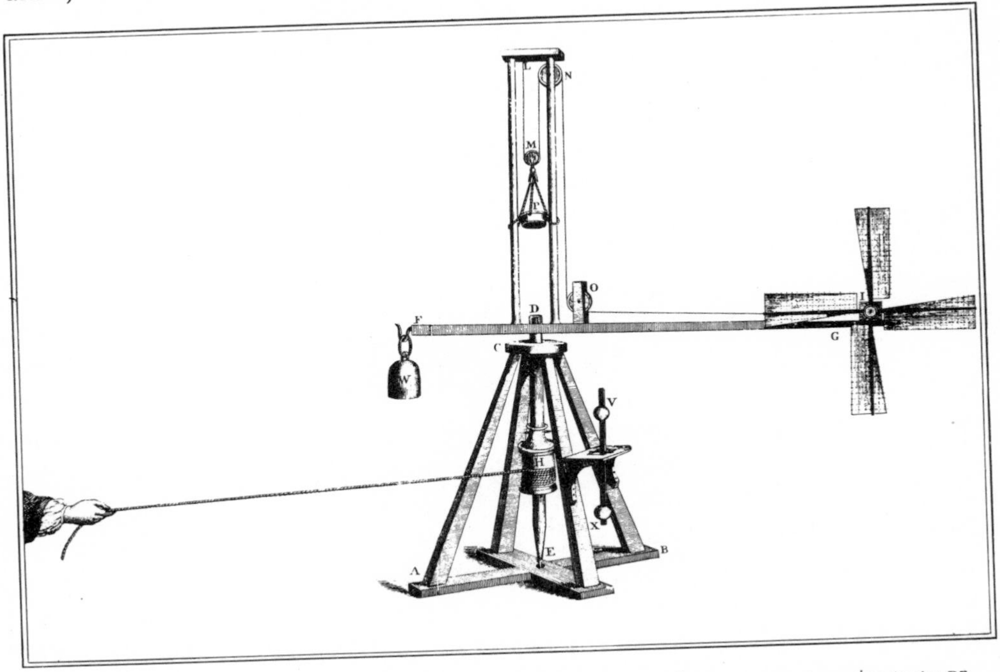

FIGURE 96—*Smeaton's model to measure the power of windmills.* ABC, *frame to support moving parts;* DE, *upright axis on which is* FG, *an arm to carry sails;* H, *barrel with cord round it to give circular motion to* FG, *allowing the sails to be directed to the wind.* L *fixes the line that goes over pulleys* MNO *and ends at barrel* I. *When the sails turn, the cord is wound up and raises* P, *a scale in which weights are placed;* VX, *adjustable pendulum for time measurement.*

Smeaton wrote:

Desaguliers makes the utmost power of a man, when working so as to be able to hold it for some hours, to be equal to that of raising a hogshead (63 ale gallons) of water ten feet high in a minute. When working at a mean rate, the 30 ft sail will be equal to the power of 18·3 men, or of 3·66 horses, reckoning 5 men to a horse; whereas the effect of the common Dutch sails, of the same length, will be scarce equal to the power of 10 men, or of 2 horses.

That these computations are not merely speculative, but will hold good when applied to works in large, I have had an opportunity of verifying; for in a mill with the enlarged sails of 30 ft, applied to the crushing of rape seed, by means of two runners upon the edge, for making oil, I observed, that when the sails made 11 turns in a minute, in which case the velocity of the wind was about 13 feet in a second, the runners then made 7 turns in a minute; whereas 2 horses, applied to the same two runners, scarcely worked at the rate of $3\frac{1}{2}$ turns in the same time.

The common Dutch windmill of the eighteenth century had a span of 100 ft and a windshaft some 45 to 50 ft above the ground. According to Smeaton's calculations it should have had an energy-output of some 10 hp, and this agrees quite well with modern measurements. The smaller Dutch windmills with 24-ft sails were found to give 4·5 brake-hp in a 20-mile wind. Interesting estimates were obtained with an old marsh-mill of the large type, built about 1648 [13]. When pumping 35 cu m of water per minute against a head of 2 m and with an average wind-velocity of 8 to 9 m/sec it produced 40 hp on the windshaft, the actual output being only 15·6 hp (39 per cent). Therefore 61 per cent of the energy derived from the wind was lost in transmission. Further experiments with modern sails and improved gear showed that the eighteenth-century mill would produce an average of 10 hp. This could be improved to 13 to 14 hp by increasing the moment of inertia of the sails, and to 18 to 20 hp by using more modern sails. Changing the gearing-system and using modern sails might raise the output to some 30 hp, but this represents the maximum attainable without changes in construction such as are to be seen in the modern wind-motor. Similar results have been obtained with other eighteenth-century Dutch marsh-mills. They needed a wind-velocity of 8 to 9 m/sec to work efficiently and they produced 10 to 12 hp, or 15 hp at the utmost, in an average wind. All this agrees well with the ratings of the various prime movers as given by Rankine and d'Aubuisson:

Man working a pump	0·036	hp
Man turning a crank	0·04–0·078	,,
Man pushing a capstan bar	0·047	,,
Horse turning a gin at a walk	0·367–0·578	,,
Various 18-foot overshot wheels	2–5	,,
Post windmill	2–8	,,
Turret windmill	6–14	,,

Smeaton used cast iron to strengthen parts of the windmill, but this practice spread slowly and the windmill remained essentially a wooden construction. Its maximum was about 50 hp on the windshaft, but it lost much of this in transmission through the use of wooden cog-wheels and pinions—though these had the advantage of damping down vibrations better than cast iron parts do. The windmill reached the upper limits of its evolution in the eighteenth century, then inevitably gave way to the steam-engine when this prime mover developed more energy more cheaply.

In the east, the windmill had the form of a circle of sails acting on a vertical axle (vol II, p 615). Wind-turbines were occasionally tried there, which is interesting in view of the later development of the turbine [14]. They are not mentioned in the Dutch handbooks on windmills of the eighteenth century, but

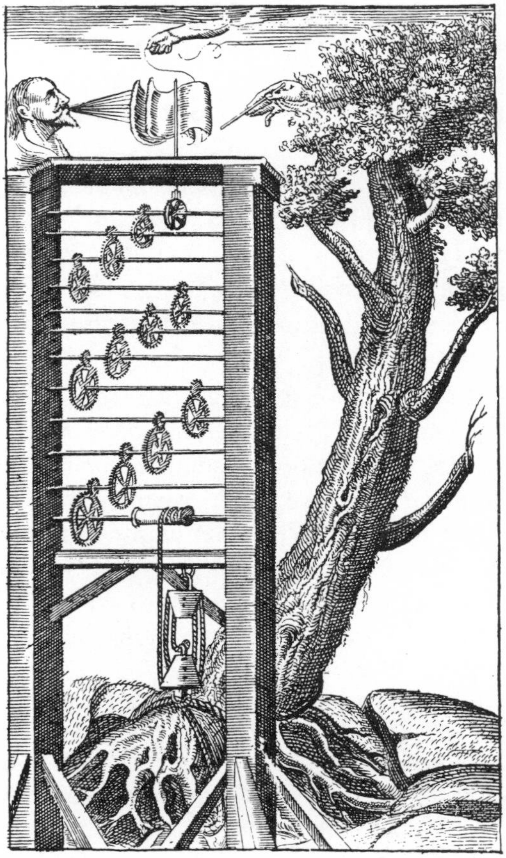

FIGURE 97—*Wind-turbine. The roots of the oak are supposed to extend over about ½ sq mile and the weight of soil on them is taken to be 4000 m lb. By means of two double pulleys and 12 wheels it was calculated that a small windmill could uproot the tree.*

Dutch patents for mills worked by wind-turbines go back to the seventeenth century (cf figure 97). The hot-air turbine, though never developing into a prime mover, occupied the attention of many a famous engineer. In the period we are discussing it took the form of the blades of a fan moved by the hot air rising in a chimney, the fan in its turn moving gears that turned a spit on which meat was roasted. Early designs are found in manuscripts of the sixteenth century from

Leonardo da Vinci onwards. It became known as the chimney-wheel, draft-mill, and smoke-jack, and is illustrated by Branca (p 168) and others (figure 98). Some even contemplated making it move a roller-mill for iron bars.

III. THE STEAM-ENGINE AS A PRIME MOVER

The coal-mines and the iron industry proved the best promoters of the steam-engine [15]. Scarcity of charcoal and limitation of water-power were economic

FIGURE 98—(A) *Proposed chimney-wheel by which hot air rising up a chimney was to work a rolling-mill.* (B) *Proposed stamp-mill, to be worked by hot air.*

threats to the iron industry of the eighteenth century. Many attempts were made to break this tyranny of wood and water. In 1757 Isaac Wilkinson took out a patent for a new machine or 'bellows . . . so that a furnace, forge or any other works may be blowed from any waterfall or falls . . . to several miles distant by means of a pipe'. This was never used and, until late in the century, iron-works continued to use direct water-power. Inadequacy in the fall of water caused a tendency to separate the smelting and the finishing of the metal. The adaptation of the steam-engine to crushing ores in iron-works discouraged this separation. More important still, Watt's engine freed the ironmasters from their dependence on constant supplies of running water for their bellows, hammers, and mills.

Before its introduction it was estimated that the average period of working in iron-works was about forty weeks a year, but a season of drought might curtail this considerably and bring financial loss to the masters and distress to the workers. Attempts at economy of water had been made with various devices; at Coalbrookdale the water that had passed over the wheel was raised above it again by a Newcomen engine, and at Furness hand-pumps had been used for the same purpose. Steam-power meant that the iron-works could be carried on with cheap mineral fuel, so that there was no reason for the separation of furnace, forge, and mill that had characterized the iron industry in the early years of the century.

By the end of the same century the coal-pits throughout the midlands had also come to rely largely on the steam-engine for their working. This meant heavy capital expenditure, since a Newcomen engine cost about £1500 to install, but the investment was well worth the while of the larger enterprises. The change had come about because Boulton had had the Kinneil steam-engine designed by Watt brought down from Scotland and had turned his Soho (Birmingham) works into the prototype of the modern factory. The first two steam-engines built by the firm of Boulton and Watt were erected at Bloomfield colliery in Staffordshire and at John Wilkinson's new foundry at Broseley, Salop, respectively.

Certain factors, however, prevented the rapid displacement of the earlier prime movers by the steam-engine. The early machine-builders were handicapped by want of skilled engineers. Their engines were built by a miscellaneous collection of blacksmiths, wheel-wrights, and carpenters, as their designs show clearly. Only too often the parts refused to work when put together. Watt found that a cylinder made by the best workmen available in Glasgow varied by three-eighths of an inch in diameter, and Smeaton told him 'that neither tools nor workmen existed that could manufacture so complex a machine with sufficient precision'. John Wilkinson, however, could tool metal with a limit of error not exceeding 'the thickness of a thin sixpence' in a diameter of 72 inches. No wonder that Watt avoided applying high-pressure steam in his engines (p 182), even though this was the only way to higher thermal efficiency and energy-output.

The builders of the first engines had therefore both to train the necessary specialists to build their machines, and to devise means of finishing their parts with sufficient precision. Prime movers had hitherto been of wood with few metal parts; steam demanded stronger and more durable material. The way to precision was to clamp the relevant tool and material firmly in a machine; then the tool could be adjusted and guided to do its work of grinding, boring, slotting, drilling, turning, or cutting (vol III, pp 334–6). Maudslay's slide-rest of 1794 was the first of a series of such fundamentally important machine-tools developed by the new engineers, but the co-operation of science and mechanical engineering was not yet sufficiently close to allow a rapid advance.

When Watt's patent expired in 1800 there were 496 Watt engines at work in Britain in mines, metal plants, textile factories, and breweries. Of these 308 were rotative engines and 164 pumping-engines, while 24 were for producing blast-air. One or two were rated at 40 hp, but the average capacity was only 15 to 16 hp and therefore not significantly higher than that of the windmill and the water-wheel. The steam-engine profited by its relative mobility and its dependence on coal rather than on the fickle elements, but it could have revolutionized technology only very slowly if it had stopped at this point.

The real development of the steam-engine into a new and stronger prime mover came between 1800 and 1850. In the earlier days of Watt the nascent theory of heat had had some influence on the development of the steam-engine, but it was not yet ready to assist in the proper calculation of such engines. The engineers themselves had by trial and error found the means of introducing high pressure, and they made the methods of transmission of energy from engine to machinery less cumbersome. Several branches of science provided new knowledge useful for the building of steam-engines. The science of applied mechanics was gradually extended after the testing of materials by such men as Coulomb and La Hire had yielded practical rules for calculating the proper dimensions of engine parts. The rise of the art of bridge-building (ch 15) contributed much to the calculation of the constructional details of steam-engines. Tools and methods were devised to measure elasticity and the different stresses acting on parts of the engine. The inquiry into friction and its importance in engine and transmission came rather later. Important also was the elaboration of the theory of gases by such men as Mariotte (1620–84), Gay-Lussac (1778–1850), and Regnault (1810–78).

Fundamental, too, was the further development of the theory of heat, not only in calorimetry and temperature measurement, but most of all in the rise of the new science of thermodynamics. The foundation of thermodynamics was laid by Sadi Carnot (1796–1832) in his 'Motive Power of Heat' [16]; he stated that the efficiency of an engine depended on the working substance and the temperature-drop between cylinder and condenser. In 1842 Robert Mayer (1814–78) calculated the work equivalent to a unit of heat. The law of conservation of energy—the first law of thermodynamics—was formulated in 1847 by Helmholtz (1821–94). Joule (1818–89) carefully measured the mechanical equivalent of heat (1843), and his work was later confirmed by Rankine (1820–72). Clausius (1822–88) finally reconciled Carnot's theory of heat and the discovered equivalence of heat and work, and was thus able to formulate the second law of thermodynamics, namely that heat cannot of itself pass from a colder to a hotter body. Only after the elaboration of these laws could real progress be achieved in designing steam-engines.

Earlier engineers found perplexity in expressing the power of their engines and comparing them. For the most part, figures are given expressing the engine's 'duty', the unit being one million ft-lb per bushel (84 lb) of coal. This allows us to calculate the thermal efficiency of the engine, but gives no accurate data on its power. The following data are reported [17]:

RECIPROCATING STEAM-ENGINES

Date	*Builder*	*Duty*	*Percentage thermal efficiency*
1718	Newcomen	4·3	0·5
1767	Smeaton	7·4	0·8
1774	Smeaton	12·5	1·4
1775	Watt	24·0	2·7
1792	Watt	39·0	4·5
1816	Woolf compound engine . .	68	7·5
1828	Improved Cornish engine . .	104	12·0
1834	,, ,, ,, . .	149	17·0
1878	Corliss compound engine . .	150	17·2
1906	Triple-expansion engine . .	203	23·0

The rapid rise in thermal efficiency in the early nineteenth century is remarkable.

Boulton and Watt speak of '20-horse engines', using a unit devised by Watt in 1783, each 'horse' being the power to lift 33 000 lb through one foot in a minute, but in fact the early engineers had great difficulty in finding a proper unit of work. Boulton and Watt built their engines in series of 4 to 30 horses and 36 to 100 horses, the '20-horse engine' being the most popular one. Thomas Young (1773–1829), discussing the efficiency of the steam-engine, said:

The daily work of a horse is equal to that of five or six men, the strength of a mule is equal to that of three or four men. The expense of keeping a horse is generally twice or thrice as great as the hire of a day labourer, so that the force of horses may be reckoned about half as expensive as that of men. . . . On the authority of Mr Boulton a bushel (84 lbs) of coal is equivalent to the daily labour of $8\frac{1}{3}$ men or perhaps more; the value of this quantity of coal is seldom more than that of the work of a single labourer for a day, but the expense of machinery generally renders a steam-engine somewhat more than half as expensive as the number of horses for which it is substituted [18].

Heat-economy and thermal efficiency were of the highest importance for the future of the steam-engine. Full exploitation required the introduction of high-pressure steam. Evans and Trevithick worked with a steam-pressure of 3·5 atm in 1810, this rising to 5 to 6 atm by 1830 (p 190). Between 1840 and 1850 many older engines were converted into high-pressure engines. However, the inter-

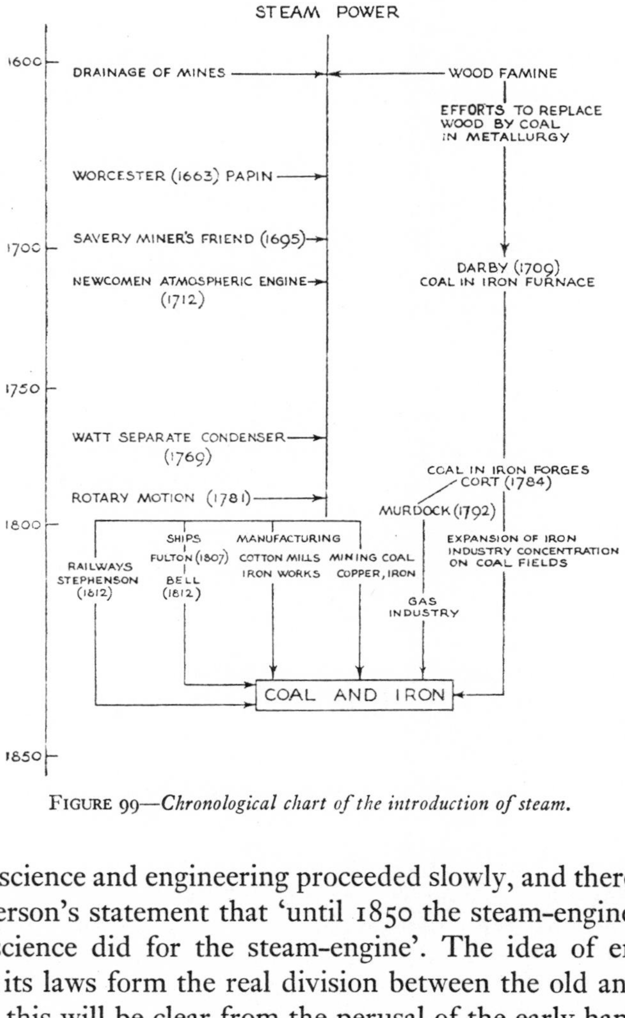

FIGURE 99—*Chronological chart of the introduction of steam.*

penetration of science and engineering proceeded slowly, and there is some truth in L. J. Henderson's statement that 'until 1850 the steam-engine did more for science than science did for the steam-engine'. The idea of energy and the recognition of its laws form the real division between the old and the new engineering, and this will be clear from the perusal of the early handbooks on the steam-engine by Farey [19] and Tredgold [20].

Hence the improvement of the steam-engine in the early nineteenth century was slow (figure 99). By 1820 Birmingham had only 60 engines with '1000 total steam-power in horses'. In 1835 Lancashire and the West Riding of Yorkshire had 1369 steam-engines and 866 water-wheels. A list of steam-engines extant in Birmingham in the same year mentions a total of 169, developing altogether 2700 hp, built between 1780 and 1835, of which 94 were ten years old or less; 275 hp was used for grinding flour, 1770 hp for working metals, 279 hp for pumping water, 87 hp for glass-grinding, 97 hp for working wood, 44 hp for paper-making, 37 hp for grinding clay, 61 hp for grinding colours, and 50 hp for other purposes. The average horse-power was still only about 15. In Prussia the engines of 1835 had an average of 31·5 hp; this increased to 55·1 by 1904.

The situation is mirrored in the annual output of coal in Great Britain. In 1700 this was about 3 000 000 tons, largely for domestic supply. The amount had doubled by 1800, owing to the introduction of the steam-engine. By 1850 it had multiplied by 20, reaching 60 000 000 tons, for by then the steam-engine was dominating industry. But even in 1824 Sadi Carnot was right in saying: 'To rob Britain of her steam-engines would be to rob her of her coal and iron, to deprive her of her sources of her wealth, to ruin her prosperity, to annihilate that colossal power.'

In certain cases we have more definite data on the power of early steam-engines [21], and the rise of the steam-engine to a significantly more powerful prime mover by 1850 can be illustrated by the following figures:

Date	*Engine*	*Power in hp*
1702	Thomas Savery's Miner's Friend	1
1717	Desaguliers' Savery engine for St Petersburg	5·5
1732	Newcomen engine for France	12
1765	Smeaton's transportable atmospheric engine	4·5
1772	Smeaton's Long Benton engine	40·5
1778	Watt engine from Soho	13·8
1781	Hornblower's reciprocating compound engine	11·5
1793	Thompson's reciprocating atmospheric engine	48
1807	Fulton's marine engine	20
1812	Evans and Trevithick's high-pressure engine	1–100
1837	Cornish engine for London Water-works	135
1846	Corliss engine (exceptional for the period)	260
1848	Cornish engines for Haarlemmermeer	40
1850	Woolf compound engine	40–50
1870	Sulzer engine	400
1876	Corliss Philadelphia Exhibition engine	2500
1881	Edison's Pearl Street power-station engine	175
1890–1900	Electric power-station engines	1000 and over

REFERENCES

[1] VOWLES, H. P. and VOWLES, M. W. 'The Quest for Power.' Chapman, London. 1931.
HARTLEY, SIR HAROLD. *Nature, Lond.*, **166**, 368, 1950.
[2] McCLOY, S. T. 'French Inventions of the Eighteenth Century.' University of Kentucky Press, Lexington, Ky. 1952.
SMITH, E. C. *Phil. Mag.*, 150th anniv. no., 92, 1948.
[3] USHER, A. P. 'A History of Mechanical Inventions' (rev. ed.). Harvard University Press, Cambridge, Mass. 1954.
[4] REULEAUX, F. 'Theoretische Kinematik', p. 38. Berlin. 1875.
[5] SMEATON, J. *Phil. Trans.*, **51**, 100, 1759.
[6] WOLFF, A. R. 'The Windmill as a Prime Mover.' London. 1885.
WAILES, R. 'Windmills in England.' Architectural Press, London. 1948.
[7] BOONENBURG, K. 'De Windmolens.' De Lange, Amsterdam. 1949.
[8] LINPERCH, P. '*Architectura mechanica* of Moole-boek.' Amsterdam. 1727.
VAN ZYL, J. '*Theatrum machinarum universale* of groot algemeen molenboek.' Amsterdam. 1761.
VAN NATRUS, L., POLLY, J., and VAN VUUREN, C. 'Groot Volkomen Moolenboek' (2 vols). Amsterdam. 1734, 1736.
[9] NOPPEN, J. 'Rapport van Proeven gedaan op de werking van een vijselmolen en een Scheprad-Molen staende aan de Westvaart onder Haserswoude.' Leiden. 1765.
[10] DOUWES, B. J. 'Verhandeling over de proporties tussen de vermogens der gewone watermolens, werkende met een staand scheprad en de nieuwelings door Gebr. Eckhardt uitgevonden hellende schepradmolens.' The Hague. 1779.
[11] GRINWIS, C. H. C. *Nieuwe Verh. proefonderv. Wijsbeg.*, **9**, 1, 1844.
[12] SMEATON, J. *Phil. Trans.*, **51**, 138, 1759.
[13] 'Het Prinsenmolenboek.' Veenman, Wageningen. 1942.
[14] BATHE, G. 'Horizontal Windmills.' Published by the author, Philadelphia. 1948.
[15] ASHTON, T. W. 'Iron and Steel in the Industrial Revolution' (2nd ed.) University Press, Manchester. 1951.
[16] CARNOT, S. 'Réflexions sur la puissance motrice du feu et sur les machines propres à développer cette puissance.' Paris. 1824.
Idem. 'Reflections on the Motive Power of Heat and on Machines fitted to develop that Power' (ed. by R. H. THURSTON). London. 1890.
[17] DICKINSON, H. W. 'Short History of the Steam Engine.' University Press, Cambridge. 1939.
Idem. 'James Watt.' University Press, Cambridge. 1935.
[18] YOUNG, T. 'Lectures on Natural Philosophy', Vol. 1, pp. 132 f. London. 1807.
[19] FAREY, J. 'Treatise on the Steam Engine.' London. 1827.
[20] TREDGOLD, T. 'The Steam Engine.' London. 1838.
[21] MATSCHOSS, C. 'Die Entwicklung der Dampfmaschine' (2 vols). Springer, Berlin. 1908.

6

THE STEAM-ENGINE TO 1830

H. W. DICKINSON

I. TO DENIS PAPIN (1647–1712)

THE earliest known contrivance operated by steam-power was the 'Sphere of Aeolus' or aeolipile devised by Hero in the first century A.D. It may be described as an elementary type of reaction-turbine, but was a mere philosophical toy yielding no appreciable power. Hero invented another heat-engine, in which the expansive force of air when heated was used to drive water from a tank up through a siphon into a suspended bucket which, as it descended with increasing weight, opened the doors of a temple against the action of a counterweight (vol II, p 635, figure 575).

Not until the seventeenth century was attention again turned to the derivation of power from heat. Giovanni Battista della Porta (1538–1615) in his *Tre libri de' spiritali* (Naples, 1606) explained not only how water could be forced upwards from a tank by pressure of steam on its surface, but also how the condensation of steam could produce suction for drawing water from a lower level. In 1615 Salomon de Caus, a French gardener, described an ornamental fountain worked by steam. A boiler was fitted with an open-ended pipe extending downwards nearly to the bottom. The pipe ended externally in a nozzle provided with a cock. When the steam-pressure was high enough, the cock was opened and a jet of water projected upwards. For the next display, the boiler was refilled and the pressure again raised. Giovanni Branca (1571–1640), an Italian architect, was the first to realize that a jet of steam could turn a wheel by acting on blades around its circumference. In 1629 he described a sort of impulse-turbine working on this principle. It was connected to a pair of drop-stamps through treble-reduction gearing (figure 98). The design was far too crude to work, and the idea lay dormant until the nineteenth century.

An important step leading to the invention of the steam-engine was the discovery of the pressure of the atmosphere. The accepted explanation of the rise of water into a vacuous space created by pumping or otherwise, was that 'nature abhorred a vacuum', but this gave no reason why the rise should be limited. It is said that because of the failure of the engineers of Cosimo de' Medici II,

Grand Duke of Tuscany (1590–1620), to make a suction-pump draw water from a depth of 50 ft (although experience had shown that a lift of about 30 ft was the limit), an appeal was made to Galileo (1564–1642). Galileo began to make experiments, which were continued after his death by his pupil Evangelista Torricelli (1608–47). Torricelli announced in 1643 that the atmosphere exerted a

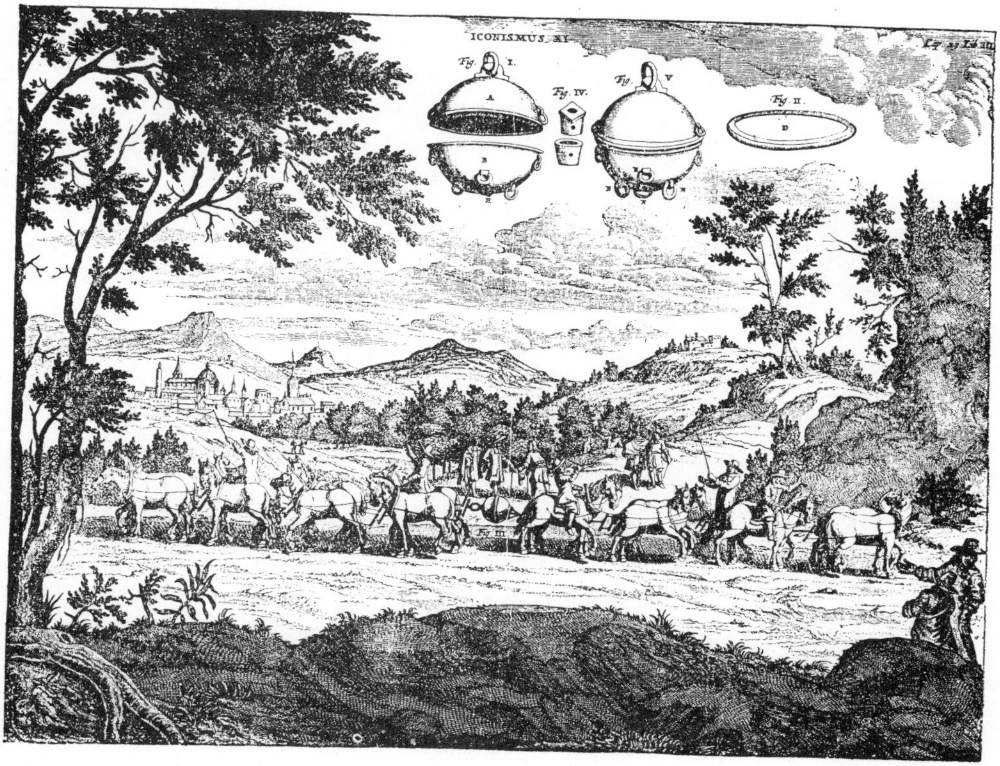

FIGURE 100—*Otto von Guericke showed in a demonstration how even sixteen powerful horses could not pull apart the two halves of an evacuated sphere. c 1654.*

pressure equal to that of a vertical column of mercury of about 30 inches in length, and that it was this pressure that determined the height to which a liquid could be made to rise by suction. Torricelli predicted that the pressure would fall with increasing altitude, and this was confirmed in an experiment suggested by Blaise Pascal (1623–62), who in 1647 had a barometer carried to the top of a 4800-ft mountain in the Auvergne. The mercury fell by about 3 in during the ascent.

The discovery suggested the possibility of using atmospheric pressure to do work on a piston beneath which a vacuum could be created. It thus led to experimental work, in many countries, that culminated in the invention of the steam-engine.

A successful attempt to create a vacuum mechanically was made by Otto von Guericke (1602–86), burgomaster of Magdeburg, who applied existing knowledge of pumps to the development of one to draw air instead of water. With its help he made spectacular demonstrations (figure 100) of the effects of atmospheric pressure. In one of them, performed at Ratisbon in 1654, he used a fixed vertical cylinder with a diameter of 20 inches in which a well fitting piston was suspended from a rope passing over a pulley. Connecting an air-pump to the cylinder he created a partial vacuum below the piston, causing it to descend in spite of the joint efforts of 50 men pulling on a rope to hold it up. He used the same apparatus to lift heavy weights. Thus it was evident that, if a vacuum could be established and re-established at will, the design of a useful engine working by atmospheric pressure would be in sight.

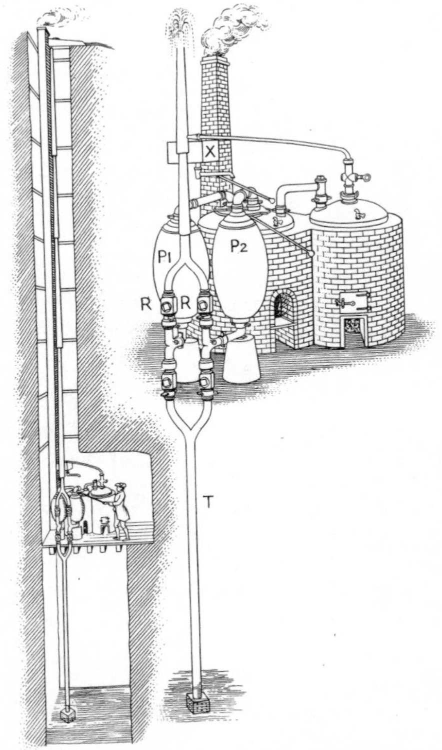

FIGURE 101—*Savery's 'Miner's Friend, or an Engine to Raise Water by Fire'. Steam is admitted to the oval vessel* P1 *and displaces the water upwards through a check-valve* R. *When* P1 *is emptied of water the supply of steam is stopped and cold water from a cistern* X *is poured on* P1 *to condense the steam there. This creates a vacuum and water is sucked through* T *and valve* R. P2 *is filled with steam while* P1 *is being cooled.*

Something of the sort was attained in 1663 by Edward Somerset (1601–67), later second Marquis of Worcester. His description is too vague for discussion here, but he certainly achieved something, and that not merely on a laboratory scale, for the French historian Samuel Sorbière (1615–70) in 1664, and Cosimo de' Medici in 1669, recorded having seen the marquis's machine at Vauxhall; it would force water to a height of 40 ft. In 1663 the marquis secured an Act of Parliament enabling him 'to receive the Benefit and Profit of a Water Commanding Engine by him invented . . . for a term of 99 years'. It failed to achieve commercial success.

Several early inventors thought of the explosive force of gunpowder as a source of power. The idea was generally to employ it to produce a vacuum and so to enable power to be derived from the pressure of the atmosphere. Thus Christiaan Huygens (1629–95) in 1680 suggested a form of gunpowder-engine in which the explosion took place in a cylinder beneath a piston held in a raised position by a counterweight, nearly all the gas of the explosion escaping through automatic relief valves. As the remaining fraction cooled, the pressure of the air forced down the piston and thus raised the weight. In his first experiments with this device, Huygens had as his assistant Denis Papin (1647–1712?), who became well known by his inventions of the 'digester' (1681) or steam pressure-cooker, and of the safety-valve which he devised as a precaution against its explosion.

Papin realized that the gas remaining in the cylinder after the explosion made it impossible to attain a satisfactory vacuum beneath the Huygens piston, and saw the necessity of using some substance that would leave no residue. In 1690 his thoughts turned to steam, and he wrote:

> Since it is a property of water that a small quantity of it turned into vapour by heat has an elastic force like that of air, but upon cold supervening is again resolved into water, so that no trace of the said elastic force remains, I concluded that machines could be constructed wherein water, by the help of no very intense heat, and at little cost, could produce that perfect vacuum which could by no means be obtained by gunpowder.

Papin's engine of 1690 consisted of a vertical tube, about 2½ inches in diameter, fitted with a piston and rod. A little water was put into the bottom of the tube and, by applying heat to the outside, the generated steam raised the piston to the top of the tube where it was held by a catch. When the steam had condensed through the cooling of the tube, the catch was released by hand and atmospheric pressure forced down the piston. The tube thus had to perform the triple duty of boiler, engine-cylinder, and condenser. Papin's engine demonstrated a principle, but was of no practical use. Nevertheless he was the first to employ steam to move a piston in a cylinder, and to indicate a cycle of operations afterwards put to practical effect by Newcomen.

II. SAVERY (1650?–1715), NEWCOMEN (1663–1729), AND SMEATON (1724–92)

In those days the need for machinery was felt most for the pumping of water. Of all patents granted during the reigns of Elizabeth I, James I, and Charles I about one in seven related to pumping. Amongst the many who devoted their attention to the subject was the military engineer Thomas Savery, a prolific inventor and the first to construct a practical steam-pump. His principle was to raise water by the condensation of steam in a closed vessel to as great a height as the atmospheric pressure would permit; to retain the water; and, by the application to it of as great a steam-pressure as could safely be employed, to force the water up to a still higher level. In practice, he used two vessels so arranged that one refilled while the other was discharging. His master patent of 1698 was taken out for a

new Invention of Raiseing of Water and occasioning Motion to all sorts of Mill Work by the Impellent Force of Fire, which will be of great Use and Advantage for Drayning Mines, Serveing Towns with Water, and for the working of all Sorts of Mills where they have not the benefit of Water nor Constant Windes.

The patent was for the usual period of 14 years, but in the following year an extension to 21 years was given by Parliament. In 1701 the rights for Scotland, to terminate at the same date as those for England, were granted to James Smith, of Whitehill in Midlothian. In his 'The Miner's Friend' (1702) Savery writes:

Though my thoughts have long been employed about waterworks, I should never have pretended to any invention of that kind had I not happily found out this new, but yet much stronger and cheaper cause of motion than any before made use of. But finding this of rarefaction by fire, the consideration of the difficulties the miners and colliers labour under by the frequent disorders, and cumbersomness in general of water engines, incouraged me to invent engines to work by the new force.

Savery made a working model of his apparatus which he demonstrated to the king at Hampton Court, and in 1699 he showed it in operation to the fellows of the Royal Society, with a drawing of his engine (figure 101) [1].

An advertisement of 1702 [2] shows that Savery was an energetic business man:

Captain Savery's engines which raise Water by the force of Fire in any reasonable quantities and to any height, being now brought to perfection and ready for publick use; These are to give notice to all Proprietors of Mines and Collieries which are incumbered with Water; that they may be furnished with Engines to drain the same, at his Workhouse in Salisbury Court, London, against the Old Playhouse, where it may be seen working on Wednesdays and Saturdays in every week from 3 to 6 in the afternoons, when they may be satisfied of the performance thereof, with less expense than any other force of Horse or Hands, and less subject to repair.

Thus Salisbury Court, between Fleet Street and St Bride's church, harboured the first workshop in the world for making steam-engines. Their employment was necessarily restricted by the pressure that boilers, piping, and displacers could withstand. Savery also had trouble with high-pressure steam, for when he used pressures up to 8 or 10 atmospheres

> its heat was so great that it would melt common soft Solder; and its strength so great as to blow open several of the Joints of his Machines; so that he was forc'd to be at the Pain and Charge to have all his Joints solder'd with Spelter or Hard Solder [3].

His engines, nevertheless, achieved considerable success for comparatively low lifts, and many were adopted for the water-supply of large buildings. They were also used to pump up water for water-wheels, and thus, indirectly, to produce mechanical power. An improvement of Savery's engine was effected by Desaguliers, who arranged for the condensation of the steam inside the displacement-chamber by a jet of water.

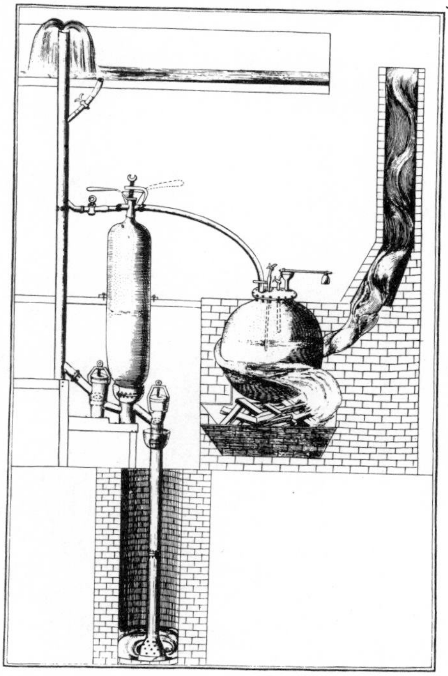

FIGURE 102—*Papin's modification of Savery's engine, 1705.*

Savery's engine fell into disuse early in the eighteenth century.[1] An attempt to improve it was made in 1705 by Papin (figure 102), but here he abandoned his earlier and promising plan of condensing steam beneath a piston in a cylinder and thus deriving power from the pressure of the atmosphere. This principle had the outstanding advantage that steam was required at only about atmospheric pressure, so that the construction of both engine and boiler was well within the capacity of the artisans of the time. The idea of proceeding along Papin's original lines was conceived independently by Thomas Newcomen, who achieved a success immeasurably greater than anything previously attained. He first established the steam-engine as a practical and reliable machine.

Newcomen left no account of the conception or the development of his invention, but the Swede, Mårten Triewald (1691–1747), who came to England in 1716 and assisted Newcomen with the erection of at least one of his engines, wrote [4]:

> Now it happened that a man from Dartmouth named Thomas Newcomen, without

[1] Its principle was revived in Hall's 'Pulsometer' (1876), which still provides a simple and useful means of emergency pumping.

any knowledge whatever of the speculations of Captain Savery, had, at the same time also made up his mind, in conjunction with his assistant, a plumber by the name of Calley, to invent a fire-machine for drawing water from the mines. He was induced to undertake this by considering the heavy costs of lifting water by means of horses, which Mr. Newcomen found existing in the English tin mines. These mines, Mr. Newcomen

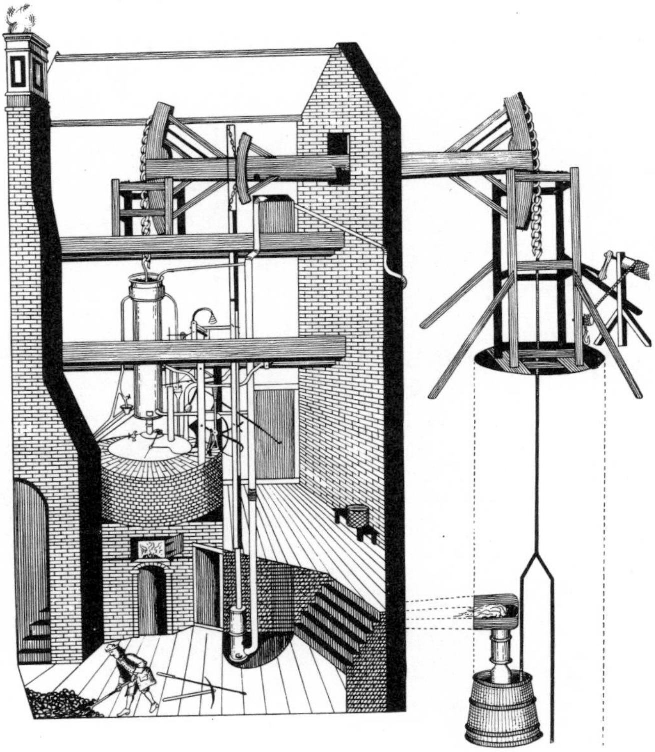

FIGURE 103—*The steam-engine erected by Newcomen and Savery at Dudley Castle in 1712.*

often visited in the capacity of a dealer in iron tools with which he used to furnish many of the tin mines.

The statement that Newcomen had no knowledge of what Savery was doing is corroborated by another writer, Stephen Switzer, who wrote in 1729 [5]:

> Mr. Newcomen was as early in his Invention as Mr. Savery was in his, only the latter being nearer the Court, had obtained the Patent before the other knew it, on which account Mr. Newcomen was glad to come in as a Partner to it.

The association of Savery and Newcomen, referred to by Switzer, is confirmed by an engraving of 1719.

Regarding the priority of this engine, we have the assurance of Triewald that 'Mr. Newcomen erected the first fire machine in England in the year 1712, which erection took place at Dudley Castle in Staffordshire' (figure 103).[1] In an engraving of the engine there is a note in a contemporary hand which tells that the beam 'vibrates 12 times in a Minute and each stroke lifts 10 galls of water 51 yds p'pendr.' This duty would require about $5\frac{1}{2}$ hp.

As regards the association of Savery's name with the Dudley Castle engine, it seems that when Newcomen, after ten years or more of experimental work, had produced a satisfactory steam-engine, he found his way blocked by Savery's master patent which covered the use of 'The Impellent Force of Fire' by any and every kind of engine. All that he could do was to come to some arrangement with Savery. By 1712 the latter must have realized that there was no future for his own engine, and that Newcomen's was vastly superior.

In Newcomen's engine, as constructed in 1712 (figure 104), the boiler with its setting was little more than a large brewer's copper, producing steam at only atmospheric pressure. When the steam was admitted to the bottom of the cylinder above the boiler, the piston rose to the top, mainly by the weight of the pump-rod hanging from the other end of the beam. The steam discharged any air or water that had got into the cylinder, through the eduction pipe and water-sealed valve, and then, after the closing of the connexion to the boiler, it was itself condensed by a jet of cold water. The resulting vacuum allowed the atmospheric pressure to force the piston back to the bottom of the cylinder, thereby raising the pump-rod. The cycle was then started again by admission of more steam. The steam-valve and the injection-cock were perhaps at first operated by hand, but, according to a story, in 1713 the boy whose duty it was to work the valves arranged for this to be done by the engine itself, by means of 'catches and strings'. There is no confirmation of this legend and since there is, on the contrary, evidence of its untruth, it may perhaps rank with the later legend of the boy Watt and the tea-kettle. There is, in fact, no reason to suppose that the method of operating the valves automatically by the motion of the rod of the injection pump, as shown on the engraving of the Dudley Castle engine, was not employed when that engine was first set to work in 1712.

The need for the water-seal was due to the impossibility, in those days, of making an accurately bored cylinder of the size required. Cannon- and pump-barrels up to about 7 inches in diameter could be bored successfully, but anything larger was beyond the capacity of the workshops. Hence at first the only way of finishing the cylinders for Newcomen's engines was to rub the inside of

[1] More precisely, Dudley Castle is in an enclave of Worcestershire.

the castings smooth with abrasives. The pistons would thus not fit very well, and the difficulty was overcome by fixing to the top of each piston a flexible leather disk and keeping it sealed with water to maintain the vacuum.

The engine at Griff colliery, near Coventry, must have been erected almost simultaneously with that at Dudley Castle. At first it was not a success, but

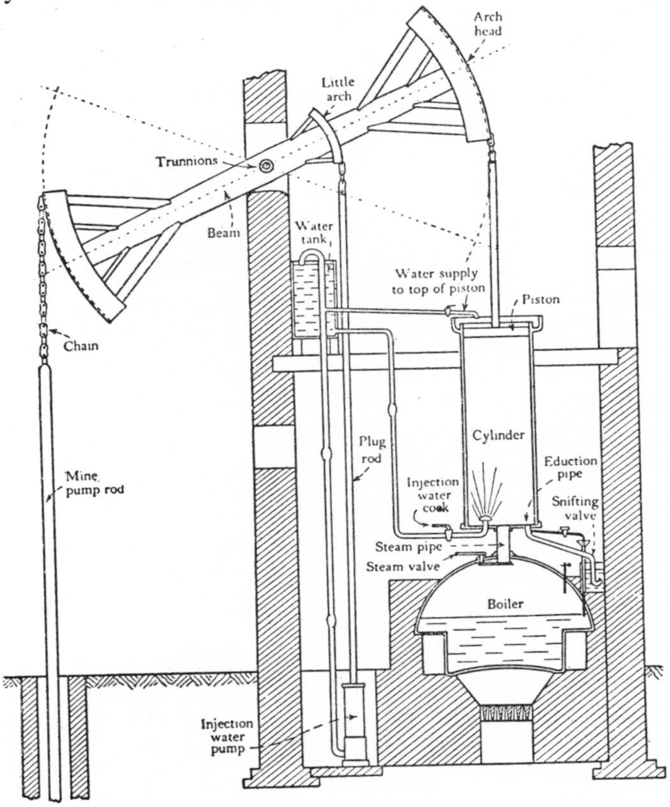

FIGURE 104—*Diagram of Newcomen's atmospheric engine, 1712.*

this was not wholly unfortunate, for thereby it aroused the interest of a local resident, Henry Beighton (1686–1754), a land-surveyor. He was the first to study the Newcomen engine scientifically and is credited with suggesting improvements to the valve-gear. It was he who provided the information about the engine which Desaguliers published in his 'Experimental Philosophy' (1744). This includes Newcomen's method of calculating the power of his engines from the diameter of the cylinder and the barometric pressure, with allowance for estimated frictional and other losses. In practice, to be on the safe side, engineers usually assumed a mean effective pressure of half an atmosphere on the piston. Beighton published a table (see below) of his recommendations for the diameters of pumps and cylinders for engines to draw water from depths of from 15 to 100 yds, in quantities from 48·51 to 304·48 hogsheads an hour.[1] In all cases the engines are assumed to have a 6-ft stroke and to make 16 double strokes per minute.

On Savery's death in 1715 his patent rights were acquired by certain 'Proprietors', who in 1716 advertised their readiness to treat for the erection of

A *Physico-Mechanical* Calculation of the Power of an *Engine*.

Diameter of the Pump inches.	Draws at a 6 Foot stroke.		at 16 St. in a Min. draws per Hour.		The Diameter of the Cylinder. The Depth to be Drawn in Yards.												
Inch	Ale	Gall.	Hogsh.	Gall.	15	20	25	30	35	40	45	50	60	70	80	90	100
4	3.	20	48.	51		Inches			9	10	11	11½	12	13½	14	15	16
4½	4.	04	60.	60				10	11	11¾	12	13	14	15	16	17	18¼
5	5.	02	66.	61			10	11	11¾	13	13¾	14	15½	16¾	18½	19½	20¼
5½	6.	26	94.	30		10	11	12	13	14	15	15¾	17	19	20	21	22¼
6	7.	22	110.	1	9½	11	12	13	14	15½	16	17	19	20½	22	23	24½
6½	8.	46	128.	54	10	12	13	14	15½	16¼	18	19	20	22	23	24½	26¼
7	9.	82	149.	40	10¾	13	14	15½	16¾	18¾	19	20½	22	24	25½	27	28½
7½	11.	32	172.	30	11	13¾	15	16½	18	19	20	21¼	23¼	25	27	28½	30¼
7¾	12.	02	182.	13	12	14	15½	17¼	18¾	19¾	21	22	24¼	26	28	29¼	31½
8	12.	82	195.	22	12½	14½	16½	18¼	19	20¼	21½	23	25	27	29	30½	32½
8½	14.	52	221.	15	13½	15¼	17¼	19	20¼	21¾	23	24	26¾	28½	31	32½	35¼
9	16.	24	247.	7	14	16¼	18	20	21½	23	24¼	25	28	30½	33	35	36½
10	20.	04	304.	48	15½	18	20	22	23¾	25¼	27	28¾	31¼	33¾	36	38¼	40

From 'The Ladies' Diary', p 22. London, 1721.

atmospheric engines, mentioning that some had already been erected in the counties of Stafford, Warwick, Cornwall, and Flint. There were in fact others in Lancashire, Yorkshire, Northumberland, and Durham, of which the 'Proprietors' seem to have been unaware. One of their agents, John Potter, erected such an engine at Edmonston, Midlothian, in 1725. Many interesting details concerning it are known, among them that the cylinder had a diameter of 29 in and a stroke of 9 ft. This and the pumps came from London, the cylinder alone costing £250. The beam of the engine came from Yorkshire and cost £82 16*s* delivered. The annual royalty was £80. For looking after the engine the engineers were to be paid £200 per annum, together with half the profits of the colliery. The licence

[1] The hogsheads were apparently the old wine measure of 63 gallons, and the exactness of the deliveries listed is academic rather than practical. The printing of the original is poor and a few of the fractional values in the table are doubtful.

was to terminate in 1733, when the English and Scottish patents for the Savery engine were due to expire. This shows that Newcomen's invention was being exploited under these patents. The client paid separately for the materials and component parts, which were assembled and erected on the site by the appropriate craftsmen supervised by an engineer.

By 1725 the Newcomen engine was coming into general use for pumping, especially for mines, and also to raise water for operating water-wheels to drive machinery. An engraving of 1726 shows an engine with valve-gear of the tappet type; and also an arrangement for feeding the boiler with the water from the eduction-pipe of the cylinder instead of from the almost cold water on the top of the piston, as was done at first. It is not known if this improvement was Newcomen's own.

The knowledge of the new power extended to the continent. The first Newcomen engine outside Britain was erected in 1722 at Königsberg, near Chemnitz in Saxony, for J. E. T. von Erlach of Vienna. He had visited England and had taken back with him an experienced workman to do the job. This man later erected several other Newcomen engines in Saxony, where he was regarded as their inventor. In France the first engine was installed in 1726, at Passy, a suburb of Paris, to supply the city with water from the Seine. One of the erectors was a member of the committee exploiting the engine on behalf of the 'Proprietors'.

Newcomen died in 1729, having lived to see his engine in use in Saxony, France, Belgium, and possibly Germany and Spain. Whether he derived much pecuniary benefit from his important invention is doubtful. It seems most likely that he had been thrust aside by the proprietors of Savery's patent, who took the major share of the profits.

In 1733 the patent expired and the employment of the engine spread rapidly, for it met a definite want and had no competitor. The coal-mining industry, particularly, benefited from its use, for it permitted far deeper mining than did pumping by animal-power (vol III, ch 3). In the deep coalfields of the north of England, where many pits had been flooded by the end of the seventeenth century, it brought about almost a rebirth of mining. As the numbers of engines increased, so did their size, though the design remained little changed. The larger engines, however, needed increased boiler-power, and two or more boilers replaced the single one of Newcomen.

In 1765, Gabriel Jars (1732–69), a French metallurgist, visited Newcastle upon Tyne, and described the engine he saw working at the Walker colliery near by (figure 57). It had been built by William Brown, a local colliery-engineer, and was the largest in the district. It was served by three boilers with another in reserve. Jars states that the boilers were of wrought iron with lead tops, except the one immediately beneath the cylinder, which had a copper top for ease of connexion. The piston was packed with hemp rope, and three water-jets were used for condensing because of the large size of the cylinder. From another source we learn that the cylinder had a diameter of 74 in and a length of 10½ ft. It weighed 6½ tons and came from Coalbrookdale in Shropshire.

For long after Newcomen's death the development of his engine was due to practical men, for the 'philosophers' seem to have considered machinery beneath their notice. The first scientific engineer to devote much attention to steam power was John Smeaton, famous as the constructor of the Eddystone lighthouse (ch 15, p 468). As a youth, he became interested in a Newcomen engine at a colliery close to his family home in Yorkshire. Later, in the course of his professional work, he grew much dissatisfied with the design and performances of the engines that he had observed. In 1767 he designed an engine to take the place of horses in raising water from the New River in London to a reservoir at a higher level. The engine did not come up to expectation, so in 1769 he constructed in his private workshop an experimental engine with a cylinder 10 inches in diameter and of 38-in stroke. He also obtained from William Brown (p 178) a list of about 100 engines in the north of England, with particulars of the performances of 15 of them having cylinders ranging from 20 to 75 inches in diameter, and collected further particulars of 18 large engines in Cornwall. From the data, he found that on the average they raised the equivalent of 5·59 m lb of water one foot high for the consumption of one bushel (84 lb) of coal. This was the way that the 'duty' of an engine was then reckoned. The average effective pressure on the pistons was only 6·72 lb to the sq in [6], which was no better than Newcomen had obtained.

In 1772 Smeaton compiled a table of proportions of the parts of engines with cylinders up to 72 inches in diameter, and in the same year designed and superintended the construction of an engine for Long Benton colliery, Northumberland, with a cylinder of 52-in diameter. Owing to improvements in details and workmanship, and especially in boring the cylinder (for which he designed a special mill at Carron Iron Works), the Long Benton engine (figure 105) could do 9·45 m ft-lb of useful work per bushel. This was a very remarkable advance on current practice. In 1775 Smeaton designed an engine with a cylinder of 66-in diameter for emptying the docks at Kronstadt, Russia, and at almost the same time he built his most famous engine—that at Chacewater in Cornwall—which had a 72-in cylinder.

Smeaton, with knowledge and manufacturing facilities unavailable to Newcomen, almost doubled the efficiency of the atmospheric steam-engine, raising its performance about as high as was possible with the type. This, however, was extremely low, mainly because of the great waste of heat in using the working

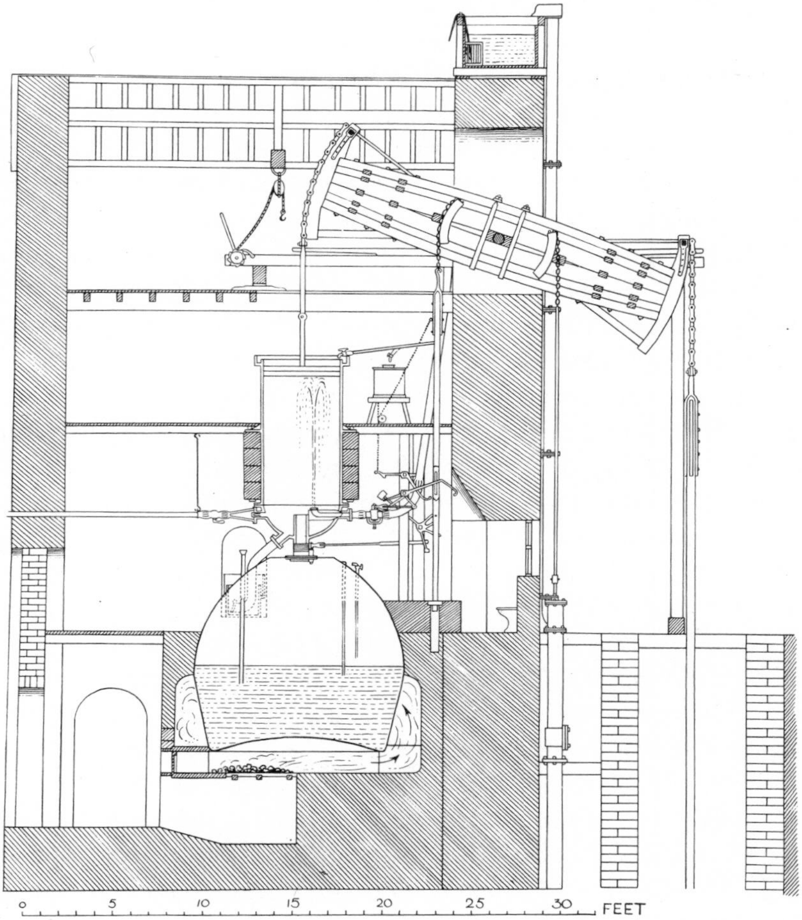

FIGURE 105—*The Newcomen engine made by Smeaton in 1772 for Long Benton colliery.*

cylinder also as a condenser. He regarded the performances of his Long Benton engine as a standard of quality; yet, if one assumes that low-grade coal of only 12 000 B.Th.U. per lb was used for raising steam, his figures show the overall thermal efficiency to have been only about 1 per cent. But, despite its enormous consumption of coal for work done, the Newcomen engine held the field unchallenged for more than 60 years. It was the main factor in the exploitation of the mineral resources of Britain, thereby laying the foundations of the industrial development of the country.

The limitations of the Newcomen engine, except for pumping, were very great. It was inherently a single-acting engine, as the chain-connexion between the piston-rod and the end of the beam precluded any thrust on the upward stroke. To obtain a rotary motion the engine could be provided with a connecting-rod driving a crankshaft and fly-wheel. In this case the beam had to be overloaded at the crankshaft end sufficiently to produce the required downward pressure on the crank-pin during the upward stroke of the piston. The arrangement, though clumsy, was often used instead of horses for winding coal from shallow pits, and survived into the nineteenth century. Alternatively, the engine could be made to pump water into an overhead tank, the water then being allowed to descend over a water-wheel that drove the machinery. This method gave the uniform motion needed in such industries as cotton-spinning. Smeaton employed it to obtain reversible drives by using a water-wheel resembling that shown by Agricola in 1556, in which one half of the width had a right-handed set of buckets, and the other half a left-handed set, the water being diverted from one set to the other as required.

III. WATT (1736–1819)

After Newcomen, the first to make any outstanding advance in developing power from steam was James Watt, who by his inventive and scientific genius made a fundamental improvement in the efficiency and mechanical design of steam-engines. Watt, the son of a master carpenter and ship-wright at Greenock, went to London as a youth to learn the craft of instrument-making. He returned to Glasgow in 1757, was appointed 'Mathematical Instrument Maker to the University', and had a workshop in the college buildings.

In 1763 he repaired a model Newcomen engine belonging to the university, and made it work, though a London instrument-maker had failed to do so. The cylinder of the model had a bore of 2 in and a stroke of 6 in, the boiler being about 9 inches in diameter. Watt found that its consumption of steam was so great that it could make only a few strokes at a time before coming to a standstill. He attributed this to the loss of heat by conduction through the cylinder-walls, the surface of which was greater in proportion to the volume than in a larger engine. To minimize this source of loss he made another working model with a wooden cylinder 6 inches in diameter with a 12-in stroke. From experiments with this model he decided that the real cause of the high steam-consumption was the cooling of the cylinder by the injection-water at every working stroke. During this research he independently discovered the phenomenon of latent heat of steam, which, unknown to him, had already been discovered by his friend Joseph Black (1728–99), then professor of chemistry in the University. In Watt's own words [7]:

I perceived that, to make the best use of steam, it was necessary, first, that the Cylinder should be maintained always as hot as the steam which entered it; and secondly, that when the steam was condensed, the water of which it was composed, and the injection itself, should be cooled down to 100°, or lower where that was possible. The means of accomplishing these points did not immediately present themselves; but early in 1765 it occurred to me that, if a communication were opened between a Cylinder containing steam, and another vessel which was exhausted of air and other fluids, the steam, as an elastic fluid, would immediately rush into the empty vessel, and continue to do so until it had established an equilibrium; and if that vessel were kept very cool by an injection, or otherwise, more steam would continue to enter until the whole was condensed.

Watt goes on to explain that he proposed to maintain the vacuum in the 'other vessel', or condenser, either by draining it through a water-sealed vertical pipe more than 34 ft long, or, preferably, by using a pump or pumps for the purpose. As soon as possible after the idea of using a separate condenser had occurred to him, he made a rough model to test its practicability, and this 'answered his expectation'. He realized that Newcomen's method of sealing the piston with cold water would have to be abandoned, because it conflicted with the principle of keeping the cylinder as hot as possible, and that the atmosphere should not act directly on the piston for the same reason. He therefore decided to provide a cylinder-cover with a hole and stuffing-box for the piston-rod to pass through, and to use steam instead of atmospheric pressure to force the piston down. He intended that the cylinder should be kept hot by a steam-jacket, the outside of which would be lagged with wood. Watt constructed a large cylinder on these lines, and experimented with it in conjunction with a surface-condenser of his own design. However, he feared that, in service, this type of condenser would become encrusted with deposits from the water, and believed that the much simpler and smaller jet-condenser would serve the purpose better. To this view he always adhered. Watt's first notion was to connect the piston-rod directly with the pump-rod which it was desired to operate, but he finally decided that the better way would be to transmit the motion of the piston through a rocking beam, as Newcomen had done.

As Watt had neither the money nor the facilities to develop his invention on a practical scale, Black introduced him to John Roebuck, an enterprising industrialist, who was interested in the drainage of coal-mines. Roebuck suggested that a patent be applied for, and in 1769 Watt was granted his historic patent for 'A new Method of Lessening the Consumption of Steam and Fuel in Fire Engines'. The essential element in this was the use of a separate condenser. In return for taking over the expenses already incurred, Roebuck came in as a partner to the extent of two-thirds. An experimental engine of the beam type with a cylinder 18 inches in diameter and a 5-ft stroke was erected at Roebuck's residence; but the matter could not be followed up vigorously, partly because Watt had begun practising as a civil engineer, and partly because Roebuck was becoming financially embarrassed.

Watt had occasion to visit London on business, and on his return, furnished with introductions from friends, he called upon Matthew Boulton (1728–1809), a leading manufacturer whose works was at Soho, near Birmingham (plate 31 A). Boulton became interested in the engine because his own works was short of water-power and he was seeking means of pumping back the water that drove his machinery. Boulton, however, was not disposed to develop the engine unless he could exploit it on a scale sufficiently large to justify a special factory for making it, and to this Roebuck would not agree. In 1773 Roebuck became bankrupt, and his share in the patent, which the receivers valued at only about a farthing, was taken over by Boulton in discharge of the debts that Roebuck owed him. Watt then brought his experimental engine to Birmingham and gave his whole time to its development, with such success that in 1774 he wrote: 'The fire engine I have invented is now going and answers much better than any other that has yet been made.' The patent, however, had only eight more years to run, and Boulton realized that it would expire before any profit could be earned. Watt therefore petitioned Parliament for an extension, which was granted in 1775, for twenty-five years ending in 1800. The famous partnership of Boulton and Watt was entered upon for a like period.

Boulton was enthusiastic about the new engine, and persuaded Watt to proceed to construct one with a 50-in cylinder for Bloomfield colliery in Staffordshire, and another with a 30-in cylinder for blowing blast-furnaces for John Wilkinson (1728–1808), an ironmaster at the New Willey Company, Broseley, Shropshire. Wilkinson had made and patented in 1774 a new type of boring-mill for making cannon (p 421). The greatly increased accuracy attainable by this machine made it invaluable for boring cylinders to the fine limits that Watt needed. Both these engines of Boulton and Watt were most successful. Their consumption of coal was less than a third of that normal at the time. Inquiries poured in from the tin- and other metal-mines in Cornwall, where coal was dear and the cost of pumping limited the depth at which mining was commercially practicable. Cornwall, indeed, provided so important a field for the engine that it became necessary for one or other of the partners to be on the spot. A royalty

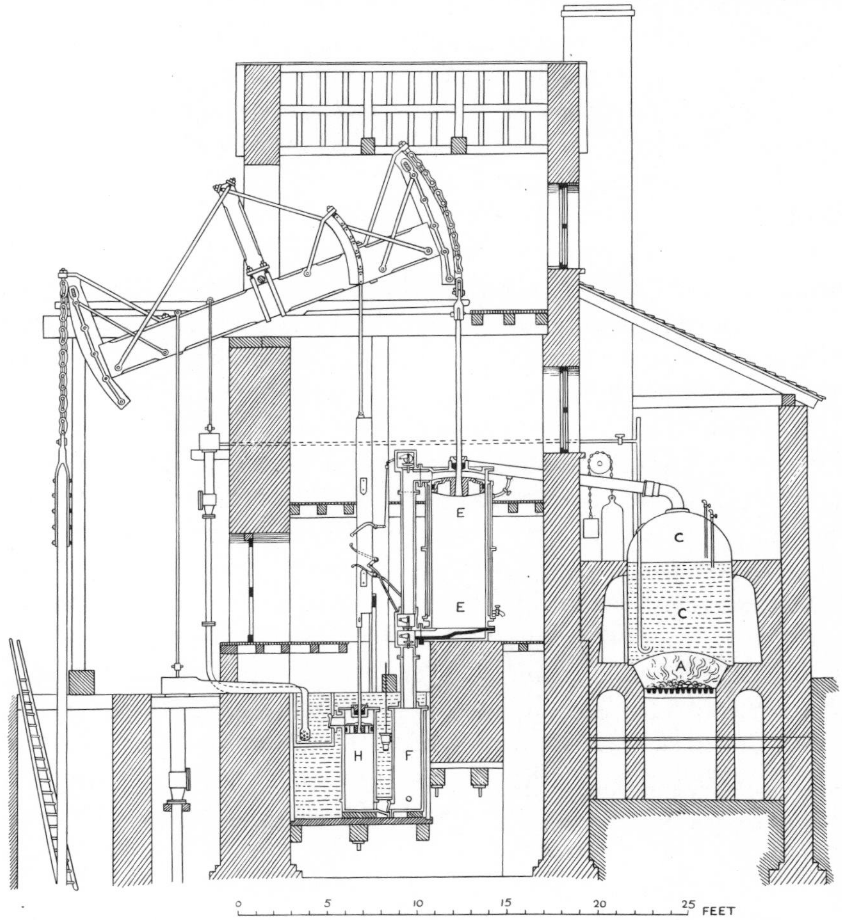

FIGURE 106—*Watt's single-acting engine for pumping water for draining mines, 1788. The boiler* C *is placed in an outhouse, and the steam passes to the cylinder* E, *which is kept hot all the time by a separate steam jacket.* F *is the separate condenser and* H *an air-pump.*

equal to one-third of the saving in the cost of fuel, as compared with that of the common engine, was charged to the users, and to determine this ratio Watt made careful tests of many existing engines both in Cornwall and elsewhere. On the basis of these trials he concluded that the effective pressure on the piston of the common engine was 7 lb per sq in, while in his own engine it was 10·5 lb.

In the final design of the single-acting engine of Watt, as used from about 1788, there were several new features (figure 106). The boiler (C) had a greater heating-surface. Noteworthy are the closed and steam-jacketed cylinder (E) and the jet-condenser (F) with air-pump (H) alongside in a hot well below floor-level. The piston was rendered steam-tight by a packing of hemp rope held in a recess around its circumference by a junk-ring fastened by studs. By the side of the cylinder was a pipe, at the head of which was the inlet valve which, when opened, admitted live steam above the piston and also to the interior of the pipe. Near the lower end of the pipe was the equilibrium valve, which allowed steam to pass from the space above the piston to that below it. A third valve, the exhaust valve, controlled the flow of steam from beneath the piston to the condenser. All the valves were of the drop type, operated by tappets.

The operation of the engine was as follows. When the piston was at the top of its stroke, the exhaust valve was opened to produce a vacuum beneath it, and the inlet valve was simultaneously opened to admit steam above it. The piston was then forced downwards by the atmospheric pressure and the pressure of the steam. When the piston reached the lower end of its stroke the inlet and exhaust valves were closed and the equilibrium valve was opened. The piston, having then an equal pressure on each side, was pulled up again to the top of the cylinder by the weight of the pump-rod.

Watt was urged by Boulton to devise some way of obtaining rotary motion from his engine, which would give it wide application in manufacturing industries. The old idea of using a crankshaft driven by a connecting-rod from the working end of the beam had occurred to Watt, but was taken up by one of his workmen and patented in another name in 1780. The patent might have been contested, but the long-headed Watt, who himself held numerous patents, was too wise to become involved in litigation of that type. He devised other expedients, which he patented in 1781. One of these, the epicyclic or sun-and-planet gear, suggested by his assistant William Murdock (p 262), came into general use. It consisted of a spur-wheel keyed to the end of the driven shaft, and geared with a similar non-rotating wheel fixed to the end of a connecting-rod hanging from the beam, the wheels being kept in gear by a link joining their centres; the shaft would thus make two revolutions for each double stroke of the engine. The sun-and-planet motion was used for all Boulton and Watt rotative engines until the expiry of the crankshaft and connecting-rod patent in 1794.

In 1782 Watt patented two very important improvements. The first made the engine double-acting, and thus able to develop twice the power from the same cylinder-volume. The second used the steam expansively, admitting it to the cylinder only during the early part of each stroke, after which it would drive the piston by its expansive force. To render the engine double-acting, the flexible chain connecting the piston-rod to the beam had to be replaced by some mechanism that would transmit a force in either direction. Watt's first notion was to extend the piston-rod by a rack which would gear with a toothed arc on the end of the beam. This was a clumsy device, and in 1784 he patented his well known three-bar straight-line motion, which he himself regarded as his masterpiece. Within a few months, he saw that he could double the length of the linear path by employing the pantograph principle. Thus he produced his elegant 'parallel motion', which characterized the rotative beam-engine throughout the century or more of its service (figure 107).

In 1787, to ensure constancy of speed with varying loads, Watt provided the engine with a conical pendulum-centrifugal governor controlling a butterfly-valve in the steam-inlet pipe (vol III, p 105, and plate 4A). Such governors were already in use for controlling the setting of the millstones in flour-mills, but Watt was the first to use them for regulating steam-engines. By this time the double-acting rotative steam-engine had become practically standardized, and remained so until the expiration of Watt's master patent for the separate condenser in 1800. Watt then retired from active work, after having not only provided industry with a prime mover of an efficiency hardly improved for the next half-century, but having also raised the performance of pumping-engines from the 9·45 m ft-lb per bushel of coal attained by Smeaton (p 179) to the 30 m ft-lb or more that Boulton and Watt could guarantee at the close of their partnership.

The further development of the beam-engine was practically confined for many years to mechanical and constructional improvements, the most outstanding of which was the control of the steam-flow into and out of the cylinder by a single sliding valve in place of the separate drop-valves employed by Watt. The slide-valve was invented and patented in 1799 by Murdock, who also devised the eccentric on the crankshaft as a means of operating it. After expiry of their master patent the first serious competitor of Boulton and Watt was Matthew Murray (1765–1826) of Leeds. He simplified and lightened Murdock's valve in 1801 by bringing the steam- and exhaust-ports of the cylinder close together in a single facing, so that they could be controlled by a comparatively small valve. About this time cast iron beams began to replace the wooden beams of Newcomen, Smeaton, and Watt, and connecting-rods of cast iron succeeded the wooden rods flitched with iron plates that had at first been used. But the beam-engine underwent no other noticeable change until 1845, when John McNaught, of Bury in Lancashire, gave it a long extension of life by his simple and effective way of converting it into a compound engine.

The persistence of the beam-type of engine is to be explained by the embryonic state of mechanical engineering in those early days. Its great size and

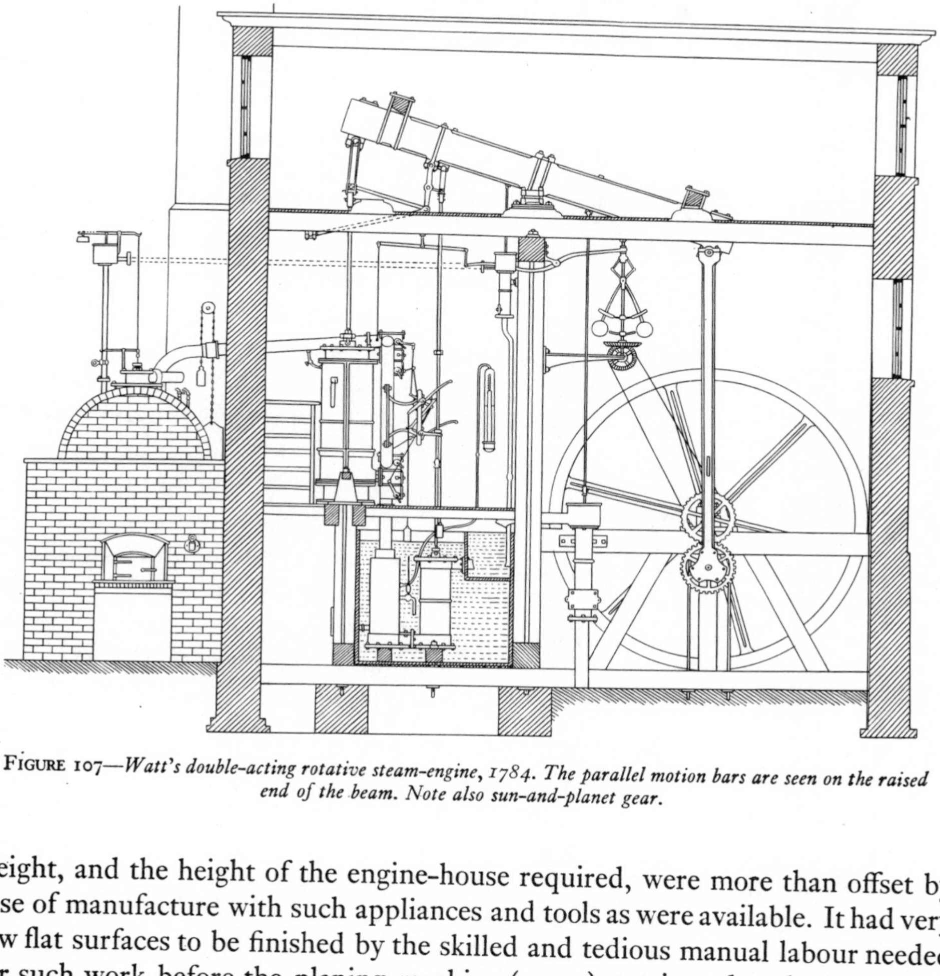

FIGURE 107—*Watt's double-acting rotative steam-engine, 1784. The parallel motion bars are seen on the raised end of the beam. Note also sun-and-planet gear.*

weight, and the height of the engine-house required, were more than offset by ease of manufacture with such appliances and tools as were available. It had very few flat surfaces to be finished by the skilled and tedious manual labour needed for such work before the planing-machine (p 433) was introduced about 1820. One of its greatest virtues was tolerance of quite appreciable misalignment, on account of the length of its beam, connecting-rod, and eccentric-rod. The cottered brasses of its numerous pin-joints also simplified any required adjustments by the operator, and the whole engine was very durable.

IV. EARLY ENGINES OF TREVITHICK

Despite the enormous improvements by Watt, the engine, as he left it, was still essentially a vacuum-engine, for he was resolutely opposed to steam-pressure higher than a few pounds above atmospheric, because of supposed danger. In his first patent of 1769, he made a claim for non-condensing engines that 'may be wrought by the force of steam only, by discharging the steam into the open air after it had done its office', but he never followed up this idea. It is, indeed, more than doubtful whether his claim would have been valid, for Jacob Leupold of Leipzig had published in 1725 a description of a non-condensing single-acting pumping-engine (figure 108) [8]. But the use of steam at a much higher pressure than Watt contemplated was very promising, and the first progress here was due chiefly and almost simultaneously to Richard Trevithick (1771–1833) in England and Oliver Evans (1755–1819) in the United States.

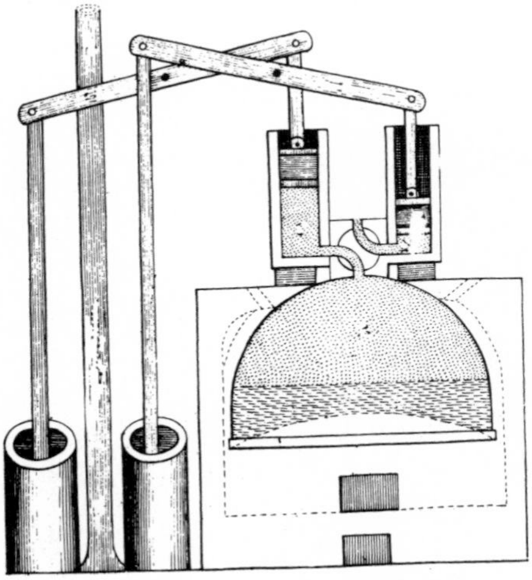

FIGURE 108—*Leupold's design for a high-pressure, non-condensing steam-engine, 1725. The steam is alternately admitted to the cylinders and exhausted from them to the atmosphere by one rocking motion of the circular valve shown between them.*

Trevithick's first high-pressure double-acting engine was one of the beam and connecting-rod type, constructed in 1800 for winding-duties at a mine in Cornwall. He next designed a steam road-carriage which was tested in 1801. This had a cylindrical, internally fired boiler, with return flue. The vertical cylinder was partly sunk into the boiler, and the piston-rod drove the rear wheels by a cross-head with slide-bars and connecting rod. The exhaust steam was turned up the chimney to increase the draught. The vehicle would carry several persons, had a loaded weight of about 30 cwt, and ran at some nine miles an hour on a level road. In 1802 Trevithick, jointly with his cousin Andrew Vivian, took out a patent for 'Improvements in the Construction and Application of Steam Engines', which covered the mechanical details of both a stationary engine and a road locomotive engine. In the former, the unit consisting of boiler and cylinder is shown oscillating on trunnions so as to avoid the need for slide-bars or connecting-rod (plate 10 A).

In 1802 Trevithick built at Coalbrookdale an experimental pumping-engine of the beam type, working at the unprecedented pressure of 145 lb per sq in. The boiler was of cast iron with a diameter of 4 ft and a thickness of $1\frac{1}{2}$ in; the cylinder was 7 inches in diameter with a 3-ft stroke. It astonished everyone who saw it by reason of its small size in relation to the power developed [9]. The next year he built another steam-carriage with a single cylinder and a pair of 8-ft wheels driven by gearing. It would carry eight or ten passengers, and made several trips in London, but excited no general public interest. Trevithick then returned to Cornwall to exploit his stationary engines, which seemed to offer a better field for his energies. While there, he undertook to build a steam-locomotive to draw a load of 10 tons over the $9\frac{3}{4}$ miles of cast iron tramway connecting the Pendarren ironworks with the Glamorganshire canal. Its trial in 1804 was completely successful, though it caused the breakage of several of the tramway plates. The engine, which weighed about 5 tons without water, would easily pull much more than its specified load, and, as Trevithick said, 'was the first and only self-moving machine that ever was made to travel on a road with 25 tons at four miles per hour, and completely manageable by only one man'.

Trevithick was thus not only the originator of the locomotive, but had proved —what was then disbelieved—that there would be sufficient adhesion between smooth wheels and rails to transmit the tractive force. His device of turning the exhaust steam up the chimney to provide an adequate draught, had he patented it, would have given him as great a control over locomotive development as the invention of the separate condenser gave to Watt in the field of stationary engines. He probably influenced locomotive history by designing a locomotive, similar to his Pendarren engine, for a colliery near Newcastle upon Tyne. This was built at Gateshead in 1805 by one of Trevithick's mechanics, and there can hardly be room for doubt that a knowledge of it must have stimulated George Stephenson in 1813 to make his first locomotive for use at the Killingworth colliery in the same coalfield.

Trevithick's incursions into locomotive work did not interfere to any extent with the development of his stationary engines. In a long letter [10] of 1804 to his friend Davies Giddy (1767–1839),[1] he spoke of nearly 50 of his engines, their tasks including driving sugar-mills, corn-grinding, pumping water, and rolling iron. He constructed them with either horizontal or vertical cylinders: the former design (1803) with his original globular boiler (figure 109), and the latter, a few years later, with his internally fired return-flue boiler.

Oliver Evans inaugurated the use of high-pressure steam in the United States about the same time as Trevithick did in England. Evans was a wheel-wright, but

[1] In 1817 Giddy changed his surname to Gilbert. He was president of the Royal Society from 1827 to 1830.

in 1780 entered into partnership with his brothers, who were flour-millers. He had already shown inventive genius, and in 1797 obtained a patent for a steam-carriage. In 1803, when there were probably not more than half a dozen steam-engines in the United States, he constructed a steam dredging-machine, and the next year built a successful direct-acting vertical stationary engine with a double-acting cylinder 6 inches in diameter and a stroke of 8 in, to run at 30 rpm. The steam- and exhaust-valves were three-way cocks operated by pins on the fly-wheel. Like Trevithick, he used a cylindrical boiler with an internal fire-plate

FIGURE 109—*Side view and section of Trevithick's high-pressure engine with horizontal cylinder and dome-topped boiler, 1803.*

and flue, and in 1805 was proposing to use steam at a pressure of 120 lb to the sq in. His enterprise received no encouragement in his lifetime, but its influence was shown by the extensive use of high-pressure steam in the United States while the Watt engine was still the prevailing type in Britain.

By 1800 several inventors had attempted to make improvements on Watt's beam-engine for mine-pumping, but all had been frustrated by their inability to use a separate condenser. Thus in 1792 Edward Bull, once an erector for Boulton and Watt, and later associated with Trevithick, put up at Dolcoath mine in Cornwall an engine of his own design. In this he had eliminated the beam and further simplified the construction by inverting the cylinder and connecting the piston-rod directly to the pump-rod below, but as he was using a separate condenser Boulton and Watt took legal action and in 1794 obtained an injunction against him.

V. HIGH-PRESSURE ENGINES

With the opening of the nineteenth century, the use of a separate condenser was free to all. The lead given by Trevithick in the use of high-pressure steam brought the compound engine definitely into sight as a practical objective. Such an engine would allow a greater range of expansion of the steam to be employed without infringing Watt's principle that a working cylinder should be subjected to the least possible temperature range, and it also made possible greater uniformity of the torque on a crankshaft.

The first to exploit the compound engine under the new conditions was Arthur Woolf (1776–1837), a versatile engineer who had been employed in the Cornish mines. In 1803 he patented an engine of this type, and experimented with the principle by adding a high-pressure cylinder to an existing Watt engine at Meux's brewery in London, where he was then working. The result was not satisfactory for, thinking that steam at a pressure of *n* lb could be expanded to *n* times its original volume without reducing its pressure to less than that of the atmosphere [11], he had made his high-pressure cylinder far too small, so that the engine would not give the power required. However, to develop his ideas, he left the brewery and entered into partnership with Humphrey Edwards, a millwright who had a workshop at Lambeth, and in time they standardized a satisfactory design. This was a beam-engine with two cylinders, side by side, both piston-rods being connected to the same pin of the parallel motion. A test of one of their compound engines in 1811 showed a saving of about 50 per cent in fuel, as compared with a simple Watt engine. In the same year the partnership was dissolved, Woolf returned to Cornwall, and a few years later Edwards went to France, where he had already erected about 100 of the Lambeth-made engines. He had secured a French patent for the engine in 1815, and in partnership with a French firm built up an important engine-manufacturing business in that country, where he remained until his death. Other firms later took up the manufacture of the Woolf engine, which was being built in France until about 1870.

Woolf's return to Cornwall was influenced by reports of the decline in performance of the engines there since Boulton and Watt had ceased to have their former financial interest in them. In 1800 the duty obtained per bushel of coal had been about 30 m ft-lb, whereas in December 1811 the average duty of 12 engines was found to be only 17 m ft-lb. Woolf foresaw here an opening for his compound engines. In 1814 he erected one to work with steam at a pressure of 40 lb and using 8- or 9-fold expansion; another was set up in 1815. Both did extremely well, but he did not have the field to himself, for by 1812 Trevithick, having been bankrupted by the failure of certain enterprises in London, had returned to Cornwall determined to retrieve his fortunes. He had sold his last interest in his engine-patent, but his faith in high-pressure steam was as great as ever. One of his first feats in Cornwall was the construction in 1812 of a high-pressure 'Cornish' beam-engine for pumping, the earliest example of a type which, on account of its remarkable efficiency and negligible cost of maintenance, held its own for waterworks-pumping until the close of the nineteenth century. It was supplied with steam at a pressure of 40 lb by one of Trevithick's internal-flue 'Cornish' boilers 26 ft long. This design of boiler is still used, almost unchanged, for small industrial duties.

Except for the high steam-pressure and expansive working, the steam-cycle was similar to that of the Watt pumping-engine (p 184). The cylinder was single-acting, with a diameter of 24 in and a stroke of 6 ft. It was not steam-jacketed, but lagged with straw and plaster. With the piston at the highest point, steam was admitted above it to force it down and thereby raise the pump-rod at the other end of the beam, the underside of the piston being open to the condenser. The steam was cut off as early as one-ninth of the stroke, the remainder of the stroke being effected by its expansion. After a pause to allow the pump-barrel to become filled with water, an equilibrium valve was opened to equalize the pressure on both sides of the piston so that the latter was raised again to the head of the cylinder by the weight of the ram and pump-rod. The duration of the pause was regulated by a 'cataract' device, in which the time required for a given weight of water to escape through an adjustable orifice determined the moment at which the valve opened.

Trevithick, however, did not confine himself to pumping-engines. Among his various activities, he built a number of engines of the self-contained type for threshing corn, grinding meal, and other agricultural purposes. One of these, supplied in 1812, continued in use until 1879 and still survives (plate 10B).

Apparently not realizing that with his 'Cornish' pumping-engine he had originated a type that was soon to have no rival, Trevithick almost simultaneously designed and built what he called a plunger-pole engine for pumping-duties. The plunger-pole was simply an iron ram, in this case 16 inches in diameter and of 8½-ft stroke, which replaced the ordinary piston. It worked through a stuffing-box at the top of the cylinder, and had the advantage of making unnecessary an accurate boring of the cylinder. The latter stood on bearers across the head of the pit-shaft. At the head of the ram was a cross-head sliding in guides, and from the cross-head side-rods descended to another cross-head below the cylinder, from which the pump-rod was hung. With this arrangement there was no need for any reciprocating beam.

This engine, of course, was of the single-acting type, the ram being raised by steam-pressure and descending by its own weight and that of the pump-rod. The air-pump for the condenser was worked by a tumbler mechanism. Steam was used at 100-lb pressure and was cut off at one-third of the stroke. Inertia of the moving parts assisted the expanding steam to complete the stroke. Trevithick wrote in 1813 that it was 'lifting 40 million pounds 1 ft high with one bushel of coal, very nearly double the duty that is done by any other engine in the County'. He took out a patent for the plunger-pole engine in 1815, and erected others on the same principle, besides compounding a number of existing Watt engines by working them with high-pressure steam which was first expanded in a plunger-pole cylinder added to the engine, thereby substantially increasing both power and efficiency.

The design of the plunger-pole engine probably reached its highest point in one erected in 1815. This worked with steam at a pressure of 120 lb, and had a plunger 33 inches in diameter making 10-ft strokes. In consequence of rumours, Trevithick had it tested in 1816 by independent engineers, who reported that its duty was 48 m ft-lb per bushel of coal, but that they had no doubt that it would do over 60 m when the bottom of the mine was reached. They found that it was operating with steam at 100 to 120 lb per sq in, and was making an average of 9¼ ten-ft working strokes a minute, with a cut-off at one-sixth of the stroke. When non-condensing the duty was 28 m.

Trevithick's patent for his plunger-pole engine had also included a claim for a high-pressure non-condensing reaction-turbine, working on the principle of Hero's aeolipile (p 168), except that he did not require the boiler to revolve. In 1815 he constructed such a machine, which he called his whirling-engine. It consisted essentially of a hollow shaft through which steam at a pressure of 100 lb was conveyed to the interior of a pair of hollow arms mounted at one end of the shaft. Each arm was 7 ft 6 in long, and had an orifice near its tip through which the steam escaped to the atmosphere in a tangential direction and thus drove the machine by its reaction. Power was taken off by a belt from a pulley on the shaft. As the shaft could not be run at much more than 250 rpm, giving a nozzle-velocity of about 200 ft per sec, the efficiency was low. Trevithick was, nevertheless, enthusiastic about the machine, mainly because of its light weight, but he did not develop it further.

A matter that aided Trevithick and Woolf in improving Watt's engines was that the mine-owners of Cornwall began from 1811 to publish regular reports on the performances of their engines, to encourage rivalry and so to promote efficiency. In the first report, the average duty of the 12 engines tested was no more than 17 m ft-lb per bushel of coal. By 1816 the average of 35 engines had risen to 23 m, and by 1826 the average of 51 engines reached 30·5 m, the increase being ascribed to new and improved engines, as well as to the spirit of emulation that developed. By 1844 the average duty of engines in Cornwall was said to be 68 m [12], though much higher figures were reported in individual cases. The best record is said to have been obtained by an engine having a cylinder 80 inches in diameter and a 10-ft stroke, erected at Fowey Consols mine, for which a duty of 125 m ft-lb per 95-lb bushel of coal was claimed in 1835. Since this would be equivalent to almost exactly $1\frac{1}{2}$ lb of coal per hp-hour, it is hard to believe.

Neither the plunger-pole engine of Trevithick nor the compound beam-

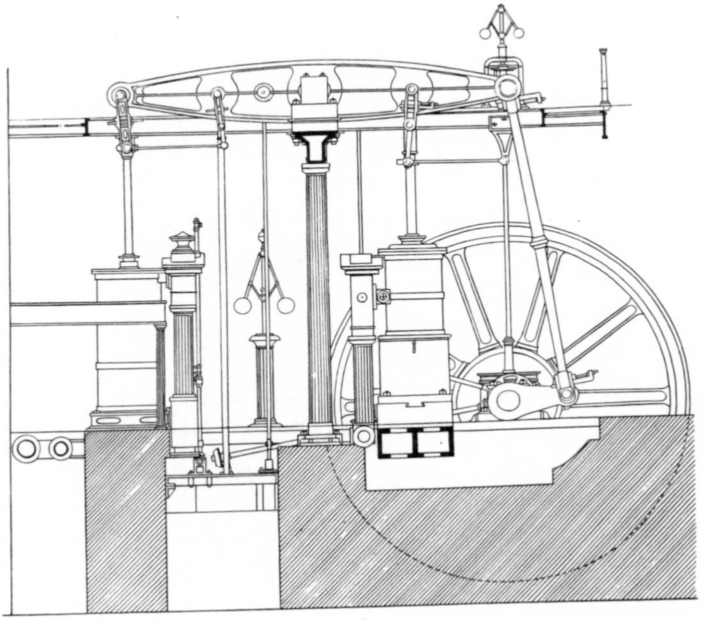

FIGURE 110—*Elevation of McNaught's 60 hp compound beam-engine, 1848. McNaught compounded many existing engines by adding a high-pressure cylinder midway along the beam.*

engine of Woolf long survived. The ram of the former was difficult to keep steam-tight, and its cooling by repeated exposures to the atmosphere was a further disadvantage. Woolf built no more of his compound engines after 1824 because, in spite of their efficiency, their greater cost and complexity made them unable to compete with the high-pressure Cornish engine of Trevithick, which held the field for heavy pumping-work without serious rivalry until nearly the end of the century.

For the heavier industrial duties, such as driving the machinery in factories and mills, the design of the rotative beam-engine held its own for many years, almost as it had been left by Watt. The only important improvement was in 1845 by John McNaught, of Bury, Lancashire, who compounded it by adding a small short-stroke high-pressure cylinder, having its own parallel motion, to act on the beam about half-way between the centre of the latter and the end driving the connecting-rod (figure 110). Many existing Watt engines were thus compounded to be operated with high-pressure steam, while for new engines the inclusion of a 'McNaught' cylinder taking steam at a pressure of 120 to 150 lb was adopted as standard.

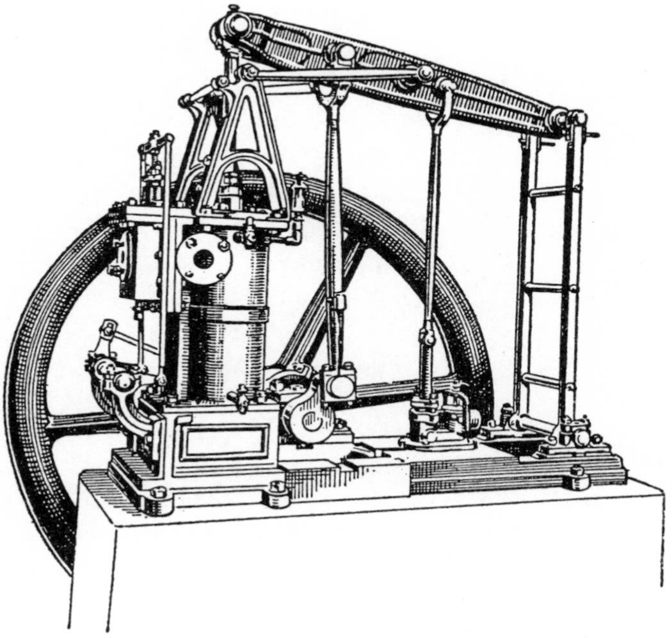

FIGURE 111—*The grasshopper engine of Easton and Amos, 1861. The name was suggested by the rocking links at the beam end.*

VI. DIRECT-ACTING ENGINES

Although when steam-engines were required for rotative duties there was no compelling reason for a cumbrous rocking beam, that type had the advantage of requiring only pin-joints for the guidance of the cross-head instead of slide-bars, which were far more difficult to make. To retain this advantage while eliminating the lengthy beam, the 'grasshopper' type was patented in 1803 by William Freemantle, the same principle being employed by Oliver Evans in America.

The grasshopper mechanism was based on the geometrical fact that if the mid-point of a straight link can move only in a circular arc by reason of a radius-rod attached to it, and if one end of the link be compelled to move in a straight path, the other end of the link will describe a second straight line at right angles to the first (figure 111). In practice, the piston-rod was attached to one end of the link, moving vertically, while the other end of the link was free to move in a small arc of circle, almost equivalent to a horizontal straight line. The mid-point of the link was held by a radius-bar. Thus the movement of the piston-rod was rendered rectilinear without need for slides.

A simpler form of parallel motion, working on exactly the same principle, but with the connecting-rod attached directly to the cross-head of the piston-rod, was devised by John Scott Russell (1808–82). This was used for many years, and a horizontal engine embodying it was driving a cotton-mill in Stockport as late as 1898.

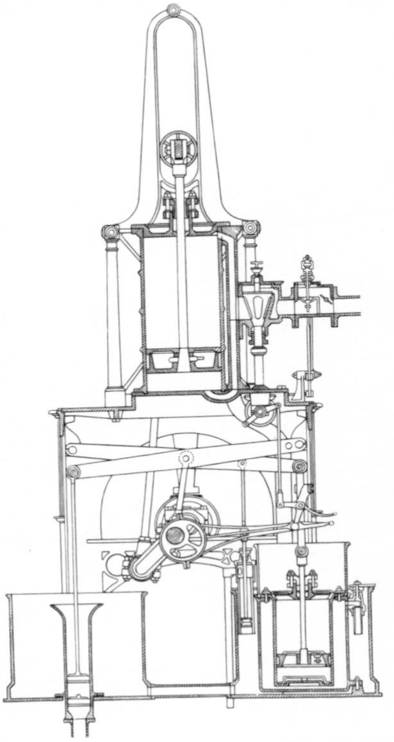

FIGURE 112—*Section of Maudslay's table engine, 1807. The beam was dispensed with and the crankshaft was driven by two connecting-rods from the cross-head above.*

The pioneer of direct-acting steam-engines without a beam was William Symington (1763–1831). In 1801 he applied such an engine to the propulsion of a tug-boat on the Forth and Clyde Canal. This engine had a horizontal double-acting cylinder 22 inches in diameter by 4-ft stroke, driving the crankshaft of the paddle-wheel directly through a connecting-rod. The simplicity of his design, however, made no appeal at the time, for the belief that a beam of some kind was essential to a satisfactory engine was deeply rooted. Stationary practice was therefore followed in marine work, though it was soon modified by replacing the overhead beam by a pair of lower beams, one on each side of the cylinder (see vol V, ch 7).

Direct-acting engines for industrial purposes had been built by both Trevithick and Evans early in the nineteenth century (p 189), but the first type to come into extensive use was the table engine of Henry Maudslay (1771–1831) patented in 1807. In this engine (figure 112) a vertical cylinder stood at the centre of a small cast-iron platform, its piston-rod carrying a cross-head having wheels running between vertical iron guides. A pair of connecting-rods from the ends of the cross-head drove a crank-shaft running on bearings beneath the platform. This engine was widely used in small factories for at least 40 years, and in a simplified form the type survived until the end of the century, especially for duties where its compactness was a consideration.

The belief that a cylinder placed otherwise than vertically would suffer undue wear from the weight of the piston was probably the reason for the tardiness in placing it horizontally. Such engines were hardly used before 1825, when Taylor and Martineau in London introduced the now familiar small open-type factory engine having its cylinder, slide-bars, and crankshaft-bearings on a horizontal cast iron bedplate of box-girder section.

To summarize the state of steam-engine practice about 1830 it may be said that the standard prime mover for the larger mills and factories was the Watt jet-condensing beam-engine using steam at little more than atmospheric pressure. In smaller establishments, the 'grasshopper' and the 'table' engines were commonly employed. For pumping at mines and waterworks the high-pressure Cornish engine of Trevithick, usually working at about 70 lb to the sq in, had no rival. For marine work, propulsion was by paddles always driven by side-lever engines, jet-condensing and working at about 4 or 5 lb to the sq in. Locomotive practice (vol V, ch 15) was in its infancy.

REFERENCES

[1] "An Account of Mr. Thos. Savery's Engine for raising Water by the help of Fire." *Phil. Trans.* **21**, no. 253, 228, 1699.

DICKINSON, H. W. 'A Short History of the Steam Engine', Pl. 1. University Press, Cambridge. 1939.

[2] *Post Man*, 19th–21st March 1702.

[3] DESAGULIERS, J. T. 'A Course of Experimental Philosophy', Vol. 2, p. 466. London. 1744.

[4] TRIEWALD, M. 'Kort Beskrifning om Eld- och Luft-Machin.' Stockholm. 1734. (Eng. trans. by R. JENKINS. Newcomen Society, London. 1928.)

[5] SWITZER, S. 'An Introduction to a General System of Hydrostaticks and Hydraulicks Philosophical and Practical', p. 342. London. 1729.

[6] FAREY, J. 'A Treatise on the Steam Engine, historical, practical and descriptive.' London. 1827.

[7] ROBISON, J. 'A System of Mechanical Philosophy' (4 vols). Edinburgh. 1822.

EWING, SIR JAMES ALFRED. 'The Steam Engine and other Heat-Engines.' University Press, Cambridge. 1926.

[8] LEUPOLD, J. *Theatri Machinarum Hydraulicarum* (2 vols). Leipzig, 1724, 1725.

[9] TREVITHICK, F. 'Life of Richard Trevithick with an Account of his Inventions', Vol. 1, pp. 153 ff.: Letter dated 22 August 1800. London. 1872.

[10] *Idem. Ibid.* Vol. 2, pp. 2 ff.: Letter dated 23 September 1804.

[11] JENKINS, R. *Trans. Newcomen Soc.*, **13**, 55, 63, 1932–3.

[12] MORSHEAD, W. *Min. Proc. Instn Civ. Engrs*, **23**, 46, 1863.

BIBLIOGRAPHY

BATHE, G. and BATHE, DOROTHY. 'Oliver Evans, A Chronicle of Early American Engineering.' Historical Society of Pennsylvania, Philadelphia. 1935.

DICKINSON, H. W. 'A Short History of the Steam Engine.' University Press, Cambridge. 1939.

Idem. 'James Watt, Craftsman and Engineer.' University Press, Cambridge. 1936.

Idem. 'Matthew Boulton.' University Press, Cambridge. 1937.

DICKINSON, H. W. and TITLEY, A. 'Richard Trevithick, the Engineer and the Man.' University Press, Cambridge. 1934.

EWING, SIR JAMES ALFRED. 'The Steam Engine and other Heat-Engines' (4th ed.). University Press, Cambridge. 1926.

FAREY, J. 'A Treatise on the Steam Engine, historical, practical and descriptive.' London. 1827.

JENKINS, R. "Savery, Newcomen, and the Early History of the Steam-Engine." *Trans. Newcomen Soc.*, **3**, 96–118, 1923; **4**, 113–33, 1924.

ROBISON, J. 'The Articles Steam and Steam-Engines, written for the Encyclopaedia Britannica.' Edinburgh. 1818.

SMEATON, J. 'Reports of the late John Smeaton' (4 vols). London. 1812–14.

TREDGOLD, T. 'The Steam Engine, its Invention and Progressive Improvement.' (2 vols). London. 1838.

See also *Transactions of the Newcomen Society.*

7

WATERMILLS *c* 1500 – *c* 1850

A. STOWERS

I. INTRODUCTION

THE origin and early history of water-power have been discussed and illustrated in chapter 17 of volume II of this work, where it was shown that the earliest form of water-wheel was the Norse mill. This had a horizontal wooden wheel with scoops rotated by a running stream; it developed, at the most, about half a horse-power. Roman engineers developed the Vitruvian mill with a vertical wooden wheel on a horizontal axle, producing up to about 3 hp. In western Europe the watermill and windmill were the main sources of motive power for many centuries until the steam-engines of Newcomen, Smeaton, and Watt were introduced in the eighteenth century.

The Vitruvian mill was constructed in two forms: (*a*) the undershot wheel, dipping into a river so that water flowed underneath and turned the paddles, and (*b*) the later overshot wheel, with a regulated stream of water directed on to the top of the wheel. These two main types revolutionized the grinding of corn, and when it was appreciated that they could be used or adapted for driving other machinery, technology was advanced on a new basis. This development took place especially after the fourth century, when the Christian religion was officially adopted in the Roman Empire and the long-established use of human power for the grinding of corn was discouraged.

Although technological progress was severely handicapped after the disintegration of the Roman Empire, the number of watermills increased, particularly in the eleventh and twelfth centuries, and by the fifteenth century they were being used for numerous industrial purposes, such as cutting and polishing marble, grinding powder and pigments, sawing timber, fulling cloth, tanning, crushing oil-seeds, and making iron and paper, as well as for irrigation.

The earliest known record of a watermill in England for grinding corn has been found in a charter granted in A.D. 762 by Ethelbert of Kent to the owners of a monastic mill east of Dover. But the most important historical landmark in this respect was undoubtedly the Domesday Survey, begun in 1080 and completed in 1086. In this were recorded over 5000 corn-mills, mostly south and east of the rivers Trent and Severn. The mills were probably of both types, Norse and

Roman, but the latter eventually predominated and most of them were situated on the eastern side of the country, which suggests that the utilization of water-power came from the European continent, first into Kent and then spreading into East Anglia, Lincolnshire, the midlands, and the south.

II. THE SIXTEENTH CENTURY

It is evident that at the opening of the sixteenth century the water-wheel was by far the most important source of motive power in Europe. It was the basis of mining and metallurgy, and hammers and bellows driven by the water-wheel were essential for the manufacture of wrought and cast iron. The hoisting, crushing, and stamping of ore, the drilling of gun-barrels, and the drawing of wire were carried out with the aid of water-wheels. Water-power had also been adopted in the mining of copper and silver.

In England, most villages and towns, which had naturally been established on favourable sites where water was available, possessed one or more corn-mills rented by the millers from the manorial lords. Towns grew in the river valleys—which appear to have been crowded with watermills—where industries, particularly those for producing iron and textiles, flourished. The expanding use of the water-wheel in industry obviously called for the concurrent development of methods of mechanical power transmission, especially the use of primitive gears for driving machines of different types in various ways and for increasing their speed and output.

In feudal times the manorial mill was a valuable source of income for the lord of the manor, providing a substantial rent from a comparatively small plot of land. Mill rentals varied considerably and the miller, who might be obliged to provide his own stones for grinding, often paid partly in cash and partly in kind. Eels from the mill pond were sometimes included in the rent. The feudal law of milling soke gave the lords the sole right of building and working mills on their estates. Peasants were theoretically compelled, according to the right of multure, to have their corn ground there. The miller levied a grist toll, usually one-sixteenth or one-twentieth of corn from every sack he ground, and this led to many grievances owing to the varying, and in some cases excessive, tolls demanded by unscrupulous millers. Penalties were imposed by landlords on peasants who secretly ground corn at home with hand-querns, or took it to a more convenient mill owing to the difficulties of transport or sometimes to shortage of water. The offending querns were frequently destroyed or confiscated.

Numerous watermills were owned by monasteries and priories, since the size of their establishments necessitated the grinding of corn on a comparatively large scale. Some mills belonged to the king and others to private owners. There are increasingly frequent references to watermills in conveyances, wills, and other legal documents. Whereas with windmills there could hardly be disputes about the use of air, many conflicting interests were involved in the ownership or use of streams and rivers. For example, men dependent on fishing for their livelihood complained that it was affected adversely by the mills; the owners of barges and boats protested that mills, weirs, floodgates, and suchlike obstructions introduced new dangers, and fatal accidents due to these causes are in fact on record. Then again, the construction of a new mill could affect the working of older mills lower down the river, especially in seasons of water shortage.

A valuable source of information is John Fitzherbert's 'Boke of Surveyinge and Improvements', published posthumously in 1539. He stated that it was common practice for corn-mills to be built not on large rivers, but at a more convenient site to which water was conveyed from the river by a man-made millstream to a weir, made of timber or stone or both, by means of which water could be stored just above the mill. P. N. Wilson considers that these mills were probably furnished with simple undershot wheels having flat unshrouded paddles rotated by the flowing water. They were convenient but very inefficient.

Fitzherbert refers in the same book to the importance of an adequate fall in the tail-race to minimize the disadvantages of back-watering, which caused the wheel to slow down owing to the building up of water below it. He wrote: 'Also there be two maner of corne mylnes, that is to saye a braste mylne and overshot mylne, and these two maner of mylnes be set and goe most commonly upon small brookes and upon greate pooles and meryres [meres] and they have always a brode bowe a fote [foot] brode and more, and the ladles be always shrouded with compost bordes on both sydes to hold in the water, and then they be called buckettes. And they most be set moche nerer togyther than the ladels be, and moche more a slope down wardes to hold moche water that it falls not out for it dryveth the wheel as well with the weight of the water as with the strengthe. And the mylner must drawe his water according to his buckettes, that they be always full and no more, for the longer that they holde the water the better they be.'

With the breast-wheel, water flowed into the buckets just above or below the level of the horizontal axle; it was consequently a type intermediate between the older undershot and overshot wheels. Fitzherbert wisely confirms the principle that more power can be produced by breast and overshot wheels, if their buckets are well filled, than by undershot wheels. The water was to a great extent prevented from leaving the buckets, before they reached the bottom position, by the building of a close-fitting breast of brick or stone, shaped to the profile of about a quarter of the wheel and only an inch or so from it. Working millers in the sixteenth century probably knew from experience that the weight of water in the buckets produced more power than the force of the same stream acting on the paddles of an undershot wheel, although there seems to have been some doubt about it. This principle was, however, confirmed 200 years later by Smeaton, whose experiments are referred to later in this chapter.

III. UNDERSHOT WHEELS

In its most primitive form the vertical wheel was used for the raising of water for irrigation of land in the Far East; the floats dipped into the river which turned them, at the same time filling bamboo tubes closed at one end, or earthenware pots lashed to the rim, the water from which flowed out at the top of the wheel into a trough or canal.

In western Europe a great advance was made, and increased power obtained, by building a dam or barrier across a stream to collect water and raise its head, as, for example, in hammer-ponds. A water-course or small canal was cut allowing the water to return to the river lower down. The wheel, which could be inside or outside the mill, dipped into the stream, and a sluice was built between the wheel and the pent-up water to regulate the flow. The water was confined between strong masonry walls supporting the bearings in which the horizontal axle turned, and was directed on to the paddles or float-boards. When the wheel was idle and the sluice shut, the level of the water rose until it reached the top of the dam, so provision had to be made for it to return to the river by overflowing a weir or waste-water sluice, which in later times was fitted with a self-acting balanced float.

These were the simplest watermills, easily made and managed. The undershot wheel supplied cheap mechanical power to drive corn-mills, fulling-mills, and forges. These were widely used by an agricultural population to supply themselves with bread, woollen cloth, and iron, the main requirements of a community where spinning and weaving were still domestic employments.

The undershot wheel was in many cases superseded by the breast-wheel in order to get the most value from the water available, but it was still useful even in the nineteenth century in remote places where water-power and timber were plentiful but mechanical skill and labour scarce. In the eighteenth century such eminent engineers as John Rennie (1761–1821) and Sir Marc Isambard Brunel (1769–1849) designed and built saw-mills with large undershot wheels and iron axles at Dartford and at Chatham dockyard. The wheel at Dartford was 16 ft in diameter by $4\frac{1}{2}$ ft wide, and worked 16 saws of various types. The wheel designed by J. V. Poncelet (1788–1867) was virtually an undershot wheel converted into a kind of water turbine (figure 113). It was used for falls up to 6 ft and its efficiency approached 65 per cent.

IV. SMEATON'S EXPERIMENTS

At the time when John Smeaton (1724–92) was born, many industries were dependent on water-wheels for the power to drive machinery. Horse-mills were inadequate, and windmills were unsuitable for processes where stoppages would ruin production, but the demand for power was accelerating. Smeaton decided, when 27 years old, to investigate scientifically how the design and efficiency of water-wheels could be improved. Having been apprenticed to a mathematical instrument-maker, he made a really good model with his own hands and tested it accurately (figures 91, 92; pp 152 and 153).

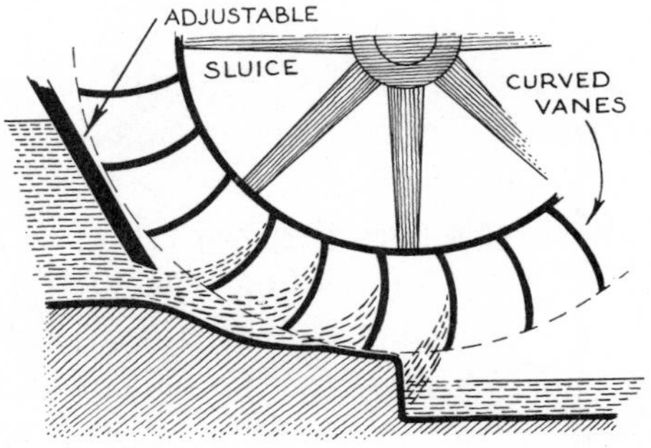

FIGURE 113—*Poncelet's water-wheel.*

The model, as originally constructed, had an undershot water-wheel, 2 ft in diameter, with flat paddles. By means of a hand plunger-pump, water was raised to a wooden storage tank, giving a 3-ft head, and then flowed through an adjustable sluice and along a channel until it struck the paddles. The output of power was measured by observing the height through which a scale-pan carrying weights was raised in one minute. The flow of water supplied to the wheel was measured by counting the number of strokes per minute of the piston in the pump needed to maintain a constant head of water in the storage tank. The water flowed round in a closed circuit, and was thus used again and again. In his second set of experiments, he employed instead a model overshot wheel with a trough to guide the water on to the top of it.

Smeaton found that the maximum overall efficiency which he could obtain from the undershot wheel was about 22 per cent and from the overshot about 63 per cent. He observed that there was a serious loss of power if a jet of water struck the flat paddles of the undershot wheel, and he proved that it was indeed more efficient to fill the buckets of the overshot wheel with water and develop power by gravity instead of by impulse. He also found there was no appreciable advantage in increasing the head of water over the top of the overshot wheel or in allowing water to strike the buckets with considerable velocity. He wrote: 'The higher the wheel is in proportion to the whole descent, the greater will be the effect;

because it depends less upon the impulse of the head and more upon the gravity of the water in the buckets. . . . It is desirable that the water should have somewhat greater velocity than the circumference of the wheel, in coming thereon; otherwise the wheel will not only be retarded, by the buckets striking the water, but thereby dashing a part of it over, so much of the power is lost.'

V. BREAST-WHEELS

On 3 and 24 May 1759 Smeaton presented two papers to the Royal Society, entitled 'Experimental Enquiry into the Natural Powers of Wind and Water to turn Mills' (published in London, 1794), detailing his results; for these he was awarded the Society's Copley medal. Before that time, the breast-wheel was little known, imperfectly understood, and regarded as a compromise by combining impulse and gravity. Although Smeaton did not test this type with a model, he stated that the same principles should be applied in these mixed cases, for: 'All kinds of wheels where the water cannot descend through a given space, unless the wheel moves therewith, are to be considered of the nature of an overshot wheel according to the perpendicular [that is, vertical] height that the water descends from; and all those that receive the impulse or shock of the water whether in a horizontal, perpendicular or oblique direction, are to be considered as undershots.' He concluded that the total effect or power of a breast-wheel would be the sum of (*a*) the effect of an undershot with a head equal to the difference in height between the surface of the water in the storage pond and the level where it struck the wheel, and (*b*) that of an overshot with a head equal to the difference between the level of impact and the surface of the tail-water. In actual practice, however, the total power was rather less than this.

VI. OVERSHOT WHEELS

If a stream flowing down a hill were directed into the earthenware vessels on the rim of a primitive irrigation wheel, they would be successively filled and the side of the wheel with the extra weight would be forced to descend, the vessels emptying themselves at the bottom. Thus rotary motion and mechanical power would be obtained, and this overshot wheel would rotate in the opposite direction to an undershot. Obviously vessels with a restricted neck would be inconvenient, so with larger streams a series of wooden troughs placed across the face of the wheel would be more effective. The stream was made shallow and nearly as broad as the wheel on to which it was directed. The wheel itself (figure 114) was constructed by fixing two sets of arms or spokes on the axle at a suitable distance apart and attaching to their outer ends wooden segments shaped to form the circumference. On to these, and across the face of the wheel, were nailed the sole-boards. On the ends of, and at right angles to, the sole-boards were fastened the two shroudings made of strong planks, a foot or more wide, and between these planks the buckets, made of lighter timber, were fixed with their ends let into the shrouding which closed them. The buckets thus resembled a triangular trough in section, with the third side open to receive the water. In later wheels only two boards were used, forming the front and bottom of the bucket. This shape was used for many years until curved iron plates were introduced.

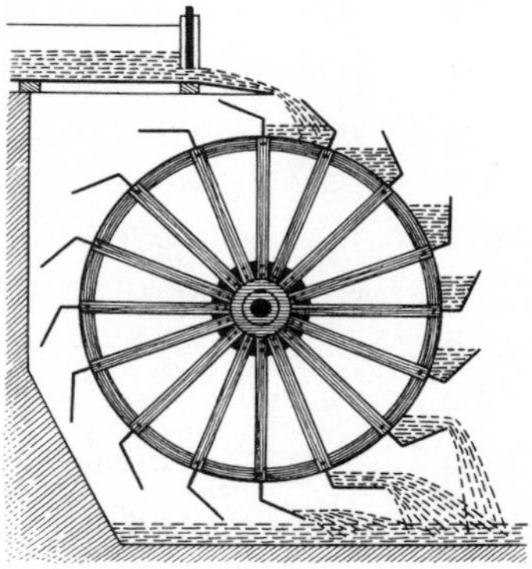

FIGURE 114—*Typical overshot water-wheel with side-shroudings removed. c 1600.*

Joseph Glynn, another civil engineer, who constructed numerous large water-wheels in the nineteenth century, wrote that 'Mr. Smeaton's experiments showed that the best effect was obtained when the velocity of the wheel's circumference was a little more than 3 ft in a second; and hence it became a general rule to make the speed of the overshot water-wheels at their circumference $3\frac{1}{2}$ ft per second or 210 ft per minute. Experience showed this velocity to be applicable to the highest water-wheels as well as the lowest, and if all other parts of the work be properly adapted thereto, it will produce very nearly the greatest effect possible; but it has also been practically shown that the velocity of high wheels may be increased beyond this rate without appreciable loss as the height of the fall and the diameter of the wheel increase, and that a wheel 24 ft high may move at the rate of 6 ft per second without any considerable loss of power.' Glynn adopted 6 ft per second in constructing several overshot wheels of iron, 30 ft in diameter or larger. By thus raising the velocity, the revolutions of a 30-ft wheel were increased from $2\frac{1}{4}$ to almost 4 per minute. The greater speed meant that less gearing was needed for driving machinery at the required rate, and reduced the load on the wheel and axle nearly in the inverse ratio of the speeds; furthermore there was a gain in the regularity of motion derived from the momentum of the quicker wheel. On the other hand, as Glynn stated, there was a limit to the diameter, for a very large overshot wheel was costly, cumbersome, and slow.

VII. SMEATON'S WATER-WHEELS

John Smeaton was one of the foremost engineers of the eighteenth century; his success in building the third Eddystone lighthouse (p 468) established his popular reputation, but during his busy working-life as a consulting engineer he carried out much work, less well known, in both civil and mechanical engineering. He was not primarily an inventor, but it was said of him that he could not touch anything without improving it. The Royal Society possesses about 1200 of his drawings, bound in 6 volumes, of which 'A Catalogue of the Civil and Mechanical Engineering Designs 1741–1792, of John Smeaton, F.R.S.' was published by the Newcomen Society in 1950.

After Smeaton's death in 1792, his manuscripts, drawings, and letter-books were purchased by Sir Joseph Banks, president of the Royal Society, with whose approval in 1795 a committee of the (Smeatonian) Society of Civil Engineers, founded by Smeaton himself, undertook to publish a selection of his reports. For many years the drawings were in the hands of John Farey (1760–1826) and his better-known son, John (1790–1851), who collected and arranged them.

Volumes I ('Windmills and Watermills for Grinding Corn') and II ('Mills for various Purposes and Machines for Raising Water') constitute a most valuable record of part of his work. From these drawings and the watermills they portray, P. N. Wilson has selected and analysed 60 schemes in a paper presented to the Newcomen Society in 1955 (see the bibliography at the end of the chapter). Where a corn-, oil-, gunpowder-, or fulling-mill was driven by a water-wheel, the plant was normally described as a 'mill', but it is interesting to note that water-wheels used for driving pumps or furnace blowers were usually described as 'engines'. The water-wheel drawings in volume III ('Fire Engines for Raising Water') are all 'engines' mainly working with a pumped supply and used for operating reciprocating machinery or for mine-haulage. 'Fire Engines' here refers to beam engines of the Newcomen type which pumped water from the tail-race to the top of the overshot wheel. Wilson has located the sites of many of the watermills but has stated that, so far as he is aware, no remains of any of Smeaton's water-wheels have been found. In many cases the mills have disappeared, but even where they still remain his original wooden wheels were probably replaced within fifty years.

Many of Smeaton's water-wheels were of the low breast type (figure 115) with flat paddles and no shrouds. The diameters varied from 12 to 18 ft, the widths from 2 to 7 ft, and the working head from 4 to 10 ft. Where the head of water was very low, the wheels were almost undershot. His only true undershot wheel was a very large example, 32 ft in diameter by 15 ft wide, constructed for London Bridge waterworks, on the Thames (p 491). It was turned by the water flowing through the arch of the bridge in which it was installed. The wheel had 24 floats, 4½ ft deep, and drove force-pumps through wooden gears. After working from 1768 to 1817 it was replaced by an iron wheel. The history of the London Bridge waterworks, originally installed by Peter Morris for supplying water to houses in the City of London, has been well described from 1582 onwards in 'Water Supply of Greater London' by H. W. Dickinson, published in 1954 by the Newcomen Society. It includes drawings of the water-wheels and pumps dated 1635, 1737, and 1768; the last was Smeaton's, referred to above.

A typical wooden breast-wheel built by Smeaton was that at Woodford Bridge artificial slate factory, Essex, with a working head of 6 ft. The wheel was 16 ft in diameter by 5 ft wide. The 6 wooden felloes on the circumference were fastened

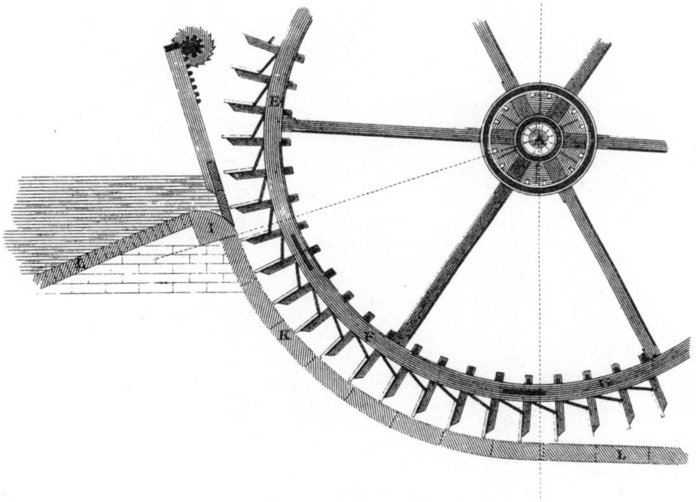

FIGURE 115—*Typical low breast-wheel, eighteenth century, designed by Smeaton. This wheel was controlled by a sluice operated by a rack-and-pinion gear.*

together with iron fish-plates and bolts. The 12 arms or spokes were mortised into the wooden axle, 2 ft in diameter, which rotated in two bearings, the iron gudgeons or journals at each end of the axle being 8 inches in diameter by 8 in long. An iron ring was fitted tightly round the axle, and 4 iron spokes, called the cross, were let into the axle and fixed by screws, the gudgeon being secured to the cross.

Smeaton built relatively few high breast-wheels, though this type became popular after 1800, but he gave much attention to overshot wheels and used them whenever circumstances permitted, owing to their higher efficiency, as proved by his experiments with models. He prepared two designs for the Carshalton corn-mill on the river Wandle, Surrey, one having two low breast-wheels 18 ft in diameter by 6 ft wide, and the other having two overshot wheels 7 ft

4 inches in diameter by 7 ft 6 in wide, for a head of 8 ft 6 in. The latter design was chosen and built.

Smeaton was consulting engineer to the Carron Company's ironworks, Falkirk, and was able therefore to experiment with, and develop the use of, cast iron parts for machinery, one of his greatest contributions to mechanical engineering. His

FIGURE 116—*Model of nineteenth-century iron breast-wheel. In this type the gearing of the wheel has been transferred to the circumference, allowing lighter construction of the axle and bearings.*

first cast iron water-wheel axle was made in 1769 for the Carron No 1 furnace blowing-engine, to replace one with a fractured wooden axle. A typical example was the cast iron shaft for the wheel at H.M. Victualling Office, Deptford, which was a single casting with two flanges to take the arms. Such shafts often ran for several years, but some gave trouble, as they were liable to break in cold and frosty weather. The fault was found to be due to the porous nature of the cast iron, in the parts where the relatively thin flanges joined the much thicker shaft. Smeaton also proposed cast iron for the rings or rims, built up in segments, of large low breast-wheels for driving boring-mills and rolling-mills. His intention was to provide a more constant speed of boring by increasing the fly-wheel effect. Cast iron gearing was used for Brook Mill, Deptford, in 1778 and frequently afterwards.

Smeaton's designs mark the end of an era of wooden water-wheel construction which had lasted for eighteen centuries. His numerous improvements enabled him almost to reach the limit of power that could be generated and transmitted by wooden wheels. His experimental and practical work marked a very important stage in the development of water-power, and fully justify his honoured place in the history of engineering and technology.

After his death, revolutionary improvements in design took place, the most important being all-metal construction (plate 11 A). Others were the fixing of the main driving gear-wheel on the circumference of the water-wheel (figure 116) so that the shaft did not have to transmit the power; ventilated buckets on high breast-wheels; and the sliding hatch or sluice of John Rennie (1761–1821), which admitted water over the top in a thin stream and thus enabled the maximum use always to be obtained from the available head.

Space does not permit the description of the relatively much less important tide mills and floating mills (vol II, pp 607–8, 610, 648), but descriptions of these, and fuller details of the types of watermill here considered, will be found among the works listed in the bibliography at the end of this chapter.

VIII. STRATFORD CORN-MILL, SOMERSET

Stratford Mill was formerly in the parish of West Harptree, Somerset, in the valley of the Chew. Originally it formed part of the manor of West Harptree Tilly, owned by Walter de Dowai at the time of the Norman Conquest. According to the Domesday Survey, this manor already had a mill for which the annual rental was 5*s*. It is not improbable that Stratford Mill was built on the site of this ancient Saxon mill. During the reign of Edward V, the manor passed out of the Tilly family and had a succession of different owners, but unfortunately the manorial records have not been discovered.

The first known reference to the present Stratford mill occurs in the local rate book of 1790, when the owner-occupier was John Collins. In 1861 Joseph Hassell became tenant and later the owner, being succeeded by his daughter. When she died in 1930, the mill was sold to the Duchy of Cornwall, and was purchased in 1939 by the Bristol Waterworks Company. The mill was very active during the war of 1939–45. The post-war construction of a large reservoir in the Chew valley made it necessary to demolish a number of buildings in the area, including the mill. Fortunately, however, a number of acts of generosity made it possible to dismantle the mill and re-erect it in the grounds of Blaise Castle House Folk

Museum near Bristol. It is in consequence possible to describe in detail the machinery of a highly developed watermill.

The existing mill machinery (figure 117) is worked by an external undershot

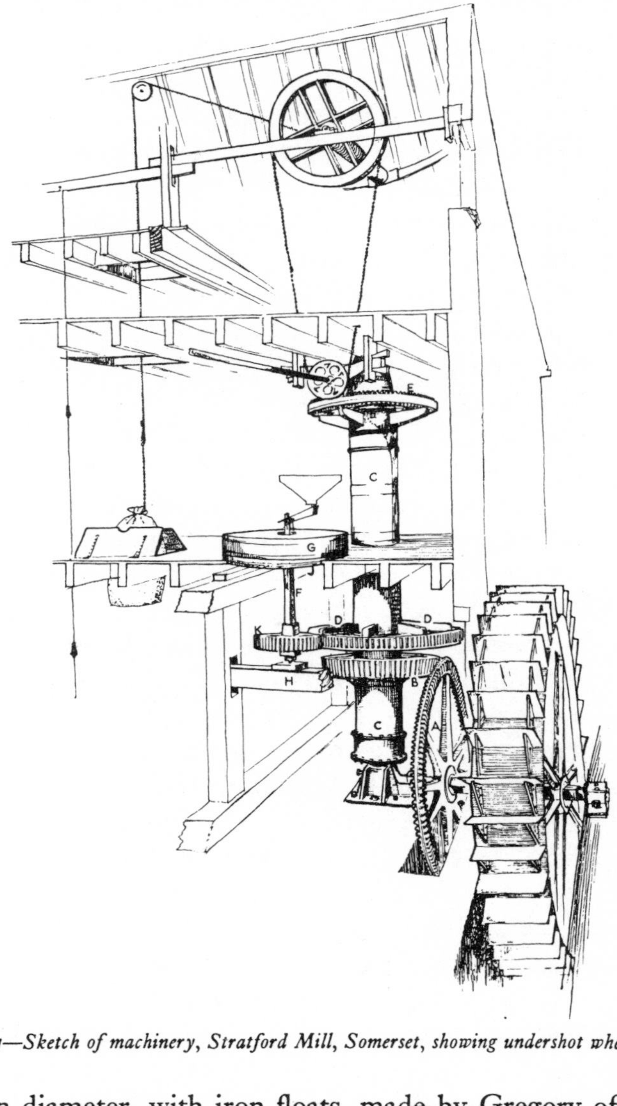

FIGURE 117—*Sketch of machinery, Stratford Mill, Somerset, showing undershot wheel and gears.*

wheel, 14 ft in diameter, with iron floats, made by Gregory of Flax Bourton, Somerset, about 1870 to replace the former wooden wheel. The flow of water, diverted from the main stream into the race, is regulated by a hatch, adjusted by a simple rod-gear operated by the miller within the mill. This in turn controls the speed of the wheel and hence of the machinery. When the hatch is in its lowest position the wheel is stopped. The horizontal iron shaft of the wheel also carries, inside the mill, the vertical pit-wheel A, driving by bevel cogs the wallower or horizontal wheel B on the main vertical shaft C. The latter is of apple wood, about 18 inches in diameter, and is supported in a bearing on the ground floor; it extends upwards through the first floor to a bearing secured to the joists of the second floor. It carries three horizontal wheels, the wallower B, the large spur-wheel D about 6 ft in diameter, and the horizontal gear-wheel E, near the top. It is interesting to note that throughout the driving mechanism the cog wheels are arranged so that metal cogs engage with timber cogs of apple or beech wood, which could be individually shaped and fitted, resulting in quieter running.

The vertical iron shaft F carries and drives the runner, that is, the upper one of the pair of stones G, and is supported in a bearing on the strong wooden bridge-tree H, adjustable at one end by a simple screw mechanism (not shown), which, by raising or lowering this beam relative to its fixed end, raises or lowers the vertical shaft and runner. The degree of fineness of the ground meal is determined by tentering, that is, adjusting the vertical gap between the runner G and the bedstone J at first-floor level. The shaft F is rotated by the stone-nut K, and can be disengaged by raising it clear of the spur-wheel D. The grain in the hopper flows down the shoe or chute and is shaken into the eye of the runner by the 'damsel' or extension on the top of the shaft F. After leaving the stones, the meal travels round inside the hurst or casing surrounding them, and originally descended inside timber chutes through the first floor to points where sacks were hung on adjustable cord supports for filling.

The hoisting of sacks is effected by the mechanism worked from the top of the vertical shaft C. Here the revolving wheel E is continuously engaged with a little vertical cog-wheel driving a horizontal shaft which carries a chain pulley. The chain passes up through the second floor and drives a large vertical wooden wheel at roof level, directly connected to a drum round which the hoisting rope is wound. The operation of this hoisting mechanism is controlled by a lever system which raises or lowers the large wooden pulley at roof level, thereby tightening the chain round the revolving chain pulley at first-floor level. The engaging of this mechanism can be effected from the ground floor by ropes passing through both floors to the levers. The hoisting rope, after passing over a small pulley mounted on the roof timbers, passes down through hinged wooden flaps in each floor which open when a full sack is hoisted and automatically close by dropping as soon as the sack has passed up. Sacks of grain can be hoisted to a platform at roof level, enabling the miller to spread the grain on the second floor, from which it can flow down timber or hessian chutes to the hoppers above the first-floor millstones. This mill originally had two pairs of stones but now has only one pair.

FIGURE 118—*Dressing millstones by hand. Some traditional designs are shown. Upper and lower stones were dressed similarly.* (A) *Late Roman;* (B) *eighteenth century;* (C), (D), (E) *nineteenth century.* (F) *and* (G) *right-handed and left-handed stones in 'four-quarter' dress.*

IX. VARIETIES OF MILLSTONE

Years ago there used to be three main varieties of millstone: (*a*) solid Peak stones, quarried in Derbyshire; (*b*) French burr stones, produced from French quarries in small blocks which were cemented together with plaster of Paris to form the required size; and (*c*) blue stones or cullin stones, which were solid German stones quarried at Cologne, whence their name. Today composition stones of emery and cement are widely used. After a long period of grinding, the millstones become dulled and have to be dressed or sharpened with double-ended steel picks and bills, wedged into the heads of wooden thrifts. There are standard patterns of master furrows running from the eye at the centre to the outer edge, with other furrows branching off from them (figure 118); the lands or grinding surfaces are either closely lined or untouched. Stone-dressing was usually done by the millers themselves, but sometimes by itinerant stone-dressers who walked from mill to mill and lived there until each job was finished.

Plate 11 B shows another old mill for grinding corn. This was Coldron Mill at Spelsbury, Oxfordshire, erected *c* 1800 and demolished in 1937.

BIBLIOGRAPHY

AGRICOLA, G. *De re metallica*, Books VI and VIII. Basel. 1556. Eng. trans. by H. C. and LOU H. HOOVER. The Mining Magazine, London. 1912.

BENNETT, R. and ELTON, J. 'History of Cornmilling', Vols 1, 2. Liverpool. 1898, 1899.

DICKINSON, H. W. 'Water Supply of Greater London.' Newcomen Society, London. 1954.

DICKINSON, H. W. and STRAKER, E. "The Shetland Water Mill." *Trans. Newcomen Soc.*, **13**, 89–94, 1932–3.

FAIRBAIRN, SIR WILLIAM. 'Treatise on Mills and Millwork' (4th ed.). London. 1878.

FITZHERBERT, JOHN. 'The Boke of Surveyinge and Improvements.' London. 1539. See also the edition of 1767.

GARDNER, EMILIE M. "Some Notes on Dutch Water Mills." *Trans. Newcomen Soc.*, **27**, 199–202, 1949–51.

GLYNN, J. 'Power of Water' (5th ed.). London. 1875.
HILLIER, J. 'Old Surrey Watermills.' Skeffington, London. 1951.
JESPERSEN, A. 'Gearing in Watermills in Western Europe.' Published by the author, Virum (Denmark). 1953.
REES, A. 'The Cyclopaedia; or Universal Dictionary of Arts, Sciences and Literature', Vol. 38: 'Water.' London. 1819.
ROSE, W. 'The Village Carpenter.' University Press, Cambridge. 1937.
SCIENCE MUSEUM. 'Historic Books on Machines', by C. ST. C. B. DAVISON. H.M. Stationery Office, London. 1953.
Idem. 'Pumping Machinery' by G. F. WESTCOTT. Part I: 'Historical Notes'; Part II: 'Catalogue.' H.M. Stationery Office, London. 1932–3.
SKILTON, C. P. 'British Windmills and Watermills.' Collins, London. 1947.
SMEATON, J. 'Experimental Enquiry into the Natural Powers of Wind and Water to turn Mills.' London. 1794.
Idem. 'Reports of the late John Smeaton (3 vols). London. 1812.
Idem. 'Catalogue of the Civil and Mechanical Engineering Designs 1741 to 1792 preserved in the Library of the Royal Society.' Newcomen Society, London. 1950.
SOMERVELL, J. 'Water-Power Mills of South Westmorland.' Wilson, Kendal. 1930.
WAILES, R. "Tide Mills in England and Wales." *Trans. Newcomen Soc.*, **16**, 1–33, 1935–6.
WILSON, P. N. "The Origins of Water Power." *Wat. Pwr.*, **4**, 308–13, 1952.
Idem. "Water Power and the Industrial Revolution." *Ibid.*, **6**, 309–16, 1954.
Idem. 'Watermills, an Introduction.' Society for the Protection of Ancient Buildings. Booklet No. 1. London. 1955.
Idem. "The Waterwheels of John Smeaton." *Trans. Newcomen Soc.*, **30**, 1955–6 (in the press).

Half-timbered watermill at Rossett, Denbighshire, built in 1661.

8

PART I

THE CHEMICAL INDUSTRY: DEVELOPMENTS IN CHEMICAL THEORY AND PRACTICE

E. J. HOLMYARD

FROM about the middle of the eighteenth century the chemical industry came to play an increasingly important role in industrial life generally, until towards the end of the period with which this volume deals it already promised to become the giant that we know today. The manner of this development was twofold. In the first place, increased demands for such commodities as glass, soap, soda, dyes, and textiles led to an intense *ad hoc* experimentation, as a result of which there were great improvements in the methods of manufacturing such fundamental substances as the mineral acids and the common alkalis. This aspect of the growth and influence of the chemical industry is dealt with in the second part of this chapter. There was, however, another development taking place simultaneously, and as this parallel line of advance gradually led to the decline of empirical methods, and finally to their almost complete abandonment in more recent times, some account of it is necessary for the balance of the picture.

The gist of the matter is that the period now under review saw a complete revolution in chemistry itself. Until the close of the seventeenth century chemistry had not outgrown alchemical ideas (vol II, ch 21), and although considerable scepticism existed about the possibility of transmuting cheaper metals into gold chemists nevertheless adhered to the basic habits of alchemical theory and practice. Thus they believed that the number of elements constituting all matter was either four (fire, air, water, earth), or three (salt, sulphur, mercury); they paid little or no attention to changes of weight occurring in chemical reactions; they did not recognize the existence of different gases; and they hardly realized the concept of chemical individuality. Such a background does not exclude the possibility of striking empirical discoveries, with which the period indeed abounds, but it is a limiting factor and, had it persisted, would have effectively prevented the astonishing development of chemical industry so characteristic of the nineteenth century and later.

The beneficial, and in the sequel exceedingly fruitful, change in chemical outlook did not take place all at once, but we can conveniently trace its first beginning to the publication in 1661 of 'The Sceptical Chymist' by Robert Boyle (1627–91). In this classic work, Boyle attacked the old ideas of 'elements' and stated that, in his view, chemists should hold no preconceived notions as to the number of elements existing but should rather regard as elements all those substances that they could not decompose into two or more other substances:

> I mean by elements, as those chymists that speak plainest do by their Principles, certain primitive and simple, or perfectly unmingled bodies; which not being made of any other bodies, or of one another, are the ingredients of which all those called perfectly mixt bodies are immediately compounded, and into which they are ultimately resolved . . . I must not look upon any body as a true principle or element, which is not perfectly homogeneous, but is further resolvable into any number of distinct substances.

This conception of a chemical element became a cardinal point of later theory, but for reasons easy to understand it did not gain adherents quickly. For one thing, it replaced the deceptively simple and elegant earlier schemes with a multiplicity of possible elements without providing or suggesting analytical means of investigation. For another, it appeared to contemporary chemists to serve no useful purpose. It thus aroused little discussion or controversy at the time, but though it lay dormant for a while it germinated in the following century when other developments had rendered conditions for its use more favourable. It was revived by Lavoisier (p 220) and then soon gained universal acceptance.

One of these new developments was an increasing interest in gases. To the alchemists there was only one gas, namely air; other aerial fluids were merely air more or less contaminated with poisonous, odorous, inflammable, or coloured impurities. Though they were certainly adept enough to have collected gases, the idea of doing so seems never to have occurred to them until towards the close of the alchemical age. The pioneering steps in the field of 'pneumatic' chemistry or the chemistry of gases were taken by the Flemish iatrochemist Johann Baptista Van Helmont (1577–1644), who was the first to perceive in these tenuous forms of matter a new and important class of substances and who in fact invented the word gas (from chaos) to designate them (vol II, p 745). Van Helmont showed that the *gas silvestre* (carbon dioxide) obtained by burning charcoal was also obtainable by fermenting sugary liquids, and he was able to detect it in the air of the Grotto del Cane, Naples. An inflammable gas from the intestines and from fermenting manure he called *gas pingue* (methane), and it is clear from his writings that he must have obtained several other gases in an impure state.

Though Van Helmont established a footing for gases on the chemical dais he did not succeed in collecting them. Boyle was more ingenious. He took a glass flask with a long neck and completely filled it with dilute sulphuric acid. He then dropped six iron nails into the flask and inverted it in a vessel containing more of the dilute acid. Bubbles of a gas (hydrogen) rose to the top of the apparatus, displacing the acid and soon filling the flask. Here was the germ of that invaluable device so familiar in the elementary laboratory, the pneumatic trough. A further advance in the manipulation of gases was made by John Mayow (1643–78), a Bath physician, who showed that a gas could be transferred from one vessel to another by filling the second one with water, inverting it in a trough of water, and bringing the mouth of the first vessel, containing the gas, under the mouth of the other: 'care being taken that the mouth of neither of the glasses is raised above the surface of the water'. Mayow further emphasized the importance, in work involving measurement of gaseous volumes, of levelling the water inside and outside a jar containing the gas, in order to get the latter at atmospheric pressure. This he accomplished by means of a siphon (figure 119, left).

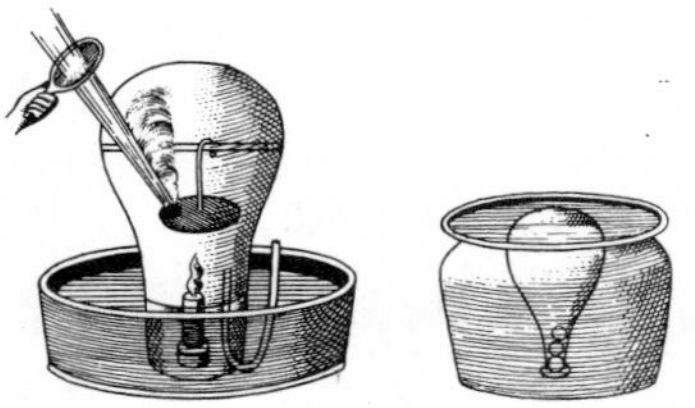

FIGURE 119—*Some of Mayow's apparatus for experiments with gases.* (Left) *Combustion in a limited volume of air. Note siphon.* (Right) *Collecting a gas (nitric oxide) obtained by the action of dilute nitric acid upon iron balls.*

The next improvement was made by Stephen Hales (1677–1761), parish priest of Teddington in Middlesex, whom Horace Walpole described as 'a poor, good, primitive creature' but who nevertheless was one of the founders of plant physiology. In his 'Vegetable Staticks' (1727) he gives an account of many experiments with gases, made in the course of his botanical work, and illustrates some of the apparatus he had devised for the purpose. Figure 120, taken from his book, shows the pneumatic trough used to collect gases evolved during the destructive distillation of vegetable matter. A final touch came with Joseph Priestley (1733–1804), who on occasion filled the trough and collecting-jars with mercury and was thus enabled to isolate several gases previously overlooked or little known owing to their solubility in water; among them were hydrogen sulphide, sulphur dioxide, ammonia, and nitrous oxide.

Investigation of the chemical properties of gases was accompanied by a determination of many of their physical and physico-chemical characteristics. Boyle had shown in 1662 that the volume of a given mass of gas varies inversely as the pressure upon it if the temperature is constant, and J. A. C. Charles (1746–1823)—the first man to make an ascent in a balloon filled with hydrogen (p 255)—discovered (1787) the complementary law that the volume of a given mass of gas at constant pressure varies directly as the absolute temperature. A few years later (1808) Joseph-Louis Gay-Lussac (1778–1850) was able to announce that, according to his experiments, gases react in volumes that at the same temperature and pressure bear a simple ratio to one another and to the volume of the product if that is gaseous: an observation that had a vital bearing on the development of chemical theory.

While the pneumatic chemists were thus establishing a new branch of chemistry,

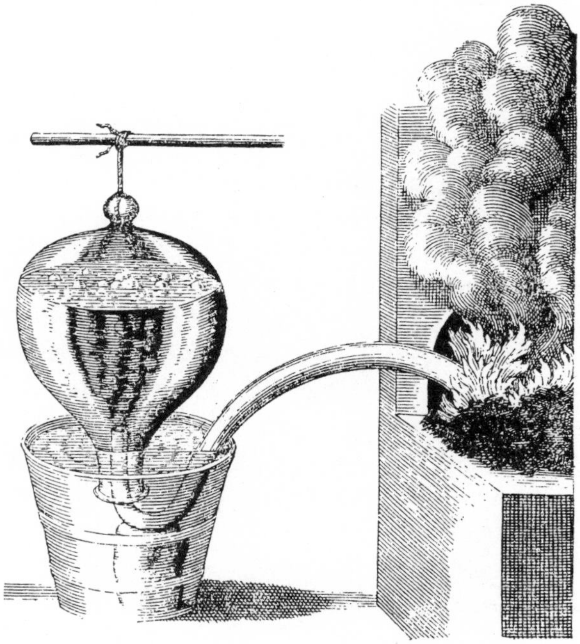

FIGURE 120—*Apparatus used by Stephen Hales to collect gases given off during destructive distillation of vegetable matter.*

fundamental progress was being made in other departments of the science. In the first place, it gradually became tacitly accepted by chemists that, in any and every chemical reaction, the total weight of the reactants is exactly equal to the total weight of the product or products—which is equivalent to postulating that matter is 'conserved', or indestructible and uncreatable. It is impossible to assign credit for this basal assumption to any single head, but the first to use it effectively was Joseph Black (1728–99). In 1756 Black published a paper entitled 'Experiments upon Magnesia Alba, Quicklime, and some other Alcaline Substances', in which, as the result of careful quantitative work, he explained the chemical relationship of limestone, quicklime, and carbon dioxide on lines that have stood the test of time. He relied on the balance at every step, and belief in the conservation of matter is implicit throughout his argument. Black's paper was indeed the first example of that logical, quantitative procedure that afterwards became the norm.

It was in a combination of pneumatic and quantitative chemistry that the modern science had its birth. In 1774 Joseph Priestley (p 216), a dextrous but dilettante experimenter, idly concentrated the Sun's rays through a burning-glass[1] on to a substance then known as calx of mercury (mercuric oxide), and was beyond measure surprised to find that mercury was formed and that a gas was given off with remarkable powers of supporting combustion. His surprise was occasioned by the fact that, in common with all other chemists of the time, he held an erroneous theory of combustion and metallic constitution. This was the theory of phlogiston, according to which a combustible body owed its combustibility to the presence in it of a fiery principle, phlogiston. On combustion, the phlogiston was lost and only an ash—the other constituent of the combustible body—was left. The more readily a substance burned, and the smaller the amount of ash left, the greater the proportion of phlogiston in the substance. The ash of a metal was known as its calx, and even a metal that could not be made to burn with a flame might yet be caused to yield its phlogiston and form a calx by continued heating. To Priestley's mind, therefore, heat should have had no effect on the calx of mercury, and one wonders what freak of thought led him to try this particular experiment. However that may be, the result was momentous, for he had discovered oxygen. Never a very clear or logical thinker—'*il se servit de ses mains, plus que de son cerveau*'—Priestley was unable to explain the reaction, but his discovery provided the missing clue to a problem that had been engaging the attention of the French chemist A. L. Lavoisier (1743–94).

Attracted by the phenomena of combustion, Lavoisier observed—as had indeed been observed many times before—that the calx of a metal weighed more than the metal from which it was obtained. Boyle, to whom this fact was well known, ascribed it to the passage of heat, which he regarded as a material substance, through the walls of the vessel from the fire to the metal. Lavoisier saw that this explanation was susceptible of experimental proof or disproof:

> If [he says] the increase in weight of metals calcined in closed vessels is due, as Boyle thought, to the addition of the matter of flame and fire which penetrates the pores of the glass and combines with the metal, it follows that if, after having introduced a known quantity of metal into a glass vessel, and having sealed it hermetically, one determines

[1] Burning-glasses were quite often used to provide heat in chemical experiments. A large one made and mounted in France is shown in plate 8 A.

its weight exactly; and that if one then proceeds to the calcination in a charcoal fire, as Boyle did; and lastly that if one then reweighs the same vessel after the calcination, before opening it, its weight ought to be found to have increased by the whole of the quantity of the matter of fire which entered during the calcination. . . .

If, on the contrary . . . the increase in weight of the metallic calx is not due to the combination of the matter of fire nor to any exterior matter whatever, but to the fixation of a portion of the air contained in the space of the vessel, the vessel ought not to weigh more after the calcination than before, it ought merely to be found partly empty of air, and the increase in weight of the vessel should take place only at the moment when the missing portion of air is allowed to enter.

There could hardly be a more lucid statement of the problem, and Lavoisier proceeded to put his views to the test of experiment. He took a weighed glass flask, introduced a weighed quantity of tin, sealed the flask hermetically, and then heated it for some hours until no further calcination appeared to be taking place. He now allowed the flask to cool, after which he weighed it. There was no change in weight. Upon opening the flask, air was heard to enter, and when the apparatus was weighed once more, an increase in weight was found. This was clearly the weight of air that had entered the flask, and Lavoisier discovered that, to within about six parts in a thousand, it was equal to the increase of weight undergone by the tin on calcination. These results made it plain that calcination, far from being a decomposition, was on the contrary a combination of the metal with air or with a gas or gases forming part of the air.

Further experiments on the same lines enabled Lavoisier to conclude:

First, that one cannot calcine an unlimited quantity of tin in a given quantity of air.

Second, that the quantity of metal calcined is greater in a large vessel than in a small one. . . .

Third, that the hermetically sealed vessels, weighed before and after the calcination of the tin they contain, show no difference in weight, which clearly proves that the increase in weight of the metal comes neither from the material of the fire nor from any matter exterior to the vessel.

Fourth, that in every calcination of tin, the increase in weight of the metal is, fairly exactly, equal to the weight of the quantity of air absorbed, which proves that the portion of the air which combines with the metal during the calcination has a specific gravity nearly equal to that of atmospheric air.

Finally, that the portion of the air which combines with the metal is slightly heavier than atmospheric air, and that which remains after the calcination is, on the contrary, rather lighter. Atmospheric air, on this assumption, would form, relatively to the specific gravity, a mean result between these two airs.

These pregnant observations and deductions show how far chemistry was now moving from alchemy. The law of the conservation of matter was here again tacitly assumed, and the balance was the irrefragable arbiter. Instead of being one of the 'four elements', air was not an element at all but must consist of at least two gases, one active in calcination (and therefore in combustion) and the other inactive.

But at this point the work was still unfinished: the problem remained of separating the active part of the air from the inactive. Here fate intervened, by effecting a meeting between Lavoisier and Priestley at which Priestley told the Frenchman about the curious behaviour of calx of mercury on heating. Lavoisier instantly perceived that his problem was solved, the key being the facts (*a*) that when mercury is heated comparatively gently in air it gradually calcines, or combines with the active portion of the air, and (*b*) that the calx on being heated more strongly decomposes into its constituents, namely, mercury and active air. On this basis, Lavoisier carried out an operation so momentous in its results as to have become familiarly known by the simple title of 'Lavoisier's experiment' (figure 121). It consisted in moderately heating mercury in contact with a limited volume of air until no further calcination could be observed. During the calcination the volume of enclosed air diminished by about one-fifth or one-sixth, and the remaining air would not allow substances to burn in it. The calx was carefully collected, and more strongly heated in an apparatus suitable for receiving the gas evolved. Lavoisier found that this gas supported combustion much better than ordinary air, and that its volume was equal to the diminution in volume undergone by the air originally taken. When it was mixed with the inactive gas left in the first operation, the mixture was indistinguishable from ordinary air.

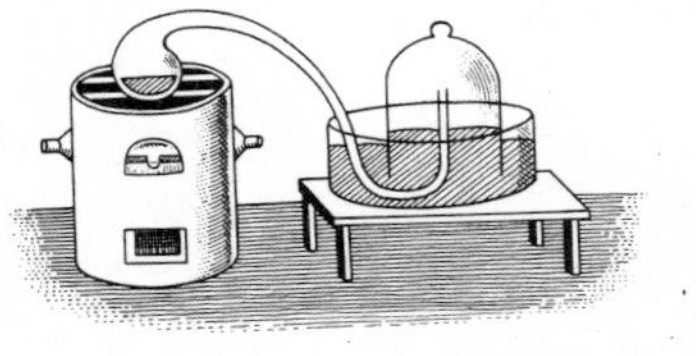

FIGURE 121—*Diagrammatic representation of the apparatus for 'Lavoisier's experiment'.*

Lavoisier had thus demonstrated the composite nature of atmospheric air in the most convincing way possible: by taking it apart and putting it together again. Further experiments firmly persuaded him, and later all other chemists, that combustion and calcination were combinations of active air with the combustible or calcinable body: phlogiston was overthrown and the modern theory of combustion established. A specific name for the active gas was obviously desirable, and since the products of combustion of sulphur, phosphorus, and carbon in the moist gas proved to be acid, Lavoisier framed the word 'oxygen', from the Greek words meaning 'acid-producer'.

In the meantime, H. Cavendish (1731–1810) had shown that when oxygen and the gas we now know as hydrogen were sparked together (figure 122), water was formed, but he put an erroneous interpretation upon his results. Lavoisier repeated and extended Cavendish's experiments and was able both to synthesize water by the explosion together of hydrogen and oxygen, and to liberate hydrogen from water by passing steam over red-hot iron. He had thus established the composite nature of two of the classical 'elements', and though 'fire'—heat or caloric—left him puzzled he had no doubt about the composite nature of 'earth'.

While this revolutionary work was going on, great extensions took place both in the repertory of known chemical substances and in the field of chemical analysis. A Swedish apothecary, C. W. Scheele (1742–86), not only discovered oxygen independently of, and slightly earlier than, Priestley, but was the first to isolate chlorine and to prepare such valuable substances as hydrofluoric, lactic, oxalic, citric, tartaric, and uric acids, glycerol, and milk-sugar. He showed that graphite is a form of carbon, and invented new methods of preparing ether, calomel, and phosphorus. His contemporary, the German chemist M. H. Klaproth (1743–1817), elaborated reliable methods for the analysis of minerals and discovered the elements uranium, titanium, and zirconium. Gay-Lussac (p 217) laid the foundations of volumetric analysis, and C. L. Berthollet (1748–1822)—one of the first chemists to adopt Lavoisier's new theory of combustion—discovered hypochlorites and chlorates.

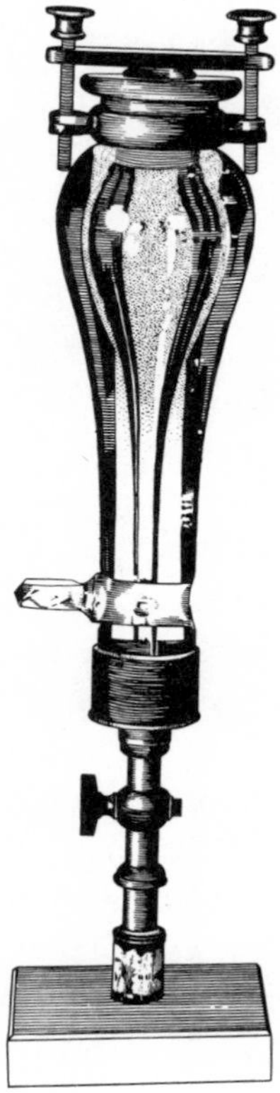

FIGURE 122—*Cavendish's vessel for the explosion of gases.*

Such activity, of which these few examples must here suffice, impressed upon chemists the urgent need for a thorough revision of chemical nomenclature. The old nomenclature was completely unsystematic and had grown up piecemeal and at haphazard; it contained such absurd names as butter of arsenic, sugar of lead, flowers of zinc, and liver of sulphur, as well as other names—powder of algaroth, colcothar, aethiops, sal alembroth, sal mirabile, and so forth—that made excessive demands upon the memory without giving any information about the substances for which they were employed. There were in addition several alchemical names, which meant one thing to the chemist and another to the layman. Given the history of the science, such confusion was no doubt inevitable, but with the rapid advance of chemical knowledge it became apparent that an orderly and reasonable nomenclature was a prime necessity. Lavoisier's work on oxygen and water provided the requisite basis for such a system, and he, together with Guyton de Morveau (1737–1816), Berthollet, and A. F. de Fourcroy (1755–1809), undertook the preparation of a nomenclature based upon scientific principles. The report of the committee was published in 1787, under the title *Méthode de Nomenclature Chimique*, and in his prefatory memoir Lavoisier observes that there are three things to distinguish in every physical science: the series of facts that constitute the science, the ideas that recall the facts, and the words that express them. The word must evoke the idea, the idea must depict the fact: they are but three impressions of one seal. The perfect chemical nomenclature would render ideas and facts in their exact verity, without suppression and more particularly without addition.

This counsel of perfection was given a more practical turn by Guyton de Morveau, who suggested (*a*) that a chemical name should not be a phrase, (*b*) that it ought not to require circumlocutions to become definite, (*c*) that it ought to recall the constituents of a compound body, (*d*) that it should not be of the type 'Glauber's salt', which conveys nothing about the composition of the substance, (*e*) that in the absence of knowledge concerning the constitution of a substance, the provisional name should be non-committal, (*f*) that new names should preferably be coined from Latin or Greek, so that their signification could the more widely and easily be understood, and (*g*) that the form of such words should be assimilated to the genius of the language in which they are to be used.

One instance will be sufficient to show how these principles were applied in the detailed system proposed, which is basically that still employed. Sulphur, says de Morveau, in combining with oxygen produces an acid. To conserve the idea of this origin and to express clearly the first degree of composition, the name of this acid ought to be a derivative of the word sulphur; but this acid exists in two states of saturation and shows different properties in each. To avoid confusion, each state must be given a name that, while conserving the root, nevertheless marks this difference. Lastly, it is necessary to consider sulphur in other direct combinations, such as with alkalis and metals. Five different terminations, adapted to the same root, sulphur, are suggested to meet these requirements:

sulphuric acid will express sulphur saturated with oxygen as far as it can be, that is, what is called vitriolic acid.
sulphurous acid will express sulphur united to a less quantity of oxygen.
sulphate will be the generic name of all salts formed from sulphuric acid.
sulphite will be the name of salts formed from sulphurous acid.
sulphide will denote all the compounds of sulphur not carried to the state of an acid.

Guyton de Morveau remarks with justice that 'no-one will fail to perceive, at the first glance, all the advantages of such a nomenclature, which, while indicating various substances, at the same time defines them, recalls their constituent parts, classes them in their order of composition, and to a certain extent draws attention to the proportions that cause the variation in their properties'.

The work of the committee was completed by a dictionary giving the old and new names of about 700 substances, in which occur for the first time such familiar terms as potassium carbonate, copper nitrate, zinc sulphate, and ammonium molybdate. The enormous improvement of the new system does not need to be emphasized, but apart from its convenience it manifests that the idea of chemical individuality—altogether foreign to the alchemists—had become so generally accepted as to be taken as axiomatic. With the oxygen theory of combustion and with the ever-growing reliance on quantitative work, the systematic scheme of nomenclature had largely effected the chemical revolution on which so much of nineteenth-century technology was to be firmly based.

Largely, but not entirely: two or three other important factors had essential parts to play, and we may consider them in turn. The first was the establishment by John Dalton (1766–1844) of a serviceable atomic theory of the constitution of matter. The operative word is 'serviceable', for atomic theories were as old as classical Greece and Rome, and had been revived on sporadic occasions throughout the centuries. They bore, however, little fruit until Isaac Newton (1642–1727) used the atomic conception to explain certain physical properties. Thus in the *Principia* he stated that 'if the density of a fluid gas which is made up of mutually repulsive particles is proportional to the pressure, the forces between the particles are reciprocally proportional to the distances between their centres. And *vice versa*, mutually repulsive particles, the forces between which are reciprocally proportional to the distances between their centres, will make up an elastic fluid, the density of which is proportional to the pressure.' This argument provides a theoretical explanation of Boyle's law (p 216), and is typical of a new attitude towards atomic speculation. Greek philosophers, or some of them, had postulated a discrete constitution of matter but could not discover any way of testing their postulate; the advance of science had suggested some such ways, and it was for Dalton to apply them particularly in the field of chemistry.

This is not the place in which to describe in detail the chemical atomic theory that gradually shaped itself in Dalton's mind, but the main points of it must be briefly noted. First, Dalton assumed that all matter is composed of a vast number of extremely minute particles or atoms, and that chemical analysis and synthesis are nothing more than the separation of particles from one another, and their reunion: in other words, atoms are indestructible and uncreatable, whence comes a theoretical foundation for the law of the conservation of matter. Next, each element has its own distinctive kind of atom, and similarly each compound has its own distinctive kind of 'compound atom', or molecule as we now say. Dalton then went on to point out that it is important, and possible, to ascertain the relative weights of different atoms; and the fact that he suggested how this might be done is a sufficient mark of his genius. Quantitative chemistry was by now well established, and, as Dalton said, 'it has justly been considered an important object to ascertain the relative weights of the simplest elements which constitute a compound'. If, therefore, one knew the relative numbers in which the atoms of the different elements combined, the relative weights of those atoms could easily be calculated from the results of the quantitative analysis. The crux of the problem lay in the 'if', and Dalton's great achievement was that he saw how the difficulty might be surmounted. In effect, he applied Occam's razor—'entities must not be multiplied beyond what is necessary'—and assumed that when elements combine to form compounds, the molecules of the compounds consist of small whole numbers of the atoms of the elements concerned, the emphasis being on the small.

It was only an assumption, but it showed the way to experimental investigation, and if the results to which it led proved to be inconsistent it always allowed room for adjustment. We may take a few examples. At that time, water was the only known compound of oxygen and hydrogen; Dalton therefore assumed its molecule to consist of one atom of each element. But gravimetric analysis showed that in water eight parts by weight of oxygen were combined with one part by weight of hydrogen. Therefore the atom of oxygen must be eight times as heavy as the atom of hydrogen. Similarly, the only compound of nitrogen and hydrogen known to Dalton was ammonia, whose molecule he thus took to consist of one atom of each element. Analysis showed that the relative weights of hydrogen and nitrogen in the gas were as 1 is to about 5, hence the nitrogen atom must weigh about five times as much as that of hydrogen. Finally, Dalton knew of two oxides of carbon, carbonic oxide (carbon monoxide) and carbonic acid (carbon dioxide); the former he considered to be a binary compound of one atom of carbon and one of oxygen, and the other a ternary compound of one atom of carbon and two of oxygen. By quantitative analysis it was therefore a simple matter to arrive at the relative weights of the oxygen and carbon atoms.

Working in this way Dalton was able to construct a table of 'atomic weights' of the elements, that is, the relative weights of their atoms taking the weight of the hydrogen atom as unity. By an extension of the figures he was able to discover the relative weights, compared to that of the hydrogen atom, of the ultimate particles or molecules of various compounds. The significant outcome of the work, which was pursued not only by Dalton himself but—with greater analytical accuracy—by the Swedish chemist J. J. Berzelius (1779–1848), was that, though various discrepancies occurred, the 'atomic' and 'molecular' weights exhibited a remarkable degree of interdependent agreement. This showed that Dalton was at least on the right track, and in point of fact he had deservedly good luck in selecting for his early investigations substances whose molecules happen to be of a very simple constitution. But his guesses at their molecular structure were not always correct, and the figures he obtained for 'atomic' weights were merely what the modern chemist knows as equivalents. They could not be taken as definitive until the appropriate molecular structures were known with certainty, and then it might prove necessary to multiply them by an integer to get the true atomic weights. Dalton was never able to solve this aspect of the problem, which was later cleared up successfully by A. Avogadro (1776–1856) and S. Cannizzaro (1826–1910), but his provisional atomic weights played an incalculably valuable role in systematizing chemistry and in consolidating the experimental advances that were now being made in rapid succession.

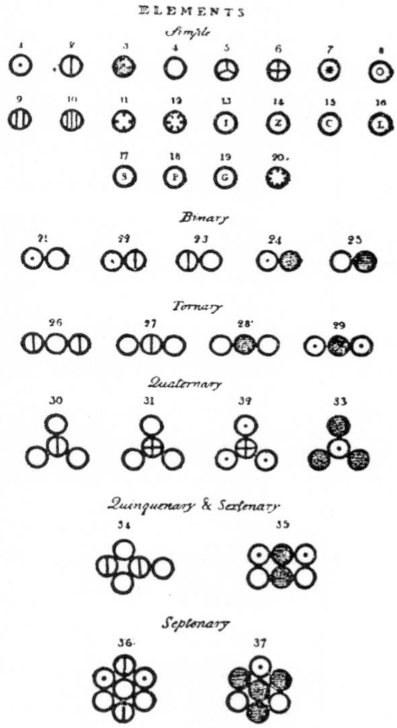

FIGURE 123—*Some of Dalton's symbols and formulae.*

Thinking always in terms of atoms, as he did, Dalton soon perceived the convenience of having a symbolic notation for them, and he constructed a scheme in which circles with lines, dots, shading, or capital letters in them were used to represent atoms of the various elements. Suitable groupings of these elementary symbols were used as formulae for the molecules of compounds. A list of some of Dalton's symbols and formulae is given in figure 123. The important difference between his signs and those in earlier chemical use is this: that whereas the old sign ♀, for instance, had signified copper in any quantity, Dalton's symbol © stood for one atom of copper and thus possessed a definite quantitative significance completely absent from the sign ♀. The formulae of compounds conveyed even more information; thus that of carbon dioxide, ○●○, showed that, in the opinion of those who adopted it, the molecule of carbon dioxide contains one atom of carbon and two of oxygen. And since (according to Dalton's reckoning) the atomic weight of oxygen is 6·5 and that of carbon 5, it is implicit in the formula that the composition of carbon dioxide is *carbon : oxygen* as *5 : 13*.

Dalton's symbols and formulae were adopted by those few chemists perspicacious enough to understand their potential value, but for the chemical world in general the system proved much too cumbersome. Fortunately, about 1814 or even a little earlier, Berzelius suggested a much more convenient notation, which is, in essentials, the one still employed. In his *Théorie des proportions chimiques* (1819; second edition 1835) he points out that the use of symbols greatly facilitates the expression of chemical facts. In order to render the usage general, it would be quite sufficient to give each element its own particular symbol, which would represent the relative weight of its atom. Berzelius then selected as appropriate symbols the initial letter of the (usually Latin or latinized) name of the element, or, when two or more elements had names beginning with the same letter, the initial letter together with another characteristic letter of the name, after the single initial had been allocated. Thus C signified one atom of carbon, Cr one of chromium, and Co one of cobalt. Juxtaposition of atomic symbols, with numerical suffixes when necessary, gave such molecular formulae as CO (carbon monoxide) and CO_2 (carbon dioxide).

This system was so simple to use, so easy to remember, and so concisely informative, that it very quickly gained universal currency among chemists. It has been modified and extended since the time of Berzelius, but his conception of a formula as a summary of experience still holds good. By a mere inspection of its formula, a chemist may gather as much about the constitution, preparation, properties, and reactions of a substance as might occupy two or three pages of prose description. Such formulae are indeed a principal medium for the expression and transmission of chemical knowledge.

All these striking upheavals in chemistry had been crammed into the space of comparatively few years—no more than a single life-time—and the tale is still not complete. On 20 March 1800, eight years before Dalton outlined the atomic theory in the first part of his 'A New System of Chemical Philosophy', the Italian physicist Alessandro Volta (1745–1827) announced his invention of the 'voltaic pile' or electric battery. The news of this invention aroused intense interest throughout Europe, and in the autumn of 1801 Volta was invited to demonstrate his battery before the Institute of France. Napoleon himself attended a demonstration and was so much impressed by what he saw that he not only made Volta a handsome gift in money, but offered a prize of 60 000 francs to encourage the study of electricity. An electric battery soon became an indispensable part of the equipment of a chemical laboratory, and in a few years it had proved its surpassing value as a scientific tool.

In May 1800, only a few weeks after Volta's original announcement, W. Nicholson and Anthony Carlisle showed that water could be split up into hydrogen and oxygen by the passage of an electric current through it. In the following September the German scientist Ritter effected an electrolytic copper-plating, and a little later Berzelius showed that, in general, an aqueous solution of a salt on electrolysis yielded the metal or its hydroxide at the cathode and oxygen or an acid at the anode. In 1806 Humphry Davy (1778–1829) advanced the hypothesis that chemical and electrical attraction are essentially identical, and expressed the belief that many substances that had hitherto resisted all attempts to split them up might possibly be decomposed if a sufficiently powerful current were passed through them. Two such substances were caustic soda and caustic potash. It is true that Lavoisier, with characteristic flair, had suspected them to be metallic compounds containing oxygen, but the suspicion had never been substantiated. In 1807, however, Davy passed a strong electric current from a battery (figure 124) through fused caustic soda and potash, and had the keen satisfaction of observing each of them to be decomposed: the soda into oxygen, hydrogen, and the soft white metal now known as sodium, and the potash into the same two gases and the similar metal potassium.

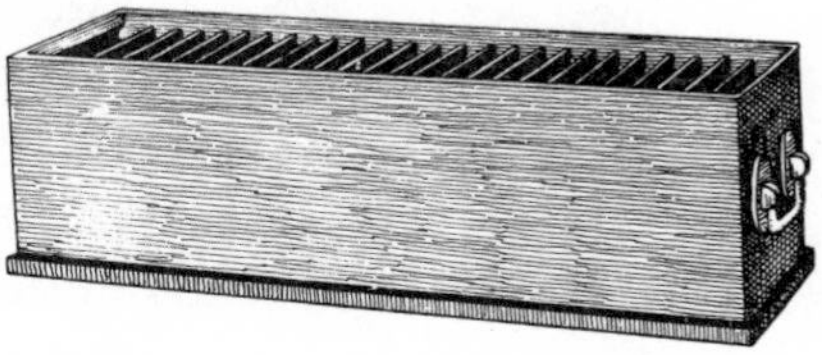

FIGURE 124—*Davy's battery at the Royal Institution, London.*

The qualitative importance of the electric battery was thus soon established, and towards the end of the period with which this volume deals the quantitative aspects of electrolytic phenomena were elucidated by Michael Faraday (1791–1867). In 1832–3 he showed that the mass of any individual product liberated in electrolysis is directly proportional to the quantity of electricity which has been passed through the electrolyte, and that the masses of the various products liberated in electrolysis by the passage of the same quantity of electricity are in the exact ratio of their chemical equivalents. These fundamental discoveries were the germ of the electrochemical industry that grew up in the second half of the nineteenth century (vol V, ch 11).

To describe or even to list any of the countless minor developments and discoveries made between 1750 and 1850 would be foreign to the purpose of this work. What this brief sketch of chemical history during that period has attempted to show is that, while the industrial revolution was taking place, chemistry was itself undergoing a revolution of comparable magnitude. The whole outlook of the science was metamorphosed. At the beginning of the period alchemy still lingered, empirical methods held undisputed sway, and such chemical theory as existed was sterile if not actually an obstacle to progress. Then a change began, at first slowly but later with gathering speed, and the foundations of the modern science were quickly laid one after another. The idea of chemical individuality led to improved methods of purification and analysis; the idea of the conservation of matter led to the establishment of quantitative chemistry; the work of the pneumatic chemists led to the discovery of the true composition of air and water and to a satisfactory theory of combustion; physical investigation of gases led to the enunciation of the atomic theory and chemical investigation to its acceptance; the atomic theory led to a better understanding of chemical reactions and to a convenient system of notation; and the discovery of the electric battery led first to wider qualitative discovery and subsequently to quantitative advances and to the development of fruitful chemical theory. From its very beginnings this spectacular growth reacted upon the chemical industry—even the mineral-water industry was initiated by Priestley—and little by little offered improvements upon old methods as well as suggesting entirely new ones. The conservatism of industrialists, still not unknown, was gradually broken down and more and more reliance was placed upon the knowledge that chemists provided. Many of the chemical manufacturers were themselves skilled in chemistry, and the ultimate importance of academic research to industry gained growing recognition. Conversely, the increased bulk and variation of industrial activity reacted upon the growth of pure chemistry by directing much research into specific channels, but the vital point is that the success of the chemical industry and in the long run of industry as a whole was very largely the result of the basic advances in pure chemistry here outlined. The history of technology since 1750 cannot be properly understood unless this fact is kept in mind. The detailed account of the chemical industry that follows shows how, in the branch most immediately affected, the new knowledge and philosophy made their influence felt.

BIBLIOGRAPHY

FREUND, I. 'The Study of Chemical Composition.' University Press, Cambridge. 1904.
HOLMYARD, E. J. 'Makers of Chemistry.' Clarendon Press, Oxford. 1931.
LOWRY, T. M. 'Historical Introduction to Chemistry' (3rd ed.). Macmillan, London. 1936.
MASSON, SIR JAMES IRVINE ORME. 'Three Centuries of Chemistry.' Benn, London. 1925.
McKIE, D. 'Antoine Lavoisier.' Constable, London. 1952.
MEYER, E. S. C. VON. 'A History of Chemistry' (trans. from the German by G. McGOWAN, 3rd ed.). Macmillan, London. 1906.
MUIR, M. M. P. 'A History of Chemical Theories and Laws.' Wiley, New York. 1907.
PARTINGTON, J. R. 'A Short History of Chemistry.' Macmillan, London. 1937.
THORPE, SIR THOMAS EDWARD. 'History of Chemistry' (2 vols). Watts, London. 1909–10.

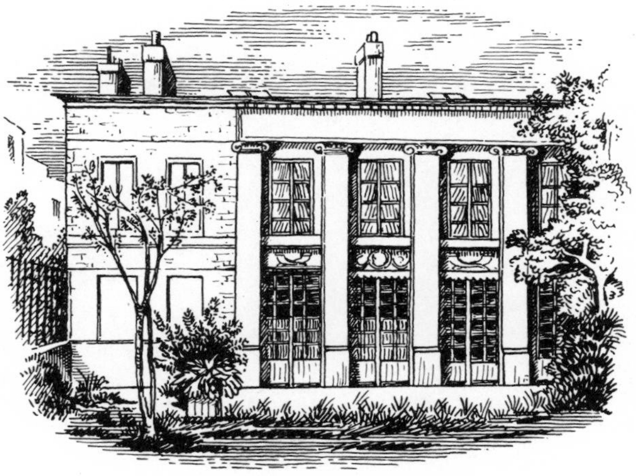

Lavoisier's house opposite the Madeleine, Paris.

8

PART II

THE CHEMICAL INDUSTRY: INTERACTION WITH THE INDUSTRIAL REVOLUTION

A. AND N. L. CLOW

THE chemical industry is the most polygamous of all industries—a description that pin-points a fundamental difference between it and practically all co-extensive industries. Not only does the chemical industry operate on a wider range of raw materials than, say, the textile industry, but its products are only rarely ends in themselves. They are in the main absorbed by other industries—sulphuric acid by the fertilizer industry, soda by glass-manufacturers, mordants by the textile trade—with the result that many products never appear as such in everyday life. But, although it may not have been obvious, chemistry has nevertheless played a fundamental role in the development of practically every branch of technology: metallurgy, textile-finishing, glass- and pottery-making, soap-making, and agriculture, to name only a few. It is this diversity that makes the chemical industry difficult to deal with in a coherent and summary form: its raw materials are many, its products varied, each manufactured by a process peculiar to itself.

Fortunately, however, this complexity can be reduced, because, while differing in detail, the number of fundamentally different techniques used is not great. These include: (*a*) furnace techniques, whereby the astonishing transformations of the metallurgical, glass, and pottery industries are brought about, (*b*) purification by crystallization, as in the production of salt and sugar, (*c*) distillation, and, as a later development, (*d*) the handling of gases. These processes enabled industrial chemists to progress towards the more sophisticated procedures of the twentieth century.

Furnace techniques go farther back than written records, and on them are centred the first observations that led to a body of chemical knowledge (figure 125): classical examples are the transformation of green malachite into red metallic copper, the firing of grey clay to give a red earthenware body, and so on. The ancients knew of six solid metals, but metallurgy was not the only furnace technique that industry of the industrial revolution inherited. The manufacture of glass and pottery (though for centuries neither product was widely used except among the upper classes) was established from China to the Baltic, and even at an early date some examples imply a high degree of technical competence. In making these products craftsmen cannot have failed to observe the profound changes taking place as their raw materials were transformed in the furnace, and they must have had the knowledge to search for, and to select, the proper materials—plant-ashes to supply alkali, sand to supply silica, and clays with the proper rheological properties.

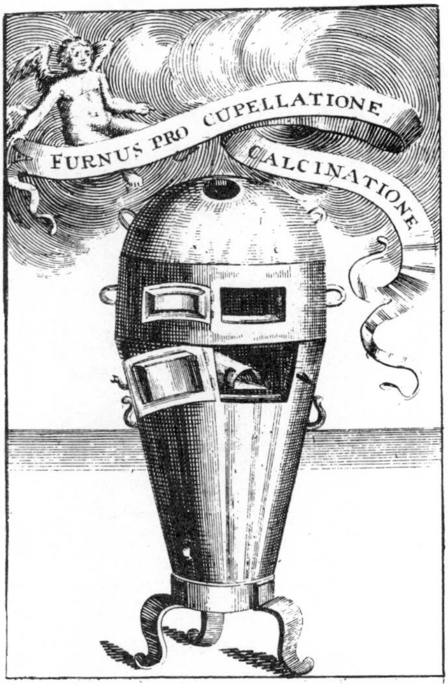

FIGURE 125—*Furnace for cupellation and calcination.*

In addition to the above (which by their use of fire undoubtedly have a dramatic quality), over many generations a body of knowledge comprising more subtle techniques was accumulated. These include tanning, involving knowledge of aluminium salts, and the production and use of mordants and dye-wares. Also, there is the part played by those chemists who saw their subject as the handmaid of medicine, the iatrochemists. By the beginning of the eighteenth century they, and the alchemists who were studying material bodies for a different purpose, had accumulated a collection of facts, as yet only loosely tied together by the most nebulous of theories, but nevertheless sufficient to play an important part in the subsequent development of chemical technology. To give only one example: there was the observation by J. R. Glauber (1603–70) of the resistance of lead to sulphuric acid, an observation that was utilized by John Roebuck (1718–94) when he began to make sulphuric acid in Britain in 1746. Glauber's observation may be considered a key discovery; its value was quite beyond reckoning. His 'Treatise on Philosophical Furnaces' was one of the outstanding collections of chemical and technological information published during the seventeenth century (vol III, ch 2).

Among the substances that attained importance in the chemical revolution were the following: *soda* and *potash*, mild alkalis derived until the end of the eighteenth century from plant-ashes (figure 126), or from natural deposits when geologic and climatic conditions were suitable. These alkalis may also have been known in the caustic condition, so rendered by the action of *lime*. By reaction with fats or oils the alkalis gave *soap* (vol III, pp 703–5), the manufacture of which, together with glass-making, may be taken as an index of an emergent chemical industry. The production of *salt* and *alum* must be similarly regarded, since the technique on which it is based, namely purification by recrystallization (figure 127), is of great importance throughout the whole of the chemical industry, as well as in the technical production of such substances as *sugar* (vol III, pp 7–8).

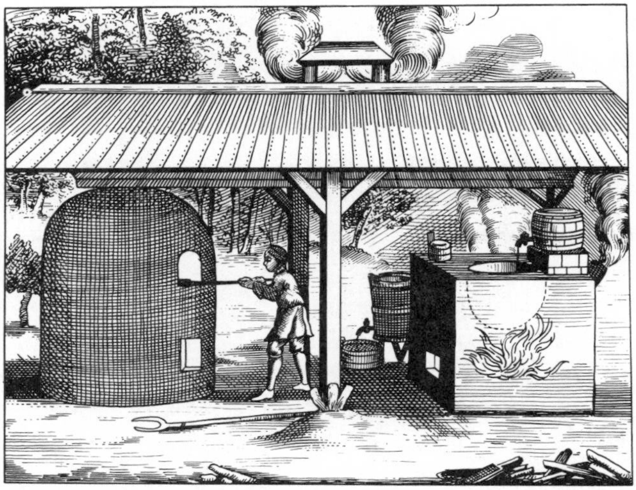

FIGURE 126—*Production of potash by the leaching of wood-ash.*

From our knowledge of the history of gunpowder it is clear that early technologists were familiar with two other chemical raw materials: *sulphur*, which occurs in the Mediterranean area and in Spain, and *saltpetre* (or nitre), mostly obtained from India and China through the East India trade, though knowledge that it could be made by neutralizing nitric acid with potash dates from the seventeenth century (vol II, pp 379–82).

The purification of sulphur and arsenic involved a knowledge of sublimation (figure 128), as also did the production of *sal ammoniac*, another substance which attained some importance from the seventeenth century onwards. Both sal ammoniac and borax were used as fluxes. A noteworthy list of substances then known was published by G. Roth in 1721.

To the above must be added an almost universal knowledge of the production of alcohol by fermentation, and the subsequent isolation of the alcohol by distillation (figure 129 and vol III, pp 11–12). Not only was it known how to produce alcohol but it was early realized that the fermentation could be taken a stage farther with the production of *acetic acid*, an acid which, together with citric acid and the salts of both, was much used in the textile industry. Glauber realized that the acids produced from wood-distillation and by fermentation were identical.

The more powerful mineral acids (sulphuric and nitric) were also known and found uses ranging from refining precious metals to the production of pharmacological nostrums. Glauber gives the preparation of hydrochloric acid from rock-salt and sulphuric acid, and fuming nitric acid from potassium nitrate and arsenious oxide.

FIGURE 127—*Crystallization of salt, illustrating early method of purification.*

The extent of the technological knowledge available at the beginning of what J. U. Nef calls the first industrial revolution may be judged by the publications then in existence. There was, for example, *De re metallica* by Georg Bauer (Agricola) (1494–1555) published at Basel in 1556. Bauer collected a mass of material about mineralogy, metallurgy, and chemical processes generally, and his work may be taken as the most complete on the chemical industry, such as it was, written before the seventeenth century. Then there is *Alchemia* of Andreas Libavius (1540–1616) of Halle, first published in 1597. The *Alchemia* is often described as the first real textbook of chemistry. It covers chemical technology, pharmacy, and metallurgy. In it the preparation of sulphuric acid from sulphur and saltpetre is rationally described. But it was a century before a publication that can justly be called a textbook of chemistry appeared. This was *Elementa chemiae* of Hermann Boerhaave (1668–1738). While professor of chemistry at Leyden, Boerhaave taught many of the men who subsequently made fundamental contributions in the application of chemistry to industry. To these works may be added four publications purely technological in origin. First is the *De la pirotechñia* of Vannoccio Biringuccio of Siena, which appeared in 1540 and is remarkable for its freedom from alchemical influence. Second comes the earliest handbook on the tinctorial arts, published by Rosetti of Venice in the same year; the sixteenth century saw new dye-wares introduced into Europe as the result of the discovery of America and the ocean route to the East, and the development of new methods of fixing dyes with, for example, iron, aluminium, and tin mordants. Lastly there are the *Art de terre* by Bernard Palissy (1510–88), in which great emphasis is laid on recourse to experiment, and the *De arte vitraria* by Antonio Neri of Florence, published in 1612.

Not only do the above treatises indicate the expansion and amassing of knowledge, but, with the founding of the Royal Society of London in 1660, we have

FIGURE 128—*Purification by sublimation, as in the preparation of arsenic.*

a further indication that time was ripening for the organized pursuit of natural knowledge. The 'Heads of Enquiries' issued by the Society shortly after its foundation reveal the interest of its founder members in the advance of technology, much of it chemical and metallurgical. This development was not confined to England: the *Académie Royale des Sciences* was founded in Paris in 1666 and its members displayed similar interests.

Among the topics of greatest interest were the substitution of coal for timber, and the need to deepen mines. The introduction of coal as a substitute for wood is a dominant factor both in the mechanical and in the chemical revolutions of the eighteenth and nineteenth centuries; it is therefore necessary to look at the position held by timber in the economy prevailing before the industrial revolution.

The structural use of wood on land and sea is obvious, but by-products of wood, particularly tar and pitch, were also essential to a maritime nation. Wood was also frequently the only fuel available. In domestic grates the substitution of coal gave rise to no particular difficulties, but for many generations wood continued to be used in industry because technologists were unable to prevent their products from being contaminated with the by-products of burning coal (vol III, ch 3).

The substitution of coal for wood in iron-smelting is associated with the name of the first Abraham Darby (1677–1717), founder of the Quaker dynasty of Coalbrookdale ironmasters, who solved this pressing economic and technological problem by converting his mineral fuel into coke before he used it in the blast-furnace (p 99). The year was 1709. The first to use coke in a blast-furnace in Germany was von Reden at Gleiwitz in 1796.

FIGURE 129—*Distillery. 1729.*

In glass-making the use of coal led to the closing-in of the top of the glass-pot, and that in turn to the evolution of flint glass, which was more easily fluxed in the covered pot (p 370). In pottery-making it led to the introduction of saggars.

The glass-maker, having solved his fuel problem, had still to face the fact that potash (the residual ash from timber or other plants) was an essential ingredient in the glass itself. So also was it indispensable to the manufacturers of soap, alum, and saltpetre. The latter when mixed with yet another timber by-product, charcoal, and with sulphur gave the only explosive known until nearly the middle of the nineteenth century. Thus we see that mining, metallurgy, and a variety of other industrial interests were competing for a dwindling supply of timber. As a result, from many quarters in the seventeenth century we have records of a timber famine, and the search for a substitute for wood was one of the dominant features in the development of eighteenth-century technology (vol III, ch 3).

The solution of the fuel problem was, however, only half the technological battle. As has been mentioned, plant-ashes supplied the alkali needed by glass-makers, soap-boilers, bleachers, and other manufacturers. Thus as a subsidiary facet of the search for an alternative to wood we have the search for a substitute for natural alkali. When the problem was solved at the end of the eighteenth century, the industries using alkali became the focus of practically the whole chemical industry, and so remained for some fifty years. At this point therefore it is necessary to discuss the rise of the alkali industry, and to consider the means whereby the solution of the problem was effected.

From an early date local supplies of alkali in Britain were insufficient to meet the growth of demand, and additional supplies were imported either in the form of crude weed- or wood-ash or as refined potash or pearl-ash. There were two sources of this alkali, namely *barilla* from the Mediterranean region, and wood-ash from northern Europe or America. But with the expanding economy of Europe, and particularly of Britain, demand continued to exceed supply. This directed the attention of technologists to possible solutions of the scarcity. Of these, four may be listed: (*a*) organized importation; (*b*) augmented domestic production of wood-ash; (*c*) the production of alkali from hitherto unexploited material, such as seaweed; and finally (*d*) synthesis. For nearly a century (1730–1830) the third of these possibilities made a major contribution to British economy, being superseded only when an adequate supply of soda came on the market as the result of the establishment in the 1830s, in the neighbourhood of the Cheshire salt-fields, of works operating the Leblanc process.

While kelping—that is, the production of alkali by the incineration of seaweed—is mentioned in Scotland as early as 1694, it is not till about 1730 that such production is generally noticed in contemporary records. Kelping is included here because it represents, in a sense, one of the roots of the British chemical industry. Its product, low-grade vegetable alkali, was absorbed by a range of manufacturers. It is in fact a good example of the point, made earlier, that most chemicals are not ends in themselves but are 'intermediates' absorbed in the manufacture of other products.

As a chemical raw material, kelp[1] was very different from the highly purified alkaline products of twentieth-century chemical industry, yet the technical skill of the era during which it was an important item of commerce was sufficient to make full use of its varied content. Kelp (ash) contains a mixture of sodium carbonate, chloride, and sulphate, magnesium sulphate and chloride, and a certain quantity of potassium chloride, and, while much of it was not alkali as such, as a chemical miscellany it was nevertheless useful to contemporary industry. Later it became of importance on account of its workable content of iodine.

From our point of view the development of the trade in kelp was nothing more than a palliative measure taken to lessen temporarily the difficulties arising from the shortage of other vegetable alkali. A more radical and scientific approach was to apply the increasing knowledge of the interaction of chemical substances in a frontal attack on the problem of making alkali.

[1] Kelp is a general name for brown seaweeds; it is also applied to the ash obtained by calcining the seaweeds.

The foundation and rise of the alkali industry represent the transition from an industry based on accumulated craft knowledge to one based on applied chemical knowledge. Although often represented as if the change happened more or less overnight, this is very far from true, and the significant events that took place in the third decade of the nineteenth century have antecedents going back for half a century at least. Moreover, while the principal product of the new industry was alkali, at the same time it yielded by-products which were absorbed by the bleaching industry and in turn revolutionized it. The new bleaching-agents also had a notable effect on the production of paper from rags. Indeed, Justus von Liebig (1803–74) described the synthesis of soda as the 'foundation of all our improvements in the domestic arts'.

At this point it is important to look at some of the antecedents mentioned above. As early as 1737 H. L. Duhamel-Dumonceau (1700–82), the originator of many technological improvements, who in the previous year had emphasized the distinction between soda and potash, was working on a process not unlike that on which the great alkali industry operated during its first century. Not long afterwards Joseph Black (1728–99) of Edinburgh (p 217) published his 'Experiments upon Magnesia Alba, Quick-Lime and Other Alcaline Substances', in which he made clear the interrelation between mild and caustic alkalis (p 217). Associated with Black in his experiments towards the synthesis of alkali were John Roebuck, the pioneer manufacturer of sulphuric acid, and James Watt (1736–1819) the engineer. Another interested investigator was James Keir (1735–1820), who was connected with the Rogers Amblecote glass-house at Stourbridge.

How successful these experimenters were we do not really know. It is reported that Black and his associates alleged that they would have gone into commercial production had it not been for the duty they would have had to pay on the salt they proposed to use as a raw material. They joined forces in 1771 to oppose a patent-application for the manufacture of soda from common salt by two London chemists, Alexander and George Fordyce. Evidence was produced that Keir had successfully synthesized soda, and at the same time Pierre Théodore de Bruges, a saltpetre manufacturer, also claimed that he had equipped a factory to make alkali.

These indications that some success had been attained in the synthesis of alkali are strengthened by the fact that in 1781 a British Act of Parliament reduced the duties on 'foul' salt 'used in the manufacture of fused fossil or mineral alkali'. That the problem was still current is evident from the remark in Richard Watson's 'Chemical Essays' (1782–7) that the subject was 'one of great national concern'. These references clearly reflect its economic importance, as also do the patents taken out for the manufacture of alkali about the same time by Richard Shannon (no. 1223 of 1779), Bryan Higgins (no. 1302 of 1781), John Collison (no. 1341 of 1782), and James Gerard (no. 1369 of 1783). A close study of these patents will repay those interested in the chemical background of the alkali problem. Some of the processes bear a marked resemblance to the Leblanc process; indeed, in 1789, Anthony Bourboulon de Boneuil referred in a patent (no. 1677) to sodium sulphate and charcoal as materials 'already used in the manufacture of alkali'.

Important though these developments undoubtedly were, it is questionable if any of them led to the real foundation of the alkali industry in Great Britain. For that it is necessary to turn to the activities of Archibald Cochrane, ninth Earl of Dundonald (1749–1831), and his associates in the Newcastle upon Tyne area.

In the 1780s Dundonald got in touch with two manufacturers, William Losh and Thomas Doubleday, who were trying to convert common salt into soda. Dundonald sent Losh to Paris in 1791. Guyton de Morveau had shown in 1782 that soda could be made from sodium sulphate. Armed with information collected in France, Losh and Dundonald, about 1796, with a number of partners, set up an alkali works at Walker upon Tyne, Dundonald having taken out a patent for the manufacture of mineral alkali (no. 2043). In essentials the process covers the production of Glauber's salt (Na_2SO_4, $10H_2O$) from salt ($NaCl$), and converting the former to sodium sulphide (Na_2S), from which soda, either mild (Na_2CO_3) or caustic ($NaOH$), could be prepared. At first their output was not high, but, considering the relatively low percentage of alkali in kelp, even a small output almost certainly had a considerable effect on the alkali market.

Following the establishment of the above co-partnership several other firms began to make alkali: Doubleday and Easterby of Bill Quay in 1808, Hutchinson of Felling *c* 1810, and Cookson of Jarrow in 1823. Similar developments took place in Scotland, particularly at Dalmuir in Dunbartonshire, where the development was associated with Lords Dundonald and Dundas (1795). From that focus the manufacture spread to several other centres in the neighbourhood of Glasgow, and to Ayrshire. In 1814 manufacture was started at Liverpool by Thomas Lutwyche and William Hill, who supplied alkali to local soap-makers.

All these developments antedate the founding of the first alkali works to operate the now much better known Leblanc process. To follow up the history of Leblanc it is necessary to return to the European scene and to the year 1775.

On the continent, as in Britain, there was an acute shortage of alkali, but the continental situation was aggravated by the warlike state of Europe. This being so, French scientists directed their attention to possible syntheses of soda. Malherbe devised a process involving the fusion of sodium sulphate, charcoal, and iron: Guyton de Morveau and Carnay were so confident of success that they erected a factory at Croisac in Picardy in 1782: de la Métherie heated sodium sulphate and coal in closed retorts: Athénas had yet another process. Then in 1787 Nicolas Leblanc (1742–1806) brought forward the process that became the core of the whole heavy chemical industry for nearly a century. Leblanc's process depended on the decomposition of common salt by sulphuric acid with the production of sodium sulphate (figure 130 (i)). This in turn was mixed intimately with chalk and charcoal and heated in a crucible. The resulting 'black ash' was leached with water (figure 130 (ii)) and the resulting soda recovered from the solution by evaporation (figure 130 (iii)). The process was patented in France in 1791, and a factory was built by Leblanc and Dizé at St Denis to work it. Unhappily the tide of revolution swept over Leblanc. His patron, the Duke of Orleans, was executed, his factory was confiscated, and a commission appointed by the *Académie des Sciences*, to award a prize of 2400 livres, decided that the processes put forward by Malherbe and Athénas were the most promising, but that none was satisfactory enough to be worthy of the prize.

As has been indicated, Leblanc's process hardly seems to have been unique in its fundamentals. It is curious therefore that the great efflorescence of industrial chemical activity in Britain in the 1820s and 1830s did not involve any of the workers or take place at any of the industrial foci so far described. In Britain, Cheshire, with its rich deposits of salt and ready access to supplies of coal and limestone, was the natural locus for the development of chemical industry, and there, and in the adjacent parts of Lancashire, in due course it did develop after an initial short phase at Liverpool. In addition to choosing perhaps one of the most favoured districts in Europe for the establishment of a chemical industry, its founder was able to benefit by the repeal of the salt-duties in 1823. The pioneer to avail himself of the opportunity was James Muspratt (1793–1886).

Muspratt was making prussiate of potash, acids, and solvents in Dublin in 1816. Six years later he settled at Liverpool, where he continued to make prussiate, and added sulphuric acid to his output. His chemical knowledge was small, but the capital acquired in the manufacture of prussiate was sufficient to enable him to embark on the manufacture of soda by the Leblanc process in 1823, a date often taken as the foundation of the alkali industry in Britain. In 1828 he was joined by J. C. Gamble (1776–1848), a Glasgow-trained chemist.

In 1825 the manufacture of Leblanc alkali was initiated at Glasgow, the pioneer in that region being Charles Tennant (1768–1838), who, as the developer of bleaching-powder, was already a chemical manufacturer of some substance.

FIGURE 130—*Manufacture of soda by Leblanc's process.*

The St Rollox chemical works, the site of the development, was in time to become the greatest chemical factory in Europe.

After a somewhat slow start, due to the conservatism of the soap-boilers who constituted their principal market, the Muspratt and Gamble enterprise flourished. But in the very year that they joined forces (1828) they had the first of numerous encounters with the law. As first introduced, the operation of the Leblanc process gave rise to very large quantities of a noxious by-product, hydrogen chloride, which the pioneer manufacturers endeavoured to disperse simply by passing it up tall chimneys. In this way, their activities caused widespread devastation to vegetation and destruction of property. Muspratt was consequently arraigned in 1828 for causing a public nuisance. While legal action did not in fact close down the Liverpool works, it undoubtedly had a considerable influence on the subsequent locus of development of the alkali industry. Already Muspratt had started a second alkali works at St Helens, where the manufacture of bottle-, crown-, and plate-glass was established, and it was there, and in such other neighbouring places as Widnes, Warrington, and Runcorn, that the great development in Britain of the heavy chemical industry and its associated manufactures took place in following years. That these districts did not suffer from intolerable industrial pollution may be attributed to the fortunate invention in 1836 of a means of absorbing the offending hydrogen chloride. This was the utilization of an old windmill packed with wet brushwood, and subsequently of towers specially built for the purpose, by William Gossage (1799–1877) a Worcestershire alkali manufacturer (B.P. no. 7267 of 1836). Another factor was the realization by the manufacturers that they were allowing a valuable material to run to waste. From the hydrogen chloride could be produced chlorine, a bleaching-agent, a development that will be dealt with subsequently.

There is not space here to go into the detail of the evolution of the alkali industry during the middle years of the nineteenth century. Economics brought about the need for improved processes and attention to the utilization of waste products; social pressure resulted in a demand for the more careful operation of the industry; and these together produced in the end a process that finally superseded Leblanc's classic one. But the developments so far described set the pattern for the evolution of the heavy chemical industry till nearly the end of the nine-

---

FIGURE 130 (*cont.*). (i) *Section of a salt-decomposing furnace. The salt and sulphuric acid were brought together in* A, *which was lead lined. After several hours, during which time reaction took place and hydrochloric acid was driven off, the mass was pushed into* C. *The reaction was completed in* D, *the hottest part of the furnace.* (ii) *Black ash vats in which the sodium carbonate was dissolved out.* (iii) *Section of the crystallizing house in Chance's alkali works, Oldbury, Worcestershire, in which soda suitable for the production of plate glass was prepared.*

teenth century, a pattern that is succinctly described by Stephen Miall in his 'History of the British Chemical Industry', pp 5, 6:

> The works of the chemical manufacturer tended to become larger and more complicated; he began to make soda, using common salt and sulphuric acid and other raw materials. After a time he started to make his own sulphuric acid by burning sulphur or pyrites; if he used pyrites, it was probably a mixed sulphide of copper and iron, and it was comparatively easy to make copper sulphate and ferrous sulphate from the roasted pyrites. The process of making sodium sulphate produced large quantities of hydrochloric acid, and, as nitric acid was required in the manufacture of sulphuric acid, the alkali manufacturer easily developed into a manufacturer of hydrochloric, nitric, and sulphuric acids, and various salts of sodium, copper, and iron. It was a very common development for the alkali manufacturer to use the chlorine he recovered so as to make bleaching-powder, and in this way he became a maker of calcium chloride and bleaching-powder, and, as demands for them grew, he made other salts of sodium and calcium required in large quantities. The manufacture of all these 'heavy' chemicals became in this way an involved process, in which one part was dependent on the others and almost every effort to prevent waste involved the manufacturer in some new product.

With this picture of the heavy chemical industry in mind it becomes necessary to look at the history of the one substance that was the kernel of the whole structure, namely, sulphuric acid.

Knowledge of sulphuric acid, or oil of vitriol, was one of the legacies of the alchemical period. It is variously described in the works of the pseudonymous Basil Valentine, Paracelsus, and Agricola, and by 1570 we have a fairly accurate description of its preparation by the distillation of green vitriol (ferrous sulphate, $FeSO_4,7H_2O$) in the works of Gerard Dorn. In this method (operated at Nordhausen from 1755) ferrous sulphate was decomposed by heat to give oxides of sulphur which were absorbed in the water of crystallization. The yield of sulphuric acid was only of the order of 10 per cent of the weight of green vitriol used, and as this was insufficient to meet a growing demand attention was turned to other methods of production, in particular to the oxidation of sulphur, a method suggested by Cornelius Drebbel (1572–1634) and probably introduced into England about 1720. In this process the sulphuric acid was said to be made *per campanam*, the operation consisting of burning sulphur and saltpetre (potassium nitrate, KNO_3) together under a variety of bell-shaped vessels. Such vessels are illustrated in the works of Lefèvre and Lémery, where they are seen to consist of glass or earthenware.

There is no record of continuous manufacture of sulphuric acid in England until a good deal later, when Joshua Ward (1685–1761) and John White began to produce 'oil of vitriol made by the bell', first at Twickenham (1736), and then at Richmond (1740). Ward and White's venture represents a transition in the production of sulphuric acid from the laboratory scale to that of the factory. They still used glass vessels—of some 40 to 50 gallons capacity—but they produced acid at about a twentieth of the former price, and so presented to industry for the first time the possibility of procuring acid at reasonable cost. Unfortunately no detailed account of all the uses to which this early acid was put has survived. Andrew Brown, in his 'History of Glasgow', recorded that before 1750 Scottish bleachers procured their sulphuric acid from England or Holland; we know that it was used in pharmacy (in making the *sal mirabile* of Glauber); and there are good indications that it was used by tinplate-makers, brass-founders, button-makers, japanners, gilders, and the refiners of precious metals. They used it either for pickling and cleaning metals, or in the form of 'stripping-liquor' (sulphuric acid containing potassium nitrate) for removing silver from copper, and it is almost certain that it was to cater for this market among the metal-workers of Birmingham that the next English sulphuric acid works was established in 1746. The pioneers were John Roebuck and Samuel Garbett (1717–1805), the owners of a refinery for precious metals in Steelhouse Lane, Birmingham.

FIGURE 131—*Manufacture of sulphuric acid in glass vessels about the time of Joshua Ward.*

The Roebuck and Garbett enterprise was not, however, just one other sulphuric acid works in an ever expanding list. Roebuck had received the best possible scientific education of his time, by studying medicine at Edinburgh and Leyden, and having decided to abandon medicine for technology he made use of Glauber's observation that lead is not attacked by sulphuric acid and built his vitriol-producing plant of that metal. This substitution of lead for glass was one of the great forward steps in the history of chemical technology: it freed the manufacturer from the use of fragile laboratory-scale apparatus (figure 131) and brought about a further fall in the price of a valuable industrial commodity.

The Birmingham Vitriol Manufactory found a ready market for its products among the trades of Birmingham. There were, however, few outlets in the midlands for sulphuric acid until it was found useful as a substitute for sour milk—till then the only acid liquor available in quantity to the bleaching-trade. It happened that for several decades the Board of Trustees for Fisheries, Manufactures, and Improvements in Scotland (founded 1727) had been subsidizing the laying-down of bleach-fields, and a bleaching-trade that catered for weavers as far away as London had been built up. Roebuck and Garbett next established a sulphuric acid works at Prestonpans, on the Firth of Forth, a few miles east of Edinburgh. Once again they brought the manufacture of their product, always a difficult one to handle, into an area where there was a profitable market. In addition there may have been patent difficulties with Joshua Ward, and, Scotland then having its own patent law, they may have thought to avoid the consequences of litigation by moving north. This does not seem to be a very cogent reason, however, since, while Francis Home (1719–1813), professor of *materia medica* in the university of Edinburgh, published the first account of the use of sulphuric acid in the souring of linen, it is generally believed that Roebuck had earlier knowledge of it and had suggested the substitution to the bleachers.

The inviolability of patent rights being dubious in the middle of the eighteenth century, Roebuck and Garbett attempted to rely on secrecy to enable them to reap the advantages of their enterprise. For history this is unfortunate, as there is now no account of the way in which they carried out their operations. It is known, however, that they imported sulphur from Leghorn and bought saltpetre from the East India Company, and that in the year after they started manufacture they were exporting sulphuric acid to Holland at $3\frac{1}{2}d$ a pound.

Within a decade sulphuric acid works had sprung up in various parts of the country—that of Rhodes at Bridgnorth (1756); somewhat later that of Skey at Dowles in Worcestershire; and that of Benjamin Rowson at Bradford, which probably dates from 1750. There were others in Edinburgh and Govan—but the Prestonpans Vitriol Works was still the greatest in Britain in 1784. Other early vitriol works were founded in Holland and at Rouen. In Germany the first works to use lead chambers was that founded by von Waitz at Ringkuhl, near Grossalmerode, Hesse.

As the industrial revolution proceeded, more and more uses were found for the cheap acid, many of them connected with the textile trade. Bleachers found it admirable as a substitute for the sour milk formerly used, and after the discovery of chlorine it became an essential in the preparation of chemical bleaches. Calico-printers also used it as a sour and in the production of citric acid. It was used by dyers to render indigo soluble, in the preparation of mordants, and in many other ways. Just how useful it was to the expanding economy of the industrial revolution may be gauged by the fact that by 1820, that is, several years before sulphuric acid began to be absorbed on a large scale in the production of synthetic soda, there were some 40 vitriol works in Great Britain: approximately two dozen were in England, and half that number in Scotland.

In spite of this evidence of industrial activity few descriptions of the process have come down to us. The following, however, gives some idea of practice at the beginning of the nineteenth century. It describes the six chambers used by Bealy, of Radcliffe, Manchester.

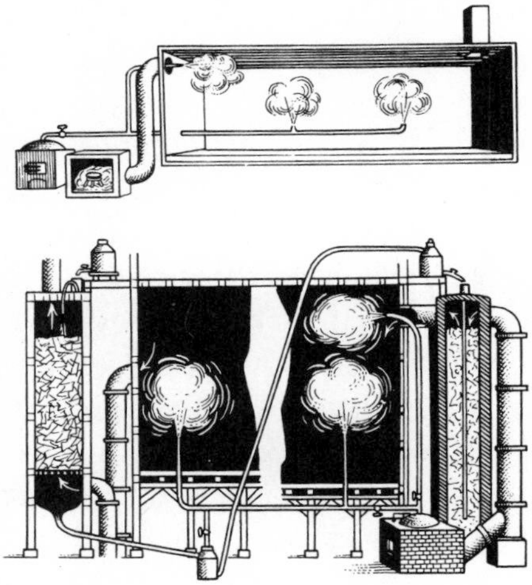

FIGURE 132—*Lead chambers in which sulphuric acid was made.*

They were ten feet square and twelve feet high, with a roof like a cottage, each house having a door, usually of mahogany, and a valve on top for ventilation between burnings. The floor was constructed to hold water to a depth of eight or nine inches. The 1 lb charge consisting of a mixture of seven to eight parts of sulphur with one of nitre was introduced upon two trays. This was lit and the doors shut for upwards of an hour until the combustion had taken place. Three hours from the time of lighting were allowed for condensation to take place, after which the doors and valve were opened to 'sweeten' the chamber. The operation was repeated every four hours day and night for about six weeks, after which the acid was withdrawn and concentrated in lead vessels. (Quoted in Clow, 'The Chemical Revolution', p 145).

We see that this is little more than the *per campanam* process writ large, with lead vessels in place of glass or earthenware. Soon, however, other changes were to be put in train. In 1803 Charles Tennant built the first lead chambers at St Rollox. These were constructed with a separate furnace for the combustion of the sulphur and saltpetre, and within ten years the water on the floor of the chambers had been replaced by jets of steam, so that the chambers remained as reacting spaces only (figure 132). The process having been made continuous by Jean Louis Holker (1770–1844), it remained virtually unaltered until the introduction of the catalytic or contact process many years later (vol V, ch 11).

Production of sulphuric acid in Britain just before the great expansion necessitated by the rise of the synthetic soda industry was of the order of 3000 tons a year. The cost of producing this sulphuric acid was about $2\frac{1}{2}d$ a pound, a figure that was further reduced when Chile saltpetre ($NaNO_3$) was substituted for the potassium salt after 1830. Pyrites was substituted for elementary sulphur after difficulties in procuring supplies of the latter had occurred about 1840.

The above account describes the manifold influences of sulphuric acid upon the European economy. Space does not permit a detailed description of the way in which, indirectly, it freed greater supplies of potassium salts for agriculture, and for the manufacture of explosives, by making available soda that could be used in place of the potash formerly absorbed in the manufacture of soap and glass, and in the textile industry. Nor is it appropriate to deal here with its use after 1845 in the production of phosphatic fertilizers (vol V, ch 11), which has since become the principal absorber of sulphuric acid. In spite of these omissions, however, it is clear that cheap sulphuric acid had a considerable influence on the cost of the bleached and printed cotton-goods that Britain exported in large quantities in exchange for colonial raw materials, and on the cost of the glass and soap she used at home. Thus the lead-chamber process for making sulphuric acid takes its place with the other great, particularly mechanical, inventions that helped to promote the industrial, chemical, and social revolution of the late eighteenth and early nineteenth centuries.

During the nineteenth century, mechanical technology radically transformed the production of textiles, by a series of ingenious devices operable on a large scale with the reliable power provided by James Watt's improved steam-engine (1769), and installed in mills lit by W. Murdock's gas-lights (1805). But there was little point in speeding up the production of textiles if the processes carried out by the finishing-trades, namely bleaching, dyeing, and printing, could not be hastened as well. Textile-printing was accelerated by the introduction of cylindrical printing by Bell in 1785, and, fortunately for the progress of the industrial revolution in Britain, her chemists also made conspicuous improvements in the chemistry of bleaching and dyeing.

Several references have already been made to improvements in the art of bleaching. Originally a domestic craft, much was done to organize it into an industry before chemical knowledge had any marked influence on the processes carried out. The different methods in operation throughout Europe do not merit discussion here, but it was at the instigation of the Board of Trustees in Scotland (p 244) that information was published which led to the first of two major revolutions in the technique of bleaching. The suggestions are contained in Francis Home's 'Experiments on Bleaching' (Edinburgh, 1754), where the author advocated the use of dilute sulphuric acid in place of the traditional sour or buttermilk. Although the change may seem somewhat trivial to twentieth-century eyes, supplies of cheap mineral acid enabled bleachers to reduce the time of souring to about a twenty-fifth of that formerly required. But even this increased rapidity of bleaching was not adequate to cope with the output of the mills, soon to be increasing by millions of yards annually.

Fortunately an entirely new bleaching agent was at hand. In 1774 chlorine was discovered by the Swedish chemist, C. W. Scheele (1742–86), and in 1785 the French chemist, C. L. Berthollet (1748–1822), discovered that it was a powerful bleaching agent. News of this was communicated to James Watt and to Patrick Copland (1748–1822). As a result, a second revolution in bleaching was initiated by the introduction of chlorine into industrial operations, first at Aberdeen in 1787, and then at Glasgow and Manchester within a matter of a year or so. From these centres the use of chlorine spread rapidly to the other textile producing areas, despite the difficulties inherent in handling the new reagent.

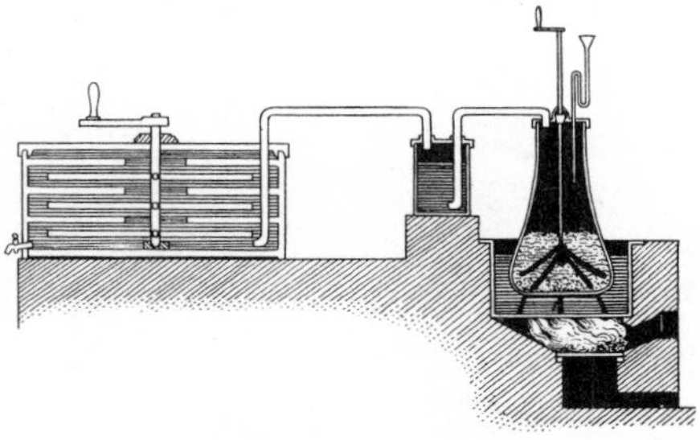

FIGURE 133—*The preparation of chemical bleach by the absorption of chlorine in water and alkali solution.*

Chlorine is a gaseous element and, at the date of its introduction into industry, pneumatic chemistry (p 215) had not emerged from the laboratory. Joseph Priestley's 'Experiments and Observations on Different Kinds of Airs' is dated 1774–7. On account of the difficulties contingent in handling gaseous chlorine, the first of a number of technical advances of great value was suggested by manufacturers at Javel,[1] who put forward the idea of absorbing chlorine in alkali with the production of dissolved hypochlorite (*eau de Javel*) (figure 133). In France the process did not succeed commercially, and its inventors emigrated to Liverpool, where lack of patent protection and the hazards of transporting their product to the bleach-fields led to the same result. In 1789 Charles Tennant (1769–1838), a bleacher of Darnley, Renfrewshire, took out a patent for the production of a liquid bleach made from chlorine and a sludge of slaked lime ($Ca(OH)_2$) (no. 2209), and simultaneously avoided the difficulty of transport by licensing manufacturers to work his patent at their own bleach-fields. He enjoyed the protection of this patent for only some four years, however, since proceedings in 1802 made it clear that the process was already widely used.

Meanwhile the Tennant company had registered a second patent, this time

[1] Javel (*not* Javelle) was a village on the outskirts of Paris, but now forms part of the XVth *arrondissement* of the capital.

for the production of an entirely dry bleaching-powder (no. 2312 of 1799) (figure 134), thus solving the transport difficulty. It was to operate this patent that Charles Tennant and Company established their chemical works at St Rollox in 1799. In the first year of its existence fifty tons of bleaching-powder were produced, which was sold at £140 a ton: by 1830 output had reached 1000 tons a year and the price had been reduced to £80.

Like the introduction of lead in the manufacture of sulphuric acid, and the production of soda from common salt, the development of bleaching-powder was one of the milestones in the evolution of Britain's chemical economy. Liebig assessed its significance in the following terms:

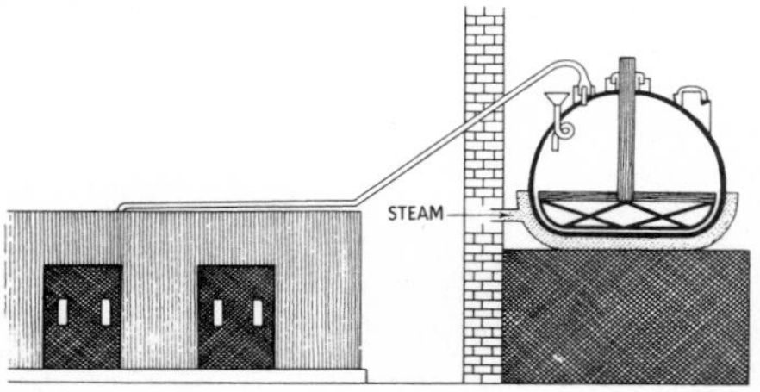

FIGURE 134—*The preparation of bleaching-powder. Lime is placed on trays in a stone chamber 8 to 9 ft high. The chlorine is produced in a large lead-lined chamber by the action of sulphuric acid on a mixture of common salt (sodium chloride) and manganese dioxide. It passes into a leaden chamber containing water (not shown) and so into the lime house. After 2 days the lime is stirred by rakes, and after another 2 days the reaction is complete.*

> But for this new bleaching process it would scarcely have been possible for cotton manufacture in Great Britain to have attained the enormous extent which it did during the nineteenth century, nor could it have competed in price with France and Germany. . . . Had not chlorine bleaching been introduced, finding capital to purchase land for the old methods of bleaching would have presented a considerable problem, especially when it is realised that by 1840 a single establishment near Glasgow was bleaching 1,400 pieces of cotton daily throughout the year (J. Liebig, 'Familiar Letters', p 28).

Although in the period under discussion no revolution comparable with that in bleaching affected the art of dyeing, contemporary scientists did help to change dyeing from a craft into an industry. In the 1660s Boyle and Hooke performed experiments on dyeing before the Royal Society, and Sir William Petty listed the dyes then in use in England. They included madder, cochineal, saffron, anatto, weld, turmeric, woad, logwood, and indigo (vol V, ch 12), and these remained among the principal dye-wares used in Europe for many generations, in spite of the fact that many of them were fast neither to light, nor to washing, nor to alkali, even when improved by the simultaneous use of mordants (vol III, ch 25). In part the difficulty lay in the chemical complexity of most of the natural colouring-matters, the diverse chemical composition of the common fibres, and in the fact that there was no sound theory of the dyeing-process. E. Bancroft (1744–1821) distinguished substantive and adjective dyes in 1794. It was not till two of the directors of the French dye industry, P. J. Macquer

(1718–84) and C. L. Berthollet, became interested that any advance was made beyond a purely mechanistic conception. Macquer introduced Prussian blue (discovered by the Berlin colour-manufacturer Diesbach in 1704) as a dye, and the enthusiasm with which it was adopted, despite its shortcomings, is a measure of the weakness of the dye department of the textile industry.

Among the more successful innovations in this field during the period under discussion were (*a*) the perfection of the dye cudbear, discovered by Dr Cuthbert[1] Gordon and developed by George Macintosh (1739–1807), and (*b*) the solution, also by Macintosh, of the problem, which faced all the western nations in the eighteenth century. of producing a fast red cotton colour equal to the 'Turkey-red' produced from madder (*Rubia tinctorum*) in the orient. At the Dalmarnock dye works, Macintosh produced the best Turkey-red on a vast scale; 5000 looms were employed in 1796 in the neighbourhood of Glasgow making pullicates[2] for the Turkey-red dyers. These became known throughout Europe as monteiths, after Henry Monteith, who acquired Dalmarnock from Macintosh.

In addition to the introduction of new dye-wares, mechanical and chemical invention added to the variety of textiles available. Goods requiring only simple patterns were produced by resist-work, in which a resistant mixture, invented by a man named Grouse, was first printed on the fabric which was then dyed, often in a blue-vat, thus producing a white pattern on a blue ground. Another process in operation from the beginning of the nineteenth century was chemical discharge. In this the cloth was first dyed uniformly, and then a design was produced on it by clamping it between lead stencil-plates through which a bleaching-solution was forced, to discharge the colour in the exposed parts. Bandannas were produced in this way. When chromium compounds became available, about 1820, they were introduced to increase the range of colour-effects, though by modern standards they were certainly less satisfactory than one would judge by contemporary acclamation. Nevertheless these and the other chemical developments described above were important in the history of the industrial revolution. To quote Edward Baines, the historian of the cotton-industry: 'Chemical science has done at least as much to facilitate and perfect the processes, as mechanical science to facilitate and perfect the operations of manufacturing.' Together they brought about so great and so rapid an expansion that it is without parallel in the annals of industry.

Another essential part of the dyeing-process is mordanting, which improves, or indeed often effects, the adhesion of the dyestuff to the fabric. Further,

[1] Of whose name cudbear is a corruption. This dye is obtained from certain lichens.

[2] Bandannas. The name pullicate derives from Pulicat, a town on the Madras coast.

different mordants produce different colours, or lakes, with the same dye, and so increase the variety of colour that can be produced from a limited range of dyes. Supplying these ancillaries was an essential part of the early chemical industry. For the most part they consisted of alums (salts of the general formula $M'M'''(SO_4)_2,12H_2O$), or copperas, that is, ferrous sulphate ($FeSO_4,7H_2O$),

FIGURE 135—*Calcining alum shale at Hurlet, Renfrewshire.*

with the addition at a later date of lead acetate, iron acetate, and aluminium acetate.

Alum has been a commodity handled by eastern Mediterranean traders since the earliest times. Indeed, the manufacture of alum has been called the earliest chemical industry. There were alum-works in England in Elizabethan times at Guisborough, some ten miles south-east of Middlesbrough. Production depended on deposits of aluminous shale, which were calcined in the open air in vast heaps (figure 135). The resulting ash was extracted with water and the solution evaporated with alkali (figure 136). It was the existence of alum shale in waste from coal-mines that enabled Charles Macintosh (son of the George Macintosh already mentioned) to start an alum-works at Hurlet, Renfrewshire, in 1797. This soon became the largest in Britain. In 1808 Macintosh, Knox and Company started a second factory at Campsie, Stirlingshire, to utilize a very pyritous alum shale, found in the coal-measures, for the production of both alum and copperas. Their output of alum reached 1000 tons a year in 1812, and 2000 tons in 1835, in which year the price was £12 a ton. But this simple and lucrative method of making alum did not remain unrivalled for long. In 1845, Peter Spence (1806–83), who had been a chemical manufacturer in Dundee, London, and

FIGURE 136—*The manufacture of alum.* (Left) *Evaporating the solution;* (right) *removing the alum from the crystallizing pans.*

Cumberland successively, took out a patent (no. 10 970) for the production of alum and copperas by digesting roasted iron pyrites and burnt shale in sulphuric acid. A second patent followed in 1850 (no. 13 335), and having settled at Pendleton, near Manchester, the firm of Peter Spence became in time the largest manufacturer of alum in the world.

The history of copperas is similar to that of alum. It was being made in Elizabethan times at Queenborough in the Isle of Sheppey; then from the middle of the seventeenth century at Deptford; and from the middle of the eighteenth in the Newcastle upon Tyne area. From Newcastle it was exported in large quantities to French dye-houses. Macintosh, Knox and Company produced it at both Hurlet and Campsie.

Advancing chemical knowledge during the eighteenth century led to the introduction of new mordants, or to changes in the methods of producing those already in use. Lead acetate, formerly made in Holland with lead imported from Britain, was made in Britain from 1790; pyroligneous acid took the place of sour beer in the production of iron acetate for the 'red liquor' of the calico printers, and in time aluminium acetate was substituted for the lead salt.

Hitherto we have considered the core of the emergent heavy chemical industry —the applied chemistry of the industrial revolution. To leave the subject at this point would, however, be to present an unbalanced picture. There were other correlative advances which, if not part of the chemical industry proper, nevertheless were very relevant to it. Chief of these is the use of coal as a chemical raw material. In this capacity the first practical development was due to the versatile and active-minded Dundonald (p 238), who, in 1781, was granted a patent (described by a contemporary as of greater importance than Watt's for the steam-engine) for the production of tar by the destructive distillation of coal in tar-ovens (no. 1291). Earlier attempts had been made by Clayton in 1738. The economic and national significance of Dundonald's British Tar Company was that it could supply an alternative to wood-tar, hitherto produced from a dwindling supply of timber. Dundonald succeeded in establishing his tar-ovens at a number of places, usually where there were already ironworks; he also narrowly missed being the inventor of gas-lighting, through failing to see the possibilities, as an illuminant, of the inflammable vapours given off in the distillation of his tar. In this he was not alone, since several experimenters had observed and recorded that inflammable vapours are produced when coal is destructively distilled.

The first practical utilization of this observation came in 1785, when J. P. Minkelers (1748–1824) tried gas-lighting (ch 9) in the university of Louvain. Independently, William Murdock (1754–1839), manager of the Boulton and Watt interests in Cornwall, lit his house at Redruth with gas in 1792 (plate 12). The senior partners of the firm appreciated the possibilities of gas for lighting the mills in which they were installing their engines. Engines were capable of working long into the night without tiring, but the mills had to be lit, and by 1805 they had installed a thousand lights in one Manchester mill. For the conception of a public supply we are indebted to Frederic Albert Winsor (p 264), the holder of four patents for 'extracting inflammable air from all kinds of fuel' (nos. 2764 of 1804, 3016 of 1807, 3113 of 1808, and 3200 of 1809), who was granted a charter to found a Gas Light and Coke Company in 1812. A gas-works was erected in London almost at once, and very soon there were gas companies in the course of formation in most large cities (ch 9).

Gas-lighting advanced with great rapidity and it is said that the suppression of vice, consequent on the better lighting of the streets, was one of the minor social revolutions of the first half of the nineteenth century. This is merely incidental to our theme, but the early gas-industry did indeed have a far-reaching influence in two widely different branches of technology.

In the first place, it was the manager of a gas works, J. B. Neilson (1792–1865), who introduced the revolutionary 'hot blast' furnace into the iron-industry, as described elsewhere (p 109) in this volume. The preliminary stages of the second of the two developments took place in Glasgow. It added a new word to the English language—mackintosh—incidentally thus mis-spelled. For the preparation of the cudbear referred to on p 249 the Macintosh company required large quantities of ammonia. Before the development of the gas-industry they made it from human urine. Then in 1819 Charles Macintosh agreed to purchase all the by-product tar and ammonia from the Glasgow gas-works. He was already in a position to absorb the ammonia, and the pitch made from the tar, and it was in seeking an outlet for the low-boiling naphtha that he hit on the idea of using it as a solvent for rubber (introduced into Europe in 1736 by Ch. M. de la Condamine), and employing the resultant solution for making a waterproof fabric (B.P. no. 4804, 1822) (vol V, ch 31). After an experimental period at Glasgow, the process was developed by Charles Macintosh and Company at Manchester.

The broad pattern of the application of chemistry during the industrial revolution has now been outlined, but there are still several subsidiary developments to be recorded. For example, during the period under discussion the soap industry benefited greatly by cognate development in the chemical industry and by the advance of chemical knowledge; then towards the end of the period the availability of sulphuric acid made possible a supply of chemical fertilizer in the form of superphosphate, and also fostered the development of the match industry.

During the 1780s C. L. Berthollet and C. W. Scheele, continuing the earlier work of Tachenius, published papers on the chemistry of oils and fats; Scheele's work demonstrated that glycerine or glycerol ($C_3H_5(OH)_3$) is a by-product of the saponification reaction. In 1797 d'Arcet, Lelièvre, and Pelletier produced a report on the manufacture of soap, and the second decade of the nineteenth century saw the publication of the classical researches of M. E. Chevreul (1786–1889). These gave, for the first time, a clear understanding of the nature and reactions of the raw materials used by the soap industry and so made quantitative working possible. Thus, with adequate alkali coming forward in the form of Leblanc soda, soap-making (figure 137) expanded greatly, and in the expansion became closely connected with, and indeed dependent on, the chemical industry. The key material in its evolution was sulphuric acid.

The same is true of the initial development of the fertilizer industry. The importance of phosphates in the economy of vegetation was pointed out during the 1780s: guano was examined in 1805,[1] and bones to the value of several thousand pounds were imported by Britain during the first three decades of the nineteenth century. At first, to promote their absorption by vegetation, they were crushed or ground into a coarse meal, but about 1840 Justus von Liebig suggested that they might be rendered more soluble by treatment with sulphuric acid. This was tried by John Bennet Lawes (1814–1900) in 1840 and 1841, with

FIGURE 137—*Soap-making in the second half of the eighteenth century.*

very satisfactory results. As a result, in 1842 he took out a patent for the manufacture of 'superphosphate'. In 1843 he started to make it in a factory at Deptford, whence the manufacture spread throughout the world. Superphosphate manufacture has ever since provided one of the principal uses of sulphuric acid.

Another industry that derived impetus, both direct and indirect, from sulphuric acid was the match industry. In 1775 Carl W. Scheele first prepared phosphorus from bone-ash by treatment with sulphuric acid and subsequent reduction with charcoal. This led to the invention of a 'phosphoric taper' about 1781, and a *briquet phosphorique* by 1786. While neither safe nor satisfactory these 'instantaneous lights' nevertheless remained in use for upwards of forty years, being joined by Chancel's 'chemical matches' (depending on a mixture of potassium chlorate and sugar ignited by sulphuric acid) in 1805. Later, friction matches (prometheans, lucifers, and congreves), with heads of potassium

[1] The first large importation was in 1835.

chlorate and antimony sulphide—the first of the kind being invented by John Walker (d 1859) of Stockton-on-Tees—all involved the use of sulphuric acid, either directly or at some stage in the manufacture of the necessary raw materials. For a time yellow phosphorus was used, but after Schrötter's discovery of red phosphorus in 1847 Böttger reintroduced phosphorus-free match-heads.

Another collateral development depending on the availability of sulphuric acid, and by no means an insignificant one in the light of subsequent events, was the rise of aerostation (ballooning) in the 1780s. Following a short period of experimentation with hot-air balloons, J. A. C. Charles and the Robert *frères* released the first hydrogen balloon (unmanned) from the Champs de Mars in Paris in August 1783. On 1 December of the same year Charles and one of the Roberts ascended from the Tuileries Gardens in a gondola attached to a similar balloon. The connexion with sulphuric acid was that the acid was used to generate the hydrogen required to inflate the large envelopes which were the means of the first practical conquest of the air (vol V, ch 17).

Reference has been made earlier to the revolution wrought in the textile industry by the introduction of chlorine-bleaching. Similar changes were brought about in the manufacture of paper. In paper technology the introduction of chlorine made it possible for the paper-maker to avail himself of supplies of printed linen rags, which by chemical bleaching could be used in the production of white writing-papers, till then made exclusively from unprinted linen. A patent for bleaching, by hypochlorite solution, rags to be used in paper-making was granted to Clement and George Taylor in 1792, but four years later the patent was disputed when it came to light that J. A. Chaptal (1756–1832) and Joseph Black had demonstrated its use, and that it had been employed at Polton Mill, Midlothian, the year before that in which Taylor's patent was granted. An English patent for bleaching rags with gaseous chlorine was granted to Hector Campbell in 1792.

A second element in the halogen group, namely iodine, was discovered in 1812. A saltpetre manufacturer near Paris, B. Courtois (1777–1838), traced the corrosion of his copper vessels to an unknown substance in the kelp lye used to decompose the product of the nitre beds. He identified it as a hitherto unknown element, which was given the name iodine on account of its violet vapours (Greek, *īodēs*, violet-coloured). While the chemical properties of iodine were not such as to make it a commodity of industrial significance comparable with chlorine, its production (vol V, ch 14) is not without importance, if for no other reason than that it helped to retain kelp as a marketable commodity after the decline of its importance as a source of soda.

On reviewing the narrative here given, it will be clear that during the industrial revolution much of the expansion of the chemical industry was indeed conditioned by the prodigious growth of the textile industry. It is, however, important to recognize that it was far from being entirely so controlled. The glass industry absorbed thousands of tons of soda. Both glass and pottery created a demand for lead oxides, the former for the production of flint-glass, the latter for glazes. Red lead and white lead, much improved by Thenard (1777–1857), were manufactured for the production of paints; an oxide of lead and antimony gave Naples yellow; a copper hydrogen arsenite was sold as Scheele's green, and a similar composition as Schweinfurt green; lead in combination with chromium compounds gave the chrome yellows. Prussian blue (p 249) was being manufactured at Newcastle upon Tyne in 1770, and by the Macintosh concern at Campsie from about 1810. A synthetic ultramarine (the natural mineral lapis lazuli had been used as a pigment since ancient times) was developed by Gonelin, Guimet, and Tessaert between 1814 and 1828.

Thus did the application of chemistry bring a little colour into the drab lives of those who were being engulfed in the festering mushroom industrial towns. Not that the influence of chemistry was confined to any narrow sphere. In 1819 W. T. Brande (1788–1866) had confessed that it was difficult to select one useful art that was not immediately dependent on chemical principles for its improvement. How much more did that become true when the full impact of the chemical revolution became apparent during the ensuing decades of the nineteenth century!

BIBLIOGRAPHY

ALLEN, J. F. 'Some Founders of the Chemical Industry.' Sherratt and Hughes, London and Manchester. 1906.

ARMSTRONG, SIR WILLIAM (GEORGE), *et al.* (Eds). 'The Industrial Resources of the District of the Three Northern Rivers, Tyne, Wear, and Tees.' London. 1864.

ASHTON, T. S. 'Iron and Steel in the Industrial Revolution.' University Press, Manchester. 1924.

BANCROFT, E. 'The Philosophy of Permanent Colours' (2 vols). London. 1813.

BECKMANN, J. 'History of Inventions, Discoveries, and Origins.' London. 1797.

BERTHOLLET, C. L. 'Essay on the New Method of Bleaching' (trans. from the French by R. KERR). Dublin. [1790?].

BRITISH ASSOCIATION FOR THE ADVANCEMENT OF SCIENCE. 'Local Industries of Glasgow and the West of Scotland' (ed. by A. MCLEAN). [Glasgow Meeting of the British Association, 1901.] Glasgow. 1901.

Idem. "On the History of the Alkali Manufacture" by W. GOSSAGE, in 'Report of the 31st Meeting . . . held at Manchester in September, 1861': 'Notes and Abstracts', p. 80. London. 1862.

Idem. "On the most important Chemical Manufactures carried on in Glasgow and the Neighbourhood" by T. THOMSON, in 'Report of the 10th Meeting... held at Glasgow in August, 1840': 'Notes and Abstracts', p. 58. London. 1841.

CHAPTAL, J. A. C. 'Chimie appliqué aux arts.' Paris. 1807.

CLEGG, S. 'A Practical Treatise on the Manufacture and Distribution of Coal-gas.' London. 1841.

CLOW, A. and CLOW, NAN L. 'The Chemical Revolution: A Contribution to Social Technology.' Batchworth Press, London. 1952.

COCHRANE, A., NINTH EARL OF DUNDONALD. 'Account of the Quality and Uses of Coal Tar and Coal Varnish.' London. 1785.

DICKINSON, H. W. "Manufacture of Sulphuric Acid." *Trans. Newcomen Soc.*, **18**, 43, 1937.

GIBBS, F. W. "The History of the Manufacture of Soap." *Ann. Sci.*, **4**, 169, 1939.

HARDIE, D. W. F. 'A History of the Chemical Industry in Widnes.' Imperial Chemical Industries, Liverpool. 1950.

HEAVISIDES, M. 'The True History of the Invention of the Lucifer Match, by John Walker, of Stockton-on-Tees, 1827.' Heavisides, Stockton-on-Tees. 1909.

HIGGINS, S. H. 'A History of Bleaching.' Longmans, London. 1924.

HOME, F. 'Experiments on Bleaching.' Edinburgh. 1754.

HUGHES, E. 'Studies in Administration and Finance, 1558–1828.' University Press, Manchester. 1934.

JARDINE, R. "An Account of John Roebuck, M.D., F.R.S." *Trans. roy. Soc. Edinb.*, **4**, 65, 1796.

KINGZETT, C. T. 'History of the Alkali Trade.' London. 1877.

LIEBIG, J. VON. 'Familiar Letters on Chemistry and its Relation to Commerce, Physiology and Agriculture', ed. by J. GARDNER. London. 1843.

LORD, J. 'Capital and Steam Power, 1750–1800.' King, London. 1923.

MIALL, S. 'A History of British Chemical Industry, 1634–1928.' Benn, London. 1931.

MORGAN, SIR GILBERT (THOMAS) and PRATT, D. D. 'British Chemical Industry. Its Rise and Development.' Arnold, London. 1938.

MUSPRATT, S. 'Chemistry, as Applied and Relating to the Arts and Manufactures' (2 vols). London. 1860.

NEF, J. U. 'The Rise of the British Coal Industry' (2 vols). Routledge, London. 1932.

PARKES, S. 'Chemical Essays' (4 vols). London. 1815.

PARTINGTON, J. R. 'The Alkali Industry.' Baillière, Tindall and Cox, London. 1918.

PROSSER, R. B. 'Birmingham Inventors and Inventions.' Birmingham, 1881.

SYKES, SIR ALAN (JOHN). 'Concerning the Bleaching Industry.' Bleachers' Association, Manchester. 1926.

TENNANT, E. W. D. 'One Hundred Years of the Tennant Companies.' Tennant, London. 1937.

URE, A. 'The Philosophy of Manufactures.' London. 1835.

WADSWORTH, A. P. and MANN, JULIA DE L. 'The Cotton Trade and Industrial Lancashire, 1600–1780.' University of Manchester, Economic History Series No. 7. Manchester. 1931.

WATSON, R. 'Chemical Essays' (5 vols). London. 1782–7.

9

GAS FOR LIGHT AND HEAT

SIR ARTHUR ELTON, Bt.

THE first public exhibition of gas for lighting and heating took place in Paris, in October 1801, at the Hôtel Seignelay (now 45–47 rue Saint-Dominique). The gas was generated by the destructive distillation of wood in two 'thermolamps', a name coined by their inventor, Philippe Lebon (1767–1804), an engineer attached to the *Service des Ponts et Chaussées*. One thermolamp warmed and lighted the interior of the house; the other lighted the garden with flames designed to take pleasing and fantastic shapes. A fountain in a grotto spouted flame instead of water.

The exhibition was continued at weekly intervals for some months, and was widely advertised in the Press. Lighting by gas thus came to be regarded as a practical possibility. Formerly, the generation and burning of 'inflammable airs' had seemed only a striking laboratory experiment. Lebon's great importance lies less in his inventiveness than in the fact that he demonstrated the practical application of principles already well known.

Ever since the discovery of *gas pingue* in the late sixteenth century by Van Helmont (1577–1644), natural and 'factitious' inflammable airs had attracted the attention of chemists and natural philosophers. In 1618 Jean Tardin studied a burning seepage of natural gas and concluded that it had something in common with the flames from burning oil or coal [1]. In 1667 Thomas Shirley (1638–78) sent a communication to the Royal Society, describing inflammable air issuing from coal-measures near Wigan. Johann Joachim Becher (1635–82) described coal-gas briefly in 1683 in his *Närrische Weissheit und weise Narrheit* or 'Foolish Wisdom and Wise Folly'.

Stephen Hales (1677–1761) stated in his 'Vegetable Staticks' (1727) that coal and other organic substances could be made to yield inflammable air by heating them in a closed vessel. In 1730 James Lowther led 'damp air' (fire-damp) through a pipe from the workings of one of his mines near Whitehaven to the surface, where it burned continuously (cf pl 6 A). He demonstrated samples of the gas, preserved in bladders, to the Royal Society, and showed that it would burn at the mouth of a tube. At about the same time, his agent, Carlisle Spedding (1695–1755), offered to light Whitehaven by exhalations from the pit, conducting the gas through pipes laid under the streets [2]. The offer was refused, but it is said that Spedding so lighted his office, and that the Whitehaven physician William Brownrigg (1711–1800) studied the gas chemically and physically.

The first detailed account of the production of gas by the destructive distillation of coal was by John Clayton (1657–1725), rector of Crofton near Wakefield. Though he made his observations in about 1684, it was not until 1739 that they were published in the 'Philosophical Transactions'. He says:

> I . . . got some Coal which I distilled in a Retort in an open Fire. At first there came over only *Phlegm*, afterwards a black *Oil*, and then likewise a *Spirit* arose, which I could noways condense, but it forced my Lute, or broke my Glasses. Once, when it had forced the Lute . . . I observed that the Spirit which issued out caught Fire at the Flame of the Candle, and continued burning with Violence as it issued out, in a Stream, which I blew out, and lighted again, alternately, for several times. I then had a Mind to try if I could save any of this Spirit, in order to which I took a turbinated Receiver, and putting a Candle to the Pipe of the Receiver whilst the Spirit arose, I observed that it catched Flame, and continued burning at the End of the Pipe, though you could not discern what fed the Flame: I then blew it out, and lighted it again several times; after which I fixed a Bladder, squeezed and void of Air, to the Pipe of the Receiver. The *Oil* and *Phlegm* descended into the Receiver, but the Spirit, still ascending, blew up the Bladder. . . . And when I had a Mind to divert Strangers or Friends, I have frequently taken one of these Bladders, and pricking a Hole therein with a Pin, and compressing gently the Bladder near the Flame of a Candle it [at] once took Fire, it would then continue flaming till all the Spirit was compressed out of the Bladder. . . .

The first person to take a firm step towards using coal-gas for illuminating a room seems to have been George Dixon, owner of a colliery near Newcastle upon Tyne. About 1760, using a kettle as a retort, he experimented with gas conducted through runs of tobacco-pipe to burners formed by piercing holes in the clay luting. He also attempted to estimate the amount of tar in a ton of coal by carbonizing it in a boiler. There was an explosion, and he decided that coal-gas was too dangerous for common use [3]. The 'Chemical Essays' (1781) of Richard Watson (1737–1816), bishop of Llandaff, contain an account of experiments made to determine the relative qualities of different varieties of coal and wood by distilling them in closed vessels. He bubbled the gas so obtained through water, and recommended converting the normal type of coke-oven into 'distilling vessels'.

Meanwhile others were studying the properties of hydrogen, which Henry Cavendish had discovered in 1766, and which was usually generated by the application of dilute sulphuric acid to chips of iron or zinc. In 1777 François Chaussier (1746–1828) stated that it could be made to burn brightly when squeezed from a bladder through a narrow pipe and ignited by an electric spark.

In 1780 F. L. Ehrmann suggested lamps using hydrogen as an illuminant, a method exploited as a novelty by James Diller, whose 'Philosophical Fireworks' were demonstrated in Paris before the *Académie Royale des Sciences* in 1787 [4], and subsequently in many parts of Europe.

In spite of Watson's suggestion, the coking industry had little influence on the development of gas-lighting, for early coking-ovens were not well adapted for the collection of gas. Nevertheless, in 1770 coke-ovens for carbonizing coal in closed retorts were erected at Sulzbach by the Prince of Nassau. They were described in detail by de Gensanne. The tar drained into a metal pot, and the gas is shown escaping to waste through a vertical pipe (figure 138). There is no indication that it was burned, though about twelve years later Archibald Cochrane, ninth Earl of Dundonald, ignited gas flames at his tar-ovens at Culross (p 252). He is said to have amused his friends by collecting the gas in a vessel 'resembling a large tea-urn', and igniting it at a nozzle [5].

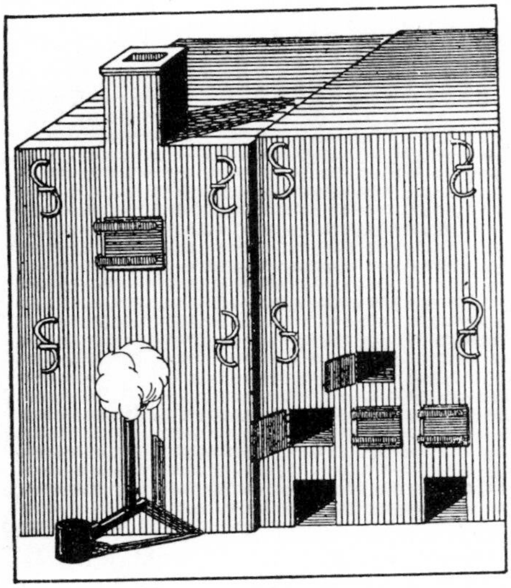

FIGURE 138—*Burning off gas from de Gensanne's coke-oven at Sulzbach.*

Perhaps the first practical use suggested for coal-gas was for the inflation of balloons. This led to some early inconclusive experiments in gas-lighting. Charles Green, in 1821, appears to have been the first person to apply coal-gas on any scale to ballooning, but Faujas de Saint-Fond had suggested its use as early as 1783, though without conviction. He proposed to rid the gas of carbon dioxide by passing it through water to which lime had been added [6]. In the same year Lapostolle, an Amiens apothecary, noted that coal-gas prepared for balloons burned with a beautiful flame [7]. In 1784, Jean Pierre Minkelers (1748–1824), professor of natural philosophy at Louvain, published his *Mémoire sur l'air inflammable* on the preparation of gas for ballooning from coal and other organic solids. Many years after his death, it was stated that, at the same time, he lighted his class-room with gas, a practice he repeated for a number of years in succession. In consequence, he has sometimes been called the inventor of gas-lighting.

At about this time, a number of others began to make rudimentary experiments in gas-lighting. None appears to have presented his work to the public at the time it was carried out. Johann Georg Pickel (1751–1838), professor of pharmacology at Würzburg, lighted his laboratory with gas in 1786 [8]; John Champion, a Bristol copper-smelter, in 1790 contemplated taking out a patent for using gas in lighthouses [9]; J. B. Lanoix, of Lyons, experimented at some time before 1792 [10]; Christian Polykarp Friedrich Erxleben (1765–1831), apothecary of Landskron, lighted his laboratory in about 1795 [11]; Wilhelm August Lampadius (1772–1842) started experiments in 1796, and demonstrated gas-lighting in the castle of the Elector of Saxony in Dresden in 1799 [12].

However, the work of only two of the early experimenters with gas-lighting, Philippe Lebon and William Murdock (1754–1839), culminated in its commercial application. The former may have started investigating gas from wood as early as 1791; the latter began to study the illuminating properties of gas from coal in 1792.

Lebon was born and brought up among the charcoal-burners of Brachay, near Joinville, and doubtless this is why he developed an interest in combustion. In a thesis written at the age of twenty-four he stated that smoke consisted of particles suspended in a colourless inflammable gas, which he proposed to pass through water or to condense in a series of water-cooled pipes. In 1797 he subjected wood to destructive distillation in an iron retort and cooled the gas produced in a vat. He thought that it could be applied to lighting, heating, and the inflation of balloons.

In an effort to persuade the French government to apply gas to public buildings, Lebon moved to Paris in 1798, and conducted experiments on a bigger scale in a house on the Île-Saint-Louis. He took out a patent on 28 September 1799, *pour des nouveaux moyens d'employer les combustibles plus utilement, soit pour la chaleur, soit pour la lumière, et d'en recueiller les divers produits*, with an extension dated 1801. The French government, preoccupied with the war with England, was not interested. It was for this reason that Lebon decided to stage at the Hôtel Seignelay the more public demonstration which has already been described.

Lebon's patent contains a sketch (figure 139) of his gas-making plant. The sheet iron retort (AA) is encircled several times by the flue (FF) from the furnace (EE). The whole is set in fire-brick. The gas, conducted from the retort through G, is to be passed through water, and the by-products—oil, bitumen, and pyroligneous (acetic) acid—are to be collected. In spite of Faujas de Saint-Fond's proposal to use lime to remove carbon dioxide, it is unlikely that Lebon hit on the same idea to remove sulphureous impurities.

Lebon states that his gas was ready to extend everywhere the most sensible heat and the softest lights and could be conducted through the smallest and most fragile pipes. The latter could be embedded in the plaster of walls and ceilings. Provided that the nozzles were of metal, the pipes themselves could be made of varnished silk (*taffetas gommé*). He proposed to burn the gas in a glass globe into which three tubes were introduced; one conveying gas, one air, and the third carrying the waste products of combustion to the open air.

Lebon's contribution to the theory and practice of gas-lighting was great, not only because he was the first man publicly to demonstrate its possibilities, but because his imaginative grasp of its potentialities guided and inspired the men who came after him. In his few writings, Lebon anticipated nearly all the applications of gas in the hundred years succeeding his death.

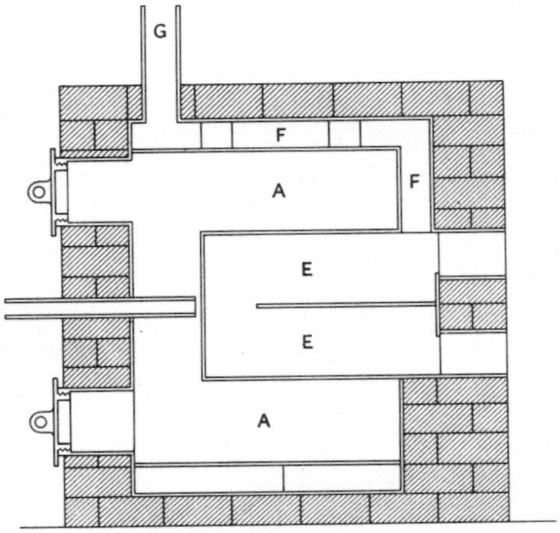

FIGURE 139—*Lebon's first gas-making plant.* (AA) *Sheet iron retort,* (EE) *furnace,* (FF) *flue,* (G) *pipe leading from retort. From his patent specification, 1799.*

William Murdock was trained as a mechanic by his father, a miller of Auchinleck, in Ayrshire. In 1777, at the age of twenty-three, he was engaged by the great engineering firm of Boulton and Watt. By 1790 he had become the firm's principal engine-erector in Cornwall. His interest in coal-gas was stimulated by a patent he took out in 1791 for 'treating certain Ores to obtain Green Vitriol, Pigments, and Compositions for preserving Ships' Bottoms'. This led him to study the destructive distillation of wood, peat, coal, and other substances. In 1792 he generated gas from coal and lighted a room in a house in Cross Street, Redruth. He began to make tests of its cost as an illuminant as compared with oil and tallow. In a paper communicated to the Royal Society by Sir Joseph Banks in 1808, he wrote:

> My apparatus consisted of an iron retort, with tinned copper and iron tubes through which the gas was conducted to a considerable distance; and there, as well as at intermediate points, was burned through apertures of varied forms and dimensions. The experiments were made upon coal of different qualities. . . . The gas was also washed with water, and other means were employed to purify it.

One burner had a number of small holes like the rose of a watering-can; in another, the gas burned in a long thin sheet. There was also a gas-burning Argand, the name at that time given to the normal type of oil lamp with a wick and glass chimney, invented by Pierre Ami Argand (1750–1803) and introduced into England in 1783. Boulton and Watt took it up in 1784. In a gas-burning Argand, air was introduced at the centre of an annular burner surrounded by a glass cylinder. In addition, Murdock collected the gas in vessels and bags of tinned iron and leather or varnished silk in an endeavour to make a portable light.

In 1798 Murdock moved to Birmingham to work in Boulton and Watt's celebrated Soho Foundry. There he continued his experiments on a larger scale,

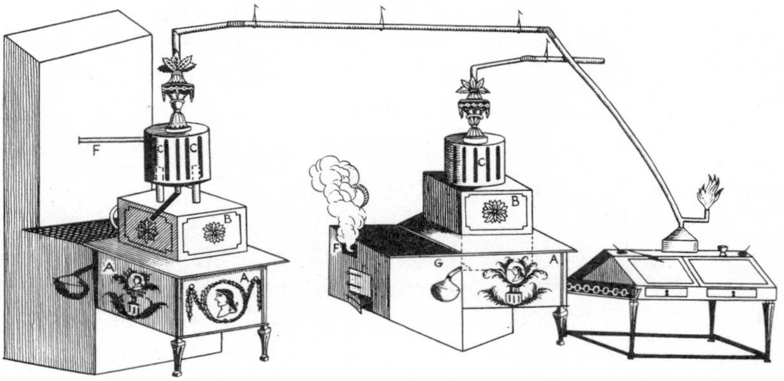

FIGURE 140—*Two forms of Daisenberger's 'thermolamp' built to the design of Johannes B. Wenzler in 1802.* (A) *Furnace,* (B) *retort,* (C) *condenser,* (F) *pipe to relieve excess pressure,* (G) *receptacle for heavy fractions.*

using for retorts upright cast iron pots 30 inches deep and 12 inches in diameter with closely fitting lids luted with clay. A charge was 15 lb and the retorts were brought to a red heat. Though the principal building was lighted by gas 'during many successive nights', the evidence suggests that these experiments had been stopped by 1801 because of the firm's lack of interest.

Murdock's particular and important contribution to gas-lighting was that from the beginning, following Watson, he investigated systematically the comparative behaviour of different classes of coal under conditions of varying temperature and time of carbonizing.

Though no contemporary picture of Lebon's thermolamp is known, it probably resembled one built by J. M. Daisenberger in 1802 to the design of Johannes B. Wenzler, treasurer to the court of Passau [13] (figure 140). Decorated to take its place in the living-room, Daisenberger's thermolamp is in three parts. The furnace is in the lowest part. Above is a rectangular sheet iron retort, from which the heavier fractions drain away. Above the retort is a circular vessel containing a worm immersed in cooling water. The gas rises into a varnished silk pipe and is conducted to a lighting jet above a writing desk.

Zachaus Andreas Winzler (1750–*c* 1830), a Moravian chemical manufacturer living in Austria, who also derived his ideas from Lebon, gave a number of dinner-parties in December 1802, at which the food was cooked on a gas stove and the dining-room was heated by gas [14]. In 1803 he published a detailed account of his methods [15]. His retorts were based on the conventional laboratory equipment of the day, but above the one illustrated (figure 141) there are spaces for heating cooking-utensils. The gas was bubbled through water (lime was not added) and could be passed to a cooker with four burners and a small oven behind, or to a holder in the form of a bellows with a small weight on top. From the holder the gas could be led to a room, where it was used both to warm a radiator and in Argand lamps.

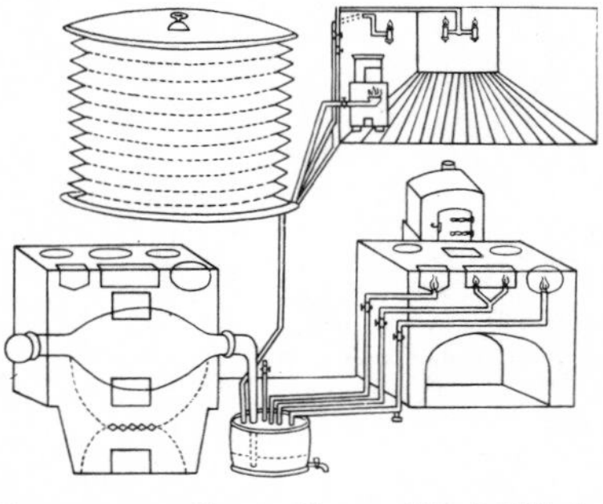

FIGURE 141—*Gas appliance of Z. A. Winzler. It is similar to the laboratory apparatus of the time and is adapted for cooking.*

Among the many people attracted to Lebon's demonstrations at the Hôtel Seignelay was an eccentric German 'professor of commerce', Friedrich Albrecht Winzer (1763–1830), who subsequently anglicized his name to Frederic Albert Winsor. Though he was in no sense a man of science and was without mechanical aptitude, he became infatuated with the idea of lighting houses and cities by gas. He failed to buy a thermolamp from Lebon, but after a great struggle succeeded in making one for himself. After attempting to peddle the idea of gas-lighting in various countries in Europe, he came to England at about the end of 1803: 'the thought of introducing the discovery, for the great advantage of the British realm struck me . . . like an electric spark'.

Another important visitor to the Hôtel Seignelay was Gregory Watt, James Watt's second son, who had managed to get to Paris even though Britain and France were still technically at war. He sent a report on Lebon's work to his brother James, stating that there was no time to lose if their firm was to gain any advantage from Murdock's experiments.

Lebon failed to persuade anyone to take up his proposals. On the evening of 30 November 1804 he was robbed and stabbed to death in the Champs Elysées. In spite of his vision, his murder at the age of thirty-seven had the effect of extinguishing for many years almost all interest in gas-lighting on the continent of Europe. Only in England was the situation favourable for its development. There were a number of reasons for this. The American and Napoleonic wars had interfered with the supply of whale-oil and Russian tallow, and the cost of lamp-oil and candles had risen steeply at the end of the eighteenth century. Further, cotton mills were peculiarly prone to fire, and insurance premiums were correspondingly heavy. In consequence, mill-owners were interested in any new source of light that was economical and safe. The incentive to overcome the difficulties in the way of generating, purifying, storing, and distributing gas was therefore great. In these circumstances the position of William Murdock was particularly favourable, for of the early experimenters with gas-lighting, he alone

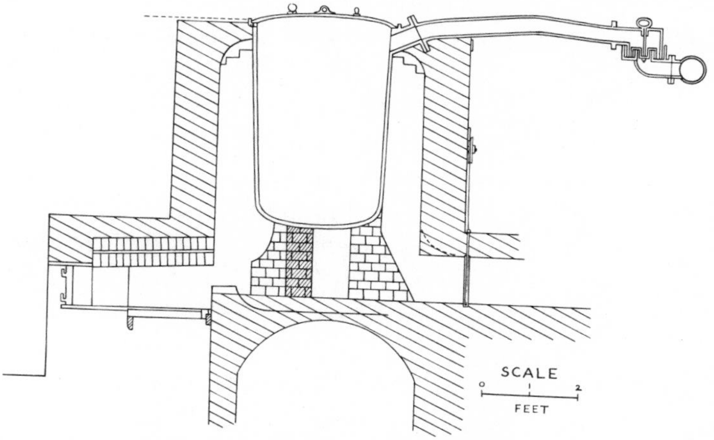

FIGURE 142—*Section of Murdock's first retort for Phillips and Lee, 1805–6. See also figure 143.*

was able to command the help of experienced mechanics and workmen. Without the Soho Foundry he would have been much handicapped.

As a result of the letter from Gregory Watt describing Lebon's demonstration, Murdock resumed his experiments late in 1801. When the Soho Foundry was illuminated to celebrate the Peace of Amiens, signed on 27 March 1802, the decorations included prominently two gas-flares, one at each end of the main building, supplied by pipes up a chimney from a small retort resting in an ordinary fireplace [16]. Statements that the whole front of the building was illuminated by gas are untrue.

From this time, encouraged by William Henry (1774–1836), the celebrated Manchester chemist, Murdock pursued gas-lighting experiments energetically, working with a variety of vertical, sloping, and horizontal cast iron retorts. Though trials were made to determine the best grades of coal to use, the relative efficiency of Argand and ordinary gas-burners, and the relative cost of illumination by gas and candles, little attempt seems to have been made to study the gas itself or methods of purifying it. By 1804 Boulton and Watt felt sufficient confidence in Murdock's apparatus to canvass for orders. Their first client was George Lee of the firm of Phillips & Lee, owners of one of the largest cotton-mills in the kingdom, at Salford, near Manchester.

The first test of the apparatus for Phillips and Lee took place with fifty lamps on the evening of 1 January 1806. Murdock reported a gratifying absence of 'Soho stink'. The first stage of the installation (plate 13 A) was completed in March. There were six retorts in the form of cast iron pots, 5 ft 6 in deep, and tapering in diameter from 3 ft 6 in to 3 ft (figure 142). They were arranged in threes under a crane which lowered into them openwork metal baskets, each holding a charge of about 15 cwt of coal. The gas was led away, past a hydraulic seal (figure 143) operated by hand, to a dry main, and thence to a vertical cylindrical air-cooled condenser about 6 ft long and 2 ft 6 inches in diameter. The tar ran into a pit, and the gas was conducted to cubical sheet iron holders, of 10-ft side, mounted in a row over water, each clumsily supported at the centre by a rope running over a pulley and carrying a counterweight at its other end.

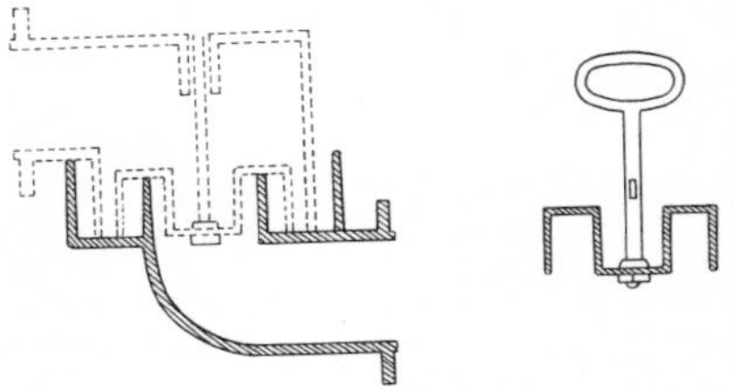

FIGURE 143—*Detail of hydraulic seal on Murdock's first installation.*

The apparatus could scarcely have been cruder. The retorts carbonized the coal badly and became encrusted with spent coke. Judging by the only available drawing, the gas was neither washed nor purified. Murdock's satisfaction at the absence of smell must have been short-lived. But, in spite of all its deficiencies, lighting-costs were much reduced and the plant was extended until, by 1807, it served the whole factory, a short stretch of private road, and Lee's residence. There were 271 Argands and 633 Cockspurs—burners consisting of three small holes in the closed end of a pipe. Single-hole burners were called Ratstails, and those with more than three holes Cockscombs.

Drawings in the Boulton and Watt collection in the Birmingham reference library show that, by 1808, Murdock had evolved what was to be, with minor variations, standard practice until the firm gave up making gas-plant a few years later. He used cast iron horizontal retorts (figure 144), 4 ft long, single-ended and elliptical in section, roughly 2 ft by 1 ft. In 1810 he also experimented with ear-shaped and other sections, but does not appear to have applied them in practice. The retorts were capped by a mouthpiece with a rectangular opening set at an angle of 45° and closed by a hinged flap. The heat from the furnace was applied to the retort through flues, and not directly as in his first designs. The crude gas rose from the front of the retort and passed to a dry main through a hydraulic seal. In some designs, the gas was led down to the seal from the front of the retort. There was no hydraulic main.

The gas was led to a vertical cylindrical condenser—sometimes air-cooled, sometimes water-cooled by the holder-water—where it met a jet of water introduced at the bottom, a design obviously based on the condenser of a steam-engine. Gas, water, and tar passed from the bottom of the condenser to a chamber whence the gas was conducted to the holder and the water and tar trickled away to a tar-pit or, in at least one case, into a canal. There was no chemical

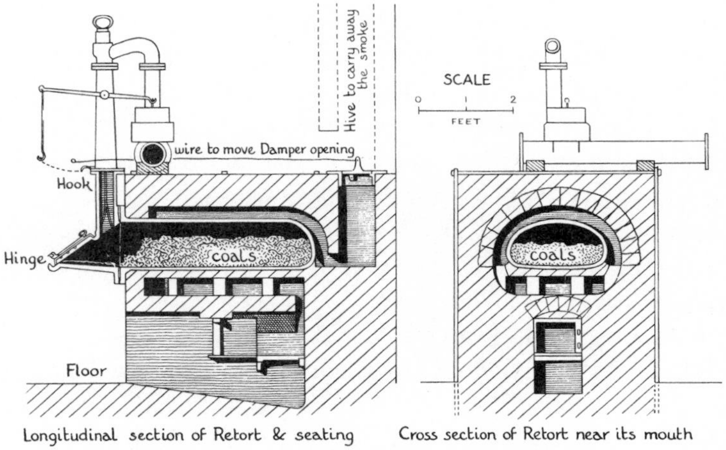

FIGURE 144—*Murdock's horizontal retort, 1808.*

purification by lime. The gas was introduced into or led away from the holder from below by vertical stand-pipes, or frequently directly through the side by pipes with unwieldy hydraulic valves at each end to allow the holder to rise and fall. The holders were rectangular, usually about 10 by 10 by 20 ft.

Though it has been said that Boulton and Watt gave up making gas-apparatus about 1814 out of pique occasioned by the success of their rivals, it seems as likely that their clients deserted them in favour of better equipment made by others. Their initial success may have been due not so much to the basic soundness of their ideas as to their prestige, their foundry and workshops, their command of capital, their salesmanship and, above all, to the well deserved reputation of William Murdock as one of the greatest mechanical engineers of his day.

At all events, Murdock was outdistanced by the first man to approach gas-lighting with something of the outlook of a chemical engineer. Samuel Clegg the elder (1781–1861), who had been educated under Dalton, soon became

Murdock's successful rival. Apprenticed to Boulton and Watt, Clegg worked on the illuminations for the Peace of Amiens, though he stated later that Murdock had refused to reveal his methods to him. He left the firm in 1805. After putting gas installations into a number of small factories, he was given an order to fit up Henry Lodge's cotton mill near Halifax, and claimed that on this contract he was a fortnight ahead of Murdock at Phillips and Lee. He was probably the first person to purify the gas by passing it through water to which lime had been added, an idea which gained him a medal from the Society for the Encouragement of Arts (later the Royal Society of Arts) in 1808. At first the lime was added to the water under the holder, and the gas bubbled through it. A separate liming machine was introduced at Stonyhurst College in 1810. Clegg invented the hydraulic main in 1811, for a batch of four retorts at Greenway's cotton mills [17]. In the next year, he installed gas in the premises and dwelling-house of Rudolf Ackerman, the famous printer and engraver in the Strand (plate 12 A). The equipment was described in detail by Frederick Christian Accum (1769–1838), lecturer in chemistry and author of the first textbooks on gas-lighting. It comprised two cast iron, horizontal, single-ended retorts of circular section. A single charge of coal weighed about one cwt. The gas passed to a hydraulic main and was cooled in a worm immersed in the water below the holder. It was purified in a wet-liming machine, agitated occasionally by hand, and was washed by being bubbled through the holder-water. The apparatus served 48 Argands and 32 Cockspurs, used both for illumination and for the heating of metal plates.

Independently of Murdock and Clegg, Frederic Albert Winsor started to demonstrate gas-lighting in London in the autumn of 1804. From the first he realized that the Boulton and Watt idea of installing gas mill by mill and house by house was unsound. He saw that consumers would have to be supplied through mains radiating from central gas-generating stations. He realized, too, that the amount of capital required for such a purpose would be beyond the resources of any single individual or group of capitalists. It would be essential to obtain a charter from Parliament to form a joint stock company with limited liability.

In 1806 Winsor was sufficiently encouraged by the results of his demonstrations to canvass the formation of The National Light and Heat Company 'for providing our streets and houses with light and heat . . . as they are now supplied with water'. Though he promised, in extravagant language, preposterous profits to subscribers, he also had what Boulton and Watt lacked—vision and a grasp of the social and economic implications of gas-lighting.

He obtained permission to display his lights along the top of the wall separating the garden of Carlton House from the Mall on 4 June 1807, the birthday of George III. In December he lighted part of the south side of Pall Mall, opposite Carlton House. For the first time the public realized that there was something more behind Winsor's frenzies than megalomania. His committee of business men, bankers, and peers, headed by the Duke of Atholl and Lord Anson, rashly announcing that anyone subscribing but £5 would receive an income of £5700 a year, decided to apply to Parliament for a charter.

To the ordinary trader, risking his private capital in manufactory and shop, such companies seemed an invasion of private enterprise, to be resisted at all costs. Boulton and Watt and many other interested parties used every trick to block the charter, but the case for a central supply of gas was too strong. The National Light and Heat Company, renamed The Gas Light and Coke Company, gained its charter early in 1812.

At the start, the chartered company was handicapped by the erratic conduct of its business by Winsor, who was neither administrator nor engineer, and whom the board ruthlessly drove out in a few months. Another failure seems to have been Accum, who had been engaged as a technical witness in the fight for the charter, and was given a position of importance as soon as the company was formed. He resigned in 1817.

The situation was saved by Samuel Clegg, who joined the company late in 1812, just in time to wrestle with the formidable problems created by the great and growing demand for gas-lighting. On 1 April 1814 the oil lamps in the parish of St Margaret's, Westminster, were discontinued in favour of gas, and crowds of curious people followed the lamp-lighters on their rounds. By May 1815 there were nearly fifteen miles of gas-main in London. By December, there were twenty-six miles. Even before this time, insurance premiums had been marked down for mills and public buildings illuminated by gas.

In Clegg's first installation for The Gas Light and Coke Company (plate 12 B), the retorts were of cast iron, circular in section, and tapering from a diameter of 12 in at the front to 10 in at the back. They were single-ended and about 10 ft long. They carbonized the coal badly and were soon given up in favour of retorts of elliptical section, with one side flattened, charged and discharged by scoops and long-handled shovels and rakes, a method that remained in use for decades.

Clegg perpetuated the inconvenient method of cooling the gas in a worm immersed in the water of the holder. It was purified in a wet-liming machine, and washed in a compartment supported on a wooden framework under the holder, but now fed with an independent supply of water.

Though the liming-machine went some way towards ridding the gas of sulphureous impurities, it produced a foul-smelling, poisonous, and useless liquid known as 'blue billy'. Some companies poured it into the sewers, polluting the rivers and killing the fish. The Gas Light and Coke Company concentrated it by evaporation under the retorts, and removed the resulting stinking mess through the streets at night.

Clegg left the company in 1817 owing to a dispute about pay. He and Accum installed gas at the Royal Mint in the same year, and the plant was notable for including a semi-continuous carbonizing system, a semi-solid liming machine, a self-acting wet meter, and a gas governor.

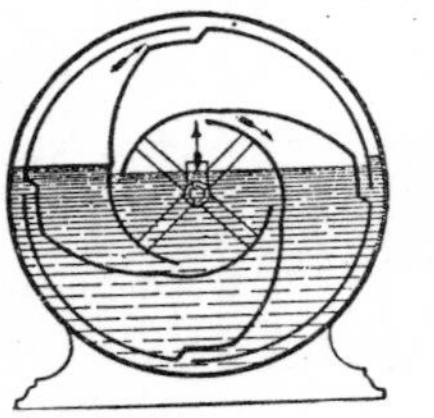

FIGURE 145—*Malam's wet meter. This consists of a paddle-wheel, with one inner and four outer chambers, revolving in a case. The gas enters the inner chambers and, in escaping through one outlet pipe in the outer case, forces the wheel to rotate.*

The carbonizing system comprised segmental trays, each charged with coal, and supported between the spokes of a horizontal wheel, rotated by hand, which carried them into the furnace. Though ingenious and in advance of its time, this apparatus was a failure owing to excessive wear in use. Clegg's wet meter took the form of a revolving cylinder divided at first into two, and later into three, compartments, alternately filled with gas and emptied as the cylinder revolved. Its complicated and mechanically unsound valve-mechanism caused it to fail, though its principle is still that used to measure the output from a works. It was greatly improved in 1819 by John Malam, Clegg's son-in-law, who was also employed by The Gas Light and Coke Company [18] (figure 145). The governor was virtually a miniature holder rising and falling with changes in pressure and actuating a valve according to its position.

Clegg's successor at The Gas Light and Coke Company, T. S. Peckston, wrote the first modern textbook on gas. He established principles that were to govern its manufacture for at least another seventy-five years. He mounted the retorts in benches of three, four, and five, though satisfactory designs to ensure even heating took years to evolve. In spite of their defects, he used cast iron retorts. Fireclay retorts, with cast iron mouths, did not become universal in Britain until the middle of the century. Presently, two banks of retorts were set back to back. By 1850, 'through' settings—that is, retorts open at each end and about 18 ft long—were coming into use at the larger works. At first they were charged and discharged through both ends by hand (plates 13 B and 14 A). Automatic and semi-automatic charging and discharging by machine were later introductions.

Reuben Phillips patented the dry-liming process in 1817. In 1823 John Malam patented the method of passing the gas through layers of quicklime, first in one direction, then in the other. This may have resulted in the marked improvement of gas said to have occurred at about this time. Lime was not given up in favour of oxide of iron till the end of the nineteenth century. Though oxide of iron stripped the sulphur from the free hydrogen sulphide, it left untouched certain other sulphur compounds, present in small quantities. Its use depended on the introduction of incandescent lighting, which led to a great reduction in the proportion of gas burned without flues.

At first, retorts were subject to back-pressure, and at high temperatures the gas was 'cracked', leaving a deposit of carbon that had to be chipped away by hand: a difficulty not overcome, by the introduction of exhausting-pumps, until the late thirties. Without these, it was impossible to lower the pressure on the retorts, and the gas could not even be passed through efficient washers and scrubbers. Before their introduction, large quantities of ammonia reached the mains, corroding copper and brass pipes and fittings, depositing a dangerous explosive compound, and giving the gas a nauseating smell.

Though wooden mains of tamarack (American larch) logs were in extensive use in the United States as late as 1878 [19], the London mains were of cast iron, first introduced for water in 1810. Their supply was less of a problem than that of the small-diameter service-pipe, which was known as 'barrel'. This term is still used by gas-fitters because the pipe was made in the same way as cheap gun-barrels, from 4-ft lengths of strip iron, bent over a mandrel and welded down the joint. For cheapness, old or rejected gun-barrels, in ample supply after the war with France, were often pressed into use. The problem of making barrel in quantity was not solved till Cornelius Whitehouse's patent of 1825 for making drawn wrought iron pipe, a process perfected in the following ten years. An early pipe for gas is shown in figure 146.

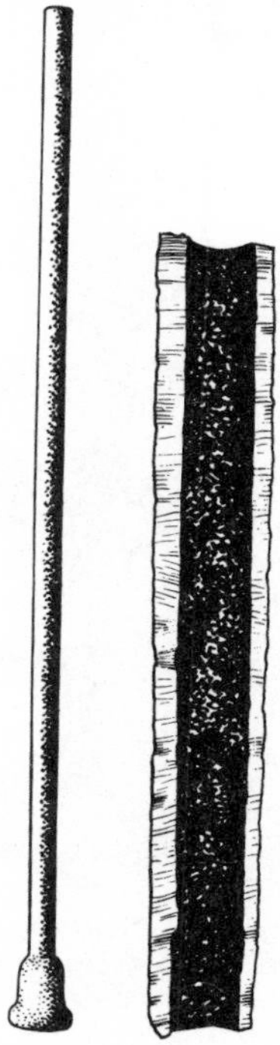

FIGURE 146—*A length of ½-in iron pipe laid in 1836 by the Cupar Gas Company.* (Left) *External view*; (right) *section* (*magnified*).

Meters were not supplied to consumers for many years, and dry meters did not become common till the fifties. Gas was often charged for not by volume, but by the number of burners in use for a given time—an arrangement leading to the theft of much gas. Some people simply lighted the gas at the open end of a pipe and let it rip; many fried-fish shops liked to have flares 10 in long. After a short time, the batswing and fishtail burners became standard. The former consisted of a long narrow slit, the latter of two jets of gas impinging upon one another, a system invented by J. B. Neilson about 1820. The greatly superior Argand never became popular. It was susceptible to changes in gas-pressure and was inclined to smoke when badly adjusted; it was expensive; and its glass chimney made it difficult to maintain (figure 147).

By 1823 three rival chartered companies were operating in London north of the Thames. Each invaded the territory of the other, and their mains writhed round each other like worms. The whale-oil interests, which had at first joined forces with those who wished to suppress gas altogether as dangerous, poisonous, or a defiance of Almighty God, later entered directly into competition with coal-gas. Animal fats and oils were cracked in heated cast iron retorts. The cast iron acted as a catalyst in the reactions, but soon became covered with carbon and so ceased to be effective. This was a fatal disadvantage, and all the oil-gas companies had failed by about 1830.

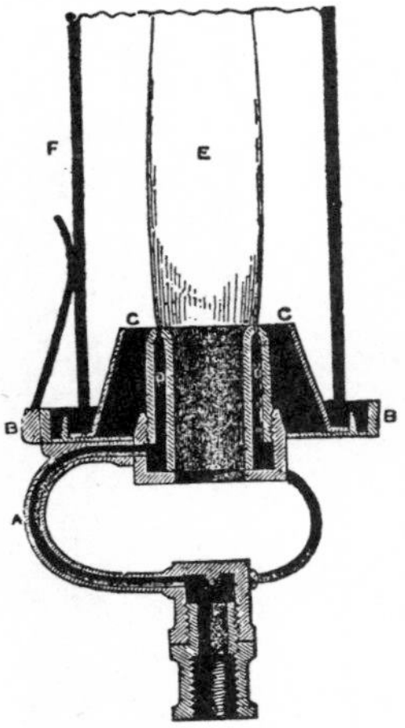

FIGURE 147—*Sugg's Argand burner, adopted as the British government standard burner in 1869.* (A) *Supply-tube to chamber of combustion;* (B) *support for chimney;* (C) *cone, outer air-supply;* (D) *steatite chamber of combustion;* (E) *flame;* (F) *chimney.*

Gas was adopted almost immediately by factories, public buildings, and shops. By 1825, churches, banks, 'The Times' printing-office, the Mechanics' Institution, East India House, Drury Lane theatre, and half a dozen London clubs were illuminated by gas. But a combination of imperfect purification, bungling fitting, leaky joints, and blackened ceilings made its use in a small room insufferable. John Martin, the allegorical painter, showed Satan presiding over the infernal council in a Hell illuminated by coronas of flaring gas-jets. Not even Accum's delightful Regency fittings, or the water-slide which William Caslon designed in 1818—a gas-bracket made of sliding tubes and a water-seal that could be raised or lowered—could dispel public prejudice. Though the Mansion House had 2062 gas lights in 1825, there was none in the Lord Mayor's parlour. As late as 1833, the 'Mechanics' Magazine' suggested that the proper way to use gas for domestic illumination was to reflect inwards light from a burner placed outside the window. In 1841 Samuel Clegg junior warned against 'sickness and oppressive headache' from gas-lights in an apartment not well ventilated, and Michael Faraday was called in by the Athenaeum in 1843 to mitigate the 'stupefying effects of gas' and to prevent the bindings of books from being spoiled. Gas was wholly excluded from the Crystal Palace in 1851 (it closed at sundown), and the industry had to have an exhibition of its own at the Polytechnic Institution [20]. It was for years common practice to fit a little ventilating pipe, called a perdifume, over each light.

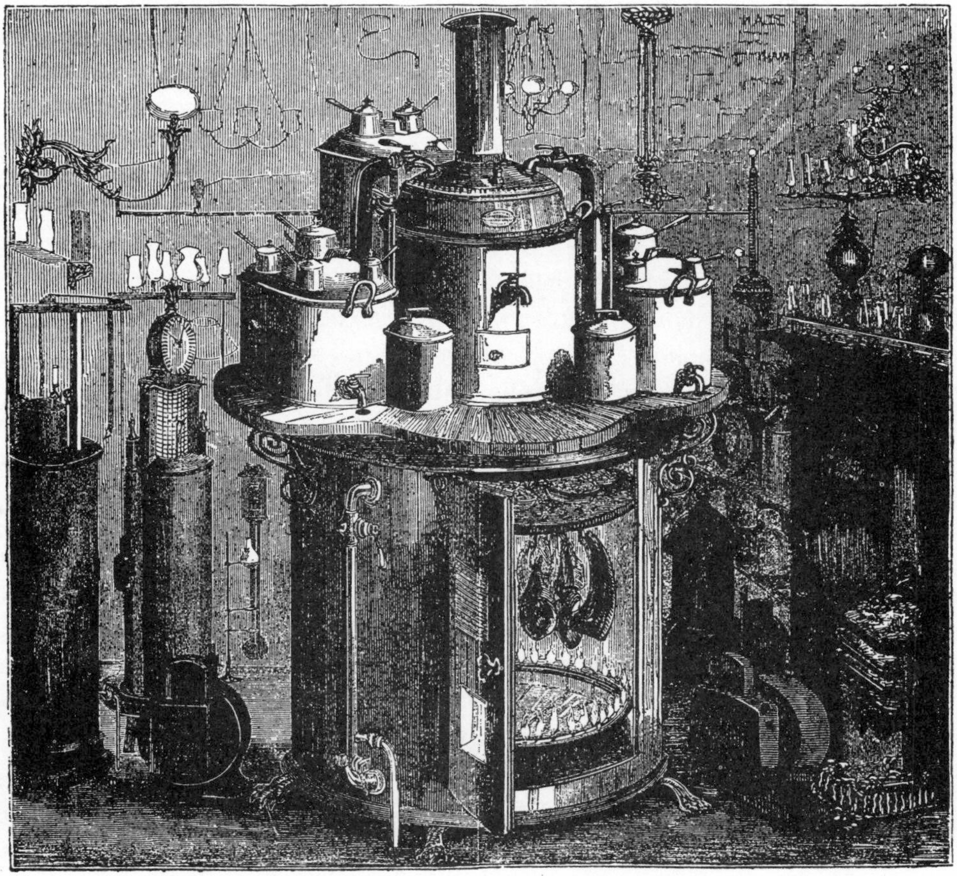

FIGURE 148—*Sharp's gas-cooking apparatus*, c *1851. It occupied a floor space 4 ft 6 in square and on top of the oven was a boiler to heat kettles and pans. It could cook dinner for 100 persons.*

Gas could not be applied efficiently till the atmospheric burner in which a supply of air was introduced into the gas stream just below the point of combustion was devised, surprisingly late, about 1840 [21]. The handy version to which R. W. Bunsen (1811–99) gave his name was designed by him for his new laboratory at Heidelberg in 1855. The gas-ring was introduced in 1867. Benjamin Waddy Maughan patented the geyser in 1865; he failed to protect the name and it came to be used by all manufacturers. Though John Maiben had suggested a gas fire in 1813, made by playing gas-flames on 'fancy figures' of cast metal, the gas fire with radiants of the type familiar today was not introduced until 1880. It did not become popular for another twenty years. Gas cooking was not common before the seventies, though the still familiar cast iron box with a hot plate over it was introduced about 1850 (figure 148). From 1880 the cooker changed hardly at all in fundamentals until thermostatic control became common about 1930.

The social and economic effects of gas can scarcely be exaggerated. Scoffing at those who claimed that sunlight was necessary for growth, Andrew Ure pronounced that children suffered no harm working twelve hours a day in mills lighted by gas. If gas must bear some of the responsibility for the intolerably long hours of labour in the early nineteenth century, it also gave the workman and his family a new life. For gas encouraged evening classes in the Mechanics' Institutes, and aided the new literacy and education. That people could congregate after their working hours in well lit halls encouraged the processes of popular government. The social, industrial, and communal life of the nineteenth century could not have developed as it did without gas-light.

So great was the impetus created by the rapid success of the early companies, that England became responsible for many of the installations on the continent of Europe and in America. An enormous export trade developed in gas-making appliances and pipes. From 1828 until the eighties the gas industry in Britain passed through a period of easy and complacent prosperity. A Board of Trade report in 1869 complained that the diversity of illuminating power from various burners and in various cities was incredible, and the waste of gas a disgrace.

Then, suddenly, gas undertakings were shaken out of their torpor, for between 1879 and 1884 the electric arc-light and the incandescent electric filament-lamp attained commercial success. Gas shares slumped, and the industry would have been in bad straits but for the Austrian inventor, Carl Auer von Welsbach (1858–1929), who patented the incandescent gas-mantle in 1885. An answer to the threat of electricity had been found, and gas was able to hold its own as a lighting-agent while the industry developed the techniques necessary for its prime function in the twentieth century—the flexible and convenient supply of heat-energy for domestic and industrial use, and of raw materials for the production of chemicals.

ACKNOWLEDGEMENTS

For much information or assistance the author is indebted to Dr M. Bouvet, President of the Society of the History of Pharmacology; Dr F. Klemm, of the Deutsches Museum; the Curator of the Boulton and Watt Collection at the Birmingham Reference Library; and the Assay Master of the Birmingham Assay Office. For information concerning Lebon he has drawn on papers quoted extensively by Amédée Fayol in *Philippe Lebon* and by Charles Gaudry in *L'Industrie du gaz en France, 1824–1924*.

REFERENCES

[1] TARDIN, J. 'Histoire naturelle de la fontaine qui brusle près de Grenoble.' Tournon. 1618.
[2] JARS, G. 'Voyages métallurgiques', Vol. 1, p. 248. Lyons. 1774.
[3] MACFARLAN, J. *Trans. Newcomen Soc.*, **5**, 53–55, 1924–5.
[4] *Obsns phys.*, **31**, 188–95, 1787.
[5] HART, J. *Mechanics' Mag.*, **40**, 410, 1844.
[6] FAUJAS DE SAINT-FOND, B. 'Description des expériences de la machine aerostatique de MM. de Montgolfier', p. 166. Paris. 1783.
[7] *J. Paris*, 24 Jan., 1784.
[8] "Über Thermolampen." *Verkündiger*, **6**, no. 35, 274, 1802.
FRIEDE, H. *Apothekerztg, Berl.*, **42**, no. 25, 369–70, 1927.
[9] Letter from John Champion to Matthew Boulton, 15 June 1790. Assay Office Collection, Birmingham.
[10] "Les premiers essais du gaz d'éclairage." *Chron. méd.*, **31**, 206*n*, 1924.
[11] FISCHER, W. "Geschichtliche Blätter aus der Apothekerfamilie Erxleben in Landskron in Deutschnöhmen" in 'Apotheker-Bilder von Nah und Fern', Pt 5, p 21. Vienna. 1912.
[12] LAMPADIUS, W. A. *J. Chem. Phys.*, **8**, 38, 1813.
[13] DAISENBERGER, J. M. 'Beschreibung der daisenbergerschen Thermolampe.' Stadtamhof. 1802.
[14] Letters from J. Du Mont de Florgy to Sir Joseph Banks. Woodcroft Collection, Patent Office Library, London.
[15] WINZLER, Z. A. 'Die Thermolampe in Deutschland.' Brünn. 1803.
[16] "Materials for a Memorium of Mr. Samuel Clegg." *Mechanics' Mag.*, **22**, 470, 1835.
[17] CLEGG, S., Sr. 'Description of an Apparatus by which Twenty-five Cubic Feet of Gas are Obtained from each Cauldron of Coal', p. 8. London. 1820.
[18] PECKSTON, T. S. 'The Theory and Practice of Gas-Lighting', pp. 322–36. London. 1819.
[19] KING, W. B. 'Treatise on the Science and Practice of the Manufacture and Distribution of Coal Gas', Vol. 2, p. 334. London. 1879.
[20] "Gas Apparatus and the Exhibition." *Expositor*, **1**, 275, 1851.
[21] ROBISON, SIR JOHN. *Edinb. new phil. J.*, second series, **28**, 291, 1840.

BIBLIOGRAPHY

ACCUM, F. C. 'A Practical Treatise on Gas-Light.' London. 1815.
Idem. 'Description of the Process of Manufacturing Coal Gas.' London. 1819.
BLOCHMANN, G. M. S. 'Beiträge zur Geschichte der Gasbeleuchtung.' Dresden. 1871.
CHANDLER, D. and LACEY, A. D. 'The Rise of the Gas Industry in Britain.' British Gas Council, London. 1949.
CLEGG, S., Jr. 'A Practical Treatise on the Manufacture and Distribution of Coal-Gas.' London. 1841.
CREIGHTON, H. "Gas-Lights." Article in Supplement to 4th, 5th, and 6th editions of 'Encyclopaedia Britannica'. Edinburgh. 1824.
KING, W. B. 'Treatise on the Science and Practice of the Manufacture and Distribution of Coal Gas' (3 vols). London. 1878–82.
MATTHEWS, W. 'An Historical Sketch of the Origin, Progress, and Present State of Gas-Lighting.' London. 1827.
PECKSTON, T. S. 'The Theory and Practice of Gas-Lighting.' London. 1819.
PECLET, E. 'Traité de l'éclairage.' Paris. 1827.

'The Gasman's Arms', from a lamp-lighter's Christmas broadsheet, c *1815.*

10

PART I

THE TEXTILE INDUSTRY: MACHINERY FOR COTTON, FLAX, WOOL, 1760–1850

JULIA de L. MANN

I. THE FIRST SUCCESSFUL MACHINES

THE industrial revolution is often thought of as having started in 1760. While this is a conventional date in a century that saw continuous change and growth in industry, it is at least true that the first successful spinning-machines, which were to transform the textile industry, were produced in the following decade. The cotton industry led the way, partly for technical reasons: of all the textile fibres cotton proved the easiest to spin by mechanical means. The industry was also experiencing a period of expansion in the early sixties and had adopted Kay's fly-shuttle in the previous decade, so that the demand for yarn stimulated a search for quicker means of spinning. As Paul's attempt was known in Lancashire, and Bourn's carding-engine (vol III, p 154) had been used there, it was natural that the possibilities of spinning by rollers should be canvassed. Arkwright was well able to take advantage of current ideas, but how far the machine that he patented in 1769 was his own invention need not concern us here; he deserves full credit for the persistence with which he carried it to success.

In 1760 the raw cotton, after being opened and cleaned, was carded by hand into a loose roll which was drawn out and slightly twisted on the spindle into a roving; the roving was spun into yarn by the same means. Arkwright's machine (figure 149) was a wooden frame at the top of which were four bobbins, placed horizontally across it, containing rovings. A roving from each bobbin passed through two pairs of rollers divided into four sections corresponding to the bobbins. The second pair of rollers moved more quickly than the first and so elongated the roving, which then passed down the arm of a flyer attached to a spindle at the bottom of the machine and was wound on the bobbin carried by the spindle. The speed of the bobbin was retarded in relation to that of the spindle by a brake in the shape of a piece of worsted twisted round its base. The winding was thus done on the same principle as that of the Saxony wheel from which Arkwright took the idea, even to the rather clumsy device of placing pins on the flyer so that the spinner could guide the thread evenly on to the bobbin. In Arkwright's specification the machine was designed to be worked by a horse, but the motive-power generally used at first was water: hence the name water-frame. Several improvements were made between 1769 and 1775, but little information about them has survived. One of the most important, patented in 1772 by Coniah Wood, one of Arkwright's workmen, was the introduction of a movable rail in place of the pins to guide the thread for winding; its movement

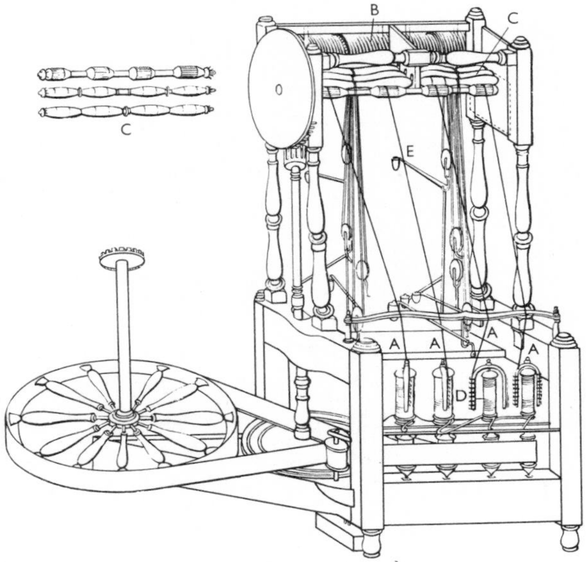

FIGURE 149—*Arkwright's original water-frame spinning-machine of 1769. The four threads* (A) *come from the roving bobbins* (B), *through the rollers* (C) *and on to the flyers* (D), *which are shown in different positions. The pairs of rollers (shown enlarged at the side) are pressed together by the weights* (E).

was later made automatic by means of a heart-shaped wheel or cam. Another pair of rollers was also added.

Almost contemporaneous with the water-frame was a hand-driven machine which owed nothing to previous experiments. This was the spinning-jenny, which reproduced the actions of the hand-spinner. James Hargreaves, a weaver of Stanhill near Blackburn, is said to have invented it in 1764, but he did not patent it until 1770, a few weeks after Arkwright. As he had sold some jennies before that date, his patent was held to be invalid. Bobbins filled with roving were placed at the bottom of a frame carrying several spindles, and a sliver from each was attached to a spindle, passing on the way between two rails forming a bar which slid back and forth on the frame. The spinner drew out the roving by moving the bar back a certain distance. The rails were then pressed together to hold the sliver fast while the backward movement of the bar, and the turning of the wheel which moved the spindles, were continued. When enough twist had been given, the bar was moved forward again and the spindles were turned slowly to wind the yarn; meanwhile the spinner pulled a lever which depressed a wire, called the faller, to push down the thread into a position where it could be wound. The jenny received several improvements, especially from Haley of Houghton Tower, soon after it came into use (figure 150).

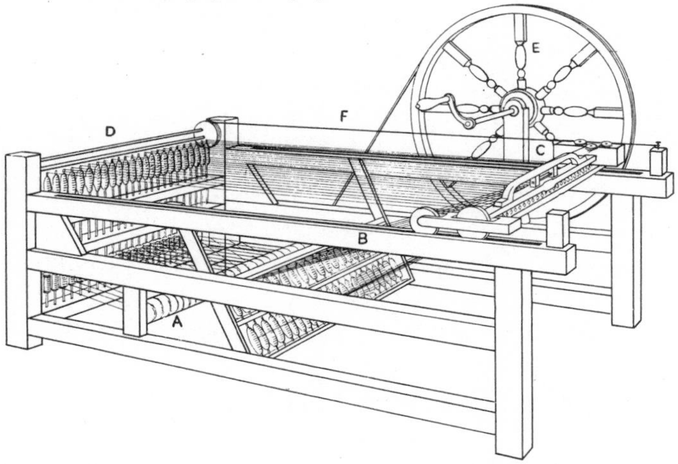

FIGURE 150—*Hargreaves's spinning-jenny after it had been improved by Haley, who made the roller* (A) *of sheet tin for the sake of lightness, and placed the wheel* (E) *in a vertical position. The thread passes from the roving bobbins* (B) *through the clasp* (C) *to the spindles* (D). *These are rotated by bands from the roller* (A), *which is turned by the large wheel* (E). *The faller cord* (F), *when pulled, presses down the transverse wire* (*below* D).

The water-frame produced a strong, well twisted yarn suited for hosiery and the warp of cotton goods. Jenny-spun yarn was at first used for warp and weft, but proved more suitable for the latter. The next machine, Crompton's mule, would spin yarn for either. It was never patented, and the only early model seems to be in France (plate 14 B). The earliest in England (in the Chadwick Museum, Bolton) dates from 1802 or later, and is a model on the lines of Kelly's patent (p 288) [1]. Crompton began experiments in 1774 and the machine was working by 1779. He combined the rollers of the water-frame with the movable carriage of the jenny by placing the spindles on the carriage and the rollers where the spindles had stood in the jenny. The spinner drew back the carriage at the same rate as the rollers gave out the sliver, until about five-sixths of the whole distance had been traversed. Then the rollers were stopped and made to act like the clasp on the jenny, while the carriage continued to recede at a much slower rate and the spindles continued to twist. At the end of the stretch the spindles were turned a few times in the opposite direction to disengage the yarn. The carriage was then pushed in again with the spindles turning slowly in the original direction to wind on the yarn with the help of the faller, as in the jenny.

For some time the great merit of the mule was thought to be the absence of strain on the roving, but in course of time spinners found that a slight stretch at this point was beneficial. Hence arose the practice, for certain types of yarn, of drawing out the carriage faster than the rollers gave out the roving—the 'gain of the carriage', as it was called [2]. The practice of turning the spindles faster during the second part of the carriage's outward journey is attributed to John Kennedy, the great Manchester spinner and machine-maker, presumably about 1790 [3]. Much of the usefulness of the mule can be attributed to the fact that it admitted such great variety in the relationship between the speed of the spindles and that of the rollers and carriage, so that every sort of yarn could be spun.

The mule was considerably improved before 1790. The horizontal roller round which the driving-belts of the spindles had passed (as in the jenny) was replaced by a vertical drum, round which the belts were fixed at different heights so that they covered the whole drum. This made it possible greatly to increase the number of spindles. The rollers were driven by a clockwork mechanism which dropped out of gear when the carriage had receded to the proper point, and the carriage itself was connected by a pulley to the rollers, so that its speed on the first stretch was controlled by them. These additions made the spinners' work easier and more accurate, but the mule was still a hand-driven machine.

The invention of spinning-machinery stimulated efforts to speed up the preparatory processes. The early carding-machines seem to have derived from Bourn's patent, and a machine of this kind is said to have been Arkwright's first model. He later substituted one on Paul's pattern, consisting of a large cylinder known as the 'swift' surmounted by a half cylinder or 'flat', the interior of which, like the surface of the swift, was covered with wire teeth. The carded cotton was removed from the swift by a doffer cylinder revolving in the opposite direction. The cards were arranged in strips across the cylinder, with spaces between each strip so that the cotton came off in short pieces. Arkwright's patent of 1775 shows him in process of experiments for making a continuous carding. By 1785 he had arrived at a solution by covering the whole of the cylinder with card-teeth, taking off the fleece of carded cotton by means of a comb working up and down on a crank, and passing it under rollers and through a funnel to narrow it to a sliver, which then fell in coils into a can. Some of his additions to the carding-engine had been made independently by others, notably the feeding-cloth for bringing the cotton to the swift, but it is now agreed that the crank and comb were his own invention, though they were claimed for Hargreaves in 1785. The machinery used for the further processes of drawing and roving was also shown in the patent of 1775, but the process was more intensive than would be guessed from the specification. The purpose of drawing was to take the place of the spinner's fingers in making the texture of the sliver uniform throughout. A number of cardings were drawn from their cans to unite and pass through two pairs of rollers, by which they were drawn out into one sliver of as many times the original length as there were cardings to be united. This process might be carried out several times, until, at the end, the sliver was given a slight twist to make the roving; this was done by rotating the can that received it (figure 151). The original model had a door through which the rovings were removed by hand, but, as handling exposed them to damage, later machines contained a box which could be lifted out.

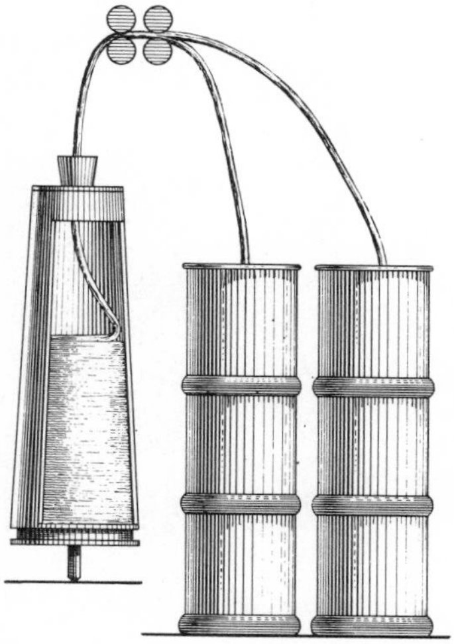

FIGURE 151—*Arkwright's roving-can, known from its shape as the 'lantern can'.*

Arkwright had thus a process for carding, drawing, and roving which was all but continuous, and his machines were driven by power. His patent of 1775 was infringed and was first declared invalid in 1781, but he persisted in challenging those who took advantage of this ruling, and the final decision against him was not given until 1785. Even so, his machines were expensive, and many attempts to find a satisfactory alternative were made in the late seventies and early eighties by men who were using the old carding-machine and the jenny. The one which proved successful, the billy, also a hand-driven machine, did not appear until 1786 (figure 152); it is not certain who was the inventor [4]. In form the billy looked rather like a jenny, but the spindles stood on the carriage and the twisting and winding took place as on the mule. In place of the rollers there was an endless cloth moving in a slanting position round two drums rotated by a weight which was attached to the upper one and wound automatically every time the carriage was moved in. The cardings, drawn in short lengths from cards arranged horizontally on the doffer cylinder, were placed side by side on this cloth and moved forward by its rotation, new lengths having constantly to be pieced to the backs of the old ones. As they moved forward they passed between two rails which acted like the clasp on the jenny to hold them while the spindles twisted them into rovings. This was a far cheaper method than Arkwright's, but it omitted the drawing and so gradually disappeared from the cotton industry—though not from the woollen—as his machines became more common. In the nineties there were many manufacturers possessing carding- and roving-machinery on Arkwright's model who sold rovings to others for spinning on the mule.

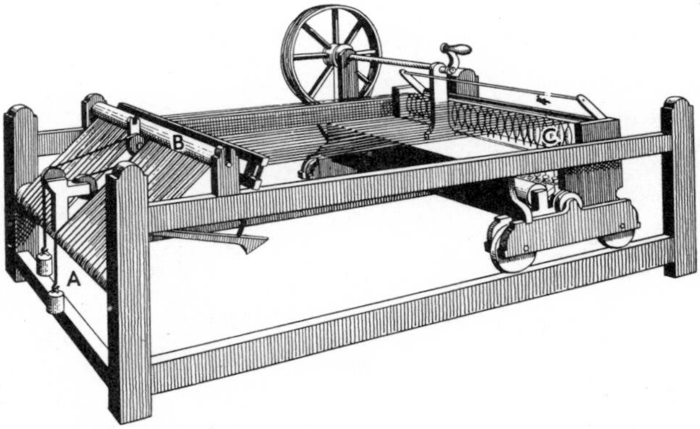

FIGURE 152—*The slubbing-billy—a combination of the jenny and the mule. The cardings were placed on the endless band of cloth* (A) *which is in a sloping position and which leads them under the roller* (B) *and so to the spindles* (C).

II. THE DEVELOPMENT OF SPINNING-MACHINERY UP TO 1850

The machines of 1790 were still crude, and the yarn they produced was imperfect. In discussing their development the different fibres must be treated separately, for it was often necessary to alter a machine invented for cotton in order to make it suit another fibre. From 1800 inventions not only in Britain but in France and the United States must be taken into account. In spite of British prohibitory laws, France acquired the first machines very quickly, mainly through emigrants, and the United States came not far behind. French contributions were made for linen and worsted, but in America attention was concentrated on designing machines of simple construction which would produce quickly and so offset high wages. Most of these machines would not spin fine yarn, but British superiority in this department was in any case too great for effective competition. Skilled mechanics, scarce in England, were even scarcer in France and America [5], and at least up to 1840 it was not uncommon for machinery invented in the last two countries to be greatly improved in Britain [6]. Early machinery was mainly constructed of wood, often by the manufacturer himself. The use of cast iron for machine-frames began in the first decade of the nineteenth century [7]—though much wooden machinery continued in use—and specialized machine-makers became more common. Steam as the motive-power was first used at Arkwright's factory at Shude Hill, Manchester, but this worked on the Newcomen principle by pumping the water which drove the machinery. The first steam-driven factory was at Papplewick, Nottinghamshire, where Boulton and Watt set up an engine in 1785. From 1790 the use of steam-power spread rapidly

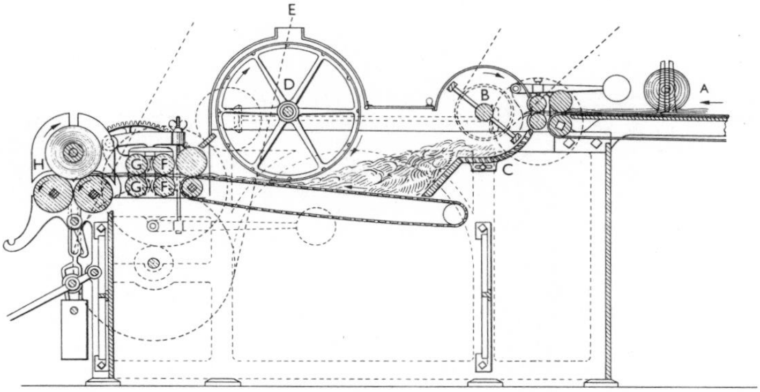

FIGURE 153—*Scutching and lap machine. The cotton was fed to the machine at* (A), *and led past the beaters* (B), *which removed the dust through a grid* (C). (D) *was a revolving cage through which more dust was sucked up the pipe* (E). *The layer of beaten cotton was then led between the rollers* (FF) *and* (GG) *and round the lap cylinder* (H). *When* (H) *was full it lifted a crank and the sliver was cut between rollers* (F) *and* (G). *In the full-scale model the parts from* (A) *to* (F) *might be repeated four to five times.*

and had the effect of concentrating mills in towns instead of dispersing them over the countryside: but many water-driven mills survived.

(*a*) COTTON. Power seems to have been applied about 1800 to the preparatory processes of willowing and batting the cotton to remove impurities and open it thoroughly. Various forms of machine were made for willowing and were found to suit different types of cotton. They all involved teasing the cotton between spikes set in a container, which was quickly rotated while the dirt fell through a grating at the bottom of the machine. For the next process, that of batting, a power-driven machine, the scutcher, was produced in Scotland by Neil Snodgrass in 1797 and improved at the mills of Arkwright and the Strutts, but it was not used at Manchester until 1808. The cotton was again beaten by revolving arms and subjected to a draught to suck up impurities. A given weight of cotton was then put on the feeding-cloth of a lap-machine, where it was passed under rollers to reduce it to a fleecy mass; this was delivered to another cloth ready to feed the carding-engine. In 1814 Crighton attached a lap-machine to the scutcher, but in the majority of factories in England the processes continued to be separate [8] in spite of the fact that by the thirties an efficient combined machine had been evolved (figure 153). In this machine the lap-cylinder revolved on friction-rollers placed below it, and was progressively lifted by a crank to allow for its increasing diameter. When it had reached a certain size the machinery behind it was thrown out of gear, thus cutting the sliver.

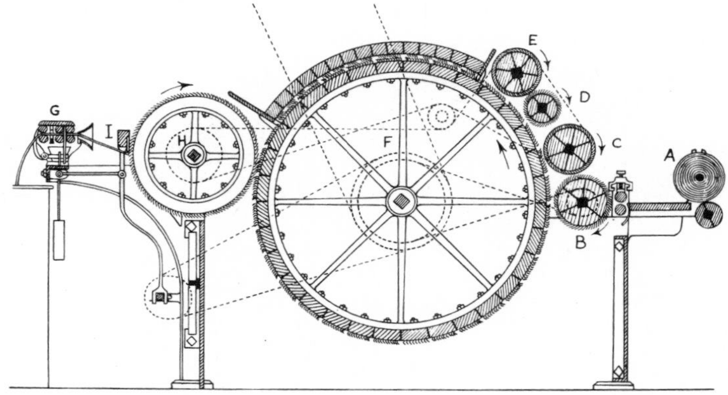

FIGURE 154—*Carding-machine.* (A) *Feeding cylinder;* (B) *licker-in;* (C), (D), (E) *urchins;* (F) *main carding-cylinder or swift;* (G) *metal plate with slit to round sliver after drawing;* (H) *doffer;* (I) *crank and comb or doffing knife.*

The carding-machine became larger and more complicated (figure 154). The cotton was fed to the swift by a small, slower-moving cylinder, the licker-in, and then carded between a series of small cylinders or urchins working on the swift. It next passed under the flats, from which it emerged with the fibres roughly parallel. The doffing took place as in Arkwright's machine, but the sliver received its first drawing, and was rounded by passing through a vertical slit in a metal plate before falling into the can. The drawback of this carding-engine was the trouble of cleaning the flats, which had to be done twice a day by hand. Various automatic cleaning processes were produced, but none was very successful owing to the delicacy of adjustment needed. A patent for revolving flats, to be cleaned by a brush attached to the machine, was taken out by James Smith of Deanston in 1834, but it succeeded only after 1850, when many improvements had been made to it.

This carding-engine was essential for fine yarns, for which the cotton was carded twice. The first machine, known as the breaker, had coarser cards than the finisher. Another type of machine, the roller-and-clearer card, without flats but with a number of smaller cards round the swift, was also in use for coarse yarns (figure 155). The cotton was carded by the action of successive cylinders placed on top of the swift; next to each large cylinder was a smaller one which cleared the cotton from it and returned it to the swift.

Arkwright's drawing-frame remained unchanged, but his system of roving was not entirely satisfactory because the coil had to be wound on a bobbin before spinning, and might be damaged in the process. It was finally superseded by the bobbin-and-fly frame (figure 156) introduced by the machine-making firm of Cocker and Higgins in 1815 and perfected by Henry Houldsworth of Glasgow in 1825 (figure 156). This machine, in appearance like the water-frame, revived Arkwright's first idea of winding the roving straight on to the bobbin by means of a flyer, but the problem of doing so with such a tenuous thread was much more difficult than with yarn. To avoid straining, it must be wound at exactly the same speed as that at which it is given out from the front rollers, but if the angular velocity of the bobbin is constant its peripheral velocity will increase as it grows larger with winding. It was therefore necessary to find a means of keeping the relative speeds of the spindle and the surface of the bobbin constant, so that winding might always go on at the same rate. This was achieved by driving the bobbins separately from the spindles by means of a strap sliding on a conical drum, an idea which Arkwright had patented but was unable to bring into action. As the strap moved from the smaller to the larger circumference of this cone, it moved at a gradually increasing speed. The cone was connected to a wheel which, by coming alternately into gear with other wheels, raised and lowered the copping-shaft on which the bobbins stood, for the rovings were too delicate to move up and down them. By the changing speed of the strap the velocity of the bobbins was gradually increased by the difference between the new speed and the constant velocity of the driving-shaft. Through a chain of wheels set in motion when the copping-shaft reached the top of its upward journey, the pulley round which the strap of the cone passed was moved backwards at each double traverse (up and down) of the copping-rail by just so much as was necessary to allow a tooth to move from one rack to the next. When the bobbin was full the tooth had reached the last rack, and by doing so set in motion a mechanism that stopped the machine.

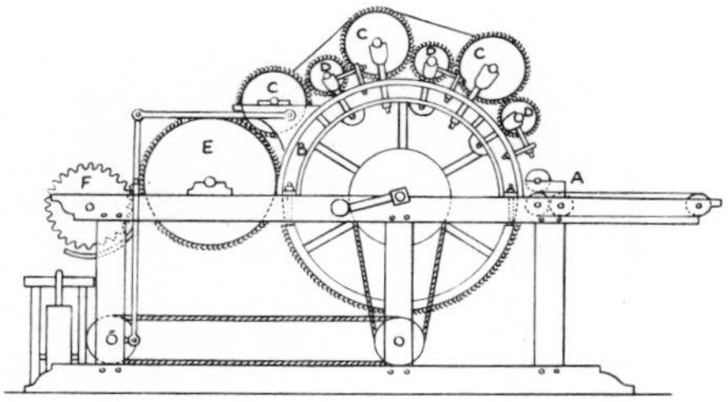

FIGURE 155—*Roller-and-clearer card.* (A) *Feed rollers;* (B) *main cylinder or swift;* (C) *rollers;* (D) *clearers;* (E) *doffing-cylinder;* (F) *fluted cylinder used for wool but not for cotton.*

This was satisfactory as long as the spindles always turned at the same rate, but if more or less twist was needed very intricate adjustments had to be made, which might involve much waste before the right relationship was achieved. Henry Houldsworth, working on an idea patented in 1823 by Green, a tinsmith of Mansfield, solved the problem by introducing a differential motion which kept the velocity of the bobbins in constant relation to that of the spindles whatever the speed of the latter might be. The same device is claimed for an American in-

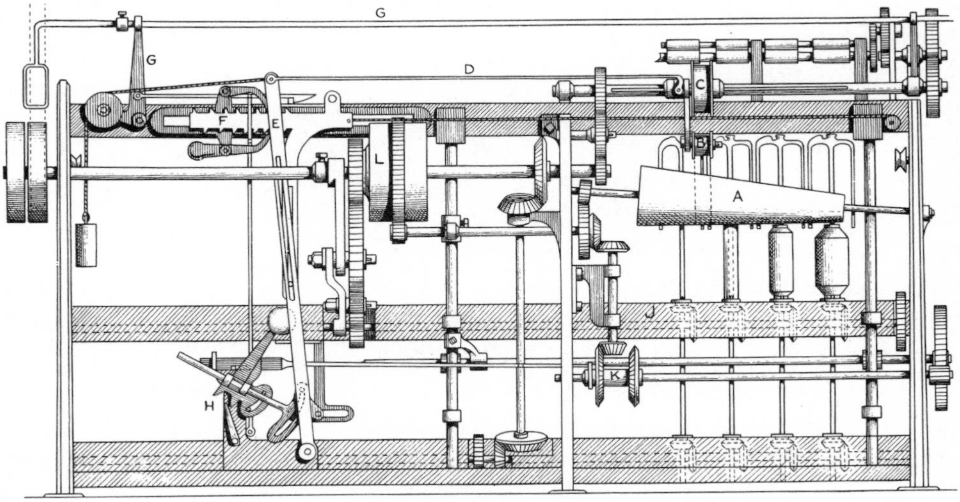

FIGURE 156—*Back view of the bobbin-and-fly frame.* (A) *Cone;* (B) *strap attached to pulley* (C), *which is connected by rod* (D) *to lever* (E); (F) *toothed shaft;* (G) *mechanism for stopping machine;* (H) *mechanism connecting copping-shaft* (J) *with lever* (E); (K) *wheels for raising and lowering copping-shaft;* (L) *Houldsworth's differential box.*

ventor, Asa Arnold, who patented it in 1822. A model of his invention was brought to England in 1825, but it is quite possible that Green and Houldsworth arrived at their solution independently.

Almost at the same time as Houldsworth's patent, an American invention—the tube roving-frame, patented by C. Danforth of Massachusetts in 1824—was introduced into England by J. G. Dyer, who obtained another patent for an improvement in it in 1829 (figure 157). In this machine the place of the spindles was taken by revolving tubes through which the roving passed. Their revolution twisted the rovings backwards to the rollers, but the twist was only transitory, serving to make them hold together on their way to the bobbins. These were placed horizontally below the tubes on iron drums which moved at the speed of the front drawing-rollers and carried the bobbins round, the change in their circumference being provided for as in the lap-machine. The tubes moved to and fro across the bobbins, and the rovings were untwisted in the act of being wound on. This frame produced a very soft roving, suitable only for coarse yarn. It was one of several speed-frames produced in the United States, of which only one other, the Eclipse Roving Frame, in which the roving was temporarily twisted by revolving leather bands, appeared in England. Both were simpler and cheaper than the bobbin-and-fly frame and gave far quicker results, but they made more waste and were eventually abandoned. The fly-frame gained much ground during the thirties, though some manufacturers continued for a time to

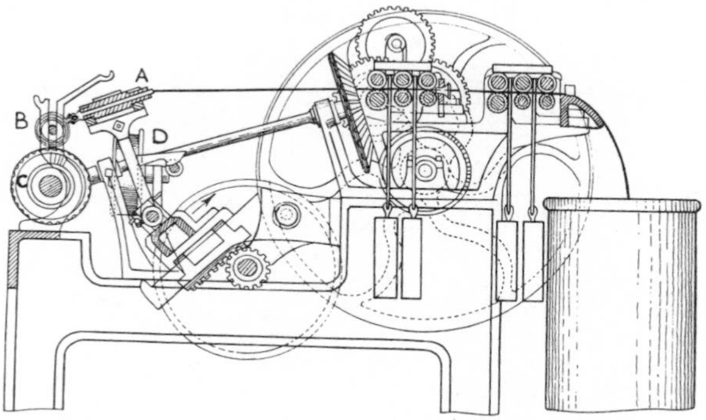

FIGURE 157—*Danforth's or Dyer's tube roving-frame. The sliver passes from the can through the two sets of drawing rollers, through the tube* (A), *and so round the bobbin* (B); (C) *friction rollers which turn the bobbin;* (D) *mechanism giving transverse motion to* (A).

use Arkwright's 'lantern' supplemented by a stretcher-frame, worked by hand on the lines of a mule, which further attenuated the roving.

The credit for making the process from carding to spinning continuous has often been given to J. G. Bodmer, a Swiss inventor who lived for many years in Lancashire [9], but Bodmer's inventions were very little used there, being found 'too complicated to be practical' [10]. This did not prevent their adoption on the continent and in America, but in Lancashire the carrying of cans from one machine to the next has always been preferred.

Spinning. There is no evidence that the jenny was ever power-driven, but for cotton it was soon superseded by the mule. Efforts to apply power to this machine were made from 1790 onwards, but the achievement of a fully self-acting mule was the work of many years. In 1790 William Kelly, manager of Dale's New Lanark Mills, applied water-power for driving the clockwork mechanism which turned the rollers and drew out the carriage for the first stretch. Immediately afterwards Wright, of Manchester, formerly an apprentice of Arkwright, doubled the number of spindles by putting the driving-gear or 'rim' in the middle of the machine. In 1792 Kelly took out a patent for a completely self-acting mule, but abandoned it on finding that it was cumbrous and brought no economic advantage, since only a comparatively small number of spindles could be used.

From 1793 onwards, John Kennedy experimented with driving the mule by steam, and in 1800 he succeeded in doing so up to the point when the spindles finished twisting at the end of the outward stretch. The change of speed for the carriage and the spindles was automatically effected by levers acted upon by the

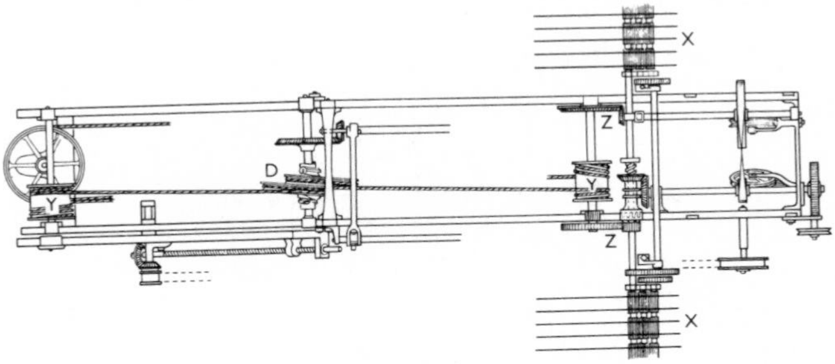

FIGURE 158—*Headstock of Roberts's mule.* (D) *Scroll pulley;* (XX) *rollers;* (YY) *drums taking carriage out and controlled by wheels of different diameters* (ZZ).

passage of the carriage, which set in motion a train of wheelwork coming into gear alternately with wheels of different diameters. The machinery was set so that the spindles continued twisting after the carriage had stopped for a length of time depending upon the twist required; the spinner then took over the winding-on, as in the hand-mule. This invention made the mule a factory-machine, but it required skilled operators, who could command high wages. Several self-acting mules were produced between 1818 and 1825, but none was successful enough to come into general use until, during the spinners' strike of 1825, Richard Roberts was asked to solve the problem. Roberts, the son of a Welsh shoemaker, had established himself as a machine-maker at Manchester after having worked with Maudslay, the great engineer, as a turner and fitter [11], but, although he was recognized as an ingenious mechanic, his works was not on a large scale. The machine that he patented in 1825 did not entirely succeed, but his second patent of 1830 was much more satisfactory. In 1828 he entered into partnership with the firm of Sharp Brothers, who had been established at Manchester as machine-makers since 1806, and they spent £12 000 in perfecting this second patent (figures 158 and 159).

The movements to which Roberts had to apply power were those of reversing the spindles to 'back off' the yarn, and of sending in the carriage and turning the spindles, both at varying speeds, in order to build up the cop in the double cone which was necessary to make it hold together: in the mule, as distinct from the water-frame, the cop was built on the spindle itself without a bobbin. He furnished the machine with three driving pulleys and two driving belts, one of the latter moving in the opposite direction to the other. Until the twisting was finished one belt drove two pulleys, which between them moved all the machinery

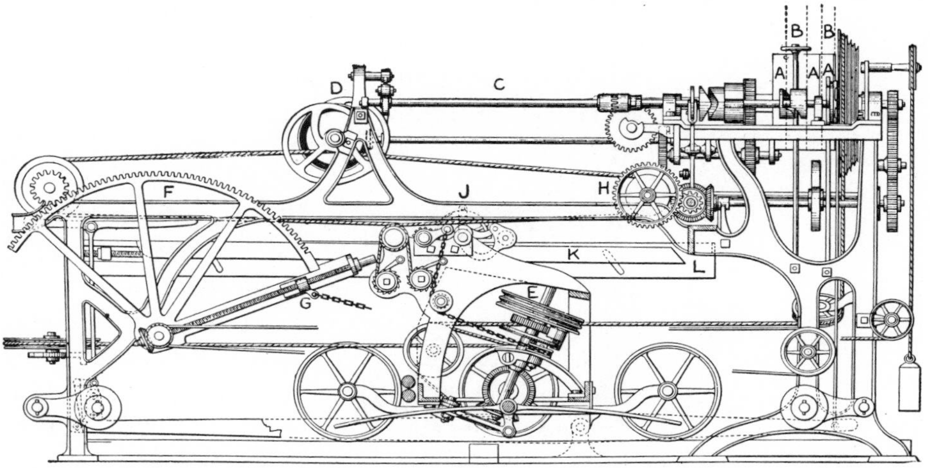

FIGURE 159—*Side view of headstock of Roberts's self-acting mule.* (AA) *Steam-driven pulleys;* (BB) *driving belts;* (C) *driving shaft;* (D) *scroll pulley for inward journey;* (E) *drum driving spindles;* (F) *toothed quadrant;* (G) *nut sliding on radial arm from which chain is attached to carriage;* (H) *wheel driving drum which takes carriage out;* (J) *self-actor governing path of faller through rail* (K), *which is guided by shaper-plates attached to the frame* (L).

needed, while the other belt revolved idly on the loose pulley. In backing off, the first belt was shifted to the first pulley and the second to the other, which drove the spindles, so that they turned in the opposite direction. When backing-off ended, the belts shifted back to their former positions. The moving-in of the carriage was done by a spiral 'scroll' pulley; this took over its control from the pulleys which moved it outwards and pulled it in, at first at an increasing and then at a decreasing speed, according to the diameter of the groove from which the rope was being unwound. To maintain the proper tension of the yarn Roberts introduced a counter-faller wire underneath it, which moved up towards the faller as soon as backing off began, to take up any slack in the yarn. Both faller and counter-faller were operated automatically by mechanism set in motion by the carriage when it reached the end of the stretch. The path of the faller, which determined the point on the spindle where the winding-on should begin, was regulated by a rail moved up and down by pins moving on two shaper-plates, which lowered the faller and raised the counter-faller to the proper position.

The problem of how to vary the speed of the spindles, which must be in accordance with the speed of the carriage and must also vary according to the state of the cop, was not solved until 1830, when Roberts added the 'quadrant' (figure 159), which finally made the machine a success. The quadrant was a segment of a toothed wheel with a grooved arm in which slid a nut attached to a chain, the other end of which was wound round the drum driving the spindles. On the outward journey the quadrant moved backwards through a quarter-circle, and the inward movement drew it forward again at speeds varying with those of the carriage. The chain attached to the nut retarded the movement of the spindles relative to that of the carriage according to the place which the nut occupied on the grooved arm. The more nearly it reached the apex of the arm, the longer were the arcs through which it turned, causing the spindles to rotate more slowly at the beginning of each stretch and more quickly at the end. The path of the nut on the screw on which it moved was guided by the shaper-plates through a connexion between the screw and the faller. When the ends of the cop were formed the range of the faller was lessened, and the nut remained fixed while the body of the cop was built up.

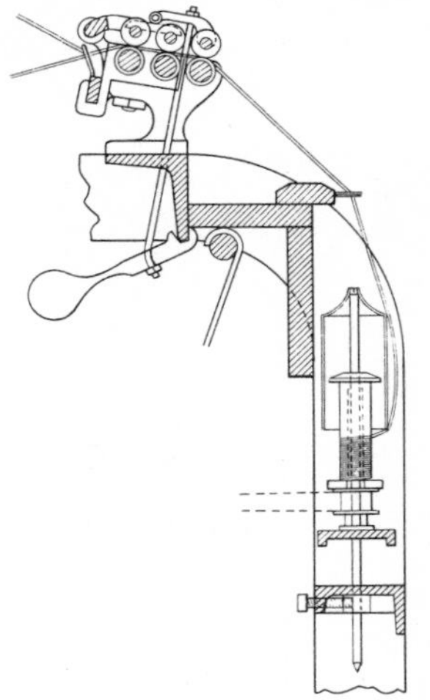

FIGURE 160—*Danforth's throstle for cap spinning; cross-section of spinning parts.*

All the motions of the self-acting mule were governed by making the driving-shaft turn through a quarter-circle at successive points in the operation. At each turn the mechanisms governing the motions which were to stop were thrown out of gear, and those which governed the next motions were engaged. When the carriage reached the roller-beam the shaft returned to its original position.

The self-actor was acclaimed as an almost perfect machine, but it did not spread quickly. By 1839 the profits had not exceeded £7000 [12], and the patent was extended for another seven years. By 1850 counts up to fifty were being spun on it. Another self-actor, invented in 1834 by J. Smith of Deanston, was also being used to some extent for counts up to thirty, but the older mule was still in use for fine yarns. Improvements in the latter, simplifying the putting-up action, made by Evan Leigh in 1832, had enabled two mules to be coupled together on either side of the headstock, thus increasing to a possible 1200 the number of spindles that one spinner could drive.

Throstle-spinning. When the mule became a factory-machine its ability to spin all kinds of yarn led to a decline in the use of the water-frame for spinning cotton. After the Napoleonic wars, when the spread of power-looms created a demand for strong yarn, the water-frame returned in the enlarged and more economic form of the throstle. Instead of having the spindles grouped four or six to a head, each head being separately driven, the frame now consisted of two long lines of spindles set back to back, all driven from one driving-belt. A copping-rail was introduced, as in the bobbin-and-fly frame, and the method of winding was simplified by allowing the thread to drag the bobbin round by its own weight, a method possible only when the yarn is strong and thoroughly twisted. The throstle therefore would not spin fine yarns. An even simpler contrivance, known as Danforth's throstle frame after its American inventor (p. 286), was patented in England by J. Hutchinson in 1829 (figure 160). There was no flyer, and the spindles were stationary but covered by a conical cap which revolved at a high speed. The bobbin, which moved up and down the spindle, and the cap rotated together, and the thread was conducted to the bobbin under the rim of the cap, the friction of which retarded its speed relative to that of the bobbin so that winding-on could take place. The value of this machine was its simple construction and its speed. It produced yarn softer and more fleecy than that spun on the throstle, but it also made more waste. In the cotton industry it never conquered more than a small part of the field held by the throstle, but it was eventually adopted for worsted spinning. There were other attempts in the thirties to speed up the process of spinning, but none survived. Ring-spinning, which was ultimately to triumph, was invented in America in 1828 and introduced into England in 1834, but it soon disappeared and did not return until after 1850.

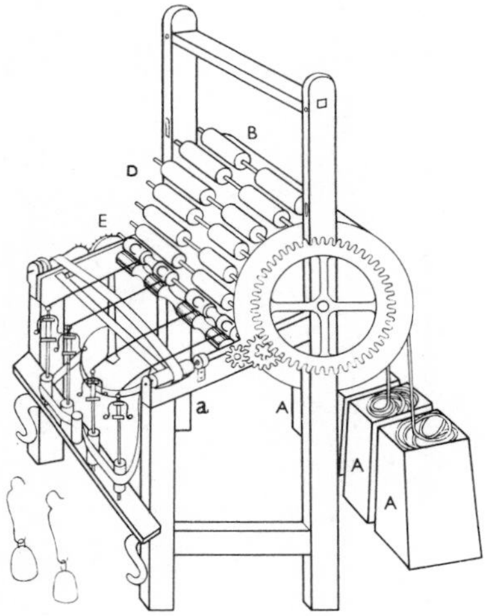

FIGURE 161—*Kendrew and Porthouse's machine for spinning flax. The slivers are drawn from the bins* (A) *over the roller* (B) *and under the heavy rollers* (D). *Weights* (a) *are hung on the rollers* (C). *The thread passes over the damp band of material* (E) *before reaching the spindles. The drawing-frame is similarly weighted.*

(*b*) FLAX. The fibres of flax are longer than those of cotton: they consist of short filaments held together by a gummy substance which must be loosened before fine yarn can be spun. Drawing and spinning flax for coarse yarn became a factory-process long before heckling, which corresponds to carding in cotton and separates the 'line' or long fibres from the 'tow' or shorter ones, which can be spun like cotton. The first patent for adapting Arkwright's machinery to spinning line was taken out in 1787 by J. Kendrew and A. Porthouse of Darlington (figure 161). The pairs of drawing-rollers had to be placed much farther apart than for cotton, and both in drawing and in spinning the flax was subjected to the pressure of heavy weights. In spinning, the thread was passed over a wet cloth just before it reached the spindles, in order to soften the gum. This machinery was worked at Darlington and in Scotland, but much greater success was gained by the commercial genius of John Marshall of Leeds, who soon substituted for it the machines patented by Matthew Murray, at that time his foreman mechanic. Murray, whose first patent was taken out in 1790, drew the flax between leather straps revolving round a pair of rollers tightly pressed together and placed in a vertical position at right-angles to a second pair (figure 162). No provision was made for wetting the thread, but dry-spun yarn proved to be more elastic and filled the web better. Both methods were in use later for coarse yarns, wet-spun being stronger and more silky in appearance.

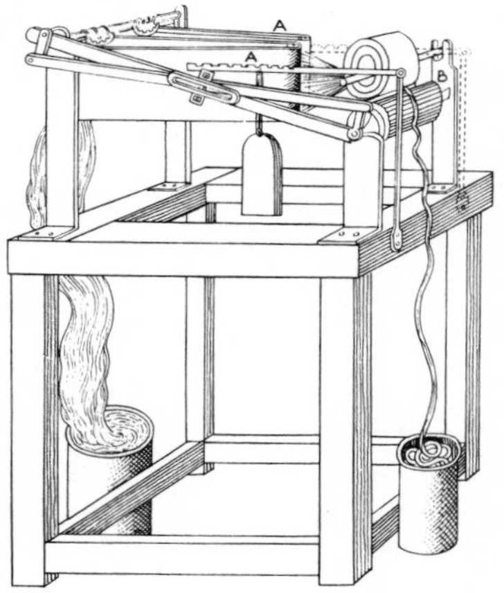

FIGURE 162—*Matthew Murray's drawing-frame for flax. The flax is drawn between the vertical leather bands* (A), *which are tightly pressed together. It is then drawn out to the proper size under the weighted roller* (B) *and drops into the bin. The spinning-frame is similar, but the first pair of rollers is placed vertically above the second set.*

These methods of applying pressure to the fibres could not produce a perfectly regular yarn. The discovery of a superior method of preparation was the work of a French inventor, Philippe de Girard (1775–1845). At the beginning of the century there had been unsuccessful efforts in France to rescue the linen industry from the competition of cotton by applying machinery to its manufacture, and in 1810 Napoleon offered a prize of a million francs for a successful process. P. de Girard produced his solution too late for the prize, and the official opinion of his methods was unfavourable. Like most new inventions, his machines needed many adjustments before they would produce good results, and his French factories were not successful. He later started others in Austria and finally in Poland, where he was employed by the government. His processes were brought to England by two of his associates and sold to Horace Hall, who patented them in 1814, but it was only several years later that his whole system was adopted.

Philippe de Girard's three innovations were the use of a hot alkaline solution to separate the fibres before drawing; the drawing of them when dry through combs or gills (probably from the French *aiguilles*); and the immersion of the roving in another alkaline solution on its way to the spindles. Of these, gill-drawing or something like it had been patented by an English inventor in 1801 but had never come into use. It straightened and levelled the fibres and produced a more even sliver by placing between the drawing-rollers a succession of bars carrying combs fixed to revolving cylinders, over which the fibres were drawn more quickly than the comb-bars moved. This process began to be employed in England between 1816 and 1820. de Girard's other processes were neglected.

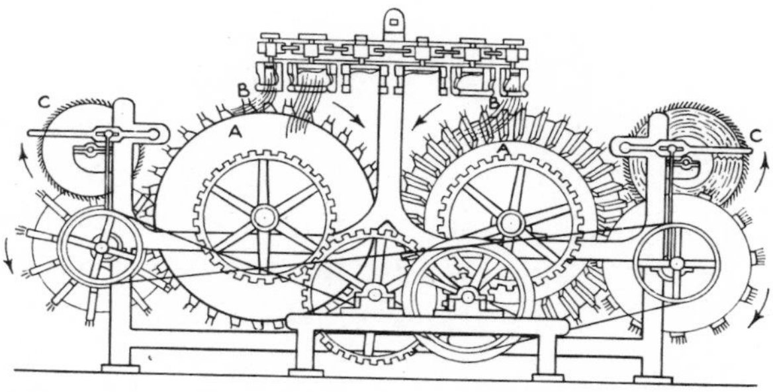

FIGURE 163—*Wordsworth's flax-heckling machine.* AA *are the two cylinders revolving in opposite directions, and the stricks of flax are held at* BB. CC *are brush cylinders to remove the tow from the machine.*

In 1825 James Kay of Preston took out a patent for macerating the roving by soaking it in cold water for about six hours before spinning, thus softening the gum so that the shorter filaments held together by it could be loosened for drawing and spinning, after which the gum would harden again and preserve the original strength of the flax. Since the spinning was done while the fibre was soft, the rollers were placed nearer to each other, as in cotton-spinning, to support the short filaments. This lost Kay the action which he brought against Marshall for infringement, since it was held not to be original and invalidated that part of the patent which dealt with maceration. de Girard pointed out that he had been the first inventor of maceration, and his claim seems to be justified. In the forties, the method of steeping the flax in hot water before drawing, and wetting the roving again on the spinning-frame by making it pass through a trough of hot water before reaching the rollers, seems to have been the general practice for finer yarns.

Gill-drawing was improved by the screw-gill patented in 1833 by Lawson and Westly, and improved by Fairbairn in 1846 and 1848. The comb-bars were made to travel forward on a pair of screw-shafts so that they might present a flat surface and approach as near as possible to the back of the drawing-rollers, each bar as it came to the end being knocked down to a lower level and carried back to the beginning by another pair of shafts.

Good spinning depended, however, on the thoroughness with which the flax was heckled. All the early heckling-machines had in common the suspension of a series of stricks (bundles) of flax, each in its own holder, to be brought into contact with a series of heckling-teeth, generally fixed on a revolving cylinder. As they combed only one side of the strick it had to be reversed by hand; and finally the strick had to be taken out of its holder and fastened in the other way, so that the other end might be heckled. Wordsworth improved on this system in 1833 by adding a second cylinder moving in the opposite direction. He also graduated the size of the heckling-teeth and provided mechanical means for reversing the stricks. Brush-cylinders at the side of the machine removed the tow remaining in the teeth of the comb, so that this had no longer to be done by hand (figure 163). In 1832 de Girard produced a machine which was brought to England by a mechanic named Decoster and patented in the name of T. M. Evans; the patent included some improvements, possibly made by Decoster [13]. The stricks of flax were hung between two vertical sheets of combs which moved in opposite directions. As they moved they drew nearer to each other and then again receded (figure 164). There was an arrangement for taking off the tow similar to that in Wordsworth's patent. In England this machine was often known as Wordsworth's heckler, as he patented an improvement to it giving an up-and-down movement to the holder which enabled the teeth to penetrate progressively deeper into the flax [14]. It was widely used, and formed the basis for several improved hecklers, but a great variety of machines was in use in 1850. At that date, however, manual labour still remained universal for flax intended for fine yarn.

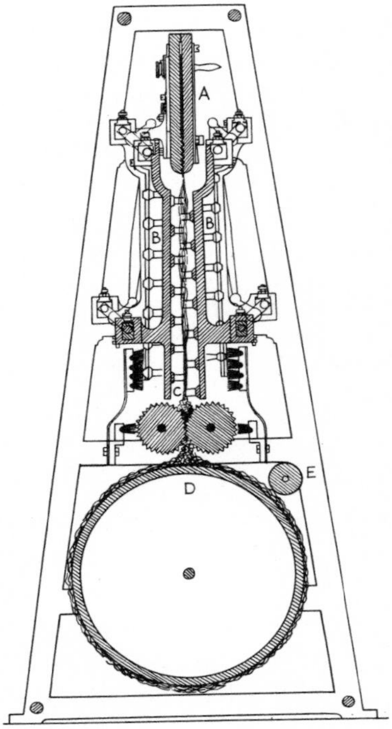

FIGURE 164—*Heckling machine derived from de Girard's.* (A) *Holder for strick;* (BB) *section of comb cylinders moving in opposite directions;* (C) *tow deposited on fluted rollers and falling to drum* (D), *round which, under pressure of roller* (E), *it forms a lap.*

(*c*) WOOL. The staple, or length of fibre, in wool ranges from under 1 inch up to 10 in or more. All wool has small curly hairs branching out from the main stem, but the number of them to an inch in a short-stapled wool is far greater than in a long-stapled one. Short wool, therefore, will felt but long wool will not; these differing properties account for differences during this period in the method of manufacture (now largely superseded by modern machinery), beginning with the fact that long wool was combed while short was carded.

Combing wool. In spinning long wool for worsted the fibres must be laid as straight as possible to produce an even thread, and Arkwright's machinery was well suited for this purpose. The first mill was at Dolphin Holme near Lancaster in 1784, but more successful attempts were made in Yorkshire from 1787 onwards. The only change in the spinning- and drawing-frames was the placing of the pairs of rollers at a greater distance from each other to suit the longer staple. For roving, the bobbin-and-fly frame was used, but without the cone or differential, the roving being strong enough to pull the bobbin round, as in spinning. In France, methods of roving without twist were preferred, and a way of rubbing the sliver to make it cohere had been invented by Dobo in 1815; but the importation of American roving-frames, as described on p 286, in the late twenties seems to have led to a greater extension of the practice. French manufacturers had also adopted gill-drawing from the linen industry in 1820 or earlier. In England an operation of this kind was in use in 1835 in what was called the breaking-frame, to which the wool was taken after being combed [15], but it was not introduced into the actual operation of drawing until the late forties. A similar difference prevailed in methods of spinning. In France the mule, and in England the throstle, were the prevailing machines, to the virtual exclusion of the other in each case. Cap-spinning (p 291) does not appear to have been adopted in England until after 1850 [16]. Many writers assume it to have been introduced in 1831, but an illustration published by James in 1857 shows merely the ordinary throstle. It was not universal even in 1870. The French use of the mule, together with their better preparatory methods, gave them a superiority in the finest worsteds.

Combing, corresponding to the heckling of flax, was the most difficult process to mechanize, and up to 1850 hand-combing held its ground for all but coarse worsteds. The first machine-comb was invented by Edmund Cartwright, of power-loom fame, in 1792 (figure 165). Slivers of wool made by hand were drawn through a tube in an oscillating frame and delivered by rollers to the teeth of a circular revolving comb; this carried them under a smaller cylinder-comb moved to and fro across it by a crank. The short fibres, called noils, were

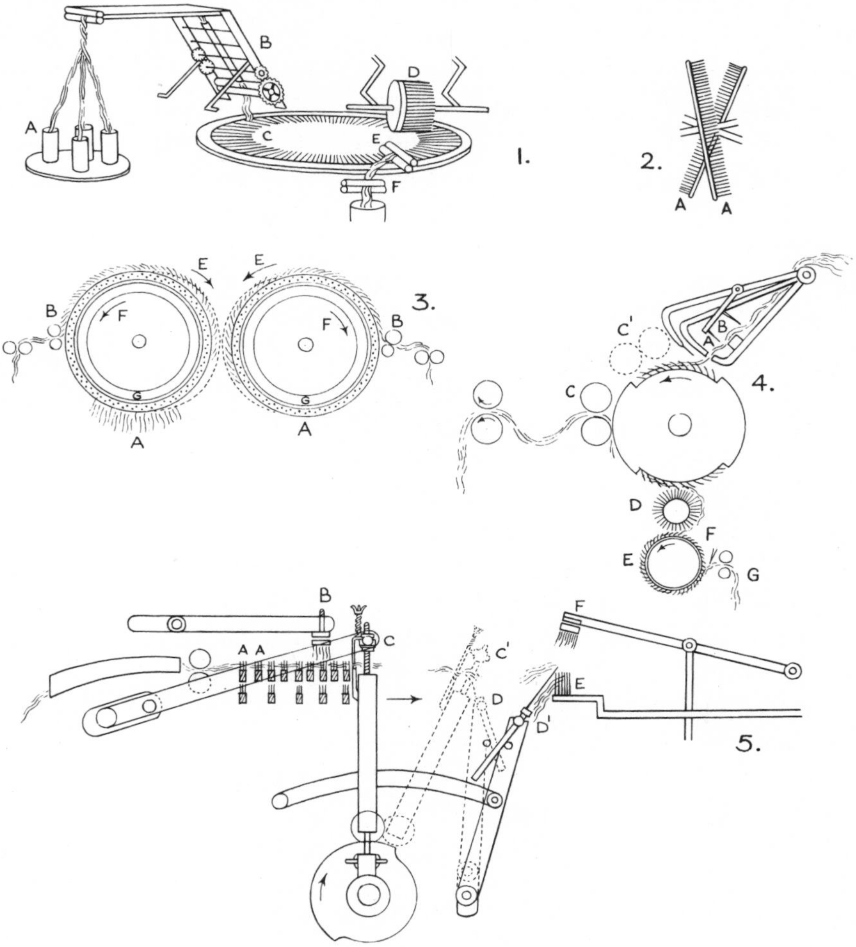

FIGURE 165—*Various combing-machines.*

(1) *Cartwright's, 1792. Slivers of wool are drawn from the cans* (A), *through a tube by the oscillating frame* (B), *into the teeth of working comb* (C), *and so to working comb* (D). *From there it is pulled through the rollers* E *and* F *into the can below.*

(2) *and* (3) *Platt and Collier's, 1827. The machine consists of two circles of combs* (A). *Wool is fed on to one comb and, as the combs are made to approach each other and rotate in the direction* E, *it is equally distributed between them. The angle at which the combs are set can be seen in figure 2. The combs are then separated and by moving in the direction* F *the top can be slipped off at* B.

(4) *Heilmann's, 1846.* (A) *The nip;* (B) *intersecting comb;* (C) *rollers which move down from* C^1; (D, E) *brush cylinders for removing noils;* (F) *knife which pushes the noils off the brush cylinder to pass through rollers* (G).

(5) *Lister and Donisthorpe's, 1851.* (A) *Gill comb;* (B) *brush;* (C) *nip moving to* C^1; (D) *porter comb moving to* D^1; (E) *section of circular comb;* (F) *brush. The taking-off rollers are not shown.*

teased out and remained in the small comb, from which they had to be removed by hand, while the long fibres which make the 'top' were carried off by rollers into a can. Cartwright himself was not successful with this comb, but it formed a basis for better machines, at which there were many attempts. None was widely used until that patented in England by Platt and Collier in 1827. This embodied a French invention by a manufacturer named Godard, of Amiens, who had obtained a first patent in 1816 in conjunction with Collier, an English machine-maker established in Paris [17]. The machine arrived in England with improvements patented in France in 1825 (figure 165). It consisted of two circles of combs, one of which was filled by hand. They moved in opposite directions and were so placed that the teeth of one circle worked into those of the other. The combs began their revolution when they were only just touching each other, and were brought closer until half the wool from the first comb was transferred to the second. Then drawing-rollers, placed on each side, were brought into contact with the combs and carried off the top. The noils remaining in the teeth had to be cleaned off by hand. This comb was not entirely superseded in France until 1845, and not in England until after 1851, though many inventors were in the field; these included Noble, whose comb was successful after 1850, and a German named Wieck, of Chemnitz, whose comb was patented in England by Preller in 1852.

In 1845 Josué Heilmann of Mulhouse produced a comb on a new principle, in response to a suggestion that if fine cotton could be combed as well as carded a much finer thread could be produced. The comb proved equally suitable for wool (figure 165). The wool was passed through a frame furnished with two jaws to nip the sliver when a sufficient length had passed through. The comb-teeth, covering a quarter of the combing-cylinder, then revolved through the sliver presented to them and were succeeded by the flat surface of the next quarter; this carried the sliver to the drawing-rollers which moved down to receive it. These in turn held it fast by the combed end while the jaws opened, allowing the other end to pass over the succeeding comb-teeth; an intersecting comb descended to comb the middle section of the sliver, which escaped the teeth of the cylinder. As the combing-cylinder revolved the noils were cleared off by a brush-cylinder at the bottom and finally by a knife and doffing-rollers. A patent for this machine was taken out in England in 1846 but it did not become generally known until it was exhibited at the Great Exhibition of 1851.

Meanwhile, in England, G. E. Donisthorpe, who had been experimenting with combing-machines from 1835, produced in 1842–3 an improved model on Cartwright's principle; this attracted the attention of S. C. Lister, a large worsted manufacturer at Bradford, who bought the patent rights. Together they arrived at a machine that resembled Heilmann's in using the nip (figure 165). The wool was fed through rollers across a gill-comb to a nip placed at the top of a crank which carried it to a porter-comb, and this again fed it to a circular revolving comb. Brushes placed above both the gill and the circular combs descended to force the wool into the teeth, and the top was taken off the latter by rollers. The noils were removed in the same way as in Heilmann's comb. Lister and Donisthorpe had several patents, but the final one, in which the use of the nip was specified, was not taken out until 1851, and Heilmann won an action against them for infringement. Subsequently he sold his rights to other Yorkshire manufacturers who resold them to Lister. Lister suppressed Heilmann's comb in favour of his own, which held the field for a considerable time in England, as Heilmann's did in France. The rights in the latter for use in cotton had, however, been bought by a group of manufacturers at Manchester, where it opened up a new era in fine cotton-spinning.

Two other innovations deserve mention. Wool was carded before combing as early as 1814 in France and 1829 in England. Cotton warps for worsteds were introduced into Yorkshire in 1834 [18] and led to a great extension of the worsted-industry.

Carding wool. The first power-driven machine in the cloth industry was the carding-engine, which was set up in Yorkshire in the early 1770s, often in existing fulling-mills where it could be turned by water. This machine was of the type patented by Bourn, which developed into the roller-and-clearer card, since the short fibres must be thoroughly interlaced and not laid straight as would be done in a machine with flats. The process was duplicated, the first carding being known as scribbling. From this machine the wool came off in a fleece; it was then weighed and put on the feeder of the carding-engine proper. Here the old arrangement of placing the cards on the doffer cylinder in parallel strips was retained, so that the carding came off in flat pieces about 3 ft long, which passed under a fluted roller to make them round. In the early twenties there were several attempts in both England and America to produce a machine that would make a continuous movement of carding and slubbing (roving). The experiments that finally succeeded were begun by John Goulding of Massachusetts about 1822. He used a ring-doffer, on which strips of card were placed round instead of across the cylinder, and the latter was given a traversing motion so that it might clear the whole of the swift. Later, a second doffer below the first, with strips of card to take off the wool in the gaps left by the first doffer, was sometimes employed. The flat, continuous strips obtained in this way were rounded by passing through revolving tubes, and wound on bobbins ready for spinning. This machine was patented in England in 1826, but neither it nor any of the machines patented by English inventors for the same purpose came into use there. Goulding's machine, with some variations, appeared in France in 1834, and in Germany after 1839; it was not used in England, and only to a small extent in Scotland [19], until it arrived in a much improved form as the condenser, after 1850.

Since short wool cannot be drawn, Arkwright's machinery was useless in this connexion, but the billy and the jenny proved to be admirably suited for slubbing and spinning. The rolls obtained from the carding-engine were placed on the feeding-cloth of the billy, where they had constantly to be pieced up by children; but in the forties this was increasingly being done by a piecing-machine known as the 'tommy'. The billies were, in general, hand-machines like the jenny. The mule could be adapted for wool by dispensing with one pair of rollers and using the other to pay out the slubbing and then to hold it during the second stretch. It was introduced at Leeds in 1816 but it did not spread quickly. In 1843 spinning was 'most often' performed by it [20], but this was either the hand-mule or the semi-power-driven one. The self-actor was not used until well after 1850. In the remoter places the use of the jenny continued, in some cases right into the twentieth century.

III. WEAVING

Apart from the Jacquard loom (p 318) only one significant improvement was made in the hand-loom after 1760. This was Radcliffe's arrangement for taking up the woven cloth by means of a ratchet-wheel connected with the batten, so that the cloth beam moved automatically. It was patented in 1805 in the name of Radcliffe's employee, Thomas Johnson, and besides speeding up the action of the hand-loom it provided a contribution towards the power-loom. The dandy-loom, as hand-looms equipped with this action were called, came into general use during the nineteenth century.

The obvious problems in applying power to the loom were to devise means of performing the motions made by the hand-weaver, namely, opening the shed for the passage of the shuttle, driving the shuttle, beating up the weft, and winding up the woven cloth. But in a power-loom further devices are necessary to stop the loom in case a thread breaks, to keep the cloth stretched in width, and to size the warp, which the hand-loom weaver did at intervals as necessary. The first English attempt to put a power-loom into action came from outside the industry and owed nothing to previous models. Cartwright made his first attempt in 1784, and after producing an unworkable model in 1785 he patented in the following year a power-loom which, with improvements patented in 1787 and 1792, was worked in his factory at Doncaster, as well as by licensees at Manchester until their factory was burnt down. He provided means for dealing with all the points noted above, and attached the warping to the loom so as to size the threads mechanically before they reached the warp-beam. Considering the primitive state of engineering technique at that time it is not surprising that the loom would not work economically. It had some serious disadvantages. The shuttle was propelled by a spring, which made its action too sudden, and the driving-force was provided by a single shaft, which made all the movements too harsh. Its great merit was to show that weaving by power was not impossible. Further attempts were made by several inventors, especially by Robert Miller of Glasgow in 1796. His loom is said to have derived not from Cartwright's but from that of Jeffrey of Paisley, who had designed a model at almost the same time. Miller's loom, known as the wiper-loom from his use of excentric wheels or wipers to drive the shuttle, was used in Scotland in the early 1800s.

The problem of sizing the warp was satisfactorily solved by Thomas Johnson, who in 1803 produced a machine that sized the threads in the warping-mill by passing them through rollers one of which was impregnated with size. The size was worked in by a series of brushes and dried by passing the threads over a current of hot air driven upwards by fans at the bottom of the machine. This machine, improved by later inventors, was not abandoned until after 1850, though it was partly superseded by the tape-sizing machine of Hornby and Kenworthy patented in 1839. In this machine the warp, divided into bands or tapes of relatively few threads, passed into a trough of size and was dried by being rolled round two heated cylinders.

Of the different looms produced during the early years of the nineteenth century the most significant was that of William Horrocks of Stockport who, among other improvements, introduced in 1813 a method of varying the speed of the batten so as to increase the period for which the shed remained open for the shuttle to pass through. He also adopted Radcliffe's method of taking up the cloth. Between 1813 and 1820 the number of power-looms in Britain increased from 2400 to 14 150, a growth that seems to have been mainly due to the merits of this loom—although there was great variety in detail. The model that appears finally to have emerged as the most practical was one constructed by Roberts, the inventor of the self-acting mule, based on Horrocks's loom. About 1822 Roberts set up a partnership for loom-making under the title Roberts, Hill and Company, and the loom he produced was known by his name, although the patent that he took out in that year was chiefly concerned with weaving twilled fabrics.

Roberts's loom (figure 166) had two shafts, the main one driving the batten while the second, known as the tappet-shaft, drove both the treadles for raising the healds and the pickers for throwing the shuttle. The main shaft had at its end a toothed wheel connected with another wheel, having twice as many teeth, at the end of the tappet-shaft, so that the latter revolved only half as fast; hence the batten moved twice (once forward and once back) for every movement of the

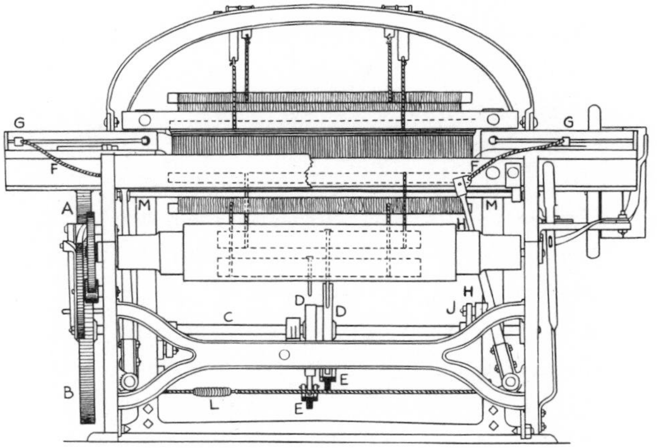

FIGURE 166—*Roberts's power loom, front view.* (A) *Wheel on main shaft, driving wheel* (B) *on tappet or wiper shaft* (C); (DD) *tappets or excentric wheels working on treadle levers* (EE); (FF) *picker cords driving pickers* (GG) *and attached to lever* (H); H *is moved by rollers* (J) *in connexion with excentrics* (DD) *and brought back by spring* (L); (MM) *'swords of the lay'* (p 302).

healds and the shuttle. The healds were connected by cords passing over the roller-beam and were raised by treadle levers moved by excentric wheels or cams set opposite each other, so that the larger side of each wheel raised its lever in turn while the heald that was drawn downwards automatically drew the other one upwards. The cords attached to the pickers which impelled the shuttle were drawn to and fro by other levers moved by rollers fixed in a slot on the excentrics; by shifting their position in this slot the point at which the shuttle began to move could be adjusted to any point in the movement of the healds, thus ensuring co-ordination in weaving any type of cloth. These levers were restored to their original position by a spring mounted on a cord uniting them. There was an automatic stop-movement, in case the shuttle was caught in the shed, consisting of a small shaft under the batten connecting with levers partly entering the shuttle-boxes. If the shuttle did not enter the box it failed to raise the other end of the shaft, which in consequence came into contact with a projection and moved it forward, stopping the machine.

The batten was supported from below by two cranks, 'the swords of the lay', attached to a mechanism moving on the driving-shaft. By adjusting the cranks the velocity of the batten could be varied to suit different types of cloth. In the model shown in the accompanying diagram (figure 167) the warp was unrolled by an arrangement of weights on the warp-beam in the same way as in the hand-loom, but several attempts were made to provide means of turning the beam to allow the threads to unroll without putting any strain on them. The woven cloth was taken up by an improved method based on Radcliffe's principle. No allowance was made for the increase in size of the cloth-beam during winding, which resulted in the tension being slacker towards the end of the cloth; but the problem of keeping a completely even tension between warp-threads and cloth was not solved before 1850.

The Roberts loom spread widely, with many variations. In 1826 it was introduced into France, where there were already several other models [21]. Loom construction in France dated back to one invented by Biard during the Empire; later, one made by Collier was patented in several countries.

A large number of improvements continued to be made, particularly in connexion with the difficult problem of obtaining exactly the right degree of force to drive the shuttle; in this respect the introduction of William Dickinson's 'overpick' or Blackburn loom in 1826 marked a step forward. Among other inventions it is possible to mention here only those relating to the two points in which Roberts's loom was deficient, namely, the lack of any device for keeping the cloth stretched in width, and of an automatic stop-motion in case of the breakage of a weft-thread. For the latter, the first successful device was patented by Ramsbottom and Holt of Todmorden in 1834; it was improved by Kenworthy and Bullough in 1841, and again in Bullough's brake, which made stoppage immediate, in 1842. In its later form it consisted of a small fork projecting through the reed over which the weft passed. If the weft failed to pass the fork fell back and set off a train of motion which stopped the machine. Out of the many devices produced for an automatic stretching-mechanism or temple, that which proved most satisfactory was the trough-and-roller temple patented by Kenworthy and Bullough in 1841, an improvement on a method that had been introduced earlier. It consisted of two small rollers with a roughened surface placed one at each side of the cloth-beam and moving with it in a trough. The cloth passed between the rollers and the trough, and was kept stretched by the adhesion of the roughened surfaces.

The above description applies to the power-loom for weaving plain fabrics, but its adaptation for a twill or fancy weave, in which the pattern is formed by the raising at intervals of different sets of warp-threads, had been made quite early. Improvements were patented by Bowman in 1820 and by Roberts in 1822. All systems involved the substitution for the excentrics of a number of circular wheels (or rollers mounted on one wheel, as in Roberts's patent) corresponding to the number of healds to be raised by means of projections on the wheels, which moved the appropriate levers. Of later patents the most important was that of Woodcroft in 1838. It was claimed that up to eight pairs of healds and eight changes of pattern could be worked by this method. It took longer to mechanize the working of the drop-box, by which shuttles containing weft of different colours could be used at will by the hand-loom weaver. The final solution was found in the endless chain, patented by Squire Diggle of Bury in 1845. This was composed of a series of plates of different thicknesses which revolved at the end of the loom under a pulley attached to a rod carrying the drop-box at its other end. As the chain revolved, the plates raised the rod to the height determined by the thickness of each plate, thus bringing the appropriate shuttle into place. These contrivances eventually gave way to the Jacquard loom, which for worsted was worked by power from about 1833. In cotton, however, where cheapness was important, the use of the 'dobby', a simpler form of Jacquard, does not appear to have become common until after 1850.

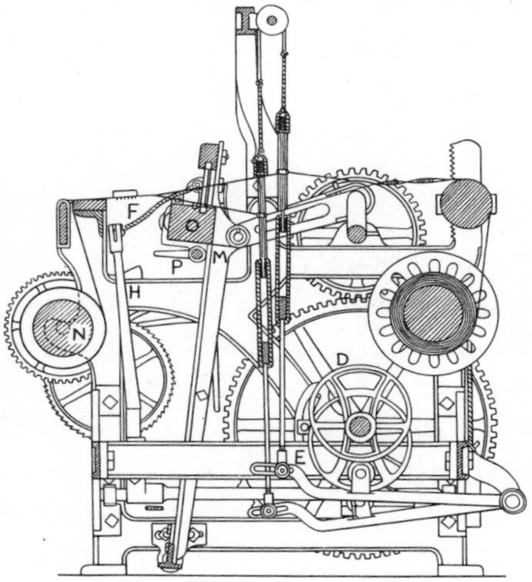

FIGURE 167—*Roberts's power loom, side view.* D, E, F, H, *and* M *as in figure 166;* (N) *cloth beam;* (O) *batten;* (P) *lever to stop loom if shuttle is caught in the shed.*

By the middle forties, therefore, the power-loom had been brought to a state which made its use much more economical. The weft-breakage stop-motion and the automatic temple eliminated the necessity for constantly watching each loom, and made it possible for one weaver to look after a number at the same time. Other inventions in the forties, especially Bullough's 'loose reed' by which the reed was dissociated from the batten when the shuttle stuck in the shed, and was thus prevented from driving it against the warp, made it possible to work with increased speed. By 1850 the power-loom was well on the way to superseding the handloom-weaver in cotton and had almost completely done so in worsted, where it had been introduced in 1824. For wool, however, the fragility of the thread made it impossible for the shuttle to move at a higher rate than in the hand-loom, so that there was little to be gained by employing it until after the improvements of the forties; but it was spreading in 1850. For linen, the lack of elasticity in the yarn meant that the thread would break under a strain where cotton or worsted would give, and a different method had to be adopted for letting out the warp. This problem was not seriously attacked until after 1850, which accounts for the very small number of power-looms at work in the linen industry at that date.

IV. FINISHING

There were numerous power-driven machines for finishing that cannot be described here, but a word must be said about the machinery for cloth-dressing, the introduction of which caused so many riots. It seems probable that the use of the gig-mill (vol III, p 172) had never been quite abandoned, and in the 1790s some Gloucestershire manufacturers began to use it with great success for fine cloth. Elsewhere it encountered stubborn resistance, especially in Yorkshire, where the Luddite riots of 1812 were mainly concerned with its destruction and that of the shearing-frame. There were a large number of patents for gig-mills, some using teasels and some wire cards, the object of the latter being to provide a more durable material than teasels, which were often scarce and dear, though they had not been superseded by 1850. There were also attempts to make the gigs work in different directions, either across the cloth or with a circular motion, but the original lengthwise direction proved to be the right one. The gig-mill was imported into France in 1802 and spread widely there after 1807, receiving many improvements. In England its success varied in different parts of the kingdom. In the west it seems to have been universally employed during the 1830s, but in 1850 there was still some hand-raising in Yorkshire.

In the production of machinery for shearing the nap, France preceded England, since the machine supposed to have been invented by Everett of Heytesbury in 1758 is a myth [22]. This machine appears in most continental histories of textile technology, owing to misleading information given to Roland de la Platière (1734–93) and embodied in the *Encyclopédie Méthodique*. The first shearing-machine was that of Delaroche of Amiens in 1784, but J. Harmer of Sheffield, who patented his in 1787, was not far behind. In these machines several pairs of shears were united by a crank and moved by power. Harmer improved his device in 1794, and there were several later patents. In some types the shears travelled across or along the cloth; in others, the cloth was drawn under them by means of rollers. At first this machinery seems to have spread more widely in France than in most parts of England, where opposition to it was strenuously maintained until the great depression of 1816. The first rotary machine was invented by an American, Samuel Dorr, and patented in England in 1794, but nothing more was heard of it here. It was improved in America, where other machines on the same principle were also produced. Introduced into France in 1812, it was improved by Collier, who patented it in England in 1818, where it was sometimes used [23]. More widespread in England, however, was the rotary machine patented by J. Lewis of Brimscombe, near Stroud, in 1815. This has generally been regarded as his own invention, though it is possible that he may have seen or heard of the American model, drawings of which were brought to England in 1811 [24]. These machines and others produced later differed in details, but all included a cylinder furnished with blades placed spirally round it, so that when the cylinder rotated they came into contact with a fixed blade underneath. The carriage on which the blades were mounted was drawn over the cloth either lengthwise or from list to list; and there were contrivances for keeping the cloth stretched and for bending it sharply at the point of contact, so that the blades might encounter the nap at the best angle. Rotary shearing-frames spread widely after 1820, but hand-shearing was not quite extinct even in the forties.

REFERENCES

[1] Dobson, B. P. 'The Story of the Evolution of the Spinning Machine', p. 81. Marsden, Manchester. 1910.

[2] Murphy, W. S. 'The Textile Industries', Vol. 3, p. 54. Gresham, London. 1910.

[3] Fairbairn, W. "Rise and Progress of Manufactures and Commerce in Lancashire and Cheshire" in Baines, T. 'Lancashire and Cheshire Past and Present', Vol. 2, p. 197. London. 1869.

[4] Wadsworth, A. P. and Mann, Julia de L. 'The Cotton Trade and Industrial Lancashire, 1600–1780', p. 496, note 2. University of Manchester Economic History Series, No. 7. Manchester. 1931.

[5] 'Report of the Committee on Artisans and Machinery', pp. 102, 300, 327, 384. London, Parliamentary Papers, Session 1824, Vol. 5.
Montgomery, J. 'A Practical Detail of the Cotton Manufacture of the United States of America', pp. 151–2. Glasgow. 1840.

[6] *Idem. Ibid.*, pp. 60, 61, 70.
'Report of the Committee on Artisans and Machinery', p. 327. London, Parliamentary Papers, Session 1824, Vol. 5.

[7] *Ibid.*, p. 385.

[8] Montgomery, J. See ref. [5], p. 28.

[9] BROWLIE, D. *Trans. Newcomen Soc.*, **6**, 86, 1925–6.
URE, A. 'Ure's Dictionary of Arts, Manufactures and Mines', ed. by R. HUNT (5th ed. re-written and enl.): Spinning. London. 1860.
[10] LEIGH, E. 'The Science of Modern Cotton Spinning' (2nd ed.), Vol. 1, p. 145. London. 1873.
[11] DICKINSON, H. W. *Trans. Newcomen Soc.*, **25**, 123–37, 1945–7.
[12] WEBSTER, T. 'Reports and Notes of Cases on Letters Patent for Inventions', Vol. 1, p. 573. London. 1844.
[13] BALLOT, C. 'L'introduction du machinisme dans l'industrie française, pp. 241 ff. Marquand, Lille; Rieder, Paris. 1923.
[14] PICARD, A. 'Le bilan d'un siècle, 1801–1900', Vol. 4, p. 199. Le Soudier, Paris. 1906.
[15] URE, A. 'The Philosophy of Manufactures' (3rd ed., with additions by P. L. SIMMONDS), p. 151. London. 1861.
[16] BAINES, SIR EDWARD. "The Woollen Trade of Yorkshire" in BAINES, T. 'Yorkshire Past and Present', Vol. 2, p. 682. London. 1877.
[17] BALLOT, C. See ref. [13], p. 206.
[18] BAINES, SIR EDWARD. See ref. [16], p. 684.
[19] CLAPHAM, SIR JOHN H. 'An Economic History of Modern Britain', Vol. 2, p. 13. University Press, Cambridge. 1932.
[20] TAYLOR, W. C. 'The Handbook of Silk, Cotton and Woollen Manufactures', p. 154. London. 1843.
[21] DOLFUS, E. *Bull. Soc. industr. Mulhouse*, **3**, 323, 1830.
[22] PILISI, J. *Industr. text.*, no. 818, 51, 1955.
[23] 'Report of the Committee on Artisans and Machinery', p. 21. London, Parliamentary Papers, Session 1824, Vol. 5.
Ibid., p. 44. 1825.
[24] URE, A. See ref. [15], p. 141.
WEBSTER, T. See ref. [12], Vol. 1, p. 126.

BIBLIOGRAPHY

ALCAN, M. 'Essai sur l'industrie des matières textiles' (2nd ed.). Paris. 1859.
BAINES, SIR EDWARD. 'History of the Cotton Manufacture in Great Britain.' London. 1835.
BALLOT, C. 'L'introduction du machinism dans l'industrie française.' Marquand, Lille; Rieder, Paris. 1923.
BARLOW, A. 'The History and Principles of Weaving by Hand and by Power.' London. 1878.
BURNLEY, J. 'The History of Wool and Woolcombing.' London. 1889.
COLE, A. H. 'The American Wool Manufacture' (2 vols). Harvard University Press, Cambridge, Mass. 1926.
DOBSON, B. P. 'The Story of the Evolution of the Spinning Machine.' Marsden, Manchester. 1910.
DODD, G. 'The Textile Manufactures of Great Britain.' London. 1851.
HORNER, J. 'The Linen Trade of Europe during the Spinning Wheel Period.' McCaw, Stevenson and Orr, Belfast. 1920.
JAMES, J. 'History of the Worsted Manufacture in England, from the Earliest Times.' London. 1857.
KENNEDY, J. "Rise and Progress of the Cotton Trade of Great Britain" in 'Miscellaneous Papers on Subjects connected with the Manufactures of Lancashire.' Privately printed. 1849.

Idem. "Brief Memoir of Samuel Crompton." *Ibid*. 1849.
LEIGH, E. 'The Science of Modern Cotton Spinning' (2nd ed., 2 vols). London. 1873.
LIPSON, E. 'A Short History of Wool and its Manufacture.' Heinemann, London. 1953.
MARSDEN, R. 'Cotton Spinning.' London. 1884.
Idem. 'Cotton Weaving. Its Development, Principles, and Practice.' London. 1895.
MONTGOMERY, J. 'A Practical Detail of the Cotton Manufacture of the United States of America.' Glasgow. 1840.
Idem. 'The Theory and Practice of Cotton Spinning' (3rd ed. enl.). Glasgow. 1836.
MURPHY, W. S. 'The Textile Industries' (3 vols). Gresham Publishing Company, London. 1910.
PICARD, A. 'Le bilan d'un siècle, 1801–1900', Vol. 4. Le Soudier, Paris. 1906.
PRIESTMAN, H. 'Principles of Woollen Spinning' (2nd ed.). Longmans, London. 1924.
Idem. 'Principles of Worsted Spinning' (2nd ed.). Longmans, London. 1921.
REES, A. 'The Cyclopaedia; or Universal Dictionary of Arts, Sciences and Literature.' London. 1819.
TAYLOR, W. C. 'The Handbook of Silk, Cotton and Woollen Manufactures.' London. 1843.
URE, A. 'The Cotton Manufacture of Great Britain.' London. 1861.
Idem. 'The Philosophy of Manufactures' (3rd ed., with additions by P. L. SIMMONDS). London. 1861.
Idem. 'Ure's Dictionary of Arts, Manufactures and Mines', ed. by R. HUNT (5th ed. rewritten and enl., 3 vols). London. 1860.
WADSWORTH, A. P. and MANN, JULIA DE L. 'The Cotton Trade and Industrial Lancashire, 1600–1780.' University of Manchester Economic History Series, No. 7. Manchester. 1931.
WARDEN, A. J. 'The Linen Trade, Ancient and Modern' (2nd ed.). London. 1867.

Penny token issued by Jackson and Lister of Barnsley, c *1811*.

10

PART II

THE TEXTILE INDUSTRY: SILK PRODUCTION AND MANUFACTURE, 1750–1900

W. ENGLISH

THE period from 1750 to 1850 saw appreciable progress towards more scientific methods in the culture of the silkworm (*Bombyx mori*), and this coincided with the transfer of more of the work from peasant homes to the filatures, or larger silk-producing establishments. In Italy, in particular, a number of painstaking scientists and agriculturists carried out experiments and made numerous observations concerning the life and habits of the silkworm—more correctly, the silk-caterpillar—in relation to the qualities and quantities of the silk produced by it, and their findings contributed largely towards increasing the efficiency of the silk-producing industry, not only in Italy but in other parts of the world.

The selection of those cocoons from which moths were to be allowed to emerge for breeding was made chiefly by reference to their shape and size, and the fineness of the silk filaments. No attempts seem to have been made to develop strains from which eggs could be obtained, although some producers preferred to buy eggs from other sources rather than continue using eggs from their own stocks. Experiments had shown that artificial heating of the compartments in which the worms were reared, in order to avoid excessive variations in temperature, was extremely beneficial. Ample ventilation and a relatively dry atmosphere were also found to be important factors in maintaining the health of the worms, and means for obtaining these conditions were provided. Count Vincenzio Dandolo (1758–1819), one of the most prominent members of the group of experimenters mentioned, did much to improve the conditions under which the silkworms were reared. He was particularly zealous in the matter of ventilation and cleanliness, having noted the unhealthy conditions under which the worms were reared in the dwellings of the Italian peasantry. He widely disseminated the knowledge he had gained from his experiments, both in his writings and in lectures. His book was published in an English translation [1] in 1825 by a chartered company—The British, Irish and Colonial Silk Company—which had the avowed purpose of developing the culture of the silkworm in Great Britain, Ireland, and certain colonies.

Disease amongst silkworms was then common; this was not surprising in view of the conditions under which silkworm culture had been carried on for centuries. One very prevalent disease was known as jaundice because of its effect on the colouring of the worms; the application of powdered lime was found to be a satisfactory preventive, if not a cure. It was about the middle of the nineteenth century that another disease, which was later given the name *pébrine*, began to cause considerable anxiety amongst the French producers. There was indeed justification for this concern, since between 1853 and 1865 the output of silk cocoons in France was reduced, through this disease, from 26 000 000 kg to a mere 4 000 000. *Pébrine* also spread to other European silk-producing countries, and even to the east, but the story of Pasteur's successful investigations of it, resulting in the restoration of the silk-industry to its former prosperity, belongs to a later period (p 320).

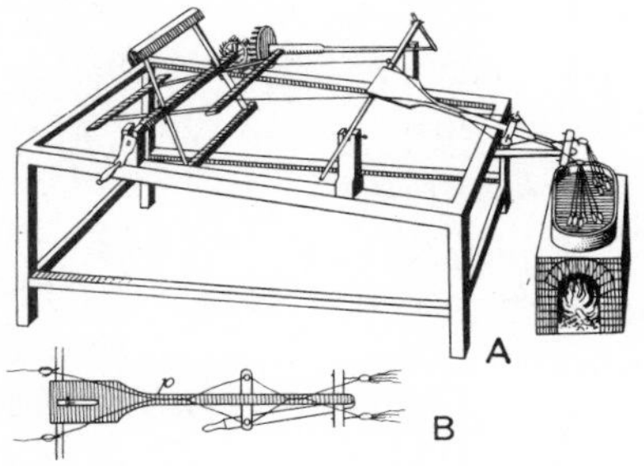

FIGURE 168—(A) *Eighteenth-century silk-reeling machine.* (B) *The double* croisure *on the silk-reeling machine.*

The East India Company was responsible for developing silk-production in India. Up to the middle of the eighteenth century Bengal silk was of extremely low quality—it was worth only one-third to one-half as much as raw Italian silk—and the quantity available for export was insignificant. In 1772 the Company sent a number of experts to Bengal, with the result that in a few years satisfactory qualities were established and exports considerably increased. The basis of most of this work appears to have been instruction in, and the adoption of, Italian methods of sericulture. Even by 1828, however, and 'notwithstanding all the attention and care which the East India Company have devoted to an amelioration of their filatures', the silk was not good enough for 'the richest qualities of broad goods' [2].

I. THE REELING OF SILK

From the viewpoint of quality, reeling—that is, the unwinding of the silk cocoon—is almost as important as the health and development of the silkworm. Careful attention on the part of the operative is a major factor, but improvements in the reeling-machines have contributed towards better results. These machines were turned by hand, and usually two separate skeins were reeled at the same time. Figure 168 A shows a side-view of the type of reel in use in the period. The water in which the cocoons were placed was heated by a fire below the basin (seen on the right of the figure), and one of the difficulties arising from this method of heating was that of maintaining a suitable temperature. The operative kept a vessel of cold water by her side to cool the heated water when necessary. Subsequently the water was steam-heated, and the expression 'steam-filature' was evolved. The filaments, collected together from several cocoons to form one group, were taken over a kind of bobbin on their way to the reel. This tended to flatten the thread, and in order to prevent the flattening, and to preserve a circular cross-section and compact construction, the *croisure* or crossing of the threads was devised. This was accomplished either by twisting adjacent threads round each other several times and then separating them, or by arranging for one thread to pass through guides which diverted it and allowed it to be twisted round itself. The arrangement also assisted in the quicker drying of the filaments by squeezing out some of the water. Figure 168 B shows in plan an enlarged view of a double *croisure*, the crossing taking place at *p*; this improvement gave a still more compact and cylindrical thread.

The traversing of the threads across the face of the reel was necessary during the reeling process, since if they had been allowed to pile up over preceding layers before the threads were dry they would have become gummed together. There were several methods of providing this traverse. In some cases a wheel on the axis of the reel drove, through a band or cord, a wheel which actuated the traverse-guide—usually referred to in the eighteenth century as a guide-stick. In other examples cog-wheels (figure 168 A) were used, giving a positive drive without risk of slip, as might happen with a band-drive. The ratio of the diameters of the wheels, or of the numbers of teeth in the cog-wheels, determined the rate of spread of the threads along the reels; S. Pullein devised a ratio which provided that the threads were not laid again in the same part of the reel until nearly 600 yds had been wound. This was at a time when the usual interval was 150 yds, and the method therefore greatly reduced the risk of threads adhering because of insufficient drying [3].

Italian reeled silks were considered much superior in quality to French silks, but so far as the reeling process affected these standards it would appear that the difference was not due to any constructional superiority in the Italian machines, or even to better technique amongst the reelers, but rather to the stricter control enforced by the Piedmontese government over those responsible for the reeling processes [4]. In 1825 John Heathcoat, an Englishman already famous as the inventor of a lace-making machine, patented a cocoon-reeling machine that was later copied and used in the Italian silk industry.

II. SILK-THROWING

The introduction of silk-throwing machinery (plate 15) into England, and its rapid early development by reason of the enterprise of John and Thomas Lombe, belong to an earlier period than the one under consideration. It is, for example, not generally realized that Lombe's silk-mill at Derby preceded Arkwright's first cotton-mill by over fifty years. What does concern us here, however, is the fact that once Thomas Lombe's patent lapsed, in 1732, and others began to use his processes, various improvements were applied to the machines. This was a somewhat gradual operation, largely because import duties on thrown-silk yarns protected the new English industry, and it was not considered necessary to aim at greater efficiency. One authority stated that very few improvements took place before 1824, and that before that year 'no machinery in Great Britain was so barbarous as that in the throwing trade' [2]. The duties were relaxed in 1826, and new and improved machines began to be installed more generally. But if British throwsters were tardy in modernizing their equipment, continental throwsters seemed to have remained at a standstill. As late as the 1830s the Piedmontese were still using the same types of machines as Lombe had copied in 1718; in France, too, at the same date, no improved machinery had 'up to a very recent period' been made for throwing silk.

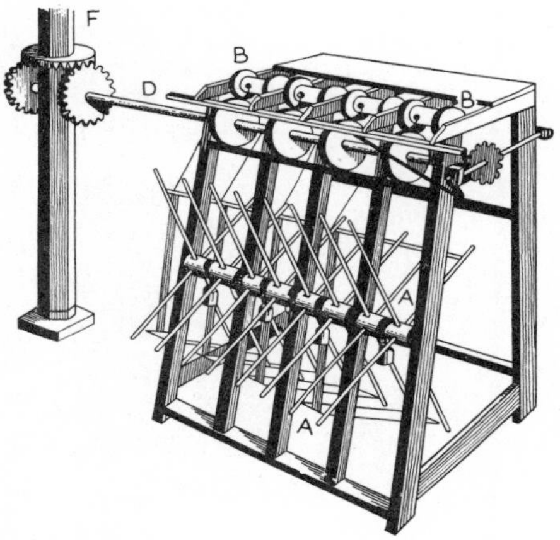

FIGURE 169—*Silk-winding machine of the early nineteenth century.* (AA) *reels or swifts, upon which skeins of silk were placed;* (BB) *bobbins for winding silk.* (D) *the layer, a light wooden rod with holes in it through which the silk was guided on to the bobbin; it was moved to the right and left by a crank.*

The improvements did not involve any fundamental changes in the throwing processes, and were mainly constructional alterations in the machinery. For example, wood was replaced by cast iron in the making of wheels, and crudely made wrought iron spindles were superseded by turned steel spindles. Similarly, metal bearings for the spindles replaced wooden shoulders. Elementary though these changes appear to be, they made an enormous difference to the performance of the machines: spindle-speeds reached 3000 rpm (the Italian and French machines operated at only about 300 to 800 rpm) and costs were reduced by almost 50 per cent.

Throwing in the wider sense of the term involves winding and doubling operations as well as the actual throwing or twisting. Figure 169 shows an early winding-machine, in which the skeins of silk, mounted on swifts (light revolving frames) AA, were transferred to the bobbins BB. Generally the machines were much longer than the one shown. Figure 170 shows a simple form of throwing-machine, in this case arranged for manual operation; by extending shaft R and gearing it to a vertical driving-shaft similar to shaft F in figure 169 the machine could be power-operated. The bobbins wound on the preceding machine now

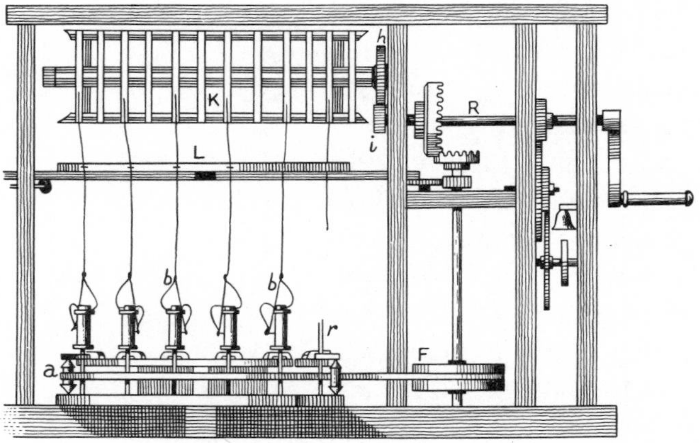

FIGURE 170—*Silk-throwing machine of the early nineteenth century, as used in the home. From the arrangement of spindles it was known as 'the oval'; normally it contained 13 spindles, of which only 6 are shown. Bobbins were placed on spindles* (r) *and thread was led through a piece of bent wire called the flyer* (b) *with an eye at each end. The thread was then led through an eye in the oval frame* (L), *which was given traversing motion by a crank, and so to the reel* (K). *As spindle and flyer revolved, twist was given to the thread, the tightness or hardness being regulated by the size of wheels* (h) *and* (i), *which were changeable.*

supplied the thread, and withdrawal of the yarn was aided by the wire flyers *b* which were free to rotate. The bobbins were mounted on spindles, which were rotated by the belt *a* driven by the pulley F. As the reel K rotated it withdrew the yarn from the bobbins and re-formed it into a skein. During the process the rotation of the bobbins caused the yarn to twist, and the degree of twisting could be varied by changing the gear-wheels. As bar L was given a rapid side-to-side motion, and as the yarn guides were fixed to this bar, the yarn was wound round the swift in a crossed formation. This spreading of the threads made the skeins easier to handle. The mechanism was patented by Nouaille in 1770. In his specification he claimed that this quick crossing of the yarn 'had never been done before' [5].

The doubling-machine was in effect another winding-machine, in which two or more single yarns on separate bobbins were transferred to one bobbin. This process was necessary when organzine[1] yarns, intended for the warp threads in

[1] From the town of Urgenj, in Turkestan, an early market for Chinese silks.

the loom, were being produced, and was a preliminary to the process of throwing or twisting the two or more yarns together. It was important that the full complement of single yarns should always be maintained, and to assist in this object a stop-motion was applied to the machine to interrupt the winding process when any of the single yarns failed. This may or may not have been applied to Lombe's original machine, although it is clear from his patent specification that there was a stop-motion on his winding-machine, where it was not so important a requirement. The stop-motion of the doubling-machine is shown in figure 171, where A is one of the supply bobbins and B is the receiving bobbin driven by the disk F, as in the winding-machine described. It will be noticed that the yarn passes through a guide *e*. This guide is free to slide up and down in a hole in the frame *f*, and the tension of the yarn is such that it keeps the guide out of contact with a lever *t*. If the yarn fails, however, the guide falls, and depresses lever *t*, so that its other end *v* enters the teeth of the ratchet formed in the flange of the bobbin B and arrests its motion.

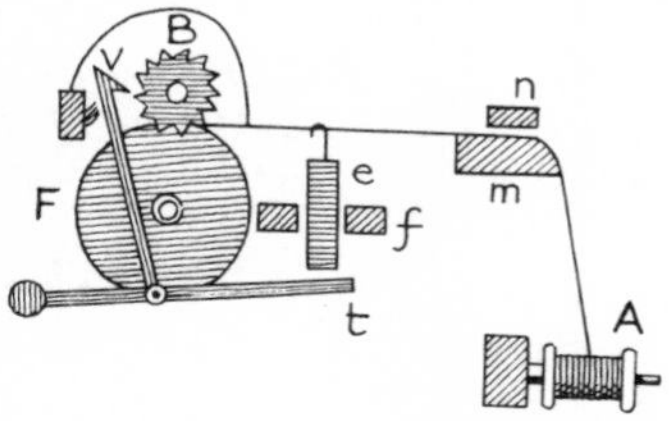

FIGURE 171—*Stop-motion silk-doubling machine, early nineteenth century. Thread from bobbin* A *is first cleaned by passage between* m *and* n. *It then passes under the hook in* e, *which slides up and down in* f. *If the thread breaks,* e *falls and depresses* t, *which allows pawl* v *to enter teeth of ratchet and prevent the receiving bobbin* (B) *from turning.*

The setting or stabilizing of the twist in thrown yarns was effected by immersing the skeins in boiling water. During the period under consideration, steaming replaced this method. This was quicker and more effective than immersion.

III. THE SPINNING OF WASTE SILK

Even today rather more than half the silk produced by the cultivated silkworm is unreelable, and it is probable that this proportion was even greater when silkworm culture and silk-reeling were less efficient. It is this unreelable silk, consisting of cocoon-remains after reeling, damaged cocoons which will not unwind continuously, and the ordinary processing-wastes resulting from silk-throwing and so on, which is described as 'waste' silk. Given suitable preparation, however, this so-called waste can be spun, the products being known as spun silk yarns to distinguish them from the thrown or nett silks. Because a specialized form of spinning has been developed within the last hundred years it is sometimes thought that silk-spinning in general is a modern conception, but this is not so. In fact, some authorities say that silk-spinning originated before silk-throwing, and in support of this view state that the moths of the wild (uncultivated) silkworms would break through their cocoons before the latter were collected. Such cocoons would of course be unreelable.

The possibilities of spinning became obvious once it was discovered that fermentation—or, alternatively, steeping in certain hot aqueous solutions—removed much or all of the gummy matter in the silk, leaving a soft, fibrous, and lustrous mass; for the fibres could then be cleaned, carded, dressed, and spun much as flax and wool. By the middle of the eighteenth century silk-spinning by means of hand carding and combing, followed by the distaff and wheel, was in consequence an established cottage industry, and the yarns were used for a wide variety of goods, such as gloves, stockings, shawls, neckerchiefs, and ribbons. E. Chambers [3] states that the degumming process consisted in steeping the cocoons for three or four days, with frequent changes of water, boiling half an hour in a lye of ashes, straining, washing, and drying in the sun. The combing or dressing operation consisted in passing heckles or combs through the silk while it was held at one end. When the fibres were sufficiently near to parallel, with short fibres and impurities removed, the tuft was reversed so that the processed portion was held whilst the other end was combed.

The gradual mechanization of spinning processes in Great Britain naturally led to attempts to spin waste silk by machinery. A number of patent specifications issued during the latter half of the eighteenth century, while primarily relating to processes involving the preparation of flax and wool for spinning, also mentioned the suitability of the machines for the corresponding treatment of silk. Amongst these were Thomas Wood's combined carding and spinning machine [6], Cartwright's comb [7], and Axon's cleaning and fining machine [8].

But although the preparatory processes of breaking, opening, and heckling required little modification to render them suitable for operating on waste silks, combing methods in use were not satisfactory. This was due to the excessively tangled and matted condition of the fibres and to the action of the combers, resulting in excessive losses of expensive silk as 'waste'. Another difficulty lay in the fact that the silk fibres were present in a variety of lengths, from very short to very long. In the successful spinning machines of the day—Arkwright's throstle-frame and Crompton's mule—the attenuation of the loose strands of fibres was done by drawing-rollers, and these rollers were spaced apart to correspond with the average length of the fibres. Any fibres that were too long would break or otherwise disturb the flow of attenuation, while those too short would tend to accumulate and create thick places in the yarn. This explains why cotton, having relatively short fibres, not too variable in length in a given quality, was successfully spun on these machines.

The obvious solution was to cut the silk fibres to shorter lengths. This was in fact done on machines made somewhat like chaff-choppers, which cut the fibres to lengths varying from 1 to 2 in, corresponding to cotton-fibre lengths.

The mechanical spinning of waste silk began in 1792 at a factory near Lancaster, and subsequently a number of other concerns were started both in Lancashire and in Yorkshire. In one or two instances existing cotton-spinning mills began spinning waste silk. These developments were confined at first entirely to Great Britain, and it was not until about the second decade of the nineteenth century that other countries began mechanized spinning, although on the continent in particular there was a very large cottage industry.

The cutting of the fibres into such short lengths was necessary in order that they could be spun on cotton machinery, but it was not long before attempts were being made to spin the material without such drastic treatment. Machinery for preparing and spinning long fibres was being developed in the flax and wool industries and it was to these sources that inventors turned for ideas. The first of them were Gibson and Campbell [9], of Glasgow (1836). In their specification they were frank enough to say that the machinery described was the same as that used by flax-spinners, and it is therefore not surprising to find that, following an action at law [10], a disclaimer regarding some sections of the patent was issued. The case also brought to light the fact that a number of spinners had been using flax machinery more or less openly for spinning waste silks before 1836. It was in connexion with Gibson and Campbell's process that the term 'long-spun' or 'long-spinning' was first applied to spun silk, to distinguish it from the cotton-system where the cut fibres were used.

Other attempts to prepare and spin the fibres without cutting them were made by Iveson [11] in 1838 and by Templeton [12] in 1841. To obviate the old method of cutting and carding the former used fluted drawing-rollers to tear the fibres apart, afterwards subjecting them to further pressure to render them softer and more pliable. It was Templeton, however, who seemed to hit on the right idea—that of carding or combing the fibres in such a way that at least two separate groups of fibres were formed, one group containing long fibres and the other short fibres.

An improvement in spinning-machines made in 1833, and intended for all long-fibre processing, ultimately proved extremely valuable in the spinning of long-fibred waste silk. This was the invention by Lawson and Westly [13], in 1833, of the screw-gill. Gills or fallers are essentially combs that move along between two pairs of drawing-rollers, so assisting in carrying forward the shorter fibres. They are an important part of the drawing operation, and the inventors applied a worm-gear drive instead of the unreliable chain-and-sprocket drive hitherto used to move the fallers along between the rollers.

Fully satisfactory preparation of waste silk for the spinning process was not achieved until a mechanical dressing-machine was devised by which the silk was separated into a number of groups, known as drafts, according to their fibre-

FIGURE 172—*Loom for weaving silk brocade, worked by a draw-boy.*

lengths. These developments took place mainly during the second half of the century.

IV. WEAVING

Nearly all improvements to looms have ultimately been applied to the weaving of more than one kind of textile material. This has been true of the Jacquard machine, but as it was originally specifically applied to the silk-loom it will be dealt with here; accounts of other developments will be found in the first part of this chapter. The weaving of more or less elaborate designs was a natural development for the enhancement of fine and lustrous silk fabrics, even though such weaving was a slow and laborious process involving the use of a draw-boy to select and lift the correct warp threads for each insertion of weft (figure 172 and vol III, ch 8). A diagram of the draw-loom apparatus is given in figure 173. It shows the comber-board, below which the cords carrying the heald[1] eyes,

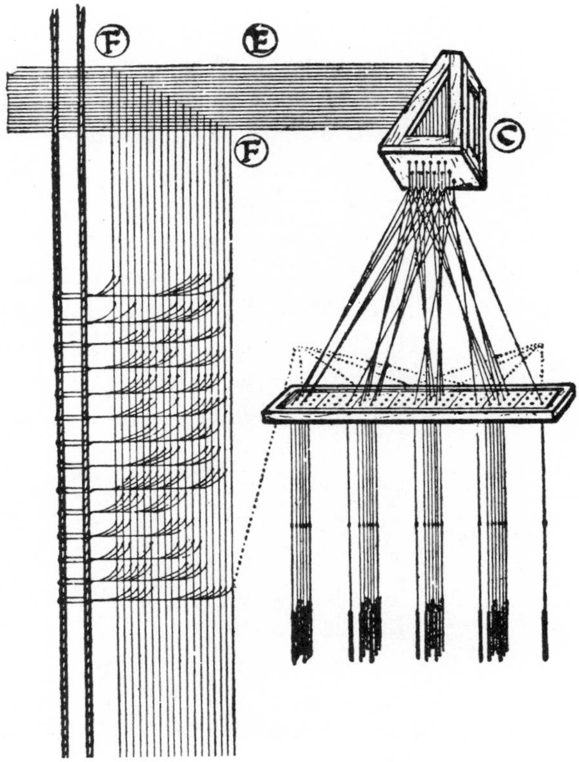

FIGURE 173—*Mechanism of the draw-loom apparatus.*

through which the warp-threads pass, are held taut by lingoes (p 318). Inside the triangular frame C are pulleys over which cords E move, the other ends being fastened to, say, a wall. It will be seen that when the draw-boy pulls one of the cords F, the corresponding heald eyes and warp-threads will be lifted. There had been attempts before that of J. M. Jacquard (1752–1834) to provide mechanism which would do the work of the draw-boy. One was patented by Joseph Mason as early as 1687, and another by William Cheape in 1779. In the meantime a number of inventors continued to apply modifications and improvements to the apparatus for selecting and lifting the warp, without actually making it automatic.

[1] Heddle.

Thus Bouchier had provided needles and hooks in 1725, and three years later Falcon replaced perforated rolls by a series of cards linked together. In 1745 Vaucanson transferred the apparatus from the side of the loom to an overhead position, and added a perforated cylinder rotated directly from the loom (vol III, pp 165–7). At the time when Jacquard applied himself to the problem, the apparatus embodied the 'harness' and 'ties', complete with lingoes,[1] comber-board, and chain of cards; the designs were transferred to squared paper, from which the cards were perforated. But the draw-boy was still needed to operate the harness, and it was Jacquard's invention, known in Great Britain at first as a draw-engine, that finally resulted in all the movements being worked from the loom. He combined the needles with the hooks, changed the cylinder to a prism (although the term 'cylinder' is still given to this part of the apparatus), and applied a lifting-mechanism operated directly from the loom.

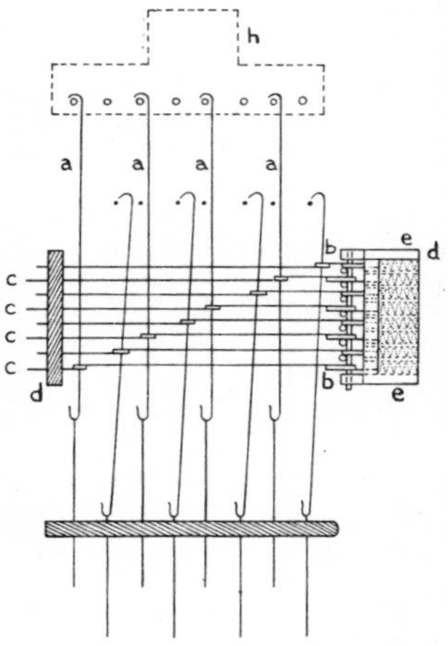

FIGURE 174—*Diagram showing the principle of the Jacquard loom.*

Jacquard's machine was invented in 1801, and eleven years later there were 11 000 draw-looms of this type in use in France. It is usually stated that they were not seen in Great Britain until the 1820s, although there is in the Science Museum at South Kensington a 'Spitalfields loom with Jacquard' which, the catalogue states, was made by Guillotte of Spitalfields about 1810. Figure 174 is taken from a work published in 1831 and will show to those familiar with the modern Jacquard machine how little the fundamentals have changed [4]. This apparatus is fitted to the top of the loom. The hooks *aa* pass perpendicularly through eyes in the needles *bc*, which are fixed in the frame *dd*. (Eight are shown but there may be many more.) The needles protrude at *c* and are kept in that position by springs *ee*. Above the frame *dd* is another frame *h*, which is alternately raised and lowered. The hooks are lifted by the bars in the frame *h* if they are retained in a vertical position. If they are thrust out of this position (as shown by the four lower hooks) the bars miss them and they remain down. The pattern of the perforations in each card as it is pressed against the needles at *c* determines which needles are thrust back and which are not; that is, a perforation allows a needle to remain stationary, and its hook vertical, so that the hook and the corresponding series of warp threads are raised. A blank in the card

[1] Pieces of lead or wire hung on the bottom of each coupling to maintain the tension.

thrusts a needle backwards, its hook remains lowered, and the warp threads controlled by the hook remain below the weft.

In the meantime, and while Jacquard's machine was being kept a close secret, several British inventors had been working on the problem. The fillover loom developed by John Harvey in the early years of the nineteenth century, which produced the Norwich fillover shawls, required the assistance of a draw-boy but appears otherwise to have been a great improvement on existing looms. Other inventors, however, worked directly on the warp-selecting mechanism; they included Clulow (1801), Birch (1804), Duff (1807), and Sholl. A few years later they were followed by Jones and Hughes (1820), and Richards (1821). Some of these draw-engines are described and illustrated in the work already referred to [4].

One important improvement devised in Great Britain was that of W. Jennings, who so rearranged the ties in the Jacquard harness that with other alterations it became possible to place the machine in a much lower position over the loom. This was a useful modification not only in connexion with factory construction, but for what was still also a cottage industry. In Coventry, for example, where there were about 600 Jacquard machines in 1832, steam-engines behind rows of cottages supplied power to the looms inside.

V. THE PERIOD 1850–1900

No outstanding developments in silk-throwing took place after 1850, while the developments in weaving were common to textiles in general. However, a political action having far-reaching consequences for the British silk industry, and important advances in three branches of the industry other than throwing and weaving, will be considered here in order to complete the picture for the nineteenth century. This political action was the Franco-British treaty of 1860, by which silk goods manufactured in France were to be imported into Britain duty-free, while similar goods made in Britain were to be subject to a duty not exceeding 30 per cent *ad valorem* at the French ports. Before the ratification of the treaty, French silk goods were subject to an import duty in Britain, while British goods were completely prohibited in France. The immediate effects on the British silk-industry were disastrous, particularly among the Spitalfields weavers and the ribbon-manufacturers of Coventry. On a longer view, however, it is probable that technical improvements were, as a result, developed in the industry at a faster rate than would otherwise have been the case.

The important advances made in the sections of the industry other than throwing and weaving were concerned with Pasteur's work on silkworm diseases, the weighting of silk during dyeing, and the development of long-spinning in the production of yarns from waste silk.

VI. THE WORK OF PASTEUR

It was in 1865 that Pasteur (1822–95) began his investigations into the causes and prevention of silkworm diseases, particularly *pébrine*. After three years' work on the problem, he had isolated the bacilli of two diseases, and expressed the opinion that these diseases were of long standing, the then recent epidemic condition having arisen owing to the unhealthy conditions under which the worms were reared. The preventives he recommended were mainly based on the adoption of small, isolated rearings of the worms with frequent checks on their condition, including the opening and microscopic examination of selected chrysalides. Having established that a satisfactory condition of health existed, the eggs from such rearings were to be used by the commercial breeders. The adoption of these methods brought about a rapid improvement in the health of the worms, and Pasteur's work restored the prosperity of the silk industry not only in France but in other silk-producing countries.

VII. THE WEIGHTING OF SILK

The dyeing of textiles is dealt with elsewhere in this work (vol V, ch 12), but there is one aspect of the dyeing of silk which may be appropriately mentioned here. This is the weighting of silk, which is usually carried out as part of the dyeing process. Weighting is possible because silk has a chemical affinity for certain metallic salts, a discovery made in the early part of the sixteenth century. Other substances also have been used, such as sugar, which was employed in England, if not elsewhere, during the first half of the nineteenth century. Metallic salts, however, remain the principal ingredients, and when they are used with discretion the resultant weighting gives to the silk fabrics fullness and firmness in handling.

In 1857, in a small dyeworks at Krefeld, a skein of silk to be dyed black was by mistake immersed in a vat prepared for dyeing a Prussian blue. It was subsequently passed on for dyeing black, and was afterwards found to be more lustrous and much heavier than it would have been had it been dyed black by the methods then normal. Further experiments confirmed that this offered a means of weighting silk far in excess of other known methods, so that ultimately black dyed silks were often weighted up to 40 oz per lb, and some spun silks as much as 150 oz per lb. For many years it was only in black dyeing that silks were so heavily weighted, but by the 1880s the practice had spread to coloured silks;

salts of iron and tin, and a number of tannin compounds, were used for the purpose.

These developments took place chiefly in Germany and France, and, since they brought about a considerable reduction in the price of silk goods, the British silk industry suffered a serious decline. Lack of technical knowledge of the processes of weighting, and in some cases refusals to attempt such weighting on the grounds of commercial morality, were the principal reasons why British dyers did not at once follow the continental practice. As to the second reason, there was a gradual acceptance of the position that not only was limited and controlled weighting not injurious to the silk, but that in fact it improved the 'handle' and appearance. On the other hand, excessive weighting, carried out mainly to cheapen the goods, was extremely injurious, and many of the imported silks were soon looked upon with suspicion by the public after some experience of their poor serviceability. In the end, British dyers had in self-defence to begin the weighting of coloured silks, and the position was well summed up by one authority, who in 1885 wrote: 'It is absolutely necessary for a dyer to be a good chemist . . . but I am sorry to say the dyer's chemistry is almost wholly needed nowadays for the weighting of silk, not for the dyeing of it. Nothing is more difficult than to weight silk to the same extent the French do. The tinctorial part, since the introduction of aniline dyes, is easy in comparison' [14].

VIII. THE SPUN-SILK INDUSTRY

The preparation and spinning of waste silk is now almost entirely done on the long-spinning system, and the outstanding developments took place mainly during the second half of the nineteenth century. Not all sections of Gibson and Campbell's patent (p 315) were invalidated, and certainly some of the sections retained in the specification were subsequently applied with success. A number of spinning concerns adopted and improved upon the processes described in the specification, and it was not long before the spinning of long-fibred silk wastes became a recognized and established business.

As has been indicated, however, the combing of silk waste on machines similar to those used for combing wool and other fibres was not a satisfactory operation, and although many improvements were made in the processes preparatory to combing which further softened and disentangled the material, the combing operation continued to be performed by hand-dressing. The wool-comber S. C. Lister (1815–1906; he became Lord Masham) and J. Warburton invented a combing-machine in 1859 intended especially for the combing of silk, but although it was possible to spin high-quality yarns from its products much expensive fibre was rejected as waste, and commercially the machine was a failure.

IX. LISTER'S SELF-ACTING DRESSING MACHINE

Some nine years earlier, Greenwood and Warburton had introduced the intersecting gill, in which two sets of gills or fallers were used, one set working upwards and the other downwards, so acting on both sides of the sheet of fibres

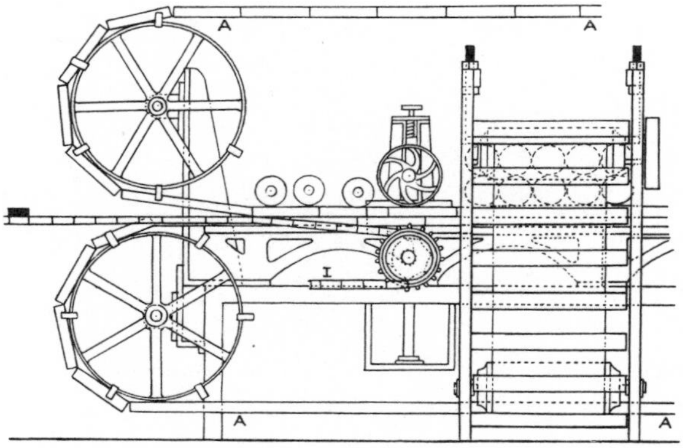

FIGURE 175—*Side view of Lister's self-acting silk-dressing machine, from the original specification.*

at the same time and ensuring better control during the attenuating process. Subsequent improvements and their application to the processing of silk waste ultimately resulted in Lister's comb becoming redundant, and Lister himself, now well established as a silk-spinner, installed the intersecting gills and reverted to hand-dressing. At the same time he began working on a dressing machine that should be automatic in operation, and in 1877 his efforts met with success. Although Lister himself claimed that his machine was the first self-acting dressing machine, de Jongh of Alsace had invented a machine of this type in 1856, and at least one authority [15] has stated that Lister's patents of 1877, 1878, and 1891 were mainly improvements on de Jongh's ideas. Certainly they made the machine workable and commercially successful. Figures 175 and 176 are taken from Lister's specification. These figures show respectively a side view and a plan of part of the machine. AA are two moving endless belts formed of wood blocks hinged together, and the silk is fed between these two belts, which hold it firmly while another endless belt carrying the cards or combs I moves alongside, as shown in the plan, and combs out the projecting tufts, straightening the longer fibres and removing the shorter ones. The cards are positioned in relation to the 'nips', as they were termed, so that the combing action is graduated, the teeth penetrating more deeply into the tufts as the combing proceeds.

An ingenious device on the machine provided for a transfer of the nips from one end of the tuft of silk to the other, so that the silk previously held could now be combed. An additional set of nips was provided for this purpose. The shorter fibres gradually accumulated on the cards; these were removed at intervals and subsequently again fed to the machine or to a similar machine. This process

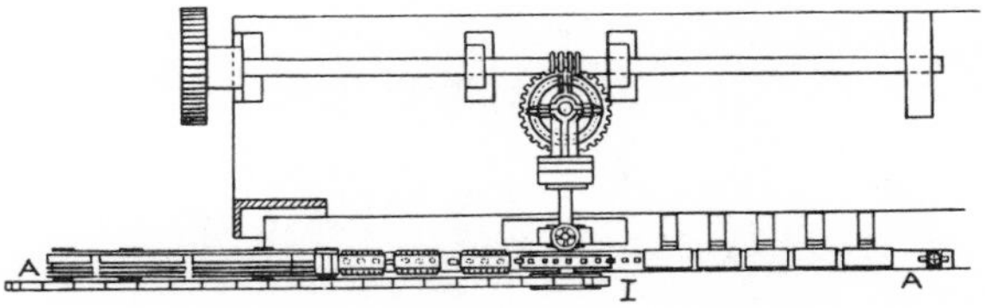

FIGURE 176—*Lister's silk-dressing machine, seen in plan.*

could be repeated as often as necessary so that finally a series of drafts of different qualities was produced.

A number of improvements were made on the machine from time to time. Fairbairn and Newton in 1856 devised an addition whereby the cards or combs operated alternately on both ends of the silk tufts 'during one passage of the holders through the machine'. Three years later they provided an intermittent feeding arrangement, while in 1865 Warburton replaced the travelling combs with cylinders. In 1889 Priestley patented an apparatus for automatically reversing the 'books' of silk, and for releasing the tufts on completion of the combing and transferring them to a delivery apron.

X. THE FLAT DRESSING MACHINE

It is not certain how many other spinning-mills adopted Lister's dressing machine. Certainly the flat dressing frames that came into general use in British mills bear very little resemblance to Lister's machine. They were probably so called to distinguish them from the circular dressing machines, which were being mainly used on the continent and for which a patent was first granted to Quinson in France in 1856, although they did not supersede the flat machine until after 1870. Greenwood and Batley, of Leeds, were making flat dressing machines as early as 1860.

A typical flat dressing machine, as used in Great Britain in the 1890s, is shown in sectional side-elevation in figure 177, the large drum and its adjacent parts being applied about 1880. An endless moving belt A carried a number of combs B and cards C. The silk, after preliminary preparation, was fed to the combs from the box or 'in-frame' E, consisting of a series of holders with screw adjustments so arranged that the silk was firmly held in position for combing. The whole box was movable vertically by the cams KK, and could be swivelled completely round on the pivot H, the whole being carried on a carriage J mounted on rails RR. The box could therefore be withdrawn from the machine for refilling; it could be turned round so that both sides of the tufts of silk could be combed; and it was raised to bring the silk gradually closer to the moving combs. Having combed the tufts in both directions, the in-frame was withdrawn from the machine while the tufts were taken out by hand and reversed in the holders so that the silk previously held could now be combed. The tufts were then removed and passed on to the next process. In the meantime the silk retained by the combs and cards was removed and prepared for further dressing, to constitute another draft with shorter fibres than the preceding one.

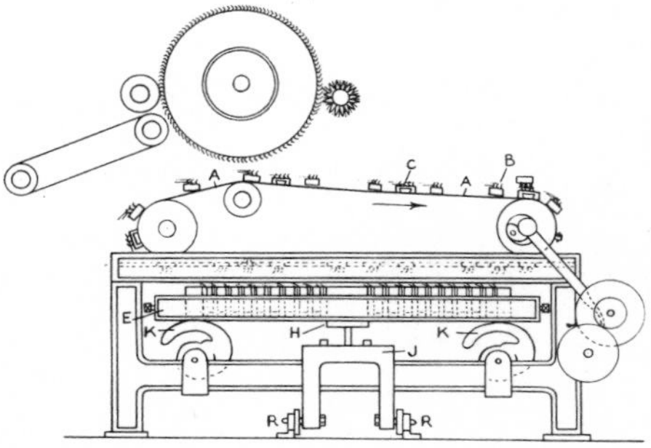

FIGURE 177—*Flat dressing machine, 1890.*

XI. BAUWENS AND DIDELOT'S DRESSING FRAME

The originators of this form of dressing were undoubtedly Bauwens and Didelot, who patented their process in France in 1821. Reference to figure 178, taken from the specification, clearly shows the similarity. The endless band *f* carries the cards or combs, while below is the table G with its nips or grippers pressed together by screws and holding the silk. The table is mounted on wheels for easy withdrawal; it is pivoted to reverse the combing action, and can be raised and lowered through the levers shown. Repetition of the operation produced several drafts. The inventors used the machine in their own factory in Paris, the motive power being a steam-engine.

Among British patents for improvements in this type of dressing machine was that of Molineaux in 1840, who, however, adapted his machine for flax and tow. Another improvement was that of Greenwood, who in 1862 introduced a variable-speed drive to the endless belt carrying the combs. It is generally accepted, however, that the main features of Bauwens and Didelot's patent remained unchanged to the end of the century—a remarkable achievement in view of the difficulties met with by the early inventors of silk dressing machines.

Although the circular dressing machine was not largely adopted in Britain until the turn of the century, it is worth noting that British inventors were concerned with improving it before that time. Thus in 1864 Greenwood and Hadley devised an arrangement of holders, mounted on a large revolving cylinder in the circular machine, which automatically slackened their grip on the silk as they approached the position where the operative was required to remove the combed tufts and replace them with uncombed ones, and then automatically tightened as they moved to the combing position. In 1881 Greenwood, with Schule, patented further improvements.

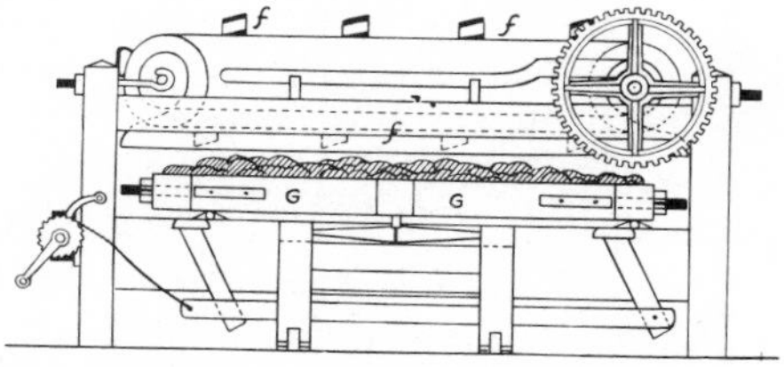

FIGURE 178—*Bauwens and Didelot's silk-dressing frame.*

XII. PROCESSES BEFORE AND AFTER DRESSING

As has been indicated, there were processes that preceded the dressing operation, and these were developed throughout the second half of the century. Thus improved degumming or discharging methods were adopted, and subsequent processes included suppling, for softening and freeing matted fibres by applying soap solutions; cocoon-beating, to free the silk of portions of chrysalis and other foreign material; and opening, to disentangle the fibrous masses further and partially to straighten the fibres. This was followed by a coarse combing operation on the filling machine, where the silk was spread uniformly over the periphery of a cylinder. This layer was next cut into strips about 7 inches in width, so that all excessively long fibres were shortened, and as these strips were removed from the cylinder they were placed between hinged boards termed book-boards, where they were firmly held and transferred to the in-frame of the dressing machine.

Processes following dressing were similar to those used in spinning other long fibres such as wool, and need not be described here. Spun-silk yarns being of a more hairy character than nett silks, it was necessary in many cases to remove these projecting fibres. Neps (very small bunches of tangled fibres) and foreign matter were also found to adhere to these yarns, and a combined gassing and cleaning machine invented by Lister in 1868 proved very effective in removing them. Each yarn was passed rapidly several times through a Bunsen flame, the yarn moving backwards and forwards round a series of bars so as to rub against itself at the crossing points; in this way the singed fibres were removed and the yarn cleaned.

About 1880, various types of the so-called wild silks, that is, silks produced by worms not cultivated and reared in the manner of the *Bombyx mori*, began to be used in the British silk-spinning industry. Tussore silk in particular, from wild Indian silkworms, was spun and woven into a popular range of fabrics. On the continent these and other waste silks were only partially degummed by a process of fermentation, the product being known as Schappe silk. The process was never adopted in this country and in fact has almost died out.

ACKNOWLEDGEMENTS

The author acknowledges with thanks the assistance given by Messrs Greenwood & Batley, of Leeds, who were actively engaged in the development of the silk-spinning machinery described, and who kindly supplied information from their early records; Messrs William Thompson & Company Limited, of Galgate, near Lancaster, the earliest known mechanical spinners of silk waste; the Textile Institute, Manchester; and Messrs T. M. M. (Research) Limited, of Helmshore, Lancashire.

REFERENCES

[1] DANDOLO, COUNT VINCENZIO. 'The Art of Rearing Silkworms. Translated from the Work of Count Dandolo.' London. 1825.
[2] BADNALL, R. 'A View of the Silk Trade.' London. 1828.
[3] CHAMBERS, E. 'Cyclopaedia.' Edinburgh. 1784.
[4] LARDNER, D. 'Cabinet Cyclopaedia': 'A Treatise on Silk Manufacture.' London. 1831.
[5] British Patent, No. 960, 1770.
[6] British Patent, No. 1130, 1776.
[7] British Patent, No. 1787, 1790.
[8] British Patent, No. 1935, 1793.
[9] British Patent, No. 7228, 1836.
[10] Law Journal Report. New Series. Common Pleas, p. 177. *Gibson* v. *Brand.*
[11] British Patent, No. 7600, 1838.
[12] British Patent, No. 9169, 1841.
[13] British Patent, No. 6964, 1833.
[14] WARDLE, SIR THOMAS. 'Report on the English Silk Industry.' Manchester. 1885.
[15] MANGOLD, F. and SARASIN, H. F. 'Société Industrielle pour la Schappe: Origines et Développement, 1824–1924.' Delchaux et Niestlé, Neuchâtel. 1924.

BIBLIOGRAPHY

BADNALL, R. 'A View of the Silk Trade.' London. 1828.
DANDOLO, COUNT VINCENZIO. 'The Art of Rearing Silkworms. Translated from the Work of Count Dandolo.' London. 1825.
HOOPER, L. 'Handloom Weaving: Plain and Ornamental.' Hogg, London. 1910.
HOWITT, F. O. 'Bibliography of the Technical Literature on Silk.' Hutchinson, London. 1946.
LARDNER, D. 'Cabinet Cyclopaedia': 'A Treatise on Silk Manufacture.' London. 1831.

MASHAM, LORD. 'Lord Masham's Inventions. Written by Himself.' Argus & Lund, Bradford and London. 1905.
RAYNER, H. 'Silk Throwing and Waste Silk Spinning' (2nd rev. ed.). Scott, Greenwood, London. 1921.
SILK AND RAYON USERS' ASSOCIATION. 'The Silk Book.' Silk and Rayon Users' Association, London. 1951.
WARDLE, SIR THOMAS. 'Report on the English Silk Industry.' Manchester. 1885.
Idem. 'A Paper on Silk read before the Society of Chemical Industry (Manchester Section).' Manchester. 1887.
WARNER, SIR FRANK. 'The Silk Industry of the United Kingdom.' Drane, London. 1921.

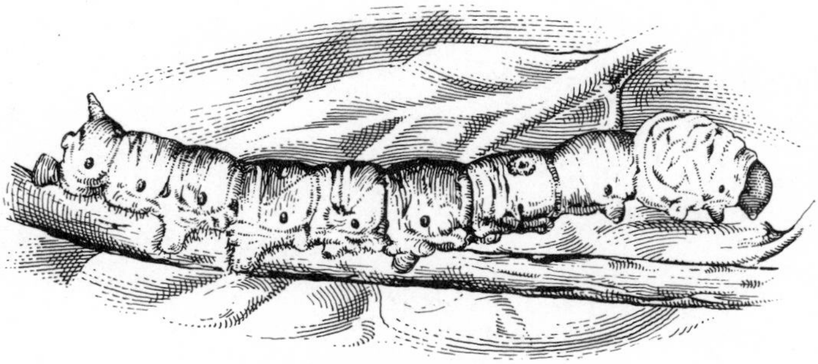

Silkworm (Bombyx mori).

II

CERAMICS FROM THE FIFTEENTH CENTURY TO THE RISE OF THE STAFFORDSHIRE POTTERIES

A. AND N. L. CLOW

I. INTRODUCTION

ALTHOUGH many of the inventions that brought about the industrial revolution of the late eighteenth century were born and nurtured in England, this was not so in the ceramic industry; several European countries had witnessed notable developments in ceramic art before the great expansion of the potteries in Staffordshire after 1750. Moreover, even these European developments were not purely regional in origin, but owed their inception to stimuli that came in the main from the Middle or Far East.

During the fourteenth century a knowledge of the materials and techniques of pottery-making, dating from the beginning of the Christian era at least, percolated into the Mediterranean area along the trade-routes of Syria and Persia. By the sea-route, the Portuguese, who had a trading-centre at Macao at the mouth of the Canton river, brought knowledge of the ceramic achievements of China to Europe, and following the establishment of the Dutch East India Company in 1609 a flood of oriental wares appeared in the European markets. Importation by the British East India Company dates from 1631. This imported china had a profound influence both on the technology and on the aesthetics of European pottery. Not only did the physical properties of the imported wares derive from techniques then unknown in Europe, but the idiom in which they were decorated became a standard of style that was widely copied and adapted to European taste. Attempts to copy both the quality and the style of the imported products stimulated experiment over many generations, and this led not only to the invention of new and discrete types of European ceramics but to the rediscovery of methods of manufacture used in the east. Thus in Europe pottery-making evolved over many centuries from a humble craft producing local ware for everyday use into a highly skilled industrial activity employing power-driven machinery and, particularly in the hands of Josiah Wedgwood (1730–95), such scientific knowledge of materials as was available. Not until this happened—and the whole process took several hundred years—did ceramic products appear in place of wooden and pewter furnishings on the tables of the artisan classes as well as on those of the wealthy. When the change did take place, Staffordshire—where potting of a sort, European in feeling, had been carried on since the middle of the seventeenth century—rapidly evolved into one of the principal pottery centres of the world. It used local coal and clay, but also imported raw materials over considerable distances even before the advent of railways. Its products were sold by English traders in all accessible parts of the world.

Wherever there was clay there were potters, and from the beginning of the fifteenth century rudely fashioned and simply decorated ware was widely made for local use. Nevertheless, without seeking to over-simplify the history of ceramics in Europe, one pre-eminent line of development can be singled out. It extends from the Hispano-Moresque pottery of fifteenth-century Spain, the best pottery in Europe from 1425 to 1475, through the tin-glazed *maiolica*[1] of Italian Tuscany (1475–1530), the hard-fired Rhenish stoneware of Germany, and the ware made by the alchemist Bernard Palissy (1510–88), to the dominant position occupied by delft, which was made at the Dutch town of that name, throughout practically the whole of the seventeenth century. In the following century Delft gave place in turn to Meissen (1710–56) and to Sèvres (1738–75). By this time European pottery was beginning to take on its modern form, and in due course the principal focus moved to Staffordshire (1775 onwards).

To pretend that this outline represents the whole development of ceramic art in Europe would be grossly misleading. While the dates given above denote the periods of pre-eminence of the types and localities named, the tradition of peasant pottery continued everywhere, with the possible exception of England, and the earlier great centres continued to operate, in some instances even to the present day. Thus, while for half a century Italian *maiolica* enjoyed an unrivalled position based on the quality and skill of its production, this position was one that, considering the universality of ceramic materials, it could not expect to occupy indefinitely. So one observes the spread of the manufacture to France, Germany, Switzerland, and the Netherlands, and its continued operation there, also over long periods. There was in fact parallel development everywhere, although—not unnaturally—success varied greatly from centre to centre, some regions being more favoured than others by the fortuitous existence of deposits of superior raw materials.

[1] The name *maiolica* is derived from Majorca, a source of the present Hispano-Moresque ware. Italian *maiolica* was made at many centres, including Orvieto, Faenza, Urbino, Deruta, Castel Durante, Gubbio, Caffagiolo, Florence, Pesaro, Forlì, Venice, Siena, Padua, and Castelli.

II. CLAYS

Unlike ores of metals, which often occur in relatively isolated lodes, the raw materials from which ceramic objects are produced are of extremely wide distribution. Moreover, it is on their rheological properties rather than on their chemical composition that the selection of clays for potting depends, although the composition decides the quality of the final product, its texture, refractoriness, colour, and so on. Even so, few clays can be used just as they are dug from the ground.

FIGURE 179—*The 'blunging' of clay. This was done by mixing the clay and water with a long-handled blade having a cross-bar as handle. These blades were usually made of ash. In the background is a sieve, through which the liquid was strained into the evaporating trough.*

The clay, or a mixture of clays, has first to be purified by levigation, that is, it is 'blunged' with a large quantity of water and the resulting suspension of fine particles sieved and run off (figure 179). The sludge has to be concentrated and dried until sufficient water has been removed to enable the potter to handle it properly. The stiff, but still plastic, clay is next wedged, that is, large pieces are slapped one on the top of the other to remove air-bubbles, which would cause deformation during firing, and to improve the rheological properties of the clay (figure 180). For countless generations all these operations were carried out by hand under exceedingly primitive conditions. Gradually, however, artificial heat was introduced for drying the clay in the vat or sun-pan, and power-operated machinery was used to mix it.

Having obtained his clay in a proper state for working, the potter can proceed in three ways. He can press the clay into a previously prepared mould (figure 181); he can throw it on the wheel (figure 182); or he may obtain the required shape by casting in a mould from a sludge of clay kept in liquid form by the addition of some such substance as water-glass. This method, introduced into England about 1750, gave the potter greatly increased facilities for the production of more complicated objects.[1]

Profound chemical and physical changes are brought about by firing. The temperature at which this is carried out, and the amount of free oxygen in the

[1] For the treatment of clays and general methods of manufacture and finishing see vol I, ch 15, and vol II, ch 8.

atmosphere of the kiln, determine the nature of the final product. In the Mediterranean area, where fuel was scarce and fuel economy important, firing did not bring about the same degree of vitrification of the clay as characterizes, for example, the stoneware of northern Europe, where abundant forests provided sufficient fuel to enable the kilns to be heated to 1200–1400° C, or even higher temperatures. It was this difference in the technique of firing that produced the distinctive Rhenish stoneware of Renaissance Germany, which was imported in

FIGURE 180—*The clay is wedged by throwing one lump of it on to another to expel any air-bubbles. The potter's wheel was turned by the man at the large wheel.*

large quantities into Elizabethan England. This ware later had an important influence on the technology of potting in Staffordshire although, as it happens, the first examples of it to be made in England did not come from Staffordshire but from the pottery of John Dwight (fl 1671–98) of Fulham, London.

While the vitrification of stoneware is sufficient to render it impermeable to water, impermeability is not achieved when products are fired at lower temperatures. Thus from very early times additional processes had to be carried out, on the one hand to render the vessels aesthetically more pleasing, and on the other to make them more serviceable.

III. DECORATION AND GLAZING

Slip decoration, the simplest of all treatments, is of great antiquity. A wash of clay-sludge is applied to the moulded or thrown article to improve its surface, and, if the slip is of a different clay, to produce a simple decorative effect by a variety of colour contrasts. A common practice was to use a whitish clay on the common red (plate 16 D). Fine early French, German, and English tiles were produced in this way, the decorative effect depending entirely on the use of different coloured clays. Designs could also be produced by scratching through the slip, thus exposing the clay of the body, and also by manipulating the clay while still wet with combs and brushes. These constitute the earliest forms of decoration.

A more satisfactory way of rendering pottery vessels impermeable to liquids is to coat the primary body with glaze, in essence a clear or coloured glass (vol II,

FIGURE 181—*Clay is moulded by first rolling it on to cloth, as by the workman on the right, and then placing it in or over a mould. The woman is fixing handles on to a moulded shape.*

chs 8 and 9). The origin of glazing is hopelessly obscure, but a siliceous glaze, consisting virtually of soda-glass, was certainly known in Egyptian times, and indeed Egypt may well have been the site of its origin; lead glaze, which had a greater adhesive power than the earlier siliceous glaze, was known from China to Rome as early as the time of the Han Dynasty (*c* 206 B.C.). In the more primitive method galena (lead sulphide) was simply applied by insufflation to the ware before firing, during which process the lead reacted with the silica in the clay body to produce on its surface a strongly adhering fusible glass. With the progress of chemical technology, artificially prepared lead compounds, such as litharge and red lead, were substituted for galena, and the production of lead compounds for potters became an important ancillary to the pottery industry.

Glazing opened up new fields for aesthetic exploration, and in time glazes became nearly as varied as the clays of the bodies they covered. The clear colourless glaze produced by the fusion of pure silica and lead oxide can be coloured by the addition of natural coloured earths containing iron, manganese,

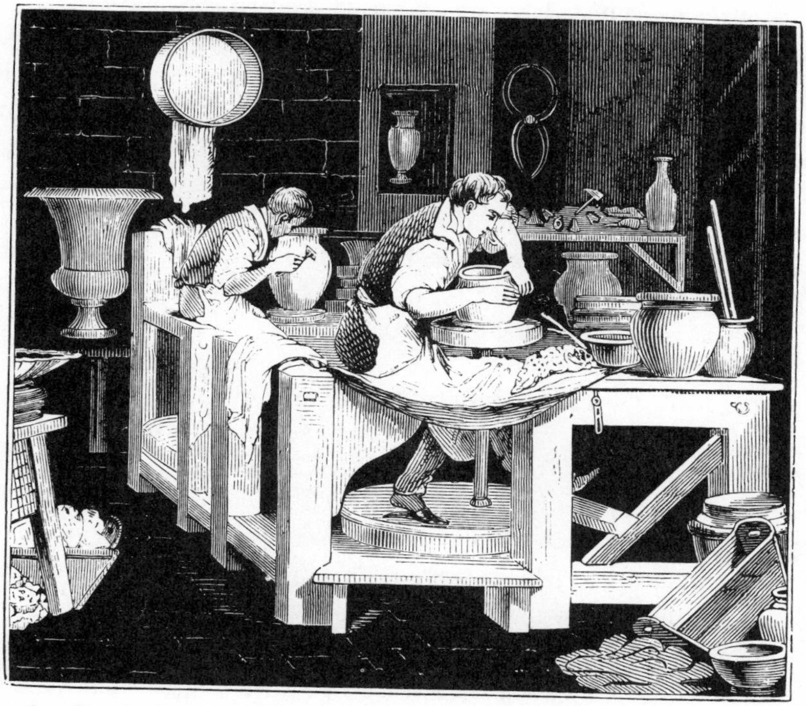

FIGURE 182—*Clay thrown on a wheel turned by foot. An apron was fastened beside the wheel to catch the wet clay and slip thrown off as the wheel turned.*

and cobalt. Although the only colours available in the Mediterranean area were yellow and brown (from iron and possibly antimony), green (from copper), purple and brown (from manganese), and blue (from cobalt), ceramic artists evolved between the ninth and the sixteenth centuries a palette of surprising diversity, and with it produced wares of the highest artistic merit.

In addition to the property of taking up traces of iron, manganese, and cobalt to form coloured glazes, lead glaze has also the useful property that it can be rendered white and opaque by the addition of tin ash (stannic oxide). The resulting tin glaze, or enamel, hid most effectively the natural dark colour of many clay bodies and produced an attractive canvas, as it were, for increasingly subtle decoration; it also satisfied a social demand for a whiter ware and in many regions took the place of the earlier slip-coated ware. This property of tin oxide was known to the ancient civilizations of the Near and Middle East, and knowledge of it was probably brought to Europe by Mohammedan invaders. Certainly in the fourteenth century the Muslim countries from Spain to Egypt, and possibly beyond, were using it to coat a body made of whitish clay and sand which was subsequently decorated with vivid pigments and lustres. The use of tin glaze was much improved by Luca della Robbia (1388–1463). Its development and perfection gave us the Italian *maiolica*, an enamelled earthenware which was the pre-eminent ceramic product of Europe throughout the period 1475–1530 (plates 16 A and C). Tin glaze was also the basis of the delft ware of the Netherlands, which held the field throughout most of the seventeenth century.

The introduction of tin enamel had, however, one disadvantage: it caused difficulties in decoration, and at first only copper-green and cobalt-blue could be used, because manganese gave black and brown instead of purple, and iron unacceptable yellows.

The problem of colour in relation to ceramics is worth considering here, since, for chemical reasons, the range of materials suitable for the ceramic artist's palette is very limited. Unlike the colours used in any other branch of art, with the exception of enamelling, those employed in pottery must be stable at temperatures of the order of at least 1000° C, a requirement that severely limits the range of suitable materials. In spite of this difficulty, the four high-temperature colours, purple, yellow, green, and blue, used alone or in combination, have enabled the ceramic artist throughout the centuries to achieve a wonderful range of decorative effects.

Most pottery clays burn to a yellowish-red, owing to the almost universal presence of iron in them. This iron-produced colour can be transmitted to lead glaze, giving the type of effect that characterizes so much peasant pottery. But, as has been mentioned, lead glaze will dissolve several metallic earths to give coloured compounds of great permanence. The production of green glaze by the addition of copper is of great antiquity: some natural copper minerals are highly coloured and so may have attracted the notice of an observant early experimenter. The fact that copper dissolves in vinegar was recorded in Roman times. In the fifteenth century copper contributed conspicuously to the decoration of the Spanish Paterna ware, and three centuries later it was again used in the production of the early green ware that was the first of Josiah Wedgwood's successful productions.

The blues, so characteristic of ceramic decoration, are produced by cobalt. Their popularity rests entirely on a technological basis, and the reason for the predominance of cobalt blue in the decoration of the 'china' of the Ming Dynasty (1368–1644) was that cobalt was the only pigment that would stand the high temperatures used in firing the true porcelain of the east.

The Egyptians knew that blue could be produced with cobalt, and purple with manganese. Oxide of manganese occurs widely as the mineral pyrolusite, but the source of early cobalt is not known. The Chinese obtained their cobalt minerals from Persia; later supplies came from the Erzgebirge, on the confines of Saxony and Bohemia, and from Sweden. Besides giving purple, manganese when suitably applied will also yield a black: it was used, for example, by Wedgwood in the production of his black basalt ware.

The fourth of the high temperature colours, yellow, is produced by antimony, which with the addition of iron oxide yields an orange. These elements furnish the brilliant colours seen on Italian *maiolica* of the latter part of the fifteenth century.

The one conspicuous omission from the early high-temperature ceramic palette is red, the reason being that no stable compound possessed this colour. For a long period the only method of producing red was by the use of Armenian bole. Usually, however, red was omitted altogether from the decoration, or was applied at a subsequent firing as a muffle colour (p 336). From late in the seventeenth century ferric oxide, obtained by calcining ferrous sulphate, was used to produce red.

The use of the above materials indicates no little skill in prospecting for raw materials to produce the required colours, since in no case does the naturally occurring oxide bear any marked resemblance to the final pottery colour. Similar skill is evidenced in the production of the copper-red lustred Hispano-Moresque ware. How this ware came to be invented is not known; it is found in the Mediterranean region from the ninth century. The interesting technological point is that its production implies an empirical recognition of the difference between an oxidizing and a reducing atmosphere in the kiln. For the latter, smoke-producing material such as damp brushwood was introduced into the kiln at the appropriate stage in the firing. The carbon particles in the smoke acted as a reducing agent upon copper oxides applied to the body, forming a film of free metal on its surface, usually of a pale or dark copper colour (plate 16 B). Produced in Spain with great, if somewhat fortuitous, success during the Hispano-Moresque period, and decorated with coats of arms or texts from the Koran, it has a continuous history up to the rise of the Staffordshire potteries.

IV. DELFT WARE

The foregoing is in outline the technical knowledge available when one of the major events in the history of ceramics took place, namely the rise of the Dutch town of Delft as a dominant centre of European pottery production. The stimulus to this expansion of potting was provided by the greatly augmented importation of blue and white Chinese porcelain into Europe during the early years of the seventeenth century. Sporadic imports had occurred earlier, but it was the development of the Dutch trade with the east, following the foundation of the Dutch East India Company in 1609, that brought about the change in fashion and established the ideal aimed at by European pottery-makers for many years to come. Imported porcelain had properties then unattainable by European techniques, but within a few years (1615) Dutch potters were imitating it, albeit crudely, in tin-enamelled earthenware, virtually a *maiolica* (cf plates 17 A, B).

By the middle of the seventeenth century the tin-enamel industry had become centred on the town of Delft (though the Italian potteries continued to flourish) and for the next century the industry there enjoyed great prosperity. Historically, delft, a soft clay body covered with tin-enamel, forms a link between the medieval Italian and Spanish wares and products deriving from the technical discoveries that led to the manufacture of true porcelain in Europe.

Chinese porcelain, as has been said, was characterized by a quality and whiteness not previously known in Europe. To emulate such excellence, Dutch potters turned their attention to the more careful preparation of their clay and to the quality of their glaze, and this new degree of refinement affords a technical distinction between *maiolica* and delft. Originally the process consisted of throwing a carefully prepared fine buff clay, drying it, and baking it to give an unglazed and absorbent biscuit. The biscuit was then dipped in tin-enamel and dried; decoration in high-temperature colour was applied to the unfired enamel, a glaze applied, and the ware fired a second time.

By the end of the seventeenth century, a similar ware was being produced in England at Lambeth, Liverpool, and Bristol, and at various centres on the continent. Of these, Lambeth was the most Italianate (plate 17 C); Bristol was characterized by its chinoiserie; and Liverpool was celebrated for its punch-bowls decorated with representations of ships. This was the first painted English pottery.

V. OTHER IMITATIONS OF PORCELAIN

In attempting to imitate some of the effects seen on imported porcelain, the delft-makers had to turn from the use of true high-temperature colours as described above to the more elaborate palette produced by muffle colours; these are applied on top of the already fired glaze and fused at a lower temperature. Careful attention to detail, and the occasional application of an additional glaze, enabled the Delft potters to maintain a leading position in European ceramics until their production fell away in the face of competition from the superior ware produced at Meissen (p 338), and from the English salt-glazed stoneware and lead-glazed white and cream earthenware.

Up to this point the line of ceramic evolution is comparatively straightforward, but from the end of the seventeenth century it takes on a new complexity. There are two main streams of development: (i) the improvement of ceramic objects generally, and (ii) the avowed attempt to produce in Europe a ware comparable

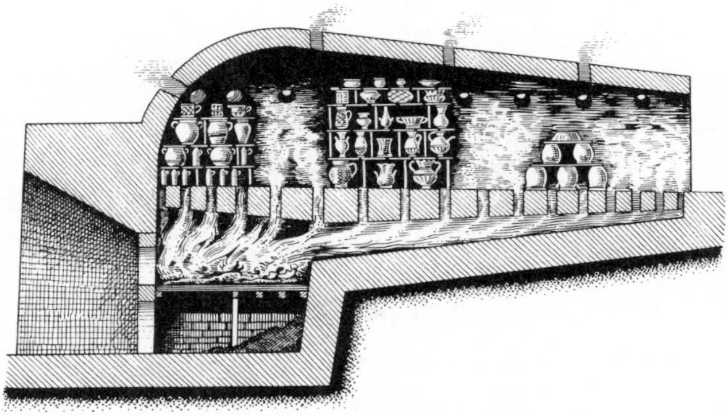

FIGURE 183—*Wood-fired furnace for porcelain.*

with imported porcelain. As a result of this latter activity ceramic evolution took place in three directions: (*a*) the production of a glassy (soft paste) substitute porcelain; (*b*) the production of a true porcelain from European materials; and (*c*) the evolution of bone-china, a peculiarly English innovation.

The introduction of porcelain into northern Europe was the result of Dutch and Portuguese trade, but knowledge of porcelain may also have reached Mediterranean Europe even earlier by the land route through Persia or Egypt. Certainly the first porcelain of any sort to be made in Europe was the famous Francesco de' Medici 'porcelain' which was made at Florence from about 1575 to 1585 (plate 17 E). It was a soft translucent paste composed of sand with Faenza and Vicenza clay fused together with a glassy frit made of rock-crystal and soda, and coated with a thick creamy lead glaze. The product was in fact more akin to opaque glass than to porcelain. After the Medici porcelain there is a long interval before the next record of any other glassy porcelain being made in Europe. This brings us to Rouen (of which the products are very rare) and St-Cloud, the first important French porcelain factory, founded in 1693. The St-Cloud body was formed from an ivory-white paste, which was inclined to crack during the process of firing. The glaze, which was greenish-white, was of good quality but prone to be marred by black specks derived from the wood used as fuel in firing it (figure 183). The manufacture of porcelain had spread to Chantilly by 1725 and to Vincennes-Sèvres by 1738 (p 339).

The Chantilly ware was made of a fine soft body. This was glazed for the first ten years with tin-enamel, but from then on with ordinary lead glaze. By contrast, the first productions of Vincennes were of a slightly grey paste covered with a good clear glaze. *Pâté tendre* was substantially a glassy frit containing chalk or marl. The ceramics from these factories were, however, not true porcelain any more than were those first made in such English centres as Chelsea, Bow, Derby, and Longton Hall, where the manufacture of soft-paste was begun slightly later than in France. Worcester ware also is an imitation porcelain based on soapstone. Moreover, these English factories soon began to add bone-ash to their clay body and so to evolve along a line peculiar to themselves, to be discussed later (section VII).

VI. THE MANUFACTURE OF TRUE PORCELAIN IN EUROPE

The rediscovery of the secret of making true hard porcelain is due to Johann Friedrich Böttger (1682–1719), who worked at Meissen, near Dresden: hence the name Dresden china. The story of how the Meissen factory with which Böttger was associated came to take the lead during the period 1710–56 is the next part of the history of European ceramics to be considered.

The porcelain factory at Meissen owes its inception to the association from 1707 of the mathematician E. W. von Tschirnhausen with Böttger, alchemist to Augustus II (the Strong), Elector of Saxony and King of Poland. First, Böttger succeeded, in 1708, in making a fine red stoneware like that imported along with tea from China, and esteemed as the proper ware in which to infuse tea. His successful technique derived from his realization that it was necessary to add a fluxing agent (alabaster or marble) to the naturally infusible Saxony clay. So hard is this red stoneware that it can easily be mistaken for jasper. By varying his raw materials, and particularly by using an earth from Aue, in the Erzgebirge, he soon succeeded in making a similar white porcelain body and so achieved the success that had eluded other European potters for many generations. Within a year he had also devised an appropriate glaze for his new ceramic body.

Founded on these important technological innovations, the Meissen porcelain works was established in 1710 and the new ware marketed in 1713. Böttger managed the works till his death in 1719, when he was succeeded by J. G. Herold (1696–1765). Herold made conspicuous contributions to the technology of ceramic production. He altered the composition of the body in 1722, making it correspond more closely to the Chinese ware it was devised to imitate, and developed suitable colours with which to decorate it.

In Böttger's method china clay (kaolin) was fused with the calcareous flux (marble or alabaster) at from 1300 to 1400° C in improved kilns. This calcareous flux was later replaced by a felspathic flux of petuntse or china-stone, which takes up the insoluble kaolin to give a translucent matrix rendered opaque by the infusible kaolin. This true porcelain is known as 'hard porcelain' to distinguish it from the earlier glassy or 'soft' porcelains of St-Cloud and elsewhere. It has a hardness of between 6 and 7 on Mohs's scale of hardness. The secrets of porcelain-manufacture were closely guarded, and Meissen was virtually a state prison.

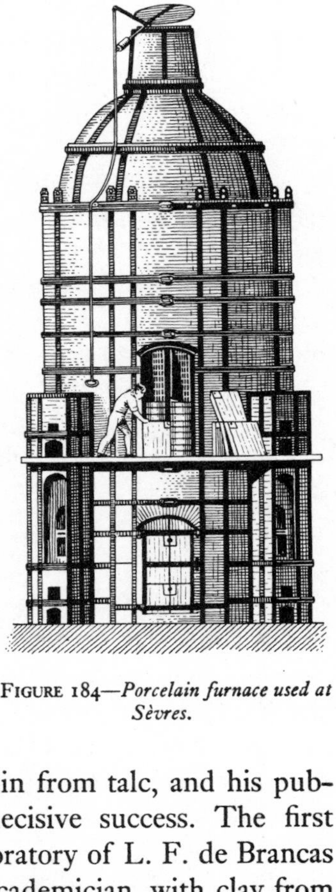

FIGURE 184—*Porcelain furnace used at Sèvres.*

Böttger was by no means the only chemist trying to make porcelain. Only a few years after Meissen porcelain came on the market, the famous French scientist R. A. F. de Réaumur (1683–1757) was experimenting towards the same end, starting with ground and powdered glass as his raw material. We also know that he received specimens of the true porcelain raw materials, kaolin and petuntse, from Père d'Entrecolles, superior-general of the French Jesuits in China, but at the time he was unable to distinguish kaolin from talc, and his publications do not indicate that he attained any decisive success. The first French hard-paste was made about 1758 in the laboratory of L. F. de Brancas (1733–1824), Comte de Lauraguais, scientist and Academician, with clay from Alençon. Having fled to England for religious reasons in 1763, he secured an English patent in 1766 (B.P. No 849) and promptly tried to sell it to Matthew Boulton of Birmingham. Only a couple of years later the manufacture of porcelain was started at Sèvres and the supremacy of Meissen came to an end.

Sèvres, the Manufacture Royale de Porcelaine de France, had been founded at Vincennes in 1738 under aristocratic patronage and utilizing technical knowledge brought by absconding workmen from earlier porcelain works. Success was long in coming, and may be said to date from the appointment of Academician Jean Hellot (1685–1766) to be chief chemist in 1745, a position he retained till 1757/9, when he was succeeded by P. J. Macquer (1718–84).

Although from the start the aim at Sèvres was the production of true hard porcelain, only soft-paste was made till about 1770, and costly experiments aimed at the production of hard porcelain were carried out for nearly thirty years. It was not till 1768, when Macquer began to use the kaolin of St-Yrieix-la-Perche, near Limoges, discovered some years before by the chemist Jean-Étienne Guettard (1715–86), that a successful hard-paste body was assured (figure 184).

The Sèvres body was difficult to work and very liable to fracture, two properties that may be reflected in the shapes that characterize this ware (plate 17 D). The glaze was extremely soft and easily fused, so that the over-glaze enamels sank into it to a greater degree than in almost any other porcelain. The ground-colours produced at Sèvres were outstanding: yellow, rich cobalt, and turquoise blue from 1753, an apple-green from 1756, and rose-pink from 1757. Many of the pieces were elaborately gilded with gold taken up in honey (p 356).

The discovery of kaolin and its exploitation by Böttger and Macquer afford yet another instance of simultaneous independent discovery in the history of science, for in the same year, 1768, William Cookworthy (1705–80), a Plymouth chemist, took out the first English patent for the manufacture of true porcelain (B.P. No 898).

Cookworthy began experimenting with Devon and Cornish clays about 1745, but not till 1768 was he satisfied that he had produced a true porcelain. His patent covered the manufacture of a ceramic body from 'moorstone' or 'growan', and 'growan clay', with a glaze made of china-stone to which lime and fern-ashes, or magnesia alba (basic magnesium carbonate), were added. With a company of Quakers, including Lord Camelford, he established a factory to exploit his discovery at Coxside, Plymouth. This was the first of the kind in England. At Plymouth, however, Cookworthy had to fire his pieces with wood, a convenient supply of coal not being available, and it was the difficulty of securing adequate supplies of fuel locally that led to his removal to Castle Green, Bristol, in 1770, only two years later.

Cookworthy's scientific skill exceeded his business acumen, and after some three years he was forced to make over his patent to Richard Champion (1743–91). Champion, however, encountered difficulties when he tried to renew and register an extension of Cookworthy's original patent in 1775 (B.P. No 1096).

This patent defines porcelain made from a wide range of proportions of clay and china-stone, and for the glaze suggests additionally magnesia, nitre, lime, gypsum, fusible spar, arsenic, lead, and tin-ash. Wedgwood and others challenged Richard Champion's patent and, following litigation, the use of kaolin and china-stone was thrown open to general use. The newly won freedom was eagerly seized by the Staffordshire potters, who applied it to improve their stoneware. In 1781 Champion himself was forced to sell the patent to a group of five potters in Staffordshire who, in the following year, began to make hard-paste porcelain at New Hall, near Shelton. This centre, and its two predecessors at Plymouth and Bristol, represent the only factories at which hard-paste porcelain, comparable with that made on the continent at Meissen, Sèvres, and other less important works, was produced in Britain. New Hall continued to operate till 1825, but from about 1810 it was turning out a product to which bone-ash had been added.

VII. ENGLISH SOFT-PASTE WARES

Having traced the evolution of true porcelain from its importation into Europe during the fifteenth and sixteenth centuries to the establishment of the small group of factories that made it in England, it is now necessary to go back a little to follow up another line of ceramic evolution: one that ultimately had a profound effect, particularly in Staffordshire. Soft-paste porcelain had been made in England considerably before 1768 as a result of experiments in which ground glass and other materials were added to the basic clay. In the successful substance, frit-porcelain, or soft-paste porcelain, the additional materials included kaolin of a sort, various calcareous minerals, and, at one particular group of English factories, ground bone-ash. These factories were at Stratford-le-Bow, Lowestoft, Chelsea, Derby, Longton Hall, and Worcester (plate 18), and while they may not be important in the history of European ceramics as a whole, they are of technological significance in that the developments they initiated led to the evolution of a hybrid ceramic species characterized by its content of bone-ash, and thus differentiated from contemporaneous continental wares.

The origin of the first English soft-paste factory, at Stratford-le-Bow, is obscure, but it is known that a patent for the production of 'a certain mineral whereby a ware might be made equal to porcelain' was registered in December 1744 (B.P. No 610) by Edward Heylyn, a Bristol copper-merchant, and Thomas Frye (1710–62), a painter and engraver from Dublin. The mineral, imported from the American colonies, is presumed to have been some sort of kaolin; it was known as *unaker* to the Cherokee Indians. A second patent was registered in the name of Frye alone in 1749 (B.P. No 649). The material patented was an earth 'the produce of the Cherokee natives' in America.

In his patent specification Frye refers to the use of 'virgin earth', derived from the calcination of animals, vegetables, and fossils. A. H. Church identified it as bone-ash (calcium phosphate). It was used to fabricate a soft-paste porcelain which was fired with wood 'in cases' (saggars) at about 1100° C. True porcelain, by contrast, requires a temperature of about 1300 to 1400° C. The Frye patent is important in that it appears to cover the first actual use of bone-ash in the production of a porcelain, although the idea had certainly been mooted in Germany a century earlier. Macquer, at Sèvres, adopted it some six or seven years after Frye.

At first the Bow paste was thick and heavy, subject to fire-cracking and warping. The yellowish glaze was soft, and so became abraded in use. It also tended to flow in the process of firing and to collect in pools round the foot of the article. With regard to decoration, the Bow blues had a greyish appearance: over-glaze printing was carried out in red, black, and puce.

The Chelsea Porcelain Works is believed to date from about the same time as Bow: bone-ash was first incorporated in the soft-paste there about 1755. Managed by a French potter, Charles Gouyn, and patronized by the Duke of Cumberland, until the 1770s Chelsea was the principal porcelain works in England, at first frankly imitating Meissen, but later developing its own style.

The Chelsea paste was soft, fragile, and creamy-white in colour, with a particularly vitreous glaze. The ingredients of the body were often badly mixed and when fused gave areas of increased translucence, which are highly characteristic of early ware. Both fire-cracking and warping are common. Most of the specimens are decorated in over-glaze enamels; following Sèvres, blue ground-colour was used from 1755, green from 1759, turquoise and crimson lake from 1760. Yellow was seldom used by the Chelsea decorators.

The Chelsea works was acquired by William Duesbury of Staffordshire in 1770. He had taken charge at Bow ten years earlier, but in 1775 he closed it down, transferring operations to Derby. Chelsea shared the same fate in 1786. The history of Derby porcelain, and of the celebrated Chelsea–Derby productions of the 1770–84 period, though well documented, does not concern us here, but one might add a note on Longton Hall, another factory with which Duesbury was associated, on account of the pioneering activities of its founder, William Littler. Longton Hall was founded in 1750 and operated till 1760, by which time it appears to have become associated with Duesbury. Its products were similar to those of Chelsea, but technically are not without interest in that

Littler was the first in Staffordshire to use cobalt blue—the so-called Littler blue, an under-glaze put on rather unevenly.

The production of the next porcelain manufactory, Worcester (founded 1751), is characterized by the presence in the paste of soapstone or steatite (a hydrated magnesium silicate). The introduction of this mineral into ceramics is associated

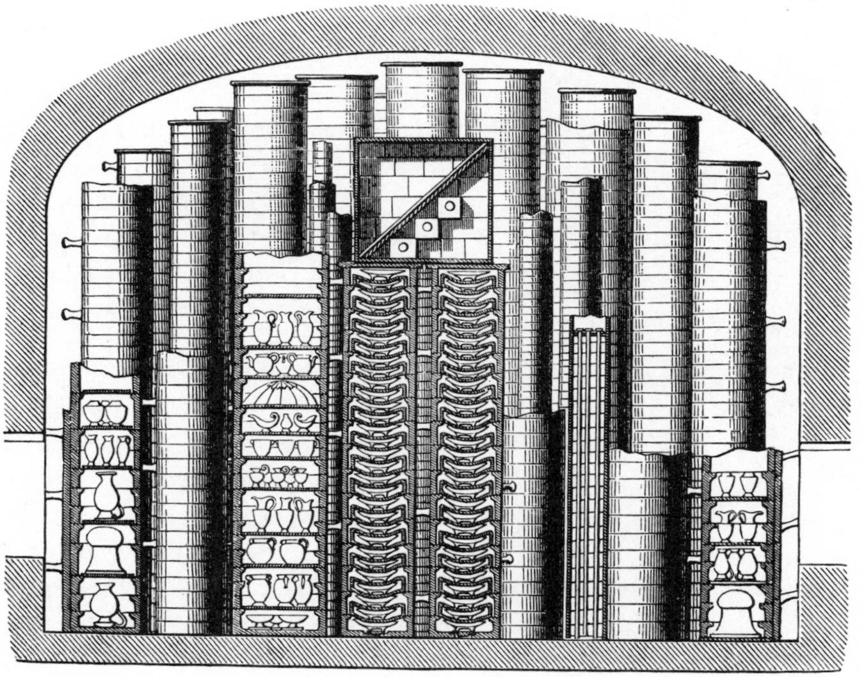

FIGURE 185—*Section of a porcelain kiln as charged at Sèvres, showing the use of saggars to prevent the smoke from coming into contact with the ware.*

with William Cookworthy, the first use of it in soft-paste having been made at Lowdin's Bristol Glass-house founded about 1700. This glass-house was an experimental one; it was transferred to Worcester in 1752 and with it the use of the new material. The resulting paste, which had a greenish tinge, was used till 1823, products of the period 1768–83 being characterized by a high proportion of steatite. On this ware an exceptionally fine glaze, containing a trace of cobalt, was brushed instead of being applied by dipping. Transfer-printing was introduced early, first in over-glaze black, red, and purple, and later (1756) in under-glaze blue (p 354).

To sum up the history of ceramic developments in England, the principal centres for delft were Lambeth, Bristol, and Liverpool; for true porcelain, Bristol, Plymouth, and New Hall (Shelton); for soft-paste, Bow, Chelsea, Derby, Lowestoft, and Longton Hall; for soapstone-paste, Worcester, Caughley, and Liverpool. The manufacture of bone-china started at Bow, spread to the other soft-paste potteries, and in time became the standard English paste, thus giving England a distinctive place in the history of European ceramics. These latter developments, many of which took place on the threshold of the industrial revolution, were, however, none of them in the direct line of ceramic evolution from the small pot-houses to the great factories such as those organized by Wedgwood and Spode. To this industrial evolution we now turn.

FIGURE 186—*Placing the saggars in the biscuit kiln. These kilns were 12 to 14 ft high and had eight fireplaces.*

VIII. THE EXPANSION OF THE INDUSTRY IN STAFFORDSHIRE

Few, if any, of the English potteries so far mentioned were advantageously situated with regard either to raw materials or to timber, and it was where fuel and clay were found in reasonably close proximity that the great industrial expansion of pottery manufacture took place. Just as with other contemporary industries, potting was influenced by the timber famine of the early eighteenth century, which in time made a shift to the coalfields inevitable. Not only did the need for coal determine the ultimate location of the great potteries, its adoption also brought in its train such technical changes as the necessity for firing wares in saggars (figures 185 and 186), which prevented the combustion products of coal from coming into contact with the ware in the oven.

The district of England in which pottery manufacture expanded most considerably was north Staffordshire, a region favoured by the occurrence of many kinds of clay, adequate supplies of coal, and an ancient potting tradition. Even in the late sixteenth century a considerable trade was carried on from Burslem and Hanley with ware made from local red-burning clay glazed with galena. Output in the early days consisted in the main of jars, bottles, and butter-pots, fired with coal dug by the potters themselves. About 1680 a second method of glazing became available when salt glazing was introduced into England from the continent, where it had been known in the Rhineland and the Low Countries since the beginning of the sixteenth century. It was introduced, it is said, although the attribution is doubtful, by David and John Philip Elers, two potters of Saxon stock who are reputed to have come to England from Delft with William of Orange. There are thus two lines of evolution, lead-glazed wares, and the salt-glazed. On the common brown clay, however, neither lead nor salt gave a product with the appeal of oriental porcelain or European delft.

The first step towards a white-bodied ware was the utilization by Thomas Miles of a pale Shelton clay to give a crude whitish stoneware. Experiment continued, and by adopting the Derbyshire crouch clay already in use in Nottingham, a brownish ware, known as crouch ware, was evolved. It dates from the end of the seventeenth century and was of a brownish or drab colour. All these wares were given a single firing which lasted for about three days, on the last of which, if salt-glaze was being produced, salt was thrown into the red-hot kiln. In the heat of the kiln, the salt reacts with the silica and alumina of the clay to form a coating of fusible glass on the surface of the hot primary body.

To the Elers brothers are also due the first attempts to improve form and finish, and to establish new standards of excellence in Staffordshire. Originally they had been silversmiths and it was probably to their previous skill in metal-working that their desire for refinement in ceramics may be attributed. According to A. H. Church the careful attention they gave to the levigation of the clay, combined with the fact that they turned the clay bodies on the lathe before they were fired, and their introduction of salt-glazing, were 'precious legacies to the Pottery District'; their technique brought about a complete revolution in potting methods in England.

From crouch ware, a white-dipped or slip-ware was evolved by treating the insides of vessels with a slip of white pipe-clay. This ware was in great demand from about 1710–40. Not only was the slip used to coat the whole inner surface of the vessel, but by slip-trailing or applying thinned-down clays of different colours, as in icing a cake, decorative effects of considerable charm were produced. This ancient technique, practised considerably in Kent, perhaps received its most perfect expression in the hands of two potters, probably father and son, both named Thomas Toft, of Leek, Staffordshire, in the second half of the seventeenth century (plate 19 A). Thirty-four of their dishes are known, two of them dated 1671 and 1677; they have been described as follows:

They were made from common clay, presumed to have been dug in the locality where the Tofts worked, to which fine sand may have been added. The pieces were wheel thrown and turned. All the decoration was executed on the ware before firing while the clay was still moist. A coating of white slip was first applied over the entire upper surface of the dish to provide a clay coating of pleasant colour and texture. The design was then drawn in by means of a trailer, resembling an oil-can, from which the liquid slip was directed. The initial outline of the design was executed in a dark brown slip made by colouring the red slip with an oxide of iron or manganese. Such decoration appears far too spidery in character unless enhanced by broad masses of another colour, and for this reason Toft filled in the main passages of decoration with slip made from different clay which fired an orange-brown colour. Finally white dots were added to the original dark brown outlines, producing a certain scintillating effect that enhances the whole design. . . .

When the decoration had been completed a coating of pulverised galena, or similar lead compound, was dusted over the ware, which was then ready for firing. There is evidence that this type of pottery was fired to 1050° C.[1]

This was a further step in the direction of a light coloured ware as a substitute for the oriental porcelain or European tin-enamelled delft which, in London and the foreign markets, was then the most sought-after table furnishing. That pipe-clay, in the first instance, was used only as a slip was almost certainly a matter of cost, since it had to be brought to the potteries from a distance, for example from Bideford in Devon, no light undertaking in the absence of cheap transport.

So obvious, however, were the advantages of this white-burning clay that it was soon incorporated in a mixture with fine grit and sand, and a light coloured stoneware was made for the first time. Its invention is commonly associated with the name of John Astbury (1688?–1743). This fine salt-glazed stoneware (plate 19 C) enjoyed great popularity from about 1710 to 1780, its evolution contributing greatly to the subsequent prosperity of The Potteries.[2] In thin pieces it was translucent and its hardness rivalled that of quartz (Mohs's scale 7): it was, indeed, almost a porcelain. Macquer described it as having 'all the essential properties of the finest Japanese porcelain', and for many years it was a fashionable substitute for that ware, particularly as it brought some of the grace and amenities of the well-to-do within the reach of those less wealthy. It is interesting to note that the production of the other substitute for imported porcelain, namely tin-enamelled earthenware, never gained a footing in The Potteries. Instead, the continued striving towards a light-coloured body, and the invention of white salt-glaze ware, anticipated one of the major changes in the whole history of ceramics. This was the abandonment, at the behest of fashion, of the common red

[1] Cooper, Ronald. 'The Pottery of Thomas Toft.' Leeds and Birmingham, 1952.

[2] The Staffordshire potteries are mostly grouped in the six towns forming the county borough of Stoke-on-Trent, and this district is commonly described as The Potteries or the Five Towns.

and buff clays rendered white by slip or tin-enamel, and their replacement by a mixture of white-burning clay and calcined flint, giving a ware that was white throughout the whole body.

The practical utilization of ground flint (silica) in the ceramic body is also attributed to John Astbury. It was effected by him in 1720, although the idea had been mooted about 1698 by John Dwight (1637?–1703) of Fulham, secretary to the bishop of Chester, and himself the owner of patents for the 'mystery of transparent earthenware' dated 1671 (B.P. No 164) and 1684 (B.P. No 234), against the infringement of which he took action against the Elers and three of the Wedgwoods. Two of Dwight's notebooks, covering experiments from 1689–98, were discovered at Fulham in 1869. Thomas Heath of Lane Delph is also said to have made the suggestion before Astbury. The flint was calcined and ground to a fine powder (plate 20 A); the first flint-mill was built at Hanley in 1726. Added to native or imported clay, it lightened the colour of the fired vessel and gave it a more refractory body, in consequence of which it could be fired at a higher temperature and so rendered harder. The body was finished by glazing with salt or lead, of which the latter became ultimately the more important.

FIGURE 187—*Flint-crushing. After being crushed, the flint was sieved and mixed with water.*

There was, however, a disadvantage in the industrial use of ground flint. It was in time realized that flint-grinding had introduced a very dangerous new industrial hazard into pottery-making. At first the flint was calcined in kilns and ground by hand in primitive stamp-mills or in large iron mortars, after which the fine powder was sieved through lawn (compare figures 187, 188). The result was that, in spite of all precautions, silica got into the lungs of the operatives. This led Thomas Benson to apply his knowledge of colour-grinding to the problem and to take out a patent in 1726 for grinding under water (B.P. No 487). Initially the grinding was effected by iron wheels and balls, but traces of iron contaminated the flint and coloured the ware in which it was used, so in 1732 Benson took out a further patent covering the use of stone balls instead of iron ones (B.P.

No 536) (figure 189). The large potteries set up their own mills, while the smaller Staffordshire establishments bought their flint as slip from mills in the Moddershall valley that specialized in this trade. These mills, together with the extended use of the lathe in the production of more accurately finished wares, mark the advent of the demand for mechanical power in the pottery industry, to be met in due course by the adoption of James Watt's improved steam-engine. It would, however, be an error to suppose that mechanical power was unknown in The Potteries before the introduction of steam. Indeed, water-power was an important prerequisite of a successful pottery: in this respect Whieldon and Wedgwood were favourably placed, and to it may be attributed some of their early successes. Wedgwood employed James Brindley (1716–72)—who was later renowned as the engineer of the Duke of Bridgewater's canals, and whose brother John had a pottery at Longport—to construct flint-mills. Many generations were to pass, however, before power was to be applied to the throwing-process and to the manufacture of flat and hollow ware.

FIGURE 188—*Flint-grinding. The flints were ground by massive stone rollers and then transferred to vessels containing water, where they were mixed to a cream.*

According to John Thomas:

> Like every industry, pottery, even in the peasant stage, needs raw materials. These must be suitably prepared, or the finished article will be poor. All these peasant potters had raw materials prepared in water-mills. These were often converted corn-mills. These flint water-mills have persisted from the seventeenth century to this day in the potteries.[1]

As changes were made in the basic raw materials, corresponding improvements were introduced in pottery processes generally. Ralph Shaw of Burslem is reputed to have introduced the drying of clay in a shallow kiln heated by flues from an external fire. This eliminated much of the contamination that inevitably accompanied the preparation of clay in the primitive sun-pan. About 1750 Enoch Booth of Tunstall introduced double firing into Staffordshire. A preliminary firing produced the biscuit stage, which was followed, after glaze and decoration had been applied, by the glost or glazing firing. Easier to operate, the double firing began to oust salt-glazing, which suffered from the additional disadvantage

[1] Thomas, John. 'The Pottery Industry and the Industrial Revolution.' *Econ. Hist.*, 3, 399, 1937.

that it was less economical. Among the first to follow Booth in the production of a cream-coloured ware were Ralph and John Baddeley of Shelton, and John Warburton of Hot Lane, Cobridge. Booth also pioneered the glazing of wares with slip instead of merely dusting them before firing with powdered galena. Unfortunately the lead glaze used increased the risks to health. Booth progressively altered his glazing process from a simple dusting with lead ore to dipping in a slip of red- or white-lead with clay and flint, and finally to lead compounds and flint according to William Littler's method. The ware was dipped in this glaze after the biscuit-firing (figure 190). The body of Booth's ware was composed of local clay to which he added white-burning clays from Devon and Dorset, as well as ground flint, as suggested by Astbury. These changes took the evolution of cream-coloured earthenware one stage nearer the form in which it superseded salt-glazed ware and tin-enamelled delft and secured a world market under royal patronage. Production expanded rapidly between 1750 and 1760.

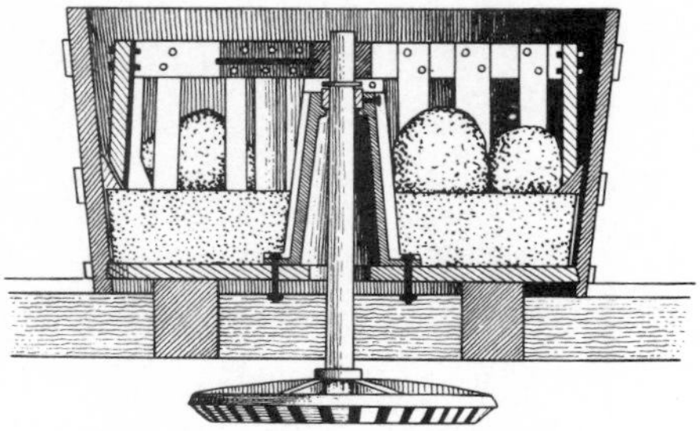

FIGURE 189—*Ball-mill for grinding calcined flints under water. The flint was burnt in a kiln like a lime-kiln and while still hot was quenched in water. The foot of the mill was a large block of chert (a flint-like quartz or siliceous rock), and large stone balls were moved round on it by oak paddles, thus grinding the calcined flints.*

A minor invention that contributed to increased output was the introduction, attributed to Ralph Shaw, of pieces of sharp-edged stoneware to separate vessels during the firing process. Several pieces could thus be stacked one inside the other and fired in the same saggar. This simple device considerably increased output from a given number of ovens.

By 1770 local clays had been abandoned in spite of transport difficulties: Staffordshire was still served by the same roads that had sufficed in the seventeenth century.

> These roads were narrow, rutty lanes, along which hard-working horses and donkeys, muzzled to prevent them from eating the hedges, carried packs or panniers filled with crates of pottery or balls of clay. It is almost incredible that five hundred separate potteries employing 7000 persons could import their clay and export their wares along such routes, for, according to the petition presented to Parliament in 1762, these wares were sent in vast quantities to London, Bristol, Liverpool, and Hull, for despatch to America, the West Indies and almost every port in Europe. The clay and flints came to Liverpool and Hull. From Liverpool they were brought by the Mersey and Weaver to

Winsford in Cheshire; from Hull to Willington in Derbyshire. From Willington and Winsford they were brought on the backs of horses and donkeys to the Five Towns.[1]

The popularity of Enoch Booth's cream-coloured ware led to a further improvement in its quality about 1765, when he adopted a glaze devised, but not

FIGURE 190—*Dipping biscuit or once-fired ware in liquid glaze.*

patented, by John Greatbach, and also when, about 1768, he added china-stone as well as china-clay to the body. It was this improved body that Josiah Wedgwood began to make when he set up as an independent potter.

Improvements were not, however, confined solely to the ceramic bodies and glazes. Ovens increased in size and were repeatedly rebuilt to modified designs in an attempt to secure an easier control of temperatures; and whole banks of ovens in due course replaced the older and more primitive single units. In 1740, John and Thomas Wedgwood invented 'pyrometric beads' which changed colour with rising temperature. Whitehurst (1749), Ellicott (1750), and Smeaton (1754) all made contributions in the same field, and Josiah Wedgwood in-

[1] Hammond, J. L. and B. 'The Rise of Modern Industry' (4th edn.), p. 169. Methuen, London. 1930.

vented the 'pyrometric cones' that have been used by the pottery industry ever since.

The revolution in the potteries consisted in the discovery by constant experiment of new bodies, new glazes, and new methods of decoration; a greater division of labour, a growth of the factory and a development of methods of control, i.e. the beginning of scientific management, cost accounting; the improvement of transportation and the opening up of new markets at home and abroad.[1]

We shall now see how this was effected at the hand of one of the greatest potters of all time, Josiah Wedgwood.

IX. JOSIAH WEDGWOOD

Josiah Wedgwood (1730–95) came of a family already well known in The Potteries. At the age of nine he started work in the family pottery, and after twenty years of work there and in partnership with Thomas Whieldon (1719–95) of Fenton, he set up in 1759 on his own account at Burslem. One of his first successes was the production of a fine green-glazed ware, but he made all varieties of Staffordshire ware. Within a few years he had evolved an improved stoneware from the older cream-coloured ware of Booth and Warburton and, having secured royal patronage, dubbed it Queen's ware. The body consisted of roughly 4 parts of ground flint and some 20 to 24 parts of the whitest Dorset, Devon, or Cornish clays. Following Booth's practice it was fired twice, and glazed with what was virtually flint glass. Production of this fine ware increased very rapidly, and in 1764 Wedgwood moved to larger premises at the Bell House. Queen's ware was easy to manufacture, was as cheap as the other wares then in use, and as a result of Wedgwood's attention to form was of considerable aesthetic appeal even in the almost total absence of applied decoration. Wedgwood having shown the way, the ware was soon being made in a hundred other potteries, and as the years passed it became one of the major products of The Potteries. Every form of table-

FIGURE 191—*Mechanical power was introduced for lathe-turning as the output of the mass-produced articles increased.*

[1] Bladen, V. W. 'The Potteries in the Industrial Revolution.' *Econ. Hist.*, I, 117, 1926.

furnishing was made from it, and in the course of time Queen's ware was in use throughout England, displacing the clumsier delft and also the much older pewter which was then still in use in many districts. With its universal acceptance the full tide of the industrial revolution had come to Staffordshire. Power was required in quantity to turn the lathes on which the refined shapes were finished (figure 191); flint had to be crushed and ground in large quantities; and the various ingredients had to be incorporated mechanically in a homogeneous mix (plate 20 B).

After the legal fight with Richard Champion in 1775 over the china-clay patent (p 341), Wedgwood visited Cornwall in company with John Turner of Lane End. In Cornwall they saw Newcomen engines in operation, and so impressed was Turner with the possibilities of steam-power that, on his return, he installed an engine to pump water back over an existing water-wheel, exactly as Matthew Boulton did at the Soho Manufactory at Birmingham. When Spode took over Turner's pottery, the engine probably passed to him. Wedgwood arranged for James Watt to survey flint-mills at Trentham and Lane End, and in particular directed him to examine the engine and mill at Spode's works. As a result, in 1782 Wedgwood ordered his first steam-engine. It was designed to supply power for grinding flint and enamel colours, to operate a saggar-crusher, and to temper or mix clay. This first order given by Wedgwood was fortunate for Boulton and Watt, since their engines had displaced many of the older Newcomen type in Cornish mines, and Staffordshire was now ripe for mechanization. The market for engines in the mills of Lancashire, and later Yorkshire, developed after the general adoption of mechanical power in The Potteries. In the pottery industry, as elsewhere, the steam-engine changed the whole pattern of activity and led to the evolution of the modern type of factory equipped with power for the preparation of the raw materials, and for facilitating the mechanical operations.

It was at Wedgwood's Etruria that these changes were first put into operation, but it must not be thought that Wedgwood's activities were confined to the scientific management of the production of vast quantities of Queen's ware, and of *objets d'art* for his royal patrons. He was an indefatigable experimenter and freely availed himself of such scientific information as he could get in the search for improved ceramic raw materials. According to John Thomas 'he elevated pottery manufacture from a matter of guess-work and procedure by rule of thumb to a matter of scientific measurement and calculation'.

By the end of the eighteenth century, as a result of Wedgwood's activities and those of many less well known potters, a wide range of ceramics was being produced in Staffordshire, which had become the leading pottery area in the world. Scientific experiment had covered all the readily available refractory materials, and kaolin, china-stone, flint, and bone-ash had found established places. The last quarter of the century saw salt-glazed stoneware, in the production of which Staffordshire had been pre-eminent, give way to fluid-glazed cream-coloured ware. The production of stoneware did not by any means stop, but it was gradually excluded from the homes of the well-to-do, who showed a preference for wares more directly inspired by oriental porcelain. Throughout Europe this preference was met by the production of a true hard-paste porcelain; only in England, with its special tradition of porcelain-making, was the new taste served by the hybrid bone-china (p 341), which became the standard English body. When Josiah Spode II (1754–1827) took over his father's works at Stoke-on-Trent in 1797, he is reputed to have established this standard body by adding both felspar and bone-ash. It is still in use today, since it is easy to work and lends itself to mass-production. Similarly, the composition of Queen's ware today is very much as the first Josiah Wedgwood left it.

In 1725 the output of The Potteries had not reached a value of £15 000, but by 1777 it had increased to £75 000. Ten years later there were no fewer than 200 master-potters with 20 000 employees.

X. TECHNICAL AIDS TO POTTING

There now remains to be discussed the introduction of several techniques, such as pressing and casting, that supplemented the changes already discussed. The first of these is the introduction of moulds. As has been described above, in making a pottery vessel the appropriate clay was initially formed by the potter's hands. In Staffordshire, about 1740–50, this simple form of throwing was supplemented by the use of moulds. The innovation is attributed to Ralph Daniel of Cobridge. The first moulds were of cast metal, from which small vessels of high precision could be stamped. It was soon found, however, that moulds of plaster of Paris had the additional advantage of absorbing moisture from the clay and so expediting the drying of the primary body. Lightly baked clay moulds, called pitcher moulds, were also used for the same reason. These were often cut in intaglio and used to make the small flower motives which were attached with slip in the production of the characteristic wares of Thomas Astbury and Thomas Whieldon. At a higher level of technical competence they were used by Wedgwood in producing his 'jasper' portrait-medallions and other similar pieces (plate 19 B).

The usual technique was to prepare in alabaster a master of the design or article required, and to make a stoneware duplicate or block of this, from which the plaster moulds were subsequently made (plate 19 D). So important was this innovation in promoting the speedy reduplication of a standard design that the block-cutter became one of the most important workers in the pottery industry. Many potters made their blocks themselves, but demand was sufficient for some designers to set up on their own. The most celebrated mould-cutter of his day was Aaron Wood (1717–85). Wood started life with Thomas Wedgwood, and his work had a lasting influence on the style of the moulded Staffordshire wares. Moulding not only called for makers of moulds, but in time caused the 'flat hollow-ware presses' (figure 192) to outnumber the traditional 'throwers'.

FIGURE 192—*Presses for flat hollow-ware such as plates and saucers were introduced to speed up the production of cheaper ware. The balance was to weigh the piece of clay to be pressed, and so standardize the finished product.*

Apart from other advantages, the use of moulds enabled the potters of the industrial revolution to move in the direction of mass-production, so converting the small craft-pottery into the factory. At the same time, moulds introduced a considerable degree of standardization, since each vessel was a copy of the master.

The necessity for increased production similarly led to the invention of a method for the rapid reduplication of decoration. This was effected by transfer-printing, one of England's principal contributions to ceramic technique. As with so many inventions in the ceramic industry, the name of the innovator is not certainly known. It may have been an Irish engraver John Brooks (1720–60), or Simon-François Revenet (1706–74) of Battersea, *c* 1752. Another possible inventor is Robert Hancock (1730–1817), who was associated successively with Battersea, Bow, Worcester, and Caughley. It is clear, however, that the new art was in use by the early 1750s, and by 1756 there was an important printed ware works at Liverpool. Its owners were John Sadler (1720–89) and Guy Green, who claimed that they had invented the transfer-printing process as early as 1749, but no patent in their names has been recorded. Printing was at first in black, red, and purple: under-glaze blue dates from 1756. John Wall (1708–76) was using it at Worcester in 1757, and Wedgwood by 1760.

The technique was to engrave the pattern on a metal plate which was then 'inked' (figure 193); the design was taken up on paper and transferred to the articles to be printed (figure 194). Initially the pattern was applied over-glaze, but after a few years it was being used for under-glaze as well. When stipple engraving replaced line drawing, 'bats' made of sheets of glue were substituted for paper. In bat-printing the design was transferred by a thick oil which was then dusted with colour and fired.

To these cheap yet reliable processes we may attribute the enormous market enjoyed by Staffordshire under-glaze blue landscapes in the early nineteenth century, when England had a clear lead over other European countries in this particular development.

A modification of transfer-printing proper enabled potters to keep pace with the growing demand for their products and yet retain some of the qualities of craft potting. This was the printing of nothing more than a faint outline guide for the artist, who subsequently developed the full pattern by hand-painting. From the 1830s this method was used particularly at Coalport (Coalbrookdale in Shropshire), and at the Rockingham works at Swinton in Yorkshire. Further developments in this field are outside the period under discussion in this chapter.

FIGURE 193—*In transfer-printing the design was first engraved on a copper plate. This was heated and rubbed with a mixture of metallic oxide and oil. The surplus was scraped off and an impression taken on special paper which had been moistened with soap and water.*

In the above discussion numerous ways in which the primary body can be decorated, and made aesthetically pleasing and technically sound, have been described: slip decoration, high-temperature and muffle colours, glazing, printing, and painting. It now remains to say something about decoration in metals, particularly gilding—an indispensable adjunct to the production of many fine ceramic products.

By far the most important of the decorative metals was gold. It was first used in the early eighteenth century in the form of size-gilding; the ware to be decorated was painted with a varnish made of linseed-oil and litharge and the gold leaf was applied to it. Being unfired, the gilt was naturally much weaker than most ceramic decorations and was easily abraded. An improvement was effected by incorporating the gold in a lacquer. In Europe a fired decoration dates from the introduction of honey-gilding. In this process gold leaf mixed with honey was painted on, a method in use throughout the greater part of the eighteenth century. This 'fired gold' was one of Europe's few ceramic contributions to the east.

Yet another method was, it is true, introduced about 1780, but it involved a serious industrial hazard in that it depended on the use of gold amalgam, from which the mercury was driven off in a low-temperature oven, to the detriment of the workers' health.

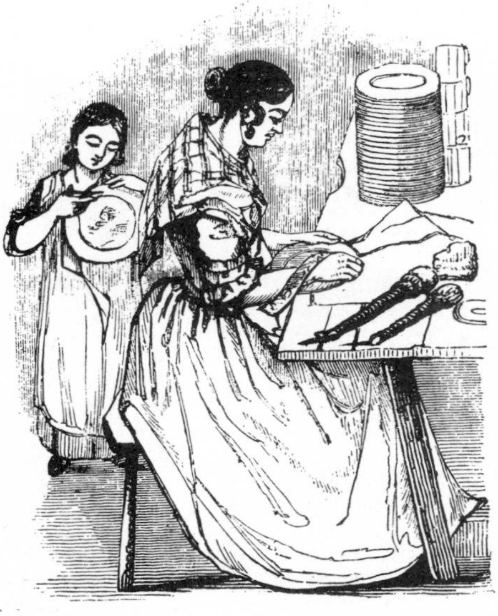

FIGURE 194—*The design was transferred from the paper to the ware by rubbing with a roller. The paper was then washed off in cold water. The ware was heated to drive off the oil, and finally glazed.*

Another process involving the use of metals in the late eighteenth and early nineteenth centuries was the production of lustre wares. Often the avowed intention of the eighteenth-century potter was to imitate a metal article. To do so, pigment containing copper, silver, gold, or platinum was applied over the glaze and the ware was fired in a reducing atmosphere. In Staffordshire, Wedgwood made particular use of this process (*c* 1800), employing the then comparatively new metal platinum. Incidentally, Josiah Wedgwood's only patent (B.P. No 939, 1769) is concerned with encaustic gold bronze. In 1810 Peter Warburton took out a patent for printing in platinum and gold, which was actually one of the earliest industrial uses of platinum.

The gradual multiplication of the processes whereby ceramic products could be produced led, as in other industries, to a marked division of labour. Josiah Wedgwood's Etruria, where the principle of specialization was first introduced, was divided into departments according to the type of ware produced: useful, ornamental, jasper, basalt, and so on. In 1790 some 160 employees were engaged in the 'useful' branch, in the following categories: slip-house, clay-beaters, throwers and their attendant boys, plate makers, dish makers, hollow-ware pressers, turners of flat ware, turners of hollow-ware, handlers, biscuit-oven firemen, dippers, brushers, placers and firemen in the glost oven, girl colour-grinders, painters, enamellers and gilders, and, in addition, coal getters, modellers, mould makers, saggar makers, and a cooper.

This long list emphasizes the contrast between the mechanized production of the textile industry where, from early in the industrial revolution, one operative had been able to concentrate on tending, say, a machine producing simultaneously a large number of threads, and the pottery industry, where, despite mechanical aids, each article has still to be handled many times in the course of production.

BIBLIOGRAPHY

BLADEN, V. W. "The Potteries in the Industrial Revolution." *Econ. Hist.*, **1**, 117, 1926.
BRONGNIART, A. 'Traité des arts céramiques, ou des potteries, considerées dans leurs histoires, leur practique et leur théorie' (2 vols and atlas). Paris. 1844.
BURTON, W. 'A History and Description of English Earthenware and Stoneware.' Cassell, London. 1904.
Idem. 'A History and Description of English Porcelain.' Cassell, London. 1902.
CHURCH, A. H. 'English Earthenware of the 17th and 18th Centuries.' Victoria and Albert Museum Handbook. Wyman, London. 1904.
CLOW, A. and CLOW, NAN L. 'The Chemical Revolution.' Batchworth Press, London. 1952.
FORTNUM, C. D. E. 'Maiolica, Historical Treatise.' Oxford. 1896.
HANNOVER, E. 'Pottery and Porcelain: a Handbook for Collectors' (3 vols, trans. from the Danish edition by B. RACKHAM). Benn, London. 1925.
HARRISON, G. 'Memoir of William Cookworthy . . . By his Grandson.' London. 1854.
HAVARD, H. 'La céramique hollandaise.' Éditions Vivat, Amsterdam. 1909.
HONEY, W. B. 'European Ceramic Art from the end of the Middle Ages to about 1815' (2 vols). Faber & Faber, London. 1949, 1952.
JEWITT, L. 'The Ceramic Art of Great Britain from Prehistoric Times down to the Present Day' (2 vols). London. 1878.
LORD, J. 'Capital and Steam-power, 1750–1800.' King, London. 1923.
MACKENNA, F. S. 'Cookworthy's Plymouth and Bristol Porcelain.' Lewis, Leigh-on-Sea. 1946.
MARRYAT, J. 'History of Pottery and Porcelain, Medieval and Modern.' London. 1857.
PARKES, S. 'Chemical Catechism' (8th ed.). London. 1818.
PLOT, R. 'Natural History of Staffordshire.' Oxford. 1686.
SHAW, S. 'A History of the Staffordshire Potteries, and the Rise and Progress of the Manufacture of Pottery and Porcelain.' Hanley. 1829.
SOLON, M. L. 'Brief History of Old English Porcelain.' Bemrose, London. 1903.
THOMAS, J. "The Pottery Industry and the Industrial Revolution." *Econ. Hist.*, **3**, 399, 1937.
TURNER, W. 'Transfer Printing on Enamels, Porcelain and Pottery.' Chapman & Hall, London. 1907.

12

GLASS

L. M. ANGUS-BUTTERWORTH

I. OPTICAL GLASS

IN the middle years of the eighteenth century both Chester Moor Hall (1703–71) and John Dollond (1706–61) were working on the solution of the optical problems resulting from the dispersion of light that, as Newton realized, always occurs on refraction (vol III, p 233). They found that by combining two types of glass in a single lens the disturbance caused by the formation of differently coloured images could be greatly reduced. The original discovery was made by Moor Hall, but its development was due to Dollond, a practical optician: he apparently learnt of the invention from George Bass, who ground the lenses for Moor Hall's achromatic combination. Following reasoning similar to that advanced in 1695 by David Gregory, Moor Hall became convinced, from a study of the human eye, that achromatic lenses were possible. After various experiments he found, in 1729, two kinds of glass of dispersions sufficiently different to enable him to realize his idea. Accordingly, about 1733, a number of truly achromatic lenses were constructed according to his specifications. The concave component was of flint glass and the convex of crown glass.

Although controversy later arose about the credit for the invention of the achromatic lens, the patent was awarded in 1758 to Dollond after he had read a paper in that year to the Royal Society under the title of 'An Account of some Experiments concerning the different Refrangibility of Light'. The mathematical theory of the achromatic objective was apparently not worked out until later, being published by Samuel Klingenstierna (1689–1785) of Uppsala in 1760. Klingenstierna had written to Dollond in 1755 to tell him that he had doubts about Newton's views on refraction and dispersion and believed further experiment to be desirable.

These discoveries were of great practical value. Until this time the lenses of telescopes and microscopes had been relatively small, and ground from thick crown or plate glass; chromatic aberration severely limited their performance. It was now found that if a convex lens of crown glass was cemented to a concave lens of flint glass, which had a higher refractive index, the chromatic effect was largely absent in the combination. Unfortunately, however, there remained a great lack of suitable glass, partly because the small demand for glass of optical quality meant that the cost of production was very high. It soon became evident that the time was ripe for advances in glass-making technology, and attention was therefore turned in that direction.

A discovery of prime significance in connexion with the manufacture of optical glass was made by Pierre Louis Guinand (1748–1824), a Swiss, at the close of the eighteenth century. His career was remarkable. He began life as a wood-worker, specializing in the making of clock-cases. From this he turned to the then very profitable work of casting bells for clocks. The metal used in bell-founding was stirred during the operation to make it homogeneous, and Guinand had the brilliant idea that in the same way the homogeneity of glass might be improved by stirring it in the crucible while still in the molten state, and that in this way better glass for making lenses might be obtained.

Guinand began to take an interest in optical glass as early as 1768, when he undertook small-scale experimental foundings. At the start, his methods did not differ from those of his contemporaries, and success eluded him. He built his first full-scale furnace in 1775, but as the stirring device had not yet occurred to him little progress could be made. It was not until the summer of 1798, after thirty years of effort, that Guinand first used a stirrer. The original form was mushroom-shaped, and was not fully effective. Other patterns followed, and in 1805 he devised the type that became universally adopted, namely a hollow cylinder of burnt fireclay, moved through the molten glass by means of a hook-ended iron rod.

The value of Guinand's discovery lay in the fact that it helped to solve many of the intractable problems associated with the making of optical glass, which calls for a higher degree of homogeneity than any other kind. If it is not of the same composition throughout, its refractive power is variable and a distorted image is formed. Thus in a flint glass—of which the essential constituents are silica, lead oxide, and potash—the relatively high density of the lead oxide causes it to be unevenly distributed through the molten material. This variation may cause veins or striae to be present, and no control of the defect was possible until the introduction of stirring.

The chief advantage of stirring was that it enabled much higher proportions of relatively heavy materials to be used in the batch mixtures, and this in turn ultimately led to a great extension of the range of composition available for optical glass. Another advantage of stirring the molten metal was that, if the operation was long continued, it became possible to release very completely the air-bubbles generated during the founding. In this way the proportion of light transmitted was increased, because previously some had been scattered and dispersed at the surface of the bubbles.

Guinand's own resources being limited, he established contact with the German manufacturer Utzschneider, founder of the Munich optical institute, and agreed to produce lenses for him. For this purpose he removed to Benediktbeuern in Bavaria, and in conjunction with Joseph von Fraunhofer (1787–1826), who was acting as Utzschneider's manager, he made considerable progress in perfecting the stirring process. Guinand returned to Switzerland in 1814.

The stirring process remained a secret one, but glass-manufacturers in a number of countries were anxious to learn details of it, especially after the death of Guinand in 1824. In France, in 1827, Georges Bontemps, a glass-maker, and J. N. Lerebours, an optician, agreed to purchase the secret from Henri Guinand, the eldest son of the inventor, for 3000 francs. Trial melts were made at the Bontemps factory at Choisy-le-Roi, and by the following year good lenses were being produced.

In England it was not until 1837 that Lucas Chance, of the Chance Brothers glass company at Birmingham, made an agreement with Bontemps to acquire particulars of his manufacturing technique. Bontemps was paid immediately a fee of 3000 francs, the same amount that he himself had paid Henri Guinand, and was to receive five-twelfths of the profits resulting from the business. Chance took out an English patent for the Guinand process in 1838, but for various reasons the invention was not fully exploited for a further decade.

In 1848 Bontemps, by then the most celebrated glass-technologist of the day, had to leave France because of the revolution. He made an agreement with Chance Brothers to devote himself exclusively to their service, and in particular 'to carry out the manufacture of Optical glass in accordance with Lucas Chance's patent of 1838'. A new plant was built for him, and in a short time the firm was producing optical glass of a very high standard in the form of 'hard crown' and 'dense flint' for telescopes, and 'soft crown' and 'light flint' for camera lenses. By 1849 London opticians were reporting that the Chance flint glass was superior even to Swiss flint, not being so easily altered by the atmosphere. In 1850 glass was sent to a number of the principal opticians in Germany and Austria, and from that time onwards steady improvements were effected in the size and quality of the lenses made.

While the main line of advance in the manufacture of optical glass has now been traced, reference should be made to the work in this connexion of Michael Faraday (1791–1867). In 1824 the Royal Society appointed a committee to consider the improvement of optical glass, especially such as would be suitable for telescope objectives. It was proposed to carry out investigations on the melting of optical glass, and Faraday took charge of this undertaking, with the assistance of Sir John Herschel, who was to determine the refractive indices, and G. Dollond (1774–1852), who was to make up the glass into lenses.

When Faraday began his investigations the glass-melting was done at the Falcon glass works of Green and Pellatt (plate 21 B). This proved inconvenient to Faraday, however, as the works was three miles away from the Royal Institution. Accordingly, in 1827, a small furnace was built at the Institution, and during the following two years Faraday devoted much of his time to the work. He left careful records of this research, which was discontinued in 1830 when supplies of optical glass began to be more freely available from other sources.

The Herschels, father and son, were greatly interested in lenses in connexion with their astronomical work. The father, Francis William Herschel (1738–1822) was a native of Hanover, a kingdom which during his lifetime was still united to the British Crown; he made four surveys of the sky of the northern hemisphere with instruments of his own construction. The son, Sir John Herschel (1792–1871), who co-operated with Faraday, extended the surveys to the southern sky.

In the first half of the nineteenth century two men were responsible, in the main, for the advances that were made in the art of optical glass manufacture, namely Fraunhofer in Germany, and William Vernon Harcourt (1789–1871) in England.

Joseph von Fraunhofer was born at Straubing in Bavaria, and at the age of twelve was apprenticed to a glass cutter and polisher at Munich. He became the manager of the optical institute at Benediktbeuern in 1818. In conjunction with Guinand he did valuable work in extending the range of dense flint and crown glasses. This investigation was on well established lines, and did not include the use of any new fluxes, but spectrometric examination of the glasses produced showed that in two cases there was decided diminution of the secondary spectrum.

Fraunhofer also spent much time on the improvement of optical instruments. He invented ingenious machines for polishing lenses and mirrors without altering their curvatures, a spherometer, a heliometer, and a micrometer. He produced some of the finest object glasses of the early nineteenth century, including the 9½-in objective of the Dorpat equatorial.

Vernon Harcourt devoted more than a quarter of a century to experiments on the composition of optical glass, making 166 trial meltings. He was greatly handicapped by lack of proper equipment and by the necessity of working on a small scale, but was finally able to produce two nearly flawless disks of titanium glass and two of borate glass. His work demonstrated the possibility of abolishing the secondary spectrum.

II. MIRRORS

The earliest mirrors were of copper, bronze, or brass. Mirrors of glass were being made at Venice at the beginning of the fourteenth century (vol III, p 238), but their manufacture was not introduced into England until early in the seventeenth century. In 1623 Sir Robert Mansell (1573–1656), in applying for a renewal of his general glass-making patent, claimed to have brought from abroad experts to make Murano crystalline glasses, spectacle glasses, and mirror glasses, the last two being new businesses. He further claimed that he then had 500 Englishmen engaged in 'making, grinding, polishing and foyling looking glasses'. Forty years later, in 1663, the Duke of Buckingham, in a petition to Charles II, asked for a further renewal of the patent, with a clause therein 'for the sole makinge glasse-plates, glasses for coaches and other glasse plates'.

In the manufacture of mirrors the first stage was preparation of the polished plate glass (plate 21 A), used also for other purposes and described elsewhere (p 368). As regards the 'silvering', the process used throughout the eighteenth century was the one using tin and mercury discovered by the Venetians. The glass plate, after being polished on both sides, was laid on a perfectly flat table or base, usually of stone and of great strength and solidity. As the mercury used was very costly, the table had a raised edge so that none of it could escape, and guttering leading to receptacles so that as much as possible of it could be recovered.

After being carefully cleaned, the upper surface of the glass was covered with sheets of tinfoil, which were rubbed down smooth. Mercury was then poured on, some of it at once forming an amalgam with the tin. Part of the excess mercury having been run off, a woollen cloth was spread over the whole surface and square iron weights were applied. A day and a night were allowed for setting, after which the weights and cloth were removed. The glass was then taken to a wooden table which could be set at a gradually increasing inclination. The object of this was to allow such mercury as had remained unamalgamated to drain completely away. The draining was allowed to continue for about twelve days. In the final product only a film of amalgam remained, coating the glass and adhering perfectly to it.

The mercurial process is still used to a small extent for the reproduction of 'antique' mirrors. Apart from this limited application, however, it became obsolete about 1840, when the chemical deposition of silver was introduced. In its early form this method of making mirrors consisted of treating the glass with an ammoniacal solution of a silver salt, such as silver nitrate, to which tartaric acid and sugar-candy had been added.

Greater care began to be taken to see that the plates used had surfaces that were truly flat and parallel, in order to avoid the distortion visible, for example,

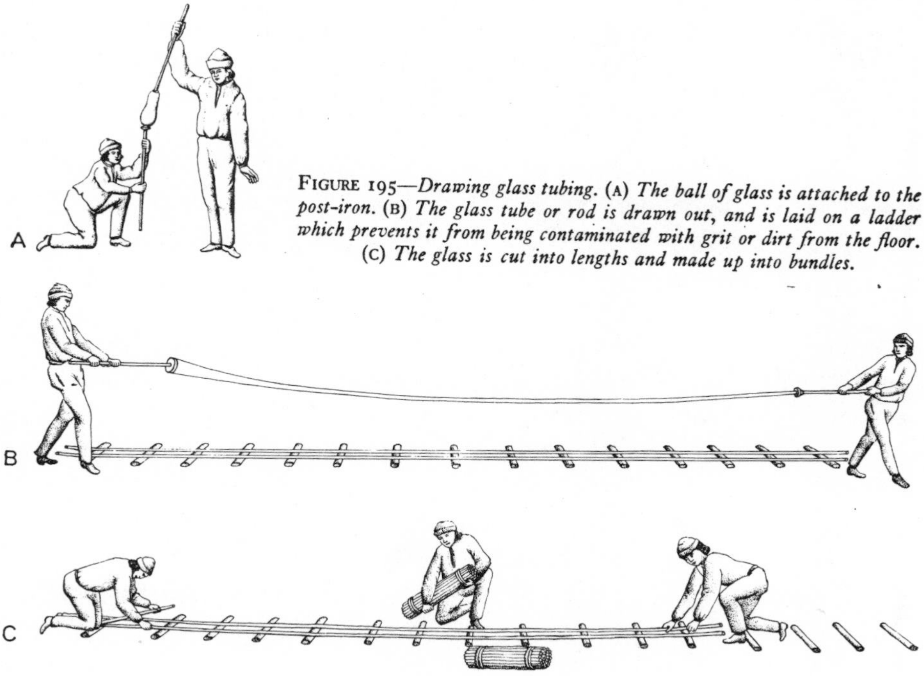

FIGURE 195—*Drawing glass tubing.* (A) *The ball of glass is attached to the post-iron.* (B) *The glass tube or rod is drawn out, and is laid on a ladder which prevents it from being contaminated with grit or dirt from the floor.* (C) *The glass is cut into lengths and made up into bundles.*

in the Galerie des Glaces at Versailles. The layer of silver deposited was very thin and delicate, and therefore had to be well protected. This was done by giving it a coating of shellac, followed by a backing of red lead, turpentine, and japan gold-size. This method continued until the introduction of copper coating in recent times.

The size of mirrors was limited by that of the blown or cast glass plates from which they were made, and until the close of the eighteenth century it was necessary to build up large wall mirrors in sections. Where the plates joined they were sometimes serrated for security; in other cases the sections had between them strips of wood supporting metal strips that overlapped the glass and held it in position—the wood was below the joint and the metal above it. The plates frequently had their edges bevelled by hand with pumice-stone, thus increasing the decorative effect,

III. GLASS TUBING AND ROD

Glass was considered such difficult material to handle in the molten state that mechanization was introduced later than in most industries (vol V, ch 28). During the early part of the industrial revolution no attempt was made to draw glass tubing and rod mechanically, and the traditional method of drawing by hand accordingly remained standard practice (figure 195).

FIGURE 196—*'Glory-hole.' A ball of glass is shown inserted into the reheating furnace. While manipulating the gathering of molten metal, the glass-maker supports his blow-iron on an iron stand.*

The process consisted of taking a gathering of glass from the crucible on a blow-iron. As gathered, the gob of glass was roughly spherical, and had to be rolled on a small iron table or marver[1] to give it a symmetrical and slightly conical shape. When hollow tubing was required the glass-maker blew air down the blow-iron, but when solid glass rod was needed the blowing was omitted.

If the draught of tubing or rod was to be long or heavy the first gathering needed to be coated with two or three layers of fresh glass to build up the quantity of metal needed, and between each gather the ball had to be marvered afresh. During these operations the glass lost heat and tended to become too stiff to work. A subsidiary furnace or 'glory-hole' (figure 196) was thus provided in which the ball could be reheated. The ancillary furnaces were fired originally with beech-wood and the like, but later with wood mixed with cobs of coal.

When reheated, the glass, retaining its symmetrical marvered form, was mounted on an iron post carried by an assistant. The gathering of glass, in its compact cylindrical form, was now supported at both ends and was drawn out by the tube-drawer, who walked backwards from the post-holder (figure 195 A, B), usually a youth. During the draw the glass was twisted slowly, and by intermittent blowing the operator maintained the air-cavity in the tubing and kept it circular.

[1] The marver was so called because when first used in France the top was of marble (*marbre*).

While being drawn the tubing was gauged by a third man armed with calipers. This assistant noted when the tube had reached the required diameter at a particular point, and then cooled it by flapping the air near it with a sheet of leather, thus causing it to set. In this way the gauger followed the drawer at a short distance, repeating his gauging and cooling operation as required. Glass rod was made in exactly the same way, except that the gathering was on a solid iron.

Drawing tubes by hand was highly skilled work, but by varying the size and shape of the gob, and by regulating the speed of drawing, an experienced man could draw tubes of various diameters with a fair measure of accuracy. Much depended upon having the glass at just the right temperature, and the drawer needed to have instinctive appreciation of the glass he happened to be working with, the behaviour of which varied according to its composition. The gathering might be from 4 to 8 inches in diameter, and from 6 to 12 inches in length. From this could be drawn tubing of $\frac{3}{32}$ to 6 inches in outside diameter, and of lengths up to 150 ft for the smaller diameters.

IV. CROWN WINDOW-GLASS

The crown window-glass process was the earlier of the two chief methods of making sheet glass by hand (figure 197), and was in common use until shortly after the end of the eighteenth century. The procedure was somewhat elaborate, the work being shared among a team of as many as ten men and boys. The earlier and simpler stages of the operation were undertaken by the younger members of the group, thus permitting the senior men to concentrate upon the stages where more skill was required, and at the same time giving the boys experience in handling the metal. Because the glass was blown, it was necessarily thin, in contrast to cast plate glass (p 368).

After the glass had been founded overnight and brought to a liquid state, it had to be cooled before working. When cooling had reduced it to a consistency something like that of treacle it could be gathered on a blow-iron. As clarity and transparency were important, a fireclay ring was floated in the melting-crucible to keep back scum or stringy metal. An assistant glass-blower dipped his pipe inside this ring, thus ensuring that he gathered only the best of the glass.

The quantity of the glass required being considerable, it could not be taken from the crucible in one operation. The first gathering after removal was accordingly cooled and a second gathering taken upon it by another assistant. Meanwhile the pipe had become too hot to handle with comfort, and so was trundled in a trough of cold water, care being taken not to splash the ball of glass. Marvering of the glass followed, the ball being rolled on an iron table or in a hollowed block of wood until it acquired a conical form.

The marvering was a two-handed operation. While a man rotated the pipe, a boy blew down it to expand the globe. As the glass was setting rapidly during this work it had to be reheated from time to time according to the judgement of the operator. Finally, when the globe was ready a pontil or solid iron rod was

FIGURE 197—*General view of a glass-house, showing the manufacture of crown glass. In the background is seen a disk of glass which has been 'flashed' from the molten metal. Note the protective masks.*

attached to it by a nodule of the molten metal directly opposite the original blow-iron, which was now broken free. The removal of the blowpipe left in the sphere an opening with slightly jagged edges.

In the final and most spectacular stage a highly skilled glass-maker took the globe and spun it in a reheating furnace. The man wore a veil or mask because great heat was required and he therefore had to stand very close to the furnace. The glass was rotated rapidly and vigorously. When it was reduced to a very soft and semi-molten state, a moment came at which centrifugal force caused it to flash into a flat disk, still adhering to the pontil by the boss in the centre (figure 197).

After flashing, the glass-maker had instantly to remove the disk from the reheating furnace. The thin, brilliant disk of fire-polished glass being still very soft when removed, he had to keep whirling it at the end of his pontil until it became cooler and stiffer. An assistant then cut it free from the pontil with shears, so that it could be taken to a kiln for annealing.

Every sheet made by this method had in the middle the bull's-eye or 'crown' from which it took its name, this being the point where the pontil had been attached. The sheets were comparatively small, and as they were circular the size was still further reduced if they were cut square after making. The sizes of the pieces of glass yielded by this process were thus severely restricted.

After the 1830s crown glass became obsolete except for a few special purposes. A limited amount, for example, continued to be made for the small slides upon which microscope specimens were mounted, as the quality of the glass was considered to render it particularly suitable for this purpose.

V. MAKING SHEET GLASS BY THE HAND-CYLINDER PROCESS

In the early years of the nineteenth century the hand-cylinder process was already well established in both Lorraine and the German states. This method of manufacturing sheet glass was brought to England in 1832 by Lucas Chance (p 360), with the help of Georges Bontemps of Choisy-le-Roi and a team of foreign workmen.

The making of sheet glass by the hand-cylinder process was essentially a development from the crown glass method. From 20 to 40 lb of glass was gathered on a particularly strong blow-iron about 5 ft long, the weight being regulated according to the size of the sheet required. After preparation of a globe of glass, as in the crown method, a further process was introduced. This consisted of swinging the hot glass in a trench up to 10 ft deep. While being swung the globe assumed an elongated form, the blower keeping it inflated meanwhile.

The cylinders produced were normally 12 to 20 inches in diameter and 50 to 70 inches in length. To form them into flat sheets two methods were adopted, the removal of the ends being the first stage in each. In one case the resulting cylinder was allowed to cool somewhat and was then slit lengthwise with a diamond tool. Reheating in a flattening kiln then caused it to fall into a flat sheet. A more careful method was to reheat the cylinder after slitting, and then pass it to a flattening-stone covered with glass, where it opened into a rather wavy sheet. A flattener rubbed the sheet with a *polissoir* or block of wood mounted on an iron rod, after which it was taken to a kiln for annealing.

The operations called for great skill and judgement on the part of the glass-makers. The gatherer had to gauge just how much metal was needed to make cylinders which, when split and flattened, would give sheets of a given size and thickness. The blower had to manipulate the molten metal by swinging and rotating it so as to ensure even thickness throughout the cylinder as well as correct overall size. For fashioning a sheet of glass in this way five types of skilled workers were required: gatherers, blowers, snappers, cutters, and flatteners. The sheets were larger than those of crown glass and were free from the boss in the centre, besides being lower in cost.

FIGURE 198—*Casting and running plate glass. c 1780.*

In 1839 Sir James Chance (1814–1902) invented a method of grinding and polishing sheet glass, thus giving it the brilliance and transparency of plate glass that had been similarly treated. The patent declared that his object was 'to remove the irregularities of surface without grinding away irregularities arising from any bending or curves which may exist in the general substance of the glass'.

This aim was achieved by supporting the sheet during operations upon a bed of moistened leather mounted upon slate, and causing it to adhere by applying suction. The adequately firm but not rigid background enabled the finishing-work to be done without the strain that was otherwise imposed through the more or less bent or buckled sheet being pressed against a hard, flat base, and also without the risk of grinding the glass thin in places.

VI. CAST PLATE GLASS

Casting was first introduced into France in 1688 when a company was given a monopoly of the home market (vol III, ch 9). The manufacture eventually settled at St-Gobain in Picardy, where the wood necessary for fuel was plentiful. By 1760 the output exceeded 1000 tons a year. A great part of the demand was for glazing windows—a practice then becoming increasingly popular among the wealthy—and carriages. In England the manufacture of plate glass by casting was introduced by Huguenots in 1773, though there had been an abortive attempt in 1691. In 1776 a British cast plate glass company began operations with a works covering about 30 acres at Ravenhead, near St Helens in Lancashire. The great casting-hall, 113 yds long by 50 yds wide, was one of the largest industrial buildings of the period. The technical processes were for a very short time under the control of Philip Besnard, but he was very soon replaced by Jean B. F. Giraux de la Bruyère (1739–87), who had received his training in France; and at the start most of the experienced workmen also were French. This firm had a very

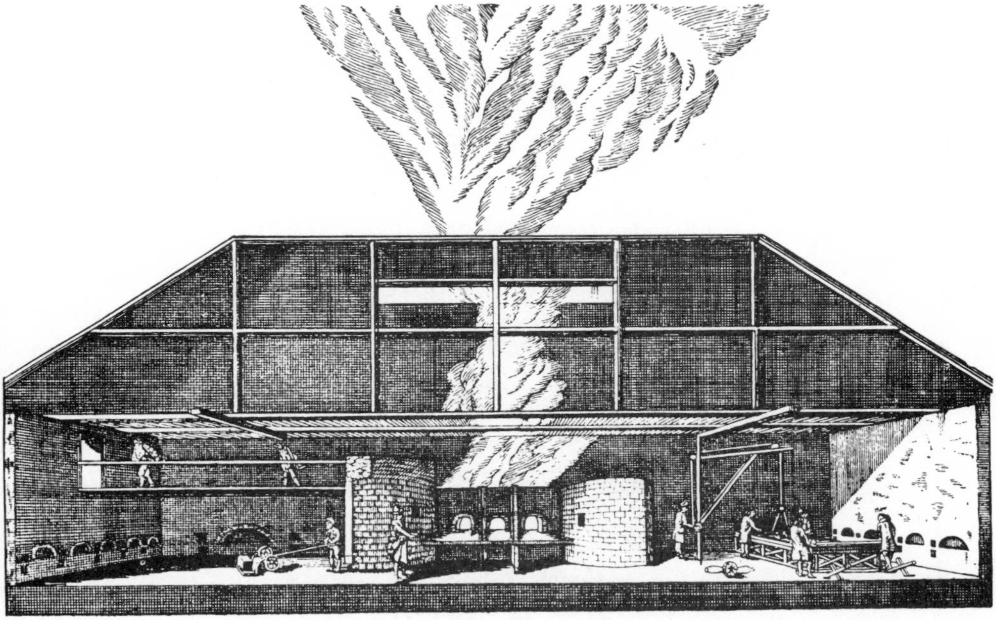

FIGURE 199—*Plate glass factory of c 1800. Smoke from the wood-fired furnace escaped through a vent in the roof. On the right is the casting-table, with the crane for inverting the container of molten glass. Along each side of the glass-house are the openings to the annealing chambers. On the left is a man with a hand-trolley for removing the hot container after it has been emptied.*

unpropitious infancy and in its early years nearly failed, the main difficulties being poor management, heavy excise duty, and—above all—a very high rate of breakage. Complete reorganization, and the removal by war of competition from St-Gobain, eventually brought it great prosperity.

The French system of casting plate glass was quite different from the method of blowing it (figure 198, and vol III, pp 238–9). Casting had the advantage of enabling larger plates to be produced. The largest plates that could be made by blowing were 50 in by 30 in, while by casting it was possible to obtain plates 160 in by 80 in. A plate glass factory of about 1800 is shown in figure 199.

At Ravenhead the first task was to decide upon a batch-mixture which would produce a good plate of glass, capable of resisting the action of air, water, and the common mineral acids. The following was chosen:

	lb
Siliceous sand, washed and sifted	720
Alkaline salt	450
Quicklime, slaked and sifted	80
Nitre	25
Cullet, or broken plate glass	425
	1700

It was calculated that this mixture would give an average of 1200 lb of good glass.

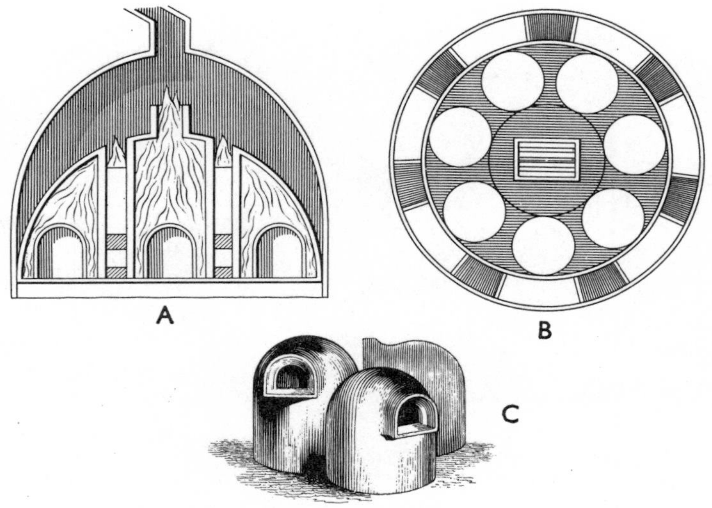

FIGURE 200—(A) *Section of the interior of a glass-furnace, and* (B) *ground plan;* (C) *covered pots for melting glass.*

The materials were prepared for use by a process known as fritting. This consisted of calcining to a sufficient extent to drive off moisture and to reduce the whole to a uniform mixture of paste-like consistency. The resulting frit was cut into square cakes, which were fed into the crucibles at intervals. This rather tedious operation was necessary because the frit was more bulky than the fused metal, and thus no new charge could be added until the preceding one had melted down. During the melting process an opaque white scum, known as glass-gall, rose to the surface, and had to be carefully skimmed away.

The materials were fused in earthern pots or crucibles standing in a high-temperature furnace (figure 200). These crucibles had to be very carefully prepared in order to withstand not only the intense heat of the fire but the solvent action of the molten glass. They were commonly made of five parts of the finest Stourbridge clay in a raw state, and one part of 'grog' or burnt clay, the latter being old crucibles ground to powder.

Until after the middle of the eighteenth century both plate and sheet glass

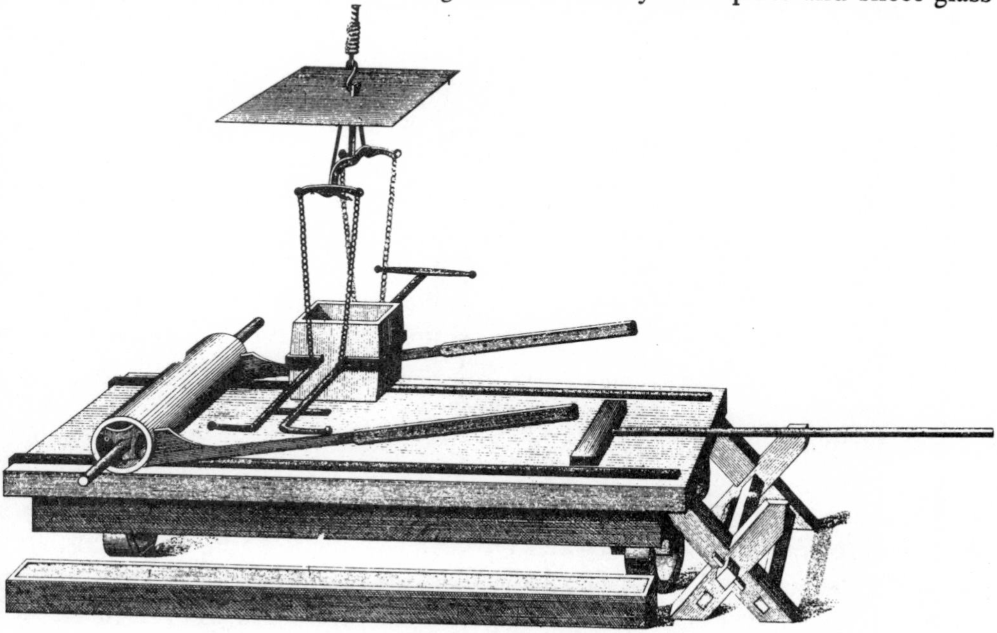

FIGURE 201—*An early form of casting-table, with the roller used for flattening the mass of molten metal. Above the table is suspended the crucible holding the glass; this container is in an iron framework with handles on either side to permit pouring.*

were founded in furnaces fired with wood. In 1763 attempts were made at the St-Gobain works to substitute coal for wood, but with such little success that as late as 1819 this French company purchased further large forests to maintain their normal fuel supplies. By 1829 the company had succeeded in melting the glass in a coal furnace, but it still needed fining in a wood furnace. At Ravenhead, Robert Sherbourne, who was appointed manager in 1792, introduced 'caped' or covered pots (figure 200 (C)) for use with coal fuel; by this means the spotting of glass by furnace soot was avoided.

The original casting-tables at Ravenhead, like those in France, were made of copper supported by solid masonry. It was considered that copper would have less effect in discolouring the molten glass than iron, but the copper was found liable to crack when the mass of molten glass was poured upon it. When this happened the tables were rendered useless—a serious matter, for great labour and expense were incurred in grinding and polishing them.

About 1843, after several accidents of this kind, the British Plate Glass Company—as it was known after reincorporation in 1798—made a trial of cast iron, although it was hard to obtain an iron plate of the dimensions required. They succeeded in casting one 15 ft long by 9 ft wide and 6 in thick. This massive table, with its frame, weighed 14 tons, and it was necessary to construct a carriage to convey it from the iron-foundry to the glass-house. It was afterwards mounted on castors (cf figure 201), so that, unlike the stationary copper tables, it could be moved to the mouths of the different annealing chambers (cf figures 199 and 203). These ovens, placed in two rows on each side of the glass-house, were each 16 ft wide by 40 ft deep, and had their floors exactly level with the casting-table.

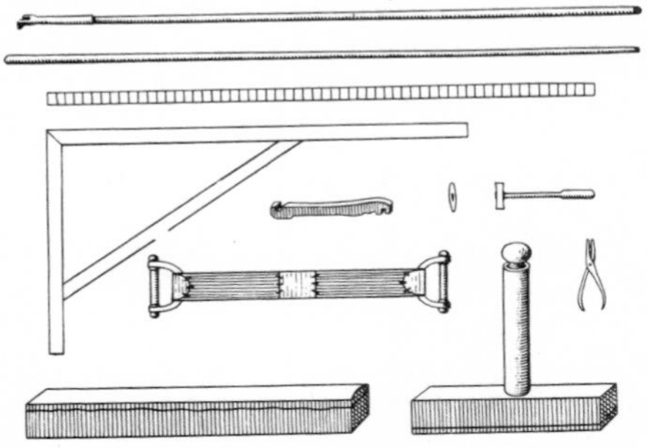

FIGURE 202—*Some tools and equipment used in the making of plate glass, including appliances for moving it, measuring it, and breaking it into sections.*

As regards the actual casting of the glass, there was a steady advance in the size of the plate produced, but while manual handling remained in force this depended mainly on using more and more men to operate the equipment, and the work was slow and laborious. Annealing, too, continued to be slow, taking about ten days. Grinding and polishing were necessary because the surface of the glass was roughened during manufacture by contact with the roller above and the casting-table below. Some of the appliances used for moving, measuring, and cutting the cast plate are shown in figure 202.

To grind plate glass it was laid on a table of fine-grained freestone, and plastered down with lime or stucco to prevent movement during the grinding. Upon the glass to be ground was laid another piece less than half its size, this upper plate being cemented to a wooden plank which in turn was fastened to a horizontal wheel made of light but hard wood. By means of the wheel the upper plate could be turned or moved backwards and forwards, thus causing constant attrition between the two glasses. To aid the process water and sand were poured in, being retained within the framework of the grinding table by a rim. Coarse sand was used first, then finer, and finally powdered smalt. This manual method continued until 1789, when for the first time a steam-engine—made by Boulton and Watt—was used to grind and polish the plates of glass.

After the grinder had done his work the polisher took over, using finely powdered tripoli stone or emery applied by a small felt roller with a double handle at each end. According to long-established practice the roller was mounted on a wooden hoop, which acted as a spring and by bringing the roller back to its original position helped the actions of the workman's arms (plate 21 A).

In Britain a great expansion in building took place in the early 1820s. Between

FIGURE 203—*Annealing arches. The doors to each annealing chamber were made to open in sections. Thus when small ware was being made the heat could be conserved by using the minimum size of opening. The lower archways were used for firing the ovens. Similar chambers were used for plate glass.*

1821 and 1825 brick-production rose from 900 m annually to 1950 m, and the demand for flat glass rose proportionately. To the existing works at Ravenhead and on Tyneside a number of others were added to meet the new demand. Thus the St Helen's Crown Glass Company was formed in 1826, and in 1832 the Smethwick firm of Chance and Hartley brought glass-makers from the continent to blow cylinder-glass. In 1836–7 the great Union Plate Glass Works (figure 204) was built at Pocket Nook, St Helens. Its casting-hall (figure 205) was nearly as big as that at Ravenhead and the equipment included two founding and two firing furnaces and twenty annealing kilns.

VII. COLOURS IN GLASS

Great advances were made in the chemistry of glass coloration between 1750 and 1850. Surprisingly good results had previously been obtained by empirical means, but subject to a wide margin of error; this, however, was of no consequence in such applications as stained glass windows, and might even prove advantageous from the artistic point of view. In the period in question the scientific basis of the colouring agents was explored much more fully than ever before, and in consequence a much closer control over their uses was gained.

Glass was coloured blue with cobalt at a very early date, but the metal was not identified until 1733, when Georg Brandt (1694–1768) named it after the German *Kobold*, a kind of malicious gnome that delighted in frustrating the work of miners. T. O. Bergmann (1735–84) examined the properties of the metal in 1780,

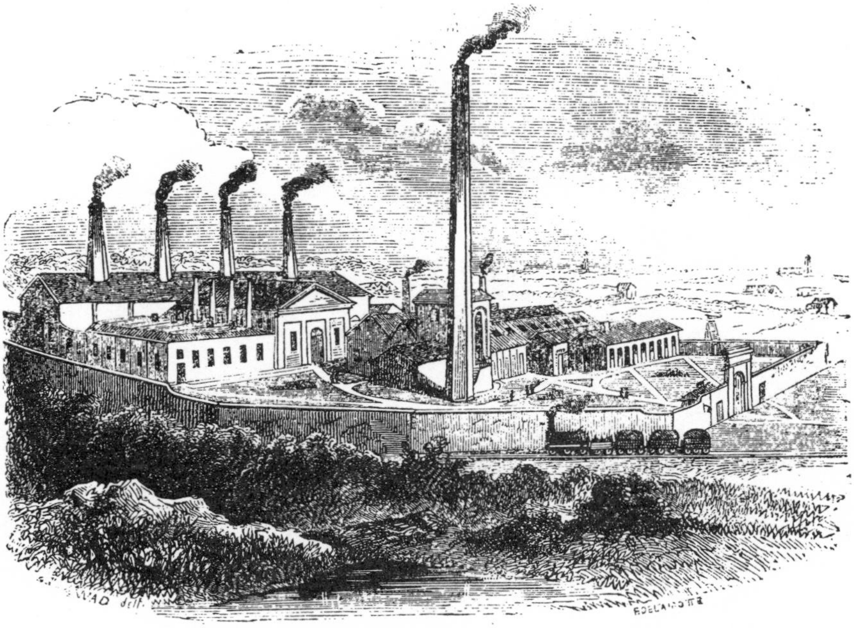

FIGURE 204—*The Union Plate Glass Company's works at Pocket Nook.* c *1843.*

and in 1802 Thénard (1777–1857) began systematic research into the chemistry of cobalt compounds.

Nickel can be used to produce a variety of colours that range, according to the composition of the glass, from brown, green, and grey to an attractive purple. The name is a shortened form of *Kupfernickel*, or copper-goblin: the nickel ore looked like copper ore but yielded no copper, suggesting the interference of a mischievous sprite. A. F. Cronstedt discovered the metal in 1751, and Bergmann investigated its properties in 1774.

In his 'Travels Through England', R. Pococke mentions that in 1751 he came to Stourbridge, 'famous for its glass manufacture, which is here coloured in the liquid of all the capital colours in their several shades'. In spite of this tribute it appears that there was one important exception, in that no good ruby glass was available. In a patent specification of 5 December 1755, for making transparent red glass, the applicant proposes to colour flint glass by melting with it an equal quantity of *Braunstein* and adding 20 grains of dissolved Dutch gold. As *Braunstein* is an impure form of manganese dioxide, and Dutch gold an alloy of copper and zinc, the resulting colour would be purple rather than ruby. The way of making true copper ruby glass seems to have been rediscovered in 1826 by Georges Bontemps.

FIGURE 205—*Casting Hall, Union Plate Glass Company, Pocket Nook. c 1843.*

In 1779 J. F. Gmelin noted that glasses containing iron became blue when founded under strongly reducing conditions, but no explanation was then possible. The colour was later attributed to a modification of ferric oxide which is stable only in the presence of ferrous oxide. This involves the existence of the metal in its two states of valency in the glass.

In 1789 M. Klaproth (1743–1817) identified a new element, uranium, in the mineral pitchblende. He obtained sodium uranate as a bright yellow solid, which soon came to be used as a colouring-agent for glass and glazes.

Glass can be given a bright green colour with chromium, discovered in 1795 in the Russian mineral crocoite, a form of lead chromate. Chromium has been used for colouring glass from early in the nineteenth century.

In 1831 Sir David Brewster (1781–1868) investigated changes of colour with temperature, and since then several studies have been made of this relationship. For example, a glass coloured with cadmium sulphide is nearly colourless when submerged in liquid air, is yellow at room temperature, and when heated changes first to orange and then to red.

Carbon is commonly used for the manufacture of yellow glasses, being introduced in the form of powdered coke, graphite, or anthracite. The true source of the colour is to be found in the sulphur compounds contained as impurities in the carbon. D. K. Splitgerber demonstrated this in 1839 when he melted two carbon-containing batches, the first of which had 1·75 per cent of sodium sulphate but the other none, and only the former developed a yellow colour. T. J. Pelouze (1807–67) was able to confirm these results by experiments he conducted shortly afterwards.

As regards the colour of glass in general use there were two well marked categories in the period under review. Bottles intended merely as containers were black or very dark green, through excess of iron and other impurities in the raw materials. In evidence before the commissioners at an excise inquiry in 1831 it was stated that the materials employed in the making of common bottles were sand, soap-makers' waste, lime, common clay, and ground bricks. For flint glass, from which table-ware was produced, a much higher standard had to be maintained, and it was stated that the materials used to give a colourless glass were pearl-ash, litharge or red lead, with Lynn or Alum Bay sand or 'Yorkshire stones burnt and pulverized'.

VIII. GLASS-CUTTING

For the making of English cut-glass the great period was from 1750 to 1810, after which the art declined until recent times. The fame of the English product was based partly on the excellence of the workmanship, but to an important extent also upon the quality of the metal. The early crystal glass consisted of sand, lime, and soda, with some potash and a very small proportion of lead oxide added as a flux.

By gradual stages more lead oxide was substituted for the lime, and in the same way the soda was gradually replaced by potash. There was no question of any sudden change or invention by one man, the development taking place slowly. In the event, however, the result was brilliant, for the power of breaking up light into its constituent colours is in proportion to the optical density of the translucent material through which the light passes.

The process of glass-cutting by hand, as carried on until the mid-nineteenth century, was simple in its elements but required a high degree of skill. Three operations were involved, namely grinding, smoothing, and polishing. For the grinding (figure 206), an iron disk was mounted on a horizontal axis and was rotated by power supplied originally by the human foot, then by water, and afterwards by steam. The wheels, larger on the average than those used for engraving, ranged from 3 to 24 inches in diameter.

The glass to be cut was pressed against the iron wheel, and was grooved by the movement of the wheel combined with the abrasive action of sand. When the patterns were completed they were smoothed with wheels of fine sandstone fed with water. Finally, the polish was restored by treating the surfaces of the cuts on a wheel of willow- or pear-wood supplied with putty-powder and water. The designs were chiefly geometrical, and interesting effects were obtained by leaving some parts of the pattern in the smooth state and bringing others back to the original brilliant fire-polish.

FIGURE 206—*Grinding cut-glass vessels.*

IX. GLASS-ENGRAVING

The engraving of glass was a handicraft skill that flourished in the earlier half of the nineteenth century but has since become almost extinct. It was found that engraving could be applied to thin blown glass-ware that was unsuitable for the deeper penetration of cutting. The treatment of the surface of the glass was lighter than in the case of cut glass, and greater freedom of design was possible. Engraved designs were delicate but sharply defined in form, and had easy-flowing curves that contrasted with the straight lines normal in cutting.

The engraver worked before a small copper wheel or disk rotating in a lathe, and used fine grades of emery made into a paste with linseed-oil as the abrasive medium. Engraving-wheels were of many different sizes, and had a variety of bevelled edges. For one design the engraver might use fifty different wheels, varying in diameter from $\frac{1}{8}$ to 4 in or more.

BIBLIOGRAPHY

ANGUS-BUTTERWORTH, L. M. 'The Manufacture of Glass.' Pitman, London. 1948.
Idem. 'British Table and Ornamental Glass.' Hill, London. 1956.
CHANCE, SIR HUGH. "Centenary of Optical Glass Manufacture in England." *J. Soc. chem. Ind., Lond.*, no. 52, 795, 1947.
DICKSON, J. H. 'Glass.' Hutchinson, London. 1951.
DIDEROT, D. and D'ALEMBERT, J. LE R. (Eds). 'Encyclopédie ou dictionnaire raisonné des sciences, des arts et des métiers.' Paris. 1751–72.
FISCHER, J. L. 'Handbuch der Glasmalerei.' Hiersemann, Leipzig. 1914.
HENRIVAUX, M. J. 'Le verre et le cristal.' Paris. 1897.
JEANS, SIR JAMES. 'The Growth of Physical Science.' University Press, Cambridge. 1947.
KRUYT, H. R. (Ed.). 'Colloid Science', Vol. 1. Elsevier, Amsterdam. 1952.
LE VIEIL, P. 'Art de la peinture sur verre, et de la vitrerie.' Neuchâtel. 1781.
MCGRATH, R. 'Glass in Architecture.' Architectural Press, London. 1937.
MARTIN, B. 'An Essay on Visual Glasses (vulgarly called Spectacles).' London. 1756.
MASON, S. F. 'A History of the Sciences.' Routledge & Kegan Paul, London. 1953.
POWELL, H. J. 'Glass-making in England.' University Press, Cambridge. 1923.
SCHULZ, H. 'Die Geschichte der Glaserzeugung.' Akademische Verlagsgesellschaft, Leipzig. 1928.

Fishergate Glass Works, York, c 1850, established by John Prince in 1794.

13

PRECISION MECHANICS

MAURICE DAUMAS

PRECISION mechanics could not come into being until certain conditions were fulfilled. It is difficult to assess the order of importance of these conditions, as their influence was exercised in a rather complex manner, about which we still know very little. Up to now the historian has limited himself to mentioning the appearance of certain perfected instruments and new machinery. He has acknowledged that a certain technical evolution, which he has even incorrectly called revolution, occurred over a relatively short period. He has studied the industrial and social consequences of these changes. But the reasons for such changes, and the course of their development, have never been very thoroughly analysed.

There has always been a relationship between the needs and wishes of the user—the scientific research worker or engineer—and the limits of technical achievement. This relationship has itself been influenced by a number of factors, ranging from the general level of transformation techniques to the political situations within various states. These influences resemble pressures exerted upon several regions of a complex network, the object of the constant transformations being to maintain the internal equilibrium of the network as a whole. The factors determining this equilibrium are still obscure, however, because their investigation would require the collaboration of specialists who have, as yet, had little occasion to meet each other.

The above remarks apply more or less strictly to technical progress as a whole, but they have a special importance in the history of precision mechanics. In this field, indeed, invention and the putting of invention into effect have been given expression only when there was some chance of a new object being attained by the users. Progress required the work of skilled craftsmen, the use of materials of the best quality, and costly instruments and machinery; in other words, it required relatively considerable human and monetary capital. If the capital thus tied up were not productive—that is to say, if there were no customers—the invention would languish for lack of means. In fact, customers were not numerous; they were not always prepared to use the new invention; and their financial state was variable.

On the other hand, the activities of the users stimulated invention by bringing new problems to the attention of those putting inventions to practical use. It was only by assessing the limits of the earlier products of the precision engineers that the user could ask them continually to exceed this limit.

Precision mechanics, which arose from clock-making, was first developed in workshops making scientific instruments (vol III, ch 23). The market for these articles was still very restricted in the eighteenth century, and the forces alluded to above must have been very closely balanced.

This is best explained by way of example. The invention of the compound sighting telescope at the beginning of the seventeenth century altered the manufacture of astronomical instruments only very slowly. The first such telescopes fitted to quadrants, for example, were more than a metre in length; the sizes of the instruments were not changed by this innovation. The problems of construction, and more particularly that of dividing the graduated limbs, were the same: the method of transversals used by Tycho Brahe was sufficient for satisfactory precision. After the invention of achromatic objectives (p 358), it was possible to shorten the sighting telescope, which then came into more general use. Observatory instruments remained large and their precision was increased; it was also possible to adapt the sighting telescope easily to instruments for geodesy and nautical astronomy. These were adopted by users because they were small and easy to handle; they were also more precise than instruments fitted with sights, because the technique of marking the scales had been improved. The vernier, the principle of which had been known for a century and a half, then came into use. Further, as large numbers of instruments were being manufactured, manual methods of division were no longer sufficient and dividing-machines were invented. With these it became possible to design new instruments and put them to practical use.

By comparing this process with that determining invention and improvements in other fields of mechanics, we can see what differences there were. If we confine ourselves to the steam-engine and to Watt's work, it is easy to see that the same factors applied, creating circumstances favourable to invention and to putting them to practical application; that is to say, causing progress. In this case, however, the pressure between the governing factors was not so acute; there was a greater opportunity for real and rapid progress.

Thus the precision mechanics industry was able to go ahead only under certain circumstances which it is not possible to analyse in detail here. An understanding of their nature, however, is sufficient to explain both the historical importance of the achievements of engineers in the eighteenth century and the manner in which these achievements stimulated an activity that has continually increased.

I. PROCESSES, TOOLS, AND MACHINES

Ever since the Alexandrian era there have always been instruments for special purposes with which it was possible to carry out operations more precisely than was feasible with common instruments, but this does not mean that the origin of precision techniques is to be found as far back as that. For clarity, it may be agreed that these techniques constituted a special field from the time when craftsmen devised and used special methods and, in particular, special tools. These tools consisted of machines which replaced manual work by mechanical work. The manual skill of expert workers was no longer used directly in making instruments, but for the construction of machines with which a craftsman of ordinary ability could execute work previously done by experts.

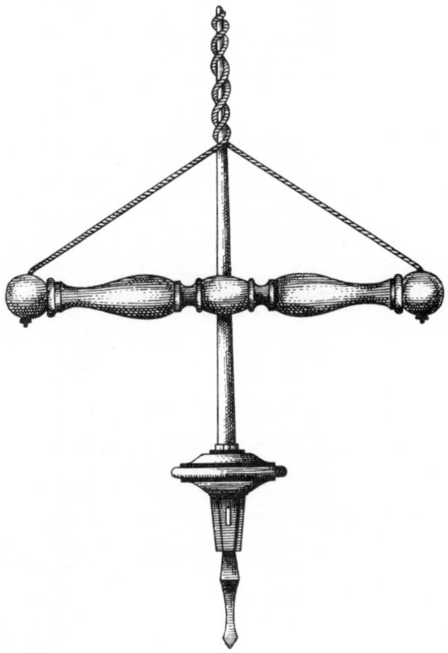

FIGURE 207—*Strap drill.*

Hand tools. The methods used by precision manufacturers up to this period were borrowed from the ancient guilds, such as those of locksmiths, sand-moulders, and tool-makers: they were allowed by the rules of the guilds to use tools of all the metal-workers. From the time that good steel began to be manufactured, namely the end of the seventeenth century, the form of these tools has not varied fundamentally. Some still used are just as they were two or three centuries ago.

Although for a long time only the strap drill (figure 207) was known, the drill with crank and bevel gearing (figure 208) came into use as early as the second half of the eighteenth century. Chisels, gouges, drills, dies, vices, and in general all hand tools used in the workshop, have hardly changed at all since then. They were adopted by instrument-makers who worked in steel, cast iron, brass, or copper. Apart from these, they do not appear to have had any special tools, except for an occasional device invented for executing a special job; some such devices have been abandoned and others adopted. An example of the latter is the machine for cutting helical teeth on wheels (figure 209).

Mathematical and engraving instruments for dividing circles and rulers were also in use very early. In each workshop there was a round table, the surface of which was carefully trued and the centre accurately marked. Solidly constructed, this table was used for the assembly and graduation of quadrants and other sighting instruments.

Little by little, machinery borrowed directly from clock-makers, or based upon those they used, was added to these standard tools. The art of the clock-maker developed only after the inventions of seventeenth-century scientists and technicians such as Huygens, Hooke, and their contemporaries (vol III, ch 24). All masterpieces made before that period, Burgi's astronomical computers for example, were individual works due to the exceptional skill of one man: they had no influence on the progress of applied mechanics as a whole. From the beginning of the eighteenth century this was no longer so. New tools and special methods of working were devised; these were not only soon adopted by all clock-makers, but were used in all workshops where precision work was carried out. Thomas Tompion (1639–1713) and his pupil George Graham (1673–1751) exemplify how precision mechanics derived from clock-making. Graham was the first great English instrument-maker of the eighteenth century; he trained Jonathan Sisson (1694?–1749) and John Bird (1709–76), and he was imitated by all the instrument-makers of that period and by their immediate successors.

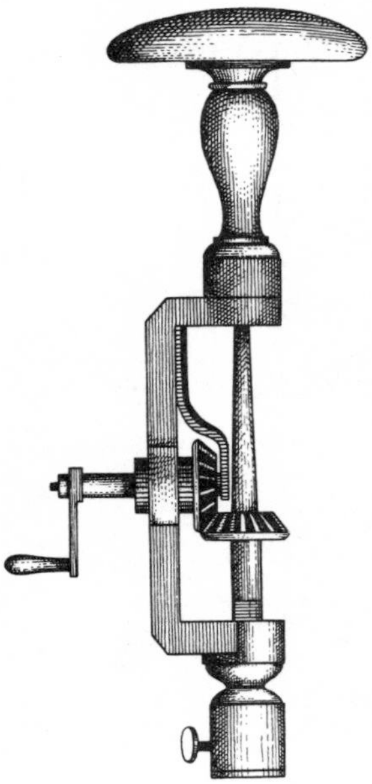

FIGURE 208—*Hand-brace with bevel gearing.*

The lathe. The first machine available to engineers, as regards both date and importance, was the lathe. This machine, which goes back to some unknown period, did not achieve popularity until the sixteenth and seventeenth centuries; it became really useful in the second half of the latter century (vol III, pp 335–6). Opticians used it for cutting lenses for astronomical telescopes, modifying a relatively rough technique for their special purposes. They gave their lathe a stronger frame in order to ensure its stability, but it was still constructed of wood, and was thus unsuitable for metal-work. It was the clock-makers who invented the first precision lathes.

Arbors and the cylindrical parts of clocks were turned on small iron lathes. These consisted mainly of an iron bar, square in section, on which were a fixed headstock at one end, and a second, loose headstock sliding the whole length of the bar (figure 210). A cylindrical opening was made in the top of each headstock, and through this a pointed rod passed to secure the work. Headstocks and centres were tightly fixed by screws. The bracket for the tool was carried by a sliding support. The part to be turned, placed between the centres, was rotated by a bow.

Large lathes were used by turners of fancy work and by cabinet-makers. Their frames were of wood and they had one or two headstocks according to whether the work was turned on the face plate or between centres: these headstocks were of iron. The main part was the mandrel, on which the part to be turned was fixed. A cord passed around the mandrel: one end of the string was fixed to the end of a flexible pole, and the other end was attached to a treadle under the table (vol III, figures 218, 220). Such a pole-lathe had an alternating rotary motion. For big jobs, turners used a lathe driven by a hemp or gut cord passing round a pulley. The driving-wheel was large; it was fixed to the ground and operated by an assistant who turned the handle. This kind of lathe employed continuous rotation.

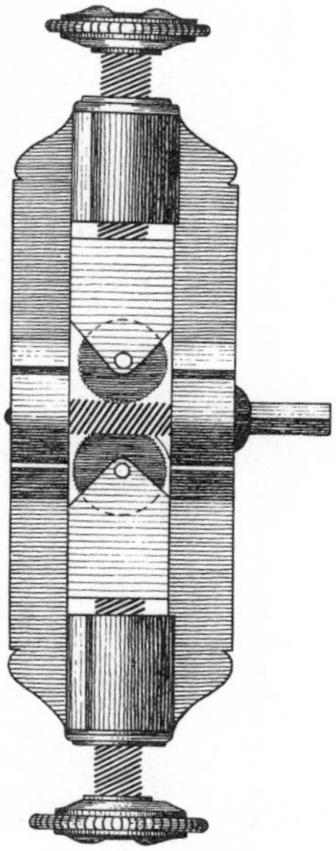

FIGURE 209—*Stock and die foı cutting helical teeth on wheels.*

From the end of the seventeenth century the pole-lathe was adopted by many amateurs who set up workshops adjoining their chemical and physical laboratories and their cabinets of curiosities. Wood, horn, and ivory were the chief materials worked. Then the working of metals became fashionable, and important improvements were made in the design of lathes. Engineers constructed them not only for wealthy and exacting amateurs but for craftsmen who manufactured for customers.

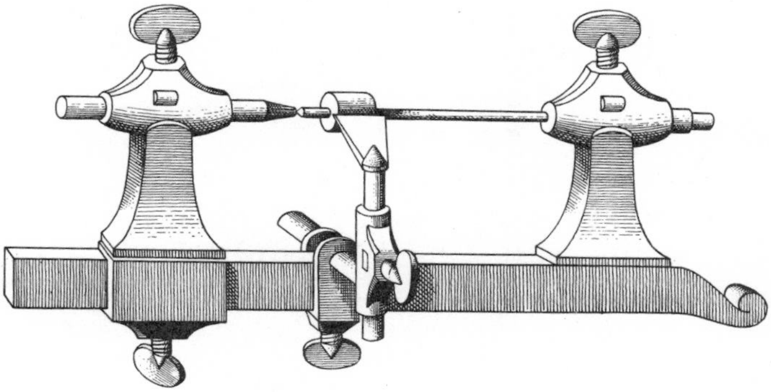

FIGURE 210—*Clock-maker's lathe.*

Cast and wrought iron, steel, and brass gradually replaced wood in the construction of lathes; this gave them greater strength and stability. The driving mechanism consisted of a heavy wheel placed on a bracket above the lathe and operated by a cord connecting a crank on the wheel to a treadle below; the transmission from the wheel to the shaft of the lathe was made by grooved pulleys with an endless cord (figure 211). Devices were added not only to regulate the tension of the cord according to the dampness of the air, but to vary the speed of rotation of the lathe as required without altering the foot-movement. A lathe constructed by the Saxon engineer Merklein, about 1775, had a screw system of great precision for this purpose.

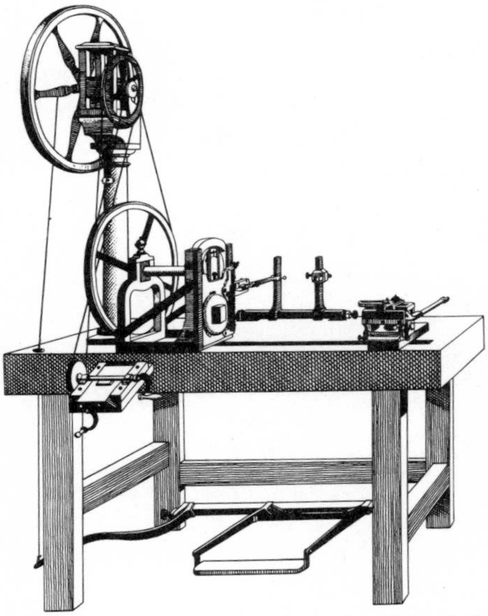

FIGURE 211—*Rotary lathe with treadle and flywheel.*

The greatest improvement was made to the tool, which until then was held in the hand. Its handle was usually bent; it was used as a lever, the bend resting on the tool-holder. The latter was only a support and it did not guide or regulate the feed. Towards the beginning of the eighteenth century, however, clock-makers began to use mechanically guided tools. Antoine Thiout (1692–1767) and Fardoïl, in France, invented machines for cutting fusees (vol III, p 656) in which the part to be turned moved in front of the fixed tool, or conversely the tool moved in front of the part. In the first model, the fusee was given the shape of a cone by inclined guides in the form of very flat isosceles triangles. The feed of the tool, which was manual, was later effected mechanically. The second model, due to Thiout, is the most interesting from the historical point of view, as without doubt it incorporated the first tool-holder carriage with longitudinal movement [1] to be constructed. It is of very simple design. The tool is fixed by a slide-block to a flat bar; movement is obtained by a kind of pantograph in which one of the bars is fitted with a collar threaded internally to take the gearing of a worm screw (figure 212). Here we have one of the earliest examples, if not the earliest, of the use of a screw drive for operating the tool of a precision machine. This device dates back to about 1750.

Jacques de Vaucanson (1709–82) was the first to adapt these methods to machinery for working on a larger scale. He devised a lathe and a drill each fitted with a tool-holder carriage moved by a threaded screw [2]: these must have been made between 1768 and 1780. He redesigned the iron frame of a shaping lathe and made it larger. He copied the idea of the lead-screw and carriage for the tool in machines for turning fusees and for guilloching.[1] His lathe measured 140 cm in length. The carriage was moved by a lead-screw placed parallel to the line of the headstock centres; it moved along a prismatic bench, a device which was used

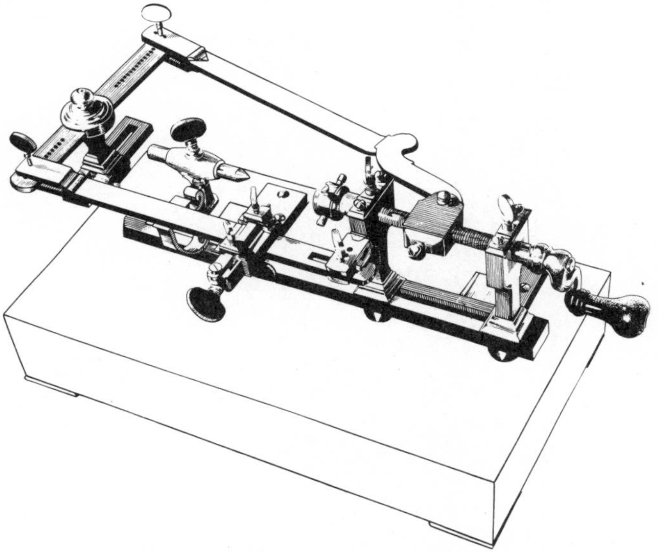

FIGURE 212—*Thiout's lathe for cutting screw-threads on spindles for clocks and watches.*

later on all machine tools. The advance of the tool was also controlled by a screw (plate 23 A).

Vaucanson's drill is even more interesting. It is a horizontal drill in which the carriage is guided by a horizontal prismatic bench; the tool-holder moves along a vertical bench similar to the horizontal one (plate 22 A). The movements are controlled by threaded guide-rods, the cranks of which rotate in front of graduated dials. There is as yet no vernier: this was used only by instrument-makers of the next generation, in the first half of the nineteenth century.

Henry Gambey (1787–1847) constructed for his own use an improved lathe, the tool of which was controlled by micrometer screws and tilted by a toothed sector with helical gearing and vernier graduation.

Screw cutting. All these working methods were adopted by precision-instrument

[1] A guilloche is an ornament in the form of interlaced bands.

makers during the last quarter of the eighteenth century, but it is not possible to find out to whom the credit for any of these adaptations is due. However, a few examples will enable us to understand how the first special engineering tools were developed.

One of the most essential operations in the construction of instruments for the measurement of angles is the cutting of an accurately threaded screw. Several methods were used to do this. With stocks and dies it was possible to obtain only levelling- and retaining-screws, or screws with large pitches. For finer and more accurate screw threads, such as the screws for the slow motion of microscopes, there was no alternative to cutting them on a lathe.

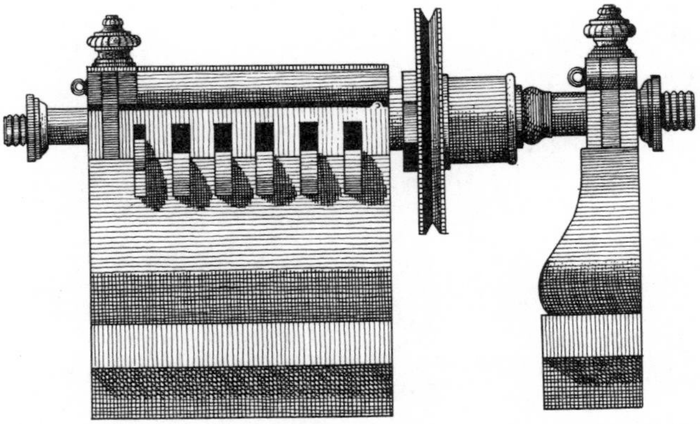

FIGURE 213—*Keyed headstock of lathe for screw-cutting. The 'keys' are the six levers on the left. The first is locked. A different thread corresponding to each is cut on the mandrel.*

With a lathe it was possible to work in several ways. The usual process was to use a headstock with a threaded chuck in which a guide-screw rotated; at the extremity of this screw was fixed, along the same axis, the rod to be threaded, supported by a second headstock. When rotating, the rod moved backwards and forwards in front of the tool according to the pitch of the guide-screw selected. In the second half of the eighteenth century lathes were fitted with keyed headstocks, which made it possible to change the pitch easily. These keys consisted of levers, integral with the headstock, each of which engaged independently in the thread of a guide-screw of a given pitch (figure 213); five or six threads of different pitch could therefore be cut on the same spindle.

For precision work, or for cutting lead-screws, the following procedure was adopted (figure 214). On a rectangular sheet of paper transverse lines were drawn, the spacing and angle of inclination of which corresponded to the thread to be traced. The paper was wound around the rod to be made into a screw and the threads were traced by following the line with a sharp file; the cutting was done first with a triangular file and finally with a steel chaser having teeth spaced to correspond with the pitch of the screw to be made.

Such methods took a long time, and the quality of the result depended entirely upon the skill of the operator. To overcome these difficulties the great English engineer, Jesse Ramsden (1735–1800), in 1770 invented two screw-cutting lathes which were certainly the first machines of this type ever constructed and which gave satisfactory results [3].

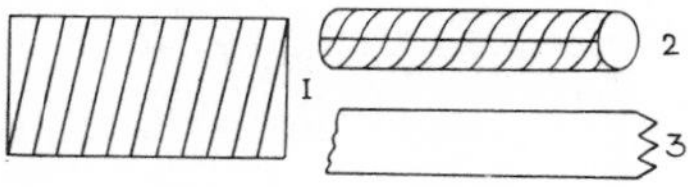

FIGURE 214—*Screw cutting by means of file.* (1) *Track of thread cut;* (2) *paper wound on the rod to be threaded;* (3) *metal comb.*

In the first of these machines the guide-screw and the rod to be threaded are placed parallel to each other (figure 215). The latter is set in motion by a crank; its motion is transmitted to the lead-screw through toothed gearing-wheels, the number of teeth being a function of the ratio between the pitch of the guide-screw and that of the screw to be cut. The lead-screw has a threaded collar which drives the tool-holder. The guiding is effected by a bar of triangular section placed parallel to the lead-screw. The tool is fitted with a diamond for cutting hard steel.

Ramsden's second screw-cutting lathe is of a more elaborate design (figure 216). The lead-screw guides the tool by means of a chuck-plate with helical teeth into which it engages. At the centre of this chuck-plate there is a grooved pulley, and the guide-bench of the tool-holder is placed more or less at a tangent to this. After being pushed back to the end of the bench the tool-holder is drawn towards the centre of the chuck-plate by a small cord which winds around the pulley when the machine is working. The rod to be threaded is placed parallel to the guide-bench. It is rotated by the driving crank of the lead-screw by means of gearing which includes an angle pinion, the two pieces in this instance not being parallel. When we consider the construction of these two machines in the light of the means available to the engineers of those days, and of other contemporary inventions, we must form a very high opinion of Ramsden's technical ability and understanding. In research and in the design of tools intended to reduce the personal factor in the making of accurate parts, the personal factor itself played a considerable part.

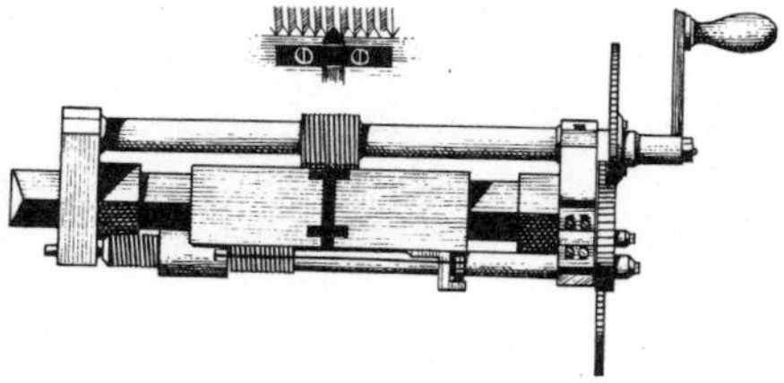

FIGURE 215—*Ramsden's screw-cutting machine with lead-screw (detail above).*

Ten or fifteen years after Ramsden, the French engineer Jean Fortin (1750–1831) had his own method for screw-cutting. Unfortunately no description of this has been handed down to us. We only know that Fortin proceeded in stages; from an original screw he cut another more uniform, then with this a third which was as perfect as could be. Several engineers at the end of the eighteenth century and the beginning of the nineteenth became past-masters of the art of threading. Among them Ramsden's old craftsman, Samuel Rhee, was reputed to be the best.

Towards the end of the century the engineering industry began to have screw-cutting lathes at its disposal, thanks to Maudslay. In 1795, the Frenchman, Senot, constructed a screw-cutting lathe for working large parts which does not appear to have been known to his contemporaries. In 1797, Maudslay designed a lathe which was widely adopted in the trade; its history is part of that of machine tools and is considered elsewhere (p 424). It is worth mentioning, however, that it is not impossible that Maudslay knew of Ramsden's lathes. The latter was an instrument-maker with an international reputation; he was a Fellow of the Royal Society; and his workshop was of very great repute. Further, the description of his lathes was published. The great English engineers who in the nineteenth century invented the principal machine tools for the engineering industry were no doubt influenced by his work.

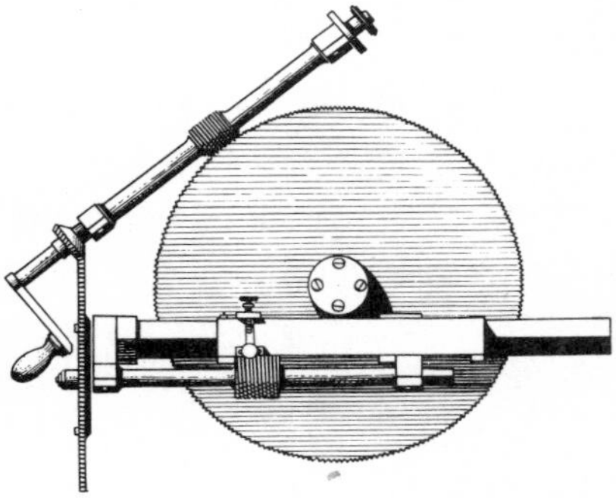

FIGURE 216—*Ramsden's screw-cutting lathe with lead-screw and toothed plate. This made it possible to make long screws from a small original.*

Division of limbs. From about 1760 precision workers had to solve another problem, that of mechanically dividing the graduated limbs of instruments and rules. For centuries previously, methods had evolved very slowly, but it took only some forty years for dividing-engines to be adopted in all workshops.

Towards the end of the sixteenth century Tycho Brahe had brought into use the method using transversals, the principle of which had then been known for about two centuries. This was replaced gradually by the traditional dividing by points, which was finally abandoned only towards the end of the seventeenth century.

The craftsmen knew the geometrical processes for dividing by means of compasses. The method with transversals consisted in tracing parallel lines cut perpendicularly by the division marks of the rule (figure 217); to obtain the tenth of these divisions a transversal was drawn, that is, a diagonal of the rectangle bounded by the first and eleventh lines and the two neighbouring dividing marks. The tenths of a unit were found by intersection of the transversal and each of the ten parallels. The reading was made by moving a pointer in front of the scale cutting all the parallels at right angles. It was thus possible to find one-hundredth of an inch or a tenth of a line (on the old measuring system 1 line = $\frac{1}{12}$-in).

On circular limbs the transversals were concentric circles. With seven concentric circles angles of ten minutes could be read. When achromatic reading telescopes were adopted and the mechanical parts of instruments were improved, sighting was made more precise and the instrument-makers had to revise their method of dividing. It was no longer sufficient to trace rectilinear transversals and equidistant arcs of circumference on the limbs. The transversals themselves had to be circular arcs passing through the centre of the instrument (figure 218). Concentric circles no longer had to be equidistant; their radii were determined by dividing into six equal parts the circular arcs serving as transversals. The geometrical methods enabling this lay-out to be effected strictly were perfected in the first few years of the eighteenth century.

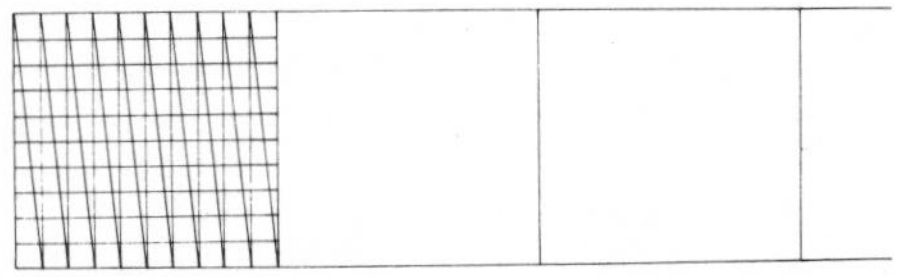

FIGURE 217—*Method of division by transversals.*

For a long time one great difficulty still remained in the principal operation, the division of an arc into 90 degrees. The only strictly accurate division which can be done with a compass is the bisection of an arc, but it was not possible to go very far with this alone; consequently various devices were invented.

First, an arc of 90° must be accurately measured on the limb to be graduated, whether this is a circle, semicircle, or quadrant. The geometrical method was to begin by striking an arc of 60° from the zero point: this was done with the dividers, since the chord of 60° is equal to the radius of the circle. Bisecting the arc gave the 30° point, and by setting off an arc of 30°, again with the dividers, beyond the 60° point, 90° was found. Bisection of these three arcs gave 15°, 45°, and 75° respectively. For the rest, the worker used a table for finding the opening of the compass corresponding to one-third of each of the chords, and then to one-fifth of the latter. When the limb was thus divided into degrees, the subdivision into ten-second intervals was made by the method of transversals mentioned above.

When limbs had to be more accurately graduated, the instrument-makers invented processes for determining a 90° arc by double sighting using a plumb-line. However, the difficulty of dividing the arc itself remained unsolved. In 1725

George Graham (p 382) devised a method using a duplicate scale with 96 units for 90 sexagesimal degrees. This enabled him to mark accurately, by repeated bisection, sections of 3 such units (instead of 5° sections, each divided into degrees); the units were in turn subdivided into 8 by bisection. A table gave the equivalence between these units and their subdivisions, and the sexagesimal degrees and seconds. Following Graham, his pupil John Bird further perfected the geometric operations required for this method.

The construction of the first machines for dividing did not do away immediately with the necessity of using a compass for large instruments. With the machines of Ramsden and his contemporaries it was possible to divide mechanically only the limbs of small instruments such as sextants and geodesic circles. The large mural circles in astronomical observatories still had to be divided by hand. It was only in the first quarter of the nineteenth century that J. G. Repsold (1771–1830) and H. Gambey (p 394) discovered how to construct machines for dividing the limbs of large instruments. Consequently the instrument-makers of the end of the eighteenth century used Bird's method, or invented ones of their own.

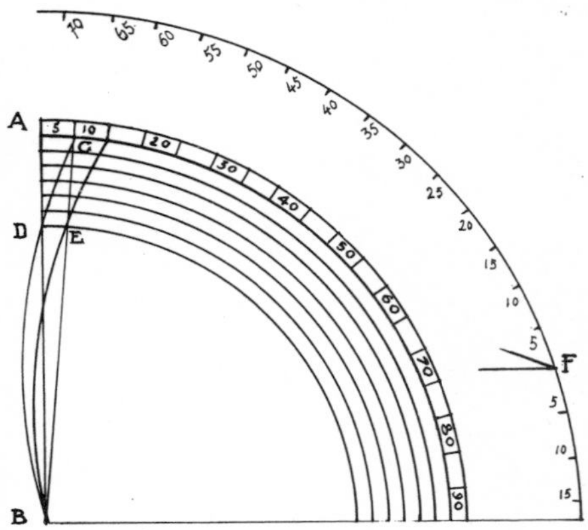

FIGURE 218—*Division of a limb by transversals. The outer curve is the geometric locus of the centres of all the arcs of the circles forming the transversals of the graduation. See p 389.*

Dividing-engines. These delicate operations were of no pecuniary interest to the instrument-maker unless they were entrusted to a specialized craftsman who executed a series of them, or unless they were included in the construction of a large instrument for which he could command remuneration. Consequently, almost throughout the eighteenth century it was only the English workshops which had a clientele abundant enough for these manufactures to be carried out satisfactorily. Besides those of Graham, Sisson, and Bird the workshops of the Adams and the Dollonds had undisputed supremacy in the whole of the market for precision instruments, because they employed numerous specialized craftsmen, each for a given operation.

Meanwhile the progress in the optical qualities of telescopes, the improvement in manufacturing materials such as brass, steel, and bronze, and above all the ever-increasing demand of users—navigators, geodesists, and surveyors—necessitated the search for new graduation processes. Geometrical methods had attained their ultimate perfection; for this reason the first tentative steps were taken towards the construction of dividing-engines.

Clock-makers had already solved the problem some time previously for their own purposes. The machines they had been using since early in the eighteenth century to cut toothed wheels and pinions consisted of a division-plate on which concentric circles were traced, each having a certain number of equidistant points incised upon them. The divisions of these circles, which had been traced by geo-

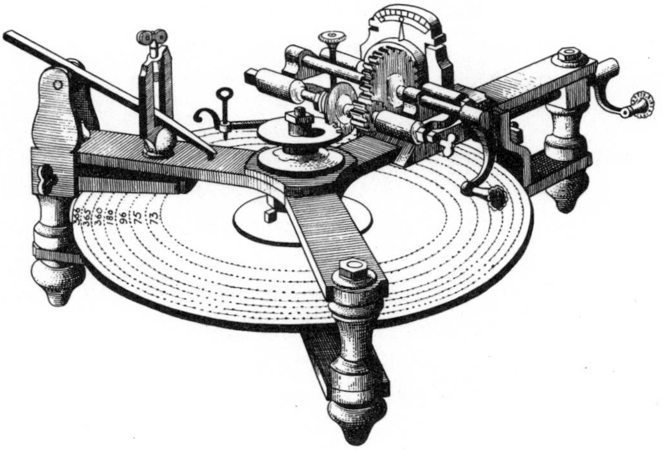

FIGURE 219—*Machine, with division-plate, for cutting clock-wheels. Cf figure 238.*

metrical methods, corresponded to the usual divisions of the wheels and pinions in clock-making. From the plate on which they had been engraved they could be reproduced at will. The disk to be cut was fixed above the division-plate and parallel to it. It was marked by a cutter moved by a crank; a pointer following the graduations on the plate, mark by mark, and moved after each cut, made it possible to turn the disk through the arc corresponding to one tooth (figure 219).

The first attempt by instrument-makers consisted in trying to adapt the clock-maker's machine for dividing scales. That of the English clock-maker Henry Hindley, made in 1739, does not seem to have led very far. Although the attempt is of some historical interest, it is probable that the technical means available at the time did not enable Hindley to obtain very satisfactory results.

A little later, in 1765, the Duc de Chaulnes (1714–69), a French academician, had two machines constructed, one for circles, the other for straight lines [4]. He used the principle of the clock-maker's division-plate, on the edge of which he cut helical teeth. This is the first example of drive by tangent screw being applied to this type of machine, but the threading of a screw with strictly constant pitch was not then practicable. For a long time to come all instrument-makers came up against this obstacle, and had to find a device for turning the dividing-plate.

The Duc de Chaulnes established empirically the correspondence between the number of turns of the crank and the angle of rotation of his plate. On the latter he traced a division by the ordinary method, but instead of using dividers he used two microscopes of his own invention, the cross-hairs of which took the place of the points of the dividers. His process of division is extremely ingenious, but it does not depend on mechanical ingenuity. Its principle was used later by other engineers, as will be seen.

A master copy having thus been prepared, the circle to be graduated was fixed above the plate and turned under a scriber; the division lines of the master were used as were the points of the clock-maker's division-plate, the microscope this time taking the place of the pointer (figure 220). In designing the mechanism serving to control the movements of the scriber the Duc de Chaulnes showed some imagination, but on examining the mechanism it will be seen that its inventor was without the experience and understanding of applied mechanics which enabled Ramsden, for example, to find effective solutions.

The machine for dividing a straight line is simpler, because the problem is simpler. A graduated master-plate was moved under a microscope at the same time as the rule to be divided was moved under a scriber. The displacement was obtained by a plate with helical teeth engaging on one side with a worm screw turned by a crank, and on the other with a toothed rack on a carriage bearing the master-plate and the rule.

The Duc de Chaulnes's tests were described and published. They drew the attention of engineers to the usefulness of adopting the tangent-screw drive and position-finding by a microscope. Ramsden was the first to use these two methods, and constructed the first dividing-engine suitable for use on an industrial scale (plate 1) [5]. His research lasted nearly fifteen years: it was during the period 1760–73 that he invented the two screw-cutting lathes mentioned above. But his enterprise could not have succeeded without progress made by the founders and turners.

One of the principal parts of the dividing-engine for circles (vol III, figure 378) was a bronze wheel, cast in one piece. This wheel, having a diameter of 110 cm, was reinforced by ten spokes, an inner ring, and ribs. Placed horizontally on three rollers, it could revolve around a vertical axle consisting of a steel shaft turned with great precision. The creation of this unit involved the co-operation of several craftsmen, each of them excelling in his own craft.

The edge of the wheel had helical teeth cut with the aid of a hardened steel worm-screw, the threads of which were sharpened to a keen edge. The operation was effected in discontinuous fractions, corresponding to 9 out of 10 teeth of the wheel, so as to distribute throughout the circumference the error arising in the cutting of the sharp screw. The wheel had 2160 teeth, each corresponding to an angular distance of 10 minutes. Ramsden reckoned that the precision of his tooth-cutting was about 2½ seconds per tooth, or 10 minutes for the whole circumference.

The other special features of the machine are the tangent screw, which turns

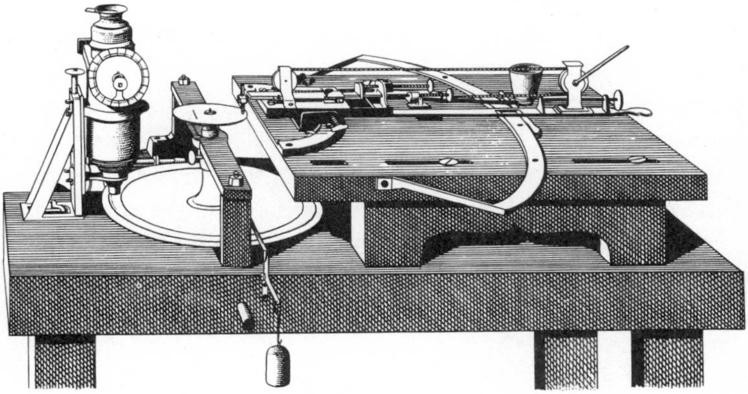

FIGURE 220—*The Duc de Chaulnes's dividing-machine fitted with dividing plate and microscope.* A *is the disk to be divided; the scriber control mechanism is at the right.*

the toothed wheel, and its method of operation. For the latter, Ramsden invented a mechanism comprising a spring drum round which a string was wound. Drawn by a foot-operated treadle, the string turned the tangent screw; the spring drum returned cord and treadle to the starting position. At each touch of the treadle the plate of the machine turned through a given angle, always the same, carrying the scale to be divided under the scriber. By a special appliance the feed could be regulated and limited to the extent of the travel of the treadle. The mechanism permitted the obtaining of automatic feeds of up to 10 seconds.

In the construction of the machine for dividing a straight line Ramsden used a screw of strictly constant pitch. This screw engaged throughout virtually the whole length of the rectilinear toothed rack of the carriage bearing the rule to be divided. In the former machine only a few threads of the tangent screw engaged with the toothed wheel, so that its irregularities had less effect. It was for the making of this important screw that Ramsden constructed his second screw-cutting lathe (figure 216). The movement of the carriage was obtained by a mechanism similar to that of the dividing-engine for circles.

Ramsden's machines aroused keen interest. The Board of Longitude in London entered into an agreement with the inventor for their application and for the publication of their description. A number of engineers of the day, among them Edward Troughton (1753–1835), constructed several examples.

From that moment the main difficulties in making dividing-engines seemed to have been overcome by all good engineers. In France several first-class engineers acquired a high reputation though unfortunately they did not, for numerous reasons, have such ample resources as their English colleagues. Some of them, however, successfully constructed dividing-engines—among them Lenoir, Mégnié, Richer, Fortin, and Jecker.

That of Étienne Lenoir (1744–1832) had a fixed plate and a movable alidade carrying the scriber round its centre. Lenoir used it for the division of reflection and repeating circles, which we shall describe later (p 401). On Fortin's machines the feed of the circular plate, or of the carriage bearing the rules, was obtained by a worm-screw operated by a crank. A buffer and graduated disk mechanism enabled this feed to be controlled accurately to a given interval; in its return movement the crank did not turn the worm. Jecker imitated but simplified Ramsden's machine.

Progress was also made by two great instrument-makers of the following generation: Georg Reichenbach (1772–1826) and Henry Gambey (1787–1847). The former constructed a machine the plate of which measured 135 cm in diameter. It was a little larger than that of Ramsden, but constructed on the same lines; it was stationary. Two superimposed alidades revolved around the centre; they could be set with a given difference. Reichenbach first traced twenty divisions corresponding to an angle of 18° between the alidades. Then he traced the intermediate divisions.

This method is based on the principle used by the Duc de Chaulnes in his method of position-finding by microscope. Gambey took it up in his turn for the construction of a machine the precision of which was better than any that had preceded it; he used it also for the graduation of the great 2-metre mural circle constructed in 1840 for the Paris Observatory [6].

The division of this great circle was a masterpiece of precision. Gambey operated as follows. The circle was placed horizontally, and the points of its vertical axis were supported by conical bearings. Four microscopes suitably contrived served first of all to mark two orthogonal diameters, and then a certain number of intermediate divisions on the circumference. In order to mark out the teeth on the circle he worked with a sharp-pitch screw by the Ramsden method, progressing by limited portions of arc in such a way as to distribute the error of tooth-cutting over the whole of the circumference. After having calculated the average error of pitch in each space, Gambey made a rectifying plate which he fixed on the pin of the tangent screw. In this way he was able by means of a crank to advance his large circle by strictly constant angles.

The division of the circle was effected with the aid of a specially constructed dividing-engine [7]. The platform for this machine had itself been toothed by an original rectification process. Two circular limbs had been superimposed and fastened to each other by screws and a first common cutting of teeth effected; the position of one of the limbs was then modified in relation to the other and the thread of the tangent screw was passed through the teeth again. This operation being repeated systematically a certain number of times, the teeth of the two limbs were corrected reciprocally, and Gambey obtained a perfectly regular pitch.

Gambey also tried to eliminate two other sources of error. The first concerned the imperfection of the centring of the circle to be divided on the machine; the second the magnification of errors arising from the fact that the circle to be divided was of a larger diameter than that of the machine. He conceived a deformable parallelogram, driven by a rectifying plate, which automatically corrected the position of the scriber for each division, causing practically all the mechanical faults to disappear. This correcting device was used after him by other instrument-makers.

We cannot give details of all the precautions that Gambey took in carrying out his operations. We will give as examples compensation for the inertia of mobile parts by judiciously placed counterweights, and remote control of the scriber in order to eliminate the effects of the body-heat of the operator. These demonstrate Gambey's sense of mechanical precision. His great mural circle, which was executed about 1840, remained in use until 1920.

Dilatometers and comparators. Clock-makers were the first to try to measure the thermal expansion of metals. The earliest instruments served to study the expansion of brass and steel rods intended for making pendulums. In 1726 John Harrison invented his bimetallic gridiron, designed to cancel by compensation the effects of variations of temperature on the length of the pendulum.

About the same time, Graham conceived the first precision dilatometer. This instrument was composed essentially of two fixed end-pieces between which was placed the metal rod to be examined; one of the end-pieces was pierced by a threaded hole, in which a micrometer screw was inserted. The desired constant temperature having been established, the screw was turned until its extremity touched the extremity of the rod. The displacement of the screw was read on a dial whose divisions indicated the thermal elongation of the rod. The experiment was repeated at a higher temperature, when a different setting of the screw was necessary to make contact with the rod. A little later, in 1754, Smeaton described a dilatometer of his own invention (figure 221) which is merely an improvement on that of Graham [8]. One of the end-pieces is hinged and moves as a result of the thrust due to thermal expansion. The elongation of the rod is then amplified

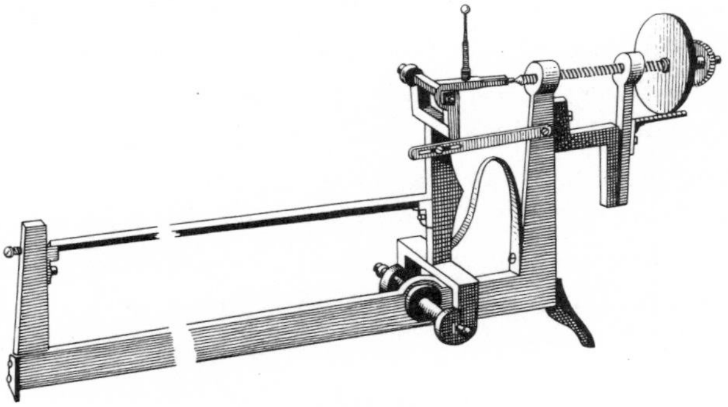

FIGURE 221—*Smeaton's dilatometer, 1754.*

and the movement of the reference point is measured by the rotation of a micrometer screw fitted with a dial and bearing on a stop carried by the end-piece.

About 1760 Berthoud made a constant-temperature enclosure in which he suspended metal rods to be studied. One extremity of these was fixed; the other rested on one arm of a small bent lever, the other arm of which carried a toothed sector engaging with a pinion, on the shaft of which was placed a pointer. A counterweight, the cord of which passed over a grooved wheel, brought the pointer back during cooling. This device for amplifying small movements has been used in nearly all instruments, both dilatometers and comparators, constructed subsequently. A common form of these instruments was the Musschenbroek dilatometer, made simply for physical laboratories and not used industrially.

Lavoisier used the same appliance, on a large scale, for the expansion measurements carried out with Laplace in 1781 [9]. The rod to be examined was placed in a large tank containing water heated to a given temperature. One of its extremities rested against a fixed glass stud, and the other on the arm of a lever bearing a sighting telescope. The inclination of the telescope was measured by means of a graduated levelling-rod placed 200 metres away. The degree of precision was of the order of 0·003 cm.

About 1784 Ramsden constructed a dilatometer for William Roy, in charge of geodesical triangulations in Kent (p 607), which in certain respects recalls that of Lavoisier and Laplace [10]. The rod to be examined, placed in a tank, rests on rollers; one of its extremities rests on a fixed stud, the other on a hinged spring. The observation is made according to a principle quite different from that described above. Ramsden used two microscopes, each placed at an extremity of the apparatus. The body of one of the microscopes being divided, the objective followed the displacement of the free end of the rod being examined, and this displacement was measured by a micrometer fitted to the eyepiece. The precision was of the order of 0·0014 in.

In 1792 Edward Troughton constructed a comparator accurate to 0·001 in. This instrument is nothing else than a beam compass, the points of which were moved by micrometer screws.

In France several comparators were constructed by Fortin and by Lenoir for the *Commission des Poids et Mesures*. Fortin's comparator was designed to measure the dimensions of cylindrical standards of the kilogram [11]. It consisted of a carriage which rested against the cylinder to be measured and was fitted with a feeler which moved in front of a graduated scale a pointer whose position was read through a microscope. The apparatus was accurate to 0·00008 in.

Under the direction of J. C. de Borda (1733–99) and Lavoisier, Lenoir made rules for measuring the bases of triangulations. These rules were of platinum; each had at one end a small graduated slide which moved in a guide in front of a vernier. Lavoisier had some years previously used a rule made on the same principle by Lenel. The thermal examination of the rules was made by transforming each of them into bimetallic thermometers; a copper foil, of about the same length as the rule, was fixed on each platinum rod at one of its extremities; and a vernier graduation was engraved on the other end in order to read the differences in the variation of the two lengths. Lenoir also made an original thrust comparator, with which the reading was made with the aid of a vernier. Later he designed another thrust and bent lever comparator; the unequal arms of the lever increased the precision of the reading [12]. Several examples of this apparatus, which was accurate to 0·00008 in, were made subsequently.

Afterwards, lever comparators and microscope comparators were used simultaneously for a long time. Gambey used a microscope for reading on the vernier the position of a sliding rule on his comparator, which was constructed on the principle of externally measuring calipers; he obtained an accuracy of 0·001 mm. He also constructed a lever apparatus. Brunner, about 1850, constructed a dual lever comparator the precision of which was about 0·001 mm. Subsequently he constructed very precise microscope comparators for the *Commission des Poids et Mesures*.

II. THE INSTRUMENTS MANUFACTURED

Astronomical instruments. We shall speak here only of the mechanical parts of these instruments and their general arrangement. Thanks to the improvement in methods, the construction of large instruments made considerable progress in the period between the middle of the eighteenth century and the middle of the nineteenth. Telescopes, which since 1755 had been fitted with achromatic objectives, continued to be used as transit instruments, meridian or equatorial telescopes, or for equipping circles or quadrants serving to determine the position of the stars. But what characterizes the period up to about 1820 is the favour that large reflecting telescopes found with astronomers.

It was not until the second quarter of the eighteenth century that the reflecting telescope began to be commonly made. Scarlett (d 1743) in England, and Paris and Passemant (1702–69) in France, were those who spread its manufacture. The instruments that came from these workshops consisted of small brass cylinders 16 inches in length, usually mounted on a folding tripod. From this period the orientation of the tube was controlled by toothed sectors engaging with a cranked pinion. The adjustment of the small mirror was effected by a knob turning a threaded rod.

These telescopes were drawing-room pieces. The first observatory telescopes were constructed by James Short (1710–68). This Scottish astronomer and instrument-maker confined himself to Gregorian telescopes, some of them being of large dimensions, up to 12 ft in length. He must have made a special study of the mechanical design. For controlling the different movements he used long mahogany handles with Cardan joints, a device fitted at this time to all instruments above a certain size. Short made the tubes of his instruments of mahogany with a polygonal section. At about the same time Dom Noël, custodian of the royal collection of physical apparatus in Paris, constructed large telescopes of the Cassegrain type; the largest had a focal length of 24 ft.

It was with Sir William Herschel (1738–1822) that the reflecting telescope became a true instrument of astronomical research. From 1785 to 1789 he devoted himself to the construction of a 40-ft instrument, called a 'front view telescope' on account of the principle on which it had been designed [13]. The main difficulty consisted in the casting and polishing of the mirror, but the mechanical equipment also demanded quite new methods. A wooden frame supporting the tube, which measured 12 metres in length and 147 cm in width, was mounted on a platform revolving on rollers.

Herschel's discoveries aroused great interest in this type of telescope. Several examples were constructed in the years that followed. In France, Carochez made one in 1800. But the success of the big refracting telescopes began soon afterwards, and for a time engaged the attention of instrument-makers and astronomers. On account of their dimensions, the mechanical problems posed by their installation were very difficult to solve; their cost was very high. It was only towards 1850 that large reflecting telescopes were built again. Lord Rosse's 52-ft telescope, constructed in Ireland in 1845, amazed his contemporaries. Léon Foucault revived this tradition in France at the same time.

The German optician Fraunhofer and his French colleague Lerebours (1762–1840) were the first to succeed in constructing large lenses for astronomical purposes when, about 1815–20, the manufacture of flint-glass became relatively straightforward (ch 12). The progress of the optician's art led to correspondingly great progress in the mechanical art. During the first half of the nineteenth century the dimensions of refractors grew steadily. The construction of stands for them, and the making of driving devices, developed rapidly. Among the problems most difficult to solve were those relating to the setting and adjustment of transit telescopes and meridian circles. The outline which has been given above of the improvement of the working resources available to engineers enables us to understand how the solutions devised could be progressively improved. Instrument-makers like Ramsden and Troughton were the first to seek entirely new appliances. They adopted the truncated-cone shape both for the telescope bodies and for the transverse arms supporting them. The mechanical strength of two frusta of a cone joined by their bases led them to introduce this structure into the construction of numerous instruments. They used a metal frame, having the shape of a long cage with four or six pillars, to hold meridian or equatorial telescopes. They abandoned the old toothed sectors and replaced them by circular plates with helical teeth engaging with tangential screws. These devices had first been used for small instruments like sextants or microscopes, but the improvement in materials and tools permitted them to be successfully used for large astronomical instruments.

Later, Reichenbach, Repsold, Airy, and Gambey used and improved these devices still further. Great progress was made in the casting of metal parts. Up to the end of the eighteenth century large parts had consisted of metal bars joined by screws. John Bird brought the manufacture of quadrants to the highest point of perfection that it could at that time attain, by determining the most suitable shape of the different elements and the best manner of assembling them.

The cage-like frame with metal pillars was abandoned for meridian instruments, and replaced by solid masonry columns, but great ingenuity and skill had then to be devoted to the supporting parts. In order to avoid bending the supports, and to reduce the strain on the driving gears, the large parts were counterpoised. It was during this period that the constructional principles of the large modern instruments were worked out.

Geodesy. The construction of instruments for geodesy and nautical astronomy developed much more rapidly than that of the larger astronomical instruments. After the end of the seventeenth century, Hadley's quadrant and octant were added to the standard instruments which had been in use for several centuries (vol III, ch 20). Whereas the quadrant was adopted fairly quickly by geodesists, sailors remained faithful to the old instruments up to the middle of the eighteenth century. Octants with sights, several types of which were invented about 1730–2, came into use only towards the middle of the century.

The octant consists of a sector of forty-five degrees; a moving alidade carries a small mirror situated in the centre of the instrument. On one arm is a sighting telescope and on the other a second fixed mirror. The height of a star is measured by noting the position of the alidade when the image of the star, reflected from the pivoted to the fixed mirror and thence into the telescope, coincides with the horizon, seen through an unsilvered portion of the fixed mirror. To permit direct reading, 30 minute divisions on the limb are numbered as degrees (vol III, figure 342).

New problems were set by the manufacture of these instruments, which are not, however, more complicated in their principle than the traditional quadrants and circles. The most difficult to solve were the optician's. In particular the manufacture of perfectly plane mirrors presented serious difficulties even at the end of the eighteenth century.

Iron, brass, and wood were for long used in combination in the making of the bodies of octants and quadrants. Much effort was devoted to the alidade and to the method of fixing it, and to the engraving of the divisions. For long, a brass plate carrying the graduations was fixed to the wooden or iron limb. In the end it was seen that this combination of materials impaired the precision of the measurements, particularly on account of the differences in expansion. Towards 1760 these instruments, the radius of which attained 40 to 50 cm, were cast in one piece. The length of the radius was reduced and that of the arc extended. The 60° sector was divided into 120 degrees and the instrument assumed the name of sextant (plate 22 B). With the addition of a vernier and an adjusting-screw it rapidly assumed the form in which it is used by sailors in our own times.

All these little manufacturing problems were relatively simple, and had already been solved in other connexions. It is, however, interesting to note that the invention of the sextant led to their systematic study with a view to finding large-scale manufacturing processes; all the workshops adopted the best available solutions, which quickly became standard ones. It has already been mentioned that it was the industrial manufacture of sextants that gave the incentive to the invention of dividing-engines.

The quadrant remained the favourite instrument of geodesists up to about 1780. In 1752 the German astronomical geometer J. T. Mayer (1723–62) thought of using a small circle and repeating the measurement of the same angle several times without reverting to zero between each measurement. The error due to the defects of the instrument was thus divided by the number of observations. About 1772 the navigator and astronomer J. C. de Borda (1733–99) took up Mayer's principle, which had remained unused, and slightly modified the apparatus of the German astronomer. He invented the instrument known as the Borda circle [14]. This instrument (figure 222) was made by the French engineer Lenoir. About ten years later the same engineer thought out the dual-telescope repeating circle for terrestrial observations.

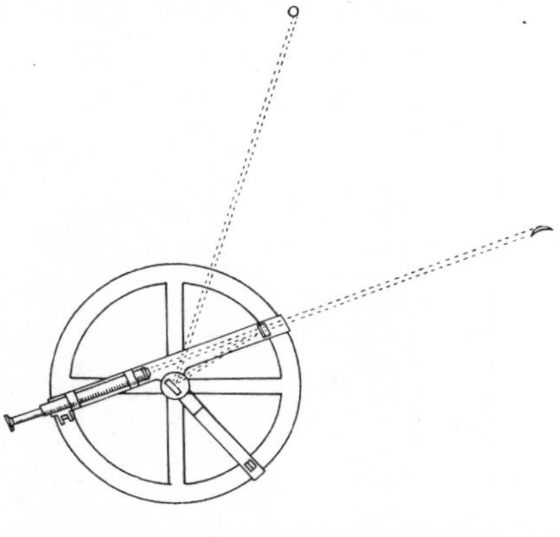

FIGURE 222—*Borda's reflection circle, constructed by Lenoir. (See figure 329.)*

The reflection circle was quickly adopted because Lenoir (1744–1832) knew how to manufacture it perfectly. The art of the engineer was here applied to the turning of the axis of the alidade, and its seating in the alidade and in the centre of the circle [15]. The circle itself was cast in one piece. The division of the graduated limb was done by machine. Numerous other details of design were executed with excellent judgement.

The repeating circle is of a much more complicated design. It is borne on a conical column resting on a plate fitted with clamping screws, alidade, and vernier, and can be orientated in every azimuth. The circle is fixed at its centre to a cylindrical axis perpendicular to its plane. This axis has at its other extremity a counterweight balancing the whole equipment; at its centre it passes through another axis, the extremities of which, turning on pivots, rest on two branches of a vertical brace surmounting the column. This shaft, turning on its pivots, enables the circle to take any inclination from horizontal to vertical. The circle has two telescopes which move independently of each other. The limb is graduated into 4000 degrees, and reading is effected by four microscopes opposite four verniers.

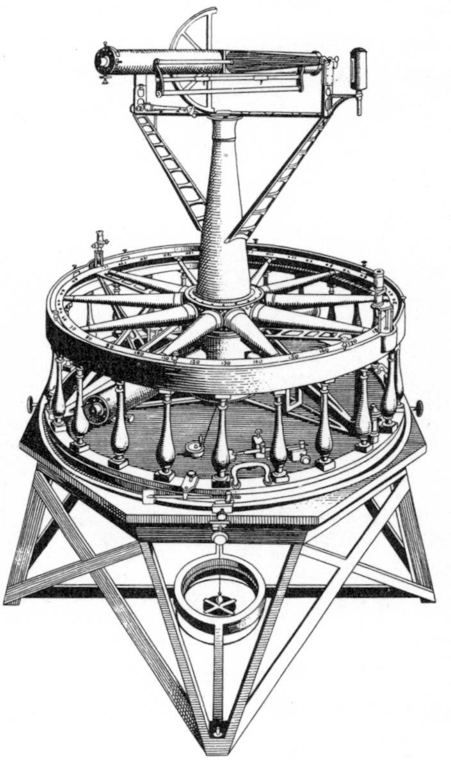

FIGURE 223—*Ramsden's first large theodolite, 1784.*

The invention and execution of these two instruments were notable events in the history of precision mechanics. Lenoir's repeating circle is in fact one of the first modern instruments for geodesy. It gave much better results than other instruments known at the time. Following the linking up of the triangulations of France and England (p 604), it enabled measurements to be made which were as accurate as those effected with Ramsden's theodolite, one of the masterpieces of the great English engineer. It was this instrument that was adopted for Mechain and Delambre's operations; the best instrument-makers of the time, Fortin, Reichenbach, and later Gambey, were inspired by its principle to construct other triangulation instruments.

The first theodolite had been described by Leonard Digges about the middle of the sixteenth century (vol III, p 541), but the instrument was not much used until towards the end of the eighteenth century, following the magnificent work of Ramsden, who between 1784 and 1790 built two large theodolites which were used for the triangulation of Great Britain [16]. These instruments are interesting because we see in them the best design of the time.

All the parts subject to mechanical stress are frusta of cones (figure 223). The cradle of the telescope consists of two parallel circles; the stability of the brace on which the cradle-shaft rests is ensured by two perforated struts. The reading is made by means of two microscopes on the zenith circles and four microscopes on the azimuth circle. The circles are operated by tangential screws. This instrument enabled bearings to be taken at a distance of 10 miles with a precision of about one second.

No theodolite of such large dimensions was subsequently constructed, but the best engineers of the nineteenth century made numerous models of similar type. The telescope with its zenith circle generally rests, through a brace, on a brass column fixed on an azimuth disk; the latter is provided with clamping-screws. These are Ramsden's solutions adapted to smaller instruments.

The instruments used by geometers and surveyors for measuring angles benefited from the optical and mechanical improvements made during this period in instruments for geodesy. Among these we shall mention only the graphometer, in which the telescope was substituted fairly late for the sighted alidade. This substitution involved a more accurate division of the semicircular limb with a vernier, and the use of the tangential screw for the two movements.

Physical apparatus. The improvement of physical instruments and the increase in their number and diversity were the consequence of many factors. We shall ignore here all the demonstration instruments with which the physical laboratories of the day were equipped: conceived during the first quarter of the eighteenth century to illustrate the laws of Newtonian physics, they were reproduced for more than a century without any mechanical improvement or any great practical advantage.

This was not so, however, as regards observational instruments, all of which received the improvements made possible by the progress of technology. Turning, adjusting, division of scales, the introduction of verniers and micrometer screws gave each of them a modern construction in the period approximately from 1780 to 1840; this is true also of barometers, thermometers, hygrometers, and microscopes, and, later, of polarimeters and the numerous optical instruments which appeared, pneumatic pumps, and electrical machines.

The increase in number and improvement in design and construction of these appliances are facts whose importance must not be underestimated. Two examples will enable us to understand how laboratory research was linked with the techniques of instrument-making from the middle of the eighteenth century.

The first is that of the construction of precision balances. The art of the scale-maker is an old one. Relatively sensitive and precise balances were manufactured very early to meet the needs of goldsmiths and money changers. In the laboratory, the assayers were the first to need good balances. Physicists used hydrostatic balances to ascertain the density of solids. But these adaptations were made without any fundamental transformation of the balance itself. The proportions of the parts were reduced to make assay balances in which the beam, with a shaft passing through its centre, rested on bearings at the end of a vertical rod. Such balances were, however, articles of ironwork rather than fruits of mechanical theory.

The method of suspension was improved, but only very slowly. The pivots of the beam were better cut, and the bearings on which the pivots rested were provided with a hard steel bushing. The true knife-edge bearing, however, was not in current use until the beginning of the nineteenth century. The suspension wires of the scale pans were lengthened to lower the centre of gravity of the system, and began to be made of brass to eliminate the influence of variations in the humidity of the atmosphere. An indicator moving in front of a scale was fixed in the middle of the balance beam. Finally, placed under a protective glass cover, the balance was fitted with a device to check the movement of the pans [17]. Such a balance was made by the clockmaker Gallonde for the chemist Rouelle about 1760 (figure 224).

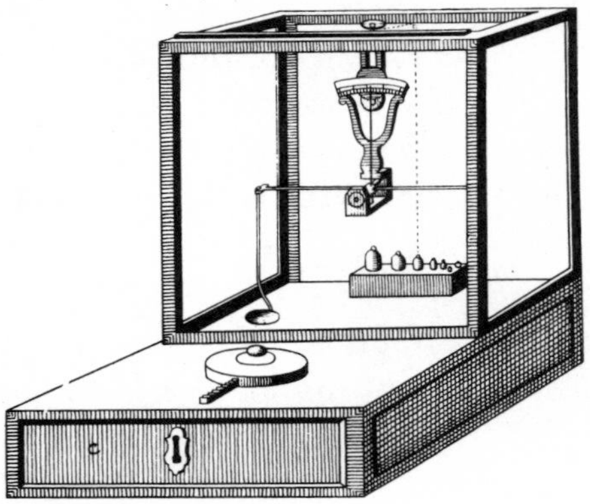

FIGURE 224—*Assayer's balance, constructed by Gallonde about 1760.*

Some years later the structure of the balance was profoundly modified and all the problems of sensitivity and accuracy were carefully studied. The first precision balance, apparently, was the one constructed by John Harrison (1693–1776) for Cavendish about 1770–5 [18]. Harrison tried to ensure the rigidity of the beam by giving it a triangular section, and adjusted the position of the centre of gravity by means of threaded rods, fixed one at each end of the beam, carrying movable nuts. For the first time there appeared a knife-edge of triangular section, and a device for raising the beam clear of it while at rest.

Several of these designs were used at the same time by the mechanical engineer Mégnié (1751 ?–1807), who made the first two precision balances for Lavoisier. Mégnié understood the need to make the central knife-edge of the beam rest on a hard steel plate placed at the top of a rigid column. The beam was raised when the balance was not in use by a cranked lever placed inside the column; this system is neater and more finished than Harrison's [19].

Two other large precision balances, one made by Ramsden about 1787 (figure 225), the other by Fortin in 1788, served as models for more than twenty years.

Ramsden made the beam in the form of two frusta of cones united at their bases, a principle widely used, as already stated, for the construction of all parts where rigidity was essential [20]. The knife-edge, whose section was diamond-shaped, rested on agate plates supported by a brass frame. The support for this frame consists of four small brass columns fixed firmly on the base.

About 1797 Troughton constructed a balance inspired by that of Ramsden [21], but great differences can be seen, which should have made Troughton's instrument superior. Although we again find the beam to be formed of two frusta of cones united at their bases, the devices for supporting the knife-edge and balance pans are designed differently. Moreover, the base of the apparatus no longer consists of a vertical cage but of a brass column of large diameter (figure 226). The advantages of this design are easily understood.

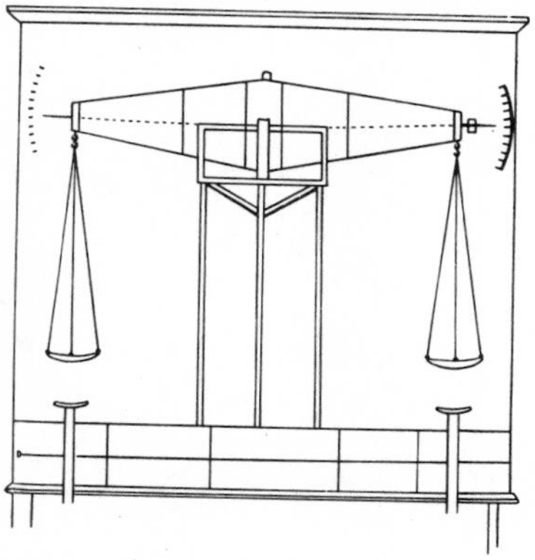

FIGURE 225—*Ramsden's precision balance, c 1787.*

In Fortin's balance, 1788, the beam is made of a strong steel blade turned on edge [22] (figure 227); the hardened steel knife-edge rests on less hard steel bushes so that the edge is not worn down. The beam is supported on a strong brass column. For thirty years Fortin remained faithful to this kind of beam and suspension. He used various devices for lifting the beam and releasing the knife-edge while at rest, each simpler and more precise in operation than the previous one. Like his colleagues, he used a long pointer to give more precise readings, which were made with a microscope. Curiously enough, the balance-makers apparently soon abandoned the microscope, and it does not reappear again until later. Fortin constructed many balances. The first was ordered by Lavoisier, others by the *Commission des Poids et Mesures*. An excellent scale-maker at the Paris Mint, Fourché, also built some balances inspired by those of Fortin.

All the precision balances at the end of the eighteenth century were designed for weighing quantities of the order of a kilogram with an accuracy of about a milligram. In general they had long beams and large pans suspended by metal attachments. To meet government requirements, scale-makers like Parent continued to make large precision balances, but for laboratories the dimensions of the balances were reduced after the Swedish chemist J. J. Berzelius (1779–1848) had shown that it was more convenient to work with small quantities.

Gambey and the engineers of his generation gave precision balances their modern appearance about 1840–50 [23]. The beam was from that period made of brass; it was in the form of a flattened lozenge turned on edge. Finally, in a balance made by Collot in 1855, we see small fractional weights or riders placed on the balance beam by a hook manipulated from outside the case by a long rod with a milled head. This device remained in use for a very long time and only recently disappeared from modern balances.

A second example of the part precision mechanics played in the construction of laboratory apparatus is provided by instruments of quite another kind constructed for Lavoisier, though not all of them can be discussed here. It is sufficient to mention only the history of the two large pneumatic bell-jars which he called 'gasometers'.

Probably during the winter of 1781–2, Lavoisier had a first pneumatic apparatus of this kind made to a fairly simple design [24]. Above a water-tank made of tin is suspended a similar, but slightly smaller tank, which can be inserted upside-down in the first. The suspension is by a cord carrying a counter-weight and passing over a pulley. Nozzles and cocks were fitted to let gases in or out. This device did not represent any particular mechanical invention, but soon afterwards Lavoisier felt the need to turn it into a measuring device. It was easy to add differential barometers (virtually manometers) and thermometers for determining the physical state of the enclosed gas.

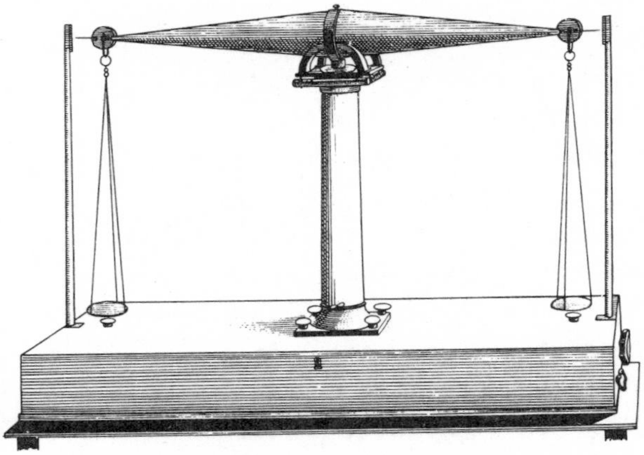

FIGURE 226—*Troughton's precision balance*, c *1797*.

It was also necessary, however, to modify the system of suspension. Meusnier, an engineer officer and member of the Académie des Sciences, who collaborated with Lavoisier in studying the industrial preparation of hydrogen, invented the first device for this purpose. The tank was suspended at the end of a balance beam by chains which would not stretch, or at least were considered not to do so. The idea for the balance beam was undoubtedly borrowed from early steam-engines of the Newcomen type. Each arm of the balance ended in an arc of a circle on which the suspension chain was supported, as in fire pumps of the day. One of the arms supported the pneumatic tank, the other a pan on which weights were placed to balance the weight of the tank. In addition, however, it was necessary to compensate for the variation in the upthrust on the suspended tank, which depended on the extent to which it was immersed. Meusnier succeeded in doing this by means of a parallelogram, whose shape would be altered by means of a screw; by adjusting the latter it was possible to vary as desired the position of the centre of gravity of the system (figure 228). In 1783 Mégnié constructed two devices based on this principle.

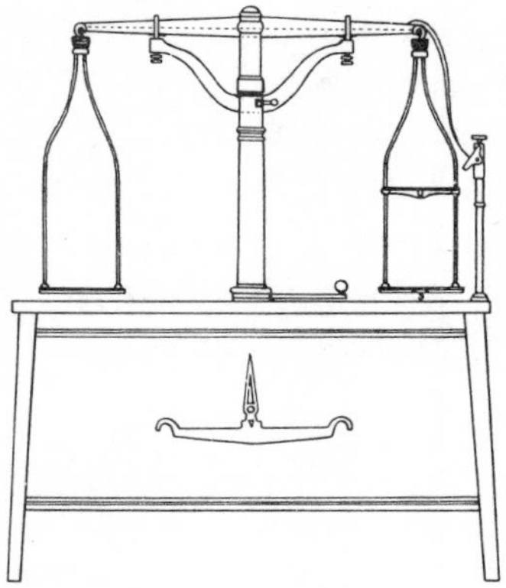

FIGURE 227—*Precision balance constructed by Fortin between 1788 and 1800.*

Two years later Lavoisier ordered from the same engineer two other 'gasometers', which were completed in 1787. It is particularly interesting to compare them with the preceding ones. The rectangular tanks were replaced by cylindrical tanks with convex bottoms. This form did not give satisfaction, however, because during use the upper bell revolved and it was difficult to remove the gaseous residues that accumulated in the top of it. Apart from this, all the other innovations seem to have been very judiciously designed. The balance beam terminated by two arcs of a circle was retained; it was made of brass and neither of its arms was cut, which certainly ensured much greater precision of the readings. Compensation for changes in upthrust was effected by means of a loaded brass ball sliding on a metal bar fixed to the middle of the balance beam, and perpendicular to it. On one side of the bar was a rack, and the ball had a toothed pinion which could be turned with the aid of a rod fitted with a milled head. The ball could thus be moved with precision. Attention was also given to the rollers on which the axis of the beam rested; the idea was borrowed from the clock-makers, who used it at that time for the construction of the most delicate movements. This structural detail, which gave the apparatus exceptional sensitivity, makes it an excellent precision instrument (figure 229).

FIGURE 228—*Lavoisier's first 'gasometer' devised by Meusnier and built by Mégnié.*

These designs are among the first, if not the first, in which it is possible to realize the value and importance of the engineer's contribution to laboratory research. It is very characteristic that it came just when engineers were beginning to develop methods which enabled them to give their work a sensitivity and precision previously unknown.

From this period, scientific research was increasingly linked with applied mechanics. Lavoisier's experiments on the composition of water gave rise to the

FIGURE 229—*Lavoisier's second 'gasometer', constructed by Mégnié, 1787.*

manufacture of apparatus constructed on the same principles as those described above. Lefebvre-Gineau at the Collège de France and Van Marum at the Teylers Museum, Haarlem, constructed 'gasometers' in subsequent years. The result of the first attempt had already borne fruit; the new types of apparatus were less cumbersome and contained less finical structures than those of Lavoisier. As time went by, the research worker had to appeal constantly to the engineer, and submit the most widely different problems to him. It is impossible here even to summarize the history of this collaboration. Having emphasized the point, we shall confine ourselves to recalling very briefly the work of Léon Foucault (1819–68) which came at the end of the period with which we are dealing.

Foucault carried out two experiments of historical importance, namely the physical demonstration of the rotation of the Earth by the pendulum and gyroscope and the measurement of the speed of light by the rotating mirror method. The success of these experiments is due chiefly to the mastery with which Gustave Froment (1815–65) constructed the apparatus designed by Foucault. Froment, who was a student at the École Polytechnique in Paris, was one of the best of the French precision engineers who worked in the middle of the nineteenth century. Almost all the French physicists of that time owed their practical achievements to his feeling for applied mechanics and his constructive skill. From 1840, in association with Dumoulin, he won a high reputation for his firm. He was the first, from 1844, to use an electric motor for driving his dividing-engines. He did not make scientific instruments only: among his achievements of great historical importance should be mentioned telegraphic equipment with a dial (1843) and the Hughes telegraphic equipment (1856).

These two examples show the extent of the application of precision engineering at this time: until then, although it fulfilled many needs, it still had only a relatively limited field of application. Engineering achievements at the beginning of the nineteenth century represented only a relatively low degree of precision: it cannot be considered, for example, that the boring of the cylinders of steam-engines then showed a very high degree of precision. Several decades later this was no longer so. The perfection of mechanisms and the industrial use of electricity, in telegraphy for example, were creating new and rapidly expanding fields.

Chronometers. Innovations in the mechanism of clocks and watches resulting from the use of the pendulum and spiral spring led clock-makers and mechanics to devote much effort to the construction of chronometers that could be used at sea. This research was of great interest in view of the difficulties, indeed the impossibility, confronting a navigator in plotting his exact position at sea if he did not know the time at the zero meridian. Since the different astronomical methods of measuring longitude gave only inadequate results, the solution consisted in finding means of constructing very accurate clocks whose working was not disturbed by the motion of the ship.

Huygens thought of making the end of the pendulum travel in a cycloidally curved path to ensure the isochronism of its oscillations, while to compensate for the motion of the sea he suggested various modes of suspension of the pendulum. The majority of clock-makers who studied the problem at this time, or later, attempted to use double balance wheels, copied from Hooke, with the idea that the irregularity of one would be offset by that of the other. Henry Sully (1680–1728) was perhaps one of the last to attempt to apply such solutions, but when his clocks were tried out at sea they did not give good results. At the same time, many other investigations were carried out; among them, for example, that of a Frenchman, de Rivaz, who used circular balance wheels fixed at the centre of a flexible steel beam stretched between two supports.

The most interesting of unsuccessful experiments was that of Pierre Leroy (1717–85), who devoted himself to the problem between 1748 and 1766 [25]. At the beginning of this period, Leroy invented a new escapement which he used in the construction of his two chronometers. Very ingenious in design, but very difficult to construct, this escapement was not used by any other clock-maker, but its principle—that of the escapement leaving the balance wheel free during the greater part of its movement—is the one used later in marine chronometers [26].

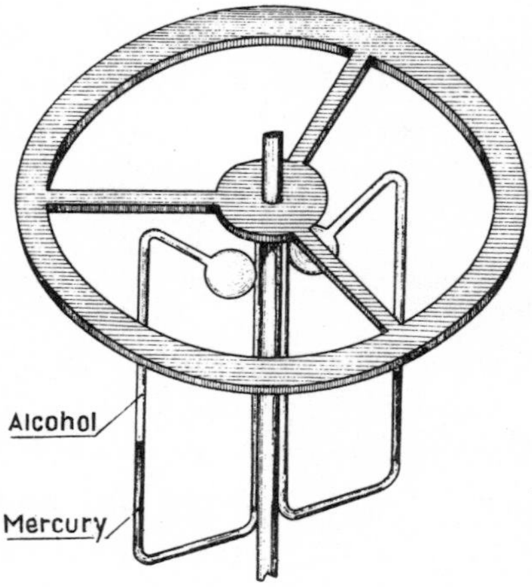

FIGURE 230—*Leroy's balance wheel with alcohol–mercury thermal compensation.*

Leroy also thought of thermal compensation for the balance wheel. For this purpose he used what were in effect two thin curved thermometers, each containing mercury and alcohol, fixed on either side of the staff of the balance wheel so that the mercury was pushed towards the staff when the temperature rose (figure 230). Finally, he obtained isochronism of the oscillations by using two spiral springs, wound in opposite directions, for the attachment of which he applied a principle which has since been known as the Leroy rule for points of attachment.

Tried out at sea during three successive voyages between 1767 and 1772, Leroy's two chronometers gave excellent results, comparable with those obtained by the English clock-maker Harrison some years earlier with his best marine watch. However, at this time Leroy had a long dispute with his rival, Ferdinand Berthoud (1727–1807), and decided to retire from the field: except for this incident his work would have had a wider result. In the event, it remained merely an episode without a sequel in the history of chronometry. Although Leroy was the first to expound clearly the principles on which marine chronometers were later constructed, none of the actual solutions which he used was adopted.

The English clock-maker John Harrison (1693–1776) was undoubtedly the first maker of a timepiece that could be used satisfactorily at sea [27]. As early as 1728 he had submitted the plans for a marine clock to Graham, who had encouraged him and advanced him £200 for further experiment. In 1735 he completed his first marine chronometer: this was tested at sea and gave results which were sufficiently good for further financial help to be granted to its maker. Harrison then began clock No 2, which he did not submit for trial, announcing that he had

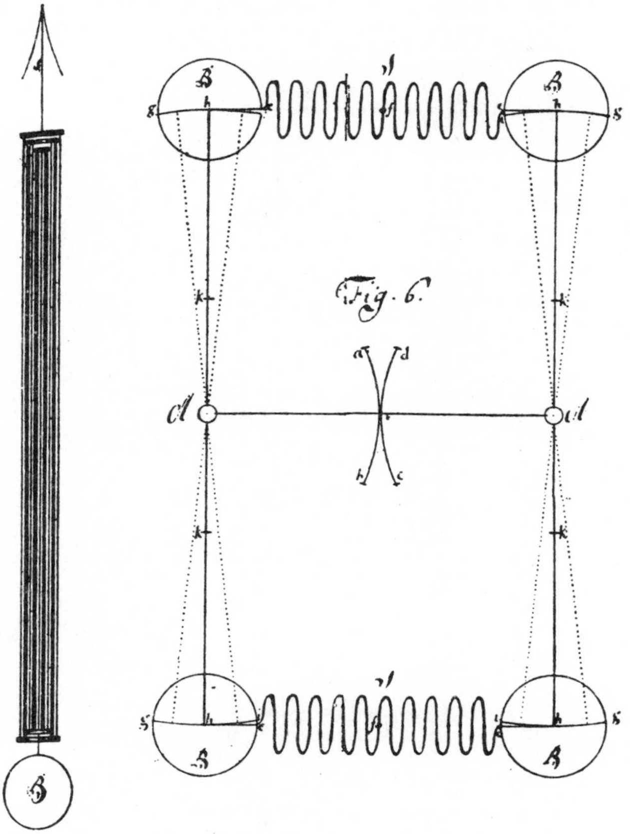

FIGURE 231—*Parts of Harrison's chronometers, according to an original manuscript, showing gridiron pendulum and rectilinear compensator.*

begun to construct, by a different principle, his clock No 3, which was completed in 1757. Finally clock No 4 was completed in 1759 [28]: only this last one was tested at sea. The responsible authorities in England (the Board of Longitude) demanded numerous trials, and caused the clock-maker Larcum Kendall (1721–95) to make a replica of Harrison's No 4; when tested this gave results as satisfactory as those of the original. It was not until 1772, however, that Harrison received the whole of the award of £20 000 which the Board of Longitude had offered since 1714 for the first marine chronometer capable of enabling longitude to be determined at sea with an accuracy of half a degree (vol III, pp 557, 672).

Throughout his work Harrison's mastery as a mechanic can clearly be seen. The son of a carpenter, he began by manufacturing wooden clocks: for a long time he used wood for certain parts of his chronometers, with the object of avoiding the use of lubricating oil. His No 4, however, was made entirely of metal.

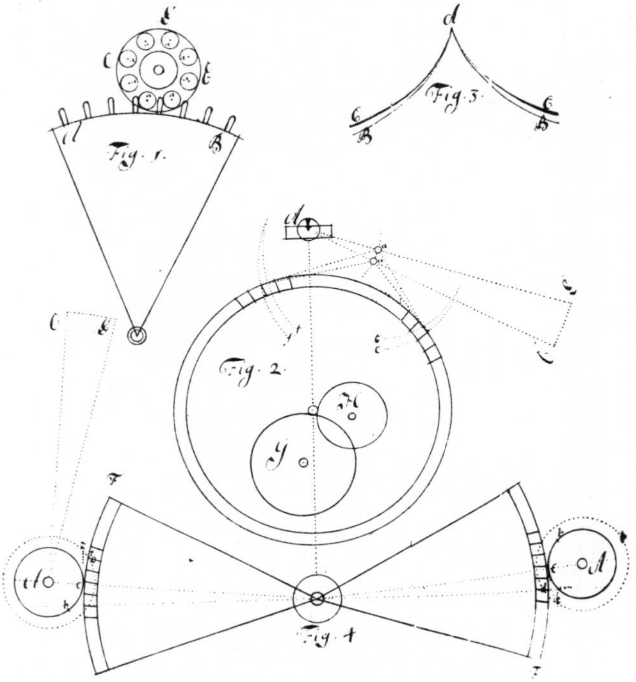

FIGURE 232—*Parts of Harrison's chronometers, from original manuscript, showing roller pinions, bevel escapement, and cycloidal guides for the balance wheels.*

In his first two clocks he used a double rectilinear balance mounted on counterpoised shafts and guided by cycloids (figure 231). On the first there is a bimetallic compensating device for thermal variations. Harrison made long investigations to perfect this device, still called the Harrison grid. The three grids of clock No 1 have the effect of displacing steel stops, and so causing the tension of the spiral springs on the balance wheels to vary. This system was simplified for clock No 2.

The modifications made in the construction of clocks Nos 3 and 4 are numerous. The most important are the abandonment of the rectilinear balances in favour of balance wheels, and the replacement of the grid by a bimetallic strip. The latter device ensured thermal compensation of the oscillations of the spiral spring in a simpler and more elegant manner.

Harrison also invented a special 'grasshopper' escapement (figure 232 and vol III, figure 411), and an original device to ensure the isochronism of the two balance wheels. He used roller bearings to eliminate friction and the need for lubrication. He introduced certain complications in his mechanism, such as a remontoir to keep the driving force to the escapement practically constant and a spring to maintain the movement during the winding of the clock.

Most of these inventions appear in John Harrison's fourth and last design, chronometer No 4, but this again is entirely different from the one that preceded it. Its dimensions are considerably reduced, and approximate to those of a watch. He abandoned the principle of a double balance wheel and the use of rollers; he remained faithful to the cycloidal correction of the movement of the balance; and he invented a new escapement with diamond palettes. Tested over long distances, including two voyages to Jamaica, chronometer No 4 consistently showed variations that involved errors in the calculation of longitudes less than the maximum of half a degree stipulated by the Board of Longitude for its full award.

Harrison had already obtained remarkable results when the Swiss clock-maker Ferdinand Berthoud began his investigations, which were conducted mainly from 1760 to 1768. Berthoud, indeed, made more rapid progress than his English contemporary. He was already a skilled clock-maker when he began to devote himself to the problem of marine chronometers, and unlike Harrison he did not have to complete his training while working. He proceeded more directly to good mechanical design. He devoted less thought and reflection to his work than Harrison did, but his work was guided by wider experience in the practice of clock-making. As with Harrison and Pierre Leroy, Berthoud's work shows outstanding practical ability.

The range of parts constructed by Berthoud is large [29], but the complete clocks made during these researches numbered only seven or eight. His clock No 1 was made in 1760, followed in 1763 by clock No 2. These two instruments are bulky, though No 2 was notably smaller than the first. In these clocks Berthoud put two circular balance wheels oscillating in opposite directions and connected with one another by means of a toothed wheel. Their axes rested on roller bearings. A bimetallic gridiron, already widely used by clock-makers since its invention by Harrison, compensated for variations in temperature by variations in the length of the spiral. The escapement was made more complicated in clock No 2, in which Berthoud introduced an equalizing remontoir. It should be noted that he at first used a spring barrel fitted with a fusee as the source of motive power; this device has been retained until the present time for the construction of marine chronometers, but Berthoud himself temporarily abandoned it almost at once. In a marine watch, also made in 1763 (watch No 3), Berthoud used a bimetallic strip for thermal compensation and a single balance wheel.

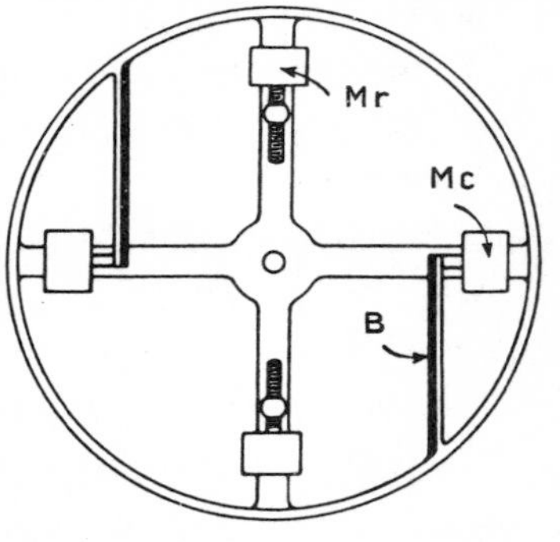

FIGURE 233—*Berthoud's compensated balance wheel.* (MR) *Adjustable slider;* (MC) *slider attached to bimetallic strip* B.

Retaining the single balance wheel suspended by a wire and guided by rollers, he returned to the gridiron method of compensation for the construction of his subsequent clocks, of which Nos 6 and 8 (1767) ensured his success. In this series the motive power derived from weights placed on a vertical metal plate which descended the length of three brass columns. An escapement with ruby cylinders replaced the escapements previously used, and all the parts were relatively compact. The mechanism was above the gridiron and the whole occupied the top part of the clock, which was enclosed in a long glass cylinder; the three brass columns guiding the descent of the weight took up almost the whole height of this cylinder. The horizontal dial covered the glass box. Clocks 6 and 8 were tested at sea in 1768 and 1769, and showed variations in their working of the order of from 5 to 20 seconds a day.

We know of only five chronometers made by John Harrison, who did not reach his goal until a fairly advanced age. Berthoud, on the contrary, was able to continue working for thirty years and it was he who gave the marine chronometer practically its modern form. Abandoning the roller suspension of the balance wheel, he adopted a pivot suspension. He came back to compensation by bimetallic strips, eliminating the cumbersome gridiron, and used a balance wheel compensated by means of four small weights. Two of these weights were fixed and the two others were carried by a bimetallic strip which moved towards or away from the arbor according to variations in temperature (figure 233). Finally, Berthoud returned almost definitively to the spring drive.

His nephew, Pierre-Louis Berthoud (1754–1813) succeeded him in his work as marine clock-maker, and began to industrialize the construction of chronometers in France. The four apprentices allowed him by the government—Motel, Gannery, Jacob, and Dumas—in their turn, with Breguet, made similar productions during the first half of the nineteenth century.

During the same period, several English clock-makers fulfilled the same function: Thomas Mudge (1715–94), John Arnold (1736–99), and Thomas Earnshaw (1749–1829). They endeavoured to simplify the construction of chronometers and to devise more efficient parts. The efforts of the two latter were devoted chiefly to constructing compensated balance wheels and detent escapements. They each invented a type of free escapement, in which they made various modifications. Earnshaw's model was finally adopted in view of the simplicity of its design and the regularity of its functioning (figure 234). Arnold, for his part, studied and recommended a particular form of helical spring to ensure the isochronism of the oscillations. His work paved the way for that of Edouard Phillips, who in 1861 published his researches on the terminal coils of spiral springs. This famous paper by the French mathematician, and later the discoveries of the Swiss Ch.-E. Guillaume, enabled marine chronometers to be given the only two improvements that clockmakers at the beginning of the nineteenth century had left for their successors to discover. The perfection of the marine chronometer was in the main established by the intelligence and skill of a relatively few men working between approximately 1730 and 1820.

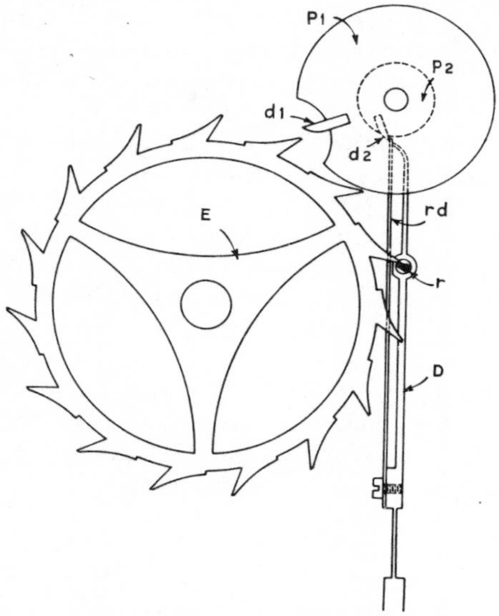

FIGURE 234—*Earnshaw's free detent escapement.* (P1) *Notched plate carrying the impulse lever* d1; (P2) *plate bearing the axle of the balance wheel and the pawl* d2; (E) *escapement wheel, of which one tooth engages with the catch* r *of the detent* D; (rd) *detent spring.*

REFERENCES

[1] Musée du Conservatoire National des Arts et Métiers, Paris, No. 1234.

[2] *Idem.*, Nos 12, 16.

[3] RAMSDEN, J. 'Description d'une machine pour diviser les instruments de mathématiques' (French trans. by J. J. LE F. DE LALANDE). Paris. 1790.

[4] CHAULNES, DUC DE. 'Nouvelle méthode pour diviser les instruments de mathématiques.' Paris. 1768.
Musée du Conservatoire National des Arts et Métiers, Paris, No. 832.

[5] RAMSDEN, J. 'Description of an Engine for Dividing Mathematical Instruments.' London. 1777.

[6] SÉGUIER, BARON A. DE. "Note . . . sur la machine à diviser les cercles de Gambey et sa méthode pour diviser le grand mural de l'Observatoire de Paris." *C.R. Acad. Sci., Paris*, **68**, 207, 1869.

[7] Musée du Conservatoire National des Arts et Métiers, Paris, No. 8323.
[8] SMEATON, J. *Phil. Trans.*, **48**, 598, 1755.
[9] DAUMAS, M. 'Lavoisier, théoricien et expérimentateur', p. 154. Presses Universitaires, Paris. 1955.
[10] ROY, W. *Phil. Trans.*, **75**, 461, 1785.
[11] Observatoire de Paris.
[12] Musée du Conservatoire National des Art et Métiers, Paris, No. 3335.
[13] HERSCHEL, W. *Phil. Trans.*, **85**, 347, 1795.
[14] BORDA, J. C. DE. 'Description et usage du cercle de réflexion.' Paris. 1816.
[15] DELAMBRE, J. B. J. and MÉCHAIN, P. F. A. 'Base du système métrique décimal', Vol. 2, pp. 160–9. Paris. 1807.
Musée du Conservatoire National des Arts et Métiers, Paris, No. 8604.
[16] ROY, W. *Phil. Trans.*, **80**, 111, 1790.
Science Museum, London, No. 1876–1203.
[17] DIDEROT, D. and D'ALEMBERT, J. LE R. (Eds). 'Encyclopédie', Vol. 2, p. 247. Article: Balance. Geneva. 1772.
[18] Royal Institution of Great Britain, London.
[19] DAUMAS, M. See ref. [9], p. 136.
Musée du Conservatoire National des Arts et Métiers, Paris, Nos 19.885, 19.886.
[20] Royal Society, London.
[21] EVELYN, SIR GEORGE (SHUCKBURGH). *Phil. Trans.*, **88**, Pt I, 135, 1798.
[22] Musée du Conservatoire National des Arts et Métiers, Paris, No. 19.889.
[23] CONSERVATOIRE NATIONAL DES ARTS ET MÉTIERS, PARIS. 'Catalogue du Musée, Section K: Poids et mesures.' Paris. 1941.
[24] DAUMAS, M. See ref. [9], pp. 143–50.
[25] DITISHEIM, P. *et al.* 'Pierre Le Roy et la chronométrie.' Tardy, Paris. 1940.
[26] Musée du Conservatoire National des Arts et Métiers, Paris, No. 1395.
[27] GOULD, R. T. *Mariner's Mirror*, **21**, 115, 1935.
LLOYD, H. A. *Suisse horlog.*, **68**, No. 3, 35, No. 4, 21, 1953.
[28] National Maritime Museum, Greenwich, London.
[29] Musée du Conservatoire National des Arts et Métiers, Paris, Nos 165, 166, 1386–93, 8802, 11.057.

BIBLIOGRAPHY

BERGERON, L. E. [pseudonym of L. G. I. SALIVET]. 'Manuel du Tourneur' (2nd ed., 3 vols). Paris. 1816.
BRITTEN, F. J. 'Old Clocks and Watches and their Makers' (ed. by F. W. BRITTEN, 6th ed.). Spon, London. 1933.
CONSERVATOIRE NATIONAL DES ARTS ET MÉTIERS, PARIS. 'Catalogue du Musée, Section B: Mécanique.' Paris. 1956.
Idem. 'Catalogue du Musée, Section JB: Horlogerie.' Paris. 1948.
DAUMAS, M. 'Les instruments scientifiques aux XVIIe et XVIIIe siècles.' Presses Universitaires, Paris. 1953.
'Encyclopédie Méthodique: Arts et Métiers.' Paris. 1784–91.
GOULD, R. T. 'The Marine Chronometer: its History and Development.' Potter, London. 1925.
REPSOLD, J. 'Zur Geschichte der astronomischen Messwerkzeuge von 1830 bis um 1900' (2 vols). Reinicke, Leipzig. 1914.

14

MACHINE-TOOLS

K. R. GILBERT

MACHINE-TOOLS are fundamental to industrial civilization, for without them the machines used in many manufacturing processes, and the engines to drive them, could not be built. Machine-tools make it possible to work metal objects of great size and to shape metals with an accuracy unattainable by hand. Moreover, the high speed of working with machine-tools makes commercially practicable processes which, even if mechanically possible, cannot be performed economically by hand. In the case of wood-working, where the necessity for great accuracy does not arise, the advantage of using machinery comes mainly from the high speeds attainable and the great saving of labour that may be effected.

The invention and development of machine-tools was an essential part of the industrial revolution. The steam-engine, the railway, and textile and other manufacturing machinery required machine-tools for their progress; and it was this demand that stimulated the great progress in the invention of machine-tools that took place in the period under review. In 1775 the machine-tools at the disposal of industry had scarcely advanced beyond those available in the Middle Ages: by 1850 the majority of modern machine-tools had been invented.

The credit for this remarkable progress belongs largely to a group of British engineers, though towards the end of the period the leadership moved to the United States. The employer–employee relationship that existed at one time or another between members of the British 'school' of inventors, was undoubtedly partly responsible for the speed of the advance. One inventive mind was stimulated by contact with another, and experience became cumulative. In figure 235 the connexions of the British machine-tool inventors with each other are set out diagrammatically.

An eighteenth-century turner's workshop is depicted in plate 28, which is reproduced from a volume of Diderot and d'Alembert's *Encyclopédie*, published in 1772. The pole-lathe shown at the back of the workshop was the typical lathe of the time, and had been used since the thirteenth century. A cord attached at the top to a springy pole passed once or twice round the lathe-mandrel, or round the work held between fixed centres, and was tied at the bottom to a treadle. On depressing the treadle, the mandrel was caused to rotate; and the cutting-tool, supported by a rest, was applied to the work by a turner. On releasing the treadle, the pole returned to the starting-position; during this time the work rotated in the reverse direction, and the tool had to be withdrawn. The process was then repeated. This intermittent method of working made it almost impossible to turn an accurate cylinder. The use of a crank and fly-wheel to give continuous rotation had been known since the sixteenth century, but lathes work-

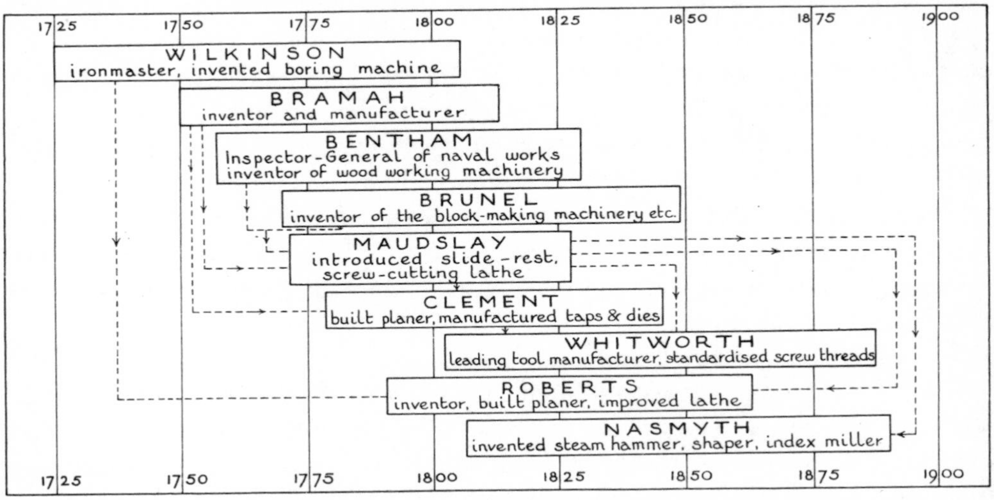

FIGURE 235—*Some important machine-tool builders of the eighteenth and nineteenth centuries. The dotted lines represent employer–employee relationships.*

ing on that principle were not so commonly used. When greater power and speed were required, the great wheel shown in the foreground was used. This provided continuous rotation, but the control of the tool, and hence the accuracy of the work done, depended entirely on the skill of the turner. These lathes were constructed of wood, and metal was used only for the centres and for some of the fastenings. The head-stock and tail-stock were often secured in the lathe-bed by wooden wedges. It must not be supposed, however, that the invention of the modern machine-tools led to the complete supersession of the earlier tools. Indeed, primitive machines like the pole-lathe and tilt-hammer still exist in use in out-of-the-way places.

Some lathes were provided with a number of guide-screws of different pitch, cut on an extension of the mandrel. It could be arranged for the mandrel to slide along horizontally under the control of one of these screws, by engaging the screw with a bearing having a threaded surface of the same pitch. A chasing-tool held against a cylindrical rod rotated in a chuck on the front of the mandrel would then reproduce the thread. A long screw could be cut in a series of short lengths. Screws were also hand-cut by the means of a screw-plate or by a die held in a die-stock: two die-stocks are shown hanging on the wall in plate 28. Screws were originated, however, by the laborious process of filing a marked cylinder (figures 213, 214).

Matthew Boulton (1728–1809), who employed between seven and eight hundred workers in his Soho factory at Birmingham, wrote in 1770: 'I have two

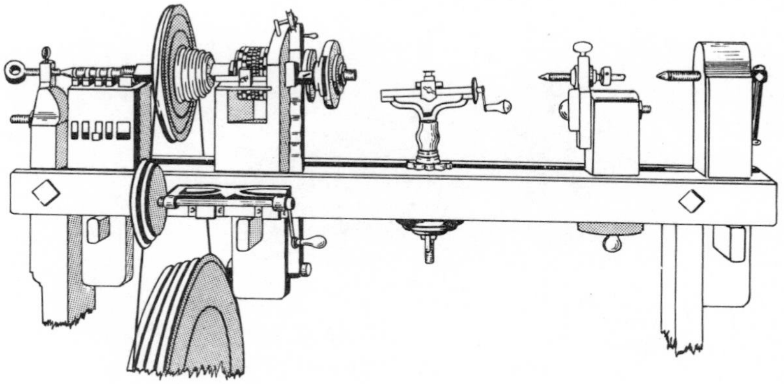

FIGURE 236—*Lathe for ornamental turning, late seventeenth century. To the left of the pulley are guide screws for the traversing-mandrel method of screw-cutting, and to the right are the rosettes for ornamental turning.* (*Cf figure 213.*)

water mills employed in rolling, pollishing, grinding & turning various sorts of Laths.' To this list of machine-tools of the period should be added the tilt-hammer. A heavy hammer was pivoted at a point about a quarter of its length from the tail, which was depressed by the action of cams set on a shaft rotated by a water-wheel. When the tail became disengaged from one of the cams, the hammer-head fell: the rotation of the wheel thus caused the hammer to deliver a succession of heavy blows. A variation was to make the cam lift the hammer at the heavy end.

This picture of the meagre equipment of the time requires qualification in two respects. There were two specialized fields in which more advanced machine-tools were used, namely ornamental turning and clock-making (see ch 13).

The interest of wealthy amateur turners led in the seventeenth and eighteenth centuries to the development of ingenious lathe accessories with which complicated patterns and shapes could be cut. One type of chuck, for example, was constructed so as to carry the work in an elliptical path. The lathe illustrated in figure 236 is a late seventeenth-century example of a lathe for ornamental turning. The mandrel can be made to oscillate laterally under the control of the rosettes to the right of the pulley, enabling patterns to be cut on the face of an object rotated in the chuck. The slide-rest with which the lathe is equipped is probably an eighteenth-century addition. This lathe is constructed partly of wood, but in the eighteenth century the use of metal throughout led to improved rigidity and accuracy, and some highly decorated and elaborate lathes were built.

Clock-makers in the first half of the eighteenth century invented several screw-

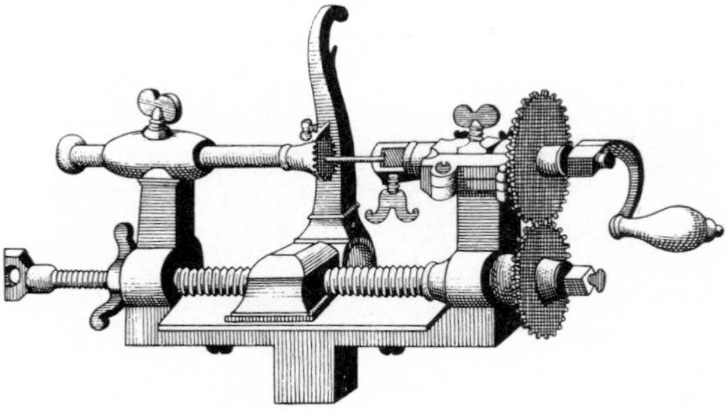

FIGURE 237—*Fusee-engine, 1741, showing the application of lead-screw and change-wheels to screw cutting.*

cutting machines for making fusees; the latter is a clock-part in the shape of a hyperboloid on which a screw-like groove is cut. The eighteenth-century tool shown in plate 27B is typical of a common type of fusee-engine. The cutter is constrained to move parallel to the screw being cut—in this illustration an ordinary screw and not a fusee—and is made to traverse as a result of its linkage with a nut threaded on the lead-screw on the mandrel. The pitch of the resulting screw depends on the leverage employed in the linkage, which may be varied by moving the fulcrum. A machine described by Antoine Thiout (1692–1767) in 1741 had a separate lead-screw, connected with the headstock-spindle by means of gear-wheels, the ratio of which determined the pitch of the thread cut (figure 237).

Robert Hooke (1635–1703) in 1671 invented a machine for cutting clock-wheels which employed a rotary file or milling-cutter to cut the teeth; these were then filed to shape by hand. In some later machines the cutter was shaped to cut the teeth in their final form. The teeth were correctly spaced by means of a divided plate, and the cutter was geared up to the handle so that it could be driven at speed. A machine of this kind, dated 1789, is shown in figure 238. In some machines the axis of the cutter could be inclined so as to cut skew teeth. That a large variety of hand-tools and some machine-tools was available to clock-makers in the eighteenth century is shown by the illustrated catalogue issued by John Wyke (1720–87), a Lancashire clock-tool manufacturer.

In 1765 James Watt (1736–1819) made his great invention of the separate condenser (p 182), but for lack of capital the construction of a large-scale steam-engine, embodying his idea, took years to accomplish. Even when this financial problem was solved, it was still necessary to overcome the great difficulty of boring an accurate cylinder. The close fitting of the piston in the cylinder, which did not so greatly matter in the Newcomen engine, was essential to the proper

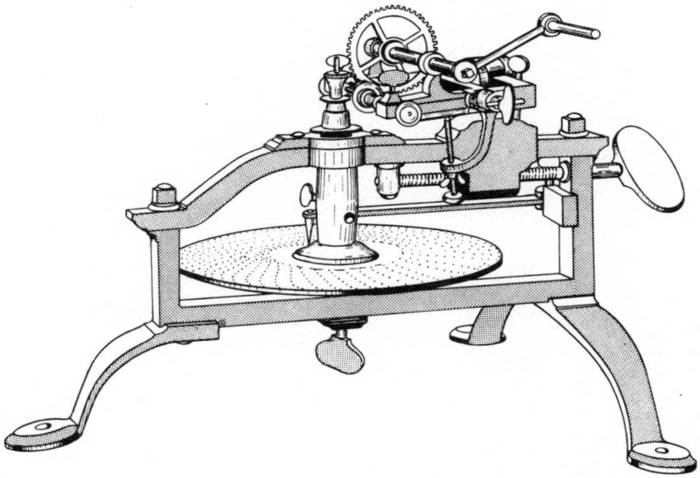

FIGURE 238—*Machine for cutting clock-wheels, 1789. The teeth are cut by a rotary cutter in the wheel blank which is mounted above the divided plate.* (*Cf figure 219.*)

working of Watt's. For want of an accurate boring-machine, the cylinder of his first engine was made of tin and hammered to shape against a hard-wood block; the gaps between piston and cylinder were sealed as far as possible with felt, paper, oiled rags, and the like. John Smeaton (1724–92), who had himself built a boring-machine in 1769, considered Watt's engine too difficult to build. The difficulty in boring a large cylinder was that the long, heavy boring-tool tended to sag and wander from the true, as it worked through the cylinder.

In 1775, however, the ironmaster John Wilkinson (1728–1808) built at Bersham a new type of boring-mill on which large cylinders could be bored with sufficient accuracy. Plate 27 A reproduces a model of this mill constructed with the guidance of contemporary records: the only part of the original mill still in existence is a boring-bar 15 ft long. In front of the water-wheel on the right are the remains of a boring-mill of the Smeaton type. Here the cylinder was mounted on a truck which could be moved along rails, and was fed over a rotating cutter-head. The weight of the cutter caused it to cut mainly on the lower part of the cylinder, and it received no guidance other than that given by the rough-casting. An attempt was made to correct this disadvantage by taking four cuts and turning the cylinder through 90° after each cut. Smeaton's apparatus, a model of which is reproduced in figure 239, was very similar to a machine for boring cannon described by Biringuccio as early as 1540 (vol III, p 367).

On the left of plate 27 A is the boring-machine invented by Wilkinson. The

FIGURE 239—*Model of Smeaton-type boring-mill, c 1770.*

large driving-wheel is keyed to the squared end of the boring-bar, which is supported in a bearing at each end. The cylinder, shown sectioned in the model, is securely fixed in a cradle. Mounted on the bar, and rotating with it, is the cutter-head, which is fed forward through the cylinder by means of a rod passing down the centre of the hollow bar and attached to the head through a longitudinal slot. The other end of the rod is prevented from rotating by a cross-bar resting on two wooden beams, and attached to a rack. The feed is given by a weighted lever acting through a pinion engaging with the rack. The success of the machine was due to the rigidity obtained by supporting the boring-bar at both ends and by securing the cylinder. It made possible the successful development of Watt's engine, and for twenty years all his cylinders were cast and bored by Wilkinson. The following tribute from Boulton, written in 1776, incidentally shows the contemporary notion of the accuracy that might be attained: 'Wilkinson hath bored us several cylinders almost without Error; that of 50 inches diam^r for Bentley & Co. doth not err the thickness of an old shilling in no part....'

Wilkinson's invention was an isolated one and his only other connexion with the machine-tool builders, to be mentioned later, was that his executors for a time engaged Richard Roberts (p 428) as a pattern-maker.

The next advance arose from the necessity of devising an economical method of manufacturing Bramah's patent lock. Joseph Bramah (1748–1814), the son of a Yorkshire farmer, was an ingenious man responsible for many inventions, including the hydraulic press, an improved water-closet (figure 285), a wood-planing machine, and a machine for numbering bank-notes. In 1784 he patented a very successful lock which he exhibited in his shop-window in Piccadilly with the notice, 'The artist who can make an instrument that will pick or open this lock shall receive two hundred guineas the moment it is produced.' Although many attempts were made, the money was not won until 1851, when a mechanic succeeded in opening the lock after fifty-one working hours. This is sufficient proof of the excellence of the lock, but it was a complicated mechanism which could be satisfactorily and economically manufactured only by a well designed series of machine-tools.

To help in building these tools Bramah engaged Henry Maudslay (1771–1831), an eighteen-year-old blacksmith employed at Woolwich Arsenal, who a year later became his superintendent. John Farey, writing some fifty years later, described Bramah's factory thus:

> The secret workshops . . . contained several curious machines, for forming parts of the locks, with a systematic perfection for workmanship, which was at that time unknown in similar mechanical arts. These machines had been constructed by the late Mr Maudslay, with his own hands, whilst he was Bramah's chief workman. . . . The machines before mentioned were adapted for cutting the grooves in the barrel, and the notches in the steel plates . . . the notches in the keys, and in the steel sliders, were cut by other machines, which had micrometer screws so as to ensure that the notches in each key should tally with the unlocking notches of the sliders. . . .

Bramah used milling-cutters mounted on the spindle of a lathe, while the part to be machined was held in an indexing-bush in a quick-grip vice mounted on the lathe-bed. These tools have been preserved in the Science Museum, London, together with a machine for sawing slots in the lock-barrels, and a spring-winding machine. This latter machine is made on the lines of a screw-cutting lathe, having a saddle that travels the entire length of the bed and is drawn along by a lead-screw. The lead-screw is driven from the headstock by change-gears which permit the relative speeds of headstock-rotation and saddle-travel to be varied, so that springs of different pitch can be made. Instead of a cutting-tool, however, the saddle carries a reel of wire which is wound on to an arbor held between centres. This machine is a forerunner of Maudslay's screw-cutting lathe, reproduced in plate 25 A.

In 1797, having been refused an increase in his wages, Maudslay left Bramah and set up in business on his own account. His firm prospered, and held a leading position throughout the nineteenth century. He was joined in 1804 by Joshua Field, formerly a draughtsman at the Portsmouth dockyard. Field was later taken into partnership and the firm continued under the well known name of Maudslay, Sons and Field. Maudslay's influence exerted through his pupils and workmen is as important as his more direct contributions to engineering. His central relationship to other important inventors is shown in figure 235.

Most machine-tools that act by cutting require the work or the tool, or both, to move in a straight line or a circle. Thus when a cylinder is generated on a lathe the tool moves in a straight line parallel to the axis of the rotating work; in the boring-mill, the rotating tool travels in a straight line through the stationary work. In the milling-machine the work moves in a straight line at right angles to the axis of the rotating tool. The rectilinear motion of a moving part of a machine-tool results from its control by two intersecting planes. Thus the cutting of a true cylinder on a lathe is brought about by ensuring the proper movement of the tool by means of the slide-rest, which is guided by two plane surfaces. The accuracy of the product of a machine-tool is therefore determined by the accuracy of its plane guiding-surfaces.

Another essential element of machine-tool construction is the screw, since it translates a rotary motion into a linear one. Thus, in the lathe the motion of the tool may be linked with the rotation of the work by means of the lead-screw. Screws are used for the correct setting and adjustment of the movable parts of machine-tools. The screw is also an essential component of the micrometer. The precision with which such screws are made is obviously unnecessary for screws used merely as fasteners.

The outstanding features of Maudslay's engineering practice were the production of accurate plane surfaces; the use of the slide-rest; the adoption of all-metal construction; and the production of accurate screws. According to Nasmyth:

The importance of having such Standard Planes caused him [Maudslay] to have many of them placed on the benches beside his workmen, by the means of which they might at once conveniently test their work. Three of each were made at a time, so that by the mutual rubbing of each on each the projecting surfaces were effaced. When the surfaces approached very near to the true plane, the still projecting minute points were carefully reduced by hard steel scrapers, until at last the standard plane surface was secured.

When placed over each other they would float upon the thin stratum of air between them until dislodged by time and pressure. When they adhered closely to each other, they could only be separated by sliding each off each. This art of producing absolutely plane surfaces is, I believe, a very old mechanical 'dodge'. But, as employed by Maudslay's men, it greatly contributed to the improvement of the work turned out. It was used for the surfaces of slide valves, or wherever absolute true plane surfaces were essential to the attainment of the best results, not only in the machinery turned out, but in educating the taste of his men towards first class workmanship.

The reason for making three surfaces coincide is that, with two only, one might be convex and the other concave, but if a third surface can be made to coincide with the first two, all three must be plane.

The earliest known illustration of a slide-rest occurs in a German manuscript of *c* 1480, the *Mittelalterliche Hausbuch* of Waldburg. It is not shown fitted on a lathe, but in isolation and without explanation. In the eighteenth century slide-rests were used on ornamental turning-lathes. About 1745 Jacques de Vaucanson (p 384) made a lathe able to turn work up to 1 metre in length; its slide-rest has two 90° V-grooves underneath and slides on two bars of square section running the length of the lathe. Yet Nasmyth, writing the appendix to Buchanan's book on mill-work in 1841, attributed the invention of the slide-rest to Maudslay. It was evidently regarded as an innovation by the practical engineers of his time.

The use of a lead-screw for screw-cutting on the lathe is found, as has been mentioned, in the fusee-engine. The idea occurs in a crude form as early as 1569 in the work of Besson (vol III, figure 217). Indeed, a screw-cutting machine with two lead-screws and complete with change-wheels was devised by Leonardo da Vinci in the fifteenth century (vol II, figure 598), but without practical consequences, since his drawing of it remained unpublished for four centuries. The screw-cutting lathe in a form similar to Maudslay's was made by Senot, a Frenchman, in 1795, and by David Wilkinson, an American, in 1798. Although the claim that Maudslay was sole inventor of the screw-cutting lathe with slide-rest, lead-screw, and change-gears cannot be sustained, he may be credited with the practical and successful introduction of these devices to engineering.

Maudslay's original screw-cutting lathe no longer possesses its gear-wheels; these would have been fixed on the three spindles on the right (plate 25 A), thus linking the lead-screw with the head-stock. The slide-rest, driven by the lead-screw, travels on two triangular bars. This lathe is notable for being made entirely of metal and marks the abandonment of wood in the construction of metal-working machines. The machine-tools Maudslay built for Bramah had wooden frames, but the exclusive use of metal in subsequent machine-tools greatly improved their rigidity and accuracy. Thereafter the use of metal throughout, for building even the largest machine-tools, became universal.

Maudslay gave much attention to the initial formation of accurate screw-threads. In the method finally adopted a hard-wood cylinder was rotated in a suitable holder against a crescent-shaped knife held obliquely to its axis. The knife in cutting into the cylinder caused it to traverse, thus generating a screw which could be copied in steel. Using an accurately made screw Maudslay was able to make a bench micrometer accurate to 0·0001 in, which served him as a workshop standard. He also effected improvements in the system of taps and dies, and standardized the pitches and diameters of the screws used in his workshop. He introduced the practice of making castings with rounded internal edges, recognizing that sharp angles were a source of weakness.

Maudslay became a leading builder of table engines—a type of stationary engine used as a power-unit in factories—and of marine engines, but his first important order was for the construction of a complete plant of machine-tools known as the Portsmouth block-making machinery.

At the end of the eighteenth century, Sir Samuel Bentham (1757–1831) was Inspector-General of Naval Works. After education as a naval apprentice at the Woolwich Arsenal, and a period at sea, he had been sent on a tour of northern European ports and had eventually taken service in Russia as a military and naval engineer and constructor. In 1791 he returned to England and the service of the Admiralty, to whom he proposed the introduction of labour-saving machinery in the dockyards. He made a study of the problem of wood-working by machinery and embodied his conclusions in his comprehensive patent of 1793. This patent included planing-machines with rotary cutters 'to cut on several sides of the wood at once'; the preparation of dovetail joints by means of conical cutters; and veneer-cutting, mortising, and moulding machines.

Bentham was particularly concerned with organizing the manufacture of pulley-blocks, of which 100 000 were required by the Admiralty each year. These were costly, as they were made by hand apart from the initial roughing out of the shells by a circular saw and the turning of the sheaves on the lathe. In 1801 Bentham was approached by Brunel with a scheme for their manufacture which he recognized as superior to his own. With characteristic lack of self-interest Bentham recommended to the Admiralty the adoption of Brunel's proposals.

Sir Marc Isambard Brunel (1769–1849) was born in Normandy and served as a naval officer until the French Revolution, when, because of his royalist sympathies, he became a refugee, first in the United States and then in England.

He made several inventions, but his best-known achievement in later years was the building of the first Thames tunnel (pp 449, 463, plate 32 A). He was the father of I. K. Brunel, the ship-builder, bridge-builder, and railway-engineer.

The block-making machinery designed by Brunel was constructed by Maudslay, who doubtless contributed to the design of the machinery. The project is of historic interest because it constituted one of the earliest examples of the use of machine-tools for mass-production. The plant was in full operation in Portsmouth by 1808, with a yearly output of 130 000 blocks. With this machinery ten unskilled men did the work of 110 skilled men, and it was estimated that for a capital outlay of £54 000 the Admiralty made a saving of £17 000 per annum. Brunel's reward was one year's saving. When first built, the Portsmouth block-machinery was one of the mechanical marvels of the time, with the fortunate result that a very full contemporary description of it was published in Rees's 'Cyclopaedia'. So well were the machines designed and built that several of them continued in use for 145 years, and examples of the more interesting of them have been preserved.

The blocks were made in three size-ranges, so that machines for certain processes were made in two or three sizes. There were altogether forty-three machines, and these carried out all the processes, except the final fitting and polishing, necessary to convert the raw material into finished pulley-blocks. They were driven through overhead shafting by a 30-hp steam-engine. The first stage in the preparation of the shells was to saw elm logs into convenient lengths by means of a reciprocating or circular saw. The latter machine was so contrived that the saw could be taken round the log and so could cut timber of almost its own diameter. The blocks of wood were then cut roughly to shape on circular-saw benches. Next, a block was placed in a boring-machine which simultaneously bored two holes at right-angles, one for the sheave-pin and the other to start the mortise for the sheave. The act of clamping the block in the boring-machine made indentations which served to fix its position correctly in subsequent machines. The block was placed in a mortising-machine which cut a slot for the sheave, and transferred to a shaping-engine which formed the outer surfaces. Grooves to hold rope were then cut in the surfaces by means of a scoring-machine. The rotating cutters of this last machine were carried in a swinging frame guided by a template, so that the cutters scored the required grooves without the exercise of any skill on the part of the operator.

The machine illustrated in plate 26 A could cut mortises in two blocks at a time. The shaft, rotating at 400 rpm, imparted a reciprocating motion to the chisels, which carried projecting tongues to clear the chips of wood. A ratchet, actuated by a cam on the shaft, engaged a toothed wheel on the lead-screw which caused the block-holder to advance after each cut. At a predetermined point the process was finished by automatically disengaging the ratchet. This machine is the earliest mortising-machine and the ancestor of the slotter or vertical shaper.

The machine reproduced in plate 26B formed the surfaces of ten blocks at a time. A cutter, guided by a former, was moved across the face of the blocks as they revolved in the drum in which they were mounted. The simultaneous indexing of all the blocks about their centres was effected through bevel-and-worm gearing mounted on radial shafts actuated by a central crown-wheel. The blocks were turned through 90°, the other former was selected, and the blocks were faced in their new position. The procedure was continued until the four sides had been shaped.

In the manufacture of the sheave a slice of lignum vitae was rounded and bored on the rounding-machine, by means of a crown-saw and a drill running coaxially. The sheave was then grooved and faced on a special lathe which had a power-driven cross-slide. Finally, three recesses for the metal bush were cut in the sheave on a milling-machine designed for the purpose. There were in addition machines for turning and burnishing the pins.

The most eminent of the engineers who at one time or another worked for Maudslay were Roberts, Nasmyth, and Whitworth. Richard Roberts (1789–1864) was born at the village of Carreghofa in central Wales. As a youth he worked in a quarry, but at the age of twenty he found employment at Wilkinson's Bradley ironworks. After various jobs he was employed for two years as a turner and fitter by Maudslay, and then in 1814 set up on his own at Manchester, his first equipment consisting of a hand-lathe and a drilling-machine.

In 1817 he designed and built the lathe illustrated in plate 24C; this has the new feature of the back-geared headstock. For direct driving the four-speed cone-pulley is connected with the spur-wheel keyed to the headstock-mandrel, but for slow-speed running they are disconnected. The countershaft is then engaged so that the pulley drives the headstock through the two pairs of gears. Another feature of this lathe is the self-acting carriage, which is traversed by a long screw driven from the mandrel through a variable-speed gear and a bevel-wheel reversing and disengaging gear. The ordinary slide-rest of the period was a self-contained appliance, clamped to the bed where required, and able, without being reset, to turn work only of the length commanded by its short screw. In this lathe the lead-screw is provided not for screw-cutting but to facilitate ordinary turning. The feed-gear consists of a divided plate with seven rings of pin-teeth which engage with a pinion sliding on the tail-end of the mandrel. Either of the two bevel wheels, mounted loosely on the lead-screw, may be connected with it by a clutch actuated by levers and a rod running the whole length of the bed and passing through the carriage; a stop placed upon this rod causes the carriage to disengage the clutch when it reaches the end of the required traverse. In the same year Roberts designed a planing-machine, to be described later.

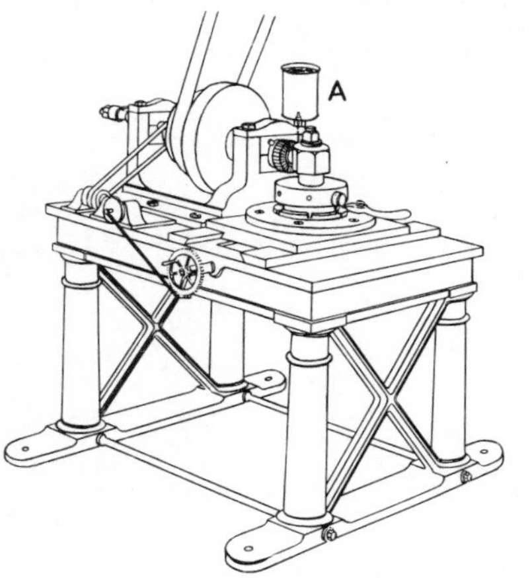

FIGURE 240—*Nasmyth's self-acting nut-milling machine, 1829.* A, *water drip. The drawing is by the inventor.*

In 1821 Roberts advertised himself as a maker of screws, division-plates, and bevel-, spur-, and worm-gears up to 30 inches in diameter. These gears were cut by milling-cutters, as was noted in his diary by Field, who visited Roberts in the course of a tour through the provinces: 'he has good lathes, screw engines, cutting engines; with the latter machine he does a good deal of work in cutting wheels for the cotton spinners both in brass & iron. His machine has the wheel held as in a lathe but not turned, being held centrally by ring on a arbor, his cutters are made of steel plate turned to the shape of the tooth. . . .'

Roberts was a most versatile inventor, but his greatest achievement was to devise the mechanism to render the spinning-mule self-acting (figure 159, p 289). His machine-tool inventions included a punching-machine for punching holes at exact intervals in wrought-iron plate. This was produced in 1847 in response to a request from the constructors of the Menai Straits railway-bridge (vol V, ch 21). Roberts's business ability unhappily did not match his mechanical ingenuity and he died in poverty, unlike the other eminent machine-tool inventors mentioned in this chapter, who were financially successful.

James Nasmyth (1808–90) was born in Edinburgh, the son of a painter, landscape-gardener, and engineer. He had a high-school education and used the opportunity afforded by his father's workshop to make model steam-engines. At the age of twenty-one his interest in the mechanical arts led him to apply for employment at Maudslay's. He was Maudslay's personal assistant for two years.

In 1829 Nasmyth built the milling-machine depicted in figure 240, in which the cutter is shown machining the face of a hexagonal nut. Water was used for cooling, as indicated at A in the drawing. The columns are typical of machines of the time, but the classical style was soon to give place to more utilitarian designs.

When Maudslay died in 1831, Nasmyth left the firm in order to open his own workshop, first in Edinburgh and then at Patricroft, Manchester. In 1836 he invented the shaper. This was the machine which is used under that name today; it is quite distinct from Brunel's shaping-engine. An early example of Nasmyth's shaper is shown in figure 241. In this machine the work is secured on a horizontal table and is cut by a tool, clamped to a horizontal ram, which is

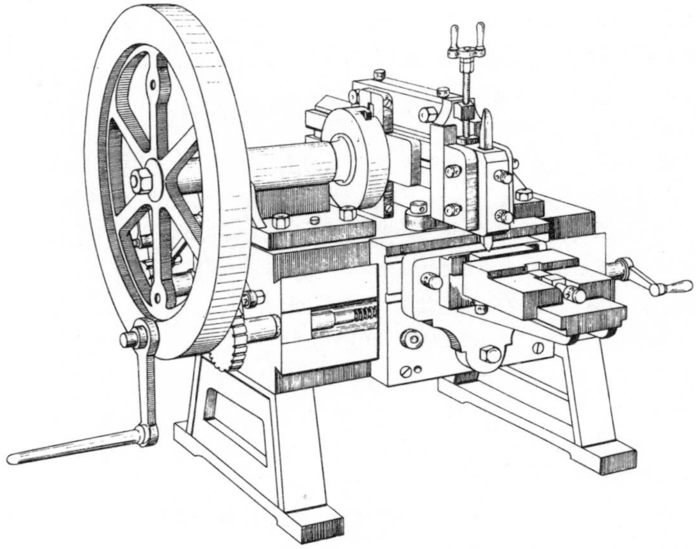

FIGURE 241—*Nasmyth's shaper, c 1850, invented in 1836. The cutter reciprocates horizontally to produce surfaces formed of straight-line elements.*

given reciprocating motion. The work-table slides on guides on the front of the main casting and is traversed by an internal screw driven either by hand or automatically by a pawl-feed motion rocked by an eccentric on the main shaft. The shaper is suitable for planing small surfaces, cutting key-ways, or producing any surface that can be formed of straight-line elements. In Nasmyth's shaper the driving-shaft ends in a disk carrying a crank-pin, to the other end of which is fitted a block sliding in a vertical slot in the ram. Whitworth subsequently improved the shaper by inventing a crank mechanism which causes the ram to make a quick return, so that a higher proportion of the working time is usefully employed in cutting.

Nasmyth's most celebrated invention is the steam-hammer. A photograph, taken in 1856, of a large steam-hammer with the inventor is reproduced in plates 24 A and 24 B. The tilt-hammer suffers from the limitation that it can be raised only a comparatively short distance. This distance and, consequently, the impact of the hammer are reduced by the thickness of the work on the anvil. Moreover, the force of the blow cannot be controlled. The designer of the engines of the steamship *Great Britain* had proposed a paddle-shaft 30 inches in diameter—though in the event the ship was built with a screw-shaft—but, finding that no one could undertake such a forging, he applied in 1839 to Nasmyth, who immediately devised his steam-hammer. The two standards that form guides for the hammer-head also support an overhead cylinder, the piston of which is connected with the hammer-head by a rod passing through the bottom of the cylinder. Steam is admitted by a valve to the cylinder in order to raise the hammer-head to the required height. The hammer falls when the steam is allowed to escape. The hammer was later made double-acting by admitting steam above the piston, so that a more powerful blow could be obtained. The description of Nasmyth's hammer in the catalogue of the Great Exhibition of 1851 states: 'This steam hammer is capable of adjustment of power in a degree highly remarkable. While it is possible to obtain enormous impulsive force by its means, it can be so graduated as to descend with power only sufficient to break an egg shell.' The steam-hammer greatly increased the size of forging possible.

Sir Joseph Whitworth (1803–87) was the son of a schoolmaster. At the age of fourteen he entered his uncle's cotton-mill to learn the business, but, being more interested in machinery than in commerce, he soon left in order to work as a mechanic with a firm of Manchester machinists. At the age of twenty-two he went to London and obtained employment with Maudslay and later with Clement (p 434). The method of making true metal plane surfaces three at a time (pp 424–5) by hand-scraping is generally supposed to have been devised by Whitworth while working at Maudslay's, but this claim is inconsistent with Nasmyth's statement, quoted earlier, that it was 'an old dodge'. Holtzapffel (1806–47), writing in 1846, attributed to Whitworth what he regarded as the essential feature of the method, namely the substitution of scraping for grinding. This does not, however, dispose of the contradiction, because Nasmyth mentioned scraping but did not refer to Whitworth.

In 1833 Whitworth rented a workshop at Manchester and displayed the sign 'Joseph Whitworth, Tool Maker from London'. The engineers who have been discussed up to this point built machine-tools primarily in order to be able to make other machines, but Whitworth built them for sale to other manufacturers. At the 1851 Exhibition he was the outstanding machine-tool maker. One, two, or even three machine-tools were exhibited by each of twenty other firms, but

Whitworth had twenty-three exhibits, including lathes and machines for planing, shaping, slotting, drilling (both plain and radial), punching and shearing, nut-shaping, screwing, wheel-cutting, and dividing. He also showed screwing-apparatus, a measuring-machine, a set of stepped gauges, and a set of internal and external cylindrical gauges. At the International Exhibition of 1862 Whit-

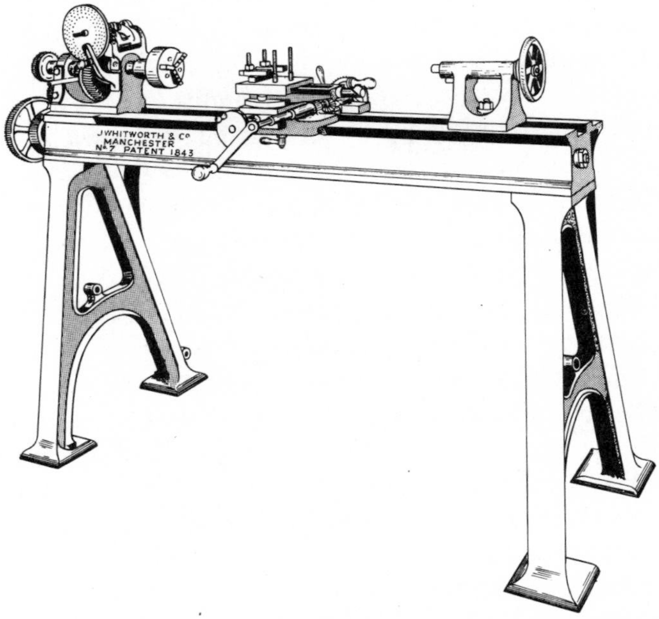

FIGURE 242—*Whitworth's lathe, 1843. Note the hollow-box construction of the bed.* (*Cf plate 25 A.*)

worth maintained his lead, for, although more than sixty firms then exhibited, his firm occupied a quarter of the total space allotted to machine-tools.

Whitworth described several improvements to machine-tools in his patent of 1839. Among them were the split nut by which the lead-screw of a lathe could be engaged at will to make the saddle traverse, and the mechanism by which the cross-feed could be actuated by the lead-screw. The lathe shown in figure 242 was built in 1843 and was in use until 1951. It exemplifies the hollow-box design of lathe-bed, introduced by Whitworth. This design makes the machine much more rigid, weight for weight, than the earlier triangular-bar construction, besides protecting the lead-screw from damage and dirt. The lead-screw passes through the split nut, which forms part of the carriage, and causes the carriage to traverse. If the split nut is disengaged, the carriage stops, and cross-feed motion is obtained through the meshing of a pinion with the lead-screw. If the cross-feed is thrown out of gear, the handle at the front, which is connected with the pinion, may be used to give rapid traverse to the carriage. In this case the lead-screw is being used as a rack.

Whitworth was responsible for bringing about the standardization of screw-threads. He collected and compared screws from as many workshops as possible throughout England and in 1841 proposed, in a paper to the Institution of Civil Engineers, the use of a constant angle (55°) between the sides of the threads, and a specification for the number of threads to the inch for the various screw-diameters. The Whitworth thread remained standard in engineering until 1948.

Whitworth also gave much attention to accurate measurement and considered end-measurement to be more satisfactory than measurement between lines. In 1834 he made a measuring machine capable of comparing yard standards to an accuracy of one-millionth of an inch. For detecting the exact point of contact he introduced the gravity- or feeling-piece. A movement of a millionth of an inch was sufficient to make a feeling-piece stand or fall. For ordinary workshop use he made measuring machines of smaller sensitivity.

Speaking in 1856, Whitworth said: 'Thirty years ago the cost of labour for facing a surface of cast iron, by hand, was twelve shillings per square foot; the same work is now done by the planing machine at a cost for labour of less than one penny per square foot, and this, as you know, is one of the most important operations in mechanics. It is, therefore, well adapted to illustrate what our progress has been.'

The invention of the planing machine for metal has been attributed to several engineers. Matthew Murray, a steam-engine manufacturer of Leeds, who died in 1826, was an important rival of Boulton and Watt. According to one of his workmen, March, who joined him in 1814 and who later became a tool manufacturer, Murray invented a planing machine for planing D-valve surfaces. March said: 'I recollect it very distinctly, and even the sort of framework on which it stood. The machine was not patented, and like many inventions in those days, it was kept as much a secret as possible, being locked up in a small room by itself, to which the ordinary workmen could not obtain access. The year in which I remember it being in use was, so far as I am aware, long before any planing machine of a similar kind had been invented.' James Fox of Derby, a manufacturer of lathes and of textile-machinery, is said to have built a planer in 1814.

The earliest planing machine still in existence (plate 25B) was made by Richard Roberts in 1817. The marks on the bed show that it was itself made without the assistance of a planer. The work is secured to a table which moves to and fro on a straight bed under a tool capable of being traversed, so that, by the two motions, plane surfaces are produced as the tool makes successive cuts. The table is moved by means of chains wound on a drum rotated by hand. The tool can be raised or lowered by means of a screw. The tool-clamp is hinged and spring-loaded, so that, although it is firm during the cutting stroke, it is free to move on the return stroke, thus avoiding damage to the tool and to the work.

The best known early planing machine was that made in 1825 by Joseph Clement (1779–1844), who set up on his own after working as a chief draughtsman, first for Bramah and then for Maudslay. Clement did much work on the problem of accurate screw-cutting, manufactured taps and dies, and introduced the tap with a small squared shank which would fall through the threaded hole instead of having to be screwed out. The table of his planing machine ran on rollers, and the machine was bedded on a massive foundation of masonry. The machine was driven by hand and had two cutters, one for each direction of travel of the bed. For ten years this machine was the only planer capable of taking large work—up to 6 ft square. Clement charged 18*s* a square foot. At this rate the machine could earn £20 per day, if fully employed, and it was his chief source of income.

Whitworth's planing machine (figure 243), made in 1842 under patents dating from 1835, was power-driven and self-acting. A lead-screw in the middle of the bed of the machine, driven by fast and loose pulleys and with a three-bevel wheel reversing arrangement, transmitted motion to the V-guided table. The cross-slide is supported on, and actuated by, two vertical screws connected by bevel-gears and to a shaft, which is hand-operated. The swivelling tool-box is on a screw on the cross-slide and is fed across the work by a ratchet and pulley. The latter is actuated by a band from a rocking pulley on the same shaft as a pinion moved by a rack-rod on the bed. This rod is moved to and fro by the table coming against stops. By means of guide pulleys, the band also reverses the tool-holder at the end of each stroke, thus cutting in both directions. In 1851 Whitworth exhibited a similar planer, and also a planer of conventional type to plane one way only, with a quick-return motion.

Work that may be done on the shaper, planer, or lathe may often be done more advantageously by milling, provided that there is sufficient repetition to justify the trouble of making a milling-cutter of suitable shape and size. The advantages of the milling process are, first, that the use of a large number of cutting edges permits high-speed machining without excessive heating, and, secondly, that special shapes can be obtained in a single operation by the use of formed cutters. The difficulty of making milling-cutters and keeping them sharp restricted their use in the early days of machine-tools.

As has already been noted, rotary cutters were first used for cutting clock-wheels, and were used for special purposes by Bramah, Brunel, Roberts, and

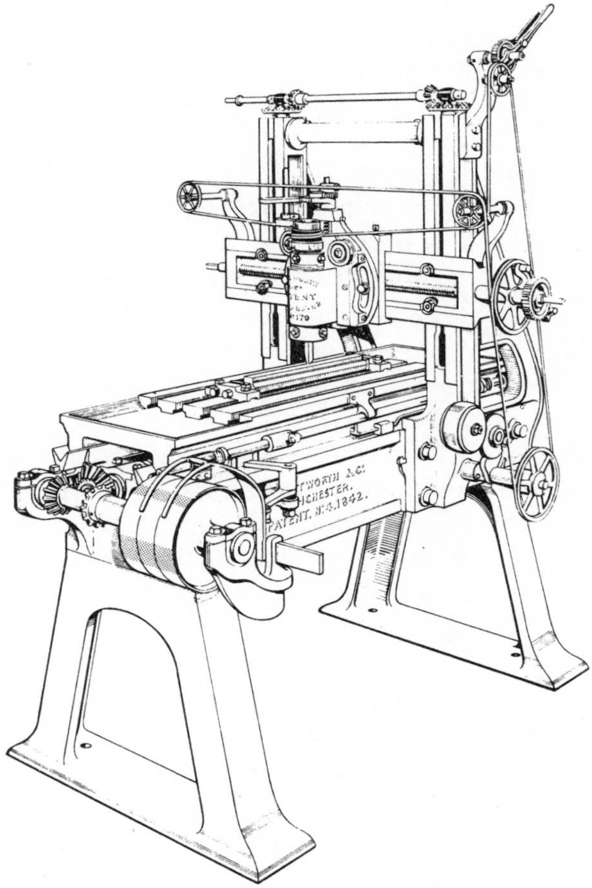

FIGURE 243—*Whitworth's self-acting power-driven planing machine, 1842. The tool is reversed after each traverse of the bed, so as to cut both ways.*

Nasmyth. The development of the milling machine for normal workshop use took place in America. Eli Whitney (1765–1825) in 1818 made a small milling machine which had a power-driven table moving horizontally below the cutter-spindle and at right-angles to it. The first milling machine manufactured for sale was designed in 1848 by Frederick Webster Howe (1822–91) for the Robbins &

Lawrence Company of Windsor, Vermont. A back view of this machine is reproduced in figure 244. The spindle, shown with a cutter in place, is driven by a cone-pulley and back-gears. The table is traversed by rack and pinion through bevel and worm gearing which can be engaged at will.

The machine-tools with cutting action so far described are used for cutting out forms derived from the circle and straight line, but several machines have also been devised for reproducing irregular forms. Their principle is that the cutter is linked with a feeler which is made to go over every point of the object to be copied.

In the medallion lathes of the eighteenth century the matrix is held in a chuck at the rear end of the headstock-spindle and the medallion blank is mounted at the front end. The spindle is free to move axially, and is pressed by a spring against the feeler which, starting at the centre of the matrix, is very slowly traversed to the edge. The cutter makes corresponding movements and cuts a reverse copy in which high points become low points and vice versa. The motion of the feeler and the cutter is derived from the spindle through gearing.

Hulot, about 1800, mounted the matrix and the blank on separate parallel spindles, geared together, and the tracer and the cutter on a bar pivoted at one end on a universal joint. With this arrangement a positive copy was made, diminished in the ratio of the distances of the cutter and the feeler from the fulcrum. A machine on this principle was built in France in 1824 for the Royal Mint; it was employed for making master punches from the designers' original medallions.

In 1845 T. B. Jordan made a machine for copying carved panels of wood and soft stone, which was used for reproducing furniture and notably in the decoration of the Palace of Westminster, then being built to replace the Houses of Parliament destroyed by fire in 1834. The tracer and two rotary cutters, for making two copies at once, moved in a vertical slide; the original and the blanks were placed on a table underneath, capable of horizontal movement in two directions at right-angles.

Between 1804 and 1819, when in retirement, James Watt improved on Hulot's principle by placing a pivoted arm between the bar and the universal joint, with the result that it was possible to under-cut and to copy objects in the round. He also used rotating cutters. Watt made two such sculpturing machines, for reducing and for copying to the same size, but they were neither patented nor generally known. A similar machine was independently invented by Benjamin Cheverton in 1826. In 1818 Thomas Blanchard of Worcester, Massachusetts, made a copying-lathe of considerable economic importance, for turning gun-stocks.

The invention of wood-working machinery, which removed the hard work from sawing and offered the possibility of high-speed working in other processes, was stimulated by the advent of the steam-engine. Reciprocating saws driven by water-wheels had, however, been used from the Middle Ages. The circular saw was probably invented in the third quarter of the eighteenth century by Walter Taylor (1734–1803) of Southampton, who had a contract for making pulley-blocks for the Royal Navy. The band-saw was patented in 1808 by William Newberry, but it was not a practical invention at the time because a steel band which would run for long without snapping could not then be made. The band-saw was successfully re-invented in the United States by Lemuel Hedge in 1849 and in France by Perin in 1855.

Bentham's comprehensive patent for wood-working machinery has already been noted. The mortising machine originates from Bentham and the block-making factory at Portsmouth. His proposals for using rotary cutters came to fruition later in the United States, in J. A. Fay's tenoning machine of 1840 and Andrew Gear's vertical-spindle moulding machine of 1853.

Bramah in 1802 made a rotary wood-planing machine for Woolwich Arsenal, and this was in use for fifty years. The wood to be planed was placed on carriages which ran on rails 40 ft long. The carriages were moved backwards and forwards by an endless chain which derived its motion from a hydraulic engine. Above the carriage was fixed the planing disk—carrying twenty-eight gouges for rough cutting and two planing-irons—which was rotated at 90 rpm by a steam-engine. In 1827 Malcolm Muir, another former employee of Maudslay, invented a machine for making flooring-boards. Planks were fed into it by an endless chain fitted with catch-hooks at intervals, and were treated by a succession of planes and circular saws which reduced them to the required dimensions and formed the tongues and grooves. This machine was improved in 1836 by John McDowall by using rotary cutters for tonguing and grooving, and by substituting for the chain-feed—which had a tendency to tear the wood—pairs of rollers under pressure at each end of the machine to feed the boards through the cutters.

In a letter written in 1785 Thomas Jefferson, then American minister to France, described as follows a visit he had paid to a gunsmith named Le Blanc:

> An improvement is made here in the construction of muskets, which it may be interesting to Congress to know, should they at any time propose to procure any. It consists in the making every part of them so exactly alike, that what belongs to any one, may be used for every other musket in the magazine. The government here has examined and approved the method, and is establishing a large manufactory for the purpose of putting it into execution. As yet, the inventor has only completed the lock of the musket on this

plan. He will proceed immediately to have the barrel, stock, and other parts, executed in the same way. Supposing it might be useful to the United States, I went to the workman. He presented me the parts of fifty locks taken to pieces, and arranged in compartments. I put several together myself, taking pieces at hazard as they came to hand, and they fitted in the most perfect manner. The advantages of this when arms need repair are evident. He effects it by tools of his own contrivance, which, at the same time, abridge the work, so that he thinks he shall be able to furnish the musket two livres cheaper than the common price.

The system of manufacture thus described is known as the interchangeable system.

In the United States interchangeable manufacture began with a contract given in 1798 to Eli Whitney, the inventor of the saw-gin for cotton. He spent two years in constructing his plant, with which he manufactured 10 000 muskets. He aimed 'to make the same parts of different guns, as the locks, for example, as much like each other as the successive impressions of a copper-plate engraving'. In 1812 he had a contract for a further 15 000 muskets. He cannot have been aware of Le Blanc's project, for he wrote that 'this establishment was commenced and has been carried on upon a plan which is unknown in Europe, and the great leading object of which is to substitute correct and effective operations of machinery for that skill of the artist which is acquired only by long practice and experience, a species of skill which is not possessed in this country to any considerable extent'. Thus the United States, with but few skilled gunsmiths to resist, perhaps, the mechanization of their craft, was a favourable ground for the introduction of the new system of manufacture, which became known in Europe as the 'American' system. The system was economical because the manufacture could be broken down into a number of operations, each of which was carried out on a special machine designed for the job. The military advantage of interchangeable gun-parts needs no emphasis.

The interchangeable system was later used for the manufacture of sewing-machines, typewriters, bicycles, motor-cars, and similar machines made in large quantities and built up chiefly from accurately fitting metal components. The system depends on the use of jigs for holding the work and guiding the tools in such operations as the drilling of accurately located holes; on accurate machine-tools; and on gauges for frequent checking during the process of manufacture.

In 1799 Simeon North began the manufacture of 1500 pistols and in 1813 he obtained a contract to make 20 000 more, the components of which were to be interchangeable. The interchangeable system was also used from 1828 onwards for the manufacture of the Hubbard rotary-gear pump. In 1835 Samuel Colt patented his revolver, but commercial success came to him only in 1846, with the Mexican war. In 1853 he built an armoury at Hartford, Connecticut, containing 1400 machine-tools. His superintendent, Elisha K. Root, devised the system of tools, jigs, fixtures, and gauges. The latter's designs included a drop-hammer and a horizontal turret-lathe. This plant probably represents the limit

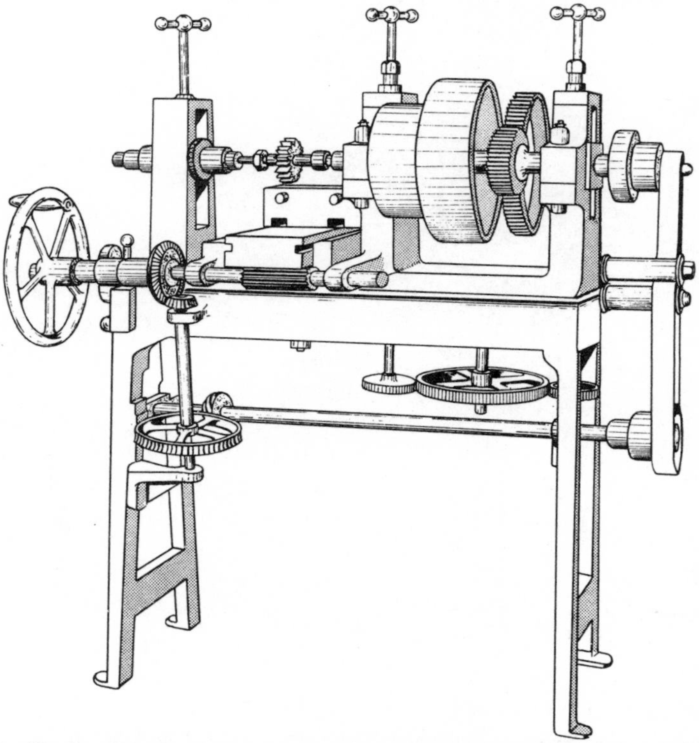

FIGURE 244—*Howe's milling machine, 1848. This was the first milling machine manufactured for sale. The cutter is not original.*

of achievement reached in large-scale precision manufacture by the middle of the nineteenth century.

One of the most influential firms in the gun business was that of Robbins & Lawrence of Windsor, Vermont, whose milling machine, designed by their superintendent, F. W. Howe, has already been mentioned (figure 244). Richard S. Lawrence, F. W. Howe, and Henry D. Stone were responsible for the modern type of turret-lathe with the vertical turret. Figure 245 shows such a lathe, made in 1855 and called at the time a screw-milling machine, because it was used for making screws. The turret-lathe was probably first made in the previous decade, both with the horizontal drum type of turret and with the vertical turret as illustrated. The turret is advanced on a slide by moving the horizontal handle to bring up in turn each of the eight tool-holders, each fitted with a tool, to the work in the head-stock. The turret is indexed by hand between operations. There is also a cross-slide with a tool-holder. It is thus possible to carry out nine predetermined operations with this machine. The skill which would be necessary

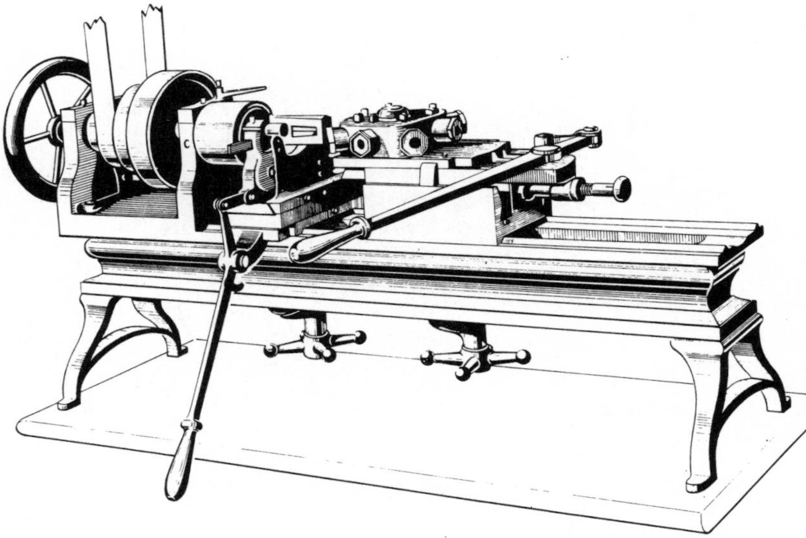

FIGURE 245—*Robbins and Lawrence's turret-lathe, 1855. The octagonal turret can carry eight tools to be used in turn.*

to do this work on an ordinary lathe is applied once only, when the machine is set up. The turret-lathe represents the most advanced stage in the evolution of the lathe in the period now under review. At the 1851 Exhibition Robbins & Lawrence showed six American army rifles, interchangeably manufactured, which attracted much attention.

In 1853 a Royal Small Arms Commission was set up under the chairmanship of James Nasmyth to advise on the manufacture of small arms, which were at that time assembled centrally from crude parts made in scattered workshops. It was resolved to introduce the American system into England. Some members of the commission visited the United States and as a result the Royal Small Arms Factory at Enfield was re-equipped. Blanchard lathes were purchased for making the gun-stocks; and for the manufacture of the metal parts of the rifle Robbins & Lawrence were given a contract for 150 machine-tools and the requisite jigs, fixtures, and gauges. The machine-tools included 57 plain milling machines, a number of universal milling machines, four- and six-spindle drilling machines, and screw-milling machines or turret-lathes. By 1857 a thousand rifles a week were being made with this machinery. Although the American system had thus been introduced into Britain, turret-lathes and milling machines do not appear in Clark's full account of the machinery exhibited in 1862. It appears, however, that steam-hammers, planers, shapers, slotters, screwing machines, punching machines, drilling machines, and radial drilling machines were obtainable in fair variety.

The smaller machine-tools were often driven by hand or foot, and even quite large machines (cf plate 28) were sometimes built for manual drive. Large machines, and workshops with several machines, were driven by water-power if available, but more usually, from about 1800 onwards, by steam-power. The power was transmitted from the steam-engine to the machines by belts and overhead shafting.

By the middle of the nineteenth century the majority of the machine-tools now in use, with the notable exceptions of automatic lathes, screw machines, and gear-cutting, broaching, and grinding machines, had been brought into existence, though not always in their modern form.

BIBLIOGRAPHY

BALE, M. P. 'Wood-working Machinery: its Rise, Progress and Construction' (3rd ed. rev.). Lockwood, London. 1914.

BUCHANAN, R. 'Practical Essays on Millwork and other Machinery' (3 vols, 3rd ed. rev., with additions by T. TELFORD and G. RENNIE). London. 1841.

CLARK, D. K. 'The Exhibited Machinery of 1862: a Cyclopaedia of the Machinery represented at the International Exhibition.' London. [1864.]

DICKINSON, H. W. "Joseph Bramah and his Inventions." *Trans. Newcomen Soc.*, **22,** 169–86, 1941–2.

Idem. "Richard Roberts: his Life and Inventions." *Ibid.*, **25,** 123–37, 1945–7.

FORWARD, E. A. "The Early History of the Cylinder Boring Machine." *Ibid.*, **5,** 24–38, 1924–5.

HUBBARD, G. "The Development of Machine Tools in New England", *Amer. Mach., N.Y.*, 1923–4.

NASMYTH, J. 'An Autobiography' (ed. by S. SMILES). London. 1883.

REES, A. 'The Cyclopaedia; a Universal Dictionary of Arts, Sciences and Literature', Article: 'Machinery for Manufacturing Ships' Blocks.' London. 1819.

ROE, J. W. 'English and American Tool Builders.' Yale University Press, New Haven. 1916.

SMILES, S. 'Industrial Biography: Iron Workers and Tool Makers' (2nd ed.). London. 1879.

15

BUILDING AND CIVIL ENGINEERING CONSTRUCTION

S. B. HAMILTON

I. ORGANIZATION AND TECHNICAL TRAINING

In the periods covered in the earlier volumes of this work no clear distinction can usually be drawn between the work of the military engineer, the civil engineer, and the architect. The same man might well serve at different times in all three capacities; Leonardo da Vinci is well known to have done, but so did many of less outstanding ingenuity and versatility.

In the latter part of the seventeenth century, however, at least in France, a tendency to specialize developed. Employment in any of the three capacities was practically a state monopoly. In 1661 Jean Baptiste Colbert (1619–83) became chief minister to Louis XIV at a time when public buildings, the improvement of communications, and the erection of fortifications were all matters of great importance. In 1664 Colbert took to himself the title of *Surintendant des Bâtiments*; he had a staff of architects, most of whom were already working on the Louvre or some other royal building. In 1666 he persuaded the king to found the Académie des Sciences, and in 1671 the Académie de l'Architecture. In 1672 Sébastien le Prêtre, Seigneur de Vauban (1633–1707), who had revolutionized the arts both of attacking and of building fortifications, was placed at the head of a formally constituted *Corps du Génie*—a body of military engineers whom he had organized and trained for such work. In 1715 the roads and bridges of France were placed under the care of a *Directeur-Général des Ponts et Chaussées*, and in 1716 a staff of engineers was embodied to work under his direction. The weakness of this organization at first was that it had no regular subordinate cadre. In 1744 it was given a small staff of draughtsmen and a registry of maps and plans. In 1747 this was enlarged to become the École des Ponts et Chaussées, the regular training-centre for surveyors and engineers under the direction of Jean Rodolphe Perronet (1708–94). In 1763 Perronet became also the *Premier Ingénieur* of the *Corps des Ingénieurs des Ponts et Chaussées*, which by then included a trained staff of all grades [1].

There was very little science applied to construction by architects, by builders, or by engineers in the early part of the eighteenth century. Henri Gautier's *Traité des Chemins* (1715) and *Traité des Ponts* (1716) are almost entirely descriptive. Gautier stated the customary proportions between the supporting pier, the arch-ring, and the span of a masonry bridge, but gave no reason for them other than tradition. Bernard Forest de Belidor (1693–1761) in *La Science des Ingénieurs* (1729) gave simple rules based on statics for checking the stability of retaining-walls and arches, and for calculating the strength of beams. He also summarized much practical information. His theory was simple and was used to reinforce, rather than to derive, practical rules. In his four-volume *Architecture Hydraulique* (1737–53) he gave full descriptions, with drawings accurate in detail, of work as it was carried out on marine structures, canals, bridges, and pumping installations, together with the plant used for various purposes.

At the École des Ponts et Chaussées there were no regular lectures, but notes were made and circulated; and there appears to have been opportunity for informal discussion between young men in training and experienced engineers, and between practical men and scholars. Some of the engineers contributed papers to be read at the Académie des Sciences, and several wrote books. Examples of their work will be considered later.

In England after the Great Fire of 1666 the rebuilding of St Paul's Cathedral and the London churches, and work on the royal palaces at Greenwich, Hampton Court, and elsewhere, was placed in the hands of Sir Christopher Wren (1632–1723), who thus attained a unique position; but in England there was never anything approaching a crown monopoly of building, still less of public works. Architecture as a profession was recognized, even in 1768, only by the inclusion of four architects at the foundation of the Royal Academy in that year.

In 1771 a group of men who were frequently called upon to prepare surveys, or to give evidence before parliamentary committees on schemes for the building of canals, docks, harbours, and the like, formed themselves into a Society of Engineers, and began to refer to themselves as civil engineers. John Smeaton (1724–92) was the recognized leader of the profession at the time. He was never the president of the society, although its surviving lineal descendant is known as 'The Smeatonian'. The Institution of Civil Engineers was founded in 1818. In 1791 a number of London architects formed an association. As with the Society of Engineers, the Associated Architects were members of a club rather than of a professional institution. The British Institute of Architects was founded in 1834; it became the Royal Institute of British Architects in 1866.

It may be said that a recognized division between military engineering and architecture—including civil engineering—took place in France in the 1670s.

The division between architecture and civil engineering began in 1715, and was practically complete soon after the middle of the eighteenth century. In England there had long been men carrying out works of drainage and river-improvement who would not have claimed to be architects in any sense, but not until 1771 did they band together as members of a common calling. Although after that time bridges and other works of an engineering character were sometimes constructed by men calling themselves architects, the practice was obsolescent.

The École des Ponts et Chaussées was, with other special schools, merged at the Revolution into a comprehensive École des Travaux Publiques. In 1795 this became the École Polytechnique, and the specialist schools, to which its courses served as an introduction, were refounded. Three innovations were made in the running of these schools, which were to serve as a precedent for technical education everywhere in the future: entrance to be by competitive examination; lectures to large classes to be given by leading scientists appointed as whole-time teachers; and practical work to be done by students in chemical and physical laboratories. The revived École des Ponts et Chaussées came under the direction of Gaspard François Prony (1755–1839), formerly closely associated with Perronet in the design and construction of some of his finer bridges. Prony wrote textbooks on mechanics and hydraulics, but the work of greatest influence in this respect was by C. L. M. Navier (1785–1836), who brought the theory of construction right up to date for students in his *Leçons sur l'application de la mécanique* (1826).

In Britain, means of instruction lagged far behind those available in France. Both John Rennie (1761–1821) and Thomas Telford (1757–1834), who, after Smeaton's death, were the most notable British civil engineers, learned French in order to be able to read Belidor and French writers on chemistry. Rennie, whose career began as a millwright, attended classes at Edinburgh University under Joseph Black in chemistry, and under John Robison in mechanical philosophy, although he did not take a degree course. Telford, who began his career as a stone-mason, made a collection of technical books, which on his death formed the foundation of the library of the Institution of Civil Engineers, of which Telford was the founder-president. There were, however, a few English books likely to be useful to a civil engineer. There was J. T. Desaguliers's 'Experimental Philosophy' (two volumes, 1734 and 1744). William Emerson's 'Fluxions' (1743) included the first explanation in English of La Hire's smooth voussoir theory of the arch. John Muller's 'Treatise concerning the Practical Part of Fortification' (1755) formed the basis of his instruction to army cadets at Woolwich Academy. His book was by no means restricted to its subject title: it included discussion of retaining-walls and arches, and of the strength and other properties of constructional materials, based in the main on Belidor. There was also a 'Treatise on Inland Navigation' (1763) by Charles Valency, which consisted of translations from Belidor and several Italian engineers, with illustrations copied from Belidor. The first English textbook on 'The Principles of Bridges', by Charles Hutton, followed La Hire and Emerson. It first appeared in 1772, and was reissued in 1801 and 1812.

In 1760 John Anderson (1726–96) was appointed to the chair of natural philosophy at Glasgow University, and from then until his death gave lectures which he invited artisans to attend in their working clothes. His work was continued at Glasgow, and later in London, by George Birkbeck. So began the Mechanics' Institutes (vol V, ch 32), many of which by the end of the nineteenth century had become famous technical colleges.

The essential engineering theory developed by the French engineers and savants in the eighteenth century was embodied by Thomas Young (1773–1829) in his 'Lectures on Natural Philosophy' (two volumes, 1807), but Young was heavy reading, and was certainly not read by many practising engineers. His ideas did, however, become known through the textbooks written by Thomas Tredgold, and through articles in the 'Encyclopaedia Britannica' by Young himself and by John Robison.

Some lectures on architecture and on engineering were delivered at University College, London, from its foundation in 1828, and at King's College, London, from its foundation in 1829. A Regius professor of engineering was appointed at Glasgow University in 1840. From 1855 that chair was held by John McQuorn Rankine (1820–72), whose subsequent comprehensive textbooks provided the English-reading student for the first time with something equivalent to the works that had long been available only in French.

Generally speaking, neither architects nor engineers placed much value on a university training for their juniors. The young man aspiring to practise either profession was articled to a practitioner already established. He paid a fee and drew no salary, usually picking up what he could from salaried assistants to whom he made himself useful. His progress depended largely on using initiative, keeping his eyes and ears open, and studying in his spare time. In an office handling important and interesting work the keen and industrious pupil could learn much, and by the end of his pupilage prove himself worthy of regular employment. If his connexions were good and his funds adequate, he could buy a partnership or open an office of his own. On the continent of Europe, towards the middle of the nineteenth century, training usually began in a polytechnic school where both theory and design were taught. The young engineer had usually acquired no actual experience of commercial or professional practice when his training ended, and in that respect he was behind his British counterpart, although his technical instruction was far more advanced. By the 1850s German designers and builders of structures and even of machinery had overcome their later start, and in many fields were competing successfully with the British and French [2].

II. MATERIALS

For the walls of buildings in towns the favoured materials were dressed masonry (ashlar) or brickwork. Since the Great Fire of 1666, buildings in London had been required to have incombustible walls and roof-coverings, and most of the provincial towns had followed the example of the metropolis. The practice in small country towns and villages depended on the locality. Where building-stone could be quarried near at hand, stone building was traditional: in well wooded parts of the country hardwood framing with daub-and-wattle infilling persisted into the eighteenth century. However, widespread clearing for agriculture, felling of timber in some areas for ship-building and building, and, in a few areas, conversion of forest to coppice for charcoal-burning, had reduced or hindered the regrowth of stands of tall, straight trees. Much of the vast quantity of timber needed for the rebuilding of London came as softwood from Norway, and once established the trade continued. Where neither stone nor hardwood was readily available, brick became the common material for walls, since more or less suitable clay was to be found in most parts of the country that were not well provided with stone. To most low-lying parts of the country coal for brick-making could be brought by the rivers, of which the navigable lengths were markedly extended during the earlier part of the eighteenth century; these waterways were augmented by canals during the last quarter of the century (ch 18). In Holland, Flanders, and north Italy building in brickwork had a much longer history. In France, as in England, the choice of stone, timber, or brick depended largely upon the local facilities.

Carved stonework is expensive, and when ornament was to be repeated it was often considerably more economical to use clay moulded to shape before burning. The Italians had long produced such work under the name of terracotta. About the middle of the eighteenth century attempts were made to popularize this material in England. The most successful makers were Coade and Sealy of Lambeth. They began in 1769 with John Bacon as designer. He also, and independently, designed statuary in stone and in bronze. Coade stone was resistant to weather and to fire, and was pleasing in colour: it won the approval of many architects and owners of buildings just at the time when large areas were being opened up for residential building in the West End of London, and its popularity continued into the Regency period. The basic material was kaolin (china-clay). The superiority of Coade's products to that of most competitors gave colour to the legend that the makers possessed a trade secret which died with the closure of the business about 1840. It seems more probable that good design and carefully controlled mixing and firing were the real foundations of its reputation [3].

The popularity of Coade stone and other such products waned with the hard times following the Napoleonic wars. For mural decoration John Nash (1752–1835), for instance, covered walls of brickwork with stucco, a mixture of lime and sand which relied for its appearance and permanence on a covering of paint. For garden ornaments and statues cast iron and pre-cast concrete were cheaper than Coade stone, which they tended to replace in just the same way as Coade stone and lead had replaced the more expensive carved natural stone. For massive features such as columns, as at Carlton House Terrace and Buckingham Palace, Nash used cast iron painted to look like stone.

Cements, mortars, and plasters. The commonest substance for use as the active ingredient of mortar is lime; but lime made by calcining natural limestones is not always pure, and its adhesive property may be improved or spoilt according to the nature of the impurity. For use as a plaster-finish a pure lime was preferred, the purest coming from marble. Realization of this fact led to the destruction of much ancient statuary by medieval lime-burners and their successors. For adhesion, however, some of the darker limes were to be preferred, and some of them had the property of setting in damp places, even under water, situations in which a purer lime remained soft or became leached out altogether. This hydraulic property of certain limes, as L. J. Vicat (1786–1861) named it, was known and utilized by the ancient Roman builders. They also knew that a volcanic earth called pozzolana when added to non-hydraulic lime could form a mixture having powerful hydraulic properties. Finely powdered clay tiles and the iron-scale from a blacksmith's forge had a similar property, as did a substance used in Holland known as trass, which resembled pozzolana.

When John Smeaton was commissioned to build the third Eddystone lighthouse (figures 263 and 264), he realized the importance of using a strongly hydraulic lime to joint the masonry, in addition to dove-tailing and dowelling the stones together. He collected samples of lime from many parts of the country, tested them for strength, and submitted them to chemical analysis. He thus discovered that this property of setting under water was always found in a lime made from a limestone that contained an appreciable proportion of clay. This discovery formed the basis of a number of 'natural' and 'artificial' cements. The natural cements were made from minerals in which calcareous and argillaceous constituents were present in roughly suitable proportions to make, when calcined and finely ground, an 'eminently hydraulic' lime. The best known of these was the so-called Roman cement, which was supposed to make mortar or concrete as hard as the best specimens surviving from the Roman occupation. It was made from nodules or *septaria* found in the London clay at Harwich and at Sheppey. It was patented by James Parker in 1796 (Brit. Pat. No 2120/1796).

The artificial cements were made by mixing together chalk or limestone and clay or mud in proportions that had to be empirically determined, because the chemical reactions involved in the setting and hardening of cement were then unknown; they are in fact highly complicated. Important pioneer work on this subject was done in France by L. J. Vicat [4]. The London clay and the chalk of the North Downs occur together in north Kent, and thus cement-works there were conveniently situated both for the unloading of coal brought by sea and for the transport of the product to London by river-barges. This important industry made Kent its home in the late eighteenth century, and it is still conducted there on a very large scale. The early work, including some of his own, was well described by Sir Charles Pasley (1780–1861), first director (1812–41) of the establishment of field-instruction at Chatham, in his book on 'Limes, Calcareous Cements, Mortars etc.' (1838). The most famous of the artificial cements was Portland cement, so named by its patentee Joseph Aspdin (1779–1855) on the optimistic assumption that the dull, grey artificial stone, or concrete, made with this cement would be an acceptable substitute for Portland stone [5]. Aspdin was a stone-mason, bricklayer, or builder in Wakefield, who in 1824 took out a patent (No. 5022) for his product. His son William, with a partner, opened works on the Thames in 1843; in 1851, with another partner, he set up a works at Gateshead. To obtain what came to be known, and is still made, as Portland cement, the calcination of the mixed chalk and clay must be taken to a sintering temperature, but of this no hint appears in Aspdin's patent specification. Aspdin may deliberately or accidentally have obtained the hard-burnt clinker and found it better than the low-temperature product he first made; he did not, however, take out a further patent, probably preferring, if he really made the discovery, to rely on secrecy. One of his rivals, L. C. Johnson (1811–1911), stated much later that it was he who had made the discovery: that what he had at one time thrown away as over-burnt and spoiled clinker, proved, when he made the experiment of grinding it fine and using it as cement, much superior in strength to the hitherto normal lightly-burnt material. However that may be, about 1850 the advantage of high-temperature calcination was generally understood by makers and users of cement, and this became the common practice. The kilns were shaped either like bottles or like truncated cones (figure 246): one dating from 1856 measured 36 ft high, 17 ft in diameter at the base, and 2 ft 9 inches in diameter at the top: it is reported to have held enough cement to fill eighty barrels. The cement-barrel, if it was the same as that used into the twentieth century for export, held 400 lb. Portland cement was thus entirely British in invention and development.

FIGURE 246—*Original kiln in the works erected by William Aspdin at Northfleet, Kent.*

The production of a fairly consistent quality of cement gave considerable impetus to the use of concrete as a structural material. The use of hydraulic-lime concrete in bridge-foundations by French engineers has already been noted (vol III, p 425). George Semple (*c* 1700–*c* 1782) mixed roach lime (fortunately hydraulic) with gravel from his excavations to form a concrete for the foundations of the Essex bridge over the Liffey in Dublin in place of the more usual grillage [6]. George Dance the younger (1741–1825) and Sir John Soane (1753–1837) made occasional use of lime-concrete in foundations. Sir Robert Smirke (1781–1867) made it a practice to use it in his larger works—such as the Penitentiary, the Customs House, and the General Post Office in London—in the form of a thick layer or raft spread evenly over the whole site. Sir Marc Isambard Brunel (1769–1849) used Roman cement in the mortar for the Thames tunnel (1826–43) (p 463); but in the concrete filling that he dumped in the bed of the Thames to stop the break-through in 1828 he used Aspdin's cement. For repairs to a defective portion of the wall at Victoria Docks, London (1850–5), Portland cement concrete was used. The first really large-scale use of Portland cement however, was in the main drainage of London, by Sir Joseph Bazalgette (p 510); 70 000 tons were used, and 15 000 tests were made during the course of the work (1858–75) [7].

A material widely used instead of lime as the basis of a plaster for walls and ceilings was made by driving off part, but not the whole, of the water combined with calcium sulphate in the mineral gypsum. Beds of this material were worked in the Middle Ages at Montmartre and it was widely used in Paris—hence the name plaster of Paris. An early reference to gypsum plaster occurs in the mid-thirteenth century, when Henry III gave orders for its use in some work at

Nottingham Castle [8]. The alabaster of the Nottingham neighbourhood is a fine form of gypsum, and the waste and inferior grades of this material came to be burnt for plaster. Gypsum is also found, and since the Middle Ages has been worked, in Dorset, Yorkshire, and many other districts.

The main use of gypsum plaster was to give a smooth, clean finish, but both in France and in England it was used structurally in floors. In Paris in the 1840s fire-resisting ceilings were constructed by supporting plaster of Paris by means of wrought iron bars and joists, between and around which it was poured as shown in figure 247. The woodwork of the floor above the ceiling was thus protected from attack by fire in the room below. In the neighbourhood of Nottingham gypsum plaster was poured over a mat of reeds supported on floor-joists. The top of the plaster was smoothed to form the surface of the floor, which required no boards.

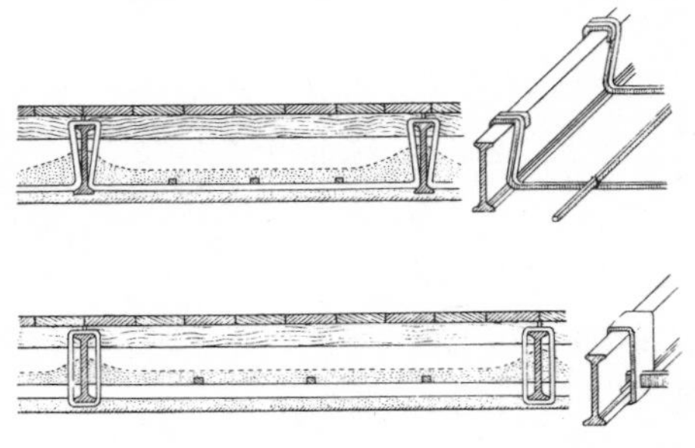

FIGURE 247—*French method of constructing iron floors. c 1840.*

Ironwork. Iron as a structural material first became important during our period, and in two forms: wrought or malleable iron, a form of the metal in which impurities were few and incidental and made no marked change in its characteristic qualities, and cast iron, in which carbon was present to the extent of from 2 to 5 per cent. Part of the carbon in cast iron forms a carbide of iron, which adds considerably to the hardness and compressive strength of the material, and part exists as plate-like deposits of graphite which, by dividing one crystal of the metal from another, introduce planes of weakness that leave the metal brittle and of low tensile strength. Wrought iron when heated to redness becomes malleable, and can be hammered or rolled into shape. Cast iron melts at a temperature (about 1200° C) lower than the melting-point of wrought iron (1500 to 1600° C) and when fused can be run into moulds. It expands slightly on solidifying and thus reproduces the details of the mould.

In the late Middle Ages, and to a greater extent thereafter, fastenings of wrought iron were used to make or strengthen the joints of large and important structural frameworks of timber, such as roof trusses, but the metal was expensive. Bars forged to link together were used for such structural members as the chains round the bases of masonry domes.

Improvements in the availability of wrought iron in the eighteenth century made little difference in England to the direct use made of it by the builder or the structural engineer. In France, however, some bold experiments were made in the structural use of wrought iron, both to bind masonry together and give it tensile strength where needed, and to form the members of roof frameworks.

The burial of ironwork in masonry had one serious drawback: masonry is not entirely impervious to air and moisture, particularly at joints, and access of damp air to ironwork leads to the formation of rust. Rust occupies a much greater volume than the metal from which it is formed, and thus tends to force apart the masonry in which the iron is embedded. The consequent open joints or cracks are liable to let in more water and air, and the rate of corrosion is accelerated, with progressive expansion, extension of the damage, and the appearance of unsightly stains. These risks, added to the high price of iron, defeated the medieval builders who used the metal to tie together some of the slender masonry in early experimental Gothic work.

FIGURE 248—*Perronet's bridge across the Seine at Neuilly. 1768–74.*

At the Great Exhibition held in 1851 in Hyde Park, London, a large beam of brickwork, reinforced with hoop-iron laid in the horizontal mortar-joints, was displayed carrying an impressive load. Sir Marc Isambard Brunel had indeed been experimenting with this combination since 1832. The plaster ceilings with embedded iron rods, as constructed in Paris about this time, might almost be regarded as a primitive reinforced concrete; but the regular use of iron as a reinforcement, to relieve masonry of tensile stresses against which its resistance is weak, had to await the development of a concrete that could be made practically impervious to water and so retain its alkaline reaction, which inhibits corrosion. Such concrete became possible with the general introduction of Portland cement in the latter half of the nineteenth century.

Cast iron was used for cannon from the mid-sixteenth century: for fire-backs in the seventeenth. In 1684 Rannequin, at the famous waterworks at Marly-la-Machine, used cast iron for pipes and pump-barrels; so did George Sorocold in 1704 in water-works at London Bridge. Smeaton used it in gearing and other millwork in the 1750s. Late in the eighteenth century cast iron became of importance as a material for structures. It assumed great prominence in the first half of the nineteenth century, and then slowly faded out of the picture as its place was taken by other materials. In its manufacture, properties, and uses it is, as previously noted, a vastly different material from wrought iron.

III. ENGINEERING CONSTRUCTION

Bridges. The century under review was one of great expansion of trade and manufacture, for which existing means of communication and transport were inadequate. A great extension and improvement of the highway system, first in France, then in Britain, and later in western Europe and North America, called for bridges in places where previously fords and ferries had been acceptable. Navigable rivers came to be supplemented in Britain, as already in Italy, the Netherlands, and France, by canals. Increase in shipping, both in gross capacity

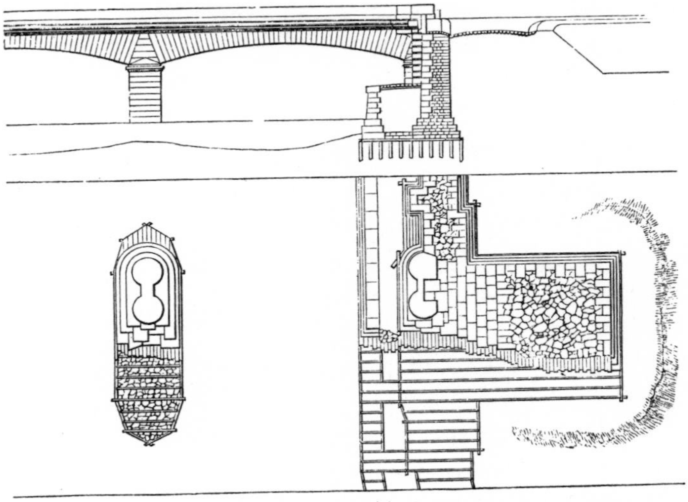

FIGURE 249—*Perronet's bridge at Ste-Maxence.* (Above) *elevation;* (below) *plan.*

and in the size of vessels, called for improved harbour facilities and justified expenditure on breakwaters, docks, and quays on an unprecedented scale. Towards the end of the period, railways, hitherto ancillary to canals, came first to rival and then to supersede them. All these developments called for construction that had to be planned, financed, and organized.

Bridge-building continued along the lines described in volume III, but with a tendency to lighter and bolder construction. The power of steam, first developed for the drainage of mines, was also available for the drainage of deep excavations, and before the end of the eighteenth century James Watt's rotative engines could be used to drive machinery, including winding- and hauling-gear. A steam-engine could be used to wind up the hammer to drive piles, or a direct steam-hammer (p 430) could be used. Without steam-power even the vast numbers of men recruited to build the railways could not have carried out the work so expeditiously, and some of it would have been impossible.

In France, from 1750 until the Revolution, many masonry bridges of advanced design and excellent workmanship were built by the engineers of the *Ponts et Chaussées* under Perronet's leadership. In comparison with the works of his predecessors, Perronet's bridges are characterized by flatter arches, shallower arch rings, and thinner piers. In these respects his work came to be regarded as bordering on the reasonably safe limit in masonry construction. The bridge across the Seine at Neuilly is shown in figure 248 as an example. Perronet was satisfied with an arch-ring of a thickness equal to about 1/24th of the span, a rise of crown above

FIGURE 250—*The centres for the bridge at Neuilly. 1768–74.*

springing at the Pont Ste-Maxence across the Oise a few miles north of Senlis of only 1/12th, and a pier-thickness of 1/10th of the span (figure 249).

Perronet's arch-centres were built up as shown in figure 250. They comprised in effect a multiple-ribbed timber arch to carry the thrust to the abutments or piers of permanent construction. The radial members were made in two pieces, halved so that when bolted together they embraced the arch-members and held them firmly in place. These centres were not well contrived to take any marked unevenness in loading, and were somewhat flexible. To strike the centre the bolts and fastenings were removed, and ropes were attached to the lower ends of the radial members. A sideways pull on the latter by winches on the banks, or in moored barges, caused the whole centre to collapse into the river.

An improved method of centring was devised by Robert Mylne (1734–1811). Mylne was the descendant of a line of masons to the Scottish crown. After qualifying as a master of his trade he studied in Rome for four years, returning in 1759 just in time to prepare the winning design for Blackfriars bridge, London, in competition with the leading practitioners. The award was undoubtedly deserved, but nevertheless aroused bitter jealousy and recrimination. Mylne's centring, shown in figure 251, embodied multiple wedges, which could be driven back when it was desired to lower the centre. Striking could be suspended if the consequent movement of the masonry aroused suspicion of weakness, whereas in Perronet's arrangement the first movement of the centre sealed its fate: there was no drawing back. The inclination of some of the members and the overall depth of the frame made Mylne's arrangement much more rigid than Perronet's, although it used less timber.

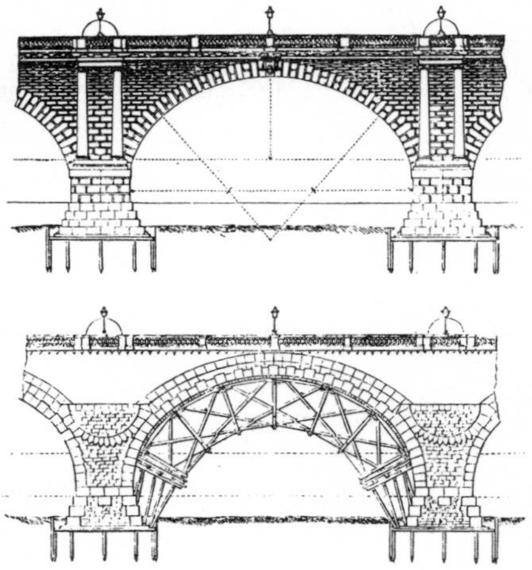

FIGURE 251—*Mylne's bridge over the Thames at Blackfriars, London. 1760–9. In the lower figure the centring is in position.*

At the outer face, the exposed voussoirs of the Blackfriars bridge were so cut as to butt against the masonry of the spandrel walls. Inside, an inverted arch was built to transmit the thrust from one span to the next. The junction between the main and the inverted arches was somewhat crude and weak, but the intention was sound. The elliptical form of the arch at Blackfriars bridge was a novelty in British bridge-building. The largest of the nine spans was 100 ft. The bases of the piers were in caissons, the bottoms of which rested on piles.

The *Ponts et Chaussées* had developed the form of contract under which a single contractor tendered a lump sum for the whole work on a bridge to a strict specification and bill of quantities, as is still customary in public works. The general contractor had not yet emerged in Britain, and Mylne had to let masonry, carpentry, smith-work, ballast-work, and so forth to different contractors. He drew 5 per cent on their bills. The bridge was opened to traffic in 1769, and only in 1869 was it replaced by the present wrought iron, arched bridge.

Before Blackfriars bridge was finished Mylne had been appointed surveyor to St Paul's Cathedral and to Canterbury Cathedral, and had designed the Jamaica bridge at Glasgow. In 1770 he became engineer to the New River Company. He also reported on harbours, canals, and water-works in various parts of the country. He was a founder-member of the Associated Architects, London, from 1791, and designed some country houses. He was the last British architect of note to be at the same time an eminent civil engineer.

John Rennie (1761–1821) graduated to bridge-building from millwrighting. He adopted and improved upon Mylne's form of bridge centring, and also the combined inverted arch and springing between adjacent spans. His most famous masonry bridges were Waterloo bridge, London—completed in 1817—(figures 252, 253 B) and the present London Bridge (figure 253 A), which in 1831 took the place of the medieval bridge. The foundations of these bridges were on piles, and were built within coffer-dams. Rennie distrusted the caisson: he preferred to see

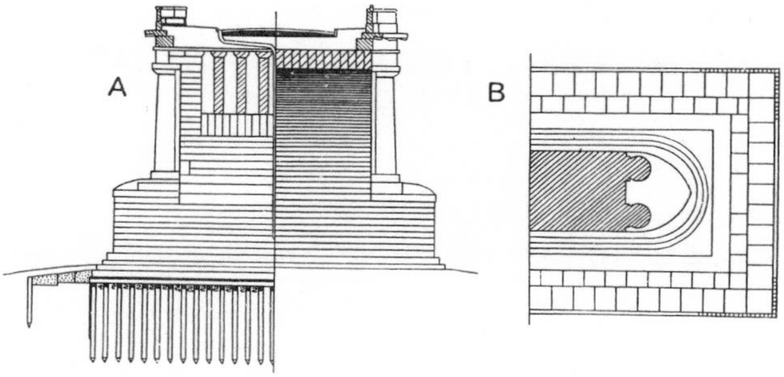

FIGURE 252—*Rennie's Waterloo bridge.* (A) *Cross-section of pier and arch;* (B) *plan through pier.*

the bottom upon which his work would rest. He built harbours, canals, and a variety of buildings, and simultaneously with Thomas Telford (p 444) developed in Britain the system whereby one main contractor undertook the responsibility for the work of all trades employed on one engineering project, however large or complex.

The first important structural use of cast iron was in the bridge that crosses the Severn at Ironbridge, near Coalbrookdale (plate 30 A). The credit for instigating this venture has usually been given to John Wilkinson, the famous ironmaster of Bersham. It is true that Wilkinson in 1775 took some of the original shares, but he sold them to Abraham Darby III (1750–91) long before the actual bridge was even designed. Credit for the design has likewise been given to T. F. Pritchard, a Shrewsbury architect. Pritchard did, in fact, produce a design for an iron bridge, but not that to which the actual bridge was built. The design, casting, and erection of the bridge were undertaken and completed by Darby, who also bore more than half the expense of the venture [9]. The bridge, of which an artist's impression is shown in plate 30 A, is nearly semi-circular. The span is 100 ft 6 in, and the rise 45 ft. There are five main ribs 12 in by $6\frac{1}{2}$ inches in section, virtually hinged at the springing and at the crown; there are also lighter incomplete ribs and connecting members. The castings for the main ribs were 70 ft long. They were cast in open sand direct from a blast-furnace, which had to be built for the purpose; the remains of the furnace, though probably altered and now partly buried in a spoil-tip, still exist (p 117, tailpiece). The parts of the bridge were so arranged as either to pass through, or to mortise into, one another, and were secured by wedges. No bolts or rivets were used. The procedure for erection was rehearsed on a wooden model, now in the Science Museum, London, for which in 1788 the Society of Arts awarded a gold medal. The main rib-castings are said to have been brought to the site by water, secured

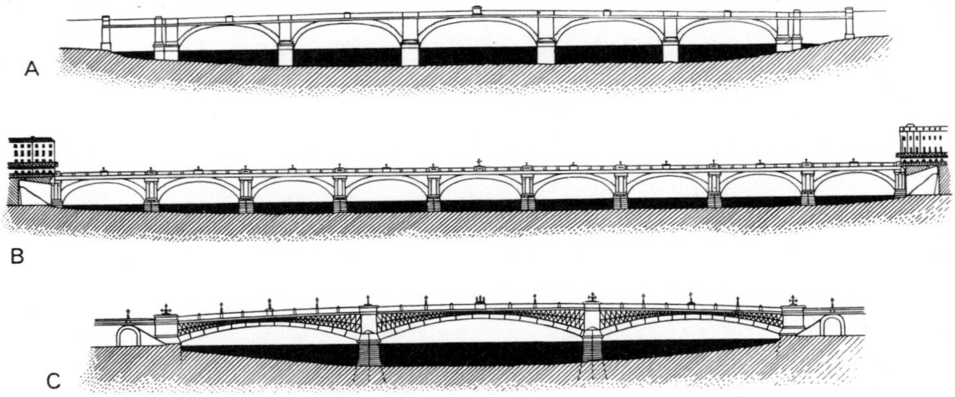

FIGURE 253—*Rennie's bridges over the Thames:* (A) *London, 1824–31;* (B) *Waterloo, 1811–17;* (C) *Southwark, 1814–19.*

in position at the foot, and hoisted up by ropes, both halves simultaneously, and joined together at the crown. The total weight of iron work, including deck, is stated by Telford to have been 378 tons. The arrangement of the secondary members shows, as would be expected for that date, no clear appreciation of their specific functions.

The abutment on the left-hand (east) side of the river is against a solid bank, and the approach for traffic is across a masonry arch. That on the right-hand (west) side is on lower ground, probably alluvial, and started to move towards the river soon after the bridge was completed. The masonry and earth-filling behind the main abutment pier were removed and wooden approach spans erected. Within forty years these were showing signs of decay, and were replaced by cast iron arch-spans which still remain, although they have been repaired. There has been some recent movement of the eastern abutment, causing cracks in the masonry which have had to be grouted. However, the bridge still stands after 180 years: a notable example of a pioneer venture and a monument to the courage and structural sense of Abraham Darby and his associates. It has been scheduled as an ancient monument, and is now used by foot traffic only.

In 1787 Thomas Telford became surveyor to the county of Shropshire, and as such assumed responsibility for the care and, where needed, the provision of bridges. Some of these he built in stone, but his curiosity was naturally aroused by the iron bridge at Coalbrookdale. When the old stone bridge of several arches at Buildwas on the Severn, a few miles above Coalbrookdale, was swept away by flood in 1795, he decided to replace it by one of iron arch construction, of the form shown in figure 254. The span was 130 ft, but the bridge weighed only 173 tons, showing a considerable economy on the Coalbrookdale design. The sup-

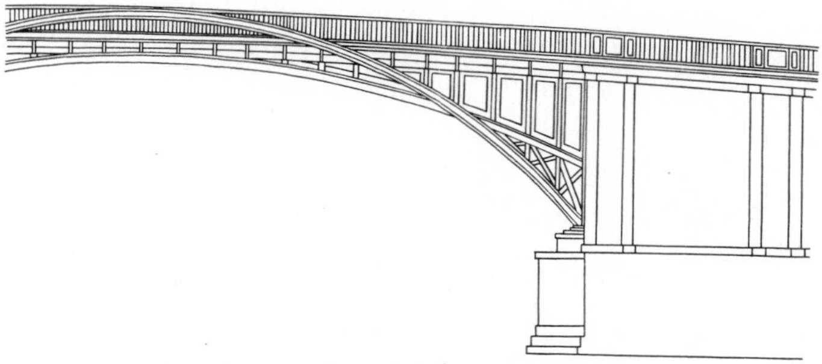

FIGURE 254—*Telford's iron bridge at Buildwas. 1795.*

port of the deck from the ribs by vertical members braced together was also an improvement, but the attempt to combine two different depths of rib was not. They behaved differently under both load and changes of temperature, cracked, and had to be repaired with fish-plates. When the plating was tightly fitted the rib cracked at some other place, until in the end the bridge had to be left alone, loosely held with fish-plates, to find its own adjustment. It lasted, however, until 1906.

A more manageable design than the solid arch rib for longer spans was the type erected in 1796 over the river Wear to connect Sunderland and Monkwearmouth. The span was 236 ft, the rise 34 ft; and the construction was of six segmental ribs each virtually consisting of 125 open-work cast iron voussoirs and wrought iron straps (figure 255 and plate 29). The builders were Walker's, the iron-founders of Rotherham, in association with Rowland Burdon—M.P. for Sunderland—who took out a patent for this type of construction (B.P. No 2066, 1795). It has often been stated that the design was due to Tom Paine, the revolutionary, who, on a mission from the United States of America, spent some time at Walker's negotiating for an iron bridge to be made by them and exported. Paine did take out a British Patent (No 1667, 1788), but he was in no sense an engineer, and the crude construction described in his patent bears little resemblance to that of the Sunderland bridge. Part of a small-span bridge to Paine's design was erected for exhibition at St Pancras, but this was broken up when he dropped his project and went to take part in the French Revolution.

In 1798 Telford, in association with James Douglas, proposed to replace Old London Bridge by a cast iron arch construction with 600 ft in a single span. It was estimated to require 6500 tons of cast iron; the abutments were to consist of 432 000 cu ft of granite and 20 000 cu ft of brickwork. How, or even whether, this vast weight could have been supported by any foundation-technique then available is conjectural. Fortunately for Telford the project was turned down, but it led to a most interesting theoretical discussion, to which reference will be made later (p 484 and tailpiece).

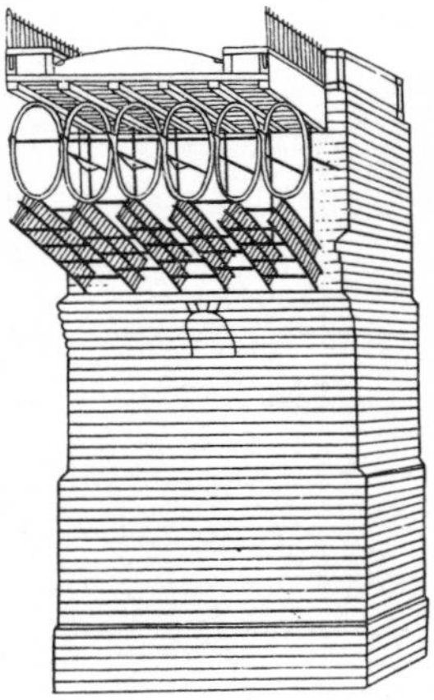

FIGURE 255—*Burdon's iron bridge over the Wear at Sunderland, showing construction. 1796.*

After a lull, caused by the wars with France, the construction of iron bridges was resumed. The general type comprised a number of parallel segmental arch ribs, with a lattice-work, or grid, of bars above to support the deck, cast either with the rib or separately, according to the size of the bridge. Cross-bracing between the parallel systems ensured stability. It was presumably realized that the rings above the ribs of the Coalbrookdale and Sunderland bridges were not an efficient device to carry a vertical load, for they were not repeated. Telford built a number of such bridges; so did John Rennie, the greatest being Southwark bridge, London, erected between 1814 and 1819, with a central span of 240 ft and two rather shorter side-spans (figure 253 C). The segmental iron ribs were of I-section, 6 to 8 ft deep and $2\frac{3}{4}$ in thick, with flanges 4 in wide. Thirteen castings, end to end, fixed to one another with taper-keys, formed each arch: they acted rather like the voussoirs of a masonry arch. The ironwork was cast by Walker's of Rotherham and weighed about 5800 tons. The bridge was replaced in 1922 by the present Southwark bridge, which is of steel arch construction.

The suspension bridge naturally attracted the attention of American bridge-builders, for at this time they had poor facilities for making large castings and forgings and yet rapidly growing centres of population were in many places separated by wide rivers. The suspension bridge with a stiffened deck seems to have been contrived by Judge James Finley (*c* 1762–1828) of Pennsylvania, who built a number of them in the first decade of the nineteenth century, and obtained a patent in 1808. One, of which the towers still stand and carry the bridge as re-built in 1909, had a span of 244 ft.

While Southwark bridge was still under construction several suspension bridges were erected in the south of Scotland, where winter floods were liable to undermine the masonry piers of arches. The greatest of these, of 300-ft span, was completed in 1820 by Captain Samuel Brown, and crossed the Tweed at Kelso. It had twelve chains consisting of iron links 2 inches in diameter and 15 ft long, with an eye-bar at each end bolted to flat links. The piers and abutments were built on rock clear of flood-level. In 1817 Brown took out a patent for flat wrought iron links. Telford had been experimenting with links consisting of bundles of small rods welded together at the ends, but on learning of Brown's links he adopted them for the chains of his famous bridge, of 580 ft span, to carry the Holyhead road across the Menai Straits.

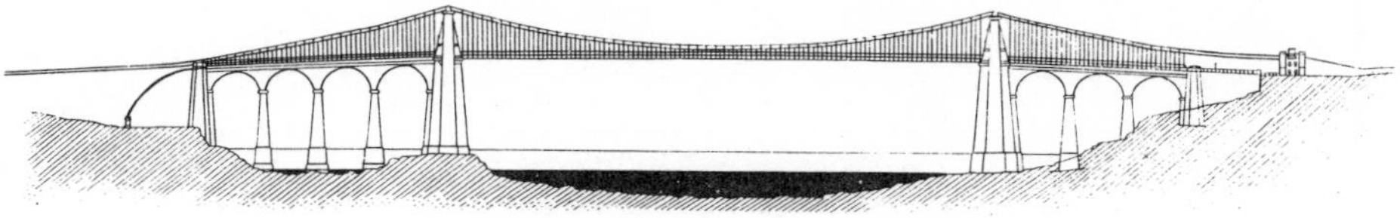

FIGURE 256—*Telford's Menai bridge, 1826.*

Work on the bridge over the Menai Straits began in 1820 and finished in 1826 (figure 256). The deck was of timber and unstiffened: it was wrecked in 1839 by a storm. A heavier timber deck lasted till 1893, when Sir Benjamin Baker reconstructed it in steel. This in turn was replaced in 1940, when the chains also were renewed in high-tensile steel; indeed, except for the towers and abutments, the present structure is a new bridge.

In 1834 Joseph Chailey, a French engineer, built a suspension bridge over the river Sarine at Fribourg, Switzerland, with a span of 870 ft; the deck was suspended by cables each comprising 1000 wires bound together with wire wrapping. It lasted 90 years.

Famous among the American pioneers in this field was Charles Ellet, who made his cables on the French system of bundles of small wires. In 1848 he broke what was then the record for length with a bridge of 1010-ft span across the river Ohio at Wheeling, West Virginia. In 1854 this bridge was seriously damaged by a tornado. Ellet's towers remained, and the rest of the bridge was rebuilt by John August Roebling, who later achieved fame by his own record-breaking activities in building long-span suspension bridges of wire cable. In 1956 the Wheeling bridge was again under repair. Ellet's towers and anchorages, and Roebling's cables and suspenders, were to be retained, but the deck was to be entirely renewed.

Although some suspension bridges were still giving good service in the 1840s, many had collapsed through the buffeting effect of winds, or even through oscillations built up by the impact of marching troops or droves of cattle. Brown had built many, and had quite a number of failures, including his bridge of 449-ft span across the Tweed at Berwick; this he completed in 1820, but it was blown down only six months later. In 1830 he had even built one to carry the Stockton and Darlington railway across the Tees, only to find that the train sank down and raised before and behind it a wave in the deck, which racked the bridge to pieces in a few years. By the use of stiffening girders, which, however, sacrificed some of the lightness that was the outstanding merit of this type of bridge, such a defect could be mitigated, but for railway work Robert Stephenson decided against it. In 1845 he joined William Fairbairn (1789–1874) in a series

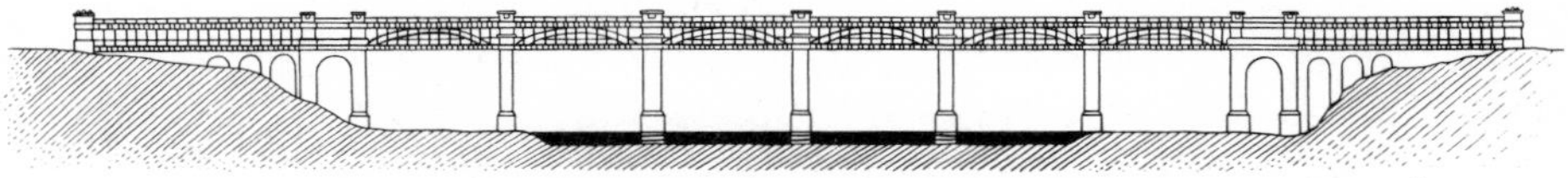

FIGURE 257—*Robert Stephenson's high-level bridge, Newcastle upon Tyne. 1846–9.*

of experiments on wrought iron girders, to determine the best form these could take for a long-span bridge, in particular for the bridge that would carry the Chester and Holyhead railway across the Menai Straits within sight of Telford's road-bridge.

Wrought iron plates and angles, riveted together, were in general use for steam-boilers at this time. There seemed no reason why this technique should not be used to build up bridge-girders of considerable size once a suitable form was decided upon. Experiments were made on tubes, and eventually it was decided to build rectangular tubes through which the trains would pass, the tops and bottoms of the tubes being themselves cellular. The test specimens worked up to a model of one-sixth of the full size before the design was made final. This bridge, however, must be regarded as the first of the next period, rather than as the last of that covered by this volume, and accordingly its construction will be described in volume V.

Although wrought iron eventually replaced cast iron as the approved material for railway-bridges before itself being superseded by mild steel, many bridges were built of cast iron in the 1840s, and some of these are still in service. There were, however, failures, and in 1848 a royal commission was appointed, which reported in 1849 upon 'The Application of Iron to Railway Structures'. Much evidence was collected, and experiments were carried out by Eaton Hodgkinson and others, but the conclusions favoured conservative design, and, in the case of cast iron, recommended adhering to the arch and beam forms of construction. There was indeed as yet no developed theory of structures upon which the design of framed girders could be based, and the commission advised against their use. This did not, however, deter the more adventurous from experimenting with these and other forms. Neuville, a Belgian engineer, had in 1846 erected a bridge with an open frame comprising horizontal top and bottom booms, joined by diagonal members set at 60° so as to form in elevation a chain of equilateral triangles. In 1848 Captain James Warren and W. T. Manzoni took out a British Patent (No 12242 of 1848) for such a construction assembled either from separate members, or from castings in which the top boom and two dia-

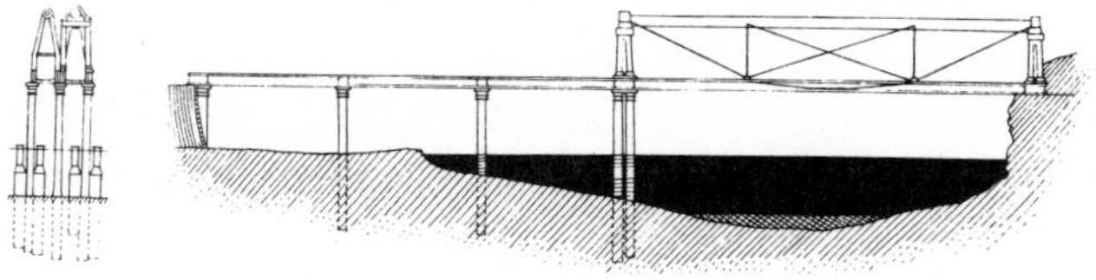

FIGURE 258—*Section and elevation of I. K. Brunel's bridge across the Wye at Chepstow, 1849–52.*

gonal members of one bay formed a triangular unit and the bottom boom in each bay was a wrought iron rod threaded to take nuts at both ends. Such girders became known as Warren girders in England, and as Neuville girders on the continent.

The most notable cast iron[1] railway-bridge is Robert Stephenson's high-level bridge at Newcastle upon Tyne, erected in 1849 (figure 257). It consists of six spans, and the distance between the centres of the piers is 139 ft. Each span takes the form of a tied arch, the railway being carried just above the crown level; there is a roadway, and there was later a tramway, at the level of the tie. This bridge still carries main-line and road traffic, now far heavier than that for which it was originally intended. The piles in the foundations were driven by means of a Nasmyth steam-hammer (p 431), which delivered one blow a second as against the one blow every few minutes previously possible.

Isambard Kingdom Brunel (1806–59), the builder of the Great Western railway, nicknamed the 'Commission on the Application of Iron to Railway Structures' the 'Commission for Stopping Further Improvement in Bridge Building'. He built many bridges in wrought iron, masonry, and timber, of which perhaps the most original was his bridge across the Wye at Chepstow (figure 258). Con-

[1] Some wrought iron was also used in this bridge: for instance, for the suspension rods concealed within the vertical cast iron members.

siderable head-room had to be left for navigation, and, as the river is subject at times to a 40-ft tidal range, ample precautions were needed against scour. He therefore made his main span across the normal river-bed 300 ft long.

The use of compressed-air caissons to permit foundations to be sunk through water-logged ground had been introduced in 1830 by Sir Thomas Cochrane, and they were used in 1851 by Cubitt and Wright to sink the cylinder-piers for Rochester bridge across the Medway to a depth of 61 ft. Brunel used the method at Chepstow in 1852 to sink the cylinders that form the piers of the bridge, six of them carrying the cast iron tower (figure 258) at the west end of the main span. The tower at the east end of this span is of masonry, built on the rock of the natural cliff. The deck is carried by four wrought iron girders, one on each side of each of the two railway tracks. These are suspended from the towers by link-chains, at distances of rather less than 100 ft from each end. The chains are continued to truss the middle part of the girders. The horizontal component of the tension in the chain is resisted by tubular top booms, 9 ft in diameter, made like huge boilers of wrought iron plate. They are slightly cambered and intermediately supported at two points. In some ways the Chepstow bridge served as a trial run for the design and methods of construction Brunel employed in the greater bridge over the Tamar at Saltash.

Tunnels. Tunnelling has long been an important branch of engineering construction, having previously been a regular practice in mining. Even before the Christian era lakes in the craters of volcanoes were drained by Roman engineers, who cut tunnels through solid lava. Medieval fortresses are known to have been reduced by tunnelling under corner towers, and then setting fire to the shoring that held up the roof. The Languedoc canal, built between 1661 and 1681, included tunnels in its course; there was a summit-tunnel over 500 ft in length cut through solid rock. Brindley adopted the same expedient in his eighteenth-century English canals. Tunnelling in rock was arduous; but the rock-face and roof, at least in small tunnels, were usually self-supporting. When a tunnel was driven through soft, wet ground, precautions to avoid collapse were imperative but sometimes extremely difficult to execute. The Tronquoy tunnel on the St-Quentin canal in France is said to have been 'the first in which a system of timbering and arching for supporting loose and soft ground had to be devised for a wide tunnel' [10].

There are several ways of tunnelling. In one, for instance, work is begun at the top: a narrow heading is driven forward from the face for a predetermined distance. A heavy timber is then drawn forward at a level just above the roof of the finished tunnel-lining. Its forward end is supported by a short post which bears on a short sill on the bottom of the heading; its rear end is wedged up from the section of roof last completed. If necessary, short boards can be driven above and at right-angles to the main timber. Other main timbers or 'bars' are placed in the same manner, until the whole roof is supported. The gaps above the completed lining, out of which the bars have been drawn forward, are packed and filled. The new lengths of arched roof and sides are built, and, if the bottom requires it, inverted arches or 'inverts' as well. Then another length of heading can be driven and the bars moved forward again, one at a time.

FIGURE 259—*A portion of the shield used by Brunel to drive the Thames tunnel. 1826–43.*

In tunnelling under a river there is the added risk that a break-through may flood the workings. Such a catastrophe brought an end to the attempt by Richard Trevithick (1771–1833) to drive a tunnel-heading about 3 ft wide by 5 ft high under the Thames with timber shoring; the disaster happened after he had cut his way for nearly 1000 ft. The feat of first tunnelling beneath the Thames was finally achieved by Sir Marc Isambard Brunel, father of Isambard Kingdom Brunel, who served him as resident engineer. Brunel made use of a shield that provided working-space for twelve men side by side at each of three levels, working on a rectangular face 38 ft wide by 22 ft 6 in deep (figure 259). Each group of three working-spaces, one above another, was within a cast iron frame, with a flat top and foot each hinged to the body; and there were two intermediate platforms. Large screw-jacks at head and foot bore against the completed masonry and held the edges of the shield tightly against the working face. Small screw-jacks bore against the verticals of the shield and held boards against the face, except where it was actually being cut.

The tunnel started from a vertical shaft 50 ft in diameter at the Rotherhithe end, and dipped slightly, on a slope of 2 ft 3 inches in 300 ft, towards the middle, where the base of the excavation was 76 ft below high-water level. The shield was placed in position on 1 January 1826, and at first worked in London clay, but within a month the workings had been carried forward into water-bearing sand and gravel not disclosed in the survey. This seriously impeded progress. As the shield worked forward 18 in at a time it was followed by a double-arched tunnel of masonry, built with Roman cement. In May 1827, and again in January 1828, the river broke in. The holes in the river-bed were attacked from a diving-bell above, plugged with Portland-cement concrete, and filled in with bags of clay; but after the second flooding the face was blocked off, and work was suspended for seven years.

After resumption of work with a heavier shield there were three more serious floodings, but at last, on 26 May 1843, the tunnel was completed and opened to foot-traffic (plate 32 A) [11]. It was ultimately taken over for the railway line that connects Whitechapel and New Cross, and is still used by the electric trains of London Transport.

IV. MARINE WORKS

Harbours were required for two purposes: to shelter ships caught in stormy weather off a lee shore, and to provide ports for the landing and embarkation of cargo and passengers. In the days of sail it was very important that there should be harbours of refuge where ships making a landfall could find shelter until the wind changed. Such harbours might also be ports, but not necessarily so: some were needed in localities where there was little or no trade. If a harbour, natural or artificial, were available, however, it would nearly always be used by, or give rise to, a local fishing industry. On a rocky, deeply indented shore some shelter could generally be found in bays partially enclosed by capes and islands, and often only a short breakwater was needed to augment existing natural protection. A port was a more complicated matter. Vessels might have to shelter there in large numbers and for long periods. Quays in still water were preferable for ships and essential for lighters. Early ports, therefore, were nearly always situated within the mouths of rivers, or even some distance upstream, where facilities were available for settlement and for land- or river-transport to other populated areas.

A breakwater, as the name implies, is intended to resist the force of the waves, so that comparatively calm water will be available for anchorage on its lee side. Resistance can be provided in one or other of two forms: a solid mass against which the waves beat and rebound ineffectively; or a long slope up which they run until their energy is dissipated in friction by rolling shingle up and down and by the interference of flow and return. In Nature these take the forms of rocky cliff and storm-beach respectively.

The force of waves depends largely on the 'fetch', that is, the direct distance from land over which the surface of the water has been exposed to a steady wind. On an ocean coast this distance may be immense, and waves of enormous height may have to be resisted. The most important 'fetch' is that of the prevailing wind. In the neighbourhood of Cape Horn waves in the Pacific Ocean have been reputed to reach a height of 50 ft with a distance from crest to crest of 600 to 1000 ft. Only vast masses of the hardest natural rock can withstand their onslaught, and only at the cost of continual erosion by the battery of stones hurled at them by the immense waves. The greatest fragments stand in the steepest

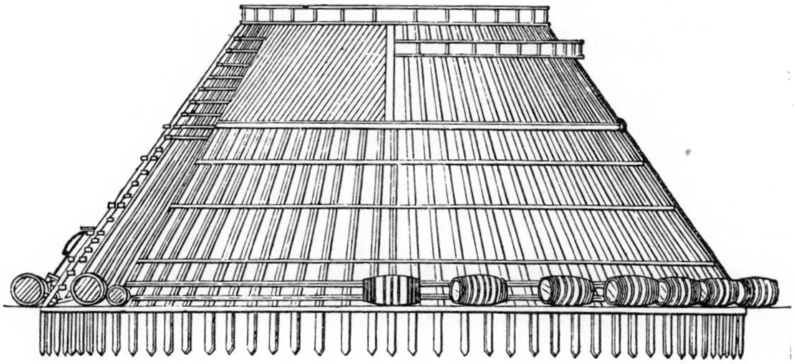

FIGURE 260—*One of Cessart's cones for Cherbourg harbour breakwater. 1780.*

heaps; the smaller are stable only on less steep slopes. Artificial breakwaters can be made to stand only on the same principles.

The port of Cherbourg is an artificial harbour, needing protection from up-Channel storms. An attempt was made by Louis de Cessart (1719–1806) to construct a breakwater of giant caissons of timber, like huge inverted tubs, floated into position by casks, and sunk by filling with rock. There was to be an open channel around both ends, but behind the breakwater the French fleet operating in the English Channel could take refuge, protected from foul weather by the breakwater, and from English privateers by the coastal defence batteries that were to be erected on it. Work was begun in 1780. The caissons (figure 260) were 70 ft high, and tapered in diameter from 150 ft at the base to 60 ft at the top. 45 000 cu ft of timber were required to build each one. They were towed into position by rowing-boats, then submerged by loading with stones and connected by a bank of stone [12].

The cost in labour and money was immense, and in 1788, when 18 cones had been placed, orders were issued to discontinue the work. The cones broke up and the stones were spilled on the sea-bed. They stood at a slope of 1 in 3 in deep water, but between high and low water the bank was dragged down by the waves to a slope of 1 in 10, and would stand no steeper however much material was added. When a stable profile had apparently been achieved, forts were built on a bed of blocks that weighed 3 or 4 tons each, but in 1812, and again in 1824, they were destroyed by storms. Eventually Vicat produced a hydraulic lime by the use of which a concrete causeway was built on top of the bank, faced and capped with coarse masonry from low-tide level to 3 metres above high-tide level. This work was successfully completed in 1850.

Nothing nearly so ambitious had been attempted off the English coast. At Dover, Hastings, and Lyme Regis small breakwaters had been made early in the eighteenth century from mounds of stones as big as could be transported on rafts made buoyant by empty casks, but their lives were short. The first breakwater of any size on the English side of the Channel was made across the natural, rock-enclosed harbour at Plymouth, leaving access round both ends. This work was undertaken by John Rennie. It had been hoped that a great mound of limestone rubble would stand with sides sloping at about 1 in 3; but such a slope was found to be stable only in deep water. Blocks that weighed about 10 tons each would stand at a slope of about 1 in 5. In the end the whole bank, when stabilized, assumed the profile shown in figure 261, similar to that finally assumed by the breakwater at Cherbourg. The mass of the interior was of smaller stones. Finally, the top was paved with granite blocks set in cement. Although a stable shape would be reached, individual stones would be dragged down the slope or thrown over the crest were such a finish omitted: consequently a good deal of replenishment of surface stones would be needed after storms. This work was begun in 1812 and finished in 1841.

FIGURE 261 — *Plymouth breakwater (section). 1812–41.*

There are, or have been, many small ports along the coasts of Kent and Sussex, but the current in the English Channel carries a considerable drift of solid matter in suspension, consisting of silt or gravel derived from the gradual erosion of coastal cliffs. Most of these ports have become choked with this matter, and their deterioration has in some cases been hastened by man. The river Rother was at one time tidal far inland, and the incoming waters flooded a wide area behind the town of Rye. On the ebb, the accumulation of water, rushing through the narrow channel beside the town, kept the course clear. Sluices and dikes designed to keep the tide from drowning the flats made it possible to reclaim valuable land for agriculture, but they robbed the port of its scouring current.

Similarly, the construction of flood-gates at Stonar to divert the storm-water that formerly scoured the bed of the Stour at Sandwich led to the silting-up of that port.

Ramsgate is an entirely artificial port, and has to be artificially kept clear. A harbour of refuge is needed on this part of the coast for shipping caught in the Roads by a northerly gale, against which the Goodwin Sands afford no protection. Labelye, and later Smeaton, were consulted regarding the harbour works undertaken at various times, and the work was eventually completed by Smeaton. The outer basin, nearly enclosed by two curved arms projecting from the coast, was rapidly choking with silt when Smeaton reported upon it in 1774. A quarter of a million cu yds had already settled, and the removal of 70 cu yds daily by two barges, each manned by ten men, was failing sadly to cope with the accumulation. The successful scheme was to enclose an inner basin of about 42 acres, let this fill with water at high tide, and discharge its contents at low tide through one or other of six sluices (figure 262). In the path of the current a barge was manœuvred so that the rush of water under and around it would scour a wide channel. At this state of tide the current passing the entrance to the harbour carried away the washings.

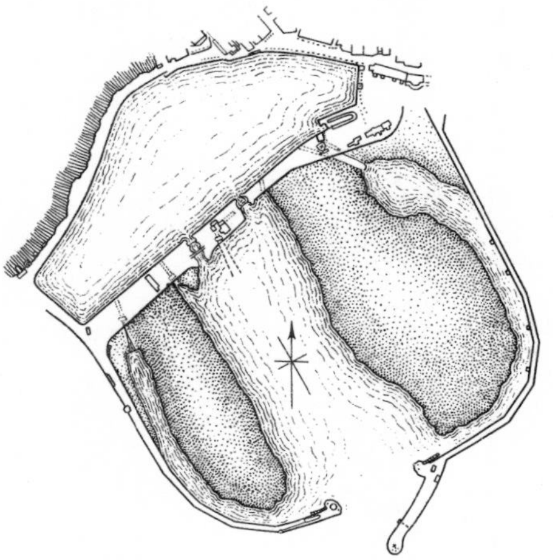

FIGURE 262—*Ramsgate harbour, c 1800. Inner and outer basins are separated by a wall through which pass two gated channels and six sluice-ducts. Water released by the sluices at low tide scours the navigable channels between which are mud-banks on which vessels lie aground.*

Until the closing years of the eighteenth century little had been done to provide docks within which vessels could ride at any state of tide. Anchored in the rivers, vessels settled at low tide on mud-banks. With the riverside open to everyone, petty thieving was rife, and on the Thames robbery on a large scale was carried out by organized gangs. The Thames Police were instituted in 1798, but their task was practically impossible until enclosed docks were built. On the Surrey side, the Howland Great Dock was completed in 1700 by John Wells for the whaling-fleet. The first on the north side, opened in 1802, were the West India Docks, constructed in Poplar by William Jessop, a pupil of Smeaton. These were followed in 1808 by the East India Docks. The London Docks in Wapping—nearer the City—were constructed between 1801 and 1805 by John

Rennie, who introduced cast iron columns and roofs for dock warehouses, and steam-operated cranes on the quayside for loading and unloading the ships.

The first dock in Liverpool, on the site of what had been the original Pool, was built by William Steers between 1710 and 1715. In 1826 it was filled in and the Customs House built over it. Smeaton was consulted about the port of Bristol, where at low tide ships lay right in the heart of the city on river mud. He recommended enclosing a long bend of the river between lock-gates and cutting a by-pass for the river Avon. This work was eventually carried out between 1803 and 1808 by William Jessop. Rennie was consulted in 1799 about the Clyde at Glasgow, where various schemes had been suggested and some river-training works constructed. Rennie recommended docks at Broomielaw, and a dredged channel thence to the sea. The dredged channel was eventually completed, but the dock scheme was not.

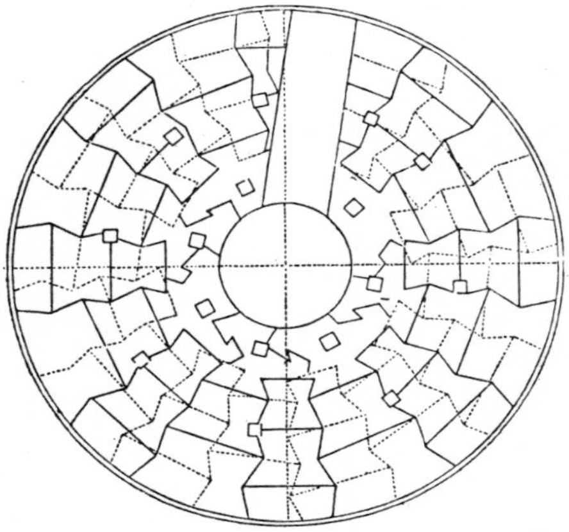

FIGURE 263—*The fifteenth course of masonry in Smeaton's Eddystone lighthouse, 1759.*

For the guidance of ships at night, whether they are making a port or avoiding a dangerous coast or reef, lighthouses are essential. Generally they are on headlands or islands; but occasionally one is needed on some isolated rock that lies too near for safety to a shipping lane or the approach to a harbour. Such was the Eddystone rock, lying about fifteen miles south-west of Plymouth. Twice before our period, lighthouses, built mainly of timber, had been built on the rock, but the first was destroyed by the exceptionally severe gales that swept along the south-west coast of England in November 1703, spreading havoc and desolation, and the second by fire in 1755.

Smeaton was asked to design and superintend the construction of the third Eddystone lighthouse. He realized that the structure must have sufficient mass to resist very heavy buffeting by storms straight off the Atlantic, and as no means could have been devised to transport single blocks of sufficient mass, he had every stone cut to dove-tail with its neighbour so that, when grouted in with a strong hydraulic mortar, every course would act virtually as a solid disk of stone (figure 263). The lower courses consisted partly of the solid rock itself. The stones of each course were also drilled and pegged to those of the course above and below by oak pegs or trenails, giving further solidity to the structure. This method, aided by the tree-like profile Smeaton gave to the tower, proved successful (figure 264). Smeaton's lighthouse tower had to be replaced in 1882, but not through any fault in the structure itself. Even by choosing the highest part of the rock for his foundation, Smeaton had had great difficulty in excavating for the lower courses in the open, because of the few hours a day during which work was possible even in fine weather. That highest part was slightly overhanging, and as erosion below proceeded with the years, fears were felt for the safety of the tower. Another has since been built alongside, using a coffer-dam and techniques not developed in Smeaton's day. Smeaton's pioneer effort has been re-erected on Plymouth Hoe as a fitting memorial to his enterprise and courage.

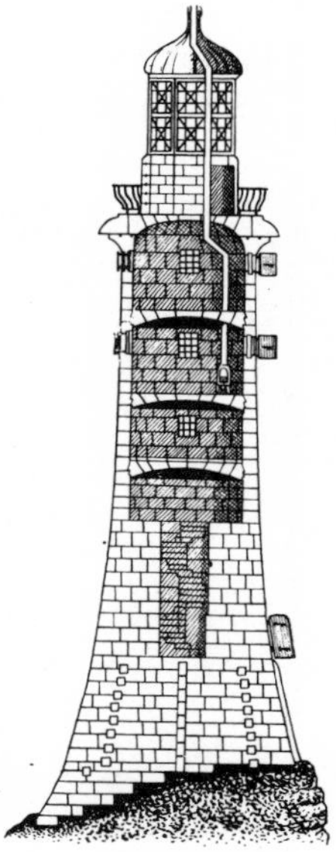

FIGURE 264 — *Smeaton's Eddystone lighthouse, 1759. Partially in section.*

V. BUILDINGS

The pages of a history of technology do not provide the ideal setting for a discussion of aesthetics, but as building, particularly in the period under review, cannot be considered without reference to architecture, and as architecture was regarded as a fine art, some reference must be made to the aesthetic attitude of those whose buildings are characteristic of their day.

The construction of the great churches, which the thought of medieval architecture immediately calls to mind, was essentially functional. The master-mason designed, constructed, and lived with his building. Whether the structural designs, growing ever bolder from the tenth to the fifteenth century, were coaxed out of the designer by the demand of the ecclesiastical patron for more daylight and more coloured glass, or whether the patron merely seized the opportunity presented to him by the designer, driven by his own desire for ever neater and more economical structural forms, could be argued indefinitely. No doubt each tendency reinforced the other, but there is nothing to suggest that either party was driven or pursued by any theory as to what would be beautiful.

With the Renaissance all this was changed. The building façade, developed by Greek architects, had been formalized by the Romans, codified by Vitruvius, and brought to perfection by designers of buildings in the high Renaissance, particularly by Andrea Palladio (1518–80). Beauty was thought to be inherent in certain geometrical forms and proportions, as it was in the harmony of musical notes the vibration-periods of which were in appropriate numerical ratio. Beauty was supposedly intrinsic in any architectural composition that embodied the rules. By the time Palladio published his great work [13], Italian architects were already tiring of the restraints imposed by these rules, but their influence persisted in France for another century. They actually became dominant in English architecture in the eighteenth century, largely through the influence of Richard Boyle, third Earl of Burlington (1695–1753), who sponsored an English translation of Palladio (1715) and acted as patron to a number of promising young men

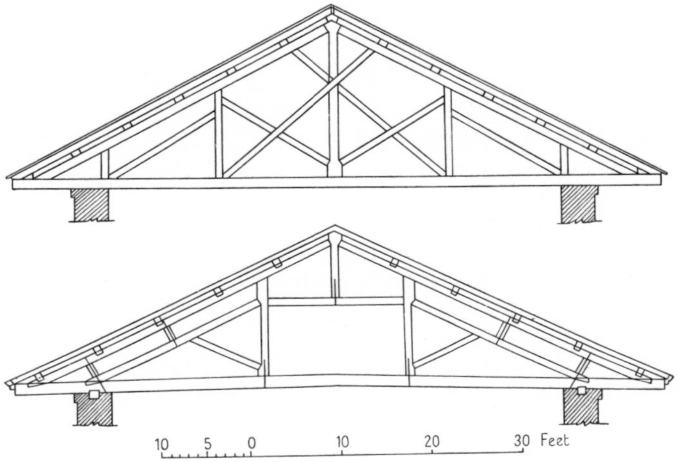

FIGURE 265—*Roof of St Paul's Church, Covent Garden.* (Above) *1636;* (below) *1796.*

such as Colin Campbell, William Kent, and Henry Flitcroft. He sent them to study, as he had done himself, in Italy, and set the fashion in England for public buildings and gentlemen's country houses in the Palladian style (plate 30 B). John Wood (1707–64) and his son of the same name (1727–82) replanned Bath in that style. It was not long before the rules were reduced to copy-book presentation by authors such as Michael Hoare (who wrote under the pseudonym of William Halfpenny) and Batty Langley, 'carpenter and architect'. With the aid of these books an ambitious craftsman could even set himself up as an architect, or at least build correctly to architect's drawings incompletely detailed.

Buildings designed in accordance with Palladio's rules were dignified, but they lacked variety or originality. Both architects and patrons tired of them in time, and in Britain early in the nineteenth century, and much sooner on the continent, movements were set on foot to adopt alternatives. Such movements involved the repudiation of the theory that beauty was intrinsic in objects: beauty was believed to be in the eye of the beholder. Objects which aroused certain associations were beautiful to those in whose minds these associations were emotionally powerful and pleasant. If certain things were widely acclaimed as objects of beauty, that was because a common outlook and culture disposed people to find the same associations pleasant. If, then, one admired Gothic buildings one need not be written down a savage; nor was it monstrous to repudiate Palladio and go back

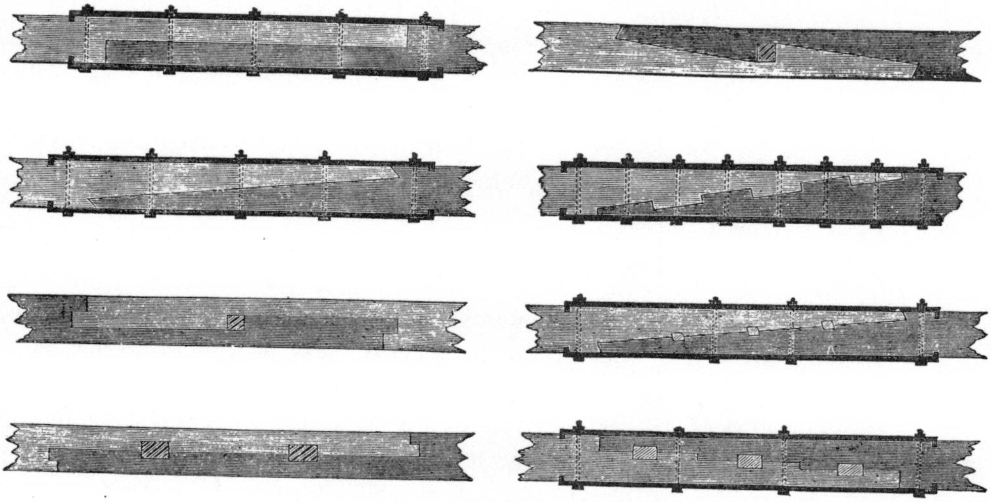

FIGURE 266—*Scarfed joints in timber ties.*

for inspiration to the original classic Greeks, who knew nothing of Palladio's rules.

The Renaissance, however, had done its work only too well, separating those who built into gentlemen and players. The architect was a scholar—a man of the drawing-board. The master-craftsman still directed the actual work of building, and the training of apprentices in his own trade, but he was no longer permitted to design. Unless he thoroughly assimilated the copy-book and took to speculative building in the growing towns, as naturally many did, he must be content to operate as a contractor. Details of construction were often left to the master-craftsman; in carpentry, for instance, the general use of sawn softwood in place of axe-dressed hardwood led to considerable modification of traditional practice. Medieval joists and purlins were often square in section, and even if oblong were often laid with the broad side flat. Galileo (1638) showed that the strength of a beam was proportional to its breadth and to the square of its depth, but Joseph Moxon (1627–1700), writing in 1677 [14], seems not to have known this fact: indeed, as a practical rule it probably diffused from the work of Wren and Robert Hooke, each of whom was both scientist and architect.

A striking example of the changed ideas in carpentry appears in Peter Nicholson's 'Carpenter's and Joiner's Assistant' (1810) in which he compares the roof of Inigo Jones's church of St Paul, Covent Garden (1631–8), with Hardwick's roof-work in the apparent replica of that building erected in 1796 to replace the original, which had been gutted by fire. Figure 265 shows both the original and the replacement. The purlins in the earlier work were 12 in wide by 10 in deep; in the latter $6\frac{1}{2}$ in wide by 9 in deep. The massive upright and diagonal timbers in the roof, halved at their crossings and all somewhat indeterminate in their function, were replaced by a neat arch consisting of two principal rafters and a horizontal bar, which met at queen-posts; from this was suspended the tie-beam, of which the main function was no longer to act as a beam but to tie in the feet of the arch. Nicholson worked out the timber-content of the two roofs (the old 298 cu ft, the new 198 cu ft), thereby demonstrating the saving that could be effected by using a properly trussed construction instead of a vague assembly of props and struts. It may be noted that Wren used trusses in the roof-work of St Paul's Cathedral and his other buildings. He may well have been the first English architect to make a clear, functional approach to the design of a timber roof-truss.

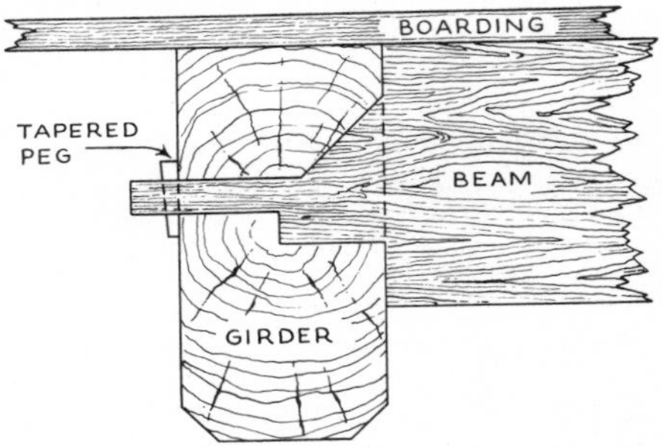

FIGURE 267—*Beam with tusk-tenon.*

The difficulty in designing a timber framework has always been to provide joints through which a pull could be transmitted. Except in such great roofs as those of Notre-Dame, Paris, and Rheims Cathedral [15] the medieval carpenter tried to avoid them, as he had to depend on mortised joints and wooden pegs or trenails. The eighteenth-century architect could afford to make freer use of smith's work. The tie-beam came to be hung from the foot of the king- or queen-post, no longer regarded as a post but as a means of suspension, by a forged strap secured by gib and cotter. With improved saws and bolts, a scarfed joint in a long tie-member became practicable (figure 266). No substantial improvement was made until the introduction in the twentieth century of toothed-ring connectors, so clamped by bolts as to bite into the flanks of the timbers that they joined, laid side by side. Meanwhile mortising, halving, and other devices, though they could be used to make sound joints, drastically reduced the useful load-bearing section of the wood. Moxon realized that a mortise-hole was less deleterious to the strength of a beam if it were made half-way down than if it removed material from near the top or bottom. This recognition led to the development

FIGURE 268—*The House of the [Royal] Society of Arts, designed by Robert Adam, 1772–4.*

of the tusk-tenon (figure 267) to join, for instance, a heavily loaded trimmer or secondary beam to a main girder, a problem frequently encountered in building the large floors of eighteenth-century mansions.

Except for improved jointing and the more economical use of wood, the altered style of building made little change in the structural design of domestic buildings: the emphasis was rather on appearance and finish. The use of smooth plaster on interior wall-surfaces and ceilings spread from large and important houses to much humbler dwellings, at least in towns; and the improvements in joinery and the use of sash-windows (vol III, p 267) also became general. Even in gentlemen's town houses and other buildings of importance, however, heavy classic features in solid masonry were less commonly adopted after the Napoleonic wars: the desire

FIGURE 269—*Regent Street, Piccadilly, designed by Nash*, c *1820*.

for elegance was undiminished, but money was scarcer. Surface decoration of exteriors was shallower than before. In this movement Robert Adam (1728–92) took an active lead (figure 268), and, as already mentioned, John Nash (p 447) often substituted cast iron for carved masonry in columns, and a smooth rendering of mortar or stucco for large surfaces of masonry (figure 269).

Reference has already been made to the use of wrought iron in the last quarter of the eighteenth century by certain Parisian architects, both in roof-work and as armature embedded in masonry. As armature to masonry Claude Perrault (1613–88) between 1667 and 1670 reinforced flat architraves and vaults at the Louvre. In 1779 J. G. Soufflot (1713–81) planned an iron frame of 15 ft 8 in span to carry a mansard roof, a coved ceiling, and a skylight 17 ft wide. It covered a hall and stairs leading from a public entrance to a gallery. The roof was completed in 1781, but disappeared when the hall was rebuilt about 1805. The framework consisted of wrought iron bars with forged ends pinned together. Soufflot also buried a framework of wrought iron bars in the masonry of the churches of Ste-Geneviève and St-Sulpice, Paris, in an attempt to break away from the dependence of masonry-work solely on thrust and weight for stability [16] (figure 270).

Iron has an advantage over woodwork in the roof—for instance, in theatres—in that it is incombustible. It is not, however, as was sometimes claimed for it, fire-proof, for if strongly heated iron loses its strength, and the structure collapses. Combined, however, with slabs made of hollow earthenware pots embedded in plaster, a roof or floor supported by iron beams offers a high degree of resistance to fire. Pots suitable for this purpose were introduced in 1785 in Paris by St-Fart, an architect who specialized in hospitals (figure 271). Soon these pots were being made also in London, where Sir John Soane used them in vaults in the Bank of England (1792). They were commended in a report of a committee of the Associated Architects on the prevention of fires (1791). William Strutt (1756–1830), a prominent mill-owner of Derby and Belper, adopted them in parts of the 'fire-proof' mills he was building at this period [17].

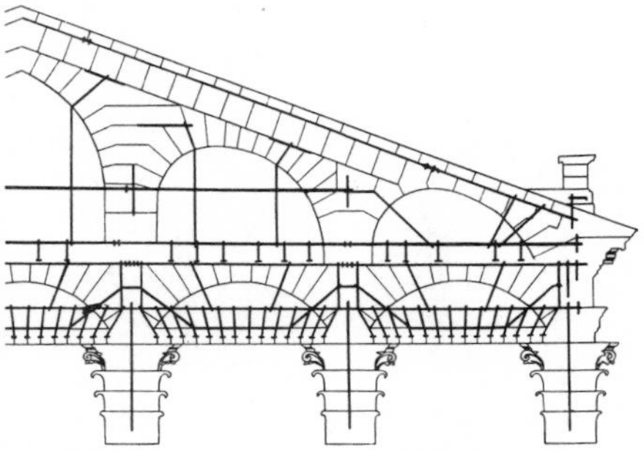

FIGURE 270—*Wrought iron armature to masonry by Soufflot at Ste-Geneviève (later the Panthéon Français).*

Until Strutt turned his mind to this problem of improving the fire-resistance of factories, the typical multi-storey mill building had solid wood-plank floors, carried by heavy beams that stretched from wall to wall. If the span was great or the loading heavy the span of each beam was divided by wooden posts jammed in between the floor below and the beam above. Heavy timbers did not easily catch fire; they tended to char and smoulder, but with naked lights everywhere a fire among inflammable goods could only too easily be started and get out of hand before the primitive fire-fighting appliances of the time could make any impression on it. In that way many valuable mills had been destroyed and lives lost. Strutt's first modification was to substitute brick arches for the wooden floor between beams (figure 272). A hardwood skewback was fixed on each side of the beam, and given some fire-protection by sheet iron on the exposed face. The underside of the beam was plastered. The supporting columns were of cast iron, spigoted into the beam. Subsequent developments were to replace the wooden beams by cast iron, and to improve the shape of the iron beam [18]. In end-spans of floors at Belper, and in the roof, Strutt used—for the sake of lightness—arches of hollow pots in place of solid bricks. Cast iron played an important role in developing the theory of construction, as its use and some failures drew attention to the lack of knowledge of the behaviour of this material under load, and of the most economical shape in which to make the castings. Up to the middle of the nineteenth century cast iron was widely used in the construction of bridges and buildings other than factories. By that time, however, the riveting together of wrought iron plates, as practised by the boiler-maker, was finding other uses, particularly in ship-building. The *Great Britain*, of the unprecedented length of 320 ft, which had in 1845 made her first Atlantic voyage to New York in fourteen days, was built of wrought iron, a fact that gave great encouragement to the use of this material in other ships and also for bridges and beams. A wrought iron beam need be only half the weight of a cast iron one of the same load-carrying capacity, and thus although the material was, weight for weight, twice as expensive, the net cost was about the same. The reduction in dead-load was therefore an advantage that cost nothing.

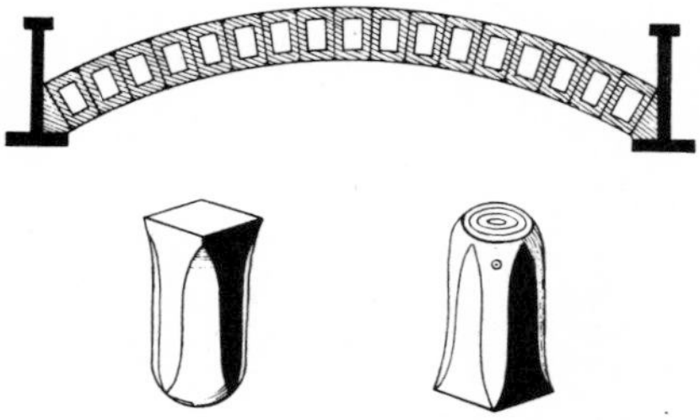

FIGURE 271—*One of St-Fart's hollow pots, showing assembly into arch. 1785.*

The extended use of wrought iron had brought into use machines for shearing plates to the size required, and for punching holes (p 429) in them. Rolled bars of T- and angle-section were available about 1820, and small I-section beams, useful for light work, were produced in Paris from 1847. Heavy I-section beams were not easily produced, as wrought iron was practically hand-made from blooms that weighed less than 2 cwt each. Though several blooms could be hammered together before rolling, the heavy work involved made the process more expensive than the riveting together of plates and angles. Heavy rolled I-section beams had to await the invention of mild steel, cast in massive ingots, in the 1860s.

One of the most remarkable buildings erected at the end of our period was the Crystal Palace, which in 1851 housed the Great Exhibition in Hyde Park, London. The idea of using a vast greenhouse to cover the whole exhibition occurred to Joseph Paxton (1801–65), a man of affairs and initiative, who, as head gardener on the Duke of Devonshire's immense estate at Chatsworth, had already experimented in buildings of iron and glass on a considerable scale. When the scheme was accepted, Paxton immediately engaged the services of Fox, Henderson and

Company, who worked out the design in detail and organized the production and delivery, within a period of months, of parts containing 3500 tons of cast iron, together with large quantities of wrought iron, glass, timber, paint, and other materials. No single foundry could deal with so large an order, so the work was split between three midland firms. All girders and other parts were to be made to

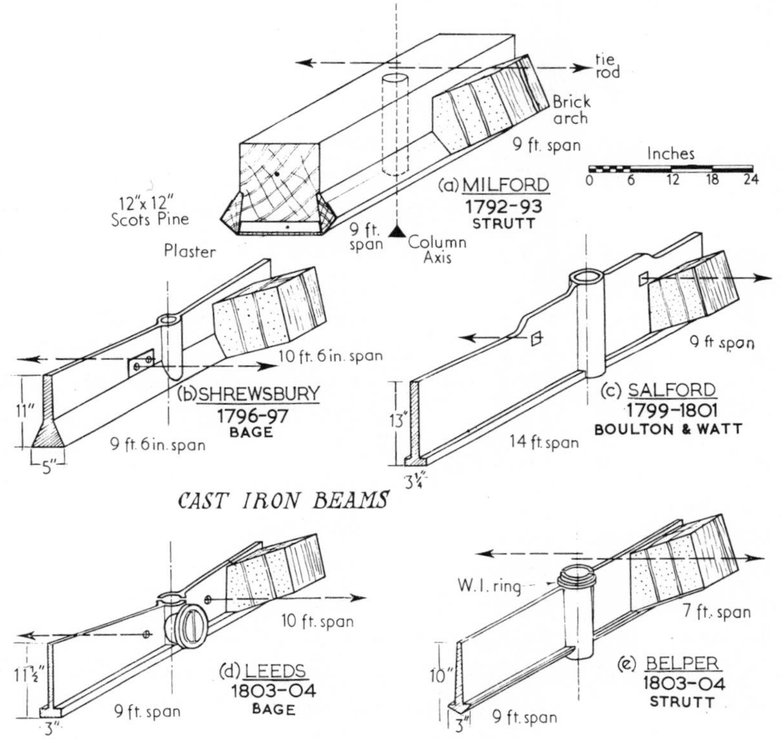

FIGURE 272—*Evolution of beam design for 'fireproof' mill buildings, 1792–1803.*

strict measurements, so that, without any fitting at the site, they should go together (figure 273). To ensure this, each girder as it arrived at the site was lifted by crane from the lorry and dropped into a frame, built to serve as a gauge, and also provided with hydraulic jacks to apply a proof-load. Testing for fit and strength took only four minutes a beam.

VI. THEORY

It will be clear from the notes on theory in the chapter (16) on bridges in volume III that up to 1750 the builders of bridges had at their disposal very little scientific knowledge. Galileo had shown geometrically that the moment of resistance of a beam rectangular in cross-section was proportional to its breadth, to the square of its depth, and to the resistance of the material to direct tension. La Hire had shown how the loading should vary across the span of an arch if the whole of the material were to be in compression and the force across any joint between voussoirs to have no shear or frictional component. Pierre Bouguer had shown in a similar manner how the weight of each course of masonry should vary with the curvature if a dome were to be stable and subject to compressive forces only [19]. If, however, a dome had been built to some arbitrary shape, and was showing signs of distress, these theories gave no assistance towards finding its actual stress-condition. This was the problem set by Pope Benedict XIV in 1742 to three notable mathematicians—Le Seur, Jacquier, and Boscovitch—when alarming cracks were observed in the dome of St Peter's, and in the masonry structure below the dome.

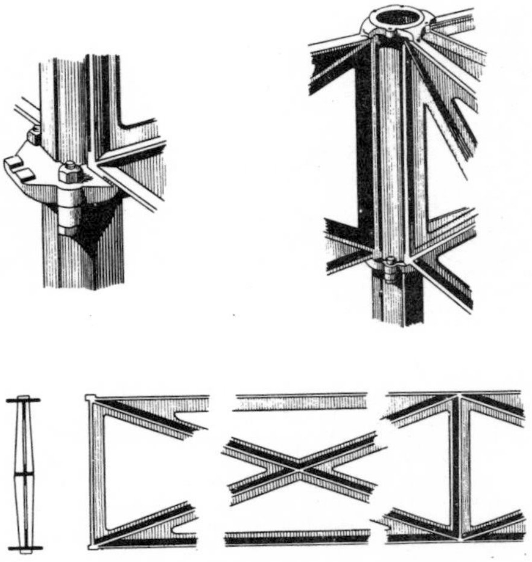

FIGURE 273—*Typical girder used in building the Crystal Palace, 1851.*

They reported in 1743. In order to reduce the problem to one of statics and of manageable form they considered the dome, and the drum on which it stood, to be arbitrarily divided into portions like the segments or liths of an orange, with a virtual hinge on the inside where the dome joined the drum. On this assumption liths of dome would tend to fall downwards, and to push out the drum, which would therefore tilt about the outer edge of its base (figure 274). The work done by a lith of dome would be the product of its weight by the amount its centre of gravity was lowered. This was partly balanced by the work done on the section of drum, which was the product of its weight by the amount its centre of gravity was raised by the tilting. The difference must be made good by the work done in stretching the retaining-chain which encircled the dome where it joined the drum. This was reckoned to be the product of (*a*) the amount by which the chain was lengthened and (*b*) the force exerted in stretching the chain. If the chain were unstressed when the tilting began, the average force resisted would be half that at the finish. The calculation showed that if stability depended on the chain the situation was serious, for the chain would have to resist three times the force which would break it, even if it were as strong as the iron wire the strength of which had been tested and recorded in 1729 by Pieter Van Musschenbroek [20]. The strength of a heavy forged and welded chain was, on the contrary, likely to be, area for area, much less than that of a fine drawn wire. No account was taken in the calculation of the energy absorbed in shear-resistance, friction, and the crushing of masonry in the movement, but the fact that a virtual work calculation was undertaken is of some interest. Further developments in that direction, combined with the studies of the elastic behaviour of materials by members of the Académie des Sciences and the *Ponts et Chaussées* were in due course to lead to powerful techniques of stress-analysis and structural design. Meanwhile the tendency was—with some plausibility—to blame earthquakes, thunderbolts, defects in workmanship, and flaws in design for the incipient failure of St Peter's. There was, however, no disagreement about the need to supply additional chains and to replace damaged masonry. These measures proved effective.

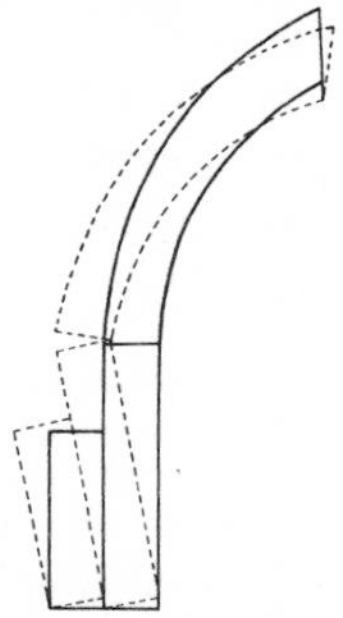

FIGURE 274—*St Peter's, Rome: stability of the dome. 1743.*

An important step in the study of the elastic behaviour of materials was undertaken by Leonhard Euler (1707–83), a Swiss mathematician. His interest lay not so much in the study of the actual materials as in that of curves into which they were bent, which could be mathematically defined. These included the curves into which laths or laminae would be bent under the action of given forces. In 1757 he derived an expression for the critical load under which a long, flexible column would become unstable. In later theory Euler's work proved of fundamental importance, but long, flexible columns were of no practical interest in the 1750s, and Euler was ignored.

Charles-Augustin de Coulomb (1736–1806) came much nearer than any predecessor to providing engineers with a working theory of the strength of materials, in a paper he presented in 1773 to the Académie des Sciences 'on the application of the rules of maxima and minima to some problems of statics relative to architecture' [21]. In forty pages he covered the theory of beams as still taught in modern textbooks, including that of shearing-forces, based on the laws of static equilibrium which he stated clearly at the outset: he developed the wedge theory of earth-pressure on retaining-walls, as still used, and the treatment of the arch. This was not a set of smooth voussoirs liable to slide one on another, but a body liable to crack, and so rotate and fold up piecemeal about virtual hinges, the position of which could be found by a method he described. At the time, however, Coulomb's work, like Euler's, appeared to be too mathematical and indigestible, and was not widely noted. Coulomb himself became interested in other things, and did not develop his work to show how it could be applied to practical examples. It was, however, studied by Gauthey (see below), Prony, and others at the *Ponts et Chaussées*, and in the fullness of time was embodied by C. L. M. Navier in his 'Lectures on the Application of Mechanics' [22], which formed the basis of instruction on the subjects of strength of materials and theory of structures to students of that famous school.

Closely contemporary with Coulomb was Emiland Marie Gauthey (1732–1806), an officer in the *Ponts et Chaussées*, and a notable writer on the theory of construction. Although of much less fundamental importance, his work was more immediately influential than that of Coulomb, because he became involved in the controversy over the dome of Ste-Geneviève—later to become the Panthéon Français, Paris.

The supports of the domes of St Peter's in Rome, and of St Paul's in London, had been conventional. In each case the dome was carried on a drum backed by buttresses, the whole carried on four great arches bearing upon and thrusting against massive abutment-towers or bastions within the body of the church at the four corners of the crossing. In the reconstruction of Ste-Geneviève, begun in 1757, the architect, Soufflot, decided to try a new scheme. He would support the great arches beneath the dome on four clusters of columns sufficient to take the vertical load. The horizontal thrust he would transfer to the main walls of the building, and so avoid the obstruction by bastions in the body of the church. In channels within the joints of the masonry he proposed, where necessary, to bury cages of wrought iron bars, linked together to form virtually a system of open-framed girders. When they realized his intention, traditionally-minded architects were scandalized and prophesied disaster. Gauthey, however, when consulted by Soufflot, approved of his scheme. Gauthey also designed and built a testing machine with a wooden frame and an iron lever 7 ft long, to apply a leverage of 24 to 1 to the specimen under test (figure 275). On this machine Gauthey tested many specimens of the selected stone to make sure that the columns would safely carry their load. So far as is known this was the first time that a testing machine had been used to provide information required in the design and erection of an actual building. Soufflot had a similar machine made, but with an iron frame; so did the *Ponts et Chaussées*. Finally Jean Rondelet (1734–1829), who worked under Soufflot and completed the rebuilding of Ste-Geneviève after Soufflot's death, improved the machine by providing a knife-edge instead of a bolt at the fulcrum, and a screw-jack to apply the load, so that the weigh-beam could be kept level while the specimen under observation was compressed [23].

Within a few years of the completion of the work ominous cracks appeared both in the dome and in the columns that carried its weight. The battle of pamphlets that had raged in 1770, and had been checked only by Gauthey's arguments backed by the results of the tests, broke out anew in the 1790s. The building itself appeared to have taken sides with Soufflot's enemies. All manner of pro-

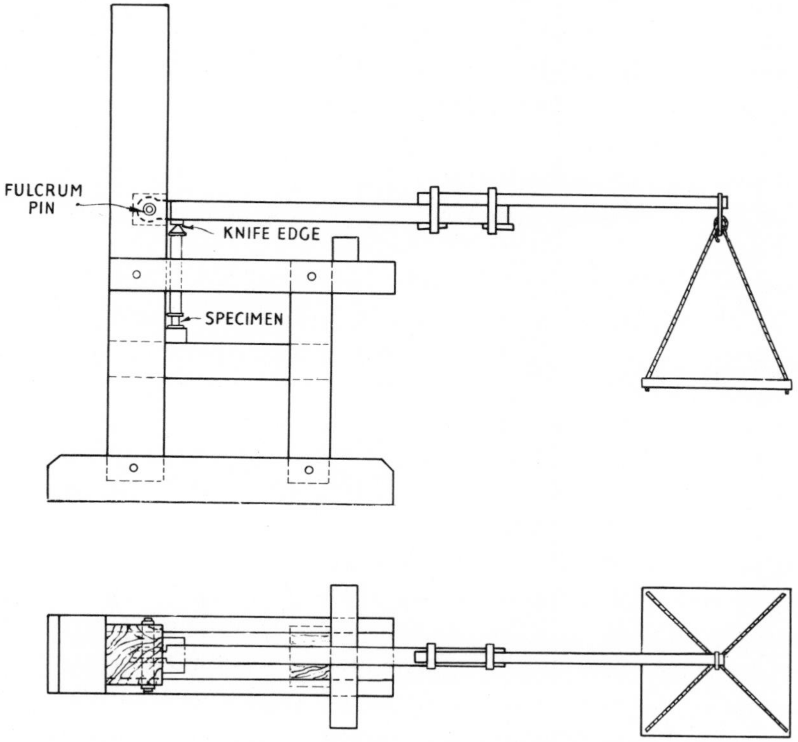

FIGURE 275—*Gauthey's testing machine, 1770.* (Above) *elevation;* (below) *plan.*

posals were made: for erecting great additional columns and buttresses inside the building, and even for pulling down the dome and replacing it by a much shallower and lighter construction. Gauthey again came to the rescue with fresh calculations, which showed that the average loading of the piers below the dome was only 28 tons to the sq ft, which was not excessive for the stone used. In erecting the piers, however, a hard stone had been used for the facing, and a softer stone for the hearting. This threw a greater share of the load on the harder, less compressible stone; and to make matters worse the masons had worked the beds to a taper, showing hardly any thickness of joint at the face but allowing a thicker bed of mortar behind. Naturally the overloaded edges of the stone had cracked and spalled. In the end, Rondelet added about 2 ft of additional stonework to two of the sides of the triangular piers, and bound them into the original masonry by means of wrought iron bars (figure 276).

This use by Soufflot of iron bars embedded in mortar, in grooves cut into the beds and joints of masonry wherever there might otherwise be a tendency for the masonry to crack or part, was in a way an anticipation of reinforced concrete. It had the disadvantage that the iron was not very effectively protected from corrosion. It was also, almost certainly, designed with only a rough idea as to the

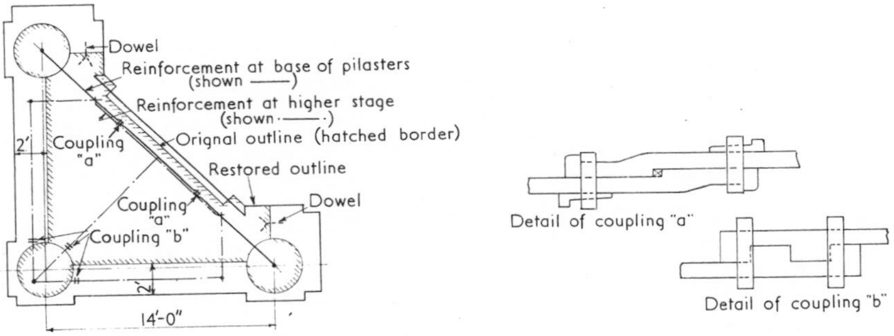

FIGURE 276—*Rondelet's additions to the piers of Ste-Geneviève. 1806–10.*

magnitude of the forces that the bars would be called upon to resist; so was the wrought iron roof-work erected in Paris about the same time and later [16].

Graphic methods of analysing the forces in a pin-jointed truss or framework were not developed until after our period, but the descriptive geometry on which they were based was worked out by Gaspard Monge (1746–1818) while professor of mathematics at the military school at Mezières, between 1768 and 1780. Later he taught at the École de Marine. When in 1794 the school was founded in Paris that in 1795 became the École Polytechnique, to give basic scientific training to cadets of all services, both military and civil, it was Monge who was called in to organize it.

Between Robert Hooke (1635–1702) and Thomas Young (1773–1829) no English scientist contributed anything of importance to the theory of construction. All overlooked Hooke's justly famous law *ut tensio sic vis*: the distortion in any material is proportional to the force that produces it. Some of the French students of the subject, notably Coulomb, had assumed such a law as a useful working hypothesis, but none appeared to be aware of the carefully conducted experiments by which Hooke had established it. The subject had also been confused by failure to distinguish between the effect of low stresses, which produce small elastic distortions in accordance with Hooke's law, and the effect of high stresses, which, in ductile materials, produce large plastic deformations. The behaviour of all materials, whether ductile or brittle, deviates markedly from Hooke's law at loadings far below the ultimate. Most tests made until well into the nineteenth century had been tests to destruction, and consequently had thrown no light on the importance of elastic movement within the range of normal working loads. Euler had introduced into his equations a term, constant for any given material, relating load and distortion, but it remained for Young to define the 'elastic modulus'[1] in a way that made it potentially useful as a means of calculating actual deflections. The word potentially is used advisedly, for Young's writings were obscure and difficult to read. They did not receive the attention which, had he expressed himself more intelligibly, their topical importance would have ensured. Young was a man of great learning, but unfortunately he never even began to realize the limits of comprehension of ordinary minds. His lectures were unintelligible to his audiences, and in printed form were, and still are, difficult reading. He was called upon to give lectures on natural philosophy at the Royal Institution. The appointment was cancelled after the second year, but Young had gone to immense trouble to prepare his lectures and decided to publish them. They appeared in two volumes in 1807 [24].

On the subject of materials of construction Young extended the work of Euler, and of Coulomb, whom he greatly admired. He introduced into beam theory the term 'neutral axis' for the trace, on the cross-section of a beam, of the neutral layer, the substance of which is neither stretched nor compressed. As he dealt with none but 'prismatic' sections he did not define its position in general terms, but he did show how its position was changed when an end-wise load was added to the normal transverse load on a beam. Euler, as has been noted, had given an equation for the load under which a long, straight, slender column would collapse through becoming elastically unstable. He had assumed a perfectly central load, and had been surprised to find that in theory no deflection was produced at all under a gradually increasing load until the load reached the critical value, when sudden collapse occurred.

Young considered the cases of a column slightly bent, and of a column eccentrically loaded. He showed that, with either of these, deflection increased more rapidly as the load increased. His equations for these two cases were rediscovered in the twentieth century, and put forward as new [25].

[1] Young's own elastic modulus was a weight equivalent to what we now know as 'Young's modulus' multiplied by the area of cross section of the material. His 'height of the modulus' was our Young's modulus divided by the density of the material.

Young's work was studied by John Robison, who was the author of an influential textbook on practical mechanics. Some of Young's ideas found their way, presumably by way of Robison, into the textbooks of Thomas Tredgold, which were widely read by engineers of the period.

The scheme put forward by Telford and Douglas (p 458) to replace Old London Bridge by an arch of cast iron in a single span of 600 ft was referred to a select committee of the House of Commons on the improvement of the Port of London, and discussed in their third report (1799 and 1800). The committee called as expert witnesses an imposing selection of mathematicians, including the Astronomer Royal, and engineers, among them Rennie, Jessop, and John Sothern of Soho, Birmingham. A list of questions was drawn up, mainly about the distribution of load through such a vast assembly of castings. Would it act as one solid object? Would the bulk of the weight be thrown on the lowest rib? How should the parts be joined? Could it crack up piecemeal? And so on. Young followed their deliberations, although he was not summoned to take part. He summed up in these words: 'It would be difficult to find greater discordance in the most heterodox professions of faith, or in the most capricious variations of taste, than is exhibited in the responses of our most celebrated professors on almost every point submitted for their consideration.' In the article on bridges that he wrote for the 'Encyclopaedia Britannica', Young attempted to answer the questions himself. The article was highly technical, and is too long to summarize here. The important features are that Young visualized the problem as one of elastic movements no less than of strength. Only Robison and John Sothern had shown any appreciation of this aspect of the problem in the evidence before the committee. Where witnesses had usually been content to make vague general statements, Young backed up nearly every answer by calculations. None had been able to give a reliable figure for the strength of cast iron; indeed, the first test-figure published was probably that obtained by George Rennie in 1818 [26]. Not to be defeated on such a point, however, Young made a simple test for himself. He filed a small prism of cast iron $\frac{1}{8}$ in $\times$ $\frac{1}{8}$ in $\times$ $\frac{1}{4}$ in long, placed it in a vice, and measured the force needed to crush it. Allowing for friction, he calculated this to be about a ton, or 64 tons to the square inch, a very fair result for such an extemporized test.

The proposal for London Bridge was in the event turned down, but strangely enough nothing was said about the abutment foundations, although these might have proved the most difficult part of the undertaking, since any appreciable settlement could easily have been disastrous to the bridge.

In none of his investigations had Young encountered the problem of the most economical shape in which to make a cast iron beam, having regard to the fact that the metal was at least five or six times as strong in compression as in tension. The problem was raised, however, when it came to be considered that a good way to improve the fire-resistance of mill buildings was to carry the floors on brick arches springing from cast iron beams (p 475). The early beams were nearly rectangular in section; but proof-tests soon showed that extra metal, provided at the lower edge to give a better support to the skewback of the arch, also increased the strength of the beam in much greater proportion than it added to the weight.

William Fairbairn adopted an inverted T-section with advantage: then, finding that Eaton Hodgkinson (1789–1861) was already making experiments on similar lines with small specimens, Fairbairn invited him to join forces, and to make use of his foundry and plant for a comprehensive series of tests. By this means Hodgkinson was able to discover the most economical section, and to devise a formula for calculating the strength of a cast iron beam. The load W, which it would carry concentrated at mid-span, was proportional to the area of the tension flange A, the depth of the beam d, and, inversely, to the span L. Expressing W in tons, and all dimensions in inches, Hodgkinson calculated [27] that for the most economical section:

$$W = 26Ad/L.$$

It was found, however, that a large beam of Hodgkinson's ideal section had so much metal concentrated in the bottom flange that the thinner parts elsewhere tended to cool more quickly, and high internal stresses might in consequence be set up in the metal. In practice, therefore, full theoretical economy was not usually attempted.

Hodgkinson continued his investigations to include the strength of columns. Unlike masonry columns, metal columns were not infrequently long and thin, and the tendency to instability—quite apart from the risk of crushing—to which Euler had drawn attention was found to be no longer negligible. Hodgkinson tried to fit his results to a formula for the collapse load, P, of the form

$$P = cd^n/L^m,$$

where c, m, and n were constants and d was the diameter. In Euler's case, where L was great compared with d, n was 4, and m was 2, but both these constants were too high for Hodgkinson's test-results. Eventually he found that no pair of constants fitted all cases, and that the best approximation to the collapse load was obtained by taking the harmonic mean between the crushing load and Euler's critical load. If the beam was very short, this coincided with the crushing load; if very long, with Euler's load. Between the extremes, the curve fitted fairly well the lower limit of the scatter of points of failure loads, plotted for intermediate values of L/d. Hodgkinson's final formula, modified by Lewis Gordon and later by William Rankine, entered the textbooks as the Gordon–Rankine formula for columns and was widely used throughout the nineteenth century.

Towards the middle of the nineteenth century, as already noted in the section on bridges (p 460), an alternative to the use of cast iron for beams arose in the form of built-up plate-girders of wrought iron. The top flange had to be stiff to resist compression: the bottom flange, which resisted tension, was less complicated. The function of the vertical 'web' plate or plates, other than that of holding the flanges in place, was not immediately recognized, but experiments on forms suitable for the Britannia bridge showed that this, too, required a certain amount of stiffening if it were not to buckle or fold into a wavy and unstable form. In these experiments, indeed, the design of plate-girders, and a theory of the way they functioned, were evolved. The investigation was made jointly by George Stephenson, William Fairbairn, and Eaton Hodgkinson.

The railway boom also aroused interest in the open-web type of girder, or truss, in which the web took the form of struts and ties, forming, with the flanges or chords (or booms as they might alternatively be called), a series of triangles. There was in Britain little experience of this type of construction, and some of that was unfortunate. The Royal Commission on the Application of Iron to Railway Structures, reporting in 1849, deprecated their use.

In 1850 W. Bindon Blood and W. T. Doyne submitted to the Institution of Civil Engineers a short paper on the calculation of the forces in these web-members; and in 1851 W. H. Bow published in Edinburgh a 'Treatise on Bracing'. That type of bridge-truss had, however, made considerably more progress in the United States, where bridges with timbers for compression-members, and wrought iron rods for at least some of the tension-members, were in common use as highway bridges. Many ingenious arrangements of bracing were tried, and some became standard practice in certain districts. The early examples were entirely empirical, but in 1847 Squire Whipple brought out 'A Work Upon Bridge Building', and in 1851 Herman Haupt 'The General Theory of Bridge Construction'. Both American and British authors resolved the forces in the members meeting at each joint as a separate system of forces in equilibrium. Graphical methods, which simplified both the problem and its solution, were not developed until the 1860s. The pioneer of graphic statics was Carl Culmann, who between 1849 and 1851 visited both England and North America: he was particularly interested at that time in the work of Squire Whipple.

REFERENCES

[1] HAMILTON, S. B. *Trans. Newcomen Soc.*, **22**, 149, 1941–2.
[2] *Idem. Struct. Engr*, **32**, no. 12, 315, 1954.
[3] *Idem. Archit. Rev., Lond.*, **116**, 295, 1954.
[4] VICAT, L. J. 'Recherches expérimentales sur les chaux de Construction.' Paris. 1818.
[5] GOODING, P. and HALSTEAD, P. E. 'Proceedings of the third International Symposium on the Chemistry of Cement, London, 1952', pp. 1–29. Cement and Concrete Association, London. 1955.
[6] SEMPLE, G. 'On Building in Water.' Dublin. 1776.
[7] *Min. Proc. Instn civ. Engrs*, **25**, 66, 1865–6.
[8] SALZMAN, L. F. 'Building in England down to 1540', pp. 155 f. Clarendon Press, Oxford. 1952.
[9] RAISTRICK, A. 'The Darbys; a Dynasty of Ironfounders.' Longmans, London. 1953.
[10] KIRBY, R. S. and LAURSON, P. G. 'The Early Years of Modern Civil Engineering', p. 167. Yale University Press, New Haven. 1932.
[11] BEAMISH, R. 'Memoir of the Life of Sir Marc Isambard Brunel.' London. 1862.
[12] CRESY, E. 'An Encyclopaedia of Civil Engineering', pp. 227 f. London. 1847.
[13] PALLADIO, ANDREA. 'I quattro Libri dell'Architettura' (4 vols). Venice. 1570.
[14] MOXON, JOSEPH. 'Mechanick Exercises.' London. 1677.
[15] CHOISY, F. A. 'Histoire de l'architecture', Vol. 2, pp. 327 f. Paris. 1899.
[16] RONDELET, J. 'Traité théorique et pratique de l'art de bâtir', Vol. 2, p. 151. Paris. 1812.
ECK, C. L. G. 'Traité de construction en poteries et fer à l'usage des bâtiments civils, industriels et militaires.' Paris. 1836.
[17] HAMILTON, S. B. 'The Structural Fire Protection of Buildings. A Historical Note'. H.M. Stationery Office, London. 1956.
[18] JOHNSON, H. R. and SKEMPTON, A. W. *Trans. Newcomen Soc.*, **30**, p. 179 ff., 1956.
[19] BOUGUER, P. *Hist. Acad. R. Sci.*, 149–66, 1734.
[20] MUSSCHENBROEK, P. VAN. *Physicae Experimentales et Geometricae*. Leiden. 1729.
WOLF, A. 'History of Science, Technology and Philosophy in the Eighteenth Century', pp. 517 f. Allen & Unwin, London. 1938.
[21] COULOMB, C. A. "Essai sur une application des règles de maximis et minimis à quelques problèmes de statique, relatifs à l'architecture." *Mém. Acad. Sci. Sav. étrang.*, **7**, 343–82, 1776.
[22] NAVIER, C. L. M. 'Leçons sur l'application de la méchanique.' Paris. 1826.
[23] RONDELET, J. See ref. [16], Vol. 3, pp. 72 f. 1805.
GIBBONS, C. H. *Trans. Newcomen Soc.*, **15**, 169, 1934–5.
[24] YOUNG, T. 'Lectures in Natural Philosophy' (2 vols). London. 1807.
[25] HAMILTON, S. B. *Min. Proc. Instn civ. Engrs*, **1**, Pt III, 379 f., 1952.
[26] RENNIE, G. "Account of Experiments on the Strength of Materials." A letter to Dr. Thomas Young published in *Phil. Trans.*, [**108**], 118–36, 1818, in which a new testing machine was described capable of applying a load of about 11 tons.
HAMILTON, S. B. *Trans. Newcomen Soc.*, **21**, 143, 1940–1.
[27] HODGKINSON, E. *Mem. Manchr lit. phil. Soc., Manchester*, second series, **5**, 407, 1831.

BIBLIOGRAPHY

CRESY, E. 'An Encyclopaedia of Civil Engineering.' London. 1847.
GWILT, J. 'An Encyclopaedia of Architecture.' London. 1842.
HANN, J., MOSELEY, H., HOSKING, W., *et al.* 'Bridges.' London. 1843.

SMILES, S. 'Lives of the Engineers, with an Account of their Principal Works' (3 vols). London. 1861–2. See also: SKEMPTON, A. W. "The Engineers of the English River Navigations, 1620–1760." *Trans. Newcomen Soc.*, **29**, 1953–5.

Modern works:

HAMILTON, S. B. "The Historical Development of Structural Theory." *Min. Proc. Instn civ. Engrs*, **1**, Pt III, 374–419, 1952.

KIRBY, R. S. and LAURSON, P. G. 'The Early Years of Modern Civil Engineering.' Yale University Press, New Haven. 1932.

STRAUB, H. 'Die Geschichte der Bauingenieurkunst.' Birkhäuser, Basel. 1949.

Idem. 'A History of Civil Engineering' (Eng. trans. by E. ROCKWELL). Hill, London. 1952.

TIMOSHENKO, S. P. 'History of Strength of Materials.' McGraw Hill, New York. 1953.

WOLF, A. 'A History of Science, Technology and Philosophy in the Eighteenth Century.' Allen & Unwin, London. 1938.

Telford's plan for a new London Bridge embodying a single 600-ft span of cast iron. This project was never started.

16

PART I

SANITARY ENGINEERING:

WATER-SUPPLY

J. KENNARD

THE period from 1750 to 1850 saw the development of modern water-supply in Britain. The influx of population to the towns from rural areas, the rapid growth of manufacture, and the introduction of railways entailed large demands for a continuous supply of clean water, not only for domestic use but for industry.

Before 1800 no reliable estimates of population were possible. The first census was undertaken in 1801, following an abortive attempt in 1753. The growth of population in England, Wales, and Scotland during the next half-century is shown in the following table:

Year	*Total*
1801	10 500 956
1811	11 970 120
1821	14 091 757
1831	16 261 183
1841	18 534 332
1851	20 816 351

The population of cities grew remarkably quickly. That of Glasgow, for instance, increased four-fold between 1801 and 1851, and the demand for water increased from 6 500 000 gallons a day in 1838 to 14 000 000 gallons a day a little over a decade later.

To meet such demands, numerous joint stock companies were constituted by private enterprise throughout Britain, under special powers conferred by private Acts of Parliament; over a hundred of these Acts were passed in the nineteenth century. Generally the companies were very successful financially. In a number of towns, however, with the encouragement of Parliament, several companies competed with each other in providing supplies. Towards the middle of the nineteenth century amalgamations were taking place, and in some cases the local authorities acquired the undertakings of the companies, especially when it was felt that the latter did not have the resources or the initiative to undertake the large works that were then considered to be necessary. In the case of Edinburgh the reverse took place: the municipality handed over its supply to a company in 1819, for the sum of £30 000.

In 1840 a Select Committee of the House of Commons was appointed to inquire into the supply of water to large towns and populous districts in England and Wales. Reference was made to the many shortcomings and the deficient supplies, sometimes polluted: out of fifty towns considered, the supply of water was regarded as good in only six. The Committee's recommendations resulted in the passing of the Waterworks Clauses Act of 1847 and the Public Health Act of 1848, which became the foundation of modern water-law in Britain. They provided that water-supplies were to be 'pure, safe, and constant', and of such a pressure as to reach the highest house within the area of supply. The Acts further dealt with the provision of compensation for loss and damage to property in developing resources, constructing works, and laying pipes, and with the method of charging for water on the basis of the ratable value of the property for domestic purposes, and by gallonage for industry. The principal object was to standardize, as far as possible, the powers of undertakings authorized to supply water, and to avoid the necessity for setting out the powers and duties in detail in each individual private Act.

The development of canal systems during the first phase of the industrial revolution, and the construction of large reservoirs for the purpose of supplying them with water, provided much valuable information and experience which were in turn applied to the construction of similar works for water-supply. Nevertheless, it was soon realized that the essential basic data necessary to enable proper consideration to be given to the hydrological aspect of reservoir-design depended on reliable records of rainfall, evaporation, and absorption-losses, and of dry-weather flows of streams and rivers. J. F. Bateman, when designing the early water-works for Manchester, deplored the rule-of-thumb and guesswork methods then in use, as did other engineers of that time, and they persuaded undertakings to set up rain-gauges on several gathering-grounds under consideration.

The first known rainfall records for the British Isles were kept by Richard Townley at Towneley, near Burnley, from 1677 to 1703. By 1788 there were ten such records, but the recording of rainfall was regarded as nothing more than a hobby of scientists and clergymen. It was not until 1847 that serious recording was started by James Glaisher; it was continued by G. J. Symons from 1860 onwards. Symons energetically recruited observers, and by the end of the century there were over 3000 of them. In 1919 the recording of rainfall became a national service undertaken by the Meteorological Office of the Air Ministry.

The importance of geology to the water-engineer was realized when James Hutton published his 'Theory of the Earth' in 1795. In 1815 William Smith published his famous 'Delineations of the Strata', with the first geological map; three years later he produced a geological atlas. Meanwhile, in 1807, the Geological Society was founded, and this society in 1835 established the Geological Survey of Great Britain, the first organization of its kind in the world. A few years later saw the introduction of ordnance survey maps on a scale of 6 in to a mile.

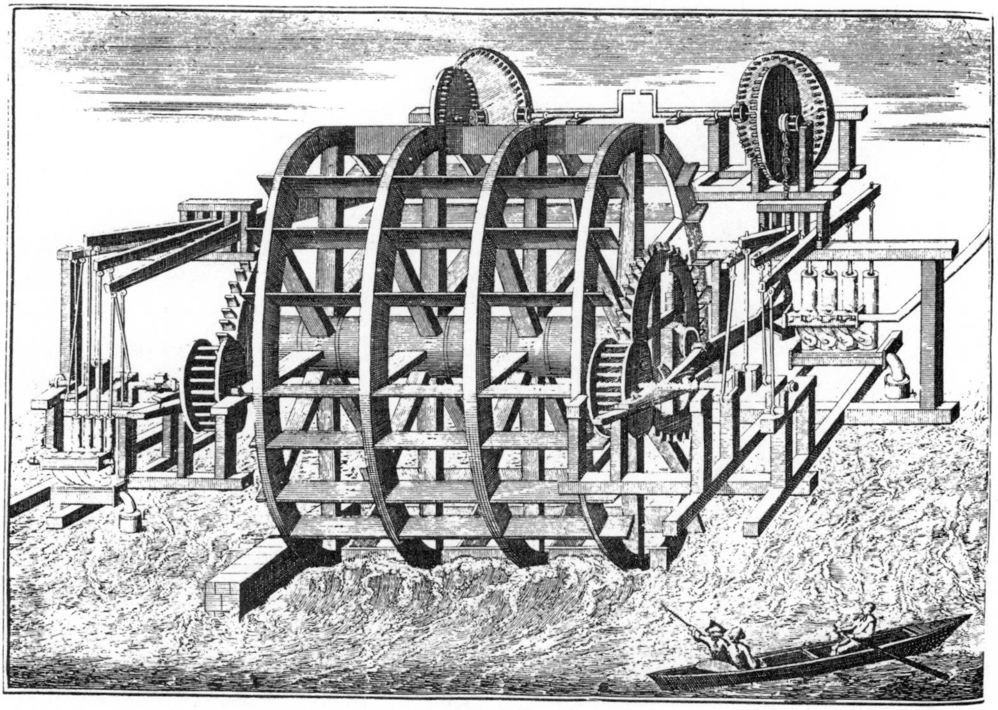

FIGURE 277—*Water-wheel and pumps at London Bridge water-works. 1749.*

No history of water-supply in this period would be complete without a brief description of that to the City of London. The first company to be established was the London Bridge waterworks in 1581; by means of pumps driven by water-wheels, water was raised from the Thames at London Bridge (figure 277). The works when fully established are stated to have been capable of furnishing a supply of nearly 4 m gallons a day, but the great fall of water occasioned by their operation endangered navigation through the bridge; an Act was therefore passed in 1822 for their removal, and for the transfer of the undertaking to the New River Company. In 1613 this company had constructed an aqueduct known as the New River, to convey water from springs in Hertfordshire to London, a distance of 38 miles (figures 278 and 279). The work was initiated by Sir Hugh Myddleton, and in 1738 the company was allowed to divert water from the river Lea into the aqueduct.

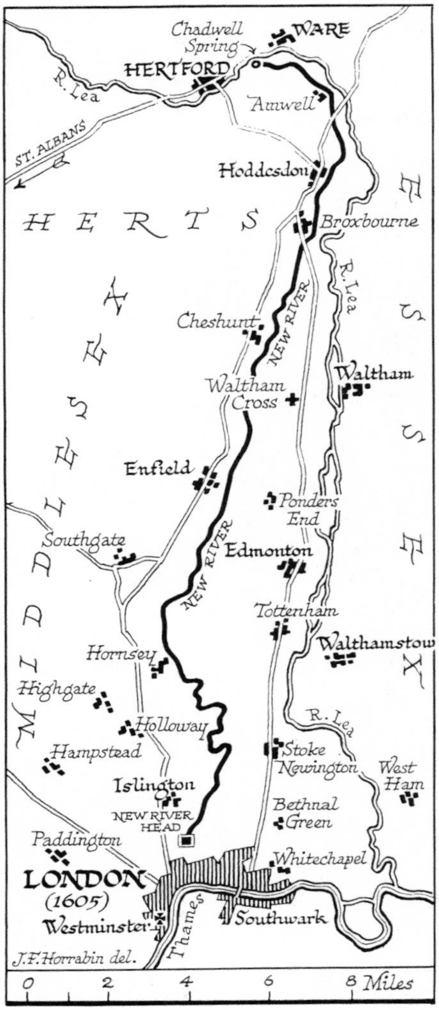

FIGURE 278—*Map of the New River cut.*

The Shadwell Company originated in works set up about the year 1669, the area supplied including Wapping and Stepney. The West Ham Waterworks originated in 1743, and was situated on an arm of the Lea at Bow; it supplied an area including Mile End and Stratford. Both these companies were subsequently acquired by the London Dock Company.

In 1692 the City leased its Hampstead Heath undertaking to certain lessees to form the Hampstead Water Company, which subsequently constructed reservoirs in the Vale of Health and at Cane Wood. These supplied an area starting from below Hampstead and reaching to Camden Town. In 1833 a well was sunk at the bottom of Hampstead Heath, followed a few years later by a second well at Kentish Town.

The excavation of a shallow well generally required little skill. With a plumb-bob to check verticality, a method of removing the excavated material, and the provision of a suitable lining to hold up the sides and to exclude pollution as much as possible, very little else was necessary. Brickwork was commonly used for the lining, but in wet ground the addition of puddled clay behind the brickwork was relied upon. In more recent times concrete and cast iron linings were developed. In a vain attempt to obtain further water a boring was made from the bottom of the Kentish Town well, but it was abandoned in 1855 after reaching a depth of 1302 ft.

In the case of deep boreholes sunk from the bottom of a shallow well the principal method of boring consisted of pounding the strata into small fragments and dust, and removing the debris as sand or mud. The boring-tool, which varied according to the nature of the work to be done, was attached to steel or wooden rods, and a vertical reciprocating motion was given to the tool, thus breaking up the material at the bottom of the hole. It was also given a circular motion in order to ensure that it did not strike the same point at each stroke. The tool was removed from time to time, to enable the debris to be removed by baling and flushing, and further rods were added.

FIGURE 279—*Water-carrier selling New River water.*

The York Buildings Waterworks Company, incorporated by Act of Parliament in 1691, owned works situated near the bottom of Villiers Street, Strand, which enabled water to be taken from the Thames. The water was raised to a cistern by means of a horse-driven engine, and delivered to Piccadilly, Kensington Gardens, Whitehall, and intervening streets. This company was the first in London to make use of steam for pumping, and about the year 1712 Thomas Savery erected for it a machine for 'raising water by fire'. The need to undertake expensive alterations to meet the increasing competition of other companies resulted in a financial loss, and in 1818 the undertaking was acquired by the New River Company.

The Chelsea Waterworks Company was established in 1723, and two ponds in Green Park were converted into reservoirs. The water was obtained from a canal extending from Pimlico to the river-bank at Chelsea, where water-wheels were used to raise the water. The first attempts to purify river-water supplies were made at Chelsea, but increase in pollution of the river caused the company, in common with others affected by the Metropolis Water Act of 1852, to move its intake beyond the tidal waters. This Act also required all water to be filtered unless drawn from wells, and all reservoirs within 5 miles of St Paul's to be covered.

The Lambeth Waterworks Company was incorporated by Act of Parliament in 1785 for supplying Lambeth and adjacent areas. Considerable works were established to meet increasing demands, and in 1848 the company procured purer sources of supply by moving its intake to Surbiton, where filter-beds (p 501) were constructed.

The East London Waterworks Company was established in 1807, and in the following year acquired the undertakings of the Shadwell Waterworks Company and the West Ham waterworks from the London Dock Company. Intake-works and reservoirs were constructed at Old Ford, but in 1829 the company decided to move its intake to Lee Bridge, which became the centre of the distribution system. By the end of the century this was the second most powerful station in the metropolitan area.

The Kent Waterworks Company was established in 1809, and obtained water from the river Ravensbourne for the supply of Deptford, Lee, Greenwich, Lewisham, and Rotherhithe. After developing a deep well at Deptford in 1856 the company abandoned the use of river-water, and the area was supplied entirely from wells. In 1811 the Grand Junction Waterworks Company was incorporated, and from 1820 drew water from the Thames at Chelsea, but subsequently the intake was removed to Kew Bridge. In 1845 the Southwark and Vauxhall Company was incorporated to amalgamate the Southwark and the Vauxhall companies, whose principal works comprised an intake at Battersea, which was subsequently moved to Hampton.

The following table gives the amount of water supplied by the nine Metropolitan companies in existence in 1848–9 (figure 281):

Company	*Total number of tenements supplied*	*Average daily supply (million gallons)*
New River	83 206	15·5
East London	56 673	9·0
Southwark and Vauxhall	34 864	6·0
West Middlesex	24 480	3·3
Lambeth	23 396	3·1
Chelsea	20 996	3·9
Grand Junction	14 058	3·5
Kent	9 632	1·1
Hampstead	4 490	0·4
Total	271 795	45·8

By the middle of the nineteenth century, almost every house in London, except the very poorest, had a cistern filled at stated times. Figure 280 shows the method of supply to houses in Piccadilly at the beginning of the nineteenth century.

Where geological conditions were favourable in gravel areas it was quite usual to sink shallow wells, from which supplies of water were obtained for individual houses and industries, and also to rely upon springs issuing at the junction of pervious strata with impervious clay. The spread of pollution, however, caused many of these supplies to be abandoned, and eventually purer, deep-seated sources were tapped by sinking boreholes.

As the lower reaches of rivers in many parts of the country were rapidly becoming polluted, and the demand for water increased beyond the capacity of wells and boreholes, attention was directed to the purer head-waters. This generally necessitated the construction of dams to form storage- or impounding-reservoirs, in order to augment the natural flow in time of drought.

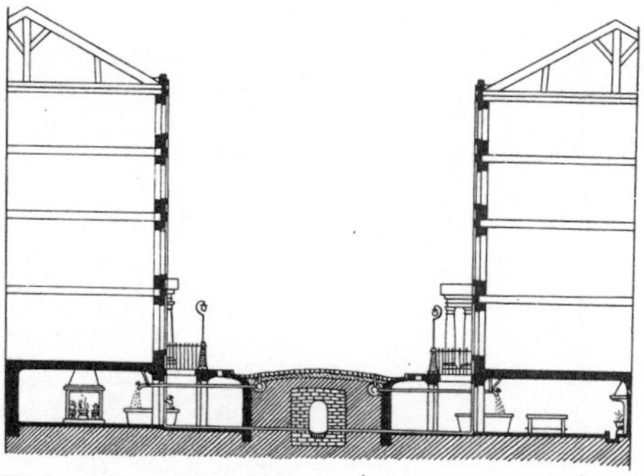

FIGURE 280—*The water-supply in Piccadilly, London, at the beginning of the nineteenth century, showing the distribution of water within each house. It also shows water from the roof drained into the main sewer running beneath the centre of the road.*

A number of nineteenth-century Acts authorizing local undertakings to construct reservoirs and take water from a river were free of restriction as to the rate of abstraction, but in others it was the practice to protect the interests of such riparian proprietors as mill- and factory-owners. The practice of providing compensation-water steadily developed, and when water-wheels were in common use for driving mills the compensation-water which had to be discharged into the river was fixed at high rates of flow. Failure by the water-undertakings to fulfil their obligations involved substantial penalties. In more recent times, as the nature of the use of rivers altered, lower rates of compensation-water were sanctioned by Parliament.

A notable example of an early waterworks-dam is the Belmont dam in the Pennines, constructed about 1827 by the Great and Little Bolton Waterworks Company. The company obtained powers to take water from springs that flowed into the Belmont brook, but in order to provide compensation-water for the mills lower down, on the river Eagley, a reservoir was necessary. The dam was built of clay, to a height of 65 ft above the stream bed, and in 1843 it was raised by 16 ft. It is still in use, although extensive repairs were carried out in 1925–6.

The success of this reservoir, and the benefits obtained by the mills owing to the evening-out of the flow of the river, led other mill-owners to construct for their own benefit the Turton and Entwistle reservoir, also near Bolton. The embankment was planned to be 128 ft high, but was completed to only 108 ft. These examples furnished reliable information for calculating the yield of reservoirs in such districts, and the data so obtained were used for the design of larger schemes, such as the Longdendale works for Manchester.

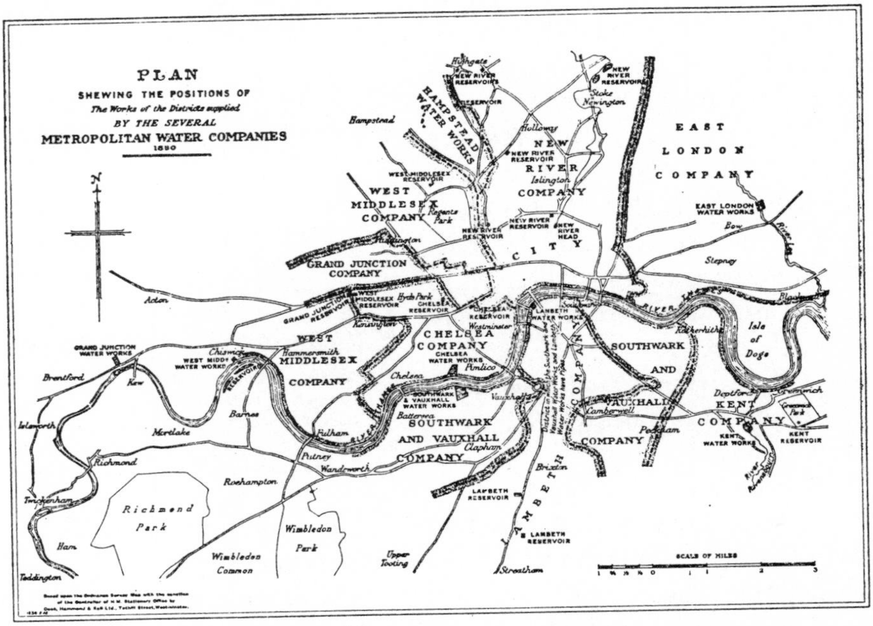

FIGURE 281—*Plan showing positions of several Metropolitan water-works in 1850.*

In 1848 Manchester Corporation obtained parliamentary powers to utilize the Longdendale Valley, about 10 miles east of the city. Five embankments were constructed forming reservoirs; two, at a low level, were used solely for storing compensation-water. The scheme was begun in 1848, and water was sent to the city in 1851. The yield of these works is 19 m gallons a day, but even by 1879 this was considered to be insufficient, and Manchester put on foot the construction of the Thirlmere scheme, to take water from the Lake District through an aqueduct 96 miles long.

The Longdendale scheme was the first important supply-scheme in Great Britain based upon impounded water. Considering the limited information and experience available at that time, the fact that such works are still in satisfactory use reflects great credit on the engineers, J. F. Bateman and G. H. Hill. These two men were also responsible for the Loch Katrine scheme for Glasgow.

Embankments were generally constructed at that time by forming a central watertight core of puddled clay, flanked on each side with suitable filling-material. The face towards the water was covered with stone pitching, and the outer face with soil, sown with grass. To prevent water from passing under the dam through permeable strata, a trench was first dug down to a watertight foundation such as shale or solid rock, and then refilled with puddled clay. This mode of construction of earth-dams is still practised in Britain, but concrete has replaced the clay below ground. It was not unusual for landslips to occur during and after construction, but by the addition of more material the dams were usually made satisfactory.

An example of the serious consequences of failure is provided by a disaster that took place in 1864, when the Dale Dike reservoir for Sheffield was filled for the first time. Within a few hours, the embankment settled and allowed the water to overflow the top, and about a quarter of the dam was washed away. The consequent release of water resulted in the loss of 244 lives and a considerable amount of damage to property. The water company was required to pay £373 000 in compensation, and a special Act of Parliament was passed to enable it to raise the money.

The early earth-dams were mainly in the Pennines, where absence of sound rock near the surface generally precluded the construction of other types of dams, notwithstanding the invention of artificial Roman cement by Edgar Dobbs in 1810. This was followed in 1824 by Joseph Aspdin's patent for Portland cement (p 448). The first large masonry dam, the Vyrnwy dam in north Wales, for supplying Liverpool, was constructed during the years 1881–92. This dam is 1172 ft long and 161 ft high.

The development of water-supply on the European continent followed a pattern similar to that experienced in England, and in some instances British practice was introduced and British capital employed. In Belgium, it was only in the eighteenth century that local authorities took an active interest in the supply of water by establishing public wells, and not until the nineteenth century were underground catchments, surface-water dams, and distribution-systems developed. Denmark was always able to draw upon its underground resources, and although the first centralized supply, with pumping-arrangements and iron pipes, was not established until 1853, at Odense, other cities followed suit a few years later. In Finland the first water-works were established in Helsinki in 1876.

At the beginning of the nineteenth century the supply of water to Paris, which then had a population of slightly over 500 000, was obtained partly from springs but principally from the Seine. From 1786 the water was sold by water-carriers, who hawked the water obtained from public tanks known as *fontaines marchandes*, but from 1819 it was forbidden to fill the water-carts from these fountains. In 1821 experiments in filtration were commenced, and during 1834–41 an artesian well 547 metres in depth was sunk in the middle of the Place de Breteuil at Grenelle. Subsequently, in 1856, Eugène Belgrand (1810–78) initiated the system of dual supply which is in use at the present time, the supply for public services being obtained from the Seine and the Ourcq canal, and the domestic supply from distant springs.

Germany in 1770 already possessed about 140 central waterworks that provided an intermittent supply, but by 1867 over 140 large towns were using modern systems, chiefly municipally owned.

In the Netherlands drinking-water supplies developed rather late, and it was not until the beginning of the nineteenth century that water was obtained from a depth. The Amsterdam works came into being in 1853, with Dutch initiative but with the aid of English experts and money. In Switzerland, about the same time, central water-supply systems were being set up in the towns.

The dams built during the seventeenth, eighteenth, and nineteenth centuries in the vicinity of the Belgrade forest at Istanbul, as well as the viaducts built by Sinan (1489?–1587), indicated remarkable foresight on the part of the Turks. It is worth recording an ingenious method used by these pioneers to determine the suitability of drinking-water. Pieces of cotton-wool were weighed, moistened with different samples of water, and dried in the sun. The water was considered the best that left the weight of the piece of cotton the most nearly unchanged.

Examples of important early European dams include one constructed in France in 1843. This arched dam, the Zola-canal dam, was built in masonry and was 118 ft high. Some masonry dams for irrigation reservoirs were built in Spain in the sixteenth and eighteenth centuries. An example is the old Puentes dam, constructed in 1785–91 across the river Guadalentin. This dam failed in 1802, because of unsatisfactory foundations.

From the seventeenth century onwards, the sinking of deep wells was practised to obtain water from pervious underground sources, and quite frequently it was found that the water would rise to the surface and overflow. This type of well, known as an artesian well, was so called because the phenomenon was stated to have been first observed in Artois in 1126.

In the London area wells were driven down to the bed of water-saturated sand that underlies the London clay, but with the increasing number of wells this source of supply soon became exhausted. Subsequent wells were driven into the chalk, where the water was under pressure. The large amount of water abstracted from this source has had the effect of lowering the water-levels considerably. An example of such a well is one sunk in 1845 to a depth of 396 ft, at Trafalgar Square, to supply water to the fountains. The water-level then was 112 ft below the surface of the ground; by 1875 it was 141 ft, and in 1911 the well was abandoned when the water had fallen to 236 ft. The water is still falling and was 283 ft down in 1937.

The development of water-supply was naturally influenced to a considerable extent by the law relating to the ownership of the water abstracted. The law with regard to the question of ownership in underground water became definitely settled, so far as Britain is concerned, by the famous case of *Chasemore* v *Richards* in 1859. The defendants had sunk a well about a quarter of a mile from the river Wandle for the purpose of supplying water to Croydon, and in so doing abstracted water that formerly flowed through the ground into the river, thus decreasing the flow past the plaintiff's mill. It was held that unless the water is flowing in a known or defined channel, such as a mine-adit, the owner of the land has an unlimited right to abstract the water by means of a well, and is not liable for any injury to those above or below him. Subject to statutory control, this general rule of law obtains today.

The driving-power of pumps during the period we are now discussing was steam, and in about 1800 a number of steam-pumps, almost all designed by James Watt, were in use (p 181). The expiration of Watt's patent in 1800 led to further developments; in 1812 Trevithick produced the first high-pressure condensing pumping-engine, known as the Cornish engine (p 188). These engines were developed primarily for removing water from mine-workings in Cornwall and elsewhere, but some were used by water undertakings. The necessity for higher pumping-heads and for pumping against variable pressure caused the development of compound rotative beam-engines (p 191), and a number were built in 1848.

The hydraulic ram (vol V, ch 22) was invented and patented by a Frenchman, J. M. Montgolfier, in 1797, but did not come into general use until 1840. In 1868 John Blake of Accrington patented an improved type of ram capable of raising up to 100 000 gallons a day.

For the distribution of water, wooden mains up to 10 inches in diameter, and generally bored from elm trees, were in common use during the seventeenth and eighteenth centuries (figure 282); they were not prohibited in London until the passing of the Metropolis Paving Act of 1817. In some of the forested areas of Scandinavia and central Europe wooden pipes are still in use. Although cast iron pipes had earlier been used in small quantities at several places—for example, by the Chelsea Waterworks Company in 1746 and in Edinburgh in 1755—this date marks approximately the beginning of the use of cast iron pressure-pipes on a large scale. As long ago as the latter half of the seventeenth century, however, cast iron had been used for the mains of the Marly waterworks installation at Versailles (figures 93 and 94). They comprised over 15 miles

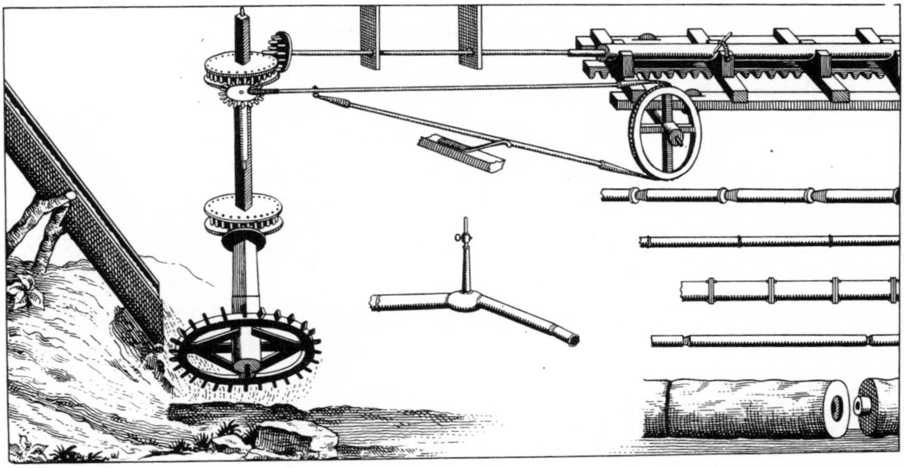

FIGURE 282—*The boring of wooden pipes, mid-eighteenth-century, showing use of water-wheel as source of power. Various methods of jointing are seen on the right.*

of piping, in lengths of about 1 metre only, having flanged joints. The diameter ranged from $1\frac{3}{4}$ to 20 in. The spigot-and-socket joint was invented by Thomas Simpson about 1785. Sandstone pipes had been tried in many towns, including Manchester (*c* 1812), but the stone was generally unable to withstand a pressure of more than 30–40 ft head of water and their use was discontinued. The West Middlesex Water Company experimented with stone pipes at the beginning of the nineteenth century, but experienced considerable leakage from them, and eventually substituted iron for wood. Until about 1850 all iron pipes were cast horizontally, but in 1846 D. Y. Stewart obtained a patent for producing vertically-cast iron pipes, and from that date the horizontal method became obsolescent. The longevity of cast iron is well known, and in Edinburgh a main of 7 to 9 in diameter, laid in 1790 to replace a wooden pipe, is still in use. In 1825, butt-welded wrought-iron tubes were introduced for distribution pipes.

Early forms of stop-valves in pipe-lines were generally very crude and inefficient, and as higher pressures were used the need for a better valve became apparent. Ball-valves were mentioned in 1748; before that the supply to cisterns had to be regulated by taps. In 1839 James Nasmyth (1808–90), at the request of the East London Water Company, produced a double-faced, wedge-form sluice-valve, and this forms the basis of valves employed today. Even earlier, in 1824, an old box-valve of peculiar design was fixed on the outlet end of a 15-in pipe-line controlling the flow from the Belmont reservoir (figure 283); it was discovered when repairs to the reservoir became necessary a hundred years later.

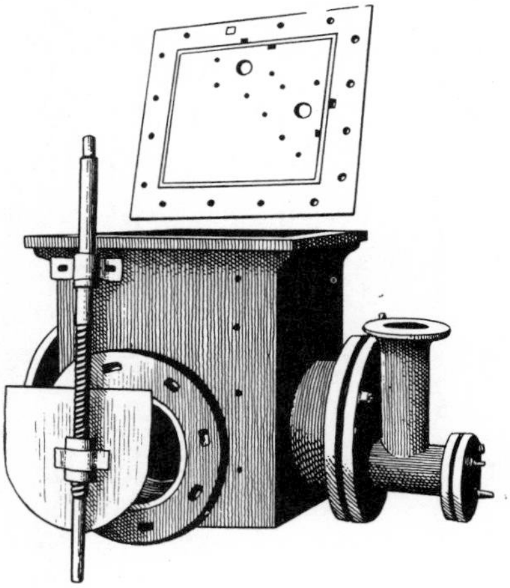

FIGURE 283—*Box-valve from the outlet end of a pipe in the Belmont reservoir. 1824.*

In 1797 Giovanni Venturi (1746–1822) postulated what is now termed the 'Venturi law', namely that in passing through converging pipes fluids under pressure gain speed and lose head, and vice versa for diverging pipes. Before 1800, it was possible to measure the rate of flow of water in open channels, but there were no means of metering flows in closed pipes. The first meter for this purpose was patented by Thomas Kennedy in 1852, and was at once used extensively by many water undertakings (figure 284). G. F. Deacon in 1873 invented a simple rising-disk meter that showed on a drum-chart the actual flow of water from hour to hour. This meter was devised to record the use and misuse of water, and is still employed. In 1887 the American engineer Clemens Herschel devised a simple instrument for the exact measurement of the flow of fluids, based on Venturi's law, and the Venturi principle is now very widely adopted for metering flows in pipes, tunnels, and channels.

The necessity for clear, clean water in the dyeing and bleaching trades prompted some Lancashire manufacturers to filter their water by passing it through beds of sand. In 1791 James Peacock (1738–1814) took out a patent for passing water upwards through beds of graded sand. Slow sand-filters were successfully constructed for treating water for public supply at Paisley in 1804, at Greenock in 1827, and at Chelsea in the same year. Later, such filters were built in many parts of Britain and elsewhere in Europe, and in the United States. Before such filters were introduced, the attempts to purify river-water consisted simply of allowing the impurities to settle in subsiding-reservoirs, but this was found to be inadequate. Water from upland reservoirs and from springs was generally considered to be naturally suitable, and was often supplied untreated in any way until after the introduction of chlorination in 1905. Early work on filters was concentrated on the clarification of turbid waters, and for a long time

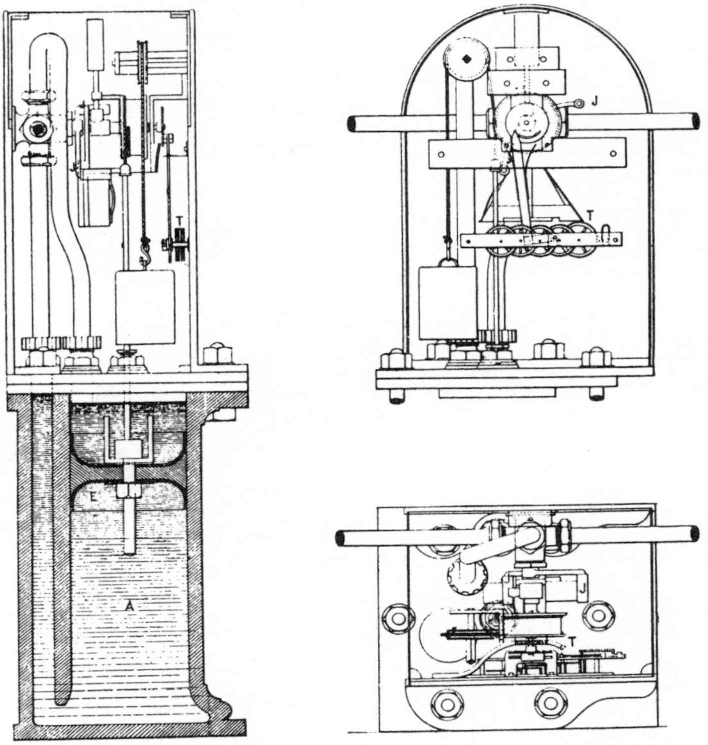

FIGURE 284—*Water-meter from the patent specification (1852) of Thomas Kennedy.* (Left) *Side view;* (top rlght) *back view;* (bottom right) *plan. This was the first meter for measuring flow in closed pipes. The quantity of water passing through the meter is recorded on the gauges at* T *by filling and emptying the chamber* A *by means of the piston* E. *The direction of movement of the piston is controlled by a valve operated by a hammer* J.

the production of a clear water was the sole test of efficiency. The action of filters was not understood until the development of the science of bacteriology. The slow sand-filter provides both a microscopic screen and an efficient biological instrument that is capable of removing bacteria from the water.

The filters designed by James Simpson for the Chelsea Water Company were the first to be built in London, and the form has not materially changed since then. Tunnels of loose bricks covered with tiles were laid on the floor; above this was placed a 2-ft layer of washed coarse gravel, and then a layer of washed fine sand. The bulk of the sediment was retained in the top 3 in of sand, which was removed, cleaned, and replaced from time to time. This bed was used till 1856, when the company's intake was moved to Surbiton. The first statutory provision for filtration was in the Lambeth Company's Act of 1834.

In 1849 and 1853–4 there were serious outbreaks of Asiatic cholera in London, which were traced by physicians to drinking-water derived from sources contaminated by excreted matter. The water from the Thames had become increasingly foul and these occurrences roused public feeling to a high pitch. The 1849 epidemic led to the passing of the Metropolis Water Act of 1852, which precluded the abstraction of water from the tidal reaches of the Thames, and made it compulsory for the water to be filtered. New sources of water were not to be tapped unless approved by an inspector of the Board of Trade.

The art of softening water was first developed in Great Britain. Although pioneer work had been done before the nineteenth century, it was not until 1841 that Thomas Clark (1801–67) was granted a patent for a 'New Method of Rendering Certain Waters Less Impure and Less Hard'. The varying action of water on soap had long been attributed to its hardness or softness, and in 1856 Clark formulated his famous scale of hardness, whereby one grain of lime or other soap-destroying ingredient in one gallon of water (or 1/70 000) corresponded to one degree of hardness. The first municipal water-softening plant in London was installed at Plumstead in 1854, but the idea of softening did not meet with great favour. In 1862, when the predecessors of the present East Surrey Water Company were constituted a water undertaking, the compulsory softening of water was first introduced in a private Act.

Sterilization of water was virtually unknown until the beginning of the twentieth century, but in 1897 Dr Sims Woodhead used calcium hypochlorite for the disinfection of water-mains at Maidstone following an outbreak of enteric fever.

BIBLIOGRAPHY

DICKINSON, H. W. 'Water Supply of Greater London.' Newcomen Society, London. 1954.
HOBBS, A. T. (Ed.). 'Manual of British Water Supply Practice' (2nd ed.). Heffer, Cambridge, for The Institution of Water Engineers, London. 1954.
ROBINS, F. W. 'The Story of Water Supply.' Oxford University Press, London. 1946.
WALTERS, R. C. S. 'The Nation's Water Supply.' Nicholson & Watson, London. 1936.

16

PART II

SANITARY ENGINEERING: SANITATION

J. RAWLINSON

IT has been recognized from the earliest times that drainage, whether natural or artificial, is essential to the health and comfort of mankind. Surplus rainfall and the waste-products of humanity must be disposed of, and as populations have increased and centres of civilization have grown it has become necessary to augment or replace natural drainage systems by large and sometimes costly engineering works.

I. ANCIENT AND MEDIEVAL DRAINAGE SYSTEMS

There is evidence that at the palace of Minos at Knossos in Crete a drainage system existed before 1500 B.C., and that in many respects it was similar to the installations of much more recent times. Excavations have revealed that stone ducts and terracotta pipes conveyed rain-water from roofs and terraces to rain-spouts in the outer walls. A latrine on the ground floor was connected to a main drain, and provision was made for flushing it with rain-water. The drainage pipes were tapered so that the narrow end of one pipe fitted into the broader end of the next.

From remains that may still be seen it is apparent that sewers were to be found in ancient Greek cities. Ruins of houses have been discovered which show that they were equipped with closets of simple design. These were made so that they could be flushed with water, and sometimes were connected to a sewer in the street.

In the sixth century B.C. Rome possessed an extensive network of sewers draining the marshy ground lying between the hills on which the city was built. Small sewers collected the water and discharged it into a larger one known as the *cloaca maxima*, of which parts still exist. This sewer was probably built about 2500 years ago as an open drainage-channel and was roofed-in about 300 or 400 years later. Its dimensions were approximately 15 ft to the top of the arch, by about 15 ft wide. After the fall of the Roman Empire little progress was made in sanitation for some centuries.

In the Middle Ages the problem of drainage was more simply solved than it is today because it was the custom merely to throw all household refuse and human excreta into the street. By-laws issued by some town authorities forbidding this practice were ignored by the populace, since there was normally no alternative method of disposal (vol II, p 532).

In the records of Paris for the year 1412 a reference is made to 'the great drain'. This was apparently the brook of Ménilmontant, into which the drainage from the gutters in the streets was discharged. No improvement to this watercourse was made until 1740, when it was walled in; some time afterwards it was arched over. In 1513 the *coutume* (common law) in Paris decreed that every house should have its own privy, but as late as the eighteenth century it was still the prevalent custom to throw refuse into the street. A survey carried out in Madrid in 1773 disclosed that the royal palace did not contain even one privy.

II. STREET-CLEANSING

In the City of London there was considerable concern about the insanitary conditions of the streets. 'The plague had recurred from time to time in England since the Black Death in 1349. Kites and ravens were protected birds and they and the pigs which roamed about grew fat on the offal in the streets. Dogs were innumerable.' In the City itself instructions were issued from time to time to secure some degree of cleanliness, but usually these had little effect. Rubbish of all descriptions continued to be deposited in the streets, and the liquid from it, augmented in time of rainfall, ran down the central gutter into the nearest stream or ditch. After the fire of London in 1666 lay-stalls, or temporary dumping-places for rubbish, were set up in the streets, and orders were given for the refuse to be deposited there for later removal. Scavengers were appointed in each ward of the City; their duties were to supervise the cleansing of the streets. The holders of this office (Izaak Walton at one time held the position) were unpaid, and much of the work was done by rakers, who corresponded to the refuse-contractors of more recent days. As the City streets became increasingly built up, sites for lay-stalls became more difficult to find, and they were later replaced by fixed or movable boxes in which refuse was thrown. A charge was made for the removal of the rubbish by the rakers, who later became paid servants of the commissioners of sewers and afterwards of the City Corporation.

For the areas of the metropolis outside the City a number of Improvement Acts were passed during the eighteenth and early nineteenth centuries, which gave to vestries or special bodies of commissioners powers in regard to paving, cleansing, or lighting. Some of these powers required the householder to cleanse the pavement in front of his premises, and enabled the authorities to make arrangements with rakers for the sweeping of the carriage-way and the removal of dirt and rubbish. The Metropolitan Paving Act of 1817, known as Michael Angelo Taylor's Act,[1] codified these various Acts and remained the statute under which these works were carried out until the passing of the Metropolis Management Act, 1855. Among other things, the former Act required 'scavengers, rakers, or cleansers' to carry away at their own costs or charges the ordinary refuse, which they were empowered to retain. In those days, and even in more recent times, scavenging-contractors were willing to pay for the privilege of sweeping the streets and collecting the sweepings and household refuse, which they were able to sell at a profit.

Some authorities, such as the town council of Liverpool, took over the control of all cleansing operations and employed staff to carry out the work. The disposal of the refuse when it had been collected was a difficult problem. In many towns the contents of privies and domestic ash-pits were collected at the same time as the street-sweepings, and in Liverpool in 1866 it was estimated that the amount of refuse which had to be removed each month was as much as 64 000 tons. Some of the refuse was sold to farmers for use as a fertilizer, and sometimes markets could be found for other of the waste products, but there still remained a large quantity to be disposed of. This was done by sending it out to sea in barges and dumping it there; by burning it in specially built destructors; or by tipping it into disused chalk-pits or on waste land.

III. LAND-DRAINAGE AND SEWERAGE IN ENGLAND

In England complaints were frequently made in Parliament about the inadequacy of the land-drainage system, and from a very early date ordinances were issued to landowners to cleanse streams and ditches and to keep the banks in good order. In 1531 a 'Bill of Sewers' consolidated the earlier enactments and became the statute from which commissions responsible for drainage drew their authority.

The problem became intensified with the rapid increase in the population. The first census, taken in 1801, returned a figure of approximately 10 500 000 for Great Britain, but in 1851 this had risen to 20 800 000 (p 489). The rapid development of the urban areas, which was among the effects of the industrial revolution, resulted in great masses of country-bred workers being flung into a miserable existence amid unhealthy living conditions in overcrowded towns. In this insanitary environment disease inevitably flourished, and the finding of means to combat it became a progressively serious and urgent problem for the authorities.

[1] Michael Angelo Taylor (1757–1834) was a barrister of Lincoln's Inn, a Member of Parliament for many years, and a privy councillor.

IV. HOUSE-DRAINAGE

By 1800 the houses of the well-to-do usually contained at least one privy, but for the poorer classes a common privy serving a number of houses was the generally accepted standard. The wealthier residential areas were comparatively well scavenged and night-soil men emptied the privies every night. Even in the poorer districts collections were made at intervals, although these were usually very irregular. Compared with modern standards these arrangements do not seem very satisfactory, but in these matters England was at the time ahead of her neighbours. Smollett complained of the scarcity of privies in France and of their filthiness where they did exist.

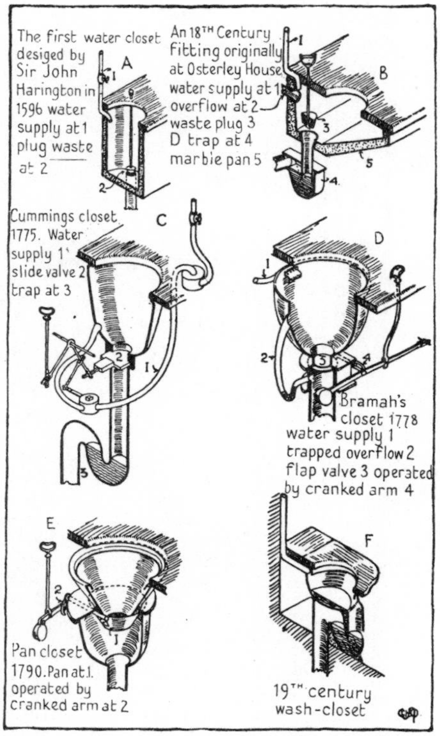

FIGURE 285—*The evolution of the water-closet.*

Collections of night-soil were still being made at the end of the century; in by-laws made in 1891 the London County Council prescribed that this should be done only between the hours of 4 a.m. and 10 a.m. from March to October and between 6 a.m. and 12 noon from November to February. This was to ensure that there was sufficient daylight to allow the work to be carried out efficiently, and to give as little offence as possible when the refuse was being transported through the streets.

By the end of the eighteenth century the water-closet in a very elementary form began to be introduced.[1] The apparatus was considered to be such an advance in sanitary arrangements that once one was installed in the house, then all difficulties of sewage-removal would at once be overcome. As, however, the closet was more often than not built into an enclosed cupboard and connected by an unventilated pipe direct to a cesspool it became a more virulent source of infection than even its forerunner had been. Foul gases were now conveyed directly into the house from the evil-smelling cesspool, usually built in the basement. In order to prevent the passage of these bad odours, traps containing a water-seal

[1] The valve water-closet was described, with figures, by Sir John Harington (1561–1612) in his book 'The Metamorphosis of Ajax', 1596.

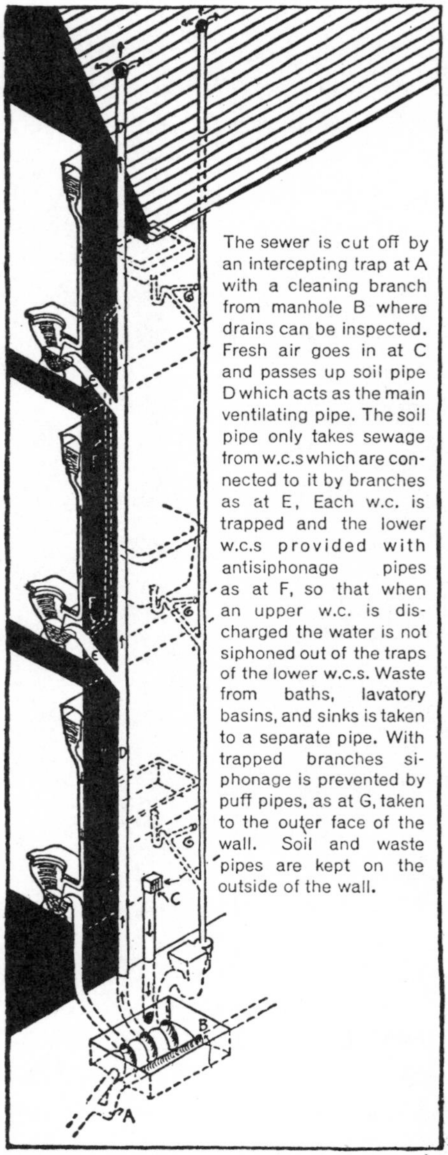

FIGURE 286—*The English two-pipe drainage system.*

were introduced. The first patent for this kind of trap was taken out by John Gaillait in 1782, for 'the invention of an entire new machine . . . a stink trap which will entirely prevent the very disagreeable smells from drains and sewers'.

Later developments and improvements in the design and construction of water-closets are shown in figure 285, but it was a long time before satisfactory methods of connecting them to the cesspool or sewer were brought into use. The two-pipe system of house-drainage shown in the diagram (figure 286), which effectively prevents all noxious odours from penetrating into the house, was coming into use in England at the close of the nineteenth century. This system requires separate pipes for the water-closet and bath- or lavatory-waste, but the contents of each pass eventually to the same drain.

Water-closets began to be installed in increasing numbers in the early 1800s, but drainage authorities frequently insisted that they should be connected to cesspools and not to the sewers. As the cesspools were seldom emptied, their contents frequently overflowed and the surrounding ground became sodden and stagnant. In spite of the veto imposed by the authorities, some cesspools were connected to the sewers in attempts to overcome the intolerable conditions. Even the sewers, however, were very often ineffective for this purpose. With their shallow gradients they retained for long periods the sewage which was discharged into them, with the result that it became putrescent and offensive. As improvements were made to the sewers, and in an endeavour to overcome the nuisance caused by the cesspools, it eventually became compulsory for all water-closets in the larger towns to be connected to the sewers.

Although this action produced beneficial results it also had the effect of greatly increasing the flow in the sewers, and as these usually discharged into the nearest river the pollution was transferred from the ground on which the houses stood to the river which flowed through their midst. A further problem was thus created which could be solved only by the execution of large-scale sewerage works.

In the latter half of the nineteenth century many large towns carried out extensive works for the better drainage of their areas. Liverpool obtained parliamentary powers in 1847, as a result of which the town council was designated the sole governing sanitary authority for the paving, sewerage, drainage, and sanitary improvement of the town. It at once proceeded to build a series of new sewers. Edinburgh constructed a trunk sewer in 1864, to which a number of the earlier sewers were connected.

FIGURE 287—*Deepening sewer under Fleet Street. 1845.*

V. DESCRIPTION OF DRAINAGE-WORKS IN LONDON

The drainage-works carried out in London between 1850 and 1900 may be regarded as typical of those executed in many other towns, and a short description of them will thus serve as an example of the schemes of sewerage that formed a feature of this period.

In 1843 the Poor Law Commissioners who had been appointed to investigate the sanitary conditions of the labouring population drew attention to the defective state of sewerage and drainage, and a commission was appointed to inquire into the means of improving the health of the people.

Some works to improve local drainage, such as the deepening of the sewer under Fleet Street, were carried out at this time (figure 287). Yet the banks of the Thames, in its wider reaches between Waterloo and Westminster bridges for instance, became covered with vast accumulations of foul and offensive mud which were exposed at low tide. Cholera epidemics in 1849 and 1853–4 (p 503), from which nearly 20 000 people died, emphasized the gravity of the problem caused by the pollution of the Thames, from which much of London's drinking-water was drawn. The accompanying illustration (figure 288) shows the Fleet river in 1844; the chutes discharging from the houses into the river may be clearly seen. Between 1848 and 1855 no fewer than six commissions were appointed, and numerous designs for improving the drainage were prepared and considered; but in spite of their efforts conditions became so intolerable that Parliament in 1855 decided to set up a new authority to deal with the problem. Under the Metropolis Local Management Act of 1855 the Metropolitan Board of Works was created. The Act provided that the Board 'shall make such sewers and works as they may think necessary for preventing all or any part of the sewage within the Metropolis from flowing into the Thames in or near the Metropolis . . .' Sir Joseph Bazalgette (1819–91) was appointed engineer to the Board, and within a year he put forward plans for complying with this order.

FIGURE 288—*The river Fleet in 1844, showing the chutes from the houses discharging directly into the stream.*

Up to this time the main sewers—which were the old water-courses and are now mostly bricked over—flowed to the Thames, mostly at right-angles to it. In order to prevent their contents flowing into and polluting the Thames, Bazalgette proposed to build large sewers running west to east, roughly parallel to the river, which would intercept the flow in these sewers and convey it to outfalls some distance down the river. There were to be three intercepting sewers on the north side of the river and two on the south, and the outfalls at Barking in Essex and Crossness in Kent were about 12 miles below London Bridge. Figure 289 shows a section of the low-level sewer on the north bank of the Thames. From Westminster bridge to Blackfriars bridge this sewer was incorporated in a new embankment, which served the triple purposes of providing a suitable route for the sewer, a wide roadway over it, and reclamation from the river of 37 acres of land which formerly consisted of evil-smelling mudbanks. The subway above the sewer was built to contain the services of public utility companies, in order to avoid disturbance of the road and footway when repairs and maintenance became necessary. Bazalgette's proposals entailed the construction of over 100 miles of large-diameter sewers, and of three pumping-stations to lift the sewage so that its flow to the outfalls could continue by gravity.

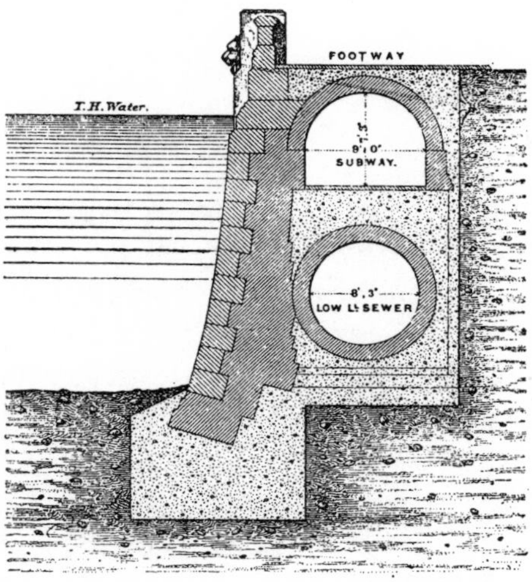

FIGURE 289—*Section of Thames Embankment, showing subway and low-level sewer.*

The design of the system of intercepting sewers provided for a daily flow of sewage to the outfalls of 5 cu ft or $31\frac{1}{4}$ gallons per head of the population, the population being taken as 2 300 000 on the north side of the Thames and 1 150 000 on the south side, a total of 3 450 000. In addition, rain-water amounting to 178 000 000 gallons a day on the north of the river and 108 000 000 gallons on the south side was allowed for. The latter quantities represent $\frac{1}{4}$-in and $\frac{1}{10}$-in of rainfall respectively, distributed over the 24 hours.

A disadvantage of the proposal was that in times of heavy rainfall the intercepting sewers would become surcharged, but provision was made for the excess storm-water—carrying with it a certain amount of diluted sewage—to flow over weirs into the old main-line sewers direct to the river. The points of intersection were so designed that the intercepting sewers, while carrying away to the outfalls any sewage coming down the old main-line sewers during dry weather, permitted any excessive flow due to rainfall to run away partly in the intercepting sewers and partly by short cuts down the old main-line sewers to the river.

All Bazalgette's plans had been carried out by 1875, and for many years few additions were made to the sewers in spite of the fact that the population and the discharge of sewage and rain-water were constantly increasing.

The effect of the new drainage system was remarkable. The condition of the Thames in the metropolitan area was considerably improved, and the unhealthy conditions, owing to defective drainage, previously suffered by many of those living on low-lying land near the river, were largely remedied.

Similar drainage-works were carried out at this time on the continent (figures 290, 291). In Paris a detailed survey of all the drains had been made in 1833, and a considerable amount of drainage-work was carried out, as the following table shows:

Year	*Total length of drains (of all kinds) in use*
1663	10 380 metres
1806	23 530 ,,
1832	40 330 ,,
1837	75 565 ,,
1863	350 000 ,,

While the new drainage-works were in progress, the opportunity was taken to regrade many of the roads. These were formerly concave in section, with a drain in the centre in which iron gratings were set at intervals to allow the water to reach the sewer below. The gratings frequently became blocked, and planks were used to enable pedestrians to cross the road; vehicles meanwhile travelled through a swamp of mud. During reconstruction the centre of the road was raised, so that it drained to gutters at each side; at the same time more headroom was provided and a sewer built beneath.

The larger of the new sewers contained sufficient room for a footpath on one or both sides of the water-channel, and in these, as well as in the smaller ones, provision was made for gas- and water-mains to be carried on brackets built into the sides or the floor (figure 290).

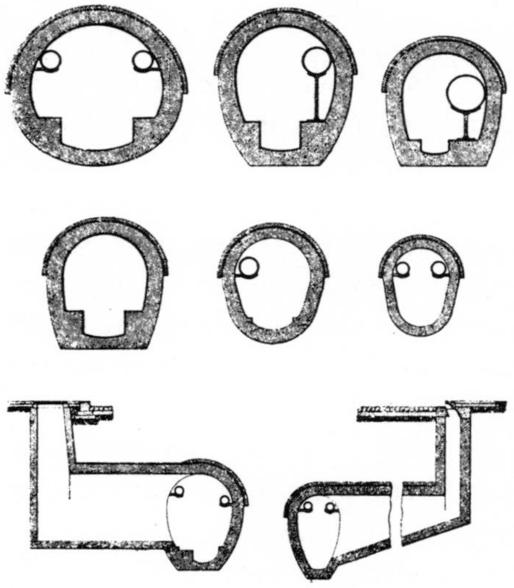

FIGURE 290—*Cross-sections of various drains in Paris.*

VI. TYPES AND SIZES OF SEWERS

Types, sizes, and shapes of sewers vary a great deal. The drainage from a dwelling-house normally passes through a stoneware pipe of small diameter, glazed to render it impervious, into a larger pipe or small brick-built sewer in the street. This in turn may connect with a larger sewer, the drainage flowing next into the main sewer and finally to the intercepting or outfall sewer. In the earlier days of their use stoneware pipes were unsatisfactory, not so much on account of defects in their manufacture as owing to the lack of knowledge and skill in methods of jointing and fixing them together. Today they are laid on a bed of concrete and benched up with the same material, a process which prevents fracture, and jointed with cement. Earlier, however, they were laid direct in the ground with no support, and the

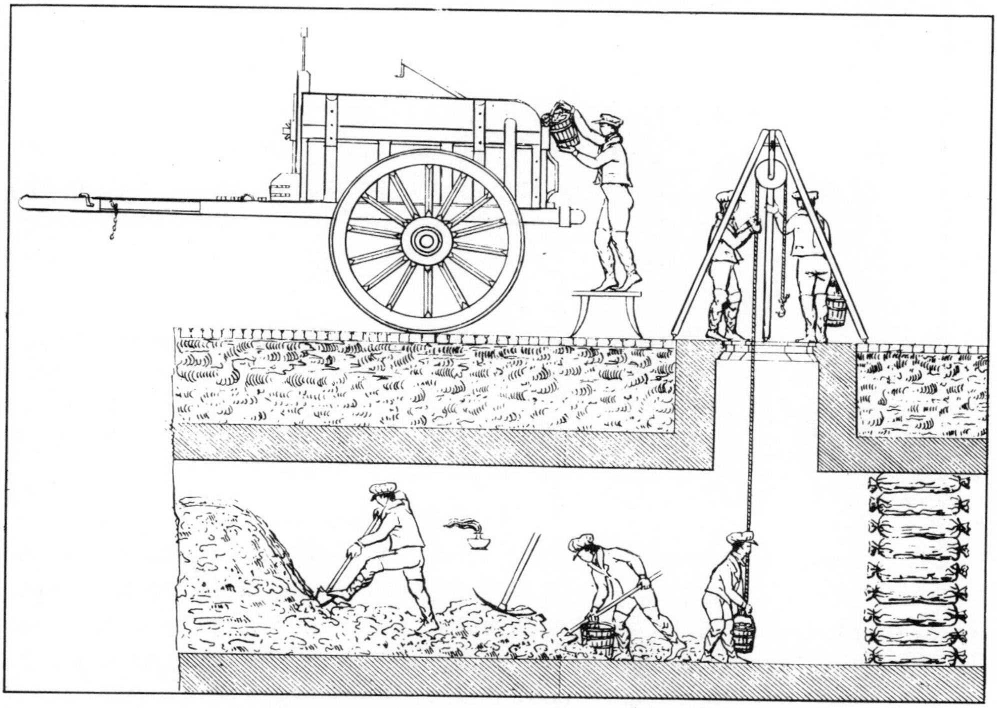

FIGURE 291—*Clearing drains in Paris, early nineteenth century.*

joints were made with clay. Frequently the joints broke apart and allowed the sewage to percolate into the surrounding ground. This gave rise to considerable controversy between those who recommended pipes—among whom Sir Edwin Chadwick (1800–90), the great English sanitary reformer, was a leading figure—and their opponents who preferred the larger brick sewers.

Brick sewers in Britain range from about 2 ft 6 in by 3 ft 9 in to about 12 ft or more in diameter. In Paris they are generally larger, the smallest being 5 ft 6 in high by 2 ft 3 in wide. For local drainage, where the flow is not constant, a sewer of oval section, with the narrow part at the bottom, is found to be more efficient than one circular in section. The reason is that in dry weather, when the flow is small, the former shape gives a greater depth of liquid and consequently greater velocity of flow and scouring-power. The broader section at the top gives greater room for the passage of storm-water, and for the workmen engaged in cleansing and maintenance. Intercepting and outfall sewers in which the flow is more constant are circular in section, a shape which combines the greatest strength and capacity with the smallest amount of brickwork, and is therefore the most economical.

VII. SEWERS: CALCULATION OF SIZES REQUIRED

In a description of his works that he gave in 1865 Bazalgette mentions some of the data on which he based his calculations in order to determine the capacity required for the various sewers in his plans. The study of hydraulics was not very far advanced at that time, and it is interesting to note an extract from Robinson's 'Theory of Rivers' which Bazalgette quoted:

> We learn from observation that a velocity of 3 inches per second at the bottom will just begin to work up fine clay fit for pottery, and however firm and compact it may be, it will tear up. A velocity of 6 inches will lift fine sand, 8 inches will lift sand as coarse as linseed, 12 inches will sweep along fine gravel, 24 inches will roll along rounded pebbles an inch in diameter, and it requires 3 feet per second at the bottom to sweep along shivery angular stones of the size of an egg.

Bazalgette stated that his own experience confirmed these observations. He regarded a mean velocity of 1½ miles an hour, in a properly protected main sewer when running half-full, as being sufficient for the minimum velocity required. By using this figure and the data regarding population and water-supply cited earlier, he was able to calculate the minimum sizes required for his main, intercepting, and outfall sewers.

London, Liverpool, and other populous cities situated on large estuaries have a combined system of drainage; that is, the same sewer conveys both sewage and rain-water. Some towns have been drained on the 'separate' system, which provides that rain-water is carried away separately to a stream or water-course, while the sewage is taken by a different system of sewers to the outfall or sewage-disposal works. The advantage of the separate system is that a smaller volume of material has to be purified and treated, a matter which will be dealt with later.

VIII. SEWERS: MAINTENANCE, CLEANSING, VENTILATION, AND REPAIRS

A well designed and well built brick sewer has a very long life. As it is below ground it is little subject to the effect of changes of temperature and to alternating wet and dry conditions. In the course of time the bottom, or invert as it is called, may become worn, but this can be repaired.

Inspection, cleansing, and maintenance of the sewers is carried out by gangs of men who regularly patrol them. In the older sewers, which, as has been stated, were frequently bricked-in streams, no alteration to the original gradients was made when they were enclosed, and consequently sand and grit are quickly deposited. This deposit is removed at suitable intervals while still maintaining the sewage-flow. It is shovelled up and placed in skeps, which are drawn up to the surface at the nearest man-hole, as in figure 291.

In order to carry out repairs to the sewer it is necessary to direct the flow into an adjoining sewer. This is achieved by using a sluice known as a penstock; it is a large iron flap or door which can completely close the sewer.

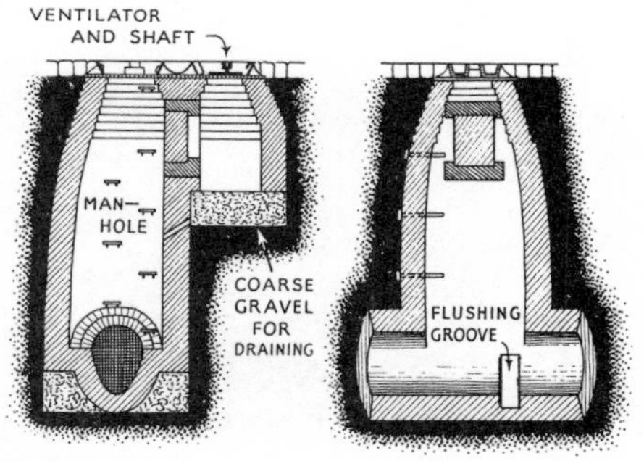

FIGURE 292—*Types of manholes and ventilating shafts on brick sewers, 1878. The covers over the manholes were airtight; those over the ventilating shafts were open and hinged so that the dirt collected at the bottom of them could be removed by scavengers.*

The safety of the men who work in sewers requires, among other things, that there should be adequate ventilation. To solve this problem without causing nuisance or annoyance has always been difficult. Sewers which took surface-water only were usually ventilated by gulleys at the sides of the streets, but this practice could no longer be tolerated when sewage was discharged into them. Until about 1830 none of these gullies contained traps, but in London during the following decade about 900 traps were formed in the surface-water gullies. The result was that, with the sewer-vents closed up, unpleasant emanations began to appear in other places. In 1852 the Board of Health proposed that openings should be made from the sewers to the centres of the roadways in order to reduce air- or gas-pressure in the sewers. The method of construction adopted in 1878 is shown in figure 292. In most towns this is still the current practice, and it has been found that the more ventilators there are the fewer are the complaints of nuisance caused by them.

In 1858 an experiment was made by Bazalgette and Colonel Haywood with a furnace built into the clock-tower of the Houses of Parliament; it was hoped that this would draw fetid air from the sewers and destroy it. It was not a success, as the radius within which the sewers were affected by the furnace was found to be very limited.

Another interesting system, devised at the end of the nineteenth century, was due to J. E. Webb: the details are shown in the illustration (figure 293). In addition to providing illumination for the streets, the gas-burners drew the air from the sewers and thus provided continuous ventilation. A number of these lamps were installed in Blackpool, where the cost at that time was stated to be £29 for installation and connexion to the gas-supply and sewer, with an annual maintenance cost of £16 10*s*. Other methods that have been tried include the fixing of pipe-ventilators to the sides of buildings, the use of the vent-pipes in the house-drainage system, the use of mechanically operated fans in conjunction with ventilating-shafts, and, on occasion, the draught created by neighbouring factory chimneys.

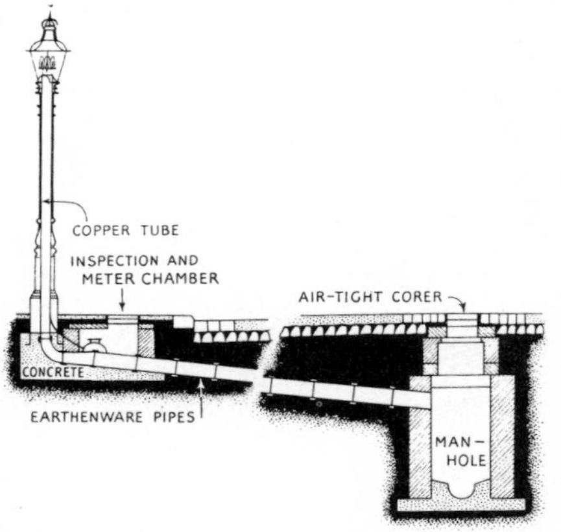

FIGURE 293—*Webb's sewer-ventilating lamp at Blackpool. The gases from the sewer pass up and through the lamp. Gas is burned at the top and the sewer gases are led through the hot zone and also burned.*

If the sewers are not ventilated there is a serious risk of explosions and of accidents to the sewermen, owing to the accumulation of explosive or injurious gases. In 1894 the London County Council obtained powers to prevent the discharge of improper substances into the sewers. Certain trade-wastes, although comparatively innocuous in themselves, may react with other wastes to produce poisonous gases. Gas from a leaking supply-pipe seeping into the sewer, and inflammable liquids, constitute additional hazards. The danger from all these causes is greatly reduced if there is sufficient ventilation.

It is interesting to record that, in spite of what might seem very adverse conditions, the health of the men who work and spend a great deal of their time in sewers is remarkably good; their sickness-rate compares well with that of other workers. There is a reference in Mayhew's 'London' to men called 'toshers', who in the early part of the nineteenth century used to search the sewers for metals, money, and valuables, referred to as 'tosh'. He writes:

> It might be supposed that the sewer hunters would exhibit in their pallid faces the unmistakable evidence of their unhealthy employment. But this is far from the fact. Strange to say the sewer hunters are strong, robust and healthy men, generally florid in their complexion, while many of them know illness only by name. Some of the older men who head the gangs are between 60 and 80 years of age and have followed the employ-

ment during their whole lives. The men appear to have a fixed belief that the odour of the sewers contributes in a variety of ways to their general health.

The hazards already mentioned are not the only ones that sewer-workers are called upon to face. A sudden storm in a distant part of the drainage system may cause a rapid rise in the height of the water, and adequate means of warning must be installed to warn the men of this danger.

Sewer-men are also liable to attacks of leptospiral jaundice (Weil's disease, *Spirochaetosis icterohaemorrhagica*), which is due to the presence of rats and is contracted through abrasions in the skin. Precautionary instructions are issued to those likely to contract this disease, and the provision of special medical facilities has reduced the number of cases of infection.

IX. PUMPING-STATIONS AND PUMPING-PLANT

In a large town the sewage collected may have to travel considerable distances before it reaches the outfall. If the contours of the land are favourable it may flow for some part of the way by gravity, but it frequently happens that the sewage has to be lifted at intervals so that it may continue to flow on again by gravity. In London four pumping-stations were built and equipped with pumps for lifting the sewage to heights ranging from 14 to 41 ft. The plant in each case consisted of steam-driven double-acting beam engines driving ram or plunger pumps. At Abbey Mills pumping-station, on the north side of the river, eight engines each of 142 hp, and each with two boilers to provide steam, were installed. Their cylinders were 4 ft 6 inches in diameter with a stroke of 9 ft. Each engine worked two double-acting pumps having diameters of 3 ft $10\frac{1}{2}$ in and a stroke of $4\frac{1}{2}$ ft. The plant at this station was capable of lifting a maximum of 15 000 cu ft per minute of sewage and rain-water to a height of 36 ft.

The 'Illustrated London News' in 1865 referred to the pumping-machines at one of these stations as 'perhaps the finest specimens of engineering work in the country' and prophesied that 'they would exist for a very long time indeed, longer than anyone now living may hope to see'. The beam-engines of the station were in fact in service until 1952.

X. SEWAGE-DISPOSAL

Even when the sewage has been conveyed away from the town to the outfall on the river or sea the problem of its disposal still remains. Before the system of water-carriage came into being the night-soil from privies was sold for use as an agricultural fertilizer, and there were many advocates of the proposal that sewage should be allowed to flow on to the land so that its value should not be lost. In ancient Greece the disposal of sewage by land-irrigation was practised, and there is mention of the same procedure in use in Germany in the sixteenth century. Where the quantity of sewage was comparatively small, and where considerable areas of vacant land existed, this method was successfully employed in Britain. Thus at Salisbury the effluent from the pipe-sewers was allowed to flow over a number of fields in rotation, and at the time this was considered to be a satisfactory method of disposal.

The adoption of land-irrigation was considered by the Metropolitan Board of Works after complaints had been made of the nuisance caused in the region of the outfalls by the discharge of the whole of London's sewage into the Thames at that point. It was decided that the acquisition of sufficient land to enable the vast quantity of London sewage to be effectually filtered through the soil without nuisance to the local inhabitants would be attended with almost insurmountable difficulty, and that the cost would be prohibitive. As an alternative, the Board constructed works for the precipitation or chemical clarification of the sewage at both outfalls.

The chemical composition of sewage when it arrives at the disposal works is rather surprising. Nine hundred and ninety-nine parts out of every thousand are water. Only 0·1 per cent, or about 1·7 cu in per 1 cu ft, consists of impurities, and this amount can be divided again into inert solids, such as sand or grit, and organic material, such as faeces, fat, and vegetable matter, in roughly equal proportions. The organic matter may be in suspension or solution, and some of the solids are neither suspended nor dissolved but in a colloidal form. If left untreated the organic matter decomposes, taking up oxygen and releasing offensive gases in the process. When discharged into a river in sufficient quantity the sewage may denude the water of oxygen and render it incapable of supporting the life of fish and plants; it may also cause the formation of mud-banks and the silting up of the river.

In Germany and the United States of America, where sewage may be discharged into large rivers or lakes, it was customary to pass it through fine screens only, or in other words to give it merely the first stage of treatment. In Britain, however, with a much higher density of population in relation to the available rivers, it was found necessary to apply one or more further stages of purification. In the late nineteenth century this was carried out by chemical precipitation; by 1894 as many as 500 patents had been taken out for chemical precipitants.

One of these was known as the A.B.C. process, a name derived from the principal ingredients of the precipitant—alum, blood, and clay. This was a process carried out by the Native Guano Company. Aluminoferric, a substance containing aluminium and iron, was another common precipitant; lime also was widely used. At the London outfall-works a mixture of lime and ferrous sulphate was used for many years.

The method adopted was as follows. On entering the outfall-works the sewage flowed first through gratings or screens to remove the larger solids. It was then passed slowly through precipitation channels, where it received 4 grains of lime and 1 grain of ferrous sulphate for each gallon passed through the channels. After a channel had been in use for about 60 hours the flow through it was stopped and the contents were allowed 2 hours in which to settle. The liquid was then drawn off and discharged to the river as effluent. A deposit of wet sludge, about 4 ft in depth, remained; this was screened and pumped into sludge-settling channels where it was treated with 20 grains of lime and 10 grains of ferrous sulphate per gallon and again allowed to settle. The top liquid was then drawn off and pumped back into the outfall sewers; the sludge, which still contained about 93 per cent of water, was pumped to specially constructed ships which took it out to sea.

A disadvantage of this system was that as the precipitation channels were rectangular in shape the sludge lying at the bottom had to be pushed or swept to the outlet by men using squeegees. To overcome this drawback a very deep circular tank was used, first at Dortmund in Germany. Its lower part was shaped like a funnel and the sludge automatically slid down to the outlet, from which it was removed as necessary. Many attempts have been made to dry sewage and use it as manure, but its high water-content has made it very difficult to reduce it to a manageable commodity; up to 1900 comparatively little of it was used for agricultural purposes.

BIBLIOGRAPHY

BAZALGETTE, J. W. "The Main Drainage of London" (ed. by J. FORREST). *Min. Proc. Instn civ. Engrs*, **24**, 26, 1865.

BUER, M. C. 'Health, Wealth and Population, 1760–1815.' Routledge, London. 1926.

CHAMBERS'S ENCYCLOPAEDIA. Article: "Sanitation". Newnes, London. 1950.

DAWES, J. C. 'Public Cleansing.' H.M. Stationery Office, London. 1929.

EDINBURGH CITY COUNCIL. 'Main Drainage of the City of Edinburgh.' Edinburgh. 1955.

FINER, S. E. 'The Life and Times of Sir Edwin Chadwick.' Methuen, London. 1952.

JEPHSON, H. 'The Sanitary Evolution of London.' Unwin, London. 1907.

LIVERPOOL CITY COUNCIL. 'A Century of Progress.' 1947.

LONDON COUNTY COUNCIL. 'The Centenary of London's Main Drainage, 1855–1955.' Staples Press, London. 1955.

17

ROADS TO *c* 1900

R. J. FORBES

I. ROAD POLICY, 1600–1775

DURING the fifteenth and sixteenth centuries roads deteriorated rapidly. Those employed to make them or keep them in repair were ignorant farmers and uncouth forced labourers. The funds for repairs were scanty and new roads were rarely made. The oldest known technical document on road-building is a police ordinance of the Jülich-Berg (western Germany) district, of 1554. It states that timber, stones, and faggots found along the road could be used for repairs. It lays some stress on drainage by ditches, and specifies that the centre of the road should be well above the level of the ditches.

The pernicious use of bundles of faggots in building and repairing roads persisted up to the eighteenth century. Such fascines were used together with stones to fill pot-holes, but in central Europe even new roads were built on layers of fascines, which were believed to improve the drainage of the subsoil and to increase the carrying capacity of the road surface. However, more and more people voiced their doubts about the use of this material, and at Glatz (now Klodzko) the use of fascines was forbidden in 1767; in other parts of Germany fascine foundations were still laid as late as 1787. Fortunately, several factors were at work to improve road-building:

(*a*) a revival of interest in scientific road-building;
(*b*) the coming of wheeled traffic and an increase in travel;
(*c*) the growth of central authorities and their need of good roads; and
(*d*) the creation of administrative bodies dealing with roads and transport.

(*a*) The revival of interest in scientific road-building was part of the consequence of the renewed study of the documents and monuments of antiquity. Prominent Renaissance architects stressed the building of better roads. Thus Andreas Palladio (1518–80) put forward a well designed road-plan for cities (figure 294). His contemporary Vincenzo Scamozzi (1552–1616) considered that rural roads should be elevated well above the subsoil water-level on each side; that they should be straight and have an ample width; and that they should be constructed of durable materials. Other Italian authors, notably Castelli (1577–

1644), wrote much on the same lines; most of their ideas were inspired by Vitruvius. A more original contribution is the essay (*c* 1587) by Guido Toglietta describing the interaction of wheel, the 'destructor', and road, the 'resistor'. Toglietta describes the construction of cobble pavements, but favours a foundation of gravel carrying a road surface of stone, sand, and mortar, a type that would demand frequent repairs, though cheaper than the solid ancient Roman roads.

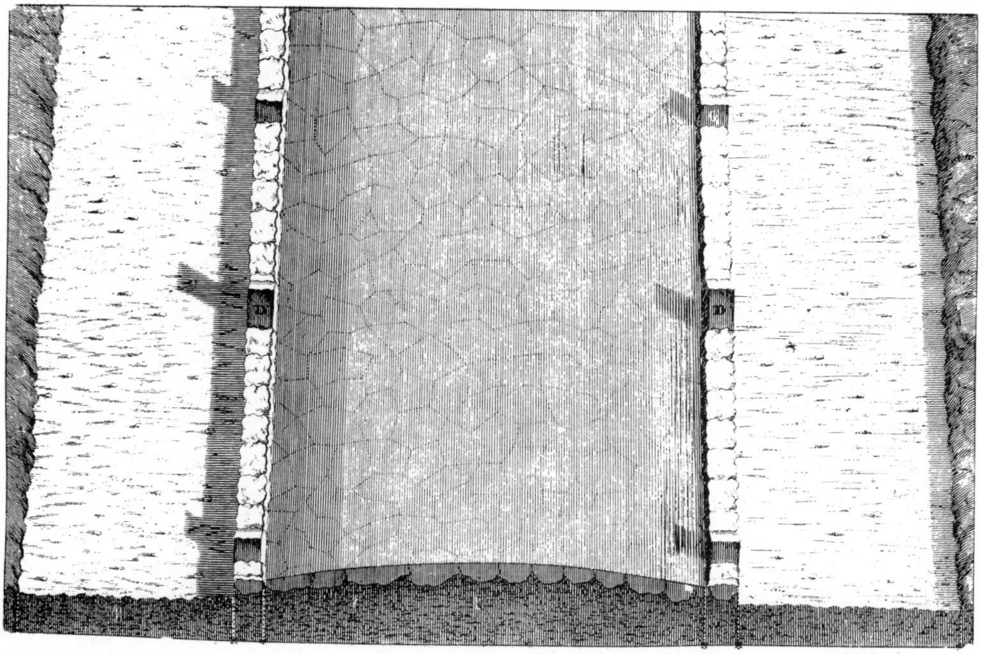

FIGURE 294—*Palladio's plan of a road. The centre, for pedestrians, was paved so that the edges of the stones met perfectly and the rain could run off. The sides, for carriages and cattle, were of sand and fine gravel. The stones along the edge were to help horsemen to mount, and the larger stones* (D) *marked the distance from Rome.*

These Roman roads stimulated engineers to invent new constructions. This started with the discovery by a Rheims lawyer, Nicolas Bergier (1567–1623), of remains of Roman roads in his garden. He studied them carefully and started to collect from ancient texts and archaeological reports data which he published in his *Histoire des grands chemins de l'Empire Romain* (plate 35) [1]. This book attracted the attention of many authorities who had for generations been plagued by merchants clamouring for better roads. The Duke of Sully, Henri IV's minister in charge of roads, was particularly interested (figures 295 and 296).

An important French handbook on road-building by Gautier (1660–1737) [2], engineer of the Corps des Ponts et Chaussées, proposed a road-body enclosed by stone walls and built from earth and hard-core, well rammed before traffic was admitted (plate 33 A). Like most French engineers of his day he paid great attention to good alignment, which was quite possible by that time since contemporary geodetical instruments were very accurate [3].

(*b*) The second powerful factor in the revival of road-building was the increase in wheeled traffic, largely due to oversea trade, which induced a notable increase in travel. Vehicles were becoming more suitable for travelling. Wagons carrying merchandise would take passengers as well. By 1500, covered wheeled vehicles called chares, cars, chariots, or whirlicotes were used, though only by ladies. The development of vehicles increased, but even in 1550 there were only three coaches in Paris, one for the queen, one for Diane de Poitiers, and one for a gentleman, too fat to ride a horse, who had the king's permission to drive in a coach. In 1555 the first coach was built in England after a continental model, and in 1556 Mary I obtained one. The state coach for Elizabeth I was imported from the Netherlands in 1564.

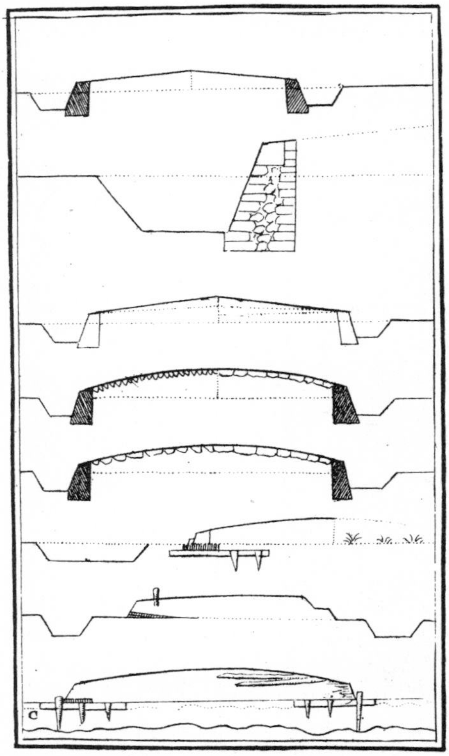

FIGURE 295—*Cross-sections of various eighteenth-century French roads.*

The early wheelwrights adopted wide-rimmed heavy wheels to minimize wear and tear from the very rough road surface. Iron tyres had been used by the Romans. In the Middle Ages it became customary to stud wheels with iron nails, in the belief that they gave a better grip on the road. The designs of the wheels were adjusted to suit the type of road surface (figure 297). The urge for rapid wheeled transport produced a host of pamphlets and books on wheel-design in the eighteenth century. Good road-building techniques were not yet forthcoming, and it was believed that better coach-construction, more wheels, and above all wider rims, would provide more comfortable travel and do less damage to the roads. During the seventeenth century coaches became so common that public services started in several towns.

The earliest steel springs bearing the body of the coach were C-shaped tempered steel strips. They were introduced about 1665. The heavy state coaches of the eighteenth century needed stronger springs. Elliptic steel springs came into use early in the nineteenth century. Then the new principle of eliminating the connecting-pole of front and rear axles and introducing cross-beds connecting the two axles with the body of the coach, discovered by Obadiah Elliot of Lambeth (1804), made more rational coach-design possible. In the later eighteenth century two-wheeled vehicles such as the cabriolet or cab were introduced, and the wheels were fitted with brakes.

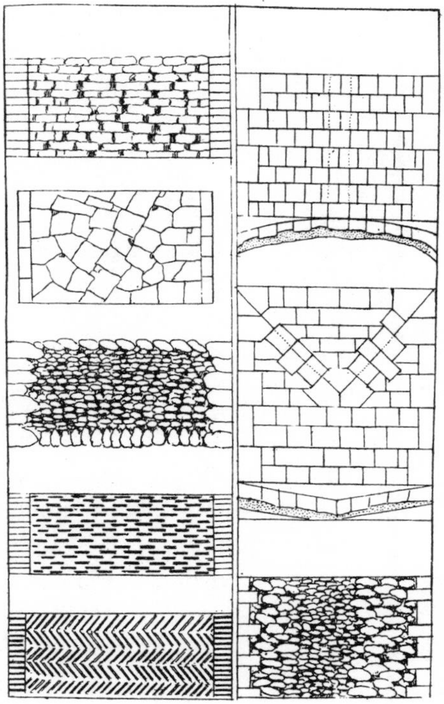

FIGURE 296—*Plans of various eighteenth-century road surfaces in Paris.*

There was as a result no longer any need to increase the width of wheels to lessen stresses on the road surfaces. Stage-wagons (plate 33 B) with 16-in tyres had been in use; in the reign of George II the average was 9 in, and they were very destructive of the poor roads. An attempt was made to control them by legislation, but the designers started to build bevelled wheels so that no more than a rim-width of 3 inches actually touched the road.

In 1845 R. W. Thomson designed the first pneumatic tyre, but the state of the roads and the imperfect rubber produced in those days prevented the success of this happy solution of the wheel-impact problem. Thomas Hancock then introduced solid rubber tyres for carts (1847), and Thévenet (1865) adapted them to the early bicycle. By 1890 Thomson's invention was so completely forgotten that Dunlop's reintroduction of the pneumatic tyre was hailed as something novel (vol V, ch 31).

(*c*) The growth of central authorities also encouraged improved wheeled traffic, and was a third important factor in the renaissance of road-building. Travelling became increasingly fashionable, and this habit promoted the publication of good guides and maps (plate 34). In 1553 Robert Estienne published his famous *Guides des chemins de France*, and other countries rapidly followed suit.

Estienne's book revealed that although France already had a road-system of some 17 000 miles it was in a deplorable state. Even the 'royal' roads were paved for only a few miles beyond the towns. Traffic consisted mostly of pack- and saddle-horses, droves of cattle, pigs, and sheep, and a few wagons and carts. The steep pack-horse bridges, often built by rich and charitable persons, showed clearly that wheeled traffic was still a minor factor.

(*d*) The creation of administrative bodies for roads and transport by the monarchs who favoured a more vigorous road-building policy encountered much opposition. Guides, often working hand in hand with robbers, exacted money from the traveller to lead him by the most practicable way. The highway, sometimes hardly recognizable from the open field, was more a right of way from place to place than a surfaced road. Innkeepers considered that travelling was becoming too fast and that they would lose by good roads. Landlords set their faces against improvement, for they enjoyed a right to seize whatever fell upon the road, such as the contents of an upset wagon.

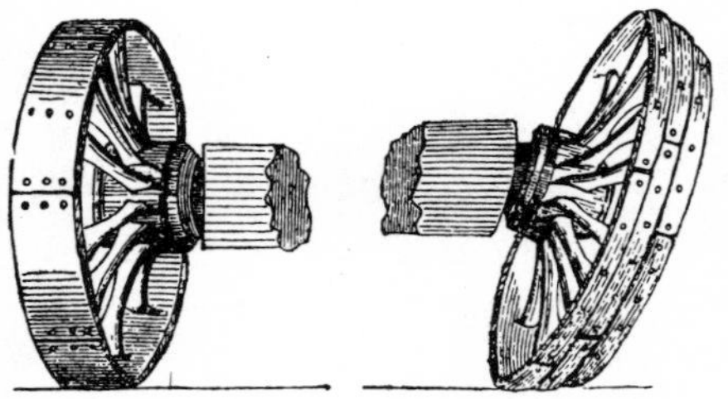

FIGURE 297—*Types of wheels;* (left) *cylindrical and* (right) *conical.*

Everywhere governments were confronted with a lack of expert labour and competent supervisors, for the roads often had to be rebuilt completely. In England, for instance, a series of statutes—all repealed and re-enacted by a codifying act of 1766—tried to cope with the difficult situation. The government, confronted with the problem of financing road-construction, wavered between a toll system and statutory labour. Queen Mary's Act of 1555, for example, laid the duty of financing the roads on the cities and parishes along them. Each parish was to appoint two surveyors and was subject to heavy penalties for neglect of the roads. This system, however, had already failed in the Middle Ages. The fact that there were so few properly paved roads proves the inability of the authorities to raise the necessary money and to enforce the four days of labour imposed by law upon each parishioner (1563), notwithstanding the heavy fines for default (1670). The surveyors obtained some legal backing from the Justices of the Peace (1654) and the extent of statutory labour and the fines were revised (1691), but it was all of little avail.

Statutory labour (plate 36 A) was universally disliked and could never be satisfactorily enforced. Efforts to supplement it by the proceeds of a rate were similarly a failure. The picture of the condition of the roads which John Ogilby draws in his 'Britannia' (1675), the first good English road-book, shows the menacing state of affairs. On the other hand, the government was greatly helped in its efforts to establish better roads by the union of the English and Scottish crowns (1603), and the establishment of the first parliament of Great Britain (1707). The seventeenth and eighteenth centuries saw a rapid growth of London and other ports, and a gradual rise of local distributive and manufacturing centres that heralded the industrial revolution.

The proper solution—the formation of a strong administrative and technical body to educate engineers and direct road-building, the fourth and final factor in the revival of road-building—was found in France. There the first organized system of trenched roads was initiated about 1720.

In France there was a complete absence of any authoritative planning in the days of Robert Estienne, who often had to indicate in his road-book that there were dangerous forests or robbers at two, three, or four miles from a particular spot. Henri IV made a brave attempt to cope with the situation. In 1599 he created the post of *Grand Voyer de France*, in order to centralize all road building and repairing activities: Sully was the first to hold it. In each province local lieutenants were nominated to deal with the situation (1604), and in 1607 the first highway code defined the duties of the Grand Voyer. The provincial Voyers were to inspect their own provinces and to report on the situation of the roads every year. The diverting of toll-money from road-repairing was strictly forbidden. The state helped the provinces in financing road-building by lending them money, to be repaid from the salt tax.

Unfortunately the post of Grand Voyer was suppressed by Louis XIII in 1621, but it was re-established in 1645. In 1661 Colbert was thoroughly impressed by the results: many roads had been repaired and new ones created, and the general state of the road-system allowed the creation of a service of state coaches in 1664. Colbert combined the functions of Grand Voyer and that of Comptroller-General of Finances, and in this dual capacity gave a further impetus to road-building. The administration of roads was entrusted to special commissioners, and royal grants were given for each new road-project. Many country roads were paved with stone setts, the so-called *pavés du roi.*

Towards the end of the reign of Louis XIV the wars demanded too much money and road-building suffered severely. The recovery under Louis XV was crowned by a very important step, namely the creation in 1716 of the *Corps des Ponts et Chaussées* (ch 15), a body of road and bridge experts and engineers formed to supervise public works. This was the first body of civil engineers in Europe maintained by a government, and it gave France the leadership in this field during the eighteenth century. Many accomplished engineers joined and led it. The early years of the *Corps* were not happy, but it was reorganized in 1726 and again in 1750 and 1754.

A training-school also was created, which was to become even more famous. Daniel Trudaine (1703–69), a French administrator, and Jean Perronet (1708–94), an engineer of Swiss origin, put into effect the royal decree of 1738 which established such a school. In February 1747 the *École des Ponts et Chaussées* was opened, with Perronet as its first director. The school was directed by the department of home affairs, and fifty promising young scholars were selected to study at it; all the famous French engineers of the eighteenth century were trained there.

Both *Corps* and *École* had the steady support of the minister Turgot (1727–81). Decrees of 1705 and 1720 had ordered the roads to be laid out as avenues. In 1730 it was decided to call upon the population and to institute statutory labour, as there was not enough labour available for road-building; but even under such trained supervisors as were now available labour of this kind was bound to fail in the long run. Turgot soon realized that only paid labour would yield adequate results and in 1776 he abolished statutory labour. He was, however, forced to resign in 1777, and this unpopular form of labour was temporarily re-established; it was finally abolished in 1789, an example that, unfortunately, other countries did not follow until many years later.

By a decree of 6 February 1776 the *routes nationales* were defined and classified. The first-class roads were those leading from Paris to the principal cities; they were to be 42 m wide 'between the fences'. Second-class, 36-m, roads led from the principal cities in one province to those in another. Third-class, 30-m, roads connected the principal towns in one and the same province. Fourth-class, 24-m, roads connected smaller towns and villages. By then, France had some 25 000 miles of highways, half of which were being rebuilt or aligned. During the reign of Napoleon this system of national roads was revised; some roads were to be financed by the state, others by the provinces and towns. There was further legislation in 1836, 1851, and 1852.

During the French Revolution (1789–99) the roads were again neglected, but Napoleon was particularly interested in road-building for strategic purposes. Even in his day, however, ordinary road-traffic found it difficult to maintain an average of 15 miles a day, and the intrinsic cost of road-transport of goods was 8 to 12 times as high as at present.

II. ROAD-BUILDING, 1775–1830

In the meantime Pierre Trésaguet (1716–94) had developed a new system of road-construction which was to be introduced throughout France about 1775 (figure 298 B). Early in the eighteenth century the French road-makers had worked under the inspiration of Bergier and Gautier, who insisted on good drainage and a solid foundation (figure 298 A). A road trench was excavated, some 18 ft wide, and two or more layers of stones were laid flat, by hand, on the bottom of the excavation. On this foundation a layer of small stones was placed and rammed down, and the surface of the road was formed and completed with a finishing coat of stones broken smaller than those immediately beneath. The depth of the causeway, protected by large stones along the sides, was some 18 in at the middle and 12 in at the sides. The use of statutory labour working only in spring and autumn made roads of this thickness necessary in order that they might last through the intervals between repairs. With less depth they would have been cut through and totally destroyed by the deep ruts formed during the intervening months.

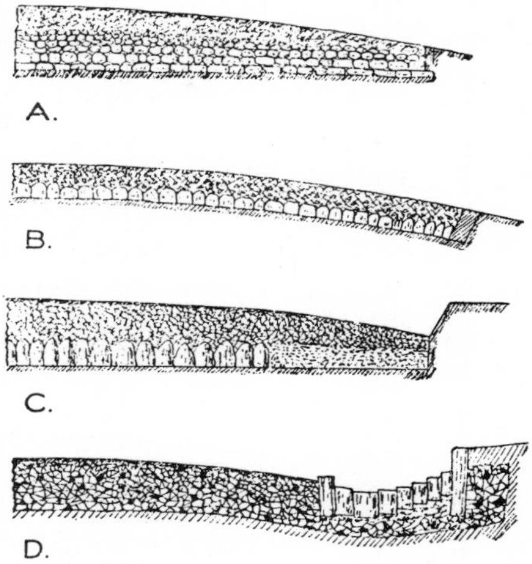

FIGURE 298—*Cross-sections of various roads.* (A) *French, previous to 1775.* (B) *Trésaguet (1764). The foundation layer, which was parallel to the road surface, was formed of large stones placed on edge and hammered in. The next layer was of smaller stones, also hammered in, and the surface, which was curved, was of small hard stones.* (C) *Telford (1824). A layer of large stones was placed edgeways on a level bed. Smaller stones were then added, to a depth of 7 in at the centre and sloping off to 3 in deep 15 ft away. The centre 4 ft were covered with small stones, well trodden down by horses. Finally the whole road was covered with 1 to 1½ in of good clean gravel.* (D) *McAdam* (c *1820*). *No large stones were used, the only foundation being the well drained natural soil. A layer of hand-broken stones, about 1½ inches in diameter and none weighing more than 6 oz, was spread over and worked in. No binding material was used.*

Such stone highways had been built in other parts of Europe also. In the 1730s several German states issued ordinances prescribing such constructions. Swabia in 1737 demanded 12-m highways, the centre part, of 8 m, to be of a construction identical with the French one. Similar constructions were introduced in Hesse (1746), Treves (1753), Westphalia (1769), Weimar (1779), and Saxony (1781).

Trésaguet was not satisfied with this heavy construction. The foundation was often laid with little attention to the level of the subsoil water. Good drainage and proper selection of materials seemed essential to him. He thought that the hard-core and rubble employed were too uneven in quality, and he disapproved of a foundation that, by not running parallel to the road surface, became unnecessarily and wastefully deep in the middle of the road. He believed that he could reduce the depth of the road-bed to 9–10 in from side to side, which would lower the cost to less than one-half. He says:

the bottom of the foundation is to be made parallel to the surface of the road. The first bed of the foundation is to be placed on edge, and not on the flat, in the form of the rough pavement, and consolidated by beating with a large hammer, but it is necessary for the stones to be even with one another. The second bed is to be likewise arranged by hand, layer by layer, and beaten and broken coarsely with a large hammer, so that the stones may wedge together and no empty space remain. The last bed, 3 inches thick, to be of pieces broken to about the size of a small walnut with a hammer on one side of a sort of anvil, and thrown upon the road with a shovel to form a curved surface. Great care must be taken to choose the hardest stone for the last bed, even if it be necessary to go to more distant quarries than those which furnish the stone for the body of the road.

The object of the lower course of large stones was to separate the wearing-surface from the sub-strata, rather than to form a foundation for the road. Trésaguet stated that in Limoges such roads lasted for ten years when constantly maintained, and that they were then as good as when first constructed. His system allowed for proper drainage of the road surface without the excessive camber that made the older roads dangerous. His system was generally adopted by the French road-engineers, and the method spread to central Europe, Switzerland, and Sweden; it was later imitated by Telford (figure 298 C), and it inspired McAdam (figure 298 D).

The rise of absolute monarchy and of economic nationalism in eighteenth-century Europe promoted road-building in other countries as well. In Germany political dissension and the division of the country into many states, each too limited financially to execute a good road-building plan and all jealous of their own rights, were the principal arresting factors. Thus even in 1816 Prussia could claim only 500 miles of good roads.

The rulers of Austria were active road-builders during the eighteenth century [4]. Charles VI (1711–40) started by having a *chaussée* built from Vienna to Trieste and another from Karlstadt to Fiume. Road-building then stopped for some time because of the wars, but it was resumed by Maria Theresa about 1760 and continued under Joseph II (1780–90), to be resumed again in Napoleonic times. The impetus came from France. The earlier roads were built by military engineers, but the state slowly built up a central administrative body of road-commissions directing the work in each of the states under Habsburg rule.

In Russia road-building was now begun. From 1720 to 1746 over 450 miles of road were built to connect St Petersburg (Leningrad) with Moscow, and in 1781 the great Siberian highway from Moscow to Perm, Tobolsk, and Irkutsk was started. The first macadam road-surface (p 532) was laid on the highway connecting Tsarskoe Selo (residence of the Czars) and Gatchine during the reign of Paul (1797).

In the Low Countries road-building was stimulated by the Austrian authorities. In the north, brick roads were often made, for the Dutch cities had already long been paved with the 'clincards'[1] that John Evelyn admired. However, organized road-building did not start in this part of Europe before the time of Napoleon.

Farther north, road-building was sporadically attempted in Scandinavia, but at that period sea-traffic was dominant, and in Sweden the use of canals postponed the development of roads until well into the nineteenth century. Little, too, was done in Italy [5], then politically divided, though several popes concerned themselves with the maintenance of the old Roman road-system, even establishing a tax to pay for such roads in the Papal States. In the Balkans and Spain road-building did not start until much later.

The Alpine roads regained their importance by the end of the eighteenth century (plate 36B). The Roman roads over the Alps had been totally neglected, but the passes with their sharp ascents and descents remained important trade-routes. The passes were used fairly continuously for foot-passengers and for pack-animals. A few monasteries and cities occasionally undertook their repair. The monastery on the St Bernard, founded in 962, yearly fed and lodged 20 000–22 000 pilgrims; that on the St Gothard, founded in 1331, roughly half as many. Driving over the Alps was impossible. The building of highways under such conditions was too much for the earlier generations of road-engineers.

In 1591 the Duke Charles Emanuel of Savoy made a mule-trail through the Tenda Pass; this was later (1782) extended into a carriage road. Then the Emperor Joseph II made the road through the Arlberg Pass (1782–5), but it had to be repaired again in 1793. The Mönchberg Pass had been made negotiable for carts and wagons by Sigismund, archbishop of Salzburg (1765–7). However, Napoleon was the first to make proper Alpine highways. Swiss engineers like Lucas Voch understood their task but funds were lacking. After the conquest of the country by Napoleon centralization set in. The Swiss engineer Guisan, inspector of roads and bridges, had effective plans for the improvement of the roads. The Montgenèvre–Mont Cenis road was taken in hand by the end of 1797,

[1] Dutch *klinker*, *klinckaerd*, a hard type of brick.

and was reconstructed between 1803 and 1810. The Simplon road was built by Nicolas Céard (1747–1821) between Brigue and Domodossola, a stretch of 48 miles on which two brigades of French engineers worked. This reconstruction period lasted until 1830. After some thirty years another two decades of building began, to be stopped by the advent of the Alpine railways (1880); the roads again received attention when the motor-car came to these regions about 1907.

III. THE COACHING AGE, TELFORD, AND McADAM

The second half of the eighteenth century thus saw a general improvement in the highway system, though it failed to meet the demands of the rapidly increasing traffic. In Great Britain there was no central educational system for engineers, and the civil engineers trained their pupils on the road itself. The industrial revolution called for cheap and rapid transport of goods. Scotland was well served by a system of military roads built by General Wade after the rebellion of 1715 (figure 299), but in England the state of the roads found many critics. In 1749 John Shapleigh, in his 'Highways . . . a treatise showing the hardship and inconvenience of presenting or indicting parishes', pointed out the difficulties of bringing negligent surveyors and other officials to book. A cartoon of the period depicts a sailor with a wooden leg beside a stage-coach. Asked whether he wants a lift, he replies: 'No, I am in a hurry!' Arthur Young in his 'Six Months' Tour through the North of England' (1770) speaks of the 'infernal' Wigan road. The costs of carriage weighed heavily on prices, and it was not exceptional for timber to take a year to reach the coast. By contrast, a German visitor like Moritz (1782) found the roads around London incomparably good.

By the time the earlier British road-statutes had been given embodiment in the Road Act of 1766 (p 524), the system of turnpikes was generally accepted, and trusts were allowed to levy tolls provided the yield was partly devoted to the maintenance of the road. The first turnpike, on the Great North Road, was authorized during Charles II's reign (1663). There were seventy-one Turnpike Acts between 1720 and 1730. By 1829, 3783 turnpike trusts had been established, covering some 20 000 miles of highways. These turnpikes were not always erected with discrimination; they were the bane of travellers and their evasion by roundabout lanes was a favourite pastime. Nevertheless the turnpike trusts were for long accepted as the best successors to the hated statutory labour system. Indeed, about 1760 the number of roads and bridges began to increase and their quality grew better. In 1809 over £2 000 000 was spent on road-repairs by the trusts. On such roads the first steam-carriages made their experimental runs.

The failure of the turnpike trusts was mainly due to wretched administration and heavy capital charges. On the London–Holyhead road 23 trusts operated. Only half of the money collected was spent on the roads, and the debts of the trusts accumulated. By the nineteenth century taxation had killed voluntary effort at road-building. In 1829 the trusts responsible for 1119 miles of roads were expending £85 a mile against a revenue of £73 a mile. Their reign was over when the General Highways Act of 1835 created a new parish organization for highway-building, abolished statutory labour, and arranged maintenance.

Whatever blame may be laid on the turnpike trusts, they did create a better road-system. This is obvious from the growth of traffic. They made regular coach services possible. The new road surfaces made by Metcalf, Telford, and McAdam reduced the camber of the roads and drained them properly. Fewer coaches now overturned, and their speed was increased in proportion to the increased safety.

By 1834 English coaches drove at an average of 9–10 miles an hour, as compared with the 6 miles of the French *malle-poste*. Severe winter weather was the only serious cause of dislocation. In 1784 a strictly scheduled mail-coach system was started; armed guards protected it from highwaymen, and great speed was effected. The mail was carried from London to Birmingham in 12 hours, to Exeter in 17¼ hours. Now at last was speed back again to the limit imposed by equine capacity.

It is curious to read of protests in 1837 against the speed of the coaches in Britain—that travelling had become as dangerous as ever owing to the loads piled on the vehicles, and that the improved roads offered a temptation to fast driving. These better road-surfaces were the creation of great English road engineers working for the turnpike trusts and for the government.

Telford (1757–1834), originally a journeyman stonemason, was one of the great engineers of his generation. He is still remembered for his beautiful bridge over the Menai Straits (p 459) on the London–Holyhead road to Ireland. He had reconstructed the Shrewsbury–Holyhead section of the road, choosing the Trésaguet system, but over the hand-laid foundation course he applied only a fairly thin set of layers of chips (figure 298 B) [6]. In his own words:

> Upon the level bed prepared for the road materials the bottom course, or layer of stone, is to be set by hand in the form of a close, firm pavement. They are to be set on the broadest edges, lengthwise across the road, and the breadth of the upper beds is not to exceed 4 inches in any case. All the irregularities of the upper part of the said pavement are to be broken off by a hammer, and all the interstices to be filled with stone chips, firmly wedged together by hand with a light hammer. The middle 18 feet of pavement is

to be coated with hard stone as nearly cubical as possible, broken to go through a 2½-inch ring, to a depth of 6 inches, 4 of these 6 inches to be first put on and worked by traffic, after which the remaining 2 inches can be put on. The work of setting the paving-stones must be executed with the greatest care and strictly according to the foregoing directions, or otherwise the stone will become loose and in time may work up to the surface of the road. When the work is properly executed, no stone can move; the whole of the material to be covered with 1½ inches of good gravel, free from clay or earth.

Telford had wide experience of road-building in Shropshire and reconstructed many of General Wade's roads in Scotland (figure 299). He was very careful in selecting the small stones for the top strata, and differed from Trésaguet in making the road-bed level and in forming the crown of the road (with a fall of 1 : 60) with the stone itself, rather than making the finished surface parallel to the base. Most of his contemporaries did not like his use of a final layer of gravel, which 'by sinking between the stone diminishes absolute solidity to the surface of the road, lets in water and frost and contributes to preventing complete consolidation of the mass of broken stones'. This is partly correct, since at that time no good rollers were available. The cost of Telford's roads was relatively high because of the heavy foundation, and because when not properly and regularly repaired the top layers proved too thin for the wear of traffic.

The next step, combining proper drainage and low cost, was taken by John McAdam (1756–1836) of Ayr, who went into business in New York (1770–83) but returned to Britain to become deputy-lieutenant of Ayrshire and a Road Trustee, often spending his own money on road repairs and experiments. He was called to Bristol in 1789 and there tried different ways of building roads. By 1814 he had thoroughly inspected 30 000 miles of roads and spent some £10 000 of his own money on road construction. In 1815 he became surveyor-general of the Bristol Road Trusts, and started rebuilding their 180 miles of road according to his own system. His basic principles were:

That it is the native soil which really supports the weight of traffic; that while it is preserved in a dry state, it will carry any weight without sinking and that it does in fact carry the road and carriages also; that this native soil must be previously made quite dry and a covering impenetrable to rain must then be placed over it in that dry state; that the thickness of the road should only be regulated by the quantity of material necessary to form such impervious covering and never by any reference to its own power of carrying weight.

He believed that he could substitute for the costly hand-laid foundation a thin set of layers, less than 10 inches in all, of broken and graded chips.

As no artificial road can be made so good as the natural soil in a *dry state*, it is neces-

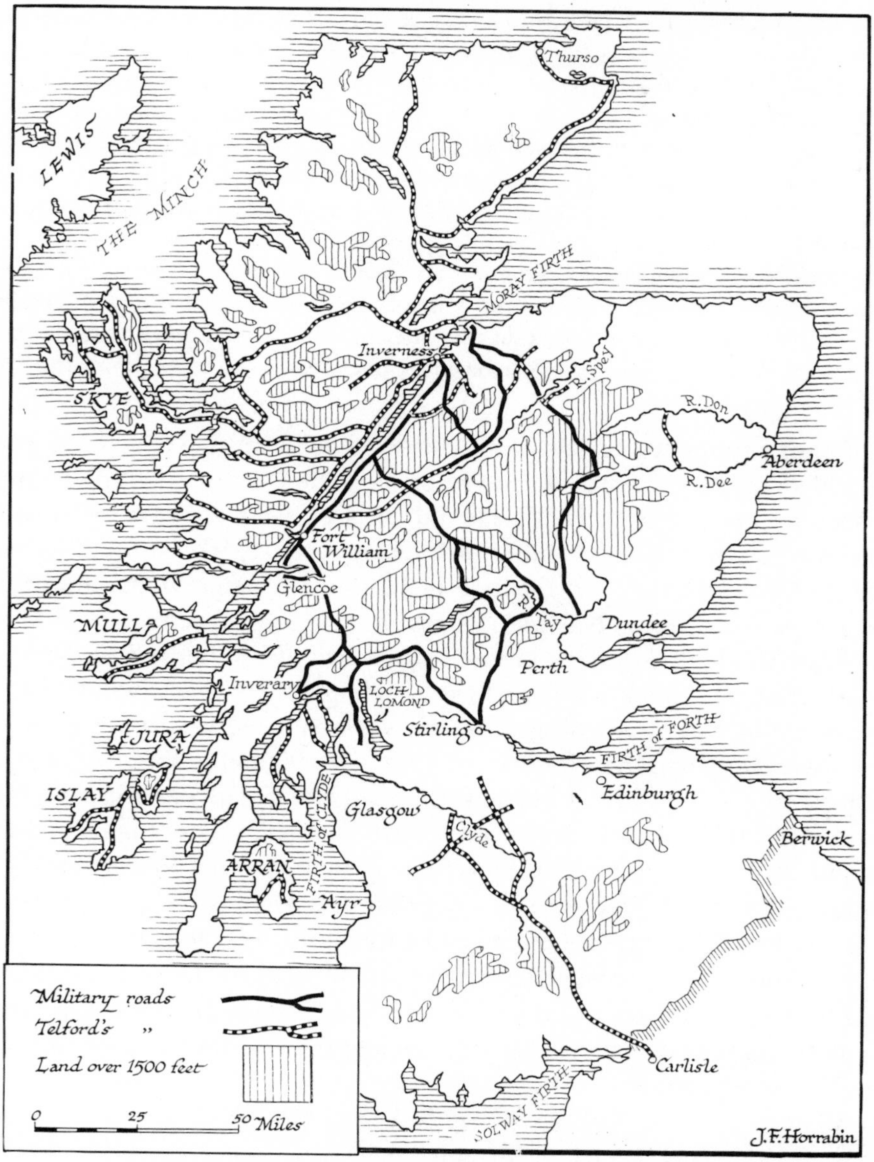

FIGURE 299—*Map of Telford's roads and military roads in Scotland.*

sary to preserve this state. The first operation should be the reverse of digging a trench. The road should not be sunk below, but raised above, the adjacent ground; that there be a sufficient fall to take off the water, so that it should be some inches below the level of the ground upon which the road is, either by making the drains to lower ground or, if that be not practicable from the nature of the country, then the soil upon which the road is to be laid, must be raised some inches above the level of the water.

Having secured the soil from *under* water, the road-maker is next to secure it from rain water, by a solid road, of clean, dry stone, or flint, so selected, prepared and laid, as to be impervious to water; and this cannot be effected, unless the greatest care be taken, that no earth, clay, chalk, or other matter, that will hold water, be mixed with the broken stone; which must be so laid, as to unite by its own angles into a firm, compact, inpenetrable body.

The thickness of such a road is immaterial; as to its strength for carrying weight, this object is obtained by a dry surface, over which the road is to be placed as a covering, to preserve it in that state: experience having shewn, that if water passes through a road and fills the native soil, the road, whatever its thickness, loses its support and goes to pieces [7].

McAdam's proposals, given in an abbreviated form above, were so revolutionary that there was a parliamentary investigation before any great sum was expended on his type of work [8]. He did not seek to lay down a rigid rule for road construction, and the number of layers was to depend on the thickness of the road. The important thing was to make the road impervious, so that water could not penetrate to its bed and destroy its carrying-capacity.

McAdam's contemporaries were well aware that he did not invent the method of breaking stones which had long been practised in Sweden, Switzerland, and other countries, but the grading of stones was welcomed by the workmen, who set their wives and children to work at breaking stones and profited byMcAdam's insistence on good grading. McAdam enforced the use of the 2-in ring for the measurement of stones, which he said should not weigh more than 6 oz. 'Every stone put into a road, which exceeds an inch in any of its dimensions, is mischievous', as it would increase the permeability and might be dislodged by wheels. As he did not use rollers he advocated applying the new stones in thin courses, allowing time between successive applications for the metal to be compacted by traffic. A three-stage application was suggested as desirable, and he particularly insisted on the necessity of keeping the road well shaped during the intervals of compaction.

McAdam sought also to keep the road as level as possible and to avoid sharp ascents and descents, which were detrimental to proper drainage. He often reconstructed older roads that had a proper foundation. Nowadays his idea of a soft, yielding foundation for the road is not accepted as good practice. But the older Telford foundations were very expensive and hence the custom of building a Telford–McAdam road grew up; that is, a road with a Telford base and a McAdam wearing-surface. For the repair and reconstruction of older roads

McAdam's system was excellent, and thus his name became attached to the 'water-bound macadam[1] road' that dominated in the nineteenth century. However, the filling of the interstices of the top layer by washing in sharp sand was not McAdam's invention and he actually condemned it. It was devised by Richard Edgeworth (1744–1817), whose road-building handbook was much praised by his contemporaries [9].

McAdam was appointed surveyor-general of roads (1827). In his first book he had indicated 'the state of the public roads, the alarmingly increasing debt, and the loose state of the accounts of the several Trusts' as the best proofs of the defects of the turnpike system. In his last book he proposed to centralize the administration and construction of roads under a committee of experts. Road-builders, he held, should not have other occupations and should be adequately paid for work that benefits agriculture, trade, and traffic. In Parliament it was suggested that the days of the road were over, now that the railways had come, but nevertheless American engineers came to study his results. His books were translated into several languages and had a profound influence in Europe. By the end of the nineteenth century some 90 per cent of the principal highways were macadamized.

The water-bound macadam system was further improved after 1876, when a third course was generally applied. The use of steam-rollers at this time effected much greater compaction, and justified the belief in the fairly light road-construction as urged by McAdam. A century of public pressure and hard work had gone by since Metcalf had obtained his first contract, but the results were encouraging:

LENGTH OF METALLED ROADS IN 1868–9

	Length (thousand miles)	*Area of country (thousand square miles)*	*Population (millions)*
United Kingdom	160	123	31
France	100	210	38
Prussia	56	140	24
Spain	11	198	16

IV. THE ADVENT OF THE RAILWAY AND THE MOTOR-CAR (1830–1900)

Many of McAdam's contemporaries feared to abolish the hand-laid foundation, and protested violently against such new-fangled methods. However, McAdam's principle of preventing water from reaching the foundation was

[1] In this form McAdam's name has become a part of the English language.

sound, and his system proved its worth. Was it necessary to keep the hand-laid foundation in the case of wet foundations? Thomas Hughes gave the proper solution in his 'Art of the Construction and Repair of Highways' (1838). The metalled surface of the road should cover not only the middle strip of the road but its full width, and the road-metal should be applied to an even depth over this full width. Proper drainage should be effected by digging ditches 5 ft deep and 2 ft wide alongside the road so that the water could be drained to the full depth of the foundation, leaving the latter in its natural state as far as possible. If necessary, drains in the form of earthenware pipes or trenches of compacted rubble should cross the road-bed to remove any water that in freezing might force the road up. His methods were applied to the macadam road with good results.

The French and English variants of McAdam and Telford's constructions spread over Europe. The older roads were mostly macadamized, stone setts or cobbles being sometimes used. Napoleon's conquests were the start of many national road-organizations in Europe, for he was very conscious of the strategic importance of roads. His ideal seems to have been a tripartite road, the middle paved with cobbles for the artillery, one side having a water-bound macadam surface for the infantry, and the other side carrying an earth-road, called the summer road, for the cavalry. Though few roads of this type were built, Napoleon certainly promoted scientific road-building between 1804 and 1814. His national roads still form the core of many highway systems and he made the Alpine roads accessible again to wheeled traffic.

Slowly the macadam road penetrated beyond Europe. In Australia there were some 275 miles of metalled roads by 1820, but the building of a proper highway system began much later. In the United States [10] the earliest roads were Indian trails. In 1632 Virginia obtained its first road-law, followed by Massachusetts in 1639. The Maryland law of 1704 provided for a 20-ft road and for road-signs. American development up to 1890 involved repairs by compulsory labour modelled on the statutory labour scheme developed in Britain. This lasted until the advent of the automobile brought more sophisticated road constructions, making skilled labour essential.

The first American turnpikes were built in Virginia, Connecticut, and Maryland. In 1785 a Turnpike Act was passed in Virginia, and a turnpike road was in operation a year later. As there was inadequate provision for repairs it was handed over to the Fairfax and Loudon Turnpike-Road Company, incorporated in 1795 to handle this road from Little River to Alexandria. The company was reorganized in 1802 and rebuilt the old road in 1805, operating it as a toll road for over ninety years. Meanwhile, other roads rapidly followed. In 1808 Albert

Gallatin, Secretary of the Treasury, could report that 770 miles of metalled road had been completed in Connecticut, and that over 3000 miles were under construction in New York State, with hundreds of miles in other states.

Such roads were usually 36 ft wide, but only 15 ft of the width was covered with gravel or pounded stones. Sometimes two courses of broken stone were applied; their size was large and there was no rolling or sprinkling. American engineers studied road-building in the Old World, and very capable men like Gillespie and Gillmore introduced better methods [11]. McAdam's principles were adopted by General Gratiot when repairing the surface of the Cumberland road east of the Ohio river in 1832.

The turnpike companies were in fact the first American public service corporations. In the beginning they made only graded roads; later, stone surfaces of water-bound macadam became the general type. By 1850 most had given up their charters as they were threatened by the canal boom (1810–40) and the railway boom (after 1840). In 1891 the legislature of New Jersey passed the first state-aid law assuming responsibility for part of the initial cost of construction. The era of modern road-building had begun.

Railways had become a serious menace to good road construction in the Old World also. As early as 1839 it was said: 'If the railways yield these supposed commercial advantages, we shall have no reason to regret their superseding stage-coaches.' By 1800 the average highway carried several thousand tons of goods a year, as compared with a thousand tons in the Middle Ages, but the real increase in traffic started only when the steam-engine began to play an important part in the actual manufacture of goods. However, by about 1875 road traffic had been largely displaced by the railways, whose load grew with the increased output of manufactured commodities.

A change came with the advent of the motor-car, which returned traffic to the roads; but before this could happen the engineers had to invent means of consolidating the road surfaces and combating the clouds of dust raised by the tyres. One solution was to secure better compaction during construction, and not to leave this to the action of traffic. The road-building equipment of the earlier phases consisted of tools such as hammers, sieves, spades, wheelbarrows, rammers, and pickaxes. Machines for proper compaction, such as rollers, had been used by the ancients, and in 1619 John Shotbolte proposed to use 'land stearnes, scowrers, trundlers and other strong massy engines . . . in the making and repairing of highways'. The first good roller is illustrated in Leupold's *Theatrum machinarum* of 1725, which pictures a horse-drawn iron roller weighing over a ton (figure 300). In Diderot's *Encyclopédie* (supplementary volume, 1777) is described a two-wheeled roller, with a box for additional stones to increase the weight when desired. In 1787 Louis Alexandre de Cessart (1719–1806) proposed a cast iron horse-drawn roller with a cylinder 8 ft wide and 36 inches in diameter, weighing about 3½ tons. Such rollers were used after 1815 in England, Hanover, and France, but it was feared that the horses or men drawing them would destroy the smooth road-surface before it was sufficiently compacted. However, horse-drawn rollers were gradually introduced in the 1830s. For the initial stage of compaction light types were used, followed by heavier ones when the road had been sufficiently compacted. During compaction sand was washed into the top layer of the macadam road.

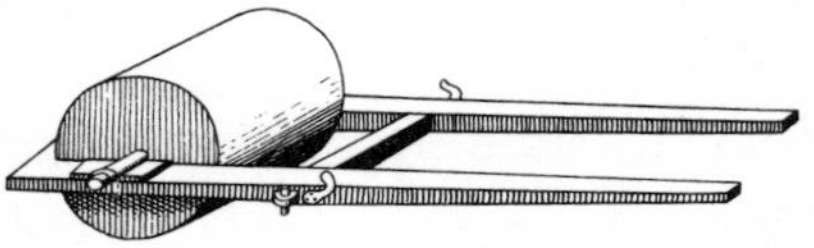

FIGURE 300—*Road-roller as drawn by horses.*

The first steam-driven roller was invented by Lemoine (1859), but its trial run was not a success (1861). Then came Ballaison (1862) with his 17½-ton roller driven by a 5-hp engine; this was produced by Gellerat et Cie of Paris from 1864 onwards, with other models of 8½ and 15 tons respectively. Despite its manifest advantages the steam-roller gained ground only gradually. The earliest British steam-roller was patented by W. E. Batho of Birmingham and W. Clark, chief engineer of the city of Calcutta, in 1863. The first American patent was awarded to Andrew Lindelof of New York in 1873. Aveling & Porter of Rochester, Kent, produced the first effective steam-rollers in 1866, and Green & Sons soon improved upon them (1879). At first glance, these steam-rollers appeared to be three-wheeled, but the roller actually consisted of a pair of cylinders set side by side: this made steering easier.

During the same period good stone-crushers were invented. In McAdam's days stones were broken by hand, and even as late as 1900 this was still economical: it cost no more than 1*s* 3*d* to 2*s* 6*d* a cubic yard. In 1858, however, Eli Whitney Blake, a kinsman of the inventor of the cotton-gin and a manufacturer at New Haven, Connecticut, constructed the first stone-crusher. This treated stones for the roads in Central Park, New York City, which were then being built. It did not meet with enthusiasm, for a prize-winning essay of 1890 still assures us that 'hand-broken stone is much superior to that crushed by a machine, which is generally of irregular shape and seldom cubical, so that it does not readily bind together'. Nevertheless the stone-crusher had come to stay.

Besides new road-building equipment, two new constructions were evolved during the nineteenth century, though they came into common use only after 1900. The first was the concrete road. This began in antiquity, but was forgotten until William Hobson took out an English patent (1827) for grouting a macadam road with lime-mortar. His system found little recognition, though it was exactly the method adopted by the Romans in certain cities. MacNeill used concrete on a stretch of the Highgate–Archway (London) road where the subsoil water-level was fairly high. A 6-in concrete foundation was built as a water-tight base for grouted chips, its surface being roughened to carry the road-surface of macadam (1829). Concrete roads proper had to wait until the invention of Portland cement (p 448).

During the 1850s several concrete roads were built in Austria. The first English concrete road was constructed in 1865. In 1872 the first concrete road in Scotland was built in Edinburgh; France followed four years later with one at Grenoble. In 1887 the Blücher Platz at Breslau received a concrete surfacing, and concrete roads were constructed soon afterwards in Vienna (1898). The first American concrete road was built in 1892 at Bellefontaine, Ohio. Cheap concrete roads were closely bound up with the evolution of machinery to build them, which was first successfully constructed by P. Jantzen of Elbing (then in Germany, now in Poland) in 1879.

The second new-comer was the asphalt road. In 1712 Eyrinis d'Eyrinis, a Greek doctor, discovered the rock-asphalt at Travers near Neuchâtel (Switzerland) and learnt how to blend the powdered rock with hot pitch, making what we now call an asphalt mastic. He also applied his mastic to the making of floors and steps, some of which were examined by Fournel in 1838 and found in excellent state. d'Eyrinis interested a banker, de la Sablonnière, in his exploitation of rock-asphalt and obtained tax-exemption for it in France (1720).

This led others to the discovery of further rock-asphalt at Péchelbronn and Lobsann, Alsace. More thick oil and rock-asphalt were found at Wietze (Hanover), Osmundsberg (Sweden), and in Hungary and Rumania. In 1797 further sources were discovered near Seyssel (France) and mastic was made of it. The earlier work of Sécretan there was revived in 1832 by de Sassenay, who mixed the powdered rock-asphalt with bitumen from natural oil seepages and thus obtained a mastic of better quality. By 1835 his sales had gone up to 1000 tons a year. This asphalt mastic was used for footpaths at Lyons (1810), Geneva (1820), Strasbourg (1822), and other places. The first trials on roads were started on the pavements of the Pont Royal and the Pont du Caroussel in Paris. These were paved with mastic, as also was the Place de la Concorde (1835). Co-operative work by de Sassenay and Équem resulted in the foundation of a company with a capital of £30 000 to exploit the Seyssel rock-asphalt. Eventually, Seyssel regularly produced some 1000 tons of mastic a month. Attempts to introduce it into England met with little success until 1869, when part of Threadneedle

Street was paved with Travers rock-asphalt. This started a boom in asphalt streets in London.

Meanwhile new methods of construction with asphalt had been discovered. In 1849 Mérian observed that powdered rock-asphalt spread from carts became naturally compacted into a good road-surface. At first, he had powdered Travers rock-asphalt brushed and rolled into the interstices of a macadam road between Travers in Switzerland and Pontarlier in France. A few years earlier de Coulaine had covered a fresh macadam surface with hot powdered rock-asphalt and rolled it into a splendid road-surface (Bordeaux–Bayonne, 1837), but the under surface was wet and the trial failed. Malo, however, discovered a way to disintegrate the Travers rock by heating and rolling the powdered rock after spreading it over the road-base. Together with Vaudry he laid over 800 sq m of compressed asphalt in the Rue Bergère, Paris (1854). Its wear over fifteen years proved less than ¼-in. By 1858 compressed asphalt was in common use in Paris.

Travers now became a serious competitor with Seyssel. Asphalt from Limmer, Hanover, began to appear on the English market and Trinidad Lake asphalt also came to the fore, the latter notably in the United States. In 1848, the Earl of Dundonald had started advocating the use of Trinidad Lake asphalt with as much fervour as d'Eyrinis had devoted to Seyssel asphalt, but except for a floor in the Merchants' Exchange Building in Philadelphia it was not used until trial stretches of paving were built of compressed asphalt in front of Newark City Hall in William Street (1871) and in Union Square (1872).

American asphalt-paving was greatly promoted by the work of the Belgian engineer E. J. De Smedt, who used a mixture of sand, limestone-powder (as a filler), and mastic from Ritchie County (Virginia), and thus made the first sand-asphalt. He found other native asphalts in the United States suitable for such mixes. He and Clifford Richardson calculated the percentage of bitumen needed to fill the spaces of the mineral substances and thus obtained a good water-tight road-construction. In Cleveland (1873) a grout consisting of a mix of coal-tar and gravel was used on macadam, but with little success. In St Louis, De Smedt introduced asphalt blocks (1873) and compressed asphalt (1883). New Orleans had its first asphalt road in 1880 and in Philadelphia a few of the streets were asphalt-paved in 1884. The first successful Trinidad Lake asphalt pavement was laid in front of the Capitol in Washington by De Smedt in 1876.

Three types of asphalt roads were thus known before the end of the century: (*a*) compressed asphalt made by rolling rock-asphalt disintegrated by heating and spread on a base; (*b*) mastic asphalt, a mixture of mastic, sand, and a filler, poured on to the road surface and trowelled into shape; and (*c*) sand-asphalt, a hot mixture of bitumen, sand, filler, and sometimes larger stones, designed to leave no voids after compaction and spread and rolled after mixing at a temperature of 150–200° C. The invention of the steam-roller was a vital factor in the making of roads of this kind; they could not otherwise have been built.

Tar also now found use as a road-building material; crude tar was being distilled for the manufacture of solvents and dyes and the residues of heavy tars and pitches became available. Tar-macadam was first made in Nottinghamshire (1832–8), and was used for a section of the London road at Nottingham in 1845. Sheffield (1875) and Liverpool (1879) followed. The first tar roads in the United

FIGURE 301—*The water-cart helped to keep down the dust in the streets of the nineteenth century.*

States were built at Cleveland (1873). At Melbourne a three-layer tar-macadam was made in 1895. This tar-macadam was usually prepared by mixing tar and stones hot, then spreading them and consolidating the road with rollers after cooling. A final coat of sand was usually applied.

Concrete, asphalt, and tar roads came into their own with the advent of the motor-car. This gave road-building a new future, provided road-engineers could produce surfaces that stood up to the new forms of impact of traffic and vehicles. Until then the hammering action of hoof and wheel had been the main form of impact. Motor-traffic, however, with its rubber-tyred wheels, exerted a suction on the road-surface that was detrimental to macadam roads. Clouds of dust consisting of the finer particles sucked up from the interstices of the macadam structure were a great source of annoyance even before this (figure 301).

The obvious course in building new roads was to make them of the dustless concrete or asphalt types. However, something had to be done to cure the dust problem on the extensive network of older macadam roads. In 1902 Guglielminetti experimentally coated with tar an old macadam road near Monte Carlo. This treatment proved excellent, and in the course of the following decades both hot bitumen and tar, or emulsified forms of these materials, were extensively used for such surface-treatments.

V. CITY STREETS AND PAVEMENTS (1730–1900)

The history of city paving runs along much the same line as that of roads; it was the rise of the cities as economic units that determined the search for better streets and the financing of paving in general. Paris started paving its streets in 1184; London made some advance during the thirteenth century, and in 1280 the supervision of paving repairs in each ward was delegated to the aldermen.

In 1443 a road in front of the Savoy Palace was 'substantially performed with Stones and Gravel'. Such loads of new road-material were usually dumped on the old pavement and thus raised its level, to the annoyance of householders. During the sixteenth century most European cities had regular paviours on their pay-roll, for it had proved unsatisfactory to leave the work to the owners of property fronting the roads.

In most German cities a city engineer supervised the repair of street pavements. Cobbles were in common use. They were laid on a foundation of 6–8 in of clean sand, which was to be free from clay or loam to prevent swelling and cracking of the pavement. Methods of levelling had been devised and rollers were sometimes employed. The paviours were generally paid by the square yard of pavement, the footpaths being usually repaired by the city at the expense of the house-owner.

By the sixteenth century increased wheeled traffic in the cities had begun to turn the unpaved surfaces into mud-pools. Each city had to cope with this traffic problem. In London, Smithfield was paved in 1614 'to remove the Scandal the City was obnoxious to on account of its ruinous and dangerous condition; whereby instead of being a service, it was rendered a common nuisance to the City'. New regulations for the paviours were drawn up in 1662. The street gutters were to be covered in; narrow streets with cobble pavements sloping from both sides to an open sewer in the middle and crossed by innumerable transverse gutters were forbidden. Wheeled traffic demanded better pavements, though there were attempts to exclude such traffic from the cities. In Paris the size of the vehicles was limited in 1624, and the number of horses and the maximum weight drawn were prescribed in 1670. In Elizabethan times the number of carts in London was restricted to 420, and most merchandise was transported on pack-horses. In Dutch cities, where water transport was often available, wheeled traffic was completely banned until the eighteenth century. However, such regulations were ineffective in the absence of officers to enforce them.

The paving materials were usually cobble-stones, easily and cheaply available. The pavement was protected by posts at intervals. Paving-stones such as were used in the principal streets of London from 1616 onwards were mostly small and badly laid; after a shower they squirted mud and water when stepped upon. London received its cobble-stones from Guernsey and Kent, its flags from Purbeck. To provide good road-materials many cities enacted ordinances commanding all wheeled traffic to bring into the city a certain number of paving-stones. Even certain American cities like Boston and Washington started to pave some streets with cobbles about 1650, though Philadelphia had no paved street before 1761. During the seventeenth and eighteenth centuries the towns, as growing centres of manufacture and distribution, began to understand the need of rational and well organized paving.

In London, unfortunately, a great opportunity was missed after the Great Fire (1666): the street pattern was not recast (vol III, pp 296–8). In 1765, however, great improvement was effected in Westminster. Signs and posts obstructing traffic were removed, and the streets were raised or lowered to bring them nearer to a level. Footpaths on each side were elevated, defined by kerb-stones, and paved like the floor of a room. Attempts were made to construct a smoother pavement by forming the stones into blocks, at first of no particular shape but giving a comparatively smooth surface. Then the carriage-ways were paved with Scottish granite, gently sloping to the channels at each side. The City of London followed suit fairly quickly, after levying a rate on the annual value or rental of the houses.

Telford, in a report of 1824 (published in the second edition of Henry Parnell's 'Treatise on Roads'), recommended for street pavements a foundation of broken stones, 12 in deep; and above this foundation rectangular paving-stones of granite. The latter were to be worked flat on the face, straight and square on all the sides, so as to fit close together, with a base equal to the face, thus forming in fact an ashlar causeway. The dimensions of the stones were to be:

	Width (*inches*)	*Depth* (*inches*)	*Length* (*inches*)
For streets of the 1st class .	6 to 7½	10	11 to 13
,, ,, 2nd ,, .	5 to 7	9	9 to 12
,, ,, 3rd ,, .	4½ to 6	7 to 8	7 to 11

Stones of dimensions comparable to these were generally employed in street-paving, and proved to possess great durability. They have now been for the most part abandoned in favour of narrower paving-stones, 3 or 4 inches in width, though many secondary streets in London and elsewhere are still paved with 6-in stones. McAdam's system was introduced in streets where the traffic was light, but it did not equal the granite paving.

In a pamphlet written by a Colonel Macirone of London in 1826, when the city had a population of 1 400 000, the author says: 'Florence, Sienna, Milan and other Italian cities have pavements with especially prepared wheel-tracks. These tracks are three feet in width, made of large and particularly well-laid stones. They are about four feet apart, and the space between paved with smaller stones.' He further states that these pavements, as well as those of Rome, are the best that he has seen, but that they would be too expensive for London. The pavements of London, even in the principal streets, were, he says, surprisingly bad, in marked contrast with the excellent turnpikes.

Although Paris had a number of pavements while London was still unpaved, it was many years before its streets were in even a decent condition. Martin Lister, writing of Paris in 1698, says: 'The pavements of the streets are all of square stones of about eight or ten inches thick; that is, as deep in the ground as they are broad on top, the gutters shallow and laid round without edges, which makes the coaches glide easily over them.' Elsewhere he says that the material was a very hard sandstone, and that all the streets and avenues were paved. A distinguished American traveller, Aaron Burr, in 1811 thus describes their condition in a letter to a friend: 'No side-walks—the carts, cabriolets and carriages of all sorts run up to the very houses. Most of the streets are paved as Albany and New York were before the Revolution, some arched in the middle and a little gutter on each side very near the houses.'

A pavement of broad, smooth, well jointed blocks of granite for wheel-tracks, with pitching between for horses, was laid in Commercial Road, London, in 1825 (figure 302). In the same year Telford recommended the use of stone blocks $4\frac{1}{2} \times 7\frac{1}{2}$ inches for street use, and 3×9 inch granite setts, with mortar joints, were laid on Blackfriars bridge in 1840. This was probably the first attempt at a modern stone pavement. In London such granite setts were not laid on concrete before 1870. In passing, it may be noted that London pavements in the 1820s suffered much from explosions of the gas-mains, for the gas industry was still young and many difficulties in the distribution of gas had to be overcome.

However, street paving was rapidly improving in the first decades of the nineteenth century, but its concomitant noise and clatter remained an affliction.

Brick pavements had been suggested, and had indeed been used in certain countries where the production of bricks was cheap. They were generally introduced in Dutch cities (p 529) during the seventeenth century, and a hundred years later in Italian cities. One of the first roads to be paved with bricks was that leading from The Hague to Scheveningen. Brick pavements had some success in the United States, where they were first introduced at Charleston (1870) and Bloomington. Bricks were of some importance in the paving of footpaths in other cities.

Wood-paving came from Russia, where Gourief first used wooden pavement-

FIGURE 302—*Paving a London road with Scottish granite.*

blocks in St Petersburg about 1820 (plate 33 C). In 1836 he wrote a book on them, in which they are described as hexagonal blocks laid and washed in with sand and receiving a coating of tar or pitch. Fink proposed to use 16-cm wooden cubes for the carriage-ways of bridges. Experimental stretches of wooden pavement were laid in London in 1838, in Oxford Street and from Charles Street to Tottenham Court Road; they included a stretch of hexagonal pine-blocks. These were later laid on a lime-concrete base. Between 1840 and 1843 Carey and others patented forms square in plan but double-wedge-shaped in section. Creosoted wood-blocks had been proposed by L. Wagner in 1829. He claimed that they were better than stone, but they did not come into use until much later. They were first employed in America on a bridge at Sunderland (1867), though wood-blocks had been applied to New York (1835) and Chicago (1856) streets much earlier. In 1839 there were 1100 sq yds of wooden pavement in London. By 1842 this had increased to 60 000, when, according to a statement in the City Council by an alderman during a controversy over the relative merits of wood and stone pavements, there were 600 000 sq yds of the latter, probably almost entirely macadam. These two items without doubt represented the total amount of pavements in a city of nearly 2 000 000 people. But traffic was rapidly increasing in London: in 1850 no fewer than 13 099 vehicles crossed London Bridge in twelve hours.

REFERENCES

[1] Bergier, N. 'Histoire des grands chemins de l'Empire Romain.' Paris. 1622.

[2] Gautier, H. 'Traité de la construction des chemins.' Paris. 1693.

[3] Schmidt, F. 'Geschichte der geodätischen Instrumente und Verfahren im Altertum und Mittelalter.' Pfälz, Neustadt a. d. Haardt. 1935.

[4] Birk, A. *Beitr. Gesch. Tech. Industr.*, **11**, 75, 1921.
Idem. Z. öst. Ing.- u. ArchitVer., **76**, 171, 1924.

[5] Caletti, P. 'Le strade da Roma imperiale all' Italia Fascista.' Bardi, Rome. 1932.

[6] Telford, T. 'Life of Thomas Telford, Civil Engineer, Written by Himself' (ed. by J. Rickman). London. 1838.
Baker, J. F. and Armitage, J. *Civ. Engng, Lond.*, **6**, 727, 1936.

[7] McAdam, J. L. 'Remarks on the Present System of Road Making with Observations Deduced from Practice and Experience' (9th rev. ed.). London. 1827.
Idem. 'A Practical Essay on the Scientific Repair and Preservation of Public Roads.' London. 1819.
Idem. 'Observations on the Management of Trusts for the Care of Turnpike Roads, as Regards the Repair of the Road, the Expenditure of the Revenue and the Appointment of Officers.' London. 1825.

[8] Barry, G. S. *Surveyor, Lond.*, **90**, 529, 1936.
Devereux, R. 'John Loudon McAdam, a Chapter from the History of Highways.' Oxford University Press, London. 1936.

[9] Anderson, R. M. C. 'The Roads of England.' Benn, London. 1932.
Ballen, Dorothy. 'Bibliography of Roadmaking and Roads in the United Kingdom. King, London. 1914.
Jeffreys, W. R. 'The King's Highway.' Batchworth Press, London. 1949.
Cookson, R. B. S. *Road Tar*, **6**, 5, 1952.
Edgeworth, R. L. 'An Essay on the Construction of Roads and Carriages' (2nd ed.). London. 1817.

[10] Labatut, J. and Lane, W. J. (Eds). 'Highways in our National Life. A Symposium', Pt I. University Press, Princeton. 1950.
Macdonald, T. H. *Proc. Amer. Soc. civ. Engrs*, 1545, 1927.

[11] Gillespie, W. M. 'Manual of the Principles and Practice of Road Making.' New-York. 1847.
Gillmore, Q. A. 'A Practical Treatise on Roads, Streets, and Pavements.' New York. 1876.

BIBLIOGRAPHY

Birk, A. 'Die Straße.' Kraft, Karlsbad. 1934.

Gregory, J. W. 'The Story of the Road, from the Beginning Down to the Present Day (2nd ed., rev. and enl. by C. J. Gregory). Black, London. 1938.

KNOLL, A. 'Geschichte der Straße und ihrer Arbeiter' (3 vols). Zentralverband der Steinarbeiter Deutschlands, Leipzig. 1925.

LAW, H. and CLARK, D. K. 'The Construction of Roads and Streets' (rev. with additions by A. J. WALLIS-TAYLER, 8th ed.). Crosby Lockwood, London. 1914.

LOESCH, K. L. VON. "Die Straße im Lebensgefühl der Völker." *Straße*, **4**, no. 17, 490, 1937.

MCCLOSKY, J. M. "History of Military Road Construction." *Milit. Engr, Wash.*, **41**, 353–6, 1949: **43**, 42–45, 192–5, 1951.

MERDINGER, C. J. "Roads Through the Ages." *Ibid.*, **44**, 268–73, 340–4, 1952.

PAGE, L. W. 'Roads, Paths and Bridges.' Sturgis & Walton, London. 1912.

PETER, A. "La route à travers les âges." *Schweiz. Z. Straßenwesen*, **17**, 325, 1931.

SHELDON, G. 'From Trackway to Turnpike.' Milford, London. 1928.

WEISE, A. 'Von Wildpfad zur Motorstraße.' Volksbund für Bücherfreunde, Berlin. 1929.

WILKINSON, T. W. 'From Track to By-Pass. A History of the English Road.' Methuen, London. 1934.

A stage-wagon with broad-dished wheels. Early nineteenth century.

18

PART I

CANALS:

INLAND WATERWAYS OUTSIDE BRITAIN

ROGER PILKINGTON

THE practice of canal-building was well established before the eighteenth century and the principle of overcoming differences in level by pound-locks had long been normal practice (vol III, ch 17). On the other hand, the great advances in hydraulic engineering that found expression in vertical lifts were not made until towards the end of the nineteenth century with the development of electrical methods and the internal combustion engine. The period from 1750 to 1850 is characterized by the great extension of the waterways themselves rather than by the introduction of important mechanical principles into their construction.

Yet during this period steam-power was gradually being developed. Thus as early as 1803 Fulton introduced a steamer on the Seine above Paris, and from 1817 a successful steamer service was run on the Mississippi between Louisville in Kentucky and New Orleans in Louisiana. This was soon to be succeeded by other packet-boats—so called because they carried not only passengers and general cargo but the United States mails. Similar paddle-wheelers were introduced on European rivers. In 1816 the London-built *Defiance* initiated the first service of powered craft on the Rhine, and the *Lady of the Lake*, built on the Clyde, began navigation on the Elbe. In 1830 steamers were plying on the upper reaches of the Danube, but the turbulence of their wash and the vulnerability of their paddles made such craft unsuitable for canal-work. A steam tug with a screw-propeller was used in 1844 on the canal from Charleroi to Brussels, but its destructive effects on the soft banks caused the temporary abandonment of such mechanical haulage.

The problem of supplying steam-power without a destructive wash was difficult, but in 1832 Tourasse and Mellet laid a submerged chain along much of the bed of the Seine between Paris and Rouen. The chain was picked up over the bows, passed round a steam-capstan on the tug, and dropped again over the stern. Unfortunately the chain proved too weak and this attempt, too, was abandoned, but many years later the idea was taken up once more and chains were employed with considerable success in a number of continental waterways. R. L. Stevenson's 'Journal of an Inland Voyage' contains an interesting account of the system in use on the Willebroek canal. In general, however, towage at this period was either by horse- or man-power, with help when possible from a sail.

The only lifting-system of any magnitude built during this period was the astonishing series of inclined planes on the Morris canal (figures 303 and 304).

FIGURE 303—*An inclined plane of the Morris canal.*

This canal was built between 1825 and 1831 to link the Hudson and Delaware rivers. It involved a rise of more than 900 ft to the summit pound at the watershed on the Alleghenies. Twenty-two locks were installed, each being at the head of an inclined plane running down to the pound below it, and descending on a gradient of 1 in 10 or 1 in 12. A 79-ft barge with a load of up to 30 tons was taken into the lock, and when the pen was emptied it came to settle on a trolley running on lines with a gauge of rather more than 12 ft. The lower gates were then opened, and the descent was made under gravity, checked by brakes. As the rails ran out into the lower pound and levelled off under water, the boat came to float again on an even keel. For the upward journey the procedure was reversed, and the cradle was hauled up the slope by a drum-and-cable mechanism, the power for which was supplied by a water-wheel. The device was remarkably efficient, and the total weight of 110 tons of cradle, barge, and cargo was raised through a vertical distance of 50 ft in $3\frac{1}{2}$ minutes for the expenditure of less than a twentieth of the amount of water required to raise a barge through a similar distance by conventional locking.

Navigation-works at this time were of several types. The simplest were concerned with improving the bed of a river which, either because of rapids or owing to silting, was unsuitable for commercial craft. The famous Iron Gates rapids on the lower Danube had impeded the use of this great river since antiquity. To by-pass them the Romans had cut a canal a mile and a half long. After the Roman period the Iron Gates remained an insuperable obstacle until 1830, when the Hungarian Count Szechenyi employed the engineer Vásráhelyi to survey the whole course of the lower river with a view to making it fully navigable. The count was tireless in his efforts to persuade the Russians and Turks to allow these improvements in the part of the river that ran through their territories, but the Russians were apathetic and the Turks actively hostile. Undaunted, he improved many sections of the river by cutting past rapids, but his scheme to by-pass the Iron Gates with a lock was abandoned.

Farther up, however, the Danube was regulated for 144 miles from Ennsmündung to Theuben, by work begun in 1849 and completed at a cost of more than half a million pounds, and by the end of the nineteenth century Hungary had nearly 2000 miles of navigable waterways. Much of this total was represented by the Danube and by the Nega canal from Themesvar to Titel, dug by the Romans and reconstructed in the eighteenth century. The Franz canal was opened in 1802 to join Bezdán and Bács-Földvár and so provide a cross-link between the courses of the Danube and the Tisza.

Navigation of the Rhône also was difficult. By 1840 the barge-traffic was in excess of 200 000 tons annually, but the splitting of the course into many winding, shallow channels was a serious impediment. The Canal de Miribel was therefore made just downstream of Lyons. By a system of dams and dikes the water was confined in this single course, but the speed of the current was so greatly increased that navigation remained difficult. Not until the middle of the twentieth century did thorough canalization of the river make upstream navigation easy for barges.

The Rhine showed a similar tendency in its Alsatian section. In 1840 the river was a maze of channels and backwaters, with shoaled reaches sometimes exceeding a mile in width. The flood-dikes were set more than a mile out to the sides, and the course was so diffuse that, although barges of 200 tons could work below Strasbourg, the river upstream of the city could accommodate only much smaller craft. At times of low water the river was sometimes impassable. Canalization of this section was begun in 1840, but once more the result was to increase the current to a degree that made upstream haulage practically impossible, and the faster flow of water scoured out the channel and obstructed the downstream reaches with silt and shingle.

The Mississippi with its tributaries drains two-fifths of the United States. Before the nineteenth century it carried considerable traffic, but only downstream, on account of swift and shallow passages. Rafts were the original form of transport, but they were soon replaced by flat boats. It was not until keeled boats were introduced that journeys up the river were at all possible, and such craft, manned by a crew of from 6 to 10, carried cargoes of 40 tons upstream by a combination of poling and warping.

Many rivers were improved by cutting off their bends, and in 1794 work was begun on the Guadalquivir which rendered it navigable as far as Seville and reduced the distance from 84 miles to 53. Making such cuts was usually accomplished by armies of workmen with pick and shovel, but at the end of the eighteenth century a labour-saving method was introduced in Germany, particularly on the Oder. This system involved digging the narrowest possible ditch along the line of the intended cut, and furnishing it with rectangular bays on either side alternately. At the time of the spring floods the upstream connexion with the river was opened through, and the torrent of flood water swirled down to erode a wide course. This simple system had its disadvantages, for, on the one hand, the flood easily got out of control and forged a channel in a direction different from that intended, and, on the other, the vast quantities of soil and subsoil swept away were sometimes deposited as banks in the lower reaches where, with increasing breadth of river, the force of the current was insufficient to dislodge them. In the nineteenth century, however, the system was much improved by laying finished banks in position beforehand, and by regulating the force of the incoming torrent.

Of all the river-improvement schemes of this period none offered greater possibilities than the work on the St Lawrence river in Canada, culminating in the drastic enlargements in the mid-twentieth century. These are to make inland navigation available to large ocean-going tankers as far as the terminus of the oil pipe-lines from Alberta, which reach the shores of the Great Lakes more than 2200 miles above the entrance to the St Lawrence. Much of the work has necessarily consisted of by-passing the rapids on the section of river between Montreal and Lake Ontario (figure 304). In 1821 the first successful cut was made between Montreal and Lachine, to overcome the Lachine rapids which had a fall of 46 ft. Originally this by-pass was limited to a depth of 5 ft, but within twenty years it was reconstructed with a minimum of 9 ft. At the time when the Lachine canal was built the sets of rapids at Les Cascades, Coteau du Lac, Mill Rapids, and Split Rock had already been overcome by a comparatively shallow canal 14 miles long and rising more than 80 ft; between 1834 and 1847 the navigable route through to Lake Ontario was completed by the Cornwall canal and the three shorter Williamsburg canals. As the lake was already connected to Lake Erie by the Welland canal (figure 304), cut in 1824–9 by a private company to by-pass the 327-ft drop of the Niagara river and falls, navigation right through to Lake Huron was now possible for grain-ships and lumber-floats of moderate draught.

A further connexion through to Lake Superior was already provided by the Sault Ste Marie canal (figure 304), since enlarged on several occasions. Though only 1 mile in length, it is today one of the busiest waterways in the world. In the first canal, opened in 1798 by the Northwest Fur Company, there was one lock only; this had a depth of no more than 1½ ft on the sill and was the first to be constructed in the American continent. It was destroyed by American troops in 1814.

In the same period a second route was begun between Montreal and Lake Huron, linking together the numerous small lakes lying to the northward of Lake Ontario to form a 224-mile waterway between the Bay of Quinte on Lake Ontario and Georgian Bay, but the marine railways involved at two points on the descent of the Severn river still limit the use of the through connexion to 20-tonners drawing not more than 4 ft of water.

Work parallel to that on the St Lawrence river was also undertaken in the first half of the nineteenth century on the Ottawa river, to provide through navigation between Montreal and Ottawa. Once again it was a matter of three small canals to by-pass the St Anne, Carillon, and Long Sault rapids (figure 304). But in 1826 the Canadian government decided to construct the Rideau Navigation from Ottawa to Kingston at the head of Lake Ontario to facilitate movements of goods and troops. This was in case war with the United States should render the St Lawrence route unusable—the boundary between the two countries passing down the river itself for a distance of nearly a hundred miles. This waterway was fortified, and crossed the summit of the watershed between the Rideau river (a tributary of the Ottawa) and the St Lawrence, and involved forty-seven locks. It exists today much in its original form, but is now more used by yachtsmen than by commercial craft, the depth having been left at the original 5 ft.

A more important route commercially was that of the St Ours and Chambly canals built between 1830 and 1850 to improve the course of the Richelieu river, which flows from Lake Champlain to reach the St Lawrence 46 miles below Montreal. By these navigations a through connexion to New York was eventually established when the 66-mile Champlain canal was constructed on the American side of the frontier to join the southern end of Lake Champlain to the Hudson River at Albany.

Quite apart from river-improvement schemes the era was one of canal-

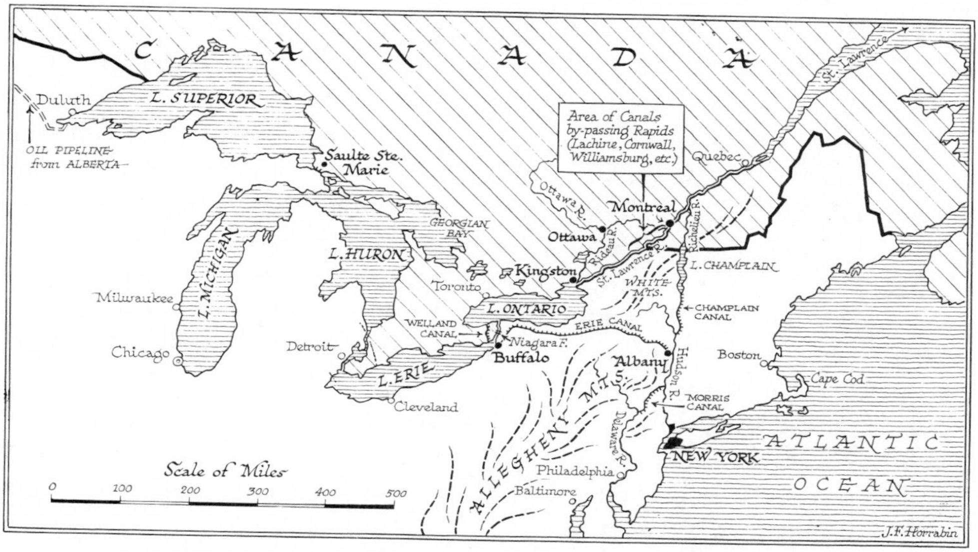

FIGURE 304—*Principal canals and waterways of the Great Lakes–St Lawrence region.*

development in many parts of the world. Some of these, such as the Franz canal of Hungary, were cut to join two already navigable river-courses, and if these flowed into different sea areas the effect was to provide an inland route to replace a lengthy sea voyage. Amongst the more astonishing projects was that of Maire, the Belgian engineer, who in 1786 planned an elaborate system of continental waterways based on Vienna and incorporating a canal that should cross the Alps and reach the sea at Fiume or Trieste, so providing a transcontinental route to the Adriatic. The Holy Roman Emperor Franz II sent his engineer Maillard to study the methods of building canals over hilly country. It was intended to cut through the highest ranges with tunnels, and, though the scheme was abortive, 40 miles of this canal were completed at the Vienna end of the line, and furnished with thirty-six locks.

As early as 1701 Peter I of Russia had begun the construction of a navigable link between the Volga and the Don, which at one point approach within 48 miles of each other. The work was abandoned because of war, but it was succeeded by two even more ambitious schemes that linked the Baltic with the Caspian Sea. The first line connected the Neva and the Volga by way of Lake Ladoga, but owing to poor water-supply it was soon replaced by the Vychnyvolotschok canal, which in spite of a draught of only 18 in at the sills of the locks was conveying more than 3000 eighty-ton craft annually in 1760. Further improvements were made between 1808 and 1811, when the Tikhvine and Mariinsk canals were cut. The former was a direct link of 57 miles between the Neva and the Volga, crossing the watershed in a total rise of 543 ft, while the latter was a more easterly route by Lake Onega, designed from the outset for craft of 165 tons and having only thirty-eight locks in 757 miles of waterway. A more direct route from the Gulf of Riga to the Black Sea was opened in 1805 with the cutting of a canal between the Beresina and Dvina rivers. This, though used for some time by timber-rafts, was eventually allowed to decline. Finally, a canal to Moscow was begun in 1825 solely to bring through from the Volga the stone required for building the Temple of Christ the Saviour, but when the railway to the capital was opened in 1844 the work was discontinued.

Owing to the number of major rivers in eastern Europe, Russia had some 50 000 miles of navigable waterways by the middle of the nineteenth century, and the average barge-haul was more than 600 miles—nearly twenty times the distance of the average haul in Britain.

In Sweden, canals with locks had been constructed as early as the late sixteenth century, but the waterway of most importance was the Gotha route, spanning the country from the Kattegat to the eastern Baltic with sixty-three locks. Constructed between 1810 and 1832, it was built partly for strategic reasons but carried considerable produce and particularly timber.

In Spain two canals, begun as far back as the sixteenth century, were completed within our period. Pignatelli completed the Imperial canal of Aragon, which had a two-step staircase lock at Casablanca. By 1795 a flourishing passenger service was operating there, and the carriage of grain was bringing in dues of a third of a million reals annually, but when the Saragossa to Pamplona railway was opened the waterway declined and was suppressed. Strangely enough it was to be reopened in 1918, the railway track being starved of materials for the repair and maintenance of the permanent way as a result of the 1914–18 war. The Castille canal from Valladolid to Medina de Rioseco, with forty-two locks, was completed in 1849.

In Germany the Ludwig canal, completed in 1845, was to form a link between the North Sea and the Black Sea by connecting the rivers Main and

Danube. Through insufficient water-supply, however, it remained virtually impassable until much later, when further works were carried out.

Some canals were constructed not only for navigation but for irrigation. Such was the Pavia canal, built under a decree of Napoleon, which connected the Naviglio Grande (a twelfth-century canal) with the Ticino by way of Milan; it was furnished with twelve locks, each of which carried a water-mill operated by the irrigation spill-over. In Egypt the dual-purpose Mehmondieh canal was dug between 1800 and 1825, to carry the waters of the Nile to Alexandria. 350 000 navvies worked on it, but the line was not marked out in advance and the result was a 50-mile course of odd straight sections connected by sharp bends which made navigation difficult. In India a magnificent project was begun in 1848 to the designs of Sir Proby Cautley, and when completed the Upper Ganges canal had a length of more than 500 miles and involved spanning the Solani river with an aqueduct 300 yds long and 50 yds broad. Other streams were carried across the top of the canal in smaller aqueducts.

The most enterprising canal on the American continent was constructed by de Witt Clinton from Albany to Buffalo between 1817 and 1824, and involved crossing two watersheds by means of seventy-two locks. This, the 364-mile Erie canal, provided an artery down which the grain from the Great Lakes could flow to New York. It was navigated by barges drawn by pairs of horses. The round trip, including the Hudson River section of the voyage, took about 4 weeks, but, being ice-bound from December to May, a barge could not deliver more than six or seven loads a year at best. Yet the volume of traffic was so great that within eleven years the cost of construction had been met by the tolls. Before 1850 double locks had to be installed to cope with the ever-increasing number of packet-boats and barges plying between the Great Lakes and New York Harbor. In the twentieth century the Erie canal was greatly enlarged, and its course came to form part of the New York State barge-canal system, navigable for vessels of 300-ft length.

The greatest developments of inland waterways, however, were taking place in France and the Low Countries. In 1810 the famous St Quentin canal was opened to link the North Sea and the Scheldt and Lys systems with the English Channel by way of the Somme, and with Paris and Le Havre by way of the Oise and Seine. This canal still carries a great volume of traffic. A system of horse-relays was organized over the whole length of the 60 miles from Chauny to Cambrai and quickly extended to the Canal Lateral à l'Oise, which led from the St Quentin canal to the Oise proper at Janville, near Compiègne. With no appreciable current on the canal section, two horses were adequate for laden barges, but on the Oise eight were often needed for the return haul upstream from Conflans St-Honorine.

The St Quentin canal incorporated two tunnels. The longer, or Grand souterrain de Riqueval, was $3\frac{1}{4}$ miles long, and when in due course the canal was opened no boatman dared to enter it. In desperation the authorities offered freedom from all canal dues in perpetuity to the first boat to pass through the tunnel, and one man volunteered. His boat was renamed the *Grand Souterrain* in celebration of the occasion, and until nearly the end of the nineteenth century it was still navigating tax-free. At that time, however, the dues on the canal were remitted entirely, and the *Grand Souterrain* retired honourably.

Other important links made at this time were the Canal du Centre (1793), constructed by Gauthey to connect the Loire at Digoin with the Saône at Chalon and thus complete the first inland route from the English Channel to the Mediterranean; the Canal de Bourgogne (1832), which linked the Seine to the Saône at a more northerly point and provided a more direct route from Paris to Lyons; the Rhine–Rhône canal (1834), completing a direct north to south route across western Europe; and the Canal de la Sambre à l'Oise, which today is part of the main trunk route from Antwerp and Liège by way of the Meuse to Paris.

In Belgian territory a canal was all but built which if completed would have vitally affected the development of both Rotterdam and Amsterdam by diverting their trade to Antwerp. As early as 1598 Spinola, the general holding the southern Netherlands for Philip II of Spain, conceived the idea of a Rhine–Meuse–Scheldt canal which would provide a route from the Rhineland to the sea passing only through territory held by the Spaniards. Work upon the canal was begun in 1626, but the Hollanders, seeing that the Rhine trade would be taken from them, destroyed the canal and wrecked the works. In 1804 Napoleon chanced to see the remnants of the works and at once planned to construct for strategic reasons the great Canal du Nord, though on a route slightly farther south. Two years later, however, the assimilation of Holland within his empire made the canal no longer necessary and work was suspended, but the completed portion in Germany was used until 1848.

Any scheme to connect the Rhineland with the Scheldt would inevitably deal a heavy blow to the Dutch ports at the mouth of the Rhine, and the idea has always been extremely unpopular in Holland. When in 1828 and again in the twentieth century the merchants of Antwerp clamoured for the canal to be finally cut, the Dutch opposed the proposal with every means in their power.

Many Belgian waterways (figure 305) have been traffic arteries for centuries. Visitors to Ghent can see the magnificent row of canal-side warehouses and note among them the tiny house of the toll-collector, next to a huge granary which from the Middle Ages was used to store the grain exacted as a toll upon the cargoes carried by barge through the city waterways. The main extension of the canals, however, took place towards the end of the eighteenth century and particularly during the first half of the nineteenth, to carry the coal of Bergen (Mons) and Charleroi southward to Paris and the areas of northern France, and northward to Brussels, Ghent, and Antwerp. In the coalfields the Mons–Condé canal

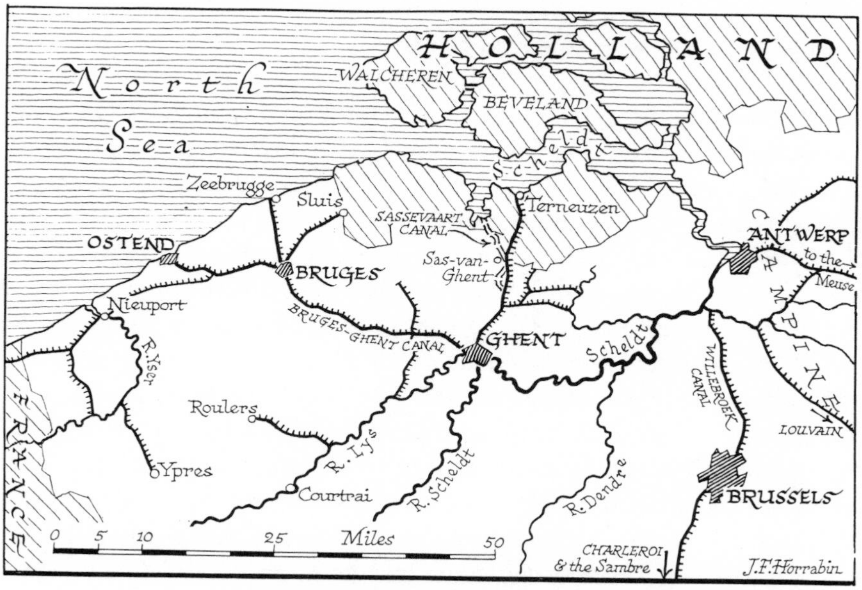

FIGURE 305—*Some Belgian canals.*

was built (1818), the Pommeroeul–Antoing canal was opened to connect the Haine and Scheldt basins (1823), the Sambre river was canalized (1828), and the Charleroi–Brussels canal was opened in 1827 as a southward extension of the Willebroek canal—known in our own day as the Brussels Ship Canal but in reality one of the oldest artificial canals in Europe. Later, the great routes of the Campine were laid down to carry the agricultural produce of that area to the port of Antwerp, and to form a connexion between the Meuse and the Scheldt (1846).

Towage on the Charleroi–Brussels canal was mostly by man-haulage, though horses could be used between lock 40 and Brussels, but since there was a great demand for both labour and horses in the mines of the area through which the canal passed, traffic was sometimes brought almost to a standstill for lack of haulage. A towing-company was formed which imported donkeys from England, but they proved difficult animals, particularly in the tunnel, and their use was discontinued. Brussels itself ran short of fuel in the hard winter of 1837–8, entirely owing to lack of haulage for the many laden coal-barges accumulating on the canal.

Not all the northward-bound supplies from the Sambre area were routed to Brussels and Antwerp, however, for the Dutch, too, extended their network of canals to link with the same industrial field. Maastricht and Liège are both on the Meuse, but the river above Maastricht was still unregulated (as it is in one section today) and the Maastricht–Luik (Liège) canal was opened in 1850; it continues to carry a great quantity of traffic. Uniting at Maastricht with the Zuid Willemsvaart, which ran northward towards Hertogenbosch and linked up with the river estuaries of the Hollandsch Diep area, it made possible the transport of stone, coal, and steel from the Meuse and Sambre industrial areas to every part of the Netherlands.

The prosperity of the great cities of Flanders had for centuries been intimately bound up with the waterways. Bruges was at one time easily accessible to the sea-going ships of every seafaring nation when, in centuries long past, a broad inlet of the sea, the Zwijn, ran deep into the Flanders country-side by way of Sluis and Damme, where it was joined by the Roya, a small river running out of Bruges in a north-easterly direction. At that time the trade of Bruges was at its height, and ships from Ireland and Germany, Poland and Venice and Russia, Scandinavia and Scotland were plying to Damme to unload into barges the rich cargoes to be taken up the Roya to the warehouses of the wealthy merchant burghers of Bruges, set on the banks of the town canals. In the fifteenth century, as many as 150 foreign vessels were clearing the port of Damme in a day, and Bruges contained the consulates of a score of countries, but today Damme has shrunk to a mere fiftieth part of its former size. Its fate was inseparably linked with that of Bruges, and both were ruined when in the early part of the fifteenth century the sea began to desert them. The banks then beginning to form south of the mouth of the Scheldt were soon to close for ever the mouth of the estuary, and the Zwijn itself silted up until navigation was impossible. The harbour at Damme was left on dry land, the Zwijn disappeared, the marshes were reclaimed, and the most prosperous city of northern Europe fell into inevitable decline.

Bruges eventually made an effort to regain her lost trade, and in 1722 the river Yperlée was canalized to form the present course of the canal from Ostend to Bruges, so that sea-going ships could once again reach the city. In the middle of the nineteenth century British schooners of more than 200 tons regularly plied to Bruges by this canal, most of them carrying cargoes of salt from the Mersey.

The Ostend–Bruges canal carried a flourishing packet-service, and when

Robert Southey visited Bruges in 1815 he travelled by the *trekschuit* or fly-boat, drawn by four horses and making a speed of 5 mph. It was a fine affair, the better of the two cabins being splendidly fitted up with crimson plush.

The anonymous writer of 'What may be done in Two Months' went by the canal boat *Élégante Messagère* on this same canal in 1834, and wrote that 'there never was a cleaner or better fitted up packet-boat: the little cabin with its beautiful sofas, mirrors and chairs, rivalled the nicest drawing room: and breakfast was served in it with so much propriety and order'. The boat was drawn by two horses at 4 mph and the charge for the trip was only 2 francs, which included the breakfast. At Bruges the passengers were taken by carriage to the Ghent packet, an equally smart boat that ran on the Canal de Bruges à Ghent.

The history of Ghent was similarly bound up with its outlet to the sea. At first sight it seems strange that this should have been a matter of concern for a city situated on the navigable reaches of the Scheldt, but the lower reaches of the river ran through states that were not always on good terms with Ghent, and the city could ill afford to remain in a position where her entire export trade could persist only on the sufferance of others. Accordingly in 1251 the Lieve canal was begun, leading all the way to Damme, which port Ghent then shared with Bruges until the disastrous silting of the Zwijn rendered it useless.

For many years afterwards Ghent used the Scheldt as an outlet, but the growth of the textile industry led to new thoughts about an alternative route to the sea, and in 1549 the Sassevaart was opened to bring sea-going ships from a point on the south side of the Scheldt estuary, opposite the island of Beveland, right into the city.

Luck was against the citizens, however, and the Treaty of Münster in 1648 gave control of the outlet of this canal, and also of the main Scheldt itself, into the hands of the Dutch. Article XIV stated that 'The rivers of the Schelde, as also the canals of Sas, Zwijn and other mouths of rivers disemboguing themselves there shall be kept shut on the side of the Lords the States'; and to make sure that their monopoly of navigation should remain unbroken the Dutch built a fort at Lillo (the present frontier-post in the estuary) to cover the Scheldt route, and another at Sas-van-Ghent to cover the canal. Nothing could pass without paying crushing dues, so the city of Ghent had once again to plan a new export route or die. This new canal was the Canal de Bruges à Ghent, begun in 1724 and reconstructed in 1751 and on three later occasions. From the outset it was designed to carry 100-ton craft, and it enabled the exports of Ghent to flow down through Bruges to Ostend and thence to such parts of Europe as were independent of Dutch control.

In 1795 the French Republican government reopened the Sassevaart for traffic, but when in 1800 an enterprising burgher named Lieven Bauwens succeeded in acquiring a Crompton spinning-mule in England and smuggling it out of the country in pieces and bringing it home to Ghent, busy cotton-mills sprang up, and the increased trade demanded something bigger and better than even the Sassevaart and the Ostend route together could provide. Accordingly, after the departure of the French the big modern Ghent ship canal was cut through to Terneuzen and opened in 1827. It followed much of the line of the old Sassevaart, but was shorter and straighter and it made certain the rise of Ghent to a flourishing port in our own day. It now passes 25 000 ships annually.

Elsewhere, two other canals for sea-going vessels were constructed. Amsterdam was accessible by way of the Zuider Zee, but the continual silting of this shallow area of water progressively made the position of the port more precarious. In 1825, therefore, a long and admirably constructed ship canal was opened, by-passing the entire Zuider Zee coast and reaching the North Sea in the Texel roads opposite the western end of the chain of the Frisian islands. Half a century later it was to be succeeded by the much shorter ship canal to Ijmuiden, but the smaller cargo-vessels still use the North Holland canal if bound from the north for Alkmaar. It was originally constructed with a minimum depth of 18 ft (as against 11 in the Zuider Zee) and the locks at each end had a length of 213 ft. Forty yards broad and fifty miles long, it was a handsome piece of canal construction across soft and very difficult land.

The other great work of the period, which was to prove so valuable when improved at a later date, was the bold stroke of making a waterway which would by-pass the Kattegat and the dangerous Skagerrak, and so give direct access from the Baltic to the North Sea. Earlier attempts had been made; the Vikings portaged their ships across a 10-mile watershed on rollers, and as early as 1398 a canal for small craft was cut by way of Lübeck on the line of the present Elbe–Trave canal. In 1784 the Eider canal was laid down between the Kiel fiord and the Upper Eider lakes, on the instructions of the Danish King Christian VII. This waterway was cut to a depth of 10 ft and had three locks (see plate 38 A) on either side of the watershed, and from where it connected with the Eider river at Rendsburg the river-course westwards was dredged and deepened. Originally intended for Danish ships only, the Eider canal (figure 306) was opened to craft of all nations in 1785, and it was not until more than a hundred years later that the increased size of modern ships made it essential for the course to be widened, deepened, and straightened to form the Kiel canal—a waterway which today carries more than 2 million tons of shipping a month.

The Kaiser Wilhelm or Kiel canal was opened in 1895, with a length of 59 miles from the locks at Brunsbüttel at the North Sea end, where there is a tidal range of some 13 ft, to the Holtenau locks in the Kiel fiord, where the tide ranges through only a few inches. Crossing low and undulating country, and with plenty of water available from the Eider (figure 306), its construction did not present any special problems, but the railway-bridge at Rendsburg is a notable feat of engineering. Sufficient height is gained by a loop of track which

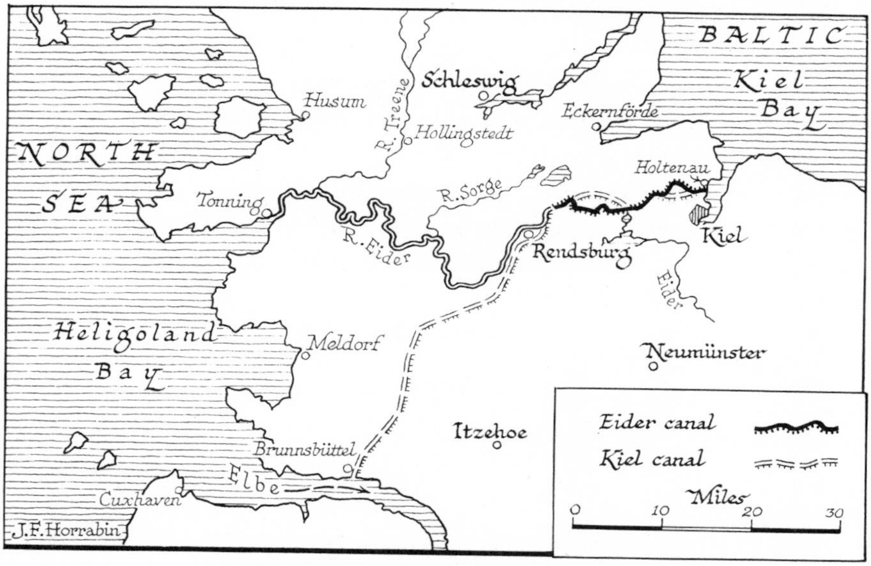

FIGURE 306—*Lines of the Kiel and Eider canals.*

encircles the city on a rising viaduct and crosses over itself before running on to the main span above the water, while the underside of the bridge serves as a carrier for a trolley from which a road transporter is suspended at bank level.

The Kiel canal not only by-passed the dangerous Skagen area of northern Denmark, where millions of tons of shipping had been lost, but cut the distance from the English Channel to the southern Baltic by several hundred miles. An even greater shortening of commercial seaways was the object underlying the construction of the two other great inter-sea or inter-oceanic canals, work on which was begun during the latter half of the nineteenth century. The scheme of a canal to link the Mediterranean with the Red Sea dated back to pre-Christian times, but it remained for Ferdinand de Lesseps (1805–94) to construct the existing Suez canal, a waterway 99 miles long and without locks at either end. Opened in 1869, this waterway was taking £2 500 000 annually in dues before the end of the century, but the deposition of sand eroded by wash or carried by the wind has made continual dredging necessary in order to preserve the depth of water (plate 38 B).

The narrow isthmus of Central America also offered attractive possibilities for a link between the Atlantic and Pacific oceans, and work was in fact started on the Nicaragua canal in 1889. It was abandoned, however, in favour of the Panama route which had already been begun by de Lesseps, but work on which had been halted by financial difficulties and the ravages of malaria and yellow fever. Connecting the Atlantic at Colon with the Pacific at Balboa, the Panama canal was eventually completed by the United States government and opened to traffic in 1914. Its construction involved six locks with bankside haulage, and a 7-mile cutting through the Culebra hills.

These three canals now carry approximately the same annual tonnage of shipping, but on account of the many vessels of relatively small size working the Baltic routes the Kiel canal handles seven times as many ships as either the Panama or Suez canal.

BIBLIOGRAPHY

ADAMS, S. H. 'The Erie Canal.' Random House, Toronto. 1953.

"A.K." 'Afloat in Belgium.' London. 1871.

Annales des Ponts et Chaussées. Paris. 1850–83.

CANADIAN DEPARTMENT OF TRANSPORT. 'The Canals of Canada.' Ottawa. 1937.

CRESY, E. 'Encyclopaedia of Civil Engineering' (new ed.). London. 1861.

DUMONT, M. E. 'Gent — een stedenaardrijkskundige studie.' Rijksuniv. te Gent, Werken uitgegeven door de Faculteit van de Wijsbegeerte en Letteren, 107e Aflevering. De Tempel, Bruges. 1951.

'The Emperor's Claims . . . together with Extracts from the Articles of the Treaty of Munster . . . whereby the Dutch found their Right to the Blocking up of the Schelde.' London. 1785.

'Haven van Gent.' Report published by the Harbour Authority, Ghent. 1955.

HOERSCHELMANN, E. F. DE. 'Aperçu historique du développement des voies navigables de l'Empire de Russie.' Kiev. 1894.

'Map of the Inland Waterways of France.' Imray, Laurie, Norrie & Wilson, London. 1950.

'Der Nord-Ostsee Kanal.' Wasser- und Schiffahrtsdirektion, Kiel. 1955.

PILKINGTON, R. 'Small Boat through Belgium.' Macmillan, London. 1957.

SOUTHEY, R. 'Journal of a Tour in the Netherlands in the Autumn of 1815.' Heinemann, London. 1902.

STEVENSON, R. L. 'An Inland Voyage.' London. 1878.

THOMAS, B. F. and WATT, D. A. 'The Improvement of Rivers and Canals' (2nd ed.). John Wiley, New York. 1913.

Verhandlungen des III Internationalen Binnenschiffahrts=Kongresses. Frankfurt. 1888.

VERNON-HARCOURT, L. F. 'Rivers and Canals' (2nd ed., 2 vols). Oxford. 1896.

'What may be done in Two Months.' London. 1834.

18

PART II

CANALS:

INLAND WATERWAYS OF THE BRITISH ISLES

CHARLES HADFIELD

BRITAIN was slow to begin building canals, but, once started, they were quickly extended as the industrial revolution developed. In 1750 there were over 1000 miles of navigable river in Great Britain (figure 308), and in

FIGURE 307—*The Duke of Bridgewater's canal crossing the Irwell.*

1850 about 4250 miles of inland navigation, in addition to a considerable mileage in Ireland (vol III, ch 17).

The first modern canals, the Sankey Brook from the St Helen's coalfield to the Mersey (1757), and the Duke of Bridgewater's from the Worsley mines to Manchester (1761) (figure 307 and tailpiece), presented few engineering problems other than the building of the Irwell aqueduct. Later canals had to surmount hilly country and, because no state finance was available, had to be cheap and bring returns quickly. The Trent and Mersey canal, for instance, was begun in 1766 and completed in 1777; it was 93½ miles long with 75 locks and five tunnels (figure 309).

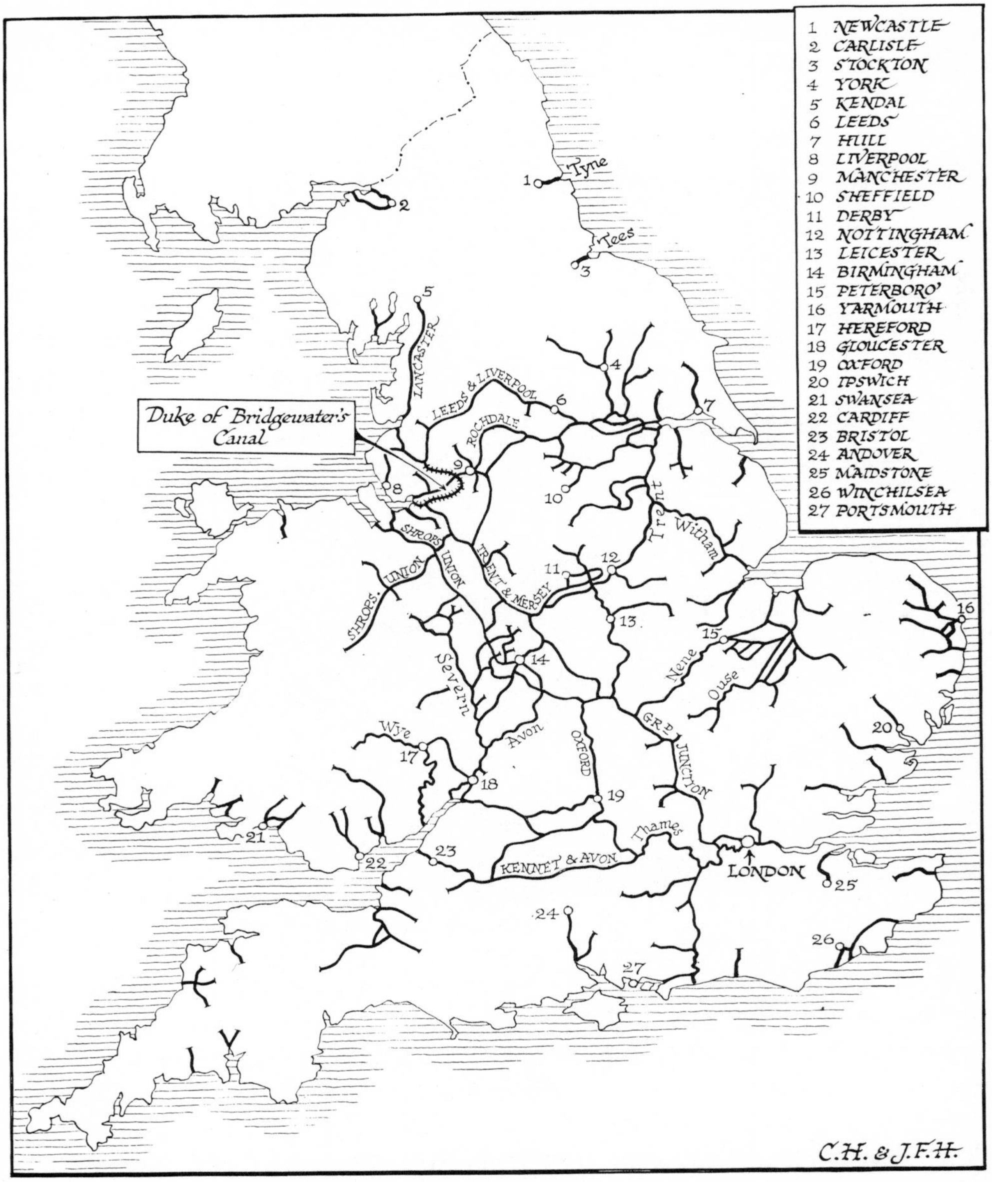

FIGURE 308—*The inland waterway system of England and Wales at its greatest extent. 1858.*

Three types of canal were developed: wide for some main lines with ambitious shareholders; narrow with 7-ft locks for cheaper routes, especially those with poor w·ter supplies; and the tub-boat canal for the steepest gradients. Wide

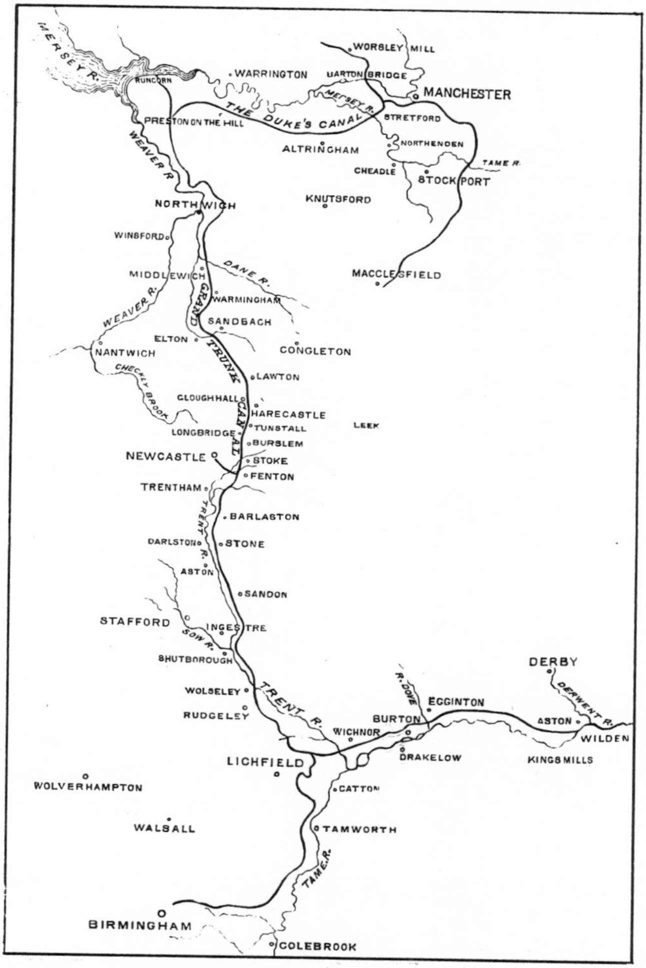

FIGURE 309—*The Grand Trunk (Trent and Mersey) and Duke of Bridgewater's canals, with early proposed extensions to Birmingham and Macclesfield. The latter was in fact continued through Macclesfield to rejoin the Grand Trunk at Lawton.*

canals were mainly in the north-east and north-west of England and in Scotland; narrow canals in south Wales and around Birmingham, the ascent to which is by flights of locks on all sides; the tub-boat canals in the south-west and in Shropshire. Within these groups variations were developed, but broadly

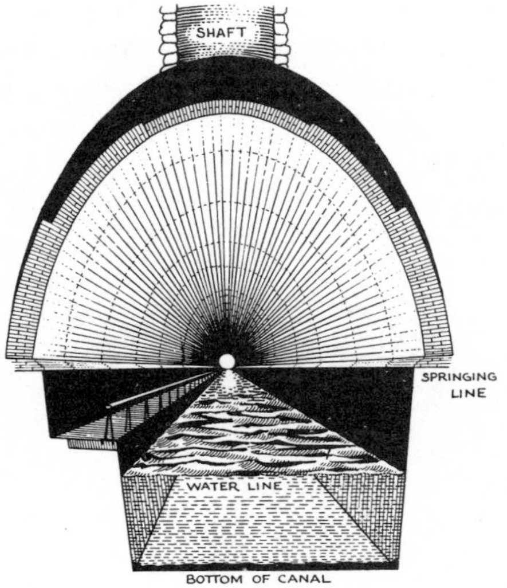

FIGURE 310—*Section of the Strood tunnel on the Thames and Medway canal.*

speaking a narrow boat 70 ft by 7 ft could travel anywhere south of the rivers Trent and Mersey except on the tub-boat canals, and a barge 58 ft by 13½ ft anywhere north of that line. Larger barges worked upon the river navigations.

As already mentioned, the early canals were built as cheaply as possible. It cost less to follow the contours than to make embankments or cuttings, and the extra length hardly mattered when boatmen's wages were low. Accommodation bridges were built when a farmer's land had to be cut in two (plate 39 B). Later, as wages rose, canals became straighter and more expensive. The Staffordshire and Worcestershire (plate 37), completed in 1772, is a typical contour canal, with hardly an embankment or cutting of any size upon it; while the Birmingham and Liverpool Junction (now the Shropshire Union main line), completed in 1835, is almost straight, with long stretches on embankments or in cuttings, including the 2-mile-long Tyrley cutting, the deepest in the country. In two cases, the Birmingham and the Oxford canals, a contour canal was later straightened.

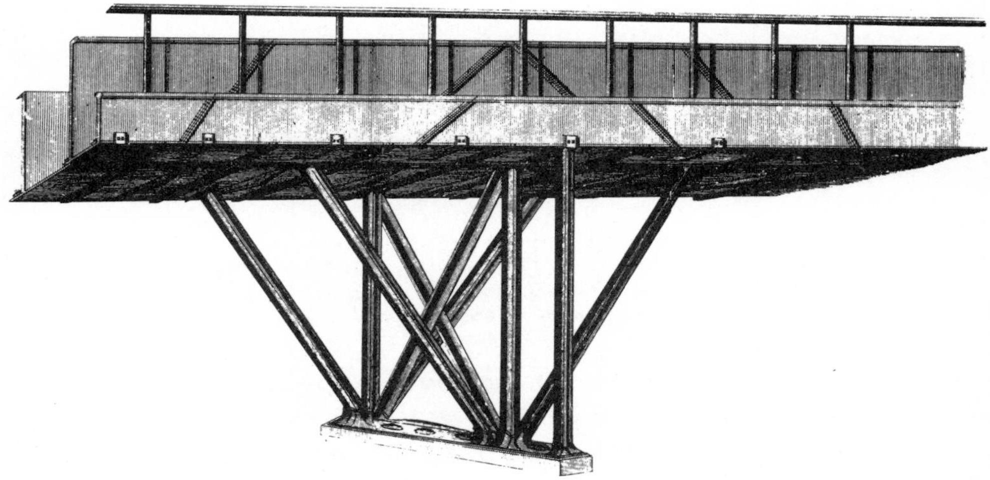

FIGURE 311—*The iron aqueduct conveying the Shrewsbury canal over the river Tern at Longdon in Shropshire.*

Where hills had to be passed, tunnels were cheaper than cuttings. About 45 miles of canal tunnel were built in Great Britain, most of them not big enough to allow boats to pass each other. Earlier tunnels, except the shortest, had no towpath, boats being legged or shafted through, or pulled with chains fastened to the walls. Paths were later provided, the first, on timber stretchers over the water, being in the Berwick tunnel of the Shrewsbury canal. Later, the bores were enlarged to take a single or double tow-path. The longest tunnel built was at Standedge on the Huddersfield canal, 5415 yds long; the largest in dimensions

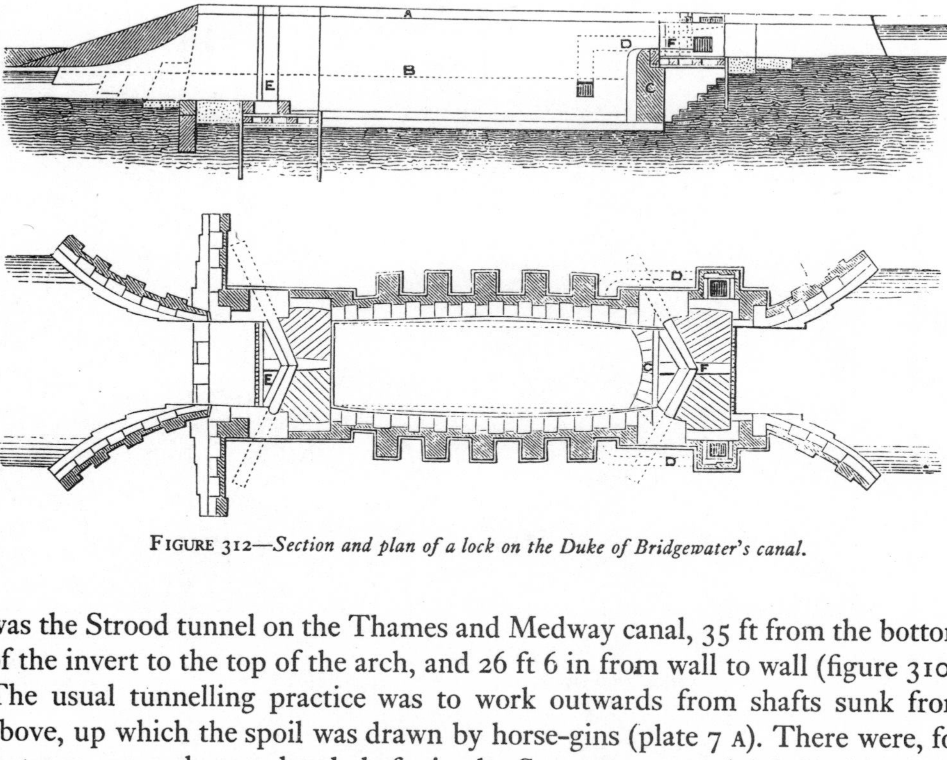

FIGURE 312—*Section and plan of a lock on the Duke of Bridgewater's canal.*

was the Strood tunnel on the Thames and Medway canal, 35 ft from the bottom of the invert to the top of the arch, and 26 ft 6 in from wall to wall (figure 310). The usual tunnelling practice was to work outwards from shafts sunk from above, up which the spoil was drawn by horse-gins (plate 7 A). There were, for instance, 25 such completed shafts in the Sapperton tunnel (3808 yds) on the Thames and Severn canal.

Aqueducts carried the canals over river valleys. Early canal engineers built them immensely strong of stone or brick, within which frame the waterway, usually narrowed, was carried in a puddled bed. A major development was the substitution of an iron trough, first used on the Longdon-on-Tern aqueduct on the Shrewsbury canal (figure 311). The most notable was at Pont-y-Cysyllte on the Ellesmere canal, the aqueduct being 1007 ft long with 19 arches, and 121 ft above the river Dee. The trough is 11 ft 10 in wide, the tow-path being carried over it on iron supports, so allowing a wider waterway than at Longdon-on-Tern, where it lay beside the waterway in a separate trough.

Locks (figure 312), inclined planes (figures 313 and 314), and lifts (figures 315, 317) were used to raise or lower boats from one level to another. The gate,

FIGURE 313—*A medium plane for use in small canals with a rise of only 20–30 ft. A water-wheel was used as a source of power on a number of planes in the West of England.*

counterbalanced by a beam, and its heel-post revolving in a quoin, was commonly used for locks, though occasionally a vertically-rising counterbalanced gate is found, as on the Shrewsbury canal or on the Stratford on Avon canal at King's Norton, Birmingham. Double locks placed side-by-side appear first to have been used on the Regent's canal in London, opened in 1820, while staircase locks, in which two or more were built together and had gates in common, were frequent, the biggest being the five-lock staircase at Bingley on the Leeds and Liverpool canal. Water was passed into or out of locks by almost every possible combination of ground- and gate-paddles. The normal arrangement was to have both the ground- and the gate-paddles on the upper gates, and gate-paddles alone on the lower, the paddles rising vertically by ratchet and pinion worked by a detachable windlass, though sideways-moving paddles and fixed windlasses are also found.

Inclined planes for moving tub-boats from one level of canal to another were used in hilly parts of the country (figure 313). Fourteen were worked in south-western England, two in south Wales, and six in Shropshire. One was built in Scotland at the end of our period, and one in Leicestershire after it, both for

FIGURE 314—*A double inclined plane, where the boats were lowered on rails. The weight was counterbalanced by a large tub of water in a pit. The tub, which was about 9 ft in diameter and 5 ft deep and contained about 8 tons of water, was filled from the upper canal. When it reached the foot of the pit, which was on a level with the lower canal, the water was released and escaped through a trough. A plane using this method was built at Hobbacott Down on the Bude canal.*

larger craft. The first incline, at Ketley in Shropshire (plate 48 C), began work in 1788, and the last, at Trench not far away, was closed in 1922. These planes were slopes upon which single or double lines of rails were laid: upon the rails the boats were carried either in wheeled caissons full of water, or dry in wheeled cradles, or ran on their own wheels (figure 314). Water was the usual, steam the occasional, motive-power. The greatest vertical height of any British plane carrying boats was 225 ft, on the Hobbacott Down plane of the Bude canal in Cornwall. In addition to the boat-carrying planes, one carrying trucks, into and out of which boxes of coal were lifted, for some years connected two pounds of the Somerset coal canal. Several others using trucks either fed canals with loads brought down from mines and quarries, as at Froghall in Staffordshire, or carried canal cargoes down to a river-wharf, as at Morwellham on the Tavistock canal, or delivered them to a works, as at Coalbrookdale on the Shropshire canal.

Lastly, a few vertically-rising lifts counterbalanced by water were built (figure

FIGURE 315—*The perpendicular lift. The cranes move the boats, and the weight is counterbalanced by the tub of water in the pit. This was an idea that never became practicable.*

315), the only ones successfully operated under working conditions being the set of eight designed by James Green for the Grand Western canal and used from 1838 to 1867. A device patented by Robert Fulton is illustrated in figure 316. Fulton wrote on canals and took out patents, but the development work on the subjects of his study had already been largely done by others. After our period a larger lift, worked at first hydraulically and later by electric power, was built at Anderton in Cheshire; it is still in use.

The craft on the canals developed little during the period (plate 39 A and figure 317). The single boat drawn by one horse or a pair of donkeys was almost uni-

FIGURE 316—*Device patented by Fulton in 1794 for conveying loaded boats from one level to another on canals.*

versal; bow-haulage by men was not unusual on rivers, and sails were sometimes used. Boats carrying boxes of goods or tramway wagons were occasionally used. Specialized boats were developed on many canals for carrying passengers by day, and on the Forth and Clyde canal there were sleeping-boats for night travel. Light passenger-boats travelling at some 10 mph were run for many years on the Glasgow, Paisley, and Ardrossan canal.

In 1789 Symington tried the second of his steam-boats on a canal in Scotland, and in 1802 his tug, the *Charlotte Dundas*, worked there for a time, till she was abandoned because of her wash. Later, many experimental steam cargo-carrying boats were run on canals, but the only regular development of the steam-boat within our period was as a tunnel-tug, one of the first being that which started work through the Islington tunnel on the Regent's canal in 1826.

Between 1750 and 1850 the great British canal engineers—Brindley, the elder Rennie, Outram, the Whitworths, the Jessops, the Dadfords, Telford, and

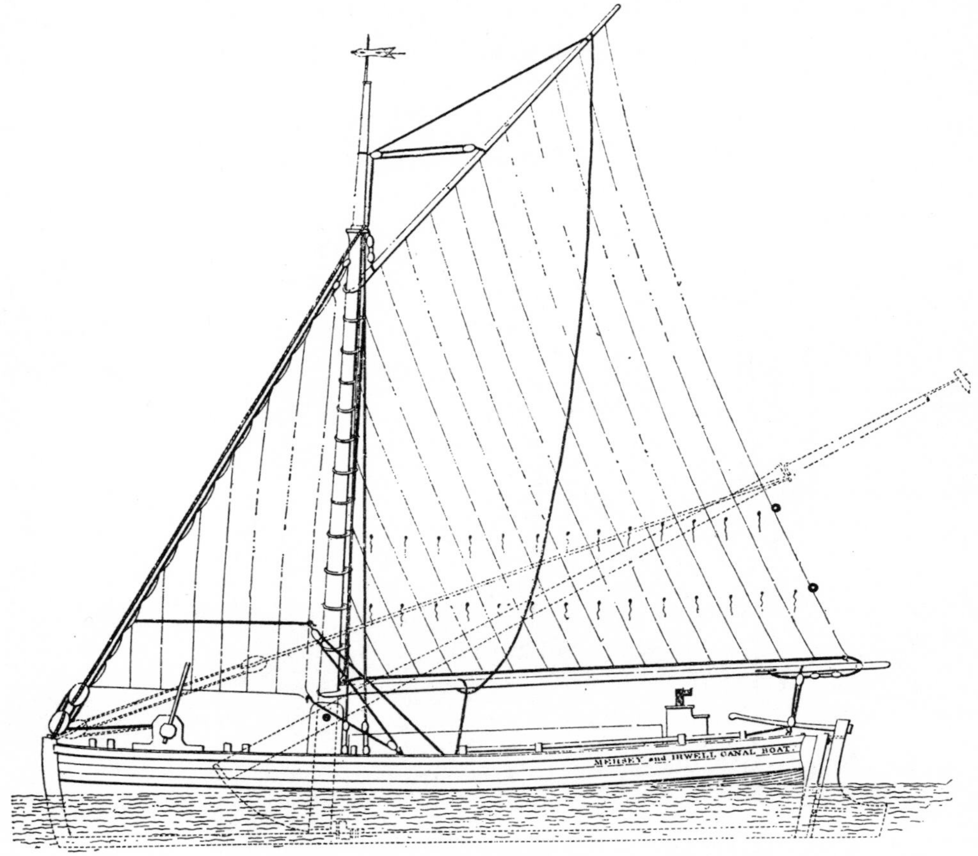

FIGURE 317—*Canal boat as used on the Mersey and Irwell navigation. The mast could be lowered.*

Green—had joined the Thames, Severn, Mersey, Trent, and Aire by trunk canals, from which many branches had been built, while a number of separate canal systems had been developed. In Wales, canals brought coal and iron from the hills to the ports; in Scotland, two great waterways had been built from sea to sea, the Caledonian in the north and the Forth and Clyde in the south; and in Ireland two crossed the country from the Shannon to Dublin. They made an invaluable contribution to the great nineteenth-century development of Britain.

BIBLIOGRAPHY

DE SALIS, H. R. 'A Chronology of Inland Navigation in Great Britain.' London. 1897.
FORBES, U. A. and ASHFORD, W. H. R. 'Our Waterways.' John Murray, London. 1906.
HADFIELD, C. 'British Canals: an Illustrated History.' Phoenix House, London. 1950.
Idem. 'The Canals of Southern England.' Phoenix House, London. 1955.
JACKMAN, W. T. 'The Development of Transportation in Modern England.' University Press, Cambridge. 1914.
PHILLIPS, J. 'A General History of Inland Navigation.' London. 1792.
PRIESTLEY, J. 'Historical Account of the Navigable Rivers, Canals and Railways throughout Great Britain.' London. 1831.
Report of Royal Commission on Canals and Waterways (12 vols). H.M. Stationery Office, London. 1907–9.
ROLT, L. T. C. 'The Inland Waterways of England.' Allen & Unwin, London. 1950.
SMILES, S. 'Lives of the Engineers with an Account of their Principal Works' (3 vols). London. 1861–2.
'The History of Inland Navigation.' London. 1766.
VERNON-HARCOURT, L. F. 'Rivers and Canals' (2nd ed., 2 vols). Oxford. 1896.

The basin at Worsley, showing the canal entrance to the coal-mine.

19

SHIP-BUILDING

GEORGE NAISH

I. PERFORMANCE AND TYPES OF SHIP

THE fact that there had been no startling progress in the development of the ship during the eighteenth century was noted by the author of the article on seamanship in the third edition of the 'Encyclopaedia Britannica' published in 1797: 'What a pity it is that an art so important, so difficult, and so intimately connected with the invariable laws of mechanical nature, should be so held by its possessors that it cannot improve, but must die with each individual.' The seaman, having no advantages of education, 'cannot think'. Yet a ship was a machine and therefore capable of improvement, and particularly during the latter half of the century the historian can trace ideas stirring in the minds of philosophers and mechanics—though attracting little public attention—that herald the remarkable changes which were to alter ships completely during the next century. If we consider the performance of certain ordinary ships in the middle of the eighteenth century, it is not difficult to condone the general apathy towards improving means of water-transport. Trade by sea was expanding as fast as wars would allow, and at the same time notable voyages of discovery were being performed by little ships otherwise undistinguished. In capable hands the wooden sailing-ship proved itself a very satisfactory machine, so that the need for improvement was not obvious. No great consideration of the new mathematical theories had gone, for example, into the design of the Whitby colliers which the British Admiralty bought in succession and fitted out carefully for the three voyages of circumnavigation (1768–80) commanded by Captain James Cook (1728–79). These colliers were described as 'cat-built barks'. Bark was a common term for a small three-masted ship, and was used by Shakespeare and Hakluyt in this sense. Cat was a word of Scandinavian origin for a type of hull, common to the maritime countries of northern Europe, having a bluff bow and straight stem, without the beak-head and figure-head common to larger ships. The broad, round stern had a narrow, flat piece above the transom, with stern windows in it looking out of the after-cabin or coach; this type of stern was called a 'pink' stern. Cat-built vessels were very roomy for their size and were not only colliers but carried goods across the

North Sea and Atlantic. They were, however, best known as colliers, and having flat bottoms could be unloaded into carts on beaches at low water. They could be sailed close to the wind, for the narrow upper part of the stern enabled the main yard to be braced sharp round. Their anchors were weighed with powerful windlasses in the bow.

Cook considered this type of ship ideal for exploring unknown coasts, and with reason. Thus when the *Endeavour* was holed on the Great Barrier Reef of Australia she was run ashore on a beach and repaired, which could not have been done with a bigger ship. The *Endeavour* (plate 40 A) was 97 ft long on the lower deck and of 29 ft beam: her burthen was 368 tons. In this vessel Cook rediscovered New Zealand, sailed round the North and South Islands, and discovered and explored the Great Barrier Reef. The *Resolution*, a similar ship, was called upon to sail in high southern latitudes, voyaging 3660 leagues in 117 days without sighting land. Yet the *Resolution* might well never have set sail, for she proved so 'crank' (top heavy) working down the Thames from Deptford before Cook's second voyage that her first lieutenant wrote: 'I think her by far the most unsafe ship I ever saw or heard of.' The Admiralty had added a poop deck in the stern to provide accommodation for Sir Joseph Banks (1743–1820) and his staff of artists and botanists, but Banks gave up the expedition. Cook wrote: 'She was a stiff ship before we got her', and advised the removal of the top-hamper, after which the *Resolution* proved herself one of the finest sea-boats of all time.

The story of Cook's ships, which were typical of the smaller European merchant ships of the day, shows that such vessels, well found and competently handled, were generally speaking incapable of being overwhelmed by heavy weather in the open sea. Shipwreck was another matter, however. For example, a gale might spring up when a ship was unloading on the sands at low water and she might be lost when the tide came in. Errors of navigation were frequent; in fact, they could not be avoided by the most skilful ship-master because of the insufficiency of the charts (ch 20). Nevertheless, Nelson once wrote cheerfully, when he commanded his favourite 64-gun ship, the *Agamemnon*: 'To me it is perfectly indifferent to what quarter of the world we go: with a good ship and a good ship's company we can come to no harm.' Cook felt equally secure in the *Endeavour*. 'Her best sailing is with the wind a point or two abaft the beam; she will then run 7 or 8 knots and carry a weather helm', he wrote. And again: 'No sea can hurt her laying-to under a main sail or mizzen ballanced.' He had had little opportunity of sailing her in company with other ships, but enough to notice that she made more leeway than most, about a point or a point and a half.

The biggest merchant ships were those trading with the east and managed by the English, French, and Dutch East India Companies (plate 42 B). At the end of the century the English company was taking up ships of three sizes, the largest being officially 1200 tons, which in effect meant anything up to 1500 tons. These ships were well armed with from 30 to 36 guns, and while not fast were well found and well manned and very safe. They usually made three voyages out and back, taking six years, and then were thoroughly repaired and perhaps taken up by the company again. Heavily built and bluff-bowed as these Indiamen were, it is on record that a naval frigate convoying three of them had difficulty in not losing company by running ahead out of sight—the frigate under bare poles and the Indiamen staggering along under a press of canvas which included studding-sails. Nevertheless, the Indiamen were outwardly almost indistinguishable from small warships. The latter, however, were built for speed rather than for cargo-space and were heavily armed, but not necessarily heavily laden, and well manned. The larger naval vessels were considerably larger than any merchant ships.

The ships of the Royal Navy were administratively divided into six rates, according to size and armament. The first three rates were deemed suitable for the line of battle. British ships were usually built a little smaller than French, Spanish, or Dutch ships of the same calibre, and this was a cause of frequent complaints by British naval officers, because the larger ship was both roomier and faster and able to fight better in a sea-way. It was a common fault—arising from attempts to put a quart into a pint pot—for English ships to carry their lower gun-ports nearer the water than was designed by the naval architect. In 1782 Great Britain had 105 ships of the line, France 89, Spain 53, and Holland 32. The financial struggle to maintain this lead was the cause of the niggardly economy of building British ships a little too small. However, a good many French, Spanish, and Dutch ships found their way into the Royal Navy.

A solitary survivor of the line-of-battle ships of those days, H.M.S. *Victory* (plate 42 A), is still in commission as the flagship of the Commander-in-Chief, Portsmouth. The *Victory* deserves our consideration as a very successful ship, so popular that she was always chosen as a flagship throughout her long and active career. She was laid down at Chatham in 1759 and launched in 1765. The length of her gun-deck is 186 ft and her beam is 52 ft. Her armament is 100 guns, the heavier firing a 32-pound ball, with two 68-pounder carronades (short guns) on the forecastle. Between 1778 and 1812 she flew the flags of fourteen admirals and took part in eight major actions, including the battles of Cape St Vincent (1797) and Trafalgar (1805). Her longevity was not due to the careful choice of her timber, because before Trafalgar she had undergone two expensive repairs, in 1787–8 and 1800–3. She was repaired again in 1814–16, and brought up to date in the light of experience gained at Trafalgar. In 1922, after being placed in dry dock, she was restored to her Trafalgar appearance. A visitor to the ship can imagine the cramped life on board, the enormous quantity of timber that went into the building of a wooden ship, and, perhaps above all, the skill and strength needed to handle such a ship under sail and to man-handle her spars, anchors, and boats. One of her officers at Trafalgar, Lieutenant Rivers, compared her with the *Dreadnought*, of much the same dimensions, launched at Portsmouth in 1801. The latter was a heavy, dull sailer, but he records that the *Victory* sailed beautifully, was very weatherly, and steered like a fishing-boat. He calls attention to a fact that was well known: two ships, even if built to the same draught, would never behave alike.

Evidence of the efforts made to improve the theory and practice of shipbuilding will be found in the number of books published on various aspects of the subject. Works by Frenchmen which were widely studied, translated, adapted, and copied were M. Bouguer's *Traité du navire, de sa construction, et de ses mouvements* (1746) and H. L. Duhamel Dumonceau's *Élémens de l'architecture navale ou traité pratique de la construction des vaisseaux* (1752). The Swiss mathematician Leonhard Euler (1707–83) wrote on the form of ships and why they sail to windward; written originally in Latin and published at St Petersburg, his books were translated and he was regarded as the great authority on ship-design. He favoured the full-bowed and clean-tailed, or cod's-head and mackerel-tail, hull. On the whole, however, the scientific reasoning of the mathematicians seems to have resulted in theories that did not work out in practice. A well laden ship with bluff bows drove before her a great swell of water which impeded both sailing and steering, not merely in stormy conditions but in fine weather and over a smooth sea. When running before the wind in bad weather she was liable, even with a good helmsman, to broach-to when yawing about, and her fine lines under the stern made her liable to be pooped by a following sea. On the other hand, a ship with wedge-shaped bows could not carry sufficient sail when upon a wind or close-hauled in a rough sea, because she would plunge dangerously deep, and the water would come on board and fill her main deck.

Ship-builders ignored the theories and strove in the light of experience to find successful designs that represented a compromise between the opposing factors. Most of the many draughts prepared for the Royal Navy during the eighteenth and nineteenth centuries have survived and can be studied (plate 41 A). While merchant ships were built with full-bodied hulls to carry the greatest amount of cargo, warships were designed with many little variations—made within very narrow limits—that represented the testing of various suggested improvements in design. Good use was made of a successful design, and it was often employed for many decades as a basis for later ones. When a ship was captured, her lines were recorded as soon as she reached a naval dockyard, and thus it is possible directly to compare English ships with those of French, Dutch, Spanish, American, and all other navies that came into conflict with that of Britain. The comparison is interesting, and shows the interest in ship-design taken by the British Admiralty. However, admiration for captured French ships was such that there was a tendency for their faults to be copied as well as their virtues. Gabriel Snodgrass, surveyor to the Honourable East India Company, wrote: 'In my opinion, a great deal too much has been said in favour of French ships. I cannot, myself, see anything worthy of being copied from them but their magnitude.'

Warships were commonly built with their top-sides pinched in, so that they had a greater beam at the water-line than at the level of the upper deck. This feature was called the 'tumble-home'. It kept the weight of the upper-deck guns inboard and the hull was supposed to be stronger because of it, but, on the other hand, the tumble-home gave less buoyancy when the ship was heeled. Straight sides also gave more room on deck. Snodgrass did not approve of the tumble-home, which was not the fashion with East Indiamen and other merchant ships. It was excessive in French warships. 'It must appear very extraordinary,' continued Snodgrass, 'that there are several line of battle ships and large frigates now building [1796] for the Government from draughts, copied from those ridiculous ships.' Snodgrass had no use for this 'absurd old fashion of tumbling in', which also wasted crooked or 'compass' timber. The British government was in this period very concerned over the timber situation, and an inquiry brought to light many interesting facts which were probably common to other seafaring countries. Keeping large supplies in the royal dockyards led to wastage because much decayed before it was used, but there need have been no shortage if the forest lands had been replanted at all systematically.

From his experience in building and inspecting ships for the East India Company, Snodgrass made suggestions that were of real practical value; they were generally adopted, though not always immediately. He thought ships should be built more strongly: 'I have no idea of a ship of war, that is properly built, foundering, or not keeping the seas in the worst weather.' His proposals included thicker planking on the bottom, from four to six inches in the case of line-of-battle ships; straight sides to give greater spread for the shrouds and to make the masts more secure; firm, flush, upper decks to strengthen the hull and prevent a weight of water collecting between decks in the waist; moving the foremast farther aft to lighten the ship in the bows; and removal of the quarter galleries to lighten the stern, which should also be strengthened with strong dead-lights in place of the weak stern windows. A great advance was his suggestion for iron knees, standards, and diagonal braces to prevent the ship from 'working'. The use of iron not only saved timber but gave greater strength. Snodgrass advised the Admiralty and other government departments from 1771 onwards, and gathered his experience from ships of all countries.

It seems probable that the urge to improve ships, which began to take effect at the end of the eighteenth century, was common to all European countries that possessed shipping. The French led the way in trying to unite theory with practice. For example, much space was given in French books on the subject to descriptions of all possible ways of rowing Greek triremes, and the canoes of the South Sea islands are fully illustrated from the descriptions of Cook and Anson. But, as has been shown by the modern use of testing-tanks, it is difficult to apply theory to ship-design, and the improvements came generally from cautious trial and error. In 1791 a privately formed group in London carried out a series of experiments in the Greenland dock, and although the society for the improvement of naval architecture which they formed got into difficulties and failed, its transactions were privately printed and given away. At the same time, Captain John Schank (1740–1823) was experimenting with sliding keels or centre-boards. Various ships were also built with peculiar hull-forms or rigs which achieved a certain amount of success but no lasting favour. Examples are the sloops *Arrow* and *Dart*, designed by Sir Samuel Bentham (1757–1831). They had sharp ends, the stem and stern-post raking, and their sides spread outwards so that they had more beam on deck than at the water-line, which was supposed to make them very stiff. They were armed with carronades mounted on non-recoil carriages. They were fairly successful and more were built. An officer of the East India Company, Richard Gower (1767–1833), built and had launched from Itchenor, in 1800, a four-masted ship, also with sides spreading out and with a rig of his own design in which the sails were very flat. This vessel, the *Transit*, was exceedingly fast sailing to windward. Such trials were followed with interest, and encouraged further practical experiments.

II. COPPER SHEATHING FOR SHIPS' BOTTOMS

Weeds and barnacles attach themselves to the bottoms of ships, and unless they are cleared off the ship is made slow and unhandy. In the tropics, the bottom of a wooden ship will quickly be destroyed by the mollusc known as the shipworm (*Teredo*) unless it is protected. In the eighteenth century it was usual to sheath the bottom of a ship with thin fir-boards over hair and tar; and when, in addition, the bottom was covered with the broad heads of nails the ship was said to be sheathed and filled. In the West Indies it was very difficult to careen ships and burn off or 'bream' their bottoms, and in 1761 the Navy Board suggested to the British Admiralty that a ship's bottom might be covered with plate copper as a protection against worm. This suggestion had been made before, for example in 1708, but it was now carried out, the frigate *Alarm* being sheathed with thin copper by way of experiment. She came home in August 1763. The copper had been on for twenty months; it had somewhat wasted away, but it was clean of weed and barnacles and had kept the caulking in place, and the worm had not got into the planking. On the other hand, much to everyone's surprise, the false keel had fallen off and the iron fastenings of the rudder were so decayed that the rudder would very soon have followed. By replacing with copper the iron fastenings on the hull below the water-line, rudder and keel were made safe, but weed grew on the copper, which was disappointing. The electrolytic action between the copper and the iron was not understood until later. In 1776 twelve vessels in the Royal Navy, all frigates or smaller, were coppered. In 1780 there was a great drive to copper ships, and in that year Admiral Rodney was sent with a coppered fleet to relieve Gibraltar.

III. THE INDUSTRIAL REVOLUTION AND THE SAILING-SHIP

Until the end of the eighteenth century the heavy labour of ship-building was being performed in England with little mechanical assistance, despite the example of the revolution that was altering the character of many industries. Foreigners, however, did not seem to think England backward in this respect. Daniel Lescallier (1743–1822) in 1791 was full of praises for the great merchant yards on the Thames where Perry and Wells were building East Indiamen and whaling-ships. At the end of the century Thomas Pennant (1726–98), on his last tour, visited Portsmouth and inspected the dockyard. He saw the anchor-smiths: 'seventy or eighty brawny fellows were amidst the fires busied in fabricating those securities to our shipping'. He saw the faultless anchor of the unfortunate *Royal George*, bearing the motto: 'Fear not; I will hold you fast.' He saw the rope-walk, 870 ft long: 'The making of a great cable is a wonderful sight; a hundred men are required for the purpose, and the labour is so hard that they cannot work at it more than four hours in the day.' The sawing was all done by hand over saw-pits, and it was sometimes cheaper to buy planks from Scandinavian countries where sawing was done in mills by wind- or water-power. Pumping water out of the dry docks was another heavy labour, in this case performed by horses.

Sir Samuel Bentham, the brother of Jeremy Bentham, had early training as a shipwright. He gained his military rank in the Russian service and had returned to England on leave when he visited the dockyards to advise on improvements in 1795. He left the Russian service, became inspector-general of naval works (a new office), and laboured with a small staff to bring the naval yards up to date. In 1798 he wrote: 'I lost no time in considering the means of enabling inanimate force to perform some of the most important of the preparatory operations subservient to naval works.' He suggested a steam-engine, but the idea found little favour. He conferred with the First Lord of the Admiralty, Lord Spencer, who

FIGURE 318—*Blockmaking. The horses work both a saw and a lathe. The parts of the block are the shell, of elm or ash; the pin, of lignum vitae, greenheart, or iron; and the wheel, of lignum vitae.*

allowed him to try out a steam-engine at Redbridge, near Southampton, where new ships of his own design were building for the Navy. The ships were ready before the engine, which he was then allowed to introduce into Portsmouth Yard.

This engine, made by Sadler, seems to have worked at about 12–14 hp; its first job, when set up by a master millwright in 1799, was to replace the horses used for pumping out a new dock, and to work saws. Sadler's engine cost £800, the pump £550, and the saws £600. The total of £1950 compared very favourably with the cost of the horse-pump for the dock alone, which was £2758. The new engine was to pump by night and saw by day. It also raised fresh water from a well and pumped water through the fire-engine hoses. A second engine was ordered from Boulton and Watt; it appears to have produced 30 hp. In 1801 there were discussions about a movable steam-engine and apparatus 'calculated to perform the work of from 30 to 40 labourers': this seems to have been equivalent to six horses. Block-making (figure 318) was an operation of great importance to the sailing Navy, and in 1802 Bentham was inquiring about the block-making contract and very shortly was submitting his own plans for making the blocks in the dockyard by steam. The blocks for the Navy were then made under contract by Dunsterville at Plymouth and Taylor at Southampton: the latter owned quite an elaborate plant driven by a water-mill. Under Bentham a large works was established for block-making machinery, but the story of this has been told elsewhere (p 426). It employed ten men and produced 160 000 blocks annually. By this time, too, the steam-engines were harnessed to both the rope-walk and the iron- and copper-works. Bentham was responsible for many other

FIGURE 319—*Sheer hulk and sheers. After a new ship had been launched at a naval dockyard she was taken alongside the sheer hulk and her lower masts were stepped. The rope was cut to the proper length and worked up into standing and running rigging on board by the ship's company, blocks were stropped and fitted, and the masts and spars sent up aloft.*

improvements in the dockyards, such as building covered slips. This had often been suggested, but he was in a position to carry it out. Some of the slips can still be seen at Chatham and Devonport dockyards.

IV. THE SAILING WARSHIP, 1800–40

The Napoleonic wars naturally focused attention on the warship, though certain merchant ships and privateers were built with a particular view to speed. The Royal Navy blockaded the coasts of Europe, and Admiral Mahan, the naval historian, has told us how 'those far distant, storm-beaten ships, upon which the Grand Army never looked, stood between it and the dominion of the world'. Admiral Cornwallis was off Brest, Collingwood off Rochefort, Pellew off Ferrol, and Nelson off Toulon. It is sufficient indication of the endurance of ships and men to mention that from 16 June 1803 Nelson did not set foot out of the *Victory* for very nearly two whole years.

Nelson must have considered the ship of the line as almost incapable of improvement. At Trafalgar the foremost ships of the two British lines were some time getting into action, and suffered much from raking fire into their bows, where the beak-head bulkhead afforded little protection from the enemy shot. As a result of this lesson, various forms of bows and sterns were proposed which

FIGURE 320—*'Hooping' a mast, that is, driving on iron rings.*

afforded better protection. Sir Robert Seppings (1767–1840), one of the surveyors of the Navy, was responsible for a much stronger round stern, which was very unpopular amongst naval officers because of its ugliness. Before this an officer fighting an action astern, as in the famous retreat conducted by Admiral Cornwallis before a superior French force in 1795, was forced to mutilate the stern of his ship in order to make gunports through which to fire at the enemy; a gun was fired from within to blow out the stern frame.

Seppings devised a new way of framing ships that was adopted in the Navy. Declaring that 'partial strength produces general weakness', he pointed out that the frame of a 74-gun ship, 170 ft long, was formed of 800 different timbers placed at right angles to the keel (plate 41 B); there the ribs were each made of several pieces, about 14 in thick, and there was a space of from 1 to 5 inches between each 'frame', as the complete rib was called. The ribs were planked within and without, and the deck beams tied the sides together and supported the deck-planking. All the timbers composing the hull were placed at right-angles to each other, which allowed the hull to work in a sea-way. Seppings devised an elaborate system of diagonal trusses to hold a ship rigid, and filled the spaces between the frames. The trusses and the fillings also prevented the ship from 'hogging', that is, sagging at the bow and stern when the middle of the ship was on the crest of a wave. Hogging came about from the want of a continued succession of support from the centre to the extremities. Seppings omitted the inside planking, called the ceiling.

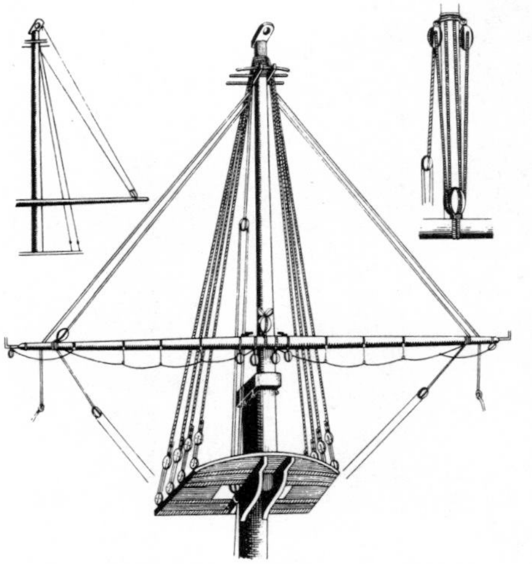

FIGURE 321—*Rigging of the topsail yard. When a ship was rigged, everything had to go on or up in the right order.*

In 1811 a school of naval architecture was established in Portsmouth dockyard. Forty-two students were educated there in a few years, though the Admiralty could employ only 25 men so highly trained and educated. The principal of the school, James Inman (1776–1859), was a brilliant mathematician, and many of the pupils became famous in later years. Once again, however, mathematics provided no short cut to improvement; the ships designed by the school were undistinguished and it was closed down as a failure in 1832. At the same time the Navy Board, the department of the Admiralty that looked after ship-building, was abolished and its administrative work reorganized under the Admiralty. A naval officer, Sir William Symonds (1782–1850), who had a flair for designing ships but no especial training, was appointed surveyor of the Navy. He built many ships, of all classes, which had a great reputation for speed and stability. They could carry a press of sail, but had a violent motion which made them bad gun-platforms; they also had a V-section which sometimes meant that stores had to be stowed on deck because there was too little room in the hold. It was suggested that while there was too much mathematics in the ships designed by the school of naval architecture, Symonds's designs suffered because he was untrained. Despite his claims to originality, such a man as

Symonds found no pleasure in designing hulls for the new steam-engines. Instead, he delighted in trying to improve the sailing qualities of the already old-fashioned wooden warship, frigate, or line-of-battle ship. The hooped masts (figure 320) would be stepped in the hull as she lay alongside a sheer hulk (figure 319); and when they had been stepped would be clothed with the appropriate standing and running rigging; then the tops and caps could be placed over the mastheads and secured. The topmasts and topgallantmasts would follow and be rigged in the proper order; after which the yards could be crossed and the sails bent (figure 321); then the spectators had the wonderful sight of the full-rigged ship

FIGURE 322—*Sails of a ship. These are named after the masts, and each mast of a full-rigged ship was in three parts: the lowermast, topmast, and topgallantmast. The squaresails on the foremast are the foresail, fore topsail, fore topgallantsail, and fore royal. The extensions to the squaresails are the studding sails. There are staysails between the masts, and the mizzen is brailed up and the spanker or driver set. The jib and two staysails are set from the bowsprit, and the spritsail-topsail and spritsail under the bowsprit.*

with her acres of canvas (figure 322), of which the individual sails had been stitched and roped by hand (figure 323) by the sail-makers sitting on their characteristic benches. The progressive rigging of a warship just put into commission was carried out by the newly raised ship's company under their own officers. It was skilful work founded on the stored experience of many generations of sailormen.

V. INTRODUCTION OF CHAIN ANCHOR-CABLE

In 1808 Sir Samuel Brown (1776–1852) of the Royal Navy proposed the use of iron cables and rigging. The iron cable came into general use in the Navy—one chain-cable to each ship—in 1811, and the fleet under Admiral Lord Exmouth which bombarded Algiers in 1816 lay at anchor with chain-cables, which could not be shot away. The original cost of the chain was not much greater than that of the hempen cable, which, in the *Victory* for example, was some

20 inches in circumference. Chain was not affected by alternate wetness and dryness, which quickly rotted hempen cables, especially in the tropics, and it did not easily part amongst rocks. The chain could be stowed in a locker, whereas the ablest men in a ship were required to coil down the hempen cable in the cable-tiers so that it would run out quickly without a kink, which might jam. The chain was, however, difficult to handle in deep water, and the hawse-holes in the ship's bows, as well as the riding-bitts, had to be cased in iron to take it. The difficult task of splicing the hempen cable, and the 'puddening' or padding of

FIGURE 323—*Sailmaking. Tools illustrated include a sail hook, used with a tackle for stretching the bolt rope when sewing it to the sail; seam rubbers and mallets; and palm and needles.*

the anchor-ring, were no longer necessary. Merchant ships gave up carrying hempen cables, though men-of-war carried two or three for laying out anchors. By 1840 chain slings for lower yards, chain topsail sheets and ties, chain gammonings, and chain bobstays were common.

VI. LAST DAYS OF THE SAILING NAVY

During the Napoleonic wars there was very little difference between the ships of the navies of the principal powers: Great Britain, France, Holland, and Spain. At the end of the wars, however, Great Britain was supreme except for a young but sturdy rival, the United States of America. In the war of 1812 the United States built large frigates which inflicted startling losses on the ships of the Royal Navy. On the other hand, the commerce of the United States was cleared from the seas and most of these powerful frigates were ultimately captured. Their lines were recorded by their captors and so have been preserved.

In 1815 it was not apparent to the directors of naval strategy that the new steam-engine, still uncertain, could be of any use for purposes of war except for powering tug-boats. Certain far-seeing officers thought otherwise, and it is not surprising to find the Earl of Dundonald and Charles Napier advocating better use of this new method of propulsion. Contemporary engines were unreliable, fuel was bulky, and early ocean-going steamships were therefore fully rigged. Paddle-wheels interfered with sailing, especially when the ship was heeled, and the screw-propeller was introduced to aid sailing-ships. Moreover, paddle-wheels were very vulnerable to gun-fire, and it was the screw-propeller that made the steam-warship practicable. In the navies of the world steam-propulsion slowly found favour, though the larger navies were more reluctant to countenance drastic changes than the smaller ones. Meanwhile the grand old wooden line-of-battle sailing-ships completed their slow development, and reached a remarkable climax to their long and steady progress. The last three-decker launched for the Royal Navy was the *Victoria* of 121 guns; this was in 1859.

A ship with a more active career, the *Queen*, of 110 guns, was launched at Portsmouth in 1839; the length of her gun-deck was 204 ft and of her keel 166 ft; her breadth was 60 ft; and her tonnage 3104. Her main truck, that is, the top of her main-mast, was 240 ft above the water-line, and her main yard was 111 ft long. Her lower-deck ports were 6 ft 6 in above the water-line. Her main armament consisted of 32-pounders, the guns on the lower decks being longer and heavier than those on the upper. The *Queen* was flagship in the Black Sea during the Crimean war; she was towed into action with the tug-boat lashed along her disengaged side, and was set on fire by Russian shells. In 1859 she was cut down to a two-decker, and fitted with engines of 500 hp. She was sold out of the service in 1871. H.M.S. *Duke of Wellington*, of 131 guns, was launched at Pembroke in 1852. The length of her gun-deck was 240 ft and her tonnage was 3771. She was one of the largest wooden warships and, although designed as a sailing-ship, was given engines on the stocks. She saw active service during the Crimean war, including service as a flagship in the Baltic campaign in 1854. She was screw-propelled, and her engines, built by Robert Napier & Sons, were of 700 hp. H.M.S. *Marlborough*, 131 guns, launched at Portsmouth in 1855, was a little larger than the *Duke of Wellington* and can therefore be regarded as the climax of the wooden warship, driven by sail and steam (plate 40 B).

In the merchant service, iron construction started with small vessels; it both saved timber and, in the case of steam-vessels, lessened the risk of fire. The navies, especially the Royal Navy, long looked askance at iron construction. A shell that could be fired from ships' guns had been invented in 1822 by the

French general H. J. Paixhans (1783–1854). Although the *Duke of Wellington* could fire shells from her 68-pounders their destructive powers on the wooden ships of the enemy received less consideration than the danger of filling them in the magazines of ships also constructed of wood. In 1853, in the preliminaries which led up to the Crimean war, a very superior Russian fleet destroyed a Turkish squadron at Sinope, firing shells from their 68-pounders against the wooden hulls of the enemy, who could retaliate only with the old-fashioned solid shot. The massacre at Sinope underlined a lesson that should have been obvious before, and the French navy immediately ordered armoured 'floating batteries' for service against the Russians.

Another lesson, that of the superiority of the steam-propelled ship, was still not so obvious. The last days of the sailing navy saw very efficient sailing-ships, smartly handled. In H.M.S. *Queen*, for example, all three topsails could be reefed together in about a minute. The sailing-ship was, however, helpless in a calm and might be prevented by a head-wind from leaving port. The existence of small steamships made surprise attacks possible. Nevertheless, particularly in England, it was unthinkable that the traditional wooden walls should be abandoned. The ship-building industry was prepared to go on building wooden ships, claiming that we should lose our advantage if there were a change.

VII. THE FULLY-RIGGED IRONCLAD, 1859

The French government had led the way in building floating batteries, armoured against shell-fire. In 1859 they had a wooden two-decker on the stocks cut down a deck, and her sides armoured. The removal of her upper deck compensated for the weight of the armour, so that the ship was not made top-heavy. The British Admiralty replied to this French ironclad, *La Gloire*, with a new design of their own, a ship iron-hulled and iron-armoured, originally planned by John Scott Russell and Isaac Watts. H.M.S. *Warrior* was epoch-making as being the first armoured ship in the Royal Navy; when put in commission she could have taken on the navies of the world single-handed. The necessity of protecting a broadside with hundreds of tons of iron slabs meant that to retain stability a ship either had to be much broader, and therefore much slower, or much lower in the water and therefore impracticable as a three-decker with the customary three tiers of guns. In the *Warrior* the answer was to increase the length and to mount the guns in one tier; thus, the old nomenclature of the Royal Navy being retained, she was rated as a frigate.

Wooden ships had already reached a limit in length, and the *Warrior* was built on an iron frame. She was divided into watertight compartments by bulkheads, and her machinery and equipment were distributed between these compartments. She was 380 ft long between perpendiculars, and her beam was 58 ft; her tonnage was 9140. A length of 208 ft of her hull was armoured, but her hand-steering gear was left unprotected. Her $4\frac{1}{2}$-in armour was backed by teak topsides and could resist the heaviest gun then afloat, namely the 100-pounder such as she herself mounted. She was rather unhandy because of her length, and her handsome beakhead with figure-head and the old-fashioned frigate-stern made her wet at sea. Her graceful head concealed a ram bow below water. She was fully rigged, unlike *La Gloire* which had a schooner-rig as auxiliary to her screw and engines. The *Warrior* had powerful engines, by J. Penn & Son of Greenwich, which drove her at over 14 knots—much faster than foreign warships. On occasions she logged 13 knots under sail. Her single screw was fitted with lifting-gear and came up into a trunk in the stern of the hull; for this operation the ship had to be hove-to and 600 men of her complement of 705 tailed on to the falls. Her anchors were weighed by hand. Her armament was three 100-pound Armstrong rifled breech-loaders on the upper deck; below, she carried eight more 100-pounders and twenty-six smooth bore muzzle-loaders on the gun deck. The government yards had no facilities for iron construction, so the *Warrior* was built on the Thames in a private yard. She was ordered in 1859 and completed in 1861. She was paid off from service in 1884, by which time she was well out of date. The armament race between warships, rightly feared by the British Admiralty, had begun.

The *Warrior* was copied and improved upon, and the screw-driven ironclad warship continued to be fully rigged with masts and sails. The warships of the European navies were always fully manned, and ready to visit distant parts of the globe away from stocks of coal. Masts and their supporting shrouds and other rigging did not get in the way of broadside ordnance, and warships were generally sailed whenever possible, to save coal. In 1861, however, during the American civil war, John Ericsson (1803–89) persuaded the Federal government to build an ironclad 'monitor', and the name was indeed a warning to all the old-fashioned navies of Europe. The features of the *Monitor* were complete armour above the water, low free-board, and a revolving gun-turret. The revolving turret made the fitting of mast and sail impossible. The *Monitor* was the first of the modern warships to be designed to carry a chosen weapon at the expense of the usual sea-going conveniences of a ship. Turret-ships were added to the Royal Navy, and in 1869 the *Captain* (plate 43B) was launched, embodying some of the features of the *Monitor* in a much bigger and sea-going ship of 4272 tons; she was fully rigged. Her armament included four 12-in 25-ton guns in two turrets. The ship's low free-board amidships was accentuated because of a mistake in her design: designed to be 8 ft it was in fact 6 ft. She capsized in a squall off Cape Finisterre in 1870 with the loss of most of her complement of 500 men, including her designer Captain Cowper Coles (b 1819). When she was heeled so that the edge of the deck went under water she quickly lost stability and capsized.

The sailing ironclad's days were numbered. The turret-ships *Glatton* and *Devastation*, both launched in 1871, each had one mast for signalling-purposes only; but until the turn of the century the Navy had use for some sailing-ships on foreign stations.

VIII. THE CLIPPER SHIP

The British East India Company enjoyed a monopoly of trade with the Far East until 1833, when its charter was revised. Even then firms such as Green & Wigram of Blackwall on the Thames and T. and W. Smith of Newcastle took over the trading responsibilities and carried on the old traditions. Their comely ships were 'snugged down' each night, that is, sail was reduced. The ships were not slow, but they were not driven; they could do 12 knots on occasion and made Calcutta in about 90 days. For example, the *Blenheim*, constructed in 1848, was frigate-built and in the event of war would have been taken into the Royal Navy. She was 175 ft long by 42 ft beam, and measured 1314 tons.

Meanwhile, however, the idea that ships must hurry was gaining ground. Queen Victoria, for instance, visited Scotland in 1842 in her sailing-yacht the *Royal George*, which was towed all the way by a naval steamer. Nevertheless the Queen found the voyage very tedious and vexatious, and came home in the *Trident* belonging to the General Steam Navigation Company, which in a head-wind soon left the *Royal George* and the naval steamers out of sight. Speedy passage was particularly desirable for passengers and mails, and the American-owned packets which sailed backwards and forwards across the Atlantic were well known for their quick passages and their regularity. An American who visited England in 1833 tells the story of a packet-ship sailing from London to New York and back and finding still sheltering in the Downs, awaiting a fair wind, an Indiaman and several other ships that had sailed in company with her from London. The Americans had studied how to build fast ships and they drove these ships hard. In 1849 Great Britain repealed the Navigation Acts which for long had made the eastern markets practically the monopoly of British ships. In reply, fast soft-wood ships which had been built in the United States set about chasing British shipping off the seas. Emphasis was placed on speed under sail at the expense of capacity for carrying cargo. The first ship each year to arrive back in Europe with the new tea crop from China earned a handsome premium. British owners took up the American challenge and turned to the ship-builders for help. The racing was very keen and captured the attention of the public.

There has been much argument as to what constitutes the clipper ship.

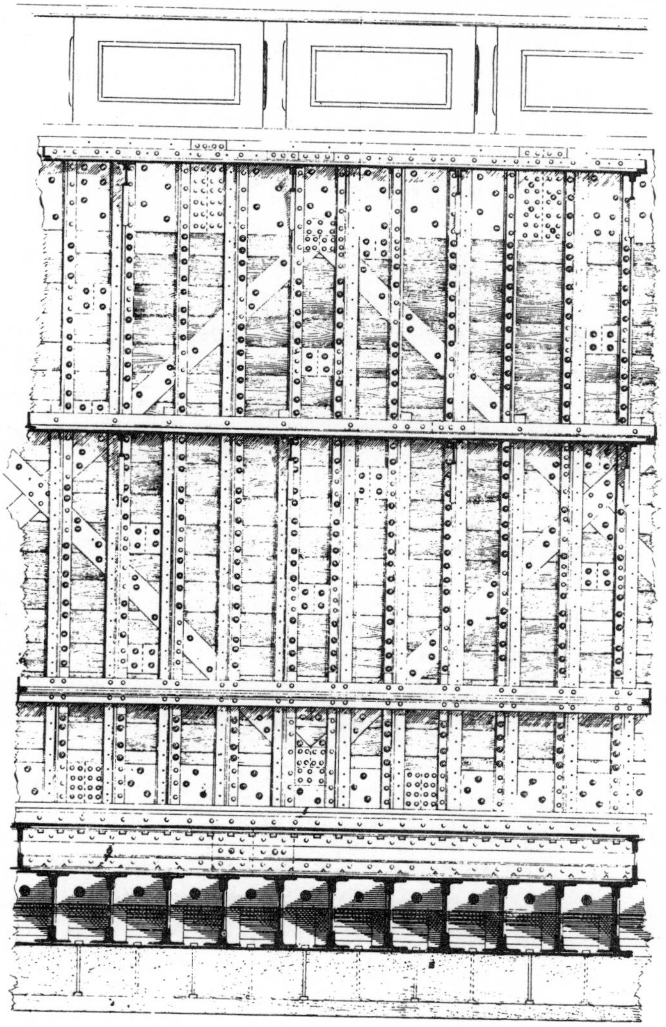

FIGURE 324—*Suggestions for the construction and classification of composite ships. Before the opening of the Suez canal many clipper ships were composite built, as it was called, that is, their bottoms were wooden planking over an iron frame, the advantage being that the bottoms of such ships could be sheathed with copper, Muntz metal, or zinc, and kept reasonably clean so as not greatly to retard their speed. However, composite building was not suitable for steamers with full engine-power, and after the opening of the canal it went out of fashion for merchant ships, though remaining in use for small naval vessels which still made passages under sail.*

Schooners built at Baltimore proved very fast as privateers in the war of 1812 and were copied in both Britain and America. The ship-builders of Aberdeen developed fast schooners whose lines were copied for larger vessels. In fact, the building of fast ships was being undertaken on each side of the Atlantic even before the repeal of the Navigation Acts in 1849. Tea clippers were ships built for that special trade. They were mostly small, of some 700 tons, and heavily canvassed for sailing through the light winds in the China Sea. Their fine ends made them wet ships, and if caught aback they might gather stern-way and be lost as a result of driving their sterns under water. Their period of fame was, however, short—from 1849 to 1875 at the most. The Suez canal was opened in 1869 and offered a shorter route to the east, practicable only for steamships. Two famous clippers built on the Clyde at Greenock were the *Ariel* and *Sir Lancelot*, both launched in 1865 and built to the same lines. Their length was 197 ft and their beam 33 ft 9 in. The lower masts of the *Ariel* were of iron. They were extreme clippers, and excelled in light winds. The *Ariel* was very seldom passed at sea—on one occasion she and the *Taeping* (plate 43 A) raced up the Channel logging 14 knots—but she was very tender, and in strong winds had quickly to be relieved of her canvas when running before the wind, as otherwise she was in danger of being pooped. She was lost in 1872 on a voyage out to Sydney and is thought to have been pooped when running her easting down in the Roaring Forties, strong winds for which she was unsuitable. The *Thermopylae*, built at Aberdeen in 1868, was a very popular ship, rather larger than the *Ariel*, being 212 ft long with a 36-ft beam. She never raced the *Ariel*, but was the better ship if not the faster, for she sailed well to windward and was also very fast and manageable when running in strong winds.

The only survivor of these famous ships, the *Cutty Sark*, is now preserved in a dry dock at Greenwich. She was very fast in strong winds, having once logged $17\frac{1}{2}$ knots. Built in the year in which the Suez canal was opened, her active career lasted until 1922. The *Cutty Sark* was composite built of iron and wood, a form of construction used for many of the tea clippers and for some small vessels, sloops and gun-vessels, of the Royal Navy (figure 324). Wooden planking on iron frames had the advantage that the bottom could be sheathed with copper and kept sufficiently clean to prevent any great retardation in the ship's sailing. Iron hulls were found to foul rapidly and were sometimes planked outside with wood and then sheathed with copper over all, but care had to be taken to prevent the copper from coming into contact with the iron, as electrolytic action would then have been set up (p 580). Iron lower masts and wire rigging were introduced, to support the heavy strains when big sailing-ships were raced. The clipper ship

Caliph, launched in 1865, had wire standing-rigging and wire lifts. Wire standing-rigging was introduced into the Royal Navy in 1838.

IX. SAIL AND STEAM

The iron hull was developed to withstand the vibration of the steam-engine, but it proved suitable for sailing-ships also, except for the fact that the bottom fouled quickly. Steamships were fully rigged as long as engines were unreliable, but as engines improved so the top-hamper of masts and yards was cut down. French steamships were often rigged with three short masts and jib-headed schooner-sails. Some British shipping-lines retained sails to steady the ship, but when ships came to steam at higher speeds square canvas was useless (plate 44 A). They steamed at a steady pace throughout the voyage, and already mail-steamers were making some 360 nautical miles a day. Hence by 1883 merchant ships favoured fore-and-aft canvas only: they had planned voyages and regular arrangements for the replenishment of fuel, so that sails became less important. Again, few ships had enough crew to see that a steamer's sails were properly set. The screw-propeller had been developed for use in sailing-ships (p 587), and naval ships with large ships' companies were able to make full use of sail and steam, but in the merchant service, where crews were relatively small, the tendency was for steamers to give up sail. The Orient Line, however, kept full rig on their ships which voyaged to the Cape and Australia. There was still a large tonnage of iron sailing-ships, which they could afford to let wait in port warehousing a cargo. A further advantage of the sailing-ship was that the hull is relatively more capacious than that of the steamship, which has a large engine-room.

At different times auxiliaries were tried, but in several ships the engines were afterwards removed. An example was the *Lancing*, a four-masted iron ship, built at Glasgow in 1866 as the steamer *Pereire*. With the engines removed, the *Lancing* was still sailing in 1924 under the Norwegian flag. Various labour-saving devices helped to improve the sailing-ship. An example was the patent reefing-gear invented by Henry Cunningham in 1850, which enabled topsails to be reefed from the deck. The topsail was bent to a smaller yard, below the topsail-yard and hanging from it, which could be rotated by means of chains so as to roll up the head of the topsail on it. The gear necessitated a split down the middle of the sail; this was covered by a laced patch called the bonnet. It was claimed that the sail could be close-reefed in heavy weather by one man and a boy in 2½ seconds. By such means small crews were able to handle large sailing-ships, such as the iron barques, often four- or five-masted, which at the end of the nineteenth century still crowded the ports of the world (plate 44 B). This was the final development of the ocean carrier, fully rigged. A five-masted ship, the *Preussen*, built of steel at Hamburg in 1902, was 433 ft long overall with a beam of 53 ft, and carried a sail area of 60 000 sq ft of canvas, divided into six square-sails on each mast and eighteen fore-and-aft sails. She could log seventeen knots and had steam-power on board for weighing her anchors and working her cargo. She was the only five-masted ship square-rigged on all five masts ever built (figure 325).

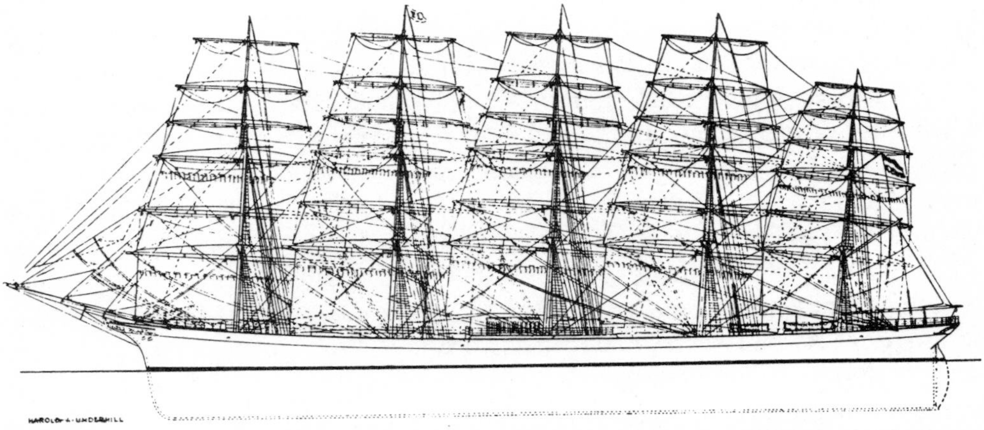

FIGURE 325—*Five-masted ship* Preussen, *the only five-masted full-rigged ship ever built. She marked the climax of the big merchant sailing-ships.*

X. LLOYD'S REGISTER OF SHIPPING

Lloyd's[1] register deserves mention here as it reflects the major changes in ship-construction during this period. The earliest register is of ships sailing in 1764, 1765, and 1766. The ships were classified according to hull and equipment, and the list was issued to subscribers for the use of underwriters, who were to regard it as private and not for publication. The list gives particulars of some 4500 ships, several of from 400 to 600 tons, two of 800 tons, and one of 900 tons. 8271 ships are classed in the register for 1800. Iron cables appeared in 1813, and a steamship, the *James Watt* (294 tons), in 1822. There were 81 steamships in 1827 and 100 in 1832. In 1834 a permanent committee representing merchants, shipowners, and underwriters was set up, and there was competition with a Liverpool register of shipping. In 1836 the description 'built of iron' first occurs, and rules for iron construction were framed in 1854, the committee co-operating with the ship-builders. Lloyd's rules for classing ships have been of the greatest

[1] From Lloyd's coffee-house, originally in Tower Street, London, where from 1687 merchants and others interested in shipping used to meet.

value in improving ship-building practice, and the testing of equipment has done much to prevent loss of life at sea.

BIBLIOGRAPHY

ABELL, SIR WESTCOTT S. 'The Shipwright's Trade.' University Press, Cambridge. 1948.
ALBION, R. G. 'Forests and Sea Power.' Harvard University Press, Cambridge, Mass. 1926.
ANDERSON, ROMOLA, and ANDERSON, R. C. 'The Sailing Ship.' Harrap, London. 1926.
'Annals of Lloyds Register, Centenary Edition.' Lloyds, London. 1934.
BENTHAM, M. S. 'The Life of Brigadier General Sir Samuel Bentham.' London. 1862.
CHAPELLE, H. I. 'The History of American Sailing Ships.' Putnam, London. 1936.
CLARK, A. H. 'The Clipper Ship Era.' Putnam, New York. 1911.
COTTON, E. 'East Indiamen.' Batchworth Press, London. 1949.
CUTLER, C. C. 'Greyhounds of the Sea.' Putnam, New York. 1930.
FALCONER, W. 'A New and Universal Dictionary of the Marine.' London. 1769. See also the enlarged edition by W. BURNEY. London. 1815.
FINCHAM, J. 'A History of Naval Architecture.' London. 1851.
GREENHILL, B. 'The Merchant Schooners', Vol. 1. Percival Marshall, London. 1951.
LESCALLIER, D. 'Vocabulaire des termes de marine anglois et françois' (new ed., 2 vols). London. 1783.
Idem. 'Traité pratique du gréement des vaisseaux et autres bâtiments de mer' (2 vols). Paris. 1791.
LEVER, D. 'The Young Sea Officer's Sheet Anchor' (2nd ed.). London. 1819.
LUBBOCK, B. 'The China Clippers.' Brown, Glasgow. 1922.
MACGREGOR, D. R. 'The Tea Clippers.' Percival Marshall, London. 1952.
DUHAMEL-DUMONCEAU, H. L. 'Elemens de l'architecture navale.' Paris. 1752.
MOORE, A. 'Last Days of Mast and Sail.' Clarendon Press, Oxford. 1925.
Idem. 'Sailing Ships of War, 1800–1860.' Halton & Truscott Smith, London. 1926.
NATIONAL MARITIME MUSEUM. 'Catalogue of Ship Models in the National Maritime Museum', by R. C. ANDERSON. H.M. Stationery Office, London. 1952.
PARKINSON, C. N. 'Trade in the Eastern Seas, 1793–1813.' University Press, Cambridge. 1937.
PLIMSOLL, S. 'Our Seamen—an Appeal.' London. 1873.
SCIENCE MUSEUM. 'Sailing Ships—their History and Development as Illustrated by the Collection of Ship Models in the Science Museum', by G. S. LAIRD CLOWES. H.M. Stationery Office, London. 1932.
SHARP, J. A. 'Memoirs of Rear Admiral Sir William Symonds.' London. 1858.
SHEWAN, A. 'The Great Days of Sail.' Heath Cranton, London. 1927.
SOCIETY OF NAUTICAL RESEARCH. *The Mariner's Mirror.* The Quarterly Journal of the Society of Nautical Research. 1911–.
STEEL, D. 'The Elements and Practice of Rigging and Seamanship' (2 vols). London. 1794.
Idem. 'The Shipwright's Vade Mecum.' London. 1805.
UNDERHILL, H. A. 'Sailing Ship Rigs and Rigging.' Brown Son & Ferguson, Glasgow. 1938.
Idem. 'Masting and Rigging the Clipper Ship and Ocean Carrier.' Brown Son & Ferguson, Glasgow. 1946.
Idem. 'Deep Water Sail.' Brown Son & Ferguson, Glasgow. 1952.
VILLIERS, A. 'The Way of a Ship.' Hodder & Stoughton, London. 1954.
WATSON, H. 'A Compleat Theory of the Construction and Properties of Vessels.' London. 1776.

20

CARTOGRAPHY

R. A. SKELTON

I. THE WORLD MAP

THE construction of the framework of an accurate world map, depending on determinations of the shape and size of the Earth and the accurate fixing of the latitude and longitude of a sufficient number of points on its surface, was the work of geodesists and cartographers of the late seventeenth century and the eighteenth century, initiated by the *Académie des Sciences* of Paris.

Jean Picard's (1620–82) measurement of a degree on the meridian of Paris in 1669, and the measurement of arcs of this meridian to north and south by Jean Dominique Cassini (1625–1712) and his son Jacques (1677–1756) between 1700 and 1718, had given a diminishing figure for the degree of latitude as it approached the pole, suggesting that the polar diameter of the Earth was greater than the equatorial. The French expeditions which measured arcs of the meridian in high and low latitudes (in Lapland and Peru) between 1736 and 1745 established the figure of the Earth as an oblate spheroid, flattened at the poles, and provided estimates for the length of a degree in various latitudes which served as the basis for eighteenth-century cartography (vol III, pp 553–4).

In the seventeenth century numerous tables of positions had been published; a geographical textbook of 1661 listed no fewer than 2200 places whose latitude and longitude were 'certain or probable'. The wide variation in the estimates made by different authors and map-makers pointed, however, to their fallibility. Without a series of accurately determined positions and, in particular, without any reliable method of ascertaining longitudes, cartographers could not lay down the land-masses and oceans of the world with any approximation to their correct extent and shape. Ptolemy's world map had been shattered by the geographical discoveries of the fifteenth and sixteenth centuries, but his acceptance of too low an estimate for the circumference of the globe was reflected in the exaggeration of longitudinal distances in seventeenth-century maps. Thus the east-to-west width of continents was generally too great, the coast of China being drawn over 25° too far to the east; and the Mediterranean, to which Ptolemy had ascribed a longitudinal extension of 62°, was still laid down 15° to 20° in excess of its true length.

From 1672, the year after the opening of the Paris observatory, French scientists were systematically making astronomical determinations of longitudes from shore stations; these were mainly derived from observation of eclipses or of the occultation of Jupiter's satellites, for which tables were published in 1668. By 1682 the latitude and longitude of 24 places on the French coasts had been established, and a corrected outline of the country could be laid down. *La Connoissance des temps*, an ephemeris published by J. D. Cassini from 1679, recorded the gradual increase in the number of positions accurately fixed: in Europe, 32 in 1684 and 83 in 1691; in the world, 40 in 1682 and 109 in 1706.

The observations thus collected were incorporated in the maps published from 1700 to 1726 by Guillaume Delisle (1675–1726), who has been called the first modern cartographer. While Delisle had little new information on the interiors of the continents, their coastal outline on his world map was notably correct, and the Mediterranean was reduced in length to 42°. Delisle also introduced a useful reform in his choice of a prime meridian. A French decree of 1634 had prescribed that longitudes should be taken from the west point of the island of Ferro (Hierro) in the Canaries; but its exact longitude from Paris was not known. Delisle ran his longitudes from the meridian 20° west of Paris—the 'reputed Ferro'; and this became the general practice until, with the publication (from 1767) of 'The Nautical Almanac' containing astronomical tables calculated for Greenwich, the Greenwich prime meridian attained gradual—though not universal—acceptance.

The critical method of appraising the cartographer's materials was applied even more rigorously by J. B. Bourguignon d'Anville (1697–1782). Rejecting all traditional data that failed to satisfy his searching collation of ancient authorities and modern travellers' reports, he re-drew the maps of the continents. The conventional Ptolemaic representation of the African river systems, as interpreted by sixteenth-century geographers, was finally discredited, and d'Anville's map (1749) became the starting-point for the exploration of inland Africa during the next century. For eastern Asia he was able to use the maps and determinations of the Jesuit astronomers established in Peking; and for the interior of North America the results of the recent French explorations from the Great Lakes to the Gulf of Mexico.

From the second half of the eighteenth century cartographers were supplied with an ever increasing volume of reliable information on positions, topography, and coastal outlines. This was due not only to activity in exploration but to refinements in the technique of exploratory survey and to the organization of systematic topographical surveys in European, and a few extra-European, countries. The voyages of Louis de Bougainville, 1767–9, and James Cook, 1768–79, drew the modern map of the south Pacific Ocean; and Matthew Flinders charted the coasts of Australia, 1798–1803. Cook, 1778–9, and La Pérouse, 1785–7, surveyed the American and Asiatic shores of the north Pacific; Malaspina, 1791–2, and Vancouver, 1792–4, its American coasts. Between 1770 and 1855 British, French, and German expeditions revealed the geography of northern Africa, and the oceanic coast-line of the continent was surveyed in 1822–6. The Antarctic continent was discovered in 1819, and by 1850 extensive sectors of its coast had been traversed. From the third quarter of the eighteenth century the traveller was equipped with lighter precision-instruments (ch 13) which, unlike the cumbersome astronomical quadrant and theodolite, could be used in a route-traverse or on the deck of a ship. The reflecting sextant—'a portable observatory'—and the chronometer allowed him to determine the latitude and longitude of his discoveries with sufficient accuracy to enable them to be re-identified from his map or chart.

For the determination of longitude on his first Pacific voyage (1768–71), Cook had only 'that great natural chronometer presented by the moon in her orbital motion round the earth'; that is, he employed the method of 'lunar distances', obtaining Greenwich time, at the moment of his sextant observations, from the tables printed in 'The Nautical Almanac'. These tables enabled the seaman, for the first time, to make his computations for longitude rapidly and in sufficient numbers to reduce, by 'meaning', the errors of individual observers and instruments. By lunar observations, 'when multiplied to a considerable number, made with different instruments, and with the sun and stars on both sides of the moon', Cook claimed to be 'sure of finding a ship's place at sea to a Degree and a half and generally to less than half a Degree'. In 1769, in fact, he determined the longitude of the north point of Tahiti within one minute of the modern reckoning (and the latitude, by meridian altitudes of the Sun, within one second); and the longitudes on his chart of New Zealand, made by a running survey in 1769–70, are seldom more than half a degree out. Although on his second and third voyages he carried chronometers made to the design of John Harrison (1693–1776), Cook and his officers continued to make lunar observations in extraordinary numbers; for instance, at Tongataboo in 1777, 131 sets of lunars were taken, 'amounting to above a thousand observed distances'. These, however, were used only for comparison with 'the Watch'; and the accurate timekeeper, designed independently by Harrison of London between 1729 and 1761 and by Pierre Leroy (1717–85) of Paris in 1766, and developed by later horologists, was to become the standard instrument for finding the longitude (ch 13).

The cartographer of the early nineteenth century therefore disposed of a vastly greater number of accurately fixed positions for his world map than were available to Delisle; in 1817 they were estimated to amount to over 6000. By the middle of the century trigonometrical surveys, proceeding from a network of

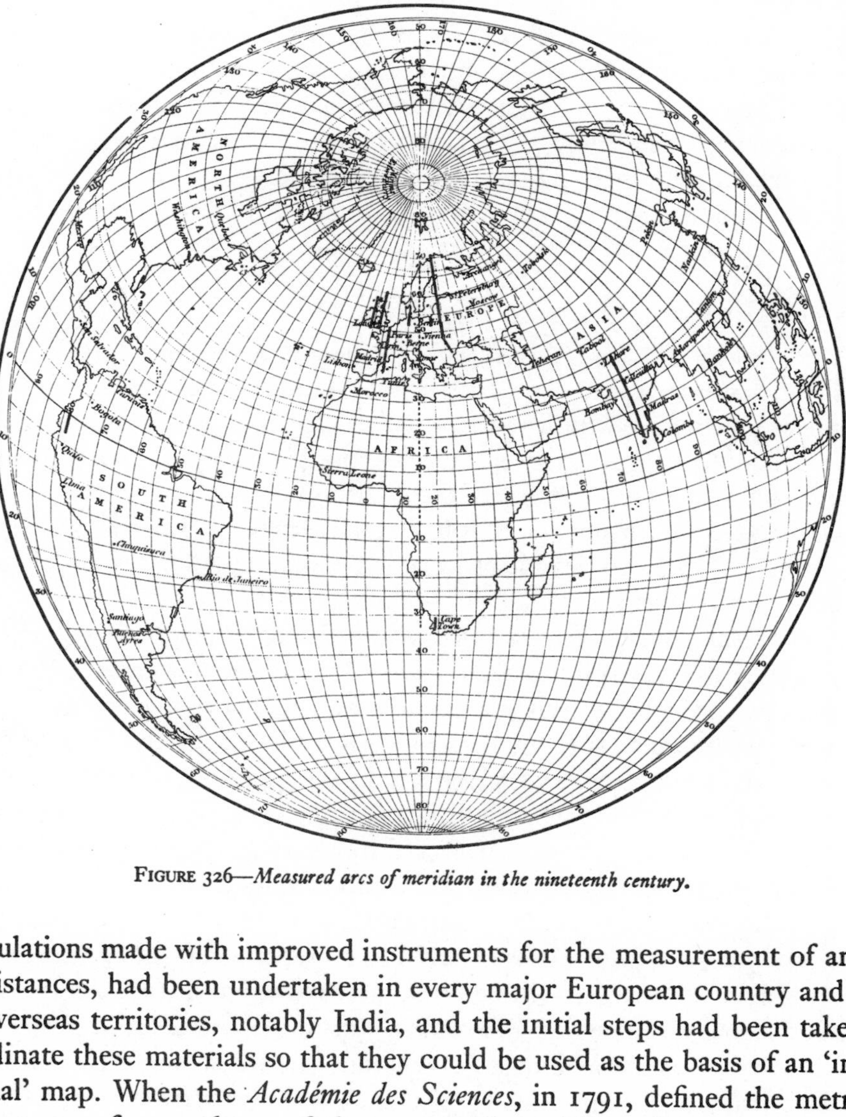

FIGURE 326—*Measured arcs of meridian in the nineteenth century.*

triangulations made with improved instruments for the measurement of angles and distances, had been undertaken in every major European country and in a few overseas territories, notably India, and the initial steps had been taken to co-ordinate these materials so that they could be used as the basis of an 'international' map. When the *Académie des Sciences*, in 1791, defined the metre as 1/10 000 000 of a quadrant of the terrestrial meridian, the various national standard measures of length could be converted into a 'natural' linear standard, the basic unit of which was proportionate to the circumference of the Earth. The adoption of the metric system led to the concept of a 'natural scale' for maps, expressed as a fraction relating one unit of length on the map to the number of like units on the Earth's surface represented by it. The 'representative fraction', which was first used in 1806 in the *Atlas national de la France*, is an international formula, being independent of local linear measures used on the ground.

These developments laid the foundation for the world map of the nineteenth century. They created both the need and the opportunity for new geodetic measurements to determine the shape of the Earth. From arcs measured in various parts of the world (figure 326), seven principal figures for the flattening of the spheroid at the poles, varying from 1/293·5 to 1/300·8, were calculated between 1830 and 1910.

II. INSTRUMENTS FOR TOPOGRAPHICAL SURVEY

The techniques of land-survey in the eighteenth century did not differ in principle from those already known, but important modifications in the standard instruments, introduced by English and French craftsmen, enabled surveys to be conducted with greater precision and speed. While surveying practice in England differed in some respects from that of the continent, the European market for scientific instruments was largely served by English makers, who were supported by a progressive engineering industry and by an ample supply of metals and optical glass.

Distance measurement. For distance measurement direct methods were commonly used: in surveys on cadastral scales, for example of estates or parks, the English surveyor had Gunter's chain of four perches (22 yds) in length, 'the land-measurer's most important instrument', while the continental surveyor employed wooden rods from 2 to 5 m long. In the mapping of larger areas or in road measurement, surveyors preferred the wheel-perambulator or hodometer, the revolutions of which were transferred by bevel-and-worm gearing to a dial (plate 23B). Regional maps, in the eighteenth century as in the sixteenth, were still generally made from road-traverses with cross-bearings taken by alidade, that is, with the plane-table or surveying compass, on points off the measured route. The private surveyor was slow in adopting more refined techniques for the indirect measurement of distances. In the second half of the eighteenth century, every English county was mapped on a scale of one inch to a mile or greater; but only six of these maps are accompanied by a diagram of triangulation.

The traditional instruments were liable to variations of length, in conditions of changing temperature or humidity, and to displacement of adjoining members when placed in contact. These defects could not be tolerated in the accurate measurement of an extended line, such as the base for a triangulation, in which the resultant angular errors would become cumulative throughout the survey. Italian and French surveyors, using copper- or brass-tipped wooden rods for the measurement of base lines, reduced the contact error by leaving an interval, which was measured with beam compasses, between adjacent rods. To mitigate and correct temperature errors, materials with a low coefficient of expansion were used, and the mean temperature of every section of the base was measured and reduced. In his triangulation of 1733–40, Cassini de Thury (1714–84) used both 24-ft wooden rods, tipped with iron, and iron bars 15 ft long. William Roy

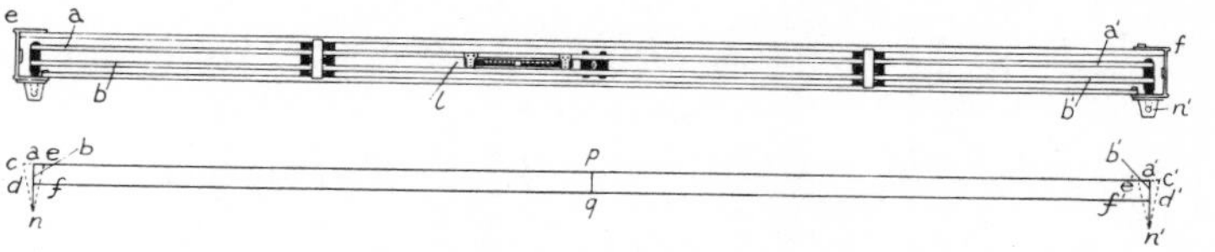

FIGURE 327—*Diagram illustrating the principle of Colby's compensation-bars.* aa′, *brass bar;* bb′, *iron bar;* pq, *steel connecting bar;* cc′, dd′, *brass bar, iron bar, at higher temperature* (62°+*n*°); ee′, ff′, *brass bar, iron bar, at lower temperature* (62°−*n*°); abn, a′b′n′, *position of steel tongues at* 62°; cdn, c′d′n′, *position of steel tongues at* 62+*n*°; efn, e′f′n′, *position of steel tongues at* 62°−*n*°; n, n′, *compensation points;* l, *longitudinal level.*

(1726–90) in 1784, taking a base of over 5 miles for his triangulation of south-east England, made a preliminary measurement with a 100-ft steel chain; and, after overlapping rods of Riga pine had proved too unstable in varying humidity, the final measurement was made with glass tubes. Roy's base of verification was measured in 1787, however, with the steel chain. Various applications of the principle of compensation, already familiar in horology, were made in apparatus for base-measurement. The French scientist J. C. de Borda (1733–99) in 1792 used bars of two metals (copper and platinum), with unequal coefficients of expansion, to determine more exactly the effect of temperature changes in different sections of the base; and F. W. Bessel (1784–1846), in his triangulation of East Prussia in 1836, employed compensated rods of iron and zinc similarly constructed. About 1825 Thomas Colby (1784–1852), director of the Ordnance Survey, invented an apparatus in which two parallel bars of brass and iron were rigidly connected at their centres and linked at the ends by pivoted metal tongues; the compensation-point marked at the extremity of each tongue was thus maintained at an invariable distance from the centre of the bar in all temperatures (figure 327). Colby's compensation-bars were used in 1827–8 in measuring bases for the primary triangulation of Ireland, and in 1849 for that of England; the average rate of measurement was six bars an hour, or 461 ft in a day, and the error in the Irish base amounted to about 1:200 000. A base-apparatus designed by F. G. W. von Struve (1793–1864) for the primary triangulation of Russia (1817–55) used spring-contact levers by which the effects of temperature could be accurately allowed for; for this a mean probable error of 1:1 240 000 was claimed.

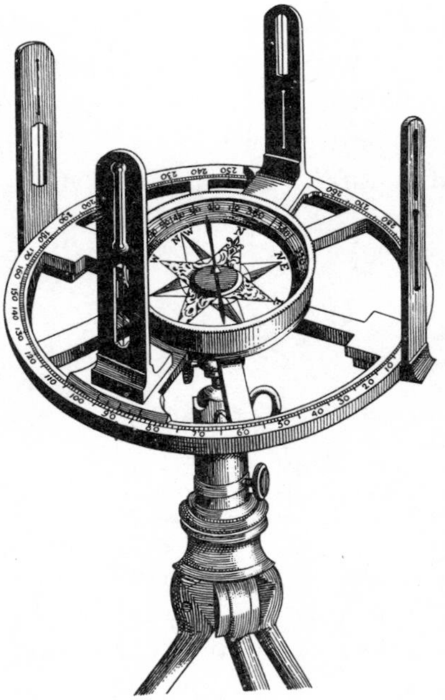

FIGURE 328—*'Common theodolite' with open sights, by George Adams. Eighteenth century.*

Tacheometry, the basic process for indirect distance measurement in modern medium-scale surveys, had been practised as early as the seventeenth century, and was first brought to the notice of surveyors by William Green (1725–1811) in a pamphlet published in London in 1778 [1]. The 'stadiometer' described by Green, like the modern tacheometer, measured the angle subtended at the optical centre of the instrument by rays from two points at a known distance apart on a staff, and thus enabled the distance of the staff, and of distant points in the same vertical plane, to be calculated. The 'anallatic' lens invented by Ignazio Porro (1801–78) in 1823 enabled the observer to read the subtended angle directly (that is, on the vertical axis of his instrument), without making allowance for the focal length of the object-glass. The tacheometer, as a combined range-finding instrument and level, became popular with engineers engaged in rapid surveys for canals (ch 18) and railways (vol V, ch 15) during the early nineteenth century.

Angle measurement. For azimuthal observations, that is, the measurement of horizontal angles, topographical instruments derived from the magnetic compass were still generally used in the eighteenth century: in England the circumferentor or surveying compass, in France the graphometer or surveying semicircle. These instruments, incorporating a compass and an alidade with open sights, allowed the surveyor to read the bearing of a line of sight; they were said to be liable to an error of 2° or more, and the early Ordnance surveyors detected in the English county maps 'an error of nearly three miles . . . in a distance of eighteen'. Other surveying circles had both fixed and movable pairs of sights and gave the angle between two lines of sight: such were the *cercle hollandais* (perhaps developed from the nautical astrolabe) and the so-called 'common theodolite', a modification of the circumferentor (figure 328). The surveying quadrant or *quart de cercle*, also with both fixed and movable sights, was widely used on the European continent. Picard, during his triangulation in 1669, had been the first to fit telescopes with micrometer-wires to his quadrants; for the smaller quadrants, of 2-ft radius, used in the eighteenth-century triangulation of France, Cassini de Thury claimed an accuracy of from 8 to 10 seconds of arc, and his detail survey was made with graphometers fitted with telescopes, in which a probable error of up to 10 minutes was expected.

Plane-tabling, by which lines of sight were directly plotted in the field, was extensively practised. English writers of the seventeenth and eighteenth centuries considered that its use should be confined to 'Townships and small Inclosures' and recommended 'in laying down of a spacious businesse [that is, a large area]' the circumferentor or theodolite [2]. The plane-table was the standard topographical instrument of military engineers employed in surveys of fortifications.

Various types of altazimuth instruments had been developed during the sixteenth and seventeenth centuries; in the eighteenth, London instrument-makers perfected the altazimuth theodolite which was to become the fundamental instrument in trigonometrical survey. This resulted from a series of improvements in the design and construction of angle-measuring instruments, affecting their optical accuracy, the mechanical trueness of the circle and alidade, and the precise division and reading of the graduated limb.

In the first half of the century Thomas Wright (1711–86) and Jonathan Sisson (1694?–1749), followed by other makers, replaced the open slotted sights of the common theodolite by a telescope with cross-hairs, which was mounted on a graduated arc so as to permit the vertical movement of the sight required to align the telescope, with its more restricted field of view, on the object. Thus the surveyor could observe horizontal and vertical angles simultaneously. The function of the compass still incorporated in the instrument was now subsidiary. Spirit-levels were fitted to level the horizontal circle of the theodolite and to bring the vertical arc to zero; the graduated circle was read by verniers. The achromatic lenses introduced by John Dollond (1706–61) in 1758 permitted shorter refracting telescopes to be constructed. John Bird (1709–76) developed a method for graduating astronomical quadrants more accurately, and Jesse Ramsden (1735–1800) (plate 1) invented circular dividing-engines in 1766 and 1775 (p 392).

The theodolites that Ramsden constructed for the geodetic and topographical surveys of England initiated by Roy and carried on by the Board of Ordnance were designed and machined to permit perfectly smooth rotation and freedom from 'central shake' [3]. Roy remarked that the 'mode of centering [was] one of the chief excellencies' of the 'great instrument', 3 ft in diameter, completed for him in 1787 (cf figure 223). The transit-telescope of this theodolite could be completely rotated round its horizontal axis; tangent-clamps and slow-motion screws enabled the telescope to be smoothly and correctly aligned; and three microscopes allowed the horizontal and vertical scales to be read to 1 second of arc—a degree of precision never before reached. Ramsden's 'great instrument', which proved itself capable, in the primary triangulation of England, of measuring angles at a distance of 70 miles to 2 seconds of arc, is the prototype of the modern theodolite.

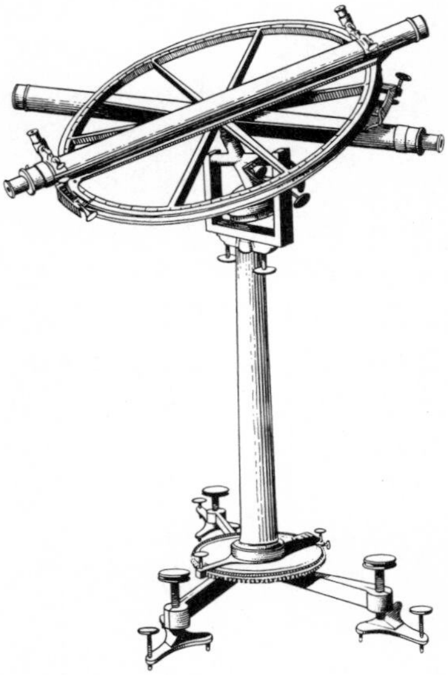

FIGURE 329—*Repeating circle, 33 cm in diameter, by Étienne Lenoir. (See figure 222.)*

In the French triangulation, continued by the fourth Cassini (Jacques Dominique, 1748–1845) and carried across the Straits of Dover to connect with Roy's in 1787, the azimuthal observations were made with a repeating circle (p 402), 33 cm in diameter, developed by Borda in 1775 and constructed by Étienne Lenoir (1744–1832) (figure 329). This employed the method of repetition of angles, using different arcs of the circle, introduced by Tobias Mayer (1723–62), so that mechanical errors were reduced by 'meaning'. Borda's reflection circle, embodying the principle of Hadley's quadrant, with repeating angles, became the preferred instrument of French marine surveyors (p 618).

Altitude measurement. In the measurement of altitude, the altazimuth theodolite gave vertical angles from which relative height could be determined; but levelling operations, at first for engineering projects and later in topographical surveys, demanded a direct method of observation. At the beginning of the eighteenth century the spirit-level (air- or bubble-level), which had been described by M. Thévenot (1620?–92) in 1661, quickly superseded the old plummet and water-level and facilitated the construction of compact levelling-instruments and clinometers. Among these was the Y-level, first made by Sisson.

Early barometric determinations of height, uncorrected for air-temperature and depending on no agreed correlation of pressure and altitude, gave widely divergent results. After 1772, when J. A. Deluc (1727–1817) published rules for the construction and use of the mercury barometer and his formula for relating pressure with altitude, the barometer enabled surveyors to obtain heights more rapidly and simply than by trigonometrical methods. Such observations, notably by H. B. de Saussure (1740–99) in the Alps, Alexander von Humboldt (1769–1859) in South America in 1799–1803, and L. Ramond (1755–1827) in the Pyrenees in 1802–3, supplied absolute hypsometric data both for topographical mapping and for the applied cartography by which the altitudinal distribution of physical phenomena was to be recorded (p 614). Deluc's comparative study of the fall in the boiling-point of water with diminishing atmospheric pressure and increasing height provided the theoretical basis for the hypsometer, developed in the early nineteenth century as the characteristic altitude instrument of exploratory survey.

III. NATIONAL SURVEYS

The eighteenth century established the general principle of modern survey, which, proceeding from the whole to the part, constructs a rigid geometrical framework of triangles before filling in the topographical detail by local observation of angles and distances. Such a system depends on no more than one linear measurement, that of the primary base-line; only the angles of the triangles are measured, and the sides are computed from them by spherical trigonometry. The survey is correctly located on the Earth's surface by astronomical observations to define the latitude and longitude of the principal stations.

France was the first country to be wholly mapped by these methods. The astronomical fixes made by Picard and P. de La Hire (1640–1718) on the coasts in 1679–81 enabled a revised outline of the country to be drawn (figure 330). This revealed errors of longitude in the older maps, which had displaced the Atlantic coast up to one-and-a-half degrees too far west, and errors of latitude in the south amounting to about half a degree in a southerly direction.

These determinations of position, to which the coastal surveys later published in the *Neptune françois* were adjusted (p 615), prompted a proposal by Picard, in 1681, for a trigonometrical survey of the kingdom. The geodetic operations of J. D. Cassini and his son during 1700–18 produced a band of triangulation along the meridian of Paris from Dunkirk in the north to Roussillon in the south; and in those undertaken in the years 1733 to 1740 by Cassini de Thury, G. D. Maraldi (1709–88), and others, as a check on the length of a meridian degree yielded by the earlier observations, triangles were run along perpendiculars to the Paris meridian and round the coasts and frontiers of France. By 1745 the country was 'enclosed' by a net of nearly 800 triangles developed from 19 measured bases. The necessary geodetic and trigonometrical data for the map of France had now been supplied, and two years later Cassini received a royal

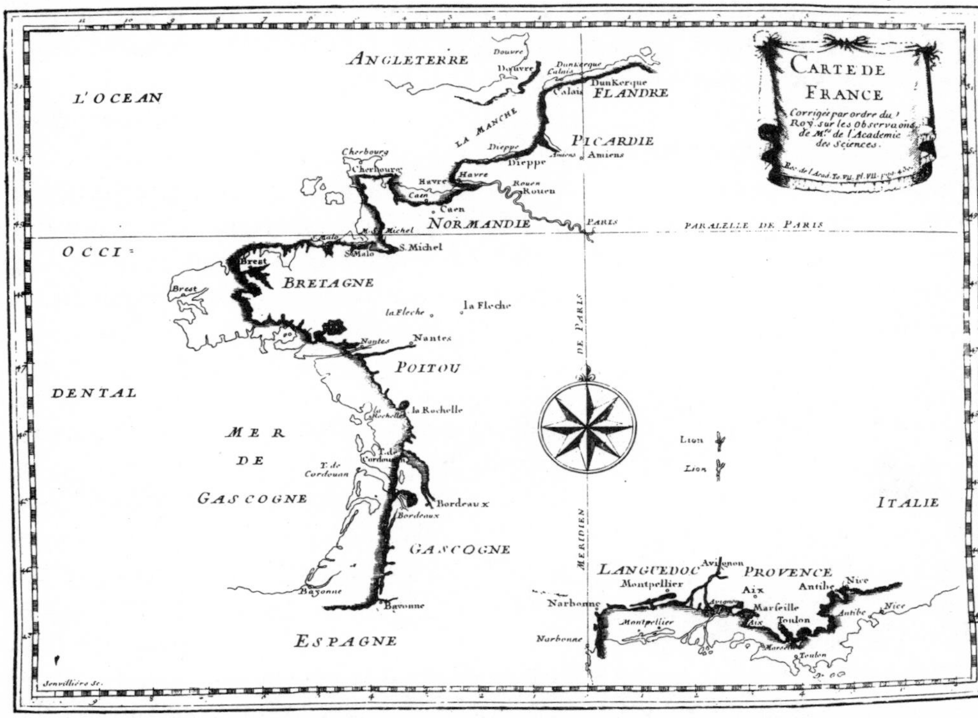

FIGURE 330—*Outline map of France by Philippe de La Hire, 1693, superimposed on that by Sanson, 1679. The new outline is shown in shaded line.*

order to map the whole kingdom. By 1783, when Cassini de Thury published his *Description géométrique de la France*, the secondary triangulation, comprising 40 000 observed triangles, and the infilling topographical survey had been completed. The *carte de Cassini*, on a scale of 1:86 400, was published in 182 sheets between 1756 and 1793. In 1818 a new survey of France was begun, and the *carte de l'État-Major*, on a scale of 1:80 000, was completed by 1878.

Cassini de Thury had in addition carried out in 1748 a 'geometrical' survey in Flanders, by which he connected the triangulation along the Paris meridian to that carried out by Willebrord Snell (1591–1626) in Holland in 1615; and in 1762 he was able to carry the triangulation along the perpendicular to the Paris meridian as far east as Vienna. Twenty-one years later he presented a memorial to the British government, proposing triangulation from London to the French coast in order to establish the difference in latitude and longitude between the observatories of Paris and Greenwich. This operation was directed by the Royal Society and executed by William Roy, who had long advocated 'a general survey of the whole island at public cost' and had already in 1783 observed a series of triangles round London. Roy's base-line was measured on Hounslow Heath in 1784, by means of glass rods, with an error of only 1/158 000 (about 2 inches in the whole length of 27 404 ft, over 5 miles). After a delay of three years while Ramsden completed his 3-ft theodolite, the principal triangulation was in 1787 carried, with the help of 'white lights' as signals, to Dover and across the Straits to the French coast; and a base of verification was measured on Romney Marsh (figure 331).

Roy's was the first accurate triangulation to be made in Britain; and it was to be, as he recommended, 'the foundation of a general survey of the British Islands'. In 1791 administrative provision was made by the Duke of Richmond, Master-General of the Ordnance, for the continuation of the trigonometrical survey and the preparation of a map of the country on the scale of 1 inch to 1 mile (1 : 63 360), a scale familiar to military surveyors. The survey was equipped with two 100-ft steel chains by Ramsden, for base measurement, and a new 3-ft theodolite by the same maker for the 'great triangles'. The secondary triangles were observed with smaller theodolites constructed by Ramsden and by Troughton and Simms; and the field survey, at 2 in to 1 mile, was made by traversing with the measuring-wheel and circumferentor. By 1825 the whole of England and Wales had been triangulated, all but the six northern counties mapped, and the triangulation of Scotland was nearly complete. Under William Mudge (1762–1820), director of the Survey from 1799 to 1820, an arc of the meridian had been measured from Dunnose in the Isle of Wight to Clifton in Yorkshire, using a zenith sector with an 8-ft telescope, made by Ramsden. This very accurate operation, while inconclusive in determining the figure of the Earth, gave a mean curvature of the meridian that served as a basis for the one-inch map. In practice, the latitude and longitude of all the principal stations were computed in relation to the Greenwich meridian; and, whenever the operations were 'extended in eastern or western directions over spaces of sixty miles from fixed meridians', the 'directions of meridians', or azimuthal bearings, of selected stations were determined by observing the maximum east-and-west distance of Polaris from the celestial pole. Unlike the French survey, Mudge's triangulation was formed not in narrow belts or chains but as a mesh gradually spreading from south-east

England over the whole country. The 'great theodolites' of Ramsden were the earliest instruments 'capable of detecting spherical excess' in terrestrial triangles; and the effects of refraction near the horizon were carefully noted, with the accompanying circumstances of temperature, air-pressure, and wind.

In 1825 the resources of the Ordnance Survey were diverted to a cadastral survey of Ireland, ordered by Parliament as a basis for land valuation, on a scale of

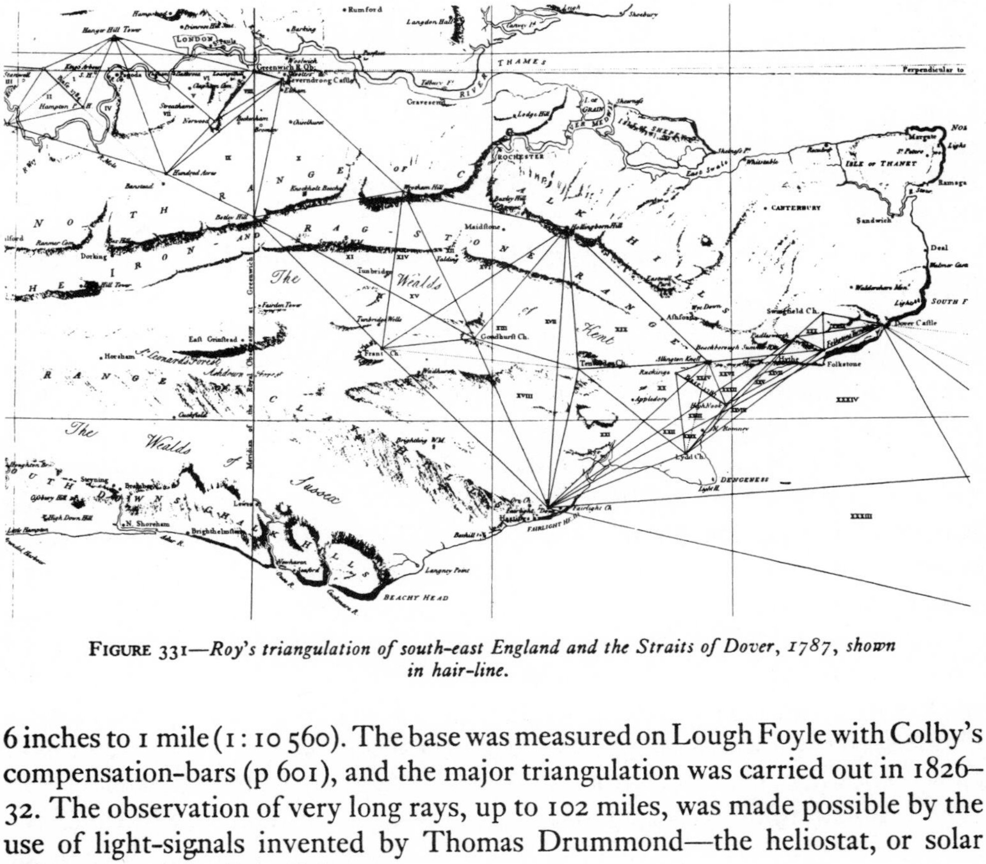

Figure 331—*Roy's triangulation of south-east England and the Straits of Dover, 1787, shown in hair-line.*

6 inches to 1 mile (1 : 10 560). The base was measured on Lough Foyle with Colby's compensation-bars (p 601), and the major triangulation was carried out in 1826–32. The observation of very long rays, up to 102 miles, was made possible by the use of light-signals invented by Thomas Drummond—the heliostat, or solar reflector, and the lime-light.

The larger scale of the Irish survey led to some important changes of practice, introduced for greater precision. In the field survey, chaining superseded traversing. From 1839 altitude measurement was carried out by levelling, based on a low-water datum in Dublin Bay. The observation of vertical angles hitherto practised was a less accurate method, which did not lend itself to continuous representation of relief and slope so readily as levelling, and the series of heights produced by the level could be easily plotted as contours. The projection of the maps of Ireland followed the system of rectangular co-ordinates adopted in the *carte de Cassini*, the origin being the point of intersection of a selected central meridian with a great circle at right-angles to it. The plotting of the curved and

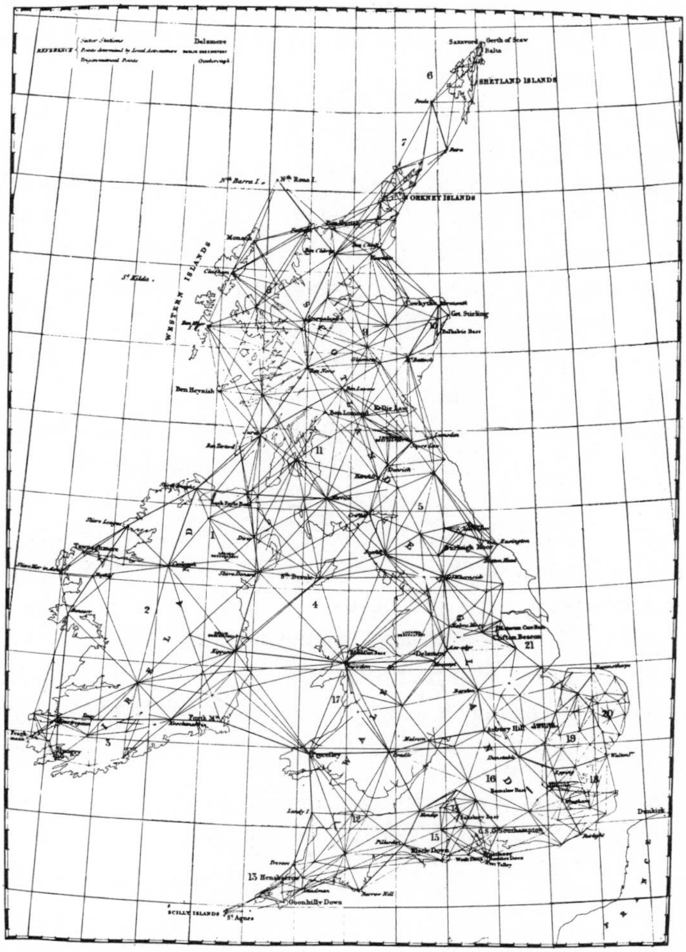

FIGURE 332—*The principal triangulation of the British Isles, completed in 1852.*

converging meridians as parallel straight lines on the map leads to an exaggeration of the scale to north and south along all meridians except the central one. While Cassini had plotted his map of the whole country on the meridian of Paris, the surveyors of Ireland reduced the contingent error by plotting the map of each county on a central meridian appropriate to it.

The survey of Scotland was resumed in 1838, and by 1852 the principal triangulation of Great Britain had been completed (figure 332). This depended on the two base-lines measured with Colby's apparatus, verified by four check bases. In the great triangles, 66 sides exceeded 80 miles in length, and the precision of the work is gauged by the difference of only 5 in between the length of the Salisbury Plain base as measured and its length as computed from the Lough Foyle base 350 miles distant.

The survey of northern England and of Scotland was conducted by the methods adopted in Ireland. The field survey was executed on the 6-in scale, from which the 1-in maps were made by reduction; the publication of 6-in maps of Great Britain was begun, the first sheet for Scotland appearing in 1843 and for England in 1846. These 6-in maps of Great Britain, like those of Ireland, were issued as 'county maps', each on its separate central meridian. The primary levelling of Great Britain, from a datum fixed at the mean level of high- and low-water at Liverpool, was completed between 1840 and 1860, and the 6-in maps, like those of Ireland, were contoured from about 1843.

The national surveys of other European states sprang from the same impulses as their prototypes in France and England. Scientists recognized that the topographical field-work of a regional map must be preceded by trigonometrical survey, and that the geodetic basis had to be established by measurement of long arcs of the meridian and other great circles. In an age of almost continuous warfare, governments appreciated the necessity for accurate maps in political and military intelligence. The new national surveys of the eighteenth and nineteenth centuries adopted the plan and technical procedures of the French and British. The progress in the mapping of Europe during this period is indicated below, where the period is shown in which primary triangulation was initiated:

1750–75: Austria-Hungary, north Italy, Brandenburg, Tyrol, Denmark, Sweden.
1775–1800: Belgium, Hanover, Norway, Saxony, south Italy, Portugal.
1800–25: Holland, Prussia, Bavaria, Baden, Hesse, Württemberg, Russia.
1825–50: Switzerland.

The earliest trigonometrical survey undertaken outside Europe was that of India. Between 1763 and 1777 James Rennell (1742–1830) had surveyed Bengal by route-traverses adjusted to observations for latitude and longitude. Triangulation, from a base line measured near Madras in 1802, was begun by William Lambton (1756–1823) with the object of measuring an arc of the meridian. By 1840 a 'great arc' of 20° of latitude, extending from Cape Comorin to the Himalayas, had been triangulated, and chains of triangles had been run across the subcontinent from east to west. These provided the framework for the Great Trigonometrical Survey of India.

IV. METHODS OF CARTOGRAPHIC REPRESENTATION

Relief. The effective delineation of relief—the third dimension in topography—by the map-maker enables the configuration of land-forms to be clearly visualized and the altitude and gradient of the land-surface at any point to be ascertained. Before the eighteenth century none of these conditions was satisfied by land-maps, which commonly employed pictographic symbols drawn in half-perspective or bird's-eye view, with hatching 'obliquely' shaded as if illuminated from the north-west. Such a method conveyed a general impression of relative elevation, but failed to disclose the plan of relief features, their absolute altitude, or their slope.

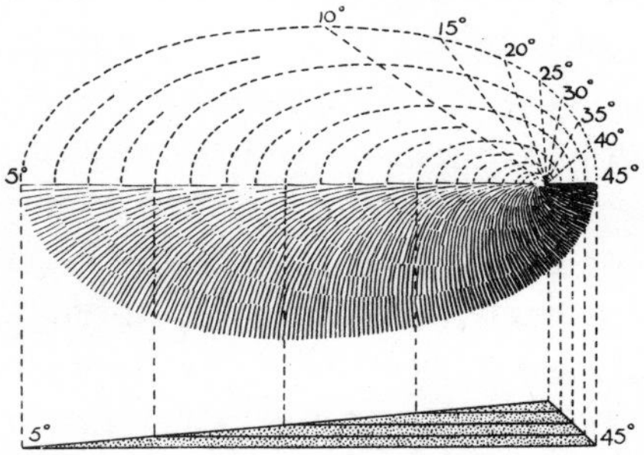

FIGURE 333—*Diagram illustrating the principle of J. G. Lehmann's graded hachures.*

Early in the eighteenth century, cartographers began to draw their hill-hatching as if vertically shaded or illuminated from a source above the object. From this method, which facilitated the representation of relief features in plan, developed hachuring by parallel lines drawn in the direction of the slope, the steepness being indicated by the thickness of the hachures and the interval between them. This convention was used with plastic effect in 1757 in the physical maps of Philippe Buache (1700–73) to illustrate the morphology of river-systems and watersheds. An original, if ingenuous, application of it was made by Christopher Packe (1686–1749) in his 'Philosophico-chorographical Chart of East Kent' (1743) to demonstrate the pattern of valleys and 'their use in draining the waters from the surface of the earth' [4].

The Cassini map of France employed an insensitive style of hachuring which suggested two levels only—erosion valleys divided by a scarp from the surrounding table-land. Cassini, who recognized the need for a comprehensive levelling of the country, had to admit the limitations of his topographical surveyors, and they were required only to sketch relief from rough field-notes, such as D or F for '*pentes douces ou fortes*'. Although Cassini's method of delineating relief was widely imitated in military and topographical surveys, it was superseded by the 'theory of mountain drawing' published by J. G. Lehmann (1765–1811) in 1799 (figure 333). In the scientific system of hachuring introduced by Lehmann the gradient was accurately represented by equidistant parallel lines, the thickness of which was made proportionate to the angle of slope. Lehmann's system was widely adopted on the continent, and in the first national survey of Switzerland —the 'Dufour map'—a notably plastic effect was achieved by emphasizing the hachures on the south and east slopes as if obliquely illuminated.

Hill-shading and hachuring, even in their most refined forms, have only a limited range in the differentiation of slopes, and unaided they cannot indicate absolute elevation. As the eighteenth-century surveyor learnt to use field-instruments for observing altitude—the surveying level, barometer, altazimuth theodolite, and tacheometer—the cartographer was supplied with determinations of height which had to be recorded on his map, though it is true that these were not yet numerous. In 1807 Humboldt noted that no more than 122 altitudes in the world had been reliably measured, nearly half of these being from his own barometric observations, and no topographical survey of a large area was accompanied by systematic levelling operations before that made for the French *carte de l'État-Major*. Cartographers of the eighteenth century, however, evolved the principal techniques that were to be used in the nineteenth for representation of absolute altitude.

Marine charts had since the sixteenth century recorded the relief of sea-bottom or river-bed by depth-figures obtained by sounding. Altitude-figures, or 'spot heights', were not marked on land-maps until the middle of the eighteenth century. Packe's map of 1743 provides the earliest English example, from barometric observations, and at about this time French military engineers began to insert altitude-figures, obtained by levelling, in their plans of fortifications.

The isometric line had been introduced into cartography by Edmond Halley's (1656–1742) chart of magnetic variation (1701), and hydrographers were accustomed to the use of form-lines on charts to indicate the coastal shelf and the limits of shoals. By an easy development, lines run through points of equal sounding produced underwater contours or isobaths. This step was first taken by the Dutch engineer N. S. Cruquius (1678–1754), in whose chart of the river Merwede (1729) depth was depicted by contours at a vertical interval of 1 fathom, referred to the low-water mark (itself a contour). A bathymetric chart of the English Channel, prepared by P. Buache in 1737 and published in 1752, drew submarine contours at 10 fathoms interval and was accompanied by a vertical section of the sea-bed (figure 334).

Contouring was not generally adopted in marine charts for over a century after the initial essay by Cruquius; it was introduced on the Russian official charts in 1834, and on the British in 1838. Meanwhile theoretical studies of its application to topographical survey had been made in France in 1771. While making a gravity survey of a Scottish mountain in 1777 Charles Hutton (1737–1823) em-

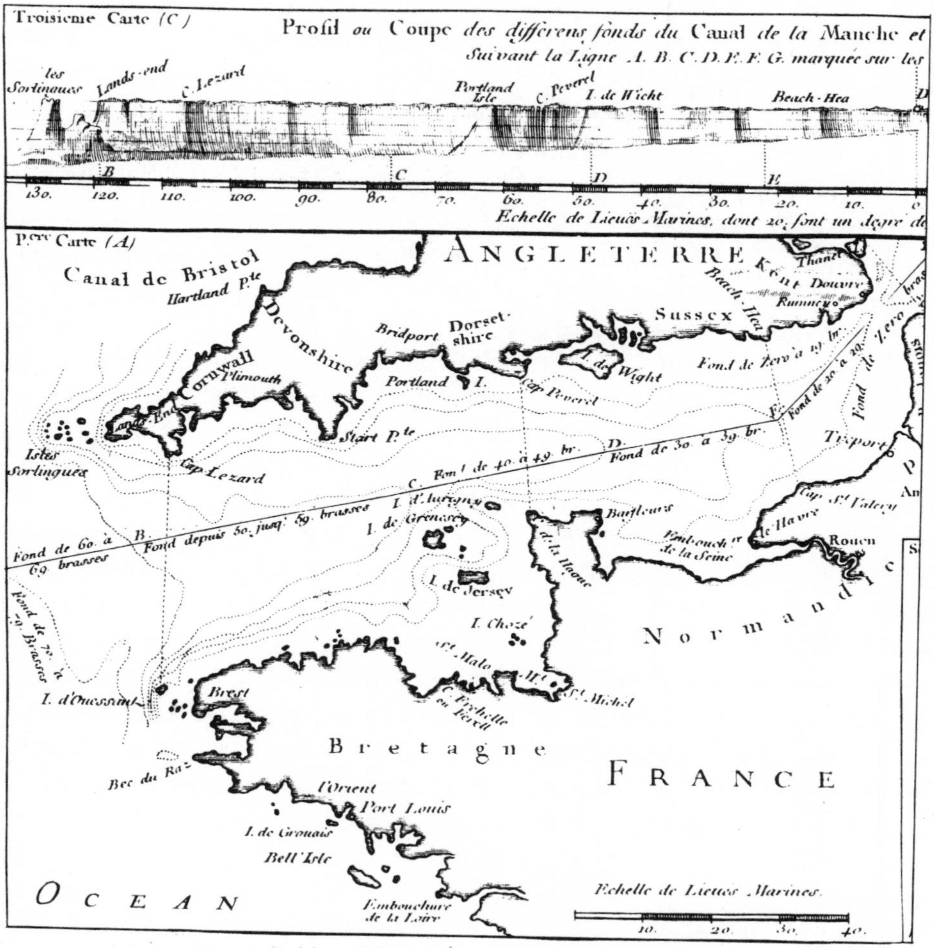

FIGURE 334—*Contoured chart and vertical section of the English Channel by P. Buache (detail), 1752.*

ployed the method, 'connecting together by a faint line all the points which were of the same relative altitude'; and the first map of a larger land-area in which it is found is that of France (1799) by J. L. Dupain-Triel (1722–1805?). Here, in an attempt to show the configuration of country '*par une nouvelle méthode de nivellements*', altitude was represented by contours above mean sea-level, at a vertical interval of 20 m, together with spot-heights, hachures with oblique shading, and a vertical section across the country.

The interest in hypsometry, or the comparative study of heights, in the early nineteenth century assumed diverse forms. The geologist and the meteorologist required accurate orographic maps on both large and small scales. The relation between altitude and the distribution of plants and other physical phenomena was illustrated in the maps of Humboldt (1769–1859) and H. C. W. Berghaus (1797–1884). Such studies called for data on elevation, which were supplied by the growing number of barometric observations and by the levelling operations associated with national surveys. Hypsometric maps of larger areas revealed their morphology more plainly; the *Esquisse orographique de l'Europe* (1824) by the Danes J. H. Bredsdorff (1790–1841) and O. N. Olsen (1794–1848) employed 1000-ft contours with hachuring, and in 1856 J. M. Ziegler (1801–84) published his *Hypsometrischer Atlas* of the world. Contouring, supplemented by spot-heights and form-lines, became the standard method for the precise recording of altitude. When combined with layer-tinting or colouring (first used in Adolf Stieler's *Hand-Atlas*, 1817–34) and with hachuring or hill-shading it became an effective graphic means of presenting the morphology of land-forms.

Land cover. From the sixteenth century, estate plans on cadastral scales had described the state of cultivation of enclosed land, but the scale of regional maps was commonly too small to show more than the limits of woodland, waste, and plantation. In Germany and other European countries the value of forests, whether for economic exploitation or for hunting, ensured their accurate mapping, with distinction between deciduous trees and conifers, which are mostly non-deciduous. In eighteenth-century topographical maps on medium scales a more ambitious attempt was made to represent vegetation and the use of land. The Cassini map of France and its derivatives drew in detail only parks, woods, and ornamental grounds; but the agrarian revolution in England, associated with active development of landed property and with the introduction of new farming procedures, called for more exact delineation of land cover. Packe's map of east Kent (1743) had distinguished arable land, downland, and marsh, and, in the English county maps of the second half of the century, the cartographers—who were usually also estate surveyors—employed a varied vocabulary of symbols, adapted from large-scale plans, for crops and vegetation cover. In the 2-inch to a mile maps of John Rocque (*c* 1704–62), for instance, appropriate conventions defined arable and pasture, hop-lands, formal and landscape gardens, parks and woodland, heath and marsh.

A more systematic technique was applied in a map of the London region published by Thomas Milne (fl 1788–1800) in 1800, from a survey made in 1795–9 and covering an area of 16 miles by 14 on a scale of 2 inches to a mile [5]. The boundaries of enclosures, unlike those of Rocque's maps, were carefully surveyed, and each field (whether open or enclosed) was marked by a characteristic letter or colour denoting its cultivation. No fewer than 17 forms of land-use were thus differentiated, and Milne's map strikingly anticipates the practice of land-utilization surveys of the twentieth century.

Special maps. The observation of the inorganic and organic phenomena of the Earth's land and water surfaces, and the investigation of their physical composition, called into being maps of special types, whose individual modes of expression are studied in a later section (p 620).

V. HYDROGRAPHY AND OCEANOGRAPHY

At the opening of the eighteenth century the charting of the seas and coasts of the world fell far short of the seaman's needs. Three factors essential to precise hydrographic survey were still lacking. The number of points whose latitude and longitude had been reliably determined was few; neither instruments nor methods for accurate survey of a coastline had come into general use; and the technique of chart-drawing had developed little since the sixteenth century.

The reformation of hydrographic survey followed that of land-survey. The sea-atlas *Le Neptune françois*, published in Paris in 1693, introduced a number of innovations in its charts of western Europe. They were drawn on the Mercator projection ('*cartes réduites*'), enabling the navigator to plot bearings as straight lines, and were graduated in latitude and longitude; the positions of many coastal stations were laid down from the astronomical determinations of Picard and Cassini; and a shore-survey, with more accurate instruments than could be used on shipboard, preceded the plotting of the marine details. The example thus set was followed in the charts compiled by J. N. Bellin (1703–72) in the Dépôt des Cartes, Plans et Journaux de la Marine between 1737 and 1752 and published in 1756 as a sea-atlas of the world with the title *L'Hydrographie française*.

The accurate graduation of charts of the world, other than the European coasts, was, however, not possible until the introduction of the reflecting quadrant and sextant, and of the chronometer, enabled the seaman to find his latitude and longitude with confidence on board ship. Throughout the eighteenth century he continued to carry compass-charts oriented to magnetic north, not graduated in longitude and seldom in latitude, and covered with the traditional network of bearing-lines radiating from centres arranged on the periphery of a circle (vol III, pp 523–6).

Before the second half of the century the methods of hydrographic survey lagged behind those of land-surveyors. Although ships of the Royal Navy were occasionally issued with survey-equipment, including theodolite, plane-table, and chain, this part of a seaman's education was neglected. As late as 1770 Cook could write of 'the few [seamen] I have known who are capable of drawing a Chart or Sketch of a Sea coast', and Cook himself received his first training in survey, in 1758, from a military engineer. A coastal survey, like that of Great Britain, 1681–8, by Greenvile Collins (fl 1669–93), whose charts remained in use to the end of the eighteenth century, was commonly constructed from compass intersections on landmarks, taken from the ends of a sailed traverse which was measured by the ship's log, that is, by dead reckoning; or, in a 'geometric' survey on land, the coastline was traversed with measuring-wheel (plate 23 B), or chain and angular observations were made by surveying-compass or theodolite.

By the middle of the century the fallibility of these methods had become apparent, and surveys were being developed through a framework of triangulation from a level base-line measured on shore (figure 335). In his survey of the Orkney Islands, 1747–9, Murdoch Mackenzie (fl 1747–97) measured two bases on land with an iron chain, observed the primary triangles by theodolite, and defined prominent points on the coast by secondary triangulation. Finally the coastline was filled in by a boat-survey, compass bearings being taken to fix the position of marks, soundings, and reefs. Between 1751 and 1770 Mackenzie charted the west coast of Great Britain and the coasts of Ireland for the Admiralty; and in the same period (1763–7) Cook was making a trigonometrical survey of Newfoundland. Cook's survey, adapted to the charting of a difficult and 'practically unknown shore', combined Mackenzie's 'stasimetric' method with that of a running survey: a harbour was carefully planned from a measured base, the triangulation was carried as far afield as possible, and the surveying ship then sailed for the next harbour, sounding and sketching-in the coastline and fixing the ship's position by quadrant angles or compass bearings on the shore stations, determined by the theodolite. Cook's work was extended southward by surveys made for the Admiralty between 1763 and 1773 by J. F. W. Des Barres (1722–1824), Samuel Holland (1728?–1801), and their deputies. Their charts, covering 1000 miles of the Atlantic coast of North America, from the St Lawrence to Florida, were published in the sea-atlas 'The Atlantic Neptune' (1777–81).

By now the reflecting sextant, developed from Hadley's quadrant in 1757, was becoming the marine surveyor's tool-of-all-work. Not only was it employed in the observation of altitudes, for which it had been designed, but it was to supersede the compass as the standard instrument for taking horizontal angles. It was, as Mackenzie pointed out, 'more portable . . . and generally more accurately . . . divided' than the theodolite; and Dalrymple remarked that Hadley's quadrant

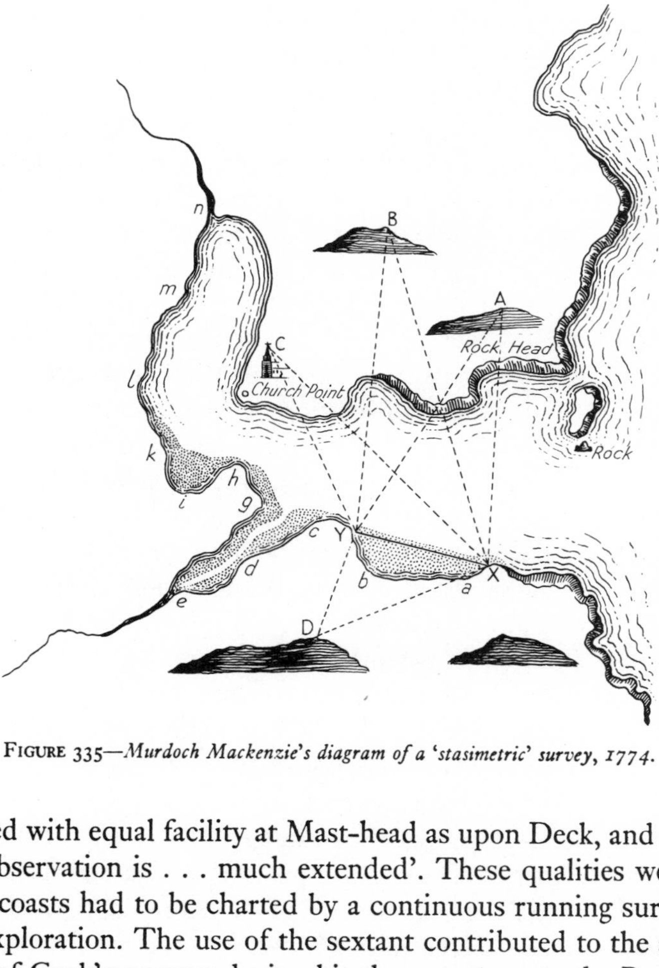

FIGURE 335—*Murdoch Mackenzie's diagram of a 'stasimetric' survey, 1774.*

could be 'used with equal facility at Mast-head as upon Deck, and therefore the Sphere of Observation is . . . much extended'. These qualities were of special value where coasts had to be charted by a continuous running survey from the ship, as in exploration. The use of the sextant contributed to the accuracy and the rapidity of Cook's surveys during his three voyages to the Pacific, the outstanding hydrographic achievement of the century. In his circumnavigation of New Zealand in 1769–70, in the course of which he charted 2400 miles of coastline in six months, Cook made no use of dead-reckoning; he plotted his track by fixing the ship's position from his courses and from intersecting rays on landmarks, adjusting it from time to time to the astronomical observations; and he 'made no farther use of the log than to connect those points of the track which the ship was in when he took his angles and bearings'. The drawing of the charts from these voyages, we may add, conformed to modern practice. Unlike those of Cook's Newfoundland survey, they were habitually graduated in latitude and longitude; the meridians were true, not magnetic, and the variation was recorded wherever it was observed; and Cook was the first navigator engaged on discovery to run his longitudes from the prime meridian of Greenwich.

Many refinements were made in the practice of coastal survey at the end of the century. Mackenzie's successors, continuing his charting of the English coasts, were able to use, for the 'landwork', the triangulation of the trigonometrical survey carried out under the Board of Ordnance, and their examination of the sea-bed off-shore became more detailed and systematic. Resection by the quadrant, that is, the fixing of a ship's position by observation of three rays on shore marks, had been described in principle as early as 1764, and this method of making 'running fixes' was practised by English surveyors, using the sextant, and by C. F. Beautemps-Beaupré (1766–1854) with Borda's reflection circle during d'Entrecasteaux's Pacific expedition of 1791–3. The station-pointer, said to have been invented by Graeme Spence (1758–1812) while surveying for the Admiralty about 1780, provided a mechanical solution which enabled the position of the survey-boat, while sounding, to be rapidly determined by resection and directly plotted on the chart. The precision of the off-shore survey was further increased by the adoption of methods of marine triangulation employing temporary beacons or floating buoys as stations. The technique had been foreshadowed by the 'quincunx' (four ships anchored in a square, with a fifth in the centre) proposed by Alexander Dalrymple in his 'Essay on the Most Commodious Methods of Marine Surveying' (1771), the first English textbook on the subject. By this method, using beacons and buoys, Admiralty surveyors charted the banks and channels of the Thames estuary in 1818–20 and 1832.

The Hydrographical Office was established by the Board of Admiralty in 1795 and was charged with the custody, compilation, and issue of charts for naval ships. About 1811 the surveying service of the Admiralty was brought under the administration of the Hydrographer, and in 1814 the first surveying-ships were entered in the Navy List. From this time British naval surveys, recorded in the Admiralty charts, were extended over the coasts and waters of almost the entire world.

The French hydrographic service had for half a century continued the work of Bellin, expanding the *Hydrographie française* into a series of 'Neptunes' (sea-atlases) compiled for the different '*navigations*'. A new survey of the coasts of France from a shore-triangulation was made between 1816 and 1836 and published in *Le Pilote français*. This was directed by Beautemps-Beaupré, as chief hydrographer; and the boatwork, using his method of fixing positions by the reflection circle and taking samples of the sea-bottom by means of a new type of sounding-rod, produced an extremely detailed survey of the marine features.

For want of suitable equipment, little physical study of the deep sea beyond coastal waters was possible before the nineteenth century. Sailors had regularly deduced the existence of surface currents from discrepancies between their dead-reckoning and their observed positions, and charts of oceanic circulation associated with the wind-systems had been produced since the seventeenth century. The introduction of the chronometer led to greater precision in records of the direction and velocity of currents, and the early nineteenth century saw the first systematic studies in oceanography, notably those of James Rennell, whose charts of the currents of the Atlantic Ocean were completed in 1827. Water-sampling instruments had been used during the eighteenth century, for instance by the scientists of Cook's expeditions, to measure the temperature and salinity of sea-water. Temperature observations to determine the limits of the Gulf Stream were made with Fahrenheit's thermometer by Benjamin Franklin (1706–90) in 1775 and Sir Charles Blagden (1748–1820) in 1776–7.

The floor of the ocean, however, could not be charted, and remained 'a sealed volume', until deep-sea sounding apparatus had been devised. In 1773 Captain C. J. Phipps, in 65° N 3° E, on his return from Spitsbergen, spliced together all his lines and, using a lead of over 150 lb, obtained 'a very fine soft blue clay' from a depth of 683 fathoms; this is the earliest deep-sea sounding recorded. On his Antarctic expedition (1839–43), Captain James Clark Ross (1800–62) made numerous deep soundings with a hemp line over 4 miles long, marked at every 100 fathoms. Lieutenant M. F. Maury (1806–73), as head of the U.S. hydrographic service, recommended a lighter line and lead—'a common twine thread for a sounding-line, and a cannon-ball (of 32 pounds) for a sinker'. With this equipment measurements of depths to over 5000 fathoms were claimed, and Maury's chart of the north Atlantic (1853) showed more than a hundred soundings in excess of 2000 fathoms. Maury also experimented unsuccessfully with echo-sounding by underwater explosions, and he introduced a deep-sea sounding rod, invented by Midshipman J. M. Brooke, which enabled specimens of the ocean-bottom to be recovered.

Maury is rightly regarded as the founder of systematic oceanography, and his textbook 'The Physical Geography of the Sea' (1855) remained in use for over half a century. During his service in the U.S. hydrographic office (1841–61), he compiled, from the tracks and observations of ships whose logs came into his hands, a series of 'Wind and Current Charts', the first of which appeared in 1847, employing an ingenious combination of colours and symbols. These charts pointed to the shortest sailing-routes, and Maury asserted that their use had reduced the average duration of the passage between New York and California from 183 to 135 days, and that between England and Australia from 124 to 97 days. In 1853 an international conference held at Brussels adopted the standard form of abstract log proposed by Maury.

VI. ATLASES AND SPECIAL MAPS

By the beginning of the nineteenth century maps on medium and large scales could describe with much greater precision the topographical elements of location, direction, distance, extent, and altitude. Of the general atlases which, continuously revised from contemporary sources, served as an index to the progress and current state of world cartography, the prototype is Adolf Stieler's (1775–1836) *Hand-Atlas.* The first edition of this was issued, in parts, between 1817 and 1834 by the great geographical publishing house of Justus Perthes (1772–1843) at Gotha, and new editions and supplements appeared regularly until 1930.

At the same time cartographic techniques were elaborated to represent geographically, in structural or spatial relationship, the data of other sciences. This enlargement of the map-maker's field embraced on the one hand the physical phenomena of the lithosphere, the hydrosphere, and the atmosphere, and, on the other, the material of various branches of human geography.

The earliest meteorological example is Edmond Halley's wind-chart, published to accompany his 'Historical Account of the Trade Winds and Monsoons' (1686). Halley drew tapering lines to indicate wind-directions, and the more familiar arrow appeared on eighteenth-century maps; the 'feathers' or lateral strokes denoting wind-strength were added after the introduction of the Beaufort scale in 1806. The isopleth, or 'curve-line' of equal value, introduced by Halley in 1701, was adapted to the representation of meteorological facts in the nineteenth century. Isotherms—lines of equal mean annual temperature—were drawn by Humboldt in mapping the distribution of plants (1817). Isobars—lines of equal mean pressure—were first plotted by Heinrich Berghaus (1797–1884), in his barometric world-chart (1838), as straight lines, parallel to the equator, drawn across the oceans to show pressure at sea level. Alexander Buchan's (1829–1907) world-maps of isobars for the months and the year, published in 1868–9, established that pressure varied with longitude as well as latitude. In synoptic weather charts, such as those of the eastern United States (1846) by Elias Loomis (1811–89), the data of winds, cloud, precipitation, atmospheric pressure, and temperature were brought together. Daily weather-charts from telegraphic reports were produced at the Great Exhibition from August to October 1851.

The association of longitude with the phenomena of terrestrial magnetism was illustrated, in the eighteenth century, by maps of magnetic declination (variation) and inclination (dip). In Halley's isogonic charts of the Atlantic and of the world, lines of equal variation for the year 1700 were drawn over the oceans, and J. H. Lambert (1728–77) in 1770 extended isogones over the land-surfaces of the globe. Isoclines, or lines of equal magnetic dip, were first used by William Whiston (1667–1752) in the maps of eastern England and north-west France published with his essay 'The Longitude and Latitude found by the Inclinatory or Dipping Needle' (1721), and in 1768 J. C. Wilcke (1731–96) produced an isoclinic world chart. On his South American travels (1799–1803) Humboldt had made observations of the decrease of magnetic intensity from the poles towards the equator, and in 1805 he drew a sketch of isodynamic zones. The earliest isodynamic maps, with lines of equal magnetic force, were those of north-west Europe (1825) and of the world (1826) by C. Hansteen (1784–1873).

The cartographic description of the physical materials of the Earth's crust also begins in the period now under consideration. Mineral resources and workings had been shown on maps since the sixteenth century, and geological sections of coal-seams in south-west England were drawn early in the eighteenth. The development of scientific agricultural methods was accompanied by an interest in soils, exemplified in Packe's physiographic map of east Kent (p 611) and in the 'soil maps' published with the reports of the Board of Agriculture (1794–1810), in which soils were characterized by their texture and fertility. The extension of geological observations, the systematic study of the sculpture of land-forms, and the classification of successive rock-formations—all these aspects of the young science of geology were to be served by a new kind of map.

In the mineralogical maps of France and north-west Europe (1746) drawn by Philippe Buache from the investigations of J. E. Guettard (1715–86), the first attempt was made to summarize the results of geological observation over a large area (plate 32 B); the pattern of rocks and sedimentary deposits was defined, and the location of fossils and minerals was indicated by distinctive symbols. At the end of the century William Smith (1769–1839), 'mineral surveyor', made his momentous correlation of rock-formations with their associated fossils, and the tables of strata which he drew up supplied the key to his geologically coloured maps, from that of the Bath district (1799) to his mature work in the map of the whole of England and Wales on a scale of 5 miles to an inch ('A Delineation of the Strata of England and Wales', 1815) and his 21 geological maps of English counties.

A geological map of the eastern United States was published by William Maclure (1763–1840) in 1809, and between 1825 and 1835 France was geologically mapped by J. B. A. L. L. Élie de Beaumont (1798–1874) and O. P. A. P. Dufrénoy (1792–1857) on the basis of the English stratification. These were independent enterprises. Geological surveying at the public expense was initiated in Great Britain. In 1814 John MacCulloch (1773–1835) was appointed geologist to the Ordnance Survey; in 1826 a geological branch of the Survey in Ireland was set up; and in 1832 H. T. De la Beche (1796–1855) was authorized to add geological colours to the 1-in topographical maps for south-west England. Three years later, when eight of these sheets had been published, the Geological Survey was established as a branch of the Ordnance Survey, with De la Beche as Director, to continue the geological mapping on the 1-in scale; this was the first national geological survey department. Before 1850 the study of the phenomena of glaciation led to the making of the earliest drift-maps.

The mapping of agricultural and mineral resources pointed the way to economic cartography. A pioneer essay in this field, anticipating work of a century later, was the map of Europe by A. F. W. Crome (1753–1833), published at Dessau in 1782. Here symbols were used to show the distribution of 56 commodities, and the principal commercial centres; and the map was accompanied by tables of the area and population of countries.

A synoptic view of the development of physical geography in the first half of the nineteenth century was presented in the notable *Physikalischer Atlas* compiled by Heinrich Berghaus (p 620) and published in parts from 1838 to 1848 by Justus Perthes. The data of the several divisions of the science—meteorology, hydrology, geology, terrestrial magnetism, the geography of plants, animals, and man—were co-ordinated and interpreted in 90 plates, accompanied by memoirs, in which Berghaus effectively applied the novel cartographic techniques introduced during the century.

In his sections on 'anthropogeography' and 'ethnography' Berghaus had treated human geography only in biological terms; but maps were already being brought into service to collate and depict quantitatively the facts of social geography, abstracted from statistical records. During the seminal period 1835–55, it has been claimed, 'almost every technique now known for representing population numbers, distribution, density and movements seems to have come into being'.

The earliest population maps were made in the British Isles, where a regular census had been instituted in 1801. The final report of the railway commissioners for Ireland, published in 1838, was illustrated by an atlas of six maps, drawn by H. D. Harness (1804–83) 'on a new design', which anticipated a num-

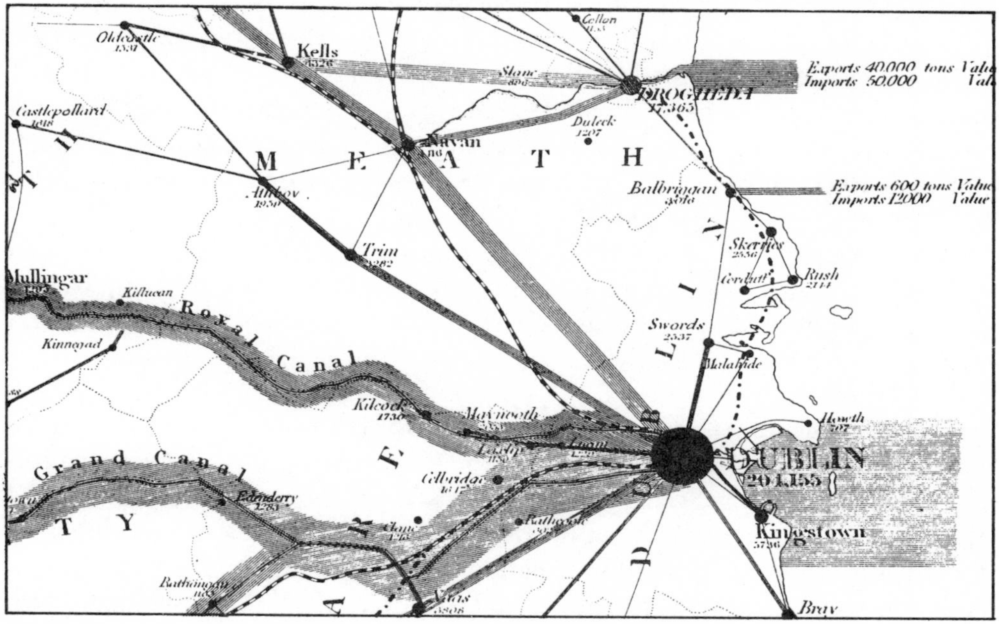

FIGURE 336—*Traffic-flow map of Ireland by H. D. Harness, published in 1838 (detail). This illustrates the use of 'flow lines' for traffic density and of graduated circles or dots for population.*

ber of modern cartographic techniques [6]. In his two traffic maps, showing the number of passengers carried by public conveyances and the volume of goods-traffic, Harness drew 'streams of shade', the thickness of which was proportional to the movements represented; this is the earliest example of the use of 'flow lines' (figure 336). In his map showing 'the comparative density of the population', as in his traffic maps, Harness indicated towns and cities by solid black circles proportional in size to the population as given by the 1831 census. The population map also represented the density of rural population by four degrees of aquatint shading, supplemented by occasional figures for the number of persons to the square mile. The density-shades are not delimited by boundaries of the administrative divisions for which the census returns were made, but correspond to zones of settlement, and Harness was thus also the first cartographer to employ the so-called dasymetric technique.

The originality of Harness's methods does not seem to have attracted attention, but it bore fruit in the maps published with subsequent census reports, such as that of 1841 for Ireland, in which similar distribution techniques were adapted to indicate population, housing, education, and agricultural property. The population maps of the British Isles (1849 and 1851) by August Petermann (1822–78) introduced into general use the practices of density-shading for distribution by area, and of graduated dots or circles for towns and cities, which had been initiated by Harness. Similarly, Petermann's cholera map of the British Isles (1850), showing the districts attacked by the epidemic of 1831–3, although not the earliest medical map, demonstrated the contribution which the cartographer could make to the geography of diseases.

Before the middle of the nineteenth century, therefore, map-makers had foreshadowed the processes now familiar for 'depicting the primary physical, economic, human and social facts' of a region.

VII. PROJECTIONS

The latitude and longitude of points on a map are defined by reference to the network of parallels and meridians on which it is drawn. This network suffers distortion, in shape or scale, when it is transferred from the curved surface of the globe to the plane surface of the map. The choice of projection depends on the qualities that are required in a particular map. In the late eighteenth and early nineteenth centuries, the initiation of accurate geodetic and topographical surveys and the extension of the applications of cartography gave a new impulse to the mathematical study of projections. J. H. Lambert laid the foundations for this study in an essay published in 1772 under the title *Anmerkungen und Zusätze zur Entwerfung der Land- und Himmelskarten*. Here he analysed the properties of the two principal methods of projection: the conformal (or orthomorphic), in which angles and the true shape of any small area are preserved on the map, and the equivalent (or equal-area), in which the area of any tract on the map is equal to that of the same tract on a globe to the same scale.

Lambert's work marked 'the beginning of a new epoch in the science of map projection', not only by its enunciation of basic principles but by the forms of projection that he devised. His equal-area conic projection, with one standard parallel, was modified in 1805 by H. C. Albers (1773–1833), who employed a cone intersecting the globe at two standard parallels; this gave a projection that greatly reduced the errors of scale in the north and south of the map and was especially suitable for areas with wide extension in longitude. The French *carte de l'État-Major* and other national surveys of the nineteenth century, however, adopted an older conic projection, also equal-area, used by Rigobert Bonne (1727–95) in 1752 and named after him. Lambert's conformal conic projection was revived for military mapping in the twentieth century.

Equivalence is plainly an essential property in the mapping of distributions or densities; but correlation of these factors with differences of latitude and climate, as required by many physical maps, is not clearly evoked by the equal-area conic projections, which have curved parallels of latitude. In the nineteenth century, projections with horizontal and rectilinear parallels were accordingly brought into use. The older sinusoidal, or Sanson-Flamsteed, projection became popular in atlas maps; and in 1805 K. B. Mollweide (1774–1825) constructed his homalographic projection, which, as specially suitable for circular hemispheric maps, came into general use in the second half of the century.

The Mercator chart, drawn on a conformal projection and therefore correctly representing angles between intersecting lines, such as parallels and meridians, had by the middle of the eighteenth century established itself as the standard navigational chart, enabling the seaman to lay off his compass course as a straight line. Its formal properties, with rectilinear parallels and meridians drawn parallel to the edges of the map, led to its adoption for some special types of map, such as meteorological charts; and its ease of construction made it the standard projection for world-maps in the general atlases of the nineteenth century.

VIII. THE PRINTING OF MAPS

From the middle of the sixteenth century the great majority of maps were printed from incised copper plates. Intaglio engraving on copper reproduced the cartographer's line with unequalled sharpness, precision, and delicacy; details could be deleted or corrected when the map required revision; and the plate if properly husbanded had a long life. These qualities recommended the process as much to the cartographer of the nineteenth century as to his less scientific predecessors, and it was employed in printing both the topographical maps of national surveys and the special maps described in a preceding section.

Nevertheless, copper-plate engraving had some disadvantages. It was a slow, highly skilled, and expensive process; in the eighteenth century the cost of engraving a medium-scale map was as great as that of surveying and drawing it. When a large number of impressions had been pulled from it, the relatively soft plate lost its sharpness unless it was reworked. Line-engraving was not suitable for the rendering of tones or surface colours, which had to be added by hand.

While few nineteenth-century cartographers doubted the superiority of copper-plate engraving, its limitations encouraged the introduction of rival or supplementary processes for map-printing. Engraving on steel plates, softened by heat to take the burin and then annealed, had a brief vogue in England and France from about 1820. This gave the fine line required by the cartographer, and the harder surface of the steel permitted larger printings, but the plate was less easily corrected than copper. Lithography, in which the design to be printed is drawn or traced on a chemically prepared stone surface, was applied to maps soon after its invention by C. Senefelder (1771–1834) about 1798. Its flexible line, although less brilliant than that of the incised metal plate, was a suitable vehicle for the cartographer's drawing, which could be applied directly to the stone without suffering the risk of corruption by the engraver. The lithographic stone was challenged, for the surface-printing of maps, by the much cheaper and lighter zinc plate, and in 1855 the Ordnance Survey adopted zincography for the reproduction of its large-scale plans at 25 inches to the mile.

Meanwhile, maps continued to be printed from engraved copper plates, as they have been to the present day. Revision was facilitated by the use of electrotypes, in which corrections or additions could be made without risk of injury to the original plate. This method, employed in Stieler's atlas from 1842, also enabled different maps to be prepared on the same topographical base; thus the Ordnance Survey issued three versions of the first edition of its 1-in map—with contours, with hill-hachuring, and with hill-hachuring and geological outlines.

Before the second half of the eighteenth century, colouring was employed principally to distinguish political divisions and the main physical features, such as water and woodland, or to enhance the decorative elements of a map. Its functions were immensely widened when maps were called into service by the physiographer (and especially the geologist) and by the social geographer. For applied cartography in these fields, the use of tones and colours was indispensable. Until the middle of the nineteenth century all colouring of maps was still done by hand; aquatint tones were occasionally used in distribution maps, such as that of Harness (1838). The introduction of chromolithography placed at the printer's disposal a process apt for reproducing flat colours, and therefore suitable for the colouring of geological maps and of layered orographic maps. Thus, while the maps in the *Physikalischer Atlas* (1838–48) of Berghaus were still hand-coloured, the layer colouring in Ziegler's *Hypsometrischer Atlas* (1856) was printed from lithographic stones. The first edition (1838) of H. von Dechen's geological map of Germany used only eight colours, added by hand, but the second edition (1869) was in 32 colours printed by lithography.

REFERENCES

[1] GREEN, W. 'Description and Use of the Improved Reflecting and Refracting Telescopes, and Scale for Surveying, etc.' London. 1778.
[2] LEYBOURNE, W. 'The Compleat Surveyor.' London. 1657.
[3] ROY, W. *Phil. Trans.*, **80,** 137, 1790.
[4] CAMPBELL, E. M. T. *Imago Mundi*, **6,** 79, 1949.
[5] BULL, G. B. G. *Geogr. J.*, **122,** 25, 1956.
[6] ROBINSON, A. H. W. *Ibid.*, **121,** 440, 1955.

BIBLIOGRAPHY

General:

CRONE, G. R. 'Maps and their Makers.' Hutchinson, London. 1953.
ECKERT, M. 'Die Kartenwissenschaft' (2 vols). De Gruyter, Berlin and Leipzig. 1921, 1925.
PESCHEL, O. 'Geschichte der Erdkunde' (2nd rev. ed.). Munich. 1877.

The World Map:

PERRIER, G. 'Petite histoire de la géodésie.' Presses Universitaires de France, Paris. 1939.
SANDLER, C. 'Die Reformation der Kartographie um 1700.' Oldenbourg, Munich. 1905.
WOLF, C. 'Histoire de l'Observatoire de Paris, de sa fondation à 1793.' Gauthier-Villars, Paris. 1902.

Instruments:

ADAMS, G. 'Geometrical and Graphical Essays.' London. 1791.
DAUMAS, M. 'Les instruments scientifiques aux XVIIe et XVIIIe siècles.' Presses Universitaires de France, Paris. 1953.
LANCASTER-JONES, E. 'Catalogue of the Collections in the Science Museum: Geodesy and Surveying.' H.M. Stationery Office, London. 1925.
LAUSSEDAT, A. 'Recherches sur les instruments, les méthodes, et le dessin topographique' (2 vols). Paris. 1898, 1903.

National Surveys:

BERTHAUT, H. M. 'La Carte de France, 1750–1898' (2 vols). Service Géographique de L'Armée, Paris. 1898–9.
CASSINI DE THURY, C. F. 'La description géométrique de la France.' Paris. 1783.
CLOSE, SIR CHARLES (FREDERICK). 'The Early Years of the Ordnance Survey.' Institution of Royal Engineers, Chatham. 1926.
MUDGE, W. *et al.* 'An Account of the Operations carried on for accomplishing a Trigonometrical Survey of England and Wales' (3 vols). London. 1801–11.

Hydrography and Oceanography:

DEACON, G. E. R. "Exploration of the Deep Sea." *J. Inst. Navig.*, **7,** 165–74, 1955.
ROBINSON, A. H. W. "The Early Hydrographic Surveys of the British Isles." *Emp. Surv. Rev.*, **11,** 60–65, 1951.
SKELTON, R. A. "Captain James Cook as a Hydrographer." *Mariner's Mirror*, **40,** 92–119, 1954.

Applied Cartography:

HELLMANN, G. 'Neudrucke von Schriften und Karten über Meteorologie und Erdmagnetismus', No. 4: "Die ältesten Karten der Isogonen, Isoklinen, Isodynamen"; No. 8: "Meteorologische Karten." Berlin. 1895–7.

WOODWARD, H. B. 'History of Geology.' Watts, London. 1911.

Projections:

AVEZAC, A. B. d'. 'Coup d'œil historique sur les projections des cartes de géographie.' Paris. 1863.

Surveyors' instruments drawn from a vignette on an early eighteenth-century map.

21

DREDGING

G. DOORMAN

WHILE the development of the European canal system (ch 18) was of great importance it was not a wholly unmixed blessing, for much dredging was necessary to keep the canals clear. Many ports, too, had to be dredged, especially as ships grew larger. In some cases fast-flowing rivers, such as the Scheldt, Meuse, and Rhine, kept the ports at their entrances free, but many towns had to move their harbours nearer to the sea. Thus Grevelingen (Gravelines) and Dunkirk became the ports for St Omer; Dixmude, later Nieuport, for Ypres; and Damme, later Sluis, for Bruges.

The various methods of deepening rivers, canals, and harbours that have been used may be classified as follows:

(*a*) removal of silt in suspension;
(*b*) scoops;
(*c*) ladle-dredgers;
(*d*) grab-dredgers;
(*e*) wheel-dredgers;
(*f*) chain-dredgers or bucket-dredgers.

(*a*) *Removal of silt in suspension.* In order to deal with local shoaling in a river it is sometimes sufficient to bring the silt into suspension merely by narrowing the river by crib-dams or, more simply, by hauling a heavy rake or harrow across the stream by means of a winch set up on the bank. Conradis [1] illustrates work of this kind during the sixteenth to eighteenth centuries, and also shows horses wading in a river to drag a harrow downstream. A defect of this method, however, is that the silt so removed will settle again farther down the river.

A similar system was the *spoelsluis* (cleansing sluice), which was applied in some sea-ports of Holland and Zeeland. Smeaton [3] saw it working satisfactorily in 1755. In this method a dock or lake was filled by the sea at high tide, and by closing a sluice-gate the water was kept there until low tide, when it was suddenly released by opening the sluice. The sudden rush of the released water carried off much of the silt (cf p 467).

This scouring effect was often increased by a special ship, called a *mol* (mole) or *krabbelaar* (scraper). A model of such a ship is seen in figure 337. The ship had a broad stern, widened by hinged lee-boards, so that it would be swept along by the current. As it moved downstream it tore up the bed of the river by means of adjustable rakes and harrows. An early *mol* with iron teeth is mentioned in the municipal accounts of Middelburg (Zeeland) for the year 1435.

Faustus Verantius of Venice, about 1600, refers to a boat similarly used on a

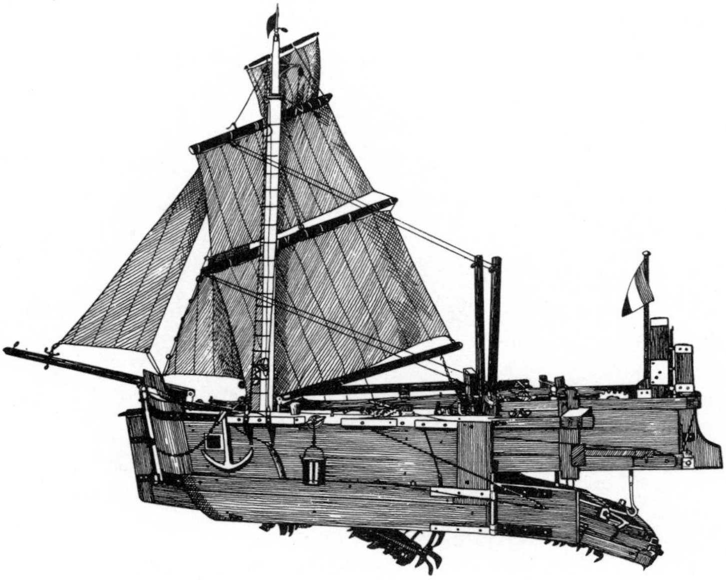

FIGURE 337—*Model of an eighteenth-century* krabbelaar *or scraper.*

river; it had a horizontal shaft carrying at each end a paddle-wheel, rotated by the stream, and in the middle a number of arms for tearing up the river-bed.

In a patent of 1589 Simon Stevin (1548–1620) claimed *inter alia* the process of conveying mud, clay, sand, or other suspended matter through tubes to deposit it on land [2]. It is remarkable that Stevin formulated such an advanced idea, for it was incapable of realization at the time. Had the patent system not then been in an immature state the States-General would have rejected the claim, since it failed to disclose the means by which it could be performed. In fact, it could be realized fully only much later, in the nineteenth century, when the steam-driven centrifugal pump reached a useful stage. An early practical solution was the 'squirting-dredger', designed for the Suez works. In this, a chain of buckets delivered the mud into a high tank, in which it was mixed with water from a centrifugal pump. The mixture was discharged through a gutter with a gradient of 1:20 and a length of 30–70 m. It is believed that this method of removing mud from the Suez canal is still adopted in principle.

Another system, also used for the Suez canal, was Bazin's steam-driven sand-pump (figure 338), a model of which was shown at the Paris exhibition of 1867. A rotating harrow beneath the forepart of the ship loosens the ground, and the resulting silt is taken up by four suction-tubes at the stern; these rest on a frame which can be adjusted in order to bring the ends of the tubes to the desired

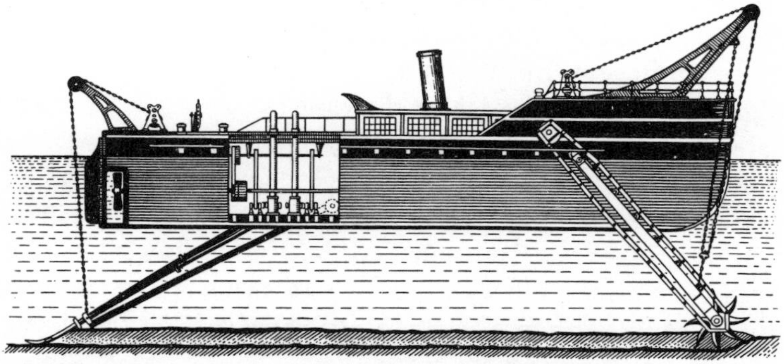

FIGURE 338—*Model of Bazin's steam-driven sand-pump. The rotating screw loosened the sand, which was then sucked up by tubes at the stern.*

height. Marcaire mentions *refoulement par une charge d'eau*, indicating that certain tubes beneath the suction-tubes (not shown) served to direct a jet of water on to the sand in order to bring it into suspension. Centrifugal pumps delivered the mixture into lighters. Such a dredger could daily lift 3000 cu m of material with a specific gravity of 1·8 to 2·0 from a depth of 8 to 12 metres. From about the same time dates Woodford's sand-pump, provided with a vertical centrifugal pump; this pump was lowered until its inlet was just above the river-bed, when it took up a mixture of water and mud.

The conduction of liquid mud by applied pressure seems first to have been used by English contractors when cutting the *Noordzeekanaal* for Amsterdam (1865–76). They worked with the Burt and Freeman sand-pump, an improved vertical pump of the Woodford type fed by a chain of buckets. The pump forced the mixture through a floating pipe-line consisting of a series of wooden tubes reinforced with iron. These tubes, each 6 m long, were joined by linen (later leather) sleeves. The pipe-line was about 100 m long and in some cases its outlet was 2½ m above the water.

From such devices have developed modern suction- and pressure-dredgers.

(*b*) *The scoop.* The simplest implement for dredging is the scoop, in Britain known also as the bag-and-spoon. The scoop is derived from the spade by bending up the edges of the blade in order to hold the semi-liquid mud. At an early stage the blade was replaced by a bag of permeable fabric, made of hemp or leather, attached to a strong metal ring. This instrument still forms a useful means for dredging; it has also been used in well-sinking. For the latter purpose, the bag was carried at the lower end of a vertical pole which was rotated from above by two men. The method was patented in 1602 by Pieter Pietersz Enten [2], who reached a depth of 232 ft with its aid. Sketches in technological works of the seventeenth and eighteenth centuries [1] show that the system was widely used; with certain improvements it still is.

For dredging purposes a bag larger than a man could handle was proposed at an early date. In his patent of 1589 Stevin claims such a device, hauled by a winch: the States-General stipulated that the exclusive right should be restricted to bags more than 1½ times as large as those up to then in use. However, for similar bags, the stress is proportional to the linear dimensions, whereas the capacity increases with the third power of this dimension, and large bags therefore wear very rapidly. Although a mechanically hauled bag was seen in Amsterdam in 1830 [1] most designers of dredgers have followed other ways, which will now be discussed.

(*c*) *The ladle-dredger.* A model owned by the *Hoogheemraadschap Rijnland* at Leiden (figure 339) shows an early design of ladle-dredger, doubtless the one patented in 1627 by Dominicus Van Wesel [2]. As indicated in the patent, this dredger was designed for cutting channels under water. It had a pontoon carrying '4, 5, 6, 8 or more instruments for clearing a broad cut of uniform depth and width with incredible rapidity'. The model shows six winches on the pontoon, each worked by hand. The cable of every individual drum has each end connected to the end of one of a pair of ladles, so that while one ladle rises, the other is lowered. After every stroke the rotation is reversed. Each of the twelve ladles is manœuvred by a man standing on one of a pair of floats; he pushes the ladle into the mud, and after it has been lifted he makes it unload into a mud-hopper or mud-scow. The cutting of polder-canals before the marsh had been drained, as is done today, may have been a novel feature of the invention. About the year 1645 Van Wesel's dredger was used by Van der Wel for land reclamation in Holland. A patent of 1603 [2] taken out by two carpenters of Hoorn shows that Van Wesel was not the first to design a ladle-dredger with winches. This earlier dredger had iron buckets 5 ft long and with a width of 3–6 ft. A dredger with a davit for bringing the bag of a ladle inboard after it had been hoisted by means of a winch seems to be typically English. A sketch of about 1760, in the Hamburg state archives (see tailpiece), reproduces such a device [1].

Little more is heard about ladle-dredgers until the eighteenth century, when the French constructed their famous pontoon-dredgers. de la Balme's design of 1718 was only a modification of dredgers already working in the harbours of Brest and Toulon. Far more complicated and effective were the French designs

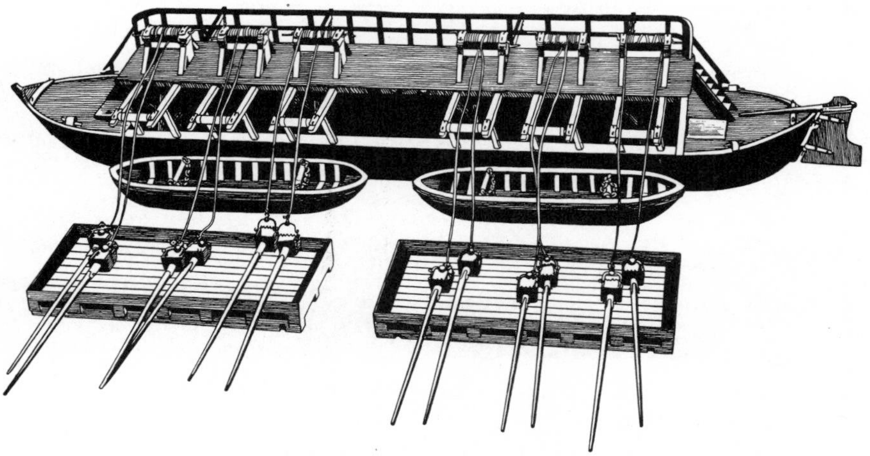

FIGURE 339—*Model of an early ladle-dredger, showing the ladles which were raised and lowered by the winches. Men standing in the small boats used the long handles to guide the ladles.*

with two treadmills, the larger one for hauling and lifting the bucket and the smaller one for its return movement. An example of such a dredger, dated 1745, is shown in figure 340 At first sight these designs are bewildering: a large bucket at the end of a heavy pole, about 14 m long, seems to move through water and air as if some giant handled the pole. It is reminiscent of Goethe's poem *Der Zauberlehrling* which inspired Paul Dukas's well known symphonic poem *L'apprenti sorcier*; in that tale, an incantation made a broom start its sweeping action without being touched by man.

In the French dredger the movements of the hand-operated device were faithfully followed when it was mechanized: such imitation in a mechanical device is commonplace in the history of invention. As in digging with a spade or dredging with a bag, the spoon was first applied to the ground, then moved forward towards the stern of the boat. The pole was tilted a little to prevent spilling during the raising of the bucket.

The two treadmills are mounted on the same boat, which has on each side a pole with a metal bucket. Each pole passes through a horizontal guiding-slot about 3 m above the water. A chain passes from each bucket over a pulley (E) on the stern of the boat and then horizontally to the shaft of the large treadwheel. Here the chains are wound on the shaft, one clockwise, the other anti-clockwise, and the last link of each chain is attached to the shaft near the nave of the treadwheel. Thus, when one bucket is hauled to the stern and finally raised, the chain

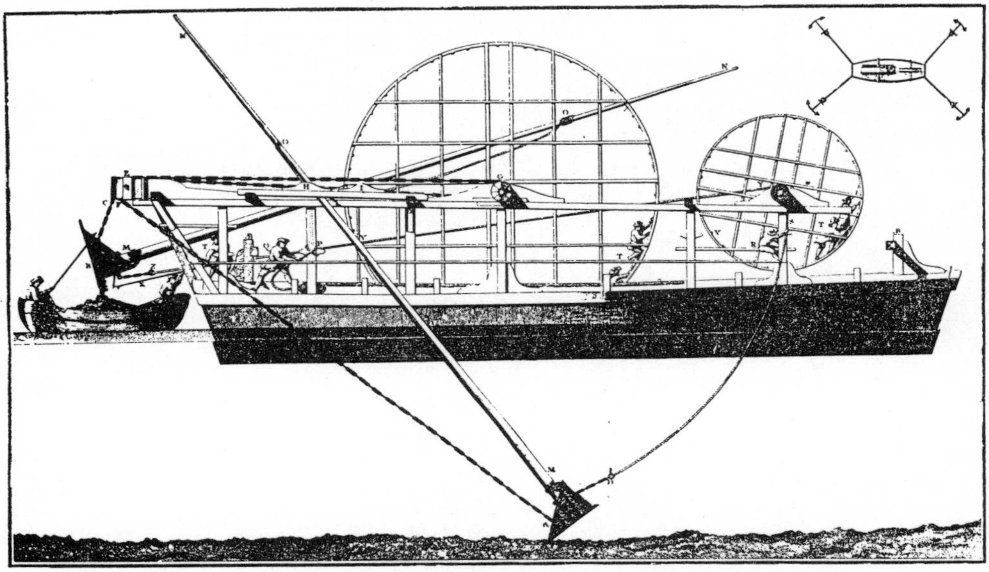

FIGURE 340—*French pontoon-dredger, with power supplied by treadmills, 1745.*

of the other one is paid out, as in Van Wesel's dredger. Cables are similarly wound on the shaft of the smaller wheel. This dredger carried a crew of six—a foreman (shown twice), two workmen in each wheel, and an ordinary seaman (S).

When on the bottom of the river, in the position shown in figure 340, the bucket is hauled to the left by the chain, and would fail to dig into the soil were it not for the fact that the foreman restricts the upward movement of the pole by means of a rope fixed to it at O. This rope passes over a pulley (H) and is controlled by the foreman at P. The pole gradually comes into a perpendicular position and then tilts from one end (H) of the guiding-slot to the other end (I). As a result the bucket comes into a position in which it will hold the mud that it has grasped. Meanwhile the smaller wheel has paid out the rope attached to the bucket, but this is then stopped, or at least checked, by the seaman, with the result that the bucket is lifted out of the water. The foreman leaves his position and opens the rear door of the bucket by releasing a catch on it with a boat-hook (X), thus discharging the mud into a mud-hopper brought under the bucket.

In both treadwheels the workmen then go to the other side (from T to V) in order to reverse the motion, bringing the bucket back to its original position relative to the boat. Before the next cut begins the boat can be moved transversely by means of the moorings, shown in the corner of the drawing.

The development of the French pontoon-dredgers cannot be attributed to a single inventor, but Antoine Macary seems to have had a great share in it. He shows the construction in its most perfect form in his Dutch patent [2] of 1763. This was for a dredger built in 1756 for deepening the canal and the harbour of Dunkirk. In a complete cycle, taking 8 to 9 minutes, it raised 72 cu ft of mud and sand from a depth of 15 ft. The smaller treadmill was mounted on a separate boat, in front of the main pontoon and connected to it by means of a wooden frame. This frame had slots for the poles of four buckets, again working in couples, each bucket containing 18 cu ft of mud. The mud was discharged into a mud-hopper brought between the two boats. Otherwise the construction was practically the same as that described above.

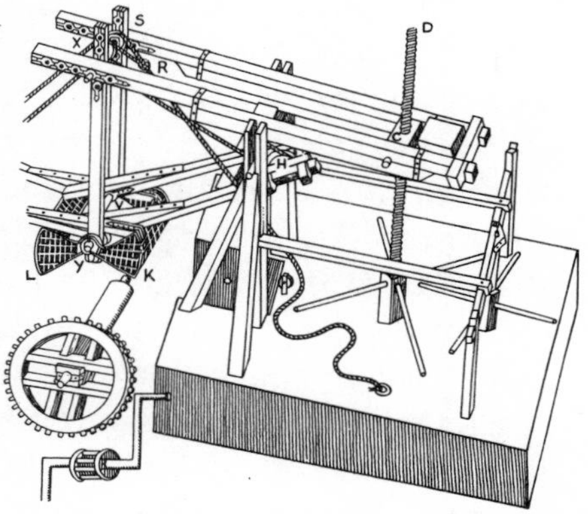

FIGURE 341—*Grab-dredger, 1597.*

Such pontoon-dredgers worked in several French harbours (for example, Toulon and Brest) and in Holland (Middelburg, Helvoet, Enkhuizen).

(*d*) *The grab-dredger.* Verantius informs us that in his time (about 1600) several devices could be seen in Venice for removing silt and sand from the bottom of the sea, but that one he had invented [1] could reach deeper and worked faster. It had two pontoons, between which was suspended a grab in the form of a pair of tongs. This could be lowered to the bottom and, after being closed by means of the cables of two windlasses, could be lifted by a winch turned by a treadmill. The mud-hopper was brought under the grab when this was lifted.

In a book of 1597 Lorini (b 1540) describes one of the Venetian dredgers improved according to his own proposals. As shown in figure 341, a wooden frame has been mounted on a square pontoon and carries a horizontal beam. Also mounted on the pontoon is a vertical screw (D) passing through a nut on the inboard end of the beam. Adjustably hinged to the outward end of the beam are two vertical bars (XY) bearing at their lower end the axle (YV) of a grab (LK). The outer half (L) of the grab has two arms reaching above the pontoon, where their ends are connected by cross-bars carrying a pulley (H). In the same way the inside half of the grab has two arms with cross-bars and pulley, though these are not included in the drawing. A rope divides (R) into two branches running over pulleys (S). One of these branches passes over the pulley (H) and its end is brought back and fixed to some point near the pulleys (S). The other branch is in the same way connected to the other half of the grab, so that by hauling the rope the grab is closed. The lifting of the grab is effected by turning the screw (D); to allow this, the nut (C) is hinged on two horizontal pins of the beam. The screw should also be able to turn slightly around a horizontal axis on the pontoon; this is not shown in the drawing but was probably well known in the art, for a similar mechanism is correctly drawn in the figure of a crane in folio 37 of Besson's *Theatrum*. The drawing shows that the front side of the pontoon has been so shaped as to allow the grab to pass with its arms and pulley.

Conradis points out that dredgers of this sort were employed over a long period, and in Venice they were still in common use in the nineteenth century. It can be proved that they were invented before 1561. In February of that year Pietro Venturino of Venice obtained in Brussels a patent [2] for the Low Countries for his art of deepening rivers and other waterways. In November of the same year he was allowed to co-operate with one or two experts who were to act as licensees under his supervision. The text of the patent of February is not known, and the additional patent of November gives no description of the new dredger. However, in 1562 the council of Kampen sent Otto Tengnagel, one of its members, to Antwerp to negotiate with an Italian dredging expert about deepening the Kamperdiep. By July, Tengnagel had accomplished his task, and on 11 September a large committee, together with the town carpenter and 'the Italians who wished to deepen', sailed out in four pilot-boats to examine the situation [4]. Again there is no description of the dredger, but at this stage a complete specification was given of the wooden planks and bars required to make the pontoon. At the author's request Mr W. Hildernisse, a shipbuilding engineer, made a drawing of the pontoon from these data, and evolved the design shown in figure 342. In this he has found a place for all the parts in the specification except one 27-ft bar which was probably intended as a spare part or to make the beam. This investigation gives us the dimensions of the dredgers then in use.

The figure shows that the pontoon has a deeper draught in the bow than in the stern; this, as stated by Lorini, serves to give the necessary buoyancy when lifting the grab. The pontoon has a flat front, not recessed for the passage of the arms of the grab as in Lorini's dredger; but Lorini informs us that his improvements consisted only in the longer beam and in the construction of the grab. It is therefore likely that Venturino was the inventor of the original Venetian dredger.

A few grab-dredgers are known from the eighteenth century, some with ingenious devices for closing the grab. Today the appliance is still widely used to remove mud from confined spaces and corners inaccessible to the bucket-dredger, and occasionally for lifting heavy objects from the water. It is now more commonly employed, however, for moving dry material such as coal and sand.

(*e*) *The wheel-dredger.* As a first example of a dredger with buckets on a rotating wheel a sketch by Leonardo da Vinci has been instanced [1], but this is evidently one of the many sketches he rapidly drew without giving much attention to how the design might be realized. It shows a horizontal shaft, driven by a handle and reduction-gearing. Mounted crosswise on the shaft are four arms ending in open beaks and reaching into the water between two boats, each carrying brackets with bearings for one end of the shaft. The mud was supposed to fall into a mud-hopper between the two boats, but much would have been spilt sideways from the open beaks during the preceding two-thirds of each revolution. There would also have been a difficulty inherent in all wheel-dredgers discharging outwardly, namely that, in order to be able to bring a mud-hopper or even a collecting-plate near enough to the rotating wheel, the latter would have to be of large diameter. In a project of de la Balme, in 1718, a wheel 30-ft in diameter was proposed. In the case of a vertical bucket-chain a movable collecting-plate was applied which was moved below each bucket as soon as it came into the unloading position, and was withdrawn again to allow the next one to pass. It is interesting to note that in Leonardo's sketch the dredging-mechanism served also for hauling on a rope fastened to a pole fixed in the canal; this device would give the whole system a slow forward movement during the dredging. The same feature is found in many later dredgers. Leonardo further conceived the idea of making the wheel-shaft adjustable in height, but he did not describe a method of doing so. A wheel-dredger is said to have been constructed in Berlin in 1630, but if this were ever more than a project it seems to have been unsuccessful.

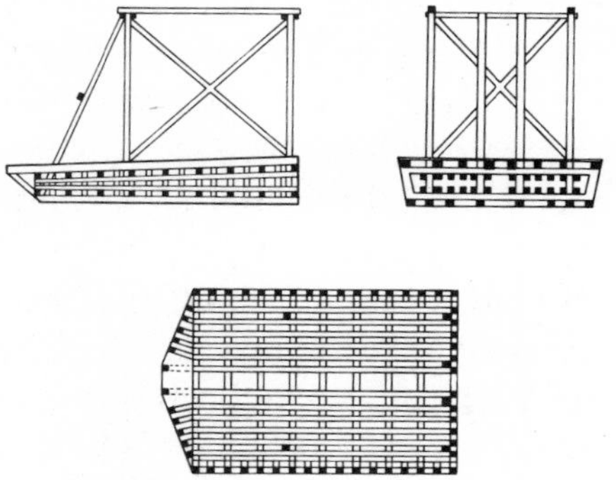

FIGURE 342—*Reconstruction of the dredger of 1562 for the Kamperdiep.*

While the discharge of buckets to the outside of a wheel was difficult, discharge to the inside had its own inconveniences. A project by M. Peltier (1742) for conducting the mud through the spokes to a hollow wheel-shaft would not have been successful, for clogging would soon have occurred. A better method was found earlier, in 1674, by the Dutch painter Jan Van der Heyden, inventor of the fire-engine with suction- and delivery-hoses. We have no drawing of his complete dredger, but there is one of a preliminary model; this forms part of a report made by Van der Heyden in 1675, now in the municipal archives of Amsterdam. As shown in plate 45 A, the wheel had eight compartments for taking up mud. The compartments were open towards the inside of the rim, but a stationary screening-segment prevented the mud escaping until it came above a second screen which sloped outwards and protected the bearing of the wheel against the falling mud. The wheel moved through an opening in the bottom of the pontoon and its shaft was supported by a frame which could be raised or lowered through a short distance: to allow for this the wheel was driven by a lantern-gear with long staves. Van der Heyden reported that he had to surmount great difficulties, but he eventually succeeded, and for some time the dredger did its work on the Voorzaan. The cost of building it was nearly 6000 guilders.

One of the last wheel-dredgers was described by Bouvier in 1831 [1, 5]. This *roue dragueuse* was used in the Beaucaire canal. To make it adjustable in depth a lantern-gear was used, as in the Van der Heyden dredger. The compartments of the wheel delivered the silt at their circumference by way of the outside of the preceding compartment and over a screen. A mud-hopper was kept as near as possible to the screen by guiding-rods that allowed some relative vertical movement.

In general the wheel-dredgers were not successful. They could be used only in shallow waters, and it was difficult to find a satisfactory way of throwing off the mud without soiling shafts and other moving parts.

(*f*) *Chain-dredgers or bucket-dredgers.* A chain fitted with buckets, each carried by a link of the chain, for raising water was known as early as 16 B.C. Marcus Vitruvius Pollio gives a sketch of such an instrument [6]. A tumbler-wheel is mounted on a horizontal shaft driven by a treadwheel. A chain with a bucket on every other link is suspended on the tumbler and its end hangs freely in the water. The buckets throw out their water when turned over by the tumbler. Drawings by Leonardo da Vinci, Agricola, Lorini, and Ramelli [6] prove that water-raising instruments of this character had continued in use.

The first known application of the chain for dredging purposes was the mud-mill, invented in 1589 by Cornelis Dircksz. Muys, the town carpenter of Delft [2].

There is a small illustration of this mill in an engraving of 1606 showing a view of Amsterdam, but a much clearer drawing, reproduced in plate 45 B, accompanied a booklet, *Grondighe Beschrijvinghe van Noort-Hollandt . . .*, annexed to the third edition of Joost Jansz.'s (Bilhamer's) map of that province. In this connexion several authors mention what they call 'an old engraving by E. Vermorcken of 1600'; however, the fact is that this Flemish illustrator lived in the nineteenth century and his drawing does not add to our knowledge of the mud-mill.

A good drawing [7] of the device was made between 1600 and 1620 by Roelandt Savery (certainly not by Pieter Brueghel the elder as assumed by the Vasari Society). The dredger consisted of a boat fitted with two treadwheels each worked by two men. These wheels were mounted aft and drove the top tumbler of a chain. The chain was guided through an inclined wooden sleeve or trough, carrying the other tumbler at its lower end. In contrast with modern bucket-dredgers, the chain moved in such a direction that its ascending part ran below the descending part. The chain had no buckets, but was furnished with flat wooden boards working as pushing-plates in the sleeve, in which they fitted as closely as the movement allowed. At its lower end the sleeve had an entrance reinforced with pointed iron plates for taking up the mud; the latter was forced upwards by the boards as they moved round the lower tumbler. The whole sleeve, with the chain, could be lowered about the axis of the top tumbler by means of a winch. During transport it could be lifted out of the slit in the bottom of the ship through which it reached the bed of the river when working.

Later drawings, for example plate 46 A, show the main parts more clearly. Here the treadwheel on the fore part of the ship is replaced by a horse-mill on the stern, driving the shaft of the top tumbler by means of gearing and a transmission-shaft below the deck. This was the ordinary arrangement, also shown in drawings of 1660, 1700, and 1761. D. Hudig & Company, at Rotterdam, and the Science Museum in London, possess models with the horse-mill carried forward. In this case the long transmission-shaft would have been unnecessary, but the mud would have had to pass below the mill. There is no evidence that such a dredger was built.

The first suggestion for placing a horse-mill on a chain-dredger came from Jacob Jacobssen of Haarlem in 1622 [2]. His construction—with 60 or 70 iron buckets, each taking up as much as half a wheelbarrowful of mud—was said to lift even hard ground, such as sand and clay, from a depth of 14 or 15 ft. This dredger would have been much like a modern bucket-dredger, but it seems doubtful whether such a heavy chain could have been driven with the mechanical means then available. Much later (1785), however, a dredger of this type was worked with a horse-mill by Grundy, at Kingston upon Hull [9].

Muys's mud-mill, with its flat boards, was meant to deal with the soft mud of canals and harbours. Although it has been much used in England, Denmark, Italy, and Germany it is generally known as the mud-mill of Amsterdam, where it did its work until well into the nineteenth century in competition with the first steam-dredgers [1]. In the eighteenth century about five mud-mills were constantly at work on the IJ,[1] each with four men and about three horses; two reserve horses were kept in a stable on board. Van Veen [8] mentions that Amsterdam levied mud-taxes to cover the expenses of dredging, and that between 1778 and 1793 the tax totalled 1 598 000 florins; this large sum gives an idea of the scale on which the dredging of the IJ was necessary. However, the bar across the Zuiderzee (Pampus) could not be removed by such means, and large laden ships could pass it only with the aid of 'camels'.

Muys obtained a patent both from the States of Holland and from the States-General, after the former had satisfied themselves that a machine which he had built in Delfshaven would be of great value to the country. They stipulated that Muys should not proceed with his invention before a committee had fixed the remuneration payable to him by towns wishing to build such dredgers during the twelve-year term of the patent. Two months later (May 1589) this committee fixed the sum as 200 carolus guilders for each of the eleven largest towns and 150 for each of the smaller.

In those days the States used to ask for some specification, drawing, or model before granting a patent. In most cases such documents are unhappily lost, but in the case of Muys they were not required, since the States had seen the dredger at work. It is only by a lucky chance that we have been able to ascertain the nature of the invention Muys had patented. Some competitors, wishing to praise their own inferior dredging-method, wrote in their patent of August 1589 that it worked much better than the dredger of a master-engineer of Delft (doubtless Muys) 'where the mud is pushed upward along planks'. For those who know the mud-mill this is a clear definition of Muys's invention.

In general terms, Muys's invention was a dredger with an inclined chain running over an upper and a lower tumbler, taking up the mud near the bottom and throwing it out above, its depth in the water being adjustable by a swinging movement of the chain around the axis of the top tumbler. Such a definition would cover all modern bucket-dredgers.

A vertical chain-dredger with buckets was designed and built in 1752 by

[1] In Dutch, IJ is a single character.

de Lonce [1]; it had one top tumbler and two below, 1 m apart. The chain had four buckets, which took up mud during their horizontal travel between the tow lower tumblers. This dredger was used in clearing foundations for bridges on the Loire. A note on a sketch preserved at the university of Leiden proves that a dredger of this type was built at Rouen in 1797.

It was also in the second half of the eighteenth century that dredgers with inclined chains began to be fitted with buckets; improved mechanical devices—especially geared wheels and steel plates for the buckets—made this possible.

In some cases the buckets were hauled over the ground by a slack part of the chain [1]; but on a trip to London in 1830 Henz, a German engineer, saw a dredger fitted with an 8-hp steam-engine in which the buckets passing the bottom tumbler-wheel were pressed into the ground by the weight of the inclined chain of buckets. This machine had guiding-bars fitted with cast iron rolls, to reduce the friction, along which the buckets moved. It was used to raise gravel for making macadam roads.

The first steam-dredger was built about 1796, when Boulton & Watt mounted a 4-hp steam-engine on an existing ladle-dredger employed in Sunderland harbour [1], in order to save the wages of the men operating the four ladles. In 1802 John Rennie advised the Hull dock company to replace the horse-mill of a bucket-dredger by a steam-engine. It was not until 1804 that this project was carried out, however, and in the meantime Oliver Evans had forestalled Rennie by building the first steam-dredger with a bucket-chain, for the Philadelphia docks. The introduction of steam raised new problems. A treadmill or the horse-mill stopped when the resistance on the chain became too strong—for example, when a bucket met a heavy stone. In the case of a steam-engine some yielding part, such as a friction-coupling or belt-drive, became necessary. An alternative was to provide some easily replaceable element which would break at a certain load; this was proposed by Jessop, who designed a steam-dredger for the Caledonian canal in 1805 [1].

Accessories. The mud-hopper, discharging from underneath, was very suitable for dumping the mud into the sea. It was proposed by Stevin in his patent of 1589 [2], and later, in 1594 or possibly 1617, Verantius claimed to have invented a mud-hopper of that type.

A drawing made in 1742 by Martin Peltier [1] shows a construction in which the side-walls of the central compartment for the mud converge to the discharging-doors in the bottom of the vessel. Buoyancy was obtained by compartments between this central one and the side of the boat. This is still a common arrangement, but it seems to some extent to have fallen out of use in the nineteenth century. In his patent of 1830 [10] a well known Dutch contractor of dredging-works, S. T. Kater Czn, says that the discharging of 40 cu m used to take 2 days, whereas it was performed in from 12 to 20 minutes by a boat that he had invented. In this boat, which was used with great success, the buoyancy compartment was at the bottom, under the floor of the mud compartment, which sloped towards doors in both sides of the boat.

It is not possible to discuss here the various means developed for the destruction of rocks, heavy trunks, or roots on the bottom of canals or rivers, but one of the earliest devices for that purpose deserves mention. The Bayerische Staatsbibliothek at Munich possesses a manuscript of Giovanni Fontana which, according to the catalogue, dates from about 1420. It contains two sketches of pontoons fitted with a spike, reaching to the bottom of the river through a central opening in the pontoon. Underwater obstructions could be broken up by repeated blows with the spike, and possibly the idea derived from contemporary agricultural practice. In one of these appliances the spike is dropped vertically. The other has an interesting mechanism, shown by Conradis [1] though without a clear description of its working. To the drawing a cryptographic note[1] has been added. The drawing shows an inclined semicylindrical sleeve hinged on a horizontal axis above the pontoon. The spike is chisel-shaped and its rounded end is guided by the sleeve. Both the sleeve and the spike are sharpened at the end. Initially the sleeve is lowered to the bottom, its hinged suspension allowing regulation of its setting with regard to both depth and inclination. The spike is then dropped several times, its downward movement being effected both by gravity and by the cable of a winch. In this way obstructions consisting of stone or wood could doubtless have been broken up.

REFERENCES

[1] CONRADIS, H. 'Die Naßbaggerung bis zur Mitte des 19. Jahrhundert.' Verein Deutsche Ingenieure, Berlin. 1940.

[2] DOORMAN, G. 'Patents for Inventions in the Netherlands during the 16th, 17th and 18th Centuries.' Netherlands Patent Board. Nijhoff, The Hague. 1942.

Idem. 'Octrooien voor uitvindingen in de Nederlanden uit de 16e–18e eeuw.' Netherlands Patent Board. Nijhoff, The Hague. 1940.

STEVIN, S. Patent G.7.

ENTEN, P. P. Patent G.68 (for his original drawing, see DOORMAN, G., *Ingenieur*, *'s Grav.*, **67**, A220, 1955).

[1] We are indebted to the Bayerische Staatsbibliothek for the text, as deciphered by Herr W. Meyer: Cavum canale dicitur opus novum eo quod cavare lectos potest aquarum ruere primo permititur unum lanceatorium deinde reliquum per illud et frangit nedum mollia sed dura similiter. ('A new work in which the beds of streams are dug out is called a hollow canal. First, a spike is allowed to fall down heavily; then the other piece [scoop] after it; not only soft material but hard likewise is broken up.')

VAN WESEL, D. Patent G.278. (For D. Van Wesel and also J. van der Heyden, see DOORMAN, G., *Ingenieur, 's Grav.*, **63**, A414–18, 1951.)

VENTURINO, P. Patent K.2. (See DOORMAN, G., *Ingenieur, 's Grav.*, **56**, A213, 1941.)

MUYS, C. D. Patents G.6 and H.5. (See DOORMAN, G., *Ingenieur, 's Grav.*, **63**, A415, 1951; **64**, A83, 1952.)

JACOBSSEN, J. Patent G.209.

MACARY, A. Patents H.250 and G., Dec. 1763. (See CONRADIS, H. Ref. [1], p. 113.)

[3] SMEATON, J. 'John Smeaton's Diary of his Journey to the Low Countries, 1755, from the original MS. in the Library of Trinity House, London' (with an introduction by A. TITLEY), p. 24. Newcomen Society Extra Publication No. 4, London. 1938.

[4] UITTERDIJK, J. N. *Bijdr. Gesch. Overijssel*, **10**, 66–73, 1890.

[5] 'Annales des ponts et chaussées, 1831 à 1840', 1831, 2e semestre, p. 352, Pl. XVI. Paris. 1843.

[6] BECK, T. 'Beiträge zur Geschichte des Maschinenbaues' (2nd enl. ed.). Verein Deutsche Ingenieure, Berlin. 1900.

[7] ZIMMER, G. F. *Trans. Newcomen Soc.*, **4**, Pl. II, 1923–4.

[8] VAN VEEN, J. 'Dredge, Drain, Reclaim', p. 78. Nijhoff, The Hague. 1948.

[9] "History of the Dredging Machine." *Mechanics' Mag.*, **39**, 307, 1843.

[10] DOORMAN, G. 'Het Nederlandsche Octrooiwezen en de techniek der 19e eeuw', figure on p. 173. Netherlands Patent Board. Nijhoff, The Hague. 1947.

Ladle-dredger, c *1760.*

22

TELEGRAPHY

G. R. M. GARRATT

IT has been said that the history of the art of communication is the history of the human race. While such a statement is perhaps too sweeping, it is undoubtedly a fact that the development of communication is an integral part of the growth of civilization. Every improvement in the speed and facility with which thoughts and ideas can be exchanged has had its social or economic effect, and we can appreciate fully the significance and trend of historical, social, and political developments only if we view them against the background of the contemporary state of the art of communication.

The hundred years with which we are here particularly concerned was one of special interest, for at its beginning the fastest means of communication over long distances was that of a rider on horseback, while by its end the electric telegraph was firmly established. Although the earliest proposal for a system of electric telegraphy was made as early as 1753, it was nearly ninety years before a really practicable scheme was evolved. The intervening period was, as we shall see, filled with suggestions and experiments, mostly of a somewhat unpractical nature but all indicative of that instinctive urge towards the improvement of communication which has been such a marked characteristic of the human race.

Before describing the stages by which the electric telegraph evolved from its earliest beginnings, it is necessary to devote some attention to a review of the system of visual telegraphs which matured in France during the Revolutionary period, and which was for nearly forty years an important factor in contemporary naval and military operations.

The scene may be set by recalling the situation in France during 1793–4. The Revolution was at its height, and France was assailed on every side by the allied forces of Britain, Holland, Prussia, Austria, Spain, the Italian States, Hanover, and Hesse. The cities of Marseilles and Lyons were in revolt, and a British fleet held Toulon. Three factors alone were on the side of the French in their seemingly hopeless position: the lack of co-ordination between the allied forces due to their inadequate lines of communication; the disunity of allied purpose; and the single-minded determination of Lazare Carnot in establishing coherence among all sections of the French army.

In this situation, the advent of the Chappe telegraph was one of the major factors that eventually turned the scale in favour of the French forces. It must not be supposed, however, that Claude Chappe (1763–1805) was the sole originator of visual telegraphs. Primitive methods of signalling were almost certainly in use 4000 years ago, and the Romans are known to have made wide use of towers for signalling purposes. The invention of the telescope did much to make visual telegraphy more practicable, and Robert Hooke (1635–1703), in a discourse to the Royal Society in 1684, gave a vivid and comprehensive outline of the requirements for an effective system. There were few practical details to which Hooke did not refer, but it was one thing to describe such an invention and another altogether to carry it through all the troubles of development, and then to operate it over hundreds of miles in the conditions existing at the close of the eighteenth century.

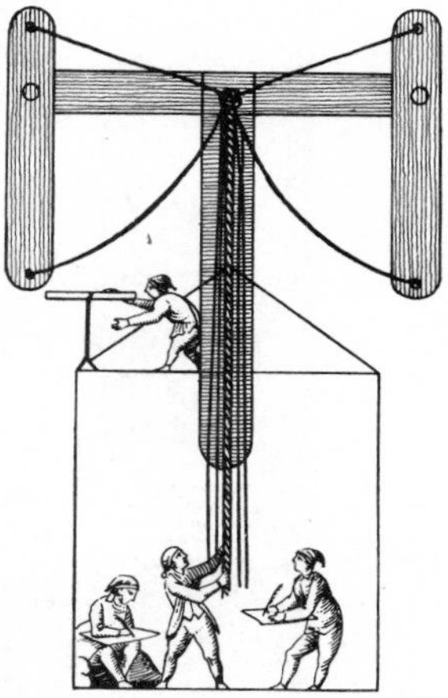

FIGURE 343—*Chappe's semaphore telegraph.*

Claude Chappe was one of a family of ten of whom only seven survived infancy. In the disturbed conditions of the times, he and his brothers found themselves without regular employment, and early in 1790 they allied themselves enthusiastically to the new cult of republicanism then sweeping the country. During a period of enforced leisure in the summer of that year, Chappe determined to devise a system of communication (figure 343) that would enable the central government to receive intelligence and transmit orders in the shortest possible time. His investigation included a study of the electric telegraph (p 651). During the next two years he experimented with several different forms of visual telegraphs. On two occasions his apparatus at the Étoile in Paris was destroyed by fanatical mobs in the belief that he was communicating with the imprisoned Louis XVI. Not discouraged by these reverses, he persevered with his experiments and by the summer of 1793 the value of his proposals had been recognized. He was accorded the title of *Ingénieur-Télégraphe* and was ordered to establish a line of telegraph stations between Paris and Lille, a distance of 144 miles. Within a year the line of fifteen stations, each within sight of the next, was complete, and the first telegram to be transmitted over such an organized system was that sent from Lille to Paris on 15 August 1794 informing the government that their forces had retaken Le Quesnoy. A fortnight later, another message, which gave rise to scenes of wild enthusiasm in the French capital, told of the recapture of Condé. The Chappe semaphore consisted of a wooden beam pivoted at its centre so that it could be rotated in a vertical plane. At each end of the beam were additional movable arms, and a large number of configurations was therefore possible (figure 344).

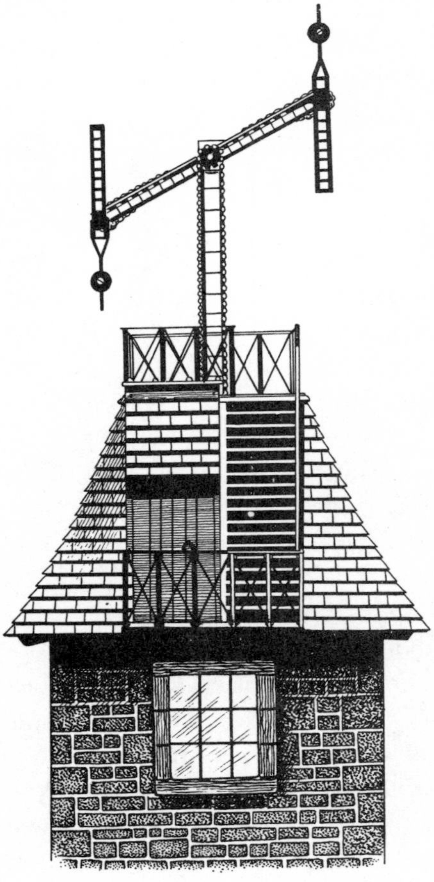
FIGURE 344—*Model of a Chappe telegraph tower.*

Lines of Chappe telegraphs were established during the next few years between Paris and Strasbourg and between Paris and Brest, but since each station in the line had to be within sight of the next—there were fifty between Paris and Strasbourg—the difficulties of administration and the wages of the staff were considerable. It is not surprising that financial troubles were incessant, at least until the service was linked with a lottery scheme.

Chappe died in 1805, probably by suicide occasioned by the strain and anxiety to which he had been subjected, but for fifty years the system of telegraphs he had instituted covered the greater part of France. In 1852, when the Chappe system was finally superseded by the electric telegraph, the network covered a total distance of more than 3000 miles and included 556 separate stations.

In England, reports of the working of the Chappe line between Lille and Paris were received during the autumn of 1794, and an illustrated description appeared in 'The Sun' on 15 November. Although it is not uncommon for similar inventions to be made quite independently yet almost simultaneously in widely different places, it seems likely that it was these reports from France that stimulated Lord George Murray and John Gamble to propose schemes for visual telegraph systems to the Admiralty early in 1795. Murray's scheme, which was adopted, was very similar to one of Chappe's earlier proposals. It employed a large wooden framework provided with six movable shutters which, exhibited in different combinations, provided sixty-three distinct signals. A chain of these stations, fifteen in all, was erected for the

Admiralty between London and Deal at an expenditure of nearly £4000—including the cost of an eight-guinea clock and two twelve-guinea telescopes at each station—and it was reported that a signal could be sent and acknowledged within two minutes.

A similar chain of ten stations was erected to link the Admiralty with Portsmouth, and some of the prominences upon which the stations were erected are still known locally as 'Telegraph Hill'. Yet another chain was projected in 1801, to link London with Yarmouth, but during the brief lull in the fighting with France marked by the Peace of Amiens (1802) the plan was postponed; it was not in fact completed until 1807. Another important chain was that between London and Plymouth, completed during the summer of 1806.

The first visual telegraph, on the semaphore principle, in the United States was built in 1800 by Jonathan Grout. It was a 65-mile line connecting Martha's Vineyard with Boston, and its purpose was to transmit news about shipping.

Between 1811 and 1814 the shutter system was gradually replaced in Britain by the superior Chappe semaphore, but with the defeat of Napoleon and his banishment to Elba all sense of urgency was lost and many of the telegraph stations were abandoned. The relaxation was but an interlude, however, for when Napoleon escaped and landed in France in the spring of 1815 the telegraph-lines were hastily restored, and were converted to the semaphore system where this had not already been done. The revival was short-lived, however, for such was the dependence of the telegraph on a state of war that upon the final defeat of Napoleon at Waterloo, and the ending of the long struggle with France, the telegraph stations were abandoned.

Within a few years an effort was made to revive them, and the line to Portsmouth was not finally closed until 1847. Essentially, however, the visual telegraphs had been an instrument of Admiralty, and it is not surprising that the service tended to fall into disuse when deprived of the stimulating effect of war. The semaphore telegraphs were extravagant in man-power, for the stations were seldom more than 8 miles apart; they were subject to interruption by adverse weather conditions; and they were of little use to the individual citizen. With these handicaps it was perhaps inevitable that they should fail to survive a long period of peace; in any case, the advent of the electric telegraph about 1840 rendered the semaphore system obsolete.

The history of the electric telegraph is generally considered to start in the year 1753, when a remarkable letter, signed only with the letters C. M. (p 649), appeared in the 'Scots Magazine' of 17 February. Before describing the proposals made by C. M., however, it is appropriate briefly to review the background against which they were made, and to bear in mind that knowledge of the science of electricity (vol V, chs 9 and 10) was still only rudimentary.

It had been known from very early times that a piece of amber, when rubbed, acquired the property of attracting small pieces of straw or paper. Such phenomena, however, attracted little attention and were considered of no practical significance until near the close of the sixteenth century, when William Gilbert (1540–1603) of Colchester collected together various scattered observations on them and, adding many of his own, laid the foundations of the science of electricity in his great work, *De magnete*, published in 1600. It was Gilbert who coined the word 'electric' from the Greek *ēlektron*, meaning amber. Some advance was made by Robert Boyle (1627–91), who in 1675 published a small book on the origin and production of electricity, but though he speculated on the causes of electrical phenomena he was no more able to offer a satisfactory explanation than the Greek philosophers had been, more than 2000 years earlier.

An important advance was made between 1660 and 1663 by Otto von Guericke (1602–86) when, in the course of some experiments that he was carrying out on another subject, he constructed a large ball of sulphur that could be rotated on a spindle. Pressing his bare hand against the ball as it revolved, he observed that it became strongly electrified, and he thus unintentionally became the inventor of the first machine to generate electricity.

Development of the frictional machine proceeded slowly. The sulphur ball was replaced by one of glass, probably by Newton in 1675. In 1733, J. H. Winckler (1703–70) mounted a leather cushion in contact with the glass to act as a rubber, and G. M. Bose (1710–61) introduced the prime conductor in 1738. In 1742 Andrew Gordon (1712–51) substituted a glass cylinder for the rather awkward globe, and thus by the middle of the eighteenth century the frictional machine was established as a fairly reliable generator of electricity.

Familiar as we all are today with the basic facts of electrical practice—that metallic wires act as conductors, and that rubber, porcelain, mica, and other such substances act as insulators—we must remember that there was once a time when even these elementary facts were unknown. It would take too long to describe here the remarkable series of experiments carried out by Stephen Gray, a pensioner of the Charterhouse, between 1720 and his death in 1736, but his discovery of the basic principles of electrical conduction and insulation in 1729 laid the foundations upon which the electric telegraph was to be built. Before his time there had been no attempt to transmit electric charges over a distance, even of a few feet.

Among Gray's many experiments were a number carried out in the summer of

1729, in which he showed that electric charges could be transmitted along such materials as moistened pack-thread and brass wire, but not along silk threads, glass rods, or sticks of resin. In the course of his experiments, he succeeded in transmitting electric charges to a distance of nearly 300 yds, and it is of interest to note that, in so doing, he had in fact set up all the essential elements of an electric telegraph: a source of electricity at the sending-end, an insulated line, some form of indicator at the receiving-end (Gray used a down feather), and an earth-return circuit, although the function of this last was not suspected at the time.

Before we come to C. M.'s electric telegraph, one further invention must be briefly mentioned—that of the Leyden jar in 1745. This was important not so much for its uses in telegraphy—to which, indeed, it had little direct application—as for the manner in which the discovery of its properties aroused widespread interest in electrical phenomena throughout Europe. For the first time, electric charges could be stored. Popular demonstrations and experiments were carried out in many places, and it became commonplace to transmit an electric shock through a circle of twenty or thirty persons, each holding hands with the next. It was shown that the shock was experienced simultaneously by all those in the circle. The experiment was repeated on a grand scale by the Abbé Nollet (1700–70), and when a shock was passed round a circle, more than a mile in circumference, in which some 200 Carthusian monks were linked together by lengths of iron wire, it became evident that the speed of transmission was exceedingly high. Here, then, were all the requirements for an electric telegraph, and it is not surprising that within the space of a few years a fully detailed proposal was published for the employment of electricity for the transmission of intelligence.

It is convenient to classify the various forms of electric telegraph proposed between 1750 and 1850 under three headings, according to the basis of their operation:

(*a*) Telegraphs employing static electricity.
(*b*) Electrochemical telegraphs.
(*c*) Electromagnetic telegraphs.

This classification serves to indicate how the development of the telegraph was influenced and stimulated by the discoveries of Galvani, Volta, Ampère, and others in the basic science of electricity.

Telegraphs employing static electricity. The name of the author of the remarkable letter published over the initials C. M. in the 'Scots Magazine' in 1753 is not known. Although it has been attributed by some to Charles Morrison and by others to Charles Marshall, the evidence in favour of either is weak and the author's identity must remain uncertain. Whatever his name, his letter constituted a fully detailed specification for an electric telegraph employing static electricity. Although it is doubtful whether he ever carried his proposals to the stage of practical experiment, it is clear that he foresaw nearly all the difficulties that would be encountered.

C. M.'s letter is too lengthy to quote in full but, briefly, he proposed that 'a set of wires, equal in number to the letters of the alphabet, be extended horizontally between two given places, parallel to one another and each of them about an inch distant from the next to it. At every twenty yards let them be fixed in glass, or jewellers' cement, to some firm body, both to prevent them touching the earth, or any other non-electric,[1] or from breaking by their own gravity. . . .' The letter goes on to explain in detail how the wires are to be connected to the prime conductor of the electric machine when it is desired to signal a particular letter. At the receiver, 'let a ball be suspended from every wire, and about a sixth or an eighth of an inch below the balls, place the letters of the alphabet, marked on bits of paper, or any other substance that may be light enough to rise to the electrified balls. . . . Having set the electrical machine a-going as in ordinary experiments, suppose I am to pronounce the word Sir; with a piece of glass or any other *electric per se* I strike the wire S, so as to bring it in contact with the barrel, then i, then r, all in the same way; and my correspondent, almost in the same instant, observes these several characters rise in order to the electrified balls at the ends of the wires. . . .'

C. M.'s letter attracted little attention at the time and, detailed though it was, it did not contribute materially to the development of practical telegraphy. Of historical and technical interest for the manner in which it proposed to apply the latest advances in the electrical art, it may have failed to find practical uses for economic reasons. Moreover, it is to be doubted whether the civilized world was yet ready for an electric telegraph, especially one which required the use of twenty-six insulated wires for its operation.

During the thirty years that followed the publication of this letter, a number of somewhat similar schemes were suggested, notably by Bozolus (1767), Odier (1773), and Le Sage (1782), but, so far as is known, none ever reached the stage of practical experiment. In 1787, however, M. Lomond in Paris gave demonstrations on a small scale, his scheme being an improvement on C. M.'s in that he employed only a single conductor, with a pith-ball electroscope as an indicator.

[1] An electric material was one which could be electrified by rubbing, that is, an insulator. A non-electric was thus what we term a conductor.

By means of a pre-arranged code, the receiving-operator was able to translate the motions of the pith-balls into letters of the alphabet, but perhaps the very slow rate of signalling discouraged development on a larger scale.

The semaphore telegraph developed so successfully by Chappe has already been noticed, but it is not generally known that before this work he had, in 1790, carried out extensive experiments with an electric telegraph. His scheme made use of two clocks, the pendulums of which were carefully adjusted to swing in unison. Around the seconds dials, he marked the numerals 1–9 and 0. Signalling was achieved by the discharge of a Leyden jar, the receiving operator noting the numeral indicated by the seconds-hand at the instant of discharge. Chappe seems, however, to have been discouraged by the difficulties he encountered in insulating the conducting wire, and abandoned his electrical scheme in favour of the visual telegraph which seemed, at that time, to offer prospects of more immediate success.

Less daunted by the apparent difficulties inherent in an electrical system was Don Francisco Salvá of Barcelona who, in 1795, put forward a multi-wire scheme in which he proposed that the discharge of Leyden jars at the transmitter should be detected as electric shocks experienced by the operators at the receiver. His proposals, which included a scheme of submarine telegraphy, were described in great detail, but in spite of the patronage of the Spanish court it does not appear that his ideas ever found more practical application than that of a purely local demonstration. There is a report that in 1798 a modification of Salvá's scheme, using only a single wire, was actually constructed between Madrid and Aranjuez, a distance of about 26 miles, but the absence of reports on the working of this line is in such striking contrast to the wealth of detail regarding the original proposals that its existence must be regarded as uncertain.

The last, and perhaps the most interesting, of the telegraphs employing static electricity which we shall notice is that described and demonstrated by Francis Ronalds in 1816. Born in 1788, and originally intended for a career in commerce, Ronalds seems to have taken unkindly to such prospects and from 1812 onwards devoted himself to chemistry and physics, experimenting in static electricity. He had probably observed the slow, cumbersome, and unreliable system of semaphore telegraphs then employed by the Admiralty, and it is evident that he devoted a great deal of time and expense during the summer of 1816 to a large-scale experiment on the use of electricity for the purposes of telegraphy.

At that time Ronalds was living at a house in Hammersmith, London, the garden of which was 600 ft long. In order to demonstrate the speed at which electrical impulses travelled, he erected a pair of large wooden frames, from the bars of which he suspended a total of eight miles of wire. To one end of the wire he connected a frictional machine which charged the line; to the other he connected an indicator in the form of a pair of pith-balls which diverged when the line was charged. At the sending-station Ronalds provided a dial which was marked with the letters of the alphabet and could rotate behind a plate through an aperture in which one letter at a time could be seen. A similar dial was provided at the receiver, and both were rotated synchronously by means of clockwork, a scheme not unlike that proposed, but abandoned, by Chappe in 1790. The line was charged continuously by the frictional machine, but was discharged by the sending-operator at the moment when the desired letter appeared in the aperture of his instrument. The receiving operator would see the pith-balls of his indicator collapse and he would note the letter which was at the same moment exposed in the aperture of his dial.

Having satisfied himself that the system would work with an overhead line, Ronalds then proceeded to construct an underground line 525 ft in length in a trench 4 ft deep in his garden. He insulated the copper wire with lengths of glass tube, which were encased in soft pitch in long troughs of wood. Many years later, in 1862, a length of this line was discovered in the Hammersmith garden, and a short specimen is preserved in the Science Museum at South Kensington.

Were Ronalds's proposals really practicable? Had they the makings of an efficient electric telegraph? In the light of later knowledge, the answers must almost certainly be in the negative, but there is no doubt that his experiments constituted a serious attempt to solve what was, at that time, a very difficult problem. Their scale and success were certainly such as to merit official investigation. It was unfortunate, therefore, that when Ronalds offered to demonstrate his telegraph to the Admiralty he was informed that 'telegraphs of any kind are now wholly unnecessary and no other than the one now in use will be adopted'.

Electrochemical telegraphs. In the closing years of the eighteenth century, the work of Galvani and Volta was responsible not only for introducing a completely new era in the field of electric telegraphy but for laying the essential foundations upon which the practical application of electricity was to be built. In consequence of their work, electricity became available in a low-pressure form, the supply of which was to prove as copious and tractable as that of static electricity had been elusive and capricious. Sooner or later, it is safe to assume, telegraphs dependent on static electricity would have developed into reasonably acceptable forms for practical use. There can be no doubt, however, that the provision of low-pressure voltaic electricity very greatly facilitated the development of convenient and simple devices for the purpose of communication, and in the telegraphs now to be described we shall see how the basic discoveries of Galvani and Volta, and later of Oersted, Ampère, Arago, and Sturgeon, were applied in the development of practical systems.

Very briefly, Galvani showed in 1791 that contact between metals and animal tissues often produced muscular contractions which seemed to be of an electrical origin; Volta showed that the effect was due to the generation of electricity arising from the conjunction of two dissimilar metals in a moist body. This led him in 1800 to the invention of his well known column or pile of zinc and silver disks, each pair being separated by pasteboard moistened with brine. Volta's pile constituted the first electric battery. It was soon observed that the maintenance of an electric current was associated with chemical action on the disks of the pile, and it was also shown (Nicholson and Carlisle, 1800) that water could be decomposed into its constituent elements, oxygen and hydrogen, by the passage of an electric current from the pile.

This association of electricity with chemical action quickly resulted in suggestions for a variety of electrochemical telegraphs, the first of which was due to Salvá in 1804. Salvá, as was mentioned earlier, had previously developed a static-electricity telegraph; he now proposed to employ the bubbles of hydrogen that appear at the negative electrode during the electrolytic decomposition of water as the indicator in a telegraph, with one of Volta's piles as the source of electricity. His proposals were published but, lacking development, they were quickly forgotten; thus it was once again shown that an inventor needs both to develop and to exploit his schemes before he can expect either acknowledgement or reward.

Prominent among other inventors of electrochemical telegraphs was S. T. von Soemmering, whose apparatus (figure 345) was described in considerable detail to the Munich Academy of Sciences in the summer of 1809 and was subsequently demonstrated on many occasions. His apparatus, which he had installed at his residence, was very similar to that proposed by Salvá, the only original contribution made by von Soemmering being the fitting of an alarm (seen on the right in the figure) to call the attention of the receiving operator; but so earnestly did he advocate his scheme over a period of several years that he has been widely regarded as its original inventor. Employing no fewer than thirty-five wires between the sender and receiver, however, it was clearly too costly and unpractical for general use, and it is not surprising that the many officials and governments whom von Soemmering approached showed little desire to adopt it.

Among those to whom von Soemmering demonstrated his telegraph in 1810 was Baron Schilling, an attaché at the Russian Legation at Munich. Greatly impressed with the possibilities of an electric telegraph, Schilling devoted much of his time during the next twenty-seven years to the development of an acceptable system. Since Schilling's instrument later provided the basis of the Cooke and Wheatstone inventions, the friendship between von Soemmering and Schilling was of the utmost consequence in the history of the electric telegraph.

Other forms of chemical telegraph were proposed by a number of inventors during the thirty or forty years following von Soemmering's demonstrations, notably those of Sharpe (1816), Coxe (1816), E. Davy (1838), Smith (1843), and

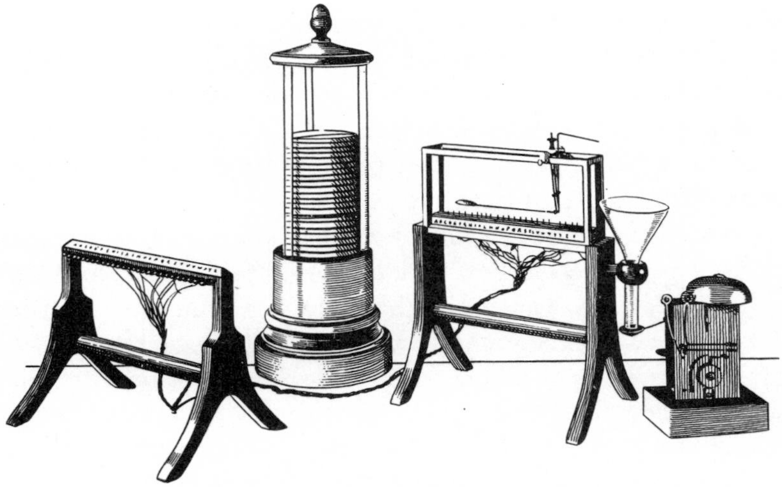

FIGURE 345—*von Soemmering's telegraph, 1809.*

Bain (1846), but none proved of practical value. With the coming of electromagnetism, telegraphy underwent a new orientation.

Electromagnetic telegraphs. For at least one hundred and fifty years preceding 1820, if not a great deal longer, the relationship between magnetism and electricity had been obscure. There were so many obvious analogies that some sort of connexion seemed certain, but in the absence of any steady source of direct current the real nature of the link between magnetic and electric phenomena had not been understood. With the invention of Volta's pile, however, and the subsequent development of various primary cells, it was inevitable that, sooner or later, the true relationship should be disclosed. During the winter of 1819–20 Hans Christian Oersted (1777–1851), professor of physics in the university of Copenhagen, made the vital observation that a magnetic needle was deflected when a current flowed through a wire above it. His observations, first published in Latin in July 1820, aroused the greatest interest, and were immediately followed up by Ampère and Arago in France; by Humphry Davy, Faraday, and Sturgeon in England; by Schweigger and others in Germany; and by Henry in America. Within a few weeks Ampère had published his first memoir on electromagnetism, and Arago had announced his discovery of the magnetizing effect of an electric current.

A few months later, an invention of the greatest importance to telegraphy—that of the galvanometer—was announced by J. S. C. Schweigger (1779–1857) of Halle. Observing that a magnetic needle was deflected in one direction by a current flowing in a wire above it and in the same direction by a reverse current in a wire beneath, he found he could obtain almost twice the deflexion if he arranged the outward-flowing current to pass above the needle and, simultaneously, the return current to pass beneath. The deflexion was doubled again by giving the wire an extra turn around the needle, while a third turn gave nearly six times the original deflexion.

Schweigger's galvanometer, or multiplier as it was first called, was a primitive device consisting merely of a small magnetic compass with a few turns of wire around it, but improvements in its construction were soon made by Ampère and others. It quickly attracted the attention of von Soemmering and Baron Schilling.

Schilling's experience in the diplomatic and military fields, and the close interest that he had paid to the subject of electricity over a number of years, enabled him fully to appreciate the possibilities of Schweigger's multiplier for the purposes of telegraphy. Details and dates in regard to Schilling's early experiments are lacking, but it seems probable that he began experimenting in his spare time about 1822. During the next fifteen years—until his death in 1837—Schilling devised a number of separate arrangements, sometimes using a single multiplier as indicator and sometimes five or six (figure 346). In the case of the single-needle instrument, he used a code, not unlike the later Morse code.

An interesting feature of Schilling's telegraph was the alarm device (figure 346 B), which bore a striking resemblance to that employed some fifteen years earlier by von Soemmering. This device consisted of an additional galvanometer-movement fitted with a horizontal arm so arranged that, when the needle was deflected, it struck a delicately balanced lever which, in falling, operated the detent of an ordinary clockwork alarm.

Although Schilling appears to have travelled widely and to have brought his telegraph to the notice of many, he seems to have made no serious attempt to put it into practical use until 1836. In that year a commission was appointed by the Emperor Nicholas of Russia with a view to installing the telegraph between St Petersburg and the imperial palace at Peterhof. Unfortunately, Schilling died before the plans could be carried into effect. In 1835, however, he had demonstrated his instruments to a Heidelberg professor named Moncke, who had a copy made for use in his own lectures. In March of the following year this instrument was seen by W. F. Cooke.

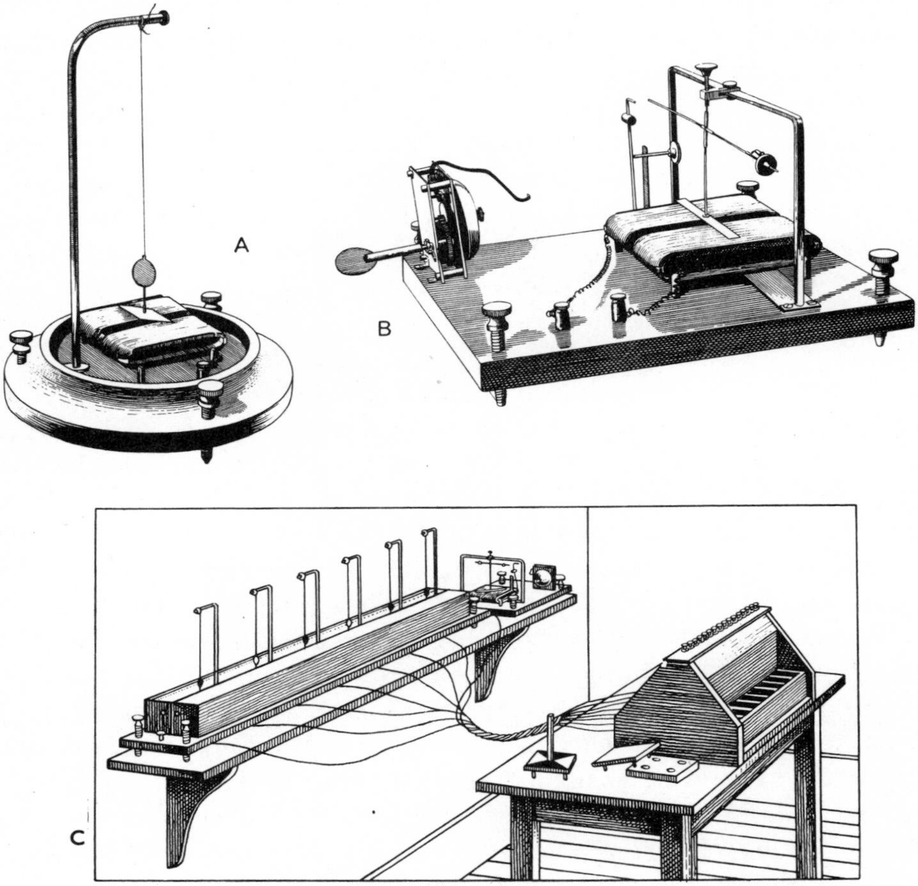

FIGURE 346—*Schilling's telegraph,* c *1825:* (A) *indicator;* (B) *alarm mechanism;* (C) *complete installation.*

William Fothergill Cooke was born in 1806, the son of a doctor, and at the age of twenty joined the East India army. Compelled to relinquish his commission on account of ill health, he had begun to earn a living by anatomical modelling, but his interest in Moncke's instrument led him to devote his whole attention to telegraphy. Returning to England in April 1836, Cooke constructed several forms of telegraph during the following months. One of these it was proposed to install on the Liverpool and Manchester railway, but he met with certain difficulties in the working of the electromagnets and as a result called on Charles Wheatstone (1802–75), professor of natural philosophy at King's College, London. Wheatstone had himself been conducting experiments with telegraphic apparatus, and in view of their joint interests they eventually decided to form a partnership. Their first patent was granted in June 1837, and in the

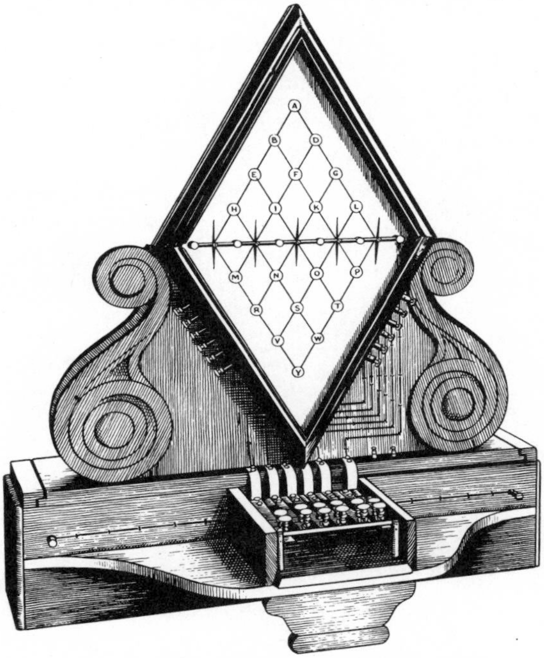

FIGURE 347—*Cooke and Wheatstone's five-needle telegraph. 1837.*

following month a demonstration of their five-needle telegraph (figure 347), working between Euston and Camden Town, a distance of about a mile, was given to the directors of the new London and Birmingham railway.

Disagreement between the directors of the railway company as to the need for a telegraph delayed further action, but in the following year, the directors of the Great Western railway company approved the installation of the telegraph between Paddington and West Drayton, a distance of about 13 miles. This was commenced in May 1838, and proved so successful that it was extended to Slough in 1842.

The instruments employed on the Paddington–Slough line were of the double-needle type in which particular letters were signalled by the momentary deflexions of the needles in accordance with a pre-arranged code (figure 348). With the exception of Schilling's telegraph, to which the needle-instruments of the Cooke and Wheatstone telegraphs bore a close resemblance, most earlier telegraphs had been of the type in which each letter had to be specifically indicated, either by a pointer, by bubbles of hydrogen, or, as in Ronalds's instrument, by the appearance of a letter behind an aperture in a dial. Wheatstone himself particularly favoured the use of letter-indicating telegraphs, and the original five-needle instrument of 1837 was of this type, as can be seen from figure 347. His ABC. telegraphs, as they were known, remained popular for many years, particularly where traffic was light and where the telegraph had to be operated by unskilled persons. In regular telegraph offices, however, where trained operators were employed, it was soon found that a predetermined code formed a far quicker way of operating; in time it became almost universal.

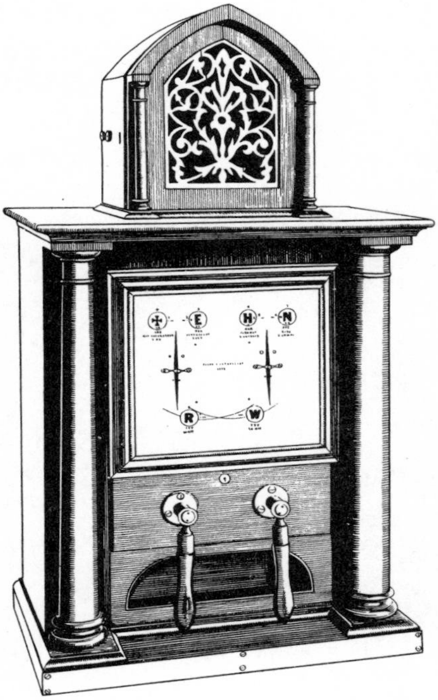

FIGURE 348—*Cooke and Wheatstone's two-needle telegraph. 1842.*

The success of the Paddington–Slough line led to rapid progress. A telegraph had already been installed on the Blackwall railway, and in the next two years Norwich was connected with Yarmouth; London with Gosport and Southampton; Tonbridge with Maidstone; and Wolverton with Peterborough. In 1846 London was linked with Dover. The rate of growth at this period may be deduced from the fact that in 1844 Wheatstone received only £444 in respect of his share of the royalties for newly laid lines, whereas in the following year he received £2775.

The telegraph had as yet attracted little public notice, but in 1845 there occurred an incident that strikingly demonstrated its possibilities. A woman was murdered at Slough and the suspected murderer was seen to board a train for Paddington. A full description of him was telegraphed to Paddington, as the result of which he was recognized on arrival, arrested, and subsequently hanged. It will be remembered that in more recent times a similar incident—the arrest of Crippen in 1910 as he was about to step ashore from an Atlantic liner when fleeing from England—drew public attention to the far-reaching powers of wireless telegraphy.

Until the close of 1845, the commercial interests of Cooke and Wheatstone remained under Cooke's personal management; he also acted as the contractor responsible for the installation of the telegraphs. Upon receiving the order for the London–Dover line, however, it seemed opportune to form a company, and the Electric Telegraph Company was incorporated early in 1846. Such was the progress of the company that by 1852 it was estimated that some 4000 miles of telegraph-lines had been completed in Britain.

Unhappily, a quarrel had persisted between Cooke and Wheatstone since the early days of their partnership, and it is beyond question that the strained relations between them retarded the technical development of the telegraph. As early as 1838, Cooke had had occasion to remonstrate with his partner about his often-repeated claim to be the exclusive inventor of the telegraph. Cooke, while not claiming to have invented the telegraph, had done more than anyone else to make it a practical device, and he strongly resented the manner in which his partner claimed all the credit for himself. The quarrel became almost childish in the manner in which charge and counter-charge were published during a period of some fifteen years. One's sympathy undoubtedly tends to rest with Cooke, but truth lies in the statement made in 1841 that 'it is to the united labours of two gentlemen so well qualified for mutual assistance that we must attribute the rapid progress which this important invention has made during the five years since they have been associated'.

With the founding of the Electric Telegraph Company, Cooke continued to be fully employed with the commercial development of the telegraph and its ever-extending lines, and he was far too busy to undertake any major technical developments. Wheatstone, however, with his academic background, had opportunities for making technical progress, and for many years he continued to devise new and improved forms of telegraphic apparatus. In 1840 he had been responsible for the first serious proposal for a cross-Channel telegraph, and in the same year he brought out the first of his many forms of ABC. telegraphs. In 1841 he invented the first type-printing telegraph, but this particular instrument was before its time and did not come into general use.

The Cooke and Wheatstone telegraph is an example of an invention that evolved more or less logically from previous discoveries and inventions. It was consequently founded upon well tried and established principles, and its success was substantially due to these circumstances. By contrast, the telegraph invented by Samuel Morse about 1835 was original, but as he was technically inexperienced his instrument was crude and unpractical (plate 47 A). His receiver consisted of a pen held in contact with a moving strip of paper. When the receiver was energized the pen was moved by an electromagnet and a notch appeared in the track drawn by the pen. Morse was an artist of some distinction—he was appointed professor of art in the university of New York in 1832—but his idea of developing an electric telegraph would have been frustrated by his lack of technical knowledge if it had not been for the assistance he received from his friend L. D. Gale, and from Joseph Henry (1797–1878), secretary of the Smithsonian Institution. Towards the end of 1837, Morse found an assistant and supporter in Alfred Vail (1807–59), who early in 1838 completely redesigned the telegraph and was instrumental in bringing it to the notice of influential congressmen. Two notable improvements were made: the introduction of relays to extend the range of transmission, and the adoption of the now well known dot-dash code (plate 47 B).

At the end of 1842, Congress was persuaded to vote 30 000 dollars for establishing a telegraph between Washington and Baltimore, a distance of about 40 miles, and this was successfully completed in June 1844. As in England, the next decade was a period during which widespread expansion of the telegraph system took place. A whole network of lines was set up, often by companies that competed with each other until their amalgamation into Western Union in 1856.

In England, as we have seen, many lines were laid down in the years immediately following 1842. The telegraph between London and Dover, opened in 1846, attracted considerable notice and can scarcely have failed to stimulate thoughts of an extension of the line across the Straits of Dover to the continent. Though Wheatstone had first proposed such a link, it fell to the two brothers John and Jacob Brett to pioneer the first submarine telegraph cable between England and France. This was laid on 28 August 1850 (figure 349), but it proved a failure on account of inadequate mechanical strength; a second and successful cable was laid in September 1851.

If the development of the electric telegraph represented one major milestone in the progress of human communications, the development of the submarine cable was another of equal importance. While the one speeded communication within countries, the other linked countries and continents overseas. With the successful laying of submarine cables across the North Sea and in the Mediterranean, it was natural that thoughts should next turn to the laying of a cable across the Atlantic.

The story of the early Atlantic cables is an epic of enterprise, courage, and perseverance in the face of heart-breaking disasters and calamitous losses. The first attempt was made in 1857, but the cable broke and was lost when nearly 350 miles had been laid. A second attempt was made in the spring of 1858, but fresh disasters occurred and it was not until August of the same year that the laying of the cable was completed. Unfortunately it was far from perfect—it had almost certainly been damaged and mishandled in the various mishaps—and although messages could at first be sent slowly over the cable, the signals became unintelligible after only four weeks; six weeks later the cable failed

FIGURE 349—*The first submarine telegraph cable ever laid: the tug* Goliah *on 28 August 1850.*

completely. A fresh attempt was made in 1865 with a cable of greatly improved design, which was laid by the *Great Eastern*, but further accidents were experienced and the cable finally broke, being lost in mid-Atlantic at a depth of 2000 fathoms. A still further attempt was made in 1866, and at last, on 27 July, a sound cable, again laid by the *Great Eastern* (plate 46 B), stretched from Valentia in Ireland to Trinity Bay in Newfoundland. Credit for this final achievement was due to many, but to none more than Cyrus W. Field (1819–92), a great American citizen whose untiring efforts had constituted the mainspring of the whole undertaking for nearly thirteen years. The *Great Eastern* rounded off this success by recovering one end of the cable that had parted the previous year and splicing a new length to it, thus providing a second complete cable. Since that time transatlantic telegraph cables have been in continuous use.

BIBLIOGRAPHY

APPLEYARD, R. 'Pioneers of Electrical Communication.' Macmillan, London. 1930.
FAHIE, J. J. 'A History of the Electric Telegraph to the Year 1837.' London. 1884.
HAMEL, J. VON. 'Historical Account of the Introduction of the Galvanic and Electro-magnetic Telegraph.' London. 1859.
SABINE, R. 'History and Progress of the Electric Telegraph.' London. 1869.
TURNBULL, L. 'The Electro-magnetic Telegraph.' Philadelphia. 1853.

The electric telegraph office, Lothbury. c *1850.*

23

THE BEGINNINGS OF THE CHANGE FROM CRAFT MYSTERY TO SCIENCE AS A BASIS FOR TECHNOLOGY

A. R. J. P. UBBELOHDE

I. CRAFT EXPERIENCE AND CRAFT MYSTERIES

UNTIL the advent of the scientific age, technological advances were based on craft experience, and the personal element in transmitting such experience from one generation to another, and from one place to another, was exceptionally strong. In these volumes several instances have already been recorded of the transportation of a technology even involving the physical movement of the craftsmen from one centre to another—as in the importation into Britain of Flemish brick-makers and of French glass-makers.

Such imported craftsmen would naturally be particularly secretive in handing on essential details of their craft, but craft skill and experience were at all times valuable personal possessions that needed to be protected by secrecy. This can be conveniently summarized by stating that ancient technologies were based on craft mysteries learnt and handed on privately, a circumstance that makes any comprehensive survey of craft technologies difficult. Other factors, discussed below, contribute to the incompleteness of our knowledge of craft mysteries, some of which involved a remarkable degree of practical knowledge.

As modern science grew in stature, roughly from the scientific renaissance of the mid-seventeenth century onwards, a basic change in the foundations of technology gradually took place. The object of this final chapter of the present volume is to describe and to discuss various aspects of the beginning of the change from craft mystery to science as the basis of modern technology. The subject will be further developed in the concluding chapters of volume V.

The permeation of craft mysteries before 1750

Different sections of this and earlier volumes have surveyed the growth and decay of various crafts in different parts of the world. Though our present knowledge is far from complete, these surveys make it clear that, in the past, copying from other communities—often by the importation of more advanced craftsmen—and local innovation have gone hand in hand, whenever the conditions of material welfare have been sufficiently stable in a community to allow wealth to accumulate.

History records many instances of the rise and fall of nations. Each such consolidation of power, stability, and wealth fostered to high levels of refinement and skill the growth of a diversity of crafts; each might serve to illustrate the permeation of craft mysteries. When the nation declined, a concomitant decline in its technology was inevitable and was often severe. Considered in space and time, world history thus exhibits zones of high-level skills separated by transition regions in which the permeation, and even the survival, of such skills was much more uncertain and obscure.

It is possible to draw contours around centres of culture in the world in successive ages to illustrate the appearance and disappearance of zones of high-level craft skills, but no complete tracing of the permeation of craft mysteries in past ages will be attempted here, fascinating though the story is. For the present survey it is sufficient to refer to the technological consequences of the rise of the Roman Empire, and of the establishment of a firmly administered *Pax Romana* over considerable portions of the world. This encouraged the permeation of craft mysteries on a quite extensive scale. Examples quoted previously (vol II) include the practices of metallurgy (ch 2), of military engineering (ch 20), of building and civil engineering (ch 12), of glass-making (ch 9), and of the production of ceramics (ch 8).

The decline of the Roman Empire led to a general dissipation of the accumulated wealth and craft experience of the ancient world. Zones of high craft-skills of the Roman Empire are, as it were, separated from the technology of medieval and modern times by a deep valley with marshy bottom not yet fully explored. The submergence of Roman civilization took place earlier in the west European fringe than in the east. As a result, when the upheavals due to barbarian invasions in the west were subsiding, east to west permeation of technological improvements, though variable in intensity, persisted in this direction at least until the Renaissance. This contrasts with technological improvements based on science, which have mainly flowed from west to east.

Craft mysteries and a managerial class

One of the unsolved problems about the handing on of craft mysteries is how supervisors and managers were trained in such of the ancient technologies as called for managerial supervision. The methods used for such training are important for the present survey, since they could provide one of the most systematic approaches to the technological foundations of ancient crafts.

By way of example, in at least two instances capital accumulation in ancient technologies reached a level which called for a class of supervisors; these were mining and metal-working. There is evidence (vol II, ch 4) that well paid mining managers were employed in Roman times to supervise slave labour, but it is not fully known in what form technical secrets were handed on within this managing class. Notwithstanding their relative prosperity, such *technites* did not enjoy full civic rights (vol II, ch 4); and for this reason only incomplete descriptions of their functions are given in ancient records.

In Renaissance mining, the Fuggers of Augsburg had founded a *Bergschule*, for instructing overseers of mines and analysts of metals and ores, at Villach in Carinthia. The father of Paracelsus, who was also town physician, taught chemical theory and practice at this school shortly after 1500 [1]. Apart from such fragmentary information, it is difficult to arrive at an understanding of the managerial foundations of ancient crafts, because of the very way in which they were practised. More is known about the various levels of recognized proficiency in medieval trade-guilds. These regularized the teaching and handing on of craft mysteries, which still remained, however, on a basis of personal skills.

Some handicaps to applied science in ancient civilizations

One essential factor in the gradual introduction of a scientific outlook and scientific procedures into modern technology was the increasingly active leadership in this direction given by men in relatively prominent social positions, especially from the seventeenth century onwards. This arose from the widespread growth of interest in natural science amongst this class, who were also concerned in exploiting new economic opportunities. Roman capitalism, and ancient capitalism generally, were greatly handicapped in this respect by the old contempt for applied science, which resulted in the supervisors of ancient craft-processes having apparently been quite out of touch with any scientific thinking.

Various authoritative statements show the general attitude of the actual leaders of ancient civilized communities towards technology. For example, Plutarch (A.D. 46?–120) [2], in his life of the Roman general Marcellus (270?–208 B.C.), has recorded various details about the life and opinions of the greatest of the Greek applied mathematicians, Archimedes (287–212 B.C.). The latter is famous amongst other things for having invented, or having had attributed to him, many highly original mechanical inventions connected with warfare. The pressing demands for increasingly effective means of attack and defence led to quite distinctive applications of science to military technology even in ancient times. Plutarch states that Archimedes

> did not think the inventing of [military engines] an object worthy of his serious studies, but only reckoned them among the amusements of geometry. Nor had he gone so far, but at the pressing instances of Hiero of Syracuse, who entreated him to turn his art from abstracted motions to matters of sense, and to make his reasonings more intelligible to the generality of mankind, applying them to the uses of common life.
>
> The first to turn their thoughts to mechanics, a branch of knowledge which came afterwards to be so much admired, were Eudoxus [fl 366 B.C.] and Archytas [428?–347 B.C.], who confirmed certain problems, not then soluble on theoretical grounds, by sensible experiments and the use of instruments. But Plato inveighed against them, with great indignation, as corrupting and debasing the excellence of geometry, by making her descend from incorporeal and intellectual, to corporeal and sensible things, and obliging her to make use of matter, which requires much manual labour, and is the object of servile trades. Mechanics were in consequence separated from geometry, and were for a long time despised by philosophers [2].

Geometry, astronomy, and similar pure sciences were relatively advanced even in Greek and Roman times, but among the intellectual leaders there was little interest in the scientific foundations of technology. The social submergence of technology in the ancient civilizations, and the social inferiority of craftsmen, can be illustrated from many old records. Ecclesiasticus [3] admirably summarizes an attitude of mind that persisted for many centuries:

> . . . every workman and master workman, that must turn night into day. Here is one that cuts graven seals; how he busies himself with devising some new pattern! How the model he works from claims his attention, while he sits late over his craft! Here is blacksmith sitting by his anvil, intent upon his iron-work, cheeks shrivelled with smoke, as he battles with the heat of the furnace, ears ringing again with the hammer's clattering, eyes fixed on the design he imitates. All his heart is in the finishing of his task, all his waking thoughts go to the perfect achieving of it. Here is potter at work, treadles flying, anxious continually over the play of his hands, over the rhythm of his craftsmanship; arms straining at stiff clay, feet matching its strength with theirs. To finish off the glaze is his nearest concern, and long must he wake to keep his furnace clean. All these look to their own hands for a living, skilful each in his own craft; and without them, there is no building up a commonwealth. For them no travels abroad, no journeyings from home; they will not pass beyond their bounds to swell the assembly, or to sit in the judgement seat. Not theirs to sift evidence and give verdict, not theirs to impart learning or to make award; they will not be known for uttering wise sayings.

Resurgence of craft technologies and the impact of science: some precursors

With the decay of Roman administration and Roman rule throughout the world, many of the more refined crafts gradually lost impetus. It is not the purpose here to describe the decay in the west of crafts derived from Greek and Roman times. The resurgence of craft mysteries under the more stable social and economic conditions of medieval times likewise does not concern us directly. Historical research is paying increasing attention to the upsurge of medieval science, but these activities of the human intellect could not properly be described as having any profound scientific influence on technology. What must be considered in some detail is the strengthened interest in natural science and in the experimental method which spread to a marked extent in the sixteenth, and particularly in the seventeenth, centuries among the very class of social leaders who had for so long held aloof from it.

By far the most complete and well documented record of this new growth of the influence of science on technology can be found in the history of the foundation of the Royal Society under the patronage of Charles II. Before discussing this it must, however, be emphasized that all strong movements in history show precursors; this can certainly be said of the precursors of the seventeenth-century revolution in pure and applied science.

Two brief biographical examples must suffice to throw light on some of these precursors. One was a Renaissance artist whose genius for applied science was at least comparable with that of Archimedes. Leonardo da Vinci (1452–1519) has left a long list of projects and inventions, which showed at least an intuitive grasp of the many technological possibilities of applied science. However, there appears to be no evidence that these inventions were based on theoretical scientific studies of anything like the same degree of advancement. The continued and urgent practical demands of the arts of war for new applications of science stimulated Leonardo to devise a number of war machines, including a breech-loading cannon, fire-arms rifled to impart a spin to the bullets, a wheel-lock pistol, and a steam-cannon, the *architronito* [4]. Leonardo is also reputed to have invented a submarine ship, details of which he never divulged because he was apprehensive of its wrongful use by tyrants.

A second precursor of those who founded the Royal Society was Sir Walter Ralegh (1552?–1618) [5]. This prominent Elizabethan followed many projects of high adventure, but when imprisoned in the Tower (*c* 1604) he spent his time in writing a 'History of the World' and in chemical experiments, probably chiefly concerned with distillation.

Foundation of the Royal Society

The history of the early years of the Royal Society is particularly important for the present chapter because it records three factors that became important in the mid-seventeenth century in promoting the shift from craft mysteries to science as a basis for technology. First, the Royal Society united a new class of men interested in natural philosophy and its applications. Secondly, it sponsored 'Histories of Nature, Arts or Works', which provided, often for the first time, scientific descriptions of craft technologies as they were practised in the seventeenth century. Thirdly, it stimulated the publication, so that all might know of them, of important new scientific and technological discoveries.

(i) *The new class of men.* A somewhat biased but historically interesting description of the 'new men', and of the shift of interest brought about by the new developments of natural philosophy, is due to Joseph Addison, writing in the 'Spectator' (No. 262, 1711): 'It draws men's minds off from the bitterness of party, and furnishes them with subjects of discourse that may be treated without warmth or passion. . . . The air pump, the barometer, the quadrant, and like inventions were thrown out to those busy spirits, as tubs and barrels are to a whale, that he might let the ship sail on without disturbance, while he diverts himself with these innocent amusements.'

An even more closely contemporary, and less patronizing, view of the new men can be obtained from a history of the Royal Society published in 1667 soon after the grant of the Royal Charter (1663) [6]. Thomas Sprat's (1635–1713) description of the wide range of interests in pure and applied science of one of the early members, Christopher Wren, refers to 'so much excellence covered with so much modesty'. According to Sprat, Christopher Wren's works included:

> A doctrine of Motion . . . an Instrument to represent the effect of all sorts of Impulses, made between two hard globous Bodies, either of equal, or different bigness, and swiftness, following or meeting each other, or the one moving, the other at rest . . . of all which he demonstrated the true Theories. . . .
>
> A History of the Seasons . . . because the difficulty of a constant observation of the Air by Night and Day seemed invincible, he therefore devised a Clock to be annexed to a Weather-cock, which moved a rundle, covered with paper, upon which the Clock moved a black lead pencil so that the observer by the Traces of the Pencil on the paper might certainly conclude, what Winds had blown in his absence, for twelve hours space. After a like manner he contrived a Thermometer to be its own Register. . . . He contrived an Instrument to measure the quantities of Rain that falls . . . many subtile wayes for the easier finding the gravity of the Atmosphere, the degrees of drought and moysture . . . new Discoveries of the Pendulum . . . many ways to make Astronomical Observations more accurate and easie. . . .

He has attempted to make Glasses of other forms than Spherical. Other works include the Theory of Refraction and Dioptrics, Observations on Saturn, Selenography, Magnetical Experiments, Studies of the Geometrical mechanics of rowing, of the dry way of Etching, of the Emendation of Water works, the devising of Instruments of respiration for straining the breath from fuliginous vapours, to try whether the same breath so purifyd will serve again, long lived lamps and registers of furnaces for keeping a perpetual temper, in order to various uses; as hatching of eggs, insects, producing Fossils and Minerals, keeping the motion of Watches equal, in order to longitudinal and astronomical uses, and infinite other advantages; and injecting liquors in the veins of Animals . . . transfusing blood.

Sprat makes it clear that some of Wren's inventions 'he did only start and design and they have since been carried on to perfection, by the Industry of other hands'. But even with this reservation, it is clear that the breadth of ideas and originality of inventions cited are in the same class as those of Leonardo da Vinci.

(ii) *Scientific surveys of craft technologies.* The 'Histories of Nature, Arts or Works' sponsored by the Royal Society included the following:

Histories of English Mines and Oars . . . of Iron making, of Lignum Fossile: of Saffron: of Alkermes; of Verdigreace: of Whiting of Wax, of Cold, of colours, of fluidity, and firmness. The Histories of Refining: of making Copperas: of making Allum: of Saltpeter: of refining Gold: of making Pot-Ashes: of making Ceruse: of making Brass: of Painting, and Limning: of Chalcography: of Enamelling: of Varnishing: of Dying:

The Histories of making Cloth: of Worsted-Combers: of Fullers: of Tanners, and Leather making: of Glovers, and Leather dressing: of Parchment, and Vellum making, and the way of making transparent Parchment: of Paper making: of Hatters: of making Marble Paper: of the Rowling Press.

The Histories of making Bread: of Malt: of brewing Beer and Ale in several places: of Whale-fishing: of the weather for several years: of Wind-mills and other Mills in Holland: of Masonry: of Pitch and Tar: of Maiz: of Vintners: of Shot: of making Gun powder: and of making some, that is twenty times as strong as the common Pistol powder.

These openly accessible surveys of contemporary craft technologies were an essential first step towards applying scientific principles to technology generally.

(iii) *The new inventions.* An impressive list of instruments is attributed by Sprat to the activities of the new Society. His list includes:

Astronomical instruments.
Clocks and watches.
Instruments for compressing and rarefying the Air.
Barometers.
Gravity scales.

Magnetic scales.
Surveying instruments.
Geological augers.
Instruments to measure the velocity of movement of objects in water.
Diving apparatus, a Diving Bell, means of supplying air to divers.
Apparatus to measure wind velocity.
Rotary-vane water pump.
Thermometers.
Corn planters.
Hygroscopes.
Water analysers.
Engines to determine the force of gunpowder by weights, springs, etc.
Do. to measure the recoiling and other properties of guns.
Several instruments to improve hearing.
Several chariots for progressive motion.
A chariot way-wiser measuring exactly the length of the way of a chariot or coach to which it is applyd.
An instrument for making Screws with great dispatch.
A way of preserving the most exact impression of a Seal, medal or Sculpture.
An instrument for grinding optick glasses.
Several excellent telescopes of divers lengths including one sixty foot long, with a convenient apparatus for the managing of them.

Seventeenth-century views about applied science

Sprat records interesting contemporary views about how far new discoveries in science could benefit the advancement of technology. He criticizes—on grounds similar to those we have already discussed—the complete failure of the Greeks and the Romans to apply science. Sprat takes a balanced view about contemporary applications. He refers to 'corruptions of Learning, which have been long complained of but never removed: The one, that Knowledge still degenerates to consult present profit too soon; the other, that Philosophers have bin always Masters, and Scholars; some imposing and all the others submitting; and not as equal observers without dependence.' He quotes as a significant defect of learning 'the rendering of Causes barren: that when they have been found out, they have been suffered to lie idle; and have been onely used, to increase thoughts, and not works. . . . To this the Royal Society has applyd a double prevention; both by endeavouring to strike out new Arts, as they go along; and also, by still improving all to new experiments.' These views about the interaction between pure and applied science remain apposite today.

In the rest of seventeenth-century Europe, this growth was paralleled under the leadership of scientists such as Descartes (1596–1650), Huygens (1629–94), Leibniz (1646–1716), and many others who openly published their scientific discoveries. Open publication, even when limited to discoveries in pure science, is in marked contrast to the concealment traditional and necessary in the writings of early alchemists and inventors. Such publication of discoveries in applied science was undoubtedly helped by the granting of limited but effective patent protection. The change in attitude to knowledge is clearly marked, for example, in the diary of John Evelyn, a Fellow of the Royal Society, covering the period 1640–1706. He records both attendances at the public experiments sponsored by the Royal Society, and the claims of contemporary alchemists who kept their methods secret from him.

II. THE FIRST OF THE NEW TECHNOLOGIES—THE DEVELOPMENT OF POWER-ENGINES

The stimulating effect of scientific ideas and methods on long-established crafts is easy to grasp. In addition, from the seventeenth century onwards entirely new technologies, without any craft precursors, were developed to meet new demands created by the reorganization of manufactures and of town and country life generally described as the industrial revolution. But often, until the economic and social pressure of these new demands became really strong, entirely new technological applications of the new scientific principles met with only limited success. In contrast with present times, money to support adequate research and development was not then readily mobilized. Methods of actually creating new demands did not appear with any prominence until the twentieth century. In the development of the earliest new technologies demand had to spring from the general economic development of a community.

For example, in the seventeenth century one pressing demand was for new sources of power to run pumping-engines for mining operations. When mines got deeper, as shallow veins of ore were exhausted, the need to pump out water and to provide ventilation systems became progressively more urgent (ch 3). Quite elaborate pumping arrangements had to be driven by humans—or horses, or even goats and lesser animals—in a treadmill. In his *De re metallica* (1556) Agricola gives rather pathetic illustrations of some mechanical contrivances recommended for harnessing the driving-power of animals of various sizes.

Even before the seventeenth century, scientists had considered various ways of harnessing the power of fire [7], but no useful application of steam-power was made in the ancient world, partly because there was no effective demand in a society organized to use the driving-power provided by men and animals.

Some mining enterprises in the seventeenth century had both the urgent need for new sources of driving-power and the money to pay for rather costly contrivances to meet this need. The incentive is clearly described in a report written in 1685 by Sir Samuel Morland (1625–95), Master Mechanic to Charles II, for the king's information: 'Water being evaporated by fire, the vapours require a greater space, about 2000 times that occupied by the Water. And rather than submit to imprisonment it will burst a piece of ordnance. But being controlled according to the laws of statics, and by science reduced to the measure of weight and balance, it bears its burden peaceably, like good horses, and thus may be of great use to mankind, especially for the raising of water.'

Many inventors in the seventeenth century were attempting to harness the power of fire and steam (ch 6). Hero's book on 'Pneumatics' had been translated from the Greek at Bologna in 1547. At least two suggestions derived from this book were to use his aeolipyle—a small steam-jet rotor—instead of dogs to turn a roasting-spit, and to use the jet of steam from a bronze kettle to drive an impulse-wheel (Branca). Another inventor with many ideas was the Marquis of Worcester (1601–67); his close collaboration with his mechanic, Caspar Kaltoff, illustrates both the increasingly active part in the development of applied science taken by socially prominent men and their dependence on collaboration with craftsmen practising traditional methods. No clear description of the Marquis's 'water-commanding engine', constructed around 1663, appears to be available; the details were no doubt kept secret deliberately.

Other scientists, such as Denis Papin (1647–1712?) and Huygens, are known to have experimented with the expansive force of gunpowder and of steam in cylinders fitted with pistons. Thomas Savery's (1650–1715) first pumping-engine for raising water was a pistonless vacuum-producing device; when exhibited to William III in 1698 it raised water to a height of about 16 fathoms. Savery was a versatile military engineer much interested in profitable inventions. He was associated with Thomas Newcomen in producing, about 1712, the first successful piston steam-engine for pumping water from the mines at Dudley Castle. The working of this stationary engine has been described by Smiles: 'the working of a Newcomen engine was a clumsy and apparently a very painful process, accompanied by an extraordinary amount of wheezing, sighing, creaking and bumping. When the pump descended, there was heard a plunge, a heavy sigh, and a loud bump. Then as it rose, and the sucker began to act, there was heard a creak, a wheeze, another bump, and then a rush of water as it was lifted and poured out.'

The Savery-Newcomen venture, though evidently economic for certain pumping stations in mines, had only limited appeal in other applications of inanimate power, because of its inefficiency and low ratio of power to weight. Its development illustrates the effectiveness of association between the craftsman Newcomen and the more theoretical inventor Savery. However, really scientific principles concerning heat and mechanical power were not applied to the steam-engine before the work of James Watt (1736–1819). Watt's development of a condenser for the steam, separated from the cylinder in which the piston moved, was closely linked up with and inspired by the scientific researches of Joseph Black (1728–99), then professor of chemistry at Glasgow University. As will appear more fully below, Black was the first to measure heat-energy quantitatively, and this led to his discovery of latent heat. James Watt began his technical work as mathematical instrument-maker to Glasgow University. His many discussions with Black, and his own scientific experiments, undoubtedly contributed to the much closer dependence of his steam-engine on scientific principles and on the theory of heat, compared with the Savery and Newcomen engine.

Application of Watt's designs of piston steam-engines was at first hampered by the difficulty of financing the necessary research and development, although Black assisted further by lending Watt £1500. This difficulty was finally overcome when Watt made a partnership agreement with Boulton: the first commercially successful Boulton & Watt engine was ordered in 1775. Subsequent applications of steam-power to requirements other than pumping water from mines developed slowly but steadily. They do not concern us in this section, which aims to trace the shift from craft to science in the foundations of power-technology, but it is worth noting that Watt's early collaboration with the scientists in Glasgow University was followed by a continued friendship and collaboration with scientists in later years. Both Boulton and Watt were members of the 'Lunar Society' at Birmingham, which included active scientists such as Erasmus Darwin, Samuel Galton, James Keir, and Joseph Priestley.

III. PERSONAL INFLUENCES FAVOURING THE PERMEATION OF TECHNOLOGY BY SCIENCE

The life of James Watt provides an important illustration of the personal influence during the eighteenth century of scientific leaders like Joseph Black. Similar instances may be found in the lives of other leading scientists of the period under review. It would be particularly valuable to have records of the kind of consulting work undertaken, since this has the most direct bearing on applied science, but unfortunately such records are often very incomplete. However, four examples relating to the period from about 1750 to about 1850 may be quoted. In addition to advising Watt, Black was also the first to recommend the use of hydrogen for filling balloons, on the basis of the specific gravity of the gas as determined by Henry Cavendish. Many instances are on record of his contributions as a scientific consultant to the bleaching industry, to the ceramic industry, to Lord Hopetoun's project for working Scottish ores, to the coal-tar industry, to distilleries, and to the malleable and cast iron industry [8]. The French chemist Antoine Laurent Lavoisier (1743–94) acted as consultant on the Paris water-supply, on the production of gunpowder in the French arsenal, on prisons, on balloons, and on the hospitals of Paris. He was also particularly active in advising on applications of science to agriculture, which was then a matter of great importance in France. In England, Michael Faraday (1791–1867) was a member of the scientific advisory committee of the Admiralty, scientific adviser to Trinity House, and a member of the committee for the improvement of glass for optical purposes [9]. The Ulster-Scottish physicist William Thomson, later Lord Kelvin (1824–1907), played an extremely active part in the development and laying of the first transatlantic cables (1856–66), and was responsible for many improvements to navigation instruments.

In addition to the instances recorded above, many other examples might be found to illustrate the permeation of technology by a scientific outlook through the personal influence of eminent scientific consultants. In the late eighteenth and early nineteenth centuries other more broadly based modes of permeation can be plausibly attributed to the influence of messianic or philanthropic concepts of the social functions of applied science. Four examples, of differing degrees of importance, illustrate the kinds of influence referred to:

(i) The work of the French encyclopaedists.

(ii) Count Rumford's philanthropic plans at the Royal Institution to promote new applications of science for the relief of poverty.

(iii) Contemporary enthusiasm for the messianic power of applied science as a liberator from the servitude of hard labour.

(iv) The formation in 1831 of the British Association for the Advancement of Science.

(i) *The French encyclopaedists.* The famous *Dictionnaire raisonné des sciences, des arts et des métiers* under the editorship of Denis Diderot (1713–84) and Jean d'Alembert (1717–83) first appeared, in 39 volumes, during the period 1751–72. Its general form is obviously inspired by earlier encyclopaedias, such as that produced by Ephraim Chambers (d 1740) in 1728. But by reason of its amplitude the French encyclopaedia, like the 'Histories of Nature, Arts or Works' sponsored by the Royal Society in the preceding century, had an important systematizing influence on contemporary technology in France, which was then in a state of transition from a craft to a scientific basis. As is well known, Diderot's encyclopaedia is also widely considered to have made an important contribution to the ferment of controversies that led to the French Revolution, but this aspect of the work does not directly concern us here.

(ii) *Count Rumford* (1753–1814), was an American born in Massachusetts of English stock, and had been concerned with a number of philanthropic schemes in Munich during his services to the Elector of Bavaria: the history of his ideas for developing applied science is of considerable interest for the present survey. In 1796 Rumford put forward proposals for an establishment in London for 'feeding the poor and giving them assistance . . . connected with an Institution for introducing and bringing forward into general use new inventions and improvements, particularly such as relate to the management of heat and the saving of fuel, and to various other mechanical contrivances by which domestic comfort and economy may be promoted . . .'.

Originally the plan was to collect 'perfect and full sized models of all such mechanical inventions and improvements as would serve these ends. . . . Cottage fireplaces and kitchen utensils for cottages, a farm house kitchen with its furnishings, and a complete kitchen with all utensils for the house of a gentleman of fortune, a laundry, including boilers, washing, ironing and drying rooms for a gentleman's house or for a public hospital . . . models of newly invented machines and implements of husbandry, models of bridges of various constructions.'

Rumford also made interesting comments about the applications of science to technology in his day. In his 'project' he refers to the causes of the slowness, indifference, and jealousy under which improvements made their way—the influence of habit, ignorance, prejudice, suspicion, dislike of change, and the narrowing effect of the subdivision of work into many petty occupations. According to him,

> between workmen and merchants comes in a class of men who have devoted themselves to the labor of observing, analysing, inventing. The movements of the Universe, the relations and habitudes of men and things, causes and effects, motives and consequences, are the powers on which they meditate for the development of truth. . . . It is the business of these Philosophers to examine every operation of Nature or of Art, and to establish general theories for the direction and conducting of future processes. Invention seems to be particularly the province of the men of science.

The immediate outcome of the founding of the Royal Institution turned out rather differently from Rumford's project. This was partly due to the fact that its members, who commissioned lectures and discourses in its early days, stemmed from a social class not at that time widely interested in technological progress or philanthropy, but keenly stimulated by the brilliant scientific discoveries made by such men as Humphry Davy and Michael Faraday in the laboratories of their Institution.

(iii) *Applied science as a liberator from servitude.* The enthusiasm that possessed some of the early technologists sprang from an almost supernatural confidence in the power of applied science to lighten the burdens that weigh down mankind. This thesis could be established in a number of ways; one of the most direct is to record two extracts from contemporary praise of the new benefits brought by applied science.

The first of them comes from 'The Philosophy of Manufactures. The Scientific Moral and Commercial Economy of the Factory System of Great Britain.' This rather pompous-sounding book by A. Ure (1778–1856) was first published in 1835: the quotation that follows is from the third edition of 1861.

> . . . tens of thousands of old, young and middle aged of both sexes, many of them too feeble to get their daily bread by any of the former modes of industry, earning abundant food, raiment, and domestic accommodation, without perspiring at a single pore, screened meanwhile from the summer's sun and the winter's frost, in apartments more airy and salubrious than those of the metropolis in which our legislative and fashionable aristocracies assemble. In those spacious halls the benignant power of steam summons around him his myriads of willing menials, and assigns to each the regulated task, substituting for painful muscular effort on their part, the energies of his own gigantic arm, and demanding in return only attention and dexterity to correct such little aberrations as casually occur in his workmanship. Magnificent edifices, surpassing far in number, value, usefulness, and ingenuity of construction, the boasted monuments of Asiatic, Egyptian and Roman despotism, have, within the short period of fifty years, risen up in this kingdom. . . .

The second extract is taken from a practically contemporary French book by Marc Seguin, *Traité sur l'influence des chemins de fer* (1839) [10].

> To increase the well-being and the enjoyment of material life is today the dominant idea of civilised nations. All their efforts are turned to industry because it is from that alone that one can expect progress. It is industry that gives birth to and develops in mankind new needs and gives them at the same time the means to satisfy them. . . . A thousand inventions are simultaneously born and lead to other discoveries and these in turn will become the starting point for new progress; all these changes concur to the profit of the whole public and tend to make well-being common property. . . . So look, everything is changed around us—the towns, the face of the countryside, the course of the rivers,

the work of the peoples, the production of the soil and industry, the distribution of property. . . .

Finally, in our own valleys and across our hills wind and spread long ribbons of iron, along which rush, rapid as thought, those formidable machines which seem to eat up space with spontaneous impatience and which seem almost alive in their breathing and their movement . . . when one remembers that these results are the work of an industry which is only very imperfect, and an art which is in its infancy, one asks what will be the last prodigies to be realised by the perfecting of this art, and one feels a noble desire to contribute to the realisation of these incalculable blessings. . . .

(iv) *Founding of the British Association for the Advancement of Science in 1831.* In civilized countries, the pursuit of science and of its applications seems almost inevitably to undergo cycles of activity that are difficult to explain. The foundation of the British Association in 1831 marks one deliberate attempt to counter, by co-ordinating the powers and enthusiasm of a band of experts, what was felt to be a contemporary decline of science in Britain. Its proclaimed objects were 'to give a stronger impulse and a more systematic direction to scientific inquiry, to obtain a greater degree of national attention to the objects of science, and a removal of those disadvantages which impede its progress, and to promote the intercourse of the cultivators of science with one another and with foreign philosophers'.

Subsequent history has recorded only fluctuating preoccupation of the British Association with applications of science to technology. Nevertheless, during the period of its existence the Association has often provided a platform for important debates, and the publicity of such debates has from time to time promoted new applications of science.

IV. SOME DEVELOPMENTS IN APPLIED SCIENCE LEADING TO NEW KINDS OF TECHNOLOGY

One of the ways in which the scientific approach to practical problems permeated age-old craft-technology was through accounts of various crafts compiled by scientists—for example, those sponsored by the Royal Society in the seventeenth century, and those by the French encyclopaedists in the eighteenth. Besides transforming long-established branches of technology, new scientific discoveries in some cases formed the basis of quite novel ones, which never had a craft ancestry, though the full efflorescence of this trend occurred after the period we are now considering. During that period, the most important fundamental advances of science that ultimately led to new kinds of technology were mainly those concerned with the study of various forms of energy.

There were also many new advances in applied science. In a short space it is difficult to list all the applied discoveries without distorting the historical perspective. Two obvious, and often quoted, examples refer to the use of coal-gas for providing artificial light, and to the controlled removal of carbon from molten iron to produce steel in bulk.

The development of the gas industry (ch 9) for the first time made it reasonably inexpensive to supply artificial light for large rooms, as in factories. Work was no longer regulated by the length of daylight, and the practicability of working several shifts made possible the use of machinery too expensive to be left idle for long.

The partial decarburation of molten iron to form steel was another extremely important new discovery, though its practical application was completed just after the period now under review. It provided cheap steel for constructional uses. The first Bessemer converter for blowing air through molten iron, to remove combustible impurities such as excess carbon, was in operation about 1856. The first Siemens-Martin open-hearth furnace, for melting iron under oxidizing conditions to produce steel in large quantities, was erected at about the same time.

As has been noted, the scientific discoveries productive of new technologies were in the main those concerned with energy changes: among these, discoveries in the field of electricity were of exceptional importance.

(i) *Electricity from chemical sources.* Up to the time of the invention of the now historic pile by Volta (1745–1827), electricity had been chiefly known and studied as produced by friction, but the quantity of electrical energy involved is extremely small in most electrostatic manifestations. Somewhat larger quantities of electricity could be studied after the invention of electric condensers or Leyden jars in the middle of the eighteenth century. Researches on electricity by Benjamin Franklin during the period 1746–52 led to his highly practical invention of the lightning-conductor for the safe discharge of low thunderclouds without danger to buildings.

The voltaic pile consisted of alternate disks of copper or silver separated from disks of zinc or tin by disks of absorbent paper soaked in brine. By building up long columns of such sequences of disks high voltages were obtained between the topmost and lowest disks, and large currents could be obtained. The voltaic pile formed a crude electric battery, and more efficient ones were later produced. They all have in common the production of electricity as a result of internal chemical changes. Electric batteries were highly important to the development of the science of electricity. By their means Davy in 1807 isolated sodium and potassium by electrolysis of the corresponding fused caustic alkalis. In this discovery were the seeds of great modern electrochemical industries, such as the aluminium industry, though they were long in germinating.

(ii) *Electromagnetism.* Studies of magnetic effects around a wire carrying a current obtained from a battery led to the discovery of a number of the basic phenomena of electromagnetism. From these stem the whole of the great electric power-generating and power-using industries of today, though again the rate of progress was very slow. In 1820 the Danish physicist, H. C. Oersted (1777–1851), first observed the magnetic field present around a copper wire carrying a current. Various laws concerning this electromagnetic force-field surrounding a conductor carrying a current were established by scientists such as A. M. Ampère (1775–1836).

The complementary discovery to that of Oersted was made by Faraday in 1831: an electric current is generated in a conductor when this is moved in a magnetic field. Faraday's observation of electromagnetic induction completed the scientific knowledge of interdependent electromagnetic phenomena associated with currents and conductors, and led to dynamos that can generate large electric currents when their coils are rotated in a magnetic field. The industrial significance of this development needs no emphasis.

In an inverted use of the dynamo, electric current is made to pass through coils of wire mounted on a movable frame in a magnetic field, so producing a force on the coils that leads to the rotation of the movable frame. This is the basic principle of electric motors, now of outstanding importance, though the development of the electric motor is again a little beyond the period now under consideration.

(iii) *Precision measurements of energy: discovery of the laws of thermodynamics.* During the first half of the nineteenth century discoveries less tangible, but quite as fundamental, as those in electromagnetism were made through precise measurements of energy. Such measurements led to a clear understanding of the laws of thermodynamics, which today permeate the whole of power-production on the one hand, and are a determining factor for large sections of chemical industry on the other. For the reasons that follow, however, these very important scientific discoveries affected technology only slowly.

It is comparatively easy to grasp how certain scientific discoveries could be applied to whole groups of craft technologies based on cognate natural phenomena. For example, the discovery of how to harden copper by adding tin affected all users of metal in the Bronze Age: the discovery of how to control the carbon content of iron accurately and cheaply on a large scale affected all users of steel in the Iron Age. But more abstract discoveries, such as those about the electrochemical production of electricity, required a considerable lapse of time before they acquired extensive technological influence. Even more abstract are the laws of thermodynamics, which were finally established during the period 1800–50.

Measurements of heat-energy and of other forms of energy are conceptually difficult compared with, say, measurements of length, because suitable standards of comparison are by no means obvious. Nevertheless, it is technologically very significant that the first steam-engine built on scientific principles was closely associated with Black's discovery of how to measure quantities of heat-energy (p 673). Black used the rise in temperature of a given mass of water as a measure of the quantity of heat it had taken up. This mode of measurement permitted fairly exact assessment of the quantity of heat-energy taken up in unit time by a steam-engine. By means of it, Black discovered that on being converted to steam at the same temperature water takes up large quantities of heat which become 'latent' in the steam. Latent heat-energy can be partly transformed into useful mechanical energy by means of a steam-engine. James Watt, working closely with Black, discovered how to measure mechanical energy, or mechanical work, in terms of the force exerted by a pulling horse lifting weights over a pulley. Combining these measurements of heat-energy and mechanical energy, Watt was the first power-engineer who could in principle determine the efficiency of his engine, that is, the ratio of the quantity of heat-energy taken up to the mechanical energy obtained; though not all these concepts were as yet clearly understood.

At this stage there was still an awkward gap in the group of basic energy-measurements relating to steam-power. Black's method for measuring heat-energy, though quantitative, was based on a standard of comparison different in kind from Watt's method for measuring mechanical energy. This gap was bridged through the experimental researches of J. P. Joule (1818–89) over the period 1840–50. Using a system of churning paddles, Joule determined the mechanical equivalent of heat by finding the rise in temperature of a known mass of water when a definite quantity of mechanical energy was transformed into heat within the water. From that time, power-production could be based on extremely accurate energy balance-sheets. Exact balance-sheets recording interchange of different forms of energy are based on the first law of thermodynamics, which states that, in any physical process, energy is neither created nor destroyed. Energy may appear in new forms but these are quantitatively equivalent to the other forms of energy that disappear.

The second law of thermodynamics, as enunciated in 1851 by R. J. E. Clausius (1822–88) and by Lord Kelvin, makes a statement which in appearance is even milder: that there is a theoretical maximum to the efficiency of any engine which converts heat-energy into useful work. Its enormous importance derives from the discovery by Lord Kelvin that the vast majority of observable transformations, if these involve heat-energy in any way, can be proved to be governed by the second law of thermodynamics. The technologies of power-production and the technologies of chemical industry both involve heat-energy in a very basic way, and so are governed by the second law of thermodynamics. This law imposes natural limits to the efficiency of any energy-transformation that can be devised, and so provides fully reliable standards whereby practical operations can be controlled.

As with many other scientific discoveries, the technological significance of the second law of thermodynamics was only slowly appreciated, despite its vast practical importance. Its formal enunciation, however, was an important event in the changing relationship between science and technology, and with it this chapter can most appropriately end.

REFERENCES

[1] HARGRAVE, J. 'The Life and Soul of Paracelsus', p. 26. Gollancz, London. 1951.
[2] 'Plutarch's Lives' (trans. by J. LANGHORNE and W. LANGHORNE): Life of Marcellus, Vol. 3, pp. 119 ff. London. 1821.
[3] *Ecclesiasticus*, chap. 38 (trans. by R. A. KNOX): 'The Old Testament Newly Translated from the Latin Vulgate', Vol. 2, p. 1053. Burns, Oates & Washbourne, London. 1949.
[4] MCCURDY, E. 'The Mind of Leonardo da Vinci.' Cape, London. 1952.
[5] CREIGHTON, LOUISE. 'Life of Sir Walter Raleigh.' Longmans, Green, London. 1902.
[6] SPRAT, T. 'The History of the Royal Society of London for the Improving of Natural Knowledge.' London. 1667.
[7] VITRUVIUS *De architectura* (Loeb ed. with Eng. trans. by F. GRANGER, 2 vols). Heinemann, London. 1931, 1934.
[8] CLOW, A. and CLOW, NAN L. 'The Chemical Revolution.' Batchworth Press, London. 1952.
[9] THORPE, SIR EDWARD. 'Essays in Historical Chemistry', ch.: "Michael Faraday". London. 1894.
[10] BERNAL, J. D. 'Science and Industry in the Nineteenth Century.' Routledge & Kegan Paul, London. 1953.

I. INDEX OF PERSONAL NAMES

Bouvier (*c* 1831), *and* description of wheel-dredger, 638.
Bow, W. A. (*c* 1851), author of a 'Treatise on Bracing', 486.
Bowman (*c* 1820), patentee for weaving devices, 303.
Boyce, Joseph (*c* 1800), *and* reaping machine, 7.
Boyle, Richard, third Earl of Burlington (1695–1753), *and* architecture, 470.
— Robert (1627–91), chemist, 215–16, 218–19, 223, 248, 648.
Bozolus (*c* 1767), *and* electric telegraphy, 650.
Brahe, Tycho (1546–1601), Danish astronomer, 380, 388.
Bramah, Joseph (1748–1814), inventor and manufacturer, 418, 423–5, 434–5, 437, 507.
Branca, Giovanni (1571–1640), architect and mechanician, 161, 168, 672.
Brancas, L. F. de (1733–1824), Comte de Lauraguais, scientist, *and* porcelain, 339.
Brande, W. T. (1788–1866), *and* comprehensive influence of chemistry, 256.
Brandt, Georg (1694–1768), Swedish chemist, 145, 374.
Bredsdorff, J. H. (1790–1841), Danish cartographer, 614.
Bréguet, A. L. (1747–1823), clock-maker, 414.
Bremoutier (*c* 1790), *and* afforestation, 33.
Brett, Jacob (*c* 1850), *and* submarine telegraphy, 660.
— John W. (1805–63), *and* submarine telegraphy, 660.
Brewster, Sir David (1781–1868), scientist, 376.
Bridgewater, Duke of (1736–1803), *and* canals, 348, 363–5, 367.
Brindley, James (1716–72), canal engineer, 348, 462, 571.
— John (eighteenth century), potter, 348.
Brooke, J. M. (middle of nineteenth century), midshipman, *and* deep-sea sounding rod, 619.
Brooks, John (1720–60), engraver, 354.
Brown, Andrew, author of 'History of Glasgow', *and* sulphuric acid, 243.
— Sir Samuel (1776–1852), engineer, 459–60, 585.
— William (*c* 1765), colliery engineer, 178–9.
Brownrigg, William (1711–1800), Whitehaven physician, *and* gas, 259.
Brueghel, Pieter, the elder (?1520–69), artist, *and* mud-mill, 639.
Bruges, Pierre Théodore de (*c* 1770), saltpetre manufacturer, 237.
Brunel, Isambard Kingdom, son of Sir Marc Isambard (1806–59), engineer, 427, 461–3.
— Sir Marc Isambard (1769–1849), engineer, 202, 418, 426–7, 430, 435, 449, 451, 463.
Brunner (*c* 1850), instrument-maker, 398.
Brunton (nineteenth century), inventor of calciner, 123.
Bruyère, Jean B. F. Giraux de la (1739–87), glass-maker, 369.
Buache, Philippe (1700–73), cartographer, 611–13, 621.
Buchan, Alexander (1829–1907), meteorologist, 620.
Buchanan, R. (1813–66), author of 'Practical Essays on Millwork and other Machinery', 425.
Buckingham, Duke of (1628–87), *and* glass-making, 362.
Budd, James Palmer (*c* 1845), of Ystalyfera iron-works, near Swansea, 113.
Buddle, John (*c* 1844), *and* haulage in coal mines, 84; *and* ventilator, 93; *and* lighting, 97.
Bull, Edward (*c* 1792), erector for Boulton & Watt, 190.
Bullough (*c* 1841), patentee for textile-machinery, 302–3. *See also* Kenworthy.
Bunsen, R. W. (1811–99), chemist, *and* gas-burner, 273, 325.
Burdon, Rowland (*c* 1796), M.P. for Sunderland, *and* bridge construction, 457–8.
Burgi, Jobst (1552–1632), Swiss instrument-maker, 382.
Burr, Aaron (1756–1836), Vice-President of U.S.A., 1801, *and* description of Paris streets in 1811, 544.

C. M. (*c* 1753), *and* electric telegraph, 647, 649–50.
Calley (*c* 1716), plumber, Newcomen's assistant, 174.
Camelford, Lord (1737–93), *and* porcelain factory, 340.
Campbell, Colin (d 1729), architect, 470.
— Hector (*c* 1792), patentee for bleaching rags, 255.
— *see* Gibson.
Cannizzaro, S. (1826–1910), chemist, 225.
Carey (*c* 1840), patentee for wooden pavement-blocks, 545.
Carl Theodore (1733–99), Elector of the Palatinate, *and* agriculture, 25.
Carlisle, Sir Anthony (1768–1840), surgeon, 227, 653.
Carnay (*c* 1782), French chemist, 239.
Carnot, Lazare Nicolas Marguerite (1753–1823), *and* semaphore telegraph, 644.
— Sadi (1796–1832), physicist, 163, 166.
Carochez (*c* 1800), French maker of telescopes, 399.
Cartwright, Edmund (1743–1823), inventor of power-loom, 151, 295–7, 299–300, 314.
Caslon, William (*c* 1818), designer of gas-bracket, 272.
Cassini, Jacques (1677–1756), geodesist, 596, 605, 615.
— Jacques Dominique, Comte de (1748–1845), astronomer, 604.

II. INDEX OF PLACE-NAMES

III. INDEX OF SUBJECTS

Jesse Ramsden (1735–1800) with his dividing engine. (pp 392, 603)

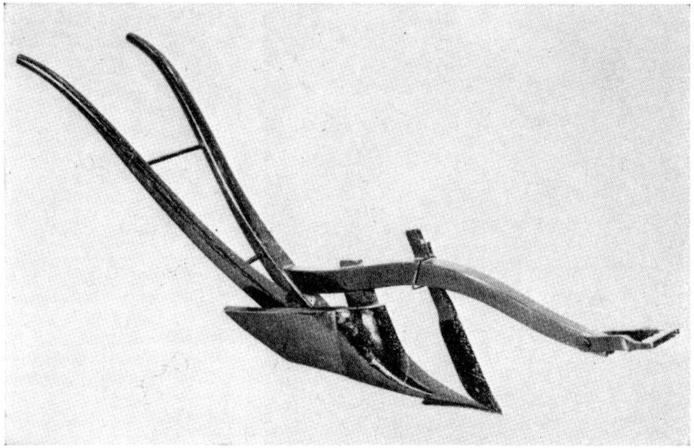

A. *Model of the Rotherham plough. Eighteenth century.* (p 2)

B. *Model of the Kent turnwrest plough. Eighteenth century.* (p 4)

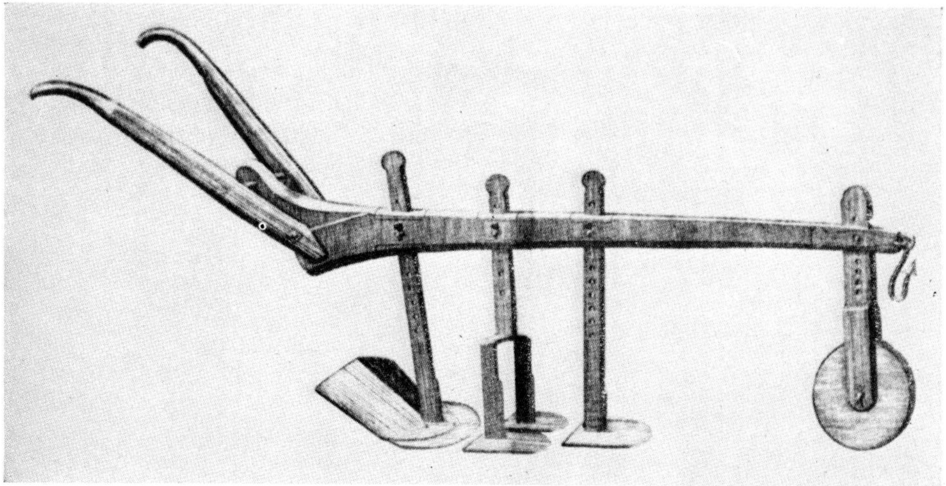

C. *Drawing of horse-hoe for weeding and earthing between plants. Eighteenth century.* (p 13)

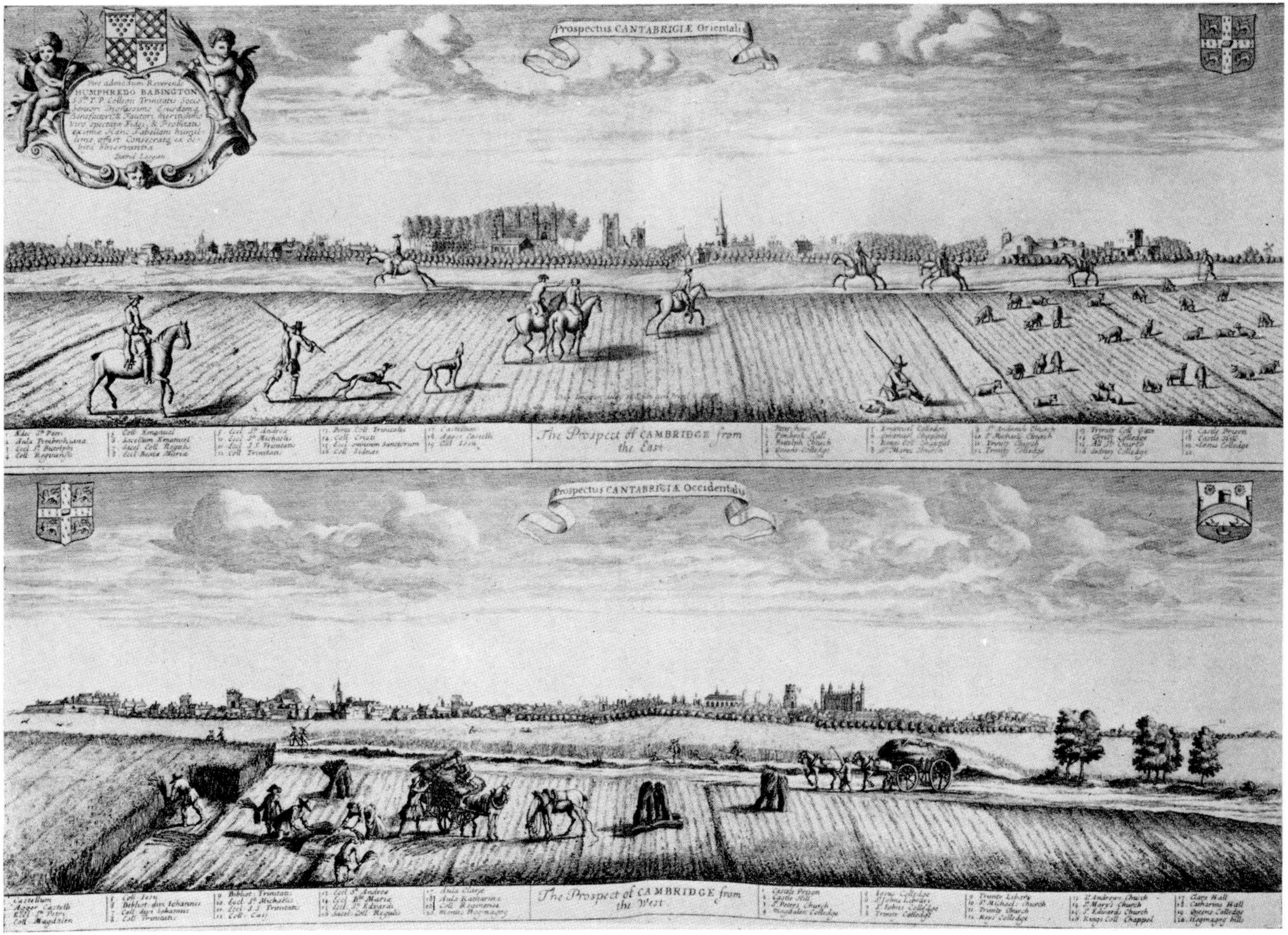

Unenclosed fields near Cambridge during and after harvest, c *1688. Note the sheep grazing on the stubble, in accordance with a custom that prevailed for very many years after this date and was one of the obstacles to improved rotations.* (p 17)

A. *Eighteenth-century whalers hunting Greenland whales with hand harpoons in the Arctic.* (p 58)

B. *Whaling in the Californian lagoons. The boats have been lowered after a school of Grey whales and the harpoons are ready. A ship in the distance is boiling oil on the deck.* (p 58)

A. *Single-, double-, and three-handed drilling downwards. Before 1850.* (p 70)

B. *Dolcoath man-engine, Cornwall.* c *1850.* (p 76)

A. *Wallsend colliery, Newcastle upon Tyne,* c *1860. Extracted fire-damp is seen burning from the chimney on the left.* (pp 93, 258)

B. *Dolcoath copper mine showing horse-whim, 'bal maidens' breaking large pieces of ore, and hoisting of ore in baskets.* c *1850.* (pp 88, 123)

A. *Removal of water was essential in many underground workings. The above illustration shows pumps erected for draining the Kilsby tunnel in 1837.* (pp 78, 567)

B. *The inside of a smelting-house at Broseley, late eighteenth century.* (p 100)

PLATE 8

A. *The great burning-glass constructed for the French Academy of Sciences under the direction of Lavoisier and others. The movable lens served to concentrate the sun's rays still further. The substance to be exposed to the action of the burning-glass was placed on an adjustable support. The operator is wearing dark glasses.* (p 218)

B. *An iron forge in 1772.* (p 116)

Blacksmith's shop, 1771. (p 106)

A. *High-pressure direct-acting engine patented by Trevithick in 1802. This was developed for stationary and locomotive use, eventually superseding the beam engine.* (p 188)

B. *Trevithick's high-pressure engine, 1811. This was used for threshing and was working in Cornwall until 1879.* (p 192)

A. *Large water-wheel at Laxey, Isle of Man, 1854.* (p 209)

B. *Coldron Mill, Spelsbury, Oxfordshire. This mill, erected* c *1800, was used for grinding corn. The illustration shows it as formerly displayed in the Science Museum, London.* (p 212)

A. *Samuel Clegg's gas-making plant for Ackerman, 1812.* (p 268)

B. *Clegg's gas-making apparatus constructed for the Gas Light and Coke Company,* c *1814.* (p 269)

A. *Murdock's gas-making plant for Phillips & Lee*, c *1806*. (p 266)

B. *Drawing the retorts at the Great Gas Light Establishment, Brick Lane, London, 1821*. (p 270)

A. *Charging retorts at Beckton, 1878.* (p 270)

B. *Mule.* (A) *Carriage with spindles,* (B) *rollers,* (C) *creel for roving bobbins.* (p 279)

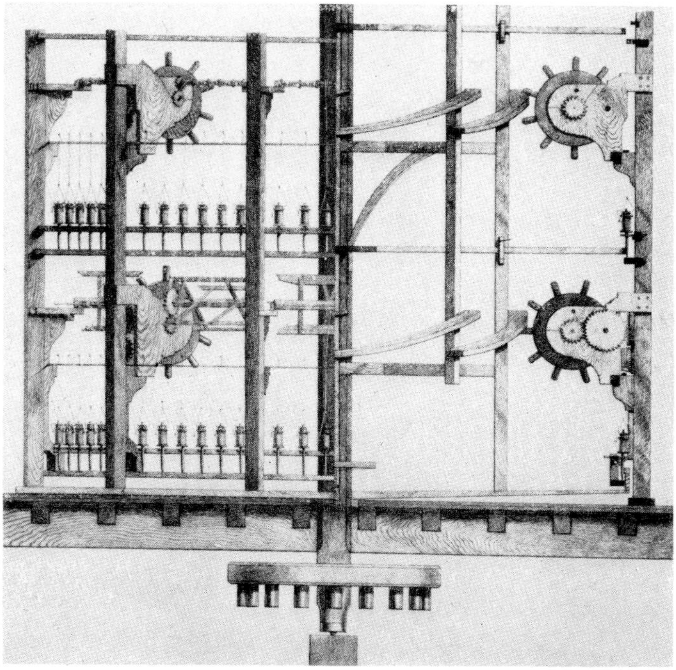

Lombe's throwing machine. The plan (above) *shows the arrangement of the swifts and bobbins in the form of a circle. The elevation* (below) *shows the lower tier with swifts to carry the skeins of silk. The silk was withdrawn from the swifts and taken to the bobbins below, first passing through the wire flyers. As the bobbins and flyers rotated, twist was inserted and the yarn wound on the bobbins. The upper tier shows a similar arrangement, except that the silk is unwound from the horizontally arranged bobbins, and is therefore receiving a second twisting.* (p 311)

A. *Maiolica: Faenza*, c 1552. (p 334)

B. *Spanish lustre ware, Valencia. Circular dish painted in lustre, an effect produced by firing in a reducing atmosphere.* (p 335)

C. *Maiolica: Castel Durante. Vase from pharmacy showing shields and coat of arms.* (p 334)

D. *Slip decoration: Staffordshire*, c *1700. Posset-pot in buff earthenware with white and brown slips under a yellow glaze.* (p 331)

A. *Delft wig-stand in manganese purple outline and blue. Dutch, late seventeenth century.* (p 336)

B. *Delft tea-caddy, black enamel painted in green and yellow in imitation of Chinese lacquer. Dutch, late seventeenth or early eighteenth century.* (p 336)

C. *Delft wine bottle with the arms of the Pewterers' Company, inscribed John Smith and Margeri, Lambeth, 1650.* (p 336)

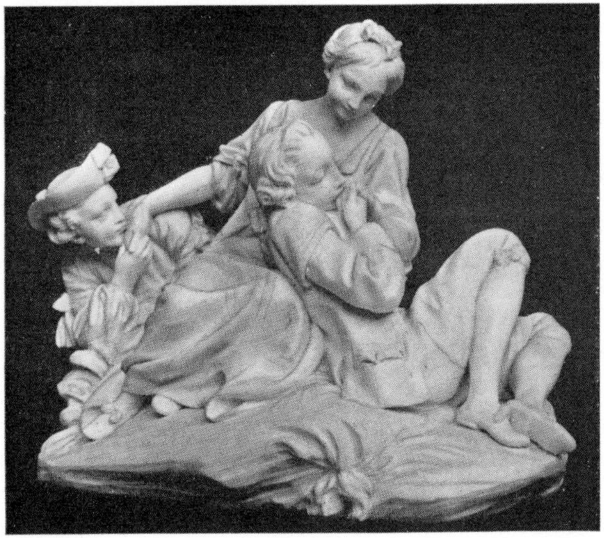

D. *Sèvres biscuit group 'Les trois Contents', modelled by Falconet. 1765.* (p 340)

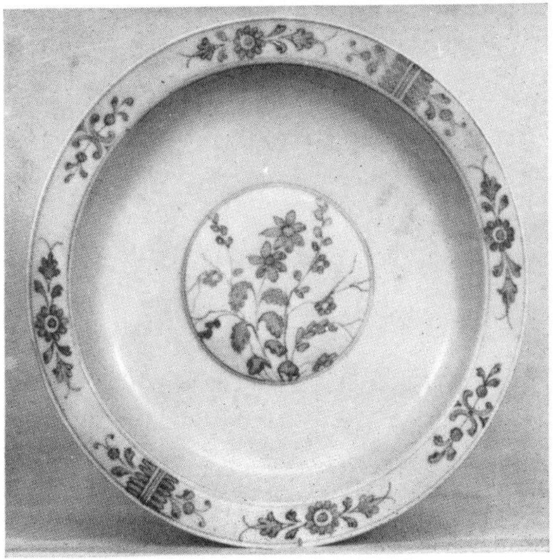

E. *'Porcelain', Florence, Francesco de Medici, 1575–85. The first 'porcelain' of any sort to be made in Europe.* (p 337)

PLATE 18

A. *English soft-paste, Stratford-le-Bow. 'The Piper.'* (p 341)

B. *English soft-paste mug. Derby*, c *1760*. (p 341)

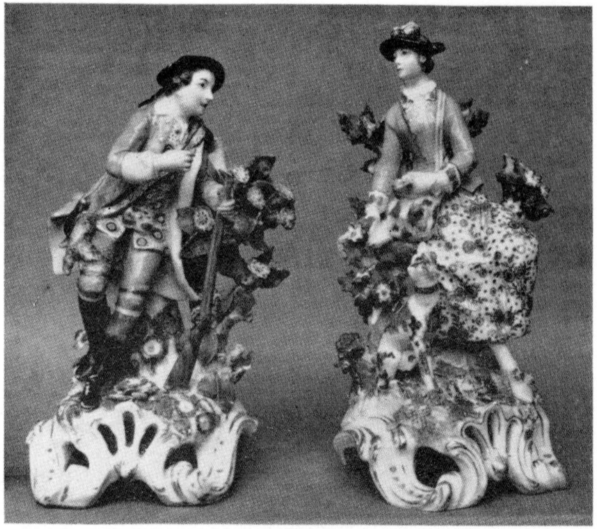

C. *English soft-paste, Chelsea. Group, 'Sportsman and Sportswoman'.* (p 341)

Longton Hall, plate 7·6 inches in diameter, c *1755*. (p 341)

E. *Longton Hall, mug*, c *1755*. (p 341)

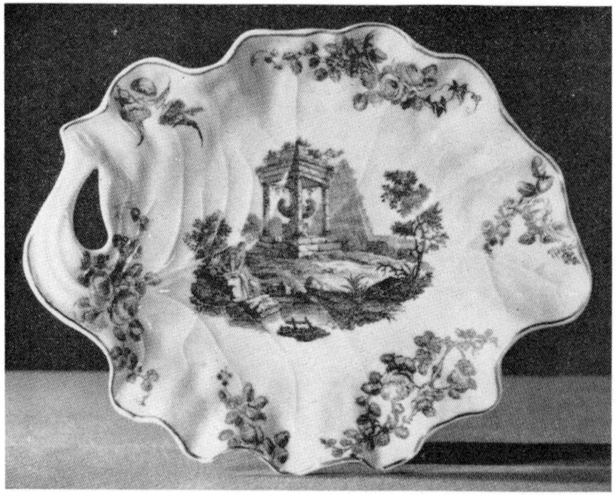

F. *Worcester: dish decorated in black and gilt, 8·5 inches in diameter*, c *1775*. (p 341)

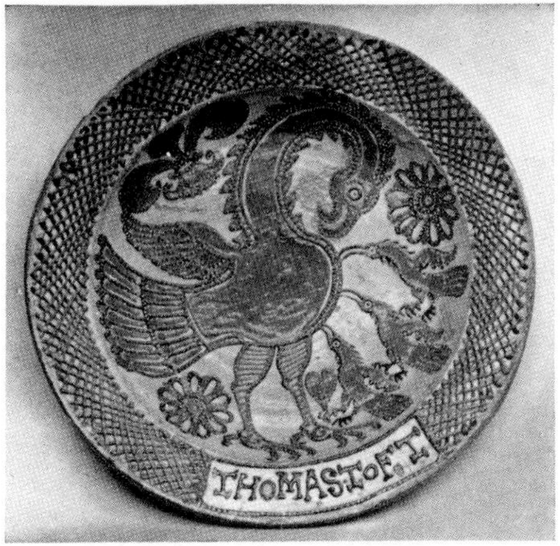

A. *Staffordshire: Thomas Toft slip-decorated dish, 'The Pelican in her Piety'. 17 inches in diameter. Seventeenth century.* (p 345)

B. *Staffordshire: Wedgwood portrait medallion of Joseph Priestley.* (p 353)

C. *Staffordshire: salt-glaze Madonna and Child, 8·3 inches high.* (p 346)

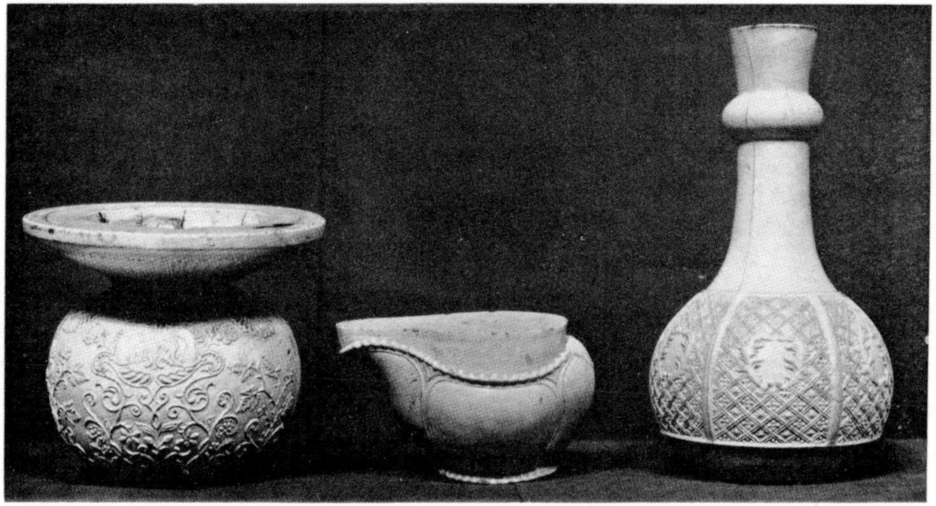

D. *Blocks for making moulds: Chinese shaped spittoon signed by Aaron Wood, 5·7 in; sauce-boat, 3·4 in,* c *1750; bottle, 9·9 in* ,c *1750.* (p 354)

A. *Preparing and calcining flint for pottery and porcelain. The flints were broken with an iron mallet* (1) *before being burned in with charcoal* (4). *They were then ground* (2) *and sieved* (3) *before being mixed with clay and water* (7). *When made* (5), *the pottery was allowed to dry* (8) *before being placed in the furnace* (6). (p 347)

B. *Mill-room for mixing ingredients for pottery.* (p 352)

A. *The final stage of buffing or polishing plate glass for mirrors is being carried out with the help of felt rollers on the ends of springs made from strong pieces of hardwood; rouge or some similar polishing medium is applied to assist the process.* (p 362)

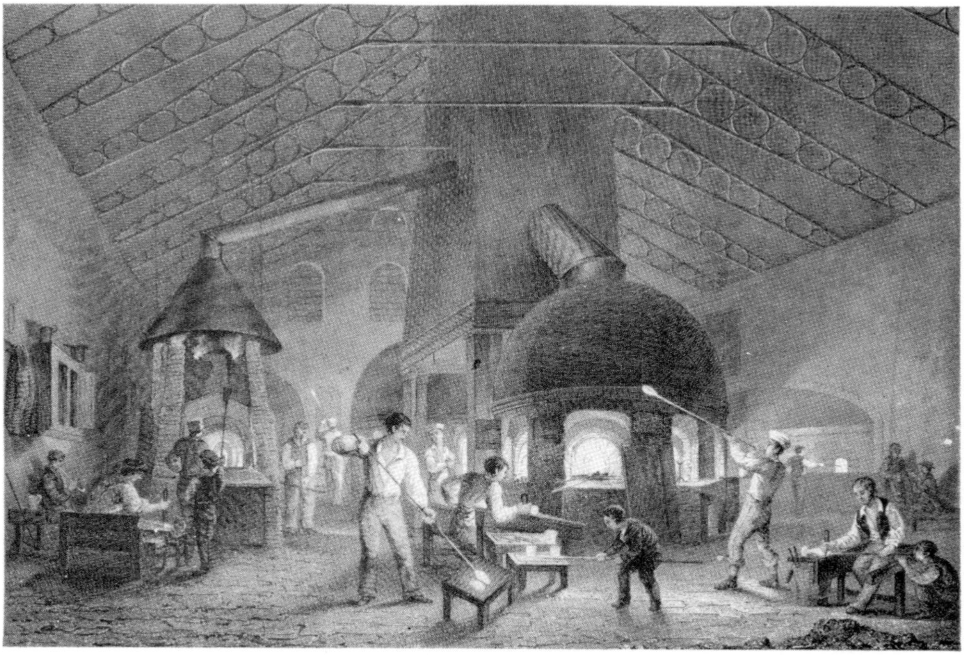

B. *Glasshouse scene: Falcon Glass House, Blackfriars. Two furnaces stand on either side of the main chimney shaft. To the left is a 'glory hole' and to the right the annealing chambers.* (p 361)

A. *Vaucanson's drill, in which the position of the tool is adjusted by two worm-screws.* (p 385)

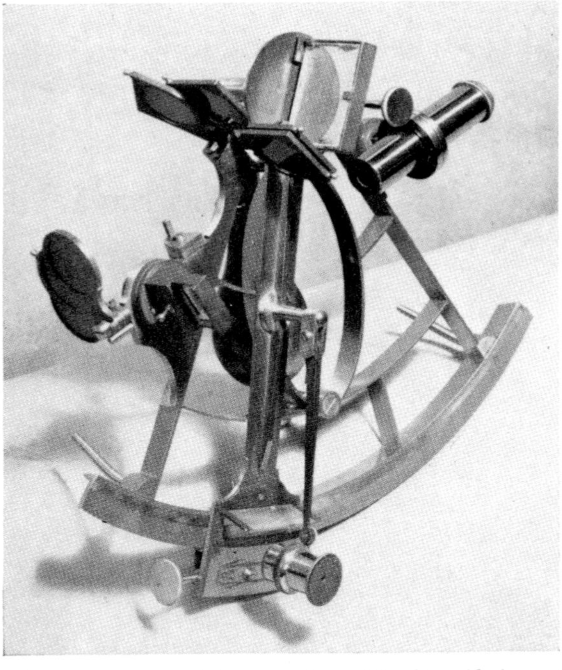

B. *Sextant constructed by Barthelemy Bianchi, mid-nineteenth century. This model represents almost the final form of this type of instrument. It is provided with a micrometer screw for adjustment of the alidade, a lens mounted on an articulated arm for reading the vernier, and coloured screens for reducing the intensity of sunlight.* (p 400)

A. *Vaucanson's lathe for traversing large jobs, with tool-holder driven by a worm-screw.* (p 385)

B. *The hodometer measured distances as it was wheeled along the ground. The distance travelled was recorded on the dial fixed to the handle.* (p 616)

PLATE 24

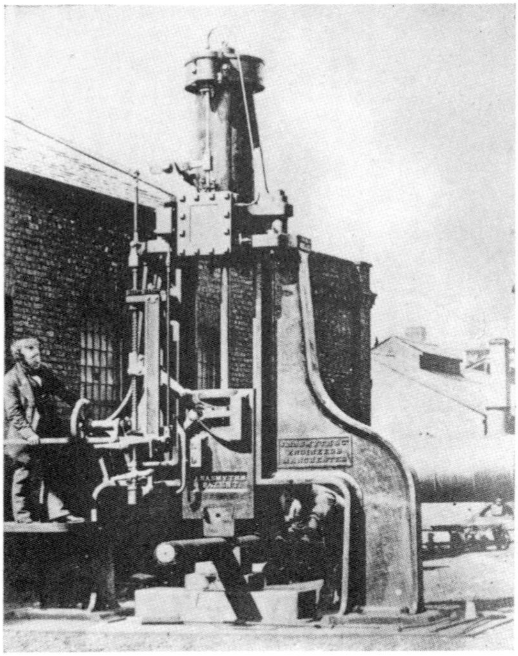

A. *Nasmyth with his steam-hammer, 1856—an improved version of his 1839 hammer.* (pp 116, 431)

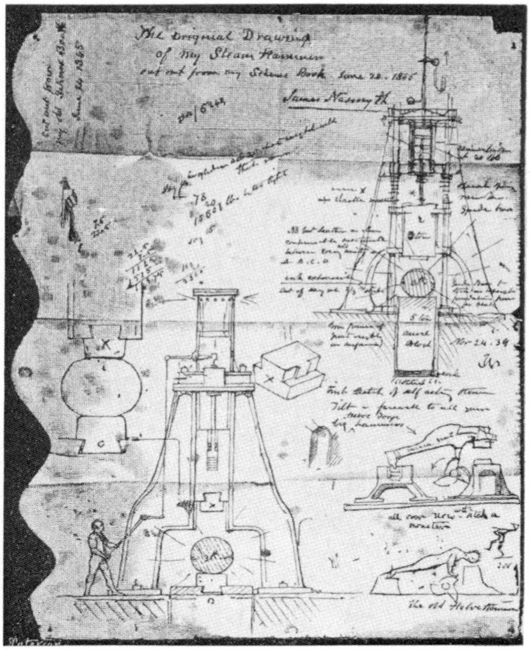

B. *Nasmyth's original sketch of his steam-hammer, 1839.* (p 431)

C. *Roberts's original self-acting back-geared lathe, 1817.* (p 428)

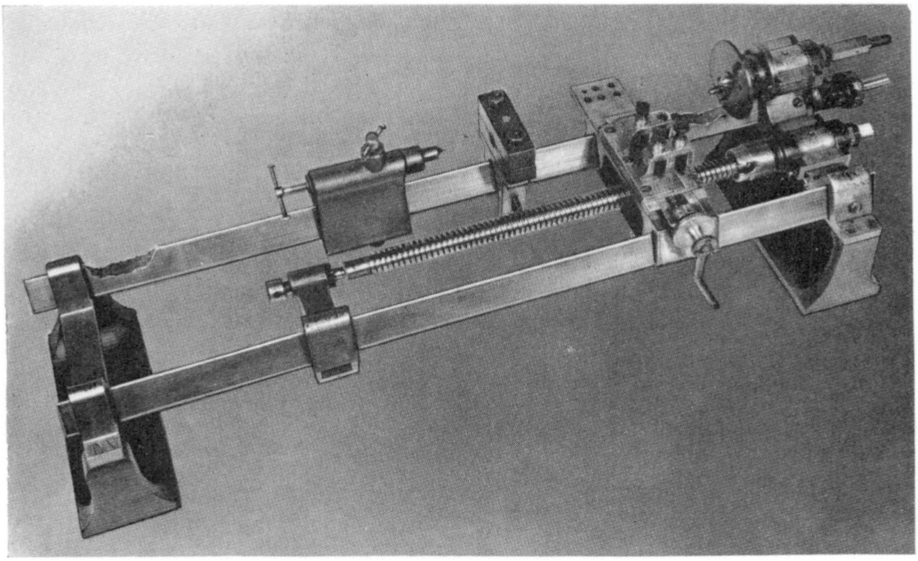

A. *Maudslay's original screw-cutting lathe*, c *1800*. (pp 424, 425, 432)

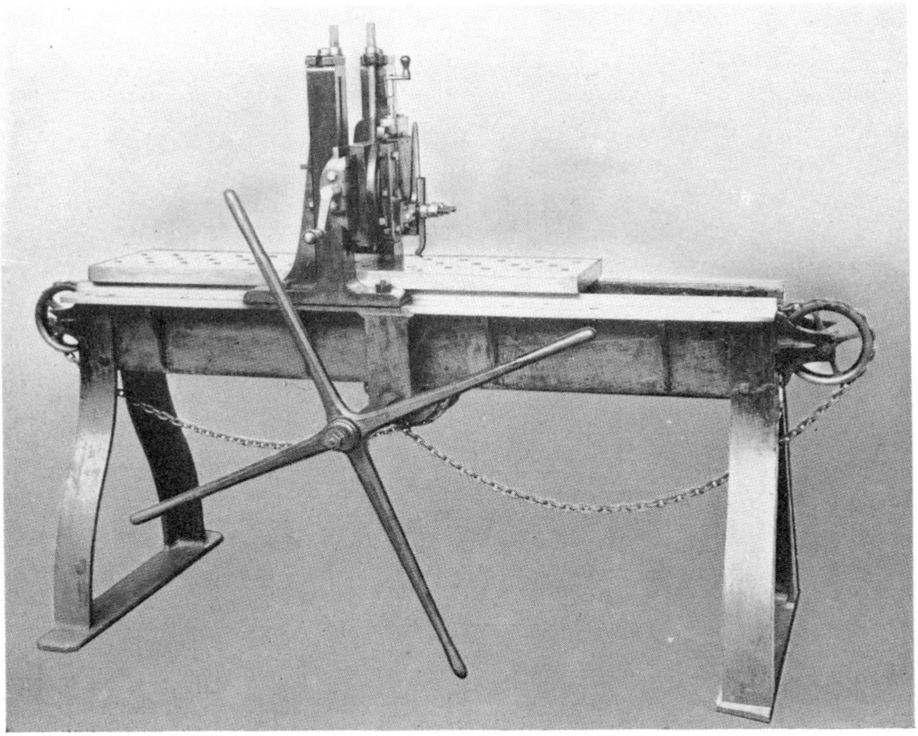

B. *Roberts's planing machine*, *1817*. *This is the earliest extant planing machine.* (p 433)

A. *Brunel's* **machmortising-ine**, *built by Maudslay in 1803, for cutting the slots in pulley blocks.* (p 427)

B. *Brunel's shaping-engine, built by Maudslay in 1804, for shaping the surfaces of pulley blocks, ten at a time.* (p 428)

A. *Model of Wilkinson's boring mill, 1775.* (pp 421, 422)

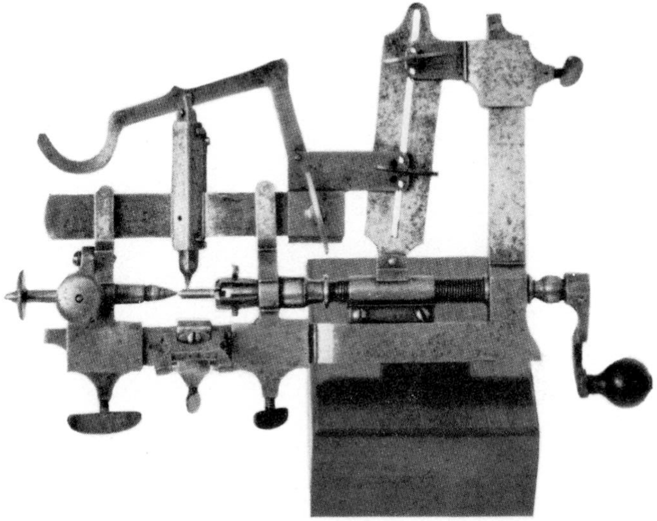

B. *Fusee engine, eighteenth century. A screw is being cut by a tool which derives its motion from a lead-screw on the chuck spindle.* (p 420)

A turner's workshop of the eighteenth century, showing the use of the pole lathe and the great wheel. (pp 417, 419, 441)

PLATE 29

Burdon's iron bridge over the Wear at Sunderland before removal of the centre, 1796. (p 457)

A. *Darby's bridge at Coalbrookdale, the first iron bridge in the world, 1779.* (pp 105, 455)

B. *Burlington House, Piccadilly, designed by Lord Burlington. The building was begun in 1715, and rebuilt in 1866.* (p 470)

A. *The famous factory of Boulton & Watt at Soho, 1798.* (p 183)

B. *The factory of Swainson & Birley near Preston,* c *1830. The contrast with Boulton & Watt's factory* (above) *is striking; the fashion of giving factories the appearance of great country houses has disappeared in favour of a more strictly practical design.*

PLATE 32

A. *The Thames Tunnel, begun by Marc Isambard Brunel in 1824. On several occasions the river broke in, and the work was not completed until 1843.* (pp 427, 464)

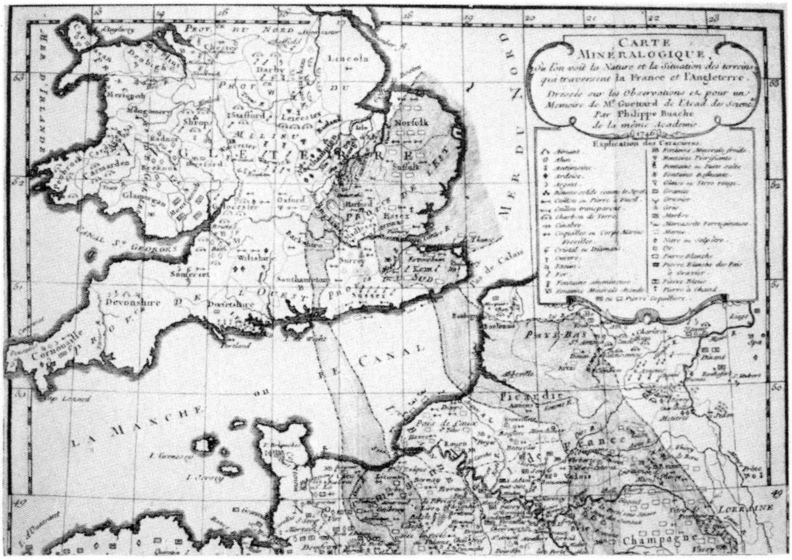

B. *Detail from a mineralogical map drawn by P. Buache 'from the observations of' J. E. Guettard, 1746, showing the key to the geological symbols.* (p 621)

A. *Early road building. The title-page from Gautier's book on road-making.* (p 522)

B. *The Edgware Road at Kilburn, London, in 1750, showing an old stage wagon.* (p 523)

C. *Wood paving in the Nevski Prospect, St. Petersburg, which was paved with small hexagons of resinous wood laid on a bed of crushed stones and sand, and covered with boiling pitch.* (p 545)

PLATE 34

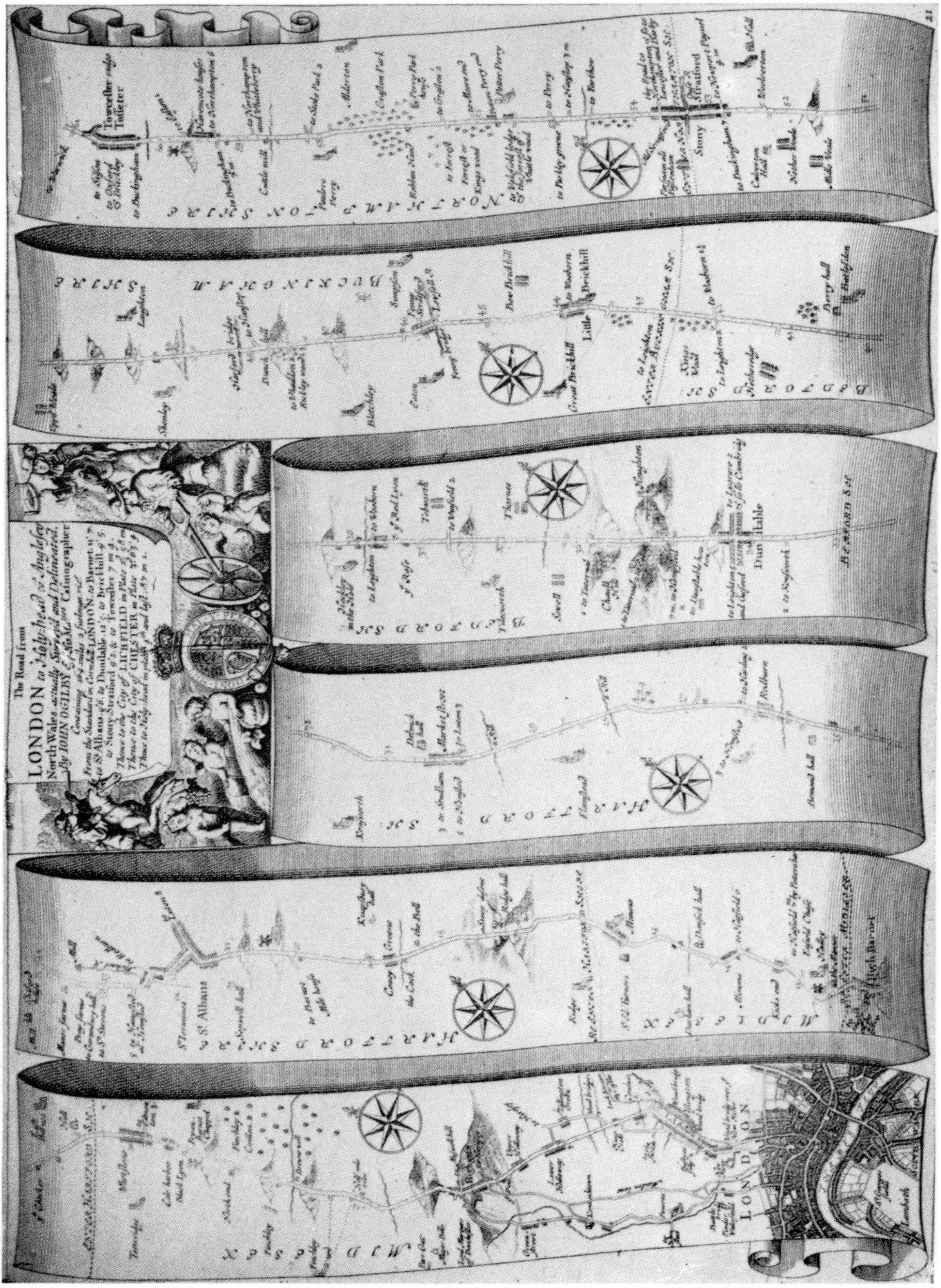

A seventeenth-century map of the road from London to Anglesey. (p 523)

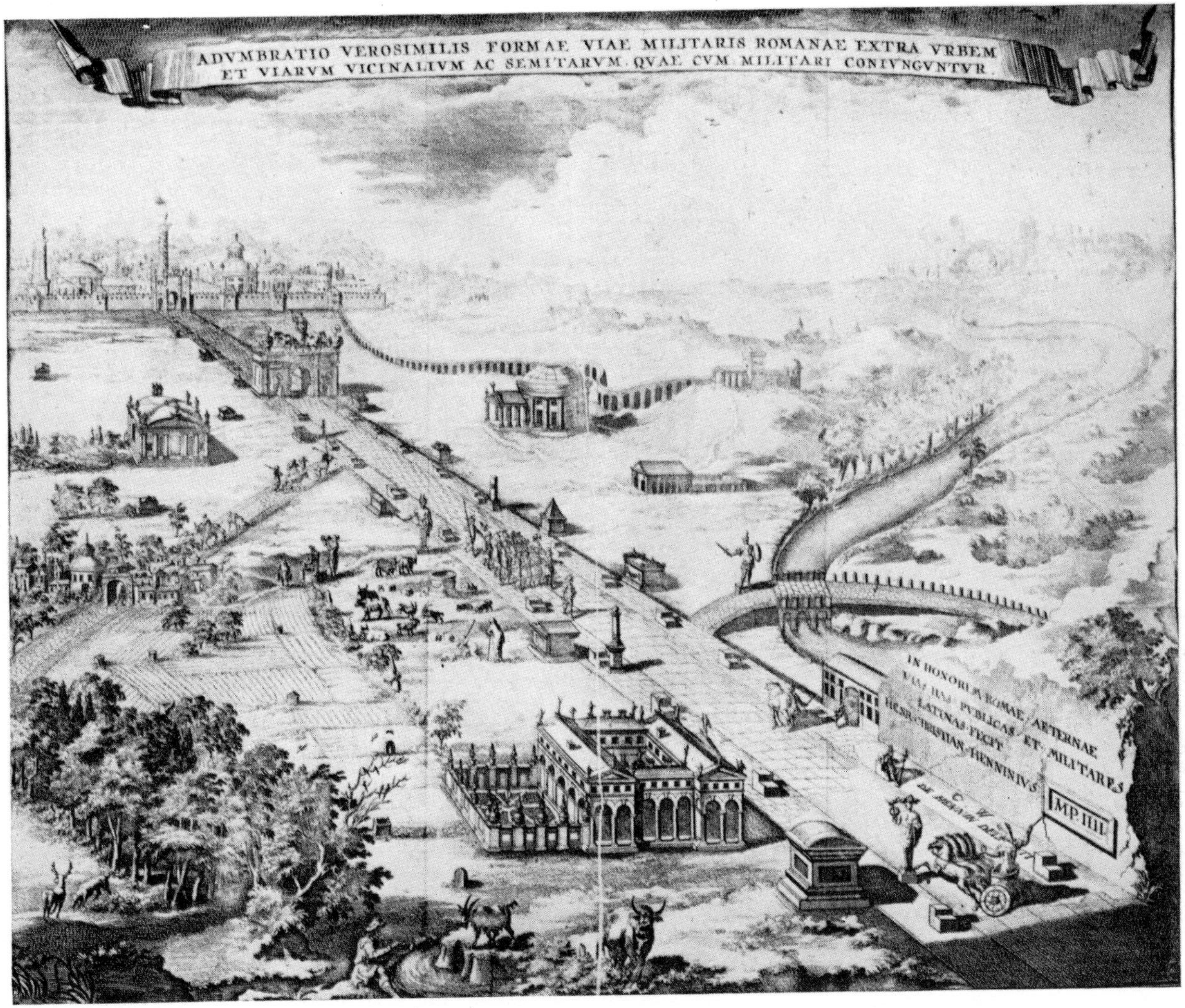

Bergier's conception of Roman highways. (p 521)

PLATE 36

A. *Newgate prisoners repairing roads*, c *1790*. (p 524)

B. *The Devil's Bridge on the St Gothard Pass through the Alps. Early nineteenth century*. (p 529)

The junction of the Staffordshire and Worcestershire canal with the river Severn at Stourport in 1776. (p 566)

A. *The Knoop lock on the Eider canal, seen from the east,* c *1800.* (p 561)

B. *The Suez canal near Kantara, 1869, showing dredgers in action.* (p 562)

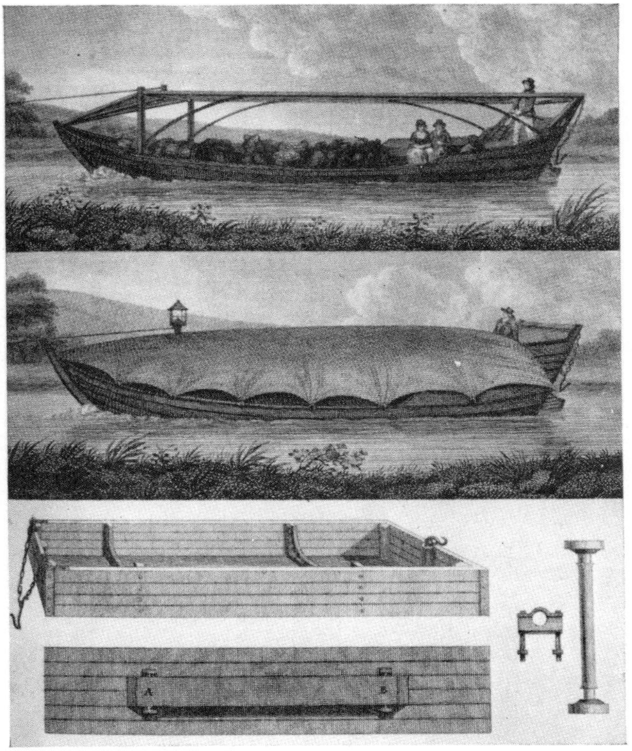

A. *Various boats for use on the canals*, c *1790*. (Above) *The market or passage boat;* (centre) *the dispatch boat;* (below) *a small tub-boat with wheels for running on the rails of inclined planes, such as those on the Bude canal.* (p 571)

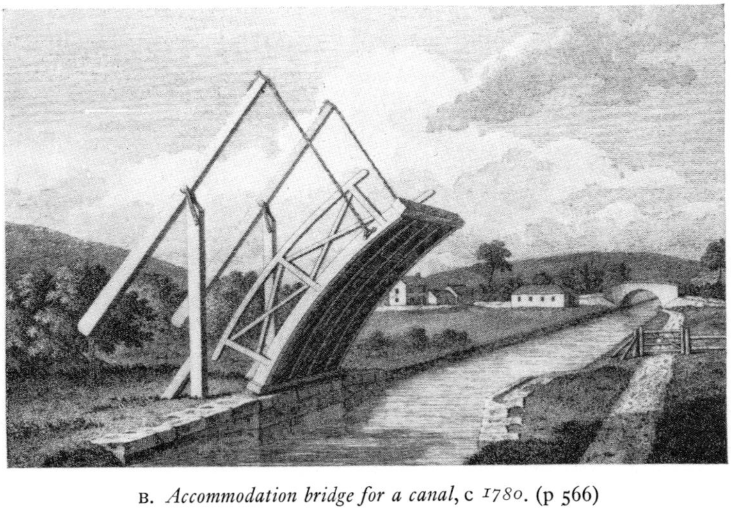

B. *Accommodation bridge for a canal*, c *1780*. (p 566)

PLATE 40

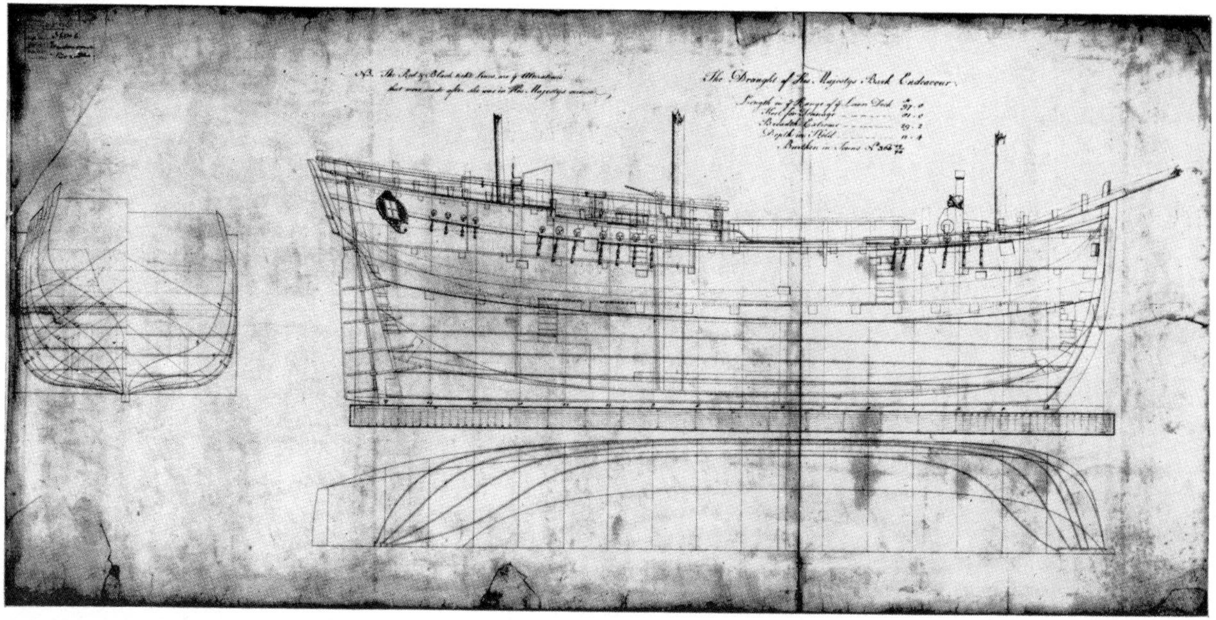

A. *'The Draught of H.M. Bark Endeavour.' The ticked lines on the sheer draught are the alterations made for James Cook's first voyage of circumnavigation. From aft, working forward on the upper deck, will be noticed the tiller and steering-wheel, with the mizzen mast between; the capstan; a pump abaft the main mast; and abaft the foremast a knighthead decorating the anchor winch, which is surmounted by the high gallows of the belfry.* (p 575)

B. *Exploded view of the* Marlborough, *with funnel up and screw down. Although called a three-decker, it will be noticed that she is practically a four-decker, the waist being decked over.* (p 587)

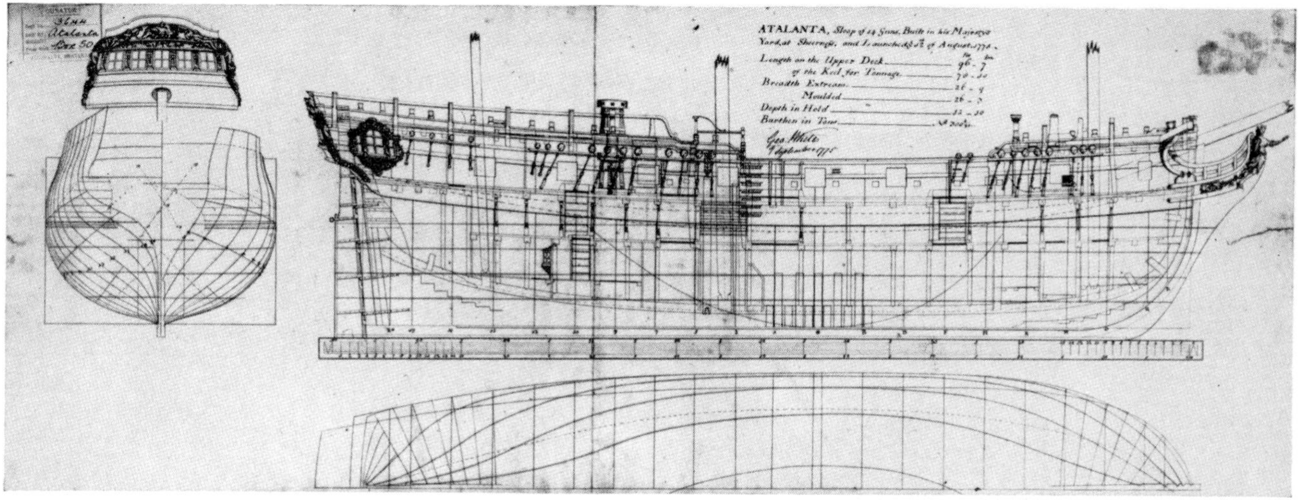

A. *Draught of the* Atalanta, *a sloop of 14 guns built for the Royal Navy at Sheerness Dockyard in 1775. This was a little smaller than the* Endeavour *and had finer lines and the usual beakhead and figurehead which the colliers did not have; note the long poop deck and forecastle with a deep waist between the main and fore masts.* (p 577)

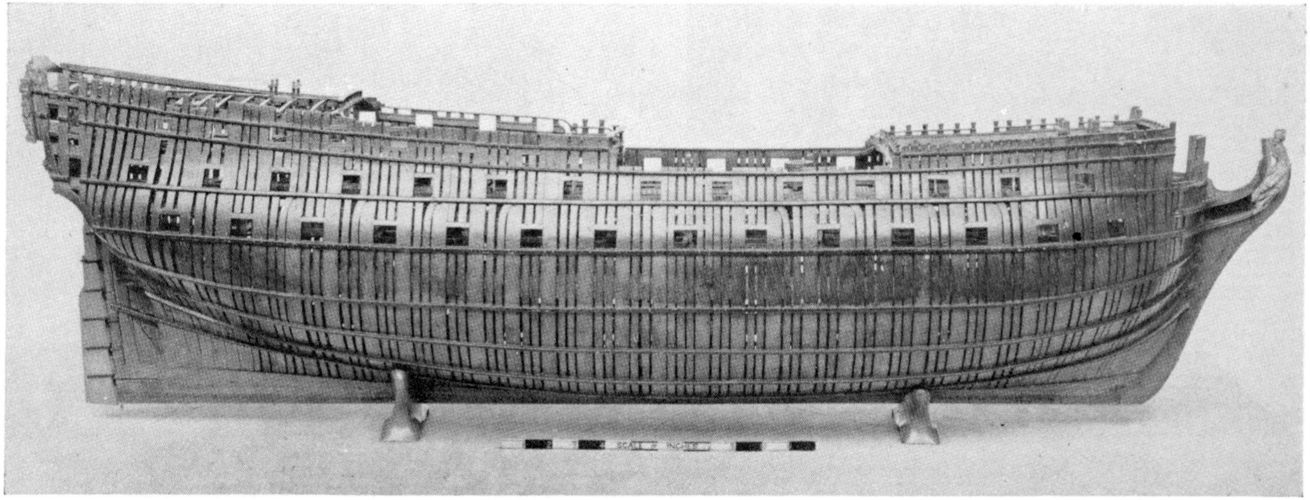

B. *The* Bellona, *74 guns, built at Chatham Dockyard in 1760. A contemporary scale model, unplanked, to show the distribution of the frame timbers or ribs, set closely together and every third frame doubled. The length of her lower gun deck was 168 ft and her beam 47 ft.* (p 584)

A. *H.M.S.* Victory *at sea, late 1790s. By the time of Trafalgar, 1805, the* Victory *had been given a flat, built-in stern without galleries. It will be noticed that she still has the old-fashioned mizzen lateen yard, but the sail is all abaft the mast. By the end of the century the lateen yard had given place to a gaff.* (p 576)

B. *The Honourable East India Company's ship* Atlas, *built in 1812 and mounting 28 guns. The Indiaman with her painted gunports, real and imaginary, was difficult to distinguish from a man-of-war.* (p 576)

A. *The* Ariel *and* Taeping *passing the Lizard in the Tea Race of 1866. Both ships have skysails set on the mainmast. The* Taeping *has double topsails.* (p 592)

B. *H.M.S.* Captain, *1869. Naval steamships remained fully rigged long after merchant steamships were beginning to discard sails.* (p 589)

PLATE 44

A. *The* Great Western, *1837, designed by I. K. Brunel. Although she was a wooden ship of 1350 tons, Brunel stressed in his design great structural strength, adequate engine power, and a supply of fuel estimated to last 26 days. Therefore he was able to cut down the ship's rig to that of a schooner, with four masts. She could easily steam at 12 knots.* (p 593)

B. *British four-masted barque, a type which became popular in the 1880s when it became necessary to build rather larger iron sailing ships to compete with steam. The vessel shown here was 287 ft long, with a beam of 42 ft, and of 2081 tons weight.* (p 593)

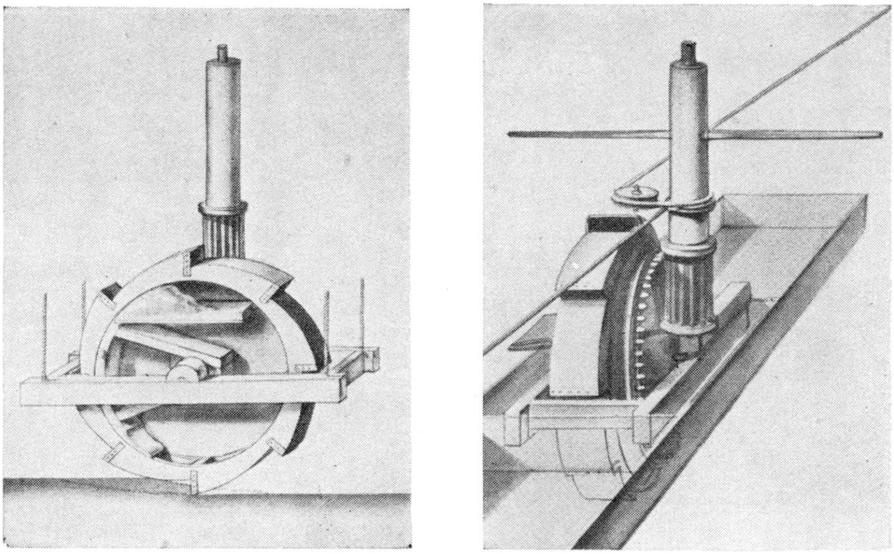

A. *Model of Van der Heyden's wheel-dredger, 1674.* (p 638)

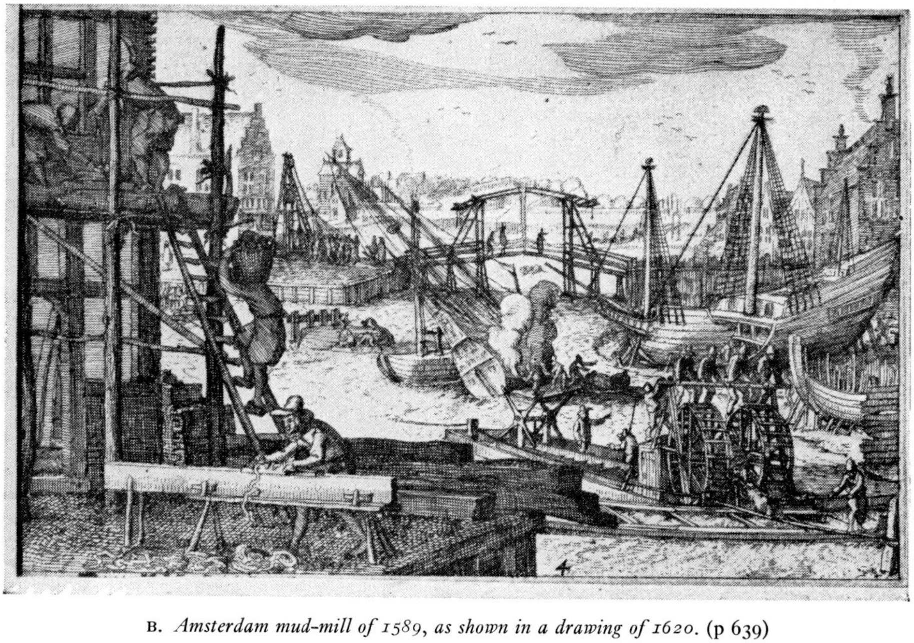

B. *Amsterdam mud-mill of 1589, as shown in a drawing of 1620.* (p 639)

PLATE 46

A. *Mud-mill of* c *1730*. (p 639)

B. *The* Great Eastern *under way, 23 July 1866*. (p 661)

Reproductions of Samuel Morse's telegraphs of 1835 (above) *and 1846* (below). (p 660)

PLATE 48

A

B

C

D

E

F

Many of the trade tokens issued at the end of the eighteenth century, mostly made in Birmingham, show scenes of contemporary technological interest. (A) *A stylized canal boat on the Basingstoke canal, 1789.* (B) *A glass-works illustrated on a Dundee halfpenny token, 1797.* (C) *The inclined plane at Ketley, 1789.* (D) *Mechanical trip-hammer in the works of John Wilkinson, 1793.* (E) *Hand-hammering of iron, 1795.* (F) *Distillation apparatus illustrated on a Perth halfpenny, 1797*